WOMEN
BUILDING
CHICAGO
1790–1990

WOMEN BUILDING CHICAGO 1790–1990

A BIOGRAPHICAL DICTIONARY

EDITORS

Rima Lunin Schultz   Adele Hast

ASSOCIATE EDITORS

Carolyn De Swarte Gifford,
Babette F. Inglehart, Mary Ann Johnson,
Cheryl Johnson-Odim, Clarice Stetter,
Margaret Strobel

SPONSORED BY

Chicago Area Women's
History Conference

Center for Research on Women and
Gender, University of
Illinois at Chicago

INDIANA UNIVERSITY PRESS
BLOOMINGTON & INDIANAPOLIS

This book is a publication of

Indiana University Press
601 North Morton Street
Bloomington, IN 47404-3797 USA

http://iupress.indiana.edu
Telephone orders 800-842-6796
Fax orders 812-855-7931
Orders by e-mail iuporder@indiana.edu

The paper used in this publication meets the minimum requirements of American National Standard for Information Sciences—Permanence of Paper for Printed Library
Materials, ANSI Z39.48-1984.

Manufactured in the United States of America

Library of Congress Cataloging-in-Publication Data

Women building Chicago 1790–1990 : a biographical
dictionary / editors, Rima Lunin Schultz, Adele Hast ;
associate editors, Carolyn De Swarte Gifford . . . [et al.].
    p.   cm.
Includes index
ISBN 0-253-33852-2 (cl : alk. paper)
1. Women—Illinois—Chicago—Biography—Dictionaries.
2. Chicago (Ill.)—Biography—Dictionaries.
I. Schultz, Rima Lunin, date   II. Hast, Adele.
HQ1439.C47 W66 2001
305.4′09773′11—dc21
00-058162

1 2 3 4 5 06 05 04 03 02 01

CONTENTS

Color plates follow p. 34

List of Illustrations

Foreword

This extraordinary volume offers a new view of the history of Chicago. One of the most vibrant cities in North America, Chicago occupies an important place in the history of the United States. Here the early trading community, incorporated in 1833, grew into a thriving metropolis by 1893, the year the city invited the world to its Columbian Exposition. Here, when the city held another World's Fair in 1933, a crop of new skyscrapers expressed its vigorous modernity. And here, by 1933, a whole new scale of growth produced one of the most confident urban cultures in the world.

Yet until the publication of *Women Building Chicago*, the history of the city's women remained largely unknown and untold. Now a team of dedicated historians of women has made it possible for us to know the city's full history. Here we see the first women settlers of European descent move into the plains beside the lake. We observe women building the city's institutional structures of churches, missions, convents, and schools before and after the Great Chicago Fire of 1871. We watch women immigrants create the city's ethnic communities in Polish, Greek, Jewish, Czech, African American, and other organizations. We witness women labor leaders shape wage earners' struggles for social justice and clubwomen vitalize the city's civic culture. We view women reformers at Hull-House transform American traditions of social welfare. We see how women reconfigured the city's legal, medical, teaching, and journalistic professions, contributed to its artistic traditions, and molded its commercial culture. We gain a new perspective on the civil rights movement. And in the twentieth century, we watch women construct institutions for communities of Japanese, Chinese, and Mexican immigrants.

This wealth of new knowledge about Chicago women has been mined in archives throughout the city. Rich holdings at the Chicago Historical Society and other historical archives have contributed substantially to the book's success. Some of these materials were known to scholars but unknown to the wider circle of readers to whom this book will appeal. Others are new to everyone. In their search for sources about women's lives, the book's editors went far beyond the familiar. Organizational records abandoned in basements and personal papers languishing in attics were brought to light and explored for the first time. Documents in convents, churches, and synagogues that chronicled women's lives were analyzed in new ways. Catalogues of exhibits highlighted forgotten achievements.

The process that created this biographical dictionary is as remarkable as the volume itself. The Chicago Area Women's History Conference began to plan the venture in 1990 and oversaw its development, especially in the early years. During the past decade the project was carried forward by its devoted editors, Rima Lunin Schultz and Adele Hast. They raised money for it. They maintained its high scholarly standards. They worked long hours, year after year. They coordinated the corps of researchers and writers who excavated materials from the city's cellars and vaults. They inspired continued support for the project from the Center for Research on Women and Gender at the University of Illinois at Chicago. They edited and rewrote unceasingly. And through all this they maintained the collective spirit of the project's origins.

A labor of love on the part of many people, *Women Building Chicago* can be used in many ways. Readers looking for a particular woman can go to the alphabetical listing of biographies or scan the index. Those interested in particular periods in the city's history can consult the list of entries organized by birth year. Teachers can use this list to construct a new approach to Chicago's history. Readers can use the index to explore themes such as labor organizing or the arts. This strategy will appeal to students of American history who are seeking to connect the national story with Chicago's history.

Women Building Chicago sets a new standard of inclusiveness for a biographical dictionary. The book offers an extensive survey of Catholic women religious, for example, embracing nuns in a variety of orders. The book's editorial commitment to diversity is evident in the many different ethnic groups represented in its pages. Protestant ministers are also strongly represented as are African American women in a wide range of occupational categories.

Although the volume is organized around biographies of individual women, it reaches far beyond those persons. The entries form points of access to the wider world of social, political, economic, and cultural life in Chicago over a century and a half of the city's history. Through these individuals we can understand the city's social movements, its social institutions, and its enormous capacity for social change.

Here, too, is a new view of the city's men—as fathers, brothers, husbands, sons, and as clients and partners in the many enterprises that women fostered. This view of the city's men helps us see the indispensable role they played in the lives of the women with whom they lived and worked. It also helps us see how women accomplished much of what they did while nurturing others at the same time.

Every major American city deserves to have a historical directory as complete and many splendored as *Women Building Chicago*. In this as in so many other ways, the city of Chicago has been blessed by the women who have called it home.

KATHRYN KISH SKLAR

Preface

Women Building Chicago 1790–1990 grew out of the need for an accurate history of Chicago. In published histories of the city, women were virtually absent, except for a relatively small number of prominent women, despite the involvement of women in diverse areas of city life. This book gives an account of the history of Chicago through the lives of 423 women. Because of the close ties between the city and its neighboring suburbs, women were selected from both Chicago and the greater metropolitan area for which Chicago was and is an economic, social, and cultural center.

The book originated in the Historical Encyclopedia of Chicago Women Project of the Chicago Area Women's History Conference, Inc. (CAWHC), a non-profit organization that holds public meetings on topics in women's history and also produces books and educational materials. From the outset of research on the book, CAWHC, through its board of directors and members, was a sponsor and supporter of the project. In 1992, when a project proposal was sent to the National Endowment for the Humanities through the University of Illinois at Chicago, the Center for Research on Women and Gender—a newly formed program—became a sponsor of the project and its home organization at the university.

The editorial board includes two editors who are historians and six associate editors from history, journalism, and literature. Ten scholars expert in women's history and related areas, including immigration history, urban history, education, and literature served as the advisory board.

In the selection of women who were involved in events in Chicago, the editors used several criteria. A woman had to have died by December 31, 1990, so that a complete picture of her life and activities could be given. She had to play a role in some way in Chicago history; she accomplished much in her areas of concern or expertise, or she left a written record of her life that showed the impact of events on her, her family, and her community. Enough information had to be available to write an entry of reference value. For many women, although their roles in the city were known, too little information existed for a biography. Some of the women in the book were much involved as social reformers and civic activists in events as the city grew and developed. They developed educational institutions at all levels and as teachers worked to create opportunities and an educational environment for women equal to that of men. Chicago, with its large immigrant population in the nineteenth and twentieth centuries, had many neighborhoods dominated by specific ethnic or racial groups, and each of these communities had women leaders whose activities needed to be placed in the historical record. Women sought reform for the betterment of society and for the equal standing of women and men in employment, wages, suffrage, and participation in government. They achieved as artists and artisans, novelists and poets, scientists and physicians. Their lives show how they responded to limitations placed on them as women and how they overcame gender discrimination. Women played many roles—in their homes, their local communities, the city at large, the state, and the nation, as well as in their professional and work activities. Viewed collectively, the biographies place the activities and experiences of women from varied backgrounds within the context of Chicago history.

Although some of the women are prominent, the search for entrants for the book yielded mostly women who have not yet been included in reference books and about whom little is known. Research to find women began in 1990 with an examination of the pathbreaking reference book edited in 1979 by Andrea Hinding, *Women's History Sources: A Guide to Archives and Manuscript Collections in the United States*. Information on a woman is sometimes found in her own papers but often resides instead in manuscript collections of organizations, institutions, or individuals other than the woman herself. Hinding's listings of manuscript collections in Chicago repositories as well as elsewhere in the country name the women about whom information exists in each collection. Since little had been published about the majority of women in the book, information had to come from primary sources, and Hinding identified manuscript collections and their locations. In the search for possible subjects for the book, the editors also read many biographical books published in the nineteenth and twentieth centuries, including directories of Chicago leaders, some including women only and some that specialized in specific professions. In addition, names were solicited from historians and others expert in various fields as well as from members of ethnic and racial groups in the area—individuals who were familiar with the work of women in their respective communities. Practitioners in fields included in the book suggested women, some of whom they had known in their professional work. The research to find women for inclusion resulted in a database of some three thousand names.

By January 1993, the editorial board had selected the first hundred entrants for the book and in 1993 conducted two workshops for potential writers. Further intensive research was needed to select the remaining biographees. Even for women who seemed appropriate choices, the editors had to confirm that sufficient source material was available for a reference article. Members of the editorial board did research on specific groups of candidates—lawyers, women religious, scientists, artists, and others—and reported their findings to the entire board, which made the final selection decisions.

For writers of entries, the editors drew on a broad group that included established scholars, graduate students, experts on specific women or subjects, and members of Chicago communities. For some immigrant communities, writers had to be able to read the language or interview informants—relatives or others who knew the subject—in a language other than English. In the search for writers, the editors contacted faculty members in history and other fields included in the book, wrote to groups in women's studies and women's history, and placed announcements in newsletters of professional associations.

The format of the biographies is generally chronological. Each entry includes discussions of both the woman's personal life and her professional or other activities. A personal description is included when available. For most of the women, research disclosed a comprehensive story on their decisions, relationships, and achievements. A majority of the biographies drew on manuscript sources, including some collections only recently made available at repositories, for example, the Hannah Greenebaum Solomon Papers at the Library of Congress and the Edith Spurlock Sampson Papers at Schlesinger Library. Some entries are less complete than others, since full information was not always available on personal relations or on some periods of a woman's life.

Cross-references to other women in the book appear within an entry in capital letters the first time they are printed in the entry. Such cross-referencing highlights the connections and interrelationships among several women, as well as their shared activities and roles as part of a larger picture. Each entry concludes with a *Sources* paragraph—a selected bibliography of materials used in the research for the entry and other pertinent publications and primary materials useful for further research.

Quotations in an entry are identified with short citations; the *Sources* provide the complete citations. Sources frequently used are abbreviated in the bibliographic paragraphs.

In terminology, the entries use current vocabulary—African American or Black, Native American or American Indian—except for direct quotations from earlier years. However, if a woman retired from a university as a professor emeritus, that title is recorded in the interests of accuracy. The text avoids gendered vocabulary where both men and women were involved; artisans are crafts workers rather than craftsmen. The accepted usage of chair or head has replaced chairman.

The biography of each woman is discussed in historical context, and the length of the entries varies depending on the information available about a woman and the amount of contextual background needed for clarity. Since many readers may not have the knowledge of history needed to understand fully the events of a life, the editors saw the importance of context for each biography.

These biographies place women in Chicago history. As a reference book, *Women Building Chicago 1790–1990* may stimulate and assist further research on the women themselves and on the many areas and activities changed by their efforts and accomplishments.

ADELE HAST

Acknowledgments

Work on the book project, which carried the working title Historical Encyclopedia of Chicago Women Project, started in 1990, and during the decade that the book was being developed, the editors received invaluable assistance from many persons and groups. Professional colleagues—librarians, scholars, teachers, and others with knowledge about women in the history of Chicago—provided expert information. Funding agencies, individuals, and organizations gave financial and pro bono support that was important to the completion of the project. Support came from more persons and groups than can be acknowledged here. Many repositories are noted in the Sources paragraphs that provide bibliography for each entry.

Archie Motley, archivist emeritus at the Chicago Historical Society, always made himself available to help both editors and writers and, through his familiarity with the collections, brought to our attention materials beyond those requested. Mary Ann Bamberger, assistant Special Collections librarian emerita at the University Library, University of Illinois at Chicago, gave us the benefit of her detailed knowledge of the contents of the Midwestern Women's History Collection and other papers and publications at the library. Joel Wurl, curator and assistant director, Immigration History Research Center, University of Minnesota, provided expertise on immigration sources for Chicago women of different ethnic communities. Mary Ann O'Ryan, OSB, gathered material on Catholic women religious in the Midwest. Brother Michael Grace, SJ, university archivist, Loyola University Chicago, helped writers and editors and presented materials that he thought would be useful. Other library professionals in the Chicago area also welcomed our writers, shared expert knowledge of collections, and made materials available on specific women: Matthew Cook, Rights and Reproductions, Chicago Historical Society; Linda J. Evans, chief cataloger, Chicago Historical Society; Eileen Flanagan and Cynthia Matthews, photography, Chicago Historical Society; Michael L. Flug, archivist, Vivian G. Harsh Research Collection of Afro-American History, Carter G. Woodson Regional Library, Chicago Public Library; Diana Haskell, Lloyd Lewis Curator of Midwest Manuscripts, the Newberry Library; Gretchen L. Lagana, Special Collections librarian, University Library, University of Illinois at Chicago; Daniel Meyer, associate curator, Special Collections, University of Chicago Library; Patrick Quinn, university archivist, University Archives, Northwestern University; Bart H. Ryckbosch, archivist, the Art Institute of Chicago.

David M. Sokol, Art History, University of Illinois at Chicago, and Susan S. Weininger, Art History, Roosevelt University, Chicago, offered suggestions in the field of art history. Lynn Weiner, History, Roosevelt University, gave assistance in developing a number of entries in conjunction with her students, who wrote biographies. Frances Freeman Paden, Women's Studies, Northwestern University, did the same with her students. Barton J. Faist, art expert, allowed researchers to use his materials. Ruth Dear, who was a source of important support to the project through her volunteer services, gave editing assistance.

In addition, the following individuals provided valuable advice and information: Ann Barzel, *Dance Magazine*; Valerie Gerrard Browne, Mundelein College Archives, Loyola University Chicago; Mark Burnette, Evanston Historical Society, Evanston, Illinois; Marjorie Buttner, Dominican Archives, Sinsinawa, Wisconsin; Jeanie F. Child, Cook County Archives; Ruth Hanold Crane, Norwegian Historical Society, St. Olaf College, Northfield, Minnesota; Anita Olson Gustafson, Presbyterian College, Clinton, South Carolina; Suellen Hoy, University of Notre Dame; Glen Humphreys, Conrad Sulzer Regional Branch, Chicago Public Library; Sister Patricia Illing, Mercy Sisters Archives, Chicago; Sister M. Vivian Ivantic, St. Scholastic Priory, Chicago; Richard Johnson, the Newberry Library; Judith Russi Kirschner, School of Art and Design, University of Illinois at Chicago; Sister Mary Grace Krieger, Maryknoll Mission Archives, Maryknoll, New York; Sabina Logisz, Polish Museum of America Library, Chicago; Odd Lovoll, St. Olaf College, Northfield, Minnesota; Arthur Miller, Lake Forest College, Lake Forest, Illinois; Steven A. Reiss, History, Northeastern Illinois University, Chicago; Margaret Rossiter, History of Science and Technology, Cornell University; E. Leonard Rubin, Gordon & Glickson LLC; Philip Runkel, Marquette University Libraries, Milwaukee, Wisconsin; Mona Scheuermann, English, Oakton Community College; Norman Schwartz, Chicago Jewish Historical Society; Dan Sharon, Norman & Helen Asher Library, Spertus Institute of Jewish Studies, Chicago; Norma Spungen, archivist emerita, Chicago Jewish Archives, Spertus Institute of Jewish Studies; Susan Taraba, Wesleyan University Library; R. Stephen Warner, Sociology, University of Illinois at Chicago.

Throughout the project, student assistants, both graduate and undergraduate, assisted with research and handled correspondence, record keeping, and computer input of text that kept the work flowing. The first research assistant on the project, Laura Magnavite, participated in editorial board meetings, did research, and performed myriad tasks for the project. Katherine Clark did much of the paperwork needed to acquire illustrations, and she and Amy Schneidhorst provided research assistance as well as computer work on edited entries. Paola Kindred and Annette Chapman-Adisho also assisted in preparing computer versions of the texts. Geraldine Franco handled correspondence with libraries and other repositories. Barbara Dobschuetz did research and helped in the final stages of preparing the manuscript. Gwen Hoerr McNamee did research on women lawyers. Martha Elena Espinoza assisted with research in the Hispanic community. Rachel Seed, Kunal Thakkar, and Tammy Lee helped with preparation of final text. Dea Shipps, Chrashawn Averette, Jennifer Ray, and Schena Harris, who were Communiversity Fellows at Chicago State University, provided assistance. The efficiency and thoughtful questions of these assistants are much appreciated.

At Indiana University Press, Joan Catapano, assistant director and senior sponsoring editor, made an early commitment to the book and provided encouragement throughout the years of work. Editor Melanie Richter-Bernburg asked perceptive questions in the course of her careful copyediting.

At the same time that professional colleagues gave assistance that helped us to define the contents of the book, several agencies provided essential financial aid. The National Endowment for the Humanities, an independent federal agency, supported the book project with two major grants as well as advice from Jane Aikin and Martha Chomiak that started at the first draft of the project proposal and continued through the years of grant support. During the early stages of book development, grants by the Chicago Foundation for Women made possible two workshops for writers. The Spencer Foundation awarded a grant for the work on women in education. The Chicago Area Women's History Conference (CAWHC) provided support and financial assistance from the outset.

Several programs at the University of Illinois (UIC) at Chicago aided the project. The Center for Research on Women and Gender at UIC, under director Alice J. Dan, with the invaluable assistance of project coordinator Mary Lynn Dietsche—who managed the budgetary tasks of the project—gave financial and logistical support. John A. Gardiner, director of the Office of Social Science Research at UIC, with the assistance of secretary Iris B. Tillman, provided office space and other support. Funds for a research assistant came from the Institute for the Humanities Grants-in-Aid Program funded by the Office of the Vice Chancellor for Research at UIC. The Women's Studies Program (renamed in 2000 the Gender and Women's Studies Program), UIC, directed by Stephanie Riger, supported the project. Women's Studies administrative secretary Wildred Hughes coordinated the bookkeeping records for student work. Margaret Strobel, as acting director of the Women's Studies Program and as a Great Cities Institute faculty scholar, donated the services of her research assistant to the project.

Individuals and groups contributed funds to support expenses. When the NEH grant required matching funds, Jean Spaay Hunt, as president of CAWHC, formed a fund-raising group, the Friends of the Historical Encyclopedia of Chicago Women Project. (Friends members are noted by * in the list below.) The Friends campaign not only met the match but also raised additional funds critically needed for completion of the project. Throughout the time that the project was in operation, the following donors provided essential support, most of them by direct financial contributions and some through in kind or pro bono service:

Charlotte Adelman; Joanne H. Alter; Ann Thacher Anderson; Phyllis Kelmanson Apelbaum; *Ann Armstrong, in honor of Jean Hunt and Rima Lunin Schultz; Elaine Arnstein; Melissa J. Auerbach; Leah Joy Axelrod; Barbara Ballinger; Mary Ann Bamberger, in memory of Hannah Byerly; Melinda Barber and Thomas Ritchie; Robert J. and Sheila Bator; Diana M. Beliard; Carol Belshaw; Elspeth H. Benton; Laura Bentz; Biederman, Stetter, Silverman & Co.; Melissa Rae Bingman; Victoria Boies;

Heather Booth; Rachael Ann Bottorff; Linda Boyle; Gerri A. Brauneis; Beatrice B. Briggs; Bliss Williams Browne; Valerie Gerrard Browne and Archie Motley; Ann C. Bryne; Lorraine A. Bucky; Ethel Burakoff; Gail Brook Burket; *Sandra K. Burns; Marie K. Burnside, in memory of Julia Kramer's mother; Debra O. Callen; Mary J. Campbell; Marifran Carlson; Gloria Carrig; Centuries & Sleuths Bookstore; Elise H. Chadwick; Chicago Teachers Union; Jeanie F. Child; Chin-ling Helen Chin; Barbara Ciurej; *Marilyn D. Clancy; Sylvia M. Clasby; Joy Clough; Elizabeth W. Colburn; Marilyn Comen; Teresa Conway; Margaret Corwin / Smith, Miller, and Franklin; Ann C. Courter and Norman M. Hirsch; Willa G. Cramton; Arlene Crewdson; Elizabeth P. Crookes; Yolande R. Crosby; Barbara Flynn Currie; Alzina Stone Dale; Alice Dan; Margot and Raoul J. Davion, in memory of Leah Emdin Glaser; Jean Dean; Mary De Cock; Ann Lewin Diament; Mary Lynn Dietsche; *Colleen Dishon; Marilyn A. Domer; Mary Therese Donnelly; Veronica Drake; Yaffa Claire Draznin; Susan Dvora, in tribute to Jean Hunt's contribution to CAWHC; Rita Lavery Eckstein; Dena J. Polacheck Epstein; Joan L. Erdman; Judith M. Erickson and Daniel Kearney; Linda J. Evans; Martha A. Farley; Ann E. Feldman; Marjorie Feldman; Mary Ann Finnegan; *Sunny Fischer; Virginia Kemp Fish; Mary Priscilla Flaccus; *Joan Flanagan; Margaret G. Fling; Etha Beatrice Fox; Katie Frankel; Helene Frankfater; Gerissa A. and R. Dean French; *Maya Friedler; Barbara A. Furlong; Frank Galati; Bernice E. Gallagher; Carol B. and Lawrence Gartner; Carolyn De Swarte Gifford; David O. Gifford; Mary Gifford; Sally M. Gifford; William A. Gifford Jr.; Sue Ling Gin; Sylvia Glagov; Connie Heaton Goddard; Sherry B. Goodman; Ann D. Gordon; Sylvia Gordon; Virginia R. Gosse; Marjorie M. Graham; Molly R. Green; Nancy Green; Karen V. Griebel / Feminist Writers Guild; Mary Griffin; Blair Perkins Grumman, in honor of Carolyn De Swarte Gifford; Charles and Yolanda Hall; Jacqueline Harper; Harris Foundation / Joan W. Harris; Cecil W. Hart; Adele Hast; Melody W. Heaps; Blanche G. Hersh; *Bette Cerf Hill / Herald Newspaper Foundation; Celia Hilliard; Stina L. Hirsch; Susan E. Hirsch; Nancy Holder; Marshall M. and Doris B. Holleb; JoAnn R. Horowitz; Mary Houghton; Sandra M. House / Greenhouse Communications; Suellen Hoy; Ellen M. Hunt and David Medendorp; Jean Spaay Hunt, in memory of Ruth Schwanke Lachman; Lester C. Hunt; Sarah M. Hunt; Jan Lisa Huttner; Fredda Hyman; Babette F. Inglehart; Devra R. Jacobson; Lenore Janecek; Linda A. B. Johanek; Angelee Johns; Bernard B. Johnson; Mary Ann Johnson; Cheryl Johnson-Odim; Dorothy V. Jones; Charlotte Josephs; Vivian M. Kallen; Kathleen and Vincent Keefe; Sister Joyce Kemp; Jacquelyn Kendall; Zoe Kiethley, in memory of Isabell Bryne Marfoefer and Mary Smith Bryne; Thelma Kirkpatrick; Jacqueline P. Kirley; Charlotte O. Kirshbaum; *Louise W. Knight; Annette Kolasinki; Emma A. Kowalenko; Iris Krieg; Ingrid Christiansen Kretzmann; Angelika Kuehn; Melinda Kwedar; Ethel P. Kyros, in memory of Ruth Schwanke Lachman; Ruth Schwanke Lachman; Susan Spafford Lane; Legion of Young Polish Women; Ann Leonard; Charles and Ruth Levy Foundation / Barbara and David Kipper; Dale K. Light; Lucia Woods Lindley; Georgia Lloyd; Regina Lopata Logan, in honor of Martha Virginia Keller; Barbara Denemark Long; *Marcena W. Love; Jane A.

Lucas; Leslie Lumberg; Philip A. and Leah Marcus, in honor of Betty Nathanson; Janet Mark; Marget S. Matchett; Mary Ann McFarlane; Mary Quinlan McGrath; Eileen M. McMahon; Sylvia McNair; Dennis J. and Gwen Hoerr McNamee; Katherine F. McSpadden; Jill S. Mesirow; June Michaelson / Hospitality Standards, Ltd.; Midwest Bookhunters, in memory of Carol Zientek; Liz Mitchell / Project Communications; Thomas G. Moher and Lynn Weiner; Terry Moon; Jo and Art Moore; Deloris J. Mosier / D. J. Mosier Financial Services; Marilyn McGrath Murphy; Lorraine and Martin Nadis; Adele S. Neems; Kathryn Sheehan Nesburg; Eleanor A. and Thomas Nicholson; Joan Nicklin Fund; Nila V. Nolan; Northwestern University Settlement Association; Norwottock Charitable Trust / Adele Simons; Walter Nugent; Doris Piccino Overboe; Francis Freeman Paden and family; Martha Palmer; Esther Parada, in memory of Leah Emdin Glaser; Sara Paretsky; Gail E. Parry; Erica Pascal; C. Diane Percival; Jean Paulson Peterman; *Eleanor P. Peterson; Paula F. Pfeffer; Carol W. and Robert J. Piper; Patricia Plautz; Playboy Foundation / Christie Hefner; Catherine L. Price; Patrick M. Quinn; Ann Rackas; Helen Ramirez / Chicago Teachers Union; Sherry K. Rasmussen; *Hedy M. Ratner; contribution in memory of Rose Markowitz Ratner; Anne Remien; Doris Rich; Ann M. Ripley; Frances M. Roach; Julia S. Rock; Priscilla H. Rockwell; Judith Cosin Roothaan; Gayle S. Rosenberg; Roslyn Group for Arts and Letters; Susan and Jeffery Rubenstein; Rowena M. Ruff; Evelyn Salk; Max and Virginia Samter; Debra Jaffe Sandroff; Florence Scala; Cathleen Ann Schandelmeier; Janet Schenk; Joan G. Schroeter; Carolyn Schulham; Rima Lunin Schultz; Esther K. Seaborne; Natalie W. Seglin; Sandra Shane-DuBow; Sherry Siegal; Peggy Tuck Sinko; Sisters of Charity BVM; Sisters of Mercy, Regional Community of America; Margie Skelly; Susan B. Slocum; Alice H. Smith; *Diann DeWeese Smith; Elizabeth Emery Smyth; Rosemary Snow; Alice W. Snyder; June Sochen; Julie Kelly Soper; Patricia J. Spadoni; Susan J. Stall; Nancy Staunton; Clarice Stetter; Ellen Ruth Stone-Belic; Margaret Strobel; Frances Sullivan; Ruth Surgal; Tal International Marketing, Inc.; Jean C. Tello; Ann J. Termenyi; Phyllis Eckardt Tholin; Judith Thomashow; Helen McMahon Tillman; Phyllis B. Toback; Anne Coulter Tobey; Barbara S. Todd; Irene W. Tracy; Eric and Katherine Jean Tyacke; Ursula Ulrich; Robert C. Vagnieres; Joan Vanderbeck / Service Web Offset Corp.; Harriet Edith Van Horn; Daniel W. Vittum Jr.; Mary Jan Vogt-Jeffries; Louise Carroll Wade; Helena Wajda; Carol Kyros Walker; Michael J. Walsh; Julie K. Ward; Patricia Spain Ward; Mary D. Watson; Natalie Weil; N. Sue Weiler; Nella Fermi Weiner; Bernard A. Weisberger; Gloria A. and Herbert C. Weiss; Janet Welsh; Rupert L. Wenzel; Thelma K. Wheaton; Helen A. Widen; Wilmette Historical Society; Muriel B. Wilson; Evelyn B. Wingate; Patricia C. Wishart; Paula Wolff; Judith and Paul Wolfman; Women and Labor History Project; Grace W. Young; Kay Forrest Zak; Joanne Kuper Zimmerman; Marge Tye Zuba.

We appreciate their confidence in the project and their support, which helped make *Women Building Chicago 1790–1990: A Biographical Dictionary* a reality. We hope that they will see in the book a fulfillment of their expectations.

Advisory Board and Liaisons to Sponsors

ADVISORY BOARD

Henry C. Binford, Associate Professor of History,
    Northwestern University
William H. Chafe, Dean of the Faculty of Arts and
    Sciences and Vice Provost for Undergraduate
    Education, Duke University
Gerald A. Danzer, Professor of History, University
    of Illinois at Chicago
Allen F. Davis, Professor of History, Temple
    University
John A. Garraty, Governeur Morris Professor of
    History Emeritus, Columbia University
Nellie McKay, Professor of English and Afro-
    American Studies, University of
    Wisconsin–Madison
Anne Firor Scott, W. K. Boyd Professor Emerita of
    History, Duke University
Barbara Sicherman, William R. Kenan, Jr.,
    Professor of American Institutions and Values,
    Trinity College
Kathryn Kish Sklar, Distinguished Professor of
    History, State University of New York,
    Binghamton
Joel Wurl, Curator and Assistant Director,
    Immigration History Research Center,
    University of Minnesota

LIAISONS TO SPONSORS

Jean Spaay Hunt, Past President, Chicago Area
    Women's History Conference
Alice J. Dan, Professor and Director, Center for
    Research on Women and Gender, University
    of Illinois at Chicago

Introduction

From these 423 biographies of Chicago women emerges a synthesis of Chicago history that provides the beginnings of a new narrative. Many volumes have been devoted to documenting Chicago's history as the quintessentially American saga of entrepreneurial development that catalyzed commercialization, industrialization, and urbanization on a vast scale. The biographies of Chicago women in this volume provide the reader with a new context for understanding the growth and development of this midwest city. The depth and scope of the contributions to Chicago of the majority of the women included here will be new to the reader and should provoke questions leading to a more inclusive and complex explanation of the factors involved in the transformation of American society and the rise of the modern city.

The historical survey that follows attempts to sketch for the reader the major themes that have emerged from a collective reading of the biographies and to provide an understanding of some of the larger themes in American history and in the growing scholarship on the history of women in the United States. As for the biographies themselves, taken individually, they inform the reader of the personal ambitions, struggles, and achievements of women from a wide variety of backgrounds in different periods of history. Taken topically, they provide the reader with histories of women's progress in various fields, including art, education, literature and the theater, politics, law, and medicine. They provide a history of the suffrage movement in the Chicago area and of women in politics and in social movements. Read collectively and interconnectedly, the biographical narratives provide an appropriate, congruent context for understanding the meaning of the individual lives and, beyond this, a new interpretation of Chicago and American history.

WOMEN CONTRIBUTE TO THE COMMERCIAL AND SOCIAL DEVELOPMENT OF CHICAGO, 1790–1860

Chicago emerged as a boomtown during a period in which the canon of domesticity contrasted the home and the world, defining the former as a sanctuary, an oasis, a place where character-building takes place and where women as wives and mothers work selflessly for the good of family and society out of religious conviction as well as republican ideology; and depicting the latter as a place of pecuniary self-interest and competition. In the heady excitement of land speculation during the transition from an economy of fur-trading to one of commercial investment and speculation, Chicago personified the masculine spirit of capitalism. In the early days, men outnumbered women inhabitants. In 1837, "of the 3,989 white persons residing in the city, more than forty-five per cent were males twenty-one years of age or over, and there were less than half as many women as men" (Bessie Louise Pierce, *A History of Chicago: The Beginning of a City, 1673–1848* [1937], I, 172). Yet gender issues are strikingly present even in the precommercial period prior to the incorporation of the town in 1833 when, with the end of the Black Hawk War and the signing of a treaty, the Potawatomi tribe was resettled. When the French and Indians began to trade in the 1600s, American Indian women were often critical to the success of such enterprises. Women such as Archange Chevallier Ouilmette acted as intermediaries between tribal groups and Europeans. They knew the languages and the social mores of the tribes; they had important skills for the fur trade itself, and alliances were made between European men and Indian or métis women that, as in the case of Archange Chevallier Ouilmette, lasted a lifetime. In 1796 or 1797, Chevallier, a métis born to a French fur trader and his Potawatomi wife, married Antoine Ouilmette, a French Canadian fur trader who came to Chicago in 1790.

A consideration of the woman's sphere in pre–Civil War Chicago indicates that home and church—traditional places for female activity—were hardly insignificant in the construction of cultural authority and influence for society as a whole. These venues in a small and new place, which Chicago was in the 1830s, 1840s, and 1850s, were significant arenas for political and social interchanges and the planning of cultural and charitable enterprises. In a world where local government was minimal and public space was not yet defined by museums, lecture halls, and other cultural institutions, the private residence retained an important, quasi-public role. Juliette Augusta Magill Kinzie, perhaps the best example of this feature of life in early Chicago, was a social leader influential in the politics at St. James Episcopal Church—established in 1834 largely through her efforts—including the hiring and firing of clergy. Without her approval it was difficult to carry on a charity event or plan a church expansion. As the wife and daughter-in-law of early settlers, Kinzie had a position as a leading citizen that came naturally but was enhanced by her education and talents—including piano playing and fluency in French—and her literary skills as the popular historian of early Chicago history.

From another perspective, private domestic space was enmeshed in the entrepreneurial development of the city in immediate and focused ways. City improvements, for example, were paid for by a special tax assessed according to the direct value a bridge, sidewalk, or sewer added to private property. If a person's property gained more value than a neighbor's down the block, the person's assessment was higher. In most Protestant denominations, church membership was determined by the purchase or rental of pews. Class exclusion as well as gender exclusion typified the privatized nature of the pursuit of culture. The first libraries and reading rooms run by the leading men in Chicago were not open to the public but based on subscription and membership dues, and privileged and educated families had private collections of books and art that made up for the embryonic cultural establishments. Refined people had performances of music and readings of poetry and plays in their own homes since public entertainment was limited to public taverns and music halls.

Matters of politics and public policy did, however, intrude into domestic space. Mary Jane Richardson Jones played a major role in the tiny community of free African Americans; she and her husband, John Jones, the first Black to be elected to a political office in Illinois, were part of an interracial abolitionist network in Chicago. Their home was one of only two Underground Railroad terminals operated by African Americans in the city. Frederick Douglass and John Brown were guests in the Joneses' home, and Mary Jane Richardson Jones maintained contacts with them and other national leaders in the abolitionist movement through her letter-writing. In a parallel way, Mary Ann Mills Hubbard, wife of meat packer and Chicago civic leader Gurdon S. Hubbard, a former antebellum mayor, held court in her own home and became known for her intelligence and knowledge of public affairs and politics. Guests in her household in the 1850s included Abraham Lincoln and Orville H. Browning, who came to visit when Gurdon Hubbard, a leader in the recently formed Republican Party in Illinois, brought his colleagues home to strategize. Memorialized by a member of the Chicago Historical Society, Mary Ann Hubbard was remembered for her remarkable and "almost masculine understanding and grasp of affairs generally" (Chicago Historical Society, *Annual Report*, 219).

While it is true that women did not participate in government or business, early Chicago women made an essential contribution to the creation of a commercial society as leaders in the expansion of literacy in the West. Many economic and social factors were involved in the settlement of the American continent; yet the process of community-building, the development of commerce and trade, and the organization of industrial and manufacturing enterprises required an infrastructure of workers with basic communication skills. For those who would be the managers of the burgeoning market system, a basic education was a requirement, not a luxury. In the context of postrevolutionary America, the development of responsible and harmonious civic life required an educated citizenry. The moral imperative to develop a virtuous citizenry required a level of literacy sufficient to sustain Bible reading.

Early Chicago developed because of the confluence of an agricultural and commercial revolution and an educational revolution for women in the United States and in parts of Europe, for example, in Ireland. Commercial development was also aided by the Second Great Awakening (1800–30) in the United States, a religious movement in which thousands of women and men committed or recommitted their lives to an acceptance of Jesus Christ as their savior. For many women, the conversion experience led to careers in moral reform and in teaching others to read so that the Gospel message would be available to them. The conversion experiences of Frances Langdon Willard in 1820 in New England and Eliza Emily Chappell Porter in Rochester, New York, in 1828, link the Second Great Awakening to Chicago's early development, since both women became convinced that their role in life was to spread the Gospel through their calling as schoolteachers in new settlements in the West. Before her marriage to Presbyterian minister and mis-

sionary Jeremiah Porter, Eliza Chappell started the first public school in Chicago in 1833, partially funded by money from the school fund. Willard was well-versed in the work of such educational pioneers as Sarah Pierce, Mary Lyons, Emma Willard, and Catharine Beecher. Both Willard and Chappell came to the West as single women and traveled without family or colleagues for support. Both women were advocates of education and education-training; they organized and founded new schools, and they mentored other women in their school teaching roles. As a missionary's wife and mother of nine children (three died in infancy), Chappell Porter established schools where her husband planted Presbyterian churches in Illinois and Wisconsin in the 1830s through the 1850s, resettling in Chicago in 1858. During their stay in Green Bay, Wisconsin, the Porter home was the last stop on the Underground Railroad before slaves crossed by boat into Canada. After the Civil War, Eliza Chappell Porter began schools for freedmen in Tennessee and Texas and, when Jeremiah Porter received a commission as an army chaplain, the Porters spent twelve years in a succession of western army camps. Wherever she went she established schools, taught in them, and trained others to teach.

Frances Willard opened a Female School in Chicago in 1836, and during a career that lasted three decades, she established schools in seven states and twenty-three towns and provided opportunities for advanced training to at least twelve hundred girls and women. Seventy-four of these young women became teachers. Willard's indefatigable efforts were commendable; her vision of what young women should learn in school, however, set the stage for the development of a female consciousness that would rebel against the constraints imposed by contemporary social mores. She taught natural philosophy, chemistry, bookkeeping, logic, and moral philosophy in addition to the frequently prescribed subjects for a girl's training. Classes in botany and calisthenics in the 1830s were unusual. Such courses, however, were increasingly popular among the new middle class of commercial settlers and their families, whose experiences with female academies in the East had whetted their appetite for a more rigorous curriculum for young girls.

SCHOOLTEACHING AND FEMALE SOCIAL MOBILITY

Chappell Porter's and Willard's biographies illustrate the ways in which single and married women participated in the opening up of the commercial frontier and took paths that were distinct from those of women and men who cultivated midwest farmland. From the earliest period of commercial settlement, the entrepreneurial frontier was a force in dislodging women from the so-called domestic sphere. Female school teachers were in great demand, since conventional mores allowed them to be paid half what their male counterparts received. Female school teachers quickly became the norm. School teaching also became an avenue for women's further professionalization. The first and second generation of women college students often taught school prior to finishing either college or advanced degrees as a way of financing further education. Since requirements for teaching school were minimal, even at normal schools, which initially had two-year programs at best, it was not unusual for a young woman to teach for a few years before going on to study law or medicine, or even before entering a doctoral program. The biographies of Sarah Ann Hackett Stevenson, Catharine Van Valkenburg Waite, and Myra Colby Bradwell, a physician and two lawyers, respectively, suggest the pattern.

No group of women illustrates this pattern of social and occupational mobility more than Roman Catholic women religious. It is a paradox that the hierarchical and patriarchal system to which they owed absolute obedience (in theory) provided independence and a degree of autonomy for immigrant and working-class women. Mother Mary Agatha O'Brien, born Margaret O'Brien in 1822 in Graigue, County Carlow, Ireland, was only twenty-four years old when she arrived in Chicago in 1846 after three years in Pittsburgh, Pennsylvania, at the first foundation of Mercy Sisters in the United States. She entered the Carlow Sisters of Mercy as a lay sister (a nun without a dowry) and worked in the kitchen until she and six others emigrated to Pittsburgh. Had she remained in Ireland, her lot in life would most likely have remained unchanged, since European religious orders retained class and status distinctions. But Margaret O'Brien had benefited from the recently developed Irish national school system. In the United States, her literacy and her natural abilities marked her as a leader, and, with no restrictions to overcome, she rose to a position of authority. O'Brien found that half the population of the booster lake port were Irish and German immigrants, the majority Catholic and working class.

Under O'Brien's leadership, three schools were opened almost immediately: St. Mary's (for girls) and St. Joseph's (for boys) were free and provided education for the children of immigrant Catholics; St. Francis Xavier Academy charged tuition and enrolled well-to-do young women from Protestant and Catholic families a decade before Chicago erected its first public high school. As with the Protestant women who taught school, the Catholic teaching sisters continued to open new schools, teach students, and create systems of teacher training and supervision. Biographies of Mother Mary Francis De Sales Monholland, a Mercy Sister and Irish immigrant; Sister Mary Agatha Hurley, Sisters of Charity of the Blessed Virgin Mary, another order predominantly of Irish immigrants and Irish American women; and Sister Walburga Gehring, Daughters of Charity, an order of German immigrant women, document the early activities of women religious in Chicago during the antebellum and Civil War period. These women, like Protestant women schoolteachers, experienced opportunities for career advancement and personal freedom through acts of moral benevolence that society had defined as woman's work. Their biographies describe the acquisition of land, successful efforts at fund-raising and financial planning, capable supervision of construction projects, and intelligent administration and counseling of staff and personnel in the running of educational programs, hospitals, orphanages, and rescue missions.

Women's roles as educators did not challenge the cultural authority of the leading men in the city, who retained their monopoly on politics and economic affairs and who were also the trustees of the school fund and in charge of public education. Teaching enabled women to rise above humble beginnings and, in some cases, to overcome a bad start in life. Such was the experience of Kate Newell Doggett. In 1853, after she buried her infant daughter and divorced her adulterous husband, Kate Newell Horton dropped her married name and at age twenty-six taught school in Cleveland, Ohio, then resettled in Chicago. In a short time "Mrs. Kate E. Newell," whom Chicagoans met as a young, well-educated, and cultivated "widow," opened her own school and soon married the wealthy, civic-minded William E. Doggett, a boot and shoe manufacturer.

WOMEN AND MORAL BENEVOLENCE IN ANTEBELLUM CHICAGO

Women's work of moral benevolence in antebellum Chicago became a training ground for the assumption of civic leadership by females during the Civil War. Among the charitable and benevolent institutions founded in Chicago in the decade of the 1850s were Mercy Hospital and Orphan Asylum (1852), the Magdalene Asylum (1858), the Providence for Working Girls (1859), St. James Hospital (1854), and the Home for the Friendless (1858). The first three were the work of Catholic Mercy Sisters; the last two were established by the efforts of Episcopalians and an interdenominational group of Protestant women, respectively. Mary Ashton Rice Livermore, Jane Currie Blaikie Hoge, and other prominent Chicagoans who founded the Home for the Friendless represented the various organized Protestant churches in the city; the home assisted friendless women and children in finding suitable employment and permanent housing, admitting them without regard to creed, color, or nationality. Women board members were responsible for fund-raising and ran the day-to-day operations, which included rescuing women and children from the streets and bringing them to the home. These efforts to provide for the health and well-being of Chicagoans were critical, since Chicago's death rate exceeded that of New Orleans, Louisiana—which was known for its epidemics—as a result of yearly epidemics of typhoid, smallpox, and cholera; tuberculosis in the city was also serious. City and county public institutions were inadequate for a municipality whose population reached 109,620 in 1860, 50 percent of it foreign born. Efforts by the mayor and fire department in 1857 to clean out an area on the North Side of the city along the lakefront known as "The Sands," which was notorious for its saloons, gambling dens, and bordellos, were inadequate; the city counted more than one hundred houses of prostitution in 1858. Both the Chicago Relief and Aid Society and the Chicago United Charities were established in 1857, when a national economic panic and depression that began that year had serious consequences in the city. As business failures dampened the booster mentality of Chicagoans, businessmen flocked to revivals where such evangelical ministers and popular preachers as Dwight L. Moody attempted to restore confidence and offer a religious interpretation of secular events.

THE CIVIL WAR AND WOMEN'S RELIEF WORK

Soon after the first battles of the Civil War awakened women's and men's sensibilities to the lack of organizations to aid Union soldiers and care for the wounded and sick, the United States Sanitary Commission was formed to assist the Medical Department of the Army with disease prevention and relief. The Chicago (later Northwestern) Branch of the United States Sanitary Commission was established in 1861; soon after, in 1862, Mary Livermore and Jane Hoge were named associate managers of the Northwestern Sanitary Commission and lent their considerable experience and leadership to the cause. As associate managers, women learned how to run mass organizations and to raise funds on a scale exceeding local ladies' auxiliary efforts. Ultimately, about three thousand aid societies came under the supervision of Livermore and Hoge, who had organized many of them personally. Other war workers in Chicago included Myra Bradwell, Kate Newell Doggett, and Eliza Chappell Porter, who provided nursing assistance on the battlefield. Helen Culver also responded to a call for nurses from the Sanitary Commission after the Battle of Stones River near Murfreesboro, Tennessee, and took charge of a forty-bed hospital. Catholic women religious made a significant contribution in the field of nursing. Sisters of Mercy from Chicago were one of the twelve orders of Catholic nuns who ministered to the wounded and sick soldiers in the North and the South. Sisters of Mercy, who had learned their nursing skills under Florence Nightingale in the Crimean War, were valued; and Mother Francis De Sales Monholland sent Mercy sisters and a group of thirty lay women assistants to Lexington, Missouri. Back in Chicago in 1863, Mother Monholland directed her sisters in nursing typhoid and smallpox patients at Mercy Hospital; Monholland and her sisters also ministered to Confederate prisoners incarcerated in Camp Douglas, Chicago. Daughter of Charity Sister Walburga Gehring worked in the ambulance corps during the war; her order tended both Union and Confederate wounded on the battlefields.

THE MOVEMENT FOR WOMEN'S RIGHTS

In the midst of relief efforts, women in Chicago were beginning to come together in a movement for women's rights, including suffrage; an end to sexual discrimination in occupations; improvement of educational and economic opportunities; and the right to work and wages. They were doing so in a highly polarized political environment in which leaders in the northern Democratic Party and Republican Party were debating citizenship issues and the political settlement of the war. In Chicago women and men who had supported Lincoln and the Union army—many of whom had been Free Soilers or abolitionists in the 1850s—saw the opportunity to bring state and federal constitutions into alignment with more inclusive notions of citizenship. For women, however, issues of social justice had a particular meaning, and questions of wages and the right to work—poverty and dependency—resonated among female war relief workers brought up in the context of gender-specific relationships to property and citizenship. Even before the end of the war, Chicago women had expanded their initial goals of raising money and supplies for soldiers to include the relief of women on the home front. Sanitary Commission workers observed the hardship and need of women and children that resulted from the dislocations occasioned by war as well as the economic problems that befell many widows. Mary Livermore and others began to question whether or not women were actually protected by the patriarchal arrangements of society and the

laws that kept married women from owning property, entering into contracts, or keeping their own wages. In the short term, the Chicago branch hired women in its offices and sewing rooms and provided them with wages. The idea that women needed training and experience outside the domestic sphere to insure the stability of family life gained adherents. Mary Livermore was radicalized by the contradictions in her legal status as a married woman unable to sign a business contract and head of a relief agency worth millions. Her abolitionist background had led to her immersion in war relief work, but before the Civil War she had opposed woman suffrage. In 1867 Livermore wrote to Susan B. Anthony, explaining that she had once believed the ballot would come to women after the right to work and wages but that she had recently decided women had to vote first and that the other goals would follow women's full realization of citizenship.

Myra Bradwell's involvement in the battle for legal equality of women began in part because of her own unsuccessful efforts to be admitted to the Illinois bar. She had read law with her husband, James Bradwell, who, in 1861, was elected judge in Cook County; in 1868 she founded *Chicago Legal News*, a legal newspaper that soon became one of the most important legal publications in the Midwest. The following year she passed the bar exam but was rejected for admission to the Illinois bar on the grounds that as a married woman she was unable to enter into contracts and, therefore, could not practice law. Her case was argued unsuccessfully before the U.S. Supreme Court in December 1872. That year Illinois women's rights activists, including Alta May Hulett, and Myra and James Bradwell, lobbied successfully for passage by the state legislature of an anti–sex discrimination act. Hulett became the first woman admitted to the Illinois bar on June 6, 1873, two days after her nineteenth birthday. In the early efforts by women lawyers to become licensed, arguments were made that combined talk about rights and citizenship with discussions about the importance of economic independence for women. By 1868, ferment among women regarding these issues as well as the debate about the proper method for achieving advancement and equality had, in the minds of a core group of activists, solidified around the belief that women had to obtain the right to vote first. This right, they argued, was central to women's struggle for political equality, and it alone made women the legal equals of men. Without the vote, women were robbed of their natural rights.

In 1855, Catharine Van Valkenburg Waite, an Oberlin graduate who taught school and was married to Charles Waite, a lawyer and freethinker, founded Illinois's first suffrage organization in Earlville, a small town west of Chicago. Her plea for political rights for women, the first to be written in the state, was published in the *Earlville Transcript* that year. The following year both Waites lectured on equal rights throughout the state. In 1859 the Illinois legislature passed a law permitting women to reclaim their maiden names after divorce. It was almost ten years before the next step was taken toward the organization of women to obtain their rights. In June 1868, a woman's association, Chicago Sorosis—after the New York Sorosis formed a few months earlier—was formed; it specifically avoided calling itself a "suffragist" society. Catharine Waite, Cynthia Leonard, and Mary Livermore attended the founding meeting and, from the beginning, women's rights issues dominated. Internal conflict split Chicago Sorosis into two competing groups, one following the leadership of Mary Livermore and the other that of Cynthia Leonard; the two groups hosted simultaneous but separate suffrage conventions in the city on February 11 and 12, 1869, at Liberty Hall (Mary Livermore) and at Crosby Hall (Cynthia Leonard). Guest speakers included Susan B. Anthony, Elizabeth Cady Stanton, and Lucy Stone, who participated in both conventions. Stanton introduced a resolution that prefigured the controversial resolution presented in New York at the Equal Rights Association (ERA) meeting in May 1869. At the New York meeting, the ERA split, with Stanton and Anthony forming the National Woman Suffrage Association. In Chicago, Stanton and Anthony argued that black and female enfranchisement had to be treated as inseparable; since the Republicans in Congress had determined in the Fourteenth Amendment to enfranchise black men but not women, Stanton and Anthony called for resolutions withdrawing support from the Republican Party. Their position was not supported in Liberty Hall, where Judges James Bradwell and Charles Waite—husbands of Myra Bradwell and Catharine Waite—spoke out against the Stanton-Anthony position. The Crosby Hall group, which brought together Spiritualists, Fourierites, freethinkers, and suffragists, passed resolutions that were more consonant with the Stanton-Anthony position. At the conclusion of the meetings, two Illinois suffrage groups emerged: the Illinois Woman Suffrage Association with Mary Livermore as president, and the Universal Suffrage Association. The former led the movement for women's rights in Illinois in association with Stanton and Anthony's national group; the latter lasted only several months.

The revolution in women's lives brought about by the opportunities for education coincided with a new understanding of the fragility of domestic relations. Women in Chicago, as elsewhere in the nation, had lived through two major economic depressions—in 1837 and 1857—prior to the upheavals of the Civil War. Great risk was associated with entrepreneurial capitalism in nineteenth-century America. In 1861, married women in Illinois obtained the right to ownership of separate property brought to a marriage and could control, transfer, and contract upon this property as they saw fit. This right was, in part, a response to the insecurities married women faced when husbands failed in business. The ability to retain inherited property gave a woman security in a volatile, unpredictable economy. A year later, lobbying efforts to secure joint guardianship of children and easier access for widows to deceased husbands' property failed to secure passage by the legislature.

With the impetus from the conventions and the creation of the Illinois Woman Suffrage Association (IWSA), women immediately turned to the state legislature in session in Springfield. The major figures from Chicago—Livermore, the Bradwells, and the Waites—lobbied successfully for the passage of legislation that would entitle a married woman to receive, use, and possess her own earnings and sue for the same in her own name, protected from the interference of her husband or his creditors. The act, passed in March 1869, made clear that it was not to be construed as giving to a wife any compensation for any labor she performed in the care of her children or husband.

Kate Doggett returned from her experience as a delegate to the September 1869 Women's Industrial Congress in Berlin, Germany, opposed to the creation of separate institutions for employment of women and critical of the idea of a separate woman's sphere.

CULTURE ON THE MARGINS: THE PARADOX OF WOMEN INTELLECTUALS

In the 1870s Doggett remained frustrated at the contradiction between women's engagement in cultural affairs in certain quarters and exclusion from membership in many of the standard societies of learning—the dilemma of the female intellectual and new professional. For example, she and other Chicago women participated in the Philosophical Society of Chicago when it was formed in 1873 by leading men and women intellectuals, including Unitarian minister Celia P. Woolley, medical doctors Julia Holmes Smith and Sarah Hackett Stevenson, liberal Protestant ministers Robert Collyer and David Swing, Liberal-Reform Rabbi Bernard Felsenthal, and prosuffragist and freethinker Judge Charles B. Waite. The group presented papers to one another on a range of topics, including the position of women in society, evolution, sacred books and mythologies, and geology. Many members of the Philosophical Society were also women's rights activists in the late 1860s and 1870s. Generally they were middle-class women (Kate Doggett was probably the wealthiest in the group) whose husbands were professionals—clergy or lawyers—and who shared the ideology of the radical Republicans, whose zeal for citizenship rights for Blacks had carried in Congress. They were liberal in their religious views and interested in the new ideas of science and social science. Also involved were the new professional women—ministers, doctors, lawyers. The Philosophical Society remained the exception to a cultural and business milieu in which Victorian mores dictated that women be excluded from membership in the newly established institutions of culture, including the Chicago Historical Society and the Chicago Academy of Sciences. Kate Doggett was elected to the Chicago Academy of Sciences only five years after its founding in 1864, even though she had curated the academy's valuable collection of plant specimens.

Doggett's achievements serve to underline the lack of inclusion of women intellectuals; caught in this paradox, she began the Fortnightly of Chicago in 1873. Originally attended by women and men, it soon became a literary society of largely self-educated women who presented serious papers on philosophy, literature, art, and women's history. Three years later the Chicago Women's Club (renamed Chicago Woman's Club in 1895) launched an ambitious agenda of education and social action that drew on six committees—reform, philanthropy, education, housekeeping, art and literature, science and philosophy. The Chicago Woman's Club (CWC) was basically the domain of privileged white women; admission of its only black member, Fannie Barrier Williams, had been controversial, and she remained the only African American in the club for the next thirty years. The CWC became a network of influential women whose overlapping memberships in other clubs and associations further strengthened the women's movement in the city. The club movement in Chicago, as elsewhere, was related to the larger movement of women, nationally and internationally, who were working to advance themselves and their gender toward full participation in the mainstream of economic, political, and social life.

Closely associated with the growth of sophisticated cultural institutions in the rising metropolis of Chicago was the interest shown by the city's elites in acquiring art, both for themselves and for public museums. Women had roles as both artists and art patrons. One exceptional woman became a major art dealer for many of the elite of Chicago. Women artists such as Cornelia Adele Fassett were accepted. She exhibited her watercolor of Abraham Lincoln, painted from life in 1860, at the Ladies' Northwestern Fair for war relief held in 1863. An accomplished portraitist, Fassett and her husband had a studio in Chicago; there he was active in the new field of photography and she painted the portraits of prominent Illinois and Chicago men. Annie Cornelia Shaw began studying at the Chicago Academy of Art and in 1873 exhibited her painting *View on the Des Plaines* at the second annual Chicago Inter-State Industrial Exposition. One year later, she opened her first studio; by 1875 both Shaw and Fassett had been elected to associate membership in the Chicago Academy of Design, and four years later the academy elected Shaw to full status as an academician.

Other late-nineteenth-century and early-twentieth-century women artists in Chicago included painters Mary Hackney Wicker and Enella Benedict; sculptors Bessie Onahotema Potter, Julia Bracken Wendt, and Nellie Verne Walker; and etcher Bertha Evelyn Clauson Jaques. Three years before the Art Institute of Chicago was incorporated by leading men cultural philanthropists, women established the Chicago Society of Decorative Art (later the Antiquarian Society of Chicago), and Sara Tyson Hallowell began her career as the leading art agent for wealthy Chicagoans, including Bertha Honoré Palmer. Alice DeWolf Kellogg and a friend, Marie Koupal, along with a handful of others, all of them female students at the new School of the Art Institute of Chicago, established the Bohemian Art Club (later the Palette Club), one of the first art associations for women in Chicago. Rose Fay Thomas and three other women launched the all-female Amateur Musical Club in the 1870s and began playing piano quartets together. The organization grew into a society of female pianists and singers with professional ambitions but few opportunities. Most of them taught music, since it was not until the 1950s that women began to appear with any frequency as orchestral performers. The careers of these women were typical: while there were gains made by individuals, women generally found it necessary to create separate female-only professional groups to support their careers.

Women remained marginalized in institutions of cultural philanthropy while men served as trustees, museum directors, and curators. Sara Hallowell's influence with the major art collectors in Chicago—the core founding fathers of the Art Institute of Chicago—was informal. She was denied directorship of the art exhibit at the World's Columbian Exposition in 1893 in spite of the strong endorsement of Bertha Honoré Palmer, a cultural and civic leader whose position as head of the Board of Lady Managers for the exposition gave her significant power. Palmer's French impressionist collection, key to the reputation of the Art Institute of Chicago, derived from Hallowell's advice and the connection this female art dealer made between Bertha Palmer and artist Mary Cassatt. Hallowell, who had been the art agent for the Inter-State Industrial Exposition from the 1870s and had traveled between European art capitals and Chicago to arrange annual exhibitions, held her final exhibition in 1890, when she showed works by Claude Monet, Edgar Degas, Alfred Sisley, Pierre Auguste Renoir, and Camille Pissaro to midwest art collectors. Museum trustees, including Bertha Palmer's husband, disregarded her innovative and bold art patronage, and Hallowell's institutional role at the museum came from her membership in the female-only Antiquarian Society. The same is true of other women art patrons whose collections were formative for the museum—Kate Sturges Buckingham, Annie Shaw Coburn, and Margaret Day Blake. Antiquarian Society member Frances MacBeth Glessner, who patronized arts and crafts artists and did silversmithing in her home studio, endorsed the museum's innovative decorative arts acquisitions. The Antiquarian Society created the groundwork for the museum's acknowledgment of the importance of decorative arts and for the appointment in 1914 of Bessie Bennett as Curator of Decorative Arts, the first woman to become curator at the Art Institute of Chicago.

THE GREAT CHICAGO FIRE OF 1871

The exclusion of women from governing boards of cultural institutions, in spite of new educational opportunities and career initiatives that were propelling women beyond the home, is evident in relief efforts after the Great Chicago Fire of 1871 that ignored women leaders of the Sanitary Commission. The Chicago Relief and Aid Society, a private charitable organization run by the city's business elite since the late 1850s, was authorized by Mayor Roswell B. Mason to become the official relief effort of the municipality and to distribute goods and supplies. Mason distrusted the elected alderman, whose narrow political interests he thought would get in the way of a scientific and prudent handling of the substantial relief fund of more than four million dollars. Instead, Mason and other supporters of the Relief and Aid Society argued that the wealthiest and most influential men of the city had no pecuniary interest and would be wise and economical in the distribution of relief. This approach also reflected the theories of scientific charity that dominated private relief agencies, whose fear of creating dependency among the able-bodied poor led to stringent rules regarding worthy and unworthy applicants for relief. In addition, the Relief and Aid executive committee privileged those individuals who had previously owned a home by providing small, prefabricated shanties; renters were sent to barracks. While the Employment Bureau of the society outfitted tradesmen who had lost their tools, jobless laborers had to take whatever jobs were available. In short, the Relief and Aid Society ran its programs so that the victims of the fire were assisted, but help was not extended to those whose economic plight was deemed unrelated to the conflagration. At the end of eighteen months of relief distribution, the Relief and Aid Society discontinued relief to eight hundred families deemed the "chronic poor," and the Relief and Aid Society used the six hundred thousand dollars left in its coffers to create a comfortable operating fund that allowed the organization to suspend all of its own fund-raising for the next decade.

The Chicago Relief and Aid Society's outreach was limited. Others, especially groups run by women, ignored or rejected the scientific charity approach and provided relief more inclusively. Sister Mary Francis De Sales Monholland and her nursing staff at Mercy Hospital assisted victims of the Chicago Fire. Sister Walburga Gehring and the Daughters of Charity took charge of the Barracks Hospital that had been set up as an emergency hospital for the fire victims.

While the Great Chicago Fire of 1871 continues to dominate the narrative of the city's history as a commercial and industrial metropolis, fire stories figure less frequently in the narratives of Chicago women. Martha Joanna Reade Nash Lamb's novel *Spicy*, published in 1872, describes women's benevolent work in Civil War Chicago, the assassination of President Abraham Lincoln, and the Great Chicago Fire. Lamb's female characters are strong and heroic in the novel and are based on the leading figures who supervised the work of the Northwestern Sanitary Commission during the war. Biographers of Cyrus H. McCormick agree that his wife, Nettie Fowler McCormick, who was twenty-six years his junior, provided the energy and will power to rebuild the McCormick Reaper plant after the fire destroyed the works. She wrote in her journal: "I constantly urge Mr. McC. to miss no opportunity to go forward with the new factory THIS YEAR (italics in original)" (Stella Virginia Roderick, *Nettie Fowler McCormick* [1956], 100). Emma Dryer, who was close to Nettie McCormick, recalled in her memoirs that the couple had prayed together on the subject and that McCormick left the decision to his wife since she would outlive him and had the children's future to consider. Nettie McCormick's decision-making in the business increased after her husband's death in 1884, when she became the chief stockholder and began writing to lawyers, financial agents, and advisers, including J. Pierpont Morgan, Cyrus Bentley, and Charles Deering. She was one of the few women in Chicago whose participation in industrial growth after the fire approximated that of male capitalists.

WOMEN AND WAGE LABOR

By the late 1870s the newly organized clubwomen in Chicago were working on two agendas: the advancement of white, middle-class women into the economic mainstream, and a reform agenda that had as a major goal the protection and assistance of working-class women and children. Efforts to protect working women came out of a shared gender experience that crossed class lines. For middle-class and working-class women, women's dependency was not an abstract concept but one that touched their lives directly. The wives and daughters of middle-class husbands and fathers were not defined by their class position in the same way that males were. Women could not be equal if they remained dependent on husbands and fathers. The movement for women's equality first had to battle for women's right to work, for married women's right to their own wages, and for acceptance in professions that initially excluded women. Women learned from experience that economic fluctuations in the market affected the security of middle-class families, as did the death of husbands.

During the post–Civil War era, American society experienced profound social, economic, and political changes. Transportation systems linked mechanized farms with urban centers in a national economy. Within a generation after the war, the United States was transformed from a predominantly agricultural to a manufacturing nation. The demographic and physical changes in urban areas shocked a generation whose childhood had been spent in pre-industrial, antebellum America. Chicago's population rose from 298,977 in 1870 to 503,185 ten years later to 1,099,850 in 1890. The annexation of surrounding towns in 1889 accounted in part for the growth. Chicago was the leading meat packer and the leading grain and lumber market in the United States. In 1860 Chicago became the center of the world's largest rail network, and by 1871 twenty-one mainline railroad tracks entered the city. The Union Stockyards opened in 1865. Thousands of Chicago workers, like their counterparts in other American cities, were employed in factories, sweatshops, and industrial plants, where they earned low wages for long hours and received no unemployment insurance or compensation for industrial accidents. Women and children worked many hours for pennies an hour in factories and sweatshops that were foul, unsanitary, and dangerous. Trade unionism was in its infancy, and there was a rise of industrial violence between organized labor, which was seeking recognition, and capital, which rejected collective bargaining. There were no child labor laws, no rules regulating the industrial workplace, and no safety nets for working-class or, for that matter, for middle-class employees.

In demanding changes in working conditions for women, middle-class clubwomen rejected the prevailing economic and social theory—the doctrine of *laissez-faire*, which dictated that the natural laws of supply and demand controlled prices and wages. The development of an alternative vision of how social and economic relations should be arranged in society was the major contribution of the post–Civil War women suffragists and reformers. Well before Progressive Era politics, middle-class women began advocating the same measures that militant trade unionists and socialists in workingmen's parties championed. Legislation to put an end to sweatshops became a rallying point for organized women across class, religion, and ethnic divisions. Women bucked the conventional thinking of the majority of Protestant clergy and benevolent workers in nineteenth-century America, whose ideas about the proper response to cases of poverty in were based on a *laissez-faire* theory that reinforced theological ideas of personal sin and conversion. Charles Darwin's theory of evolution was translated by conservative economists and social theorists into a Social Darwinism that supported the *laissez-faire* concept. Progress demanded that a government assume only minimal responsibility for the welfare of the citizenry; workers' demands for minimum wages, the eight-hour day, or even child labor restrictions and other kinds of protective legislation for women and children had to be rejected because such legislation interfered with the natural laws of the market system. Unscientific kinds of charity were especially suspect since indiscriminate, sentimental almsgiving created dependency and interfered with the laws of supply and demand. Attempts by workers' unions to bargain collectively for better wages and hours were also rejected. Middle-class and wealthy women who were engaged in reformist activities in the Chicago Woman's Club redefined their class position substantially enough to advance a critique of unregulated capitalism and to offer counterproposals for the way in which decisions about compensation for a person's labor should be made. These views did not mean, however, that middle-class and wealthy women who allied with working-class women agreed completely with the latter's positions and tactics. Nor did it mean that cross-class alliances among women were without tensions and conflicts. Yet many privileged women responded affirmatively to the call for a shorter work day, for regulation of factories, for minimum wages, and for an end to child labor—even though businessmen of their own class fought these reforms.

It is easy to understand why working-class women and men in trade unions and workingmen's parties rejected the rhetoric of the ruling elite. Clashes between labor and capital increased during the 1870s and 1880s, as did the incidence of state-supported violence against striking and demonstrating workers. In 1877 radical women workers participated in street activities in Chicago during the Railroad Workers' Strike that had spread across the United States and that reached Chicago in July. The following year, Alzina Parsons Stevens, Elizabeth Flynn Rodgers, Elizabeth Morgan, Lizzie Swank Holmes, and Lucy E. Parsons joined Chicago's first labor organization for working women, Working Women's Union No. 1 (WWU), with Stevens as the first president. The WWU was conceived by leaders of the Chicago Council of Trades and Labor Unions and the Socialist Labor Party, who thought it was time to organize yet unorganized women workers. Membership included workers from the Scandinavian, German, and English-speaking women's sections of the Socialist Labor Party. Many of the first generation of women trade union leaders in the city came out of the WWU. Elizabeth Flynn Rodgers, for example, served as a delegate to the Knights of Labor State Trades' Assembly of Illinois in 1880, and the following year she led one of the Knights of Labor's first all-women assemblies. Lucy Parsons, whose experiences with trade unionism and electoral politics in the Workingmen's Party (later the Socialistic Labor Party of North America) transformed her into a revolutionary socialist and one of the leaders of the new International Working People's Association (IWPA), wrote for the *Alarm*, which was edited by her husband, Albert Parsons. Her "To Tramps," published on the front page of the first issue, reflected her intense anger at social injustice as the unemployed and homeless died of hunger and exposure during the severe winter of 1883–84. She had come to believe that wage slavery would be defeated in the same way chattel slavery had been ended, and she adopted the ideology of propaganda by the deed in response to the state-sanctioned violence used against workers organizing for better wages and the eight-hour day.

For anarchist women such as Parsons and Lizzie Swank Holmes, the suffrage convention held in Chicago in 1884 had little meaning. Holmes, writing in the *Alarm* in 1885, debated whether or not socialist women should engage in the struggle for woman suffrage. She argued that the ballot was not the cure for women's problems, agreeing with Lucy Parsons and others who believed that the revolutionary workers' movement took priority and was, ultimately, the only way to improve conditions of women and men. Holmes and Parsons became involved with

the nationwide eight-hour-day campaign, and on May Day 1886, hundreds of working women participated in the Chicago parade of eighty thousand workers. Two days later a clash between strikers and police took place at the McCormick Reaper Works. In response to the incident at the McCormick plant, protesters called a meeting at Haymarket Square for May 4. The peaceful crowd was about to conclude its speeches and disperse when a contingent of 180 police arrived. Moments later a bomb exploded, sparking a police riot. Eight policemen died as a result of the bombing and the crossfire among police. In the disorder, an undetermined number of demonstrators lost their lives. The identity of the bomb thrower remained unknown, but eight anarchists, including Lucy Parsons's husband, Albert, were tried and convicted of conspiracy to murder a policeman. Four of them, including Parsons, were sentenced to death; a fifth condemned anarchist killed himself in jail; and three others stayed in jail until released in 1893 by Illinois governor John Peter Altgeld, whose pardon message contained a bold indictment of the trial.

MIDDLE-CLASS WOMEN ADVANCE A REFORM AGENDA FOR THE CITY

During the 1870s and 1880s, activist middle-class women also tried to make sense of the industrial city and found themselves repelled by the disorder, immorality, corruption, and violence. While women suffragists in the 1860s had been interested in protecting dependent women and children (Susan B. Anthony organized her radical Working Woman's Association in 1866), the leaders of the suffrage movement began to articulate a reform agenda in the late 1870s that became more fully developed in the Progressive Era. One of the first groups to assert the new agenda was the Illinois Social Science Association founded in 1877 by Elizabeth Boynton Harbert. An affiliate of the American Social Science Association, the Illinois group under Harbert argued that social progress would occur when women's moral influence was combined with up-to-date knowledge of the new industrial conditions in urban America. They also thought that traditional charity and moral reform directed at individual salvation were inadequate to solve the problems of modern society and that scientific charity organizations were limited responses to social concerns. Harbert had no confidence in the political system's ability to solve urban problems. She expressed her repulsion of men's abuse of power in ways that resembled the rhetoric of local temperance crusaders, whose protest against public drunkenness and political corruption had gathered support in small towns throughout the Midwest and in 1874 had led to the formation of the Woman's Christian Temperance Union (WCTU). In 1878 Mary E. McDowell heard Frances E. Willard address a group of young women in Chicago; impressed, the young McDowell joined in the temperance work and by 1887 was the national director for the WCTU's Young Woman's branches in Illinois and other states. With Willard's assumption of the presidency in 1879, the WCTU began advocating many of the same reforms that Harbert called for in her column, "Woman's Kingdom," which first appeared in 1879–80 in the Chicago *Inter-Ocean*, a daily newspaper. The column reported news about suffrage campaigns, reform movements, temperance, education, and health and offered a critique of existing societal institutions.

As secular clubwomen moved toward a new definition of their role in public affairs (and in turn redefined an expanded role for the state in an industrial democracy), women in traditional fields of benevolent work also redefined their roles and explored new avenues of service (and in turn redefined and expanded the sphere of woman's work and woman's ministry in religion). The Woman's Presbyterian Board of Missions of the North-West was organized in December 1870; under the leadership of Jane Hoge, it expanded from 70 auxiliaries in eight states to more than 1,430 auxiliaries in eleven states by 1885. The focus of the work was on the Christianization of heathen women and the support of female missionaries. Also in 1870, the Reverend Augusta Jane Chapin, the second woman to be ordained in the Universalist denomination, served on the Universalist General Convention, the denomination's governing body; and the following year she formed, with other activist Universalist women, the Woman's Centenary Association of the Universalist Church, the forerunner of the Association of Universalist Women. Emma Dryer came to Chicago in 1870 to take up benevolent work for women and children and became a leader in the Ladies' Christian Union; after the Chicago Fire of 1871, this organization engaged in relief work and changed its name to the Women's Aid Association. By 1873 it had reorganized as the Women's Christian Association after having affiliated with the Young Men's Christian Association. One of the outcomes of Dryer's leadership was the establishment of a home for "self-dependent girls." In 1871 Mary Jane Richardson Jones and three other women organized the Workers for the King, a religious group that offered aid to the growing African American poor population in the city. Rumah Avilla Crouse became the founding president of the Women's Baptist Home Missionary Society in 1877; run by women, its purpose was to develop missions within the United States rather than in foreign countries. Considered a controversial departure, it was a direct response to the pleas of women missionaries in the field who faced poverty, racism, and social problems from rapid urbanization and immigration. Women from a conservative religious tradition tended to identify differently with the problem of the unmarried working girl in the city, the so-called "woman adrift," than did secular social reformers, although from the 1880s through 1900s the common ground that united all middle-class and privileged women was a deepening anxiety over women who lived alone in the city and worked in factories, department stores, or sweatshops. There was growing alarm about the loss of innocence of young immigrant women and migrants from small towns and, worse, a fear that such women would become victims of the sex trade. The range of responses to the problems of youth in the city and the potential for corruption and exploitation of young women and men included those of Matilda Carse, a WCTU leader who, in 1882, helped open the Rehoboth, a refuge and alcohol recovery home, at a mission in an African American neighborhood on Chicago's South Side; Sister M. Theresa Dudzik, a Polish immigrant and founder of the Franciscan Sisters of Chicago, who opened a rescue mission in the 1880s; urban evangelist Mary Everhart, who opened the Olive Branch Mission in 1893, which continued a longstanding tradition of ministering to the homeless; and women such as Louise deKoven Bowen, whose interest in protecting youth in the cities was directed to legislation to close dance halls. Providing an increasing number of independent women workers with appropriate housing and recreation also had moral overtones, even when such projects were undertaken by social reformers who advocated the emancipation of women. Ina Law Robertson established Eleanor Clubs, low-cost boarding houses for single working women that provided safe homes and a Christian atmosphere. In the African American community, clubwomen Elizabeth Lindsay Davis and Fannie Emanuel, a medical practitioner, provided black single working women with housing in the Phyllis Wheatley Club, which opened in 1896.

THE CLUBWOMAN AS CAREER PROFESSIONAL: THE CASE OF PHYSICIANS

Characteristic of the emerging woman's culture of the 1880s was the way in which the first generation of women in the fields of law, journalism, medicine, religion, and in the academy maintained connections with women's organizations not related to professional advancement per se as well as with the suffrage movement. Women physicians, lawyers, and university professors played prominent roles in the Chicago Woman's Club. Conversely, such organizations as the Illinois Woman's Press Association, founded in 1885, or the Cordon Club, founded in 1915, while focused on the advancement of women's careers in journalism and art, respectively, had a broad membership of women from the larger woman's movement. Another way of looking at the cross membership of women is the way in which middle-class women supported women's trade union organizations, for example, the Women's Trade Union League (WTUL), founded in 1903. Trade union women such as Agnes Nestor played important roles in the suffrage movement in Illinois and in the League of Women Voters of Illinois after the passage of the Nineteenth Amendment in 1920. There were serious divisions and class conflicts, however, that made such alliances precarious and often short-lived. An examination of the way in which the first generation of women physicians participated in the social and political ferment of the woman's movement helps define the nature of the first wave of feminism in the United States.

Women doctors' intellectual achievements and consummate professional work ethic could not compensate for the conventional attitudes of both women and men to female practitioners. They constructed careers as physicians out of the women's movement in which they were activists. Clubwomen offered them support, both financial and in terms of acceptance and status; they in turn provided professional expertise and were able to guide women's political culture toward women's and children's health care agendas. Women's culture campaigned for public health programs, and clubwomen (career volunteers) raised funds to establish nursing schools and hospitals where women doctors could practice. Women physicians such as Sara Hackett Stevenson, Julia Holmes Smith, Frances Dickinson, and Lucy Waite, and women lawyers, artists, and social activists established the Queen Isabella Association in 1889. Stevenson, Dickinson, Smith, and Waite were leaders in the Chicago

Woman's Club. Stevenson became president of the medical staff of the Frances E. Willard National Temperance Hospital when it opened in 1886. She had joined the WCTU in 1881 and served as the first superintendent of its department of hygiene, responsible for publicizing the negative effects of alcohol on health. Julia Holmes Smith was president of the Chicago Woman's Club, presided over the biennial meeting of the Association for the Advancement of Women in Chicago, and served on Julia Ward Howe's Woman's Committee at the World's Industrial and Cotton Centennial Exposition in New Orleans in 1884–85. She became director in 1886 of the Illinois Training School for Nurses, founded in 1880 by a group of clubwomen led by Lucy Coues Flower to train working women for a profession and to supply trained nurses to the poor.

In the field of medicine the career pattern for women differed substantially from that of men. Mary Harris Thompson graduated from New England Female Medical College, Boston, Massachusetts, in 1863 and selected Chicago as a place of opportunity where an ambitious new doctor could overcome the disabilities of her sex; Thompson promoted the education of women doctors. Not only were women denied access to most male schools of medicine, but those who were able to graduate from the minority of schools in the United States that took both women and men or who had the opportunity to study abroad where there were opportunities for women, were refused hospital privileges. Women graduating from female colleges of medicine often sought another M.D. degree from either a European school of medicine or a coeducational school in the United States perceived to be more "reputable." The first and second generations of women doctors were activists in establishing hospitals and schools of medicine for women, in creating separate societies for women physicians, and in pushing for removal of the limitations that kept them on the margins of male-dominated institutions. They were also activists who participated in the new woman's movement, taking leadership roles in clubs and reform societies and volunteering their expertise and time in clinics and agencies to protect and care for women and children. They wrote textbooks, delivered scientific papers, and published their findings on medical issues and public health. Mary Harris Thompson's initial involvement in Chicago was with the Sanitary Commission, where she became convinced that the city needed a hospital for women and children. Through her efforts the Chicago Hospital for Women and Children (in 1895 renamed the Mary Thompson Hospital of Chicago for Women and Children) was opened May 8, 1865.

Following the pattern of many women in medicine, Thompson sought advanced training at Rush Medical College, but like Catharine Van Valkenburg Waite, who had been rejected by Rush in 1866, Thompson was turned away. Rush's rival, Chicago Medical College, was willing to accept Thompson as a result of the efforts of a liberal faculty member, Dr. William H. Byford. He encouraged Thompson to establish a women's medical college in connection with the Chicago Hospital for Women and Children and, in 1870, under Byford's direction, the Woman's Hospital Medical College opened (it was renamed Chicago Woman's Medical College in 1879). Thompson taught hygiene and obstetrics and gynecology. Marie Josepha Mergler also graduated from the Woman's Medical College; but

although she finished first in the exam for appointment as intern at the Cook County Insane Asylum at Dunning, she did not receive the appointment. She went to Switzerland for postgraduate work in clinical medicine and pathology at Zurich. Frances Dickinson interned at Women's and Children's Hospital under Mary Harris Thompson and studied at the Illinois Eye and Ear Infirmary, then at the Royal Ophthalmic Hospital, London, where women had just been admitted in 1883. She then worked with Dr. Adolph Weber, an internationally known ophthalmologist in Darmstadt, Germany.

In a world where the professionalization of medicine was itself in flux, women could make strides in alternative medicine. Julia Holmes Smith completed her medical education at the Chicago Homeopathic College and practiced homeopathic medicine for the next forty years. Homeopathy was a more hospitable field for women and in the late nineteenth century was considered by many to be a legitimate alternative to allopathic medicine. Alice Stockham also graduated from the Chicago Homeopathic College. Smith and Stockham were critical of standard medicine, especially the treatment of women's diseases. Stockham's book, *Tokology: A Book for Every Woman* (1883), was a manual on women's health and pregnancy that sold 160,000 copies by 1891 and, six years later, was in its forty-fifth edition.

Sarah Hackett Stevenson's career, on the other hand, was equal to that of many men in the medical field. Initially benefiting from Thompson's pioneering efforts, Stevenson graduated with highest honors from Woman's Hospital Medical College in 1874. The next year she traveled extensively in Europe for postgraduate study, visiting several hospitals in Dublin and London; while in the latter city, she studied under scientists Thomas Huxley and Charles Darwin. Back in Chicago in 1875, she was appointed to the physiology chair at the Woman's Hospital Medical College and elected to membership in the Illinois State Medical Society. Illinois Governor John Beveridge sent her as a delegate to the First Sanitary Conference in Vienna. In 1876 she attended the convention of the American Medical Association (AMA) in Philadelphia as an alternate delegate and, when the delegate was unable to attend, took his place and became the first woman member. An exception was made for Stevenson, and she remained the only woman in the AMA until it formally accepted women members in 1915. Stevenson was the first woman appointed to the staff of Cook County Hospital in 1881.

BLACK WOMEN PROFESSIONALS IN THE 1880S AND 1890S

The biographies of two of the first generation of new black women professionals demonstrate that race rather than class or education predetermined the outcomes for African Americans in this country. In 1894 Ida Platt became the first African American woman to earn her Illinois law license. African American men were allowed to enter the legal profession four years before white women were, yet the number of black men admitted to practice law in Illinois increased slowly. Platt remained the sole African American woman lawyer in the state until 1920, when Violette Anderson graduated from Chicago Law School (later

Kent College of Law). In 1887 Harriet Rice was the first African American woman to graduate from Wellesley College. She earned her medical degree at the Women's Medical College of New York Infirmary for Women and Children in 1891 and, after postgraduate work in New York and Philadelphia, resettled in 1893 in Chicago, where she took up residence at Hull-House. Both Platt and Rice had experienced little race prejudice as children and young adolescents; they came from black families with long traditions of freedom and professionalism in communities where they were part of a small minority. Rice and Platt had little reason to doubt that they would be judged by their individual achievement and were not prepared for the realities of race discrimination and prejudice that they experienced as professional women. They were not, however, willing to become "race women," as the generation of black clubwomen saw themselves. Rice and Platt both resisted working in all-black institutions or for black clients.

THE ILLINOIS WOMAN'S ALLIANCE

By the 1880s and 1890s, women's professional organizations, clubs, benevolent missions, trade unions, and political equality organizations were an indication of the scope of women's participation in public affairs and the mainstream economy. Much remained to be accomplished, however. The Seneca Falls declaration had been conceived in the world of agrarian America at the dawn of urban, industrial society. The rights discussions in which women engaged in the 1880s reflected the changed context; in addition to their continued interest in legal or political rights for themselves, the vast majority of women had begun to think about the ways in which women and children were disproportionately damaged by industrial and urban conditions. An agenda of protection emerged in the 1880s: Frances E. Willard introduced an entire platform of demands under the heading "Home Protection"; Ellen Henrotin and Sarah Hackett Stevenson of the Chicago Woman's Club created the Protective Agency for Women and Children in 1886, and by 1889 it had become an independent institution functioning as a legal-aid bureau successfully filing court claims in cases of wife abuse, desertion, and divorce. By 1896, with the help of women lawyers, the agency had collected $1,249,000 in fraud, injustice, and divorce cases from 7,197 complaints.

Concern for the well-being of working women reached a peak in the summer of 1888 when a series of exposés on the city's sweatshops appeared in the *Chicago Times*. Responding to a call from two socialist women, Elizabeth Morgan and Corinne Stubbs Brown, leaders of the Ladies' Federal Labor Union No. 2703, members of the Chicago Woman's Club, and around thirty other women's organizations had formed the Illinois Woman's Alliance (IWA), a cross-class coalition, by November. The IWA put forward counterproposals that questioned *laissez-faire* capitalism and called for the state to take responsibility for minimal standards of public welfare. The groups represented in the IWA reveal how the movement for women's rights and professional opportunities had now expanded to include in its agenda a strong social justice component. The first coordinating committee included Corinne Brown as chair, representing the

Ladies' Federal Labor Union (LFLU). The daughter of a skilled worker, Brown was a former teacher and principal in the Chicago public school system who had married a prominent banker; her involvement in the LFLU was part of a pattern of support and participation by middle-class women in the early organization of women's trade unions in Chicago. Caroline Alden Huling, of the Cook County Suffrage Association, was a new career woman who arrived in Chicago in 1884 to attend a national suffrage convention and remained to make her way as a self-supporting journalist. Her father had owned a newspaper and publishing firm in upstate New York, and the family's political connections to then-governor Grover Cleveland made possible Caroline Huling's appointment as notary public. She was one of the first women to hold the position in the state. Huling had just attended the International Council of Women conference held in Washington, D.C., in March 1888 and was a link between Chicago and the women's movement internationally. Fannie Barrier Williams, a leader in the black clubwoman movement in Chicago, also participated in the IWA; between 1891 and 1894, she held almost every office including vice-president and secretary. In 1894 she was head of the Alliance's Committee on State Schools for Children. Her participation in the IWA is noteworthy since her proposed membership in 1894 in the Chicago Woman's Club took fifteen months to confirm because of bitter debates among the all-white membership.

The IWA's practical agenda endorsed a variety of legislative initiatives and city programs that, taken together, aimed to eliminate the sweatshop system. The women understood that factory inspection alone could not end some of the worst aspects of the system. It was necessary to remove children from the workplace and put them in schools, and demands were made for new schools, compulsory education laws, and the prohibition of child labor. The IWA also addressed the issue of police victimization of prostitutes and demanded an end to the double standard under which women were convicted of prostitution while the men who engaged in sex for money remained anonymous and went unpunished.

In 1892 the Alliance broadened to include Hull-House residents Alzina Parsons Stevens and Florence Kelley; the former had returned to Chicago where earlier she had organized the Working Women's Union; the latter, the daughter of a prominent Pennsylvania industrialist and politician, had become a socialist while in graduate school in Zurich, Switzerland, and had recently moved to the city from New York. The Chicago Trades and Labor Assembly, Hull-House residents, the IWA, and well-known radicals such as Henry Demarest Lloyd successfully pressured the state legislature to pass the Illinois Factory and Inspection Act (also known as the Sweatshop Act) in 1893; the act set sanitary standards for the workplace, prohibited the employment of children under age fourteen in any manufacturing enterprises, limited the daily working hours of females to eight, and increased the enforcement powers of factory inspectors. Governor John P. Altgeld appointed Kelley chief inspector and Stevens assistant inspector. Although the Illinois Supreme Court overturned the eight-hour clause of the 1893 Sweatshop Act in 1895, the legislation was a significant victory for organized women workers and social reformers. In 1894 the IWA dissolved over internal tensions between working-class and middle-class segments of the organization. There would be other attempts at alliances between working-class women and middle-class allies, notably in the Women's Trade Union League; but issues of class presented serious challenges to the vision of a united womanhood. Male-dominated trade unionism showed ambivalence if not outright distrust of efforts to organize women, especially those engaged in unskilled jobs. First-wave social feminists such as Mary E. McDowell, Margaret Dreier Robins, and Florence Kelley argued that their support was crucial in the early years of women's trade union organizing.

While the IWA did not last, it was, for women in Illinois, one of the first expressions of a political and social philosophy that would be most extensively implemented during the Progressive Era. The IWA's three fundamental principles—written in 1891—summarize the philosophy of the social feminists who became the leaders of organized women in Chicago from 1890 to 1920: first, "the actual status of the poorest and most unfortunate woman in society determines the possible status of every woman" (Meredith Tax, *The Rising of the Women: Feminist Solidarity and Class Conflict, 1880–1917* [1980], 71). This concept of reciprocal social responsibility and an awareness of interdependence between labor and capital, rich and poor, immigrant and American-born was further elucidated and implemented through the leadership of Jane Addams. With Ellen Gates Starr, Addams had founded the Hull-House Settlement in 1889. The second concept was the belief that "the civilization of the future depends upon the present condition of the children" (p. 71). As a consequence of this view, different branches of organized womanhood sought to accomplish their goals through the education of the child in the broadest sense, an education that included the construction of appropriate moral and physical environments in which children and adolescents would thrive. The third principle held that "public money and public officials must serve public ends" (p. 71). Rejecting the idea of a limited role for government, women's organizations demanded that public monies be spent appropriately and efficiently for the common good. Women had to involve themselves in the political process; woman suffrage had become a vehicle for achieving reform of society rather than an end in itself.

THE WORLD'S COLUMBIAN EXPOSITION OF 1893: ISABELLAS AND LADY MANAGERS

Women looked to the World's Columbian Exposition of 1893 as an opportunity to demonstrate their intellectual and cultural accomplishments. The exposition was also an opportunity to forge connections nationally and internationally with likeminded women.

How and in what context women would participate in the World's Columbian Exposition became a divisive issue for different groups, and it reflected many of the tensions and growing pains of the women's movement itself. Did married, white, privileged clubwomen such as Bertha Honoré Palmer and Ellen Martin Henrotin speak for all women? Were black clubwomen to be included on boards and committees? Should Jewish women participate on a religious basis or as another "branch" of women's clubs? Should women have their own separate build-

ing at the fair or participate in all of the exhibits alongside men? Women had begun to plan for their participation in the exposition as early as 1889, when the Queen Isabella Association was established. Drs. Julia Holmes Smith, Sarah Hackett Stevenson, and Frances Dickinson, lawyer Catharine Van Valkenburg Waite, and poet and Catholic art expert Eliza Allen Starr were active Isabellas and argued that women's representation at the exposition should be integrated into all the exhibition halls and displays along with the works of men, not separated into a building solely for woman's work. Starr's Isabella of Castile was published in 1889 and made the case for the significance of the female ruler of Spain in the exploration and discovery of the New World. As the Isabellas worked toward their goal of inclusion and integration, Bertha Palmer had the inside track on control of women's representation. She and her husband, well-known business leader Potter Palmer, had been busily engaged with other influential Chicagoans in making certain that their city was the site chosen for the Columbian Exposition. Bertha Palmer steered a moderate course in her role as head of the Board of Lady Managers. The women had been appointed by the Fair Commission in 1890 and had as their major task approval of applications for exhibition space in the women's pavilion.

Palmer resolutely held fast to the concept of a separate woman's building where exhibits by women would be displayed without a political context or any discussion of suffrage or the women's rights movement. Unable to persuade Palmer and the managers to integrate women's work into men's exhibits, the Isabellas, through their Physicians Publishing Company, financed the construction of their own building, the Isabella Hotel and Club House. In the end, the lawyers and physicians who were Isabellas and had fought for full and equal inclusion of women were as removed from the major exhibits as was the Woman's Building. Dr. Julia Holmes Smith, when the Isabellas lost their argument, organized a model hospital and emergency clinic for women and children at the exposition. This exhibit had a building of its own with a model hospital, up-to-date operating room, diet kitchen, office and reception room, a section of a children's ward and women's ward, and a private room for patients. Julia Smith, Dr. Sarah Stevenson, and others recruited volunteer women homeopathic, allopathic, and eclectic doctors, as well as nurses from the Illinois Training School for Nurses to staff the clinic, which treated more than three thousand patients during the exposition. Every attempt to penetrate male-dominated organizations forced women into the creation of separate associations. Julia Smith was the only woman on the committee that was organizing the Homeopathic Physicians and Surgeons Congress and eventually became the head of the Woman's Committee of the same congress. Women lawyers experienced a similar fate. Attorney Ellen Martin, a vice-president of the board of directors and chair of the legal department of the Isabellas, organized a meeting of women lawyers in August 1893; fourteen prominent women attorneys spoke on a variety of topics. Martin, whose private practice in downtown Chicago was a model of achievement even by male professional standards, felt it necessary to cofound the National League of Women Lawyers to promote the interests of women in the practical work of the legal profession and also to found the Chicago

Political Equality League with Catharine McCulloch and other Chicago Woman's Club activists.

The organizational politics and representational dilemmas of women in 1893 clarified for many equal rights activists and professionals the need to battle for advancement in every arena. The case of women artists makes this clear. By 1893, membership in the all-women Palette Club included more than seventy women, one-third of whom had studied abroad. The World's Columbian Exposition served as a vehicle for success for individual members as well as for the club as a whole. The all-male jury, established to select work to be exhibited in the Palace of Fine Arts, chose 520 painters and sculptors, 104 of whom were women. Of these women, eight were members of the Palette Club.

AFRICAN AMERICAN WOMEN AND THE WORLD'S COLUMBIAN EXPOSITION

Other divisions among women also surfaced. There were no African American board members, and no provisions were made for the inclusion of exhibits from black women. An ad hoc group of black women requested that an office be established to collect exhibits from "colored" women in the United States. Instead of creating the proposed office, the Fair Commission appointed a black woman, Chicagoan Fannie Barrier Williams, to assist in supervising the installation of exhibits in the Woman's Building. Williams also served as secretary of the art department of the women's branch of the congress auxiliaries held in conjunction with the World's Columbian Exposition. While Ida B. Wells expressed outright criticism of the exclusion of black Americans from the exposition—at the exposition Wells distributed her pamphlet *The Reason Why the Colored American Is Not in the World's Columbian Exposition*—Williams's connections with white clubwomen and more conciliatory approach were evident in the two addresses she delivered at the exposition, the first at the World's Congress of Representative Women, the second at the World's Parliament of Religions, where she was one of five African American women to speak.

THE WORLD'S PARLIAMENT OF RELIGIONS

Since 1848, when one of the resolutions at Seneca Falls called for overthrowing the monopoly of the religious pulpit by men, women had continued to exercise marginal leadership at the ministerial level in religious institutions dominated by men. Events in 1893 may have provided a falsely optimistic picture of progress in women's long struggle for equality in the polity and ministry of the different Protestant denominations and in the liberal movement in Judaism because so many women engaged in the World's Parliament of Religions and related congresses. They included Universalist ministers Augusta J. Chapin and Olympia Brown and Universalist lay leader Julia Ward Howe; ordained Unitarian women Celia Parker Woolley, Ida Hultin, and Marion Murdock; lay Methodist leader and Woman's Christian Temperance Union president Frances E. Willard. Clubwoman Fannie Barrier Williams spoke on "Religion's Duty to the Negro." Two Jewish women, Josephine Lazarus and Henrietta Szold, addressed the parliament, and the Congress of

Jewish Women, organized by Hannah Solomon and Sadie American, was held in conjunction with the parliament. Solomon and American favored the ordination of women as rabbis and both had delivered lectures from the pulpit at Chicago Congregation Sinai, a leading temple in the liberal Reform movement in Judaism. On the recommendation of Chapin, as chair of the Woman's Committee of the World's Congress Auxiliary, women members of the Theosophical Society spoke at the Theosophical Congress held at the World's Parliament of Religions. Emma Curtis Hopkins's students in the Hopkins Metaphysical Association formed the Columbian Congress of Christian Scientists (New Thought) to interact with the women's organizations affiliated with the Queen Isabella Association.

NATIONALIZING TRENDS IN WOMEN'S ORGANIZATIONS

The 1893 World's Columbian Exposition accelerated trends already emerging in the multifaceted infrastructure of women's organizations. The General Federation of Women's Clubs (GFWC), with a membership of 185 clubs located in twenty-nine different states, had its first biennial convention in Chicago in 1892. The exposition became a vehicle for the implementation of nationalizing trends in women's separate organizations: Sadie American presented a speech, "Organization," on the final day of the Congress of Jewish Women, in which she elaborated a plan for an organization called the National Council of Jewish Women; the first official meeting of the International Kindergarten Union was held during the exposition; the National Convention of Women's Amateur Musical Clubs met (Rose Fay Thomas was head of the Committee on Representation of Women's Amateur Musical Clubs); Ellen Henrotin, whose belief in the power of women's associations was strong, helped to found several organizations at the 1893 women's congresses, including the National Household Economic Association, the National League of Roman Catholic Women, the International League of Lutheran Women, and the League of Superintendents of Manual Training Schools. Under the aegis of the Woman's Branch of the Congress Auxiliary of the Columbian Exposition, 210 congresses were scheduled; Bertha Palmer was president of the body of congresses, but Ellen Henrotin served as vice-president and chief executive. The women's congresses, like the women's clubs, were divided into departments, with Mary Wilmarth running education, Lucy Flower heading moral and social reform, Jane Addams coordinating social settlements, and Ellen Henrotin managing the labor congress.

WOMEN AND WORK

One of the messages that ran through many of the congresses and meetings of women was that women were in the labor market to stay—as factory workers, professionals, and even as financial investors and owners of property—with the potential to influence the relationship of labor and capital. Ellen Henrotin, who became president of the General Federation of Women's Clubs in 1894 and during her presidency supported uniform state labor legislation, improvement of the state educational systems, the eight-hour working day for women, and women's business clubs committed to cooperation and self-support, called for financial independence for women. In a speech, "The Financial Independence of Women," Henrotin elaborated on a theme she had introduced earlier: wealthy women had responsibilities in society and should use their privilege to effect moral and social reform. She explained that women were emerging from the domestic sphere and entering the business and labor market, earning money, and investing hundreds of millions of dollars in building and loan associations and real estate. Instead of depicting women as victims of discrimination or as selfless benevolent workers, Henrotin argued that women had power that they had not yet marshaled and used. Women needed to vote their own stock, to become corporate directors, and to learn to manage their own financial affairs. Even Bertha Palmer, still sitting on the fence regarding support of woman suffrage in 1893, took the opportunity of her opening remarks at the dedication of the World's Columbian Exposition, October 21, 1892, to promote women's material interests and women's industrial equality and to call for equitable compensation for services rendered. Such statements reflected the growing reality that women were, in fact, a presence in the labor force.

Historian Joanne Meyerowitz has estimated that 3,800 wage-earning women lived independently in Chicago in 1880 and that the entire female labor force in the city that year was 35,600. By 1910 the number of wage-earning women living independently in Chicago had grown to approximately 31,500, and the percentage of women heading households had increased from 5 percent in 1880 to 13 percent in 1910. The steady increase in women entering the work force continued. From 1880 to 1930, the female labor force in Chicago increased more than 1,000 percent; this rate of increase was three times as great as the rate of increase of the female labor force for the nation as a whole.

In addition, between 1900 and 1910 more than six million immigrants arrived in the United States, adding to the millions of immigrants who had settled in America between 1860 and 1900. No more than one-third of the immigrants went into farming or related activities after 1900; instead, they went to the already congested cities. In cities like Chicago, immigrants and their children were the overwhelming majority of residents. Citizenship questions were immediately apparent to women activists, whose engagement in suffrage and women's legal rights advocacy made them sensitive to the ways in which immigration law affected women and children differently from men. Social control issues in urban areas seemed more complicated and threatening to so-called American values because of high rates of immigration. From this viewpoint, urban America did not resemble the New England village or the midwest town.

WOMEN AND MODERNIZATION

For many women the way to deal with industrial America was to educate young women and mothers in scientific methods of child development, household economy, and sanitation, and to obtain legislation to build healthy environments in the city.

Not only did women see themselves as entering the mainstream of economic life, they defined their contributions to society in the broadest sense as a belief in progress. Women demonstrated not only receptivity to modernization but leadership in forging an industrial society in which technology and innovation would be used not only to build private fortunes but to create the good society. The sources for women's interest in modernizing the American city were diverse. The tradition of Christian moral benevolence, reshaped to include trained deaconesses and churchworkers, led to the institutional expansion of modern health care in the United States and abroad. New women professionals created training schools and modern institutions to deal with urban industrial problems. And, as noted, the merging of social science and social reform in the approaches of the varied organizations that made up the women's political movement in the Progressive Era advanced the trends of modernization a thousandfold in the cities of the United States.

Women on the political Left contributed to the modernization of industrial society. Mary Walden Kerr's monthly column of advice, "The Home," published in Charles H. Kerr's *New Times*, emphasized the need for rational action in the life of each and every home. A socialist, Mary Kerr's approach was reminiscent of the writings of such other women reformers as Mary Livermore, whose article "Cooperative Womanhood in the State," in the *North American Review* (1891), postulated a new period of progress and harmony in which women and men would adopt more nurturing, harmonious, and rational or scientific solutions in both the public and private spheres. So extensive was the acceptance of the need for social planning among leaders in the progressive women's political culture that the major antisuffrage leader in the Midwest, Caroline Fairfield Corbin, was initially sympathetic to the woman suffrage movement. Her first book, *Rebecca, or A Woman's Secret*, published in 1867, supported women's rights. In 1888 she had a change of heart and wrote two pamphlets addressed to Frances E. Willard, whose leadership of the Woman's Christian Temperance Union had merged temperance reform with advocacy of woman suffrage and, in her agenda to reform society, introduced socialism to otherwise conservative, middle-class white married women. Willard's Christian socialism, an expression of the Social Gospel, was widely held by many women who found Edward Bellamy's utopian novel *Looking Backward: 2000–1887* (1888) the expression of a possible new cooperative order for society. According to Bellamy, private enterprise, shown as a wasteful system fostering inequality and poverty, would give way to the collective organization of the state in an evolutionary, nonviolent, rational process in which women were equal and involved in the leadership of society. Nationalist Clubs—advocating the transformation of American society along the lines of Bellamy's vision of a cooperative order—flourished in the 1890s with significant women's membership and leadership. In post-Haymarket Chicago, Corbin, however, associated socialism with the anarchists and Marxists whose views, she believed, were potentially violent and lured women from the home. Corbin, who founded the Illinois Association Opposed to the Extension of Suffrage to Women in 1897, was a Social Darwinist who believed that the progress of society depended on the differentiated roles of men and women within the family.

MUNICIPAL HOUSEKEEPING AND MODERNIZATION

Chicago and other American cities engaged in a modernization process of great breadth and scope. Women's clubs and political organizations and coalitions forged alliances that promoted modernization.

In the area of education, women activists engaged in political activity to advance women's involvement in the administration of public schools and in support of child labor laws; women were leaders in curricular innovation that included kindergartens, household arts, vocational education for girls as well as boys, physical education, parenting education, sex education, special education for handicapped children, occupational therapy, "Americanization" classes for immigrants, vacation schools, and school gardens. Agnes Nestor was named to the federal Commission on Vocational Education that shaped the Smith-Hughes Act of 1917; the act provided the first federal aid to vocational education. Structural innovations in the field of education included visiting nurses, visiting teachers, school physicians, vocational guidance, employment bureaus, development of schools as community centers, and school libraries. And there were efforts to address physical concerns: better school buildings, sanitation in schools, and better design, decoration, furnishing as a means to aesthetic development.

In the category of public health, women's political activity included support for the federal Children's Bureau; regulation of milk supplies; pure food and drug legislation; slaughterhouse monitoring; regulation of perceived health hazards, including cigarettes; and support for housing legislation and studies of occupational health hazards. In 1892 Ada Celeste Sweet founded the Municipal Order League of Chicago and served as its first president. Sweet was dedicated to cleaning up the city and successfully lobbied for a department of street cleaning, instead of private contractors, and for municipal incineration of garbage. In 1911 Ethel Sturges Dummer financed a trip to European cities by Mary E. McDowell, who studied those cities' waste disposal procedures. Upon McDowell's return, she put together a coalition of supporters drawn from the male City Club and Citizens' Association, the University of Chicago faculty, the Chicago Woman's Club, and the new Woman's City Club. They demanded that Chicago improve its method of collecting trash and garbage and build either incinerators or reduction plants to dispose of waste. After Chicago women secured municipal suffrage in 1913, Mayor Carter Harrison appointed a City Waste Commission that included McDowell and promised money to hire sanitary engineers to devise a solution to Chicago's garbage disposal problem. The commission's recommendations were followed and open dumps were finally phased out.

Women also founded hospitals, premature infant stations, dental clinics, free dispensaries, well-baby clinics, ambulance services, tuberculosis sanitariums, open-air schools, district nurses, baby-saving conferences and expositions, school lunch programs, public baths, and public laundries.

Related to the issue of public health was the campaign against infectious diseases and the "social evils" of prostitution and venereal disease. Women supported the work of the Chicago Vice Commission (on which Ellen Henrotin served),

the scientific study of prostitution and venereal disease, laws to raise the age of consent, and laws to close houses of prostitution. Sadie American represented the National Council of Jewish Women at the International Anti-White Slavery Conference. Rejecting the sexual double standard, women monitored judicial decisions relating to prostitutes and threatened the recall of judges whom they took to be prejudiced against women. Institutions that dealt with issues of prostitution included the Immigrants' Protective League, the Juvenile Protective League, detention homes for delinquent girls, and committees on sex hygiene.

Women offered positive approaches to the prevention of juvenile delinquency and fought for legislation to regulate dance halls and motion pictures and to support public financing of recreation. They advocated the building of playgrounds, formed working girls' clubs and societies, and recreation centers for working women. They developed drama and pageant as alternative forms of recreation. Women worked in corrections and prevention as probation officers, police matrons, and policewomen. They advocated the creation of juvenile courts and reformatory institutions, and they conducted investigations of prisons and advocated prison reform.

Women social reformers also took up the issue of race relations in American society. They studied foreign cultures, surveyed the industrial and educational problems of immigrant communities, studied the conditions of African Americans in cities, and held conferences on Americanization. Institutions such as settlement houses, the Immigrants' Protective League, and—in Chicago—the Frederick Douglass Center, the Abraham Lincoln Center (where Thyra Edwards was active), the Urban League, and the National Association for the Advancement of Colored People developed programs for assimilation and the improvement of race relations.

Women reformers pioneered in the expansion of social services. Organized women were the political force behind support for mothers' pensions. Women developed the National Consumers' League, state and national conferences for social service, Associated or United Charities, Jewish communal services, public health exhibits, and schools of social work.

Women were active in city planning. They demanded city parks and public beaches, creation of municipal art commissions, preservation of natural areas, and creation of city planning boards and metropolitan planning districts. In 1905 Helen Culver made a major donation to the City Club of Chicago to pay for the Merriam investigation of municipal government in Chicago. Civic Federation participants included Bertha Palmer, Jane Addams, and Ellen Henrotin.

HULL-HOUSE

The institution in Chicago that took a central role in linking all of the different elements of the progressive women's agenda was Hull-House. When Jane Addams and Ellen Gates Starr began to think about founding a settlement in a Chicago immigrant neighborhood, they presented their plans to leaders of the Chicago Woman's Club (CWC) in meetings at the homes of CWC leaders Mary J. Hawes Wilmarth and Lydia Coonley-Ward, where they received enthusiastic support for their proposal. Jane Addams and the Hull-House women were the "daughters," literally or figuratively, of the first generation of organized womanhood that included Mary Wilmarth and Lucy Flower. While some, like Addams, personally fought the "family claim," the women of her generation who sought careers and a different, more expanded relationship with public affairs were not necessarily in opposition to their mother's generation. Addams and her generation, however, wanted to express their commitment to social justice and religious values in new ways, and this required carving out new institutions in which women could legitimate their interests and lifestyles outside traditional family arrangements. Addams and Starr wanted to have an impact on the industrial and political problems of their society; in the context of Victorian society, they had to overcome conventional boundaries and leave the traditional sphere of women's activities. Historians, including Kathryn Kish Sklar, Helen Horowitz, and Robyn Muncy, have shown how Hull-House became, among other things, a new space for women.

Within a short time, Hull-House became a central link between the larger movement for women's advancement in society and the new social science disciplines (political science, sociology, psychology, and anthropology). One result of this interaction was the development of new practical schools for training in social work, public health, occupational and recreational therapy, and pedagogy. Hull-House women had a significant role in creating these institutions. Addams and Starr were soon joined by Julia C. Lathrop and Florence Kelley. After 1900, Edith Abbott, Alice Hamilton, Sophonisba Breckinridge, and Grace Abbott became residents. Lathrop and Kelley were, like Addams and Starr, educated women without professional jobs or affiliations. Kelley had graduated from Cornell University but had to go to Europe to pursue graduate studies; Lathrop graduated from Vassar College, then returned home and read law informally in her father's office. At Hull-House they functioned the way social policy specialists interested in gender and class issues might operate out of a university-affiliated institute, a government agency, or perhaps, a foundation or not-for-profit interest group. Hull-House provided the collective authority for innovation. Abbott, Hamilton, and Breckinridge later brought the Hull-House point of view back to the university and, as a result of the historical conditions present there, were reasonably successful in creating "institutional space" for the production of research and scholarly books noteworthy for their focus on women's issues. But they were forced to do so in separate women's departments such as household economy (home economics) rather than in the economics and political science departments where they had been awarded doctorates. Still, much of what we know about women in the labor market and women's legal disabilities as immigrants comes from the work of Abbott and Breckinridge. Hamilton developed the field of occupational medicine and industrial toxicology and was the first woman on the faculty of Harvard University. One could make the case, however, that it was Hull-House and its climate of research combined with social activism rather than the medical school community that was most influential in Hamilton's understanding of the relationship of the environment to disease. While conducting research on antibodies and on scarlet fever and other diseases, she concentrated at Hull-House on public

health efforts that allied her with progressive medical and lay circles. In 1909 she studied sixteen hundred working-class families and found that high infant mortality rates correlated with high birth rates. Hamilton worked in the initial phase of the Chicago birth control movement, led by gynecologist Rachelle Yarros. These experiences provided the context for Hamilton's growing awareness of the environmental causes of disease.

Breckinridge and Abbott received their advanced degrees at the University of Chicago; the former received a Ph.D. in political science in 1901 and a J.D. degree in 1904; the latter completed her dissertation, "The Wages of Unskilled Labor in the United States, 1850–1900," and received a Ph.D. with honors in 1905. Despite Breckinridge's graduation summa cum laude in both political science and law, no academic position was offered to her, while male students went to positions on college or university faculties. Her opportunity for research and teaching came first through Hull-House, where the new Chicago School of Civics and Philanthropy (CSCP), an early social work school (later the School of Social Service Administration at the University of Chicago), was housed. In 1908 it moved to larger quarters adjoining the Immigrants' Protective League office, another Hull-House spin-off. This arrangement facilitated interaction as well as collaborative research between the two agencies. In 1907 Julia Lathrop, temporarily the director of research at CSCP, asked Breckinridge to take that position. Edith Abbott accepted their offer to be assistant director of research at CSCP.

Universities did not have a monopoly on social science research in the 1890s or the first two decades of the twentieth century. Hull-House, for example, was able to produce an extraordinarily successful work of scholarship in 1895 with the publication of the historic *Hull-House Maps and Papers*. Kathryn Kish Sklar has called the book a work of "female social science," since it was the product of the Hull-House women and reflected the new women's agenda. In it the social feminist women of Hull-House began to define an agenda for social science as well as a plan of social activism that overlapped with the Chicago Woman's Club's agenda; but they were doing something new. They were staking out a new realm for the production of knowledge in society; twenty years later, the existence of this alternative place for the development of social policy initiatives would influence the shaping of academic departments and professional schools at the University of Chicago. These women also implicitly established the value, indeed the necessity, of a relationship between the realms of knowledge and of politics and practical activity. Five of the ten articles in the Hull-House book focused on what might be called female-specific issues: sweatshop labor; Cook County charities; child labor; labor organizations for working women; a description of the work of Hull-House residents. The maps themselves were based on data collected by agents employed by the U.S. Department of Labor under the direction of Florence Kelley.

The fact that this work emanated from Hull-House gave it independence from the male-dominated departments at the University of Chicago and allowed for a focus on women and children. Residents of the Hull-House settlement believed that research was done to serve those in need and to heal social problems. The opposite, pure research removed from any social content, would not have been valorized by Addams and the other residents, who commented negatively on those who did not have "the settlement spirit" and worked individualistically or for personal gain.

Hull-House was a place for women who remained marginalized in the university environment. But the settlement was not the full extent of the connection university women maintained with organized womanhood and the woman's movement. Women were better educated by the late nineteenth century, but they remained underemployed. The discrimination against women physicians, lawyers, and Ph.D. holders and their virtual exclusion from employment in male-controlled institutions meant that college graduates and professionals continued to participate in the agencies of organized womanhood, such as the Chicago Woman's Club, and to be involved in the politics of the woman's movement. Activist members of the Chicago Woman's Club's ranged from birth control advocate and physician Rachelle Yarros to the first woman elected judge in Cook County, Mary Bartelme. She became president of the Chicago Suffrage Club in 1907, nine years after her appointment as public guardian of Cook County. Julia Lathrop retained her membership in separate woman's organizations before and after she was appointed the first director of the U.S. Children's Bureau in 1912, and she was one of the founders of the League of Women Voters. Jane Addams and other prominent settlement leaders were active, and university-attached women such as Sophonisba Breckinridge and Edith Abbott retained memberships in the separate woman's movement organizations long after they became professors at the University of Chicago.

Hull-House continued to support the research its women residents undertook; it also grew institutionally as an outcome of the implementation of social policy derived from the research. The Immigrants' Protective League and the Juvenile Protective Association were special interest agencies designed to deliver services. They were also part of the system of investigation, policy formation, and advocacy that characterized Hull-House enterprises. National legislation on immigration policy (the Cable Act) was influenced by the Immigrants' Protective League, and the Juvenile Protective Association spoke authoritatively on juvenile delinquency and its prevention.

Hull-House's encouragement of research into new areas led to the growth of the physical campus. The first building in the early years was adequate for readings in literature and the establishment of clubs; but soon the opening of a kindergarten and interest in art, theater, and music all required new space. The original Hull mansion was joined by a series of buildings that made up a complex of educational and philanthropic enterprises. When Addams and Starr moved in, they occupied only the second floor of the old building and had the use of the drawing room on the first floor. By spring they were able to lease the entire house. In 1891, they erected the Butler Art Gallery on adjacent property to the south. The building was a two-story structure that housed a branch of the public library and the art gallery and had space for clubs and classes. In 1892, the donation of dilapidated buildings—owned by businessman turned progressive reformer William Kent—in the immediate vicinity of Hull-House, made it possible to demolish the structures and construct the first public playground in Chicago, which was opened on May 1, 1892. In 1893 a second building was constructed with

a coffee house below and a gymnasium above. A third story was added to the Butler Art Gallery building in 1896 to provide rooms for men in residence; in 1898 a special building was erected for the Jane Club, a cooperative residence for working girls. A new coffeehouse, with a theater above it, was built in 1899, while the old coffeehouse and gymnasium were moved and remodeled. The next year the Hull-House Labor Museum was established. In 1908 the last of thirteen Hull-House buildings opened. Included in this complex were the offices of the Immigrants' Protective League and the Juvenile Protective Association; these "institutions" reflected the degree to which Hull-House initiated new areas of social enterprise.

Hull-House also made a lasting contribution to the University of Chicago: in 1920, Breckinridge and Abbott, who were convinced that a university was the proper place for a professional social work school, negotiated to move their school to the University of Chicago. In 1924, the new School of Social Service Administration (SSA) became a permanent entity of the University of Chicago and Edith Abbott was appointed dean. In 1927, Abbott and Breckinridge initiated the social work profession's first scholarly journal, *Social Service Review*, which published articles on social policy, social work research, and advances in social programs.

Between 1890 and 1920, social feminists in Chicago brought about a significant number of reforms that benefited women and children, including the establishment of the juvenile court system, minimal protection for women in industrial jobs, and the introduction of recreational and occupational therapy for inmates of institutions. They also produced some of the first works of research on gender topics. They had a permanent influence in the academy through their insistence on the necessity of a research component for the study of social work. They did not, however, bring the study of gender and women into the core social science departments of the university or rearrange the humanities curriculum; this assault on male-dominated disciplines of higher learning was left to Second Wave Feminists.

Considerable space has been given to Hull-House because so many activist women were either directly participating in the daily life of this settlement or had important connections to it. Additionally, many nationally prominent reformers, labor leaders, university and governmental policymakers, innovators in public health, and contributors to the arts were, in part, a product of the Hull-House experiment. Here, too, was a place where woman's culture interfaced with the male worlds of politics and labor. Here women reformers talked on equal terms with the leaders of male trade unions; with the male leaders of the Democratic, Republican, and Bull Moose (Progressive) Parties; with male philosophers and sociologists from the University of Chicago; and with distinguished male visitors from abroad. When women entered government at the city, state, or federal levels, they were often women whose associations with Hull-House were formative and lasting.

MADONNA CENTER

There were yet other arenas where women developed woman's culture. At the Guardian Angel Mission, which became the Madonna Center, the wealthy, Catholic, Amberg family attempted to be "good neighbors" to Catholic immigrants in the same geographic area in which Hull-House was located. Mary Amberg became resident director in 1914 and remained its head until her death in 1962. She flourished as a capable administrator and developed a model of independent social service outside the convent for Catholic single women. When Mary Amberg attended the Academy of the Sacred Heart run by the Mesdames of the Sacred Heart, a French order of nuns, she was taught about Catholic stewardship along lines that paralleled the stewardship and Christian womanhood model inculcated in Protestant women attending such institutions as the Rockford Female Seminary, which Jane Addams and Ellen Gates Starr attended.

After a soul-searching experience at age thirty-eight, when she confronted what she perceived as her lack of involvement in useful, productive work, Amberg struggled with values of womanhood, marriage, and career. She renounced marriage but did not seek a religious vocation. Instead she announced plans to join her friend Catherine Jordan and share an apartment in rooms above the classrooms of St. Francis School near Guardian Angel Mission. Amberg maintained friendly relations with Jane Addams but saw the institution's secular worldview as a challenge. The ultimate goal of Amberg's mission was to promote Catholic religious values; she broadened the center with funding from Chicago Catholics, including Frederick Siedenburg, dean of the Loyola University School of Sociology. Guardian Angel/Madonna Center accepted people of all faiths into its programs, but Catholic values permeated. It taught so-called "middle-class" habits of cleanliness, nutrition, and child care, but its clubs were religious and the classes began with prayer. Amberg attempted to Americanize Catholics and to reinforce traditional Catholic faith and allegiance to parish institutions at the same time. Amberg's ideas on women's issues were conservative. She condemned birth control; yet, as one of the first laywomen to spend her life doing social work, she pioneered this career for Catholic women. Madonna Center became a training center for Catholic students in social work, medicine, and domestic science.

GADS HILL CENTER

At Gads Hill Center, southwest of Hull-House, Ruth Inez Austin was head resident from 1914 to 1947. She wrote a textbook for teaching English to immigrants that showed enormous compassion for the immigrant woman's situation, and she used poetry written by women for women.

Gads Hill established some interesting group work with neighborhood "gangs" and children in the community, somewhat different from what Hull-House was doing. Austin instituted a myriad of social clubs for neighborhood children, young adults, and adults. Believing in the benefits of self-governance for the clubs as a preparation for citizenship, Austin established a governing board, the House Cabinet, and every social club elected three representatives to attend its monthly meetings. Gads Hill clubs worked out their annual budgets for recreational activities and other programs, set and collected dues, and took responsibility for themselves.

CATHOLIC WOMEN RELIGIOUS

In Chicago's Polish community in the St. Stanislaus Kostka parish, and in the German Catholic and Lithuanian ethnic neighborhoods, Catholic women religious were involved in the development of a religious culture that included both a belief system and a cultural heritage. They were also preparing their students for success in the American economy and were obliged to teach the ways of American citizenship. Little is known about the way in which parochial schools dealt with dual cultures, Americanization, and the preservation of ethnic culture and religion. Discussion of the diversity of ethnicity among Catholics has tended to center around the Irish American hierarchy's attempt to dismantle national/ethnic parishes and the reaction among different ethnic groups to this forced homogenization of practice and language. Many high-powered women religious (for example, Sister M. Cecilia Himebaugh, Mother Maria Kaupas, Sister Mary Innocenta Montay, Mother Imelda Fischer, and Sister Dolores Schorsch), whose work was largely in teacher training, curriculum development, and school administration, were engaged in fashioning programs that attempted to preserve cultural identity and to accommodate their students' needs to modern American society.

Nuns developed bilingual education and worked in a variety of media to encourage the education of immigrant children in two cultures, thereby bridging the worlds of Europe and America. The educational work done in parish schools and academies influenced the worldview of thousands of students and families; the involvement in teacher training also gave these nuns enormous opportunity to influence future generations of parochial school teachers and to model educational curricula along ideological and philosophical lines that they had considerable power to delineate.

In the case of the Franciscan Sisters of Chicago, a Polish order led by Sister M. Theresa Dudzik, the congregation of nuns (most of whom were immigrants themselves) focused on the training of new members and on their own charitable institutions; but the dramatic increase of Polish immigrants in Chicago and other urban centers brought the early Polish Catholic sisterhoods a new challenge—the education of children. Leaders of the growing Polish Catholic parishes wanted teaching sisters to educate students in the Catholic faith and in Polish history and language as well. Public school teachers were called in to prepare Franciscan sisters for placement in the expanding parochial elementary school programs. The sisters were also instructed by Polish scholars in the Polish language, literature, and culture. It was a strenuous program, and many of the young sisters were not much older than the students they taught.

CATHOLIC WOMEN AND EDUCATION

By the time of the World's Columbian Exposition in Chicago in 1893, Catholic Chicago's progress in establishing a system of parish schools was substantial. The archdiocese's displays at the exposition included a Catholic educational exhibit to which different parochial schools contributed examples of students' work. A chartered train took more than one thousand students enrolled in the Holy Family schools on Chicago's West Side to the fairgrounds to celebrate Catholic Education Day, September 2, 1893. After the exposition, Holy Family parish, one of the largest parishes in the world, was one of the popular Chicago sights that Catholic dignitaries visited.

Two Approaches to Secondary Education for Young Women:
St. Mary High School and Lucy Flower Technical
High School

In 1899 the Sisters of Charity of the Blessed Virgin Mary (BVM) were pioneers in developing secondary education for Catholic girls in Chicago and in the United States. The sisters' initial decisions about the goals of St. Mary High School had outcomes that were significant for the social mobility of an emerging American Catholic middle class and for American Catholicism.

St. Mary High School was inaugurated at the height of the debate over urban education and the role of the schools in the preparation of immigrants for the workplace and for their involvement as citizens. Institutions of secondary education were inadequate at the beginning of the twentieth century in both the public and the Catholic systems. In 1885 only 7 percent of American fourteen-to-seventeen-year-olds attended high school. At the turn of the century, secondary education remained an option for only a small segment of the population, whether American-born or immigrant. By 1904 Catholic educators had begun to focus on secondary education needs. If the Catholic school system was to meet the challenge of preparing future generations to compete in the increasingly interdependent and technologically changing national economy, a whole new system of secondary education had to be inaugurated. Otherwise Catholics would send their children to the rapidly expanding public high school system. St. Mary High School remained, however, the single central Catholic girls' secondary institution in Chicago, and by 1912 only fifteen central Catholic high schools existed in the United States.

The public high schools in the United States grew more than 1,000 percent from 1900 to 1930. Civic and business leaders in the early twentieth century debated what shape the new schools would take, who would attend, and what mission or function they would serve. While Lucy Flower Technical High School, which opened in 1911, was not the only institution Chicago's young women students could attend, it was inaugurated as an answer to the specific educational needs of the city's females from working-class and middle-class homes, from all ethnic and racial backgrounds, a population similar to the one St. Mary's was designed to serve. Flower Technical High School principal Dora Wells taught history and civics at Medill High School on Chicago's West Side, where most of her students came from the surrounding immigrant neighborhood and many of the male students went on to successful careers. Wells worked with Chicago's first woman superintendent of public schools, Ella Flagg Young, in developing Lucy Flower Technical High School for Girls as an equivalent education to that provided for Chicago boys in the city's two large technical high schools—Richard T. Crane and Albert G. Lane.

Wells and Young came up with two different curricula for Lucy Flower. For the minority of girls who would become teachers or whose families could afford to keep them at home until they married, there was a four-year home economics course that included college preparatory work. The majority of girls enrolled in the two-year vocational course, which prepared them for jobs in sewing, dressmaking, and millinery—occupations close to traditional female household skills. Both the academic and the technical programs assumed a lifetime of marriage and childrearing for the vast majority of women.

In contrast, St. Mary High School immediately identified college and careers in education as the major goal for its students, many of whom were the daughters of Irish immigrant women who had worked as laundresses, seamstresses, and domestics. When commercial courses were introduced in 1902, they realistically prepared St. Mary's students for the sector of the economy in which jobs for women were expanding rapidly: the commercial office. Courses in bookkeeping, typing, business arithmetic, and soon stenography, set the tone, with the goal for many graduates of attending business college. The number of female clerical jobs increased 1,400 percent between 1900 and 1930, with stenography and typing moving from the eighth largest occupational category for women in 1910 to the third largest in 1930. At Lucy Flower, stenography and typing were not included in the early years. The curriculum at Lucy Flower, perhaps the result of American-born social reformers' concerns about assimilation and acculturation of immigrant women, focused on domestic science education and disseminated technical information about running a home. Although St. Mary's instituted home economics in the 1920s, it did not occupy the central position of such courses at Lucy Flower.

By the mid-1920s, there were 550 students at Lucy Flower, the vast majority attending for only one or two years, and only about a tenth completing the four-year course. In contrast, St. Mary High School students—with enrollment reaching around 900 in the mid-1920s, were completing four-year programs and many were going on to college or commercial schools.

ETHNIC COMMUNITIES

Irish Women

Irish American girls had a variety of female role models to contemplate. Their mothers, immigrant women, often became the primary breadwinners for their families as domestics, laundresses, and needle workers. At the 1893 World's Columbian Exposition, young Catholic women visiting the fair could view the statue of Queen Isabella, paid for by Catholic and protestant women of the Isabella Society. A leading member, Eliza Allen Starr, a Protestant convert to Catholicism and Chicago's foremost authority on Catholic religious art, wrote for the Catholic weekly newspaper New World, conducted an art studio and salon in her home located near Holy Name Cathedral, and lectured on Catholic art at St. Mary High School. There were the BVMs and the Mercy sisters, who taught in parish elementary schools, convent schools, academies, and now were principals and teachers in newly established secondary institutions. For the significant percentage of Irish American Catholic girls who attended public schools, an increasing number of their teachers were also Irish Catholics. The handful of Catholic high schools were producing disproportionate numbers of successful female graduates able to pass the entrance exam to the Normal School. Irish Americans Margaret Haley and Catharine Goggin were Chicago public school teachers who organized the Chicago Teachers' Federation in 1897, the first union of elementary school teachers. Helen Maley Hefferan, clubwoman, educator, and Chicago school board member for eighteen years, was president of the Illinois Catholic Women's Association and a trustee of Rosary College. In 1900 she helped establish the Illinois Congress of Parents and Teachers (later renamed the Illinois Parent-Teacher Association).

Czech and Bohemian Women

The varied experiences of Czech women immigrants in Chicago reflect the complexity of ethnic settlement in that city. For example, in 1894 fifty Bohemian women in the Pilsen area began operating the Bohemian Women's Publishing Company. They published *Zenske Listy, or Women's Record: The Only Czech Weekly in America Devoted to the Interests of Women*, edited by Josefa Humpal-Zeman. Educated in both Prague and the United States, Humpal-Zeman rejected the freethinking tradition of her father and converted to Protestantism through exposure to the Czech-speaking chapter of the Women's Christian Temperance Union. Jane Addams supported Humpal-Zeman's efforts and encouraged her writing about the Bohemians in Chicago. Her strong ties to feminists in Prague gave Humpal-Zeman an international viewpoint. This approach was not uncommon for educated immigrants of different nationalities who lived in Chicago or other American cities but retained interest and even involvement in the country of their birth. Humpal-Zeman's work was published in *Hull-House Maps and Papers* (1895). Her advocacy of progressive reform, women's rights, and Americanization as a way for Czech and Bohemian women to gain autonomy and advancement placed her at odds with different political groups among people from her home country in Chicago.

Not far from the Bohemian Publishing Company, Czech immigrant Božena Salava and her family became members of the Bethlehem Settlement, a mission to Bohemian immigrants run by the Congregational Church. A talented young woman, Salava soon became a teacher of Bohemian children and was sent by the Congregational Church to the Bethlehem Missionary Training School in Cleveland, Ohio, where she prepared for a lifelong mission among the Bohemian people in Chicago. At its high point there were more than a thousand children in the Bethlehem Sunday school. From time to time, when there was no minister to attend to the church, Salava gave the sermons and conducted the services. Although encouraged to prepare for the ministry by fellow church workers, Salava remained a lay church worker. However, as a result of her missionary zeal, Bethlehem became one of the largest institutional churches maintained by the Congregational denomination in Chicago.

By 1918 there was a rich institutional ethnic subculture for Czechs, with ninety-one benevolent societies, 125 building and loan associations with fifteen million dollars in assets and thirty thousand members, fifteen fraternal orders, many gymnastic societies (*sokols*), and four daily newspapers.

Another aspect of the Czech community that was shared by most other ethnic communities was the important role that homeland conditions and politics continued to play in the communal lives of immigrants. Vlasta Vráz, member of a prominent Chicago Czech family, became a journalist and wrote articles on the Czech independence movement. Vráz and her family returned to Czechoslovakia when the first Czechoslovak republic was established in 1921. She was a foreign correspondent for the Chicago Czech paper Svornost. Vráz returned to Chicago from Czechoslovakia after the invasion by Hitler and the country's occupation by the Nazis. She became an editor and copublisher of Svornost and aided the Czech government in exile. In 1940, she organized two thousand Czech American women into Czechoslovak units of the American Red Cross.

Polish Women

At the same time that middle-class and upper-class American-born, Protestant women were joining clubs, promoting social reform, contributing to community organization, entering the professions, and establishing new institutional structures and occupations for themselves, women in many of the ethnic communities in Chicago were active in similar ways. In the Polish community, for example, Lidia Pucińska was a mediator between the culture of the ethnic enclave and the culture of the metropolitan area. She contributed to the kind of cosmopolitanism that defined Chicago. Pucińska was an actress and journalist who had her own Polish American radio hour; she was involved in a vast array of community activities, promoting Polish culture, Polish theater, and contributing to the cause of Polish freedom fighting/war relief in Europe. As a radio star, she helped other Polish-American women define their identities.

Stefania Chmielińska was one of the leading activists in Chicago Polonia. She was a founding member of the Polish Women's Alliance (PWA), and in 1899 she became the organization's first president. Her presence was instrumental in shaping the PWA's goals and activities for the next twenty years, during which she founded local branches and established a library and the PWA newspaper, *Głos Polek*, in publication to this day. Chmielińska was also the first women's instructor in the Polish Falcons, and she fought for women's equal membership in that organization. In addition, she was a successful businesswoman.

Stefania Laudyn's social activism and feminism began in Europe. She studied in Moscow and took part in the women's pan-Slavic movement before emigrating to the United States around 1909. In 1910 Laudyn became editor of *Głos Polek*, turning it from a monthly into a widely circulated weekly. She first held this influential post until 1912, when she resigned under a cloud of controversy, then again from 1914 to 1921. Her views on subjects such as women's rights, the international women's movement, the education of immigrant children, and the role of Polish immigrant women in America, found voice in the editorials she wrote and the news items she reprinted.

Swedish Women

Swedish-born Othelia Myhrman, who came to Chicago in 1875 and was employed as a domestic for several years, became active in the Swedish National Association of Chicago; it had been formed in 1894 primarily for the purpose of procuring the conviction of two members of the Chicago Police Department who had murdered a Swedish American citizen. The organization opened a free employment bureau with Myhrman in charge in 1894; she remained in charge until 1912. During that period nearly one hundred thousand men and women were given employment through this agency. She also served as president of the Swedish Woman's Club of Chicago for twenty years. After leaving the Swedish National Association of Chicago's employment bureau, she began her own business, the Swedish National Employment Bureau, in Chicago.

Dutch, Norwegian, Italian, and Greek Women

Physician and social reformer Cornelia De Bey was born in Holland and emigrated to the United States with her family. Her father was a minister and a leader in the Dutch community in Chicago, and De Bey's civic and professional leadership went beyond the boundaries of her ethnic community. Active with the Women's Trade Union League, she served on the Chicago Board of Education in 1905. Petra Dahl was the daughter of Norwegian immigrants, became a medical doctor, and worked for public health reforms in Chicago. A leader in medical women's groups, Dahl organized the Medical Woman's Club of Illinois, established a free woman's clinic, and unsuccessfully ran for local political office. Dahl was active in the Norwegian Woman's Club. Rosamund Libonati Mirabella was a clubwoman and civic leader who bridged the gap between Italian American organizations and the mainstream women's clubs, including the Chicago Woman's Club and the General Federation of Women's Clubs. Presbytera Stella Petrakis was a community leader and philanthropist who organized volunteer war relief and many other charitable activities. She was involved in providing aid and relief to fleeing Greek refugees from Asia Minor who were being uprooted from their ancestral homeland by the Turks; her activity extended over many years, even after she came to America. In Chicago she founded such organizations as the St. Helen Philoptochos Society, the Koraes School Mothers Club, the Young Ladies' Hellenic Society, Asia Paraskeve, and the St. Constantine Red Cross Unit.

German and Eastern European Jewish Women

German Jewish women participated in local and communal institutions that they ran primarily to aid working-class and poor fellow coreligionists who had come from Eastern Europe during the period of mass immigration from the 1880s through the 1910s. These women also participated in the mainstream club movement and reform political culture of the Progressive Era. Hannah Greenebaum Solomon was welcomed by the Chicago Woman's Club. Rose Haas Alschuler, Stella Levinkind Counselbaum, Jennie Franklin Purvin, and Esther Loeb Kohn identified both with Jewish affairs and the larger issues that made up the municipal housekeeping agenda of progressive women reformers. Esther Weinshenker Natkin was a community organizer, clubwoman, and advocate for Chicago's Eastern European Jewish immigrant community; she was also founding director of the Chicago Hebrew Institute. Natkin had been born in Moghilev, Russia, and she came to Chicago with her family in 1886. She was one of the first women in Chicago to promote Zionist causes at a time when assimilated German Jews in the Reform movement of Judaism tended not to embrace the cause. She wrote about the tensions that existed between German and Eastern European Jews that derived from class and cultural differences. Many of the former were upper-class and middle-class professional and business people whose appearance and religious practices reflected their successful assimilation to the dominant culture in the United States. The latter spoke Yiddish and generally were workers; many observed Orthodox religious practices. Sadie American and Minnie F. Low forged careers in social work and developed relationships with both Jewish communal professional organizations and with mainstream groups.

Working-class Jewish women had major roles in the trade union movement and in radical social movements. In the 1910s young Bessie Abramowitz led her comrades out of the garment factories and sweatshops in Chicago to forge a labor movement that culminated in the founding of the Amalgamated Garment Workers' Union. In the 1920s, 1930s, and 1940s, Lillian Herstein and Mollie Levitas were labor activists in the Chicago Federation of Labor as well as in the Women's Trade Union League. In the 1930s, 1940s, and 1950s, Myrna Siegendorf Boredelon Kassel developed worker education programs. Annie Livshis settled in Chicago after an unsuccessful experiment at socialistic farming in the Lasker Colony, Kansas; in Chicago in the 1900s, her home became a center for anarchists and a place of refuge from time to time for Emma Goldman, Voltairine de Cleyre, and Lucy Parsons. Raya Dunayevskaya, a philosopher and activist who had witnessed the Russian Revolution of 1917 in her native land, immigrated to Chicago with her family in 1922. She joined the communist youth organization but later became critical of events in the Soviet Union and of the Communist Party. By the 1940s she had begun to develop Marxist-Humanism, and in 1955, she formed News and Letters Committees. Tobey S. Prinz had roots in the secular Jewish community and in the labor movement in which she led the drive to strengthen and consolidate the different teachers' organizations into the Chicago Federation of Teachers in 1937.

Diversity of Immigrant Women

The biographies of immigrant women provide an understanding of the ways in which immigrant communities formed stratified, complex, social and cultural entities. The biographies defy easy generalization and, in the case of the interpretation of gender roles, it is important to consider the context of both Old World circumstances and New World opportunities. It has been noted that working-class Irish and Polish women were able, in the context of congregations of women religious in America, to achieve social mobility and educational and career advancement. In judging the gender roles, then, it is possible to see women in male-dominated, authoritarian systems achieve advancement nonetheless and have a sense of autonomy and even a perception that as women they had achieved progress. This progress also existed for women's cultural self-expression. For example, there were Polish, Lithuanian, and Czechoslovakian women and men whose nationalistic aspirations were unmet in Europe. In Chicago immigrants could express their cultural, religious, and national identities more fully and freely than they had been allowed to in their homelands, where they had suffered political, religious, and cultural oppression. This is why Maria Kaupas and four other Casimirite sisters resisted attempts by the Irish American dominated hierarchy of the Roman Catholic Church to assimilate Lithuanian immigrants in Chicago. Taking over the administration of the Lithuanian parochial schools and the training of teachers, Mother Kaupas developed curriculum to teach Lithuanian language, literature, history, folklore, and culture to the children of the immigrants. Many were able to learn from material not available to them in Europe.

The biographies of the immigrant women included in this volume bear close reading; in the details of the immigrant experiences it is possible to see patterns of cultural formation that identify the agency of immigrants and recognize the interplay of assimilative forces versus self-determining countermeasures. They offer perspectives on career development, identity, and gender issues.

WOMEN'S PARTICIPATION IN POLITICS AND THE SUFFRAGE MOVEMENT, 1891–1920

Women's political influence and activity in the larger political sphere in Chicago grew steadily from the 1890s. In 1891 the Illinois legislature passed a school suffrage bill allowing women to vote in school elections. It was a small victory, but it established the precedent that the state could act affirmatively on women's suffrage demands. That year Lucy Flower was appointed to the Chicago Board of Education, on which women had been allowed to serve since 1873. As a Republican and a woman, Flower was not reappointed in 1894 when Democratic mayor John Hopkins was elected.

Having acquired the right to vote in school elections, women then set their sights on winning seats as trustees of the University of Illinois. Both Republican and Democratic women began to organize, and both parties slated female candidates from Chicago—Julia Holmes Smith for the Democrats, Lucy Flower for the Republicans. Hopkins's decision not to reappoint Flower to the Chicago Board of Education aided in the organization of women voters, and Flower won the election. She was the first woman elected to a statewide office in Illinois. (Smith was appointed to fill the vacancy left by another trustee of the University of Illinois just prior to Flower's inauguration.)

Women's organizations in all communities in Chicago had provided practical schools of civics and politics even among ethnic groups, where talk of suffrage and women's rights was still controversial. By developing moral benevolence societies, church auxiliaries, and ethnic clubs women had planted themselves firmly in the politics of their communities well before women achieved the vote. Demands for inclusion in ethnic, religious, and professional organizations had not been successful for women, and in most cases they had formed separate associations. For the cause of suffrage to succeed, however, the core suffragist leadership had to convince uncommitted women to join the movement and to organize a broad coalition that would demand legislative action by the male-controlled political system of the United States. The suffrage movement in Chicago and Illinois worked in a number of arenas as efforts were made to increase women's political influence and activity and to garner support from women's groups not yet part of the coalition.

The Chicago Woman's Club (CWC), for example, did not initially embrace the suffrage cause outright; Susan B. Anthony's reception by the club in 1888 was noted by its historian as the first formal recognition extended to the leading voice for suffrage by a woman's club. Suffrage activists within the CWC, including Catharine McCulloch and Ellen Henrotin, formed the Chicago Political Equality League in 1894 as a separate organization but ruled that in its first year of existence, all officers of the league had to be members of the CWC. The Illinois Federation of Women's Clubs, organized in 1894, included seventy-seven women's clubs in its first year; by 1904 it represented 246 clubs with a total membership of twenty-four thousand women. It attracted fairly conservative middle-class women but supported child-related issues, the domestic science movement, and the professionalization of teacher training. Only after 1900 did the federation gradually become involved in more controversial issues; it began to mention suffrage in its proceedings after 1902 and by 1910 was a major segment of the new alliance seeking the vote. The Woman's City Club of Chicago, formed in 1910 by such upper-class women as Louise deKoven Bowen, Lydia Coonley-Ward, Hannah Solomon, Mary J. Hawes Wilmarth, and Ruth Hanna McCormick, and such social reformers as Mary E. McDowell and Rachelle Yarros, immediately focused on attaining suffrage.

Black Clubwomen and Suffrage

The suffrage movement had been almost exclusively white. Yet in Chicago there was, from the 1890s, a substantial black clubwoman movement. As in its white counterpart, the membership was made up of middle-class, well-educated married women whose husbands were leading businessmen and professionals. The first generation of black clubwomen included Mary Fitzbutler Waring, a physician married to Frank Waring, an educator. Mary Waring was a leader in the National Association of Colored Women, founded in 1896, where she worked on health issues in the black community. Ida Bell Wells-Barnett, a journalist and one of the cofounders of the National Association for the Advancement of Colored People, married Ferdinand Barnett, a lawyer and journalist. Known best for her antilynching campaign, Wells-Barnett organized the Negro Fellowship League in Chicago, a social settlement for young black men. Fannie Barrier Williams and her husband, S. Laing Williams, an attorney with a thriving practice in Chicago, launched the Prudence Crandall Study Club, an elite literary society that attracted some of the city's most socially prominent African Americans. Williams supported Provident Hospital and Training School, the only nursing school in Chicago that admitted black women. She played an active role in the founding of the National League of Colored Women in 1893 and was involved in the establishment of its successor, the National Association of Colored Women. Elizabeth Lindsay Davis, the daughter of well-to-do African American settlers in Peoria, Illinois, was married to William H. Davis, a chiropodist who was active in community affairs. Elizabeth Davis became the secretary of the Ida B. Wells (Wells-Barnett) Club organized in Chicago in 1893 with Wells as president. Davis and other women organized the Phyllis Wheatley Club in 1896, envisioning it as a neighborhood betterment organization. Davis was a leader of the Illinois State Federation of Colored Women's Clubs that were affiliated with the National Association of Colored Women. Except for Fannie Barrier Williams, there were no cross-race memberships for black women in the infrastructure of the white club system.

The segregation in the clubwoman movement was not unlike that found in the settlement movement and in such organizations as the Young Woman's Christian Association, the Woman's Christian Temperance Union (WCTU), and professional organizations that women formed. The exception that proved the rule was the Frederick Douglass Center, which was founded by a white woman, Celia Parker Woolley, as a place where middle-class Whites and Blacks could interact and promote better relations. It was not a conventional settlement house but a center situated geographically on the edge of the Black Belt, the segregated area in which the black elite and the black working class lived, the boundaries demarcated by the discriminatory behavior of the white neighborhoods and a real estate market that systematically upheld the maintenance of segregated housing patterns. (Housing discrimination continued to exist through the 1960s, and Martin Luther King Jr. came to Chicago in 1966 to protest de facto segregation in northern cities.)

Both Fannie Emanuel and Ida B. Wells-Barnett initially participated in the Frederick Douglass Center, although tensions and conflicts immediately developed. When Wells-Barnett, who had served as vice-president of the center's woman's club, sought the presidency, she was denied the position. It went, instead, to Emanuel; Wells-Barnett discontinued her relationship with the center. Emanuel was not satisfied either. She began to plan for her own settlement by taking a year-long course in 1908 in the newly opened Chicago School of Civics and Philanthropy. Emanuel Settlement was not established as a center for middle-class interactions on matters of race; rather, it was situated in the heart of the Black Belt and offered one of the few kindergarten classes in the city in which African American children could enroll; a medical clinic; an employment bureau; literary, art, cooking, and sewing classes; and a nursery and reading rooms. It lasted only three years. Wells-Barnett's Negro Fellowship League also struggled and had a short existence. There was not enough financial support in the black community for such endeavors. At the same time, African Americans were not welcomed in settlements designed to serve white ethnics. While Jane Addams, Mary E. McDowell, Harriet Vittum, Graham Taylor, and others had concerns about the plight of the new arrivals from the South in the Great Migration of Blacks to Chicago, they were participants along with the rest of white America in a status quo that upheld segregation as the norm.

Anticipating passage in Illinois of the Presidential Suffrage Bill, Wells-Barnett organized the Alpha Suffrage Club in January 1913. It was Illinois's first black woman's suffrage organization. Wells-Barnett traveled to Washington, D.C., to attend the National American Woman Suffrage Association's parade in March 1913 and discovered, once she arrived, that the national organizers did not want Blacks to march with Whites. They were afraid that an integrated parade would alienate Southern white suffragists. Wells-Barnett waited for the parade to begin, then suddenly appeared from the crowd and took her place in the middle of the other Illinois suffragists.

Wells-Barnett and the Alpha Suffrage Club went block by block canvassing the predominantly black wards to get women registered to vote in the aldermanic primary in Chicago in 1914. They succeeded in registering three thousand women in the 2nd Ward; Alpha Suffrage supported a black independent instead of the regular machine candidate and nearly brought him an upset victory. The close call for the regular candidate got the attention of the political establishment. The Republicans (Blacks had not yet switched to the Democratic Party) told Wells-Barnett and the Alpha Suffrage women that if they supported the party regular, the Republicans would fill the next vacancy with a black candidate. In 1915, with the help of organized black women, Oscar De Priest became the first black alderman in the history of Chicago.

Maternalist Argument for Suffrage

Jane Addams's article "Why Women Should Vote," published in the *Ladies' Home Journal* in 1910, expressed the maternalist argument that by this time had become the dominant rhetoric of the suffrage movement. She believed that women had a special role in transforming society and fighting social, economic, and political injustice; and she focused on the collective utility of woman suffrage in the movement to eradicate the evils of economic inequality in American society. Respecting the work women did as nurturers, she argued that woman's political equality was the inevitable result of contemporary government's involvement with the basic human interests with which women had traditionally been concerned. She made a strong argument for woman suffrage on the basis of traditional definitions of woman's role. Society had developed to a point where protection of the family required mothers to be engaged in public life. Traditional family life would be protected as a result of women's having the vote and being included in organizations, political parties, and labor unions. This view was an extension of the arguments first advanced in the 1870s by Elizabeth Harbert, when suffragists in Chicago had already begun to depart from liberal, individual rights arguments and were theorizing about women's differences from men and women's unique and natural capacity for civilizing and moralizing social life.

Trade Union Women and Suffrage

A second component in the suffrage alliance was the involvement of working-class and immigrant women. Settlement house workers and social reformers had forged coalitions with trade union and immigrant women starting with the Illinois Woman's Alliance in the late 1880s and continuing with the Chicago chapter of the WTUL. The cooperation of allies (middle-class and upper-class women) with trade union women was possible when both sides saw eye-to-eye on protective legislation such as eight-hour-day laws, minimum wage legislation, child labor laws, and factory inspection laws. Florence Kelley, Margaret Dreier Robins, Jane Addams, Ellen Henrotin, Ellen Gates Starr, and Mary E. McDowell were leaders in the WTUL.

The WTUL did not endorse woman suffrage until 1907, when Margaret Dreier Robins was president and was able to forge an effective alliance with such trade union women as Elisabeth Christman, Mary Anderson, Agnes Nestor, Margaret Haley, and Elizabeth Maloney. In May 1907 Margaret Dreier Robins led a parade of some twenty thousand working women and men through Chicago to protest the arrest of International Workers of the World leader William "Big Bill" Haywood and two other labor leaders. They had been forcibly transferred from Colorado to Idaho and placed on trial for the murder of a former governor of Idaho, a charge of which they were eventually cleared. The demonstration of solidarity was important in winning the respect of labor for the cause of woman suffrage. That same year, as a result of pressure by social reformers Mary E. McDowell, Sophonisba Breckinridge, and Edith Abbott, President Theodore Roosevelt initiated a federal investigation into the conditions of working women and children. The Bureau of Labor began its study on working women and in 1910 published the first volume in the multi-volume series *Report on Conditions of Women and Child Wage-Earners in the United States* (1910–13). Using this information, Mary E. McDowell and other progressives lobbied for state legislation to restrict the hours of work for women and children and to establish minimum wages for women in industry. In 1908 Margaret Dreier Robins, as president of the Chicago WTUL, became a member of the executive board of the Chicago Federation of Labor, which had a male majority. Two years later, Agnes Nestor joined a group of suffragists on the Suffrage Special train to Springfield, Illinois, to speak in favor of a state suffrage bill; there she began organizing groups of labor union women to push for the passage of the Illinois suffrage legislation.

Shortly after the 1913 victory in the Illinois legislature, and seven years before the passage of the federal suffrage amendment, problems between suffragists and trade unionists exploded in Illinois. Suffrage leaders had accepted publisher William Randolph Hearst's offer to print a special suffrage edition of the *Chicago Examiner,* with the proceeds going into the suffrage treasury. However, the Hearst papers were on organized labor's list of employers engaged in unfair labor practices, and the Chicago Federation of Labor sent the suffrage organizations a series of resolutions condemning Hearst. The WTUL informed Trout and the Illinois Equal Suffrage Association that they would not continue to affiliate if Hearst's offer was accepted. A meeting with suffrage and WTUL leaders was arranged, but the Chicago Political Equality League and the Illinois Equal Suffrage Association representatives did not show up. The Hearst edition went forward. Mary McDowell was dismayed by the failure of suffrage leadership to embrace the cause of working women. "Our sisters of the suffrage movement who worked so splendidly for us because we are women failed to understand the struggle we must make because we are workers" (quoted in Steven M. Buechler, *The Transformation of the*

Woman Suffrage Movement: The Case of Illinois, 1850–1920 [1986], 179).

Chicago Political Equality League

In 1910, under the leadership of Grace Wilbur Trout, a relatively conservative clubwoman who had the ability to combine public relations and modern technology, the Chicago Political Equality League forged a more broad-based campaign focused on convincing state legislators that their political careers depended on their votes in favor of suffrage in Illinois. In Chicago, suffragists persuaded male trade unionists to support the cause. Settlement house workers campaigned among male voters, and the Cook County Suffrage Alliance organized on a ward and district basis. The WTUL distributed prosuffrage literature to every labor union in the city. Despite these efforts, Chicagoans defeated the resolution by almost two to one in a nonbinding popular vote on woman suffrage in 1912.

Many of the leading suffragists and social reformers joined the Progressive (Bull Moose) Party in 1912 and actively campaigned for Theodore Roosevelt. Everyone got involved, from Jane Addams and Mary J. Hawes Wilmarth, both of whom were on the platform at the convention and seconded Roosevelt's nomination, to Republicans such as Ruth Hanna McCormick, who broke ranks with the regulars. On the local level, women supported Progressive Party and Independent reform candidates, including Alexander McCormick (no relation to Ruth McCormick) for county commissioner and Charles Merriam for alderman. In both cases women's support made a difference and the reformers won; this was also true when reformer William E. Dever was elected mayor of Chicago.

In 1913 Grace Wilbur Trout was elected president of the Illinois Equal Suffrage Association, bringing the same upper-class connections and money that dominated the Chicago Political Equality League to the entire statewide effort. There were more than one hundred affiliated suffrage clubs throughout the state focusing their efforts on the legislators in Springfield. Trout hired paid staff workers for the first time. Having organized twenty-nine of the thirty-two state senatorial districts outside of Chicago, the Illinois Equal Suffrage Association established permanent headquarters in the state capitol in 1913 and carefully watched the floor proceedings. In June 1913 the Chicago WTUL formed its own Wage-Earners Suffrage League to organize working-class women en masse. The Illinois legislature passed the Presidential Suffrage Bill in 1913. It permitted Illinois women to vote for all national offices and virtually all municipal, county, town, and village offices.

Illinois women now faced the challenge of national enfranchisement. Activists worked on two fronts. They continued to campaign for the federal amendment, and they organized to use the vote in local elections. At Jane Addams's urging, Harriet Vittum, head resident at Northwestern University Settlement and president of the Woman's City Club of Chicago in 1913, ran as an Independent for the 17th Ward aldermanic seat. The following year, having lost her bid for the aldermanic seat, Harriet Vittum and Mary E. McDowell ran for the Cook County Board of Commissioners on the Progressive Party ticket. They lost the election because of a last-minute judicial ruling that women could run for county offices but could not vote in county elections. Nearly one hundred thousand registered women were denied participation.

THE NEW WOMAN IN THE PROFESSIONS AND ARTS

In the 1890s there was a significant increase in the choices available to young, single women for constructing a life of economic independence in urban America. The New Woman was initially more closely identified with economic independence than with sexual liberation. New ideas about marriage, female sexuality, and reproduction, however, were necessarily woven into the arguments in favor of women's economic independence. Women physicians took the lead not only in providing models of economic independence but as students of anatomy and physiology whose perspective as females was different from that of male doctors. They began to alter the conventional wisdom about women's physical and mental capacities. Physician Alice Stockham was labeled by the Chicago *Inter-Ocean* newspaper the "original 'new woman' of the West" (May 21, 1905) for her rejection of Victorian conceptions about women's anatomy, physiology, and mental capacities. Stockham's *Karezza: Ethics of Marriage* (1896) was one of the first marriage manuals that dealt with sexual relations from a female point of view. She was one of several women gynecologists, including Lucy Waite and Marie Mergler, who wrote manuals and textbooks to reform the treatment of women's diseases and to educate women and young girls about their bodies.

Women in nontraditional religions also contributed to a questioning of conventional attitudes about women's roles. These women began by rejecting the patriarchal message in the male interpretation of Christian Scripture. They focused on the ways in which Christianity subordinated and oppressed women and contributed to the sexual double standard in society. New Thought religious leader Ursula Gestefeld's novel *The Woman Who Dares* (1892) compared wives with prostitutes and fought for a woman's right to determine her own sexual and emotional life. Elizabeth Boynton Harbert's theosophical novel Amore (1894) argued that traditional Calvinist theology produced the evils it tried to eliminate while religions based on the principle of love led to harmony in society.

Putting her theories into practice, Spiritualist Ida C. Craddock opened a sex counseling service in Chicago's central business district in 1893. She supplemented her lectures and personal consultations with pamphlets that advocated the shocking (for the time) notion that there should be mutuality in sexual intercourse and that female sexuality was normal and respectable. Stockham's and Craddock's mail order pamphlets and tracts on sexuality brought them into federal courts for violation of the mail obscenity law.

Women in the freethinking and socialist movements also contributed to the reformulation of conceptions of womanhood. Lucy Waite, a freethinker, combined a scientific approach to female reproduction with radical ideas about marriage. Waite's novel *Doctor Helen Rand* (1891) critiqued religious morality that stigmatized children of unmarried parents. Socialist and anarchist Lizzie Swank Holmes's *Hagar Lyndon; or, A Woman's Rebellion* (1893) exposed the evils of traditional marriage and, at the same time, showed that women had limited opportunities under existing capitalist conditions to lead alternative, independent lives.

A growing number of educated women born before the Civil War did not want to marry. Instead, physicians Mary Harris Thompson and Sarah Hackett Stevenson, businesswoman Helen Culver, poet and art teacher Eliza Allen Starr, lawyer Ellen Annette Martin, dramatics and speech teacher Anna Morgan, artist Annie Cornelia Shaw, and educator Mabel Slade Vickery pursued careers and found new space in which to live autonomous, independent lives. Caroline Huling became an associate editor of a trade journal in Chicago in 1884 after answering a want ad for the job with the ambiguous signature, "C. A. Huling." She obtained an interview and then convinced the editor that her experience working on her family's newspaper was more than adequate preparation. In Huling's novel *The Courage of Her Convictions* (1896), the heroine wants to have a child and is artificially inseminated because she is disillusioned by the character of men. After giving birth she marries her male doctor (who is really the father of the baby) because she realizes a child needs both parents. Huling never married and supported herself as an editor and journalist all her life.

For many the break with their family's expectations was traumatic. Jane Addams experienced emotional and physical crises after graduation from college. Addams's modest inheritance allowed her to cofound, with Ellen Gates Starr, Hull-House settlement, a new enterprise that influenced the way in which early twentieth-century women reconfigured their roles as nurturers and caregivers in society. Starr may serve as a more realistic model for the New Woman who emerged by the 1890s. She had completed only one year of college before she was forced to support herself and began teaching at Miss Kirkland's School in Chicago, a position she held for ten years before joining Addams to establish Hull-House. Frances E. Willard went through a soul-searching experience in which she broke off her engagement to a young man. She remained a member of her family household and lived with her mother while pursuing her career as organizer of the temperance movement, lecturer, publicist, and writer.

Jane Addams went so far as to claim that the subjective necessity for the settlement movement came out of the personal needs of a generation of college-educated women and men whose desire to be useful was as significant a drive in establishing neighborhood centers such as Hull-House as was the discovery of urban poverty and social injustice, which represented the objective necessity for settlements. She wrote about the pull of family and how difficult it was to forge ahead in an independent direction.

In Addams's case, her friendship with Ellen Gates Starr was significant, even critical, in releasing the energy necessary to implement her yearnings to be independent and to be useful. Starr, however, was not to be Addams's long-term partner. Addams and Mary Rozet Smith did develop a lifelong relationship. Everyone who knew them well understood that Smith and Addams had a unique relationship of deep emotional and psychological attachment. Smith, ironically, honored her "family claim" and was a dutiful daughter to her aged parents, maintaining her primary residence in her family home in Chicago.

She traveled extensively with Jane Addams and was a daily member of the Hull-House community, a confidante of Addams, and one of the major financial contributors to Hull-House until her death one year before Addams died.

Other women lived together quietly and unflamboyantly. Such long-term attachments were acknowledged among women settlement residents. When Gads Hill Center settlement was looking for a new head resident, Mary E. McDowell of University of Chicago Settlement recommended Ruth Austin for the job. McDowell reminded the Gads Hill board that there was an additional advantage in hiring Austin: her friend Neva Leona Boyd, recreational training specialist, would be living with Austin and therefore be available to provide her expertise. Boyd and Austin had a long-term partnership as did Frances E. Willard and Anna Gordon; the younger Gordon "became an integral member of the household" and was Willard's "beloved companion" (see the entry for Anna Adams Gordon, below). Cornelia De Bey and Kate Starr Kellogg lived together, the former a physician and prominent reformer, the latter an educator and administrator in the Chicago public schools. Helen Culver lived with her companion Martha Ellen French for more than thirty years. Theologian Georgia Harkness and musician Verna Miller were partners who shared a home for thirty years until Harkness died in 1974. Other women couples included rare-book dealers Margery Barker and Frances Hamill and artists Kathleen Blackshear and Ethel Spears. The latter couple probably met in 1926 at SAIC and remained together until Spears's death in 1974; the former also met in 1926 and remained together until 1980, when Barker died. Botanist Margery Carlson and Kate Staley, an instructor in physiology, were companions for more than forty years.

Other women also took advantage of the growth of economic opportunities to lead independent lives. Ada Celeste Sweet, a government pension agent, businesswoman, and journalist, was manager in 1911 of the newly organized Woman's Department in the Chicago office of the Equitable Life Assurance Society, where she sold insurance to career women like herself. The city was a place of employment for an ever-increasing number of young women factory workers, office workers, department store clerks and salesgirls, schoolteachers, domestics, and nurses. It was also a magnet drawing in young women with aspirations to become novelists, poets, reporters, painters and sculptors, performing artists, and playwrights. In the 1880s through 1940s, most students at the School of the Art Institute of Chicago (SAIC) were women. (The number of men enrolled began to equal the number of women only after World War II.) In 1909, 3,222 students were enrolled at SAIC; and in 1922 there were 4,521 students. First generation New Woman artists Bessie Potter Vonnoh, Nellie Verne Walker, Bertha Jaques, Enella Benedict, Clara Barck Welles, Edith de Nancrede, Bessie Bennett, and Laura Van Pappelendam, and second generation New Woman artists Gertrude Abercrombie, Frances Strain, Jane Heap, Beatrice S. Levy, Julia Thecla, Kathleen Blackshear, Macena Barton, and Ethel Spears studied at SAIC. Benedict, Bennett, Van Pappelendam, Spears, and Blackshear also had careers as SAIC faculty.

A number of craftswomen opened shops in Chicago. Clara Barck Welles had studied at SAIC in the late 1890s and later exhibited her work at the Art Institute of Chicago. She was influenced by Arts and Crafts movement ideals and was the founder of Kalo Shop in downtown Chicago near Bessie Bennett's silver shop. Welles closed her downtown shop after marrying George Welles in 1905 and opened the Kalo Art Craft Community in the Chicago suburb of Park Ridge. She held design classes and ran an apprenticeship program in metalsmithing for women and men. Her classes were attended mostly by young women, many of whom she hired.

Many first generation new women in the arts also advocated making high cultural forms accessible to working-class and immigrant neighbors, a major goal of Hull-House from its inception. The settlement's Butler Art Gallery opened in 1891. Hull-House's art studios were run by Enella Benedict, a painter who agreed with Addams and Starr that there was a connection between art and social reform. As Starr became a leader in the Chicago Arts and Crafts Society, Benedict applied many of the principles of that movement to the studio arts. Benedict also taught at SAIC, and she was an important bridge between the two institutions. She brought professionals to the neighborhood, and she encouraged talented students at Hull-House to continue to study at SAIC. Ellen Gates Starr dedicated herself to the principles of the Arts and Crafts movement and was a catalyst in bringing together architects and crafts people who shared a critique of industrial society's ugliness and the alienation of the crafts worker that resulted from the factory system.

Laura Dainty Pelham became the director of the Hull-House Players, an ensemble of fourteen neighborhood residents who were amateur actors and worked regular jobs during the day. They learned from the local little theater movement in Chicago and performed the latest in American and European drama, including works by George Bernard Shaw, Henrik Ibsen, and John Galsworthy. Pelham concentrated on new Irish drama, including plays by John Millington Synge; the Abbey Players attended performances of the Irish plays done by the Hull-House ensemble.

Hull-House resident Eleanor Smith composed vocal music and pioneered in the field of music education. Under her direction, the Hull-House Music School was an important cultural and artistic force in Chicago. It presented regular choral, orchestral, and chamber music performances as well as solo voice and instrumental recitals. Smith was interested in pedagogical theory and practice and worked with John Dewey. Her *Hull-House Songs* (1915) expressed the social outlook of Hull-House. Charlotte Chorpenning, who was influenced by Professor George Pierce Baker's famed 47 Workshop in playwrighting and directing at Harvard, and she wrote and produced plays for community groups. Neva Leona Boyd of the Recreation Training School of Chicago learned of Chorpenning's work and asked her to become drama director of the school. Chorpenning expanded her work to include group dramatics with children.

Edith de Nancrede helped create a network of clubs at Hull-House that integrated the arts and social contact by using drama and other arts to encourage group cooperation, to acquaint young people with the works of high culture, to teach proper elocution, and to draw on immigrant culture for theatrical inspiration. Nancrede saw the theater as a means of developing social relationships and a sense of community in the neighborhood. Jane Addams encouraged the different settlement groups to work together. The Hull-House Dramatic Association (later the Hull-House Players) was a troupe of actors selected from all of the young people's clubs and classes. When they did a play, Nancrede directed, Harriet Monroe might write it, its music was scored by Eleanor Smith, and its set was designed by Enella Benedict. Mary Wood Hinman and Rose Marie Gyles, who taught movement and gymnastics classes, also helped in the staging.

Women's involvement in the performing arts, including movement, gymnastics, and folk dance, was part of a new conception of what normal, healthy females should and could undertake in their physical development toward mature young women. Mary Wood Hinman—a leader in pageantry and recreation and a folk dance specialist—had been influenced by Melvin Ballou Gilbert, who taught "aesthetic calisthenics." Hinman combined an emphasis on women's capacity to bear children and engage in physical and mental activity with the discovery of folk culture and a new appreciation of the diversity of cultural expression. Hinman introduced dance at Hull-House in 1898.

The major departures for creative women in the 1890s were in the little magazines and little theater movements. Born in 1860, the same year as Jane Addams, poet and editor Harriet Monroe described her childhood as restrictive; and like many Victorian young women, she suffered from an overwrought nervous condition. She embarked on a career in journalism writing art criticism; in 1888 she moved to New York City, from which she sent back freelance articles on art as a correspondent for the Chicago Tribune. Monroe's interest in writing was not unusual for a woman of her time. In fact women wrote for newspapers and magazines throughout the nineteenth century. The Illinois Woman's Press Association, founded in 1885, included a wide variety of women publicists; journalists; editors of legal publications; writers of utopian New Woman novels; writers on literary subjects, religious topics, and practical manuals on a variety of subjects; and writers of medical texts. In the 1890s Amy Leslie began her long career as the drama critic for the Chicago Daily News, a position she held until her retirement in 1930. She wrote from two to three reviews and feature articles on theater a week. A self-proclaimed New Woman, she advocated a more liberated egalitarian lifestyle for women. She wrote about the double standard, divorce, and the working conditions of young girls and children.

Just as wealthy women had subsidized the reform and research efforts of Progressive Era women activists, well-to-do patrons of the arts funded new little magazines, little theater, and avant-garde art galleries. Kate Sturges Buckingham, Bertha Honoré Palmer, and Edith Rockefeller McCormick were among the rich Chicagoans who financially guaranteed Harriet Monroe's Poetry: A Magazine of Verse in its first five years. Patronage was important in the African American community as well. In 1921 Nora Douglas Holt founded and became the editor of Music and Poetry, a magazine that featured the original musical scores of Holt and a number of contemporary composers; she received financial support to keep the magazine afloat from several wealthy Chicago families.

Monroe was also a member of the Little Room group. It rep-

resented a transition stage between the Victorian world and modernism. Made up of many Fine Arts Building residents and their friends, including sculptor Bessie Potter Vonnoh; writers Henry Blake Fuller, Clara Louise Root Burnham, Hamlin Garland, Elia W. Peattie, and Edith Wyatt; and playwrights Mary Aldis and Alice Gerstenberg, the group had considerable influence in shaping Chicago's art world. Critic and novelist William Dean Howells noticed Edith Wyatt's "Three Stories of Contemporary Chicago" in McClure's (1900) and encouraged her to write more along those lines; a year later she published twenty-one short stories in one volume, Every One His Own Way (1901). Howells announced that Wyatt should be included with Chicago writers Henry Blake Fuller, Will Payne, George Ade, and Robert Herrick as a defender of realism. In 1903 she produced her first novel, True Love, in which she attempted to define how women's roles were changing. Wyatt's heroine seeks equality, honesty, and compatibility in marriage.

Another art arena for the expression of New Woman attitudes was the little theater movement. In 1898 Anna Morgan opened the Anna Morgan Studios on the eighth floor of the Fine Arts Building. Her suite of eight rooms had a small stage and an equipped gymnasium. Her program was intended for women, although men could participate. She promoted expressive skill, health, physical grace, and mental well-being at a time when women were just beginning to participate in athletics and physical fitness. Alice Gerstenberg studied at her school. Many Chicago artists and craftspeople were tenants in the building and socialized on the building's upper floors, forming a community that met daily and that regularly entertained visitors. In the 1910s Maurice Browne and Ellen Van Volkenburg opened the Little Theatre, which was housed in the Fine Arts Building. Mary Reynolds Aldis, an upper-class matron who had homes on Chicago's Gold Coast and in affluent Lake Forest, Illinois, built the Play House with her husband, Arthur Aldis, on their Lake Forest property in 1911 and began to produce plays with a group of amateur actors. These productions were social affairs as well as theatrical experiences.

THE NEW WOMAN, SEXUAL LIBERATION, AND FEMINISM

Women's gains were increasing by 1900; that year the majority of high school graduates were women. More women than ever before had access to higher education: 80 percent of the colleges, universities, and professional schools in the nation admitted women. The percentage of women in the work force increased from 15 percent in 1870 to 20 percent by 1900. From the 1870s to the 1920s, between 40 and 60 percent of women college graduates did not marry; this was at a time when only 10 percent of American women remained single. The use of the word "feminism" was rare before 1910 but frequent by 1913. As a result of advances in medicine, there was a significant drop in the birth rate, from 7 children per family in 1804 to 3.56 in 1900.

By 1910 there were significant numbers of New Woman adherents. While women in the 1890s who did not marry had advanced the argument that self-development was a legitimate goal, only an agenda of women's freedom from sexual subservience and oppression in marriage, not one of sexual liberation, had been advocated. The second generation New Woman of the 1910s and 1920s thought about sexual autonomy and advanced the idea that sexual experimentation and self-expression was a positive, natural aspect of women's identity. Margaret Anderson, who left small town life in Indiana for Chicago, where she "could live and breathe" (Margaret Anderson, *My Thirty Years' War* [1930], 16), took a leading role in the Chicago Renaissance and experienced both a sexual and an artistic awakening. The movement to advance literary modernism in the United States took hold in Chicago with Floyd Dell and his wife, Margery Currey, Tennessee Mitchell Anderson and Sherwood Anderson, Eunice Tietjens, Maurice Browne, Ellen Van Volkenberg, and other literary figures. Margaret Anderson's innovative magazine the *Little Review* was launched in 1914. Jane Heap, initially an art student at SAIC, joined Anderson's *Little Review* staff; the two, who identified themselves as lesbians, fell in love. Anderson wrote "here was my obsession—the special human being, the special point of view" (*My Thirty Years' War*, 107–108). In the 1920s, attorney and gay and lesbian rights activist Pearl Hart lived with Blossom Churan, an aspiring singer and actress.

WORLD WAR I AND THE WOMEN'S MOVEMENT

The outbreak of World War I divided the coalition forged by suffrage and progressive reform issues. Jane Addams and Lola Maverick Lloyd cofounded the Woman's Peace Party and were two of the forty-seven American women who traveled to the International Congress of Women at The Hague. There they joined European women, all of whom had come as representatives of local women's organizations. After the conferences, Alice Hamilton, who had also attended, accompanied Addams on her peace mission to several warring nations. Labor leader Elisabeth Christman also attended the International Congress and helped found the International Committee for Permanent Peace; at the WTUL convention she supported a resolution requesting an embargo on arms and war supply exports. Addams and Lloyd persisted in their refusal to support the war and continued to hold this unpopular position after the entry of the United States into the conflict. When the United States entered the war and labor supported it, Margaret Haley and the Chicago Teachers' Federation withdrew permanently from the ranks of the American Federation of Teachers and from the American Federation of Labor.

Women, War Work, and the Eighteenth and Nineteenth Amendments

Another flank of the coalition not only supported the war but, after the United States became involved, used the Women's Committee of the Council of National Defense, Illinois Division—chaired by Louise deKoven Bowen from 1917 to 1919—as a vehicle to implement a variety of progressive reforms. For example, Rachelle Yarros delivered lectures for the Council of National Defense on social hygiene and the eradication of venereal disease. Mary E. McDowell became a member of President Woodrow Wilson's Committee on Women in Industry; the committee's charge was to see that laws restricting hours of work for women and children and establishing minimum wages were implemented in the defense industries. Elisabeth Christman, who had opposed the war, found herself chief field representative for women workers in the Women in Industry Service formed in the Department of Labor. Mary Fitzbutler Waring organized classes for black Red Cross nurses, and Ada S. McKinley worked as a hostess to black soldiers at War Camp Community Services, a government project organized by the Chicago Urban League. This work led to her continued efforts to provide programs for Blacks in the community and to the establishment of the South Side Settlement House (later Ada S. McKinley Community Services). In 1920 the Women in Industry Service was transformed into the Women's Bureau of the Department of Labor and given permanent legal status. Eleanor Slagle trained volunteers in occupational therapy techniques for the Chicago Red Cross chapter and then persuaded the U.S. Surgeon General's office to appoint her a consultant to the army, charged with training aids to work with returning soldiers.

The Woman's Christian Temperance Union began a major lobbying effort for prohibition during the World War I period. Anna Gordon, elected National WCTU president in 1914, brought to the Judiciary Committee of the U.S. House of Representatives a scroll containing a plea for prohibition, signed by representatives of twelve thousand organizations. The heightened campaign for prohibition occurred simultaneously with the unabated efforts of the national suffrage movement. Five thousand women marched through pouring rain—the rainy day suffrage parade—in Chicago on June 7, 1916, to show their support for Grace Wilbur Trout and three other National American Woman Suffrage Association representatives who brought the suffrage plank appeal to the Platform Committee at the Republican National Convention at the Chicago Coliseum. The Republican delegates placed a suffrage plank in their platform. The following year the WCTU and other temperance groups lobbied Congress for war prohibition. The signatures of six million women were gathered for a food conservation petition, which requested that, in a time of government food rationing, grains and fruits not be used for the production of alcoholic beverages. Congress voted to forbid the use of foodstuffs in distilled liquor and, in December 1917, passed a resolution to submit a national prohibition amendment to the states. Even after passage of the Eighteenth Amendment in January 1919, Anna Gordon continued the work of the WCTU, focusing on Americanization, "Scientific Temperance Instruction," and child welfare. By 1924 the WCTU's membership was approaching five hundred thousand.

After the passage of the Nineteenth Amendment, Alice Paul's National Woman's Party began its campaign for an Equal Rights Amendment (ERA). In Chicago and Illinois, however, the dominant leadership of the postsuffrage and social reform movements rejected the National Woman's Party and the ERA. At the victory convention of the National American Woman Suffrage Association in Chicago, February 14, 1920, women voted to create the League of Women Voters, a nonpartisan, educational organization geared to preparing women to use the franchise. By October the Illinois League of Women Voters had been formed, and Flora S. Cheney had become its first president. Under her leadership the league began publishing a newsletter, which by the end of 1922 was issued monthly and had a circulation of about twenty-two thousand.

WOMEN AND MODERNISM IN LITERATURE AND ART

New thinking about art and individual freedom led to discussions of new roles for women in society and a new conceptualization of womanhood. Artistic modernism smashed traditional aesthetic axioms such as tonality in music and classical perspective in painting and replaced them with a variety of self-consciously invented and individual standards. In terms of form, instead of representations of external reality that could be recognized by the viewer, artists rendered original forms that were individualistic and not recognizable. Etcher Beatrice Steinfelt Levy was one of the Chicago women artists who embraced postimpressionism. Catholic liturgical artist Margaret Dagenais, who studied at SAIC, would later incorporate material objects from different non-Western cultures in her collages. Alice Roullier, a cofounder of the Arts Club of Chicago with Rue Winterbotham Carpenter, was interested in postimpressionist paintings and sculpture and did much to stir up the conservative art world of Chicago in the 1910s and 1920s. Following the 1913 AIC *Post-Impressionist Exhibition* (the name given to the New York City Armory Show when it came to Chicago), the majority of art students, teachers, and patrons in the midwest city rejected the advant-garde modern art of Henri Matisse, Pablo Picasso, Georges Braque, Marcel Duchamp, and Constantin Brancusi. Alice Roullier became a leader in changing the climate in Chicago and in providing a new context for a positive reception for the new art. As the head of the Exhibitions Committee of the Arts Club from 1918 until 1941, she brought not only postimpressionist art to Chicago but also new music, poetry, and dance. In a sense, the Arts Club became a safe corridor through which controversial art could migrate into the conservative museum world without the latter's engaging in too much risk. Many of Roullier's Arts Club exhibits occurred in rented gallery space at AIC.

Helen Gardner taught the first art history survey course at SAIC. Her book *Art through the Ages: An Introduction to Its History and Significance* (1926) was one of the first texts to acknowledge the historical context in which art was produced yet consider each work of art on its own merits. She analyzed what she believed were the universal design elements in each work. This approach provided a new strategy for understanding art across cultures and historic time periods. Artist Kathleen Blackshear began teaching the survey of art history at SAIC in 1926, and the two worked together for the next twenty years. They encouraged students to study natural history, anthropology, and the sciences so that they could detect the universal patterns in the natural world and in manufactured objects.

In the 1920s, etcher Beatrice S. Levy and other rebels formed an "art for art's sake" group that believed in no particular school or movement. Russian painter Nicholas Roerich named them the Cor Ardens (burning center) Society on one of his visits to Chicago. Modernists found gallery space in the Thurber Gallery and Raymond Katz's Little Gallery, located in the Auditorium Theater building. Painter Fritz Brod joined the Chicago No-Jury Society and served as its vice-president.

The Association of Arts and Industries was established in 1922 and was dedicated to forging an alliance between artists and industrialists to promote the cause of good design in manufacturing through a school of industrial art. Norma K. Stahle was chief fund-raiser and administrator from 1922 to 1937. Artist Laura Van Pappelendam and photographer and artist Eva Watson Schütze were involved in advancing a modernist agenda in the Renaissance Society, which held lectures, concerts, and exhibits that were in keeping with the idealist approach to art of Charles Hutchinson, Martin Ryerson, and Lorado Taft.

Pianist Djane Lavoie-Herz's teaching studio/salon was a focal point for avant-garde music in Chicago in the 1920s, at a time when there were few venues for young composers in the city. Her studio served as a meeting place for composers and performers traveling through Chicago as well as for her own students. She filled her apartment-studio with Oriental, medieval, and Renaissance art as well as with contemporary art. Ruth Crawford Seeger dedicated her "Piano Preludes" of 1924–28 to Lavoie-Herz.

In the 1920s, Fanny Butcher's bookshop in downtown Chicago acquired the atmosphere of a literary salon. It was the first store in the United States to be owned by a literary critic. In 1928 Margery Barker and Frances Hamill opened Hamill & Barker, a rare-book store that placed them among the first women rare-book dealers in the United States. They acquired and dealt in the papers of Virginia Woolf and other members of the Bloomsbury group.

By the late 1920s and early 1930s, Chicago's Black Metropolis was experiencing its own cultural renaissance. Vivian Harsh had begun to develop the Special Negro Collection (renamed the Vivian G. Harsh Research Collection of Afro-American History and Literature), housed in the new Hall Branch Library that opened in 1932. She acquired books, pamphlets, clippings, and photographs from friends in the association for the Study of Negro Life and History. In 1933 Harsh started a Book Review and Lecture Forum that attracted such speakers as Richard Wright, Langston Hughes, Zora Neale Hurston, Arna Bontemps, Gwendolyn Brooks, Horace Cayton, William Attaway, Margaret Walker, St. Clair Drake, and Alain Locke. The library became a research site and a meeting place for young black writers, artists, and social scientists.

Children's librarian Charlemae Rollins, music critic and journalist Nora Holt, and symphony composer Florence Price were part of a social and cultural world that was based in Chicago's Black Metropolis. Marita Bonner Occomy, an essayist and short story writer who had been involved in the Harlem Renaissance, came to Chicago, where she wrote her "Frye Street" stories about the Chicago ghetto. Lovie Austin was a blues pianist and composer, and Lil Hardin was a pianist and composer who led her own jazz band. Estella C. Bonds was an organist at Berean Baptist Church and was prominent in the musical world of Chicago. She was the first piano teacher to her daughter, Margaret Allison Bonds. Margaret Bonds became a composer and concert pianist. Sculptor Richmond Barthe, poets Langston Hughes and Countee Cullen, soprano Abbie Mitchell, and composer Will Marion Cook all visited the Bonds' home. Margaret Bonds also studied with Florence Price, in whom she found a friend, mentor, and collaborator. Bonds's mother was a founding member of the National Association of Negro Musicians, established in Chicago in 1919. Its local branch was the Chicago Music Association. Playwright Lorraine Hansberry, born in 1930, spent her childhood and adolescence in the rich cultural environment of Chicago's Black Metropolis; her father and mother entertained W. E. B. Du Bois and Richard Wright in their home.

CONSERVATIVE WOMEN AND MODERNISM

Not all women embraced cultural diversity, modernism in literature and art, or ideas of sexual freedom and self-expression. Anne Shaw Faulkner Oberndorfer was a music educator whose music appreciation textbook, *What We Hear in Music*, was published in 1913; it was one of the first books for music appreciation used in the public schools. In the 1920s, Oberndorfer introduced the first program classes in connection with the Chicago Symphony Orchestra (although never officially affiliated with the symphony itself), and from 1920 to 1926, she headed the music division of the General Federation of Women's Clubs. Her publications for music educators during her tenure with the federation reflected the contemporary debate over music. What was American music? Should all folk songs be sung in English? Should composers assimilate music from other countries into the music from America? Oberndorfer sought an American music that somehow consolidated the different traditions; she believed that music should promote and correct morals, values, and virtuous action. Along with many women's groups, she opposed jazz, citing so-called medical studies that showed the demoralizing influence of the persistent use of syncopation. She saw jazz as disorganizing, stimulating listeners to engage in extreme deeds and to break with all rules and conventions.

In the art world, conservatives split from the Chicago Society of Artists and formed a new organization, the Association of Chicago Painters and Sculptors, leaving the modernist core to run the Chicago Society of Artists. Josephine Logan's Sanity in Art organization, founded in 1936, attacked the aesthetics of modernism; Eleanor Jewett, art critic for the Chicago Tribune, shared Logan's point of view and labeled the works of Paul Cezanne, Paul Gauguin, and Vincent van Gogh brutal, primitive, and childish.

WOMEN'S POLITICAL CULTURE AFTER 1920

The post–World War I "Red Scare" dominated political culture, and the restrictionist path taken in 1915 culminated in immigration quota laws in 1924. Cultural pluralists such as Caroline Hedger began to write less on topics of Americanization when the increasing conservatism of the Americanization movement made them uncomfortable. Pearl Hart had spent her early years as an attorney enmeshed in the women's political culture of the 1910s and 1920s. She dealt chiefly with cases of child abandonment, bastardy, child abuse, and with women criminals designated prostitutes. She worked with the Committee on Social Work and the Woman's City Club of Chicago to defend the rights of poor women in the Morals Court and became one of the first public defenders in the renamed Women's

Court in 1929. Hart found herself defending the rights of aliens, radicals, and eventually, gays and lesbians in the 1920s through 1960s. Increasingly, progressive women and men were attacked by conservative politicians and publicists. Two of the most significant accomplishments won by the progressive women's political reform coalition—the juvenile court system and federal aid for prenatal and infant health care—were successfully attacked. The Sheppard-Towner Maternity and Infancy Act was not renewed by the U.S. Congress in 1929, and in 1935 the Illinois Supreme Court ruled that the original 1899 juvenile court legislation was unconstitutional. The courts criminalized children older than ten, placing them outside the scope of the juvenile court and in contact with adult criminals.

In the 1920s the work of progressive women continued, even though the broad coalition formed in the struggle for suffrage no longer existed. One of the vehicles for the expression and implementation of the pre-1920 agenda after passage of the Nineteenth Amendment was the League of Women Voters. The nonpartisan nature of the league was disarming to those who felt threatened by the introduction of millions of potential new voters into the political process. The establishment of the league has often been interpreted as a move away from activism and women's involvement in realpolitik. However, on the basis of the historical record of women's political involvement in Illinois in the three decades following the achievement of the Nineteenth Amendment, a case can be made for the central role of the League of Women Voters in the support of women politicians and the continuation of the progressive reform agenda. The league stayed out of party politics and did not endorse candidates. However, its issue-oriented approach distinguished those candidates that loyal and intelligent league members should support. A reading of the Bulletin, later called The Illinois Voter, demonstrates the public policy concerns that made the League of Women Voters the successor and major institutional structure through which the women's political culture of the Progressive Era continued.

Initially the officers and leadership of the Illinois League of Women Voters were drawn from the WTUL, the Chicago Woman's Club, the Illinois Equal Suffrage Association, the settlement movement and the social science think-tank connections of Hull-House. The connection was vividly on display when thousands of Illinois women arrived in Springfield, Illinois, on January 3, 1923, for Lottie O'Neill's inauguration as 41st District State Representative. She was the first woman elected to the Illinois state legislature. Julia C. Lathrop, who had headed the U.S. Children's Bureau, was president of the Illinois League of Women Voters, and she presided at the evening banquet held in honor of O'Neill. The press coverage of the election of O'Neill trivialized the enormous victory women political activists and progressive reformers experienced by focusing on the lack of a ladies' bathroom near the legislative chambers. Such human interest stories along with photographs of elected women in maternalist poses with their families contributed to the growing popular idea that while women had gained the right to vote, they were not a political force. Few women were elected, and those who were elected to office were marginalized.

Efforts made by elected women to put the progressive women's agenda in place through legislation contributed to the idea that women were a different breed of politician. In her first term, O'Neill sponsored several bills that became law: funding for the education of crippled children; an amendment of the inheritance property act to provide for a widow to receive one-third of the real estate of her deceased husband in place of the dower right to a share in the income of his real estate during her lifetime; a moratorium on the purchase or sale of certain wild flowers in danger of extinction. These were seen as women's issues, and they represented a continuation of maternalist politics. Those women who ignored women's issues were also criticized, however.

Material for a new narrative of the history of women in politics in Chicago is provided by the biographies of state representatives Lottie O'Neill, Flora S. Cheney, Bernice Van der Vries, and Marjorie Pebworth; state senator Anna Wilmarth Ickes; state representative and state senator Esther Saperstein (later the first female alderman in Chicago); congresswomen Winnifred Mason Huck, Ruth Hanna McCormick, and Marguerite Stitt Church; League of Women Voters activist Laura Hughes Lunde; Cook County Commissioner Lucy Palermo; Republican committeewoman Irene McCoy Gaines. These elected women differed from one another in substantial ways. For example, Lucy Palermo, an Italian American whose interest in services to the aged and sick in Cook County gave rise to her political career, joined the conservative "We, the Mothers" group, the largest isolationist mother's organization active during World War II. Its leader was Elizabeth Dilling, who was known for her virulent attacks on first wave feminists and the progressive social reform agenda represented best by the Hull-House women. Of the elected women, only Winnifred Huck supported the first ERA amendment.

There were also personal struggles among the elected women. Republicans Lottie O'Neill and Ruth Hanna McCormick publicly challenged each other's authority and, in a primary, O'Neill ran against McCormick; both women lost their bid for a place on the ballot in U.S. congressional elections.

The issues advocated by the Illinois League of Women Voters from the 1920s through 1950s included the basics of the progressive reform agenda: prohibition of child labor; protection of women workers; expansion of educational programs, including day care; reform of married women's inheritance and other property laws; modernization of the structures of government. In 1924 the Illinois league's Child Welfare Committee organized an Illinois Joint Committee to urge the ratification of the Child Labor Amendment. Reorganized two years later as the Illinois Child Labor Committee, it included Esther Loeb Kohn, Grace Abbott, Sophonisba Breckinridge, Agnes Nestor, and Edith Abbott. In 1924 Laura Hughes Lunde became secretary of the Illinois Women's Conference on Legislation, a coalition of women's organizations (including the League of Women Voters) that had been established to research and pool information about legislation of interest to member organizations.

Many of the peace activists of the Progressive Era continued their efforts between the two wars. In 1923, Zonia Baber served as the Illinois delegate to the Women's Committee for Recognition of Russia, affiliated with the Women's International League for Peace and Freedom, which urged the recognition of the Soviet Union. Alice Hamilton served on the Health Committee of

the League of Nations from 1923 to 1930 and became a League of Nations advocate. Sister Vincent Ferrer Bradford of Rosary College served as an officer of the Catholic Association for International Peace, founded at Catholic University in 1927. The award of the Nobel Peace Prize in 1931 to Jane Addams was in recognition of work she began in 1915. After her death in 1935, the organization that she had initiated and guided, the Woman's International League for Peace and Freedom, adopted a people's mandate to government to take joint action for peace by reduction of arms and peaceful settlement of ongoing conflict. That year Anna Wilmarth Ickes presided over a peace movement rally in Washington, D.C., which was attended by two thousand supporters who had come to mark the twentieth anniversary of the Women's International League for Peace and Freedom. Anita McCormick Blaine and Lola Maverick Lloyd were also engaged in peace activism.

POPULAR CULTURE AND WOMEN

Radio and television images had enormous power, and women initially took leadership roles in the emerging broadcast industry. Women promoted educational uses of broadcast media in the same ways that they had developed programs from kindergarten through adult education in the context of schools, settlements, public health services, recreation, libraries, museums, and religious institutions. In all of these venues women had utilized the local infrastructure of the club movement to aid them in the dissemination of information about literacy, child care, nutrition, sanitation, social hygiene, and citizenship. Women's use of print material continued unabated in the 1920s and 1930s, often in conjunction with the new medium of radio. A link between maternalism and consumerism had already been made in the nineteenth century, when women organized to use their purchasing power to advance political change and social transformation. This resulted, for instance, in the boycotts of products produced by slave labor during the abolitionist movement in a strategy that Florence Kelley's aunt, Sarah Pugh, embraced; later, Florence Kelley "mobilized consumers' political activism on a much broader scale" (Kathryn Kish Sklar, *Florence Kelley and the Nation's Work* [1995], 22) through the National Consumers' League.

Another connection between maternalism and consumerism was made by proponents of scientific motherhood, the Progressive Era movement that had both academic and popular culture aspects. University of Chicago professor and dean Marion Talbot studied under Ellen Richards, a key figure in the home economics movement that attempted to transform household management into a social science. Believing that the majority of women students would become homemakers, she identified the need for educating them "both to administer their homes and to become involved in social reform work [municipal housekeeping] in the community" (see the entry for Marion Talbot, below). The home economics movement, whose leaders included Katharine Blunt and Lydia Roberts, saw scientific motherhood as a golden opportunity to improve future generations and solve many of society's problems. This use of modern medical, technological, and even psychological and sociological information to develop better methodologies for the prenatal and postnatal care of children was an extension of the larger reform projects of women through the nineteenth and into the twentieth centuries. These ideas formed the core of the U.S. Children's Bureau approach advocated by Julia C. Lathrop; the kindergarten movement promoted by Alice Putnam, Elizabeth Harrison, and Edna Dean Baker; and the municipal housekeeping efforts of a wide range of women, including Ada Celeste Sweet, Lucy Flower, Caroline Hedger, Rachelle Yarros, Harriet Vittum, Edna Foley, and Harriet Fulmer. The latter two used the Chicago Visiting Nurse Association to teach mothers, in the context of home visits, how to care for infants and children.

The boundary between selling products and disseminating information about useful products was less well defined in the early years of radio and newspapers, which used women experts to give advice to a mass audience of homemakers. The use of a female persona to educate the public about new products was an effective marketing device. Leona Krag Malek was one such writer/journalist, and she used the persona Jean Prescott Adams. Her fellow home economist Ethel Kemper was "Virginia Page" of Sears, Roebuck, and was the company's domestic science editor. In 1925 Leona Malek became "Prudence Penny" for the *Herald and Examiner*, writing the daily home economics column. She invited her readers to attend her lectures on home economics, which were held at Chicago's Balaban and Katz Theater, and to listen to her weekly radio program broadcast on Chicago's station KYW.

In 1928 Martha Crane joined the radio mail department of the *Prairie Farmer*, one of the leading farm newspapers in the Midwest and owner since 1924 of radio station WLS. Crane became "Uncle Toby," preparing and editing a weekly children's page for *Prairie Farmer* and later hosting the paper's *Homemakers' Hour* on radio. By 1929 Martha Crane hosted the daily morning *Radio Bazaar* on WLS, taking the role of helper assisting her audience with everyday homemaker activities. Her afternoon show was *Homemakers' Hour* and offered music, inspirational talks, poetry, and informal chats by a number of women broadcasters on topics of interest to homemakers. From 1928 to 1930, nearly three hundred speakers appeared on the program, addressing such topics as dental clinics for school children, running water in homes, hot school lunches for rural children, rural recreation, good books, and baby care. In 1935, Martha Crane did a new show on WLS, *Feature Foods*; the show limited its sponsors to food and grocery advertisers, all of whom allowed Crane to write commercials for the program.

In the 1920s Anna J. Peterson began broadcasting from radio station KYW fifteen-minute daily *Table Talks*, short cooking demonstrations that were most likely the first cooking programs broadcast in America. Home economists such as Peterson, working in utility-sponsored home service departments, played a vital role in boosting the sales of gas and electric products while also promoting do-it-yourself housewifery. By 1923 consumer demand for neighborhood-based services prompted Peoples Gas to open eight branch stores; home service was integral to the mission of these neighborhood stores, which featured spacious auditoriums designed for cooking classes and demonstrations, alongside bill-paying centers and appliances for sale. Anna Peterson and her staff extended the reach to Polish, Italian, and Colored Mothers' Clubs, the Urban League, and community and settlement houses.

The commercialization of radio, that is, the sale of radio time to sponsors, did not happen all at once. For example, in 1922, Judith Cary Waller went to work for the radio station WCU, recently acquired by the *Chicago Daily News*. Typically radio stations at this time were owned by newspapers and were seen as outlets for reporters to air their stories and features. Waller became the first general manager in this new and untested medium at a time when women had opportunities to become managers, producers, writers, and announcers. Throughout the 1920s, Waller had a free hand to determine the nature of the shows that were broadcast since there were no sponsors. Waller featured classical music on her station while the other Chicago radio station played popular music and jazz. She produced innovative shows, broadcasting collegiate sports, a major league baseball game, the inauguration of Calvin Coolidge in 1925, and that same year, a transatlantic news broadcast from London by *Chicago Daily News* foreign correspondent John Gunther.

Chicago Historical Society librarian Caroline McIlvaine, showing that she understood the impact of radio in reaching new audiences, began to make live broadcasts in 1925 concerning services the society could offer to the citizens of Chicago. Judith Waller offered to broadcast talks on CHS and on Chicago history. McIlvaine's resulting broadcast about the Great Chicago Fire in 1871 was accompanied by a "Radio Photologue" in the *Chicago Daily News* on October 10, 1925, so that listeners could view photographs of sites she described. In the vanguard of what later was termed "outreach," McIlvaine organized special tours with docents/interpreters for subscribers to Polish newspapers, promoted the museum by advertising in streetcars, and displayed objects from the collection at Orchestra Hall in downtown stores and office buildings. She also established a Junior Auxiliary for CHS members' children and prepared lectures, entertainment, and special exhibits for them.

Judith Waller also experimented with broadcasting as a service to public schools by producing a series of programs for an elementary school in Chicago in 1926; by the end of the year, eleven schools were tuning in to what was the forerunner of the *American School of the Air*, broadcast by the Columbia Broadcasting System (CBS) a few years later. In 1927 Caroline McIlvaine worked again with Judith Waller to broadcast a series of talks on notable Chicagoans, directed to the city's primary schools. In her capacity as NBC's education director, Judith Waller developed educational programs and, in the 1930s, two to three hundred schools participated, including some in the five states adjoining Illinois. Ruth Harshaw became the director of the new Educational Services Bureau at Carson Pirie Scott & Company, a major department store. From 1933 to 1949 she developed innovative marketing programs for Carson's including a monthly mail-order children's book club, Hobby Horse Book Foundation, in which books of her selection were advertised.

Chicago was considered the capital of the daytime radio serials and home to many favorite soap operas. In 1929, Irna Phillips created a storyline for a WGN family serial aired for ten minutes daily, five days a week; it was called *Painted Dreams* and ran through 1931. Phillips's *Today's Children*, the renamed version of *Painted Dreams*, ran from 1932 to 1938 on NBC. By 1938 it had become the most popular daytime serial on radio. She also created *The Road of Life* and *The Guiding Light*. While Irna Phillips lived an unorthodox life as a single woman who adopted two children at age forty, her soap opera characters followed the genre's basically conservative portrayal of women's roles in society. Virginia Payne starred in *Ma Perkins*, a show that attracted millions of listeners, most of them women; the show was broadcast from Chicago through 1947 and portrayed a folksy character whose life was very different from Payne's own activist life as a union organizer in the broadcast industry. Other women in broadcasting were Ireene Wicker and Marion Claire.

Immigrant women also used the broadcast media to disseminate cultural, political, and social ideas about ethnic identity and acculturation. Lidia Pucińska hosted the popular radio program *Sunshine Hour-Godsina Słoneczna* from 1933 to 1984. Broadcast in Polish, it aired Polonia news, commentary on cultural and theatrical events, literary readings, practical household and childrearing tips, and current events in Poland.

BLACK AND WHITE CLUBWOMEN AND ACTIVISTS
BETWEEN TWO WARS, 1919–1941

The World War I period was one of expanded opportunities for African Americans and, at the same time, an era of increased tensions and racial violence against Blacks in both the South and in the industrial cities of the North. Between 1916 and 1919, fifty thousand Blacks migrated to Chicago from the South in what became known as the Great Migration. Whereas in the nineteenth century a small black population had attended white public schools and lived in different neighborhoods, in the 1920s the response by white residents to the increased numbers of rural Blacks in the city was to impose a strict policy of segregation. This policy consigned most migrants to the Black Belt on Chicago's South Side to housing that was substandard and soon overcrowded. Similarly, the public schools in the Black Belt were crowded and inadequate. Segregated health facilities did not meet the needs of the population, and the mostly poor and unskilled Blacks faced discrimination in the job market. The housing shortage in the Black Belt became acute by 1919 and contributed to mounting racial tension in the city. Conflicts surrounding employment of returning white servicemen who viewed the black newcomers as competitors in the period of readjustment from a wartime to a peacetime economy also strained race relations.

On July 27, 1919, a race riot erupted in Chicago. While swimming at a Lake Michigan beach at 29th Street on Chicago's South Side, a young African American man had accidentally crossed the imaginary racial dividing line and found himself in a whites-only section. He was stoned by Whites and drowned. Reactions to the drowning by African American youths and assaults by Whites on African Americans precipitated four days and nights of turmoil and violence. When order was restored, thirty-eight citizens were dead, more than five hundred injured, and thousands left homeless. During the riots, Jane Addams, Mary E. McDowell, and Harriet Vittum contacted African American settlement head resident Ada S. McKinley and worked with her to restore order in the neighborhoods. They took to the streets and linked arms in solidarity with McKinley and then began organizing job placement programs for Blacks.

Although significant individual progressive reformers, including McDowell and Addams, worked with Blacks in interracial coalitions, the majority of Whites continued to perpetuate segregationist policies; and whether or not these conditions disturbed them, they were reluctant to fight for integration. Rather, they assisted Blacks in operating their separate institutions. Leaders in the black community were caught in a dilemma. They opposed segregation and had no desire to contribute to it. Activist Blacks faced the question of whether to continue to work with white activists under the circumstances. When African Americans realized how desperate was the need for services and economic help for their community, they tended to compromise and work within the system. In addition, black elite and middle-class leaders had mixed feelings about the race riot. There were some who experienced embarrassment and hostility toward migrants whose existence appeared to threaten the progress that had been achieved among educated, professional Blacks in Chicago. African American middle-class clubwomen, including Fannie Emmanuel, Mary Fitzbutler Waring, Maudelle Bousfield, and Fannie Barrier Williams, generally believed that the Southern black migrant family needed to be educated and socialized.

Black clubwomen debated what role they should take in an environment in which even those Whites who wanted to work for better race relations and economic improvement continued to accept segregation as part of the American way of life. Former National Association of Colored Women (NACW) president Mary McLeod Bethune felt that the organization's priorities were misplaced and began in 1928 to recruit supporters to form a new national organization. Plans for this group, which became the National Council of Negro Women (NCNW), were underway; in Chicago Mary Fitzbutler Waring disagreed with this initiative and feared the proposed NCNW would weaken the national black women's club movement. Waring, who was national president of the NACW in 1933, continued to emphasize the traditional concerns of women that centered around home, family life, employment, and health; she also used *National Notes* to speak out against lynching and discrimination, and in response to the Scottsboro case, urged NACW members to actively support the antilynching measure that was pending in the U.S. Senate and to join efforts to make segregation illegal; but she did not join Bethune's NCNW.

Another aspect of the tension in the black community over strategies to achieve economic justice and full citizenship in the United States came from the class and status structure that developed as some Blacks made gains in their personal careers and financial standing. Often they did so in the context of the segregated community itself or as a result of a political system that incorporated Blacks who accepted the general rules of white majority control in order to gain minor appointments and patronage for their cooperation. Attorney Violette Anderson was appointed an assistant city prosecutor in 1922. Fannie Barrier Williams became the first Black and the only woman appointed to the Chicago Library Board in 1924. In the context of segregated facilities, Blacks emerged as leaders and managers of programs. In 1926 Maudelle Bousfield was appointed Dean of Girls at Wendell Phillips High School, the first African American to hold that position at a Chicago high school. The South Side Settlement House grew with support from Whites and Blacks. Soon it was providing social services to more than twenty-five thousand people. McKinley was an active member of the Social Workers Round Table, an organization comprised of forty-seven members that met regularly at the South Side Settlement House to plan and provide educational seminars. McKinley was an early supporter of the League of Women Voters of Chicago and one of the organizers of the Douglas branch of the league, an all-black chapter. Irene McCoy Gaines became industrial secretary to the first "Negro" branch of the Young Women's Christian Association in Chicago. Florence Chapman Williams organized a Negro health institute in 1937. Working within the constraints of Chicago's racially segregated health and school systems, Williams had to contend with the fact that since its opening in 1915, the Municipal Tuberculosis Sanitarium, the city's largest and best tuberculosis (TB) hospital, had been closed to most Blacks. Provident Hospital attempted to serve the South Side of Chicago, but the TB ward at Cook County Hospital was the last stop for most black Chicagoans with advanced TB.

At the same time that they participated in the segregated, racially discriminatory institutions in Chicago, black women professionals and activists in the club movement began to challenge the prejudices and social inequalities of a society that conferred second-class citizenship on all African Americans. As early as 1931, Maudelle Bousfield's master's thesis, "A Study of the Intelligence and School Achievement of Negro Children," based on research she conducted at the Keith Elementary School in Chicago, drew conclusions about the testing of African American children that later would be acknowledged by the broader academic community. She found that tests had to be devised that were not culturally biased, that is, that did not depend on the manners, customs, or background of the child. As a member of the book selection committee of the Children's Department of the Chicago Public Library, Charlemae Rollins educated her white colleagues on the detrimental effects of ethnic and racial stereotyping. She agitated against racism in children's books. She protested the 1931 publication of Lucy Fitch Perkins's *The Picaninny Twins*. In 1937 Rollins succeeded in having Elvira Garner's *Ezekiel* pulled from the Chicago Public Library's selection list because the black child Ezekiel was portrayed offensively as a pickaninny, an unkempt and uneducable black child.

WOMEN AND LABOR BETWEEN TWO WARS, 1919–1941

Women continued to pursue goals of social justice in the economy and the protection of women and children in the workplace. During the 1920s the WTUL sponsored four women workers a year to attend their Chicago Trade Union College. There, worker-students enrolled in classes on labor problems and trade unionism. Alice Henry directed the training program in the 1920s. She had been involved with the Bryn Mawr College summer school for women workers in 1921. One of the trainees was Fania Cohn, who later became educational director of the International Ladies Garment Workers' Union.

Chicago Federation of Labor delegate Lillian Herstein taught at the famous Bryn Mawr School for Women Workers in Industry founded by M. Carey Thomas. Agnes Nestor, who served as president of the WTUL, maintained a relationship with the old Progressive Era coalition of trade union women and middle-class allies through the WTUL; it continued to exist through the 1950s. She also worked with the League of Women Voters, for which the eight-hour day law for women and the child labor amendment remained top priorities.

In 1933, when the Chicago Board of Education voted drastic cuts in curriculum and services to schools, high school teacher and union activist Mary Herrick organized a mass rally of twenty-seven thousand teachers, parents, and concerned citizens to protest the cuts. The same year, Herrick and Laura Hughes Lunde were among the organizers of the Save Our Schools committee, which soon became the Citizens Schools Committee, a progressive coalition engaged in depoliticizing and reforming the Chicago school system. Helen Maley Hefferan was a featured speaker at the 1937 rally. Her presence linked the old progressive coalition with the new labor union activists. Herrick, Tobey Silbert (see the entry for Tobey Silbert Schein Prinz, below), and Lillian Herstein were charter members of the Chicago Teachers Union (CTU), Local #1, of the American Federation of Teachers. CTU was the product of a merger of various teacher union locals in an effort to consolidate power in the depths of the depression when Chicago teachers were being paid in tax anticipation warrants, which they could cash for only three-quarters of their value. Herrick, a high school teacher, had chaired the Joint Board of Teachers Unions, a coalition that forged the CTU in 1937. Lillian Herstein was instrumental in arguing for affiliation with the American Federation of Labor (AFL) rather than the Congress of Industrial Organizations (CIO). She reasoned that the Chicago Federation of Labor had supported their organizing efforts, but she also challenged the AFL's discriminatory policies toward African Americans.

Catholic women on the Left increased their participation in working-class politics and supported trade unionism in the 1920s and 1930s. Many Catholic women religious and lay activists were influenced by the 1931 papal encyclical Quadragesimo Anno, the central theme of which was the dignity of the human person and a concern for social order, including a more just distribution of wealth. Sister M. Vincent Ferrer Bradford, who taught history at Rosary College (now Dominican University), located in the Chicago suburb of River Forest, was an early participant in the Catholic Conference on Industrial Problems, organized in Chicago in 1922 to explore how American industrial problems could be solved through the application of Catholic teachings on social justice. Bradford invited Dorothy Day of the Catholic Worker movement to the River Forest campus during the 1930s. Like Herstein, she was an early supporter of industrial unionism and the CIO. Beginning in 1937, Bradford was an annual member of the teaching staff of the summer institute for women workers sponsored by the National Council of Catholic Women and held at the National Catholic School of Social Service, Washington, D.C. Bradford worked with Frances Perkins, Secretary of Labor in the Roosevelt administration, as well as with many union leaders, including Agnes Nestor and Elisabeth

Christman. The summer institutes continued even during World War II. Bradford also taught at the Sheil School of Social Studies, Chicago, the center of progressive social thinking among Catholic educators, clergy, and women religious in Chicago. Bradford and others connected with Sheil School encouraged students to engage personally in social activism; to volunteer to work in youth programs in inner-city Catholic parishes; and to work at the Chicago branch of Friendship House, an experiment in interracial community building begun in Harlem, New York, in 1938.

For many Progressive Era settlement head residents, the Great Depression seemed to bolster a determination to work with working-class groups in efforts to relieve unemployment immediately and to achieve passage of labor legislation and support unionism. In 1932, after holding hearings to publicize the conditions of the unemployed, Harriet Vittum of Northwestern University Settlement and other reformers and settlement workers formed the Chicago Workers Committee on Unemployment (CWCOU), a group motivated by the extreme social dislocations. Vittum was a member of CWCOU's Advisory Committee, which included Jessie Binford and Lea Demarest Taylor. After the early relief measures and New Deal programs were put in place, CWCOU created grievance committees to investigate the complaints of the unemployed so that those who were victims of administrative errors or oversights could have their situation rectified.

The Great Depression created a climate in which federal social initiatives toward recovery and emergency relief allowed for advances in the progressive women's reform agenda. For example, Rose Alschuler was appointed staff director for the Works Progress Administration (WPA) nursery schools in Chicago; eventually the WPA supported eighteen nursery schools scattered throughout the city. The following year Edna Dean Baker was involved on the national level in establishing emergency nursery schools as a member of the National Advisory Committee for Works Progress Administration (WPA) Nursery Schools. Lea Taylor became the first woman to be appointed to the Metropolitan Housing and Planning Council; when federal funds made public housing possible in the 1930s, Taylor advocated an open housing policy and resident support services.

By 1934, although women politicians had retained connections with the postsuffrage coalition represented by the League of Women Voters, women remained a tiny minority in state and national office. In Illinois that year Bernice Van der Vries was one of two women representatives in the Illinois General Assembly. She had been reelected ten times, but few other women were joining the ranks of political officeholders. In 1937 the Woman's Eight Hour Bill was passed finally by the Illinois legislature. In 1941 Van der Vries became the first woman to head a standing committee in the Illinois General Assembly when she was appointed chair of the legislative committee on municipalities. Lucy Palermo was elected to the thirteen-person Cook County Board of Commissioners; she was one of three women, all of whom were Democrats.

Women achieved leadership roles as well as funding for their work as artists in the Federal Art Project of the Works Progress Administration (WPA/FAP). Increase Robinson (after her husband's death, Josephine Dorothea Reichmann took his

name) became the midwest regional director of the Public Works Art Program (1933–34), an adviser to the Treasury Relief Art Project (1935–39), and administrator of the Illinois Art Project of the Works Progress Administration's Federal Art Project (WPA/FAP) (1935–43). Artists Julia Thecla, Ethel Spears, Macena Barton, Frances Foy, and Fritzi Brod participated in the Illinois Art Project of the WPA/FAP.

THE GREAT DEPRESSION AND THE AFRICAN AMERICAN COMMUNITY

Among Chicago's black workers, the Great Depression was disproportionately severe. While unemployment for Chicago's white workers doubled in 1931, it tripled for Blacks. Although Blacks made up less than 10 percent of the city's population in 1931, African Americans comprised 16 percent of the total unemployed and 25 percent of the city's relief cases. The black community's relationship with organized labor had a complicated history. In the early years of the Great Migrations to northern industrial cities, Blacks had been brought in as scabs to cross the picket lines of striking white workers. Prominent black businessmen, preachers, and civic leaders had encouraged poor and relatively unskilled migrants to place their trust in the paternalism of capitalists who owned the Pullman Company in Chicago. There was a legacy of anti-union sentiment in the black community that also came from the prejudices and racist behavior of workers and a reluctance by unions to accept Blacks into their apprenticeship systems. A. Philip Randolph, the leader of the Brotherhood of Sleeping Car Porters and Maids, had to raise the consciousness not only of workers but of the community as a whole in his efforts to develop a strong union. Recent scholarship by Beth L. Bates indicates the central role of black clubwomen and social reformers, including Ida B. Wells-Barnett, Irene McCoy Gaines, Thyra Edwards, and Halena Wilson in supporting Randolph's efforts and in transforming the negative image of unions in the black community. By 1935, even conservative clubwoman Mary Fitzbutler Waring had come to accept the view that the central concern of the black community had to be jobs. Her address, "Women in Industry," at the 1935 biennial convention of the National Association of Colored Women, reflected her continuing concern with the impact economic depression and the high level of black unemployment had in the black community and for black women workers; she advocated hiring Blacks as salespersons and attendants in the parts of the community where Blacks predominated.

Just as white trade union organizers had advocated leadership training of working-class women in worker colleges, black and white union organizers raised money to send black factory workers from Chicago to labor school. Talented social worker Thyra Edwards received a fellowship to attend the International People's College in Elsinore, Denmark. During her six-month stay in Europe, she made independent field investigations of low-cost housing developments in Sweden, Finland, Russia, Germany, France, and England.

Having assisted A. Philip Randolph in organizing the Chicago Brotherhood of Sleeping Car Porters by speaking at mass rallies in the 1920s and 1930s, Lillian Herstein was prepared to support him at the convention in a battle to force the AFL's Brotherhood of Railway Clerks, a white-dominated union, to admit Blacks as full members, not auxiliary members with no voting rights. The discussion never came to the floor.

The disproportionate misery African Americans experienced during the Great Depression radicalized many in the black community and focused the attention of leaders on economic issues. Thyra Edwards was a leader of the National Negro Congress when in February 1936 more than five thousand men and women attended its first convention. She chaired a committee at the Abraham Lincoln Center in Chicago called The Negro in Industry, which focused on how to open employment opportunities for more Blacks. Delegates to the first national conference of local women's economic councils officially formed the International Ladies' Auxiliary of the Brotherhood of Sleeping Car Porters. The original Colored Women's Economic Council was formed in New York in 1925, in Chicago in 1926. In Chicago, Halena Wilson was a leader, serving as president of the Chicago branch in 1931 and becoming the president of the newly formed auxiliary. A number of Pullman maids were members, as were wives, partners, and daughters of Pullman porters. The object of the auxiliary was to advance the economic, social, moral, and intellectual welfare of porters and their families through the promotion of women's involvement in brotherhood affairs and fund-raising. Women were involved in membership-building; and from the 1930s through the 1950s, they also engaged in civil rights activism. In 1939, Irene McCoy Gaines was one of the founders and president of the Chicago Council of Negro Organizations, a group formed to secure the civil rights of Chicago's black population. In 1941, Irene McCoy Gaines led a group of fifty Chicagoans to Washington, D.C., where they met with others and protested racial discrimination in federal employment. This effort was an important precursor to that of A. Philip Randolph who, four months later, threatened a massive march on Washington to protest the very same thing. That year, President Franklin D. Roosevelt issued Executive Order 8802 forbidding employment discrimination by businesses holding government contracts.

WORLD WAR II AND WOMEN

Wartime measures at home once again made possible some progress in the implementation of the women's agenda. Securing federal money for day care or early childhood education was difficult, if not impossible, in peacetime but made easier by war. Women's employment in sectors of the economy traditionally closed to them became available in wartime. In 1941, with America's entry into World War II, Lillian Herstein was appointed the woman's consultant for the War Production Board. Her job was to advise the board on child care and problems of absenteeism among women workers in war industries. She was sent to Los Angeles, California, where the Lockheed, Vega, Douglas, and North American plants and large shipyard all had women workers. Congress passed the Lanham Act that provided grants for child care to communities with war-related plants. Rose Alschuler was hired in 1943 as a consultant to the Federal Public Housing Authority to plan activities and services for children in housing projects. She served in this capacity for the rest

of World War II, using her consulting fees to support research projects of the National Association of Nursery Education. Psychologist Helen Koch supervised wartime nurseries in Chicago.

America's entry into World War II expanded career opportunities for women. Alice Bright graduated second in her University of Chicago Law School class of 1941 and was the first woman hired by Sidley & Austin, one of only three women then at major Chicago law firms. Bright was headed for a position in military intelligence in Washington, D.C., and Sidley & Austin was willing to interview her because of the shortage of male applicants.

For African American women, World War II offered opportunities for personal advancement and, with the involvement of labor unions and professional organizations, a way to demand the end of discriminatory practices in different industries. Carrie E. Bullock, who promoted the professional advancement of African American nurses, worked to equalize opportunities for white and black nurses in the Army Nurse Corps. She launched a letter-writing campaign to protest discrimination against black nurses in the Army and Navy Nurse Corps, and in 1945 the U.S. Navy dropped the color bar against black nurses. Sylvia Woods, who migrated to Chicago in the 1930s from New Orleans, Louisiana, had found it difficult to secure any better job than one in a commercial laundry; she later obtained a skilled job at a Bendix Aviation plant on the West Side of Chicago during World War II. Initially hired at the factory in one of the lower skilled jobs—those generally assigned to African Americans—Woods eventually became a drill press operator. She helped organize United Auto Workers Local 330.

For Japanese Americans living on the West Coast, World War II was a nightmare of injustice and dislocation. Wartime production requirements, however, offered some Japanese Americans in internment camps an opportunity for resettlement in the Midwest. About thirty thousand Japanese Americans who had been internment camp residents came to Chicago. In 1943, Chicago became the largest Japanese American resettlement center in the forty-eight states. Among those who came in the summer of 1944 were the Arais. Akira Arai arrived first, having accepted a job at International Harvester to recruit Japanese Americans. About a month later, Joan Arai and her son joined him, and she found employment as a clerical worker with the Chicago YWCA. Imayo Suzuki and her family resettled in Chicago after she and her husband and their three children were imprisoned in the Minidoka Camp located in Idaho. Research scientist Chiyo Murakami came to Chicago in 1943 after spending one year in a relocation camp. She became a staff member of the Mt. Sinai Hospital laboratory, where she assisted with the development of the blood bank and worked on the new method of typing blood by its Rh factor.

Women in Chicago's ethnic neighborhoods were organized to aid their homelands. Stella Petrakis was active in the Greek War Relief Association, sold Defense Bonds, and founded and headed the Greek-American Star Mothers who prepared and sent food and gift parcels to American servicemen. Czech immigrant Vlasta Vráz organized two thousand Czech American women into Czechoslovak units of the American Red Cross. She also worked with the Voice of America and with Radio Free Europe and played an active role in relief work for Czechoslovak refugees. Lidia Pucińska promoted war bond sales in Chicago's Polonia through her radio programs.

PROGRESSIVE WOMEN IN POSTWAR AMERICA, 1945–1960

Women in Chicago who taught school, worked in YWCAs, were social workers and probation officers, lawyers and research scientists, who staffed settlement houses and community centers, were nurses and doctors in hospitals, made candy in factories, worked as clerks in offices and waitresses in restaurants lived a reality different from the suburban lifestyle portrayed in television programs, consumer advertisements, and magazine articles. Stay-at-home mothers in suburbia were a real phenomenon, but even here the image of life in the postwar bedroom communities ignored the process of community-building in which many women were engaged. Women in the suburbs organized for library and education bond issues and for expanded community services; they established League of Women Voters chapters and Parent Teacher Associations, and a minority began to question the proliferation of nuclear armaments, Strontium 90 in the milk supply, the use of DDT, and the disturbing images of Jim Crowism in the South. In postwar suburban Riverdale, Illinois, Marjorie Pebworth became active in the Department of Social Relations in her local Episcopal church and worked on open-housing issues; she also served on the board of Benton House, a neighborhood settlement house. In 1958 Pebworth was the first woman elected in suburban Cook County to the Thornton Township High School and Junior College Board, on which she was instrumental in getting the first black teacher hired in the Thornton district. In 1965 she was one of seven women elected to the Illinois legislature, where she worked on open housing initiatives. Although a state fair housing law was never achieved, in July 1966 Governor Otto Kerner did issue an open occupancy order that called for revocation or suspension of licenses of brokers who listed any property that the owners did not want sold or rented to Blacks or minority religious groups.

In Chicago, a great urban center whose metropolitan population had grown to nearly 5,600,000 in 1950, the number of city residents had begun to decline in proportion to the increase in the number of residents in the suburban metropolitan area. The city's black population doubled between 1940 and 1950 and increased another 65 percent between 1950 and 1960 (from 492,000 to 813,000). The Congress of Racial Equality was founded in Chicago in 1942. One of its major campaigns was to integrate public facilities, including lunchrooms, public accommodations, and transportation. But the fault line of racial tension in Chicago remained the area of housing.

A period of urban renewal brought high-rise housing projects to the city's segregated neighborhoods and maintained the segregated patterns. Between 1945 and 1954, nine major racial riots related to housing took place in Chicago. Lorraine Hansberry's autobiographical play *Raisin in the Sun*, the poignant story of the Younger family's dream of owning their own home in a quiet, uncongested, tree-lined Chicago neighborhood, is bracketed by the hopelessness of ghetto life and the potential violence that awaits them when they become the first black family to move into a white neighborhood. Public housing official

Mary Bolton Wirth—who had witnessed the 1919 Chicago Race Riot while attending the University of Chicago—was appointed a supervisor in the Community and Tenant Relations Division of the Chicago Housing Authority in 1953. It was apparent at that early date that building maintenance at the CHA projects was inadequate, that tenants felt hopeless, that vandalism and crime were not being controlled, and that the demolition of slums and provision of new housing was not sufficient "to cure the ills of the relocated slum dweller without additional welfare services" (see the entry for Mary Bolton Wirth, below). Lea Taylor voiced similar concerns. She had been appointed in 1946 to the Metropolitan Housing and Planning Council's Committee on Race Relations. Taylor helped to organize a conference on civil rights and social welfare in 1949; as Chicago's racial strife worsened, she served on the Citizens Committee to Fight Slums.

Public schools shared the problems associated with segregated housing patterns, overcrowding, and inadequate facilities in South Side and West Side black neighborhoods. Black educators, librarians, and civic leaders had advocated curriculum reforms and a variety of programs to combat the growing racial intolerance and polarization in the school system from the 1920s. In 1942, staff members at Hall Branch library and William Johnson, superintendent of the Chicago Board of Education, collaborated on a research project to choose materials for the preparation of black history courses to be included in the regular school curriculum. Charlamae Rollins and Vivian Harsh started a Reading Guidance Clinic for parents. Stella Counselbaum began promoting human relations extracurricular clubs devoted to creating interracial understanding and interaction in Chicago-area public and Catholic schools. The Chicago Council against Racial and Religious Discrimination, of which Counselbaum was a member, sponsored an Institute on College Quotas; the findings confirmed there was discrimination in Chicago and Illinois schools against members of racial and religious minority groups. Counselbaum established the Women's Council for Fair Education Practices of Illinois in 1948 and served as secretary of the organization. The group unsuccessfully lobbied for passage of the Illinois Fair Practices in Education bill.

In 1948 Annabel Carey Prescott was appointed assistant principal in charge of the new freshman-sophomore Cregier Branch of Crane Technical High School. It had an enrollment of African American, Italian, Mexican, and Caucasian students from the racially changing nearby neighborhoods on the West Side; in addition to poverty, the West Side was experiencing serious racial tension as the second wave of black migration from the South settled there. The other ethnic groups attending Cregier came from neighborhoods resisting integration.

Organizations such as the National Association for the Advancement of Colored People, the Urban League, the Anti-Defamation League, the National Conference of Christians and Jews, and government commissions on human relations—including the Chicago Commission on Human Relations, the Human Relations Committee of the Chicago Public Schools, and ad hoc groups such as the Citizens Committee to Fight Slums—attest to the formative development in the 1940s of the civil rights movement in the North and in Chicago. The African

American community had always struggled for civil rights and economic justice, as illustrated by the biographies of Chicago women beginning with Mary Jane Richardson Jones in the antebellum period; Ida B. Wells-Barnett, Fannie Barrier Williams, and Elizabeth Lindsay Davis in the Progressive Era; and Ada S. McKinley, Irene McCoy Gaines, Maudelle Bousfield, Annabel Prescott, and Thyra Edwards in the interwar and postwar periods.

Events in Europe during World War II that led to the establishment of a war crimes tribunal for the first time in human history formed the broader context for human rights activists such as Lillian Herstein, Tobey Prinz, Stella Counselbaum, Sister Mary Ellen O'Hanlon, Annetta Dieckmann, Rose Hum Lee, Raya Dunayevskaya, Sylvia Woods, Pearl Hart, Thyra Edwards, and Edith Sampson. Anti-Semitism and racism had dominated events inside the United States and abroad. Sociologist Rose Hum Lee studied Chinese immigrant communities, and her interest in issues of race and human rights led to her appointment to Chicago's Commission on Human Relations. Edith Sampson, the first African American woman to serve as judge in Cook County, toured Europe after World War II, lecturing on human rights; she was made an alternate delegate from the United States to the United Nations. Herstein, Prinz, and Edwards had been radicalized in the 1930s when they took the side of the Loyalists in the Spanish Civil War (1936–38). Sylvia Woods had been influenced by the Pan-Africanism of the 1920s and 1930s. For Edwards, Woods, and Prinz, the Communist Party in the 1930s and 1940s expressed their commitment to socialism, internationalism, interracialism, and antifascism.

For Catholic educator and scientist Sister O'Hanlon, the shock of recognition of racism in American institutions, including the Roman Catholic Church, occurred during a period of postgraduate study in Europe prior to the outbreak of World War II. In her work as a college biology teacher in the 1940s and 1950s, she wrote textbooks that countered racial stereotyping with sound biological information. Dieckmann and Hart drew on their experience in the field of civil liberties in advocating human rights. The former directed the South Parkway YWCA's industrial programs for black women workers and took a progressive stand on social and economic issues; the latter was, in 1937, a founding member and the first national secretary of the National Lawyer's Guild. Counselbaum had forged interfaith and interracial relationships through her work with the Anti-Defamation League in the Midwest. On the national level she worked with Mary McLeod Bethune in shaping an interracial dialogue between black and white women.

Russian immigrant and founder of the Marxist-Humanist News and Letters Committees Raya Dunayevskaya had written for the *Negro Champion*, the newspaper of the American Negro Labor Congress. *News & Letters* was edited by African American revolutionary Charles Denby, and the black liberation movement was at the core of interest for Dunayevskaya and the News and Letters Committees. Of the women active here, Dunayevskaya was the most self-consciously engaged in theorizing about the liberation of women. She had rejected the Soviet system by the 1930s, had even broken with Leon Trotsky in 1939 when he insisted that Russia was still a workers' state; and she began to argue that the transformation of the relationship

between women and men was fundamental to a Marxist concept of a new society. Only Stella Counselbaum had deep roots in the network of women's organizations that had been so important for the activism of the Progressive Era and the period between the two wars. Most of the networking took place in radical circles; in the organizations established to defend civil liberties; in the coalitions to promote understanding among different racial, ethnic, and religious groups; with organizations dedicated to civil rights; and in labor unions.

The experience of Annabel Prescott illustrates how modest programs for interracial understanding and integrated schools could be attacked as subversive and anti-American. At Cregier High School, Prescott's father, African Methodist Episcopal Bishop Archibald J. Carey, member of a prominent and prestigious old-settler black family of Chicago's Black Metropolis, found that white flight turned integrating schools all black and made black children feel a sense of rejection; their resentment ultimately turned into hostility toward learning. Prescott identified the same pattern among Mexican students who experienced prejudice and rejection. Prescott condemned the practice of passively permitting this ghettoization of schools. In the 1950s, under the superintendency of Herold Hunt, a reform-minded school leader, Prescott's programs were initiated; she was able to stabilize Cregier, at least temporarily. Prescott received awards for her work, but the Chicago school superintendent responsible for attacking segregation throughout the system came under an intense red-baiting attack. Hunt was labeled a communist by the *Chicago Tribune* because he had attended Columbia University in New York City, identified as communist-led. His tenure with the Chicago school system was over by 1953.

Much of the energy of activists in the 1940s and 1950s was turned toward defending themselves and others accused of being communists or of participating in communist-front organizations. In 1947 the Taft-Hartley Act precipitated organized labor's purge of radical trade union leaders. Taft-Hartley's non-communist affidavit requirement stipulated that unions whose local or national officials were communists or affiliated with communists could not enter into collective bargaining agreements. Unions purged their ranks of accused and suspected communists to comply with the act. Taft-Hartley provisions also established a sixty-day cooling off period in which strikes could not be declared, outlawed mass picketing, and provided for the suing of labor unions for unfair labor practices. Between November 1949 and August 1950, the CIO kicked out ten unions, including the United Electrical, Radio and Machine Workers of America (UE), one of its original affiliates, in a defensive response to the Taft-Hartley Act and the anticommunist red-baiting. Florence Criley was an organizer for UE in the Chicago area and, with her husband Richard Criley, became an ardent champion of the civil liberties of radicals and a foe of the McCarthy-type red-baiting tactics of the cold war era.

The passage of the McCarran Act in 1950 began a period of deportations and raids to sweep up immigrants accused of being communists. In 1952 Title I of the Walter-McCarran Act identified the U.S. Communist Party (CP) as a clear and present danger to national security; CP members were required to register, and the law barred members from holding federal jobs and from receiving passports; it tightened existing espionage laws and denied entrance to aliens who were CP members or associated with the CP. Title II mandated detention of likely spies, though they could appeal to a review board. In 1952 aliens suspected of CP affiliation were to be deported or, in the case of naturalized citizens, their citizenship was to be revoked. Pearl Hart, who had responded to the growth of racism in the United States and the repression or restriction of the activities of trade unions, civil rights advocates, and immigrants by insisting that the Constitution of the United States protected all of these activities, advocated a strong civil liberties approach. She entered a period of legal work defending immigrants and radicals. By the 1960s, the McCarthy-like tactics and proceedings of the House Un-American Activities Committee (HUAC) had extended to the pursuit of activists in the civil rights movement and in the antiwar movement. Hart was the legal counsel for the Chicago Committee to Defend the Bill of Rights, which was part of a national movement, the American Committee to Defend the Bill of Rights. These groups publicized HUAC's abuses and other oppressive government actions.

Radicals like Tobey Prinz learned to function in the context of red-baiting and conservative unionism. Prinz pragmatically signed a teachers' loyalty oath so that she could continue as a public school teacher but retained her membership in the CP. Prinz established the ad hoc Committee on Community Relations within the Chicago Teachers Union as well as the Concerned Rank & File Teachers. These groups kept alive integrationist goals. Prinz also worked for international acceptance of the Stockholm Peace Appeal aimed at stopping nuclear war; she worked with other activists in her local Parent Teacher Association to reject the national organization's proposed endorsement of a universal military draft in peacetime. Her involvement in grassroots organization never faltered. She worked for tenants' rights, local progressive politicians, and to save the beaches along Lake Michigan in the Rogers Park neighborhood in which she lived. In all these efforts she worked in coalitions with neighbors, social justice Catholics and Jews, antimachine political organizations, the homeless, and the unemployed.

Protestant theologians began to call for desegregation of the all-white Protestant churches in America. Theologian Georgia Harkness opposed the merger of the Methodist Church with the Evangelical United Brethren Church, arguing that no union should take place until the all-black Central Jurisdiction of the Methodist Church was integrated into the new United Methodist Church. The segregated jurisdiction would not be eliminated until 1972, four years after the merger.

PROFESSIONAL WOMEN AND SUBURBAN SETTLERS, 1945–1960

From the earliest days of Chicago's corporate history, women engaged in economic and social activities that were integral to the growth of the city. Immigrant, African American, and white American-born women were innovative educators, municipal reformers, social scientists, physicians and lawyers, artists and writers, broadcasters and journalists. In their struggles to enter the mainstream of the American economy in Chicago—one of the fastest growing business and industrial cen-

ters in the country—they emerged as shapers of modern culture. As modernizers, most women reformers prior to World War II shared an uncritical belief in the potential efficacy for society of technology, science, and knowledge of human nature—a faith in progress shared by men.

By the 1950s, such women as Irene Kawin, Charlotte Towle, Mary Bolton Wirth, Lea Demarest Taylor, and Jessie Binford realized that the problems of inadequate housing, segregation, poverty, and juvenile delinquency were more intractable than they had initially thought. As social workers whose careers spanned the Progressive Era and the New Deal, they came to understand that the professionalization of the field of social work had produced its own problems. Struggles with the political system prevailed, and interest groups emerged that confounded efforts to implement programs offering hope for rehabilitation or prevention of society's ills. In Chicago, the persistence of racism stymied many efforts to improve housing, education, and the standard of living for African Americans.

One of the strengths of *Women Building Chicago 1790–1990: A Biographical Dictionary* is its recovery of biographies of women whose major activities and careers are situated in the period from 1945 to 1960. These biographies provide evidence for the continuation of women's efforts in politics and the professions at the same time that they provide the political and social context for understanding the attacks on women's advancement in these decades. Postwar women in suburbia in the 1940s and 1950s were told that women's role as homemaker was the appropriate one. Individual women like lawyer Soia Mentschikoff, who successfully pursued careers, denied the need for a women's movement to fight for equal rights and argued that their achievements were based on merit. The disengagement from women's organizations by career women who attempted to define themselves according to the masculine image of lawyer, doctor, or scientist made it difficult for the majority of college-educated women to understand what opportunities and constraints actually existed for them in the economy. Women's alienation from one another's plight in this period is evident from a reading of the biographies of such scientists as Mary Alice McWhinnie, Chiyo Murakami, Maud Slye, Margery Claire Carlson, Margaret Morse Nice, Dorothy Price, Libbie Hyman, and Maria Goeppert Mayer, and of mathematician Mary Catherine Bishop Weiss. It was difficult for women to advance in careers in science and mathematics, regardless of the significance of their work. The biographies of psychiatrist Therese Benedek, lawyers Dorothea Blender and Alice M. Bright, opera company director Carol Fox, merchandising executive Edith Grimm, anthropologist Frances Shapiro Herskovits, psychologist Helen Lois Koch, and sociologist Rose Hum Lee begin to fill in the details of women in the period between the two waves of feminism—the first women's movement that emerged after the Civil War and ended at about the time the Nineteenth Amendment was passed, and the second wave that began around 1963 and continued through the late 1970s. Our understanding of both women's movements will be enriched, and even transformed, by this new knowledge.

SECOND WAVE FEMINISM IN CHICAGO

The majority of women activists in second wave feminism in Chicago are still alive and therefore are not included in this collection of historical biographies. Those women who died young, by December 31, 1990, and are included here begin to tell the story of this period. As recent books indicate, the leaders of the women's liberation movement in the late 1960s and early 1970s were a mixture of college-age women whose involvement in civil rights and antiwar movement politics placed them in the center of great political, social, and cultural upheavals and older women activists, whose longstanding commitments to social change also located them in the movements for social justice, civil rights, and peace.

An indication of the onset of the second wave was the 180-degree change in attitude toward the Equal Rights Amendment (ERA). The old progressive coalition had opposed the ERA because they feared that the hard-won protections of women and children would evaporate in challenges by conservative forces if the ERA was approved. By the time Esther Saperstein first introduced bills in the Illinois General Assembly requiring equal pay for men and women and the repeal of the Eight Hour Day Law (which effectively prevented female workers from working more than eight hours a day), the second wave of feminism had reconfigured the debate. In 1961 Illinois Republican Congresswoman Marguerite Stitt Church, as a member of the House Judiciary Committee, introduced a resolution proposing an amendment to the U.S. Constitution providing equal rights for men and women. In 1963, State Representative Esther Saperstein established a Commission on the Status of Women and used it to launch legislation to achieve women's equality. The U.S. Congress passed the Equal Pay Act of 1963 and the Civil Rights Act of 1964, the latter containing a prohibition against sex discrimination in employment. In 1963 Saperstein introduced her bills requiring pay equality and the repeal of the Eight Hour Day Law; though the bills failed to pass, she reintroduced them in each new session. In 1969 Saperstein secured passage of the first grant-in-aid bill to provide for day-care centers in Illinois.

After the U.S. Congress passed the Equal Rights Amendment in 1972, identical ERA ratification bills were introduced in both houses of the Illinois legislature; Esther Saperstein was sponsor in the State Senate. Saperstein cosponsored ERA bills through 1974, but none passed; Illinois remained the only northern state to fail to pass ERA. Ironically, after the progressive social reform coalition succeeded in obtaining passage of the federal Sheppard-Towner Maternity and Infancy Act in 1921, Illinois was one of the handful of states that did not create the matching legislation and funding to participate in the program. Illinois also retained anti-abortion laws after many northern states had made provisions for legal abortion. In a radical departure, women activists in the Chicago Women's Liberation Union began an underground abortion service called "Jane." Only with the Supreme Court decision in Roe v. Wade in 1973 did Illinois women gain the right to choice. Congressman Henry Hyde, the author of the Hyde amendment, is from suburban Illinois and continues to use the power of appropriations in the House of Representatives to prevent the use of public funds for abortions for women with low incomes.

Outside the Illinois legislature, women activists had mounted a substantial movement for ERA. The coalition that supported ERA reflected deeper changes in the construction of womanhood that had occurred in the postwar period. For example, an entire segment of Catholic women religious and lay Catholic women emerged as militant feminists in the 1960s. Their involvement with women's liberation politics was one aspect of a revolutionary change occurring in the American Catholic Church, the repercussions of which are still not fully clear. In 1968 Sister Marjorie Tuite and others founded the National Assembly of Religious Women, a Catholic feminist social justice ministry based in Chicago; it was the first of many Catholic feminist groups that emerged after Vatican II. Founded originally to provide a national and public voice for women in religious congregations, it opened its membership in 1983 to all Catholic women. When Sister Albertus Magnus McGrath was asked in 1974, "Are women oppressed in the Church?" she answered with a resounding yes. She turned a critical eye on the institutional structures of the church as they affected women's struggle for self-determination. In her book *What a Modern Catholic Believes about Women*, published in 1972 (reprinted as *Women and the Church* [1976]), McGrath reveals the contempt with which women have often been treated in clerical circles, despite declarations by the church hierarchy of the equality of women and men as children of God. In the book's final chapter, "Women as 'Niggers' of the Church," McGrath characterizes the Catholic Church as "overprotective of women on the one hand, and, on the other, as the land of the perpetual putdown of the feminine" (see the entry for Sister Albertus Magnus McGrath, below).

McGrath was a member of the National Organization of Women and an ardent proponent of the Equal Rights Amendment; she went public with her endorsement of ERA in an advertisement in the Chicago *Sun-Times* that featured her photograph and quoted her as saying, "Sometimes I think Illinois seems almost past praying for when it comes to equality for women."

When U.S. Steel denied Alice Melickian Peurala a promotion because of her sex, she made a complaint to the Equal Employment Opportunity Commission (EEOC), invoking the 1964 Civil Rights Act. EEOC investigated Peurala's complaint and, two years later, in 1969, found probable cause. Since U.S. Steel refused to reverse itself, Peurala sued the company for sex discrimination. In 1974, U.S. Steel settled with Alice Peurala and she was given the job previously denied her.

Undeterred in her efforts to democratize the steel union and press for equal treatment for women, Peurala won a seat on the grievance committee of Steelworkers Local 65 in 1976; she developed a reputation as a fighter for the rights of all workers. She began meeting with other women in Local 65 and they pressured the executive board and union president to appoint a women's committee. Alice Peurala ran successfully for president of Steelworkers Local 65; in 1979 she became the only woman in the nation to head a basic steel unit. Defeated for re-election in 1982, Alice Peurala regained the presidency of Local 65 in 1985. Peurala had initially opposed the ERA but realized, through her own experience, that the provisions of the so-called protective laws were used against her. She came to support the ERA and believed that equality of opportunity on the job was crucial, as was having an effective union willing to stop the continuing harassment of women by male bosses.

In the late 1960s Iris Barbara Merrill helped found the Black Labor Leaders of Chicago, a precursor to both the Coalition of Labor Union Women (CLUW) and the Coalition of Black Trade Unionists. The founding members were African American officers in a number of Chicago unions who wanted to advocate for more black leadership in the local unions. Following the assassination of Martin Luther King Jr. and the ensuing riots in 1968, black leaders organized union contributions toward the rebuilding of Chicago's West Side. They also worked with the local office of the Southern Christian Leadership Conference.

The CLUW emerged after a meeting of eight female union leaders who convened in Chicago in 1973. Cofounders Addie Wyatt of the Amalgamated Meatcutters Union and Clara Day of the Teamsters immediately invited Iris Barbara Merrill to join the organizing activities; Merrill became one of the coordinators of the Midwest Conference of Union Women, a prototype of the national organization. Two hundred women from eighteen states representing twenty national unions participated in the regional conference held in 1973. A year later, Merrill helped coordinate the founding national conference, at which Florence Criley and other trade union women created the CLUW. Some three thousand women delegates came to the founding meeting; soon afterward its Chicago chapter was created. The Chicago chapter of CLUW ran a speakers bureau, conducted educational classes, organized nonunion women, supported striking workers, lobbied for passage of the ERA in Illinois, and held demonstrations in support of a full employment bill.

In the 1900s the WTUL had played a significant role in developing the women's movement of the Progressive Era, the first wave of feminism. A comparison of the WTUL with the CLUW of the second wave of feminism illustrates some of the continuities and differences in the two women's movements. It also offers some final insights into Chicago history. The WTUL emerged from a cross-class alliance; its early leadership was in the hands of prominent women social reformers that included Margaret Dreier Robins, Ellen Gates Starr, Jane Addams, and Mary E. McDowell. Trade unionists, including Agnes Nestor and Mary Kenney O'Sullivan, achieved significant leadership roles as well. CLUW included women who were experienced union activists; their efforts were directed toward democratizing and integrating the male-dominated, gradualist unionism that prevailed in American labor after 1945 and after the purges of Left-oriented leadership. Iris Barbara Merrill, by creating a coalition of workers and community organizations, helped found a union for public employees in Chicago at a time when Cook County party politics controlled labor contracts. CLUW came together without the assistance of middle-class activists; rather, as Merrill and others liked to point out, union women, influenced by the women's movement, wanted to join the fight for the ERA as trade unionists; at the same time, they sought more power and recognition within their unions as women. Socialist and trade union women in the first wave of the women's movement voiced their concerns as they attempted to define their role and identity in relationship to the suffrage campaign. In this sense, issues of class and race always differentiated women from each other and created the internal politics of women's movements.

NEW IMMIGRANTS IN THE POST-WAR PERIOD

Chicago continued to receive new immigrants in the postwar period. Displaced persons from Europe came in the 1950s, Hungarians and Cubans in the 1960s, Indo-Asians and Middle Easterners in the 1970s. Native Americans from more than forty tribes lived in Chicago, making up a population of ten thousand. The biographies of Amy Leicher Skenandore and Chauncina Yellow Robe White Horse are accounts of the experiences of Chicago's modern Native American population.

One of the largest groups of immigrants in the post-1945 period were the Mexicans. Nearly 275,000 Mexican immigrants arrived legally in the United States in the 1950s. By the 1960s and 1970s, there was a vital Chicano (Mexican American) movement in the United States. Maria del Jesus Saucedo, community activist in Chicago, came to the United States during this period and with her family settled in Pilsen, a growing Mexican American neighborhood. Saucedo graduated from Northeastern Illinois University, where with fellow students she founded the Chicago Student Union in 1974. Saucedo also founded and edited *Contra la Pared* (*Against the Wall*), a newsletter that addressed Chicano issues. She was part of the Compania Trucha, a street theater in Pilsen that was an outgrowth of the community's political activism. In the context of the larger women's liberation movement, Saucedo used the Compania Trucha to address women's issues. She did not call herself a feminist and she did not see the Latino male as the primary problem for Latinas; she believed in a unified struggle involving both men and women. She taught school after graduating from college and cofounded the Mexican Teacher's Organization.

Social worker Maria Diaz Martinez was one of the founders of Mujeres Latinas en Acción (Latin Women in Action), the first Latina women's agency in Chicago. A rebellious adolescent who was pregnant at age fifteen and forced to marry her child's father, Martinez had a second chance when she enrolled in the University without Walls, an outpost of Northeastern Illinois University in Chicago that enabled Chicanos who had not completed their education to continue their studies. Martinez received a bachelor's degree in social work and served as a crisis intervener and counselor with Mujeres Latinas en Acción. Returning to school, Martinez enrolled at Roosevelt University, Chicago, where she received a master's degree in social work.

Chicago's history is intimately tied to the transformation of the nation from a largely agricultural society to one dominated by industrial cities. It is also closely bound up with the peopling of these cities by migrants from the American countryside and small towns and by immigrants from foreign countries. Here new American forms emerged even as neighborhoods retained cultural institutions adapted from those of the Old World. When the latest immigrants to occupy Pilsen developed Compania Trucha, they dipped into their Mexican heritage and styled their contemporary street theater after Teatro Campesino, which had been used by Cesar Chavez and Luis Valdes. Now secular and focused on current events, these street and political theaters drew upon a long tradition of religious theater in Mexico and other Latin American countries. Earlier in the 1940s, Mexican immigrant Angelina Moreno Rico had brought a traditional dance to the West Side of Chicago to encourage young Mexican American children to look with pride on their traditions. In the 1970s, Martinez and Saucedo explored their identities as women, as Latinas, and as Americans. As in earlier periods of immigration, they coalesced with other women of their ethnic background and developed organizations of self-help and social outreach.

Following the pattern of women in nineteenth-century Chicago, immigrants to the city in the last part of the twentieth century continued to create opportunity for themselves by using education as the major source of social mobility. Through the process of education, women trained themselves and returned to their own communities to develop ways to live in urban settings that promoted the well-being of the next generation. Just as Catholic women religious had forged structures of education designed to foster balance between assimilative and autonomous goals for immigrants and their children, immigrant Mexican women found ways within their own traditions to accomplish similar agendas. In the process, women achieved economic autonomy for themselves and established new pathways for female social mobility.

These biographies provide a new context for understanding contemporary culture and society. The diversity of the women's lives presented in the following biographies illustrates the ways in which women are differentiated by class, race, and culture distinctions and suggests that much research in the field of the history of women remains to be undertaken. There are many ways to read these biographies, and new patterns and interpretations are bound to emerge to further expand our understanding of the role of gender relationships in urban society.

RIMA LUNIN SCHULTZ

Abbreviations for Sources

BWA = Darlene Clark Hine, ed., *Black Women in America: An Historical Encyclopedia*, 2 vols. (1993)

CHS = Chicago Historical Society

CPL = Chicago Public Library

CT = *Chicago Tribune*

diss. = dissertation

Hist. Soc. = Historical Society

NAW (1971) = Edward T. James, Janet Wilson James, and Paul S. Boyer, eds., *Notable American Women 1607–1950: A Biographical Dictionary*, 3 vols. (1971)

NAW (1980) = Barbara Sicherman and Carol Hurd Green, eds., *Notable American Women: The Modern Period: A Biographical Dictionary* (1980)

NCAB = *National Cyclopaedia of American Biography* (1891–1984)

NL = The Newberry Library, Chicago

NYT = *The New York Times*

SL = The Arthur & Elizabeth Schlesinger Library on the History of Women in America, Radcliffe College, Cambridge, Massachusetts

Spec. Coll. = Special Collections

UC Spec. Coll. = Department of Special Collections, University of Chicago Library

UIC Spec. Coll. = Special Collections, The University Library, University of Illinois at Chicago

Univ. = University

Biographies A–Z

a

ABBOTT, EDITH
September 26, 1876–July 28, 1957
SCHOLAR, EDUCATOR, SOCIAL REFORMER

Edith Abbott, born in Grand Island, Nebraska, was one of four children of Othman Ali and Elizabeth (Griffin) Abbott. Second born, her siblings included an older brother, Othman A. Jr., a younger sister, GRACE ABBOTT, and a younger brother, Arthur Griffin Abbott. Her mother's family settled in Illinois in the late 1830s. Her father, born in Canada, came to the United States at age eight and was raised in Illinois. Othman Abbott and Elizabeth Griffin met in high school and after a lengthy courtship married in 1873. Upholding his family's antislavery position but in opposition to their pacifist beliefs, Othman Abbott served in the Civil War. In 1867, he and his brother traveled West, settling in Nebraska, where he established a law practice. Othman Abbott continued the family's traditional interest in social reform and political involvement, becoming Nebraska's first lieutenant governor. Elizabeth Griffin's family were staunch abolitionists and were active participants in the Underground Railroad. She graduated from the Rockford Female Seminary in Illinois in 1868 and became a high school teacher and a respected high school principal. Although Elizabeth Griffin was raised in a Quaker household and Othman Abbott in a Protestant home, neither was an active member in any organized church. Their children attended church services and functions as part of community involvement rather than on the basis of any specific spiritual commitment.

Both of Abbott's parents valued education highly, and school and the enhancement of knowledge were prominent in her life. She began attending school on an informal basis at the age of three and often received books as gifts. Her parents endeavored to bring both culture and the outside world into their home by providing piano lessons and access to scholarly magazines. In 1889, at age twelve, Edith Abbott was sent to Brownell Hall, an Episcopal girls' boarding school in Omaha, from which she graduated in 1893. During this period hard times fell upon the country. The farmlands of the Midwest succumbed to a drought, resulting in years of crop failures. Dependent on the success of farming, Othman Abbott's business enterprises, including the bank that held Elizabeth Griffin's inheritance, failed. Unwilling to declare bankruptcy, Othman Abbott liquidated as many assets as possible and paid off the family debts over the next several years. Unable to attend college due to the family's financial constraints, at age sixteen Edith Abbott took a teaching post at Grand Island High School, beginning a lifelong career in education. Determined to further her education, Abbott took correspondence courses over the next several years from the University of Nebraska and attended summer sessions there. She entered the University of Nebraska as a full-time student in 1899, became a member of the Delta Gamma sorority, and graduated Phi Beta Kappa in 1901. For the next two years she taught in the Lincoln school system. In the summer of 1902, Abbott attended a summer session at the University of Chicago and met SOPHONISBA BRECKINRIDGE, an assistant professor in MARION TALBOT's Department of Household Administration. Breckinridge and Abbott spent the next forty years in close collegial and personal association. Breckinridge had received a Ph.D. in political science in 1901 from the University of Chicago and during the summer of 1902 was studying for a J.D. degree. Abbott was excited about the atmosphere at Chicago, and, stimulated by her talks with Breckinridge about their mutual research interests in the legal and economic role of women, she eagerly accepted a small fellowship and returned as a full-time student in 1903 in economics. She completed her dissertation, "The Wages of Unskilled Labor in the United States, 1850–1900," and received a Ph.D. with honors in 1905.

Breckinridge, a charter member of the Chicago branch of the Women's Trade Union League (WTUL), helped Edith Abbott obtain her first employment after graduation as secretary of the Boston branch of the WTUL and, at the same time, as a re-

FIG. 1. *Edith Abbott and Sophonisba Preston Breckinridge, founders of the School of Social Service Administration, University of Chicago.*

searcher with the American Economic Association (AEA), analyzing wages and prices and women's work. Abbott lived at Denison House settlement among residents active in the Boston area labor movement. Her research was impressive, and in 1906 the Carnegie Institution, already funding the AEA project, offered Abbott a research position to investigate the employment of women. This position allowed Abbott to pursue research questions first raised in Breckinridge's course at the University of Chicago. She left Boston for New York, living at College Settlement and studying working women and tenement conditions on the Lower East Side. While in New York, she completed a substantial part of the research for her book, *Women in Industry*, sections of which were published as a series of articles in the *Journal of Political Economy* that was started in 1906. That year Abbott won a competitive fellowship to study abroad from the Association of Collegiate Alumnae (forerunner of the American Association of University Women) and, with additional funds from Carnegie, did postdoctoral study at the London School of Economics and the University of London's University College.

In London, Abbott met Beatrice and Sidney Webb, leaders of the socialist Fabian Society, and their influence was second only to that of her mentor and friend, Sophonisba Breckinridge. The Webbs were conducting social investigation and advocating reform of the English poor laws. Their strong reform spirit, shared by the Fabian Society, came from a belief that men and women have a moral responsibility to improve the social order. This view made sense to Abbott, and she embraced Fabian intellectual and practical strategies. She spent time at St. Hilda's, a settlement house, as a way to further her understanding of the people reported on by the Webbs in their research. Abbott re-

turned to the United States in 1907 to a teaching position at Wellesley College, an elite women's college in Massachusetts.

In 1908, after one year of teaching economics at Wellesley, with the urging of Sophonisba Breckinridge and Hull-House resident JULIA LATHROP, Abbott returned to Chicago. Part of her decision to leave Wellesley came from her conviction that coeducation provided equal educational opportunities, whereas women's colleges offered a lower standard of education. The staidness of Wellesley College also created a constrained atmosphere, and Abbott wanted to be in a place where she could gain firsthand experience of the social issues she researched. The return to Chicago represented a challenge and opportunity to build a future with other social activists. She was eager to have the opportunity to blend her scholarship with her interests in social action. She took up residence with her sister Grace at Hull-House, already a center for experimentation in social science research and social reform initiatives. She realized that the nation's welfare needs were too vast to be met through private philanthropy. Abbott supported the expansion of state functions, believing the state should promote human welfare. She viewed access to public services as an integral part of U.S. citizenship.

In 1908 Abbott joined Breckinridge and Lathrop on the faculty of the Chicago School of Civics and Philanthropy (CSCP) as assistant director of the research department. CSCP, founded in 1908 under the direction of the Reverend Graham Taylor, head resident of the Chicago Commons settlement, had grown out of a series of lectures given in 1903. Called the Institute of Social Science, it was attended by workers in charitable institutions. Julia Lathrop of Hull-House and the State Board of Charities, Taylor, and Charles Henderson of the University of Chicago were the first faculty. Renamed CSCP, it was funded in 1907 by an annual grant of ten thousand dollars obtained from the Russell Sage Foundation by Breckinridge, who was the director of the research department. CSCP initially had been an adjunct of private social service agencies and emphasized fieldwork, offering courses by prominent social workers based on their own experiences.

Abbott was critical of Taylor's casual style and repeatedly voiced her desire for a more rigorous structure and a curriculum based on social theory and social research. She wanted to raise social work to the professional level attained in schools of medicine and law. As the number of schools of social work increased, Abbott recognized the need to develop standards for social work education. In 1919, with Breckinridge, she initiated the establishment of the first national association for social work education, the American Association of Schools of Social Work.

Financing problems plagued the school from 1915 until 1920, when CSCP received its final grant from Russell Sage, which was then phasing out its funding of social work training schools. In this context change was essential, and Breckinridge and Abbott were convinced that a university was the proper place for a professional social work school. They took the opportunity and negotiated to move CSCP to the University of Chicago. The move was highly criticized by Taylor and other social work practitioners, who feared the potential loss of autonomy and identification with the agencies served by social workers. Abbott firmly believed professional social work must utilize new scientific knowledge, methods of social research, and ideas from studies in the liberal arts. This approach could only be accomplished through affiliation with a university that would support a blend of academics and field work. In 1924, the new School of Social Service Administration (SSA) became a permanent entity of the University of Chicago, with Edith Abbott appointed as dean.

In 1927, Abbott and Breckinridge initiated the social work profession's first scholarly journal, *Social Service Review,* which published articles on social policy, social work research, and advances in social programs. Breckinridge and Abbott also launched a Social Sciences Series of ten books published by the University of Chicago Press on contemporary social problems that caught the interest of other social scientists. The first in this series was Abbott's *Immigration, Select Documents and Case Records* (1924).

A prolific writer, Abbott's publications included scholarly articles, book reviews, government reports and critiques, letters to the editor on matters of social concern, and numerous papers presented at national and international conferences during a period of nearly fifty years. Her topics were broad, ranging from labor issues, women's and children's rights, crime, immigration, housing, public assistance, and social work education to memoirs of the two most significant persons in her life, Grace Abbott and Sophonisba Preston Breckinridge. Grace and Edith Abbott both lived at Hull-House in their early years in Chicago and had interrelated careers: the former became head of the innovative Immigrants' Protective League, Chicago, and then served as the second head of the federal Children's Bureau, Washington, D.C.; the latter wrote extensively about immigration and children and women in the labor force. Close from childhood, their individual experiences reinforced each other's reform efforts. Af-

ter Grace Abbott's tenure with the Children's Bureau from 1921 to 1934, she rejoined her sister, becoming a professor of public welfare at the School of Social Service Administration.

Edith Abbott was fine featured, slender, and tall, with blond hair and brown eyes. Like many contemporary professional women, Abbott did not marry or have children. Instead, she committed herself to a life of scholarly pursuit, viewing marriage and children as a hindrance to professional growth. Abbott had a great appreciation for her midwestern roots, seeing the region as a land with its own beauty, built from the dedication and tenacity of the pioneers of the prairie. Somewhat unsociable, she did not engage in what she considered the trivia of life. Instead, she was intense, focused, disciplined, and direct to the point of abruptness. She possessed an inquiring mind and an insatiable thirst for learning and knowledge. Abbott was observant of complexities, analytical, and a keen assimilator of facts and nuances that provided a strong foundation to her scholarly pursuits.

The death of her sister Grace in 1939 left Edith Abbott adrift and lonely, and she opened her home to her longtime friend and colleague, Sophonisba Breckinridge. Abbott retired as Dean of the School of Social Service Administration in 1942 but remained on the faculty. She cared for Breckinridge until her death in 1948. Increasingly lonely, Abbott moved back to Hull-House in 1949. In 1953, she retired from the university. No longer able to care for herself, Abbott returned to her family home in Nebraska to live with her brothers for the rest of her life.

Abbott viewed social work practice as both an art and a science that included social planning, agency administration, and social research. She felt strongly that to attain professional status, social work must blend together scholarship, social action, and public social service. Although Abbott eschewed the growing prominence of social casework offered by other schools, through her association with CHARLOTTE TOWLE she came to accept the place of psychiatric theory in the curriculum. Group work, however, did not fare as well. Abbott continued to show little interest in what she viewed as mere "recreation" that offered nothing to professional social work. Based on her belief that the university had a responsibility to prepare men and women to provide leadership in social agency administration, she developed a curriculum that included courses in history, social economics, law and policy, social treatment, social research, and public administration. Abbott also believed that schools of social work must offer an academic curriculum, clinical fieldwork, and research in order to meet the labor demands of social service agencies and develop and promote the profession of social work. During her twenty-nine years at the School of Social Service Administration, Abbott gained recognition and remained a renowned scholar and leader in social work education.

Edith Abbott was a scholar dedicated to scientific inquiry and the advancement of knowledge. Her books are classic works that provide documents and case studies still relevant to scholars in the social sciences and history fields. A woman of untiring vision and action, her most significant achievement was the development of a foundation for the professionalization of social work and the design of a graduate curriculum for students dedicated to the improvement of social welfare services and administration. Present-day curricula of schools of social work have been built upon her broad-based approach and innovation.

Sources. Collections of Abbott's professional and personal papers are held in the UC Spec. Coll.; the Archives of Social Welfare History, Univ. of Minnesota; and the Nebraska State Hist. Soc. Abbott's significant publications include *The Wages of Unskilled Labor in the United States, 1850–1900* (1905); *Women in Industry* (1909); *The Delinquent Child and the Home* (with Sophonisba Preston Breckinridge, 1912); *The One Hundred and One County Jails of Illinois and Why They Ought to be Abolished* (1916); *Truancy and Non-Attendance in the Chicago Schools* (1917); *The Tenements of Chicago, 1908–1935* (1936); *Immigration, Select Documents and Case Records* (1924); *Public Assistance, American Principles and Policies* (1940); *Historical Aspects of the Immigration Problem: Select Documents* (1929, reprint 1969); and in the *Social Service Review,* "Grace Abbott, a Sister's Memories," September 1939; "Sophonisba Preston Breckinridge Over the Years," December 1948; "Grace Abbott and Hull House, 1902–21," September 1950 and December 1950. Abbott's career is chronicled in three entries of the *Social Service Review:* "Three Against Time: Edith and Grace Abbott and Sophonisba P. Breckinridge," March 1954, by Helen R. Wright; "Edith Abbott's Contributions to Social Work Education," March 1958, by Elizabeth Wisner; and "Scholarship in the Quest for Social Welfare: A Fifty-Year History of the *Social Service Review,*" March 1977, by Stephen J. Diner. Rachel Mark's topical annotated bibliography of Abbott's signed and published articles, "The Published Writings of Edith Abbott, A Bibliography," is found in *Social Service Review,* March 1958. The most complete history of Abbott, including a comprehensive listing of her published works, is Lela Costin, *Two Sisters for Social Justice* (1983). Abbott is listed in *NCAB* (1930), *Current Biography* (1941), *NAW* (1980).

JOAN R. RYCRAFT

ABBOTT, GRACE
November 17, 1878–June 19, 1939
SOCIAL REFORMER, SETTLEMENT RESIDENT, CHIEF OF FEDERAL AGENCY

Grace Abbott, who would become the second chief of the federal Children's Bureau, was born in Grand Island, Nebraska, four years after her older brother Othman Jr., two years after her sister EDITH ABBOTT, and only sixteen months before their youngest sibling, Arthur. Both of her parents, Othman Ali and Elizabeth (Griffin) Abbott, grew up in English-descended, Republican families in Illinois. Othman Abbott migrated to Nebraska in 1867, following his service in the Civil War, to take up the practice of law and eventually business. The Quaker Elizabeth Griffin graduated from Rockford Female Seminary in Rockford, Illinois, in 1868 and became a teacher. When, at age twenty-eight, she decided to marry, she was a high school principal and ardent suffragist.

Although the Abbotts enjoyed prosperity and prominence during the high-flying 1880s, their economic fortunes took a turn for the worse during the depression of the 1890s. Indeed, Othman Abbott's business ventures failed to such an extent that the family had to sell virtually everything it owned; because they refused to declare bankruptcy, the whole group had to pull together to work itself out of debt.

In the midst of this misfortune, Grace Abbott managed to get enough education to start a first career. Having begun her secondary education at a private boarding school, she graduated from Grand Island High School in 1895, then from Grand Island College in 1898. After one year of teaching in Broken Bow, Nebraska, illness forced her to return to Grand Island, where in 1899 she began teaching at the local high school.

Between 1899 and 1907, Grace Abbott longed for something more adventurous than living with her parents in the town where she grew up. Like many women of her generation, she also wanted to reach beyond the traditional women's profession of teaching. During the summers, she took occasional trips with friends and eventually enrolled in summer school at the University of Chicago, where her sister, Edith, had earned a graduate degree. That experience convinced her that she, too, wanted to relocate to the city and to continue her studies.

In 1907, she moved to Chicago, and entirely new vistas opened for her. She earned a master's degree in political science from the University of Chicago in 1909, after having moved, in 1908, into Hull-House, the famous social settlement founded nearly twenty years earlier by JANE ADDAMS and ELLEN GATES STARR. This innovative institution provided living quarters for well-educated women and men who wanted to explore and help to solve urban problems. By offering women an alternative living arrangement to marriage, it also afforded them a degree of independence they could hardly have achieved otherwise. This independence clearly appealed to Abbott, for she continued to live at Hull-House until 1917 and never married.

By the time Abbott moved into Hull-House, the settlement was renowned as the home of some of the country's most influential women, many of them deeply involved in progressive reform. They worked tirelessly to improve working conditions for the laboring classes; to better the housing, diet, and child care of Chicago's recent immigrants; and to provide education, recreation, and political opportunities for the city's wage-earners. The ultimate goal of these progressive reformers was to ease the worst suffering caused by the increased pace of industrialization, urbanization, and immigration at the turn of the century. The methods they chose for ameliorating the distress of the working classes often created new kinds of jobs for the reformers themselves. Grace Abbott's career exemplified this dynamic.

Once Abbott was swept into the reforming circles swirling around the social sciences at the University of Chicago and Hull-House, her intelligence, buoyancy, and gift for administration assured her positions of responsibility and visibility. In 1908, as Chicago's reformers were organizing Illinois's Immigrants' Protective League (IPL), they approached Abbott about directing the new private agency. She agreed and served as director of the IPL until 1917.

In this capacity, Abbott expanded her world. She researched the experience of immigrants arriving in Chicago, and she agitated for legislation and built institutions to protect new arrivals. In particular, she struggled to end abuses of immigrants by shady employment offices, to stop deportations, to improve medical care for immigrants, to halt the campaign for immigration restriction, and to unite fresh arrivals with their families. She traveled in eastern Europe, the better to understand the cultures from which many of Chicago's immigrants came, and she published the findings of her research and experience not only in academic journals but also in the popular press.

So well known did she become in the field of immigration

FIG. 2. *Grace Abbott, Hull-House resident and head of the Immigrants' Protective League; she later became director of the federal Children's Bureau.*

Abbott's professional focus changed dramatically in 1917, when JULIA LATHROP, former Hull-House resident and then Chief of the Children's Bureau in the federal Department of Labor, convinced her to serve as director of the bureau's new Child Labor Division. Abbott thus moved to the nation's capital to begin implementing the first federal child labor law, passed in 1916. To the dismay of child labor reformers, the U.S. Supreme Court declared the groundbreaking legislation unconstitutional in 1918. Abbott returned to Chicago the following year as director of the Illinois Immigration Commission.

She remained in Illinois for only two years, however, as a new opportunity—or obligation—beckoned her back to Washington in 1921. Lathrop wanted very much to retire from her position as Chief of the Children's Bureau, but she demurred until she could find a suitable replacement. She believed that there was a great deal at stake in the appointment of her successor. Created by Congress in 1912, the Children's Bureau was the first federal agency ever headed by a woman; it was the jewel in the crown of women reformers and especially child welfare advocates. From her position at the head of this agency, Lathrop engineered passage in 1921 of the country's first federal social welfare legislation, the Sheppard-Towner Maternity and Infancy Act, a cherished goal of many female reformers. The act provided federal funds to the states for the creation of maternal and infant health services and education. Successful implementation of this program meant the world to Lathrop and to literally hundreds of thousands of women across the country who had lobbied for it, who would gain valuable health education from it, or would be employed by it. Lathrop could not entrust the promise of this program to just anyone; Abbott was her number one choice.

Abbott herself would have preferred to steer her career onto some other path. She wanted especially to return to Nebraska to run for political office, and she dreaded the confinement of public administration. However, the pressure from her mentors and colleagues was so great that she agreed to let Lathrop put her name forward as a candidate for the position of Chief of the Children's Bureau, and Lathrop got what she wanted. Abbott moved back to Washington, where she headed the bureau from 1921 to 1934.

In implementing the Maternity and Infancy Act, Abbott drew enormous praise from the reform community and from rural mothers who benefited from the medical checkups and health information they received as a result of the program; but she also endured terrible hostility from the growing numbers of congressmen and conservatives who opposed the legislation. She was vilified by right-wing women and men who insisted that Abbott and all of her reforming network were in the employ of Russian Bolsheviks; other opponents maliciously attacked the women in the Children's Bureau by drawing on the newly circulating ideas of Sigmund Freud to suggest that unmarried, working women were psychologically damaged and should not be allowed to advise anyone on the rearing of children. Abbott faced her opponents with grace and aplomb; indeed, she seemed at times to enjoy having a round with one of her more outrageous accusers at a congressional hearing. Even so, this opposition combined with that from the American Medical Association and a miserly Congress to cut off funds for maternity

that Massachusetts hired her, in 1913–14, to direct a study of immigration that resulted in a powerful report, *The Immigrant in Massachusetts* (1915). The next year, she spearheaded the organization of a conference on "oppressed nationalities" in Washington, D.C.; in 1917, her first book appeared, *The Immigrant and the Community*.

While developing a national reputation for her expertise in immigration, Abbott involved herself in numerous other reform initiatives. In 1910–11, for instance, she joined striking Chicago garment workers on their picket lines; in 1912, she campaigned for Progressive Party presidential candidate Theodore Roosevelt; in 1913, she celebrated the victory of partial suffrage for women in Illinois; and in 1915, she accompanied Jane Addams to The Hague for an international conference of women devoted to peace.

and infancy programs in 1929, despite continued support from organized women all over the country.

During the 1920s, as she administered the Children's Bureau and worked to keep the Maternity and Infancy Act alive, Abbott also took on new domestic responsibilities. In 1925, her older brother's twelve-year-old daughter, Charlotte, moved in with her. Charlotte's mother had died during a flu epidemic in 1918, and the Abbott family had rushed to care for the child; but her favorite caretaker was her warm and attentive Aunt Grace. The niece and aunt remained devoted to each other through the rest of Grace Abbott's life.

The final decade of Abbott's life coincided with the Great Depression. Sadly, the 1930s saw this public administrator, policymaker, and activist reach the pinnacle of her career simultaneously with the deterioration of her health. In 1927, a first bout with tuberculosis forced Abbott to leave Washington for several months of recuperation in Colorado. From that point, her health was always a concern. Nevertheless, when Franklin Delano Roosevelt won the presidency in 1932, he considered Grace Abbott a candidate for Secretary of Labor. Nursing dreams of running for office from Nebraska, Abbott declined consideration for the spot and urged her supporters to push for Frances Perkins's appointment.

As she was turning over leadership of the Children's Bureau in 1934, Abbott moved back to Chicago to live with her sister and to take on several new jobs. She became a professor of public welfare at the University of Chicago's School of Social Service Administration, where her sister was dean; she agreed to edit the *Social Service Review*, founded and previously edited by her sister, and she accepted appointment to President Roosevelt's advisory council to the Committee on Economic Security.

In the latter office, Abbott helped to shape the Social Security Act of 1935. Along with colleagues in the Children's Bureau, she drafted programs that would find their way into this keystone of the U.S. welfare state: Aid to Dependent Children, services for disabled children, and a limited version of the maternal and infant health programs originated in the 1920s. Abbott's long-held hope for a federal prohibition of child labor was also partially realized in the Fair Labor Standards Act (1938).

For all of the success that this New Deal legislation represented for Abbott and her reforming friends, the security it offered was not nearly enough to satisfy them. As a professor and editor, Abbott continued to critique existing social programs and to suggest farther reaching ones. In 1938, Abbott published two volumes of documents on laws pertaining to children, *The Child and the State*; after her death, her sister compiled many of Abbott's lectures and articles from the 1930s for a volume titled *From Relief to Social Security: The Development of the New Public Welfare Services and Their Administration* (1941).

In 1938, doctors diagnosed Abbott with multiple myeloma, and she died of this cancer the next year at age sixty. At her death, she was living with her sister in Chicago. She was cremated, and her ashes returned to Grand Island for burial.

Grace Abbott, daughter of the Great Plains, became one of the early twentieth century's most important public administrators. By implementing the federal government's first piece of social welfare legislation and playing a central role in formulating the Social Security Act, Abbott helped to pour the foundation of the U.S. welfare state. As one of her graduate school professors observed of her as a student: "She had then a remarkably clear, clean, and incisive mind. . . . She was not aggressive or unpleasantly self-assured, not irritatingly complacent; but she did have, I think, assurance or at least a calm confidence, and, as you looked at her, you felt that she had her hand on the tiller and her eyes on the light at the masthead" (quoted in Edith Abbott, "Grace Abbott and Hull House," September 1950, 375).

Sources. Her personal papers, the papers of Edith and Grace Abbott, are in UC Spec. Coll., and much of her life's work is documented in the Children's Bureau Records, National Archives and Records Administration, Washington, D.C. Although Grace Abbott was more an activist than a scholar, she published quite a lot. Her earliest publications appeared after her move to Chicago, and they focused mostly on immigration. These include "The Chicago Employment Agency and Immigrant Worker," *American Journal of Sociology*, November 1908; "The Treatment of Aliens in the Criminal Courts," *Journal of the American Institute of Criminal Law and Criminology*, 1911; and "The Midwife in Chicago," *American Journal of Sociology*, March 1915. Her first book, *The Immigrant and the Community*, appeared in 1917, and her last book, *The Child and the State*, in 1938. Like so many reformers and public officials, Abbott articulated her positions on public issues in frequent testimony before Congress, in the many speeches she delivered before professional and voluntary associations, and in the articles she wrote for popular magazines. Abbott compiled reports on the Children's Bureau from 1922 to 1934. Her biographer, Lela B. Costin, wrote *Two Sisters for Social Justice: A Biography of Grace and Edith Abbott* (1983). Memories by the sister with whom she worked very closely are in Edith Abbott, "Grace Abbott: A Sister's Memories," *Social Service Review*, September 1939, and in a two-installment series, "Grace Abbott and Hull House, 1908–21," *Social Service Review*, September and December 1950. Another rich testimony by a personal acquaintance is that of Helen Wright, "Three Against Time: Edith and Grace Abbott and Sophonisba Breckinridge," *Social Service Review*, March 1954. One view of Abbott's contributions to the Social Security Act is laid out in Edwin Witte, *The Development of the Social Security Act* (1962). An entry on Abbott appears in *NAW* (1971).

ROBYN MUNCY

ABBOTT, MERRIEL
April 27, 1893–November 6, 1977
CHOREOGRAPHER, DANCE EDUCATOR, HOTEL ENTERTAINMENT DIRECTOR

Merriel Abbott was born into an orthodox Jewish family to Russian immigrants Benjamin and Frieda (Heyman) Abbott; she was the youngest of three children and the only one born in the United States. Abbott began studying dance in Chicago at the age of fifteen. While a student of Andreas Pavley and Serge Oukrainsky, she worked as their teaching assistant. Her parents would not allow her to dance on the stage, considering any profession connected with the theater to be disgraceful, but they did permit her to go to New York to study.

When Abbott returned to Chicago, she attended National Kindergarten and Elementary College (now National-Louis University), from which she graduated in 1918. She taught kindergarten at National until 1920 and then at a Montessori school—based on an educational approach of self-motivation by children—on Chicago's South Side. Her real love, though, was dancing, and she soon left kindergarten teaching to open a dance school in downtown Chicago. Here she taught hundreds of girls, including such soon-to-be stars as Ginger Rogers and June Taylor (of the June Taylor Dancers). She brought in experts in all types of dance to teach her students, who came from a range of economic backgrounds—from neighborhood community centers to wealthy homes in Hyde Park, the south Chicago neighborhood in which she grew up.

On May 21, 1921, Abbott married Dr. Philip Lewin, an orthopedic surgeon and inventor of the Lewin splint for finger injury. They had met when one of Abbott's students broke her wrist during a dance class and Abbott had rushed her to Lewin's nearby office. The two had an unconventional marriage, with Abbott pursuing her career and the couple living in various hotels.

Her school became "a dance center for study and employment in the Midwest" (Cohen-Stratyner, 1). Abbott directed dance revues, known as Prologs, performed in Chicago's Paramount /Publix movie theaters, a chain with headquarters in the city. The performers were the Merriel Abbott Dancers, informally known as the "Abbott girls," who were chosen from the students at her school. They did precision acrobatic acts as well as standard group dance routines. With a troupe of about one hundred dancers, Abbott also sent performance lines to theaters in Europe and Latin America, and she herself did the choreography and costuming. In the late 1920s, she directed a male dance team for Prolog work.

Abbott supervised the activities of the women dancers, setting standards of behavior that she deemed desirable. She arranged for their education to continue when they were in Europe. She left them for a month or two at a time with a woman in Paris, who taught them French language and culture. She provided extensive courses in grooming and etiquette. Abbott was strict about virtually every aspect of the dancers' lives, not even allowing them to date musicians or other show business personnel.

In 1933, shortly after the Empire Room of the Palmer House Hotel in Chicago opened, Abbott introduced her dancers to the room. Four years later she became booking agent for the Empire Room, selecting and hiring performers. When Conrad Hilton acquired the Palmer House in 1945, he was so impressed with her work that he appointed her director of entertainment for Hilton Hotels worldwide. Abbott traveled frequently to Europe and elsewhere to find and book talent.

Abbott brought in many singers and dancers who were famous and others who were unknown but later became stars, such as Liberace, whose first important appearance was in the Empire Room. She was able to recognize talent in young performers. Maurice Chevalier, Edith Piaf, and Jimmy Durante were all brought to the Empire Room by Abbott very early in their careers. She featured singers Tony Martin and Hildegaard and dancers Cyd Charisse and the Jose Greco Company. She also booked the same performers into Hilton Hotels all over the world.

The Abbott Dancers performed as the opening act of each show. The young women lived in the hotel when performing, so they would not have to go home unescorted after the show. They studied dance and continued their schooling, with Abbott con-

stantly reminding them that they would not be able to dance all their lives. They had to weigh in before every performance, and any dancer who was over her limit had a fine extracted from her salary; the money was ultimately used for a party for the dancers. Respected by both her dancers and the solo performers as a strict disciplinarian and a fair person, she earned the nickname "Teach" for teacher.

She was in charge of all activities in the Empire Room and later in the Boulevard Room at the Conrad Hilton Hotel (now the Hilton and Towers), even getting involved with how food was served. On prom night, high school students came to the Empire Room. She instructed the waiters to let the students take their minimum charge in food, since no drinks could be served to them. She watched over the details of the service.

Abbott "became the dean of the nation's chorus lines" (*Chicago Tribune*, November 7, 1977) by extending her involvement beyond Chicago. Through her friendship with Barney Balaban, owner of Chicago theaters where the Abbott line performed, Merriel Abbott worked in Hollywood in the late 1930s and early 1940s. She choreographed three Jack Benny movies, using the Abbott Dancers in *Man about Town* and *Buck Benny Rides Again*. Abbott did the choreography for *Broadway Melody of 1938*, with William Powell, and for George White's *Scandals*. She worked with comedian Eddie Cantor and Busby Berkeley, a film dance director, and choreographed routines for Mickey Rooney and Judy Garland. She also supplied dancers for a number of Broadway theater productions, including *Rain or Shine* and *Fine and Dandy*.

Between 1942 and 1945, Abbott left the school in order to join her husband, who was in military service. After World War II, many of the dancers no longer performed because they married. By about 1955, Abbott had no dancers whom she had trained. She hired "outside girls" (Abbott notes, Newberry Library), but felt that they lacked the training and elegance of the Abbott Dancers. She ended the dance act at the Empire Room in 1957 but continued to engage other performers.

In 1948 Abbott and Lewin bought a home in Highland Park, a northern suburb of Chicago. Three years later a new element was introduced into their lives after Lewin began treating a six-week-old infant who was paralyzed by polio. His teen-age parents could not afford the extensive surgeries and medical treatments needed for his recovery. The biological parents allowed Abbott and Lewin to take over their son Frank's care and eventually to adopt him.

One of the conditions of the adoption was that the child receive at least three years of Catholic education because his biological parents were Catholic; Abbott helped him with these studies. According to Frank Lewin, Abbott was completely devoted to him. After Philip Lewin died on May 13, 1960, Abbott and her son remained in Highland Park for about two years and then moved back to the city, to the Edgewater Beach Hotel.

In her direct manner, Abbott taught Frank about life in show business. He had a band while he was attending Francis Parker High School, and Abbott became the manager. She went with them when they played school dances and birthday parties. She called in a choreographer to show the boys how to stand with their instruments, and she took a cut of their earnings.

In 1958 Abbott retired briefly from the Hilton position at age sixty-five and was immediately appointed by Conrad Hilton as an independent agent. She received a pension and kept the same office at the Palmer House. Besides booking the Empire Room, she choreographed and booked ice shows at the Boulevard Room of the Conrad Hilton Hotel and booked the Polynesian Room at the Edgewater Beach Hotel during the time she lived there. She worked for the Hilton Hotels worldwide until shortly before her death at eighty-four years of age.

Abbott became an executive at the Empire Room while the country was still in the throes of the Great Depression, at a time when women were rarely seen in this role. She used her knowledge of dance and her choreographic skills to develop an entrepreneurial domain as the director of entertainment for the Hilton hotel chain. Frank Lewin summed up his mother's life as a woman working in a "male-oriented . . . organization. It was virtually unheard of in those days, to get that kind of respect and that kind of power and responsibility, where Conrad Hilton would say, 'Whatever you want to do, you just do'" (Lewin interview).

Sources. Brief autobiographical notes by Merriel Abbott in the Barzel Dance Collection at NL focus on her work with the Abbott Dancers. Important information comes from interviews by Norma Libman in 1995 with Abbott's son, Frank Lewin; Ann Barzel, Chicago dance historian; Renee Sax, a former student and friend; and Ken Price, public relations director for the Palmer House Hotel. A short biography appears in Barbara Naomi Cohen-Stratyner, *Biographical Dictionary of Dance* (1982). Abbott talks about her work in Roger Simon, "Her Hotel Hideaway Is Full of Chorus-Line Tales," *Chicago Sun-Times*, October 18, 1977. An obituary in the *CT*, November 7, 1977, summarizes her career.

NORMA LIBMAN

ABBOTT, NABIA
January 31, 1897–October 15, 1981
SCHOLAR, AUTHOR

The first woman faculty member appointed at the Oriental Institute of the University of Chicago, Nabia Abbott specialized in the reading of obscure papyrus documents written in early Classical Arabic scripts and pioneered in scholarship on the position of women in the Islamic Middle East. Abbott was born to a Christian family in the late years of the Ottoman Empire, in the town of Mardin (now in southwest Turkey). The original family name was Kuselias. Her ancestors had migrated to Mardin in the late 1700s from Tbilsi, Georgia. Her father, Aboud Kuselias, a Christian, was born about 1870. Her mother, Bidour Eshoo, is thought to have been Persian, Armenian, and Arab in heritage. In 1901, as the Turks began to persecute the Armenians, the affluent Kuselias family felt threatened by the violence and chose to migrate to the South. Some time before the age of six, Abbott traveled with her sister and parents in a covered wagon with a caravan of nomad horsemen down to Mosul (in present-day northern Iraq), where they stopped briefly and then continued on by river to Baghdad, leaving the threat of persecution behind. In 1904, Charles, the oldest of Abbott's two brothers, was born. The family moved to Bombay in 1907 for unknown reasons.

The family name was changed sometime between 1907 and 1910 from Kuselias to Abbott, an adaptation of the father's name, Aboud. An English surname guaranteed entry into good schools, and Bidour Abbott wanted to enroll her children in the excellent English/Indian schools. Nabia Abbott attended Isabella Thoburn College for Girls in Lucknow, India. In 1915, she took and passed the Overseas Senior Matriculation Examination of Cambridge University, the colonial equivalent of being accepted to Cambridge.

Because World War I broke out, she stayed on in India and returned to Lucknow from Bombay, where she taught at her alma mater, Thoburn College. In 1919, she received a B.A. degree with honors from this school, which was an affiliate of the degree-granting University of Allahabad.

Possibly because of her knowledge of Arabic and her British certificate, she was asked in 1919 or 1920 to come back to Iraq, recently made an independent kingdom after the war, to set up a program of girls' education there. She became principal of the first school for girls in that country. Her family also came to Baghdad at this time, leaving the youngest son, Joseph, who was born in 1910, in school in India.

Charles, the third child of the Kuselias/Abbott family, left the Middle East in 1920 and moved to Boston. In 1923, the family, with the exception of the father, who stayed in the Middle East, followed Charles to Boston. Two years later, Abbott attained an M.A. degree at Boston University. Eager to pursue her career as an educator, she accepted a job offer at a small Christian college—Asbury College—in Wilmore, Kentucky, and the family followed her. She began her college teaching career in the Department of Education, but, soon after arriving, she moved to the Department of History, which she chaired for several years. Abbott was a meticulous and strict teacher. It is said that she flunked both her brothers for not working hard enough in her class.

At the age of twenty-eight, Abbott began to study what would become her life's work. After her family moved to Chicago, she took summer classes under Dr. Martin Sprengling, professor of Classical Arabic at the Oriental Institute of the University of Chicago, starting in the summer of 1925. He was reputed to be astonished by her skill in reading Arabic and her consummate intelligence. He urged her to continue her studies, and she earned a Ph.D. under his guidance in 1933. She had a natural flair for the time-consuming and often frustrating work of deciphering the scripts on fragments of old documents, some religious and others commercial or literary. Her talent and dedication impressed Dr. Sprengling who, despite the severe restraints on the Oriental Institute budget during the depression era, persuaded the director to hire the young woman.

Abbott began her formal connection with the Oriental Institute as a research assistant on July 1, 1933. She assisted Dr. Sprengling as he worked on editing and assessing the value of the early Islamic documents housed at the institute. Written in barely decipherable scrawls on parchment, papyrus, and paper, the contents of these scraps were of immediate interest to historians of the early Islamic period of the seventh and eighth centuries. Abbott's devotion and skill in reading the papyri earned her a research appointment. However, because of financial constraints and, perhaps, gender discrimination, she was paid a very low salary, which continued to plague her, because future salary increments were percentages of this low base. Her mother and sister were living with her, and she was the primary breadwinner for the household, even though her sister also worked as a secretary in the institute until she died in 1958.

In 1937, Abbott's rank was raised to research associate but with little salary advancement. It took six years for her to move from research assistant to research associate to assistant professor in both the Oriental Institute and the Department of Oriental Languages and Literatures in 1939. Now she added teaching to her job duties. Her book, *The Rise of the North Arabic Script and Its Kuranic Development with a Full Description of the Kuran Manuscripts in the Oriental Institute*, published by the University of Chicago Press in 1939, was well received by scholars in the United States and Europe. It detailed, via the extensive inclusion of plates, the development of the writing system of early Arabic. In 1944 she was promoted to associate professor with tenure.

Despite her avid interest in its history, Abbott did not relish traveling in the Middle East. She returned there only once, in 1946–47, in the midst of political unrest. In Egypt, the populace was expressing dissatisfaction with both the monarchy and the continued presence of British troops. In Palestine, tension among Jews, Arabs, and the British representatives charged with governing the area as a League of Nations Mandate produced an atmosphere of fear among visitors. Counseled not to travel to Jerusalem, she went anyway after spending several months in Cairo. Once in the area, she was eager to revisit the old haunts of her youth.

During her stay in Egypt, the dual handicaps of gender and religion hampered her search for new documents relating to the early days of Islam. She had no trouble accessing manuscript archives in museums, but as a Christian woman, she was barred from the holiest places of Islam and had to settle for photographs and secondhand reports from Muslim men willing to help her survey holdings.

In 1949, the result of one of her most exciting discoveries was published in an article in the *Journal of Near Eastern Studies*. In "A Ninth Century Fragment of the Thousand Nights: New Light on the Early History of the Arabian Nights," Abbott described her reading and identification of the marks on a scrap of paper in the Oriental Institute collection that antedated by five centuries all other known manuscripts of the famous tales. The artifact was also the earliest known extant evidence of any paper book outside the Far East and helped to establish the existence of early contact between Middle Eastern and Chinese cultures.

In her publications, Nabia Abbott followed two major passions—the challenge of deciphering obscure epigraphy and the desire to illuminate the world of women in the Middle East. She was clearly conscious of her gender and perceived that the Islamic world overlooked its women. Hence, in addition to her scholarly works on Arabic epigraphy and paleography, she published two works and several articles related to women that were intended for a more general readership. The first, *Aisha, the Beloved of Mohammed* (1942), deals with one of the wives of Mohammed and her pivotal relationship with the rise of early Islam. Written in a readable style, it is nevertheless quite detailed and therefore difficult for someone unfamiliar with Islamic studies to follow and appreciate.

The second, entitled *Two Queens of Baghdad: Mother and*

Wife of Harun al-Rashid (1945), describes the lives and influence of the mother and the wife of Harun al-Rashid, the famous Abbasid Caliph of the eighth and ninth centuries A.D. On the whole, scholars found these books too "light" for their taste; but in them Abbott details the intrigue and politics with which these women were involved. Her devotion to rescuing these women of early Islam from obscurity is evident in her letter to the director of the Oriental Institute during her trip to Egypt in 1946. In it she indicated that she had three books floating in her brain on the Muslim royal women of Egypt, Spain, and India. For some reason, they were never written.

After returning to Chicago, she was appointed full professor in 1949. Her publishing slowed until the 1957 publication of the first volume of her projected three-volume work on Arabic papyri. Entitled *Studies in Arabic Literary Papyri*, volume one appeared in 1957, volume two in 1962, and volume three in 1972. In the three volumes, she published more than seven hundred pieces of the papyri collection of the Oriental Institute and other archives, dating from the first five centuries of Islam.

During the period 1949 to 1955, Abbott exchanged acrimonious memos with the director of the institute over her salary. Two money issues upset Abbott. One was her struggle to get the institute to pay her the salary equivalent to the men of her rank and productivity. The other was the suggestion of someone from the university, after her retirement in 1963, that she make the university the beneficiary of her estate, since she had no immediate family. (By that time, her mother and sister had died and her brother, Joseph, who lived close to Chicago, was caring for her financial affairs.) She was incensed. For years, she felt, the institution had treated her unfairly; now it was asking her to be generous and give back her hard-earned assets. She refused.

Nabia Abbott retired at the mandatory retirement age with a very small pension. The university granted her the title of professor emerita. She continued to work for the Oriental Institute for two more years, after asking for more time to finish the trilogy on Arabic papyri. She kept her office into the 1970s, as was the custom of the institute. Her colleagues at the Oriental Institute considered her a "scholar's scholar," high praise from men not given to flattery.

Nabia Abbott died at the age of eighty-four after several years of slow mental and physical decline. The *Journal of Near Eastern Studies*, a house publication of the Oriental Institute, dedicated an issue to her; she was able to see the first of its two parts a few weeks before she died. She was buried in Munster, Indiana, near her brother Joseph.

Nabia Abbott's work on the position of women in the Islamic Middle East and her thorough examinations of Arabic literary papyri were both pioneering and revolutionary. She is credited with ceaselessly and painstakingly studying and publishing many of the Oriental Institute's early Islamic documents, helping it to acquire others, and expanding its library holdings. A resolute scholar in her field, Abbott paved the way for future scholars while unveiling mysteries of early Islamic culture.

Sources. In addition to works cited above, Abbott's published works include *The Kurrah Papyri from Aphrodito in the Oriental Institute* (a revision of her dissertation) in 1938; numerous scholarly articles published in journals, including *American Journal of Semitic Languages and Lit-*

eratures, *Ars Islamica*, *Journal of Near Eastern Studies*, *Journal of the American Oriental Society*, *Journal of the Royal Asiatic Society of Great Britain and Ireland*, and *Zeitschrift der Deutschen Morgenländischen Gesellschaft* throughout the 1930s, 1940s, and 1950s. A file at the Oriental Institute regarding Abbott and containing memos and reports provides biographical material as does a memorial issue of the *Journal of Near Eastern Studies*, vol. 40, 1981, which also evaluates her contributions to the field. Personal correspondence between Carolyn G. Killean and two nephews—Michael and Robert Abbott—in 1994 provided additional details.

CAROLYN G. KILLEAN

ABERCROMBIE, GERTRUDE
February 17, 1909–July 3, 1977
PAINTER

Gertrude Abercrombie was a painter who made portraits, still lifes, landscapes, and interior scenes that translated a private vision into the concrete terms of this world. Her paintings, called "magic realist" or "surreal" by critics, were psychic self-portraits that grew out of an unusual personality as well as the regional mentality that conditioned much of Chicago art in the early twentieth century. Her occasional forays into sculpture or woodcut prints were thematically similar to the painting that was her dominant medium.

Abercrombie was the only child of Tom and Lula (Janes) Abercrombie, who were performing with a traveling opera company in Texas at the time of her birth. Abercrombie's mother went to stay in Austin with her sister, Gertrude, when the time to give birth was near. Shortly after the birth, Abercrombie's family resumed traveling, settling in 1912 near Ravinia, north of Chicago, where her mother (who used the stage name Jane Abercrombie) was a prima donna in a legitimate opera company. In 1913, the family went to Berlin, where Jane Abercrombie had been offered an opportunity to study opera; her husband worked for the Red Cross, and Gertrude Abercrombie achieved fluency in German. The advent of World War I forced the family to return to the United States. They arrived on Christmas eve, 1914, and set out for Aledo, the small western Illinois town where Tom Abercrombie's family lived.

Gertrude Abercrombie was firmly rooted in the Midwest. Her mother's family were the Wisconsin Janes after whom the town of Janesville was named. By the time she was enrolled in school at six years of age, Abercrombie was already familiar with Aledo, Illinois, having been left in the care of her relatives numerous times. Aledo was home to an extended family of aunts, uncles, and cousins to whom Abercrombie remained close all her life. At about this time, Jane Abercrombie developed a goiter that threatened both her voice and her life. With Jane Abercrombie's career at an end, Tom Abercrombie took a job as a salesman, and the family moved to the Hyde Park neighborhood of Chicago where Abercrombie, aside from eagerly anticipated summers in Aledo, spent the rest of her life.

After graduating from Hyde Park High School in 1925, Abercrombie attended the University of Illinois at Urbana-Champaign, where she earned a B.A. degree in romance languages in 1929. Although she took numerous art courses in college, the visual arts were not a clear career choice. Not only was she gifted in foreign languages, she also displayed a talent for writing and a musical aptitude that, among other things, included perfect pitch and the ability to whistle and hum simultaneously in harmony. Although Abercrombie eventually made painting her career, language and words fascinated her; she loved word games and crossword puzzles.

Returning to Chicago in 1929, Abercrombie enrolled in classes at the School of the Art Institute of Chicago and the American Academy of Art, studying commercial techniques and figure drawing. Although she had not yet defined herself as a painter, the exigencies of coming of age during the Great Depression may have encouraged her to take her first job in 1931 as a commercial artist at the Mesirow department store, followed by a similar job at Sears in 1932. It was during this time that she met artist Tom Kempf, whose brother, sculptor Tud Kempf, Abercrombie credited with encouraging her to become an artist.

She exhibited her work publicly for the first time in a 1932 exhibition called *Portraits of Chicago Artists by Chicago Artists* at INCREASE ROBINSON's Studio Gallery in Chicago, a progressive venue supportive of local artists. In the next three years, she exhibited with the Chicago Society of Artists (the oldest continuously exhibiting artists' group in Chicago) and the more radical Chicago No-Jury Society of Artists, a group offering exhibition opportunities to anyone who paid the small yearly membership fee; in a number of short-lived but nontraditional commercial venues; and in the important Grant Park Outdoor Art Fair of 1933, an egalitarian undertaking that was profoundly important to Abercrombie socially as well as artistically. A setting where she met numerous artists from a variety of backgrounds, the fair offered her a sense of community that she felt was missing elsewhere in her life. In 1935, she exhibited for the first time in Chicago's most prestigious noncommercial venue, the juried annuals at the Art Institute of Chicago (AIC). She exhibited in all three in 1935: *Artists of Chicago and Vicinity*, *International Watercolor Exhibition*, and *American Painting and Sculpture*. In 1936, she was one of a very few Chicago artists to be shown at the most progressive commercial gallery in the city, the Katharine Kuh Gallery, which opened in late 1934. In the same year, she won the Joseph Eisendrath prize at the AIC Chicago and Vicinity Annual for her painting *There on the Table* (1935).

In 1933, Abercrombie was appointed to the Public Works of Art Project, the first, short-lived federal project providing support for artists during the depression. She subsequently worked for Illinois Art Project of the Works Progress Administration, for which she produced easel paintings until 1940. The appointments validated her as an artist and also gave her the financial independence to move into her own apartment in the Weinstein Building in Hyde Park; it was occupied by numerous artists and writers. During this period she began the friendships that were to last the rest of her life. She met writers Thornton Wilder, Wendell Wilcox, and James Purdy (who immortalized her as Eloisa Brace in his novel *Malcolm*) and the painters Charles Sebree and Karl Priebe, who began introducing her to black jazz musicians in the 1930s. Her passionate interest in jazz continued throughout her life, and her musician friends included Dizzy Gillespie, Charlie Parker, Max Roach, and Sonny Rollins.

For Abercrombie, the 1930s were a period of happiness during which she achieved economic and physical independence from what she perceived as an oppressive life dominated by her rigid and inflexible mother. She had a group of artistic and literary friends and was embarking on a successful career. During this period Abercrombie also developed the themes that occupied her artistic imagination throughout her career. A series of objects that functioned as personal emblems begin to appear— the cat, the owl, Victorian furniture, gloves, carnations, bunches of grapes—along with a mysterious woman, always a self-portrait, in a spare Victorian interior or an otherwise uninhabited landscape. Her still lifes, landscapes, and interiors were personalized with ordinary objects invested with significance because they belonged to Abercrombie; moreover, the objects themselves came to signify the artist without her presence in the image.

In 1940, Abercrombie married attorney Robert Livingston, and in 1942 her only child, Dinah, was born. In 1944, she moved to a house in the Hyde Park neighborhood that became the site for Saturday night parties and Sunday afternoon jam sessions that included jazz musicians, writers, and artists, along with liberal amounts of alcohol. It was here that Abercrombie functioned as the self-appointed "Queen of Chicago," as she was known to her friends and relatives, presiding imperiously over the revelry. In 1948, she and Livingston divorced and she married Frank Sandiford, a writer and former small-time criminal who had served time for burglary.

Abercrombie was productive and successful in the 1940s and 1950s. She exhibited regularly in Chicago and in New York; in 1952, a particularly prolific year, she had five one-person shows, exhibited at the AIC American Annual, and participated in at least four additional group shows. In 1951, she began making tiny paintings of subjects taken from her established repertoire of motifs—self-portraits, still lifes, cats, owls—and had them mounted as brooches. These and other small-scale paintings were highly salable and provided her with a regular income, which supported her family. She was comfortable exhibiting in commercial venues and was a fixture at the Hyde Park Art Fair from its inception in 1947, setting her work up against the side of one of the three old Rolls-Royces she owned at various times.

Even Abercrombie's most conventional work, her early portraits *Elinor Porter Carlberg* (1934) and *Martha Parsons (Cousin Martha)* (1937–), and her landscapes *The Pump* (1938) and *Horse and Blue House* (1942–), have an idiosyncratic quality. The early landscapes share the regionalist exaltation of the American Midwest that prevailed in the 1930s all over the United States. Abercrombie always identified proudly with her midwestern origins: on the rare occasions when a male figure appears in her work, he almost always looks like Abraham Lincoln, even if he remains unidentified (*Pink Visit* [*Lincoln Paying a Call, The Visit*], 1945; *Levitation*, 1967). Although she exhibited regularly in New York in the 1940s and 1950s, she never considered moving away from Chicago and rarely traveled, never going to Europe as an adult despite her language proficiency. By the late 1930s, the more traditional qualities in her work yield to the personal and eccentric: dark landscapes and still life paintings replete with her own possessions, which function as personal emblems (*Objects of the Night*, c. 1943; *Search*

for Rest, 1951; *Pink Carnations*, 1939; *Marble Top Table*, 1944; *Bowl of Grapes*, 1945).

Her most resonant works are the series of empty interior spaces that she began to do shortly after moving into the Weinstein Building. Sometimes Abercrombie appears, as in *Where or When (Things Past)* (1948), surrounded by her real possessions. The cat and the conical shape of the upturned phonograph speaker, suggesting a peaked witch's hat, are among numerous references to witchcraft and sorcery that appear in Abercrombie's work. Along with the powerful persona of the queen, she consciously and repeatedly presented herself as a witch, in life and in art, using these roles as a way to control and manage a conflicted inner life. She was willing to endure the pain of being identified as a witch by neighborhood children or strangers in order to feel the sense of power that the role brought. Her paintings, particularly the impenetrable, fastidious, and austere interiors, also ordered the world in a way that gave her control over it.

In a characteristically disingenuous way, Abercrombie attributed the "picture in a picture" device that she used frequently to extend or enhance the meaning of a painting to the image on the old Quaker Oats box. The same association with the popular and prosaic is seen in Abercrombie's frequent references to her lack of formal training and her assertion that art is about ideas, not technique. Even her predilection for the innovative and improvisational qualities of jazz over the more conventionally pleasing forms of classical music is part of her pervasive preference for the popular and idiosyncratic. Abercrombie began to suffer from a series of illnesses in the late 1950s. Although she lived until 1977, she had numerous health problems that were intensified by her addiction to alcohol, making her a virtual invalid for most of the last decade of her life. Financial difficulties and problems with her second marriage (which ended officially in 1966 but actually several years earlier) added to her troubles. The creative work of the last decade of her life was her self-named, unpublished "Joke Book," a collection of personal anecdotes, stories, and one-liners that Abercrombie found humorous. Like her painting, each of them had deep personal significance, often involving herself as protagonist.

She died in Chicago, leaving a will that provided that the art in her estate (which included excellent examples from all phases of her career, some of them repurchased by Abercrombie from earlier owners) be donated to museums or other not-for-profit organizations. In this way, she attempted to exert control over the future perception of her career.

Abercrombie was beset with internal conflicts all her life. She was able, however, to transform her own psychic pain into works of art of great power, mystery, and resonance. Her private and eccentric vision reflected the marginal position she occupied as a Chicago artist and a woman. At the same time, the idiosyncratic nature of her work linked her to the well-known Chicago imagists, a group that emerged in the late 1960s, many of whom felt a connection to Abercrombie. Her enigmatic work continues to attract new viewers, demonstrating its ongoing resonance and appeal.

Sources. Abercrombie's papers are located in the Archives of American Art, Smithsonian Institution, Washington, D.C., and are available on microfilm. The papers contain correspondence, photographs, exhibition announcements and catalogs, information on specific works of art (including a card file, which is extremely helpful though incomplete), and versions of Abercrombie's "Joke Book." The artist Karl Priebe's papers at Marquette University, Milwaukee, Wisconsin, include correspondence from Abercrombie to Priebe. The most important secondary source is the catalog of an exhibition curated by Kent Smith and Susan S. Weininger, *Gertrude Abercrombie* at the Illinois State Museum, Springfield, Illinois, 1991, with an essay, exhibition history, and excerpts from the "Joke Book"; the notes and bibliography provide complete references to earlier sources. Interviews with a number of Abercrombie's friends and family provided biographical and other information for the essay. The most important of these were with Dinah Livingston, Abercrombie's daughter (1983); Wendell Wilcox (1980); and Elinor Porter Carlberg, Abercrombie's cousin (1983), all conducted by Susan S. Weininger. Other oral sources included a 1977 taped interview that Studs Terkel broadcast on WFMT, and taped interviews made with Abercrombie in 1971 by her friend, Dale Bernard. Several exhibitions since 1991 include *Abercrombie: Thinking Modern: Painting in Chicago, 1910–1940,* curated by Susan S. Weininger at the Mary and Leigh Block Museum of Art at Northwestern University, Evanston, Illinois, in 1992; and Susan S. Weininger, *The "New Woman" in Chicago, 1910–1945: Paintings from Illinois Collections* (1993) for the exhibition at the Rockford College Art Gallery, Rockford, Illinois, 1993. Both exhibits situate Abercrombie within the broader context of Chicago art of the early twentieth century.

SUSAN S. WEININGER

ADDAMS, JANE
September 6, 1860–May 21, 1935
SOCIAL REFORMER, SETTLEMENT HOUSE FOUNDER AND
HEAD RESIDENT, SOCIAL THEORIST, PEACE ACTIVIST

Jane Addams towers over Chicago history like a mythical Amazon of social reform. Rising to prominence in the years between 1889 and 1910, she became the central figure in that pantheon of reform notables who created the "progressive" response to industrial capitalism. Her stature extends beyond her prodigious civic activism. While the list of her accomplishments was long and the breadth of her concerns wide, Addams shared her activist burdens with thousands of other Americans who were similarly anxious to bring equity, dignity, and peace to industrial relations and urban life. What distinguished Addams was her singular ability as a writer and public speaker to endow the progressive movement with ideological coherence and to give the movement a humane but challenging voice. Addams became a central figure in the era's domestic reform circles and a leader of international renown, because her compelling use of language made her the conscience of the nation, the industrial age's secular priest. The first key to understanding Jane Addams's reform career lies in recognizing that she was the most effective and prolific writer of her generation of reformers. The second key lies in understanding that she supported many different reforms in public policy but persistently advocated for only one thing: democracy won through peaceful means. Her writing survives as a reminder that Jane Addams was a social theorist as well as a social reformer.

Born in the fall of 1860, a few weeks before Abraham Lincoln's election to the presidency, Jane Addams grew up amidst the rolling hills and rich wheat fields that surrounded the farming village of Cedarville, Illinois, just north of Freeport. At one level, hers was a privileged childhood. Her father, John Huy Addams, had achieved success and esteem in the region as a miller, a banker, and an investor in the local railroad. In the decade before Jane Addams (named Laura Jane Addams) was born, John Addams had become the richest man in the county, built the largest home in Cedarville, and won election to the Illinois State Senate on the new Republican ticket. But alongside the wealth and status, there were tragedy and family complexity. When Jane Addams was two years old, her mother died from complications due to pregnancy. When she was six, an older sister died of typhoid fever. When she was eight, her father remarried, bringing the fascinating but volatile Anna Haldeman and her two sons—Harry and George—into the family circle.

As a child, "Jennie" was closely mothered by her eldest sister and her stepmother, and she doted upon her "dignified" (*Twenty Years at Hull-House,* 7) Pa. When disillusionment with Reconstruction politics caused John Addams to leave the state legislature in 1870, he had more time for community and business affairs, his demanding new wife, and Jennie, his youngest—and brightest—child. In early adolescence, Jane Addams was tutored in politics and history by an attentive, if emotionally reserved, father. John Addams believed deeply in classical liberalism's tenets of individual rights but just as deeply in the republican merit of community stewardship by a virtuous elite. As a Republican legislator, he had advocated government sponsorship of private enterprise but had also voted for public provisions for the needy. John Addams actively supported the two Protestant churches in Cedarville but was not a "professing Christian" (Jane Addams to James Weber Linn, February 2, 1935, Jane Addams Memorial Collection). He was devoted to hard work and ethical conduct but placed more faith in this life than the next. The young Jane Addams absorbed these lessons from her father, alongside lessons from her stepmother about the social graces, the arts, and the culture that wealth can buy.

Jane Addams enrolled in Rockford Female Seminary, which was located thirty miles from her home in Cedarville, in the fall of 1877. At age seventeen, she was her father's daughter by temperament and ideology. Her four years at seminary did little to change that. She resisted the school's Christian evangelism and diplomatically skirted its most femininizing and domesticating influences. At the same time, Addams was the undisputed star of the campus. She excelled in the classroom, led the school's first science club and one literary society, served as president of her class for all four years, was editor of the *Rockford Seminary Magazine* in her senior year, and was valedictorian of the class of 1881. When Rockford became a college the year following Addams's graduation, she was among the select group of scholars who received the school's first bachelor's degrees.

Presaging patterns in her later life, Addams enjoyed the devotion of her peers at Rockford while maintaining a distinctive aura of privacy and personal dignity. Only to ELLEN GATES STARR, the Rockford Seminary friend with whom Addams would later found Hull-House, did she reveal her doubts about Christianity and her struggle to imagine a life's work that could accommodate her nascent ambition to be a female steward without church affiliation.

The ideology of stewardship that Jane Addams crafted for herself in college was not, however, a preview of her adult con-

FIG. 3. *Jane Addams, about the time she cofounded Hull-House.*

FIG. 4. *Hull-House complex, 1905–10.*

FIG. 5. *Hull-House residents celebrate the 40th anniversary of the settlement. Seated, left to right, Dr. Alice Hamilton, Rose Marie Gyles, Jane Addams, Enella Benedict, and Edith de Nancrede. Standing, left to right, Jessie Binford, Rachelle Yarros, Esther Kohn, Victor Yarros, Ethel Dewey, George Hooker, and Adena Miller Rich.*

victions about democratic process and the power of the social environment to limit or liberate human potential. As a young woman, Addams absorbed the works of John Ruskin, Ralph Waldo Emerson, and, above all, Thomas Carlyle. She identified with their masculine, heroic ideals and wrote numerous essays and editorials at Rockford extolling the power of individuals "destined" for greatness. The young Jane Addams admired men who could lead through force of will, triumphing over any obstacles society placed in their path. In sharp contrast to her predecessors and successors at *Rockford Seminary Magazine*, Addams avoided all discussion of the woman question in her editorials. And when she preached to her classmates about women's unique public role as "Bread Givers" ("Opening Address," *Rockford Seminary Magazine*, April 1880, 110–11), she emphasized women's strengths, not men's prejudices. She placed her adolescent faith in the ability of unique individuals to rise above all, and she imagined herself among that elite.

The life that Jane Addams lived after graduating from Rockford forced her to revise drastically her romantic, heroic dreams of elite stewardship. In the eight years that intervened between graduation and the founding of Hull-House, events in her personal life and the realities of nineteenth-century social life gave Addams a new humility and a respect for the power of circumstance. This experience turned her away from belief in individual heroism and toward the practice of cooperative democracy.

Within weeks of her graduation from Rockford Seminary in June of 1881, Jane Addams's father died, leaving her without her proud, doting champion. His death also forced her to cancel her ambitious plans to study at Smith College in preparation for medical school. Finally, it designated her—the family's young, spinster daughter—as the companion to her stepmother, who was now a lonely, needy widow. In the subsequent eight years, Addams tried to combine family duty with personal ambition by moving to Philadelphia with her stepmother and attending the Women's Medical College of Pennsylvania. That effort failed after a semester. She then tried studying French and German and art history on a tour of Europe with her stepmother between the fall of 1883 and the spring of 1885. Addams's debility from a back ailment, combined with persistent demands from her stepmother and her siblings, and Addams's own doubts about a career, made all of these efforts seem fruitless. In one of those "moments of deep depression" to which she would later refer in her autobiography, Addams wrote to Ellen Gates Starr from Geneva that all her activities in the three years since graduation had "gained nothing and improved nothing" (June 8, 1884, Starr Papers).

During these same years of apparently aimless wandering, however, Jane Addams was making the important observations about economic class, charity work, and women's opportunities that would ultimately shape her life purpose. Her letters and diary entries from Europe and from two winters spent with her stepmother and stepbrother in Baltimore indicate that Addams was pondering the inequities in the lives of the rich and the lives of the poor, and she was questioning the social utility of both female higher education and of philanthropy that merely gave alms to the needy. At the same time, she noticed that her own brief involvement with charity work in Baltimore engaged and energized her in a way that medical school, aesthetic studies,

and European travel had not. Moreover, as she grew closer to Ellen Gates Starr, she was more intrigued by Starr's wish that they "do some work together." "I believe," said Starr, "we should work well" (November 28, 1885, Starr Papers).

When Jane Addams went on a second tour of Europe in 1888, she was accompanied by Ellen Starr rather than her stepmother. During this trip, Addams first encountered Toynbee Hall, a new "settlement house" in the East End of London staffed by young, male graduates of Oxford University and presided over by Samuel and Henrietta Barnett. Toynbee Hall reflected all the currents of the day: the desire of the educated elite both to teach and learn from the poor; the zeal of liberal Christians like the Barnetts to uplift but not evangelize; the social reformers' disdain for almsgiving; and the conviction that modern, urban poverty was best addressed through cross-class fellowship. The Barnetts' settlement house appealed to Addams's background as a steward of society, her nonconvert's respect for Christian principles, and her now humble desire for community cooperation over heroic leadership. Before their return to the United States in the summer of 1888, Addams and Starr had devised what they called a "scheme." They would combine Addams's inheritance of sixty thousand dollars from her father with the Chicago contacts Starr had cultivated through her aunt ELIZA ALLEN STARR and Miss Kirkland, and they would open a social settlement in a working-class section of the Midwest's booming industrial center.

In the subsequent decades, Addams and Starr would grow apart, although both continued to live at Hull-House. But in the early years at Hull-House, they were an effective team. Starr attended to many organizational details and deferred, as she always had, to Addams's public charisma. When they were just launching their settlement effort in the early fall of 1889, Starr wrote to her cousin, "Everybody who comes near Miss Addams is affected by her. It is as if she simply diffused something which came from outside herself, of which she is the luminous medium" (Starr to Mary Allen, September 15, 1889, Starr Papers).

When Jane Addams appeared on the Chicago scene, the city already had a well-developed organizational infrastructure for philanthropy and social reform. That infrastructure was led as much by Chicago women as by Chicago men, for the women in the city's leading families had, since the 1860s, taken an active role in civic affairs. The existence of an independent female network in Chicago proved invaluable to Addams's success. From the beginning, it gave her independence from any religious affiliation. Though her settlement project drew interest from several of Chicago's missionary-based men, Addams chose to affiliate Hull-House with the city's secular, reform-oriented women.

Ellen Starr's contacts and Addams's own status as the educated daughter of a former state senator gave the two women entrée into the influential Chicago Woman's Club, where their project quickly won the endorsement of civic leaders such as ELLEN HENROTIN and MARY WILMARTH. Their own reform work prior to 1889 made these club women open to new ways of improving urban life. Jane Addams's settlement house scheme had great appeal, because it promised a useful social role for the educated daughters and sons of the privileged as well as useful social services for the needy. Jane Addams was made a new club member with unusual rapidity.

The welcoming community of elite, activist women who provided immediate support for Hull-House stood in stark contrast to Addams's own family, which saw her Chicago adventure as an abandonment of filial duty. When Addams wrote, in later years, of the conflict reform-minded young women faced between the "family claim" and the "social claim" ("The Subjective Necessity," 14) she drew from painful, personal experience.

Support from the activist women of Chicago helps to explain Addams's virtually instantaneous success in the fall of 1889. She and Starr found a suitable house—the decaying Hull mansion at Halsted and Polk streets—and secured a lease from its owner, HELEN CULVER. After a modicum of remodeling and furniture installation, Addams and Starr established themselves as "neighbors" to the diverse immigrants in the community. Within days of opening in September, they were offering classes and providing direct services such as child care. Within weeks they had attracted favorable newspaper coverage and a considerable number of upper- and middle-class volunteers to the enterprise.

By 1893, the thirty-three-year-old Jane Addams was describing herself, somewhat pridefully, as "the grandmother of American settlements" (Addams to Alice H. Addams, February 10, 1893, Jane Addams Memorial Collection); and, indeed, she was. In the years between 1890 and 1895, when fledgling settlements were opening around the nation, Hull-House stood as the flagship. It expanded beyond the Hull mansion to include an art gallery, coffee house, and gymnasium. Addams had learned quickly what her neighbors wanted and had responded with a rich, daily menu of meeting times for children's programs, ethnic clubs, labor organizations, women's clubs, political discussion groups, and classes in English, government, literature, and art. By 1895, these programs were attracting thousands of Chicagoans to the settlement every week.

The programs at Hull-House were popular and effective, but they alone were not what distinguished Jane Addams's settlement house from the other settlements in Chicago or elsewhere in the United States. It was Addams's published writings and her leadership style that brought to Hull-House its national prominence and its remarkable staff of residents and volunteers. In the six years between 1893 and 1899, Addams published thirty-five articles in which she set forth her conviction that members of the privileged classes gained as much as they gave by engaging in work with what she called "the industrial classes." Addams told her largely white, middle-class readers that approaching any sort of community work with an attitude of self-sacrifice was dishonest and harmful to the efforts. She argued for a spirit of mutual respect in all cross-class endeavors. Implicit in all of these articles was the assumption that cooperative work across class was imperative if the nation was to solve the social problems created by industrial capitalism.

A commitment to democratic process informed Addams's early writings, but Jane Addams was still a steward at heart and always a charismatic individual. These qualities coexisted with her democratic philosophy in shaping Addams's unique leadership style at Hull-House. Unlike most other settlements, where the head resident and the board of directors dictated the organi-

zation's agenda and activities, the Hull-House residents and volunteers had a strong voice in designing the settlement's program. Addams had founded Hull-House to provide young women and men, but especially young women, with an opportunity for creative, socially responsible work. By 1900, there were twenty to thirty residents at the settlement at any one time. Addams fulfilled her aim by encouraging each of these residents to identify a need in the community and invent a programmatic response. Her authority lay in guiding residents' initiatives in directions she thought most productive, not in making rigid, daily assignments. The result of Addams's agility at mixing an egalitarian attitude with tremendous personal influence was that Hull-House residents stayed longer than residents at other settlements, and Addams attracted a notably independent, creative staff. Within its first decade, Hull-House became a haven for educated, ambitious American women who sought a base for their operations and a community of like-minded females. FLORENCE KELLEY, JULIA LATHROP, ALICE HAMILTON, and GRACE ABBOTT were just the most prominent names on a list of women residents for whom Addams provided the space and opportunity to pursue their own interests in labor legislation, asylum reform, public health, and child welfare. These residents were joined by nonresident volunteers from the larger Chicago community, who responded to such Hull-House innovations as the Juvenile Court, the Immigrants' Protective League, and the University of Chicago Extension. Reformers such as Henry Demarest Lloyd, the Reverend Jenkin Lloyd Jones, and Clarence Darrow; unionists such as MARY KENNEY (see O'SULLIVAN), MARGARET DREIER ROBINS, and Abraham Bisno; and civic leaders such as ANITA McCORMICK BLAINE, Lyman Gage and Julius Rosenwald were all drawn into Addams's circle of influence. None of these individuals agreed with Jane Addams on every public issue of the day, but all of them encountered in her a person who strove to be as democratic in her organizational style and programming as in her writing.

Jane Addams's personal inheritance made it possible for her to open Hull-House on her own, but it did not allow her to sustain or expand the settlement. Throughout her career, she was engaged in constant fund-raising for one building or special project after another. Vital to the settlement's survival and growth were two wealthy Chicago women, LOUISE deKOVEN BOWEN and MARY ROZET SMITH. It was their financial generosity that made it possible for Hull-House to expand so noticeably in size and function. By 1907, it comprised thirteen buildings covering an entire square block of the city. This expansion gave Hull-House a physical and programmatic presence unequaled by any other settlement house in the nation.

The warm friendship Addams enjoyed with Louise deKoven Bowen and the loving partnership she built with Mary Rozet Smith helped Addams to create a life in which the personal and the political were comfortably integrated. Smith and Bowen were at the center of a circle of friends including Kelley, Hamilton, Julia Lathrop, and Lillian Wald of the Henry Street settlement in New York City. Over the years, these women created an extended family network that embraced various sons and daughters and nieces and nephews. Ellen Starr was a valued but less intimate member of this circle. Jane Addams's own relatives—her stepmother, sisters, and stepbrothers—held themselves aloof from the settlement for a variety of personal and political reasons. One sister's death gave Addams guardianship of a niece and two nephews. Her attentions to those children and her close ties to her other nieces gave Addams some experience juggling parental duties and the demands of a public career.

The dinners Jane Addams presided over every evening in the Hull-House dining hall reflected her integration of public life and private. On any given evening, Mary Smith might be sitting across one table from the University of Chicago philosopher John Dewey, who could be seated next to an Italian socialist or a visiting member of the Russian nobility or an aspiring ballerina from Kansas. Enlivening the conversation at each table would be the Hull-House residents, young women and men from all over the country who had come to live and work under Jane Addams's guidance. Her own quiet humor tended toward the wry and self-effacing, but Addams must have enjoyed a good laugh, because her dearest friends were known as much for their biting wit as for their political savvy.

Sentimental expression was never Addams's style, but she was extravagantly attentive to friends and relatives, knitting sweaters for former residents' babies, researching used car prices for her nephew, collecting autographs of the famous for Louise deKoven Bowen's grandson, sending carefully selected gifts of clothes and books to nieces and grandnieces. Mary Smith's money allowed the two women to go on extended foreign tours and to buy a summer home near Louise deKoven Bowen's in Bar Harbor, Maine. It also made possible their lifelong contributions to the support and education of their own nieces and nephews and allowed them to help Florence Kelley, a single mother, pay for her three children's college education.

For all the good fellowship that Addams fostered between neighbors, residents, and volunteers, she never protected Hull-House from the tensions and controversies of the day. Just four years after settling into Hull-House, Addams had to cope with the devastating economic depression of 1893 and the bitter Pullman Strike of 1894. Hull-House was designed to provide programs, not direct aid; but the depression forced Addams to confront her neighbors' immediate, dire needs. And while Addams's aim was to encourage cross-class understanding, George Pullman's intransigence during the strike and his cold rebuff of her offers of mediation forced Addams to realize that capitalists would not soon embrace her vision of economic cooperation. Passage of the Illinois Factory Law in 1893, under Florence Kelley's leadership, was a great victory; but shifts in state politics soon scuttled its enforcement. And even though her Hull-House neighbors admired Addams's commitment to democratic methods, they did not join her unsuccessful campaigns in 1896 and 1898 against the ward's corrupt boss, Johnny Powers.

Defeats such as these did not weaken Addams's commitment to building a more democratic community. If anything, they strengthened her determination to make comfortable Americans understand that individuals' living conditions and working conditions were fundamental to their ability to participate in democracy. "As the very existence of the state depends on the character of its citizens," she reasoned, "it becomes possible to deduce the right of state regulation . . . [when] industrial conditions are forcing the workers below the standard of de-

cency" (*Twenty Years at Hull-House*, 229). With increasing sharpness, Addams argued for a fundamental reform in Americans' concept of the role of the government. In an era of urban industrialism, citizens needed a more activist, regulatory government. Experience, combined with the political education she received from Florence Kelley, Henry Demarest Lloyd, and others, convinced Addams that legislative efforts were required if there was to be fundamental change in labor-capital relations, factory conditions, urban housing standards and services, public health, education, or recreation. A small, private, local institution like Hull-House could not enact permanent change in these matters, but it could provide the social science research and the lobbying energy necessary to produce such changes in the structure and function of American government.

In the years between 1900 and 1915, Hull-House residents continued to offer its neighbors a full range of daily programs and services; but other residents, and Jane Addams herself, were increasingly involved with state and national efforts to increase government involvement in the regulation of economic life and the provision of social services. Even though unionists were skeptical of state regulations and employers vehemently opposed them, Addams served during these years on numerous national committees whose purpose was to build citizen support for child labor laws, housing and factory regulations, protective labor legislation, vocational education, public health services, and public recreational facilities. In addition, Addams's outspoken support for the National Association for the Advancement of Colored People and for the National American Woman Suffrage Association served to telegraph her belief that every citizen's access to direct participation in the state was vital to national progress.

As she expanded her public purview, Addams also widened the audience for her reform message. She was in constant demand as a public speaker and was able to maintain personal contacts with reform colleagues around the nation through paid speaking tours. Most importantly, she lobbied the American people through her writing. In the first decade of the twentieth century, almost 150 articles appeared under Jane Addams's byline. Articles, as well as reprints or excerpts or revisions of articles, appeared in all sorts of publications, from the *Annals of the American Academy of Political and Social Sciences* to the *Ladies' Home Journal*; from the *American Journal of Sociology* to the *Machinists' Monthly*; from the *Atlantic* to the *Bulletin of the Chicago Federation of Teachers*. She was, quite consciously, spreading her message in order to create a constituency that would support legislative transformation of economic and social relations.

Jane Addams founded Hull-House out of a democratic urge to participate in mutual, cross-class education. Her experiences in the 1890s in Chicago persuaded her that such education had to be accompanied by state regulation of industrial capitalism and urban life. The philosophical result of her evolution is evident in the discussions of social theory that she published between 1900 and 1925. Two assumptions shape all of this writing. Addams assumed, first, that only a democratic process can create a stable, prosperous, healthy society; that democracy was "not merely a sentiment" but a "rule of living"; and that the "cure of the ills of Democracy is more Democracy" (*Democracy* and Social Ethics, 6, 11–12). Second, she assumed that only a peaceful process could produce democracy's desirable goals: "the great task of pushing forward social justice could be enormously accelerated if primitive methods as well as primitive weapons were once and for all abolished" (*Newer Ideals of Peace*, 212). Long before she resisted American participation in World War I, Addams had read the philosophical writings of the Russian author, Leo Tolstoy. She accepted his argument for "non-resistance," which meant not combating evil in an aggressive way but steadfastly and peaceably adhering to alternate principles.

Throughout her adult life, Addams was convinced that competitive hostility in international relations, labor relations, judicial relations, and even personal relations was inherently undemocratic because it precluded the process of participatory dialogue. No matter how worthy the cause for which people might be fighting, said Addams, the pain and bitterness resulting from the fight would render meaningless any victory.

Addams set forth these principles most clearly in her first two books, *Democracy and Social Ethics* (1902) and *Newer Ideals of Peace* (1907). In both works, Addams expressed her disdain for idealism that was "afraid of experience" and for elite stewardship that was "in reality so contemptuous" (*Newer Ideals of Peace*, 32, 49) of the masses. As she addressed concrete problems in municipal government, charitable efforts, the labor movement, the classroom, and the household, Addams deftly guided her readers to an appreciation of the living connection between the most prosaic realities of daily life and the most elevated ideals of democracy and pacifism. "The social passion of the age," she argued, was bent toward "the complete participation of the working classes in the spiritual, intellectual, and material inheritance of the human race" ("A Modern Lear," *Survey*, 136).

Addams was just as disturbed by the imbalances of power in political relations, class relations, gender relations, and racial and ethnic relations as any radical democrat of her day. But, unlike most of her allies in progressive movements between 1890 and 1918, Addams did not believe that heroic defeat of the powerful would bring peace and democracy. She argued that only peace and democracy would bring peace and democracy. In addition, she argued that permanent, lasting reform required appeals to citizens' interest in the common good, not appeals to self-interest. "We cannot hope to attain a sane social development," she wrote in *Newer Ideals of Peace*, "unless we subordinate class interests and class feeling to a broader conception of social progress" (p. 119). For Addams, this approach meant that workers had to be as generous of spirit and as peaceful in conduct as they wished employers to be.

Consistent with this position, Addams used her considerable diplomatic talents to act as an interpreter across class and cultural boundaries. The genius of the *Spirit of Youth and the City Streets* (1909), *Twenty Years at Hull-House* (1910), and *A New Conscience and an Ancient Evil* (1912) lay in Addams's ability to make vividly clear the internal logic motivating the behavior of the juvenile delinquent, the corrupt policeman, the ward boss (and the voter who supported him), the prostitute, the capitalist, the anarchist, and the cocaine addict. She asked that her readers understand the thief without condoning theft, because she believed that citizens could engage in peaceful

processes of change and achieve democratic ends once they recognized a fundamental, human similarity in diverse people's hopes, desires, and fears.

Having dismissed class warfare as a viable political strategy, Addams's work pointed toward a sanguine future that included an active, legitimate, peaceful labor movement cooperating with a capitalist class that understood its social responsibility to prevent poverty, not simply ameliorate it. Her work pointed as well toward a pluralistic society in which ethnic and racial identities informed America's international relations and gave citizens daily practice in the democratic work of negotiating across differences.

The problem Addams faced was how to get from the reality of early twentieth-century urban, industrial America to the peaceful, democratic, social ideal she envisioned. Her challenge was to create a population of healthy, educated, stable citizens when the existing state was not democratic. Addams disdained the path of social philosophers who never tested their theories in real life; "the standard of social ethics," she said, "is not attained by traveling a sequestered byway" (*Democracy and Social Ethics*, 6). But Addams's temperamental and ideological recoil from conflict sometimes limited her effectiveness as a participant in contentious democratic movements. There is a profound irony in this limitation, one that has shaped history's view of Addams: on the one hand, people applauded her insistence on mediation in all matters and admired her ability to "set a subject down, unprejudiced, and walk all around it" (Gilman, 184). Indeed, partisans often valued Addams's reputation as the ultimate honest broker because her acknowledgment alone could confer legitimacy on a cause. On the other hand, advocates caught up in the heat of battle often resented Addams's cool distance and felt her failure to champion their side as a hypocritical abandonment of her democratic principles.

Addams's disappointing tenure on the Chicago School Board between 1905 and 1909 reveals the personal and political dilemmas she faced when she tried to enact her ideals of mediation and fair-mindedness in real life. At the time of her appointment to Mayor Edward Dunne's "reform" school board, the conservative newspapers disdained Addams as a partisan of the teachers' union. At the same time, MARGARET HALEY, the union's fiery leader, expressed hope that Addams's moderate manner would produce more results than Haley's bombast. When Addams agreed to a compromise plan on teacher promotions that violated the union's basic goals, however, Haley denounced her as unprincipled. Later, when Addams declined to resign from the school board because the mayor had fired her progressive allies, she came under more bitter attack. In this situation, as in others, Addams was ill-prepared for the heat that would singe her disinterested stance. At the height of a school board crisis in 1906, Addams told another board member that she simply could not understand "where all the emotion comes from" (Addams to Anita McCormick Blaine, December 27, 1906, Jane Addams Memorial Collection). For all her talent at seeing everyone's ideological point of view, Addams was often insensitive to—or disdainful of—the depth of partisan emotion. She regarded Margaret Haley's intransigence in the same unworthy light as she viewed the newspapers' sensationalism and the school superintendent's "commercialistic ideal" (*Twenty*

Years at Hull-House, 334). To Addams, they all blocked democratic dialogue. By confessing later that she "certainly played a most inglorious part in this unnecessary conflict" (p. 335) on the school board, Addams took her share of blame but made clear her frustration at others' unnecessary and, to her, immoral rigidity.

Typically, Addams avoided the discomfort of the school board conflict by distancing herself from organizational squabbles. Though she was a valued public speaker for the woman suffrage movement, and even served as a vice-president of the National American Woman Suffrage Association from 1911 to 1914, Addams kept her distance from the strategic battles being waged between suffrage organizations in the years between 1900 and 1920. She made a temporary foray into partisan politics by seconding Theodore Roosevelt's nomination for president on the Progressive Party ticket in 1912 and campaigning enthusiastically for Roosevelt; but Addams withdrew from the intraparty bickering that followed Roosevelt's defeat. By situating herself, institutionally, within Hull-House and, ethically, within the democratic pacifism she outlined in her writings, Addams was able to serve in an advisory capacity to numerous organizations without ever becoming embroiled in their internal disputes. For years, this pattern served her political, philosophical, and emotional needs while performing a valuable, if sometimes irritating service: Addams's mere presence on a board or executive council was supposed to remind members to put aside their petty quarrels and consider the good of the whole.

World War I marked the end of Addams's freedom to rise above the partisan fray as the unassailable advocate of peace and reason. In wartime, pacifists are unwitting partisans, and in the years between 1914 and 1918, Addams became increasingly radical in the cause of mediation. She had belonged to peace organizations since the 1890s, had spoken out against the imperialism of the Spanish-American War, and had thoroughly grounded her social activism in pacifist principles. The war brought no change in her convictions, but it thoroughly transformed her public image. Addams sacrificed her status as a beloved female figure when she challenged the bellicose climate of the day and criticized European belligerence, American preparedness efforts, and, ultimately, American participation in the war. Her leadership in organizing and then chairing the Woman's Peace Congress at The Hague in 1915, and her subsequent tour of European capitals to urge mediation, coincided with Americans' increasing militance. At best, Addams's critics regarded her as a dangerous traitor; at worst, they saw her as a silly, sentimental woman with no business interfering in the international affairs of men.

So stunning and vitriolic were the attacks on Addams during the war and in the postwar Red Scare, that it is easy to imagine her alone and isolated in the decade between 1914 and 1924. It is true that Addams lost many friends during the war and was temporarily shunned by many others. It is also true, however, that Addams still enjoyed tremendous national and international influence and was actively involved in expanding circles of friends and colleagues in the peace movement. During the war, Herbert Hoover, who was head of the United States Food Administration, recruited Addams to raise funds for his agency's war relief work because, he said, of "people's unbounded confidence in you" (Herbert Hoover to Addams, March 2, 1918, Swarthmore College Peace Collection).

Pacifist women in the suffrage movement, for example, Lillian Wald and Crystal Eastman, also turned to Addams to lead their antiwar protest precisely because of her reputation for "dispassionate and marvelously detached impersonal judgement" (Mary C. Percy to Addams, February 19, 1918, Swarthmore College Peace Collection/Women's International League for Peace and Freedom Collection). Before the war, Addams had been less a leader of the women's movement than an exemplar of its ideals. This nonpartisan status made her valuable for legitimizing the image of feminist pacifism. She had previously preferred mixed-sex organizations for pursuing social reform, but during the war Addams became convinced that the peace movement needed a separate women's organization to counter "masculinist" thinking (Addams to Anita McCormick Blaine, January 17, 1917, Jane Addams Memorial Collection). The war inspired in Addams greater feelings of gender solidarity than she had ever expressed before. Though her personal circle had always been composed chiefly of women, and though her public circle continued to include valued male colleagues, the war convinced Addams that women simply cared more about life than men did. The war strengthened her resolve to see that women, as women, would have a powerful voice in all political affairs. This subtle shift in emphasis emerged in her most prominent publications of the time: *Women at The Hague* (1915), *The Long Road of Women's Memory* (1916), "The Devil Baby at Hull-House," *Atlantic* (October 1916), and *Peace and Bread in Time of War* (1922).

The organizational affiliations that Addams formed as a result of World War I, the Women's Peace Party and, out of that, the Women's International League for Peace and Freedom, dominated her public activity for the rest of her life. She continued to administer Hull-House and to serve on numerous boards concerned with such domestic issues as child labor, old age pensions, and unemployment relief. She also continued to write and speak out on domestic concerns. In the decade after the war, she lent her much-sought-after endorsement to several unpopular civil liberties cases. She also chastised a conference of social workers in 1926 because the profession had stopped challenging "the construction of society itself" and had obeyed the public's postwar "desire to conform and play safe" ("How Much Social Work Can a Community Afford?" 200). But at the center of Addams's attention and activity was her international work for peace.

Addams chose to serve as the president of the Women's International League for Peace and Freedom (WILPF) rather than as president of the United States section of the organization. This decision allowed her to skirt the bitter disputes that plagued the American unit of WILPF and to maintain a comfortable distance from the squabbles at the International's office in Geneva. Her focus was on doing what she could do better than any other woman of her day: speaking, writing, fundraising, and organizing for WILPF chapters around the globe. Building on the international perspective she had developed as a result of living in an immigrant neighborhood and traveling often with Mary Rozet Smith, Addams, now a woman in her sixties, embarked on a whole new career. Her time in the 1920s was devoted to corresponding and meeting with peace activists from many nations, lobbying for relief to Germany, Russia, Poland, and Armenia, affiliating with liberation movements in Ireland and India, and encouraging women's independent activism in Latin America, Mexico, China, and Japan.

In recognition of these endeavors, Jane Addams became the first American woman to win the Nobel Peace Prize, in 1931, at the age of seventy-one. By that time, most people had forgotten that she had been called a "traitor," a "slacker," a leader of the "spider web" of vicious subversives during World War I and the reactionary twenties. When the Nobel Prize was announced, five hundred congratulatory telegrams poured in from friends and organizations in twenty different countries, all singing her praises as one of the spiritual forces of the age. Few knew, at the time, that she received these telegrams from a hospital bed where she was recovering from surgery on an ovarian cyst. Addams had long been plagued with kidney problems and recurrent bouts of bronchitis, but her health had not begun to deteriorate seriously until 1923, when she had a mastectomy in Tokyo, Japan. Three years later, at age sixty-six, she had suffered her first heart attack and was thereafter under strict orders, enforced by Mary Rozet Smith, to slow down. In the last decade of her life, Addams had, grudgingly, trimmed her schedule; and she spent more time away from Hull-House at the summer home she shared with Smith in Bar Harbor, Maine, or at Louise deKoven Bowen's home in Tucson, Arizona. She never retired, however. Members of Franklin D. Roosevelt's New Deal administration actively sought her advice right up to the end, as did the residents charged with running Hull-House. So, too, devoted members of WILPF sought Addams's general guidance in the face of encroaching Nazism; and frightened members of the Jewish community sought—and received—her support. But increasingly in the 1930s, Jane Addams's attention centered on her life with Mary Rozet Smith and the lives of her nieces and nephews and their children. Her own dear friends were dying: Florence Kelley and Julia Lathrop died within weeks of one another in 1932; and, most painfully, Mary Rozet Smith, who died early in 1934, following close on the heels of Addams's second heart attack.

Addams worked virtually up to the day of her death. She sent off the manuscript of her last book, *My Friend, Julia Lathrop*, in early March of that year; traveled to Berkeley, California, to receive an Honorary Doctor of Laws degree at the University of California; and went to Washington, D.C., in mid-May for a dinner, hosted by Eleanor Roosevelt, to celebrate the twentieth anniversary of WILPF and to honor Addams's career. Friends and physicians expended so much worry on Addams's weak heart and the loss of Mary Smith that it came as a great surprise when she was diagnosed with abdominal cancer on May 18, 1935; she died of the disease just three days later.

When she was a young woman, Jane Addams displayed the talent to be a fine scholar. But she wanted "to live in a really living world" (*Twenty Years at Hull-House*, 64), she said, and gambled her health, her fortune, and her family ties to do so. In an age of industrial and reform giants, Addams rose to a stature never before enjoyed by any American woman. She did it with tireless work in her neighborhood, in city, state, and national reform movements, and in the relationships she cultivated with people from all walks of life. But woven throughout her active engagement with the real life of social reform was an artistic and scholarly thread, always observing, analyzing, pulling back for perspective, always directing her audience's eye to the larger ethical tapestry on which she was working. Just days before Addams's death, a colleague in the peace movement wrote to say, "you have been like a North Star guiding us" (Harriet Laidlaw to Addams, May 1, 1935, Swarthmore College Peace Collection). The timeless, compelling nature of her writing has made it possible for Addams to continue guiding generations of readers seeking a vision of peaceful, democratic society.

Sources. The Jane Addams Paper Project has collected, from more than six hundred different repositories, the surviving correspondence and documents related to Jane Addams's life and career. This massive collection is currently available in an eighty-two-reel microfilm edition titled *The Jane Addams Papers* (Microfilm Edition, 1985). The first twenty-six reels of the microfilm are devoted to the surviving personal and professional correspondence; the remaining reels include documents on Hull-House, the Women's International League for Peace and Freedom, and Jane Addams's various other organizational activities, as well as her clippings file and copies of her published and unpublished books, editorials, essays, and speeches. Those interested in the microfilm collection are advised to consult *The Jane Addams Papers: A Comprehensive Guide*, ed. Mary Lynn McCree Bryan (1996). The two main repositories for Jane Addams's papers are the Swarthmore College Peace Collection and the Jane Addams Memorial Collection, UIC Spec. Coll. UIC also has the papers of the Haldeman-Julius family. There are additional Addams-Haldeman Papers at the Lilly Library, Indiana Univ. Ellen Gates Starr Papers are in the Sophia Smith Collection, Smith College, Northampton, Massachusetts. Jane Addams published a dozen books over the course of her career. Those books are *Residents of Hull-House, Hull-House Maps and Papers: A Presentation of Nationalities and Wages in a Congested District of Chicago* [1895]; *Democracy and Social Ethics* (1902); *Newer Ideals of Peace* (1907); *The Spirit of Youth and the City Streets* (1909); *Twenty Years at Hull-House* (1910); *A New Conscience and an Ancient Evil* (1912); *Women at The Hague* (1915); *The Long Road of Women's Memory* (1916); *Peace and Bread in Time of War* (1922); *The Second Twenty Years at Hull-House* (1930); *The Excellent Becomes Permanent* (1932); *My Friend, Julia Lathrop* (1935). The *Jane Addams Papers: A Comprehensive Guide* includes a detailed bibliography of all of Jane Addams's published and unpublished writings. A less complete but still extensive bibliography of her writings can be found in John C. Farrell, *Beloved Lady: A History of Jane Addams's Ideas on Reform and Peace* (1967). See her early writing on woman's role in society in "Opening Address," *Rockford Seminary Magazine*, April 1880. A short list of Addams's most significant and influential articles would have to include "A New Impulse to an Old Gospel," *Forum*, November 1892; this article is more commonly known as "The Subjective Necessity for Social Settlements," the title given to it when it was published in *Philanthropy and Social Progress*, ed. Henry C. Adams (1893). Addams republished the same article as chapter 6 of *Twenty Years at Hull-House*. Additional, significant articles are "Why the Ward Boss Rules," *Outlook*, April 2, 1898, which was an excerpt from "Ethical Survivals in Municipal Corruption," *International Journal of Ethics*, April 1898; "The College Woman and the Family Claim," *Commons*, September 1898, and "The Subtle Problems of Charity," *Atlantic Monthly*, February 1899 (both reworked as chapters in *Democracy and Social Ethics*); "Trade Unions and Public Duty," *American Journal of Sociology*, January 1899; "A Function of the Social Settlement," *Annals of the American Academy of Political and Social Science*, May 1899; "Child Labor Legislation: A Requisite for Industrial Efficiency," *Annals of the American Academy of*

Political and Social Science, May 1905; "Why Girls Go Wrong," *Ladies' Home Journal*, September 1907; "Why Women Should Vote," *Ladies' Home Journal*, January 1910; "Charity and Social Justice," *Survey*, June 11, 1910; "Why I Seconded Roosevelt's Nomination," *Woman's Journal*, August 17, 1912; "Pragmatism in Politics," *Survey*, October 5, 1912; "The Progressive Party and the Negro," *Crisis*, November 1912; "My Experiences as a Progressive Delegate," *McClure's Magazine*, November 1912; "A Modern Lear," *Survey*, November 2, 1912; "Pen and Book as Tests of Character," *Survey*, January 4, 1913; "Need a Woman of Fifty Feel Old?" *Ladies' Home Journal*, October 1914; "Larger Aspects of the Woman's Movement," *Annals of the American Academy of Political and Social Science*, November 1914; "The Revolt Against War," *Survey*, July 17, 1915; "The Devil Baby at Hull-House," *Atlantic*, October 1916; "How Much Social Work Can a Community Afford?" *Survey*, November 15, 1926; "Social Consequences of the Depression," *Survey*, January 1, 1932. To date, the two most reliable biographies of Jane Addams are Allen F. Davis, *American Heroine: The Life and Legend of Jane Addams* (1973), and James Weber Linn, *Jane Addams: A Biography* (1935). See, too, Victoria Bissell Brown, "Jane Addams," in *American National Biography*, ed. John A. Garraty and Mark C. Carnes (1999). For other perspectives on Addams, see Mina Jane Carson, *The Settlement Folk: Social Thought and the American Settlement Movement, 1885–1930* (1990); Kathryn Kish Sklar, *Florence Kelley and the Nation's Work: The Rise of Women's Political Culture, 1830–1900* (1995); Leila J. Rupp, *Worlds of Women: The Making of an International Women's Movement* (1998); Mary Jo Deegan, *Jane Addams and the Men of the Chicago School, 1892–1918* (1990); Christopher Lasch, *The New Radicalism in America, 1889–1963: The Intellectual as Social Type* (1965); and John C. Farrell, *Beloved Lady: A History of Jane Addams's Ideas on Reform and Peace* (1967). Charlotte Perkins Gilman discusses Addams in *The Living of Charlotte Perkins Gilman: An Autobiography* (1935).

VICTORIA BISSELL BROWN

AHERN, MARY EILEEN
October 1, 1860(?)–May 22, 1938
LIBRARIAN, EDITOR

Mary Eileen Ahern, a leader of the public library movement in the United States, was born on a farm in Marion County, Indiana. She was the second daughter and second of three children of William and Mary (O'Neill) Ahern. Ahern's parents, both natives of Ireland, met and married after each had emigrated to the United States and settled in Indianapolis. In 1870, the Ahern family left the farm and moved to Spencer, Indiana, a small town northwest of Bloomington. When Mary Eileen Ahern was twelve years old, her mother died. Although she was raised by a Catholic father, Ahern chose to attend a Presbyterian church in adulthood. Ahern graduated from Spencer High School in 1878 and from Central Normal College in Danville, Indiana, in 1881. For the next eight years, she was a public school teacher in Spencer, Peru, and Bloomfield, Indiana.

Ahern's lifelong career dedicated to library service began in Indiana in 1889. Interested in librarianship because of her experiences as a teacher, Ahern decided to run for the office of Indiana State Librarian. She was not elected but was chosen to be one of the assistant state librarians. During her four years in this position, Ahern cataloged the book collection of the state library and worked on improving public document availability. Ahern's work with library organizations started with her involvement in the establishment of the Indiana Library Association in 1889, which she served as its first secretary. She continued to take a leadership role

in the association for the next seven years, including a term as president in 1895. She remained an honorary member of the Indiana Library Association throughout her lifetime.

Supported by Democrats, Ahern was elected by the state legislature for a two-year term as Indiana State Librarian in 1893. Believing that the state library would greatly benefit from having continuity of leadership and service and that the position of state librarian should be removed from the political sphere, Ahern successfully lobbied during her tenure for a bill placing the state library under the control of the Indiana State Board of Education. In 1895, after her term as state librarian expired, Ahern decided she would attend library school in order to prepare herself better for library work.

In September 1895, Ahern enrolled as a student in the Department of Library Economy at the Armour Institute of Technology in Chicago. Established just two years prior to Ahern's enrollment by KATHARINE SHARP, a student of the library science pioneer Melvil Dewey, Armour's Department of Library Economy was the first library school founded in the Middle West. Ahern received a certificate upon graduating from Armour in April 1896.

Prior to her graduation, Ahern was offered the editorship of a new journal to be sponsored and published by Library Bureau's Chicago office. Library Bureau, a library equipment and supply business, had been established by Melvil Dewey, creator of the Dewey decimal classification system. The committee of librarians and officials who selected Ahern believed that there was a need for an inexpensive journal that would provide information, advice, and technical instruction to the many newly established small public libraries, especially those in the Middle West. Interest in libraries and their use had been generated by exhibits relating to libraries at the World's Columbian Exposition held in Chicago in 1893. Beginning in the 1880s, the number of public libraries in the United States increased dramatically, in large part due to the philanthropy of steel magnate Andrew Carnegie. Ahern was an ardent supporter of Carnegie's public library philanthropy. Ahern was hesitant to accept the new journal's editorship due to her inexperience, but the committee convinced her that their selection demonstrated good judgment and should be trusted. In May 1896, one month after Ahern's graduation from Armour, the first issue of *Public Libraries* was published. Ahern remained the sole editor of *Public Libraries* (changed to *Libraries* in 1926 to reflect its broadened scope) for the next thirty-six years.

Published monthly except in August and September, *Public Libraries* contained an overview of library matters and methods. The journal printed editorials, information on meetings and conferences, news of national and state library associations, library and personnel news, letters, reprints of speeches, and articles. The pages of *Public Libraries* provided a forum for Ahern's beliefs. Her views on library service were also expressed in articles that she published in other professional journals as well as in speeches given before associations, clubs, societies, and library schools.

Ahern actively encouraged women to enter the profession of librarianship. As early as the 1850s, women were employed in libraries. With the rapid growth of libraries in the 1890s, the number of female librarians significantly increased due to the heavy demand for trained librarians. Library work was considered well suited for women, who, with expanded educational opportunities, were increasingly entering the workforce. In her writings and personally, Ahern gave advice and encouragement to many young female librarians, guiding them in their librarianship and in career advancement. Ahern advised women to develop executive ability and a knowledge of business methods. In the June 1899 issue of *Public Libraries*, Ahern wrote, "One of the first and most important lessons which a woman who enters the business world needs to learn, is the seeming paradox, to forget she is a woman and at the same time keep ever before her that she is a woman" (p. 258).

As a service to libraries and to librarians, Ahern functioned as a one-person personnel service. She offered her assistance to library trustees and to librarians to find the best available person for a particular job. She counseled women to value their work and to ask for an increase in the relatively low salaries paid to librarians. In the June 1899 issue of *Public Libraries*, Ahern wrote, "I have my doubts about sending a girl's name for a position, who is willing to work for nearly nothing, for I cannot help thinking her talents are not in demand in the market, or else she does not intend to carry out her contract, and her work will be worth no more than she asks for it" (pp. 260–61).

Ahern belonged to the Chicago Woman's Club and the Woman's City Club of Chicago, organizations that advocated an expanded role for women in public affairs. Unlike the majority of clubwomen who made up the membership roles, Ahern, like many women librarians, did not support suffrage for women. In her view, supporting advancement for women in the library profession was not a contradiction, since librarianship was an acceptable enlargement of ideas for women, akin to the field of education. Support of a woman's right to vote was seen as a challenge to well-established norms that many women, including Ahern, were unwilling to make.

From the 1890s, Ahern was an active member of the Chicago Library Club. It brought together librarians from all types of libraries, initially to promote the professional interests of its members and to increase the efficiency of the city's library system. In the first decade of the 1900s, the group changed focus as it became aware of Chicago's social problems and the potential service that librarians provided by collecting and circulating books to children and to immigrants. The club began promoting neighborhood branch libraries, special children's rooms, and book collections in the native languages of immigrants. The Chicago Library Club was instrumental in the development of jail libraries for adult criminals and juvenile offenders. Ahern served as treasurer of the club in 1897; as president for two terms, 1904–1906; as first vice-president, 1918–19; and as a member of various committees. Ahern's activities in the club supported her philosophy that the public library was a democratic educational institution and that humanitarian service was part of librarianship.

In 1897, Ahern also served as secretary-treasurer of the Illinois Library Association (ILA). In that same year, *Public Libraries* was made an official organ of ILA. She continued to volunteer her expertise and enthusiasm to ILA by serving as its president in 1908, 1909, and 1915, and by heading numerous ILA committees throughout her career.

In addition to participation in local and state organizations, Ahern was also active on the national level. Believing in the educational benefit of cooperative work between schools and libraries, she was largely responsible for the formation of a library department within the National Education Association in 1896. She served as the department's secretary from 1896 to 1907. Ahern was one of forty-four charter members of the American Library Institute, a national group of experienced librarians who met to study and discuss library issues. She served as its secretary from 1912 to 1916. Ahern was a life member of the American Library Association, the oldest and largest national library association in the world, which moved its headquarters from Philadelphia to Chicago in 1909. She served on the American Library Association Council, the association's governing body, for fifteen years and was the head or a member of numerous committees. She traveled throughout the United States as well as to England, Canada, Belgium, Scotland, and Italy to attend more than forty American Library Association conferences. In 1919, Ahern went to France as publicity agent for the American Library Association War Library Service, a program to raise funds and collect books for distribution to soldiers in the United States and overseas. She also served as an advocate for public library service in France. The trip heightened Ahern's interest in developing international library cooperation. She returned to England and France in 1927 to study the organization and administration of their libraries.

When failing eyesight forced Ahern to give up the editorship of *Libraries* in November 1931, Harry Datz and H. R. Sampson of Library Bureau's Chicago office decided that Ahern was irreplaceable and that it was impossible to continue the journal without her. The last issue of *Libraries*, dated December 1931, contained parting words from Ahern and tributes to her by colleagues in the United States, Canada, and England.

In May 1938, weakened by arteriosclerotic heart disease, Ahern died on a train near Atlanta, Georgia, while en route to Chicago from Orlando, Florida. Ahern had never married. She was buried in Indianapolis where her sister resided.

Ahern was internationally known for her pioneering work in the public library movement in the United States. In the December 1931 issue of *Libraries*, W. E. Henry described Ahern's advocacy for high ideals and public library service: "Miss Ahern has been a devout supporter of the public library because she believes so strongly in the individuality of people. She has been a democrat of the positive and elevated type, believing in educating the entire group by the help of the free public library" (p. 444). During her lifetime, Ahern saw the number of public libraries increase to more than 6,230 libraries serving approximately 63 percent of the American population. Both *Libraries* and its editor played a significant role in supporting and recording the development of these public libraries. Ahern provided guidance, inspiration, and information to thousands of librarians.

Sources. The Mary Eileen Ahern papers, part of the American Library Association Archives, are at the Univ. of Illinois Library at Urbana-Champaign. A major source of information on Ahern is *Public Libraries* (became *Libraries* in 1926), published from May 1896 to December 1931. Ahern's writings appear throughout the journal's thirty-six volumes. Notable articles include "The Public Library Is an Integral Part of Public Education," August 1896; "Women as Librarians in the Business World," June 1899; "Ideals for a State Library," November 1931; and "A Time to Begin and a Time to End," November 1931. "The Business Side of a Woman's Career as a Librarian" in *Library Journal,* July 1899, is an example of Ahern's writing published in another library journal. Ahern's portrait is the frontispiece and her life is highlighted in the *Bulletin of Bibliography,* May–August 1925. The final issue of *Libraries,* December 1931, contains a number of articles about Ahern's life and career. Ahern is named in a list of forty leaders of the library movement in *Library Journal's* "A Library Hall of Fame," March 15, 1951. Ahern is included in *NCAB* (1930), *NAW* (1971), *Dictionary of American Library Biography* (1978), and *World Encyclopedia of Library and Information Sciences* (1993). Carolyn M. Mulac's Ph.D. dissertation, "Librarian Militant: Mary Eileen Ahern and *Public Libraries*" (Univ. of Chicago, 1978), provides information about Ahern and analyzes the content of the journal. Obituaries appear in the *CT,* May 24, 1938; *NYT,* May 25, 1938; *Bulletin of the American Library Association,* June 1938; and *Library Journal,* June 1, 1938. Dee Garrison's "Women in Librarianship," in *A Century of Service: Librarianship in the United States and Canada,* ed. Sidney L. Jackson, Eleanor B. Herling, E. J. Josey (1976), provides historical information on the status of women librarians.

GAYLE SOSIN ROSENBERG

ALDIS, MARY REYNOLDS
June 9, 1869–June 20, 1949
WRITER, PRODUCER, THEATER MANAGER

Mary Reynolds was born in Chicago to attorney and investor William Collins Reynolds and Marie Antoinette (l'Hommedieu) Reynolds. She was educated at St. Mary's School in Knoxville, Illinois. The family moved frequently during Mary Reynolds's childhood, eventually settling on Chicago's fashionable Near North Side. There, as a young woman, she met Arthur Taylor Aldis, who lived down the street. They married on June 8, 1892.

Arthur T. Aldis was born in St. Albans, Vermont, in 1861, to Judge Asa Owens Aldis and Nancy (Taylor) Aldis. He attended Harvard University as a law student but left to travel to Wyoming, where he ranched from 1885 to 1889. In 1890, he moved to Chicago to join his brother Owen in the real estate firm of Aldis, Aldis and Northcote (later Aldis & Co.). Their firm, pioneering in the construction of skyscrapers, "collaborated with Peter and Shepard Brooks of Boston to build some of Chicago's finest buildings, including the Rookery, the Marquette Building, and the Monadnock Building" (Kimbrel, 19–20). Arthur Aldis also helped to develop the town of Lake Forest, Illinois. After the marriage of Mary Reynolds to Arthur Aldis, they commissioned the respected architecture firm of Holabird and Roche to design a home for them on North Lake Shore Drive. Mary Aldis was intent on living in a replica of a Venetian Gothic palazzo. The building, with its patterned brickwork and traceried balconies, was completed in 1896. The Aldises soon found the layout of the three-story building too narrow and crowded for their entertainment needs, and within several years they moved to an apartment on East Chicago Avenue in Chicago's Gold Coast neighborhood. Their only child, Arthur Graham Aldis, was born in Chicago on November 12, 1895.

The Aldises became part of an upper-class cultural and social set and, like many other wealthy families, established a sub-urban residence in one of the North Shore communities conveniently linked to Chicago by commuter railroad lines. The Aldises had visited friends in Lake Forest, Illinois, and kept their horses at the exclusive Onwentsia Club there before they established a summer home in 1902. In that year they moved to Lake Forest to an estate at the corner of Deerpath and Greenbay Roads, where they summered for many years.

In Lake Forest, year-round and summer residents engaged in amateur and professional artistic activities that mirrored those in Chicago. Bored by the routine of recreational sports, cards, and partying, and increasingly aware of the possibilities of the little theater movement that was developing in Chicago, Mary Aldis soon became involved in the open-air amateur theater productions at various Lake Forest homes. Mary Aldis's interest in producing, directing, and acting in little theater productions increased during these early years of the century, until in 1911 she decided to create her own permanent theater on the estate. The Aldis compound, as it was called, consisted of a main house with a paddock, several small cottages, various storage buildings, and an ice house. After numerous additions, her next step was to convert a building to a permanent theater.

Both Mary and Arthur Aldis were already important figures in the arts in Chicago as patrons and participants. The Aldises' strong interest in theater mirrored the desire in Chicago to create little theater that would serve to challenge the shallowness of commercial offerings. In 1906, Arthur Aldis founded The New Theatre in Chicago, a resident professional company playing in the Whitney Opera House; the theater closed within a year for lack of support.

The Aldises' attention then focused on new initiatives in Irish theater. They worked to develop connections with playwrights and players from Ireland. In May 1909, Arthur Aldis and novelist Hobart Chatfield-Taylor invited guests to attend a performance of John M. Synge's *Playboy of the Western World* at the Winter Club in Lake Forest. Arthur Aldis's interest in founding his own theater resurfaced that year when he saw a performance of Mrs. Fiske's players in Synge's *The Shadow of the Glen* at the Illinois Theatre. He announced his intention to produce it in an amateur way at his summer home in Lake Forest, with a cast of summer residents. In Mary Aldis's capable hands, this dream was to become a reality within two years.

The building of Mary Aldis's Play House began in 1911 while her husband was on a journey in Europe. In her preface to *Plays for Small Stages* (1915), Aldis describes how, in the spring of 1911, she "cast an affectionate and calculating eye upon a small frame house next door." After rejecting an architect's plan to create a Greek-style theater for upwards of three thousand dollars, she hired a local carpenter to transform one of the cottages into a playhouse. The theater could seat one hundred people and had a stage that added 8 × 18 feet to the existing platform of 14 × 10 feet (formerly the kitchen). Aldis supervised the renovation and spent only three hundred dollars. From the outside the theater looked like a faded red barn; inside it was cozy, and its brown oak-leaf wallpaper resembled the oak trees outside. The Play House, as it was called, opened on June 11, 1911, with a performance of Helen Dudley's one-act play, *The Winged Shrine,* followed shortly by *The Noble Tzigane,* a Romanian folktale transposed by Frances Wells Shaw.

The Play House now a reality, Mary Aldis was ready to present Irish theater on her own terms. She had hosted a sumptuous reception in Chicago for Lady Augusta Gregory and the Irish Players of the Abbey Theatre in February 1911; now on July 15, 1911, Mary Aldis invited the Hull-House Players to perform two Irish plays by Lady Gregory, *The Rising of the Moon* and *Spreading the News*, at the Play House. Soon after, Aldis presented productions of William Butler Yeats's *A Pot of Broth* and Synge's *The Shadow of the Glen*. In the fall of 1911, the Aldises were instrumental in bringing the Irish Players of the Abbey Theatre along with playwright Lady Gregory to Chicago as part of a national tour.

The Play House productions were social affairs as well as performances, and admission was by invitation only. Dinners often accompanied the openings and were hosted by various friends and supporters. Ironically, during that first summer season, much of the credit for bringing serious theater to Chicago audiences was given to Arthur Aldis. Although Mary Aldis's name was sometimes included, she clearly was not seen as the driving force. But by the following summer, columnists and critics referred to "Mrs. Arthur Aldis's private playhouse in Lake Forest" (*Chicago Tribune*, August 24, 1912) and reported on the plays that were being produced. The theatrical evenings were seen as an important part of the cultural and social scene in the North Shore suburbs. Mary Aldis established her place as the founder, producer, playwright, and often the lead actress for the Lake Forest Play House from 1911 to 1920.

In 1912, a year after Mary Aldis opened her Play House in Lake Forest, Maurice Browne and his wife ELLEN VAN VOLKENBURG opened the Little Theatre in the Fine Arts Building in Chicago. The Aldises had supported the couple's efforts, providing them a place to live on their estate in Lake Forest. Although Browne credited himself with founding the Little Theatre movement, in fact several developments, including Mary Aldis's Play House, preceded him. ANNA MORGAN's theater and school in the Fine Arts Building in 1898 and the reorganization of the Hull-House Players by LAURA DAINTY PELHAM around 1900 were also important in providing a foundation for the renaissance of theater in Chicago in the early years of the twentieth century. Both Mary and Arthur Aldis had supported Morgan and Pelham, and Browne himself acknowledged Pelham as being "the true founder of the American Little Theatre Movement" (*Too Late to Lament*, 128). The cross-fertilization of the arts during the Chicago Renaissance period was exemplified by the figure of HARRIET MONROE. Known mainly for her poetry and editing, Monroe also wrote five verse plays for Anna Morgan's theater group. Correspondingly, the plan to finance Monroe's innovative *Poetry* magazine was hatched by novelist Hobart Chatfield-Taylor, a close friend of the Aldises, while Monroe was a visitor at their Lake Forest estate. Monroe was part of the same cultural and social group that gathered there and in Chicago.

Keeping the Play House "amateur" was important to Mary Aldis. She states in her preface to *Plays for Small Stages*: "Amateurs have one great advantage, they give a play only once or twice and so attain a freshness and spontaneity that it would take years of technical training to enable them to keep up through a long run" (p. xiv). The Aldis Play House became the summer home for the players on a regular basis for the next ten years and sporadically for years thereafter. In 1913, the group took the name the Lake Forest Players; by that season Mary Aldis was widely regarded as their guiding spirit. Before Aldis and her husband sailed to Europe for the summer, she suggested that the Aldis Play House remain open under the direction of an executive committee of three selected to run the Play House until her return. A company of players was thus formally established and a highly successful season ensued. When Aldis returned, she took up the reins again and produced three plays. One of her most popular plays, in which she also starred, *Mrs. Pat and the Law*, was presented on September 14, 1913.

During the first three years, the Lake Forest Players company gave forty-eight performances of forty-two different plays, forty at the Play House and eight in other venues. On one occasion, in December 1913, they left the Chicago area and traveled to Boston to perform five plays at the Toy Theatre, where they received rave reviews; however, concerned husbands back in Chicago soon ended these trips. The Lake Forest Players' season, generally extending from June to October, consisted of two or three productions each month. Each program usually presented two one-act plays. Many plays were repeated each year, especially those written by Aldis herself, including *Mrs. Pat and the Law* and *Extreme Unction*, as well as the plays of Synge and Yeats. The last full season was 1915. Activity at the Play House continued sporadically until the late 1920s.

Aldis drew on the creativity of her talented neighbors as actors, playwrights, and designers. Among those regularly appearing in Aldis's productions were Chauncey McCormick, Charles Atkinson, SYLVIA JUDSON HASKINS, Dorothy Linn, Isabel McBirney, Richard Little, Dorr Bradley, and MARGARET AYER BARNES. Occasional appearances by son Graham Aldis, novelist and playwright ALICE GERSTENBERG, Little Theatre innovator Ellen Van Volkenburg, and the Countess Gizycka (Eleanor Patterson) indicate the rich mix of prominent and wealthy leaders of Chicago society, its writers, theater people, and artists who came together at the little theater in Lake Forest. Despite their social nature, Mary Aldis's productions increasingly were taken seriously. They were reviewed by the critics in most of Chicago's newspapers, thus raising the level of the productions well beyond the realm of private theatricals.

Although Aldis had the central role in producing the plays, she did not direct them. The Lake Forest Players, a group of individualists, decided not to have a single designated director. Aldis recalls, "Our composite results are obtained by a process of mutual suggestion and recrimination" (preface, *Plays for Small Stages*, xiv–xv). Another key to their success was the absence of rules: only two were posted in the Green Room—"Keep Your Temper" and "Return Your Manuscripts" (p. xv).

The plays performed in Lake Forest, chosen primarily by Aldis, were avant-garde, and quite different from those available in the commercial theater of the period. They were written by amateurs as well as by established playwrights; by local, national, and international figures; by poets, novelists, socialites, and businessmen. Some were adapted from short stories, some translated from the French, and some used the dialects of the new immigrant populations in Chicago. Among European playwrights, she chose Yeats, Synge, and George Bernard Shaw;

among the Americans, Upton Sinclair, W. D. Howells, Zoe Akins, Floyd Dell, and Susan Glaspell. Local playwrights, many of them friends and neighbors, included Helen Dudley, Frances Wells Shaw, Joseph Medill Patterson, Gertrude Robins, novelist JANET AYER FAIRBANK, poet Arthur Davison Fiske, Cleves Kinkead, and Alice Gerstenberg. Mary Aldis's knowledge of French permitted her to produce a large number of French plays adapted in English either by Aldis herself or by other translators. She also favored works by George Middleton, J. M. Barrie, O. Henry, G. K. Chesterton, and Ernest Dowson. In most of her selections, women characters outnumbered men, and she tended to favor the work of women playwrights. Alice Gerstenberg's famous one-act poetic comedy *Overtones* (believed by many to have prepared the way for Eugene O'Neill's Freudian epic *Strange Interlude*) was to have one of its earliest productions at the Play House on November 29 and 30, 1915. The audience on the night of the play's performance in Lake Forest included Harriet Monroe, who reviewed it favorably in the January 1916 edition of *Poetry* magazine.

While generally Mary Aldis's choice of the modern classics overlapped with those of Maurice Browne's and Ellen Van Volkenburg's larger and more influential Little Theatre in Chicago, Aldis did more modern, socially relevant plays than did Browne and Van Volkenburg. Aldis's choices reflected social issues that were far outside her own personal experience and that of the majority of her audience. Her own "problem plays," as she called them, included *Mrs. Pat and the Law, Extreme Unction, The Harlem Tragedy* (based on an O. Henry story), and *The Unawakened: A Problem Play.* Plays by other writers extended these interests; such plays included Joseph Medill Patterson's *By-Products,* set in a tenement house of a large city.

Many of Aldis's own plays had their debut at the Play House; five of these were reprinted in her volume *Plays for Small Stages* in 1915. *Mrs. Pat and the Law* seriously confronts the issue of domestic violence, alcoholism, and poverty in the Irish tenements of a large city. *Extreme Unction* tackles the issue of infanticide, guilt, and atonement in the character of a young prostitute dying in a city hospital ward. *Drama Class* examines the issue of "wifely duty" and the meaning of marriage in the middle-class setting of an amateur drama group and pits the "progressive" women against the more conservative members. *The Letter* is about a love triangle in the upper classes; similarly, *Temperament* examines modern marriage in the same milieu. Influential theater teacher and producer Anna Morgan, in her 1918 autobiography *My Chicago,* credited Aldis with having done "more good along these general lines than any other Chicago woman" (p. 180). Although the repertoire and actors of the Play House changed from season to season, many favorites were brought back again and again. In all, the repertoire of the Play House reflected the tastes and talents of one woman, Mary Aldis, as dramatist, translator, and actor.

Besides producing the plays for the Lake Forest Players during this period, Aldis further supported the development of little theater by giving access to the Play House to many other groups, especially the Hull-House Players. During 1911 and 1912 they produced two Irish plays by Lady Gregory and one by John Masefield. Indeed, one critic noted that "since the open-

ing of the Play House almost every Saturday has found the Hull-House Players in whom Mr. and Mrs. Aldis find especial interest, occupying the stage in a presentation of one of the unusual plays they delight in producing" (*Chicago Tribune,* July 18, 1911).

In addition to her leadership in cultural affairs, Mary Aldis also participated in the social reform movements of the Progressive Era. She combined her concerns for authentic amateur theater with an agenda of social justice, and she often used theater as a fund-raising vehicle for benevolent projects in which she was active. Mary Aldis brought her productions to Hull-House and other venues where she could raise money for social causes. She produced a benefit performance for the Grove Home for Convalescence at the Ravinia Park Theatre in September 1912. Another benefit, for the Infant Welfare Society, brought Aldis and members of her group to the Marquette Hotel in Chicago, where she directed four plays and raised two thousand dollars for the society. The hit of this benefit was Joseph Medill Patterson's *By-Products,* starring his sister Cissy (the Countess Gizycka). The program that night opened with a performance of *Somewoman,* a suffrage-morality play. Written in blank verse by Chicagoans Mrs. James Keeley and Mrs. Horace Martin, it was described as "the tale of Somewoman's quest for the vote, of her uncertain position on the fence the while she listened to the arguments pro and con" (*Chicago Tribune,* February 15, 1912). In March 1913, the Lake Forest Players performed at the University of Chicago in a benefit for the Equal Suffrage League and were lauded by Professor Robert Morss Lovett as "one of the best amateur companies in the country" (*Chicago Maroon,* undated). In December 1913, the Players performed at the Fine Arts Theatre in a benefit for the Chicago Equal Suffrage Association. Favorable commentary came from at least half a dozen columnists, including critic Richard Henry, who exulted: "It was not only the best amateur performance ever given on a Chicago stage, but . . . there are few professional performances that could excel it for sincerity, attention to details and wonderful characterizations." The plays were *Mrs. Pat and the Law, The Stronger* (with Countess Gizycka as Madame Y, who "left nothing to be desired") (*Inter-Ocean,* December 9, 1913), and *How He Lied to Her Husband.*

In 1913, the Lake Forest Players also presented three plays at the Hull-House Theatre before the Social Service Club, with Aldis putting in play form an experience of a district nurse in the Chicago Visiting Nurse Association in *Mrs. Pat and the Law.* The other two plays were Patterson's *By-Products,* also a play of tenement life, and *Which One?* Both the Infant Welfare Society and the Chicago Visiting Nurse Association were special interests of Aldis, who served as a director of the former and was president of the latter.

In the mid-teens, Mary Aldis maintained an apartment in New York's bohemian neighborhood, Greenwich Village, where she spent periods of time away from Chicago and Lake Forest. "She had lived a lifetime . . . in a conventional pattern, bringing up her son and co-promoting with her husband, demands made by the community," her friend Alice Gerstenberg wrote, "but now at last she felt free to be on her own" ("Autobiography" manuscript, 229). "The social surface," Gerstenberg continued, "dutifully endured, covered a longing to paint, to write, to act, in all of which she was gifted" (p. 230).

Mary Aldis expressed herself in media other than theater. In 1916, she published her only volume of verse, *Flashlights*. In 1918, she published *Princess Jack*, an adult fairy tale with strong feminist overtones. The main character, Princess Jack, defying the rules of the kingdom where only men may serve as monarchs and only men can vote, proves herself capable of excelling in male activities; ultimately she prefers to live as a woman, combining male logic with female intuition and finally becoming queen. In 1918, Aldis also published *Drift*, her only adult novel. The work drew attention to her concerns about the lives of the social elite. She raised the issue of what wealthy women might best do with their time and resources. The heroine, Eileen Picardy, "drifts" from art school to settlement work to marriage and finds them all unsatisfactory. Hers is the restlessness of the postwar woman who leads a selfish and aimless life. The novel also contains an interesting and extended portrait of the labor problems surfacing in the company town that Picardy's husband owns. This same theme is approached by Aldis in her 1924 play *Heir at Large*.

In 1917, Chicago's Little Theatre closed, but Aldis's connections with Browne and Van Volkenburg continued. Mary Aldis briefly followed them to Seattle, Washington, where the couple took positions in 1918 at the Cornish School of Drama, Music, and Dance, established by Nellie G. Cornish. Aldis predicted, correctly, that when the wealthy patrons of the school acquired control, they would commercialize its offerings and force Cornish to resign. Aldis also continued to be a witness to the unorthodox relationship between Browne and "Nellie Van," who remained business partners and intimates after their divorce in 1926. She gave lodging to Van Volkenburg at her apartment in Greenwich Village, but she disapproved of the relationship of the divorced couple.

Although the activities of the Play House had virtually ended by 1920, Aldis continued her interest in writing for the theater. Two plays appeared in 1924: *An Heir at Large* and *Two Plus Two* (or *Two and Two Make Four*). *An Heir at Large*, a play based on the cartoon story by John T. McCutcheon published in the *Chicago Tribune* during 1921 and 1922, was produced at the Goodman Theatre in Chicago from December 1925 through January 1926. In the play, a romantic comedy of appropriate marriages is secondary (but parallel) to the plot of appropriate relations between capital and labor in a one-industry steel town. Like Aldis's novel *Drift*, it is an argument for enlightened ownership of industry and for enlightened marriage. Aldis suggested producing the play in the same style as the cartoon, all black and white. The sets were drawn by McCutcheon. *Two Plus Two* was produced by Gerstenberg's Playwrights' Theatre in 1924 and again in 1930–31. It depicts the boredom, financial dependency, and lovelessness in the lives of two married women in the 1920s.

Arthur Aldis was injured in an automobile accident in Paris in 1925 and never completely recovered. In 1928, the Chicago Avenue house burned down; the senior Aldises, together with their son Graham, his wife Dorothy (an author of books for children), and their four children moved to the Lake Forest estate. The senior couple moved into the Play House, leaving the main house to their children and grandchildren. The arrangement did not work well. Soon Mary and Arthur Aldis were spending more time at their winter home in Winter Park, Florida.

In May 1930, Mary Aldis's three-act play *Flying Blind* was entered into competition at the First Annual National Long Play Tournament at the Waldorf Theatre in New York. On November 6, 1930, it was presented at the Playwrights Theatre of Chicago, founded by Alice Gerstenberg. Five years later Samuel French published Aldis's *No Curtain: Suggested Themes for Impromptu Plays*. These eight short sketches, all comedies, reflect Aldis's belief that impromptu plays were "the most taxing, the most developing, and the most fun of all kinds of dramatic entertainments" (foreword to *No Curtain*, 7). A common thread present in this collection is that of dissatisfaction and discontent in the lives of rich and poor, the misunderstandings, antagonisms, and jealousies that prevail. One of the sketches, *Baubles and Beans*, was performed at the Lake Forest Play House on June 28–30, 1926.

In the 1930s, Mary Aldis's attention also turned to painting. Arthur Aldis, always interested in modern art, learned of Chicago artist and teacher Hubert C. Ropp, whose abstract and surrealistic paintings (and those of his students) raised the ire of Chicago's traditionalist art community. The Aldises established the Ropp School on the third floor of their home on Chicago Avenue, where it continued to prosper until its merger with the Art Institute of Chicago in 1937. During the summers, Ropp taught art classes at the Red Bird cottage on the Aldises' Lake Forest estate. It was here that Mary Aldis pursued her interest in painting watercolors; her works were soon exhibited at galleries in Chicago, New York, and Florida.

Arthur Aldis died at the Aldises' winter home in Winter Park, Florida, in 1933. Mary Aldis continued to live in both Chicago and Florida until her death in 1949 when she was in Milwaukee. The last recorded presentation at the Play House was on September 29, 1939; it was a performance by the Lake Zurich Players of Oliver Goldsmith's *She Stoops to Conquer*. The Aldis compound was razed in 1969.

Mary Aldis was a pioneer of the little theater movement in the United States. Her Play House opened in 1911, a year before Chicago's more famous Little Theatre in the Fine Arts Building in Chicago, and its cofounder Maurice Browne respected her contributions to the movement. He described Aldis as coming "from a different world. Dark, with perfect bone-structure and carriage . . . gifted alike as poet, dramatist and painter, she had a brilliant mind and, when she chose to exercise it, a devastating wit" (*Too Late to Lament*, 150). As a society woman, she transformed her role as social hostess into one of theater patron, playwright, and producer. In so doing, she was part of a tradition of women doing similar work to enhance the role of serious theater in the United States. What began as a summer frolic quickly developed into one of the most significant parts of her life. She developed a new repertoire of one-act plays that could be performed by groups in their homes or small theaters. She influenced the little theater movement nationally when Susan Glaspell and George Cram Cook, her fellow participants in the development of the little theater movement, took these ideas east and helped establish the famed Provincetown Players, introducing the work of Eugene O'Neill to the American stage. Aldis brought new energy to the amateur theater, developing a new seriousness of purpose and sophistication to counter the commercialism of popular theater. She was an influential force in the development of the modern theater in America.

Sources. A conflict exists about Mary Aldis's year of birth. Dawn Kimbrel, *The Aldis Compound* (1994), lists it as 1869. Earlier sources had indicated 1872. By far the most useful sources on Aldis are the two Mary Aldis Scrapbooks held at the CHS, containing newspaper articles, clippings, and programs of the Lake Forest Play House. Lake Forest College Library has some additional materials, in particular copies of Aldis's published works. Arthur Aldis's papers are at the UIC Spec. Coll. Additional primary sources, including correspondence between Aldis and Ellen Van Volkenburg, are in the Ellen Van Volkenburg Papers at the Univ. of Michigan, Spec. Coll. Library. The manuscript of Alice Gerstenberg's unpublished autobiography, in the Alice Gerstenberg Papers, CHS, is a good source of relevant information. A small collection is found in the Modern Poetry Collections, Mary Aldis Papers, at UC Spec. Coll. Mary Aldis's published works include *Plays for Small Stages* (1915), *Flashlights* (1916), *Princess Jack* (1918), *Drift* (1918), and *No Curtain: Suggested Themes for Impromptu Plays* (1935). Scattered critical references to Aldis are found in many sources, including Maurice Browne's *Too Late to Lament* (1956) and Anna Morgan's *My Chicago* (1918). Others include Karen J. Blair, *The Torchbearers: Women and Their Amateur Arts Associations in America, 1890–1930* (1994); Donald F. Tingley, "Ellen Van Volkenburg, Maurice Browne and the Chicago Little Theatre," *Illinois Historical Journal*, Autumn 1987; and Douglas Clayton, "Yesterday's City: Temple of a Living Art," *Chicago History*, November 1993. Constance D'Arcy Mackay's early volume *The Little Theatre in the United States* (1917) contains a short chapter on the Aldis Play House. The most recent and comprehensive study of the Aldis Play House appears in Dawn K. Kimbrel, *The Aldis Compound* (1994).

BABETTE F. INGLEHART

ALLISON, FRAN HELEN
November 20, 1907–June 13, 1989
RADIO AND TELEVISION BROADCAST PIONEER

Fran Helen Allison, star of the popular television show *Kukla, Fran and Ollie,* was born in LaPorte City, Iowa, the first child and only daughter of Jess L. and Nan (Helpin) Allison. A brother, Lynn, was born two years later. The Allisons were second generation Irish-American Catholics. They kept a small grocery store and were socially active in their rural community. Allison grew up immersed in midwestern small town life. Years later, she used this experience to develop her radio and television characterizations.

Allison's parents both became seriously ill while she was still in grade school. Her father developed a paralysis and her mother contracted tuberculosis. Allison took on many adult caregiver responsibilities. The family's religious faith was strong, and this childhood test was the first in which Allison later credited her faith as an essential factor in pulling her through personal crises.

Allison graduated from LaPorte City High School in 1924 and entered Coe College in Cedar Rapids, Iowa, in the fall of that year. She majored in music and education and, as a member of the college glee club, made her radio debut in an era of crystal receiver sets with headphones. Her father never fully recovered from his illness, and after two years she left college because of financial problems. The ensuing seven years took her

through many hit-and-miss job experiences that seem in retrospect to have nourished her later achievements. For four years she taught in small, low-paying rural schoolhouses before trying department store sales, singing contests, and a theatrical group that shortly failed.

Lynn Allison became the catalyst for his sister's broadcast career, when in 1932 he invited her to sing with his band on WLT, a fledgling radio station in Waterloo, Iowa. She rapidly became the station's "girl," doing spot announcements, songs, and cooking lessons, as well as canvassing downtown businesses for advertising.

It was during this period in the mid-1930s that Allison coalesced the elements of her broadcast talent. In addition to her singing and acting, her hands-on apprenticeship in the business and technology of radio, and her diplomacy with listeners and advertisers, she rapidly molded her own distinct performing persona—the key ingredient of which was her incredible ability to improvise. One day the announcer for the *Cornhuskers' Variety Show* tried an impromptu prank, announcing that his dear old Aunt Fanny was just entering the studio for a chat. Allison, on the spot to perform, startled everyone with her instant creation of a garrulous small-town spinster. Aunt Fanny had an immediate following and sponsors, and became a staple in Allison's permanent repertoire. This impromptu success also established her as a performer who worked better and more often without a script than with one.

Allison's burgeoning regional fame was barely underway when, in December 1933, she was critically injured in an automobile accident that left her life in doubt for the next three weeks. Her mother prayed continuously, recruiting others to do the same. Recovery was slow, with lingering pain and extensive facial scars, altering the wholesome prettiness that was part of her initial popularity. Allison, however, was profoundly grateful to be left physically whole with her vision and vocal powers intact.

Inspired by her mother's example of courage and confidence, she returned after several months to the microphone. At a time when most radio broadcasts didn't have studio audiences, she hoped to maintain a career in which she could remain largely out of sight. Feeling self-conscious and timid, she declined some interviews and personal appearances. Photographs before and during the 1930s indicate that she was, though changed, still attractive and photogenic in a more mature way. The more lasting effects of the accident were connected with residual physical discomfort and emotional sensitivity. As soon as she was well enough to resume broadcasting, her popularity continued to climb.

Allison's regional following became so strong that in 1937 she was invited to audition for the National Broadcasting Company (NBC) in Chicago. Her success was immediate. She continued to do a variety of bits for commercials and songs as needed. She also began her regular appearances on major programs such as Ransom Sherman's *Club Matinee* and, most important for her career, Don McNeill's *Breakfast Club.* The McNeill program pioneered the concept of an unscripted variety format and was ideal for the spontaneous talkiness of Aunt Fanny. Allison continued to appear with McNeill on and off in later years, until his show closed in 1968 after thirty-five seasons.

FIG. 6. *Fran Allison with puppets Kukla and Ollie.*

During this period Allison met a young puppeteer named Burr Tillstrom. He had gained considerable notice as a Works Progress Administration (WPA) performing artist. One day, as Allison emerged from the Wrigley Building on Chicago's North Side, she joined the crowd lined up on the broad sidewalk in front of Tillstrom's puppet stage. Allison soon found herself in conversation with Kukla, Tillstrom's lead puppet (and, according to legend, his alter-ego). Their chemistry was spontaneous and effortless. Tillstrom concluded the show by having Kukla say he'd like to kiss a certain pretty girl. When Allison assented, Tillstrom appeared from behind the stage and bestowed the kiss himself.

In 1947, seeking to establish a postwar television presence in Chicago, the Radio Corporation of America (RCA) asked Burr Tillstrom to develop a children's program. RCA had worked with Tillstrom on earlier broadcast experiments. They agreed with him that a human presence in front of his puppet stage could help connect viewers with his puppet troupe, the Kuklapolitan Players. Tillstrom and WBKB, then the local affiliate of the American Broadcasting Company (ABC), agreed Allison was perfect for the role.

Kukla, Fran and Ollie premiered on Monday, October 13, 1947, live from WBKB, and was aired nearly every weekday evening for the next ten years. The show won rapid popularity and critical acclaim for its artistry, intelligence, and the ability to entertain children and adults. Tillstrom and Allison claimed it was not aimed solely toward either children or adults and disliked the industry's insistence on categorization. Among the famous adult fans who shared this view were Orson Welles, Arturo Toscanini, Helen Hayes, and John Steinbeck. Starting as a local, then a regional presentation, by 1951 it was aired across the country.

The program was the perfect showcase for Allison's and Tillstrom's genius for improvisation: it was unscripted and unrehearsed, except for a brief brainstorming of possible topics and themes just before air time. The chemistry between Allison and the puppet characters, talking and singing together, was one of the show's strongest elements. To the degree that she herself experienced them as real, she conveyed that sense to viewers. For her they had a credibility that did not change substantially offstage; after the show ended, she refused to see her "friends" on display in an exhibit at the Chicago Historical Society. As interviewers noted, and Allison herself insisted, her own off- and onscreen personality was essentially the same, giving viewers the sense that they might easily know her socially. "What's . . . amazing is the utter believability of Fran" ("Puppet Regime"), wrote critic Rick Kogan.

This feeling of believability carried over to the rest of the Kuklapolitans through the medium of Allison's own engagement with them. The cast members, charismatic on their own merits, were an eclectic group. The principals were Kukla, a red-nosed, balding little man of great intelligence and curiosity, and Oliver J. Dragon, with a single tooth, wild orange mane, and smooth baritone voice. Other regulars included Beulah Witch; Mme. Ophelia Ooglepuss, a former opera singer who remained a diva; and Fletcher Rabbit, the postman whose job opened many avenues of news and conjecture.

Allison's extraordinary relationship with Tillstrom was at the

Allison's move to Chicago also brought about her meeting with Archie Levington, a music publishing representative who regularly visited the major broadcast studios. The two formed a fast friendship. In Chicago, Allison worked briefly at the Columbia Broadcasting System (CBS) in 1939 and the early 1940s. Her popularity continued as a staff singer, actor, and announcer. A series of cosmetic and structural surgeries, in 1940, completely restored Allison's handsome facial features. The procedures were repetitive and painful, but she at last felt more inclined to respond to increasing demands for personal appearances.

Allison and Levington were married at a small private ceremony on February 21, 1942, shortly before Levington left for Army duty in World War II. The happiness of marriage and her successful operations was marred by another life-changing ordeal. The Levingtons expected a baby early in their marriage, after which Allison planned to retire and devote herself to their home life. She miscarried and was unable to bear children thereafter. This loss, on the heels of her long medical tribulations, was extremely difficult. She credited her husband, her mother, and her Catholic faith for imparting to her the will to return to a functioning life.

Allison was fully enough recovered during the remainder of the war years to maintain a full schedule, somewhat compensating for her losses and Levington's long absences. She presented her new face at bond rallies, radio appearances, and almost anything else that was requested of her.

root of the show's verisimilitude. The two were likely to improvise at almost any time. They would sit together when traveling and pretend to be two strangers, conversing and gesturing in character to the end of the trip. In the increasingly competitive world of commercial television, they refused to have a written contract with each other, any more than they would consent to have a script. Allison once said, "It was such a fortunate meeting of minds; we thought alike. We remembered things from our childhoods which were astoundingly alike. And the other characters I just came to love because they were friends" (audiotape reminiscences, April 1, 1986, Museum of Broadcast Communications).

In addition to their regular shows, the cast appeared in a number of acclaimed specials. Notable among these was the *Kukla, Fran and Ollie* version of *The Mikado*, which they performed in seven different interpretations over the years. Another considerable achievement was an original short opera on the theme of St. George and the Dragon, composed by *Kukla, Fran and Ollie*'s music director, Jack Fascinato, collaborating with Allison and Tillstrom on the libretto. It was notable also as the first coast-to-coast color transmission of any program and was telecast from NBC's New York studio, with Arthur Fiedler conducting the studio symphony.

Despite these and other triumphs, network executives decided in 1957 to discontinue *Kukla, Fran and Ollie*. An avalanche of protest mail, calls, and telegrams caught them off guard, but did not alter the decision. Throughout the sixties and early seventies, the Kuklapolitans returned for various appearances: a series of five-minute shows, a stint on public broadcasting, syndicated reruns, and more specials. From 1967 to 1979 *Kukla, Fran and Ollie* hosted the unique CBS Children's Film Festival, providing greetings and brief commentary on an educational series of foreign films. But there was never again a sustained series of regularly scheduled programs. The original show, encores, and specials earned many awards and citations, including the "Emmy" for the 1953 and 1970–71 seasons and Peabody Awards in 1949, 1964, and 1967.

In addition to the show's reprises, Allison did many projects on her own. She often made *Breakfast Club* appearances as Aunt Fanny. In 1958 she appeared with the actor Mickey Rooney in a televised adaptation of *Pinocchio*, and in 1967 in *Damn Yankees*.

Allison and her husband began to spend more of each year away from Chicago traveling to Detroit (for his business), Iowa, and California, where they settled in 1976. She remained active into the 1980s, including volunteer work and appearances for charitable and civic causes. A priority among these was concern for the elderly, which was the focus of her show *Prime Time*, on KHJ-TV in Los Angeles.

After a long and happy marriage Allison was widowed in 1978. Her friend and costar, Burr Tillstrom, died in 1985. Allison died in 1989 after suffering from leukemia for about six months. She was buried in Cedar Falls, Iowa.

Allison lived to see her long career acknowledged. There were retrospective tributes at museums and articles and interviews about her own and the industry's past. Her pioneer role in the early days of both radio and television and her own immense range of talent secured her historical place as a woman in

broadcasting. *Kukla, Fran and Ollie* was her crowning achievement, shaping the second half of her professional life and securing her permanence in the topmost echelon of broadcast annals. *Kukla, Fran and Ollie*'s durability was again confirmed after fifty years: its silver anniversary was commemorated by the announcement of a 1997 home video release, initially offering thirty-nine episodes in color, fully restored and digitally enhanced.

Sources. The Fran Allison Collection at the Museum of Broadcast Communications (MBC) Archives, Chicago, has a forty-five-minute audiotape interview of Fran Allison by Jim Conway, conducted for the MBC. The MBC also has more than 100 audio and videotapes of *Breakfast Club* radio shows, *Kukla, Fran and Ollie* television shows, and various interview and variety broadcasts with guest appearances by Allison and/or Burr Tillstrom. The Coe College (Cedar Rapids, Iowa) alumni office has a small collection of newspaper and magazine clippings on Allison from the late 1930s, as well as documents from her college years. The Burr Tillstrom papers, CHS, have correspondence, press clippings, and artifacts, including his puppets. The March 20, 1953, Fran Allison segment of NBC's *This is Your Life* is owned by Gloria Van Allison, her sister-in-law. Two articles of particular interest are Carol Hughes, "Kukla and Ollie's Real-life Heroine," *Coronet*, October 1951, which focuses on the period surrounding Allison's automobile accident and early marriage, and Nora Ephron, "Fran Allison of the Kuklapolitan," *New York Post*, April 8, 1967, which gives a broad retrospective and contemporary view of Allison's personality and work. See also Rick Kogan, "Puppet Regime," *CT*, October 24, 1996. June Skinner Sawyer, *Chicago Portraits* (1991), has a biographical entry on Allison. Several reference books on radio and television are useful, including John Dunning, *Tune in Yesterday* (1976); Tim Brooks and Earl Marsh, *The Complete Directory to Prime Time Network TV Shows 1946–Present* (1979); George W. Woolery, *Children's Television: The First Thirty-Five Years, 1946–1981. Part II: Live, Film, and Tape Series* (1985); and Alex McNeil, *Total Television* (1991). An excellent overview of Chicago's crucial role in the early "golden age" of television is Joel Sternberg, "Television Town," *Chicago History*, Summer 1975. Obituaries include Jack Hovelson, "Kukla's Fran Allison Returns Home to Iowa," *Des Moines Register*, June 21, 1959; Susan Heller Anderson, "Fran Allison, 81, the Human Side of Kukla, Fran and Ollie Show," *NYT*, June 14, 1989.

NANCY TAYLOR POORE

ALSCHULER, ROSE HAAS
December 17, 1887–July 4, 1979
EDUCATOR, AUTHOR, PHILANTHROPIST

Rose Haas was the third and last child born to Charles and Mary (Greenebaum) Haas. A cattle salesman born in Stadtecke, Germany, Charles Haas came to America at age two with his family. Mary Haas's maternal uncles and grandfather, Michael Greenebaum, had emigrated from Germany in the 1840s and 1850s. Settling in Chicago, they started a variety of businesses and eventually became prominent bankers, philanthropists, and civic leaders. A leading nineteenth-century German-Jewish Reform family, they valued education and pursued cultural interests in Germany and America. At age thirteen, Rose Haas's mother, Mary, was sent to boarding school in Frankfurt, Germany, where she developed interests in education and art. Haas's aunt, HANNAH SOLOMON, was a founder and leader of the National Council of Jewish Women and a social reformer in Chicago.

Rose Haas went to the Southside Academy, one of three schools that combined in 1903 to become the Laboratory School of the University of Chicago; she was in the first class to graduate from the Laboratory School. She attended the University of Chicago from 1904 to 1905, then transferred to Vassar College. She spent only one year at Vassar because, as she later recalled, "I felt that I should miss more in being separated from all that home offered me, than in missing the year at College" ("Mayma," 12). The following year she again enrolled at the University of Chicago.

In 1907 she met Alfred Alschuler, a young architect, and they married on her twentieth birthday. After a European wedding trip, the couple stayed with her family for several months until they found an apartment in the Hyde Park neighborhood. Two years later they bought a house nearby. Alfred's career flourished, and in 1915 they moved to Winnetka, an affluent northern suburb of Chicago, where Alschuler lived for twenty-six years. Alschuler considered motherhood to be a profession and by 1917 had five children, Marion, Frances, Alfred, Richard, and John. When the family moved to Winnetka, there were few other Jewish families there. By 1921 the Alschulers decided to help establish a Reform Jewish congregation and were instrumental in starting the North Shore Congregation Israel in Glencoe of Sinai Temple, Hyde Park. They both served on the board, and Rose Alschuler taught the first group of Sabbath school children. In 1927 the cornerstone was laid for the building that Alfred Alschuler designed.

Rose Alschuler's interest in early childhood education grew out of her own parenting experiences. While living in Hyde Park, she realized the value of preschool education and established a small class in her home for her own and neighborhood children. She also organized a study group that met weekly in her home to learn about childhood development. When the family moved to Winnetka, she again sponsored a home study group. In 1920 she participated in the parent education group for the North Shore Country Day School, which her children attended.

In 1922 her interest in child development led her to open a nursery school called Children's Community School with her cousin, Charlotte Kuh. Located near the Francis Parker School on Chicago's Near North Side, it was one of the earliest nursery schools in Chicago. In 1925 a member of the Chicago Board of Education visited and asked Alschuler to set up a nursery school in a public school. In September 1925, with partial funding by the Chicago Woman's Club, the Franklin School nursery school opened. It was only the second public nursery school in the country. Alschuler realized that the school should do more than teach, so she arranged for other agencies, including the Elizabeth McCormick Memorial Fund, to provide the service of dieticians, physicians, and mental health experts to help evaluate the child in both home and school environments.

In 1926 the superintendent of schools in Winnetka heard Alschuler speak and asked her to set up a nursery school there. When it opened in 1927 there were ninety applications for sixteen spaces. To meet the growing demand, a new junior-kindergarten nursery was built at Winnetka's Skokie Junior High. The Alschulers donated the money to pay for the addition, and Alfred Alschuler designed it. In 1929 she was asked to plan nursery school programs for the Michigan Garden Apartments, a South Side housing project. Because of her wide experience in establishing and running nursery schools, Alschuler was appointed staff director for the Works Progress Administration (WPA) nursery schools in Chicago. Eventually the WPA supported eighteen nursery schools scattered throughout the city in schools, settlements, and other sites where Alschuler could find space. Alschuler later wrote of the sense of adventure she felt in the 1920s and 1930s as these first programs for nursery schools in the United States were being established.

While Alschuler was actively establishing nursery schools in the Chicago area, she was also prominent in national groups that were defining the field of early childhood education. In June of 1925 she was one of twenty-five people invited to Columbia University to plan the first national conference on nursery schools. The conference, held in February 1926, led to the creation of the National Association of Nursery Education, for which Alschuler later served as both secretary and vice-president. From that point on, she served on the boards of numerous educational organizations and participated in many conferences on early childhood education. She participated in the White House Conference on Child Health and Protection in 1930 and the MidCentury White House Conference on Children and Youth in 1950.

After her husband's death in 1940, Alschuler moved to Washington, D.C., to chair the National Commission for Young Children, a group formed to promote child welfare among public and private agencies. In that capacity Alschuler traveled throughout the country, lecturing at conferences, leading informal discussions at colleges, and visiting children's facilities. The group disbanded in 1943 and became a part of the National Association of Nursery Education. In 1943 Alschuler was hired as a consultant to the Federal Public Housing Authority to plan activities and services for children in housing projects. She served in this capacity for the rest of World War II, using her consulting fees to support research projects of the National Association of Nursery Education. In 1946, Alschuler moved to New York City, where she spent two years on the editorial board of the magazine *Two to Six*. During the 1940s, Alschuler wrote numerous articles for parenting magazines as well as educational journals.

For several years after leaving New York she divided her time between a winter home near Tempe, Arizona, and houses she rented on Chicago's suburban North Shore. Then in 1950 two of her sons designed a house for her in Highland Park, where she lived until her death. In 1953 Alschuler visited Israel. When she came back, she devoted her energies to fund-raising for the new state. She was active in Israel Bond drives and supported various projects in Israel, including the Technion, an Israeli training institute for engineers, which awarded her a citation of achievement. Even though her fund-raising efforts largely focused on Israel, she continued to give financial support to a wide variety of American charities and educational organizations through the Alschuler Philanthropic Fund. In addition to her many cash donations, Alschuler also presented art work to the Art Institute of Chicago and art groups in Tempe. In 1964 Alschuler once more helped establish a nursery school, serving as a consultant for the Horizon House Nursery School in the Parkway Gardens housing project.

Throughout her life Alschuler received numerous awards and citations honoring her work. In 1944 she was given a University of Chicago alumni citation for public service. She received the Eleanor Roosevelt Award in December 1966 from the North Shore Committee for the State of Israel Bonds. The Chicago Association for the Education of Young Children honored her on three different occasions for her work with children. Roosevelt University honored her four times for her support of that institution. She died in her home at the age of ninety-two.

Alschuler established some of the first public preschools in the United States. They served as models for schools around the country and provided a training ground for a generation of educators. Through her work with national organizations, such as the National Association of Nursery Education, she helped to define the field of early childhood education. Universities around the world recognized her expertise, even though she was largely self-taught, and invited her to give lectures. Her many books and articles helped educators and scholars understand the educational needs of the preschool-age child, while her work on publications like *Two to Six* explained early child development to parents.

Sources. The Rose Haas Alschuler papers are at UIC Spec. Coll. They contain correspondence, reports, newsletters, financial records, programs, family memorabilia, Alschuler's publications, her handwritten notes, and other papers relating to her career and personal life. The Asher Library at the Spertus Institute of Jewish Studies, Chicago, also has papers of Alschuler. *Bits and Pieces of Family Lore*, reminiscences and essays on Alschuler's family, including her essay, "Mayma: A Portrait of My Mother for My Children," was privately printed in 1962. Of great value to researchers is a booklet based on an interview by Mary Lynn McCree in 1973, *Oral History Interview with Rose Haas Alschuler*, edited in 1985 by Richard H. Alschuler. Books by Alschuler include: *Two to Six: Suggestions for Parents and Teachers of Young Children* (1933, reissued 1937, 1947); *Children's Centers: A Guide for Those Who Care for and about Young Children* (1942); coauthored with LaBerta Hartwick, *Painting and Personality: A Study of Young Children*, 2 vols. (1947, reissued 1969); and coauthored with Christine Heinig, *Play—the Child's Response to Life* (1937).

CATHLYN SCHALLHORN

AMBERG, MARY AGNES
August 6, 1874–August 28, 1962
SETTLEMENT-HOUSE DIRECTOR, MISSIONARY

Mary Agnes Amberg was resident director of the Madonna Center, a settlement house and Catholic mission to Chicago's Italian immigrants, from 1914 until her death in 1962. Settlement work offered many middle-class women in the Progressive Era a route to independence from their families, but Amberg's experience was just the opposite. She came to it out of a sense of duty to her family. Her parents, William A. and Agnes (Ward) Amberg, were central figures in the Chicago Catholic community. Her mother, one of the founders of the Madonna Center and its de-facto head until her daughter became resident director, was a role model for Amberg, who called herself a "shy wren" (Mary Amberg, *Madonna Center*, 194) and modestly thought of herself as carrying on her mother's achievements. Yet in reality she flourished in her new position and made it her own. She be-

FIG. 7. *Mary Agnes Amberg with her mother, Agnes Ward Amberg, shortly after the Guardian Angel mission was founded, 1899.*

came a capable administrator, winning the admiration of other social work professionals and the respect of her immigrant neighbors.

William Amberg was the son of a master tailor who immigrated from Albstadt, Bavaria. According to Mary Amberg, her father was born in Virginia, but an obituary for her grandfather gives Bavaria as William Amberg's birthplace. Agnes Ward was from a prosperous Chicago family of Scotch-Irish descent. The Ambergs married in 1869 and had three children, Mary,

Genevieve, and John. William Amberg rose from bookkeeper to partner in a series of stationery firms and then established Amberg File and Index Company, which manufactured his patented office aids. He invested in a granite mill in Wisconsin and an iron company in Michigan, and his increasing wealth allowed him to move his family from the West Side to a stately home on Chicago's Near North Side and a vacation home on Mackinac Island, Michigan.

Money also connected the Amberg family to the growing Catholic elite in Chicago. The Amberg home was a "sort of way station" (*Madonna Center*, 27), where visiting priests and bishops were accommodated and talk of church politics and Catholic culture provided an education for daughter Mary. Situated between an affluent neighborhood and a more modest one, and equipped with a spacious yard, swings, slides, and other kinds of play equipment, the Near North Side Amberg mansion was constantly full of local children. Young matron Agnes Amberg put her administrative skills to good use caring for these young neighbors. Mary Amberg thus grew up in an atmosphere much like the settlement house she would run in her adulthood.

William Amberg was president of the Chicago Union Catholic Library Association in 1875 and a trustee of St. Mary's Training School in Des Plaines, Illinois, which housed and educated poor children. He was a member of the Columbus Club of Chicago, a Catholic laymen's organization, and a supporter of the Illinois Catholic Historical Society. Agnes Amberg was active in the Catholic Women's League and the alumnae organization of the Academy of the Sacred Heart, both in Chicago. She also supported the Christ Child Society, a charity that provided baby clothes to poor mothers, and the nuns of the Cenacle, who promoted spiritual retreats for Catholic laywomen.

As her mother did before her, Mary Amberg attended the Academy of the Sacred Heart on Taylor Street, reinforcing her growing social conscience. The Academy was run by the Mesdames of the Sacred Heart, a French order of nuns who specialized in teaching the daughters of the Catholic elite. The Mesdames attempted to inspire their charges with a sense of *noblesse oblige* appropriate to their future importance in Chicago's Catholic community.

In 1898 the Mesdames encouraged members of Sacred Heart alumnae to found a Sunday school for Italian immigrants on Chicago's West Side. Specifically, they hoped to reach the Italian community that was growing on the fringes of Holy Family parish, to which many of the alumnae belonged. The alumnae secured the use of two rooms for the mission in an abandoned parochial school in the neighborhood. With help from their daughters, they cleaned away many years of grime from the rooms and created a chapel using donated furniture. Mary Amberg taught catechism, played the organ, and helped to keep the books.

The mission, originally named Guardian Angel Mission, grew so quickly that a parish was soon created to care for its flock. Holy Guardian Angel church was built in 1899. About the time the church was constructed, the mission became a full-fledged social settlement with a night school and English classes for adults, as well as a summer school for children with classes in

home economics for girls and manual arts for boys. Mission staff also reviewed the children's academic progress during the school year.

Amberg's benevolent activities did not become her life work until she was thirty-eight years old, when a family friend suggested she take over her mother's leadership role and supervise Guardian Angel. The mission had grown substantially, with close to 1,500 children attending Sunday school and 115 volunteer assistants teaching catechism and Bible. Night school classes for adults and a summer vacation school expanded the religious-oriented settlement's scope. Agnes Amberg had supervised staff and volunteers and raised funds. Now Mary Amberg confronted what she termed her own "self-indulgence" (*Madonna Center*, 73), for she had spent her young adulthood searching for health in visits to resorts and in stays at relatives' homes between casual bouts of settlement work. She wrote, "I was well on my way to becoming that silliest of creatures, a society bird of passage, without strong home ties and ever eager to seek a new roost among distant friends and acquaintances far from Chicago" (*Madonna Center*, 73).

During the period of turmoil, which she referred to as her "dark night of the soul" (*Madonna Center*, 80), she struggled with doubts and anxieties. In the context of ideal American and Catholic attitudes about womanhood, marriage and career were mutually exclusive choices. She had to renounce the possibilities of marriage and motherhood, which she had not put aside completely. She was concerned about the financial insecurity of Guardian Angel and its location in the shadow of the famous Hull-House. Influential lay and religious leaders close to her mother, including William J. Bogan, a Catholic who later became Chicago's public school superintendent, encouraged her to take charge. She read Pope Leo's *Rerum Novarum*, with its social teachings, and accounts of Toynbee Hall, Samuel A. Barnett's settlement in England under Anglican auspices. Finally, a new book by Father Agnew of St. Ignatius College put her life in perspective, and she announced plans to join her friend Catherine Jordan and share an apartment in rooms above the classrooms of St. Francis School near the settlement, thus choosing the settlement life as her professional career. The *Chicago Tribune* reported, "Miss Mary Amberg Leaves Home of Wealth for Slum Work" (quoted in *Madonna Center*, 88).

When she chose the settlement life, in 1914, she felt a profound sense of peace, saying, "At last I was among my children. For the first time I felt that I really belonged" (*Madonna Center*, 88). With this new sense of peace, Amberg flourished. Her health problems seem to have disappeared. Soon after, Marie Plamondon joined in the mission's work on a volunteer basis, becoming a permanent resident in 1922 and later co-resident director with Amberg. Amberg envisioned the Guardian Angel Mission in part as a rival of Hull-House. She maintained friendly relations with JANE ADDAMS but saw the institution's secular worldview as a challenge. The ultimate goal of Amberg's mission was to promote Catholic religious values, and the sacredness of the mission made up for its small size and facilities. Since many of the mission's Italian neighbors were Catholic, Guardian Angel appealed to them in a way that secular institutions could not.

One of Mary Amberg's first innovations was to broaden the funding for Guardian Angel from a primarily Amberg family project to a cause for all Chicago Catholics. Establishing an auxiliary, Amberg called on William Bogan; Bishop A. J. Mc-Gavick of Holy Angels Church; Reverend Frederick J. Siedenburg, S.J., dean of the School of Social Work, Loyola University; HARRIET VITTUM, head resident of the Northwestern University Settlement; Judge Edward E. Brown, former justice of the Appellate Court; Leonora Z. Meder, head of the social service agencies of Cook County; and others, including her parents, to speak at the first auxiliary meeting in the Auditorium Building in 1919. The auxiliary was so successful that by 1922 the mission was able to buy a substantial building that provided for day care, kindergarten, after school care, sports, and recreational activities. With the move to South Loomis Street, the Guardian Angel Mission changed its name to Madonna Center.

Madonna Center accepted people of all faiths into its programs, but Catholic values permeated the daily activities. The center offered clubs and classes and tried to teach its neighbors middle-class habits of cleanliness, nutrition, and child care. Unlike secular settlements, several of its clubs were religious, and the classes began with prayer. From Amberg's point of view, Madonna Center had a special mission with Italian immigrants and, in direct contrast to Hull-House, sought to develop an Americanization process that reinforced rather than competed with traditional Catholic faith and allegiance to parish institutions. Particularly among the children, the center strove to "lay a groundwork of adherence to the faith" (*Madonna Center*, 129) that would remain with them throughout their lives.

Amberg's views on women's issues were conservative. She agreed wholeheartedly with the church's condemnation of birth control, and Madonna Center worked to convince local women to reject it. Yet, as one of the first laywomen to spend her life doing social work, she pioneered this career for Catholic women. For Catholic girls, she promoted the Girl Scouts, saying that, in the slums, "A boy can rove to his heart's content. A girl . . . has no such escape" (*Madonna Center*, 148). During the 1920s, Madonna Center organized Girl Scout troops throughout the West Side Italian community, and Amberg served as a board member of the Girl Scouts of Chicago from 1921 to 1928.

Amberg never married. Her closest relationships were with members of her family, especially with her parents and her sister Genevieve. She also had a deep and lasting relationship with her longtime friend, Marie Plamondon. Through her long years of service Amberg won the respect and friendship of many prominent leaders in Chicago social work circles. For example, she became friends with the Reverend Frederick J. Siedenburg, founder of Loyola University's School of Social Work, because the Madonna Center served as a training center for Catholic students in social work, medicine, and domestic science. As a result of Amberg's professionalization of the Catholic settlement, Madonna Center joined the Chicago Federation of Settlements, a secular agency with few Catholic member organizations. Amberg consciously steered her settlement along a course that gained from the advance in mainstream social work at the same time that the central mission of Catholic outreach remained the chief focus. In practical terms, it meant that Madonna Center turned down an offer from the Chicago Public Library for a branch library within the walls in order to retain control of the kinds of books their small library would have on its shelves. Madonna Center rejected any family planning clinics but supported regular clinics for prenatal care.

Amberg was recognized for her contributions to the field of social work in 1928, when Loyola awarded her an honorary degree of Doctor of Laws. From 1937 to 1942, she served as director of the Council of Social Agencies, and from 1926 to 1956 as director of the House of the Good Shepherd. In 1950 she accepted an honorary degree from Rosary College that, for unknown reasons, she had turned down in 1942. That same year, she shared with Marie Plamondon a Citation for Distinguished Service from the Alumnae Association of the Sacred Heart at Barat College. In 1957, she received the Jesuit Centennial Citation awarded to one hundred distinguished Chicagoans.

During the 1930s and 1940s the Madonna Center complex on Loomis Street was the site of many community programs, including St. Ann's Day Nursery, a medical clinic, Boy Scout and Girl Scout troops, drama, dance, and music classes, intramural clubs, sports teams, and summer programs. Students and faculty from Catholic high schools and colleges, including Loyola University and Mundelein College, were volunteers. Although significant numbers of Italian Americans remained in the neighborhood, in the 1940s and 1950s increasing numbers of African Americans moved in as well. Amberg opposed racism as unchristian, but the settlement was never able to forge the kind of close personal relationships with its new neighbors that it had with its old ones. The Madonna Center closed permanently when Amberg died in August 1962.

For nearly a half century, from 1914 to 1962, Mary Amberg directed Madonna Center, a settlement house that served its Italian immigrant neighborhood. While focusing on Catholic religion, Amberg developed a broad program that included activities also found in secular settlements.

Sources. The Madonna Center Papers are housed in Memorial Library of Marquette Univ. in Milwaukee, Wisconsin. Their main value is a record of the day-to-day activities of the center, beginning in 1898 when it was known as the Guardian Angel Mission, and continuing into the 1950s and 1960s. They contain some personal documents of the Amberg family, including a limited amount of correspondence, newspaper clippings, and several honors and awards. One notable source they contain is a travel diary that Mary Amberg kept on a journey to Europe and Northern Africa with her parents in 1899. The richest source of information about Mary Amberg's life and of insight into her character is her book, *Madonna Center: Pioneer Catholic Social Settlement.* Written in 1942, the book is most widely available in a 1976 edition. The activities of the Madonna Center can be traced in the newspaper of the Archdiocese of Chicago, *New World.* Rivka Lissak, in *Pluralism and Progressives: Hull House and the New Immigrants, 1890–1919* (1989), discusses the Madonna Center as part of a Catholic strategy to diminish Hull-House's attractiveness to immigrants by providing competing services. Margaret Mary McGuiness, in "Response to Reform: A Historical Interpretation of the Catholic Settlement Movement 1897–1915" (Ph.D. diss., Union Theological Seminary, 1985), argues that Catholic settlements such as the Madonna Center were rare in Chicago because the archdiocesan hierarchy expected immigrant groups to create institutions to provide for their own needs.

DEBORAH ANN SKOK

Color Plates

PL. 1. Pottery Salt-Glaze Vase with Blue
Geometric Flower Fret, n.d.
by Susan Stuart Goodrich Frackelton

PL. 2. *Raphael Fassett*, 1867
by Cornelia Adele Fassett

PL. 3. *Landscape with Haystack*, 1878
by Annie Cornelia Shaw

PL. 4. *My Blue Eyed Model*, n.d.
by Mary Hackney Wicker

PL. 5. *Landscape with Bridge*, n.d.
by Mary Hackney Wicker

Pl. 6. *Brittany Children*, c. 1892
by Enella Benedict
Oil on canvas
31 5/8 × 24 1/8 in.

PL. 8. Portrait bust of *Edward B. Butler*
by Julia Bracken Wendt
Bronze, 1918

PL. 7. *The Young Mother*, modeled 1896, cast 1903
by Bessie Potter Vonnoh
35.6 × 38.1 cm

Pl. 9. (FACING PAGE) *Mary Rozet Smith*, n.d.
by Alice Kellogg Tyler

Pl. 10. (TOP) *Cornelia De Bey*, n.d.
by Alice Kellogg Tyler

Pl. 11. (BOTTOM) *Macena in Red*, 1925
by Macena Barton

PL. 12. *From My Studio Window*, c. 1927
by Pauline Palmer
Oil impasto on canvas; 31 × 25 in.

PL. 13. *Cottage at Provincetown*, n.d.
by Pauline Palmer
Oil on canvas; 20 × 24 in.

PL. 14. *A Boy Named Alligator*
by Kathleen Blackshear
Oil on canvas, 1930
56.2 × 46 cm

PL. 15. *Portrait of Frances Strain,*
1932
by Frances Foy

PL. 16. *Self-Portrait*, 1934
by Fritzi Brod

PL. 17. *Jenny (at Old Lyme)*,
c. 1935
by Ruth Van Sickle Ford

PL. 18. *Self Portrait*, 1936
by Julia Thecla

PL. 19. (FACING PAGE) *Self Portrait in Green*, 1938
by Gertrude Abercrombie

PL. 20. *Around the Bird House*, c. 1943
by Laura Van Pappelendam

Pl. 21. *In Fragments*, 1973
by Margaret Dagenais

Pl. 22. Two Religious Figures in Stone, n.d.
by Margaret Dagenais

AMERICAN, SADIE
March 3, 1862–May 3, 1944
CLUBWOMAN, SOCIAL REFORMER

Sadie American was an influential clubwoman engaged in social reforms during the Progressive Era. As a self-defined modern Jewish woman, she practiced liberal Judaism and advocated an expanded role for women in the Jewish community and synagogue. Dedicated to improving the conditions of coreligionists who had come to the United States as immigrants and settled predominantly in major cities, Sadie American honestly confronted the specific problems of immigrant women—single and married—including such controversial issues as prostitution and pregnancy outside of marriage. Not satisfied working solely in the context of the Jewish community, American was successful in her work with the major women's political and reform organizations, which were dominated by middle-class and upper-middle-class Protestants.

Sadie American was born in Chicago, Illinois, the only child of Oscar L. American, a German immigrant and successful merchant, and Amelia (Smith) American of New York. Oscar American ran a dry goods business with a partner, I. J. Smith. Sadie American was raised in Chicago and attended public grammar and high schools. She had hoped to attend college, but her conservative parents felt this was too extreme a move for their daughter.

After she graduated from high school, American served an "apprenticeship" as a civic activist in Chicago, first working as a club leader with Jewish immigrants from eastern Europe at the Maxwell Street Settlement. In 1882, she helped form the Young Ladies Aid Society and was elected its treasurer at the first regular meeting. In 1896, it was renamed the Chicago Woman's Aid. The organization's founding members adopted a benevolent philosophy toward those in need. In its early years, committees were appointed to visit, on a regular basis, Michael Reese Hospital—established by German Jews to meet the needs of Jews and others on the Near South Side of Chicago—and the committees provided blankets and other items to people in need. "Later the club's interests included aid for the blind and visually handicapped, improvement of public schools, the provision of birth control facilities at Jewish social agencies, and sponsorship of children's facilities at the [Michael Reese] Hospital and programs for senior citizens" (Hinding, 248). American and the other women communal leaders in the Chicago Jewish community were aware of the clubs and the benevolent work undertaken by Protestant clubwomen in the city and, like their non-Jewish counterparts, began to study the conditions that led to the poor health of women and children, to crime and prostitution, and to juvenile delinquency. In the 1880s organized clubwomen in Chicago critiqued the limited social services available for the poor and for immigrants, identified areas where reform and new programs were necessary, and innovatively advocated a juvenile court system, playgrounds and recreation for children, improved work conditions for adults, and better housing conditions for families.

American was a member of Chicago Sinai Congregation, where Reform Rabbi Emil G. Hirsch served as religious leader. Established in 1861, Chicago Sinai was influential in the Reform movement of the nineteenth century; under the leadership of Hirsch, it stood in the radical camp of the Central Conference of American Rabbis. The Reform movement sought to modify traditional Judaism better to express the prophetic philosophy and ethics of the religion for modern Jews. Radical and moderate Reform leaders "were firmly committed to rationalism . . . [and] placed their emphasis on the moral aspects of Judaism, dismissing the ritual and ceremonial laws as out of date" (Blau, 23). Where the radical and moderate wings of Reform Judaism differed was in the "readiness of the radical group to transfer the observance of the Sabbath from Saturday to Sunday to conform to the prevalent patterns of employment in American economic life" (Blau, 23). Hirsch advocated having the major weekly worship service on Sunday, since many businesses operated on Saturday, the traditional day held for Jewish worship. Many Jews in both the traditional and liberal branches of Judaism objected to what they perceived as an adoption of the Christian Sabbath. Hirsch argued that Reform Jews at Sinai and elsewhere no longer observed the traditional Sabbath laws and were not attending Saturday services regularly. He reasoned it was better to hold services on Sunday, a time when the preponderance of the congregation's families could attend and had the freedom to fully participate. "We . . . do not disguise the fact that originally . . . Sunday [Sabbath] was a symbol of ideas antagonistic and antithetical to those which Judaism distinctively entertains" (Blau, 43), Rabbi Hirsch wrote. "And still with all this, and perhaps all the more on account of this difficulty," Hirsch continued, "we would give this, our *de facto* day of rest, a Jewish religious character and celebrate it with true Jewish fervor" (p. 43). Sadie American supported Rabbi Hirsch's Reform Judaism and the introduction of a morning service on Sunday.

American taught in the Sinai Sunday school from 1894 to 1899 but felt that Jewish women should have a more expanded role in congregational and religious life. In 1897 American spoke from the pulpit at Chicago Sinai Congregation, a privilege generally reserved for men, but occasionally extended to women as it had been on February 14, 1897, to HANNAH SOLOMON. American favored the ordination of women as rabbis, and believed women should not only study Judaism but work in its name. She argued that women's duties should extend beyond the home and serve the social needs and concerns of the community at large.

One of the more significant positions American assumed was her role in the founding and development of the National Council of Jewish Women (NCJW). In 1891, ELLEN HENROTIN, vice-president of the Board of Lady Managers of the World's Columbian Exposition, asked Hannah Solomon to gather Jewish women in an effort to include them in the Woman's Branch of the World's Congress Auxiliary to be held at the same time as the World's Columbian Exposition. Later that year, Solomon formed the Jewish Women's Congress for the World's Parliament of Religions and appointed sixteen women to serve on a committee to organize its program, including the thirty-year-old Sadie American. The committee developed a four-day program and scheduled lecturers to speak on a variety of themes relating to Judaism, modern woman's role in the synagogue, and also secular topics including women as independent wage earners, and issues surrounding Jewish immigration.

Sadie American presented her speech, "Organization," on the final day of the Congress of Jewish Women. In it she laid out a plan for an organization that was to become the National Council of Jewish Women (and in the early years was also called the Council of Jewish Women). She called for the new organization to have four goals: to study Judaism, provide religious education for the poor, undertake philanthropic work, and act as a forum for the exchange of ideas among all Jewish women. American wanted women to extend their activity from the home to the community and Jewish women to take an active part in representing Judaism as a whole. While Solomon was noted as being reserved, appeasing, graceful, and "ladylike," American was described as brusque, strong-willed, and dominant. Solomon was raised in a tightly knit upper-middle-class family. She was married with three children. A great deal of her time was invested in her husband and family, and she volunteered her free time to the NCJW. She served the NCJW as an administrator and maintained a hands-off approach to helping the less fortunate. In contrast, American was single, dedicated a good deal of her time to the NCJW, and believed that it was Jewish women's duty to help people learn how to help themselves. Their most significant difference arose in the approach to the organization's mission. While Solomon wished to maintain its religiousness, American saw its mission becoming increasingly more philanthropic. There were other issues involved underneath, however. Solomon had been displeased when in 1900 American spoke in public on the controversial subject of the observance of the Sabbath on Sunday at Sinai Temple. Solomon, who also observed the Sunday Sabbath personally, was disturbed because it appeared that American endorsed the practice as an official representative of the NCJW. The correspondence exchanged by the two women reflected a deeper rift or antagonism and, as well, a distrust that American felt regarding Solomon's support of her work. The two were reelected to serve NCJW and worked together, although a year later American relocated in New York City, where she continued to serve as corresponding secretary of NCJW.

American, like Solomon, also engaged in reform work in the larger community through association with the Protestant-dominated Chicago Woman's Club. American's name was proposed for membership to the Chicago Woman's Club (CWC) in 1895 and supported by Solomon (already a member), Anne Sweet Dennis, Mariette A. Dow, Juanita Stafford, and JANE ADDAMS. American was an active member of CWC until 1901 and served on its committees for education, playgrounds, and vacation schools. American advocated vacation schools, and in 1895, she visited New York to study vacation schools, where she met a single mother who worked during the winter months to support her family. The mother complained to American that during the summer months she had to stop working as her children could not attend school. American promoted vacation schools—schools organized during the summer months to provide children with scheduled activities such as trips to the country, crafts, and recreational sports. American attributed the need for such activity to the growth and crowded conditions of American cities, where children's vacation time did not allow them the freedom to experience nature and instead exposed them to the dangers of traffic. Trips to the country afforded chil-

dren the opportunity to climb trees, chase butterflies, and otherwise interact with nature. Vacation schools liberated urban mothers from the worry of protecting their children. In 1896, American formed the Permanent Vacation School and Playgrounds Committee of the Chicago Woman's Club and in 1898 secured funds from the Chicago City Council to develop temporary small parks. She was also instrumental in having the education law of Illinois amended to enable vacation schools to be supported with public funding. By 1898 she published "The Movement for Small Playgrounds" in the September issue of the *American Journal of Sociology*. She supported the idea that playgrounds alleviated the evils of urban dwelling. American wrote that children's character could be refined by recreation and that supervised playgrounds taught children respect for other's rights and property. She stressed that open space provided children with a place where they could exercise their "natural expression of physical energies" (p. 166). She cited police reports in areas where playgrounds existed and noted that teenage boys who were given the alternative of organized activities in parks did not enter saloons or play in the streets where their activities would lead to arrest. In November 1898, American published "The Movement for Vacation Schools" in the *American Journal of Sociology*, identifying the special problems that the end of the school year presented to poor families.

In 1900, her father became a patient at the Eastern Illinois Hospital for the Insane in Kankakee, Illinois. The following year, she and her mother moved to New York City, where she became president of the local branch of the NCJW. American refused to accept a salary from the council and voluntarily served in varying capacities for twelve years. In 1905, she became the first paid employee of the council, appointed executive secretary the year that Hannah G. Solomon declined to serve as president.

American also continued her work in the fields of play and recreation and expanded her concerns to provide programs for children with disabilities. In 1906, she became founding member of the board of directors of the Playground Association of America (PAA) and served on the Committee on Play in Institutions. Devoted to populations of children who were visually or hearing impaired, she served on the Committee on the Normal Course on Play, which created a curriculum guide for professional recreation workers that included information for people with disabilities in a section entitled "Play in Institutions." She established public playgrounds in immigrant neighborhoods and was active in the early years of PAA from 1906 through 1910.

Sadie American's work with the New York branch of the NCJW brought her into closer contact with leaders in the organizations involved with Jewish immigration. She "was instrumental in establishing the organization's reputation as an effective agency for assisting Jewish immigrants" (Katz-Hyman, 38). Concerned with providing new eastern European immigrants with tools that would help them become American citizens, Jews of German descent designed programs that sought to maintain Judaism in a largely Protestant community. The NCJW—dominated by a German Jewish membership—was especially concerned with the well-being of women and girls who came to America and were unfamiliar with the English language and

American customs. In New York, the NCJW sent members to meet girls and women at Ellis Island and provided the new immigrants, among other things, with living quarters, informational pamphlets, jobs, and training as they entered the United States. By 1916, the council's activity provided assistance to the blind, guidance for girls released from correctional institutions, care for convalescents, care of insane aliens, and religious education—especially in Reform Judaism—for women and children.

During a nationwide panic created by the media, white slavery or the forced prostitution of young women became a concern of many social reform organizations. The NCJW, like other groups, developed programs designed to protect young women. In 1908, American was asked to organize a campaign to help prevent white slavery. She forced the Jewish community to examine this social problem and urged NCJW members to support a campaign against the trade in the United States. In 1911, she represented the NCJW at the International Anti-White Slavery Conference and in 1913 wrote to the editor of the New York Times and defended the stage drama The Lure. The play was under investigation by the grand jury because of its frank examination of the white slavery problem. It was written by George Scarborough and was based on his experience as an agent for the federal government. Earlier, in 1908, Sadie American had openly acknowledged the existence of prostitution among Jewish women instead of hiding it, as some coreligionists, who feared the rise of anti-Jewish sentiment, had advocated. That year she had called upon the Jewish community to address the problem, encouraging Jewish women to take political action to prohibit the traffic of women for the purpose of prostitution.

In 1913, Sadie American founded and served on the board of the Lakeview Home for Girls, an agency whose objective was to "care for first offenders" (Kneeland, 272) and provide services to girls, single mothers, and children, in Staten Island, New York. The home provided unwed mothers with support before their children were born and career and vocational training postpartum so that women could financially provide for their families. That same year at the annual meeting of the NCJW, American reported on the council's work with immigrant girls, particularly the establishment of English classes which, that year, served two thousand women. Three thousand children were taught in religious schools run by the council.

In the years 1905 through 1914, American served as executive secretary to three council presidents. Beginning in 1911 she began to be criticized by the membership. Initially, her use of funds as executive secretary came under scrutiny by the Baltimore state section of the NCJW; but eventually she was criticized by the officers, including Solomon, for her strong will and her approach to council matters. She was viewed as being difficult to work with and accused of abusing her position as executive secretary. She resigned in 1914 rather than forfeit her power as executive secretary to the officers of the organization. At the time, her salary as secretary was four thousand dollars annually. In 1916, Sadie American officially ended all her connections to the organization.

On an international level, American served in a number of capacities. In addition to writing conference papers, she worked as a delegate to the National Congress of Women in London in 1899 and in 1910 attended the Jewish International Conference in London. She founded a Jewish women's organization in Germany in 1904. She acted as a consultant on the prevention of "white slavery" to the Spanish royal government in 1910 and published a letter in the New York Times in 1914 to the women of Mexico on behalf of the International Council of Women, asking them to work with Americans for peace. She worked for the International Council of Jewish Women in 1923.

American never married. Throughout her life, she was active and supported many organizations including the Art League of Chicago, General Federation of Women's Clubs, the International Council of Women, the Illinois Consumers' League, and Jane Addams's Women's Peace Party. At the end of her life, she resided at the Graystone Hotel on New York's Upper West Side. She died at the age of eighty-two at Aurora Sanitarium in Morristown, New Jersey.

As a social reformer working within the Jewish community, American persuaded women to move beyond their prescribed role in the home and family to carry out social reform work for issues that affected women, Jews, and society at large. Influenced by the work of reformers such as Jane Addams, American believed there was a need to create social and economic conditions that would provide a healthy environment in which to develop the next generation of United States citizens. Her work provided care for Jews, especially those populations that stood outside the larger community—mentally ill aliens, delinquent girls, prostitutes, and single mothers. Concerned with solving social problems beyond surface action, she developed programs that investigated the roots of problems and provided guidance, alternative choices, and lasting solutions.

Sources. The American Jewish Archives, Cincinnati, Ohio, have papers of Sadie American. Information about American can also be found in the Chicago Woman's Aid Papers, UIC Spec. Coll. The American Jewish Hist. Soc., Waltham, Massachusetts, holds two folders on American in the social workers archives. She is also mentioned in the Woman's Club Papers, CHS, and has correspondence in the Hannah G. Solomon Papers at the Library of Congress. American's published articles include "The Movement for Small Playgrounds," American Journal of Sociology, September 1898, and "The Movement for Vacation Schools," American Journal of Sociology, November 1898. Ellen Sue Elwell, "The Founding and Early Programs of the National Council of Jewish Women: Study and Practice as Jewish Women's Religious Expression" (Ph.D. diss., Indiana Univ., 1982), is helpful. Information on Sadie American is included in Karen Blair, The Clubwoman as Feminist: True Womanhood Redefined, 1868–1914 (1980); Linda Gordon Kuzmack, Woman's Cause: The Jewish Woman's Movement in England and the United States, 1881–1933 (1990); Faith Rogow, Gone to Another Meeting: The National Council of Jewish Women, 1893–1993 (1993); Martha Katz-Hyman, "Sadie American (1862–1944)," in Jewish Women in America: An Historical Encyclopedia, ed. Paula E. Hyman and Deborah Dash Moore (1998); and in "History of Special Recreation—Miss Sadie American, 1862–1946: America's First National Leader in Special Recreation for Disabled Children and Youth," Special Recreation Digest, ed. John A. Nesbitt, Winter–Spring 1988. Information on Sadie American's role in vacation schools and playgrounds is also found in Mary A. Logan, The Part Taken by Women in American History (1912). Andrea Hinding, ed., Women's History Sources: A Guide to Archives and Manuscript Collections in the United States, 2 vols. (1979), includes a description of the Chicago Woman's Aid. George J. Kneeland, Commercialized Prostitution in New York City (1913), discusses the Lakeview Home. See Julia Wood Kramer, "'Paradise Was Not Perfect without Woman': World's Fair Women of 1893 and the Founding of the National Council of Jewish Women," a paper given at a meeting of the Chicago Jewish Hist. Soc., April 18, 1993. For information on Chicago Sinai Congregation and Reform Judaism, see Emil G. Hirsch, "The Philosophy of the Reform Movement in American Judaism," in *Reform Judaism: A Historical Perspective. Essays from the Yearbook of the Central Conference of American Rabbis*, ed. Joseph L. Blau (1973).

ELIZABETH M. HOLLAND

ANDERSON, MARGARET CAROLYN
November 24, 1886–October 19, 1973
EDITOR, WRITER

Margaret Anderson founded the literary journal *Little Review* in Chicago in 1914, helping to advance literary modernism in the United States. Born in Indianapolis, the daughter of Arthur Anderson, an executive with Interurban Electric Lines, and Jessie (Shortridge) Anderson, the daughter of a prominent Indianapolis family, Margaret Anderson was the eldest of three daughters.

Enraptured with music and literature as a young woman, Anderson dreamed of becoming a concert pianist. She pursued higher education at Western College for Women in Oxford, Ohio, but left after three years in 1906. Returning to Indiana restless and bored, Anderson wrote a letter to Chicago editor and columnist CLARA LAUGHLIN (later the author of travel books for young women), and asked how a "perfectly nice but revolting girl could leave home" (*My Thirty Years' War*, 16). Much to her astonishment Laughlin replied and invited her to Chicago for a visit. Accompanied by her father, Anderson was captivated by Laughlin's stories of stage stars and life in the big city. "Here was a place," she later wrote in her autobiography, *My Thirty Years' War*, "where I could live and breathe" (p. 16).

Laughlin, impressed by Anderson's enthusiasm, offered her a job writing book reviews for the religious journal *Interior* (renamed *Continent* in 1912) and offered to look after Anderson and her sister Lois, who would make the trip with her. On the train ride to Chicago, Anderson thought, "Chicago: enchanted ground from the moment Lake Michigan appeared in the window. I would make my beautiful life here" (*My Thirty Years' War*, 13). Ensconced in the Young Women's Christian Association on Michigan Avenue, Anderson and her sister soon found themselves in trouble over cigarette smoking. Arthur Anderson was sent for by Laughlin to retrieve his delinquent daughters.

Back in Indiana, Anderson initiated a letter-writing campaign designed to convince both Laughlin and her father to give her a second chance. When Laughlin relented, Anderson returned alone and restarted her life in Chicago in 1909.

Francis Hackett, the Irish Fabian editor of the *Friday Literary Review* of the Chicago *Evening Post*, hired Anderson to write book reviews that same year. Anderson also got a job at Browne's Bookstore, owned by Francis F. Browne, publisher of the prestigious *Dial* magazine, whose offices were next door. *Dial* was published in Chicago from 1880 until 1919; when Browne hired Anderson to work on *Dial*'s printing staff, she learned invaluable skills that would assist her in her own career as a publisher. Anderson was soon in trouble again, however, when she

wrote in *Continent* a favorable review of Theodore Dreiser's *Sister Carrie*, a novel that many readers, including the editor, saw as "immoral" (*My Thirty Years' War*, 34).

Frustrated by such constraints and feeling generally discouraged with her career, Anderson decided to begin her own magazine, a difficult undertaking for a young woman with limited resources. Nevertheless, she successfully established the *Little Review*, in part due to fortuitous timing in literary history. Chicago in the early twentieth century was experiencing an artistic awakening that came to be known as the "Chicago Renaissance." Writers, authors, playwrights, and critics were engaged in breaking new ground in arts and letters; they were specifically interested in shattering Victorian themes, models, and taboos. These new militants expressed an affinity for radical politics, atheism, and sexual rebellion.

Anderson became acquainted with the major figures of this movement when Floyd Dell took over the editorship of the *Friday Literary Review*. Anderson was invited to the literary gatherings hosted by Dell and his wife MARGERY CURREY, where she met some of the leading members of the Chicago Renaissance and earliest contributors to the *Little Review*—Theodore Dreiser, Maxwell Bodenheim, Ben Hecht, Sherwood Anderson, EUNICE TIETJENS, Maurice Browne, ELLEN VAN VOLKENBURG, and Vachel Lindsay.

It was at the Dell home that Anderson announced the founding of her new journal, to be based on the very latest in the arts. She was able to convince Chicago's artistic rebels of her vision because of her infectious enthusiasm and magnetic attractiveness. Dell wrote that she was "austerely idealistic, matching her starry-eyed, unearthly young loveliness which was too saint-like" (*The Homecoming*, 228). The Chicago poet Eunice Tietjens, who heard the announcement, later wrote, "Anyone who could resist Margaret Anderson was granite and cold steel" (*The World at My Shoulder*, 64).

Working in Room 917 of the Fine Arts Building in downtown Chicago, Anderson published the first issue of the *Little Review* in March 1914. The early years of the magazine were dedicated to a wide variety of literary and political movements. Anderson published the poetry of T. S. Eliot, W. B. Yeats, H. D. (Hilda Doolittle), and Amy Lowell, while also running articles analyzing Friedrich Nietzsche and writing editorials supporting experimental literature, the labor movement, and feminism. In her debut editorial, Anderson wrote, "Feminism? Any right thinking magazine can only have one attitude and the degree of ours is ardent" ("Announcement," 2).

Part of Anderson's radicalism sprang from her self-identification as a lesbian. In 1915 she wrote an editorial in the *Little Review* analyzing a speech made by Edith Ellis, wife of the famous British sexologist Havelock Ellis, which, in Anderson's view, made insufficient reference to the question of homosexuality. Anderson complained that Ellis had issued a statement before her talk that her discussion would refer to "those people who, through perverted or inverted sexual tendencies, faced the problem of having to turn their abnormality—perhaps their gift of genius, if we understood these things better—into creative channels" ("Mrs. Ellis's Failure," 16). Anderson concluded her essay, "With us love is just as punishable as murder or robbery. Mrs. Ellis knows the workings of our courts; she knows of boys and girls, men and women, tortured or crucified every day for their love—because it is not expressed according to conventional morality" (p. 19). This editorial has been identified as "the earliest militant defense of homosexuality known to have been published by a lesbian in the United States" (Katz, *Gay/Lesbian Almanac*, 363–64).

Anderson's political sympathies included anarchism. By the third issue in May 1914, she had come under the sway of Emma Goldman and wrote in her autobiography, "I just had time to turn anarchist before the presses closed" (*My Thirty Years' War*, 54). Her support of Goldman, who had become a personal friend, led to investigations from authorities and reduced the number of subscriptions. Many of Anderson's *Little Review* essays were extremely bold in their pronouncements, such as when she wrote in December 1915 in "Toward Revolution," "Why doesn't someone shoot the governor of Utah before he shoots Joe Hill?" (p. 5). At one point Anderson and her small group of followers had so alienated subscribers that they had to camp for the summer on the beach of Lake Michigan at Lake Bluff, Illinois, due to lack of funds for housing. Although her anarchist ardor cooled as time went on, Anderson remained steadfast in her support of Goldman, attending her 1917 Conscription Act trial and seeking funds for her support in Goldman's exile years.

Anderson viewed the *Little Review* as a magazine based on conversation between editor, contributors, and readers. One of the biggest boons to the magazine in this regard was her meeting JANE HEAP, a woman Anderson called "the world's greatest talker" (*My Thirty Years' War*, 103). Jane Heap was an artist and member of Maurice Browne's Little Theatre, which was also housed in the Fine Arts Building. Anderson and Heap became romantically involved and had a stormy relationship. Heap was a major influence in the magazine after accepting Anderson's plea to become coeditor. She wrote most of the pithy rejoinders to letters to the editor and by the early twenties led the magazine to focus more on the visual arts. Together Anderson and Heap pushed the bounds of rebellion in the Chicago Renaissance beyond a mere challenge to the genteel tradition. They attacked prevailing notions of culture, leading the charge of modern consciousness.

In 1917 Anderson and Heap left Chicago for New York in an effort to make the journal "an international organ" (*My Thirty Years' War*, 136). The move meant fewer contributions from Chicago-based writers and more from New York and European-based writers, including Djuna Barnes, William Carlos Williams, Ford Madox Ford, and Wyndham Lewis. When their foreign editor, Ezra Pound (based in London), secured chapters from James Joyce's *Ulysses*, both Anderson and Heap recognized the value of the work and began serializing it in the *Little Review* from 1918 to 1920. The novel attracted the attention of the New York Society for the Suppression of Vice, and several issues of the *Little Review* were confiscated and burned by the U.S. Post Office. In 1921 Anderson and Heap were charged with obscenity, convicted, and fined.

After the *Ulysses* trial, the *Little Review* struggled on, first becoming a quarterly and then appearing only sporadically due to the lack of money and the end of the relationship between Anderson and Heap. Heap more or less took over the magazine,

emphasizing the visual arts, especially international movements such as surrealism, constructivism, and Bauhaus.

Anderson and Heap remained friends, and in 1924 they sailed to France to investigate the teachings of Russian-Armenian mystic George Gurdjieff, whose work had attracted many New York intellectuals and artists. Gurdjieff influenced both women for the rest of their lives. Heap eventually moved to London, where she became a teacher of Gurdjieff's philosophy; Anderson remained in France. The *Little Review* ceased publication in 1929. The two women met in the Hotel Bonaparte in Paris to put the final issue together.

Anderson spent the majority of her post–*Little Review* years writing the three volumes of her autobiography—*My Thirty Years' War* (1930), *The Fiery Fountains* (1951), and *The Strange Necessity* (1969)—as well as editing *The Little Review Anthology* (1953, 1970) and writing a book on her spiritual beliefs, *The Unknowable Gurdjieff* (1962). After her relationship with Heap ended, Anderson had two long-term relationships, one with the Belgian opera singer Georgette Leblanc and the other with Dorothy Caruso, widow of opera singer Enrico Caruso.

Although alone and suffering from emphysema by the 1960s, Anderson continued to exhibit a vital attitude toward her life as it was coming to a close. She wrote, "The blessings I wanted were love and music, books and great ideas, and beauty of environment. I have had all, and to a degree beyond my asking, even beyond my imagining" (*The Strange Necessity*, 222). Anderson died of heart failure in Le Cannet, France, and was buried next to Georgette Leblanc in the Notre Dame des Anges Cemetery.

By publishing European writers in America and assisting the careers of pioneering American modernists, Anderson played a crucial role in establishing modernism as a literary movement in the United States. An early twentieth-century feminist, her autobiographies have found new audiences among scholars of women's history, literature, and sexuality.

Sources. Margaret Anderson papers are found in the Flanner-Solano Collection at the Library of Congress; the Allen Tanner Collection, Univ. of Texas at Austin; and the *Little Review* Collection at the Univ. of Wisconsin–Milwaukee. Smaller collections are at UC, the Houghton Library of Harvard Univ., and NL. Anderson's writings include her three-volume autobiography, *My Thirty Years' War* (1930), *The Fiery Fountains* (1951), and *The Strange Necessity* (1969). Important editorials published in the *Little Review* by Anderson include "Announcement," March 1914; "Mrs. Ellis's Failure," March 1915; "Toward Revolution," December 1915. Anderson edited *The Little Review Anthology* (1953, 1970). Her autobiographies have recently been supplemented by an autobiographical lesbian novel, *Forbidden Fires* (1996), that Anderson wrote in the 1950s but could not get published. See Jackson Bryer, "A Trial-Track for Racers: Margaret C. Anderson and the *Little Review*" (Ph.D. diss., Univ. of Wisconsin–Milwaukee, 1965), and Holly Baggett, "Aloof from Natural Laws: Margaret C. Anderson and the *Little Review*" (Ph.D. diss., Univ. of Delaware, 1992). The autobiographies of two contemporaries, Floyd Dell, *The Homecoming* (1933), and Eunice Tietjens, *The World at My Shoulder* (1938), have comments on Anderson. Jonathan Katz, *Gay/Lesbian Almanac: A New Documentary* (1983), is useful. See Holly Baggett, "The Trials of Margaret Anderson and Jane Heap," in *A Living of Words: American Women in Print Culture*, ed. Susan Albertine (1995), for a detailed account of the obscenity trial of Anderson and Heap.

HOLLY A. BAGGETT

ANDERSON, MARY

August 27, 1872–January 29, 1964

UNION ORGANIZER, LABOR LEADER, FEDERAL OFFICIAL

Mary Anderson, labor organizer, Women's Trade Union League activist, and longtime official of the U.S. Department of Labor, was born on a farm outside the village of Lidköping, Sweden. She was the youngest of seven children and the fourth daughter of Magnus and Matilda (Johnson) Anderson. Anderson received her only formal education there at a Lutheran elementary school. When Mary was sixteen, the Andersons lost their farm. Years of soil erosion, in combination with high taxes assessed by the crown, left them unable to support a family on the farm. With Northern Europe in the grip of a similar agricultural crisis, more than one million Scandinavians chose to emigrate to the United States between 1880 and 1900. In 1889, Mary and her sister Hilda Anderson bought steerage tickets for their cross-Atlantic journey, landing at New York's Castle Island. From there they boarded a train to the logging camps of northern Michigan, where their eldest sister, Anna, had settled two years earlier. Sixteen-year-old Mary soon found work washing dishes in a lumberjack's boardinghouse.

It was the first in a series of marginal jobs that Anderson held during her early years in the country. After three years of domestic work, Anderson left for Chicago. There she worked briefly at a garment shop but soon found the trade that would carry her through the next fifteen years—stitching shoes and boots. Though she developed quickly into a skilled bootmaker, work was scarce after the economic crash of 1893. For more than a year Anderson was forced to move from shop to shop and town to town in Illinois and Wisconsin looking for work. Late in 1894 Anderson found a permanent position at Schwab's, a large Chicago shoe factory. She remained there for seven years, during which time she was drawn into the labor movement.

In 1899 Anderson joined the International Boot and Shoe Workers Union. She was attracted to trade unionism for the same reason as many young immigrant women of that era; she was lonely and looking for a sense of community. Like a select group of immigrant women in cities across the United States—Russian Jews, Italians, Irish, Germans, and Swedes, among others—Anderson quickly realized that she had found her calling as a union organizer.

Union responsibilities soon filled Anderson's life. Before and after her long days of stitching boots, Anderson leafleted, spoke to women workers about their grievances, and met with union officials. Firm in her support of workers' rights but an avowed moderate who adhered to no ideology, Anderson quickly won the admiration of women workers, male union officials, and employers. Within a year of joining, Anderson was elected president of the all-woman Boot Stitchers' Local 94. Shortly thereafter, she was appointed to represent her union at meetings of the Chicago Federation of Labor. In 1906, Anderson was elected to her union's national executive board, achieving a position rare for women in the labor movement at the time.

By 1905, union work had brought Anderson into the circle of progressive women reformers that surrounded Hull-House founder JANE ADDAMS. Anderson met Addams through fellow bootmaker Emma Steghagen, who left a union position to become secretary of the infant Chicago Women's Trade Union League—a branch of the National Women's Trade Union League (WTUL) founded in 1903 to facilitate union organizing among women workers. The WTUL exemplified the cross-class collaboration that occurred during the Progressive Era in many organizations between working-class women and allies of the middle and upper classes. Anderson was appointed to its executive board.

Anderson, who never married, found her emotional home in this community of women reformers. She greatly admired Addams and the Chicago WTUL's first president, MARY McDOWELL, of the University of Chicago Settlement. In social reformer MARGARET DREIER ROBINS, who led the Chicago branch from 1907 to 1913 and the national organization from 1913 to 1922, Anderson found a lifelong friend and mentor. These three women helped convince Anderson that, along with organizing unions, it was necessary to work for legislation to regulate the conditions under which women workers lived and labored. Anderson's political beliefs were also shaped by the friendships she made among the other working-class activists in the league—particularly Steghagen and glovemakers AGNES NESTOR and ELISABETH CHRISTMAN. The mixture of intimacy and collegiality that Anderson found among these women became the basis of a lifelong commitment to the Women's Trade Union League.

In 1910, as a WTUL representative, Anderson played an important role in the massive strike of Chicago men's garment makers. In September of that year, thousands of young women workers in the men's garment trade walked out of their factories to protest wage cuts and dangerous working conditions. Within a month, more than forty thousand workers from non-union garment shops across the country joined them. The strike paralyzed Chicago garment manufacturing and humbled the city's largest clothing firm, Hart, Schaffner, and Marx, which boasted forty-eight factories and nearly ten thousand employees.

Anderson and her colleagues at the Chicago WTUL worked tirelessly to sustain solidarity, despite cold and hunger among the strikers, many of whom had been working for subsistence wages. WTUL members formed committees to provide food, organize picket lines, protest police brutality, and publicize the importance of the strike. Although the WTUL had a significant role, the garment workers were represented by the United Garment Workers' Union (UGW) at the bargaining table; unfortunately, the strike was only a partial success because UGW had little interest in signing with the city's myriad small garment shops. Its sole target was Hart, Schaffner, and Marx. Still, the agreement was one of the first settlements with a major firm that recognized the right of workers to organize and created a permanent arbitration committee of workers and employers. Anderson was on the committee that negotiated the groundbreaking settlement and years later cited its pioneering collective bargaining agreement as the most important achievement of her lifetime.

In the strike's aftermath, flush with their success and with the excitement of picket lines and demonstrations, Chicago garment workers began staging small wildcat strikes over every grievance. Worried that such actions would endanger the union contract, the WTUL asked Mary Anderson if she would accept a paid position to quiet strike spirit and explain to the striking workers the importance of labor-management arbitration. Challenged by the prospect and attracted by a higher salary than she had ever earned, Anderson accepted. She never returned to the shop floor.

FIG. 8. *Women's Bureau head Mary Anderson christens the Liberty ship* SS Anna Howard Shaw *in 1943.*

For the next four years, in the employ of the Chicago WTUL, Anderson organized women workers in a wide variety of trades. Though she traveled through the Midwest and along the Atlantic seaboard for the league, she focused most of her energies on Chicago women workers. Following the league's philosophy, Anderson reached out to women who had largely been ignored by the established unions: department store clerks, candy makers, and stockyard workers. During these years, Anderson worked with native-born Whites, African Americans, and immigrants of all backgrounds.

With the entry of the United States into World War I, organized labor became a partner with government to coordinate domestic industrial work as part of the war effort. Women's heightened role in industry brought WTUL leaders to the forefront of economic planning and policy making. For Mary Anderson, it was an opportunity to take a national role in advancing the cause of women workers. Initially, Samuel Gompers, president of the American Federation of Labor, failed to appoint a single trade-union woman to the Advisory Commission of the United States Council of National Defense, the coordinating vehicle whose subcommittee dealt with issues of wages and working conditions for men and women. There was an outcry, especially among WTUL leadership, and Anderson was one of those who wrote to complain. In response, Gompers invited her to Washington, D.C., and appointed her to a subcommittee on women in industry. It was here that Anderson met Mary Van Kleeck, longtime WTUL activist and director of industrial studies for the Russell Sage Foundation.

For about a year, Anderson commuted back and forth from Washington to Chicago, working on the subcommittee in the former city and also continuing her organizing of stockyard workers in the latter. Van Kleeck convinced Anderson she could do more for women workers by staying in Washington than by returning to Chicago.

In 1918, Van Kleeck persuaded President Woodrow Wilson to establish a Women in Industry Service to regulate and smooth relations between the Department of War and women working in defense industries. Van Kleeck was appointed director. She chose Anderson as her assistant. When Van Kleeck resigned in 1919, she helped Anderson get the post of director. In 1920, Congress converted the Women in Industry Service to a permanent Women's Bureau of the U.S. Department of Labor, and Mary Anderson was appointed chief. The first rank-and-file working woman to sit in a director's chair of a federal agency, Anderson retained that position for almost a quarter century.

During Anderson's first decade at the Women's Bureau, she functioned as a powerful advocate for minimum-wage, maximum-hour, and safety legislation for women workers in the face of a strong challenge against these laws by an odd coalition of conservative judges and politicians, businessmen, and National Woman's Party (NWP) pro-Equal Rights Amendment feminists. Hoping to settle the question of labor legislation for women, Anderson commissioned bureau researcher Mary Winslow to coordinate a massive study of the effect of labor legislation on working women in the eleven states with the most women workers. The report concluded that labor legislation was far more beneficial than harmful to the vast majority of women workers. The NWP—citing Anderson's close ties to the WTUL and her long-time support of labor legislation—condemned the report as fixed, and some historians have argued that Women's Bureau researchers marshaled evidence to support Anderson's own views. It is possible that Anderson's subordinates at the Women's Bureau felt obliged to toe a particular political line, but the study seems to have been deeply and carefully researched. In any case, Anderson's unwavering support of labor legislation for women helped to preserve those laws into the 1930s, when New Deal legislation extended protections to male as well as female workers.

Anderson was active in the framing of Franklin Roosevelt's 1933 National Industrial Recovery Act. Though she condemned wage and hour codes that discriminated on the basis of sex and race, she argued that the New Deal did so much for working women that its weaknesses could not overshadow its accomplishments. She enjoyed the friendship and the ear of the Roosevelts throughout the 1930s and used that closeness to argue that women workers deserved a permanent voice in federal policy making; but by the late 1930s Anderson was growing restive.

When WTUL activist Eleanor Roosevelt came to live in the White House, Anderson had assumed that she would now have increased access to power as well as increased funding for the Women's Bureau. These changes never materialized. President Roosevelt's Secretary of Labor Frances Perkins, a longtime ally of the New York WTUL, seemed uncomfortable with Anderson and failed to consult her on many major decisions. At the time of the WTUL's greatest influence in Washington, Anderson felt increasingly marginalized. She feared Perkins planned to disband the Women's Bureau. Her frustration grew after 1941. Concerned that women workers were being given short shrift in World War II planning, Anderson asked for an expansion of bureau resources to enable it to manage the massive influx of women into the workforce. When Perkins refused to grant Anderson's request, she decided it was time to retire. In 1944, Anderson left public service with great fanfare, looking forward to a quiet retirement.

After twenty-seven years, Washington had become her home, and Anderson chose to live out her life there. From 1919 until 1934, she had made a home with her eldest sister, Anna. After Anna's death, she lived mostly alone, although for a few years here and there she lived with government colleagues. During her long retirement, she was much honored by women's and labor organizations. In her last years, Anderson completed her memoirs and spoke on occasion at labor, women's, or government functions, expressing satisfaction at the great changes she had helped to bring about. She died of a stroke at the age of ninety-two.

As the first trade-union woman appointed to an executive position in the federal government, Mary Anderson's long career reflected the changing relationship between government and the woman worker during the first half of the twentieth century. From her young adulthood as an immigrant bootmaker in Chicago, through a decade of work for the Chicago Women's Trade Union League to a twenty-four-year tenure as director of the federal Women's Bureau, Anderson dedicated herself to the cause of improving wages, hours, and working conditions for wage-earning women in the United States. She fought for equal pay for equal work and for government guarantees of workers'

right to organize. A keen labor organizer, a pioneer in labor-management arbitration, and a staunch advocate of state and federal labor legislation, Anderson was a key figure in the development of twentieth-century U.S. labor policy.

Sources. Anderson's papers are housed at the SL, as are those of her close colleague, Mary Winslow. SL has a taped interview with Anderson by Esther Peterson, director of the Women's Bureau during the John F. Kennedy administration. The most extensive sources on Mary Anderson's life and career are contained in the *Papers of the Women's Trade Union League and Its Principal Leaders,* which include Anderson's personal papers as well as those of Margaret Dreier Robins and the Chicago Women's Trade Union League. All of these collections contain information about Anderson. The only other major source is Anderson's autobiography, *Woman at Work* (1951). Sister John Marie Daly, R.S.M., wrote a biographical study, "Mary Anderson, Pioneer Labor Leader" (Ph.D. diss., Georgetown Univ., 1968).

ANNELISE ORLECK

ANDERSON, TENNESSEE CLAFLIN MITCHELL
April 18, 1874–December 20(?), 1929
SCULPTOR, MUSIC TEACHER

Tennessee Claflin Mitchell Anderson, a sculptor and supporter of the arts in Chicago, was born in Jackson, Michigan, the oldest of three daughters of Martha C. (Woodhull) and Jay P. Mitchell, a postal clerk. She was the namesake of Tennessee Claflin, who, along with her sister Victoria C. Woodhull, was a famous radical of the times. The name was a source of both pride and embarrassment to Tennessee Mitchell. As a youth she was so sensitive to the Claflin association that she changed her name to Tennis C; she was, in fact, listed thus in city directories, and some of her friends years later used that form of her name. Linked with an activist family, she developed an independent spirit. After graduating from high school and having become proficient as a pianist, she chose to work as a piano tuner, and a few years later, following her mother's death and her father's remarriage, she moved to Chicago, taking along her sister Amber, who died soon after of meningitis.

In Chicago, Tennessee Mitchell continued her piano tuning and later gave lessons in piano and dance. She became popular with her wealthy clients and often during vacation periods traveled or visited with them. Most of her friendships were with writers and artists. She was considered to be physically attractive, if not beautiful, and was known for her sophisticated charm and wit. She was also a stylish dresser with a flair for distinctive hats, scarves, and earrings.

From 1909 to 1910 Mitchell had an affair with Edgar Lee Masters, a lawyer and emerging writer, while Masters was married to his first wife. The sporadic relationship was painful for both Mitchell and Masters and ended after he decided that he was unable to break off with his wife. Sometimes disdainful of Mitchell in later years, he nevertheless acknowledged that she had a significant impact upon his creative ability. He referred to her in numerous poems, including "Ballade of Ultimate Shame: T.M., August 20, 1909–May 23, 1911," in *Songs and Sonnets, Second Series* (1912). Two of his plays, *Eileen* and *The Locket,* both written in 1910, were influenced by his relationship with Mitchell.

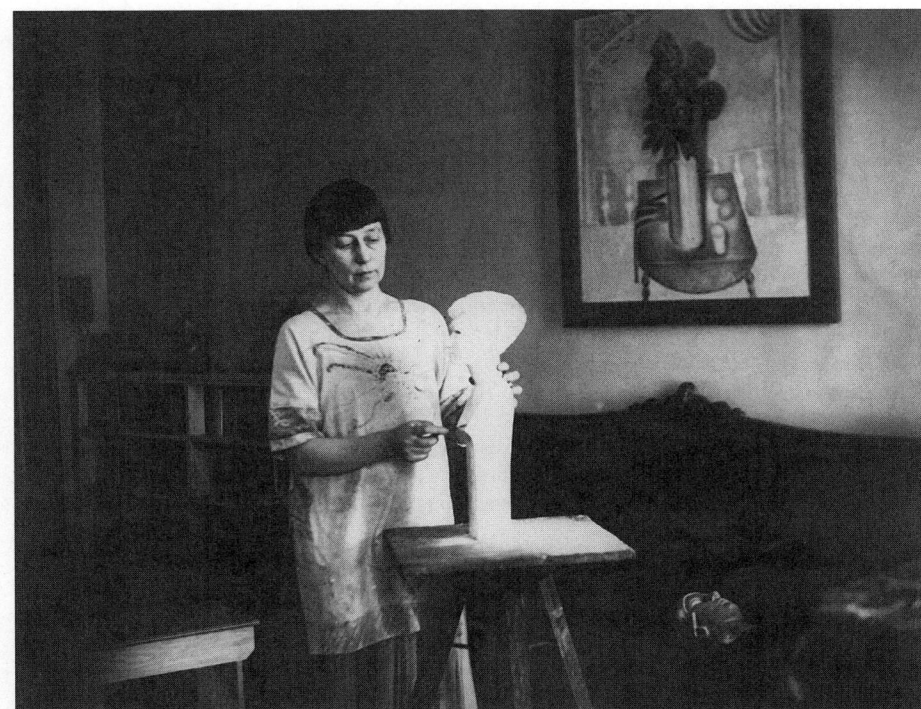

FIG. 9. *Sculptor Tennessee Claflin Mitchell Anderson in her studio.*

A few years later, she developed an important relationship with author Sherwood Anderson. In 1913 Anderson, having left his business in Elyria, Ohio, came to Chicago to pursue a writing career. In 1914, he separated from his wife Cornelia and their three children and met Tennessee Mitchell. She meanwhile became interested in eurythmics, a style of modern dance taught by a friend, Alys Bentley, who had a camp at Upper Chateaugay Lake, near Merrill, New York. Mitchell and Anderson stayed at the lake for much of the summer of 1916, and it was there on July 31, four days after his divorce from Cornelia became final, that they were married. Years later Anderson was to claim that he proposed the marriage in order to save Mitchell from scandal resulting from her affair with Masters. Whether this reason was indeed a motivation is questionable, but there is no doubt that the marriage was unconventional. After their return to Chicago, he often stayed at her apartment on Division Street; but he kept his own apartment nearby in accordance with an understanding that they would freely come and go. They kept this arrangement during much of their marriage, with Sherwood Anderson maintaining separate residences and making frequent trips without her.

Throughout their marriage, Tennessee Anderson experienced periods of illness and depression. By the spring of 1920, Sherwood Anderson reported to a literary friend, Van Wyck Brooks, that she was better than she had been for several years. "She is getting better and is happier than I have ever seen her" (*Letters*, 54), Anderson announced. He had spent the previous winter by himself in Mobile and Fairhope, Alabama. She had joined him at Fairhope, where she rested, and attracted to the colorful clays of the area—

red, yellow, and blue—began to experiment with sculpture. For Sherwood Anderson, her work, as a self-taught artist, was remarkable and promising. As her husband he delighted in the new personal well-being that resulted: "What new joy in life that approach towards beauty coming in a definite form out of herself has given her. [I] go about whispering to myself, 'She is going to be well. She is going to be well'" (*Letters*, 54–55).

At the same time, however, Sherwood Anderson was contemplating his escape from life as a twosome, since he planned to work alone during the following winter. By the fall of 1920 he faced the complication of his wife's wanting to devote herself to her newfound art form. The marriage had been predicated not only on an unconventional openness toward others, but on the two of them earning their own livelihoods. Sherwood Anderson wrote friends that "[d]own in Alabama [Tennessee] got some beautiful clay in her hands and turned out some remarkable character heads. The result is she doesn't want to be an honest working woman any more, but has the same disease that has caught the rest of us" (*Letters*, 64). The disease was ambition to focus on one's own creativity.

Sculpturing soon became her primary artistic medium. One year later she began modeling figures, and photographs of her pieces were used to illustrate a new collection of Sherwood Anderson's stories. In 1921, he published *The Triumph of the Egg*, which began with "Impressions in Clay by Tennessee Mitchell," photographs of seven sculptures, three of which were representations of characters in the stories.

During the summer of 1921, the Andersons traveled with Sherwood's friend Paul Rosenfield to Europe, staying mostly in

Paris, where they met such literary figures as Gertrude Stein and James Joyce. The Andersons separated in 1922; he spent the winter alone in New Orleans and in the summer made a permanent break from Chicago, moving to New York and then to Reno, Nevada, where he awaited a divorce, which became final on April 4, 1924. They had no children.

Tennessee Mitchell Anderson remained in Chicago, residing in a studio apartment on the Near North Side that was elegantly furnished with a grand piano, antique furniture, and art works. She was active in many cultural organizations, such as the Arts Club, the Romany Club, the Chicago No-Jury Society, and various theatrical groups. She maintained a wide circle of friends in the arts, including HARRIET MONROE, Bernardine Szold Fritz, EUNICE TIETJENS, and Aaron Copeland. She continued to develop her talents in sculpting and began showing her work in the summer of 1924 at a small gallery in Woodstock, New York.

More exhibitions followed, and she soon attracted critical interest. Blanche C. Matthias, in the Chicago *Evening Post*, November 24, 1925, wrote an admiring review of her work and included photographs of three sculptures: *Negro Mask, Listening to Bertrand Russell,* and *Suggested by Mrs. Untermeyer.* In 1927, following a show at the Whitney Studio Club in New York, Ernestine Evans, writing in the *Nation,* commended the unconventional liveliness and humor of Anderson's work. An article by Marian Maxwell Goss in the *Chicagoan* in 1928, illustrated with a Rudolph Weisenborn portrait of Anderson, praised her amusing depictions of American types in works such as *School Teacher, Labor Leader, Well Fed, At the Opera, In a Street Car, Club President,* and *Chicken Farmer.* Goss also noted Anderson's continuing interest in African American subjects, citing two recent examples: *Negro Madonna* and *Hallelujah.* The sensuality of the latter work, however, was controversial and was deemed indecent by conservative critic Eleanor Jewett in the *Chicago Tribune* of April 22, 1928. The following year, Anderson humorously satirized such puritanical attitudes in one of her last works, *Fig Leaves,* which consisted of five nudes using various objects—flowers, a fan, a heart, a mask, and carrots, to cover themselves. Anderson joined artists Emil Armin, Charles Biesel, FRANCES FOY, George Josimovich, Fred Biesel, Gustaf Dalstrom, FRANCES STRAIN, U. M. S. Hannell, and Emile J. Grumieaux, known as The Ten, in an *Exhibition of 10 Artists* in the Marshall Field and Co. gallery, January 7–9, 1929. Modernists all, The Ten were leading advocates of no-jury and were, like the literary crowd Anderson also frequented, openly hospitable to experimentation in the arts. She had found her place.

Tennessee Mitchell Anderson's personal problems came to a head in 1929. In 1928, Anderson had begun an autobiography, which briefly sketched her life from childhood through her affair with Masters. On October 8, 1929, she wrote to Sherwood Anderson to ask if he had any objection to her bringing him into it. There is no record of a response from him, and she did not resume the autobiography. She had in the meantime fallen into a period of depression, as she sometimes tended to do during the holiday season. She was taking sedatives and, in a letter to Bernardine Szold Fritz on December 5, 1929, complained of a recent "horrible slump" in her productivity. She wrote that she had "no desire to work" but was "not contented not to." Anderson came to Chicago in early December, and they spoke on the telephone but did not meet before his departure for Florida on December 17.

Her death probably occurred during the night of December 20, 1929; she was last seen that evening. Her body was discovered by police, who broke in on the evening of December 26. The police reported that she had died from hemorrhaging in the lungs, possibly caused by an overdose of sleeping pills. It was suspected by some of her friends that her death was a suicide, the result of continued heartbreak over the failure of her marriage. She was buried at Graceland Cemetery in Chicago.

Tennessee Mitchell Anderson's accomplishments took many forms. She was strong in her influence on two major midwestern writers, Edgar Lee Masters and Sherwood Anderson, just as their careers began to flourish. Sherwood Anderson recalled that she had a following of young aspiring authors who often came to her apartment to read and discuss their works with her. She was also a strong supporter of the arts in Chicago, including music, dance, and theater. Her own most important artistic expression was sculpture, which she began untutored at the age of forty-six and continued to develop until her death just nine years later. A eulogy published in *Art Digest,* "Dying, She Made a Fling at Prudery That May Be Immortal," observed that, especially in *Fig Leaves,* she approached major status as a sculptor. Indeed, her life was marked by such proximity to renown. In her own brief career as an artist, she never achieved the artistic development that she might have. At the same time, she gave selfless encouragement to others.

Sources. The manuscript of Tennessee Mitchell Anderson's unfinished autobiography is at NL. Also at NL are a few letters from her to Sherwood Anderson and Bernardine Szold Fritz and the sculptures photographed in *The Triumph of the Egg.* The most extensive sources of information on Anderson are Dale Kramer, *Chicago Renaissance* (1966), supplemented by his notes at NL; and William Sutton, *The Road to Winesburg* (1972). Other discussions are John H. and Margaret Wrenn, "'T.M.': The Forgotten Muse of Sherwood Anderson and Edgar Lee Masters," in *Sherwood Anderson: Centennial Studies,* ed. Hilbert H. Campbell and Charles E. Modlin (1976); and Kim Townsend, *Sherwood Anderson* (1987). Edgar Lee Masters's account of his relationship with Tennessee Mitchell Anderson, whom he called Deirdre, in *Across Spoon River* (1936) is unreliable. Comments on her by Sherwood Anderson may be found in his *Memoirs* (1969) and the collections of his letters: Howard Mumford Jones, ed., *Letters of Sherwood Anderson* (1953); Charles E. Modlin, ed., *Sherwood Anderson: Selected Letters* (1984); William A. Sutton, ed., *Letters to Bab* (1985); and Charles E. Modlin, ed., *Sherwood Anderson's Love Letters to Eleanor Copenhaver Anderson* (1989). *The Old Guard and the Avant-Garde* (1990), ed. Sue Ann Prince, has a few references to Tennessee Mitchell Anderson. Articles about her include Blanche C. Matthias, "Character Studies, Grotesques and Portraits," Chicago *Evening Post,* November 24, 1925; Ernestine Evans, "A Lively Sculpture," *Nation,* February 16, 1927; "Dying, She Made a Fling at Prudery That May Be Immortal," *Art Digest,* February 1, 1930; and Marian Maxwell Goss, "Chicagoans: Tennessee Mitchell Anderson," *Chicagoan,* November 3, 1938.

CHARLES E. MODLIN

ANDERSON JOHNSON, VIOLETTE NEATLEY
July 16, 1882–December 28, 1937
ATTORNEY, CLUBWOMAN, SOCIAL REFORMER

Violette N. Anderson, an African American attorney, broke both racial and gender barriers. Born in London, England, to Richard E. and Marie (Jodi) Neatley, Violette Neatley was the only child of her German mother and West Indian father.

Immigrating to Chicago with her parents at an early age, Neatley attended public school. At North Division High School (1895–99) she earned her way by giving music lessons for fifty cents per hour. She was a member of St. Thomas Episcopal Church, where she sang in the choir. Founded in 1879, the church was the first predominately African American church in Illinois and had many prominent African Americans in its congregation.

Although Violette Neatley married three times, nothing is known of the last two marriages. She married Amos Preston Blackwell in 1899 and ended the marriage in a well-publicized divorce in 1906, citing extreme cruelty, both physical and verbal, as the reason. She then married Dr. Daniel Hale Anderson, a pharmacist, a few months after the divorce. She later married Albert E. Johnson on August 14, 1920, although she retained the name Anderson professionally.

After graduating from high school, Neatley was employed as a stenographer in a lawyer's office and worked her way up to court reporter. By 1905, she established a stenography and court-reporting agency in downtown Chicago, the only public stenographic office to employ African American women. In her daily visits to the courts she became interested in studying law. Anderson entered Chicago Law School (later Kent College of Law) in 1917. She continued operating her business while attending classes in the evening. The only woman in her class, Anderson graduated on June 20, 1920, with honors for her scholarship and for her thesis on marriage and divorce. Anderson was the second African American woman admitted to the Illinois bar. IDA PLATT had received a license to practice law in 1894.

By the time Anderson received her law degree, she was already established in the Chicago legal arena. During 1920, Anderson briefly authored a weekly column called "Legal Hints to Women" that appeared in the *Chicago Whip,* a militant "race paper" founded in 1919. She shared a downtown law office with Edward H. Wright, a prominent African American attorney and politician who was active in the Republican Party.

Anderson's legal skills were often applauded in the African American press. One of her most noted cases involved a woman accused of murdering her common-law husband. Warned by other attorneys to plead guilty to manslaughter, Anderson successfully pleaded self-defense on behalf of her client, noting that her client had been severely beaten and threatened. She conducted the entire case alone, "preferring to trust 'woman's intuition' rather than man's skill" ("Woman Lawyer Wins Her First Murder Case," *Chicago Whip*, July 29, 1922).

In December 1922, at a time when women began to play a greater role than before in political and civic affairs, Anderson was appointed assistant city prosecutor. During her service in the prosecutor's office, she became the first African American woman lawyer admitted to practice in the U.S. District Court,

Eastern Division. In 1926, she was admitted to practice before the U.S. Supreme Court.

Parallel to Anderson's rise as an attorney came the growth of the African American population in Chicago, particularly in the Grand Boulevard/Douglas Park neighborhood, an area known as Bronzeville. Migrants from the South were moving to Chicago in search of a better life. Racially segregated, African Americans established their own churches, businesses, and institutions. An African American middle class emerged; some, like Anderson and LIL HARDIN ARMSTRONG, purchased homes at the black resort town of Idlewild in central Michigan. African American lawyers were needed to serve the growing population. Excluded from membership in the Chicago Bar Association and the American Bar Association, African American lawyers established the Cook County Bar Association in 1914 and the National Bar Association in 1925. These newly formed bar associations provided a support system for African American attorneys, a base from which they influenced law and politics and that enabled such women as Violette Anderson to wield power and influence on behalf of women. Anderson held the office of first vice-president in the Cook County Bar Association from 1920 to 1928. She spoke on behalf of women attorneys at the 1926 National Bar Association convention.

After serving in public office, Anderson conducted a successful private practice. She did not limit her practice to domestic cases, feeling that although a woman lawyer was more sympathetic and understanding in domestic cases, such cases were not sufficiently lucrative.

Known as Mrs. Johnson in her private life, Violette Anderson juggled the demands of her domestic responsibilities and her legal career. She thought that law was a good field for the woman who could devote her full time to it but doubted "whether any but the superwoman can do justice to law and a home at the same time" (Johnson, 9). Journalist I. Marie Johnson portrayed her as just such a superwoman: "By no means submerged beneath that capable legal personality or beneath that of the practical social worker is the personality of the real woman, warm, sympathetic, human—the devoted daughter who cares for her aged mother . . . ; the model housewife who takes an occasional fling at interior decorating and does it like an artist . . . ; the woman who thinks enough of clothes and style to stage fashion shows and to make her own clothes; the unusually busy woman who still finds leisure for quiet evenings in her beautiful library . . . or for an evening with friends" (Johnson, 9).

In May 1926, Anderson was honored by the Esther Social Register, a club organized to recognize achievement. She was chosen because club members had "watched [Anderson] grow in spite of a legion of handicaps" ("Social Register Honors Attorney," *The Light and "Heebie Jeebies,"* May 8, 1926). Anderson was among the first wave of African American professional women who considered themselves "race women." They strove for both racial and gender equality through public service and social reform. Anderson was an adamant believer in service to others. She served as president of the Friendly Big Sisters League from 1926 to 1928, an organization of about two hundred African American women. The league was made up of women who "worked, not for public approbation or praise, but because of the help and service they could be to others" ("President's Annual Report," 1927). The league operated the Mary C. Home, an eight-room cottage located on the South Side of Chicago. The home, run in cooperation with the Juvenile Court to care for pregnant young women and delinquent girls, sheltered thirty-two women and girls in 1926.

That year, Anderson joined the Zeta Phi Beta Sorority. The sorority sponsored social and civic activities centered around college and professional women. Anderson became the national president of the sorority in 1933. She emphasized social reform rather than social recreation. She encouraged her sorority sisters to become women of achievement.

Within women's clubs, Anderson used her legal skills to educate women about their rights. She headed the legal department for the Chicago and Northern District Federation of Colored Women's Clubs. She chaired the department of government and legal status of women within the Douglas League of Women Voters. Composed of such middle-class African American women as Anderson, ADA McKINLEY, and EDITH SAMPSON, the chapter was unusual in the otherwise largely white league. She used her position in the Douglas League as a platform to educate women. In 1935 she led a discussion of the public and private rights of women in Illinois. She wrote and directed a play, "Women Wise and Otherwise," which dealt with the status of women.

Anderson complemented her local activity with national work. At the 1935 National Bar Association convention, Anderson led a discussion in which she stated, "In the matter of civil rights our colored citizenry has not pressed sufficiently for adjudication, matters which deal with their civil rights. This is largely true, but I have noted an increasing number of evidences in the courts of Illinois, particularly, of an awakened and progressive interest in civil rights" (Adams, "Lawyers Elect").

In 1936 Anderson used her position as head of Zeta Phi Beta to lobby for the successful passage of the Bankhead-Jones Farm Tenant Bill, which established the Farm Security Administration to aid farm tenants, sharecroppers, and those who had lost farms during the depression. She toured Arkansas and Texas campaigning for the bill and wrote letters to Illinois congressional representatives. Anderson's effort was part of a larger movement among African Americans to ease the plight of southern tenant farmers. In this campaign, Anderson worked with Claude Barnett, founder of the American Negro Press.

During the last years of her life, Anderson worked out of her home on the South Side. She was active in Zeta Phi Beta until her death, saying on her deathbed, "Tell the girls to keep on going ahead" (quoted in *Pittsburgh Courier*, January 1, 1938). Anderson died of colon cancer following a brief hospitalization in Provident Hospital. She was buried in Lincoln Cemetery in Chicago.

Violette Anderson's life personified the social, political, and career engagement of "race women." Breaking gender and racial barriers as an attorney, she used her legal knowledge to promote the work of such organizations as the League of Women Voters and the Zeta Phi Beta Sorority.

Sources. Original source material is very limited. In the Chicago African American press, *Chicago Defender*, *Broad Ax*, *Chicago Whip*, and *The Light and "Heebie Jeebies"* are excellent sources of information. Ander-

son's January 1, 1927, "President's Annual Report," typescript, for the Friendly Big Sisters League, is found in the Irene McCoy Gaines Papers at CHS. The Illinois League of Women Voters Papers at UIC Spec. Coll. contain the papers of the Douglas League of Women Voters. Anderson's correspondence concerning the Bankhead-Jones bill is included in the Claude Barnett Papers at CHS along with memorabilia from Zeta Phi Beta and the National Bar Association. I. Marie Johnson's "Finds Law Good Field for Women," in *The Light and "Heebie Jeebies"* of October 1, 1927, is an excellent profile on Anderson. Both Edith Sampson, *Chicago Defender*, May 4, 1935, and Sadie Alexander, *National Bar Journal*, 1941–44, mention Anderson in writing about African American women attorneys. Julius J. Adams, "Lawyers Elect Lawrence Head of National Bar," *Chicago Defender*, August 10, 1935, quotes Anderson's discussion of civil rights. *The Making of the Black Lawyer, 1844–1944* (1993) highlights Anderson along with other African American attorneys. She is listed in *Who's Who in Colored America* (1928–29); Romer B. Garrett, *Famous First Facts about Negroes* (1972); *BWA*; and Frederic H. Robb, ed., *1927 Intercollegian Wonder Book, or, 1779—The Negro in Chicago—1927*, vol. 1 (1927), published in Chicago by the Washington Intercollegiate Club of Chicago and located at the Vivian G. Harsh Research Collection of Afro-American History and Literature, Carter G. Woodson Regional Library, CPL. An obituary appeared in the *Pittsburgh Courier*, January 1, 1938.

TABITHA R. OGLESBY

ARAI, JOAN FUJISAWA
June 24, 1908–August 18, 1976
EDUCATION ACTIVIST, COMMUNITY ORGANIZER

Joan Fujisawa Arai, a Nisei (second-generation Japanese American), for whom a middle school in Chicago's Uptown area is named, was born in Los Angeles. Joan Fujisawa was the second of four daughters of Toyomatsu and Midori (Mukai) Fujisawa, first-generation Japanese immigrants who ran a fruit stand in Los Angeles. Her parents were part of a major wave of Japanese immigration that began at the end of the nineteenth century.

Joan Fujisawa entered the University of California, Los Angeles (UCLA) in 1926, majoring in education; she was a volunteer member of the Young Women's Christian Association (YWCA) of Los Angeles. In her junior year at UCLA, however, her mother became ill with cancer, and Fujisawa left school to take care of her mother and younger sisters, Alice and Doris. When her mother died, Fujisawa gave up the pursuit of a bachelor's degree and got a job as a clerical worker in a Japanese wholesale-produce firm in Los Angeles.

While working in this firm, Joan Fujisawa met Akira Arai, a Nisei from Hawaii. Arai worked in a Japanese firm owned by the husband of Fujisawa's elder sister, Connie. Fujisawa and Arai married in 1933, and their only child, Harold, was born three years later.

When the United States entered World War II, Joan Arai's life, like that of thousands of other Japanese Americans, changed drastically. In 1942, the United States government removed all persons of Japanese descent, including citizens, from the Pacific Coast states to ten relocation camps in the interior of the country, where more than one hundred thousand Japanese were detained behind barbed wire. The Arais were put in Camp Amache near Grenada, Colorado, in September 1942. From the inside, Joan Arai kept in touch with YWCA members on the outside who helped her set up a recreational program for children in the camp. Educating the youth in the camps was one of the greatest concerns for Japanese American parents, not only because they did not want their children to miss years of schooling but also because the sense of alienation and injustice felt by interned Japanese American children had to be treated carefully. Children also needed activities to fill their time in the closed environment. Arai's program with the YWCA was her response to this concern. Becoming known for her work, she obtained special permission to leave Camp Amache to attend a YWCA leadership conference in the Chicago area in 1943.

Although the internment camps were in operation until the end of 1945 (with the exception of Tule Lake, which remained in operation until 1946), some camp residents, mostly Nisei, were able to resettle in areas outside the restricted West Coast region beginning in June 1942. Between 1943 and 1950, more than thirty thousand camp residents came to Chicago, where some evacuees found jobs in war industries, which had a shortage of labor. Chicago was soon to become the largest Japanese American resettlement center in the forty-eight states. Among those who came in the summer of 1944 were the Arais. Akira Arai arrived first, having accepted a job at International Harvester to recruit Japanese Americans. About one month later, Joan Arai and their son joined him, and she found employment as a clerical worker with the Chicago YWCA.

Until 1944 Chicago had only a small population of Japanese, who were employed mostly in small shops and restaurants, with work for the firms of Mikimoto Pearls and Nippon Shipping Company the only exceptions. There were few incidents of overt anti-Japanese sentiment, and even the local newspapers were free of the kind of attacks Japanese experienced on the West Coast. In this climate Joan Arai was able to become part of the larger Chicago community relatively soon after her arrival. Through the YWCA she met prominent Chicagoans and community activists with whom she formed a women's group that discussed social issues. She left the YWCA after a few years to further supplement the family income, since their goal was to purchase a home. She worked for A. W. Mendenhall Co., where she was employed as the account manager supervisor until she became ill in 1975.

Arai's belief in education and citizen participation continued after she moved to Chicago. After purchasing a house, she devoted time to community work and education in Uptown, an area on Chicago's North Side, where the Arais and many other Japanese American families resided. After the war, Uptown was a culturally and ethnically rich but economically deprived community. Originally developed as an elegant residential area, Uptown was one of Chicago's most successful business areas at the beginning of the twentieth century and was also known as a center of film production in the early 1920s. With the rapid popularity of automobiles, however, the flow of people and capital started bypassing Uptown for the suburbs. Never having recovered from the Great Depression, Uptown's economy steadily declined, and once fashionable buildings turned into tenement houses for newcomers to the city: Appalachian Whites, Native Americans, East and Southeast Asians, and Hispanics. By 1970, Uptown was Chicago's area of greatest transience, and its schools and housing declined.

As in other declining urban neighborhoods, Uptown in the 1960s saw a high level of citizen participation. Many community organizations in Uptown were working on the area's economic, social, and physical problems; and Arai started attending meetings of various organizations, including the YWCA Uptown center. As part of federally funded urban renewal programs of the 1960s, Uptown was designated one of four Model City areas in Chicago. Arai was appointed in 1968 by Mayor Richard J. Daley to the Lake View–Uptown Model Cities Area Council, where she served as head of the education committee until her death. This initial appointment was based on her community's recommendation, acknowledgment by coworkers of her civic commitment. In 1970 when the community elected the council, Arai was reelected; and in 1973 she was again appointed by Mayor Daley to the position. She was also a member of the District 24 Education Council that consisted of parents and community members; and she was an executive board member of the Region V Citizens Council, which served six midwestern states, including Illinois.

As a member of the Model Cities Area Council, she worked to secure funds for new educational institutions and made sure that education programs were running smoothly. Programs included the Stockton CoPlus and Stockton Child Parent Center, cooperatively planned urban schools; Disney Magnet School, with an emphasis on performing arts; Urban Gateway arts and education programs; and Operation Head Start, a preschool program for poor and disadvantaged children. She was instrumental in founding the Uptown Neighborhood Health Center and also served on area scholarship award boards in the Lake View, Uptown, and Edgewater areas.

Those who knew Arai described her as quiet but determined. "She would go after things in her quiet way and wouldn't give up until she reached her goal" ("Uptown Honors Woman," *Chicago Tribune*, August 5, 1976), a friend recalled. At home, she was a devoted wife and mother. She accorded her son's education high priority among family affairs.

Arai was instrumental in the establishment of a middle school, which opened in September 1974. In 1968, when she was appointed chair of the education committee of the Lake View–Uptown Model Cities Council, there was only one secondary school in Uptown, with serious overcrowding in its classrooms. Concerned about high rates of juvenile delinquency and dropouts among the area's high school students, Arai organized community people and fought from 1969 to 1974 to secure the land and funds for a new school at a time when very little school construction was taking place on the North Side. She believed that students from the sixth to eighth grades needed a school that was separate from both elementary and high school. The new middle school was to provide homemaking and manual arts training for both boys and girls, along with a regular academic curriculum.

When the school was finally established, community groups petitioned to have it named after Arai. The school board, however, ruled against naming schools after living persons and named the school Hazel-Wilson Middle School after the streets that bounded it. Arai died of cancer after a year of illness. She was buried in Chicago's Montrose Cemetery. Within a week, the Chicago Board of Education unanimously voted to rename Hazel-Wilson the Joan Arai Middle School, honoring the education activist. A memorial ceremony held for Arai at Truman

City College was attended by many residents of Uptown, members of the Japanese American community, and leaders of civic organizations and city agencies.

Arai had a strong commitment to children's education; as a Nisei whose world was wider than the immediate Japanese American community, her goal was to improve education for all. "Japanese-Americans need to become more involved in the activities of the larger community," a Japanese American community leader commented after her death. "She was a good model of this, a good example to follow" ("Japanese Honored," *Sunday Star*, August 29, 1976).

Sources. The records of the organizations that Joan Arai belonged to during the 1960s and 1970s are found in UIC Spec. Coll. Included are the reports of Model Cities Councils, District 24 Education Council, and CoPlus programs. Interviews were conducted by Hiromi Mizuno during the summer of 1994 with Akira Arai, Arai's husband; Nathan Lofton, former principal of the Joan Arai Middle School; and Tom Teraji, who was formerly on the Chicago Board of Education. Information also came from correspondence between Harold Arai, Arai's son, and Hiromi Mizuno in March 1996. Arai and her accomplishments were featured in newspaper articles in *CST*, April 21, 1974; *Sunday Star*, July 18, 1976, and August 29, 1976; and *CT*, August 5, 1976. A city resolution to recognize Arai for her accomplishments, a plaque presented to her by the Lake View–Uptown Community Council, and other awards and honors she received are at the Joan Arai Middle School. For discussion of the situation Uptown was facing when Arai was active, see Elizabeth Warren, *Chicago's Uptown: Public Policy, Neighborhood Decay, and Citizen Action in an Urban Community* (1979), and Ed Marciniak, *Reversing Urban Decline: The Winthrop-Kenmore Corridor in the Edgewater and Uptown Communities of Chicago* (1981). Efforts of Japanese Americans for education in the relocation camps are described in detail in Thomas James, *Exile Within: The Schooling of Japanese Americans, 1942–1945* (1987). Masako Osako, "Japanese-Americans: Melting into the All-American Pot?" in *Ethnic Chicago*, ed. Peter d'A. Jones and Melvin Holli (1981), outlines the general history of the Japanese American community in Chicago after World War II.

HIROMI MIZUNO

ARMSTRONG, LILIAN HARDIN. *See* HARDIN ARMSTRONG, LILIAN (Lil)

ASHER, VIRGINIA HEALEY
December 18, 1869–February 2, 1937
REVIVALIST, SINGER, WOMEN'S ORGANIZER

Virginia Healey Asher, a prominent revivalist for evangelical Protestantism in the late nineteenth and early twentieth centuries, was born in Chicago. Her parents were of Irish Catholic descent. At the age of eleven the young Healey attended a revival at the Chicago Avenue Church, later renamed the Moody Church after its founder, Dwight L. Moody. At the revival, Healey was converted to Protestantism and began to direct her life toward evangelistic work. Prior to her admission to church membership in 1883, she participated in Chicago Avenue's active youth program; and she frequented the Pacific Garden Mission, a shelter for the homeless and indigent, with members of her Sunday School class. Music was a central part of her evangelistic experience and outreach. Healey attended the Chicago Conservatory of Music, where she received training for her contralto voice. These involvements strengthened Healey's religious commitment and

she "decided to consecrate her singing as well as her speaking voice to the Service of the King" (Buffalo Campaign Account, March 18, 1917, Billy Sunday Papers). These dual aspects of her career, singing and revivalism, continued throughout her life, beginning with her preaching and singing in saloons and brothels and later in churches and in large urban revivals.

In 1887 Virginia Healey married William Asher, a Scottish immigrant who also attended the Chicago Avenue Church. William Asher's family owned a bakery on Clark Street that was a popular gathering place for many of Chicago's urban missionaries, including rescue mission directors as well as saloon and brothel evangelists. The contacts she made through her marriage further expanded Asher's evangelistic network. In 1893, Dwight L. Moody selected Virginia Asher, along with eleven other young women, to participate in his World's Fair Revival, which was organized to parallel Chicago's World's Columbian Exposition of 1893. Asher evangelized primarily on the Midway, the public center for the exposition's amusements. Her moral presence and religious outreach on the Midway contrasted with the more secular and oftentimes notorious entertainment of that highly popular area of the exposition. While the Moody revival taught that women belonged in the home and far away from the corrupting influences of the Midway, the evangelistic campaign was willing to place Virginia Asher and other women evangelists there strategically for the ultimate good of redeeming sinful urban America. In this way the evangelistic campaign used the moral and social authority of womanhood, even as Asher began to redefine and expand the role of women as religious leaders.

In October 1897 Virginia Asher enrolled along with her husband in the Chicago Bible Institute (renamed Moody Bible Institute after Moody's death in 1899), the premier training school for evangelical workers. By the latter part of the nineteenth century, nondenominational Protestants had realized the importance of providing systematic training for women and men in order for both to be prepared adequately for Christian work. Asher's education at the institute was part of a larger professionalization process that prepared students for a wide variety of opportunities. The Bible Institute's 1897 student body, of which Virginia Asher was a part, numbered 400 permanent students, 160 of whom were women. Asher trained as an urban missionary. Her practical experience was directed toward home visitation and women's and children's activities, including cottage prayer meetings and Sunday school organization.

Asher's Bible Institute education encouraged interaction with other women and groups from Chicago's evangelical community, particularly the Young Women's Christian Association (YWCA) and the Woman's Christian Temperance Union (WCTU). Women from the Bible Institute led weekly Bible studies for the Chicago YWCA, and Virginia Asher evangelized in Chicago's slums with Jessie Ackerman of the WCTU. Virginia Asher began her career in Chicago and benefited from the training and support she received within the city's evangelical subculture. Chicago's Protestant churches as well as the Bible Institute encouraged women to exert the spiritual and social power of evangelical womanhood, an ideal that provided Virginia Asher with a secure arena from which to launch her early work. Her career as a singer and revivalist made her known na-

FIG. 10. *Revivalist Virginia Asher, against tree, with colleagues, including Billy Sunday, standing and wearing suit, and Helen Sunday, sitting by dog.*

tionally, but the strong imprint of Chicago evangelicalism remained.

William Asher trained as a saloon evangelist at the Chicago Bible Institute, and both husband and wife were asked to join the staff of the Jefferson Park Presbyterian Church, then pastored by Frank Talmadge. Virginia Asher organized the women's work and music, while her husband served as an assistant pastor. In 1900 the Ashers moved to Duluth, Minnesota, to supervise the Duluth Bethel, a rescue mission for miners and lumbermen. Drawing on her Chicago training and experience, Virginia Asher became the matron of the mission and was primarily responsible for its relief work to women. Virginia and William Asher also began a "Bowery Work," saloon evangelism that featured the saloon preaching of William Asher and the songs of Virginia Asher accompanying herself on a small folding organ. Virginia Asher also played an autoharp, and she frequently sang "My Mother's Prayer," a hymn that seemed to be particularly effective because it evoked the memory of the mother's prayer to the child to remember her moral influence. In response, many men sobbed that if they had their mother's influence near them they could lead a different life.

Soon after their marriage, Virginia Asher bore a child who died at birth. Even though she was without children and would lead a career independent of home and family, Asher skillfully incorporated evangelical concepts of motherhood and domesticity into her ministry. Working first with Duluth's prostitutes and their offspring and later through her participation in urban revivals, Asher persistently "took in the world of lost souls and mothered them with a divine love" (Sanders, 6). Asher's physical presence reinforced this maternal spirituality. Descriptions

of Virginia Asher focused on her motherly characteristics, her ample figure, wavy silver hair, and most important her mellow voice, all of which convinced countless audiences of the nurturing yet authoritative role of evangelical womanhood.

In 1905 Virginia and William Asher left Duluth to join the staff of revivalists J. Wilbur Chapman and Charles Alexander. Following in the steps of their predecessor Dwight L. Moody, the Chapman-Alexander team was one of several groups that conducted large urban revivals in the early decades of the twentieth century. These revivals were primarily directed toward defining the social and religious values of an emerging urban middle class. The Ashers, however, attempted to bring this same brand of morality to those they defined as needing moral uplift. They were particularly involved in organizing revival meetings in saloons and brothels. In 1910, Virginia and William Asher returned to Chicago as part of the Chapman-Alexander Simultaneous Evangelistic Campaign, an effort committed to canvassing and converting the city to the evangelical cause. Chicago evangelicals welcomed the 1910 revival with open arms. They were especially entranced with Virginia and William Asher, who were known as Chicago natives and who also pledged to bring evangelical religion and social order to the city's underclass.

Virginia Asher's effort was directed toward Chicago's large population of underpaid female factory workers as well as prostitutes who worked the city's streets. Virginia Asher organized and led a variety of noontime and evening revival meetings for these female workers throughout the city. In the Chicago Stockyard's chipped beef room, the Garrick Theater, and the famous brothel owned by ADA and MINNA EVERLEIGH, Asher's reputation as a revivalist of "delicacy and tact," particularly to the city's "outcast and delinquent classes," won her the reputation of "angel of the slums" (*Chicago Examiner*, October 30, 1910). The Ashers remained with the Chapman organization for seven years, evangelizing in cities across the country as well as in eighteen countries around the world.

In 1912, William Asher left the revival circuit to assume a pastorate. After a bout with illness, Virginia Asher joined the staff of Billy Sunday in Chicago. He was emerging as the leading revivalist of that period. Virginia Asher had met Billy and HELEN SUNDAY through their participation in the Jefferson Park Presbyterian Church. Within the Sunday revival organization, Virginia Asher professionalized her ministry. Music provided a highly visible role for Virginia Asher, and she frequently sang at the widely publicized revivals held in tabernacles, which were temporary wooden halls constructed for these meetings. Her solos, as well as duets with campaign song leader Homer Rodeheaver, were very popular. Asher eventually recorded numerous revival songs such as the "Old Rugged Cross" and "Tell Me the Story of Jesus."

Asher's ministry encompassed both working women and those of middle-class status. Prior to a revival, Asher enlisted the support and participation of middle-class women by organizing a preliminary Women's Invitation Committee. A specific message was directed to these women, who were told they had an obligation to be role models for working women and to live up to their social and moral responsibilities. "Speaking to a churched audience at the Epworth Methodist Church, Virginia Asher reminded her middle-class listeners of their social and moral responsibility" (Caldwell, 193). She told her listeners, "If the church members would do their duty there would be fewer girls and women in the 'red-light' district of Chicago" (quoted in Caldwell, 193). The committee canvassed business and industrial areas to encourage both employers and workers to attend revival meetings. There was a specific message to working girls also. The female evangelists' message of patronizing empathy toward working women underlined female victimization by both the industrial system and men. "Speaking to female workers at the Kirk Soap Company, Virginia Asher said: 'The working girl of this city needs sympathy more than anything else. At the base of all my talks lies sympathy. She has battles to fight that the woman in better circumstances knows nothing about. If she knows that the world is in sympathy with her struggle it aids her in carrying on the battle'" (quoted in Caldwell, 194).

In 1922 the original Invitation Committees in cities throughout the nation, plus the recent revival converts, formed the Virginia Asher Businesswomen's Councils. The first organizing meeting for the nationwide council was held in Virginia Asher's home in Winona Lake, Indiana. The goals of the council were to perpetuate revival commitments through Bible study and to provide friendships after the revival itself had ended. The councils also supported a variety of evangelical programs, including the Virginia Asher Hospital for Lepers in Soonchun, Korea; aid to Polish Jews; the Cumberland Mountain Mission in Virginia; and a recreation cottage in Winona Lake that was made available to working women. The Virginia Asher Businesswomen's Council, in conjunction with the Chicago YWCA, rented rooms in Chicago's business district that were ample enough to accommodate its four hundred members, who met twice a week for lunch. The rooms were also open on Thursday nights for council members. It is not clear how long the council functioned in Chicago, but in other cities, such as St. Louis, the council continued to meet regularly until the 1950s.

Virginia Asher remained with the Billy Sunday revival organization for seventeen years. During that time she participated in more than ninety revivals across the country, each of which lasted at least a month. Ill health finally forced Virginia Asher to retire from the Sunday staff. She died in Winona Lake and was buried in Warsaw, Indiana.

As a speaker for evangelicalism, Virginia Asher preached a belief that was principally defined by an individual conversion experience and a subsequent willingness on the part of the convert to lead a moral life. Like most evangelicals, Asher expressed her faith through nineteenth-century ideals of domesticity and maternity, ideals that equated godliness with motherhood and heaven with the domestic sphere. Virginia Asher pursued a revival career independent of her husband while extolling the virtue of marriage and motherhood; she traveled widely for years, yet emphasized the value of hearth and home. Her commitment and training, which were forged in Chicago's evangelical Protestant culture, reflected a central contradiction for evangelical women—how to convert the world without participating in it. For Virginia Asher, her commitment to evangelicalism led her to a public career that far surpassed her domestic message.

Sources. The Virginia Asher collection at the Archives of the Billy Graham Center in Wheaton, Illinois, includes pictures, two of Asher's diaries (1919, 1927), correspondence, instructions for the Businesswomen's Councils, and Lena Sander's *The Council Torchbearer* (1936)—a summary of Asher's life and a tribute to her work. Numerous references to Asher are found in the J. Wilbur Chapman papers, located at the Graham Center Archives, and the Papers of William Ashley and Helen Amelia Sunday at the library of Grace College and Theological Seminary in Winona Lake, Indiana. These files include newspaper coverage of various revivals throughout the country and offer summaries of Asher's evangelistic work. Her early days at the Chicago Avenue Church and Chicago Bible Institute are documented in the records of the church held by the Billy Graham Archive and in the archive of the Moody Bible Institute in Chicago. The institute also has a scrapbook, "The Story of the Memorable Chapman-Alexander Revival as Told by the Press," compiled in 1910 by the Layman's Evangelistic Council of Chicago. The scrapbook presents the day-to-day coverage of the 1910 revival and includes extensive documentation of the work of Virginia and William Asher. Other revivals in the city, such as the 1893 World's Fair Revival and Billy Sunday's 1918 campaign, received daily coverage in the city's newspapers. The Northeast Minnesota Hist. Soc., University of Minnesota–Duluth, has the *Bethel Record*, which explains Virginia Asher's early work with Duluth women. Thekla Ellen Caldwell, "Women, Men, and Revival: The Third Awakening in Chicago" (Ph.D. diss., Univ. of Illinois at Chicago, 1991), has information on Virginia Asher and other Chicago women in the evangelical movement.

THEKLA ELLEN CALDWELL

AUSTIN, LOVIE (Cora Calhoun)
September 19, 1887–June 10, 1972
PIANIST, COMPOSER, ARRANGER, CONDUCTOR

Lovie Austin was an African American female blues pianist who was popular during the Chicago Jazz Age of the 1920s. Lovie

Austin, whose name at birth was Cora Calhoun, was born in Chattanooga, Tennessee. There is scant information on her family and upbringing and on her beginning years. Austin was a college-trained musician, rare for her time. She studied theory and piano at Roger Williams University in Nashville, Tennessee, and also attended Knoxville College in Knoxville, Tennessee.

By the early 1900s Lovie Austin had married a movie house operator named Delaney, in Detroit, Michigan. Lovie Austin worked during these early years for vaudeville companies. Her husband was a variety artist with whom she traveled and performed as accompanist. Prior to moving to New York, Lovie Austin traveled with an Irving Mills show called *Blues Babies*. Playing the blues was Austin's forte. As a black female piano accompanist in a male-dominated profession, she was breaking gender barriers, earning respect in the musical field for her "strong pianistic support for gifted soloists, both instrumental and vocal" (Handy, 166). In Harlem, she performed at the Club Alabam, a black nightclub. At this popular club, Austin had two musical shows, *Sunflower Girls* and *Lovie Austin's revue*, which she composed, arranged, and directed. She also toured with the Theatre Owner's Booking Association (TOBA) circuit for a few years. In 1923, Austin recorded with such female jazz singers as Ida Cox on Paramount records. With Cox she recorded "Weary Way Blues." With Alberta Hunter she composed two hit records, "Nobody Knows You When You're Down and Out" and "Down Hearted Blues." Bessie Smith was famous in 1923 for her version of the latter song. Afterwards, Lovie Austin herself wrote "Graveyard Blues" for Smith. She also worked with Ma Rainey, Edmonia Henderson, Viola Bartlette, and Ethel Waters.

During the 1920s she organized the Blues Serenaders, her own band. Austin toured the Midwest and the South with her band. Throughout this period band members changed, but Lovie Austin's Blues Serenaders was the name of the band that recorded with her in the 1920s during the era of race records—music produced for the black community. Lovie Austin's second husband was Tommy Ladnier, a cornetist who was also at times a member of her Blues Serenaders. In 1924 and 1925 Ladnier's name appeared on several recorded sessions under the Paramount label as a member of Lovie Austin's band. Other members of her band were jazz musicians Johnny Dodds, Kid Ory, Jimmy O'Bryant, and Natty Dominique.

Lovie Austin moved to Chicago, a center for blues recording in the 1920s, and became the house pianist for Paramount Records. Under the Paramount label she recorded many songs as a piano accompanist for other artists, but she also played with her own band. By the 1930s Lovie Austin worked for the Chicago Monogram Theater. Austin remained at the theater for twenty years, arranging pieces for orchestra and serving as musical director. When her career at the Monogram ended, she worked at the Joyland Theater for nine years. During World War II Austin did some work at a defense plant and later some touring with her own shows. She returned to theater work, and by the late 1940s she was the pianist at Jimmy Payne's Dancing School in Chicago.

Austin's musical style was definitive of the music of the twenties. In two pieces she recorded for Paramount in the 1920s, "Steppin' On Blues" and "Traveling Blues," she performed with her Blues Serenaders. She wrote both musical pieces in a "boo-

gie romp style" (Zaimont, 198), and according to a review of her performances on the recordings, they exemplified her ability to function as the "entire rhythm section" (Schenker).

Lovie Austin's particular skill was to perform backgrounds for blues singers. Performing artists and the public alike respected her work. The significance of her musical style to other performers of the period was expressed in a 1926 *Chicago Defender* review article about local black women band leaders in which the writer highlighted Austin's presence at the Monogram: "Miss Lovie Austin [is] well known by all musicians of Chicago and theater-goers of the South Side. . . . Vaudeville artists look forward to their engagements here, knowing well that their accompaniments will be well rendered." Lovie Austin also developed a prominent name for herself and the Serenaders as recorders of phonograph records for many of the leading recording companies in Chicago.

Black female jazz pianist May Lou Williams, who as a child witnessed Austin working at the TOBA theater in Pittsburgh, Pennsylvania, later remembered Austin "sitting in the pit and conducting a group of five or six men, her legs crossed, a cigarette in her mouth, playing the show with her left hand and writing the music for the next act with her right. *Wow!* I never forgot this episode. . . . My entire concept was based on the few times I was around Lovie Austin. She was a fabulous woman and a fabulous musician too. . . . She was a greater talent than many men of this period" (quoted in Handy, 165).

In 1946, Lovie Austin played piano for Chippie Hill on a recording for Circle Records. Her career waned in the 1950s. Later, in 1961, her work appeared again on an album she recorded with well-known jazz musicians. She died in Chicago, having received no royalties from her reissued music.

Lovie Austin's life paralleled the development of the blues and jazz tradition in the South through its popularity in the North in the 1920s. Her skill at playing the piano and writing orchestrations opened up a demand for her style. Convincingly manifesting her accompaniment skills, she refuted stereotypes associated with female band leaders and became an integral part of music life in Chicago.

Sources. Short biographies on Lovie Austin can be found in *BWA*; Arnold Shaw, *The Jazz Age* (1987); and Antoinette D. Handy, *Black Women in American Bands and Orchestras* (1981). Biographical material on Lovie Austin appears in William Howland Kenny, *Chicago Jazz* (1993); Linda Dahl, *Stormy Weather: The Music and Lives of a Century of Jazzwomen* (1984); Judith Zaimont, *The Musical Woman: An International Perspective* (1983); Sally Placksin, *American Women in Jazz: 1900 to the Present, Their Words, Lives, and Music* (1982); and *Chicago Defender*, June 12, 1926. A collection of her recordings from the 1920s has been published as part of a series of the Chronological Classics Records of France, entitled *Lovie Austin: 1924–1926* (1994), with notes by Anatol Schenker.

GLORIA YVONNE

AUSTIN, RUTH INEZ
December 16, 1884–October 14, 1990
SETTLEMENT HOUSE ADMINISTRATOR, SOCIAL REFORMER

Ruth Inez Austin was born on a fruit farm in Hamlin, New York, to James and Ruth Rhonda (Smith) Austin. The family home had been a stop in the Underground Railroad that spirited escaped slaves from the American South to freedom in Canada. This history of the struggle for liberty, with its message of social responsibility for those already free, resonated in Ruth Austin's life. Austin was the last child of four, including William Sumner, Nellie Lois, and George Irving. She spent her youthful years on the fruit farm, which was nestled in an area that still had some American Indians as neighbors. Ruth Austin's mother told stories of local Indian lore. One of the first graduates of the State Normal School, Oswego, New York, she taught school before her marriage in 1869 to James Austin.

Ruth Austin, who was hearing impaired from childhood, attended Hamlin's public schools through eighth grade. She attended Miss Lattimore's School, Rochester, New York, for one year. Her sister contracted tuberculosis and was sent to live with a farm family in Colorado. Since the Austins did not want her to live in Colorado alone, Ruth and her mother traveled to Colorado by train to be with Nellie Lois. Later, it was feared that Ruth Austin had tuberculosis; she was sent to Florida for a year and lived with a cousin in Jacksonville. Ruth Austin had to overcome initial images of herself as frail and handicapped. Her brother, William, an electrical and mechanical engineer, who graduated from Cornell University in 1896, encouraged his sister to follow her dreams. William Austin, then working in New York City, took his sister to an ear specialist (c. 1900). The doctor had no treatment and thought she should go back to the farm, but her brother told her not to allow the doctor to keep her from what she wished to do.

Ruth Austin came to Chicago around 1900 to study at the Chicago Kindergarten Institute. It appears that she met a number of Chicago reform women associated with the settlement movement before she returned to New York State, where she graduated from the Buffalo Kindergarten Institute. She worked for the Chautauqua movement in upstate New York for a short time. Later, Austin took courses at Teachers College, Columbia University, New York City.

Austin's rural foundations seem to contradict her dedication to urban problems. In reality Austin merged rural and urban philosophies by using the neighborhood as the geographical and social unit on which all settlement work was based. Years after leaving the farm, she liked to visit for a few days at a time, "but soon yearned for the City, where the families needed to be served" (Bloodworth letter to Raymond Brod).

In 1910, at age twenty-six, Austin was appointed the assistant head resident of the Lenox Hill Settlement in New York City and became part of the Progressive Era reform women's culture led by such reformers as FLORENCE KELLEY and Lillian Wald. While at Lenox Hill, Austin taught English to foreign-born women. She experimented with different kinds of reading materials, aware that the instructional books available were about men's experiences and ignored the realities of working-class women immigrants. Austin learned about these experiences firsthand, when she joined with trade union women and was arrested for assaulting a police officer with a muff during a garment workers' strike. The charge was dismissed, but the experience was significant. She obtained a post as special investigator with the Consumers' League in New York City and Buffalo, gaining employment in factories to experience the working

conditions of women. On one occasion Austin sued an employer for harassment because of sexual overtures.

With the "brashness of youth" (Bloodworth letter), Austin sought a publisher for the lessons she had written for her English classes. Austin's *Lessons in English for Foreign Women for Use in Settlements and Evening Schools* was published in 1913. Her book stressed practical applications of the English language to women's everyday activities. There was a chapter titled "A Day's Work in a Cigar Factory," and Austin included poetry by women for women to supplement the lessons.

Austin moved permanently to Chicago the year her book was published. Her first job was to teach English to women workers at the McCormick, Deering, and W. D. Allen companies. Eventually, the public schools conducted classes along the lines begun by Austin. She taught classes in English for the foreign-born at Northwestern University Settlement, University of Chicago Settlement, the Young Women's Christian Association, and the Women's Trade Union League (WTUL). This teaching gave her a quick introduction to the Chicago social reform scene and its leaders, including HARRIET VITTUM, MARGARET DREIER ROBINS, and MARY McDOWELL. She was secretary briefly to Margaret Robins, the WTUL leader. Ruth Austin also met the Hull-House circle and developed what would be a long-lasting friendship with NEVA BOYD, who was pioneering in the field of recreation and play.

In fall 1914, Gads Hill Center needed a new head resident. The settlement, established in 1898 in the Pilsen neighborhood, a short distance to the west and south of Hull-House, served Polish, German, and Bohemian immigrants. Unlike Hull-House, it had a religious affiliation, the Presbyterian Church, and had been founded by Leila Martin, "an acquaintance and contemporary of JANE ADDAMS, sharing many of her . . . ideas about women's suffrage and social justice, and adding another idea to the purpose of the settlement house—that of temperance" (Margaret Brod, 1). Mary E. McDowell recommended Ruth Austin and told the Gads Hill trustees that if "Miss Austin is selected Miss [Neva] Boyd who is in charge of the Playground Department of the School of Civics and Philanthropy and is a friend of Miss Austin's, will come with her to live at Gads Hill, and the playground will get the benefit of their practice students" ("Minutes," October 1, 1914, Gads Hill Center records). Harriet Vittum told the trustees that "Austin has more spontaneity which is greatly needed in such work" ("Minutes," n.p.). Austin was hired and received an annual salary of fifteen hundred dollars.

When Austin became head resident, Gads Hill Center was located in a small store that originally contained a saloon. At times, inebriated ex-patrons would wander into the center, disappointed at finding sewing machines instead of the bar. By 1916, Austin and her board had raised sufficient funds to build a new facility a few blocks east of the old store. I. K. Pond, of Pond and Pond, was the architect, and shortly after completing the new structure, he became a center director. (His brother, Allen Pond, had a similar close relationship with Hull-House.) One year later, more than fifty clubs and classes had been established, with staff and volunteers engaging in such activities as traveling to prisons, providing homemaking care for sick mothers, assisting neighbors with medical needs, and lending money to families for necessities.

After the United States entered World War I, Austin and Gads Hill Center members hosted many activities related to the social impact of the war on the neighborhoods. Americanization classes were initiated also. The "Patriotic Service League for Girls" was formed, and 150 active members assisted with various Red Cross activities.

At this time, Austin began developing her philosophy of settlement work. "Our job was plainly to offer opportunities which should awaken in young and old a desire for education and for clean recreation, and above all a consciousness of their relationship and responsibility to society at large—in other words, Citizenship. With this in mind . . . we have tried to put the responsibility for the individual back on the group whenever possible and have provided opportunities for the advancement of the group rather than of the individual" (Austin, *Gads Hill*, 8). Austin instituted a myriad of social clubs for neighborhood children, young adults, and adults. Believing in the benefits of self-governance for the clubs as a preparation for citizenship, Austin established a governing board, the House Council, and every social club elected three representatives to attend its monthly meetings. The representatives carried reports back to their clubs. The social clubs all belonged to a federation of clubs. Austin was proud in 1920 when one report cautioned club members, when electing anyone for any kind of political office, to "always vote clean, don't sell your vote for it means selling your happiness" (*Annual Report*, 1920, n.p.). Gads Hill clubs worked out their annual "budgets" for recreational activities and other programs, set and collected dues, and took responsibility for themselves.

In a paper she delivered to a conference for activities program workers in institutions, Austin outlined the ways in which she had worked to change antisocial gang behavior. She formed a social club of twenty young men ranging in age from eighteen to twenty-five. They were from a typical neighborhood gang, dominated by an aggressive, self-appointed dictator, or boss. The group had been outlawed from attending several recreational centers in the community. They came to Gads Hill and applied for membership solely to be eligible for the gymnasium privileges. These were granted only to organized clubs that participated in the federation of clubs and the House Council. The group was admitted with certain conditions; a staff leader was appointed and the "club" was required to have a democratic organization. Austin stated, "The change-over from a dictatorship [the gang] to a democracy was, as always, slow, uphill going. Acceptance of domination by an individual or a faction constitutes what might be termed an admission of mental, physical and spiritual laziness. . . . The remedial agents . . . were dynamic staff leadership, membership, in a democratic club, and a federation of clubs where the group experienced 'freedom under law'" (Austin, "Basic Principles," 2–3). The ills of democracy were to be treated by the application of democratic principles.

The 1920s were a period of growth for Gads Hill. By 1929, the year of the stock market crash, the center recorded an attendance figure of more than one hundred thousand, almost twice the number that had attended in 1919. The Gads Hill Nursery School was supported by the Gyro Club of Chicago, and a new group had been formed, the Polish Alliance School for children six through fourteen years of age, which met every Saturday. The nursery school operated with concurrent parent education. A roof playground emphasized child development through group play.

Soon the neighborhood was challenged by the economic dislocation and unemployment of the Great Depression. In 1930, Governor Emmerson designated Gads Hill a subagency for the state Commission on Relief and Unemployment. As the depression deepened, the bread lines at Gads Hill lengthened. Governor Emmerson's commission supplied bread.

In 1933, forty of the Center's young men joined the federal government's Civilian Conservation Corps reforestation project. The next year, a Public Works Administration grant of $250,000 paid staff salaries at settlement houses in Chicago, including eight workers at Gads Hill.

World War I and the Great Depression tested the spirit and resources of the settlement house staff. It changed the direction of funding and permanently brought the involvement of all levels of government in the affairs of the neighborhood. Austin continued to believe that it was the neighborhood, not the nation or the city, that remained the "practical medium for social effort. . . . The settlement, as a permanent part of the community, is probably the agency best fitted to initiate community endeavor for social betterment" (Maschek, 177). As a measure of self-help and protection from loan sharks, a Credit Union was started by club members and families in 1937. Still, the involvement of all levels of governmental bureaucracy in local affairs became the normal routine after the 1930s. The Gads Hill staff reacted accordingly, assisting patrons in adjusting to the new range of programs with new groups such as the Old Age Assistance Club, which included some of the first Social Security recipients in 1938.

By 1939, thirty-nine neighborhood youth clubs met at Gads Hill, where 123 groups met weekly and 128,235 persons used the facilities yearly. The library had books in thirteen languages. Gads Hill had also had a part in the founding of the Arden Shore Camp at Lake Bluff, Illinois, and the Naperville Tuberculosis Sanitarium.

During World War II, Gads Hill Center's staff accommodated such federal programs as the draft for military service and Red Cross training. Day care and after-school programs became important to support the new influx of women who entered the industrial work force. Gads Hill club members initiated a successful fund drive, which financed the addition of a fourth floor on the center building to accommodate more children. Austin wrote letters to soldiers and maintained the connection between Gads Hill and those serving overseas.

Austin became sensitive to the vast social transformations occasioned by World War II. At home, industrial and social organization for war preparedness changed the scope and direction of the government and of industry. Abroad, American soldiers experienced both the horrors of war and the expansion of their horizons that came from foreign travel and a mingling with people from different cultures, including Americans whose backgrounds varied. She addressed her concern about reorganizing Gads Hill to expand education and recreational opportunities so that the settlement's facilities could compare favorably with those of the U.S.O. (United Service Organizations) and the Red Cross. She turned to the House Council of the Federation of Social Clubs to make a five-year plan to raise money to upgrade the settlement's gymnasium.

Austin was also concerned about the changes in the general area that Gads Hill served; in 1945 and 1946 the settlement worked to incorporate the Southwest Central Improvement Association to better local conditions. Members included business and professional men, clergy, union officials, and residents of the district.

Ruth Austin retired in December 1946 as head resident of Gads Hill. She continued to work in the settlement movement, from 1947 to 1949 directing an experimental school for adolescents with learning disabilities at Hull-House. Neva Boyd, a longtime Gads Hill resident volunteer, friend, and confidant of Austin, also retired. Austin served on the Gads Hill board of trustees until 1954. She moved to Portland, Oregon, where she lived in a retirement home until her death at age 105. Her ashes were interred in the family plot in Lakeside Cemetery, Hamlin, New York.

At age 102, "Ruth Austin's only regrets [were] in what [had] been lost in the kind of community work to which she dedicated her life: 'Old settlement workers have been engulfed by case-workers. The old intimacy has been lost. If you asked a boy what he knew about Jane Addams, he would say, "She likes pie." There was that kind of intimacy'" (Heynen, 7). She had dedicated her life to an ideal of individualism and democracy that came out of teaching the young and the old how to work together to solve local and national problems. For more than fifty years Ruth Austin advocated group interactions, either in play or in committee work, to reconcile differences, teach respect, and develop citizenship.

Sources. Biographical information about Ruth Austin was provided by her niece, Gladys Austin Bloodworth, in a letter to Raymond Brod dated May 20, 1992. Twenty-seven document cases make up the materials on Gads Hill Center (1898–1963) at the CHS; they include correspondence, minutes, reports, financial and other agency records, news clippings, and articles. See Ruth Austin, "Basic Principles of Group Organization for Recreative Workers," manuscript, n.d., copy held by Raymond Brod. Two histories of Gads Hill are part of the CHS collection: Ruth Austin, *Gads Hill Center: The Story of One of Chicago's Outposts, 1898–1924* (n.d.); Burrell J. Maschek, "A History of Gads Hill, 1898–1924," manuscript, n.d. See Margaret A. Brod, "The Gads Hill Center: A Microcosm of Twentieth Century History," manuscript, June 1991, in possession of Raymond Brod. A brief biographical essay of Ruth Austin is found in Jim Heynen, *One Hundred Over One Hundred* (1990). The *Oregonian* ran her obituary October 15, 1990.

RAYMOND BROD

BABER, ZONIA
August 24, 1862–January 10, 1956
GEOGRAPHER, EDUCATOR, SOCIAL ACTIVIST

Zonia Baber, a progressive educator and a founder of the Geographic Society of Chicago, was born Mary A. Baber. Her parents, Amos and Nancy Rebecca (Lycan) Baber, farmed near Kansas, Illinois. Baber had an older sister, Laura, and a younger brother, Amos. She also had relatives throughout the area, both the Babers and the Lycans being well-established families there.

Little is known about Baber's early life. By 1870 Baber's father had died and her mother had married James Smith, also a farmer. Baber and her brother and sister lived with their mother and stepfather. The Smiths had a daughter, Sylvia, around 1876. As a child, Baber attended the country school near her home. Her own explorations of the family farm ignited a lifelong interest in nature and geography. In order to attend high school, Baber left home to live with an uncle in Paris, Illinois, graduating in 1882. By this time she had adopted the first name "Zonia." She taught in a county school 1882–83. In pursuit of further education, she studied at the Cook County Normal School (CCNS), graduating from the Professional Training Class in 1885 and continuing with graduate courses. At the time of Baber's attendance, well-known progressive educator Colonel Francis W. Parker headed this institution. Parker's methods emphasized the individuality of each child's learning and encouraged hands-on active teaching, including observations and field trips. He departed from memorization and drills and instead encouraged students to think independently. He promoted the study of geography in his curriculum, and in particular, geography fieldwork. Baber enthusiastically adopted this progressive method of teaching. In addition, she became close friends with the Colonel and his wife, Frances Parker.

Following completion of graduate work in 1886, Baber became principal at the Hillside Street School in Youngstown, Ohio, where she stayed until 1887. She returned to CCNS and in 1889 became head of the Department of Geography, a position she held through 1899. After her return she recommended adding to the CCNS teaching staff FLORA COOKE, a teacher she had supervised in Ohio.

Baber's work at CCNS showed her interest in hands-on active teaching of geography. Several pamphlets created during her tenure as head of the geography department were included in the 1896–97 *Chicago Normal School Yearbook*; directions for field trips to Dune Park, Indiana, and to the Des Plaines River provided the Professional Training Class with complete instructions for conducting such a trip and instituting classroom follow-up. Also included was a series of pamphlets called "Outlines of Geography," which provided the prospective teacher with ideas on combining activities such as painting, drawing, reading, sculpting, and field trips in order to convey the basic concepts of geography to third-grade through eighth-grade children.

CCNS went through a number of upheavals. Colonel Parker's progressive methods attracted not only attention but, in some cases, censure from the governmental bodies in charge of the school. In 1896, in a cost-cutting measure, the Cook County commissioners gave the school to the city of Chicago. Renamed the Chicago Normal School, its work continued, but Colonel Parker remained under fire.

Meanwhile, in 1898, Baber helped found the Geographic Society of Chicago. A suggestion from her that Chicago should have a geographic society that included both laypersons and geographers bore fruit in a meeting on February 26, 1898. Baber presided, and a resolution was passed to start a "society for the increase and diffusion of geographic knowledge" (Geographic Society of Chicago Minutes). The first official meeting was held in April 1898. Baber served as vice-president until 1899 and then as president through 1904. During these years she frequently contributed to the programs of the society. In 1901 she gave a lecture on the teaching of geography illustrated by her students. More often she led excursions to such sites as Starved Rock or the Indiana Dunes or presented illustrated slide lectures.

Baber left the Chicago Normal School in 1899, when Colonel Parker accepted an offer from ANITA McCORMICK BLAINE to endow the Chicago Institute of Pedagogy, a private institution at which he might continue his work without the interference of politics. Baber, like most of the teachers at the Chicago Normal School, resigned soon after Parker in order to accept a position at Chicago Institute. Although the school building was unfinished, the teachers were paid salaries and given the next year as a sabbatical. Baber traveled during this year, undertaking a voyage around the world, concentrating on the study of Asian countries.

The Chicago Institute included not only a teacher-training department but also a demonstration school that would operate as a private school for children. However, not long after it opened, William Rainey Harper, president of the University of Chicago, invited Colonel Parker to bring his training institute and demonstration school to the university, to be combined with John Dewey's Laboratory School to form the School of Education. Parker and the Chicago Institute faculty moved to the University of Chicago in 1901. The school they left continued for a time as the North Side Branch of the demonstration school. It would later become the Francis Parker School, a private school.

Zonia Baber was appointed to the faculty of the University of Chicago along with other members of the Chicago Institute in June 1901 and began duties as Associate Professor of the Teaching of Geography and Geology in July. The following year she was chosen to act as principal of the elementary school in the School of Education for a year. She undertook course work at the university and was awarded the S.B. (Bachelor of Science) degree in 1904.

Through the courses Baber taught at the School of Education from the early years of the 1900s, she continued to train teachers using the active teaching style that she had developed at the normal school. She taught chalk modeling, a method of creating relief maps, to demonstrate land formation, and conducted field trips and industrial excursions. The students at the demonstration school learned firsthand the workings of some of the forces of nature. Ida Heffron, a fellow teacher, recalled classes held in an "out-of-door laboratory" where, in "an excavated depression . . . in the school yard, with a waterhose [sic] to provide the water for the river and the lake" (*Francis Wayland Parker*, 84), a student could experiment in creating landforms by the forces of erosion.

She also published articles about her methods. Her 1907 article in the *Elementary School Teacher,* "A Lesson in Geography—from Chicago to the Atlantic," described a month-long field trip in which she led fourteen teachers through Kentucky, West Virginia, Virginia, and Washington, D.C., studying various land formations and the effects of glaciers, underground water, rivers, tides, vegetation, and humans on the land. She noted that "the relative merits of teaching geography from books alone or from the earth itself is no longer a debatable question. . . . 'Things before words' has become axiomatic" (p. 458). Baber again exhibited her interest in the use of concrete examples in

teaching in the 1917 pamphlet published by the Geographic Society entitled *Stony Island: A Plea for Its Conservation.* Here, she urged the preservation of this Chicago limestone reef in its natural state, enumerating the excellent opportunities it provided for demonstrations to students.

Baber's course offerings demonstrated Colonel Parker's belief that there were only two comprehensive subjects to study, humans and nature, and they were united by geography; each subject explained the other. The impact of geography on human beings was a new and exciting idea, which Baber's courses explored. "Geography in the Primary Grades" included the study of "peoples whose habits show marked geographic control." Her course in political geography discussed the "distribution and concentration of people; relation to topography, climate, life, minerals, and other peoples." The "Geography of Eurasia" considered "the physical, climatic, and life conditions of the continent; relation to human occupations and industries" (Annual Register of the University of Chicago, 1908–1909).

In a 1916 article, "Lost Opportunities in Teaching Geography," Baber expressed her belief in the ability of the geographer to help the cause of internationalism and the eradication of race prejudice. Disparaging the common belief that one's own nation or tribe is superior to others, she stated that because geography "is the only subject that brings one into contact with all the living peoples of the world," the geography teacher "more than any other has the opportunity of erasing race prejudices" and "establish[ing] an intellectual habit of justice, which is the only true basis of amity" (p. 297).

She took every opportunity to observe other nations and peoples. Her courses and Geographical Society of Chicago lectures drew on her own experiences as a world traveler. She visited Bermuda in 1898, and in 1899 she went around the world. She studied glaciology in Spitsbergen, an island in the Arctic Ocean, in 1910, and in 1914 she traveled with the British Association for Advancement of Science to the South Seas, New Zealand, Australia, Tasmania, and Tahiti. The winter of 1920 found her in Mexico City, where she taught graduate students at Mexico's National University. Other trips took her to South America, Africa, India, and Palestine.

She retired from the University of Chicago in 1921, at her own request, because of a physical disability from injury in an accident some years before. In spite of health problems, the years of retirement were productive ones. She continued to serve on the board of directors of the Geographic Society of Chicago and was an active member of many other organizations, including the Chicago Woman's Club and the Wild Flower Preservation Society, of which she was a founder.

Baber continued to pursue the goal of erasing racial prejudice. In 1927, she chaired a project, "The Negro in Art Week," originated by the Chicago Woman's Club and cosponsored by a number of other Chicago associations. Organized to improve race relations by educating the public about African accomplishments in the arts, the project included an exhibition at the Art Institute of Chicago of historic African sculpture, modern paintings and sculpture, and applied art and books.

In 1940, she cochaired the Commission on Intercommunity Relations of the Hyde Park–Kenwood Council of Churches and Synagogues with Rabbi Morton M. Berman. The commission reported on "The Negro Problems of the Community to the West." She wrote for the report an essay on "Moral Issues," which urged more communication between members of different races as equals. She noted that "playing the part of 'Lady-Bountiful' to ones believed to be inferiors may be delightfully flattering to the actor, but it solves no urban racial problems." Declaring that there were "many opportunities of equals, white and colored, meeting," she suggested that religious organizations take a first step of sending delegates to the Chicago Urban League board meeting each month. "Synagogues and churches," she concluded, "*cannot, must not* fail in solving this local, national, and international problem of 'Color Prejudice,' one of the most stupid and most wicked of human conceptions" (p. 28).

Baber served on the board of the Chicago Urban League during the 1940s. The Urban League's annual report in 1947 described the organization as "common ground between Chicago's white and Negro citizenry" (n.p.), working to erase the discrepancy between the increased opportunities that African Americans had hoped to find in the North and the often harsh realities they discovered upon their arrival.

Baber opposed nationalism as a cause of war and of mistaken belief in the superiority of one race over another. In her "Lost Opportunities" article she stated that the "*ideal* of internationalism must be realized if society is to avoid constant reversions to barbarism" (p. 295). In this cause she devoted a great deal of time to the Women's International League for Peace and Freedom (WILPF). In 1923, she served as the Illinois delegate to the "Women's Committee for Recognition of Russia," affiliated with the WILPF, which urged the recognition of the Soviet Union as morally necessary and basic to Europe's economic stability. In 1937 she served on a WILPF committee to revise the state constitution of Illinois. She became interested in public monuments and symbols of peace and began collecting photographs and information on them, eventually becoming head of the Peace Symbols Committee of the WILPF and in 1948 publishing *Peace Symbols*, a booklet of her collected photographs. She also served as the head of the Latin America Committee for WILPF. She was the U.S. Representative of Liga Social Sufragista de Puerto Rico (League of Women Voters of Puerto Rico). She frequently gave lectures on her travels as well as on human geography and international instruments for peace.

The Geographic Society of Chicago honored her at a dinner on its fiftieth anniversary in 1948, presenting her with the society's gold medal, inscribed "In grateful tribute to The Founder who initiated the organization of the Society" (Baber, *Peace Symbols*, 4). In the 1990s, the society was still active in Chicago, and Baber's portrait hung in its office.

Baber lived in the Hyde Park neighborhood of Chicago until the late 1940s. She died at the age of ninety-three in East Lansing, Michigan, at the home of her niece, Helen Baber Muncie.

Baber's teaching inspired two generations of teachers. Both her classes and her writings vividly demonstrated the use of things before words in geography instruction. At a luncheon in her honor held in 1944, her colleagues united in expressing admiration for her pioneering work in educational geography. The honor in which she was held at the Geographic Society of Chicago testified to her skill and enthusiasm at conveying geographical knowledge to the nonspecialist. Her interest in the earth's peoples, as well as its surface, was clearly reflected in her work for such organizations as the Women's International League for Peace and Freedom and the Chicago Urban League.

Sources. Zonia Baber is listed as "Mary Baber" in the U.S. Census Report, Kansas, Illinois (1870). The records of the Francis W. Parker School, at CHS, include letters from Francis and Frances Parker to Baber. UC Spec. Coll. provides information in the Rollin Salisbury Papers; College of Education Records—Correspondence of Dean's Office; Minutes of the University of Chicago Trustees meetings; Annual Register of the University and Circular of Information, Department of Arts, Literature, and Science. Details on her work for the Geographic Society of Chicago are contained in the minutes, yearbooks, and other papers of that organization, which are maintained in society offices. The Lola Maverick Lloyd Papers at the New York Public Library contain correspondence on Baber's work for Women's International League for Peace and Freedom. She published two articles in the *Elementary School Teacher*, "A Lesson in Geography—from Chicago to the Atlantic," April 1907, and "The Teaching of the Continent of Eurasia," May 1907. In the *Journal of Geography*, she published "Lost Opportunities in Teaching Geography," April 1916. Her article, "Oceans: Our Future Pastures," appeared in *Science Monthly*, September 1916. She published two pamphlets, *Stony Island, a Plea for Its Conservation* (1917) and *Peace Symbols* (1948). She contributed an essay, "Moral Issues," to the report of the Hyde Park–Kenwood Council of Churches and Synagogues, "The Negro Problems of the Community to the West," January 24, 1940, a mimeographed pamphlet held by Northwestern Univ. Library. A biographical entry is included in Agnes and Gertrude Gilman, *Who's Who in Illinois, Women Makers of History* (1927). *Annual Report: Chicago Urban League 1916–1947* lists Baber as a member of the board of directors. The following biographies of Colonel Francis Parker have information on Baber: (n.a.), *Francis Wayland Parker: His Life and Educational Reform Work* (1900); Ida Cassa Heffron, *Francis Wayland Parker: An Interpretive Biography* (1934); and Jack Campbell, *Colonel Francis W. Parker: The Children's Crusader* (1967). Newspaper articles include Irene Steyksa, "Geografic [*sic*] Society Will Observe Its 50th Anniversary," *Chicago Sunday Tribune*, February 15, 1948, and Baber's obituary, *CT*, January 12, 1956.

LESLEY A. MARTIN

BAKER, EDNA DEAN
August 27, 1883–March 20, 1956
EDUCATOR, COLLEGE PRESIDENT

Edna Dean Baker, president of National College of Education from 1920 to 1949, was born in Normal, Illinois, to Joshua Edmund and Olive (Clark) Baker. Her sister, Clara Belle, was born in 1885. When Edna Baker was six, her family moved to Bellingham, Washington, where her father was a banker. They stayed there until Edna Baker graduated from high school in 1902 as salutatorian and president of her class. The family then moved to Evanston, Illinois, a northern suburb of Chicago, so she could attend Northwestern University. She began as a classics major, but her studies took a new direction in the spring of her junior year, 1905, when her father died after a long illness. Aware that she must secure a job to help support her family and increasingly convinced that she wanted to work with little children, Baker decided to become a kindergarten teacher (known then as a kindergartner). As a child, she had enjoyed attending a private kindergarten and had seen for herself in her various early school experiences the difference between dry, empty instruction and rich learning by doing, learning through play—self-active learning such as kindergartners promoted.

Because it had no kindergarten program, Baker could not stay on at Northwestern University. She and her mother visited the Chicago Kindergarten College (CKC) in Chicago's downtown area, where they met president ELIZABETH HARRISON and business manager RUMAH CROUSE. Impressed, Baker applied directly to CKC. Her Northwestern professors counseled her to "continue her original plan of becoming a Latin teacher, believing that the kindergarten field was below the dignity of a young woman of intelligence" (p. 115), she remembered in *An Adventure in Higher Education.*

Baker's creative work with children earned her a student teaching assignment at a private kindergarten in Evanston, headed by CKC graduate Laura Ella Cragin. In Baker's second year there, she was a junior assistant, earning fifteen dollars a month, "the first money that [she] had earned and no other check was ever to be so important" (Baker, *Adventure*, 121). Baker continued to teach at Cragin, and after her graduation in 1908, the ailing Cragin arranged for Baker to take over the school as her own. Baker and her sister Clara ran the school from 1909 to 1917, renaming it the Evanston Elementary School and expanding it to include six grades.

During this period, Baker was already playing different and important roles at her alma mater. She always taught at least one CKC course after graduating. In 1913 she received a bachelor's degree from the college, renamed National Kindergarten College, and soon became the registrar. In 1915 during president Elizabeth Harrison's illness and convalescence, Baker was named assistant to the president, and in 1918 she became acting president of what was then known as National Kindergarten and Elementary College. When Harrison retired in 1920, she asked that Baker be her successor. The governing board agreed, and Baker became president.

Her first task was to obtain consensus that National's campus move to a location both larger and safer than the old campus on Michigan Avenue on the city's Near South Side. That part of Chicago was experiencing growing racial tensions as large numbers of African American migrants from the South sought adequate housing and were met by discrimination and, finally, violence. In 1919, the school found itself located in the middle of a race riot, its five old mansions and carriage houses in the center of a cordon the military drew around the mob-ridden area, its students flinching at pistol shots ricocheting in the alley behind the college buildings. Baker found the perfect location for the college in Evanston. As plans for the move took shape, she proved to be an excellent fund-raiser, eventually raising almost one million dollars in a building campaign she called "The Business of Childhood."

In February 1926, with the new Harrison Hall and Marienthal Residence Hall ready for occupancy, National moved to Evanston. That the move took place in the depths of winter in the middle of the school year suggests the urgency with which Baker viewed the need to relocate. Elizabeth Harrison wrote in a letter to Baker from Texas, "You have shown surprising ability in business lines and extraordinary courage and faith in the future. With all my heart I congratulate you and am proud of having had insight enough to encourage you to prepare for the position of head of the school. But I frankly confess I don't yet see how you made your dream become a reality *so soon*" (Harrison Collection, October 18, 1926).

After guiding the college through the financial labyrinth of the building campaign, Baker had to ease a heavily mortgaged institution through the financial exigencies and low enrollments of the Great Depression. During this era many colleges folded. Kindergarten colleges were especially hard hit, because so many school districts cut their kindergarten programs to save money, creating a teacher surplus, and because so many families looked at a college education for their daughters as the first thing to cut in the family budget. Nevertheless, Baker and her board of trustees kept National alive by cutting salaries, reducing faculty and staff, and retrenching. She was able to make such drastic cuts work because she drew around her faculty and staff who were equally committed and loyal to the mission of the college.

Baker led National College through World War II, when resources were scarce and so many products were rationed that even securing an order of paint brushes and stencils required wartime priority rating. During the war, teachers' colleges in Illinois and throughout the United States lost 60 percent of their enrollment, but National lost only 20 percent. "In some war years," Clara Belle Baker wrote in the spring of 1949 in *Our Guidon*, the college's alumnae magazine, "National . . . graduated more elementary teachers than all five state teacher colleges combined" (p. 14). By 1947 President Baker had seen to it that the Marienthal Residence Hall was purchased, the Harrison Hall mortgage paid off, and two neighboring houses bought for needed campus expansion.

At the same time Baker faced these financial hurdles, she worked to strengthen National's academic program. In 1930, when two-year teaching programs were the national standard, she introduced a four-year undergraduate teaching curriculum, the first in Illinois and one of the first in the country. That same year the college changed its name to National College of Education (NCE). Baker guided NCE through its first accreditation processes, earning full accreditation from the American Association of Teachers Colleges in 1942 and the North Central Association of Colleges and Secondary Schools in 1947. In 1942 the state of Illinois called upon her to serve as chair of the committee to establish certification requirements for all kindergarten and primary teachers, the first such requirements in the state.

With her sister Clara, Edna Dean Baker founded the Baker Demonstration School at NCE in 1918. The school began as a preschool and eventually grew to include eight grades as well. It emphasized the "learning by doing" philosophy that kindergartners had helped introduce into child education methods. When NCE moved to Evanston in 1926, its Demonstration School brought the first nursery school to Chicago's northern suburbs. In 1929 Baker backed Louise Farwell Davis, an NCE faculty member, in creating the Guidance Center to conduct research and provide clinical help in identifying and correcting reading and learning disabilities at the Demonstration School and, later, at the college.

At the same time, the college continued its work with inner-city children, when Baker joined efforts in 1925 with JANE AD-

DAMS, head of Chicago's Hull-House settlement, to found the Mary Crane Nursery School at Hull-House, a program of parent and early childhood education for children of diverse backgrounds. Several generations of NCE students did their practice teaching at Mary Crane Nursery School.

During the depression, Edna Dean Baker held important national posts in early childhood education. In 1930 she was named to President Herbert Hoover's Preschool Committee of the White House Conference on Child Health and Protection; from 1933 to 1935, she was the president of the Association for Childhood Education International; from 1934 to 1936, she served on the board of the National Council of Parent Education. Between 1933 and 1938, Baker was intensely involved in establishing emergency nursery schools as a member of the National Advisory Committee for Works Progress Administration (WPA) Nursery Schools. From 1939 to 1941, she was a member of the National Advisory Committee for Family Life Education, WPA, which included nursery schools, homemaking, and parent education; Baker was responsible for supervising the development of emergency nursery schools in Illinois, Indiana, and Kentucky.

During World War II, she boosted the morale of working mothers and unemployed teachers by providing mothers with care for their children and teachers with jobs in emergency nursery schools. She was also one of the original members of Chicago's Child Care Committee and head of the Committee on Training Student Aides for War Nurseries, overseeing training of volunteer aids for wartime nursery programs. From 1942 to 1944 she served on the Illinois Advisory Committee on the Child Protection Program, WPA. From 1945 to 1956, Baker eagerly took on the college's appointment as an Inter-American Demonstration Center of the United States Office of Education, a reflection of her efforts to encourage foreign students to enroll at NCE. Since the early 1930s, she had served on the board of Japan's Kobe College Corporation, advising on the selection of exchange students and teachers. When National's alumnae gave a scholarship in Baker's name, it was originally earmarked for a deserving student from another country in recognition of her deep and abiding interest in children and teachers of all lands.

In addition to earning her teaching credentials at CKC, Baker earned bachelor's and master's degrees in 1920 and 1921 from Northwestern University, where she was named to Phi Beta Kappa. She also did graduate work at Teachers College, Columbia University. Her pioneer work in early childhood education was recognized by three honorary degrees: the D.Litt. degree from Georgetown College, Kentucky, in 1941; the D.Ed. degree from Western Michigan University in 1949; and, in 1954, the D.Humane Letters from her own institution.

Edna Dean Baker carried the work of the college across the country through her publications, lectures, and national committee work, as well as through the efforts of NCE's thousands of alumnae. Usually her lectures were to parent-teacher groups, teacher associations or church groups, to Rotary, Kiwanis and Lions Clubs, and to women's clubs and commerce associations throughout the country and abroad. Although she wrote a history of NCE and coauthored three successful Bobbs-Merrill early readers series with her sister, she was best known for her

books and her numerous articles on character and religious education; her articles appeared in magazines such as *Childhood Education*, *National Parent-Teacher*, and *American Childhood*. Her books included *The Beginner's Book in Religion* (1921), *The Kindergarten Method in the Church School* (1925), and *A Child Is Born: The Story for Little Children* (1932), which later came out in a special issue for the Woolworth stores that sold hundreds of thousands of copies.

Her books suggest the importance Baker placed on religious life. Active in Evanston's First Methodist Church, she served as director of the beginners' department from 1910 to 1922, the junior department, and finally the board of religious education. For many years she acted as advisor to the interdenominational Mothers' Circle sponsored by her church. She also taught religious education in the Demonstration School and at the college. Baker considered NCE in the vanguard in offering character education and religious education courses, "both in methods of teaching religion to children and later in guidance of religious development" (Baker, *Adventure*, 239). From 1941 to 1946 the college hosted annual interfaith conferences with the aim of fostering social responsibility in young people. Baker was convinced that "a new day of cooperation, social justice, and brotherhood is coming to the world through constructive beginnings in the early years" (Memorial, *Edna Dean Baker, 1883–1954*, frontispiece).

After nearly three decades as NCE president, Edna Dean Baker, affectionately called "Ever Dearly Beloved" by many students and faculty, retired in 1949. At her retirement ceremony, one college trustee described Baker's administration as a miracle. No one disagreed, for she had brought the college through a major building program, the Great Depression, and World War II without an endowment and without wealthy alumnae to offer support. She had built a strong institution committed to an excellent teachers' education program.

In 1952, when Clara Belle Baker retired from NCE, the two sisters moved to Riverside, California. Four years later, Edna Dean Baker died. Her longtime NCE colleague, Trustee President Henry J. Brandt, saluted Baker's spirit and commitment, which had carried National College through difficult times. He counseled that in the future the trustees and administrators would do well to be guided by Baker's example of sane thinking, wise decision making, and courageous spirit during her twenty-nine year presidency.

Sources. A collection on both Edna Dean Baker and her sister, Clara Belle Baker, can be found in the archives of National-Louis Univ., Evanston, Illinois (formerly National College of Education). The material includes copies of their books, yearbooks, articles in alumni magazines, speeches, photographs, correspondence, memorials to each, and other memorabilia. In addition, the Elizabeth Harrison Collection, including letters, in the archives of National-Louis Univ., is useful. Edna Dean Baker's NCE history, *An Adventure in Higher Education: The Story of National College of Education* (1956), provides autobiographical details. She wrote many books for and about young children; besides those mentioned in the entry, she was coauthor of *The Bible in Graded Story* (1921) and author of *Parenthood and Child Nurture* (1922) and *The Worship of the Little Child* (1927). See also Clara Belle Baker, "Beliefs We Have Cherished" in *NCE News*, October 1960; and Alberta L. Meyer, "Edna Dean Baker, 1883–1956, Clara Belle Baker, 1885–

1961," in *Childhood Education*, May/June 1985. For a history of NCE from its inception to its centennial year, see Janet Graveline Messenger, "The Story of National College of Education, 1886–1986" (1985), manuscript deposited in the National-Louis Univ. archives.

JANET GRAVELINE MESSENGER

BARBE, LIZZIE T. SPIEGEL
October 30, 1856–September 29, 1943
CLUBWOMAN, COMMUNITY LEADER

Lizzie T. Spiegel Barbe, who was active in Jewish communal work for more than fifty years, was born in East Liberty, Ohio. Her mother, Caroline Frances Hamlin, an American Quaker, married her father, Marcus Spiegel, born in Abendheim, Germany, in a civil ceremony in Alliance, Ohio, in 1852. After their marriage, they moved to Chicago so that Lizzie Spiegel's mother could learn German and prepare for her conversion to Judaism. Caroline (Hamlin) Spiegel was the first person to convert to Judaism in the city of Chicago. Her conversion on August 21, 1853, was noteworthy, since conversion to Judaism during this time period was uncommon.

After the conversion, the Spiegels returned to Ohio. While in Ohio they had five children, Hamlin, Lizzie, Moses, Hattie, and Clara. Lizzie Spiegel's father was a dry goods entrepreneur and a famous Union colonel in the Civil War. His untimely death, on May 4, 1864, as a result of an ambush aboard the *City Belle* on the Red River in Louisiana, created a hardship for Lizzie Spiegel's mother, who was almost thirty years old and pregnant with her fifth child at the time of her husband's death. In 1865, Caroline Spiegel and her children moved to Chicago, where Marcus Spiegel's relatives helped her to establish herself. Marcus Spiegel's family provided a home as well as rental property for the widow and her children.

Lizzie Spiegel's education began in the public school system in Millersburgh, Ohio. While residing in Chicago, she attended the Zion Temple School for two years. When that school closed, she went to the neighborhood public school. In addition to public school, she attended religious school and was confirmed in 1871, a ceremony established by the Reform movement for young men and women of high school age.

After the Great Chicago Fire of 1871, the family rented out its house and temporarily relocated to Akron, Ohio, for approximately two and a half years. In Ohio, Lizzie Spiegel attended public high school. When the family returned to Chicago, her mother had her assist with the daily housework, and Lizzie Spiegel never completed her high school education.

On October 4, 1876, Lizzie Spiegel married Martin Barbe, a wholesale clothing merchant who was born in Cincinnati, Ohio. Fourteen years older than Lizzie Spiegel, Barbe had been raised in Chicago and had attended the first public high school in the city. The Barbes had four children: Ella Rachel, born 1877; Alfred Marcus, 1879; Myrtle Agnes, 1880; and Walter Spiegel, 1883. Barbe's household initially included a cook and a housemaid and was continually open to several relatives and boarders who stayed with them at various times.

In May 1889, Barbe, her husband, four children, and a servant began an extensive European trip that lasted two years. Shortly after the family returned from Europe, Martin Barbe experienced dramatic financial difficulties that lasted until his death in 1914. The Barbes' primary residence, as well as other properties, had to be sold. The family had to take in tenants in order to supplement its income. For the time after Martin Barbe's death, Lizzie Barbe's source of income is unclear. Throughout the rest of her life, Barbe traveled extensively with friends and family members and continued to work exclusively in a volunteer capacity for the Jewish community.

Barbe's lifelong devotion to volunteerism in the Jewish community was a result, in part, of her experience within the Reform German-Jewish community of Chicago, and the progressive and liberal leadership of Emil G. Hirsch, the rabbi of Sinai Congregation from 1880 to 1923. She was also influenced by her relationship to the extended Spiegel family, including the Greenebaum relatives, a prestigious pioneer Jewish family. HANNAH SOLOMON, the founder of the National Council of Jewish Women (NCJW), was her first cousin and lifelong friend. Hannah's mother, Sarah Spiegel Greenebaum, was Marcus Spiegel's sister. Lizzie Spiegel Barbe was singled out as being an extraordinary lifelong friend by Hannah Solomon in her autobiography, *Fabric of My Life* (1946).

Barbe had a wide range of involvement within the Jewish community in terms of both leadership positions and types of organizations. Like many other German-Jewish clubwomen, her main focus was providing help to the newly arriving Russian Jewish immigrants. Shortly after her marriage, she joined a sewing society, a women's group in her local synagogue. She was elected an officer of the short-lived Women's Auxiliary of Hebrew Union College (HUC). HUC, in Cincinnati, Ohio, where a large group of German Jews had settled and embraced the Reform movement in Judaism, was the first, and for the nineteenth and most of the twentieth centuries, the only seminary in the United States that prepared Reform rabbis. The auxiliary, founded in 1877 to support HUC's efforts, lasted fewer than ten years. Barbe served as both secretary and treasurer for most of the auxiliary's existence.

In 1880, Chicago Sinai Congregation's Industrial School was founded, and Barbe was astonished to be elected its president. The school's goal was to teach young immigrant girls sewing and miscellaneous housekeeping skills for their improvement and assimilation into American society. In 1888, a group of philanthropists began to plan a more ambitious industrial and vocational agency to train young men and women, and a substantial sum of money was donated. Barbe remained president through the transition period but then stepped down from her leadership role because she felt "the proposed school would be too great a responsibility for a woman" (Lizzie Barbe, *Memoirs*, 36). The institution was renamed the Jewish Training School and opened in the fall of 1890.

Barbe played an active role in Johannah Lodge No. 9, the first Chicago chapter of the United Order of True Sisters, originally established in 1846 in New York City; it was "the only national Jewish women's organization to predate the NCJW" (Elwell, "The Founding and Early Programs of the National Council of Jewish Women," 95). In 1874 Johannah Lodge No. 9 became the first United Order of True Sisters lodge to be established outside the East Coast. Members were Chicago Jewish women of German ancestry who initially kept their minutes in German. Barbe was financial secretary in 1891 and was president for three separate terms—1892–95, 1906–1909, and 1914–17. The Johannah Lodge No. 9 is credited with initiating programs that the general community eventually adopted. The primary goal of the organization was to provide help to the destitute Jews of Chicago by raising money and providing services such as penny lunches at primary public schools, sewing circles, programs to help the blind, after school classes, vacation classes, kindergarten classes, soup kitchens, and scholarships for financially needy students.

A milestone in the history of American Jewish women in the nineteenth century was the gathering of Jewish women at the Jewish Women's Congress. This was part of the Congress of Religions held in Chicago during the World's Columbian Exposition of 1893. Barbe was a member of Hannah Solomon's committee, which was responsible for inviting and organizing the delegates from around the United States. As a direct result of this assembly of women, the National Council of Jewish Women (NCJW) was created. Barbe is credited with being one of its founding members and was a dedicated participant in practically every triennial meeting during her lifetime. Barbe was the third president of the Chicago Section of NCJW from 1902 to 1905, and she also held various leadership positions on the national executive board.

One of the first social programs undertaken by the NCJW was an effort to provide summer vacation camps for Jewish children, the sons and daughters of poor Jewish immigrants. These children were employed in sweatshops and factories; they lived and worked with their families in dangerous tenements, ill-ventilated breeding places of disease. Barbe and other NCJW women devoted themselves to the summer camp program; Barbe spent more than thirty years of her life in the administration of Council Camp. The *Bulletin* of the Chicago Section of NCJW called Barbe the "guiding spirit and genius of Council Camp" (Mrs. Jacob Lifschutz, "Report of the April Meeting," *Bulletin*, Chicago Section, May 1923, 10) and stated that "the workers at the Administration Building for the Associated Jewish charities call the work of Mrs. Martin Barbe and her Committee 'the best work and the one which has the most far reaching effect done by any organization'" ("Council Camp," *Bulletin*, November 1922, 6).

Barbe played a minor role as a board member in another organization, the Miriam Club, that also helped young immigrant girls. The Miriam Club, established in 1905, provided affordable subsidized housing with a home environment for young women trying to be self-supporting.

In 1895, Hannah Solomon spearheaded the creation of an umbrella organization that would unify the Jewish women's organizations within the city of Chicago. Barbe was appointed the first president of the Conference Committee of the Jewish Women's Organizations. This consortium originally included twenty-six diverse Jewish women's organizations and remained viable until the Jewish men of Chicago created the Associated Jewish Charities in 1900. The goal of the consortium was to link together the presidents of the Jewish women's organizations to avoid replicating the services each of them provided to the community. Ten years later, the Jewish women of Chicago re-created the group under a new name, the Conference of Jewish Women's Organizations, chartered in 1910 and still in existence.

The Chicago Sinai Congregation Sisterhood was established in 1914, and Barbe was one of its founding members. The goal of the newly established sisterhood was to create and support social and educational projects and generate enthusiasm in the Sabbath schools. Barbe was the sisterhood president from 1917 to 1925. When, in 1923 in a progressive move, the constitution and by-laws of Sinai Congregation were amended to allow the election of two women to the board of directors, Barbe was elected.

The National Federation of Temple Sisterhoods (now called the Women of Reform Judaism), the organization that created an affiliation among Reform movement sisterhoods, was established in 1913 and represented fifty-two Reform congregations. Barbe held an unusually lengthy term on the national executive board, from 1923 to 1931.

In 1918, the Woman's Auxiliary Board of Michael Reese Hospital (later named the Woman's Board of Michael Reese Hospital and Medical Center) was formed as a compromise to women's requests to be included on the board of directors. This new organization was limited and controlled by the men who sat on the board of directors. Barbe was asked by the president of Michael Reese Hospital, Gustav Freund, to be the first auxiliary board president. During her presidency (1918–24) her committees were restricted to traditional women's areas. As the male-dominated hospital board permitted, she cautiously expanded the role of the organization.

After a long illness, Barbe died at age eighty-seven. She is buried alongside her husband and his family in the family plot in Rosehill Cemetery, Chicago.

Throughout the later years of her life, Barbe was recognized as an important asset to the leadership of the Jewish community of Chicago. When she died, she was an honorary member of almost every organization with which she had ever been associated. In contrast to her cousins and some of her peers, she chose to commit her time and energy exclusively to the Jewish community and thus is viewed as a "Jewish clubwoman" by modern historians. The Chicago Jewish clubwomen of her time were responsible for founding many of the organizations that formed the essence of the Jewish community of Chicago in the twentieth century. These groups prospered and expanded despite the limitations that were imposed on them by a predominantly male Jewish leadership in Chicago and by society in general.

Sources. Lizzie Spiegel Barbe's autobiography, *Memoirs: Lizzie T. Barbe 1856–1943* (privately printed, 1943), can be found in the Spiegel Family papers at the Chicago Jewish Archives (CJA) at Spertus Institute, Chicago. A few items about Barbe can be found in Hannah Solomon's scrapbook, which is available on microfilm through the American Jewish Archives (AJA) in Cincinnati, Ohio. A small collection of papers from the National Council of Jewish Women (NCJW) Chicago Section can be found at CHS and the AJA. The main collection for the NCJW is at the Library of Congress. The CJA have some of the papers from the Johannah Lodge No. 9, the Conference of Jewish Women's Organizations, the Women's Auxiliary Board of Michael Reese Hospital, and the Jewish Training School. The AJA have the Sinai Congregation collection and an assortment of documents from the National Federation of Temple Sisterhoods. The office of the Women of Reform Judaism in New York City has retained a small archive. A handful of documents from Sinai Congregation can be found at the CHS. Barbe is cited in a few books located in the rare book collection of Asher Library, Spertus Institute, including Mrs. Oswald Stein, ed., *Leading Women in Social Service: A Review* (c. 1914), *The Chicago Jewish Community Blue Book* in two different versions (c. 1917–18), and *Papers of the Jewish Women's Congress* (1894). Helpful are the *Bulletin* of the Chicago Section NCJW, November 1922 and May 1923. Brief biographical sketches can be found in the following books: *The American Jewish Year Book 1905–1906*; H. L. Meites, *History of the Jews of Chicago* (1924, facsimile edition reprinted 1990); *The American Jewish Year Book 1944–1945*; Jacob Rader Marcus, ed., *The Concise Dictionary of American Jewish Biography*; and Faith Rogow, *Gone to Another Meeting: The National Council of Jewish Women 1893–1993* (1993). Barbe is also mentioned in Frank L. Byrne and Jean Powers Soman, eds., *Your True Marcus: The Civil War Letters of a Jewish Colonel* (1985), and Hannah G. Solomon, *Fabric of My Life: The Autobiography of Hannah G. Solomon* (1946). Ellen Sue Levi Elwell, "The Founding and Early Programs of the National Council of Jewish Women: Study and Practice as Jewish Women's Religious Expression" (Ph.D. diss., Indiana Univ., 1982), highlights Barbe as an example of a delegate to the Congress of Jewish Women and one who helped to establish the NCJW. For additional information on the Johannah Lodge No. 9, refer to Mildred L. Braun, *A History of Johanna No. 9 United Order of True Sisters* (privately printed, 1955). Charlotte Baum, Paula Hyman, and Sonya Michel, *The Jewish Woman in America* (1977); Jacob R. Marcus, *The Jewish American Woman, 1654–1980* (1981); and Linda Gordon Kuzmack, *Woman's Cause: The Jewish Woman's Movement in England and the United States, 1881–1933* (1990), should be consulted for a comprehensive overview of Jewish women in America. See also Joyce Anther, *The Journey Home* (1977), and Paula Hyman and Deborah Dash Moore, eds., *Jewish Women in America: An Historical Encyclopedia*. Barbe's obituary is in the *CT*, September 30, 1943.

SANDRA K. BORNSTEIN

BARKER, MARGERY
January 8, 1901–May 6, 1980
RARE-BOOK DEALER

HAMILL, FRANCES
March 30, 1904–October 21, 1987
RARE-BOOK DEALER

Chicago rare-book dealers for more than fifty years, Margery Barker and Frances Hamill were the first in their field to acquire and deal in the papers of Virginia Woolf and other members of the Bloomsbury group, introducing these collections to an American audience. They were among the first women rare-book dealers in the United States, opening their business in 1928, the beginning of an enduring business and personal relationship.

Margery Barker, born in Michigan City, Indiana, grew up with her older brother, Wallace, on a forty-acre estate in that city. Her father, Norton W. Barker, worked for his uncle, John Henry Barker, president of the Haskell & Barker Car Company, the world's largest manufacturer of freight cars, which, in 1922, merged with George Pullman's company. Her mother, Marjory (Clark) Barker, was socially prominent and active in many volunteer efforts.

Frances Hamill, daughter of Robert W. and Katharine (Lyon) Hamill, grew up on an estate in Clarendon Hills, Illinois, the youngest of four children, including Robert Jr., Emily, and Katharine. Known throughout her life as "Doll" or "Dolly"

by family and friends, she enjoyed riding horses (which were stabled in a three-story structure that housed a basketball court and was crowned by a large windmill). Her father, a Chicago businessman, and her mother, an active suffragist and supporter of Margaret Sanger's birth control movement, supported the reform work of JANE ADDAMS, a visitor to the Hamill home.

Although both young women received their early education in their home towns, each went East in her adolescent years for private schooling: Barker, to prepare for admission to Bryn Mawr College, Bryn Mawr, Pennsylvania, and Hamill, following her sisters, to Miss Porter's in Farmington, Connecticut. In the early 1920s, Hamill took business courses at Northwestern University's Chicago campus.

Margery Barker began her freshman year at Bryn Mawr College in 1920. By the spring of her second semester in 1921, however, she was told to leave the school and not come back. Having had conversations with Bryn Mawr administrators about petty thefts in her dormitory but never being formally accused of any wrongdoing, Barker attempted to find out why she was being "expelled" (although the term was not used) and demanded the right to clear herself of suspicion. The college refused to make any formal charges, hold a hearing, or reinstate her. Barker's mother initiated legal suits, first in the Court of Common Pleas, Montgomery County, Pennsylvania, and later in an appeal to the Pennsylvania Supreme Court. Both suits were denied on narrow, technical grounds rather than any consideration of the facts of the case. The Court of Common Pleas determined it had no jurisdiction in the case. The Pennsylvania Supreme Court ruled that the college, as a private institution, was entitled to ask a student not to return and that the court had no role. Hence, the incident ended without redress for Barker, who returned to Michigan City for a brief period.

Barker began her bookselling career in 1922 as a clerk in FANNY BUTCHER's bookstore. Butcher was the *Chicago Tribune*'s chief book reviewer and a central figure in Chicago's literary world. Irish poet William Butler Yeats and English novelist W. Somerset Maugham visited the store. Within three years, Barker moved to the position of store manager, and the next year, in 1926, she hired Frances Hamill.

Hamill and Barker became friends and began to think about going into business together. When Butcher's employers at the *Chicago Tribune* decided her bookstore represented a conflict of interest with her book reviewing, they gave her an ultimatum: either sell the store or resign from the paper. Butcher decided to sell the bookstore. Hamill and Baker wanted to buy it, but in late 1927 Butcher sold to the Doubleday Company. At the time Hamill and Barker felt betrayed, but Butcher's decision started them on a new path, the rare-book business.

In early 1928, Barker and Hamill set out for Europe to learn about rare books and to buy inventory. After eight months, they returned to Chicago, where they opened up a bookstore on Chicago's North Side, announcing that Barker would supply imagination and Hamill practicality. The first catalogs, issued from 1928 thru 1936, listed two works by Virginia Woolf: a first edition of *Mrs. Dalloway* in 1933 at $6.00, and *Jacob's Room* in 1934 at $8.50. Barker and Hamill formed a legal partnership in 1941, with the former contributing two-thirds of the capital, and both agreed to share equally in the profits and losses.

Wartime efforts on the home front during World War II soon occupied center stage, and Hamill and Barker decided they, too, should join the ranks of the tens of thousands of women employed in factories. By mid-1943 they had closed Hamill & Barker, storing their inventory of books in the dance hall that Barker's parents had built on the Michigan City estate. Both women went to work as tool grinder trainees at the General Motors Electro-Motive Division in La Grange, Illinois. Often putting in fifty hours per week, they worked the night shift, standing for long periods and coping with flying particles and dust in poorly ventilated spaces. On August 6, 1945, they quit the plant and, the following year, reopened their bookstore in Chicago at a new location.

The 1950s were important years for the firm and for Frances Hamill personally. She was elected president of the Antiquarian Booksellers Association of America in 1953, the first woman and first midwesterner to lead that organization. In 1955, her essay, *Some Unconventional Women before 1800: Printers, Booksellers, and Collectors*, was published by the Bibliographic Society of America. She had read the essay in Chicago on May 13, 1955, and, after detailing many facts about women in the book profession, quipped that Jose Glover shipped the first printing press to the United States in 1638, using his wife's money. It took many years before she gained membership in the prestigious bibliophilic clubs, the Grolier Club in New York City and the Caxton Club in Chicago. Neither admitted women to membership until the mid-1970s.

It was in the 1950s when, arranging to meet Leonard Woolf on one of their annual summer buying trips to England, Barker and Hamill began their long association with Woolf and other members of the Bloomsbury group. The purchase of Virginia Woolf's diaries took thirteen years to complete, from 1957, when they bought the 25 volumes containing 2,253 pages, until 1970, when they received the diaries. They were not on a first-name basis with Leonard Woolf, in contrast to most of their clients. They liked him but found him frustrating, mostly because of the drawn-out diary deal resulting from the fact that Woolf wanted easy access to the diaries during his lifetime.

Other purchases over the years, many of which went to the Berg Collection in the New York Public Library, included manuscripts of Virginia Woolf's *The Voyage Out, Jacob's Room, To the Lighthouse*, and hundreds of letters, including those from Virginia Woolf to her sister Vanessa Bell and her friend Vita Sackville-West. Hamill and Barker were attacked for raiding British treasures. Most of the material was kept together, however, in the Berg Collection. Barker and Hamill recognized the importance of the Woolf material even before a biography of Virginia Woolf was published.

During the same decade, Hamill & Barker purchased a large and outstanding collection of books and manuscripts amassed by George A. Poole of Lake Forest, Illinois, owner of Poole Brothers, Inc., a Chicago printing firm. Purchased for $265,000 in 1958, the collection encompassed rare books from the fifteenth to the twentieth centuries from Europe, the United States, and China, and manuscripts from as early as 800 A.D. The collection, which was later sold to Indiana University's Lilly Library, included such treasures as one volume of a two-volume Gutenberg Bible and a 1484 printing of Chaucer's *Canterbury Tales* by William Caxton, the first printer of books in English.

Hamill & Barker attracted attention in 1973 when, at Chicago's biggest rare-book auction, at the Hanzel Galleries, they outbid a well-known New York dealer for the manuscript of Arthur Conan Doyle's *The Sign of Four*, part of the Thomas Gage Joyce Collection. Hamill & Barker paid $51,000 and were dubbed "the big guns from Boul Mich [Michigan Avenue]" by book critic and dealer Van Allen Bradley ("New Records Set," 1227–28). They spent $300,000 on literary treasures that included a farewell letter from Lord Byron to his wife and the manuscript of the Arthur Conan Doyle romance, *The White Company*.

The same year as the Hanzel Galleries auction, Hamill and Barker inadvertently made national news and lost money because six atlases they unwittingly purchased had been stolen from the Yale University library. Yale University learned of the theft when Hamill & Barker offered two of the atlases for sale to the university. Barker and Hamill offered to help in the FBI investigation that ensued, eager to identify the culprits, but acknowledgment of their assistance was belated and lukewarm.

Margery Barker and Frances Hamill were partners in business and in life. For many years they shared an apartment in the Mies van der Rohe buildings on North Lake Shore Drive.

Margery Barker died of cancer and was buried in the family plot at Pine Lake Cemetery in LaPorte, Indiana. Frances Hamill died of a stroke and was buried in the Lyon family plot at Graceland Cemetery in Chicago.

Generous in giving their time and energy to serious book people, they also gave books to, among others, the fledgling University of Illinois at Chicago in the late 1960s. As highly-regarded book dealers, they brought a wide range of important literary works, including the Bloomsbury group and a rare Gutenberg Bible, to the American book scene. In doing so they established an international reputation for their integrity and knowledge of books.

Sources. The papers of Hamill and Barker are in Spec. Coll., Northwestern Univ. Library. These include business correspondence, newspaper clippings, Frances Hamill's essay, and her eightieth birthday scrapbook. Also important are their personnel records at the General Motors Electro-Motive plant in La Grange, Illinois. Terence Tanner, employee and friend of Hamill and Barker and owner of Hamill & Barker Antiquarian Booksellers, Evanston, Illinois, since 1987, gave many interviews to Ruth B. Hutchison as well as access to documents, including transcripts of the Bryn Mawr lawsuit. Van Allen Bradley's article, "New Records Set at Great Chicago Sale," *American Bookman's Weekly*, October 15–22, 1973, focuses on the Hamill and Baker purchases at the Hanzel galleries auction.

Ruth B. Hutchison

BARNES, MARGARET AYER
April 8, 1886–October 25, 1967
NOVELIST, SHORT STORY WRITER, PLAYWRIGHT

Margaret Ayer Barnes gained widespread attention in 1931 when her first novel, *Years of Grace*, won the Pulitzer Prize in Letters. Her father, Benjamin Franklin Ayer, came from a distinguished New England family. Moving to Chicago in 1857, he worked as general counsel and board director for the Illinois

Central Railroad and participated in professional, social, and civic organizations. Her mother boasted a comparable background. Janet (Hopkins) Ayer was the daughter of a New York state senator and later Wisconsin federal judge. An Episcopalian and Republican, she held memberships in the Fortnightly of Chicago, the Daughters of the American Revolution, the Colonial Dames of America, and the Illinois Association Opposed to Woman Suffrage. Margaret Ayer was born in Chicago, the youngest of five children. She recalled the advantages of childhood on the Near North Side in a 1934 essay, "The Town We Grew Up In." She remembered a "village life, pleasant, provincial and prejudiced" (p. 455), with days of running in and out of neighbors' houses and playing jacks or hopscotch. If she and her peers heard nothing of class struggle and social injustice, she reflected, they were thoroughly steeped in the personal virtues of "sympathy, fair play, honesty, generosity, and unselfishness" (p. 456) and were taught a "social responsibility" (p. 457) that would lead to service on boards of orchestras, museums, hospitals, parks, and universities. Recognition of a larger sphere also developed. Her father's railway position provided the family with passes for travel to the Rockies, San Francisco, and New Orleans. Thus, this young Chicago girl grew up with a sense of "the nation and the neighborhood" (p. 456).

She was educated formally at the University School for Girls in Chicago and graduated in 1904, but learning at home enhanced the lessons of the private school. Hers was a household where the family "really did read aloud, around the living-room lamp, the two-volume novels of the Victorians" ("The Town We Grew Up In," 456). As an adolescent on vacation in Lake Geneva, Wisconsin, Margaret Ayer discovered a love for the theater while reading Edmond Rostand's classics with the future playwright Edward Sheldon. Her literary leanings led to a concentration in English and philosophy at Bryn Mawr College, Bryn Mawr, Pennsylvania, from which she graduated in 1907.

A pretty woman with brown eyes and dark hair, Margaret Ayer was a vivacious, witty, and charming socialite, a desirable partner at the glittering dinners and dances of a select Chicago set. On May 21, 1910, she married Cecil Barnes, a lawyer who had graduated from Harvard College, Cambridge, Massachusetts, and Northwestern University Law School in Chicago. They established an eighteen-room home on Chicago's North Side. She had three sons—Cecil Jr. (1912), Edward Larabee (1915), and Benjamin Ayer (1919). Although she resisted a social calendar, preferring reading and writing or camping and climbing with her family, she joined the Arts Club, the Friday Club, and the Fortnightly. She was a member of the Cosmopolitan Club of New York City as well. For these groups, she offered an occasional paper or acted in a skit.

When the little theater movement reached the North Shore suburbs of Chicago, and MARY ALDIS converted her summer home into a private theater compound for entertaining the social, cultural, and professional elite, Barnes joined the Lake Forest Players. From 1912 through 1916, she appeared in productions that showcased plays by Aldis and such international playwrights as George Bernard Shaw, August Strindberg, and John Millington Synge. A well-publicized 1912 benefit for the Infant Welfare Society had Barnes portraying Conservatism in "Somewoman: Her Quest of the Vote. A Morality Play by Pro and Con."

Although never identifying herself as an activist, Barnes had been influenced by Bryn Mawr College president M. Carey Thomas, a feminist who encouraged women to assume public roles. In 1920, Barnes accepted a three-year post as the Bryn Mawr alumnae director. During her tenure, the school started its Summer School for Women Workers in Industry. Barnes served on the Joint Administrative Committee that designed a summer program for women factory workers and raised scholarship funds. Courses were offered in literature, composition, labor economics, and political history in this innovative adult education and leadership training program for women in the labor movement.

An automobile accident in France during a 1925 touring holiday left Barnes with a broken back. This event redirected her professional life. During the months of recuperation she again met Edward Sheldon. At his urging, and following the lead of her older sister JANET AYER FAIRBANK, she began to write short character sketches, proving herself an apt protégée. Her leading men rejected conservative banking and legal establishments for creative employment as novelists or architects just as they left their wives and children for high-spirited mistresses. Her leading women, on the other hand, limited to preservation of home and family, were keenly aware of the penalties for straying from conventional roles. They too yearned; but they resisted. Fashionably decorated homes in Chicago and manicured estates along the North Shore graphically laid out the economic as well as social stakes. Reviewers thought her work refreshing and sophisticated. In 1928, eight stories that had appeared in *Pictorial Review*, *Harper's Magazine*, and *Red Book* were collected in the volume *Prevailing Winds*.

Impressed by her skill, Sheldon convinced Barnes to develop a script for Edith Wharton's novel, *The Age of Innocence*. Its successful Broadway run, starring Katherine Cornell, prompted Sheldon and Barnes to collaborate on the uninspiring *Jenny*, a 1929 comedy about a business attorney who took an actress as his mistress in response to a wife who had taken a Russian lover. In 1930, Sheldon and Barnes undertook a murder mystery based on the real case of an 1857 Glasgow, Scotland, woman who murdered her lover out of fear that he would betray her to her prospective husband. Even a brilliant Cornell in the lead could not save *Dishonored Lady* from savage reviews.

Barnes gained distinction with these Broadway plays, but it was her novel *Years of Grace* (1930) that took the Pulitzer Prize and thrust the relative newcomer into the national spotlight. The prize committee, ignoring Ernest Hemingway and William Faulkner, chose Barnes over Elizabeth Madox Roberts and Dorothy Canfield. This Chicago novel had met the criteria for a representative American experience that explored changing attitudes toward love, sex, and marriage yet upheld moral standards and promoted social improvement.

In contrast to the sweep of a modernist literature that reveled in disturbingly chaotic, experimental, and open-ended forms, *Years of Grace* stood out as a witty and well-constructed narrative. Chicago's urban setting gave birth to the responsible and respectable family that cultivated "dignity and decency and decorum" (*Years of Grace*, 577). Barnes demonstrated how bonds first fashioned in the drawing rooms of Pine Street, Rush, and Huron on Chicago's fashionable North Side were affirmed later in the comfortable suburban "Lakewood" estates. Artistic, cultural, and religious events reflected hallowed institutions—the Art Institute, the Auditorium Theater, and Holy Name Cathedral.

To preserve the sense of her age, Barnes carefully chronicled the years from the World's Columbian Exposition of 1893 through World War I and into the jazz age. Meticulous detail authenticated the historical fabric, while the sensitive portrayal of female self-definition added a modestly feminist subtext. The novel explored the economic forces that were changing the context for conservative Victorian attitudes and mores. Barnes's examination of women's lives mapped out the boundaries of intellectual, imaginative, and emotional growth imposed by their positions of leadership.

While the protagonist crafted by Barnes never strayed far from societal norms, her flirtations with impropriety projected an unflattering picture. In the second novel, *Westward Passage* (1931), a seven-day trans-Atlantic voyage reduces female intellectual engagement to an argument between life with the flamboyant, passionate former husband-artist from the East Coast and her current stolid spouse from the Midwest. The debate measuring emotional adventuring against the comforts of home and family turns on an economic pivot. Critics found themselves equally at the center of a disequilibrium—praising the classic weighing of alternatives while lambasting the protagonist as provincial, indecisive, and superficial.

Barnes explored the fuller impact of economic conditions through a female figure from a banking family. The historical context for *Within This Present* (1933) extends from 1914 to 1933 and includes World War I, the 1929 stock market crash, the Great Depression, and Chicago gangster wars. Another three-generational Gold Coast family represents the quintessential American heritage. On the eve of European war during an opening dinner speech, the family matriarch offers Chicago history as the national exemplar; she recalls how the Des Plaines River flood, a cholera epidemic, and the Chicago Fire of 1871 challenged and reinvigorated their forebears. Disappointed in a family life enervated by success, she believes that although the pioneering spirit withers as financial security flowers, it revives under adverse conditions.

Barnes never rejected the economic system that supported her own privilege, but the later novels grew increasingly disenchanted with its impact on women. The fourth novel directly confronted the alienation and isolation triggered by the pursuit of the American Dream. In *Edna His Wife: An American Idyll* (1935), the issue of class reorders the narrative vantage point. A plump and pretty young girl from a working-class Chicago-area railroad family runs away with a parentless young man determined to improve his station as a rising attorney. From the 1890s to the mid-1930s, they move up—from a Chicago flat to Gold Coast apartment, Washington, D.C., house, and finally New York City penthouse. Each step up the ladder takes the woman, but not her spouse, further from meaningful relationships and purpose. This challenge to the social order from a protagonist with limited intelligence, little political insight, and no activist inclination drew the ire of some reviewers and later prompted

one scholar to deem Barnes a good novelist of manners but an unsatisfactory social critic. Nevertheless, the story of female debilitation attracted a small following and in 1937 played to mixed reviews when adapted as a one-woman theatrical evening.

In her last novel, *Wisdom's Gate* (1938), Barnes resumed the family saga initiated in *Years of Grace*. Erosion of family integrity, a peripheral theme earlier, surfaces in full force. Quick divorces, fast remarriages, and easy extramarital affairs disrupt family lines. Political and economic turmoil are reduced to background for the serene, suburban "Lakewood" world being slowly dismantled by marital infidelity and mistrust. Women of this generation agonize over the support of family unity, as did their foremothers.

Barnes wrote no novels after *Wisdom's Gate*, which completed the cycle. She remained socially active well after the death of her husband in 1949. She sold their Chicago home and moved east in 1958 to be nearer her children. Barnes died of a heart attack at age eighty-one in Cambridge, Massachusetts, and was buried near her summer home in Mount Desert, Maine.

The literary achievement of Margaret Ayer Barnes remains open to debate. Over the years, her fiction has been dismissed as inconsequential genteel romance, then praised as documented social history. Her work has been accused of justifying a social elite, reprimanded as mere representation of manners, then upheld as a feminist critique of twentieth-century sexism and capitalism. Still Barnes remains an untapped resource, for beneath the age-old struggle between the community and the individual lies a neglected but intriguing inquiry into the social and economic underpinnings of women's intellectual, imaginative, and emotional growth.

Sources. Typescripts of Margaret Ayer Barnes's plays are available in the Berg Collection of the New York Public Library; copies are housed in the Katharine Cornell Collection at the State University of New York at Buffalo. Miscellaneous correspondence exists in several manuscript collections: Alice Gerstenberg papers at the NL, Cornelia Lynde Meigs Papers at Dartmouth College, and the Houghton Mifflin files at Harvard University. Her novels are *Years of Grace* (1930), *Westward Passage* (1931), *Within This Present* (1933), *Edna His Wife: An American Idyll* (1935), and *Wisdom's Gate* (1938). In addition to the books mentioned in the entry, Barnes collaborated with her sister Janet Ayer Fairbank on the introduction to *Julia Newberry's Diary* (1933), a journal of 1870 Chicago life written by the young daughter of a prominent family. Barnes outlined her family background in "The Town We Grew Up In," *Survey Graphic*, October 1934; she explained the purpose of her fiction in "Period Novel," *What Is a Book?: Thoughts about Writing*, edited by Dale Warren (1935). Lloyd C. Taylor Jr., *Margaret Ayer Barnes* (1974), is the only full-length biography. Lennox Bouton Grey, "Chicago and 'The Great American Novel'" (Ph.D. diss., Univ. of Chicago, 1935), establishes Barnes in a Chicago writing tradition that he labels dynastic. Margaret Lawrence, *The School of Femininity* (1936), situates Barnes in a matriarchal tradition. See also Thelma J. Shinn, "Margaret Ayer Barnes," *American Women Writers: A Critical Reference Guide from Colonial Times to the Present* (1979); Grace Eckley, "Margaret Ayer Barnes," *Dictionary of Literary Biography: American Novelists, 1910–1945* (1981); Clarence A. Andrews, *Chicago in Story: A Literary History* (1982). The years as a playwright are mentioned in Eric Wollencott Barnes, *The Man Who Lived Twice: The Biography of Edward Sheldon* (1956).

KAY HOYLE NELSON

BARTELME, MARY MARGARET
July 24, 1866–July 25, 1954

JUDGE, LAWYER, CHILD ADVOCATE, SUFFRAGIST

Mary Margaret Bartelme was an intelligent, visionary, and courageous woman who broke numerous barriers to fulfill her mission to assist and protect children. A committed suffragist and women's rights advocate with a highly skilled legal mind, Bartelme was Illinois's first woman to be appointed Public Guardian and first woman elected to the Circuit Court bench. As a teacher, a lawyer, and a judge, Bartelme devoted most of her life to assisting children in need.

Born in Chicago in a farmhouse, Bartelme, her brother Alfred, and her sister Adeline were raised by their Alsatian immigrant parents, Balthazar and Jeannette Theresa (Hoff) Bartelme, in River Forest, Illinois. Bartelme excelled in her studies, first in the Chicago public schools, where she graduated from West Division High School; then at Cook County Normal School; and subsequently under a private tutor. She became a schoolteacher when she was nineteen, teaching at Armour Street and Garfield Park schools in Chicago. In 1891, after her mother died, Bartelme described herself as so deeply saddened by her loss that she was unable to continue teaching and decided to seek a new career.

Bright and undaunted by challenges, Bartelme decided to enter one of the learned professions. Because of her aptitude for chemistry, she first thought of entering the medical profession. However, while she was investigating the opportunities for women doctors, a female physician suggested she consider the law and directed her to seek the counsel of MYRA BRADWELL. Bradwell, who had studied law since the 1850s and had been a well-established legal journalist and editor for more than twenty years, was instantly taken with Bartelme and encouraged her to pursue a career in the law. Bartelme, equally impressed with Bradwell, followed her advice and in 1892 began her studies at Northwestern University School of Law.

In keeping with the trend toward law school rather than apprenticeship in a law office, Bartelme chose a law school known at the turn of the twentieth century for its support of women students, though she was the only woman in her class. Bartelme excelled in her studies, demonstrating a superior legal ability. She graduated and was admitted to the Illinois bar in 1894 (just months after Bradwell died of cancer). In her final year she won a prize for her thesis on spendthrift trusts, which Bradwell's husband published in the *Chicago Legal News*, and a prize from the *American Law and Register Review* for a case annotation.

Bartelme immediately opened a law office—Barnes, Barnes and Bartelme—with two male partners and began practicing probate law, working at the same time toward the advancement of women in the profession. In 1894 Bartelme was one of the founders of the Chicago Business Woman's Club. This organization, which was first organized after the 1893 World's Columbian Exposition, was created to support women professionals in their work and to provide basic services they needed but could otherwise not obtain. Through a successful fundraising campaign in 1902, the year Bartelme was president, the Chicago Business Woman's Club was able to establish a clubhouse that contained exercise and shower facilities for the women, reading rooms, lounges, and dining rooms. Through such clubs, women who were excluded from male fraternal organizations were able to form their own networks of support, opportunity, and reform. The cost of the club, however, proved overwhelming, and within a short time they were forced to declare bankruptcy and disband. Bartelme lost almost three thousand dollars that she had invested personally.

Bartelme was an active suffragist. She was a member and officeholder in the Chicago Suffrage Club and used her position as a lawyer to advocate for women's full citizenship rights. Shortly after being admitted to the bar, Bartelme wrote a response to a query posed by the *Chicago Tribune* asking if women wanted the vote. The *Tribune* published Bartelme's letter (the *Chicago Legal News* republished it), which argued straightforwardly that since women were subject to all the laws of their country as well as to criminal penalties for violating them, they should have a voice, through the vote, in determining the nature of those laws.

It was not long into Bartelme's legal career that she chose to focus her work on advancing and protecting the rights of children. Bartelme's practice in the probate court caught the attention of Judge Christian C. Kohlsaat. The Cook County probate judge was so impressed with Bartelme that he encouraged Governor John R. Tanner to appoint Bartelme Public Guardian of Cook County and urged her, in turn, to accept. In 1897 Bartelme became the first woman to hold that position, which she kept for sixteen years under four governors. Traditionally, the responsibilities of this office were to decide questions of custody and handle the estates of minors who were wards of the state. Bartelme expanded these duties significantly, using state resources to improve the quality of life of these children. She recognized their rights as individuals and sought to protect them from assault on their person or property. Whatever the time or weather, Bartelme would go to the homes of children in need, even taking them into her own home if necessary. She always kept donated clothes in her office for women and children in need. Bartelme was so genuinely devoted to her work and to these children that she and her sister took into their home and raised as their own two young orphaned sisters whose foster parents had died.

Other judges and agencies quickly came to respect Bartelme's efforts and expertise, using her as a resource to assess home-finding associations and seeking her advice in divorce cases involving child custody. During her first years as the Public Guardian, Bartelme became involved in the campaign to establish a juvenile court. In her official capacity, Bartelme attended the meeting organized by JULIA LATHROP at the State Board of Charities. She assisted Lathrop, LUCY FLOWER, and a group of women reformers in their fight to secure the first juvenile court in the United States. Once the court was established in 1899, Bartelme joined with LOUISE deKOVEN BOWEN, Sara Hart, and other women reformers in founding and operating a detention home as an alternative to jail for juveniles who came before the new court.

By 1912, the Cook County Juvenile Court had worked through some of its initial challenges in establishing an effective system to process cases, house the children, and develop disposition options in line with its philosophy of helping rather than punishing the child. The Juvenile Court remained, however, in need of continued financial assistance, legal expertise, and on-

FIG. 11. *Women reformers, including Harriet E. Vittum and Catharine Waugh McCulloch, standing to the left and right, supported the successful 1923 campaign to elect Mary Bartelme, seated, the first woman judge of the Cook County Juvenile Court.*

going support. One of the new problems facing the court was what to do with the increasing number of female juveniles who appeared before it. Presiding Judge Merritt W. Pinckney determined that there was a need to have a woman judge hear these cases, and Bartelme was chosen unanimously by the circuit court judges to fill this position. In 1913, Pinckney appointed Bartelme his assistant judge, and this marked a significant restructuring of the juvenile court. For the first time, cases involving juvenile girls were heard behind closed doors. Additionally, all the participants, from the judge to the police officers, were women.

Once appointed, Bartelme immediately began to introduce new court practices to address the needs of girls who entered the justice system. She began with the quest to find alternative dispositions for the large number of girls who came before the juvenile court for committing only slight wrongdoings. Since many of these girls came from abusive homes or lived on the street, Bartelme could not send them home; but she often found that their offenses did not justify committing them to the state institution. To provide a third alternative, Bartelme established the first "Mary Club" in 1914, donating her own home in Chicago's Austin neighborhood as a place where the girls could live with other girls and trained workers until they could be properly placed. The home was well received by the press and, according to Bartelme, by the girls. Because of the growing number of girls who came through the courts and the small size of the residence, "Mary Club B" was established two years later. Both of these clubs were for white girls only. In 1921 the Mary Club Board worked with the middle-class black women reformers who made up the board of the Friendly Big Sister's League. Together they established a third home, "Mary Club C,"

for girls of color. By 1923, more than twenty-six hundred girls had passed through these homes.

Bartelme soon extended her approach, which she began developing in the Public Guardian's office, to all aspects of her judicial work. In addition to founding the Mary Clubs, Bartelme, in collaboration with women's volunteer organizations, instituted a program that provided a suitcase of clothes and necessities to girls who came through the juvenile court and then resided in a girls' home. These girls often appeared in court with no possessions other than the clothes they were wearing. Bartelme relied on women's clubs to furnish the suitcases and their contents. The Chicago Woman's Club (CWC) formed a Service Council specifically for this purpose, and a club of ten women in Evanston met once a week to make dresses to order for the girls, sewing approximately 150 dresses a year. This program was widely praised in the press and earned Bartelme the nickname "Suitcase Mary."

Despite the popular support Bartelme's programs received, there were some who challenged her authority. In 1915 the grand jury created a committee to investigate allegations that Bartelme was acting as a judge, though she had not been elected to that office. After examining Bartelme's methods, the committee reported that Bartelme's work was a milestone in the treatment of juvenile girls. They lauded her programs and urged that the juvenile court be given absolute jurisdiction over the cases of juveniles. The grand jury adopted the report and joined in the committee's praise of Bartelme's work.

Women's clubs in the county, and particularly the CWC, strongly supported Bartelme throughout her career, both in the programs she initiated and in her personal aspirations. Cognizant of the importance of these relationships, Bartelme was an active member in the CWC, and she held memberships in the Cordon Club, the Woman's City Club of Chicago, and the Every Day Club; she was an honorary member of the Chicago College Club and the Big Sisters. She accepted countless invitations from civic and religious organizations to speak about her work. Bartelme always brought along a list that specified ways her audience could assist in the programs of the court.

The work Bartelme carried out as an assistant judge of the juvenile court initially provided the kind of middle-class services for girls that middle-class and upper-class men's organizations had provided for boys. Bartelme explained that boys who went through the juvenile court system had always had a man to preside over their cases, and they received many philanthropic services through such organizations as the Union League Boy's Club, the Rotary Club of Chicago, the Kiwanis Club, and the Knights of Columbus. However, there was no similar system of support for juvenile girls. Bartelme and the women's associations filled that void.

In 1923 Judge Thomas Windes died in the second year of a six-year term as Cook County circuit court judge, creating a vacancy on the juvenile court bench. Bartelme, still presiding as an assistant judge in the court, decided to run for the position. Bartelme had earned the respect of the Chicago bar. She was a member of the American Bar Association, the Illinois State Bar Association, the Chicago Bar Association, and the Women's Bar Association of Illinois, a long time suffragist and a member of the League of Women Voters. Bartelme's friends and colleagues, including Juvenile Court Judge Victor Arnold and VIOLETTE ANDERSON, a leading black woman lawyer in Chicago, supported her candidacy. Sara Hart, Bartelme's dear friend and juvenile court advocate, agreed to be Bartelme's campaign manager. Bartelme and her supporters understood the important effect that holding a judicial seat would have on her mission to establish and protect the rights of all women and children. With full judicial authority, Bartelme believed, she could expand her program to assist the girls who came before the court. In 1923, by a margin of fourteen thousand votes, Bartelme was elected judge in the Circuit Court of Cook County and was assigned to sit in the juvenile court.

Bartelme viewed her election as both a personal victory that brought recognition for her expertise and as a victory for all women. The day following her election, Bartelme told a journalist, "I hope my election will act as an incentive in interesting women in their government, both local and national, and in everything that pertains to the welfare of their country and the world. The day is coming, I believe, when women will share equally with the men the burdens of our courts. . . . Though I may not be living at that time, I expect a woman to some day be president of the United States" ("Miss Bartelme Back at Work after Victory").

As an elected judge, Bartelme continued to employ an innovative, comprehensive approach that included a cooperative courtroom style, collaboration with social science experts, and support of public programs directed at juveniles. In her courtroom, Bartelme embraced a philosophy that rejected the established adversarial methods of practicing law, since she did not believe they facilitated the work of the juvenile court. Expand-

ing the practices of other early juvenile court judges who often heard children's cases privately in their chambers, Bartelme would not allow attorneys to raise objections in her courtroom. In talking to the children directly, she employed a direct and sympathetic approach for discerning the facts and the issues and administering justice. As Bartelme explained, this method caused her to buy handkerchiefs "by the gross" (Ernest, "Juvenile Court Aids Girls Who Are Friendless") to hand out to the many children who came to tears during their hearings.

In deciding what resolution would most benefit the child, Bartelme collaborated with the new social scientists who were studying the causes and treatment of delinquency and the child welfare experts who were trained in the new field of social work. Bartelme supported the work of philanthropist and social activist ETHEL STURGES DUMMER who, in 1909, persuaded psychologist William Healy to come to Chicago and found the Juvenile Psychopathic Institute to aid the juvenile court in its work. Healy evaluated the children and made recommendations to the court based on what he believed would most directly help the child. Bartelme was also assisted in this work by the efforts of lawyer, scholar, and social reformer SOPHINISBA BRECKINRIDGE. As one of the founders of the Chicago School of Civics and Philanthropy (after 1921 the University of Chicago School of Social Service Administration), Breckinridge and her colleagues trained social workers in the methods needed to investigate the social and economic conditions of children's lives. These findings were then provided to the juvenile court and used to assess the best approach to meeting the needs of the children.

The final element in Bartelme's innovative approach to dispensing justice was her emphasis on providing public services to children. The services were intended to prevent delinquency by providing alternative activities for the children as well as teaching them the skills the court believed would allow them to lead productive lives. For example, Bartelme championed reforms that would keep children in school, including a law that set the minimum age for women's employment at sixteen years. She also worked with the Juvenile Protective Association and the Chicago Park District to increase the number of parks and expand public amusement programs. To win public support for these programs, Bartelme chaperoned a dance at a westside Chicago public park in 1925, and the following year she organized the Service Council for Girls to help her in this work.

Bartelme's approach won her local, national, and international acclaim. In 1926 the Queen of Romania, on a visit to the United States, spent a day in Bartelme's courtroom to observe her methods. In 1927 Bartelme was reelected to the bench for a full six-year term. She then became the presiding judge over the juvenile court and began hearing the cases of both boys and girls. She handled the boys' cases as she did the girls' and sought to establish for them some of the same services she had established for girls.

Bartelme wielded tremendous power over the lives of children and their families. In her work she fused her belief that all children were good and should be treated as individuals with her belief that middle-class American values would benefit most children. She encouraged most of those who came before her to adopt many of the white middle-class values prevalent during her tenure, at the same time valuing the children as individuals who had rights and were entitled to certain protections. For example, Bartelme consistently encouraged immigrant children and their parents to speak English and learn American ways. Because Bartelme viewed these children as growing up in a different world than the one their parents understood, a world with American temptations that differed from those of "the old world," she encouraged foreign parents to join American religious and secular organizations to help them understand the modern American world in which their children lived. Yet Bartelme consistently admonished the children to obey and respect their immigrant parents. Similarly, Bartelme encouraged young girls who wanted to get married and have children to learn the new "scientific" methods of housekeeping and childcare; but she also encouraged girls who wanted careers to pursue them.

Bartelme held equally complicated positions on racial issues in her role as judge of the juvenile court. While she approached each case individually, treating all races with equal concern, Bartelme did order services and placement according to race. For instance, Bartelme followed the established juvenile court practice of assigning black probation officers to black children. The underlying theory was that a black probation officer could be more effective than a white probation officer in working with the child and the family. Acknowledging the extreme racial barriers that existed in Chicago, the black community showed some support for this practice and for Bartelme herself.

During a placement crisis for African American children in the late 1920s, Bartelme, with the support of the Chicago Council of Social Agencies (in 1948 the Welfare Council of Metropolitan Chicago, after 1976 the United Way of Metropolitan Chicago), ordered the Joint Services Bureau to create the Department of Child Placing. The task was to provide foster care for black children in need of placement. Despite persistent efforts, and faced with the increased strain of the depression, the department reported to the court by 1932 that it could not meet the needs of the children under its supervision. Bartelme, who had often turned to the community in times of need, arranged a meeting of Protestant organizations and agencies, intending to persuade them to assist in providing foster care for these children. In her address, Bartelme noted that the juvenile court took responsibility for all dependent children but encouraged religious groups to undertake care of dependent children of their faith; she referred specifically to the responsibilities taken on by the Archdiocese for Roman Catholic children and by the Jewish Child Welfare Council for Jewish children. She then emphasized the need of the Protestant organizations to provide for all Protestant children, both black and white. Bartelme explained that this responsibility involved active and immediate participation, strongly suggesting that each Protestant organization create a case committee that would meet weekly to address the needs of each homeless child and then make a presentation to the juvenile court. To her disappointment, only a few organizations agreed to help the court.

The Great Depression would ultimately end Bartelme's efforts. Her attempts to assist black children met with only limited success, and her work was strained further as the depression grew more serious. In 1931 two group homes that together housed 177 white boys closed their doors due to inadequate funding; the state refused to provide care for the boys that were released. Bartelme attempted to turn to her women's association networks for support, but they too were struggling to survive. Though Bartelme did set up a committee of business leaders and social reformers to address the crisis, the severity of the depression and the lack of community support made it difficult for the court to maintain its mission to address the needs of each individual child. When her term expired in 1933, Bartelme decided to retire. She expressed her disappointment in a speech she gave in 1932 in tribute to her dear friend and longtime colleague, Sara Hart, noting that she "had hoped to do some really constructive things during her term of office" (speech, May 26, 1932, Bartelme Papers). When Bartelme retired, the Chicago Bar Association and all those affiliated with the juvenile court held a civic dinner in her honor. The Chief Judge of the Cook County Circuit Court praised Bartelme for her work as did JANE ADDAMS and fellow juvenile court associates.

Bartelme spent the last two decades of her life in Carmel, California, where she lived with her brother, until his death, and his daughter. Bartelme's sister, Adeline Tilt, lived nearby. During her retirement years Bartelme became a member of the Christian Science Church, and she spent much of her time tending her flower garden. She did make several trips to Chicago during these years to visit friends and family. After a short illness, Bartelme died at the age of eighty-eight. One of her last requests was that anyone wishing to send flowers should instead make a contribution to the Mary Bartelme Clubs.

Throughout her career Bartelme was sincere in her belief that middle-class reformers could help guide all children who came before the court toward a "better" life. Bartelme also understood that not all children needed or wanted the same things. She crossed race, class, and ethnic lines in her legal and social reform efforts, but she stopped short of embracing racial integration. Like most of the women lawyers of her day, Bartelme believed in the legal and political equality of all women and fought for the rights and protection of all children. Her position as a lawyer and a judge and her work in the juvenile court gave her the tools to influence the legal profession and the law and its administration in a manner consistent with her vision.

Sources. Bartelme's own writings, including copies of many of her speeches and correspondence, reports of the grand jury investigation of Bartelme's appointment to the juvenile court, as well as numerous news clippings are included in the Mary Margaret Bartelme Papers, UIC Spec. Coll. Helpful is a clipping file at Northwestern Univ. Archives that includes alumni records on Bartelme. The Grace Harte Papers, Mary Earhart Dillon Collection, SL, include an unpublished biography of Bartelme by Catharine Waugh McCulloch. The Virginia Hugo Collection, CHS, has an unidentified news clipping, "Exhausted by Her Effort to Save a Woman's Club," that details the demise of the Chicago Business Woman's Club. Sketches of Bartelme include "Mary Margaret Bartelme," in Agnes Geneva Gilman and Gertrude Marcelle Gilman, *Who's Who in Illinois, Women Makers of History* (1927); "Judge Mary M. Bartelme," in E. F. Dunne, *Illinois, the Heart of the Nation*, vol. 5 (1933); "Mary Bartelme First Woman Judge in Illinois Courts," in *Journal of the Illinois State Historical Society*, vol. 17, 1923; and *NAW* (1980). Articles on Bartelme's law school career include "Miss Mary M. Bartelme's Graduating Thesis" and "Miss Mary M. Bartelme

Takes the First Prize," both in *Chicago Legal News*, vol. 27, 1894; and "Mary Margaret Bartelme," *Chicago Legal News*, vol. 26, 1894, which also contains information on Bartelme's relationship with Myra Bradwell. Further descriptions of the relationship between Bartelme and Myra Bradwell are in "The Myra Bradwell School Commencement," *Chicago Legal News*, vol. 32, 1900, and Mary O'Connor Newell, "Guardian, Political Iconoclast, and Now Chicago's First Feminine Jurist," *Chicago Record-Herald*, June 16, 1912. Articles on Bartelme's work as Public Guardian include "Miss Bartelme Appointed Public Guardian of Cook County," *Chicago Legal News*, vol. 29, 1897; Edith Brown Kirkwood, "'There Were Three Old Maids,'" *Farmer's Wife*, March 1919; and "One Woman's Duties," Chicago *Evening Post*, August 28, 1897. Articles on the need for Bartelme's appointment, the appointment itself, and her work as an assistant to the judge include Merritt Pinckney, "The Delinquent Girl and the Juvenile Court," in *The Child in the City*, ed. Sophonisba Breckinridge (1912); "A Court for Girls with a Woman Judge," *Collier's: The National Weekly* (c. 1913); "Juvenile Court Judge—Woman to Be Offered Assistant Judgeship," *Chicago Legal News*, vol. 44, 1912; "Personals," *Survey*, May 17, 1913; "Women Who Are Making Good in Public Office," *Current Opinion*, August 1913; Ellen Tracy, "The Mother of Ten Thousand Children," *McCall's Magazine*, June 1913; and Anne Shannon Monroe, "When Women Sit in Judgment," *Good Housekeeping*, April 1920. Information on the grand jury investigation of Bartelme's appointment includes "Vindication of Juvenile Court," *Chicago Herald*, August 27, 1915. Information on Bartelme's adoption of the two sisters is in "For Miss Bartelme," *Oak Parker*, November 1923. Articles on Bartelme's judicial election and judgeship include Betsy Greenbaum, "The Court of 'Another Chance' Where Judge Mary Bartelme Presides," *Woman Citizen*, August 1927; Genevieve Forbes, "Mary Bartelme 'Real Judge' Now and Real Human," *CT*, November 8, 1923; "Women Cheer Bartelme Victory," *Chicago American*, January 7, 1923; June Sawyers, "Way We Were: 'Suitcase Mary' Leads a Crusade for Needy Girls," *CT*, n.d.; "Mary Bartelme: An Honor to Chicago," *Chicago Herald Examiner*, November 5, 1923; "Woman Expert with Juveniles May Win Judgeship," *Christian Science Monitor*, October 30, 1923; Violette N. Anderson, "Woman's Place in the Judicial Campaign," *Colored Women's Exchange News*, October 1923; "Miss Bartelme Back at Work after Victory," *Chicago Daily Journal*, November 7, 1923; "'Pretty Clothes' in a New Suitcase, Cheer Girl in Juvenile Court," unidentified clipping, October 14, 1923; "Chicago's Young Delinquents Find Woman Judge 'Big Sister,'" *Christian Science Monitor*, January 2, 1924; and "Personal Glimpses: Women Who Help Boss Us," *Literary Digest*, January 17, 1925. Evidence of the African American community's opinion of Bartelme is in C. M. Cunningham, "The Juvenile Court of Cook County," in *The Negro in Chicago 1779 to 1929: The Wonder Book*, vol. 1–2 [*sic*], ed. Frederic H. Robb (1929). Articles on Bartelme's reelection as judge include "The Juvenile Court," *Herald Examiner*, September 3, 1927. Descriptions of the work of Bartelme during the Great Depression include Gifford Ernest, "Juvenile Court Aids Girls Who Are Friendless," *Chicago Daily News*, May 2, 1930; Gifford Ernest, "William Runs Afoul of the Law, 'Gets Breaks,'" *Chicago Daily News*, May 1, 1930; Gwendolyn Hart, "Clubs and Societies," *Chicago Daily News*, September 2, 1931; Judge Mary Bartelme, "The Financial Crisis in Cook County and What It Has Meant to the Children of the Juvenile Court," *Young Citizen*, April 1930; [n.a.], "Seek to Provide for Boys County Will Not Keep," *Chicago Record Herald*, June 22, 1931; and [n.a.], "Miss Bartelme Tells of Mary Clubs' Work," *Evanston Daily News*, October 1, 1937. Obituaries are "Mary Margaret Bartelme Memorial," *Chicago Bar Record*, vol. 36, 1954; "Judge Mary Bartelme, 88, Dies in West," *Chicago Daily Tribune*, July 26, 1954; "Mary M. Bartelme, Aided Needy Girls," *NYT*, July 26, 1954; and "Judge Mary Bartelme," *Monterey Peninsula Herald*, July 26, 1954.

GWEN HOERR MCNAMEE

BARTON, MACENA ALBERTA
August 16, 1901–May 30, 1986
PAINTER

Macena Barton was an active member of the Chicago art community from the mid-1920s until her death. The daughter of Henry James and Jessie (Rodgers) Barton, she was born in Union City, Michigan. Her father was an attorney, and her mother was a printer. Barton had at least one sister, Rosana, also an artist. Rosana Barton was a frequent subject for Macena Barton's painting. Little more is known about Barton's family.

Barton was educated in the public schools in Battle Creek, Michigan, and came to Chicago in 1921 to study at the School of the Art Institute of Chicago (SAIC). On her own financially, Barton first worked at Continental Commercial Bank as a clerk and later as a proofreader for R. R. Donnelley, the printing and publishing company. These jobs paid for her education at SAIC. After art school, in order to survive as a young and unknown artist, Barton continued to work as a proofreader.

Graduating in 1924, Barton spent one year in postgraduate studies with Wellington Reynolds, John Norton, Allen Philbrick, and Leon Kroll. All were important artists, but perhaps the best known was Kroll. He considered a nude Barton painted in his class "the best he had seen since he had been in Chicago" (C. J. Bulliet, "Artists of Chicago, Past and Present"). Barton extracted something from all of her teachers while never copying them, in the end creating a style that was unique. Kroll introduced his students to the moderns, encouraging them to see the value in Paul Cezanne and Pierre Auguste Renoir at a time when resistance to modern art still dominated the classrooms at SAIC. Promodernist art critic Clarence J. Bulliet wrote that "Kroll gave Macena Barton new eyes—eyes to see the subtleties of Cezanne's coloring, the glorious flesh tones of Renoir" ("Artists of Chicago").

Barton's work began to receive attention immediately after art school. She exhibited regularly at the juried Art Institute annual exhibition, beginning in 1926. That year, Barton had two paintings accepted. She was to exhibit in all but three Art Institute of Chicago annual exhibits between 1926 and 1945. Although she received much positive critical attention, Barton was never able to support herself entirely as an artist. She kept her proofreading job at R. R. Donnelley most of her adult life and joined the Chicago Typographical Union. It was said that she read copy at night, slept in the mornings, and painted in the afternoon.

Barton began her lifelong interest in painting the female nude when she was a student at SAIC. One of her first nudes was *Salome*, and she was intrigued with this theme. Kroll encouraged her to paint nudes at a time when many contended that a woman was not capable of painting a great nude. Rebellious, Barton engaged an African American female model to pose for her; Barton's completed portrait, *Mitzi*, caused a sensation when exhibited in the No-Jury Show of 1931. The painting *Mitzi* toured the United States in an Art Institute of Chicago traveling exhibition.

Barton kept a studio at the Tree Studios, then and now a popular location for artists. She was a member of the Chicago Society of Artists, the Woman's Artist Salon of Chicago, the Association of Chicago Painters and Sculptors, and the Arts Club.

Barton also associated with the No-Jury Society, a group dedicated to promoting contemporary art through exhibitions open to anyone who paid a minimum membership fee. The No-Jury Society was organized in 1922 in response to the juried Art Institute annuals that often excluded the more innovative or experimental works that No-Jury hoped to encourage. Barton exhibited with the No-Jury Society and served as president in 1939.

Chicago was not an easy place for modernists to work. Outside the small art community there was very little support for the avant-garde. Chicago artists were divided into two distinct groups, the modernists and the conservatives. The former associated with the No-Jury Society, and the latter were often with the juried Art Institute annuals. The two groups were bitter rivals. As an artist, Barton did not fit easily into either group, exhibiting with both. "The 'moderns' sense her as an individualist," art critic C. J. Bulliet commented, "an egoist, going her unique way, untrammeled by the 'schools.' The 'conservatives' recognize her technical equipment and note her contempt for the 'isms'" ("Artists of Chicago"). Yet Barton was often a controversial figure. Not only did she become known for her nudes, which were bold for the period, but her personal life was also unconventional. She had a highly publicized affair with Bulliet, Chicago's champion of the modernist movement. During their long friendship and love affair Bulliet wrote numerous favorable articles about Barton and her work. Many other artists felt his appraisal of her work was biased by their personal relationship.

Barton's work was characterized by naturalistic forms, expressive color, and psychological drama. Her portraits often had "auras" or hazy areas of color surrounding the figures. The meaning of the auras is unclear, but different sitters were highlighted with different colors. The auras have been described as Barton's interpretation of the inner character of the sitter or subject. Barton's ability to create a close likeness to her sitters was highly praised. She often tried to engage her sitters in conversation to gain their confidence and relax them. She also insisted that her sitters wear vibrant colors when they sat for her portraits. To insure that the portrait had the quality of a painting, not a photograph, Barton emphasized the most characteristic feature of the person. One of Barton's most famous portraits is *Clarence J. Bulliet* (c. 1933). Bulliet was a large man, and Barton does not hide his size. He appears almost larger than life, perhaps Barton's statement about his power in the art world. He is shown seated, though the chair is only visible just above his right shoulder, and he appears to be floating. This arrangement, and the red aura surrounding him, give Bulliet an unearthly quality. His skin tones are beautifully painted as are his soft elongated hands. Barton alludes to Bulliet's book *Apples and Madonnas* (1927) by seating him next to a still life of apples and including a painting of a Madonna and Child above his figure. A portrait with Barton's signature aura (probably a copy of a painting by Barton that was owned by Bulliet) is drawn above Bulliet's left shoulder. Barton's keen sense of both humor and aesthetics is visible in the Bulliet portrait.

Barton was best known as a portrait painter, but she also had a reputation as a painter of nudes, including ones of herself. Her *Untitled (Nude Self-Portrait)* (c. 1930) has soft naturalistic forms, and the painter subject confronts the viewer without any display of modesty. Barton gives herself a warm blue aura, which makes the cool tones of her skin seem to jump off the canvas. "Fond of painting realistic female nudes in a period when conservative tastes in Chicago favored a more academic and refined treatment, Barton was able to follow her own vision because of her isolation and marginalization, rather than in spite of it" (Weininger, *The "New Woman" in Chicago, 1910–1945*, n.p.).

Barton had a long and prolific career, exhibiting in many commercial galleries, including Knoedler Galleries (1930) and Findley Galleries (1933–36), both in Chicago. She exhibited in the following museums: Art Institute of Chicago; Virginia Museum of Fine Arts; Boston Museum of Fine Arts; Kansas City Art Institute; Carnegie Institute, Pittsburgh; Minneapolis Institute of Art; and the Los Angeles Museum of Art. In the early 1930s, Barton was offered the opportunity to exhibit between twenty and thirty paintings in the Netherlands at the Modern Museum in Amsterdam and then The Hague. She declined the offer because the cost of shipping her work to Europe was prohibitive.

Barton was honored with prizes, including the August Peabody, Art Institute of Chicago, 1927; the Chicago Woman's Club Prize, Art Institute of Chicago, 1932; and the Chicago Galleries Association First Prize (1945–56). Her work was selected for the 1933 Century of Progress *Exhibition of Paintings and Sculpture* and the AIC *Half Century of American Art* exhibition.

On January 17, 1953, she married Robert Francis McNeilan in a Presbyterian service. McNeilan, an architect, ran the McNeilan Gallery, presenting works of Macena Barton. In 1974 McNeilan died of lung cancer. Barton never remarried. Barton died at age eighty-four; she had painted until age eighty-one.

Difficult to label during her lifetime, today Barton is most often associated with the modernist movement in Chicago. Barton was a strong woman with an individual style, both in life and in art. Her work is still represented in Chicago galleries, including Robert Henry Adams Fine Art. In 1993 her work was included in the exhibition *The "New Woman" in Chicago, 1910–1945: Paintings from Illinois Collections* at the Illinois State Museum, Springfield, and at Rockford College, Rockford, Illinois.

Sources. The Macena Barton papers are in the Archives of American Art, Smithsonian Institution, Washington, D.C., and are available on microfilm at the Ryerson Library, Art Institute of Chicago. They include clippings, reviews of her exhibitions, letters, photographs, and other personal papers. Barton is listed in *Who Was Who in American Art* (1985); Esther Sparks, "A Biographical Dictionary of Painters and Sculptors in Illinois, 1808–1945" (Ph.D. diss., Northwestern Univ., 1971); and Louise Dunn Yochim, *Role and Impact: The Chicago Society of Artists* (1979). She is profiled in C. J. Bulliet, "Artists of Chicago, Past and Present," *Chicago Daily News*, May 13, 1935. She is also discussed in Susan S. Weininger, *The "New Woman" in Chicago, 1910–1945: Paintings from Illinois Collections* (1993).

EDEN JURON PEARLMAN

BAUER, SYBIL
September 18, 1903–January 31, 1927
SWIMMING CHAMPION

Sybil Bauer won national acclaim by establishing and breaking all swimming records in the women's backstroke, in which she was never defeated. Bauer held twenty-three world records, won an Olympic gold medal, and was the first woman to break a male swimming record, before cancer claimed her short life. She was born in Chicago, the third of four children. She had two older brothers, Walter and George, and a younger sister, Dorothy. Her parents, Mr. and Mrs. Carl Bauer, were of German-Norwegian descent. The family lived in the Logan Square neighborhood on the city's Northwest Side, where Bauer attended Monroe Public School. At Carl Schurz High School, Bauer blossomed as an athlete. Earning top grades in physical education, she also distinguished herself on the girls' intramural teams. She led her team to victory in basketball, and in one baseball game scored a run each time she came up to bat. In a girls' swimming meet in 1921, she scored twenty-five of her team's total of thirty-five points. The ongoing debate among physical education and health professionals over the value of competition for women limited Bauer to such intramural events. She sought greater challenges outside the restrictive school environment, but such opportunities were limited by the prevailing views of physicians and educators that strenuous exercise was harmful to women.

In 1921 Bauer entered the Chicago River Marathon, a 1¼-mile swimming competition sponsored by the *Chicago Journal* newspaper. The surprising victory of a high school student brought Bauer to the attention of Chicagoans. She began competing for the Illinois Athletic Club (IAC), whose swim team coach, Bill Bachrach, had produced many of the country's top swimmers over the previous decade. The partnership produced immediate results. That year, Bauer twice broke Ethelda Bleibtrey's record in the 100-yard backstroke and won the Amateur Athletic Union's national championship. It proved to be the first of six successive national titles.

The following year Bauer challenged not only the swimming record but social convention as well. Her backstroke record while still in high school bettered that of the boys' interscholastic champion. Upon graduation in 1922, she traveled to Bermuda with the IAC team, where she broke Stubby Kruger's 440-yard men's record, trimming four seconds off the mark. Bauer garnered both the indoor and outdoor championships of the United States, setting three more records in the process. Such feats often met with disdain; many males, physicians, and middle-class female physical educators who eschewed the competitive female athletic model charged that such ventures harmed women's more delicate constitutions or diminished their femininity. Yet Bauer, a slim 5'6" blonde, was described as gentle, graceful, and feminine.

Bauer continued her education and her athletic success at Northwestern University, where she enrolled in the School of Speech. There she presided over the Women's Athletic Association and participated in student government and the Gamma Phi Beta sorority. She also starred in basketball, field hockey, and swimming; but the lack of formal intercollegiate competition for women forced her to seek such challenges through the IAC.

Bauer continued her record onslaught in 1923. On a summer tour of the East, she swam in three meets in New York City, drawing more than 12,000 spectators to the Starlight Park Natatorium in the Bronx in July. She did not disappoint them, setting two new records at 50 and 200 yards. She swam the backstroke "as methodically as a machine . . . without deviating a foot from her course" (*Tri-Color*, "Sybil Bauer," August 1923, 26). On a midwestern tour, another 5,000 fans turned out at De Kalb, Illinois, to watch her tie her own 50-yard record in August. By the end of the year Bauer held 17 world records in women's backstroke at distances from 50 yards to 440 yards.

Swimming for the IAC, in early 1924 Bauer continued to lower her own records. At the national championships in Miami she established seven new world records without the benefit of other competitors or even pacers, as she swam unopposed. The *New York Times*, March 9, 1924, speculated that "the discussion prior to the 1924 Olympics was whether Bauer would swim against women or men. So remarkable is her speed that she may be allowed to swim against the men contestants at the Olympic games in Paris" (quoted in Evans, 151). The issue of competition for women remained unresolved with the Olympic committee, however, and few sports were offered to women. The women's backstroke was limited to a 100-meter event. Despite poor accommodations and awkward practice schedules, Bauer won easily, setting a new world record in the trials and bettering it in the finals. After her Olympic victory Bauer toured Norway and the eastern United States, where she engaged in a series of swim meets. By the end of the year she had broken eighteen American records.

Shortly thereafter, at the national championships at St. Augustine, Florida, in February 1925, Bauer garnered her fifth straight national backstroke title, remaining undefeated during that time. She took second place in the medley, a test of all-around ability. Following the St. Augustine meet, Bauer sustained an injury when the driver of a car in which she was riding mistakenly started the vehicle while she was still alighting. The resultant fall broke both of her wrists and curtailed her swimming exploits temporarily.

By mid-year Bauer resumed her assault on the record books. Traveling to Toronto, she and Ethel Lackie, the other member of the Illinois Athletic Club's two-person women's team, both broke the Canadian records. In St. Louis, Missouri, Bauer broke the existing record for the 200-meter backstroke. When Lackie was stricken with scarlet fever, Bauer stepped in to win both the backstroke and freestyle championships at the Central Amateur Athletic Union meet at the Great Lakes Naval Base near Chicago. She followed that performance with another appearance in the Chicago River Marathon. An estimated crowd of 18,000 lined the riverbanks and watched her break her own record of 1921. She bettered the mark by more than thirty seconds in yet another victory, but it signaled the twilight of her astonishing career.

In the fall of 1926 Sybil Bauer was diagnosed with intestinal cancer. She spent three months at Chicago's Michael Reese Hospital before dying at the age of twenty-three. She was to have been married that summer to Ed Sullivan, a New York sportswriter, who later became a famous television personality. A funeral service was held at the family home and at the First Lutheran Church in Chicago. In addition to her parents, brothers, and younger sister, the entire Gamma Phi Beta sorority of Northwestern attended. The top male swimmers in America, all friends and teammates—Johnny Weissmuller, Ralph Breyer, Dick Howell, Hugo Miller, Robert Skelton, and Weston Kimball—served as pallbearers for the interment at Mount Olive Cemetery.

In 1949 a Northwestern University sportswriter declared Bauer to be that institution's most outstanding athlete of the half century. She was inducted into the International Swimming Hall of Fame in 1967, the year that it was established. She was a superstar during the 1920s, the so-called "Golden Age of Sport" in the United States, when sportswriters lionized athletic achievements. Her athletic feats challenged contemporary notions of female debility and inferiority and gave promise of opportunities for women in sport. As a star athlete Bauer was feted at banquets, entertained by socialites and dignitaries, and accorded travel opportunities similar to those of male counterparts. Bauer's accomplishments gave hope and promise to girls, who took to sport in increasing numbers during the next decade. Nevertheless, her early death fueled the ongoing, albeit unsubstantiated, controversy over the strenuous effects of competitive sports on women.

Sources. Schurz High School in Chicago maintains Bauer's personal and scholastic record, and its yearbooks, *Shurzone*, provide a partial account of her activities through her junior year. The most comprehensive and contemporary treatment of Bauer's athletic exploits is found in the Illinois Athletic Club's monthly journal of club activities, *Tri-Color* magazine, 1923–26, including "Sybil Bauer Breaks More World's Records," August 1923, housed at the CHS. Chicago newspapers of the period covered her swimming feats, and the *CT* provided coverage of the funeral in some detail over a three-day period, February 1–3, 1927. The Archives of Northwestern Univ. Library maintain a file with a few clippings, including Bob Lefley's tribute, "Tragic Hero Found in Quest for NU's Greatest Athlete," *Daily Northwestern*, February 17, 1949. Buck Dawson, *Weissmuller to Spitz . . . An Era to Remember: The First 21 Years . . . The International Swimming Hall of Fame* (1988) provides a short biographical sketch. Virginia Evans, "The Status of the American Woman in Sport, 1912–1932" (Ph.D. diss., Univ. of Massachusetts, 1982) places Bauer within the social context of the period. Jerry Bowles, *A Thousand Sundays: The Story of the Ed Sullivan Show* (1980), provides some insight into Sullivan's relationship with Bauer, but contains factual errors as to the date and place of her death.

GERALD R. GEMS

BENEDEK, THERESE FRIEDMANN
November 8, 1892–October 27, 1977
PSYCHOANALYST, PSYCHIATRIST

Therese Friedmann Benedek's work on the psychobiology of women "anticipated by thirty or forty years the current work being done on physiological correlates of emotional states" (Dr. H. P. Coppolillo interview, October 19, 1995). Her work, done with Dr. Franz Alexander of the Chicago Institute for Psychoanalysis, made a significant contribution to the field of psychosomatic medicine. Benedek joined Alexander and his staff in April 1936 and remained an active clinician and researcher with the Institute for more than forty years.

Therese Friedmann was born in Eger, Hungary, to Ignatz and Charlotte (Link) Friedmann. Her father worked as a businessman and her mother as a homemaker. She had two older siblings, a brother Soma, and a sister, Elizabeth, as well as a younger sister, Ilus. Both of her parents, Orthodox Jews, valued intellectual achievement for their children. The family lived in the town of Eger, a regional Catholic cultural center, until 1898, when they moved to Budapest.

In Budapest, Therese Friedmann began to pursue the goal of a scientific career, even though it was difficult for a girl to obtain the education that would make such a career possible. At that time, a female student had to be exceptionally talented to be admitted to a gymnasium (the equivalent of high school), and only those young women who graduated with an A average were able to enroll in medical school, Friedmann's goal. Friedmann met the requirements and began medical school at the University of Budapest in 1911, graduating with a medical degree in 1916. She was the first member of her family to obtain an advanced degree.

Friedmann's interest in psychology had its roots in her days at gymnasium, where she found that she had a talent for the subject. This skill was remarkable, because psychology and psychoanalysis, her particular focus, were just becoming established fields of study. While a student, she attended lectures of the Hungarian pioneer in psychoanalysis, Sandor Ferenczi. Friedmann was also drawn to the study of child development and children's illnesses. In medical school, along with her interest in psychology, she developed "an equally great interest in pediatrics" (Thomas G. Benedek, 7). She trained in pediatrics, working as a resident and intern in Budapest hospitals from 1916 to 1919, but soon realized that her attraction to the specialty was really an interest in "the childrens' psyche alone" (p. 7).

She had been reading the works of Sigmund Freud. "Stimulated by these and other psychoanalytic observations on children," Friedmann planned to use the clinical material that was available to her to make "systematic psychoanalytic observations on a larger scale" (Thomas G. Benedek, 7). It was in this period that she did her first analytic experiments (dream analyses on adults and analyses of children) and, in her various hospital positions, was able to observe many severely hysterical and also healthy children. She had begun to see relationships between physical and psychological findings, an approach she adopted throughout her career. She also obtained brief formal training in psychoanalysis during these years.

On April 19, 1919, Therese Friedmann married Tibor Benedek, the son of a vintner and a fellow student, who received a medical diploma a few weeks before their wedding. They had begun medical school together, but military service had delayed his graduation. She was working at Pressburg University when the town of Pressburg, then in Hungary (now Bratislava, Slovakia)—near the Czechoslovakian border—was occupied by the Czechs. Disturbed by the political instability in Pressburg and Hungary, the Benedeks relocated in Leipzig, Germany, in February 1920. Tibor Benedek secured a residency in dermatology at the University of Leipzig Medical School, and Benedek became an assistant physician at the psychiatric clinic at the same institution. Benedek focused on a psychoanalytic career and immediately perfected her German so that she could continue her clinical studies. One year later she opened a private practice in psychoanalysis and began a correspondence with Dr. Karl Abraham, the founder of the Berlin Psychoanalytic Society.

In September 1922, with Therese Benedek's leadership, a

small circle of budding psychoanalysts in Leipzig began to meet together for study and discussion of their research and clinical findings. It was one of the early psychoanalytic study groups in Europe: Sigmund Freud had founded the Vienna society in 1907, Karl Abraham the Berlin society in 1908, and Sandor Ferenczi the Budapest society in 1913. By 1923–24 the Leipzig group was established and active; Benedek was president and had given five lectures on the theory of neuroses. The group studied Freud's more recent works and was in touch with the Berlin society.

Benedek's career began to flourish. In November 1923 she presented a paper at the Berlin Psychoanalytic Society, "The Development of the Organization of Society," and Karl Abraham wrote to Freud commending her paper. The following year, December 2, she presented another paper at the Berlin society, "Notes from the Analysis of a Case of Erythrophobia," and it became her first publication (*Internationale Zeitschrift für ärztliche Psychoanalyse*, 1925). Abraham again wrote Freud, commenting on the excellence of her work: "She is of great value in her ability to attract young people as well as in her excellent practical work" (Benedek, "A Psychoanalytic Career Begins," 14). She became a member of both the German Psychoanalytic Society and the International Psychoanalytic Association, serving as a lecturer and training analyst for the former.

As Benedek's career grew, so did her family. A son, Thomas, was born in 1926, and a daughter, Judith, in 1929. During this period of her life she established a pattern that she would adhere to for years to come. She was wife and mother to her family, analyst to her patients, and researcher and teacher to colleagues and students.

Benedek began research into the interactions and correlations between physical and psychological processes in humans. This topic remained a focus of her work throughout her career. One of her earliest papers, "Mental Processes in Thyrotoxic States" (1933), explored the relationship between thyroid disease and the emotional states predictably found in the presence of the illness. During the last three years in Germany (1932–35), in addition to her work in Leipzig, she was a member of the faculty of the Berlin Psychoanalytic Institute and generally spent three days a week in Berlin.

In 1935, it became clear to Benedek and her husband that the political situation in Germany rapidly was becoming unstable. Tibor Benedek journeyed to the United States in November 1935 and visited Chicago in preparation for the family's emigration. They decided to emigrate to the United States and arrived in Chicago in April 1936. Benedek had secured a position with the Chicago Institute for Psychoanalysis, and her husband joined the faculty at the Northwestern University School of Medicine. Much of the first year for both of them was consumed with preparing to take the Illinois medical licensure examination and, especially for her, learning English. She passed her exams on the first try.

Benedek settled into her work at the Chicago Institute for Psychoanalysis, an institution whose primary goals are to provide psychoanalytic services to patients and to train therapists in psychoanalytic technique. The Institute also provides staff members a forum for conducting and sharing research. Benedek was fully involved in all facets of the Institute's mission,

teaching a number of courses to the Institute's analytic trainees and maintaining a thriving clinical practice. The analytic work with patients formed the basis for groundbreaking research in psychobiology and the psychology of women.

During these early years at the Institute, Benedek continued her work on the interaction between physical and psychological processes in human beings, particularly in women. This interest in the relationship between biological and psychological states is the focus of the field of psychosomatic medicine, a field which many late-twentieth-century researchers believe was founded, in part, upon Benedek's early research at the Institute and the work of Franz Alexander. Defined loosely, psychosomatic medicine concerns the interactions between psychological processes (thoughts, feelings, and fears, for example) and physical processes, such as hormonal activity or disease onset and progression. By the 1990s, the field was largely focused on understanding the psychological processes that may contribute to physical illness, but much of the early research sought to understand the connection between mind and body in nonpathological functioning as well. Benedek's major contribution to this field was her work on the psychology of the human sexual response, where she eventually focused on the psychological correlates of the menstrual cycle and childbirth in women.

In 1942, Benedek coauthored with Boris Rubenstein *The Sexual Cycle in Women: The Relation between Ovarian Function and Psychodynamic Processes*. She reported that women's hormonal and emotional cycles vary together in a predictable way. Benedek's data was drawn from her own patients, women that she met with daily. She recorded the thoughts, dreams, and fantasies of her patients as they emerged during the psychoanalytic sessions and then compared that emotional material with readings of hormonal levels gleaned from daily blood tests. Benedek was able to predict ovulation on the basis of emotional activity alone and reported this finding in *The Sexual Cycle and Personality* (1951).

Benedek's research on the psychobiology of women, as well as on more general issues in psychoanalysis, brought her recognition and acclaim in professional circles. In 1950 she was elected president of the Illinois Society for Personality Study, the first woman to hold this position. Benedek also served as president of the Chicago Psychoanalytic Association.

Benedek argued that traditional psychoanalytic theory did not adequately account for the behavior of women. In "The Organization of the Reproductive Drive," *International Journal of Psycho-Analysis* (1960), Benedek noted that the traditional model of the reproductive drive in human beings explained men's reproductive behavior, which essentially consisted of engaging in the procreative act. Women, she pointed out, had a much more protracted role in the reproductive process. Not only did they engage in the sexual behavior that results in conception; they carried the child during gestation, gave birth to it, and nurtured it after birth. Sexual intercourse, the act around which prior theories of reproductive behavior centered, was only the preparatory phase in Benedek's model of female sexual behavior. Traditional psychoanalytic theory, in its failure to account for differences, was limited in its ability to explain women's behavior.

Benedek's work also sought to improve upon traditional psychoanalytic theories of personality development, which postulated development ending in late adolescence, when an individual became sexually mature. Benedek's research suggested that personality development continued beyond adolescence and was spurred by the acts of conceiving, delivering, and parenting a child.

Therese Benedek was active professionally well into her eighties. As she grew older she suffered from a hearing impairment that made it difficult for her to hear in the presence of any background noise. To compensate, she continued to work with patients in quiet settings where her hearing was not disrupted. During this period of her life she also suffered the loss of her husband Tibor, who died in 1974. At age eighty-four, Benedek suffered a heart attack while in a taxi on the way home from her office. She was hospitalized at Illinois Masonic Hospital, where she died ten days later. Services were held November 6, 1977, at the Bond Chapel, University of Chicago.

Therese Benedek was a pioneer in many ways during her long career. She is perhaps best remembered as a prolific and insightful researcher, whose work on the psychobiology of women was innovative and in advance of her field. Her research on the relationship between biological processes and psychological states in human beings won her enormous respect among her colleagues and secured her place as one of the founders of the field of psychosomatic medicine. Her papers and books are still widely quoted and referenced in current psychiatric research.

Sources. The papers of Therese Benedek can be found at the Chicago Institute of Psychoanalysis; they include drafts and reprints of journal articles and book chapters, syllabi from her courses, lecture notes, case notes, data collection sheets, and personal correspondence. A full listing of Benedek's books, articles, and chapters can be found in A. Grinstein, ed., *Index of Psychoanalytic Writings* (1956–58, 1964). Among her most important books are *Insight and Personality Adjustment* (1942); with Boris Rubenstein, *Sexual Cycle in Women: The Relation between Ovarian Function and Psychodynamic Processes* (1942); edited with E. J. Anthony, *Parenthood: Its Psychology and Psychopathology* (1970). She also wrote many journal articles and book chapters, including "Toward the Biology of the Depressive Constellation," *Journal of the American Psychoanalytic Association,* July 1956; "Psychological Aspects of Pregnancy and Parent-Child Relationships," *Emotional Problems of Childhood,* ed. S. Liebman (1958); "Parenthood as a Developmental Phase: A Contribution to Libido Theory," *Journal of the American Psychoanalytic Association,* July 1959. See Therese Benedek, *Psychoanalytic Investigations: Selected Papers* (1973) for a collection of her publications from 1931 to 1968, together with accompanying discussions that place each paper in the context of the development of Benedek's research and of psychoanalysis. Recent journal articles identify Benedek's contribution to current research, including Barbara Fajardo, "Parenting a Damaged Child: Mourning, Regression, and Disappointment," *Psychoanalytic Review,* Spring 1987; Marjorie Frank and Shlomit Hoek, "Kitchen Therapy in Action," *Journal of Social Work Practice,* November 1985; and B. M. Robertson, "The Psychoanalytic Theory of Depression: I. The Major Contributors," *Canadian Journal of Psychiatry,* June 1979. Further information came from interviews conducted by Catherine Coppolillo in October 1995 with Benedek's son, Dr. Thomas G. Benedek, and with Dr. Henry Coppolillo, one of Benedek's former students at the Chicago Institute for Psychoanalysis. Benedek's obituary appears in *NYT,* October 28, 1977, and in *CT,* October 29, 1977. A useful article is Thomas G. Benedek, "A Psychoanalytic Career Begins: Therese F. Benedek, M.D.—A Documentary Biography," *Annual of Psychoanaly-*

sis, 1979, which details the early years of Benedek's career in Hungary and Germany. See also Doris Weidemann, "The Life and Work of Therese Benedek: Feminine Sexuality and the Psychology of Women" (Ph.D. diss., Univ. of Cologne, Germany, 1988).

CATHERINE M. COPPOLILLO

BENEDICT, ENELLA
December 21, 1858–April 6, 1942
ARTIST, TEACHER, SOCIAL REFORMER

Enella Benedict was an artist and a resident social reformer at Hull-House, the settlement house established in 1889 by JANE ADDAMS and ELLEN GATES STARR. Despite the constraints of being a female professional artist in a male art world, Benedict created a position of influence for herself that enabled her to bring the visual arts to a diverse population and a diverse population to the visual arts.

Benedict shared a similarity of family background with Addams and other Hull-House women reformers from white, upper-middle-class, Protestant families with politically active fathers. Her father, Amzi Benedict, was a Chicago merchant as well as a founder and mayor of the elite Lake Forest suburb. After studying at the School of the Art Institute of Chicago and in New York, Benedict traveled to France to receive a higher level of professional training, despite the isolation there of female art students, who paid higher fees and received less rigorous instruction. Returning to America, she found opportunities for artists were limited, especially for women.

The 1893 World's Columbian Exposition celebrated the four hundredth anniversary of the arrival of Columbus in North America. The specially constructed White City on Chicago's lakefront showcased the commercial and cultural progress of urban America. The Woman's Building featured arts that were rooted in domesticity, but it also reflected the conflicts that women faced in society. Women were able to emphasize their accomplishments, but only in a segregated space.

Women working in the arts in the 1890s concentrated on either the fine arts or applied art for decoration and industry. The Woman's Building featured both but limited the number of paintings and drawings in order to provide space to exhibitors from foreign countries. Therefore, many American women artists exhibited in either the state buildings or in the Palace of Fine Arts. In one of the seventy-four galleries of the Palace of Fine Arts, Illinois women artists displayed two hundred juried selections. One contemporary described Benedict's picture *Counting the Ships:* "a Dutch peasant girl sits on a rocky promontory, wistfully looking out to sea. Her blue dress against the grey of the rocks produces a pretty color note. Miss Benedict is a draughtswoman of great promise. She also uses pigment with judgment. It will be remembered *The Singing Spinner* by this artist was awarded the first prize at the fifth annual black-and-white exhibition of the Chicago Society of Artists" (Cameron, 298–99). When Benedict created the image of a Dutch peasant child looking out to sea, it is likely that she did not realize that in her own life she would help many poor European immigrants to learn to see the world differently and to expand their horizons.

Besides exhibits, a series of congresses during the exposition addressed social issues as well as women's work and progress.

Jane Addams spoke about the double burden of working-class women in factories and the household. The shared life in Hull-House freed women from the claims of family life and the demands of housekeeping while offering them a supportive and creative setting in which to pursue their goals. During the World's Columbian Exposition, Benedict became a resident of the Hull-House settlement, taught fall classes there, and became the director of the studio arts program.

Hull-House cofounders Addams and Starr shared with Benedict a vision of the interdependence of art and society and of the role of the arts in improving the lives of the urban poor while renewing the dignity of labor. Benedict met Addams in early 1889, shortly after Addams arrived in Chicago to promote the "scheme" that would become the famous settlement house. They lived in the same rooming house across from Washington Square Park, north of the central business district. After the two attended meetings, went calling, and attended a Bible class together, Addams wrote to a relative that "dear Miss Benedict is very good to me. Ellen [Gates Starr] insists that we are positively intimate" (February 12, 1889, Jane Addams to Mary Catherine Addams Linn, Jane Addams Collection, Swarthmore College Peace Collection). Later Addams often gave Benedict's works as gifts to friends and relatives.

From the beginning, Hull-House maintained an art studio. Benedict was delighted with the models there and traveled weekly to the settlement house to paint. Starr promoted the arts at Hull-House through lectures and exhibits, for "the hungry individual soul which without art will have passed unsolaced and unfed, followed by other souls who lack the impulse this should have given" (quoted in Addams, 372). Hull-House was an art center in social reform, preserving art and extending it to everyone. Before the end of the second year, a new building with an art gallery and studio provided better accommodations for artists and attracted many neighbors to view the loaned artwork in the first permanent art gallery in an industrial quarter.

While Starr became a leader in the Chicago Arts and Crafts Society and an active craftswoman, Benedict applied many of the same concepts of art's uplifting power to the studio arts. Under Benedict's leadership, the Hull-House art studios expanded and changed to meet the needs of a changing neighborhood and to appeal to all age groups. A number of teachers, including sculptor Lorado Taft from the School of the Art Institute of Chicago, taught during the initial years of the settlement house. When Benedict became a resident and developed the studio art department, she taught drawing, painting, and clay modeling, and she sought to bring in other teachers and artists-in-residence. She taught drawing, painting, and anatomy at the School of the Art Institute of Chicago in the morning and then attended to her duties at Hull-House. From the 1890s to the 1920s, Benedict served as an important link between the Art Institute of Chicago and the Hull-House art studio as she brought professionals to the industrial neighborhood and encouraged talented locals to continue their education at the museum's school. While the Art Institute gave students a program that integrated school and museum activities, Hull-House provided a program that integrated the art studio into neighborhood activities. Both sites stressed the importance of exhibiting the works of masters and students.

During the first twenty years, the art studio moved three times within the complex; in 1910 it occupied the entire top floor of the Smith Building, just north of the original Hull-House mansion. After years of working by gas light, the artists were delighted to have natural lighting from above. The studio was open day and evening for painting and printmaking as well as for classes, lectures, demonstrations, and exhibitions. By World War I, linoleum printing, etching, lithography, freehand and mechanical drawing, lettering, and cast and model drawing enhanced the curriculum. Two Hull-House programs emerged from the art studio: the Hull-House Art School for children and the Hull-House Kilns. A systematic program of advancement exposed children to a variety of media, starting in beginner classes for the very young to more advanced classes in technique and composition for the older children. A pottery program in the art studio appealed to older children and especially to potters from the Mexican population of the neighborhood.

In the 1920s, many commercial artists worked under Benedict in the studios. Many of the students and artists-in-residence also became noted painters in Chicago while teaching and exhibiting at Hull-House; they included Emily Edwards, Michael Gamboni, Sadie Ellis, Leon Garland, William Jacobs, Norah Hamilton, William Savin, and Morris Topchevsky. On Tuesday and Thursday evenings live models posed, and any artist in the city was welcome to work in the studio for a contribution. Benedict was especially proud that in America there was "probably no other life class where anyone can go paying 15 cents each time" (August 13, 1931, Enella Benedict to Jane Addams, Jane Addams Collection, Swarthmore College Peace Collection). Benedict brought books, magazines, pictures, and reproductions to the studio to share. The studio atmosphere offered each artist an opportunity to find self-expression while exchanging ideas with other artists. The art studio had become a center for creative aesthetic work, not just a site for art instruction.

The walls of Hull-House's art departments displayed work that was "helpful to the life and mind and soul" (Hull-House Scrapbook, 1889–1894). By 1900, in the Labor Museum at Hull-House, Benedict's colored sketches of workers in the northern Michigan copper foundries, hung in the metal department, portrayed the artistic dimension, while the textile department displayed her sketches of North Carolina mountaineers shearing and spinning. Benedict traveled summers throughout the United States and Europe, but most often to her summer cottage in Westport Point, Massachusetts. On her return to Chicago, she exhibited the results of her summer's work and held a homecoming tea at the Hull-House art studio. Her oil paintings were impressionistic in style, and the subjects ranged from rural to urban settings and neighborhood scenes, still lifes, and portraiture. Her drawings, pastels, and watercolors were more realist in style and featured portraits and Chicago views. Whether tired workers walking home in grey silence, a proud immigrant mother holding her newborn, or a farm wife gazing through an open door, her renderings offered the imagination powerful stories.

Her teachers in Paris, Jean-Paul Laurens, Jules Lefebvre, and Benjamin Constant, were realists—fine draughtsmen and colorists who produced historical works and portraits. As realists, they instilled in Benedict a style of precision but also a philosophy of the relevance of art to the social, political, and economic events of the time. Benedict took the concept of realism as a moral art and applied it to her teaching and artwork, creating her own realism appropriate to urban, industrial America. She exhibited seascapes and rural landscapes at Hull-House. She showed over forty different works at the Art Institute of Chicago in the *Chicago and Vicinity* and *Watercolors by American Artists* shows. She exposed Chicagoans of different cultural backgrounds to images beyond their experience and helped them see familiar views from a new perspective and to find beauty in everyday life. She portrayed both public and private space, taken from everyday life.

As a Hull-House resident, Benedict had additional obligations that ranged from overseeing the front door and gymnasium to giving stereopticon lectures to serving as banker of the Provident Penny Bank savings plan. She beautified the quadrangle, worked on mapping, and helped with sets and costumes for plays, dances, and the Christmas Cantata. An avid reader, she opened a library in the Clubhouse and guided children's reading. She had a reputation for diligent and dedicated work. Once she asked the dining room to provide "for numerous bills of fare that our palates may be tickled with more varied substances and concoctions" ("Residents Minutes," January 7, 1895). Her room in the Women's Quarters on the second floor of the original Hull-House building was simply furnished. In later years, she moved to a studio on the Boys' Club roof. After Addams died in 1935, Benedict became the resident storyteller, telling tales of Addams and the early years at Hull-House.

During the Great Depression and after Jane Addams's death, Hull-House suffered from a loss of residents and participants as well as from reduced finances. The Art School Committee asked the Hull-House Board of Trustees for support rather than face the elimination of the programs. Benedict traveled to Mexico to persuade Emily Edwards to return to Hull-House as the art department head and to reorganize and expand the Hull-House Art Center and Design Workshops. In May 1938, Hull-House opened a new permanent art gallery on its main floor with a retrospective exhibition of Benedict's paintings. Named in her honor, the Benedict Gallery was lost with the demolition of the Hull-House complex in the mid-1960s.

Benedict lived continuously as a Hull-House resident longer than anyone except Addams. She was patient, warm-hearted, broad-minded, principled, and often rather frank. As "one of the chief art mentors at Hull-House for nearly a half century" (*Hull-House Yearbook*, 1939), she encouraged artists to find their own self-expression even if it differed from her traditional approach. *The Chicago Evening American*, in a review of Hull-House's fortieth anniversary art exhibition, noted, "That most of the names connote an association with advanced methods in painting is a fact of further interest, pointing to Hull-House as perhaps the fountainhead of the modernist movement in Chicago" (Hull-House Scrapbook, May 1930). As a Hull-House pioneer and founder of many of its fine arts programs, Benedict worked in community with other women reformers to create new careers and visions for themselves and the urban poor. The 1893 World's Columbian Exposition provided a model for urban planning amidst urban decay. Hull-House offered a living model for urban self-help that continued throughout the twen-

tieth century, and Benedict's lifework provided the pattern for connecting people with the aesthetic arts and with each other. After a funeral service in Benedict Gallery, she was buried in Rosehill Cemetery just a short distance from the grave and statue of Charles Hull, whose Halsted Street mansion served as her home and as a center for the arts and for hope in the slums of the 19th Ward of Chicago.

Sources. Benedict's life at Hull-House is documented in the Jane Addams Memorial Collection, UIC Spec. Coll., through *Hull-House Bulletins, Hull-House Yearbooks*, newsletters, minutes, scrapbooks, and letters. The Lake Forest–Lake Bluff Historical Society has information on her family background. Jane Addams's correspondence is available in the Jane Addams Collection, Swarthmore College Peace Collection. The CHS, the Hull-House Museum, the National Museum of Women in the Arts, and the Ryerson Library of the Art Institute of Chicago contain documentation on Benedict's artistic and teaching career. Publications on Hull-House include Jane Addams, *Twenty Years at Hull-House* (1910); Allen F. Davis and Mary Lynn McCree, *Eighty Years at Hull-House* (1969); and Kathryn Kish Sklar, "Hull House in the 1890s: A Community of Women Reformers," *Signs*, Summer 1985. Information on Benedict's art career is in William E. Cameron, *The World's Fair, Being a Pictorial History of the Columbian Exposition: Containing a Complete History of the World-Renowned Exposition at Chicago* (1893), and Peter Hastings Falk, *The Annual Exhibition Record of the Art Institute of Chicago, 1888–1950* (1990).

CHERYL R. GANZ

BENNETT, BESSIE
March 7, 1870–March 23, 1939
MUSEUM CURATOR, ARTIST, TEACHER, PHILANTHROPIST

Bessie Bennett was one of the most energetic women of Chicago's art world during the first half of the twentieth century. She put her stamp on the local arts and crafts scene, was the first woman to become curator at the Art Institute of Chicago, guided the development of its important decorative arts collections, as well as those of private collectors, and transformed the practice and methods of exhibition design in museums nationwide.

Bennett was born to a prestigious and affluent Cincinnati, Ohio, family. She was the second of five children and the first of two daughters of Augustus Alexander and Delia (Gurley) Bennett. On May 21, 1867, Augustus Bennett, a prosperous firearms dealer in Cincinnati, had married Delia Susan Gurley, whose father was a preacher, newspaper publisher, colonel in the U.S. Army, and finally a politician, serving two terms (1858–62) in Congress from Ohio's second district.

Little more is known about Bessie Bennett's childhood, except that she attended school in Cincinnati and Boston. In the summer of 1895, at the age of twenty-five, Bessie Bennett with her twenty-one-year-old brother, Augustus A. Bennett, moved to Chicago. Augustus led a fairly unheralded life as an electrician who occasionally assisted his sister in the manufacturing of her jewelry designs. Their mother, once widowed, left Cincinnati around 1910 and spent the last years of her life with her children in Chicago.

Bessie Bennett attended the School of the Art Institute of Chicago (SAIC) where, in September 1895, she enrolled in the design curriculum of Louis J. Millet, the New York-born nephew of the great French painter Jean-Francois Millet. Louis Millet's influence on Bessie Bennett was immense. Millet had received his architecture and design education at the École des Beaux-Arts in Paris. He formed a partnership with one of his fellow students, George L. Healy, son of portrait painter George P. A. Healy. In the 1880s and 1890s, their interior decorating and design firm became one of the most celebrated Chicago crafts companies, specializing in stained glass, glass mosaics, ornamental tiles, and frescoes.

Millet's courses in decorative design were conducted in a studio setting, five days a week, six hours per day, allowing for highly individualized instruction geared toward preparing graduates for careers as professional designers in one of Chicago's many manufacturing industries. Millet's courses differed from those offered in most art schools.

On June 17, 1898, Bessie Bennett graduated first in her class from SAIC with a certificate in decorative design. Several of Bennett's fellow students gained national renown: CLARA WELLES, founder and owner of the Kalo Shop in Chicago; Clara C. Finn, Hope McMaster, and Margery Woodworth of the Tre'O Shop in Evanston; and George Mann Niedecken of the interior design firm Niedecken-Walbridge. Niedecken designed and manufactured interior furnishings for a dozen of Frank Lloyd Wright's commissions, including the Coonley House and the Robie House.

A few months after Bennett completed her studies, the Art Institute of Chicago (AIC) received a large monetary gift from art patron and museum trustee Martin Ryerson for the construction of a new library for the museum and school. For the first time in the institution's history, a full-time librarian, Jessie Forrester, was hired. Bennett was appointed part-time assistant librarian, combining the post with another newly created part-time position, exhibition clerk in the office of the museum's director. Bennett also lectured on decorative design to the students of SAIC's Normal Department, a training program for art teachers.

Over the next few years, Bennett's responsibilities and duties toward the library diminished. By 1906 she was the assistant of museum director William French, entrusted with the administration and direction of all temporary exhibition and permanent collection matters. Bennett continued to teach decorative design until 1912. LAURA VAN PAPPELENDAM was one of Bennett's students who became a successful artist and an influential teacher at SAIC from 1909 to 1959.

Outside the museum and school, Bennett attained modest fame and success as a jewelry designer. She participated in every AIC arts and crafts exhibition between 1902 and 1915, winning the medal for best piece of local craftswork, a copper buckle, in 1907. Bennett designed a variety of jewelry pieces such as hair pins, brooches, necklaces, rings, combs, as well as ornamental lamps, trophy cups, crosses, and silk weavings. She occasionally executed her designs herself but more often had them manufactured by specialized craftspeople: in 1902 Augustus A. Bennett; from 1902 to 1908, Juergens & Anderson; and from 1909 to 1914, Essie Myers.

Bessie Bennett was frequently referred to as "General Curator" of AIC. The Board of Trustees formally awarded her the title Curator of Decorative Arts on December 15, 1914. During her nearly twenty-five-year tenure, Bennett dedicated her time to furthering the cause of decorative arts in the museum. She directed numerous special exhibitions, oversaw the expansion of the collection of decorative art and the enlargement of the exhibition space, and publicized the work of midwestern artists and artisans.

Bennett wrote for the *Bulletin of the Art Institute of Chicago*, presenting new major acquisitions to the museum's membership and highlighting key pieces in the collections. Bennett contributed to the *Sketch Book*, first published on February 20, 1902, a monthly magazine of literary and artistic contributions from students, alumni, and SAIC faculty. Bennett was a frequent contributor in 1902 and 1903, describing the arts and crafts scene in Chicago and writing a series of biographies, "Western Artists," profiling Charles Francis Browne, Albert Fleury, Louis Millet, and Frederick Richardson.

From 1905, efforts were made to expand the *Sketch Book*'s readership to students in every art school in the country, and in the process, the concentrated focus on the local Chicago art scene ended. As the Chicago emphasis diminished, so did Bennett's contributions. The *Sketch Book* folded after the 1907 December issue.

Another approach by Bennett to drawing more attention to the craftspeople and designers of the West was the formation of an alumni association of Louis Millet's design students. Called the Alumni Association of Designers, their first meeting took place May 15, 1902, and Bessie Bennett was elected secretary and treasurer. From December 16, 1902, to January 11, 1903, the Alumni Association of Designers staged an extensive exhibition at AIC, *The First Annual Exhibition of Original Designs for Decorations and Examples of Art Crafts Having Distinct Artistic Merit*. Invitations to participate were circulated nationwide, and the response was overwhelming.

Individual decorative designers, craftsmen, and craftswomen exhibited pieces alongside works produced by commercial companies such as Tiffany, Rookwood, and Teco. The inclusion of the companies was controversial; critics acknowledged that the exhibit was "varied and diversified" but felt that the presence of commercially produced articles "virtually [made] the Art Institute an agency for private retail concerns" ("Gleenings from American Art Centers," 311) and the galleries, since pieces were for sale, salesrooms. The arts and crafts show, which later became an arts and crafts exhibition, was so popular, however, that AIC Director William J. French made it an annual event organized under the auspices of the museum.

One of Bessie Bennett's contributions as museum curator was to deviate from the standard museum practice of using neutral, white walls, instead installing exhibitions of paintings, sculpture, and decorative arts in rooms with different wall backgrounds. She varied scale, color, and texture from room to room, depending on the nature of the items on display. For instance, black and white paneling was used to dramatize the visual effect of a 1915 exhibition on lace. In an adjoining room, blue textiles and orange terra cotta were displayed against a checkered backdrop of orange and blue. Old manuscript books and illuminations were installed in a cool gray room. Bennett's intent was to make each room a unit of design.

Bennett traveled extensively in Europe and on the East Coast to visit museums, study their decorative arts collections, and observe various display and lighting techniques. An eloquent speaker, she also took numerous trips throughout the Midwest, rarely declining an invitation to speak. She gave countless lectures to art students, art craft clubs, women's clubs, and other organizations on a wide variety of subjects such as "Industrial Art in the United States," "Color in Household Decoration," "Historical Silver," and "The Ancient Art of Weaving." In addition to organizing and installing numerous exhibitions, Bennett also sat on the selection juries of dozens of shows that were staged at AIC by organizations such as the Chicago Ceramic Art Association, the National League of Mineral Painters, and the Atlan Ceramic Art Club. Bennett continued to organize, install, and promote these annual arts and crafts shows until 1925, when the *Applied Arts 23rd Annual* was held as the last event of this series.

After 1925 Bennett concentrated her efforts mainly on developing and attracting large-scale thematic exhibitions. In 1927 Bennett arranged an outstanding exhibition of Swedish decorative arts at AIC, which resulted in a better understanding in the United States of the Swedish fine arts in general. On December 28, 1928, King Gustav V of Sweden presented Bennett with the Golden Wasa Medal, one of the highest possible distinctions given to a non-Swedish national. During World War I she curated an exhibit on French design and was decorated in 1919 by the French government for her efforts to promote French design and decorative arts.

Robert Harshe, director of AIC between 1921 and 1938, did not entirely share Bessie Bennett's passion for decorative arts. He also found Bennett's limited formal academic training problematic, although he acknowledged and respected her unusual talent for designing and installing exhibitions. At an annual meeting of the governing members, where the director introduced each department head to give a report of accomplishments, he referred to Bennett as "the lady curator of everything, the person who could put a dishrag on display and make it look like a museum piece . . . and often does" (Zolberg, 25).

During her thirty-nine-year career at the Art Institute—a tenure that spanned five directorships—Bennett relentlessly sought to add to the museum's decorative arts collections as well as to increase the exhibition space reserved for them. The new Allerton Wing, exclusively built for the Decorative Arts Department, was nearing completion at the time of Bennett's death in 1939. With the addition of the new wing, approximately one-third of the museum's floor space was occupied by decorative arts exhibits. The current collections of European Decorative Art, Textiles, African and Amerindian Arts, and a portion of American Arts found their origin in Bessie Bennett's Decorative Arts Department.

Robert Allerton was a prime example of a wealthy art patron whose interest, taste, and generosity were influenced by Bessie Bennett. Raised in wealthy surroundings, Bennett moved comfortably in Chicago's elite social and financial circles, developing connections and striking up friendships with famous collectors such as KATE BUCKINGHAM, Martin Ryerson, and Robert Allerton. They sought Bennett's advice and expertise in developing and expanding their own personal art collections.

Gradually, most of these private collections were donated to AIC through bequests or outright gifts. Martin Ryerson gave hundreds of objects to the museum, ranging from Renaissance furniture to French stained glass and Italian and Dutch faience—earthenware with colored opaque glazes.

Bennett's influence was also evident in her involvement with the Antiquarian Society, a group of elite women with a shared interest in decorative arts that predated the establishment of AIC. Gradually, the society evolved into a support group for the Art Institute's American Arts and Decorative Arts departments. Though not officially a member of this society, Bessie Bennett was the guiding force behind it for nearly three decades. She advised the leadership and convinced its members to provide funding for numerous AIC acquisitions of decorative art objects.

In 1924, Bennett made her first financial contribution and donation of art objects to the Art Institute. By 1927 she was named a benefactor to the museum, when she donated securities valued at twenty-five thousand dollars. In her will she bequeathed money to AIC for the establishment of the Bessie Bennett Fund, the income of which was earmarked for decorative arts acquisitions. The museum made its first purchase in 1942, a Queen Ann side table, and over the next half century, forty-three pieces followed.

Bessie Bennett suffered a stroke, collapsed, and died instantly after a meeting with the president of the Antiquarian Society. Funeral services were held in a chapel on Stony Island Avenue in Chicago's South Shore community, where she had lived with her brother Augustus. She was interred at the Spring Grove Cemetery in her birthplace, Cincinnati, Ohio. On April 19, 1939, a memorial service was held, appropriately in the decorative art galleries of the Art Institute by the museum administration and the Antiquarian Society, honoring her nearly four decades of long association with the institution.

Bessie Bennett was a transitional figure in a period of rapid growth for the Art Institute of Chicago. When she first arrived at AIC, all curatorial, registration, public relations, and educational tasks were the responsibility of director William R. French and his one-room administration. By 1939 AIC's workplace had grown to several hundred employees, with five curatorial departments and separate offices for museum registration, public affairs, education, and publications. Bessie Bennett was the museum's last stereotypical connoisseur-curator of the late nineteenth and early twentieth centuries, an individual with an artistic background and limited academic credentials who was largely a self-taught generalist motivated to educate the public and who supported wealthy and socially prominent patrons through personal relationships. She was at the same time the first female upper-level professional at the museum, an example to other women who were gradually moving into positions of responsibility in Chicago's cultural institutions.

Sources. Bessie Bennett's family history can be reconstructed through genealogical records at NL. Cincinnati census data and Chicago city directories provide further personal data. Information on Bessie Bennett is found in several collections at the Art Institute of Chicago. The institutional archives contain Bennett's curatorial papers, which include a limited amount of business correspondence, in-house memos, and exhibition information. Her gradual rise in the museum's hierarchy can be traced in the correspondence of the director's office, the minutes of the board of trustees meetings, museum catalogs, bulletins and press releases, annual reports, school prospectuses, and faculty personnel files. Information on the Bessie Bennett fund and Bennett's influence on several Chicago collectors lies in the archival records of the development office, office of the secretary of the corporation, and the museum registrar's files. Annual reports and minutes in the Antiquarian Society Papers document the role she played for the organization. The Ryerson Library of the Art Institute has a full run of the little-known serial publication, *Sketch Book*, which reveals details on Bessie Bennett's concurrent careers as jewelry designer, librarian, teacher, and administrator. Periodic press coverage of Bennett's exhibitions, lectures, and other activities is located in the *Scrapbooks on Art and Artists in Chicago*, which also contain her obituaries. Sharon Darling's *Chicago Metalsmiths* (1977) and *Chicago Ceramics and Glass* (1979) provide information on the art scene in Chicago during Bennett's time. "Gleanings from American Art Centers," *Brush and Pencil*, January 1903, describes the first annual exhibition of art crafts at the Art Institute of Chicago. Vera Zolberg's "The Art Institute of Chicago: The Sociology of a Cultural Organization" (Ph.D. diss., Univ. of Chicago, 1974) offers valuable insight into various social dynamics and how they affected the museum's evolution. Polly Ulrich's "Women in the Arts and Crafts Movement of Chicago: 1877–1915" (master's thesis, School of the Art Institute of Chicago, 1994) has a refreshing perspective, although it contains some factual inaccuracies. Bruce Robert Kahler's "Art and Life: The Arts and Crafts Movement in Chicago, 1897–1910" (Ph.D. diss., Purdue Univ., 1986) succinctly describes Bennett's environment and her influence and provides a thorough philosophical and art historical framework.

BART H. RYCKBOSCH

BEST, MARJORIE AYRES
August 20, 1874–February 12, 1942
FOUNDER, ADMINISTRATOR OF AMATEUR DRAMA LEAGUE

The Drama League of America deserves credit as the major force, from 1910 to 1930, in generating popular enthusiasm for amateur theater in America. The organization was developed by an ingenious Evanston, Illinois, woman, Marjorie Ayres Best.

The Drama League of America was the brainchild of a women's amateur drama club, the Riley Circle, founded in 1901 in Alice C. D. Riley's Evanston home. For almost twenty years its women members met regularly as the Drama Club of Evanston to study plays and sponsor theater projects in their community. In April 1910, the group called a conference of representatives of similar women's drama clubs in the Midwest to create the Drama League of America. This influential organization was originally conceived as a means to make social change through uplifting drama, to educate the general public to the importance of theater, and to lobby for higher standards of commercial theater. Marjorie Best's organizational talents helped to launch this significant theater network, which was instrumental in shaping national attitudes about the theater in the era from 1910 to 1930. Although Riley inspired the founding of the Drama League, she quickly retired to serve in minor roles. Leadership fell to Marjorie Ayres Best, who directed the association for the entirety of its twenty-year history. Marjorie Ayres was born in Truro, Cape Cod, Massachusetts, the daughter of oil magnate Marshall Ayres and Louise (Lombard) Ayres. She spent most of her first twenty-five years in New York City, educated by governesses and at private schools and summering on Long Is-

land. At the age of sixteen, she entered Smith College, where she became active in extracurricular drama productions. She graduated in 1895. The next year she married Albert Starr Best, grandson of the founder of Best Department Store in New York and himself the founder of A. Starr Best Department Store in Chicago. They raised two sons, Marshall and Albert, and two daughters, Marjorie and Barbara, in Evanston, Illinois.

In the capacity of acting president of the Drama Club of Evanston, Best hosted the 1910 conference of theater clubs in Chicago that culminated in the creation of the Drama League of America. The new organization's mission was twofold: to stimulate an interest in good drama and to enlighten the American public to the social and educational value of high level, moral, dramatic art. Best served as the first president of the Drama League of America from 1910 to 1914 and built the organization rapidly. Representatives from sixty-three existing drama societies, with a membership of ten thousand, had attended the founding convention. Within a year and a half, the league had attracted twenty thousand members in thirty-five states. By 1913, eighty thousand members had joined; by 1914, ninety thousand; and by 1915, membership peaked at one hundred thousand.

Believing women to be more naturally sympathetic toward the arts, Best felt it necessary to put special efforts into attracting male membership to the organization. She succeeded in awarding the Drama League presidency to a succession of men from 1914 to 1930, including Dr. Richard Burton, Percival Chubb, and Francis Nielson. These celebrities in the popular theater movement reigned only as figureheads and left Best to serve as the power behind the throne. Their presence, however, misrepresented the steady volunteer labor that women offered in keeping the organization growing, vital, and responsive to American theater needs.

Although she never officially served as president after 1914, Best supervised the league's growth and development until the organization folded in 1931. In its initial stages, Best publicized the goals of the Drama League of America and invited its natural allies, women's literary and civic clubs, to embrace theater projects. To do so, she spoke before the biennial conference of the General Federation of Women's Clubs in 1910 and before conventions of many other women's organizations. She initiated the *Drama Quarterly* in 1911 (later changing the title to *Drama Monthly*, 1919, and finally to *Drama Magazine*, 1931). The periodical, initially edited by Theodore B. Hinckley, became a regular publication of the league. Best hosted national conventions of her organization in Chicago in 1912 and 1921, and in Evanston, Illinois, in 1922.

Best shaped the Drama League into a national alliance of local drama league circles or chapters, based in Chicago. Each chapter provided bulletins evaluating the quality of local theatrical productions available through professional touring companies and publicized the results through public libraries, clubs, and neighborhood centers.

Soon, as the scope of the organization widened to include the nurturing of amateur theater companies, local chapters drew on new resources developed at the national office in Chicago. The Drama League headquarters sponsored and disseminated bibliographies about theater topics for study clubs. The league held annual conventions to acquaint little theater groups with modern trends in community drama. It held competitions and awarded prizes for new plays; sponsored the publication of plays with Samuel French, a New York publisher; and offered theater tours to Europe. The league also supported a bureau that served as a clearinghouse for theater questions, even providing advice, patterns, and seamstresses for difficult costumes.

In summer 1917, the Drama League created the Children's Civic Theater on Chicago's Municipal Pier, a lively drama program that lasted into the 1920s. The league assisted amateur theater groups in celebrating the Shakespeare Tercentenary of 1916 and the Pilgrim Tercentenary of 1920 with celebratory theatrical productions.

Best herself was active in state and national Young Women's Christian Association (YWCA) volunteer work, Liberty Bond drives during World War I, and theater education. She was an avid gardener, golfer, and horsewoman. She took special interest in religious drama and in 1916 founded both the Pilgrim Players and the Junior Pilgrim Players at the Evanston Congregational Church. She also lectured on religious drama at the Garrett-Evangelical Theological Seminary, Evanston, Illinois, and taught religious drama at the Drama League's Summer Institute in Chicago in the 1920s.

The Drama League of America succeeded in inspiring countless community theater clubs to produce plays with and for local neighborhoods. By the 1930s, however, many forces conspired to eliminate the league. There were fund-raising problems. Additionally, many secular theater clubs objected to the league's alliance with a religious theater organization. There were also the allure of radio and movies and the desire of member clubs for more autonomy in their activities. After 1931, only the New York Drama League circle, with connections to a vital professional theater world, remained; it was still operating in the 1990s.

Best suffered a stroke in 1933 soon after the breakdown of the Drama League of America. She died nine years later and left instructions for her ashes to be scattered over Lake Michigan. Her husband's headstone commemorates her at Dutchess County Community Cemetery in Pine Plains, New York.

For two decades Marjorie Best's Drama League of America provided leadership, focus, and practical assistance in support of the general public's enthusiasm for amateur dramatics and the call for higher standards in the quality of professional theatrical offerings.

Sources. A small collection of Marjorie Best materials can be found at the Evanston Hist. Soc. Marjorie Best wrote "Echoes," *Drama,* June–August 1922; "Drama League of America, 1914," *Drama,* February 1914; "Drama League of America," in the *Biennial Report of the General Federation of Women's Clubs* (1910); and "A Decade of Experiences in Religious Drama," *Drama,* November 1929. See Genevieve Wheeler Simpson, "Mrs. A. Starr Best," *Our Congregational Heritage* (1976), and Marjorie Starr Best (Mrs. Stuart) Abby, "Mrs. A. Starr Best, 1874–1942," in *Program of Dedication of the Women's Terrace of Ladd Arboretum* (1976). Christopher Wenn Craig, "Drama League of America: Its Conception, History, and Contribution to the American Theater, 1909–1931" (master's thesis, Univ. of California, Los Angeles, 1965), is pertinent, as is chapter 6 in Karen J. Blair, *The Torchbearers: Women and Their Amateur Arts Associations in America, 1890–1930* (1994).

KAREN J. BLAIR

BEY, CORNELIA BERNARDA DE. *See* **DE BEY, CORNELIA BERNARDA**

BIESEL, FRANCES STRAIN. *See* **STRAIN BIESEL, FRANCES**

BINFORD, JESSIE FLORENCE
January 20, 1876–July 9, 1966
CHILDREN'S ADVOCATE, SETTLEMENT HOUSE RESIDENT, COMMUNITY ACTIVIST

Hull-House resident and advocate for children's welfare Jessie Florence Binford was born in Marshalltown, Iowa, the daughter of Thaddeus and Angie (Beasley) Binford. Her father, a successful attorney, was the son of an Ohio Quaker, although the family belonged to the Methodist Church and Binford remained a Methodist throughout her life. While Binford was in high school, JANE ADDAMS came to Marshalltown to lecture on her work at Hull-House in Chicago. She spent the night with the Binford family. Young Jessie Binford remembered how "after the lecture she sat in our living room and talked about the children in Chicago's streets. . . . Before she left I knew what I wanted to do with my life" (Detzer, n.p.).

Binford graduated from high school in 1893, and in the fall enrolled at Rockford College, Jane Addams's alma mater, in Rockford, Illinois. There she was editor of the college's monthly magazine. She spent her sophomore year (1895–1896) at Smith College, Northampton, Massachusetts, returning to Rockford to graduate in the spring of 1898. After graduation, Binford returned to Marshalltown, where she did volunteer work with needy children, went on two grand tours of Europe, and spent her summers volunteering at Hull-House in Chicago. In 1902 Binford moved into Hull-House and became a full-time resident; she lived there until 1963.

During her first days as a resident at Hull-House, Binford asked Jane Addams what she should do to help. Addams told her, "Don't do anything for a while. Just get acquainted and look around. Maybe you will see things to be done which none of us have thought of" ("Acceptance of Citation," n.p., Binford Papers). Soon after, the police brought a confused girl they had found wandering on the streets to Hull-House for protection. Following up on something the girl said, Binford visited the state prison at Joliet in an attempt to locate the girl's father. The visit launched her lifelong concern for "children and youth and adults . . . who go through our police stations, jails, courts, prisons, and reformatoria" ("Acceptance of Citation").

In the summer of 1904, Binford assisted Hull-House resident and physician ALICE HAMILTON in an investigation into the sale of cocaine to young boys in the surrounding neighborhood. Hamilton directed the investigation, while Binford gathered evidence. Binford subsequently became director of a new outpost of the Legal Aid Society, established at Hull-House in 1906, where she worked to suppress cocaine traffic in the neighborhood. Her experiences awakened her to the potential of citizen action in controlling social conditions that were hazardous to and exploitative of youth.

In 1907 a Hull-House district branch of the newly established Juvenile Protective League was organized with Binford as secretary. The Juvenile Protective League's goal was to prevent

FIG. 12. *Juvenile Protective Agency director and longtime Hull-House resident Jessie Florence Binford at work in 1951.*

dependency and delinquency of children. An extension of the work of the Cook County Juvenile Court (established in Chicago in 1899), its strategy was to remove those conditions that harm children and to foster those institutions, conditions, and agencies that support a nurturing environment for children. Binford was the first special investigator of community relations of the league and served as protective officer of the Hull-House district for seven years. In 1909 the agency was reorganized and its name changed to Juvenile Protective Association (JPA). A permanent location for the association was established at Hull-House with LOUISE deKOVEN BOWEN as president of its expanded twenty-seven member board. The Juvenile Psychopathic Institute, the world's first child guidance clinic, financed by ETHEL STURGES DUMMER, was also created in 1909 to support the work of the Juvenile Court and the JPA.

From 1911 to 1916 Binford and the JPA fought for the establishment of specialized courts to serve specific groups of offenders in Chicago. This effort resulted in the Court of Domestic Relations, 1911; Boys' Court, 1914; and Morals Court (later called Women's Court), 1916. A JPA study, "What Should Be Done for Chicago's Women Offenders" (1916), recommended a central detention center for women and a state reformatory for

women. Binford and her backers fought for and won a police-women's division and specially trained officers to handle juvenile cases. Binford rose in the JPA ranks, serving first as assistant superintendent and then acting superintendent, succeeding Amelia Sears, who had served as superintendent of JPA from 1914 to 1916. Binford was appointed general superintendent (executive director) in November 1916, a position she held until her retirement in 1952.

During World War I, Binford's work focused primarily on the newly emerging field of social hygiene. In 1917 she supervised the central district of the national Committee on Protective Work with Girls, organizing girls' protective bureaus near military encampments and the Girl's Protective Bureau in Chicago. In 1918 she became the midwest district supervisor for the United States Interdepartmental Social Hygiene Board, whose purpose was to support uplift and reformative work with women. In 1919 Binford urged the Juvenile Protective Association formally to take up protective work with girls in Chicago—against Louise deKoven Bowen's wishes—and during this period regarded the protection, reformation, and rehabilitation of wayward girls a primary responsibility of the agency and her work. Bowen had focused on child protective casework rather than social hygiene issues among young adults. Binford pulled the JPA in the direction of the latter, while dealing with the heavy burden of casework the former still required.

During the 1920s Binford organized a series of investigations of vice conditions in Chicago, with special emphasis on roadhouses and white slavery, that is, the luring of young women into prostitution. The findings alarmed Bowen, who became more supportive of Binford's concerns with vice and social hygiene issues. In a 1922 survey of prostitution in the city, Binford cooperated with the U.S. Social Hygiene Board to prepare and submit a report to a special grand jury impaneled in 1923 to analyze the evidence. The JPA study revealed that prostitution flourished in various parts of Chicago and suggested that the police and government officials were in collusion with owners of the brothels. The political consequences of the study's revelations were dramatic; fearing impeachment, the police commissioner closed every house of prostitution in Chicago, while the mayor, William "Big Bill" Thompson, was compelled not to seek a third term.

During this period and into the 1930s, Binford represented the JPA at national forums and conferences and published her findings in journals such as *Survey* and *Journal of Social Hygiene*. Through these activities and publications, she achieved wide recognition and came to personify the association in the minds of many.

While her home was in Chicago, Binford returned periodically to Iowa, where she owned and managed a farm as well as other business and real estate interests. She was also co-owner of a ranch in Texas.

The Great Depression brought scarce funding and necessitated a reorganization of social service agencies in Chicago into a comprehensive system with agency specialization. At the same time, new trends in social work that emphasized casework, professional training, psychoanalytic theory, and group work with delinquents were creating alternative approaches to protective agencies such as JPA. In 1936, the JPA was evaluated by a Loyola University affiliate; the report concluded that the agency did not use a "casework approach" and that association workers sometimes tried to "frighten or coerce clients" (Anderson, 461) rather than help them understand all the factors in their situation. By the late 1930s, the Chicago Council of Social Agencies, the central body for allocating casework responsibilities among Chicago's private agencies, urged the JPA to specialize in cases of child abuse and neglect, in many instances those cases that the newer agencies were declining to accept.

Binford continued to believe in the need to combine casework with community work. She contended that it was as important, if not more important, to transform the "fundamental community conditions which so affect[ed] so many more children and youth than the comparatively few helped by . . . casework agencies" (Anderson, 532). As she had fought the corrupt conditions that had allowed prostitution to flourish in the 1920s, from the mid-1930s Binford focused her attention on the effect that excessive alcohol consumption had on children and family life. During this time she supervised the investigation of thousands of taverns in Chicago and helped organize the Chicago Committee on Alcoholism, which had been created to develop treatment facilities for alcoholics.

In 1949 the trend toward professionalization of child welfare work eclipsed the approach of Binford and the JPA. The American Humane Association began to demand professional standards for protective agencies. At this point, the JPA's board was urged by the Welfare Council of Metropolitan Chicago to hire a new executive director for the agency.

At the time Binford was embarking on her latest crusade: a campaign against the widespread sale of heroin to minors and their addiction to the drug. Her study *Dope and Chicago's Children* was published in 1951. The JPA worked with the *Encyclopaedia Britannica* staff to produce a film, *Drug Addiction*, that became a standard in high school health classes.

Binford retired as executive director of the JPA on July 31, 1952, after thirty-six years of leadership. "I have no thought of giving up or 'retiring,'" Binford wrote to Miriam Van Waters, a California juvenile court judge, in June 1952, "for I feel as well as ever, and there is so much one has to do. And of course I will continue to live here at Hull House" (Binford Papers).

Throughout her long career Binford maintained good relations with the press as well as with many public officials. In 1950 she was interviewed by Keith Wheeler of the *Chicago Sun-Times* for an article, "Friend of the Poor—Miss Binford Fights for Social Justice," which appeared on April 26. In it Binford identified herself not as a social worker but as a resident of Hull-House and a citizen of the area around Taylor and Halsted Streets in Chicago who was interested in the welfare of her community and of the city and state at large. Wheeler went on to describe Binford at the age of seventy-four: "Her face has grown lined, but her eyes are clear and alert and her hands are as strong and sure as ever. She wears glasses only for reading. Probably the only concession she has made to age or nervous pressure is to smoke a denicotinized brand of cigarette."

Binford continued to speak publicly on behalf of JPA after retirement but soon became discouraged by the new director's emphasis on professional training and casework. She eventually became concerned about the agency's increasing "exclusion of leadership in relation to those fundamental community conditions which so affect . . . children" (Anderson, 532).

In 1961, Binford emerged from retirement to join the struggle of neighbors around Hull-House to preserve the area as a residential community. The city of Chicago designated a section of the area as the site for a new urban branch of the University of Illinois. In the spring of 1961, Binford became co-chair, along with Florence Scala, of the Harrison-Halsted Community Group established to protest this decision. Scala, a young woman of Italian descent, had grown up in the neighborhood and attended Hull-House classes as a child. Now in her eighties, Binford fought a vigorous campaign to block establishment of the university campus in the neighborhood. In spite of their best efforts, which included personal appeals to the Hull-House board of trustees and to government officials and formal appeals that went all the way to the Illinois Supreme Court, the decision to build the University of Illinois in the area prevailed. The Hull-House organization moved its settlement programs from the Halsted Street location in April 1963, decentralizing its services into several centers throughout the Chicago area. Binford, Scala, and a few others remained in Hull-House until June 1963. Finally the wrecking ball came to raze eleven of the thirteen Hull-House buildings, leaving behind two to be restored as a museum and historic site. When it was obvious that the battle was lost and it was no longer safe to stay in the buildings, Scala persuaded Binford to leave and find another home. While unsuccessful in this neighborhood, Binford and Scala's efforts to preserve the Harrison-Halsted area attracted wide media attention and raised public consciousness in the early 1960s. As a result, the "Harrison-Halsted struggle" became a symbol of citizen resistance to external encroachment on local communities and eventually led to increased government sensitivity to residential input in future urban renewal projects.

After the relocation of Hull-House in 1963, Binford returned to Marshalltown, Iowa, to live, taking up residence in the Tallcorn Motor Hotel. Here she maintained an active correspondence with Florence Scala and others, continuing to contribute financially and emotionally to the causes of child protection and those of the Harrison-Halsted group.

During the 1960s she maintained an avid interest in the civil rights movement and was pleased that her friends and associates participated in the March on Washington in 1963. Her ongoing interest in young people and their concerns was expressed by her support of the protest movement to end the war in Vietnam. She reiterated this abiding concern in an interview with Studs Terkel, Chicago author and radio personality, conducted at the Tallcorn Motor Home in the mid-1960s. The interview was published as the epilogue to Terkel's book *Division Street: America*, in 1967. "We've forgotten the spirit of youth, in things we permit to happen to them," Binford said; "if we're ever going to fulfill the possibility of life for all men, the spirit of youth must not be neglected. It must not be injured" (p. 381).

Binford died in Marshalltown. She was buried in Riverside Cemetery.

Binford's life and work represent the clearest example of the Hull-House tradition—living (settling) in the community, providing concrete services to meet the immediate needs of people in trouble, extensive use of research as the base for advocacy for social change through legislation and improved service delivery. Binford never rejected her role as good neighbor when she found herself inhabiting an increasingly specialized, bureaucratic, social work field. That connection to the community was a source of strength. As Binford recalled, "Miss Addams didn't start with any blueprints. She didn't start out with getting money from a foundation. Everything grew from the bottom up. We lived where we worked. And the place belonged to everybody. You learned life from life itself" (quoted in Terkel, 380).

Sources. Jessie Binford Papers, UIC Spec. Coll., include much of her correspondence, publications, and materials related to her directorship of the Juvenile Protective Association. Included is her "Acceptance of Citation" manuscript [1964]. The Juvenile Protective Association Records are also at UIC Spec. Coll. Binford's articles include "Community Protective Social Measures" and "Making the Community Safe for the Child," *Proceedings of the National Conference of Social Work,* 1924 and 1926, respectively; "May We Present the Roadhouses?" *Welfare Magazine,* 1927; "Cook County (Illinois) Roadhouses," *Journal of Social Hygiene,* 1930; "Community Responsibility for Recreation Facilities," in *Our Common Cause, Civilization,* Report of the International Congress of Women, Including the Series of Round Tables, July 16–22, 1933, Chicago, Illinois; "Don't Forget the Children," *Rotarian,* 1943; and the pamphlet, *Fifty Years of Pioneering* (1961), a twenty-two-page chronology of the Juvenile Protective Association. See Karl Detzer, "Miss Jessie Fights for the Kids," *Christian Herald,* December 1950, and the abridged version in the *Reader's Digest,* December 1950; Studs Terkel, *Division Street: America* (1967); Keith Wheeler, "Friend of the Poor—Miss Binford Fights for Social Justice," *Chicago Sun-Times,* April 26, 1950. Alice Hamilton, *Exploring the Dangerous Trades: The Autobiography of Alice Hamilton* (1943), gives the story of the Hull-House campaign against cocaine. For information on the Juvenile Protective Association, see Paul Gerard Anderson, "Juvenile Protective Association," in *Social Service Organizations,* ed. Peter Romanofsky, vol. 1 (1978), and Paul Gerard Anderson, "The Good to Be Done: A History of the Juvenile Protective Association of Chicago, 1898–1976" (Ph.D. diss., Univ. of Chicago, June 1988).

WYNNE SANDRA KORR

BLACKSHEAR, KATHLEEN
June 6, 1897–October 14, 1988
ARTIST, EDUCATOR

The first woman to wear pants in her small southern hometown, Kathleen Blackshear was not only daring and outrageous in her physical appearance but also bucked convention in every aspect of her life. Born in Navasota, Texas, Kathleen Blackshear was the only child of Edward Duncan and May (Terrell) Blackshear. Both the Terrells and Blackshears had settled in Texas in the 1850s. May Terrell was a member of the Daughters of the American Revolution and the Daughters of the Republic of Texas and was active in cultural and musical clubs in Navasota. She played piano and organ for the Baptist Church. Edward Duncan Blackshear worked as vice-president of the Swanson Grocery Company, a local wholesale grocer, and was superintendent of the Baptist Sunday School. Kathleen Blackshear spent her childhood summers at the country residences of both her maternal and paternal grandparents. Defying the social conventions imposed on a white child growing up in the South, Blackshear made friends with the African Americans who picked cotton on a large farm owned by the Terrells. These childhood friendships

influenced Blackshear's later career as both an artist and teacher, when she would make many sketches of Texan African Americans.

Blackshear entered Navasota Grammar School in 1904 and began studying art and music in her early teens. In her senior year at Navasota High School, she became the art editor of the yearbook, *Sachem.* The following fall, in 1914, Blackshear enrolled at Baylor University in Waco, Texas. In addition to her full-time studies, she continued to take art and music lessons. She also worked as art editor of the Baylor *Annual* and, during her senior year, designed costumes for a play, *Everysenior.* Blackshear graduated in 1917 with a B.A. degree in modern languages after completing a thesis entitled "Art Criticism in English Literature," which examined writings about art in the published works of Robert Browning, William Hazlitt, Sir Joshua Reynolds, and John Ruskin.

Blackshear then shifted her focus from writing about art criticism to pursuing her own artistic endeavors. Enrolling at the Art Students' League of New York, she spent a year (1917–18) studying sculpture with Solon Borglum, drawing with George Bridgeman, and portraiture with Frank Vincent Du Mond. Blackshear became unhappy with the school after being told by her chief instructor that "she belonged to 'the doughnut school of painting.'" The instructor explained that "she found the outer rim of a face more intriguing than the nose and mouth" (Bulliet, 24), referring, perhaps, to the simplified forms, radical foreshortening, and strong geometric shapes that were typical of Blackshear's modernist figuration. After leaving New York, Blackshear spent the next six years traveling and exploring various career options in Los Angeles, New Orleans, Europe, and Mexico while continuing to make photographs, paintings, prints, and sculpture.

Blackshear came to Chicago in 1924 and enrolled at the School of the Art Institute of Chicago (SAIC) in the Department of Drawing, Painting, and Illustration. The following year she studied art history with HELEN GARDNER, a teacher who proved to be a profound influence. In a letter to former student and faculty member Harold Allen, Blackshear recalled her initial encounter with Gardner: "She was a wonderful person. The first day in her class I knew she was giving us the information I had needed all my life. She had an academic background and so did I. But she had an understanding of Art that was more than academic" (Art Institute of Chicago Archives, April 13, 1965). In 1926, Blackshear was hired by SAIC as a member of the faculty to teach the Survey of Art History. As a teacher, Blackshear actively promoted vanguard ideas. Lecturing on subjects such as the importance of emotional content and formal relations over subject matter, she taught her students how to identify and appreciate new arrangements of form, shape, and color. As stated by fellow student, long-time faculty member, and former dean Norman Rice, "If there was any innovator on the faculty at that time, it was Kathleen" (*Oral History,* 11). In the same year that Blackshear began teaching, the first edition of Gardner's book, *Art through the Ages,* was published. This book was one of the first texts that acknowledged the underlying conditions and religious beliefs within historical periods yet considered works of art apart from their particular economic and political contexts. Gardner's achievement was to analyze the universal design elements inherent in each work, offering a key by which an understanding and appreciation of art from all cultures and historic periods could begin. Blackshear followed Gardner's philosophy in her own teaching.

She shared with Gardner an interest in non-Western art. Blackshear's 1926 self-portrait, *Gallery Notes*, depicts her taking notes in front of two paintings in the Helen Birch Bartlett Memorial Collection at the Art Institute. By choosing, in her self-representation, to directly engage the viewer and to position herself in relation to paintings by Vincent van Gogh (*Madame Roulin Rocking the Cradle*, 1889) and Paul Gauguin (*The Day of the God*, 1894), Blackshear revealed her interest in art that used non-Western sources in order to challenge convention and expand visual possibilities.

Blackshear chose to reveal herself and her feminist sentiments the same year through the writing of a play founded on Hindu mythology. Titled *Swayamvara [The Own-Choice Ceremony]: An East Indian Festival*, the play was presented at the Goodman Theatre for the Art Students' League Thirty-Second Annual Mardi Gras. This play told of a woman whose choice of suitor did not meet her father's approval; when the father acted out in protest, his head was turned into that of a goat because his decision was unjust, implying, perhaps, Blackshear's own struggle with the dictates of patriarchy.

In an era when much non-Western art was studied from an anthropological rather than from a visual art standpoint, Blackshear's and Gardner's interest broke new ground. Both took their students to such sites as the Field Museum of Natural History, the Oriental Institute, the Shedd Aquarium, the Lincoln Park and Brookfield zoos, the Adler Planetarium, and the Museum of Science and Industry. Studying objects in collections that were primarily anthropological and scientific, students were encouraged to see these objects as art and as everyday, utilitarian artifacts. With their pan-disciplinary, cross-cultural approach to teaching, Gardner and Blackshear fostered a sensitivity in students to systems of abstract patterning in the natural world and in manufactured objects. Divorced from their strictly utilitarian or natural settings, these objects became means by which students could appreciate the equivalences among objects, reconfigured from one cultural or historical genre to another as unique variations on universal patterning themes. In Gardner's and Blackshear's view, this learning process expanded Western conventions of art by challenging the ritualistic and restricted place of art in society. The objects were liberated from their display as specimens to stand as beautiful tools that served the agricultural, administrative, medical, and spiritual needs of the societies in which they originated. The radicalizing effect of these objects on the cognitive and imaginative process of the students was in the study of these objects as sites of design rather than sites of use. Freed from both the museum case and from their pragmatic place in space and time, these objects became charged lessons in the interactive roles of object, art, and community. The outcome of this lesson was construction of contemporary art production with the same integrated function.

By introducing their students to the art of non-Western cultures, Gardner and Blackshear also provided students and successive teachers at SAIC, such as Whitney Halstead, with unconventional source material for their own art making and teaching. This exposure contributed to the rise of a distinctive Chicago art style that gained prominence in the 1940s and 1950s and was associated with a group of artists known as the Monster Roster: Leon Golub, Theodore Halkin, Seymour Rosofsky, Evelyn Statsinger, and others. In part following Halstead's instructional lead, a later group, the Chicago imagists, was influenced by nontraditional sources.

Blackshear also shared Gardner's interest in using visual analysis to understand works from a formal point of view. To demonstrate how art could be deciphered and appreciated cross-culturally and transhistorically, Gardner incorporated analytical drawings in *Art through the Ages*; Blackshear drew most of these images for Gardner's revised (1936) edition and contributed drawings to the third edition (1948), which, together with Harold Allen, she saw through completion following Gardner's death in 1946.

In her own teaching, Blackshear took Gardner's analytical approach even further, most likely because Blackshear, unlike Gardner, was an artist. As artist Jack Beal noted, Blackshear "taught Art History as Art, not as history" (Kind, 6). Blackshear encouraged projects that required students to design art objects incorporating the materials, tools, and techniques used by artists in different cultures and historical periods. Termed "in-the-manner-of" (Harold Allen, 14) projects, these assignments offered students an opportunity to see how artists in both Western and non-Western cultures organized such visual elements as line, shape, value (light and dark), texture, and color in their art-making processes. A favorite assignment among the students was to design a portrait in the style of the eighteenth-century Japanese printmaker Toshusai Sharaku using a contemporary character as subject matter.

Blackshear's approach to teaching art history was complemented by her own work as an artist. Playing an integral role in the Art Institute's Gallery of Art Interpretation, Blackshear composed analytical drawings for companion exhibitions on Picasso's and Goya's works. Helen F. Mackenzie's book based on an exhibit, *Understanding Picasso: A Study of His Styles and Development* (1940), included Blackshear's sequence of drawings showing a drinking glass in various stages of cubism in order to demonstrate Picasso's methodical process in constructing a new image.

Described in 1954 by art critic Copeland C. Burg as "one of Chicago's most talented and least appreciated artists," Blackshear enjoyed a prolific artistic career. While she is perhaps best known for her portrayals of African Americans in a series of photographs, paintings, prints, and sculpture spanning sixteen years (1924–40) of her artistic career, Blackshear's later work was particularly influenced by the non-Western art that she so revered.

In response to changes imposed on the art history department by a new administrator at SAIC, Blackshear resigned from her teaching position and as head of the department in 1961. Joined by partner and fellow faculty member ETHEL SPEARS, Blackshear returned to Navasota. Although it is unknown when the two women began their relationship, Blackshear's biographical notes suggest that they first met in 1926 when Spears was a monitor for John Norton's class at SAIC. In Navasota, both women continued to lecture and create and exhibit their artwork. In 1968, Blackshear was designated Professor Emeritus by the School of the Art Institute of Chicago in recognition of her distinguished teaching career.

In the years following Spears's death in 1974, Blackshear became increasingly confused and disoriented. She was admitted to Canterbury Villa Nursing Home, where she spent her remaining years and died in her sleep. Blackshear was buried in Oakland Cemetery in Navasota next to the graves of Ethel Spears and Spears's sister Lilly May. A fourth plot was devoted to a lone oak tree that Blackshear had earlier planted.

Blackshear embodied the pioneering spirit of modernism and through her art and teaching she imparted its excitement to others. On the faculty of SAIC for thirty-five years, Blackshear was a highly influential presence, leaving her mark upon Chicago artists and successive teachers at the school.

Sources. Kathleen Blackshear's papers are available through the Archives of American Art, Smithsonian Institution. Additional information was obtained from the Department of Archives and the Ryerson Library at the Art Institute of Chicago; Harold Allen; and Jane Terrell, wife of William J. Terrell Sr., executor of the Blackshear estate. Work by Blackshear is in the permanent collections of the Art Institute of Chicago; Southwestern Univ. in Georgetown, Texas; the Modern Art Museum of Fort Worth; the Museum of Fine Arts in Houston; and a number of private collections in Chicago, Navasota, Houston, and San Diego. In 1990, an exhibition was held at the School of the Art Institute of Chicago to honor Blackshear and her legacy. Portions of this essay originally appeared in the exhibition catalog, *A Tribute to Kathleen Blackshear* (1990), by Carole Tormollan, and are reprinted here with permission of the School of the Art Institute of Chicago. C. J. Bulliet, "Artists of Chicago No. 97: Kathleen Blackshear," appeared in the *Chicago Daily News,* July 29, 1939; Copeland C. Burg, "Art and Artists: Chicagoans' New Work on View," is in the *Chicago Herald American,* February 13, 1954. Harold Allen briefly discussed Blackshear in "Centennial of Helen Gardner's Birth," *Crumbs,* March 28, 1978. Her influence at SAIC is noted in Roger Gilmore, ed., *Over a Century: A History of The School of the Art Institute of Chicago, 1866–1981* (1982), and Joshua Kind, "100 Artists 100 Years: Reflections on the School," *New Art Examiner,* April 1980. Carole Tormollan, *Oral History of Norman Rice* (1994), is available at the Art Institute of Chicago.

CAROLE TORMOLLAN

BLAINE, ANITA EUGENIE McCORMICK
July 4, 1866–February 12, 1954
PHILANTHROPIST, SOCIAL REFORMER, PEACE ACTIVIST

Anita McCormick Blaine, millionaire philanthropist, was an advocate of progressive education, founding the Francis Parker School and donating funds for the University of Chicago School of Education. She was a patron of such figures as Presidents Woodrow Wilson and Franklin D. Roosevelt and presidential candidate Henry Wallace. Often controversial in her philanthropic choices, Blaine gave one million dollars in the late 1940s for the creation of the New World Foundation for World Peace.

She was born in Manchester, Vermont, to Cyrus Hall and NETTIE FOWLER McCORMICK. She was the fourth of seven children and the second of three daughters. Only five children survived to adulthood: Anita, her older sister Mary Virginia, and brothers Cyrus Hall Jr., Stanley, and Harold. Her father was the renowned inventor and manufacturer of the reaper, who came to Chicago from Walnut Grove, Virginia, in

1848. He amassed considerable wealth since he benefited from the tremendous economic opportunities that Chicago and the expanding midwestern frontier offered. Her mother was a supporter of Protestant causes, including seminary education, evangelism, and missionary activities. She was a model of philanthropic giving for her daughter, although the objects of their giving differed. Anita McCormick was educated by tutors and governesses for much of her schooling; when the family returned from an extended stay in Europe in 1879, McCormick attended the Kirkland School in Chicago, an elite girls' preparatory school, graduating in 1884, two months after her father's death.

McCormick's serious nature and sense of family loyalty helped her assume family responsibilities thrust upon her at an early age by her mother, who was involved in managing the family's extensive business and philanthropic concerns before and after her husband's death. McCormick managed her sister Virginia's emotional health problems and financial affairs throughout her life and took on responsibilities as a young woman for her two younger brothers.

Anita McCormick met her future husband, Emmons Blaine, after her social debut in 1887. Blaine, the son of Republican Senator and presidential candidate James G. Blaine, was an administrator with a railroad and had lived in Chicago since 1880. The wealthy, Democratic McCormicks were particular about their daughter's choice of a husband. She had inherited a considerable fortune and her mother was concerned about the amount of control Blaine might have over her daughter's money once they were married. After establishing a trust from which Anita McCormick would receive an allowance, the family gave its approval, and the couple was married in Richfield Springs, New York, on September 26, 1889. Despite the problems of fame, wealth, and family concerns, Anita Blaine was deeply in love with her husband and he with her. Their marriage was tragically cut short by his untimely death of blood poisoning in 1892, less than two years after the birth of their son, Emmons Jr., known as Em.

A widow at twenty-six, Blaine was concerned foremost for the welfare and education of her child. As a young teenager, Blaine had already begun to formulate her ideas about education. She was concerned about the problems that traditional educational methods posed, with their overemphasis on competition and rote learning. In 1894, as her son was nearing school age, Blaine met John Dewey and Colonel Francis Parker. Both men were reforming educators who had gained attention for their controversial views on child-centered education. Parker was the head of the Chicago Normal School, and Dewey directed the Department of Pedagogy at the University of Chicago. Blaine was especially drawn to the education focused on practical experience offered at Parker's school. In 1897, she enrolled her son in the Chicago Normal School and for a time attended classes herself. In 1899, she provided funds for Parker to establish the Chicago Institute to train teachers and to found two schools—a private school near her home on Chicago's North Side that her son would attend and a free school for the education of poor children. Both used Parker's educational methods. The original plans were ambitious and included funding for faculty training, salaries, and construction of a new facility. Blaine eventually contributed more than one million dollars to the project.

When the financial needs of the Chicago Institute went beyond what Blaine was willing to fund, she came to an agreement with Parker, Dewey, and University of Chicago President William Rainey Harper. The pedagogy school of the Chicago Institute was transferred to the university, and, through Blaine's financial contribution, the University of Chicago School of Education was founded. At the same time, Parker's school on the North Side was built on land donated by the University of Chicago.

After Parker's death in 1902, the school was named in his honor. Blaine became even more involved in the financing and the management of the school and for a time in 1906 acted as assistant principal. FLORA COOKE, one of Parker's students, became principal in 1901 and remained in that position until her retirement in 1937, with Blaine's support. Blaine's contribution to the school totaled more than three million dollars and was one of her most significant and lasting philanthropic achievements.

After her first venture into educational reform, Blaine subsequently enlarged her own horizons and created a public life in which her talents, wealth, and growing interest in reform could be applied. She joined the emerging social reform network in Chicago headed by JANE ADDAMS and others. These new causes eventually became her lifework, and her wealth and social position gave her power and influence to bring about social change in Chicago and, eventually, worldwide.

Her continuing interest and involvement in educational reform led Mayor Carter Harrison to appoint her a member of the Chicago Public School Board in 1905. During her two-year tenure, she served on the board's juvenile court and truancy committees and created a school textbook trust to which she contributed more than one hundred thousand dollars for books to be used in the first five grades of the public schools. Her additional educational contributions over the years were extensive, amounting to more than four million dollars. Her interests included the Henry B. Favill School of Occupations, one of the first schools for occupational therapy in the country, named for one of her most trusted friends and advisers; the Harvard Medical School in China; the University of Wisconsin Agricultural School; and forty others.

In the early twentieth century, issues of labor reform, poverty, and tenement housing were being addressed in a new way, which was described as scientific philanthropy. Blaine and others believed that society's complex problems required scientific investigation, bureaucratic organizational structures, and social reform legislation. The residents and supporters of Chicago's Hull-House settlement were at the forefront of these organizing and investigative efforts and Blaine's friendship with Jane Addams, Hull-House's head resident, led to her involvement with social reform institutions advocating scientific philanthropy, such as the University of Chicago Settlement directed by MARY McDOWELL, Graham Taylor's Chicago Commons Settlement, and the Chicago School of Civics and Philanthropy (CSCP), founded by Taylor, and headed by Hull-House resident JULIA LATHROP. Blaine served on the board of trustees of the CSCP, providing more than thirty thousand

dollars for the school, which eventually became the School of Social Service Administration at the University of Chicago. In 1899, Blaine served on the executive committee of the Chicago Board of Charities and later on the board of United Charities, a national organization. By the end of her life, Blaine had contributed more than one hundred thousand dollars to the local charity board, which helped needy individuals become independent. In 1900 she and Addams created the City Homes Association to address the inadequate housing available for Chicago's poor. Blaine became chair of the association's tenement committee, which sought to provide better, affordable housing.

Blaine's activism included involvement in labor struggles and party politics. In 1899, Blaine and Addams helped striking workers in the garment trade. They both incurred the wrath of the Merchant Tailors' Association, which accused them of being socialists. Blaine took labor reforms such as the eight-hour day seriously, even applying it to her own household staff. In 1912, she joined other Chicago reformers working to organize and fund the campaign of Progressive Party candidate Alexander McCormick (no relation) in his successful bid for the Cook County Board presidency.

In 1917, with the entry of the United States into World War I, Blaine's philanthropic interests shifted from the local to the national and international scene. Her son volunteered to serve in the army but was denied a military commission because of his poor health. When he died in the 1918 influenza epidemic, Blaine was distraught. During the war, she had begun to realize the urgent need for world peace and determined that her own personal loss could have meaning through her commitment to this cause. She had been in regular correspondence with Woodrow Wilson throughout the war and, at its close, began to contribute time and money to help him bring about his vision for a League of Nations. After Wilson's death in 1924, Blaine pledged ten thousand dollars to the newly formed League of Nations Non-Partisan Association and served in the local branch of the association. By the late 1930s, with the failure of the League of Nations and the beginning of World War II, Blaine stepped back from her commitment to the establishment of world peace and urged President Franklin Roosevelt to support the allies and persuade Congress to declare war on the axis powers. Concerned for the plight of China during the war, in 1943 she gave one hundred thousand dollars to Madame Chiang Kai-shek, wife of China's president. Blaine presented her gift to Madame Chiang in person, turning over to her a suitcase full of International Harvester stock during Madame Chiang's visit to Chicago, to be used in any way she wished to aid the Chinese.

After the war was over in 1945, she turned once again in earnest toward her dream of a world government. She had been a supporter of the World Association for the Advancement of World Citizenship, contributing more than one hundred fifty thousand dollars toward this association's efforts. With the founding of the United Nations in 1945, the association changed its name to the American Association for the United Nations (AAUN). Blaine became a board member and then vice-chair. She also represented the AAUN at the United Nations Relief and Rehabilitation Administration.

Blaine's national political interests took a controversial turn with her large financial commitment to the 1948 presidential campaign of Progressive Party candidate Henry Wallace. Wallace, who had been secretary of agriculture in Roosevelt's cabinet and then vice-president from 1944 to 1948, ran for president to fight what he saw as the Democratic Party's shift to the right. He opposed the party's rigid anti-Communist cold war stance and its abandonment of labor issues, civil rights, and other liberal Democratic goals. Blaine supported Wallace in his estimate of the Democratic Party, and she particularly admired his belief in the possibility of world peace through a world governmental organization. She served on the board of Wallace's Progressive Party and contributed nearly eight hundred thousand dollars to the unsuccessful Wallace presidential bid. After the election, Blaine continued to promote Wallace and his political views by funding several political newspapers that Wallace wrote for and edited. From 1948 until her death in 1954, she contributed more than a half million dollars to two of these papers, the *Daily Compass*, which advocated world government, and the *National Guardian*, a more radical paper whose objective was to be a dissenting voice against the government's cold war policies.

Discouraged by the failure of the League of Nations to move toward world government earlier in the century and by Wallace's defeat in 1948, Blaine became interested in the Foundation for World Government. She gained national attention when she pledged one million dollars to the organization, committed to limiting national sovereignty, enforcing world law, and controlling atomic development. The foundation eventually contributed more than four hundred fifty thousand dollars to world government organizations, international government research, and legislative lobbying efforts to promote world government.

Besides funding organizations, Blaine often supported individuals with whose work and aims she sympathized. One such person was W. E. B. Du Bois, founder of the National Association for the Advancement of Colored People (NAACP). In 1948 Du Bois sought Blaine's financial support on the advice of Henry Wallace. The aging African American intellectual had been dismissed from the NAACP without a pension because of his increasingly radical views, and he needed support for himself and his invalid wife. Blaine provided a pension of five thousand dollars a year for Du Bois and continued to correspond with him until her death.

In December 1949, Blaine underwent intestinal surgery from which she never fully recovered. After several years of ill health, she died of bronchial pneumonia. By the end of her life she had given more than ten million dollars to many causes and individuals. At her death, twenty million dollars of Blaine's thirty-five million dollar estate was put into the New World Foundation Trust, dedicated to peace, education, and the eradication of poverty, continuing the commitments of her long career of philanthropic giving.

Sources. The papers of Anita McCormick Blaine are at the Wisconsin State Hist. Soc., Madison, Wisconsin. They are extensive, consisting of more than eleven hundred boxes, and include correspondence, journals, and financial records. Margaret R. Hafstad, ed., *Guide to the McCormick Collection of the State Historical Society of Wisconsin* (1973), is a useful aid to understanding the scope and content of Blaine's papers.

Sources for Blaine's involvement in Chicago reform activities are found in the Jane Addams Memorial Collection, UIC Spec. Coll.; the records of the Francis W. Parker School at CHS, with materials on Flora Cooke; and the Alexander McCormick Papers, NL. CHS has a newspaper clipping file on Blaine. Two full-length studies of Blaine have been written: *A Timeless Affair*, a biography by Blaine's grandson-in-law, Gilbert Harrison (1979), mainly concerned with McCormick family relationships, and William White, "The Philanthropy of Anita McCormick Blaine" (master's thesis, Univ. of Wisconsin–Madison, 1959). An entry on Blaine appears in *NAW* (1980).

BARBARA DOBSCHUETZ

BLAKE, MARGARET DAY
February 20, 1875–September 29, 1971
ART PATRON, PHILANTHROPIST, REFORMER, CLUBWOMAN

Margaret Day Blake's activism as a young woman prepared her to assume important leadership positions on the governing boards of the Art Institute of Chicago and as an elected trustee of the University of Illinois. Born Margaret Pynchon Day in Springfield, Massachusetts, she was the fourth of five daughters of Albert Morgan and Fanny Forsythe (Pynchon) Day.

In 1876 the Days moved their growing family to Chicago, where the staunchly Republican and Presbyterian Albert Day became a highly respected civic leader and president of the Chicago Stock Exchange. He headed the brokerage firm of Counselman & Day. His commitment to a tradition of civic involvement was taken up later by his daughter, Margaret. The Days moved to the affluent suburb of Lake Forest in 1892.

Called Daisy by family and friends, Margaret Day boarded at Dobbs Ferry, a private high school in New York state. Photographs show an attractive young woman with strong features and dark hair. Day disliked feminine clothes and small talk and preferred the company of men. Smart, funny, full of ideas, she refused to conform. In a daringly unconventional move after high school, Day left Lake Forest to live as a single woman in Chicago. She became involved with Chicago's Hull-House, a center of cultural activity and social reform initiatives. It was at the settlement that she probably met her future husband, Tiffany Blake, a journalist. Leaving her family home to live in Chicago was remembered by a relative as "an act of rebellion" (transcript of interview with Pauline Rogers, May 14 and 27, 1995, 2). She took a maid with her as a chaperone and proceeded to take classes at the University of Chicago.

In 1905, at the age of thirty, Day married Tiffany Blake, the forty-year-old *Chicago Journal* drama and music critic who later became literary editor and chief editorial writer for the Chicago *Evening Post*. In 1908 he was named chief editorial writer for the *Chicago Tribune*. Both Blakes had a sense of humor, but Tiffany was scholarly, gentle, and physically frail while Margaret Blake was vigorous, talkative, and strong-willed. Blake and her husband had no children; she took an active interest in her sisters' children and grandchildren. They, in turn, admired her and craved her approval.

Influenced by her Hull-House experience, Blake became active in the Women's Trade Union League (WTUL), an organization that brought together women of the working class and the middle and upper-middle classes. The Chicago WTUL initially met at Hull-House, and its leaders included MAR-

GARET DREIER ROBINS, AGNES NESTOR, and MARY McDOWELL. The WTUL advocated labor organization, improvement in the conditions of women's employment, and social reforms for the betterment of women and children. Leaders were concerned about protecting the lives of young immigrant women, many of whom became laborers in factories and manufacturing plants. In response to a request from the New York City Women's Municipal League and the National Council of Jewish Women, the Chicago WTUL formed an Immigration Committee in 1907, which included Margaret Blake, RACHELLE YARROS, Amelia Sears, and Harriet Van Der Vaart, the chair.

Overwhelmed by the massive wave of new arrivals, the WTUL and civic leaders formed the Immigrants' Protective League (IPL) in 1908. Blake served as the first IPL membership chair, was on its executive committee, and sat on its board. Hull-House resident GRACE ABBOTT became the IPL's director, and the organization gained support from the Chicago Woman's Club, the major women's reform organization in the city. Blake was active in the Chicago Woman's Club as well as IPL and the Chicago WTUL.

Blake's advocacy of a women's reform agenda in the Progressive Era included her commitment to winning suffrage for women. She was the founder and first president of the North Side Suffrage Association in 1909. Both the Chicago Woman's Club and the Woman's City Club of Chicago—organizations in which Blake participated—endorsed suffrage and encouraged women's role in civic affairs, including politics. Already able to vote for school officers, Illinois women had elected trustees for the University of Illinois since 1894. In 1913, the Illinois legislature gave women the right to vote in presidential and municipal elections. Remaining active in the suffrage movement, Blake helped to organize the victory convention of the National American Woman Suffrage Association (NAWSA) held in Chicago in February 1920. On February 14, 1920, NAWSA became the League of Women Voters, a non-partisan, educational organization geared to preparing women to use the franchise they had won.

During World War I, the major Illinois women's organizations volunteered to help in the war effort and were organized under the Woman's Committee of the National Council of Defense, Illinois Division. Blake sat on this committee representing the Woman's Land Army and was president of the executive board of the Illinois Training Farm in Libertyville. The Land Army sought to train women to take the place of men in such jobs as planting and harvesting, if the war continued. It was thought that farmers' wives needed support first, and the sole project of the Land Army became the Training Farm. In its only year of existence, the farm trained fifty-five women to assume a variety of agricultural jobs. Following the end of the war, an agreement was reached with Blackburn College in Carlinville, Illinois. The farm stock and equipment were given to the college in exchange for a promise to encourage women to take agriculture classes. Blake hoped more women would take advantage of the growing demand for skilled farmworkers.

In November 1918 Blake was elected trustee of the University of Illinois (UI) on the Republican Party ticket. Before setting foot on campus, she angrily protested the cover on the magazine the *Illinois Agriculturist,* a student publication. She thought the cover, which pictured two young women as farmers, ridiculed women in farm work. Blake served as a University of Illinois trustee from 1919 to 1925 and chaired the Campus Plan Commission, which culminated in the construction of a library, a stadium, and two other buildings. She worked with UI President David Kinley for increased university funding and encouraged her husband to advocate that the editors of the *Chicago Tribune* endorse a state tax increase to support UI.

Living on a newspaper writer's salary, Margaret and Tiffany Blake had little money. In the 1920s Blake decided that she was tired of being poor, took her father's wedding gift of $8,000, and began to invest in stocks. She studied the market, called her broker every morning, questioned corporate moguls at social events, and could see the potential in technological advances. Her successful investments funded all of her philanthropy. She boasted that she never spent any of the capital her father left her. She was also able to minimize her losses in the crash of the stock market in 1929.

Blake and her husband traveled often for pleasure or to educate themselves and, in 1925, Blake's increasing wealth enabled them to begin the first of several long journeys. Their six-month tour of the Orient was physician-prescribed to relieve Blake's stress and restore Tiffany's health. In late 1927 they began a five-month journey through the Middle East.

Family duties also kept Blake busy. After her mother died in 1926, she ran her parents' Lake Forest estate. She and Tiffany lived there during the four to six months each year when her father was in town. Blake again served as a University of Illinois trustee from August to December 1930, having been appointed to fill a vacancy. That fall she ran for trustee again, on the Republican ticket, but lost the election.

Margaret Blake was a major donor and trustee of the Chicago World's Fair, the 1933–34 Century of Progress. She was also a member of the fair's fine arts exhibition committee, which worked with representatives of the Art Institute of Chicago (AIC).

The final third of Blake's life was devoted to the AIC. When her husband died in 1943 and left the museum fifteen thousand dollars, Blake offered to make additional funds available if she and two museum officials could agree on the purchase of a specific work. This agreement showed both her generosity and her need to keep control.

Carl O. Schniewind, who had joined the AIC's Department of Prints and Drawings in 1940 as its first professional curator, helped to educate Blake and collaborated with her on acquisitions. She and Pauline Palmer—the wife of Potter Palmer II—were escorted by Schniewind and his wife on several European acquisition and teaching expeditions. Blake and Palmer served on two AIC committees together. Blake also read and traveled on her own to see collections in the United States and Europe.

At the time, the print and drawing collection at the Art Institute was haphazardly acquired and considered second-rate. Blake and Schniewind decided to search for master drawings, the best of a specific artist's work. Few in the art world thought a major collection could still be assembled. But within two years Blake had purchased important drawings by Paul Cézanne, Edgar Degas, Jean-Honoré Fragonard, Paul Gauguin, Édouard

Manet, Henri de Toulouse-Lautrec, and Vincent van Gogh. By 1947 she had added the museum's first authentic Rembrandt drawing, a major Theodore Géricault portfolio of sixty-four drawings, and modern drawings by Fernand Léger, Max Beckmann, and Oscar Kokoschka. Other major artists included Anibale Carracci, Mary Cassatt, Honoré Daumier, Eugène Delacroix, James Ensor, Jean-Auguste Dominique Ingres, Paul Klee, Amedeo Modigliani, Auguste Rodin, Giovanni Battista Tiepolo, Anthony Van Dyck, and Benjamin West. A Pablo Picasso drawing, *Embrace of the Minotaur,* was considered by Harold Joachim "the greatest 20th century drawing in the Art Institute" (p. 2) in his introduction to the 1970 exhibition catalog, *A Quarter Century of Collecting: Donations Given to the Art Institute by Margaret Day Blake, 1944 to 1970.* Joachim had succeeded Schniewind as curator of prints and drawings; he, too, had a close relationship with Blake. Today, the Margaret Day Blake Collection is a major part of the Department of Prints and Drawings, and Blake's donations have helped it take a premier place among the world's great print and drawing collections.

Blake was an unusual donor because she bought works only for the Art Institute, not to hang on her own walls. She was the first woman on the prints and drawings committee and chaired a subcommittee on contemporary art. She established a fund for drawings by contemporary artists and used friendship to acquire such donations as a sizable collection of drawings by *Chicago Tribune* political cartoonist John McCutcheon.

In 1952 women active in the Emergency Campaign, a major AIC fund-raising effort, were asked by the museum trustees to organize a Woman's Board. Margaret Blake became the first president and had specific goals; under her leadership the board initiated changes to make the museum feel more comfortable to the general public who visited it. According to Associate Curator Sam Carini, the Woman's Board "opened up the institution" and "made the museum accessible to the masses" (transcript of interview with Anselmo (Sam) Carini, January–March, 1995, 2). Blake had "formative" (p. 2) ideas and, in addition to her leadership of the Woman's Board, she was able to lead the way to major changes in the museum as the first woman trustee of the Art Institute. She sat on the board of trustees from 1952 to 1955, when her term as Woman's Board president ended.

Woman's Board projects that Blake helped to initiate included the Community Associates, a suburban outreach project; a May festival with an auction and tours; and the Junior Museum. The women initiated greater emphasis on educational programming and expanded the docent and volunteer programs. To make the work of Chicago artists both affordable and accessible to the public, in 1954 the Woman's Board organized and ran the Art Rental and Sales Gallery. Blake served on the organizing committee and was one of the original project underwriters.

By the late 1950s, heart disease had made Blake dependent on oxygen and forced her to remain at home. Always planning ahead, she began to make major gifts to relatives and institutions and spoke of these contributions as a way to ensure that her many visitors would return, hoping for more. To some nieces and nephews she gave antique furniture and jewelry; to those in need she gave money. Major contributions at this time included the 1960 endowment of the Ferdinand Schevill Distinguished

Service Professorship at the University of Chicago and four hundred thousand dollars to Presbyterian St. Luke's Hospital in 1962 for a cardiovascular research and education fund in her father's name. Blake loved being with artists and was a major donor to the Skowhegan School of Painting and Sculpture in Skowhegan, Maine. In 1960 the Woman's Board commissioned a drawing of Blake by a Skowhegan artist friend, Jack Levine. Blake also belonged to American Friends of China, the Orchestral Association, Friends of Opera, and the Illinois Republican Women's Club. She was a member of the Arts and Casino Clubs in Chicago and the Cosmopolitan Club in New York, where she stayed when visiting that city. In addition, Blake was a director of the Hitchcock Foundation, a hospital in Hanover, New Hampshire, with which a physician nephew was connected.

At the end of her life Blake was bedridden but still buying art for her beloved museum. Frail and in pain, she planned to die when her pacemaker failed, which it did on September 29, 1971. There was no funeral. A nephew scattered her ashes over Lake Michigan.

Two major exhibits of Blake's contributions to the Department of Prints and Drawings were held during her lifetime. The 1954 exhibit highlighted Jean-Antoine Watteau's masterpiece, *Four Studies of Italian Actors,* and the 1970 exhibit looked at her contributions over twenty-five years. In his 1970 catalog introduction, Joachim called Blake's donations "a miracle" (*A Quarter Century of Collecting,* 3) in their effect on the department.

A 1954 estimate valued Blake's print and drawing donations alone at more than two million dollars. Her entire estate, including her Astor Street apartment and its furnishings, was left to the museum, and a clause in her will enabled reconstruction of the Prints and Drawings Department. As of January 1995, more than one-third of the 328 items in the Blake Collection, including Endowment Fund acquisitions, were prints and drawings. Blake was also active in other areas of the museum. She contributed to the textile, Oriental, and decorative arts departments and to the libraries; chaired the textile committee for seventeen years; and was active on the school and other committees. The Art Institute named Blake an Honorary Trustee in 1955 and a Life Trustee in 1971. In 1955 she was named Woman's Board Honorary President for the first time; she remained a Woman's Board member until her death. She was named a Benefactor in 1956 and a Major Benefactor in 1965.

Blake's involvement with the governing bodies of the Art Institute was as significant to its development as her monetary donations. Her social and political activism influenced Blake's work for museum policies that emphasized outreach, accessibility, and education.

Sources. The papers of the Board of Trustees and of the Woman's Board, the Print and Drawing Committee Minutes, and the Registrar Collection Records all have information related to Margaret Day Blake's activities and art patronage and are found in the Archives of the Art Institute of Chicago (AIC). There is a Blake Correspondence File in the Department of Prints and Drawings, Archives of the AIC. Also in the AIC archives are photographs, letters, newspaper clippings, speeches, and exhibition catalogs; Florence Lowden Miller, "The Woman's Board of the Art Institute of Chicago," a 1967 unpublished paper; and Jean Nevitt, "A History of the Art Rental and Sales Gallery, 1954–1987," an undated typescript. The Ryerson Library, AIC, has newspaper clippings. A computerized list of Blake's donations is on file in the Office of Museum Registrations, AIC. Albert Morgan Day, "Day Family Record," manuscript, July 17, 1918, is at the CHS; so is Day's "To My Children," typescript, 1924. The CHS clipping file has a Blake folder. The microfilm collection of the Women's Trade Union League Papers is at CHS as are some of the Annual Reports of the Immigrant's Protective League (IPL). Other IPL reports and other materials are in the IPL papers. UIC Spec. Coll. University Trustees' Papers, including correspondence between Blake and the president, are in the University of Illinois Archives, University Library Urbana. There are Tiffany Blake letters in the Henry B. Fuller Papers, NL, and there is a Margaret Day Blake letter to John and Evelyn McCutcheon, February 3, 1945, in the John McCutcheon Papers, NL. The NL has a scrapbook of Tiffany Blake articles, April 13, 1901–January 30, 1919. Interviews were conducted with the following people between January and June 1995: Anselmo (Sam) Carini, Associate Curator of the Department of Prints and Drawings, AIC; Mary Ward Wolkonsky, who served on the Woman's Board with Blake; greatnephew Francis Farwell; nephew James Gamble Rogers Jr.; great-niece Edith Van Slyck; Pauline Rogers, who was married to a Blake nephew; and nephew Leeds Mitchell Jr. There is a transcript from an interview of Edith Van Slyck's mother and Blake's niece, Katharine Rogers Van Slyck, which was taped in the summer of 1986. For Illinois women's role in World War I, see Marguerite Edith Jenison, *The War-Time Organization of Illinois*, vol. 5, *Illinois in the World War* (1923), and *Final Report of the State Council of Defense of Illinois, 1917–1918–1919* [n.d.]. See Harold Joachim, A *Quarter Century of Collecting: Donations Given to the Art Institute by Margaret Day Blake, 1944 to 1970* (1970).

JAN GINSBERG FLAPAN

BLENDER, DOROTHEA PEARL
November 25, 1908–October 10, 1972
LAWYER, PUBLISHER, ACTIVIST

Dorothea Blender was the first woman vice-president of Commerce Clearing House, Inc., a legal loose-leaf publisher. During her forty-year career, she helped promote the advancement of women lawyers through her organizational work.

Blender was born near Carthage, Hancock County, Illinois, the second child of the physician who delivered her, William Blender, and Meda May (Kloty) Blender, a nurse, both children of German immigrants. In 1917, Blender's parents moved so her father could practice medicine and surgery in Peoria, Illinois. She had an older brother, Thomas, and a younger brother, William; the three children were encouraged to set high standards for themselves. The emphasis on selflessness and excellence was a strength that Blender applied to all of her later accomplishments.

Blender attended local public schools, then Bradley University, Peoria, from 1926 to 1929; while at Bradley, she won the first place prize for oration in Illinois. She completed her bachelor of philosophy degree at the University of Chicago in 1930 and her Doctor of Jurisprudence at the Law School of the University of Chicago in 1932. Blender's generation of newly graduated professional women and men faced the difficult task of finding employment during the depths of the Great Depression.

Hired as a legal editor by Commerce Clearing House, Inc. (CCH), in Chicago in 1932, she worked there until retiring as vice-president of development in 1972. CCH was a legal publisher of ring-bound, loose-leaf books, called "reporters," which allowed for the easy and frequent supplementation required by annual changes in the law. Blender produced a book on the

Banking Law of 1934 in about ten days. The book was extremely profitable and contributed greatly to the company's success. Blender was promoted to full-time editor. In 1939 she was promoted again, becoming assistant to the president for public relations. She worked closely with the managing editor and sales manager at CCH to develop new products. At the close of World War II, when she hired the first head of her fledging News Bureau, Blender had performed many jobs for the company. The News Bureau was an innovation that made CCH a leader in tax- and business-law reporting. Blender also helped launch products such as the *Banking Reporter*, the *Bankruptcy Reporter*, and *Tax Guides* for CCH.

Blender became CCH's vice-president for business development in 1957 and served on the firm's executive committee. During the time of her employment, the company expanded from eight topical reporters to more than one hundred fifty. A decade later, the number of vice-presidents had increased to ten, and by 1975, there were as many as sixteen vice-presidents in the company.

Blender's work took her to many places. As assistant to the president, she did public speaking on the CCH topical system and other technological developments. She used her travels and talks to promote both CCH and the Women's Bar Association, an organization in which she took a leadership role.

Blender vigorously supported women's economic advancement. She maintained that the best advertisement for a woman lawyer was a good woman lawyer. She also supported the legal rights of women generally. Blender became active in the National Association of Women Lawyers (NAWL), founded in New York City in 1899, and often worked on organizational projects with her good friend and fellow Chicago lawyer HELEN CIRESE. Blender was elected NAWL's Illinois state director for the 1944–45 term. Later that year, she became associate editor for the *Women Lawyers Journal*, the organization's publication. Blender was a drafter and advocate of the NAWL Model Divorce Law, upon which modern uniform divorce law is patterned. It provided protections for the rights of children of divorce and for the non-wage-earning spouse.

Blender was elected president of the Women's Bar Association of Illinois in 1946–47. That year Blender took part in an American Bar Association (ABA) sponsored debate on the proposed Equal Rights Amendment (ERA). First introduced in 1923, the ERA read: "Men and women shall have equal rights throughout the United States and every place subject to its jurisdiction." Proponents of the ERA, members of the National Woman's Party, "sought to end forever all distinctions between men and women in laws affecting family law, possession of property, political rights, and employment opportunity" (Rosenberg, 79). The ERA was rejected from the 1920s through the 1940s by almost all women's organizations in the country that feared the loss of hard-won protective legislation.

Professional women, including lawyers, were also divided over the issue of the ERA. They debated in their associations about the best way to advance the cause of women's rights and opportunities. The NAWL had debated the ERA, and Blender had been one of the architects in 1941 of an alternative amendment—the sex-disqualification removal amendment—which was introduced in the United States Senate and referred to the

Senate judiciary committee. It was hoped that the sex disqualification removal amendment, by preventing the enactment of laws that restricted married women, would address the inequities women faced without endangering any protections. At the NAWL convention in 1941, members voted two to one in favor of this alternative amendment.

Thus, it was not surprising when Blender argued against the ERA in the ABA debate in 1946. Blender feared that the ERA was not a solution to all of women's legal and economic disabilities and might, in fact, create problems. Nor was it a contradiction when Blender advocated electing women to office. As president of the Women's Bar Association of Illinois, she campaigned to elect a woman lawyer to a Cook County judgeship. She was joined by the Illinois Federation of Business and Professional Women's Clubs, along with other leading women in this educational effort. At that time, the only female judge in Illinois, MARY BARTELME, had been elected to the Cook County Circuit Court in 1923. She remained the singular example, however.

In 1947 Blender became known nationally when she published her first review of legal periodicals in the *Women Lawyers Journal* (*WLJ*). The same year she became editor-in-chief of the *WLJ*. Her prominence as a spokeswoman for her profession was to continue for two decades.

Blender's editorial interests were evident in the *WLJ*. In the post–World War II era, *WLJ* covered many international issues. *WLJ* reported on the attempt of the United Nations Commission on the Status of Women to obtain information in 1948 concerning, and to recommend improvement in, the rights of married women and children living in foreign countries. The commission looked into the problems of statelessness and dual nationality. Blender used her editorial space in the *WLJ* to cover the proposed United Nations Human Rights Declaration. The journal debate continued with a later presentation of arguments pro and con. Blender also highlighted the history of women attorneys.

Blender was attuned to legislative change as part of her work at CCH. Publication of legal loose-leaf services required following and anticipating changes in the law to predict new legal publications. The *Legislation Report*, a feature of the *WLJ*, included notes on the newly introduced equal pay and antidiscrimination bills pending in the U.S. Congress, reflecting Blender's interests.

In early 1950 Blender was appointed to the ABA's Standing Committee on Publications, and she held that committee membership for two years. Other women had occasionally been appointed to ABA committees at least as early as 1938.

By the fall of 1952, Blender had moved from the position of vice-president of NAWL to that of president. During her presidency, with the assistance of state delegates and an active membership chair, membership in the NAWL began to increase. Blender's efforts to help elect women to public office continued through her presidency. In 1953 NAWL endorsed Chicago woman attorney B. FAIN TUCKER in her campaign for circuit court judge. A bipartisan women's campaign effort was successful. During Blender's second term as president, the NAWL invited the nation's three women federal judges to address that organization's fifty-fifth annual convention.

Blender oversaw the annual NAWL convention in 1954, which was held in conjunction with the annual ABA convention. The ABA had recently completed its headquarters, and NAWL contributed a large sum of money for a sculptural entrance wall. Blender highlighted the work of her term: public relations and membership, international legal issues, and keeping the organization's finances on track.

Blender acknowledged the importance of her personal contacts and travels in her NAWL efforts. She also noted the crossover between her role in public relations at CCH and that of her NAWL presidency. Blender advocated that her successors overhaul the structure of NAWL to streamline operations, specifically suggesting they solicit membership from high quality and prominent women attorneys and remember that younger women attorneys might turn away from membership in the women's bar association as women lawyers participated in the men's bar associations. Blender continued to argue that a separate organization was necessary. "Our endorsement of women for public office is certainly important and resultful [*sic*]" ("President's Annual Report," WLJ, Fall 1954, 12), she maintained. She urged, "We must put our best foot forward, for inevitably you, I and all other women lawyers are judged by the individuals we thrust into the limelight" (p. 12). For Blender, the emphasis was always on quality. Blender continued to serve as the NAWL delegate to the ABA from 1954 to 1957. One of her causes during this period was to support the appointment of an ABA delegate to the United Nations.

Over the years Blender remained close to her family and took an active and generous interest in her many nieces and nephews, encouraging them and assisting their education financially. Her close friends within the legal profession included Elsa Beck, Helen Cirese, and Judge Tucker. Like other women professionals in her circle, Blender could afford to travel in Europe. Blender lived in the Gold Coast area of Chicago and later in Glenview, Illinois.

Blender's last few years with CCH were marred by illness. Diagnosed with a brain tumor in the late 1960s, she eventually had surgery that was not helpful. Her health continued to deteriorate, and by 1971 she came to work in a car-pool driven by her admiring coworkers. In 1972, when she became too ill, she retired; she died that year in Evanston, Illinois.

Dorothea Blender devoted her legal career to building and leading Commerce Clearing House, Inc., a publishing house central to the growth and success of the legal profession. At the same time, she worked to improve professional opportunities for women lawyers in both women's and men's bar associations.

Sources. Interviews were conducted with Blender's cousin, Kathleen Williams; Richard T. Merrill, a coworker at Commerce Clearing House; and Thelma Brook Simon. Articles by Blender include "Topical Law Reporters in the Law Library," *Law Library Journal*, November 1945; "The Common Market and the Law Library," *Law Library Journal*, November 1963; "President's Annual Report," *Women Lawyers Journal*, Fall 1954. Issues of the *Women Lawyers Journal*, 1938 to 1955, are a key source of information for Blender's organizational work. See Eleanor March Moody, "Dorothea Blender," *Women Lawyers Journal*, Fall 1949. For background on women's politics, see Rosalind Rosenberg, *Divided Lives: American Women in the Twentieth Century* (1992).

CYNTHIA L. BARNES

BLUNT, KATHARINE
May 28, 1876–July 29, 1954
CHEMIST, RESEARCHER, UNIVERSITY EDUCATOR, COLLEGE PRESIDENT

Katharine Blunt was born in Philadelphia, the eldest of three daughters of Stanhope English and Fanny (Smyth) Blunt. Her father had a successful military career that included positions as an instructor of mathematics and ordnance at West Point Academy and commander of the Frankford Arsenal in Philadelphia, the Rockford Arsenal in Illinois, and the Springfield Armory in Massachusetts. He authored several books and articles on gunnery and small arms. In 1912 he retired from the army at the rank of full colonel.

Growing up in an affluent family, Katharine Blunt enjoyed educational opportunities granted to relatively few young women of the time. She entered Miss Porter's elite girls' preparatory school in Springfield, Massachusetts, and in 1894 enrolled at Vassar College, Poughkeepsie, New York, the first woman in her family to go beyond finishing school. Blunt focused her studies on chemistry, devoting her spare time to athletics and to editing the *Vassar Miscellany*, in which she occasionally published essays. She graduated in 1898 with a B.A. in chemistry.

At the insistence of her family, Blunt spent the first four years after graduation at home, engaging in church and community work and studying chemistry for a brief time at the Massachusetts Institute of Technology and Columbia University. In 1902 she continued her studies in chemistry at the University of Chicago. The next year she accepted a position as an assistant in chemistry at Vassar College. In 1905 she moved to the University of Chicago to study with the noted chemist Julius Stieglitz and earned a doctorate in organic chemistry in 1907. After spending a year teaching chemistry in the domestic science department at Pratt Institute in Brooklyn, New York, Blunt returned to Vassar, where she served as chemistry instructor until 1913. At Vassar, she taught what she called "sanitary chemistry, . . . applications of chemistry to food and sanitation" ("Teaching of Sanitary Chemistry," 324), based on organic chemistry. That year she accepted a position as an assistant professor in home economics at the University of Chicago.

Blunt's appointment to the home economics department of the university could not have come as a surprise to a woman trained in chemistry, a field still thoroughly dominated by men. Home economics emerged as an academic discipline, primarily for women, at the turn of the twentieth century, an era of growing faith in the capacity of science to solve the broad range of social and public health problems that accompanied rapid industrialization and high immigration rates. It was a period of heightened visibility of the nation's women's rights movement and the accompanying discussion about women's demands for suffrage and for political and social equality. Also discussed were the consequences that equality might have for women's traditional domestic roles. Public officials, educators, and activists (including many women) argued that the modern woman had to be trained in the "domestic sciences"—including sanitation, nutrition, food chemistry, textile science, child psychology, and even bacteriology—in order to raise healthy children and maintain an efficient household. Blunt argued that the "foundations of health, behavior, character, happiness and social, civic and moral ideals are found in early home care, training and experiences. Education for intelligent home-making, therefore, is the most logical, fundamental, and effective method of attacking these problems of human betterment" (quoted in Dye, *History of the Department of Home Economics*, 357–58).

For Blunt, however, home economics was not only a training program for housewives and mothers but also a particularly feminine branch of public service. In keeping with the Progressive Era belief in the need for educated women to engage in social reform work, Blunt urged women to bring their new scientific expertise to bear in rural areas, medical dispensaries, infant welfare societies, poor relief organizations, schools, and commercial and industrial cafeterias.

The entry of the United States into World War I presented Blunt with an opportunity to demonstrate the public usefulness of home economics. In 1917, she was granted a leave of absence from the university to serve as a nutrition expert for the Department of Agriculture, where she oversaw the production of a series of widely distributed pamphlets on wartime food and nutrition problems. At the request of the U.S. Food Administration, she collaborated with Florence Powdermaker, who worked in the Department of Agriculture, to prepare lessons for colleges on food conservation and nutritional guidelines for food substitutes. The curriculum was sent to seventy-five colleges, intended for courses geared to women students. The lessons were published in 1918 under the title *Food and the War* and adapted for younger students and the general public in *Food Guide for War Service at Home*. During the war, Blunt also served in the Conservation Department and as head of the Education Department of the Woman's Committee, State Council of Defense of Illinois; and the Woman's Committee, Council of National Defense, Illinois Division, as part of a team of women interested in health, food, and quality of life issues on the home front.

Blunt remained at the University of Chicago for sixteen years, advancing to the rank of associate professor in 1918, when she became unofficial head of the department, and to full professor and department chair in 1925. A staunch advocate of home economics as a profession for women, Blunt helped build the department's reputation for rigorous scientific training with an eye to practical application. As head of the department, Blunt stressed the importance of research in such areas as food chemistry and the biochemistry of nutrition (her personal research interests), household economics, household organization and equipment, clothing and textiles, and child development and parent education.

Blunt's reputation as an expert in food chemistry and nutrition attracted growing numbers of graduate students to the University of Chicago home economics program, including CHI CHE WANG, who went on to run hospital research programs, and LYDIA ROBERTS, who succeeded Blunt as chair of the department. Although Blunt complained repeatedly of lack of funding and facilities, the program continued to expand throughout her tenure. By 1925, Blunt reported that University of Chicago alumnae were employed either as heads or as staff members in at least eighteen state university home economics departments, another eighteen state agricultural colleges, and a number of private colleges. In addition, a program graduate served as chief of the national Bureau of Home Economics and another alumna was Home Economics Specialist of the Federal Board of Vocational Education.

Blunt's vision of the profession was captured in an April 1923 article in the *Journal of Home Economics,* in which she noted that experts in home economics practiced "the highest intellectual labor, imaginative constructive thinking of the highest order . . . at the same time . . . they may be making a direct contribution to wholesome living" (quoted in *Current Biography,* 1946, 58). The citation for a Wesleyan University honorary degree awarded to Blunt in 1936 credited her with developing "in the graduate school at Chicago one of the best departments of home economics in our American universities" (quoted in *Current Biography,* 1946, 58). Her status as a leader in the field was confirmed in 1924 when she was elected president of the American Home Economics Association, a position she held for two years after serving three years as vice-president of the organization. She was also president of the Illinois Home Economics Association from 1921 to 1922.

During Blunt's years in Chicago, she produced her most important scientific work, centering on nutritional chemistry and the basal metabolism of women and children. In a 1921 article published in the *Journal of Biological Chemistry,* for example, Blunt and her student Marie Dye argued that women experienced no regular variation in their basal metabolism during the menstrual period. A later study published in the same journal compared the nutritional value of evaporated and pasteurized milk for children and adults. Blunt also published numerous articles on food chemistry and nutrition in the *Journal of Home Economics.* Her best known work, coauthored with Ruth Cowan, was a book-length summary of research on the subject *Ultra-Violet Light and Vitamin D in Nutrition,* which appeared in 1930.

In September 1929, Blunt left Chicago to become the first woman president of Connecticut College in New London. Founded in 1915, the liberal arts institution offered at the time the state's only four-year college degree for women. Under Blunt's leadership, every department added new courses, and the school authorized a master's degree in 1930. Phi Beta Kappa installed a chapter at the college in 1935. Blunt presided over the expansion of the college's faculty and economic resources. The teaching staff of forty grew to seventy-three by 1942, and faculty salaries increased by 68 percent. Research and study resources were greatly enhanced by major additions to the college library and the creation of a fund for faculty research. The institution attracted several major corporate research grants and began publishing a monograph series for scholarly research. The physical capacity of the college also expanded greatly and included the construction of new science laboratories, a nursery school for students of child development, a music facility, an arboretum, and seven new student dormitories. By the time Blunt retired in 1943, the school boasted twenty-one buildings, a faculty numbering more than one hundred, and a student body of about seven hundred fifty, and it stood on solid financial footing. She returned to the presidency briefly for the academic year 1945–46, when she retired permanently, a month shy of her seventieth birthday.

As college president, Blunt worked to put into practice her deeply held belief in the need for students, and women in particular, to use their education and their privileged social status to serve the public good. The rise of fascism in Europe during the 1930s sharpened Blunt's conviction that women must become involved in politics and public service so that their "desire" (Blunt, "How About the Women?" 19) to be of use would become carefully planned action. In a speech delivered in 1937 at the dedication of the Maxwell School of Citizenship and Public Affairs at Syracuse University, she observed that "it may be that women, with their belief in the force of education, their fresh political energy, can do much to serve the democracy which has helped them, at this moment of its extreme peril. Our colleges must do all they can to give women the consuming desire for public service, the necessary knowledge, and power to think on public questions . . ." ("How About the Women?" 20). In keeping with this model of the educated woman, Blunt brought numerous prominent women to the Connecticut College campus, including Eleanor Roosevelt, JANE ADDAMS, Amelia Earhart, Dr. ALICE HAMILTON, Judge Florence Allen, Lillian Gilbreth, and Frances Perkins.

Public service was an important aspect of Blunt's life. In addition to her membership in professional societies, including the American Association for the Advancement of Science (where she was a fellow), the Biochemical Society, and the American Chemical Society, she served on the Connecticut Board of Education from 1931 to 1940, was head of the New London Red Cross War Fund from 1944 to 1945, and held officer positions in the League of Women Voters and the American Association of University Women. She traveled extensively in South America, Europe, and the Middle East, participating in meetings of the International Council of Women and the International Federation of University Women. Although committed to public life, Blunt remained devoted to practicing and promoting the highest standards of scholarship. It was for her work as scholar, educator, and activist alike that she was awarded honorary degrees from Mount Holyoke College (1937), the University of Chicago (1941), and Connecticut College (1943), in addition to the earlier Wesleyan University award. In 1954, the American Chemical Society honored her for her research work.

Despite failing eyesight, Blunt remained active in retirement. In New London, she took a leading part in a campaign of the League of Women Voters to establish moderately priced rental homes. She also gave radio speeches and participated in legislative hearings to promote a project for low-rental housing. She continued to travel, visiting Israel and Turkey in 1950. She died of a pulmonary embolism in July 1954 after suffering a broken hip.

At a time when home economics was perceived as a feminine area of study, Katherine Blunt's changes in the Department of Home Economics at the University of Chicago enabled students to prepare for careers in a professional field that offered many job opportunities. She developed an outstanding graduate curriculum that included scientific training and research. She also trained educated women who would be running households to use home economics education as a route to public service.

Sources. Blunt's writings on the education of women range from "The Teaching of Sanitary Chemistry in a Woman's College," *Journal of Home Economics,* October 1912, to "How About the Women? Their

Part in Public Service," *Journal of the American Association of University Women*, October 1938. Blunt discusses her government work in "The Food Administration," *Vassar Quarterly*, July 1918. Her research articles on various aspects of nutritional chemistry are listed in the indexes to the *Journal of Biological Chemistry* 1916–33 and in *Chemical Abstracts* indexes 1907–36. Marie Dye, *History of the Department of Home Economics, University of Chicago* (1972), gives an account of Blunt's work at the university. For a full description of her administration at Connecticut College, see Irene Nye, comp., *Chapters in the History of Connecticut College during the First Three Administrations 1911–1942* (1943). A brief discussion of the Connecticut years appears in Gertrude Noyes, "Dr. Katharine Blunt: Educator, Administrator, Public Servant," *Pioneer Women Teachers of Connecticut 1767–1970*, ed. Helen M. Sheldrick (1971). Biographical essays are found in *NCAB*, vol. B (1927); *Current Biography* (1946); and *NAW* (1980). Obituaries are published in the *NYT*, July 30, 1954, and the *Journal of Home Economics*, September 1954.

KATRIN SCHULTHEISS

BONDS, MARGARET ALLISON
March 3, 1913–April 26, 1972
COMPOSER, CONCERT PIANIST, TEACHER, EDITOR

Although she gained distinction early in her career as a concert pianist, Margaret Allison Bonds has come to represent the second generation of black women composers. Through her own perseverance and through mentoring by more established African American musicians and composers, she became one of the pioneers in breaking down the color and gender barriers that existed in classical music circles. She produced more than eighty-five known compositions, including art songs, spiritual arrangements, choral works, popular songs, and music for piano and orchestra. Her music was often commissioned and continues to be performed by many important African American vocal artists, including Leontyne Price, William Warfield, Martina Arroyo, Betty Allen, Jessye Norman, and Kathleen Battle. As a recitalist she performed throughout the United States and Canada, and she appeared as soloist with several symphony orchestras. In addition, she served as accompanist for such performers as Etta Moten, and she maintained a strong commitment to the music education of African American children throughout her life. Although she lived in Chicago for only twenty-six years of her life, those years had a great impact on the development of her work as a musical artist.

Bonds was born in Chicago into a family that immersed itself in the Black Renaissance occurring in Harlem and other major cities in the United States from around 1917 through 1935. Her mother, Estella C. Bonds, was an organist at Berean Baptist Church and prominent in the musical circles of the African American community. She served as Bonds's first piano teacher and was an early musical influence for her. Bonds wrote that because of her mother she had "actual physical contact with all the living composers of African descent. My mother had a collector's nose for anything that was artistic . . ." ("A Reminiscence," 192). The sculptor Richmond Barthe, poets Langston Hughes and Countee Cullen, soprano Abbie Mitchell, and composer Will Marion Cook all passed through the Bonds home. These encounters had a profound impact on Bonds's musical style as well as her lifelong dedication to the music and literature of the black experience.

At age five, Bonds composed her first piece, a song for piano entitled "Marquette Road Blues." During the same year, she received a scholarship to study music at the Coleridge Taylor School of Music, where she was a student of Martha B. Anderson. Between ages eight and nine she won a scholarship in piano at the Chicago Musical College. Later she returned to the Coleridge Taylor School as a pupil of T. Theodore Taylor, who also served as music director at the prominent Grace Presbyterian Church on Chicago's South Side.

While a student at Parker High School, Bonds was sent by her mother to study composition with William L. Dawson and composition and piano with FLORENCE PRICE. (Dawson later departed Chicago in 1930 to become music director at the Tuskegee Institute.) In Price, Bonds found a friend, mentor, and collaborator in significant performances over the next several years. She recalled fondly, "we used to sit around a large table in our kitchen—manuscript paper strewn around, Florence and I extracting parts for some contest deadline" ("A Reminiscence," 192).

During the 1920s, Bonds became a charter member of the junior division of the National Association of Negro Musicians (NANM). Bonds's mother was a founding member of the organization, established in Chicago in 1919 for the purpose of preserving, encouraging, and advocating African American music. Bonds continued her connection with NANM and its local branch, Chicago Music Association (CMA), throughout her life. It provided an important forum for the nurturing of her considerable talents and gave her exposure to many important African American musicians. By age sixteen, she regularly appeared as an accompanist at the multitude of concerts and other performances held at black churches throughout Chicago's South Side.

During her teens, Bonds's close association with Abbie Mitchell helped her understand the important relationship between text and music. Working with the singer also expanded her knowledge of vocal repertoire to include both European art song and the music of African American composers such as Harry T. Burleigh and Will Marion Cook. The music of both Burleigh and Cook served to influence Bonds's early compositional efforts. She copied the part for Cook's choir when they performed on the National Broadcasting Company (NBC) radio.

In 1929, Bonds entered Northwestern University, studying with Emily Boettcher. During this period she received consecutive scholarships from Alpha Kappa Alpha, the black sorority (1929 and 1930), and a scholarship award from NANM (1931). During this period Bonds first read the poetry of Langston Hughes. She described sitting in the basement of the Evanston Public Library and discovering his poem, "The Negro Speaks of Rivers." This poem later provided the text and title for her first published art song in 1942. Hughes's poetry provided the text for many of her most successful works. Bonds attended Northwestern at a time when African American students were not allowed to occupy campus housing, and she commuted by train from the South Side to the Evanston campus, using this time as an opportunity to write down her compositional ideas. Completing a bachelor's degree in music on June 17, 1933, she continued her studies at Northwestern on a Rosenwald Fund Fellowship. She received an M.M. degree in 1934.

The next several years represented a flurry of activity in Bonds's artistic life in Chicago. In 1932 she was the recipient of a $250 prize awarded by the Rodman Wanamaker Memorial Foundation. This represented one portion of a $1,000 prize established in August 1929 by Captain John Wanamaker, head of a Philadelphia department store, in honor of his father. Bonds won the song competition for "Sea Ghost," written for voice and piano. That same year her teacher, Florence Price, was awarded first prize in two categories—one for her symphonic work, *Symphony in E minor* ($500) and the other for her *Piano Sonata in E minor* ($250).

One of the most significant events at this time was Bonds's appearance as piano soloist with the Chicago Symphony Orchestra conducted by Dr. Frederick Stock. The concert was arranged by the Chicago Friends of Music and performed as part of the American Series for the Century of Progress Exposition at the Auditorium Theater. Roland Hayes, tenor, and probably the leading African American male classical singer of the period, headlined the event, which also included a performance of Price's *Symphony in E minor*. Bonds performed "Concertine" by John Alden Carpenter, a noted Chicago composer and philanthropist who had attended the rehearsal earlier that week. Not only was this the first time a major American orchestra had performed a symphony by a black woman composer, but the first time the Chicago Symphony had engaged an African American as a guest soloist. For the first time, Bonds's expertise as a classical pianist was provided a showcase by a major cultural institution in the city. The music critic for the *Herald-Examiner*, Glen Dillard Gunn, wrote of her performance, "Miss Bonds['s] vivid style and able techniques, together with a rhythmic instinct which may be racial or musicianly, and doubtless is both made Mr. Carpenter's graceful work glow with a fire [a] more experienced pianist well might envy" (quoted in *Chicago Defender*, June 17, 1933).

This concert elevated Bonds's prominence in Chicago's African American musical community. In September 1933, she was asked to appear at the exposition's Indiana Hall in the Court of States to unveil a bust of Clarence Cameron White, a leading African American musician and composer of the opera *Ouanga*. In the September 16, 1933, issue of the *Chicago Defender* she is pictured with her mother, Noble Sissle, and Camille Nickerson, and described by *Defender* music critic Maude Roberts George as "Chicago's musical gift to A Century of Progress."

During August 1934, Bonds performed as a guest artist at the Michigan Gardens Music Festival under the direction of J. Wesley Jones, conductor of the Metropolitan Community Church Choir. Later that month she and Florence Price represented the CMA at the NANM convention held that year in Pittsburgh. With Bonds playing the orchestral transcription, Price performed her *Concerto in D minor* for the organization's National Artists Program. Bonds also appeared on a program for the R. Nathaniel Dett Club at the same convention.

The Pittsburgh performance of Price's concerto served as preparation for its official premier on Thursday, October 18, 1934, at the Chicago Century of Progress Exposition with Bonds as piano soloist. The Women's Symphony Orchestra, under the direction of EBBA SUNDSTROM, performed in the Ford Symphony Gardens.

Some time during the 1930s, Bonds established the Allied Arts Academy. The academy provided instruction in dance, visual arts, and music. Bonds served as director and teacher. The academy also served, at least occasionally, as a meeting place for CMA. Bonds continued to maintain the academy throughout the depression. As late as June 1939, the Allied Arts Guild, an arm of the organization, made plans to publish a yearbook in December that would serve as "a directory of Negroes in the arts" (*Chicago Defender*, June 2, 1939). During this period Bonds continued her private piano studio. One of her piano students was a young Hyde Park resident and future composer, Ned Rorem.

In April 1939, Bonds presented a recital at Curtiss Hall in the historic Fine Arts Building. The performance featured the work of Brahms, Carpenter, Price, Bonds, and Coleridge-Taylor. Bonds's composition, "A Spanish Mother," was choreographed and danced by Posie Flowers. Grace Tompkins's column "Music News" in the *Chicago Defender* indicated that "the audience was generous with applause, flowers and bravos" (May 5, 1939). Bonds also appeared as a performer at the *Defender's* Achievement Congress Tea, which annually highlighted the accomplishments of "colored women" (May 27, 1939).

Moving to New York in 1939, Bonds worked briefly as an editor for a music publishing company, published several of her more popular songs, and continued to pursue her piano studies with Henry Levine and composition with Robert Starer at the Juilliard School of Music. She studied composition privately with Roy Harris and Emerson Harper and was the recipient of a Roy Harris Fellowship. As Bonds began to develop new professional and personal relationships, her Chicago roots continued to provide support for her musical activities. In May 1940 she performed a joint recital with Theodore C. Stone, noted Chicago baritone and an official with both CMA and NANM, at the Baha'i Center in New York.

She was married in 1940 to Lawrence Richardson of New York, a probation officer with the New York State Supreme Court. This marriage produced one daughter, Djane, who was named after her piano teacher at Juilliard, DJANE LAVOIE-HERZ.

In New York, Bonds formed the Margaret Bonds Chamber Society, dedicated to presenting the works of African American composers, and toured as a piano duo with Gerald Cook, one of her students. In addition, she worked on radio and gave her Town Hall debut in 1952, the same year she became a member of the American Society of Composers, Authors and Publishers (known as ASCAP). She also taught at the American Theatre Wing and developed a music education program for young people at a church in Harlem.

In the 1960s Bonds moved to California. There she worked as music director of the Inner City Repertory Theater, taught piano, and arranged choral works for the Los Angeles Jubilee Singers. Most of her important compositions were written after leaving Chicago. Besides those already mentioned, they include *The Ballad of the Brown King* (1954), *Three Dream Portraits* (1959), both with text by Langston Hughes, "Troubled Water" (1967), "You Can Tell the World" (1964), and "I Got a Home In That Rock" (1968). Her music is characterized as "very pianistic" (Green, 50), blending jazz and black folk idioms within more traditional European musical forms. Particularly in her vocal music, the vocal line with piano accompaniment demonstrates craftsmanship in its balance of rhythmic complexity and melodic simplicity.

Although Bonds left Chicago to work in New York and later California, the city and the rich cultural life of its African American community made an indelible mark on Bonds's artistry. On January 31, 1967, she was honored with an All-Margaret Bonds Concert, held at her mother's church, Berean Baptist. During that same year she also received the Alumni Medal from Northwestern University. This award represented an important achievement for Bonds.

Margaret Bonds died in Los Angeles, California, at age fifty-nine. Her *Credo* for chorus and orchestra was premiered that year by the Los Angeles Symphony Orchestra conducted by Zubin Mehta. She had succeeded in her struggle to have African American musicians and their unique contributions to the field of music recognized by the wider community, especially in the area of classical music.

Sources. The Black Music Research Center, Columbia College, Chicago, is a repository for papers related to the history of NANM and CMA. The Harold Washington Library (CPL) has the *Chicago Defender* (1929–40), which carried regular columns reporting the musical activities of churches, schools, NANM, and CMA. "A Reminiscence," by Bonds is in *International Library of Negro Life and History: The Negro in Music and Art* (1967). Mildred Denby Green, *Black Women Composers: A Genesis* (1983), is valuable. An extensive listing of Bonds's works can be found in *Fifteen Black American Composers: A Bibliography of Their Works* (1981), edited by Alice Tischler with the assistance of Carol Tomasic. In addition, Eileen Southern's *Biographical Dictionary of Afro-American and African Musicians* (1982); Raoul Abdul's *Blacks in Classical Music* (1974); and an article by Barbara Garvey Jackson, "Florence Price, Composer," in the *Black Music Perspective*, Spring 1977, provide some insight. Maude Roberts George, in "Roland Hayes Triumphs in Recital Here—Noted Tenor and Miss Margaret Bond [*sic*] Star with Symphony," *Chicago Defender*, June 17, 1933, quotes Glen Dillard Gunn's praise of Bonds's performance. Bonds's music is published in *Art Songs and Spirituals by African American Women* (1995), *Black Women Composers: A Century of Piano Music, 1893–1990* (1992), and *Art Songs by Black Composers* (1981). Recordings of her music include *Art Songs by American Composers* (1991), *Black Diamonds: Althea Waites Plays Music by Afro-American Composers* (1993), *Watch and Pray: Spirituals and Art Songs by African American Women Composers* (1994), and *Art Songs by Black American Composers* (1981).

BARBARA SUGGS MASON

BONNER OCCOMY, MARITA
June 16, 1899–December 6, 1971
SHORT STORY WRITER, PLAYWRIGHT, ESSAYIST, TEACHER

Marita Bonner was a writer of a distinct genre of community-centered narratives about people and places undergoing radical change. Writing in the early decades of the twentieth century and situating many of her narratives in Chicago, Bonner was acutely aware of a need to create new visions of cultural and social identity, to construct new patterns of filiation and affiliation, in short, to map new literary landscapes to accommodate the experience of those black urban migrants or European immigrants who peopled her texts.

Marietta Odette Bonner was born in Brookline, Massachu-

setts, one of four children of Joseph Andrew and Mary Anne (Noel) Bonner. She grew up in a close-knit family and community, where her interests in music and literature were nourished. Bonner's early life was not unusual for a bright and talented African American child growing up in New England in the early twentieth century before the arrival of successive waves of black migrants from the South. By the time she was in high school, she was already writing stories for publication and became one of the regular contributors to Brookline High School's literary magazine, the *Sagamore*. Her first story, "Going to the Dogs," appeared in May 1914 when Bonner was fourteen. Bonner also wrote the music for the class song and graduated in 1917. Her talents and abilities gained her admission to Radcliffe College in 1918, where she studied English and comparative literature. While at Radcliffe, Bonner was a student in Charles T. Copeland's prestigious writing seminar. Deeply involved in student activities at Radcliffe, she won two campus song composition competitions, in 1918 and 1922.

Bonner turned to school teaching while still in college, working at a high school in Cambridge. After graduation in 1922, Bonner taught in Bluefield, West Virginia, and in Washington, D.C. During the years she spent in Washington, D.C., from 1922 to 1930, Bonner was actively writing and publishing. In 1925 she published an essay, "On Being Young—a Woman—and Colored," in the *Crisis*, a journal that showcased the work of African American intellectuals. In this essay, which won first place in the *Crisis*'s 1925 literary contest, Bonner explores racial and sexual discrimination. In terms of sexual discrimination, Bonner hits upon a paradox. On the one hand, one is awakened to the gender barriers that one ultimately hopes to bring down; on the other, however, the way one brings down these barriers is limited, based on society's gender assumptions. In other words, one must not be too angry or too loud when one cites gender inequality.

During her years in Washington, D.C., Bonner was a member of writer Georgia Douglas Johnson's "S" Street Salon. Other salon participants included Langston Hughes, Countee Cullen, Alain Locke, Jessie Redmon Fauset, and Jean Toomer, all leaders in the Harlem Renaissance. (Harlem Renaissance refers to the cultural and literary developments and activities of African American writers, artists, and musicians during the 1920s in several areas of the country, including Washington, D.C., and Philadelphia, as well as New York's Harlem.) Having served her apprenticeship with these talented and productive writers and playwrights, Bonner was then positioned to have a brilliant career.

While living in Washington, D.C., Bonner grew increasingly more active as a writer. In addition to the essay "On Being Young—a Woman—and Colored," she wrote another, "The Young Blood Hungers," published in the *Crisis* in 1928. This essay warns its audience that poor race relations will soon bring violence. In addition to these essays, Bonner also wrote three plays. Each play treats an explicitly racial or social theme. *The Pot Maker*, published in *Opportunity*, another leading African American journal, in 1927, criticizes infidelity; *The Purple Flower*, published in the *Crisis* in 1928 and by far her most popular play, depicts generational conflict about racial inequality and, at the same time, calls for a revolution to fight racism; *Exit—An Il-*

lusion (*Crisis*, 1929), examines the complexities of miscegenation. She also wrote and published five short stories: "The Hands: A Story" (1925), "The Prison-Bound" (1926), "Nothing New" (1926), "One Boy's Story" (1927), and "Drab Rambles" (1927).

In 1930 Bonner married William Almy Occomy and moved to Chicago. They had three children: William Almy Jr., Warwick Gale, and Marita Joyce. Bonner's early years in Chicago were productive ones in terms of her writing. Between 1930 and 1941 she wrote seventeen short stories, several of them literary prize-winners, known collectively as "the Frye Street Stories," set in Chicago. The hypothetical community known as Frye Street, which Bonner had introduced in 1926 in "Nothing New," became by 1930 the unifying symbol for all her fiction of this period. In Bonner's stories, the Frye Street community is enclosed within a white bourgeois construction. It is cornered between "Grand Avenue," implicitly a defended neighborhood "on the white kids' side," patrolled and policed by white youths demanding, "'Stay on your own side!'" (*Frye Street*, 75–76), and the curve of the river. Within this enforced cul-de-sac, Frye Street's imprisoned inhabitants periodically strike out against each other in frustration like "hard, jaggered pebbles" in a tin can, or exhausted, shrink into themselves like peas in a sealed pod which "[do] not touch each other" (*Frye Street*, 119, 148).

Bonner's Chicago stories chronicle changes in the city. White urbanites begin their exodus from the metropolis to the suburbs, abandoning the city to the evils perceived within its streets and to African Americans from the South migrating in search of work. The concept of the city itself, then, undergoes a transformation as dramatic as the change in the notions of selfhood of migrant peoples taking possession of its street during this period of historical transition. Bonner's text, *Frye Street and Environs*, interrogates the difference and development within the African American community ensuing from this turbulent moment of migration, while revealing strands of continuity linking the present to the past.

This search for cultural continuity is important for Bonner, because it calls attention to the relocation process and the vacuum within the soul that is created when one is uprooted from home, family, and friends during the quest for material advancement. Many find "the houses on Federal Street . . . just as grey, just as bare of color and comfort as the hut they had left in Mississippi" (*Frye Street*, 188). For too many the solution for the ache of homesickness is "unreal living"—intense consumerism funded on the "never-never" (*Frye Street*, 188, 161), creating a nightmare of debt, bad company, alcohol—the lure of the trivial and superficial. Moreover, Bonner investigates the dynamic behind the contemporary economics of urban exploitation and finds that here, too, the roots of bitterness are deeply embedded and common to both exploiter and exploited.

Frye Street's fictional universe portrays disintegration, reconstruction, individual isolation, and community centeredness across class and gender lines. The Frye Street stories permit Bonner to exert her imaginative influence over her new environment and other people's lives at the same time that she brings to bear a new perspective on the changing American landscape. Her stories celebrate communal life, castigating those who neglect or deny their ancestry, but they also show concern with

racial and cultural survival and the challenges presented by a new urban environment. An example is her short story, "Hongry Fire" (1939), where there is a generational conflict between Ma, who points with determination toward the necessity for present and future accomplishment, and Jule—the ultra-modern "Jazz baby"—whose hardened attitudes toward life negate Ma's version of racial pride.

Although Bonner recognized and warned of the dangers of the city, she was nevertheless optimistic about the potential the new environment offered a dispossessed people. In the short story "High-Stepper" (1938–40), Sadie intuits that the limits of the mind and the limits of the city are one and the same, suggesting that to overcome the one is to deny power to the other.

By the time Bonner's third child was born in the late 1930s, Bonner apparently found it difficult to continue the pace of her writing and attend to the responsibilities of a family and household. She held a variety of teaching jobs but frequently gave up working outside the home to care for her children. Her daughter Joyce Occomy Stricklin, in her introduction to *Frye Street and Environs: The Collected Works of Marita Bonner* (1987), described her mother as "one who had seen worldliness. . . . She protected her children physically, mentally, and morally, and yet created a household life in which [they] were encouraged to spend time alone regularly and develop . . . independence" (p. ix). From 1941 until her death, Marita Bonner did not seem to have written or published anything more. She died at age seventy-two of injuries sustained in a fire in her apartment.

The posthumous reputation of Marita Bonner has gradually been gaining prominence in the wake of emerging scholarship on African American writing, especially that by women. *Frye Street and Environs*, a collection of her writings from the 1920s to 1941, was not published until 1987 in the wake of that new scholarship. This publication, as well as research on her earlier writing, has shown her to be a pioneer writer of experimental fiction and plays who prefigured and inspired the works of several African American writers who followed her. Bonner was a diligent observer of human nature whose compassion for her subjects was real. She was among the earliest African American writers and perhaps the first African American woman writer to use fragmented narrative sequences that present composite perspectives of multiple lives. Although written more than a half century ago, Bonner's Frye Street stories do not seem dated except in certain specific details; many of the problems that the changing urban environment of Chicago posed for its inhabitants during the 1930s still challenge city dwellers at the end of the twentieth century. Her portrayal of the tensions and struggles of Frye Street residents remains fresh and insightful.

Sources. A collection of Marita Bonner's papers is at the Radcliffe College Archives, Cambridge, Massachusetts. In addition to Bonner's works mentioned above, she wrote "A Possible Triad on Black Notes" (1933), "A Sealed Pod" (1936), "Black Fronts" (1938), "Hate is Nothing" (1938), "The Makin's" (1939), "The Whipping" (1939), "Patch Quilt" (1940), "One True Love" (1941), "On the Altar" (1937–40), "Stones for Bread" (1940), "Reap It As You Sow It" (1940–41), and "Light in Dark Places" (1941). The latter two works were not published but were found only in a worn notebook, along with two fragmentary sketches, in the Marita Bonner Papers, Radcliffe College Archives. There is as yet no full-length biography of Bonner, but Joyce Occomy Stricklin and Joyce Flynn, eds.,

Frye Street and Environs: The Collected Works of Marita Bonner Occomy (1987), contains an introduction by Bonner's daughter Stricklin with biographical information. Elizabeth Brown-Guillory, ed., *Wines in the Wilderness: Plays by African-American Women from the Harlem Renaissance to the Present* (1990), includes work by Bonner. Diane Isaacs has written an entry on Bonner in Bruce Kellner, ed., *The Harlem Renaissance: A Dictionary for the Era* (1984), and Elizabeth Brown-Guillory has an entry on Bonner in *BWA*. Cheryl A. Wall, *Women of the Harlem Renaissance* (1995), is useful for the context in which Bonner wrote; Wall also briefly analyzes some of Bonner's writings.

MARYEMMA GRAHAM

BOUSFIELD, MAUDELLE BROWN
June 1, 1885–October 14, 1971
EDUCATOR, EDUCATIONAL REFORMER, CIVIC AND
COMMUNITY LEADER

Maudelle Brown Bousfield, the first African American principal of a Chicago public school, was born in St. Louis, Missouri, the daughter of Charles Hugh and Arrena Isabella (Tanner) Brown. Her father worked in education for fifty years, both as teacher and administrator, retiring from the profession as principal of L'Ouverture School in St. Louis. Her mother, also a teacher, was from a prominent African American family. She was the niece of Bishop Benjamin Tanner of the African Methodist Episcopal Church and a cousin of Henry O. Tanner, a well-known painter during the first decades of the twentieth century. Brown had four siblings: Nell, Charles, Howard, and Elmer Alfred.

Along with her siblings, Maudelle Brown attended public school in St. Louis, graduating from both Sumner High School and the Charles Kunkel Conservatory in St. Louis in 1903. Embarking on what would be a long line of "firsts" in breaking racial barriers to education, Brown was the first African American to be admitted to the conservatory. Also in 1903, Maudelle Brown entered the University of Illinois, graduating with honors in 1906 with a double major in mathematics and astronomy, the first African American woman to graduate from that university. An outstanding scholar, she was invited back to the University of Illinois in 1965 for induction into the chapter of Phi Beta Kappa, established after her graduation.

Following graduation, Maudelle Brown taught for one year at Lincoln High School in East St. Louis, Illinois, in 1906. From 1907 to 1913, she taught mathematics at Baltimore Negro High School in Baltimore, Maryland, during which time she traveled extensively in the United States and Europe. She returned to St. Louis, Missouri, in 1914 as a teacher of mathematics at Sumner High School. Later that year, she stopped teaching to marry Colonel Midian O. Bousfield, M.D., and subsequently became the mother of a daughter whom she named after herself, Maudelle Brown Bousfield.

After relocating with her family to Chicago, Illinois, Bousfield resumed her education career, moving eventually from teaching to administration. The schools to which she was assigned both as teacher and administrator were ones that contained an almost solidly African American population, in accordance with the Chicago public school administration's policy at the time not to assign black teachers to schools with a majority of white students. In January 1921 she began to teach mathe-

matics at Wendell Phillips High School, remaining in that position until 1926. Bousfield was then appointed dean of girls at that high school, the first African American to hold that position at a Chicago high school. In 1928, she was named the first African American principal in Chicago, accepting an appointment at Keith Elementary School. She became principal of Stephen A. Douglas Elementary School in 1931 and served there until 1939. From 1939 until her retirement in 1950, she was principal of Wendell Phillips High School, the first African American high school principal in Chicago.

While Bousfield was teaching at Wendell Phillips High School in the mid-1920s, she decided to go back to school to enhance her education and academic career. She entered the University of Chicago Graduate School and received an M.A. degree in 1931. To fulfill her graduation requirements, she combined both her professional and academic knowledge in writing her thesis, "A Study of the Intelligence and School Achievement of Negro Children," basing it on research she conducted in a Chicago elementary school.

During the second decade of the twentieth century, thousands of African Americans migrated to Chicago from the south, seeking a better life for themselves and their families. By 1930 African Americans, nearly 234,000 in number, constituted 6.9 percent of Chicago's population. The growth in Chicago's African American population meant a corresponding increase in the number of black children attending the Chicago public schools. Like other African American educators across the country, Bousfield was concerned about the kind and quality of education that growing numbers of African American children were receiving.

In the late 1920s and 1930s, intelligence testing became increasingly popular in school systems across the country. Some African American educators viewed this kind of testing as a means often used by school systems to subordinate African American students and began to question the value of standardized tests for determining the intelligence of black children. Bousfield's master's thesis addressed this issue by looking at how Chicago's public schools measured the mental ability and achievement of African American children. She carried out her thesis research while she was teaching at Keith Elementary School, testing 222 students in the fifth through eighth grades.

All students in her study were given questionnaires to fill out detailing information about their personal lives and home situations. The questionnaire was used to determine "certain environmental and economic conditions of the group, especially poverty and home mal-adjustment" (Bousfield, "Intelligence of Negro Children," 389). The students were also given three different intelligence tests in order to compare the results. She noted that the results of intelligence testing varied widely, depending on which standardized intelligence tests were given; while students in her study tested below average on tests that depended heavily on reading ability, they scored average or above on a test that did not depend on reading skills. She also found that testing revealed differences in ability in math and reading between sexes, girls sometimes showing greater proficiency in reading and boys in math.

Bousfield published her thesis research in the *Journal of Negro Education* in 1932. The acceptance of her article in this scholarly quarterly devoted, as its masthead read, to "a . . . review of the problems incident to Negro education," marked her as an educational theorist as well as teacher and administrator. She wrote in the article: "indication of homes lacking ordinary indices of normal living are so scattered over the entire group that conclusions as to the relationship between mentality, achievement and home conditions cannot be drawn with any degree of certainty" ("Intelligence and School Achievement of Negro Children," 395). She called for further research to develop testing techniques that would better determine "which particular home factors affect mentality and achievement and to what extent" (p. 395). She also concluded that more valid tests should be devised, ones that did not rely so heavily on linguistic skills and did not depend on "manners, customs or background of the individual" (p. 395).

Committed to research and to the improvement of education for African Americans, Bousfield proposed sweeping changes in the education of African Americans. In "Redirection of the Education of Negroes in Terms of Social Needs," an article published in the *Journal of Negro Education* in 1936, she advocated better education for African Americans so that they could succeed in American society, segregated and prejudiced as it was. The effect of the Great Depression, she wrote, was felt disproportionately by African Americans with the result that "eventually the Negro will be forced to live on scant charity. His morale will be entirely broken, his outlook utterly without hope. Economically he is poor; educationally his training is inadequate; politically he is powerless in most Southern states; socially he is being rapidly reduced to a state of parisitism" ("Redirection of Education," 413). In order for African Americans to address their desperate situation and enable themselves to survive, Bousfield spelled out a number of areas she thought crucial to develop. She urgently called for improvements in health education, adult education, the education of gifted children, vocational training, teaching of African American cultural traditions and history, and, most importantly, teacher training.

In addition to her work in the field of education, Bousfield's commitment to the African American community was shown in her involvement with many civic betterment organizations. In 1921 she was initiated into the Beta Chapter of Alpha Kappa Alpha Sorority (AKA). AKA, established at Howard University in 1908, was the first Greek-letter organization founded by African American women. Bousfield transferred to the Theta Omega graduate chapter when it was organized in 1921. In 1929, in recognition of her leadership and service to AKA, she was elected Sixth Supreme Basileus or national leader of AKA. She expected high morality, scholarship, and community service from the members of the sorority.

In 1932, at the public meeting of the fifteenth Boule, the national convention of AKA, Bousfield spoke on the topic of health. In her speech, she set the stage for the AKA-sponsored Mississippi Health Project, begun in the summer of 1935. This nationally recognized project set up mobile health units, staffed by twelve visiting doctors, nurses, and other health care providers, who gave immunizations and medical attention and distributed health information pamphlets. Bousfield was a member of its advisory committee.

In the 1940s and 1950s, Bousfield continued to serve in a number of civic and educational positions. During World War II, she was the only African American member of the Women's Advisory Committee of the War Manpower Commission. Later, she was vice-president of the board of directors for Provident Hospital, an institution that served the black community, and a member of Mayor Richard J. Daley's Committee on Juvenile Delinquency and of the Community Fund of Chicago. She was the first African American to serve on the Board of Oral Examiners of Chicago, conducting principal's examinations from 1946 until retirement from her position as principal of Wendell Phillips High School in 1950. During the 1940s, Bousfield's husband was the first African American appointed to membership on the Chicago School Board. For a time she was principal at Coolidge School in southern Cook County, and she continued to tutor mathematics after she retired from that position. An active Episcopalian, she served from 1947 to 1959 as president of the board of trustees of St. Edmund's School, an Episcopal institution affiliated with St. Edmund's Church, which she helped to found.

Along with her many other activities, Bousfield maintained her interest in music, graduating with a B.A. degree from Chicago's Mendelssohn Conservatory of Music in 1950. She was a charter member of the National Association of Negro Musicians, which was formed in Chicago after World War I.

A gardening enthusiast in her retirement years, Bousfield wrote a weekly column, "Let's Grow a Garden," for the *Chicago Defender,* the city's leading African American newspaper. She also hosted a radio program for women, "Maudelle Bousfield Chats." Although her activities were somewhat curtailed by failing eyesight in her later years, she maintained her interest in educational, church, and community issues and activities. Bousfield died at the age of eighty-six.

Bousfield raised significant questions about the use of intelligence testing for evaluating children. As a teacher, a researcher, and an administrator, she worked for the improvement of education for African American children. In honor of her achievements, her portrait hangs in the social room of Wendell Phillips High School.

Sources. Bousfield's master's thesis, "A Study of the Intelligence and School Achievement of Negro Children" (Univ. of Chicago, 1931), and two articles published in the *Journal of Negro Education,* "The Intelligence and School Achievement of Negro Children," October 1932, and "Redirection of the Education of Negroes in Terms of Social Needs," July 1936, give a good understanding of her educational theories and the reforms for which she called. Bousfield also wrote "In High School," an article in *Ebony,* December 1950. Roi Ottley, "Woman Leads Way for Negro in Education," *CT,* October 29, 1955, is about Bousfield. She has an entry in *Who's Who in Colored America* (1950). Obituaries for Bousfield were published in *CT,* October 17, 1971, and in *Jet,* November 4, 1971. Two volumes on Alpha Kappa Alpha, both written by Marjorie H. Parker, include information on Bousfield: *Alpha Kappa Alpha in the Eye of the Beholder* (1979) and *Alpha Kappa Alpha through the Years, 1908–1988* (1990). Parker also authored *African-American Women Heritage Series* (1995), which has information on Bousfield. See the entry on Alpha Kappa Alpha in *BWA* for information on the Mississippi Health Project. For information on the situation for African Americans in the Chicago public schools during much of the time Bousfield worked as teacher and administrator in them, see Michael Homel, *Down from Equality: Black Chicagoans and the Public Schools, 1920–1940* (1984). Harold Gosnell, *Negro Politicians* (1937), provides a further description of the status of education in Chicago's African American community during the 1930s. For background on the development of Chicago's African American community, see Allan H. Spear, *Black Chicago: The Making of a Negro Ghetto* (1967), and James R. Grossman, *Land of Hope: Chicago, Black Southerners, and the Great Migration* (1989).

DENISE TRAVIS

BOWEN, LOUISE deKOVEN
February 26, 1859–November 9, 1953
SOCIAL REFORMER, POLITICAL ACTIVIST, CLUBWOMAN

Louise deKoven Bowen, a wealthy Chicago socialite, represented the epitome of noblesse oblige and the exercise of power for the benefit of the larger community. Her longtime positions as president of the Juvenile Protective Association and treasurer of Hull-House had a significant impact both on these organizations and on the history of Chicago. Bowen's tenure as president of the Woman's City Club coupled with her activism for woman suffrage and municipal reform demonstrated her ability to use her influence to merge issues in both partisan and nonpartisan ways. Bowen's appointment to mobilize the war effort during World War I reflected a recognition of her elite status, her organizational skills in philanthropic work, and her wide network of women activists. Throughout her long career of public service and activism, Bowen's uppermost goals were the welfare and betterment of women, children, and their families.

The granddaughter of Fort Dearborn pioneers, deKoven was the only child of John and Helen (Hadduck) deKoven. Her large inheritance "derived from her maternal grandfather, who built a large fortune from real estate that later became the heart of Chicago's . . . [downtown]" (Sklar, 107). At the age of sixteen, having been one of twelve honors graduates of Dearborn Seminary, deKoven refused the opportunity to present her graduation speech because her father thought that making such a speech in a crowded church would appear "unwomanly" (Bowen, *Growing Up with a City*, 18). Upon graduating, deKoven embarked on church work as an acceptable outlet for her interest in community service. She taught a Sunday school class of boys in need of guidance and direction. During the eleven years she taught at St. James Episcopal Church, she visited the boys' families, talked with them about their circumstances, and through her network of friends, assisted the boys in finding jobs. Realizing the need for recreational opportunities, deKoven at first invited the boys to her home to play billiards; but she later established and ran the first Chicago boys' club, the Huron Street Club. DeKoven continued this activity until the time constraints of marriage and motherhood prevailed.

Married at twenty-seven in 1886 to a prominent manufacturer and banker, Joseph Tilton Bowen, Louise deKoven Bowen had four children in the next six years: John deKoven Bowen in 1887; Joseph T. Bowen Jr. in 1888; Helen Hadduck Bowen in 1890; and Louise deKoven Bowen in 1892.

Mindful of her civic responsibilities, Bowen, while still a mother of young children, became board member and then president of Maurice Porter Memorial Hospital, later named Children's Memorial Hospital. She soon became vice-president of the Woman's Board of St. Luke's Hospital and then president of the Woman's Board of Passavant Hospital.

Bowen's long-term friendship with JANE ADDAMS and involvement with Hull-House originated when Addams invited her to join the newly formed Hull-House Woman's Club and to assist neighborhood women in using parliamentary procedures at club meetings. First Bowen had to learn parliamentary rules herself. She began her seventeen-year involvement with the club, eventually becoming secretary and then president. Bowen gained both public speaking expertise and an understanding of contemporary issues. With the expansion of membership, Bowen helped Addams and the Hull-House trustees fund a new building, Bowen Hall, to house an auditorium and library for use by the Hull-House Woman's Club. Bowen continued to forge connections between her elite social class and the poor of the Hull-House neighborhood, all the while developing as a person. Sharing Addams's vision of service and sense of social justice, Bowen became a major financial contributor to Hull-House and the primary solicitor of Hull-House funding. "Over a period of thirty-four years, between 1895 and 1928, Bowen contributed a total of $542,282, averaging $15,049 annually. No other donor came close to her record" (Sklar, 107). In 1911, as a memorial to her husband who died that year, Bowen gave the settlement seventy-two acres of land in Waukegan, Illinois, to establish the Joseph T. Bowen Country Club. In addition, she provided an endowment to maintain the site as a summer boys' camp for children from the Hull-House neighborhood.

Jane Addams spoke to the heart of the relationship between Bowen and her husband at the Bowen Country Club's opening. She recalled Joseph T. Bowen's "whole-hearted cooperation, to the last detail, in everything that came to Hull-House through his wife" (*The Excellent Becomes the Permanent*, 87). Years later, Bowen commented that her husband "was proud and sympathetic about everything I did" (*Survey Midmonthly*, April 1939, 106).

By the late 1890s, her involvement in Hull-House broadened both Bowen's concerns for children's welfare and her strong sense of social responsibility. Bowen brought her considerable energies and skills when she joined with other social and child welfare activists in developing a reform agenda for women and children's protection and betterment. By 1898, a coalition of county judges, the Chicago Bar Association, and women reformers including LUCY FLOWER, JULIA LATHROP, MARY BARTELME, and Louise deKoven Bowen successfully lobbied for a new juvenile court in Chicago—the first juvenile court in the United States. It opened in 1899 and handled delinquent children separately from adult criminals, though no provision had been made to pay probation officers. To meet this need and make certain the system did its job, the women reformers organized a Juvenile Court Committee (JCC) whose major initial goal was fund-raising for probation officers' salaries; Bowen first served as vice-chair, and by 1904 chaired the committee. Soon JCC extended its purpose to include finding suitable homes for dependent and delinquent children. Toward this end, Bowen led efforts to establish a Juvenile Court Building and Detention Home by obtaining commitments from the City of Chicago to provide the land and from the Cook County Board to provide funding for construction.

With the completion of this project, the JCC was "disbanded" in 1907 "but at the same time absorbed a small organ-

FIG. 13. *In 1922 Louise deKoven Bowen, a leader in the campaign for woman suffrage, was influential as Hull-House's treasurer and as a leader of the Juvenile Protective Association.*

FIG. 14. *Louise deKoven Bowen, seated third from right, member of the Woman's World's Fair Board, 1926; other members included politician Ruth Hanna McCormick, seated second from right.*

FIG. 15. *Louise deKoven Bowen remained a leading force at Hull-House until her death in 1953, long after the death of her friend Jane Addams in 1935.*

ization called the Juvenile Protective Association, started by Judge [Julian] Mack, Mr. Hastings Hart and Miss Minnie Lowe [sic]" (*Growing Up with a City*, 115) (see MINNIE LOW). Bowen became president of the Juvenile Protective Association (JPA). Following the approach of *Hull-House Maps and Papers* (1895), studies were published as inexpensive pamphlets widely distributed to social welfare activists, public officials, and the public-at-large. Bowen authored many of the studies and demonstrated an acute understanding and analysis of the need for both local and state government action and intervention to prevent juvenile delinquency.

The JPA studies identified aspects of urban life that had negative consequences for unprotected and unsupervised children whose family circumstances forced them into the city's streets and created an environment that promoted delinquency. Public dance halls and theaters were areas where liquor and prostitution flourished. Children were also at risk when they were employed in street peddling. Bowen led the campaign for laws to prohibit liquor sales in public dance halls and to regulate street peddling. In 1912, a city ordinance regulating peddling by boys and girls was passed during the administration of Mayor Carter H. Harrison Jr., who cooperated with Bowen and the JPA's reform agenda. When William "Big Bill" Thompson was elected mayor, the political climate for reform worsened. Political bossism, corruption, and the incompetence of Mayor Thompson's administration made adequate enforcement of the 1912 ordinance difficult. Bowen shifted from a private letter-writing campaign criticizing Thompson to public denunciation of the mayor. Later, using one of her pamphlets as campaign literature, Bowen was able to get a bill prohibiting liquor sales in public dance halls introduced and referred to a legislative committee in 1917.

Bowen was one of the first reformers in Chicago to become aware of the need for Chicago's African American community to have "an equal chance for work, for living accommodations, and for recreation" ("Annual Report," 1912–13, 48, JPA Records). In 1913 Bowen authored *The Colored People of Chicago*, one of the first social investigations into the social and economic conditions of Blacks in the city. Bowen concluded that Chicago's African American children's lives were "so circumscribed on every hand by race limitations" (*Speeches, Addresses, and Letters*, vol. 1, 275) that action was necessary against the deep-seated and extensive injustice first before the JPA could itself help the children. The JPA published the in-depth study of racial prejudice and discrimination in education, employment, housing, law enforcement, and entertainment as one of its pamphlets.

To fund JPA activities, Bowen contributed significant sums of her own money. In addition, because no one else would accept the responsibility, Bowen became the long-term chair of the organization's finance committee in 1910. In this capacity, she solicited corporate as well as individual contributions. Among the major individual benefactors were BERTHA PALMER, from Bowen's own elite circle, and Augusta Rosenwald, Julius Rosenwald's wife, from Bowen's elite and social welfare contacts. Nevertheless, Bowen was aware of the JPA's continual funding problems. In 1919, when the JPA executive director JESSIE BINFORD wanted the organization to do pro-

tective work with girls and not just with boys, Bowen knew that the association was already overextended financially because of child labor work assumed from the defunct Illinois Consumers' League. Facing a JPA budget of $27,000 and a deficit of $1,100 in October 1918, Bowen was rightly concerned. By 1929, when the budget was $40,000, Bowen resigned from the presidency because of the difficulties of funding a budget "about $12,000 more than I can raise and be moderately sure of" (JPA Board "Minutes," October 11, 1929, JPA Records). Yet, within three months, Bowen was back as president with a presumably lowered budget.

Bowen was also involved with the woman suffrage movement. Her initial support for woman suffrage resulted from her sympathies for the ardent English suffragettes and their commitment rather than from Jane Addams's influence. Yet, once Bowen became a suffragist, she and Addams worked together organizationally, with Bowen as vice-president of the Illinois Equal Suffrage Association, president of the Chicago Equal Suffrage Association, and auditor of the National American Woman Suffrage Association.

Supporting woman suffrage as a means of social reform and municipal and state housekeeping, Bowen argued that women were victims of taxation without representation. Refuting the ecclesiastical and physiological arguments of women's innate inferiority, Bowen proudly asserted women's equality with men in sharing civic responsibility. Bowen labeled as "manifestly absurd" (*Speeches, Addresses, and Letters*, vol. 1, 163) the domestic and social arguments that women, if given the vote, would precipitate marital discord and neglect of the family. Bowen further noted the inconsistency between praise by men for women as philanthropists and criticism of women when those same activities were no longer "considered philanthropy but politics" (*Speeches, Addresses, and Letters*, vol. 1, 163). In her argument in support of a federal amendment, Bowen noted that, with the opposition of the "liquor interests and disrespectable politicians who fear the moral influence of women at the polls," and "with so much money and organization opposing woman suffrage, it . . . [is] almost impossible to get . . . [woman suffrage] fairly before the voters" (*Speeches, Addresses, and Letters*, vol. 1, 478) on a state-by-state basis.

When, in 1912, the Republican Party refused to endorse woman suffrage and Theodore Roosevelt as the Progressive Party presidential candidate made such an endorsement, Bowen campaigned for Roosevelt. In 1913, women in Illinois gained a limited franchise and the right to hold certain offices. With encouragement from her network of activist supporters, Bowen became a Progressive Party candidate for Cook County Board in 1914, along with MARY McDOWELL and SOPHONISBA BRECKINRIDGE; Bowen had to withdraw her candidacy due to serious illness.

Simultaneous with Bowen's partisan activities as a suffrage supporter was her 1914–24 presidency of the nonpartisan Woman's City Club. Resigning the presidency of the Hull-House Woman's Club to accept this new position, Bowen felt that she would now be able to extend her sphere of influence beyond the Hull-House neighborhood, since the Woman's City Club had a citywide membership. Beginning with her presidency, the Woman's City Club's views on public policy were sought out by both city of Chicago and Cook County officials. Bowen led the Woman's City Club in expanded activities to promote citizenship education and to monitor the city administration's enforcement of laws. In the March 1915 Woman's City Club *Bulletin*, Bowen strongly encouraged women to vote in the April 1915 mayoral election because "women [hold] the balance of power" (p. 1) in that election.

In 1916, when Republican presidential candidate Charles Evans Hughes endorsed a federal amendment for woman suffrage, Bowen supported Hughes. During the June 1916 Republican convention in Chicago that nominated Hughes, the Chicago Equal Suffrage Association headed by Bowen organized a parade of five thousand women to march two miles down Michigan Avenue to the Coliseum.

During World War I, in recognition of Bowen's elite social status and the key position she held in political and civic circles, Illinois Governor Frank Lowden appointed her to the Illinois State Council of Defense; she was the only woman member. As appointed chair of the Woman's Committee of the Governor's Council and as elected chair of the Woman's Committee of the Council of National Defense, Illinois Division, Bowen worked with the heads of Illinois women's organizations. It was Bowen who spearheaded the establishment of an intricate statewide organization that mobilized women for the war effort. That effort included registering women for war work, raising funds to finance the war, and demonstrating techniques of food conservation. A statewide network of trained women speakers carried "the war message to people in every part of the state" (Bowen, "The War Work," 95). Bowen and her committees assisted women in finding job training and wartime employment and in training farm women to maintain their family farms.

During this war effort, Bowen's friendship with Jane Addams became more strained because of Addams's pacifism and refusal to support the United States in World War I. Compounding the rift were not only Addams's ideological position and Bowen's formal role in the war effort, but also the fact that Bowen was most anxious about her two sons fighting overseas. Years later, Bowen referred to "that horrid time of the war when we differed so radically" (Bowen to Addams, February 26, 1926, *Jane Addams Papers*).

After World War I, in 1920, as president of the Woman's City Club, Bowen took an active part in getting large numbers of women registered to vote in the presidential election, a right Illinois women were able to exercise because of the 1913 state suffrage law. Bowen believed the example of women voting in large numbers would move ratification of the proposed Nineteenth Amendment forward. With the passage of the Nineteenth Amendment, the National American Woman Suffrage Association held its spring 1920 convention in Chicago and became the League of Women Voters. At that convention, Bowen was one of several prominent speakers as well as a recipient of a Certificate for Distinguished Work in the Cause of Woman Suffrage. When the Illinois Equal Suffrage Association met in October 1920 to organize the Illinois chapter of the League of Women Voters, Bowen was elected one of its directors.

With the end of the war and ensuing high prices, Bowen was appointed the Woman Fair Price Commissioner for Illinois by U.S. Attorney General A. Mitchell Palmer. Bowen found it difficult to get sufficient money to pay clerks' salaries, was inundated with advice about how to manage and organize, and became the object of public disapproval; she resigned after about a year.

Bowen argued in favor of women's running for public office as both an exercise of the newly achieved "privileges and responsibilities" (Woman's City Club *Bulletin*, December 1921, 8–9) of their full citizenship and as an influence in the "new social order" (pp. 8–9). Advocating participation in both "party councils and government activities," (pp. 9–10), Bowen strongly urged women to run for office because of the contributions and leadership qualities that women could bring to public service in a democracy.

Joining the newly established Woman's Roosevelt Republican Club and soon becoming its vice-president and later its president, Bowen insisted that she detested politics and everything associated with it. Yet, she argued that because of political party domination in the United States, if one cared for "good government" (*Speeches, Addresses, and Letters*, vol. 2, 689), women had to relinquish nonpartisanship, join political parties, become loyal party supporters, and thereby influence both the nomination and election of qualified reform-minded male and female candidates. Such partisan activity would demonstrate "the power of women's votes" (*Speeches, Addresses, and Letters*, vol. 2, 689) and work toward good government. However difficult it was for Bowen to compromise by endorsing an entire Republican ticket that included a few less-than-qualified male candidates, Bowen and the Woman's Roosevelt Republican Club were instrumental in supporting the nomination and election of Mary Bartelme, the first woman judge in Cook County. Years later, while at times refusing to endorse certain Republican candidates, Bowen and the organization endorsed and helped to elect RUTH HANNA McCORMICK to the U.S. House of Representatives.

It was because of Bowen's political, social, and reformist networks and demonstrated leadership that there was some discussion in 1923 of a Louise deKoven Bowen candidacy for mayor of Chicago. Bowen's strengths as a mayoral candidate included publicity as a woman candidate, appeal to the women's vote, refusal to build a political machine, and lack of association with the Ku Klux Klan, which was in its heyday in Chicago. Though Bowen later insisted that she "had no idea whatever of running for mayor" ("Chicago's First Woman World's Fair Closes Its Successful Exposition," 215–16), she did note, "Had I been 20 years younger I would have liked to try it" (pp. 215–16) because campaigning would have produced activity and publicity for her municipal program. Yet Bowen was especially satisfied that, because she delayed her response on her possible mayoral candidacy and because newspapers and others publicly and privately debated the possibility, both the Democratic and Republican parties nominated "good" (*Speeches, Addresses, and Letters*, vol. 2, 702) mayoral candidates. Shortly after, Bowen was appointed one of three women on the Republican National Committee.

In April 1925, Bowen chaired the eight-day Woman's World's Fair held in Chicago, organized by the Illinois Republican Women's Club and the Woman's Roosevelt Republican Club. The plan was to demonstrate women's achievements in the trades, professions, and the arts, and to do so by holding annual fairs. While President Calvin Coolidge opened the exposition via a radio address, Vice-President Charles G. Dawes, an Illinoisan, closed the fair in person. Bowen herself emphasized the nonpartisan aspect of recognizing women's achievements. In describing the exposition luncheon given for "famous women" ("Chicago's First Woman World's Fair," 453), Bowen noted that Jane Addams, who sat to her left, was a "prominent LaFollette worker" (p. 453). Bowen headed the organizing group in 1926; fairs were also held in 1927 and 1928.

In 1935, when Jane Addams became seriously ill, she was taken to Louise deKoven Bowen's home, where she remained until she was hospitalized for the last time and died. Bowen resigned from the JPA presidency after thirty-five years to devote more time to Hull-House. Appointed acting president of the settlement, and then president in addition to her position as treasurer, Bowen began to work with ADENA MILLER RICH, the newly appointed head resident. From the start, Bowen voiced reservations about Rich's half-time appointment to a position she felt was a full-time task. Rich, who was also director of the Immigrants' Protective League, contributed her time as head resident and did not receive a salary. Bowen remained critical; she was concerned that Rich was not accessible to Hull-House residents, to people in the Hull-House neighborhood, and to Bowen herself. Additionally, Bowen faced fund-raising problems and found it difficult to fund Hull-House's $100,000 annual budget, especially in the midst of the Great Depression. Bowen recognized the need for additional members on the Hull-House board and hoped that the appointment of one or two businessmen with financial expertise would assist her in the management and investment of Hull-House's $640,000 endowment.

The apparent tension between Rich and Bowen was in large part due to Bowen's habit of spending all her mornings at Hull-House, while Rich did her part-time work there in the evenings. Although the settlement seemed to be functioning well, Bowen knew very little of the day-to-day operations, unlike her practice at Hull-House, which she managed during Jane Addams's frequent absences. Though the budget was balanced, Bowen was concerned that to receive Community Fund financial assistance, Hull-House would have to hire a full-time head resident with a salary. Finally, Rich resigned, voicing her own concern about the "respective functions" (Trustee "Minutes," April 2, 1937, Hull-House Association Records) of Hull-House trustees and Hull-House residents.

Rich was replaced by Charlotte E. Carr, who had been executive director of the Emergency Relief Bureau of the city of New York during the Great Depression. Bowen was confident Carr would "again put Hull-House on the map" (Bowen to Dr. Taylor, November 10, 1937, Margaret Dreier Robins Papers). While Bowen admired Carr's hard work, strong character, and dynamic personality, Bowen nevertheless remained concerned about financial support. With the passing of Jane Addams and her generation of supporters, Bowen recognized that invoking Addams's name to solicit contributions was no longer effective. Working with Carr, Bowen and the Hull-House Association Board increased its number of trustees, retained some additional Community Fund support, and planned a fiftieth anniversary celebration for publicity to raise funds. Bowen herself, by personal letters to nearly twenty-nine hundred people, raised tens of thousands of dollars each year and in 1941, with a projected budget of more than $131,000, personally raised almost $51,000.

Within a short time, Bowen considered Carr a friend who had appropriately taken Addams's place. Likewise, Bowen was proud of Carr's political activities and contacts in Washington, D.C., and her interest in labor relations; but Bowen remained concerned. In 1940, Bowen commented: "I hope she will not be too violently for Roosevelt because almost all the money which supports the [Hull] House comes from Willkie supporters and they would not like our endorsing Roosevelt" (Bowen to Margaret D. Robins, October 1, 1940, Robins Papers). Carr was interested both in reinstating Hull-House as a "pacemaker" (Trustee "Minutes," December 21, 1942, Hull-House Association Records) in the settlement movement and in changing the conditions of the Hull-House neighborhood. Bowen and the board were concerned about the divisiveness of politics should the Hull-House director take a "leading roll [sic] in a political campaign" (Trustee "Minutes," December 21, 1942). There was concern for reduced and canceled contributions because of Carr's "partisan political activities" (Trustee "Minutes," December 21, 1942). Bowen herself was also worried that during Carr's tenure $125,000 were spent from unrestricted endowments, with $80,000 of this amount used to cover the yearly budget deficits. Ultimately, the problem with finances intertwined with politics and the future of Hull-House. Carr resigned, and shortly after, Russell Ballard became head resident. Bowen was made honorary president, though she continued as treasurer until 1953.

Even with Ballard as head resident of Hull-House and Bowen as honorary president, the eighty-four-year-old stalwart continued to guard the traditions and reputation of Hull-House and Jane Addams. Bowen admonished Ballard for suggesting that board members serve as employees of the board. She emphasized to Ballard the importance of Hull-House policies that were neutral on "politics, party affiliation, religion and labor unions" (Bowen to Ballard, February 8, 1946, Russell Ballard Papers). She herself had made up the difference in lost contributions when Jane Addams had appeared "too much in sympathy with working people," ("First Citizen of Chicago," Louise deKoven Bowen Scrapbooks, vol. 3, 27), but times had changed. Bowen objected to Ballard's use of the Jane Addams Memorial Room in the settlement's original building as his office; she tried to maintain it intact in order to preserve Addams's historic contributions. Almost six years after Ballard's appointment, Bowen voiced concern that he was becoming too involved in politics, and she referred to Charlotte Carr's involvement with the 1940 National Democratic Convention in Chicago that nominated Franklin Roosevelt. It had resulted in a crucial loss of contributions to Hull-House.

Perhaps compounding Bowen's continuing concern and involvement with the finances of Hull-House was her own personal situation. Years earlier Bowen and her husband had acquired Baymeath, a nineteen-bedroom summer estate in Bar Harbor, Maine. In the decades after her husband's death, Bowen spent most of her summers at Baymeath, where friends and family members stayed both for short and long visits. In part because of failing health, but also because she could not afford its upkeep, Bowen decided to sell Baymeath in 1940. Although she was used to contributing large sums to Hull-House, even Bowen lamented in the 1940s that she was "sadly hampered by the thought that I would better be careful" (Bowen to Ada Hicks, July 10, 1940, Ballard Papers); by then she had given more than one million dollars to Hull-House.

During most of the period of Bowen's activism with Hull-House, she had also been an organizer and longtime board member (1909–50) and vice-president (1912–50) of United Charities in Chicago. Jane Addams had also been a board member of United Charities. Attempting to facilitate cooperation among Chicago's charitable organizations, United Charities investigated the extent of Chicago's poverty and helped find jobs for the needy.

In the early 1900s, Bowen and Addams were board members for the Visiting Nurse Association (VNA), whose major goal was to bring nursing care to poor families. As with United Charities, the VNA conducted investigative studies of the needs of the poor. As a result of Bowen's initiative, the Chicago Board of Education, and later the city of Chicago for a period of time, assumed financial support for visiting school nurses who were sent to sick children's homes.

Always a political activist, in the last twenty years of her life Bowen continued to speak out on political issues and to support both Republican and Democratic candidates she felt were worthy. As a Republican woman, she endorsed Ruth Hanna McCormick for U.S. Senate in 1930. As a member of an independent nonpartisan committee, Bowen endorsed Democrat Anton Cermak as the Chicago mayoral candidate in 1931. Years later, as a Republican who considered herself independent-minded, Bowen supported Illinois Governor Adlai Stevenson, the newly nominated Democratic presidential candidate. In 1952 he gave his first postnomination speech from the balcony of Louise deKoven Bowen's Astor Street home. Regarding issues, Bowen opposed the Equal Rights Amendment out of fear that it would abolish the protective labor laws she had long supported and fought to obtain for women. This was the position of the majority of women's organizations from the 1920s through the 1940s. Yet, starting in 1914, for almost forty years she lamented that not enough women were in public life.

Louise deKoven Bowen died at the age of ninety-four. She is buried in Graceland Cemetery in Chicago. Through almost a century of social, political, and cultural changes, Bowen remained active until a few months before her death. No understanding of Chicago history from the turn of the twentieth century is complete without knowledge of Bowen's participation in the reform movements of the Progressive Era, especially in the efforts to advance women's citizenship rights, and in the organizations that she helped build, run, and sustain, including Hull-House, the Juvenile Protective Association, and United Charities.

Sources. Louise deKoven Bowen Papers, 1864–1953, including Louise deKoven Bowen's Scrapbooks, vols. 1–4, and Woman's City Club of Chicago records, are at the CHS. The CHS also has a clipping file for Louise deKoven Bowen. The Margaret Dreier Robins Papers are available at CHS in the microfilm edition of *Papers of the Women's Trade Union League and Its Principal Leaders* (1981). At UIC Spec. Coll. are the Hull-House Association Records; the Russell Ballard Papers; the Juvenile Protective Association Records; the Adena Miller Rich Papers; the Jane Addams Memorial Collection; and *The Jane Addams Papers* (Microfilm Edition, 1985). Bowen's published writings include *Safeguards for City Youth at Work and Play* (1914); *Growing Up with a City* (1926); *Speeches, Addresses, and Letters of Louise deKoven Bowen: Reflecting Social Movements in Chicago*, 2 vols. (1937); Mary E. Humphrey, ed., *Open Windows: Stories of People and Places* (1946); and *Baymeath* (privately printed 1945). Bowen's articles include "Colored People of Chicago," *Survey Midmonthly*, November 1, 1913, originally published as a Juvenile Protective Association pamphlet, *The Colored People of Chicago* (1913); "The War Work of the Women of Illinois," *Transactions of the Illinois State Historical Society*, 1919; "Chicago's First Woman World's Fair Closes Its Successful Exposition," *Journal of Illinois State History Society*, July 1925. Articles by Bowen were published frequently in the Woman's City Club *Bulletin* and *Survey Midmonthly*. Jane Addams's chapter on Joseph T. Bowen in *The Excellent Becomes the Permanent* (1932) is helpful for an understanding of the Bowens' marriage. Kathleen D. McCarthy, ed., *Lady Bountiful Revisited: Women, Philanthropy, and Power* (1990), has an essay by Kathryn Kish Sklar, "Who Funded Hull House?" that discusses Bowen's financial contributions to the settlement. Paul Gerard Anderson, "The Good to Be Done: A History of the Juvenile Protective Association of Chicago, 1898–1976," 2 vols. (Ph.D. diss., Univ. of Chicago, 1988), provides important background. See Sharon Z. Alter, "A Woman for Mayor?" *Chicago History*, 1986.

SHARON Z. ALTER

BOYD, NEVA LEONA
February 25, 1876–November 21, 1963
SOCIAL GROUP WORK THEORIST, PLAY MOVEMENT THEORIST, EDUCATOR, SETTLEMENT WORKER

Neva Boyd developed her basic ideas on group work and play in the political environment of Progressive Era Chicago and in the innovative atmosphere of the settlements. At a time when reformers were attempting to rescue children from the worst conditions of industrial society, specifically child labor in sweatshops and factories, Boyd underlined the need for recreation with her conclusion that play was the most important "work" that children undertook. She discovered that "the intensive group life of childhood and youth is largely the play life. It is in the interplay of group life that social qualities are born and social relationships are wrought out" (Boyd, *Play and Game Theory in Group Work*, 39).

Neva Leona Boyd, the eldest daughter in a family of six children, was born in Sandborn, Iowa, to Richard M. and Eliza (Swecker) Boyd. Her father was of Scotch-Irish descent and had immigrated to the United States in 1853. After serving in the Civil War, where he was wounded and discharged in 1864, he became postmaster of Sandborn for a short time. In 1866 he married Eliza Swecker and the two set up a homestead where they began raising a family. One of Boyd's brothers, Melville, went to Alaska to prospect during the gold rush. Her other siblings remained in the Midwest, one brother becoming a builder in the Sandborn area.

Upon graduation from high school, Boyd enrolled in the Chicago Kindergarten Institute, where she was trained to work with both children and young adults. After completing this program, she took a job in Dallas, Texas, where she supervised a large kindergarten comprised primarily of children from low-income families. In 1904, she moved to Buffalo, New York. There she worked at the Welcome Hall Settlement house as the kindergarten supervisor and also taught courses to staff workers in the Buffalo Kindergarten Association. As a result of these early experiences, Boyd began developing ideas about the relationship between play and the education and development of children. These formative experiences led to her conviction that the socialization of children should be guided by planned activities and not left to chance.

In 1908 Boyd returned to Chicago, continuing her education through courses at the University of Chicago, while she put her ideas into practice through volunteer activities at various settlement houses in the city. In 1909, the Chicago Woman's Club successfully petitioned the West Chicago Park Commissioners to hire Boyd to organize social clubs, direct dramatics, and supervise social dances and play activities at Eckhart Park, in the heart of a Polish immigrant neighborhood and near the Northwestern University Settlement. Boyd's efforts were successful, and soon the commission began promoting similar activities in other Chicago playgrounds and parks. Her approach, which emphasized social interaction and group relations, was a departure from the more traditional view of recreational activities that regarded play as physical exercise alone.

In 1911 Boyd moved to formalize her educational ideas by establishing the Chicago Training School for Playground Workers, the first such training school in the United States. The school, codirected by Boyd and Marie Huef Hoper, an extension worker from Columbia University, New York, was housed at the Abraham Lincoln Center, a settlement house established by Unitarian minister and reformer Jenkin Lloyd Jones in 1905. Boyd's new school, based on the belief that recreation workers should be professionally trained, offered courses in the theory of play activities and emphasized the psychological aspects of folk arts and dances, drama and games. Its curriculum was innovative and practical, fusing theory with fieldwork.

The Chicago Training School for Playground Workers expanded rapidly during its first three years. In 1914, the school was integrated into the Chicago School of Civics and Philanthropy, becoming its Department of Social Group Work with Boyd as its head. The Chicago School of Civics and Philanthropy had been established in 1908 by Graham Taylor, director of the Chicago Commons settlement house, to train settlement house and other social service workers. Boyd's curriculum included classroom studies as well as field work assignments carried on by students in various Chicago settlement houses including Hull-House, Chicago Commons, and Gads Hill Center, then under the direction of RUTH AUSTIN, a close associate and friend of Boyd. In 1914 Boyd took up residence at the Gads Hill Settlement.

Boyd's techniques worked well with children who came to participate in the social clubs and recreation activities offered through the settlement houses and park programs. Boyd found that the use of play and recreational activities had value for the mentally ill and with individuals in custodial homes, hospitals, and correctional institutions. In 1917 an experiment in recreational therapy was undertaken by graduates of the Recreation

Training School in the Chicago State Hospital. Initially, the superintendent and staff were hostile to Boyd's methods. Soon they became supporters, and her work was introduced in other state hospitals for persons with mental illnesses.

In 1920, when the Chicago School of Civics and Philanthropy was incorporated into the University of Chicago as the new School of Social Service Administration, Boyd's educational program remained independent from the university, moving instead to Hull-House. There it was reorganized and named the Recreation Training School of Chicago. Although not officially connected to Hull-House administratively, Boyd's Recreation Training School became popularly known as the "Hull-House School."

Boyd advocated her theories widely; she joined a Chautauqua circuit, touring nearly eighty towns in Michigan, Illinois, and Wisconsin and lecturing on the importance of play in the healthy socialization of children and adolescents. She also lectured in colleges and universities. Boyd conducted a special program in Paris, France, at the invitation of the International Federation of Settlements. According to Ellen Coolidge, secretary of the Boston Social Union and Boyd's sponsor at the international conference, Boyd gave practical demonstrations that impressed the Europeans. The following year the Boston Social Union invited Boyd to conduct a six-week summer session in that city.

In 1927 the Recreation Training School was absorbed as the Group Work and Recreation Division of the Department of Sociology, Northwestern University. There Boyd was appointed an assistant professor, a rank and position she retained until her retirement in 1941. Boyd continued to develop programs and train students for positions in both group work with children and adolescents and group work in treatment and therapeutic institutions. In 1929 she conducted a summer recreational program at the Lincoln State School. She taught the staff at the Geneva (Illinois) School for Girls during 1932 and 1933, putting in place a program that served as a model for modernizing reformatory procedures.

Boyd had an important role in defining group work as a legitimate field of social work. Group work involves conducting activities for a number of clients with similar needs together. During the period in which she taught at Northwestern, group work slowly became recognized as an integral part of social work. It was gradually separated from its earlier ties to recreation, adult education, and progressive education. This transformation was aided when the National Conference of Social Work created a section on social group work; Neva Boyd was an influential member of the committee. She had presented a paper in 1935 at a national forum that marked the beginning of this section. The American Association for the Study of Group Work was formed in 1936 and worked to define the meaning of group work and to develop some common methodological principles for the profession. Boyd wrote *Social Group Work: A Definition with a Methodological Note* (1937) as part of this movement in the social work field. Boyd continued to recommend the use of group work in treatment and therapeutic institutions, but this approach did not achieve widespread application until after World War II.

Boyd embarked on several new endeavors while she was actively bringing her play and recreation theories to mainstream social work theory and practice. She became involved with the National Association of Cooperatives and promoted rural recreation in the United States. She introduced a series of institutes that she conducted in the Cooperative School for Group Organization and Recreation. The school, sponsored by the Cooperative League of America and the U.S. Farm Bureau, met for two-week sessions each summer in various midwest camps and conference centers.

At age sixty-five, Boyd retired from Northwestern University; her work now focused on therapeutic programs in state institutions. She became a consultant to the Active Therapy Department of the Illinois Department of Public Welfare in 1941. For the next twenty-two years she worked with the Department of Public Welfare. Additionally, she served as staff consultant for the Manteno State Hospital, implementing therapeutic programs of play for the patients. Boyd lectured around the country and remained active in national organizations. She also continued to advocate for programs in rural recreation. Always deeply interested in children's games, Boyd compiled *Handbook of Games* (1945).

In 1959 Boyd was elected a fellow of the American Sociological Society. Neva L. Boyd Recreation Hall was named in her honor at the East Moline State Hospital in Illinois.

After her colleague, confidant, and longstanding friend Ruth Austin retired as head resident of Gads Hill in 1947, Neva Boyd moved to Hull-House, where she lived until 1960; that year Boyd took an apartment on the Near North Side of Chicago, where she continued to work on her papers until her death three years later.

Former students and colleagues carried the memory of Boyd's informally run classes, where they learned games and folk dances of different countries for use with the children in Chicago's diverse neighborhoods. Later, Boyd conducted sessions around the discussion table, where these activities were analyzed and understood as means for social education and reeducation. Whether her students were destined to work with the young or old, individuals with disabilities and mental disease or children and adolescents whose poverty and social conditions put them at risk, they brought to institutions and programs a positive, constructive approach that emphasized the whole patient, not just a specific illness or behavior problem.

Sources. The Neva Leona Boyd Papers, UIC Spec. Coll., include letters, notes, diary entries, clippings, an unpublished manuscript, and case studies. Among Boyd's published works are *Handbook of Games* (1945, reprinted 1975); *Schoolroom Games* (1919, reprinted 1932); *Hospital and Bedside Games* (1930, revised edition 1945); *Descriptions of English and American Country Dances: Music and Description of European Games and Dances* (n.d.); *Lithuanian, Polish and Russian Folk Dances* (n.d.); *Old Square Dances of America,* coauthor Tressie Dunlany (1932); *Description of Morris Dances, Pavane and Highland Fling* (n.d.). Her theoretical writings include *Social Group Work: A Definition with a Methodological Note* (1937, reprinted 1949). A compilation of her scholarly papers, *Play and Game Theory in Group Work: A Collection of Papers,* ed. Paul Simon (1971), includes a lengthy biographical sketch of Boyd's life and work. An obituary is found in the *American Sociological Review,* August 1964.

DINA L. STEPHENS

BRADFORD, SISTER M. VINCENT FERRER
(Ann Helen Bradford)
March 8, 1889–November 30, 1972
EDUCATOR, SOCIAL ACTIVIST

Ann Helen Bradford entered the Dominican order of women religious at a propitious time in the history of American Catholicism. She moved beyond the traditional boundaries that had constrained nuns and, as an academician and activist, engaged in the political, economic, and social issues of her time, becoming a nationally recognized spokesperson on Catholic social teachings.

Bradford was born in Madison, Wisconsin, to Benjamin Franklin and Margaret (Hayes) Bradford. She had one sister, Margaret. Her mother was a Catholic and had Ann baptized into the faith April 21, 1889. Her father remained true to his Protestant heritage until late in his life, when he converted to Catholicism.

Bradford attended St. Raphael School and Wisconsin Academy in Madison. In 1910, she graduated from the University of Wisconsin–Madison with a B.A. degree. She entered the Dominican order in 1912 and took the religious name Sister Vincent Ferrer in 1914. After teaching for three years at St. Clara College, a woman's college in Madison run by the Dominican religious order, Bradford began graduate work at Catholic University, Washington, D.C., completing an M.A. degree in history in 1918. She returned to St. Clara, and four years later, when the Dominicans relocated their college to River Forest, Illinois, Bradford was one of the original charter faculty of the renamed Rosary College (later Dominican University). She became a professor of political science and economics.

Bradford's professional career began during a period in which the American Catholic Church was redefining its mission. By the 1920s, church membership had grown to an estimated twenty million Americans, making it the single largest religious denomination in the country. Immigrant restriction laws implemented during this decade ended an era in which the church's primary energy was directed toward the care of poor and ethnically diverse immigrants. Many Catholic ethnics, particularly Germans and Irish, had become part of the American middle class and sought higher education for their children and an enlarged role in American society for the Catholic community. They began to see their religion as the true inheritor and champion of American values, including the ideals of progress, democracy, and human reason.

American Catholic thinkers were aided by a growing liberalism in church teaching. In 1891, Pope Leo XIII sympathetically analyzed the condition of the laboring classes and devised a program of social reform based upon Catholic concepts of the dignity of labor and social justice. Like many of her coreligionists, Bradford took to heart the social justice message of the church and began to translate these ideals into public service. Bradford became an early participant and lecturer at Catholic Conference on Industrial Problems (CCIP) meetings. CCIP had been organized in Chicago in 1922 to explore how American industrial problems could be improved through the application of Catholic teaching. It was the same year that Rosary College opened its River Forest campus. Bradford was excited by the intellectual ferment and commitment to social justice.

She was a speaker at CCIP regional conferences in Indianapolis, Chicago, Dubuque, Davenport, Detroit, St. Louis, Atlanta, Columbus, Pittsburgh, Kansas City, San Francisco, and Butte, and at national conferences in Milwaukee and Cleveland. The attendance at these meetings was never fewer than three hundred and at some exceeded a thousand, as Catholics came together in an emerging social movement of major importance to the shaping of modern Catholicism. Bradford realized that at the same time that hundreds of people were awakening to issues of social justice related to the industrial world, they were also "made conscious of the fact that women wearing the religious habit and 'living behind convent walls' need not be isolated from but deeply concerned with the society in which they work" ("Forty Years After," 14).

Bradford also pursued international peace concerns. She served as one of the first vice-presidents of the Catholic Association for International Peace (CAIP), founded at Catholic University in 1927. CAIP advocated the application of the principles of natural law and Christian charity to the international problems of the day. At a time when the League of Nations was a weak world organization and many in the United States took an isolationist stance in response to the emerging tensions among European nations, CAIP advocated the creation of a world police force, an international bill of rights, a federated Europe, and the establishment of funds for technical aid to countries in need.

Economic issues also loomed internationally as a worldwide depression engulfed Europe and the United States, putting traditional ideas about capitalism into question. Bradford and other Catholics in CCIP, already sensitive to the deep social inequalities in American society, now faced the immediate economic crisis and addressed its meaning for Catholic social thinking. In 1931 Catholic leaders, intellectuals, and lay persons were further encouraged in their quest for social justice by a papal encyclical, *Quadragesimo Anno*, the central theme of which was the dignity of the human person and a concern for the social order. The encyclical addressed specific issues such as wages, working conditions, unemployment, and a more just distribution of wealth.

The Catholic Worker movement under the leadership of Dorothy Day had a great influence on Bradford. Day came to speak at the River Forest campus in 1933, the same year that the movement was inaugurated. (Day subsequently addressed the Rosary faculty and student body in 1936 and 1937.) Bradford was also influenced by theologian Peter Maurin, whose ideas had shaped Day. Maurin came to Rosary in 1933. Both Maurin and Day emphasized "Christian Personalism . . . with emphasis on personal sanctity and commitment . . . [and] voluntary action in the service of the poor and the worker" ("Aspects of Catholic Thought and Action," 27). In addition, the spirit of *Quadragesimo Anno* and the work of the CCIP had broadened Bradford's awareness of working-class issues. Bradford became an early supporter of the Congress of Industrial Organizations (CIO) when it formed in 1935. Among the leaders in the labor movement and the CIO in the 1930s were American Communist Party (CP) members and rank and file on the Left who sympathized with the CP. In an attempt to make common cause with Catholics, CP leader Earl Browder embraced Bradford's advocacy of rights for women workers, and the Catholic nun was

quoted in a CP pamphlet he authored. Bradford argued for strong trade unionism but rejected communism. She good-naturedly let it be known that she considered communists her brothers and would pray for them. She was determined to develop a social justice movement grounded in Catholic teachings and in opposition to Marxism.

Bradford also courageously denounced Father Charles Coughlin, the radio priest from Royal Oaks, Michigan, whose anti-Semitism and radical denunciations of President Franklin D. Roosevelt's New Deal programs preyed upon the fears and insecurities of ordinary men and women who struggled to survive during the depths of the Great Depression.

Keenly aware of the rising tide of fascism in Europe, Rosary College hosted the Catholic Association for International Peace's regional meeting in 1936. First lady Eleanor Roosevelt was one of the conference's speakers, and fifteen hundred were in attendance.

In 1937 the National Council of Catholic Women sponsored a summer institute for women workers that was held at the National Catholic School of Social Service in Washington, D.C. The institute educated women workers about their role in the economy and provided them with a firm foundation in Christian teachings. "As leaders," Bradford later wrote, "they could go back to their jobs prepared to take active and constructive participation [*sic*] in formulating and controlling the action of their union in securing justice for the workers. In this way they would spread Christian influence as well as combat Marxism" ("Aspects of Catholic Thought and Action," 5). Young women, Catholic and non-Catholic, from across the country enrolled in the program. Most of them came on scholarships covering full expenses, which were provided by the National Council of Catholic Women, other organizations, individual labor leaders, and some labor unions. Bradford influenced successive classes of young women for more than a decade as a regular member of the teaching staff. During her summers in Washington, she became acquainted with Frances Perkins, Secretary of Labor (1933–45) in the Roosevelt administration, as well as with many union leaders. In particular, she met many women in the labor field, including ELISABETH CHRISTMAN, Mamie Santora, Esther Peterson, and AGNES NESTOR, president of the Chicago branch of the Women's Trade Union League.

As the economic and social conditions of Europe continued to deteriorate and Germany's invasion of Poland resulted in a declaration of war by Great Britain and France, Bradford attended the 18th International Congress of Pax Romana, a student organization founded in 1921 to further the establishment of a Catholic international student movement. More than three hundred delegates from forty foreign countries met in Washington, D.C., between August 28 and September 2. The next week the group moved to New York City, where meetings were held at Fordham University. Bradford remembered the emotions experienced by the group when, in the midst of the meetings of prayer, study, and socializing, the young men from the European delegations were called home, perhaps to be sent in a few months to kill each other on the battlefields of Europe. Bradford wrote, "It is not surprising that this experience converted me into a non-violent pacifist and to work zealously with all groups to prevent another war" ("Aspects of Catholic Thought and Action," 17).

Bradford continued to teach at the labor education summer institutes. She lived in the dormitory with the young women attendees and continued to surprise many "'that a nun should have a wide interest in economic problems and so much information of the subject'" ("Aspects of Catholic Thought and Action," 7). In 1944, the summer institute was held at Rosary College. Courses on labor problems, social legislation, the social encyclicals of the Catholic Church, the practices and principles of trade unionism, labor's participation in industrial relations, and public speaking and parliamentary law were offered for the young women who were members of labor unions, including the International Ladies' Garment Workers' Union, the Typographical Union, and the Chicago Federation of Labor.

Bradford taught at the Sheil School of Social Studies, Chicago, established by Bishop Bernard J. Sheil in 1943. Sheil School was a project of the Educational Department of the Catholic Youth Organization. The school, while coming from a Christian social justice orientation, was open to all creeds, races, and economic groups and gave courses in American political and economic history with the goal of promoting human dignity and equality. By 1945, thousands of people attended Sheil School classes, lectures, and exhibitions. Bradford taught at the Sheil School for eight years from 1943 to 1951. In 1944 she received the first Pope Leo XIII Award, given by the Sheil School for outstanding work in Christian social education. Bradford inspired many of her Sheil and Rosary College students to engage personally in social activism; they volunteered to work in youth programs in inner-city parishes, and in the innovative Friendship House.

Through Bradford's leadership, Rosary College had a connection with Chicago's Friendship House from the 1940s. In 1938, Russian émigré and Catholic convert Catherine De Hueck founded Friendship House in New York City's Harlem. Committed to the principles of interracial and economic justice, and grounded in her religious faith and opposition to Soviet communism, De Hueck created an urban center that ministered to the poor through social service. She saw her work as an alternative to the American Communist Party, whose members were active in the black community. At the same time, she chastised the Catholic Church for its failure to educate against racism and to minister to African Americans. Friendship House was not a formal religious community, but it stressed the value of a shared life centered around prayer, commitment to voluntary poverty, and acts of charity among the African American poor. In 1942, a house was established in Chicago. Sister Vincent Ferrer and her Rosary College colleague SISTER MARY ELLEN O'HANLON taught there. When the group was required to leave its original building on the South Side, Rosary College loaned Friendship House five thousand dollars for three years without interest. Graduates of Rosary College became staff members and others did volunteer work at Friendship House.

During the 1940s the Catholic Association for International Peace became more ecumenical in direction. In 1943 Chicago Archbishop Samuel Stritch asked Bradford and other faculty at Rosary College, including Sisters Thomas Aquinas O'Neill,

Mary Aquinas Devlin, and Gilbert Kelly, to prepare a pamphlet on world peace that could be used in study groups and popular forums. *Patterns for Peace* (1944) outlined seven basic principles for world peace and was a digest of Pope Pius XII's many statements on peace and commentaries on these papal statements written by Dr. Gonella, an Italian priest and scholar. *Patterns for Peace* was adopted by the Federal Council of Churches in America, a mainly Protestant body, the Synagogue Council of America, and the National Catholic Welfare Conference. Bradford participated in a "sort of 'ecumenical experiment'" ("Aspects of Catholic Thought and Action," 10) on the University of Wisconsin campus in 1945. The two-week summer school course was conducted under the auspices of the University of Wisconsin School for Workers. It was an industrial relations institute for Christian religious and lay leaders in key church activities.

Moving beyond religious circles, in the 1940s Bradford was invited to give two lectures at Hull-House, one to the Woman's Club about problems in which women as citizens should be interested; the other was an evening lecture to an adult education class of men and women. This lecture was announced in the Chicago daily papers and Bradford received many letters. Concerned about the publicity and about the rumors that Hull-House harbored communists, Bradford consulted Bishop Sheil about whether or not she should speak there. He replied, "All the more reason I want you to go" (quoted in "Aspects of Catholic Thought and Action," 26).

Bradford continued to attend conferences and educate students in the 1950s and 1960s. In 1969 she wrote a thirty-page memoir, "Aspects of Catholic Thought and Action in the Thirties and Forties Foreshadowing Future Development," that outlined her pioneering efforts. She left Rosary College in April 1972 for St. Dominic Villa, Dubuque, Iowa, and seven months later died there.

Edward A. Marciniak, writing on the rise and decline of Catholic social action in 1970, included Sister Vincent Ferrer Bradford with such luminaries as Dorothy Day and Peter Maurin as one of the men and women in the decades between the first and second World Wars who "crystallized a body of Catholic social thought, characteristically American, ecumenical in outreach and attractive to the laity" (Marciniak, 511). As an educator, Bradford identified her "students" in the broadest sense, including those enrolled in college, workers at summer institutes, adults taking occasional courses, women's groups, and the community at large. As a Catholic, she believed in the value of ecumenism. As an American, she was a proponent of democracy and warned against the forces of totalitarianism presented by the Soviet Union and Germany under Hitler. Her concern for the oppressed and downtrodden made her aware too of "the insidious dangers which modern capitalism has constituted for all spiritual values" (quoted in the *Rosarian*, November 16, 1961, 1). She battled poverty and racism in the United States in forty years of social action.

Sources. The Sinsinawa Dominican Archives, Sinsinawa, Wisconsin, have a small amount of material on Sister Vincent Ferrer Bradford, including her unpublished paper, "Aspects of Catholic Thought and Action in the Thirties and Forties Foreshadowing Future Development" (1969). Articles about Bradford include Charles Harbutt, "Chicago," *Ju-*

bilee, September 1956; n.a., "Forty Years After . . . (a social actionist reminisces)," *Exchange*, December 1971; Cherie Bauch and Pat Bachluber, "This Teacher Knows the Tempo of the Times," *Rosarian*, November 16, 1961; Ralph McGill, "One Word More," *Atlanta Constitution*, February 10, 1943; Louise McGuire, "Near-Miracle of Social Service," *Catholic Action*, July 1932; Edward A. Marciniak, "Catholic Social Action: Where Do We Go from Here?" *America*, December 12, 1970.

EILEEN M. McMAHON

BRADLEY, MARY HASTINGS
April 19, 1882–October 25, 1976
WRITER, EXPLORER, GAME HUNTER, CLUBWOMAN

Mary Wilhelmina Hastings, the daughter of William Fitzbacchus and Lina (Rickcords) Hastings, was born in Chicago. Her father, who came to the city from Kentucky prior to 1871, died before she was born. Her mother was a Chicago native of New England background. In 1893 Lina Hastings married Arthur Mills Corwin, and their daughter, Sylvia, Mary Hastings's half-sister, was born January 17, 1894.

Two childhood pleasures—learning about Africa and writing stories for publication—influenced the direction of Mary Hastings's life. Her great-grandfather piqued her interest in Africa by reading aloud to her Sir Henry Stanley's *In Darkest Africa*. At twelve, her first story, one concerning animals, won a *Chicago Daily News* short story contest. Two years later the *Chicago Tribune* published another of her stories in serial form.

After schooling in Chicago, Hastings attended Smith College, receiving a B.A. degree in 1905. Later, graduate study at Oxford University in England enabled her to concentrate on historical research that provided material for her first novel, on Anne Boleyn, *The Favor of Kings* (1912).

A mutual interest in Africa led to the friendship and subsequent marriage of Mary Hastings and Herbert Edwin Bradley, a Canadian-born Chicago attorney, on June 21, 1910. Herbert Bradley came to Chicago in 1896, earned an LL.B. degree at Chicago Law School in 1899, and was a partner in the firm of MacChesney, Becker and Bradley before he established a practice in his own name. Their daughter Alice was born August 24, 1915. A second daughter, Mary Lee, died in infancy.

One of Herbert Bradley's clients was a staff member of the American Museum of Natural History (AMNH) in New York City, Carl F. Akeley, who, with his wife Delia Akeley, was a leading explorer of Africa. Through this connection, the Bradleys joined an AMNH expedition to the Belgian Congo in 1920–21. The expedition sought mountain gorillas and covered territory that no Americans had explored previously. The expedition's efforts were successful, both in photographing wild gorillas for the first time and returning with a number of specimens for exhibit at the museum.

Besides carrying a Springfield rifle, Mary Bradley traveled with a portable typewriter and prodded herself to write every spare moment to record details. Sketching and drawing maps also reinforced her memory.

Bradley, a fearless game hunter, dauntlessly participated in adventures, such as climbing the volcano of Nyamlagira in the Congo during its state of eruption. Although she hunted only dangerous game—elephants, buffalo, and lions, most of which provided the expedition's food—she was publicly criticized in

1923 by the Dean of St. Paul's Cathedral, London, who declared that "nothing would give me greater pleasure than to know that Mrs. Bradley had been killed by a gorilla" ("I Hope a Gorilla Kills You!"). In a widely published response, Bradley denied she had killed gorillas and pointed out that medical schools and universities, as well as the AMNH and the public, benefited from the expeditions.

In 1924 and 1925, the Bradleys were in the first European expedition to walk more than thirteen hundred miles through the mountains west of Lake Edwards in the Congo. Bradley detailed this expedition in *Caravans and Cannibals*, published in 1926. From Africa, the explorers continued on to Sumatra in the Netherlands East Indies (now Indonesia) before going on to Indochina in southeast Asia to hunt tigers.

On a third expedition to Africa in 1930–31, the Bradleys studied Pygmy and Mangbetu peoples as the expedition traveled from Africa's west coast to its east coast. One purpose of this expedition was to determine whether an entire Pygmy village could be transported to Chicago for the 1933 Century of Progress Exposition, but the estimated expense made the idea impractical.

In all, Bradley made six expeditions to Africa. She and her husband took their last African trip together in 1951. Her writings, lectures, travels, and the decor of her home reflected her lifelong fascination with Africa. Visitors to her home in Chicago's Hyde Park neighborhood were awed by the bungalow located on top of the three-story apartment building, called the African Room. The room's furnishings included nine-foot-long elephant tusks, lion skins, buffalo heads, African pottery, and other mementos of her travels, a collection she loaned for display at the Los Angeles Art Museum in 1969. In the African Room, Bradley did much of her writing. She also enjoyed entertaining friends and famous visitors there with decorations, food, and entertainment that duplicated those of a typical African safari.

Bradley became a member of the International Society of Women Geographers in 1926 and was elected a fellow of the Royal Geographical Society (London) in 1928. When the National Geographic Society's 5,000-seat auditorium opened in 1928, she was the first woman to address an audience there. At the 1928 Woman's World's Fair held in Chicago, she was among a select group of attendees at the Famous Women's Breakfast. Theta Sigma Phi, a national journalism organization (now Women in Communications) elected her to honorary membership at its national meeting in 1929.

Bradley's daughter Alice accompanied her parents on expeditions from age six. Pictures Alice Bradley drew on African trips illustrated two of Mary Bradley's children's books, *Alice in Jungleland* (1927) and *Alice in Elephantland* (1929).

In forty-three years, Bradley wrote twenty-three books, including adventure tales, romance novels, mysteries, and children's stories, and frequently contributed to popular national periodicals. Reviewers varied in their enthusiasm for Bradley's writing. FANNY BUTCHER, a leading Chicago reviewer, praised *On the Gorilla Trails* (1923) for presenting a record of a scientific expedition as an exciting adventure. A collection of four short romances, entitled *Old Chicago*, published in 1933, was patterned after Edith Wharton's *Old New York*. While

Butcher wrote in the *Chicago Daily Tribune* that Bradley delved meticulously into Chicago's past and wrote the record with fidelity and the skill of an experienced novelist, *New York Times* critic Fred T. Marsh panned it. Although Bradley's books entertained readers with their light-hearted, easy-to-read style, they contained few messages of consequence or reflections on Chicago during the era in which she lived. Today few public libraries have her fiction on their shelves.

Her earliest magazine fiction was a 1913 serial for *Woman's Home Companion*, and from then on her short stories and articles appeared frequently in *Saturday Evening Post*, *Harper's*, *Harper's Bazaar*, *Cosmopolitan*, *Collier's*, *Redbook*, and others. Three of Bradley's books, *Palace of Darkened Windows* (1914), *The Fortieth Door* (1919), and *I Passed for White* (1955) were made into movies.

Because her daughter served as a Woman's Army Corps (WAC) officer during World War II, Bradley took an interest in that branch of the service. She became a special correspondent for *Collier's* with War Department credentials to cover WAC activities in Eastern, Far Eastern, European, and Mediterranean war zones. Her 1945 whirlwind tour of battle theaters included stops in North Africa, Italy, France, Germany, and England.

Bradley was active in journalism and writers' groups, including the Illinois Woman's Press Association and the Society of Midland Authors, serving as president of the latter from 1944 to 1945. She was an active member of the woman's club Fortnightly, where large attendance at her lectures attested to her popularity. For the Fortnightly's seventy-fifth anniversary in 1948, Bradley wrote its commemorative history, *Seventy-Five Years of "Best Girls."* By then, she had been a member for more than half a century. In addition, she belonged to a number of other clubs, including the Arts, the English Speaking Union, the National Society of the Colonial Dames of America, and Women's University Club. She was one of the last persons admitted to the famed Little Room, a loosely organized group of eminent Chicago artists and writers that existed from 1893 to the early 1900s.

Bradley extended her activities to teaching and public events. As a member of the reception committee of the 1933 Century of Progress Exposition, she entertained journalists and introduced them to Chicago writers. In 1938, Bradley spoke at a benefit for the Theta Sigma Phi student chapter at the University of Illinois. Her ability to attract a crowd to the event enabled the financially weakened chapter to achieve solvency and remain in good standing with its national office. During the 1940s she taught courses for the Midwestern Writers conferences, usually focusing on novel writing.

Mary Hastings Bradley died at the age of ninety-two and was buried at Graceland Cemetery in Chicago. Although she was a member of the Congregational Church, her final order was that there be no services of any type.

Bradley observed that she could not imagine living without writing. She reflected in an article in the *Matrix* that to a writer, "every life about you is an unwritten book; each man and woman of us lives in struggle and difficulty and renewed hope; in the deep and secret places of the heart we face the irrevocable poignancy of love and death. To tell the truth of this, . . . to enter into all experience with sympathy, without prejudice, with hatred for nothing but cruelty and oppression, with the compassion of a fellow traveler as well as the interest of a recorder, that, as I see it, is the goal of writing—that, and nothing less" ("The Desire to Write," 6).

Sources. The Mary Hastings Bradley Collection is held at UIC Spec. Coll. The 171 boxes comprising the Bradley collection include family genealogy records, diaries, correspondence, manuscripts, texts of lectures, scrapbooks, African artifacts, photographs, and article clippings, which include Bradley, "The Desire to Write," *Matrix*, August 1937, and "I Hope a Gorilla Kills You!" *Cape Argus*, Cape Town, South Africa, September 24, 1923. Marion P. Schaefer provided information in an interview with Jane Lord on June 23, 1994. See above text for Bradley's books.

JANE LORD

BRADWELL, MYRA COLBY
February 12, 1831–February 14, 1894
LAWYER, PUBLISHER, WOMEN'S RIGHTS ADVOCATE

Myra Colby Bradwell, founder and editor of the *Chicago Legal News*, and a tireless advocate of women's rights and other legal and social reforms, was born in Manchester, Vermont, the youngest of the five children of Eben and Abigail Hurd (Willey) Colby. Both parents were of New England stock and belonged to the Baptist faith. Shortly after Myra Colby's birth, the family moved to Portage, New York. In 1843 the family moved to the township of Schaumberg, Illinois. Myra Colby received part of her education in Kenosha, Wisconsin, then attended finishing school in Elgin, Illinois; she taught for several years in local schools.

On May 18, 1852, Myra Colby married James Bolesworth Bradwell of Palatine, Illinois, the son of poor English immigrants. The couple moved to Memphis, Tennessee, where they taught and opened their own private school. James Bradwell also began studying law, and in 1854 the Bradwells moved to Chicago. Earlier that year, before arriving in Chicago, their first child, Myra, was born; three more followed. Only two survived, Bessie (1858), and Thomas (1856). James Bradwell continued his legal education and in 1855 was admitted to the Illinois bar. He entered into a partnership with a brother-in-law, built up a large practice, and in 1861 was elected a Cook County judge.

Since the early years of their marriage, Myra Bradwell had been reading law under her husband's guidance. In 1868 she undertook the publication of a weekly newspaper called the *Chicago Legal News*. At the same time, the Bradwells also set up a printing, binding, and publishing company that worked in tandem with the newspaper. In 1869 Bradwell applied for admission to the Illinois bar. Her application was accompanied by a document certifying that she had passed the bar examination and by a brief in which she stated that the only question involved in the case was whether or not being a woman disqualified her from receiving a license to practice law.

The Illinois Supreme Court promptly denied her petition and based its decision not on the grounds that she was a woman but that she was a married woman. Under the law of coverture, a principle under which the husband and wife's legal existences merged into one, a married woman would not be bound by contractual obligations made between herself and her clients. Bradwell countered by re-petitioning and filing a brief arguing that most married women's legal disabilities had been removed by recently enacted laws. The Illinois Supreme Court again denied her petition, this time not because she was a married woman but simply because she was a woman.

Bradwell appealed the decision to the United States Supreme Court and retained Senator Matthew H. Carpenter of Wisconsin, one of the country's ablest constitutional lawyers, as her attorney. As Carpenter prepared his case, he realized that the greatest obstacle to a favorable judicial decision was the widespread fear that if women were declared constitutionally entitled to practice law, it might follow that they were also constitutionally entitled to vote. This specter of nationwide woman suffrage was far more terrifying to the populace than was the threat of women being admitted to the bar. Carpenter thus took great pains to distinguish Bradwell's constitutional right to practice law from the establishment of woman suffrage. Carpenter based his argument upon the Fourteenth Amendment's Privileges and Immunities clause, arguing that Illinois could not abridge the right of citizens to practice their chosen professions. Nevertheless, in 1873, the United States Supreme Court denied Bradwell's claim, stating that the right to practice law was not a privilege covered under the Constitution.

As a result of these court decisions, the *Chicago Legal News* became the focal point of Bradwell's legal career. A brilliant success from the start, the *Chicago Legal News* quickly became the most important legal publication west of the Alleghenies. Known for its broad and judicious coverage of the legal news of the entire country, it carried more advertising than any other paper in the state. It became a platform for reform even as it served to record and publicize important legal cases. For twenty-five years Bradwell discussed and evaluated opinions of lawyers and the courts as well as new legislation. She advocated such reforms as regulation of railroads, reform of local zoning ordinances, improved court procedures and courtrooms, and implementation of new and better standards in the legal profession. Bradwell also addressed such issues as temperance, prison reform, and the rights of women.

Bradwell's *Chicago Legal News* became an arena in which vying concepts of woman's place and power were argued and developed. On the one hand, the rhetoric of domesticity led nineteenth-century women to argue for participation in the political world as an extension of their role within the separate, private sphere of the household. On the other hand, the rhetoric of women's civil rights led others to argue for increased power within society based upon the belief that there were no inherent differences between men and women sufficient to justify women's second-class citizenship; they argued for a public role for women based upon citizenship and equality.

Drawing from these two views, Bradwell proposed that although men and women were different, this difference should not be defined by domesticity or woman's sphere but by women's capabilities in the public sphere. She insisted that women deserved a greater role in influencing the society around them, arguing that to do otherwise would be an indication of immoral and irresponsible behavior on men's part in particular and society's on the whole. Women were rational, civic citizens, whose sense of duty was equal to that of men.

Advocating women's legal equality meant changing existing statutes, especially those concerning married women, through such new laws as Illinois's married women's property acts. Through a statute passed in 1861, married women were guaranteed the right to ownership of separate property brought to a marriage; they could control, transfer, and contract upon this property as they saw fit. Bradwell sought to extend this control to income acquired during marriage. In 1869, with the support of her husband, nationally known suffragist Elizabeth Cady Stanton, and others, including CATHARINE WAITE and KATE NEWELL DOGGETT, Bradwell lobbied successfully for this amendment. She also secured passage of a law giving a widow an interest in her husband's estate in all cases.

As the drive for women's rights increased, suffrage became of increasing importance to Bradwell. The advances in married women's property rights gave her the necessary foundation for the advancement of woman suffrage. After expansion of women's legal independence, Bradwell was certain that women would start to cross the lines of the household and demand recognition and participation in politics. In 1868 the franchise for women was a radical notion. Most men clung to the tradition of a separate, domestic sphere for women and could not see the logic in allowing women to vote, especially in public. As one contemporary male admonished, "My wife shall never vote—the idea of her making herself ridiculous by crowding up to the polls on election day"; and his companion, echoing his beliefs, affirmed, "I would not *allow* my wife to vote" (Anonymous, *Chicago Legal News*, November 7, 1868). Bradwell, who had recorded and published this episode in the *Chicago Legal News*, was quick to note that "we felt like asking the gentleman if his wife ever rode in street cars or attended matinees. . . . The very expression that this man used, shows that he regarded the poor being who was unfortunate enough to be selected as the companion of his life, more as his cringing slave than his wife" (Bradwell, *Chicago Legal News*, November 7, 1868).

As with married women's property rights, the march toward the franchise for women was often fragmented and contradictory. Bradwell strove for a middle ground, trying to piece together a moderate, national coalition of suffragists, which included such eminent leaders as Lucy Stone and MARY LIVERMORE. Closer to home, Bradwell was for many years a member of the executive committee of the Illinois Woman Suffrage Association, where she worked closely with fellow Chicagoan Catharine Van Valkenburg Waite. Bradwell also was careful to record progress in other states and territories, praising Wyoming and its politicians, for example, for allowing women to vote. In 1891 in Illinois, a statute was finally passed allowing "school suffrage," a partial franchise that allowed women to vote on local school issues. Predictably, Bradwell had lobbied hard through the *Chicago Legal News* for its passage. The law was immediately contested in the courts, but with a new result. For the first time in Illinois history the Supreme Court of Illinois had decided a women's rights case in favor of women. In 1893 Bradwell voted for the first time, casting a ballot in a Chicago school board election.

The *Chicago Legal News* also became a forum for discussions of asylum reform. Bradwell had developed a keen interest in the issue from firsthand knowledge of the sufferings of Mary

Todd Lincoln, a longtime friend of the family, who had been committed to the Bellevue Place Asylum by her son, Robert. Concerned about his mother's overspending and the consequent effect on her estate, he initiated committal proceedings that ended in her incarceration in 1875. Bradwell, answering Mary Todd Lincoln's pleas for help, was successful in getting her released, but only after a protracted battle with Robert Lincoln and the asylum's resident physician.

Myra Bradwell continued to edit and publish the *Chicago Legal News* until the end of her life. In addition to her contributions to married women's property rights, the woman suffrage movement, women in the legal profession, and asylum reform, she advocated the advancement of women in many public offices, believing that there was no occupation that women should be barred from solely on account of either their gender or their marital status. These professions included the office of notary public; elective offices in the public school system; and the position of master in chancery or assistant to a judge presiding over a court of equity. Bradwell was successful in opening many professional doors for future generations of women. Although she never practiced law, in 1890—when she was fifty-nine—the Illinois Supreme Court, acting on her original motion of 1869, admitted her to the practice of law in that state; two years later she was admitted to practice before the Supreme Court of the United States. She died at the age of sixty-two and was buried in Rosehill Cemetery, Chicago. Her newspaper continued under the management of her husband and then of her daughter, Bessie Bradwell Helmer, until 1925.

In the first issue of the *Chicago Legal News*, Myra Bradwell wrote, "One thing that we do claim—that a woman has the right to think and act as an individual—believing that if the Great Father had intended it to be otherwise, he would have placed Eve in a cage and given Adam the key" (*Chicago Legal News*, November 7, 1868). Through her sustained challenge in the courts to practice law, and in her political activities, legal journalism, and suffrage advocacy, she forcefully argued for women's equality and full citizenship.

Sources. There is a small collection of items in the Myra Bradwell Papers in the Illinois State Historical Library, which includes a letter to the governor of Illinois in 1870 outlining her efforts to advance the legal status of married women. Other primary sources include some sparse correspondence in the Authors and Editors Collection at the CHS. Bradwell's *Chicago Legal News* is available through the CPL, the Illinois State Library in Springfield, Northwestern Univ. Law Library, and the UC Law Library. For a recent useful study of Bradwell, see Jane M. Friedman's book, *America's First Woman Lawyer: The Biography of Myra Bradwell* (1993). For information on female lawyers in Illinois, see Charlotte Adelman, *The Women's Bar Association of Illinois—The First 75 Years* (1992). A number of articles and essays are also quite valuable, including Ellen Carol DuBois, "Taking the Law into Our Own Hands: *Bradwell, Minor,* and Suffrage Militance in the 1870s," in *Visible Women: New Essays on American Activism,* ed. Nancy A. Hewitt and Suzanne Lebsock (1993); Meg Gorecki, "Legal Pioneers: Four of Illinois' First Women Lawyers," *Illinois Bar Journal,* October 1990; Nancy T. Gilliam, "A Professional Pioneer: Myra Bradwell's Fight to Practice Law," *Law and History Review,* Spring 1987; and Herman Kogan, "Myra Bradwell: Crusader at Law," *Chicago History,* Winter 1974/75.

CAROLINE K. GODDARD

BRECKINRIDGE, SOPHONISBA PRESTON
April 1, 1866–July 30, 1948
RESEARCHER, SOCIAL REFORMER, SOCIAL WORK EDUCATOR

Breckinridge, who cofounded the School of Social Service Administration at the University of Chicago with friend and colleague EDITH ABBOTT, was born of a distinguished family in Lexington, Kentucky. "Nisba" to her family and friends, she was the daughter of William Campbell Preston Breckinridge, Confederate colonel, journalist, member of Congress, and lawyer, and his second wife, Issa (Desha) Breckinridge. Breckinridge was the second of five living children with an elder sister, Ella, a younger sister, Curry, and two brothers, Desha and Robert.

Breckinridge graduated from Wellesley College in 1888 and was retroactively elected to Phi Beta Kappa when a chapter was established on campus. While she was an undergraduate, female academics such as President Alice Freeman Palmer and Helen Schafer, her mathematics instructor, served as role models whom Breckinridge emulated. Breckinridge taught mathematics in a Washington, D.C., high school after graduation from college and returned to Lexington after the death of her mother in 1892.

Breckinridge's relationship with her father, whom she dearly loved and wished to please, was complex. Although her father repeatedly urged her to uphold the family reputation for thinking and speaking courageously, he did not support her stand for woman suffrage or her desire to become a lawyer. Further, he caused his family great anguish after a breach-of-promise suit was filed by a woman with whom he had a long affair. Thus, as her unfinished autobiography attested, Breckinridge experienced a period of trauma and uncertainty about her life plans when she finished college. Her father finally agreed to support her desire to learn law, and she read law in his office. Breckinridge passed the bar exam in 1895, the first woman in Kentucky to do so, but her practice did not prosper, and she felt "baffled and discouraged" (Cook, 35).

In 1895, during a visit to a former Wellesley classmate, May Estelle Cook, in Oak Park, Illinois, Breckinridge met MARION TALBOT, Dean of Women at the University of Chicago, with whom she began a long, fruitful friendship. "I was a miserable person almost down and out," Breckinridge later recalled (autobiography, n.p.). She remained grateful to Talbot, who not only found Breckinridge a clerical job in her office and made dormitory living arrangements for her but later "snatched for me a fellowship in political science which a man student had resigned" (autobiography, n.p.).

Breckinridge received a Ph.D. in political science in 1901 and a J.D. degree in 1904 from the University of Chicago. Despite her graduating summa cum laude in both programs, no position in political science or economics awaited her, while male students went to positions on college or university faculties. Talbot provided further support by asking Breckinridge to organize courses dealing with the legal and economic aspects of family life in the new Department of Household Administration that Talbot headed. Between 1904 and 1920 Breckinridge regularly taught in the department, including a course on the legal and economic position of women. In 1912 she and Talbot collaborated on a textbook, *The Modern Household,* which was intended for housewives and college students to help them adapt to social changes affecting the home. They saw the modern household as a complex center of consumption that had lost its social value as a productive unit.

Breckinridge, who called herself an independent Democrat, was a staunch supporter of women's rights and worked toward this goal in several organizations. She served as vice-president for the National American Woman Suffrage Association in 1911 and was also an early member of the Chicago branch of the Women's Trade Union League (WTUL). WTUL recruited a cross-class alliance concerned with issues such as equal pay for equal work and the eight-hour day. Breckinridge was also an early president of the Woman's City Club of Chicago and a national officer of the American Association of University Women.

After the outbreak of World War I in 1914, Breckinridge helped organize the Woman's Peace Party (WPP), with headquarters in Chicago, in 1915. Along with JANE ADDAMS, who chaired the WPP, GRACE ABBOTT, and ALICE HAMILTON, Breckinridge was part of a delegation from the United States that attended the International Congress of Women (ICW) at The Hague in 1915.

Breckinridge's deep friendships with a circle of women—Grace and Edith Abbott, JULIA LATHROP, FLORENCE KELLEY, and Alice Hamilton—were an increasingly meaningful part of her life. All six lived for varying periods at Jane Addams's Hull-House, a settlement house on Chicago's West Side, and were involved with each other and with Addams in research, reform, and social activism. Two of the many organizations that particularly interested this circle of friends were the Immigrants' Protective League (IPL), founded in 1908 to eliminate exploitative practices toward immigrants, and the Chicago School of Civics and Philanthropy (CSCP), an early social work school, which was housed originally in Hull-House.

In 1908 the CSCP moved to larger quarters that adjoined the IPL office and had a connecting door. This arrangement facilitated interaction as well as collaborative research between the two agencies. Julia Lathrop, temporarily the director of research at the Institute of Social Sciences, the precursor of the CSCP, asked Breckinridge in 1907 to take the research directorship. During that same period the two women journeyed to Wellesley where Edith Abbott, who had been a student of Breckinridge in the university's Department of Household Administration, was teaching. Abbott accepted their offer to be the assistant director of research at the CSCP and returned to Chicago to live in Hull-House.

Thus began a long, meaningful, personal friendship and a professional collaborative relationship between Breckinridge and Edith Abbott. Their friendship was remarkable for its lack of personal competition; thus, it is often difficult to distinguish the individual contributions of each. Their collaborative efforts included *The Delinquent Child and the Home* (1912), which documented the problems faced by urban youth; and *The Tenements of Chicago, 1908–1935* (1936), dedicated to the memory of Lathrop, a massive study based upon house-to-house canvassing of 151 Chicago blocks with some of the research done by students of the two women. Their approach to urban behavior research was based on recognition of the need to use a scientific method and to collect data about a particular problem

before appropriate social policy or programs could be formulated.

Breckinridge's first major book on women, *New Homes for Old* (1921), was an account of the difficulties facing immigrant women in American society. *Family Welfare Work in a Metropolitan Community* (1924) examined strains on the modern family, such as widowhood and illness, and *Social Work and the Courts* (1934) showed how law shaped the definition and resolution of social problems. These studies were part of the University of Chicago Social Service Series in which Abbott and Breckinridge selected materials to reveal the social construction of community issues. Finally, *Marriage and the Civic Rights of Women* (1931), a classic statement in the sociology of law, discussed the relationship between marital status and citizenship.

Breckinridge and Abbott held considerably different views from Graham Taylor, director of the CSCP, regarding the philosophy of the school. In 1920, while Taylor was on leave, Breckinridge played a significant role in moving the CSCP to the University of Chicago, where it became the School of Social Service Administration (SSA). Both women ultimately had distinguished careers within the SSA, which reflected their philosophy that social work should become the science of social policy in which academic and fieldwork were combined. The two were also instrumental in establishing the first scholarly journal for the profession, the *Social Service Review* (in 1927), which became a leading publication in social work. Abbott was the editor, with Breckinridge a senior editor who served until her death in 1948. Initially, much of the editorial work and writing fell to the two women, who viewed the journal as a way of strengthening the educational program of the SSA. The journal covered a remarkable range of topics, including a section with analyses of public documents, reflecting Breckinridge's legal training and her conviction that such materials were indispensable to social workers but sorely neglected in other publications.

In 1925 Breckinridge was promoted to professor of social economy, after Talbot and two other female professors wrote a lengthy letter to the president and Board of Regents of the university detailing various discriminatory practices toward women faculty. In 1929 she became the Samuel Deutsch Professor of Public Welfare Administration. Breckinridge's concerns roughly encompassed three areas: improving the lives of children, promoting research on and reform of the urban world, and expanding the political and economic equality of women. She worked diligently to abolish child labor and also prepared a report on the first ten years of Chicago's pioneering juvenile court movement.

Breckinridge repeatedly championed the rights of African Americans. She served as an early member of the National Association for the Advancement of Colored People. At the University of Chicago she unsuccessfully attempted to reduce racism. In 1907, as assistant to Marion Talbot, Breckinridge allowed a black woman student to live in a dormitory. After several white women moved out, the university president called in Breckinridge and told her that the dormitories were for white students only, forcing her to reverse her decision. In a tenement survey for the Chicago Department of Health in 1910, she insisted on doing a canvas in neighborhoods where African Americans lived, and she described the racial prejudice that resulted in segregated substandard housing. The report Breckinridge's students prepared in 1919 after collecting data for the Chicago Commission on Race Relations stood as a comprehensive assessment of race relations in the northern United States.

Breckinridge's and Abbott's reform and social activism programs meshed with their research, which was representative of the early work done in urban sociology at the University of Chicago. Breckinridge's writings provided insights and baseline data in areas that are still the concern of social scientists: work and occupations, especially those affecting women; ethnic groups; delinquency and crime; poverty; and the legal rights of women. Her *Women in the Twentieth Century* (1933), one of a series of monographs written for President Hoover's Committee on Social Trends, represented a landmark effort that delineated the status of women from 1890 to 1930. Breckinridge played an active role as a theorizer and producer of knowledge who not only helped to legitimate the place of women in the public sphere but also considerably expanded the social space for women.

Breckinridge epitomized the professional, progressive approach to reform. In seeing the role of the state as a necessity for social welfare undertakings, she was far ahead of her time. Individualistic, pathological explanations for social phenomena were still commonplace among social workers. Breckinridge, however, looked beyond the individual to social processes and structural factors to explain behavior. Her work at the SSA played a major role in her professionalization process and enabled her to function effectively as she moved from local and state levels to national and international ones. She perfected not only her research skills at the SSA but also more intangible ones, such as coalition building.

In appearance, Breckinridge, a Presbyterian who never married, was deceptively frail, with a slender frame and delicate features. She combined toughness with sensitivity, and her quiet voice concealed an iron will. Although the peak of her academic activity occurred between 1912 and 1936, she remained professionally active from her retirement in 1942 until her death. In 1939 she moved into Edith Abbott's house after the death of Abbott's sister Grace. Breckinridge died in Chicago from a perforated ulcer and long-standing arteriosclerosis. Her cremated remains were interred in Lexington, Kentucky.

Upon her death, Breckinridge's former students articulated her place in the SSA. "She imparted to students, through her teaching, her own intellectual honesty . . . and a rare blend of kindness, brilliance, and sympathetic insight" (Abbott, "Breckinridge: Over the Years," 422). Breckinridge, whose work led to landmark legislation, was a champion of the rights of the poor and oppressed and an advocate for the rights of minorities and women. The Social Security Act and formation of the United States Children's Bureau are traceable to the social policy that Breckinridge and Abbott helped write into law. Breckinridge's belief that the state must be the most effective instrument for the promotion of human welfare was translated into the curriculum they developed for the SSA. She had little use for the idea that those interested in social welfare should be divided into the doers and the thinkers or the teachers. Rather, she saw each activity—research, teaching, and participation in the welfare services—as enriching the others. Her own actions demonstrated

the value of this threefold approach. Her work embodied the approach of present-day feminist scholars who see an interconnection between thinking and acting about the world.

Sources. The Breckinridge Family Papers are deposited in the Library of Congress. They include forty containers of her correspondence, speeches, and articles from 1873 through 1948. UC Spec. Coll. has the Sophonisba Breckinridge Papers, including her fragmentary autobiography. Marion Talbot's autobiography, *More Than Lore* (1936), details her attempts to enhance the place of women (faculty and students) in higher education. Edith Abbott, "Sophonisba Preston Breckinridge: Over the Years," *Social Service Review*, December 1948, a tribute to her friend, is part of a special issue devoted to Breckinridge. *NAW* (1971) and *NAW* (1980) give chronological histories of both Breckinridge and Abbott and their long friendship. While focusing upon the Abbotts, Lela Costin's *Two Sisters for Social Justice* (1983) provides insights into their friendship and work with Breckinridge. Virginia Kemp Fish, "The Hull-House Circle," in *Gender, Ideology, and Action*, ed. Janet Sharistanian (1986), discusses the six members of the circle and the intermeshing of their lives in the public and private spheres. May Estelle Cook, "Sophonisba Preston Breckinridge: 1866–1948," in *Wellesley*, October 1948, is a memorial in the alumnae magazine of Breckinridge's college. Walter I. Trattnor, ed., *Biographical Dictionary of Social Welfare in America* (1986), contains an excellent bibliography of Breckinridge's writings. Ellen F. Fitzpatrick, *Endless Crusade: Women Social Scientists and Progressive Reform* (1990), examines four female social scientists at the University of Chicago, including Breckinridge. Catherine Altany, "Power in the Midst of Powerlessness: The Contributions of Sophonisba P. Breckinridge to Social Work during the Formative Years of the Profession" (Ph.D. diss., Case Western Reserve Univ., 1992), is a biographical case study of Breckinridge that examines the nature of women's influence on establishing and shaping the profession of social work. Mary Jo Deegan, ed., *Women in Sociology: A Bio-Bibliographical Sourcebook* (1991), has a fine bibliography and strong analysis of Breckinridge's life.

VIRGINIA KEMP FISH

BRENNER, SISTER M. REBECCA
(Marie Pauline Brenner)
December 15, 1906–August 4, 1978
TEACHER, SOCIAL ACTION LEADER

Marie Pauline Brenner was born in St. Paul, Minnesota, the youngest of nine children of Aquilin and Rosa (Weber) Brenner. Aquilin Brenner, from Steinbach, Bavaria, emigrated to the United States in 1874 and settled in the St. Paul area, where he farmed and was a tanner. Rosa Weber, from Sulz, Switzerland, emigrated in 1884. She married Brenner in 1890. Rosa Brenner was widowed in 1911.

Marie Brenner was educated in St. Paul. In 1926, she followed her older sister Rose's example and joined the School Sisters of St. Francis, entering St. Joseph Convent, Milwaukee, Wisconsin. Now Sister M. Rebecca, Brenner began teaching grades four through seven at St. Nicholas School, Aurora, Illinois. At the same time, following the typical pattern of women religious, Brenner continued her own education and graduated with an A.B. degree in 1933 from DePaul University, Chicago. She majored in social science.

After college, Brenner returned to St. Joseph's Convent, Milwaukee, where she began to train young women preparing for religious life. Many of the novitiates were as young as fourteen years; some had come to the School Sisters of St. Francis because family economic hardships during the Great Depression made religious life an attractive option. Until 1937 she also taught grades six through eight in School Sister elementary schools in Wisconsin, including St. Thomas in Waterford, Holy Ghost in Milwaukee, and St. Mary's in Fennimore.

Sister Rebecca Brenner returned to Chicago in 1937, when she began to teach in Alvernia High School, administered by the School Sisters of St. Francis, Milwaukee. She taught religion, Latin, and American history. In addition, she initiated one of the first courses in sociology in a Catholic high school, the first taught at Alvernia. Her approach to teaching sociology was unusual. She believed that a classroom education needed to be supplemented by active involvement of students in the community. Instead of writing assignments, students investigated and reported on the conditions of Chicago public housing, child care centers, Cook County prison and court facilities, and the Bridewell Hospital for prison inmates. One student, who later became a School Sister and a science teacher, commented that her investigations of the women's house of corrections and the tenements that housed the poor taught her "that the women and the poor were no different from us but that only their circumstances were different" (interview with Sister Leona Truchan, April 8, 1994).

While teaching at Alvernia High School in Chicago, Brenner began graduate school at the University of Notre Dame, South Bend, Indiana. She studied sociology and American history and wrote her master's thesis, "Churchgoing among Our Catholic Immigrants," in April 1944, concluding that "abandonment by civic and ecclesiastical superiors" (p. 110) was the primary cause of Italian immigrant apostasy. She received an M.A. degree in 1944. As the daughter of immigrants, Brenner understood the spiritual, material, and physical disadvantages of the immigrant. She advocated a more aggressive and more inclusive role for the clergy. The church had to minister to immigrants, understanding how cultural shock, lack of education, and traditional anticlericalism exacerbated the poverty of recent arrivals.

By 1945, Sister Brenner had become increasingly sensitive to the needs of inner city youth. She taught her sociology students about the causes of poverty and crime, which she perceived to be outcomes of the racism, isolation, and apostasy of urban America. For Brenner, the Great Depression and World War II had challenged democracy and Christianity internationally and at home. Roman Catholics had to find ways to solve problems of poverty, crime, and racism through the application of Christian social action in a world where Nazism had been defeated but an antireligious materialism was on the rise.

Because of racism, traditional Catholic ethnic neighborhoods resisted efforts to deal with urban problems. Whites resisted attempts to place public housing for African Americans and other working poor in their neighborhoods. Catholic parishes and schools did not embrace integration. Sister Rebecca hoped that Alvernia High School, situated on the city's perimeter, could act in an affirmative way to counter the segregationist trends in the neighborhoods. Located in an all-white section of Chicago, the high school sought to recruit students from black neighborhoods. It was faced with the problem of transporting the students safely. Brenner encouraged her students to respond

positively regardless of whether the school was successful in its plan to integrate. Her students were encouraged to provide food and clothing for inner city families.

At Alvernia Brenner instituted a program of field trips that brought her students out of the classroom and into the community. She combined book knowledge with practical life experience. Her sociology classes spent time volunteering in the public housing projects and the prisons of Cook County. When Sister Claire Marie Sawyer, a graduate of Alvernia High School, became director of educational services for the National Catholic Conference for Interracial Justice, she remembered the work begun by Brenner. Writing to Brenner in 1965, Sawyer recalled how, at a time when it was not popular or secure to be fighting interracial injustice, Brenner was on the scene. Brenner had made inroads into the prejudice of her white students and had begun the hard work of teaching them how they were connected to the whole of humanity, not simply their own small group.

In 1952, after establishing the sociology curriculum at Alvernia, with its emphasis on field work, Brenner was called back to Milwaukee, where she became an instructor in history and sociology at Alverno College, also an institution directed by the School Sisters of St. Francis. She continued her own education during summer terms at Marquette University, Milwaukee, Wisconsin; Catholic University of America, Washington, D.C.; and St. Louis University, St. Louis, Missouri.

At Alverno, Brenner developed the sociology courses and was an adviser to a variety of student organizations, including the Intercollegiate Council, the Sociology Club, and the Alverno Interracial Club. The Sociology Club was practical in orientation, following Brenner's concept that deeds were essential for Christian faith and belief. Students were to acquaint themselves with the realities of the social world through social service agencies. They were encouraged to do social service during their college careers. The Interracial Club's purpose was to learn, apply, and promulgate the Catholic principles of interracial justice and charity.

In 1961, at age fifty-five, Brenner went back to high school teaching at St. Joseph Convent High School, Milwaukee. In a period of great change in Catholic life, St. Joseph decided to close its school in 1966. During the five years she taught there, Brenner brought the emerging women's movement to the young female students, teaching them about the power of the vote and the importance of women as activists in the political and social world.

From 1966 to 1968, a time when many women religious began to look self-critically at their traditional roles and to seek change and new direction, Brenner did social service research for St. Anthony's Hospital, Milwaukee, in an effort to discover ways in which her sisterhood could alleviate tensions from racism and economic inequality that plagued the city. She became a part-time instructor for the Sisters of St. Francis at St. Joseph LaFarge Lifelong Learning Institute, stressing self-development and community service. At age sixty-two she learned to drive so that she could chauffeur the retired sisters in a secondhand station wagon she had obtained.

Retiring from teaching in 1971, Brenner devoted herself full time to social work, participating in Milwaukee's urban renewal and interracial justice programs, including the Central North

Community Council. In 1972 she worked on the Education Task Force for the Harambee Revitalization Project and took a personal and active interest in the care and well-being of the children of interracial and interethnic marriages, providing them with food and clothing and bringing them to school and church. Her work in Milwaukee's 3rd Ward included publishing a local newspaper and participating in Pentecostal prayer groups. This ministry returned Brenner to many of the concerns in which she was first engaged when a young teacher of sociology in Chicago.

Sister Rebecca Brenner died of cancer at age seventy-one. She was living at Maryhill Nursing Home in Milwaukee. She was buried at Mt. Olivet Cemetery, Milwaukee.

For more than half a century, Brenner was at the forefront of the transformation of Catholic life in the Midwest, prodding her own religious order and the Catholic hierarchy to adopt interracial policies and work for social justice. Described by colleagues and students as a tall woman who strode into the room, with large and deep-set eyes, a deep and low voice, and an unusual sense of humor, she empowered their social consciences and helped them through their daily lives.

Sources. Biographical information comes from the Archives of the School Sisters of St. Francis and the Archives of Alverno College, both in Milwaukee. Helpful were oral interviews conducted in April and May 1994 with Professor Bernardin Deutsch; Sisters Austin Doherty, Maureen Hartnett, Christopher McNaney, and Leona Truchan; Dorothy Durkin; and Frank Zeidler, former mayor of Milwaukee. For information on Brenner's religious order, see M. Francis Borgia, OSF, *He Sent Two: The Story of the Beginning of the School Sisters of St. Francis* (1965).

TERRY J. MICHELSEN

BRIGHT, ALICE MARY
September 18, 1917–October 25, 1982
ATTORNEY

Alice Bright was the first woman attorney to be hired by Sidley, Austin, Burgess & Harper (now Sidley & Austin), one of the largest law firms in the United States and among the oldest in Chicago. "When she accepted employment . . . at $150 a month, [she] . . . was quite a rarity as one of only three [women] lawyers then [1942] at major Chicago law firms" (Kogan, 160). In 1957 she was the first woman to become a partner at that firm, at a time when few, if any, women were partners in major legal firms in the country. Born in Homewood, Illinois, she was the first daughter and fourth of five children of Orville T. Bright Jr. and Mary (Griggs) Bright. Both Alice Bright's father and her paternal grandfather were teachers in the Chicago public schools. Her father served as superintendent of schools for the Flossmoor, Dolton, and Lake Bluff districts and was briefly assistant Cook County Superintendent of Schools, and her grandfather had been the superintendent of Englewood schools and Cook County Superintendent of Schools. Mary Bright, a graduate of the University of Chicago, had studied Latin and Greek.

Homewood Elementary and Thornton High School provided the foundation for Alice Bright's education. In the fifth grade, the same year she researched and wrote an ambitious paper on American Civil War generals, Bright decided she would become a lawyer. Never distracted from that goal, she attended the University of Chicago, where she received a partial scholarship. Along with one other woman, she received her undergraduate and law degrees in a concentrated six-year program, earning an A.B. degree in 1939 and a J.D. cum laude in 1941. Bright was admitted to the Illinois Bar November 6, 1941. She clerked in a small law office from November 1941 through May 1942 but continued to seek other employment where the pay would be better and there would be opportunities to specialize in estate work.

America's entrance into World War II expanded career opportunities for women. In October 1941 George F. James, assistant dean of the University of Chicago Law School, recommended several candidates, including Alice Bright, for a job in Kansas City, Missouri. He explained that, if they would consider a woman, Bright was intellectually better than the men he was recommending. Her standing was ninth in her class. In April 1942 Dean James again wrote on her behalf, for a job at Sidley, Austin, Burgess & Harper. He was pleased to recommend her, assuming that the firm would have a woman. Bright was headed for a position in military intelligence in Washington, D.C., when she received a call from Paul Harper, "who, like other senior partners [at Sidley, Austin, Burgess & Harper] was on the lookout for bright draft-exempt prospects" (Kogan, 160).

Initially, Bright's assignments were in the field of probate, but, due to the firm's short-handedness during wartime, the scope of her duties broadened to include wills, trusts, estate planning, real estate, and contract matters and, eventually, domestic and adoption cases. She became a proficient litigator who was well known in the Chicago legal community for several of her dramatic and high profile courtroom cases. More importantly, she was known and respected by her peers for her high standards and her competence and effectiveness as a trial attorney.

During her early years as a practicing attorney, Bright was active in the Illinois Women's Bar Association, serving as its president from 1955 to 1956. When her term expired, she resigned from the association because she thought the cause of women lawyers could be better advanced without a separate organization. Bright was helpful and supportive of women attorneys in general, but her recommendations that the Women's Bar Association should disband and that its members should become active in the traditional, male-dominated organizations was resented by some of her fellow female attorneys.

Bright dealt with the discrimination she encountered on a regular basis by ignoring it. For example, the Mid-Day Club was in the same building as her law firm, and many of the firm lawyers lunched there with clients. The club's male-only policy excluded Bright, who conferred with her associates about a client's case and then took her meal elsewhere. Bright's client then lunched with the firm's male lawyers at the club. Apparently, she did not discuss these impediments with her peers or close friends.

Bright's subsequent activities in bar associations and other legal organizations reflected her expressed convictions. She was a member of the Chicago Bar Association (CBA), serving on its legislative and adoption committees and chairing the probate committee in 1956.

Bright became the first woman partner at Sidley & Austin in 1957. Regarded by her associates as a strong and aggressive attorney, she was also highly principled, intractable, and uncompromising when she believed she was right. These traits, plus her vigorous and assertive advocacy techniques, led to the perception that she was one of the toughest attorneys at Sidley & Austin. Some opposing counsels considered Bright overly aggressive or "unlady-like," as her courtroom demeanor was not gentle or deferential, and she was capable of interrupting when necessary.

Bright successfully argued two contested adoption cases. The first, *Huebert v. Marshall*, was decided in 1971, and the second, *Polales v. Catholic Charities*, in 1979. Both illustrate Bright's success in arguing before the Illinois appellate courts. Bright's client in the first case had signed a consent for the adoption of her thirteen-day-old infant daughter. Bright argued that the appellate court should reverse the decision; her client's consent was invalid since it had been obtained while she was under duress and undue influences. Similarly, Bright argued that Catholic Charities had placed an infant for adoption without securing a valid consent from its unwed mother. The child, now two and a half years old, was returned to the birth mother. The highly publicized suit, with its dramatic overtones and important legal implications, had taken two years, culminating in forty days of trial during a four month period. The judge announced his finding of fraud against Catholic Charities in a packed courtroom.

Like many successful male attorneys, she was a hard-nosed practitioner who defended her position and made her points emphatically. She was a particularly effective negotiator, who was more inclined to litigate than settle. Her handling of several legal matters for the wealthy and prominent Wrigley family of Chicago reflected these professional traits and attributes. When in 1977 Philip and Helen Wrigley died within two months of one another, their estates were handled by a team of Sidley & Austin attorneys led by W. Sterling Maxwell and Bright. Bright was able to secure a favorable valuation of Wrigley Company stock for the estates. Philip K. Wrigley was the son of William Wrigley Jr., the founder of the chewing gum empire and the owner of the Chicago Cubs, the professional baseball team. Bright represented William Wrigley III (Philip Wrigley's son) against his wife, Joan, in a long, complex, and bitter domestic dispute that resulted in the annulment sought by Wrigley after seven years of marriage.

Bright belonged to the Illinois State Bar Association (probate and trust section), the American Bar Association (real property, probate, and trust law sections), the American College of Probate Counsel, and the American Judicature Society. She gave speeches and lectured for the Illinois Institute for Continuing Legal Education.

After her profession, Bright's attention and energy were focused primarily on her family. She remained single, and she and her younger sister, Jane, lived with and cared for their mother in the family house until the latter's death in 1968. Bright and her sister Jane enjoyed literature and music and, in particular, were devotees of opera, attending Lyric Opera productions regularly and amassing an extensive record collection of operatic works. Bright was an avid reader of all varieties of books, including the

romance novel. She did not participate in sport activities and was a heavy smoker. She had a fondness for animals and owned German shepherd dogs.

After their mother's death, the Bright sisters moved to Wilmette, where their father, separated from their mother since 1940, joined them in 1970. Alice Bright took care of her father until he died in 1981 and of her sister, who was an invalid for many years but outlived Bright. In addition to being a caretaker, Bright was also the family's historian, its adviser on legal and business matters, and its principal hostess.

Bright died from cancer at Evanston Hospital at age sixty-five. Funeral services were held at St. John's Lutheran Church, Wilmette, Illinois, and burial was at Memorial Park Cemetery, Skokie, Illinois.

Bright was popular with law clients, always willing to listen, to help, and to advise. Her office desk grew stacks of paper so high that eventually Bright had to confer with clients and attorneys in a conference room. Her legendary messiness and aversion to administrative tasks were attributed to her preference for dropping the paperwork in hand to listen to another's problem. She was thoroughly imbued with the work ethic and thrived on professional activity. "She was not only a superior lawyer," said a partner at Sidley & Austin, "but also tenaciously loyal to the cause of her clients. During a period when it was not easy for a woman to be accepted, much less [be] overtly aggressive for her client, she managed to do so with both dignity and force" (*Chicago Daily Law Bulletin*, October 27, 1982).

Sources. Information about Alice M. Bright can be found in her student file, the University of Chicago Law School. Biographical and career information was obtained from interviews with coworker James Carroll, May 24, 1994; brother Frank Bright, June 6, 1994; and classmate Delcome B. Hollins, June 14, 1994. See Herman Kogan, *Traditions and Challenges: The Story of Sidley & Austin* (1983), to learn about the firm and Bright's role there. Obituaries appeared in the *Chicago Daily Law Bulletin*, October 27, 1982; the *CT*, October 27, 1982; and *Wilmette Life*, October 28, 1982.

NANCY CANAFAX

BRIMSON, ALICE WORTHINGTON SMITH
April 19, 1884–October 11, 1981
CAREER CHURCH WORKER, ADMINISTRATOR, TEACHER

Alice Worthington Smith Brimson, president of the Baptist Missionary Training School (BMTS) in Chicago during the late 1920s and 1930s, was born in Lafayette, Indiana, the third and last child of William George and Susan (Smith) Brimson. Her father, an English immigrant, started work on the railroad as a telegrapher and, though he had little formal education, worked his way to an executive position. Her mother was a homemaker.

When Brimson was eleven, the family moved to the Englewood area of Chicago. Her father continued his duties as vice-president and general manager of the Quincy, Omaha, and Kansas City Railroad. The family participated in worship, education, and social life at the Englewood Baptist Church. For many years Brimson's father was the Sunday school superintendent, and she taught a class for young boys. Spiritual life continued at home where each day started with family prayers.

After graduation from Englewood High School in 1901,

Brimson attended Smith College, earning a B.S. degree in 1905. She took courses in zoology and botany as well as history, and she served as president of the Biological Society in her last year. After graduation she returned home to Chicago with no particular plans. She chose not to have a party for "coming out" into society such as her older sister Mary had.

For nearly ten years, Brimson devoted herself to domestic duties. Her sister married Fred Grow in 1906, and the couple lived in the seventeen-room Brimson home. When their mother died in 1911, the two sisters assumed the running of the household. Alice's nephew, Brimson Grow, was born in 1909, and she became a second mother to him.

William Brimson purchased property near Alexandria, Minnesota, which the family made a vacation destination. The tents used the first years were soon replaced by a cabin. Brimson loved the summer place, often organizing picnics and long walks. The family invited church friends to come as summer guests, with swimming, fishing, and hiking to fill the days. Brimson also helped run this household, with hired help from daughters of nearby farmers. She shared her love of birds and flowers with all the guests, planning long hikes around the lake to enjoy the flora and fauna.

In the first two decades of the twentieth century, immigrants from central and southern Europe were pouring into Chicago. The men worked in the stockyards, while the children attended school. The women were usually at home, doing their best to cope with their families' marketing and household needs without knowing much English. In the late 1910s, inspired by a missionary talk by Helen Barrett Montgomery, nationally prominent Baptist leader of a women's missionary movement, about the importance of home missions and the opportunities for Baptists, Brimson realized that the world was coming to Chicago and that she could be of service to others, particularly foreigners. She began to help run the Worldwide Guilds, Baptist service groups for young people, working as a volunteer. She was touched by the difficulties of the immigrants and searched for ways to help them.

Work with the Worldwide Guilds led to Brimson's appointment as the first secretary for Christian Americanization of the Women's American Baptist Home Mission Society (WABHMS). From 1877, when the WABHMS was organized by RUMAH CROUSE and other founders, until the end of the second decade of the twentieth century, most of the work was done by volunteers, often middle-class married women. By creating the position of Christian Americanization secretary, Baptist women were acknowledging the need for trained leadership to give the many volunteers the direction needed in outreach. Brimson was not expected to do everything herself but to help women in their own churches and neighborhoods break down class and race prejudices that surfaced as communities changed. With her leadership, Baptist women organized efforts to befriend immigrant women, teaching them English and providing classes and parties as well as sponsoring Bible studies and other religious activities. Outreach to African American women continued to be an important part of this work. As she viewed the difficulties and problems of the city, also seeing the rich heritage the newcomers brought, Brimson believed the church had an important role. She wrote in her 1925 report to WABHMS,

"Within our land race prejudice stalks more blatantly than ever, and many strangers, chilled by its horrid glare, have retreated more than ever into their foreign groups. Only love that expresses itself as brotherhood can make the America that is to be a strong united land" (*National Baptist Convention Annual Report*, 674). While she expressed discouragement that so many women were blind to the opportunities, she reiterated her belief that every Christian could become a missionary without leaving home.

To supplement her practical work, Brimson entered the University of Chicago School of Social Service Administration and earned an M.A. degree in 1927, writing a thesis, "The Effect of Immigration on Religion." She surveyed a number of immigrant groups—Italians, Poles, Greeks, Czech-Slovaks, Lithuanians, and Jews—highlighting the ways the immigrant experience affected their lives. She found that the immigration experiences varied so widely that one could not generalize from group to group.

Offices for Christian Americanization were housed at the Baptist Missionary Training School. The first school of its kind, BMTS offered a three-year course of study for young women who wished to become missionaries. In 1926 Brimson became president. The school emphasized practical work; in addition to studies in Bible, students had field assignments in various community clubs and churches. For example, in 1928 she reported that community work included regular hospital visiting, a Sunday school at the Japanese Young Men's Christian Association, community classes for African American boys and girls, and work at the Polish Baptist church.

Brimson brought many changes and improvements to the academic program. She arranged with Denison University in Granville, Ohio, to accept credits from BMTS so students would need only one year more of study to earn a B.A. degree. In 1936 she completed efforts to make the training school education a four-year college program in which students could earn either a B.A. degree or a Bachelor of Religious Education. Some faculty came from the University of Chicago to teach specific courses in the sciences and literature. These men from the university as well as pastors who came in to preach added diversity to the female institution. Despite the financial difficulties of the depression, enrollment doubled during her tenure.

Brimson also gave thought and direction to the spiritual needs of the students. On Thursday nights the community met together for prayers. She set aside a special prayer room with a key. Students who wished to be alone could hang the key outside the door so that others would know not to disturb them. With memories of the happy times at the family's vacation home in Minnesota, she also instituted faculty-student retreats at Lake Geneva and a special Dunes Day in the fall when there were no classes and everyone packed up to spend a day at the Indiana dunes. Brimson always spoke at Friday chapel, with an emphasis on practical, helpful messages. Her assistants thought her especially gifted in diplomatically handling students with problems. Using vivid imagery she reported to the Baptist Convention and spoke to women's groups about the difference that home mission work could make in helping immigrants combat the difficulties they faced.

Living in an apartment at the school, Brimson kept in touch

with her sister and the rest of the family; but because all of the students needed financial help, her free time was limited. In addition to duties at the school, she visited state women's organizations and persuaded them to give money. Her personality and management skills impressed many people, some of whom made substantial gifts. Even during the Great Depression of the 1930s, Brimson kept BMTS solvent.

In spare moments, despite frequent severe headaches, she nurtured her love of flowers, poetry—especially Shakespeare—and painting, all of which provided outlets of creativity from her management duties. She also enjoyed the travel opportunities she received, both to speak on behalf of the school and to visit mission sites. In 1930 she visited Japan, continuing the interest in Asian culture that had begun years before in her immigrant work.

In 1937 she moved to New York City to become the executive secretary of the WABHMS. Her reports reflected growing concern with the state of the world. In 1940 she noted the need arising from the increasing number of Jewish immigrants fleeing from crises in Europe. She reported on farm problems, including drought, that merited concern. Brimson led Baptist women in working ecumenically with other church women to meet these needs, but finances remained a problem. She recognized that since more money could not be raised to enlarge the work, it must be "deepened spiritually." She feared that financial problems existed "not because the Baptists have less ability to give, but because they have less interest in giving" (*National Baptist Convention Annual Report*, 1940, 779). In 1942 she called attention to the race prejudice that was rising rapidly in the United States and the suffering of Japanese Americans in internment camps. Baptist women, with Brimson's leadership, took these concerns seriously, sending Christmas presents to the camps and working to free Japanese Americans whom they knew.

In 1947 she retired and moved back to Chicago near BMTS. She and her sister lived in nearby apartment buildings, reestablishing a close relationship. She taught foreign missions at BMTS and served as a delegate to the 1950 Northern Baptist Convention. After her sister moved to St. Petersburg, Florida, in the early 1950s, she spent the winters with her.

Brimson continued in vigorous service to home and church. She still loved walking and being outdoors, and friends remembered her striding energetically down the street, petticoats sometimes showing. When her sister suffered a stroke in 1959, she nursed and cared for her until her death three years later. In the summer of 1966, at age eighty-two, she embarked on a trip to Europe and the Near East. On her return she purchased a home in Atherton Homes, a Baptist retirement community in Alhambra, California. There she became active in the First Baptist Church of Pasadena and gave time to growing roses and other flowers. When she moved to an apartment in the complex, she deeded her home to the retirement community. In turn, the community dedicated the gardens to her, naming them "Brimson Gardens." In 1980, she broke her hip and died several months later at the age of ninety-seven. She was buried near Alhambra, California.

Brimson, like other women of her generation, worked through the church to have an effect on society during a time of increasing immigration and urbanization. Like many of these women, she began as a volunteer but pursued skills and education, turning volunteer work into a career. In both the BMTS and the WABHMS she gave the leadership necessary to leave them stronger institutions than she found, carving out a solid place for professional women within the denomination.

Sources. Brimson's published writings include her master's thesis, *The Effect of Immigration on Religion* (1927), Univ. of Chicago; *Every Foreign Woman* (1923); and *Witnessing to the Light* (1940). The American Baptist Historical Society, Rochester, New York, has annual reports for the National Baptist Convention, where Brimson's yearly reports are recorded. A taped interview with her nephew, Brimson Grow, by Linda Gesling on December 12, 1994, provides biographical information. Faith Coxe Bailey, *Two Directions* (1964), has information on the history of the Women's American Baptist Home Mission Society.

LINDA J. GESLING

BROD, FRITZI SCHERMER
June 16, 1900–December 1, 1952
PAINTER, LITHOGRAPHER, DESIGNER, WRITER OF ART BOOKS

An active member of the Chicago art community in the second quarter of the twentieth century, Fritzi Brod was born Frederika Schermer in Prague, Bohemia, then under Austrian rule (now Czech Republic). One of three children of a wealthy Jewish family, her father was a Sephardic Jew, and her mother came from a prosperous Austrian family of farmers and brewers. Primarily a housewife and lady of leisure, Fritzi Schermer's mother also dabbled in decorative painting of china and fans. Fritzi Schermer was educated at private schools and later studied art in Prague at the Lycee and the Art Institute of Prague and in Vienna at Kunstgewerbeschule. Her mother encouraged her daughter's interest in art, and the Schermers traveled extensively during summer vacations, visiting centers of art and culture in Austria and Germany.

It was on holiday that Fritzi Schermer met her future husband, Oswald "Ozzi" Brod, a native Austrian who was a naturalized American citizen. Brod was in Austria on a buying trip for his employer, the New York bookstore Brentano's. After a two-year courtship in Europe, Ozzi Brod returned to America in order to maintain his citizenship, and he was soon sent to Chicago to run the art department at Kroch's and Brentano's bookstore. Interested in modern art, Ozzi Brod, the chief buyer of art books at the store, made certain that Chicagoans had a wide selection of the latest books on modern art, which he made available to local artists by offering reasonable discount rates. When Fritzi Schermer joined him in Chicago, she became part of this emerging community of modernist artists. The two were married in 1924.

The young Fritzi Brod arrived in Chicago already an accomplished textile designer. She embarked immediately on a continuation of her design career, and her patterns were among the first of a modern style to be displayed at the Marshall Field store. Brod's design talent found commercial application in the decorative painting she did for the Balaban and Katz movie theaters throughout Chicago. Although she was successful as a designer, Brod sought a more fulfilling expression of her art talents in painting and lithography. She had studied painting in Europe but began to paint seriously in Chicago under the tutelage of

Hungarian-born painter, illustrator, and graphic artist Raymond Katz, who was active in the new art movements of the city. It was in the context of this vital world of experimentation and advocacy for the avant-garde that Fritzi Brod emerged as a painter.

From the 1920s and their arrival in Chicago, the Brods participated in the informal, independent Chicago artist movement, whose members were rebellious and individualistic and were striking out on their own in a city still cold to the post-impressionist art first seen when the 1913 New York Armory Show, *International Exhibit of Modern Art*, came to the Art Institute of Chicago (AIC). Independent associations of artists—the introspectives, the Cor Ardens, and the Chicago No-Jury Society—rejected the conservatism of the major art institutions and galleries. Even the oldest local art association, the Chicago Society of Artists, founded in 1887, split in 1923, with the conservatives forming a new organization, the Association of Chicago Painters and Sculptors, leaving the modernists' core to run the society. First the modernists found gallery space in such new venues as the Thurber Gallery and Raymond Katz's Little Gallery, located in the Auditorium Theater building and established in 1932. That year Brod began to take art lessons with Raymond Katz and to exhibit regularly at the Little Gallery. She joined the Chicago No-Jury Society of Artists formed in response to the juried Art Institute annuals that often excluded the more progressive work the society hoped to encourage. Brod not only exhibited with the No-Jury Society, she also served as vice-president.

Brod's unique form of modernism suggests the influence of Austrian expressionism. This expressionistic character appears natural, considering her European background and education. Flattened forms and vibrant colors are characteristic of work, for instance, her *Self-Portrait* (1936). Her subject's hard, almost chiseled features add psychological drama to the work, as does the sitter's far away glance and anxious expression. The sitter in *On The Balcony* (1935) also has a faraway gaze. She stares out from her seat behind an iron balcony, which also serves as a decorative barrier. The background of the painting is an intricate tapestry-like design and owes much to her early work as a designer of textiles. This design adds a decorative quality to the work. The sitter's hands are oversized, and she appears to be wringing them. The deep red background suggests a relationship to Austrian expressionism. Pensive women, often alone and seemingly lonely, recur in her work.

A departure from her usual subject matter, *Untitled (Trapeze)* (c. 1938) looks like pastel both in color and technique, although it is an oil painting. Brod seems to be experimenting with standard painting conventions. There is also an interesting hatching pattern visible throughout the painting, perhaps a result of her extensive work as a printmaker. The composition is modernist in feel; the compressed space is almost uncomfortable, and the viewer looks at trapeze performers from an unusual bird's eye view. The use of performers as a subject was introduced by the impressionists in the 1870s and 1880s; some examples were already in the Art Institute of Chicago's collection in the 1930s. Brod not only uses this characteristic impressionist subject matter, she also shows an interest in the nineteenth-century technique of pointillism, exemplified in Georges Seurat's masterpiece *Sunday Afternoon on the Island of La Grande Jatte* (1884–86), acquired by the Art Institute in 1936. Brod would surely have been familiar with the painting, since it had a great impact on the Art Institute and Chicago immediately upon installation.

Brod worked with proficiency in many media. In addition to oil painting she worked in watercolor and many graphic media. Many of her lithographs were influenced by the highly tactile nature of her textiles; the precise lines are from this tradition as well. Her lithographs also reflect ideas seen in her paintings. In *Attitude* (c. 1938) a woman sits alone with a faraway glance. She wears a shawl over her head, and there is an intricate pattern within the shawl owing to Brod's proficiency as a designer of textiles. In this work, too, the sitter's hands are prominent. In one hand she holds a handkerchief and in the other, a small book, perhaps a Bible. There is an underlying sadness in many of her prints. Brod was regularly included in various art calendars, including a 1937 *American Block Print Calendar* published in Milwaukee, in which she shared space with such famous artists as Grant Wood and Stuart Davis. She participated actively in the easel and mural division of the Illinois Art Project (IAP) part of the Works Progress Administration (WPA) during the 1930s.

Brod's work was recognized by a few open-minded critics, for example, C. J. Bulliet, art critic for the *Chicago Times* and *Chicago Daily News*. In the 1930s he wrote a series of articles in the *Chicago Daily News*, "Artists of Chicago Past and Present"; Fritzi Brod was featured on August 1, 1936. He praised the "emotional content" and the "explosive, exuberant, mad energy" in her work. Bulliet was one of the few to recognize her uniqueness and talent. Some critics of the time praised her for the decorative qualities of her work, entirely missing or minimizing its modern aspects. One critic referred to Brod as a "highly decorative painter working with figures" ("Art Institute News," July 14, 1936). Other critics recognized the modernist quality in her work and were critical of it. A reviewer described her work as "ruthlessly and sometimes cruelly (distorted) especially in her pictures of nudes" ("Fritzi Brod Will Show Controversial Works," January 7, 1936).

Fritzi Brod's painting career took off relatively quickly after the Little Gallery. From 1936 through 1951, except 1937, 1945, and 1947, she exhibited at the juried AIC annual *Chicago and Vicinity Exhibitions* for local artists. Brod's work was shown regularly at local commercial galleries, including those at the Palmer House Hotel and Mandel Brothers department store. Her paintings were also included in museum group shows nationally and internationally, including the Pennsylvania Academy of Fine Arts (1934, 1935, 1937, 1938, 1940–45); Detroit Institute of Arts (1939); Milwaukee Art Institute (1939); Cornell University (1938); Albright Art Gallery, Buffalo, New York (1938); Dayton Art Institute, Dayton, Ohio (1944); the National Academy of Design, New York (1942, 1945, 1946); the Toronto Art Gallery (1939); and the Kansas City Art Institute (1940).

In the 1950s, as modernism became more acceptable, Brod's work was more widely praised by critics. On September 21, 1951, Eleanor Jewett, a *Chicago Daily News* critic who was generally opposed to modernism, called her "an exceptional artist [whose] exhibit is too good to miss." Copeland C. Burg of the *Chicago American* recognized her work as "having emotion, vitality and depth" (June 15, 1953).

Brod was honored with the bronze medal from the Chicago Society of Artists in 1937 and the silver medal in 1939. Her lithograph *Woman Asleep* was selected by the Library of Congress as one of the fifty best prints of 1944. Brod was also the author and illustrator of *200 Motifs and Designs* (1945) and *Flowers in Nature and Design* (1947). In both books, Brod combines her artistic skills with her earlier interest in design. She also illustrated *A Child's Book of Birds* (1951). Art works by Brod are in several public collections, including the Art Institute of Chicago; Spertus Museum of Judaica, Chicago; Mary and Leigh Block Museum, Evanston, Illinois; and the Tel Aviv Art Museum in Israel.

Brod's death from cancer in 1952 cut short her prolific and successful career. In June 1953, a memorial exhibition cosponsored by the Renaissance Society of the University of Chicago and the Chicago Society of Artists was held at the Mandel Brothers Department Store Gallery in Chicago. The importance of the sponsors of this exhibition speaks to her impact. Her work continues to be included in group exhibitions, especially those with modernist and/or feminist themes. Brod is remembered as an artist who not only created exciting, unique, and aesthetically pleasing work in a wide variety of media but was also a leader in the fight for modernism in Chicago.

Sources. The Fritzi Brod Papers are in the Archives of American Art, Smithsonian Institution, and are available on microfilm at the Ryerson Library of the Art Institute of Chicago. They include clippings, reviews of her exhibitions, a résumé, and other personal papers. Brod authored and illustrated *200 Motifs and Designs* (1945), *Flowers in Nature and Design* (1947), and illustrated *A Child's Book of Birds* (1951). Brod is listed in *Who Was Who in American Art* (1985); Esther Sparks's "A Biographical Dictionary of Painters and Sculptors in Illinois 1808–1945" (Ph.D. diss., Northwestern Univ., 1971); George J. Mavigiliano and Richard A. Lawson, *The Federal Art Project in Illinois 1935–1943* (1990); and Louise Dunn Yochim, *Role and Impact: The Chicago Society of Artists* (1979). She is profiled in C. J. Bulliet's "Artists of Chicago Past and Present," *Chicago Daily News*, August 1, 1936. Brod is also discussed in Susan S. Weininger's *The "New Woman" in Chicago, 1910–1945: Paintings from Illinois Collections* (exhibition catalog) (1993). Critics described her work in "Art Institute News: 19 One-Man Shows to Open," *Evanston Illinois News Index*, July 14, 1936; and "Fritzi Brod Will Show Controversial Works at Art Association Show," *Rockford Morning Star*, January 7, 1936. Reviews of Brod include Bulliet, mentioned above; Eleanor Jewett, "Review," *Chicago Daily News*, September 21, 1951; and Copeland C. Berg, "Review," *Chicago American*, June 15, 1953.

EDEN JURON PEARLMAN

BROWN, CORINNE STUBBS
December 14, 1849(?)–March 15, 1914
CLUBWOMAN, LABOR REFORMER, SOCIALIST

Corinne Stubbs Brown was a key figure in the creation of alliances between working women and middle-class women in Chicago at the end of the nineteenth century and was prominent in the Socialist Party at the beginning of the twentieth century. Born and raised in Chicago, she was the daughter of an immigrant mother and a New England father. Jane McWilliams was born in England into a family of radicals and came to the United States at age seventeen. She met and married Timothy R. Stubbs, a skilled craftsman, raised in Maine. Corinne

was one of several daughters educated in the city's public schools and reared in the Swedenborgian faith.

Having grown up under strict, if unorthodox, religious instruction, Stubbs later boasted of defying her father to read fiction as a child. Her education continued through graduation from a city high school, and she put that training to work for thirteen years as a school teacher and six as a principal. Her career lasted until her marriage to Frank E. Brown, a banker employed by the First National Bank. At their south Chicago home in Woodlawn Park, the Browns enjoyed what friends described as a very compatible marriage until Frank Brown's death in 1906. Corinne Brown gave birth to at least one daughter.

Corinne Brown's route into social reform has been variously charted. By an account in the *Chicago Times*, September 2, 1894, she heard the call in an Ethical Culture Society lecture in 1885. By another account, in *Woman of the Century* and elsewhere, the Haymarket bombing in Chicago in 1886 and the subsequent arrest of radicals awakened her to the need for radical social reform. Her biographies also indicate that she began as an adherent of economic reformer Henry George's single-tax theory until she concluded that it fell short of promising to break up the immense concentrations of wealth around her. These diverse accounts need not contradict each other. She was clearly alert to the economic problems of the late 1880s, and the city provided ample opportunity to explore alternative corrections. The *Chicago Times* article (an imperfect source) also quoted Brown as saying that she met Thomas J. Morgan, Chicago Socialist leader, and learned her socialism from him and the books he recommended.

However she got there, Corinne Brown burst upon the scene as a leader in the circles of women reformers by 1887. In that year, she affiliated the Woodlawn Reading Club with the new Protective Agency for Women and Children and served as the club's delegate to its governing board. A citywide group, with representatives from nineteen clubs and societies, the agency was founded "to afford the full support of the law to those whose poverty prevents them from invoking its assistance" (*Second Annual Report*, 9). Through her club, Brown raised significant sums to fund the agency's legal aid in suits that recovered women's wages, protected their limited property rights, intervened against abusive husbands, and even helped them win divorces. This middle-class alliance met Brown's strict standard for philanthropy, as she defined it in her inaugural address as president of the Woodlawn Woman's Club in 1895: it should "break down the artificial social caste that is sapping the life of society" and "condemn the offense and condone the offender, especially if the offender be a woman" (Woodlawn Woman's Club, *First Calendar*, 25).

Reform attracted Brown more than philanthropy. During her two years on the agency's board, she explored a more radical route to emerge as the head of the Ladies' Federal Union No. 2703, where she worked closely with the socialist organizer, ELIZABETH MORGAN. The union enabled women in unskilled jobs and unorganized industries to affiliate with the American Federation of Labor and gain representation in the Chicago Trade and Labor Assembly. That, Brown told the National Council of Women in 1891, gave women direct access to twenty-five thousand votes. Brown found sympathy and inspiration for her own convictions among the experienced women of the city's socialist labor movement, and she joined the Socialist Labor Party. By 1888, writing for woman suffrage journals, she advocated governmental control of the means of communication and transportation—essentially, an anti-monopoly program—and urged women to sign on for "the coming struggle . . . between the two systems of competition and cooperation" (*Woman's Journal*, September 22, 1888).

The Illinois Woman's Alliance (IWA) was born out of Brown's collaboration and experimentation with Elizabeth Morgan and was one of the city's most significant contributions to the political history of late nineteenth-century women. Precipitated by journalist Nell Nelson's shocking exposure of conditions in Chicago's sweatshops, the IWA placed women at the local center of reform, leading investigations and broad campaigns for legal action to improve public education, housing, child labor, women's work, and safety in factories and workshops. Formed in November 1888, the IWA followed the model of the Protective Agency as an affiliation of clubs and societies and stretched it to embrace a varied group of twenty-five organizations, including delegates from the Trade and Labor Assembly. Its slogan promised "Justice to Children—Loyalty to Women," and it created great agitation on the topics it investigated. At its peak, the IWA could muster five hundred women to pack a city council meeting. The first president, CAROLINE HULING, came from the Cook County Woman Suffrage Association; Brown acted first as corresponding secretary and later served as president. Temperance unions, physiological societies, clubs, and the Knights of Labor also sent delegates.

At the end of one year's work, the IWA had standing committees on factory inspection, free baths for women and children, evaluation of public institutions, the need for a government-run industrial school, school necessities, and ward work. Campaigns initiated by these committees attracted wide support, not only from women, but also from men. Brown often traveled to Springfield to lobby for the legislation the IWA proposed. By the start of 1891 the women won enforcement of the existing compulsory education law, the appointment of truant officers—half of them women, and a new law that lengthened the required school year. Allied with teachers, they corrected a practice that allowed the schools to delay paying salaries. The landmark Illinois Factory Inspection Act of 1893 culminated campaigns against child labor and sweatshops begun by the IWA in 1888.

Brown also identified herself with the woman suffrage movement, augmenting that small cadre of nineteenth-century suffragists who raised the concerns of working women and the need for economic reform in debates over political rights. Her letters and articles appeared in Chicago's suffrage paper, *Justitia*, and in the nationally distributed *Woman's Journal*. She represented Illinois at national meetings and aided efforts to win endorsements of woman suffrage from national labor unions. When Chicago women had the opportunity to be candidates and vote for trustees of the University of Illinois in 1893, Corinne Brown was nominated as the Socialist Party candidate.

Brown persisted as a clubwoman while she adopted radical ideas about social reform and she thus bridged disparate elements of the woman's movement. To prepare for the 1893 World's Columbian Exposition, she was active both in the Queen Isabella Association with professional women who advocated woman's equality and in the committee that planned congresses concerned with labor and industry. She belonged to groups where her own radical ideas could develop, such as the Nationalist Club she led. Here, committed reformers and socialists studied the implementation of the ideas in Edward Bellamy's *Looking Backward*, which advocated a system of public ownership of industry and equality of the sexes. At the same time, she started groups where conservative women could begin to experience the lessons of cooperation and solidarity, such as the Woodlawn Woman's Club, founded in 1895. There, the study of art and literature at first attracted more members than either philanthropy or reform. Early in the twentieth century, she was a national figure in both the General Federation of Women's Clubs and the Socialist Party.

These were not separate tracks for Corinne Brown. The "Isabellas" and the labor reformers applied parallel pressure on the Exposition's Board of Lady Managers to recognize the economic realities of women's lives. The three hundred members of the Woodlawn Woman's Club eventually carried on where the IWA left off by working for some of its causes: limits on child labor, free textbooks in the schools, and appointment of more women to the school board. In the General Federation of Women's Clubs, Corinne Brown was the first head of a new industrial committee.

To Brown, the good that came of organization and solidarity among women transcended class. In her inaugural address as president of the Woodlawn Woman's Club in 1895, she explained that in a club, women learned the value of the law of cooperation. "At home she but gives the word—at the Club she must win the majority." She learned that her privileges were limited by others' rights. In a parallel construction, Brown wrote in the Chicago Populist weekly, the *Vanguard*, June 11, 1892, that lives "governed by the petty rules and fines of the shop and factory" also grew from the experience of cooperation and responsibility.

By the middle of the 1890s, the cross-class alliances that Brown helped to develop were increasingly difficult to sustain in Chicago. Events such as the Pullman strike in 1894 made clear the deep division between the forces of capital and those of organized labor. Class conflict made it hard for women either to imagine or to effect a role for their sex independent of their social class, while men hardened their class positions and obstructed women's alliances and leadership. Brown did not give up the old ideas, even if they would not again mobilize a city. She continued to believe that women were the natural leaders in the redistribution of wealth, and she took that conviction with her into the twentieth century and the new Socialist Party of America in 1901.

Brown welcomed this new organizational form for her dream of a cooperative society and served as one of the small group of women delegates to the party's founding convention. She was pleased with the party's inclusion of equal civil and political rights for women in its platform; in 1889 she had argued with Socialist Party leaders about their vision of economic change that could, she believed, leave women economically dependent in a socialist society. The struggle for socialism and women's rights had to be simultaneous. Brown's political career had also been driven by a conviction that women's cultural experience both necessitated their autonomy in the movement and informed their moral critique of competitive society. She advocated independent socialist organizations for women, while a younger generation of activists opposed separate clubs and wanted their perfect equality to begin within the party structure. As official policy their views prevailed. This debate about separatism exposed how grounded in her own historical experience Brown's ideas and expectations were. She remained active in the Socialist Party and was hailed by Eugene Debs as a friend and comrade at the time of her death. Corinne Brown moved to New York in 1913, when her daughter enrolled in Columbia University Teachers College; she died there the next year.

Chicago's Socialist Woman's League conducted her memorial service. Through the somewhat inflated praise spoken there, certain themes of her personality stood out. According to her friends, she never gave up being a teacher, and an intellectual vitality drew people into her orbit. They described her as a "live wire" and a "dynamo," whose "intense enthusiasm passed into her audience and roused that audience of many as one" (*Memorial for Corinne Stubbs Brown*, 7). With wage earners and clubwomen alike she had "revealed women to each other" and "demonstrated to them the royal good time of being together" (*Memorial*, 12). When "ancient platitudes or sentimental slush" threatened to sink a woman's club meeting, "she would sail in, to the great relief of some of us, and clear the atmosphere as might an electrical storm," said one friend (*Memorial*, 3). A reporter once caught a flash of that storm when she wrote in the May 27, 1893, *Vanguard* about a meeting at the 1893 World's Columbian Exposition on the conditions of wage-earning women and children. "Mrs. Corinne S. Brown, socialist, of this city, was presiding, and to the suggestion of one of the audience that the meeting close with singing 'Praise God from whom all blessings flow,' Mrs. Brown promptly responded, 'But we haven't got the blessings'—and the gavel fell." Corinne Brown's vision of women's agency in bringing about a new and just social order bridged the city's class divisions for nearly two decades and informed some of its most significant reform societies during the critical period from the Haymarket incident to World War I.

Sources. Articles by Corinne Brown appeared in many newspapers during the 1880s, 1890s, and the first decade of the twentieth century. These included the *Vanguard* (Chicago), *Justitia* (Chicago), *Woman's Journal* (Boston), *Railway Times* (Chicago), *Labor Advocate* (Providence), and *Workman's Advocate* (New York). Accounts of her speeches at the National American Woman Suffrage Association and the National Council of Women, both in 1891, can be found in the proceedings of those organizations. Her inaugural address as club president in 1895 was printed in Woodlawn Woman's Club, *First Calendar* at the CHS. Information about her work can be gleaned from the histories of organizations, including the annual reports of the Protective Agency for Women and Children, 1887–90, at the CHS. The Illinois Woman's Alliance is well documented in the Thomas J. Morgan Papers, Illinois Historical Survey, Univ. of Illinois at Urbana-Champaign, and in the Chicago Trade and Labor Assembly Collection, CHS. *The Book of Woodlawn* (1920), available at the CHS, relates the history of the Woodlawn Woman's Club. Biographical material is found in Frances E. Willard and Mary A. Livermore, eds., *A Woman of the Century* (1893); "Work of the Sex," *Chicago Times*, September 2, 1894; Gertrude Bres-

lau Hunt, "Corinne Brown," *Socialist Woman*, February 1908; obituary, *NYT*, March 16, 1914; *Memorial for Corinne Stubbs Brown* (1914), available at the CHS. Useful too are Meredith Tax, *The Rising of the Women: Feminist Solidarity and Class Conflict, 1880–1917* (1980), and Ralph Scharnau, "Elizabeth Morgan, Crusader for Labor Reform," *Labor History*, Summer 1973. Brown's role in the Socialist Party is ably told in Mari Jo Buhle, *Women and American Socialism, 1870–1920* (1981).

ANN D. GORDON

BUCKINGHAM, KATE STURGES
August 3, 1858–December 14, 1937
CULTURAL PHILANTHROPIST, ART PATRON

Kate Sturges Buckingham, patron of the arts, philanthropist, and last member of an eminent Chicago family, was born in Zanesville, Ohio. Her family was of English ancestry, the Presbyterian faith, and Republican political allegiance. She was the second of three children and the eldest daughter of Ebenezer and Lucy (Sturges) Buckingham. Her brother, Clarence, was born in 1853 and her sister, Lucy Maude, in 1870. Both paternal and maternal ancestors were prominent in colonial affairs and Connecticut history before moving west to Ohio. Kate Buckingham's grandfather, Solomon Sturges, settled in Zanesville in 1815; the Buckinghams resided in nearby Putnam. Over a forty year period of Ohio residency, the two families, wealthy through a national chain of grain elevators in Ohio, Pennsylvania, and along the route of the Erie Canal, became increasingly intertwined in business partnerships and intermarriages.

In the 1850s, expanding agricultural markets in the West beckoned to wealthy and enterprising Easterners, many from Ohio. The Buckinghams and Sturgeses sought a collective family fortune in Chicago before the Civil War, when Chicago was a small town. Partnerships, habits, and family traditions continued there. In Chicago, Kate Buckingham's great uncle, Alvah Buckingham, built the first grain elevator, known as the Fulton Elevator, in 1850. Her maternal grandfather, Solomon Sturges, an astute businessman, was at the helm of the family's more extended Chicago enterprise, a storage elevator business, founded in 1855. He was soon joined by relatives who were his business partners, including Kate Buckingham's father, Ebenezer, and her uncles George Sturges and John Buckingham. The Ebenezer Buckingham home on the North Side was the location of large family gatherings. A Thanksgiving family reunion was held there in 1870 with all living relatives in attendance. Buckingham reunions were significant events, sometimes commemorating the centenary of a deceased relative's life decades after the individual's death, reinforcing family attachment and continuity.

The Buckingham home on Chicago's North Side was destroyed in the Great Chicago Fire of 1871. An economic depression in 1873 and the aftermath of a second fire in the city caused misery for many citizens. Initiated into upper-class benevolent activities, young Kate Buckingham gave a Christmas party with gifts for children in the Cook County Hospital.

The Sturges and Buckingham elevators and warehouses, also destroyed, were rebuilt and expanded. A new Ebenezer Buckingham family home on Prairie Avenue, about to become Chicago's most prestigious street, was finished in 1877 when

Kate was nineteen. The family attended the Second Presbyterian Church, a block from the Buckingham home, which replaced the historic First Presbyterian Church destroyed in the fire.

Kate Buckingham lived a privileged and sheltered life. At a time when many wealthy girls were sent away to school and several female members of the Buckingham family had supported female education (the Putnam Female Seminary, Putnam, Ohio, was established by the sisters' grandmother and great aunts), Kate and Lucy Maud Buckingham were educated at home.

The family kept its private affairs outside the public eye. Perhaps this was in reaction to the high visibility achieved by the family's increasingly more profitable grain business. J&E Buckingham monopolized an important sector of the Midwest's leading agricultural market by controlling storage facilities and by engaging in lucrative arrangements with railroad and canal lines. J&E Buckingham, one of the largest grain warehouses in the nation and a major force on the Chicago Board of Trade, made headlines because of speculative grain deals or "corners" of the grain market, which determined the price of corn, wheat, and pork and affected the fate of producers and consumers nationally and internationally. The Chicago press editorialized against J&E Buckingham and other combinations, portraying them as rapacious and greedy enemies of farmers and consumers. Populist protest against such combinations attacked the whole system, while even more moderate voices in the Chicago press editorialized against the unethical practices of the Board of Trade dealers and called for reform. Kate Buckingham grew up in this culture of public criticism; later in life she argued forcefully that capitalism had been a positive influence in the growth of the republic and in the well-being of individual Americans.

By the mid-1880s, many of Chicago's wealthiest citizens began to migrate to permanent homes in the northern suburbs, especially to Lake Forest, where many already had summer homes and where Chicago's old line Presbyterian upper class had historic connections. In 1882 Ebenezer Buckingham built a home in Lake Forest on a bluff overlooking Lake Michigan. Unlike many Prairie Avenue residents, the Buckinghams did not move permanently to Lake Forest; the main family residence continued to be in the city. Perhaps this was because of the death of Kate Buckingham's mother, Lucy Sturges Buckingham, on July 6, 1889. Kate Buckingham, at thirty-two, became the female head of the household. Clarence (age thirty-six) and Lucy Maud (age nineteen), both unmarried, continued to reside in the Prairie Avenue family home. Lucy Maud had health problems and increasingly lived as an invalid, cared for by her family and, especially, Kate Buckingham. Ebenezer and Clarence had expanded into banking, insurance, steel, and real estate.

In the 1890s, municipal leadership shifted from Chicago's wealthy businessmen to politicians, and wealthy men began to exhibit their civic leadership through the support of cultural institutions. Wealthy Chicagoans began to accumulate art collections for their private homes and for the museums they founded. The Buckinghams were part of the circle of art patrons in the city. Kate Buckingham's association with the Art Institute of Chicago (AIC) began at this time through her brother, Clarence, who was an AIC trustee. Clarence Buckingham had created an outstanding Japanese print collection starting in the mid-1890s after admiring Japanese art at the World's Columbian Exposition of 1893. Frederick William Gookin, a bank employee of the Buckingham family and print collector since the 1880s, became Clarence Buckingham's full-time art advisor for the Japanese collection.

Ebenezer Buckingham died in 1911, leaving a fortune of more than $4 million to his children, all residents of the Prairie Avenue home where they lived along with William Buckingham, a lawyer cousin of Ebenezer, who spent much of his time traveling in the West. On February 12, 1912, Kate Buckingham bought an eighty-one acre tract of land, Bald Hill Farm, in the Berkshires near Lennox, Massachusetts. She had a neocolonial mansion built, eventually expanding the grounds to 160 acres. By 1913, Kate, Clarence, and Lucy Maud Buckingham were spending part of their time at Bald Hill, part in the Prairie Avenue mansion, and part in the Lake Forest residence. On August 28, 1913, Clarence Buckingham died, just two years after his father's death. He left a $1.5 million estate and his valuable Japanese print collection to his sisters.

In 1914, the two sisters sold the Lake Forest estate to Clayton Marks, who razed the house and redeveloped the property. The sisters kept the family home on Prairie Avenue as their Chicago residence. Kate Buckingham's exposure to art was through her mother, who had traveled in Europe as a young woman, and from observation and involvement in the development of her brother Clarence's collection. "Her earliest recorded purchases were a selection of snuff bottles and miniature figures in jade, lapis, amber and porcelain in 1915 . . . purportedly bought to please her invalid sister" (Pearlstein, 38). That year, just two years after her brother's death and her involvement with the print collection, Kate Buckingham "was the first woman to join a formal committee" (McCarthy, 133) at the Art Institute.

Kate Buckingham's decorative art purchases reflected the kind of art patronage women embraced during the late nineteenth and early twentieth centuries, but with a difference in degree and kind of bequest. As a result of her control of the family fortune, she made substantial decorative arts purchases and loaned or donated them to the AIC directly rather than through the Antiquarian Society. That society, composed of Chicago's elite women, had become a major support group for decorative art acquisitions at the AIC. These were purchased by the society, with its members fund-raising or making contributions or donations. Buckingham's personal involvement with the Antiquarians was peripheral, in keeping with both her enormous wealth and her personal style; she was not an organization woman or clubwoman and did not take a leadership role in any groups.

On August 4, 1920, Lucy Maud Buckingham died in Lenox, Massachusetts. She left a $2.5 million estate to Kate Buckingham who, in 1923, demolished the Prairie Avenue family home, now in a deteriorating neighborhood. She moved into an apartment in a cooperatively owned luxury building designed by Chicago architect Howard Van Doren Shaw and located in Chicago's Lakeview neighborhood. Each apartment was custom-designed; while in Europe looking for furnishings and artifacts, Shaw identified two medieval rooms that were available for purchase. He knew that Buckingham had already begun to collect artifacts from this period. Contacting Kate Buckingham, Shaw suggested that one of the rooms could be used in her new apartment. Buckingham purchased both rooms. She bought one for the apartment and the other one as a gift to the Art Institute of Chicago. She lived in the Shaw-designed apartment for the remainder of her life, spending part of her time in Massachusetts.

Kate Buckingham grew into the role of art patron after the deaths of her father and brother, Clarence, who had been a governing member of AIC for thirty years and a trustee for twelve. She continued to purchase Chinese art works after the death of her sister. "Kate's taste for Song ceramics developed to encompass striking examples of Jun, Jian and Longquan wares and a few extraordinarily refined examples of Cizhou ware" (Pearlstein, 38). By the time of Kate Buckingham's death, the Lucy Maud Buckingham Collection of Chinese Ceramics included more than four hundred pieces and represented more than 260 years of Chinese history, from the Han to the Qing dynasty. But her "most distinctive legacy . . . was a significant assemblage of Chinese ritual bronzes, incrementally presented to the museum in Lucy's name" (p. 39). The Lucy Maud Buckingham Collection of Asian Art, a memorial to her sister, included "forty aesthetically and historically important" (Pearlstein and Ulak, 8) Chinese ritual bronzes and formed the foundation of the AIC's Asian art collection.

Kate Buckingham donated her collection of medieval sculpture, tapestries, and decorative arts to the AIC in 1924 as the Lucy Maud Buckingham Memorial Gothic Room in honor of her sister. This was during the period in which the Art Institute installed a number of period rooms, including galleries in British, French, Dutch, and American styles.

Kate Buckingham had loaned her brother's Japanese prints, numbering fourteen hundred sheets, to the AIC, and Frederick Gookin was appointed to oversee them. In 1925 Kate formally presented the collection to the Art Institute as a memorial to Clarence, along with funds to expand, house, exhibit, and maintain the collection, which today includes more than twelve thousand sheets.

Kate Buckingham was brusque on the surface, but she was a sensitive woman who had a charitable outlook from childhood and recognized the great gulf between her wealth and that of the average person. As a young woman, and throughout her life, she was benefactress to hundreds of poets, painters, musicians, and charities. Her largest benefactions were made after the deaths of her father and brother, beginning when she was in her mid-fifties, when she had full control of a great fortune. Her greatest public visibility also began at this time. She is remembered as a tall, regal, white-haired woman, eccentric, with a carefully cultivated public persona. The same attitude pertained on many levels to her donations to the Art Institute. She suggested modes of display to the curators and received commendation for her creativity. Her involvement with the terms of her artifact loans created legends that contributed to her reputation for eccentricity. Sometimes objects were loaned for years before she permanently donated them. Although it was her intention to present particular objects as gifts from the day of deposit, she carefully staged the accession dates she permitted the institute

to record, tailoring her donations to fit her tax needs. Careful record keeping on art deposits corresponded to her meticulous recording of investments and apartment rentals, where she posted daily profits and percentages.

Her major gifts were always given in memorial, never in her own name. Along with the art collections for the Art Institute described above, Buckingham also donated art for public spaces, her best known gift, the Buckingham Fountain, memorializing her brother Clarence. Buckingham hired architect Edward H. Bennett, of the Chicago firm of Bennett, Parsons and Frost, as the principal designer of the fountain project. It "consists of three circular basins, one above the other, of Georgia pink marble carved in the Beaux-Arts manner with shells and other sea life motifs" (Bach and Gray, 21). In the middle of a "base pool 280 feet in diameter" are "four identical pairs of highly original bronze 'sea horses' placed in quadrant positions and representing the four states that border on Lake Michigan" (Bach and Gray, 21); they were designed and crafted in France by Marcel Loyau. The fountain, located in Grant Park, was dedicated on August 26, 1927, and cost $750,000. Kate Buckingham also established a $300,000 trust fund to maintain it. Her second outdoor project, the Alexander Hamilton commemorative monument in Lincoln Park, is less well known than the fountain.

Kate Buckingham was ill with spinal arthritis the last several years of her life. During the final year, she was crippled and in pain; her involvement with her gifts was apparent when she was brought through the Art Institute in a wheelchair to examine and critique her collection.

She died at her apartment on the North Side of heart disease at the age of seventy-nine. She is buried in Woodlawn Cemetery in Zanesville, Ohio, alongside her parents, brother, and sister and many Buckinghams and Sturgeses, a number of them Chicagoans.

Kate Buckingham, reserved, brilliant, quick-witted and with a sense of comedy, was beloved by her associates. Charles Fabens Kelly, Art Institute curator, wrote that she "was one of the rare people of earth, difficult to get to know, but worth the effort" ("Kate S. Buckingham as a Collector," 5). Chauncey McCormick, at the dedication of the Alexander Hamilton Memorial on July 6, 1952, said that Buckingham had a "possessive" (*Hamilton Memorial Dedication*, 1) love for Chicago, and she wanted to beautify the city for the people.

Sources. The Kate Sturges Buckingham Papers and Ledgers, including correspondence, are in the Art Institue of Chicago (AIC) Archives. See also the Antiquarian Society Papers, AIC Archives, including Minutebooks, 1896–1930. Accounts of Kate Buckingham include "Kate Sturges Buckingham," *Art Institute of Chicago Newsletter* (1926); Chauncey McCormick, "Kate Sturges Buckingham," *Alexander Hamilton Memorial Dedication* (1952); and Patricia Erens, *Masterpieces: Famous Chicagoans and Their Paintings* (1979). Genealogical and family history can be found in James Buckingham and Mary J. Tilton, *Ancestors of Ebenezer Buckingham Who Was Born in 1748 and of His Descendants* (1892); Ebenezer Buckingham, *Solomon Sturges and His Descendants: A Memoir and Genealogy* (1907). Published descriptions of Kate Buckingham's collections and gifts are Charles Fabens Kelley, "Kate S. Buckingham as a Collector," *Art Institute of Chicago Bulletin* (1945); Elinor Pearlstein and James T. Ulak, *Asian Art in the Art Institute of Chicago* (1933); Daniel Catton Rich, *Handbook to the Lucy*

Maud Buckingham Collection (1945); Charles Fabens Kelley and Ch'en Meng-chia, *Chinese Bronzes from the Buckingham Collection* (1946); Elinor Pearlstein, "The Chinese Collections at The Art Institute of Chicago: Foundations of Scholarly Taste," *Orientations*, June 1993. For information on public art donated by Buckingham, see Ira J. Bach and Mary Lackritz Gray, *A Guide to Chicago's Public Sculpture* (1983). Information about upper-class Chicago families in the late nineteenth century and early twentieth century can be found in *Social Register of Chicago* (1896–1937); Emmet Dedmon, *Fabulous Chicago* (1953); Edward Arpee, *Lake Forest, Illinois: History and Reminiscences 1861–1961* (1963); Helen C. Callahan, "Upstairs-Downstairs: The Glessner Household," *Chicago History*, Winter 1977–78. For information about Buckingham's Tanglewood connection, see May Callas, *Profiles of Tanglewood Families* (1995). Kathleen McCarthy's *Women's Culture: American Philanthropy and Art, 1830–1930* (1991) discusses women's art patronage, especially in the decorative arts movement, and its relationship to the formation of the modern museum. Obituaries of Kate Buckingham are "Miss Buckingham, Patron of the Arts," *NYT*, December 15, 1937, and "Miss Kate Sturges Buckingham Dies at the Age of 79," *Lake Forester*, December 15, 1937.

MARGARET W. NORTON

BULLOCK, CARRIE E.
June 16, 1887–December 31, 1962
NURSE, NURSING LEADER

Carrie E. Bullock, who promoted professional advancement for African American nurses, was born in Laurens, South Carolina, to William Wade and Mary (Crisp) Bullock. Bullock was two years old when her mother died; her father died six years later. She was raised by her ex-slave grandparents, Thomas and Myra Crisp.

She attended St. Lawrence High School in the village of Laurens, South Carolina, and for another two years she attended a Presbyterian mission school in Aiken, South Carolina. In 1904, she graduated from Scotia Seminary Normal Department in Concord, North Carolina. After graduation, she taught school in a rural area at Cross Hill, South Carolina, for two years. She had dreamed of a career in nursing for a long time and decided to leave teaching. She entered the Hampton Nurse Training School at Dixie Hospital in Hampton, Virginia, in 1906. Dixie, along with Spelman, Provident, and Tuskegee, were the four earliest nursing schools for Blacks, having been established between 1886 and 1892. Although she loved the people at Dixie Hospital and the community life in Hampton, she wanted to train in an area that offered more opportunities. Bullock left Dixie Hospital after a few months and entered Provident Hospital in Chicago on October 6, 1906. Provident Hospital Training School (PHTS), was founded in 1891 by Dr. Daniel Hale Williams, a black surgeon and superintendent of the hospital, to train "colored women for the profession of nursing" (Coles, 29). PHTS was accredited and earned a national reputation for providing a high quality education that enabled black nurses to fill leadership positions across the nation. Provident students worked with patients through Chicago's Visiting Nurse Association but were limited to assignments in black neighborhoods. Bullock completed her nursing training at PHTS in 1909.

Upon graduation from PHTS, she was invited by the superintendent of the Chicago Visiting Nurse Association (VNA) to join the staff on a probationary basis. After a few months, she was accepted as a regular public health staff nurse with the VNA. Bullock was assigned to a VNA substation located in the heart of Chicago's Black Belt on the South Side since the de facto segregation in the North meant that the nurses served only the members of their own racial group. Bullock demonstrated much enthusiasm and love for public health work. In addition to providing nursing care to the black residents in her area, she frequently brought clothing to needy families.

Issues of discrimination were faced by black nurses at every juncture in their quest for professional acceptance and advancement. Black women were consistently denied admission to many of the leading graduate nursing programs and kept from challenging career opportunities in supervisory or administrative positions in nursing. The vast majority of black graduate nurses worked in private-duty jobs and had to suffer the injustice of unequal pay as well. The "denial of membership in the American Nurses' Association was the most visible and demeaning manifestation of professional ostracism" (Hine, *Black Women in America*, 889). The American Nurses' Association's exclusionary practices motivated black nurses to organize the National Association of Colored Graduate Nurses (NACGN) in 1908.

During her first ten years of service with the Chicago VNA, Bullock was a staff nurse, then the assistant supervisor; in 1919, she became supervisor of Chicago VNA black nurses, the first black nurse to serve in that position. She continued to improve her education by reading nursing literature and taking courses at the Chicago School of Civics and Philanthropy and the extension program at the University of Chicago.

In 1922, as a tribute to her contribution to the Chicago VNA, Bullock was awarded the Harriet McCormick scholarship to attend the NACGN's thirteenth annual convention in Kansas City, Missouri. As the Chicago delegate to the meeting, the Chicago VNA had charged her with inviting the NACGN to Chicago the following year. In 1923, the Chicago Local Nurses' Association and the Chicago VNA made that convention one of the largest ever held in the history of the NACGN. Bullock was elected vice-president of NACGN at that convention.

In August 1926, Bullock was elected president of NACGN at the convention held in Philadelphia, Pennsylvania. She brought an energetic personality and strong leadership to the organization and worked tirelessly to promote the ideas of the organization. During her presidency from 1927 to 1930, she focused on two key issues: opening lines of communication between black nurses and fostering postgraduate education for black nurses. To reach this goal, Bullock established the *National News Bulletin*, the official monthly publication of the NACGN, and edited the first issue in February 1928. The bulletin featured educational offerings and a section for student nurses. Bullock was also instrumental in seeking funds from the Julius Rosenwald Fund to support education and health programs for black nurses. She assisted in the establishment of the Julius Rosenwald Fellowship Program for black graduate nurses to encourage black nurses to pursue postgraduate education.

In 1928 Bullock and Adah B. Thoms coauthored an article, "Development of Facilities for Colored Nurse Education," which expressed interest in expanding the care given by black nurses to the "sick public—white as well as colored" (p. 723).

The authors appealed to the American Nurses' Association (ANA) for greater cooperation and more intimate professional contact with ANA leaders to bridge the gap between black nurses and the delivery of care to white patients.

In 1938, NACGN awarded Carrie Bullock the Mary Mahoney Award for outstanding achievement in nursing and human service. She was the second recipient, the first having been Adah B. Thoms. The award was named after Mary Mahoney, the first black woman to graduate from a nursing school in the United States. Mahoney had graduated in 1879 from the New England Hospital for Women and Children, Boston, Massachusetts.

During World War II, Bullock worked to equalize opportunities for white and black nurses in the Army Nurse Corps. Nursing groups of all races were encouraged by Bullock to write letters and send telegrams protesting the discrimination against black nurses in the Army and Navy Nurse Corps. Bullock served on the NACGN committee that promoted recruitment of black nurses. As a result of the efforts of this committee, the U.S. Navy dropped the color bar against black nurses on January 25, 1945.

In August 1949, members of NACGN voted to dissolve the organization at the annual convention in Louisville, Kentucky, and to merge with the American Nurses' Association (ANA). The NACGN decision to dissolve came as a result of the ANA's action in 1946 to eliminate discrimination against racial groups and the 1948 vote to extend membership to all black nurses excluded from any state association. After the merger of NACGN and ANA, Bullock worked for unity within the integrated association.

In 1956, Bullock retired after serving almost forty-seven years with the VNA. As a Provident Hospital alumna, she was very active in the alumnae association. At different times, she held all of the offices of the association.

During her retirement, Bullock worked with underprivileged children through the outreach programs of Grace Presbyterian Church on Chicago's South Side. Bullock was a member of the congregation. She also volunteered at Provident Hospital. In the winter of 1962, after a short stay in Billings Hospital, Bullock died from heart disease at age seventy-five. Her funeral was at Grace Presbyterian.

Bullock dedicated her life to improving the status of nursing and, particularly, that of the black nurses through her work as a public health nurse and as a leader in nursing organizations, where she held important leadership positions. She worked to open equal professional opportunities for black nurses and to promote integration of black and white professional nursing associations. Today's modern nursing profession, composed of all races and serving all races, was built on the early efforts of Carrie Bullock.

Sources. An article by Bullock, coauthored with A. B. Thoms, "Development of Facilities for Colored Nurse Education," can be found in the *Trained Nurse and Hospital Review*, vol. 80, 1928. Biographical summaries on Carrie Bullock can be found in "Nursing Portraits: Carrie E. Bullock, R.N.," *National News Bulletin*, vol. 8, 1936; *BWA* (1993); M. E. Carnegie, *The Path We Tread: Blacks in Nursing* (1986); and T. Yensen, ed., *Who's Who in Colored America* (1933). Darlene Clark Hine, ed., *Black Women in the Nursing Profession: A Documentary History* (1985), includes A. B. Coles, "The Howard University School of Nursing in Historical Perspective," and M. K. Staupers, "The Negro Nurse in America." Darlene Clark Hine, *Black Women in White: Racial Conflict and Cooperation in the Nursing Profession, 1890–1950* (1989), is useful. Susan L. Smith, "The Black Women's Club Movement: Self-Improvement and Sisterhood, 1889–1915" (master's thesis, Univ. of Wisconsin–Madison), includes a chapter on Provident Hospital and Nurses Training School that is informative. See obituary, "Miss Bullock, Widely Known Nurse," *CT*, January 2, 1993.

CARRIETTE WEDDLE

BURNHAM, CLARA LOUISE ROOT
May 26, 1854–June 21, 1927
NOVELIST, SHORT STORY WRITER, POET, LYRICIST

Clara Louise Root Burnham, an immensely popular author whose literary career spanned more than forty years, lived most of her life in Chicago, where she wrote numerous poems, lyrics, short stories, and twenty-six novels that sold over half a million copies. Burnham's work was usually advertised as bright and entertaining, perfect fare for a lady's summer reading; and her reputation as a humorous and insightful story-teller persisted well into the twentieth century. More important, her fiction eventually developed maturity and clarity in style and characterization and increasingly dealt with a number of serious subjects, many of them weighty social issues facing women of her time.

Born in Newton, Massachusetts, Clara Louise Root was the oldest daughter of George Frederick and Mary Olive (Woodman) Root. Mary Root was a talented musician and singer, and George Root was a famous composer who produced more than seventy-five music books and wrote a number of cantatas, gospel songs, and war songs, including "The Battle Cry of Freedom" (1861) and "Tramp, Tramp, Tramp, the Boys Are Marching" (1864). Clara Root spent the first nine years of her life with her mother and siblings at Willow Farm, the Root family home near North Reading, Massachusetts, and attended the New Church School in Waltham. Throughout the 1850s, George Root traveled widely and directed choirs in Maine, Massachusetts, and New York. Around 1860, he began to visit Chicago, where his brothers had opened the music publishing company of Root and Cady. In 1863, George Root moved with his family to Chicago.

Chicago was a new and growing city, with unpaved and muddy streets. Nine-year-old Clara, her two older brothers and three sisters, and their parents lived in the city for only a short time. The Root family soon relocated in Groveland Park, a country-like setting where Clara Root attended public school and studied music. The family also began to establish the tradition of spending summers with family and friends in New England at a cottage called "The Mooring" on Bailey's Island, Casco Bay, Maine.

In 1871, the Root and Cady offices were destroyed in the Great Fire, but their book plates were preserved in a safe. George Root, his two sons, and his brother soon established the music publishing house of George F. Root and Sons. Except for Charles Root, who resided in New York, all the Root siblings lived in Hyde Park, at this time located outside Chicago's city limits. The family often gathered at the Hyde Park Yacht Club, where they were members and kept "catboats." Clara Root's sister, Mary Ruth Root Kern, would become a talented musician and faculty member of the University of Chicago. A niece, Josephine Kern, would become a well-known sculptor.

In 1873 nineteen-year-old Clara Root married Walter Burnham, a Chicago lawyer (not related to Daniel Burnham). No information is available about how they met, but there is speculation that they separated after a year. Walter Burnham died a short time later, and Clara Burnham resided for most of her life with her father in Chicago, first at the Elms Hotel and later at the Cooper-Carlton Hotel. During the 1870s, John M. Stahl, president of the Farmer's National Congress and later a member of the Society of Midland Authors, lived near Burnham on the eleventh floor of the Elms. In his autobiography, *Growing with the West* (1930), Stahl describes Clara Burnham as very "ladylike" (p. 471), the kind of person who was always going out or entertaining guests. Others describe the author as tall and slender, with light hair and blue eyes, vivacious and outgoing, "the life of the party" (*New York Times*, June 22, 1927). Following in her family's tradition, Clara Burnham's chief interest at this time was music, but a major change would soon occur in her life. In *The Women Who Make Our Novels* (1918), Grant M. Overton quotes Burnham's advice, "If a young person aspiring to print should ask me whether there is a definite way to begin, I should tell him to start by catching a big brother" (p. 271).

Clara Burnham's older brother, Frederick Woodman (F. W.) Root, had studied in Europe and was pursuing a musical career. A member of the Cliff Dwellers and the Little Room, he served as president of the Chicago Literary Club. Frederick Root's literary interests led him to encourage his sister to write, but Clara Burnham at first resisted. "I suppose the reason I did not wish to write was that music satisfied me," she wrote. Her brother was very persistent, however, and, "with no conscious preparation I was like a ship ready to be launched. Fred pushed me off into deep water" (quoted in Overton, 272).

Burnham's first literary efforts, novelettes, were rejected; and when the aspiring young author hired a professional reader, she was advised to give up writing. In 1880, she finally had a poem published in *Wide Awake* and began to see her stories and poems appear in such magazines as *St. Nicholas* and *Youth's Companion*. In 1881, Houghton Mifflin published Burnham's first novel, *No Gentlemen*, which was followed by an amazing output of five more novels by the end of the decade: *A Sane Lunatic* (1882), *Dearly Bought* (1884), *Next Door* (1886), *Young Maids and Old* (1888), and *The Mistress of Beech Knoll* (1890).

Most of Burnham's novels are light romances with predictable outcomes in which lovers are first separated and then finally united. They are usually set in pleasant surroundings, but a sense of place is not crucial to the story's success. Instead, like EDITH WYATT and many other women authors of her time, Burnham uses urban and rural settings, small towns and large cities, as backdrops for the drama of competing social values. Characters discuss such important contemporary issues as the migration from country to city, urban poverty, philanthropy, inheritance laws, unwise financial investments, unfaithful husbands, female independence, neurasthenia, educational opportunities, fair employment, suffrage, the post–Civil War surplus of unmarried women, career versus marriage, and the tension between traditional morality and rising materialism.

While her fictional characters debated these important issues, Burnham herself seems to have developed a strong sense of her place in life as a professional writer in Chicago. Her travels were limited: two trips to Europe and one visit to Yellowstone Park. Burnham spent most summers at her home on Bailey's Island in Maine, describing it as a "small green hill in the superb sweep of the Atlantic" (quoted in Overton, 269); but she also found it "uninspiring" (p. 269). Throughout the 1880s and until her death in 1927, Burnham wrote during the winter months in Chicago, a place she found particularly congenial for work, "the nicest place in the world" (*Young Maids and Old*, 43). "Lake Michigan explains why I have not followed the tide of successful writers to New York. I love Chicago, with all its soot and wind" (quoted in Overton, 270).

In 1894, Burnham published *Sweet Clover*, a novel that vividly illustrates some of the tensions shared by author and readers alike, at the same time providing "one of the most favorable imaginative treatments" (Smith, *Chicago and the American Literary Imagination*, 144) of the 1893 World's Columbian Exposition. *Sweet Clover: A Romance of the White City* tells the story of Clover Bryant, a young Hyde Park resident who finds love and romance at the Fair. At the same time, however, the novel uses Chicago and its residents to illustrate the sharp contrasts of nineteenth-century American life as exemplified by the fair. One of Burnham's characters describes the Midway as "some dirty and all barbaric. It deafens you with noises; the worst folks in there are avaricious and bad, and the best are just children in their ignorance" (p. 201). The exposition itself is much different, as the same character notes, for "you pass under a bridge—and all of a sudden you are in a great beautiful silence. The angels on the Woman's Building smile down and bless you, and you know that in what seemed like one step, you've passed out o' darkness into light" (pp. 201–202). The novel is filled with sentimentality for middle-class ideals and hopes for Chicago, but in the end the exposition is proven unreal, a magic kingdom dedicated to the ideals of purity, order, and beauty, which eventually burns to the ground. Love still survives, of course, as Clover and the other confused lovers eventually pair off and live happily ever after. Burnham defends this and other "safe" stories against any possible charges of sentimentalism. "Do tell me, what is the use of writing books to make one cry? I hold that a man or woman who publishes a book, has a great responsibility. He or she has no right to make people miserable, even if it is only temporary misery. The better the writer, the greater the responsibility" (*No Gentlemen*, 130).

Many of Burnham's conflicting beliefs were reconciled when she embraced the Christian Science religion. Novels such as *The Right Princess* (1902), *Jewel* (1903), *The Opened Shutters* (1906), and *The Leaven of Love* (1908) are saturated with the spiritual principles of Mary Baker Eddy. Burnham continued to stress Christian Science beliefs in her later works and even collaborated with Robert A. Dempster, a New York actor, who, in 1912, helped her rewrite *The Right Princess* as a stage play entitled "The Moon Calf."

As late as 1916, Burnham continued to write about the quest for a happy and peaceful life in *Instead of the Thorn*. The novel opens in Chicago, where the main characters meet at the "South Shore Club"; but this luxurious setting is soon forsaken when the heroine's father suffers financial ruin. The young girl leaves Chicago for New England, where a simple and quiet village setting restores mental poise and happiness, at the same time providing a suitable mate for the heroine.

Burnham's own life, both literary and personal, seems to have been peaceful and relatively happy, despite the fact that she never remarried and perhaps because she dedicated herself to her work. When asked whether she had a "method" in her writing, Burnham replied that writing came easily to her, but she disciplined herself to write for three hours every day. Burnham seldom revised her novels and said, "my mother used to say that I wrote just as other people hemmed handkerchiefs. Writing has never meant any struggle to me" (quoted in Overton, 276).

Over the years, Burnham's novels always received brief but favorable notices in magazines and newspapers. Reviewers praised her fine plot structures and clear style, the "pleasant" nature of her work, and its pervasive, yet not oppressive, strain of Christian Science philosophy. Along with her novels, many of which were translated into foreign languages, Burnham continued to produce stories, poems, and novels for children, such as *Uncle Benjamin's Christmas Gift* (1894) and *Flutterfly* (1910). With her father, Burnham wrote and published several songs that were immensely popular in both England and the United States, including "The Waif's Christmas" (1886) and "Judge Santa Clause" (1887), as well as cantatas for children such as "Santa Claus' Mistake or The Bundle of Sticks" (1885), "Snow White and the Seven Dwarfs" (1888), and "Santa Claus and Company" (1889). Several of Burnham's novels were adapted for the screen, and shortly before her death she sold the film rights for *The Lavarons* (1925) to a Hollywood producer.

Throughout her career, Burnham enjoyed a large and devoted audience for her work and became an influential Chicago writer. Along with important literary figures, including Indiana poet James Whitcomb Riley, Wisconsin novelist Zona Gale, and editor HARRIET MONROE, Burnham helped found the Society of Midland Authors in 1914. She was a member of the Little Room and the Chicago Circle of Bookfellows, as well as a personal friend of notable Chicagoans such as novelist George Barr McCutcheon and his brother John McCutcheon, a cartoonist; journalist George Ade; and playwright Charles Klein. Burnham enjoyed good health all her life and died peacefully in her sleep at "The Mooring" on Bailey's Island, Casco Bay, Maine, at age seventy-three. Her death was attributed to heart disease. Funeral services were held at the Christian Science Mother Church in Boston, of which Burnham was a member, and the Boston Crematory.

Most of Burnham's novels remained in print throughout her lifetime and continue to be valuable as vivid examples of the particular tensions that preoccupied late-nineteenth-century and early-twentieth-century Chicago women writers and their female readers. One hundred years later, Burnham's greatest contribution exists in *Sweet Clover*, one of the most accurate and complete accounts of the Columbian Exposition written in novel form. In *Chicago and the American Literary Imagination, 1880–1920* (1984), author Carl S. Smith acknowledges that Burnham presents her readers with a unique view of her time and place, an alternative vision to those of such male writers as Henry Adams and Henry Blake Fuller.

Sources. The Clara Louise Root Burnham Papers are at Knox College, Galesburg, Illinois. They include correspondence dated 1921–24, to George Steele Seymour and his wife, Flora Warren Seymour. The content of these letters is primarily concerned with Burnham's current reading, social plans, health status, and address changes. In addition to those works cited in the text, Burnham wrote *Clever Betsy* (1910); *The Golden Dog* (1913); *A Great Love* (1898); *Heart's Haven* (1918); *How to Keep Your Child from Fear* (1909); *In Apple-Blossom Time; A Fairy-Tale to Date* (1919); *The Inner Flame* (1912); *Jewel's Story Book* (1904); *The Key Note* (1921); *Miss Archer Archer* (1897); *Miss Bagg's Secretary, A West Point Romance* (1892); *Miss Pritchard's Wedding Trip* (1901); *Phyllis, the Farmer's Daughter: An Operatic Cantata with Words by Clara Louise Burnham and Music by George Frederick Root* (1892); *The Queen of Farrandale* (1921); *The Quest Flower* (1908); *The Right Princess: A Play (in three acts)* (1917); *The Right Track* (1914); *Tobey's First Case* (1926); *A View of Christian Science* (1912); *We, Von Aridens*, by Edith Douglas (a pseudonym) (1881); *Wenonah's Stories for Children*, with coauthor Warren Proctor (1918); *A West Point Wooing, and Other Stories* (1899); *The Wise Woman* (1893). See Sidney H. Bremer, "Lost Continuities: Alternative Urban Visions in Chicago Novels, 1890–1915," *Soundings*, Spring 1981, and Bremer, "Willa Cather's Lost Chicago Sisters," *Women Writers and the City* (1984). Biographical information is contained in Bernice E. Gallagher, *Illinois Women Novelists in the Nineteenth Century: An Analysis and Annotated Bibliography* (1994), and Grant M. Overton, "Clara Louise Burnham," *The Women Who Make Our Novels* (1918). Also informative are Carl S. Smith, *Chicago and the American Literary Imagination, 1880–1920* (1984), and John M. Stahl, *Growing with the West* (1930). Reference works to consult include Lina Maniero, *American Women Writers* (1979); Allen Johnson and Dumas Malone, eds., *Dictionary of American Biography* (1964); and Stanley J. Kunitz and Howard Haycraft, eds., *Twentieth Century Authors* (1942). Burnham's obituary appeared in NYT June 22, 1927.

BERNICE E. GALLAGHER
NOELLE WATSON

BUTCHER, FANNY AMANDA
February 13, 1888–May 14, 1987
LITERARY EDITOR AND CRITIC

Fanny Butcher, longtime literary editor of the *Chicago Tribune*, was born in Fredonia, Kansas, the only child of L. Oliver and Hattie May (Young) Butcher. Her father was a colorist of photographic portraits who aspired to higher artistic achievement. Some time in the early 1890s the Butchers moved to Chicago so that he could attend night classes at the School of the Art Institute of Chicago. After a dental mishap that nearly killed him and left him effectively disabled, the family settled into a life of genteel poverty and quiet disappointment, with the child Fanny as the beleaguered bridge between two unhappy parents.

Fanny Butcher graduated from McKinley High School in 1906. With money earned from academic odd jobs, she was able to attend Lewis Institute (now Illinois Institute of Technology), where she received an A.A. degree in 1908. With additional help from a wealthy patron she continued her education at the University of Chicago, which granted her an A.B. degree in 1910. Throughout her student years she was propelled by an obsessive love of books. She always said this passion had been kindled by a childhood Christmas gift from an adopted aunt, a deluxe copy of *Black Beauty* bound in red silk. She read her way through the library shelves at school and church, and one of her college jobs was reading aloud an hour a day to a blind woman, Mrs. French, who had

FIG. 16. *Fanny Butcher knew the major literary figures in Chicago. Seated, left to right, are Mrs. Carl Sandburg, Carl Sandburg, Julia Peterkin; standing, left to right, are Mrs. Carl Hendrickson, Fanny Butcher, and Harriet Monroe, in 1933.*

graduated first in her class at Mt. Holyoke College, South Hadley, Massachusetts. Mrs. French wanted to hear history, biography, and philosophy. She never wasted time on mediocrity, Butcher once remembered, and if asked to name a single person who had most encouraged her love of the printed word, it was Mrs. French.

Fanny Butcher served five months as principal of a high school in rural Indiana; she then returned to Chicago. She worked in the Fine Arts Building as secretary to the Little Theatre, selling tickets, paying bills, and pouring tea for nervous actors. She also wrote feature stories for two short-lived magazines, *Morrison's Weekly* and *Chicago,* receiving bylines but no pay. She persuaded Floyd Dell at the Chicago *Evening Post* to let her review a few books for that paper's literary supplement. The batch he gave her included novels by Jack London and Willa Cather. He invited her to picnics he hosted on the beach, and over several months she met the cream of Chicago's talented young literati.

Through her magazine work Butcher became eligible for membership in the Illinois Woman's Press Association. Presiding at the first meeting she attended was Mary Eleanor O'Donnell, women's editor of the *Chicago Tribune.* After the program O'Donnell called Butcher aside and asked about her current employment. Afraid that her qualifications were being questioned, Butcher tried to back away; but O'Donnell wanted to know if she would like to write a column for the *Tribune,* "How to Earn Money at Home." Butcher gladly accepted the job. This meeting appeared to have taken place some time in August 1912, though the *Tribune's* records indicate that her full-time employment there began officially on June 11, 1913.

From that single column Fanny Butcher branched out to write for nearly every department at the paper. She covered society, beauty, fashion, etiquette, clubs, and Sunday afternoon concerts at Orchestra Hall, in addition to politics, Morals Court, and a few murder trials. She was one of perhaps two dozen women writers and editors at the *Tribune,* colleagues who shared a free-for-all atmosphere of excitement and opportunity, much of it promoted by Mary King, Sunday editor and one of the most progressive newswomen of her day. Fanny Butcher's gentle appearance and modest style belied her sturdy resourcefulness and lifelong habit of hard work. She was of medium height with chestnut brown hair and eyes of the same color, and she usually wore a suit with pearls or a good pin. She lived at home with her parents, who had moved from the West Side to Hyde Park, and supported them as well as herself on a salary of $18.75 a week. She accepted almost every assignment that came her way, whether it interested her or not; but all the while what she really wanted to write about was books.

Before World War I, the chief literary critic of the *Tribune's* Saturday book page was ELIA PEATTIE, an imperious bluestocking; she was succeeded by her temperamental opposite, the brash and irreverent Burton Rascoe. Around 1915 Fanny Butcher suggested to Mary King that the paper run additional literary news on Sunday. In contrast to the highbrow tone of Saturday's coverage, this new Tabloid Book Review could feature lively notes on writers and the publishing world, plus spot reviews of the latest bestsellers. Butcher offered to write the copy for it in her "spare time" (*Many Lives—One Love,* 115). Mary King said yes. With this official pulpit, Butcher gained a base from which she could begin to discuss modern literature as it was published and personally cultivate its celebrated authors. In time she developed a wide readership, and after Burton Rascoe was booted from the *Tribune* for one too many ill-considered jibes, she was appointed at last in 1922 to the job of her dreams.

Butcher came into this coveted post on the Saturday book page during a great period in American letters. The dominance of British authors, who still made regular lecture tours in the United States, was fading. Fresh new American voices emerged in fiction and poetry, flourishing by way of New York's many independent publishing houses. As editor in charge, Butcher covered a wide range of printed material, from serious literature to what she called "hammock novels" (*Chicago Tribune*, May 6, 1931), travel guides, Wild West stories, the occasional cookbook, and children's classics. Once she reviewed a manual on rifle shooting. She read a book a day for most of her life. She assigned reviews to others as well and used the book pages to discuss useful reference works, events at the public library, literary prizes, and magazine articles of unusual interest. She took hold of every opportunity to promote reading. She had charge of a booth at the Woman's World's Fair in 1925, appeared at writers' conferences, and spoke often to journalism classes and ladies' clubs. For one year in 1934 she interviewed authors on her own fifteen-minute radio program.

Fanny Butcher liked to say that a newspaper review was primarily a news story about a new book that aimed to intrigue a general audience. She was adamant that it was not a scholarly essay or a demonstration of the critic's intellectual superiority. To this end Butcher's reviews were consistently intelligent, balanced, and readable. In the relatively short space of a news column she was able to convey the flavor of the book under discussion. P. G. Wodehouse stories tripped along like a musical comedy. Lytton Strachey's new biography of Queen Victoria was a "cruelly real" picture of "that figure which was so bulky against the sky of English history that it shadowed the sun of sixty years" (*Chicago Tribune*, June 26, 1921). Butcher was quick to spot the trite or clichéd. She told readers that Fannie Hurst's *Back Street* would "twang the heartstrings" (*Chicago Tribune*, January 2, 1931). Her technique was often to describe a work rather than to impose a sweeping judgment, but she did not dissemble. When an important writer was performing below par, she said so. About one of Arnold Bennett's later sad concoctions she remarked, "It is obviously written with a pair of scissors and a pot of paste" (*Chicago Tribune*, May 1, 1921). She was always generous to Chicago authors. This approach was warranted in the case of writers like Carl Sandburg and Ring Lardner, but other lesser lights enjoyed her favor too. She felt it was a matter of loyalty to the city.

Her taste was sometimes dismissed as too conservative. One of her colleagues reported: "At the Public Library it has been said 'When Fanny Butcher recommends a book we get many inquiries for it from shop girls'" (Hansen, 199). She did write that Sherwood Anderson had no sense of the music of words, John Dos Passos's *Three Soldiers* was more propaganda than literature, and in a poem like *The Waste Land* T. S. Eliot was simply dumping the disorganized contents of his mind onto paper: "He sees a pile of ideas and he yanks one out" (*Chicago Tribune*, February 4, 1923). On the other hand she sensed the promise of writers like Eugene O'Neill, F. Scott Fitzgerald, and Carson McCullers with their first appearance in print. She was uncom-

fortable with the carnal and the violent. That was her bias. Yet she found a way to appreciate those qualities in the novels of Ernest Hemingway, who remained her enduring favorite.

Fanny Butcher never lost her star-struck enthusiasm for books and authors. She liked writers and she listened to them carefully. An important component of every review was to divine the author's intent and then assess how well it had been realized. Writers repaid her sympathetic understanding with gratitude, affection, and candid accounts of their hopes and defeats, many of their expressions recorded in letters they wrote to her as often as once a week. Willa Cather was a lifelong confidante. She inscribed an early photo of herself "For Fanny Butcher who wrote the first discriminating review of my first novel" (inscription to Fanny Butcher, Willa Cather portrait photo, Fanny Butcher Papers). EDNA FERBER described their friendship as "a continuous live river" (Gilbert, 419). The mystery writer Mignon Eberhart declared, "You are one of the Basic Rocks of my existence" (Mignon Eberhart to Butcher, March 1940, Fanny Butcher Papers). Butcher's most important literary bond was probably with Sinclair Lewis, the first American to win the Nobel Prize for Literature. She met the gangly red-haired writer when he was still a manuscript reader in New York, eager to make a mark, scratching out his novels while on transcontinental train journeys. He called her "little sister" (Sinclair Lewis to Butcher, undated letter, c. 1916, Fanny Butcher Papers) and huddled in her attic studio to advise about men friends and her own nascent hopes to write fiction, nourishing a tie that blossomed through a long and intimate correspondence.

An interesting sidelight in Butcher's early career was a bookshop she opened in 1920 in the Pullman Building on Adams Street. It was the first such store in America owned by a literary critic. Designed by RUE CARPENTER, the tiny space exuded bohemian charm. It was stocked with a mix of new publications and literary classics, and purchases were wrapped with bright yellow paper and orange tape, a sort of trademark packaging that was recognized instantly by other shoppers in the city. The store was patronized by the carriage trade, downtown bankers and lawyers, and a long list of cultural celebrities who had read about it in American and English newspapers. It acquired the atmosphere of a literary salon, and when Butcher sold out in 1927 to Doubleday Page Book Shops, her customers were desolate. In an atypically extravagant gesture she used a large part of the ten thousand dollar proceeds to finance a couple of first-class jaunts to Europe, where she arranged for introductions to such luminaries as Edith Wharton, Gertrude Stein, James Joyce, George Bernard Shaw, and Colette. She first met Ernest Hemingway when he was a virile young star of the American colony in Paris.

In the course of time Fanny Butcher became one of the most influential literary editors in the United States. She was a great favorite of Colonel Robert R. McCormick, the *Tribune*'s publisher, and was featured regularly in the paper's advertisements. It was said that she could make a book. Merchants attributed increased business to her spirited reviews. One of her columns was credited with selling two thousand copies of a single novel. Carl Sandburg called her "Miss Chicago, Lady Midwest" ("Homage to Fanny Butcher"). H. L. Mencken said, "I'd no more think of visiting Chicago without waiting on you than I'd think of visiting Rome without leaving my card on His Holiness" (Mencken to Butcher, May 1932, Fanny Butcher Papers).

In 1935 she married Richard Drummond Bokum, a fifty-year-old bachelor from an old Chicago family. He was a good-looking man of grace and humor. As a friend put it, he "had lived for his mother until she died" (Lloyd letter to his aunts, February 13, 1935, Fanny Butcher Papers), and once she was gone, he put Butcher on a pedestal in her stead. Dick Bokum captivated the literary community with his easy charm, and most of its members assumed that Fanny Butcher had now come into wealthy circumstances. In fact, he had a small income from a family trust and was largely content to let his wife carry the financial weight of the partnership. They were good companions, and she supported him in every way for the rest of his life, sometimes at an emotional cost entirely unsuspected by her closest colleagues and friends.

Throughout the 1920s and into the 1930s the *Tribune* book page appeared on Saturdays. Later it was featured on Wednesdays. In 1942 management decided to establish a separate Sunday book section. Butcher had pushed the idea for years, polling booksellers and turning in regular suggestions to broaden and enliven coverage. At 1,300,000, Sunday circulation was at an all-time high. Nevertheless, the change came about only after the new *Chicago Sun* announced its own weekend book supplement. In the harshest blow of her career, Butcher was passed over for the editorship of this new Sunday venture, the job going instead to a genial reporter from the travel section. She pressed her qualifications to those in charge. She was stonewalled and then, worse, assigned to write a weekly column on society. It was then hinted that doing double-duty on the book pages might prove too much work for one person. In retrospect, Butcher probably lost out for a mix of reasons, most of them impersonal. She was fifty-seven years old, and a new generation of managers was moving its own team into place. The book trade was more commercial than it had been, and the chief qualification for the new section's editor-in-chief was the ability to sell advertising. Then too, she was a woman. By way of announcing the change, the question the *Tribune* bosses put to every New York publisher they visited was, "What would you think of a man?" (Bennett Cerf to Butcher, October 2, 1942; Harold Latham to Butcher, October 2, 1942). This rejection sent Butcher into a period of crushing despair. In private notes she scribbled the nearly unthinkable: "Wish I could leave Trib" (private notes, December 17, 1942, Fanny Butcher Papers).

In the end she soldiered on, refusing to relinquish a presence on the book pages. For several years she wrote the lead review every Sunday. Later she was obliged to share that slot with other contributors. She produced a weekly column called "The Literary Spotlight," a blend of book world gossip and reminiscence that drew heavily on her friendships with longtime stars of the literary firmament. She also retained the title of "literary editor." Though the title was now stripped of any real authority inside the *Tribune* offices, Butcher kept her hold on the public's imagination. In 1945 one reader wrote her, "I always go to books. Somehow or other I unconsciously give you credit for the best of everything I read there" (Oliver R. Barrett to Butcher, 1945, Fanny Butcher Papers). Following orders, for fifteen years she wrote a society column that she signed "Thalia," after the Greek muse of comedy. (It ended after Butcher collapsed from overwork.) She never talked about this part of her job, but she

managed to use its travel opportunities to tuck in more visits with authors on their home ground. A trip to interview box holders at the Hialeah race track in Florida meant a chance to see Marjorie Kinnan Rawlings in her cottage at Cross Creek. In Chicago Butcher was a great host herself. Several writers said that their warmest memories of the city were evenings at her North Side townhouse, a bottle of bourbon planted on the sideboard while Dick Bokum whipped up plates of scrambled eggs and toast.

As she grew older, Fanny Butcher was celebrated as the dean of Chicago literary critics. In 1953 she was the first woman to be honored by the Friends of the Chicago Public Library, an organization she subsequently served as president for ten years. She was elected a Patron Saint of the Society of Midland Authors, and the University of Chicago chose her as Communicator of the Year in 1964. She was continually feted by the book trade and showered with awards from women's groups and civic associations. Much later, at the age of ninety-two, she was inducted with ten other alumni into the first Hall of Fame at the Illinois Institute of Technology. The year after that she was inducted into the Chicago Press Club's Hall of Fame.

Fanny Butcher retired from the *Chicago Tribune* in December 1962, a few months short of her fifty-year anniversary at the paper. Her husband died the following November. In 1972 she published an autobiography titled *Many Lives—One Love*, which documents her long career and many literary friendships. The book was hugely gratifying to her former colleagues, though it does not match the thrill of meeting the legends of prose and poetry in their own letters to her. Butcher lived quietly in a sun-filled apartment on Astor Street, surrounded by first editions, double-shelved in every room. She was sustained by a continuing exchange of letters and gifts with aging friends and the antic companionship of a series of white poodles, all named Bobo. In lonely circumstances she managed a gracious equanimity. She died at the age of ninety-nine. Her body was cremated and her ashes were brought to the Laurel Hill Cemetery in Philadelphia, where they were placed in her husband's crypt.

Fanny Butcher succeeded in her ambition to live in the world of arts and letters. The sheer power of her role as lead critic at the largest newspaper in the Midwest necessarily drew the regard of writers and publishers and gave her a superb public platform. In Chicago, at least, she established an invincible persona, a virtual brand name that she used unstintingly to connect books and readers. Probably she was less critic than collaborator in the enterprise of literature. Her talent as a reporter lay in her ability to perceive an author's essential intention and convey it in a few words for an audience she understood well. Her enduring sympathy with the struggle of putting words on paper drew the grateful trust of two generations of writers in this country and abroad. She saved most of the letters they wrote to her over a period of seventy-five years. Intimate, revealing, full of confusion and doubt, this cache of correspondence offers an affecting picture of artistic striving. It is the visible remains of an extraordinary bond and is, in itself, Fanny Butcher's most important achievement. Bequeathed to the Newberry Library at her death, the letters constitute a rich resource for those interested both in literature and in the workings of the cultural marketplace in twentieth-century Chicago.

Sources. The Fanny Butcher Papers at the NL include correspondence, personal notes and engagement diaries, photographs, miscellaneous news and magazine clippings, and family documents and memorabilia. Included is Carl Sandburg's unpublished "Homage to Fanny Butcher," April 1953. This material includes a large group of inscribed first editions. Her book reviews can be read in her own bound albums in the CPL Spec. Coll. Besides her autobiography, *Many Lives—One Love* (1972), Butcher wrote a few scattered pamphlets and some magazine articles on various topics. In the latter part of her professional career and into her retirement years she gave occasional interviews to newspapers and trade magazines. She is mentioned briefly in some accounts of the Chicago Renaissance. She does figure in the biographies of several important American writers of the 1920s and 1930s, but the material used is taken largely from her own papers, which remain the best source of information about her. Useful books include Julie Goldsmith Gilbert, *Ferber: A Biography* (1978), and Harry Hansen, *Midwest Portraits* (1923). Obituaries include "Fanny Butcher Dead: Literary Critic Was 99," *NYT,* May 17, 1987; "Fanny Butcher; Knew Giants of Literature," *Chicago Sunday Tribune,* May 17, 1987; "Fanny Butcher, 99; *Tribune* Literary Editor for 40 Years," *Chicago Sun-Times,* May 16, 1987.

CELIA HILLIARD

BUTLER TALLEY, ISABELLA MAUDE GARNETT. *See* GARNETT BUTLER TALLEY, ISABELLA MAUDE

C

CARIS, MARTHA CRANE. *See* **CRANE CARIS, MARTHA**

CARLSON, MARGERY CLAIRE
November 21, 1892–July 5, 1985
BOTANIST, PROFESSOR, CONSERVATIONIST

Margery Claire Carlson, noted for both her research expeditions into Mexico and Central America and her diligent conservation efforts in Illinois, was born in rural Arthur, Illinois, the eldest of three children, to John E. and Nellie Marie (Johnson) Carlson. She traced her love of nature back to childhood summers spent looking for wildflowers along the nearby Vermilion River. With her brother Harry and sister Helen, Carlson attended LaSalle–Peru Township High School, where the principal encouraged her to continue her studies in college. Her father's salary as an optician, however, could not finance her education, and Carlson taught two years in a country school near Ottawa, Illinois, and sold cookbooks door-to-door to earn money for college.

In 1912, Margery Carlson entered Northwestern University on a scholarship and was the school's first female botany major who would continue on toward a doctorate. Carlson struggled hard to combine a heavy load of course work and a series of part-time jobs. Although a good student, she failed to qualify for the academic honor society Phi Beta Kappa, a disappointment she still remembered in 1936 in an autobiographical sketch.

Carlson received a B.S. degree in biology from Northwestern in 1916 and embarked on a series of high school teaching positions to pay off her college debts. She began full-time graduate studies in 1919 at the University of Wisconsin–Madison, where she received an M.S. degree in 1920. She then taught at Wellesley College in Massachusetts for two years and returned to the University of Wisconsin in 1922. She received a Ph.D. in 1925. It was most likely at Madison that Carlson met Kate Staley, who became her lifelong friend and traveling companion.

Staley received an M.S. degree in Medical Sciences from the University of Wisconsin in 1925 and continued there as an instructor in physiology in the medical school.

In 1925, Margery Carlson was awarded a highly coveted two-year post-doctoral position at the Boyce Thompson Institute for Plant Research in Yonkers, New York. She stayed there until 1927, when she returned to the University of Wisconsin for two more years as a research assistant. Carlson then joined Northwestern University's botany department as an instructor, one of five women on Northwestern's faculty. In 1930, Carlson was promoted to assistant professor, a rank she held for more than twenty years. Watching her male colleagues promoted ahead of her, Carlson was stung with a sense of "mild outrage" (interview with Burger). Carlson commented that she held the record at Northwestern University for length of service as an assistant professor. Yet she chose to suffer the injustice silently, wearing the slight as a badge of honor, testifying to a strong sense of intellectual and personal independence. Women students saw her as a role model who inspired them to pursue graduate study. In 1954, Carlson was belatedly promoted to associate professor in biology, a title she retained as an emerita after her retirement from Northwestern in 1958.

During her long stay at Northwestern, Carlson matured as a botanist and delineated the research areas that would define her place in the field of botany. Her earliest interest was in the cultivation and regeneration of orchids. By 1935, Carlson had successfully cultivated thirty-five varieties of domestic orchids, gathering seeds from the swamplands bordering the southern tip of Lake Michigan. Outside interest in her work was more than academic; orchids were then a popular, though expensive and scarce, retail flower. Attempting to domesticate the wild orchids she found near Lake Michigan, Carlson anticipated the day when she could document and research the physiological process of orchid regeneration and distribution in its native tropical regions in Mexico and Central America.

She traveled eighteen thousand miles in the United States in 1940, studying and photographing plants. Desiring to put her botanical knowledge to practical use, Carlson chaired the Evanston Victory Garden Committee from 1941 to 1948, encouraging patriotic Americans to help the war effort by growing their own food. Under Carlson's guidance, more than twenty-five hundred Evanston families farmed on individual or community plots.

Following World War II, Carlson eagerly embarked on her first expedition abroad to collect tropical flora. She chose the mountains of El Salvador, becoming the first woman to lead a plant-collecting expedition into that country. Kate Staley, who had retired in 1940 from a teaching position at the University of Wisconsin–Madison, accompanied Carlson on this first and later excursions, serving simultaneously as secretary, research assistant, traveling companion, and confidant. Staley had moved to Evanston in 1940 to live with Carlson, who never married. The first trip was exceedingly difficult; they traveled by oxcart down steep ravines and up treacherous precipices seeking the wild orchids that clung to the sides of the mountains. Though Carlson was fond of retelling an incident when farmers, armed with machetes, threatened her and Staley, Carlson trusted the local people they met. A colleague recalled the event in the October 1985 issue of the *Field Museum of Natural History Bulletin*: "Sizing up the situation quickly (these were two poor farmers and not dangerous bandits), Margery proceeded to admonish them in Spanish: 'Don't you realize you could have scared us to death? And if that had happened you would never go to heaven!' Whereupon she invited them to have some lunch—which they did" (Burger, "Margery Carlson," 5). The El Salvador trip covered more than three thousand miles and netted more than four thousand plants from twelve hundred different species, including one hundred distinct varieties of orchids.

Claiming she was bitten by wanderlust, Carlson made a ten-thousand-mile trip into southern Mexico to study cloud forest vegetation in 1949; completed a five-thousand-mile trip into Honduras in 1952; returned to Mexico in 1953, 1954, and 1961; collected plants in Hawaii in 1962; visited Costa Rica in 1956; traveled sixteen thousand miles in Europe in 1959 to examine collections of Central American flora; and then made periodical return trips to Mexico and Honduras into the early 1970s. She discovered new plants on nearly every trip to Central America. Carlson made more than a dozen trips to Mexico and Central America between 1945 and the mid-1970s, under joint sponsorship of Northwestern University and the Field Museum, where she was named an associate in 1954 and promoted to research associate in 1963.

Carlson took most of her early trips during the Christmas season, timing her collecting to accommodate both her teaching schedule and the end of the tropical rainy season. January brought dry, sunny weather to Mexico and Central America, ushering in an explosion of wildflower blossoms and offering dry roads to facilitate travel. Carlson remarked many times that she and Staley traveled compactly on their expeditions, like a snail, with their home (and plant presses, blotting papers, and packing boxes) on their backs; Carlson fittingly dubbed their paneled truck *El Caracolito*, the little snail.

Once back at Northwestern, Carlson drew upon her collections for her research. She published extensively in the *Annals of Botany* (1927), the *Botany Gazette* (1929, 1938, 1940, 1945), the *Journal of Botany* (1938), *Zonta International* (1946), the *Chicago Naturalist* (1947), and the *American Journal of Botany* (1950). Her most important research accomplishment was her 1957 "Monograph of the Genus *Russelia* (Scrophulariaceae)," published in the Field Museum's *Fieldiana: Botany* journal. It was a ground-breaking classification of twenty-one new species of *Russelia*, a member of the snapdragon family. In honor of her friendship with Kate Staley, Carlson named the twenty-first specimen *Russelia Staleyae* Carlson.

Carlson combined her foreign travels and research with an equally rigorous schedule of activities at home. Planning ahead to her retirement, Carlson started to supplement her teaching and collecting duties with a deep-seated commitment to local conservation. In 1958, she directed the wildflower nature trail and educational center at the Grosse Pointe Lighthouse in Evanston, a project she had helped start in 1934. She served as a tour guide there to elementary school children. She went on the local lecture circuit, addressing Chicago area garden clubs, sororities, professional women's groups. Carlson also taught adult evening classes in an effort to heighten community awareness of nature conservation. Also in 1958, she spearheaded fundraising to preserve two of the last remaining bogs in Illinois, near Volo and Wauconda in Lake County. In February 1964, Illinois Governor Otto Kerner appointed Carlson to a newly formed advisory board, the Illinois Nature Preserves Commission, to work with the state Department of Conservation on proposed sites for parks and nature preserves. Carlson had actively lobbied for the appointment, creating an "imposing physical presence" (Burger, "Margery Carlson") with her shock of white hair, her steady gaze and voice, and her proudly erect pose. She had used her authoritarian demeanor as part of her strategy, continually reintroducing herself to the governor at conservation meetings so that he would consider her when filling spots on the commission. Kerner also placed her on the governor's advisory committee for Illinois Beach State Park, which recommended ways to preserve the park's wild life and plants. From 1964 to 1967, Carlson was secretary of the Illinois Chapter of the Nature Conservancy, which she had helped establish in the early 1950s, and was instrumental in the conservancy's acquisition of nature preserves in the state at Pine Rock, at Berkeley Prairie in Highland Park, and at the Big Bend area along the Vermilion River in LaSalle County.

It was the last of these, the Big Bend Project, that brought Carlson full circle as a botanist and conservationist, for it was in that stretch of riverbed near LaSalle-Peru where Carlson had first experienced the joys of studying wildflowers as a young girl. In September 1976, the Illinois Nature Preserves Commission and the Nature Conservancy formally recognized Carlson's contributions by renaming the Big Bend Preserve the Margery C. Carlson Nature Preserve. It was, said Carlson, "the only memorial I'll have" (Snyder, "Great Teachers").

That honor, however, was only one among many that Carlson earned for her professional and civic accomplishments. Two of her most prominent honors were awarded to her by the Garden Club of America. The Eloise Payne Luquer

Medal, awarded in 1952, praised Carlson for her achievement in botany, and the Sarah Gildersleeve Fife Memorial Award in 1954 commended Carlson for her exceptional publications in research as well as her service and achievements in gardening.

Margery Carlson was active well into her eighties, continuing her vocal advocacy of local conservation. Her travels tapered off after Kate Staley became ill, and she and Carlson moved together to the Presbyterian Home in Evanston in late 1974. Margery Claire Carlson died at the Presbyterian Home at the age of ninety-two. She is buried in Oakwood Cemetery in LaSalle, Illinois, her childhood hometown. Kate Staley, Carlson's companion for more than forty years, died shortly thereafter in December 1985.

Carlson's significance rests both in her contributions to the field of botany and in her lifelong commitment to local nature conservation and preservation. Carlson was among the first women faculty members at Northwestern University, although women had been working as botanists for many years. She and Staley were intrepid explorers, even well into their later years, and Carlson contributed to the discipline an important understanding of cloud-forest plant life frequently overlooked by other collectors. In addition, Carlson's collections, especially those of Mexican flora, comprise a significant part of the Field Museum's botanical holdings. Margery Carlson's contributions to the preservation of natural prairie, bog, and wildflower sites across the state of Illinois and her eagerness to teach others the importance of conservation testify to her commitment to nature in all its manifestations, confirming, as she herself said, that "Nature is my middle name" (*Evanston Review*, June 8, 1970).

Sources. The archives at the Evanston Hist. Soc. and at Northwestern Univ. Library have significant collections of biographical sketches, newspaper clippings, and memorials detailing Carlson's professional life and accomplishments. These papers include two detailed autobiographical sketches by Carlson in typescript, one at Northwestern Univ. [1953?] and one [1974] at the Evanston Hist. Soc. The documents only lightly touch upon Carlson's childhood and personal life; few documents remain to shed light on her early years and personal beliefs. The Evanston Hist. Soc. has the scrapbooks that Carlson kept during her years as Victory Garden chair, and Northwestern Univ. holds certificates of merit that Carlson received as well as typescript press releases from the Northwestern University News Service for December 19, 1945, and April 11, 1946. Her botanical collections are housed at the Field Museum of Natural History in Chicago. In addition to her research reports, mentioned above, Carlson wrote two articles about her travels: "Plant Hunting in El Salvador," *Zontonian*, June 1946, and (with Kate Staley) "In the Cloud Forests of Chiapas," *Americas*, April 1953. Throughout Carlson's career, the *Evanston Review* reported on her work; these articles include "N.U. Botanist Finds, Corrects Errors in Europe Collections," September 3, 1959, and Lorraine Bannon, "Botanist Is Wild about Lighthouse Center," June 8, 1970. Memorials written after Carlson's death include Alice Snyder, "Great Teachers," *Northwestern Alumni News*, September 1985; "Remembering Pioneer Margery Carlson," *Conservator*, fall 1985; and William C. Burger, "Margery Carlson, 1892–1985," *Field Museum of Natural History Bulletin*, October 1985. Kathleen D. Toerpe interviewed William C. Burger and Margaret Martling, two former colleagues of Carlson, on May 3, 1994.

KATHLEEN D. TOERPE

CARPENTER, HELEN GRAHAM FAIRBANK
January 13, 1868–June 28, 1945
CLUBWOMAN, FAMILY PLANNING PIONEER, GIRLS'
ORGANIZATION COMMISSIONER

Helen Graham Fairbank was born in Chicago, the oldest daughter among eight children. Her mother was Helen Livingston (Graham) Fairbank, the only daughter of three children of John Andrew and Helen Smith (Beeckman) Graham. The Graham family was of Scotch-Irish descent. Fairbank's father was Nathaniel Kellogg Fairbank, a grain merchant who came to Chicago in 1854 from New York and became one of the leading businessmen in the city.

The young Helen Fairbank, "something of a tomboy" (Jachimowicz, 2), revealed in a diary she kept how much she liked playing with her two brothers. She enjoyed music and reading in her father's library, including books of poetry, philosophy, and medicine.

Helen Graham Fairbank married Benjamin Carpenter on September 18, 1893, in an Episcopal ceremony at the fashionable Grace Church, Chicago. Carpenter, the son of Elizabeth Curtis (Greene) Carpenter and George Benjamin Carpenter, was born in Chicago in 1865 and graduated in 1888 from Harvard University, Cambridge, Massachusetts. His father was one of the pioneer businessmen who forged a thriving commercial metropolis in Chicago. Benjamin Carpenter joined his father's firm, George B. Carpenter & Company, ship chandlers and manufacturers and jobbers of railroad, mill, building, and vessel supplies.

In 1895, two years after the couple married, Helen Carpenter found herself responsible not only for her own household but for her father's as well when her mother died suddenly, following an appendix operation. Soon after losing her mother, Helen Carpenter also suffered the loss of her maternal grandmother Fairbank, who had helped her mother run the Fairbank household. The Carpenters moved in with Nathaniel Fairbank and his six living children, and Helen Carpenter oversaw her siblings' activities. In 1896, Helen Carpenter gave birth to the first of her four children, Benjamin Jr.; the next three soon followed: Cordelia Fairbank, born 1898; Elizabeth Webster, 1900; and Fairbank, 1902. Despite her wealth and the availability of household servants, Carpenter knew firsthand the responsibilities of contending with a large, extended family. She managed the Chicago household as well as a summer home in Lake Geneva, Wisconsin.

As a society matron, Carpenter had both the time and the money to work on social causes she favored, even while she ran a large household. She joined the auxiliary of St. Luke's Hospital, an Episcopal-affiliated institution begun by a small group of women, including her own mother, who attended Grace (Episcopal) Church.

In 1902, the Carpenters moved into their own home in Winnetka, Illinois. The following year Nathaniel Fairbank died, and Helen Carpenter brought her two sisters to Winnetka to join her own children. It was a pleasant suburban existence for the four young Carpenters and the two young Fairbank women. The entire family traveled abroad in 1907.

The cause with which Carpenter was most associated was the birth control movement. Clubwomen and female professionals such as RACHELLE YARROS, a gynecologist and obstetrician who had lived at Hull-House for twenty years, had long been concerned about the health of women and children. Yarros had lectured for some time to the Chicago Woman's Club and the Woman's City Club on the need for birth control. The issue gained support, however, after Margaret Sanger spoke to a Chicago audience in 1916 in a hall in the crowded working-class and immigrant Stockyards neighborhood. Civic leaders, professors from the nearby University of Chicago, and local free speech advocates made up the audience of fifteen hundred people.

After the Sanger talk, a group called the Parents' Committee formed to advocate the cause of birth control in Chicago. Members included university professors, clubwomen, and physicians. University of Chicago economist and demographer James A. Field served as the first president of the Illinois Birth Control League, formed out of the Parents' Committee's initial meetings in 1917. The league prevented the passage of a very drastic anti-birth-control law by the state legislature.

World War I intervened, and the Illinois Birth Control League lapsed into inactivity after its founding. Benjamin Carpenter was commissioned as captain and later major, on active duty July 1917 to February 1919. Helen Carpenter became cochair of the Chicago headquarters of the American Fund for French Wounded, a society devoted to making hospital dressings and raising money for supplies to be used in French hospitals.

Helen Carpenter became interested in the 1920s in the work of physician Clara M. Davis, Children's Memorial Hospital, Chicago. Davis established a small nursing home for infants and toddlers to illustrate her theory that if children were allowed to select their own diets their nutrition would be improved. "The experiment proved highly successful; the health of all the children improved markedly" (Jachimowicz, 4). The nursery closed in 1929, but the experiments influenced books on child rearing.

In another child-oriented endeavor, Carpenter participated in the Girl Scouts of Chicago and Cook County during the early 1920s. She worked with her daughter Cordelia to establish a permanent campsite for the organization in Elkhorn, Wisconsin. Carpenter served as the first commissioner of Girl Scouts in the Chicago and Cook County area.

Carpenter continued to work with the birth control movement in Illinois. The Illinois Birth Control League was revived in 1923. "When the League decided to open a free clinic, we had wonderful plans and high hopes which were all dashed by the refusal of the Health Commissioner [Dr. Herman N. Bundesen] to grant us the necessary license" ("Annual Report," April 29, 1925, 1), Carpenter wrote. Her name and reputation was attached to the case, *Helen G. Carpenter* v. *William S. Dever* in 1923. "We took the matter into court and received a decision in our favor from Judge Fisher, but the case was immediately appealed" (p. 1). At the time, Carpenter was vice-president. In 1927, Helen Carpenter became president of the league, a position she held until 1937.

To work around public sentiment against dispensing birth control and to stay within the law, the league decided to abandon its idea of a free clinic, which required a license, and instead planned to open an office where patients could pay for health services. The league was accused of indiscriminately handing out birth control information, an act that some believed to be immoral. Carpenter emphasized that women coming to the clinic were making voluntary visits. "The true picture is very different," Carpenter wrote in April 1925 ("Annual Report," 2). "Our offices . . . have very little publicity. We do not advertise . . ." (p. 2).

Carpenter championed the educational work that was essential for the acceptance of birth control methods among the poor. Chicago in the mid-1920s had a population of more than 2.7 million, and many were immigrants. The birth control clinic served many European immigrant women who were familiar with abortion. The league hoped to expand its informational services to introduce the idea of family planning to poor families, limiting the need for abortion.

Carpenter, a wealthy woman who at the time lived in the fashionable Astor Street neighborhood on Chicago's Near North Side, wrote with sympathy for the poor women the clinic served. "The young girls under 20 [who come to the clinic] are not school girls; they are rather weary, discouraged little mothers with two and three children, who seem to us to be entitled to information which will give them a few years rest in which to recuperate before they bear more children" ("Annual Report," 3). Carpenter argued against the popular notion that women who wanted to use birth control were selfish or were so-called modern women who wanted to "leave their homes and go into industry" (p. 3). Instead, she found that almost all of the women who came to the clinic gave their occupations as "housewives" (p. 3), although many worked to contribute financially to their families. While most of the husbands worked, many were also ill, drinkers, and gamblers. Even though families had many reasons for not wanting more children, "the foundation of the trouble is economic, but it is nearly always complicated with other things" (p. 4), Carpenter wrote. The clinic reached many nationalities. "I think it would be simpler to say what nationality we do not reach" (p. 2), Carpenter commented. The women were of all ages, from sixteen to forty, the largest number being between the ages of twenty-five and thirty.

One particular case was especially poignant to Carpenter. A young German Protestant woman, married at age sixteen, had given birth to ten children. Nine were still living and her husband was an alcoholic. She came for birth control information because she was too poor, worn out, and tired. "When one stops to think that this reason is given by a young woman of 29," wrote Carpenter, "it seems to me sad beyond words" (p. 5). Worse yet, she thought this particular case was not atypical.

The Illinois Birth Control League was supported by many women, including Carpenter, from old and respected families. The league's work, however, continued to be hampered by legal fights, and progress was slow. Carpenter remained optimistic: "I hope that our friends will stand by us and give us the help of their enthusiasm as well as their money," she wrote. "It is hard to fight in an unpopular cause" (p. 6).

Because she was a society matron, Carpenter's way was made smoother by money, and she had time to devote to her interests. The family home on the shore of Lake Michigan in Winnetka provided outlets for swimming, boating, and tennis. The Carpenters kept horses and dogs. Both Benjamin and Helen

Carpenter were accomplished amateur musicians and gathered weekly with friends to play chamber music.

After Benjamin Carpenter died in 1927, Helen Carpenter continued to work on projects that interested her. A member of the American Genealogy Society, Carpenter worked in the 1930s and 1940s on sorting and cataloging materials for a book on the genealogy of the Graham family. She traveled extensively for her work on the book, which was published in 1942.

Helen Carpenter died at age seventy-seven. She is buried on the grounds of Christ (Episcopal) Church, Winnetka, Illinois.

The organization that Carpenter devoted much of her time to changed its name from the Illinois Birth Control League to Planned Parenthood Federation of America in 1941. Though surrounded by wealth, Helen Carpenter was also the product of a culture that encouraged noblesse oblige on the one hand, and on the other, endowed womanhood with a special responsibility to actively pursue the welfare of women and children. She dedicated many years of her adult life to a controversial, unpopular cause, aiding poor women so that they could choose birth control as an option. She was one of a small group of Chicago reformers responsible for opening the country's second birth control clinic.

Sources. "The Annual Report of the Illinois Birth Control League," typescript, April 29, 1925, written by Carpenter, as well as other reports and letters by Carpenter, are at CHS. The records of the Planned Parenthood association are in the Medical Library, UIC. The Winnetka Public Library has clippings about the Carpenter family. See Helen Carpenter, *The Reverend John Graham of Woodbury, Connecticut and His Descendants* (1942). See Bernice J. Guthmann, *The Planned Parenthood Movement in Illinois* (1975), for a history of the birth control movement in Illinois. A short biography of Carpenter is found in Elizabeth Jachimowicz, *Eight Chicago Women and Their Fashions 1860–1929* (1978).

MARY E. ADAMI

FIG. 17. *Portrait of art patron Rue Winterbotham Carpenter by Constantin Brancusi, charcoal and graphite, n.d.*

CARPENTER, RUE WINTERBOTHAM
November 15, 1876–December 7, 1931
ART PATRON, INTERIOR DECORATOR

Rue Winterbotham Carpenter, a founder and president of the Arts Club of Chicago and an influential cultural force in the city, was the second of four children born to Joseph Humphrey and Genevieve (Baldwin) Winterbotham in Joliet, Illinois. Her father, an energetic entrepreneur, moved the family to Chicago in 1892, where he established several successful businesses, including manufacturing and mortgage financing. His sons, John and Joseph Jr., entered the family business after attending Yale University. Nothing is recorded about Rue Winterbotham's formal education. Both she and her sister, Genevieve, traveled to Europe, where Rue Winterbotham began to develop her lifelong interest in the visual and performing arts.

On November 20, 1900, Rue Winterbotham married John Alden Carpenter. Like his bride, Carpenter hailed from a prominent Chicago family. George B. Carpenter and Company were ship chandlers and dealers in railway and contractors' supplies. John Alden Carpenter, a graduate of Harvard University, Cambridge, Massachusetts, was company vice-president as well as a promising musician and composer. He had studied music in Rome with Sir Edward Elgar, among others, and would earn in-

ternational renown for modern and jazz compositions. Two years later, Rue Carpenter gave birth to a daughter, Genevieve.

The family traveled frequently to Europe, where Rue Carpenter continued to explore art galleries and museums, developing an informed and sophisticated aesthetic, which served as the basis for her activities as an interior decorator. She was an accomplished linguist and through her facility with languages was able to form important friendships with dancers, musicians, painters, and sculptors of the European avant-garde. Sources do not indicate whether she received formal instruction in painting, but her skill was considerable; her work was later compared with that of French artists Marie Laurencin and Berthe Morisot. "Had she been more selfish as a painter," wrote Mary Hoyt Wiborg in the *New York Times* on December 12, 1931, after Carpenter's death, "developing her talents, [she] could have stood alone today as one of the best women artists in America."

Instead, Carpenter devoted herself to charitable causes, becoming especially a model of patronage and support for art and artists. She channeled her own artistic impulses into altruistic enterprises such as painting a mural at Children's Memorial Hospital, where she joined the auxiliary board in 1904, and creating grand decorations for charity balls in New York and Chicago. Similarly, she took great care furnishing her home: the residence rented by the Carpenters from Cyrus Hall McCormick in the late teens became known in Chicago society as the epitome of distinction and charm. Through all these efforts, Carpenter gained recognition for her superb taste and elegant interior designs. Among the significant commissions she received as a decorator were the Casino Club, the Fortnightly, and the Racquet Club in Chicago and, in New York, Elizabeth Arden's salon and the Double Six Club at the Waldorf Astoria Hotel.

Carpenter's greatest impact was through the Arts Club of Chicago, a center for the presentation and discussion of avant-garde art in what was, in the early twentieth century, a highly conservative cultural enclave. An example of Chicago's aversion to new artistic styles was the hostile reception of the International Exhibition of Modern Art, or Armory Show, when it traveled to the Art Institute of Chicago from New York in 1913. Local papers reviled the cubist, expressionist, and futurist works on view with a ferocity unprecedented in New York reviews, and a group of art students demonstrated their indignation toward the exhibition by attempting to burn Henri Matisse in effigy. Despite the burgeoning collections of the Art Institute, the presence of some thirty commercial galleries in the city, and the attention given to cultural events in the press, in Chicago emphasis on the arts was decidedly traditional. Carpenter identified a need for a forum in which contemporary art could be introduced and promoted; she began, shortly after the Armory Show, to formulate plans for an association of collectors, curators, artists, and cultural devotees who would come together in support of experimental work in the visual arts as well as in poetry, literature, music, and dance.

According to Carpenter's vision, the Arts Club would have facilities for exhibitions, concerts, lectures, and social events, where members could engage ideas in a comfortable and gracious environment. By 1916, the club was incorporated, with a board of directors and headquarters in the Fine Arts Building on Michigan Avenue. Carpenter's cofounders included artist Grace McGann, who served as the club's first president; ALICE ROULLIER, who worked with her father at his art gallery; realtor Arthur Aldis, the enlightened Art Institute trustee most responsible for bringing the Armory Show to Chicago; Frederick Clay Bartlett, an artist, collector, and benefactor of the Art Institute; financier Charles Hutchinson, president of the Corn Exchange National Bank and of the Art Institute's board of trustees; Dr. Frederick Stock, conductor of the Chicago Symphony Orchestra; and other members of the city's cultural elite. Carpenter was head of the art committee and succeeded McGann as president of the club in 1918. She retained the post for the rest of her life.

Arts Club exhibitions opened to the public that year in galleries at the club. Working with architect and fellow board member Arthur Heun, Carpenter designed and furnished the club rooms in a style characterized by great refinement, combining choice antiques in an ambiance of modern restraint. She then embarked on an ambitious exhibition program with Roullier, who was crucial to the realization of the club's progressive mission. Roullier served as director of the exhibition committee for more than twenty years, applying her knowledge of the interna-

tional art market and her fluency in French to the task of bringing an awareness of contemporary art to Chicago. Together the two women arranged the first major Chicago showings of works by Constantin Brancusi, Georges Braque, Laurencin, Fernand Léger, John Marin, Pablo Picasso, Auguste Rodin, Jacques Villon, and others. The francophilia informing this roster was balanced by exhibitions of traditional and non-Western art that Carpenter and Roullier understood to have relevance to modern movements: African sculpture, Egyptian and medieval art, Chinese bronzes, Tibetan painting, Persian carpets.

Some of these selections were installed in the Arts Club Exhibition Room at the Art Institute, where, from 1922 to 1927, Carpenter, Roullier, and their committee presented a series of exhibitions in addition to those offered at the Arts Club itself. In 1924, the club moved to larger quarters, again designed by Carpenter and Heun, in the Wrigley Building. All the while the various Arts Club committees under Carpenter's leadership organized dramatic and musical performances, dance recitals, and poetry readings. Guest artists and authors included Martha Graham, Arthur Honegger, Archibald MacLeish, Edna St. Vincent Millay, Serge Prokofiev, Bertrand Russell, Carl Sandburg, and Igor Stravinsky. Carpenter rallied attendance at these events and wielded her influence to increase artistic appreciation at every opportunity. When the Moscow Art Theater played to meager audiences at Chicago's Great Northern Theater in 1923, she addressed a letter to the entire club membership, urging them to patronize the troupe; otherwise, she feared, Chicago risked being omitted in the future from the itineraries of international traveling productions of great merit.

It was not just apathy against which Carpenter regularly struggled; contempt and mockery were regularly heaped upon the early Arts Club exhibitions by an antagonistic press and public. Nevertheless, many of the objects exhibited were sold to club members and patrons. With the establishment of the Arts Club Gift Purchase Fund in 1923, a number of works were also acquired and donated to the Art Institute and to the Field Museum of Natural History. In this way, Carpenter's endeavors permanently enriched Chicago collections, both public and private. She played a critical role in the 1927 purchase by the Arts Club of sculptor Brancusi's extraordinary polished bronze, *Golden Bird* (1919/20). When Brancusi had an extensive exhibition at New York's Brummer Gallery in 1926, Carpenter brought an abbreviated version of the show to the Arts Club the following year. A portrait drawing inscribed "Hommage à Madame Carpenter" in the Art Institute's collection probably dates to 1926 or earlier and documents Brancusi's sensitive appreciation for his intelligent and sympathetic patron.

In 1921, with an initial gift of fifty thousand dollars, Carpenter's father established a fund at the Art Institute for the acquisition of European paintings. After Winterbotham's death in 1925, Carpenter and her brother John supplemented the endowment to seventy thousand dollars.

Such was Carpenter's contribution to the cultural life of the city that when she died suddenly of a cerebral hemorrhage on December 7, 1931, the *Chicago Daily Tribune* carried the news the next day in a front-page headline. At the time of her death, in addition to her ongoing activities at the Arts Club, Carpenter was in charge of decorations for a charity ball at the Auditorium to benefit the Joint Emergency Relief Fund and was a member of the board of directors of Chicago's Century of Progress Exposition scheduled for 1933. After private funeral services were held for Carpenter at Graceland Cemetery, presided over by an Episcopal minister, she was interred at the family's summer home in Charlotte, Vermont.

Searching for a suitable means of honoring Carpenter's memory and of maintaining something of the vitality she imparted to programs at the Arts Club, the board of directors adopted a resolution in January 1932 establishing the Rue Carpenter Arts Club Memorial Fund with an investment of twenty thousand dollars. The income from this endowment would be used to underwrite lectures on contemporary art. Not limited to the Arts Club, these lectures could also be presented by the Art Institute, Field Museum, or by the Oriental Institute or other arts organizations at the University of Chicago. Interpreting problems in contemporary art in a tradition begun by the club's founder, the lecture series continues to this day.

Carpenter was eulogized by two critics for the Chicago *Evening Post* who recognized her significant legacy to the city. On December 15, 1931, Inez Cunningham singled out Carpenter's courage in "Mourn for a Gallant Art Leader," reminding Chicagoans of the way she had stood up to criticism and ridicule to maintain good taste. The following year, Clarence Bulliet remembered Carpenter for her keen intellect, international vision, and above all for her unmatched fearlessness in defying a theory that equated modernism with Bolshevism. The ramifications of Carpenter's diligent sponsorship of modern art were evident in the positive response elicited by the 1933 Century of Progress exhibition at the Art Institute, which included works by Brancusi, Braque, Marcel Duchamp, Wassily Kandinsky, Léger, Matisse, Joan Miró, Picasso, and others who had premiered in Chicago at the Arts Club. The dramatic contrast between the 1913 Armory Show's local reception and the popular success of the challenging art exhibition at the Century of Progress Exposition twenty years later was due in large part to Rue Winterbotham Carpenter's commitment to broadening the appreciation of the art of her time.

Sources. The papers of the Arts Club of Chicago, including a bound scrapbook of clippings and tributes to Carpenter titled "In Memoriam— Rue Winterbotham Carpenter, President," are preserved at NL, Chicago. Three exhibition catalogues published by the Arts Club of Chicago contain useful histories of the club's early years under Carpenter's leadership: *Drawings 1916/1966: An Exhibition on the Occasion of the Fiftieth Anniversary of The Arts Club of Chicago* (1966); *The Arts Club of Chicago: Seventieth Anniversary Exhibition* (1986), with an informative essay by James M. Wells, "Portrait of an Era: Rue Winterbotham Carpenter and the Arts Club of Chicago 1916–1931"; and *The Arts Club of Chicago: Seventy-Fifth Anniversary Exhibition 1916–1991* (1992). See also Sophia Shaw, ed., *The Arts Club of Chicago: The Collection 1916–1996* (1997). For the patronage of the Winterbotham family, Lyn Delli Quadri's "A Living Tradition: The Winterbothams and Their Legacy," in the Art Institute's *Joseph Winterbotham Collection: A Living Tradition* (1986), is an excellent reference. Carpenter is briefly acknowledged in an important volume establishing a context for her efforts to bring modern art to the city: Sue Ann Prince, ed., *The Old Guard and the Avant-Garde: Modernism in Chicago, 1910–1940* (1990).

SUE TAYLOR

CARSE, MATILDA BRADLEY
November 19, 1835–June 3, 1917
TEMPERANCE ADVOCATE, BUSINESSWOMAN, SOCIAL REFORMER

Matilda Bradley Carse, as president of one of the most active Woman's Christian Temperance Unions in the nation, established and supported a multitude of social welfare programs. Matilda Bradley was born of Scotch-Irish parentage in Saintfield, Ireland, near Belfast. Her father, John Bradley, was a linen merchant, and her mother, Catherine (Cleland) Bradley, reared at least three children. Matilda Bradley emigrated to the United States in 1858 and resided on the West Side of Chicago. There, on October 8, 1861, Bradley married Thomas Carse, a successful railroad manager. During the next several years the Carses had three sons, David Bradley, John Bradley, and Thomas Alexander.

Thomas Carse contracted tuberculosis, and in 1869 the family moved to France, where they hoped to find a more beneficial climate for his illness. Nevertheless, he died in June 1870. Now a thirty-four-year-old widow with enough of an inheritance to sustain herself and her children, Matilda Carse returned to Chicago with her three young sons, all of whom were under the age of seven. She joined the Union Park Congregational Church, which was located on the city's West Side, on January 1, 1871, and began actively participating in benevolent enterprises.

Carse focused on temperance reform in 1874 when a drunken cart driver ran over and killed her youngest son, Thomas. That year Carse joined the Chicago Central Woman's Christian Temperance Union (WCTU) and served on its executive and finance committees. In that capacity she raised money to provide a salary for FRANCES E. WILLARD, the president of the Chicago WCTU and future president of the National WCTU (NWCTU). Carse, already committed to woman suffrage, maintained a lifelong friendship with Willard, who once characterized Carse as very persistent, "a woman of remarkable financial ability, . . . a favorite in society" (*Minutes NWCTU*, 1893, 100), possessing a dominant will. Carse succeeded Willard as president of the Chicago Central WCTU in 1878. The handsome, energetic woman, of sturdy stature and with strong features and a generous mouth, remained in that office thirty-five years, until 1913. During the following four years she was the honorary president of the Chicago Central WCTU.

During Carse's presidency the Chicago Central WCTU expanded its temperance agenda to encompass an ever widening circle of social services. Carse, who reveled in the "building up of tangible things" (*Minutes NWCTU*, 1887, cclxxi), was instrumental in establishing and supporting two of the first day nurseries in the city for the children of working mothers, a mission for "wayward" girls, Sunday and industrial schools, two medical dispensaries, and a low-cost lodging house and restaurant. She worked with other organizations to obtain matrons for female inmates placed in Chicago police stations.

In May 1882, in an effort to provide shelter for prostitutes and alcoholic women, Carse helped to open the Rehoboth, a refuge and recovery home, at a mission in an African American neighborhood on Chicago's Near South Side. The facility accommodated approximately thirty-five residents and was addi-

FIG. 18. *Woman's Christian Temperance Union (WCTU) Temple Building, located at the corner of LaSalle and Monroe Streets, Chicago; its successful completion owed much to the efforts of Matilda Bradley Carse*

tionally used as a daytime kindergarten classroom and an evening gospel temperance meeting room. Chicago Central WCTU members read Bible passages and led services at gospel temperance meetings and encouraged intemperate men and women to sign pledges to stop drinking alcohol and to help eliminate trade in liquor.

The Chicago Central WCTU hired Carrie Moffatt to be resident supervisor at the Rehoboth refuge. The WCTU intended the facility to be "self-supporting" (*Signal*, July 13, 1882, 4) and planned to require "the inmates to earn their own living by laundry-work, needle-work, and such other woman's work" (p. 4). In May 1883, the Rehoboth lodging was discontinued by the Central Union because of expense.

Carse and the Central Union relocated its Near South Side mission to nearby South Clark Street, Chicago's vice district, and opened the Bethesda Mission on November 13, 1883. In this one-room mission the Chicago Central WCTU maintained a free kindergarten, a medical dispensary, and Sunday and industrial school classes. There were regular gospel temperance meetings and a children's temperance group named "Band of Hope." During the winter months the mission served as a daytime shelter as well.

The goals of most of the Bethesda programs were practical

assistance and instruction. According to Mary Bannister Willard, Frances Willard's sister-in-law, the Chicago Central WCTU hoped to teach the neighborhood women how to make their homes "neat, clean, and attractive; how to cut out and make garments, and how to prepare their scanty supplies so as to furnish the greatest amount of nourishment, and in the most palatable manner" ("Minutes," Chicago Central WCTU, 1883, 26–27). Likewise, in the kindergarten the teachers spoke "a great deal about keeping the faces and hands clean" (pp. 26–27). The medical dispensary offered free medicine as well as medical advice and services along with a gospel message. As one worker explained, "Ours was designed through the body to reach the soul—to be a three-fold mission, healing the body, reclaiming the drunkard, and saving the soul" ("Minutes," Chicago Central WCTU, 1883, 2).

Carse's establishment of nurseries' and mothers' meetings for poor and immigrant women was consistent with the NWCTU's goal of preventing the formation of bad habits and protecting children from harmful influences. These two programs allowed WCTU members to inculcate middle-class child-rearing attitudes and methods in the children of the poor and immigrant working classes. WCTU nurseries provided day care for the babies of low-income, working mothers, while mothers' meetings disseminated information on prenatal, infant, and child care. During 1884 and 1885 the Central Union WCTU opened two of the first day nurseries in Chicago, the Bethesda Nursery and the Talcott Nursery, both near the downtown area. According to the women reformers of the WCTU, prior to the establishment of nurseries, young children were often left at home alone or with a "drunken and worthless husband and father" ("Twelfth Annual Meeting of the Central Union of the W.C.T.U.," newspaper clipping, n.d., Frances Willard scrapbook 29, Willard Memorial Library). The Talcott also housed a free kindergarten and medical dispensary. By 1892 the Talcott facility also provided nearly fourteen thousand free meals for the district's poor. In 1894, the Chicago Central WCTU added an industrial school to the Talcott facility and, by 1896, converted it into an overnight shelter for women and children.

In 1886, Carse launched two additional ventures, a home for "wayward" women and a men's lodging house. The Anchorage Mission for women was located, according to Carse, on a "street then noted for its unsavory condition, the resorts of vile men and lewd women" (quoted in Bliss, *A Glimpse of Shadowed Lives in a Great City*, 63). Prior to its opening, Chicago Central WCTU members canvassed the neighborhood and passed out cards signed by Matilda Carse and corresponding secretary Helen Hood that read: "Christian Meetings. . . . Everything Free, for Women Only" (*A Glimpse of Shadowed Lives*, 63). All women were invited to visit the Anchorage to "read, to rest, to drink a cup of coffee, to counsel with friends when in trouble" (p. 63). After additional rooms for lodging were acquired, the Anchorage provided a temporary home for young women "in trouble for any cause" (*Annual Report of the State of Illinois WCTU*, 1892, 79). Residents were provided "plain nutritious food" and "comfortable and healthful apartments for sleeping, additional clothing when needed, . . . real home life" (*A Glimpse of Shadowed Lives*, 60), and religious counseling. Matilda Carse intended that the Anchorage be a refuge where young women could find "Christian sympathy and help" (*Annual Report of the State of Illinois WCTU*, 1888, 119). It was a place where "wayward and fallen girls . . . are given a home and a chance to reform and begin life over again" (*Annual Report of the State of Illinois WCTU*, 1896, 108).

In July 1886, Carse established the Bethesda Inn, a low-cost lodge and restaurant for men, which offered beds and baths for ten to fifteen cents. Wealthy meat packer Philip Armour and Evangelical philanthropist NETTIE FOWLER McCORMICK, the wife of Cyrus H. McCormick, the reaper king, loaned Carse fifteen hundred dollars to establish the inn, which consisted of 256 beds, 5 bathrooms, and reading rooms stocked with newspapers and games. The inn accommodated more than fifty thousand men annually until it closed in 1892, most likely because of financial pressures.

The social welfare agencies run by the WCTU cost approximately ten to fifteen thousand dollars annually. Carse personally raised a substantial portion of that amount through subscriptions and donations. Her successful fund-raising for Chicago Central WCTU projects propelled her toward larger efforts on behalf of the NWCTU. In 1880 she founded the Woman's Temperance Publishing Association (WTPA), an exclusively female-owned stock company. Carse served as its president for eighteen years. The WTPA published temperance and reform literature and periodicals, including the *Union Signal*, the NWCTU's weekly newspaper. By 1890 the enterprise employed more than one hundred women, published more than 125 million commercial and temperance pieces annually, and posted an impressive 7 percent dividend to its stockholders.

Matilda Carse created the Woman's Temperance Building Association (WTBA) in 1887 in order to underwrite the construction of a projected twelve-story office building in downtown Chicago, the Woman's Temple. The building would provide office and meeting space for the Chicago and NWCTU as well as rental income that would be used to retire the bonds issued to pay for the construction. Eventually the rentals would generate income for the NWCTU. Carse leased a lot on the corner of LaSalle and Monroe streets from Marshall Field, the department store magnate. She hired Chicago architect John W. Root, of Burnham and Root, to design the building, a French Gothic structure of red granite and terra cotta.

The WTBA funded the construction through the sale of stocks and bonds to local capitalists, including Philip Armour, William Deering, and Marshall Field. Though the WTBA was financially a separate entity from the NWCTU, emotionally the project was deeply ingrained in the minds and hearts of the membership. Countless individual members and local unions pledged money toward the construction and took pride in the finished product. The temple building symbolized women's accomplishments and the WCTU's prominence among women's organizations.

What should have been a spectacular success for Carse and the NWCTU turned into a debacle as a result of the financial panic and subsequent national economic depression that began in 1893. The ensuing cancellation of leases and lack of rental income forced the WTBA to appeal to the WCTU membership for cash. The financial pressures, coupled with internal

NWCTU power disputes, intensified and solidified opposition to the WCTU temple. Throughout the controversy Frances Willard supported Carse and the temple project. However, immediately following Willard's death in 1898, the NWCTU voted to disaffiliate from the venture. That act barred Carse from soliciting contributions from the membership through WCTU vehicles such as the *Union Signal* newspaper. Nevertheless, for more than a decade, Carse continued to head the temple's board of managers and to raise money in an unsuccessful attempt to secure ownership of the capital stock of the temple.

Besides WCTU activities, Carse was connected with a number of other reform agencies. In 1886, she joined the Chicago Woman's Club, serving on its Equal Suffrage Committee. Carse also served on the boards of several of Chicago's free kindergartens, and in 1889, she became the first woman to be appointed to the Cook County School Board. Carse organized the aid society for the Chicago Foundling's Home and directed its procurement of hundreds of thousands of dollars. She was a member of the Board of Lady Managers of the World's Columbian Exposition of 1893 and founder of the Woman's Dormitory Association of the Exposition, an organization that secured lodging for working women who attended the exposition. By 1911 Carse was a member of the Chicago Political Equality League, the group that linked woman suffrage to a larger agenda of social reform and was the offshoot of the Chicago Woman's Club's suffrage activities.

Matilda Carse retired in 1913. She spent the last year of her life with her son David in Park Hill, New York. She died at age eighty-two of heart disease. Her remains were returned to Chicago and interred at Rosehill Cemetery.

Personal tragedy propelled Matilda Carse into a career of temperance reform. At the helm of the Chicago Central WCTU, Carse realized her tremendous organizational and leadership abilities. She inspired and mobilized the diverse membership and skillfully tapped the financial resources of the city's elite in order to support a plethora of social programs to protect and assist women and children.

Sources. Woman's Christian Temperance Union (WCTU) records provide the most comprehensive and detailed account of Matilda Carse's temperance career. Frances E. Willard materials at the Frances E. Willard Memorial Library, National WCTU Headquarters, Evanston, Illinois, include Willard scrapbooks and correspondence concerning Carse's activities with the WCTU temple. The Samuel Willard Papers and the Illinois Woman's Christian Temperance Union Records, Illinois State Historical Library, Springfield, Illinois, have material on Carse. Papers of the Union Park Congregational Church, at CHS, include a few biographical details about Carse's mother. The papers of the Chicago Woman's Club, CHS, include material about Carse's membership. The CHS also has *History of the Home Protection Petition and Legislation in Pursuance Thereof* (n.d.) authored by the WCTU. "Minutes" for the Chicago Central WCTU are published in *Annual Report of the Central Woman's Christian Temperance Union of Chicago, Illinois*; annual reports for various years between 1874 and 1887 are at the CHS. Information for various years can be found in the *Annual Report of the State of Illinois WCTU*, located at the Illinois WCTU headquarters in Springfield, Illinois. *Minutes of the National Woman's Christian Temperance Union* are available on microfilm or bound at the Frances E. Willard Memorial Library, Evanston, Illinois, and have information on Carse's involvement with the publishing company and the

WCTU temple project. WCTU periodicals provide additional, albeit scattered, information on Carse. The Willard Library holds copies of the early Illinois WCTU newspaper, the *Signal*, and the National WCTU newspaper, the *Union Signal*, both of which contain various references to Carse and Chicago Central WCTU activities. During the early twentieth century the Illinois WCTU published a monthly newspaper called the *Illinois Watch-Tower.* It frequently reported on the activities of the Chicago Central WCTU. The Illinois State Historical Library, Springfield, Illinois, has a partial collection of this periodical. Contemporary works with information about Carse and the WCTU include Frances E. Willard, *Glimpses of Fifty Years: The Autobiography of an American Woman* (1889), N. S. Bliss, *A Glimpse of Shadowed Lives in a Great City* (1913). Biographies of Carse are in Frances E. Willard and Mary A. Livermore, eds., *A Woman of the Century: Fourteen Hundred–Seventy Biographical Sketches Accompanied by Portraits of Leading American Women in All Walks of Life*, 2 vols. (1893), and *NAW* (1971). Ruth Bordin, *Woman and Temperance: The Quest for Power and Liberty, 1873–1900* (1981), and Mark Edward Lender, *Dictionary of American Temperance Biography: From Temperance Reform to Alcohol Research, the 1600s to the 1980s* (1984), provide background. For discussion of temple history, see Rachel E. Bohlman, "Our 'House Beautiful': The Woman's Temple and the WCTU Effort to Establish Place and Identity in Downtown Chicago, 1887–1898," *Journal of Women's History*, Summer 1999.

NANCY WADDELL DAFFNER

CARTER, VIVIAN
March 25, 1921–June 12, 1989
DISK JOCKEY, RECORD STORE OWNER, RECORD COMPANY
FOUNDER

Vivian Carter made her name as a pioneering radio disk jockey in Chicago and in Gary, Indiana, and cofounded, in 1953, Vee-Jay Records, "the country's largest black-owned record company" (Pruter, *Doowop*, 103) prior to the legendary Motown Records. She was born in Tunica, Mississippi. Her parents, Ludie and Minnie Carter, moved to the thriving, yet segregated, steel town of Gary, Indiana, in 1924, where Vivian attended school until her graduation from the prestigious all-black Roosevelt High School in 1939. An active student, she participated in school plays, oratorical contests, and sports. She next entered Cortez Peters Business College in Chicago, then went to work for the Quartermaster General's Office in Washington, D.C. She returned to Chicago in 1942 until her transfer to the Signal Corps. She left the Signal Corps to become a waitress at Club DeLisa, a thriving Chicago South Side night spot.

Her start in show business came in 1947, when she won a talent contest sponsored by Chicago disk jockey (deejay) Al Benson of radio station WGES. As a result, she became the city's first black female disk jockey, hosting a fifteen-minute program. Soon discontented, she returned to Club DeLisa for another stint as a waitress until returning to Gary in 1948. She quickly landed an on-air job at WJOB in Hammond, Indiana; she moved to WGRY in Gary in 1952 and, finally, to neighboring WWCA in 1953. Broadcast in Carter's "'booming, rapid fire, throaty' deejay delivery" (Henry Farag quoted in Kostanczuk, "Label Matriarch"), her popular show *Livin' with Vivian* became a staple for local black and white teen music fans. Not content to remain in the cramped radio studio playing records, she broadcast every Thursday night from various city night spots, and from one of them, Upshaw's Famous Door, on Saturday afternoons. She was on the air four hours a day, six days every

FIG. 19. *Vivian Carter, pioneering radio disk jockey in Chicago and Gary, Indiana; cofounder in 1953 of Vee-Jay Records, a black-owned record company.*

week. Meanwhile, she had met James Bracken in Chicago in 1944, and they opened Vivian's Record Shop in 1948 in Gary's Midtown neighborhood (with a branch later in Chicago). The shop gave her increasing access to the latest records, usually obtained from Chicago distributors, as well as upcoming local rhythm and blues performers. Carter and Bracken married in late 1953.

Not content just to sell or play records, in 1953 Vivian Carter and James Bracken produced one of their first singles on their recently christened Vee-Jay Records label, the Spaniels' recording of "Baby, It's You," which reached the Top Ten of the national rhythm and blues (R&B) charts. The Spaniels' "Goodnite, Sweetheart, Goodnite," called the ultimate '50s doo-wop ballad, quickly reached pop stardom when released in March 1954. (Sung by the McGuire Sisters, it became a million record seller.) The Spaniels rehearsed in Carter's mother's garage, now converted to a studio, and recorded at Universal Studios in Chicago. Carter became the group's legal guardian and manager. A group of five Gary youngsters just out of high school, led by James "Pookie" Hudson, the Spaniels wrote as well as sang their own songs.

Best known for a string of R&B recordings (soon termed Rock 'n' Roll), Vee-Jay released a single by Jimmy Reed, an earthy bluesman, simultaneously with the original Spaniels' record, indicating an increasingly eclectic approach to black popular music. Vee-Jay also marketed white artists, unusual for black record companies. With such early success, they decided to move to Chicago's South Side in 1954, first to a converted garage, and finally to their own plush office building on South Michigan Avenue. The company originally included Carter's brother Calvin and soon added Ewart Abner as chief administrator. Following the Spaniels, Vee-Jay signed the El Dorados, the Dells, the Kool Gents, and numerous other regional black doo-wop groups. Quickly branching out, they added bluesman John Lee Hooker and a proliferating number of gospel acts, including the Staple Singers, Swan Silvertones, Harmonizing Four, and Highway QCs. By the late 1950s they had also added a jazz line, including Wynton Kelly, Wayne Shorter, Eddie Harris, and Lee Morgan.

As Vee-Jay Records gained fame and fortune, with both singles and albums, Vivian Carter was increasingly pushed to the sidelines, although she managed to lead the high life as long as possible. The big time came with Gladys Knight and the Pips, Dee Clark, Gene Chandler's 1962 hit "Duke of Earl," Jerry Butler, Betty Everett, the Four Seasons, even briefly the Beatles before they became an American sensation in 1964 and were released by Capitol Records. Reaching for the stars, the company briefly moved its headquarters to Los Angeles in early 1964 and had sales of fifteen million dollars; but in late 1965 the head office was returned to Chicago. Bankruptcy came a few months later, and in 1967 the company's property, including the record shop, was auctioned to pay its debts. Off the record, "friends and former business associates" explained the bankruptcy by "Carter's affinity for extravagance, her generosity, lack of business acumen and the enemies she made with what some called a ruthless business style" (Barry Saunders). After the company folded, Carter returned to WWCA as a late-night gospel deejay, ran unsuccessfully for Gary city clerk in 1967, and served as a clerk and supervisor in the Calumet Township Trustee's office from 1976 to 1982, when her health began to fail. She "suffered a stroke and underwent multiple amputations . . . to stem the spread of diabetes" (*Post-Tribune*, June 14, 1989) before her death in 1989 in Wildwood Manor Nursing Home. (James Bracken had died in 1972.) Services were held at First African Methodist Episcopal (AME) Church in Gary.

Vee-Jay is considered the first successful black-owned record company in the United States, predating Motown by a few years. Vee-Jay's "true figurehead" (Kostanczuk, "Vee Jay") was seen to be cofounder Vivian Carter. She played a singular part in its rather brief history, particularly during the early years, in developing, for example, the Spaniels and El Dorados. A vital and dynamic presence, always seemingly optimistic, Carter nonetheless felt used and pushed aside by the various men in her life, particularly by her husband James Bracken, brother Calvin, Ewart Abner, and the others who increasingly made Vee-Jay's corporate decisions. Moreover, James "Pookie" Hudson blamed her for depriving the Spaniels of much of their royalties, a grievance that long simmered. She shrewdly promoted Vee-Jay records on her radio show and sold them from her shop, creating an expanding local market. Never a mother, she threw herself into her professional life, a lone black woman in the heady atmosphere of the highly competitive music industry.

Sources. There is little written about Vivian Carter aside from various histories of Vee-Jay Records, often with erroneous dates and other information. Her autobiography, written with the assistance of Yjean [*sic*] Chambers, yet unpublished, will supply much information and insight into her public and private life. A brief obituary appeared in the Gary *Post-Tribune*, June 14, 1989, and *Chicago Sun-Times*, June 15, 1989. Other articles appeared in the *Post-Tribune*, including Barry Saunders, "'Livin with Vivian' Just the Beginning"), May 14, 1989, and Bob Kostanczuk, "Vee Jay: Record Label's Fall Was as Meteoric as Its Rise" and "Label Matriarch Turned to God after Collapse," November 17, 1991. Histories with discussions of Vee-Jay, with passing reference to Vivian Carter, include Arnold Shaw, *Honkers and Shouters: The Golden Years of Rhythm & Blues* (1978); Robert Pruter, *Chicago Soul* (1991); Robert Pruter, *Doowop: The Chicago Scene* (1996); and Richard Carter, *Goodnight Sweetheart, Goodnight: The Story of the Spaniels* (1994). Mike Callahan published an extensive history of Vee-Jay in *Goldmine*, May 1981; portions were republished in the booklet with the three-CD boxed set *Vee-Jay: Celebrating 40 Years of Classic Hits, 1953–1993* (Vee-Jay Limited Partnership).

RONALD D. COHEN

CASSETTARI, ROSA
February 2, 1866/1867–1943
STORYTELLER, CLEANING WOMAN

ETS, MARIE HALL RODIG
December 16, 1893–January 17, 1984
SOCIAL WORKER, WRITER AND ILLUSTRATOR OF
CHILDREN'S BOOKS

Rosa Cassettari, storyteller and cleaning woman, and Marie Hall Rodig Ets, social worker and children's story writer, met in 1918 at the Chicago Commons, a neighborhood settlement house established in the late nineteenth century to encourage interaction between immigrants and Americans. The twenty-five-year-old, white, well-educated, middle-class, Protestant Commons worker Marie Hall Rodig (later Marie Hall Ets) had just left a career in interior design after the untimely death of her first husband, Milton Rodig. Despite differences in ethnicity, class, education, and age, the two women were drawn together by experiences of social injustice and by their belief in the possibility of bridging differences through storytelling. The result of their friendship and collaboration, *Rosa, the Life of an Italian Immigrant*, was published in 1970.

Rosa Cassettari (Rosa Cavalleri in *Rosa*) was born in Milan's foundling hospital. Initially, the infant was cared for by a hospital nurse whose mother-in-law became so enamored with the child that she convinced her daughter-in-law to bring Rosa home. When the nurse became too busy with her own baby, her mother arranged for a peasant couple who lived in Bugiarno (Cuggiono in *Rosa*), a small village outside Milan, to become Rosa's foster parents. At age four, in addition to participating in Bugiarno's main livelihood, the production of silk, Rosa recited Latin prayers for the older villagers. Through listening to the stories of her foster mother and other villagers, she developed a talent for storytelling and distinguished herself with a growing repertory of tales. When Rosa was seven, her real mother, an Italian actress and singer (whose identity Rosa withheld even from Ets), returned to the foundling hospital to retrieve her daughter. To join her mother meant escaping peasant life, plus an opportunity to become a public entertainer. It also meant using her storytelling talent to earn money rather than to participate in the communal and religious culture of her adopted community. Her pious foster mother had instilled piety and religious devotional values in Rosa. Despite a court ruling in her favor, Rosa's biological mother finally agreed to leave her daughter in Bugiarno with the couple Rosa considered her real parents.

Rosa's foster parents were fortunate to own a small restaurant and a piece of land in the village, yet high taxes necessitated their sending Rosa to work in exchange for room and board. From the age of six to nine Rosa worked at local silk mills. At ten she went to a convent in Cannolio (Cannobio in *Rosa*) for three years where, in addition to working silk, she daily received two hours of instruction in mathematics, geography, and Latin. Despite punishment from nuns who did not think some of her stories appropriate, Rosa told folk tales and tales she made up to amuse the other girls. At fourteen she returned to Bugiarno, and soon after, married an older but seemingly financially stable man chosen by her foster mother. Around 1882, Rosa had her first child. In 1884, she immigrated to the United States to join her husband, who had already left Italy to work in an "iron mine in Missouri" (*Rosa*, 166).

Although Rosa and her husband had two more children together, repeated bouts of verbal and physical abuse convinced Rosa to leave him and take the children. With the help of Louis Cassettari, another Italian immigrant, she moved to Chicago in 1887 and obtained a divorce. She found piecework she could do at home while watching her children. Eventually she married Louis Cassettari. The Cassettari family was forced to move from its apartment in an Italian immigrant neighborhood on Chicago's Near North Side when the Reverend Graham Taylor founded the Chicago Commons Settlement in 1894. As his daughter LEA DEMAREST TAYLOR later recalled, "The building had a big front porch and was set back from the street. The rear section was a wooden, two-story building with a long hall and rooms on either side of the second floor, where twelve Italian families were living" (*Lea Demarest Taylor*, 7). Rosa Cassettari first interacted with the Commons not to participate in its activities or programs but to admonish the new residents for leasing the house in which her family had an apartment and which they were forced to leave. Turned away from vacancies because she was Italian, Cassettari had no choice but to rent a tiny basement that frequently flooded, endangering her small children. The Commons responded to her complaint by helping her acquire better accommodations and offering her part-time work as a cleaning woman.

Marie Hall, the daughter of Walter Augustus and Mathilde (Carhart) Hall, was born in North Greenfield, Wisconsin, "in a town that isn't there any more—it got lost in the city of Milwaukee" (Ets, autobiographical sketch, 115). She attended Lawrence College in Appleton, Wisconsin, for a year, then left in protest when a sorority denied admission to a poor girl. Against her parents' wishes, she became a student in the New York School of Fine and Applied Arts (now the Parsons School of Design) and majored in decorating and interior architecture. She finished the two-year degree in one year and, in 1917, went to Los Angeles, California, to sketch for interior designers at D.N. & E. Waters & Company. Hall followed one of the Wa-

ters's designers to San Francisco, California, and continued designing. As a volunteer teacher of English to immigrants in San Francisco's Little Italy, Hall met Milton Rodig. They married on November 30, 1917. Two months later her husband died suddenly of pneumonia.

On the advice of friends, Marie Rodig left art and began a career in social work. She moved to the Chicago area, volunteering for the U.S. Navy (she was stationed in Waukegan, Illinois), and for United Charities in Chicago. In 1919 she enrolled at the Chicago School of Civics and Philanthropy (after 1921 the University of Chicago's School of Social Service Administration). For the service component of her degree, Rodig chose Chicago Commons settlement house rather than the well-known Hull-House, founded by JANE ADDAMS, because it was "smaller and had a more familylike atmosphere" (*Rosa*, 3). The Commons provided an intimate space in which immigrants interacted with Americans. Soon after Rodig's arrival, she met Italian immigrant Rosa Cassettari. In addition to supervising toy making and street games for children, for the next thirteen years Rodig listened to Rosa Cassettari's tales and transcribed the oral stories about her life in Italy and America.

Marie Rodig married Harold Norris Ets in 1930 and moved to New York City. She took with her a draft of Rosa Cassettari's life story based on the woman's anecdotes. Ets attempted to publish the manuscript in 1931, but publishers did not share her enthusiasm for the collaborative effort the work represented. When chronic illness (due to the misapplication of vaccine shots in 1921) made her career in social work impossible, Marie Ets began writing and illustrating children's books. Ets would return to Rosa Cassettari's story and the unpublished manuscript in the late 1960s.

Her first children's book, *Mister Penny* (1935), is based on a man from Ets's "own childhood who had a whole family of animals. Grownups warned the children not to go near this old man but [Ets's] sympathies were all with him" (Arndt, 10). Since the economic crisis of the 1930s made color illustrations unfeasible, Ets invented a modified form of the Java batik dying method to create vivid black and white illustrations. For *Mister Penny*, "droll, loose-limbed, a little ragged at the edges, the illustrations set the tone. As pictures they have the merit—and the appeal to children—of being at once filled to the frame, uncluttered and distinct" (Bader, 167). Ets is celebrated for creating books with "deceptively simple" (Higgins, 326) text and illustrations.

Ets chose subjects seldom portrayed in children's books. In *The Story of a Baby* (1939), she based her detailed illustrations of an embryo's development up to birth on the human embryos exhibited at the 1933 Century of Progress Exposition held in Chicago. Her concern for accuracy in representation made her open to collaboration. For *My Dog Rinty* (1946), Ets consulted with writer Ellen Tarry about family life in Harlem and used the work of Alexander and Alexandra Alland, professional photographers. Ets spent two summers in Mexico City to draw urban children from life for *Nine Days to Christmas* (1960) and collaboratively wrote the narrative with Aurora Labastida, children's librarian at the Benjamin Franklin Library in Mexico City. In 1960 Ets received her greatest recognition, the Caldecott Medal for *Nine Days to Christmas*.

That same year Ets had the opportunity to fulfill the promise made to Cassettari to publish her life story. While conducting research for his dissertation on Chicago's Italian immigrants, Rudolph J. Vecoli discovered the original manuscript Ets had left at the Chicago Commons. Aware of the dearth of documentation of Italian immigrant women, Vecoli contacted Ets and convinced her to revise and submit her manuscript to the University of Minnesota Press. In 1970 the life story was published as an autobiography entitled *Rosa, the Life of an Italian Immigrant*, with an introduction by Ets.

Rosa traces the life of Rosa "Cavalleri" from birth, when she was left by her mother at Milan's foundling hospital in the 1860s, to her retirement as a cleaning woman at Chicago Commons in the 1930s. Writing Cassettari's life story ultimately involved more than word for word transcription. Ets undertook extensive research to verify every reference made by Cassettari, from the name of her village to the circumstances of her divorce. The earliest draft of Cassettari's life story (which Ets recorded in dialect) includes comments by Cassettari that represent the collaborative nature of the narrative and attest to the friendship between the two women: "Don't you go away, Miss Mary! You the only friend I got left in Neighbor House now" (typescript drafts, 413). The comments also reflect the agreement between the two women that any profit from the collaboration would fund a trip they would take to Italy. "Oh, 'is woanderful [*sic*], those churches! We go and see that too, if we go in Italia, no?" (typescript drafts, 44). Ets visited Rosa Cassettari regularly until Cassettari's death in 1943. Unfortunately, they never made the trip to Italy.

Although the University of Minnesota Press editor, John Ervin Jr., was interested in the manuscript, he would not agree to Ets's wish to share credit for its creation with Cassettari. Ets conceded omission from the final version of the "autobiography" all reference to her informal publication agreement with Cassettari that they were "coauthors," but she persisted in her desire to donate to the Chicago Commons Association the equivalent of royalties that Cassettari would have received. Ervin refused Ets's request and demanded instead that she accept an indemnification clause to warrant against libel and invasion of privacy. To do so meant Ets would have to claim sole proprietorship of Cassettari's life story. When she refused, Ervin replied that without her acceptance of his conditions, he had to leave the book project. On April 7, 1969, Ets finally relented, and Ervin approved publication.

Despite her concessions, Ets wanted to show in the book that she and Rosa were good friends. She changed the copy for the book jacket from "Marie Hall Ets, a social worker who knew Rosa Cavalleri" to "Marie Hall Ets, a former social worker and friend of Rosa Cavalleri" (Ets to Salisbury, February 28, 1970). In her final piece of correspondence with the press in July 1972, Ets wrote of her hope that the book would be widely read. Ets thought highly of Rosa Cassettari and wanted other people to love her as she did.

Ets published twenty-one children's books from 1935 to 1974 and received three major awards besides the Caldecott Medal in 1960. The New York *Herald Tribune* gave her the Children's Spring Book Festival Award for *Oley, the Sea Monster* (1947) and *Gilberto and the Wind* (1963). She received the Hans Christian Andersen International Award in 1956 for *Play*

with Me (1955), Ets's first color picturebook about a little girl who discovers that if she stays still, the animals in the forest will move closer to her. Ets's last recognition for her contribution to books for children was the University of Minnesota's Kerlan Award in 1975. After suffering years of chronic illness, she died at age ninety in Inverness, Florida.

Marie Hall Ets initially found Rosa Cassettari's stories worthwhile; she retained a lifelong commitment to bringing these tales, filled with "the fears and superstitions and beliefs of the people of her village" (introduction, *Rosa*, 7), to a wide readership and hoped to do so without obliterating the authorship of the immigrant woman whose stories had intrigued her during the twelve years the two had been friends at Chicago Commons. Historian Rudolph J. Vecoli concludes that "in *Rosa* we have an authentic expression of the immigrant experience. Its value is enhanced by the fact that the story is told by a woman. . . . the charm of Rosa's story derives from the candor with which it is told" (foreword, *Rosa*, vi). This realism came from the collaboration of two women—Rosa Cassettari and Marie Hall Ets.

Sources. Marie Hall Ets's papers, research notes, and the early typescript drafts of Rosa's life story are at the Immigration History Research Center, Univ. of Minnesota. The proof sheets for *Rosa, the Life of an Italian Immigrant* (1970), the editor's notes to the author, and drafts of the introduction are at the Univ. Archives, Univ. of Minnesota. The Univ. of Minnesota Press has files on the editorial process and marketing of *Rosa*; these include correspondence between the editor and Ets and others related to the project. See the Kerlan Collection at the Wilson Library of the Univ. of Minnesota for an autobiographical sketch written by Ets on which her Viking editor, May Massee, based "Marie Hall Ets: Biographical Note," in *Newbery and Caldecott Medal Books, 1956–1965* (1965). Preceding the note is Ets's "Caldecott Award Acceptance" speech. In addition, the collection has drafts of her children's stories, notes related to them, and original illustrations. For additional information on Ets, see James E. Higgins, "Ets, Marie Hall," *Twentieth-Century Children Writers* (1995); Jessie Ash Arndt, "Illustrator Sees through Child Eyes," *Christian Science Monitor*, May 23, 1960; Ruth R. Irvine, "Marie Hall Ets—Her Picture Storybooks," *Elementary English*, May 1956; Marguerite Schumann, "She Writes Books: For Young Eyes Only," *Sunday Post-Crescent*, January 8, 1967; Barbara Bader, *American Picturebooks from Noah's Ark to the Beast Within* (1976). Karen Nelson Hoyle's entry, "Marie Hall Ets," in the *Dictionary of Literary Biography*, vol. 22, ed. John Cech (1983), contains a complete list of Ets's publications. For background information about the Chicago Commons settlement, see *Lea Demarest Taylor: Her Life and Work between 1883 and 1968* (1968), a published transcription of an autobiographical tape recording of Taylor; the transcript was done by the Training Center of the National Federation of Settlements, Chicago, under the direction of Arthur Hillman. Univ. Library, UIC, has a copy.

BARBARA L. CICCARELLI

CATHERWOOD, MARY HARTWELL
December 16, 1847–December 26, 1902
NOVELIST, SHORT STORY WRITER, POET

Mary Hartwell Catherwood earned an important place in American literary history as the first nationally recognized woman fiction writer born and educated in the Midwest. A lifelong resident of the region who researched and wrote much of her fiction in Chicago, Catherwood published twenty books and scores of short stories. Her work was widely read and critically acclaimed for effectively combining autobiographical reflection and historical data in new fictional forms.

Born in the village of Luray, Licking County, Ohio, the eldest child of Dr. Marcus and Pheba (Thompson) Hartwell, Mary Hartwell moved with her family to Milford, Iroquois County, Illinois, in 1856. Within the year both parents were dead. Doctor Hartwell succumbed to pneumonia and Pheba Hartwell died in childbirth. Hartwell and her younger siblings, Roxana and Marcus, were left penniless and returned to live with their maternal grandparents in Hebron, Ohio, where ten-year-old Mary Hartwell published her first literary work, a poem entitled "Willetta," in the public school newspaper. At thirteen years of age, she earned a teaching certificate, at fourteen began working in a rural school, and by fifteen had already published numerous short poems and local news items in the Newark, Ohio, *North American*. In 1864 her story "The Hospital Nurse" was published in the *North American*, and Hartwell began to write primarily in the popular local color genre.

From 1865 to 1868 Hartwell worked her way through Granville (Ohio) Female College, and in 1869 she and her college roommate, Anna Hoff, accepted teaching positions in Danville, Illinois. During these years, Hartwell primarily wrote children's stories, often using the pen name of "Lewtrah," a variation of her last name. Her works were published in such magazines as *Leslie's*, *Ladies' Repository*, *Golden Hours*, *Lippincott's*, *Wide Awake*, and *Youth's Companion*; in 1871 she won a one hundred dollar prize for a story in *Wood's Household Magazine*. When the 1873 panic forced many children's periodicals out of business, Hartwell decided to write for more mature readers.

Mary Hartwell was busy and successful as a rural school teacher, but she yearned for a full-time literary career. In 1874 she stopped teaching and began work as a free-lance writer, first in Newburgh, New York (1874–75), and later in Cincinnati, Ohio (1875–77). Her earliest novel, *A Woman in Armor* (1875), was serialized in *Hearth and Home*, but she continued to struggle to support herself as a writer, especially during the period 1874 to 1877.

It was in Hoopeston, Illinois, about 115 miles south of Chicago and home to Hartwell's two aunts, that Hartwell met James Steele Catherwood and married him on December 27, 1877. Shortly after their wedding, the couple relocated near Indianapolis, where James started a grain business and Mary found new opportunities to study midwestern life and promote her writing. Marriage brought financial ease, and the author joined literary societies and met several popular American writers. Of special importance was poet James Whitcomb Riley, who became a close friend and began his lifelong support of Catherwood's literary efforts.

Riley had just begun to achieve recognition and invited Catherwood to collaborate with him on a romance called *The Whittleford Letters*, a story of two young writers whose careers and meetings resembled their own. The novel was left unfinished, however, and as Catherwood explained it, "The substance of the fictional romance suddenly became too real for both" (Price, *Indiana Authors and Their Books*, 55).

From 1879 to 1882 Catherwood wrote drama reviews for the *Saturday Review*, an Indianapolis newspaper; she published sketches in *Lippincott's* and the *Atlantic Monthly*; she wrote three book-length serials, two novels, numerous short juveniles, seven short stories, and a large miscellany, and continued to gain recognition as a fiction writer. In Indianapolis, Catherwood also met Benjamin S. Parker, the American consul at Sherbrook, Canada, and as a result of visiting his family and witnessing the St. John's Day celebration, the author secured important data for her first critically acclaimed novel.

The Romance of Dollard (1889) took three years to write and was initially rejected by *Harper's*. Riley then forwarded the manuscript to Richard Watson Gilder, editor for the Century Company. Catherwood was ambitious and impatient, but when she traveled to New York and confronted Gilder in his office, the editor said, "There is just as much chance of your being struck by lighting [*sic*] as there is of the acceptance of your work and publication as you desire it. Why, we have here in our safe enough manuscripts of that nature to last us five years" (Wilson, *Biography*, 61). Catherwood responded fiercely: "I have no manuscripts to lie in your safe for five years. . . . I will remain in New York, Mr. Gilder . . . until you accept or reject that work" (p. 62). After only a few days, Gilder notified the author that "lightning had struck" and advised her to call at his office to collect her check.

In his preface to *The Romance of Dollard*, historian Francis Parkman justifies Catherwood's fascination with the past by arguing, "The realism of our time has its place and function; but an eternal analysis of the familiar and commonplace is cloying after a while, and one turns with relief and refreshment to . . . Mrs. Catherwood's animated story" (p. 3). Catherwood continued her Canadian visits, studied documents, observed landscapes, noted representative characters, and began to achieve fame as a writer of historical romances.

From 1882 to 1899 the Catherwoods divided their time between Chicago and Hoopeston, where their daughter Hazel was born in 1884. Her first child, a son, had died in infancy. Catherwood was an active worker in Hoopeston's Universalist Church and Sunday School and in various organizations including the Mary Hartwell Catherwood Club, a literary group that still exists. In 1886 Catherwood helped Riley to organize the Western Association of Writers, a group she worked with throughout her life.

Catherwood's circle of professional friends widened, and she began to spend more extensive periods of time in Chicago, giving regular readings of her work to city and suburban literary societies, including the Chicago Historical Society. She used the city as a place to write in private. In correspondence with her friend Eleanor Ruthrauff, Catherwood wrote, "One week I went into the city, shut myself up at hotel with hired typewriter, and worked literally day and night, finishing an important piece of work" (February 6, 1896, Catherwood Papers). She also became involved in political events in the city. Catherwood mentioned, "We were in Chicago when Mr. [William Jennings] Bryan was nominated, and he gave Hazel one of his badges. He is a relative of our intimate friends. But we are *not* silver democrats" (Letter to Eleanor Ruthrauff, August 31, 1896, Catherwood Papers). Using an assumed name and the admission ticket of a friend, Catherwood attended the 1901 Chicago trial of Leon Czolgosz, the assassin of President McKinley, and later based her short story "The Queen Bee" on this event.

During the summer months Catherwood regularly traveled north by rail from Chicago to seek the cool air of Mackinac Island, Michigan, where she often wrote in an outdoor study. She was usually accompanied by her daughter, and *Mackinac and Other Stories* is dedicated "To my daughter Hazel, the companion of all my travels." In 1891 Catherwood and Hazel toured England, Scotland, France, and Germany; and in 1894 the author, her husband, and her daughter traveled to France, where Catherwood researched the life of Joan of Arc. Her article on this subject was published in the *Century* at the same time that Mark Twain's series on the same topic appeared in *Harper's*. Catherwood eventually published *The Days of Jeanne D'Arc* (1897), writing that the novel was "the outcome . . . of journeys over the Maid's country, following her path from Domremy to Rouen, in voitures, in carts, and on foot; of careful study of the fifteenth century" (quoted in Wilson, 49). Additional research for the novel was done at the Newberry Library in Chicago.

During the 1893 World's Columbian Exposition in Chicago, Catherwood participated prominently in the Congress of Authors, a part of the Literature Congress. George Washington Cable delivered the first address on "The Uses and Methods of Novel Writing," and Catherwood followed with a paper, "The Technic of Fiction, or Form and Condensation in Novel Writing." Although her early work was marked by realistic portrayals of contemporary midwestern life, by 1893 Catherwood was best known for her historical romances and had become chief spokesperson for conservative writers. She argued for the "aristocratic" in literature and was vigorously attacked by Hamlin Garland and other young proponents of realism.

During the 1890s, while James Steele Catherwood worked at the successful real estate development business of Wallace and Catherwood in Hoopeston, Mary Hartwell Catherwood's literary career continued to flourish, and she began to spend more extended periods of time near her Chicago publishers. Her literary activities were regularly interrupted by domestic duties, however, and once she stopped writing for an entire year.

In 1899 Hazel Catherwood enrolled in the Female Seminary at Lake Forest College, and Mary Hartwell Catherwood took a suite at the Beach Hotel in Chicago. In 1900 she moved to the Plaza Building in Lincoln Park and placed her daughter at Kirkland School for Young Ladies. Shortly thereafter, Hazel Catherwood entered the Kenwood Department of the University of Chicago, and Catherwood secured a large and permanent home on the city's West Side, where she resided for the rest of her life. James Catherwood visited his wife on weekends or more often, talked with her about her work, and listened as she read to him from her recent writings.

From 1899 until her death, Catherwood resided primarily in Chicago and produced a voluminous amount of work, including one of her most popular historical romances, *Lazarre*. The novel is based on the story of Eleazar Williams, supposedly the "Lost Dauphin" who escaped from the Paris temple and was raised by the midwestern Mohawk and Oneida tribes. Otis Skinner dramatized the novel and first performed in the title role at the Green Bay, Wisconsin, Opera House on September 8, 1902. *Lazarre* received rave reviews after it was performed at Chicago's Grand Opera House, and following a national tour the production returned to the Chicago stage in December 1902. In the

meantime, Catherwood had begun work on "Tippicanoe," a historical romance based on the beginnings of the New Harmony Colony in Indiana and its founder, Gilbert Dale Owen.

Catherwood's hopes for future literary achievement came to an abrupt end when she died of intestinal cancer at her Chicago home. Following funeral services at St. Paul's Episcopal Church in Kenwood, Catherwood's body traveled by Chicago and Eastern Railway to Hoopeston, where she was eulogized by numerous personal and literary friends. Otis Skinner accompanied the Catherwood family on their journey from Chicago, and James Whitcomb Riley praised the author for her "fine mental endowment," deeming her death "a distinct loss to the fraternity of letters" (quoted in Wilson, 85). Hobart Chatfield-Taylor emphasized Catherwood's "unique place in American literature, because of her inclination toward the historic features regarding the early settlement and exploration of the Middle West and Northwestern portion of America" (quoted in Wilson, 89).

In her own time Catherwood's literary achievement was recognized by contemporaries, including William Dean Howells, Eugene Field, George Cable, and Joseph Kirkland. In 1915 Fred Lewis Pattee reevaluated Catherwood's fiction in *A History of American Literature since 1870*, pointing out her distinction in two important categories. First, Catherwood's early stories of the 1880s detail the manners, customs, speech, and everyday incidents of life in the corn belt, compressing color and form in realistic pictures reminiscent of northeastern writers Sarah Orne Jewett and Mary Wilkins Freeman. Her historical romances of the 1890s provide a poetic representation of historical data and reflect her belief that American readers were "harking back more and more to their past, for a deeper comprehension of their present" (Catherwood, *The Story of Tonty* [1890], 8). Pattee insists that Catherwood's best fiction possesses a "Hardy-like power to catch the spirit of a locality" (Pattee, 260).

Critic Kenny J. Williams notes that the desire of late-nineteenth-century Chicagoans to examine their cultural roots and "codify their definitions of themselves" (*Prairie Voices*, 40) led to the rise of the Chicago novel. Catherwood's contributions in this regard were significant. "As she looked backward toward the seventeenth century and to the days of New France, Mrs. Catherwood discovered that a gracious culture was finally destroyed through greed for money. Does she mean to imply that such a destruction might serve notice on Chicago?" (p. 37). Williams faults Catherwood for concentrating primarily on the usable past and avoiding treatment of negative features; at the same time, she acknowledges that the author believed in honor, the life of the spirit, and the possible "union of Commerce and the Cross" (p. 41). These same beliefs were held by many nineteenth-century women authors and their readers and made Catherwood one of the most widely read writers of her day.

Catherwood's work is rich and complex, moreover, because it reflects the complexities and dualities of American culture. There is a tension between "romantic" structure and "realistic" material, between the author's desire to write a romance and the need to be honest about experience. Catherwood's fiction depicts the concrete realities of daily life, demonstrates continuities between past and present social conditions, and stresses the development of society. Catherwood captures history and local color, but she also unfolds, through dramatization, the complex implications of reality and the difficulties that characterize everyday life. In the end, she is reluctant to let go of romantic idealism. Mary Hartwell Catherwood's achievements in critical realism, regional sketches, and historical romance continue to assure her place as one of Chicago's most important early authors.

Sources. The Mary Hartwell Catherwood Papers are at NL. They include photographs; scrapbooks; travel journals; newspaper articles; notes on historical research; typed and handwritten manuscripts of poetry, short stories, and novels, including the unfinished manuscript of "Tippicanoe"; letters to Seba Green Taylor, Eleanor Ruthrauff, and others; and memorabilia. In addition to those works cited in the text, Catherwood wrote *The Dogberry Bunch* (1879), *Craque-o-Doom* (1881), *Rocky Fork* (1882), *Old Caravan Days* (1884), *The Secret at Roseladies* (1888), *The Lady of Fort St. John* (1891), *Old Kaskaskia* (1893), *The White Islander* (1893), *The Chase of St. Castin and Other Stories* (1894), *The Spirit of an Illinois Town* (1897), *Bony and Ban: The Story of a Printing Venture* (1898), *Heroes of the Middle West: French* (1898), *The Queen of the Swamp and Other Plain Americans* (1899), and *Spanish Peggy* (1899). For discussion of her work, see Fred Lewis Pattee, *A History of American Literature since 1870* (1915); Robert Price, "A Critical Biography of Mary Hartwell Catherwood" (Ph.D. diss., Ohio State Univ., 1943); Kenny J. Williams, *Prairie Voices: A Literary History of Chicago from the Frontier to 1893* (1980); and Milton H. Wilson, *Biography of Mary Hartwell Catherwood* (1904). Useful articles are found in the following reference works: Allen Johnson, ed., *Dictionary of American Biography* (1929); Robert Price, "Mary Hartwell Catherwood," in *Indiana Authors and Their Books 1816–1916*, ed. R. E. Banta (1949); *NCAB*, vol. 9 (1899); *NAW* (1971). See also Robert Price, "Mrs. Catherwood's Early Experiments in Critical Realism," *American Literature*, May 1945; Price, "Mary Hartwell Catherwood: A Bibliography," *Journal of the Illinois State Historical Society*, March 1940; and Bernice E. Gallagaher, *Illinois Women Novelists in the Nineteenth Century: An Analysis and Annotated Bibliography* (1994).

BERNICE E. GALLAGHER

CHAPIN, AUGUSTA JANE
July 16, 1836–June 30, 1905
MINISTER, WOMEN'S RIGHTS ADVOCATE

Augusta Jane Chapin was born in Lakeville, New York, the eldest of eleven children of Almon Morris and Jane (Pease) Chapin. The family moved to Chapin Station (later called Eden), Michigan, in 1842, where her father was a sugar bush farmer as well as the postmaster. Almon Chapin, educated as a doctor, was a Universalist who strongly believed in education and brought books to the pioneer town. He taught school at different times during his life. Taking great pride in his daughter's intelligence and aptitude for learning, which he believed confirmed his theory that children were never too young to learn, Almon Chapin began Augusta Chapin's formal education at age three. She studied at the local schoolhouse and received considerable attention, since there were few other children enrolled and she was such an "apt" pupil (E. R. Hanson, 433). "Her father, who was a man of liberal culture, gave her much instruction at home" (Willard and Livermore, vol. 1, 167). Like so many fathers of the early women suffragists in the United States, he believed in educating his daughters as well as his sons. Augusta Chapin read John Bunyan's *Pilgrim's Progress*, the New Testament, and *Robinson Crusoe*. That book "became a volume

of unfailing interest to her. She read and re-read it until the pages were worn and soiled, until the covers were gone . . . and finally all remonstrances failing to wean her from the book, it was seized and burned in her presence, to her great dismay and grief, before she was ten years old" (E. R. Hanson, 433–34). She also attended simple Sunday schools in the rural area in which they lived and was rewarded for memorizing the Gospels and large portions of the rest of the New Testament.

By age fourteen she had completed a college mathematics course, studied Greek, Latin, French, and German; and had taught one term of public school. Having been denied admission to the University of Michigan, which did not accept applications from women at the time, in 1852 she taught one more term of public school before enrolling in Olivet College, Eaton County, Michigan. Olivet was a Congregational college and rigorous in its religious training. Augusta Chapin had never been exposed to the conservative, Calvinistic religious doctrine to which Congregationalists at Olivet subscribed. Nor could she manage to experience the kind of religious conversion anticipated in that environment as a requirement for membership in the Congregational Church. Instead, she struggled to come to her own truth about religious belief and her own faith. At seventeen she concluded that the Congregationalist dogma was not true; she emerged with a belief in Universalism, a doctrine she felt had biblical truth but also conformed to the laws of nature and reason. Chapin later reflected, "I have no recollection of ever considering the question of whether I would preach or not. . . . From the moment I believed in Universalism it was a matter of course that I was to preach it" (quoted in E. R. Hanson, 434).

Chapin then attended Michigan Female College. She planned to enroll at Lombard University, located in Galesburg, Illinois, although it did not yet have a divinity school. Begun by Universalists in the 1850s, it admitted young women from its first days. They attended the same classes and were eligible for the same degrees as men, and two of the six recipients of the B.A. degree, first awarded by the university in 1856, were women. (Eventually Lombard University's trustees became part of the Meadville Theological Seminary, Chicago, now Meadville/Lombard Theological School.) Chapin, however, did not attend Lombard but began a period of itinerant preaching, giving her first sermon in Portland, Michigan, May 1, 1859.

After 1859, she continued to preach. She was the second woman to be ordained by the Universalist denomination, in Lansing, Michigan, December 3, 1863, the same year in which Olympia Brown became the first woman ordained by the denomination. The Universalist church's policy of automatically allowing ordination to anyone who had preached a year, and therefore had obtained Letters of Fellowship, worked in Augusta Chapin's favor in her efforts to become ordained. Although Olympia Brown had been challenged initially in her attempts to be ordained as a Universalist minister, Chapin's application was made three years after she began preaching, and her request was granted immediately by a unanimous vote May 4, 1862. "During her subsequent career, in addition to much itinerant preaching, often undertaken during her vacations, she held a succession of settled pastorates" (*NAW* [1971], 320), beginning with

Portland, Michigan (1864–67), and continuing at Mount Pleasant, Iowa (1868–69).

In 1868 when the trustees at Lombard University awarded her an honorary M.A. degree, Chapin delivered a commencement address advocating liberal education for women. That same year Chapin became involved in the formation of the American Woman Suffrage Association and, along with Julia Ward Howe, Lucy Stone, Amelia Bloomer, and MARY LIVERMORE, signed the charter of the new organization.

From the start, Chapin understood that her activism within the Universalist church was related to the advancement of women, and she joined with other women's rights advocates. In 1868 she was a charter member of the New York Sorosis, one of the earliest clubs for women in the United States. In 1873 Chapin was a member of the executive committee of the Association for the Advancement of Women (AAW), a national organization of suffragists, advocates of higher education for women, and leading female professionals in medicine, law, the ministry, and science. Among the early members of the AAW were amateur botanist KATE NEWELL DOGGETT, astronomer Maria Mitchell, and journalist Mary Livermore. At the AAW's first meeting, held in New York in 1873, Augusta Chapin gave a paper, "Woman in the Ministry."

Augusta Chapin, "an effective preacher" (NAW [1971], 320), was pastor of a Universalist church in Iowa City, Iowa, from 1870 to 1874. She also began writing for the Universalist press and became known in the denomination. Chapin was among the early women recognized by the denomination. As a ministerial delegate from Iowa to the Universalist Centennial Convention at Glouster, Massachusetts, in September 1870, she offered an amendment to a proposed law on a system of fellowship, discipline, and government, and her amendment was adopted. She was the first woman on the convention's council and was one of the activists "who formed the Woman's Centenary Association of the Universalist Church (1871), the forerunner of the Association of Universalist Women" (NAW [1971], 320). There was conflict between Universalists who believed in the equality of the sexes and those who wished to maintain the traditional patriarchy. "In 1870, only five women had sought a place alongside the 600 male liberal clergy. Twenty years later, the Universalists and Unitarians together had ordained only about seventy, and far fewer actually had a chance to use their credentials in full-time, paid pastorates" (Tucker, 3). Opportunities were better for women in the Middle West, however, than in the more settled East. Chapin was one of the pioneering ordained Universalist ministers who spoke out forcefully for equality and set forth her conviction that "in Christ there is neither male nor female" (Hanaford, 372–73).

Detailed information about Chapin's experience over the ensuing decade is scant. She ministered in San Francisco, California, in 1874, where she may have been the first woman to perform marriages west of the Rockies. She raised funds for the denomination in Pittsburgh, Pennsylvania (1875–76), and had pastorates in Blue Island, Illinois (1876–78), Aurora, Illinois (1879), Lansing, Michigan (1881–83), and Hillsdale, Michigan (1884–85). Positions in Milwaukee, Wisconsin (where a newspaper reporter was amazed that she commanded a man's salary), and Allston, Massachusetts, are listed without dates.

While she was in Michigan, a number of ministers, including Chapin, formed the Michigan College of Ministers (1881). Chapin was director. She also returned to university study, enrolling at the University of Michigan (1882–84) "after it had opened its doors to women, studying modern languages and rhetoric; she received the A.M. degree in 1884" (NAW [1971], 320).

In December 1885, Augusta Chapin became the minister of Unity Church, Oak Park, Illinois. The village, just west of Chicago on the Chicago and Northwestern Railroad line, had been settled by prosperous business people eager to develop a community of Protestant churches, substantial residences, and no taverns or liquor stores. During Chapin's pastorate, her close friend Anna Lloyd Wright and her three children—one of whom was Frank Lloyd Wright—came to live with her. (Years later Frank Lloyd Wright, then a beginning architect, rebuilt Unity Church after the original building was destroyed in a fire begun by a lightning strike.) Chapin stayed in Oak Park as Unity's pastor until October 1891; it was her longest pastorate.

Chapin continued to teach literature at Lombard University as a nonresident lecturer from 1886 to 1897. She championed the concept of the university extension program—college courses for credit offered to nonresident students—and was also an extension lecturer in English at the University of Chicago from 1892 to 1897. She combined a pastorate in Omaha, Nebraska (1894–96), with her lectureship in the extension program the University of Chicago offered in Omaha the same years. There she offered a survey course in American literature, assigning her students readings in the major works of American fiction and poetry as well as works of historians, theologians, essayists, and literary critics. Innovative was her inclusion of works by American women writers, including African American poet Phillis Wheatley, essayist and women's rights advocate Margaret Fuller, and novelists Louisa May Alcott, Harriet Beecher Stowe, and Frances Hodgson Burnett. She also served on a revising committee for Elizabeth Cady Stanton's The Woman's Bible, published in two volumes in 1895 and 1898.

In 1893, at the World's Parliament of Religions congresses held during the World's Columbian Exposition in Chicago, Augusta Chapin's efforts to advance the cause of women in all spheres of human endeavor came together. As chair of the Women's Committee, Chapin addressed the opening session of the Parliament of Religions. Other Christian women addressing the Parliament included Olympia Brown, Universalist minister; Julia Ward Howe, active with Chapin in the Association for the Advancement of Women; FANNIE BARRIER WILLIAMS, African American clubwoman and reformer—and the only African American woman to address the Parliament; Unitarian minister CELIA WOOLLEY, a founder of the Frederick Douglass Center, Chicago, a settlement uniquely focused on the goal of interracial harmony in Chicago; and FRANCES E. WILLARD, president of the Woman's Christian Temperance Union. Chapin also read Antoinette Brown Blackwell's address, "Women and the Pulpit." Fannie Williams spoke on the topic, "Religion's Duty to the Negro." Chapin adopted an inclusive, progressive approach in defining speakers and topics. On her recommendation, members of the Theosophical Society, including Annie Besant, F. Henrietta Muller, and Isabel Cooper-

Oakley, made presentations at the Theosophical Congress, held in conjunction with the World's Parliament of Religions. Two Jewish women, Josephine Lazarus and Henrietta Szold, addressed the World's Parliament of Religions; the Jewish Women's Congress, organized by HANNAH SOLOMON, was held in conjunction with the Parliament. Augusta Chapin was a symbol of the strong link between the struggle for woman's equality in religious institutions and the larger women's rights agenda. "In recognition of her contribution Lombard University, which had earlier awarded her an honorary M.A. (1868), conferred on her the honorary degree of Doctor of Divinity (1893), reputedly the first conferred on a woman in this country" (NAW [1971], 321).

In 1897, at age sixty-three, Augusta Chapin was one of the main speakers at the annual National American Woman Suffrage Association. After her stint in Omaha, Nebraska, she had moved to her last pastorate in Mt. Vernon, New York, a suburb just north of New York City. Defying all stereotypes of Victorian womanhood, as a single woman and one of the few women to be ordained in a Protestant denomination, Chapin had traveled extensively, always maintaining an active ministry, teaching students college courses in English and American literature, and lecturing on woman suffrage. A biography of Chapin published in 1893 estimated that she had "delivered more than four-thousand sermons and public addresses, ha[d] baptized and received many hundreds of persons into the church, ha[d] attended some two-hundred funerals, and ha[d] officiated at many marriages" (Willard and Livermore, vol. 1, 167). She had visited and preached in more than half the states in the United States, had traveled twice to Europe, and had published articles in the magazines and journals of the denominational press.

Augusta Chapin died of pneumonia in Mt. Vernon, New York, on the evening before she was to embark on a European trip. She was buried in Mason, Michigan.

As a young college student she had rejected Congregationalist dogma for belief in Universalism. Her struggle to find an independent, autonomous identity as an intellect and a minister in the Universalist denomination brought to a national forum concerns regarding the role of women in religion and in American society. "Within a dozen years of . . . [her] death the [Universalist] denomination had as many as seventy women preachers" (NAW [1971], 321).

Sources. Univ. of Chicago Annual Calendar, 1892–97, has listings of Augusta Chapin's extension lectures. Augusta Chapin's one-page history of her father, Almon Morris Chapin, 1879, is deposited in the Lansing Historical Museum, Lansing, Michigan. Augusta J. Chapin, General Survey of American Literature: Syllabus of a Course of Six Lecture-Studies, printed brochure (1895), is at UC Spec. Coll. Biographical details about Augusta J. Chapin are found in Phoebe A. Hanaford, Women of the Century (1877); E. R. Hanson, Our Women Workers: Biographical Sketches of Women Eminent in the Universalist Church for Literary, Philanthropic and Christian Work (1882); Frances E. Willard and Mary A. Livermore, eds., A Woman of the Century, 2 vols. (1893); and Ernest Cassara, "Chapin, Augusta Jane," NAW (1971). See also Gilbert W. Chapin, The Chapin Book of Genealogical Data (1924). For a record of her pastorates, see Universalist Register, 1864–1906. The Christian Ledger, February 22, 1894, July 5, 1894, and May 9, 1895, mention Chapin's University of Chicago extension department courses.

Useful is her obituary in Universalist Leader, July 15, 1905. Russell Miller, The Larger Hope: The First Century of the Universalist Church in America 1770–1870 (1979); Cynthia Grant Tucker, Prophetic Sisterhood: Liberal Women Ministers of the Frontier, 1880–1930 (1990); and Catherine Wessinger, ed., Religious Institutions and Women's Leadership: New Roles Inside the Mainstream (1996), are useful for background. For information about the World's Parliament of Religions see John Henry Barrows, The World's Parliament of Religions, vol. 1 (1893); J. W. Hanson, ed., The World's Congress of Religions: Addresses and Papers Delivered before the Parliament and an Abstract of the Congresses Held in the Art Institute, Chicago, Illinois, U.S.A., August 25 to October 15, 1893, under the Auspices of the World's Columbian Exposition (1894); May Wright Sewell, The World's Congress of Representative Women, 2 vols. (1894); and Mary Kavanaugh Oldham Eagle, The Congress of Women Held in the Woman's Building, World's Columbian Exposition (1894).

GLORY SOUTHWIND

CHENEY, FLORA SYLVESTER
March 11, 1872–April 8, 1929
CIVIC LEADER, POLITICAL ACTIVIST, STATE LEGISLATOR

Flora Sylvester Cheney, first president of the Illinois League of Women Voters, was born near Fond du Lac, Wisconsin, the daughter of Seth Sylvester, a farmer and owner of a stone quarry, and Emily (Rose) Sylvester. Flora Sylvester attended the nearby country school and then spent two years at the high school in Fond du Lac, where she boarded with the family of her future husband, Henry W. Cheney, who was home at the time.

Sylvester spent the next two years in her home district school, teaching pupils from kindergarten through the first year of high school. Among them was her younger brother Harland. For the following year she lived in New York with an artist aunt; Sylvester did a great deal of painting before returning to her country school to teach for another year.

In 1896, Flora Sylvester married Henry Cheney, a recent graduate (1892) of Northwestern University Medical School. The couple settled in the Woodlawn neighborhood on the South Side of Chicago, where Dr. Cheney set up practice; Flora Cheney devoted her energies to their two children, a daughter, Kathryn Winifred, and a son, Harold Sylvester.

In 1907, Cheney began to play an increasingly active role in the community. She demonstrated a strong commitment to public service and a talent for organizational leadership, as her sphere of concern expanded gradually from her immediate neighborhood to the city and beyond.

She first took on the task of reorganizing three struggling women's groups at her church. Under her direction, the Woman's Circle of the Woodlawn Baptist Church set new fundraising records and established a strong presence in the community. Cheney also pursued a variety of neighborhood improvement projects. Among these were campaigns to organize supervised school playgrounds in Woodlawn, improve the caliber of children's movies shown at local theaters, and establish a public bathing beach in Jackson Park. Cheney also served as PTA (Parent Teacher Association) president at Ray School, which Kathryn and Harold attended.

Passage of the Illinois Presidential and Municipal Suffrage Bill in 1913 gave women the right to vote for all national offices and virtually all village, town, county, and municipal offices and propelled Cheney into increasingly active involvement in politics. She believed that the ballot was a powerful tool for civic improvement and, once it was available to her, diligently put it to use in a succession of campaigns for high-caliber candidates in her ward, the city, and eventually the state.

Charles E. Merriam, professor of political science at the University of Chicago and candidate for alderman from the Woodlawn area, received Cheney's support. A reform Republican and a member of the Progressive Party, Merriam was an advocate of women's rights as well as of a broad range of social, economic, and electoral reforms. His 1913 campaign for 7th Ward alderman marked the beginning of Flora Cheney's practical experience with politics, as she assisted her husband, chair of the successful campaign.

Cheney took an active part in Merriam's subsequent campaigns as well as those of other able candidates for municipal office. In each case, the cause of good government rather than party allegiance guided her choice of candidate. Thus, although a Republican herself, Cheney supported Democrat William Dever's 1927 bid for reelection as mayor with a reform agenda.

Complementing Cheney's partisan activities was her involvement in the continuing struggle to secure full suffrage for women. Although the suffrage bill of 1913 had given Illinois women broad rights not enjoyed in most other states, much hard work remained. To demonstrate their commitment to the franchise, women's organizations joined forces for a voter registration campaign aimed at a strong turnout in the 1914 municipal elections.

In Chicago, much of the organizing work for this and other suffrage efforts took place at the ward level where Cheney played a leadership role for several key women's organizations. One of these was the 7th Ward Auxiliary of the Illinois Equal Suffrage Association, which in 1914 numbered more than one thousand members. Another was the Chicago Political Equality League (CPEL), organized in 1894 as an auxiliary of the Chicago Woman's Club to promote the political rights of women and by 1912 an independent organization and the largest suffrage league in Illinois. In 1915, Cheney was named president of the 7th Ward Auxiliary and served as head of the 7th Ward civic committee for the CPEL as well.

The following year brought tragedy to the Cheney family when twelve-year-old Harold was killed by lightning on July 16, 1916. His death came as Flora Cheney was bringing local civic, social, church, and business organizations together to establish a community center for Woodlawn. By January 1917 the Woodlawn Community Center was in operation at Hyde Park High School with some eight hundred adults enrolled in a wide range of classes. The center became for Cheney a memorial to her son and was her most enduring contribution to her neighborhood. For the next twelve years, she served as chair of the center's executive committee and also served as first president of the Public School Community Center Association of Chicago.

During this period, Cheney was also active in the campaign to establish a branch library in Woodlawn, another collaborative effort of the community that resulted in the dedication of a new building in 1917. That same year the Cheneys' second daughter, Carol Eleanor, was born.

Active service in leading women's civic organizations occu-

pied much of Cheney's attention in the remaining years of the suffrage campaign. In 1917, Cheney was elected to a three-year term on the board of directors of the Woman's City Club, an organization dedicated to civic improvement and good government. Her involvement in the CPEL continued as well. In a final demonstration of support for suffrage, these and other major women's groups joined together in the spring of 1920 to launch a massive campaign to get "Every Woman at the Polls" for the fall national elections. Cheney served on the executive committee for that campaign and was chair for the 7th Ward.

The ratification of the Nineteenth Amendment in 1920 proved to be a pivotal event for Cheney, because it resulted in the transformation of the National American Woman Suffrage Association into the League of Women Voters (LWV), an organization to which she would dedicate most of her civic energies for the remainder of her life. The *Woman's City Club Bulletin* described the LWV's dual mission: "to foster education in citizenship and to increase the effectiveness of women's votes in furthering better government" (Ward, 9). For Cheney, this mission matched her own vision of how best to promote the common good.

The need for the new organization was not universally recognized, and strong voices were raised against the formation of the Illinois League of Women Voters (ILWV) at the final convention of the Illinois Equal Suffrage Association in October 1920. Some women insisted that existing organizations could do the ILWV's work. A majority of delegates agreed, however, that a nonpartisan educational organization was needed to assist the new woman voter and provide unbiased information on governmental issues. Cheney was nominated by the CPEL and the Woman's City Club and became the ILWV's first president.

To Cheney and her board fell the task of overcoming the opposition stirred up by the convention, creating a plan of work, recruiting members and organizing league groups across the state, raising operating funds, and establishing a place for the fledgling organization among the network of existing women's groups. They moved quickly to demonstrate the league's potential with an intensive, two-week School of Citizenship, held in January 1921 in cooperation with the University of Chicago, and attended by more than five hundred women. Hundreds of one-day citizenship schools followed during the next few years, providing technical instruction on voting and information about the structure of government and key policy issues of the day.

Initially limited to organizational affiliates, the ILWV saw steady growth as Cheney launched a campaign to recruit individual members. Under her guidance, the league began publishing a newsletter, which by the end of 1922 was issued monthly and had a circulation of about twenty-two thousand. First as president and then as editor until 1928, Cheney established the *Bulletin* (later called *The Illinois Voter*) as an important source of news of league activities, solid discussion of public policy concerns, and extensive preelection information on candidates.

Stepping down from the state ILWV presidency in November 1922, Cheney turned her attention to coordinating and strengthening the organization's work in Cook County. She guided the formation of the Cook County Council of Leagues of Women Voters and was named its first president, a position she held from 1923 to 1928. Cheney also served on the board of the Chicago League of Women Voters' Forum, successor to the CPEL and sponsor of monthly educational programs for league members and the public.

In 1924 and again in 1926, Cheney was the campaign manager for her closest friend of twenty-five years, Kathryn Hancock Goode, in her successful candidacy for the state legislature from the fifth senatorial district. Cheney also became active at this time with the Municipal Voters' League, an independent political organization dedicated to electing honest and able public officials. She was elected to its advisory committee in 1924 and then to a three-year term on its executive committee in 1925.

Following Kathryn Goode's death in office early in 1928, Cheney ran for and was elected to her friend's seat in the state legislature. Cheney served just three months in the General Assembly, leaving Springfield ten days before her death from Hodgkin's disease. She died at home at the age of fifty-seven.

During her brief tenure in office, Cheney introduced legislation to create a state commission to study and recommend revisions to the patchwork of election laws of Illinois. After her death, the "Cheney bill" was quickly approved. Cheney's vision of a permanent voter registration system, with safeguards against fraud, was subsequently endorsed by the Commission on the Revision of Election Laws and became law in 1936.

In June 1929, the ILWV placed the names of Cheney and Kathryn Goode on a roll of honor established by the National League of Women Voters to celebrate its tenth anniversary. The special contributions of Cheney and Goode were further commemorated with a large stone bench and sundial in Chicago's Jackson Park, dedicated in the spring of 1932.

To Flora Cheney, the ballot offered the most effective means of promoting the common good, and she took a leading part in those organizations of her day whose mission championed citizen education and good government. Her vision of an active and informed citizenry together with her ability to unite people around a common goal galvanized and ensured the success of the new Illinois League of Women Voters.

Sources. Flora Cheney's 1922 convention address describing the challenges of the Illinois League's first two years is reprinted in the November 1922 issue of the *Illinois League Bulletin.* Personal reminiscences about Cheney were published in a June 1929 memorial issue of *The Illinois Voter* and in a typescript two-page biography of Cheney written in June 1982 by her daughter, Kathryn Cheney Merriam. Early issues of the *Bulletin* and the *Voter,* as well as a small collection of Cheney memorabilia are at the office of the Illinois League of Women Voters in Chicago. A few documents concerning Cheney are included in the Woodlawn Community Collection in the Neighborhood History Research Collection at the Harold Washington Library, CPL. The CHS has papers of the Illinois League of Women Voters from this period, including considerable material relating to its campaign for permanent voter registration. The collection also includes a few papers of the Cook County League. Papers of the Chicago Political Equality League are stored with those of its successor organization, the Chicago League of Women Voters, at UIC Spec. Coll. The early years of the Illinois League are also the subject of *The First Ten Years of the Illinois League of Women Voters* by Edith Rockwood (1930) and *Thirty Years of Faith and Work* (1952) by Katharine Dummer Fisher. The league is described in Estelle Frances Ward's article, "The Illinois League of Women Voters,"

Woman's City Club Bulletin, November 1920. Events of the last decade of the suffrage campaign are documented in "Side Lights on Illinois Suffrage History" by Grace Wilbur Trout in *Transactions of the Illinois State Historical Society for the Year 1920* and also in the *Woman's City Club Bulletin* for those years.

ELEANOR REVELLE

CHMIELIŃSKA, STEFANIA
March 16, 1866–February 24, 1939
BUSINESSWOMAN, WOMEN'S RIGHTS ACTIVIST,
SOCIAL ACTIVIST

Stefania Schneider was born in Warsaw, only three years after the failure of a bloody insurrection against foreign rule in that Russian-controlled area of partitioned Poland. Her patriotism, formed in the wake of this upheaval, would lead her to a life of leadership among Polish immigrant women in America.

A seamstress by profession, in September 1883 she married Prussian Pole Józef Chmieliński, some twenty years her senior, who preceded her to America. In 1891 Stefania Chmielińska and her parents, Karol and Anna Schneider, joined Chmieliński on Chicago's Near West Side. (Her contemporaries report that this entourage included Chmielińska's young daughter, Ludwika. Census reports, however, suggest that Ludwika was born in the United States nearly a decade later.) Settling in the Wojciechowo neighborhood near St. Adalbert's Roman Catholic church (in Polish, St. Wojciech), the couple established a successful florist shop. This long-standing family business was also well known for creating the distinctive flags, banners, sashes, and uniforms required by the patriotic societies that were so vital a part of Polish immigrant society.

The Chmielińskis contributed to more than the outer trappings of organizational life. Stefania and Józef Chmieliński were both linked to the early history of Polish American fraternals and sororals as business owners and as activists and organizers. Józef Chmieliński was a national officer with the Polish Falcons, who were devoted to serving Polish national interests through physical and military training. The Falcons were similar to the German Turners or Czech and Slovak Sokols. First organized in Europe and then brought to America, a group of Falcons emerged within the Polish National Alliance in Chicago in 1886; by 1894 a separate Polish Falcons of America had been organized. Its members obtained social insurance for themselves and developed a group identity in America at the same time that they kindled a strong commitment to the establishment of an independent Poland, working to provide actual humanitarian aid for Poles in Europe. Stefania Chmielińska's earliest organizational experience in this country was also with the Falcons, as its first female instructor in the United States. In 1895, Chmielińska organized and directed the women's and children's gymnastic exercises at the national Falcon gathering, held in Chicago. Falcon chronicler Artur Waldo reported that, in reaction to cheers for the male instructors, the women's voices rang out, "Long live Chmielińska!" (Waldo, 61).

Women, however, did not enjoy equality as Falcon members. At an 1897 meeting a contingent of women, including Gabriela Laudon, Maria Rokosz, TEOFILA SAMOLIŃSKA, and Stefania Chmielińska, spoke out against their auxiliary, nonvoting status. Falcon officers argued that since women could not serve as soldiers, their position in what was essentially a paramilitary group was necessarily secondary. Chmielińska countered by reminding them of women soldiers who had fought in Poland's insurrections. "By the examples of Emilia Plater and Henryka Pustowójtówna," she insisted, "each Woman Falcon should gain the right to consider herself a soldier of the Polish Republic, equal with men. Otherwise the role of a Woman Falcon is inferior" (Waldo, 119). Nevertheless, the petition for equal standing was denied.

In reaction to women's secondary status in powerful immigrant organizations like the Falcons, the Polish National Alliance, and the Polish Roman Catholic Union, Stefania Chmielińska held a meeting at her home on May 22, 1898, and the Związek Polek w Ameryce (ZPA)—the Polish Women's Alliance—was born, with Maria Rokosz as president and Chmielińska as treasurer. While the ZPA was not the first or only Polish immigrant women's organization, it became the most successful and long lasting. Chmielińska envisioned a consortium of local groups united in defense of Polish immigrant women's economic, social, and political interests, with strong ties to Polish national ideals and with an interest in the status of women worldwide.

At Chicago's Pulaski Hall in November 1899, the fledgling organization brought several women's societies together in just such a consortium, electing Chmielińska president. For the next thirty years Chmielińska served the ZPA in various executive capacities, including four terms as president (1899, 1901, 1906, and 1908) and three as vice-president (1900, 1916, and 1918). She also assumed the presidency in 1900, during then-president Genowefa Zółkowska's prolonged stay in Poland.

Most active in the Alliance's formative first twenty years, Chmielińska established several vital programs, including a lending library and an auxiliary membership plan for young girls, thus ensuring the organization's continued growth beyond the first immigrant generation. In 1902 the ZPA began electing an official physician, always a woman. Also under Chmielińska's leadership the influential ZPA newspaper, *Głos Polek,* was founded. Edited at first by Franciszek Wołowski, whose wife, Łucja, was a ZPA activist, the paper struggled and faded from existence for several years, until in 1910 it was reestablished under the editorship of newly arrived woman of letters STEFANIA LAUDYN. The paper continued in the 1990s, though reduced in circulation, scope, and frequency. In addition, Chmielińska was instrumental in the 1910 purchase of the second ZPA headquarters and served on the education committee, which organized nightly classes and lectures, fresh-air camps for children, and weekend lessons in the Polish language.

In addition to cultural projects, educational work, and political lobbying on behalf of Poland and of Poles in America, the ZPA, like the male fraternals, concerned itself with the financial protection of its members. Given the uncertainties of immigrant working-class life, from its very inception the Alliance operated its own life insurance program. In 1898, for an initial fee of fifty cents and monthly dues of five cents, members were entitled to as much as five hundred dollars in life insurance. From its earliest days under Chmielińska, the ZPA carried out its varied programs and managed its own financial affairs. At the time of her death in 1939, the ZPA's leadership was managing assets of five million dollars in real estate, loans, bonds, and cash deposits.

Although the ZPA was administered for the most part by well-educated women who, like Chmielińska, belonged to Polonia's professional and entrepreneurial class, its rank and file was made up of women from all strata of the immigrant community. Thus the new organization soon became the official voice of Polish immigrant women. Chmielińska herself, although a business owner and civic leader, was not removed from the common experience of the women whom she represented. Like most of them, she was involved in her parish, even acting in its popular amateur theatricals. As was common, she helped support an extended family of newly arrived relatives.

Chmielińska's experience as an immigrant woman and her duties as a public representative led her to social activism on behalf of numerous immigrant and Polish national issues. The ZPA quickly made its peace with the male-dominated fraternals and cooperated with them on projects like the 1910 construction of monuments in Washington, D.C., to honor American Revolutionary heroes Tadeusz Kościuszko and Kazimierz Pułaski. Chmielińska represented the ZPA at that dedication and, as a member of the education committee at the first Polish National Congress, called for the introduction of Polish language, history, and literature classes into American public schools. Two years earlier, she had served as vice-president of a group organized to protest restrictions on Polish language and culture in the Prussian territories. In 1917, along with Anna Neumann and Emilia Napieralska, Chmielińska paid an official visit to the Polish immigrant troops encamped in Canada at Niagara-on-the-Lake, Ontario. These soldiers would fight for the Polish cause as part of General Haller's Polish Army in France. In addition to her national duties, Chmielińska remained a grassroots organizer, founding four local ZPA chapters, including one later renamed in her honor.

After the death in 1918 of her mother, whose patriotism and activism had greatly influenced Chmielińska and who had herself been a force in the creation of the ZPA, Chmielińska withdrew from her administrative role in the organization. The year 1925 brought the death of Józef Chmieliński, who had also encouraged and supported his wife's public activities. Failing health finally led her to move into the South Side home of her daughter, Ludwika (Łucja) Kurzawska. Despite this less active role, and despite some debate over which of the early organizers could rightly be called the "mother" of the Polish Women's Alliance, in 1931 Chmielińska was elected its first honorary president and was generally acknowledged as the organization's founder.

When Chmielińska died in February 1939, her funeral became a public event. She lay in state at the ZPA hall. Polonia's leaders attended the funeral, and Polish Consul General Gawroński posthumously awarded her the Gold Cross of Service. ZPA President Honorata Wołowska eulogized that the organization stood as a monument to Chmielińska's work. She is buried at St. Adalbert's Cemetery in Niles, Illinois.

Chmielińska's death offered an opportunity to reflect on the passing of the immigrant "old guard." *Dziennik Chicagoski* artist Walter Krawiec portrayed Chmielińska as a model for future generations of Polish American women. In his cartoon, reprinted on the front page of *Głos Polek* (March 9, 1939), Chmielińska's tombstone, naming her as founder of the Polish Women's Alliance, social activist, patriot, and neighborhood leader, is superimposed on the ZPA's impressive building with its Polish flag waving. The shadowy figure of an elderly woman stands in the background; a young girl gazes up raptly at Chmielińska's image, while her mother admonishes, "Naśladuj ją! (Follow in her footsteps!)" Three generations are joined and the American and Polish nations linked in this tribute to Chmielińska's guiding vision for Polish American womanhood.

Sources. Information on Stefania Chmielińska's life and work must be gleaned from various sources. In Polish, back issues of *Głos Polek* and other Polish immigrant newspapers contain occasional articles about her activities, as well as information about the Polish Women's Alliance in general. Many studies of American Polonia also refer to Chmielińska, usually in a perfunctory manner and sometimes erroneously, as in Francis Bolek, *Who's Who in Polish America* (1943). The most detailed discussion is found in volume two of Artur L. Waldo, *Sokolstwo, przednia straż narodu: Historja idei i organizacji w Ameryce* (The Falcons, advance guard of the nation: The history of an idea and organization in America) (1956). The official ZPA history, *Historia Związku Polek w Ameryce* [The history of the Polish Women's Alliance in America], issued in three volumes under various authors between 1938 and 1981, has some information. Donald Pienkos's forthcoming English-language history may provide a closer look at Chmielińska. She is also discussed briefly in his earlier works, *One Hundred Years Young: A History of the Polish Falcons of America, 1887–1987* (1987) and *For Your Freedom Through Ours: Polish American Efforts on Poland's Behalf, 1863–1991* (1991). Several articles put Chmielińska's work into historical and ideological context: Thaddeus Radzilowski, "Immigrant Nationalism and Feminism: *Głos Polek* and the Polish Women's Alliance in America, 1898–1917," *Review Journal of Philosophy and Social Science*, vol. 2, 1977; and William J. Galush, "Purity and Power: Chicago Polonian Feminists, 1880–1914," *Polish American Studies*, vol. 47, 1990.

KAREN M. MAJEWSKI

CHORPENNING, CHARLOTTE BARROWS
January 5, 1873–January 7, 1955
PLAYWRIGHT, DIRECTOR, TEACHER, AUTHOR

Charlotte Barrows Chorpenning achieved international recognition as an educator, director, teacher, and playwright. She is best known for her work as director of the Children's Theatre at the Kenneth Sawyer Goodman Memorial Theatre in Chicago and as a leading youth theater dramatist.

Charlotte Barrows and eight siblings were born to Allan Campbell and Laura Barrows. Her father's first career was as a clergyman in Kent and Cleveland, Ohio. He later became a professor of English literature at Iowa State Agricultural College (now Iowa State University) in Ames and then moved to Ohio State University, Columbus, where he initially held the position of associate professor of English literature and subsequently was appointed dean of the College of Arts, Philosophy, and Science. Her mother was an accomplished pianist. Because of her desire to "run and find out" about things, Barrows was nicknamed "Rikki-tikki-tavi" (quoted in Rubin, "Literary and Theatrical Contributions," 16). She entered Iowa State Agricultural College, developing an interest in chemistry and physics. She transferred to Cornell University, Ithaca, New York, where she studied history and received a Bachelor of Letters degree in 1894.

Barrows then taught literature in Springfield, Ohio, where she met John Charles Chorpenning. The couple married and had one daughter, Ruth, who was born in Springfield on February 11, 1898. John Chorpenning developed tuberculosis and moved his family to Denver, then moved alone to a Mexican plantation. His wife did not wish to take her young daughter to Mexico. In 1904, Charlotte Chorpenning and daughter Ruth moved to Winona, Minnesota, where Chorpenning taught literature at the State Normal School.

In 1913, Chorpenning was one of twelve people accepted into Professor George Pierce Baker's 47 Workshop at Harvard University, Cambridge, Massachusetts. This course gave Chorpenning her first experiences in playwriting and directing. *Between the Lines*, the play she wrote at the workshop, was produced at a later date in Boston at the Castle Square Theatre. John Chorpenning expected to rejoin his family in Cambridge, Massachusetts, but died in Mexico in 1916.

Chorpenning returned to Winona, Minnesota, and continued to develop her theatrical interests, writing and producing plays for community groups in Winona and Minneapolis. NEVA BOYD of the Recreation Training School of Chicago heard of these endeavors and asked Chorpenning to meet with her. Boyd's school had moved to Hull-House in 1920 but was not officially connected to the settlement. Chorpenning became drama director of the Recreation Training School, popularly known as the "Hull-House School" because of its location. At Hull-House, Chorpenning worked in dramatics with both adults and children.

The Recreation Training School remained at Hull-House until 1927, when it was incorporated into the sociology department of Northwestern University. Boyd joined the sociology department, and Chorpenning became a member of the university's School of Speech. At Northwestern, Chorpenning began two undertakings that influenced the course of her life. The first was the opportunity to direct student-developed scripts written in the playwriting course given by Theodore Hinckley. This work gave her practical experience in revising new scripts. The second activity was working with WINIFRED WARD, the leading force in the child drama movement. Ward was involved in organizing resources of the university and the Evanston PTA (Parent Teacher Association) to establish a children's theater. Knowing Chorpenning's experience in community dramatics, Ward invited her to take part in the organizational meetings.

In 1928, Ward asked Chorpenning to do some rewriting on a *Wizard of Oz* script. Soon afterward, again at Ward's request, Chorpenning wrote *The Emperor's New Clothes*, her initial script earmarked for audiences of children. Maurice Gnesin at the Goodman Theatre in Chicago, after seeing the play, hired Chorpenning in 1931 to direct children's plays for the Goodman. Chorpenning made her mark as a director, playwright, and teacher at the Goodman, drawing attention nationally to its programs in children's theater through the high quality and enormous energy that distinguished her work. She produced about eighty productions, expanded the repertory of plays designed for children with the dramatizations she wrote, and taught playwriting. She observed children's reactions in the audience; had discussions with parents, colleagues, and theater staff; and tried various approaches for directing and writing plays of quality for the child audience.

As a playwright, Chorpenning believed that plays were not written but rewritten. She advocated expending any amount of effort if the result brought satisfaction to a child. She dramatized fairy tales, folk tales, historical episodes, and original concepts. Her plays treated both simple and complex ideas. Chorpenning sought material that appealed to both children and adults and often featured a child as the hero or as a major figure in the development of the story line.

Some of these presentations were unequaled in quality when they first appeared and still enjoy the respect and interest of audiences. The Children's Theatre of Evanston, the Curtain Pullers of Cleveland, the Nashville Junior League Theatre, Children's Theatre of the Texas State College for Women at Denton, and the Federal Children's Theatre Project staged Chorpenning's plays. In 1966, 188 of the 943 titles published by Anchorage Press (formerly the Children's Theatre Press) were Chorpenning plays. Titles representative of her work include *The Emperor's New Clothes* (1932), *Jack and the Beanstalk* (1935), *Hans Brinker and the Silver Skates* (1938), *Radio Rescue* (1938), *Cinderella* (1940), *Rumpelstiltskin* (1944), *Many Moons* (1946), *The Sleeping Beauty* (1947), *Flibbertygibbet (His Last Chance)* (1952), and *Lincoln's Secret Messenger* (1955).

From 1932 to 1957, the Goodman was primarily a school for those aspiring to professional theater careers. Chorpenning worked with advanced students at the school. While directing, she moved about the theater continually, observing from various sections of the auditorium. If she felt something was not right, she took to the stage to fix it. When a show was in performance, she observed audience members as they watched the show. Her writing was influenced by audience response. Further, if she saw that a child was frightened, she would take the child backstage to meet the cast.

Dedicated to the cause of child drama, Chorpenning worked with organizations engaged in theatrical activity. She assisted the Ohio Farm Bureau in founding a National Cooperative Recreational School. Chorpenning had a major role in establishing the Children's Theatre Conference (now American Alliance for Theatre and Education), which became the national organization for child drama professionals. She assisted Sara Spencer, getting the Children's Theatre Press into operation and serving as a member of its advisory board. She commuted between Chicago and New York in 1947, when her plays were scheduled for the opening season of the professional Children's World Theatre company. Chorpenning adapted seven of her plays for television for the Children's Theatre Series, *The Magic Slate*, on NBC.

In the summer of 1949, Chorpenning's health failed. After a serious breakdown, she was taken east for recuperation at a health camp. Continuing to maintain her active engagement in advocating child drama, in 1950, with colleagues Burdette Fitzgerald and Sara Spencer, Chorpenning prepared a special report, "The Value of the Theatre in the Emotional Development of Children," for the Mid-Century White House Conference on Children and Youth held in Washington, D.C. The report was used by the American government in reeducating German youth. Although she returned to Chicago and stayed with the Goodman Theatre until 1952, she did not recover fully. From 1949 to 1952, she lived in an apartment near the University of Chicago with former student Mary Dodge. When she retired, her achievements were recognized through an honorary Doctorate of Fine Arts given by the Art Institute of Chicago.

The definitive text of the Chorpenning philosophy is *Twenty-One Years with Children's Theatre* (1954). Because Chorpenning completed the work so near the end of her life, it is regarded as her final statement on the art of children's theater, a summary of her career, and a statement of her creed. As published, the book is divided into two sections, "How the Children Taught Me" and "How I Used What the Children Taught Me," and includes a "Coda." She presents principles for youth theater playwrights to follow, including, most importantly: the story must never stop; show it, don't tell it; the three elements of a play are story, character, and meaning; have a clear idea of purpose when writing; and write with a free imagination.

Chorpenning's final years were spent with her daughter and son-in-law, Jim Norris, in the Warwick Valley in New York. By the fall of 1955, her health was poor. Her death came two days after her eighty-second birthday.

Chorpenning's plays became a staple for children's theater nationally from their initial appearance in the 1930s. Her influence can be seen in the plays of such youth theater notables as Geraldine Brain Siks, Aurand Harris, and Martha King. As a tribute to her, in 1956, the Charlotte B. Chorpenning Cup award was established to honor outstanding achievement in playwriting for youth theater. The award is given annually by the American Alliance for Theatre and Education.

Chorpenning's contributions spurred national growth and enthusiasm for youth theater. Her guiding spirit helped to build a discipline, and her influence continues to exert itself within this field. Her legacy is more than her scripts and writings; it is also her dedication and inspiration, as evidenced by the respect she is still accorded and the stature assigned her work by child drama practitioners and scholars. She was addressed by many names, "Chorpy," "Charl," "Haley," "Senorita," and "Daisy," but she is remembered, not by title, but as the modest, energetic, understanding, and creative author of plays that became the cornerstone of the youth theater movement in America.

Sources. Materials relevant to Charlotte Chorpenning's life and career are in the American Alliance for Theatre and Education and the Child Drama Collection, Arizona State Univ., and the Winifred Ward Collection, Northwestern Univ. Archives. The Anchorage Press (formerly the Children's Theatre Press) maintains script publication records. Articles by Charlotte Chorpenning include "Dramatics and Personality Growth," in Progressive Educational Association, *Growth and Development: The Bases for Educational Programs* (1936); "The Special Audience," *Theatre Arts*, September 1949; "Adults in Plays for Children," *Educational Theatre Journal*, May 1951. Published plays by Chorpenning, in addition to those mentioned above, include *The Indian Captive* (1937); *Rip Van Winkle* (1938); *Little Red Riding Hood* (1948); *The Three Bears* (1949); *King Midas and the Golden Touch* (1950); *Robinson Crusoe* (1952); *The Prince and the Pauper* (1954); *Rama and the Tigers* (1954); *Hansel and Gretel* (1956); and *Alice in Wonderland* (1959). Janet E. Rubin, "The Literary and Theatrical Contributions of Charlotte B. Chorpenning to Children's Theatre" (Ph.D. diss., Ohio State

Univ., 1978), is based on unpublished personal correspondence, oral interviews, an unpublished autobiography by Chorpenning, and a biographical sketch by Chorpenning's daughter, Ruth Chorpenning Norris. Additionally, a useful source is Janet E. Rubin's "Charlotte Barrows Chorpenning," in *Notable Women in the American Theatre: A Biographical Dictionary*, ed. Alice M. Robinson, Vera Mowry Roberts, and Milly S. Barranger (1989). See also Marjorie Chandler, "An Analytical Study of the Published Plays of Charlotte B. Chorpenning, Based on Criteria Established by Mrs. Chorpenning and Others in the Field of Children's Theatre" (master's thesis, Univ. of California, Los Angeles, 1967); Claribel Baird Halstaed, "Women Leaders of ATA: Beginning to 1955," *Theatre News*, vol. 10, 1977; Nellie McCaslin, *Creative Dramatics in the Classroom* (1974); Thelma Rantilla, "Week-End Commuting by Air Just in Day's Work for Children's Dramatist: Children's World Theatre in New York Drafts Mrs. Charlotte Chorpenning to Direct Her Play," *Christian Science Monitor*, November 5, 1947; and Dorothy Schwartz, "A History of the Children's Theatre Conference, 1944–1955" (master's thesis, Univ. of Alabama, 1956).

JANET E. RUBIN

CHRISTMAN, ELISABETH
September 2, 1881–April 26, 1975
LABOR ORGANIZER, REFORMER

Elisabeth Christman dedicated her life to the improvement of working conditions for women. Her organizing skills were forged in the Chicago factory milieu, where she worked as a young teenager, and honed in the national unions, where she became one of the few women to achieve a leadership position.

Born in Germany, Elisabeth Christman immigrated to Chicago in 1884 with her parents, Henry and Barbara (Guth) Christman, both born in Germany. Christman was the eldest of six children. Henry Christman was a laborer who earned extra income by playing the clarinet in a union band. Barbara Christman ran a laundry service from her home.

Elisabeth Christman attended a German Lutheran school until the age of thirteen. She then left school to become a glove worker at the Eisendrath Glove Company located in Chicago. Learning all aspects of the glove-making process, Christman labored ten hours a day, six days a week. She paid for the power supplied to her sewing machine and purchased her needles and machine oil. After four years of long hours and continual harassment from supervisors, Christman joined a strike led by her coworker AGNES NESTOR in the spring of 1898. The strikers demanded pay raises, a union shop, and an end to paying rent for their sewing machines. They won a victory after ten days on the picket line. Long before this triumph, Christman had learned the merit of unionization. She took pride in her father's membership in the Musician's Union and lived in a neighborhood where organized labor had a strong history. This early exposure to unions helped to give Christman the impetus to become active in the labor movement.

In 1902, after another strike at the Eisendrath factory, Christman and Nestor organized a glove operators union which later that year became a local of the newly formed International Glove Workers' Union of America (IGWU). Over the years Christman served in many capacities for this local. She was a shop steward from 1905 to 1911, president from 1912 to 1917, and head of the grievance committee. In 1913, she was named secretary-treasurer of the IGWU itself, serving in this capacity

until 1931. Christman was one of the few women at the time to hold such high office for a national union. From 1931 to 1937, she served as vice-president of the IGWU.

A popular young woman with brown hair and brown eyes, Christman was extremely energetic. Although she was at one time engaged, she never married. Her lifelong friendships with labor and social service activists included MARY ANDERSON, Agnes Nestor, and Pauline Newman.

The greatest outlet for Christman's organizational talents was the Women's Trade Union League (WTUL). Founded in 1903 by reformers and trade unionists, its members were working women and middle-class and upper-class women allies. This cross-class alliance made the WTUL a unique federation; although affiliated with the American Federation of Labor (AFL), its leadership went beyond the issues of wages and hours to advocate labor legislation and to develop educational programs for working-class women. Prior to becoming secretary-treasurer on the national level, Christman was on the executive board of the WTUL Chicago branch between 1910 and 1929. Through these eventful years, Christman and the Chicago WTUL participated in a series of strikes supporting women in the garment trades. The Chicago WTUL allies were part of the Hull-House reform culture, advocating education and legislation to improve the conditions of women workers.

WTUL leaders recognized the need to teach women about unions, and the approach the league took brought together educational and organizational work. In so doing, they developed a "redefinition of the process of union organizing" (Hyman, 34). Following the initial garment strikes in Chicago in the years after 1910, officers of the Chicago WTUL saw an urgent need for training women organizers. In 1914, the national WTUL, whose headquarters were now in Chicago, worked closely with the Chicago league in organizing and directing a new Training School for Women Organizers. It was the first full-time labor school in the United States offering field training as well as academic training. Colleges and universities also developed schools for training women in labor organization leadership. Through the league, Christman became involved in the Bryn Mawr Summer School, which offered scholarships to women for training in labor organization leadership. From 1914 to 1926, she was a member of the joint administrative committee at Bryn Mawr as well as of the executive committee of the American Labor Education Service. Later she served on the University of Wisconsin Summer School Committee. Christman considered this leadership education among the league's greatest achievements and pointed with pride to hundreds of women who were national and local union officials trained by the WTUL.

The dual role of working with the WTUL and IGWU never presented a problem for Christman. She represented both organizations, for example, during the 1915 canvas glove makers strike at the Herzog Manufacturing Company in Chicago. The dispute concerned unequal pay; thirteen of the young women who participated in a picket were arrested. During the strike Christman helped to organize a dramatic meeting of more than eight hundred workers, many of whom did not speak English; she succeeded in bringing the conflict to a successful resolution.

Christman also became involved in international women's reform activities. In 1915, she traveled to Holland as a delegate

FIG. 20. *Young women trade unionists; seated, left to right, Mame Butler, Rosa McGovern; standing, left to right, Mary Nestor, Elisabeth Christman, Margaret Blake, Agnes Nestor. Milwaukee, Wisconsin, 1909.*

to the International Congress of Women. There she helped found the International Committee for Permanent Peace and at the WTUL convention worked for a resolution requesting an embargo on arms and war supply exports. The Chicago delegation, including Christman, presented this resolution to Congress and President Woodrow Wilson.

When the United States entered World War I, opportunities widened somewhat for women. In 1916, at an American Federation of Labor convention, Elisabeth Christman and Mary Anderson introduced a resolution to form a federal women's bureau, but the proposal was not supported. However, in 1918 the Women in Industry Service (WIS) was formed in the Department of Labor, and Christman was named its chief field representative for women workers. Answering calls from all over the country, she watched for possibilities of strikes so that she could settle grievances. She spoke to factory workers and supervisors, pushing for improved standards in health and safety, equal pay, and a decent minimum wage. In 1920 the WIS was transformed into the Women's Bureau of the Department of Labor and gained permanent legal status.

After the war, in 1919, Christman was appointed to the National Executive Board of the WTUL. In 1921, she was elected secretary-treasurer of WTUL and retained this position until the organization dissolved in 1950. Christman moved with the WTUL in 1930, when its headquarters changed from Chicago to Washington, D.C. Through this work, she forged a vital link with women organizers and workers across the country. At that time, she also began to edit the league's influential bulletin, *Life and Labor*, and gained further national prominence.

Christman's stature and expertise were recognized by several presidential administrations. In 1921, she was appointed by President Warren Harding to the Unemployment Conference. President Herbert Hoover selected her to serve on the Vocational Guidance and Child Labor Subcommittee of the White House Conference on Child Health and Protection in 1929,

and as a representative to the 1933 Unemployment Relief Committee. In 1936, Christman was named to President Franklin Roosevelt's Commission on Vocational Guidance.

Elisabeth Christman increasingly represented the position of trade union women that protective labor legislation was necessary for the well-being of women workers. In 1923 she was concerned over a recent decision of the U.S. Supreme Court, *Adkins v. Children's Hospital*, which invalidated a minimum wage law in the District of Columbia that benefited women. She voiced her opposition to the Equal Rights Amendment (ERA), first introduced to Congress by the National Woman's Party in 1923; Christman believed that although the ERA could lead to legal equality, it could not insure protection for women in the work place nor lead to economic parity. She traveled to Vienna in 1923 for the Third International Congress of Trade Union Women and in 1928 attended the Pan-Pacific Women's Conference in Honolulu. After assisting Chicago dressmakers during an eighteen-week strike in 1927, Christman helped to avert a strike of the Waist and Dressmakers Union in Philadelphia by successfully negotiating a contract. In the late 1920s, she participated in efforts to bring industrial women workers from the southern states into trade unions.

Despite tonsillectomy surgery in 1932, Christman continued her hectic schedule, as she fought for women's equal rights in the workplace. At the 1933 AFL convention, she pleaded with delegates to organize the five million women employed in industry and business—particularly semi-skilled and unskilled workers—into unions. She brought forth a resolution for the formation of a board of men and women to bring unions into industries that had been resistant to labor. At the time the resolution was not voted on, but one year later John L. Lewis of the United Mine Workers argued in its favor. As a result, a compromise version of Christman's earlier resolution was adopted.

During the Great Depression, Christman served in New Deal agencies representing labor. She was named the first woman member to the Code Authority of the National Recovery Administration and also served on an advisory board of the National Industrial Recovery Act (NIRA) of 1933. The NIRA established production quotas, prices, and resources for each industry. Under the code authority for the leather and woolen-knit glove industry, Christman investigated conditions and wages and testified at hearings that dealt with industries hiring women.

Opposition to women workers during the depression faded quickly as World War II began and growing numbers of the male labor force disappeared into the armed services. As the need for women's labor increased, some aspects of women's protective labor laws were ignored. Provisions against night shifts and longer hours were waived. Eager to have Christman's expertise, Secretary of Labor Francis Perkins asked for her services in 1942.

As a special agent of the Women's Bureau, Christman concentrated on "issues of equal pay" (*American National Biography*). Displaying her forceful yet diplomatic nature, she pressured General Motors to agree to give women equal pay by stressing the harm unequal pay would do when the soldiers returned home. In 1942, Christman remarked that "peacetime and wartime wages for women have a common denominator—women earn less than men" (Foner, 359).

Issues of pay were not the only concerns for Christman during World War II. In West Virginia, she convinced the United Mine Workers to allow women into the union. At the United Aircraft's Chance-Vought plant in Connecticut, she solved the dispute over women wearing for warmth what men considered to be tight-fitting and provocative sweaters. Using tact and diplomacy, she reached an agreement with management to supply free jackets to wear over the sweaters and convinced the young women to accept this compromise.

Christman resumed her duties with the WTUL before World War II ended. Contributions from wealthy patrons had kept the league in operation over the years, but these funds had steadily decreased since the retirement of MARGARET DREIER ROBINS as national president in 1922. Robins had been politically influential, and without her the league lost some of its donations. The economic difficulty of the depression years impacted the WTUL further. League president Rose Schneiderman maintained in 1947 that the WTUL could not survive without Christman. Despite efforts to raise funds, the situation became so desperate that at times Christman did not draw her own salary. Still, she stayed on until the WTUL ran out of money in 1950. Christman then became the legislative representative for the Amalgamated Clothing Workers of America, which had absorbed the Glove Workers' Union.

In 1952, Christman retired. She never stopped paying union dues or advising women in labor disputes. In later years, she suffered from diabetes and blindness. She died at the age of ninety-three in Delphi, Indiana, of cerebral arteriosclerosis.

All through her life, Elisabeth Christman applied persistent and effective organizing efforts. Although her work took her to Washington, D.C., and elsewhere, she kept in touch with the Chicago labor community. She was widely respected for her contributions to reform and to trade union efforts.

Sources. Little can be gleaned about Christman's personal life from any sources. U.S. Census records for 1900, 1910, and 1920 present conflict-

ing information regarding Christman's place of birth and year of immigration. However, most sources indicate Germany as her birthplace and 1884 as the year of her immigration. The most important information can be found in the Agnes Nestor Papers and the Chicago branch Women's Trade Union League Papers at the CHS and in Mary Anderson, *Woman at Work* (1951); Agnes Nestor, *Woman's Labor Leader* (1954); and Rose Schneiderman, *All for One* (1967). Other helpful books include Gladys Boone, *The Women's Trade Union Leagues in Great Britain and the United States of America* (1942); Philip S. Foner, *Women and the American Labor Movement* (1980); James J. Kenneally, *Women and American Trade Unions* (1978). Colette A. Hyman's chapter, "Labor Organizing and Female Institution Building: The Chicago Women's Trade Union League, 1904–1924," in *Women, Work and Protest: A Century of U.S. Women's Labor History*, ed. Ruth Milkman (1985), is helpful for understanding the women's labor culture in which Christman was a participant. In addition, short biographies published on Christman in *Current Biography* (1947); Gary M. Fink, ed., *Biographical Dictionary of American Labor Leaders* (1974); and *NAW* (1980) help verify the facts of her service and contributions. See also Marilyn Perry's "Elisabeth Christman," John A. Garraty and Mark C. Carnes, eds., *American National Biography* (1999). Interviews with Lillian Herstein in 1970 and 1971 conducted by Dr. Elizabeth Balanoff of Roosevelt Univ. add insight into Christman's personality. Obituaries appeared in the *CT*, April 17, 1975, and in the *Washington Post*, April 29, 1975.

MARILYN ELIZABETH PERRY

CHURCH, MARGUERITE STITT
September 13, 1892–May 26, 1990
CONGRESSWOMAN

Marguerite Stitt Church, who was the Republican congresswoman from the 13th District from 1951 through 1963, was born in New York City, the daughter of William J. and Adelaide (Forsythe) Stitt. She and her older sister, Edna, grew up in the New York metropolitan area; were raised within a prosperous, closely knit, conservative Methodist family; and traveled abroad every summer with their parents. In 1910 Marguerite Stitt graduated from St. Agatha School, where she had played basketball and participated in forum discussions. Four years later she received a B.A. with highest honors at Wellesley College, Wellesley, Massachusetts, where she had majored in psychology and minored in the fields of economics and sociology. She had been a member of the college debating society, the Intersociety Council, and president of the Zeta Alpha sorority. Elected to Phi Beta Kappa in her junior year, she was a Durant Scholar in her senior year. Although she was reticent as a child, her college experience transformed her into an effective and sought-after speaker.

Stitt taught for a year at Wellesley College before entering graduate school at Columbia University in New York City. She received an M.A. in political science in 1917. During World War I, Stitt worked as a consulting psychologist with the State Charities Aid Association in New York, where she became involved with the settlement house movement.

On December 21, 1918, Marguerite Stitt married Ralph Edwin Church, a Chicago lawyer and Republican state representative serving in the Illinois legislature (1916–32), and the couple moved to Evanston, Illinois. They had three children: Ralph Edwin Jr., born in 1920; William Stitt, born in 1924; and Marjory Williams, born in 1929. In 1934 Ralph Church was first elected to the U.S. House of Representatives; he served from 1935 to 1940 and again from 1943 to 1950. During her husband's tenure in public office, Marguerite Church was active in various social service organizations, including the Family Welfare Association of Evanston, the Evanston Receiving Home of the Illinois Children's Home and Aid Society, and the North Shore Auxiliary of the Chicago Maternity Center. In 1935 she was selected to be the woman speaker at the Institute of World Affairs in California and spoke on "Feminine Force in a Changing World." Four years later she accompanied her husband to the Interparliamentary Union Conference in Oslo, Norway, where he was a delegate from the U.S. Congress.

Marguerite Church was prominent in Republican political circles. Her talent for public speaking was noted by party officials, and she was assigned to nationwide speaking tours on behalf of the National Republican Committee in the presidential campaigns of 1940 and 1944 and on behalf of the Brookings Institution, a Washington, D.C., think tank, during the 1940s. She was elected president of the Congressional Club (1948–50), Washington, D.C., whose membership was restricted to the wives of current and former members of Congress, the cabinet, and the Supreme Court. At the request of her husband in 1949, Church toured Europe to study postwar conditions.

In March 1950, during the second session of the 81st Congress, Ralph Edwin Church died, and the Republican Party nominated Marguerite Stitt Church as the best qualified candidate to succeed him on the ticket. No one completed his term of office, and, because her husband had died just a few weeks before the primary, she ran under his name. Since Marguerite Church won by a narrow margin, a nominating convention had to be called; selected as the regular candidate, she ran in the general election in November. She was taken seriously as a candidate, receiving praise from Senator Paul H. Douglas, Democrat of Illinois, and Congressman Dewey Short, Republican of Montana. In accepting the party's nomination, Church stated that she would "make no apologies for being a woman, nor ever seek office on the basis of being a woman" (Luft). Church waged a campaign in which she made an average of seventeen speeches a week. Women's groups in Lake and Cook counties worked on her behalf. She also garnered support from both Democrats and Independents and received the largest number of votes recorded for a House candidate in the 13th District. She received the largest number of votes among House candidates nationwide in 1956 and 1960. At age fifty-eight, Church became one of eight women—six of whom were Republicans—elected to the 82nd Congress. She served six consecutive terms.

During her first session in Washington, D.C., Church established a friendship with Congresswoman Vera Buchanan, Democrat from Pennsylvania. Buchanan also had succeeded her late husband and both women understood the double burden of being women in public office and of being widows with their husbands' reputations to uphold, if not surpass. Congresswoman Edith Rogers, Republican from Massachusetts, also served as a role model for Church. Church respected Rogers for her humanity. "I remember the time last year [1960] when she cast a vote with great political courage, and coming up to me afterwards . . . said, 'I hope that vote did not disturb you. You

know, I cannot refuse to spend mere money when I know that people need it'" (Congressional Record, 1961, v. 107, pt. 1, 787). In this connection, Church supported Congresswoman Kathryn Granahan's House bills on issues concerning child welfare, civil rights, and equal pay for women. Although Church was a Republican and Granahan a Democrat from Pennsylvania, both believed that government had a moral and legal responsibility to represent and protect all of its citizens.

Church consistently introduced and supported legislation to make government accountable for its policies and procedures. As a fiscally conservative Republican, Church advocated efficiency and economy in government and worked successfully to establish cost-accounting in government. She insisted that government could and should be run like a business in the private sector, because a sound defense policy could only be built upon a sound fiscal policy. Her foreign policy positions were based on a philosophy of creating international cooperation without compromising the security of the United States or the efforts of subject peoples to achieve freedom and liberation from dictatorships. In the cold war political climate, she consistently affirmed that the Republican Party was the party of freedom and carried the burden of responsibility for the fight against communism or the enslavement of people. As a member of Congress who also sat on the House Committee on Foreign Affairs, she advocated a bipartisan approach. Rather than hold to a party line for the sake of politics, she believed that foreign policy was of such importance that it was essential to promote honesty rather than partisan gamesmanship in any committee deliberations.

As a crusader for economic and political freedom, she fought unsuccessfully against passage of an amended Mutual Securities Act in 1954. She argued that the funds were being used to cultivate allies rather than aid in the development of the economy of a foreign country; also, she was reluctant to establish markets for American-made products in countries where freedom, peace, and security had not yet been established.

Church served ten years on the House Committee on Foreign Affairs and four years on the House Committee on Government Operations. She also served on the subcommittees on Foreign Economic Policy, Far East and Pacific Policy, and Science and Astronautics. Her committee responsibilities, which she took seriously, included first-hand investigations into the economic and political conditions of developing countries and the effectiveness of U.S. foreign policy. The investigations led to her fight for revised legislation that did not put "dollars over human values" or "provide guns instead of understanding" (Congressional Record, 1961, v. 107, pt. 15, 19,503) but would send aid only to countries with economic and political systems in line with the U.S. form of government and capitalist or free market system. A lifelong friend of fellow Wellesley College graduate, Madame Chiang Kai-shek—wife of the president of Taiwan—Church fought against admission of Communist China into the United Nations. She argued, "The United Nations shall not be threatened by the admission of a nation which defies our principles of freedom" (Congressional Record, 1961, v. 107. pt. 13, 17,770). In 1962, President John F. Kennedy appointed Church a delegate to the 16th General Assembly of the United Nations; as a result of her investigations in South Africa, she was one of the first public leaders to denounce its apartheid policies.

Church was conscious of being a woman in the male-dominated fields of politics and government; in accepting the Republican nomination in 1950, she stated, "If a man had been nominated and made a mistake, you would have said he is stupid. If I make a mistake, you will say she is a woman" (Luft). Like many women of her generation in the Congress, including Senator Margaret Chase Smith, Church believed that women serve "not as women but as fellow congressmen, in the generic sense of the word" (*Congressional Record*, 1961, v. 107, pt. 13, 17,262). However, she also regretted that women had not achieved equal numbers and acceptance. In 1953 she was the only woman member of the Republican Party's Policy Committee. President Dwight David Eisenhower appointed her to be one of two delegates from the House of Representatives to the presidential inauguration in Mexico in 1958, and in 1960 she was a delegate to the White House Conference on Children and Youth. In 1959 Church began pushing for legislation to prohibit wage discrimination on account of sex. Two years later, in 1961, as a member of the House Judiciary Committee, she introduced a resolution proposing an amendment to the U.S. Constitution that would provide equal rights for men and women. She also introduced a resolution to amend the Railroad Retirement Act of 1937 to eliminate the requirement that a husband or widower have been dependent upon his wife in order to qualify for a spouse's or widower's annuity on the basis of her wage record. Church argued for equal pay from the economic standpoint that whether women supported themselves or their families, their incomes reflected the general health and strength of the nation's economy.

In addition to her congressional activities, Church was a member of the League of Women Voters; the Business and Professional Women's Clubs of America; the American Association of University Women; the Women's Advisory Committee of the National Safety Council; the national board of directors, Girl Scouts of the United States of America; and the Women's Board, University of Chicago. In 1960, Civic Affairs Associates, Incorporated, awarded Church the Merit Award for Service, citing her work on behalf of economic and political freedom in the world; and in 1962, Loyola University Chicago presented Church with its Founders' Day Award.

In 1963, at age seventy, when her congressional district was redrawn, Church determined it was time to retire from Congress after twelve years and eleven thousand roll call votes. She had missed only four roll calls. In her retirement she continued to attend Republican Party conventions, campaign for Republican Party candidates, and encourage college women to enter politics. Congresswoman Frances Bolton, Republican from Ohio, paid tribute to Church, stating, "I do not know just where we shall find another [congressional representative] who will be as fair, as just, as honest in her criticisms and in her efforts to build more constructive programs" (*Congressional Record*, 1962, v. 108, pt. 17, 23,245).

Marguerite Stitt Church died in her Evanston home at age ninety-seven. She is buried in Memorial Park Cemetery, Skokie, Illinois. She was remembered as a leader who was "principled and committed, gentle but firm in her beliefs" (Luft).

Sources. A family record was filled out by Marguerite Church for the Evanston Hist. Soc., February 14, 1967. The society also has clipping files on both Marguerite and Ralph Church. An interview was conducted with Church's daughter, Marjory Church Barnum, June 14, 1996. The *Congressional Record*, 1950–62, provides information on committee assignments and legislation and includes speeches and remarks indicating Church's political and personal values and principles. *Congressional Directory* (1935–62) is useful. See Kerry Luft, "Marguerite Church, Ex-congresswoman," *CT*, May 27, 1990; [n.a.], "Marguerite Church Is Waging Brilliant Speaking Campaign; Able, Distinguished Candidate," *CT*, October 12, 1950. Biographical entries on Church are in Hope Chamberlain, *A Minority of Members: Women in the U.S. Congress* (1973); and Office of the Historian, U.S. House of Representatives, *Women in Congress 1917–1990* (1991), a biographical reference book prepared under the direction of the Commission on the Bicentenary of the U.S. House of Representatives.

TERRY J. MICHELSEN

CIRESE, HELEN MATHILDE
December 1, 1899–October 10, 1983
LAWYER, ACTIVIST, LOCAL POLITICIAN

At a time when women were not yet permitted to sit on juries in Illinois, Helen Mathilde Cirese enthusiastically embarked on her legal career, arguing both criminal and civil cases successfully. She wholeheartedly devoted herself to her law career when few women were entering the professions. The third of nine children, Cirese was born in Marion, Indiana, where her Italian immigrant parents, Joachim Phillip and Providence Mary (Graziano) Cirese, initially settled in 1892. The family moved to Chicago in 1907 and then in 1912 settled permanently in Oak Park, a Chicago suburb where Cirese lived her entire adult life. The community was known for its wealth, prohibition of liquor, and Protestant churches. The Cireses owned their own home and attended St. Giles, the local Roman Catholic church. Cirese's father supported his large family by working as a South Water Street commission merchant in Chicago, buying and selling produce as a wholesaler, while her mother raised the family and was active in church, civic, and charity work.

Helen Cirese attended Oak Park–River Forest High School, where she was associate editor of the school newspaper and worked with fellow editor Ernest Hemingway. Cirese's initial ambition was to be a newspaper reporter, but upon graduation from high school in 1917, she enrolled in the College of Law of DePaul University (now the DePaul University School of Law). The college had been formed in 1912 when DePaul University became affiliated with the Illinois College of Law. A college degree was not yet a prerequisite for law studies.

Cirese was one of five women in a class of sixty-seven students. She was vice-president of her class and an associate editor of the DePaul newspaper, *Minerval*. She delivered the salutatory address at the graduation ceremony in the spring of 1920. She was only twenty years old when she received her LL.B. degree. She never married and continued to live with her family in their Oak Park home.

In February 1921 Cirese passed the Illinois Bar exam, one of the youngest women ever to do so. Ironically, women, who had practiced law in the state since 1873, had only just gained suffrage and were still denied the right to sit on juries in the state of Illinois. Cirese's first career opportunity came from a friend of her father. He had promised her a position in his law firm, but when she learned the position was not as an attorney, but rather as a stenographer, she opened her own office for the general practice of law in downtown Chicago.

Shortly after opening her office, Cirese was invited into partnership with two other lawyers, one of whom was a former De-Paul classmate. During the first year of the new partnership of Boneli, Quilici and Cirese, Helen Cirese became involved in a highly publicized case. She defended an Italian-American woman, Sabelle Nitti, who had been convicted by a Cook County court for the murder of her husband, a truck farmer in Stickney, Illinois. The woman was sentenced to hang. Cirese was one of a group of Italian-American lawyers who volunteered their services to appeal the sentence before the Illinois Supreme Court. On April 21, 1924, the Illinois Supreme Court reversed and remanded the previous conviction on the ground of insufficient evidence and inadequate representation. Unstated issues of ethnicity and class were at work in the publicity surrounding the case. Cirese and the other attorneys realized that Nitti's ethnicity and image as a crude and uneducated woman hurt her. She "had the dubious distinction of being the first woman sentenced to death in Cook County" (*Chicago Tribune*, October 13, 1983) during a period of conservative politics and conflict over gender roles. It was also a time when the foreign-born faced discrimination and deportation, as the U.S. immigration policy was changed to limit the numbers of southern and eastern Europeans who came into the country. In an interview after the victory, Cirese described the defense's strategy: "We simply re-conditioned her. I got a hairdresser to fix her up everyday. . . . We taught her to speak English. . . . You wouldn't have known her" (quoted in the Philadelphia *Evening Bulletin*, September 6, 1940). The success of this case established Cirese's reputation in criminal law, but thereafter she primarily concentrated on civil law.

Helen Cirese and other women lawyers faced serious challenges in the early 1930s. The Great Depression added additional stress to the problems of employment of women in the field of law. Sadie Turak, a lawyer in New York, recalled that "the Depression gave law firms still another excuse for not hiring . . . [women]" (quoted in Morello, 203). She was asked at interviews "how I could possibly expect to be considered when there were men out there with families to support" (p. 203). In 1930, after Cirese's former partners accepted judgeships, she and her older brother, Charles, opened their own law office. (In 1943, her younger brother, Eugene, joined the firm.) Working in a family firm as a single woman offered Cirese advantages, but she was keenly aware of the plight of other women lawyers and of married women in general. As a leader in the National Association of Women Lawyers (NAWL), she argued against the attempt by state legislatures to pass laws prohibiting the employment of any married women whose husbands' income exceeded a certain amount.

Helen Cirese became active in many legal and professional organizations. She dedicated her energy to making inroads into male-dominated legal organizations and to strengthening organizations that worked for the special interests of women. In 1930 she was elected president of the Women's Bar Association of Illinois. She actively campaigned for the right of women to be jurors in the state of Illinois. As the pressure mounted to pass leg-

islation, Cirese argued, "There are women lawyers, women court attorneys, women judges, therefore, is it not absurd that women should be excluded in acting as jurors? Such exclusion is a lingering discrimination which does not belong in this century" ("Women on Juries"). The injustice was even more stinging because other states had already provided for women's participation as jurors. Passage of a state law was delayed by legislative maneuvers and court cases until 1939.

Cirese also participated in the male majority Chicago Bar Association. From 1933 to 1935 Cirese chaired the Chicago Bar Association's (CBA) Committee on the Defense of Indigent Prisoners. She was the first woman to chair a committee of the CBA. This committee was responsible for successfully lobbying for the passage of the Public Defenders Act in Illinois.

It was also during the 1930s that Cirese became increasingly involved in the NAWL, an organization founded in 1899 with only twelve members. Its membership expanded from the initially East Coast base to a national one, with regional directors and state organizations. "The time may come, and we hope it will not be long off, when our interests as women lawyers will be identical with the men and problems which are still peculiarly ours will disappear" (Cirese letter to Lillian M. Kohlmetz, July 26, 1941, Cirese Papers), she wrote. Although she continued to work with the predominantly men's professional associations as well, Cirese argued in the 1930s and 1940s that "there . . . [was] still considerable place for a 'National' Women's Bar to effectively safeguard the civil rights of women in, as well as out of, the professions" (Cirese to Kohlmetz, July 26, 1941, Cirese Papers).

After holding a number of positions within the organization, Cirese became NAWL president in 1939. As president she worked tirelessly to bolster its membership and its credibility within the greater legal community. She wanted the NAWL to be truly representative of women lawyers. NAWL took positions during this period against discriminatory policies women faced in the job market. At its 1939 convention, the NAWL went on record as strongly disapproving the trend in state legislatures to enact discriminatory legislation against the employment of married women. Related to this issue of sex discrimination in employment was the highly political debate over the proposed Equal Rights Amendment. Women lawyers were in a particularly sensitive place regarding issues of discrimination and rights. They participated in a male-dominated legal system; yet they were often leading activists for women's rights and the expansion of opportunities of women attorneys. They worked inside and outside the system—organizing separate associations and attempting to join the men's professional groups.

The Equal Rights Amendment (ERA), first introduced in the U.S. Congress in 1923, remained a topic of heated debate among women lawyers. Cirese was part of a group of Illinois women attorneys, including DOROTHEA BLENDER, who were members of the Women's Bar Association of Illinois. They opposed the ERA, arguing that if passed it would not accomplish its intended purpose. Instead they offered a different "equal rights" amendment, the sex-disqualification removal amendment. This amendment aimed "at removing disqualifications on account of sex or marriage" and would, "eliminate the systematic efforts of certain groups to have various states enact laws restricting married women from gainful occupations"

("Senate Receives Amendment"). Chicago attorney and chair of the political and civil equality section of the legislative committee of the Women's Bar Association of Illinois (WBAI) Grace H. Harte argued that the WBAI sex-disqualification amendment offered by the women attorneys would break the twenty-year "deadlock between proponents and opponents" ("Senate Receives Amendment") of the ERA endorsed by the National Woman's Party (NWP). Women's groups had argued against the so-called "blanket" ERA ("Notes of the Women's Bar Association") championed by the NWP because they feared that its wording, considered too ambiguous, would endanger hard-won legislation that protected women. Harte's leadership was endorsed by Helen Cirese, Dorothea Blender, and other activists in the WBAI.

At the same time that the ERA was at a stalemate, incursions against women's rights to employment opportunities mounted. In 1940, for example, the City Council of Akron, Ohio, passed a resolution requesting the school board, the local department stores, and the tire companies to discharge all married women workers. The city councils of Columbus, Cincinnati, and Cleveland, Ohio, were considering similar resolutions. This was a national trend, begun in the 1930s with the decline of the economy in the depths of the Great Depression. The NAWL, at its convention in Oakland, California, in 1940, "went on record strongly disapproving the trend of legislation discriminating against married women as not only undemocratic but as an opening wedge to start other class discrimination" (Cirese to Grace B. Doering, April 18, 1940, Cirese Papers). This was the context for the NAWL's discussion of the ERA.

Cirese, as NAWL president in 1941, brought to the national organization the controversy of which amendment to support. NAWL had initially approved the NWP-endorsed ERA at a convention in 1935. Debate over the issue did not end, however, and disquiet over the position continued. From Cirese's standpoint, NAWL's position—adopted at a meeting in Los Angeles where "there were not more than 30 to 35 members present at the time the resolution was adopted"—(Cirese to Florence K. Thacker, June 11, 1941, Cirese Papers) was an obstacle to many women lawyers who were not joining NAWL because they disagreed with the ERA. In her capacity as president, Cirese had pushed for a growth in membership and contended that some kind of polling of the opinions of members was necessary on vital policy issues such as supporting or rejecting the ERA. She had campaigned for president on the platform that polling of all the members would be the way to eliminate control of the organization by "small cliques" (Cirese to Thacker, June 11, 1941, Cirese Papers). While some NAWL members wanted to avoid conflict, Cirese urged that a polling of the membership take place so that the organization could adopt an official position on the ERA.

After heated debate, with NWP activists present, NAWL endorsed the alternative sex-disqualification amendment two to one at its national convention in 1941; it was introduced in the U.S. Senate and referred to the Senate Judiciary Committee, becoming Senate Res. 72. Neither of the proposed amendments, however, was ever adopted.

From 1939 on, Cirese encouraged the NAWL to interact with the American Bar Association (ABA). After her term as president in 1941, she urged the organization to send delegates to ABA yearly conventions. ABA's primary criterion for organizational membership in its body was that a prospective affiliate already have at least 25 percent of its members as ABA members. In 1943, when the 25 percent mark was achieved, the NAWL became an ABA affiliate. Cirese served as an NAWL delegate to the ABA House of Delegates in 1959.

The outbreak of World War II engendered patriotic service among many Americans; often, first-generation Americans became sensitive about any perceived questioning of their loyalty. In the case of the children of Italian immigrants, Italy's Fascist government and aggression as a member of the Axis made public demonstrations of patriotism relevant. Cirese was an active member of a speaker's bureau that raised money for the War Fund Drive. She also participated in the Citizens Defense Corps, coordinating fund-raisers.

Cirese continued to live in Oak Park and to participate in the local village's politics. At the age of twenty-six she had campaigned unsuccessfully to be elected justice of the peace. In 1925 there were only two examples in Illinois of women judges—CATHERINE McCULLOCH, justice of the peace in Evanston, and MARY BARTELME, judge of the Cook County Circuit Court—and Cirese promoted her own and other women's election to the judiciary. She was the first woman to be elected justice of the peace and police magistrate in Oak Park in 1945. She was reelected in 1949, 1953, and 1957.

Cirese's interests in politics and the judicial system were not limited to Oak Park. In 1950, during the administration of President Harry S. Truman, Cirese was endorsed by the NAWL and the WBAI to be appointed by the president to fill a vacancy as a federal judge in the Northern Illinois District. Cirese actively pursued this appointment, conferring with state and county Democratic Party leaders, although she had not been a party stalwart or even much of a party supporter. She met with U.S. Senator Paul H. Douglas in January 1951 to discuss the vacancy; he made it clear that the selection had already been made and that Cirese was not the choice. How much this decision was a result of her lack of party affiliation or her sex is difficult to determine. The record on women judges in 1951 was grim, however. "In 1930 only twelve states had at least one woman judge. In 1950 there was at least one woman judge in thirty-nine of the states. It was not until 1949 that a woman was appointed to the federal district court" (Morello, 219).

In the postwar years Cirese became the first woman president of the West Suburban Bar Association (1949). She was also involved in the Immigrants' Protective League and chaired its Italian Committee in 1952 and 1954, organizing fund-raising concerts to benefit the league's work. She was also a founding member of the Justinian Society of Italian Lawyers, a member of Lex Legio of DePaul University, and a member of the American Foreign Law Association.

In 1961 Cirese ran again for justice of the peace of Oak Park Township. Her supporters came from the women's network she had earlier constructed in her days as an activist in the NAWL and WBAI. They included Dorothea Blender, whom she called upon to prepare letters to women and set up ads in the local newspapers, adding "I do appreciate this Dorothea. I like the way you use the English language" (Cirese to Blender, February 21, 1961, Cirese Papers). Special committees of the Central Business and Professional Women's Clubs and the Women's Bar Association of Illinois were established to assist in the campaign; NAWL found her eminently qualified and endorsed her for reelection. The competition had become more difficult with the reorganization of the Illinois judicial system. Cirese, who was running in a field of many candidates from whom only three justices of the peace would be elected, lost her bid for reelection.

Cirese continued to live in Oak Park in her family home; in 1969 at age seventy she moved her law offices from downtown Chicago to Oak Park. In her later years she was a trustee of the Celia Howard Foundation Trust of the Illinois Federation of Business and Professional Women's Clubs. She traveled with her sister Josephine Cirese, who also remained unmarried. Shortly before she would have turned eighty-four, Cirese died. Her funeral service was held at St. Giles Church, Oak Park, and she was buried at St. Joseph Cemetery.

Helen Cirese dedicated herself to a professional career in the law and, with many of the pioneering group of women attorneys in the 1920s through 1940s, fought political and legal battles to complete the unfinished work of removing women's legal disabilities that had begun with the campaign for woman suffrage in 1848 but that had by no means been accomplished by the passage of the Nineteenth Amendment in 1920.

Sources. The Helen M. Cirese Papers are at UIC Spec. Coll. They focus on her professional life and her involvement in a variety of organizations, including the National Association of Women Lawyers. There is an article by Grace H. Harte, "Notes of the Women's Bar Association," unknown newspaper clip, October 28, 1941, Cirese Papers, that is important for an understanding of the debate over the ERA in the National Association of Women Lawyers. Clippings include "Senate Receives Amendment for 'Equal Rights,'" *Chicago Daily News*, c. October 1941. The Women's Bar Association of Illinois Papers, CHS, include information about Cirese's work with that organization. Cirese's article, "Women on Juries," first printed in *Women Lawyers Journal* in 1939, was reproduced in the *70th Anniversary Calendar*, Women's Bar Association of Illinois, 1985. Issues of the *Oak Leaves*, an Oak Park village newspaper, can be found at the Oak Park Public Library and are a source of information on Cirese's campaigns for justice of the peace and her organizational activities in the western suburbs. "Beauty Aids Saved Woman's Life," Philadelphia *Evening Bulletin*, September 6, 1940, describes her high-profile criminal case. Karen Berger Morello, *The Invisible Bar: The Woman Lawyer in America 1638 to the Present* (1986) is helpful in providing background. Her obituary appears in the *CT*, October 13, 1983.

HOPE E. SHELDON

CLAIRE, MARION COOK WEBER
February 25, 1904–February 24, 1988
OPERA SINGER, RADIO EXECUTIVE

Marion Claire (her stage name) won acclaim on the operatic stage, delighted audiences as a singer of light operetta, and brought her art and talents into the homes of millions of Americans through her involvement in the early days of radio. She was born Marion Cook in Chicago to Horace Wright Cook, a successful lawyer and attorney, and Grace (Minkler) Cook, an accomplished pianist and organist. Her parents provided a secure upbringing as well as an early introduction to music and

FIG. 21. *Opera singer Marion Claire discusses her solo for the Grant Park Concert with her husband, Henry Weber, director of WGN's symphony orchestra; Grant Park, July 1937.*

the arts. Cook began her musical career as a child prodigy. Having started violin lessons at age six, by age ten she was featured as child star and soloist with the Chicago Symphony Orchestra in a performance of Henryk Wieniawski's *Faust* violin concerto at Ravinia Park, Highland Park, Illinois.

Pursuing a liberal arts education first at Ferry Hall, Lake Forest, Illinois, and then at National Park Seminary, Washington, D.C., Marion Claire balanced academic studies with engagements as a concert violinist. At the age of twenty-one, however, Claire made a self-discovery that set her career on a different path: "I possess a musical, a singing voice and enjoy using it" (Towerman, 5). Serious vocal training began in Chicago with Ettore Titta, brother of the famous baritone Titta Ruffo. Claire's natural musical abilities again proved prodigious, and by late 1925 she traveled to Milan, Italy, to learn the basic operatic repertory from the distinguished Mario Malatesta. After only several months of coaching in Milan, Marion Claire made her operatic debut in Venice singing the role of Mimi in Giacomo Puccini's *La Bohème*.

Favorable reaction to Claire's debut performance landed her an invitation to sing with the Berliner Staatsoper (Berlin State Opera) early in 1927; she appeared as Sophie in Richard Strauss's *Der Rosenkavalier*. Claire quickly won the hearts of

Berlin audiences, received a reported twenty-seven curtain calls after her debut, and succeeded in obtaining contracts with the Staatsoper for the next four consecutive seasons. For Berlin she added new roles that helped set the ground for appearances in leading opera houses throughout Germany, Italy, and France. Her new roles included Desdemona in Giuseppe Verdi's *Otello*, Elsa in Richard Wagner's *Lohengrin*, Nedda in Ruggiero Leoncavallo's *I Pagliacci*, Eva in Wagner's *Die Meistersinger* and Elizabeth in *Tannhäuser*, Violetta in Verdi's *La Traviata*, Marguerite in Charles Gounod's *Faust*, and Liù in Giacomo Puccini's *Turandot*. She sang the title role in Jules Massenet's *Manon* as well as other substantial parts in *Carmen, Das Rheingold, Götterdämmerung,* and *Don Quixote*.

Following a Berlin performance in 1928, Marion Claire met fellow American Henry George Weber, conductor of the Chicago Civic Opera Company and the youngest conductor of grand opera in America, who happened to be in Europe scouting vocal talents. Astounded by Claire's voice and struck with her beauty, Weber proposed marriage and the opportunity for Claire to return to Chicago where she might sing with such performers as MARY GARDEN and ROSA RAISA.

Claire's Chicago debut, portraying Mimi in *La Bohème* at the Auditorium Theater, came on November 1, 1928, the second night of the season. This performance was eclipsed by a subsequent portrayal of Elsa in Wagner's *Lohengrin* on November 4. Here, Claire was electrifying, having gained distinction even among the rest of the notable cast. That same season she recreated her roles as Desdemona in *Otello* and Nedda in *I Pagliacci*. With the 1929 Chicago production of Jacques Offenbach's *Tales of Hoffmann*, Claire assumed the dual roles of Giulietta and Antonia (a challenge for any soprano) and later assumed the part of Cherubino in a risk-taking "modernistic" adaptation of Wolfgang Amadeus Mozart's *Marriage of Figaro*—surprising at least some of the operagoers, yet not without some success.

Perhaps the greatest surprise of the Chicago opera season came at noon on January 21, 1929, when Marion Claire married Henry Weber in her suite at the Congress Hotel. The simple Protestant ceremony was witnessed by only sixteen of the couple's closest family members and friends. That evening, Claire and Weber left for Boston, where they joined the opera's touring company in a production of Wagner's *Lohengrin*, which was scheduled to open in one week's time. News of their "secret" wedding was publicized from Chicago to New York City in the next morning's papers.

Boston heralded the newlyweds' arrival, and their performances drew music critics from up and down the East Coast. Claire's performance in *Lohengrin* met with much acclaim. Critic H. T. Parker described "her voice . . . the voice of Elsa . . . [as] young, clear, shimmering, dream-haunted, reticent until the hour of fate" (Wielich, 13). Soon after the Boston success, accompanied by her conductor-manager-husband, Claire returned to Berlin and Italy to complete her scheduled European appearances.

Claire and Weber returned to New York on July 12, 1931, and embarked on a leisurely automobile trip back to Chicago where they made a home together in the North Shore suburb of Lake Bluff, Illinois. Claire was delighted about their return, "the sight of beautiful Michigan Boulevard with all its great build-ings, bustle and thrilling splendor. It was wonderful being home" (Towerman, 16). Their only child, Henry George Jr., was born November 20, 1932. Claire combined duties as a mother and homemaker with concert engagements with the Chicago Symphony Orchestra, the Cleveland Symphony, and other leading philharmonic societies throughout the United States. Claire enjoyed traveling and found much pleasure away from performing in such outdoor activities as horseback riding and swimming.

On January 13, 1934, Claire returned to Chicago's operatic stage in the title role of Massenet's *Manon*. Other appearances found her sharing the spotlight with Lotte Lehmann in Richard Strauss's *Der Rosenkavalier* and as Liù, with Rosa Raisa, in Puccini's *Turandot*. In July 1936 Claire gave an orchestral *Lieder* recital at the Ravinia Festival with Weber conducting. The couple had a large following in Chicago, and Claire moved gracefully within the city's social circles. Henry Weber enjoyed prestige as a member of the then all-male Cliff Dwellers Club, an elite gathering of important artists, businessmen, and members of Chicago society. Claire did not hesitate to accept guest appearances throughout the Midwest in support of various clubs and rallies that shared her Republican Party views. On December 15, 1937, Marion Claire made her farewell stage performance before Chicago operagoers, choosing to sing Mimi opposite Swedish tenor Jussi Björling's Rodolfo in *La Bohème*—the very role with which she had launched her career.

From the mid-1930s through the 1940s, Marion Claire expanded her singing repertory to encompass operetta and the lighter musicals that were capturing the enthusiasm of Chicago as well as national audiences. She took principal parts in such shows as Noel Coward's *Bittersweet*, Sigmund Romberg's *Desert Song*, and many others. Her appearances in Max Gordon's *The Great Waltz* at the Center Theater of New York's Radio City Music Hall in 1934–35 helped to earn the show its reputation as the spectacle of the century. Claire's film debut, singing "Music in My Heart" in a Hollywood release of *Make a Wish*, came soon afterward in 1937.

Claire's increasing popularity within the fields of operetta and American musical theater drew her to the attention of radio hosts and program directors. Those millions of Americans unable to see her on stage or screen thrilled to Claire's radio broadcast performances on programs sponsored by General Motors, Chevrolet (sponsor of *Hour of Smiles*), Sears and Roebuck, Lucky Strike, Kraft (sponsor of *The Kraft Music Hall*), and Lux soap (sponsor of *Lux Theater*). In 1940, Claire was featured soloist for the inaugural broadcast of the *Chicago Tribune Symphonic Hour*, with the Chicago Symphony Orchestra directed by Frederick Stock.

Prospects of reaching, entertaining, and educating vast numbers of eager listeners via the new medium of radio were intriguing to both Marion Claire and her husband. Weber became director of music for station WGN in 1934, while Claire took a great interest in a WGN experiment that sought to unite the beauty of operatic arias and musical numbers with the straightforwardness and dramatic potency of spoken dialogue. The result was the uniquely creative *Chicago Theatre of the Air*, aired first on October 5, 1940; it held its prime time position on Saturday evenings from 9:00 to 10:00 P.M. for fifteen years. From

1940 to 1947, Marion Claire was the show's featured prima donna for the many hundreds of opera and operetta renderings brought to its devoted listeners. She also served later in a managerial role. The program was received across the nation via the Mutual Broadcasting System and opened with a presentation of Rudolph Friml's operetta, *The Vagabond King,* with Claire opposite romantic baritone Conrad Thibault.

As leading lady, Claire was joined by guest singers from the Chicago, New York Metropolitan, and San Carlo opera companies. Claire's leading men included such luminaries as Richard Tucker, Giorgio Tozzi, Igor Gorin, and Robert Merrill. George Bizet's *Carmen,* Gounod's *Faust,* Puccini's *La Bohème,* Verdi's *Rigoletto,* Johann Strauss's *Die Fledermaus,* and Gioacchino Rossini's *Barber of Seville* were but a few of the program's offerings. Operettas included Romberg's *The Student Prince* and *Maytime,* and Victor Herbert's *Mlle. Modiste.*

Marion Claire retired from her singing career in 1947 and became the full-time director of WGN's FM station, WGNB Radio, with offices in the Tribune Towers in downtown Chicago. Busy with her increased duties as a radio executive, Claire still found time to remain with *Chicago Theatre of the Air* as the program's production supervisor. She came to realize that her dual position offered marvelous opportunities to encourage and assist hopeful young singers at the start of their careers. Claire sought out budding talents in the Chicago area and routinely heard auditions of young vocalists from all over the country. She used a portion of *Chicago Theatre of the Air* time called "Career Performance" to introduce new singers to the radio public. Furthermore, Claire took personal interest in young people's musical aspirations and great pride in offering them every opportunity. "You can't realize what personal gratification comes from the discovery of an unknown artist, ready, waiting for a break. . . . It's a full time job; however, it's our responsibility to see that these young people get that chance they justifiably deserve" (Towerman, 5).

Claire served as executive director of WGNB until the station closed in 1953. The *Chicago Theatre of the Air* broadcast its final show, appropriately enough with a presentation of Coward's *Bittersweet,* on May 7, 1955. Claire retired with her husband to Fort Lauderdale, Florida, where she could look back upon a success-filled and varied career and enjoy visits with her three grandchildren. Marion Claire died in Fort Lauderdale.

Music critics universally applauded Marion Claire throughout her career. Some said she sang "with bells on her tongue" (Crimmins). The beauty of her voice, its resiliency and flexibility, enabled her to champion many styles ranging from Wagnerian music drama to show tunes. Her glamorous physical appearance, graceful demeanor, and sense of style were attested to by the many photographs that often accompanied reviews of her singing. Long after her retirement from the stage and radio, Marion Claire helped establish new generations of opera singers.

Sources. Sample recorded programs of Marion Claire and the *Chicago Theatre of the Air* are available at the Museum of Broadcast Communications Archives, Chicago. Jay Hickerson, *The New Revised Ultimate History of Network Radio Programming and Guide to All Circulating Shows* (1996) has information on a private collection of *Chicago Theatre*

of the Air recordings. Claire shared much information with columnist Sidney Towerman in an interview published as "Marion Claire: Lady of the Airwaves," *Music News,* November 1949, which features a full-size photograph of Claire on the issue's front cover. Another important article on Claire is Ludwig Wielich, "Behind the Curtain: A New Yorker Goes to Boston to See the Opera from Chicago," *Musician,* March 1929. Reviews of Claire's singing career are in *CT, NYT,* and other U.S. and European newspapers from 1928 to 1947, as well as in such studies as Edward C. Moore, *Forty Years of Opera in Chicago* (1930). Claire's appearances and roles on the Chicago opera stage may also be traced in the detailed appendix to Ronald L. Davis, *Opera in Chicago* (1966). K. J. Kutsch and Leo Riemens, *Concise Biographical Dictionary of Singers,* translated by Harry Earl Jones (1969), and *Grosses Sängerlexikon* (1987) provide information on the three recordings Claire made of operetta arias for Victor Records. For the *Chicago Theatre of the Air,* see entries in Frank Buxton and Bill Owen, *The Big Broadcast: 1920–1950* (1972), as well as John Dunning, *Tune in Yesterday—The Ultimate Encyclopedia of Old-Time Radio: 1925–1976* (1976). Her obituary, "Marion Weber," by Jerry Crimmins, appeared in *CT,* February 25, 1988.

MICHAEL A. NEALON

CLARK, HERMA NAOMI
October 25, 1871–November 26, 1959
NEWSPAPER COLUMNIST, MONOLOGIST, POPULAR HISTORIAN

Herma Clark was born on a farm in Bureau County, Illinois, the daughter of Major Atherton Clark and Jerusa (Whitmarsh) Clark. Clark's father was a Civil War soldier and farmer. Her mother taught school before her marriage. Clark had an older brother and sister, Hubert Atherton and Lora Harriet, and a younger sister, Alice. Another baby girl died in infancy. When she was ten, Clark and her family moved to Princeton, Illinois, where she attended school and graduated from Princeton High School. After attending Oberlin College, Oberlin, Ohio, for one year, Clark left and taught school in Seatonville, Illinois, a small mining town near Princeton. She hated the town and the teaching experience, remaining only one year.

In 1897, at age twenty-six, Clark moved to Chicago, where she hoped to make a living as a freelance writer or as a newspaper woman. She lived at the Young Women's Christian Association (YWCA) and wrote some free-lance articles for the Chicago *Evening Post* on women's work and shopping. These were "mainly contributions to the Woman's Column" (Clark, "Adventures of a Columnist," 2). She also took a part-time job reading several hours a day to an elderly Chicago business pioneer, William Blair. Blair had established the first wholesale hardware business in the city. Following his death a few months later, Clark agreed to stay on as companion and secretary to Blair's widow, Sarah. Clark's decision to live in the Blair household and work for Sarah Blair gave Clark the opportunity to hear her employer's stories about the culture of early Chicago and about the pioneer families whose efforts had been instrumental in the city's growth and prosperity in the nineteenth century. She also met many of Sarah Blair's "large circle of friends . . . many of the people who had helped to build Chicago . . . and their descendants" ("Adventures of a Columnist," 2). Clark recorded the details in small notebooks. Sarah Blair died in 1923 at the age of ninety-six.

After twenty-five years of employment and tutelage with

Blair, Clark found herself, at age fifty-two, without a position. She continued to write as a Chicago correspondent for the New York periodical, *Town and Country*, but this work alone was insufficient to support her financially. Clark turned to the real estate business, working first in Chicago and later in Florida. While in Florida she began to write society news about Chicagoans living in Miami for the *Chicago Tribune*.

In 1929 Clark returned to Chicago with plans for a new writing career. She convinced the editors at the *Chicago Tribune* to experiment with a feature column that would be based on letters written by a fictitious nineteenth-century Chicagoan, Martha Freeman Esmond, to her school friend Julia Boyd, of New York. This format allowed Clark a vehicle to use the social history material she had gathered in her years as social secretary for Sarah Blair. The first column of "When Chicago Was Young" appeared in the *Tribune*'s Sunday edition, September 15, 1929. The first letter was dated "Chicago, October 27, 1854" and began, "Dear Julia, Father has gone to a political meeting to be addressed by someone I never heard of before—the Honorable Abraham Lincoln of Springfield, Illinois, capital of our state" (*Chicago Tribune*, June 15, 1933).

That opening sentence began a *Tribune* tradition that continued each Sunday for the next thirty years. Through Martha Freeman Esmond's letters, Clark wrote of events in Chicago history and of the socially prominent Chicagoans of that time. The columns began in 1854 when Martha Freeman was a young woman living in her parents' home. They followed Martha's life as she fell in love, married, had a family, and was part of the growing, changing Chicago. Readers mourned after President Lincoln's death, followed Chicago's rich and poor as they fled the Great Chicago Fire in 1871, and got a glimpse of prominent city leaders as they attended the opera, entertained in elaborate homes, and talked the politics of the day.

Readers were convinced that Martha Esmond had actually lived and wrote to Clark asking where she had found Martha's letters, inquiring whether Esmond was still alive, or, if not, where she was buried. The realism of Clark's writing came from the stories she had gathered while working in the Blair household and from additional information she researched in historical archives. Clark was always careful to reply to readers' questions, saying that the events described by Martha Esmond were true but that Esmond and her family were a fictitious vehicle created to tell the story.

Subject matter in the column was not limited to the social affairs of Chicagoans but included the election of James Garfield as United States President, transportation developments in Illinois in 1841, the Women and Children's Hospital in the city, the Chicago kindergarten movement, and the death of author Louisa May Alcott. Footnotes that traced family connections of real people mentioned by Martha Esmond added to the interest of the column. In a series on Chicago houses and buildings, Clark requested that readers send in stories about old houses still standing. Columns describing elegant banquet feasts and old Chicago cooking carried a request for favorite recipes. Responses from enthusiastic readers provided Clark with factual material for future columns.

Soon Clark's interest in and her knowledge of Chicago history opened the way for other projects on early Chicago. In

1932, Clark joined with local playwright ALICE GERSTENBERG in writing *When Chicago Was Young*. The historical play began with a prologue set in 1673 on the banks of the Chicago river. The play moved on to the Lincoln-Douglas debates in 1858, then to the Great Chicago Fire of 1871, and ended with a lavish ball set in the Potter Palmer residence in 1893, the year of the World's Columbian Exposition, when BERTHA HONORÉ PALMER debuted as the premier hostess of the city. The play, which anticipated the 1933 Century of Progress Exposition, was performed at the Goodman Theater for a three-week engagement.

Long before the genre of women's history became popular, Herma Clark's interest in social life and customs led her to include many of Chicago's prominent women professionals and activists, as well as society leaders, in her presentations. In *The Elegant Eighties: When Chicago Was Young*, Clark wrote about HANNAH SOLOMON and the Chicago Woman's Club, Drs. MARY THOMPSON and SARAH HACKETT STEVENSON, and concert pianist FANNIE BLOOMFIELD ZEISLER.

In 1933 the popularity of Clark's column inspired the publication of *Dear Julia*, a collection of some of the columns written over the previous five years. The activities surrounding the 1933 Century of Progress Exposition and the exhibit rooms that Clark helped design provided additional publicity for the book. During this period, Clark offered a series of history puzzles in her column. She received more than four hundred letters, including telegrams and special delivery responses to her quiz, "Distinguished Cities of Illinois." Winners of the quizzes were sent autographed copies of *Dear Julia*.

Herma Clark began a second career as a public speaker and monologist in the 1930s. Standing five feet nine inches with red hair and grey eyes, she dressed in Victorian period costume. She gave presentations at the Drake Hotel, Orchestra Hall, the Chicago Woman's Club, and the Cordon Club, where she was a member. "Bustles and Bangs," a light-hearted description of the customs and manners of the 1880s, was one of her most popular programs. One fan wrote that Clark's "skill as a pantomimist makes one truly see the imaginary cloth she measures and the amazing decorative gadgets she pulls out of her (also imaginary) telescope" (Mrs. William Tuttle, note to Clark, March 6, 1939, Clark Papers). Clark's speaking career included the new medium of radio, which was especially popular in Chicago during the 1930s. In her radio broadcasts, she read "Dear Julia" letters, described the elegant eighties for her radio audience, and gave a series of historical monologues, "First Ladies," on the wives of the American presidents. Clark's second book, *The Elegant Eighties: When Chicago Was Young* (1941), was a collection of "Dear Julia" letters that her fictitious heroine, Martha Esmond, had written in the 1880s. The book further solidified Clark's reputation as a historian of Chicago society and cultural life. Clark completed *Victorian Keepsake* in 1941, an anthology that contained a collection of old prose and poetry popular during the Victorian era. She patterned the book after the early English annuals, gift books that contained "a miscellany of moral observations, anecdotes of the great and sentimental poetry" (*Victorian Keepsake*, 10).

In 1943, Clark collaborated again with Alice Gerstenberg in

an updated version of their 1932 play *When Chicago Was Young* under a new title, *Port of Chicago*. It was produced in celebration of the fiftieth anniversary of the World's Columbian Exposition. Once again, the dramatization of important people and events in Chicago's early history was brought to life for a new theater audience. In May 1946, after seventeen years of bringing local history to Chicago audiences through her newspaper columns, books, radio broadcasts, and monologues, Herma Clark was given an award for her contribution to the field of literature by the Friends of Literature, a Chicago society dedicated to supporting writers.

During and after World War II, Clark found that social clubs and the general public were more interested in the war and postwar events than in people and events in the 1800s. There were fewer requests for monologues and public appearances. While she continued to write her weekly columns, Clark needed to increase her income and undertook some new writing projects with mixed success. A proposal for a book on "women who influenced Chicago" (Clark letter to Rosemary B. York, March 29, 1943, Clark Papers) never moved past the planning stage, and an attempt at a Chicago historical cookbook was judged too limited by a prospective publisher. In 1947, Clark did find a market for a pamphlet, *Let's Walk Along Rush Street*, which was popular with both local historians and Chicago tourists. Another small publication, *Keys for Happiness*, was published in 1948 and offered Clark's method of achieving satisfaction in life. It included the optimistic premise that happy people are successful people, and the door of opportunity opens for them.

In the Cold War climate of the 1950s, Clark became an advocate for the Republican Party and strongly campaigned for Republican presidential candidate Dwight David Eisenhower. She had become concerned that millions of voters had not voted in the 1948 presidential election and, in preparation for distribution before November 1952, Clark coauthored with Alice McClanahan a one-act play designed to show the importance of voting. Called *America vs. Mary X Public*, it was directed at women voters. The play was read at the women's headquarters of the Republican Party's National Convention and was heard in condensed form over the *Chicago Tribune*'s radio station WGN.

In 1950, just a few months short of her eightieth birthday, Clark, who was still writing her column, seeking new projects, and living on her own, fell and broke her arm. After a three-week hospital stay, Clark spent time recuperating under the care of her niece in Glencoe, Illinois, a suburb north of Chicago. There she received close attention from her family, including two grandnieces who thought their rather famous aunt was quite elegant and special.

Clark had never married but stayed close to her married sisters and brothers and their families. Clark's city friends and associates and her many relatives made up the extended family network important to her over the more than fifty years she lived and worked in the city. In 1953 Clark traveled back and forth to Princeton, Illinois, as she went through the process of dismantling the family home. That same year, she was forced to cut back on her speaking engagements because of high blood pressure. The Society of Midland Authors honored Clark in 1954, the silver anniversary of her column.

The death of her sister Lora Clark Gossard in 1957 was especially difficult for Clark. Through the years the two sisters had visited each other regularly and had written and published a few songs together, including the patriotic "God Bless Our Home." Two years later Herma Clark died suddenly of a heart attack. At age eighty-eight, she had been living at the Bethany Methodist home in Chicago and had continued to work at the *Chicago Tribune* up to the time of her death, working in the editorial offices the day before she died. A funeral service was held at Fourth Presbyterian Church.

Herma Clark invented a career when she was fifty-seven years old. An independent woman who was largely self-educated, Clark learned to market her skills and create interest among the general public for local history subjects. Without using a strident tone, she managed to educate the public through writing about a great variety of women activists, including Bertha Honoré Palmer; Drs. Sarah Hackett Stevenson, JULIA HOLMES SMITH, and Mary H. Thompson; Methodist churchwoman LUCY MEYER, who founded the Deaconess Training School; clubwomen FANNIE BARRIER WILLIAMS and Hannah Solomon; and pioneer Juvenile Court Judge MARY BARTELME. Her resourcefulness made it possible for Clark to succeed as a freelance writer and career woman in a highly competitive commercial world.

Sources. The Herma Clark Papers at the CHS include a typescript of her undated autobiographical sketch, "Adventures of a Columnist"; business and personal correspondence; fan mail; and drafts of columns and articles covering her thirty-year career. An interview with Katrina Schmidt Pfutzenreuter, of Glencoe, Illinois, was conducted March 10, 1997. The column "When Chicago Was Young" appeared weekly in the *Chicago Sunday Tribune* from September 15, 1929, through November 22, 1959. Clark's books include *Dear Julia* (1933), *The Elegant Eighties: When Chicago Was Young* (1941), *Victorian Keepsake* (1941), and *Keys to Happiness* (1948). Clark wrote three plays: *When We Were Young*, coauthored with Alice Gerstenberg (1932); *Port of Chicago*, coauthored with Gerstenberg (1943); and *America vs. Mary X Public*, coauthored with Alice McClanahan (1952). Articles about Clark include two in the *CT*: Ruth Crary, "A Beloved Column Has a Birthday," September 12, 1954; and Anne Clark Fischer, "A Tribute to 'When Chicago Was Young,'" December 13, 1959. See also n.a., "A Deceiving Woman: Herma Clark Writes of Yesteryear Society," *Editor and Publisher*, November 13, 1954. Clark's obituary appeared in the *CT*, November 27, 1959.

CLARICE STETTER

CLEARY, KATE McPHELIM
August 22, 1863–July 16, 1905
NOVELIST, SHORT STORY WRITER, POET, HUMORIST

Kate McPhelim Cleary, whose short stories, sketches, articles, and poems appeared frequently in the *Chicago Tribune*, the *Chicago Daily News*, and the *Chicago Record Herald* as well as in major American periodicals from the 1880s until her death in 1905, was born in Richibucto, New Brunswick, Canada. Her father, James McPhelim, born in Ireland and educated at the University of Louvaine in Belgium, immigrated to New Brunswick, where he began a lumber and shipping business and served as the High Sheriff of Kent County. Margaret (Kelly) McPhelim, her mother, born in Ivy Lodge, County Tipperary, Ireland, moved to New Brunswick following the death of her father, a physician, when she was fourteen. James and Margaret McPhelim married in 1856 and had four children: Edward Joseph, 1860; Kate Theresa, 1863; Frances Albert, 1865; and Catherine Chrystal, who died as an infant.

When Kate McPhelim was two, her father died. The family remained in New Brunswick, and she attended the Sacred Heart Convent in St. John, where she studied classics and began writing poetry. Financial difficulties forced her mother to return to Ireland sometime during this period to live with relatives at Ivy Lodge and the Mall, Templemore. Eventually, Margaret McPhelim decided to try her chances in America and immigrated to Philadelphia with her three children in the late 1870s.

Kate McPhelim, her mother, and her brother Edward worked together to support the family on the income they made from writing poetry for the newspapers, family periodicals, and story magazines proliferating at the time. Kate McPhelim also sold paintings and sketches, but when *Saturday Night* published her first short story, "Only Jerry," when she was fifteen years old, her writing career began in earnest. Under the pseudonym K. Temple More, after her Irish homeland, her stories began to appear regularly. Her first stories and poems were typical of popular literature of the time with sentimental themes and pastoral settings; however, even at this young age, her sense of humor and her love of irony glimmered through. She continued to use pen names, usually K. Temple More, Kate Ashley, and Kate Chrystal.

In 1880, Margaret McPhelim and her children moved to Chicago. A strong Catholic, Margaret enrolled her daughter in St. Xavier Academy, which was run by the Irish-Catholic Mercy Sisters. The McPhelim family wrote to support themselves, selling poems for thirty-six dollars a dozen. Margaret wrote poetry; Frank, news reports; Kate, short stories; and Edward, older than Kate, began working full time for the *Chicago Tribune*, becoming one of the city's leading literary and drama critics.

In her autobiographical short story entitled "Why We Didn't Hear Nilsson," Kate McPhelim describes her early Chicago years in their "French flat" as ones in which they were "disgustingly poor, . . . absurdly poor" (*Chicago Tribune*, March 19, 1899). Yet the family rose to the challenge, using humor and wit to assail their condition and realizing that "intellectually [they] were wealthy" (*Chicago Tribune*, March 19, 1899). Following a tradition established by Finley Peter Dunne in his weekly newspaper columns about Mr. Martin Dooley, the aging, philosophical barkeeper in the Irish neighborhood of Bridgeport on Chicago's South Side, humor and satire became strong elements in Kate McPhelim's writing throughout her career. An urban local colorist like Dunne, she provided a female voice for the Irish immigrant experience, not only in urban Chicago but also in the rural Midwest.

Kate McPhelim met Michael Timothy Cleary sometime around 1882–83, perhaps at a dance hosted by the Irish-American Club at the Palmer House, for his name is penciled in for the third set on a dance card in the family scrapbooks. Michael Cleary was born in Clonmel, Ireland, in 1855, and served as a member of Company B of Chicago's First Regular Infantry of the Illinois National Guard. Since their immigration to Chicago in 1863, Michael Cleary and his father, James Mansfield Cleary, a liquor wholesaler, had been working to bring the rest of the family from Ireland to Chicago. When Kate McPhelim met her future husband, he was considering relocating in the West because of health problems, presumably tuberculosis. Traveling to Nebraska where his brother-in-law John Templeton had established several lumber businesses, he decided to begin M. T. Cleary Lumber and Coal in the newly created community of Hubbell on the Nebraska and Kansas border. He returned to Chicago, and he and Kate wed on February 26, 1884. The next month the Clearys and Margaret McPhelim arrived at the dull red depot in the frontier village to begin a new life.

Within the first year of marriage, thanks to the mushrooming growth of the new community and materials from Michael Cleary's lumber business, the family was able to build a new two-story Victorian-style home. That same year, using the pen name of Kate Chrystal, Cleary wrote *The Lady of Lynhurst*, published by Street and Smith for their Leading Novel series. Unfortunately, no copies of this text have been found. In 1887, under the pseudonym of Mrs. Sumner Hayden, Cleary wrote *Vella Vernell; or, an Amazing Marriage* for Street and Smith's Select series, a book that the editors promoted as a true story occurring in a major western American city—Chicago.

The plot, a comedy of manners, centers on the twins Vella and Voyle Vernell and their wealthy uncle, the historic "lucky colonel of Chicago," who is raising them. The plot twists and turns around arranged marriages, mistaken identities, train wrecks, stolen inheritances, and a grisly murder caused by driving a nail into a man's ear. Although the novel provides a predictably happily ending for the twins, the work rises above formula fiction in the unusually drawn characters and in Cleary's excellent local color description of the city, especially the palatial estates of Chicago, the magnificence of the city's Inter-State Industrial Exposition, and the commerce and hustle of State Street. Cleary describes the characters walking past the "stately brown-stone *Tribune* building" and down Clark Street, "with its glittering jewelry stores, its numerous fruit-stands, its theaters, its gaping rows of pawn-shops, its glaringly placarded Dime Museum" (*Vella Vernell*, 116). She contrasts the opulence of the city to "its physically and morally inodorous slums" which exist "out of elbow room of the great stores and pleasure temples" (p. 116).

Cleary describes a wealthy matron's fashionable apparel, noting that "every crackling fold of her stiff silk gown protest[ed] against man's inhumanity to woman" (*Vella Vernell*, 99). Later she pokes fun at a pretentious middle-class Chicago home "with a carpet of pseudo Brussels, in which the colors swore at each other" (p. 150).

The Clearys had six children within ten years: James Mansfield, 1887; Marguerite, 1889; Gerald Vernon, 1890; Rosemarie Catherine, 1892; Vera Valentine, 1894; and Edward Sheridan, 1897. Marguerite and Rosemarie died within a four-month period from December 1894 to March 1895. Cleary herself nearly died from childbed fever after the birth of her daughter Vera Valentine, born on Valentine's Day. During these childbearing years, she became a close friend and confidant of ELIA PEATTIE, who was living in Omaha with her husband at the time.

How Peattie and Cleary met is unknown, but they may have

become acquainted through Cleary's brother, Edward McPhelim, and their Chicago newspaper ties. The earliest surviving letter from Peattie to Cleary is dated June 7, 1891, but the tone is already familiar. Peattie was only one year older than Cleary, and the two women shared not only personal intimacies as friends but advice on caring for children and husbands and support for publishing ventures. They corresponded and visited often, sometimes leaving their older children to play with one another for several weeks during the summer. This friendship proved crucial to Cleary in later years.

The Hubbell, Nebraska, years produced an eclectic assortment of writing: domestic articles published in *Good Housekeeping*, humorous sketches and poetry in *Puck* magazine, realistic and naturalistic short stories about the West for the *Chicago Tribune* and *Belford's Monthly*, and children's stories and poems in *St. Nicholas* and the *Youth's Companion*. Mrs. Henry Fisk read two of Cleary's poems for the opening ceremonies for the Nebraska Building at the World's Columbian Exposition in Chicago in 1893, since Cleary was uncomfortable reading her own poetry in public. "The Corn" emphasized the accepted belief of the West as a Garden of Eden, employing the metaphor of the rows of corn as an army conquering the Plains, typical of the myth of Manifest Destiny. The other poem, "Nebraska," depicted a darker side of the pioneering venture. The narrative described a family of ten living in a sod house and their despair when the mother became pregnant again. When the baby was born, its laughter lightened the family's burdens; however, when it died, the mother continued to rock and rock and rock the cradle with the dead baby in it.

In 1896, Cleary also became involved in the presidential campaign between Republican William McKinley and Nebraska Democrat William Jennings Bryan, as well as in the heated debate over the Gold or Silver Standard. Seven months pregnant, Cleary contented herself with politicking on the sidelines and by proxy, writing political speeches and poems upholding the Republican nominees that her son Jim, age nine, recited before enthusiastic crowds. Jim became a state and national celebrity because of his unusual abilities in the political arena, and he was nicknamed "The Boy Orator of Hubbell." Accompanied by his mother, Jim also headed parades, proudly carrying "Old Glory" and leading marchers in "Shouting for McKinley," a seven-stanza song with a repeated chorus written by Cleary.

Cleary's "Prairie Sketches," printed in Chicago newspapers, also were popular. Comparing Cleary to her writer friend, Elia Peattie, a Chicago *Evening Post* critic commented on her "keen Irish perception" and her graphic depiction of the "terrors of frontier life" ("Woman and Her Ways"), anticipating that her forthcoming novel, *Like a Gallant Lady*, also dealing with Nebraska life, would be a success. Set in Bubble, Nebraska, the novel's romantic plot involves an insurance scam in the tiny frontier community. The protagonist is the cultured Ivera Lyle, who comes from Chicago to visit her brother Rob and to find out about her fiancé's supposed death. Ivera Lyle resolves this complicated mystery and returns to Chicago where she belongs, not in Nebraska with the "awful, oppressive, overwhelming silence of the prairies" (p. 266). Again, the novel is saved from mediocrity by Cleary's colorful characters, her subtle satire and humor, and by her depiction of the small frontier community and its inhabitants.

With *Like a Gallant Lady*'s publication in 1897, Cleary's reputation grew. She became known as a humorist and was described as a "genuine bohemian, loving freedom and unconventionality as more ordinary women love matters of dress and household adornment" ("Women Who Have Humor," *Chicago Chronicle*). In her private life, however, there was tragedy and domestic conflict. Births and deaths were recorded with frequency. Kate and Michael Cleary both suffered ill health. In February 1898, Michael sold his Nebraska lumber business and tried to find a better opportunity farther west; however, he returned to Chicago in May 1898, to be followed by Kate Cleary and their children in July.

The Clearys moved to the Austin neighborhood on Chicago's West Side. Just incorporated into the city, village-like Austin was a strongly Irish community. Returning to the literary scene in Chicago in the midst of a great explosion of regional writing, Cleary began writing her strongest realistic short stories. *McClure's* featured two of her naturalistic stories in 1901: "The Stepmother" (September), a pioneer tale set in Nebraska, and "The Mission of Kitty Malone" (November), a story of an Irish couple in Chicago.

"The Mission of Kitty Malone" is set the week before Thanksgiving on the Southwest Side of Chicago, "along one of the poor streets that lie south of Van Buren and east of Blue Island Avenue" (p. 89) in the old Nineteenth Ward. Destitute but proud, the elderly Irish couple inhabit "the barest, poorest, shabbiest, cleanest little room" (p. 89). Dennis Malone's pneumonia has taken all of their resources. Too proud to ask even their grown children for help, Kitty Malone turns as a last resort to public relief. Ashamed to even tell her husband of forty-nine years of their dire need, she walks "down town" to the unwelcoming County Agent's office on Clinton Street. Humiliating her further, the Agent informs her that she cannot have any food until he sends someone to her home to investigate her case.

Shamed, she realizes that "she had asked for and received charity for the first time in all her cheerful, uncomplaining, hard-working, heroic old life. And the knowledge stung her. . . . She had begged—she!" ("Kitty Malone," 95). The Thanksgiving story ends happily, albeit sentimentally. Rody, their son, who has been wounded in the war in the Philippines, arrives home in time to save his parents from the disgrace of "begging" for food or from being sent to the state home at Dunning.

In this story, Cleary empathetically describes honest and proud Irish neighbors like the ones she knew in Austin: the Irish Catholic priest of the neighborhood parish, the street-smart "Celtic Shylocks" ("Kitty Malone," 90), and the women of the "Married Ladies' Sodality" [sic] (p. 91). Having experienced poverty herself, Cleary understood firsthand the gnawing of hunger and the shame of charity.

Financial woes and ill health continued to plague the Clearys. From 1900 to 1903, as Michael tried job after job, moving the family from one address to another, Cleary had to give up her serious writing to keep the pot boiling. She resorted to writing formula fiction, stories she could churn out daily without revision, for the *Chicago Tribune*, *Chicago Daily News*, and the short story syndicates.

In 1903, while moving to yet another apartment, Cleary collapsed and was admitted to the Elgin Insane Asylum to be cured of morphine and alcohol addiction. In 1894, when Cleary had been suffering from childbed fever, the Hubbell village doctor, a morphine addict himself, had first given her morphine for pain. Cleary continued to use the drug in the following years, when the loss of her mother and her two daughters as well as her husband's long absences contributed to her addiction.

Since antibiotics were unknown until the 1930s and most frontier doctors had little or no medical training, quinine, morphine, and laudanum were therapeutic mainstays for most "female complaints." Although it cured nothing, morphine relieved physical pain as well as emotional anxiety. Countless multi-drug patent medicines, containing morphine, laudanum, cocaine, heroin, and alcohol, were easily purchased through the mail or at any general store. Most users were respectable middle-aged, white, middle-class women, doctors, or white southern males, all of whom used the drugs for medicinal purposes and obtained their drugs legally.

Cleary's specific treatment while at Elgin will never be known, but widely diverse drug treatments proliferated at the turn of the century, including the Keeley Gold Cure, the St. George Association, the Turvey Treatment, and Dr. Kane's De Quincey Home Method. When the Bayer Company in Germany introduced heroin, a derivative of morphine, in 1898, chemists recommended it as a safe treatment for morphine addiction. Cleary remained in the Elgin hospital for treatment from October 13, 1903, until she was released into the supervision of her friend, Elia Peattie, on February 5, 1904. Michael Cleary had refused to sign for her release from Elgin. After successfully completing her three-month probationary period with the Peatties, Kate Cleary found a room for herself; her children were already in boarding schools. She supported herself and her family by writing popular fiction, and she began work on another novel about Nebraska. She also wrote a series of feature articles on Chicago mayor Edward Dunne and his family to help him campaign for election for governor of Illinois. Dunne's wife was Kate Cleary's cousin. "I'm holding my own, and paying my way," Cleary had declared in a 1903 letter to her son, Jim, but added, "If I had done more writing and less housework I would be better off in every way today" (George, 91).

Cleary's last story, "On the Highway," was published in the *Chicago Daily News* April 29, 1905. Two months later, on July 6, 1905, Michael Cleary petitioned the Cook County Court to have his wife committed again to the Elgin Asylum for the Insane. This was a terrible blow to Kate Cleary; although the two had determined to live separately, they had celebrated their twentieth wedding anniversary a year before. Dragged into court, Kate Cleary was declared not insane by a jury of seven men. Released and free to leave, Kate Cleary returned to her room in the Monarch Hotel on the corner of Indiana and Clark, where she remained confined to her bed. Ten days later, Michael Cleary brought two of the children to visit her. The husband and wife argued outside the Stoltz and Grady Drug Store below her room; disturbed, Kate Cleary left abruptly and climbed the stairs to her third floor room, followed by her little boy. As she reached her doorway, she fell dead at her son's feet. At age forty-two, she died of heart failure. Her family buried her with other family members in Calvary Cemetery in Evanston, Illinois.

The sensationalized account of Cleary's addiction and death made front-page headlines in the Chicago newspapers. Shortly before her death, Houghton Mifflin had been negotiating the publication of a collection of short stories. After her death, however, a novel she was working on was lost, and her collection of stories was not published. A few unpublished manuscripts survive. She combined several sketches that she wrote around 1903 under the title "State Street Stories." All reveal her strong appreciation of irony. One sketch, entitled "Contentment of a Kind," describes two working girls, "evidently shop or factory girls out of work" (p. 2, Cleary Collection), among a crowd of people who have stopped to admire a marvelous display of the newest fall styles in a large State Street dry-goods store. Dressed pretentiously for their class, Cleary describes them as "having stumbled up, rather than having been brought up." The two eye the goods, then declare, "I never could abide velvet" (p. 2, Cleary Collection). Another sketch, "As Ithers [*sic*] See Us," presents a weary, young mother in the waiting room of the Union depot, trying to fill the nursing bottle for her baby. The cork has broken off in the bottle of milk, so she approaches two "clerical-looking" men, Brother Bendenwacker and Brother Webster, who are "plunged in conversation" (p. 1, Cleary Collection). When she asks them for a corkscrew, they vehemently assert that they are "prohibitionists" (p. 2). Upon explaining that she only wants it to open her baby's milk, both men promptly produce the tool, then realize their duplicity. After they depart, she laughs to herself, "What hypocrites these mortals be!" (p. 2).

Cleary's life and writings present a fresh and often humorous look at the joys and sorrows of life in the Midwest and serve as cultural documents of the turn of the century. Cleary's popular newspaper fiction fulfills the accepted myths of female domesticity while subtly satirizing the society that promoted it, and her novels and short stories excel in local color depiction. "Her best work establishes Kate Cleary as an Irish-American, Chicago-bred literary realist of great promise," states Charles Fanning in *The Irish in Chicago*, who "deserves to be remembered as a good writer and a courageous woman" (p. 116).

Sources. Memorabilia, unpublished manuscripts, and letters belonging to the Cleary family are in the private collections of Marguerite Cleary Remien, Aileen Bullard Droege, and Joel Bullard, which together make up the Kate M. Cleary Collection. These and extensive research in Chicago and Nebraska newspapers and local archives form the basis of *Kate M. Cleary: A Literary Biography with Selected Works* (1997) by Susanne K. George. Cleary's books and stories are discussed above. Her children also published, in 1922, a collection of their mother's, grandmother's, and uncle's writings, in *Poems by Margaret Kelly McPhelim and Her Children, Kate McPhelim Cleary, Edward Joseph McPhelim*. Her son James Mansfield Cleary collected some of his mother's western works in 1958 in *The Nebraska of Kate McPhelim Cleary*. Charles Fanning, in *The Irish Voice in America: Irish-American Fiction from the 1760s to the 1980s* (1990) and "The Literary Dimension" in Lawrence J. McCoffrey et al., *The Irish in Chicago* (1987), discusses Cleary's writing. Articles that discuss her writings include "Woman and Her Ways," *Chicago Evening Post*, November 8, 1897, and "Women Who Have Humor: Here Are Three in Chicago Who Refute the Popular Idea," *Chicago Chronicle*, July 21, 1898.

SUSANNE K. GEORGE

COBURN, ANNIE SWAN
April 16, 1856–May 31, 1932
ART COLLECTOR, ART PATRON, PHILANTHROPIST

Annie Swan Coburn exercised a significant influence on the direction taken in acquisition by the Art Institute of Chicago with her gift of over seventy works in oil and watercolor along with a $165,000 fund for the maintenance and expansion of the collection. She was born in Fremont, Illinois. She moved with her family to Chicago before the Great Fire of 1871 and married Lewis Larned Coburn, an established patent attorney, in Brooklyn, New York, on June 23, 1880. Coburn, a native of Vermont and a graduate of Harvard University, Cambridge, Massachusetts, had settled in Chicago during the 1860s. By 1880 he was recognized as the leading patent attorney in the city, having pioneered in the field at the time that the United States was industrializing. Wealthy and community-spirited, he was serving as the president of the Union League Club of Chicago, of which he was a founder in 1879, when he married Annie Swan.

The Coburns lived in a fashionable neighborhood outside the business district, on south Michigan Avenue. In 1910 Lewis Coburn suggested that they move to the Blackstone Hotel being built by the Drake family in the city, but he died on October 23, 1910, before such a move could be made. A grief-stricken Annie Swan Coburn moved to the Blackstone with her mother shortly thereafter and remained there until her own death two decades later.

Soon after her husband's death, Coburn began to collect paintings by American artists. Little is known about Annie Coburn's childhood or educational background; and it is not possible to explain her interest in art collecting except that her mother, Olivia Shaler Swan, dabbled in watercolor painting and Coburn's husband had served as a trustee of the Art Institute of Chicago before his death, although he did not collect art. When asked about her interest in art, Annie Coburn sometimes noted that her mother did watercolors. Olivia Swan accompanied Coburn on her initial trips to France prior to 1900, when the work of the impressionists was still subject to ridicule in an art community accustomed to the muted colors and clearly delineated forms of masters such as Jean Ingres. On these early trips, and prior to Lewis Coburn's death, the two women bought nothing but spent a great deal of time looking, an activity that became central to Coburn's life as a collector.

Though Annie Coburn dismissed laudatory inquiries into her collecting strategies by asserting that she bought what she found "pretty" (Erens, 52), the confining chronology of the collection—works painted from 1860 to 1902—and the high incidence of early works that signaled significant shifts in the styles of the artists represented belie that assertion. Daniel Catton Rich, the curator of paintings at the Art Institute of Chicago at the time of Annie Coburn's death and the bequest of her collection, noted her "remarkable ability to select outstanding pictures which have a true significance in the history of art" (quoted in "Mrs. Coburn Leaves," 5). Casting Coburn's self-proclaiming proclivity for the pretty in far more commendatory terms, Rich called the paintings in her collection "the most beautiful pictures that were ever painted" in their "direct and joyous handling of paint on canvas," and he praised her ability to consistently recognize these qualities (quoted in "Mrs. Coburn Leaves," 5).

Full recognition of Coburn as a conscious, conscientious collector of art has been left to later generations of art historians and critics. Focusing on the dramatic turn taken in art collection in Chicago in the early twentieth century, Stefan Germer includes Coburn among the "Modernist Five" who shaped Chicago's collection of modernist paintings. Germer notes a radical departure from late-nineteenth-century and early-twentieth-century norms of art collection, such as the ostentatious display of established artists or works known to be worth vast sums of money, in Coburn's careful selections. At this time, art historians Arthur Jerome Eddy, Roger Fry, and Clive Bell shifted attention away from subject matter and technique in painting to focus on the emotional register of art works. Their ideas were particularly influential at the turn of the century; Germer cites Eddy's critique of the works exhibited at the World's Columbian Exposition of 1893 as one of the foundations of the post-impressionist paradigm that would govern the subsequent modernist bent in art collecting undertaken by connoisseurs such as Coburn.

Such a high level of connoisseurship necessarily implies sufficient means and leisure to both cultivate and indulge a refined artistic sensibility. As one of the sole inheritors of her husband's considerable estate, Coburn had access to both the means and the leisure. Long a lover of impressionist painting, Coburn apparently coupled her instinctive tastes with careful consideration of the formalist criticism of Fry and Bell, concentrating her energies on amassing a coherent collection of foundational pieces in the oeuvres of a select group of pivotal European artists. Claude Monet, Jean Renoir, Édouard Manet and Edgar Degas are the central figures in Coburn's collection, and her careful selections from among their varied works indicate her firm grasp of artistic paradigms that were newborn at the time she was actively collecting.

Likewise, Coburn's acquisition of works by Henri Toulouse-Lautrec, Paul Gauguin, Paul Cezanne, and Vincent van Gogh reveals a clear sense of the contiguity of impressionist paintings that so captured her imagination on her early European trips with her mother and post-impressionist and modernist trends that followed. In keeping with those early days of aesthetic pleasure, Coburn devoted a great deal of time to simply being with a painting, examining and interacting with it before consenting to purchase it. She frequently had works that she was considering purchasing sent to her rooms and spent as much as six to ten months studying them before consenting to buy.

Reporters from the society columns and art curators from around the world marveled over the huge amount, quality, and variety of art Coburn contrived to hang, prop, and stash in the Blackstone. Photographs of her rooms show paintings almost obscuring chests of drawers, leaning against the curtains in the window seat, and sitting on every available chair. She used Degas's *Uncle and Niece* as a fire screen and stored van Gogh's *Sunny Midi, Arles,* under her bed because its brighter color scheme was not in keeping with the lush sobriety of many of her other pieces.

The Coburns had no children, and many contemporary commentators noted that "her" paintings stood in their stead. Her contemporaries had a habit of linking her with the works in her collections as if she had produced them herself rather than simply purchased them. References to the "Coburn Renoirs," or "Coburn's portrait" (to signify not a painting of her but one that she owned) abounded in the society pages of the Chicago dailies as well as in art columns and museum publications. Coburn referred to the paintings that she kept clustered around her as "good company" (quoted in Fenberg).

The Antiquarian Society of the Art Institute, which counted Coburn among its members, succeeded in persuading her to loan sixty-three of her paintings and watercolors to the Art Institute in the spring of 1932. In a clear testimony to her artistic acumen, Coburn oversaw both the selection of the paintings to be exhibited and their arrangement in galleries fifty-two and fifty-three of the Art Institute. Crowds thronged to the exhibit and critics marveled at the coherence of the collection, expressed both in the careful selection of works from within a single artist's oeuvre and in the contrasts between and among the representative works of a variety of important artists.

Coburn devoted a great deal of attention and energy to the exhibition, in spite of her increasingly frail health. She battled heart disease in the later years of her life and was accompanied by her personal nurse to the formal tea given by the Antiquarian Society in her honor in April 1932 to mark the opening of the exhibit. The tea was attended by wealthy matrons whose interest in developing the museum's collections was an aspect of their own connoisseurship; several, including EDITH ROCKEFELLER McCORMICK and KATE BUCKINGHAM, were women like Annie Coburn whose art selections, although paid for by their husbands' or families' wealth, reflected self-conscious and often daring patterns for their eras. At the Antiquarian Society tea, Edith McCormick's Napoleonic gold urns and compotes were brought out of storage at the Art Institute so they could be used on the tea table and Kate Buckingham greeted friends from a wheelchair; another member of this group of wealthy women donors, BERTHA HONORÉ PALMER, president of the Antiquarian Society, was in Florida, and did not attend the event. In response to the outpouring of praise for the collection, Coburn repeatedly emphasized that it was a loan and expressed some distress that the paintings would not be there when she went home.

She died without their companionship, succumbing to heart disease. Her funeral was held June 2, 1932, in the chapel of the Graceland Cemetery; the trustees of the Art Institute acted as honorary pall bearers. All of the Chicago dailies printed obituaries mourning her loss and celebrating her contributions to the art world, as did the *New York Times* and a number of art journals.

This praise was repeated when the contents of her will were divulged later that summer. A good portion of the paintings Coburn loaned to the Art Institute in the spring of 1932 never left but stayed to form the basis of the Mr. and Mrs. Lewis Larned Coburn Collection and to substantially expand and influence the Art Institute's holdings.

Coburn's bequests constitute a guide to the significant people and events in her life. She left the vast majority of her estate to the Art Institute, including fifty watercolors and a $50,000 fund for their care and maintenance in memory of her mother. The most celebrated bequest to the Art Institute was that of twenty-two specified paintings along with the balance of her French holdings not otherwise bequeathed and a $165,000 trust fund to be added to an existing $35,000 fund for the upkeep of the collection. This endowment marked the founding of the Mr. and Mrs. Lewis Larned Coburn Collection of the Art Institute.

Ever loyal to the memory of her husband, Coburn also left important works by Toulouse-Lautrec, Degas, Cezanne, Manet, and Monet along with $25,000 for their maintenance to the Fogg Museum of Harvard University, Lewis Larned Coburn's alma mater. She also bequeathed $50,000 to Harvard for scholarships in the law school and made an identical bequest to the law school at Northwestern University in Chicago. Smith College also received a group of nine paintings under Coburn's will, along with a $10,000 trust fund for their maintenance, and she made monetary gifts of $25,000 and $100,000 to the Brainard Memorial Library in Connecticut and the Hampton Institute in Virginia, respectively. The latter gift founded the Swan Memorial Fund, in memory of her parents.

Coburn was described as quiet and withdrawn, and the life she lived with her paintings was a rather eccentric, highly reclusive one. Nevertheless, the Coburn Collection includes some of the very paintings that art lovers come to Chicago to see and from which the Art Institute derives a considerable part of its image and identity.

Sources. The Art Institute Archive, Office of the Registrar, has Annie Swan Coburn's papers, including receipts for all of the pieces in the Coburn Collection, the Coburn Collection Estate Papers, and a copy of Coburn's will. The Archive also has the *Art Institute Bulletin* and *Weekly Newsletter,* which frequently discuss Coburn's acquisitions in detail and offer lengthy commentary on the 1932 exhibition and her bequests. Her correspondence with art curator Daniel Catton Rich is filed with his papers. The article, "Mrs. Coburn Leaves 83 Pictures, $200,000 Fund, to Chicago" in the *Art Digest,* July 1, 1932, provides succinct information about Coburn's biography, the specifics of her will, and excellent contemporary comment on her person, personality, and artistic acumen. Bertha Fenberg's "Mrs. Lewis Coburn Plans to Give City Famous Collection," interview with Coburn, *Chicago Daily News,* June 11, 1931, includes photographs of both Coburn and her art-cluttered rooms at the Blackstone as well as quotes from Coburn herself. The *Chicago Herald and Examiner* and *CT* coverage of the Antiquarian Society Tea, April 7, 1932, provides excellent period contextualization, and the *Chicago Daily News* analysis of the art in the exhibit, April 12, 1932, rounds out the coverage. *Art News* printed both an obituary, June 11, 1932, and a detailed description of Coburn's bequest to the Fogg Museum at Harvard, June 26, 1932. The most succinct description of the entirety of Coburn's estate and its distribution appears in *NYT,* June 29, 1932. Coburn is the subject of two quite different book chapters. Patricia Erens's article on Coburn in *Masterpieces: Famous Chicagoans and Their Paintings* (1979) focuses on the social role played by Coburn and her art and is written in a chatty manner; Stefan Germer's study of Coburn's role in shaping the course taken by art collection in Chicago in Sue Ann Prince, ed., *The Old Guard and the Avant-Garde: Modernism in Chicago, 1910–1940* (1990), is a much more sophisticated analysis of her artistic sensibilities and their origins.

REGINA M. BUCCOLA

COFFEY, SISTER MARY JUSTITIA
(Alice Marie Coffey)
June 30, 1875–November 5, 1947
EDUCATOR, ADMINISTRATOR

Alice Marie Coffey was born in Hadley, Massachusetts, the daughter of John and Mary (Powers) Coffey, both of Kilbeggan, West Meath County, Ireland. She had one brother. After completing her primary education in a North Hadley grammar school, Alice Coffey attended Northhampton High School, from which she graduated in 1893. Mount Holyoke College in South Hadley, founded in 1847 by Mary Lyon, was nearby, and the young Alice Coffey was aware at an early age of expanding academic and career possibilities for young women.

Alice Coffey began her teaching career in Worcester, Massachusetts, in 1894 and subsequently moved with her family to Granville, Iowa, at a time when the Sisters of Charity of the Blessed Virgin Mary (BVMs) were teaching in parochial schools a short distance from Granville in LaMars and Marcus, Iowa. It is possible that Alice Coffey became acquainted with the BVMs at these schools and may have taught at one of them in the late 1800s.

Having decided to join the Sisters of Charity BVM, and in accordance with the order's requirements, Alice Coffey asked the Reverend John Adler, pastor of St. Joseph's parish, Granville, to recommend her. She was accepted and entered the novitiate in Dubuque, Iowa, on July 13, 1900, and was given her religious name, Sister Mary Justitia. During her novitiate from 1902 to 1903, she served as school directress and teacher of Latin, English, history, and geology at St. Cecilia Academy in Holden, Missouri.

In 1903, Sister Mary Justitia taught at St. Mary High School on Chicago's West Side. Opened in 1899 by the BVMs, St. Mary was the first central Catholic high school for girls supported by a religious community. The BVMs had been teaching in Chicago's parochial schools since 1867, when SISTER MARY AGATHA HURLEY first arrived in the city with a group of teaching sisters. They taught in the Holy Family parish grammar school and later in the parish high school, St. Aloysius, before establishing St. Mary nearby. JANE ADDAMS had already opened Hull-House in the same neighborhood in 1889, and a growing number of Catholic parishes had attracted many first generation immigrants whose children were attending the local parochial schools.

Her experience at St. Mary placed Sister Justitia in one of the most innovative academic high schools for Catholic girls in the country. Conceived to be the equal of the best academic public high school in the city, it offered courses to prepare its graduates to excel in the entrance exam for the Chicago Normal School so that Catholic girls could become school teachers. Girls at St. Mary studied algebra, plane geometry, solid geometry, trigonometry, and commercial arithmetic. They studied English composition and literature; Latin, Spanish, and French languages; ancient, medieval, and modern history. They read English history, civics, United States history, economics, and economic history. By 1902, St. Mary also offered commercial courses and realistically prepared students for the sector of the economy where jobs for women were expanding rapidly, the commercial office.

FIG. 22. *Sister Mary Justitia Coffey and Mother Isabella Kane were responsible for the construction of Mundelein College, North Sheridan Road, Chicago. The college opened on September 30, 1930, with 300 commuter students.*

At the same time that they were creating educational institutions to prepare Catholic girls for secular careers, the BVMs were developing themselves as educators and leaders in establishing and running institutions of higher education. The congregation began sending sisters to graduate schools all over the United States. In 1911, Sister Justitia left St. Mary and entered Catholic University of America in Washington, D.C., becoming one of the first women to study at that institution. Pressured by the BVMs and other women's congregations, Catholic University in 1911 initiated a temporary arrangement enabling sisters to live and take university classes in a nearby Benedictine convent. This was a first step in the direction of a proposed sisters' college. In addition to the regular college curriculum, Sister Justitia and five BVM companions took courses in Greek, Latin, philosophy, and French. They stayed on through the following school year, when they were tutored by university professors. Sister Justitia graduated with a B.A. in philosophy in 1914. She completed an M.A. degree in education at Loyola University (now Loyola University Chicago) in 1922.

In 1921, Sister Justitia was named superior and principal of The Immaculata, the second BVM high school for girls, which opened initially in the Greenlee Mansion at Irving Park and the lakefront in Chicago. With her hand-chosen faculty, she drew up the curriculum of basic academic requirements and served as the school principal from 1921 to 1926. Two hundred and twenty-five students registered that first year. To assuage neighbors who had objected to the presence of the school in the residential area, Sister Justitia and her faculty set down rules that became a tradition at the Irving Park site. For instance, at dismissal time each day, the students marched in silent pairs, accompanied by one of the sisters, down Irving Park Road to the streetcars on Broadway, two blocks west. No student broke ranks; it was strictly forbidden for any girl to enter a store or other establishment in the vicinity of the school. Such discipline eventually won over residents, who realized that they need not fear neighborhood disturbance by unruly young people.

By 1922, seven hundred students had enrolled in a newly constructed building. Before Sister Justitia left the school in 1927, more than one thousand girls were enrolled at what was then the largest Catholic girls' high school in the country. It was a chartered institution, accredited by the Chicago Teachers' College and the University of Illinois.

In 1927, Sister Justitia was named BVM Provincial Superior. Two years later, she resigned from this office, having been asked to assume responsibility for the construction of Mundelein College, planned for a location on North Sheridan Road in Chicago.

Consideration of opening a college in Chicago had begun in February of 1916 when Mother Mary Cecilia Dougherty, Superior General of the congregation, and two sister companions, made a courtesy call to George W. Mundelein, newly appointed Archbishop of Chicago, two weeks after his inauguration. After offering the new prelate their congratulations, they told him of their desire to open a House of Studies for their sisters in Chicago on property that they already owned. Mundelein in turn introduced them to his plan for three Chicago-area women's colleges, to be affiliated with St. Mary of the Lake Seminary. He then offered his help with Rome in disposing of their property and invited their cooperation in opening a college for women on the north side of Chicago. After discussing some of the problems connected with opening such an institution, Mother Cecilia took the invitation under consideration. After having consulted with her order's Councillors in Dubuque, Mother Cecilia informed Mundelein that "while all desire to have a college in Chicago, the time is not opportune" (Dougherty letter, May 16, 1916, Mundelein College Archives). One of the inopportune factors was the disapproval of the venture by Bishop James J. Keane, Archbishop of Dubuque.

Though the BVMs delayed plans for a women's college, Cardinal Mundelein never abandoned the idea and continued to press his point. He envisioned a commuter college built as a modern skyscraper and requiring a small parcel of land, since city property was expensive. Its location should be near Jesuit-run Loyola University, which was also close to public transportation lines. When Mother Isabella Kane became Superior General of the BVMs, Cardinal Mundelein met with her to discuss the possibilities for a college. Mother Isabella was concerned about the cost of lakeshore property, which had tripled in value since the congregation had purchased land for Immaculata High School in 1920. However, Mother Isabella decided

to complete the plans postponed by her predecessor, Mother Cecilia Dougherty. Consequently, in March 1929, the BVMs purchased 250 feet of prime lakefront land on North Sheridan Road next to Loyola University. Behind the planning of the college were Mother Isabella and Sister Justitia, who was named BVM representative. An accomplished artist, Mother Isabella sought the advice of two architects, Joseph W. McCarthy of Chicago and Nairne Fisher of Dubuque, Iowa. McCarthy, a leading Catholic architect in the Midwest, had designed Cardinal Mundelein's St. Mary of the Lake Seminary. McCarthy and Fisher designed a fifteen-story Art Deco–style skyscraper, faced with grey limestone. The new geometric design, which had won acclaim in France where it was introduced, was an immediate success. Art Deco motifs were implemented in both exterior and interior areas of the building and in the design of the chapel, radiator gratings, doorways, elevators, and lamps.

With Cardinal Mundelein's support, the BVMs obtained financing from the Continental Bank in Chicago. Groundbreaking for the college began November 1, 1929, two days after the great stock market crash. The Great Depression made fundraising difficult, and the BVM sisters mortgaged the Immaculata and St. Mary high schools and virtually starved their smaller foundations to meet the annual $90,000 interest payment on the $2,375,000 cost of constructing the college.

The Great Depression, however, had one advantage. Since labor was readily available, the construction teams worked day and night shifts. The skyscraper was completed in little less than a year, and it opened on September 30, 1930, with three hundred commuter students. Sister Justitia became president. The financial community in Chicago was impressed with the business-like manner in which the BVMs dealt with their debt and carried out their project.

Sister Justitia sought out a well-qualified faculty of BVM sisters and lay persons. She arranged for many of the sisters assigned to teach at the college to pursue doctoral studies at some of America's leading universities, including Catholic University of America, Columbia University, Notre Dame, Creighton, Loyola, Marquette, American Conservatory of Music, and state universities in Illinois, Michigan, and Colorado. From the start, the philosophy of the college was to give women a superior education that was grounded in the liberal arts but also geared to career preparation and personal growth through cultural and intellectual development. Its curriculum was developed from the one then being offered at the University of Illinois in Champaign-Urbana. Many students became teachers or secretaries, and Mundelein College provided appropriate education for both fields.

Mundelein College also provided cultural programming and introduced its students to the world of writers, dancers, musicians, thespians, and artists. Shane Leslie, Maisie Ward Sheed, Catholic University's Touring Black Friars Theater Group, and the Von Trapp Family Singers visited the campus. Under Sister Justitia's leadership students created prizewinning publications, including a newspaper, a quarterly literary magazine, and an annual book of verse. Music and drama productions were encouraged; actress Mercedes McCambridge made her debut as a freshman on Mundelein's stage.

In 1936, in accordance with canon law for religious orders, which required a superior/president to retire from office at the close of a six-year term, Sister Justitia left Mundelein and joined the staff of Clarke College, Dubuque, Iowa. In 1939 she was reappointed president of Mundelein.

Sister Justitia's role as an educational leader went beyond the world of Catholic higher education. She chaired a committee at the sixteenth annual meeting of the American Historical Society in 1935, was a member of the executive committee of the Federation of Illinois Colleges in 1942 and, in the same year, was appointed by Governor Dwight Green to serve on a public educators division of the Illinois State Council of Defense.

During World War II, Sister Justitia initiated a series of programs that included lectures by foreign correspondents, scientists, authors, and political analysts. She placed Mundelein's facilities at the disposal of the government as a Chicago-area training center for women. The college was prepared to train dietitians, chemists, bacteriologists, and laboratory technicians.

In her final report in 1945 as president of the Mundelein Board of Trustees, Sister Justitia reflected on the goal of a Catholic college: to train its students in a two-fold citizenship for temporal and eternal life. This theme of preparing women to meet the challenges of life and work in peacetime and wartime, as well as to meet the needs of personal spiritual development, was carried out programmatically in all the BVM institutions of secondary and college education.

Two years later, Sister Justitia died at Mundelein College. She was buried in Mount Carmel Cemetery, Hillside, Illinois. The Justitia Coffey Assistance Funds Award was created in her memory to enable adult, nontraditional women students to earn their B.A. degrees. Awards provide financial aid to qualified students over the age of twenty-three who attend Loyola University's Mundelein College. The fund, initiated during preparation for the 1991 Loyola-Mundelein alliance, reflects the heritage and educational mission of the Sisters of Charity of the Blessed Virgin Mary and of the vision implemented by such leaders as Mary Justitia Coffey.

Sources. Information about Sister Mary Justitia Coffey is found in the Records of the Mundelein College Archives, Gannon Center of Loyola University Chicago; further information about the Sisters of Charity, Blessed Virgin Mary (BVMs) is in the congregation's archives, Mt. Carmel BVM Center, Dubuque, Iowa. M. Jane Coogan, *The Price of Our Heritage, 1869–1920,* 2 vols. (1978); James W. Sanders, *The Education of an Urban Minority: Catholics in Chicago, 1833–1965* (1977); and Edward R. Kantowicz, *Corporation Sole: Cardinal Mundelein and Chicago Catholicism* (1983), provide background.

SISTER MARY RITA BENZ
SISTER MARY SHARON ROSE

COLEMAN, BESSIE
January 20, 1896–April 30, 1926
AVIATOR

As the first African American woman to become an aviator and acquire an international pilot's license, Bessie Coleman promoted careers in aviation for other African Americans. She began her flying career before the "well-publicized flights of Charles Lindbergh and Amelia Earhart" (Turner, 120). She used her popularity as a barnstormer to fight segregation in public gathering places.

FIG. 23. *Aviator Bessie Coleman and her manager in front of her airplane.*

She was born in Atlanta, Texas, to George and Susan Coleman, who had thirteen children. When Bessie was very young her family moved from Atlanta to Waxahachie, a small railroad town with an economy based on cotton growing. Her parents were able to buy a quarter acre of land, where her father built a three-room house and her mother planted flowers and vegetables. Even so, "racial barriers" and "depressed economic conditions" (Turner, 123) had a great impact on the family.

Her father was of African American and Choctaw Indian ancestry. Upon hearing of good living conditions and U.S. government assurances of land in the Indian Territory, he decided to move to Oklahoma. He tried to persuade his wife to join him, but she chose to remain in Texas.

Susan Coleman found work as a cook-housekeeper. She and the children supplemented her earnings by picking cotton and by taking in laundry. She could not read but had business sense. She assigned her daughter Bessie the task of maintaining a written record of their earnings.

In the evenings Bessie Coleman read to her mother and brothers and sisters. As an observant Baptist family, the Colemans read the Bible to each other. Coleman did not have a local library available to her, but one or two times each year a traveling library passed through town, and her mother rented books. Bessie Coleman especially enjoyed reading biographies of black achievers.

Bessie Coleman went to a segregated school four miles from her home. She had dreams of going to college at the Colored Agricultural and Normal University in Langston, Oklahoma, known as Langston Industrial College (now Langston University) after the uncle of poet Langston Hughes. Her mother encouraged her ambition but could not afford to pay tuition. She allowed Coleman to save the money she earned by doing laundry. Bessie Coleman was able to attend the Teacher's College at Langston, but her money ran out and she had to return home after less than a year.

She began again to do laundry but did not wish to continue such unfulfilling work. She decided to join her brothers John and Walter, who lived in Chicago, and came to the city within the period 1915–17. Refusing to be restricted by the jobs open to black women—domestic service or factory work—she enrolled in Burnham's School of Beauty Culture to learn the beautician's trade. She got a job as a manicurist at a barbershop across from Comisky Park, the White Sox baseball field. Coleman became so proficient that she won first prize in a competition for the best black manicurist, an event described in the *Chicago Defender* newspaper. She worked in the black neighborhood on State Street known as "The Stroll," an area of shops, nightclubs, restaurants, and other businesses. By 1917 she was able to send for her mother and other family members who were still in Texas.

Working as a manicurist for men, she heard stories about airplane pilots in World War I and the respect received by African American aviators serving in the European theater with U.S. Armed Forces and with French units. Bessie Coleman read every related article she could find. After the war, Bessie's brother John, who was himself a veteran, heightened her interest with stories of women in France flying airplanes. Bessie Coleman soon learned that some American women were pilots, despite a prevailing attitude that flying was socially inappropriate and even physically impossible for women.

Bessie Coleman decided that she wanted to learn how to fly and that it was a realistic goal. Hoping to increase her earnings to pay for aviation school, she gave up the manicure work and opened a chili parlor. Around 1919, she began to contact flying schools. This was a time when race riots were erupting in Chicago and other U.S. cities as African Americans moved north and sought decent housing and jobs. When she applied to aviation schools, she was turned down because of prejudice against her race and gender.

Refusing to give up, she sought advice from Robert Abbott, publisher of the *Chicago Defender*. At his suggestion, she studied French and then applied to an aviation school in France, which had become the center of the world of aviation. Two African American philanthropists, Robert Abbott and Jesse Binga, head of the Binga State Bank, provided financial support to supplement Coleman's savings.

Coleman enrolled in France's most famous flight school, École d'Aviation des Frères Caudron at Le Crotoy. She found the school to be all and more than she could have hoped for. She flew the most advanced aircraft of the time and studied with such accomplished European flight instructors as famed Dutch aircraft designer Anthony G. Fokker.

On June 15, 1921, she received her pilot's license from the Fédération Aéronautique International (FAI), the first African American to be so licensed. The FAI was the only organization whose recognition granted persons holding that license the right to fly anywhere in the world. Of the sixty-two candidates to earn FAI licenses during that six-month period, Bessie Coleman was the only woman. She wanted to interest other African Americans in entering aviation as a field of opportunity. Before heading back to the United States, she attended the Second Pan-African Congress in Paris. The congress was led by American black leader W. E. B. Du Bois.

She returned to the United States as a celebrity. Reporters from the *Air Service News*, *Aerial Age Weekly*, and the *New York Tribune* interviewed her. Her return was a front-page story for the *Dallas Express* and most other black weeklies. The cast of *Shuffle Along*, an all-black musical being performed in Manhattan, made her the honored guest at a performance.

Consistent with her desire to make flight training readily accessible, she set a new goal for herself—to open a flight school. In an interview for the *Chicago Defender* on October 8, 1921, she explained her goals of flying and of training black aviators: "We must have aviators if we are to keep up with the time. I shall never be satisfied until we have men of the Race who can fly" (quoted in Rich, 36). When she returned to Chicago, Coleman, rejected because of prevailing attitudes toward African Americans and women, was unable to support herself by flying or to purchase an airplane to start a school.

Feeling a sense of urgency to open a flight school, Bessie Coleman decided to earn money by becoming a barnstormer, an aviator who traveled around the country entertaining spectators with such death-defying feats as wing walking and parachute jumping. She sailed to Europe in May 1922 for advanced training in stunt flying and parachute jumping in France, Holland, Germany, and Switzerland. In Holland, she flew as a test pilot for Anthony Fokker. She returned as a barnstormer with the *Chicago Defender* as her sponsor; her performances were booked at the newspaper's offices in New York City. Her first exhibition took place in Garden City, Long Island, on Labor Day weekend 1922, when the Curtiss Airplane Company provided the plane and an airfield. She was delighted with the response. The event drew large, enthusiastic crowds, and some of the spectators expressed interest in learning to fly. A month later she gave her first air show in the Chicago region at Checkerboard Airdrome in suburban Maywood. Considerable publicity in the *Chicago Defender* attracted thousands to see the triumphant return of their hometown heroine. She also gave successful exhibitions throughout the Midwest.

Coleman returned to Chicago for an exhibition before beginning a tour in towns across the South. She planned to barnstorm and to lecture to African American audiences about careers in aviation. Wherever she went she attracted large crowds of curious onlookers.

Always seeking capital to purchase an airplane and open a training school, she worked in Santa Monica, California, for a tire manufacturing company, flying a plane bearing advertising. She then purchased her plane from a U.S. Army surplus depot in Los Angeles. During the flight from Santa Monica to the fairgrounds, where she was to perform, the plane nose-dived and crashed to the ground. She suffered broken bones and other injuries. When she was able, she returned to Chicago. She was out of action for more than a year, recuperating and then seeking work as a flyer.

By May 1925, she was able to arrange a series of exhibitions and lectures in Texas. At her talks, she showed films of her own flights in Europe and the United States. In the lectures, given at schools, theaters, churches, and recreation centers, she focused on African American women, asking them to become involved in aviation. While her lectures were a source of income, she allowed students to come without charge, seeing them as potential pilots. At an exhibition in her childhood town, Waxahachie, Texas, in 1926, she insisted that black and white spectators be allowed to use the same entrance to the show, although seating was still segregated. In Austin, at a dinner in Coleman's honor after a performance, the hostess was the state's woman governor, Miriam A. "Ma" Ferguson.

During a lecture series in Florida in 1926, Coleman met Reverend Hezakiah Hill, a Baptist minister, and his wife, Vivian Hill, in Orlando. She developed a close relationship with the Hills and "became a 'born-again' Christian, professing her belief in public" (Rich, 101).

In Orlando, Coleman continued her campaign against segregation at public entertainments. She refused to do an air show for the Orlando Chamber of Commerce when she learned that African Americans would not be allowed to attend. Although racial segregation was the norm, the chamber agreed to allow African Americans to be in the audience. Edwin M. Beeman, son of the manufacturer of Beeman chewing gum and "a member of Orlando's white aristocracy" (Rich, 105), gave Coleman money to transport her plane from Dallas, Texas, for a barnstorming to be held in Jacksonville, Florida, on May 1, 1926. The event was to be a fund-raiser for the Negro Welfare League. Coleman again believed that she was on the verge of opening a school.

She did not live to see her plan materialize. On April 29 she went to all of the African American public schools in Jacksonville to speak to the students. The next day, she and her copilot, William D. Wills, took off in their open-air plane on a tryout flight, with Wills at the controls. Uncharacteristically, Coleman had not fastened her seatbelt. Once aloft, the airplane malfunctioned. Coleman was catapulted out of the plane and killed. Her copilot was killed in a crash landing.

The *Chicago Defender* immediately put out a special edition with photographs of Coleman. Services were held in Jacksonville and Chicago. An interracial group of mourners in Jacksonville paid tribute to her. In Chicago her funeral was held at Pilgrim Baptist Church. Coleman was buried at Lincoln Cemetery in Alsip, Illinois.

The memory of Bessie Colman has been kept alive. Every spring, near the anniversary of her death, black pilots from around the nation gather to stage a flyover, dropping "a wreath of flowers to be placed on her grave" (Turner, 132). This tradition was begun in the 1930s by Cornelius Coffey and the Challenger Air Pilots Association. It was "continued by the Chicago American Pilots Association under the direction of aviation historian Rufus A. Hunt" (Turner, 132). In addition to the Bessie Coleman tribute, the event now honors women who followed her example. In 1977 African American women pilots organ-

ized the Bessie Coleman Aviators Club. Commercial pilots landing at Chicago's O'Hare Field are guided through the Bessie Coleman Intersection by air controllers. Passengers and others coming into the airport pass Bessie Coleman Drive, named in 1990. A Chicago Public Library branch named for her was dedicated in 1993. In 1995 the U.S. Post Office issued a stamp in the Black Heritage series in honor of Coleman. Coleman's accomplishments in her short life became an example and an inspiration for African American men and women to enter the field of aviation.

Sources. Several birthdates for Coleman appear in sources. The official date listed on her passport and international pilot's license is January 20, 1896. These documents are on permanent display in the Tuskegee Airmen exhibit at DuSable Museum of African American History in Chicago. They are pictured in a biography by Doris L. Rich, *Queen Bess Daredevil Aviator* (1993). Coleman's sister, Elois Patterson, in her *Memoirs of the Late Bessie Coleman, Aviatrix*, privately published in 1969, gives January 26, 1893. Rich's *Queen Bess* has a birthdate of January 26, 1892, based on family information. The *Chicago Defender* reported on Coleman's career in numerous articles, including "Aviatrix Must Sign Away Life to Learn Trade," October 8, 1921; "'Queen Bess' to Try Air October 15," October 7, 1922. The *Pittsburgh Courier* reported on her death in "Practice Flight Fatal," May 8, 1926. A brief biography appears in Enoch P. Waters, *American Diary: A Personal History of the Black Press* (1987). For biographical essays, see Jessie Carney Smith, ed., *Notable Black American Women* (1992); *Follow in their Footsteps* by Glennette Tilley Turner (1997); and *BWA*. Elizabeth Amelia Hadley Freydberg's biography, *Bessie Coleman: The Brownskin Lady Bird* (1994), includes a discussion of Coleman's role in American entertainment.

GLENNETTE TILLEY TURNER

COOKE, FLORA JULIETTE
December 25, 1864–February 21, 1953
PROGRESSIVE EDUCATOR

Flora Cooke, the founding principal of the Francis Parker School and a leader in progressive education, was born in Bainbridge, Ohio, the fourth of six children of Sumner and Rosetta (Ellis) Hannum. When she was five years old, her mother died, and her father sought to place the children with relatives. The other children were quickly taken in, but Flora, an active child who was seen as difficult, was in six different homes within a year before being sent to live with her mother's close friends, Charles and Luella Cooke of Youngstown, Ohio. Her life with the Cookes was happy, and they legally adopted her in 1881.

She attended elementary school in Youngstown and graduated from high school in 1884, beginning her long career as an educator by teaching in a rural schoolhouse the year after completing high school. In her second year of teaching, she found a job in Youngstown as a first grade teacher with 125 children in her classroom. Recalling her own restlessness and boredom in school and wanting to occupy the majority as she worked with smaller groups in turn, she bought materials for the children to cut and paste, borrowing from friends and family alphabet blocks for them to play with and finding a barrel of sand and a bucket of clay. In providing activities for her students, she seems to have anticipated the educational approach that was to become the focus of her life.

Cooke was fortunate in her principal, ZONIA BABER, who

FIG. 24. *Flora J. Cooke, seated in the center of the third row from the top, with other faculty members of the Cook County Normal School, c. 1889. Left to right, starting at the top:* Miss Weaver, Mary Woodruff, Frank Woodruff; Emily J. Rice, Mrs. F. W. Parker, Ida Cassa Heffron, William M. Giffin; Helen Maley Hefferan, Flora J. Cooke; Anne Allen, Zonia Baber, Colonel Francis W. Parker *(on the right next to the bannister, straw hat in hand);* Sarah Griswold, Viola Derat, Wilbur S. Jackman; *and* Walter Kenyon.

had recently graduated from Cook County Normal School (CCNS) in Englewood, Illinois (annexed to Chicago in 1889), at the time the most famous teacher training institution in the country. Baber endorsed Cooke's methods and taught her more. The two became lifelong friends. Since Cooke lived at some distance from the school and Baber lived near it, Cooke roomed with Baber when the weather was bad. Cooke recalled years later in a speech honoring Baber that she had "two years of intensive professional training (most of it given after midnight)" (October 21, 1944). When Baber moved to Chicago in 1887 to teach at CCNS, she left Cooke as her replacement as principal. In 1889, as head of the geography department at CCNS, Baber persuaded Col. Francis Parker, dynamic advocate for activity-based education and head of CCNS, to ask Cooke to teach there. Parker agreed, on condition that Baber "would take full

responsibility for the success of her protege" (Cooke, "Opportunities and Episodes of a Teacher's Life," 3). At the end of the year, Parker declared her the best primary teacher he had ever seen. Another observer noted that, as a young teacher, she encouraged "every effort toward genuine expression on the part of the child" and was "full of freedom and spontaneity in her work" (Hofer, 183).

At CCNS, Flora Cooke found a training program based on the same approach to children's learning that she had begun on her own. Parker's central beliefs were that children learn when they are active, when the activity and the learning have meaning to them, and when their natural impulse toward sociability is integrated into the learning process. These ideas, building on those of European education theorists Johann Pestalozzi and Friedrich Fröbel (also Froebel), had achieved some currency in America through the kindergarten movement but were new as applied to the elementary school. When John Dewey, who was later to be famous as the founder of progressive education, came to Chicago in 1894, he found a school where his emerging philosophy of education was already in practice. His son Fred was enrolled in Flora Cooke's first grade class in 1894–95 and his daughter Evelyn, the following year. Carleton Washburne, later a famous exponent of progressive education in the north suburban schools of Winnetka, Illinois, was also enrolled in Cooke's first-grade class.

As a first-grade teacher and "critic teacher" at CCNS, Cooke was assigned, in addition to her forty first graders, about twenty student teachers who observed her classroom for an hour a day and then spent another hour teaching children under her supervision. Besides teaching both a class of children and the student teachers, CCNS teachers were expected to take part in the many activities of the school, including parents' meetings, and to participate in community life, attend conferences, and speak at institutions. According to Cooke, Parker functioned as a strict father in his relations with his mostly female teaching staff, demanding commitment to the development of each student and constant revision of teaching methods. In spite of his sometimes peremptory manner, his belief in children aroused passionate loyalty on the part of his staff. Cooke remained faithful to his vision throughout her career. The most important lesson she learned from him was never to lose her faith in a child. Perhaps the strength of her conviction, which was borne out in many later incidents, was based too on her own difficult childhood experiences.

Superficially, Cooke could hardly have been more different from Parker. While he was large, noisy, and imposing, she was small and quietly self-assured, with a round face and a sympathetic expression. A friend described her as "the brown wren of the education world—so simple, so unassuming that her power is as astonishing as is the rush of melody that fills the woodland from the throat of that tiny singer" (Wygant, 1).

Cooke specialized in the teaching of reading while at CCNS. She believed that reading should be learned by children as readily as talking and that reading and writing should draw on the natural sociability of children. Her standard format for the teaching of reading was to engage the children in writing "reading leaflets" about an experience; each child, with the help of the other children, dictated sentences to be written by the teacher on the blackboard. The teacher then edited the whole account into a form she believed would hold the interest of the children, and they made illustrations so that their parents and other children who had not had the experience might have a clear idea of what happened. Sharing the leaflets with other first graders, she found, awakened a desire to read. Later, as principal of the Francis W. Parker School, she made this approach to reading a basic part of the school's program, with teachers using reading leaflets instead of standardized textbooks.

Cooke taught at CCNS for ten years. In 1895 she published a book for children, *Nature Myths and Stories for Little Children*, that became popular across the country. She gained considerable acclaim as a speaker at teachers' institutions; she lectured in twenty-eight states, taught for a month in Salt Lake City, and conducted a six-week summer institute in Hawaii. On many of what she called "institute jaunts," she and Zonia Baber traveled together. She recalled years later that "it was a liberal education to go with Zonia Baber into a new region" (Cooke, speech, February 8, 1945, 3).

Francis Parker believed that public schools were the best means of education for future citizens in a democracy, but for many years he had been at odds with the county and, after 1896, with city officials who supervised the normal school. He was persuaded to accept ANITA McCORMICK BLAINE's offer in 1899 of funds to begin his own private school, the Chicago Institute, as a laboratory of his ideas. Then in 1901, the University of Chicago absorbed the institute into its College of Education, and Blaine undertook to provide funds for another school, on the North Side, that would also follow Parker's philosophy. Parker asked Flora Cooke to head the new school. For thirty-three years she was principal of the Francis W. Parker School, leading it to a position of national renown as a model of progressive education.

Like Parker, Cooke believed that the existence of a private school like Francis Parker was only justified if it served as a laboratory for curriculum and teaching methods that could be applied in public schools. In order to insure that the school served the same variety of students as those in public schools, as well as to provide students with a democratic experience, Cooke always sought to maintain an ethnically and economically diverse student body. Anita Blaine subsidized the school throughout the period when Cooke was principal, so that many students were able to attend at reduced or no tuition.

In contrast to Parker's paternalistic style, Cooke maintained essentially democratic relationships with her teachers. She believed that not only should students have the opportunity for "free and spontaneous all-round growth," but that teachers "must have the same kind of freedom for creative cooperation and the same responsibility for good results" (Wygant, 1). With Cooke's leadership, teachers tried new teaching approaches and wrote curriculum materials; many of the materials were published in *The Francis W. Parker Studies in Education* (1912–34), a twelve-volume series. Only when she believed teachers were forgetting their obligation to students did Cooke draw the line. For example, when the school became overcrowded, and a teacher suggested getting rid of some of the more difficult children, Cooke said, "If their homes are as sordid as you say and their parents as blind to our vision of education and the children

as unpromising, certainly their only hope of glimpsing something better is this school" (Wygant, 1).

Cooke was also prepared to stand up to parents. During World War I, the school newspaper published an article by a student speaking against the war, and a vocal group of parents demanded the student's expulsion. Cooke spoke at a parents' meeting, saying she could not consider interfering with the student's rights to his point of view, and that doing so would violate all that the school attempted to teach. She left the meeting not knowing whether she would have a job the next day, but the parents' association sent her flowers and praised her courage.

Neither Parker at Cook County Normal School nor Dewey at the University of Chicago Laboratory School had developed a high school, but Cooke began the Parker School with the assumption that it would include twelve years. Looking back on the effort in 1930, she said that in 1901 the school had "innocently and ignorantly assumed that it could carry forward the same school procedure that was proving so successful in the lower school" ("Making the Secondary School Progressive," 2) but was immediately confronted with three major difficulties. These were that high school teachers were not trained in pedagogy and did not necessarily understand adolescents, that the high school curriculum was bound by college entrance requirements, and that there were no experimental colleges functioning on progressive principles to which graduates of progressive high schools could aspire.

Cooke found teachers who were sympathetic to adolescents but continued to feel that outside pressures prevented her school from providing a fully progressive education at the secondary level. Still, she took pride in the fact that Francis Parker School provided many opportunities for students to engage in the expressive and community activities she believed were central to progressive education and full human development. For example, the school required students to take work in the arts throughout high school and included many extracurricular activities such as writing, debate, dramatics, music, and charitable efforts that were "considered by the faculty to be the most truly educative features of the school" ("Making the Secondary School Progressive," 3).

Cooke's concern with the difficulties of building a progressive high school, given the limitations imposed by college entrance requirements, led to her enthusiastic acceptance of the invitation for Parker to participate in the Eight Year Study (1933–41). This national research project, sponsored by the Progressive Education Association, followed thirty public and private high schools as they tried more student-centered curriculum innovations.

Generally, progressive education, with its emphasis on active learning, educating the whole child, and responding to individual differences, found greater acceptance in private than in public schools. Some urban school districts attempted to promote progressive education in at least some elementary schools during the 1920s and 1930s, but overall little changed at the high school level. During the early years of the century, the child population of the country, and especially of the cities, grew dramatically, and changes in the economy led to children's staying in school longer. The result was that public schools had to accommodate vast numbers of children and to deal with them for longer periods of time. Under the circumstances, active, child-centered education, though accepted in theory by many leaders, seemed impossible to implement in public schools, at least in cities. Flora Cooke, however, never abandoned her conviction that the Parker School should pioneer arrangements and teaching methods that might be adopted in public schools.

At the same time, some proponents of progressive education distorted Dewey's and Parker's ideas, exaggerating the notion of freedom for children and adopting an anti-intellectual stance that left the movement vulnerable to critics. Cooke herself said in 1930 that under the wings of progressive education many types of schools had sheltered "some wild birds, some grotesque fledglings, some weak species hitherto unknown" ("Making the Secondary School Progressive," 1).

Cooke remained intensely loyal to the ideas of Francis Parker, editing his *Talks on Pedagogics* in 1937 and writing in several articles about his influence on her and on her school. In her recognition of Parker's influence, she was too modest about her own contribution to the progressive tradition. She went far beyond her mentor, extending his dream of progressive education to the secondary level. Under thirty-three years of Cooke's leadership the Parker School became a nationally recognized model of the best of progressive education.

To her regret, Cooke never completed a bachelor's degree, though over the years she accumulated about three years of college credit by taking University of Chicago Extension courses and science courses at the Armour Institute. In 1931 she was awarded an honorary M.A. degree by Lake Forest College.

After she retired in 1934 at the age of seventy, Cooke continued to be active in the educational life of the city and in national liberal organizations, including the American Civil Liberties Union, Americans for Democratic Action, and the Women's International League for Peace and Freedom. She was a member of the board of trustees of the Parker School and played an important role in the establishment of the North Shore Country Day School in Winnetka, Illinois; the Graduate Teachers College of Winnetka, in existence 1932–54; and Roosevelt University, a school named for Franklin and Eleanor Roosevelt that had the aim of making advanced education available for the many Chicago students who could not afford the distant state university or the private local universities. In 1945 she was honored, along with her friend of sixty years, Zonia Baber, by the Chicago Teachers College, successor to the Cook County Normal School. In the same year, at the age of eighty, she engaged in a spirited public correspondence with Senator Theodore Gilmore Bilbo of Mississippi, attacking with logic and historical evidence as well as passion his filibuster in opposition to a law prohibiting discrimination in employment based on race.

Flora Cooke died in Chicago of a heart attack at the age of eighty-eight and was buried in Buffalo, New York. Active to the end of her life, she was remembered with affection by generations of Parker students and with deep respect by proponents of progressive education.

Sources. The records of the Francis W. Parker School at the CHS contain materials on Cooke, including news clippings, drafts of speeches, letters, and published articles. The records include two manuscripts by Flora J. Cooke: "Making the Secondary School Progressive" (type-script), June 1930, and "Opportunities and Episodes of a Teacher's Life in America during the Last Half Century—Born 1864—Teaching Life 1884–1934—Present Date 1941" (typescript). Two speeches in the Parker Papers, one honoring Zonia Baber, October 21, 1944, and the other celebrating the history of the Cook County Normal School, February 8, 1945, contain interesting anecdotes of Cooke's life. The Parker records have considerable material on the administration of the school. Published works by Flora Cooke include: *Nature Myths and Stories for Little Children* (1895); "Colonel Francis W. Parker as Interpreted through the Work of the Francis W. Parker School," *Elementary School Teacher*, May 1912; "Fundamental Consideration Underlying the Curriculum of the Francis W. Parker School," *Twenty-Sixth Yearbook of the National Society for the Study of Education* (1926); "Problems of the Progressive Secondary School," *Progressive Education*, Autumn 1928; "Colonel Francis W. Parker as I Knew Him," *Illinois Teacher*, June 1936; "Colonel Francis W. Parker and His Influence on Education," *Chicago Schools Journal*, Spring 1938. In 1937 she edited a reissue of Francis W. Parker's *Talks on Pedagogics* (1894). Biographical information can be found in Carol Lynn Gilmer, "Flora Cooke: Grand Old Lady of Education," *Coronet*, October 1947; in Elsie A. Wygant, "Flora J. Cooke," *Bulletin National Council of Primary Education*, vol. 13, 1930; in *NAW* (1980); and in Nancy Stewart Green, "Flora Juliette Cooke," *American National Biography*, ed. John A. Garraty and Mark C. Carnes (1999). Information concerning Cooke's approach to reading at Cook County Normal School is included in Amalie Hofer, "Chicago Normal Training School—A Dream Come True," *Kindergarten Magazine*, November 1896. Obituaries appeared in the *NYT* and the *CT*, February 22, 1953.

NANCY STEWART GREEN

COONLEY-WARD, LYDIA
January 31, 1845–February 26, 1924
ARTS PATRON, WRITER, POET

Lydia Arms Avery Coonley-Ward, participant in and promoter of social and cultural activities in Chicago and in Wyoming, New York, grew up in a close and loving family that was influenced by her mother's activism in social and political movements: suffrage, tax reform, abolition, free coinage of silver, and anti-imperialism. Although Lydia Avery, as the oldest child, was close to her mother, the daughter was not the fiery radical her mother, Susan (Look) Avery, was but chose instead to influence society in traditional female pursuits such as hospitality, charity work, and poetry. Lydia Arms Avery was born in Lynchburg, Virginia. Five years later, the Averys moved to Louisville, Kentucky, where her father, Benjamin Avery, started Avery Plow Works, which became a profitable business. The family, sympathetic to the abolitionist cause, raised the first Union flag in Louisville. In support of the Union cause, they converted their factory to a hospital for Union soldiers; Susan Avery did volunteer nursing there.

In this dynamic atmosphere, Lydia Avery spent her childhood. She shared family life with her five younger siblings, Samuel Look (born 1846), Gertrude Arms (1848), George Capwell (1852), Helen Blaisdell (1855), and William Sidney (1858). She was educated at schools in Louisville, Utica, and Philadelphia.

On December 24, 1867, Lydia Avery married John Clark Coonley in Louisville. She had met him while she was visiting an uncle in Aurora, New York, the same village where her parents had met. John Coonley was born in 1838 in Aurora, New

York, the son of a middle-class farmer. He had studied law, which he practiced in St. Louis, but decided to go into another business soon after their marriage because of ill health. John and Lydia Coonley lived in St. Louis from 1867 to 1868, then moved to Louisville, where he worked in her father's plow business from 1868 to 1873. In 1873, he and three partners established the Chicago Malleable Iron Company, of which he was the president. That year, John and Lydia Coonley moved to Chicago with their three children, Mary Letchworth (born 1869), Avery (1870), and John Stuart (1872).

The Coonleys had three more children, Sarah Oliphant (1874), Howard (1876) and Prentiss Loomis (1880). Lydia Coonley was a devoted mother, concerned about all aspects of her children's development. She encouraged her children to write poetry by giving them five cents per stanza. Coonley had begun writing in 1878 when she submitted articles regularly to *Home and Farm*, a semimonthly journal that her father had founded in Louisville. Her essays were an emotional response to nature and the people around her. She wrote under the pseudonym Lois Catesby. Coonley also wrote many letters to the *Wyoming Reporter* about life in the country. She published a book of poetry in 1895, *Under the Pines and Other Verses*. Literature was recreational for Coonley, and she pursued her writing between a busy family life and a hectic social schedule. Her poetry shows strong interest in nature, family, life cycles, and spirituality. The poetic form most often contains regular stanzas with even metrical lines and end rhyme. She uses a great deal of description, especially nature imagery, but few metaphors. She draws on conventionally acceptable ideas.

The Coonley family lived a lively social and intellectual life, which was overshadowed by the death of John Coonley in Indianapolis on October 6, 1882. On March 3, 1885, Lydia Coonley was again in mourning, this time for her father. After these deaths, Coonley spent more time at Hillside in the village of Wyoming, New York, during the summer months but still had her main residence in Chicago.

Lydia Coonley became active in the cultural and social activities of Chicago, where her home on LaSalle Street became a center of learning. JANE ADDAMS was a friend and frequent guest. She discussed Lydia Coonley in her book, *The Excellent Becomes the Permanent*. Addams remembered Coonley's home as a place for intellectual discussion on a variety of issues by moral thinkers. She recalled parties, art exhibits, and musical recitals, all arranged and supported by Lydia Coonley. Addams was impressed with Coonley's range of support for social and intellectual activities in Chicago, as well as her ever-present encouragement of people involved in these pursuits. In 1889, Addams talked about her plans for the establishment of Hull-House at Coonley's Chicago home, where the news was received with enthusiasm and praise.

Lydia Coonley had always been interested and involved in the Chicago community both in cultural and social activities. During the years 1895–96, she was president of the Chicago Woman's Club as well as a member of the Cordon Society, Society of Midland Authors, the Fortnightly, and the Little Room, which were founded to foster the social, literary, and cultural interests of members in the Chicago community.

On March 18, 1897, Coonley married Professor Henry Augustus Ward in Chicago. He was a renowned geologist and collector of natural history specimens and a graduate of Middlebury Academy in Wyoming, New York. The couple had met at a World's Fair Committee, planning for the 1893 World's Columbian Exposition in Chicago. He was sixty years old. He wooed her aggressively by sending her love letters, going to parties, and organizing a trip to Mexico, all of which were atypical of his normal behavior. She refused him. On a visit to India, where he was doing scientific research, he wrote her a letter about the Taj Mahal, describing how it was built by Shah Jahan as a mausoleum for his wife, a monument to his great love for her. After this letter, Coonley accepted Ward's proposal, and they were married. She became Lydia Coonley-Ward. They lived in her palatial home on Lake Shore Drive in Chicago. She arranged a study for him, and from this room he began his plans for a meteorite collection and the expeditions to find them. She supported her husband's scientific research by helping to finance *The Catalogue of the Ward-Coonley Collection of Meteorites*. The collection itself is in the Geological Hall of the American Museum of Natural History in New York City.

Coonley-Ward's involvement with her husband's scientific research did not preclude her own activities. Her Chicago home was a center for musical groups and after-dinner readings. She had also started to write again. In 1896, she wrote the words for Dr. George F. Root's cantata, *Our Flag with the Stars and Stripes*. In 1897, she published *Singing Verses for Children*, a collection done with several friends. She expressed her youthfulness and joy for life in the collection *Love Songs*.

Henry Ward was accidentally killed by an automobile in 1906 while visiting Buffalo, New York. After her husband's death, Coonley-Ward stayed in Chicago until 1911, when she sold her house and moved permanently back to Hillside, the family residence that defined her idea of family and community. Six generations of the Avery family had lived here at one time or another from 1858 to 1928. At Hillside, Coonley-Ward was interested in village life and put together a lecture series that included women's rights advocate Susan B. Anthony. Other famous visitors also came to Hillside to be entertained and to enjoy Coonley-Ward's legendary hospitality. Her guests might stay for a week or as long as the entire summer. They included her mother's friends—Carrie Chapman Catt, MARY LIVERMORE, and Alice Stone Blackwell—as well as others, such as Booker T. Washington, Charlotte Perkins Gilman, and Edna St. Vincent Millay.

Coonley-Ward's home at Hillside was always open to young, struggling artists. She began a summer school in 1914, in operation in 1916 and 1917 as well, for young, aspiring artists and teachers. In 1914, she hosted the Portmanteau Players at the summer school to give actors a chance to play a variety of parts, including Shakespeare. She also gave back to Wyoming by establishing a community hall, which was dedicated on October 4, 1902. Starting in 1914, she sent a series of descriptive letters about Hillside to the *Chicago Daily News*. In 1921, a collected version of her poems in three volumes was published: *The Melody of Life, The Melody of Love, The Melody of Childhood*. These volumes expressed her lifelong interests in music, children, nature, and human relationships.

Two of Coonley-Ward's children died in 1920, and she expressed her grief in poetry. These deaths, like those of her father and her husbands, affected her deeply. Near the end of her life, Coonley-Ward suffered intermittent depression, which she shared in correspondence with her beloved friend Grace Ellory Channing Stetson. Coonley-Ward's mental state kept her at Hillside, away from family and friends. During the last three months of her life, however, she felt well enough to visit Chicago with her companion, Eleanor Rudd. She came for the wedding of her grandson John Stuart Coonley Jr. and stayed when she developed problems with her eyes and had to be hospitalized for several weeks. She died in February 1924. A simple service was held at Graceland Chapel in Chicago, conducted by Wyoming, New York, minister Reverend Francis J. Malzard with a tribute by Jane Addams.

Lydia Coonley-Ward is remembered for her life of community service, both artistic and human. She wrote that her two fondest desires were for a large and loving family and for a home where people could come together. She was prominent in cultural and civic causes, delighting in the use of her Chicago and Hillside homes as meeting places for talented people. She urged others to create works of art and gave them the encouragement and the environment to succeed.

Sources. In addition to what is listed above, Coonley-Ward wrote articles and letters that span nearly half a century for *Home and Farm* (starting in 1879), *Wyoming Reporter,* and *Chicago Daily News* (1914). Several of Lydia Coonley-Ward's letters can be found at NL in Chicago. An important series of letters to Grace Ellery Channing Stetson is at the SL. Articles written about Coonley-Ward include "Lydia Coonley Ward's Two Dearest Wishes," in Irene Beale's *Genesee Valley Women* (1985); Waldo Ralph Browne, *Chronicles of an American Home: Hillside (Wyoming, New York) and Its Family, 1858–1928* (1930). There are several entries on Coonley-Ward and her life with her second husband in Henry A. Ward and Rosell Ward, *The Rochester Society Publication,* vol. 24 (1948). Henry A. Ward, *Catalogue of the Ward-Coonley Collection of Meteorites* (1904) contains material on Coonley-Ward. She is profiled in *The Dictionary of American Biography,* vol. 19 (1936). Her obituary is in the *CT,* February 24, 1924.

BARBARA PITLICK LOVENHEIM

CORBIN, CAROLINE ELIZABETH FAIRFIELD
November 9, 1835–March 27, 1918
ANTISUFFRAGE LEADER, AUTHOR

Caroline Fairfield Corbin, founder and president of the Illinois Association Opposed to the Extension of Suffrage to Women (IAOESW), was this organization's primary spokeswoman, creating numerous pamphlets and articles published by the group. Caroline Fairfield was the fifth of eight children born to Jason Williams and Hannah Dana (Chandler) Fairfield and was the only daughter to survive to adulthood. Born in Woodstock, Connecticut, she grew up with three brothers on the Chandler homestead, just outside the town of Pomfret, Connecticut. Caroline Fairfield, or Carrie, as she was frequently called, attended public schools in Pomfret until her father moved the family to Williamsburgh, Long Island, New York. While in New York, she attended the Brooklyn Female Academy (now the Packer Institute). In the Academy's Collegiate Department, she studied a wide range of subjects, including trigonometry, astronomy, phi-

losophy, English literature, theology, physics, chemistry, and logic. She graduated in July 1852, receiving a special commendation from the teacher of composition for a piece entitled "Life's Undying Records."

After graduation, Fairfield continued to write. By the end of 1855, two of her short stories, "Cora Wentworthy, or Twice a Bride" and "Genevieve: A Christmas Story," had been published in *True Flag,* a Boston weekly newspaper. From November 1855 through July 1861, Fairfield had forty-three short stories published in its pages. She also wrote *Our Bible Class and the Good That Came of It* (1860), the first of several volumes she wrote for children. The Fairfield family moved back to Pomfret in 1856.

During a visit to an aunt living in Alton, Illinois, Fairfield met Calvin Rich Corbin, who was living in Chicago. He was originally from Charlton, Massachusetts, and, like Fairfield, was descended from English immigrants. He worked in Chicago as a merchant's agent. The two were married on July 4, 1861, in Thompson, Connecticut. Caroline Corbin's first child, daughter Grace, was born in Pomfret on July 2, 1862, but lived only nine months. By the time her son Frank Nichols was born in 1864, the Corbins had a permanent home in Chicago. Corbin continued her writing, and in 1867, *Rebecca, or a Woman's Secret,* was published. At that time, Corbin was in sympathy with the woman suffrage movement. The story line not only supports women's rights, but the dedication of the novel reads, "To John Stuart Mill, the Author would hereby express her Admiration and Gratitude, for his noble efforts in behalf of the Enfranchisement of Woman."

The year 1867 also brought the birth of fraternal twins, Calvin Dana and Caroline. Caroline died in March 1870. On May 2, 1870, Corbin gave birth to John Rich, who grew up sharing his mother's interest in writing and later held various editorial positions. In 1874, Corbin published *His Marriage Vow,* and two years later, at age forty, she gave birth to her last child, Lawrence Paul. She published a children's book, *Belle and the Boys,* three years later.

The year 1886 marked the beginning of Corbin's antisuffragist publications. Her fourth book, *Letters from a Chimney Corner: A Plea for Pure Homes and Sincere Relations between Men and Women* was published in that year. Originally a series of letters published in the Chicago *Inter-Ocean,* this book detailed Corbin's belief in the fitness of continuing the division of roles between women and men and notes that, "until society is cleansed of the moral foulness which infests it, and which . . . lies beyond the reach of civil law, women have no call to go forth into the wider fields claiming to be therein the rightful and natural purifiers" (*Letters,* 22). She admitted that the women's movement had been invaluable in its ability "to make women stronger, more self-respecting, to give them a broader outlook upon the world's affairs, and larger opportunities of measuring their capabilities, intellectual and otherwise, with the world's needs"; but she felt that its effects were detrimental in that it caused women to denigrate their roles as wives and mothers, "the foundation of what is highest and purest" (*Letters,* 28).

Her views on suffrage had changed since *Rebecca, or a Woman's Secret* had been published. In 1888, she described her change of heart in regard to the woman suffrage movement in two pamphlets addressed to FRANCES E. WILLARD, then president of the Woman's Christian Temperance Union and champion of woman suffrage. In *An Open Letter to My Dear Friend and Sister Frances E. Willard* and *A Rejoinder to Frances E. Willard*, she explained that, though she had once looked favorably on woman suffrage as a means to "open a wider door for woman," she became concerned that "false ideals were luring women from the natural and holy ministries of the home, and promoting a coarse and selfish individualism" (quoted in Camhi, 238–39). She traced this problem to the connection of woman suffrage with socialism, an ideology that she felt regarded the individual rather than the family as the basic unit of society.

An encounter in November 1886, which Corbin later described in *One Woman's Experience of Emancipation* (c. 1900), seemed strongly to have affected her beliefs about woman suffrage. She attended a lecture in Chicago given by socialists Edward Aveling and Eleanor Marx, daughter of Karl Marx. On a lecture tour of America, Aveling spoke on behalf of the men convicted of conspiracy in the Haymarket Affair. Corbin's views on Aveling and Marx may have been influenced by their advocacy of these men. However, in her pamphlet, she deals only with the couple's views on love and marriage. She reprints an account of their lecture from the *Chicago Tribune*, quoting the couple's statement that "love is the only recognized marriage in Socialism, consequently no bonds of any kind would be required; . . . divorces would be impossible, as there would be nothing to divorce, for when love ceased, separation would naturally ensue" (Corbin, *One Woman's Experience*, 1). Corbin took issue with this philosophy, which Aveling and Marx admitted could lead to the practice of polygamy or the desertion of old, sick wives for young, healthy ones. Corbin's concerns were reinforced later when she heard reports that Aveling had an invalid wife in England and that Eleanor Marx, who lived as his common-law wife for many years, had committed suicide when Aveling married another woman upon the death of his invalid wife.

A fear of socialism appeared again and again in Corbin's antisuffrage literature. Since she was the wife of a well-to-do merchant, Corbin's support of the existing social order was perhaps to be expected. Labor unrest in the 1880s and 1890s awakened fears of socialism in many. In *The Position of Women in the Socialistic Utopia* (c. 1901), Corbin examines the background of socialism and a number of socialist communities that she regarded as failures, such as Robert Owen's New Harmony in Indiana and the Oneida community in New York. She believed that socialism would fail because, rather than believing in "struggle" and "the uplift of humanity," as she felt Christianity did, socialism "would improve the condition of the poor, the incompetent, the evil disposed by bringing the rich, the strong, the successful down to a common plane" (*Position of Women*, 7). Once women received equal rights and equal pay and the vote, then care of children, Corbin felt, must necessarily fall to the state and "what is left of marriage and the Christian home?" (*Position of Women*, 10). Corbin believed in the Victorian ideal of separate spheres, a division of labor. Proponents of this ideal believed that women should work in the home while men took care of business in the outside world. Corbin believed that

this division best suited society as a whole, that men "represent us in the corn-field, on the battle-field, and at the ballot-box, and we them in the school-room, at the fireside, and at the cradle" (IAOESW *Bulletin*, no. 1, n.p.). Like many of the late-nineteenth-century antisuffragists, Corbin was a Social Darwinist, believing that society constantly evolved toward a more sophisticated and effective organization and that the differentiated roles of men and women within the family and in society exemplified this progress.

In 1897 Corbin founded the Illinois Association Opposed to the Extension of Suffrage to Women. One of a number of organizations that sprang up around the country to fight the gains the suffrage movement had achieved in that decade, it developed out of a group that had been working unofficially as the Remonstrants of Illinois. The primary role of the organization was the production and distribution of antisuffrage literature. The IAOESW was one of the first organizations specifically created to oppose woman suffrage, and it helped delineate many arguments later used by antisuffragists throughout the country. Much of the literature was signed by Corbin, and she was doubtless the author of many of the anonymous pieces as well. In addition, she gave occasional lectures, though in general the group refrained from public appearances. The bulletins of the IAOESW frequently touched on the antisocialism theme as well as the belief in separate spheres for men and women. Other arguments included the belief that women's role in the home did not allow them time to act as informed voters; that the women's vote in the western states was not successful; that some women's votes, like some men's, could and would be bought by corrupt politicians. Mentioned, but not emphasized, was the belief of many early-twentieth-century antisuffragists that without the vote women represented an unbiased group untouched by partisan politics and therefore more forceful in promoting reform.

Corbin remained president of the IAOESW until at least 1911. Her niece, Jessie Fairfield, who lived with the Corbin family in Chicago, acted as secretary for a time. In 1912, the IAOESW joined with similar organizations in Massachusetts, New York, Maryland, Pennsylvania, Oregon, Rhode Island, and the District of Columbia to form the National Association Opposed to the Extension of Suffrage to Women (NAOESW). The Illinois Association continued to issue bulletins as late as 1913, the year in which the Illinois legislature granted women in the state limited suffrage; by 1914, IAOESW admitted defeat and went out of existence.

Corbin's husband died in 1913 at eighty-one. Corbin continued to live in their home in Chicago with her youngest son, Laurence Paul, and her niece, Jessie Fairfield. In 1915, all three moved to a home Corbin and her husband had built in Harbor Springs, Michigan. Three years later Corbin died there at Petoskey Hospital at age eighty-two. She was buried with her husband and young children in Rosehill Cemetery on Chicago's North Side. Caroline Corbin was a persuasive advocate for the antisuffrage viewpoint and was an able opponent for the suffragists.

Sources. Corbin's children's writings are noted above. Her antisuffrage articles and pamphlets were published primarily by the Illinois Association Opposed to the Extension of Suffrage to Women; they included "To the Voters of the Middle West," *Bulletin*, no. 1, September 1909, and other bulletin numbers. NL has the most complete collection. In addition to the books mentioned in the text, Corbin wrote the novel, *A Woman's Philosophy of Love* (1892). Summaries of two of Corbin's novels (*Rebecca* and *His Marriage Vow*) appear in Bernice Gallagher, *Illinois Women Novelists in the Nineteenth Century* (1994). Additional general information on Corbin's antisuffrage work can be found in Manuela Thurner, "Better Citizens without the Ballot: American Anti-Suffrage Women and Their Rationale during the Progressive Era," in *One Woman, One Vote: Rediscovering the Woman Suffrage Movement*, ed. Marjorie Spruill Wheeler (1995); Jane Camhi, *Women against Women: American Anti-Suffragism* (1994); and Aileen Kraditor, *The Ideas of the Woman Suffrage Movement, 1890–1920* (1965), chapter 2, "The Rationale of Antisuffragism." See Steven Buechler, *The Transformation of the Woman Suffrage Movement: The Case of Illinois, 1850–1920* (1986), and Catherine Cole Mambretti, "The Battle against the Ballot: Illinois Woman Antisuffragists," in *Chicago History*, Fall 1980, for discussions of the Illinois movement against woman suffrage.

LESLEY A. MARTIN

CORY, BERNICE LLOYD TUCKER
June 26, 1899–April 21, 1973
RELIGIOUS EDUCATOR, EDITOR, PUBLISHER, LECTURER

Bernice Tucker Cory was cofounder and editor of Scripture Press, a fundamentalist religious publishing company. She wrote books and developed teaching aids for children, was active in numerous associations, and was a popular lecturer. Bernice Tucker, the first child of Lloyd Byron and Frances (Campbell) Tucker, was born in Denver, Colorado. Two other daughters were born, Ruth and Gene. The Tuckers moved from Denver to Milwaukee when Bernice and Ruth were young. They then settled in Chicago, living in the Austin neighborhood on the city's West Side. Lloyd Tucker was a credit manager for a meat corporation. Frances Tucker, the daughter of a physician who became a mining entrepreneur, had attended Washington College, Seattle, Washington. She became a dressmaker in Chicago.

The Tucker children attended Sunday school at Austin Methodist Episcopal Church, although their parents were not active members. Tucker was especially close to her father and was a second mother to her youngest sister. A good student who liked school, Bernice Tucker graduated from Austin High School and entered the University of Chicago with the goal of becoming a high school English teacher. She transferred to the University of Denver in 1917, where she and her family had moved to help her father's sister and brother-in-law operate a lumber business whose rapid growth was stimulated by the economic boom during World War I. The Tucker family returned to Chicago at the end of the war and Bernice Tucker resumed her studies at the University of Chicago, graduating in 1920 with a B.Phil. degree.

In the 1920s, Bernice Tucker's maternal aunt, Jennie Campbell Rader, invited the Tucker family to attend North Shore Church, a nondenominational fellowship influential in the rising fundamentalist religious movement. The Tuckers became active in the congregation. Bernice Tucker attended social events and the Christian Endeavor group, a society promoting Christian lifestyles and church involvement among young

adults. She met Victor L. Cory, her future husband, at North Shore Church.

Victor Cory, raised in Ohio, earned a B.S. degree from Heidelberg College, Tiffin, Ohio, and a second B.S. degree from Case Western Reserve University, Cleveland, Ohio, in electrical engineering. Cory moved to Chicago after World War I to look for work and found a job with the Commonwealth Edison Company. Raised a Methodist, he started attending the North Shore Church shortly after his arrival in the city.

Bernice Tucker initially disagreed with the fundamentalist teachings of North Shore Church, including its prohibitions against the worldly activities of dancing, attending movies, and theater. She had enjoyed these activities as a young adult and did not consider them sinful. However, while attending a Valentine's Day party in 1920 at the home of her aunt, Jennie Rader, where Rader read numerous Bible verses and talked about how a person could not love both the world and God, Tucker finally was convinced of her need to give up worldly activities and attitudes. In a young people's periodical published by Scripture Press she is later quoted about how, on that eventful night, she decided to "jump the fence" and receive the "Lord Jesus into her heart" (Adair, 3). Victor Cory also attended the party and became a committed fundamentalist Christian the same night.

After their conversions, Tucker and Cory pursued Bible study and taught Sunday school. Victor Cory led a Christian Endeavor group. Tucker and Cory's relationship had become serious, but after graduating from the University of Chicago in 1920, she decided to follow through with her dream of becoming a high school teacher. Tucker moved to Charleston, Illinois, and taught for the academic year 1920–21. She continued her relationship with Cory through letters and periodic visits. The two decided to marry, and Tucker returned to Chicago and briefly helped with her mother's sewing business. Tucker and Cory were married June 16, 1922, in a Sunday school room at the North Shore Church.

Early in their marriage the Corys spent four nights a week leading gospel street corner meetings. They set up a portable organ and a folding chair, gave testimonies, and handed out tracts and copies of the Gospel of John. On holidays they traveled to Elmhurst, Illinois, a western suburb of Chicago, to distribute pamphlets. The Corys had four sons: Lloyd Orrin (born 1923), Paul Russell (born 1926), Daniel Lyell (born 1927), and Philip Victor (born 1932). In 1941 the Corys moved to Wheaton, Illinois, becoming active members of the Wheaton Bible Church, a nondenominational, fundamentalist congregation like North Shore Church.

With their conversion to fundamentalism, the Corys embodied a major religious and social movement in North America during the twentieth century. Disagreements among Christians about how to interpret the Bible and what authority was to be given to scientific knowledge continued from the late nineteenth century. Those in the liberal camp accepted biblical higher criticism, geological dating of the earth, and scientific information about the evolution of species. Conservative theologians and practitioners—fundamentalists—were literalists who rejected both higher criticism and the authority of science and, instead, treated the biblical text as inerrant. Their views were labeled antimodernist and, after the 1925 Scopes Trial of a teacher who taught evolution, fundamentalists found themselves separated from both moderate and liberal voices in the Protestant denominations nationally.

Fundamentalists soon sprouted a network of institutions that supported their antimodernist views. Schools, Bible colleges, camps where conferences for children and adolescents were held, and Christian radio stations provided the infrastructure for a growing fundamentalist subculture. Chicago became an important center of fundamentalism with the fundamentalist school for church workers, Moody Bible Institute, and suburban Wheaton College providing centers for the training of young leaders in the movement.

In 1925, radio evangelist and Chicago Gospel Tabernacle director Paul Rader asked Victor Cory to enter full-time Christian work, leaving behind his secular engineering career. Rader was Jennie Rader's brother-in-law. With the support of his wife, Victor Cory became manager of the Tabernacle Publishing Company, although he had no previous experience. Two years later, he became assistant manager of the Bible Institute Colportage Association (later called Moody Press). Through this work, Victor and Bernice Cory met Clarence Benson, professor of Christian Education at the Moody Bible Institute. Benson and his students were writing new graded Sunday school lessons suitable for children being raised in the fundamentalist subculture, to replace the lessons prepared by the liberal Religious Education Association (REA). REA was founded in 1903 by William Rainey Harper, president of the University of Chicago, and other liberal pedagogues, including John Dewey. The Corys welcomed Benson's curriculum because it was graded, biblically focused, and fundamentalist in its emphasis on the inerrant truth of the Bible.

When in 1930, as the nation headed into the Great Depression, Victor Cory lost his job with the Moody Press, he and an associate opened a printing company called Scripture Press. It folded in the fall of 1933. With the financial backing of William R. Thomas, a Chicago businessman who was also a member of North Shore Church, Victor Cory reopened Scripture Press (SP). The new SP had the sole purpose of preparing and publishing the materials written by Professor Benson and his students. The new curriculum was called the All-Bible Graded Series (ABGS), and the company's motto became "The Whole Word for the Whole World" ("The Road to Tomorrow," 3). Initial writers included Mary and Lois LeBar, young educators who later taught at Wheaton College. The first graded lessons covered junior, intermediate, and senior levels and were published in October 1934.

Scripture Press started in the Corys' kitchen and was a family affair from the beginning. Victor Cory was president and responsible for sales and distribution; Bernice Cory was editor, though Benson was the first editor-in-chief. Cory had been taught the rudiments of editing by her husband and quickly became adept at proofreading. Her father, unemployed due to the depression, did the bookkeeping, helped with shipping, and wrote collection letters. The Cory children collated advertisements and were paid an hourly wage according to their age.

Despite financially precarious early years, SP expanded, doubling its distribution of materials every five years. In 1934, SP moved out of the Cory home and into a one-room office in Chicago. Five years later SP moved a second time to larger quarters and in 1947, rented more space on South Wabash Street, eventually expanding to five floors in three buildings at this location. In 1956, SP built its own facility in Wheaton, Illinois. In addition to a full All-Bible Graded Series curriculum, SP now published daily vacation Bible school materials, teaching resources, and books. From 1935 to 1955, SP sales rose from less than $10,000 annually to almost $2.5 million. The press supplied resources to more than fifty different Protestant groups, including individual congregations within the Methodist, Presbyterian, Mennonite, and Brethren denominations, and to nondenominational congregations. Scripture Press became the largest independent publisher of Sunday school materials with offices in California, Canada, and England. Its ABGS curriculum was translated into Chinese, an attempt by SP to evangelize Asia.

Bernice Cory played a central role in SP. In 1935, she hired a housekeeper, Esther van Fleet, who lived with the family for about twenty years. With Cory freed from most household duties and daily mothering responsibilities, she became a full-time editor, though not on a paid salary for the first few years. A short, stocky woman, Cory was known for her strong personality and often blunt criticism of her writers' work. She was a perfectionist who, as her son Lloyd Cory said, "took great pains and gave them to others" (interview). She worked long hours even though she suffered from back problems and, for many years, received cortisone injections.

Cory was dedicated to her work at SP, though she found it tedious at times. She wrote in a 1962 Christmas letter, "Editorially, I haven't had much opportunity for soaring, creative flights. I find that editing is about 10 percent creative and 90 percent just plain hard work" (Scripture Press Archives). Cory edited SP curriculum for doctrinal correctness as well as for grammar and punctuation. When she found that a writer used liberal rather than fundamentalist terminology, Cory made the corrections. "One writer particularly," Cory wrote, "who had a year at McCormick Theological Seminary, used modernistic terminology" ("The Story of Scripture Press Told by Bernice Cory," 6). Cory knew the writer to be in harmony with the philosophy of SP; her changing the terminology illustrated how much editing for "doctrine and just good theology" (p. 6) became a core part of her job.

Cory attended meetings at many churches and at teachers' meetings, where she presented the ABGS curriculum and spoke on Sunday school education. She developed and published visual aids called flannelgraphs. They were biblical characters made of paper and flannel that were attachable to flannel covered easels so that teachers could illustrate Bible stories for young children by moving figures on the flannelboard.

As an outgrowth of her work with Scripture Press and her commitment to spreading the fundamentalist Christian message, Bernice Cory belonged to the Sunday School Association, the Children's Reading Round Table, and the National Council on Family Relations. She and her husband regularly attended a number of conservative religious events, including meetings of the National Association of Evangelicals, Keswick Conferences of conservative Christians in both the United States and Canada, and conferences on prophecy and the evangelization of Jews. The Corys attended the Christian Book Sellers' Association annual conventions and met with colleagues in the fundamentalist publishing industry, including Henrietta Mears, founder of Gospel Light Publications. Gospel Light and SP materials were alike in their emphasis on Bible teachings, yet both also utilized the latest in educational pedagogy. In addition to these national affiliations, the Corys were central figures in the Chicago fundamentalist community through their numerous associations with faculty and staff at the Moody Bible Institute, Wheaton College, and the Pacific Garden Rescue Mission. Bernice Cory's sister, Gene, was married to Harry Saulnier, longtime superintendent of the mission.

Bernice Cory wrote four books that focused on early childhood faith development—*The Christian's Birth and Growth* (1947), *The Christian's Walk and Talk* (1948), *The Christian's Time and Talents* (1949), and *Your Baby* (1959). She emphasized the necessity of Christian parents' raising their children with a strong sense of morality and, from the earliest days, instilling in them biblical knowledge and truth. Cory and SP used the King James Version of the Bible, believing that the Revised Version, first printed in 1952, was a modernist adaptation of biblical truth. In the 1950s, Bernice Cory's writings, containing strong anticommunist rhetoric, emphasized patriotism and the "American Way." In 1959 Biola College (Bible Institute of Los Angeles) awarded Cory an honorary Doctor of Literature degree in recognition of her contributions in the field of Sunday school education.

On June 2, 1968, Victor Cory suddenly died of a heart attack. A year earlier Bernice Cory had written, "One thing we can never doubt—that the Lord Himself meant Victor and me to be a team. With grateful hearts, we magnify the Lord together" ("From Fickle to Faithful," 7). The Corys did little socializing; their lives centered on SP, an organization they viewed not only as their business but as their ministry. Cory continued with her work at SP after the death of her husband. Since she had not learned to drive a car, she found a companion to provide transportation.

In April 1973, while preparing for her sixth trip to the Holy Land, Cory was diagnosed with cancer. She spent only eight days in a nursing home before she died. She is buried next to her husband at the Wheaton Cemetery, and their tombstone reads, "Scripture Press: Co-Founders and Co-Workers."

Bernice Cory was a powerful presence in SP for more than forty years. Her work reflected the expanded professional role assumed by fundamentalist Christian women in the field of education. Although the Corys worked in a partnership in which they were complementary equals pursuing a joint calling, Bernice Cory made a unique contribution with her innovative, Sunday school materials designed to communicate conservative truths about the Bible to children living in an increasingly sophisticated media environment.

Sources. Scripture Press Archives, Scripture Press Publications, Wheaton, Illinois, contain material that documents the biography and career of Bernice Tucker Cory; correspondence and unpublished manuscripts about the history of the press include "The Story of Scripture Press, Told by Bernice Cory," typescript, n.d.; n.a., "The Road to Tomorrow . . . ," typescript, n.d.; and two unpublished pieces by Victor

Cory: "Scripture Press, Historical Survey," October 19, 1948, and "Abbreviated Sketch of the Scripture Press History," July 26, 1955. Scant materials on Scripture Press can be found in the Billy Graham Archives, Wheaton, Illinois, and at the Archives of the Moody Bible Institute, Chicago. An interview by Eleanor J. Stebner with Bernice Cory's son, Lloyd Cory, May 9, 1994, provides insights. Bernice Cory, "From Fickle to Faithful," *Power for Life*, February 12, 1967, tells about her life with Victor Cory. Articles about Bernice Cory include Wendy Bergman, "SP's Winning Formula: Prayer, People, Planning and Product," *Bookstore Journal*, April 1975, and James R. Adair, "Aunt Jennie's Valentine Party," *Power for Living*, February 14, 1965. Clayton Jacob Hunt Jr., "A Historical Study of the Development of Scripture Press Ministries and Scripture Press, Inc." (Doctor of Religious Education diss., Temple Baptist Theological Seminary, 1984), explores the development of SP, with some reference to Cory. For general overviews see Dorothy Jean Furnish, "Women in Religious Education, Pioneers for Women in Professional Ministry," in *Women and Religion in America*, vol. 3, ed. Rosemary Radford Ruether and Rosemary Skinner Keller (1986); Kenneth Gangel and Warren Benson, *Christian Education: Its History and Philosophy* (1983); George Marsden, ed., *Evangelicalism and Modern America* (1984); Jack Seymour, *From Sunday School to Church School* (1982); and Marvin J. Taylor, *Changing Patterns of Religious Education* (1984). Obituaries for Bernice Cory appear in the *CT*, April 24, 25, 1973.

ELEANOR J. STEBNER

COUNSELBAUM, STELLA LEVINKIND
May 3, 1896–March 8, 1979
CIVIL RIGHTS ACTIVIST, EDUCATIONAL REFORMER, HUMAN RELATIONS EXPERT

Stella Levinkind Counselbaum was an early activist for civil rights, improved relations among Christians and Jews, and elimination of racism, beginning in the 1930s and continuing for some thirty years. She worked for the removal of barriers that kept qualified minority youth from obtaining higher education.

She was the daughter of Hyman and Dora (Rabinovich) Levinkind and the younger sister of Jenni. Her parents came from Russia, meeting and marrying in Chicago. Her father operated a small store on the South Side, while her mother attended to the domestic affairs of the family. Levinkind grew up in a Jewish household that fostered an attitude of respect for others regardless of race, creed, or religion. In later years, she recalled her father's influence in developing values that helped her fight bigotry. While attending Bowen High School (1909–13), Levinkind helped form a social club for girls during her sophomore year. "I happened to mention there was one Negro girl in the school. . . . I said she seemed sad and lonely and that nobody had asked her to join a club. My father said, 'well'; then 'so?' 'Do you mean, I ought to ask the girls to take her into our club?' I asked. He answered . . . , 'what else?' The next day we asked her to join and she did" (quoted in Anderson, "Her Only Prejudice").

Levinkind went on to the University of Chicago, which she attended for two years, 1913–15. Convinced that she was not suited for academics, she enrolled at the Pestalozzi-Froebel Teachers College and received a teaching certificate in 1917. Levinkind never pursued a career as a teacher. After she had "a serious little talk with myself" (quoted in Walker, "Makes a Career of Human Relations"), she went to work in 1919 as an assistant to the supervisor of the Jewish People's Institute, a community center with educational, social, and a variety of cultural activities.

In 1922 Levinkind began activities that influenced the direction of her life. A close friend, Dorothy Kahn, was stricken with a debilitating illness that left her paralyzed and led to an early death. Levinkind and twelve other young women were so moved by the tragedy that they founded the Dorothy Kahn Club for Crippled Children with Levinkind as president. Their goal was to inform the public of the need for a convalescent home for children in similar circumstances. The program of the club changed as its goals were met by other groups. Eventually the Dorothy Kahn Club affiliated with Michael Reese Hospital and established a nursery school. In 1949 the club became the Spastic Children's Center. The ability to organize people for a practical goal would remain one of Levinkind's strengths, as she later moved into the areas of civil rights and promotion of understanding among people of different races and religions.

In 1923 she married Alexander Counselbaum, a clothing manufacturer. She spent the next fourteen years as a homemaker and community volunteer. In 1937 the volunteering switched to professional work, when she was hired as the first paid staff member of the Chicago Round Table of Christians and Jews, which became the Midwest Division of the National Conference of Christians and Jews (NCCJ). She functioned as program director, developing a speakers' bureau and arranging several thousand presentations. She remained with the organization for eight years, until her husband became terminally ill. The NCCJ cited Counselbaum for her work in fostering better relations among Christians and Jews. Involved in the Jewish community, Counselbaum belonged to Chicago Sinai Congregation, a liberal Reform synagogue with members involved in various social reform activities. She was a member of the Sinai Sisterhood and the American Jewish Congress and served as secretary of the Jewish Book Council of America.

After her husband's death in 1945, Counselbaum was asked by Richard Gutstadt, executive vice-chairman of the Anti-Defamation League (ADL) National Commission, to join the staff of ADL, which was part of the Jewish fraternal organization B'nai B'rith. The Great Depression saw a rise in anti-Semitism in the United States, epitomized by the popularity of the anti-Jewish radio broadcasts of demagogue Father Charles E. Coughlin. Counselbaum accepted the position of Director of Community Affairs for the Midwest Area of ADL, and she organized programs promoting dialogue among diverse groups. One of her major concerns was the ending of discriminatory practices in higher education, both against Jews and other minorities, in admissions, housing, employment, and membership in student organizations.

In the course of her work, Counselbaum became actively and visibly involved in the civil liberties movement that emerged after World War II. Mary McLeod Bethune, an outstanding figure in the African American community, was a major influence on Counselbaum's activities. Bethune, determined to create educational opportunities for African Americans, founded Bethune-Cookman College in Daytona Beach, Florida; it was accredited as a junior college in 1932 and within ten years became a four-year college. She established the National Council of Negro Women (NCNW), which united major

associations of black women. Bethune and Counselbaum shared a focus on racial discrimination, international relations, and national liberal causes. Counselbaum met Bethune in 1945 and joined NCNW.

During the years after World War II, racial tensions grew both in the South and the North. While African Americans experienced discrimination in housing, employment, and school enrollments, housing was the major origin of racial conflicts. From 1940 to 1960, the African American population of Chicago increased greatly in number and proportion of population, while available housing was decreasing. In the years 1945–54, nine major racial riots related to housing took place in the city. Against this background of racial turmoil, Counselbaum worked to promote interracial understanding through her work with ADL.

In June 1946 the Chicago Council against Racial and Religious Discrimination, of which Counselbaum was a member, sponsored an Institute on College Quotas, which attracted thirty-six local organizations. The findings confirmed discrimination in Chicago and Illinois schools against members of racial and religious minority groups but could prove discrimination in admissions policies only by statistics on minority enrollment. President Harry Truman appointed a President's Commission on Higher Education (CHE) to assess the role of higher education in the postwar era. In December 1947 the CHE issued its report, which found admission quotas and racial segregation in colleges. The commission's report focused on equality of opportunity in higher education and removal of discriminatory practices in college admissions. Counselbaum seized the moment, and with resources available through ADL and her involvement in NCNW, she began to organize. The Chicago Women's Aid Organization, which was connected to NCNW, met in March 1948 to discuss the CHE's report. As a result, Counselbaum established the Women's Council for Fair Education Practices of Illinois and served as secretary of the organization. The purpose of the council was to promote public support for the passage of the Illinois Fair Practices in Education Bill, but Illinois never enacted such a law. In 1948 Counselbaum was cited by NCNW in recognition for her accomplishments in race relations, an award given directly by Mary McLeod Bethune.

Continuing her work in education, Counselbaum initiated and promoted the first national conference of educators to address the problems of discrimination highlighted in the CHE's report. The conference was cosponsored by the ADL and the American Council of Education. At the two-day conference, held in Chicago in November 1949, one hundred educators from twenty-five states adopted a set of guiding principles that would aid in the elimination of discrimination from all aspects of college and university life.

In 1949–50 Counselbaum wrote a column for the Chicago edition of the *Pittsburgh Courier*. Bethune had contributed a weekly column in the 1930s. The *Courier*, established in 1910, was America's leading African American newspaper by 1937. Counselbaum used her column to promote and discuss the various human rights activities in which she and her colleagues were involved and to encourage an atmosphere of interracial understanding. The column on November 11, 1949, saw the conference of educators as the beginning of a solution to the problem of discrimination. Her articles focused on anti-Semitism as one form of bigotry. She expressed her basic belief that "the pattern of discrimination remains the same . . . whether it is against the Jew, the Negro, the Nisei or a member of any so-called minority group" (untitled, *Pittsburgh Courier,* March 12, 1949).

Counselbaum recognized that in order to address the injustices of the world, it was necessary to start in the family and build outward into the community. She was dismayed by the self-segregation that seemed to be growing within American society and cautioned that the only way that world understanding could come about was in developing compassion for and acceptance of one's neighbor. In her *Pittsburgh Courier* column on November 4, 1949, "The Dangers of Segregation," she deplored anti-Semitic stereotypes, citing similar anti-black prejudices.

Counselbaum received an honorary degree of Doctor of Laws from Bethune-Cookman College in 1950. The award recognized that Counselbaum, in her leadership and organizational work, achieved international recognition for her contribution to worldwide friendship and to understanding among people of different races. Afterwards, Bethune hosted a reception for Counselbaum in her own home. It was, according to Counselbaum, an event "that would have gladdened the hearts of all who believe that we can, through the democratic process, achieve equality" ("Upon Winning an Award from Bethune," *Pittsburgh Courier,* June 10, 1950). For Counselbaum, the reception itself was an affirmation of the world to come.

Counselbaum also worked in an international arena. In the summer of 1947 she attended the Workshop on Catholic, Protestant, and Jewish relations, sponsored by the International Council of Christians and Jews. The conference, held in Seelisberg, Switzerland, with representatives from seventeen countries, focused on anti-Semitism, especially toward the 250,000 Jewish displaced persons—survivors of concentration camps—living in camps in Germany. In a press conference held on her return, Counselbaum described the workshop as the first effort in Europe to bring Jews, Catholics, and Protestants together to seek mutual understanding.

In 1949 she attended a meeting of the Canada Council of Christians and Jews (CCCJ), traveling with two other women, a Catholic and a Protestant. They found considerable discrimination against Jews in the country. An aftermath of the visit was the establishment of a women's council to work with CCCJ.

In 1958 Counselbaum traveled abroad under the auspices of ADL. The purpose of her tour, which took her to Hong Kong, Thailand, Japan, India, Pakistan, Ceylon (now Sri Lanka), Iran, South Africa, and Israel, was to gather information on social and racial problems throughout the world. Upon her return, she reported her findings in a talk given at the Annual Human Relations Conference held at Central State College, Wilberforce, Ohio, in 1959. She saw human relations—the ability of people to get along with each other—as the "most essential issue in the world today" ("Human Relations around the World," 483). Counselbaum spoke with individuals in each country; in Hong Kong, she gave a lecture at a Chinese-American college. She felt that American behavior in human relations was a factor in peace or war and that the United States was not presenting a good example to other countries. Criticizing the resistance of American

society to integration, Counselbaum concluded that if Americans were to lead the world in striving for equality, they had to practice what they professed to believe.

Changes in discriminatory educational practices were slow in coming, and Counselbaum continued to work in that area in the 1950s and 1960s. In 1954, student leaders at Northwestern University drew on her expertise in organizing the Conference on Human Relations at Northwestern University. The conference dealt with all aspects of discrimination at the institution. The students' concern and activism helped to bring about gradual changes on campus. On the state level, in 1960 she was executive secretary of the Illinois Committee on Human Rights in Higher Education, which sought to set standards for colleges and universities for eliminating discrimination.

In addition to Counselbaum's involvement with colleges, her work at ADL included programs for high-school students—extracurricular clubs devoted to creating interracial understanding and interaction. She began promoting such clubs in Chicago-area public and Catholic schools in 1947. Her article in *Education,* November 1947, cited examples of the positive effects of such clubs. In 1958 she developed a program for Chicago high schools, Human Relations around the World. By her retirement from ADL in 1968, she had initiated the formation of ninety Human Relations clubs among high school students.

Counselbaum was the recipient of many citations and awards from African American, Jewish, and civic organizations. Among them was the Thomas H. Wright Award given in 1954 by the Chicago Commission on Human Relations. In 1960 the Chicago Committee of One Hundred gave her its Good American Award in recognition of her work in the area of higher education and her leadership internationally in the field of civil rights.

Stella Levinkind Counselbaum died shortly before her eighty-third birthday of complications resulting from Alzheimer's disease. Her legacy to the American civil rights movement and her tireless efforts on its behalf were summed up in a tribute by her friend and colleague, Percy L. Julian, a noted chemist and civil rights activist in Chicago. He and his family had been targets of anti–African American bigotry when the house they bought in Oak Park, Illinois, in the late 1950s was bombed. He praised Counselbaum's character: courageous enough to fight to the end for her beliefs, loving and compassionate to others. In the years before the post–World War II American civil rights movement brought about important changes, Stella Counselbaum acted as a leader and a catalyst to end discrimination in education and to further interracial and interreligious contacts and understanding.

Sources. The Stella Levinkind Counselbaum Papers at the CHS contain biographical information; correspondence, including letters from Mary McLeod Bethune; certificates of award; and clippings of articles. Aron Kahn provided information in an interview with Edna Jan Jacobs in July 1993. Counselbaum's articles in the *Pittsburgh Courier* 1949–50, also in the CHS collection, include an untitled description of her Canadian trip, March 12, 1949; "Dangers of Segregation," November 4, 1949; and a discussion of student opposition to discrimination in "Upon Winning an Award from Bethune," June 10, 1950. Her speech, "Human Relations around the World," appears in a shortened version in the *Jour-*

nal of Human Relations, Summer 1959. She describes her secondary-school program in "Building Democracy through Extra-Curricular Clubs," Education, November 1947, and in an unpublished memorandum in the CHS papers written with Hans Adler, "Program for Secondary School Education," December 15, 1958. Two articles in the Chicago Sun-Times discuss her work: Betty Walker, "Makes a Career of Human Relations," November 20, 1952; and David Anderson, "Her Only Prejudice," July 29, 1968. For background on discrimination against African Americans, see Arvrah E. Strickland, History of the Chicago Urban League (1966).

E. JAN JACOBS

CRADDOCK, IDA C.
1857(?)–October 17, 1902
SEXUAL REFORMER, SEX EDUCATOR, SPIRITUALIST

Ida C. Craddock was an enigmatic martyr to a social agenda that challenged prevailing standards of sexual propriety and of acceptable female behavior. Craddock was born in Philadelphia about 1857 to parents of Quaker ancestry. Her father, Joseph Craddock, was a wealthy Philadelphia merchant. Her mother, Lizzie Craddock, was a committed member of the Woman's Christian Temperance Union with a longstanding interest in spiritualism—a social fad and quasi-religious movement embraced by many respectable middle-class adherents during the nineteenth and early twentieth centuries. Spiritualists believed that an individual continued to exist after death and that living persons could communicate with spirits. Shortly before his death, Joseph Craddock denied all religious belief and had his wife promise not to provide religious instruction to their two-year-old daughter. Lizzie Craddock soon broke this promise, enrolling Craddock in a Quaker school and teaching puritanical, strict habits at home.

Although the surviving record of Craddock's childhood is sparse, she appeared to have been a precocious child considerably influenced by her mother and her Quaker teacher. By age eighteen Craddock had become a teacher of phonography, the Pitman form of shorthand, about which she already had written a textbook. In 1887, Craddock moved to California, where she taught in a business college and pursued her interests in religion, folklore, occultism, and sexual reform. She supported a single sexual standard for women and men, and she argued for the respectability of female sexuality.

Like her mother, Craddock was attracted to spiritualism. By 1893, Ida Craddock's sexual reform agenda took her to Chicago, where she opened a sex counseling service in an office in the central business district. Craddock offered her clients, who knew her as Mrs. Craddock, lectures and personal consultations supplemented with privately produced pamphlets that promoted her personal vision of correct sexual behavior. Craddock never married, and only her mother and close friends knew that her professed mate was a "spiritual husband" named Soph—not a flesh-and-blood spouse but a member of the spirit world she "visited" almost daily as a spiritual medium. Nevertheless, even a "spiritual husband" shielded her from having to explain how a single woman became so knowledgeable in sexual matters. Craddock's pamphlets, Letter to a Prospective Bride, Advice to a Bridegroom, The Wedding Night, and Right Marital Living, em-

phasized the necessity of gentleness, patience, and mutuality in sexual intercourse. She repeatedly argued for open public dialogue about subjects often considered too intimate to be discussed. "I need make no plea for the propriety of my subject," she wrote. "What concerns us all is eminently fit for discussion by all, and too much light cannot be thrown upon it" (Untitled ms., Craddock Papers).

Clients who did not come to Craddock's small office could subscribe to her mail-order course, Regeneration and Rejuvenation of Men and Women through the Right Use of the Sexual Function. For a ten-dollar fee, Craddock sent to the subscriber two pamphlets and a list of questions. Craddock answered with two letters providing instructions; further letters were five dollars. Additional copies of the pamphlets were sent by mail for fifty cents each. This use of the federal postal service brought Ida Craddock to the attention of Anthony Comstock, the nation's foremost censor, paid by the New York Society for the Suppression of Vice as the U.S. government's special agent to enforce the federal mail obscenity law, commonly known as the Comstock Law of 1873. She clashed with Comstock in the years to come.

When the World's Columbian Exposition opened in Chicago in 1893, Fahreda Mahzar, who assumed the stage name "Little Egypt" when she performed, soon became the exposition's most publicized attraction. Wearing a gauze shirt and long skirts, Mahzar danced with an undulating movement that critics termed indecent. Little Egypt's performance was one of the most popular attractions on "the Midway Plaisance, a noisy, mile-long promenade of beer gardens, camel rides, and facsimiles of foreign locales" (Burton, 86). Promoters described Little Egypt's performance on "A Street in Cairo" as the danse du ventre (belly dance), a presumably genteel version of the dance, but Anthony Comstock called it the "hootchie cootchie" (Brown and Leech, 66) and demanded it be closed. In the flurry of controversy that followed, Ida Craddock sent to BERTHA HONORÉ PALMER, head of the exposition's Board of Lady Managers, a four-page defense of the dance, describing it as "a religious memorial inculcat[ing] purity and self-control" (Weimann, 258). While Little Egypt avoided censorship, probably because the performance was too popular to close, Ida Craddock did not. Continuing her defense of the performance, Craddock wrote The Danse du Ventre, which Anthony Comstock declared unmailable, although no court action was taken against her.

Craddock's defense of the danse du ventre was in part based upon her personal ideology of moral reform. She promoted a single standard of sexual conduct for women and men. Like Comstock, she "advocated marital fidelity and . . . condemned prostitution, masturbation, oral sex, contraception, and abortion" (Burton, 88); but in her pamphlets, Craddock insisted that both women and men had sexual impulses needing resolution, a point of view few men or women shared at this time. She advocated both nudity and active female participation in sexual relations. Disagreeing with reformers who would limit sex to procreation, Craddock assured her clients that moderate, self-controlled sexual activity did not diminish or weaken the body but reinvigorated and revitalized it. Still, she advised limiting the frequency of sexual relations through self-control. Like Dr.

ALICE STOCKHAM, Craddock believed that men should be responsible for birth-control techniques.

Ida Craddock next confronted Anthony Comstock in 1899, when a quasi-medical journal, the *Chicago Clinic*, published the text of her pamphlet, *Right Marital Living*, as an article. Although the paper drew little public reaction, it attracted Comstock's attention, and he determined that Craddock be stopped.

On October 27, 1899, Craddock was indicted in Chicago federal court for violating the mail obscenity law; she avoided jail when criminal lawyer and free speech advocate Clarence Darrow posted her $500 bond. The indictment quoted only excerpts from the offending pamphlet because it was, according to the court, too obscene to be entered into the official record. Craddock pleaded not guilty. The prosecution subpoenaed Anthony Comstock as a witness. Sensing that her cause was lost, Craddock changed her plea to guilty in return for a suspended sentence. For the next week she was so depressed that she considered suicide.

Soon after her Chicago ordeal, Craddock moved to New York City, Anthony Comstock's bastion and headquarters of the New York Society for the Suppression of Vice. She deliberately defied Comstock, hoping to beat him in court. With the penchant of a reformer she wrote, "I am making this stand not for my own liberty—that is only incidental—I am standing for the liberty of the press and freedom of religion. I have an inward feeling that I am really divinely led here . . . to face this wicked and depraved man Comstock in open court and to strike the blow which shall start the overthrow of Comstockism" (*The Clinic*, 410).

It was not victory, however, but Craddock's martyrdom that was at hand. On March 5, 1902, she was arrested under New York's "little Comstock law," the local supplement to the federal obscenity law that many states subsequently adopted. The court refused to admit as evidence letters of support from two Social Gospel leaders, minister W. S. Rainsford in New York and English journalist William T. Stead, a critic of urban industrial society in *If Christ Came to Chicago* (1893), who had employed Craddock when she spent some time in England in 1894. The Social Gospel movement merged religious and secular values in seeking reform of urban problems and social justice, especially for poor immigrants and factory workers.

After reading Craddock's pamphlet *The Wedding Night*, the New York judge declared, "I have never before known of such indescribable filth, I cannot believe that this woman is in her right mind"; he then found her guilty and sentenced her to three months in the City Prison Workhouse on Blackwell's Island. Craddock "took her sentence in stoic silence, and looked neither to right nor left as she was led across the bridge to the Tombs" (*New York Times*, March 18, 1902). After completing her sentence, Craddock was released then immediately re-arrested under the federal Comstock Law. She secured a continuance to work on her defense and wrote a description of conditions on Blackwell's Island.

In 1902, when Craddock's case came before the New York Circuit Court, she was once more found guilty. On the morning she was to be sentenced, Craddock drank lamp oil and slashed her wrist. In a note to her mother printed by the *Chicago Tribune* on October 12, 1902, Craddock wrote, "I maintain my right to die as I have lived, a free woman, not cowed into silence by any other human being."

For a time, free speech advocates rallied behind Craddock's martyrdom. A physician, Juliet H. Severance, expressed shock and outrage in a public letter in the *Truth Seeker* in October 1902: "Ida Craddock was a pure-minded, intelligent woman, working with a clean conscience for the good, as she believed, of humanity. . . . She has been hounded to the death by these blood-hounds of the law" ("Thoughts on the Death of Ida Craddock"). Craddock's prosecution and indignation were instrumental in the creation of the Free Speech League—a predecessor of the American Civil Liberties Union—by Theodore Schroeder shortly after Craddock's death.

Although Craddock has been recognized as an advocate of sexual reform, her views have been criticized and her sanity questioned. Even Theodore Schroeder, who defended Craddock's right of free speech, characterized her in 1917 as an "erotomaniac" ("The Philosophy and Moral Theology of an Erotomaniac"). Craddock was a militant critic of the Victorian era's double standard concerning sexuality. In her efforts to achieve sexual reform, she journeyed beyond conventional efforts to protect womanhood and attempted to bring the message of sexual equality to men and women.

Sources. The Ida Craddock Papers, located in Spec. Coll., Morris Library, Southern Illinois Univ., Carbondale, contain manuscripts, correspondence, diaries, clippings, printed matter, a few photographs, and miscellaneous material. Included are writings by Craddock: *The Clinic* (c. 1902); "The Tale of the Wild Cat," which appeared in the *Journal of American Folklore*, October 1897; and manuscripts of her publications, *Letter to a Prospective Bride* (1897); *Advice to a Bridegroom* (n.d.); *Right Marital Living* (1899); and *The Wedding Night* (1900). There are also several unpublished manuscripts. Theodore Schroeder's outdated psychological analysis, "The Philosophy and Moral Theology of an Erotomaniac," manuscript (c. 1917), is in the Craddock Papers. Articles of special interest include "Mrs. Craddock Sentenced," *NYT*, March 18, 1902; "Thoughts on the Death of Ida Craddock," *Truth Seeker*, October 1902; and "Chose Death Before Prison," *NYT*, October 18, 1902. Craddock receives passing mention in Paul S. Boyer, *Purity in Print* (1968) and in Hal D. Sears, *The Sex Radicals: Free Love in High Victorian America* (1977). Her story is presented more completely in Heywood Broun and Margaret Leech, *Anthony Comstock: Roundsman of the Lord* (1927) and George E. McDonald, *Fifty Years of Freethought* (1929–31). For excerpts from Craddock's letters and a reprint of *Right Marital Living*, as well as discussion of her views, see Taylor Stoehr, *Free Love in America: A Documentary History* (1979). An excellent scholarly analysis is a two-page account in Carl Degler, *At Odds: Women and the Family in America from the Revolution to the Present* (1980). Craddock figures prominently in Shirley J. Burton, "Obscenity in Victorian America: Struggles Over Definition and Concomitant Prosecutions in Chicago's Federal Courts, 1873–1913," (Ph.D. diss., UIC, 1991). Anna Louise Bates, *Weeder in the Garden of the Lord: Anthony Comstock's Life and Career* (1995), describes Craddock's conflict with Comstock. Information on Little Egypt can be found in *The Fair Women* by Jeanne Madeline Weimann (1981).

SHIRLEY J. BURTON

CRANE CARIS, MARTHA
June 1, 1907–June 20, 1986
BROADCASTER, CIVIC LEADER

Martha Crane, a mainstay of Chicago broadcasting for more than forty years, was one of three children born to George Eber and Elsie (Perrine) Crane in Mount Pleasant, Iowa. In her early years, she worked in her family's hardware store and attended Mt. Pleasant High School, graduating in 1926. As a student at Iowa Wesleyan College, Mount Pleasant, from 1926 to 1927, she received newspaper training as Wesleyan reporter for the *Mt. Pleasant News*. The next year she transferred to Northwestern University's Medill School of Journalism, Evanston, Illinois, where, after a year of study, she joined a university journalism group for a four-month tour of Europe. Returning to Chicago, on October 15, 1928, Crane accepted what she thought would be a temporary position with the *Prairie Farmer*, one of the leading farm newspapers in the Midwest. The owners of the paper had expanded their media holdings in 1924 with the purchase of radio station WLS and began a thirty-six-year history of farm service programming and entertainment. The crusading *Prairie Farmer* supported the often financially distressed American farm community as the nation headed into the Great Depression. Crane began her affiliation with the company as a radio mail sorter. Not content with the day-to-day routine of the job, she quickly worked her way into the company's editorial department, where she became "Uncle Toby"—preparing and editing a weekly children's page for *Prairie Farmer*. Lois Schenck, women's editor of the paper, was then hosting the *Homemakers' Hour* on WLS in addition to her editorial work. Crane often substituted for Schenck, and in 1929, when the latter left the radio show, Crane was next in line.

On September 14, 1929, Crane married her hometown sweetheart, Raymond Caris, also living in Chicago, and began her life as wife and broadcaster. Presiding over the daily morning WLS *Radio Bazaar*, Crane, in combination with WLS staff, took the role of helper, assisting her audience with everyday homemaker activities. The program provided valuable information on the health, care, and education of children and offered dramatic sketches depicting incidents centering on child adoption, a relatively new approach to the problem of orphans.

Crane's daily afternoon *Homemakers' Hour* program offered music, inspirational talks, poetry, and informal chats by a number of women broadcasters on topics of interest to homemakers. In the earliest days of the show, during canning season, it was not unusual for Crane to receive more than twenty thousand letters above and beyond the usual volume of *Homemakers' Hour* mail. From 1928 to 1930, nearly three hundred speakers appeared on the program in connection with a variety of projects, including dental clinics for school children, running water in homes, hot school lunches for rural children, rural recreation, good books, and baby care. These programs were important to Americans who were struggling to survive during the depression years.

Crane remained in charge of the *Homemakers' Hour* until October 1934, when she left for Iowa to relax during her first pregnancy. Her first son, Crane, was born on April 2, 1935. As she later recalled, pregnant women did not work in those days, but her time off was short-lived. She was encouraged by the Mitchell-Faust Advertising agency to return to work at WLS,

and she started a new *Feature Foods* program in the fall of 1935. She was teamed with Helen Joyce, who had been selected from more than one hundred women who had auditioned for the program. The show limited its sponsors to food and grocery advertisers, all of whom allowed Crane and Joyce to write their own commercials for the program.

On September 13, 1937, the *Feature Foods* program moved to Chicago's WGN radio station, owned by the *Chicago Tribune*, and began a thirty-minute Monday through Saturday morning broadcast under the sponsorship of a variety of food sellers. Rotating topics by days of the week, the program focused on home improvement and beautification tips, interviews, homemaker questions, a review of new food items, and music. The series, also broadcast occasionally on the Mutual Broadcasting System, remained at WGN until fall 1938, when it returned to WLS. A year later, on April 7, 1939, Crane's second son, Barry, was born. This time, however, her time off was practically nil.

Continuing as a team, Crane and Joyce did notable WLS broadcasting during World War II. Their work on behalf of national defense earned them Navy Certificates of Merit. They provided a forum for organizations such as the Red Cross, introduced war heroes to their midwest audience, and in one of their special wartime projects broadcast a sixteen-month series of reports from a homemaker in London focusing on British life during the blitzes of 1944 and 1945. Crane also helped support a Dutch orphanage during this period, adding to her growing list of charitable causes.

In 1946, Crane's and Joyce's *Feature Foods* efforts were cited by the *Billboard* trade magazine as being "tops in daytime home-help programs" (quoted in "The Public Service Story," 18)—the only women's program so designated by radio editors in the nationwide poll. As much a fixture "as the cook stove or the kitchen sink," WLS noted in its annual yearbook for 1946 that Crane's and Joyce's "outstanding success is based on a simple, direct and completely practical approach to daily household problems. There's nothing of the 'artiste' about either one, but they know what they're talking about. This attitude has won approval of housewives" ("Martha and Helen," *WLS Family Album*, 1946, 39).

In the early 1950s, Joyce left the longtime partnership, and Crane carried on successfully with a shorter version of the *Homemakers' Hour* and a ten-minute *Household Hints* program with hints provided by her listeners. Her popularity remained strong as did her public service work. On February 11, 1957, she was selected Chicago's Woman of Distinction by the Women's Advertising Club of Chicago. In a nomination by the Chicago Chapter of American Women in Radio and Television; the Publicity Club of Chicago; and the Chicago Chapter of the professional journalism sorority for women, Theta Sigma Phi, Crane was cited for creating, writing, producing, and broadcasting the oldest continuous woman's daily radio program in the United States. Noting her recognition by *Radio-TV Daily* as "one of the finest of interviewers" ("Fact Sheet for the Press," February 12, 1957, unpublished release, Women's Advertising Club of Chicago Papers), the Women's Advertising Club also cited her continual support of local charitable campaigns and organizations; her work with civic, educational and cultural groups; and her interest in national and international affairs. The club also cited her two-year presidency of the Highland Park High School Parent Teacher Association and her work with the Highland Park Presbyterian Church. On February 17, 1957, Crane was awarded the Iowa Wesleyan Alumni Association Merit Award. She later served the college as a member of the Science Board of Visitors and the Alumni Association Board of Directors, and in 1961 she was awarded an honorary Doctor of Science degree.

The *Chicago Tribune Sunday Magazine* of November 17, 1957, noted that Crane had three existences. As a broadcaster, she was a friend to thousands of midwest wives. As Mary Blaine, a name created by the National Livestock and Meat Board, she narrated a daily fifteen-minute all-women show on the use of meat, which broadcast on more than two hundred stations. As Mrs. Raymond Caris, she was a leader in school and civic activities. A popular pioneer in a new field at a time when many women were full-time wives and mothers, it was important to Crane that she successfully manage her career, civic duties, and motherhood. She never missed a broadcast due to illness and always managed to be home when her children were home.

On February 4, 1959, Crane premiered one of the more important broadcast series of her career, *Unto Her a Child Is Born*. The Wednesday morning fifteen-minute documentary explored the preparations and adjustment that must be made by a young wife expecting her first baby. Prepared in conjunction with the American College of Obstetricians and Gynecologists, the series featured once-a-week discussions with the mother-to-be and her husband as they made plans to accommodate the infant in their lives and household. The five-month series ended with an on-the-scene account of the birth of the baby with information relayed to Crane from the labor and delivery rooms at Evanston Hospital, Evanston, Illinois. For Crane's work on this series, *McCall's* magazine gave her its prestigious Golden Mike Award for 1960. As the May 1960 issue of *McCall's* reported, Crane "taught women listeners that pregnancy and childbirth can be wonderful and free from fear" (p. 46).

Continuing her WLS duties, writing for *Prairie Farmer*, and taping broadcasts for small radio stations in need of women's programming, Crane became increasingly active in the 1960s on the national scene. She had been a charter member of American Women in Radio and Television (AWRT) and president of the Chicago chapter in 1957–58 as well as central area vice-president and a member of the national board. She believed strongly that the field of communications offered women a greater opportunity and a greater responsibility than almost any other field. On May 6, 1962, she was installed as national president of AWRT, presiding over a membership that had grown to sixteen hundred. Her activities with the organization brought increased travel, including participation in the first Congress of American Women Leaders in Washington, D.C. Organized by the National Federation of Business and Professional Women, the Congress met in October 1962 to discuss mutual goals and ambitions, mutual problems of organization and professional growth.

On July 29, 1962, *Chicago Tribune* critic Larry Wolters cited Crane as the "most durable of women broadcasters" ("Few Can Match Martha's Career"). She had been on the air practically every weekday since 1929, and Wolters said it would take an electronic brain to figure her actual on-air total. However, with the sale of the *Prairie Farmer*–owned station to the American Broadcasting Company on May 2, 1960, WLS changed its "rural" format to rock and roll. Crane's style did not fit the new station image. It was difficult for her, but she was kept at the station as a way to maintain a Federal Communications Commission (FCC) obligation for public affairs programming. She was also retained to maintain a hold on the old WLS–*Prairie Farmer* audience as well as because of her reputation as a civic and philanthropic leader. During this time, she was airing three one-and-a-half-minute celebrity interviews between 10:00 in the morning and noon. But, regardless of time slot or length, Wolters observed that Crane's broadcasts were still guided by four basic principles: "That they be mature, intelligent, informative, and of service to women" ("Few Can Match Martha's Career").

Service to women led Crane to service for her country. In 1962, she was appointed to the board of the Civil Defense Planning Commission under President John F. Kennedy, and, recalls her son Barry Caris, she also served as a member of Kennedy's National Defense Executive Reserve via the Federal Emergency Management Agency (FEMA) (interview, January 13, 1996). In the event of nuclear attack, Crane's gentle, reassuring voice would be heard by America's radio listeners. In an addition to her growing list of awards, in November 1965 she was named regional winner of the Robert E. Eastman award for outstanding contributions in the field of radio—a first for the east central region of the country.

Crane celebrated her fortieth anniversary as an on-air personality in October 1968, the longest continuous broadcasting career for a woman in the United States. The following January, she began *Martha Crane's Chicago*—a thirty-minute Sunday morning show dedicated to news makers, cultural events, and happenings. However, her time on air was coming to an end, and in the summer of 1969 she retired. WLS listed her as the station's women's director until 1972, but in 1969 she returned to Mount Pleasant, Iowa, and removed herself from the Chicago scene. Her husband had died in June 1965, and Crane now took up residence with her sister Helen and brother George in the house in which she had been born. She remained active in Mount Pleasant civic affairs and pursued her hobbies of rug making and gardening.

Martha Crane died of an apparent heart attack—possibly the result of an earlier aortic aneurysm. Crane's charitable work and community and humanitarian activities "chronicled America's contemporary sociological history" ("Martha Crane's 40th Anniversary Sets Broadcasting Record," 4). A pioneer woman in a field heavily dominated by men, she began her radio work in 1928 in Chicago with WLS-AM and continued as an on-air personality well into the frenetic rock and roll era of the late 1960s. During her career, she interviewed more than twelve thousand community leaders, authors, celebrities, housewives, politicians, and international leaders. One of the most honored women in broadcast history, she became a role model in her support of charitable and civic causes and provided leadership on the national level for American women working in radio and television.

Sources. There is little detailed information about Martha Crane. Interviews with Carol and Barry Caris were conducted January 13, 1996. Information on Crane's life and work is found in promotional material developed by WLS-AM and in brief reports of her work in the daily press. WLS promotional materials and station schedules are located at the CHS. UIC Spec. Coll. has the Women's Advertising Club of Chicago papers. American Women in Radio and Television information is available from the national chapter located in McLean, Virginia. Crane is cited briefly in two works: James F. Evans, *Prairie Farmer and WLS: The Burridge D. Butler Years* (1969), and Marion Marzolf, *Up from the Footnote: A History of Women Journalists* (1977). A more longitudinal, albeit brief, view of her career may be obtained by examining the *WLS Family Album*, published between 1930 and 1956; some albums are available at the Broadcast Pioneers Library of American Broadcasting at the University of Maryland, College Park. The rating of *Feature Foods* by radio editors is found in "The Public Service Story," *Billboard*, March 16, 1946. Chicago newspapers also track Crane's career, most notably focusing on her Woman of Distinction award on February 11, 1957. Fuller accounts of her work are available in Marcia Winn, "Radio's Friendly Martha Crane," *Chicago Sunday Tribune Magazine*, November 17, 1957; and Larry Wolters, "Few Can Match Martha's Career," *CT*, section 8, July 29, 1962. Crane's series with a pregnant woman and her husband is discussed in "Nine Women in Radio and TV Win McCall's Mike," *McCall's*, May 1960. Additional biographical information is available in Pearl Cochran, "String of Pearls," *Mt. Pleasant Iowa Free Press*, February 14, 1952; and Lloyd Maffitt, "A Record 'Temporary' Job," *Burlington Iowa Hawk-Eye*, June 10, 1962. See also "Martha Crane's 40th Anniversary Sets Broadcasting Record," *WLS Off-Mike*, February–March 1969.

JOEL STERNBERG

CRILEY, FLORENCE LOUISE ATKINSON
1915–May 29, 1976
LABOR ORGANIZER, CIVIL LIBERTIES ACTIVIST

Florence Louise Atkinson Criley, labor organizer and civil liberties activist, worked for Local 11 of the United Electrical, Radio and Machine Workers of America. Criley spent her professional life working as a labor organizer, devoting much of her personal life to protecting the rights of laborers, women, African Americans, and immigrants. She worked tirelessly with the rank and file, distributing fliers, fighting plant raids, and promulgating values of racial and religious equality.

Born into a working-class family in Barberton, Ohio, the eighth of thirteen siblings, Florence Atkinson spent her childhood and adolescence near Akron, Ohio. Atkinson's father was a laborer who had worked on many jobs, including one as a bootleg-beer truck driver, to survive and support the Atkinson family. Due to his death in 1932, in the midst of the Great Depression, Atkinson went to work while still a high school student. She was able to complete the requirements for a high school diploma. Development of a strong work ethic at such a young age helped condition Atkinson's perseverance as well as her drive. As a young woman Atkinson worked at the A&P supermarket and other jobs, including "torch" singer, waitress, social worker, and eventually on the assembly line in a rubber plant. This work brought about her first experience in the labor movement. In 1936, during the successful campaign of the Congress of Industrial Organizations (CIO) to unionize workers in Akron, Ohio, the center of the rubber industry in the United States, Atkinson coordinated sit-down strikes and picketing efforts.

Sometime in the late 1930s, Florence Atkinson moved to San Francisco with her family. She continued to build her career in the labor movement of the Left, working as office manager for Harry Bridges at the International Longshoremen's and Warehousemen's Union (ILWU) in San Francisco. At this time she also participated in various student organizations of the Left, including the San Francisco Youth Legislature, where she met her future husband, Richard L. Criley. They were married in January 1942.

That same year Criley's husband was drafted into the United States Army and was assigned to officer's training school at Fort Custer, Michigan. Shortly after, Florence Criley accepted the position of midwest director of the International Longshoremen's and Warehousemen's Union. They were able to see each other on weekends until Richard received his orders to go to North Africa in March 1943. During the war period, American trade unions agreed to forego the use of strikes in the spirit of patriotic cooperation with the national effort. Not all trade unionists agreed, however. Criley was opposed to her union's no-strike policy but initially attempted to uphold it. Her efforts resulted in physical abuse from some militant pro-strike workers, the only time in her career. Ultimately, her disagreement with the no-strike policy led to her dismissal from the ILWU in 1945.

Criley was then hired by Ernest DeMaio, district director of the United Electrical, Radio and Machine Workers of America (UE) on May 7, 1945, as field organizer pro tem. She held this job for thirty years. Founded nearly ten years earlier, in 1936, the UE expanded rapidly and at this time was at its apogee. Initially, Florence Criley organized for UE in the Chicago area. She was "the chief woman trouble-shooter in virtually every district of the union" (Richard Criley, "Notes," 4). Among her shops in the Midwest was AM Forge on Chicago's Far South Side. The work was heavy and dangerous, and the shops generally were exclusively male. When Florence Criley was first assigned to them, the shop leaders "protested that they did not want to be represented by a 'dame'" ("Notes," 4). The union district director insisted that Florence Criley be given a six-month trial period. "She borrowed asbestos clothing as required to protect from fragments of molten iron, and spent days in the shop studying each operation" (p. 4). As a result of her approach, she won the loyalty and confidence of the workers. She "became the top UE specialist on forge/hammer shops" (p. 4). The problem of winning acceptance of a leadership role as a woman, at a time when few women were in the workplace in heavy industry, was expected. Criley found that even in shops where women workers were in the majority, "women were so used to male leaders that they tended to feel short-changed if the union representative assigned was a woman" (p. 5). Criley was a model for other women workers and inspired them to be local officers and shop stewards.

The late 1940s and 1950s were a divisive period for the labor movement, as the political coalitions of the New Deal era shattered. Cold war politics challenged the Left and progressive politics in general. Anti-Communist efforts focused on defeating labor unions considered "Left" or Communist-infiltrated. The Taft-Hartley Act of 1947, with its non-Communist affidavit requirement, greatly weakened the UE. For two years UE leaders fought this requirement (and the Congressional Hartley Committee, which, in turn, targeted the UE); this resistance took enormous time and resources. In these two years there were more than five hundred "raids" of UE shops by other unions that sought to sign on former UE union members. An alternate or splinter electrical workers union, the International UE, was founded to challenge the UE in its strongholds in Lynn, Massachusetts; Schenectady, New York; and elsewhere. These plants employed thousands of women workers, and female labor leaders were crucial in the battles. Florence Criley spent time traveling in New England, the Middle Atlantic states, and the South advocating support for UE locals in union elections. The battle between the two unions weakened them both, causing a bargaining power shift from the union to the corporations. The UE ultimately left the CIO, wanting to maintain an independent stance.

The UE stood its ground firmly against any red-baiting, while other unions purged their ranks of accused and suspected communists. Criley was steadfast in her support of the UE position. Criley's first assignments as field organizer for the UE were to lead organizing efforts at Bell & Howell, Republic Drill and Latrobe Twist Drill plants.

In 1947 Criley requested release from her position as field organizer for the UE, explaining "at the present time I could contribute more to the workers in the Union and to the organization itself, as a shop worker" (letter to James J. Matles). Criley next went to work at the Chicago Transformer Corporation. She was officially reinstated as a field organizer on July 20, 1950, in District 11 because of her work at the Cinch Manufacturing Plant, where she had assisted in signing three hundred additional union members during a union drive. She continued to work at Chicago Transformer until 1951, even as she resumed her organizing efforts. Criley rejoined the UE international staff on April 15, 1951, in her former capacity of field organizer. Her first unionizing effort upon her return was at the Sunbeam shop, but Criley also maintained shops at several other Chicago area plants. She tended to all union-related duties, including handling grievances, mobilizing workers, and fighting back raids. In 1955 Criley spearheaded negotiations for a union shop at the American Brake Shoe Company, reaching an endorsed settlement for the UE.

In 1958 Criley was made an international representative, a promotion that kept her working as an organizer yet recognized her skills and value to the organization in other arenas. Criley was the first woman to hold this position.

In 1959 Criley played a central role in a struggle to re-take the GHR foundry in Dayton, Ohio. In this campaign to bring the GHR foundry back into the ranks of the UE, Criley maintained discipline within the ranks of militant workers: "My job this Sunday will be to try to keep blood from flowing in the streets and to keep some of our guys out of jail," she wrote. "Steel is running a meeting and our fellows want to invade and start a riot" ("Dear Troops" letter). Recognizing that the solidarity of African American workers was the key to bringing back the plant, Criley circulated fliers emphasizing the UE's devotion to equality. Moreover, Criley delivered speeches at black churches in the Dayton area, explaining the efforts of the UE. The battle over which union would represent GHR Foundry workers was vitriolic, with the United States government clearly on the side

of the AFL-CIO, whose leaders opposed the former CIO-affiliated UE. Analyzing situations under these competitive and political conditions between electrical unions was one of Florence Criley's strengths. Two other key victories after GHR Foundry were in turning back raids at the Sylvania plants in Emporium, Pennsylvania, and Salem, Massachusetts.

In addition to her work for the UE in the 1950s, Criley and her husband were involved in such organizations as the Civil Rights Congress, the Committee for the Protection of the Foreign Born, the Chicago Joint Committee to Defeat the Smith Act, and the National Lawyers Guild. Through these affiliations, they protested against Jim Crow; the execution of American Communists Julius and Ethel Rosenberg, who were convicted and executed as spies in 1953; and the jailing and conviction of Communist Party members, including Paul Robeson and Claude Lightfoot, head of the Communist Party in Illinois. Both Criley and her husband were under intense government surveillance throughout their lives. Richard Criley was not able to work because he had been blacklisted. Florence Criley became the breadwinner of the family. They lived in the Lawndale neighborhood of Chicago, a predominantly black working-class and poor community, as a conscious choice to participate socially and politically on a grassroots level in their fight for social justice.

In 1962 Criley was active in the strike at International Harvester, continuing her role as official and ideological organizer and leader. She took this role again in 1969–70 in the long strike at the Ashland, Massachusetts, General Electric plant.

In the 1970s Criley became involved in the feminist movement. Criley was not at first a proponent of the Equal Rights Amendment (ERA) because the UE, like most trade unions, was not in favor of the amendment, and she felt that the ERA would mainly benefit middle-class white women and would threaten hard-won protective legislation. Criley would never break with the UE even though she had experienced male prejudice against women within it. Even in the most enlightened unions, male union leaders often saw females as "cheer leaders on picket lines, and helpful for their clerical skills but not . . . as policy makers for the union" (Criley, "Notes," 5), Richard Criley recalled. "Florence was never willing to cede to male supremacy" ("Notes," 5). As time went on, however, she changed her views. She realized that trade union women needed their own organization and all women needed the ERA.

Criley played a key role in the national organizing committee engaged in the creation of the Coalition of Labor Union Women (CLUW) in Chicago in 1974. The new organization had four goals: to organize the millions of unorganized workers, to seek affirmative action in the work place, to strengthen the role and participation of women within their unions, and to encourage union women to play an active role in the legislative and political processes of their unions and the nation. Some three thousand women delegates came to the founding meeting of CLUW instead of the anticipated eight hundred. With the founding of CLUW, and its Chicago chapter, Criley again faced the difficulties of being part of a left-leaning union, the UE, which was not an affiliate of the AFL-CIO. In spite of this connection, she became a leader in the national and the Chicago Chapter. Criley was on the CLUW National Executive Committee and treasurer of the CLUW Chicago Chapter at the time of her death.

When Criley died at age sixty from a sudden heart attack, she had been suffering from crippling arthritis for some time but continued to work for the UE. There was not enough room for all those who wished to attend her memorial service held at the Automobile Mechanics Hall in Chicago on June 6, 1976. Criley is memorialized in a mural at UE hall in Chicago and through the Chicago CLUW Florence Criley Award Night held every International Women's Day (March 8) since 1980.

Criley was known for her friendliness, work ethic, intelligence, and convictions. As a member of UE's committee on women and minorities, she helped to set national policy to combat both racial and gender discrimination. Criley always worked to win equal pay for women in all the plants she serviced. In the face of McCarthyism, government surveillance, and a demanding career as an organizer for a progressive union, Criley found peace in her incontrovertible convictions and a good marriage with a person who shared and supported her ideals.

Sources. Records from Florence Louise Atkinson Criley's career at the United Electrical, Radio and Machine Workers (UE) are in the UE Archives, Archives of Industrial Society, Univ. of Pittsburgh. They chiefly contain reports and correspondence including her letter to James J. Matles, June 10, 1947, and her "Dear Troops" letter, August 7, 1959; the UE Archives also contain fliers and organizational documents. For Criley's work in helping to create the Coalition of Labor Union Women (CLUW), as well as biographical sketches, see CLUW Records, Archives of Labor and Urban Affairs, Wayne State Univ., Detroit. Criley's husband, Richard L. Criley provided background, family, and career information. See Richard L. Criley, "Notes on Florence Louise Atkinson Criley," manuscript, a response on April 26, 1996, to questions posed by Nancy L. Webster regarding Florence Criley. An oral interview with Frank Rosen, retired head of UE Local 11, and his wife Lois Anne Rosen, CLUW executive board, conducted by Nancy L. Webster in June 1996, provided important details. Pamphlets published by the UE in the 1940s and 1950s housed in UIC Spec. Coll. put Criley's life and work in a larger perspective as an employee of a progressive union during the Cold War. Criley is also referred to in the papers at CHS of the Chicago Committee to Defend the Bill of Rights, whose office was headed by Richard L. Criley, 1960–76. General works on the UE include Ronald W. Schatz, *The Electrical Workers: A History of Labor at General Electric and Westinghouse, 1923–1960* (1983), and Gerald Zahave, "Passionate Commitments: Race, Sex, and Communism at Schenectady General Electric," *Journal of American History*, September 1996.

NANCY L. WEBSTER.

CROUSE, RUMAH AVILLA HULL
August 17, 1836–November 5, 1915
WOMEN'S FOREIGN MISSIONARY SOCIETY LEADER,
KINDERGARTEN EDUCATOR

A pioneer in both religious and secular education, Rumah Avilla Hull Crouse founded the Women's Baptist Home Missionary Society (Chicago) and cofounded and served as business manager of the Chicago Kindergarten Training School. Little is known about her family or early life in Clinton, New York, except that in the mid-1850s her name appeared on a membership list of the Clinton Baptist Church and as a student at the Clinton Liberal Institute, a coeducational Universalist-sponsored school.

After her schooling was over, Rumah Hull taught young

women until 1870, when she married John Nathan Crouse. The newlyweds settled in Chicago, where her husband resumed his recently established dental practice and Crouse managed their home on Prairie Avenue, a wealthy neighborhood on Chicago's Near South Side. The couple had two sons, Daniel Howard and Dean. The domestic life of a socially prominent matron did not impede her twin interests in religion and education or her engagement in the world. By her early forties, she found an opportunity to use her leadership skills to develop the cultural and social life of Chicago.

An active member of the prestigious Michigan Avenue Immanuel (First) Baptist Church, she was known as a woman of strong faith. Because of her status within the American Baptist (Northern Baptist) denomination, Crouse was asked to lead a new society that would reflect women's superior moral power in action. In February 1877, after months of pondering her call, Crouse became the founding president of the Women's Baptist Home Missionary Society (WBHMS), a position in which she served for thirty years. Stirring controversy because the organization was run by women, WBHMS was to develop missions within the United States rather than in foreign countries, as was more usual for Protestant denominations at the time. Christianized homes were to be a goal of missionary work and women reaching women, the means.

The Northern Baptist women's home missionary society was one of the first groups to form women's missionary societies financially and organizationally independent of a male-run missionary society. Baptist women had a strong tradition of organizing: in 1800 they had founded the first women's missionary society. However, such financial and organizational matters as the selection, training, and support of missionaries were normally handled by the American Baptist Home Mission Society, run by men. By 1877 women missionaries in the field were repeatedly asking Baptist women to support their work among African Americans in the South, American Indians in the West, and immigrants in the exploding urban centers. The WBHMS was formed in direct response to the urging of women missionaries in the field, who daily faced the issues of poverty, racism, and dispossession among those whom they served, as well as the social problems arising from the rapid urbanization and immigration the nation experienced during the last third of the nineteenth century. By 1881, through Crouse's leadership, the Chicago-based WBHMS developed a national network with eighteen state societies and more than four hundred local societies.

In 1880 Crouse took a tour of the missions the WBHMS supported to observe what women missionaries encountered in their work. She found that they were expected to do a variety of things, from teaching Bible to demonstrating techniques for good health and nutrition. She also discovered that many were unprepared for the tasks they were called upon to perform. Crouse became convinced that mission work was "too responsible and too holy to be entrusted to novices." She insisted: "Not everyone that has zeal has knowledge. . . . While enthusiasm, consecration, and a tender sympathy with the victims of vice and degradation are indispensable to success, not less so is a practical knowledge of certain lines of labor and methods of work" (*Baptist Missionary Training School Catalog*, 7).

Seeing that further training of women missionaries was vital, Crouse challenged the executive board of the WBHMS to propose, at the society's annual meeting in May 1881, the founding of a women's missionary training school. It was a bold proposal, since the Baptists only trained young men for Christian service. Furthermore, the meeting was just weeks away; but a plan was created in time, and the founding of a women's missionary training school was approved. The announcement of its founding quickly generated one thousand monetary pledges, and the professionalization of women missionaries began.

In September 1881 the Baptist Missionary Training School (BMTS) rented a house on Chicago's Near South Side, close to Crouse's home, and enrolled eighteen students, fourteen of whom were experienced missionaries. Crouse continued her involvement with women's missionary education by serving on the board of BMTS, which oversaw the development of curriculum and faculty. Bible faculty were drawn from Chicago Baptist ministers and, later, from the faculty of the newly founded Baptist institution, the University of Chicago. Within a decade BMTS outgrew its original facility. A larger site near the first building was purchased in 1890.

The training school curriculum eventually covered many fields, including religious and biblical studies, sociology, physical and vocal culture, economics, medicine, and temperance work. Students were also expected to do field work among the immigrant populations in Chicago. From the beginning, Crouse and her fellow organizers understood evangelism to be both personal and social. They prepared missionaries to evangelize individuals and to improve the educational, social, and economic situations of the fields in which they ministered. From its inception, the school attracted women from diverse class, racial, and ethnic backgrounds, committed to self-improvement and the spiritual and material uplift of the destitute. The school fulfilled the vision Crouse and her WBHMS colleagues had at its founding of "preparing Christian young women for efficient leadership in the missionary service of Jesus Christ" (Bailey, 19). BMTS existed for eighty years on the South Side of Chicago before merging with Colgate Rochester Divinity School in Rochester, New York, in the 1960s.

Crouse's vision for education was not limited to mission work. In 1885, she attended a mothers' class on the kindergarten movement offered at the Loring School, an elite private school on the South Side, which her sons attended. She was aware of the innovative methods of child training known as the kindergarten movement from her work with the WBHMS; however, this class was focused on mothers and their role in education. The class was taught by kindergartner ELIZABETH HARRISON, a dynamic and compelling speaker. (A kindergartner was a person who taught kindergarten-aged children or trained their teachers.) Harrison explained the Froebelian theories of early childhood education, named for German educator Friedrich Fröbel (also Froebel), who pioneered in childhood education; these theories emphasized a holistic approach to children's development—the integration of body, mind, and spirit—facilitated by what kindergartners termed "scientific" or "conscious" motherhood. Inspired, Crouse recognized a kindred spirit in Harrison but was dismayed that only two mothers attended, although twenty-one had been invited. Crouse in-

formed Harrison that "a hundred mothers ought to have heard what you said this afternoon." After a pause, while she undoubtedly envisioned a plan drawing on her organizational and promotional prowess, Crouse added, "They shall hear it" (quoted in Harrison, 107). These words signaled the beginning of a nearly three-decade partnership for promoting the kindergarten movement in Chicago.

Within a week of meeting Harrison, Crouse made good on her word. Bridging the worlds of church and school, she personally persuaded many of the women from Immanuel Baptist Church to hear Harrison speak. On the evening of the talk, two large church parlors were filled with women. The meeting was well received and stimulated excited conversation. Seeing a new educational opportunity, Crouse announced that a class would begin the next week at the cost of two dollars and fifty cents, a portion of which would benefit the church's Ladies Aid Society. To Harrison's surprise and delight, forty-five women enrolled.

A year later Crouse and Harrison formalized their relationship and founded the Chicago Kindergarten Training School. By 1888 the school needed more space and was moved into the basement of the original Art Institute in downtown Chicago. Several moves later, in 1906, the Chicago Kindergarten College (CKC) was incorporated (now National-Louis University, located in the northern Chicago suburb of Evanston).

Throughout her twenty-five year career at CKC, Crouse primarily played a behind-the-scenes role. She managed the day-to-day business of running a school, including tasks as varied as fund-raising, student recruitment, management of housing, and all financial responsibilities. She consistently donated her salary back to the college and unhesitatingly solicited wealthy friends for funds when finances were tight. She also promoted and developed Harrison's lecture circuit.

Equally as interested in theories of education as in the organization of programs and management of the college, Crouse sailed to Europe with her sons and Harrison in 1890 to visit two well-known kindergartners, Frau (Mrs.) Schrader of Berlin and Baroness von Marenholz-Buelow of Dresden. In 1893 Crouse assisted in the organization of the kindergarten exhibit sponsored by the International Kindergarten Union and housed in the Woman's Building at the World's Columbian Exposition. Crouse also served as an honorary president during the World's Congress of Representative Women held at the exposition, a reflection of her stature in the broader Chicago cultural and social reform world.

Although the charismatic Harrison gave the preponderance of public talks on the kindergarten, Crouse also promoted the movement through speeches. In March 1892 she gave a lecture to the Chicago Federation of Women's Clubs in which she reminded her audience of the battle kindergartners waged to convince the public that learning is "a drawing out rather than a pouring in process" (Crouse, 13). She urged her listeners not to trivialize their roles as mothers or teachers of young children, pointing out that the "kindergarten . . . was created for *character building*. Underneath every game which is played, every story which is told, every song which is sung, every gift and occupation which is given, there is, or should be, a deep, underlying, spiritual truth intended to aid in unfolding the child's nature" (Crouse, 17). Crouse believed intensely in what she called the "full conception of womanhood and motherhood" (Crouse, 23). The path to the ideal woman of the future, the concept of conscious or scientific motherhood, was through education and proper training of both mothers and children. The physical, intellectual, and spiritual constraints that hamper and narrow women could be unlearned, she believed.

A year after the excitement and energy generated by the World's Columbian Exposition, Crouse and Harrison created another opportunity for learning. After a conversation with Harrison on how best to bring mothers and public educators together, Crouse orchestrated a national gathering in a matter of weeks. She envisioned a convocation for mothers on the benefits of kindergarten education as well as on prenatal care and home education. In fall 1894, nearly twelve hundred women and men from all over the northern United States arrived in Chicago by buggy and train. The convocation was such a success that another was held in 1895 and again in 1896. As a result of these gatherings, the National Congress of Mothers (later called the Parent Teacher Association) formed the following year.

Crouse lived during an exciting time, an age dominated by full-time volunteer reformers like herself who embraced the task of civilizing humanity with optimism and vigor. For Crouse, civilizing was both spiritual and practical, and the education of missionaries, mothers, and teachers was her chosen means for societal uplift. After giving thirty years of active service to the WBHMS and twenty-five to the CKC, Crouse retired in 1907, due to ill health. She continued to be honorary president of the WBHMS, however, from 1908 until her death. Crouse died from cancer of the uterus at age seventy-nine. A memorial service was held at her South Side home and a funeral at her church, Immanuel Baptist, with cremation at Graceland Cemetery.

Remembered as a dynamic, attractive, and dignified woman who successfully promoted the educational causes she believed in, Crouse was honored by both institutions she helped to found; each named its library after her. Her kindergartner colleague, Elizabeth Harrison, remembered her as a woman who sacrificed a comfortable life for one of service and recalled Crouse's words: "[Women] are so blind that they do not see the value of organized effort" (Messenger, 31). Her colleagues at BMTS and CKC admired her relentless pursuit of excellence and her dedication to women's full development through service.

Sources. Crouse has one extant writing: *The Kindergarten and Its Opportunities for Women: A Paper Read before the Federation of Women's Clubs in Chicago, May 13, 1892* (1892). There are no focused studies of her life; the little that is known can be found in Elizabeth Harrison's autobiography, *Sketches Along Life's Road* (1930); Sandra F. Branch, "Elizabeth Harrison and Her Contribution to the Kindergarten Movement in Chicago, 1880–1920" (Ph.D. diss., Loyola Univ., 1992); and two histories of National-Louis University: Edna Dean Baker, *An Adventure in Higher Education: A Story of National College of Education* (1956), and Janet Graveline Messenger, "The Story of National College of Education, 1886–1986" (1986), manuscript in the archives, National-Louis Univ. Library. Some additional details can be found in Gertrude Barnum, "The Chicago Woman and Her Clubs," in *The Graphic*, May 27, 1893, and in an obituary in the *Chicago Sunday Tri-*

bune, November 7, 1915. Correspondence of February 3, 1995, from Philip E. Munson to S. Sue Horner indicates that Crouse's middle name sometimes appeared as "Arvilla." See Bertha Grimmell Judd, *Fifty Golden Years: The First Half Century of the Woman's American Baptist Home Missionary Society, 1877–1927* (1927); Faith Coxe Bailey, *Two Directions* (1964); Wendy J. Deichmann, "Domesticity with a Difference: Woman's Sphere, Women's Leadership, and the Founding of the Baptist Missionary Training School in Chicago, 1881," in *American Baptist Quarterly*, September 1990; *Baptist Missionary Training School Catalog* (1908–1909); and *Annual Report of the Board of the women's missionary society* (1915) for descriptions of Crouse's role in Baptist missionary education work.

S. SUE HORNER

CROW, MARTHA FOOTE
May 28, 1854–January 1, 1924
EDUCATOR, AUTHOR, POET, ADVOCATE OF HIGHER
EDUCATION FOR WOMEN

Martha Emily ("Mattie") Foote Crow, was part of the first generation of women to use undergraduate and graduate degrees in coeducational colleges and universities to pursue academic and literary careers. She was born in Sacket's Harbor, New York, the second child and first daughter of the Reverend John Bartlit Foote, a Methodist minister, and Mary (Stilphen) Foote, both descendants of early New England settlers. Mary Foote died in 1859 giving birth to another son, who also died. This loss left a permanent imprint on the sensitive and imaginative child, whose father became a powerful force not only in "the storm and stress of [her] young days" (Crow, *Ministry*, 89) but in her later life.

In addition to the loss of her mother, the remarriage of her father to Louisa Young in 1860, and the arrival of three more sisters and a brother, Martha Foote's childhood was marked by constant moving among the revivalist church stations of upper New York State. Camp meetings, anti-slavery and temperance sermons, hymns, and religious books were the fabric of her tumultuous young years. The family mourned the sudden death of the oldest son, Osman Baker Foote, a student at Wesleyan University in 1870.

In 1872, Martha Foote entered the new coeducational Syracuse University, Syracuse, New York, one of twenty-seven women in a class of eighty men. The same year she and nine other women students, who found themselves unwelcome in classes in a male-run institution, founded the Michaelean Society (Alpha Phi), an all-female secret society, patterned after male fraternities. They incorporated with the help of their mentor, Professor Wellesley Coddington, who urged them to make pure homes as noble wives, and, if they desired a career, enter the acceptable profession of literature. Martha Foote's literary and social reform inclinations were also energized by the words of FRANCES E. WILLARD, at the time corresponding secretary of the newly formed Woman's Christian Temperance Union, and others at the Third Woman's Congress of the Association for the Advancement of Women held in Syracuse in 1875. At the end of the Congress, the Alpha Phi Society initiated Frances Willard into its new organization.

Martha Foote received her bachelor's degree from Syracuse in 1876 and immediately began teaching at Ives Seminary in Auburn, New York. The next year she became "lady principal" at Waynesburg College, Pennsylvania, and returned to Syracuse in 1879 for a master's degree. From 1879 to 1882, Martha Foote taught German and history at Newton High School in Massachusetts, where she was part of the women college graduates' network in Boston. Out of this network, Alice Palmer, a founder of the Association of Collegiate Alumnae (ACA, which became the American Association of University Women in 1921) and new president of Wellesley College, recruited Foote to become her assistant and teach history in the new all-female institution.

Martha Foote left Wellesley in 1884 to marry but continued to work with Alice Palmer in the ACA, serving on committees on collegiate information, childhood development, college endowment, and progress of collegiate education. She was ACA vice-president from 1887 to 1891, president from 1892 to 1895, and president of the Chicago chapter in 1894.

On August 7, 1884, Martha Foote married John McCluskey Crow, a Pennsylvania-born, U.S. and European educated professor of Greek and classics at Iowa College, later Grinnell, at the First Methodist Episcopal Church in Syracuse, with her father officiating. The two met in 1878, when John Crow returned to Waynesburg to visit his former fellow instructors; they were engaged for three years before marrying. They returned to Iowa College, where Martha Foote Crow taught German and lectured on literature and poetry of the Elizabethan age. She received a Ph.D. from Syracuse in 1885, a degree first given to an American woman in 1877. By 1900 only 228 American women had received Ph.D.s.

The students at Iowa College were alternately awed and charmed by the mercurial Martha Foote Crow, who marched briskly ahead of her husband, added an "e" (Crowe) to her married name, and taught a course in matrimony. In her six and a half years at Iowa College, she moved 79 percent of the women (who made up half of the student body) away from "ladies' courses," which were undemanding literary lectures, into degree work.

John and Martha Crow's daughter, Agatha, was born in 1888. In 1890, the family went to Colorado in search of a cure for John Crow's tuberculosis. There, within a month of each other, John Crow and baby Agatha died. They were buried in Grinnell.

Resigning from Iowa College in February 1891, Martha Foote Crow went abroad in the fall to study at Oxford University and do research for the United States Bureau of Education and the ACA on opportunities for higher education for women abroad. In June 1892, Alice Palmer, now dean of women at the University of Chicago, recommended Crow to its president, William Rainey Harper, who needed qualified women faculty for the newly founded coeducational private school. Although Palmer thought Crow was best suited to be a fellow, lecturer, or secretary, Harper named Crow an assistant professor in the Department of English Language and Literature and Rhetoric with the same pay as male professors of equal rank.

Crow lived at the home of her friend, HARRIET BRAINARD (see MOODY), rather than in the women's dormitories. Brainard, a school teacher with a wide circle of friends, ran a catering business from the top floor of her home. It was here that Crow later brought a young colleague, poet William Vaughn Moody, who eventually became Brainard's husband.

Here, too, Brainard and Crow operated the Wind Tryst Press, a small hand press from which they published Crow's poems and Brainard's high school students' essays.

In the fall of 1892, Martha Foote Crow taught a full schedule of classes and seminars in Elizabethan literature, drama, and poetry in her usual magnetic manner. Yet, as early as May of 1893, Dean Palmer was receiving criticisms of Crow's work, particularly from two male faculty members. The university trustees voted to demote her, reducing her salary by half, and assign her half time to University Extension lectures outside the university. Crow objected so strenuously that Harper and the trustees eventually reinstated her salary and courses.

By 1897, the aesthetic teaching of English literature was being challenged by those who wished more emphasis on linguistics and grammar—something between the "lifeless scholarly" and the "vague, gossipy" approach (Professor W. D. McClintock to William Rainey Harper, April 10, 1897, President's Papers). Crow's hero-worshiping style and allegations of her slovenly scholarship in her four-volume book, *The Elizabethan Sonnet Cycles* (1896–98), put her at risk in a university that often ranked research over instruction. When Harper hired a research-minded Shakespearean scholar and philologist to head the department, Crow's schedule and pay was cut so drastically that she asked Harper to define her relationship to the university.

Harper, who was always ready to give his faculty another chance, responded by naming Martha Foote Crow head of the Dearborn Seminary, a finishing school for girls and new affiliate preparatory school for the University of Chicago. During 1899 she initiated a three-year course on Elizabethan drama for the women of the Chicago Woman's Club (CWC) and also organized Sunday afternoon teas for working women, known as the Sunday Open Door, at the CWC.

In 1899, Northwestern University offered Crow the job of dean of women, and she accepted. Although this position had appeal to a woman of Crow's culture and scholarship, the dean of women was the head of only one of the women's halls, with little responsibility for the overall admission or guidance of women at the university. Despite this limitation, Martha Foote Crow advocated more physical education facilities for women, better dormitories, electric lights, a science hall, and chapel. Although she made little progress in reaching these goals, the women's dormitory was renamed "Willard Hall" after Frances Willard, the first Northwestern dean of women, upon Crow's suggestion. As a professor, she taught drama and the development of the novel.

By 1905, however, the Northwestern administration was in transition, the number of women students in the university had increased, and Willard Hall was operating at a loss. The trustees hired Ellen Smith Richards, pioneer in the development of the field of home economics, to make a scientific study of the conditions in the women's dormitory. She recommended extensive repairs and replacing the longtime matron, a friend of Crow, with a woman more scientifically educated. Martha Crow immediately resigned in sympathetic outrage. The board of trustees decided that it was time to have a dean of women who was less intellectual and had more executive and administrative gifts as well as what they considered sympathy and good judgment.

The fifty-one-year-old Crow left Evanston and Chicago with an overwhelming sense of injustice. Twice she had fallen victim to the new professional era in which the literary woman of cultured intellectuality and enthusiastic idealism was out of fashion. After a rest in Syracuse, Crow settled in New York City with her sister, a city librarian.

In her later years, as she struggled to support herself, Martha Foote Crow finally found a role that best suited her talents and gifts. After 1908, she turned out well reviewed biographies of *Elizabeth Barrett Browning* (1908), *Harriet Beecher Stowe* (1913), and *Lafayette* (1916). In 1915, she wrote *The American Country Girl*, an uplifting book showing rural girls the importance of education and culture. At the end of her life she was preparing a biography of Frances Willard. She was a popular lecturer, especially before women's groups, with subjects ranging from "The American Woman and Her Foreign Critics" to "The Pilgrim Mothers and Their Daughters of Today."

From 1917 to 1920, Crow was an active member of the Poetry Society of America, preparing lists of poetry for libraries. She compiled anthologies of poems on various social problems, such as immigration, working conditions, parentage, and war as a world crisis, and published a collection, *Christ in the Poetry of Today* (1917). She founded an organization called the Schola Poetarum Americana to teach and criticize the work of budding poets. She was the poetry adviser for the General Federation of Women's Clubs and a member of the League of American Pen Women. She remained active in the affairs of the growing Alpha Phi, a sorority, where long-term close friendships sustained her.

Martha Foote Crow also remained close to her family and the Methodist religion. The end of her own life was hastened by the successive deaths of her father, beloved half-brother, half-sister, and stepmother, the last three within a three-year period from 1920 to 1923. Virtually penniless, Crow returned to Chicago and Harriet Brainard's home in 1921, where she was cared for by her friend until her death from arteriosclerosis and heart blockage. She was buried in Oakwood Cemetery in Syracuse, New York.

Martha Foote Crow never lost her belief that higher education for women was the foundation for achieving wider rights. She defied the societal norms of her generation by pursuing higher education and an academic career and by encouraging the "sisterhood" of college women.

Sources. Although Martha Crow added an "e" to her name, historical sources continue to use Crow. Records of Martha Foote Crow, mostly from the 1915–20 period, are found at E. S. Bird Library, Syracuse Univ. Grinnell College Archives has valuable information about John Crow. UC Spec. Coll. has records in the Presidents' Papers, 1889–1925; the Alice Freeman Palmer Papers; the English department files; the Harriet Moody Papers; *Poetry* Magazine Papers; and the Board of Trustees Minutes and Registers. Northwestern Univ. has a small file on Martha Foote Crow, as well as Board of Trustees Minutes; the Onondaga Historical Association, Syracuse, New York, has material about the Foote family. NL has records of the Blue Sky Press, publisher of *The World Above* (1905). The archives of the American Association of University Women in Washington, D.C., contain early records of the Association of Collegiate Alumnae (ACA); the CHS has records of the Chicago chapter of the ACA and records of the Higher Education Congress at the World's Columbian Exposition. The Alpha Phi International Fraternity Executive offices in Evanston, Illinois, have memorabilia, including photographs. Besides the books, poems, and articles mentioned in the above entry, Crow published the following: "Will the Co-Educated Co-Educate Their Children," *Forum*, July 1894; *Arcana* (1897); *The Ministry of a Child: A Book of Verses* (1899); *The World Above; a Duologue* (1905). Numerous newspaper biographies appeared at the time of Crow's appointment to the Univ. of Chicago, Dearborn Seminary, and Northwestern Univ., including: "Knows Her Shakespeare: Portrait and Sketch of Mrs. Martha Foote Crow," *Philadelphia Ledger*, January 1905; Jane A. Stewart, "Women Deans of Women's Colleges," *Chautauquan*, August 1901.

JULIA WOOD KRAMER

CULVER, HELEN
March 3, 1832–August 19, 1925
PHILANTHROPIST, BUSINESSWOMAN, TEACHER

Helen Culver, an influential Chicago philanthropist and businesswoman, was born in Little Valley, New York, the fourth and youngest child of Lyman and Emeliza (Hull) Culver. Culver's mother died in 1838, and the four children were cared for by her father's sisters until Lyman's remarriage to Sarah Price, with whom he had two additional children. Lyman Culver was a prosperous farmer, who also bought, cleared, and sold parcels of land.

Culver attended the district school as a child, taught at a country school at the age of fourteen, and enrolled in the Randolph Academy and Female Seminary in Randolph, New York. In 1852, her studies were interrupted by her father's abrupt death from typhoid. His estate went to his widow and their two youngest children, and Culver faced the prospect of earning her own living upon graduation.

After graduating in 1852, Culver and her brother Robert headed west to DeKalb, Illinois, where their grandfather, Noah Culver, had recently settled. Culver later described opening a successful "select" school in an abandoned schoolhouse, while newspaper accounts suggest that she taught at the Dow Academy, in nearby Sycamore, Illinois. The schedule of both day and evening classes proved exhausting to Culver, however, and in 1854, she and Robert left for Chicago.

In Chicago Culver served as an administrator in two primary schools and eventually was appointed to the city's new public high school on the West Side. During this time, Culver became reacquainted with her cousin, Charles Jerold Hull, who had built a home on South Halsted Street, also on the West Side. Hull's wife, Melicent, died in 1860, and Culver left teaching to move into the Hull household to serve as manager of the home and instructor to the two Hull children, Charles and Fredrika. In 1863, during the Civil War, Culver answered a call for nurses from the United States Sanitary Commission after the battle of Stones River near Murfreesboro, Tennessee. Here she was put in charge of a one-room, forty-bed hospital, where she remained for several months before returning to Chicago.

In 1866, Hull's son Charles died after a brief bout with cholera. The family moved out of the Halsted Street homestead but retained ownership of the property. Two years later, Culver expanded her role in the Hull family, becoming an assistant to Hull in his extensive real estate business. Hull bought, subdivided, and sold property within Chicago and in several outlying states.

Culver worked in the Chicago office and, in addition, taught in the office night school that Hull had established for the benefit of street-trade boys. Hull and Culver did not view their business as a part of the rampant land speculation that characterized Chicago real estate at the time. For Hull, an advocate of the temperance movement, ownership of property was essential to good citizenship, and he considered the sale of land, primarily to the poor, a public service. Nonetheless, the business was profitable, and the office bought and sold property in about twenty different subdivisions.

In the winter of 1869–70, Hull purchased considerable land on the outskirts of Savannah, Georgia, and encouraged African Americans to buy lots and build their own homes. Culver often traveled to Savannah to oversee this business and to teach in the office night school, opened there in the winter of 1871–72, which eventually served more than three hundred African American students of all ages. Culver shared Hull's philosophy of the philanthropic goals of their business but remained realistic. "Our duty seems to be mainly in loving our neighbors and selling and renting them as many houses as possible," she wrote to him. "The loving portion of the task would be comparatively easy if we could only choose our neighbors" (Hull-Culver Papers, March 32, 1878).

After the death of his daughter Fredrika on June 16, 1874, Hull spent increasing amounts of time away from the Chicago office. To aid in her new responsibilities, Culver became a notary public on July 1, 1875, one of the first two Illinois women to gain this commission. At this time, Culver communicated with Hull in letters that were a mix of detailed business transactions, news from the Chicago real estate market, and the latest municipal scandals. She also wrote him her thoughts on spiritual and scientific lectures that she was attending. Her growing admiration and affection for Hull were evident. "Indeed, I love you too much to be 2000 miles away," she wrote him on March 17, 1878, "but I will try to do my work and not think about you all the time" (Hull-Culver Papers).

In 1884, Hull became ill with Bright's disease (nephritis), and a home was established in Chicago. Hull and Culver were joined in this residence by Martha Ellen French, former teacher and Oberlin classmate of Fredrika, who became a live-in companion and assistant to Culver.

In 1889, Charles Hull died, leaving his entire estate unconditionally to Culver. Hull believed that inherited money was soon squandered by those who had no role in earning it. His final bequest was an acknowledgment of Culver's contribution to the business. Although more than a dozen of Hull's relatives contested the will, Culver quieted their claims by agreeing to divide $212,500 of the estate among them.

Upon Hull's death, Culver inherited approximately 224 Chicago lots. Much of this property was located in the new immigrant neighborhoods of the city's West and North sides as well as in Chicago's business district and the suburb of Cicero. In addition, Culver now owned 1,155 lots of land in outlying states. Newspapers estimated the value of the estate at three to four million dollars, although Culver's own estimate was not above two million dollars.

Culver continued to run the business out of Hull's former of-fices in a bustling Chicago commercial area of coal yards and livery stables. The sign outside now read: Miss Helen Culver, Successor to C. J. Hull, Real Estate. Culver kept up a regular schedule, supervising rent collection, repairs, construction, property sales, tax and assessment payments, and investments with the help of two or three clerks, generally women. Her brother Robert was hired to oversee the Baltimore and Savannah enterprises. Culver had an excellent memory for details and made decisions only after carefully weighing the benefits to both parties. Once decided, she was seldom swayed. She devoted herself wholeheartedly to business, rarely taking a vacation and avoiding Chicago social life.

Culver was convinced that Charles Hull had intended to use his wealth for the public good. As the business prospered, she searched for ways to carry out the responsibility she believed she had inherited. Her first opportunity came when JANE ADDAMS and ELLEN GATES STARR became interested in the old Hull homestead on south Halsted Street as a site for Chicago's first settlement house. In September 1889, Addams sublet a portion of the building and opened it to the surrounding immigrant neighborhood as a settlement house. By the following spring, the settlement occupied the entire building, now named Hull-House in honor of Charles Hull and in gratitude to Culver, who had agreed to waive the rent. In addition, Culver owned lots surrounding the house, and through the years a series of leases was negotiated with Addams that allowed the settlement to expand its physical facilities into existing and newly constructed buildings. In 1895, Culver negotiated an agreement that influenced the settlement's formal administrative structure. In order to secure a twenty-five-year lease on the property, Addams agreed to incorporate the settlement and to appoint Culver to its newly formed board of trustees, conditions that were written into the lease. Culver remained on the Hull-House board until 1920, serving as a vice-president for many years.

Culver was generous but cautious in her relationship with Hull-House, tending toward reciprocal agreements in which she provided partial funds or land for projects but expecting in return matching efforts by other donors or the settlement itself. In an 1891 letter, Culver revealed her reservations. She praised the unselfishness of the Hull-House workers and welcomed the opportunity to contribute to a potentially worthy cause but expressed concern about Jane Addams's "great mingling of economy and lavish expenditure" (Culver to Nelly, January 19, 1891, Hull-Culver Papers); she was worried that the enterprise might possibly be transitory.

Culver's cautious attitude toward Hull-House may also have been prompted by the fact that she was exploring other avenues for her philanthropy. In December 1895, she offered the University of Chicago one million dollars in property, proceeds from the sale of which were to be used to fund expansion of the study of the biological sciences. The gift came at an opportune time for the fledgling university, whose science departments were underfunded and scattered throughout various buildings. Culver's gift stipulated that one half the total sum be used for departmental expansion with the remainder to be reinvested and used as a fund for research, instruction, and publication. Four new laboratory buildings were constructed on the university campus, all connected by cloistered passageways. Eventually, Culver donated an additional $253,000 to cover cost overruns and the failure of some of the properties to realize their estimated value.

Culver oversaw her donation, insisting that no parcel of land be sold below its appraised value without her consent, recommending her nephew and new clerk, Charles Hull Ewing, be hired as property manager, and offering her own suggestions on fund management. At her request, the new buildings were named the Hull Biological Laboratories and the courtyard they enclosed became known as Hull Court. Culver insisted that she had acted only as an emissary of Charles Hull in making this bequest and expressed relief to be finally free of the responsibility she had inherited. In 1900, however, the gift became a source of embarrassment when the city building department condemned the unsafe and unsanitary conditions of many of the structures included in the bequest and demanded that several be torn down immediately.

Culver's gift to the University of Chicago engendered confusion and resentment at Hull-House; the settlement had to reassure its own supporters that it had not been given away to the university. At the same time, Culver had refused Hull-House's request for additional land. Still, Culver's relationship with Hull-House was far from over. She continued to make contributions of cash, bonds, and interest-free loans, generally earmarked for building needs. In 1898, Culver finally agreed to sell land to Hull-House, a concession about which Addams wrote, "She at least could never give it away to the U. of C . . ." (Jane Addams to Mary Rozet Smith, March 23, 1898, Jane Addams Papers). In 1906, Culver donated the property on which the primary Hull-House buildings were located, in addition to the site (and a $50,000 endowment) for a new Boys' Club building. In 1920, Addams persuaded Culver to donate to Hull-House during her lifetime what she planned to leave the settlement upon her death. Culver's gift of $250,000 in bonds (later revalued at $175,000) was the largest single donation the settlement had received. At the time, Culver was elected honorary president of the Hull-House board, and at her request, her nephew, Charles Hull Ewing, replaced her as an active member.

Through leases, sales, and gifts, Culver helped Hull-House expand into a thirteen-building complex providing a wide range of neighborhood services. Although sometimes exasperated by Culver, Addams still admired her feistiness and loyalty. In 1922, Addams dedicated *Peace and Bread in Time of War* to her: ". . . in affectionate gratitude to Helen Culver whose understanding mind and magnanimous spirit have never failed the writer either in time of war or peace."

Near the end of her commercial career, Culver consolidated her business for easier management and turned it over to Charles Hull Ewing, although Culver insisted on management oversight. When called upon to transact some detail, she often remarked how good it felt to do business again.

Culver retired from business in 1900 and built "Rookwoods"—an estate in Lake Forest. She raised eyebrows there by riding her bicycle throughout the town and scrupulously paying taxes in excess of her far wealthier neighbors. When over seventy years of age, she continued a lifetime of study by learning to read Italian. With Martha Ellen French she traveled to Europe and

Cuba and in 1907 endowed the Helen Culver Gold Medal to be awarded by the Geographic Society of Chicago to distinguished scholars and practitioners in the field.

Culver's interest in urban issues was not diminished by retirement. Long convinced of the need for municipal reform, she financed an investigation in 1905 sponsored by the City Club of Chicago, a non-partisan civic reform organization. The study was conducted by Charles E. Merriam, a University of Chicago political scientist. Its conclusions were published as *The Municipal Revenues of Chicago* in 1906. Ironically, on the day Culver's donation was reported to the City Club, the all-male membership also voted down a request to admit women members.

For many, the most pressing urban problem of the day was immigration. Culver, an owner of property within Chicago's immigrant neighborhoods, established the Helen Culver Fund for Race Psychology in 1908 to explore this issue. The fund made available fifty thousand dollars to sociologists W. I. Thomas and Florian Znaniecki to collaborate on a study that resulted in the five-volume publication, *The Polish Peasant* (1922–24). This influential work, which employed the life history method, was theoretically and methodologically innovative and was considered the most significant sociological study of its time.

In 1913, because of failing health, Culver established a winter home in Sarasota, Florida, and Rookwoods was turned over to her nephew. In 1918, her companion of over thirty years, Martha Ellen French, died of heart failure. Culver's sight had begun to fail, and blindness was followed by loss of hearing, hallucinations, and, finally, confinement to bed with a broken hip. Helen Culver died at the age of ninety-three from malnutrition and was buried in Rosehill Cemetery. Her estate contained property in Arkansas, Colorado, Texas, and Nebraska and stocks, bonds, mortgages, and notes totaling almost $1,800,000. Culver left bequests to twenty-three distant relatives and to charitable and educational institutions, including the University of Chicago.

Helen Culver's early life had followed traditional paths open to women of her generation. She later entered business, persevered, and became a successful and influential, though often invisible, presence within the traditionally male field of real estate and commerce. Her wide-ranging philanthropy supported the cause of Hull-House and shaped the direction of science and social science research at the University of Chicago.

Sources. Jane Addams's correspondence with and about Culver as well as account books, leases, deeds, and newspaper clippings that detail Culver's interaction with the settlement are in *The Jane Addams Papers* (Microfilm Edition, 1985), UIC Spec. Coll. Culver's correspondence with Charles Hull, Charles Hull Ewing, and additional family members can be found in the Hull-Culver Papers, UIC Spec. Coll. The Hull-Culver Papers include Culver's obituaries as well as miscellaneous pieces pertaining to both her and Charles Hull. Culver's correspondence with President Harper is in the Presidents' Papers, 1889–1925, UC Spec. Coll.; details of fund management can be found in the UC Board of Trustees Minutes, 1891–1943, UC Spec. Coll. The most complete printed source for Culver is Thomas Wakefield Goodspeed, "Helen Culver," *The University of Chicago Biographical Sketches*, vol. 2 (1925), a thorough and detailed portrait of Culver's early life, her role as a business woman, and her philanthropy. In addition, see Goodspeed,

"Charles Gerald Hull," *The University of Chicago Biographical Sketches*, vol. 1 (1922). Culver is treated in Kathryn Kish Sklar, "Who Funded Hull-House?" in Kathleen D. McCarthy, ed., *Lady Bountiful Revisited: Women, Philanthropy, and Power* (1990).

PEGGY GLOWACKI

CURREY, MARGERY (Helen Marguerite)
May 27, 1877–August 15, 1959
LITERARY SALON HOSTESS, JOURNALIST, ARTS PUBLICIST

Helen Marguerite Currey—always called Margery—provided an essential gathering place and encouragement for known and emerging Chicago writers in her literary salon. She is mentioned as an important figure by almost every writer of the Renaissance period (c. 1910–20) in Chicago. She was born in Evanston, Illinois, north of Chicago, the eldest of seven children. Her father, Josiah Seymour Currey, was a founder, director, and president of the Evanston Historical Society and a longtime director of the Evanston Public Library. On November 24, 1875, he married Mary Ella Corell, the daughter of a school superintendent. He became district manager of an insurance company in 1895. In addition, he wrote several histories of Chicago and Illinois.

As a child, Margery Currey was close to her father. She accompanied him to the opera, to the state fair, and on a trip to New Orleans. While she was in grade school, her parents gave her Giorgio Vasari's *Stories of Early Italian Artists*, which began her lifelong interest in art. She attended Evanston Township High School and graduated in 1896, winner of a coveted Latin Prize in her senior year.

In the fall of 1896, she entered Northwestern University but remained only one year. The next year she enrolled as a first year student at Vassar College in Poughkeepsie, New York; she graduated in 1901. From September 1901 through 1909 she taught at several high schools in the Midwest and in 1906 at Rockford College, Rockford, Illinois. In September 1907 she returned to high school teaching at Davenport, Iowa, where she remained for two years. The stay in Davenport became a turning point in her life.

In the early twentieth century, Davenport, a Mississippi River town, had already developed a cultural and intellectual life. A number of well-known writers and intellectuals lived there, including George Cram Cook, novelist; Arthur Davison Ficke, lawyer and poet; Susan Glaspell, novelist; Ralph Cram, editor; and Floyd Dell, poet and journalist, then working on George Cook's farm. By 1908 Currey and Dell were involved in a courtship. "Margery," Dell wrote, was "small, attractive, dark haired. . . . She wore her brown hair like a coronal" (*Homecoming*, 179–80). Well-educated and well-read, intelligent and witty, she conversed with ease. By the late spring of 1909, when Currey's school term ended, Dell was in Chicago as assistant editor of the Chicago *Evening Post*'s new *Friday Literary Review*. With its initial publication on March 5, 1909, it gave, Dell wrote, "expression to a growing youthful body of American literary taste" (*Homecoming*, 194–95), which it encouraged and helped formulate.

In the summer Currey returned to Evanston. At thirty-two, Currey was ten years older than Dell, and with her classical education, urban background, and years of teaching experience, she was an intellectual with social advantages that Dell had never had. She encouraged his writing and helped him achieve sophistication in his stories.

On August 25, 1909, they were married at Currey's family home in Evanston. As a gesture of defiance to conventionality, they asked their friend from Davenport, Rabbi Fineshriber, to perform a Jewish ceremony, although neither was Jewish. Currey became a high school teacher in Evanston. For the next few years, their apartment in the Rogers Park neighborhood served as a meeting place for new writers and artists from Chicago's growing bohemia, the beginning of Margery Currey's literary salon. The new writers were sensitive to the quickening changes of social ideas and reform and to the youthful and rebellious spirit that impelled them; and they were militant in their thinking and uninhibited in their life styles. What literary historians later called the Chicago Renaissance began in 1909 with the *Friday Literary Review*, according to Burton Rascoe, book editor of the *Chicago Tribune*. Assistant editor Floyd Dell and Margery Currey found themselves at the center of the new excitement.

"Margery," wrote EUNICE TIETJENS, "was one of the . . . most gifted people for friendship whom I have known" (Kramer, 114). Like her fictional counterpart in Dell's novel, *The Briary-Bush*, Currey remained "wild and sweet and witty," believing that "this marriage will be one final defiance and farewell to the particular tribe to which I belong" (*Briary-Bush*, 119). Both Margery Currey and Dell's heroine wanted a modern marriage, one given to all kinds of freedom and to new ideas. As "the idealist and deeply thoughtful one," Currey had the task of coping with the sometimes "materialistic and frivolous people" whom she began to meet. She did so with an ease that added zest to both their lives. "Her gifts created an atmosphere in which ideas could dance and sparkle" (*Homecoming*, 201).

Their friends and salon guests were mostly those with interests and ambitions in the arts (*Homecoming*, 201). Their circle included novelist and playwright Susan Glaspell; Mabel Reber, journalist, and her sister, writer Edna Kenton; Martha Baker, a miniaturist; Ephra Vogelsang, an aspiring opera singer; and Marjorie Jones, an art photographer. Currey's father often joined them. They read poetry and talked ideas. In 1910 their circle of friends widened to include George Cram Cook, now in Chicago; poet Eunice Tietjens; and Vachel Lindsay, depressed over the public's reception of his poetry. Currey's understanding and tact raised the latter's spirits. Others came: Lucian Cary, book reviewer, and his wife; Maurice Browne, writer and lecturer, soon to found the Little Theatre with his actress wife, ELLEN VAN VOLKENBURG. The group came to be known as "the bohemians."

In October 1911, when Dell went on an annual publishing trip to New York, Currey accompanied him. She met Theodore Dreiser, whose writing she greatly admired. She asked to read the manuscript of *The Genius* and encouraged him. When he came to Chicago in December 1912 to seek material for *The Titan*, he was a frequent guest at the Currey apartment. MARGARET ANDERSON, yet to publish the *Little Review* and the editor of a religious magazine, came to their home seeking conversation. Anderson recalled that Currey "had created a sort of salon for Floyd . . . , relieved him of all social responsibility and presented him as an imperial being whose only function in life was to talk" (Kramer, 229).

Currey was also finding other interests. The year 1912 in Chicago was one of political conventions. A friend of feminist Charlotte Perkins Gilman and later her agent on the lecture circuit, Currey joined a suffrage parade in Chicago in support of Theodore Roosevelt's candidacy for president. Here she met piano teacher Tennessee Mitchell (see TENNESSEE MITCHELL ANDERSON) and invited her to join the bohemians. At one of Currey's parties, Mitchell met Sherwood Anderson, whom she later married. By November, the Little Theatre, which Currey and Dell had long supported, was under way.

For months Currey was aware of Dell's growing number of affairs with other women. In April 1913, they each moved to a separate studio on Chicago's South Side near Jackson Park, the location of homes and studios that writers and artists had created out of stores and concession stands on Stony Island Avenue.

The arrival of Currey and Dell brought a new vitality to the bohemians. From all appearances the couple were true, freedom-loving bohemians, but in reality they were already separated. During the summer of 1913, Currey's studio quickly became a center of activity, and Currey herself more and more the central figure of the salon. Her gift for friendship and her sensitivity as a hostess created an atmosphere of easy hospitality for local and visiting writers and artists alike; she welcomed new neighbors from the artists' colony, old friends from Rogers Park and the *Friday Review*, and new friends from the Little Theatre and *Poetry* magazine. Theodore Dreiser, in and out of Chicago, came often; Carl Sandburg, bringing poems, visited less frequently. The not-yet-published Sherwood Anderson joined the salon, and he and Currey became fast friends.

Currey involved members of the salon in support of Margaret Anderson's *Little Review*. At the salon, Anderson met Dewitt C. Wing, editor and agricultural journalist, who agreed to pay printing costs and office rent.

By late summer 1913, Currey knew that her marriage had ended. Dell resigned from the *Friday Literary Review* and moved to New York. At his farewell dinner, Currey announced that she was a reporter on the *Chicago Daily News*. There she worked with Henry Justin Smith, the news editor. Under Smith the *News* became a center of freethinking and new ideas, with such reporters as Ben Hecht, Maxwell Bodenheim, and Vincent Starrett. Currey was not only learning about reporting; she was also, as Starrett wrote in *Born in a Bookshop*, "the paper's capable sob sister" (p. 166). Starrett, Hecht, and Bodenheim became frequent visitors at Currey's salon.

When Margaret Anderson's *Little Review* first appeared in March 1914, Currey's book review, "A Feminist of a Hundred Years Ago," proved both provocative and personal. Reviewing Ellen Key's *Rahel Varnhagen: A Portrait*, a study of the German feminist whose salon in Berlin had attracted the notables of the day, Currey found that Varnhagen's influence was mainly through "the richness of her personality, the glowing warmth of her sympathy, her understanding, and the wisdom of her heart" (p. 26). It was the role that Currey was playing. Much of the review was an expression of Currey's own feelings. She wrote, "The woman who has been filled with joyful new amazement

on finding that her only reliance is on herself . . . will know how to value [Varnhagen]" (p. 25). Currey's second article in the *Little Review*, "John Cowper Powys on War," appeared in November 1915, a report on the debate between Powys and Maurice Browne of the Little Theatre. Powys extolled the glories of war; Browne declared against violent combat. Currey's ironic comments and rational insights ably caught the spirit of Powys's propaganda crusade for a Europe already at war.

By 1916 Margery Currey had been granted a divorce. She continued to live in the Stony Island studio at least through 1919. The parties were as lively as ever. The place, Harry Hansen wrote, was "a shrine of art, to which men made their pilgrimage" (*Midwest Portraits*, 101).

By 1917 Currey left the *News* and joined the staff of the *Chicago Tribune*. Although a society editor, she also covered important social and civic events under her own byline. Currey showed a special knack in reporting on war benefit programs during World War I. In these two- and three-column stories, Currey described the main event and included the names of prominent movers and organizers, usually women. Currey's vivid and detailed reporting caught the spirit and enthusiasm of Chicago's war effort. She had become a competent newswoman.

For the freedom-loving Currey, newspaper work became very demanding. She decided to leave the steady job at the *Tribune*, because the all-night hours were taking too great a toll. By mid-1917 she was working with a child welfare campaign for the Children's Bureau of the Child Welfare Department of Illinois, a job that involved doing publicity throughout the state. During World War I, in support of the war effort, she served on the Woman's Committee of the Council of National Defense.

Currey worked in publicity from 1917 to 1930, with interruptions. She left Chicago for a year or so in 1920, living briefly in California and Seattle and attempting to support herself through teaching and publicity work. The attempt was not successful, and she returned to Chicago in search of employment.

Currey's job experience in Chicago in the mid-1920s is not clear. She joined the American Art Bureau, where she began by doing publicity and promotional work on art in daily living. By 1925 the bureau published two of her pamphlets, "Pictures for Schools" and "The Pictures in Your Home," and by March 1930 she was educational director of the bureau. She had turned a longtime interest in art into a professional career. In such articles as "Pictures People Like," *Woman's Home Companion*, March 1930, which named museums that loaned pictures and identified those that people liked best, and in "How to Hang Pictures," *Better Homes and Gardens*, November 1931, the promotion of art was her chief concern. Other articles on similar topics, informative and educational, showed Currey's continued interest in making art and art projects available to the public, especially to children.

By June 1930 she had left Chicago, and for the next thirty years she lived in and around New York City, moving often from one address to another. The details of her activities in New York are not fully known. During the 1930s, she engaged in various publicity and promotional activities that included the Art Adventure League, the National Art Society, Art Expression for Amateurs; in 1936, the National Association of Art Education;

and in 1937, the Shaw Studio of Finger Painting. By 1938 she had left New York for Tamworth, New Hampshire, where she intended to establish a private school; she was unable to do so. She returned to New York, working for Art Education, Inc. She also gave talks on art subjects and on home furnishings. From 1940 until her retirement in 1950, she directed the Associated Teachers Agency, a placement bureau for teachers seeking employment. At the same time, she continued writing lively articles for magazines, promoting art and entertainment at home. In 1956 she established her own writing service.

Currey died at age eighty-two after a long illness and was buried in New York. In September 1959 she was honored with a memorial service at the First Congregational Church in Evanston.

Currey had a central role in the Chicago literary revival of the 1910s and 1920s, not as a writer but as one of its leading spirits. Her literary salons not only encouraged individual artists but for more than a decade also gave the movement much of its vitality, urbanity, and sophistication.

Sources. Currey's letters and information about her are at NL in the Floyd Dell Collection, the Eunice Tietjens Papers, and the Harry Hansen Collection. The J. Seymour Currey collection at the Evanston Hist. Soc. includes family photographs, pages from his diary, informational forms, and newspaper clippings. The Vassar College Alumnae Register Office and the alumnae directory of Vassar College for 1937 contain minimal personal information. Currey's writings in *Little Review* and elsewhere are described above. Her articles in the *CT* include "Fears New War unless Subject Races Are Freed," March 4, 1917, and "Blind Little Joe Opens Public Eye to Midwife Evil," March 10, 1917. Margery Currey is best known from the writings of those who knew her. Useful are Floyd Dell, *The Briary-Bush* (1921), and *Homecoming, An Autobiography* (1933); Harry Hansen, *Midwest Portraits* (1923); Margaret Anderson, *My Thirty Years War* (1930); Ben Hecht, *Gaily, Gaily* (1963); Vincent Starrett, *Born in a Bookshop* (1965). See also Bernard Duffey, *The Chicago Renaissance* (1954); Dale Kramer, *Chicago Renaissance: The Literary Life in the Midwest 1900–1930* (1966); Kim Townsend, *Sherwood Anderson* (1987). *NYT* published an obituary on August 17, 1959.

JOHN E. HART

d

DAGENAIS, MARGARET MARIE
January 20, 1922–June 4, 1983

ARTIST, EDUCATOR, LITURGICAL REFORMER

As an art educator and as an artist, Margaret Marie Dagenais devoted her life to the art apostolate, the idea that both appreciation and creation of art by the laity enhances an appreciation of Catholic life. Margaret Dagenais was born in Montreal, Canada, the only child of parents who died during her childhood. After the death of her parents, Dagenais was raised by her grandmother, who lived in Chicago. Little is known about her early life. At the end of her teenage years, Dagenais prepared for a career in teaching. She received a B.Ed. from Chicago Teachers College in 1942 and taught in the elementary schools of Chicago for four years and then in a high school art department.

In 1944, while she was teaching in public schools, Dagenais began taking courses at the School of the Art Institute of Chicago (SAIC). Dagenais was already interested in the connection between her artistic talent and her Catholic faith. In 1947 she wrote an article, "A Sculptor Mediates," for the Catholic magazine *Liturgical Arts,* published by the Liturgical Arts Society. The sculptor was Sister Mary Thomasita, OSF, of Cardinal Stritch College, Milwaukee, Wisconsin; Dagenais saw her as an example of a "modern religious artist who [was] using to-day's language to express Christian truths in art" (n.p.). She personified the kind of artist Dagenais hoped to become. "Art, if a pure and human work, will honor God and should be directed to Him and His service and praise," Dagenais continued. "The function of art is to minister to fellow man, not only for his own sake and satisfaction, but also for the honoring of God and the bringing of others to glorify Him" ("A Sculptor Mediates," n.p.).

Dagenais had grown up in the Chicago Catholic Church during a period of liturgical reform popularized by Reynold Hillenbrand, who was rector of St. Mary-of-the-Lake Seminary. The movement, begun in Europe, sought to use the corporate spirit embodied in the Eucharist as the model for social action.

Hillenbrand rejected liberal individualism, which he credited with responsibility for the Great Depression, in favor of a communal life based upon the unity of worship and of social reform. He identified lay activism as the linchpin of the reform movement, using as a model Jeunesse Ouvrière Chrétienne, a movement founded in Belgium in 1925 by Joseph Cardinal Cardijn. Cardijn had created small groups or cells of both students and young workers who would minister to others like themselves. Hillenbrand developed a similar model in Chicago. Additionally, Hillenbrand insisted that the liturgy be aesthetically beautiful. The liturgical reform movement's ideals—both individual and collective effort, unity of liturgy and social action, and aesthetic beauty in the service of the Catholic church—guided Dagenais's artistic practice and pedagogy throughout her life.

In 1950, still enrolled at SAIC, she began to teach part-time at both Loyola University Chicago, and Cardinal Stritch College, Milwaukee, Wisconsin, where Sister Thomasita headed the fine arts department. She earned a B.A.E. in art education and ceramics in 1951 from SAIC and, the following year, an M.A.E. in art education and painting from the same institution. That same year, 1952, she began teaching art education and art courses full-time in the education department at Loyola University. She continued to study with artists, to take postgraduate courses, and to investigate other cultural and religious traditions through study and extensive travel. As a result of her willingness to learn new methods, Dagenais could teach art education, art appreciation, design and composition, ceramic sculpture, serigraphy, flat pattern design, calligraphy, lettering and layout, backgrounds to Christian art and liturgy, basic drawing and painting, textile design, materials composition, and crafts, including pottery. Along with her classes, Dagenais made educational videos that were shown on Loyola University's television program, *Learning Brings Adventure.*

Dagenais wrote about art and the art apostolate in Catholic periodicals, including *Salve Regina,* a publication of the

Catholic University of America; *Liturgical Arts*; and *Catholic Art Quarterly*. She was art editor of *Salve Regina* from 1958 to 1960 and used this forum to present a series of ten articles on contemporary religious artists, including Sister M. Thomasita, Irene Kilmurry, and Egon Weiner. As a writer and editor she was at the forefront of the Catholic church's post–World War II efforts to both define and support modern sacred art. She was the art adviser for the St. Benet Library and the Chicago Cana Conference. Exhibits of her sculpture, caligraphs, lithographs, and designs were shown in a variety of liturgical arts exhibitions in the Middle West.

As Chicago Catholic institutions grew and matured and urban Catholics moved into suburbs after the war, the Catholic Church began a period of physical change and expansion. The associated demand for new buildings and interior furnishings afforded Margaret Dagenais numerous commissions, including works for chapels and churches in Chicago, Downers Grove, Aurora, Hillside, Niles, St. Charles, and River Grove. Dagenais was awarded commissions for church art in many Episcopal Church parishes in the Chicago area as well.

In 1955, Dagenais designed and constructed a new crucifix for the Lewis Tower Chapel located on the downtown Loyola University campus. Made from wood, she hoped "to express the spirit of the redemption . . . to be strong, yet tender" ("Crucifix in LT Chapel Holds Added Meaning"). When the chapel of St. Timothy's (Episcopal) Church, Chicago, was destroyed by fire on the eve of Ash Wednesday, 1955, the priest, Father Peter Powell, and the members of this struggling mission reached out to Dagenais. She made a gift of her talent and time to design and execute the major part of the reconstructed chapel's interiors and the outside hall that led to it. The new altar of blond oak was decorated with tiles in a loaves and fishes motif, designed and painted by Dagenais. In 1959, Dagenais completed the first of three commissions for St. Cyprian (Catholic) Church, River Grove, a life-size sculpture, *Jesus and the Children*, depicting Christ teaching children. Later she created a pair of panels depicting the Virgin Mary and St. Joseph and designed and constructed twenty individually sculpted crucifixes for classrooms, the convent rooms, and the adjoining rectory.

St. Cyprian's parish priest, Father Arthur Douaire, a leader in the liturgical reform movement, commissioned the works of regional American Catholic artists, including Dagenais, her teacher, Sister Thomasita, and Raymond Toloczko, who had studied at SAIC. Toloczko designed the full-size drawings from which the stained glass windows would be fabricated. Renowned religious artist Jean Charlot, a native of France who had studied in Mexico in the 1930s with Diego Rivera and Jose Clemente Orozco, contributed his *Stations of the Cross* (1935–38), which he had originally painted in Mexico, to St. Cyprian.

Her numerous commissions for seminaries, chapels, convents, schools, and monasteries made Dagenais an interpreter of the faith for countless Catholics. For example, in the early 1960s, Dagenais designed and created a series of sixteen crucifixes hanging above the altars in the Jesuit residence chapel on the lakeshore campus of Loyola University Chicago. She designed two eight-foot altar panels for the Servite Priory Chapel, Anaheim, California, in 1963. She also sculpted both a four-foot Madonna in gold anodized aluminum and a three-foot corpus of Christ the King for St. Michael's Monastery, Oyama, Japan. In 1965 she was named to membership on the Servite Inter-Province Commission on Liturgy, Art, Architecture, and Music. She had just completed three statues, of St. Francis of Assisi, Mary and the Christ Child, and Pope John XXIII, that were installed in St. Pascal convent and school, Chicago, after they had been sent to Italy to be reproduced life-size in marble.

For many years she had encouraged all Catholics to participate in the creation of religious art for themselves and for their homes. Education in art and liturgy, in her mind, was not reserved for women and men religious, or for professional artists and art educators. Perhaps no ecclesiastical project better demonstrates Margaret Dagenais's dedication to the art apostolate than the redecoration of the Cook County Jail Chapel in 1958–59. She donated one year of service to this project, working at least two days a week with approximately thirty male inmates in order to establish a nondenominational center for religious activity at the jail. Dagenais and her work crew transformed the space—a basement room near Death Row—by repainting both walls and ceiling, refinishing pews, and installing additional lighting, thereby creating a suitable backdrop for the sacred art designed by Dagenais and executed by the prisoners under her direction. These ecclesiastical furnishings included the stations of the cross in mosaic and an altar design consisting of a three-panel mosaic depicting Christ Crucified, the Virgin, and St. Dismas (patron saint of prisoners and thieves). In addition, the work crew disguised the plain, barred windows with stained glass.

Both materials and methods used to refurbish the Cook County Jail Chapel reflected the 1950s revival of nineteenth-century Arts and Crafts movement ideals, specifically the use of traditionally disdained craft materials and methods, such as mosaic and stained glass, in order to make both production and consumption of art accessible to untrained artists ranging from inmates to suburban homemakers. In addition, the movement espoused the rehabilitative power of beauty, especially that found in the decorative arts. The Arts and Crafts movement's assertion of the transformative power of the decorative arts dovetailed with the liturgical reform movement's emphasis upon both participatory religious experience and aesthetic beauty in the service of the church. The Cook County Jail Chapel embodied Dagenais's belief, predicated upon principles both aesthetic and religious, that art was for everyone. She explained, "Esthetic response is in the very fibre of each person—not as a luxury, but as a need placed there by God to lead us to Him" ("Art Is for Everyone," 2).

It was this belief that made her advocate the creation of a fine arts department at Loyola University, not only for art majors but to give all students an opportunity to study art. For Loyola, Dagenais argued, the need to provide such a program had an additional goal: to teach and create an environment for the development of Christian art and artists. Loyola needed to equip graduates "to compete not only technically with secularly-educated people, but to excel in idea and content" ("Art Is for Everyone," 3). Margaret Dagenais rose in rank from assistant professor in 1955 to associate professor in 1960, and in 1971, to full professor. In 1972, she began her tenure as the chair of the fine arts department, which she had established. Dagenais designed the curriculum, selected faculty members, and planned studios and galleries for both campuses. Dagenais had developed a small program into a department with rapidly increasing course enrollment and more than sixty majors. Dagenais articulated her motivation for establishing the department: "I have tried to bring the fruits of my own creative work to my classes in sharing the joy of creativity and the discipline and skill necessary in making art happen at any level . . . [to] serve the students and the school with professional skill and dignity" (Memo to Father McNamara, November 24, 1971, Dagenais Collection).

A one-semester sabbatical in 1970 had initiated change in Dagenais's work as she determined to "find the sacred in the secular" (Memo to Father McNamara, November 24, 1971, Dagenais Collection). Accordingly, Dagenais completed thirty-three oil paintings, which she exhibited as *Dagenais '70* at the E. M. Cudahy Memorial Library Gallery, Loyola University. Thereafter, Margaret Dagenais mounted a series of one-artist shows, exhibiting mixed-media interpretations of world cultures—including mask forms, totems, and the image of the word—which demonstrated, in her words, "the impact of primal message in primitive art" (Small Research Grant Proposal, April 4, 1977, Dagenais Collection).

Dagenais's focus upon the spiritual foundation uniting world cultures, the primal message, indicated a broadened application of the tenet underpinning the art apostolate, that the Christian artist manipulated matter in order to evince the spiritual meaning of the visible world. Dagenais began to use art as both process and product to investigate world cultures. She was influenced, at least in part, by the revisionist theology of her husband, John Dominic Crossan, a theologian and professor at DePaul University, Chicago, whom she married in 1969. Dagenais's pan-cultural approach to art complemented Crossan's revisionist theology, which used both cultural studies and textual analyses. Crossan, like Dagenais, posited that Christianity, and all other religions, embrace what he termed an ultimate referent, or what Dagenais identified as a primal message.

In 1973, her exhibit of sculptured paintings, *In Fragments*, captured traces of ancient cultures and their artistic efforts at communication. The exhibit was the result of two years of research and work after extensive travel in Europe and the Middle East.

The research for *In Fragments* led Dagenais to a new theme: a study of mask forms in history, "how one hides and reveals oneself behind or within masks" (Grant Application to National Endowment for the Humanities, November 26, 1973, Dagenais Collection). She developed this theme into an exhibit, *Mask* (1976), reinterpreting masks in contemporary form, including paintings in oil and collage on canvas, in bas-relief, and in three-dimensional construction. A further exploration of this theme, *Messages: Mask, Shield, and Totem*, an exhibit of mixed media, was presented in 1981.

Dagenais's last project brought her back to more familiar territory. She had taught calligraphy and design for many years. Now she turned once again to the historical alphabets of the Roman Empire, the Middle Ages, and the Renaissance for sources of modern calligraphy. She took seminars in heraldry, calligraphic design, and Baroque writing at the Newberry Library,

Chicago, and with the Chicago Calligraphy Collective. These studies convinced her of "the rich potential of medieval manuscripts as a source of inspiration for Contemporary Art" (Abstract of Project, Initial, Contemporary Art Inspired by Medieval Manuscripts, n.p., Dagenais Collection). Having received a two thousand dollar grant from the Bunker Ramo Foundation to assist in travel expenses, she traveled to Dublin, Ireland, where in 1981 she did research in the manuscript collections of Trinity College, the Royal Irish Academy, and the National Museum of Ireland.

Margaret Dagenais pursued her artistic and educational endeavors until her death two years later. She is buried at Calvary Cemetery, Evanston, Illinois. Dagenais's belief in the art apostolate enabled her to establish the fine arts department at Loyola University and also to teach art in unconventional settings, ranging from the seminary to the jail. Always she believed that the practice of art benefited the amateur as well as the professional artist. Margaret Dagenais, guided by the precepts of the Catholic liturgical reform movement in the twentieth century, promoted art for life's sake, believing not only that art was for everyone but also that art, as a manifestation of faith, must come from everyone.

Sources. The Margaret M. Dagenais Collection, Loyola Univ. Chicago Archives, has personal papers and copies of articles by Dagenais, including "A Sculptor Mediates," *Liturgical Arts Quarterly*, November 1947; "Speaking of Art," *Salve Regina*, October 1952; "Art Is for Everyone," *Loyola Alumnus*, November 1955; "The Role of the Artist Serving the Church," *Catholic Art Quarterly*, February 1956; "Contemporary Design in Church Art," *Anno Domini*, July–August 1964. Exhibit catalogues by Dagenais are *In Fragments* (1973), *Messages: Mask, Shield, and Totem* (1981). The Dagenais Collection has correspondence, memos, and grant applications written by Dagenais, including Small Research Grant Proposal, April 4, 1977; Grant Application to the National Endowment for the Humanities, November 26, 1973; personal photographs, slides, and photographs of artwork. Walter P. Krolikowski, SJ, was interviewed August 1995. Articles about Dagenais include n.a., "The Work of a Christian Artist," *Franciscan Message*, January 1963; n.a., "Crucifix in L[ewis] T[owers] Chapel Holds Added Meaning," *Loyola World*, December 9, 1955. See Steven M. Avella, "Reynold Hillenbrand and Chicago Catholicism," in Ellen Skerret, Edward R. Kantowicz, and Steven M. Avella, *Catholicism, Chicago Style* (1993), for information about the liturgical reform movement. John Dominic Crossan, *Who Killed Jesus? Exposing the Roots of Anti-Semitism in the Gospel Story of the Death of Jesus* (1995), discusses the revisionist theology influential in Dagenais's art.

KRISTIN U. FEDDERS

DAHL, PETRA MARIE
August 24, 1878–January 24, 1951
PHYSICIAN, EDUCATOR, MUNICIPAL REFORMER, PUBLIC HEALTH REFORMER

Petra Marie Dahl, who practiced medicine in Chicago, was born in Calmar, Iowa. She was the second of four children of Peter and Anna Joanette (Mikkelsen) Dahl, both native Norwegians. The family emigrated to the United States shortly after the birth of their first child, Dora, in 1872. The Dahls were among the first settlers of Calmar.

Dahl's intellectual abilities were recognized by her mother, who regularly referred to her daughter with an old Norwegian saying, "It is God's fault she is so smart." Dahl went to elementary and high school in Calmar. She then took a teacher's training program at the Valder School in nearby Decorah. Returning to Calmar, Dahl alternated between teaching and studies, receiving a B.S. degree in 1902, with considerable work in German, at Valparaiso University in Valparaiso, Indiana. This degree made it possible for Dahl to enter educational administration. She became assistant principal at the Winchester High School in Illinois, near Springfield, and then moved on, as principal, to the high schools at Ashland and Petersburg villages in the coal mining area.

In 1908 she returned to Valder for two years as principal of the school. A desire for further education took her back to Valparaiso University, where she earned a B.A. in music and an M.A. in teaching, both in 1912. Dahl became an assistant in the English department at Valparaiso and taught for a short time. Already interested in political issues, she gave a speech at the university supporting woman suffrage and discussed equality between men and women. A newspaper account referred to her smooth style, rich humor, and incisive wit.

When rheumatic fever forced Dahl to give up teaching, she decided to enter medical training. In the fall of 1912 she enrolled in the Chicago College of Medicine and Surgery, which was affiliated with Valparaiso. She received an M.D. degree in 1916, a year before Loyola University took over the college. Dahl interned at the Mary Thompson Hospital in Chicago and was licensed in 1916 to practice in Illinois. A year later Dahl took part in the most well-publicized event of her medical career when she delivered Rose Prusinski of healthy triplets.

Petra Dahl supported herself as a general practitioner in Chicago for twenty-five years, beginning in 1916. She joined the staff of Belmont Hospital in 1927, shortly after its opening. Throughout these years she focused her energies on issues of social reform. Dahl became an activist in a number of areas, including public policy affecting health care, responsibilities of women physicians, political reform in Chicago, and state programs in education.

In 1918–19 Dahl served as Acting Assistant Surgeon for the U.S. Public Health Service, playing an active role in fighting the great influenza epidemic. For four years she worked as a health officer in Chicago and pushed for improvement in public health programs. Later Dahl was the first woman to be elected president of the Chicago Health Officers Association.

While a school physician in Chicago for several years around 1920, she fought both the city health commissioner, Dr. John Dill Robertson, and the mayor, William Hale Thompson, over the use of physicians in the Chicago Health Department on temporary sixty-day appointments rather than with civil service status.

Dahl's father had died in 1909; her mother came to Chicago in 1923 and lived with Dahl for the remaining two years of her life. Dahl's niece, Esther Barlow, then moved in and lived with her aunt until Dahl's death.

Dahl supported programs encouraging good health, especially for the poor, and in 1930–31 published several short promotional articles in the *Bulletin of the Medical Women's Club of Chicago*. In "Health Audit and Health Savings," published in November 1930 in the bulletin, she described a personal health savings plan to take care of medical costs. Dahl felt that citizens—from childhood on—should regularly pay money into a health savings plan for periodic health audits and necessary health care.

Hospitals and medical schools, she firmly believed, should teach health, not disease. A reorganization of Cook County Hospital proposed in 1931, Dahl felt, overlooked the hospital's main purpose: providing care for the indigent sick. The hospital's obligation was to the county's taxpayers, not to the medical schools seeking teaching programs there.

The Medical Women's Club of Chicago, which carried out social and medical projects, occupied much of Dahl's time and effort; she served as its president 1930–31. In the latter year Dahl discovered questionable practices by the treasurer before Dahl had taken office. The ensuing dispute split the club, and Dahl founded the competing Medical Women's Club of Illinois as a result. She served as president of the club for two years. Under Dahl's leadership the Illinois club initiated a Woman's Diagnostic Clinic that operated before and during the Century of Progress Exposition in 1933.

Non-medical organizations also drew on Dahl's skills. She served as a director of the Woman's Progressive Club and as treasurer and trustee of the Business and Professional Woman's Club. After several financial scandals had occurred in the city, Dahl, in 1931, organized the Vigilance Forum of Chicago and served as its president until 1937. The forum tried to protect small investors from dishonest bankers and promoters.

Dahl sought better government in Chicago through her own political activism. In 1929 she ran for alderman on the Chicago City Council as an independent candidate in Chicago's 41st Ward. She was among the earliest women to run for local office. Although women were elected to state and national office, it was not until 1971 that a woman was elected to the city council. Stressing proper ward administration, Dahl spoke out for strict law enforcement to provide adequate police protection to residents, clean streets and alleys, and elimination of waste and graft in politics. Her reform platform dealt with problems in medicine, public transportation, and education. The city's health department, she urged, should stay out of the practice of medicine and not compete with private physicians. She objected to the use of portable classrooms in public schools, citing the need for additional school buildings. Dahl believed that both women and men should be active in municipal housekeeping, and she proposed that each ward have two aldermen, one man and one woman. In the election she obtained about eight hundred votes, well behind both regular party candidates.

Five years later Dahl worked for educational reform as a New Deal supporter, when she ran on the National Progressive Party slate for state superintendent of public instruction. She proposed expansion of curriculum to include the study of human anatomy, good health practices, and foundations of law. Dahl urged use of state school monies for adult education and cultural programs, especially in educationally deficient communities. Her views were partly derived from her earlier experiences as a high school principal in the poor coal-mining area of Illinois. Dahl's platform sought to widen educational opportunities for both adults and children. In the election Dahl received more than six thousand votes to finish fourth in a six-person race.

Norway and Norwegians found a hard-working and persistent supporter in Dahl. She encouraged both Chicago Mayor Edward J. Kelly and Governor Henry Horner to recognize contributions of Norwegians to the United States. Partly as a result of her efforts, these officials proclaimed a Norwegian Week in the city and state for several years, beginning in 1935, and later celebrated as American-Scandinavian Educational Week. During the week of celebration in October 1939, at the start of World War II, Dahl gave a radio talk on WCFL, "Scandinavian Contribution to American Development and Culture," in an effort to promote legislation in Congress for national observance. She pointed out that Scandinavians had spoken out against the great powers' greed and vicious arms races. Although a bill was passed in the Senate in 1940, it never went further.

Dahl served as president of the Norwegian Woman's Club of Chicago in 1935 and 1936. While in this position she acted as unofficial host for visiting Norwegian dignitaries. Dahl was the second physician to preside over the club, following Dr. Helga Ruud.

By 1941 heart problems caused Dahl to leave medical practice. She then carried out a project in which she had been interested for many years; she established a nursing home in the Logan Square area for patients suffering from rheumatism and arthritis. Eight years later worsening health forced her to close the home. Dahl died from the debilitating effects of chronic myocarditis and was buried in Memorial Park in Skokie, a suburb of Chicago.

Petra Dahl's major efforts with medical organizations focused on improvement of women's health. She took an active role in the lives and well-being of many citizens through her work with several watchdog and business groups. Her desire for reform in Chicago government and in educational policies led her into politics on the city and state levels. Dahl's intense interest in her Norwegian heritage caused her to promote city, state, and national recognition for Norwegians and other Scandinavians.

Sources. William K. Beatty's "Petra Marie Dahl—Physician, Social Activist, and Norwegian," *Proceedings of the Institute of Medicine of Chicago,* January/March 1990, lists some of Dahl's articles and cites the Petra Dahl Papers, held by Palma Barlow Lindholm and Joseph and Harry Andersen, which include correspondence, Dahl's published articles and a radio address, and newspaper clippings. For Dahl's views on the goals of Cook County Hospital, see "Cook County Hospital Re-Organization Plans," *Bulletin of the Medical Women's Club of Chicago,* April 1931. Helpful information on the splitting of the Medical Women's Club of Chicago is found in its *Bulletin* for October 1931. Obituaries appear in the *Chicago Sun-Times,* January 25, 1951, and the *Journal of the American Medical Association,* March 17, 1951.

WILLIAM K. BEATTY

DAVIS, ELIZABETH LINDSAY
January 8, 1855–July 22, 1944
WRITER, CLUBWOMAN, SOCIAL REFORMER

Elizabeth Lindsay Davis was the eldest of six children of upper-middle-class parents, Thomas H. and Sophie Jane Lindsay, who were early African American settlers in Peoria, Illinois. Thomas Lindsay was born in McConnelsburg, Pennsylvania, and died in Peoria after acquiring considerable real estate holdings. He served as the first African American market master in Peoria, administering the laws pertaining to the markets in Peoria. He was also well known as a social activist. Sophie Lindsay, a homemaker, was born in Kentucky.

A precocious child, Elizabeth Lindsay started school at age four and by the age of ten had learned all she could in a segregated one-room schoolhouse. Her parents sent her to the Bureau Country High School, an integrated school in Princeton, Illinois, where she, as one of the first three African American students, graduated with high honors.

Lindsay's later contribution as author of works chronicling the history of African American women's clubs was foreshadowed in her early interest in writing. She authored the "Aunt Peggy" letters to girls, published in the *Gate City Press* in Kansas City, Missouri, for a number of years. She wrote essays for local newspapers and magazines. In later years she contributed to the *Chicago Defender* and made regular contributions to the National Association of Colored Women's *National Notes.*

After high school Lindsay taught in Iowa, Illinois, Indiana, and Kentucky; she stopped when, in 1885, she married Dr. William H. Davis. A chiropodist, he was active in civic, social, religious, and educational affairs of the community. The couple had no children.

Perceiving myriad needs in their community, black women across the United States in the 1890s organized women's clubs directed at the social, economic, educational, and political advancement of African Americans. Because of the heightened pervasive racism of the period, these "colored" women's clubs paralleled the white women's club movement. The Ida B. Wells Club was organized in Chicago in 1893 with activist Ida B. Wells (see IDA B. WELLS-BARNETT) as president and Davis as secretary. Davis and other women founded the Phyllis Wheatley Club on March 17, 1896, the second African American women's club in Chicago, in lieu of forming a woman's auxiliary, as they were invited to do by the men who organized the Frederick Douglass League shortly after the famous abolitionist's death. The Phyllis Wheatley Club was envisioned as a neighborhood betterment organization, working initially to force the closing of a tavern near which schoolchildren had to walk. They also ran a sewing school attended by eighty to one hundred children of all nationalities every Saturday morning. Davis served for twenty-eight years as president.

In 1896, the National Federation of Afro-American Women merged with the Colored Women's League of Washington to become the National Association of Colored Women (NACW). At the invitation of Davis, the second biennial convention of the NACW was hosted in Chicago in 1899 by the Magic Seven. The Magic Seven, who later that year formed the Illinois Federation of Colored Women's Clubs (IFCWC), were the pioneer African American women's clubs in Chicago and included the Ida B. Wells Club, the Phyllis Wheatley Club, the Civic League, the Progressive Circle of King's Daughters, the Ideal Women's Club, the G.O.P. Elephant Club, and the Julia Gaston Club. JANE ADDAMS read about the NACW convention in the daily papers and invited the officers to lunch with her; the *Chicago Times Herald* reported the event to be the "first time that colored women have been given the decided recognition in a social way by a woman of lighter skin" (quoted in Wesley, *History of the National Association of Colored Women's Clubs*, 14). Davis assumed the position of national organizer for the NACW from 1901 to 1906 and again in 1912 to 1916. Under her leadership, more than 289 clubs were added, including the Elizabeth Lindsay Davis Club of Johnstown, Pennsylvania, named in her honor.

In 1924 Davis started compiling the history of the NACW. To get information for the book, she sent out one thousand letters, two hundred questionnaires, and one hundred "outlines" of the proposed contents of the book to women all over the country. When the book, *Lifting as They Climb*, was rushed to publication for the Century of Progress Exposition in Chicago in 1933, it was criticized for typographical errors, misplaced photographs, and the absence of an index. Despite these problems, the book contained materials that could not be found in other publications at the time. This history was not superseded until the publication of Charles H. Wesley's history in 1984.

Davis's national work was rooted in her statewide and local activism. At the local level, she organized clubs in Chicago and Peoria in 1896 and 1899, respectively, and served as president, historian, and organizer for the IFCWC. Davis was also very active in church work. A long-time member of St. Mark's Methodist Episcopal Church, she held many positions in the church and sang in the choir.

Davis and others understood the importance of combining forces. In March 1906, the presidents of fifteen Chicago area women's clubs, including Davis representing the Phyllis Wheatley Club, came together to discuss plans for a closer cooperation of African American clubwomen, which came to be known as the City Federation of Colored Women's Clubs. Its objectives included promoting education and welfare of women and children, raising the standards of the home, securing and enforcing civil rights for minority groups, and fostering interracial understanding so that goodwill might prevail among all people. In 1918 the State of Illinois was divided into three district federations: Chicago and Northern, Central, and Southern. In 1921 the City Federation was incorporated under the name of the Chicago and Northern District. The name of the organization was changed in 1931 to the Illinois Association of Colored Women and again, in 1953, to the Illinois Association of Women's Clubs.

In 1908, Davis established the Phyllis Wheatley Home. Prior to the home, no social agencies in the Chicago area served African American girls who migrated to Chicago and found themselves excluded from the Young Women's Christian Association (YWCA) and similar white organizations. There were no YWCAs for African American girls in Chicago until about 1914. The Phyllis Wheatley Home Association, an organization that grew out of the Phyllis Wheatley Club, had the responsibility for running the home, which specialized in the housing, health, vocational guidance, recreation, and religious education of young African American women. From a small beginning with only $150 with which to make a down payment on a piece of property in 1908, the home eventually outgrew two other buildings. There was no endowment fund to support the home; it had the distinction of being the only institution of its kind in Chicago that was managed and supported almost entirely by African American people.

While Davis was serving as the fourth president of the IFCWC in 1910–12, she helped to organize the Gaudeamus (Let Us Rejoice) Charity Club, which was formed in 1911. The club gave scholarships and supported other African American institutions. During World War I, the club adopted Company C of the 8th Illinois Infantry and the 370th Infantry.

Davis's support for woman suffrage derived from her commitment to improving conditions of African Americans, women in particular. In 1913 when the Illinois Suffrage Bill was passed, Davis was among the first women to register, and she became very active in politics. W.E.B. Du Bois, the prominent intellectual and editor of the *Crisis*, invited Davis in 1915 to write on voting rights for women. She chose as her topic "Votes for Philanthropy," writing that women, who had always been in the forefront for social uplift and racial and community development, were a very important factor in the political world: "[Woman] is demonstrating at all times her fitness for her duties and responsibilities by study; by insistent investigation of all candidates . . . ; by an intelligent use of the ballot . . . ; by persistent agitation to arouse civic consciousness" (p. 191).

Davis and other clubwomen realized that politicians from both parties were seeking favors from them. They were aware of their inexperience with political matters and were determined not to be exploited. Therefore, in their clubs throughout the state, they instituted regular classes in citizenship to give them the background they needed to be able to act for themselves in selecting the best man or woman to fill a political office. These women were determined that no one party could say that it had the African American women in its "back pocket" or could take them for granted. In 1923 Davis was one of twenty-seven graduates of the first citizenship training class of the Woman's City Club. She was also a member of the Chicago Forum League of Women Voters. A Republican, Davis was very active in 2nd Ward politics and interested as well in state and national politics. In 1934 she identified her political struggles with a long line of pioneer sisters, including Susan B. Anthony, Harriet Tubman, Sojourner Truth, and Harriet Beecher Stowe; she wrote, "Now that we are full fledged citizens let us remember days of yore and not misuse our power today" ("Facts to Be Remembered," *National Notes*, December 6, 1934, 18).

When World War I began in 1914 and the United States entered the war in 1917, Davis became involved with the State Council of National Defense and was in charge of the war office opened for the 2nd Ward at the Frederick Douglass Center. The Frederick Douglass Center Women's Club had been organized in October 1904 by CELIA WOOLLEY, a white Unitarian minister, and had as members both African American and white women. The center's office involved women in local defense activities, worked with men seeking draft exemptions, ran a Red Cross auxiliary, collected packages to be sent to soldiers overseas, and helped during the 1918 influenza epidemic.

Although Davis was busy with her war duties, she did not neglect club work. In 1918 Davis was appointed historian of the IFCWC and wrote *The Story of the Illinois Federation of Colored Women's Clubs, 1900–1922*. In 1914–15, she participated in the IFCWC's successful efforts to create a Northwestern Federation linking western and midwestern clubwomen.

Davis was honored for her achievements. She was chosen as one of two hundred prominent women to march down the aisle of the Chapel of the University of Chicago in 1929 in recognition by the National YWCA of the leadership of women. In 1936 IRENE GAINES named her one of the ten living African American women who had contributed most to the advancement of African Americans. In 1963 her name was also placed on the Women's Honor Roll of the Century by the Women's Auxiliary of a Century of Negro Progress Exposition.

Elizabeth Lindsay Davis died at the age of eighty-nine. She was buried at Mt. Glenwood Cemetery in Glenwood, Illinois.

Davis was a pragmatist. The only way for her to change society was to become part of it. She chose to infiltrate a defective system and institute changes from within. She was an effective communicator, diplomat, and spokeswoman for her cause. She demanded excellence from those around her in the same way she pushed herself. Part of her success with clubs came from her creativity and zero tolerance for pettiness. Davis truly believed in the principle: we must strive to "lift as we climb." She thought that African American women should climb in such a way as to guarantee that all of their sisters and brothers, regardless of social class, would climb together.

Sources. Family information can be found in the manuscript by Romeo B. Garrett, "The Negro in Peoria, Illinois" (1973), and census and cemetery records in the Spec. Coll. Center, Bradley Univ. Library, in Peoria. Davis's involvement in club activities is documented in her books, *The Story of the Illinois Federation of Colored Women's Clubs* (1922) and *Lifting as They Climb: History of the National Association of Colored Women* (1933). Her involvement with the NACW is found in the *Records of the National Association of Colored Women's Clubs, 1895–1992*, including the *National Notes*, on microfilm at Northwestern Univ. Library, Evanston, Illinois. An important article by Davis is "Votes for Philanthropy," *Crisis*, August 1915. Information on Davis and the Phyllis Wheatley Home can be found in *1927 Intercollegiate Wonder Book or 1779—The Negro in Chicago—1927*, ed. Frederic H. Robb, vol. 1 (1927), and *The Negro in Chicago 1779 to 1929: The Wonder Book*, vol. 1–2 [*sic*] (1929). See also Charles H. Wesley's *The History of the National Association of Colored Women's Clubs: A Legacy of Service* (1984); Anne Meis Knupfer, *Toward a Tenderer Humanity and a Nobler Womanhood: African American Women's Clubs in Turn-of-the-Century Chicago* (1996). Sylvia G. L. Dannett wrote about her in "Profiles of Negro Womanhood," *Educational Heritage* (1964); biographies appear in *BWA* and Jessie Carney Smith, ed., *Notable Black American Women* (1992).

ADLEAN HARRIS

DE BEY, CORNELIA BERNARDA
May 26, 1865–April 3, 1948
PHYSICIAN, SOCIAL ACTIVIST, EDUCATIONAL REFORMER

Cornelia De Bey, while working as a physician, devoted her energies to social reform in education, labor relations, and other areas. De Bey, anglicized from De Beij, was born in the province of Groningen, the Netherlands, the daughter of Reverend Bernardus and Anje (Schuringa) de Beij. She was the youngest of the De Beij family's six children, with three brothers (Willem, Gerard, and Henry) and two sisters (Alberdina and Catherine). Bernardus de Beij was a minister who began his religious career as a member of the Secession, a religious movement challenging the state church in the Netherlands. He studied theology at the University of Groningen, a center of religious training. Anje Schuringa was also a part of the Secession, in which her father became a minister. Both families were relatively well off. During Bernardus de Beij's years as pastor in the town of Middelstum he helped found a Christian primary school and worked to assist poor children who wanted to get an education, areas of concern that his daughter would later adopt. In 1868 the De Beij family migrated to Chicago, where Bernardus had accepted a call to serve a church of Dutch Americans, many of them from Groningen. As was often the case among Dutch immigrant ministers, almost half of the congregation migrated with him, and others soon followed. The De Beij household became a center of the Dutch Reformed Church in Chicago. Bernardus de Beij gained nationwide stature in the denomination, partly for theological views that stressed allowing the church to adapt to new times and surroundings, as was evident in Chicago in his support for the use of English in his church and for women praying aloud in public. Cornelia De Bey's moral progressivism took shape in this setting.

Little is known about Cornelia De Bey's childhood, but a fictionalized account appears in LUCY FITCH PERKINS's children's book, *Cornelia: The Story of a Benevolent Despot* (1919). Perkins, author of a series of books featuring children from various ethnic backgrounds, based her story of a Dutch girl on childhood anecdotes told her by an adult Cornelia De Bey. The book portrays a strong-willed child with a vigorous social conscience. De Bey's father described her in 1884 as a good student in science and art, whom the family would support to continue her studies. She attended Cook County Normal School, where students were trained to become elementary or high school teachers. She studied under the principal, Colonel Francis Parker, graduating in 1889.

Early in her life, De Bey became involved in social reform through political action. In 1890 she worked closely with John Meyers, a member of the Illinois state legislature and a friend of the De Bey family, to secure passage of a bill that legalized kindergartens within the Illinois public schools. She also successfully led a campaign to defeat a bill that would prohibit married women from teaching in public schools. De Bey, like many educated women of her time, never married.

After teaching briefly in the Chicago schools, De Bey went on to study at the Art Institute and at Northwestern University before matriculating at Hahnemann Medical College and Hospital. Her interest in medicine came partially through two of her brothers, one a doctor, the other a pharmacist. She received an M.D. degree in 1895 as a doctor of homeopathic medicine, a pharmacologically based system that cured disease by use of an infinitesimal dose of a drug that would cause symptoms of the illness in a well person. She opened an office in downtown Chicago and began the practice of medicine. She was connected with the Hull-House settlement, and much of her medical practice was with the poor and with immigrants in Chicago's neediest neighborhoods. Ernest Poole, a reporter who approached JANE ADDAMS for information about health conditions, was sent to De Bey, "and through her I found countless men, women and children, sick or crippled from their work in sweatshops, factories and mills" (*Giants Gone*, 219). De Bey was a member of the Chicago Homeopathic Medical

Society, the Chicago Pathological Society, and the Chicago Woman's Club.

De Bey was very tall and "thin almost to the point of emaciation" (Haley, 103), energetic, and opinionated. She typically wore somewhat masculine attire; as one contemporary stated, this slight woman with delicate features "might have seemed a candidate for a convent if she hadn't been careful . . . to wear a man's collar and tie and a fedora hat" (Hard, 482). Her clothing set her apart in many settings, including a formal reception in Chicago for Russian humanitarian and revolutionist Catherine Breshkovskaia in 1904. Breshkovskaia, who herself tended to simple dress, upon seeing De Bey in her tailored suit amid the formal gowns and tuxedos, reportedly "made a bee line for the doctor, whom she never had seen before, threw her arms around her and whispered urgently in her ear, 'I want to go home with you!' Needless to say, she went" (Peck, 142).

In 1903 De Bey worked for passage of an Illinois Child Labor law, speaking at the state legislature in support of the bill. During the next year she came to the attention of Chicagoans for her role in settling a strike in the meat-packing industry. A lengthy strike against the Armour Corporation by meat packers had reached an impasse; the strikers were willing to come to terms, but Jonathan Ogden Armour refused to meet with their leaders. Although De Bey did not know Armour, she called on him to plead the case of the women and children who were suffering because of the strike. "Mr. Armour submitted. He had read the newspapers with equanimity, but a strange lady who knew exactly what he ought to do was too much for him" (Hard, 482). The strike was settled, with De Bey earning the friendship of both Armour and Michael Donnelly, president of the Amalgamated Meat Cutters and Butcher Workmen Union. An indication of De Bey's own acerbic style was her comment to friends before she approached Armour: "There must be one man among all these men a little more of a man and a little less of a fool than those around him. I'm going to find out who that man is, and when I've found him I will know how to move him" (*Chicago Teachers' Federation Bulletin*, September 16, 1904, 4).

De Bey was again involved in settling a labor dispute in 1905, when she, together with Jane Addams and three local religious leaders, Rabbi Emil G. Hirsch, Reverend Jenkin Lloyd Jones, and Bishop Charles P. Anderson, was appointed by Mayor Edward Dunne to a citizens' committee to try to resolve a citywide teamsters' strike. Their efforts were unsuccessful, and the strike continued for several weeks. One side effect of the strike was a rash of sympathy strikes by Chicago school children objecting to the delivery of coal to the schools by non-union drivers. The Board of Education sent the leaders to juvenile court; De Bey was among the civic leaders who spoke out publicly in support of the board's action.

Three months later, Mayor Dunne asked De Bey to become a member of the Chicago Board of Education. De Bey was recommended by MARGARET HALEY, leader of the Chicago Teachers' Federation and one of Dunne's strongest supporters in his mayoral campaign. Dunne had been elected on a Democratic reform platform that sought municipal ownership of the streetcar system and that supported organized labor. De Bey became one of an unprecedented number of four women on the twenty-one member board, along with Dunne appointees Jane

Addams and ANITA McCORMICK BLAINE, and Mrs. W. C. H. Keough, an attorney who had come onto the board in 1904. De Bey explained her goals in joining the board: to make administration of the school system democratic, to change the process of buying textbooks, and to modify the existing procedure for teacher promotion.

Chicago's newspapers regularly identified De Bey as the spokesperson on the Board of Education for the Chicago Teachers' Federation. She was a close friend of Margaret Haley and for many years shared her home with Kate Starr Kellogg, an activist teacher and later principal at Chicago's Lewis-Champlin School. Kellogg was the sister of artist ALICE DeWOLF KELLOGG TYLER. One of De Bey's first actions on the board was her enthusiastic support of ELLA FLAGG YOUNG as the first woman principal of the Chicago Normal School. In November 1905 she made a proposal to the School Management Committee, of which she was a member, that divided the board and provoked vehement hostility from the Chicago press. The De Bey Plan called for an expanded role for teachers in the management of the schools and provided for abolition of the system of district superintendents, replacing them with smaller school districts to be comprised of elected representatives of teachers and principals. The press derided the plan as "democratization," an undesirable "leveling" (quoted in Schiltz, 98), and De Bey's ideas were criticized as "socialistic" and "anarchistic" (*Chicago Record-Herald*, November 18, 1905). Opponents of De Bey's plan saw it as an attempt by Haley and the Teachers' Federation to "secure control of the school system" (*Record-Herald*, November 18, 1905). Much of the criticism also linked De Bey's ideas with Mayor Dunne's moves toward municipal ownership of transportation and utilities, a concept at variance with traditional business dogma. A report issued the following year on De Bey's plan recommended a system of teachers' councils that would have a direct advisory relationship with the board. The board approved this concept, but its membership changed in 1907 and the councils were never implemented.

In February 1906, De Bey and Jane Addams spoke out to the board against a proposal to continue an experiment in gender segregation at Englewood High School to solve the problem of students dropping out of school. De Bey argued that such segregation was retrogressive, that radical changes in the system were needed: smaller class sizes, better equipment, and most important, greater initiative permitted to the teaching staff. Despite public opposition by De Bey and Addams, the board approved the experiment.

In June 1906 De Bey precipitated another public controversy when she proposed a resolution that the board not consider any bids from textbook vendors "unless accompanied by an affidavit that the bidder was in no way a party" (Schiltz, 109) to any arrangement that might deny to the city the advantages of competitive bidding. The ensuing press furor lasted for months, with debates about the role of textbook companies; but ultimately there was no real change in the purchasing process.

De Bey also introduced a resolution concerning the "secret marking" (*Chicago Tribune*, April 18, 1906) of teachers as part of the promotion process. Teachers were not permitted to view their own evaluations. De Bey's resolution asked that the marking system be investigated and recommendations submitted to the board. At this point, Chicago's newspapers, which had been increasingly critical of the "radical" nature of some of the board's actions, lashed out at Mayor Dunne for his appointments to the board. A *Chicago Tribune* editorial on October 10, 1906, referred to some of the board members as "freaks, cranks, monomaniacs and boodlers." De Bey, with her eccentric mode of dress, was a particular target of cartoonists as well as of editorial writers who objected to many of her positions.

Mayor Dunne was defeated in his bid for reelection in 1907. One of the first acts of his successor, Republican Fred Busse, was to send policemen bearing blank resignation forms to the homes of several members of the Board of Education, including De Bey. Some signed, but eight denied the legality of Busse's action and refused. Busse, however, appointed new members in their place. De Bey and others fought the dismissal through legal venues. The Cook County Circuit Court turned the matter over to the Cook County state's attorney, a political ally of the new mayor, who refused to do anything. The state attorney general also refused to take action. In December 1907 the Illinois Supreme Court ruled that Busse had violated the law in removing the trustees. De Bey and the other seven were restored to the board, where they served for the remainder of their terms. By this time, however, the balance of power on the board had tipped so that none of the reforms contemplated by the Dunne-appointed board were put into effect.

Around the same time De Bey was active in other political fields. During hearings for a new Chicago Charter in 1906, De Bey spoke in support of including woman suffrage. Her address, published in the *Record Herald* and reprinted in the *Chicago Teachers' Federation Bulletin*, explained that suffrage was "not the outgrowth of a fad among feminine idlers but is a right demanded by modern conditions" (*Bulletin*, April 6, 1906, 5). De Bey conceded that many women did not yet want the vote but then argued that votes for women would benefit society on two grounds: first, because women were more moral than men, and second, because women's brains would evolve. "Brains are developed only by experience, and there is no such thing as the vicarious absorption of mentality" (*Bulletin*, April 6, 1906, 5). De Bey was in contact with Anna Howard Shaw, head of the National American Woman Suffrage Association, and through her gained news of the suffrage campaign in the Netherlands.

In 1913, De Bey was an early member of the Chicago Peace Society and became known as a radical pacifist. Although never charged with violating a law, she was summoned into court four times during World War I because of her public utterances against war of any kind, holding it to be futile and not human.

De Bey began writing short stories containing moral lessons for the *Chicago Magazine* in 1911. No longer in the limelight, she continued to practice medicine in Chicago until 1928. She lived briefly in California. In 1940 De Bey moved to Grand Rapids, Michigan, close to several members of her family; a niece described her as a lovable but stubborn lady. She died at eighty-two years of age of a cerebral hemorrhage and was buried in the Pilgrim Home Cemetery in Holland, Michigan.

While De Bey's proposals for educational reform in Chicago were not acted upon during her lifetime, teachers' councils and teachers' access to their own performance evaluations later became institutionalized not only in Chicago schools but also in other school systems nationwide. The variety of De Bey's life experiences—as educational reformer, physician, peace advocate, suffragist, and general gadfly on issues of social concern—made her an outstanding activist during the Progressive Era.

Sources. The Bernardus de Beij manuscript collection at Calvin College in Grand Rapids, Michigan, provides information about De Bey's early life. The *Chicago Teachers' Federation Bulletin*, September 16, 1904, February 23, 1906, November 4, 1904, September 8, 1905, April 6, 1906, at CHS and articles in Chicago newspapers (*Chicago Daily News*, November 18, 1905, May–December 1907; *Chicago Record-Herald*, various articles 1904–1906, June 17, 1911; *CT*, April 18, 1906, October 10, 1906) describe and comment on De Bey's public activities. *Public*, vols. 8–12, 1905–1909, edited by her fellow Board of Education member Louis Post, is helpful for her work in educational reform, as is the manuscript of Post's unpublished reminiscences, "Living a Long Life Over Again," in the Louis Post Papers at the Library of Congress; a copy was provided by Dominic Candeloro. Mary Pieroni Schiltz's Ph.D. dissertation, "The Dunne School Board: Reform in Chicago 1905–1908" (Loyola Univ. Chicago, 1993), provides analysis of De Bey's educational work. William Hard's "Chicago's Five Maiden Aunts," *American Magazine*, September 1906, details De Bey's involvement with J. Ogden Armour. Margaret Haley's *Battleground: The Autobiography of Margaret A. Haley*, ed. Robert L. Reid (1982), discusses De Bey's school board work and provides information on the Chicago Teachers' Federation. A biographical sketch appears in *NCAB*, vol. C (1930). Ernest Poole, *Giants Gone: Men Who Made Chicago* (1943), briefly describes De Bey's contact with Hull-House. Mary Gray Peck, *Carrie Chapman Catt*, describes De Bey's unconventional dress. Suzanne M. Sinke's paper, "Mommy State, Daddy State: Social Welfare in International Perspective," given at the Social Science History Association meeting in November 1993, places De Bey in the context of Dutch American women and reform. Amry Vandenbosch's *The Dutch Communities of Chicago* (1927) provides a history of the group but has inaccuracies. An obituary is in *Grand Rapids Herald*, April 3, 1948.

MARY PIERONI SCHILTZ
SUZANNE M. SINKE

DICK, GLADYS ROWENA HENRY

December 18, 1881–August 21, 1963

PHYSICIAN, BACTERIOLOGIST, RESEARCHER IN INFECTIOUS DISEASES

Born in Pawnee City, Nebraska, to William Chester and Azelia Henrietta (Edson) Henry, Gladys Rowena Henry had an older sister, Edith, and a younger brother, Ed. Her father, a cavalry officer during the Civil War, had moved into the Nebraska territory, where the government was offering land to veterans. Shortly after his second daughter's birth, he moved his growing family to the ranch he had established in Lincoln. He was an attorney, a grain farmer, and a breeder of carriage horses in Lincoln, where he attended sessions of the state legislature while his children went to the city's schools. Life on the family ranch was more patrician than primitive, and it probably contributed to Gladys Henry's lifelong attachment to animals, especially horses. An accomplished horsewoman, she continued to ride regularly well into her fifties.

Gladys Henry attended the University of Nebraska, receiving a B.S. degree in 1900. While an undergraduate, she participated in military drill, which was offered to women as a sport, an activity of which she often spoke approvingly in her later years. She had hoped to enter medical school, but her mother opposed this plan. Though women enjoyed growing opportunities for medical education both in the United States and abroad during the late nineteenth and early twentieth centuries, the practice of medicine was looked down on as an inappropriate career for a conventionally reared young woman. In Henry's case, opposition delayed but did not scuttle her training. She initially acquiesced to her mother's wishes and instead of entering medical school, taught high school biology in Kearney, Nebraska, for a year. She then returned to the University of Nebraska and took graduate courses, principally in zoology. Her determination and sense of purpose finally prevailed, and in 1903 Gladys Rowena Henry entered the Johns Hopkins University School of Medicine, Baltimore, Maryland.

Astute business judgment and entrepreneurial energies manifested themselves early in her life. She quickly assumed a leadership position among her female colleagues at Hopkins, organizing them and arranging the purchase of a house for them to share, since the university did not provide living accommodations for women students.

Following her graduation from Hopkins medical school in 1907, Gladys Henry served a two-year internship there and took a year of postdoctoral study in Berlin, but the exact chronology of these events is unclear. During this period, her focus on biomedical research and pathology began to assert itself.

In 1911, when she moved to Chicago to be near her mother, who had moved to the city, Henry began, at the University of Chicago, to conduct research in biology that was to occupy most of her professional life. It was also the beginning of her forty-year medical collaboration with Dr. George F. Dick, a young faculty member. By 1912 they had begun investigating the etiology of scarlet fever while also pursuing research on kidney pathology. They were married January 28, 1914. During that year, Gladys Dick worked as a pathologist at Evanston Hospital in the northern suburbs, then joined her husband on the staff of the Memorial Institute for Infectious Diseases in Chicago, with which she remained affiliated until her retirement in 1953. Founded in memory of John Rockefeller McCormick, and also known as the John McCormick Institute for Infectious Diseases, it was rededicated and renamed the Hektoen Institute for Medical Research in 1943 in honor of its founding director, Ludvig Hektoen. He was an eminent Chicago pathologist whose uncompromising standards and sense of fair play made him an early champion of women in the sciences. Gladys Dick was one of several women he appointed to his staff and encouraged at every turn.

During World War I, Dick worked as a bacteriologist with the United States Public Health Service. She also filled in for George Dick on the staff of St. Luke's Hospital in Chicago while he served as a major in the United States Army from 1917 to 1919. Her most substantial contributions to the fields of medical microbiology and epidemiology, however, coincided with the postwar expansion of scientific research. The Dicks' 1923 report on the discovery and isolation of the hemolytic streptococcal organism responsible for scarlet fever was followed by further refinements of their research in 1924. Their discovery of the streptococcus-induced toxin of scarlet fever, development of an antitoxin, and application of the Dick Test to pregnant women as an indicator of susceptibility to puerperal infection brought them international attention.

Although the Dicks were mentioned as possible candidates for the Nobel Prize in 1925, no award for medicine was made in that year, and the matter was dropped. Other honors came their way, however. They were invited to deliver the first Hektoen Fund Lecture at Chicago's Institute of Medicine in 1923; they received the University of Toronto's Mickle Prize in 1926; and in 1933 the University of Edinburgh awarded them the Cameron Prize for practical therapeutics, only the third time that Americans had been so honored. Gladys Dick received several honorary degrees: Sc.D.s from the University of Nebraska, the University of Cincinnati (both in 1925), and Northwestern University (1928), and an LL.D. from the University of Nebraska (1938). She was named an honorary Kentucky Colonel in 1929, presumably for her loyal service to Berea College, to which she traveled regularly to inoculate students.

Controversy erupted in the medical community when the Dicks, claiming the need to protect the integrity of their product, patented the scarlet fever toxin and antitoxin they had developed in 1924 and 1926 and also their method of producing it. In a precedent-setting lawsuit against the Lederle Antitoxin Laboratories in 1930, their claim of patent infringement was upheld by a federal district court, protecting the patentability of both their antitoxin and its production process. When penicillin revolutionized the treatment of streptococcal throat infections in the 1940s, however, the Dick vaccine—and the litigation it engendered—vanished into obscurity.

Dick's interest in child welfare led her to become a board member of the Cradle, the private infant adoption agency begun by her friend and fellow Evanstonian FLORENCE WALRATH in 1923. Less a public oriented social service agency than a nursery dedicated to supplying healthy babies to would-be parents who were generally financially secure and often celebrities as well, the Cradle prided itself on its low infant mortality rate. It was especially demoralizing, therefore, when a fatal enteric epidemic struck in 1927. Gladys Dick, working with George Dick and Dr. J. Lisle Williams, tracked down and analyzed the probable cause of this outbreak of infant diarrhea. She recommended that the powdered infant milk formula be altered so that it could be boiled without curdling in order to kill the living streptococcus organisms it harbored. The triumphant results of her bacteriological detective work were published in the *American Journal for the Diseases of Children* in December 1927. Discovery of the streptococcal culprit, and the Dick Aseptic Nursery Technique instituted by Gladys Dick to eradicate it and other disease-carrying organisms, restored Walrath's confidence in the practical wisdom of continuing to operate the agency. By isolating each infant and all its food and supplies and insisting on strict personal asepsis among nursery caregivers, the handborne spread of infant diarrhea from baby to baby was effectively halted. As a consequence, the mortality rate among infants at the Cradle dropped and remained well below national and worldwide averages. Other institutions in Chicago and elsewhere began using modified versions of the Dick technique, bringing Gladys Dick a measure of national acclaim.

Described by those who knew her as petite and a great beauty, Dick was a woman of uncommon energy—disciplined, well organized, and goal oriented. She adopted two infants from the Cradle when she was forty-nine years old—a two-month-old son, Roger, in September 1930, and five months later a three-month-old daughter, Rowena. Any disruption that children might have created in either the Dicks' professional or household routines was mitigated by a domestic staff consisting of a cook, a maid, and a governess. Thus Dick continued to run a Saturday clinic at which she performed skin tests and immunizations at ten cents per visit. During World War II she worked at the Great Lakes Naval Training Station, refining inoculation procedures.

Gladys and George Dick were research and writing collaborators. Their book, *Scarlet Fever*, published in 1938, and the many articles they wrote for the *Journal of the American Medical Association* and the *Journal of Infectious Diseases*, among others, document their accomplishments. Dr. Gladys Dick's generally robust health began to deteriorate in 1953 with the onset of cerebral arteriosclerosis, and she and her husband retired to Palo Alto, California. She died of a stroke in neighboring Menlo Park.

A respected scientist, Gladys Dick was dedicated to epidemiological research. She addressed public health concerns relating to childhood illness by successfully finding causes and preventative measures for specific diseases. Dick was best known for her work on scarlet fever. In addition, her research on infectious diseases of childhood involved her in measures to control epidemics of diarrheal illness that were prevalent among infants and children in institutional settings.

Sources. Except for their book, *Scarlet Fever* (1938), and the Cameron Prize Lecture, reprinted in the *Edinburgh Medical Journal*, 1934, the Dicks' writing was confined to articles in medical journals. These include "Anaerobic Cultures in Scarlet Fever," *Journal of Infectious Diseases*, 1914; "Immune Reactions in Scarlet Fever," I and II, both published in the same journal in 1916; "The Etiology of Scarlet Fever," *Journal of the American Medical Association*, 1924; and "The Bacteriology of Dried Powdered Milk Preparations Used in Infant Feeding," *American Journal of Diseases of Children*, 1927. A complete bibliography has yet to be compiled, but citations to Gladys Dick's most significant papers can be found in the principal biographical sources: the *NCAB* (1969); *NAW* (1980); and the *Dictionary of American Medical Biography* (1984). The case against Lederle heard in the Federal District Court in New York on May 10, 1930, *Dick et al. v. Lederle Antitoxin Laboratories*, can be found in the *Federal Reporter*. Additional biographical information was gathered from interviews done by Jean Gottlieb with Dick's son, Roger H. Dick, and her daughter, Rowena D. Kelley, in 1995. Information on the McCormick Institute, later the Hektoen Institute, can be found in the Chicago Medical Soc., *History of Medicine and Surgery and Physicians and Surgeons of Chicago* (1922); and in "Cook County Hospital: Hektoen Institute for Medical Research," in the *State of Illinois Medical Center District Fact Book* (1948).

JEAN S. GOTTLIEB

DICKINSON, FRANCES
January 19, 1856–May 19, 1945
OPHTHALMOLOGIST, EDUCATOR, WOMEN'S RIGHTS
ADVOCATE, CLUBWOMAN

Dickinson was born in Chicago, the ninth of ten children and the fifth of five daughters of Albert Franklin and Ann Eliza (Anthony) Dickinson, New England Quakers who brought their family to Chicago in 1855. Dickinson's father, a commission grain merchant, was a speculator who made and lost at least three fortunes during her childhood. Her mother, who was the aunt of women's rights leader Susan B. Anthony, mortgaged the family home and took in boarders to make ends meet.

Frances Dickinson, named Fannie as a child, was two years older than her brother, Charles, and twelve to twenty years younger than the four other children who lived to adulthood: Hannah, Albert, Melissa, and Nathan. Always a close family, the children remained friends with their famous cousin, Susan B. Anthony, and eventually owned her birthplace in Adams, Massachusetts. After graduation from Central High School in 1875, Dickinson became a teacher in the Chicago public schools. In 1878–79, after attending a series of lectures in physiology given by Dr. SARAH HACKETT STEVENSON at Chicago Woman's Medical College, Frances Dickinson decided on a medical education for herself. Encouraged by her father, who believed that women had characteristics that would make them good doctors, she entered Woman's Medical College in 1880. Her tuition was paid for by her brothers and sister, Melissa, who together had successfully reorganized the Albert Dickinson Seed Company after the Great Chicago Fire of 1871.

Dickinson graduated with high honors from medical school in February 1883 and, after interning at the Chicago Hospital for Women and Children under Dr. MARY HARRIS THOMPSON and studying at the Illinois Eye and Ear Infirmary, resolved to become an ophthalmic surgeon. During the fourteen months she spent abroad in 1883–84, accompanying her brother Charles, who was recovering from a nervous breakdown, Dickinson took advantage of the clinical education offered only in Europe. She first studied in London at the Royal Ophthalmic Hospital, where women had just been admitted and the male students treated her agreeably. She also attended clinics in the Royal Free Hospital, London, and in Darmstadt, Germany, at the private clinic and sixty-bed hospital of Dr. Adolph Weber, an internationally known ophthalmologist.

Frances Dickinson, armed with organizational skills and an enthusiasm for causes, wholeheartedly entered her profession and the network of women professionals and clubwomen active in Chicago in the 1880s. When Dickinson joined the Chicago Woman's Club in 1886, she was sponsored by fellow doctors Sarah H. Stevenson and Lelia Bedell. In 1887, she and Dr. LUCY WAITE organized women doctors into the Illinois Medical Women's Sanitary Commission, which sent two of its members to Johnstown, Pennsylvania, to help the victims of the devastating flood that occurred in May 1889. In September 1887, Dickinson attended the ninth session of the prestigious International Medical Congress in Washington, D.C., where she was one of eleven female members in a previously all-male organization.

Dickinson, an early board member of the Protective Agency for Women and Children, became active during the 1880s in Ladies Federal Union 2703 and the Illinois Woman's Alliance, both founded by ELIZABETH MORGAN and CORINNE BROWN to agitate for improved working and living conditions for women and children. Dickinson, head of the Ward and Precinct Committee of the Illinois Woman's Alliance, envisioned women as a "vigilant committee" (*First Annual Report*,

27) in their wards, responsible for the inspection and enforcement of laws on sanitation and education.

By the 1890s, Dickinson, despite her frail appearance, was at the peak of her public and professional powers. She was a member of state, local, and national medical societies. She taught ophthalmology at the Chicago Post Graduate School of Medicine and was consulting oculist to the Erring Woman's Refuge and Mary Thompson Hospital. Most of the women doctors in Chicago referred their patients to her.

Because of her reputation as both a doctor and reformer, Dickinson was named in 1890 as one of nine local members of the Board of Lady Managers for the approaching World's Columbian Exposition. Although this board, headed by social leader BERTHA HONORÉ PALMER, was only to award prizes to articles produced by women workers, their plans soon escalated to include a separate woman's building at the fair for display of women's work. This plan was vehemently opposed by Frances Dickinson and the Queen Isabella Association which she, JULIA HOLMES SMITH, and CATHARINE WAITE had founded in 1889, for the purpose of erecting a statue of Queen Isabella and promoting the interests of women, especially wage-earners, at the fair. The mostly professional and business women of the Queen Isabella Association, who met at Dickinson's office, felt that competition for prizes should be on merit, that women's labor should compete equally with that of men and not be relegated to a sideshow.

The Isabellas, under suspicion of being prosuffrage and pro-Catholic, lost the argument over a separate building to Bertha Palmer and her supporters, who preferred to present womanhood as domestic, literary, cultured, and Protestant. Dickinson, fellow women doctors, and Corinne Brown responded by financing the construction of their own building—the Isabella Hotel and Club House—through a forty-five thousand dollar stock offering in their Physicians Publishing Company, incorporated in 1891.

Frances Dickinson also vehemently disagreed with President Bertha Palmer's decision to fire Phoebe Couzins, a lawyer, suffragist, and the duly elected secretary of the Board of Lady Managers, and to name an executive committee without consulting the board. Dickinson gained notoriety by angrily telling M. H. DeYoung, a fair official and prominent San Franciscan, that he had acted meanly in cutting off her objections in a public meeting.

After the fair, Dickinson combined her interests as a doctor and an educator by taking over Harvey Medical College, a struggling, coeducational, night medical school, incorporated in 1891. By 1895, the college was capitalized at fifty thousand dollars, with Dickinson as secretary and dean; she was designated president in 1902. For ten months each year, more than two hundred men and women attended Harvey medical school, where they participated in lectures and laboratory work for three hours each evening. The school also included a twenty-bed hospital, free dispensary, a training school for nurses, a "Dime Drug Store" (Dickinson, "History of Harvey Medical College," 495) and an outpatient clinic. Dickinson, who introduced embroidery to the surgical classes, recruited and retained respected and capable faculty, including a number of women.

By 1904, however, contemporary medical opinion, fueled by the American Medical Association's (AMA) campaign to regulate and control medical education, was running against evening and stockholder-owned medical schools. When the AMA began publishing statistics about graduates of medical schools, Harvey's record compared unfavorably with more established Chicago schools such as Northwestern University Medical School and Rush Medical College. Dickinson defended herself and her school at a Physician's Club meeting in December 1904, acknowledging that "medical education at night was a radical idea" (*Illinois Medical Journal*, January–June 1905) but that medical education should be available to all as a means of gaining social position and professional advantage. This argument did not succeed. Harvey Medical College graduated its last class in 1905.

The demise of the Harvey medical school was a turning point for Dickinson, who did not practice medicine or teach full-time in Chicago after 1907 or 1908. She moved to Orange City, Florida, where she lived from 1909 to about 1915. Dickinson never married, and she had a circle of close friends and family who visited her in Florida. The many cottages in Orange City, built by the Dickinson family after 1882, were available for Dickinson's vacationing friends from Chicago, including CATHARINE GOGGIN, of the Chicago Teacher's Federation, and Corinne Brown. Dickinson, who was called "Dr. Frances" or "Aunt Fan," was a local celebrity in Florida, where she edited a small newspaper, was active in the Village Improvement Association, and became a successful real estate agent. Dressed always in black, the diminutive but formidable figure traveled the back roads to provide medical care for poor black and white families.

Dickinson, who had always been close to her younger brother, Charles, sided with him in his extensive litigation with family members over control of the seed company. In 1911, she joined her brother as a trustee of the Chicago Academy of Sciences, where she served, usually as the only woman, until her death in 1945. She shared Charles Dickinson's enthusiasm for aviation and was not only a member of the Aero Club, which he organized, but gathered much publicity for herself in 1927 by taking a flight in an open cockpit plane in rough flying weather from Florida to Chicago. In the 1930s she purchased land in Florida, which she named the Betsy Ross Airport, for the use of women pilots.

From 1915 to the 1930s, Dickinson spent the summers in Chicago and the winters in Orange City. In 1914, Corinne Brown died, and Dickinson headed the memorial committee for the Chicago service. Two years later, Catharine Goggin died in a traffic accident. The deaths of these close friends and activist allies were significant losses for the aging but still vital Dickinson.

In 1923–24 Dickinson, who had been an early supporter of the National Woman Suffrage Association (and later, the National American Woman Suffrage Association) and the Chicago Political Equality League, a women's suffrage organization founded in 1894, served as the Illinois state chair for the National Woman's Party. Her task was to promote state legislation for women's equal rights by whatever strategies she and her coworkers could devise, including dropping leaflets over the city from an open cockpit plane commissioned by Dickinson and her brother. In her will, Dickinson left a small bequest to the party to support the Equal Rights Amendment before Congress. From the 1930s until her death, Frances Dickinson lived full-time in Orange City, Florida. She died of arteriosclerosis at age eighty-nine in Orange City, after an illness of five months. After cremation, her ashes were sent to the family plot in Rosehill Cemetery, Chicago. The last ten years of her life had been spent living on several small annuities and trying to sort out her own voluminous records and those of her brother Charles. Their papers, along with twelve cadavers, filled an entire warehouse in Chicago, and their co-mingled estates were not resolved until the 1950s.

Frances Dickinson was devoted to the idea that education and medical care should be available to all classes, and for a decade she owned and operated a coeducational night medical school. Throughout her life, she fearlessly walked into places previously unknown to women, using her fierce intellect, egalitarian beliefs, and her family's prosperity to break down economic, educational, and political barriers for Chicago's working and professional women.

Sources. CHS holds a variety of material on Dickinson, including records of the Board of Lady Managers, the Chicago Teacher's Federation, and the Aero Club. The Chicago Academy of Sciences has a Dickinson file. The Dickinson Memorial Library Association Archives, Orange City, Florida, have photographs and information on the Dickinson family, including the Village Improvement Association's *Our Story of Orange City, Florida, 1894–1966* (1966). Documents from the estates of Frances Dickinson, Charles Dickinson, Melissa Dickinson, and Albert Dickinson are at the Probate Court of Cook County, Daley Center, Chicago, Illinois. Both CHS and SL have records of the Queen Isabella Association. Illinois Woman's Alliance information, including the *First Annual Report* (1890), is in the Caroline Alden Huling Papers at UIC Spec. Coll. Corporate information on Harvey Medical College, the Illinois Woman's Alliance, the Queen Isabella Association, the Albert Dickinson Seed Company, and the Physician's Publishing Company is in the Corporate Department of the Secretary of State, Illinois State Archives, Springfield, Illinois. Information about Harvey Medical College can be found in the "Medical Education" and other articles in *Journal of the American Medical Association* for 1901–1905 and in Frances Dickinson's "History of Harvey Medical College," H. D. Cutler, ed., *Medical and Dental Colleges of the West* (1896). Dickinson's discussion at the Physician's Club is in *Illinois Medical Journal, Containing the Official Record of the Proceedings of the Illinois State Medical Society and the Papers Read at the Meeting at Rock Island, May 16, 17, 18, 1905,* January–June 1905. Biographical information is in the *McDonough Medical Directories* and in F. N. Sperry, comp., *A Group of Distinguished Physicians and Surgeons of Chicago* (1904).

JULIA WOOD KRAMER

DIECKMANN, ANNETTA MARIA
February 24, 1888–October 16, 1974
INDUSTRIAL REFORMER, WOMEN'S RIGHTS ADVOCATE,
CIVIL LIBERTIES ADVOCATE

Annetta Maria Dieckmann worked for nearly three quarters of a century educating people to improve their lives through the democratic process. She supported educational progress for working women and became a leader in advocating better work conditions for women.

Dieckmann was born in Titusville, Pennsylvania, to Henry and Louisa (Klipfel) Dieckmann. When her father, an Evangelical and Reformed minister, died in 1897, his wife had two young children to support. She studied and became an osteopathic doctor and subsequently practiced many years in her hometown, Buffalo, New York. After graduating from Masten Park High School in Buffalo, Annetta Dieckmann earned her A.B. degree from Cornell University in Ithaca, New York, in 1909; she was a member of Phi Beta Kappa.

With an initial motivation of helping her mother support the family, Dieckmann took her first position working in public welfare as an inspector for the New York Board of Charities from 1910 to 1915. Inspectors examined conditions in charitable institutions and made recommendations. This was an eye-opening experience for the young woman. Attending a dinner for social workers in Buffalo, she received inspiration when the speaker rejoiced that they were all "fortunate because their work called for them to make life more meaningful to other people" (Dieckmann speech, July 30, 1972). From 1915 to 1918, she was educational secretary of the Young Women's Christian Association (YWCA) in Honolulu, Hawaii. She left this position and returned to New York City in 1918 to work with the YWCA's Industrial Department and its first group of industrial secretaries, who were sent to assignments in the Middle Atlantic states. The Industrial Department of the YWCA grew out of the organization's Industrial Clubs, formed early in the twentieth century as a forum for working women to discuss wages, safety, and other concerns. The first industrial secretary of the National YWCA, Florence Simms, was a heroine of Dieckmann and started her on what she considered her real vocation in industry and the labor movement.

In an attempt to gain an understanding of society's role in these problems and to develop solutions, Dieckmann enrolled in the sociology department at Columbia University and completed a Master of Arts degree in 1923. In the early 1920s she wrote a seventy-six page paper, "The Effect of Common Interests on Race Relations in Certain Northern Cities," which included sections on the growing isolation of the races; the race riots of both East St. Louis, Illinois (1917), and Chicago (1918); racial policies of the American Federation of Labor and other labor unions; and the effect of industrial contacts between the races. Dieckmann and others observed that the violence against Blacks occurred where the migrations of Southerners to Northern cities in search of jobs in industries created new tensions. These strains in race relations were exacerbated after the return of soldiers at the end of World War I. Dieckmann came to believe that strong unions of black and white workers would protect both groups and that, with education, individuals would come to see their commonality more than their differences.

In 1928, Dieckmann moved to Chicago and began a twenty-year career as the YWCA's industrial secretary, directing the Industrial Department in its efforts to provide educational programs for working women. She agitated for women workers' interests, including wages, hours, and job security. Among many other accomplishments in this position, she developed programs for immigrant and unskilled women workers, which provided them strategies to improve their workplace situations. Most of the women were between eighteen and twenty-five years of age, had little formal education, and worked in factories, institutions, and as domestics in private homes. During these years she stopped thinking of herself as a social worker and identified herself instead as an "adult educationist" (Dieckmann speech, July 30, 1972).

In 1930, Dieckmann lobbied the Illinois General Assembly for the Eight Hour Day Bill and brought with her working women who testified for the need of this legislation and also for a minimum-wage law. As a result of these efforts and many others, the Chicago YWCA was recognized as a leader in the field of advocacy for women workers. Interested in expanding the limited list of occupations covered by the pathbreaking New Deal Social Security Act, Dieckmann studied unemployment insurance and started programs for young working women in Evanston, Illinois, initiating a voluntary agreement with employers to cover household workers in private homes.

Dieckmann's concern for working women included the African American community in Chicago as well as the white. During the 1930s, the South Parkway Branch of the Chicago YWCA, located on the South Side where a high concentration of Blacks lived in segregated, substandard housing, had programs for black female industrial workers. Dieckmann was credited "for the progressive stand the South Parkway YWCA was able to take on social and economic issues" (Bates, 268). Educational programs taught the women self-confidence and encouraged them to learn to speak up for themselves. During Dieckmann's years with the Chicago YWCA, the organization "supplemented its labor education program by selecting a few potential leaders each year and sending them to Bryn Mawr's integrated summer college for workers. A larger group attended summer camps in Wisconsin" (Bates, 269). When a group of African American women factory workers employed in a garment plant in Chicago organized and went on strike, Dieckmann supported them. "Although the Y's approach did not advocate joining any particular union" (Bates, 268), unionization was valued.

Upon her retirement from the Industrial Department of the YWCA in 1948, a tribute from the Industrial Committee stated, "She had built her own strength into the life of the Association [YWCA]. She has, for each of us, opened new vistas of understanding and new opportunities for service. She has shared with us her high concept of the role of the Industrial worker in the life of the Young Women's Christian Association" (*Newsreel*, January 12, 1948). During the 1930s and 1940s the rise of the Congress of Industrial Organizations (CIO) was steady, and this union made working-class women's concerns a primary focus. In 1949, the YWCA abolished its separate industrial women's assemblies. However, before unions spoke for workers and Social Security, the Industrial Departments of the YWCA performed a very important function for women workers, and Dieckmann was a significant leader.

Throughout her life Dieckmann had regular contact with her brother and his family of three daughters. She spent many Christmases with her mother and brother, opening cards from friends and acquaintances from all over the world. She had traveled extensively, and in Dieckmann's younger years, her mother, Louisa Dieckmann, went along on these trips. In later years, when her mother became disabled, Dieckmann cared for Louisa in her Chicago home until she died in 1944.

In 1948 Dieckmann became project director of the St. Louis (Missouri) Labor Education Project for the American Labor Education Service, a national organization that had functioned since 1928. It was the educational arm of the labor movement and its services were used by the American Federation of Labor (AFL), adult education groups, government agencies, and universities. Dieckmann produced "Report of the St. Louis Labor Education Project," which included the history and characteristics of St. Louis race relations and some recommendations to the city and the labor unions for using educational programs to prevent discriminatory attitudes and actions. The Democratic Rights of Members Committee evolved from this study, and the members resolved to educate the union members more fully about the benefits of not tolerating racial and ethnic discrimination. Dieckmann was lauded as a "pioneer in the labor education movement" ("St. Louis Loses Pioneer") when she left St. Louis in 1950.

From 1950 to 1952 she was the Labor Standards Investigator for the Illinois Department of Labor. Her article, "The Union Makes Use of the Social Scientist," published in 1952, summarized a study that dealt with the attitudes of union members about the intermixing of races. A sociologist, Arnold Rose, from Washington University in St. Louis, found that although officially the union was "color blind" (p. 343), it was the "*mores* of the community rather than the policies of the Union [that] so largely determine[d] the attitudes of the rank and file membership" (p. 343). This finding was a disappointment to union leaders, who had hoped that larger percentages of the members would have become friendlier and more accepting of Blacks.

After her official retirement, Dieckmann became a full-time volunteer for the American Civil Liberties Union (ACLU) in Chicago and was editor of their publication, *Brief*, from 1951 to 1961. She served on the Illinois Board of the ACLU from 1953 to 1974. One of her major accomplishments was the expansion of the organization in Illinois throughout the state by establishment of ACLU chapters outside the Chicago area. When the national director said that the Illinois ACLU was "statewide in name only" ("Freedom Fighters in the Heartland," 2), Dieckmann launched "Operation Downstate." Within months she and the new state director, John McKnight, had put together civil liberties chapter groups in Springfield, Peoria, Champaign-Urbana, and DeKalb-Sycamore. Her own pride in this achievement is reflected in her statement referring to the four new chapters, "Only a beginning. But what a promising beginning!" (quoted in "Freedom Fighters in the Heartland," 2). Later these chapters successfully defended Illinois against attempts by the state's General Assembly to pass "the infamous Broyles Bill that attempted to make McCarthyism the law of Illinois" (McKnight, "Remembering Annetta Dieckmann," 5) and replicate the kinds of activities generated by the House Un-American Activities Committee in Washington, D.C.

McKnight remembered her work on the Illinois ACLU education committee. "She was absolutely convinced that freedom of a people does not reside in the courts. She insisted that if freedom is not in the hearts and minds of the people, there is no law, no lawyer, and no court that can protect liberty. So it was that she committed herself to the civil liberties education of the citizens of Illinois" ("Remembering Annetta Dieckmann," 5).

Dieckmann was "the Illinois ACLU's most famous volunteer in the 1950's and 1960's" (p. 2).

In 1963, the United States Department of Labor gave Annetta Dieckmann a special award for her contributions to the education and welfare of working women. The Illinois chapter of the ACLU gives the Annetta Dieckmann Award to the volunteer who has done the most to advance civil liberties. Dieckmann was an active member of the University Church of the Disciples in Hyde Park beginning in 1926, when she had temporary work assignments in Chicago. She and another social activist, MARY HERRICK, cochaired the Social Action Committee for many years. Longtime friends, together Dieckmann and Herrick were fearless in attacking injustice. They even took on the Chicago Police Department in the 1960s and were responsible, in part, for a *Chicago Sun-Times* article that exposed the "Red Squad," a covert unit assigned to spy on "radicals" and "subversives" and gather intelligence on their activities. Dieckmann also worked for peace in Vietnam. When a new minister arrived at University Church in 1967, she summoned him to her house and wasted no time in asking him what he planned to do to end the Vietnam war. His immediate answer did not satisfy her, and she challenged him to do more.

Dieckmann lived in the Kenwood-Oakland area in Chicago for most of her life and had some involvement with the Kenwood-Oakland Community Organization (KOCO) of that neighborhood. Believing strongly in participatory democracy, she served as secretary for the Committee on Kenwood-Oakland for the Council of Hyde Park and Kenwood Churches and Synagogues in 1966. This committee reported on neighborhood developments, including opposition to new public housing projects because of preexisting overcrowding of schools and playgrounds and resulting segregation. The committee also dealt with welfare rights and other neighborhood concerns that were the result of a changing population.

Annetta Maria Dieckmann died at age eighty-six. Her memorial service was held at the University Church of the Disciples. She was cremated, and her ashes were placed in the Memorial Garden of the University Church with a plaque.

Her friends and fellow congregants had not waited until her death to commemorate her life. On June 19, 1973, the University Church of the Disciples honored Dieckmann by appointing her an honorary official board member. Charles H. Bayer, minister of the congregation, said Dieckmann was a person who "epitomized the real spirit of University Church. Her enveloping concern for what happens to human beings has put her life at the center of humanizing activities, yet with a broad theological impetus" ("The Minister's Moment"). He noted that one of her core characteristics was that she had not gotten "stuck years ago with a set of conclusions" but had remained "open to new truth, new perceptions, new theories, and new possibilities" ("The Minister's Moment").

Sources. The Annetta Dieckmann Collection, UIC Spec. Coll., has material documenting her years with the Young Women's Christian Association (YWCA), the Illinois chapter of the American Civil Liberties Union, and reports and articles by Dieckmann, including "The Effects of Common Interests on Race Relations in Certain Northern Cities" (c. 1920) and "Report of the St. Louis Labor Education Project" (April 1950). Charles H. Bayer, "The Minister's Moment," *Messenger,* June 19, 1973, is in the Dieckmann Collection. The Young Women's Christian Association Papers, UIC Spec. Coll., include newsletters about the industrial programs in which Dieckmann participated. Biographical information on Dieckmann is on file in the Division of Rare and Manuscript Collections, Cornell University Library, Ithaca, New York. The Church Archives, University Church of Disciples of Christ, Chicago, have material that includes an untitled speech delivered by Dieckmann July 30, 1972, at University Church. Eleanor Campbell taped the speech and it was transcribed and edited by Mary Herrick then given to Dieckmann's friends on the occasion of her eighty-fifth birthday. The speech is autobiographical and gives insights into her motivation for social activism. Annetta Dieckmann published "The Union Makes Use of the Social Scientist," *Journal of Educational Sociology,* February 1952. Articles written about Dieckmann include "St. Louis Loses Pioneer in Labor Education Movement: Miss Dieckmann Is Leaving," *Midwest Labor World,* April 26, 1950; and two articles from the Illinois ACLU newsletter, the *Brief:* John McKnight, "Remembering Annetta Dieckmann," November 1974; "Freedom Fighters in the Heartland," January–February 1984. Historian Carolyn De Swarte Gifford interviewed Charles Harvey and May Sweet Lord, longtime friends of Annetta Dieckmann, November 17, 1994. Melinda Kwedar interviewed Betty Jane Dieckmann, Dieckmann's niece, December 2, 1994. The Industrial Committees newsletter, *Newsreel,* describes Dieckmann's important achievement in "Editorial," January 12, 1948. Susan Lynn, *Progressive Women in Conservative Times* (1992), provides background for the YWCA's industrial work. Beth Tompkins Bates, "The Unfinished Task of Emancipation: Protest Politics Come of Age in Black Chicago, 1925–1943" (Ph.D. diss., Columbia Univ., 1997), describes Dieckmann's work with African American women workers in Chicago. Dieckmann's obituary appeared in the *Chicago Sun-Times,* October 18, 1974, and in the *CT,* October 18, 1974.

MELINDA KWEDAR

DILLING, ELIZABETH ELOISE KIRKPATRICK
April 19, 1894–April 29, 1966
WRITER, SPEAKER, ANTICOMMUNIST CRUSADER

During the 1930s and 1940s, Elizabeth Dilling led anticommunist, anti–New Deal, and anti-Semitic mass movements comprised of women. An isolationist, she inspired thousands of women to protest against American participation in World War II. Dilling was born in Chicago and spent her entire life there and in the North Shore suburbs of Kenilworth and Wilmette. She was the daughter of Dr. Lafayette Kirkpatrick, a surgeon, and Elizabeth (Harding) Kirkpatrick. Her father came from a family with English, Irish, Scottish, and French roots that had fled political persecution in Ireland to settle in Virginia in the 1800s. Her mother grew up in Ohio and moved to Chicago. Dilling had one brother, Lafayette, born in 1887, who became a wealthy realtor and world traveler before his death in 1948.

Her father died when she was six months old, and her mother supported the family by selling real estate. Dilling's early education was in private and parochial schools. She attended the Chicago Normal School and two other private secondary schools in Chicago, the Catholic Academy of Our Lady and the Starrett School for Girls, from which she graduated. In 1912 Dilling enrolled at the University of Chicago, where she studied music and French; she left school after three years without a degree. Dilling's ambition was to play the harp in a symphony orchestra. She studied under Walfried Singer, the Chicago Symphony Orchestra's harpist, and Alberto Salvi, an internationally known musician. As a girl she was an avid student of the Bible and sometimes wrote forty-page letters about the Scriptures to her friends. Although Dilling was raised an Episcopalian and remained one the rest of her life, she retained an affinity for Catholicism.

In the summer of 1917, Elizabeth met Albert Wallwick Dilling, a consulting engineer who was studying law in night school. Born in Salt Lake City, Utah, in 1892, Albert Dilling attended the Chicago–Kent College of Law in 1917 after earning an engineering degree at the Armour Institute of Technology (now Illinois Institute of Technology) in Chicago. After further study at the University of Chicago, he was admitted to the Illinois bar in 1917. The couple was married in a civil ceremony in LaPorte, Indiana, in May 1918, followed by an Episcopal service in Chicago three months later.

The Dillings bought a home in Wilmette and prospered. Albert obtained a position as the chief engineer of the Chicago Sewerage District, and Dilling inherited money from her mother and two aunts. Their son, Kirk, was born in 1920, followed by the birth of a daughter, Elizabeth Jane, in 1925. The Dillings shared political and religious beliefs, but their marriage was turbulent. In 1920 Dilling discovered that her husband was keeping a mistress, and he paid her one hundred thousand dollars not to divorce him. Albert later acquired two additional mistresses, and the Dillings twice separated in the late 1920s and early 1930s.

Before she took up anticommunism, Dilling's avocation was world travel. She and her family went abroad ten times between 1923 and 1939 to Europe, Asia, Africa, South and Central America, the Middle East, and the Caribbean. A trip to the Soviet Union with her husband in 1931 changed Dilling's life. The Soviet experiment with communism disgusted her as she saw impoverished people, begging children, wretched transportation, and official atheism. She was particularly repelled by antireligious museums established by the Soviet government.

When Dilling returned to Chicago, she began reading intensively about communism. She became a student of Iris McCord, who taught at the Moody Bible Institute and broadcast a radio program over station WMBJ in Chicago. Dilling began showing movies she had taken in the Soviet Union and speaking to many groups, including North Shore chapters of the American Legion and the Daughters of the American Revolution. Dilling developed a network of anticommunist friends, including Harry Jung, director of the American Vigilant Intelligence Federation in Chicago, and Nelson E. Hewitt, director of Chicago Advisory Associates, a clearinghouse that collected anticommunist material. She also developed a close relationship with Francis Ralston Welsh, an anticommunist Philadelphia businessman, and Colonel Edwin Marshall Hadley of Chicago. In 1932, Dilling and Hadley organized the Paul Reveres, an anticommunist organization headquartered in Chicago with local chapters in other major cities. It dissolved within a year but marked a major commitment by Dilling to crusade against communism.

The organization coincided with the beginning of Dilling's publishing career. In 1932 she wrote a series of articles on communism for a local newspaper, the *Wilmette Announcements*,

which were collected and published as a pamphlet, *Red Revolution: Do We Want It Here?* She warned that unless Americans returned to fundamental Christian principles, communism would take over the United States from within. Dilling's crusade soon evolved into a full-time job at which she worked from early morning until midnight seven days a week. She dropped all other activities and limited her friendships to other anticommunists. Cataloging every communist and procommunist organization in America became her mission. Ultimately she collected more that one hundred thousand file cards, each containing the name of a person or organization with procommunist affiliations. She also collected a voluminous library about politics, history, law, and Jews.

Early in 1933 Dilling began compiling a list of communists, anarchists, socialists, and pacifists whom she labeled as Reds. She intended to write a pamphlet, but it grew into a book that she published in 1934 as *The Red Network: A Who's Who and Handbook of Radicalism for Patriots*. More a compendium than a narrative, it accused some 460 organizations and more than 1,300 individuals of being Reds. Although Dilling's book was praised in the right-wing press and sold about 16,000 copies over the next ten years, it was considered unreliable by most reviewers.

Dilling became a vehement critic of President Franklin D. Roosevelt, whose New Deal she considered communistic. Two weeks before the presidential election of 1936 she published her second book, *The Roosevelt Red Record and Its Background*, which she claimed documented the communist connections of the president and prominent New Dealers. Like her first book, this compendium unfairly accused liberals and even some conservatives of being communists. It did not affect the presidential election and did not sell as well as *The Red Network*.

By 1936 Albert Dilling had given up his law practice to help his wife in her work, and the Dillings faced a financial crisis. Because she was losing money in her crusade, Dilling sought the financial support of wealthy businessmen who opposed communism. She also solicited small contributions from her readers and began charging fees for some of her talks. She received money from auto magnate Henry Ford; Henry B. Joy, a retired Detroit industrialist; and Dean Solenberger of Cleveland, whose company manufactured piston rings for automobiles.

In February 1938, Dilling founded the Patriotic Research Bureau to consolidate her activities. Employing several assistants, she published a monthly *Bulletin* and dozens of pamphlets and solicited contributions.

In the late 1930s Dilling became increasingly opposed to Roosevelt's foreign policies, which she blamed on a conspiracy of Jews, New Dealers, and communists. An anti-Semite from the beginning of her crusade against communism, by 1939 anti-Semitism was the primary focus of her energy. She believed Jews were slandering Adolph Hitler, who had done much good for Germany, and were seeking to involve the United States in a war against Germany to save European Jews. However, she did not believe Hitler intended to harm Jews, only to prevent them from dominating Germany. In 1939 Dilling traveled to Germany as the guest of the German government and was hosted by prominent Nazis. She returned to publish her third book, *The Octopus*, in 1940, concerned primarily with what she considered the

Jewish threat. Realizing the book would be considered anti-Semitic, she wrote it under the pseudonym of the Reverend Frank Woodruff Johnson. Dilling wrote that Jews stretched their tentacles into every corner of the American government and were the evil genius behind the New Deal.

From the beginning of World War II in Europe in September 1939 to the bombing of Pearl Harbor on December 7, 1941, Dilling devoted most of her energies to activities to keep the United States out of the war. She opposed the Roosevelt administration's repeal of the arms embargo, conscription, and aid to Britain. Dilling was anti-British as well as anti-Semitic. Furthermore, she believed the Soviet Union was the chief threat to world peace, not Germany. Dilling became one of the leaders of the mother's movement, consisting of a loosely knit network of organizations, such as We, the Mothers; Mobilize for America; and the National Blue Star Mothers, which attracted millions of women to the cause of maintaining American neutrality. The movement peaked in March 1941, when Dilling led six hundred women to Washington to demonstrate against passage of the Lend-Lease bill.

Dilling's continued opposition to the war after Pearl Harbor led to her indictment, along with other leaders of the isolationist right, for sedition in July 1942, and to two subsequent indictments. Her trial began in 1944, but a mistrial was declared when the presiding judge died. The case languished until 1947, when all charges were dismissed.

In 1943 Dilling and her husband were divorced. She initiated a divorce suit in 1942, and after a tumultuous trial, the couple reconciled. However, the following year her husband filed for divorce in Reno, Nevada, and Dilling did not contest it. The two remained friends, and their son practiced law with his father, who continued to represent his former wife in legal affairs.

In the postwar era Dilling never attained the prominence she had achieved in the 1930s and 1940s. Her research turned increasingly to anti-Semitism. Considering herself an expert on the Talmud, she also relied heavily on a notorious anti-Semitic forgery, *The Protocols of the Elders of Zion*, published in late-nineteenth-century czarist Russia.

In 1948 Dilling married Jeremiah Stokes of Salt Lake City, a Mormon elder, anti-Semite, and anticommunist, who died in 1954. That year she also published her last book, *The Plot against Christianity*, which purported, like *The Protocols of Zion*, to show that Jews intended to destroy Christianity and rule the world.

After Dilling's second husband died, she sold her home and lived with her son Kirk, who aided her research and writing. She was troubled by poor health but continued to do research and write until her death at seventy-two.

Dilling evolved from a suburban housewife to a crusading anticommunist to an anti-Semite. With her flaming red hair, spitfire speeches, and flamboyant personality, she took her place with Father Charles E. Coughlin and Gerald L. K. Smith as one of the demagogues of the 1930s. Women had been foot soldiers in the movements of far-right male leaders, but Dilling was one of the first women on the far right to command a movement of her own. Her books are still sold by bookstores catering to the far right.

Sources. Dilling's papers are at the School of Christian Liberty in Arlington Heights, Illinois. More than three thousand pages about Dilling are available from the Federal Bureau of Investigation under the Freedom of Information Act. Other material on Dilling is in the Gerald L. K. Smith papers and the Henry B. Joy papers at the Bentley Hist. Library, Univ. of Michigan. The Mothers of Minnesota Collection of the Jewish Community Relations Council papers at the Minnesota Hist. Soc., St. Paul, has extensive material on Dilling. The best sources for Dilling's beliefs are her own books: *The Red Network* (1934); *The Roosevelt Red Record* (1936); *The Octopus* (1940); and *The Plot against Christianity* (1954). Her career is well covered in contemporary newspapers, the *CT* and the *NYT*. Some material on Dilling can be found in John Roy Carlson (pseudonym for Arthur Derounian), *Under Cover* (1943), and Carlson (Derounian), *The Plotters* (1946). The best account of Dilling's career up to 1942 is Stasia Von Zwisler, "Elizabeth Dilling and the Rose-Colored Spyglass, 1931–1942," (master's thesis, Univ. of Wisconsin–Milwaukee, 1987). An account of Dilling's career in the context of the mother's movement is in Glen Jeansonne, *Women of the Far Right: The Mothers' Movement and World War II* (1996).

GLEN JEANSONNE

DOGGETT, KATE NEWELL
November 5, 1827–March 13, 1884
AMATEUR BOTANIST, LITERARY FIGURE, WOMEN'S RIGHTS ACTIVIST, SUFFRAGIST

Kate Newell Doggett was a leader in the post–Civil War women's rights movement, locally with MARY LIVERMORE and MYRA BRADWELL, nationally with Susan B. Anthony and Elizabeth Cady Stanton, and internationally with Jenny P. d'Héricourt and André Léo. In 1873 Kate Newell Doggett established the Fortnightly of Chicago, one of the earliest women's clubs in the United States. An ardent activist for women's equality whose arguments were based on women's natural rights, Doggett could claim leadership alongside Chicago's men of culture and learning as one of the founders of the Philosophical Society of Chicago and as the first woman elected to the city's Academy of Sciences.

Kate Newell was born in Charlotte, Vermont, to George and Caroline (Bradley) Newell. Her mother was a widow with two sons when she married George Newell. Kate Newell's father died when she was four years old, and her mother remarried three years later. At the age of seven, Kate moved with her mother and new stepfather to Cleveland, Ohio. Another daughter, Kate Newell's half-sister Mary, was born in Cleveland. Her mother's death when Kate Newell was twelve disrupted the young girl's life once more, and she was sent to live with relatives in Vermont, where she briefly attended a seminary in Castleton before enrolling at the Albany Female Academy in New York State. Although unfortunate in the loss of both parents at an early age, Kate Newell had the opportunity few young women in the nineteenth century experienced when she attended Albany Female Academy, one of the early institutions for women where, by the time of her enrollment, a rigorous curriculum was in place and a tradition had been established based on the belief that women's intellect was the equal of men's. Albany (later the Union School) was founded in 1814 and incorporated in 1821, thereafter becoming increasingly more rigorous in its curriculum; by 1825 girls were studying Latin as well as mathematics, natural science, philosophy and religion, and history. Graduating in 1845, Kate Newell had studied natural philosophy, ancient and modern geography, ancient and modern history, French and Latin, rhetoric and composition, algebra, botany, geometry, chemistry, trigonometry, natural philosophy, physics, geology, physiology, and astronomy, thus beginning her lifelong interest in the natural sciences and languages, in which she excelled.

Without parents or any inheritance, Kate Newell faced limited opportunities when she graduated. In 1845, writing her half-sister Mary, who had remained in Cleveland to marry businessman W. B. Castle, eighteen-year-old Newell described herself as an old maid with only two options, teaching or marriage, "and from the last-mentioned catastrophe preserve me until I am twenty-five at least" (quoted in Beadle, *Addendum*, n.p.). On August 12, 1846, one year later, however, she married William L. Horton. They settled in Malone, New York, just across the Vermont border, and a daughter Minnie was born in 1847. (She died in childhood, though the exact death date is unknown.) By 1850 the educated Kate Newell Horton complained to her half-sister about the dullness of life in Malone. Within two years the Horton marriage collapsed when William's adultery became known to Kate, who had been pregnant in 1851 or 1852 and had miscarried. Both husband and wife had complaints: he accusing his wife of using "means to rid herself" (*Addendum*, n.p.) of the pregnancy he had desired, she uncompromising in her refusal to reconcile after his infidelity. A witness to William Horton's adultery made it possible in 1853 for Kate Horton, after agreeing to relinquish any alimony claims, to obtain a divorce. Horton did not contest the divorce. At age twenty-six, she returned to Cleveland, where she lived with Mary and W. B. Castle and taught school until 1855, when she resettled in Chicago.

By 1857 she had opened Kate E. Newell's School in Chicago and met Chicagoan William E. Doggett, a well-to-do boot and shoe manufacturer and civic leader, whom she married February 22, 1858, in St. John's Episcopal Church in Cleveland. A son, George Newell Doggett, was born December 19, 1858. After his mother's death, George Doggett recalled that he never knew the name of her first husband and, in fact, knew of this marriage and the birth and death in infancy of her first child only from Kate Doggett's sister Mary. Few people in Chicago knew her history.

Kate Newell Doggett's marriage to the wealthy and cultured William Doggett gave her the security and support she needed to develop her intellectual interests. She pursued her own intellectual ambitions in the context of a heightened awareness within herself of the educational and legal disabilities faced by women. At every opportunity, Doggett attempted to establish her intellectual competence. For example, during the Civil War years, the Doggetts engaged in relief and pro-Union activities. She became known not for traditional female handicrafts, the kind many women produced and then donated to be auctioned at fairs for the Union cause, but for collections she put together that reflected her intellectual connections and scientific interests. She collected autographs of distinguished persons, including Edward Everett, Oliver Wendell Holmes, and Henry Wadsworth Longfellow, with whom she corresponded, and put them in an album, donating it to the Western Illinois Sanitary Fair, Quincy, Illinois, in 1864 to raise money in support of Union

troops. Continuing the interest in botany that had begun during her student years, she studied and collected flora, preparing an herb collection, labeled and mounted, that brought a substantial price at the second sanitary fair held in Chicago under the auspices of the Northwestern Sanitary Commission. Her husband was one of the original incorporators of the Chicago Academy of Sciences and a vice-president in 1864. She classified and arranged the academy's valuable collection of plant specimens but was not elected a member initially, waiting a full five years for that recognition.

The Doggett home became a favorite location for a literary and social crowd. There was, however, more on Kate Doggett's agenda than social entertainment. Her home became one of the leading private salons where women engaged freely and equally with men in intellectual dialogue at a time when Americans and Europeans were debating whether or not women were the intellectual equals of men. Among the Europeans who became frequent guests was "the French woman writer and medical practitioner, Jenny P. d'Héricourt, who published *La femme affranchie: réponse a MM. Michelet, Proudhon, E. de Girardin, A. Comte et aux autres novateurs modernes* [1860] . . . [which] soon appeared in English translation as *A Woman's Philosophy of Woman, or Woman Affranchised: An Answer to Michelet, Proudhon, Legouve, Comte, and Other Modern Innovators*" (Offen, 144). Doggett was "Héricourt's friend and apparent sponsor in Chicago" (Offen, 148, note 11). Héricourt came to Chicago around 1863 and met Doggett's circle, which included abolitionist Mary Livermore, who had come to Chicago in 1857 with her husband Daniel to publish the Unitarian-Universalist weekly *New Covenant*. (Livermore founded the *Agitator* in 1869 and Doggett became a correspondent for it.) Kate Doggett's gatherings included men and women who looked to her for intellectual leadership as she held readings of Molière, Jean Racine, Voltaire, and other French classics, staged plays by Alfred de Musset, and regularly ran Saturday night theatricals with plays in Spanish, Italian, French, or German, but never in English. During one season men and women met at Kate Doggett's to read the works of Dante Alighieri in the original Italian.

Doggett asserted woman's moral and intellectual equality with men and advocated that women take every opportunity to study the sciences and the humanities. In fact, Chicago women were enlarging their scope of study in the 1860s. Doggett publicized such activities in the *Agitator*; she described botany and physiology classes attended by women. One particular male teacher, Dr. Gatchell, a professor of the Hahnemann Medical College, advocated women's admission to medical schools. Doggett argued for women's admission into all-male medical colleges and opposed the creation of women's medical schools. In an address to the American Institute of Homeopathy, which met in Chicago in June 1869, Doggett criticized male homeopaths who thought they could solve the demands of women to become members of homeopathic institutes and to enter medical schools by the creation of separate female facilities and societies. "Now is it not passing strange," she told them, "that men writhing under the obloquy which, as we all remember, attached to the name of homeopath, smarting under the discourtesy of the old-school in refusing to meet them upon terms of equality, feeling the injustice of having been excluded from the army because of their medical faith, should, in the same breath in which they give thanks for 'the first legal recognition of their [homeopathic] school . . .' deliberately give their votes for the exclusion of another class from the rights they had just conquered for themselves?" ("Homeopathy and Woman," 1).

Kate Doggett's reputation as an enlightened, knowledgeable advocate of modern education for women as well as men brought her into contact with a circle of Americans, including Massachusetts educator Horace Mann and his wife, who were advising the government of Argentina on plans for a public school system in that country. The Argentinean minister of education, Domingo Faustino Sarmiento, consulted with Kate Doggett in Chicago and maintained a correspondence with her from 1866 to 1868. He wrote Mrs. Horace Mann enthusiastically about Doggett's circle. Doggett recommended American teachers of high quality for Argentina's new schools.

Interested in educational and cultural affairs as well as in botany, Doggett participated in a variety of enterprises, including her appointment, as the only woman, to the Board of Examiners for the Chicago High School, the city's only secondary school in 1869. She fought for equal pay for women teachers in the high school, writing for the *Agitator* about the "worst instance" (June 19, 1869, 8) of discrimination in the matter of wages. Attending the high school graduation in 1869, Doggett commented on the injustice to the girl graduates who, even from the richest families, would not be encouraged to continue their education: "They have not learned enough of any science to fathom the mysteries unaided, they have not learned enough of any language to conquer its difficulties and, unless endowed with more decided tastes and more perseverance than usually characterizes sixteen or eighteen years, they will not get far from their present intellectual position" (*Agitator*, July 10, 1869, 1). Boys, on the other hand, were encouraged to attend colleges and professional schools, to specialize in a single branch of education, and to be instructed by experts. That same year she became the only female member of the Chicago Academy of Sciences.

After the war, Doggett continued to associate with women who became leaders in Chicago's women's rights movement of the late 1860s, including Mary Livermore and Myra Bradwell. It was a heady environment, filled with talk about efforts by women to break the educational barriers constraining them from entering colleges and professional schools. In 1868 she joined them in establishing a Chicago branch of Sorosis, a women's literary club. Only two months earlier, the New York Sorosis held its first regular meeting. The New England Women's Club's first meeting was also held only a few weeks before the Chicago group met. Stimulated by the expansion of women's benevolent work during the Civil War and energized by Reconstruction debates about citizenship, women had resumed their demands for equal rights and the vote, initially voiced in the Seneca Falls Platform of 1848. From the beginning, women's rights were a major topic of discussion among the Chicago Sorosis members, and the women planned for a major suffrage convention to be held in the midwest city.

Late in 1868 a dispute over organizational matters precipitated a split that led to the formation of two separate suffrage groups in Chicago. Doggett remained with Livermore and Bradwell and established the Illinois Woman Suffrage Associa-

tion. They planned the Chicago suffrage convention held February 11 and 12, 1869, to coincide with the Illinois State Constitutional Convention. Elizabeth Cady Stanton and Susan B. Anthony were the major speakers. The *Revolution*, February 25, 1869, described the leading women at the February convention, including Doggett, "a fine French and German scholar," who has the "reputation of being the best botanist in Chicago" (p. 116); Mrs. Willard of Chicago, the author of *Sexology*, "a book which is praised and vilified about equally" (p. 116); Myra Bradwell, "the bright and pretty editor of the Chicago *Legal News*, whose admission to the bar as a practitioner of law, one of these not far-off days, will throw the legal community into a catalepsy of astonishment for a time" (p. 116); CATHARINE WAITE, "the author of the *Mormon Prophet*, a book which was the outcome of her observation and experience in Utah, during the five years her husband was governor of that territory" (p. 116); the Reverend AUGUSTA CHAPIN, "who in ten years has worked her way noiselessly from an obscure little [Unitarian-Universalist] parish in Northern Michigan, to the pastorate of the Milwaukee Society, who pay her a salary of $2,000 as they would a man. All these and many more, of whom time fails us to tell, threw their strength into the Convention, and made it a success" (p. 116). The other suffrage group held its convention simultaneously in Chicago and formed the Universal Suffrage Association of the State of Illinois, an organization that lasted only one year.

At the convention, Myra Bradwell's husband, Judge James Bradwell, introduced a resolution that a committee of three men and three women be appointed to visit Springfield, Illinois, to lobby for legislation to reform the laws pertaining to women's right of property and control or custody of their children. He reminded the convention, "If a wife dies, possessing property in her own right, the husband has a life interest in the whole. If a husband dies, the wife has an interest in one-third only. If the wife is independent and earns her living, the husband can garnishee and rob her of all her lawful wages" (*Revolution*, February 25, 1869, 113). The resolution carried and Judge Bradwell, Kate Doggett, Myra Bradwell, Rev. E. J. Goodspeed, Judge C. B. Waite, and Rebecca Mott were appointed the lobbying committee.

During the convention Susan B. Anthony introduced what would soon become a divisive element in the woman suffrage movement—criticism of the Fifteenth Amendment. "The new amendment of the Constitution of the United States was a mistake," Anthony contended, "as it did not include Woman Suffrage"; and she "hoped that the Convention would speak in thunder tones to the legislatures of the Northwest" (*Revolution*, February 25, 1869, 113) in criticism of it. By summer, Stanton and Anthony formed the National Suffrage Association, and in opposition, Lucy Stone created the American Woman Suffrage Association. The second Chicago convention, planned for September 1869, with Livermore, Bradwell, and Doggett organizing the troops, contended with the fallout from the national split. Doggett found herself in the middle because she had arranged for Anthony to be her house guest in September and also, at the request of Livermore, traveled to Boston to urge Lucy Stone to come to Chicago and share the platform with her opponent. Doggett was successful, and all the national leaders shared the platform September 9 and 10, 1869, at the Western Female Suffrage convention. She served as treasurer of the meeting. Aware of the discord between the two factions, Doggett had offered a simple resolution in favor of passage of the proposed Sixteenth Amendment enfranchising women without reference to the Fifteenth Amendment already a part of the U.S. Constitution. The Lucy Stone faction attempted to pass a resolution offered by Henry Blackwell, that "rejoice[d] in the extension of the franchise to classes hitherto excluded from political power . . . whether based upon property, nativity, color, race or sex" (*Agitator*, September 18, 1869, 5)—in essence an endorsement of the Fifteenth Amendment. Casting a wide net, Susan B. Anthony and her supporters opposed the resolution, contending that the only question for the convention was "Woman Suffrage, and Woman Suffrage alone" (p. 5). Stone contended that Anthony "was at war" with those who favored "the enfranchisement of the blacks" (p. 5). Kate Doggett, acting as mediator, argued that it was unnecessary to vote a specific resolution in favor of the Fifteenth Amendment, since western women had already opposed "resolutions offered . . . at the [February 1869] Chicago Convention, by Mrs. Stanton and Miss Anthony" against the Fifteen Amendment. Stanton and Anthony "were compelled by the pressure to withdraw them," Doggett reported. "Western women stood firmly for the Fifteenth Amendment" (p. 5). Not persuaded, the convention reconsidered the Blackwell resolution, and, when put to the vote, it passed.

Doggett fully endorsed all the resolutions that advocated the vote for women and the full extension of equal rights to the female sex. She joined Livermore in staffing the new suffrage paper published in Chicago, the *Agitator*, and at the September convention was appointed a delegate to the Women's Industrial Congress in Berlin, Germany. Filled with enthusiasm for equal rights for women, Doggett was critical of some delegates to the Berlin meeting who defined the work that women did as "woman's work," and the way that speakers promoted a separate "woman's sphere" and supported a "woman's culture" (Doggett "Letter," *Agitator*, November 1869, 4) with separate schools for women and even women's savings banks. Doggett argued that European women were spending too much time and resources in creating separate institutions and should, instead, fight to open the doors of those already established. Women were too fearful of men's criticisms. "They do not accept the idea that the real question is not what men wish women to do and be, but what women themselves wish to do and be" (Doggett "Letter," *Agitator*, November 1869, 4), she wrote from Berlin. Doggett rejected arguments of women's moral superiority and women's different nature also being put forward by men and women in America and in Europe. Only by asserting women's natural right to equal treatment under the law and by arguing that women had the same intellectual potential as men would there be any progress or advancement for females. Remaining in Europe after the Berlin meeting, Doggett met with French feminist André Léo (Léodile Béra), author of *La femme et les moeurs, liberté ou monarchie*, and she "translated parts of . . . [the] book for *The Agitator* and for *The Revolution*" (Offen, 148, note 11). It was during this trip to Europe that Doggett attended André Léo's salon.

Doggett's thinking on the woman question came from her reading of eighteenth- and nineteenth-century women feminists, including Mary Wollstonecraft, Margaret Fuller, André Léo, and Jenny P. d'Héricourt, as well as her contemporaries in the woman's movement in the United States. In Paris in the 1860s she had been impressed with the salon idea as developed by Mme. de Rambouillet. Doggett's knowledge of classical texts and the history of ancient civilizations was substantial. She searched for information about women intellectuals in past times, including Artemis and Aspasia. She also absorbed information about other cultures and the roles of women in non-Western societies from frequent travels abroad, especially after her husband was appointed "Consul de La Sublime Porte a Chicago" to Turkey from 1866 to 1875. The Doggetts traveled extensively in Europe and the Ottoman Empire and also spent time in Havana, Cuba. While in Cuba she observed the struggle for independence from Spain. Sporadic revolts increased in number in the nineteenth century, and civil war broke out in 1868, beginning a Ten Years' War that brought death to more than two hundred thousand Cubans and Spaniards. Although there was agitation in the United States for intervention in the struggle on behalf of the Cubans, the movement was unsuccessful. In the April 17, 1869, edition of the *Agitator*, Doggett appealed to American women to support the Cuban revolution against Spain and published a letter from Cuban women to "the Ladies of the United States" which begged that "the American ladies, using their well-known and powerful moral influence with the people of the United States, may obtain from the new President Grant . . . the recognition of General Cespedes, and the Cubans . . ." (p. 2).

In the United States the Doggetts traveled frequently to Washington, D.C., and also in Florida, establishing a vacation home in Palatka, just north of Gainesville. The Doggetts had been in England in October 1871; their house was not damaged by the Great Fire, but the Doggett warehouse and its entire inventory went up in smoke, at a loss of one hundred fifty thousand dollars.

Back in Chicago, Doggett taught a course in botany at the old University of Chicago in 1872–73. (The old or first effort to establish a University of Chicago began in 1856 and the school closed in 1890.) She wrote a book review of George Sand's *M. Sylvestre*, did some translation from the Greek of the pre-Socratic philosopher Heraclitus, made some notes on her thoughts about Plato's philosophy, and wrote an essay on the philosophy of history. But she craved social intercourse with others. Marginalized and doing their mental work outside the academic world, women intellectuals like Doggett needed more permanent organizations for their intellectual activities and advancement. Doggett joined the Association for the Advancement of Women (AAW), established in 1872. Years later at an AAW congress, she commented about those who could not understand why women were not content with quiet labor "each in her own household, or, at most, each in her own neighborhood." She retorted with sarcasm, "There has existed for several years a 'National butter and egg Association,' perhaps it is not . . . vanity to think women and their needs of as much consequence" ("Association for the Advancement of Women Address," Fortnightly Papers). Her friend Mary Livermore had instigated the group's formation and was its first president, followed by Maria

Mitchell, the astronomer. AAW held annual congresses with programs that covered a wide range of subjects including literature, art, and philanthropy, as well as suffrage and allied topics.

Doggett required more than the annual AAW meetings could provide. One year after AAW's founding, Doggett sent invitations to women friends and associates to attend a meeting at her home "for an hour's talk of a project that greatly interest[ed] . . . [her]," but, as she put it, "ha[d] no connections with flannel for the Fiji-islanders" (Doggett invitation, May 14, 1873, Fortnightly Papers). Determined to distinguish this society from the benevolent Christian missionary groups to which women were ordinarily relegated, Doggett and the eleven women who attended began a different kind of project. It would be more like a salon, the kind Doggett had visited in Paris and had imagined when she read about Aspasia's salon in ancient Greece. Amelia Gere Mason described the first years as devoted to "enlarging the mental horizon as well as the knowledge of women" ("A Glimpse of Mrs. Doggett and Her Work," 12, Fortnightly Papers). Doggett wanted to cultivate a place of social space where privileged women would be prevented from simply being "society" leaders without any incentive to study and to think about social conditions but men were not initially excluded. They were called upon to read and to speak, as well as to listen, with the other members. Doggett served as president for seven years. Her goal was to have members whose abilities were varied. "Not only were there to be literary women, but women of forceful and executive power, women who could plan and carry to complete success, civic entertainments" (Emily McVeagh, Members' Memories, Thirtieth Anniversary, 21–22, Fortnightly Papers). It was to be a "powerful Salon," a place where "everything worth knowing" could be talked about, and "everybody worth hearing" (p. 23) could find an intelligent and sympathetic audience.

The same year that Doggett called together the Fortnightly, she had a leading role, serving as a vice-president, in the newly organized association in Chicago where men and women engaged in lively and controversial dialogue on intellectual issues, the Philosophical Society of Chicago. Women activists including Unitarian minister CELIA WOOLLEY, physicians JULIA HOLMES SMITH and SARAH HACKETT STEVENSON, and the head of the Chicago Bible School, EMMA DRYER, participated. Among the men were ministers Edward Beecher, Robert Collyer, David Swing, H. W. Thomas, and C. H. Fowler—all of a liberal brand of Christianity. Pro-suffragist Judge C. B. Waite and Liberal-Reform Rabbi Bernard Felsenthal were also active. The group, on the whole, advocated women's rights. Kate Doggett's paper, "The Position of Women under Other Religious Systems and under Our Own as Indicated by the Sacred Books and Mythologies," was given special attention by conservative clergy who thought she ought to be excluded from public debates because she was so "malignant [an] assailant of Christianity" (Rev. George Clement Noyes, Letter to Dr. Samuel Willard, February 25, 1879, Samuel Willard Papers). Doggett gave her paper on numerous occasions from 1875 to 1879. In it Doggett blamed religion for many of the crimes that "disgraced humanity" and, specifically, for "the subjugation of women" ("The Position of Women . . . " November 26, 1875, Fortnightly Papers). In words that would be echoed by many

of the contributors to Elizabeth Cady Stanton's *The Woman's Bible* more than a decade later, Doggett argued that men, not any divinity, usurped power and assigned duties to women. Men had manipulated religion for their own power and, in the process, distorted Christianity's original message, the early respect paid women.

Doggett continued her own intellectual projects; she translated Alexander Blanc's *Grammar of Painting and Engraving* (1874) from the French, winning the five hundred dollar prize offered by the publisher for the translation. The same year the book was published, Doggett took to the lecture circuit, offering talks on art, history, women's issues, and her controversial critique of patriarchal Christianity. She spoke at the Philosophical Society of Chicago; the Christian Union; the Woman's College of Evanston; Ferry Hall, Lake Forest; and St. Mary's Academy, Indiana. The last three were women's schools.

William Doggett died April 3, 1876, at the Doggetts' home in Palatka. Kate Doggett's closest friends agreed that the loss was great. ELLEN HENROTIN remarked that "when Mr. Doggett died she lost the main spring of her life" (Members' Memories, Thirtieth Anniversary, 30–31, Fortnightly Papers.) In part the general impression that she was now more vulnerable came from the realities of her financial situation after her husband's death. With her second marriage to a wealthy and generous man who shared her viewpoints, she had achieved great freedom as an intellectual, but she remained in a state of financial dependency. After his death, still not capable of earning her own living, she depended on her husband's estate, but when creditors sued for payment of money owed them and other legal entanglements held up the dispersal of funds, Kate Doggett faced immediate financial insolvency and years of legal red tape.

From 1878 to 1881, when Kate Doggett left Chicago to live in Havana, Cuba, she devoted herself to the AAW, serving as president during those three years, and to her lecture circuit. At the same time she continued to cope with a multitude of legal and financial problems. Doggett told the AAW in 1879 at the organization's sixth congress that "[a] few days ago I asked a lawyer who assured me a woman had no right to the smallest part of her maintenance from her husband's estate till it was entirely settled, what widows should do" ("Association for the Advancement of Women Address," c. 1879, n.p., Fortnightly Papers). His reply was that such a woman should "keep boarders or teach school." All the legal reforms for which she had fought had not addressed adequately or fully the continuing oppression of women and their economic dependence. Her own experience as a widow entangled in a legal web awakened her to a deeper understanding of the needs of her own sex, the majority of whom were close to poverty should a husband or father die. She urged the AAW "to develop a definite plan of work . . . to redress the sorrowing and the suffering experienced by women" ("Association for the Advancement of Women Address").

In 1882, Kate Doggett attended the American Association for the Advancement of Science's annual meeting in Montreal. Two years later, her health failing and probably suffering from tuberculosis, she told her friend Ellen Henrotin that she wanted to return to Havana, Cuba, where she and her husband had spent some wonderful times. "She would never come back," she told Henrotin, "and . . . she wanted to be buried where she died, in the southern country among the beautiful flowers" (Members' Memoirs, Thirtieth Anniversary, 32, Fortnightly Papers).

Worn out from endless legal battles concerning the Doggett estate, Kate Doggett traveled with her son George to Havana in January 1884 and died there two months later at age fifty-seven. She was buried there. At the time, the Cuban authorities reserved the right to open a grave at the end of ten years and place thereon another body. Some time before 1894, the widow of her son traveled to Havana and brought Kate Doggett's remains back to Chicago, where they were re-interred in a permanent grave in Oak Woods Cemetery. The Fortnightly attended the service in a body.

"I remember one day [Kate Doggett] came in from a wedding, dressed in a beautiful gown, and she changed this for a short cloth dress," Fortnightly member Mary Matz wrote, recalling a visit to the Doggett's home. Matz remembered how Doggett proclaimed, "'Now I feel myself again; I am the teacher; I am going to the University; that is where I belong'" (Members' Memoirs, 35, Fortnightly Papers). Her Fortnightly colleagues knew that Doggett enjoyed her brief interlude as a botany professor at the old University of Chicago more than any other achievement. In the classroom she was a useful intellect, an example that women were inherently the intellectual equals of men.

Kate Doggett did not choose to limit her activities to the sphere of women's culture emerging after the Civil War. Her feminism was grounded in natural rights theory and was enriched by the literary and philosophical writings of European feminists as well as the ideas of the women's movement of her own country. Initially, she viewed Chicago, a raw midwest commercial center hankering after culture and refinement, as ripe for her activities. She hoped to demonstrate the value of establishing Paris-like salons in the young city so that an environment for radical ideas about the role of women in society could evolve and influence the newly rich entrepreneurs and their wives—the leading citizens—to take up the challenge of advancing the cause of women's education and equality of opportunity. With time, however, Doggett's feminism developed a sharp edge, the result of her personal experiences with the reality of a woman's legal, social, and economic disabilities. She realized that even a woman of privilege needed the strength of sisterhood in a patriarchal world.

Sources. The Fortnightly Papers are at the NL and hold Kate Doggett's two Letter Books (1869–70) containing letters Doggett wrote about her travels in Europe; book reviews, including one written in French reviewing George Sand's M. Sylvestre, January 20–February 2, 1872; some untitled and undated notes on Greek philosophy; a translation by Thomas Davidson of a stanza from Herakleitas [sic]; "History," n.d.; an undated, untitled essay on art and artists; eight copy books with lectures on art and culture; her handwritten manuscripts, including "Aspasia," February 27, 1874; "Notes for Short Talk at First Annual Meeting of the Fortnightly," June 5, 1874; "Margaret Fuller Ossoli, Her Precursors, What Influence Has She Exerted upon the Thought of Her Time. One of her Precursors Mary Wollstonecraft," January 8, 1875; "Association for the Advancement of Women Address," c. 1879 (Sixth Congress of the Association for the Advancement of Women, 1879); "The Position of Women under Other Religious Systems and under Our Own as Indicated by the Sacred Books and Mythologies," November 26, 1875. Ma-

terials in the Fortnightly Papers that concern the early years of the group are Kate Doggett's original invitation to founding members, May 14, 1873, and members' remembrances of Doggett, including Ellen Henrotin, Emily McVeagh, Ellen Martin, Amelia Gere Mason, Mary L. Matz; "Addresses"; Members' Memoirs of Mrs. Doggett; all given at the Celebration of the 30th Anniversary of the Fortnightly of Chicago, June 4, 1903. Anita S. Darrow's talk, "Digging for Doggett's," Presentation to the Winnetka, Illinois, Fortnightly, 1974, representing Darrow's research into the pre-Chicago years of Kate Doggett's life, was also given at the Fortnightly, Chicago, in 1974, and reread at the 115th Anniversary, Fortnightly, April 1989. There is also a copy of Muriel Beadle, Addendum to 'The Fortnightly of Chicago'; May, 1975, a printed brochure that draws on the research by Darrow on Doggett's early years to correct the biographical material that appeared in Beadle's history of the organization published in 1973. The CHS has the William E. Doggett Papers, describing his activities as consul to Turkey; the Doggett File in the Clipping Files, largely about W. E.; several letters of Domingo F. Sarmiento, Minister of Education, Argentina, to Mrs. Horace Mann, March 9, 1868–August 6, 1868, discussing his meetings with Kate Doggett in Chicago, are in the Herma N. Clark Papers, CHS. Rev. George Clement Noyes, Letter to Dr. Samuel Willard, February 25, 1879, Samuel Willard Papers, CHS, is critical of Doggett's position on Christianity. Printed material from the Philosophical Society of Chicago can be found in the Miscellaneous Pamphlets Collection, CHS. The William E. Doggett Estate Probate Papers are at Probate Court of Cook County Records, Chicago. Kate Doggett's published essays, articles, and letters to the editor are in women's rights journals, including "Homeopathy and Woman," June 19, 1869; Doggett "Letters," October 13, 1869, November 1869a, November 1869b, January 1870, in the Agitator, and others sporadically from April 1869 to November 1, 1869; letters and articles January 8, 1870–March 5, 1870, Woman's Journal. Articles about Doggett and the woman suffrage movement in Chicago include February 25, 1869, Revolution; June 19, 1869, July 10, 1869, September 18, 1869, April 17, 1869, Agitator. Aside from the Addendum mentioned above, biographical information about Doggett is in D. B. Cooke & Co., Directory of Chicago (1858); Samuel Bradlee Doggett, A History of the Doggett-Daggett Family (1894); Marriage License of Wm. E. Doggett and Miss Kate E. Newell, Cuyahoga County Probate Court, Cleveland, Ohio. There is a biography of Kate Doggett in Appletons' Cyclopaedia of American Biography, vol. 2 (1888), ed. James Grant Wilson and John Fiske. Louis A. Haselmayer, "The Doggett-Crane Manuscript Album," Annals of Iowa, Spring 1960, discusses Doggett's contributions to the U.S. Sanitary Commission fairs. John T. McClintock, "Albany and Its Early Nineteenth-Century Schools," A Research Report for Dr. Robert L. Church, Harvard University Graduate School of Education, Summer 1967, and Albany Female Academy, Circular and Catalogue, 1845 (1845), describe the school Doggett attended and the curriculum she studied. William Kerr Higley, Historical Sketch of the Academy (Chicago Academy of Sciences, Special Publication no. 1, January 1, 1902) and Historical Sketch of the Chicago Academy of Sciences . . . Lists of Officers and Members (1877) are printed materials available in the NL. See Muriel Beadle, The Fortnightly of Chicago: The City and Its Women, 1873–1973 (1973) for a history of the association. An important article documenting the relationship of French feminist Jenny P. d'Héricourt with American women including Kate Doggett is Karen Offen, "A Nineteenth-Century French Feminist Rediscovered: Jenny P. D'Héricourt, 1809–1875," Signs, vol. 13, 1987. Lucie Manoussoff, "Inalienable Right: Kate Newell Doggett, Natural Rights Feminist," Associated Colleges of the Midwest/GCLA Seminar in the Humanities, manuscript, 1993, NL, is based on materials in the Fortnightly Papers. Obituaries for Doggett are in the Inter-Ocean, March 29, 1884, and the CT, March 29, 1884.

RIMA LUNIN SCHULTZ

DRYER, EMMA
1835–April 16, 1925

RELIGIOUS EDUCATOR, CHARITY WORKER, BIBLE INSTITUTE
FOUNDER

Emma Dryer was the daughter of John M. and Lucinda Dryer of Victor, New York. She graduated in 1858 from Ingham University at Le Roy, New York, a women's college affiliated with the Presbyterian Church. There she taught astronomy and mathematics for two years before moving to Knoxville, Illinois, to become principal of the recently chartered Ewing Female University (later St. Mary's School). From there, in 1864, she took the position of preceptress at the Illinois State Normal University (now Illinois State University) in Bloomington, where she stayed until 1870. Upon resigning her position at the Normal school, Dryer moved to Chicago to undertake benevolent work among "wayward" or "fallen" women, often unmarried and pregnant or working as prostitutes. Boarding in a private home, she attended religious services at the Illinois Street Church founded by Dwight L. Moody, and there she met the pastor, Reverend William J. Erdman, who converted her to dispensational premillennialism.

Dispensational premillennialism became an important movement within evangelical Protestantism in the United States. In the 1870s dispensational premillennialism was introduced to American Protestantism via the works and ministry of John Nelson Darby. Believing that the second coming of Jesus Christ would occur before Christ reigned on earth for one thousand years, dispensational premillennialists were conservative, placing a high value on biblical scripture, evangelism, and missionary work. Dispensational premillennialism quickly spread into conservative Evangelicalism in the 1870s and the 1880s through the Bible conference movement, Bible institutes, journals, and the Scofield Bible. Bible conferences were two-week sessions held in resort settings where evangelicals gathered to ruminate on the Bible. The dispensational premillennialists showed up at the prototype conference at Niagara Falls in 1876, and Erdman himself was one of the conference organizers. Subsequently, dispensational premillennialists promoted Bible institutes to which laymen and clergy alike could come for practical training in Christian work. Emma Dryer may have been attracted by dispensational premillennialism's focus on evangelism and missionary work.

After the Chicago Fire of 1871, Dryer helped with victim relief while conducting Bible work for members of the Illinois Street Church—the building having been destroyed by the fire—and, on weekdays, holding mothers' meetings and sewing schools for girls. To make ends meet in 1872, she also worked as an agent of the *Christian Union* magazine, and the following year, she was the secretary for the Woman's Aid Association. By 1873, one of Dryer's workers, Ella Stevens, was able to write that she had 123 students in her infant Sabbath school class plus 100 girls enrolled in sewing classes. In the afternoons, these missionaries visited neighborhood families to find out how they lived and what could be done to make their lives more cheerful. In May 1873, the Chicago Avenue Church, which had replaced the Illinois Street Church, hired Dryer as a teacher and superintendent for its Bible school. Called the Bible Work of Chicago

(BWC), by 1876 her school was a successful operation supported entirely by voluntary contributions.

The Chicago Bible Society (CBS), a branch of the American Bible Society, was responsible for the day-to-day operations of the BWC. An interdenominational Protestant organization, the CBS supplied Bibles to mission Sunday schools, public schools, hotels, jails, poorhouses, steam and sailing vessels, railroad depots, soldiers, and the poor and destitute of every class, color or language. Dryer's BWC was responsible for educating and maintaining CBS's Chicago missionaries. The BWC's constitution included terms regarding the prayerful reading and study of the Holy Scriptures with individuals in their homes and through cottage meetings. Such visits and meetings were to be conducted by persons trained specifically for such work. Dryer's field assignments included the downtown Young Men's Christian Association (YMCA) and the neighborhoods of Near West Side Chicago, the area west of the Chicago River that included the Haymarket area of industrial plants and workers' housing and a previously upper-class residential area known as Union Park.

While Dryer worked with the CBS, she also maintained a close association with Dwight L. Moody. A New Englander by birth, Moody had come to Chicago in 1856 to work as a shoe salesman for Charles E. Wiswall and in four years was a prosperous businessman in the boot and shoe industry in the Midwest, acquainted with successful entrepreneurs and industrialists. In his spare time, he joined the YMCA and conducted a street ministry in the slums, which soon turned into a very successful Sunday school. In 1864 Moody had founded the Illinois Street Church. He recruited Emma Dryer to run the Bible Work at his church and, it appears, she anticipated having a significant role in developing a full-fledged Bible workers' training institute. Moody's career as a revivalist took off, however; Dryer, determined to found Moody's and her training school, continued to make plans.

Committed to developing the Bible Work of Chicago into a comprehensive Bible institute or college, in 1876 Dryer traveled to New York City, where Moody was appearing at the Hippodrome, to further her case for the establishment of a permanent school in Chicago. In July 1876, Moody came back to Chicago in order to dedicate his Chicago Avenue Church and at a meeting at the YMCA made a plea for a Bible institute. Dryer and her supporters concluded that a school was imminent and, at the least, that she would be in charge of the women's department. Those closest to Moody, however, were aware that he was undecided about where to establish his base of operations, Chicago or his home town, Northfield, Massachusetts. Later Dryer wrote, "It was then his [Moody's] plan to return, in one year, and make this his first work. In our Lord's providence, his 'first work' has been appointed elsewhere . . ." ("Bible Work in Chicago"). Meanwhile, she continued her own education by spending a year (1879–80) in Mildmay, England, attending Bible conferences and observing the Christian work of the London Deaconess House and YMCA. The Mildmay style was similar to that employed by the Salvation Army; all Mildmay's efforts were directed toward reaching the urban poor.

During the 1870s and 1880s, Dryer was also a colleague of

Sarah Clarke, cofounder with her husband Colonel George Clarke of the Pacific Garden Mission in 1877. Dryer and Sarah Clarke visited local jails, bringing scripture to comfort inmates.

By 1878, Dryer had seventeen people engaged in her Bible Work of Chicago. A pamphlet published by the CBS during these years described the training of Bible workers as a year of study and experimental services, with the workers living at home or in the house directed by the Woman's Council and under the supervision of Dryer. Along with instruction and training by Dryer in Bible study, Bible history, and methods of Christian work, lectures were given by pastors, evangelists, physicians, and others. The workers-in-training made house-to-house visits with Bibles and helped at cottage meetings, churches, Sunday schools, mothers' meetings, classes for Bible study, children's Bible meetings, and other similar Christian practices among the destitute. (Destitute in this case referred to anyone lacking the Word of God, not to financial condition.) Requirements for acceptance to the training course included good health, a fair education, good judgment, aptness in teaching, a ready acquaintance with the Bible, and the best methods of Christian work. Dryer also required her workers to submit weekly reports on the number of visits made, meetings held, tracts distributed, Bibles given and sold, number of persons attending the meetings, number of errands run for the poor, and the number of persons brought into regular Bible study.

In September 1883, during his Chicago campaign, Moody again raised hopes for the establishment of a training school. Those interested began to hold weekly prayer meetings on its behalf. Dryer herself looked for more tangible support. Charles Blanchard, president of Wheaton College in Wheaton, Illinois, who was preaching at Chicago Avenue Church in 1883, found himself quite interested in the adult Bible classes taught by Dryer and others. "I had only begun my acquaintance with Miss Dryer, when she began to speak of the Bible Institute and to express her regrets that something was not done to start it" (Blanchard to A. P. Fitt, November 16, 1910, Charles A. Blanchard Papers), he wrote. Dryer felt that "trial sessions" of a Bible institute-type class should be conducted, and if they were a success, Moody could be persuaded to enlarge the Bible Work of Chicago in the direction she envisioned. Blanchard finally asked Dryer "how much was required to make these tests" (*President Blanchard's Autobiography*, 123) and she replied that five hundred dollars would be enough to support the class sessions and to demonstrate to Moody the viability of the idea. Blanchard contacted Moody's regular supporters and easily raised five hundred dollars. Dryer, in turn, engaged teachers, including William Gallogly Moorehead, a Presbyterian minister who taught at Xenia Theological Seminary in Xenia, Ohio. Fifty male and female students enrolled for the first winter session held at the YMCA.

The second session, held in winter 1884–85, attracted seventy-five students and elicited a response from Moody. On January 22, 1886, he spoke to Chicagoans and said that if $250,000 were raised, he would come and found a Bible institute. E. F. Ensign and others were in charge of fund-raising, but although many of Moody's supporters made generous pledges, nothing concrete was done in 1886. Moody returned to Chicago in Jan-

uary 1887 for a late winter campaign. On February 5, he met with Cyrus McCormick Jr., T. W. Harvey, N. S. Bouton, E. G. Keith, John Farwell, Emma Dryer, and NETTIE FOWLER McCORMICK to found the Chicago Evangelization Society (CES).

For the next two years there were conflicts among the board members regarding money and methods. Finally, in April 1889, Moody instructed the CES to convene a short-term training school in Chicago. At that time, he managed to raise enough money to ensure the opening later that year of the Bible Institute for Home and Foreign Missions of the Chicago Evangelization Society. On May 16, Dryer, along with one or two other board members, resigned and took her Bible Work to the Chicago Bible Society. In September, she wrote a letter to Nettie Fowler McCormick commenting on her relief at being out of the turmoil within Moody's Chicago Avenue Church. When the CBS incorporated itself in 1889, Dryer's Bible Work became one of its departments.

In its annual report for 1900, the Bible Work department of the CBS noted that during 1899, Dryer and her thirteen workers had made 13,324 home visits, had held or addressed 1,306 meetings, and had brought 140 persons into regular Bible study. In 1901, the CBS Woman's Council noted that her efforts had met the needs of the poor, sick, and needy via house visits. Her methods were models in the teaching of the Bible, its doctrines, its historical and geographical facts, and had made the Bible's vital truths practical for the family setting.

Dryer retired from active service in 1903 after supervising the Bible Work for nearly thirty years. She was then elected superintendent emeritus with the privilege of residence at the Bible Workers' Home. Dryer died at ninety years of age and was buried in Wheaton, Illinois.

By the turn of the century, due to Dryer's efforts, the CBS boasted a strong force of young women trained to serve among the immigrants of the city as well as in foreign missions. Their studies included Bible geography, history, music, the life of Christ, preparation and teaching of Sunday school lessons, methods of dealing with the unbelieving, and use of the Bible in field work.

Sources. Archival collections include a biographical file for Emma Dryer, Archives, Moody Bible Institute, Chicago; Charles A. Blanchard Papers and Jonathan Blanchard Papers, College Archives, Wheaton College, Illinois. The papers of Nettie Fowler McCormick are in the McCormick family collection at the Wisconsin State Historical Library, Madison, and include her correspondence with Emma Dryer. Published *Annual Reports* of the Chicago Bible Society, 1874–1901, have important information about Dryer's activities; they include "Bible Work in Chicago," *37th Annual Report of the Chicago Bible Society 1877–78, Including an Abstract Report for the Years 1878 and 1879,* April 18, 1880. See [n.a.], *Ingham University: Fifty Years* (1885), for information on Dryer's education. A letter from Lynne Belluscio, director, Le Roy Hist. Soc., May 26, 1993, Le Roy, New York, provides information about Dryer's teaching experience at Ingham University. Charles A. Blanchard, *President Blanchard's Autobiography: The Dealings of God with Charles Albert Blanchard, for Many Years a Teacher in Wheaton College, Wheaton, Illinois* (1915), describes Dryer's interest in developing a Bible institute. James F. Findlay Jr., *Dwight L. Moody: American Evangelist 1837–1899* (1969), discusses Dryer's relationship to Moody.

See also Lyle Dorsett, *A Passion for Souls: The Life of D. L. Moody* (1997). Thekla Ellen Joiner Caldwell, "Women, Men, and Revival: The Third Awakening in Chicago" (Ph.D. diss., Univ. of Illinois at Chicago, 1991), and Janette Hassey, *No Time for Silence: Evangelical Women in Public Ministry around the Turn of the Century* (1986), discuss gender and evangelical culture.

CYNTHIA L. OGOREK

DUDZIK, SISTER M. THERESA
(Josephine Dudzik)
August 30, 1860–September 20, 1918
FOUNDER OF RELIGIOUS ORDER

Josephine Dudzik, who founded the Franciscan Sisters of Blessed Kunegunda (renamed Franciscan Sisters of Chicago in 1968), "the first religious Sisterhood founded in the city . . . and the first Polish-American Sisterhood founded in the United States" (Knawa, *As God Shall Ordain*, xxii), was born in Plocicz (Ploetrig), Poland, near the industrial city of Poznan, the third of six children and the third of five daughters of John and Agnes (Polaszczyk) Dudzik. Her father was the son of peasant farmers. Since their village was located in a part of Poland that was controlled by the Prussian government, Dudzik attended a small elementary school where classes were conducted in German. She then enrolled in a vocational school run by the Sisters of St. Elizabeth to learn sewing and needlework.

Josephine Dudzik was already a competent seamstress helping to support her family when, in 1881, at age nineteen, she and her parents, her brother Joseph, and her youngest sister Katherine, emigrated to America and settled in St. Stanislaus Kostka parish in Chicago. The Dudzik family joined Josephine's two oldest sisters, Rosalie and Marianne, who had already emigrated to Chicago in 1873 and had married Polish immigrants. Another sister, Frances, had emigrated to the United States in 1880.

The Dudziks settled in a rapidly growing immigrant Polish neighborhood on Chicago's near Northwest Side (called West Town or Stanislowowo-Trojcowo by the Polish immigrants) and participated in the benevolent societies, parochial schools, and social activities that made up the ethnic-religious community that centered around St. Stanislaus Kostka church.

In her native Poland, Dudzik had grown up in a family and church community that was defined by Polish folk and Roman Catholic religious traditions, while at the same she attended a public school where Polish studies and the Polish language were prohibited by the Prussian government. Once in Chicago, her interest in Polish history and culture was able to blossom, and she focused on the lore of saints and patrons, including the Blessed Kunegunda, wife of Boleslaus V, King of Poland, "a model of Christian charity and [the] patroness of Poland" (Knawa, *As God Shall Ordain*, 69). Dudzik's family formed a close relationship with the Catholic Church. Her mother worked as a housekeeper at St. Stanislaus Kostka's large parish rectory. Two Dudzik sisters joined religious orders—Frances, the Congregation of the School Sisters of Notre Dame; and Katherine, the Congregation of the Sisters of Charity of the Incarnate Word. Nuns from these orders staffed Polish Catholic schools in Chicago.

Josephine Dudzik eagerly joined the benevolent and devotional societies that made up the heart of religious activities for the men and women of the parish. She was a leader in the Young Ladies' Rosary Society, which performed charitable works. In 1885, with the aid of the parish priest, Vincent Michael Barzynski, she cofounded the Archconfraternity of the Immaculate Heart with two friends, Rosalie Wysinski and Josephine Kopciak. Established "to promote devotion to the Immaculate Heart of Mary" (Knawa, *As God Shall Ordain*, 55), Dudzik and the other women decorated the altars, sewed altar linens, and led the church congregation in the singing of prayers to the Virgin Mary. Later, Dudzik would write that she "was constantly occupied with the thought of how [she] . . . could be of service to the needy and the poor" (quoted in Knawa, *As God Shall Ordain*, 8). More than forty young women entered religious life from this archconfraternity.

There were numerous opportunities for devotional life and service in the parish; a chapter of the Third Order of St. Francis was founded in 1886 and Dudzik joined. The Third Order of St. Francis, modeled after the example of St. Francis of Assisi, "did not bind its members, who were young women of the parish, by any vows, but was a true religious order with a novitiate, Rule, profession, daily Office, and a habit. . . . Third order societies . . . were aimed at lay men and women who sought to deepen their lives" spiritually (Knawa, *As God Shall Ordain*, 55). For Dudzik, the association became her seminary or religious preparatory academy and left a deep and lasting impression. She, like the other working-class women members, labored during the day and came together in the morning for meditation and at night for a conference.

Josephine Dudzik's spiritual journey did not take her away from the immigrant neighborhood of friends and family. Her work as a seamstress continued, and, after her father's death in May 1889, she moved with her mother and brother to a small house owned by her married sister. After her brother's marriage in 1891, Dudzik and her mother lived alone in their house. Dudzik "began to shelter . . . homeless and needy women in her small, inadequate home much to the growing displeasure and discomfort of her mother" (Knawa, *As God Shall Ordain*, 64). Dudzik's parish priest, Father Barzynski, encouraged her outreach work, which dovetailed with his need to find help for dependent people in the parish. Without established social service institutions, charitable endeavors were largely individual or confined to the activities generated by fraternal organizations. Perhaps with a vision of future expansion, he guided Dudzik toward a vocation of working among the poor and sick, sensing her deep need to care for the needy through an implementation of the social gospel of Jesus.

A similar religious spirit motivated many of the late-nineteenth-century women social reformers who shared with Dudzik concerns for the well-being of women and children, the homeless and the sick, the uprooted and abandoned. Protestant and Roman Catholic women in Europe and the United States were finding models of spirituality and service in the religious orders of earlier times. In Chicago, LUCY RIDER MEYER renewed the ancient deaconess order in the Methodist Episcopal Church and established a training school. In the American Episcopal Church, ELLEN GATES STARR and Vida Scudder were founding members of the Society of the Companions of the Holy Cross, a lay order influenced by examples of medieval Catholicism. Starr's and Scudder's activism in the settlement movement was, in part, a function of the renewal of interest in the social activism of men and women religious in the past.

For Dudzik, the social and economic problems of the neighborhood—apparent during the severe periods of unemployment in the 1890s—made a lasting impression. She wrote, "I felt the misery and sufferings of others, and it seemed to me that I could not love Jesus, or even expect heaven, if I were concerned only about myself" (quoted in Knawa, *As God Shall Ordain*, 65). In a manner that resembled the efforts of other idealistic young women who hungered for useful and spiritually meaningful work, in 1893 Dudzik gathered around her women who desired to join her in a common life of prayer, labor, and service in order to form the Third Order of St. Francis.

The original inspiration to combine a life of common prayer with community service was Josephine Dudzik's. The actual establishment of a community of women had, however, to be guided by a priest who acted as a spiritual director. In this case, Father Barzynski played this role. In 1894 Josephine Dudzik—now Sister M. Theresa—and six other young women, moved into the Dudzik family home and began a four-year period of preparation before they were formally admitted as candidates for the new religious order, the Franciscan Sisters of Kunegunda. They placed all their savings and property into a common fund, earned money as seamstresses, sewing custom-made dresses in their convent home, and as domestics, doing housekeeping, washing, and ironing for as many as twelve resident priests and scores of visiting priests, newly arrived from Europe and temporarily lodged in the rectory of St. Stanislaus Kostka. Their modest earnings were used to operate their convent home for themselves and for the homeless and crippled they had taken in as residents. Whatever funds remained were placed in a fund for a permanent home for the aged and crippled that they hoped to build. In addition, Dudzik and the other sisters followed the mendicant model of the medieval Franciscans and begged for alms in the Polish neighborhood for the construction of this permanent institution.

Throughout the four-year probationary period, the newly founded order was plagued with internal tensions and problems. In part the problems stemmed from Father Barzynski's involvement in local Polish Catholic church politics. One of the original members, Sister Frances, left in support of the anti-Barzynski faction and encouraged others to follow her lead in establishing another sisterhood. The difficult physical work involved in their daily chores affected the health of the sisters. Some missed any personal comforts, and others found it difficult to abide by the religious rules strictly adhered to by Dudzik. Outside the small sisterhood, the Polish parishes were focused on their own fund-raising and offered little support for the Franciscans. Instead, false rumors circulated about Dudzik's plans. She was accused of purchasing lots to build a fine house for herself, not a charitable institution.

The sisterhood also experienced successes. They saved enough for a down payment on property for St. Joseph's Home for the Aged and Crippled. The Woman's Rosary Society and the Young Ladies' Rosary Society assisted in paying the debt on these lots. Father Barzynski was able to obtain a loan for the

community, and in March 1898 the Franciscans were able to move into the newly constructed St. Joseph Home for the Aged and Crippled in Avondale, at the time an undeveloped area on the Northwest Side of Chicago, about six miles from Chicago's downtown. The Franciscan sisters and their charges moved in. The new neighborhood had no paved roads, and city gas, sewer, and water lines had not yet been extended. The home, a three-story brick building, served as an institution for the aged and as a motherhouse for the young community of eight sisters. A small chapel was assembled for their devotions. There was still no "guaranteed income from any source" (Knawa, *As God Shall Ordain*, 109), but the sisters had lost their chief income from dressmaking and domestic work when they moved to the largely uninhabited area of Avondale. The sisters farmed in the convent garden, did all the cooking and housekeeping for themselves, and even cared for the animals.

As difficult as their lives were physically, it was easier to acquire property and build institutions than it was to create a spiritual community. The same year that St. Joseph's Home opened, Father Barzynski suddenly announced the removal of Sister Theresa as superior of the community. Although Polish Catholic immigrant women achieved an unusual degree of independence in their lives as women religious—raising funds, planning the building of social service and educational institutions, supervising the agencies they created—their relationship with the hierarchical and patriarchal Catholic Church was inherently subordinate when it came to issues of religious sacraments and governance. The women needed a constitution and their internal leadership needed definition. At this crucial moment, during the group's celebration of the feast of St. Francis of Assisi, October 4, 1898, Father Barzynski, who had not been able to celebrate mass that day, arrived unexpectedly and "to everyone's surprise . . . announced the removal of Sister Theresa as superior of the community. Offering no apology or explanation, . . . [he] deposed Sister Theresa and appointed Sister Anna Wysinski . . . to succeed her as the new superior" (Knawa, *As God Shall Ordain*, 110). The order's historian, Anne Marie Knawa, concludes that Dudzik's removal from office was deemed necessary by Barzynski because the parish critics who had questioned her motives for fund-raising continued to spread false accusations even after the group moved into the Avondale building. Barzynski, himself a subject of controversy who was engaged in the internal politics of the Polish neighborhood, wanted to end the rumors about the Franciscans. The Franciscan sisters accepted his decision passively and obediently, and some may have agreed with his judgment about Dudzik's leadership.

There was one more item of tension between Barzynski and Dudzik, however. It had to do with Dudzik's increased concern for her own and the other sisters' daily spiritual exercises and devotions. In December 1898, the small group of Franciscans finally began their formal preparation to take religious vows after four long and hard years of community building and physical labor. Barzynski, learning that some of the sisters complained about Dudzik's exacting demands for following their religious rules, urged her to relax them. Dudzik, who was in charge of religious training, resisted any compromise when it came to the community's religious practice. Barzynski, in poor health, increasingly failed to provide the kind of spiritual guidance Dudzik needed, but when he died in 1899, she felt saddened that he did not live to see the pioneer sisters received into the sisterhood. "We needed Father Vincent [Barzynski] more than ever since we still did not have the habit. We were busily preparing to receive it and had hoped to receive it from his hands" (quoted in Knawa, *As God Shall Ordain,* 122), Dudzik wrote. "My success," she asserted, "while still in the world, was due to his directing me on the road of self-denial" (p. 122).

Father Andrew Spetz became counselor to the Franciscans, and they began their formal novitiate in May 1899. The original pioneer sisters took their vows June 3, 1900, and "Sister Theresa was officially appointed and called the mistress of novices and postulants" (Knawa, *As God Shall Ordain,* 140). It had been a long process and complicated spiritual journey for the Polish immigrant women who had started to seek their vocation in 1894 and finally had attained a degree of autonomy and identity six years later.

Yet there was no harmony within the congregation; instead there was rebellion in the ranks against Dudzik. There were difficulties in the spiritual formation of the new candidates; in part it was a hard life and the community had undertaken major projects from the beginning. Additionally, the immigrant women lacked a strong national identity as Poles because they had lived in the different regions of partitioned Poland. Many first-generation members of the congregation had little or no schooling; often they were older than the typical entering age and had worked and lived reasonably independent lives prior to joining the community.

The community focused on its training of new members and its charitable institutions, but the dramatic increase of Polish immigrants in Chicago and other urban centers gave the early Polish Catholic sisterhoods a new challenge—the education of children. Leaders of the growing Polish Catholic parishes wanted teaching sisters to educate students in the Catholic faith and in Polish history and language as well. Public school teachers were called in to prepare Franciscan sisters for placement in the expanding parochial elementary school programs. Initially the Chicago public school teachers had to educate the nuns in English as well as in pedagogy so that they would be able to teach religion, reading, writing, history, arithmetic, and geography. The sisters were also instructed by Polish scholars in the Polish language, literature, and culture. It was a strenuous program, and many second-generation sisters were not much older than the students they taught. Dudzik had to deal with the fact that her need to demand attention for the spiritual formation of the sisters competed with the need to train them to be employed as schoolteachers. By 1903, the Franciscans staffed three schools, including one in Cleveland. The following year they expanded their work into Wisconsin, teaching in Berlin, a little town west of Oshkosh with a large Polish population.

In 1904, the Franciscans opened St. Elizabeth's Day Nursery to care for the children of working mothers. A small daily fee was charged and children as young as four months of age were boarded for the day. Two hot meals were served, and in the evening, the sisters held classes for young girls and married women who learned cooking, sewing, and other household arts. In 1911 a free health clinic was opened in the building. The medical staff members donated their services. An Infant Welfare Station where mothers received instruction in nutrition and childcare was also instituted. The nursery closed in 1915 because of financial troubles. (It reopened in 1920 and continued to operate until 1959.)

Dudzik remained at the heart of the Franciscan community. In 1905 she served as assistant to Sister M. Vincent Czyzewski, who replaced Sister M. Anna Wysinski as mother superior. Dudzik continued to head the training of novices, manage the laundry, and care for the aged residents. After an illness, Dudzik no longer ran the laundry or offered immediate care to the elderly, but she continued to work with the novices. The following year she was admitted to St. Elizabeth's Hospital, where she underwent a hysterectomy.

By 1909, Franciscan Sisters from the Chicago community were staffing schools in Spring Valley and East St. Louis, Illinois; in Chicago neighborhoods including Hegewisch; in Whiting, Indiana Harbor, and Gary, Indiana; in Youngstown and Cleveland, Ohio; and in St. Louis, Missouri. The demand for teachers continued. The community had also sent a group of sisters to the Mercy Sisters, Chicago, for nurses training.

The time was ripe for a new level of organization of the sisterhood. The original pioneer sisters, including Dudzik, prepared to take their perpetual vows in 1909. Additionally, in January 1909, Father Spetz appointed Dudzik mother superior of the community until the permanently established chapter would select a mother general (superior) by themselves. A new advisory council, appointed by Spetz, worked with Dudzik to develop the structure necessary for the Franciscans of Kunegunda to emerge as an autonomous, established congregation. "As a consequence of the First General Chapter, a newly elected mother general would emerge who would govern the congregation with the advice of her general council" (Knawa, *As God Shall Ordain,* 237).

The delegates chose Sister M. Anna Wysinski the superior general (mother general) August 12, 1910. Council members were then elected for a six-year term. "Conspicuously absent was the name of Sister M. Theresa Dudzik on the roster of council members" (Knawa, *As God Shall Ordain,* 248). Once again her leadership was rejected. However, Dudzik was appointed by Father Spetz to head the Commission on Spiritual Affairs and to help formulate a Book of Customs for the Franciscans.

Dudzik spent the last years of her life working in the garden and greenhouse, the laundry, and the sewing room. She saw her vocation primarily in spiritual terms. Later church leaders have come to emphasize her spiritual vision. When she died, she had been a religious for twenty-three years. In her lifetime she was known as Sister Theresa, since she never served as the superior general of the congregation. The title of "Mother" was given after her death "as a gesture of recognition and respect" (Knawa, *As God Shall Ordain,* xxiv).

Sister M. Theresa Dudzik died of cancer at age fifty-eight. Her funeral took place in the chapel of St. Joseph Home. She is buried in St. Adalbert's Cemetery, Niles, Illinois. "Sister M. Theresa was laid to rest on the left side of a cemetery marker. On the right side lay her friend, Mother M. Anna Wysinski" (Knawa, *As God Shall Ordain,* 368). The two had been together at the formation of the Franciscan order and had been the leading lights for more than two decades.

A poor and immigrant woman, Sister Theresa Dudzik was a pioneer in the development of social agencies and schools that became the core institutions of the Roman Catholic Church in urban America. In a period of rapid economic and social change, she created modern structures to address problems of immigration, industrialization, and social dislocation. At the same time, both her inspiration and her method came from a vision of Scripture and Catholic traditions harking back to St. Francis of Assisi and St. Theresa of Avila. She was also empowered by the freedom that American society gave to the immigrant in search of ethnic identity. For Dudzik, America and the streets of Chicago were places where she could express her Polish identity and connect with the literature and folk culture of her oppressed homeland. She became an American who led in the creation of peculiarly American Catholic institutions at the same time that she expressed herself as a person of Polish heritage. Her work in the formation of new members of the Franciscan sisterhood was also a new adaptation that strengthened both traditional values and democratic goals. Largely self-taught, Dudzik found her "university" in the religious voluntary associations that proliferated on the Northwest Side of Chicago. Admitting poor and largely unlettered women for training as novices, Dudzik and her generation of women religious brought elements of democracy and gender equality to a patriarchal and hierarchical church.

Sources. The records of the Franciscan Sisters of Chicago (originally Franciscan Sisters of Kunegunda) are found in the Archives of the Congregation, Lemont, Illinois. Included is Theresa Dudzik's unpublished manuscript, "The Chronicle of the Franciscan Sisters under the Patronage of St. Kunegunda in Chicago, Illinois," 1910 (translated from the Polish). Two articles, Sister Clarent Marie Urbanowicz, "Mother Mary Theresa Dudzik," *Polish American Studies,* vol. 19, 1962, and Sister Anne Marie Knawa, "Jane Addams and Josephine Dudzik: Social Service Pioneers," *Polish American Studies,* vol. 35, 1978, are valuable. The most complete history of the Franciscan Sisters of Chicago, including biographical material on Dudzik, is Knawa, *As God Shall Ordain: A History of the Franciscan Sisters of Chicago, 1894–1987* (1989).

RIMA LUNIN SCHULTZ

DUMMER, ETHEL STURGES
October 23, 1866–February 25, 1954
EDUCATION AND MENTAL HEALTH REFORMER,
PHILANTHROPIST

Ethel Sturges Dummer, education and mental health reformer, was born in Chicago, the first daughter and third of nine children of George and Mary (Delafield) Sturges. Her father was president of the Northwestern National Bank and her mother was interested in social welfare issues. In 1885 Ethel Sturges completed her education at the private Kirkland School, where ELLEN GATES STARR, cofounder of Hull-House, was one of her favorite teachers. Three years later she married William Francis (Frank) Dummer, vice-president of the Northwestern National Bank. They had four daughters: Marion, Katharine, Ethel Sturges, and Frances. A son, William Francis, died in infancy.

During the 1890s and early 1900s, as her daughters were growing up, Dummer's life was primarily focused on raising her children. Both she and her husband attached great importance to education, and they assisted the family's tutors with their daughters' education through planned constructive activities. In addition, Ethel and Frank Dummer were at the center of a large intergenerational clan of relatives who congregated at the family's summer home in Lake Geneva, Wisconsin, and, from 1917 on, at their winter home in Coronado, California. Ethel Dummer was busy managing three households and a staff of servants, and entertaining friends and relatives, often for extended periods of time. The Dummers also organized elaborate excursions with their children, camping in the Far West and traveling in Europe. Their children often accompanied them to meetings and conferences that their parents thought might be of interest to them.

In the mid-1890s Dummer's mother felt that her daughter needed to broaden her interests beyond her children and urged her to join in the social welfare activities of the Kirkland Alumnae Association. Dummer helped with the association's lunchroom for saleswomen in Chicago's downtown department stores and its canteen serving inexpensive meals to workers at the Western Electric factory. As she worked with her preparatory school alumnae association, Dummer entered Chicago's lively reform community. She soon became part of an existing network made up of civic-minded members of Chicago's upper class, social reformers, welfare workers, and settlement house residents. Prominent in this network, and among those with whom she worked closely over the years, were JANE ADDAMS, head resident of Hull-House settlement; MARY McDOWELL, head resident of the University of Chicago Settlement; and LOUISE deKOVEN BOWEN, president of the Juvenile Protective Association.

Like many other Chicago women of her class and era, Dummer worked alongside professionals—both women and men—who were just beginning to create and establish the fields of sociology, social work, and mental hygiene (later mental health) for reform of Chicago's educational, health, and juvenile justice systems. At this time the lines were not clearly drawn between professional and non-professional; all were welcome to participate in a great variety of efforts to make Chicago a more habitable environment for its citizens. Dummer, however, was distinguished from many women playing leading roles in these circles by her lasting concern to theorize as well as to act. This interest in theory led her to continued interaction with academic social scientists and personal contributions to the emerging field of social science. Reflecting on her role after a lifetime of reform activities, Dummer wrote: "My social work was in *thinking* and the sharing of thought" (*Why I Think So,* 113).

Early in her reform work, Dummer evidenced a talent for bringing together people working on different angles of a problem. She described herself as "acting as a switchboard, connecting people and ideas" (Platt, 25), an apt metaphor for her way of tackling issues in which she had a vital interest. She was not merely active in committee work; she sought out experts in fields she was concerned with and disseminated their contributions through symposia, practical demonstrations, and exhibits, by funding travel to learn from expertise elsewhere, and in publications that she sponsored and often circulated.

In the early 1900s, as Dummer's educational interests broadened, she began to promote many improvements in Chicago public schools. Concerned to provide wholesome after-school activities for children, she worked with a school principal to set up a pilot recreation program, arranging with the Chicago Board of Education to keep two schools open in the evenings, offering recreation for both children and adults. After the program had been running successfully in the pilot schools, she held a dinner for the board to report on the results of the program and push its expansion. The board was impressed and quadrupled its appropriation for social activities in schools.

Dummer became interested in the progressive education ideas of ELLA FLAGG YOUNG, superintendent of Chicago's schools from 1909 to 1915. During Young's tenure, Dummer studied and encouraged progressive methods that recognized the child's need for education based on experience rather than rote learning and for free movement in the classroom rather than confinement at a desk for many hours a day. When Young was not reappointed as superintendent, Dummer searched for other ways to keep progressive educational ideas in the public school system. She organized the Joint Committee on Education, bringing together people from many civic and women's groups who were interested in creating the best education possible for the city's children. As program chair of the committee, Dummer arranged for a number of lectures by eminent biologists, psychologists, sociologists, and psychiatrists, asking them to bring the expertise of their disciplines to bear on the issue of education. She then persuaded a major publishing company to issue the papers from one well-attended lecture series; the result was an influential volume, *Suggestions of Modern Science Concerning Education* (1925).

From the mid-1920s on, Dummer searched for the answer to the question: What is thought? Drawing once again on the work of researchers from many social science disciplines, she sought to discover educational theories and methods that would encourage the fullest functioning of the human mind. Believing that mental health workers (then called mental hygienists) focused too exclusively on pathology, she began to push for work that would describe the processes capable of producing healthy, socially conscious human beings in whom mind and body development were integrated for optimal creativity. She wondered what role the unconscious, just becoming a topic of scientific research, played in the development of thought and began to gather information about the unconscious.

For many years she had been exploring the theories of late-nineteenth-century English educational philosopher Mary Everest Boole. Like many intellectuals of her day, Boole was concerned to reconcile Darwinian biology, progressive education, and religion. She posited the theory that organized play helped to develop the conscious mind—God's gift to humanity. It was through the conscious mind that the unconscious found expression. For healthy human beings both levels of consciousness must be integrated. Dummer found Boole's thought congenial, because it allowed her to come to a modern understanding of religion, one that did not deny the discoveries of a new scientific age. In an effort to introduce Boole's thought to a wider audience in the United States, Dummer had Boole's collected works published in 1931 and later authored a pamphlet,

Mary Everest Boole: A Pioneer Student of the Unconscious (1945).

Wishing to see more research on the relationship between the unconscious and conscious thought, Dummer worked to further investigation on this topic. Her honorary membership in the newly formed American Orthopsychiatric Association (AOA), a group that shared Dummer's belief in cross-disciplinary research, and in the Illinois Society for Mental Hygiene (ISMH, of which she was a founder) provided her with two arenas in which to accomplish the research goals she advocated. In 1927 she organized a meeting on the unconscious under the auspices of the ISMH, inviting as speakers scholars she had met through the AOA and other groups. The lectures were collected in *The Unconscious: A Symposium* (1928). Dummer edited and wrote a preface for this pathbreaking volume, which presented the latest research of social psychologists, neurologists, biologists, and psychiatrists.

During the mid-1910s, Dummer's work as the head of a committee on "feeblemindedness" had led her to investigate the teaching of so-called subnormal children in Chicago's public schools. She continued to mull over this aspect of education, finding very few existing methods she considered adequate to the challenge of teaching developmentally disabled children and adults. Still pursuing this interest in the 1930s, she met NEVA BOYD, Florence Beaman, and several other talented women who were introducing techniques of games and dance into their teaching of inmates at state facilities for both the developmentally and emotionally disturbed. Dummer organized and often helped fund classes for teachers taught by these women throughout Illinois.

During the late 1920s and into the 1930s, Dummer continued to work for the integration of progressive education methods into public schools and teacher training. She served as chair of the Committee on Progressive Education of the Citizen's Advisory Council appointed by School Superintendent William J. Bogan. In conjunction with the Education Department of the Chicago Woman's Club (of which she was a member), she arranged for several lecture series, bringing as speakers nationally recognized leaders in progressive education. When the depression made it difficult to fund such meetings, Dummer created an education center in her Near North Side home. She turned the room housing her private collection of materials on education and the social sciences into a free lending library and reading room for teachers and principals. Demonstration classes on innovative learning techniques were held in what had been the Dummer family dining room, and lectures, meetings, and informal discussions were held in the former living room. In the 1940s, Dummer sponsored child development courses at Northwestern University, introducing the work of Swiss child psychologist Jean Piaget on children's intellectual growth.

Another major area of Dummer's work stemmed from her membership on the board of Chicago's Juvenile Protective Association (JPA). In 1905 she was moved by reading articles about the abuses of child labor to accept an invitation to join the JPA. Initially she worked to help raise money for a detention home after a law was passed for its establishment without the necessary financial appropriation. The success of this activity led to her appointment as a member of the JPA's Research Committee on Delinquency, Its Causes and Prevention.

As Dummer reviewed and discussed case studies of individual delinquents with other committee members, she began to challenge the traditional view that delinquency was hereditary, maintaining instead that environmental influences, particularly poor childhood nurture, were responsible for much delinquency. For several years the JPA was not receptive to her idea that many juvenile delinquents needed psychiatric treatment and rehabilitation rather than incarceration. On the suggestion of JULIA LATHROP, her colleague on the JPA, she approached psychiatrist William Healy, a professional scholar who agreed with her theory and agreed to undertake research in support of this new viewpoint about the causes of delinquency. Dummer funded his work, establishing in 1909 the Juvenile Psychopathic Institute associated with Chicago's Juvenile Court. The institute became a model for later child guidance clinics throughout the country. In 1915 Healy published his findings in *The Individual Delinquent*, a volume that greatly influenced future treatment of juvenile delinquents.

Increasingly recognized as a valuable colleague by mental hygiene professionals and social and juvenile justice workers, Dummer was appointed to several posts that allowed her to work on her reform interests from the 1900s through the 1920s. She became a member of the board of the National Probation Association, a trustee of the University of Chicago Settlement, and, in 1908, a founder and trustee of the Chicago School of Civics and Philanthropy (later the University of Chicago School of Social Service Administration).

Dummer considered herself a feminist, and her work for many years on behalf of enlightened treatment of unwed mothers and prostitutes became her contribution to the cause of feminism. She initially became troubled by the attitude toward unwed mothers and their children that she had observed in her work with the JPA during the 1910s. She began to study unwed mothers, first by extensive reading and next by making a trip to Europe in 1913–14 to investigate how other countries were dealing with them. As a result of her studies, Dummer came to believe that forcing young women into what were all too often loveless marriages or putting their children up for adoption was unjust and inhumane. Instead she advocated the type of policy she had seen in Norway, where young unwed mothers were allowed to keep their children and some form of governmental support was provided for them. Dummer realized that such an enlightened view was not yet welcome in the United States. She contented herself for a time with circulating copies of Norway's Castberg Law at her own expense to sympathetic colleagues in the social work and mental hygiene movement, waiting for a better moment to introduce her ideas on unwed mothers. Eventually she worked with Chicago groups to try to get a law similar to Norway's introduced into the state legislature, thus getting the topic on the agenda for public discussion.

During World War I, Dummer became involved in the reform of the treatment of prostitutes through her work on a Committee for the Protection of Girls. Attention to the issue was heightened during wartime because of the fear that girls near military camps would be drawn into prostitution, contract venereal disease, and infect troops. Dummer was irate at the unfairness of contemporary venereal disease legislation, which led to the arrest of many women merely suspected of being prostitutes or having venereal disease, and their arrest and detention without trial, while no such legal action was taken against men who were actually infected. Besides campaigning against unfair legislation and for reform of the treatment of prostitutes, Dummer commissioned former University of Chicago sociologist Willam Isaac Thomas to undertake research on unwed mothers in order to understand their behavior and develop methods of rehabilitation that would not stigmatize them. She not only paid Thomas to undertake the study but elicited through her contacts a large number of case studies upon which he drew and provided a stream of ideas for his work. It was eventually published as *The Unadjusted Girl* (1923), with a preface by Dummer. ("Unadjusted" was, at the time, a euphemism for promiscuous.) In their correspondence, Thomas acknowledged significant intellectual influence from her on his work.

Through Dummer's interest in the fair treatment of unwed mothers and young prostitutes, she met and became a friend and colleague of Miriam Van Waters. Van Waters, a referee of the Juvenile Court of Los Angeles, also ran El Retiro, a pioneering, therapeutically oriented correctional facility for young women delinquents, including a number of prostitutes and unwed mothers. Dummer gave financial support to El Retiro in the years just after World War I, and also funded Van Waters's published studies of delinquent girls in the 1920s. Dummer and Van Waters corresponded extensively over the next decades, discussing areas of mutual interest. Like many of Dummer's colleagues, Van Waters appreciated Dummer's ability to encourage colleagues to expand their thought about problems as they searched for creative solutions. "The unique thing about talking with Mrs. Dummer," Van Waters said, "was that she took your idea without controversy, almost without question, lifted it and sent it winging some place. You always went away with something developing not only within you but in your thoughts" (Dummer memorial service, March 9, 1954, Dummer Papers).

During the 1910s and 1920s, Dummer established and maintained an informal, but crucial, relationship with the University of Chicago's Department of Sociology. The department was the national leader in the field and pioneered in introducing empirical research on contemporary society into academic sociology, often in cooperation with the social work and reform circles to which Dummer belonged. She had been a member of the American Sociological Society (ASS), based at the University of Chicago, since 1910. Seeing the ASS as a forum for presenting the need for reform of the treatment of the delinquent girl, she organized a roundtable on the subject at one of its meetings in 1921. She arranged for contributions from Van Waters and other prominent women social workers at the roundtable, providing them with a national forum for their new and controversial ideas on the treatment of delinquent girls. At its conclusion, she had the lectures printed and widely distributed among the mental hygiene and social work community.

Dummer was involved in the founding of the ASS's Section on the Family, and during 1925–26 was secretary of that section. In 1925 she was in charge of one of its sessions and reported on progress in the study of the family. She served on the ASS's executive committee from 1927 to 1930 and published an article in 1933 in the *American Journal of Sociology* on the philosophy motivating the first Soviet Five-Year Plan. For many years she corresponded with academic social scientists in Chicago and elsewhere, drawing to their attention publications she thought important to their work and finding venues where they could present their research.

Beginning in the 1910s, Dummer spent increasing amounts of time at her southern California home for her health. By the late 1940s, crippled with arthritis, she moved from her main residence in Chicago to live with her daughter Katharine (Dummer) Fisher in Winnetka, Illinois. Dummer died of a stroke at age eighty-seven; after cremation her ashes were scattered at her beloved Lake Geneva, Wisconsin, summer home. In spite of Dummer's tendency to shun publicity, preferring always to stay in the background, she was well recognized in Chicago for her reform activities over the years. She received many public tributes, including election as a Citizen Fellow of the (Chicago) Institute of Medicine in 1937 and an honorary doctorate from Northwestern University in 1940.

Only a short while before her death, Dummer participated in a ceremony dedicating Chicago's William Healy Residential School, a treatment and research facility for emotionally disturbed children from all over the state. Reunited on the platform with her old friend and colleague Healy, Dummer reminisced about the early days of the JPA and the efforts of Chicago's social reform community to found the pioneering Juvenile Psychopathic Institute. Characteristically, she failed to mention her key role as a catalyst in its beginnings. Yet Chicago's reform community remembered. The auditorium of the newly built Healy Residential School was named for Ethel Sturges Dummer. This was a fitting way to honor one who had, over the course of her life, brought so many people together in similar surroundings to hear lectures, demonstrations, and roundtables presenting the new research that would ground mental hygiene and educational reform efforts during the first half of the twentieth century.

Sources. The Ethel Sturges Dummer Papers are at SL. The collection contains a large amount of correspondence with leading figures of the period as well as with family members, speeches and writings of Dummer, tributes and memorials to her, and family documents. There is a detailed inventory of the collection by Kathleen Marquis (1979). Ethel S. Dummer, *Why I Think So: The Autobiography of an Hypothesis* (1937), is Dummer's rich account of her intellectual development as well as a detailed discussion of the network of colleagues that she built over the years when she was active in the fields of education and mental hygiene. It vividly presents her mode of working to create new solutions to social problems. Dummer wrote pamphlets and articles, including *The Evolution of a Biological Faith* (1943); *What Is Thought* (1943); *Mary Everest Boole: A Pioneer Student of the Unconscious* (1945); and "The Philosophy Back of the Five-Year Plan," *American Journal of Sociology*, January 1933. Dummer wrote prefaces to W. I. Thomas, *The Unadjusted Girl* (1923); C. M. Child et al., *The Unconscious: A Symposium* (1928); and E. M. Cobham, ed., *The Collected Works of Mary Everest Boole* (1931). See Jennifer Platt, "'Acting As a Switchboard': Mrs. Ethel Sturges Dummer's Role in Sociology," *American Sociologist*, Fall 1992, which focuses on one area of her interests and describes her relationship to the field of sociology. There are biographical entries on Dummer in *NAW* (1980) and Walter Trattner, ed., *Biographical Dictionary of Social Welfare* (1986). Relevant background information for understanding

Dummer's life is available in Louise deKoven Bowen, *Growing Up with a City* (1926); Karen J. Blair, *The Clubwoman as Feminist* (1980); Steven J. Diner, *A City and Its Universities* (1980); Mary Jo Deegan, *Jane Addams and the Men of the Chicago School* (1978); and Kathleen D. McCarthy, *Noblesse Oblige: Charity and Cultural Philanthropy in Chicago, 1848–1929* (1982).

JENNIFER PLATT

DUNAYEVSKAYA, RAYA
May 1, 1910–June 9, 1987
PHILOSOPHER, AUTHOR, REVOLUTIONARY ACTIVIST

Raya Dunayevskaya was a philosopher and activist who developed an original philosophy—Marxist-Humanism—and throughout her life searched for paths to liberation, paths she saw in the struggles of women, African Americans, youth, and labor. Adrienne Rich called her a "major thinker in the history of Marxism and of women's liberation—one of the longest continuously active woman revolutionaries of the twentieth century. . . . A core theme of [Dunayevskaya's] writing . . . [was] the inseparability of experience and revolutionary thinking, the falseness of the opposition between 'philosophy' and 'actuality'" (Rich, foreword to Dunayevskaya, *Rosa Luxemburg*, xi). She proposed that the radical movement return to the works of Karl Marx and study his roots in the philosophy of Georg Wilhelm Hegel; and she rejected the thinking, in both the United States and the Soviet Union, that identified "Marxism, a theory of liberation," with what she termed "its opposite, Communism, the theory and practice of enslavement" (Dunayevskaya, introduction to *Marxism and Freedom*, 21). She "attempted to realize the unity of theory and practice, which she took to be the core of revolutionary Marxism" (Kellner, 206).

Raya Osipovna Dunayevetskaya (Dunayevskaya in America) was born on May Day in Ukraine, then part of tsarist Russia, in the town of Yariishev near the Romanian border, the youngest child in a family of four sisters and two brothers—Zipporah, Sonia, Bessie, Maurice, and Samuel. Her father, Osip, was a rabbi, and her mother, Brina, was a homemaker. Dunayevskaya spent her early years with her family in a Jewish ghetto. The experience that transformed her life and set her on the path of revolutionary philosophy and activism was the Russian Revolution of 1917 and the ensuing civil war, which she witnessed as a young girl. Escaping her parents' arms, she ran through the streets and saw the destruction of the village and the rapes and beheading of townspeople by counter-revolutionary troops retreating from the Bolsheviks. That the Bolsheviks were welcomed as liberators shaped her actions when the family settled in Chicago in 1922 after fleeing the famine in Russia the year before. In Chicago's Near West Side Jewish neighborhood, Dunayevskaya and her sister Bessie traversed Maxwell Street, the major shopping district of the immigrant section, looking for the sign of the hammer and sickle, indicating support for the Bolshevik revolution. When they saw it in a poster at a fruit stand, the girls asked the owner if they could join the Communist Party (CP).

Although Raya Dunayevskaya was too young to be a CP member, she joined the communist youth organization soon after. Already angered by anti-Semitism, injustice, and poverty, Dunayevskaya felt such revulsion at reciting the pledge of allegiance at school that at age thirteen she contributed her own version to the CP youth journal, the *Young Comrade*. It concluded, "One aim throughout our life / Freedom to the working class!" (Comrade Sunny, "Comrade Sunny's Column," 1). A year later, she led a student strike at Cregier Elementary School against anti-Semitism and corporal punishment by the principal. The strikers, who came to the picket line on roller skates, demanded, unsuccessfully, that the principal be fired. Dunayevskaya took an active part in the life of the Workers (Communist) Party—distributing the CP shop paper, *Harvester Worker*, to employees at the gates of the McCormick Reaper plant in Chicago.

Because Dunayevskaya viewed her childhood in Russia and Chicago as the crucible for a radical life, it becomes part of the biography of the idea of freedom. As she put it in 1978, "I come [*sic*] from Russia 1917, and the ghettos of Chicago, where I first saw a Black person. . . . You're born in a border town—there's a revolution, there's anti-Semitism. . . . It isn't personal whatsoever! If you live when an idea is born, and a great revolution in the world is born—it doesn't make any difference *where* you are: *that becomes the next stage of development of humanity*" ("The Dialectic of Today's Crises and Today's Revolts," *News & Letters*, September 2, 1978, 27). It was her experiences in Russia, compounded by her recognition of similar injustices in Chicago, including her shock at seeing African Americans and realizing that they could never hide from racism, that convinced Dunayevskaya to take responsibility for helping humanity realize freedom.

Her activities were unusual: as a teenage white woman she had determined to immerse herself in revolutionary work with African Americans. She carved out a place for herself, working with the *Negro Champion*, the newspaper of the American Negro Labor Congress, whose editor was Lovett Fort-Whiteman. The *Negro Champion* office was located in the heart of Chicago's Black Metropolis. She wrote book reviews that were published widely in African American newspapers and journals. When she graduated from Medill High School in 1928, her date with an African American classmate created a protest that threatened to cancel the scheduled prom. The case was taken up by the National Association for the Advancement of Colored People (NAACP).

Dunayevskaya began to question the CP's policies and actions after the expulsion of Leon Trotsky from the party in 1928. Trotsky was the only serious revolutionary opposition to the dictator Joseph Stalin, who took power in Russia in the mid-1920s. When Dunayevskaya suggested that her local comrades hear Trotsky's response to his expulsion, she was literally thrown down a flight of stairs and kicked out of the Young Workers League. At eighteen, out of high school and recently expelled from the youth section of the CP, Dunayevskaya began a revolutionary sojourn that took her from New York City to Los Angeles. In New York, she married the actor Shimon Ruskin, who was well known in Yiddish theater. It was the first of her four marriages and was short-lived. She married Mark Sharron in 1934, Bernard Adams in 1940, and John Dwyer in 1953. Except for Dwyer, with whom she lived from 1947 until her death, the marriages were brief. Moving to Boston in 1929, Dunayevskaya met Antoinette Bucholz Konikow, a birth control advocate who spoke out for legal abortion and had formed a group of independent Trotskyists—almost all women—who had been thrown

out of the CP. Dunayevskaya had undergone an illegal abortion in the late 1920s.

Throughout the Great Depression, Dunayevskaya remained politically active; this was a period of intense labor struggle in the United States and movements on the Left gained support as workers faced unemployment and struggled to stay alive. Back in New York, she became secretary to Trotskyist leader James Patrick Cannon, who was one of the founders of the Socialist Workers Party in 1938 and its national secretary until 1953. Dunayevskaya did not stay with Cannon very long but traveled to workers' strikes at various sites. Not having enough money for transportation, she hitchhiked across the country in 1934, a year during which labor strikes were characterized by intense class conflict. When she arrived in San Francisco, the general strike of July 16–19, 1934, had begun. It has been described as "an epic moment in the history of the American working class" (Nelson, 672). More than one hundred thousand workers in San Francisco and Alameda Counties stopped work in support of longshoremen and seamen who had gone on strike along the entire West Coast. Dunayevskaya was shot at by police during a street battle that was part of the "widespread police and vigilante violence" (p. 672). The next year she was in Los Angeles, where she taught Karl Marx's *Capital* and worked as an organizer for the Spartacus Youth League. She was employed as a script typist for the movie studio 20th Century Fox. By 1936, Dunayevskaya had moved to Washington, D.C., where she worked with Ralph Bunche on the Washington Committee to Aid Agricultural Workers.

In 1937, hearing that Leon Trotsky needed a Russian language secretary, Dunayevskaya wrote him directly and left for Mexico without obtaining permission from the U.S. branch of the Trotskyist party. Trotsky was in exile in Mexico, trying to escape assassination by Stalin, who was methodically jailing and executing his past revolutionary comrades. Dunayevskaya worked with Trotsky in Coyoacan, Mexico, during the years when Stalin waged the infamous Moscow trials. She helped Trotsky respond to the trials' fantastic slanders against him, many times with only two hours' notice. In 1938, the deaths of her father and brother forced Dunayevskaya to return to Chicago.

Dunayevskaya was still in Chicago in 1939 when she broke with Trotsky over his insistence that Russia was still a "workers' state" ("Marxism-Humanism, an Interview with Raya Dunayevskaya," 16) even after Stalin made a pact with Adolf Hitler. Dunayevskaya herself saw the pact as telling socialists that they should fight for fascism. Twenty-nine year old Dunayevskaya disagreed with Trotsky, the man she considered the greatest living revolutionary. She lost her power of speech for two days. Then began what she later asserted was "my real development" (p. 16). Dunayevskaya had thrown herself into activism. The realization of Trotsky's error, a mistake that limited the total revolutionary change that Dunayevskaya envisioned, forced her to immerse herself in economics, revolutionary theory, and philosophy, a development that transformed what Marxism would come to mean for her. Driven to understand the true nature of the Soviet Union, Dunayevskaya began a rigorous study, utilizing Russian economic statistics, Marx's *Capital* (1867), and his then little-known *Economic-Philosophic Manu-*

scripts (1844). In 1941, Dunayevskaya wrote "The Union of Soviet Socialist Republics Is a Capitalist Society." She soon met a Trotskyist from Trinidad, Cyril Lionel Robert (C. L. R.) James, who had also written a position paper on state capitalism. Dunayevskaya and James formed the State-Capitalist Tendency (SCT) within the Workers Party; Dunayevskaya was active in the Harlem, New York, branch of the party. From 1940 to 1951, SCT produced bulletins and, "as an independent entity, they published the newspaper *Correspondence* from Detroit to express workers' own views" (Kellner, 205).

By 1944 Dunayevskaya's critique of Russian theoreticians, "A New Revision of Marxian Economics," published in the *American Economic Review*, reached beyond the publications of the Left and was reported on the front page of the *New York Times*. She criticized Russian theoreticians who had declared that the law of value—which Marx said was a defining feature of capitalism—operated under socialism. Will Lissner discussed her article in "Soviet Economics Stirs Debate Here" in the *New York Times*, October 1, 1944. From then on, Dunayevskaya never separated activism from her deepest delving into philosophy.

Moving to Pittsburgh, Pennsylvania, in the late 1940s, she became active in the coal miners' general strike of 1949–50 in West Virginia. At the same time she was translating Vladimir I. Lenin's *Abstract of Hegel's Science of Logic* and working on a book on state capitalism. Her activity and studies in the Hegelian-Marxian dialectic culminated in her 1953 letters on Georg Wilhelm Friedrich Hegel. Dunayevskaya referred to these letters as a determinant for her subsequent development of the philosophy she came to call Marxist-Humanism. In Dunayevskaya's view, original thinkers had profound moments of insight that could be called the philosophic moment. With Marx that was his *Economic-Philosophic Manuscripts of 1844*; with Hegel it was his work, *The Phenomenology of Mind* (1807).

In the midst of cold war politics in the 1950s, C. L. R. James was expelled from the United States for passport violations; he moved back to England after breaking up the SCT, whose Correspondence Committees had been listed as subversive by the U.S. Attorney General in 1954. James dissolved the group rather than fight the listing as Dunayevskaya desired. Immediately after the dissolution, in 1955, Dunayevskaya, together with most of the worker members of the Correspondence Committees, formed News and Letters Committees as a "unique combination of workers and intellectuals" (Dunayevskaya, "What Is News & Letters?" *News & Letters*, March 1969, 5). Although Dunayevskaya would have preferred the new organization's center to be in Chicago, it was first established in the Detroit, Michigan, home of the African American worker-editor Charles Denby.

Detroit was a proletarian center and New York, a cultural center; but Chicago was both, as well as a center of African American thought and activity. For Dunayevskaya, moving her headquarters to Chicago remained a goal. She made yearly speaking trips to Chicago and deepened relations with such activists as Fred Thompson, worker-leader of the anarchist Industrial Workers of the World (IWW). She encouraged members of News and Letters Committees to take trips and do research on Chicago history.

In 1958, Dunayevskaya published her first book, *Marxism and Freedom, from 1776 until Today*, with an introduction by Marxist philosopher Herbert Marcuse. Marcuse had published *Soviet Marxism: A Critical Analysis* the same year. Dunayevskaya's *Marxism and Freedom* aimed "to re-establish Marxism in its original form, which Marx called 'a thoroughgoing Naturalism, or Humanism'" (p. 21) and included her translations of Lenin's *Philosophic Notebooks* (1914) and two of Marx's 1844 *Economic-Philosophic Manuscripts*—the first time those essays were published in English.

Dunayevskaya worked with an array of U.S. and international movements throughout the 1960s, traveling to Europe, Africa, Hong Kong, and Japan. In 1969, she made the first donation of her writings to the Wayne State University Archives of Labor and Urban Affairs, believing one could learn as much from the process of development of theory as from the result. Her manuscript collection included voluminous correspondence with such Left theoreticians as Herbert Marcuse; Erich Fromm; Iring Fetscher and Maximilien Rubel; the Scottish worker Harry McShane; the African leaders Leopold Senghor and Nnamdi Azikiwe; and a host of women writers, including Natalia Trotsky; Sheila Rowbotham; the Portuguese revolutionaries Maria Barreno and Isabel do Carmo; and Americans Meridel LeSueur and Adrienne Rich.

The crises of the 1960s revolutionary movements compelled Dunayevskaya to work on a book that would clarify revolution theoretically. She did so with *Philosophy and Revolution: From Hegel to Sartre and from Marx to Mao* (1973). In her opinion, the failure to make a revolution in 1968 revealed the limitation of any social movement whose practice was not grounded in philosophy. "Now the one thing we learned from the turbulent 1960s was this: without a philosophy of revolution, near revolutions abort! It is a fact that because those near-revolutions had ended so disastrously, in particular France 1968, that the New Left finally ended their delusion that 'theory can be picked up en route' and a deeper look into Marx's philosophy of revolution was begun by some" ("Marxist-Humanism, an Interview with Raya Dunayevskaya," 17).

The women's liberation movement was not exempt from these difficulties, but rather than castigating it as a diversion from revolution, as most of the Left initially did, Dunayevskaya sought to make explicit its revolutionary character. She wrote in her third book, *Rosa Luxemburg, Women's Liberation, and Marx's Philosophy of Revolution* (1982), that the uniqueness of the liberation movement is that "not only did it come out of the left but it was *directed against it*, and not from the right, but *from within the left itself*" (p. 99). This work separated Marx's Marxism from that of all his followers. Dunayevskaya argued that the transformation of the relationship between women and men was fundamental to a Marxist concept of a new society. Dunayevskaya's analysis of the women's liberation movement remained relevant; a 1991 edition of *Rosa Luxemburg* had a foreword by Adrienne Rich. Dunayevskaya demonstrated "the relevance of Marx and Luxemburg for the women's liberation movement" (Kellner, 206). During the 1983 Karl Marx Centenary, Dunayevskaya, then seventy-three, undertook a three-month nationwide book tour, giving forty-six lectures.

When Charles Denby, editor of *News & Letters*, died in

1983, one strand that had tied the organization to Detroit was loosened. The next year Dunayevskaya moved herself and the headquarters of News and Letters Committees back to Chicago. Chicago had remained central to Dunayevskaya, not only because of her activity there as a youth and young woman in the labor movement, but because of the city's rich radical history and its role as a center of African American culture and politics. In Chicago, Dunayevskaya remained active in every aspect of News and Letters Committees. She continued to write a monthly column for *News & Letters* and spoke at meetings around the city. She met with members, helping them develop their ideas and talents, and chaired the meetings of the Resident Editorial Board, which took responsibility for the organization. She took on ever-increasing amounts of correspondence with intellectuals and activists and wrote articles and reviews for other publications. She published her fourth book, *Women's Liberation and the Dialectics of Revolution: Reaching for the Future* (1985), a collection of essays written over a thirty-five-year period, which sought to articulate "Marxist-Humanist views over the entire post–World War II world in a way that will . . . confront unfinished revolutions" (letter by Dunayevskaya, "Dear Friends," September 27, 1984, Raya Dunayevskaya Memorial Fund).

In November 1984, Dunayevskaya suffered a stroke, but by March 1985, she gave a lecture at the Wayne State University Archives of Labor and Urban Affairs, the first given by a living person whose collection the library housed. Looking over her life's work, she spoke at length about her youth in Chicago because she saw that in talking of her personal life, she could show through her biography the way in which her ideas had developed over the past seventy years. At both the beginning and end of her life, the Chicago experience remained crucial. That fact is seen clearly in her last years, which were dominated by studies for a book with the working title, "Dialectics of Organization and Philosophy: The 'Party' and Forms of Organization Born out of Spontaneity." In Chicago she also began the work of transforming *News & Letters* into a biweekly publication. In the midst of this activity, Raya Dunayevskaya died of an abdominal hemorrhage after surgery for a broken leg. Her husband of thirty-five years, John Dwyer, decided that she would be buried in Forest Home Cemetery, Forest Park, Illinois, with her grave facing the monument commemorating the revolutionaries who were falsely convicted in August 1886 of throwing a bomb in Chicago's Haymarket Square on May 4, 1886.

Since Dunayevskaya's death, all her books have been republished by university presses and translated and published in numerous countries. The Raya Dunayevskaya Memorial Fund published two collections of her writings, *The Philosophic Moment of Marxist-Humanism* (1989) and *The Marxist-Humanist Theory of State-Capitalism* (1992). Forthcoming is a collection of her philosophic writings, *The Power of Negativity*. As of 2000, the headquarters of News and Letters Committees remained in Chicago and its paper, *News & Letters*, published in each issue a column of Dunayevskaya's writings. Raya Dunayevskaya lived freely when women were not free and was fierce in her determination to transform a world she viewed as brutally inhuman into one where everyone could experience self-development and freedom.

Sources. The Raya Dunayevskaya Collection—Marxist-Humanism: A Half-Century of Its World Development—is housed at Wayne State Univ. Archives of Labor and Urban Affairs, Detroit, Michigan. The collection was arranged under Dunayevskaya's direction, and the *Guide to the Raya Dunayevskaya Collection* (1986) is itself a resource since it includes three introductions she wrote for volumes 1–10, 11, and 12. After she died, additional volumes were prepared by the Raya Dunayevskaya Memorial Fund. Bound volumes of *News & Letters* contain her articles and columns. Her youthful article under the pseudonym Comrade Sunny, "Comrade Sunny's Column," *Young Comrade*, was published in January 1924. Dunayevskaya's published works include *Marxism and Freedom: From 1776 until Today* (1958; reprinted 1964, 1971, 1982); *Philosophy and Revolution: From Hegel to Sartre, and from Marx to Mao* (1973); *Rosa Luxemburg, Women's Liberation, and Marx's Philosophy of Revolution* (1982, second edition 1991) with a foreword by Adrienne Rich in 1991; *The Philosophic Moment of Marxist-Humanism: Two Historic-Philosophic Writings* (1989); *The Marxist-Humanist Theory of State-Capitalism: Selected Writings* (1992), which includes "The Union of Soviet Socialist Republics Is a Capitalist Society." Discussions of her thought appear in numerous works, including Adrienne Rich, "Living the Revolution," *Women's Review of Books*, September 1986; Patricia Altenbernd Johnson, "Women's Liberation: Following Dunayevskaya in Practicing Dialectics," *Quarterly Journal of Ideology*, vol. 13, 1989; Susan Easton, "Raya Dunayevskaya, 1910–1987," *Bulletin of the Hegel Society of Great Britain*, Autumn/Winter 1987; Kevin Anderson, *Lenin, Hegel, and Western Marxism: A Critical Study* (1995); and Margaret Randall, *Gathering Rage: The Failure of 20th Century Revolutions to Develop a Feminist Agenda* (1992). "Marxist-Humanism, an Interview with Raya Dunayevskaya" (interviewer identified as CLR) appears in *Chicago Literary Review*, March 15, 1985. See Douglas Kellner, "Raya Dunayevskaya," in *Encyclopedia of the American Left*, ed. Mari Jo Buhle, Paul Buhle, and Dan Georgakas (1992); Kent Worcester, "C. L. R. James," in *Encyclopedia of the American Left* (1992); and Bruce Nelson, "San Francisco General Strike," *Encyclopedia of the American Left* (1992).

TERRY MOON

DUSTER, ALFREDA MARGUERITA BARNETT
September 3, 1904–April 2, 1983
COMMUNITY LEADER, EDITOR

Alfreda Barnett Duster documented African American history by editing the autobiography of her mother IDA B. WELLS-BARNETT, a journalist and antilynching crusader. In addition to the many years she devoted to this task, Duster was a mother of five children and managed, despite economic and racial obstacles, to see that all her children graduated from college.

The youngest daughter of Wells-Barnett and attorney Ferdinand L. Barnett, Alfreda Barnett was born in Chicago and had one older sister, Ida, two older brothers, Herman and Charles Aked, and two half-brothers from her father's first marriage, Albert and Ferdinand. Barnett's parents were politically and socially involved with the plight and struggle of African Americans, and Barnett grew up in an activist environment.

Alfreda Barnett graduated from Frederick Douglass Elementary School and Wendell Phillips High School, Chicago. She earned a Bachelor of Philosophy in 1924 from the University of Chicago. She was one of four African Americans in her class. Segregationist policies kept her from participating in tennis or swimming on campus, although she was talented in each sport.

After graduating from college at the age of twenty, Barnett

worked for a year in her father's law office, where she met Benjamin C. Duster, a man ten years her senior. He was working there as a law clerk after a few years of study at the University of Illinois, where he had been a friend and classmate of Alfreda Barnett's brother Herman. Barnett and Duster married on July 9, 1925, against her parents' advice. Although the marriage caused a strain in the family relationship with her mother and brother Herman, Duster made an effort to maintain positive interactions with her family, and she remained close to her brother Charles Aked and sister Ida.

Shortly after they were married, the couple experienced financial hardship. Benjamin Duster continued to work in his father-in-law's firm for a short time but, after leaving the firm, did not pursue a law career nor did he teach school, although he had a teaching certificate from Indiana State Normal School. Instead, he was content to take odd jobs, including painting, wall papering, and washing walls, sometimes for money and other times as a form of payment for another person's service.

Despite their limited income, the couple had two children before the Great Depression of the 1930s plunged the country into a period of unemployment. Benjamin Duster's unsteady employment continued, and his withdrawal from the white-collar world increased. The family grew, however, and the Dusters lived in apartments until 1935 when they moved with their four children into Ferdinand L. Barnett's house. Ida B. Wells-Barnett had died in 1931, and Ferdinand lived with his daughter Ida. A year after the move, Ferdinand Barnett died, leaving the Dusters and Ida Barnett in the family residence. Shortly afterward, the Dusters had their fifth child. Benjamin Duster continued to take temporary jobs; he also became active in local politics in the 2nd Ward regular Republican organization and in later years served in the Secretary of State Examiner's office.

Although Benjamin Duster was cynical about the work world, he was optimistic about the political and social situation generally, and he was a devoted father and husband. The Dusters had little money, but they structured activities so that the family spent time together. Alfreda Duster wanted the family to be close emotionally but also sought a better life for her children. With four boys and one girl to raise on a meager income, she became resourceful. She decided that the only way out of poverty was to ensure that each one had an excellent education. She made it her mission to make sure her children would qualify for college scholarships that were based on merit. She devised a routine for study according to which the plan for advancement would be a collective effort. The children came straight home from school, played for a short time in the backyard, ate dinner, washed dishes, then did their homework together around a table. After finishing their schoolwork, they played educational games that helped them in mathematics, spelling, and grammar. All of the children had library cards, and they all learned typing from their mother. In addition to encouraging the children to do their own schoolwork, Alfreda Duster became involved with the local Parent Teacher Association (PTA) and spent time at the schools that her children attended. She was elected president of the PTA for several terms, and in 1950 became the first black woman in Chicago to receive the organization's Mother of the Year award.

Benjamin Duster died in 1945 at the age of fifty-four, leaving Alfreda Duster with Benjamin, seventeen; Charles, fifteen; Donald, thirteen; Alfreda, eleven; and Troy, nine. She became a secretary at the Southside Community Committee (later Woodlawn Community Services Agency), where she had volunteered for years. Her sister, Ida Barnett, took care of the children. Duster's secretarial position allowed her to work flexible hours close to home. She continued to be involved with youth programs, ranging from entertainment activities with her children to work with probation and parole officers in the community. One of the special features of Duster's job was working with a summer camp that provided one of the few opportunities for children in the neighborhood. The Duster teenagers worked as camp counselors for several summers.

Alfreda Duster earned a modest income from her camp job that she supplemented with clerical work at night. She also filled out income tax forms for neighbors and offered her typing and mimeographing skills to ministers and students. Sometimes the entire Duster family helped assemble, staple, and stamp the materials Alfreda Duster prepared for clients. She made it fun by having the children play word and math games while they worked.

In 1953, after eight years with the Southside Community Committee, Duster became the secretary of Illinois State Representative Charles Jenkins, a Democrat and one of the few African Americans in the state legislature. Jenkins was chairman of the appropriations committee. Duster worked with the state legislature in Springfield, Illinois, during the week, returning home on weekends, while her sister continued to care for the children. In addition, Duster took court reporting classes so that she could take minutes during governmental meetings.

After many years of struggle, five Dusters graduated from Wendell Phillips High School—three as valedictorians and two as salutatorians. All five were awarded scholarships—three to the University of Illinois at Urbana-Champaign, one to the University of Michigan, and one to Northwestern University. They became respectively an attorney, professor, architect, business administrator, and special education teacher.

Duster encouraged other children from the neighborhood to achieve educational goals, informally offering them guidance and encouragement in their applications to college. She maintained a thirty-year relationship with a woman who later became a director of educational programs at the Art Institute of Chicago. The relationship began when the young woman was twelve years old. She and Duster developed a friendship over their shared interest in history and literature.

Duster began working on her second lifelong goal: to complete the editing of her mother's autobiography. Duster felt that Ida B. Wells-Barnett's life was an important part of history that needed to be brought to the public's attention. She edited and researched the manuscript for many years in the evenings and on weekends. In the early 1960s she and Ida Barnett purchased a co-op apartment in the Woodlawn neighborhood. After retiring in 1965, Duster dedicated her full attention to the editing of her mother's autobiography. Ida B. Wells-Barnett had written her memoirs in her later years and had relied on her memory. Duster followed leads as far as Mississippi and Tennessee to make sure the book was as accurate as possible; then she reedited the book. There was surprisingly little interest by publishers to produce the completed manuscript, but Duster was persistent. In 1970, following the nation's awakening to its long history of racism, a result of the civil rights movement, there was heightened interest in the autobiography of Wells-Barnett. John Hope Franklin, professor of history at the University of Chicago and senior editor of a series for the University of Chicago Press, provided the needed support, and in 1970 *Crusade for Justice: The Autobiography of Ida B. Wells* was published. Franklin, an authority on the history of African Americans in the United States, wrote the preface. In all, Duster had worked more than twenty-five years on her mother's memoir. The book continues to have a strong impact on the academic and African American community. It was an important source for the 1989 public broadcasting documentary film, *Ida B. Wells: A Passion for Justice*, directed by William Greaves. Subsequent works on the history of African American women in the United States, including the pathbreaking book by Paula Giddings, *When and Where I Enter: The Impact of Black Women on Race and Sex in America* (1984) draw heavily on *Crusade for Justice*, since scant materials beyond this work have survived from Ida B. Wells-Barnett's papers. A fire in Wells-Barnett's home several years before her death destroyed most of her papers.

After the publication of the book, Alfreda Duster began speaking at universities and public forums. In the public eye after years of consciously avoiding such exposure, Duster overcame her qualms about celebrity because of her enthusiasm to spread the story of her mother's determination, vision, and unrelenting work. Duster, in keeping with her mother's efforts, raised the consciousness of the American people about the struggles of African Americans.

Duster worked for the Woodlawn Community Services Agency's Catalyst for Youth program from 1947 to 1965. She was also president of the Wesleyan Service Guild of the Woodlawn United Methodist Church. In 1970, Mayor Richard J. Daley appointed Duster chairperson of the Mid-South Model Cities Area Council, which funded agencies in her community. She had been a member of the council since 1968 and had served as a member and subcommittee chairwoman for education.

Duster received many awards for her community service, including the Opportunity Centers of Chicago's Bootstrap Award in 1970 for her contribution to the Woodlawn community and in 1973 the University of Chicago Alumni Association's Citation for Public Service. In 1974, Duster was honored at the Harriet M. Harris Young Men's Christian Association as one of the senior black women of the community, and in 1978 she received an honorary doctorate of humane letters from Chicago State University.

Duster continued her mother's clubwoman tradition; she founded the Alfreda Wells Duster Civic Club; belonged to the Greenwood West Ladies Auxiliary, Delta Sigma Theta Sorority, the National Federation of Colored Women's Clubs, and Women's Board of the University of Chicago; and was a life member of the National Association for the Advancement of Colored People. She was an honorary member of the Rust College Alumni Association—the college in Holly Springs, Mississippi, where, in the Reconstruction era, Ida Wells and her family immediately took advantage of their newly won freedom and enrolled in classes.

Duster died at the age of seventy-eight from a cerebral hemorrhage after briefly suffering from heart problems and a mild case of diabetes. In keeping with her interest in helping others, she donated her body to science. A memorial service was held April 9, 1983, at the Woodlawn United Methodist Church, where she had been an active member for more than twenty years.

Alfreda Barnett Duster managed to rise above the hard times of the Great Depression, World War II, and young widowhood and provide a rich educational foundation for her five children. She was also a source of inspiration for many children and adults who were her neighbors. As the editor of her mother's manuscript, *Crusade for Justice: The Autobiography of Ida B. Wells-Barnett*, Alfreda Duster made a lasting and unique contribution to our nation's history of the struggle for freedom.

Sources. The Black Women Oral History Project, SL, contains a tape and transcript of an interview conducted with Alfreda Duster in 1978. Additional information was gathered from oral interviews in April 1994 with Duster's children—Benjamin, Donald, Troy, and Alfreda Duster Ferrell—and Duster's friend, Ronne Hartfield. Articles about Duster include Selig Adler, "Widow Tells How She Put Her 5 Children through College while Living in Poverty," *National Enquirer*, July 12, 1970; Margaret Carroll, "Her 5 Challenges Now 5 Successes," *Chicago Today*, May 5, 1970; Sandra Pesman, "All of Woodlawn Her 'Family' Now," *Chicago Daily News*, May 29, 1971; "Alfreda Duster Coordinator of Model Cities in Woodlawn," *Observer*, May 5, 1970; "Pioneer Chicagoan to Be Honored," *Chicago Defender*, June 15, 1974; "Long List of Achievements for Retiring Career Woman," *Woodlawn Booster*, February 11, 1965; "Woodlawner Cited for Services to Community," *Woodlawn Booster*, May 5, 1970; "Mother of the Year," *Woodlawn Booster*, May 12, 1970; and Donald L. Duster, "Rites for Alfreda B. Duster, 'A Pillar of the Community,'" *Chicago Defender*, April 4, 1983. Duster's biography is in *BWA*.

MICHELLE DUSTER

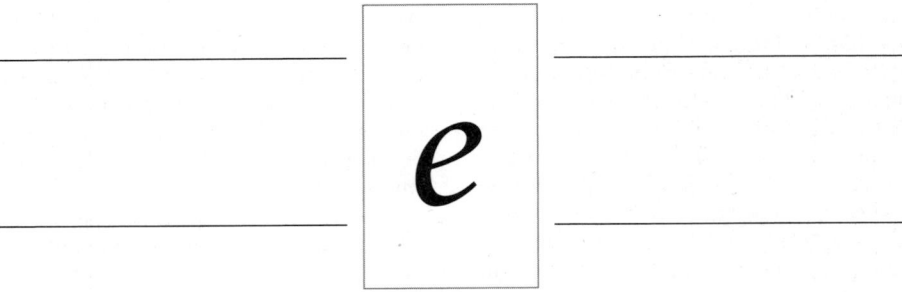

EDWARDS, THYRA J.

December 25, 1897–July 9, 1953

SOCIAL WORKER, JOURNALIST, CIVIL RIGHTS ACTIVIST

Thyra J. Edwards, whose work in the field of social welfare motivated her to become a national and international activist on public housing, health, child welfare, and interracial issues, was born and raised in Wharton, Texas. Her maternal grandmother Johnson, a slave and daughter of a cook in the plantation house of a Missouri slaveholder, was a nursemaid who secretly taught herself to read. Grandmother Johnson "stepped out of slavery" (Edwards, "A Thread from Every Man") at age eighteen when she escaped to Galesburg, Illinois, with the man she married, also a slave, and Thyra Edwards's grandfather. They traveled to freedom by way of the Underground Railroad and ultimately settled in Texas. Edwards was influenced by her vivid memories of Grandmother Johnson, a "strong, secure" ("A Thread from Every Man") woman who undermined the dynamics of the system of slavery by her act of learning to read. Johnson taught herself to write at age sixty.

Thyra Edwards's parents, Horace F. and Anna Bell (Johnson) Edwards, both teachers, were married in San Antonio, Texas, and then moved to Wharton, where Thyra was born, the second daughter of four. Edwards was educated in the segregated Houston public schools. Her father was employed in routine work as a clerk in the post office, the last African American in Houston appointed to such a position in the increasingly segregated Jim Crow South. She began to relate her father's "irratic [*sic*] moods" ("A Thread from Every Man") at home to larger social and economic forces that frustrated Blacks.

After graduating from the Houston (Colored) Public High School in 1915, she became a teacher. She first taught in the Houston public schools (1915–19), and then moved to Gary, Indiana, where she lived with her sister Thelma, also a schoolteacher. Edwards taught for one year in the Gary schools. It was one year after the Chicago Race Riot of 1919, when "bombings of black rentals and properties were every day occurrences" (Douglas, 315). During a race riot in Houston in 1917, black soldiers, taunted beyond endurance by local residents, turned on their "tormenters" (Sterling, 111), killing a number of whites. Nineteen soldiers were hanged following a "summary court martial that allowed no appeal" (Sterling, 111), and many more were sentenced to imprisonment without appeal. Journalist and antilynching activist IDA B. WELLS-BARNETT took up their cause and publicized a memorial service held in Houston for the "martyred Negro soldiers" (Sterling, 111). Edwards later described how she was "radicalized" ("A Thread from Every Man") in this period. She became aware of the economic underpinnings of this racial violence against Blacks. "Returning soldiers, many heading for Chicago for the first time because they did not want to return to former homes in the South, added to the already large numbers of black southerners who had entered the labor market during the last months of World War I" (Bates, 101). Employers frequently exacerbated racial prejudices when they threatened white workers with replacement by black laborers. Often the white workers were engaged in trade union activity, and, as African Americans were generally excluded from white labor unions as well as from most skilled occupations, they became strikebreakers, agreeing to work for less money.

Edwards enrolled in the Chicago School of Civics and Philanthropy (later the School of Social Service Administration, University of Chicago) in the summer of 1920 and studied family case work, child welfare, and labor problems. In Gary, where she continued to reside, Edwards worked as a playground director for the Gary Public Schools for one year and then, from 1921 to 1925, she was a probation officer for the Lake County (Indiana) Juvenile Court. Aware of the racial issues in Gary's child welfare system, Edwards engaged in politics and in 1924 aided a state senator in the organization of one of the first interracial commissions in Lake County. She served as general secretary of

FIG. 25. *Thyra J. Edwards worked with African Americans in support of the pro-Loyalist forces during the Spanish Civil War, 1936–38, contributing to the American Medical Bureau to Aid Spanish Democracy.*

this commission until 1929. Edwards organized a Business and Professional Women's Club, served as secretary of the Gary Community Council, and was an officer of the City Welfare Association.

Edwards continued to take courses in this period: psychology in the Indiana University Extension program (1921); forensics, contract and agency, social literature and economics at the Kent College of Law, Chicago (1925). From 1926 to 1928 she was an agent for the Lake County Board of Children's Guardians, making placements for dependent children; she then became the director of the Lake County Children's Home, residing there until 1931.

The Great Depression pushed African Americans further into poverty. By 1931, the initial programs to provide general emergency relief were put into effect. Edwards became a caseworker for the Joint Emergency Relief Commission and the Illinois Emergency Relief Commission intermittently from 1931 to 1933. In the Chicago black community, efforts to organize workers and fight for economic justice that began in the 1920s with A. Philip Randolph and the Brotherhood of Sleeping Car Porters (BSCP) continued throughout the Great Depression. IRENE McCOY GAINES, secretary of the BSCP Citizens' Committee, pulled together a group of women activists to co-

operate with the Brotherhood to work for economic change. Thyra Edwards and HALENA WILSON, president of the Colored Women's Economic Council, the auxiliary of the BSCP, were active with Gaines. Edwards began to work with Milton Webster, the Chicago BSCP leader, on the problems faced by black labor.

In this same period Edwards continued to take courses, this time at University College of the University of Chicago, where she enrolled in psychiatric social work and psychoanalysis. She reported that she studied social work, political science, and the economic and labor history of Europe and America at Brookwood Labor College, although she did not give the location of the college. Summer labor schools were popular in the 1930s among trade unionists and community activists. The South Parkway Young Women's Christian Association (YWCA) on Chicago's South Side had been sending large groups of Chicago women workers to summer labor schools since 1926. The BSCP helped raise money for these efforts. In 1933, even though raising money for workers' education was a challenge in the heart of the depression, BSCP raised money to help South Parkway send factory workers from Chicago to attend labor school. Already held in high esteem, Thyra Edwards was recommended by the BSCP for a fellowship to attend the International People's College in Elsinore, Denmark. She spent six months there, becoming familiar with Danish social legislation, adult education, and modern European politics. The conditions of working people, and especially African Americans, in the United States, however, were her main focus, and she wrote about worker powerlessness. "There are more men than jobs," she wrote. "Employers take advantage of this, using the black labour excluded from white unions as a threat against strikes. Thus the problems of white labour and black labour are inextricably interwoven" ("The Economic and Social Status of the American Negro," 3–4). Edwards continued traveling after her stay in Denmark and made independent field investigations of low-cost housing developments in Sweden, Finland, Russia, Germany, France, Vienna, and England.

Edwards returned from Denmark to Chicago's South Side in August 1934 and made her home at the Abraham Lincoln Center, an interracial social settlement founded in 1905 by Jenkin Lloyd Jones, Unitarian-Universalist minister and progressive social activist. It was one of the few community centers or settlements located within and accessible to Chicago's black community at that time. In the mid-1930s she continued doing casework for the Illinois Emergency Relief Commission and served with the housing division of the Public Works Administration as an assistant supervisor.

Edwards had observed the treatment of syphilis in Denmark in 1934, visiting with physicians who had started a state-subsidized commune for children with congenital syphilis. Back in Chicago she emphasized the strong correlation between poverty, lack of access to treatment, and poor health; those who were very poor, badly housed, and living in overcrowded conditions were more likely to experience a high incidence of disease. Treatment facilities were often not available to the Chicago black community.

Longstanding discrimination against Blacks in housing had confined the growing African American population in Chicago to congested, segregated, inadequate tenements and flats. In 1934 an interracial couple, Herbert and Jane Emory Newton, was evicted from a Chicago apartment in a white neighborhood. She helped organize the "Newton Defense Committee," formed in 1935 to publicize and protest the eviction. That same year Edwards, who had begun to write articles for Claude Barnett's Associated Negro Press, became involved in the efforts of local factory workers to organize at the Sopkins Apron plant. Edwards wrote an article for the *Crisis*, the magazine published by the National Association for the Advancement of Colored People (NAACP), which described the plight of unorganized black workers at Sopkins, who had attempted to organize a local through the International Ladies' Garment Workers Union (ILGWU). When Ben Sopkins, owner of the factory, heard that an ILGWU organizer was talking to his workers, he successfully brought in local politicians to aid him in an anti-union drive. In the name of "loyalty" to Sopkins, who had hired Blacks, Edwards reported on the irony of a misguided "Negro" leadership, "still clinging to the frayed skirts of the employer" ("Let Us Have More Like Mr. Sopkins," 82) that called for a "company union" instead of affiliating with the ILGWU. Most of the workers at Sopkins were black women, and Edwards sadly concluded that they represented "the great uninformed mass of unskilled labor caught between the nether stones of unscrupulous employers and uninformed and unscrupulous race leadership" (p. 82).

African Americans were deeply divided, however, on whether or not labor unions dominated by whites offered black workers any better protection than did white employers. In cities like Chicago, early rejection by and prejudice and violence from white workers and union officials left lingering doubts; on the other hand, the small black middle class, in conjunction with many religious leaders whose prominent pulpits were influential in shaping community opinion, cautioned Blacks to be loyal to the employers whose factories provided jobs. Increasingly, Blacks like Edwards, BSCP leader A. Philip Randolph, and NAACP cofounder W.E.B. Du Bois, who left the group in 1934 because of its too moderate stands and acceptance of small gains, rejected what they came to define as accommodation. In 1934, Edwards voiced this emerging militant stance in "An Open Letter to Ishmael Flory," a local leader. Agreeing with Flory's critique of separatist education supported by liberal philanthropists, Edwards considered him courageous. "Education that encourages this subordinate and humiliating status [separate and unequal] is worse than ignorance and illiteracy," she contended. She believed that the new era would reject the gradualist approach and demand full citizenship and manhood/womanhood for African Americans.

Edwards had coalesced with a group of Chicago black activists, including labor organizers, Communist Party members, and BSCP's Citizens Committee leaders, who called for a militant program of mass demonstrations, picketing, boycotting, and mass protest in the face of devastating economic conditions experienced by African Americans. In part, this "new crowd" of leaders was reacting to the more "elitist" (Bates, 319–20) strategies of the NAACP in the face of severely diminished economic opportunity for Blacks in northern cities and increased discrimination. Expressing the new militancy in Chicago, Thyra Edwards became one of the leaders of the National Negro Congress (NNC), when in February 1936 more than five thousand men and women came to the first convention. Edwards became a member of the national executive council of the NNC.

Edwards also continued to study at the University of Chicago in the mid-1930s, taking courses in social science, sociology, political science, and economics. She completed comprehensive exams in these fields in 1935–36.

Edwards chaired a committee at the Abraham Lincoln Center in 1936 called The Negro in Industry, which focused on how to open employment opportunities for more African Americans. Edwards noted the particular dilemma of the postwar black workers who were being replaced by white workers not only in the industry jobs African Americans had obtained during the war but also in jobs "traditionally" held by Blacks, such as cooks, waiters, and hotel workers. She continued to see the problem of race in America as primarily and essentially a problem in economics. Edwards emphasized the need for organized African Americans to receive training and education to allow them to compete for standard wage jobs. She came into conflict with the Chicago Urban League in 1937 when it was unwilling to meet her request to form a subcommittee of the Council of Social Agencies on the Negro in Industry to further explore ways to raise low wage standards for Blacks.

Thyra Edwards increasingly saw the problems of African Americans not only in economic terms but in the context of international developments. She served as a foreign correspondent for Claude Barnett, whose news service distributed national and international news of concern to the black community to journals and newspapers across the country. Edwards's articles appeared in well-known black newspapers and periodicals, including the *Chicago Defender*, the *Pittsburgh Courier*, the *Amsterdam News*, and the *Crisis*. She saw herself in a "strategic position" to lead Claude Barnett's American readers "from their parochial introversion to some grasp of their relations on a world scale" (Letter to Barnett, May 18, 1944, Barnett Papers).

Edwards persisted in bringing global news, particularly concerning minorities, home to America. She brought news of America and the issues of the black working class to Europe, as a challenge to the stereotypes prevalent in mainstream European papers. She chastised the American and foreign press for universal stereotyping of the African American "as a clown and a buffoon" ("Negro Literature Comes to Denmark," 141), and spoke of the need for Blacks to tell their own story.

Edwards was interested in the issues relating to women in the United States and in countries such as the Soviet Union which, she believed, were inaugurating new programs. At home she chaired the woman's section of the NNC. Drawn to the socialist experiment in the Soviet Union, in the summer of 1936 she led a summer tour of American students and educators to Russia and Europe, where such famous civil rights advocates as Paul Robeson and William Patterson gave talks. That summer she studied and wrote about the problems of women and children among national minorities in the Soviet Union. As a contributing editor for the *Woman Today*, a trade union magazine run by a group of black and white women in New York City, she wrote on various topics, including the Moscow Theatre for Children and new Soviet laws concerning abortion. Edwards also served on the editorial council of the magazine *Soviet Russia Today*. By 1942, such activities and writings made her an object of federal investigation as a subversive by the Federal Security Agency; she responded in her typically outspoken and independent way.

Edwards wrote exhaustively about the rise of fascism in Italy, Germany, and Spain. As always, she linked the question of the international struggle against fascism to her concern for the "Negro and his civil liberties" (February 1939 clipping, scrapbook, Edwards Papers). While in Paris in 1937, her tour group attended a conference of the World Committee against War and Fascism. She wrote, "The crisis in Spain is the crisis of democracy and of minority races" (February 1939 clipping), and said that the liberation struggles in America and Europe were part of the same struggle. In October 1937 she went to Barcelona and Catalonia as a delegate of the Social Worker's Committee to Aid Spanish Democracy. She sent articles to Barnett's Associated Negro Press on the colonies established for displaced children in war torn Spain and about the air raids in Barcelona. Back in the United States, Edwards served on the Negro People's Committee with the Medical Bureau and North American Committee to Aid Spanish Democracy. In 1938 she toured twenty-one American cities with Salaria Kee, the first African American nurse sent to Spain, as part of a nationwide campaign to raise funds for an ambulance from "American Negroes" to send to Republican Spain. She was part of the collective protest against the American embargo against Republican Spain.

By 1938 Edwards and others working with the Medical Bureau began to organize to deal with the devastation caused by the Spanish Civil War. More than half a million Spanish refugees, including many children, were living in camps in France. Edwards wrote about severe conditions in the camps. When Mexico volunteered to receive these refugees, Edwards traveled there to report on resettlement plans for the Santa Clara Valley. Edwards's many visits to Mexico resulted in a series of stories for the Associated Negro Press. Always aware of the relationship of the struggle for equality in the United States and elsewhere, her reports on attending bullfights led to one cryptic headline about American tourists: "Can Stand Lynching But Bullfight, No."

Edwards battled the racism of Hitler's German expansion programs and organized against his demand for African colonies. She was appointed executive secretary of a national organization, United Effort against Hitler, which became the National Negro Stop Hitler and Hitlerism Committee.

During World War II, Edwards returned to the social work field and the basic conditions that confronted Chicago Blacks. In 1942 she worked with the Chicago Venereal Disease Control Program as the director of the in-service training section for field investigators. The program was co-sponsored by the U.S. Public Health Service, the Chicago Board of Health, and the Work Projects Administration. The objectives were to locate cases of venereal disease, provide access to medical care, and create preventive measures through medical, educational, and legal channels.

In 1943 Edwards left Chicago and moved to New York City. She became the general manager of the *People's Voice*, a newspaper started that year by civil rights activist Adam Clayton Powell Jr., who in 1945 became Harlem's first elected congressman.

Thyra Edwards married Murray Gitlin in the summer of 1943. He was an official of the United Jewish Appeal. She also continued in journalism, reporting in 1944 on the International Labor Conference. Edwards criticized the American Federation of Labor for not including black labor representation; she chastised the African American community for not providing leadership either. Her own perspective came, as it had in the past, from direct experience with the conditions of Blacks in America. In 1944 she served as assistant director of education and public relations of the Congress of Industrial Organization's (CIO) National Maritime Union, formed for black seamen of the East Coast who had been excluded from the American Federation of Labor's International Seamen's Union. The same year in a series of six articles on the "subject of race relations' advisors in federal government departments," she saw race relations committees as "an easy substitute for action, a technique of short circuiting Negro pressure groups from direct action on state legislatures and city councils" and concluded that such approaches prevented unity between Blacks and Whites "in common cause programs" ("Are Race Relations Advisors Helping or Hindering?" April 10, 1944).

Murray Gitlin became director of the American Joint Distribution Committee's programs in Italy. In 1948 the Gitlins moved to Italy, where Edwards spent the last five years of her life. She organized the first Jewish child-care program in Rome. Little is known about her personal life; she had been reluctant to marry in what she termed "the routine way" (untitled, Folder 3, Edwards Papers). As Thyra Edwards Gitlin she continued to write and to fight for her ideals. She learned to speak Italian, mingled with peasants, clergy, and intellectuals, and became an active participant in Jewish communal life in Rome. Quite late in her life, while in Italy, she took up painting; and she was writing a book on nature and philosophy when she became ill.

Edwards died at age fifty-six following a long illness. She had returned to the United States. Her funeral was held in St. Philips (Episcopal) Church in New York City. Her ashes were scattered over the Atlantic Ocean.

Thyra Edwards traversed the globe from Houston, Texas, to Europe, Scandinavia, and the Soviet Union. Long before the concept "think globally, act locally" became an anthem for an antiwar, anticolonial generation, Edwards saw in the most intimate details of the struggle for African American liberation a connection to all minority peoples struggling against oppression. She took up the causes of the unemployed worker in the United States, the dispossessed people of Spain, and the displaced Jewish orphan in Rome with equal conviction and saw the interconnections among these struggles.

Sources. The Thyra Edwards Papers, CHS, have correspondence, a scrapbook, unpublished and published articles, including an unpublished paper, "The Economic and Social Status of the American Negro," February 1934; typescript, "An Open Letter to Ishmael Flory," April 11, 1934; and a manuscript autobiographical sketch, "A Thread from Every Man in the Village," February 1940–February 1941. Also important is Edwards's correspondence with Claude Barnett in the Claude Barnett Papers, CHS. See folders on the Abraham Lincoln Center in the Welfare Council Papers, CHS. Articles written by Edwards include "Let Us Have More Like Mr. Sopkins," *Crisis*, March 1935; "Negro Literature Comes to Denmark," *Crisis*, May 1936; "Can Stand Lynching But

Bullfight, No" *Afro-American*, January 21, 1939; "Are Race Relations Advisers Helping or Hindering the Advance of Negroes?" six-article series, 1944, n.p., Barnett Papers; "The ILO and Postwar Planning for the African Colonies," *Crisis*, July 1944. See Beth Bates, "The Unfinished Business of Emancipation: Protest Politics Come of Age in Black Chicago, 1925–1943" (Ph.D. diss., Columbia Univ., 1997); Ann Douglas, *Terrible Honesty: Mongrel Manhattan in the 1920s* (1995); and Dorothy Sterling, *Black Foremothers: Three Lives* (1979), for background. Linda J. Evans, "Claude Barnett and the Associated Negro Press," *Chicago History*, Spring 1983, is useful for a description of the agency for which Edwards wrote.

GWYNNE GERTZ

EMANUEL, FANNIE HAGEN
July 31, 1871–April 7, 1934

PHYSICIAN, REFORMER, CLUBWOMAN, SOCIAL LEADER

Fannie Emanuel, a leading member of Chicago's African American elite, was born Fannie Hagen in Cincinnati, Ohio, in 1871. She graduated from Gaines High School, moving to Chicago with her parents in the mid-1880s. No other information is available concerning her family or childhood. She married William Emanuel on February 27, 1888. He was born in 1862 in Macon, Georgia. His family moved to Arkansas, where his father achieved some modest prosperity. In 1878 in New York City, William Emanuel took a course in chiropody, a medical specialty for treatment of ailments of the hands and feet. He settled in Chicago in 1886, where he and Hagen met.

During the 1890s, Fannie Emanuel's time was devoted to her young family. She bore six children, three sons and three daughters, but only her three sons survived. Later the Emanuels adopted a daughter, Juanita. Her three sons, William Harrison, Floyd Saunders, and McKinley, would all join in the family business, while Juanita would go on to pursue a career in education. The family attended St. Thomas Episcopal Church.

Emanuel was also trained in chiropody, and for many years she worked alongside her husband in the practice. The Emanuels quickly joined the ranks of leaders of Chicago's African American community and were frequently listed in newspaper reports of major social events, charity balls, clubs, and parties. Portraits reveal an extremely attractive woman with a somewhat shy and unassuming demeanor. Julius Taylor, a lifelong supporter and great admirer of the Emanuels and editor of the *Broad Ax*, one of Chicago's leading African American newspapers, frequently featured front page photos of both Fannie and William Emanuel, praising their accomplishments and social activism. In 1907 the couple was profiled as among the community's most well-known social leaders.

By 1900, Fannie Emanuel was a prominent clubwoman. She was one of the original members in 1893 of the Ida B. Wells Women's Club, the first club established in Chicago among African American women. Black women faced extreme discrimination, and Chicago's white women's clubs were adamantly opposed to integration. The membership of black clubwoman FANNIE BARRIER WILLIAMS in the influential Chicago Woman's Club was the exception that dramatized the overall exclusion. Moreover, African Americans were excluded from almost all social service institutions and charitable organizations. Thus, whether the need was for settlement houses, or-

phanages, hospitals, old-age homes, or recreational facilities, the African American community was forced to provide for itself. By 1900 Chicago had a half-dozen "colored" women's clubs devoted to philanthropy and self-help, and many other clubs had formed throughout Illinois. Fannie Emanuel quickly became active at both the local and state level with the newly formed Illinois Federation of Colored Women's Clubs. She maintained her activism with the federation throughout her life, serving in many different positions, including those of recording secretary (1901), chair of the Social Settlement Committee (1910), officer (1912), and head of the Publicity Committee (1923) and the Social Hygiene Committee (1924).

In 1905 Fannie Emanuel turned her energies in a new direction, supporting the first settlement house established to serve the African American community, the Frederick Douglass Center. The center, founded by a white woman, Unitarian minister CELIA WOOLLEY, was dedicated to "promoting a just and amicable relation between the white and colored people" (quoted in Spear, 104). The settlement, established on the edge of Chicago's segregated Black Belt (Philpott, 318), attempted to provide an interracial setting in which middle-class, educated members of both races could work together while providing social services to those in need. However, racial and political divisions quickly erupted. Julius Taylor, in the *Broad Ax*, sharply condemned the center for not truly being located "among the neediest and poorest class of Colored people" (June 23, 1906) and argued that the center failed to provide any real services for the poor. Moreover, he claimed that all the heads of the center's departments were white. He further reported that Woolley was widely quoted as saying that African American women, no matter how highly educated, "lack executive ability and are incapable of leading off in any reform movement or serving as Presidents of the various departments" (*Broad Ax*, July 7, 1906).

Conflicts increased when IDA B. WELLS-BARNETT, who had served as vice-president of the Frederick Douglass Center's woman's club, sought to become president. In her autobiography Wells-Barnett described the political "double dealing" (p. 286) that denied her the club's presidency. Instead, Fannie Emanuel was elected president and served two terms (1906–1908), while Wells-Barnett left the center and never returned. Despite these criticisms, the Douglass Center continued to "command the loyalty of 'the cream' of black society in Chicago" (Philpott, 318) until Celia Parker Woolley's death in 1918, when it came under Urban League management and faded away.

Fannie Emanuel, however, was not satisfied with the limited work of the center and quickly became disenchanted with its vision of interracial cooperation. In 1908 she began laying the groundwork for her own settlement house, taking a year-long course in social science at the recently established Chicago School of Civics and Philanthropy. Emanuel began offering a series of luncheons at her home to raise money for a projected "Friends and Neighbors House" (*Broad Ax*, May 9, 1908). In October 1908, the Emanuel Settlement, as it came to be called, opened on Chicago's South Side. Fannie Emanuel explained her philosophy: the settlement was deliberately located in a "congested district of colored people, known as the 'black belt'. . . . We bar no one, although our work is chiefly among colored people" (quoted in Woods and Kennedy, 47). Elsewhere, in a veiled criticism of the Douglass Center, she reemphasized that "the Settlement is a great benefit to the young people of this neighborhood because it is located where it is most needed" (*Broad Ax*, October 2, 1909). The settlement offered an ambitious range of services and activities, including a nursery, employment bureau, medical clinic, reading rooms, boy's club, young woman's Christian circle, and music club, along with sewing, cooking, literary, and art classes. The settlement also offered a kindergarten class, thus providing one of the few opportunities for African American children to attend in the city at a time when education for five-year-olds was experimental and not part of the public school system. Most privately run kindergartens were for whites only. In 1910 the settlement had two full-time women workers but was otherwise staffed entirely by African American volunteers. Fannie Emanuel undertook the daunting task of completely funding the project on her own for its first year and attempted to run the settlement almost single-handedly for several years.

The Emanuel Settlement generated insufficient support within either the white or African American communities. The fate of the settlement followed a familiar pattern. Between 1900 and Chicago's 1919 race riot, nine settlements opened in the African American community, and all but one closed. All of these fledgling efforts divided and drained the very limited financial resources of the African American community.

Moreover, in 1909 William Emanuel was forced to declare bankruptcy, thereby seriously undermining Emanuel's ability to support the settlement through her personal finances. She then turned to major fund-raising efforts. For two years she served as the organizer and manager of the annual New Year's Charity Ball, the biggest social event in Chicago's African American community. This ball raised one hundred dollars each for the Emanuel Settlement, Old Folks Home, and Amanda Smith Orphanage. The sum was insufficient to support the ambitious program of social services and activities that Emanuel had envisioned; the settlement survived until 1912.

With the closing of the Emanuel Settlement, Fannie Emanuel turned her energies toward pursuit of a dream that had long beckoned her. She had studied at Jenner Medical School briefly in 1909, but finally, in 1912, at the age of forty-one, she entered the Chicago Hospital College of Medicine, a school designed for working adults, graduating with honors in 1915. Dr. Emanuel spent the next decade engaged in developing her medical practice, specializing in the treatment of women and children. She was one of sixty-five African American women physicians in the country in 1920. She also became active in supporting the expansion of medical opportunities for other African Americans, serving on the Women's Executive Advisory Council of the campaign committee to raise money for a new "colored" hospital and "colored" nurses training school. The 1921 plan to raise one hundred thousand dollars for a "Greater Fort Dearborn Hospital and Training School for Colored Nurses" (*Broad Ax*, September 17, 1921) was never realized. In 1930 she donated a generous amount for the building campaign of Provident Hospital, which was originally established in 1891.

In the 1920s, Emanuel continued her extensive club and charity work. In 1906 the Phyllis Wheatley Home for Girls had been established as a joint project by Chicago's African American women's clubs. It was intended to provide safe lodging, a proper environment, social services, classes, and an employment bureau for African American women migrating to Chicago. The idea quickly became popular among African American club women nationally, and Phyllis Wheatley Homes were eventually opened in seventeen cities across the United States. Fannie Emanuel served on the board of directors of the Chicago Phyllis Wheatley Home from 1922 to 1927. Reflecting Emanuel's philosophy, the board represented an organization of African American women that did not have affiliation with or support from white organizations. Emanuel was also a charter member of the newly established "colored" women's branch of the Young Women's Christian Association and served as president in 1918.

William Emanuel died in 1930 after a short, unknown illness. A few years later Fannie Emanuel married Dr. J. E. Carter, but nothing is known of this brief, second marriage. At the age of sixty-three, Fannie Emanuel died of an infection resulting from a diabetic condition. She was buried alongside her first husband at Holy Sepulchre Cemetery in Worth, Illinois, south of Chicago.

Fannie Emanuel devoted her life to philanthropic projects designed to benefit the most disadvantaged members of her community. A pioneering clubwoman, she actively supported a broad range of self-help institutions developed within the African American community. Dissatisfied with the patronizing attitudes of white reformers, she single-handedly founded her own settlement house. Finally, she graduated with honors from medical school, establishing a successful medical practice in the last two decades of her life.

Sources. The only authored statement by Emanuel was her first annual report on Emanuel Settlement, found in the *Broad Ax* newspaper, October 2, 1909. The contours of Emanuel's life can only be pieced together from fragmentary articles and listings in the *Broad Ax*, where she was frequently profiled. Major, but still limited, articles and photos were printed in the following editions: December 28, 1907; December 25, 1909; May 29, 1915; September 7, 1918; and February 2, 1924. Her name appeared frequently under listings of various club activities and in the social events columns 1904–25. Both her medical school graduation and death were also featured on the front page of the *Chicago Defender*, May 30, 1915, and April 7, 1934. The Emanuel Settlement was listed with a brief description in *The Handbook of Settlements* by Robert A. Woods and Albert J. Kennedy (1911) and more fully described by Thomas Philpott in *The Slum and the Ghetto* (1978). Philpott also offered a comprehensive description of the settlement house movement in Chicago's African American community. Allan H. Spear, *Black Chicago: The Making of a Negro Ghetto, 1890–1920* (1967) described the black women's club movement. Very brief biographical entries appeared in the following works: Elizabeth Lindsay Davis's *The Story of the Illinois Federation of Colored Women's Clubs* (1922), *Simms Blue Book and Directory* (1923), and *Who's Who in Colored America* (1927). She was mentioned in passing in Ida B. Wells-Barnett's autobiography, Alfreda M. Duster, ed., *Crusade for Justice: The Autobiography of Ida B. Wells* (1970), and was listed in the reference guide, *Black Biography, 1790–1950: A Cumulative Index*, ed. Randall K. Burkett, Nancy Hall Burkett, and Henry Louis Gates Jr. (1991).

L. MARA DODGE

ETS, MARIE HALL RODIG. *See* CASSETTARI, ROSA

EVANS, MARY GREEN
January 13, 1891–April 12, 1966
PASTOR, ADMINISTRATOR

Operating in a sphere that was asserted to be the province of men, Mary G. Evans was able to confront and overcome religious and social mores intended to define and limit women's roles in the church. The third of Alfred and Lucy (Anderson) Green's four living children, Evans was born Mary E. Green in Washington, D.C. Her father, who was born just after the Civil War in 1866, also in the District of Columbia, was a laborer in 1891 and a clerk by 1900. Her mother, who was born in Culpeper County, Virginia, in 1853, could not read or write. She was a laundress.

Following the death of both parents, ten-year-old Mary Green went to Louisville, Kentucky, to live with her maternal aunt, the wife of J. J. Evans, an itinerant minister of the African Methodist Episcopal (AME) Church. This event severed Green's ties to her three siblings. By 1903, when she preached her first sermon at an AME church in Chicago, Mary Green had assumed the use of her uncle's surname.

Changes of assignments were frequent for Reverend Evans. In 1904 he was appointed to serve at Davis Memorial AME in LaGrange, Illinois. The family took up residence in Evanston, Illinois. There, Evans completed her education in the public schools of Evanston and Chicago, where she graduated from Wendell Phillips High School.

In her aunt's household, Evans's nascent interest in a religious vocation continued to blossom. At age fourteen, Evans was licensed to preach by a Chicago reverend. A year later, after joining the Indiana Conference of the AME Church, Evans was issued an evangelist license by the local bishop.

After graduation from high school, Evans had to work before being able to continue her education. She then enrolled in Payne Theological Seminary at Wilberforce University, in Wilberforce, Ohio, where she completed a three-year course of study. With financial assistance from her aunt, the Federal Clubs of Indiana, and the AME Church's Indiana Conference, Evans was able to secure a bachelor's degree in divinity in 1911.

Evans attended the World's Seventh Sunday School Convention in Zurich, Switzerland, in 1913, as the delegate of the State Association of Indiana. She was one of two African American delegates selected to make a trip to Palestine. Evans thus accomplished her ambition to be baptized in the River Jordan. Upon her return to the United States in 1914, after six months of visiting countries in Europe and Africa, Evans spent the next two years preaching in almost every state, lecturing about the trip and her travels. Anchored in her career as an evangelist, Evans forged a solid reputation as an outstanding speaker, inspiring preacher, and accomplished fund-raiser. Early in 1917, Evans served the congregation of Wayman Chapel in Indianapolis, Indiana, when its newly appointed minister died. Later that same year she was employed as a Special Worker for Colored Schools with the national Young Women's Christian Association from September 1917 to January 1918. Beginning in 1924, Evans pastored St. John AME Church in Indianapolis, which was formerly Wayman Chapel. While there, she was able to build a new church and parsonage. She introduced tithing by members—giving a tenth of one's income to support the church instead of fund-raising. Evans ended her affiliation with the AME Church when she left St. John to move to Chicago to take over leadership of the nondenominational Cosmopolitan Community Church.

Evans did not give a reason for making a risky career change during the Great Depression. At St. John, she worked under restrictions that came from the AME Church's stance on the role of women in the ministry. The AME Church, oldest of the major black religious denominations, had a tradition of active female preachers, but its organizational response was reactive rather than proactive regarding the inclusion and acceptance of women into the ordained ministry. An 1888 conference ban on ordaining women to the order of deacon or elder would not be stricken from the AME Discipline until 1948. Yet Evans, like AMANDA BERRY SMITH and others who laid the groundwork before her, tenaciously persisted in pursuing and executing her calling. She faced entrenched opposition from male colleagues while at St. John AME Church. Further, the denomination had complete control over clergy appointments as well as over a congregation's finances. Her break with the AME denomination in the early 1930s represented a major decision by Evans to continue to be self-defined and in control of her ministerial vocation.

In Chicago, she took on the challenge of piloting a small, debt-ridden congregation. The minister, John Russell Harvey, had founded Cosmopolitan Community Church in 1923 after leaving the leadership of St. Mary AME Church. Cosmopolitan was part of an alliance of nondenominational churches that operated without a bishopric. When Harvey was about to retire in 1931, Evans was tapped for the position after she ran a successful revival to raise money to reduce the church's debt. From the time she became pastor in 1932 until her death, Evans was instrumental in carving out a substantial sphere of influence for Cosmopolitan Community Church on Chicago's South Side. The church's inherited debt of thirty-six thousand dollars was retired in 1936. Membership increased nearly tenfold and remained stable throughout her administration.

At Cosmopolitan, Evans had the freedom to broaden the congregation's activities in keeping with her concept of a church responsibility in the community that went beyond religious observance. Growing to maturity during the Progressive Era, Evans must have been aware of many reform issues and activities in the social and political landscape of early-twentieth-century America. Women in secular and religious settings had come together to agitate for improvements in education, health care, housing, and working conditions. Evans placed social action and assistance to residents of the community within the scope of her church. She instituted a wide range of secular programs and activities, including a day nursery for the children of working mothers, free health clinics, educational and recreational facilities and programs for youth, and highly successful subscription and membership drives for *Ebony* magazine and the National Association for the Advancement of Colored People (NAACP).

Under Evans's direction, Cosmopolitan undertook a number of building programs. In the 1930s, the church's interior and exterior were remodeled. Construction of a four-story facility, known as the Community House or the "House That Faith Built," was completed in 1948. It provided office and storage space and housed the day nursery and kindergarten, health clinics, a kitchen, and a gymnasium. Another crowning accomplishment for Evans was the church's completion of the Home for the Aged, also called the "Home That Love Built," which opened in 1963. Cosmopolitan's facilities were open to all in the community, whether or not they were members of the church.

It was the tithing instituted by Evans rather than the usual fund-raising events (teas, dinners, raffles) that enabled the church to undertake such endeavors and to meet its financial obligations. Evans organized her congregants into Calendar Clubs based on their birth month. Each club was assigned responsibility for a given expense or project. Through Club 13, which she headed, Evans always outmatched the contributions of the other clubs. Club 14 had only one member, entrepreneur Marjorie Stewart Joyner, one of the founders of the church.

Evans ran Cosmopolitan's worship services with strict discipline. The services she conducted were short, lasting less than ninety minutes; punctuality was stressed and latecomers were not seated; announcements were not made from the pulpit. Despite her strict rules, Evans inspired others by her example and was able to garner their cooperation. The common sentiment was that Evans was as giving as she was demanding, if not more so. Evans knew the name of every church member and gave all members a very early call on their birthdays.

Remembrances of Evans suggest polarities in her character and personality. She was described as being strict and austere and at the same time caring and gentle. Of average height, she carried herself well. Frugal as a rule, Evans at one time declined to buy any clothing until full funding for the Home for the Aged was secured. During that period, she made do with one shiny black suit. When Evans took time for personal pursuits, she indulged herself by traveling.

Evans, who never married, shared a residence for many years with the director of the church's day nursery, Edna Cook. Cook was the daughter of Reverend William Decatur Cook, who helped to organize Chicago's black community churches. After the Home for the Aged was built, Evans lived there for a brief period at the end of her life.

Evans had a close relationship with Jean Jones, the daughter of Dr. William Jones, who headed the church's health clinics. Evans considered Jean her adopted child. Jean (Jones) Crawford recalled that Evans was like a grandmother who spoiled her. After writing a letter to Mamie Eisenhower following the 1952 election, eleven-year-old Jean Jones received an invitation to attend the president's inauguration and was accompanied by Evans. When Jones went away to college, it was an established routine for her to receive a call from Evans every Sunday evening.

Jean Jones did not receive her expected birthday call from Evans in 1966. On that day, Evans died in Chicago's Presbyterian St. Luke's Hospital at five in the morning of a pulmonary embolus due to congestive heart failure. As she had requested, Evans was cremated and her remains were inurned and placed in the cornerstone of the Cosmopolitan Community Center.

Her alma mater, Wilberforce University, had recognized her achievements, granting her an honorary doctorate in 1960. In 1991 Cosmopolitan Community Church commemorated Evans's hundredth birthday. When the church's new facility was completed in 1996, space was reserved for a Mary G. Evans Memorial Library. These memorials attest to Evans's legacy as a church and community leader. She broadened the role of her church to include social action and community assistance at the same time that she expanded the responsibilities of parishioners to fund new programs through tithing.

Sources. The Marjorie Stewart Joyner Papers at the Vivian G. Harsh Collection of Afro-American History and Literature at the Carter G. Woodson Regional Library, CPL, contain materials from Cosmopolitan Community Church (annual reports, financial statements, brochures). Members of Cosmopolitan Community Church and others who knew Evans provided information to Caroll A. Hibler. Evans is listed in Richard R. Wright Jr., ed., *The Centennial Encyclopaedia of the African Methodist Episcopal Church* (1916). Her accomplishments are described in Dorothy Shelton, *The History of Cosmopolitan Community Church 1923–1993* (1993). Newspaper and magazine articles profiling Evans have useful information but contain inconsistencies in names, dates, and events and have a hagiographic cast; see "Lady Preacher," *Ebony*, September 1949; "Woman of God," *Our World*, February 1951; Wesley South, "Her Faith Reclaims a Needy Church," *Chicago American*, June 3, 1957; Robert Colby Nelson, "Tithing Church Aids," *Christian Science Monitor*, January 2, 1960; "God's Saintly Servant," *Now!* January 6, 1962. Obituaries for Evans appeared on April 13, 1966, in *Chicago's American, Chicago Daily News, Chicago Defender, Chicago Sun Times, CT,* and in *Jet* on April 28, 1966. Titles useful for gaining a fuller understanding of the milieu that nourished Evans and her predecessors and contemporaries are William L. Andrews, ed., *Sisters of the Spirit* (1986); C. Eric Lincoln and Lawrence H. Mamiya, *The Black Church in the African American Experience* (1990); and Dorothy Salem, *To Better Our World: Black Women in Organized Reform, 1890–1920* (1990).

CAROLL A. HIBLER

EVERHART, MARY JANE
February 13, 1853–April 3, 1928
EVANGELIST, URBAN MISSIONARY

Mary Jane Everhart operated the Olive Branch mission on the Near West Side of Chicago for almost forty years; hers was a religious mission, without the institutional support provided by such denominations as the Roman Catholic Church or the Salvation Army. Everhart, a licensed Free Methodist evangelist, raised all the funds necessary to support its work. Even while supplying the usual social services, she averaged one religious conversion per day.

Mary Jane Everhart was born on a farm near Lickingville in Clarion County, Pennsylvania. She was the only child of John and Jemima (Gilfillan) Everhart and the granddaughter of a Scottish Methodist preacher. She graduated from a normal college in Edinboro, Pennsylvania, in the late 1860s and then taught school in Pennsylvania for twenty years.

Raised in the Methodist Episcopal Church, she was converted to Free Methodism at an 1882 revival conducted by Rev. D. B. Tobey at Newmansville, Pennsylvania, just three miles from her family's farm. Free Methodists had separated from the Methodist Episcopal Church to return to what they considered were the original doctrines and lifestyle of Methodism. They condemned the worldliness of the well-established Methodist churches, opposing the practice of selling pews and advocating free pews for all, an issue that in part gave them their name. They especially emphasized the Wesleyan teaching of the sanctification of life by means of grace through faith.

Everhart became a regularly licensed conference evangelist of the Oil City (Pennsylvania) Conference of the Free Methodist Church and held church membership at Tidiout, Pennsylvania. She moved to Chicago, Illinois, in October 1890 in answer to a call for teachers from the Chicago Industrial Home for Children. Dependent children under twelve years of age went to orphanages; industrial schools, similar to orphanages, were for older dependent children up to the age of sixteen. Industrial schools received public support, while orphanages did not. At the suggestion of its superintendent, T. B. Arnold, she also began volunteering at Rachel A. Bradley's Near West Side mission. Everhart saw that the need for her help was great, not only because of the desperate plight of the clientele, but because Bradley herself was in poor health.

Bradley had started a mission around 1876. In mid-1893, as Bradley lay dying, Everhart agreed to purchase all the mission's equipment and carry on the work. Naming it the Olive Branch, Everhart reopened the mission August 30, 1893. In the first year, she gave out 2,782 garments, in addition to bedding, 883 loaves of bread, and 40 baskets of provisions; she served 1,168 meals. There were 1,067 people who attended services and sought communion. These statistics were printed in the first issue of the *Olive Branch: The World for Jesus*, a four-page monthly newspaper that Everhart began publishing in September 1894, writing virtually all of the copy herself.

By July 1895 Everhart reported more than one thousand subscribers who paid twenty-five cents per year to receive the monthly. These subscribers, from across the country, but concentrated in the Midwest, were one of two sources of support for the mission. The other came from Free Methodist camp meetings, primarily in Ohio and Michigan. After speaking at a summer gathering, Everhart would take up a collection to fund the Olive Branch. These train trips to the countryside, an escape from the "noisy, wicked city of Chicago" (*Olive Branch*, vol. 4, no. 1, 1), also afforded a brief vacation, but Everhart's work was never far from her mind: "As the train left the smoke, filth and saloons behind and swept out into the fresh air, by green fields and forests, past country homes and school-houses, my eyes looked out at the beauties through which I was passing, but my thoughts went back to DesPlaines Street, its sights and sounds which formed a very dark background to the beautiful picture of nature before me" (*Olive Branch*, vol. 1, no. 12, 2).

Conditions around the mission were abysmal. On the same block were pawnshops, brothels, and lodging houses as well as thirteen saloons. The street was filled with "crowds of poor, half-starved, ragged, wretched humanity jostling, cursing and fighting" (*Olive Branch*, vol. 1, no. 1, 3). Here, amid the stench and pollution of an industrial slum, Everhart worked among prostitutes, abandoned women and children, drunkards and opium addicts, as well as among those who had left Christianity and the unchurched children of Christians. The "cursing, quarreling, gambling and beer-drinking people" (Olive Branch, vol. 5, no.

8, 2) of the neighborhood did not deter mission workers. One volunteer assured readers of the *Olive Branch* that "the singing of the redeemed and the praying of the faithful make up fully for the odors you meet on your way" (*Olive Branch*, vol. 1, no. 4, 4).

Living conditions for Everhart and her coworkers were not much better than for those they served. At first, they slept behind a curtain partitioning the mission. Then they moved to a single third-floor room above a saloon. In May 1902, a residence for mission workers was purchased near the mission. In 1911, the mission bought a house about two miles west of the Olive Branch; Everhart and her co-laborers walked to and from the mission each day.

Daily life at the Olive Branch varied little over the forty years. It was an endless round of feeding and clothing the poor, visiting the sick and those in prison, evangelizing in saloons and barrelhouses, conducting religious services both in the mission and on street corners, providing temporary housing for homeless women and children, listening to confessions of sin and tales of woe, soliciting funds, tracking and acknowledging donations, recruiting and training volunteers, and handing out religious tracts. She wrote, "When we cease because completely exhausted, the many things we see to do rise mountain high and the cry for help echoes and re-echoes through not only our head but our very soul until we wish for the strength of ten that we might succeed in helping all" (*Olive Branch* vol. 6, no. 9, 2).

In addition, Everhart wrote most of the copy for each monthly newspaper; coworkers set the type and printed it on site. Then, each was prepared and mailed. By 1900, the mission also printed the religious tracts it distributed. Each issue of the *Olive Branch* opened with an uplifting or moral poem, gave thanks for help and asked for more, provided a testimonial from a saved soul, included letters from supporters, especially children, and listed donors and their gifts. Everhart called her newspaper the only financial agent the mission ever had.

Every contribution was accepted, from money to fresh flowers, which were distributed to hospitals. Always welcome, food was frequently solicited by direct appeals: "Dear readers, we have to pay twenty-four cents per pound for butter. Don't some of you want to send us a five-quart pail full by express?" (*Olive Branch*, vol. 1, no. 12, 1). Occasionally the appeals were tinged with sarcasm: "It would surely be very convenient if the Olive Branch Mission family could do without food during the summer months (our famine time, as we call it) for foods of every kind are so highly priced it takes a small mint of money to buy enough of any kind to keep soul and body together" (*Olive Branch*, vol. 26, no. 9, 2).

Contributors were thanked by name in each issue, often with reference to the Christian obligation to help the poor: "Butter! butter! Yes, a jar of fine, fresh butter from Mrs. Harvey Hawkins wonderfully astonished and very, very greatly delighted the Olive Branch Mission workers. This precious co-laborer believes in giving to the toilers in this little corner of the Master's vineyard a part of God's share of her fresh butter (real cow's butter), something we could not buy here even if we had plenty of money" (*Olive Branch*, vol. 26, no. 10, 2).

Everhart was disappointed that her denomination did not consider her work on a par with overseas missionaries. Her conversions were primarily among the immigrant poor, and she kept meticulous records to prove her successes in converting Swedes, Germans, Norwegians, English, Danes, and Russians. However, she never was successful in convincing the denomination's governing body to contribute money to the Olive Branch. The Free Methodists did, however, provide visiting ministers so that services with the sacraments could be held at the mission. When Everhart incorporated the mission in 1896, six of the nine members were Free Methodist ministers.

Everhart campaigned relentlessly against taverns, and in the *Olive Branch* she raged that men and women were "ensnared into the hell-holes which curse this city" (vol. 6, no. 9, 1). Like many of the thousands of members of the Woman's Christian Temperance Union, the largest women's organization in the United States during this period, she abhorred alcohol use and believed that drunkenness turned harmonious homes to places of unhappiness, poverty, and shame. Considering whiskey a trap set by the Devil, Everhart rhetorically asked in the *Olive Branch* in 1912, "Oh, how can men vote to license the sale of that which so wrecks our brothers and sisters for whom Christ died!" (vol. 18, no. 9, 2). The enactment of Prohibition in 1919 did not end her crusade, since illegal liquor remained available.

The work of the mission expanded with the population of immigrant poor, and Everhart documented every service provided. At the 1900 annual meeting she reported that during the year the mission had given out 4,225 garments and 452 baskets of food, made 2,482 visits and calls to individuals and families, visited 1,730 saloons and 392 lodging houses, and had distributed 64,812 tracts and 15,509 papers. Although a building fund was started that year, there was not enough money to purchase a new building until 1927.

Because Everhart was an only child who never married or had children, those working at the mission with her over the years became her extended family as well as her colleagues. She purchased a burial plot with space for six interments in Arlington Cemetery at Elmhurst, Illinois, and erected a pink granite headstone. At the top is the legend "Olive Branch Mission Workers," and, at the bottom, "They rest from their labors and their works do follow them." After Everhart, the names inscribed are Mabel E. Lane (superintendent from 1929 to 1939), Katie V. Hall (superintendent from 1939 to 1952), Violet B. Harp, Clara B. Spencer, and Geraldine Bower.

Throughout much of her life, health problems, exacerbated by the heavy workload and polluted environment, plagued Everhart. Healing prayers were requested in the *Olive Branch* when she was seriously ill in May 1897 and again in September 1897, after she was struck down by a group of bicyclists who were participating in a race as she crossed the street on her way to church. Increasingly weakened by illness, she developed severe eye problems in 1910 and was bedridden for several months in 1921 and again in 1922. By 1925 she was seldom well enough to work at the mission. She died in her bedroom at the mission workers' home of chronic nephritis, mitral valve insufficiency, and senility. Services were held in the newly built mission hall on the West Side.

Praise for Everhart filled the May 4, 1928, edition of the *Free Methodist* newspaper written by some of the same church officials who had refused over the years to approve funds for her urban evangelism. J. T. Logan, the editor, added his byline to her

official obituary. In a memorial tribute in the *Free Methodist*, May 4, 1928, Bishop Walter A. Sellew noted, "The one, great, consuming passion of her soul was to help up those who were down—to rescue the submerged" (p. 15).

Sources. A set of bound copies of the *Olive Branch: The World for Jesus*, edited by Everhart from 1894 to the late 1920s, is in the CHS. The newspaper has statistics enumerating the mission's work, fund-raising pleas, and descriptive narratives of life in her corner of Chicago's slums. An obituary and other memorial tributes to Everhart are in the May 4, 1928, edition of the *Free Methodist* newspaper, which can be found in the Free Methodist Church of North America World Headquarters in Indianapolis, Indiana. Ralph Woodworth included information on Everhart in *Light in a Dark Place: "The Story of Chicago's Oldest Rescue Mission"* (1978). A brief derivative overview of the mission is included in *One Part Honor: Stories and Faces of Chicago's Olive Branch* (1993), with text by Jack Dierks and photos by Sharon Smith and Wally Wright.

SUSAN McKEE

EVERLEIGH, ADA
February 15, 1876–January 5, 1960
BROTHEL OWNER

EVERLEIGH, MINNA
July 13, 1878–September 16, 1948
BROTHEL OWNER

The Everleigh sisters together owned the Everleigh Club, a sumptuous turn-of-the-century Chicago brothel that catered to many wealthy men, including such visiting celebrities as Prince Henry of Prussia. Ada and Minna Lester, born in a small town near Louisville, Kentucky, were the daughters of a financially comfortable lawyer who gave his two daughters a private school education with music and drama lessons. Like many other young upper-middle-class women of the late nineteenth century, the Lester sisters seemed destined for wealthy matrimony. Both were artistically accomplished. Both were also slender and pretty, though Minna, a blue-eyed redhead, was more outgoing than her quiet, blond sister.

The Lester sisters married a pair of brothers, but neither of them was destined to live as a traditional southern matron. Minna Lester, who married in 1897, was almost strangled by her groom on her wedding night, while Ada Lester was abandoned by her husband soon after her slightly later marriage. Together, the sisters fled to Washington, D.C., where they joined a traveling theater troupe.

In 1898, after a year on tour, the company arrived in Omaha, Nebraska. The Lesters decided that Omaha would be a good place to settle down. Solidly buttressed by a joint nest egg of thirty-five thousand dollars that they had received on their father's death, they began to look around for a suitable investment opportunity. They soon found it in the upcoming Trans-Mississippi Exposition, which was sure to be attended by many affluent out-of-town men. Reasoning that a large number of them would be traveling alone, the sisters identified their business opportunity.

As a first step toward the anonymity they assiduously pursued for the rest of their lives, Ada and Minna Lester dropped their own last name and adopted the name "Everleigh," taken from the closing phrase "Everly yours" (*Dictionary of American*

Biography, 255–56) that ended their grandmother's letters. They then bought an unprofitable brothel near the fairgrounds, spent some of their money on redecorating it and equipping it with excellent food and wines, and reopened it for business.

The Everleigh sisters proved to be gifted madams. By the time the Exposition's closing dried up their tourist trade, they had doubled their investment to seventy thousand dollars and were looking around for a new business venture. Cleo Maitland, Washington, D.C.'s most prosperous madam, suggested Chicago as a base for them to establish a permanent bordello. Maitland assured the sisters that Chicago was a large city with a rollicking reputation and a thriving area called the Levee, in which gambling dens, dance halls, and cheap brothels operated unchecked. In fact, Maitland said, there was even a madam on the verge of retirement, who was trying to sell an existing operation. For the moderate sum of fifty-five thousand dollars, the Everleighs bought the lease, the furnishing, and the staff of a South Dearborn Street house from Lizzie Allen and Effie Hankins, who had operated their brothel for ten years. Without delay they emptied the building, fired the employees, and started again from the bare walls.

They refurnished their establishment, adding all the luxurious touches for which the Everleigh Club later became famous. The club contained a well-stocked library; a fifteen thousand dollar, gold-leaf piano; and a series of gold, silver, Moorish, and other parlors, all appropriately furnished and adorned with erotic paintings. A catering staff of twenty-six provided exquisite meals at fifty dollars and up. As Herbert Asbury recalled in *Gem of the Prairie*, the club also had a newly minted corporate philosophy that any would-be patron could understand. As Minna Everleigh crisply put it, "The Everleigh Club has no time for the rough element, the clerk on a holiday or the man without a checkbook" (quoted in Asbury, 40).

The luxurious bordello opened its doors on February 1, 1900. On this frigid winter night, competitors found their twenty-five cent whiskies and ten-cent pints of beer selling briskly. Still, their businesses were no match for the Everleigh Club, where awed customers gladly paid fifty dollars for companionship and at least twenty-five dollars per bottle for costly wines and champagnes. By the end of the first evening, profits in the new establishment had reached a thousand dollars, and its two co-owners were firmly established as brothel-industry leaders.

The Everleigh sisters remained front-runners throughout the eleven years of their club's operation. By all accounts, their success was shaped partly by extremely high standards of service, decor, and catering, and partly by a supply of would-be prostitutes so steady that it totaled more than six hundred over the years of the brothel's existence.

The economics of the early 1900s contributed to making the Everleigh Club a popular place of employment. Six million American women worked outside their homes in 1900. Most of them worked in mercantile establishments with an average wage of six dollars per week—not nearly enough to provide them with nourishing food, comfortable and safe shelter, and warm clothes. All of these necessities were abundantly supplied by the Everleigh Club, whose owners also considered a 50 percent commission on each client no more than a just reward for the previous experience that was a rigid condition of each pros-

titute's employment. Other privileges included designated "beau nights," when the women were permitted to entertain their gentlemen friends in the public rooms to the sound of classical chamber music groups that was an elegant contrast to the raucous banjo pluckings popular in the neighboring bordellos. In addition, the Everleigh sisters were determined to protect the club from the drugs, pimps, and stealing that ravaged the Levee area, and they paid hefty protection money to 1st Ward alderman "Bathhouse" John Coughlin. A second precaution lay in the club's prices, which were deliberately set high enough to discourage all but the wealthiest guests.

New recruits soon found, however, that these benefits did demand a high standard of behavior. In return for their generosity, Ada and Minna Everleigh expected perfect grooming from their staff members. Furthermore, they made it clear that liberal use was to be made of their in-house library, and that only the most ladylike behavior would be acceptable.

Carefully planned and meticulously executed, these clearcut rules were often put to the test by the Everleigh sisters' love of publicity. To draw attention to their establishment, they dashed around town first in a handsome carriage, later in an eye-catching yellow automobile with a bunch of artificial flowers on its hood. They also courted newspaper reporters, giving them the run of the house as long as they did not go upstairs to the boudoirs. In return, they received just the kind of half-shocked, half-awed newspaper coverage that continued to bring in the customers.

Friendly to all, the sisters even set aside afternoons for antivice crusaders, allowing them to come into the club to distribute their tracts and pray for the prostitutes' souls. On one of these visits, an amused Minna Everleigh was buttonholed in her kitchen by antismoking reformer LUCY GASTON. "Minna! Your girls are going straight to hell! You must stop them!" "What can I do?" Everleigh asked. "Stop them smoking cigarettes!" responded Gaston (quoted in Asbury, 254).

The Everleigh sisters' tolerance toward reformers proved to be a sign of overconfidence in their own political connections and their seemingly secure position. Antiprostitution crusaders had been active long before the Everleigh Club opened its doors. They gained an ally in 1873 when the international medical profession urged all nations to check the spread of venereal disease by establishing compulsory antiprostitution supervision in their seaports. Physicians and reformers were not alone in their stand. Other activists included church organizations, Salvation Army divisions, and women's groups who saw prostitution as an example of male domination taken for granted in all political, social, and economic spheres.

By 1910 these same interest groups in Chicago zeroed in on the Levee area in general and on the Everleigh Club in particular. In unison, they demanded that Mayor Fred Busse form a vice commission to study the problem and suggest ways of combating Levee vice. The mayor responded at once, appointing philanthropist Julius Rosenwald, Bishop C. T. Shaffer, club-woman and suffragist ELLEN HENROTIN, Dr. Anna Dwyer, Judge M. W. Pinckney, and twenty-five others to the commission.

The commission was still working on its report when Minna Everleigh herself delivered the coup de grâce to her business with an ill-advised publicity campaign. In the summer of 1911, she published an illustrated brochure listing the delights of the Everleigh Club, which she described as one of Chicago's most unforgettable sights. By late-twentieth-century standards, the brochure was quite tame, and fewer than five hundred copies were printed. But newly elected Mayor Carter H. Harrison Jr. was given a copy by an acquaintance, which proved enough to close the Everleigh Club within twenty-four hours.

The end came on October 25, 1911, after a final party that ended in tears from the prostitutes. The sisters, however, remained dry-eyed. They chose not to fight the city, for an examination of their ledgers showed them that the good news far outweighed the bad. Despite the $120,000 they had spent on protection, their bank account held almost a million dollars. Other assets included $200,000 in jewels, plus at least $150,000 in artwork and Oriental carpets, furnishings, and rare books.

Ada and Minna Everleigh left on a six-month tour of Europe to give their notoriety time to fade. Unfortunately, they returned to Chicago to find themselves as well-known as ever. After a half-hearted, unsuccessful attempt at a comeback, and yearning to return to the arts-oriented lifestyle of their youth, the sisters, now in their thirties, returned to the family name of Lester.

They retired to a fashionable apartment in New York City, where they could indulge their passions for classical music, the theater, and poetry writing. They seldom entertained anyone other than the members of their poetry circle. They welcomed their guests graciously, however, serving them delicate teas from teapots of antique silver and cosseting them with dainty confec-tionery. They attributed their financial resources to an inheritance from a much loved but rather crude grandfather, who had struck it rich in the California gold rush. Minna Everleigh died in 1948. Ada moved to Virginia, where she died in 1960.

The fame of the Everleigh sisters, at least in histories of Chicago, exceeded that of the vast majority of women who were their contemporaries, whether as working women, entrepreneurs, or reformers. Their financial success, as much as their privileged upbringing, differentiated them from other women involved in prostitution.

Sources. Contemporary descriptions of prostitution in Chicago and the Everleigh sisters are Chicago Vice Commission, *The Social Evil in Chicago* (1911, reprinted 1970); and "Starts Vice War; Mayor in Fight to Clean Up City," *CT*, October 24, 1911. Biographical information is found in Charles Washburn, *Come Into My Parlor: A Biography of the Aristocratic Everleigh Sisters of Chicago* (1936), and Irving Wallace, *The Sunday Gentleman* (1965), but these are based on interviews given in the sisters' final years and are of questionable accuracy. See articles in *Dictionary of American Biography* (1974) and *NAW* (1971). Obituaries are *NYT*, September 17, 1948; *CT*, January 6, 1960. See Charles Washburn, "Closing the Book on the Everleigh Sisters," *CT Magazine*, November 1, 1953. General sources include Herbert Asbury, *Gem of the Prairie: An Informal History of the Chicago Underworld* (1942); Lloyd Wendt and Herman Kogan, *Lords of the Levee: The Story of Bathhouse John and Hinky Dink* (1943); Barbara Meil Hobson, *Uneasy Virtue: The Politics of Prostitution and the American Reform Tradition* (1990).

GILLIAN M. WOLF

EVERLEIGH, MINNA. *See* EVERLEIGH, ADA

FAIRBANK, JANET AYER
June 7, 1879–December 28, 1951

SOCIAL AND CIVIC LEADER, NOVELIST

Janet Ayer Fairbank was a social, civic, and political force in Chicago from the early 1900s through the 1940s. Festive gatherings at her North State Street brownstone and at the Lake Geneva, Wisconsin, family estate attracted celebrities from the worlds of theater, art, music, and literature in addition to imposing figures from the business, professional, academic, and political communities. Although she considered her efforts on behalf of the Chicago Lying-In Hospital as her primary occupation, she cultivated her passion for writing and research in novels that reflected the ideological conflicts engendered by an upper-middle-class milieu.

Her father, Benjamin Franklin Ayer, came from a distinguished New England family. Educated at Dartmouth College and Harvard University, he practiced law in New Hampshire before election to the state legislature. In 1857, he moved to Chicago, where he became corporation counsel to the city. Janet (Hopkins) Ayer, her mother, was the daughter of a New York State senator who later became a Wisconsin federal judge. An Episcopalian and a conservative Republican, she joined the Daughters of the American Revolution, the Colonial Dames of America, the Illinois Association Opposed to Woman Suffrage, and the Fortnightly.

Janet Ayer was born in Chicago, the third of five Ayer children, the youngest of whom was Margaret Ayer (see MARGARET AYER BARNES). In the early 1880s, her family lived on Chicago's exclusive South Side, where she enjoyed all the advantages of wealth and prominence. She was educated in private schools in Chicago and at Miss Ely's in New York. From 1899 to 1900, and periodically thereafter, she took courses at the University of Chicago.

On May 29, 1900, Janet Ayer married Kellogg Fairbank, a Harvard-educated attorney who came from a similar family background of privilege and civic involvement. His father, Nathaniel K. Fairbank, grain merchant and oil and lard refiner, succeeded during Chicago's greatest period of growth and was a supporter of the Union cause. Kellogg later administered his father's affairs.

During the first decade of marriage, while raising three children, Janet (born 1903), Kellogg Jr. (1907), and Benjamin Ayer (1909), Janet Fairbank managed a host of social, civic, and literary activities. Her affiliations included several Chicago clubs: Scribblers, Woman's City, Friday, Arts, Casino, Fortnightly, and Pen; she also held membership in the Cosmopolitan Club of New York. Distinguishing herself as a manager and fund-raiser, by 1908 she became head of the board of directors of the Chicago Lying-In Hospital, a position she held for twenty-four years. For this favorite cause, she once arranged a celebrity circus at the Chicago Coliseum. With friends pressed into service, the "Pageant of the East" was billed as "Chicago's Four Hundred on Parade—Six Thousand Performers!" (Meeker, 177–78). Fairbank dramatically entered the ring astride an elephant, dressed as Scheherazade. Her tireless efforts on behalf of Lying-In culminated in its 1928 alliance with the University of Chicago Hospital complex.

Frequently associated with the charity balls of BERTHA HONORÉ PALMER, Fairbank was lauded as one who raised more money than any other woman in the city. She worked equally hard in the political arena, supporting Theodore Roosevelt and the Bull Moose Campaign and chairing the western division of the Women's Finance Committee of the Progressive Party. When World War I required a concerted national effort, Fairbank joined the Woman's Committee of the State Council of Defense, a statewide coalition of women's organizations dedicated to fund-raising, conservation, and morale building. From 1917 to 1918, she chaired its Speakers' Bureau before moving to the Woman's National Liberty Loan Committee, where she organized five Liberty Loan drives.

In contrast to her mother's involvement with the antisuffrage movement, Fairbank steadfastly sought voting rights. In the early 1920s, she switched to the Democratic Party, which she believed better recognized the contributions of women. From 1924 to 1928 she served as the Illinois Democratic National Committeewoman, speaking throughout northern Illinois. "How to Make Politics Vital to Women" was more than another speech title. During the violent era of the notorious Chicago Republican Mayor William Hale "Big Bill" Thompson, Fairbank worried publicly about government ties with criminal elements and a political machine that fostered ethnic isolation and racial mistrust under the guise of voting empowerment. Thompson had benefited from African American support when he first ran for mayor and had appointed many black citizens to positions. Reformers, including critics in the black community aware of his inclusion of Blacks in his political machine, still condemned his politics of patronage. In the July 1927 issue of the *Woman Citizen*, her article, "What's Wrong with Chicago?" condemned a widening cronyism beginning to infect the judicial system. The rebuke, however, was modified by her fascination with the growing city, which she compared to a well-fed, lazy, unthinking teenager full of promise and potential yet different from its parent because still unseasoned and untried.

Fairbank had initiated her writing career early, at the time of a rapidly growing popular press. As a young debutante, she sold column-long romances for five dollars to "The Evening Story," a long-standing feature of the *Chicago Daily News*. Later she published stories in *Leslie's Weekly*. In 1910, she regularly contributed brief dialogues to "The Tea Table," a column in the *Sunday Record-Herald*. From "Success" and "The Pursuit of Pleasure" to "The American Husband" and "Woman and Superwoman" to "Socialism," the repartee from a select circle in an upper-class drawing room circulated abbreviated arguments on social and cultural issues. The presiding widow rendered final judgment in this refined court of public opinion. Like Fairbank, she stood foremost as an exponent of freedom, rejecting control over the individual, whether it came by social convention or governmental policy. Admiration of the individual who took action induced Fairbank to approve opportunity to anyone from any class. At the same time, a fear of intolerance moved her to chastise even the hard-working suffragist, if she rejected out of hand the traditional roles for women. At the heart of these dialogues, however, lay a disturbing, unremarked circumstance: the speakers seemed not to hear each other. These dialogues, twenty-one of which were collected as *In Town & Other Conversations* (1910), laid out the themes that would be more fully explored in later Fairbank novels.

World War I activities interrupted her writing plans, and in 1922 Fairbank published a first novel, *The Cortlandts of Washington Square*. The press marveled at yet another accomplishment from the socialite already familiar as hostess and fundraiser, swimmer and horsewoman, drama critic and political correspondent, essayist and fiction writer. Inspired by old letters found in the family attic, Fairbank rendered contemporary female experience through the prism of an earlier era. The imaginative escapades of an orphaned, middle-class girl, Ann Byrne, adopted into a sophisticated, upper-class family, were set against the competing tensions of American and European customs and values. Byrne moved with assurance from carefully designed New York City boulevards to chaotic Civil War battle zones, then out to the muddy flats of Chicago. Her journey also represented the spirited national development that Fairbank so admired. New York libraries, where Fairbank did extensive research, yielded local color; Gettysburg gave a sense of the battlefield. Reviewers acknowledged the enrichments of a reinvented fairy tale but did not mention the gender issues implicit in a convention-defying heroine.

In writing and in speeches, Fairbank repeatedly pressed for recognition of women's multiple talents. She challenged the stereotyped views of the "romantic heroines" of the 1860s and the "money getters" of 1917 in an interview in the *Chicago Daily News*, September 29, 1922. Fairbank charged that her generation of women had been dissuaded unfairly from a personal involvement in the World War I effort even while encouraged to raise money. Civil War women, on the other hand, although not deemed suited to fund-raising, had been urged to minister to the departing and returning soldiers. Although mistaken about the fund-raising activities of women during the Civil War, she had clearly targeted the female yearning for participation in local, national, and international affairs.

In her next novel, *The Smiths*, which placed second for the 1925 Pulitzer Prize, Fairbank traced the emergence and suppression of these urges within the confines of marriage and child rearing. She identified the conventions that directed women's creative drives to social and cultural venues rather than to activities associated with empire building. To show the folly of this restriction, *The Smiths*, a sequel to *The Cortlands of Washington Square*, incorporated Chicago history from the 1860s to the 1910s—Lincoln's funeral cortege, celebrations at the end of the Civil War, the Great Chicago Fire, financial panics of the 1890s, the World's Columbian Exposition, Progressive Era rallies. These events spanned three generations and added texture to the family chronicle and dimension to a woman's life. With protagonist Ann Smith, Fairbank recast the deep-rooted conflict between personal freedom and social responsibility that could pass undetected in a woman of social position.

The hidden burdens of social and cultural leadership had been implicit in the Chicago generational and dynastic novel, first modeled in *Wau-Bun: The "Early Day" in the North-West* by JULIETTE AUGUSTA MAGILL KINZIE (1856), then cultivated in the novels of Martha J. Lamb, Mary Healy Bigot, Margaret Horton Potter Black, and Katherine Keith. The Fairbank contribution to this tradition was hailed by Chicago critic and novelist Henry B. Fuller. He typified the response with praise of *The Smiths* as a "social document" valuable in a way that only a "lady novelist" might make it, masculine in its "fully informed" references to business and politics, yet "a free, frank femininity comes to the top when the requirement arises" (Fuller, 663). Like other critics, he did not dwell on the ambivalence inherent within the legacy of the matriarchal figurehead.

In *The Lion's Den* (1930), Fairbank changed her focus to a young progressive Wisconsin farmer who went to Washington for a year as a congressional replacement only to find himself in a den of women, a challenge to his wholesome midwest values. Romantic infidelities and political intrigues climaxed in financial throes at the height of the October 1929 stock market crash. This succinct interplay of three vital lines of human affairs, applauded by critics for its realistic politics and entertaining social comedy, dramatized the excesses that could threaten social harmony and national integrity.

In *The Bright Land* (1932), Fairbank returned to the family chronicle. Once more, a rebellious young woman defied her family and eloped to the West to establish a family line in Galena, Illinois, this time against a backdrop of an expanding Mississippi River transportation system, energizing California gold rush, and conflicting Civil War sentiments. Abby-Delight Flagg, like Ann Smith, resisted confronting the constraints of social responsibility. Although Fairbank attempted to disclose motivation by way of a suffrage theme, the critics complained of the lack of character analysis in this novel.

Rich Man, Poor Man (1936) returned to the Smith family. Rebelling against the established old Chicago family, grandson Hendricks Cortland Smith Jr. joined, then left, progressive politics just as he fell in love with, married, then finally left an inspiring but inflexible suffragist. His wife, from the American heartland, was first energized by political belief, then radicalized by her feminist fervor. Even a couple skilled in oratory could not surmount the difficulty of communication between the sexes. Fairbank reiterated an earlier theme of the inability of individuals to hear each other's words, first explored in her earlier *In Town & Other Conversations*.

The unexpected death of Kellogg Fairbank in 1939 initiated a decline in Fairbank's health and curtailed her writing. A sixth historical novel set in Marietta, Ohio, never reached completion. Nevertheless, her political involvement continued. Still considering herself a Democrat in 1940, Fairbank nevertheless supported Republican Wendell Willkie's bid for the presidency. She staunchly opposed Roosevelt and the New Deal, which to her violated all the principles of individualism and freedom and hard work that she valued. She joined the controversial America First Committee and served on its executive committee, although her enthusiastic espousal was seen more as an expression of her longstanding opposition to New Deal reforms than as a declaration of a noninterventionist stance. In 1947, her health declining, Fairbank entered a sanitorium in Wauwatosa, Wisconsin, where she remained until her death. She is buried near her family in Graceland Cemetery.

Janet Ayer Fairbank has been remembered as a "towering blond woman with a laugh like a trumpet and the kindest grey eyes in the world" (Meeker, 177). Arthur Meeker, an intimate of the Fairbank circle, eulogized her as "nearer to *being* Chicago than any other woman of her time[,] . . . generous, whole-souled, an energizing sun bringing life and warmth and friendliness to all who crossed her orbit" (p. 192).

Sources. The Lake Geneva (Wisconsin) Public Library maintains a Fairbank estate file with items on Janet Ayer Fairbank; that library also holds microfilm of the local and regional newspapers, which report activities of summer residents. The Bobbs-Merrill collection, Lilly Library, Indiana Univ., Bloomington, Indiana, has seventeen folders of Fairbank correspondence with the publisher; the materials from 1922–36 include pictures, promotional materials, and typescript reviews of the first three novels. Her five novels are noted above. Early stories first published in newspapers are collected as *In Town & Other Conversations* (1910).

Fairbank also wrote political articles, dramatic reviews, and cultural commentary for several Chicago and New York newspapers and magazines, including "What's Wrong with Chicago," the *Woman Citizen*, July 1927. Some of Fairbank's shorter romances were collected in *Idle Hands* (1927). A description of her impulse to write and the early efforts appeared in "I Wonder Why I Write" in the *Chicago Daily News*, January 28, 1931. In 1933, Fairbank collaborated with her sister, novelist Margaret Ayer Barnes, on the introduction for *Julia Newberry's Diary* (1933). In 1935 the two sisters finished and published the mystery novel *The Alleged Great-Aunt* started by their good friend Henry Kitchell Webster. Excellent information on the Fairbank and Ayer families is available in the *Biographical Dictionary and Portrait Gallery of Representative Men of Chicago and the World's Columbian Exposition* (1892), and Janet Ayer Fairbank's genealogy appears in *NCAB* (1954). Other helpful articles are "Society Leader Makes Debut as Novelist," *Chicago Herald and Examiner*, September 10, 1922; Charles Collins, "Janet Fairbank Defies Tradition in First Novel," *Chicago Post*, September 23, 1922; "Compares Women in Two American Wars," *Chicago Daily News*, September 29, 1922; Vera Brady Shipman, "An Ideal Social Leader," *Social Progress*, December 1923; and "Janet Ayer Fairbank," *Wilson Bulletin: For Librarians*, December 1933. The only extensive, personal portrait appears in a chapter bearing her nickname "Birdie" in Arthur Meeker, *Chicago, with Love: A Polite and Personal History* (1955). The major reviews of the novels can be tracked through *Book Review Digest*. These include Henry B. Fuller, "The Smith Family Populates a Western Novel," *International Book Review*, September 1925. A brief survey of her novels appears in Lina Mainiero, ed., *American Women Writers: A Critical Reference Guide from Colonial Times to the Present*, vol. 2 (1980).

KAY HOYLE NELSON

FASSETT, CORNELIA ADELE STRONG
November 9, 1831–January 4, 1898
ARTIST

Cornelia Adele Fassett became a successful artist, painting portraits of many prominent political figures in the second half of the nineteenth century. She was born in Owasco, New York, to Captain Walter and Sarah (Devoe) Strong. The Strongs moved their young family westward around 1839, settling in Jefferson, Ohio, in the region known as the Western Reserve, where Walter Strong was a proprietor of the American Hotel. Cornelia Adele Strong was the third of six children.

On August 26, 1851, Cornelia Adele Strong married Samuel Montague Fassett, originally of Ashtabula, Ohio, who at the time of their marriage was living in Beloit, Wisconsin. The ceremony took place at Trinity Episcopal Church in Jefferson, Ohio. Shortly after the couple's marriage they moved west to Chicago, Illinois, where Sam Fassett, an aspiring daguerreotypist, set up his studio, the Fine Arts Gallery, in the commercial district. They lived in a fashionable section of Hyde Park, a village bordering Chicago and incorporated into the city in 1889, and became the parents of eight children: Walter (who died before 1880), Flora, Montague, Raphael, Adele, Arthur, Clara, and Violet.

Although Fassett's early life was spent developing musical talents, after her move to Chicago she turned to painting miniature portraits on ivory. In 1852 she went to New York to study watercolor painting with the Scottish artist James B. Wandesforde. From 1852 to 1855, she was in Rome and Paris studying oil painting with Giuseppe Castiglione, Georges de La Tour, and

FIG. 26. *Photograph of artist Cornelia Adele Fassett as she sketches one of the more than 200 members of the U.S. Congress for her historical painting* The Electoral Commission of 1877.

Gabriel Mathieu. In 1866 Fassett returned to Europe with her husband, children, and a maid. The Paris International Exposition in 1867 afforded the couple an opportunity to see the latest developments in science, technology, and the arts. Their daughter Adele was born in France.

Chicago changed markedly during the two decades the Fassetts lived there. Chicago of the early 1850s had virtually no art exhibitions to speak of, and the Fassetts created their own in the windows of the Fine Arts Gallery. The *Chicago Daily Democratic Press* of October 9, 1855, noted that the couple devoted their talents to producing works of art. Although art works had been exhibited at state and county fairs in the fifties, the first exhibition of art in Chicago was the Art Exposition held at the Burch's Building on May 9, 1859. Several expositions followed, but the most noteworthy early exhibition of art in the city was the Sanitary Commission's Art Gallery of the Ladies' Northwestern Fair, held in November 1863. Sanitary fairs were instituted in many cities in the eastern part of the country to raise money for wounded Civil War soldiers, and Fassett generously donated a watercolor of Lincoln that was raffled at the close of the fair. Fassett painted this portrait of Lincoln from life in 1860, showing

him as a beardless, unimposing man. Fassett's husband took a photograph of Lincoln at approximately the same time that was very close to the watercolor she painted.

As the century progressed, the opportunity to exhibit works of art in the emerging metropolis increased. The Chicago Academy of Design was initiated in 1866 to "promote and foster taste for the fine arts" (Andreas, 557). Exhibitions were hosted by members of the academy, who also offered classes in painting, drawing, and modeling. In 1868 Fassett entered portraits of her son and the paintings *Montague Fassett, Mr. C. A. Spring, Miss Kitty Spring,* and *Innocence* in the academy's exhibition held at Crosby's Opera House. She was admitted to the Chicago Academy of Design as an associate member in 1874, shortly before moving to Washington, D.C. (The first woman to become a full Academician was ANNIE SHAW, in 1879.)

During the seventies, major exhibitions of art were staged at the Chicago Inter-State Industrial Exhibitions, and at agriculture and industrial fairs that included art displays. Fassett and her husband both loaned numerous works to these multifaceted shows. The sitters in her portraits included some of Chicago's most notable men—William Wirt Smith, John High Dunham, Jonathan Young Scammon, Charles Hammill, H. W. Hibbard, and Dr. Alvin Edmond Small. She also painted the portrait of William Butler Ogden Jr., a nephew and namesake of Chicago's first mayor, when he was a child. The 1875 Industrial Exposition was the last regular exposition Fassett entered in Chicago.

The Fassetts' collections were burned out in the Great Fire of 1871 and a later fire in 1873, and the family subsequently moved to Washington, D.C., in 1875. Fassett may have exhibited at other public and private shows in Chicago from the seventies to the end of the century, but extant records on her participation are available only for the First Annual Exhibition of American Oil Paintings at the Art Institute of Chicago in 1888 and the World's Columbian Exposition of 1893.

Shortly after moving to Washington, D.C., she exhibited her portrait *Chief Justice Morrison Waite* at the 1876 Centennial Exhibition in Philadelphia. In 1879 at a Washington, D.C., exhibition, *Decorative and Fine Art,* presented by the National Fair Association, Fassett showed her *Head of Moscovite Zingana* and *Portrait of Mr. Justice Miller.* In addition, she entered paintings in shows organized by the Washington Art Club, of which she was a member. Fassett was also received into the membership of the prestigious Washington Literary Society. The artist included socializing in her busy schedule, and her studio soirees were well known in Washington society.

The Fassetts moved to Washington, D.C. at the same time that Ohio politicians were rising to power. The connections the couple had from childhood in the Buckeye State, and those of their families who remained there, served them well in their new locale. Before long, Fassett executed the portraits of presidents Hayes, Grant, and Garfield. She also painted portraits of Vice-President (under Grant) Henry Wilson, Charles Foster (governor of Ohio, 1880–84), and other nineteenth-century notables, including Clara Barton and the historian MARTHA JOANNA LAMB, editor of the *Magazine of American History.*

Fassett is perhaps best known for her historical painting the *Electoral Commission of 1877,* purchased by Congress in 1886.

The commission had been established to deal with disputed electoral college votes from the states of Louisiana, South Carolina, and Florida, in the 1876 presidential election between Republican Rutherford B. Hayes and Democrat Samuel J. Tilden. Fassett painted herself in the center of a group portrait of more than two hundred members of congress, their wives, and members of the press, in a pose captured by the Chicago photographer, H. Rocher. Of the other approximately 250 portraits she included, Fassett claimed that all but a few were painted from life sittings. She had attended the commission, where she sketched the format of the painting, placing the individual portraits in at a later date. The painting has been severely criticized as having historical but not artistic merit. Critics claim that too many figures were crowded into too small a space, and as a result the painting is stilted. She was also complimented, however, on the realistic depictions of the portraits. The historical merit is questionable, since the wives Fassett included on the floor of the Old Senate Chamber would certainly not have been in attendance at the hearing. The inclusion of women reporters is a different story; Fassett placed them in the galleries, and it is likely they did attend the commission proceedings. Fassett identified each person in the picture in an inclusion key to the painting. In the end, although the painting created a good deal of controversy, Fassett was paid $7,500 for the work, roughly equivalent to $127,000 in the 1980s.

The *Electoral Commission* was not Fassett's only group portrait. She executed a crayon drawing of the justices of the Supreme Court. It is likely that she also painted individual oil portraits of these men, since there are extant examples—Morrison Waite and Samuel Freeman Miller. Because she painted life portraits, the close relationship that Sam Fassett's photographs have with many of Fassett's paintings made some viewers wonder whether he was snapping the pictures for the convenience and aid of his artist wife. Although there is no evidence of such activity, he did assist her by acting as an intermediary with her male sitters. In letters to Chief Justice Waite, Sam Fassett arranged for sittings with Cornelia Fassett.

Although portraiture was the genre upon which Fassett relied for regular income, she also worked as a history painter, in order to be considered a serious artist. Titles of some known but unlocated paintings other than her portraits include *On the Campagna, The Three Graces, Saying Grace,* and *Innocence.* Although Fassett painted the faces of her own children, she is not known for sentimental mother/child depiction.

People in Chicago continued their interest in Fassett even after the artist moved to Washington. The *Chicago Tribune,* September 18, 1881, lamented the choice of the portrait Fassett had entered in a recent exposition but went on to praise the portraits she had recently completed of young women, preferring them for exhibition. Two of the young women were daughters of the governor of Ohio, and the newspaper also singled out three small portraits of the daughters of the Chicagoan "Mrs. Colonel Mulligan" for praise. The portrait of "Mr. Austin," deputy-collector of customs of Chicago, was mentioned as a fine "crayon portrait."

Fassett died of a heart attack in Washington, D.C., while walking to a reception with her daughter Violet. The *Washington Post* obituary stated that she was "one of the best known artists and portrait painters in the United States" when few women worked as professional artists (January 5, 1898). At the time of her death she was at work on a series of miniature portraits of presidents' wives. She was a dedicated worker who persevered in order to carve out a career at a time when women received little encouragement to do so. While many women artists had artist fathers, brothers, husbands, or lovers to help direct their careers, such was not the case with Fassett. Sam Fassett was a photographer when the profession of artist was more prestigious than that of photographer. Assertive in gaining advanced art training in Europe as a married woman traveling without her husband, Fassett was taken seriously as an artist in an era when women's work was defined by the responsibilities of home and family.

Sources. Archival material on Cornelia Adele Fassett includes papers on her mural, *Electoral Commission of 1877,* in the Office of the Architect of the Capitol, Washington, D.C.; vertical file, CHS; vertical file, library, National Museum of American Art (Smithsonian Institution), Washington, D.C. Information concerning the Strong and Fassett families is in the Alice Bliss Collection, Jefferson Public Library, Jefferson, Ohio. See also Katherine Fassett Schuster, *The Fassett Genealogy: Descendants of Patrick and Sarah Fassett* (1974). Fassett's obituary appeared in the *Washington Post,* January 5, 1898. Information about Fassett's paintings is available in *The Inventory of American Paintings* (National Museum of American Art, Smithsonian Institution, Washington, D.C., n.d.); the accession file for her portrait of Abraham Lincoln, Spec. Coll., Harold Washington Library Center, CPL; James L. Yarnall and William H. Gerdts, *Index to American Art Exhibition Catalogues,* vol. 2 (1986), for a listing of the exhibitions Fassett entered prior to the centennial of 1876. Her portraiture is discussed in *CT,* September 18, 1881. Other publications to consult about Fassett's place in American art include C. E. C. Waters and Laurence Hutton, *Artists of the Nineteenth Century and Their Works* (1897); C. E. C. Waters, *Women in the Fine Arts* (1904); Charles E. Fairman, *Art and Artists of the Capitol of the United States of America* (1927); *Art in the United States Capitol* (1976); and Penny Dunford, *A Biographical Dictionary of Women Artists in Europe and America since 1850* (1989). The Chicago Academy of Design is discussed in Alfred T. Andreas, *History of Chicago,* vol. 2 (1884). Fassett's portrait *Clara Barton* is located at the Universalist Memorial Church, Washington, D.C. The portrait *Mrs. Martha J. Lamb in Her Library* is at the New York Hist. Soc. The portrait of Lincoln is at the Harold Washington Library Center, CPL; Garfield's portrait and the *Electoral Commission of 1877* are at the U.S. Capitol. The portrait *President Hayes* is in the collections of his presidential library in Fremont, Ohio. There are two Fassett portraits of Morrison Waite, one at the Ohio State Capitol, the other at the Supreme Court building in Washington, D.C. Many portraits are unlocated, including those of Ulysses S. Grant and a number of Chicagoans.

MARIANNE BERGER WOODS

FENBERG, MATILDA
July 4, 1888(?)–October 23, 1977
ATTORNEY, LEGAL REFORMER

Matilda Fenberg championed women's rights on a personal and professional level. She was one of the first women to attend Yale Law School, worked with famous Chicago criminal lawyer Clarence Darrow, and used her legal skills to promote jury service for women, the Equal Rights Amendment (ERA), and a Uniform Divorce Bill.

Fenberg was born in Grajewo, Poland (then Russia), the second surviving child and eldest daughter of William and Rachel

(Michitsky) Fenberg. Fenberg's exact birth date is not known, but July 4, 1888, is the date Fenberg used. She chose July 4 because that was the day of the annual Fenberg family picnic, and her birthday was celebrated as part of the festivities.

Fenberg's father came to the United States in 1891, leaving his wife, Matilda, and three sons behind. William Fenberg joined his brother Isaac in Findlay, Ohio, bought a horse and wagon and became a junk dealer. Within a few years, he sent for his family, and they joined him in Findlay in 1894. They were one of a few Jewish families in this small northwestern Ohio community.

Fenberg was an excellent student, attending Central Elementary School and graduating from Findlay High School in 1906. A fourth grade incident recalled by Fenberg portended her future career: a policeman came to her class asking for the Fenberg girl. He took her to the courthouse to act as an interpreter for a neighbor charged with theft, since Fenberg was the only one in town who spoke Yiddish, German, and English. She defended the man so fervently that the district attorney prophesied, "She'll be another Clarence Darrow" (Fenberg, "I Remember Clarence Darrow," 216). After that incident, Fenberg vowed she would become a lawyer, and for the next ten years she clipped and pasted newspaper articles about the famous trial lawyer with whom she would later work.

Fenberg was recruited to attend the University of Chicago, a relatively new institution founded in 1892. She was offered a scholarship to cover her tuition, but initially she did not have enough money for room and board. She taught in Findlay for two years before matriculating at the university in 1908 and completing the A.B. degree in 1911, taking a classical course of studies. She lived in the Englewood neighborhood of Chicago and tutored students to make ends meet. While at the university, Fenberg took courses in the history and philosophy of religion from George Burnhan Foster, who had debated with Clarence Darrow on the Chautauqua lecture circuit on the subject, "Is Life Worth Living?" They frequently met after class to discuss Clarence Darrow and his ideas.

Although Fenberg's mother did not believe that women should have an education and, in fact, had destroyed Fenberg's scrapbook of articles about Darrow, Fenberg not only pursued her own education but insured that three of her sisters had the resources to graduate from college and become teachers. From 1911 to 1919, Fenberg taught school in the Ohio towns of McComb, Wapakoneta, and Akron, and in Monticello, Indiana, sharing her income with her sisters. After her sisters had completed their college work, Fenberg could finally fulfill her dream of becoming a lawyer. She enrolled in a six-week summer law course at Columbia University, New York City, in 1919. At the time Ivy League law schools did not admit women, although the law schools at New York University, Boston University, and the state universities in the Midwest and West had been admitting women since the late nineteenth century. While enrolled at Columbia, Fenberg heard that Yale University's law school would open its doors to women that October. Fenberg took "the night boat [to New Haven] that very night (fare $1), and next morning . . . stood in line on the campus green, hanging onto my valise" ("I Remember Clarence Darrow," 217). She became one of the first women to attend Yale Law School.

Still needing to find ways to support herself, Fenberg began teaching nights in the New Haven public high schools. At Yale, she quickly became friendly with several of the male law students who were returning to school after serving in World War I. They called her their "sister in law" (Weiser, "Matilda Fenberg" 5). Fenberg completed her studies in 1922, but her grade average was three-tenths of a percentage point below the required average. Yale refused to factor in her grade from the Columbia course, which would have brought her average up to the required level. As a result, she did not receive her degree until forty-one years later, in 1963, when Yale Law School belatedly awarded her a diploma. In 1922 it was not necessary, however, to have a law degree to practice law, and Fenberg passed the Ohio Bar in 1922. She started her legal career that year at a Findlay, Ohio, law firm.

On a trip to Chicago to visit friends, she decided she could not leave the city without meeting her hero, Clarence Darrow. She described bursting into his office unannounced, saying "Mr. Darrow, do you think life is worth living?" "Oh hell yes," said Darrow. "Come on in. Sit down. Let's talk" ("I Remember Clarence Darrow," 216). In the course of their conversation, they discovered they had a number of things in common. Both were from Ohio, and both had taught school to earn money to continue their law studies. Fenberg missed her train back to Findlay that day but left Darrow's office with a job offer.

Fenberg moved to Chicago in April 1923 and Darrow "generously set aside a corner of his spacious desk" ("I Remember Clarence Darrow," 217) for her. She passed the Illinois Bar that year and moved to the Hyde Park area, where she lived for the next fifty-one years. She began her career in Chicago as a court-appointed criminal defense lawyer, handling shoplifting, larceny, armed robbery, and murder cases. Fenberg worked with Darrow on a number of cases and maintained a friendship with him until his death in 1938.

After three months in her own practice, Fenberg had not yet had the opportunity to try a case before a jury when Darrow called to ask her to assist him with a case of armed robbery. On the first day, Darrow insisted that Fenberg pick the jurors with occasional advice from him. The newspaper headline read, "Matilda Fenberg Trying the Shaffer Case Assisted by Clarence Darrow" (Weiser, "Matilda Fenberg," 6). The next day, Darrow sent word that he was ill, and Fenberg successfully tried the case without him. Fenberg was very proud of the fact that in her fifty-year legal career, she never lost a jury case.

In 1929, Republican Mayor William Hale Thompson appointed Fenberg assistant corporation counsel, a position she held for two years. She also began to take part in professional organizations of women lawyers. Through these groups she worked for the Equal Rights Amendment for women, for the right of women to serve on juries, and for reform of divorce laws. Women were able to vote, to hold political office, to engage in the legal system as lawyers and as judges, but they could not serve on juries in many states, including Illinois. From 1929 to 1939 she lobbied for legislation to allow women to serve on Illinois juries. After 1939, when jury service was opened to women, Fenberg wrote a booklet, *Women Jurors and Jury Service in Illinois*, to explain the importance of jury duty. In 1947 she shifted her attention to the national level and chaired the Committee on Jury Service of the National Association of Women Lawyers (NAWL), whose goal was to obtain the right to serve on a jury for women in the fourteen states that still excluded them from jury duty because of their sex.

When Mayor Thompson left office in 1931, Fenberg returned to private practice, specializing in divorce law. In the 1930s, Fenberg became involved in local politics as a precinct captain in the 5th Ward. Containing the Hyde Park neighborhood where many University of Chicago professors lived, the 5th Ward was known for independent, reform politics, and was the home of a series of reform candidates. One of the first in this tradition was independent Republican Charles Merriam, who taught political science at the university, served as 5th Ward alderman, and ran unsuccessfully as a reform mayoral candidate. Fenberg ran for the Illinois State Assembly on the Republican ticket in 1940 but lost in the primary.

Fenberg became an early advocate of no-fault divorce and the use of mediation and reconciliation in divorce cases. At the time, in Illinois and the majority of states in the United States, the only way to secure a divorce was to allege that the other party to the marriage had committed one or more of the acts enumerated in the applicable state statute as grounds for divorce. Typically the grounds were adultery, bigamy, or physical cruelty, although the grounds differed from state to state. One party had to be found guilty and the other innocent. She advocated passage of a federal uniform no-fault law that would eliminate the adversarial character of divorce actions. Instead, she believed there should be a conciliatory process that would best serve both parties and their children. Fenberg was active in NAWL's Uniform Divorce Bill Committee from its inception in 1947 and chaired the committee until 1961. She coauthored the original draft of the Uniform Divorce bill with other NAWL members. Later, she coauthored the final draft with members of the Chicago Bar Association's Matrimonial Law Committee. In the course of lobbying for the bill, Fenberg was effective in getting the American Bar Association to organize a Family Law Section and chaired the section's subcommittee on migratory divorce. She was later awarded honorary membership in the American Academy of Matrimonial Lawyers for her work on the Uniform Divorce Bill. Although the bill was never adopted, all the states eventually enacted no-fault divorce laws, and many courts now require mediation in divorce cases.

Fenberg sought to eliminate legal discrimination suffered by American women. She argued that without an equal rights amendment to the U.S. Constitution, that document guaranteed to women "nothing considered fundamental by men except the right to vote . . ." ("Blame Coke and Blackstone," 10). In fact, there were "over one thousand state laws discriminating against women, mainly against married women, their rights of inheritance, guardianship, earning, jury service and other laws" (p. 10). Fenberg agreed with the approach of the National Woman's Party (NWP), which had, since 1923, proposed to every session of Congress the Equal Rights Amendment that read: "Equality of Rights under the Law shall not be denied or abridged by the United States or any State on account of Sex" (quoted in "Blame Coke and Blackstone," 10). As the nation moved toward the hundredth anniversary of the 1848 Seneca Falls women's rights meeting, those groups that advocated passage of the NWP's ERA stepped up their campaigns. Fenberg spoke before the Democratic platform committee in 1944, on behalf of NAWL, in favor of a plank promising equal rights for women. NWP members were approaching both political parties, state governors, clergy of all denominations, and national women's organizations to gain support. Fenberg served as the Illinois chair of the NWP.

Fenberg was a hearing officer for the State of Illinois Civil Service Commission from 1942 to 1948 and from 1955 to 1956, as well as an adviser to the Illinois State Commerce Commission from 1952 to 1955. However, she maintained her office in downtown Chicago while she was in public service.

Fenberg remained active in professional associations at both the state and national levels. She served as the Illinois representative to NAWL from 1959 to 1961 and was a member of the executive committee of the Illinois Bar Association's matrimonial law committee.

In 1974, Fenberg retired to Findlay, Ohio, and three years later died of arteriosclerosis and complications from a fall. She was cremated and her ashes scattered in her sister's backyard in East Cleveland, Ohio. Matilda Fenberg's legal career, which spanned more than fifty years, included many successes as a trial lawyer and as a legal reformer.

Sources. Rita Spilka Permut, *Borkowski Nowalski Fenberg Family Genealogy* (1993) has biographical information about Matilda Fenberg. The Hancock (County) Historical Museum, Findlay, Ohio, has a typescript, "Matilda Fenberg," prepared by archivist Paulette Weiser in 1994 in conjunction with an exhibit about five prominent women from Findlay. [N.a.], *Herstory: Voices from the Past, Women in the History of Hancock County, Ohio* (1996) has a biographical sketch of Fenberg by Paulette Weiser. In July 1995 Elizabeth Berman interviewed Clarence Darrow biographer Lila Weinberg. Fenberg's publications include *Women Jurors and Jury Service in Illinois* (1940); "Status of Children: Divorce and Separation Cases," *Chicago Bar Record*, June 1956; and the following articles published in the *Women Lawyers Journal*: "Jury Service for Women," Spring 1947; "Blame Coke and Blackstone," Spring 1948; "Our Uniform Divorce Bill," Summer 1961. Fenberg's remembrances of Clarence Darrow were the subject of several articles, including "Lawyer's Dream," *Chicago Bar Record*, March 1959; "The Most Unforgettable Character I've Met," *Reader's Digest*, April 1959; "Clarence Darrow at His Best," *Chicago Bar Record*, June 1960; and "I Remember Clarence Darrow," *Chicago History*, Fall–Winter 1973. Her obituary, "Matilda Fenberg, Darrow Associate and Advocate of Women's Rights," appeared in *NYT*, October 25, 1977.

ELIZABETH K. BERMAN

FERBER, EDNA
August 15, 1885–April 16, 1968
NOVELIST, SHORT STORY WRITER, PLAYWRIGHT, JOURNALIST

Edna Ferber is known above all for her best-selling novels about America: stories about middle- and working-class people of the Midwest and South. Ferber was born in Kalamazoo, Michigan, but the family moved to Chicago shortly after her birth. She was the second of two daughters, her sister Fannie having preceded her by three years. Although Ferber's parents were both Jewish, they came from very different worlds. Her mother, Julia Neumann Ferber, was the daughter of Harriet and Louis Neumann. Louis Neumann, the descendant of an upper-class family of bankers and merchants, left Germany in the 1840s to escape political persecution. Born in Milwaukee, Julia Neumann was raised in comfortable surroundings on Chicago's North Side. Ferber's father, Jacob Charles Ferber, came from a more humble background. He grew up in the small village of Oylso, near Eperye, in Hungary, which he left at age seventeen to come to America.

Shortly after their marriage, Jacob Ferber took his bride to Kalamazoo in the hope of establishing a dry-goods business. The business did not thrive, however, and the high-spirited and fashionable Julia Ferber was clearly out of place in the small Michigan town. The Ferbers soon became parents of Fannie, then Edna. Within three years of Edna's birth, they returned to Chicago to live with Julia Ferber's parents. They stayed only a year, and though Ferber was little more than a baby at the time, she would later describe Chicago as exciting and the Neumann household as extravagant. She remembered her grandfather Louis Neumann as a scholarly gentleman who always carried a gold-headed ebony cane and loved to tell stories and present plays and operas to the delight of his grandchildren. Ferber became stagestruck as a result of Neumann's presentations.

Unable to create a profitable business in Chicago, Jacob, to his wife's dismay, decided to move his family to Ottumwa, Iowa, a small coal-mining town, where they remained for seven years. Ferber bitterly recalled taking her father his midday meal when he was too busy to come home for lunch and being subjected to the taunts of anti-Semitic adults and children who called her "sheeny" and jeered at her as she passed. Though still a child, she resolved to show up her persecutors by becoming rich and famous.

Both parents worked in the family's dry-goods store, Ferber's Bazaar, and a housekeeper helped at home. Despite hard work and lack of money, the family regularly went to the theater and Ferber read voraciously. Because of lack of business success and Jacob Ferber's developing eye problems, the Ferbers moved back in with the Chicago Neumanns. A while later, in 1896, they settled in Appleton, Wisconsin, which Ferber always remembered as a lovely little town. "Unlike Ottumwa, Appleton had a Reform synagogue, where Ferber studied Jewish history, sang in the choir, and participated in services; whatever Jewish education she managed to obtain during the course of her life came from these experiences" (Antler, 163). At age thirteen, she entered Ryan High School, where she spent four happy years, distinguishing herself by winning first place in the Wisconsin State Declamatory Contest in Madison. She described herself in high school as a "plump and ugly girl in eyeglasses perched atop a high-bridged nose inherited from my father" (*Peculiar Treasure*, 97)—a girl who compared unfavorably to her handsome sister Fannie.

Ferber hoped to go on to the Northwestern University School of Elocution and become an actress. By the time she graduated in 1902, however, her father was blind, her mother was working at Ferber's Bazaar to support the family, and there were limited resources. Determined to help support her family, Ferber, at age seventeen, became the first female reporter on the *Appleton Daily Crescent*. She earned three dollars a week, covering a regular news beat, writing the weekly society column, and eventually serving as Appleton correspondent for the *Mil-*

waukee Journal, writing features and covering sports. Ferber's career on the *Appleton Daily Crescent* came to an abrupt end, however, when a new city editor was hired who disliked her, criticized her style, and finally fired her. She later viewed this event as a stroke of luck, because she was soon invited to become a newspaper reporter for the *Milwaukee Journal* at fifteen dollars a week, a position she held for five years. One morning she fainted and was taken home for what was supposed to be a month, but she never returned. Suffering from severe anemia and recuperating from what appeared to be a nervous breakdown, she began to write and soon completed her first novel, *Dawn O'Hara*. Efforts to find a publisher, however, failed.

With the death of Jacob Ferber in 1909, Julia Ferber and her two daughters moved back to Chicago, where she invested in real estate and Ferber continued to write stories. She also tried to get a job on the *Chicago Tribune*, but she was told that they were not interested in a small-town girl. She focused on writing fiction to earn money, and in 1910 her first story, "The Homely Heroine," was accepted by *Everybody's Magazine*. Other stories followed, but still not convinced that she could earn a living writing fiction, she again tried to find a steady job at the *Chicago Tribune*. There, Burns Mantle told her flatly that they did not use women reporters. Shortly thereafter, in the spring of 1911, Ferber's writing career was finally launched when the Stokes Company offered to publish *Dawn O'Hara*, which sold ten thousand copies.

Although the three-room apartment on Chicago's South Side that Ferber shared with her mother and sister afforded little privacy for a serious writer, Ferber seems to have enjoyed life there, and she wrote exuberantly of the stimulation of the city: "Just to be out on the Chicago streets, with their smoke-blackened apartment houses and their bedlam of Loop traffic; their misty green lakeside parks and windswept skyscrapers—the stink of the stockyards from the west side, and the fresh tang of Lake Michigan from the east side—this was to know adventure" (*Treasure*, 174). Her love of Chicago was expressed in a number of short stories about its residents—stories of working people. Stories that were quickly sold to magazines included "The Kitchen Side of the Door," about a kitchen checker in a Chicago Loop hotel; "One of the Old Girls," about a woman buyer in a Chicago department store; and "What She Wore," about a clerk in a discount shoe store. A collection including many of the Chicago stories, *Buttered Side Down*, was published in 1912.

Soon thereafter Ferber embarked on a story about a traveling saleswoman named Emma McChesney, who was based on her mother's account of a woman drummer (salesperson) who had come to the store in Appleton to sell mousetraps. The fictitious Emma sold underskirts for a petticoat company and was clearly based on the strong figure of Julia Ferber. *American Magazine* was enthusiastic about the story because the American business woman in fiction had rarely been done, and they asked for a series about Emma McChesney. Ferber eventually completed about thirty McChesney stories, which were sought by magazines and acclaimed by a large readership. Three volumes of McChesney stories appeared in 1913, 1914, and 1915.

Chicago continued to fascinate her during this period. She called it "one of the most vital, unformed, fascinating, horrible, brutal, civilized, and beautiful cities in the world" (*Treasure*, 180). Though she intended to do a novel about the Chicago stockyards, she managed only a short story, "Blue Blood," which became a source of pride when it was used in an English course at the University of Chicago.

Ferber knew many writers in Chicago, including Carl Sandburg, Susan Glaspell, Sherwood Anderson, and Ring Lardner, but she claimed she saw them rarely. Her closest Chicago friend was Lillian Adler, a dance teacher and professional social worker, who became one of the chiefs in the United Charities of Chicago. Adler was eventually recreated in Ferber's 1920 novel, *The Girls*.

After the marriage of her sister, Ferber moved to New York in 1912 and soon began to travel extensively, although she spent at least half of each year of the following twelve in Chicago. After her first winter in New York, she explained her return to Chicago: "This turning my face westward was the unconscious urge to get nearer the earth" (*Treasure*, 195).

Back in New York after her first trip to Europe in 1914, Ferber oversaw the production of *Our Mrs. McChesney*, a dramatization of the McChesney stories, starring Ethel Barrymore. She found that she loved working in the theatre.

In 1916 she settled down for what she termed "the long pull of novel-writing" (*Treasure*, 223). Her second novel, *Fanny Herself* (1917), was an autobiographical account of a Jewish family in Wisconsin. Another collection of short stories followed, and then in 1921 she wrote *The Girls*, a novel about three generations of "old maids" in Chicago. Although she was disappointed with the sales, she remained pleased with what she considered a mature novel and her best work up to that time. While the characters are fictitious, the inspiration for the novel's matriarch was surely Julia Ferber, and the account of the joys and limitations of single women are probably based on her own experiences and those of Lillian Adler, to whom the book is dedicated.

After a trip to Europe with her mother, Ferber began to work in earnest on *So Big*, her novel about a middle-aged woman living on a truck farm in High Prairie, the Dutch district southwest of Chicago. Ferber had agreed to publish the book serially in the *Woman's Home Companion*, but on its completion she had reservations about publishing it as a novel, fearing that it would damage both her reputation and that of Doubleday publishers. Her editor disagreed, and *So Big* rapidly became a best seller, winning the Pulitzer Prize in 1924.

Soon thereafter she began her collaboration with George S. Kaufman on a number of plays, including *Minick* (1924), *Royal Family* (1927), *Dinner at Eight* (1932), *Stage Door* (1937), *The Land is Bright* (1941), and *Bravo!* (1948). In 1940 she briefly realized her childhood ambition to be an actress, making her first and last stage appearance as Fanny Cavendish in *The Royal Family*, a demanding role in which, according to the *New York Times*, she did well.

From 1912 to 1939 Ferber lived mainly in New York, sometimes socializing with the members of the Round Table who gathered at the Algonquin Hotel, a group Ferber admired and enjoyed despite her reluctance to take time from work to join the others at lunch. In addition to writing, she spent time on research for her novels, including *So Big*, *Show Boat* (1926), *Cimarron* (1930), *American Beauty* (1931), and *Come and Get It* (1935).

In 1939 she built Treasure Hill, a large estate in Connecticut, which was her home until she sold it in 1950, shortly after the death of her mother, and returned to New York. The house was testimony to her financial success—her triumph over the chaos of her early years. Photographs of Ferber at this time in her career reveal a short, slim, meticulously dressed woman with carefully coifed hair and manicured nails.

Ferber's life increasingly focused on her work, and while she had many friends, particularly in the world of theater, she seemed to have had little time for intimate relationships. She claimed to have written a thousand words a day, 350 days a year. By the time she died, she had completed twenty-four volumes of fiction, two autobiographies, and nine plays. She remained single and explained, "Unmarried female writers have one advantage over their wedded female contemporaries. They can lavish more time and energy on their children, of which I, as a spinster, have had thirty-two—or is it thirty-three: one loses count" (obituary, *New Haven Register*). When she died of cancer at the age of eighty-three, she was living on Park Avenue in Manhattan. Services were held at Frank E. Campbell's Funeral Chapel. There was no burial; she was cremated according to her wishes. She left an estate of more than one million dollars to her sister and nieces.

Despite her enormous readership, Ferber complained that her work was misunderstood. She claimed that her books had power, theme, and protest, but that neither readers nor reviewers acknowledged these characteristics. Reviewers saw instead a writer with a sure sense of place who was able to bring to life various regions of America. Even this praise was incomplete. Ferber never understood why critics did not consider her a Chicago writer or appreciate the importance of her Chicago books. Writing to literary critic FANNY BUTCHER, Ferber complained, "For years I've been true to that town [Chicago]. And it would have none of me. For years I've lived in it the greater part of the year, and I've written books and short stories about it that are (and I say it without shame) the best books and short stories that have been written about Chicago in ten years" (quoted in Butcher, *Many Lives—One Love*, 343). Ferber cited *The Girls* as a realistic representation of Chicago and put her short stories "Old Man Minick," "Home Girl," and "The Gay Old Dog" in the same category. Yet she did not get on Chicago critic Harry Hansen's list of Chicago writers or of those who wrote about Chicago subjects. *So Big* garnered the most praise, and there was considerable interest in *Show Boat*, *Cimarron*, *Saratoga Trunk*, and *Giant*. *Show Boat* became a landmark musical by Oscar Hammerstein and Jerome Kern after its great success on stage in 1927 and was revived in 1930, 1946, 1948, 1966, and 1994. Film versions were released in 1929, 1936, and 1951. Both *Saratoga Trunk* and *Giant* also became successful films, although Ferber herself had no interest in working on any of the films. While the *New York Times* obituary acknowledged that Ferber was considered by critics of the 1920s and 1930s to be "the greatest novelist of her day," the *Times* suggested that her books, though vivid and sociologically sound, were not profound.

In recent years more attention has been paid to two of Ferber's central concerns, her Jewishness and her interest in independent women. While her fiction is rarely about Jews, it is about the underdog and the outcast, the pioneer and the survivor—all of whom succeed in their own terms against the odds.

Thus, Ferber turned the burden of anti-Semitism into the privilege of being a Jew.

As Carolyn Heilbrun has pointed out, Ferber's originality lies in her portrayal of "strong, ambitious women" (*NAW*, [1980], 228). Basing many of her protagonists on Julia Ferber, whom Ferber called an "iron" woman, she created women who were characterized by "strength, ingenuity, perception, initiative" because the "American female . . . is stronger in character, more ingenious, more perceptive and more power-possessing (potentially) than the American Male" (*A Kind of Magic*, 283).

A citizen of the world, Ferber nonetheless treasured memories of Chicago and the Midwest and West throughout her life. Five years before her death, she contrasted herself with a nation of itinerant Americans traveling the country, affirming, "For me, the journey began only in Chicago. The Midwest, the West, these were what I wanted for refreshment" (*Magic*, 324).

Sources. The largest and most important collection is the Edna Ferber Papers (1910–77) at the State Hist. Soc. of Wisconsin, which includes correspondence, manuscript drafts, notes, reviews, and scripts of plays and movies; the society also holds her personal book collection. Clipping files and some letters are available at the Beinecke Library, Yale Univ.; the Manuscripts and Archives Division of the New York Public Library; and the Billy Rose Theatre Collection of the New York Public Library. In addition to the titles mentioned above, Ferber's novels and short story collections include *Roast Beef, Medium: The Business Adventures of Emma McChesney* (1913), *Personality Plus: Some Experiences of Emma McChesney and Her Son, Jock* (1914), *Emma McChesney & Co.* (1915), *Cheerful by Request* (1918), *Half Portions* (1920), *Gigolo* (1922), *Mother Knows Best: A Fiction Book* (1927), *They Brought Their Women* (1933), *Nobody's in Town* (1938), *No Room at the Inn* (1941), *Great Son* (1945), *One Basket: Thirty-One Short Stories* (1947), *Your Town* (1948), and *Ice Palace* (1958). In addition to the plays written with George S. Kaufman mentioned above, in 1920 she wrote *$1200 a Year* with Norman Levy. Two autobiographies, *A Peculiar Treasure* (1938) and *A Kind of Magic* (1963), are the most useful sources about Ferber's life. The only full-length biography is *Ferber: A Biography* (1978) by Ferber's great-niece, Julie Goldsmith Gilbert. A bibliography by Vito J. Brenni and Betty Lee Spencer, "Edna Ferber: A Selected Bibliography," appears in *Bulletin of Bibliography*, 1958. Entries on Edna Ferber are found in *Contemporary Authors*, vols. 5–8, first revision (1969), and in *Dictionary of Literary Biography*, ed. James J. Martine, vol. 9 (1981). An entry on Ferber appears in *NAW* (1980) and in *Jewish American Women Writers: A Bio-Bibliographical Critical Sourcebook*, ed. Ann R. Shapiro (1994). DeWitt BoDeen contributed "Edna Ferber into Film," *Films*, June–July, 1978, which includes a filmography. Mary Dearborn in *Pocahantas's Daughters: Gender and Ethnicity in American Culture* (1986) and Diane Lichenstein in *Writing Their Nations: The Tradition of Nineteenth-Century American Jewish Writers* (1992) discuss Ferber as a Jewish woman writer. For discussion of Ferber's Jewish identity, see Steven P. Horowitz and Miriam J. Landsman, "The Americanization of Edna: A Study of Ms. Ferber's Jewish American Identity," *Studies in American Jewish Literature*, vol. 2, 1982, and Joyce Antler, *The Journey Home: Jewish Women and the American Century* (1997). Other brief accounts of Ferber or her work include Grant Overton, "The Social Critic in Edna Ferber," *The Bookman*, October 1926; William Allen White, "A Friend's Story of Edna Ferber," *English Journal*, February 1930; Elizabeth R. Duval, "Edna Ferber Rings Down One Curtain," *New York Times Magazine*, September 1, 1940; Lewis Nichols, "In and Out of Books," *NYT*, June 16, 1963; obituary, *NYT*, April 17, 1968; obituary, *New Haven Register*, April 17, 1968; "Edna Ferber Is Eulogized Here as Champion of Great Causes," *NYT*, April 19, 1968; Annabel

Douglas McArthur, "Edna Ferber," State Hist. Soc. of Wisconsin, Women's Auxiliary, *Famous Wisconsin Women*, vol. 4 (1974). Information on Ferber's plays can be found in Miles Kreuger, *Show Boat: The Story of a Classic American Musical* (1978); and Malcolm Goldstein, *George S. Kaufman: His Life, His Theatre* (1979). Comments on Ferber's career can be found in Fanny Butcher, *Many Lives—One Love* (1972).

ANN R. SHAPIRO

FERMI, LAURA CAPON
June 16, 1907–December 26, 1977
AUTHOR, SOCIAL ACTIVIST

Laura Capon was born in Rome, Italy, the second daughter of Augusto and Constanza (Romanelli) Capon. Her father was an Italian naval officer and in retirement was made an admiral. Her mother managed a large household, often in the absence of her husband, whose career dictated much travel. Laura Capon (called "Lalla" by her family) had three siblings: Anna, Paola, and Alessandro. The Capons were an upper-middle-class Jewish family. During the early twentieth century, Jews in Italy were largely assimilated into mainstream Italian culture, and the Capons were no exception.

After completing the *Liceo* (the Italian equivalent of high school), Laura Capon began a course in general science at the University of Rome, the only one of the three sisters who attended university. Capon and her sister, Anna, had a shared social life. Anna was an artist and sometimes found Laura's desire to meet with a group of physicists and mathematicians a bit boring, dubbing the group the "logarithms." It was among the "logarithms" that Laura Capon met Enrico Fermi, a brilliant young physicist who became a professor at the University of Rome in 1926, at age twenty-five, and whom she married in 1928. When she married she had finished two years at the university, and her formal education ended. Nevertheless, drawing on her general science studies, Fermi began a writing career that extended throughout her life. Together with her friend, Ginestra Amaldi, wife of Enrico Fermi's colleague Edoardo Amaldi, she wrote *Alchimia del Tempo Nostro* [Chemistry for our time] (1936), a book explaining their husbands' work for a lay audience. According to Fermi, the book was successful but quickly became dated because of new discoveries that changed atomic science.

The Fermis had two children, Nella, born in 1931, and Giulio, born in 1936. Both children were baptized Catholic (the faith of their father's family) on the advice of Laura Fermi's mother, since anti-Semitism was on the rise in Italy by the mid-1930s and families with any Jewish background were endangered. In the summer of 1938, Laura and Enrico Fermi decided to move their family to safety in the United States. Enrico Fermi had taught there during past summers and had several offers of university jobs that he had declined at the time. Now he wrote, circumspectly for fear of censorship, that the reasons for declining no longer existed. Several offers were renewed, and he accepted a position at Columbia University in New York. Late in 1938, Enrico Fermi was awarded the Nobel Prize in physics. The Fermis left Italy in December 1938 and arrived in New York City in early January 1939. On the journey, the family stopped in Stockholm, Sweden, where Enrico Fermi received the Nobel Prize. Felicitously, the award money associated with the Nobel Prize allowed the Fermis to begin life in America comfortably.

The move to the United States posed a serious challenge to the development of Laura Fermi's writing career: the difficulty of learning to write articulately in a foreign language. She later wrote that her children helped her master the contemporary English used by Americans. She described the process as painfully slow; it took ten years for her to begin to write again. Family responsibilities, as well as difficulty with a new language, slowed Fermi's writing career. From the late 1930s until the mid-1940s, her husband's career and his involvement with the war effort necessitated several moves around the country. As professor of physics at Columbia University beginning in 1939, Enrico Fermi did theoretical and experimental work in nuclear physics, particularly the study of fission and atomic energy. After the Japanese bombed Pearl Harbor, Hawaii, in December 1941, the U.S. government became very interested in Enrico Fermi's research, and he began doing war work for the government. The Manhattan Project, secret work to develop an atomic bomb, was developing at the University of Chicago, and Enrico Fermi accepted an appointment in the physics department there in 1942. In the summer of 1944, Enrico Fermi's work on developing the atomic bomb for the Manhattan Project took him to Los Alamos, New Mexico. The Fermi family stayed there for a year and a half, until the Allies dropped the atomic bomb on Hiroshima and Nagasaki.

In 1945, after their stay in Los Alamos, the Fermis moved back to Chicago, to the University of Chicago neighborhood of Hyde Park, on the city's South Side, where Laura Fermi spent the rest of her life. Enrico Fermi returned to academic work at the University of Chicago. For several years, Laura Fermi was occupied in caring for her family and doing a good deal of entertaining, hosting gatherings for her husband's colleagues and students. She also found time for volunteer work, joining the local League of Women Voters, a group in which a number of her friends were active. She brought home the League's recommendations on issues, and often these determined how both she and her husband voted. The Fermis had become naturalized U.S. citizens in 1944.

After her children went away to college, Laura Fermi resumed writing, producing a number of short sketches that were never published. When someone suggested that she write a biography of her husband, she replied, "My husband is the man I cook for and iron shirts for. How can I take him that seriously?" (*Atoms in the Family*, ii). Nevertheless, Fermi did follow the suggestion and wrote *Atoms in the Family: My Life with Enrico Fermi*. The book was published in 1954 as Enrico Fermi was dying of cancer. *Atoms in the Family* enjoyed immediate success, and Enrico Fermi had the satisfaction of seeing Laura's book on the *New York Times* best seller list before he died on November 28, 1954. The book is lighthearted; Fermi wrote it before anyone suspected that her husband would soon die. Though she included chapters on her husband's work, which she explained in lay terms, most of the book was of a more personal nature, and she spoke with wit and charm of herself, her husband, their friends, and family. The book was translated into a number of foreign languages, including Italian and Japanese. Reviews of *Atoms in the Family* were generally positive. Reviewers praised the book for describing Enrico Fermi's historically significant

work from a subjective and human point of view and for presenting a readable picture to a lay audience.

Fermi's next book was *Atoms for the World: United States Participation in the Conference on the Peaceful Uses of Atomic Energy* (1957). She had been invited to write this book as historian for the Atomic Energy Commission, a position she held in 1955–56. The conference Fermi described in the book was held in Geneva, Switzerland, in August 1955 and was attended by delegates of seventy-three countries, including the Soviet Union. The delegates included both scientific and political figures.

In 1961, Fermi published three books: *The Story of Atomic Energy*, a book for young people; *Galileo and the Scientific Revolution*, written with Gilberto Bernardini; and *Mussolini*. For the first book, she hired a consultant—an eleven-year-old boy who gave her advice in exchange for a dollar and lunch.

Fermi's final published book was *Illustrious Immigrants: The Intellectual Migration from Europe, 1930–41* (1968), for which she won the Friends of Literature prize. The most scholarly of her works, it documents the lives and contributions of many of those who fled Fascism and Nazism and came to the United States. She interviewed many of the immigrants whom she profiled in the book and commented on her own immigration to America in the context of the larger influx of European refugees. "I realized that our coming to America had been part of a large phenomenon of historical importance, that had depleted Europe of brain-power and had benefited America in many ways. It had also benefited the immigrants themselves, who in this country found great intellectual resources and opportunities. . . . Under these circumstances, they became much more productive than they would have been at home" (quoted in Commire, *Something about the Author*, vol. 6, 78). Reviews for *Illustrious Immigrants* praised the book as informative, well-balanced, encyclopedic, and readable, though not always successful in its ambitious goal of chronicling the immigrant experience.

Contemporaneously with her return to scholarly writing, Fermi became increasingly involved in community activism. In April 1959, along with Alice Kimball Smith, Fermi founded the Cleaner Air Committee of Hyde Park–Kenwood (CAC). The committee had seven charter members, all women, all but one of whom were wives of University of Chicago faculty members. Fermi and the other founders of the CAC recognized the threat that air pollution posed to the environment years before air pollution became a nationally recognized issue.

From 1959 through 1972, committee members met once a month to educate themselves and community residents on the impact of air pollution in their community and to enlist citizen help in improving the physical quality of life in their living environment. Committee members furthered this goal through various activities. These included monitoring local buildings for smoke violations and reporting them to the City of Chicago Air Pollution Control Department, holding public meetings to inform the public about air pollution and related legislation, pressuring landlords of private and public buildings to convert from coal-burning equipment to gas heat, and testifying in public hearings both locally and nationally. The CAC members also published and distributed educational materials, spoke before school audiences and community groups, and served as observers at court hearings on pollution violations.

As the CAC further researched the causes and effects of air pollution, Fermi began to publish articles on the subject. Fermi wrote "Cars and Air Pollution" for the October 1969 issue of the *Bulletin of Atomic Scientists.* Her article explored the problem of air pollution caused by cars and discussed such possible alternatives as electric cars, improved public transportation, allowing only small cars within cities, and substitutes for gasoline. In 1963 and 1966, she wrote articles for the journal *New City* describing the CAC's efforts since 1959 to combat air pollution and to educate the community about pollution's hazards. Fermi was also a member of the Air Pollution Control Committee of the City of Chicago from 1959 to 1968 and of the Northeastern Illinois Metropolitan Area Air Pollution Board in 1962–63.

By 1971, partly due to the CAC's efforts, Chicago saw mass conversions of coal-burning furnaces to gas or oil, and the burning of garbage in apartment boilers had been outlawed. As a result, Hyde Park–Kenwood became a cleaner, more pleasant place in which to live. Moreover, in part due to the CAC's efforts, cleaner air had become a national concern by this time. Consequently, Fermi began to direct her energies toward another concern, gun control, and gradually withdrew from the CAC, which disbanded in 1972.

As she lessened her involvement with fighting air pollution, Fermi became increasingly concerned with the problem of gun violence and began devoting much effort toward gun control. As she had with air pollution, Fermi pioneered community activism in this area, since gun control was not a widely recognized issue at the time. In November 1971 Fermi cofounded the Civic Disarmament Committee (CDC) with other Chicago southsiders. As far as Fermi and her cofounders could determine, the CDC was the nation's first gun-control group. The CDC was founded out of personal experience, in response to recent handgun homicides committed on the South Side of Chicago by very young teenagers. The CDC worked on many fronts: it launched educational campaigns, promoted handgun legislation at both the state and federal legislative levels, and studied the possibility of improving enforcement of existing gun laws.

The CDC began legislative action in 1972, when it played an instrumental role in convincing the Chicago City Council to adopt a resolution petitioning the U.S. Congress to ban private handgun possession. The CDC sent copies of the resolution to mayors of the one hundred largest U.S. cities, urging them to take similar action. The U.S. Conference of Mayors adopted a similar gun control resolution in 1973.

Also beginning in 1972, the CDC repeatedly testified on gun control, both in person and in writing, before committees of the U.S. Congress and the Illinois General Assembly. In 1973 and 1975 CDC members lobbied for state legislation in Illinois to ban private possession of handguns and in 1975 helped organize and spoke at the Chicago hearings of the U.S. House Subcommittee on Crime. In 1976, the CDC lobbied for Bill H.R. 11193, which cleared the Subcommittee on Crime and the full House Judiciary Committee but was then shelved. The CDC also maintained a continuous correspondence with members of Congress, urging them to introduce and to support legislation banning the possession of handguns by private citizens, as well as other handgun control legislation.

On the national organizing level, the CDC was involved in planning and launching the National Council to Control Handguns. As handgun control groups were formed in other states, the CDC established contact with them and participated in conferences with these groups. Fermi was active in the disarmament committee almost to the end of her life. After Fermi's death, the CDC contributed about two thousand dollars in her honor to the National Council to Control Handguns.

In Fermi's later years, she began researching and writing a book on fifteenth-century Italian women. According to Fermi's notes and draft manuscripts of individual chapters, the aim of the book was to examine the ways in which middle- and upper-class Italian women were increasingly able to inhabit nonstereotypical female roles in fifteenth-century Italian society. In her research, Fermi collected biographical information on 135 women, grouping them as scholars, poets and writers, warriors, rulers and patrons of the arts, Saints and "the Blessed," and other categories. The book was to include a chapter entitled "Eve on the Battlefield," profiling Italian noblewomen who were career warriors who hired themselves out to fight for various princes and nobles, and others who administered and militarily defended their husbands' estates while the husbands were away at war. Another chapter, "Eve in the Quattrocento," examined the way in which the Humanist movement of the fifteenth century increased women's opportunities to study and become learned. Unfortunately, the inaccessibility of research sources in Italy and Fermi's failing eyesight prevented her from completing the book before she died. In the 1960s Fermi was afflicted with a lung disease, kept under control with medication but not cured. In 1977, she died in Chicago of pneumonia, complicated by her lung condition.

Like the women Fermi researched, she was herself a kind of "Renaissance woman," successfully combining a writing career with pioneering community activism. She and her colleagues combated air pollution and civilian gun violence, bringing both issues to the attention of local and national lawmakers long before most Americans became aware of their importance.

Sources. Fermi's papers are in UC Spec. Coll. These papers include research notes for and manuscripts of her books, including her unpublished mystery story, "Death in Atom City," and an unfinished nonfiction work, "Italian Women of the XVth Century"; a number of unpublished articles and short stories; book reviews; and miscellaneous items. "A Guide to the Laura Fermi Papers" by Leslie A. Morris (typescript, 1979) includes a brief biography of Fermi and describes the collection. Two archives in UC Spec. Coll. contain papers pertaining to the Hyde Park–Kenwood Cleaner Air Committee and the Civic Disarmament Committee, including minutes of the committees, letters, publications, and other materials. Extensive excerpts of speeches given by Emilio Segre, Alice Kimball Smith, and Ruth Grodzins at Fermi's memorial service are published in *Bulletin of Atomic Scientists,* May 1978. There is a brief introduction by Emilio Segre to the 1987 edition of *Atoms in the Family.* Anne Commire, *Something about the Author,* vol. 6 (1974), contains a sketch on Fermi including an extensive autobiographical quote. Anne Commire, *Something about the Author,* vol. 28 (1982), has an obituary.

ELIZABETH L. INGLEHART
NELLA FERMI WEINER

FISCHER, MOTHER IMELDA
(Elizabeth Fischer)
March 14, 1877–October 3, 1954
EDUCATOR, LITURGIST, ADMINISTRATOR

FISCHER, SISTER CELESTINE
(Susanna Fischer)
October 11, 1872–May 25, 1953
MUSICIAN, ARTIST

Susanna and Elizabeth Fischer were born in Bavaria, the daughters of Franz and Elizabeth (Weiss) Fischer. They were the youngest members of a family of five daughters and one son. When the sisters were young, the family planned to emigrate to the United States. Franz Fischer died of tuberculosis just before the trip, but Elizabeth Weiss Fischer undertook the journey. The family arrived in Chicago around 1885 and settled in a German immigrant neighborhood on the Near West Side.

The Fischers attended St. Joseph Catholic Church, a German-speaking parish. The four Fischer daughters were enrolled in St. Joseph Parish school, where they were taught by the Benedictine Sisters. Later they attended Saint Benedict and Scholastica Academy, also taught by the Benedictine Sisters, a congregation from Eichstatt, Bavaria, that had settled in Pennsylvania in 1852. Members of the order had first arrived in Chicago in 1861 to minister to the educational and communal needs of Catholic German-speaking immigrants. The Chicago Benedictines had established the Academy of Saint Scholastica in Canon City, Colorado. Chicago Benedictine sisters were serving as teachers and administrators of several schools in Colorado that had been established in 1886 by their order.

In Chicago, the Benedictine Sisters named their academy after Saints Benedict and Scholastica, the brother and sister who founded the men's and women's orders in Europe. Both had followed the monastic tradition, living according to the Rule of Benedict written in the sixth century. In America, the Benedictines were challenged to transform a solely monastic life into a combination of practical work in the community with an interior life of communal prayer. Two of the Fischer sisters made significant contributions to this process of modernization in the context of a renewed expression of Benedictine liturgy and spirituality.

Several members of the Fischer family, including the mother, a brother who had begun to study for the priesthood, and an older married sister died from tuberculosis. The four remaining daughters, now orphaned, found homes in the institutions of the Catholic Church: two (Catherine and Barbara) joined the St. Joseph's Convent; two (Susanna and Elizabeth) were boarders at the Academy of Saints Benedict and Scholastica.

Susanna Fischer had shown artistic ability from childhood; the Benedictines encouraged her to study under well-known artists, with a different teacher for each field of art: watercolor; portraiture; oil painting, which she studied with Will Feld in Germany; and miniature work on porcelain and ivory.

Susanna Fischer joined the Benedictine community in 1891, taking the name Sister Celestine. She taught both piano and art during her early years in the convent. After an illness affected her hearing, she focused on painting and teaching art, continuing her art education at the Art Institute of Chicago and the University of Notre Dame.

Elizabeth Fischer was an outstanding student at the Academy of Saints Benedict and Scholastica in Chicago. During her last year at the school she earned a normal school diploma and was certified to teach. In 1895, after graduation, she joined the Benedictine community and took the religious name, Imelda. Like many in the community, Sister Imelda contracted tuberculosis. She was sent to Colorado where the climate proved beneficial. Sister Imelda organized the high school program of the Academy of Saint Scholastica and graduated the first class in 1901. She provided courses in Latin, German, science, music, and the commercial and domestic arts. Imelda also initiated a program of teacher certification. Soon she took on administrative responsibilities and, in 1909, was appointed directress of the academy, a position she held until 1921.

By 1917 Sister Imelda's work in the Canon City academy was well known, and she was sent as a delegate to a meeting of the American Benedictine Sisters held at Sacred Heart Convent, Lisle, Illinois. For many years, the American communities of Benedictine sisters had attempted to establish a congregation that would unite the motherhouses under a common superior, a practice associated only with monasteries of monks. Sister Imelda was convinced that forming such a congregation was crucial for the future of the Benedictine sisterhoods. The Benedictines gathered in Lisle to draw up their resolutions and elect officers. They sought the permission of their local bishops and sent their constitution to Rome. Finally, in 1917, Pope Benedict XV, himself a Benedictine monk, approved a seven-year trial and final approval for the congregation followed. Sister Imelda always served in leadership positions with the Congregation of Saint Scholastica.

Her leadership was again recognized when she was elected prioress of the Chicago Benedictine community in 1921, taking the title "Mother." The Benedictine Rule of Life calls for the community to live and work together as a family under the direction of an elected superior. Mother Imelda returned to Chicago to begin her duties at the motherhouse, the residence of teaching sisters, of the novices and postulants, and of the sisters who were ill or retired. Other community members under her supervision lived in Chicago-area parishes where they worked, and one-third lived in Colorado.

The 1920s were a time of expansion and renewal for the Chicago Benedictines. The community and its school had outgrown the 1907 motherhouse, which had been built on a narrow strip of wooded land in the northwestern section of Chicago on Ridge Avenue. Half of this old building was used for the convent and the other half for the academy and the boarding school. Especially inadequate was the chapel, which the sisters described as a "box" (Harrison, 115). Mother Imelda closed the boarding school to relieve the overcrowding in the motherhouse. She also closed a second building, the original Academy of Saints Benedict and Scholastica, which was situated on Orleans Street on Chicago's West Side, where she had attended school. The sisters resisted the move from the old Ridge convent, but Mother Imelda was determined to begin implementing her plans for a new structure that would include a chapel, student dormitories, a gymnasium, and classroom space for grades one through twelve.

The Benedictine community needed permission from the local archbishop, George Mundelein, to begin the building project. Money had to be raised for the new construction by the

FIG. 27. *Sister Celestine, on far right, and Mother Imelda Fischer, second from right, Benedictine sisters at St. Scholastica Priory, Chicago; the two were biological sisters. Celestine was an artist and illuminator of religious texts, Imelda an administrator and educator.*

women. The community sold the western section of their Ridge Avenue property, the Orleans Street building, and land that was owned in Waukegan, Illinois. Mother Imelda spent three years fund-raising, negotiating contracts, and gaining permission from Archbishop Mundelein. In the meantime, three wooden classroom buildings were constructed for temporary use on Ridge Avenue. Her persistent efforts were successful and ground was broken for the new structure on May 7, 1924. The completed building, the Academy of Saint Scholastica, located on the remaining Ridge property, was dedicated on December 6, 1925.

The new chapel, appropriately situated at the point where the convent and the new school building came together, was the center of all the community's activity and the spiritual heart of the Benedictines's lives. It was also the beginning of the renewal of Benedictine spirituality in the New World. The Benedictines were initially called to the United States to serve the pressing needs of immigrant Germans, and the early years of their community life had left little time for the full expression of the daily schedule of prayer, called the Divine Office. In Chicago, the practice of the Divine Office had been discontinued in 1904 by the superior of the community. The saying of the Divine Office was reinstated in 1916 by Mother Imelda's predecessor, but during World War I communication with Germany was difficult, and the new books necessary for the liturgy did not arrive until 1921. Over the years, there had also been a loss of skill and knowledge in the use of traditional Gregorian Chant. Mother Imelda and the Benedictine community in Chicago became part of a world revival of interest in liturgy, theology, spirituality, and art. Gregorian Chant was being recovered from Benedictine monasteries in Europe. Mother Imelda believed that a Benedictine house like St. Scholastica could become a liturgical center. She read widely on the subject and invited European scholars and teachers to the motherhouse to bring their new perspectives on the traditional prayers and to train the sisters in singing Gregorian Chant. The first teacher she hired was Marie

Pierik, who was trained at Solesmes, France, the leading monastery in the renewal of Gregorian Chant.

In 1921, Sister Celestine was appointed by Mother Imelda to begin her work with the young novices in the convent. She taught classes in religious doctrine and Gregorian Chant and led the study of the Rule of St. Benedict. Both Sister Celestine and Mother Imelda realized that the easiest way to introduce new ideas was to begin with the community's youngest members. Under Sister Celestine's direction, the novices spent many hours learning the intricacies of Gregorian Chant. They produced English translations of the Divine Office, the Roman martyrology, and other important works. Years later Mother Imelda reiterated her belief in the centrality of celebrating the Divine Office. "For us Benedictines, this is the motor which puts in motion and keeps going all our other community activities" ("Mother's Letter," *Our Community*, February 1, 1930, 3).

Sister Celestine, as an artist and enthusiast for liturgical renewal, had envisioned a return to a more complete liturgical life in a chapel designed to teach the Benedictine Rule through its art. From 1910 to 1922, she created rare paintings on porcelain of the Stations of the Cross. Beautifully executed, they were recognized by Pope Pius XII. When Mother Imelda unveiled the plan for the new complex of buildings, Sister Celestine began fund-raising to decorate the chapel appropriately. The fund-raisers successfully accumulated enough money to pay for the initial decor of the chapel. Sister Celestine designed the altars and communion rail and made sketches for the stained glass windows. She spent time in Washington, D.C., studying the design and composition of stained glass windows, which, after her plans were complete, were fabricated in Munich, Germany, and installed in 1926. The walls of the chapel remained blank until the chapel fund was replenished more than a decade later.

The new building proved to be a financial hardship for the community and a heavy burden for Mother Imelda, to whom the women looked for leadership. Her financial acumen was substantial, however, and the loans taken to pay the more than six hundred thousand dollar building cost were met. The building debt had been assumed during the boom years of the roaring twenties; the loans were paid off during the Great Depression. Guilds, clubs, auxiliaries, and individual benefactors contributed significant sums, but the heavy responsibility to raise the funds and pay off the balance belonged to the community. The community paid sixty thousand dollars on the principal within the first three years. "This along with the heavy interest had strained every nerve of the small body" (*Our Community*, 1929, n.p.), Mother Imelda recalled. The repayment was a struggle in the financially troubled year of 1929, when the community needed to make payments of fifty-eight thousand dollars from an income derived from altar bread sales and the small salaries of the Benedictine sisters who taught in parish schools. These women, who were paid about twenty-five dollars a month, turned their salaries into the general community fund. This practice of aggregating the salaries of teaching sisters to fund the community's existence and to pay loans for expansion or unusual costs was common in most women religious congregations. The community also had income from students' tuition at the academy, which was one hundred dollars annually.

In the 1920s, anti-German sentiment in the United States presented a different kind of challenge for the Benedictines. Mother Imelda also understood that the community's work had to move away from the more narrow ethnic focus of its early years and assume a new, broader, American perspective. She urged all the sisters to become citizens, insisted they be fluent in English, and allowed only English to be spoken in the convent. Sister Celestine became a citizen in Canon City, Colorado, in 1921, and Mother Imelda in Chicago in 1924.

There was also a need to improve the quality of education in the Benedictine-run schools. By 1921, the community's teaching responsibilities, in Colorado and Illinois, included ten parish schools, two high schools, and twenty-five vacation Bible schools. Twenty years later five more parish schools were added. Critical to the quality of education was the preparation of women religious as teachers. Mother Imelda raised the standards of teacher preparation by insisting that all the teaching sisters in Chicago and Colorado complete high school and college. For the first time they were offered the opportunity to study for master's degrees. Mother Imelda enrolled at DePaul University in Chicago and received a B.A. degree in 1925 and an M.A. in 1927.

Weekends became school time for all the teaching sisters in the community. At first Mother Imelda and SISTER DOLORES SCHORSCH taught the sisters on Friday evenings, and professors from Loyola and DePaul universities taught the sisters on Saturday mornings. Later, when it became acceptable for the sisters to appear in public, they went by school bus to their classes on the university campuses. Sisters continued their studies during summer break; even week nights were often occupied with continuing education.

Catholic education was, from Mother Imelda's viewpoint, "beset by grave and subtle dangers not only from without, but also from within" ("Mother's Letter," *Our Community*, February 1, 1930, 2). External standardizing agencies required that Catholic schools adjust their training of teachers and their curriculum. Secular teachers were employed more frequently in Catholic institutions so that the new demands could be met. For Mother Imelda, unless sisters were truly "women of prayer" (p. 2), they could not detect the dangers that lurked in secularism. Thus the liturgical renewal undertaken by the Benedictines was critical and had to exist alongside new trends in education.

Overall, the female students attending the community's two high schools benefited from the upgrading of the educational preparation of the sister schoolteachers. Music, theater, and art programs were added to the curriculum. St. Scholastica High School received full accreditation from the North Central Association of Colleges and Secondary Schools and the University of Illinois.

In 1929, Mother Imelda introduced a monthly newsletter, *Our Community*, to bring news of the motherhouse and of all the missions to every Benedictine sister scattered in Colorado, Illinois, and now Kansas. She served as editor for more than thirteen years; Sister Celestine provided the art work. Ten issues were published each year, often running from twenty to thirty pages and including pedagogical materials for teachers and a personal letter from Mother Imelda.

By the 1930s, the Chicago Benedictine community was alive with creativity and activity stimulated by Mother Imelda's leadership. The publication of translations of the Matins readings for Sundays and feast days, the *Roman Martyrology* in English, and Columba Marmion's *Christ the Ideal of the Monk* with character formation guides by Sister Celestine under the title of *Elevations* were all part of the liturgical renewal begun in the 1920s. Gregorian Chant masses were sung every Sunday and feast day as were Vespers and Compline. Throughout the 1930s, many liturgical scholars, including Dom Adrian Eudine, a monk from Solesmes, France, who revolutionized church music throughout the world, came to St. Scholastica to teach in the liturgical school that was held during the summers. By 1935, sufficient money had been raised to commission Joseph Steinhage, an artist from the Maria Laach Monastery in Germany, to paint the walls of the chapel that had been left blank. He began the work, which took many years to complete, "frescoes . . . in the distinctive and bold Beuronese manner for which the German abbey had gained artistic and liturgical acclaim" (*Chicago Tribune*, December 13, 1992). The organ was installed in 1937, and with it, Mother Imelda had fulfilled one of her most important obligations as a Benedictine prioress. She had successfully provided a beautiful and unique chapel to the community for its prayer and liturgy. "Intuition born of love can outstrip the farthest reaches of mere thought" (*Our Community*, April 1936, n.p.), she proclaimed at its dedication.

Also in the 1930s, Sister Dolores Schorsch and her brother, the Reverend Alexander P. Schorsch, CM, began a long collaboration and published a unique catechetical program used throughout the United States and internationally. SISTER M. CECILIA HIMEBAUGH began writing for *Orate Fratres* and other liturgical publications. Her leadership in the Chicago Inter-Student Catholic Action (CISCA) promoted social action among St. Scholastica High School students who visited Chicago's Friendship House, the Little Sisters of the Poor, and St. Vincent Infant Asylum.

In the 1940s, after fifty years as a painter and designer, Sister Celestine became interested in the medieval art of illuminated manuscripts. Benedictines of the Middle Ages had elaborately illustrated the prayers, hymns, and other holy writings of the Church. Celestine dedicated herself to mastering this ancient art form. At the age of seventy, she began the most outstanding example of her work, a fourteen-page manuscript to commemorate the life and death of St. Benedict and the origin of the Divine Office. Only advanced arthritis stopped her artisanship at the age of seventy-six. She died of cancer at age eighty after a prolonged illness and was buried in Calvary Cemetery, Evanston, Illinois, near the statue of St. Scholastica, which she had designed years before.

Mother Imelda had been elected to her first six-year term as prioress in 1921 and was reelected three times. Because her health was failing, she resigned in 1941 before beginning a fourth term. In 1921 the community had numbered approximately one hundred and by the time she retired it had doubled. St. Scholastic High School enrolled fewer than one hundred pupils when Imelda began her work; at the time of her retirement, there was an enrollment of more than 550 students and a citywide reputation for high scholastic standing. By the mid-1950s the enrollment was approximately one thousand. She continued her work for her congregation as a member of the visitation team, making regular visits to parish schools where Benedictine sisters taught and to missions. She also continued teaching mathematics but needed a substitute more and more often because of her health. Finally, illness forced her to retire completely. She died at age seventy-seven and was buried near her natural sister in Calvary Cemetery. All four of the Fischer sisters, immigrants from Bavaria and women religious, were buried in Calvary Cemetery.

Mother Imelda and Sister Celestine were a harmonious team. They shared a zeal for the Benedictine order and the lifestyle that Benedict envisioned more than thirteen hundred years ago. They were able to use their pragmatic talents to make this vision function in twentieth-century North America. Both were dedicated to liturgy, prayer, and the education of Catholic women.

Sources. Biographical material, correspondence, and writings of Celestine and Imelda Fischer are in the Archives of the Benedictine Sisters of Chicago, St. Scholastica Monastery, Chicago. See copies of the *St. Scholastica Priory Archives Newsletter* edited by Sister M. Vivian Ivantic, OSB, and copies of *Our Community*, edited by Mother Imelda Fischer, all in the archives. The chapel contains much of Sister Celestine's artwork. See Genevieve Harrison, *Where There Was Need* (1960), a history of the Benedictine community in Chicago.

MARY ANN SAVARD

FISCHER, SISTER CELESTINE (Susanna Fischer). *See* FISCHER, MOTHER IMELDA (Elizabeth Fischer)

FLOISTAD, BERTHA GRIMSTAD
June 2, 1882–June 6, 1989
CLUBWOMAN, COMMUNAL LEADER, CHORAL SOCIETY MEMBER

"A cornerstone of the Norwegian Chicago colony" (*Decorah Posten*, June 15, 1967), Bertha Grimstad Floistad was born and raised on a remote farm in the district of Nordmøre in western Norway. She left her home in 1901, at age nineteen, to make her way to the new land of America, like many young Norwegian women at the turn of the twentieth century. After working as a hired girl on a farm in northeastern Iowa, she married a school friend from Norway, Peder Floistad. They settled on their own farm near the Norwegian American stronghold of Decorah, where she bore many children; the number varies in different sources, from twelve to fourteen. Bertha Floistad sewed and knitted for the Red Cross during World War I. In 1927 Peder Floistad accepted a job as a cattle buyer for a meat packer, and the family moved to Chicago.

Bertha Floistad joined ethnic organizations in order to maintain ties to her place of origin in Norway and to cultivate her connections with people from her home region. Like many rural and some urban immigrants, she joined *bygdelag*, or homeland regional associations, societies that sponsored regular reunions of people from particular Norwegian regions. By doing so she formalized her opportunities to meet old friends and speakers of her dialect. Floistad joined the *Nordmørslag*, made up of immigrants from Nordmøre, and the *Trøndelag*, comprised of immigrants from the neighboring Norwegian district of Trøndelag. *Bygdelag* members were looked down on by some urban Norwegian Americans as Norwegians who felt more connection to their home districts within Norway than to the country of Norway as a whole. Floistad may have considered this a false distinction; she was apparently able to blend her rural background in Norway, her years on an Iowa farm, and her urban life in Chicago without relinquishing any of her past.

In Chicago in the late 1920s Floistad joined women's organizations in particular. Along with other women of the immigrant first generation and Norwegian-speaking second generation, she joined the Anna Kolbjørnsdatter lodge of the Daughters of Norway in 1928. There is some evidence that a number of the members came from the same region of Norway that Floistad called home, which would reinforce the sense of regional loyalty conveyed by her *bygdelag* memberships. The Daughters of Norway was a fraternal/sororal society started in Minneapolis in 1897 that offered a modest death benefit, a type of insurance, to people of Norwegian descent with good health and good moral character who were between the ages of sixteen and fifty-five. (Men were also welcome to join, but the organization's name reflects the sex of almost all of its active members.) During the fifty-three years of its existence the Daughters of Norway chartered more than seventy lodges in the Upper Midwest and on the East Coast. Many of the lodges were named for female figures in Norwegian myth. Three Chicago lodges were distinctive in taking names of notable historic women: Anna Kolbjørnsdatter, a Norwegian patriot who had helped defeat the Swedes in a battle in 1716; Camilla Collett, a nineteenth-century Norwegian author and feminist; and JANE ADDAMS, the American reformer and advocate of international peace. In addition to providing insurance, organizing social occasions, and raising funds for good ethnic causes, the Anna Kolbjørnsdatter lodge sponsored a women's drill team and a chorus named Oselio, after Norwegian opera singer Gina Oselio. Over time, Floistad held every office in the lodge, including president.

Her engagement with the Oselio women's chorus was perhaps even more intense than her lodge activity. Organized in

1896, Oselio was one of the first women's choruses in Chicago. Before moving to the city, Floistad had been a delegate to the 1926 Minneapolis convention at which choruses from several midwest cities joined to found the Norwegian Women Singers' League of America. Like the lodges, women's choruses spent a lot of time and energy raising money for several purposes: to help pay for concert tours, to host choral conventions in their towns, or to donate to a variety of good causes. Floistad was deeply involved in all of these activities on Oselio's behalf.

In addition to her secular activities, Floistad and her family joined St. Peter Evangelical Lutheran Church in 1931. During the 1930s and 1940s, Floistad became active and then moved into leadership positions in organizations with both women and men members, notably Chicago's Norwegian National League (NNL), an umbrella organization begun in 1899. By the time of Floistad's energetic involvement, the league had organized dozens of ethnic member societies promoting temperance, sports, religion, women's activities, politics, workers' rights, theater, and other causes, and was promoting activities celebrating May 17, Norwegian Constitution Day, and October 9, the anniversary of Leif Erickson's discovery of America. According to an ethnography of the Norwegian National League in the Norwegian-American Historical Association Archives, by the 1930s and 1940s the league's officer positions had been carefully apportioned between men and women, with women serving as the NNL's first and third vice-presidents. Floistad attained the job of first vice-president of the league in 1943. Her responsibilities in that post were to fill in for the president in his absence, to head the committee for the Museum of Science and Industry's Norwegian Christmas party, and to lay the wreath at the Leif Erickson statue on the Sunday nearest Leif Erickson Day. It was not all pomp and festivities, however; Floistad worked hard on less glamorous organizational tasks, such as selling advertisements for commemorative program booklets. Her responsibilities at the Museum of Science and Industry were perhaps her main effort to present Norwegians to the larger Chicago community. There she led a program that not only decorated a Christmas tree in Norwegian style but also featured drill teams, children in old-country costumes, and folk dancing.

During World War II, Floistad's American and Norwegian patriotism were both manifest. She was active in American Red Cross work and had four sons in the armed forces. One, Pershing Victor Floistad, was killed in Africa. Norwegian community sources show that she was also a member of the Camp Little Norway Club of Chicago, which supported a Canadian camp training Norwegian airmen for service in the war, and that she worked for the American Relief of Norway.

After the war she continued her activities with her lodge, her chorus, and the NNL. In 1948 the Chicago and Evanston lodges of the Daughters of Norway combined to host the national meeting of their organization, raising funds for that purpose by arranging parties and having sales. That year's membership in the Anna Kolbjørnsdatter lodge, which met monthly on North Kimball Avenue, was 153, down from 337 in 1933. A brief two years later, moved by the exigencies of the insurance business, the Daughters of Norway merged into the Sons of Norway—despite vehement protests by many Daughters. Floistad perse-

vered, becoming active in the North Star lodge of the Sons of Norway. In 1951, the year after her husband died, Floistad led the members of the NNL program committee in selling ads for the printed program for Leif Erickson Day. During one of her fourteen years as president of Oselio, she organized the chorus's tour of Norway in 1952, when the chorus sang for King Haakon, among other listeners. Floistad was a popular figure in the Norwegian American press, which credited her with extensive welfare work in the ethnic community, especially from the mid-1940s to the mid-1950s. She was described as "virtually a committee of one for welfare work in cooperation with the Norwegian-American Hospital, the Norwegian Lutheran Bethesda Home for the Aged, and the Norwegian Old People's Home of Norwood Park" (*Viking*, Chicago, February 23, 1956).

For a woman whose public life was almost entirely bound up in the Norwegian American community, Floistad's displays of symbolic ethnicity may have been few. Unlike Chicago's Grieg Ladies Chorus, which in 1950 dressed in a version of the Hardanger dress that had become a Norwegian national costume, the women of Oselio performed in long dark dresses with short white jackets. Each wore a large treble clef on her right lapel. In photographs of Floistad with her fellow lodge and chorus members and her fellow officers of the Norwegian National League in the 1950s and 1960s, neither she nor any of the other women wore anything that symbolized Norwegian ethnicity, not even the traditional Norwegian brooch called a *sølje*. It was all the more significant, then, when "in [Chicago's] 17th of May parade in 1955 she rode in a car with her daughter, granddaughter, and great-granddaughter—all in Norwegian costumes. The sign on her car read: 'Great Grandma came from Norway, but we are all Americans'" (*Viking*, February 23, 1956). The sign may have had as much to do with the challenges of celebrating ethnic origins in cold war America as with the assimilation of this particular family, but the display of the symbolic ethnicity of costumes and parades reinforces the work Floistad had done to build a bridge between her adopted country and her homeland.

In 1956 the government of Norway honored Floistad's years of work by awarding her the St. Olav Medal at the Chicago Norske Klub during that year's installation of officers of the Norwegian National League. The Royal Norwegian Consul General, Knut Orre, presented the medal to Floistad, who was further honored by the inclusion in the day's program of several selections by the Oselio Ladies Singing Society. The benediction was given by her pastor, the Reverend Freeman Kunz. The St. Olav Medal, one of Norway's great honors, is awarded for the advancement of connections and cooperation between the Norwegian diaspora and the homeland. Never one to rest on her laurels, in 1959 Floistad, then vice-president of the Norwegian Women Singers' Association of America, led a committee that hosted a grand Women Singers Gathering (*damesanger stevne*) in Chicago.

In many ways Floistad was not atypical of Chicago's middle-class Norwegian American women. She lived near Logan Square in a Norwegian and German neighborhood on the northwest side of the city, attended a Lutheran church, and was a member of numerous ethnic organizations. Floistad may have been less typical of Chicago Norwegian activist women in that she and her Norwegian-born husband began their American lives as Iowa farmers. Perhaps she found the life of a city house-wife relatively uneventful after her busy life on the farm, leading her to pursue good works by the organization route. Floistad aspired to and achieved leadership roles within many of the organizations she supported. Although she was a church member, the organizations in which she was most active were secular. Historians of Norwegian America have pointed out the tension that often existed between *bygdelag*, or homeland regional associations, and pan-Norwegian groups exemplified in Chicago by the Norwegian National League. Urban and rural Norwegian Americans often expressed their old-country loyalties differently: urban immigrants honored the country as a unit, especially after Norway won its independence from Sweden in 1905; rural immigrants often had little connection to the national government before emigrating and directed their loyalties toward the Norwegian district of their birth and dialect. Floistad was notable partly for her participation in a range of Norwegian American organizations that spanned a variety of connections to the homeland.

Bertha Floistad walked an interesting line, as perhaps many middle-class women volunteers did in the early and middle part of the twentieth century, between domestic accomplishment and formal community contribution. As the mother of a large family, her domestic arrangements must have consumed considerable time, even though she moved to Chicago after her childbearing years were nearly over. Her career as a female leader of Chicago's Norwegian American community is also distinctive because, unlike many of the community's prominent women, she did not achieve her status by her association with a prominent husband. Peder Floistad's work as a cattle buyer for a meat packer was a good job, but it was not a high-status one. Nor was Bertha Floistad one of the much smaller group of highly educated women in the ethnic community, which had a notable number of women doctors, for example, who played leading roles in several organizations. In addition to her decades of leadership in Chicago and national women's organizations, Floistad seems to have met the challenges of evolving gender roles in organizations where both sexes were members. Many Chicago women served as bridges between their communities and the larger society of Chicago. The bridge Floistad built did help to span the gulf between Norwegian Chicagoans and other city residents. In addition, Floistad's volunteer activism linked Norwegian Chicagoans with each other and with their past, with Norway, the place where Floistad was born and grew to young womanhood.

Sources. The Norwegian-American Historical Association Archives (NAHA), St. Olaf College, Northfield, Minnesota, has articles on Bertha Floistad from the Norwegian American press, including *Decorah Posten*, Decorah, Iowa; *Minnesota Posten*, Minneapolis; *Viking*, Chicago; and *Duluth Skandinav*, Duluth, Minnesota. Other resources at the NAHA are the Norwegian National League of Chicago Papers, the Daughters of Norway Papers, the Hermana Rye Haugan Papers, the Women Singers League of America folder in the Norwegian Singing Societies Papers, and several files on Norwegian Clubs in Chicago. Other primary sources are a run of the *Daughters of Norway* newspaper, 1938–51, in the Minnesota Hist. Soc., St. Paul. Odd Lovoll, *A Century of Urban Life: The Norwegians in Chicago before 1930* (1988), is valu-able, as is Lovoll's *A Folk Epic: The Bygdelag in America* (1975). Floistad's obituary appeared in *CT*, June 8, 1989.

DEBORAH L. MILLER

FLOWER, LUCY LOUISA COUES
May 10, 1837–April 27, 1921
EDUCATIONAL AND SOCIAL WELFARE REFORM LEADER,
POLITICAL ACTIVIST

Lucy Flower demonstrated an astute ability to advocate on behalf of powerless groups in society and to convince political leaders that it was appropriate for government—federal, local, and state—to respond to the needs of such groups. She accomplished this feat at a time when women did not have the vote and when government took a laissez-faire approach to the consequences of industrial conditions. She specifically fought to advance public education and equity for women and to improve the lot of children who were impoverished and/or delinquent.

Lucy Coues was the adopted daughter of Samuel Elliott and Charlotte Haven (Ladd) Coues. Charlotte Coues traced her lineage to John Mason, who was the original grantee of New Hampshire. Samuel Coues was a successful merchant in Portsmouth, New Hampshire, and an avid social reformer. He was well connected politically and in 1853 accepted an appointment from his friend, President Franklin Pierce, to work in the Patent Office in Washington, D.C. Lucy Coues grew up in a family of eight children.

Coues was educated in Portsmouth until 1853 and went to the Packer Collegiate Institute in Brooklyn, New York, in 1856 and 1857. Due to family illness she was not able to complete the program. She spent a short time working in the Patent Office in Washington, D.C., and in 1859 moved to Madison, Wisconsin, where she taught in the Madison Public High School, which was at that time a preparatory school for the University of Wisconsin. In 1862, budget problems forced the city schools to close, and Coues was authorized to use the facilities to conduct a private school during the 1862–63 school year.

In 1862 Lucy Coues married James Monroe Flower, a Madison attorney. Over the next eleven years she had three children: Elliott, Harriet Dean, and Louis Bertram. In 1873 the family left for Chicago, where James Flower formed a successful law firm and was influential in Republican Party politics.

After her arrival in Chicago, Lucy Flower began to lead an active public life. By 1875 she was on the charity committee at St. James Episcopal Church and became a board member of the Half-Orphan Asylum. Later she sat on the board of the Home for the Friendless. These were the traditional activities of middle- and upper-class Protestant women of her era. For Flower and a significant group of her generation, serving on boards of charities was the first stage in developing a critique of these institutions. Just as JULIA LATHROP launched her career as a child advocate and social reformer out of her experiences as trustee of the Illinois State Charities Board, Flower went beyond the model of personal noblesse oblige when her experiences doing charity work made her question the way in which dependent children, delinquents, and the sick were treated. She joined with other women in activities to advance a reform agenda for

FIG. 28. *Lucy Louisa Coues Flower was one of seven women who spearheaded a drive in 1880 to establish the Illinois Training School for Nurses, pictured here between 1888 and 1912.*

women and children through a variety of innovative associations run by women. The Chicago Woman's Club (CWC), established in 1876, was at the center of this female reform culture in late-nineteenth- and early-twentieth-century Chicago. Flower was an active member and served as president in 1890. The CWC worked to advance a women's agenda and to place women in politically influential positions long before they were able to vote.

In 1880 Lucy Flower was one of seven women who spearheaded a drive to establish the Illinois Training School for Nurses (later the Cook County School of Nursing). The founders of the Illinois Training School for Nurses (ITSN) had two goals: to improve patient care and to make nursing a respectable occupation for women. They sought to establish standards and credentials for the nursing profession and a school to provide the necessary training. County officials opposed this endeavor because it intended to replace the political patronage system of hiring county hospital and insane asylum nurses with credentialed candidates. The founders engaged in a political struggle with county officials and eventually prevailed. Flower served alternately as either the president or vice-president of the school from 1885 to 1904.

In the fall of 1885, various women's associations came together to develop a united effort to aid dependent women and children. The Protective Agency for Women and Children, initially connected directly to the CWC, was run by moral reformers, suffragists, and philanthropists, including Lucy Flower, Dr. SARAH

HACKETT STEVENSON, and ELLEN HENROTIN, who had become concerned with a wide range of problems that confronted poor and immigrant women daily. By 1889, the agency, which was functioning as a legal-aid bureau, became an independent institution. Four years later, as a result of the Protective Agency's legal-aid bureau, women and children had collected $1,247,000 in damages from fraud, injustice, and divorce cases.

In October 1888, Flower and temperance reformer FRANCES E. WILLARD formed the Woman's League of Chicago, an outgrowth in part of the International Council of Women and in part, "a spontaneous growth from the feeling permeating all circles of organized womanhood, that the greatest efficiency depends upon co-operative action" ("The Woman's League of Chicago," *Union Signal*, October 11, 1888, 8). The league was a coalition of fifty-seven existing women's organizations and leaders, including the Chicago Woman's Club, the Woman's Christian Temperance Union (WCTU), and the Illinois Woman's Press Association. Organized womanhood, harnessed by the league, could "work reform in school matters; can open churches, not one day in seven, but every day in the week; can enforce legislation on the tenement house question, the liquor saloon, the Sabbath question . . . and when present enactments prove insufficient, can secure better laws" (p. 8). Its woman's agenda was clear: "make life better for working girls and women, sweeter and safer for little children" (p. 8). This was Lucy Flower's agenda.

Among her projects related to young people, Lucy Flower

proposed and fought for solutions to juvenile delinquency. In the late 1880s she worked with a coalition of groups in support of a measure in the Illinois legislature to provide a state industrial school for homeless boys. The 1887 bill that proposed state standards for such institutions generated opposition from religious and private groups that ran their own orphanages, and the bill was defeated. With the help of funds from the Chicago Woman's Club, Flower opened a private industrial school in Glenwood, Illinois, in 1889.

In 1891 Lucy Flower was appointed to the Chicago Board of Education, where she served until 1894. In Illinois, women had been allowed to serve on school boards since 1873; but they only obtained a limited franchise in 1891 to vote in elections for school officers. Flower worked to make education more relevant to poor children. Largely on her initiative, kindergartens, manual training, and sewing classes were introduced into the public school curriculum. Flower successfully instituted a program that provided bathtubs for tenement children.

As a board member, Flower supported improved teacher training and higher salaries for experienced teachers; she fought for equal rights to promotions based on merit for men and women. In particular, she publicly supported a highly qualified female candidate over a mediocre male candidate for the principalship of Humboldt High School in 1892.

Flower was active in the 1893 World's Columbian Exposition. She served as chair of the World's Fair Congress of Moral and Social Reform and was instrumental in the Illinois Training School for Nurses project at the Fair. The ITSN ran a model emergency ward in the Woman's Building at the Columbian Exposition. At a time when hospitals and nurses were still suspect in the minds of many, the trained nurses, representing different nursing schools, presented to the skeptical public a practical demonstration of their work. They also afforded relief and assistance to those requiring medical care while visiting the exposition.

In 1894 Flower helped found the Chicago Bureau of Charities and served as the first vice-president. She was not, however, interested in the expansion of a state bureaucracy that maintained persons, especially children, in large institutional structures. Flower and other reformers of her generation were critical of the state-run institutions where dependent people were warehoused rather than rehabilitated. Ideas of prevention and rehabilitation were new. For Flower, institutional structures were stopgaps. She hoped that children would be placed in homelike situations, and she believed that the best interests of society were served through the adoption or boarding of children in families. She thought that bureaus or boards of charities should establish state or county schools with ample provision for placing the children in homes as soon as possible.

In 1894 the Democratic mayor of Chicago, John Hopkins, did not reappoint Flower to another term on the school board. His reasons were clear: he wanted no Republicans and no women. The mayor's decision caused a flurry of protest and reopened gender issues that had characterized Flower's term on the school board.

Women were able to vote in school elections in 1894 as a consequence of a limited state franchise bill passed in 1891. Gender became a key issue in the Chicago area when it became apparent that women could win seats as trustees of the University of Illinois. Both Republican and Democratic women began to organize in preparation for the forthcoming election. Both parties ran female candidates from Chicago, women prominent in the woman's political culture of the city. JULIA HOLMES SMITH was the Democratic candidate, Lucy Flower the Republican. Mayor Hopkins's decision not to reappoint Flower to the Chicago school board energized Republican women on behalf of her candidacy.

Lucy Flower was the first woman elected to the University of Illinois Board of Trustees; she received 184,000 votes and won by a plurality. Flower was the first female elected to a statewide office in Illinois. Women's groups in Chicago celebrated the victory. As a University of Illinois trustee, Lucy Flower advocated that the institution operate on the principle of inclusivity for women. Flower and Julia Smith, who lost the election in 1894 but was appointed a trustee in 1895, used their contacts with the Illinois Federation of Women's Clubs to organize support for their projects within the Illinois legislature. The two women sent a joint letter in 1896 to University of Illinois alumnae soliciting their support for women's facilities.

Although major gains were won, women reformers found that they had to remain vigilant against political patronage even after reform legislation was enacted. Flower, for example, continued successfully to protect the county nursing profession from a return to patronage control. In 1896, Cook County Board President Daniel Healy recommended no renewal of the contract between the county and the ITSN. Healy sought revenge on Flower and JANE ADDAMS for their exposure of the adverse effects of patronage workers on the care of the insane at the Dunning Asylum.

Flower was increasingly concerned about the problem of juvenile delinquency. The concept of treating juvenile offenders separately and differently from adult criminals emerged in the late nineteenth century as progressive reformers, including Flower, Addams, Sara Hart, MARY BARTELME, and LOUISE deKOVEN BOWEN, sought ways to deal with problems associated with youth in industrial society. Flower and her colleagues brought a multifaceted approach to the problems of youth. In general, they opposed child labor and advocated compulsory school attendance laws; they wanted children under the age of sixteen to be separated from adults in courts of law and to be treated with strategies of rehabilitation rather than punishment. Initially, employers, criminal courts, and even parents opposed any laws that would change the status quo. In order to improve the conditions of children and to foster the development of productive, healthy citizens in the future, progressive reformers worked on all fronts.

Flower pushed hard for a compulsory school attendance law, which was eventually enacted in 1897. She linked school attendance and a reduction in delinquency, her basic premise being that children needed an education and a decent home in order to prepare themselves to be productive, self-sustaining citizens. Flower also came to understand that when boys and girls got into trouble, the problems were encased in weak or abusive families, truancy, and sweatshop employment. A new kind of "court" was needed to mediate these issues and to bring about an appropriate resolution that would create a better environment for the child. Flower was a leader in the coalition that worked to establish a juvenile court system in Cook County during the 1890s. By 1898 she had garnered support from Illinois social welfare leaders, the Chicago Bar Association, and county judges. In 1899 a bill was passed establishing the Cook County Juvenile Court, which was the first of its kind in the world.

There was more work to be done, however, and Lucy Flower formed a committee of citizens called the Juvenile Court Committee. Julia Lathrop was its first president, and Jane Addams served as president in 1900. The law that established the juvenile court had not provided for the salaries of probation officers, nor did it provide for a place of detention. The Juvenile Court Committee raised the money for the salaries of the probation officers and maintained a detention home where children could be housed until the court made its final decision. From 1898 to 1907, the Juvenile Court Committee raised and spent one hundred thousand dollars to sustain the juvenile court system. It secured the passage of a law that established the probation officer system as part of the juvenile court system, to be maintained by the county authority. It succeeded in persuading the county and the city governments to cooperate in the erection of a children's building, which housed both the court and the detention home. Once the work of the Juvenile Court Committee had been accomplished, a new organization, the Juvenile Protective Association (JPA), was created to look after children who were already in the care of the court. JPA raised money for protective officers who worked to prevent children from getting into the care of the court.

Flower continued to focus on the state's responsibility to delinquent youths by exposing, in 1900, the deplorable conditions at the John Worthy Reform School. She linked the conditions and poor management of the facility to political patronage and continued to advocate for the creation of institutions designed to provide delinquent youths with a trade.

Flower continued as a trustee of the University of Illinois and was instrumental in the creation of a woman's department at the university in 1897 and the appointment of a dean of women the same year. Flower advocated a curriculum for women, including a department of household science. She pushed to have women students admitted to medical school and to have female faculty hired. Flower was not nominated for re-election in 1900, however, due to conflicts with Governor Tanner and competition within the Republican Party.

Although Lucy Flower was clearly an independent thinker, her accomplishments were largely the result of collaborating and networking with various groups of women reformers. She argued and demonstrated that women should and could be agents for change who exercise political influence in the public domain, with or without suffrage rights. Essentially she did not see suffrage as the means to achieving gender equality. She believed women had the right and the responsibility to be agents for change regardless of what the laws provided. Lucy Flower modeled this philosophy throughout her life with compassion, zeal, and courage.

In 1902, Lucy Flower moved to Coronado, California, with her husband, James, who was sick. He died seven years later, and she soon became an invalid. In 1921 she died of a cerebral hemorrhage in Coronado; her body was cremated.

Sources. The Lucy L. Flower Papers, CHS, include Flower's own writings and speeches as reported, usually verbatim, in newspapers. Flower's correspondence as a trustee of the University of Illinois is found in the Andrew S. Draper Papers, Univ. of Illinois at Urbana-Champaign. Her article, "Women In Public Life," *Outlook*, June 7, 1895, expresses her beliefs about equality of the sexes and the role of women in the public sphere. Three books provide the histories of organizations and projects in which Flower was critically influential: Henriette G. Frank and Amalie H. Jerome, *Annals of the Chicago Woman's Club for the First Forty Years of Its Organization, 1876–1916* (1916); Grace Schryver, *A History of the Illinois Training School for Nurses* (1930); and Jane Addams et al., *The Child, the Clinic and the Court* (1925), chapters by Ben B. Lindsey, Julia C. Lathrop, Mrs. Joseph T. Bowen, and Timothy Hurley. The entry in *NAW* (1971) is particularly useful.

JEAN C. TELLO

FOIN, YOKELUND WONG
March 8, 1889–June 27, 1986
SOCIAL ORGANIZER, HOMEMAKER, SEAMSTRESS

A widow raising six children during the Great Depression, Yokelund Foin was a role model in the Chinese immigrant community at a time when there were very few Chinese women in Chicago. Born in California to Quock Shee, a nineteen-year-old native of California and Wong Duck, a thirty-year-old male immigrant of Xinhui, in southern China, Yokelund was the eldest of five children. Quock Shee raised the children at home, while Wong Duck worked as a tailor.

Yokelund Wong and three of her siblings grew up in San Francisco and attended schools set up by Protestant missionaries. Yokelund Wong was trained according to Chinese tradition. The Confucian concept of the role of woman—to obey father, husband, and, as a widow, the eldest son—was ingrained in her. Within this context, men ruled the family and women managed the household. Yokelund Wong had slightly more exposure to Western culture than did her mother, since she and her siblings were the second generation to attend schools of Protestant missionaries. Because the Cantonese family structure and obligations prevailed, however, Yokelund Wong was matched and married when she was fifteen years old. Her husband, Chin Foin, was a twenty-six-year-old merchant who recently had emigrated from Canton, China, leaving his first wife and children behind to tend the ancestral hearth, as was customary in traditional Chinese culture, while he conducted business in China and the United States. Because of his merchant status, U.S. immigration law allowed him to travel freely between the United States and China. Beginning in 1882 and extending until 1943, the American government passed a series of exclusion acts specifying that only merchants and their families, students, and visitors were allowed into the United States from China.

When Yokelund Wong married Chin Foin, she became part of his family in China. In 1905, Chin Foin took her back to Canton to meet his family. According to Chinese custom, Foin might have requested that Wong, along with his first wife, remain in China with his children; but he had decided before making the visit to his homeland that he wanted to make a home in the United States with his second wife and children. In the years after Wong and Foin settled in Chicago, at least one child by his first wife came to live in the Wong household.

About twelve Chinese families were living in Chicago in 1890. When Wong and Foin arrived sixteen years later, there were a few more families, but the numbers were still very small.

FIG. 29. *Seamstress and homemaker Yokelund Wong Foin, seated with her baby on her lap and a young child by her side; Chicago, 1911 or 1912.*

In 1906 Wong accompanied Foin to Chicago, where he intended to set up a restaurant business. Foin was bold. He began with a partner, and together they opened one restaurant. After they closed this restaurant, Foin opened up his own restaurant, the Mandarin Inn, one of the first Chinese restaurants in downtown Chicago. It was the first modern Chinese restaurant in Chicago that catered to operagoers (in the 1990s, the site of Jimmy Wong's restaurant). Although Foin hired many Chinese to work in his restaurant, he chose as his assistant, secretary, and business manager an Irish immigrant woman, Molly O'Farrell.

Foin worked tirelessly and amassed great wealth for his family, enabling Wong to live the life of a merchant's wife. She stayed at home, out of sight, raising her children and managing the household. She dressed in fashionable Western clothing and employed a Chinese housekeeper and a non-Chinese chauffeur. Around 1913, Wong's mother died at the age of forty-two. Since her father, Wong Duck, found it extremely difficult to take care of both the tailor shop and his children, he brought two of Wong's brothers and two of her sisters from San Francisco to Chicago to live in the Chin Foin household. One of her brothers and her father later returned permanently to Xinhui, China.

Wong had her first child, Theodore, in 1907, the same year that her own mother gave birth to her youngest sister, Yokechun (or Jenny). Wong had two daughters, Frances in 1908 and Gladys in 1911. Two years later, after her mother died, Wong took care of her siblings, had another son who died of polio three years later, and, in that same year, had another daughter, Louise. One of her closest friends, Dr. MARGARET LIN, a Chinese medical student attending the University of Illinois, lived in Wong's household in the 1910s. Wong had her last two children, Victor and Warren, in 1919 and 1921. By the 1920s, Wong's household included her children and her siblings, her father and her husband and, occasionally, Chinese students who needed housing.

Eventually, the family moved to a larger house away from the Chinese enclave in a well-to-do section of the North Side of the city. As a wealthy businessman who lived in the city, Foin was obligated to join Chung Hua, a hierarchical, merchant-based association in Chinatown; but he did not restrict himself to hiring working-class Chinese men. He also hired Chinese who came from all over China to the United States as students. These students were not accepted by the Chinese community in Chicago because they were not from the same district in southern China, Toishan, where the ancestors of the vast majority of Chicago's Chinatown population had lived. They were also excluded from other housing when white landlords, aware of anti-Chinese sentiment in Chicago, refused to rent to Chinese students. In an unprecedented move, Wong and one other family opened up their homes to them.

Their intense interest in education may account for Wong's and Foin's unusual decision to break with ancient taboo and invite students from outside their ancestral region in China to board in their home. New ideas, perhaps the result of Foin's interactions with mostly white, upper-class operagoers who frequented his successful restaurant may also account for his divergence from customary Chinese community mores. At the time Foin was one of a handful of Chinese in Chinatown who spoke English fluently. He amazed white Chicagoans because of his determination to adopt American culture. At the same time, their Chinatown connections were vital to the Foin/Wong family. It was a delicate balancing act they maintained between their American adaptations and their adherence to Chinese traditions.

While well respected by many in Chinatown, Foin's great fortune produced wonderment and speculation as to the real nature of his business. Some Chinatown residents speculated that Foin must have been involved in drug smuggling. Wong was not involved in any of the business activities; until the 1920s she maintained the traditional role of the Chinese household manager and with her family attended Chinese operas and pantomimes in Chinatown. However, she also associated with other well-to-do Chicagoans, vacationing at a popular summer resort at Paw Paw Lake in Michigan. In this era, her association with people from other ethnic communities outside Chinatown was unusual but also part of the aspirations of many Chinese.

Bridging the two cultures, Wong arranged to send her eldest child and two sisters to China to attend school. Most entrepreneurial Chinese families believed that their children needed both an American and a Chinese education in order to find a job in the United States. The employment options were either in restaurants or import/export trade. One of Wong's sisters, Grace, finished her education at the University of Chicago and married a classmate. Grace and her husband accompanied Wong's eldest son, Theodore, and other sister, Jenny, to Canton, where they attended high school and later, Lingnam University. Grace's husband prospered as a banker in China and was thus able to take care of Theodore and Jenny. The outstanding characteristic of Wong's personal life was that she worked very hard on behalf of others—her father, husband, children, siblings, and even the Chinese foreign students, managing to maintain a somewhat altered but definitely Chinese household. She wanted her children to be self-disciplined and to be able to live in two cultures.

In 1924, Wong's busy but formulaic life changed dramatically with the death of her husband. Chin Foin fell down an elevator shaft in the Mandarin Inn and died of a brain concussion. His assistant, Molly O'Farrell, ran the restaurant for about a year before deciding to return to Ireland. Wong again decreased the size of her household by sending her two eldest daughters, one of whom had attended Frances E. Willard Elementary School in Chicago, to China. She was left with three children to support.

With the stock market crash of 1929 and the Great Depression, the family's fortune plummeted. Wong did not know how to manage finances, and the family savings depleted rapidly. In 1932, at age forty-two, Wong was compelled for the first time in her life to find work outside the home to support her children. Shortly after the death of her husband, she had moved into a smaller house; but her options for working outside the home were as limited as those of a new immigrant. Her understanding of English was limited. Fortunately, Wong found a friendly upholstery-shop owner who was willing to hire her to do sewing and mending, the very same work that her father had pursued as an immigrant. Wong worked there for seven years. Eventually, she was able to move back into the role of household manager for her grown children.

Just as maintaining a Chinese household was a primary value, so was obtaining education and striving for upward mobility. All six of Wong's children graduated from college, a singular accomplishment. Although Wong's children were relatively independent and self-supporting, Wong took care of her grandchildren for several years while one of her daughters worked as an interpreter for the U.S. Department of Immigration in New York. She lived with another daughter for twenty years after that before living on her own for twenty more years in a condominium near Chicago's Chinatown. She died at the age of ninety-seven.

Perhaps the most significant aspect of Yokelund Wong's life was the strength she demonstrated in maintaining Chinese traditions while simultaneously adapting to an American lifestyle. She was not a visible social activist in Chinatown but a role model in a time when there were very few Chinese women in Chicago.

Sources. Regarding names, the Chinese form places the surname (e.g., Wong or Foin) first; the American form places it last. Under Chinese custom a wife retains her father's surname; under American custom, a wife traditionally takes her husband's surname. Information about Yokelund Wong Foin comes from interviews by Peggy Spitzer Christoff in 1993 with members of Wong's family and of the Chinatown community. They include Gladys Chen Wong, Gun Hsing Wang, Nancy Wang-Kikuchi, Eunice Tom Wong, and Lucy Moy Lee. Susan Lee Moy verified historical facts on the development of Chicago's Chinatown. Information on Chinese Americans can be found in Betty L. Sung's *Mountain of Gold: The Story of the Chinese in America* (1967); Yuan Liang's *The Chinese Family in Chicago* (1951); Judy Yung's *Chinese Women in America* (1987); Yuan-li Wu's *The Economic Conditions of Chinese in America* (1980); Tin Chiu Fan's *Chinese Residents in Chicago* (1925); Ruthanne Lum McCunn's *Chinese American Portraits* (1988); and Susan Lee Moy's "The Chinese of Chicago: The First One Hundred Years," in *Ethnic Chicago,* ed. Melvin G. Holli and Peter d'A. Jones (1995).

PEGGY SPITZER CHRISTOFF

FOLEY, EDNA LOIS
December 17, 1878–August 4, 1943
NURSE, PUBLIC HEALTH ADMINISTRATOR

Born of Irish-American parents, William R. and Matilda (Baker) Foley, in Hartford, Connecticut, Edna Foley graduated from Smith College in 1901 and the Hartford Training School for Nurses in 1904. Her education was unusual. Few nurses were college educated at the turn of the century. By the time she completed postgraduate work at the Boston School of Social Work in 1908, she was one of the best educated nurses in the country.

Foley worked on the East Coast for several years after finishing school: one year each as head nurse at Hartford Hospital in Connecticut; chief nurse at Children's Hospital in Albany, New York; and night supervisor at Children's Hospital in Boston. Following those stints, she was introduced to visiting nursing—serving the sick poor in their homes—when she became a municipal tuberculosis visiting nurse in Boston for two years. She moved to Chicago in 1909 to become the supervising nurse at the Chicago Tuberculosis Institute.

The inspiration for the institute had been provided by the Tuberculosis Committee of the Chicago Visiting Nurse Association (VNA). Foley's work among the tubercular poor was heroic, as the disease carried a tremendous stigma. For most of the nineteenth century people believed tuberculosis was inherited. Since eugenics was fashionable, revulsion for tubercular patients was common. After it was accepted that tuberculosis was caused by bacteria that could and would attack anyone, the onus fell on the poor as the source of the infection, since their weakened condition, caused by crowded and unsanitary living conditions, poor diet, and health-destroying jobs, made them the likeliest to get sick. Foley continued her work with tuberculosis victims after promotion to superintendent of the Municipal Tuberculosis Sanitarium nurses in 1911.

Foley became superintendent of the Chicago Visiting Nurse Association the following year. She replaced longtime superintendent HARRIET FULMER, who was fired after the VNA's board of directors decided the organization needed a superintendent trained in social work. Foley's education and work experience fitted perfectly with the board's new vision for the association.

Foley joined an organization with a long history. The VNA, established in 1887 to care for the sick poor, gratis, in their homes, emphasized the teaching of sanitation and cleanliness. The association, run by a volunteer board of directors composed of Chicago's wealthiest women, was supported largely by charitable contributions. The most generous donors each paid for the services of a specific nurse and received monthly descriptions of her work in return. Foley, as superintendent, was the bridge between the wealthy who ran and paid for the work of the VNA and the poor for whose care they paid. As such, she was always diplomatic. In one letter she soothed a contributor upset by the monthly reports describing the work of the nurse she supported. "I am sorry that we seem to be sending you particularly harrowing ones," Foley wrote of the reports. "Instead of letting them distress you, will you not feel that your support is of tremendous assistance to them, for without it we could not do a great many of the pleasant things that we are able to give them" (letter to Mrs. Theodore Sheldon, January 12, 1924, VNA Papers).

"Harrowing" may not have been the best word to describe the work of VNA nurses, but the sheer arduousness of their work cannot be exaggerated. The VNA divided the city into districts; each district was assigned to one nurse. Nurses traversed their districts to homes often far from the streetcar lines. They traveled almost always without automobiles, though by 1931 the VNA did have thirteen automobiles at their disposal, thanks to generous donors. The streets they walked in their ankle-length skirts were unpaved and frequently muddy. Indeed, homes, even in the city, were sometimes in the middle of prairies. Since most of the families served by the VNA had few possessions useful for the care of the sick or newborn, nurses often carried with them on their long walks not just medical supplies but also baby clothes, towels, and sheets. The homes they visited rarely had running water and often had dirt floors.

The VNA, as a matter of policy, never worked independently of physicians. Nurses made initial visits on patient request, but they only made follow-up visits after receiving explicit instructions for treatment from a physician. Foley immediately recognized this procedure as a problem. Since physicians were often difficult to contact, care was sometimes delayed. To remedy this situation, Foley sought and received "Standing Orders for the Visiting Nurse Association of Chicago," approved by the Chicago Medical Society in 1913. Foley continued to standardize the work of Chicago's visiting nurses by writing a *Visiting Nurse Manual* in 1914. Intended as a guide for all new visiting nurses and a reference manual for nurses in general, it became a model text for visiting nurse associations throughout the country.

Foley introduced other innovations as well. In 1913, she began teaching VNA nurses about the nutritive value of specific foods and how to shop for inexpensive foods high in nutrition. Nurses passed their knowledge on to the women they cared for, preventing susceptibility to illness caused by poor diet. In the fall of 1916 the VNA organized the Committee on After-Care and Study of Infantile Paralysis to supply innovative follow-up care to those stricken with polio in the previous summer's epidemic. By 1920 the VNA employed twelve nurses to work under the guidance of an orthopedic physician.

Foley also pioneered public health internships for nurses, encouraging hospitals to send their student nurses to the VNA for two months. Foley urged the long internship after it became

evident that the hospitals' practice of sending their nursing students on one-day rounds with the VNA was having a detrimental effect. Foley explained in 1924, "The average student nurse saw only the dirt, the over-crowding, the messiness, the ignorance, the selfishness, or what seemed to her the preventable illness and the indifference of the patients. When one goes merely as a visitor . . . there is danger that one will not recognize the human being in the patient, that the study of character under adversity remains a sealed book to the visitor" ("Affiliation of Training Schools," 2).

The preventive medicine practiced by the VNA yielded results. In 1917, as the city's infant morbidity and mortality rates dropped, the VNA's baby tents—set up each summer since 1905 to care for sick infants in poverty-stricken neighborhoods—were discontinued. For these improvements in health, the VNA credited its work among the city's poor. Foley herself noted in the VNA *Annual Report* for 1917, "We feel that at last our long years of teaching are bearing fruit and that the preventive work, which has been our aim from the first, is showing good results in our second generation families" (p. 28). She believed that the VNA's preventive medicine program was priceless, its cost ultimately negligible.

In addition to the highly visible work in Chicago's neighborhoods, the VNA placed nurses in industry. In 1913, Foley placed a nurse at the Illinois Steel Works and the Armour and Company meat-packing plant, increasing the number of VNA industrial nurses from seven to nine and the corporations that used the VNA nurses from three to five. Foley never hesitated diplomatically to battle employers who wanted to use her nurses as spies. In one of many similar letters she wrote to industry heads, she explained in 1918 to an officer at the Federal Reserve Bank, "If the information is circulated among the employes [*sic*] that they have the privilege of Visiting Nurse service during illness, they usually appreciate it and ask for it when reporting illness. If, on the other hand, employes [*sic*] are caught staying home to clean house or recover from Sunday indiscretions, the nurse making this report to the firm gets our whole service in disrepute . . . and we are not able to help the sick ones who really need us" (letter to Mr. F. Batemen, May 23, 1918, VNA Papers).

The Metropolitan Life Insurance Company also offered the services of visiting nurses to its policyholders. In 1912 Foley spoke out vehemently against a Metropolitan Life Insurance Company proposal to force VNAs to use practical nurses, who were low-paid, untrained workers, to care for chronically ill policyholders. Although Metropolitan Life was a major VNA financial supporter, Foley made it clear in a 1912 *American Journal of Nursing* article that she would not compromise health care quality for anyone. "Our responsibility is to our patients first, to our contributors last, and we will not deserve the support of either if we neglect our duty, which is to give our best service to all the sick," she wrote. "The poor are at the mercy of too many half-trained and counterfeit workers as it is" ("Concerning the Employing of Practical Nurses," 329–30).

Foley continued to defend excellence in health care. In 1918 the governor of Illinois appointed her to a commission formulating legislation governing health insurance in Illinois. Foley was asked to contribute a report on nurses and their relationship to health insurance. Using VNA statistics, Foley noted that in 1917, 71 percent of VNA visits were made free of charge, that is, not paid for by the patients, employers, or insurance companies. Of those families receiving free nursing care, only half were known previously to any philanthropic agency. Therefore, she argued, most families helped by the VNA only needed assistance during illness. Nursing care paid for by health insurance would invariably lessen, not increase, philanthropic and municipal relief-giving expenses.

In 1918 the Visiting Nurse Association faced one of its greatest challenges when an influenza pandemic hit Chicago. The VNA's workload increased 400 percent that fall as its nurses shared care of the city's sick with fifty municipal tuberculosis nurses. A member of the VNA board of directors described Foley's efforts during the crisis as superhuman. World War I duties made the work even harder, since more than sixty VNA nurses went overseas to work for the U.S. Army or the Red Cross. In 1919 the VNA gave Foley a year's leave to work with the Tuberculosis Commission of the American Red Cross in Italy as its chief nurse.

Foley encouraged the training and hiring of African American nurses; the VNA had nine on staff by 1928. African American nurses, however, only worked with African American patients, white nurses with white patients. In a 1918 letter to a patron who had long supported a nurse in a district now largely African American, Foley urged her to support another district. "District 3, which has been supported in your father's memory for so many years, is now almost entirely given over to colored people and we have very little work in it for our white nurse," she wrote. "Do you mind if we transfer the support of District 3 to District 5 . . . ? There are comparatively few colored people there, a good many Italians, and a great many poor people" (letter to Miss Helen V. Drake, March 27, 1918, VNA Papers).

Foley held an array of prestigious national positions in nursing, including the presidency of the National Organization for Public Health Nursing from 1920 to 1922. In 1929 President Herbert Hoover appointed her to two committees of the White House Conference on Child Health and Protection. In 1934 Foley was the first woman to be made a Citizen Fellow of the Institute of Medicine in Chicago.

Until well into the Great Depression, Foley believed strongly in the charity-driven public health work that the VNA provided. This support was the norm in the late nineteenth and early twentieth centuries, when wealthy urban women devoted time and money to a variety of charities. Foley praised their efforts, writing in 1932 that the personal service offered by volunteers was less expensive and more attentive than services offered by publicly funded medical groups. As the Great Depression continued, however, Foley's attitude changed. She blamed overcrowding and poor housing for disease, labeling illness a national calamity, not a personal misfortune. She suggested that public health nursing become a community service rather than a philanthropy. By the end of her life of service, she believed that the causes of the high maternal and infant death rates in the United States were economic and called for adequate wages to end the ongoing public health crisis. Foley retired from the VNA in January 1937.

Edna Foley never married. She was killed in 1943 in a fall from the window of her sister's apartment in New York City. Police deemed the fall accidental. During her life Foley conveyed to colleagues and laymen not only a knowledge of public health needs but an immeasurable passion for them. When she received an honorary Doctor of Science degree from Smith College in 1928, Foley was described as "a skilled nurse and teacher of nurses, a wise and rigorous administrator, an authority on public health and social welfare, a large-hearted and keen-sighted student of human nature" ("A Deserved Honor," 698).

Sources. The Chicago Visiting Nurse Association Papers, at CHS, contain Edna Foley's business correspondence, speeches, unpublished writings, descriptions of the work done by the organization while she was superintendent, and minutes of meetings; included in her manuscript writings is "The Affiliation of Training Schools with Public Health Nursing Agencies," May 9, 1924. Foley's "Superintendent's Report" for each year is found in the *Annual Report: The Visiting Nurse Association of Chicago*, also at CHS. Foley published articles in professional journals, including "Concerning the Employing of Practical Nurses by Visiting Nurse Associations," *American Journal of Nursing*, vol. 12, 1912, and "Fifty Cents Worth of Nursing Care," *Public Health Nurse*, vol. 15, 1923. She also wrote for the journals *Modern Hospital* and *Hospital Social Service*. A biography of Foley appears in Vern L. Bullough, Olga M. Church, and Alice P. Stern, eds., *American Nursing: A Biographical Dictionary*, vol. 1 (1988). Her work is described in *Chicago Daily News*, March 2, 1935, and "A Deserved Honor," *American Journal of Nursing*, vol. 28, 1928. *American Journal of Nursing*, vol. 43, 1943, contains her obituary.

JACQUELINE H. WOLF

FORD, RUTH VAN SICKLE
August 8, 1897–April 18, 1989
ARTIST, ART EDUCATOR, ADMINISTRATOR

Ruth Van Sickle was born in Aurora, Illinois, the only child of Charles P. and Anna (Miller) Van Sickle, who were from Dutch and German backgrounds, respectively. They owned a restaurant in Aurora—the Rookery. Van Sickle studied art at the Chicago Academy of Fine Arts, a commercial art school, from 1915 to 1918. She was one of the star pupils of Carl Newland Werntz, who had founded the academy in 1902. Werntz's other notable students included Walt Disney, Ezra Winter, and Carl Oscar Erickson of *Vogue* magazine. Van Sickle attended the New York Art Students League in the summers of 1916 and 1917, where she studied with John F. Carlson, founder and director of the Carlson School of Landscape Painting, Woodstock, New York.

On February 18, 1918, Ruth Van Sickle married Albert G. Ford in a military wedding. Albert Ford was a civil engineer, who later worked for Northern Illinois Gas and Electric Company. After the wedding, he went abroad with the military during the last months of World War I. Ruth Van Sickle Ford soon realized she was pregnant. During an emergency trip to Ogden, Utah, to visit a troubled friend, she gave birth to the couple's only child, daughter Barbara, on October 21, 1918. The family was eventually reunited in Aurora.

In Chicago, Ruth Van Sickle Ford studied privately with George Bellows, noted for the social realism of his paintings featuring city scenes, children at play, and his family and friends. Bellows's themes were similar to ones that appeared in Ford's art. Ford also studied with Guy Wiggins and Jonas Lie, artists whose work was representational. Inspired by her teachers and absorbing elements of their styles, Ford went on to develop her own style.

Ford's training at the Chicago Academy of Fine Arts prepared her for a career in commercial art. She was employed for a time as a commercial illustrator, but she despised the job and resigned, although uncertain of her reception in the field of fine art, where for months her paintings had been rejected by galleries. Within two weeks of leaving the commercial position, she had a painting accepted for a gallery show. Soon her paintings were regularly included in local art shows; she gained notice when her work was exhibited in 1921 at the American show at the Art Institute of Chicago.

Ford painted primarily in watercolor, but she also worked in oil. Her subject matter included landscapes, urban scenes, and portraiture. She painted from life, often selecting "time-worn residential districts, markets and wharfs" as subjects. As she put it, "Things which have been lived in for years and years have character, and the same is true of people: The most interesting ones are older people, who have . . . [done] a great deal of living" (quoted in Plummer, "Busy Woman Plans Routine"). Ford traveled throughout the United States, Haiti, Bermuda, and Mexico. On these trips, she often drove into the country and painted scenes from life. In her watercolors, her style was consistently representational, but she tended to simplify a scene in order to expose its essential qualities. This technique is evident in her most important early work, *State Street*, an award-winning painting shown in 1932 at the Art Institute of Chicago. The watercolor depicts an elevated view of a busy street corner. Each figure is clearly delineated, yet the figures remain featureless. Ford's composition emphasizes the space at the edge of the intersection. Rather than focusing on any single figure, Ford conveys the sense of atmosphere and motion in the busy street.

Ford's works reflect the color and vibrancy of the locations she chose. C. J. Bulliet, noted art critic for the *Chicago Daily News*, complimented the color in Ford's 1949 exhibit of watercolors done in Haiti, especially her market scenes of Port au Prince: "Life in the market places of Haiti is presented with vigor and with all the glamour of tropical sunshine and color" ("Ruth Ford's Paintings Full of Vigor"). Ford's modernistic use of color, which became bolder and brighter as her career progressed, was the most significant change in her painting. She remained grounded in realism and spoke publicly against artists who deviated too far from representational work. Bulliet, who welcomed many forms of modernism, commented, Ford "is opposed to Modernism as it expresses itself in the empty, abstract doodlings that have followed Picasso" ("Paintings Full of Vigor").

Ford taught at the Chicago Academy of Fine Arts from 1930 to 1937 and continued to teach after she became president and owner of the academy from 1937 to 1960. Under her direction the Chicago Academy of Fine Arts continued to ground students in the traditional skills of drawing from life; they spent the first year of study on drawing and composition. Even if a student envisioned a career as a cartoonist, Ford and her faculty demanded rigorous training in drawing and composition. When cartoonist Bill Mauldin—who would later win a Pulitzer Prize—began as a first-year student and balked at the introductory courses, Ford told him that even Picasso learned

his academic ABCs before he started his departure into modernism.

Ford combined teaching and painting throughout her career. "I get a stimulation out of teaching that helps me in my own painting. . . . Some artists would be crushed by a teaching job. But it happens to be the best way I work" (*New York Sun*, October 20, 1938). Ford was described as a particularly dedicated and insightful educator by Del Peterson, a Chicago commercial artist, who recalled, "Some instructors can only teach in their own style. . . . Mrs. Ford has the ability to relate to any individual's style" (Doty, "Portrait of an Artist as a Marvelous Devil"). Ford was outspoken and offered salty criticism to students in order to get them to improve their work.

After selling the academy in 1960, she taught at a number of locations, including Aurora College (1964–70), Aurora Wesley Methodist Church, and the Glen Ellyn Young Men's Christian Association. Barbara Turner, Ford's daughter, observed that her mother enjoyed teaching; when the amputation of one leg in 1978 made it difficult for her to teach, she continued to instruct students in her home.

In the 1960s and 1970s she spent the summers in Rockport, Massachusetts, where she was a member of the Rockport Art Association. There she tried to complete a painting every day. Ruth Van Sickle Ford was able to combine the activities of artist, educator, and administrator with family life. Her worldwide painting tours were solo, since her husband disliked travel. When questioned about her independent stance, she answered, "I think if a woman has the desire to do something, she should do it. But this business of being liberated just to be liberated is stupid—very stupid" (Doty, "Painting Portrait of Life among the Famous"). Ruth Van Sickle Ford explained that her family supported her goals. Strongly individualistic, the Fords for many years lived in a round house designed in 1949 by Bruce Goff; called the umbrella house, it was inspired by a Tibetan tent and caused a sensation, with gawkers driving by. Barbara (Ford) Turner recalled how the family counted five thousand cars one Sunday. The house had a gallery and an art studio; Goff chose coal for the color of the walls because Ford wanted a black background on which to display her watercolors, which featured bright colors on white.

Ford had several one-person shows during her career, including a 1934 exhibit at the Art Institute of Chicago and a 1947 show at the Grand Central Galleries in New York City. She received a number of awards: the Art Institute of Chicago Fine Arts Building Prize of 1931; the Chicago Woman's Aid Club Prize, 1935; and the Palette and Chisel Academy Gold Medal Award for Oil Painting, 1963. Ford was the first woman to be a member of the Palette and Chisel Club (later Palette and Chisel Academy of Fine Arts) and was the first woman member from Illinois of the American Watercolor Society. Aurora College awarded her an honorary doctorate of fine arts in 1974. In addition to her paintings and watercolors, Ruth Van Sickle Ford illustrated books and accepted art commissions from corporations. She died at age ninety-one in Mercy Center Hospital in Aurora.

Ford increasingly is seen as a regional artist of minor importance but one who is noteworthy for her urban realism and bold representations. She continued to paint largely representational art, while the art world moved toward greater abstraction. Ford's greater significance was as an educator and art school proprietor in the years from 1937 to 1960, when she was the driving force of the Chicago Academy of Fine Arts as president and director.

Sources. The Ruth Van Sickle Ford Papers, Archives of American Art, are available on microfilm at the Ryerson Library, the Art Institute of Chicago. The papers include biographical information, correspondence, notes, photographs, and printed materials documenting Ford's artistic and teaching activities. Information on Ford is in the Chicago Academy of Fine Arts Scrapbooks located at the Ryerson Library. Additional information came from an interview with Ford's daughter Barbara Turner on December 6, 1995. Her work is discussed in numerous newspaper clippings in the Ford Papers, including the following articles: "Woman Director of Chicago Art Academy Is Here on a Painting Spree," *New York Sun*, October 20, 1938; Mary Elizabeth Plummer, "Busy Woman Plans Routine," *Salisbury North Carolina Post*, May 8, 1941; C. J. Bulliet, "Ruth Ford's Paintings Full of Vigor, Color," *Chicago Daily News*, May 13, 1949; Marie Doty, "Portrait of an Artist as a Marvelous Devil," *World of DuPage and Will Counties*, March 31, 1977; and Doty, "Painting Portrait of Life among the Famous," *Suburban Trib Fox Valley*, May 13, 1979. Ford is listed in Esther Sparks, "A Biographical Dictionary of Painters and Sculptors in Illinois, 1808–1945" (Ph.D. diss., Northwestern Univ., 1971). A brief biography of Ford can be found in *Who's Who in American Art* (1986). Her obituary appeared in the *CT* April 22, 1989.

DENNIS H. CREMIN

FOX, CAROL
June 15, 1926–July 21, 1981
FOUNDER AND MANAGER OF OPERA COMPANY

Carol Fox, founder and general manager of the Lyric Opera of Chicago, was the only child of a wealthy Chicago couple. Her father, Edward Fox, was an office supply company executive. Her mother, Virginia (Scott) Fox, encouraged her daughter to follow her heart, which seemed drawn to the theater and music. Her mother made sure Fox had lessons in dramatics and elocution, in ballet, piano, and singing, and in foreign languages (Italian, German, and French). Fox attended Girls Latin School on Chicago's Near North Side, where she played leads in theater productions.

Fox's father was not so sure about her heavy emphasis on arts education. He wanted her to attend college and pursue a more rounded course of study. He urged his daughter to take the entrance exams for Vassar College; she did so and passed. In exchange, he permitted her to skip Vassar and enroll for acting studies at the Pasadena Playhouse in California.

Soon after her studies in California, Fox began taking voice lessons from Edith Mason and Vittorio Trevisan in Chicago. She continued studying voice in New York City with Virgilio Lazarri and Giovanni Martinelli and was coached by conductor Fausto Cleva in operatic repertory. When Martinelli returned to his native Italy, Fox went with him to continue her studies. She spent two years at the Martinelli homes in Rome and near Lake Como and, during this time, improved her vocal skills and mastered Italian. With her teacher's help, she found opportunities to sing some minor roles, mostly in amateur opera productions.

FIG. 30. *Carol Fox, cofounder of the Lyric Opera of Chicago in 1954.*

She then faced two truths: first, that she loved opera and desired to make it her career, and second, that she did not have a good enough voice to be successful as a singer. Hating mediocrity, she decided that a third-rate career was not acceptable to her. Almost jokingly at first, she began to tell people that she was going to start an opera company. She thought that there was no place better than Chicago in which to do this. In the early 1950s, she obtained some seed money from her father and, with insurance broker Lawrence Kelly and conductor Nicola Rescigno, began the planning and work that led to the founding of what was then called the Lyric Theater of Chicago.

They gathered together a group of thirty people, most of them fairly young like Fox herself, to handle promotion and fund-raising. The group named itself the Lyric Guild. Fox led the Guild; she also took charge of hiring, running the office, negotiating with singers and unions, choosing repertoire, and working with the opera company's board of directors, when it was formed.

When Fox and her colleagues founded their new opera company in the early 1950s, cultural and civic leaders insisted that, despite a glowing if somewhat sputtering history of operatic performance, Chicago no longer could or would support a resident opera company. They had plenty of evidence on their side. Since 1946 there had been no Chicago opera company at all. Prior to that time, six opera companies had come and gone in succession over a period of just thirty-six years. Chicago did not seem a promising place for opera; but Fox refused to accept this view, deciding to plunge ahead in what she later described as the naïve faith of herself and her colleagues Kelly and Rescigno that opera could be successful. The three went ahead and founded what would come to be known as the Lyric Opera of Chicago. As Claudia Cassidy, music critic for the *Chicago Tribune*, wrote, it was "Kelly for ideas, Rescigno for music, [and] Miss Fox for an implacable desire to get the thing done" ("Garden to Fox," 17).

Following more than a year of planning and fund-raising, the curtain of the Civic Opera House rose on February 5, 1954, on the opening scene of Wolfgang Amadeus Mozart's *Don Giovanni*, the premier production of the Lyric Theater of Chicago. "We . . . had hoped to begin with four weeks of performances," Fox explained some years later, "but the opera-house management did not believe we had the money or the talent for something that ambitious. They agreed to rent us the building for one night" ("Chicago Retrospect," 950). This arrangement did not satisfy Fox, but she felt that it was a start. She went ahead and signed the most outstanding performers that she could get. "We had to go for the best," Fox insisted. "We could not afford new scenery. All of our eggs, so to speak, went into one vocal basket" ("Chicago Retrospect," 950).

Tribune critic Cassidy, like others in the sold-out theater, could not believe what she heard and saw. "Conjured out of the air of dreams," she wrote, "it was a true *Don*, a vastly amusing entertainment, incomparably rich in its wealth of song and the moods that song reflects—the noble, the joyous, the mischievous, the satanic, the shadows and the glint of light" ("Carol Fox," 26).

The first performance was a huge success and it resulted in a second, sold-out performance. Fox believed that the Lyric Opera was on its way and she left immediately for Europe, hoping to lure some major artists to Chicago for what she and her colleagues planned to make a three-week fall season in 1954. Her chief goal was to persuade soprano Maria Callas to make her American debut at the Lyric, reasoning that Callas would be the ideal person to launch the Lyric in its first full season. Callas, at that time the world's most sought-after soprano, would be the perfect symbol, Fox believed, to link Chicago's new resident opera company with the traditions of what she referred to as Chicago's earlier golden opera age. She was able to sign Callas and continued to bring outstanding opera singers and conductors for appearances with the Lyric in subsequent years. In fall 1954, the Lyric offered Chicagoans an eight-opera, three-week season, filling the three-thousand-seat opera house to 84 percent of capacity level. In later years, those percentages would rise to sell-out proportions.

Early in the Lyric's existence, Fox faced a major crisis when her colleague Nicola Rescigno asked for a long-term contract and absolute musical control. Lawrence Kelly sided with him. Fox refused, and the ensuing dispute was taken to court. Ultimately Rescigno and Kelly left for Dallas, Texas, where they created that city's Civic Opera. Fox gained sole control as general manager of what was henceforth to be called the Lyric Opera of Chicago. The company was reorganized with a full board of directors. During the initial seasons of the opera, Fox had doubled as board president. Kelly, Rescigno, and three friends served with her. There would be no such small-scaled, informal arrangement in the future.

In 1957, Fox married C. Larkin Flanagan, a physician and early supporter of her plans for the Lyric Opera. They became parents of a daughter, Victoria, and later were divorced. Fox maintained a close and loving relationship with her daughter.

The Lyric Opera became the focus of Carol Fox's life; its triumphs and crises defined her existence. Under her leadership, it grew steadily. Seasons were lengthened carefully. The repertoire, although still heavily Italian in emphasis, began to expand to include operas from non-Italian composers, including Richard Strauss, Richard Wagner, Sergei Prokofiev, Maurice Ravel, and Benjamin Britten. Production values, sets, and stage direction became more important.

In an effort to modernize staging while holding down costs, Fox initiated both a lend-lease program that brought stellar sets from Europe to Chicago and a cooperative arrangement in which costs for new productions were shared with other companies, ranging from London's Covent Garden to the San Francisco Opera. To sustain quality and give breadth to the repertoire, she hired Pino Donati and Bruno Bartoletti as artistic codirectors in 1964. Bartoletti, a seasoned conductor, was particularly interested in widening the company's repertoire and increasing public interest in new works, but Fox remained conservative on this latter issue. The Lyric's job, she told a reporter, "is to content the public, to get them to come, and bit by bit to indoctrinate them to the new. It takes some time to make someone enjoy an unknown piece, even a new boom-boom-boom piece" ("Carol and Co.," 14).

Fox weathered a union crisis in 1967, an unsettled contract dispute concerning salaries and season lengths that caused the season to be canceled. The dispute lasted into 1968, threatening the life of the company. At that point, Chicago Mayor Richard J. Daley stepped in to mediate and the 1968 season went on.

In 1973 Fox presided over the birth and development of Lyric's apprentice artist program, designed to train professionally ten promising young singers each year. She was instrumental in bringing Lyric performances to a wider public through the radio, coming to terms in 1973 with station WFMT-FM, which broadcast the operas not only locally but later in syndication to a much wider audience.

In 1974, Fox wooed the Fourth International Verdi Congress to Chicago as part of the Lyric's twentieth anniversary celebration. In honor of the congress, the Lyric created a new production of Giuseppe Verdi's *Simon Boccanegra*. To help mark the American Bicentennial, Fox commissioned Krystof Penderecki to write an opera for the company. That project became a major factor in Fox's downfall at the Lyric. Some observers quickly criticized her decision to give the award to a Polish rather than an American composer. Within the company itself, the problem was financial. Penderecki's opera, *Paradise Lost*, was two seasons late being delivered and, although initially underwritten, ran up sizeable debts. The Lyric's board of directors was forced to draw more than one and one half million dollars from reserves to help pay the debts. Over three years, the two and one half million dollar endowment was dissipated, the result of delays on Penderecki's opera and other budget overruns.

In the meantime, Fox's health had deteriorated. A 1977 mugging in Florence, Italy, had forced her to wear a neck brace. A 1978 fall in a hospital caused a debilitating hip fracture. She suffered from asthma, emphysema, sciatica, and diabetes. During the last year of her Lyric leadership, she conducted much of her business from her bedroom at home, which had been converted into an office. When she was able to come to her regular office, she often had to use a couch set up for her backstage. As Fox's health became worse, Ardis Krainik, her assistant manager and, after Fox's death, manager of the Lyric, had to assume much of the day-to-day operation, while at the same time having to wait for Fox's decisions on crucial matters. Fox became increasingly unable to make such decisions.

As Fox's health worsened, the financial situation of the Lyric worsened as well. By the end of the 1980 season, the opera company, while not legally bankrupt, was almost without assets, except for a warehouse of sets, costumes, and props. The board of directors asked for and received Fox's resignation. She lived only six months longer, dying of a heart attack at her Near North Side home.

Robert C. Marsh, longtime music critic for the *Chicago Sun-Times*, noted Fox's contribution to the city's cultural history in an appreciation following her death. "Her place on the honored list of women who have left a permanent mark on the city had long been assured," he wrote. "She was one of those persons who had the audacity to dream great dreams, unconcerned whether they are practical or businesslike, and the skill and willpower to make them realities" ("Carol Fox, Appreciation").

From the 1950s through the 1970s, Fox won numerous honors for her work in making the Lyric Opera into a major Chicago cultural institution. The Women's Advertising Club named her Woman of Distinction in 1960. In 1976, she was named Chicagoan of the Year for bringing many seasons of fine opera to Chicagoans. She won the Illinois Governor's Award for the Arts in 1979 and the Grand Ufficiale del'Ordine al Merito from Italy, also in 1979. Over the two and one-half decades Fox managed the Lyric Opera, she revived, sustained, and enhanced a tradition of excellent opera in Chicago.

Sources. A collection of newspaper clippings, press releases, and other material can be found in the media files of the Lyric Opera of Chicago. Fox wrote an article, "Chicago Retrospect," in *Opera*, October 1979. Interviews were conducted with Danny Newman, publicity director of the Lyric Opera, June 1995; and with Ardis Krainik, general manager, Lyric Opera, June 1995. Many newspaper and magazine articles have been written about Fox, including Speight Jenkins, interviewer, "Carol and Co.," November 1972; Claudia Cassidy, "Garden to Fox," November 1973; and Claudia Cassidy, "Carol Fox," October 1981—all in *Opera News*; Margaret Carroll, "With an Aria in Her Heart," July 5, 1973; and Bess Winakor, "Fox, the Omnipotent," September 1974—*Chicago Today*; Mary Knoblauch, "The Most Powerful Women in Chicago," January 11, 1976; and John Von Rhein, "Opera Today," October 1, 1978—*CT*; and Patricia Moore, "Lyric Opera's Brightest Star" (date unknown); and Robert Marsh, "Carol Fox, Appreciation," July 22, 1981—*Chicago Sun-Times*. Entries about Fox appear in *Current Biography* (1978) and *The Annual Obituary* (1981).

PETER P. JACOBI

FOY, FRANCES M.
April 11, 1890–November 15, 1963
PAINTER, MURALIST, ETCHER

Born in the Chicago suburb of Oak Park, Frances M. Foy, a professional artist and portraitist, was the daughter of James A. and Honora (Murray) Foy. Although raised a Roman Catholic, Foy did not remain religiously active. She attended Oak Park and River Forest Township High School. There she received early recognition and encouragement for her artistic abilities when she won a prize during her freshman year; in a biographical sketch she wrote in 1940, she recalled using the prize money to purchase her first formal art lessons. She graduated from high school in 1908. Foy trained as an artist at the night school of the Art Institute of Chicago (AIC), working with Fred De Forrest Schook, Wellington J. Reynolds, and George Bellows from 1916 to 1918. By 1921, Foy had her own studio, where she painted and did some commercial work.

On June 23, 1923, Foy married Gustaf Dalstrom, also an artist and a student of George Bellows. During 1927–28 she and Dalstrom went to Europe, where they studied independently, traveling in Sweden, France, Italy, and Germany. Their son Lars Michael was born on September 4, 1931.

Foy's work earned national recognition during the 1920s and 1930s. Her oil and watercolor paintings and etchings were featured in one-artist exhibitions at the Chicago Playhouse Theatre (1928); AIC (1929 and 1940); Illinois Wesleyan University in Bloomington, Illinois (1933); Chicago Woman's Aid Club; Increase Robinson's Gallery; the Romany Club; and the Walden Gallery, among others. Many group shows included her work, among them, *A Century of Progress Exhibition of Paintings and Sculpture* at AIC (1933); *International Watercolor Exhibition*, AIC (1934); Delphic Studios exhibition, New York (1935); New Jersey State Museum exhibition, Trenton, New Jersey (1936); *Artists of Chicago and Vicinity* exhibitions (1936, 1949); the Museum of Modern Art's *16 Cities*; exhibits of the Chicago No-Jury Society (1925–38); an exhibit of prominent Chicago artists at Marshall Field Gallery during the 1930s; and others. She won a gold medal from the Chicago Society of Artists (1929) and four awards from AIC: the Marshall Fuller Holmes prize (1929, awarded for her painting *Boating*); the Jule F. Brower prize (1931, for a portrait entitled *Betty*); the Mr. and Mrs. Frank G. Logan prize, 1932; and a 1943 prize.

During the 1930s, she was awarded five mural commissions by the Treasury Section of Fine Arts (known as the Section). Funded under the New Deal by a provision that reserved one percent of federal construction budgets for "embellishments" to decorate buildings, the Section was not a relief agency, although it was often confused with the Works Progress Administration's Federal Art Project. Instead, artists were awarded commissions on the basis of anonymous competitions or after they had successfully done jobs for the agency. Commissions varied from $240 for works in small and modest post offices to $25,000 or $45,000 for sculptures or mural series in monumental public buildings; they averaged $700. Contracts stipulated that artists would cover their own supplies and other expenses. In bulletins announcing competitions, the Section suggested subjects that either memorialized local history or the history of the post office or depicted scenes of work and leisure typical of the place where the building was located. Artists were encouraged to consult with local people as they designed their submissions.

Foy was one of 162 female artists who won Section commissions (19 percent of the 852 Section artists were women). Foy executed her commissions promptly and well, and the Section recognized her work by offering additional commissions. She received five commissions in all; only about one-fifth of all Section artists received three or more commissions.

Foy worked largely within the regionalist style of the 1930s, characterized by its commitment to representational art and American subjects and exemplified in the work of Grant Wood, Thomas Hart Benton, and John Steuart Curry. Between 1936 and 1943, she installed murals commissioned by the Section in public buildings in Illinois, Indiana, and Wisconsin. These works included two panels, *Wisconsin Wild Flowers—Spring* and *Wisconsin Wild Flowers—Autumn*, mounted in West Allis, Wisconsin, in 1943. Two of her color sketches for the West Allis murals were selected for display by the architect of the east wing of the White House, built during the New Deal.

Foy belonged to a number of local and regional professional organizations, including the Chicago Society of Etchers, the Chicago Society of Artists, the Arts Club of Chicago, and the Artists League of the Midwest. She marketed her work actively, with the help of an agent, Grace Hamill, who sought to place her art in galleries where it would receive notice, find patrons, and advance her reputation. Marshall Field's department store and Walden bookstore took her paintings on consignment. Foy also consigned four of her paintings to an interior decorator in Cincinnati, though none of these were sold. She did commercial work for the J. Walter Thompson advertising agency and for the Scott, Foresman textbook publishing company.

Foy was also known as a portraitist. In her 1940 biographical sketch for the Section, she noted that she had completed thirty such commissions. Section administrator Edward Rowan was impressed with her work and requested photographs of her portraits on behalf of a friend looking for someone to paint his sons. Foy sent photographs and noted in her accompanying letter to Rowan, "I prefer to use oil for portraits, and since I paint in a high key, it seems appropriate for children, and I have done many. I have not worked in pastel. As to price, around $500 for a 26 X 30, up and down according to size" (May 29, 1940, Correspondence of Frances M. Foy).

Foy and Dalstrom shared professional interests as artists, and their correspondence with the Section offers a few intriguing glimpses of Foy's work and family life. The two collaborated in 1938 on a job at the Chestnut Street Postal Station in Chicago; as Foy acknowledged her commission, she wrote to Edward Rowan that it was a pleasure for her husband and her to be painting for the same building. Each received a $1,000 commission, and they designed murals that suggested a historical narrative— Dalstrom's *Great Indian Council, Chicago 1833* and Foy's *Advent of "The Pioneer," 1851*. On one occasion they traded commissions. When Dalstrom went to St. Joseph, Missouri, to paint his Section-commissioned series of twelve frescoes, Foy moved with him. Their letters hint at warm mutual regard and a sympathetic partnership of two artists.

At the same time, their letters also reveal the disadvantages under which Foy labored as a woman artist. She was unable to work for the Federal Art Project (FAP) of the Works Progress Administration (WPA), the large relief project that employed many artists during the New Deal. As she explained in a 1935 letter to the Section, Foy had applied for possible FAP funding that would have enabled her to plan a more elaborate design for the post office in East Alton, Illinois, but she learned that she could not be so employed because Dalstrom was already working for the FAP. Foy was disqualified for FAP employment under the married person's clause, which stipulated that only one family member could collect WPA funds. Given pervasive expectations of men as the exclusive or primary source of family income, this policy meant in practice that women had less access to the WPA.

Dalstrom and Foy both established successful careers as artists; they collaborated and they accommodated one another in the travel required for installing finished murals. They would have been highly unusual, however, if their partnership included full sharing of household and child care duties, and one telling incident suggests that it did not. As Foy and Dalstrom worked to complete their commissions for the Chestnut Street Postal Station, Foy fell behind and had to request an extension. On March 30, 1938, she wrote to Rowan, "Due to serious illness in the family I had a very bad winter—much of it spent in quarantine with my little boy—and this delayed my getting the charcoal cartoons ready for the photographer. In order to simplify things Gustaf kindly waited for me, so now both of us need more time" (Correspondence of Frances M. Foy). Foy assumed most of the responsibility for caring for Lars as he recuperated from scarlet fever. Her letter suggests further that she expected and accepted this division of labor without resentment.

Foy worked within the realist style that dominated American art until World War II. In her own biographical note, she indicated that flowers and people were favorite subjects. The women artists of the Section did not produce a body of work that was distinct from the work of male artists. Like male artists, they were more likely to paint male than female figures; when they did include female figures, the girls and women were shown as daughters, wives, and mothers or included in communal gatherings of men and women together. Of the hundreds of murals and sculptures commissioned by the Section, many celebrated masculinity in representations of men working on the land or in craft and industrial labor; by contrast, only about a dozen showed women without men or as the main subjects of the composition.

Foy's Section murals were among the very few that did offer more prominent treatment of female figures. In *The Letter*, painted for East Alton, Illinois, in 1936, two older women share a letter over a white picket fence, framed by trees and tall sunflowers. In contrast to historical genre paintings that generally emphasized male subjects, Foy's *Hiawatha Returning with Minnehaha*, installed in 1939 in Gibson City, Illinois, includes a prominent female protagonist. *Preparations for the Autumn Festival* (1941) in the post office in Dunkirk, Indiana, shows women gathering the large squashes produced on local farms. Female figures dominate the foreground of this harvest scene: three women pick and arrange the vegetables in the foreground, and an older woman holds a sheaf of corn in the background, with a bearded man beside her. Moreover, in a proposed mural, Foy planned to celebrate a prominent political accomplishment of women: *Establishment of the Children's Bureau* was to honor the unit that represented the most influential arena of female re-formers in the federal government. Submitted for the presti-gious Justice Department competition—by invitation only, in contrast to the open competitions for most Section commis-sions—the sketch was not selected for a commission.

Foy exhibited actively through the 1940s. She continued to fulfill portrait commissions and to produce easel paintings through the 1950s, but her work did not gain the attention and honors of the earlier years. The last public notice appeared in 1952, an announcement of an exhibit featuring the work of five husband-wife teams of artists. After World War II, the center of American art moved from regionalism to abstract expression-ism. Many painters working in more realistic modes lost their audiences, and perhaps Foy was among those eclipsed in the shift to a new style. Foy began to falter mentally in 1960, and she died three years later.

Productive and successful in a career that spanned at least three decades, Foy has been largely forgotten in an art history still dominated by the narrative of the triumph of modernism in abstract expressionism. Her paintings remain to attest to her work, however; they may be found still in private collections and galleries. Her murals remain in the post offices of East Alton and Gibson City, Illinois; Dunkirk, Indiana; and West Allis, Wis-consin. The Illinois Wesleyan University collection includes her work. In the records of private life, her work survives on the Christmas cards she designed each year, many of which fea-tured plants and flowers rendered in closely observed detail.

Sources. The Archives of American Art, Washington, D.C., hold the pa-pers of Frances M. Foy. The National Archives and Records Adminis-tration, Washington, D.C., holds the Correspondence of Frances M. Foy, Treasury Section, Records of the Commission of Fine Arts (Record Group 66); and letters from Foy and Dalstrom give some sense of their relationship and working lives. Lars Dalstrom's July 23, 1995, interview with Barbara Melosh provides further information on Foy's life. Brief en-tries on Foy are included in a number of biographical sources, among them *Who's Who in American Art*, vol. 3 (1939–40). A detailed sketch is in Louise Dunn Yochim, *Role and Impact: The Chicago Society of Artists* (1979). See also the entry in Esther Sparks, "A Biographical Dic-tionary of Painters and Sculptors in Illinois 1808–1945," (Ph.D. diss., Northwestern Univ., 1971). For information about the history of the Treasury Section of Fine Arts, see Barbara Melosh, *Engendering Cul-ture: Manhood and Womanhood in New Deal Public Art and Theater* (1991), and Marlene Park and Gerald E. Markowitz, *Democratic Vistas: Post Offices and Public Art in the New Deal* (1984).

BARBARA MELOSH

FRACKELTON, SUSAN STUART GOODRICH
June 5, 1848–April 14, 1932
ARTIST, INVENTOR, CLUBWOMAN

Susan Stuart Frackelton parlayed her expertise in china paint-ing, a typical nineteenth-century "lady's accomplishment," into a self-supporting enterprise that gained her national and inter-national renown as an artist, inventor, and educator. Beginning her career in Milwaukee, Frackelton relocated to Chicago in 1899. She was a leader in Chicago art pottery circles until 1909, when she turned her talents to book illumination.

Susan Goodrich, the eldest of five children, was born in Mil-waukee to Edwin H. and Mary Stewart (Robinson) Goodrich.

Both parents had moved to Milwaukee from the East Coast in the mid-1840s. Her father, initially engaged in railroad con-struction, subsequently became involved in banking and the ownership of several brickyards. The young Susan Goodrich was privately educated in Milwaukee by the Wheelock sisters and attended finishing school in New York. On July 9, 1869, she married Richard G. Frackelton, who had come to Milwaukee from England to establish a business importing crockery, china, and glassware. The couple, who were to divorce after thirty years of marriage, had four children: William (1870), Albert (1876), Felix (1878), and Gladys (1888). Felix did not live to adulthood, drowning in 1893 when his sailboat capsized on the Milwaukee River. Richard Frackelton's father, William, also lived with the family, as did varying numbers of household servants.

Although it was quite common for upper- and middle-class families to have servants who were involved with child rearing and household chores, it was less common for young matrons to work outside the home. Nonetheless, shortly after their marriage, Susan Frackelton began to work with her husband as a buyer in his import business. She also studied painting with Heinrich Vianden, a German artist who had moved to Milwaukee from Cologne in 1849, and used this skill to perfect her technique in the decoration of porcelain. This latter activity came to be an im-portant financial contribution to the family business, because porcelain blanks (undecorated white ware) were much less ex-pensive to import than was decorated porcelain ware. In August 1877 the Frackeltons expanded their import business to include a china decorating works. This aspect of the firm not only pro-duced painted china for sale but also included classes run by Su-san Frackelton and Adolph Boes, an accomplished painter and finisher. The Frackelton China Decorating Works drew praise, and Susan Frackelton's decorated china sets won awards at the International Cotton Exposition in Atlanta in 1881 and the Primera Exposición Veracruzana in Orizaba, Mexico, in 1882.

A talented artist and inventive artisan, Susan Frackelton be-came responsible for the business end of the Frackelton China Decorating Works when her husband's debts overwhelmed the otherwise successful firm. In May 1881 control of the firm was signed over to his father, William Frackelton, who had invested heavily in the company. He disposed of the stock of crockery and sold what remained of the business to Susan Frackelton, who re-portedly paid him out of her private funds. She subsequently managed and operated the firm independently of her husband until it closed in 1891. During the 1880s Frackelton effectively cornered the market for porcelain decoration in Milwaukee. She gave classes that drew students from Detroit, Pittsburgh, Buffalo, New York, Duluth, Chicago, and Atlanta; published *Tried by Fire*, an 1886 manual for aspiring china painters; patented a portable gas-fired kiln; and invented odorless paint colors that made it easier for painters to work at home.

In the 1890s, Frackelton's creative production became fo-cused less on china painting and more on art pottery. Unlike most other art potters who combined several different types of clay for a single vessel, Frackelton constructed pots entirely out of Milwaukee cream clay. Instead of the underglaze painted mo-tifs that were favored in art pottery, Frackelton applied molded or incised decoration. However, her biggest innovation was the use of salt-glaze on art pottery. This process, wherein a surface

FIG. 31. *Susan Stuart Goodrich Frackelton, ceramics artist and inventor of the portable gas-fired kiln, in her studio, 1901.*

glaze is created during firing by the interaction of sodium (from salt added to the kiln) with the silica and aluminum of the clay, had previously been used only in commercial potteries for production of utilitarian objects such as jugs, crockery, and drainage tiles. Frackelton's "discovery"—making art pottery out of salt-glazed stoneware—was in all probability a matter of personal necessity, since there were no other art potteries (but many commercial potteries) in Milwaukee at the time. Her choice of forms—steins, loving cups, punch bowls, and jugs—may also have been influenced by the utilitarian objects produced at the commercial potteries.

Frackelton's salt-glazed stoneware was exhibited in the Woman's Building at the 1893 World's Columbian Exposition in Chicago, where it garnered eight medals. Ceramics historian Edwin Atlee Barber, in his 1894 book *Pottery and Porcelain of the United States*, acknowledged Frackelton's unique accomplishment by noting that "to her belongs the credit of elevating the common salt-glazed stoneware to a place beside the finer ceramic wares in this country" (p. 512). One of her pieces was the first object sold from the Woman's Building at the World's Columbian Exposition; it was purchased by one of the directors of the Pennsylvania Museum and School of Industrial Art. This work, known as the *Olive Jar*, subsequently received a great deal of publicity and was pictured and discussed in many periodicals and texts about ceramics. Frackelton also exhibited and sold work at the other major international expositions of this era, receiving awards at the Antwerp International Exposition in 1894, the Paris International Exposition in 1900, and the Pan American Exposition in Buffalo in 1901.

Frackelton was a founder in 1892 of the National League of Mineral Painters, established to bring mineral artists in the United States together to develop a national school of ceramic art. The league held annual exhibits, and Frackelton traveled widely on its behalf, organizing local chapters and helping to set up china decorating schools as well as schools of ceramic art. At the same time Frackelton was active in the General Federation of Women's Clubs and chaired the art committee for the federation's fifth biennial held in Milwaukee in 1900, one of her last activities before leaving for Chicago in 1902. That year Frackelton's acrimonious divorce was final. She moved to the Hyde Park neighborhood with her fourteen-year-old daughter, Gladys.

Frackelton exhibited her ceramic pieces at the Art Institute of Chicago's applied arts exhibitions in 1902, 1906, and 1908 and had a one-person gallery exhibition in 1909, where one hundred of her ceramic pieces were shown. In a 1903 interview published in *Sketch Book*, Frackelton emphasized that her ceramic work was all thrown upon the wheel and not molded; molding was common practice for larger pottery operations in the early 1900s. Although she worked alone, Frackelton visited other art pottery studios such as George Ohr of Biloxi, Mississippi; Rookwood of Cincinnati; Newcomb of New Orleans; and Gates Pottery of Terra Cotta, Illinois.

In 1905–1906, Frackelton, a well-known and respected authority, was commissioned to write a series of definitive articles on American potters and potteries for *Sketch Book*. She also lectured on art pottery and other types of craft production before women's clubs, teacher's institutes, and Chautauqua assemblies. Comments on her lectures invariably mention her being a progressive spirit in art circles as well as her dramatic personality, large hoop earrings, brightly colored clothing, and cultured Bohemianism.

Frackelton gave up her ceramics studio in 1909 and turned her attention to book illumination, another craft popular with Chicago artisans of the early twentieth century. Her first such work, completed in 1913, was a memorial volume for John Plankington, pioneer Milwaukee meat packer. Frackelton subsequently illuminated a variety of secular and sacred texts, including a guest book and book of donors for the Chicago Woman's Club. Several of these volumes were collaborative projects with various Chicago metal workers and book binders, most often Monastery Hill Bindery. Frackelton received recognition in this realm as she had in ceramics, exhibiting her illuminations at the Art Institute of Chicago's applied arts exhibitions in 1916, 1917, and 1918 and winning Municipal Art League of Chicago prizes in both 1917 and 1918.

Frackelton also volunteered her time to chair the Sunday Open Door Committee of the Chicago Woman's Club, which provided edifying entertainment and refreshments in its club rooms every Sunday from November through March for non-club members. The Sunday Open Door, established in 1898 by MARTHA CROW, an English professor at the University of Chicago, was originally intended for young working women. However, during World War I, Frackelton received permission from the Woman's Club administration to extend the program season and to expand the audience to include soldiers and their families. Although attendance remained high, the Woman's Club's interest in the Sunday Open Door programs waned after World War I. By the depression in 1929, when cost-cutting was a primary concern, a suggestion was made to drop the programs. However, Frackelton, then eighty-one years old, vehemently opposed this suggestion by pointing out to the board of directors that the programs were done with volunteer entertainers at little cost to the organization. The Woman's Club continued the Sunday Open Door under Frackelton's direction until her death from heart disease in April 1932. The final report of the Sunday Open Door Committee, by Frackelton's daughter Gladys Frackelton Seeley, with whom she had lived in Kenilworth, Illinois, since 1923, was presented to the Woman's Club on April 27, 1932. Frackelton's funeral, held at the Episcopal Church of the Holy Comforter in Kenilworth, was followed by her burial in Forest Home Cemetery in Milwaukee.

Susan Stuart Frackelton had a long, productive life marked throughout by creative experimentation, shrewd business and marketing skills, and a strong desire to make her work and knowledge available to others. Her early work as a china painter and founder of the National League of Mineral Painters not only earned her a national reputation but also led her to write a manual and invent tools that made it easier for others to practice this art. Her salt-glazed art pottery gained her fame and international recognition and simultaneously proved that modest materials and facilities could yield rewards.

Sources. The Susan Stuart Frackelton Papers are at the Milwaukee County Hist. Soc., Milwaukee Public Museum, and in the Spec. Coll. department of the Univ. of Wisconsin–Milwaukee library (on loan from the State Hist. Soc. of Wisconsin). Records of the Chicago Woman's Club, including Frackelton's reports for the Sunday Open Door Committee, are at CHS. Frackelton's works include: *Tried by Fire: A Work on*

China Painting (1886; 2nd edition 1892; 3rd edition 1895); "Our American Potteries, Teco Ware," *Sketch Book,* September 1905; "Our American Potteries, Maratta's and Albert's Work at the Gates Potteries," *Sketch Book,* October 1905; "Rookwood Pottery," *Sketch Book,* February 1906; "Our American Potteries, Newcomb Pottery," *Sketch Book,* July 1906; "The Monastery Hill Bindery," *House Beautiful,* March 1914. There is an interview with her by Anne Warringdon in *Sketch Book,* September 1903. Her life and work in Milwaukee are discussed in George Weedon, "Susan S. Frackelton and the American Arts and Crafts Movement" (master's thesis, Univ. of Wisconsin–Milwaukee, 1975). Edwin Atlee Barber, *The Pottery and Porcelain of the United States* (1894), contains Barber's evaluation of Frackelton's work at the World's Columbian Exposition. Frackelton's ceramic work can be found in the collections of the Milwaukee County Hist. Soc., the Milwaukee Public Museum, and the State Hist. Soc. of Wisconsin. Her illuminated books for the Chicago Woman's Club are housed in the NL.

NANCY OWEN

FREER, ELEANOR EVEREST
May 14, 1864–December 13, 1942
COMPOSER, SINGER, CLUBWOMAN

Eleanor Everest Freer, founder and guiding spirit of the American Opera Society of Chicago (AOSC), encouraged American composers and musicians to find an authentic music vocabulary from their own national heritage at a time when the European tradition set the standard. Her greatest contributions to American music began in Chicago, where she took leadership in the movement to provide music education and critical support for American composers and musicians.

Eleanor Everest was born in Philadelphia, Pennsylvania, to Cornelius and Ellen Amelia (Clark) Everest. Her parents, from families with seventeenth-century New England roots, were raised in Connecticut. Although her paternal grandfather was a Presbyterian clergyman, Eleanor Everest was raised as an Episcopalian. Her family was musical, and Eleanor Everest's childhood home in Philadelphia formed a comfortable environment in which her talents could blossom. Her father was a theory and choral professor at the Girls' Normal School in Philadelphia and published three instructional books containing vocal exercises as well as a collection of hymn tunes and chants, *The Sabbath.* He was also a church organist and vocal coach to many famous singers of the time, including Theresa Tietjens and David Bispham. Her mother, primarily a homemaker, possessed a beautiful soprano voice. Everest's only sibling, DeWitt Everest, studied violin.

Eleanor Everest began her musical life at the age of five, when she taught herself how to play the piano. As she grew up, she gradually became responsible for accompanying her brother, mother, and herself in the musical activities that occurred daily in their home. Everest penned her first composition at age thirteen, a piano solo, *Polka Facile,* which was published in 1880.

Musical and literary guests were frequent in the Everest household. One of her mother's best friends, the playwright, novelist, and orator Anna Dickinson, commissioned Eleanor Everest to compose an overture for her play *Aurelian.* The result was Everest's second musical work, *The Aurelian March,* composed in 1878. Another family guest, the famous soprano Christine Nilsson, heard Everest sing and insisted that she be sent to Europe for vocal instruction. Following Everest's graduation

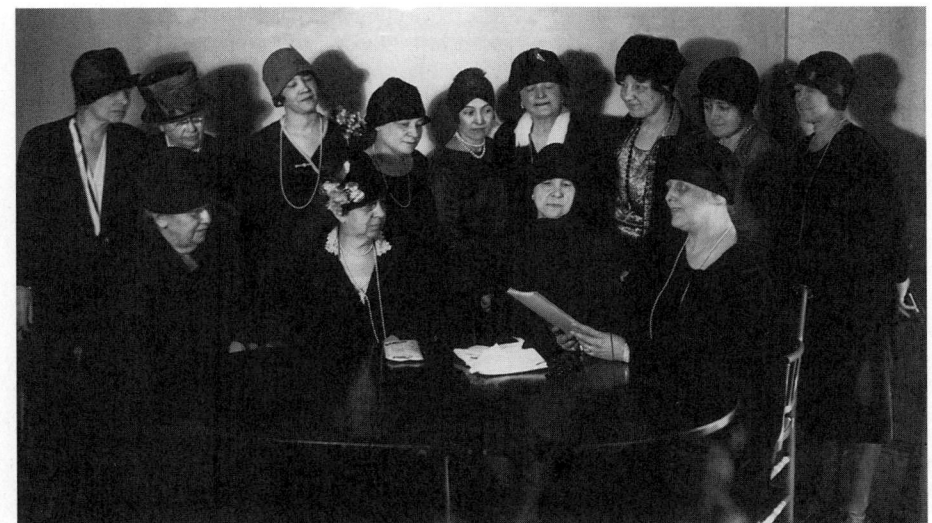

FIG. 32. A meeting of the American Opera Society of Chicago, 1928; seated, left to right, Mrs. Albert J. Ochsner, Eleanor Everest Freer, Edith Rockefeller McCormick, and Mrs. Louis E. Yager (president).

from Girls' Normal School in 1883, Nilsson arranged with friends to help pay Eleanor Everest's bills for tuition and living expenses while abroad. She set sail for Paris with a chaperone to study with Mathilde Marchesi, one of the most respected singing teachers in Europe.

During her long journey, Everest began to articulate, if only to herself, her resentment at having to leave her comfortable home to become a respected member of the music world. Why, she wondered, did the public believe it was impossible to receive adequate musical training in America? She resolved to investigate the matter as well as she could and then bring back to the United States any advanced teaching method she encountered in Paris. It was this plan to elevate American musical education that served as the central force of her musical activities throughout the remainder of her life.

At the École Marchesi, where she spent three years, Everest learned French, German, and Italian, and in addition to voice lessons, studied theory and diction with Benjamin Godard. Famous singers, including Emma Nevade, Emma Eames, and Nellie Melba attended the École Marchesi while Everest was there and, as a result, she fostered some close friendships with these divas. One of the most beneficial aspects of studying with Mathilde Marchesi was that she was very well respected by contemporary composers, who came to Marchesi's annual recitals to hear her students perform and even offered to coach those students who wished to learn vocal technique from the composers themselves. Consequently, Everest sang for, and studied with, Charles Widor, Jules Massenet, Franz Liszt, Charles Gounod, Léo Delibes, and Charles Camille Saint-Saëns. She even had the opportunity to perform a selection from Mozart's opera *Cosi Fan Tutti* before Giuseppe Verdi, the well-known Italian opera composer.

At the beginning of her third year of studies, in October 1885, Everest's father died. She was then forced to make the choice of staying and completing her degree or returning home. Upon deciding to remain in Paris, she found it necessary, since

her family could no longer support her financially, to take on odd jobs such as copying music, providing piano accompaniment for opera classes, and working as Marchesi's teaching assistant. Her assiduousness earned her, in 1886, the only certificate awarded that year by Marchesi that permitted a student to teach the Marchesi Method.

Following graduation that year, Everest returned to Philadelphia. From 1886 to 1891 she ran a voice studio at which she taught more than sixty students per week. In 1889 she also traveled twice weekly to the National Conservatory of Music of America in New York City, where she served as the Marchesi Method representative and coached several voice students.

Eleanor Everest met Archibald Freer, a wealthy young doctor from Chicago, on a short trip to Paris in 1887. They were married four years later, on April 25, 1891, in St. George's Church in New York City. Following the death of Dr. Freer's father in 1892, the couple moved to Leipzig, where Archibald Freer studied medicine. While in Leipzig, Eleanor Freer read extensively and learned to speak German fluently. On April 3, 1894, Eleanor and Archibald Freer had a daughter, their only child, whom they named Eleanor.

In 1899, the Freer family moved to Chicago and by 1901 had settled in a house on the fashionable North Side. Eleanor Freer, now age thirty-seven, contacted Bernard Ziehn, a well known professor of theory and composition, and arranged to study with him. She remained his student until 1907 but corresponded with him about her compositions long after that year. At first, she wrote only music for piano, but she quickly realized that her true calling lay in setting English verse to music. One of her most popular collections was a song cycle entitled *Sonnets from the Portuguese*, in which Freer set to music the poems of Elizabeth Barrett Browning.

Freer's career as a composer did not proceed uninterrupted. In 1907 she became very ill and was not able to compose during her long convalescence. Instead, she translated into English ten Italian librettos, an activity in which she engaged as part of her ongoing battle to prove that opera could be rendered as artfully in English as in any other language.

Composition was also impossible between the years 1914 and 1918 due to her wartime efforts. Among the many committees with which she was associated were the Paris-Chicago Hospital Foundation, the American Ambulance Fund, and the London French Red Cross Committee. She helped raise more than eighty thousand dollars in relief funds. For her efforts she was awarded the Silver Cross of the *Association des Dames Françaises* and the Medal of Gratitude by the French government, and the Medal of Queen Elizabeth by the Belgian Government. Archibald Freer, also recognized for his generous donations, was awarded the Order of Leopold for his work in the rehabilitation of Belgium after World War I.

When she was not composing or volunteering, Eleanor Freer devoted her energies to women's clubs, both local and national. She was active in the Fortnightly, the Chicago Woman's Club, the Friday Club, the Melodists, the Arts Club of Chicago, and the Illinois Woman's Press Association. In addition, the National Federation of Musical Clubs appointed her an honorary member in 1915. For these organizations she arranged musical events, wrote for their newsletters, and headed various committees, both musical and otherwise.

By 1921 she returned to composing and completed her first chamber opera, *Legend of the Piper*. She dedicated this opera to her five-year-old granddaughter, Eleanor Wilson, who had drowned while on vacation with her parents. In total, Freer composed 163 songs, 11 chamber operas, 19 solo piano works, and approximately 13 choral pieces, most of which she published in her lifetime.

Freer made one of her most important contributions to the music world in 1921 when, with the help of two friends, Marion Ochsner and Narcissa H. Yaeger, she founded the Opera in Our Language Foundation (OOLF). The primary objective of this organization was to foster an operatic tradition that was wholly American. Freer, as a founder and president, insisted that all productions sponsored by the OOLF be performed in English by American singers, instrumentalists, and conductors, with only limited use of international artists. If the OOLF wished to produce an opera originally written in another language, Freer demanded that its libretto be translated adequately into English. Furthermore, rather than hire European stars—a costly practice common in U.S. opera houses—Freer and other members of the OOLF strove to employ only American singers. Consequently, the OOLF's operas were more economical to produce, offering performances at less expense to the audience. Indeed, the OOLF's impulse to make opera an accessible art to the whole public reflected a broader trend sweeping the United States in which American music was perceived as one of the most crucial tools through which a nation might strengthen its cultural enterprises. In 1924 the OOLF was incorporated into the American Opera Society of Chicago (AOSC). Freer remained president of the AOSC until 1927 and was active in the organization for the rest of her life. The influence of the AOSC quickly spread across the United States as well as abroad. The most important achievements of this group were to encourage American composers and musicians to remain in the United States to study and to write operas based on English texts and American topics.

In 1921 Freer, and other members of the OOLF, established a fund in memory of dramatic baritone David Bispham. The OOLF, and later AOSC, awarded the David Bispham Memorial Medal to American composers who had written successful operas in the English language. Freer won the medal in 1926 for her opera, *Legend of the Piper*. Among other recipients were George Gershwin for *Porgy and Bess* and Virgil Thomson for *Four Saints in Three Acts*.

Even though Freer possessed a deep reverence for all Western art music, she remained deeply convinced that the American public needed to encourage and cultivate its own musical potential. She insisted that Americans, to participate in international art, had to develop music at home in the English language. She maintained the belief that musical art was the greatest asset a nation possessed and that only by nurturing this element could the United States become a powerful historical force. Freer remained active in the music world throughout the final twenty years of her life, writing articles and reviews for such journals, magazines, and newspapers as *Musical America, Music and Letters,* and the *Chicago Tribune*. Her compositions were performed during meetings of the OOLF and the AOSC. As a tribute to her lifelong commitment to American music, the editors of *Music News* established the Freer Music Fund, which encouraged singers and pianists to perform her chamber operas, songs, and piano works. Eleanor Everest Freer died in Chicago at the age of seventy-eight.

As a musician, Eleanor Everest Freer devoted her life to making opera more accessible to the American public. During a time when consumption of this art in the United States was dominated by western European works and performers, Freer encouraged American composers to create operatic works with English texts, as she challenged American audiences to support these endeavors.

Sources. Freer's compositions are located in the Library of Congress, Washington, D.C. Her published autobiography, *Recollections and Reflections of an American Composer* (c. 1922), in which she discussed the events of her life through the founding of the OOLF, is at the CHS. The scrapbooks of the American Opera Society of Chicago at NL, compiled by Eleanor Dawes Peters, contain articles by and about Freer, as well as programs and reviews of concerts and operas sponsored by the AOSC. Freer's biography was written by her friend Agness Greene Foster, *Eleanor Everest Freer—Patriot and Her Colleagues* (1927). Sylvia Miller Eversole documented Freer's life in "Eleanor Everest Freer: Her Life and Music" (Ph.D. diss., City Univ. of New York, 1992). Freer is listed in *NCAB* (1920), *Women in American Music* (1978), and *New Grove Dictionary of Opera* (1992). For general information pertaining to opera in Chicago and throughout the United States during Freer's time, consult John Dizikes, *Opera in America* (1993). For gender issues, see Karen Blair, *The Torchbearers: Women and Their Amateur Arts Associations in America, 1890–1930* (1994).

HILARY PORISS

FULMER, HARRIET

1877(?)–November 27, 1952

NURSE, PUBLIC HEALTH ADMINISTRATOR

Before antibiotics and inoculations, when infectious diseases were still a ubiquitous threat to Chicagoans, Harriet Fulmer was a pioneer in developing public health programs.

Fulmer was born in Fulmerville, Pennsylvania, where her

FIG. 33. *Staff nurses with the Chicago Visiting Nurse Association, 1905.*

FIG. 34. *Staff nurses with the Chicago Visiting Nurse Association outside their headquarters.*

wealthy and influential parents, John Roericke and Emma Jane (Beardsley) Fulmer, virtually owned the town. Fulmer's mother wanted a genteel daughter immersed in a musical education and insisted that Fulmer practice the piano four hours a day. Fulmer rebelled. Encouraged by an uncle and three cousins, all physicians whom she admired, she moved to Chicago to study at St. Luke's Hospital Training School for Nurses. It was there, before public acceptance of hospitals as safe places, that Fulmer discovered most nurses worked in the homes of the wealthy. "I was determined to go to the others where I felt I was most needed" (Fisher, 3), she reminisced years later.

Fulmer's determination permeated her life. Her aggression and tiny stature, so evident and incongruous, drew many comments. The *Chicago Tribune* called her "a small nurse with big ideas" (October 28, 1951). One incredulous witness to the Iroquois Theatre fire in 1903 recalled seeing a frail woman carrying body after body out of the burning theater, in a frenetic attempt to save lives. That woman was Fulmer.

After her graduation from St. Luke's in 1895, Fulmer went to work for the Chicago Visiting Nurse Association (VNA), becoming its superintendent in 1898. The VNA, established in 1887, cared for the sick poor in their homes free of charge and taught poverty-stricken families about disease prevention and sanitation. Before 1903, when the VNA placed its first industrial nurse at a workplace, the association was funded exclusively by charitable contributions. Composed by 1902 of thirty-two of Chicago's wealthiest women, the VNA board of directors solicited contributions and managed and invested the VNA's growing endowment. The daily activities of the VNA were left to Fulmer.

Visiting nurse work was both rewarding and unspeakably exhausting. Nurses walked on unpaved streets in ankle-length skirts to care for patients in filthy homes that one nurse described years later as "not unlike one-story chicken-coops" (Edna Foley, "Superintendent's Report," *Annual Report,* 1921, 27). In one VNA annual report Fulmer described a visiting nurse's not atypical day. Discovering her first patient critically ill with typhoid pneumonia, the nurse persuaded her, after some time, to go to a hospital. Finding a hospital and summoning an ambulance took even more effort. First the nurse had to walk to a drugstore to find a telephone. After three phone calls, one hospital finally agreed to admit the indigent patient. Then, since an ambulance would not come in response to a phone call, the nurse walked to the nearest cooperating physician's office to obtain a permit so the police would release an ambulance. After phoning the police, and knowing help was on the way, she walked back to the patient's home to prepare her for the trip to the hospital. Since the patient had several small children, the nurse's next task was to find a safe place for them. She walked again to the drugstore, this time to phone the Home for the Friendless. Assured that the home had space for the children, she returned to care for them. Only after the Home for the Friendless had picked up the children did the nurse continue her rounds—in this case to see nine more patients.

The titanic effort was succeeding. The VNA's preventive work was influencing the city's response to public health problems. At Fulmer's behest, for example, the VNA's Tuberculosis Committee was created in January 1903 to compile statistics on the extent of tuberculosis (TB) in Chicago and to arouse public interest in its prevention. Within three weeks, the committee conducted a well-attended meeting of physicians, charity workers, and nurses. The volunteer services of ten physicians were obtained to hold regular office hours for TB patients in a space rented by the VNA and in eight district offices of the Bureau of Charities. All patients received follow-up care by visiting nurses. The VNA Tuberculosis Committee's central office soon warehoused patients' histories and elaborate maps showing the location of every TB case in Chicago. The committee also sponsored lectures on the prevention of tuberculosis held in public schools, neighborhood halls, and settlement houses.

In 1905 the committee was disbanded as the more far-reaching and powerful State Association for the Prevention of Tuberculosis and Chicago Tuberculosis Institute took over its work; but Fulmer's VNA Tuberculosis Committee was acknowledged as the forerunner. The Chicago Tuberculosis Institute went on to establish a free dispensary and an open air camp for TB patients, an information bureau on TB care and prevention, and a testing station for experimentation with inoculations against the disease. Fulmer served on its board of directors.

Fulmer's involvement with tuberculosis care and prevention went further. Since fresh air, sunshine, and rest were thought to be the best treatment for tuberculosis at the time, Fulmer arranged for the establishment of a small tent colony in 1905 in Glencoe, a wealthy suburb north of Chicago, to house some of Chicago's tubercular poor. Patients were cared for there each summer by visiting nurses and physicians and were educated in tuberculosis prevention before they went home in the fall to share their new knowledge with the community.

Another treatment utilized by Fulmer was summertime neighborhood baby tents—portable hospitals to care for sick infants—staffed by visiting nurses. The infant mortality rate soared in the summer at the turn of the century, since few mothers had access to ice or refrigeration and milk and food spoilage was likely. As a result, thousands of infants died between June and September of dehydration from diarrhea. Started in the summer of 1905, baby tents were sponsored jointly by the Chicago Relief and Aid Society, which furnished the tents and equipment; the Northwestern University Settlement, which gave space on its grounds that first summer; and the VNA, which provided health care workers. Baby tents were soon established in many congested Chicago neighborhoods from June to mid-September each year. In the summer of 1910 alone, more than four thousand babies were cared for in the tents. Open from 8 A.M. to 6 P.M. every day unless a baby was critically ill, in which case the tent remained staffed the entire night, the baby tents brought medical treatment to infants whose parents mistrusted hospitals. VNA nurses worked in the tents and, after patients' release, went to their homes to teach their mothers about infant care. At least one doctor was in attendance at each location. Seven cities—New York, Cincinnati, Cleveland, Minneapolis, Nashville, Rochester, and Hartford—soon set up baby tents in poor neighborhoods during the summer, modeled after the baby tents in Chicago.

The VNA's efforts were not limited to the street and home. Under Fulmer, the VNA placed its first industrial nurse at the

McCormick Works of the International Harvester Company in 1903. Visiting nurses in industry combined their usual home health care and education in sickness prevention with worker advocacy. They lobbied employers to construct lunchrooms, rest rooms, libraries, and first aid stations in factories—anything to enhance the comfort and health of workers. By 1912 the VNA placed eight industrial nurses. In 1909 the Metropolitan Life Insurance Company also contracted with the VNA to send nurses to care for their sick policyholders.

The use of visiting nurses continued to spread. Thanks to Fulmer's incessant campaigning, visiting nurses were placed in the public schools in 1906. Fulmer argued convincingly that public school nurses would stop the spread of disease among children, promote personal hygiene, instruct mothers, ferret out and assist egregious cases of poverty and neglect, and foster a better understanding of students via home visits. As a result, the Chicago Board of Education agreed to use visiting nurses financed by the VNA on a trial basis. With just ten nurses, the VNA decreased students' sick days dramatically by entering homes and teaching mothers of sick school children about hygiene and illness prevention. In 1906 Fulmer authored a pamphlet regularly distributed to Chicago's public school children at the end of the school year. "How to Be Healthy This Summer" included tips on bathing, dental care, diet, and personal and home hygiene. The Chicago City Council was so impressed that in the fall of 1908 the city agreed to pay for forty public school nurses supplied by the VNA.

Fulmer's foremost concern was always with disease prevention. She was outspoken about housing reform, having targeted poor housing early in her career as a primary source of illness and misery. She lobbied long and hard for criminal charges to be brought against slum landlords. "Could this be brought about," she argued, "two-thirds of the work of this Association would be done away with" ("Report of Nurses Work 1907," *Annual Report* 1907, 34). She saw the ramifications of substandard housing everywhere. Describing the work of her nurses at the baby tents she noted, "Each baby returning to its home was supervised . . . and again the home conditions were proven the real cause of the baby's illness. This baby, from the disease-breeding tenement, is the outward and visible sign that Chicago must hasten putting into effect sane tenement house laws" ("Report of Nurses Work for the Year 1908," *Annual Report* 1908, 32). In an article, "The Housing Problem and Its Relation to Other Reform Movements," in *Alumnae*, Fulmer wrote, "Why pour water into a sieve by being content to let greedy or indifferent landlords, ignorant and careless municipal authorities, politics and what-not interfere with the human work of tenement house reform?" (October 1908, 2).

Fulmer's forthright, controversial opinions might have cost her her job. In June 1911, after she requested and was granted an eight-month vacation from the VNA, the wealthy women on the board of directors voted to fire her. They acknowledged Fulmer's years of service but felt that the association needed a superintendent "to whom should be entrusted the executive affairs of the Association and the proper direction of the nurses and their work in the districts." They went on to agree later in the meeting that "the Association's welfare absolutely demanded a leader scientifically trained to social work" ("Minutes of June Meeting 1911," VNA Papers). By October they had Fulmer's resignation, effective the following March.

Fulmer went on to become secretary of the Illinois State Association for Prevention of Tuberculosis in 1913–14. In 1915 she coauthored a health survey of White County, Illinois, under the auspices of the Illinois State Association for the Prevention of Tuberculosis. She became the first director of the Cook County Rural Health Nursing Service in 1917, retiring from there in 1942. She was the founder and first president (1926) of the Illinois State Nurses' Association, founder (1905) and editor of *Visiting Nurse Quarterly* until it ceased publication, and one of the founders and a member of the editorial staff of *American Journal of Nursing*. Fulmer was also a charter member of the St. Luke's Alumnae Association, elected its president fifteen times between 1896 and 1932. She helped organize visiting nurse associations in many cities—Dubuque, Madison, South Bend, Cleveland, Columbus, Moline, Peoria, Minneapolis, Marquette, Denver, Milwaukee, Des Moines, and Grand Rapids—all modeled after her Chicago Association.

Fulmer never married. She died at St. Luke's Hospital in Chicago in 1952. Assessing the value of a nursing career, she told graduates of the Michael Reese Training School in 1906, "No woman comes into any profession which holds for her greater privileges and richer opportunities than the one of nursing." She urged any nurse who wanted to hone her skills to work with the poor, amongst whom, she was sure, the nurse would learn more than in any hospital or private practice. "You will have incentives to keep in touch with the very latest and best methods" when working with the poor, she told her colleagues. "You will have an incentive to do your best nursing work" ("Editor's Miscellany," *American Journal of Nursing*, January 1906, 261–62).

Sources. The Chicago Visiting Nurse Association Papers, including minutes of meetings, Fulmer's unpublished writing and business correspondence, and descriptions of the work of the VNA while Fulmer was its superintendent, are at the CHS, as are annual reports (*Annual Report: The Visiting Nurse Association of Chicago*) and all issues of Fulmer's *Visiting Nurse Quarterly*. The Rush Presbyterian–St. Luke's Medical Center Archive in Chicago houses *Alumnae*, which often featured Fulmer, her work, and writing; the *St. Luke's Alumni Association Yearbook*; and a small clipping file on Fulmer. Harriet Fulmer also published articles in *American Journal of Nursing*, *Visiting Nurse Quarterly*, *Charities and Commons*, and *Survey* throughout her career. Numerous articles appeared in Chicago newspapers about her work, including a lengthy one, "Miss Fulmer: A Small Nurse with Big Ideas," in the *CT* on October 28, 1951. Biographies of Fulmer appeared in Lucy B. Fisher, "A Character Sketch of Harriet Fulmer," *Alumnae*, February 1931; Martin Kaufman, ed., *Dictionary of American Nursing Biography* (1988); and Vern L. Bullough, Lilli Sentz, and Alice P. Stein, eds., *American Nursing: A Biographical Dictionary*, vol. 2 (1992).

JACQUELINE H. WOLF

g

GAINES, IRENE McCOY
October 25, 1892–April 7, 1964

POLITICAL ACTIVIST, CLUBWOMAN, SOCIAL REFORMER

Irene McCoy Gaines represents what used to be referred to as a "race woman," that is, a woman who was involved in the struggle to end racial discrimination and who concurrently strove, both by personal example and public activism, to see to it that woman's full potential was realized in both the workplace and the home. A wife and mother, Gaines worked outside the home for wages all of her adult life even though her husband was a well-educated professional, a common circumstance in the African American community of her time. In addition she was a member of several social reform organizations and was active in electoral politics. As with other "race women" of the era, she took seriously a commitment to public service and was actively engaged in the civic arena for nearly half a century.

McCoy was born the second child of Charles Vivien and Mamie (Ellis) McCoy in Ocala, Florida. Her older sister died in childhood. Her parents were divorced, and she and her mother relocated to Chicago. During this time Chicago's African American population was increasing as Blacks from a number of southern states migrated in search of increased political and economic opportunities. McCoy attended public Mission Kindergarten and graduated from Wendell Phillips High School. From 1905 to 1910 she was a student at Fisk Normal School in Nashville, Tennessee. While at Fisk she was often in correspondence with her uncle, George Washington Ellis, who served with the U.S. delegation to the West African nation of Liberia between 1902 and 1910. This correspondence sparked her interest in international affairs, and she would later call upon women to see the global nature of their concerns.

Upon graduation from Fisk in 1910, Irene McCoy returned to her home in Chicago. Despite (or perhaps because of) the increasing numbers of black residents, turn-of-the-century Chicago was rife with racial discrimination. The young Irene McCoy was very discouraged by her initial search for work. Though well qualified to teach or do clerical work, she was only offered housekeeping chores, which she reluctantly accepted. She later wrote of this time: "It was a dreadful struggle: I spent many days and nights seeking employment. . . . Whenever I answered an advertisement for work that I felt I could do, I was told colored help was not wanted. . . . There were times when I felt dreadfully discouraged" (quoted in Smith, 384). During this time, McCoy became even more aware of her struggle as an African American and as a woman. It was the conjunction of being black and female that she felt disqualified her from all but housework. Finally she landed a job as a stenographer in the complaint department of Chicago's Juvenile Court. She became active in the community and between 1910 and 1914 won three oratorical essay contests, honing the skills that would serve her later in her many leadership roles.

On October 7, 1914, Irene McCoy married Harris Barrett Gaines, a lawyer, realtor, active Republican, and civic leader. He would later serve two terms in the Illinois legislature beginning in 1928. The couple had two children, Harris Jr. (born 1922) and Charles Ellis (born 1924). The birth of her children posed the dilemma for Gaines of whether to stop working at her job outside the home or cut back on her civic work. She did neither, continuing with the proverbial balancing act that challenges women activists. In June 1932 she received a poignant letter from her son Harris Jr., then ten years old and staying with his grandmother in the black middle-class resort at Idlewild, Michigan; he wrote in part, "Money and letters will do no good . . . I just want you" (Gaines Papers, Chicago Historical Society).

Gaines was involved in many political and social reform activities, all the while holding a number of wage-earning jobs. In 1917–18 she was director of the Girls' Work Division War Camp Community Service in Chicago, a position that she had been encouraged to accept by Mary Church Terrell, another well-

FIG. 35. *Social reformer and clubwoman Irene McCoy Gaines became president of the Illinois Federation of Republican Colored Women's Clubs in 1924.*

FIG. 36. *Irene McCoy Gaines, president of the National Association of Colored Women's Clubs, with others on steps of the U.S. Supreme Court, Washington, D.C., c. 1950s.*

known "race woman." During this time Gaines was also active in the Urban League; she also helped recruit black women for the Women's Trade Union League, of which she was a member. Between 1918 and 1921 she studied social work at the University of Chicago. She was active in the African Methodist Episcopal (AME) Church as well as the Theosophical Society—a mystical society that believed in karma and reincarnation—and corresponded and met with several adherents in nearby Evanston, Illinois.

From 1924 to 1935 Gaines was president of the Illinois Federation of Republican Colored Women's Clubs, a group that she helped to organize. In this capacity, during 1928 and 1930 she was active in the congressional campaigns of RUTH HANNA McCORMICK, for whom she helped coordinate black women's support all over the state. By 1930 she was Republican Committeewoman of the First Congressional District of Illinois; in that same year she served as secretary of the Chicago

Northern District Federation of Colored Women's Clubs. She worked with black clubwomen to support women's right to serve on juries and to provide literacy classes for black domestic workers. She was also interested in prison reform and carried on a correspondence with at least one black woman prisoner at Joliet Prison in Illinois, Adelaide Lauretta Johnson, who was incarcerated due to a conviction for "bouncing" checks. Gaines attempted to secure Johnson's freedom and to get her a job, but the ultimate disposition of this effort is unclear.

In 1920 Gaines became industrial secretary to the first "Negro" branch of the Young Women's Christian Association in Chicago. By the late 1920s she was also a member of the Woman's City Club of Chicago and a life member of the Chicago Art Institute. It may have been this latter membership and interest that spurred her during the 1920s to begin a program known as Negro in Art Week that sought to encourage artistic development and training of black youth.

In the 1930s, while employed by the Cook County Welfare Department as a caseworker, Gaines formed clubs for black youth. As a member of the Citizens' Advisory Committee, she worked throughout the 1930s for the integration of Chicago public schools and to provide for the education of pregnant teenagers. In 1930 President Herbert Hoover appointed her to his Housing Commission.

From 1939 to 1953 she was president of the Chicago Council of Negro Organizations (CCNO), a group formed to secure the civil rights of Chicago's black population. In 1941, under the aegis of the CCNO, Gaines led a group of fifty Chicagoans to Washington, D.C., where they met with others from around the United States, split into smaller groups, and visited offices of government agencies and elected officials to protest racial discrimination in employment, particularly that involving government defense contracts. The group also protested discrimination against Blacks by the Federal Housing Authority, the U.S. military, the Civilian Conservation Corps, the Works Progress Administration, and various labor unions. The group issued a report on the march, "The Right to Work Is the Right to Live." This effort was an important precursor to that of A. Philip Randolph who, four months later, threatened a massive march on Washington to protest the very same discrimination. This earlier effort may have lent credence to Randolph's threat and certainly helped to convince President Franklin D. Roosevelt to issue Executive Order 8802 forbidding employment discrimination by businesses holding government contracts. Executive Order 8802 led to large numbers of black women in the urban North moving out of employment as domestic workers and into industry for the first time.

In the 1940s Gaines made several unsuccessful bids for electoral seats. In 1940 she became the first black woman to run for a seat in the Illinois legislature and in 1948 was the first black Republican candidate for the Board of County Commissioners from Chicago. Though she lost, she received one million votes, more than any of the other Republican candidates on the ballot in Chicago. In 1947 Gaines, as vice-president of the Chicago-area Congress of American Women, read a statement before the Secretary General of the United Nations in which she protested the "inferior status" accorded the "colored women of America . . . [and] of the world" (*Notable American Women*, 259).

Gaines was involved in black women's club work for more than two decades. As a member of the National Association of Colored Women's Clubs (NACWC), an organization founded in 1896 to give unity and cohesion to the hundreds of black women's clubs all over the United States and in Hawaii and Haiti, she served as historian and recording secretary. In 1952 at the national convention she was elected president of the organization, a position in which she served three terms. Under her leadership the NACWC established new headquarters in Washington, D.C., restored the Anacostia, Maryland, home of well-known abolitionist and self-described "women's rights man" Frederick Douglass, and produced a film chronicling Douglass's life (*The House on Cedar Hill*) that won a Freedom's Foundation Award. Douglass had been among the small number of male supporters who attended the Seneca Falls Women's Convention in 1848. In 1956 Gaines helped the

NACWC secure a fifty thousand dollar grant from the Sears Foundation to sponsor a neighborhood improvement contest. Gaines also attempted to increase the NACWC's international exposure by calling upon the organization to undertake a one-world program that would allow it to become more visible as part of a global sisterhood. By the late 1950s the NACWC had more than three hundred thousand members in fifteen hundred clubs spread over forty-two states, Alaska, and Hawaii, as well as Haiti.

In a December 2, 1957, interview of Gaines by Bernice Stevens Decker that appeared in the *Christian Science Monitor*, Gaines, in her role as president of the NACWC, commented on the struggles of African Americans against discrimination: "We have to break down barriers of hate and prejudice," she stated, and committed the resources of the NACWC to enforcing the 1954 U.S. Supreme Court decision (*Brown v. Board of Education, Topeka, Kansas*) that outlawed racial segregation in public schools. This decision was widely viewed as a reversal of the 1896 *Plessy v. Ferguson* decision, which established the so-called "separate but equal" doctrine; the Brown decision was held to have broader application than only school desegregation. In the same *Christian Science Monitor* interview, Gaines anticipated the "gender, race, class" analysis of a later generation when, in reminding the interviewer that the NACWC was sixty-two years old, she continued, "Our founders were farsighted. They recognized the handicaps of all women in social, industrial, and educational opportunities. But, they were especially interested in the problems of *women* of color who had the added disadvantage of discrimination of *race* and *economic status*" [emphasis added].

Gaines was elected "Woman of the Year" in 1951 by three organizations: Sigma Gamma Rho Sorority, the Woman's Division of the AME church, and the Chicago and Northern District of Colored Women's Clubs. In 1958 she received the George Washington Honor Medal from the Freedoms Foundation at Valley Forge. In 1962 she received an honorary degree from Wilberforce University in Wilberforce, Ohio, and in 1990 was honored by the General Alumni Association of Fisk University.

Gaines died of cancer at age seventy-two. She is buried in Lincoln Cemetery, Chicago.

Irene McCoy Gaines dedicated her life to the struggles of African Americans, particularly women and youth, and fought against discrimination that attempted to proscribe their lives and dreams. She did so while working full-time outside the home and fulfilling her roles as wife and mother. Through her work she touched the lives of the dispossessed of various classes and races in Chicago, the nation, and around the world.

Sources. The papers of Irene McCoy Gaines are at the CHS and at the Univ. Library, Univ. of Illinois at Urbana-Champaign. Though incomplete, they provide general information on her life, including personal correspondence, numerous newspaper articles, copies of some of her speeches, and other memorabilia. Gaines's biography is included in Jessie Carney Smith, ed., *Notable Black American Women* (1992) and in *NAW* (1980). There is an interview of Gaines by Bernice Stevens Decker, "Negro Women See Progress," in the *Christian Science Monitor*, February 2, 1957.

CHERYL JOHNSON-ODIM

GARBE, RUTH MOORE. *See* **MOORE GARBE, RUTH**

GARDEN, MARY
February 20, 1874–January 3, 1967
LYRIC SOPRANO, OPERA COMPANY DIRECTOR

Mary Garden, legendary prima donna and self-styled "creatrice" who brought modern French opera to the United States and, most notably, Chicago, was born in Aberdeen, Scotland, the second of four daughters of Robert Davidson and Mary (Joss) Garden. Both parents were descended from prosperous Scots families. Her father was an engineer who wanted to see America, and when Mary was six, the family followed him to New York, living first in Brooklyn and then Chicopee, Massachusetts. After a brief return visit to Scotland, the family settled in 1887 in Hyde Park, a suburb about to be annexed to the city of Chicago. Her father was then an official of the Pope Manufacturing Company, manufacturers of Columbia bicycles.

By her own account, Garden was a spirited child who loathed dolls, loved playing the heroine in pretend adventures that were "tragic and awful" ("The Climb," 1), and was frequently asked to sing songs and perform for guests at home and church events. A member of the church choir, she was about sixteen when she began to focus on singing as an outlet for her restless energies. Her father arranged for her to study with Sarah Robinson Duff, an outstanding teacher of voice culture, who presented her pupils at many paying engagements in local theaters, clubs, and private homes. Attractive and charming, Duff also took the girls around town to operas and plays. Young Mary found her "so everything that I had dreamed of, and never seen in my life" (Garden and Biancolli, 9). At some point Garden's father allowed her to drop out of Hyde Park High School so she could give all her time to her music.

Duff recognized Garden's strong dramatic instincts early and devoted exceptional attention to her voice. Finally she recommended further training abroad. Since Robert Garden did not have the money for such a venture, she helped persuade Florence Mayer, wife of a wealthy merchant (and also a Duff pupil) to finance a few years' study in Paris. In May 1896 Garden, with Sarah Duff as chaperone, sailed to Europe. They arrived in Paris at three o'clock in the morning. Years later, in a memoir she wrote for *Ladies Home Journal*, Garden remembered that as their cab passed by the majestic Opera House, just emerging out of a gray mist, Duff told her, "That is the place you will some day sing" ("The Climb," 1).

Quickly rejecting such celebrated teachers as Sbriglia and Marchesi, whose methods she thought wrong for her voice, Garden studied mostly under Jules Chevalier, Lucien Fugere, and most importantly, Antonio Trabadelo. After Duff's return home, Garden lived with a French family and then in a pension, avoiding the American colony in order to master the French language and concentrate solely on her work. After three years, the Mayer family ended its support. Fearing her parents' pressure to return home, which to her meant failure, a distraught Garden was rescued by Sybil Sanderson, a prominent and well-connected American soprano. Sanderson gave Garden a room in her own apartment and introduced her to Albert Carre, director of the Opera-Comique, who invited Garden to watch rehearsals and then hired her as an understudy at one hundred francs a month.

On April 10, 1900, Marthe Rioton, star of Charpentier's new opera *Louise*, became ill during a performance, and Carre asked Garden to step into the third act. She was quickly pinned into an oversize costume and led to the wings. As the curtain rose, she walked upstage and turned her back to the audience, saying to herself, "It's your time now or it's never going to be your time" ("The Climb," 5–6). The conductor struck the first note of the opera's great aria, "Depuis le Jour." "My first note came out free and clear," she later recalled. "When I walked off the stage that night I was no longer an unknown" (Fellowes, 14).

That fortuitous debut propelled Garden to instant celebrity. Two years later her artistic territory and style were firmly established when she created the most important role of her career in *Pelleas et Mélisande*. Claude Debussy's only opera, the work is a masterpiece of lyric symbolism, featuring impressionistic orchestration and understated recitative in place of the conventional big arias. Garden's portrayal of the lost and frightened heroine was a triumph of musical intelligence. Though this difficult work was met at first with cat calls and laughter by both audience and critics, it was eventually accepted as a landmark of modern French opera.

Over the next five years Garden consolidated her international reputation, creating roles in a series of new operas, including *Le Fille de Tabarin*, *La Reine Fiammette*, *Hélène*, *Aphrodite*, and a work Massenet wrote especially for her, *Cherubin*. When she sang the role of the licentious courtesan in *Thais* at Aix-les-Bains, King George I of Greece, one of Garden's greatest admirers, predicted it would be one of her most sensational successes, and throughout her career *Thais* remained, as she wrote in her autobiography, "the war horse that brought in all the money" (Garden and Biancolli, 113). During this period she fully developed her singular gift for characterization, fusing all aspects of her interpretive art—voice, gesture, pose, costume, stagecraft—into one integrated whole. So different and convincing was her projection of each role, it was hard to recognize her face from one stage photo to the next. She seemed to prefer histrionic, often "scarlet," parts, though in private life she retained her hardy Scottish temperament. Some time during her Paris years, she subtracted three years from her age.

In 1907 Oscar Hammerstein I brought Garden to the United States as one of the stars of his new Manhattan Opera Company. Knowing American audiences might find her style and repertory strange and hard to comprehend, she insisted that he import whole cast and production ensembles from the Opéra-Comique in Paris as well. Together Garden and the fiercely competitive impresario, resplendent at every opening with his tall silk hat and big cigar, opened a new era of opera in this country. Garden learned the use of newspaper publicity as a star tool, and it kept her name in the headlines for thirty years. Her forte was the dockside interview. Every autumn she literally sailed into town, carrying a swagger stick, tossing her Russian furs, showing a peek of lemon-colored stocking. A *New York Times* reporter wondered how she got along with Oscar Hammerstein. "Treats me worse than a chorus girl." Had she married? "I am wearing a wedding ring, but I can't talk about the man now. You must wait until he comes over to carry me to his

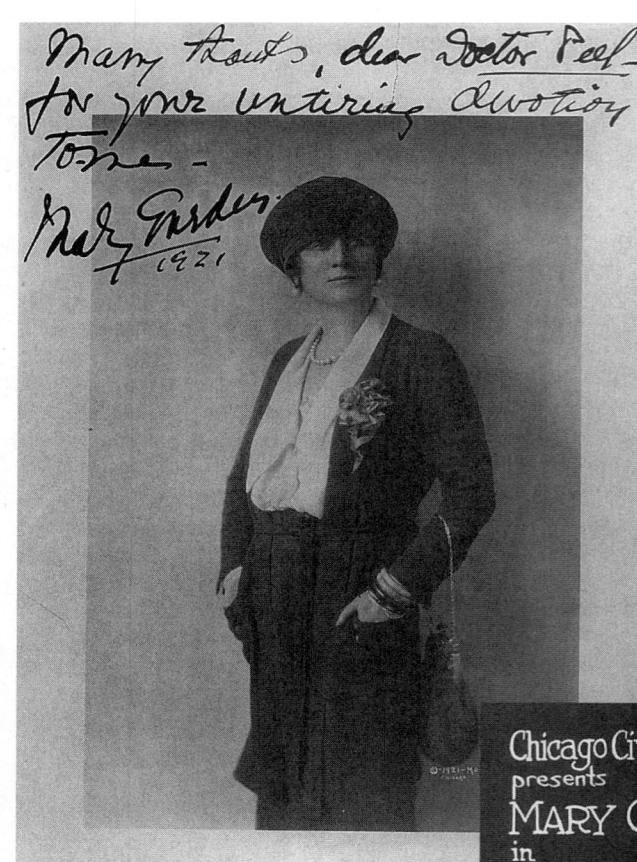

FIG. 37. *Opera diva Mary Garden, pictured in 1921, also served as the director of the Chicago Opera Company.*

FIG. 38. *This poster of Mary Garden as Salome advertised the opera singer's controversial 1921 performance with the Chicago Civic Opera Company.*

mountain fastnesses" (October 26, 1910), she explained. The *Chicago Tribune* wanted her opinion on Prohibition? "I hope the world goes dry" (December 26, 1920).

During the Hammerstein era the debate was joined about Garden's voice. "Yes, but can she sing?" was the question of the hour, with critics sharply divided between those who worshipped her with a cult-like fervor—"Mariolatry" they called it—and those who declared her voice completely gone, if she ever had one. Though Hammerstein laughed off the controversy as good for business, Mary Garden maintained to the end of her career that most critics were "dried up old men" (*Evening Post*, May 8, 1920), but she did not care, since it was only the public that mattered.

Following the Manhattan Opera's third season, the company was bought out and moved intact to Chicago, where a group of wealthy opera devotees, headed by Harold and EDITH ROCKEFELLER McCORMICK were forming the Chicago Grand Opera Company. This new entity assumed responsibility for the Manhattan's scenery, costumes, scores, copyrights, and contracts with several artists, including Mary Garden.

Garden made her first Chicago appearance with this company on November 5, 1910, opening in *Pelleas et Mélisande*. It was a courageous choice, for just as in Paris, the audience was puzzled by this moody ambiguous music-drama. Yet the public and such local critics as Glenn Dillard Gunn all understood that, culturally, "Chicago is on trial before the world" (*Chicago Tribune*, September 11, 1910), and they were prepared to give this prestigious new enterprise their unqualified support. Later that season this civic enthusiasm was put to the test when Garden appeared as the corrupt princess in Richard Strauss's *Salome*. Swathed in spangled orange veils, her perverse and lustful eyes burning below a cropped dark wig, Garden performed the Dance of the Seven Veils herself, apparently doing unmentionable things with her body and later with the severed head of John the Baptist. The Chicago Chief of Police pronounced it disgusting. "Miss Garden wallowed around like a cat in a bed of catnip," he told reporters (*Chicago Tribune*, November 29, 1910). Arthur Burrage Farwell, President of the Chicago Law and Order League, denounced her as a "great degenerator of the public morals" (quoted in Moore, 75). Garden replied, "Any one whose morals could have been corrupted by seeing 'Salomé' must already have degenerated" (quoted in Moore, 75). The chief offered to back off if she would "'tone down' her Dance of the Seven Veils" (p. 75), but Garden adamantly refused, and the whole production was withdrawn after two performances. However, by the end of this controversial first season, Garden was firmly established as the dominant personality of the new Chicago Grand Opera Company, and somehow her artistic authority and flamboyant self-confidence had now transferred to the city itself. Thereafter she was always "Our Mary" (*Chicago Tribune*, November 29, 1910).

For the next two decades, except for a few years during World War I when she remained abroad to raise money for French hospitals, Garden was the mainspring of the Chicago opera stage. Critic Vincent Sheean asserted that, with the collaboration of two superb conductors, Cleofonte Campanini (1910–19) and Giorgio Polacco (1921–31), she retained discretionary powers over every production in which she appeared.

Among her favorites were *Monna Vanna, Resurrection,* and *Le Jongleur de Notre Dame,* in which she sang the role of a young boy juggler. Critics raved over her performance as Flora in *L'Amore dei Tre Re.* Her *Carmen* interpretation was always debated. Some found it frigid. She sang in French whenever possible, though she was a good sport about singing English in Victor Herbert's light opera *Natoma.* She was always a champion of new music and untried composers, most prominently Hamilton Forrest and his Debussean jazz opera *Camille,* which the Chicago Civic Opera staged at her behest in December 1930.

Her fans said Garden was the best press agent Chicago ever had. By some accounts she made 1,225 touring performances with the Chicago opera, not counting her many solo concert appearances in convention halls, stadiums, and even vaudeville houses, where she vamped the crowds in her backless "gown of a thousand mirrors" (*New York Times*, November 20, 1919). During the 1922–23 season she began to broadcast on radio. She made two movies for Sam Goldwyn (*Thais*, 1917, and *The Splendid Sinner*, 1918), though her operatic allure failed to translate on screen. Meanwhile, her name became a familiar trademark. There was Parfum Mary Garden, Crane's Mary Garden Chocolates, a dessert called Peche Mary Garden, even a new road leading to the Mt. Rushmore Memorial named the Mary Garden Highway. Everywhere she raved about Chicago. Arriving at Union Station, she declared to the *Chicago Tribune,* "I want to breathe the smoke and hear the rattle and bang in the streets. There's no place in the world like home" (November 24, 1913).

Probably the peak of her Chicago opera career was the 1921–22 season, when she served as the company's general manager—or "Directa," as she preferred to be addressed. On the brink of divorce, Harold and Edith Rockefeller McCormick announced the end of their regime as principal guarantors. Wishing to make a last magnificent gesture, they insisted that only Mary Garden could orchestrate a suitably lavish finale to their dozen years of patronage. Other members were hesitant about a woman impresario, but her election was cheered by the general public. The papers proclaimed her "Mary the First!" During her tenure, however, Garden received various assassination threats, which she fearlessly publicized. The worst was a pistol and a box of cartridges, which arrived with a note that the sender hoped soon to be "seeing your body floating down the Chicago River" (*Chicago Tribune*, January 7, 1922).

In a decision that foretold some of her difficulties, she declined any pay for her administrative duties but assigned herself eighteen performances at her usual fee of twenty-five hundred dollars each. She gave a glorious season, bringing Giorgio Polacco from Italy as chief conductor (though Arturo Toscanini was her first choice) and presenting a glittering vocal roster that included such new singers as Claire Dux and Edith Mason. She staged the first American performances after World War I of Richard Wagner's operas in German, revived Giacomo Puccini's *Girl of the Golden West* for ROSA RAISA, and reappeared herself as the contentious Salome. Perhaps the season's highlight was the December 30, 1921, sumptuously produced world premiere of Sergei Prokofiev's *The Love for Three Oranges.*

While artistically successful, it was a turbulent year backstage. Many expensive singers had been signed on, and some of them appeared on the program only once or twice. New music required many costly rehearsals with full orchestra. Garden's dual role as manager and artist stoked dressing room intrigue and petty feuds. The company ended the year with a "deficiency" (her term) of $1.1 million and Garden concluded, "My place is with the artists, not over them" (*New York Times*, April 24, 1922). Samuel Insull, new president of the now renamed Civic Opera Company, accepted her resignation with the acknowledgment that Miss Garden throughout had been "really manly" (*New York Times*, April 25, 1922).

The stage was Mary Garden's life. Though she had a compelling effect on men and women alike, her private life was a largely solitary matter. For most of her Chicago years she lived alone in a large suite at the Blackstone Hotel, and she managed to avoid local society almost entirely. Her eating and drinking habits were ascetic, supplemented by a nightly glass of milk diluted with ten drops of iodine, which she believed toned the nervous system. Many summers were spent in a villa near Monte Carlo in Monaco, where she liked boating and swam nude in the Mediterranean. She reveled in the excitements of the casino and frequently bet on prize fights.

Mary Garden never married. During her lifetime her lurid stage roles gave rise to rumors of illicit passions, and Garden certainly exploited the publicity value of this gossip, expounding on a whole cast of lovestruck suitors. She did write of a man she called her longest romance, a handsome married millionaire with whom she enjoyed some poignant communion before his drinking and jealousy poisoned the affair. Several contemporaries convincingly identified this man as J. Ogden Armour, the Chicago meatpacker. It is doubtful, however, that Garden maintained any emotional or even sexual partnerships in the ordinary sense. She told the readers of *Ladies Home Journal* that marriage and children, while a fine adventure for some women, were "not for the great artiste" (September 1930, 180). Nor was this decision a sacrifice. In her prime her sexuality was completely at the service of her stage performances and was surely at the root of her profound dramatic impact. She once told a reporter, as applause drowned the opera hall, "When a man can do *that* to me, . . . I will marry him" (quoted in Armitage, 59). There is some suggestion that later on, in her fifties and sixties, she made tentative advances toward attractive younger men and was rebuffed.

Mary Garden retired from Chicago opera in 1931 and sang her last performance at the Opera-Comique in 1934. The following year she gave a series of master classes at the Chicago Musical College and served for a time as a talent scout and musical adviser to MGM movie studios. Her generosity and kindness inspired a long list of protégés, in whom she tried to rouse her own native stage intelligence. In June 1940, as the Germans neared Paris, she took her mother home from that city to Aberdeen, where she lived for the duration of the war. Aberdeen remained her principal residence for the rest of her life. In the late 1940s and early 1950s Garden returned to the United States for a series of lecture-reminiscences. She published an autobiography widely criticized as a gushy pastiche that obscured the real distinction of her career.

Garden's last years were spent in the theaters and tearooms of Aberdeen. After a fall in 1962 in which she broke both arms, she entered a hospital and then a nursing home, where she died of pneumonia at the age of ninety-three. She was cremated in Aberdeen, and her ashes were scattered there in the Garden of Remembrance.

During her lifetime Mary Garden was celebrated as the consummate singing actress who advanced the modern French repertory and style, most notably in her creation of Debussy's poetic Mélisande. Over the years her reputation has devolved in some quarters to the rank of "operatic personality." Critics then and now fault her voice, which was never opulent, though intense and sonorous in the lower registers. "I used my voice to color my roles" (Garden and Biancolli, 289), she said in her autobiography. Her recordings, therefore, can only convey one aspect of her interpretive art. Perhaps her achievements were more tellingly compromised by a kind of naive self-absorption, which probably played a part in her preference for the exotic roles so frequently found in second-rate musical vehicles. At her best, she was a hypnotic and thrilling stage presence, and she put her unique print on every role she played. To Chicago she brought artistic verve and continental glamour at a time when the city hungered for cultural standing.

Sources. Unpublished materials are available in the special collections of NL (including the Auditorium Theatre scrapbooks), CHS, and Northern Illinois Univ. (the depository of records from the variously named Chicago opera companies from 1910 forward). Mary Garden wrote the first substantial account of her life in a six-part autobiographical series in *Ladies Home Journal*, which appeared in the January through September 1930 issues, including "The Climb," March 1930. *Mary Garden's Story* (with Louis Biancolli) was published in 1951. Myles Fellowes's profile, "Here Is Mary Garden," appeared in *Étude*, April 1952, with a vivid account of her debut and a summary of her advice to young singers. The first general biography, *Mary Garden*, was written by Michael Turnbull (1997). She is much discussed in some general books about the American opera scene, including Edward Moore's *Forty Years of Opera in Chicago* (1930), John Frederick Cone's *Oscar Hammerstein's Manhattan Opera Company* (1964), and Ronald L. Davis's *Opera in Chicago* (1966). She is an admired fixture in the critical writings of William Armstrong, Richard D. Fletcher, James Gibbons Huneker, Vincent Sheean, Oscar Thompson, Virgil Thomson, Carl Van Vechten, and Edward Wagenknecht. Charles L. Wagner, who managed many of her concert tours, describes her in *Seeing Stars* (1940), and his associate, Merle Armitage, who frequently accompanied her on tour, wrote a brief but shrewd appraisal in *Accent on America* (1944). The triumphs and crises of Garden's career were extensively played out in the daily press, including many articles in CT and NYT, and in the major musical periodicals of the day as well. Selected articles are cited above. See the CT November 26 through December 7, 1910, for many stories about the Salome controversy discussed in the text. Issues of the NYT, January 7 through April 1922, cover events surrounding her resignation as director of the Civic Opera Company. She rebukes the critics in the (New York) *Evening Post*, May 8, 1920. Selections from Garden's acoustical recordings (Pathe—1903, G&T—1904, Edison—1905, Columbia 1911–12) and her complete electronic recordings for Victor (1926–29) are currently available on compact disc, and a complete discography (together with a comprehensive list of her performances) can be found in the June 1996 issue of the *Record Collector*.

CELIA HILLIARD

GARDNER, HELEN
March 17, 1878–June 4, 1946
ART HISTORIAN, AUTHOR, EDUCATOR

Born in Manchester, New Hampshire, Helen Gardner was the youngest of four children. Her mother, Martha Washington (Cunningham) Gardner, was born in Swanville, Maine, and her father, Charles Frederick Gardner, was born in Hingham, Massachusetts. Gardner and her two sisters, Effie and Louise, never married. Her brother, Edward L. Gardner, died in the year of his birth.

Gardner's family moved from New England to the Hyde Park neighborhood of Chicago around 1890. (She retained her New England accent throughout her life.) The Gardner family transferred to the Hyde Park Baptist Church from the Memorial Baptist Church, Chicago, in September 1892. Gardner remained an active member of the church and a Hyde Park resident for the next fifty-four years. Gardner's father was a "merchant tailor and a Baptist deacon" (Allen, "Helen Gardner," 14). He owned a men's clothing store in downtown Chicago that featured imported textiles from England. In 1893, he formed the partnership Gardner and McMillen and subsequently relocated his new business nearby.

From 1894 to 1897, Gardner attended Hyde Park High School. Gardner was a member of the Ray Literary Society, a debate and public speaking club, and of the King's Daughters Union Society, a young women's Christian organization. Gardner's early studies in Latin and Greek at the school set the intellectual framework for what would later emerge as an insightful appreciation of classical cultures.

Receiving a scholarship in 1897, Gardner continued her studies at the University of Chicago and graduated in 1901 with an A.B. degree with honors in Latin and Greek. Among her activities as a student, Gardner was a member of the Renaissance Society; Phi Beta Kappa; the Spelman House, a young ladies' religious organization; and the Women's Graduate Club. She was also treasurer for the YWCA in 1900 and 1901.

After graduation, Gardner began teaching at the Brooks Classical School, a private girls' school, on Adams Street in Chicago. Gardner's sister Effie was principal at the school, and her sister Louise was an instructor. Gardner was promoted to assistant principal in 1905 and remained in this position until 1910.

Gardner's interest in art may have resulted from her travels to Egypt, Greece, and Europe during the next five years. Though the source of Gardner's interest cannot be confirmed, she returned to the University of Chicago in 1915 to embark on the study of art history. She "received a master's degree in 1917, writing as her thesis 'A Critical Chart of Florentine Painting of the Fifteenth Century,' and was awarded a fellowship in the department of art history for 1917–18" (Allen, "Helen Gardner," 14). She then continued to take art history courses in the department until 1922.

"About 1919 . . . Gardner was appointed head of the photograph and lantern-slide department at the Ryerson Library of the Art Institute of Chicago" (Allen, "Helen Gardner," 14). The following year, she was hired by the School of the Art Institute of Chicago (SAIC) to teach the first art history survey course at the school. Gardner subsequently resigned from the library position in 1922 and began to develop an art history curriculum.

Responding to the lack of an adequate art history survey text, Gardner wrote *Art through the Ages: An Introduction to Its History and Significance*, which was published in 1926. This book was one of the first texts to acknowledge the underlying conditions and religious beliefs within historical periods yet also consider works of art apart from their particular economic and political contexts. Gardner's achievement was to analyze the universal design elements inherent in each work, offering a key with which to open up an understanding and appreciation of art from all cultures and historic periods. As described by former student and SAIC professor emerita Andrene Kauffman, Gardner "had an uncanny ability, it seemed, to give you the essentials of every period so that you could compare one civilization with another and really see what made them the same, not only different, but what made art the core of human expression" (quoted in *Over A Century*, 84).

In the same year that *Art through the Ages* was published, KATHLEEN BLACKSHEAR began teaching the survey of art history at SAIC. Gardner and Blackshear subsequently developed a close relationship that lasted for twenty years. Both teachers took their students to such sites as the Field Museum of Natural History, the Oriental Institute, the Shedd Aquarium, the Lincoln Park and Brookfield Zoos, the Adler Planetarium, and the Museum of Science and Industry. Studying objects in collections that were primarily anthropological and scientific, students were encouraged to see these objects both as art and as everyday, utilitarian artifacts. With their pan-disciplinary, cross-cultural approach to teaching, Gardner and Blackshear fostered a sensitivity in students to systems of abstract patterning in the natural world and in manufactured objects. Divorced from their strictly utilitarian or natural settings, these objects became means by which students could appreciate the equivalences among objects, reconfigured from one cultural or historical genre to another as unique variations on universal patterning themes. In Gardner's and Blackshear's view, this learning process expanded Western conventions of art by challenging the ritualistic and restricted place of art in society. The objects were liberated from their display as specimens to stand as beautiful tools that served the agricultural, administrative, medical, and spiritual needs of the societies in which they originated. The radicalizing effect of these objects on the cognitive and imaginative process of the students began with study of the objects as sites of design rather than sites of use. Freed from both the museum case and from their pragmatic place in space and time, these objects became charged lessons in the interactive roles of object, art, and community. The outcome of this lesson was contemporary art production with the same integrated function.

This approach to making and viewing art was complemented in the programming philosophy of SAIC's industrial arts division. Charles F. Kelley, dean and assistant director of the Art Institute of Chicago (AIC), noted in 1933 that students are in training for "aesthetic engineering" (McDowell). These students are "not merely designers of pretty patterns which have no practical purpose . . . [but are artists] specializing in design as it is applied to . . . books, printed textiles and wall paper . . . as well as interior architecture and architectural sculpture" (McDowell). Kelley's assertion, made in the midst of the Great Depression, was shaped by the interactive influence of two opposing curricular philosophies then current at SAIC. For although the mission of the curriculum was shared by both camps, its implementation took two distinct courses. Concerned with the power of art as a constructive and beneficial impetus to cultural progress, one camp built its arguments around the transcendental claims of pure aestheticism; the other camp aligned with the economic imperatives of the day, which demanded productive, pragmatic careers of its graduates.

This split was nowhere better illustrated than in two dramatic Chicago art events of the decade: AIC's 1926 acquisition and exhibition of the Helen Birch Bartlett Memorial Collection and the founding of Josephine Logan's Sanity in Art organization in 1936. Purchased by Chicago painter and museum trustee Frederic Clay Bartlett, the Birch Bartlett Collection was one of the most public embodiments of aesthetic art. Consisting of twenty-three paintings by modern French artists, including Georges Seurat, Paul Cezanne, Vincent van Gogh, and Paul Gauguin, this collection was revolutionary because it legitimized modes of non-Western perception even as it appropriated these modes for Western sensibilities. The Sanity in Art Group not only attacked the aesthetics of modernism explicit in the Birch Bartlett Collection but also advocated a particular aesthetic that was traditional, realistic, and well-crafted. Logan's disdain for modern art was shared by Eleanor Jewett, art critic for the *Chicago Tribune*, who several years earlier "labeled Cezanne, Gauguin, and Van Gogh 'brutal, primitive, and childish'" (Prince, 105). Jewett viewed "modernist works as products of insanity, which reflected a diseased mind or worse yet, a diseased soul" (Prince, 112). Logan and Jewett turned the pure aesthetics of the Birch Bartlett Collection into tools with which they defamed artists who did not make the "right" kind of art.

During this decade, Gardner published a second book, *Understanding the Arts* (1932), and was also busy preparing a revised edition of *Art through the Ages*. In the second edition, published in 1936, Gardner "went far beyond the first, including and expanding on arts from the non-Western world, the great civilizations of the Orient, and the arts of Africa, Oceania and aboriginal America" (Halstead, 5). The broader compass of Gardner's revised edition of *Art through the Ages* was almost certainly in response to a longstanding and increasingly vociferous dismissal of "insane" art. As suggested by Gardner's and Blackshear's successor, Whitney Halstead, Gardner's "achievement was to make clear the underlying formal basis which gave meaning to the prehistoric axe as well as to the Picasso" (Halstead, 5). Through the use of descriptive text and analytical drawings by Blackshear, Gardner showed how such realistic objects as an axe and aesthetic art by artists such as Picasso are formally equivalent. She thereby demonstrated how artists of all times, cultures, and aesthetic persuasions share the same universal principles in their art-making processes. In so doing, Gardner not only suggested a resolution for the debate between proponents of aesthetic art and its critics but also established a precedent for museum education practices later employed by Katharine Kuh in her crusade for modern art at the AIC's Gallery of Art Interpretation.

Gardner's aesthetic theory gained popular support both inside and outside the classroom. Her publisher, Harcourt, Brace and Company, sold more than one hundred sixty-one thousand copies of the second edition of *Art through the Ages* as textbooks and in general bookstores. In 1944, the second edition was also reprinted as a special two-volume paperback edition for the United States Armed Forces Institute. Harold Allen, SAIC photography teacher and a former student of Gardner, recalled "her fascinating fusion of cultivated scholar and warm, sensitive, generous person. Part of her charm was her uninhibited response to nature, which she loved with all the warmth and wonder she brought to art" ("Helen Gardner: Quiet Rebel," 163). A January 9, 1960, "Talk of the Town" column in the *New Yorker* described her as a "small, brown-eyed woman, . . . a quietly gay person who had conservative principles, a subtle sense of humor, and prodigious energy" (p. 17).

In March 1943, Gardner took an eighteen-month leave of absence from SAIC in order to write an expanded third edition of *Art through the Ages*. Gardner's writing was interrupted shortly thereafter by the discovery of metastatic cancer to her spinal vertebrae following a previous diagnosis of breast cancer and a mastectomy in 1942. In an effort to control her great physical discomfort, Gardner underwent a second surgical procedure in February 1944 that involved an injection to the root of a spinal nerve. The procedure proved unsuccessful and Gardner subsequently resigned from her position as professor of the history of art at the end of her eighteen-month leave. Gardner was retained by SAIC in an advisory capacity in exchange for a yearly pension of seven hundred dollars. Despite her failing health, Gardner continued to work on *Art through the Ages* with the assistance of Harold Allen, whom she hired in January 1946. When Gardner entered Presbyterian Hospital in Chicago on April 6, 1946, the third edition of *Art through the Ages* was in galley proof. Gardner remained hospitalized until the time of her death from bronchopneumonia. Survived by her sisters, Gardner was buried next to her parents in the family plot at Oak Woods Cemetery, Chicago.

Following Gardner's death, Allen, with the assistance of Blackshear, continued to work with Harcourt, Brace and Company on the third edition of *Art through the Ages* until it was published in 1948. Gardner's sister, Louise, subsequently sold Gardner's research papers, slides, and the rights to *Art through the Ages* to Harcourt, Brace and Company. A fourth edition of *Art through the Ages*, revised by the Department of the History of Art, Yale University, was published in 1959 and revised again in 1970, 1975, 1980, and 1986.

Helen Gardner's aesthetic theory, which validated modern and non-Western art, influenced many cohorts of students inside and outside SAIC. Indeed, her impact extended decades beyond her death.

Sources. Helen Gardner's papers and Harold Allen's papers are at the Department of Archives at the Art Institute of Chicago. Additional information was obtained from Kathleen Blackshear's papers, the Archives of American Art, Smithsonian Institution; the Ryerson Library at the Art Institute of Chicago; from Harold Allen; and from Jane Terrell, wife of William J. Terrell Sr., executor of the Blackshear estate. Further information is available from transcripts of oral interviews with Norman Lewis Rice and Harold Allen, conducted by Carole Tormollan in 1994 and copyrighted by the Art Institute of Chicago. Helen Gardner's published works include *Art through the Ages: An Introduction to Its History and Significance* (1926, revised edition 1936, 1948); *Under-*

standing the Arts (1932). Biographical information about Gardner can be found in the School of the Art Institute of Chicago, *Over a Century: A History of the School of the Art Institute of Chicago, 1866–1981* (1982); "Centennial of Helen Gardner's Birth," *Crumbs*, March 28, 1978, and April 3, 1978; Harold Allen, "Helen Gardner," *NAW* (1971). See Malcolm McDowell, "Art Engineering Latest Entrant in Professions," *Chicago Daily News*, December 14, 1933; Sue Ann Prince, "'Of the Which and the Why of Daub and Smear': Chicago Critics Take on Modernism," in *The Old Guard and the Avant-Garde: Modernism in Chicago, 1910–1940*, ed. Sue Ann Prince (1990); Whitney Halstead, "Art History Department," *Quarterly 12*, Spring 1976. Additional information is in Carole Tormollan, *A Tribute to Kathleen Blackshear* (1990); Harold Allen, "Helen Gardner: Quiet Rebel," in *Sacred Spaces and Other Places: A Guide to Grottos and Sculptural Environments in the Upper Midwest*, ed. Lisa Stone and Jim Zanzi (1993); "The Talk of the Town," the *New Yorker*, December 5, 1959, and January 9, 1960.

CAROLE TORMOLLAN

GARNETT BUTLER TALLEY, ISABELLA MAUDE
August 22, 1872–August 23, 1948
PHYSICIAN, HOSPITAL FOUNDER AND ADMINISTRATOR

HILL, ELIZABETH WEBB
November 28, 1898–May 3, 1978
PHYSICIAN, HOSPITAL CHIEF OF STAFF

Isabella Garnett and Elizabeth Webb were involved in the founding and growth of Community Hospital in north suburban Evanston, Illinois, where they worked together for fifteen years. Hospital care became increasingly segregated after 1910, and Community Hospital was established to provide the place needed for African American patients and staff. Garnett's role centered on the initial development of the hospital, while Hill carried on the work at the later stages.

Isabella Maude Garnett was born in Evanston, Illinois, to Daniel F. Garnett, a shoemaker, and Hannah B. (McDuffin) Garnett. One of the first African American families to settle in Ridgeland Village (later part of Evanston), the Garnetts emigrated to Illinois from Kentucky, possibly as early as 1850. In November 1870, Garnett's parents and six other African American couples founded the Second Baptist Church of Evanston in the Garnett's home. Isabella Garnett was one of seven children. She had three known brothers: William, a dentist; Dexter Mills, active in the Evanston Republican organization of Ward Five, where the majority of Blacks lived, and the first African American appointed to a political job in Evanston; and John, a machinist; and at least two sisters: Emma Georgiana, who in 1885 was the first African American to graduate from Evanston Township High School; and Grace, a hairdresser. Two years after Garnett's birth, her mother died. In 1878, her father married Mary E. Parker of Chicago.

Garnett attended Evanston Township High School but did not graduate. She left Evanston around 1890 and took courses for two years at a business college in Minneapolis, Minnesota, where she lived with an older sister. From 1892 to 1894, she also worked in Minneapolis as a printer for the Western L Rub Company.

In 1894, Garnett returned to Illinois and entered Provident Hospital and Nurses Training School on Chicago's South Side.

Provident, established as an interracial institution that would provide nursing training for black women who were not admitted to existing nursing schools, was the only institution in Illinois where an African American could receive medical training. Controlled by African Americans, Provident was founded in 1891 by heart surgeon Daniel Hale Williams. While at Provident, Isabella Garnett worked under Williams.

After receiving her nursing degree in 1895, Garnett returned to Evanston and worked as a school nurse. She had long before determined that she wanted to become a doctor and had taken up nursing to work her way through medical school. She credited her brother William Garnett with influencing her to pursue the long and difficult studies.

From 1897 to 1899, Garnett attended Harvey Medical College in Chicago, completing the first two years of course work. Harvey was a coeducational night school, geared to students who worked during the day. Her courses were certified by the school's secretary, Dr. FRANCES DICKINSON, who later became president and owner. While enrolled at Harvey, Garnett received, on July 5, 1898, a Certificate of Entrance to Medical College, documenting that she had passed an examination on required premedical courses given in high school or college. The Illinois State Board of Health had made such certification a requirement under the Medical Practice Act of January 4, 1898. She was then accepted at the College of Physicians and Surgeons (now the University of Illinois at Chicago College of Medicine), from which she received an M.D. degree on July 1, 1901, making her one of the first African American women physicians in Illinois. She did her internship and hospital work at Provident. Garnett then entered private practice on Chicago's South Side. By 1904, she moved her practice to Evanston, where she shared office space with her brother William Garnett.

Three years later, on January 5, 1907, Garnett married Arthur DeLyon Butler, a medical student who had come to Evanston in 1904 from Atlanta, Georgia. Garnett continued in private practice while her husband attended school, receiving his medical degree from Northwestern University Medical School in 1909. About that time they adopted a son, Arthur Garnett Butler. During all of her years of practice, she maintained her maiden name, always being known professionally as Dr. Garnett.

During the early part of the twentieth century, the number of African Americans living in Evanston continued to grow. Their proportion and numbers increased from 1,160 black residents in 1910 (5 percent of the total population), to 2,522 in 1920 (7 percent) to 4,938 in 1930 (8 percent). After 1910, hospitals in Evanston would not admit black patients except for emergency conditions. African Americans needing hospital care had to go to Provident Hospital, Cook County Hospital, or the Research Hospital of the University of Illinois, all on Chicago's South or Near West Sides.

To meet the needs of the African American population in Evanston, and to realize her longtime goal of having her own hospital, Garnett and her husband received a permit from Evanston on May 12, 1914, to open the Evanston Sanitarium and Training School in their frame house on Asbury Avenue. The house became a hospital, and they lived in a cottage behind it. Butler did surgery, and Garnett was in general practice, delivering babies and administering anesthesia for the surgeries. While the fourteen-bed hospital received some outside financial aid, including a few monetary gifts from community clubs, it was supported largely by income from Garnett's and Butler's private practices.

Tragedy struck in April 1923 when Butler contracted what was believed to be tuberculosis. In January 1924 he underwent surgery at St. Francis Hospital in Evanston, where a growth was removed from his lung. His health worsened, and on March 27, 1924, he died at age forty-four in the Evanston Sanitarium. He was buried in Rosehill Cemetery in Chicago. The next year, in December 1925, Garnett's brother William, an active Republican, died of a heart attack after delivering a political speech in Chicago. He was interred in the recently opened Sunset Cemetery (now Sunset Memorial Lawns) in Glenview, Illinois, where several months earlier Garnett had been among the first to purchase lots for a proposed cemetery exclusively for African Americans.

From 1924 to 1928, Isabella Garnett carried on the management of the hospital alone. She perceived that she could not continue to operate her establishment much longer without proper funding. The facilities at the sanitarium were limited, and seriously ill patients still had to endure the long trip to Cook County Hospital in Chicago.

In 1924 a group of women from the First Methodist Church of Evanston who were concerned with health requirements of the black community had established the Inter-Racial Cooperative Council. Two years later the council formed the Booker T. Washington Association, under President Clyde D. Foster, to work toward a hospital. The association soon became the Community Hospital of Evanston. In 1928, the council, a biracial group, commissioned Dr. William W. Walsh of Chicago to study the need for a hospital to serve Evanston's African American community. Walsh's report found that, except in rare circumstances, African Americans in Evanston were dependent for hospitalization on only four institutions—the three Chicago hospitals and Garnett's small sanitarium in Evanston. He noted, however, that Dr. Garnett's institution lacked up-to-date technical equipment and funds for maintenance.

Garnett expressed to Dr. Walsh a desire to surrender the charter of her hospital to any group that was willing to assume responsibility for the inauguration of a hospital program that would serve the medical needs of Evanston's growing African American population. Garnett believed that if a suitable hospital were established for the care of African American patients, it would be well patronized. Walsh recommended that a hospital for African Americans with a minimum of fifty beds be built in Evanston. Finally, on April 17, 1928, the two organizations— Community Hospital and Evanston Sanitarium—merged. Clyde D. Foster as president of Community invited Garnett to continue as superintendent, and she accepted.

The onset of the Great Depression prevented funding from being obtained for the proposed fifty-bed hospital. However, in 1930, Dr. A. Rudolph Penn, a well known African American physician, leased his home on Brown Avenue in Evanston to Community Hospital as an interim location. Anna Shuman Elliot, who with her husband Frank had given money to build Evanston Hospital, gave a gift of five thousand dollars for Com-

munity. The hospital was formally dedicated on December 7, 1930, and Garnett opened the doors the next day. In addition to two operating rooms, the building also had an X-ray department. While a great improvement over the original facilities, the new building had only an eighteen-bed capacity.

With the future of the hospital seemingly assured, Dr. Garnett turned attention to her personal life. On February 5, 1930, she married Rev. James Rayford Talley, a Baptist minister who was born in Augusta, Georgia. Talley was an organizer of the Emerson Young Men's Christian Association in Evanston and served as its first executive secretary.

In 1931, Dr. Elizabeth Webb Hill, who shared with Isabella Garnett a commitment to the African American community, joined the staff of Community Hospital. Born in Evanston, Hill was the daughter of Helen M. and James Preston Hill, a mail carrier and a horticulturist. During World War I he taught scientific gardening and the planning of "victory" gardens. She became interested in medicine when she was sixteen and worked as a secretary for a local physician after graduating from Evanston Township High School. Hill received a bachelor's degree from Northwestern University, then attended the University of Illinois medical school, graduating in 1929. She interned at Provident Hospital in Chicago. Because she was an African American, she was not able to obtain a residency, despite a two-year search. Instead, she borrowed fifty dollars for medical equipment, returned to Evanston and the yellow frame house her father had built, and set up her own practice. During these early depression years, Hill regularly accepted food in lieu of payment for services from patients who had no money. In addition to supplying medical services, Hill's house calls often included delivering buckets of coal to families who had no other means of heating their homes.

During the 1930s, lack of money continued to be a problem for Community Hospital. The number of hospitalizations increased, with fewer patients able to pay, and voluntary contributions, which the hospital needed to meet a greater part of its expenses, became more limited. At one point, the situation became so desperate that even though the hospital staff worked without pay for a number of months, the governing board believed closing was certain. Garnett convinced the board to keep the hospital operating under her management. In 1933, the Community Chest accepted responsibility for raising operating funds. Further help arrived in 1936, when Anna Shuman Elliot left Community Hospital fifty thousand dollars in her will. In 1937, the hospital used Elliot's bequest to purchase the building and grounds from Dr. Penn. Nevertheless, funding continued to be a problem.

In 1939, Elizabeth Hill founded a Woman's Auxiliary to help raise operating funds for the hospital. The auxiliary aided the hospital and worked for its improvement through numerous activities, including rummage sales, bazaars, and raffles. In later years, the auxiliary became the hospital's primary money raiser.

When not working at the hospital, Garnett was involved in a number of community activities. She was a member of the National Association for the Advancement of Colored People (NAACP), the Community Chest, the Old Settlers' Association, and the Second Baptist Church that her parents had cofounded. She organized an Illinois Club in the Second Baptist Church.

When the club held a tea in her honor, the donations were enough to pay off Second Baptist's mortgage. In the early 1940s, Garnett served as president of the Iroquois Club, an organization created in 1917 to provide a safe home that working African American women could afford. Known as North Shore Community House, the home opened in 1924.

In 1945 Hill became the hospital's chief of staff and a member of the board of directors. As Hill increased her responsibilities, Garnett confined her hospital duties to those of anesthetist and acting superintendent. She had hoped to return to private practice so that she could travel; but ill health, aggravated by constant exposure to anesthetics, prevented her from doing so. In early fall of 1946, Garnett retired as superintendent. After retirement, she spent most of her time at her home in Idlewild, Michigan, a town settled by Chicago-area African Americans as a summer resort.

In early 1948, the final day of National Negro Health Week was dedicated to Garnett. In a wheelchair, Isabella Garnett came to the podium to address the Evanston medical community. She died that year in Community Hospital as a result of uremia and hypertension associated with heart disease. Funeral services were held at the Second Baptist Church, and she was buried at Sunset Cemetery.

Meanwhile Hill, as chief of staff and continuing head of the Woman's Auxiliary, began a campaign to build a new hospital. By the mid-1940s, the hospital was outgrowing the Penn building, which required numerous repairs. The operating room was next to the furnace, raising fears of explosion if anesthetics other than ether or sodium pentothal were used. Under the federal Hill-Burton Act, which provided funds for hospital construction, Community received a grant of four hundred seventy thousand dollars in 1949 as matching funds to money raised, and a campaign was begun for funds to build the fifty-bed hospital envisioned since Walsh's report in 1929.

However, the project for a new hospital aroused controversy. The NAACP and some members of the Inter-Racial Council opposed the plans on the grounds that an all black hospital perpetuated segregation. When the hospital requested a lease from the Sanitary District of Chicago—the sewage disposal agency— for two acres in Evanston, J. B. Martin, a black member of the district board, objected to the lease because he saw Community as a "Jim Crow" Hospital. Elizabeth Hill contended that the sick could not wait for desegregation and fought the NAACP and others who would prevent the construction of a new hospital. Evanston Hospital was accepting African Americans only as outpatients. St. Francis Hospital, which had inpatient service only, did not allow any African American patients except for rare emergencies. After three weeks of controversy, the Community board agreed that the hospital would be interracial for both patients and staff. On October 5, 1952, the new fifty-six-bed Community Hospital was dedicated as an interracial facility. Elizabeth Hill remained chief of the medical staff of twenty-two physicians. Under Hill's leadership, the hospital expanded its service to include patients coming from Chicago, who found the city clinics crowded and impersonal.

Hill saw community action as a necessary aspect of health care and served on several Evanston city commissions, including those dealing with planning and human relations. Concerned over the lack of adequate housing available to African American families in Evanston, she purchased and renovated numerous houses and apartments, renting them at affordable prices to African American families. She also supplied her neighbors and patients with fresh vegetables from her own garden. She was totally devoted to medical practice and never married; as her colleague Dr. Warren Spencer explained, "She just felt that the men she met didn't have the kind of dedication she demanded" (quoted in Gordon).

Hill's achievement as founder of the new hospital was honored beyond Evanston when, in 1969, Wilson College in Chambersburg, Pennsylvania, presented her with its Centennial Citation in recognition of her service to the community. In 1975 she was appointed to the faculty of Northwestern University School of Medicine and became a senior attending physician in internal medicine on the medical staff of Evanston Hospital. By then Evanston and St. Francis hospitals had become interracial for both patients and staff.

Hill remained chief of staff and continued to practice medicine until she suffered a stroke in March 1978. She never recovered and died three months later. Her funeral was attended by so many friends, patients, colleagues, and members of the community that the services had to be moved from her own St. Andrews Episcopal Church to the larger Ebenezer A.M.E. (African Methodist Episcopal) Church. She was buried at Sunset Cemetery just a few yards from Dr. Garnett.

At a time when hospital care in Evanston, Illinois, was virtually closed to African Americans, Isabella Garnett and Elizabeth Hill were leaders in developing hospital facilities for their community. In serving the needs of a growing African American population, Garnett moved from a small sanitarium to a community hospital, which, under Hill, ultimately provided service to all patients, regardless of race. In 1975, Evanston dedicated sixteen acres near Community Hospital as the Isabella G. Butler Park. Two years after Hill's death, Community Hospital, suffering chronic financial difficulties, closed. With other hospitals in Evanston open to African Americans, fewer black patients and physicians were coming to Community. In 1986 the building became a not-for-profit apartment complex for physically handicapped adults, where photographs of Hill and Garnett memorialize their accomplishments.

Sources. The Evanston Hist. Soc. has files on Isabella Garnett Butler and Elizabeth W. Hill, including numerous newspaper articles and personal recollections. The collection on Garnett has a brief typescript autobiography as well as a short history of the sanitarium and the hospital that she wrote on June 28, 1947. Information on Community Hospital can be found in both the files of the Evanston Hist. Soc. and the Evanston Public Library. The article, "Interracial Health," *Newsweek,* November 17, 1952, describes the controversy over funding Community Hospital. Historical information on the African American community of Evanston is found in W. H. Walsh, *Report of a Study of the Need for Hospital Accommodations for the Colored of Evanston, Illinois* (1929); the National Urban League, *Economic and Cultural Problems in Evanston, Illinois as They Relate to the Colored Population* (1945), a study done for the Evanston Council of Social Agencies; D. L. Goggins, *Pathways to an Era's Past: A Look at Evanston's West Side History* [1978]; and Kevin Barry Leonard, "Paternalism and the Rise of a Black Community in Evanston, Illinois: 1879–1930" (master's thesis, Northwestern Univ.,

1982). *Evanston Newsette,* August 27, 1948, contains an obituary of Isabella Garnett. Bill Gordon's obituary for Hill, "Doctor's 'Children' Say Goodbye," appears in the *Suburban Tribune,* May 8, 1978.

MARIANNE DREGER
PATRICIA C. WISHART

GARRETT, ELIZA CLARK
March 5, 1805–November 24, 1855
PHILANTHROPIST

Eliza Clark Garrett, the first woman to found a theological seminary, expanded women's traditional role in Christian benevolence. Clark grew up on a farm near Newburgh, New York, in a family with strong religious ideals. She had at least one brother, Jeremiah; but beyond that little is known about her family.

In 1825 she married Augustus Garrett, an enterprising young man who soon chafed under the limitations of sharing family farms with other siblings. After the birth of a daughter, Imogene, in 1830, the young couple left New York seeking a better life. The Garretts first tried to seek their fortune in Cincinnati, but they became so deeply in debt that they left the city to escape their creditors. Their next move was to New Orleans; although the city was rapidly expanding, becoming successful there often required the support of a tightly knit ethnic or kinship group, and the Garretts could claim no such affiliation.

Imogene died of cholera in 1833 and was buried in an unmarked grave along the Mississippi River. The next year she was followed by her brother Charles. The Garretts had a third child, John, whose birth date is not known. After realizing that New Orleans was closed to them, Eliza Garrett returned to Newburgh, while her husband tried his luck in Chicago.

Chicago was a rapidly growing town: when Augustus Garrett arrived in 1834, Chicago had only 400 residents; in 1856, shortly after Eliza Garrett died, the population had reached 86,000. Augustus Garrett established himself as a flashy auctioneer. He also dealt in real estate and fire and marine insurance and was a partner in a dry-goods firm. By 1835, when Eliza Garrett arrived from Newburgh, Garrett had already sold $1,800,000 worth of real estate. Eliza Garrett herself apparently acquired skills in the real estate business, for her letters to Methodist Bishop Leonidas Hamline and his wife, Melinda Hamline, indicated that she was working on real estate ventures on their behalf.

The Garretts were among the leaders of the expanding community. Augustus Garrett became the seventh and ninth mayor of Chicago in 1843 and 1845, in an era when businessmen were the city's political as well as commercial leaders. He was elected the eighth mayor in 1844, but he lost in the rerun when the election was contested.

Eliza Garrett became an active, loyal member of Clark Street Methodist Episcopal Church (now known as Chicago Temple, First United Methodist). The couple converted under the ministry of the Reverend Peter Borein. Borein was an impressive preacher, drawing large crowds to hear his compelling sermons. He was self-conscious about his poor education and expressed the need for more training. Borein's circumstances introduced Eliza Garrett to the problem of providing adequate formal training for Methodist ministers in the West.

Although often moved by Borein's message, Augustus Garrett was unable to maintain his high resolve to make a significant contribution to the church. With little warning, Augustus Garrett died of what was diagnosed as congestion of the brain on November 30, 1848, after an illness of only six days. Although there were times when he was alert and conscious enough to make arrangements for his funeral and disbursement of some personal items, he died without making any arrangements to endow a Christian institution, much to the disappointment of his wife. Despite her association with the worldly people who were part of her husband's political and business scene, she could be relied upon to support her church.

Garrett received nearly half of her husband's assets. She used a good portion of her allowance of one thousand dollars a year to pay off his debts resulting from fires that plagued Chicago. She was concerned that the debt be paid off for the economic well-being of the biblical institute she had decided to found. She moved into the house of friends, the W. S. Gurnees. This move enabled her to place herself on a budget of four hundred dollars a year, half of which she gave to charitable causes.

Garrett was introduced to the issues of the day through her participation in Clark Street Church. Her mentor and lawyer was Grant Goodrich, friend of Lincoln, supporter of abolition, and a founder of Rush Medical College and Northwestern University. He supported Garrett in her benevolent concerns and encouraged her interest in establishing a biblical institute.

In imagining the future of the West, Garrett foresaw the need for an educated clergy and for education for young women. In 1853, with the assistance of Grant Goodrich, she wrote her will, setting aside funds sufficient for the establishment of a biblical institute and providing room, board, and books for its students. Garrett directed that any proceeds left over from this venture be used to start a college for women. Because of Augustus Garrett's debts, such money was not available as she had hoped it would be. However, North Western Female College, a girls' preparatory school, was established near the university in 1854.

The founding of the biblical institute became a source of contention in the Rock River Annual Conference, the regional policy-making body of the Methodist Church. Garrett's support, especially her financial contribution, became crucial in the church's acceptance of the biblical institute. A contingent of the conference feared that too much education would cause a corrupted clergy. They also argued that there was no money to pay for such enterprises. At this point Garrett came forth and allowed her name, previously not used, to become associated with the institute. The association of her name with the institution as its benefactor became a decisive factor in the conference's acceptance of the institute.

An additional issue developed in 1853 when John Dempster, a Methodist preacher and educator from New England, arrived in Chicago. When Dempster passed through Chicago he was planning to go on to Bloomington, Illinois, to establish a seminary. He had previously founded the first Methodist seminary in the United States, the Biblical Institute of New England, in Vermont (later the Boston University School of Theology). When he arrived in Chicago on his way to Bloomington, he met the "Friends of Biblical Learning," a small group of Chicago Methodists, including Grant Goodrich, who supported the founding of a seminary in their area; and he discovered that Eliza Garrett had already formed the vision and made provision in her will for a theological seminary.

On December 26, 1853, Dempster met with the Chicago group and learned they had decided upon Evanston, a small farm community just north of Chicago, as the location for the new theological seminary. Evanston had the advantage of being far enough away from the city to avoid what were perceived as the temptations of the city. The 1853 meeting took place without the presence of Garrett, although none of the plans could have been realized without the leadership, vision, and financial support she provided.

Because of his experience in the East, Dempster felt the need to begin immediately. A delay, he feared, would heighten the chances of those who wished to abort the founding of the institute. Haste was also in order since Garrett, still a young woman, could have remarried. Had a remarriage taken place, under Augustus Garrett's will she would have lost her inheritance. By January 1, 1855, Garrett Biblical Institute had opened. Eliza Garrett and other Chicagoans came out in sleighs on New Year's Day to celebrate the joyous occasion.

The following November, Garrett came down with bilious colic, which caused congestion of the bowels. Although she had not been ill long, she sensed the approach of death. Goodrich was with her as she lay dying. As Goodrich described her death, she lifted up her hands and exclaimed "Bless the Lord, O my soul" (quoted in Buoy, 290).

Garrett's funeral was held at the Clark Street Methodist Episcopal Church. The *Northwestern Christian Advocate,* weekly newspaper of the Methodist church in the Midwest, carried a lengthy account of the funeral in its November 28, 1855, issue, describing the procession to Rosehill Cemetery on Chicago's northern outskirts as "one of the longest that ever moved from our city." It included the entire student body and faculty of Garrett Biblical Institute with its president, John Dempster, joined by faculty and students from Northwestern University and many notable Methodists and other Chicagoans who honored Garrett with their presence.

Eliza Clark Garrett found a way to shape the future of charitable giving. She provided a strategy for using her funds to found an institution that addressed issues facing the church in her day. Her concern for an educated ministry offered a means for women to help shape ministry in the developing Midwest.

Sources. Material on Eliza Garrett, including *The Letterbook of August Garrett* (1843–45), are in the Northwestern Univ. Archives. The Garrett-Evangelical Theological Seminary Archives have correspondence between Garrett and Bishop and Melinda Hamline, letters among early faculty, the will of Augustus Garrett, and early school catalogs. Short biographies of Garrett can be found in Frederick A. Norwood, *Dawn to Midday at Garrett* (1978); Abel Stevens, *Women of Methodist* (1866); A. D. Field, *Memorial of Methodism in the Bounds of the Rock River Conference* (1886); Charles Wesley Buoy, *Representative Women of Methodism* (1893). Ila Alexander Fisher, "Eliza Garrett—To Follow a Vision," in *Spirituality and Social Responsibility*, ed. Rosemary Skinner Keller (1993), draws upon all available material on Garrett.

ILA ALEXANDER FISHER

GASTON, LUCY PAGE
May 19, 1860–August 20, 1924
ANTI-CIGARETTE ACTIVIST

Lucy Page Gaston, who devoted her life to an anti-cigarette movement, was born in Delaware, Ohio, and raised in Lacon, Illinois. Her father, Alexander Hugh Gaston, was a nonsmoking, teetotaling abolitionist, who gained local fame as a horticulturist, planting the prairies with mulberry, elm, and cottonwood trees. Her mother, Henrietta (Page) Gaston, was an active member of the Woman's Christian Temperance Union (WCTU).

Gaston grew up in a home in which the spirit of reform was a strong presence. She began teaching Sunday school at thirteen; at sixteen, she was elected president of the Marshall County [Illinois] Sunday School Association. As a student at the Illinois State Normal School in Bloomington in 1881, she led raids on local saloons and gambling halls, smashing fixtures in a style that her friend, Carry Nation, the hatchet-wielding prohibitionist, would make famous. Her younger brother, Edward Page Gaston, was lecturing on the evils of drink by the time he was sixteen; he later became a prominent prohibitionist in Great Britain.

Gaston taught school in several small towns in Illinois during the 1880s. Her interest in cigarettes as a social issue dated from this period. She was disturbed by the number of boys she saw sneaking behind the schoolhouse to smoke; they developed a "cigarette face" (Warfield, 244), she said, and invariably failed their examinations. She wrote a pamphlet for the WCTU, warning that "thousands" of boys were "smoking like chimneys and headed straight for the saloon" (*Children's Temperance Work in Illinois*, 5). Gaston came to believe that furfural, an element in cigarette smoke, irritated the nervous system to such a degree that the smoker would invariably seek relief through alcohol, morphine, or other drugs. From there, it was a short path to poverty, crime, and moral collapse. In addition, she thought cigarettes caused heart disease and other health problems.

Early in 1893, Gaston moved with her parents to Harvey, Illinois, then being developed on the outskirts of Chicago by lumber magnate Turlington Harvey and evangelist Dwight L. Moody as a haven for the temperate and the devout. She left the schoolroom for journalism, working first as the woman's editor of the Harvey *Headlight* and later as managing editor and copublisher of a rival newspaper, the Harvey *Citizen*. When a saloon opened in 1895, defying town covenants, she condemned the operators as "hardened sinners" and recommended that their enterprise be subject to the "hatchet plan" ("Harvey's Danger," *Union Signal*, August 22, 1895). She also used the legal system, in one case winning an injunction to overturn an ordinance to permit saloons in Harvey. When the Cook County commissioners issued a saloon license despite the injunction, Gaston tried to have them arrested.

Her work attracted the notice of FRANCES E. WILLARD, the charismatic president of the WCTU in the 1880s and 1890s. Writing in the *Union Signal*, Willard applauded the "intellectual force and moral courage" that Gaston had demonstrated in Harvey during her "great struggle with the powers of darkness" (Willard, *Union Signal*, January 30, 1896). When Gaston's press was damaged, possibly by someone who took issue with her anti-saloon stand, Willard sent a personal check to help repair it.

FIG. 39. *Lucy Page Gaston,*
superintendent of the Anti-Cigarette
League.

Later, she recommended Gaston for an important position as national superintendent of the WCTU's Department of Christian Citizenship.

Gaston responded to this personal interest by becoming even more active in the WCTU. At the same time, she took steps to claim as her own an issue that the reform community had ignored: cigarette smoking. She was in her mid-thirties, unmarried, with some education, a gift for expression, and an evangelical spirit. Temperance work would have been a logical outlet for a woman with her background, interests, and ambitions. However, that field was a crowded one, with an abundance of generals. The opportunity presented by a largely unclaimed target seemed to have been the deciding factor in calling Gaston to what became her life's work.

In 1896, Gaston was named managing editor of the *Christian Citizen*, published in Chicago by the National Christian Citizenship League. The league was a nonpartisan effort to apply "Christian principles" to public affairs. Her brother, Edward Gaston, was a member of the executive committee. She endorsed woman suffrage, joined the Prohibition Party, and ran as the party's candidate for trustee of the University of Illinois. She finished eighth in a field of eighteen candidates for three positions. Gaston made no further forays into electoral politics until 1920, when she attempted a quixotic run for the presidency.

Increasingly, she devoted her energies to suppressing cigarettes. Recent developments in mass production and mass marketing had greatly increased the availability and lowered the cost of cigarettes, although they still accounted for less than 1 percent of total tobacco consumption. Gaston argued that the industry was both vulnerable, because it was relatively new, and danger-

ous, because it was expanding. She began haunting legislative and civic halls, demanding laws to ban the cigarette not only for minors but for everyone. She won a victory in 1897, when the Chicago City Council passed an ordinance prohibiting the sale of cigarettes containing "opium, morphine, jimpson [*sic*] weed, belladonna, glycerine or sugar" (*Proceedings of the City Council of Chicago*, 1714–15). As an added discouragement, the ordinance also required retailers to post a five hundred dollar bond and pay an annual license fee of one hundred dollars to sell a product that typically sold for five cents a package. She had less success in the Illinois legislature, where an anti-cigarette bill was approved by the House but defeated in the Senate.

Gaston became a full-time, professional activist in 1899, when she convinced a group of Chicago businessmen to organize the Anti-Cigarette League, with herself as superintendent. She attracted support by depicting cigarettes as conduits to other social problems, particularly to alcohol abuse. She also promised a swift victory, arguing that since cigarettes were less entrenched than many other evils plaguing humankind, they would be easier to dislodge. The prospect of success against one foe, no matter how small, had considerable allure for people interested in moral reform.

Gaston had a knack for garnering public attention and influential backers. Henry Ford and Thomas Edison both lent their names to the cause, as did John Harvey Kellogg, the health reformer and founder of the breakfast cereal dynasty; Benjamin B. Lindsey, a well-known juvenile court judge; Irving Fisher, a leading economist; Harvey W. Wiley, first director of the Food and Drug Administration; David Starr Jordan, first president of Stanford University; and other notable progressive reformers.

Perhaps her greatest triumph came in 1907, when she finally convinced the Illinois legislature to prohibit all commerce in "any cigarette containing any substance deleterious to health, including tobacco" (*Laws . . . Illinois*, 265). When the state Supreme Court declared the law unconstitutional six months later, she initiated a campaign to recall the judges. Failing that, she tried to revive the law. Between 1908 and 1917, the Illinois legislature considered twelve anti-cigarette bills, each one promoted by Gaston and the league.

In other states she was highly visible and indefatigable in campaigning against cigarettes. She traveled widely in the East and Midwest, lobbying, giving speeches, attending conferences, and seeking contributions and converts. She also promoted a stop-smoking "cure" that involved painting the smoker's throat with silver nitrate. The chemical reacted with elements in cigarette smoke to produce extreme nausea. Penitents who might be tempted to backslide were supplied with gentian root, which supposedly had tonic qualities when chewed. She took to carrying a supply of gentian root with her at all times, to be thrust upon any unwary smokers she chanced to encounter.

Eventually, Gaston's zeal undermined her effectiveness. Several key supporters changed their minds about the value of coercive measures, especially those aimed at adults. Gaston, a self-described extremist, remained committed to legislating cigarettes out of existence. To doubters, she offered a pamphlet titled *Why the Manufacture and Sale of Cigarettes Should Be Prohibited by Law* (1914). Conflict over the goals and tactics of the Anti-Cigarette League came to a head during World War I. Gaston was appalled by the distribution of cigarettes to American soldiers. "People seem to be entirely swept off their feet," she wrote to Newton D. Baker, secretary of war, "and the general impression prevails that as soon as a man puts on the uniform he must begin to dope up. . . . This, of course, is the greatest folly." If soldiers had to die, she added, they should do so "clean"—free from "an enslaving habit" whose effects "closely resemble the use of opium" (July 18, 1917).

This intemperate tone was a source of embarrassment for many of Gaston's former allies. It seemed unpatriotic, and it was certainly impolitic, to attack a commodity military leaders said was necessary to the victory of good over evil. Still, she had enough support within the league to hold onto her position until the end of the war. In 1918, however, she was forced to resign.

She made several attempts to set up a rival organization, but her sources of funding—lean under the best of circumstances—had all but vanished. Rebuffed in Chicago, she found a refuge with the Anti-Cigarette League of Kansas, in Topeka. However, she was soon wrestling with that group's board of directors over whether its mission would be to discourage or prohibit the use of cigarettes. Her pronouncements became even more shrill. "I know many oppose the work I am doing," she told the *Topeka Capitol*, "but I am like Jesus Christ. I will forgive and forget the past if the people will try to do better in the future" (reprinted in *Tobacco*, December 9, 1920, 33). After little more than two months on the job, she was fired again. She returned to Chicago, where she cobbled together a new organization, called the National Anti-Cigarette League. Six months later, this group, too, fired her, saying, "Miss Gaston's methods were more drastic than the methods approved by the league Board of Managers" (*New York Times*, August 27, 1921).

With no regular salary, Gaston was forced to rely on handouts from relatives and charities. Her brother recalled that she often walked for lack of money to take a streetcar. She lived mostly on graham crackers, supplemented by a daily five-cent glass of milk from a lunch room and an occasional holiday food basket from the Salvation Army. Even in these reduced circumstances, she continued to pass out news releases and gentian root. Incensed by press reports that Queen Mary of Great Britain was fond of a cigarette after lunch, she wrote to the queen, scolding her for setting an "exceedingly unfortunate" example (*New York Times*, August 21, 1924).

She had promised an unrelenting fight against the cigarette, and she kept it up until January 1924, when she was run over by a streetcar while on her way home from an anti-cigarette rally in Chicago. She died six months later, of throat cancer, at age sixty-four. As she had requested, her body was cremated and the ashes taken to her adopted hometown of Harvey.

Her illness and death attracted the notice of newspapers around the country. Reporting on her funeral, the *New York Times* for August 23, 1924, noted that "of the thousands of friends Miss Gaston had made during the long years of her work, only a handful were present at the simple rites." Among them were four children, who knelt by her coffin and solemnly pledged to never smoke cigarettes. Gaston was a key figure in a movement that succeeded in prohibiting the sale of cigarettes in fifteen states between 1893 and 1921. By the time of her death, however, cigarettes were nominally illegal in only one state, Kansas.

Sources. Very little of Lucy Page Gaston's correspondence has survived. Gaston's correspondence with Newton D. Baker is from the Commission on Training Camp Activities, Records of the War Department General and Special Staffs (Record Group 165), National Archives and Records Administration, Washington, D.C. The best sources are the David Starr Jordan Papers, Stanford Univ. Libraries, Stanford, California, and the Herbert F. Fisk Papers, Northwestern Univ. Archives, Evanston, Illinois. The Frances E. Willard Memorial Library, Evanston, holds several pamphlets written by Gaston, including the undated *Children's Temperance Work in Illinois*, along with copies of the Anti-Cigarette League's national magazine, *The Boy*. The library also is a repository for the *Union Signal* newspaper and the *National Meeting Minutes of the Woman's Christian Temperance Union*, both of which chronicle her activities. The Chicago ordinance is found in *Proceedings of the City Council of the City of Chicago* (1896–97); the Illinois law is in *Laws of the State of Illinois* (1907). See *Tobacco*, December 9, 1920, and *NYT*, August 27, 1921, for discussion of her approach. Obituaries appeared in the *NYT*, August 21, 1924; *CT*, August 21, 1924; *Union Signal*, September 4, 1924. *NYT* reported on her funeral on August 23, 1924. Frances Warfield, "Lost Cause: A Portrait of Lucy Page Gaston," *Outlook and Independent*, February 12, 1930, is a valuable profile. Robert M. Sobel presents a lively but inflated assessment in *They Satisfy: The Cigarette in American Life* (1978). See also Cassandra Tate, "In the 1800s, Antismoking Was a Burning Issue," *Smithsonian Magazine*, July 1989.

CASSANDRA TATE

GEHRING, SISTER WALBURGA (Eva Gehring)
January 25, 1832–July 3, 1883
FOUNDER OF HOSPITAL AND FOUNDLING HOME

Eva Gehring, founder of St. Joseph Hospital of Chicago and St. Vincent Infant Asylum, an orphanage for abandoned babies in Chicago, was one of two known children of Frederick and Theodora (Steigher) Gehring of Bavaria. Her father was a tradesman. It is unclear when Eva Gehring emigrated to America, and whether she came alone or was accompanied by the brother known to have relocated to the United States. The nature of Eva Gehring's formative years, family life, and education is unknown. Since Bavaria was one of the Catholic German states, it is probable that Gehring was raised a Catholic. She had very little formal education in English when she was received into the Emmitsburg, Maryland, religious community of the Sisters of Charity. In November 1848, Eva Gehring received her religious name of Walburga. She remained in Emmitsburg as a postulant and undertook her novitiate there. At age seventeen, Walburga Gehring began her service as set forth by the community's constitution.

The order of the Sisters of Charity of Saint Joseph was founded in 1809 by Elizabeth Bayley Seton, later Mother Seton, who adopted the name in the hope of affiliating with the Daughters of Charity in France. The rules of the American order were modeled on those given by Saint Vincent de Paul to the Daughters of Charity, to serve the poor. This service took various forms as communities of the order spread, evolving from Seton's teaching mission to the establishment in 1814 of the first Catholic orphanage in the United States in Philadelphia to the caretaking of the ill, invalids, and the insane.

Although the original mission of Seton's Emmitsburg community had begun with a free school for the poor, by 1849, the order ran various far-flung hospitals. Gehring's novitiate service was as a nurse in the Midwest. Her first assignment in 1850 was at St. Peter's orphanage in Cincinnati. In early March 1852, she was transferred to Milwaukee.

Walburga Gehring and five companions had an arduous journey to Milwaukee. At one point, they were stranded in Erie, New York, until a passenger boat was finally available to take them across the Great Lakes; but the vessel became caught in the lake ice and was trapped for days. It became clear to Gehring that if nothing were done, they would starve within sight of land. She took the initiative and led her religious sisters across the frozen lake. When the other passengers observed their safe arrival on shore, they followed her example.

After an uncomfortable overland journey, the twenty-year-old Gehring began her service in Milwaukee. The novitiate years 1852 and 1853 were difficult for her. Tensions between Gehring and her Sister Servant (her religious superior—the supervisor of the community and of St. John's Infirmary) led to her transfer to St. Rose Orphan Asylum. More importantly, Gehring began to question whether she was worthy of taking her final vows. This unhappy period ended in January 1854 with her reassignment to the order's St. Louis hospital.

In St. Louis, Gehring found a supportive mentor in Mary Alexis Rayhice, Sister Servant of Mullanphy Hospital. Gehring's faith and self-confidence blossomed under Rayhice's auspices, culminating in permission for Walburga Gehring to take her final vows.

FIG. 40. *Sister Walburga Gehring founded St. Joseph Hospital and St. Vincent Infant Asylum.*

As Sister Walburga, Gehring worked at Mullanphy Hospital until the outbreak of the Civil War, when she asked for and received permission to serve in the ambulance corps. An affiliation with the French order had taken place in 1850, when the Sisters of Charity officially became the Daughters of Charity. The approximately 230 Daughters of Charity of Saint Vincent de Paul who served on the battlefields tended both union and confederate wounded. At the close of the war, the Daughters of Charity resumed their peacetime nursing missions. Gehring and Rayhice returned to St. Louis.

In 1868, at the behest of Bishop James Duggan of Chicago, the Daughters of Charity undertook to establish a hospital there. The next year, Gehring was chosen to head this new mission. By her own account in her "History and Testimonials of her Life," many Catholics in Chicago were initially unenthusiastic, even cold, to her leadership. Bishop Duggan, in poor health, both physically and mentally, "seemed no longer disposed to fulfil the fair promises he had made" (p. 27) guaranteeing his support for the project.

Gehring and two other Daughters of Charity assigned to

the project spent six months collecting and preparing bedding and the physical accoutrements for the proposed Providence Hospital. Since they did not enjoy Bishop Duggan's favor, their efforts to solicit financial contributions proved an uphill battle. Despite these obstacles, Gehring persevered, seeking an affordable rental property that could serve as the base for their little Chicago community and the hospital. At the end of June 1869, Gehring and her companions moved into a former summer residence beyond the city limits that they had refurbished.

On July 7, Providence Hospital opened its doors to patients. While staffing the hospital, converting the cookhouse into a chapel, and performing their own household duties, the sisters managed to garner sufficient donations in 1870 to purchase a parcel of land. Fortunately, Bishop Duggan's successor, Bishop Thomas Foley, enthusiastically supported the hospital project. Foley initiated the hospital's name change to avoid confusion with two already existing Chicago institutions that bore the Providence name. Walburga Gehring recalled Foley saying, "You had better call your new hospital after St. Joseph, as there is no special good work dedicated to him in the city" (Gehring, "History and Testimonials," 28).

Construction began in August 1871, and Gehring had to address the problem of supervising the new building and getting her sisters to mass while staffing Providence. "One of our Lady [sic] friends begged a gentle horse for us and our wagon came to be known and was called 'Black Maria.' Two of us knowing how to drive made us feel quite independent" (Gehring, "History of St. Joseph," 6). "Black Maria" was important to Gehring's activities during and after the Great Chicago Fire of 1871. Gehring provided a vivid account of the fire, writing: "On the night of October 9th, 1871, at 3 o'clock in the morning we were waked up. A wagon loaded with children and all kinds of furniture drove into our yard. The children told us that the city was all on fire. We could see the great light, the sky was red with it" (Gehring, "History of St. Joseph," 10–11). Nuns and clergy from other orders in the city sought refuge at St. Joseph Hospital.

Gehring and her five nursing sisters went into the city in order to aid fire victims. "As we advanced," she wrote, "we found the heat so great and the wind so high that we were obliged to stop and then turned back. The people came flocking to our house in crowds all day, famished for a drink of cold water, as the Water Works was one of the first things destroyed by the fire. The car tracks were warped, standing up and consumed by the great heat. Horses and cows were lying dead, people rushing here and there trying to find their own, as some were separated and burned to ashes" (Gehring, "History of St. Joseph," 11).

The fire spread rapidly toward Gehring's hospital and the sisters evacuated their patients, moving west. Toward midnight, the wind shifted and the fire went toward the lake, away from the nurses and patients huddled on the prairie west of the city.

The partially completed St. Joseph Hospital was spared from the flames, but construction came to a standstill. The resulting privation in the city effectively preempted continuing contributions to its building fund. Bishop Foley stood surety for a bank loan, which Gehring reluctantly took out after obtaining permission from the head of her order.

In the aftermath of the fire, barracks were established for the populace, including a hospital that Gehring sought and obtained permission to oversee. The Daughters of Charity now divided their time between two overcrowded facilities. Additionally, Gehring continued supervising the erection of St. Joseph. Cost overruns exhausted their loan monies, and Gehring was unable to secure additional loans. She applied to the Relief Society, established by the city in the aftermath of the fire, which had provisioned both Providence and the Barracks Hospital. In recognition of Gehring's dedication to ministering to all the injured and ill during a postfire epidemic, regardless of religious affiliation, and her distribution of provisions to the dispossessed based on need alone, the Relief Society responded by providing the funds to build St. Joseph to completion.

In the spring of 1872, Walburga Gehring's hard work was rewarded. On April 29, the Daughters of Charity moved into their new headquarters, and patients from both the Barracks Hospital and the now-superseded Providence Hospital were transferred to the new medical facility dedicated to St. Joseph. In her "History of St. Joseph Hospital," Gehring herself marveled at its successful realization: "Indeed, it is more than I can tell when I consider that we did not have one dollar to begin our work in time of trouble and disappointments from all sides, the Bishop insane, everyone doing—God knows what!" (p. 27).

With the continued support of the relief committee, St. Joseph flourished under Gehring's dedicated supervision. With its routine established, it no longer required all her attention. Gehring's concern now focused on Chicago's orphans. Concern for their care and salvation caused Gehring to embark on a new project: establishing a Catholic foundling home in Chicago. To this end, she involved friends and supporters in locating a suitable rental property. Like her earlier search for the hospital, the typical response was refusal by owners to rent their property to such an institution.

In late 1880, Gehring's demanding regimen took its toll and her health failed. By 1881, however, she had sufficiently regained her strength to resume her orphan project. Through the intercession of Episcopalian realtor, W. D. Kerfoot, Gehring's staunch friend, the owner of a building on North Orleans street was persuaded to rent his property to the Daughters of Charity. Mother Superior Euphemia sent Gehring four sisters from Maryland to staff the home that opened in August. In September, the Chicago Police began channeling foundlings to St. Vincent's. By the time forty infants, and some of their mothers, wed and unwed, were being housed in the frame cottage, it was clear that larger quarters were needed.

Gehring planned to sell a parcel of land that belonged to the Daughters of Charity, hoping to purchase a larger building with the proceeds of the sale. When the land did not sell, she successfully appealed to the Chicago community for help. Before the end of the year, St. Vincent's had moved to a larger former private residence, donated to the order by its owner.

Gehring, however, seems not to have recovered fully from her illness of 1880, which left her virtually deaf. At the end of 1882, she returned to the Mother House in Emmitsburg to be nursed for a large tumor of the throat. By spring of 1883, she felt well enough to request a return to active nursing. This brief period of well-being ended in June, when Gehring returned to her sickbed in the Mother House. From the symptoms described, it seems likely that she developed dropsy in addition to her tumor. After a painful month, Walburga Gehring died at St. Joseph Central House in Emmitsburg, Maryland.

As a religious who had taken a vow of poverty, Sister Walburga Gehring left no material estate, but her legacy to Chicago was a rich one. St. Vincent's orphanage, incorporated as St. Vincent Infant Asylum in 1888, eventually expanded in 1930 to a seven-story, $1,200,000 facility that served the city's children until orphanages fell out of fashion. St. Joseph Hospital continues in the Lakeview neighborhood as one of Chicago's major health care centers.

Sources. The most important sources for Gehring's life, in the East Central Province Daughters of Charity Archives, Mater Dei Provincialate, Evansville, Indiana, are her own "History and Testimonials of her Life," found in the record *Deceased Sisters, 1880–84* (privately printed, n.d.); "History of St. Joseph Hospital," an undated manuscript partially written by Gehring; and documents cataloged as "Histories of St. Vincent Infant Asylum, Chicago, Ill." These archives also contain materials from St. Joseph Hospital in Chicago and the Provincialate in Emmitsburg, Maryland. Although Gehring is not the focus of Ellen Ryan Jolly, *Nuns of the Battlefield* (1927), an account of the activities of Daughters of Charity in the ambulance service of the Civil War, she is included in the list of participants.

MICHAELA M. TOMASCHEWSKY

GERAGHTY, HELEN TIEKEN
November 16, 1902–August 12, 1987
THEATRICAL PRODUCER, DIRECTOR, TEACHER

Helen Tieken Geraghty was the leading proponent of large-scale historical drama in Chicago from the 1930s through the 1950s. She staged pageants at major expositions beginning with the Century of Progress Exposition in 1933. She also taught drama, produced numerous industrial shows, and staged charitable extravaganzas. She was born in Chicago, the first child of Dr. Theodore and Bessie (Chapman) Tieken. Her father was born in Oldenburg, Germany, but was educated in Chicago. He was a physician and professor at Rush Medical College and the University of Chicago and was on the staff of various Chicago hospitals. Her mother Bessie Chapman, the daughter of German immigrants who settled in Siegel, Illinois, devoted herself to her family and her interest in the arts, serving on the boards of various cultural institutions, including the Art Institute of Chicago, the Field Museum, the Chicago Historical Society, and the Renaissance Society. An educated woman, she graduated from the Illinois Training School for Nurses (ITSN) in 1901 and later attended the University of Chicago, where she received a Ph.B. and an M.A. in art history. She was president of the Chicago Public School Art Society for ten years and also served on the Board of Managers of the ITSN.

The family lived on Chicago's West Side. Helen Tieken had two brothers, Robert, born in 1904; and Theodore Jr., born in 1909. A somewhat frail child, Tieken grew strong from exercises on an outdoor gymnasium in the backyard and from the circus tricks her father taught the children. She later claimed that her ability to work sixteen-hour days came from "a childhood matching brain and brawn with two brothers who were six feet four inches" (Perrigo). She attended Lewis Institute (now Illinois Institute of Technology) in 1916–17 and 1920–21. She then went to the University of Chicago, where she intended to study medicine. Her father strongly disapproved of women physicians, calling them "hen-medics" (Madigan). Tieken turned instead to an interest in the arts that had developed from childhood visits to the Art Institute of Chicago when her mother attended meetings there. Tieken graduated Phi Beta Kappa in the spring of 1924.

After graduation, she went to Europe to study for a summer at Oxford University, then in 1926 at the Sorbonne in Paris. Deciding that she was most interested in the theater, she returned in 1927 to Chicago to study at the Goodman School of Drama at the Art Institute. She received an M.A. in English from the University of Chicago in 1928. Her thesis was on Max Reinhardt, the German director famous for producing both intimate indoor drama and massive outdoor spectacles, and his influence on the American stage. After receiving her degree, Tieken went to Germany to work with Reinhardt. She managed to get a job as a stagehand in 1929 and worked in his theaters in Salzburg, Berlin, and Vienna. In November 1929 she was back in Chicago, working with the Junior League to create a touring National Children's Theater. Her production of Maurice Maeterlinck's *Blue Bird* opened November 1, 1930, in Chicago. Tieken toured with the play in fifteen cities around the country.

Chicago was the site of the Century of Progress Exposition in 1933, a world's fair held to honor the centennial of the city's founding and highlight the technological advances during those one hundred years. Helen Tieken was hired by the fair management in 1932 to direct plays for children at the Junior League's Enchanted Island concession. Fair planners wanted the exposition to include historical pageantry, a fad that had swept the country beginning in the teens, in which enthusiastic amateurs would enact the history of their town in dramatic outdoor plays. They decided to stage a professional pageant of transportation that would highlight the history of transportation in America. With her background in directing and her work on Max Reinhardt's spectacles, Tieken was the logical choice to stage the pageant, *Wings of a Century*. Although often described as a slight woman with a quiet voice, Tieken had the authority and energy to manage a cast of 150 professional actors, horses, thirteen trains, automobiles, boats, stagecoaches, wagons, fire engines, and even a model of the Wright Brothers' airplane. *Wings* was a critical and popular success, attracting as many as ten thousand people a day. *Billboard* and *Variety* gave it positive reviews, as did *Chicago Tribune* critic James O'Donnell Bennett. In 1934 she coordinated revisions of the pageant for its second season but before production began was hired by España Touristica to create a pageant for its Spanish Village at the fair. She wrote, planned, and directed the pageant, *Hispañana*, another success. Critics and audiences alike considered it one of the highlights of the fair's second year.

On April 15, 1933, just six weeks before *Wings* opened, Helen Tieken married Maurice Patrick (Pat) Geraghty, president of Textile Craft Company. Their wedding trip had to be postponed while Geraghty worked twelve- to eighteen-hour days, her new husband watching the pageant every night. She later told a reporter, "Pat knew I just had to continue with my career

FIG. 41. *Helen Tieken Geraghty with Richard Humphrey and Isaac Van Grove before the musical production* Adam to Atom, *Chicago, 1953.*

and agreed. He's been completely co-operative ever since" (Madigan). In the fall of 1934, after the Century of Progress ended, Geraghty was appointed general assistant to Max Reinhardt for his Chicago performances of *A Midsummer Night's Dream* at the Auditorium Theatre. The following year Geraghty spent at home, caring for her first child, Betsy.

In 1936 Geraghty resumed work in the theater. She was appointed director of the Actor's Guild at Hull-House. The first plays she directed, John Galsworthy's *The Sun* and *The First and the Last,* were performed in November of that year. In her first two years there she produced ten plays, working with numerous ethnic theater groups as well as with the Actor's Guild. In 1937 Geraghty taught a course, "Techniques of Dramatic Production," at the University of Chicago's University College in downtown Chicago and advertised her availability as a lecturer on various topics related to the theater.

When Charlotte Carr became director of Hull-House in 1937 (after JANE ADDAMS's death in 1935 and the brief appointment of ADENA MILLER RICH), she decided to restructure its administration. Among the changes she ordered was the consolidation of the multitudinous theater groups, and in 1941 she chose to limit activity in the drama field. Geraghty left Hull-House in 1940, one of several directors who quit.

Her second daughter, Helen, was born in 1940, and Geraghty again opted to remain at home. Her third daughter, Molly, was born in 1942. The following year Geraghty began teaching drama and staging plays at the Francis Parker School. Her daughters attended the private school, noted for its progressive education philosophy and programs. She staged an average of twenty plays every year at the school and taught there until 1957.

In 1948 Chicago was the site of a lakefront fair sponsored by thirty-nine railroad companies to commemorate one hundred years of transcontinental rail transportation in America. Planners decided to include an outdoor spectacle that would be one of the major attractions of the fair. Because of her success at the Century of Progress, Geraghty was hired to produce and direct the show, *Wheels a-Rolling.* In the planning stages she sent her family to their farm near Galena, Illinois, so she could work long hours. When the show opened, she managed to combine family and career by having her children appear in several scenes, a practice she continued in later productions. Like her earlier production, *Wheels* was a huge outdoor drama with a large professional cast and props that included authentic railroad equipment. It was another critical and popular success and ran a second summer at the 1949 Railroad Fair. Dudley Pictures filmed *Wheels* and it was shown on WGN television April 16, 1949.

Civic leaders recognized the success of the Railroad Fair and decided to sponsor another exposition at the same site in the summer of 1950. Geraghty was preparing to leave on vacation when the president of the Chicago Fair called and asked her to create a pageant with a patriotic theme. Geraghty researched and wrote *Frontiers of Freedom* and worked with architects to design the stage in addition to her usual duties of directing; planning the budget, costumes, and music; arranging to borrow antique vehicles; and filling in for actresses on occasion. It was estimated that the pageants in 1948, 1949, and 1950 were seen by three million people, thus establishing Geraghty's reputation as Chicago's "pageant lady."

In the early 1950s historical pageantry enjoyed a brief revival in popularity as part of cold war pro-America sentiment to combat the perceived threat of world communism. Geraghty's pageants, unlike the earlier fad of amateur plays, were polished, professional productions with equity actors and union musicians. Her understanding of Reinhardt's spectacles enabled her to produce colorful shows that brought history alive to the audience and reinforced American values. She was one of few women active in the field. Reporters who wrote about her were amazed that a woman of her small physical stature could manage such a complex operation, calling her a "diminutive whirlwind" (Perrigo).

In 1952, Chicago's Museum of Science and Industry hosted a centennial of engineering to commemorate progress in engineering since the founding of the American Society of Engineers in 1852. It featured exhibits and a conference of international engineering societies, but the centerpiece was an indoor pageant, *Adam to Atom*, staged by Geraghty. *Adam to Atom* highlighted the role of invention and engineering through history from the cave dweller to splitting the atom and was designed to educate and entertain the general public. It played fifteen times a week from July 12 to September 28, 1952, and was seen by more than one hundred twenty thousand people. It was probably Geraghty's best expression of the values of the time, focusing on the role of progress in improving life while stressing the importance of freedom.

Geraghty's last outdoor pageant was also her only out-of-state production. She told an interviewer that she had been offered jobs in both Hollywood and on Broadway but turned them down to be with her family. She was able, however, to spend the summer of 1953 commuting between Chicago and Columbus, Ohio, to stage *The 17th Star*, a pageant depicting Ohio's history for that state's sesquicentennial celebration. The pageant was performed at the Ohio State fairgrounds from August 27 to September 7, 1953.

Geraghty began to stage smaller dramas for businesses or organizations beginning in 1949, with *Indian Trails to Iron Rails* for the Burlington Railroad. Observing the enormous popularity and success of her large-scale spectacles, other businesses commissioned her to produce dramatic histories of their companies for conventions or business meetings. Although most of these shows were not intended for mass audiences, her *Song of Mid America*, produced in 1951 for the Illinois Central Railroad, was made into a forty-five minute film and distributed by the railroad for publicity. Geraghty was one of the first to produce these industrial shows, and her unusual talents provided entertainment for the Studebaker Company (*A Family Portrait*, 1952), Rotary International (*Anniversary Album*, 1955), and for the American Red Cross (*Banner High*, 1956).

She also staged special events as fund-raisers for nonprofit organizations, including the Arthritis and Rheumatism Foundation, Illinois Children's Home and Aid Society, the Lyric Opera, and Passavant Hospital. Her *Gala* in 1969 was sponsored by the American Institute of Architects to celebrate the reopening of the Louis Sullivan–designed Auditorium Theatre after extensive renovation.

In 1957, the Chicago Association of Commerce and Industry sponsored a trade fair at Navy Pier. Geraghty served as director of entertainment and cultural activities. Since pageantry was no longer in fashion, she staged *The Big Show*, a circus-like entertainment with acts from around the world. Part of Geraghty's job was to travel and find these acts. The International Trade Fair was held annually until 1963. In 1961 it moved from Navy Pier to McCormick Place, the new exhibition and convention hall.

Helen Geraghty was appointed general manager of Ravinia Park, in the northern suburb of Highland Park, in November 1963. Although hired primarily to oversee the park's first Shakespeare festival, Geraghty found herself doing a variety of tasks and working her usual twelve-hour days. She coordinated bookings for soloists to appear with the Chicago Symphony Orchestra and negotiated contracts with the orchestra members and their union. She was also responsible for the physical upkeep of the park, supervising remodeling of the restaurant and administrative and ticket offices, and planning new parking facilities.

Geraghty's last professional position was her appointment in November 1966 as chief of the arts program for the Illinois sesquicentennial celebration from December 4, 1967, to December 3, 1968. She approved programs for each of the 102 counties in the state. Governor Otto Kerner believed the celebration could be a catalyst for a cultural renewal in the state and identified the arts program under Geraghty's guidance as central to this transformation. Geraghty coordinated the efforts of existing arts groups and provided encouragement for new endeavors through a series of competitions for one-act plays, longer drama, and literary works. Ironically, Geraghty's expertise in producing spectacles was not used. While she selected an official sesquicentennial pageant, it was never staged by her and seldom performed at all; it reflected the chaos of the 1960s and was therefore a rather dissonant and unpleasant drama lacking the unifying themes of earlier pageantry.

Geraghty retired from public life after the sesquicentennial, living quietly at the family home in Chicago. After her husband died on October 4, 1980, at their summer home in Washington, Massachusetts, Geraghty went to live with her daughter Molly. When her health failed, Geraghty moved into a nursing home in Palo Alto, California, where she died at age eighty-five.

Geraghty spent her entire career in the theater, teaching and directing from 1936 to 1957. She was best known, however, for the five major pageants she staged. She had a rare talent for piecing together a disparate mix of actors, technicians, equipment, music, and even animals to create a show that would, as she put it, "take shape like some crazy quilt pattern coming into focus" ("Note," n.d., Geraghty Papers). Her career blossomed in the 1950s. Her productions aptly reflected the heightened patriotism, faith in progress, and optimism of the post–World War II years.

Sources. Helen Tieken Geraghty Papers, UIC Spec. Coll., contain photographs and newspaper articles, including John Madigan, "Are Career Girls Happy?" *Chicago Herald-American*, February 10, 1950, and Lucia Perrigo, "Today's No. 1 'Barnum'—A Girl," *King Features Syndicate*, August 23, 1950. The bulk of the collection consists of detailed material relating to her productions. There is additional information in the

Lenox Riley Lohr Papers, Century of Progress Collection, and the Chicago Railroad Fair Collection, UIC Spec. Coll. The UC has student yearbooks that list information about Geraghty's college years. Stuart Joel Hecht, "Hull-House Theatre: An Analytical and Evaluative History" (Ph.D. diss., Northwestern Univ., 1983), discusses Geraghty's work at Hull-House. A twenty-eight minute video of the 1949 *Wheels a-Rolling* pageant is available from Interurban Films.

CATHLYN SCHALLHORN

GERSTENBERG, ALICE
August 2, 1885– July 28, 1972
PLAYWRIGHT, DIRECTOR, NOVELIST, CLUBWOMAN

A native-born Chicagoan whose grandparents, German on both sides, had emigrated to Chicago in the 1850s, Alice Gerstenberg was very much a product of the city and a shaper of its culture. She was a playwright, director, theater founder, occasional actress, active clubwoman, socialite, and feminist. Her father, Erich, was a prosperous grain merchant who held a seat on the Chicago Board of Trade, inherited from his father. Her mother Julia (Wieschendorff) Gerstenberg belonged to Chicago's cultured elite and was active in theater and music circles. Both strongly encouraged their daughter to pursue her talents. Gerstenberg was raised in a vibrant social milieu as a prominent debutante. The family's social affairs in its luxurious home and garden were often featured on the society pages of Chicago newspapers.

From an early age, while still at Bryn Mawr College, Bryn Mawr, Pennsylvania, Gerstenberg was finding her place as a dramatist. Her work in the theater was to be done primarily in Chicago, which was home to the earliest stirrings of the little theater movement: in LAURA DAINTY PELHAM's Hull-House Theatre, in the ANNA MORGAN studios in the Fine Arts Building, in MARY ALDIS's playhouse at her estate in Lake Forest, and most prominently in the Little Theatre in the Fine Arts Building. The Little Theatre, founded by Maurice Browne, who was English, and his Chicagoan wife, ELLEN VAN VOLKENBURG, was the most widely recognized and influential manifestation of the movement.

Educated first in Chicago at the Kirkland School and then at Bryn Mawr College, where she took leading parts in dramatic productions, Alice Gerstenberg began her work as a playwright in 1908 with the publication of *A Little World*, four college playlets for girls, three of which were performed at the Anna Morgan Studios. During the next two years, she continued to write sketches and plays that had amateur productions at clubs and societies. These early plays were produced in the Grace Hickox Studios in the Fine Arts Building, at the Petit Gourmet restaurant (run by HARRIET MOODY), and the Player's Workshop in the art colony on Fifty-seventh Street, founded in 1916 by Elizabeth Bingham, a disgruntled member of Browne's Little Theatre. Gerstenberg performed in the early productions of the Little Theatre as an original member of the company. Her mother was one of the Little Theatre's original founders and financial supporters.

In the years that followed, Alice Gerstenberg's one-act plays were produced in little theaters all over Chicago. In addition to the Hickox and Morgan Studios, they were presented at the Ravinia Workshop; the Jack and Jill Theatre; Mary Aldis's the-

ater in Lake Forest; at the Romany Club during the 1920s; and, the play *Latchkeys*, even on the staircase of the Gerstenberg home on Lake Shore Drive. Later, in 1931, *Latchkeys* was performed at the Goodman Theatre and at the Playshop Theatre at the Edgewater Beach Hotel. More ambitious productions were mounted at the Hotel Sherman and the Studebacker Theatre as well as at the Fine Arts Theater. A number of productions found their way to New York. But by the 1950s, Gerstenberg's plays would again be performed primarily at the Alice Gerstenberg Experimental Workshop, her career thus coming full circle.

During the same years that she was working on her plays, she completed two novels. *Unquenched Fire* (1912) contains a fictionalized portrait of producer David Belasco and chronicles the experiences of a young, socially prominent Chicagoan who is lured to New York to be an actress. The novel bears some similarity to Gerstenberg's own life at this time. It expresses themes of women's independence and desire to escape from stifling tradition. The heroine of *Unquenched Fire* is a would-be actress who turns to the stage as a revolt against the husband-hunt that occupies most of the time of her contemporaries in upper-class Chicago society. But the heroine's career in the theater is not all she hopes for and not all that she needs to secure happiness. The novel contains a satirical view of upper-class Chicago society in the 1920s. Gerstenberg's second novel, *The Conscience of Sarah Platt*, appeared in 1915 and deals with the plight of the woman of moderate means who does not marry. One reviewer of the novel called it a simplified view of feminism.

Gerstenberg's career on the professional stage took a decided turn from strictly amateur productions to the professional stage when, in 1915, her *Alice in Wonderland* dramatization of episodes from the Lewis Carroll novel was produced first in Chicago at the Fine Arts Theater and then at the Booth Theatre in New York. It then enjoyed a long run in both cities and around the country. Critic David Sievers wrote, "It remained for Alice Gerstenberg . . . to give Broadway its first really authentic glimpse into unconscious life" (Sievers, 49). The year 1915 was to be a watershed for Gerstenberg. In that same year another play, *Overtones*, was produced on November 8 at the Bandbox Theatre in New York by the Washington Square Players. It turned out to be one of her most original and influential plays. *Overtones* was chosen to represent American one-act plays on a bill of four comparative comedies by Schnitzler and other European playwrights. The play was a psychological fantasy in which two veiled figures represented the alter-egos of the two women characters. One line of action revealed the outer lives of two women, while the other, in ironic contrast, revealed their subconscious selves. The device of dramatizing the unconscious was so original and striking that it was later used by Eugene O'Neill with great success in his play *Strange Interlude* (1928). O'Neill did not acknowledge the debt to Gerstenberg and she felt that he had "copied" it ("Come Back with Me," 642). *Overtones* was produced for many years, including a long run in vaudeville with Helen Lackaye at the Palace Theatre in Chicago in 1916 and in London with Lily Langtry in 1917–18. It was Gerstenberg's most important and influential "serious" play and was later rewritten as a three-act play, premiering at the Powers Theatre in Chicago in 1922 and performed widely. Sievers said of this production, "It marks the first departure from realism for the purpose of dramatizing the unconscious" (p. 51).

Gerstenberg always seemed ready to try experimental techniques in writing and staging her plays. She continued throughout her life to write plays that explored her interest in the forces shaping the personality and that demonstrated her interest in psychoanalysis. Another experimental play, *Sentience* (1933), presents a man, a woman, a chair, and a vase and gives the inanimate objects personalities and voices that the woman is able to hear. Of this new technique in psychological drama, Gerstenberg commented, "I hope Eugene O'Neill will read my play so that he may write similar ones for the next 10 years" (undated article, "New Psychology Appears in Play of Gerstenberg," Gerstenberg scrapbooks). Other Gerstenberg plays in which the influence of Freud is apparent are *Alice in Wonderland, The Buffer* (1916), *Beyond* (1917), *The Attuned* (1917), and *The Unseen* (1918).

Many of Gerstenberg's plays, especially those in one act, were published either singly or in anthologies and thus made available to groups, both amateur and professional. They popularized the experimental plays of the little theater, plays that could be produced at home as well as on the stage. Her published volumes of one-act plays were *Ten One-Act Plays* (1921), *Four Plays for Four Women* (1924), and *Comedies All* (1930). *Ten One-Act Plays* included some of her most popular plays: *The Unseen*; *He Said, She Said*; and *The Pot Boiler*. In the introduction to *Four Plays* she suggests that these plays may be given in any drawing-room or on any platform, without scenery, a view of producing one-act plays that she held throughout her career. In addition, she outlines her philosophy of presentation: "The plays aim at simplicity of production, at lack of business because of limited setting, and rely for their sustained interest upon mental action, heart emotion, and unforced resemblance to everyday life" (preface, *Four Plays*). *Comedies All* contained ten short plays, including *Latchkeys*.

Gerstenberg was influential in promoting the opening of small theaters in Chicago and around the country. Among the first was the Players Producing Company on the main floor of the Fine Arts Building in Chicago, where *Alice in Wonderland* was produced as dramatized by Gerstenberg. This theater group featured professional actors and productions. *Alice* proceeded to success on the New York stage. Gerstenberg's commitment to amateur and experimental theater expressed itself most importantly in her founding of the Playwrights Theatre of Chicago in 1922, with a performance of the three-act version of *Overtones*. She writes of the founding of this theater: "Its function is to encourage and develop playwrights and to give experimental productions of plays to enable the authors to see and hear their scripts in action, and thereby to avoid long years of waiting for Broadway to accept or reject manuscripts" (introduction, *Overtones*, 4). It was designed to give local playwrights a chance to produce original, and often experimental, plays. She also intended the Playwrights Theatre to be a place where new plays could be given a rehearsal production with an audience and eventually a public performance. The theater's venues included the Arts Club, private homes, clubs, and small theaters.

In 1936 a somewhat different version of the Playwrights Theatre emerged in an old coach house on the Near North Side. With Alice Gerstenberg on the executive committee, a group of local radio actors and actresses came together to give live performances before an audience of up to 150 people so that the professional actors would hold the inspiration they receive from a live audience. Many residents of the Gold Coast, an upper-class neighborhood on the Near North Side, were seen in the audience.

Gerstenberg remained in charge of the Playwrights Theatre until 1945, giving support and encouragement to several generations of playwrights. In the process she brought the art of theater to the attention of Chicago's business and social community. She was able to bridge this gap because she was of both worlds herself. As late as 1955 to 1958, Gerstenberg remained an active participant in experimental theater. The Alice Gerstenberg Experimental Theatre Workshop, founded by Paul Edward Pross and Otto E. Anderson to honor the now renowned playwright, included a play-writing clinic, where writers received constructive and creative group criticism, and also a practical production department that cast plays for presentation. Plays were produced in a variety of venues. During the 1956–57 season Gerstenberg's plays *Rhythm* and *At the Club* were presented. In the 1957–58 season her one-act play *Attuned* was presented at their workshop studio, and in the 1958 season her one-act play *The Unseen* was presented on the stage of the Art Institute's Fullerton Hall.

Gerstenberg might have forged an important career in the New York theater if her desire to be with her family and to be part of Chicago society had not limited her aspirations. Nevertheless, in 1948 she closed her apartment in Chicago for a while and moved to New York. There she attended as many plays as she could but was disappointed with what she found on Broadway. The rising costs of producing a play were pushing new and experimental plays to off-Broadway, and she concluded, "This is not a Broadway that I can write for" ("Come Back with Me," 636). She returned to Chicago and settled down to write once more, producing a three-act play, *Concordie*, which dramatized some abstract psychic ideas; *The Hourglass*, about several wealthy widowed women expressing their hidden personalities in modern ways; and *On the Beam*, a play with a religious slant that introduced the idea of keeping oneself in harmony with the Divine Overall Consciousness. While Gerstenberg did not marry, she led an active social life and did not seem to regret being single, particularly when she observed the unhappiness of many of her married friends, a state that she chronicled in a number of her plays.

In addition to her family connections within Chicago society, Gerstenberg was an inveterate clubwoman. Her memberships ranged from the political—the Chicago Equal Suffrage Association; to the literary—the Cordon Club, the Little Room, the Arts Club (where she was chair of the Dramatic Committee in 1919), the Society of Midland Authors, and the National League of Pen Women; to the social—the Woman's Athletic Club, the Bryn Mawr Club, the Junior League, the Casino Club, and the Opera Dance Club of Chicago. By means of these various memberships and associations, Gerstenberg crossed traditional class and aesthetic boundaries. She, along with a number of other women and men of her class, including HARRIET MONROE, Mary Aldis, Kenneth Sawyer Goodman, and Hobart Chatfield-Taylor, were members of Chicago's affluent community but also functioned as artists and as patrons of the arts. It was this group that maintained close ties to Maurice Browne's Little Theatre and thus had much to do with the establishment of the little theater movement in Chicago. They combined avant-garde taste and creativity with the fiscal resources necessary to perpetuate theater. They acted in little theater productions at homes, in private clubs, and in small theaters. They supported theater financially and, in the case of Aldis, Gerstenberg, and Goodman, wrote plays—mainly short ones, without which the little theater movement in Chicago could not have thrived. These plays eventually appeared not only on Chicago's little theater stages but nationwide. Among these Chicago authors drawn from high society, Gerstenberg was one of the most successful and influential.

After World War I Gerstenberg became active in the Arts Club of Chicago. The club's goals included developing high standards of art and promoting the mutual acquaintance of art lovers and art workers. Many of Chicago's leading families were active among its earliest leaders, including the Palmers, Ryersons, Bowens, Rosenwalds, and Aldises. Gerstenberg and her mother each served, at different times, as head of the club's entertainment committee. In 1919 the Club produced several plays by Kenneth Sawyer Goodman, who had died during the war, and continued to sponsor new plays for several years. Gerstenberg's Playwrights Theatre regularly performed plays at the Arts Club, thus maintaining the link between the avant-garde world of the aspiring playwrights she brought to the stage and the polite and affluent society that was represented at the Arts Club. Gerstenberg remained active in the Arts Club through the 1950s. By bringing many of her affluent friends to the board of the Playwrights Theatre, she helped to guarantee that it would continue, as it did until 1945.

Another example of the way in which Gerstenberg successfully bridged the gap between the arts and the affluent society of which she was a part was through membership in the Junior League. In 1921, the league, then ten years old, was presided over by Annette Washburne, a future doctor of psychiatry and daughter of a former mayor. Wanting to establish an acting group within the league to give one-act plays along the lines of the Little Theatre, Washburne called upon Gerstenberg to chair the group. More importantly, there were no theaters giving plays for children. Professional theaters did not offer children's theater because of the expense and limited financial returns. The answer, it was clear to the two women, was to establish a children's theater under the auspices of the Junior League. This theater would be a leader in a significant movement of wholesome entertainment for children across the country.

The first play they decided to do was Alice Gerstenberg's own adaptation of *Alice in Wonderland*. Plans were made to present the first Chicago production of the acting group not in an intimate setting such as a home or clubroom but in a downtown theater, the Playhouse in the Fine Arts Building where *Alice* had originated in 1915. This location gave the production the advantage of a real stage and professional equipment. The production was a major event, the beginning of the Junior League Theatre for Children. Junior Leagues in other cities took up and adapted the model to their own local needs.

Alice opened in November 1921 and played Saturday mornings through February 1922. It was published in *A Treasury of Plays for Children* (1921) and again in *Plays New and Old* in 1929. Although Gerstenberg stepped down as director after the second season and went on to a number of other important projects, the Junior League held to the pattern of presenting children's theater on Saturday mornings in downtown theaters. Other plays for children presented nationally under league sponsorship included Gerstenberg's dramatization of Charles Kingsley's *Water Babies* in 1930.

Gerstenberg continued to write and produce plays during the decades of the 1930s, 40s and 50s. Under the auspices of the Playwrights Theatre and of the Alice Gerstenberg Experimental Workshop, her now well-known plays were presented in venues that included the Romany Club, the Fine Arts Building, the Village Summer Theater in Hinsdale, and the Studio Players (*Something in the Air*, written with Maude Fealey, performed in 1942). The play she cowrote with journalist HERMA CLARK, *When Chicago Was Young*, was presented in 1932 and again in 1937. A collaboration with Clark produced a revised version, *Port of Chicago*, which was presented by the Uptown Players between 1943 and 1951. A radio series entitled *Lake Front*, part of the WPA (Works Progress Administration) adult education program, presented six scripts dramatizing historical time periods and events in Chicago between 1845 and 1939, including the World's Columbian Exposition of 1893, the building of the Auditorium Theatre, and Montgomery Ward's fight to keep buildings out of Grant Park. Gerstenberg won the Chicago Foundation for Literature Award in 1938 in recognition of her work as playwright and producer.

During these years Gerstenberg's plays were also produced outside of Chicago. In 1931, the New York Guild Players produced *At the Club* and *Mere Man*. The Boston Repertory Theatre presented *Water Babies* in 1929 and again in 1932. Her later years in theater saw productions of *Victory Belles* (1943), *The Hourglass* (1955), *Our Calla* (1956), and *On the Beam* (1957) in Chicago.

Alice Gerstenberg died in Minneapolis of a heart condition at the age of eighty-six. She was a cultural pioneer whose artistic efforts brought Chicago to the forefront of the theater movement in the first half of the twentieth century. She was one of the earliest creators of psychological drama in this country and a representative figure of the Chicago Literary Renaissance of the 1910s and 1920s. An understanding of the tensions and currents in her life demonstrates how upper-class women forged social and artistic connections in their communities through their social and club affiliations and used these to create a richer cultural climate for Chicago.

Sources. The two main archival sources for Gerstenberg's papers are the NL's Alice Gerstenberg Collection of correspondence and papers and the Alice Gerstenberg Papers at the Chicago Hist. Soc. The latter include her long, unpublished autobiography entitled "Come Back with Me" as well as several scrapbooks filled with programs and newspaper articles documenting her career. Both collections include copies of Gerstenberg's plays. Gerstenberg's publications, in addition to the collections, miscellaneous plays, and novels mentioned above, include *Alice in Wonderland* (1915); *A Patroness* (1917); *Ever Young* (1920); *Overtones: A Play in Three Acts*, with Lorin Howard (1920, 1929); *Tuning In*

(1931); *Within the Hour: A Short Play in Seven Scenes* (1934); and *When Chicago Was Young* (1934). She wrote several articles about her work in little theater, including "The Players Workshop of Chicago," *Theatre*, September 1917; "The Playshop, Chicago," *Little Theatre Monthly*, September 1917; "Chicago Junior League Theatre," *Drama*, January 1928; and "The Children's Junior League Theatre," *Drama*, March 1928. Her series, "Hope of the Little Theatre in Chicago," appeared in *Townsfolk* magazine in December 1947, January 1948, February 1948, and March 1948, and offered an insider's view of three decades of little theater in Chicago. "When the Arts Club Was Born" appeared in *Townsfolk* in May 1950, and "Something on My Mind" was in *Drama Critique*, Winter 1966. Works about Gerstenberg include Constance D'Arcy Mackay, *The Little Theatre in the United States* (1917); Anna Morgan, *My Chicago* (1918); W. David Sievers, *Freud on Broadway* (1955); Marilyn Atlas, "Innovation in Chicago: Alice Gerstenberg's Psychological Drama," *Midwestern Miscellany*, vol. 10, 1982; Sidney H. Bremer, "Willa Cather's Lost Chicago Sisters," in *Women Writers in the City: Essays in Feminist Literary Criticism*, ed. Susan Merill Squier (1984); Babette Inglehart, *A Reader's Guide to Illinois Literature* (1985); Stuart Hecht, "The Plays of Alice Gerstenberg: Cultural Hegemony in the American Little Theatre," *Journal of Popular Culture*, Summer 1992. Biographical essays are found in *The Biographical Cyclopedia of American Women*, vol. 1 (1924); *American Women Writers*, vol. 2 (1980); and *Notable Women in American Theatre* (1989). Shorter entries can be found in *American Women 1935–1940: A Complete Biographical Dictionary* (1940), and *Who Was Who among North American Authors* (1976).

BABETTE F. INGLEHART

GESTEFELD, URSULA NEWELL
April 22, 1845–October 22, 1921
FOUNDER OF A RELIGIOUS SYSTEM, AUTHOR, TEACHER

Ursula Newell Gestefeld, who achieved national prominence as an author and leader within the turn-of-the-century New Thought movement, was born in Augusta, Maine. The child of an invalid mother, Ursula Newell was herself a sickly child. Newell reached maturity, married Theodore Gestefeld, and had four children. By 1878 the family moved to Chicago, where Gestefeld's husband held positions as the city editor of the *Staats-Zeitung*, the leading German-language newspaper in the city, and as a reporter for the *Chicago Tribune*.

Gestefeld's ill health persisted into middle age. A turning point was reached in the early 1880s, however, when a friend loaned Gestefeld a copy of a religious healing tract, *Science and Health*, written by Christian Science founder Mary Baker Eddy. Gestefeld was impressed by Eddy's book, which claimed that meditation upon the power of spirit over matter could restore physical health; and she decided to heal her own illness through Eddy's principles. Her efforts were rewarded; Gestefeld reported that within three months she had attained the good health that had eluded her until then.

In May 1884, Mary Baker Eddy came to Chicago to offer instruction in Christian Science healing. Gestefeld signed up for the class and soon established herself as a metaphysician and healer. For the next four years, Gestefeld practiced, wrote, and taught Mental or Christian Science healing in Chicago, which in the mid-1880s was host to a vibrant and volatile metaphysical community. Prominent Chicago mental healers included strict followers of Eddy, rivals to Eddy, and others who had studied briefly with Eddy but were now independently de-

veloping Eddy's basic principles. Gestefeld fell within this latter camp.

Gestefeld counted herself a loyal follower of Eddy until 1888, when Gestefeld published *Ursula N. Gestefeld's Statement of Christian Science*. Gestefeld advertised her pamphlet as a key to Eddy's *Science and Health*. Eddy, however, believed that her work needed no key and soon published a series of articles denouncing Gestefeld. When Gestefeld fought back with a second pamphlet, *Jesuitism in Christian Science* (1888), she was expelled from Eddy's Christian Science Association. In response, Gestefeld claimed simply to have outgrown Eddy's work. Over the next two decades Gestefeld evolved her own system, the Science of Being, which she described as the "legitimate and necessary successor to Christian Science" (Patterson, 252).

After her expulsion from Eddy's Christian Science Association, Gestefeld aligned herself with a growing movement of mental healers or metaphysicians who, by the early 1890s, were joining in a loose national federation under the umbrella term "New Thought." New Thought, like Christian Science, began as a religious healing faith; and like Christian Science, New Thought particularly appealed to white, middle-aged, middle-class women. The numerous churches and schools that made up the New Thought movement were united by their shared insistence that human nature contained a spark of the divine. New Thought teachers and writers identified this divine inner spark with the creative power of thought, and they believed that people could shape and direct the divine inner power through the practice of "affirmations" and "denials." Heralding the power of words, New Thought authors claimed that people could create the world they desired through verbal or mental affirmations of situations they wanted to occur and denials of things they wished did not exist.

Like scores of women of her generation, Gestefeld quickly turned her personal experience of Christian Science healing into an independent New Thought career. New Thought was open to women who were able—based on credentials ranging from independent home-study to correspondence courses to attendance at eight-week New Thought "colleges"—to present themselves as certified New Thought healers, teachers, traveling proselytizers, or pastors. Gestefeld pursued all these options and more in her rise to leadership in the New Thought movement. Immediately after taking a class with Eddy in 1884, Gestefeld began her own career as a metaphysical teacher; she taught, gave lectures, and contributed to the local metaphysical press. After breaking with Eddy in 1888, Gestefeld broadened her scope, offering low-priced courses to anyone who had studied Christian Science with any teacher.

During the 1890s, Gestefeld divided her time primarily between Chicago and New York while also lecturing and teaching at New Thought centers across the nation. Gestefeld's Science of Being diverged from most New Thought teachings primarily in its reliance upon the Bible as an allegorical map of psychic development. Possibly as a result of her fascination with the Bible, Gestefeld became a member of the Revising Committee that worked with Elizabeth Cady Stanton, women's rights and woman suffrage leader, to publish the *Woman's Bible* in 1895. Gestefeld herself contributed one commentary to the *Woman's*

Bible in which she briefly summarized Science of Being principles. Gestefeld also published two novels and a number of tracts about the Science of Being during the 1890s. A photograph of Gestefeld published in that decade showed an attractive, determined-looking woman with large eyes, thin lips, a square face, and dark wavy hair.

By 1898 Gestefeld had settled again in Chicago, where she started the *Exodus*, a monthly magazine devoted, as its masthead read, "to the systematic exposition of the Science of Being and to the Leading Questions of the New Thought Movement" (quoted in Satter, 367–68). Ursula Gestefeld was the magazine's editor, publisher, and regular—and sometimes sole—contributor. Gestefeld also created the Exodus Club, a group whose members studied the Science of Being. Club membership cost twenty-five dollars a year; club members were economically comfortable. Gestefeld also sold high-priced correspondence courses on the Science of Being. By 1902, at least three hundred people were members of the Exodus Club, and up to eight hundred people gathered weekly to hear Ursula Gestefeld preach.

Gestefeld was a founding member of the Illinois Woman's Press Association. In 1893, Gestefeld participated in the World's Congress of Representative Women, where she spoke on "Woman as a Religious Teacher." Yet, outside of New Thought circles, Gestefeld was probably best known for her 1892 novel, *The Woman Who Dares*. On the surface, *The Woman Who Dares* was a typical "New Woman" novel. These feminist protest novels of the 1890s took the hypocrisy of marriage as their theme. While New Woman novels disagreed as to the importance of woman's own sexual desire (some heralding this desire and others denying its existence), they all pointed to the kinship of married women and prostitutes and discussed the ways that male-dominated society used all means at its disposal—legal, political, economic, and religious—to enforce women's sexual subservience to men. Gestefeld's novel echoed these concerns quite closely. It told the story of a pure woman, Murva Kroom, who naively insisted upon her right to refuse her husband's sexual demands but soon discovered that this basic right was viewed by all authorities, including her husband, a male doctor, and a male minister, as a rebellion against the laws of marriage, medicine, and religion. Gestefeld's heroine then recognized how male-defined ideologies provided interlocking support for male power. Kroom concluded that "religion, science, politics, however antagonistic . . . to each other" all nevertheless stood "arrayed in solid phalanx" (*The Woman Who Dares*, 252) to support male sexual access to women.

In *The Woman Who Dares*, Gestefeld faced the dilemma of many New Woman novelists. They wished to portray a world in which women had power to determine their own sexual and emotional lives yet knew that in contemporary society such independence by women would lead to ostracism and suffering. Some New Woman novelists dealt with this dilemma by insisting upon the conventional values of their heroines, thus blunting the edge of their protest; others maintained a commitment to realism, and so portrayed both rebellion and its costs, which ranged from personal rejection to madness and death. *The Woman Who Dares* was both a New Woman novel and a New Thought novel. According to New Thought beliefs, women and men could control reality by meditating upon affirmations or statements of how they wished the world to be. Change came primarily from altering one's pattern of thought, and only secondarily from direct action in the world. Through New Thought, Gestefeld found a way out of the dilemma faced by New Woman novelists. Gestefeld could realistically discuss the consequences of rebellion (Kroom was accused of insanity and thrown out of her home for refusing to sleep with her husband). At the same time she softened those consequences by demonstrating how, through New Thought–style adherence to an inner, higher truth, Kroom could pass through emotional, financial, and even physical threats unscathed. The political consequences of this reliance upon inner thought were mixed, however. Although Kroom's understanding of the nature of women's lives under patriarchy was devastatingly clear, her response to this understanding was oddly passive. Kroom simply held to her ideals and waited for the world—and her husband—to change accordingly.

By the turn of the century, Gestefeld began to publish books about how to use New Thought affirmations to bring not physical health but material wealth. In so doing Gestefeld was following the lead of countless New Thought authors, both male and female. Indeed, by the early twentieth century the reader addressed by New Thought tracts had shifted from the invalid woman seeking physical and spiritual uplift to the independent young businessman who could draw upon "thought-force" in order to make his way in a competitive business world. For women, however, such advice challenged long-standing cultural prohibitions on women's self-assertion.

The tension between commitment to older views of women's passivity, on the one hand, and the attempt to make New Thought understandings of mental power relevant to a larger male audience, on the other, showed in Gestefeld's popular 1901 tract, *How to Control Circumstances*. This book contained oddly contradictory advice on how one ought to respond to downward mobility. On the one hand, Gestefeld argued that poverty was a spur to effort and greatness: with confidence in one's thought-power, one could "gird up [one's] loins" and "meet and conquer" (p. 68) all exigencies. On the other hand, Gestefeld continued to promote a power through passivity more typical of her earlier work. Describing the fate of a person who must leave a "handsome house and live in a small one in an unfashionable neighborhood" (p. 40), Gestefeld advised not aggressive action but a passive acceptance and retreat into one's own inner world, where nothing could hurt one.

While appealing to wider audiences through books like *How to Control Circumstances*, Gestefeld continued to build up her position within the New Thought movement. In 1903, Gestefeld began to call her Science of Being congregation "The Church of 'The New Thought.'" For the next ten years Gestefeld worked to organize a national federation of New Thought churches. She addressed New Thought congresses and held prominent positions within the National New Thought Alliance.

In 1914, the sixty-nine-year-old Gestefeld traveled to London for the inauguration of the International New Thought Alliance. By then, branches of her Science of Being had spread to Great Britain, and several of her works had been translated into German. Gestefeld continued to write and lecture on the Science of Being throughout the 1910s. She died in 1921, from toxemia, at the home of her nurse in Kenosha, Wisconsin. Her cremated remains were interred at Graceland Cemetery, Chicago.

Gestefeld's writings and career demonstrate the complexity of "positive thinking" religious practices for women. The New Thought industry was quite welcoming to women and provided producers of New Thought material with an independence and respect not easily found in other fields. New Thought healing, teaching, or writing was an ideal career for the woman of comfortable background but currently uncertain economic status. Gestefeld's New Thought writings both recognized male dominance and women's personal, sexual, and economic vulnerability and sought to convince women that the safest and best response to that vulnerability was to live in their thought worlds. This mixed strategy of both acknowledging the consequences of social inequality and promoting a nonconfrontational cushion against the psychic effects of such inequality was the ambiguous legacy left by leaders such as Gestefeld to later metaphysical or positive thinking movements in the United States.

Sources. In addition to the works mentioned above, Gestefeld's writings include *What Is Mental Medicine?* (1887), *A Chicago Bible Class* (1891), *How We Master Our Fate* (1897), *The Builder and the Plan* (1901), *The Master of the Man* (1914), and a second New Thought novel, *The Leprosy of Miriam* (1894). Scattered copies of Gestefeld's journal *Exodus* are available at the CHS. Charles Brodie Patterson wrote a short biography of Gestefeld in *Mind* magazine, January 1902. A biographical entry on Gestefeld appears in *NAW* (1971). An analysis of Gestefeld's novels and a discussion of her New Thought career appear in Beryl Satter, "New Thought and the Era of Woman, 1875–1895" (Ph.D. diss., Yale Univ., 1992). See also Beryl Satter, *Each Mind a Kingdom: American Women, Reform and the New Thought Movement, 1875–1920* (1999).

BERYL SATTER

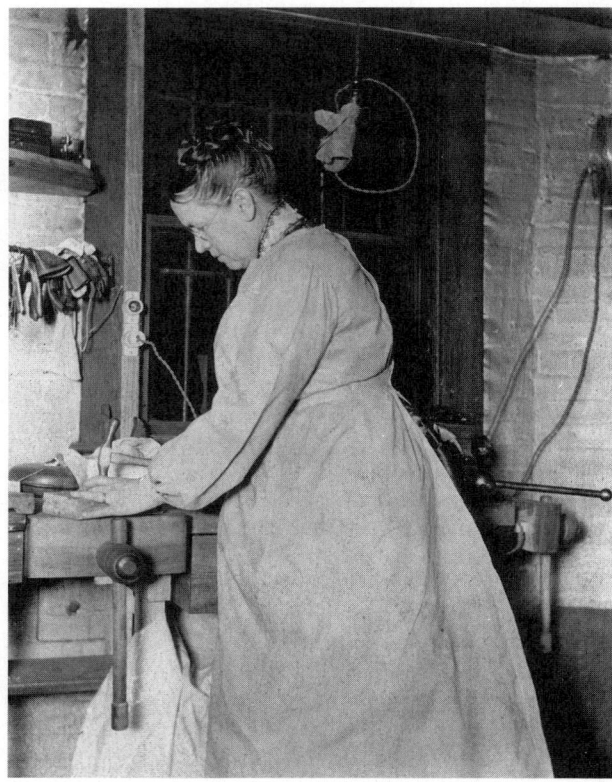

Fig. 42. *Arts patron and craftswoman Frances MacBeth Glessner silversmithing in her home studio in the basement of her Prairie Avenue mansion.*

GLESSNER, FRANCES MacBETH
January 1, 1848–October 20, 1932
CULTURAL PHILANTHROPIST, SILVERSMITH, CLUBWOMAN

Born to a family of modest means, Frances Glessner became a leading collector of aesthetic and Arts and Crafts movement decorative arts, a major patron of the Chicago Symphony Orchestra, and a skilled metalworker. Sarah Frances MacBeth was born in Urbana, Ohio, the youngest of six children of James Reid and Nancy (Bayard) MacBeth. James Reid MacBeth owned one of five general stores in Urbana in the 1840s. A literate man, skilled woodworker, and fiddle player, he and his wife instilled in their children a lifelong love of music and crafts.

Frances MacBeth was only two or three years old when the family was forced into bankruptcy. Mother and children moved into a small cottage owned by Frances MacBeth's grandfather, while her father left to seek his fortune in California mining. After a three-year absence, James MacBeth's prospecting had yielded only poppy seeds and a garnet. His separation from his family became permanent when he became general agent for the Adams Express Company in New York; he visited his family only twice yearly.

Education was valued by the MacBeths for both females and males. MacBeth's eldest siblings, Charles and Helen, were enrolled at Urbana Seminary, and Frances MacBeth probably at-

tended as well. Urbana, the nation's second coeducational institution of higher learning, was the first college-level institution in America to be affiliated with Swedenborgianism. Frances MacBeth probably then attended Oxford Female Institute (later Oxford Female College) in Oxford, Ohio, where she was exposed to the liberal "New School" theological views of Presbyterian minister David Swing, later a controversial religious leader in Chicago and lifelong friend of Frances MacBeth. Another sister, Anna, eight years older, was educated at Western Female Seminary, also in Oxford, Ohio.

The MacBeths moved to Springfield, Ohio, where Frances's mother, Nancy, took in boarders to support the family. By 1865 Nancy MacBeth's failing health required Frances MacBeth, then seventeen, to run the boarding house. She and her sister taught school in Jeffersonville and Brookville, Indiana.

Though Frances MacBeth was soft-spoken and plain in appearance, her humor and wit caught the attention of John J. Glessner, who had moved to Springfield in 1868 to work for the farm machinery manufacturer, Warder & Child, and boarded in the MacBeth home. Soon he "inspired the love of Frances" (*Family Reunion*, 314), and they married in 1870, the year Glessner was made a partner in the firm. Theirs was to become an unusually egalitarian marriage, and the couple remained intensely devoted to each other throughout their lives. They moved to Chicago that same year so that John Glessner could supervise the expanded firm of Warder, Bushnell & Glessner.

In Chicago Frances and John Glessner departed from nineteenth-century convention of men and women operating in separate spheres and pursued a shared interest in art, hosting a variety of cultural activities in their first home, a rented house on the city's Near West Side. Stimulated by contemporary debates about style and taste, they read Eugène Viollet-le-Duc, Charles Eastlake, William Morris, and John Ruskin—leaders of an aesthetic movement in decorative design. The Glessners, too, came to believe that an artfully designed house elevated the moral fiber of those who lived within it.

Frances Glessner purchased new furnishings, including a piano, reflecting her great passion and talent for music as well as the social convention of the period. John George MacBeth Glessner, their first child, was born in 1871, within days of the Great Chicago Fire. Their rented home and neighborhood were outside the range of the destructive blaze. In 1874, the Glessners purchased a large Italianate frame house nearby. A daughter, Frances, was born in 1878, and the couple began to employ several servants, whose services freed the Glessners to turn their attention to the burgeoning cultural activities of the city.

Frances and John Glessner met two individuals in 1876 who would influence their decorative choices throughout their lives: noted Chicago art historian and dealer E. L. Waters and talented furniture craftsman Isaac Elwood Scott. That year the couple also decided to begin collecting decorative objects, visiting the Philadelphia Centennial Exposition to further inform themselves. Soon the Glessners became regular patrons of Waters, whom they commissioned to buy objects during his European trips, and Scott, whom Frances Glessner commissioned to create furnishings and architectural embellishments for nearly every room. Scott began in the library, which was becoming the functional and symbolic focal point of the Glessners' domestic and social life. Here they pursued their interests in education and art, acquiring by 1886 approximately twenty-five hundred books. They were also becoming leaders in elite cultural circles.

In 1878 the Glessners commissioned Scott to design a coach house for their Chicago home. Five years later they hired him to design their summer estate in New Hampshire, "The Rocks," and a new headquarters building for Warder, Bushnell & Glessner in Chicago. Soon, Scott shared a place in the Glessners' intimate circle of friends, often joining the family for weeks during summer visits to New Hampshire, where he designed other buildings, including Frances Glessner's bee house, in which she pursued her hobby of beekeeping. Frances Glessner became Scott's lifelong patron, often attempting to help sell his work by taking his elaborately carved picture frames with her when making social visits. The journals kept by Frances and John Glessner throughout their marriage—about family life, social and cultural events, and art patronage—detail their collection of decorative objects during the 1870s. While these journals strongly indicate that John Glessner was included in these collecting decisions, he attributes the selection of objects entirely to her. Frances Glessner preferred only British or European-made handcrafted objects, many of which replicated the forms of me-

dieval Europe. She gathered steel engravings and plaster or bronze busts of celebrated and learned figures from ancient through contemporary times. For each engraving, Scott was commissioned to make a unique, elaborately carved frame. Glessner collected vases that were Japanese made or influenced, chargers (large flat platters), and bronzes as well.

Glessner also continued her cultural pursuits in other arenas, hosting lectures on music and art in her home and attending many other lectures on a wide range of subjects. In 1880 she was elected to the Fortnightly of Chicago, devoted to literary studies and self-improvement. Founded in 1873 by KATE NEWELL DOGGETT, the Fortnightly included among its members Chicago's best-educated and most socially prominent women. Intensely private and modest, Frances Glessner declined the offer of presidency of the Fortnightly, later explaining that she "knew it was better to be on the Nominating Committee" (interview with Martha L. Batchelder). On several occasions, however, Frances Glessner presented papers before this group.

Only four years after redecorating their Near West Side home, the Glessners decided to build a new residence that would reflect their elite status as well as declare them practitioners of the most progressive ideas in home design. They purchased the last lots available on Chicago's most fashionable residential street, Prairie Avenue. With great deliberation, the couple began the process of selecting an architect, resulting in the commission of Boston architect Henry Hobson Richardson. The Glessners traveled to Boston on three different occasions to meet with the renowned European-trained architect. Both husband and wife reviewed and approved Richardson's architectural drawings for their new home. On at least one occasion, Frances Glessner's recommended changes to Richardson's design—in this case in the servant quarters—were immediately accepted without question.

Richardson further stimulated and educated the Glessners in decorative theory and design, carefully leading these like-minded, educated clients toward the more advanced design of Arts and Crafts movement practitioners. On several occasions, Richardson invited them into his home, where he introduced them to the inner circle of designers and craftsman with whom he worked. His assistants took the couple on shopping trips to select appropriate furnishings for their new home. Less than ten years after purchasing a household of furniture from Isaac Scott, the Glessners commissioned a household of new furniture to better fit into the minimally ornamented oak rooms Richardson was creating for them. Supervised by Richardson's assistants, Francis Bacon of A. H. Davenport and Company, one of the most popular design houses in the country, created custom-designed furniture for the library, parlor, and dining room. Friendships with artists and other collectors also led to additions to the Glessners' collections. They had met British painter Sir Hubert von Herkomer through Richardson and purchased two of the artist's watercolors.

During the construction of their new house, the couple weathered a barrage of criticism regarding its architecture. Frances Glessner endured the critics with humor, keeping careful track of each negative and the few positive remarks about their house in her weekly journal entries, including speculation by some that the fortress-like style of this city mansion was so contructed, not long after the Haymarket incident, as a refuge against urban unrest and violence. Planned well before the Haymarket bomb, their home did, however, depart dramatically from the norm of the day. Windowless, dense walls faced the neighbors to provide privacy and respite from city noise and street traffic, with interior windows reserved for the space that opened onto a large garden-like courtyard. Despite what might have been for some a disastrous introduction into Chicago society, Frances and John Glessner exhibited a well-developed confidence in their choice of design. These short, wiry individuals of firm step, somber dress, orderly routine, low pleasant voice, and unhurried, quiet, and kindly manner soon charmed their peers with their devotion to culture and the arts.

In 1890, Frances and John Glessner traveled to England, France, and Italy to collect appropriate decorative objects for their new home, returning with several small sculptures from Italy that replicated ancient or Renaissance works. Frances Glessner exchanged notes for sources of fine European antiques with Boston art collector Isabella Stewart Gardner. The two even purchased nearly identical Italian oil lamps in Europe.

By 1891 Frances Glessner had become a significant leader among Chicago women decorative arts collectors. A member of the Decorative Arts Society (later the Antiquarian Society of the Art Institute of Chicago), Frances Glessner served as a director during the 1890s and from the 1910s through 1920. Her agenda, sometimes considered controversial, was to forge a decorative arts' selection policy that relied on professional expertise. Increasingly focused on selection and purchase of decorative arts pieces of the highest quality for display at the Art Institute, the Antiquarians transformed a private aesthetic into museum policy as they shaped and influenced the emerging collections of decorative arts at the Art Institute.

Eager to support a professional symphony in Chicago, John and Frances Glessner were among a group of civic leaders who invited Theodore Thomas to Chicago to begin an orchestra. In 1891 the Chicago Symphony Orchestra was founded with Thomas as its first conductor. Frances Glessner raised money for the symphony among her wealthy friends and developed a close relationship with the symphony's conductors. She and her husband entertained Theodore Thomas and ROSE THOMAS, his wife, and symphony guest artists, including Sergei Rachmaninoff, Ignace Paderewski, and Enrico Caruso, at Friday night dinners. She continued this practice with Frederick Stock, Thomas's successor, who wrote *Symphony in C Minor* at the Glessner's New Hampshire home and dedicated the work, and its first performance in concert on January 2, 1910, to the Glessners.

By the time of the opening of the World's Columbian Exposition of 1893, esteem for Frances Glessner among cultured circles allowed her unusual access to the exhibits. She was hosted by the Exposition's architects—Daniel Burnham, Stanford White, and Charles McKim—on private tours of the fair grounds. She watched the illumination of the opening night from the private suite of the Exposition's president, Harlow Higenbothem, and during subsequent visits purchased decorative objects for her home. These included a silver tea service from the British exhibit, a silver urn-shaped bowl and tray replicating

Pompeiian objects from the Italian exhibit, and an ornate Thai punch bowl and ladle.

Following the closing of the Exposition, William Rainey Harper, president of the University of Chicago, asked Frances Glessner to start an intellectual activity for the wives of university professors. She founded the Monday Morning Reading Class in 1894. Up to fifty socialites and professors' wives gathered each Monday at her Prairie Avenue home to listen to two hours of reading: serious works, usually histories, during the first hour, and lighter works during the second. The Monday Morning Reading Class met continuously for thirty-six years with many of its original members, disbanding when Frances Glessner became too ill to continue as its host.

Frances Glessner's creative activities expanded in 1904 to include the craft of silversmithing. For many years she had lived out the Arts and Crafts ideal of a deeper human instinct of workmanship by embroidering art linens for use in her home, most of which were from designs created by Isaac Scott. As a member of the Decorative Arts Society, she stitched William Morris designs onto silk and velvet portieres and piano throws for her parlor. By venturing into silversmithing, she entered a creative territory typically reserved for men, although there were several outstanding women metalsmiths in Chicago, including Madeline Yale Wynne and CLARA WELLES. Glessner became an accomplished metalworker under the tutelage of Hull-House jewelry maker A. Fogliati. She set up a workbench in her Prairie Avenue home at which she worked for hours at a time, creating fine silver bowls, pitchers, salt dishes, and jewelry, most of which she gave as gifts to family and friends. She also commissioned Fogliati to craft fine Art Nouveau–styled jewelry. Her metalwork displayed more wide-ranging style than her art purchases, often encompassing Art Nouveau and even the simplicity of new Scandinavian styles.

As a woman in her seventies, Frances Glessner continued to be active in the Antiquarian Society. The Glessners were one of the last Prairie Avenue families to keep a residence in the city. Frances Glessner maintained her home and had close relations with her son and daughter. Both children married and lived with their families in two houses built close to their childhood home on Prairie Avenue.

Frances Glessner died of pneumonia at the age of eighty-four. On the evening of her death, conductor Frederick Stock added her favorite musical work, Bach's *Chorale Prelude*, to the Chicago Symphony Orchestra's performance, after which the orchestra and audience stood in silent memorial. She was buried in Graceland Cemetery, Chicago.

Frances Glessner found in the theories of aesthetics popularized by the Arts and Crafts movement a way to meld her individual talents with her roles as wife and mother. Described by her husband as "a woman of strong individuality, a rare character" (*Frances M. Glessner*, 14), she made significant contributions to artistic life in Chicago.

Sources. The Glessner Family Papers, CHS, include her journals (1871–1932), which contain occasional entries by her husband, and a diary kept from 1872 to 1880 by Frances Glessner's sister, Helen Mac-Beth. Materials in the Glessner House Museum Collection include a photography collection (1887–1923) and a recorded interview with

Martha L. Batchelder (1991). Privately printed materials have biographical and genealogical information: John Glessner Lee and Percy Maxim Lee, *Family Reunion: An Incomplete Account of the Maxim-Lee Family History* (1971); John J. Glessner, *Frances M. Glessner* (1932); and John J. Glessner, *The Story of a House* (1923).

CAROL J. CALLAHAN

GOGGIN, CATHARINE
1855–January 4, 1916
SCHOOL TEACHER, LABOR LEADER

Catharine Goggin, primary school teacher and cofounder, early president, and secretary of the Chicago Teachers' Federation (CTF), was born in upstate New York to Irish immigrant parents. In 1868, her father, Patrick Goggin, a laborer, moved the family to Chicago. Goggin studied under ELLA FLAGG YOUNG at the Chicago High School, where she graduated in 1872. She began teaching that fall at the Clarke School. Later, she transferred to the King School and finally, in 1881, to the Jones School. She remained at the Jones School for more than two decades before taking a full-time position with the CTF. She served the CTF as its president from 1899 to 1901 and as its secretary until her death in 1916. She never married.

Goggin's role as an organizer grew from two complementary pressures: her daily experiences as a classroom teacher and her family background among unskilled and semiskilled workers. Goggin's household displayed a consistent pattern of employment: women could choose between being homemakers or teachers, while men worked at one of a variety of trades and crafts. A paternal uncle, James Goggin, a lawyer and, between 1872 and 1875, Chicago school board member, was a notable exception. Teaching was the one career path open to her that promised a semi-independent lifestyle, but it in no way separated her from the daily experiences of her relatives and neighbors.

After twenty years of teaching, Goggin had attained both the depth of experience and the breadth of professional contact to articulate a critique of school management on behalf of Chicago public school teachers. In 1892, she became active in a movement to petition the legislature for a teachers' pension fund, a movement that met with success in 1895. The following year, Goggin was elected to serve as the teachers' representative on the pension board, succeeding her mentor, Ella Flagg Young.

The pension movement challenged some widely held assumptions about the teaching profession. It implied that teaching would be a lifelong vocation. Many contemporaries assumed that teaching was merely a way for young women to support themselves before marriage, and the Chicago school board actively debated whether married women should continue to teach. Pensions also carried an implication of tenure, and in this respect the pension movement directly challenged the existing hierarchy of the education system. All teaching contracts were annual, expiring at the close of the school year and subject to renewal only at the discretion of the school board. The pension movement implied a limitation on the power of the board to hire or release teachers at will.

More importantly, the pension movement revealed a concern for teachers' self-interest, which may have been its most radical aspect. Most teachers' organizations were pedagogical and emphasized the teacher's responsibility to the children.

Goggin saw things differently. She, her sisters Margaret, Mary, and Kittie, and many of her friends, had devoted their lives to teaching, not merely as a prelude to marriage but as a career. Teachers, Goggin believed, deserved the same respect and remuneration afforded other workers. Goggin also believed that the way to secure that goal was through the model provided by organized labor.

In the spring of 1897, Goggin and ten other women called a meeting at the Central Music Hall to organize the Chicago Teachers' Federation. The CTF was unique among teachers' organizations for two reasons. First, membership was limited to teachers; principals, administrators, and other school board supervisory personnel were excluded. As Goggin later explained, "Experience has shown that where all branches of the service were represented in an organization the opinions and personalities of the supervising force dominated the rank and file" (Reid, 42); by limiting membership to teachers, the CTF hoped to create a space for women to realize their own goals and ambitions.

Second, the guiding principle of the CTF was, in Goggin's words, "that *material* interests would be a powerful lever in arousing the hitherto unorganized body of the grade teachers to realize the benefits which might result from united action" (Goggin, "Chicago Teachers Federation," 254). The CTF did not deny that teaching involved an obligation to the children, only that the obligation was total. Teachers' concerns as workers were as important as pedagogy. For best results teachers needed to be paid adequate salaries to relieve their anxiety about finances, and the salaries could not be subject to decreases during the year. While active in debates over the proper means of educating children, the CTF was also concerned with the needs of the teachers.

The CTF's first objective was an increase in teachers' wages. The CTF noted that most teachers had not received a salary increase in nearly twenty years. Teachers, moreover, were overwhelmingly female, while administrators, who were disproportionately male, had secured significant raises. To rectify the imbalance, the CTF petitioned the school board for an increase in pay. When the effort was rebuffed, the CTF returned in the fall of 1897 with a grass roots organizing effort. By the spring of 1898, the CTF had gathered 3,567 signatures on its petition and 2,564 dues-paying teachers on its membership rolls, from a teaching body that was no larger than 5,000. In the fall of 1898, the teachers got a raise.

The CTF rewarded Goggin for her guidance and dedication by electing her to its presidency in the spring of 1899. Her inaugural speech outlined clearly her sense of the social order and the teachers' proper role within that order. "These are the days of great opportunities and great responsibilities; the days when great industries and concentrated capital have made necessary the organization and combination of the workers of every grade of society; the days when competition and organization of capital have resulted in the sudden appearance of gigantic trusts in almost every branch of industry; the days when immense corporations dominate even our municipal, state and national government. The public school stands as a great barrier against these evils and through them and from them must come the remedy, teaching as they do, the fundamental principles of our government, the greatest on this earth, resting on that bulwark of our liberties, the consent of the governed" (Goggin, "Inaugural Address," 309). Goggin's reliance on material interests as an organizing tool and her condemnation of huge trusts as evils suggested a radical perspective, but her solution, a better educated electorate, located her within reformist circles.

Goggin's resolve was immediately tested, as the increase in pay was short-lived. The following year, the school board announced that it lacked the funds to pay the increased wages and reverted to the old scale. To investigate the shortage, the CTF formed a Tax Committee consisting of Goggin and MARGARET HALEY, a vice-president of the CTF who became a close friend and colleague of Goggin. The cause of the shortage, Goggin and Haley discovered, was that many large businesses evaded property taxes entirely by valuing their net worth at impossibly low amounts. If these businesses paid their taxes, the school board would not face a shortfall. Since the board itself was uninterested in collecting all it was due, the CTF took on the task itself.

Goggin responded to the school board decision to rescind the pay increase in a manner typical of her ingenuity and determination. In 1901, Goggin, with Haley, as representatives of CTF, sued the State Board of Equalization to enforce a reasonable valuation. Her suit displayed a keen sense of the relationship between legal actions and public affairs and of the intricacies of constitutional law. She limited her complaint to the undervaluation of property owned by some two dozen public utilities—corporations that were unable to relocate if their taxes increased and that owed their existence to a government charter. From a public relations perspective, these corporations were the easiest to attack, while any legal ruling against them could equally apply to privately controlled businesses.

She grounded her claim in the Fourteenth Amendment's guarantee of substantive due process. An argument that the due process clause protected property as well as individual liberties had been developed primarily by large businesses; and for years, corporations had used the substantive due process argument to avoid public scrutiny and what they termed excessive and arbitrary regulation. Goggin's argument turned the tables, effectively arguing that underregulation was also arbitrary and unconstitutional, as it added to the burden of other taxpayers. On October 24, 1901, the Illinois Supreme Court ruled in Goggin's favor, forcing the State Board of Equalization to collect the proper taxes.

The Teachers' Tax Suit, as it came to be called, firmly established the CTF as a major player in the Chicago educational system. It also earned attention beyond the schools. Progressive groups around the city expressed their admiration of the CTF for single-handedly challenging the supremacy of big business and winning. The businesses that saw their tax breaks evaporate resented the CTF. The school board, embarrassed by the actions of the upstart teachers' organization and smarting at the direct challenge to their authority, refused, again, to pay the increased wages, instead allocating the new money to building maintenance. It would take another lawsuit to compel the school board to honor their past agreements and pay the wages specified in the contract.

At the close of the tax suit, the CTF voted to affiliate with the Chicago Federation of Labor (CFL). The move was an obvious one in some respects. The CTF had organized itself along the general outlines of a labor union since its inception. Under Goggin's leadership, the CTF had opened an office in the Unity Building, which also housed the CFL. The CFL had provided key tactical and political support throughout the tax suit. The affiliation vote was overwhelming, but the affiliation provoked further outrage from the business community, which maintained that teachers had no right to strike during the school year.

The right of children to an education had long been used as a bludgeon to deny teachers' rights, and Goggin's response evidenced her understanding that education and organization went hand in hand. When Mayor Carter H. Harrison briefly entered the wage issue in 1900, for example, he claimed that the only two options open to the school board were to revert to the old scale, which would harm the teachers, or shorten the school year at the children's expense. Given that choice, Harrison would side with the school children. The CTF denied that it ever intended to strike against the interests of the children; indeed, the CTF articulated a position that neatly combined unionism and teaching. Goggin believed that the teachers' cause was the same as that of the worker, and both causes were one with that of the children. The CTF remained true to its principles. By 1903, in addition to its other work lobbying for better teaching conditions and curriculum improvements, the CTF was raising money and supplies for striking anthracite coal miners in southern Illinois.

Sometime during the Teachers' Tax Suit, Goggin began to reassess her role in the CTF. She had left teaching in 1901 to work full-time for the CTF, serving in highly public roles as president, secretary, and leader of the tax suit; but her interests began to drift elsewhere. In Margaret A. Haley she had found a talented organizer, eager and capable of assuming the highly public role that Goggin had played. Goggin and Haley became close coworkers and roommates, and much of the early success of the CTF traced to the friendship between the two women. As Haley took on the task of representing CTF positions to the public, Goggin turned her attention to the internal needs of the organization: recruiting members, soothing egos, training and developing the next generation of leaders. For the next thirteen years, Goggin dedicated herself to building the CTF into an organization capable of weathering assaults and advancing its causes.

Goggin's dedication to the CTF remained unwavering. On January 4, 1916, although hospitalized with bronchitis, Goggin insisted on attending a routine CTF meeting. While walking back to the hospital, she was struck and killed by a Marshall Field's delivery truck. Her sudden death at the age of sixty-one came as a severe blow to the CTF and to the city and state in which she lived. Her body lay in state in City Hall, and dignitaries, including the governor, the Roman Catholic archbishop, and the heads of various labor unions and educational groups from across the nation, sent their condolences. Goggin's gift was to bridge alliances among people with apparently disparate interests and to make such alliances seem unsurprising.

Sources. The Chicago Teachers' Federation (CTF) Papers at the CHS contain much of Goggin's personal correspondence and the "Brief History of the Chicago Teachers' Federation," which is ascribed to Goggin in a penciled notation. Also in the CTF Papers are Arvilla C. DeLuce's

"Brief Account of the Pension Movement" (typescript) and the CTF's official history, the *Report, Showing the Results of Fifteen Years of Organizing to the Teachers of Chicago* (December 8, 1908). Despite Goggin's highly public role in her first decade with the CTF, her published writings are few, limited to "The Chicago Pension Law," *School Journal*, May 1, 1897; "The Report of the Educational Commission," *Chicago Teacher*, February 1899; "The Chicago Teachers' Federation," *Chicago Teacher and School Board Journal (CTSBJ)*, May 1899, reprinted in *Chicago Teachers' Federation Bulletin (CTFB)*, June 13, 1902; "Inaugural Address," *CTSBJ*, June 1899; and a few minor notices in the *CTFB*. The Teachers' Tax Suit reached the Illinois Supreme Court, titled *The State Board of Equalization et al. v. The People ex. rel. Catherine Goggin et al.* (1901). Secondary sources generally focus on Goggin through her friendship with Margaret A. Haley. Robert Reid's "The Professionalization of Public School Teachers: The Chicago Experience, 1895–1920" (Ph.D. diss., Northwestern Univ., 1968) takes the position that the CTF was about professionalization and middle-class respectability, while Marjorie Murphy's "From Artisan to Semi-Professional: White Collar Unionism among Chicago Public School Teachers, 1870–1930" (Ph.D. diss., Univ. of California, Davis, 1981) claims that the CTF was a nascent labor union. Also of general interest is Olive Orton Anderson's "The Chicago Teachers' Federation" (master's thesis, Univ. of Chicago, 1908).

DAVID MORRISON

GORDON, ANNA ADAMS
July 21, 1853–June 15, 1931
TEMPERANCE REFORMER, AUTHOR, HYMN WRITER

Anna Adams Gordon, fourth president of the National Woman's Christian Temperance Union (NWCTU), was born in Boston to James Monroe Gordon, bank executive, and Mary Elizabeth (Clarkson) Gordon, homemaker. Anna Gordon was the youngest of four sisters and had three younger brothers. When she was a small child, her family moved to Auburndale, a Boston suburb. She attended the nearby Newton, Massachusetts, public schools and graduated from Newton High School. She went to Mount Holyoke Seminary (now Mount Holyoke College) 1871–72 and, for a time, to Lasell Seminary (now Lasell College) in Auburndale, finishing her formal education in 1875.

The Gordon family was vitally interested in the foreign missionary movement since James Gordon was, for many years, the treasurer of the American Board of Commissioners for Foreign Missions. Missionaries home on furlough, and those about to journey to foreign mission fields, were often guests in the Gordon home while Anna Gordon was growing up. Her sister Alice (Gordon) Gulick had married a missionary, and Gordon spent 1876 in Spain visiting her sister, who founded and ran a girls' secondary school there. Gordon's early knowledge of and interest in other lands would stand her in good stead as she traveled to Europe and South America on behalf of the Woman's Christian Temperance Union (WCTU) from the 1890s through the 1920s.

Back in the United States by early 1877 and planning to study music, Gordon attended a revival in Boston held by famous evangelist Dwight L. Moody. She went to a women's meeting led by FRANCES E. WILLARD, former corresponding secretary of the WCTU and temporarily working with Moody. When Willard's organist failed to appear, she asked for a volunteer from the audience, and Anna Gordon came forward and accompanied the hymn singing, having taken her first or-

FIG. 43. *Anna Adams Gordon, on the left, with Frances E. Willard; Evanston, Illinois, 1880.*

gan lesson only a short time earlier. She and Willard became good friends, and Willard quickly discerned in Gordon a talent for organizing and detail work. She asked if Gordon would become her personal secretary. Gordon agreed, and for twenty-one years, as Willard rose in the leadership of the WCTU (becoming president in 1879), she served as Willard's indispensable assistant. She arranged Willard's increasingly busy schedule, traveled with her several thousand miles each year on speaking tours as the two women organized local WCTUs throughout the United States, handled her voluminous correspondence, and, during the 1890s, as Willard became ill, took care of her.

Anna Gordon became an integral member of the household at Rest Cottage, Willard's home in Evanston, Illinois, taking primary responsibility for its smooth running. For Willard's mother, Anna Gordon was like another daughter, and Frances Willard regarded her as a much younger sister. Gordon was not only an efficient secretary; she was Willard's beloved companion who devoted her life to the internationally famous reformer. When Willard died in February 1898, Anna Gordon was devastated but rallied quickly in order to be of assistance to Lillian M. N. Stevens, vice-president-at-large of the WCTU, whom

Willard had tapped to be her successor as president. At the WCTU Annual Convention in 1898, the organization chose Gordon to fill Stevens's former position, and the two WCTU officers quickly formed a close working relationship. Willard had stipulated in her will that Gordon could live in Rest Cottage until her death, and she chose to do so. But she spent several months each year in Maine, where Stevens lived, helping to plan WCTU activities and carry out the organization's aims.

Because Willard was a reform leader of international stature at the time of her death, her organization wished to memorialize her in suitable ways. At the request of the NWCTU, Gordon took upon herself the task of memorialization. The year of Willard's death, she wrote *The Beautiful Life of Frances E. Willard* (1898), a memorial volume intended to inspire temperance workers to continue their efforts in the reform Willard led for so many years. Gordon also persuaded the Illinois legislature to choose Willard as one of two persons to represent their state, placing her statue in Statuary Hall, the Capitol Rotunda, Washington, D.C., in 1905. She was the first woman so honored, and Gordon was almost single-handedly responsible for the honor.

While Willard was alive, most of Gordon's time had been taken up with her secretarial duties. Yet she managed to carve out a niche for herself in the WCTU agenda, working with children, her special love. She composed many marching tunes and songs for the Loyal Temperance Legion (LTL), the organization's juvenile arm; and with her encouragement, children's singing and parading became important features of WCTU mass meetings and rallies. During the 1910s and 1920s, Gordon also compiled several volumes of children's temperance songs and the *White Ribbon Hymnal* (1911) for use by adult temperance organizations. In 1891 Gordon became superintendent of juvenile work for the World's WCTU (WWCTU), the international women's temperance organization founded in 1883 by Willard and organized in 1891. Under the slogan Gordon devised: "Tremble King Alcohol, we shall grow up," she worked with WWCTU leaders to organize LTLs in more than two dozen countries to educate children and young people about the dangers of alcohol abuse.

Over the first two decades of the twentieth century, public sentiment for prohibition was steadily gathering strength as more and more cities and states went "dry" and a variety of organizations began to endorse the reform. Yet prohibition forces faced a formidable enemy in the politically powerful and well-funded liquor industry. The WCTU continued, as it had for many decades, to work for prohibition through legislation, opposing the efforts of the liquor industry. Over the years the WCTU had become skilled at lobbying state legislatures and Congress for prohibition, woman suffrage, and many other reforms. During the 1910s, when it became clear that national prohibition by constitutional amendment would be the most effective way to ensure a dry America, Gordon, along with President Stevens and the WCTU's paid lobbyist, Margaret Dye Ellis, stepped up pressure on Congress. The WCTU and its leadership also worked with other organizations, including the newly powerful Anti-Saloon League, toward a prohibition amendment. But they continued to support campaigns for state and local prohibition laws and ordinances. Gordon played a crucial role in Maine, which had been seen as the flagship prohibi-

tion state since the 1850s, when it passed the Maine Law, a prohibitory measure. In 1910–11, as Maine temperance leaders prepared for the resubmission of prohibition to a statewide referendum, Gordon originated and organized the "Young Campaigners for Prohibition." At the direction of Gordon and other LTL leaders, thirty-five thousand children circulated flyers and marched and sang at prohibition rallies. They were credited by the WCTU with helping to keep Maine a dry state.

In 1914, as the WCTU undertook concerted lobbying efforts in Washington, D.C., President Stevens died. Anna Gordon, as acting president, attended hearings before the house judiciary committee and presented a scroll containing a plea for prohibition, signed by representatives of twelve thousand organizations. She was elected NWCTU president later that year and continued her lobbying efforts. At a congressional debate on prohibition in 1915, she and other WCTU leaders unrolled a petition with five million signatures around the House gallery, which WCTU members and other prohibition supporters packed. During the 1910s the WCTU also worked for woman suffrage as it had since the 1880s, by this time arguing that women voters would strengthen enforcement laws once the prohibition amendment was passed.

Gordon's presidential addresses at the annual WCTU conventions regularly listed gains, both small and large, in the fight for prohibition. She claimed in her 1915 address, with some justification, that the WCTU's scientific temperance education over the past three decades—in public schools, Sunday schools, and the LTL—had virtually created the generation of temperance supporters that were now supporting a prohibition amendment and voting in state and local dry laws.

As the nation prepared to enter World War I, Anna Gordon called for her organization to support the war effort, coining the slogan: "Every White Ribboner a Prohibition Patriot" (Tyler, 168). Because she was president of a major women's organization, Gordon was asked to be on many war-related government and citizen-initiated committees, including the Woman's Committee of the Council of National Defense and the Advisory Board of the Women's Liberty Loan Committee. The WCTU and other temperance groups lobbied Congress for what they termed war prohibition (temperance) and worked for several measures to achieve this goal. In 1917, Gordon directed the gathering of signatures of six million women for a food conservation petition, requesting that, in a time of government food rationing, grains and fruits not be used for the production of alcoholic drinks. This petition was presented to Congress along with a letter from Gordon to President Wilson, urging his support for this wartime measure. The prohibition forces' goal was partially achieved; Congress did vote to forbid the use of foodstuffs in distilled liquor. Like many other women's organizations, the WCTU, with Gordon's encouragement, also participated in numerous activities to aid American troops and civilians suffering in the war. They raised funds for ambulances sent to battle zones and for relief work among refugees, set up temperance recreation centers in army and navy bases, and pressured the government to ensure safe conditions for the many women who worked in factories during wartime.

While mobilizing for these war-related activities, the WCTU did not let up in its push for total prohibition. By December 1917, Congress passed a resolution to submit a national prohibition amendment to the states, with WCTU supporters attending. WCTU lobbyist Margaret Dye Ellis organized the intense effort to persuade members of state legislatures to vote in prohibition; and Gordon spent the winter of 1917–18 in Washington, D.C., working closely with her. Ellis lauded Gordon for being a tower of strength in the final days of prohibition campaigning. A year later, on January 29, 1919, the Eighteenth Amendment for National Prohibition was proclaimed; and the following January, prohibition went into effect. Later that year, the Nineteenth Amendment giving women the vote was passed; the two goals that the WCTU had struggled toward for nearly half a century were finally accomplished.

After the passage of the Eighteenth Amendment, many prohibition organizations disbanded. Anna Gordon, however, announced to her constituency that the work of the WCTU had just begun. As early as 1915, she had proposed to celebrate the organization's fiftieth anniversary—the jubilee year of 1924—by raising a million dollars and building the membership to one million. The money collected was earmarked for salaries for the directors of the Departments of Americanization, Scientific Temperance Instruction, and Child Welfare, areas on which Gordon wished the organization to focus during the 1920s. The money raised would also provide for an Americanization Center in New York City to train WCTU women for work in light of the new wave of immigration Gordon predicted would occur after World War I. A large grant would be given for a Child Welfare Research Station to be set up at the University of Iowa. Although the WCTU did not achieve the fund-raising and membership goals it set for itself for its jubilee year, the organization did raise a substantial sum of money and its membership neared the five hundred thousand mark by 1924.

Calls for repeal of the Prohibition Amendment began almost as soon as it was passed, and they increased in intensity over the 1920s and into the 1930s. Gordon was alert to the danger of possible repeal, and her presidential addresses during the 1920s featured extensive lists of the benefits prohibition had brought to the nation. At the same time, the success of American prohibitionists encouraged temperance reformers internationally to look toward the possibility of worldwide prohibition. To aid in making this goal a reality, in 1920 the NWCTU commissioned Gordon to make a survey of WCTU work in Europe. She visited European countries, encouraging prohibition work. In 1921, as vice-president of the WWCTU, she toured five South American republics, again surveying WCTU work there and encouraging national prohibition. She was elected president of the WWCTU in 1922 and visited Mexico that same year to gauge progress toward prohibition there. In 1925, she resigned as president of the National WCTU in order to devote herself fully to her duties as president of the WWCTU. She presided over WWCTU conventions in Edinburgh, Scotland, in 1925, and in Lausanne, Switzerland, in 1928. As the acknowledged leader of women's international prohibition activity, Gordon served, during the mid to late 1920s, as an officer of the World Wide League against Alcoholism.

Gordon's stature in international prohibition reform and her long service in the cause of temperance brought her recognition. In 1898 the NWCTU proclaimed her birthday—July 21—as LTL Day, to be celebrated by children's temperance groups in many countries. She received an honorary degree from Northwestern University in 1924. Even with all her duties for the NWCTU and the WWCTU, she still managed to be an active member in many national and local organizations, from the National Council of Women, of which she was an officer, to the women's society of the Evanston Methodist Church, which she had joined in the 1870s when she came to Rest Cottage to live with Frances Willard.

Although Gordon had kept up a whirlwind of travel during the 1920s, by the end of the decade she was, in her mid-seventies, slowing down and becoming more frail. After the Lausanne conference, she stayed at the Castile, New York, sanatarium where she had taken Willard for rest and recuperation during her last years. Gordon's sister Elizabeth accompanied her to Castile, helping to care for her there. Ill health kept Gordon from attending the 1929 NWCTU convention. She hoped to attend the WWCTU convention in 1930 in Toronto but was unable to make the trip. She died of myocarditis at age seventy-seven in Castile, with her sister at her bedside. She was cremated and her ashes interred in the Gordon family plot in Mount Hope Cemetery, Mattapan, Massachusetts. WCTU members around the world mourned their beloved leader, who had played a crucial role in achieving prohibition in the United States and who looked so hopefully toward a world without alcohol.

Sources. Eight boxes of material on Anna Gordon, including correspondence, typescripts of speeches, pamphlets written by her, a typescript of her memorial service, and memorabilia, are deposited at the Frances E. Willard Memorial Library, National Woman's Christian Temperance Union (NWCTU) headquarters, Evanston, Illinois. The library also holds copies of the hymnals, song books, and other volumes authored by Gordon, including *The Beautiful Life of Frances Willard* (1898), her memorial volume for Frances Willard, commissioned by the Woman's Christian Temperance Union (WCTU). Gordon's Annual Addresses as president of the World's Woman's Christian Temperance Union (WWCTU) are in bound volumes at the Willard Memorial Library, and there is also at the library a brief diary kept by Gordon at the time of Willard's death. The microfilm collection, *Temperance and Prohibition Papers* (1977), Randall C. Jimerson, Frances X. Blouin, and Charles Isetts, eds., contains material on Gordon in Series III–WCTU and Series XXI–*The Union Signal* (the weekly newspaper of the WCTU). The WCTU series contains films of the bound WCTU Annual Meeting volumes, which include Gordon's presidential addresses, and the *Union Signal* series contains many items about and by Gordon from the 1880s until her death in 1931. The June 27, 1931, issue of the *Union Signal* is a memorial to Gordon. Julia Freeman Deane, *Anna Adams Gordon, a Story of Her Life* (n.d., but probably 1931), a memorial biographical booklet, commissioned by the WCTU, is useful for insights into Gordon's personality, early life, and work with children. For Gordon's accomplishments as president of the WCTU and the WWCTU, see Elizabeth Putnam Gordon (Anna Gordon's sister and longtime president of the Massachusetts WCTU), *Women Torchbearers: The Story of the Woman's Christian Temperance Union* (1924), a history commissioned by the WCTU for its fiftieth anniversary; and Helen E. Tyler, *Where Prayer and Purpose Meet, the W.C.T.U. Story, 1874–1949* (1949), another volume commissioned by the WCTU for its seventy-fifth anniversary. For background on the NWCTU and Willard's and Gordon's friendship and working relationship, see Mary Earhart, *Frances Willard: From Prayers to Politics* (1944), and Ruth Bordin, *Frances Willard, A Biography* (1986) and *Woman and Temperance: The Quest for Power and Liberty,*

1873–1900 (1981). See also Carolyn De Swarte Gifford, ed., *Writing Out My Heart: Selections from the Journal of Frances E. Willard, 1855–1896* (1995), for the friendship of Gordon and Willard. For general information on the WWCTU, see Ian Tyrell, *Woman's World, Woman's Empire: The Woman's Christian Temperance Union in International Perspective, 1880–1930* (1991). For a history of the prohibition movement in the United States, see Norman H. Clark, *Deliver Us from Evil: An interpretation of American Prohibition* (1976).

CAROLYN DE SWARTE GIFFORD

GRIDLEY, MARION
November 16, 1906–October 31, 1974
AUTHOR, PUBLICIST, LECTURER

Marion Gridley, editor of the *Amerindian* and author of numerous books on American Indians, was the daughter of William Thomson and Ada A. (Robertson) Gridley. According to Gridley, her ancestors founded the town of Farmington, Connecticut, in 1640, and were friendly with the Tunxis Indians. Born in White Plains, New York, Gridley later moved to Chicago with her family.

Gridley's lifelong commitment to American Indians began when she was a child playing cowboy and Indian games: "It got to the point where the boys in the neighborhood never wanted to play with me because I always insisted the Indians should win" (quoted in "Action Line"). In 1923, her parents helped to found the Grand Council Fire, a national organization of Indians and non-Indians. Its name was changed in 1932 to the Indian Council Fire (ICF). Gridley's father was "Chief Medicine Man" or grand marshal until 1934, supervising the organization's finances, while her mother served as program chair and later helped with publicity. At sixteen, Gridley became executive secretary (Chief Storyteller), a position she held until 1969. The Grand Council Fire and later the ICF provided a forum for discussing Indian problems, sponsored social activities, and gave assistance to Chicago Indians. Among the many projects Gridley originated to benefit Indian people were scholarship programs, an exhibit devoted to Indian progress at the Chicago Century of Progress Exposition in 1933 and 1934, and the Indian Achievement Award presented annually since 1933 to Indians of distinction. During the Chicago Century of Progress Exposition, she and her mother worked to find jobs for Native Americans.

During his term as president of the Grand Council Fire (1923–25), Francis Cayou adopted Gridley into his tribe, the Omaha, giving her his mother's name, Me-Un-Ba-Tay (Little Moonbeam). As Gridley explained, "I had to belong to some Indian tribe to make it okay, so the president, an Omaha, adopted me in a real ceremony with our blood mixed and tribal dress" ("Author Bases Expertise on Indians," 16).

On May 15, 1932, she married Winnebago (now Ho-Chunk) Indian Robinson Johnson (Whirling Thunder), a lecturer on and teacher of Indian lore who worked as an instructor with the Chicago Park District. After their marriage, Robinson Johnson arranged for her to be adopted by the Ho-Chunks. She was given the name "Glory of the Morning," after a noted Ho-Chunk woman of early times. Discussing her 1947 divorce Gridley commented that "the Indian-white gap became unbridgeable" (quoted in "Author Bases Expertise on Indians").

Gridley was indefatigable in her efforts on behalf of the ICF. She persuaded many prominent Chicagoans to join this organization or support its projects. Both she and her mother served as liaisons with the Illinois Federation and General Federation of Women's Clubs, who sponsored the ICF. In 1954–55, she attended Northwestern University. In 1952, Gridley founded *Amerindian*, a not-for-profit bimonthly informational news bulletin. By the 1960s, issues of *Amerindian* stated that its purpose was "to present the Indian people with human dignity" and in terms of "accomplishment and endeavor."

Gridley described her editorial approach as "one of objectivity without political alignment or bias" ("Meet the Editor-Publisher," 3). Gridley later added an advisory board of distinguished Native Americans, many of whom were Indian Achievement Award winners. By 1974, the bulletin had increased its original four pages to eleven. Despite occasional lapses into stereotypical language, Gridley's *Amerindian* was, in the 1950s and 1960s, an important source of information about Indian achievement and contemporary issues.

Gridley increased the native voice in the journal by adding editorials by prominent Indians. *Amerindian* had features on the activities of Native American women, including a survey of the women in responsible tribal posts (September–October 1954), an article on Indian Women's Clubs (September–October 1955), and Indian "Lady Marines" (January–February 1971). It included brief notes on new books by and about Native Americans. By 1964 the bulletin was in most state and large university libraries and many public libraries across the country. It was distributed by the National Council of the Episcopal Church to its missionaries and ordered by the Mississippi Choctaw Reservation for text material. Typical of the letters of praise cited in the "Tipi Talk" column in the *Amerindian* in 1963 was a comment by the librarian of the University of Oklahoma that it was a very welcome publication on their shelves. The Illinois Woman's Press Association awarded *Amerindian* the second-place Mate Palmer Award for 1971–72 for a publication edited by a woman.

By the 1970s, *Amerindian* was being superseded by journals written and published by Native Americans. Anthropologist Beatrice Medicine (Lakota), who first met Gridley around 1957, said that *Amerindian* "really shows the interests of [American Indian] people during that time" (interview). She counts among the journal's achievements the inclusion of items about Alaskan natives, which "at that early time was not even thought of" (interview). Gridley always "tried to feature how Indians were doing things for themselves" (interview). For Medicine, one of Gridley's major accomplishments in *Amerindian* was to present news about Native Americans written by them or from their point of view.

The Gridleys and non-Indians dominated the Grand Council Fire and ICF at least through the 1950s. Willard LaMere (Ho-Chunk), whose father, Oliver, was a vice-president of the Grand Council Fire and who himself served two terms as Council Fire president (1961–67, 1977–82), stated that "Marion Gridley was always one of the people in charge of everything, you know, you didn't make a decision with her, she made the decision" ("History of Indians in Chicago," n.p.). According to LaMere, Gridley had difficulty adjusting to increased Indian assertiveness. She was hostile to the establishment of the American Indian Center, chartered in 1954, which she refused to recognize. When Robert Reitz became director, she softened her opposition around 1957 and "attached herself to it, like an ally" ("History of Indians in Chicago").

As a result of the federal government's efforts to terminate reservation status in the 1950s, Native American leaders became much more activist and then militant in their efforts to improve Indian status and life. Controversial organizations like the American Indian Movement captured headlines with their protests, and Indian organizations began publishing their own journals and newspapers. Although the Chicago community was never as militant as other urban Indian communities, individuals did become more conscious of the need to establish their own priorities and speak in their own voices.

The growing desire of the members of the ICF to take greater control of its activities led to a bitter dispute with Gridley. The two immediate causes were a Donner Foundation grant of twenty-five thousand dollars to the ICF for the publication of *Indians Today*, a collection of short biographies written by Gridley, and the fact that the ICF Illinois charter had been allowed to lapse. Because the grant had been made to her, Gridley informed the board she was going to reorganize ICF with a group loyal to her and tried to get the Illinois courts to set aside the state's reinstatement of ICF's charter. In two issues of the *Amerindian*, Gridley declared that she had established Indian Council Fire Publications, Inc., to publish *Indians of Today* (May–June 1970) and that she had arranged for an Illinois charter for the Indian Council Fire Achievement Award, Inc. (September–October 1970). Thereafter, the new organization gave its award in Washington, D.C., while the original ICF gave its award in Chicago. On April 22, 1970, the ICF formally relieved Gridley of her responsibilities as executive secretary. The controversy was not settled until 1976, when the two organizations, both of which included Indian and non-Indian members, merged. Undoubtedly part of the problem was Gridley's leadership style. ICF celebrated its fiftieth anniversary in 1982 and was active until 1989.

Although *Amerindian* covered the growing incidents of Indian militancy in the 1970s, Gridley had little patience with its leaders, who, she believed, often indulged in "a large dose of posing" ("Author Bases Expertise on Indians"). Gridley, however, stressed that whites "must try to understand the valid complaints and frustrations that lie beneath Indian militancy" ("Author Bases Expertise on Indians"). In accordance with her will, *Amerindian* ceased after her death in 1974.

Gridley also became exasperated with Chicago and urban Indian politics: "Indians in cities often become pathologically jealous—it's an absolute curse" ("Author Bases Expertise on Indians"). She concluded that this situation was "a development of their relations in white society. On the reservation, they had nothing to be jealous about, certainly not about their chiefs, who were advisers rather than dictators" ("Author Bases Expertise on Indians")—a comment that more accurately reflected Gridley's naive romanticism than the reality of reservation politics.

In demand as a lecturer on Indians and consultant for the government and others, Gridley won honorary citations from European academic societies for her work and writing. She received the Illinois Woman's Press Association Merit Award (1939–40) and in 1965 was named its woman of the year. In 1971 Gridley received a certificate of commendation from President Richard Nixon, "In recognition of exceptional service to others" (quoted in *Amerindian*, March–April 1971, 1).

A member of the Daughters of the American Revolution, the Geographical Society of Chicago, and Society of Midland Authors, Gridley was especially active in the Illinois Woman's Press Association, which she joined in 1923, three years after her mother became a member. In addition to serving on many of its committees, she was also elected as third vice-president (1940–41) and second vice-president (1950–55). She presented programs on American Indians in 1947–48 and in February 1972. From 1955 to 1956, she was regional vice-president of the National Federation of Press Women.

Throughout her career, Gridley held a series of jobs as director of publication relations, some of which overlapped. In her various autobiographical accounts and in the Illinois Woman's Press Association *Year Book*, she listed the Young Men's Christian Association (1946–49), Illinois Heart Association (1948–59), the National Society for Medical Research (1949–51), Illinois Heart Association (1948–59), Chicago Medical School (1949–50), Passavant Hospital (1953–54), Children's Memorial Hospital (n.d.), and Francis W. Parker School (n.d.). In her later years she was primarily a freelance writer who supported herself by editing.

The author of the children's book *Jamie's Dog* (1961), she is best known for her books on American Indians. Those written for young people include *The Story of Pocahontas* (1942), *Hiawatha* (1950), *Indian Nations* (5 volumes, 1969), *Pontiac* (1970), *Osceola* (1972), and *Maria Tallchief* (1973). Her most important books on Indians were several collections of biographies. Her *Indians of Today* went through several revised editions (1936, 1947, 1960, sponsored by the ICF; 1970, Indian Council Fire Publications). Equally valuable were her *Indians of Yesterday*, sponsored by the ICF (1940), and *Contemporary American Indian Leaders* (1972). Her *American Indian Women* (1974) was probably the first collection of short biographies of Native American women. Although Gridley's biographies brought to public attention the achievements of many hitherto unknown Native Americans, her accounts were often skimpy and inaccurate. Among Gridley's other books on American Indians were *Indian Legends of American Scenes* (1939), sponsored by the ICF; *America's Indian Statues* (1966), short sketches that originally appeared in *Amerindian*; *American Indian Tribes* (1974); and *American Indian Tribes of America* (1973 and 1976).

Summarizing Gridley's contributions to American Indian affairs, Medicine emphasized her sincerity: "She really was interested in doing something positive for Indian people" (interview, January 29, 1995). Medicine stressed that Gridley did "very well at the time in terms of trying to put forward an image of the Indian people that was positive" (interview). Gridley's *Indians of Today* "really did something to build a ground work on which other people could build" (interview). For more than four decades, Gridley worked to educate the public about American

Indians and their cultures. Through her work with the Indian Council Fire, she helped to provide a forum for discussing Native American problems and achievements. Unfortunately, she was unable to adjust to Native Americans' growing demand for greater control of their lives and of organizations devoted to Indian interests.

Sources. Information about Marion Gridley and her family can be found in the records and correspondence of the Grand Council Fire and Indian Council Fire (ICF) in Century of Progress files, UIC Spec. Coll., and the ICF files, Spec. Coll., NL; the latter also has the minutes of the Indian Council Fire, *Amerindian,* and most of Gridley's books for adults on American Indians. The Archives of Native American Education Services (NAES) College, Chicago, Illinois, include material on Chicago Indians, the Grand Council Fire and the Indian Council Fire, Marion Gridley, and Willard LaMere's October 9, 1979, lecture, "History of Indians in Chicago," transcript of tape. Copies of A. LaVonne Brown Ruoff's interview with Beatrice Medicine on January 29, 1995, are in Spec. Coll., NL, and the Archives, NAES College. The latter also has many of Gridley's books on Indians. Information about Gridley and her mother is also contained in the Illinois Woman's Press Association materials, CHS. Articles on her life include "Meet the Editor-Publisher," *Amerindian,* September–October 1960; "Author Bases Expertise on Indians on 23 Books," *Lerner Newspapers,* November 26, 1972; and "Action Line," *CT,* March 17, 1975. See as well *Something about the Author,* vol. 26 (1971); *Contemporary Authors,* vols. 45–48 (1974) and 103 (1982); an obituary, "Gridley," *CT,* November 2, 1974. References to Gridley are found in Rosalyn LaPier, "Chicago's American Indian Community Organizations, 1923–1934" (master's thesis, DePaul Univ., June 1994); Donna Duesel de la Torriente's unpublished booklet at CHS, "So We All Can Be Heard: A History of the Illinois Woman's Press Association, 1885–1987" [1987]; and Lola Hill, "In Appreciation, Marion E. Gridley," *The Indian Achievement Award of the Indian Council Fire* (Chicago: Indian Council Fire, 1982). Reviews of her books are reprinted in *Book Review Digest* (1937, 1973, and 1974). Gridley included a profile of her husband, Robinson Johnson (Whirling Thunder) in *Indians of Today.*

A. LaVonne Brown Ruoff

GRIFFIN, MARION LUCY MAHONY
February 14, 1871–August 10, 1961
ARCHITECT, COMMUNITY PLANNER, DELINEATOR

Born and raised in Chicago, Marion Mahony Griffin worked as an architect in the United States, Australia, and India. Her active professional career spanned fifty years (1894–1944) in three distinct periods: the early years as a young architect in turn-of-the-century Chicago (1894–1914), the middle years in Australia and India (1914–38), and her later life in Chicago (1938–61). As a progressive young architect in Frank Lloyd Wright's Oak Park studio, Marion Mahony Griffin contributed, through her drawings, to the development of the Prairie School that revolutionized American architecture and to the worldwide dissemination of its ideas.

Marion Mahony, the second of five children born to Jeremiah and Clara Hamilton (Perkins) Mahony, grew up in a female-headed household from the age of eleven. Her father, who migrated from Ireland to Illinois as a child, was a school principal, a journalist, and a poet. He died in 1882, and Marion Mahony's aunt Myra and her grandmother moved in with the family. Her mother and aunt were members of a Unitarian

congregation, and Marion was steeped in the ideas of liberal Protestantism. Two of the congregation's "covenants of faith"— that we ought to work for the good of humanity, to make the world better, and that we hold fast to the freedom of the spirit for ourselves and for all people—appear to have been principles by which Marion Mahony lived her life. Her mother, a respected educator, was for many years principal of the Komensky school, so named for Jan Amos Komensky (known also as Johann Amos Comenius), the seventeenth-century educational reformer and theologian. Through her mother's circle, Mahony came in contact with a network of influential women that included educational reformer ELLA FLAGG YOUNG and MARY WILMARTH, an active suffragist and Hull-House trustee, who would support Mahony's studies at the Massachusetts Institute of Technology (MIT), Boston. Mary Wilmarth's daughter, progressive reformer ANNA ICKES, was a lifelong friend. In this environment, Mahony developed a rebellious, inquiring, and passionate spirit, which in her adult professional and personal life also became a commitment to democracy.

Marion Mahony graduated from Chicago West Division High School and passed the MIT entrance exam in 1890. The architecture course was modeled on the École des Beaux Arts school in Paris and her design thesis, "A House and Studio for a Painter," was supervised by the French architect Constant Desire Despradelle. She also studied languages, literature, political history, political economy, and anthropology. In 1893 Mahony visited the World's Columbian Exposition in Chicago. There she likely saw the printmaking and timber construction of the Japanese Pavilion, prints and screens in the Japanese Parlor in the Woman's Building, and Mayan and Aztec geometric design forms. All were significant to her artistic and professional development. In 1894 she graduated from MIT, the second woman architect to graduate after Sophia Hayden, architect of the Woman's Building for the 1893 exposition. As the first registered woman architect in Illinois, Mahony helped pioneer women's professional participation in architecture in the United States.

On graduation her first job was with her architect cousin, Dwight Perkins, a reform-minded architect and environmentalist, who saw the potential of architecture to address social issues. At the time the recently founded Hull-House provided an important practical and intellectual focus for many reform-oriented professionals, including architects. The Chicago Arts and Crafts Society (founded 1897), of which Mahony, Perkins, the brothers Allen and Irving Pond, and Frank Lloyd Wright were charter members, met at Hull-House. There Wright gave his 1901 address, "The Art and Craft of the Machine." It was at Hull-House that Mahony met and made a lifelong friend of Australian feminist writer Miles Franklin, who would later introduce her and Walter Griffin (her future husband) to the progressive community in Sydney, Australia.

With Perkins, Mahony worked on the twelve-story Steinway Hall (now demolished) in downtown Chicago. From 1895, the loft space in Steinway Hall was home to progressive architects Perkins, Wright, Mahony, Griffin, Allen and Irving Pond, Myron Hunt, and others. The Steinway Hall group debated ideas, reading the work of Henry George, the advocate of the single tax, and Herbert Spencer, the English sociologist and philosopher. They encountered Louis Sullivan, the spiritual father of the Prairie School of architecture, and the transcendental ideas of Ralph Waldo Emerson and Walt Whitman. Like others of her generation whose encounter with the ills of industrialism initiated efforts to reestablish humanistic connections with the environment and work, Mahony was intrigued with progressive as well as religious ideas as they came together in a coherent personal and professional philosophy. Theosophy, for example, appealed to a broad artistic community that included Chicago architect and acquaintance Claude Bragdon. His book on sacred geometry, *The Beautiful Necessity: Seven Essays on Theosophy and Architecture*, was published in 1910. For Marion Mahony, involvement in the search for alternatives to materialism was part of her lifelong personal and professional development, most evidently so from the 1930s.

In 1895 Mahony began a long, if intermittent, employment with Frank Lloyd Wright. From 1900 to 1909, Wright, the principal architect of the Prairie School, completed about 120 commissions in the Midwest. Marion Mahony, who worked for Wright for more than thirteen years by her account and eleven according to his calculations, was the longest serving staff person engaged with these designs. Wright's studio, located in the Oak Park suburb on Chicago's western border, was run unconventionally. Historian Grant Carpenter Manson in *Frank Lloyd Wright to 1910* (1958) observed that if the studio had been more conventional Mahony would have had the position of head designer. Wright held "informal competitions" for parts of projects, for example, murals, fireplaces, windows, furniture, even complete interiors. Mahony often "won" these competitions, and for more than eleven years she worked on many projects, including the moon children fountain in the Susan Dana Lawrence house (1902) in Springfield, Illinois. From these years she is best known for her Japanese-inspired renderings of Wright's designs, many of which were first exhibited at the Chicago Architectural Club in 1907. In 1910 *Ausgeführte Bauten und Entwürfe von Frank Lloyd Wright* (Studies and executed buildings by Frank Lloyd Wright, known as the Wasmuth Portfolio) was published by Wasmuth in Germany. It became one of the most influential architectural publications of the twentieth century. Of the one hundred plates in the Wasmuth Folio, Mahony prepared more than half the underlays. Drawings of well-known buildings included Unity Temple and the Cheney house in Oak Park. The Como Orchard perspective and others carried her characteristic MLM (Marion Lucy Mahony) monogram. Her intellectual contribution was described by studio member Barry Byrne: "I can well remember welcoming her advent because it promised an amusing day. Her dialogues with Frank Lloyd Wright, who as we all know is no indifferent opponent in repartee, made such days particularly notable" (quoted in Rubbo, "Marion Mahony Griffin: A Portrait," 18). Her best-known private commission in the Wright years was her 1902 All Souls Church in Evanston, Illinois, which was demolished in 1961.

Mahony met Walter Burley Griffin professionally in 1901. Their personal relationship developed in 1910 while they were exploring the lakes and rivers of Illinois by canoe. Walter Griffin worked for Dwight Perkins upon graduation; from 1901 to 1906 he was a member of Wright's Oak Park studio. After a disagreement with Wright, he started his own practice. In 1909, when Wright left his studio and family, Mahony refused his offer to direct the studio. She joined Herman von Holst as head designer when he took over the practice and established an office in Steinway Hall. She is credited with the David Amberg house, Grand Rapids, Michigan (1909–11); the Adolph Mueller house, Decatur, Illinois (1910); and drawings for the Henry Ford house in Detroit. Walter Burley Griffin worked with von Holst and Mahony as a landscape consultant. Marion Mahony and Walter Burley Griffin were married on June 29, 1911, in Michigan City, Indiana. Years later, in "Magic of America," she wrote, "With that man of mine I was possessed. . . . I was devoted to my work . . . but when I encountered W.B.G. I was first swept off my feet by my delight in his achievements in my profession, then through the common bond of interest in nature and intellectual pursuits and then with the man himself" (quoted in Rubbo, "Marion Mahony Griffin: A Portrait," 16). They had no children.

The Griffins had a long and productive artistic partnership until his death in 1937. Working with her husband, but always as second fiddle by her choice, Marion Mahony Griffin prepared drawings for a number of Griffin commissions in Chicago, including the Hurd Comstock house no. 1, Evanston (1912); the Mess house, Winnetka (1912), with fireplace mural design by Marion Mahony Griffin; Trier Center, Winnetka (1912); their own house in Winnetka (1913, unbuilt); the Stinson Memorial Library, Anna, Illinois (1914); and the virtuoso aerial perspective in colored inks on satin of Rock Glen, Mason City, Iowa (1912), held by the Art Institute of Chicago.

In 1911 the Griffins collaborated on a competition entry for the design of Australia's new Federal Capital, Canberra, and Marion Mahony Griffin prepared the exquisitely rendered satin drawings in the loft in Steinway Hall. In 1912 it was announced that Walter Burley Griffin had been awarded first prize. The design is generally seen as an embodiment of democratic principles employing popular nineteenth-century city beautiful and garden city ideas; a more recent, but somewhat doubtful interpretation, suggests the presence of an esoteric spiritual schema.

In 1914 Marion and Walter Griffin moved to Australia, where they lived for more than twenty years. They were accompanied by Roy Lippincott, who had assisted with the Canberra project, and his wife, Walter Griffin's sister. Shortly after arriving in Sydney, Marion Mahony Griffin published two articles on "Democratic Architecture" in Sydney's foremost architectural magazine, *Building* (June and August 1914). In 1915 she spoke to the National Council of Women in Sydney on women as architects. The Griffins moved to Melbourne in 1916, where they had some major commissions: Newman College at Melbourne University (1915–17), the Cafe Australia (1915, now demolished), Capitol House (1921), and the Eaglemont community plan (1916–23). In 1919, working weekends, they built themselves a small house in Eaglemont using the prefabricated "knitlock" building system designed and patented by Griffin in 1918.

The development of the Canberra plan was plagued by political problems, and Walter Griffin resigned as federal director of Design and Construction in 1920. In 1921 the Griffins purchased 650 acres of land in Castlecrag, Sydney, and Walter Griffin formed the Greater Sydney Development Association (GSDA) to purchase and develop the site. He had a controlling share. The aim was to develop this spectacular peninsula with its four miles of water frontage as a model community. In its development, road layouts followed contours, site planning and building location enhanced the natural landscape, natural materials were used, and native species were planted. The GSDA placed covenants on building heights protecting views for all residents and providing pedestrian right-of-ways between building lots, allowing easy access to the water. The Griffins created an outdoor amphitheater (the Haven Scenic Theatre) to promote community life. As in Canberra, they had constant battles with planning authorities.

Like many other artists of the period, the Griffins were drawn to syncretic spiritual movements. From 1930 on, she was influenced by the teachings of Rudolf Steiner, who developed the spiritual school of Anthroposophy, an offshoot of Theosophy. Mahony Griffin joined the Sydney Anthroposophical Society in 1930, Griffin in 1931. In 1935, through theosophical connections, Walter Griffin was invited to India to design a library for Lucknow University. Marion Mahony Griffin followed in 1936 to help with this and other projects, leaving their Australian partner Eric Nicholls in charge in Sydney. Their architectural practice was as busy as it had been in the early days in Chicago and Melbourne—residences, university buildings, a building for the Pioneer Press, and the entire United Provinces Exhibition of Industry and Agriculture. When Griffin died suddenly in 1937, his widow returned to Australia.

In 1938, Marion Mahony Griffin returned to Chicago. Two years later she lectured to the Illinois Society of Architects on her Australian experience and on Anthroposophy. Billed as an architect and community planner, she spoke on India at a World Federation Round Table in 1942. LOLA MAVERICK LLOYD, peace activist and founder of the Campaign for World Government, gave Griffin two commissions, a World Fellowship Center in Conway, New Hampshire (1942), and the Hills and Rosary Crystals subdivision near Boerne, Texas, for the Maverick Lloyd family (1943). The Texas plan for the Hills and Rosary Crystals subdivision revived earlier approaches to community planning. The 388-acre site for the World Fellowship Center offered Mahony Griffin the opportunity to once again explore ideas about community planning and democracy. Neither proceeded following Lloyd's death. A third project, a plan for South Chicago (1944), also stalled.

In addition to her professional architectural work, Marion Mahony Griffin was involved in horticulture, painting, and theater. Her artwork included portrait miniatures; a large mural with an avowedly pedagogical and anthroposophical purpose, *Fairies Feeding the Herons*, in a Rogers Park school in Chicago (1931); and paintings of Australian trees on silk. In Castlecrag, Sydney, she had revived her interest in theater (begun at MIT in 1893) and had been involved in production, set, and costume design for more than twelve plays in the Haven Scenic Theater.

Until her death, she lived in Rogers Park with her niece Clamyra Hayes and helped care for her niece's children. In 1949, she completed "The Magic of America," a memorial to her life with Griffin and his life's work. The manuscript is organized into four sections or "battles": the Empirical Battle (India), the Federal Battle (Canberra), the Municipal Battle (Castlecrag), and the Individual Battle (the Griffins' relation-

ship). She died in 1961 at Cook County Hospital, and her ashes were placed at Graceland Cemetery. In 1997 her ashes were reinterred at Graceland Cemetery with a new memorial plaque.

Separating out Marion Mahony Griffin's individual contribution to architecture is a difficult task, working as she did in a collaborative way and with extraordinary men in a male-dominated profession. The work the Griffins completed together was greater than either of them achieved independently. In the late 1940s, however, she carefully inked Walter Burley Griffin's name from a significant number of drawings, and she never lost her bitterness toward Wright. This bitterness arose, in part, over his alleged treatment of Walter Griffin and conflict over attribution for ideas. The joint professional work of Marion Mahony and Walter Burley Griffin amounts to some 280 architectural, planning, and landscape projects, of which approximately 180 were built. In the United States, 76 of 114 projects were realized; in Australia, 95 of 130, and in India 7 of 37. Houses and planned communities made up the bulk of the American commissions. In their twenty-one years in Australia (1914–35) the range of their work was greater and included Canberra, five new towns, several suburban communities, three campus plans, houses, industrial buildings (primarily incinerators), and some commercial buildings.

Sources. In the United States, Marion Mahony Griffin's drawings are available at the Avery Library, Columbia Univ.; Mary and Leigh Block Museum, Northwestern Univ.; Burnham Library, Art Institute of Chicago (AIC); Massachusetts Institute of Technology Museum (thesis drawings and statement). In Australia, her work is found at the Australian Archives, Canberra (competition drawings); Willoughby Council, New South Wales; State Library of Victoria; Art Gallery of Victoria (furniture); and Newman College (furniture). Copies of her unpublished manuscript, "Magic of America," 1949, are available at the Burnham Library, AIC, and New York Hist. Soc. Other useful archival sources are the Frank Lloyd Wright Home and Studio, Oak Park, Illinois; Mark Peisch Papers, Avery Library, Columbia Univ.; Willoughby Public Library, New South Wales, Australia; Peter Harrison and D. L. Johnson Papers, Australian National Library, Canberra. Mark Peisch, *The Chicago School of Architecture: Early Followers of Sullivan and Wright* (1964), is an important general source, as is H. Allen Brooks, *The Prairie School: Frank Lloyd Wright and His Midwest Contemporaries* (1972). Studies of her life and/or work are in H. Allen Brooks, "Frank Lloyd Wright and the Wasmuth Drawings," *Art Bulletin*, vol. 47, 1966; David Van Zanten, "The Early Work of Marion Mahony Griffin," *Prairie School Review*, vol. 3, 1966; Susan Fondiler Berkon and Jane Holtz Kay, "Marion Mahony Griffin, Architect," *Feminist Art Journal*, Spring 1975; Susana Torre, ed., *Women in American Architecture: A Historic and Contemporary Perspective* (1977); NAW (1980); P. Larson, "Marion Mahony and Walter Burley Griffin: The Marriage of Drawings and Architecture," *Print Collector's Newsletter*, vol. 13, 1982; Anna Rubbo, "Marion Mahony Griffin: A Portrait," in *Walter Burley Griffin: A Review*, ed. J. Duncan and M. Gates (1988); James Weirick, "Marion Mahony at M.I.T.," *Transition*, Winter 1988; and Janice Pregliasco, "The Life and Work of Marion Mahony Griffin," in *The Prairie School: Design Vision for the Midwest* (1995). Additional studies are Jill Roe, "The Magical World of Marion Mahony Griffin: Culture and Community in Castlecrag in the Interwar Years," in *Minorities in Cultural Diversity in Sydney*, ed. Shirley Fitzgerald and Garry Wotherspoon (1995); Anna Rubbo, "Marion and Walter Burley Griffin: A Creative Partnership," *Architectural Theory Review*, vol. 1, 1966; Anna Rubbo, "The Numinous World of Marion Mahony Griffin," in Ross Mellick and Peter Waterhouse,

Spirit and Place: Art in Australia 1861–1966 (1996); Anne Watson, ed., *Beyond Architecture, Marion Mahony and Walter Burley Griffin: America, Australia, India* (1998). Jeffrey Turnbull and Peter Navaretti, *The Griffins in Australia and India: The Complete Works and Projects of Walter Burley Griffin and Marion Mahony Griffin* (1998). Useful information about Theosophy and Anthroposophy are in Jill Roe, *Beyond Belief: Theosophy in Australia, 1879–1939* (1994), and Claude Bragdon, *The Beautiful Necessity: Seven Essays on Theosophy and Architecture* (1910).

ANNA RUBBO

GRIMM, EDITH RAMBAR
January 17, 1908–September 28, 1984
BUSINESS EXECUTIVE, MERCHANDISE CONSULTANT

Edith Grimm, a vice-president of Carson Pirie Scott department store in Chicago, was born in Seneca Falls, New York, the second of three daughters of Mitchell and Florence (Kutner) Rambar. Her father left his native Lithuania at fourteen years of age to begin a new life in New York. He left Europe because, as a Jew, he would most certainly have been persecuted after being drafted for duty in Czar Alexander III's Russian army. Mitchell Rambar began his merchandising career as a peddler but soon was hired to work in a clothing factory. He opened a men's clothing store in Seneca Falls, and his career and entrepreneurial spirit greatly influenced his daughter. Edith Rambar's mother was the daughter of well-to-do parents of German descent. After marrying Mitchell Rambar and settling in Seneca Falls, Florence Rambar devoted her life to raising her three daughters, Dorothy, Edith, and Ann.

Although Edith Rambar was very bright (she skipped three years of grade school), she was not bookish, and her older sister Dorothy paid her a nickel a page to read her first book. When she was twelve years old, Rambar began selling clothes in her father's store, and her true talents began to take shape. She did well enough to be hired in another store where some of her friends worked. The man who ran this store eventually let her friends go because Rambar was doing more business than all of them. When she learned of his plans, this spunky teenager pulled the owner's derby over his ears and walked out, leaving the man without his star salesperson.

In 1920, Mitchell Rambar sold his store and moved the family to Highland Park, Michigan, a suburb of Detroit, and became a partner in a real estate business. While attending high school, Rambar worked as a buyer for a group of teenagers who sold candy to raise money for a trip to Washington, D.C. She also sold buttons, bows, and men's clothing on weekends. She began college at City College of Detroit (now Wayne State University). There she excelled at debating and public speaking, winning awards and even teaching a public speaking class to automobile sales people while she was a sophomore. She transferred to the University of Chicago, where she majored in English and excelled in nearly everything without trying too hard. She also became an accomplished tennis player and skier. Although she began a premedical program and a graduate program in English, she decided to return to Detroit and teach algebra in public schools.

Edith Rambar met her future husband, Dr. Emery Grimm, while she was attending the University of Chicago. Twelve years her senior and originally from Hungary, Grimm was a noted endocrinologist at Wesley Memorial Hospital (now Northwestern Memorial Hospital). The couple married in 1929 while on vacation in upstate New York, had a wonderful marriage, and associated with many artists, doctors, diplomats, fashion gurus, and other movers and shakers of the city.

Although she certainly did not have to work, Edith Grimm quickly found herself bored with playing bridge—a game at which she was quite accomplished and which she even taught—and keeping house. During the Century of Progress Exposition in 1934, she applied for a part-time comparison shopping position at Marshall Field & Company, and was paid seven dollars a week to write reports (seven each week) on imported gifts in connection with the Exposition. She was soon offered a full-time job, but the position was not appealing to her. Instead, she went down the street to Carson Pirie Scott & Company, where she immediately turned a coincidence into success. While waiting for her interview, she overheard some executives in a panic because they had not been able to persuade any of the city's foreign dignitaries to attend a luncheon the next day. Since the Grimms were well acquainted with many of the foreign consuls, Edith Grimm interrupted the executives' conversation and said that she would be able to persuade many of the diplomats to attend the luncheon. She did so and was hired right away as head of the mail order department.

She studied the mail and telephone ordering process of many different stores and businesses on the East Coast and worked with telephone engineers to devise a revolutionary telephone order board, which became a model for department stores. During her first years, she increased Carson's mail-order business to more than one million dollars by instituting more personalized service and faster delivery time and offering better merchandise.

After her success with the telephone order board, Grimm went on to revolutionize merchandising in nearly every department at Carson's. During World War II she became director of the interior decorating department, where she created a popular eighteenth-century village using inexpensive antiques. Antiques and furniture in general were hard to come by during the war, but she and her assistant traveled the country and brought back affordable finds that had thousands of customers clamoring at the store on the exhibit's opening day.

After several men asked her to select and buy clothing and accessories for their ladies in 1936, Grimm came up with the idea of a men-only shop during the holidays, where saleswomen of all sizes would be able to help bashful men choose gifts. Coffee and refreshments were to be served, and most importantly, no women (except store employees) would be permitted. The For-Men-Only Shop did three thousand dollars in sales its first holiday season; several years later, the shop was bringing in almost one hundred times that amount, and representatives from other department stores across the country traveled to Carson's to learn more about this innovation and apply it in their own stores.

A full-service bridal department and wedding gift shop—where a bride could order everything including the bridesmaids—was the brainchild of Edith Grimm. Professional attendants would be sent to a wedding with everything that was possibly needed, and any emergency, such as a dress not fitting properly or a defective or missing accessory, could be remedied on the spot. Grimm and her wedding staff saved the day on many occasions. One North Shore bride who had ordered dresses from Neiman-Marcus in Dallas, Texas, was on the verge of extreme disappointment as her dress and that of her bridesmaid had been lost somewhere during shipping. Although duplicate dresses were available, they were not the right size, so Grimm sent a team of professionals to alter the dresses. Neiman's president, Stanley Marcus, wrote to say how impressed and grateful he was for Grimm's and Carson's generosity and professionalism. In 1960, Carson Pirie Scott counted five thousand brides a year as customers. When Grimm conceived of her idea the store served only eleven brides.

Grimm created the once popular college shop for young women and coined the term "casual clothes" to market women's sportswear. Both of these ideas were extremely successful and copied in department stores everywhere. The concept of resort wear to sell bathing suits and summer apparel in the dead of winter also originated at Carson's with Grimm. She often held swimsuit fashion shows outside in snowy, freezing weather. The models were kept warm under special heat lamps. The spectacle attracted many passersby on State Street, and swimsuit sales soared, even though it was cold and dreary in Chicago. Edith Grimm once said, "Merchandising is like show business: It demands a stage designer playing mood music and lighting on the merchandise" (quoted in Canepa, 4). This philosophy is embraced today by nearly all successful marketers in a variety of fields.

Perhaps one of Edith Grimm's most crowning achievements was the import fair she staged in 1955. From a two-month buying trip to eleven countries in Europe, Grimm brought back everything from ashtrays to an old London taxicab. She also wrote to many European mayors in hopes of securing travel-type posters representing their cities and villages. About five thousand posters were displayed throughout the store and on the street-side glass display windows. The fair was a success, increasing Carson's import business by 140 percent and establishing the store as a true competitor in imported goods.

Although she was a manager from day one, she delighted in returning to the sales floor at every opportunity and never lost sight of what made customers happy. Grimm inspired her employees and urged them to reach their potential through creativity and hard work. One such employee was British-born Andrew Smithson, who called Edith Grimm his mentor and remembered her compassion as well as her patience.

Edith Grimm gave generously of her time to support the local community and the retail industry. Her status as one of the highest ranking female executives in Chicago and her uncanny knack for motivating others to greater personal success were the reasons that she became a role model for aspiring, career-oriented young people in the city of Chicago. During the early 1950s, Grimm teamed up with the Chicago Board of Education to present a series of seven radio broadcasts tailored especially for high school juniors and seniors. Some of the broadcast titles included "Poise without Noise"; "Facts and Frolics for Young Career Woman"; and "How to Be Hired, Not Fired" (Sarah Varco interview). Grimm was also the regional director of the Fashion Group, a prestigious, national industry organization made up of the top women in the retail business.

Grimm was promoted to vice-president of merchandising in 1963. She was the first woman to reach that level in Chicago's retail industry. Her reputation was well known throughout the country, and she was a featured speaker at many large and prestigious merchandising conventions. The National Retail Merchants Association voted her one of the top women in retailing in 1969, and she appeared on NBC–TV with David Brinkley in 1970. At the time, Carson's chair of the board, Norbert F. Armour, said, "Mrs. Grimm has proved there is room at the top for women" (quoted in Canepa, 4). In 1972, the YWCA honored her with its first outstanding achievement award for women in business and industry. She was honored by both the Italian and Israeli governments for her promotional work with these countries during Carson Pirie Scott's notable import fairs.

After retiring from Carson Pirie Scott at the end of 1972, Grimm started her own lecturing and consulting business. Her client list was impressive and included the American Management Association, American Marketing Association, *Brides* magazine, Illinois Bankers Association, Minnesota Mining and-Manufacturing, Northwestern University, University of Chicago, and University of Wisconsin–Madison.

During a special luncheon in January 1984, Dennis Bookshester, chair and chief executive officer of Carson's Department Stores, presented Edith Grimm with a newly created award to honor employee excellence. The award was named for her.

Edith Grimm died tragically on September 28, 1984, while visiting her former employee Andrew Smithson and his wife, Judy (also a Carson's employee), in Columbus, Indiana. She and her good friend Dr. Bina Rosenberg, a staff psychiatrist at St. Joseph Hospital in Chicago, were killed while crossing a four-lane highway. A well-attended memorial service was held at the Arts Club of Chicago, of which Edith Grimm was a member, on October 26, 1984. Grimm's trailblazing career as both a top executive and an innovator of successful merchandising concepts paved the way for others—men and women alike—to advance by thinking creatively and following their dreams. The fact that many of Edith Grimm's concepts are still thriving is testament to her ingenious understanding of the everyday consumer.

Sources. Many of the facts were gathered through telephone interviews with business associates or relatives of Edith Grimm. These include Ed Clark, Grimm's brother-in-law, of Dallas, Texas; Sarah Varco, a former secretary of Mrs. Grimm and personnel manager of Carson Pirie Scott, of Lincolnwood, Illinois; and Dorothy Fuller, director of the Apparel Center at the Merchandise Mart in Chicago, who also worked with Grimm in the Fashion Group. The most comprehensive profile of the professional Edith Grimm is offered by Norma Lee Browning, "They Say She Can Sell Anything," *Saturday Evening Post,* September 3, 1960. The Carson Pirie Scott employee newsletter, *CPS News,* December 22, 1972, profiles Grimm in "Our Centerfold Is Edith R. Grimm," shortly before her retirement; author Mary Ann Canepa took much of her information from the *Saturday Evening Post* article. Another article by Leona Toppel, appearing in the *Downtown News,* December 27, 1984, also draws from the *Post* article, although the story contains new information about an upcoming luncheon to honor Grimm's remarkable achievements. Grimm herself kept her biographical sketch on file and wrote her own promotional brochure when she started her merchandising consulting business. Sarah Varco supplied this information and has the most extensive file on Grimm available. Another valuable source is

Andrew Smithson's remarks given at Grimm's memorial service, October 26, 1984, typescript, Arts Club of Chicago. The *CT* obituary, "Edith Grimm, Dr. Bina Rosenberg; Killed while Crossing Indiana Highway," September 30, 1984, provides a brief account of Grimm's accomplishments.

CAROL EVANS POYNTER

GYLES, ROSE MARIE
July 29, 1868–October 1, 1949

PHYSICAL EDUCATION TEACHER, SETTLEMENT RESIDENT

Rose Marie Gyles was an early teacher and advocate of physical education for women and children. She also encouraged and coached competitive sports teams for girls and women at a time when the idea of sports rivalry among women was not well received. Gyles lived at Hull-House settlement for forty-five years. Her work there was a second vocation; the Hull-House community was her extended family.

Gyles was born in Chicago, the third of six children, to Henry J. Gyles, an English immigrant, and Catherine (Sauer) Gyles, a German immigrant. Arriving in America in 1857, Henry Gyles began work as a butcher and, by 1868, owned a meatpacking business. His business destroyed in the Chicago Fire of 1871, Gyles migrated West and, in 1878, homesteaded in Ford County, Kansas, bringing farm implements to start his new enterprise. In 1879, his six children, wife, and his wife's father joined him. Henry Gyles eventually became a successful cattle rancher, accumulating approximately two thousand acres of land.

In 1892, Rose Marie Gyles earned a degree from Rockford Female Seminary, Rockford, Illinois. The seminary, chartered in 1847 to provide education and religious instruction for young women, became Rockford College the year Gyles finished her program. She remained to complete newly established college requirements and received a B.A. degree in 1893. She had already studied at the Sargent School of Physical Education, Boston, Massachusetts, during the summer of 1892.

Gyles moved to Hull-House settlement after her graduation from Rockford College. By November 1893 she had become the first director of the settlement's new public gymnasium that had opened the same year. The building, one of the earliest of its kind in the United States, was one of the first gymnasiums to be built in Chicago. In addition to a large space for exercising and showering, it contained a public coffeehouse, lunchroom, a kitchen, and a men's club room outfitted with billiard and card tables. Use of the gymnasium was divided between women and men, girls and boys, with the evenings typically reserved for the men. When first constructed, it was the largest building in the settlement complex and was used also as an auditorium and as a reception and ballroom for different Hull-House clubs.

Gyles was gymnasium director for fourteen years. She taught women's and girls' physical education classes at the settlement and directed the gymnastics program at Hull-House summer school held in Rockford, Illinois. She also supervised activities at the Hull-House playground, constructed in 1893, the first public playground in Chicago.

Physical education was a growing field in late-nineteenth-century America. Organized gymnastics sessions were becoming the core of physical activity programs for children and adults. Two systems of gymnastics predominated—the German and the Swedish. The former was particularly popular in the Midwest, partly because many German immigrants settled there. It stressed freestanding exercises, apparatus work, sports, games, and rhythmic work. The latter system, preferred and taught by Gyles throughout her career, appealed overwhelmingly to American female physical education teachers. Several American women had studied the Swedish system in Stockholm, Sweden. The Swedish system required a knowledge of human anatomy and stressed remedial or corrective work; measurements were taken and particular exercises were prescribed to correct spinal curvature, bad posture, or other physical problems. A student followed daily routines progressing from light to more strenuous activity, performing each movement on command and concentrating on holding correct positions.

Gyles continued to learn the latest physical education theories by enrolling in evening classes at area colleges and studying at summer schools that specialized in physical education. She studied human anatomy at the University of Chicago in 1895–96 and spent a second summer at the Sargent School of Physical Education. She also attended the Chautauqua Summer School of Physical Education, Chautauqua, New York, in the 1890s, and Teachers' College, Columbia University, New York City, in summer 1923.

Gymnastics were a popular activity at Hull-House, where Gyles taught women's classes "marching and fancy steps, dumb bells and Indian club drill, free movements, gymnastics, Swedish movements and games" (*Hull-House Bulletin*, June 1897, 2). Gyles introduced team competition in women's sports at a time when most of her professional colleagues discouraged such activities. In 1896, she coached a women's basketball team at Hull-House, most likely the first organized in Chicago. Although it is not known whether Gyles was the catalyst for forming the team, she was listed as the director of team practices, which were held weekly. The June 1897 *Hull-House Bulletin* reported the girls' basketball team victorious in every contest it played that season. The best game of the season, against Englewood High School (then located in the Chicago suburb of Englewood, soon to be annexed to the city), was "fast and exciting" (*Hull-House Bulletin*, June 1897, 5) and played between two equally prepared and experienced teams. The Hull-House team won by a score of five to three.

Gyles also instructed teachers in Swedish gymnastics at the Chicago Froebel Association's Kindergarten Training School, headquartered at Hull-House. The association's major goal was to instruct kindergarten teachers in child socialization methods. Gyles hoped kindergarten teachers too would use Swedish gymnastics to identify and correct their students' physical handicaps. In addition, from 1898 to 1901, she taught physical education at the Jewish Training School, an agency located on Chicago's West Side that offered classes in manual training to immigrants.

All Hull-House residents took responsibility for guiding the different clubs and activities offered by the settlement. Gyles supervised the Aloha-Vesperian Club, a group of girls who met to read short stories and do embroidery. She also taught classes in English language and United States citizenship to immigrant neighbors. Hull-House residents ate meals together in the settlement's dining room and lived in nearby apartments. They ex-

FIG. 44. *Director of Hull-House women's sports and gymnasium program Rose Marie Gyles, seated on a chair, with the Hull-House women's basketball team, the first in Chicago.*

changed ideas about their work and were introduced to the innovative theories of an unusual array of guests who were drawn to the creative and stimulating milieu created by Hull-House cofounder JANE ADDAMS. In this environment, Gyles found support for her ideas about physical education for women and children.

In 1907, after fourteen years of residency, Gyles resigned as director of the Hull-House gymnasium to become the first physical education teacher hired at J. Sterling Morton High School, Berwyn, Illinois, a suburb of Chicago settled by immigrants from central and eastern Europe. These ethnic groups had already developed communal activities focusing on physical culture, exercise, and sport. Maintaining her ties with Hull-House, she continued to live at the settlement and to teach physical education and other evening classes there. During her first year at Morton High, Gyles taught twelve girls daily in a garage constructed of wood that had a sawdust floor instead of the innovative Hull-House gymnasium. Consistent with Swedish physical education theory, she included corrective gymnastics and nutrition classes in the curriculum.

Practitioners of physical education programs continued to debate which system was the correct one to employ in their classes. In the nineteenth century, the debate had centered on the correct approach to gymnastics itself, with the German and the Swedish schools the dominant and competitive approaches. By the early twentieth century the debate was whether to teach gymnastics, sports, dancing, or a combination of the three. Continuing the approach she had adopted at Hull-House, Gyles exposed her students to the latest trends. She favored a program that combined gymnastics, sports, and dancing. Gradually Mor-

ton High School was recognized as offering one of the finest physical education programs in Illinois. By the early 1920s, the school had both a boys' and a girls' gymnasium, a swimming pool, a track and field the size of a city block, and a large room for corrective gymnastics exercises. The school's girls' teams in 1923 included hockey, baseball, basketball, and track. Clearly, Gyles believed some competition was good for women. Swimming classes also were offered. Dance was a major part of physical education for girls, and an hour each week at Morton was devoted to dance, including folk, character, interpretive, and social dancing. Each year the girls demonstrated their dance and sports skills at a spring exhibition.

By 1928, Gyles directed a staff of six teachers for the girls' physical education programs at Morton High School. She and her staff coached girls' teams in basketball, soccer, hockey, swimming, tennis, and baseball. Corrective gymnastics were still offered, as were fancy and special dance. Gyles encouraged her students to join the Illinois Girls' Athletic Association. After becoming a member, a girl could work toward local and state awards for athletic achievement and attend a summer sports camp. In addition to directing the girls' physical education program, Gyles taught civics classes at Morton High School, a subject she also taught for years at Hull-House.

In 1933, Gyles retired as director of girls' physical education at Morton High School. For the first few years of her retirement, she traveled in Italy, the Scandinavian countries, Greece, England, and France. In summer 1938 she studied at the University of Perugia in Italy. That same year she moved from Hull-House to an apartment in Chicago, but remained committed to the ideals of the settlement movement, volunteering three days a week at the Immigrants' Protective League (IPL). Begun in 1908 by Hull-House reformers, including SOPHONISBA BRECKINRIDGE and GRACE ABBOTT, the IPL investigated the treatment of immigrants, offered services to unite separated families, and helped new immigrants find jobs, legal advice, and medical help. The IPL offered immigrants civic and language classes similar to the kind Gyles had taught at Hull-House and at Morton High School.

Gyles died at age eighty-one in a hospital in Denver, Colorado. She was buried alongside Gyles family members at the Maple Grove Cemetery, Dodge City, Kansas.

Gyles began her career in physical education at a time when custom and medical attitudes converged to keep women corseted and in sedentary lifestyles. Participation in competitive sports was considered detrimental to women's physical and mental health. Gyles became part of that generation of women who rejected these constraints and embraced the notion that physical exercise promoted the health and well-being of girls and women. Gyles worked to include the urban working class and poor in recreation and physical education classes. She advocated the extension of citizenship to immigrants and taught civics, English language, and physical education to the new arrivals, many of whom had come to Chicago with different European cultural traditions that already embraced physical improvement, culture, and sports.

Sources. Hull-House Association Records, Jane Addams Memorial Collection, UIC Spec. Coll., include copies of the *Hull-House Bulletin*, newspaper clippings, and scrapbooks with information about the settlement's residents and activities. The Robert Teeter Collection, UIC Spec. Coll., has material on sports at Hull-House and a memorial to Rose Marie Gyles. The Alumni papers, Rockford College Archives, Rockford, Illinois, include a file on Gyles. Biographical information about the Gyles family can be found at the Kansas Heritage Center, Dodge City, Kansas. Gyles's work at J. Morton Sterling High School is documented in annual editions of the *Mortonian*, the school yearbook available at the school library, Berwyn, Illinois. The University of Chicago Archives have records of Gyles's enrollment in two anatomy courses and other materials describing the kinds of curriculum offered in the Division of Physical Culture and Athletics in the late nineteenth century. Ann Dolores Harvilla's thesis on women's physical education at the University of Chicago, "An Essay Submitted to the Faculty of the Collegiate Division of the Social Sciences in Candidacy for the Degree of Bachelor of Arts," (Department of History, May 1979), is in the Archival Biographical File on Gertrude Dudley, UC Spec. Coll. Information on the physical education movement and Hull-House programs is provided in Mabel Lee, *A History of Physical Education and Sports in the U.S.A.* (1983); John E. Nixon and Ann E. Jewett, *An Introduction to Physical Education* (1969); and Mary Lynn McCree Bryan and Allen F. Davis, eds., *100 Years at Hull-House* (1990).

SUSAN R. SCHWENDENER

_h_

HALEY, MARGARET ANGELA
November 15, 1861–January 5, 1939

TEACHER, LABOR UNION ACTIVIST, SUFFRAGIST

Chicago teacher and activist for teachers Margaret A. Haley was born in Joliet, thirty miles southwest of downtown Chicago. Her parents had been immigrants, father Michael Haley from Canada, mother Elizabeth (Tiernan) Haley from Ireland. Both were self-consciously Irish in their ethnic identity, an identity that they passed on to their daughter. Haley spent her childhood on farms and in small towns in Illinois as her father tried his luck—often bad—at various small business ventures supplemented by farming. He was also a politician and labor union activist. Her mother gave birth to eight children, six of whom survived to adulthood. Margaret—Maggie to her family and friends—was the second child, becoming the oldest when her brother Tom drowned at the age of twelve. She never married.

Haley's political consciousness had been born when she was a child listening to her parents' outrage at the injustice accorded workers in Ireland and in the United States. "My father's and my mother's people," she wrote in her autobiography, "had left Ireland in order that they might have . . . independence of mind" (Haley, 23). Haley's Irish heritage was always a founding principle of her reform impulse. "The fighting Irish" thrilled her, along with their Irish nationalist heroes, "the Tones and the Emmetts [_sic_] and the Parnells" (Haley, 8). Her belief in the importance of education also emerged in her childhood. Her mother fostered her daughter's intellectual development "as only the Irish, who had been denied the full measure of education, could value it," by teaching her the Irish maxim, "Educate [yourself] in order that your children may be free" (Haley, 14).

Haley was thrust into teaching when, in 1877, at the age of sixteen, she needed to find paid work after her father lost his business. Having just graduated from St. Angela High School in Morris, Illinois, Haley's first job was in a nearby one-room school. She loved the work from the moment she arrived in the classroom. Nevertheless, she was not content to remain in one place for long, and she spent the next several years taking teacher training courses at Illinois Normal University (now Illinois State University) in Bloomington and also at Cook County Normal School (now Chicago State University) in Chicago. During these years, she moved up the career ladder to ever larger school districts until, in 1882, she made the leap to Cook County. In 1884, she took a job teaching the sixth grade in the Hendricks School in the Stockyards District. The area was incorporated into the city limits in 1889, making Haley a Chicago public school teacher at last.

Conditions at the Hendricks School added to her lifelong outrage against undeserved power. Despite having eager students, Haley's teaching efforts were hampered by an incompetent and dictatorial principal. Although she remembered herself as being a conformist rather than a rebel in those days, she also stressed that, "never in my life have I feared anything or anyone, least of all established authority" (Haley, 24). Her "forty fighting years" (Haley, xxxi) as a school reformer had begun.

After almost a quarter century in the classroom, Haley left teaching in 1901 to become the paid business representative and vice-president of the Chicago Teachers' Federation (CTF). She remained on the CTF's staff until her death in 1939. The CTF had been organized in 1897 to protect the recently enacted elementary school teachers' pension plan that the Chicago Board of Education was threatening to dismantle. The CTF was an unusual teachers' organization for its time because it limited its membership to elementary school teachers, excluding from its ranks all secondary school teachers and school administrators. Since elementary teachers were mostly female, and upper-level teachers and administrators were mostly male, the CTF was a pathbreaking association of women fighting for their professional and economic rights. In the CTF, Haley had found the platform for her crusade against the entrenched powers she believed were undermining public education. "Only

FIG. 45. *Chicago Teachers' Federation leader Margaret Haley, telephone in hand, campaigns against the proposed 1922 Illinois Constitution in November 1922.*

through the freedom of their teachers could children remain free . . . ," she explained; "I had no choice to make. It had been made for me" (Haley, 40).

Haley's first major battle on behalf of the CTF came in 1900, when the Board of Education reneged on a promised salary increase for the city's elementary teachers on the grounds that sufficient funding for the increase was not available. Rejecting this explanation, Haley and CATHARINE GOGGIN, president of CTF, campaigned as the two-member Tax Investigating Committee to restructure the city's tax base so that high profit corporations would be forced to pay their rightful share of property taxes, the revenue assigned to support the public schools. Haley and Goggin took these corporate giants to court and won. On appeal by the corporations, the U.S. Supreme Court upheld the lower court's decision. As a result, in 1907, a city-wide tax reassessment collected a windfall of current and back taxes from some of Chicago's richest corporations, providing the city's teachers with their pay raises and the schools with a stronger financial foundation than they had ever had before.

Haley's efforts to improve the economic well-being of Chicago's public school teachers was also seen in the CTF's affiliation with the Chicago Federation of Labor (CFL) in 1902. This controversial alliance of the mostly lower-middle-class female CTF with the mostly working-class male CFL embodied Haley's position that teachers had to recognize that they were not too genteel or too professional to fight for their rights as workers by joining a labor union. She also realized the value to pre-suffrage women teachers of an alliance with vote-wielding labor union men.

Haley also worked to liberate the only nationwide professional organization for teachers at the time, the National Education Association (NEA), from the control of male university presidents and school administrators when, in 1901, she became the first woman ever to speak from the floor at an NEA annual meeting. Her motivation, she later wrote, stemmed from her belief in the right of women, the majority of the NEA's membership and of the nation's teaching force, to have an equal voice within the organization. In 1904, she became the first woman ever to make a formal address at an NEA annual meeting. Her speech, "Why Teachers Should Organize," was a call to arms against the entrenched powers controlling public education.

By being the pioneer of an independent teacher voice in the NEA, Haley forced the organization to give attention for the first time to issues affecting the classroom teacher. In 1910, she further advanced the cause of women teachers by leading the successful campaign that made Chicago school superintendent ELLA FLAGG YOUNG the first female president of the NEA. "We've been fighting for years in the N.E.A. to keep the organization from growing more reactionary," Haley wrote. "We have tried to put some breath of democracy in it" (Haley, 144). At last, it seemed, she was winning this battle.

Haley's activities on behalf of women were not confined only to issues directly connected to the public schools. She was also a great admirer of the "New Women" of her day and rejoiced that she was able "to come to maturity just when women were struggling for political, economic, and social independence." If women, she realized, were "to win rudimentary justice, [they] had to battle with brain, with wit, and sometimes even with force" (Haley, 3). As a result, Haley campaigned for woman suffrage. Women needed the vote, Haley believed, because women teachers could not teach their students how to exercise their democratic rights unless the teachers themselves were enfranchised. In 1913, her work on behalf of woman suffrage was instrumental in making Illinois the first state east of the Mississippi to grant the vote to women. Throughout her career as a reformer, however, one premise underpinned all of Haley's activism: American society could not be democratic unless teachers in the public schools were truly free.

Despite her victories on behalf of the women teaching in Chicago's public schools, Haley was almost constantly fighting against attempts made by several hostile mayoral administrations and business interests to circumscribe these advances. Several factors united against Haley's reform program, beginning with the Harper Commission, named after the commission's chair, University of Chicago president and school board member William Rainey Harper. Charged by Mayor Carter H. Harrison in 1898 to draw up a plan for school reform, the Harper Commission urged school reorganization along the lines advocated by the administrative progressives of the day, that educational experts, university-based like Harper himself, should manage the schools from the top down. Teachers were to be hired hands, trained to carry out the dictates of their superiors on a day-to-day basis in the city's classrooms.

From the beginning, the influence of the Harper Commission report was felt at all levels of the educational world in Chicago. By 1903, the fledgling teachers' councils, designed to foster teacher autonomy in curriculum and discipline matters, were abolished. Although these councils were later reinstated by Ella Flagg Young after she became the first female superintendent of the Chicago schools in 1909, the overall thrust of school reform in the first three decades of the twentieth century was away from Haley's teacher democracy and toward Harper's administrative hierarchy.

Teachers' ties to organized labor also came under attack when, in 1915, the school board passed the infamous Loeb Rule, named after school board president Jacob Loeb. At issue was the vastly enhanced power of the CFL-backed CTF in its contract negotiations with the now outflanked Board of Education. The Loeb Rule was designed to end this affiliation between public school teachers and organized labor by forbidding a teacher to join a labor union or any "teachers' organizations which have officers, business agents, or other representatives who are not members of the teaching force" (Haley, 171). Since the CTF was affiliated with the CFL and since CTF business agent and vice-president Margaret A. Haley had left the classroom in 1901, the intent of the Loeb Rule was evident. In order to keep their jobs, Chicago's teachers would have to give up their membership in the CTF. Thirty-eight teachers who refused to resign from the CTF were dismissed in June 1916. Haley and the CTF challenged the Loeb Rule in the courts, but in October 1916 the Illinois Supreme Court sustained the board's power to pass the rule. However, under a bill passed by the Illinois legislature in 1917, all eligible teachers in the city's schools were given permanent tenure. As a result, the CTF left the CFL, and the teachers who had lost their jobs for being tied to organized labor through their membership in the CTF were reinstated.

Haley's prototype CTF had served as Local Number One

when the American Federation of Teachers (AFT) was organized on a national basis in 1915. Nevertheless, the entry of the United States into World War I put an end to Haley's allegiance to organized labor. She came to believe that labor had been duped by British propaganda into supporting the war effort. Her intense Irish nationalism as well as her labor pacifism were deeply offended and, as a result, Haley and the CTF withdrew permanently from the ranks of the AFT and therefore from its parent organization, the American Federation of Labor.

Other separations followed, made all the more poignant by the deaths of such staunch friends and colleagues as Catharine Goggin in 1916 and Ella Flagg Young in 1918. Despite these losses, however, Haley continued to fight throughout the 1920s and 1930s against a variety of trends that threatened teacher rights and democratic education. She protested against the "payless paydays" teachers endured as funding for public education plummeted in the Great Depression years. She denounced the new vocational high schools as "scab hatcheries" designed to mold docile workers. She was adamantly opposed to the new tests of teacher conformity in the form of loyalty oaths, and she continued to work for an end to differential pay scales based on gender and grade level that discriminated against female elementary teachers. In each of these campaigns, Haley remained true to her lifelong commitment to the rights of the female schoolteacher. By the end of her life, however, her battles ended mostly in defeat. National teacher unionization was in disarray, the administrative progressives were once again in the forefront of educational policy, and economic depression had doomed further economic advance for the elementary school teacher. By 1937, even her beloved CTF had ceased to exist, having been absorbed into the recently organized Chicago Teachers Union. Her autobiography, written over a period of three decades, found no publisher.

At the time of her own death in Chicago at age seventy-seven from heart disease, Haley viewed her work on behalf of Chicago's teachers as at best unfinished, or at worst, undone. She was wrong in this pessimistic self-assessment. Instead, she was a groundbreaking pioneer in organizing the city's and later the nation's elementary schoolteachers into an effective political force on behalf of their own rights as workers and on behalf of the public school children under their care. She was known as the "Patrick Henry of the classroom teacher movement" (Haley, xxxi), and her efforts were fundamental to the growing economic and professional freedom of public school teachers in the early years of this century.

Sources. Although no scholarly biography of Haley yet exists, her autobiographical manuscript has been published as Margaret A. Haley, *Battleground: The Autobiography of Margaret A. Haley,* edited and with an introduction by Robert L. Reid (1982). This volume also contains the text of her NEA speech, "Why Teachers Should Organize." The Records of the Chicago Teachers' Federation and the Records of the Chicago Teachers Union, located at the CHS along with the Chicago Teachers' Federation *Bulletin* and *Margaret Haley's Bulletin,* also contain important material, often in Haley's own words, about her activities. An excellent bibliography can be found in the Haley listing in *NAW* (1971). The following provide insights into Haley's activities on behalf of public education: George S. Counts, *School and Society in Chicago* (1928); Mary J. Herrick, *The Chicago Schools: A Social and Political History* (1971); Marvin Lazerson, "If All the World Were Chicago: American Education in the Twentieth Century," *History of Education Quarterly*, 1984; Lazerson, "Teachers Organize: What Margaret Haley Lost," *History of Education Quarterly*, 1984; David Tyack, *The One Best System: A History of American Urban Education* (1974); Julia Wrigley, *Class Politics and Public Schools: Chicago, 1900–1950* (1982); and Marjorie Murphy, *Blackboard Unions: The AFT and the NEA 1900–1980* (1990).

JANET NOLAN

HALLOWELL, SARA TYSON
December 7, 1846–July 19, 1924
ART ADVISER, AGENT, EXHIBITION ORGANIZER

In the late nineteenth century, an era that saw expanding opportunities for women in myriad professional fields, Sara Tyson Hallowell took advantage of the new climate to create a career for herself as the first American woman to organize and manage large and significant art exhibitions. She was the fourth of six children and the first daughter of Caleb W. Hallowell, a Philadelphia merchant, and his wife, Mary Morris (Tyson) Hallowell. Hallowell's father descended from English Quaker John Hallowell (who died in 1706), while her mother, who traced her roots to both Philadelphia and Baltimore families, came from equally well-established Quaker stock, including among her ancestors the English Anthony Morris, the Irish Christopher Marshall, and the German Rhiner [Tisen] Tyson. Unfortunately, Hallowell's father died of tuberculosis when she was eleven. This loss deprived the family of a level of financial support that ordinarily would have been theirs. The prominence of her family was, in part, responsible for her having access to the highest levels of society in her art work, despite the economic reversals of her immediate family.

Little is known about Hallowell's early years. She claimed that she developed her knowledge of art while studying at the Pennsylvania Academy of the Fine Arts, but there is no record of her attending classes. Precisely when the Hallowell family moved to Chicago is not known, but by 1870 Mary Hallowell and five of her six children were living in this city.

Sara Hallowell's name appeared in the 1878 art catalog of the Chicago Inter-State Industrial Exposition as an art agent. The exposition, begun in 1873, was an industrial and agricultural fair with an art component. While her initial responsibilities with this organization appeared modest, the five-foot six-inch, dark-haired, blue-eyed Hallowell was quickly promoted. In 1879 she became an assistant clerk and in 1880 clerk of the art committee. For the next decade, with the exception of 1886, when she was in Europe for an extended stay, Hallowell was responsible for organizing each of the Inter-State art exhibitions, which usually consisted of four hundred to six hundred works of art. No more exhibitions were held after 1890, for the exposition building was subsequently demolished to make room for the present Art Institute of Chicago.

Under Hallowell's direction, the Inter-State exhibitions increasingly focused on the work of new and young American artists and also presented work by both European and American artists who had won prizes at the Paris Salon. Numerous paintings by such artists as William Merritt Chase, Thomas Eakins, Childe Hassam, and Edmund Tarbell, which were later exhibited at the 1893 World's Columbian Exposition in Chicago as examples of outstanding American art, were included in these shows. Hallowell's final exhibition in the fall of 1890, which featured works by Claude Monet, Edgar Degas, Alfred Sisley, Pierre Auguste Renoir, and Camille Pissarro, was notable for bringing art by French impressionists to the Midwest.

Hallowell used the Inter-State expositions to establish a relationship not only with artists but also with collectors, dealers, and museum professionals. Her knowledge of contemporary art, her managerial experience, and her myriad contacts in the field, both in America and abroad, prompted her to consider herself a primary candidate for the director of art at the World's Columbian Exposition in 1893. Her campaign for this position began shortly after she opened the last of the Inter-State exhibitions on September 3, 1890. She first called on August G. Bullock, an exposition commissioner from Massachusetts who chaired the commission's fine arts committee, which was charged with the task of nominating the director of fine arts. Bullock informed Chicagoan James Ellsworth, a member of the art committee that reported to the fair's board of directors, that Hallowell received the strong endorsement of almost every one in the country whose name might be expected to lend legitimacy to her petition, including leading American and foreign artists and presidents of art museums, such as Henry G. Marquand of New York and Martin Brimmer of Boston. Her candidacy was endorsed in numerous letters from critics and collectors; by a petition from sixty artists that included the signatures of sculptors Augustus Saint-Gaudens and Daniel Chester French, and painters William Merritt Chase, as president of the Society of American Artists, Daniel Huntington, as president of the National Academy of Design, and John Singer Sargent; by a petition from the exposition's Board of Lady Managers; and by the indefatigable support and political maneuvering of BERTHA HONORÉ PALMER, president of the Board of Lady Managers. Nevertheless, Hallowell did not secure this appointment. As the October 24, 1890, *New York Times* noted, she "possessed many qualifications . . . [but] her sex was an insuperable objection." Hallowell, however, was not one to accept meekly a decision based on gender rather than on skill and experience; and over the next four months she waged an intense crusade to obtain the position. By late March 1891, it was apparent that Halsey G. Ives, director of the museum that is now the Saint Louis Museum of Art, would be appointed director of fine arts for the World's Columbian Exposition.

Disappointed by her loss of this prestigious position, Hallowell sailed for France in the spring of 1891, where she remained until her return to America the next year. While in Paris, she used her various art-world contacts to assist her long-time friends, patrons, and professional champions, Bertha and Potter Palmer, in continuing the development of their art collection. Hallowell's advisory relationship with the Palmers, who were in Europe in the spring of 1891 and 1892 on behalf of the 1893 World's Columbian Exposition, seems to have begun about 1889. Through Hallowell, the Palmers met various artists and dealers, and over time and under her guidance, they acquired, through such dealers as Boussod Valadon, works by Claude Monet, August Renoir, Camille Pissarro, Alfred Sisley, Jean-François Raffaëlli, and Edgar Degas.

Hallowell also introduced Bertha Palmer to the American expatriate artists Mary Fairchild MacMonnies and Mary Cassatt, whom Palmer, as president of the Board of Lady Managers, commissioned to undertake the two major murals, *Primitive*

FIG. 46. Portrait de Mlle S. H. (Sara Tyson Hallowell), *by Mary Fairchild MacMonnies, 1886, oil on canvas.*

Women and *Modern Women*, for the Woman's Building at the 1893 exposition. During the summer and fall of 1892, Hallowell served as the liaison between the two artists and Palmer as they negotiated aspects of the contract and the design of the murals. Hallowell's informal involvement with Bertha Palmer and the art in the Woman's Building continued with her essay on "Women in Art," which appeared in 1893 in *Art and Handicraft in the Woman's Building.*

Hallowell returned to America in September 1892 to begin work on an exhibition of foreign masterpieces from American collections to be shown in the Fine Arts Building at the exposition. She had been offered this position as an assistant chief of the art department in June 1891, but the governing board of the exposition was reluctant to pay her three thousand dollars, the salary they ultimately agreed to pay her and the other assistant chief, Charles Kurtz, who was in charge of the exhibition of contemporary American art. While Kurtz's salary dispute was settled in July 1891, this issue was not resolved to Hallowell's satisfaction until April 1892.

Hallowell's loan exhibition consisted of 132 objects, mostly paintings that were borrowed from collectors such as Jay Gould, Cornelius Vanderbilt, and Henry O. Havemeyer of New York; Alexander Cassatt of Philadelphia; and Susan Cornelia Warren and Isabel Stewart Gardner of Boston. Chicago lenders included Potter Palmer, Robert H. McCormick, Charles T. Yerkes, Albert Munger, Martin A. Ryerson, and Florence Lathrop Field, who had inherited the collection of her recently deceased husband, Henry Field. This show was notable not only for the distin-

guished list of lenders but also for the way it both traced the major developments in nineteenth-century European art and showcased work by the French impressionists. While the exhibition organized by Charles Kurtz sought to establish the parity of American artists with their European peers, Hallowell's exhibition sought to prove that American collectors were as sophisticated and knowledgeable as their European counterparts.

In March 1894, after her responsibilities at the World's Columbian Exposition ended, Hallowell returned to France. From 1895 to 1914 and the outbreak of World War I, Hallowell served as the agent of the Art Institute of Chicago in France. Her primary task was to assemble the work of American artists living abroad for the museum's annual exhibition of contemporary American art. Thus, for the next two decades she remained a part of the American expatriate art world, maintaining in particular the friendships she had established in the 1880s. Her friendship with Bertha Palmer continued until the latter's death in 1918. Her contact with Mary Cassatt was lifelong. Hallowell had developed a friendship with Auguste Rodin about 1892, when she sought to interest Bertha Palmer and other American collectors in his works; she was in periodic communication with him until his death in 1917.

In 1910 Hallowell purchased a house in Moret-sur-Loing, France, a small town about an hour's train ride southeast of Paris, near Fountainebleau, where she had been a frequent visitor since about 1891. Here she lived with her mother and her niece Harriet, who subsequently inherited the home from her.

During World War I, when Hallowell could no longer serve the American art community, she assisted a local order of nuns in running Auxiliary Hospital No. 26. Hallowell, who died from heart failure in 1924, is buried in Moret-sur-Loing.

Sara Hallowell used her knowledge of contemporary American and European art to advise collectors, particularly Chicagoans Potter and Bertha Honoré Palmer, and to assist the Art Institute of Chicago from 1895 to 1914 in selecting works from abroad for annual exhibitions. By the time of Hallowell's death, most of those whom she had championed—and those who had championed her—were dead. With the ascent to prominence of a new generation of artists and patrons came the demise of Hallowell's reputation. In the 1990s, however, growing scholarship in the history of American art of the late nineteenth century and in women's studies has led to a reexamination of Hallowell's role and significance.

Sources. Manuscript material related to the career of Sara Tyson Hallowell can be found in the Ellsworth Papers, Spec. Coll., CPL; Board of Lady Managers Papers and Palmer Papers, CHS; William M. R. French Papers, Archives of the Art Institute of Chicago; Perot Papers, the Hist. Soc. of Pennsylvania; Rodin Archives, Musée Rodin, Paris, France; and the National Archives and Records Administration, Washington, D.C. Further information on Hallowell is in several publications: Hallowell's "Women in Art," in *Art and Handicraft in the Woman's Building of the World's Columbian Exposition,* ed. Maud Howe Elliot (1893); *Catalogue of Paintings, Engravings, Designs and Casts in the Art Hall of the Inter-State Industrial Exposition* (1873–90); John D. Kysela, "Sara Hallowell Brings 'Modern Art' to the Midwest," *Art Quarterly,* vol. 27, 1964; Jeanne Madeline Weimann, *The Fair Women* (1981); Carolyn K. Carr, "Prejudice and Pride: Presenting American Art at the 1893 Chicago World's Columbian Exposition," in C. K. Carr et al., *Revisiting the White City: American Art at the 1893 World's Fair* (1993); and Carolyn K. Carr and Sally Webster, "Mary Cassatt and Mary Fairchild MacMonnies: The Search for Their 1893 Murals," in *American Art,* Spring 1994. For discussion of Hallowell's candidacy for director of art at the World's Columbian Exposition, see "World's Fair Anomalies," *NYT,* October 24, 1890.

CAROLYN KINDER CARR

HALPERN, DINA
July 15, 1909–February 18, 1989
ACTRESS, DIRECTOR

Dina Halpern was born in Praga, a suburb of Warsaw, Poland, the eldest of Isaak and Dobbe Devoira (Dachfan) Halpern's six children. Her father was an electrical engineer, and her parents were part of Warsaw's intellectual community. She also came from a rich theatrical background. Her great-aunt, Esther Rachel Kaminska, dominated the Yiddish stage in Warsaw until her death in 1925, and her cousin Ida Kaminska starred in the American award-winning film, *The Shop on Main Street.* Another cousin, Joseph Kaminsky, became a composer and concert master of the Israel Philharmonic. By the time Dina Halpern was ten years old, she was part of the dancing troupe in Kaminska's Yiddish theater in Warsaw.

Her career took off quickly. While she was in her teens, her uncle, Abram Halpern, an impresario, became her manager. As early as 1935 she was acting, singing, and dancing, both in operettas and serious drama. Since the Warsaw Yiddish Art The-

ater performers toured the larger cities in Poland and the Baltic states, she had the opportunity to perform for diverse audiences. Her talents were quickly appreciated throughout the Jewish communities of the area. Even though she was busy in the theater, she also managed in 1936 to attend classes in literature at the University of Warsaw, where she was forced, together with other Jewish students, to sit in a section segregated from the Polish students. Because of her theatrical commitments, however, she was not able to conclude her studies and never earned an academic degree.

Although Dina Halpern's professional efforts were devoted to the stage, her life was not dedicated to acting alone. Warsaw before World War II was a center of Jewish culture. There were several daily newspapers in the Yiddish language, an active group of writers, some of whom would gain worldwide prominence, numerous literary journals, and an enterprising Yiddish book publishing industry. Hebrew and Yiddish learning flourished, and members of the Jewish community were actively espousing political philosophies and Zionism. Warsaw was an emerging, vital city, full of life, and Dina Halpern was one of its most active citizens. Her work in the theater brought her into contact with journalists, writers, musicians, and artists, and she was an integral part of Warsaw's Yiddish literary and artistic community.

She enjoyed great popularity as an actress. She was able to play a variety of roles, and her repertory ran the gamut from drama to musical comedy, from roles for young girls to those of old women. So widespread was her reputation that when she came to Vilna (now Vilnius), Lithuania, to play the lead in Itzig Manger's adaptation of Abraham Goldfaden's play, *Die Kishevmacher'n* [The witch], a school holiday was declared, and children came to the train to meet her.

Yiddish theater was at its zenith in Europe during the 1930s. Many of the world's classic dramas had been translated into Yiddish, and Dina Halpern played such versatile roles as Esmeralda in Victor Hugo's *The Hunchback of Notre Dame,* Frosina in Jean-Baptiste Molière's *The Misanthrope,* and Eliza Doolittle in George Bernard Shaw's *Pygmalion;* as well as many female roles in the plays of Peretz Hirschbein, David Pinski, Jacob Gordin, and Sholem Aleichem, well-known writers of Yiddish drama. The year 1937 was a stellar one for Halpern. She made two movies, *The Dybbuk,* based on the play by S. Ansky, and still considered one of the great films of European cinematography, and *The Vow.* She also appeared in Abraham Goldfaden's *The Witch,* which was very popular with audiences. She played to full houses for a year at the two-thousand-seat Nosvotstye Theater in Warsaw. During 1937 she also began to give poetry recitals, and these she continued until the end of her life. Through her efforts the works of such Yiddish poets as Kadya Molodowsky, Abraham Sutzkever, and Rachel Boymvol became well known.

In 1938 Dina Halpern accepted an invitation from the Second Avenue Yiddish Theater in New York to come to the United States for an eight-month engagement. Until then she had never left Europe. Her career was at its zenith, and professional commitments did not allow for a lengthy absence. She had every intention to return to Warsaw after the expiration of her offer and had even set into motion a schedule for future roles. The outbreak of World War II determined otherwise. She remained in America, and this step saved her life from the fate of her immediate family. Not until 1945, when the fighting in Europe had ceased, did she learn that her entire family—parents, siblings, aunts, and uncles—as well as many close friends had been killed at the Treblinka death camp.

Early in 1939, when her contract with the Second Avenue Yiddish Theater ended, Dina Halpern joined Maurice Schwartz's Yiddish Art Theater in New York and starred opposite him in *Shylock and His Daughter* and *It is Hard to Be a Jew*. She continued to live in New York until 1948, and during those years she also acted in Jacob Ben-Ami's New Art Theatre, either in New York or on tour. With both groups she performed in the larger cities of both North and South America.

After the war she was able to add Western Europe and Australia to her North and South American tours, and she visited major cities, including London, Paris, Buenos Aires, São Paulo, Rio de Janeiro, Montreal, Chicago, and Los Angeles, performing in Yiddish plays or giving recitals. Although Yiddish theater waned in the United States during the post–World War II years, Jewish communities in Canada, France, Argentina, and Australia, many of them with large numbers of survivors from Eastern Europe, made serious efforts to preserve their Yiddish heritage. Members of these groups made up Dina Halpern's audience.

In 1948, while touring with Maurice Schwartz, she met Daniel Newman, a theater impresario, in Chicago. Later that year they were married in London, where she was working as a guest star/director. Chicago became her home, and here she gave some of her most memorable performances. Her productions at the Douglas Park Theater of *Anna Lucasta* in 1949 and *The Little Foxes* in 1950 got glowing reviews. Sam Lesner of the *Chicago Daily News* compared her to the young Lynn Fontanne, and S. Zamd called her an actress of the highest quality in the *Forward*. S. B. Komaiko from the *Sentinel* thought her acting was as great as that of Sarah Bernhardt. Her early successes in Chicago were in Yiddish translations of American plays, a reflection of the changing tastes of American Jewish audiences.

In 1962 Dina Halpern and her husband established the Yiddish Theater Association, and for the next eight years she was busy in Chicago with this nonprofit, semi-professional theater company. During those years the classics of Yiddish drama were performed at the Eleventh Street Theater and at a community center. Dina Halpern did all the directing of the plays and the training of the actors. The first production was *Die Kishevmacher'n*, in which Halpern repeated the role she had done in Warsaw thirty years earlier. In 1963 she selected Sholem Aleichem's comedy, *Dos Groise Gevins* [The grand prize], and in 1964 she produced *Mirele Efros* by Jacob Gordin. The 1965 production was *Donna Garcia Mendes* by Kadya Molodowsky, a Yiddish and Hebrew poet and personal friend of Halpern. Three more plays were presented during the next four years. Although they were well received, the audiences dwindled, making it more and more difficult to produce Yiddish plays. During the 1970s Dina Halpern remained active in Chicago with Yiddish poetry recitals and dramatic readings of Yiddish literature because there were fewer opportunities to act in Yiddish theater. As

the Yiddish-speaking population in the United States decreased, opportunities to act in Yiddish theater declined.

In 1965 the Polish Arts Ministry invited Dina Halpern to return to Poland for a seven-city tour of Yiddish poetry recitals. The halls were packed, and her performances were well received. These, however, were to be her last professional appearances in her native country. After the Israeli victory in 1967, Poland reverted to waves of anti-Semitism, and the Yiddish theater that remained became a state-controlled enterprise. Jewish artists from other countries were barred from these productions.

Many honors came her way. In 1985 the World Council for Yiddish and Jewish Culture invited her to Jerusalem to recite classic works as well as modern Jewish poetry. Later that week Bar Ilan University, Ramat Gan, Israel, launched the Dina Halpern Institute, devoted to the study of classic and contemporary Yiddish poetry. The following December she was named honorary professor by the American Association of Professors of Yiddish. In March 1986 she received the "Goldie," the Abraham Goldfaden Award, for her outstanding career and for her interpretation of Yiddish poetry. A year later Spertus College of Judaica in Chicago honored her for her contributions to Yiddish culture. In May 1988, she toured Israel in a one-woman show, and the following month she was in Paris performing to a full house. It was her last performance. Two days later in Chicago she was hospitalized.

In 1987 the B'nai B'rith Women's Council sponsored a tribute to Dina Halpern as their idea of a Jewish woman, noting her work in maintaining Jewish tradition and identity. The Illinois Senate conveyed to her a resolution of appreciation "for her distinguished and brilliant career on the International Yiddish Stage."

Dina Halpern died of cancer and was buried at Rosemont Park Cemetery. She had suffered from the disease for several years but kept active until the last months of her life.

Dina Halpern was a product of the pre–World War II Jewish cultural world, where Yiddish was the language of daily life. This world no longer exists. Although she witnessed the decline of that language and the life it reflected, she never lost her optimism that somehow Yiddish would survive. Throughout her lifetime she had an active correspondence with many of the Yiddish writers who had survived the Holocaust, including Abraham Sutzkever, Kadya Molodowsky, and Rachel Boymvol. As long as it was possible to interest an audience in Yiddish theater, literature and poetry, she gave of her talents enthusiastically.

Sources. Biographical information about Dina Halpern's life was made available during an interview by Sophie K. Black with Danny Newman on October 12, 1994. Additional discussion of Halpern is found in the playbill for the Sixth Annual Jewish Film Festival of Metropolitan Chicago, *The Dybbuk*, March 1990. Dan Santow's article "Theater" in *Chicago*, July 1989, describes Halpern's theatrical contributions. Biographical facts are included in *Consecrate Every Day: The Public Lives of Jewish American Women, 1880–1980* (1981) by June Sochen and in Zalmen Zilbertsveig's Yiddish-language *Leksikon fun Yidishen Theater*, vol. 4 (1963). A tribute to Halpern is found in the Illinois "Senate Resolution no. 375," *Journal of the Senate*, June 12, 1987. Halpern's personal library is in Spec. Coll., Harold Washington Library Center, CPL.

SOPHIE K. BLACK

HAMILL, FRANCES. *See* BARKER, MARGERY

HAMILTON, ALICE
February 27, 1869–September 22, 1970
PHYSICIAN, INDUSTRIAL TOXICOLOGIST, SOCIAL REFORMER

Alice Hamilton, pioneering specialist in industrial toxicology and a founder of the field of occupational health, was the second of four daughters born within six years to Montgomery and Gertrude (Pond) Hamilton; the only son was many years younger. Born in New York City, she grew up in Fort Wayne, Indiana, at the family compound presided over by her widowed paternal grandmother, whose husband, a native of northern Ireland, had made a fortune in the frontier community. Alice Hamilton, her sisters, and cousins flourished in this protected environment in which books, religion (Presbyterian), and each other's company played the most important part. Educated at home by both parents in ancient and modern languages, literature, and history, Hamilton attended Miss Porter's School in Farmington, Connecticut (1886–88).

Eager to do good work and also impelled by the failure of her father's wholesale grocery business, Alice Hamilton chose medicine as a career that would afford her a life of usefulness and independence, both cherished values. Her patrician family preferred her older sister Edith Hamilton's choice of classics—their father's avocation. Alice Hamilton studied science at the Fort Wayne College of Medicine and in 1893 received an M.D. from the University of Michigan. Inspired by several outstanding laboratory researchers, she turned from her initial goal of combining medical and charitable work to a career in science, then an unusual choice for men or women. After interning at the Northwestern Hospital for Women and Children in Minneapolis and the New England Hospital for Women and Children in Boston (1893–94), she pursued postgraduate study in pathology and bacteriology at Michigan, the universities of Leipzig and Munich, and Johns Hopkins Medical School. In 1897 she moved to Chicago to begin work as professor of pathology at the Woman's Medical School of Northwestern University; she took up residence at Hull-House.

The encounters with Hull-House and JANE ADDAMS were the most critical of her adult life. An eager but unformed young woman when she arrived, under the nurturing aegis of Addams, the tutelage of FLORENCE KELLEY and JULIA LATHROP, and daily acquaintance with the poverty and brutality endured by her immigrant neighbors, Hamilton gradually climbed down from the political fence. She stayed on at the settlement for nearly four decades, becoming one of Addams's closest colleagues. At first she took on everything from teaching evening classes in art, anatomy, and composition to running a well baby clinic. She felt the inadequacy of these efforts and for a decade struggled to integrate laboratory work with settlement life. When the Woman's Medical School closed in 1902, Hamilton accepted a position as bacteriologist at the new Memorial Institute for Infectious Diseases headed by Ludvig Hektoen, a distinguished pathologist and bacteriologist.

While conducting research on antibodies and on scarlet fever and other diseases, at Hull-House she concentrated on public health efforts that allied her with progressive medical and lay circles. Following her investigation of a 1902 typhoid epidemic that disproportionately affected the Hull-House district, a campaign by settlement residents against the Chicago Board of Health led to appointment of a new chief sanitary inspector. Hamilton was also prominent in residents' efforts to end the cocaine traffic: a three-year campaign resulted in a 1907 law providing stiffer penalties against drug dealers, though it was soon nullified by the courts. Cooperating with the Visiting Nurse Association and other groups, she took part in the first, information-gathering phase of Chicago's campaign against tuberculosis: she reported in 1905 on a house-to-house survey in the Jewish district near Hull-House, identified the major occupational causes of the disease for *Charities and The Commons* (1906), and studied fatigue as a predisposing factor in young women factory workers. She also served on a joint committee of the Chicago Medical Society and Hull-House that in 1908 recommended closer state regulation of midwifery to improve standards of training and conditions of practice. Probably her most important contribution during this period was a widely cited 1909 study of sixteen hundred working-class families that correlated high infant mortality rates with high birth rates. Viewing birth control as the sole alternative to abortion, which she opposed, Hamilton participated in the initial phase of the Chicago movement, led by gynecologist RACHELLE YARROS. Collectively, these endeavors provided the context for her growing awareness of the environmental causes of disease.

In the Hull-House manner, she studied occupational diseases, publishing her first article in 1908 in *Charities and The Commons*. That year Governor Charles S. Deneen appointed her to the Illinois Commission on Occupational Diseases; in March 1910 Hamilton became medical director of a nine-month survey, the first to combine modern laboratory investigation with field work. Her meticulous study of lead poisoning documented more than seventy industrial processes that used lead and 578 cases of lead poisoning, many of them severely disabling. The study prompted passage of a state occupational disease law in 1911, the year Hamilton became president of the Chicago Pathological Society.

Hamilton became special investigator for the United States Bureau of Labor in 1911; two years later her venue changed to the Bureau of Labor Statistics in the new Department of Labor. In this capacity she conducted pioneering investigations of lead poisoning in the white-lead, pottery, porcelain enameled sanitary ware, smelting, and storage battery industries, among others; during World War I, she investigated toxic substances in munitions plants. By combing hospital and dispensary records, visiting workers in their homes, and searching European sources for clues, she demonstrated high morbidity and mortality rates, something American factory owners had previously denied. She had no authority to enter plants, let alone force compliance; but moved by the plight of the mainly poor and foreign-born workers in the dangerous trades, she presented her findings to owners and persuaded many to institute simple safety precautions. While avoiding the sensationalism of the muckrakers, she did everything she could to publicize industrial diseases, particularly among her medical colleagues. Crisscrossing the country, she enjoyed both her freedom and the returns to Hull-House. Her sister Norah Hamilton, who taught art at the settlement, often joined her there; so, for a time after her husband's death, did her mother Gertrude Hamilton, to whom Alice Hamilton was especially close.

For Hamilton, disregard of workers' health was only one component of a general pattern of class exploitation. By this time, she had aligned herself with the social justice wing of the progressive movement, endorsing measures that would guarantee every American a life of decency, including a living wage, an eight-hour day, and a home, as well as compulsory state health insurance, a proposal opposed by many physicians. Her political transformation was complete when she became a pacifist during World War I. She attended the International Congresses of Women in The Hague in 1915, when she accompanied Addams on her peace mission to several warring nations, and in Zurich in 1919, after which she and Addams investigated the devastating famine in Germany with a group of English and American Quakers.

In the fall of 1919, Hamilton became assistant professor of industrial medicine at Harvard Medical School, the first woman named to a professorial position in the university. By then the most prominent authority on lead poisoning in the United States, she accepted Dean David L. Edsall's invitation to join the new industrial hygiene program only after securing her own terms, chief of which was a half-time appointment that enabled her to return to Hull-House each spring. She was a triple outsider at Harvard—by virtue of her gender, her politics, and her conception of her work, which transcended a narrow professional model—but her professional and public influence continued to grow. Two acclaimed textbooks, *Industrial Poisons in the United States* (1925) and *Industrial Toxicology* (1934), demonstrated her unsurpassed knowledge of European as well as American research and consolidated both the field and her leadership of it. Working with the lay public as well as professionals and in the continued absence of government regulation, Hamilton served as watchdog and clearing house on matters concerning industrial poisons. She raised funds for research, followed up requests to identify obscure cases of illness, kept after owners to clean up their plants, and promoted public efforts to control industrial diseases. She was in the forefront of those urging the Surgeon General to call national conferences to address the dangers of two new industrial poisons, tetraethyl lead in 1925 and radium in 1928; in the latter case she collaborated with the National Consumers' League, an organization concerned with working conditions for women and children, and with its secretary Florence Kelley.

Hamilton remained active in the women's reform and peace network; she was a convincing advocate of progressive welfare measures, including prohibition of child labor, protective legislation for women, and workers' compensation. More closely associated with workers and unions than most settlement residents, she understood the class bias of prohibition; unlike Addams, she endorsed presidential candidates Alfred E. Smith in 1928 and socialist Norman Thomas four years later. As a member of the President's Research Committee on Social Trends (1930–32), a landmark of social science research, she was more critical of capitalism than her younger male colleagues. Hamilton's wartime experiences left her with a consuming interest in international affairs. After serving on the Health Committee of the League of Nations (1924–30), she became a pro-League advocate. She was an outspoken opponent of Nazism following a trip to Germany in April 1933, shortly after Adolph Hitler's rise to power; subsequently, she helped many refugees settle in the United States. She continued to contest rearmament but did not oppose United States entry into World War II.

Her retirement from Harvard in 1935, coinciding with Jane Addams's death, propelled her once again in new directions. Hamilton, who had assumed special responsibility for Addams's health and was with her when she died, turned down a request from residents to head the settlement. Instead, she returned to the Department of Labor as a consultant in the Division of Labor Standards, recently established by Frances Perkins to promote industrial health and safety. Remaining a presence in her profession for another decade, she revised her text, *Industrial Toxicology* (1949) with Harriet L. Hardy, a younger specialist in occupational medicine. In *Exploring the Dangerous Trades* (1943), her engaging but impersonal autobiography, Hamilton took pride in the advances in workers' health since she first entered the field and expressed optimism about the future. Although alert to the obstacles to change, she was, like Addams, a bridge builder who was "willing to accept half a loaf rather than no bread" (Sicherman, *Alice Hamilton*, 360).

In retirement, Hamilton remained vitally engaged in the issues of her time. As president of the National Consumers' League (1944–49), she continued to oppose the Equal Rights Amendment, which she feared would undo protective legislation for women; she withdrew her opposition in 1952, once satisfied that New Deal gains would stand. An anti–Cold War liberal, Hamilton vigorously protested the nation's obsessive anticommunist foreign policy and the infringements on civil liberties at home in letters to newspapers, policy makers, and friends, among them Felix Frankfurter, whose Supreme Court opinions on civil liberties and the deportation of aliens deeply distressed her. In 1963, she urged withdrawal of United States forces from Vietnam.

Hamilton's deepest ties were to her family, especially her sisters, with whom she purchased a house in Hadlyme, Connecticut, in 1916; none of them married. After 1935, she lived there year round with her sister Margaret Hamilton, a retired teacher, and Clara Landsberg, a former Hull-House resident. Physically active through her eighties, Alice Hamilton died at home of a stroke at the age of 101 after several years of invalidism. She is buried in Hadlyme near her mother and sisters.

Hamilton's preeminence in the field of occupational health is a remarkable achievement for a woman who worked mainly in the male world and shunned institutional power. An unlikely blend of "crusader and scientist" (quoted from C.-E. A. Winslow in Sicherman, *Alice Hamilton*, 1), she mediated between the worlds of profession and reform. Her reputation rests not on particular studies, which have long been superseded, but on the persistence and ingenuity with which she advanced the cause of workers' health. As the *Detroit Medical News* proclaimed in 1934: "The name Hamilton parallels the building up of the awareness and the study of poisoning in industry" (quoted in Sicherman, *Alice Hamilton*, 312).

Sources. The principal manuscript repositories are the Alice Hamilton Papers and the Hamilton Family Papers, both at the SL, and the Alice

Hamilton Collection at the Connecticut College Library, New London. There are also important manuscript materials and a taped interview in the Francis A. Countway Library of Medicine, Harvard Medical School. Hamilton's autobiography, *Exploring the Dangerous Trades* (1943), concentrates on her professional and reform activities; it can be supplemented by *Women at The Hague: The International Congress of Women and Its Results* (1916), coauthored with Jane Addams and Emily Greene Balch, and "Nineteen Years in the Poisonous Trades," *Harper's*, October 1929. For her opposition to the Equal Rights Amendment, see "Protection for Women Workers," *Forum*, August 1924. Hamilton's surveys include [Illinois] *Report of Commission on Occupational Diseases* (1911) and bulletins of the United States Bureau of Labor Statistics. The fullest historical treatment of Hamilton's life and work is Barbara Sicherman, *Alice Hamilton: A Life in Letters* (1984), a mixed-genre of biography and letters that lists major archival sources; see also Barbara Sicherman, "Working It Out: Gender, Profession, and Reform in the Career of Alice Hamilton," *Gender, Class, Race, and Reform in the Progressive Era*, ed. Noralee Frankel and Nancy S. Dye (1991) and *NAW* (1980). There are two useful Ph.D. dissertations: Wilma Ruth Slaight, "Alice Hamilton: First Lady of Industrial Medicine" (Case Western Reserve Univ., 1974), which has an excellent bibliography of Hamilton's writings; and Angela Nugent Young, "Interpreting the Dangerous Trades: Workers' Health in America and the Career of Alice Hamilton, 1910–1935" (Brown Univ., 1982), which focuses on her career. See also the revealing contemporary appraisal by Elizabeth Shepley Sergeant, "Alice Hamilton, M.D., Crusader for Health in Industry," *Harper's*, May 1926; the special issue of the *Journal of Occupational Medicine*, February 1972, ed. Harriet L. Hardy; and Penina Migdal Glazer and Miriam Slater, *Unequal Colleagues: The Entrance of Women into the Professions, 1890–1940* (1987).

BARBARA SICHERMAN

HANSBERRY, LORRAINE VIVIAN
May 19, 1930–January 12, 1965
PLAYWRIGHT, ACTIVIST

Contemporary dramatist Lorraine Vivian Hansberry was a literary warrior. In her brief life, she exhibited a spirited insurgency against all oppressors of humanity; but she was especially indignant at the second-class citizenship accorded to Blacks in America.

Hansberry was born on the South Side of Chicago, the youngest of four children, to parents of pioneer spirit. Her father, Carl Augustus Hansberry, was a successful real estate broker, U.S. Marshal, candidate for Congress, and active member of the National Association for the Advancement of Colored People (NAACP) and Urban League. Her mother, Nannie (Perry) Hansberry, who was equally committed to political and social reform, relinquished a career as a schoolteacher to make a greater political impact as a Republican ward committeewoman. Hansberry graduated from Betsy Ross Elementary school in 1944 and enrolled in Englewood High School, where she was elected president of the debating society in 1947.

In a selection of her memoirs, *To Be Young, Gifted and Black*, adapted by Robert Nemiroff, Hansberry offers a disturbing portrayal of the educational system that was provided for black children in Chicago. She remembers Betsy Ross as a school of "substandard quality" (p. 35) that had been earmarked for African American ghetto children and existed "*not* to give education but to withhold as much as possible" (p. 35). She also reflects on the violence that occurred on "the day of the race riot

and strike" (p. 35) at Englewood High School and counts herself among the "well-dressed colored students" (p. 45) who stood by amusedly trading taunts and insults with the "mob of several hundred striking whites" (p. 45) rather than engaging in physical confrontation; thus she was stunned when the "unqualified oppressed" (p. 46), the black students from neighboring high schools, came to defend them. Carloads of students from Wendell Phillips and DuSable High Schools, who were "veteran" (p. 45) fighters, came from "the bowels of the ghetto" (p. 46), armed with baseball bats and fighting slogans, and actually "fought back" (p. 46) for them. While her father's stature as a successful businessman distinguished Hansberry as a "rich girl" (p. 36) to her ghetto classmates, by contrast, they won her admiration for their willingness to fight back. She writes, "My mother sent me to kindergarten in white fur in the middle of the depression; the kids beat me up; and I think it was from that moment I became a rebel" (p. 36).

Hansberry's willingness to engage in conflict was also born of the early battles she witnessed when her family attempted to integrate an all-white neighborhood near the University of Chicago. In 1938, when Hansberry was eight years old, her father taught her the meaning of commitment and conflict by challenging Chicago's restrictive real estate covenants. After the large influx of black southerners during the migrations after World War I, Chicago's white, South Side property owners became increasingly agitated by what they feared was a mass invasion of black residents. As a result, many property owners joined the Woodlawn Property Owners' League and signed covenants that barred them from renting or selling to Blacks who would be owners. These restrictive covenants were upheld in the state courts and thus provided legally sanctioned discrimination in Chicago's segregated neighborhoods. Nevertheless, Carl Hansberry challenged the covenants when he purchased a home in an all-white community near the University of Chicago and moved his family in, to the chagrin of his white neighbors.

Carl Hansberry, with the assistance of the NAACP, took his case to the U.S. Supreme Court and had the covenant legally struck down, although actual discrimination practices in Chicago continued unabated. While the case was being argued in court, the family fell prey to the violent aggressions of their bitter neighbors. During one of the nights of constant harassment, young Lorraine Hansberry was a near victim when a brick tossed through a window barely missed her head. Nannie Hansberry patrolled the home, armed with a gun, to protect her young children from further incidents. But even after the ruinous financial sacrifices, the traumatic physical attacks, and the legal complexities, housing discrimination persisted in Chicago. Finally, an embittered Carl Hansberry prepared to move his family to property he owned in Mexico, but he died of a cerebral hemorrhage in Mexico before his plans could be realized. For young Lorraine, the memory of her family's historic case, *Hansberry v. Lee* (1940), etched a lesson in pride, resistance, and pain that would inform her later stance in political confrontations with Attorney General Robert Kennedy and entertainment figure Otto Preminger. In addition to the influence of her father, whom she remembered as an "educated soul" (*Young, Gifted and Black*, 20), Hansberry's uncle, William Leo Hansberry was another contributor to her early education and one who enlarged her view of the world. He was a professor at Howard University and one of the first African American scholars to make critical assessments in the study of African antiquity and history. Hansberry's early immersion in African history, culture, and politics was augmented by her exposure to her uncle's visiting African students, scholarly contemporaries, and foreign diplomats, all of which clearly influenced her dramatic renditions of violent revolution in contemporary Africa in *Les Blancs*, the last play she worked on in the 1960s before her death. Her views on worldwide issues of humanity were also molded by the social and intellectual atmosphere of the Hansberry home. Her parents often entertained businessmen, politicians, educators, activists, and entertainers, including Langston Hughes, Paul Robeson, Walter White, Duke Ellington, Jesse Owens, and W. E. B. Du Bois.

To augment the early conditioning in racial pride, individual resistance, and the global oppression she witnessed under the tutelage of her family, Hansberry exercised her right to rebel when, in 1948, she enrolled at the University of Wisconsin rather than at Howard University, a parental choice. Her interest in playwriting was stimulated when she made a chance visit to a rehearsal of Sean O'Casey's play *Juno and the Paycock*; she later talked in glowing terms about O'Casey's willingness and ability to universalize his characters by casting them in the full realm of their humanity, from drunkard to braggart to liar to hero. Two years later, when Hansberry's interest waned at Wisconsin, she returned to Chicago and briefly studied at the Art Institute of Chicago and Roosevelt University, then in Guadalajara, Mexico.

But it was in 1950, when she ventured to New York, that Hansberry's commitment to fighting for the rights of African American people became evident. Although she had been exposed to social activism throughout her life, her own emerging radicalism was an outgrowth of her involvement with Paul Robeson's new, radical, and short-lived black journal, *Freedom*. While on staff as a reporter and an associate editor, she worked with actress-writer Alice Childress; Harlem writers John Oliver Killens and Julian Mayfield; and editor Louis E. Burnham, who was also a noted journalist and former executive secretary of the Southern Negro Youth Congress. W. E. B. Du Bois aligned himself with Robeson in the endeavor and contributed an article to the first issue in December 1950.

In this climate of social and political activism, there was a strong move on the part of many African Americans, especially artists and intellectuals, to join the Communist Party as a means of furthering the cause of black equality in America. Although Hansberry never became a member of the Communist Party, she worked with those, like Robeson, who did eventually join. While she was sympathetic to the Communist Party's efforts on behalf of black people, its stance against homosexuality, in the face of her newly emerging lesbianism in the late 1950s, prevented, at least, in part, her full participation. She did, however, opt to project her radicalism through writing and speaking.

From 1950 to 1953, she wrote book and drama reviews for *Freedom*, but more importantly, wrote news stories that addressed the social and political issues of the day on both the national and international levels. Her articles included "No More Hiroshimas" and "Gold Coast's Rules Go: Ghana Moves to

Freedom," forerunners of her later, more radical essays urging her contemporaries to activism, including "The Negro Writer and His Roots: Toward a New Romanticism" (*Black Scholar*, March/April 1961), "A Challenge to Artists" (*Freedomways*, Winter 1963), and "The Black Revolution and the White Backlash" (*National Guardian*, July 4, 1964). In a 1964 *Black Titan* tribute to Du Bois, she expressed her support for socialism. During the 1950s, Hansberry also participated in rallies, spoke on street corners, and raised money in support of gaining social, political, and economic equality for black people.

In 1952, her interest in world affairs accelerated when she represented Robeson, a passionate outspoken advocate of racial equality, at the International Peace Congress in Montevideo, Uruguay, after the U.S. State Department denied him a passport. Though the turbulent flight left her physically debilitated, she was energized by firsthand exposure to international perspectives on world peace, dictatorships, and poverty. The congress also afforded her the opportunity to forge cross-cultural alliances with other women of color.

In 1953, Hansberry married Robert Nemiroff, a Jewish intellectual and member of the Communist Party, whom she met when they were in a picket line protesting discrimination. At the time, Nemiroff was an aspiring writer and student of English and history at New York University. Nemiroff's financial support from the sale of his 1957 hit song, "Cindy, Oh Cindy" (written in conjunction with Burt D'Lugoff), enabled Hansberry to work full-time on her first play, and his theatrical connections opened the door to the stage production of the play. They divorced in 1964 but continued their artistic collaboration.

Hansberry's inspiration for her play, *A Raisin in the Sun*, was her awareness of the plight of working-class black tenants, visible in those who had rented kitchenette apartments from her father. She saw the stifling conditions of their lives expressed in Langston Hughes's poem "Lenox Avenue Mural"; the subsection of the poem "Harlem," from which she took the title for her play, posed questions about a dream that was postponed. Although the theme of black life was considered so risky that major Broadway producers initially rejected the play, Hansberry and her colleagues were confident that the play would be favorably received by audiences. Thus, her producer, Phil Rose, a friend, music publisher, and a former employer of Nemiroff, and coproducer, David S. Cogan, agreed to make test runs in other cities before approaching Broadway theaters again. They raised their own funds, took the show on the road, and gained success in New Haven, Connecticut; Philadelphia; and Chicago theaters. Finally, armed with a track record of successful showings, they convinced Broadway producers to stage the play in New York. *A Raisin in the Sun* opened at the Ethel Barrymore Theatre on March 11, 1959, and immediately elicited the enthusiasm of both audiences and critics.

Hansberry became celebrated as a dramatist in May 1959 when she won the New York Drama Critics' Circle Award for Best Play of the Year for *Raisin in the Sun*. She was the youngest person, the fifth woman, and the first African American to win the award (and additionally, opened the door for the first black Broadway director, Lloyd Richards). It is worth noting that Hansberry's competitors for the award included seasoned playwrights Tennessee Williams, Eugene O'Neill, and Archibald

MacLeish. Since that time, *Raisin in the Sun* has secured its status as an American classic and has also won international fame. The play has been translated into more than thirty languages, a testament to its broad appeal, and has been produced in France, England, the Soviet Union, and Czechoslovakia. It has been successfully rendered in two film versions and achieved acclaim in its twenty-fifth anniversary celebration production in 1984.

When she died of cancer in 1965 at the age of thirty-four, Hansberry had completed her second play, *The Sign in Sidney Brustein's Window*, produced in 1964. The play, a rebuttal of the societal apathy of liberal New Yorkers, closed on the eve of her death to mixed critical reviews, although Hansberry's own literary coterie repeatedly rallied with financial and inspirational support to insure the continued production of the play through 101 performances. In her next work, *The Movement: Documentary of a Struggle for Equality* (1964), Hansberry created the text for a graphic pictorial account of the violent and brutal living conditions, including lynchings, for Blacks in the South during the early days of the civil rights movement; the material had been compiled by the Student Non-Violent Coordinating Committee (SNCC).

Three of Hansberry's plays, written in the 1960s, *Les Blancs, The Drinking Gourd*, and *What Use Are the Flowers?*, were published posthumously by her literary executor Robert Nemiroff in *Les Blancs, The Collected Last Plays of Lorraine Hansberry* (1972). *The Drinking Gourd* (1960), commissioned by NBC–TV but never produced there, is an unflinching condemnation of slavery that depicts the stultifying effects of slavery on both races. *What Use Are the Flowers?*, written in 1961, reflected her disdain for the prevalent existentialist themes in literature. In 1967, three scenes from *What Use Are the Flowers?* were recorded for the radio program "Lorraine Hansberry in Her Own Words"; one scene was featured in the play *To Be Young, Gifted and Black*. Nemiroff published a mosaic of Hansberry's life in the "informal autobiography" (Carter, *Hansberry's Drama*, xii), *To Be Young, Gifted and Black* (1969), with selected material from her recordings, published and unpublished articles, plays, letters, and journal entries. *Les Blancs*, a forceful drama of impending revolution in Africa, was unfinished at her death. It was completed by Robert Nemiroff and staged at the Longacre Theatre in New York to mixed reviews in 1970 and revived in 1988 at the Arena Stage in Washington, D.C.

Though Lorraine Hansberry's life was cut short by her untimely death and critical assessment was truncated, recent analyses of her published and unpublished works suggest new critical perspectives, especially related to the characterization of women. In the August 16, 1983, publication of an excerpt from Hansberry's unpublished novel manuscript "All the Dark and Beautiful Warriors" in the *Village Voice*, Thulani Davis perceptively positions Hansberry in the tradition of black women writers and suggests that stronger connections can be made when scholars and critics gain greater access to her unpublished works. As a commentary on Hansberry's view of the strength and leadership potential of women, recent critical analyses by Adrienne Rich, bell hooks, and Margaret Wilkerson reveal Hansberry's clear feminist focus and support her characterization of strong women as pivotal to the movement and meaning of the plays *A Raisin in the Sun, Les Blancs*, and *The Drinking Gourd*.

The intellectual weapons that enabled Hansberry to engage the controversial issues of the day in a forthright and compelling manner included an astute political perspective, an uncompromising sensibility for equality, and a world view of humanity that balanced caring and candor. She chose the theater as her artistic battleground and forcefully dramatized the racism, colonialism, sexism, and homophobia that persistently threatened humanity. By age thirty-four, she had already established her place as a major playwright of her generation.

Sources. Two of Lorraine Hansberry's plays, *Raisin in the Sun* (published in 1959) and *The Sign in Sidney Brustein's Window* (published in 1965), were edited and reprinted by Robert Nemiroff in 1987 and enhanced by the addition of material restored from early manuscripts as well as critical essays by Amiri Baraka and John Braine. The uncompleted *Toussaint* is included in Margaret B. Wilkerson's *9 Plays by Black Women* (1986). Selected essays by Hansberry include "All the Dark and Beautiful Warriors," *Village Voice*, August 16, 1983; A "Tribute" to W. E. B. Du Bois in *Black Titan: W.E.B. Du Bois*, an anthology by the editors of *Freedomways* (1964); "The Negro Writer and His Roots: Toward a New Romanticism," *Black Scholar*, March/April 1981; "Village Intellect Revealed," *Village Voice*, October 11, 1964; "A Challenge to Artists," *Freedomways*, Winter 1963; "Willie Loman, Walter, and He Who Must Live," *Village Voice*, August 13, 1959. Numerous critical articles have been written on the works of Hansberry. One full-length analysis of her work is Steven R. Carter's *Hansberry's Drama: Commitment and Complexity* (1991). Encyclopedia articles appear in *BWA* and *Notable Black American Women*, ed. Jessie Carney Smith (1991). Her 1959 interview with Studs Terkel, "Make New Sounds: A Conversation with Lorraine Hansberry," was published in *American Theatre*, November 1984. Recent articles on Hansberry's interest in women's issues include bell hooks's "'Raisin' in a New Light," *Christianity and Crisis*, February 6, 1989, and Adrienne Rich's "The Problem with Lorraine Hansberry" in a *Freedomways* special edition, "Lorraine Hansberry: Art of Thunder, Vision of Light," Fourth Quarter, 1979. One recording of Hansberry's speeches is *Lorraine Hansberry Speaks Out: Art and the Black Revolution*, ed. Robert Nemiroff, produced by Caedmon Records (1972); it includes the essay, "The Black Revolution and the White Backlash," which is also published in the *National Guardian*, July 4, 1964, and in *Black Protest: History, Documents, and Analyses, 1619 to the Present*, ed. Joanne Grant (1968). For the Langston Hughes poem, "Lenox Avenue Mural," that inspired Hansberry, see Arna Bontemps, *American Negro Poetry* (1974).

B. J. BOLDEN

HARBERT, ELIZABETH BOYNTON
April 15, 1843–January 19, 1925
REFORMER, SUFFRAGIST, AUTHOR

Elizabeth Boynton Harbert was born in Crawfordsville, Indiana, to Abigail (Sweetser) Boynton (originally from Boston) and William H. Boynton (originally from Nashua, New Hampshire). She attended the Female Seminary in Oxford, Ohio, and subsequently graduated from the Terre Haute [Indiana] Female College with honors in 1862. When she sought additional education from the all-male Wabash College (along with several other female students), she received special permission to attend lectures but was denied admission to the school. Boynton wrote about the experience in 1865 for the *New York Independent* and received her first income (ten dollars) as a writer.

Boynton published her first novel, *The Golden Fleece*, at the age of twenty-two. Over the next two years, she became actively involved in the woman suffrage movement by serving as the vice-president of the Woman Suffrage Association of Indiana and delivering her first speech on this cause at a woman suffrage convention in Crawfordsville in 1869. The next year, she met and married William Harbert, a former army captain embarking on a career in law. In 1871, they moved to Des Moines, Iowa, where Elizabeth Harbert served as president of the Iowa Woman Suffrage Association. During this time, she persuaded the Republican Party of Iowa to include a woman's plank in their party platform.

It was also in 1871 that Harbert published her second novel, *Out of Her Sphere*. The book provides insight into her views as a women's rights activist and a baseline for understanding subsequent shifts in these views. This novel traces the lives of two girlhood friends who grew up to experience very different lives as adult women. The heroine resists attempts to confine her to the domesticity of "woman's sphere" and enjoys a happy and fulfilling life, while her friend succumbs to societal pressures, conforms to stereotypic expectations, and suffers a disastrous marriage and a lifetime of dependence on others. Harbert's novel is a morality play about the dangers of female socialization and the ideology of separate spheres, which she faulted for both economic and moral reasons. In the process, she distinguished between femininity (a pejorative category) and womanliness (a positive category), thereby claiming a middle ground between conventional femininity and free-love sexual radicals and suggesting that political empowerment would not jeopardize womanliness but rather allow its fullest expression.

In 1874, the Harberts moved to Evanston, Illinois, where they lived for almost forty years and raised a son and two daughters. Their proximity to Chicago allowed Harbert to deepen her involvement in social reform. She had already participated in the founding conventions of the American Woman Suffrage Association in Cleveland and the Illinois Woman Suffrage Association (IWSA) in Chicago in 1869. She subsequently became disenchanted with the single focus of the American Association, and her sympathies came to rest with the rival National Woman Suffrage Association headed by Susan B. Anthony and Elizabeth Cady Stanton. When Harbert was elected president of the IWSA in 1876, she did not hesitate to bring the organization into close affiliation with Anthony's organization. She remained active in suffrage work at both the national and state levels for many years, presiding over the state association until 1884 and again from 1889 to 1890 and from 1900 to 1901. As the leader of the major woman suffrage organization in Illinois during this period, Harbert maintained close ties with Susan B. Anthony as both women sought to sustain the momentum of the suffrage movement in the absence of any immediate prospects for success.

Late in 1876, Harbert had requested a ten-minute audience with William Penn Nixon, the publisher of the Chicago daily paper *Inter-Ocean*. She convinced him of the need for a column devoted to the diverse interests of women, and the first installment appeared on January 6, 1877. Harbert's column, the "Woman's Kingdom," addressed a wide variety of issues through this forum. It is most revealing for its emerging philosophy of social reform that reflected a feminist orientation, a maternalist accent, and a distinctly middle-class consciousness. Writing at a time when the American middle class was defining itself between the increasingly antagonistic poles of capital and labor, Harbert's writings stressed the need for social harmony, reciprocity, and balance. In Harbert's view, it was the role of the middle class, and of middle-class women in particular, to move society toward social harmony, and the granting of woman suffrage was presented as one method for achieving this goal. In these articles Harbert argued that women had a distinctive role as mothers in nurturing future generations.

Harbert's approach to reform was reflected in her involvement in founding the Illinois Social Science Association in 1877. As the first state affiliate of the American Social Science Association, the Illinois organization endorsed the goals of social equilibrium, symmetrical harmony, and organic interdependence. Taking organic metaphors literally, reformers reasoned that social problems were diseases that required state-administered solutions, or, better yet, preventive measures. This broad social philosophy provided an additional rationale for woman suffrage, which the association endorsed as a means of implementing these reforms. For two years she served as president of the Illinois Social Science Association.

Harbert's critical orientation to male-dominated, organized religion was part of her reform agenda. As early as the 1870s, Harbert advocated an equal role for women in organized Christianity; churches were always seeking women's financial support, she commented, while denying them any voice on issues of theology and policy. She was also critical of otherwise liberal clergy whose views on women's roles in church and society remained very traditional. In a more positive vein, it is evident that Harbert viewed progressive religious currents (as expressed in Social Gospel, New Thought, and Theosophy) as providing a model for dealing with class divisions and social reform. In addressing the first meeting of the Illinois Social Science Association, Harbert noted that fashionable and luxurious churches had departed from the teachings of their founder and had lost any dedication to the practical work of "healing the sick, feeding the hungry, and preaching a plain, yet beautiful and practical morality to the poor" ("Woman's Kingdom," October 4, 1878). She proceeded to define the role of social science in religious terms. "What relation has social science to religion? For an answer, we refer you to the sermon on the Mount, and answer one question by asking another, is not social science twin sister to religion—aye, is it not religion itself?" ("Woman's Kingdom," October 4, 1878). While Harbert continued to be critical of much of organized religion, she also continued to draw on religious themes in fashioning her approach to social reform.

A similar pattern was evident in the temperance movement. Before 1880, most temperance leaders avoided woman suffrage as too radical, but they soon learned that women had little political clout without voting rights and hence came to endorse woman suffrage as a means of implementing the temperance agenda. Suffragists like Susan B. Anthony remained wary of such an instrumental approach to women's voting rights, but Harbert and many others had little hesitation in melding the two causes. While these developments undoubtedly recruited more mainstream women into the suffrage cause, they also displaced the earlier rationale for voting rights on the grounds of justice and equality. In 1878 the Woman's Christian Temperance

Union (WCTU) passed a resolution seeking voting rights for women on saloon openings but carefully specified they were not affiliating with suffragists. Harbert's "Woman's Kingdom" column protested this refusal to endorse woman suffrage. With FRANCES E. WILLARD's election to the presidency of the WCTU in 1879, the organization moved in the prosuffrage direction. Indications of a rapprochement between suffrage and temperance surfaced as early as 1879, when Willard wrote Harbert with qualified endorsement of the woman suffrage movement. Harbert had a growing interest in the cause of temperance, and she attributed a wide variety of social ills to drinking. This issue eventually became so central to her that in 1884, when an *Inter-Ocean* editorial criticized the National WCTU for its efforts to form a Prohibition Party, Harbert resigned her position as a columnist.

The year after she resigned from her weekly column, Harbert helped to found the Illinois Woman's Press Association, an organization of women writers, editors, journalists, and publicists whose advocacy of suffrage and the advancement of women in the professions brought them together across disciplines. Early members included pioneer doctors and lawyers as well as women whose primary interest was journalism, all of them engaged in publicizing the cause of women's rights. That same year, she began publishing a newspaper called the *New Era*. The title reflected Harbert's interest in the New Thought religious movement, when the enfranchisement of women would herald a "new era." The paper consistently argued for the compatibility of woman suffrage and temperance as parallel reforms. Arguments for both causes were ultimately grounded in assumptions often stated by Harbert about "God-given woman nature" that now led her to accept the notion of woman's sphere while simultaneously seeking a role in governance beyond the home. The paper also ran a number of articles bemoaning the lack of social control and the need for a "higher order of amusements" (*New Era*, January 1885, 14), as well as practical advice on how to deal with the slowly emerging antisuffrage movement. The paper folded in less than two years.

In the later 1880s and 1890s, Harbert turned to community- and institution-building, anticipating the role of women in Progressive Era reform. In 1889, Harbert was one of the founders of the Evanston Woman's Club. During her eight-year tenure as president, the club assisted in establishing Evanston Hospital, in organizing the first Mother's Club in the Evanston schools, and in establishing the Association of Evanston Charities and the Evanston chapter of the Visiting Nurse Association. Harbert also served on the board of the Evanston Girls' Industrial School during this period.

In 1889, Harbert was the featured speaker at the graduation exercises of the Christian Science Theological Seminary, where she celebrated the fact that twenty of the twenty-three graduates were women—symbolizing the kind of institutional transformation she sought across a great many social organizations that were lacking a womanly influence. An acknowledgment of her leadership in advancing the cause of women came in 1891 when Ohio Wesleyan College conferred on her an honorary Ph.D. degree.

She was an active participant in the World's Columbian Exposition of 1893 in a variety of capacities, including involvement in the World Parliament of Religions, serving as chair of the Woman's Committee on Religious Parliament Extension. Leaders of world religions from both Eastern and Western traditions converged in Chicago in a liberal and ecumenical spirit. Approaching the new century, speakers were optimistic about religion healing social ills; marginal religions such as Christian Science and Theosophy, of interest to Harbert and other women reformers, received attention. The next year Harbert published a theosophical novel entitled *Amore*. The book is a morality tale in which traditional Calvinist theology produces the evils it strives to eliminate, whereas religions based on the principle of love lead to harmony in society and personal acts of kindness and respect in the home.

In 1896, Harbert returned to the theme of women's rights in a speech, "The Philosophy of Suffrage," that illustrated both the continuity and change in her thinking since her early critique of woman's separate sphere. While the emphasis on womanliness continued, the rationale for female enfranchisement had shifted from an argument for women's equal rights to one that emphasized how women's votes were necessary for the passage of a reform agenda and the establishment of a politics based on morality rather than greed and personal power. She endorsed some of the sex-specific notions of woman's sphere that she had criticized in her 1871 novel, *Out of Her Sphere*, arguing in 1896 that women's duties to family and society were more important than women's rights. The concern for women was now a concern for humanity as a whole, with society's problems solved through a spirit of cooperation in which women had a distinct role to play as "mothers of the race" (quoted in Buechler, "Elizabeth Boynton Harbert and the Woman Suffrage Movement," 83). Harbert's shift from directly emphasizing women's rights to indirectly doing so through an ideology of benevolent harmony and cooperation was increasingly evident in the larger suffrage movement. Harbert believed that a properly loving and harmoniously Christian household held the key to the development of a new citizenship for men and women, based on respect and the Golden Rule. On these lines Harbert became interested in the new domestic science movement that was founded on the principle that a properly run household was fundamental for human social development. She was the founder and president of the National Household Economic Association.

Although Harbert retained her catholic interests in social reform, literature, poetry, and philanthropy, she became somewhat less active after the turn of the century in the many organizations and groups she helped to create. Around 1910, the Harberts moved to Pasadena, California, where she lived until her death in 1925. Over the course of several decades, Elizabeth Harbert blended private and public life, interwove religious and secular approaches to reform, and established numerous organizations. In all these efforts, Harbert remained dedicated to infusing social institutions with a strong sense of "womanliness" that would draw on women's distinctive traits and turn those traits in the service of a larger public good.

Sources. Elizabeth Harbert's papers are found in the Huntington Library, San Marino, California, and the SL. SL also has scrapbooks with copies of most of her "Woman's Kingdom" newspaper columns in *Inter-Ocean*. Both *Inter-Ocean* and Harbert's *New Era* are available at NL. A more detailed account of Harbert's involvement in the woman suffrage movement may be found in Steven M. Buechler, "Elizabeth Boynton Harbert and the Woman Suffrage Movement, 1870–1896," *Signs*, Fall 1987, and in Buechler, *The Transformation of the Woman Suffrage Movement* (1986).

STEVEN M. BUECHLER

HARDIN ARMSTRONG, LILIAN (Lil)
February 3, 1898(?)–August 27, 1971
COMPOSER, PIANIST, BANDLEADER

Lil Hardin Armstrong, pioneering jazz recording artist, was born in Memphis, Tennessee. Little is known about her pre-Chicago days. Her mother, Dempsey Martin, worked as a cook for a wealthy Memphis family and struggled to support the family. Lil Hardin's father, Will Hardin, had run a restaurant on Lower Main Street in Memphis but died of tuberculosis when she was two. Although Dempsey Martin's situation was difficult, she managed to provide adequately for her daughter, for example, sending her to study at Fisk University in Nashville before they moved to Chicago. Hardin described her family as middle class and ascribed to her mother and grandmother attitudes toward popular music, idleness, and sin consistent with that status. Lil Hardin emerged in the context of turn-of-the-century African American aspiration for security and respectability.

Hardin's earliest music education, at three or four years of age, was informal but indicative of unusual aptitude for music. She described an early ability to pick out melodies on the piano keyboard, a talent encouraged by her mother. She received formal music lessons in the first grade. The lessons were not especially rigorous technically, but they allowed her time to develop on her own. Throughout her elementary school years, she played piano for school bands and concerts and also developed skill on the organ, which she played at Lebanon Baptist Church. Prior to arriving at Fisk, her only other formal musical education was at the Hooks School of Music in Memphis, where she received a musical education that was diverse though lacking in technical rigor. At Fisk, a black institution with a long tradition of musical excellence, from 1914 to 1916, she studied piano and enrolled first in the preparatory program and eventually in the college school. As a member of the Mozart Society, Lil Hardin came in contact with key African American classical musicians Roland Hayes and Harry Burleigh. She never completed her program at Fisk, however, and rejoined her mother, who had remarried and moved to Chicago in August 1918.

Lilian Hardin took a job at Jones Music Store as a "demonstrator." At this time profits in the music business were made through the sale of sheet music. The bigger music shops employed individuals—usually accomplished, flamboyant players—to play music for customers. The Jones shop was a gathering place for African American musicians so that, in addition to the education provided by regular practice and performance, Hardin learned much about the new emerging jazz through conversation, listening, and imitation.

The proprietor of the shop, Jennie Jones, eventually sent Hardin for an audition with a band, the New Orleans Creole Jazz Band. She was hired by the band and played throughout Chicago, most importantly at the Dreamland Cafe and Royal Gardens Theatre. In 1921, she joined trumpeter King Oliver's band, one of the most important of the pioneering jazz combos, and briefly toured nationwide with them before returning to Chicago to perform on her own and with a variety of local bands. In late 1922 she rejoined the Oliver band, which had recently hired Louis Armstrong as cornetist and second trumpet. Hardin and Armstrong eventually developed a relationship, and they were married on February 5, 1924. (Hardin had been previously married to another musician, singer Jimmy Johnson.)

This early period in her life showed the accomplishment of an early-twentieth-century African American woman in popular culture. Most profound was the way in which she challenged her mother's resistance to her pursuit of a musical career. Family tradition was to view the popular arts as degenerate and of lesser importance than sacred music. Therefore, Hardin's early pursuit of a professional musical identity in jazz was an attempt to achieve security, mobility, and status, while risking the censure of those figures most able and most likely to provide support if she failed. She risked complete loss of the social status hard earned by her family in the Jim Crow South. The social milieu of early jazz—the nightclub, the speakeasy, travel with all-male groups across country—meant that Hardin violated the conventions of appropriate behavior and aspiration for women.

Soon after their marriage, Hardin Armstrong encouraged Louis Armstrong to leave Oliver, who she felt was holding him back. This decision proved momentous. The recordings made between 1925 and 1927 by the Armstrongs and other prominent early jazz musicians—usually known as the "Hot Fives" and "Hot Sevens"—laid the foundation for much of the music known as jazz and dramatically influenced its trajectory. At Hardin Armstrong's insistence, Louis Armstrong became a dynamic and charismatic soloist. Moreover, he benefited from her formal musical training and strong rhythmic piano playing. While the collaborative and improvisatory nature of jazz as an art form makes it difficult to ascertain the specific contributions of individuals to the seminal recording sessions, it is reasonable to assert that the professionalism and drive of Lilian Hardin Armstrong accounted for much of their success. It is likely that a significant portion of the music for the sessions was written by Hardin Armstrong. She later battled Louis Armstrong in court for copyright control of specific songs; the unique character of jazz composition as a collective process complicated easy attribution of authorship.

Details are scant about Hardin Armstrong's formal education, which continued throughout the 1920s. In 1928 she obtained a degree from the Chicago College of Music and in 1929 a postgraduate degree from the New York College of Music. Louis Armstrong's increasing success and popularity strained their marriage, and in 1931 they separated. They were eventually divorced in 1938.

Hardin Armstrong attempted to establish a professional identity separate from Louis Armstrong. Almost all accounts of her life effectively end with her separation from Louis Armstrong (a full forty years before the end of her life), implying that her importance is solely in her relationship to this acknowledged giant of the jazz world. Careful consideration of the latter period of her life suggests, however, that Hardin Armstrong had her own goals and aspirations.

Most important in the establishment of this new individual identity were the bands she led in the late 1920s (with Freddie

FIG. 47. *King Oliver Jazz Band with Lil Hardin at the piano, Chicago, c. 1923.*

Keppard) and 1930s. She led two all-women groups in the early 1930s and an all-male band that lasted from 1933 to 1935. The latter group was a musical success but did not make any financial headway. To make matters worse, the band's agent insisted on promoting her as "Mrs. Louis Armstrong." After the breakup of this band, Hardin Armstrong became the house pianist for the Decca Recording Company. While with Decca, she participated in five recording sessions between 1936 and 1940 in which she led a group usually called "Lil Armstrong and Her Orchestra." A composition of this period, "Just for a Thrill," eventually became a big hit for Ray Charles and later provided Hardin Armstrong with an important source of income.

At the same time, she challenged social convention (through divorce and a court case against her ex-husband), as did other African American women struggling to make careers in the burgeoning entertainment industry. During the late 1920s and the 1930s, her small business ventures, her extended education, and her efforts at bandleading and composing showed an entrepreneurial spirit. By the late 1920s, she purchased a South Side home, where she lived for the rest of her life, and land at Idlewild, a Michigan resort town developed by African Americans.

Beginning in the mid-1940s, she was briefly a restaurateur and, on a more sustained basis, designed and marketed her own line of clothing. She remained a regular on the Chicago music scene, performing at the Three Deuces and other clubs. In 1952, she toured Europe, likely taking advantage of the revival of interest in New Orleans–style music and, while there, participated in recording dates in Paris. In 1959, Riverside Records recorded an oral history of her early days called *Satchmo and Me*; a second Riverside recording, in 1961, *Chicago: The Living Legends*, featured Hardin Armstrong and her music. Throughout this period, she also improvised a living by performing short

stints at clubs in Chicago and New York and by occasionally teaching piano and French. She hinted at one point that she was also able to supplement her income significantly by playing at the parties of wealthy white socialites.

Her career and life ended in pathos. On August 27, 1971, she performed in Chicago's Civic Plaza a musical tribute to Louis Armstrong, who had died just a month earlier. In the middle of her enthusiastic and energetic performance at the piano, she had a massive heart attack and died instantly.

In her life and career Hardin Armstrong developed a professional life in a field in which there were no models. She played down the idea of herself as any kind of musical innovator and celebrated instead the accomplishments of such jazz modernists as Thelonius Monk and Bud Powell. Yet she composed more than 150 pieces of music in her lifetime. Many compositions remain part of the standard jazz repertory. She participated in the coalescence of a new musical form, and she endured in a harsh business. She survived to claim a distinct personal identity for herself, after the individual with whom she was most closely associated became an American icon.

Sources. There has been some dispute about the exact date of Lil Hardin Armstrong's birth, but the most recent historical research suggests that the 1898 date is more reliable than the 1899, 1900, 1902, and 1903 dates often suggested. At the time of her death, *Downbeat,* the premier jazz periodical, described her as sixty-nine years of age, whereas the *NYT* obituary, August 28, 1971, listed her as seventy-three years of age. Although some of the most useful information about Hardin Armstrong is to be culled from liner notes of record albums, most are out of print. The Institute of Jazz Studies at Rutgers University maintains extensive clippings files on individual jazz musicians and possesses the most substantive collection of recordings, including the rare 1959 Riverside Records oral history *Satchmo and Me.* The second Riverside Recording *Chicago*

Legends has recently been reissued by Fantasy Records. The William Hogan Ransom Archive of Jazz at Tulane University has significant collections related to the early history of jazz. Hardin Armstrong has been treated substantively in *BWA* and in Barry Kernfeld, ed., *New Grove's Dictionary of Jazz* (1988). More importantly, she is treated in the two major feminist jazz monographs: Linda Dahl's *Stormy Weather: The Music and Lives of a Century of Jazzwomen* (1984) and Sally Placksin's *American Women in Jazz: 1900 to the Present* (1982). Useful information is also to be found in Nat Shapiro and Nat Hentoff, *Hear Me Talkin' to Ya* (1966), and James Lincoln Collier's *Louis Armstrong: An American Genius* (1983). Significant magazine and journal articles include Chris Albertson, "Lil Hardin Armstrong—A Fond Remembrance," *Saturday Review*, September 25, 1971, and Max Jones, "Lil Armstrong: Royalties and the Old Songs," *Melody Maker*, April 8, 1967. Hardin Armstrong's efforts at fashion design are noted in "She Uses a 'Hep' Needle," *Chicago Sun-Times*, March 13, 1949.

JAMES C. HALL

HARKNESS, GEORGIA ELMA
April 21, 1891–August 21, 1974
THEOLOGIAN, SOCIAL JUSTICE AND WOMEN'S RIGHTS
ADVOCATE

Georgia Harkness was the first professional woman theologian in the United States. She was born in northeastern New York in the Adirondacks on a farm that had belonged to her father's family since 1801. The tiny village of her birthplace, Harkness, was named after her grandfather, Nehemiah Harkness, who cleared land for a railroad to be built through the hamlet. Of Scotch-Irish descent, her parents, Warren and Lillie (Merrill) Harkness, had two daughters and two sons, Georgia being the youngest, and her sister, Hattie, the oldest.

Harkness's mother was a homemaker; her father was a community and church leader and his daughter's primary role model. A prosperous and successful farmer and land surveyor, his larger interests lay in social responsibility: he brought a normal school to nearby Plattsburgh, founded the county Grange (a farmers' association), gained rural mail delivery for the area, and taught the adult Sunday school class at the Methodist Episcopal Church for sixty years.

Georgia Harkness began school at age five in the one-room village schoolhouse that doubled on Sunday as the Methodist Church. Her family and church upbringing gave her a strong evangelical heritage, with emphasis on personal salvation. When Georgia was five, her seventeen-year-old sister died of diphtheria. The sisters had inherited their father's intellectual curiosity and abilities. The mantle of both father and sister fell with great weight upon Georgia, who felt called "to be as smart as Hattie Harkness" (quoted in Keller, *Georgia Harkness*, 64).

Attending high school in nearby Keeseville, Harkness graduated at fourteen. She agreed with her parents that she was too young socially to enter college and took postgraduate high school courses at Keeseville for the next two years.

Harkness's parents sought for her the best education available, at Cornell University, in Ithaca, New York, one of the nation's earliest coeducational institutions. She won the county scholarship, matriculated at Cornell in 1908, and graduated in 1912 with Phi Beta Kappa honors.

"Shy, green and countrified" (quoted in Keller, *Georgia Harkness*, 83), Harkness felt like a social misfit. However, the campus Christian group, the Student Volunteer Movement (SVM), became home to her. Like thousands of other students of her day, she took the SVM pledge to become a foreign missionary, if God permitted.

After graduation from college, foreign missionary service did not seem a realistic possibility for Georgia Harkness because of family responsibilities. For two years, she taught high school Latin, French, and German, in two small New York towns, Schuylerville and Scotia. During this time, she learned of a new program in religious education, a profession that was opening for women, at Boston University School of Religious Education and Social Service. She entered the program the next year, resolving that "'if I could not be a missionary,' the new profession of religious education 'was my calling'" (quoted in Keller, *Georgia Harkness*, 102).

While working on a master's degree, Harkness took philosophy classes in the graduate school of Boston University under Professor Edgar S. Brightman. She entered the doctoral program, believing that teaching philosophy of religion and religious education would be the fulfillment of both her calling and career. Brightman became her most significant lifelong mentor, except for her father.

During these years, Harkness came to value her mother more highly than she did as a child. On one occasion, she considered giving up her graduate program and returning home to tend the family farm. Her mother insisted that Harkness lead her own life and continue her career.

After passing Ph.D. qualifying exams in 1921, Harkness joined the faculty of Elmira College in central New York the following year as assistant professor of philosophy and religious education. In 1923, she completed her dissertation on T. H. Green, an English proponent of philosophical idealism.

Harkness remained at Elmira for fifteen years. By 1925, she led a successful faculty fight for a major curriculum revision to raise the academic standards of the institution. During these years, she became a leader for social justice in the Methodist Church and in the ecumenical movement, nationally and internationally. The drive for equal opportunities for women in the Methodist Church, including full conference membership for ordained women and rightful treatment for employed and volunteer lay women, became a primary cause. She developed a lifelong commitment to pacifism after touring Europe to study the devastation to war-torn countries following World War I.

By the late 1930s, she had received several distinctions: *Time* magazine cited her as a famous woman theologian; she was the first female member admitted to the American Theological Society; she was selected by the *Christian Century* to write an essay in its series by notable religious leaders on "How My Mind Has Changed"; and she was one of the few women delegates to attend the conference of the International Missionary Council at Oxford, England, in 1937 and Madras, India, the following year, as well as the Board of Strategy of the Provisional Conference of the World Council of Churches held at Geneva, Switzerland, in 1939.

In 1937, Georgia Harkness joined the faculty of Mt. Holyoke College, South Hadley, Massachusetts. In 1888, Mt. Holyoke had become the first female seminary to provide young women with the equivalent of college training. The move thereby enabled Harkness to maintain her commitment to the advancement of women as well as to teach in a department of religion at a distinguished college.

Harkness remained at Holyoke for only two years. Many faculty members were critical of her political involvements and her commitment to pacifism. The positive reason for Harkness's departure, however, was the opportunity to become professor of applied theology at Garrett Biblical Institute (now Garrett-Evangelical Theological Seminary) in Evanston, north of Chicago. After teaching for seventeen years in undergraduate institutions for women only, she made a major transition to a graduate seminary of the Methodist Church whose major vocation was to prepare men for ordained ministry. Drawing students from a wide range of denominations, the institute was closely affiliated with the Chicago Training School, which trained women and a small number of men to be Christian educators in local churches and deacons in home and foreign mission work.

The ten years Harkness spent at Garrett were the most consequential era of her life, both privately and publicly. She became the first full-time woman professor in theological studies in a Protestant seminary in the United States. Of all the institutions at which she taught, Garrett, Harkness felt, was her academic home, and she willed her large collection of private and public papers to the seminary.

Two pivotal events defined the significance and change in Georgia Harkness's identity while in Chicago. The first was the death of her father in 1937, and the second was a period of spiritual depression beginning in 1939 and extending to the mid-1940s. The deepest underlying cause of the depression was a sense of being cut off from God, of seeking but not finding the source of strength and support she most needed. She suffered severe and painful physical problems, which were exacerbated by the strain of overwork and accelerated by her drive to succeed as a lone woman in a male-dominated profession.

Harkness never married, but part of her healing came from the entrance of a partner into her life. In 1943, Ernest Fremont Tittle, Harkness's pastor at the First Methodist Church in Evanston, introduced her to Verna Miller, a musician and member of the congregation, believing that they would provide an enriching friendship for each other. Miller and Harkness soon decided to share a home together and maintained that relationship for the next thirty years until Harkness died in 1974.

Her recovery from spiritual depression led to a profound change in Harkness's vocational direction. As she moved into theology, she abandoned the quest for philosophical objectivity and the work of abstract theology and found her vocational identity by writing straightforward, short books directed both to laity and to clergy. Some of the most important and earliest of these volumes came while Harkness was at Garrett: *Understanding the Christian Faith* (1947), *Prayer and the Common Life* (1948), and *The Gospel and Our World* (1949). Harkness defined her new stance as that of an evangelical liberal, emphasizing both personal salvation and a social responsibility to address the structural evils of society, including sexism, racism, militarism, and classism.

By the late 1940s, Harkness gained her widest national and international distinction and was greatly sought after as a lecturer both within the church and the academy. At this time, she received a particularly hard blow when Garrett's president, Horace Greeley Smith, failed to name her to the chair in systematic theology, vacated by the retirement of Harris Franklin Rall. Though not promised the position, Harkness felt when she was hired that Smith had insinuated that she would be her colleague's successor. Smith had difficulty relating to women, and persons close to Harkness believed that the president was jealous of her fame. Harkness did not receive a raise, even when Smith increased her male colleagues' salaries.

Harkness never shared her hurt publicly, but it was a factor in her acceptance of an invitation to join the faculty of the Pacific School of Religion in Berkeley, California, in 1950. She worked out a part-time teaching appointment, enabling her to have more time free for lecturing, writing, and gaining balance between the personal and professional sides of her life. She sought to remain at Garrett, but President Smith was not open to a more flexible policy to enable his senior faculty member to scale down her professional responsibilities as she neared retirement. Harkness and Verna Miller took up residence in Berkeley, and she remained on the faculty until she retired in 1961.

Harkness continued to hold the church responsible for taking prophetic stances for the elimination of racism, sexism, and militarism within its body and society. Along with distinguished male theologians Reinhold Niebuhr, Paul Tillich, John C. Bennett, and Robert Calhoun, she served as the sole female member of the Dun Commission, appointed by the Federal Council of Churches of Christ in America in 1950 to study the moral implications of obliteration bombing for mass destruction. Only Harkness and Calhoun maintained the unconditional pacifist stance that such weapons should not be used under any circumstances.

Further, she opposed the merger of the Methodist Church with the Evangelical United Brethren Church in 1968, arguing that no union should take place until the all-black Central Jurisdiction of the Methodist Church was integrated into the new United Methodist Church. The segregated jurisdiction would not be eliminated until 1972, four years after the merger.

While at Garrett, Harkness lobbied and strategized vigorously for full clergy rights for women in the Methodist denomination. The Methodist General Conference did not grant such rights to women until 1956. At that conference, the delegates rose to give Harkness a standing ovation, recognizing her as the person who had done the most over many years to bring justice in this cause for women.

Harkness lived heartily and actively in her late years in the retirement village of Pilgrim Place in Claremont, California. She continued to write a book each year and to lecture widely, returning to Garrett, and traveling to Alaska twice during the last months of her life. In 1972, two years before her death, Harkness was a delegate to her final General Conference of the United Methodist Church. She spoke on the Conference floor, commending the members for establishing a General Commission on the Status and Role of Women for the denomination. Death came unexpectedly of a stroke. Harkness was buried in her family's plot in the Harkness, New York, cemetery.

Harkness had a fruitful professional life as a pre-feminist pioneer in a field dominated by men. She wrote almost forty books on theology, ministry of the laity, spiritual life, and the responsibility of the church to combat war, discrimination against women, and racism. Harkness was one of the most distinguished and outspoken leaders in Protestant churches, and particularly her own Methodist Church, during the second and third quarters of the twentieth century.

Sources. The collection of fourteen boxes of Georgia Harkness's Papers is in the United Library at Garrett-Evangelical Theological Seminary. They include letters, published and unpublished articles, sermons, poems, hymns, lectures, course syllabi, and newspaper and journal clippings, as well as a twenty-five page autobiographical essay written for the Pacific Coast Theological Group in the 1950s. The Edgar Brightman Papers in the Mugar Library at Boston University contain two hundred letters exchanged between Harkness and Brightman from the 1920s to the 1940s. Copies of many are in the Garrett-Evangelical collection. Harkness's books on ethics and philosophical idealism, reflecting her early period, include *Conflicts in Religious Thought* (1929), *John Calvin: The Man and His Ethics* (1931), *The Resources of Religion* (1936), and *The Recovery of Ideals* (1937). More definitive of Harkness as a mature applied theologian are *The Dark Night of the Soul* (1945), *Toward Understanding the Bible* (1954), *Christian Ethics* (1957), *The Church and Its Laity* (1957), *Women in Church and Society* (1971), and *Mysticism* (1973). Representative devotional books are *Holy Flame* (1935), *The Glory of God* (1943), and *Be Still and Know* (1953). Many articles by Harkness on theology, women in the church, pacifism, social justice, and ecumenism are published in religious journals including *Christian Century*, *Christian Advocate*, and *Zion's Herald. Georgia Harkness: For Such a Time as This* (1992), by Rosemary Skinner Keller, is the one comprehensive biography of the theologian. On Harkness's thought, see Martha Lynn Scott's "The Theology and Social Thought of Georgia Harkness" (Ph.D. diss., Garrett-Evangelical Theological Seminary, 1984). Articles include Mary Elizabeth Moore, "The Theological Agenda of Georgia Harkness," *Quarterly Review*, Fall 1993; Rosemary Skinner Keller, "Georgia Harkness: Theologian of the People," in *Spirituality and Social Responsibility: Vocational Vision of Women in the United Methodist Tradition*, ed. Keller (1993); and Keller, "Vocational Journey and Vocational Identity in the Life and Work of Georgia Harkness," in *Papers of the Canadian Methodist Historical Society: 1989* (1990). A biographical essay appears in *NAW* (1980).

ROSEMARY SKINNER KELLER

HARRISON, ELIZABETH
September 1, 1849–October 27, 1927
PRE-SCHOOL EDUCATIONAL THEORIST, KINDERGARTEN TRAINING SCHOOL FOUNDER

Elizabeth Harrison was one of the leading figures in the kindergarten movement, a new approach to early childhood education based on the theories of German philosopher and educator Friedrich Fröbel (also Froebel) (1782–1852), whose ideas found sympathetic reception among a generation of American women. Dedicated to the theory that the new science of pedagogy could (and should) be taught not only to educators but also to all mothers, insuring from the earliest moments the most beneficial environment for the development of the child, Harrison and her colleagues found allies among the social feminists of the woman's reform culture. The conscious or scientific mother of the kindergarten movement had a parallel model in the municipal housekeeper who also envisioned a new dawning for society as a result of the influence of organized, educated womanhood on public policy.

FIG. 48. *Founding president Elizabeth Harrison, Chicago Kindergarten College, on the left, with her successor Edna Dean Baker; Evanston, Illinois, 1918.*

Elizabeth Harrison, founder of the Chicago Kindergarten Training School, the first professional institution to train kindergarten teachers in the United States, was born in Athens, Kentucky, to Isaac Webb Harrison, a dry-goods merchant, and Elizabeth Thompson (Bullock) Harrison, a housewife. Shortly after Harrison's birth, the family moved to Midway, Kentucky, where they lived for seven years. A growing family and business reverses necessitated another move, in 1856, to Davenport, Iowa, where Harrison's father became a land agent.

Elizabeth Harrison first attended school in Davenport at age eight. At seventeen, she graduated high school with honors. Greatly disappointed to learn that her father's financial problems meant his promise of higher education for her would have to be postponed, she stayed in Davenport and did volunteer work. After the death of Harrison's mother in 1875, she kept house for her father for several years. When he took a small apartment in Davenport, Harrison moved to Marshalltown, Iowa, to live with her sister Mary and her family.

In 1876, Harrison visited the Philadelphia Centennial Exposition and saw a world of art she had previously only read about, along with other exhibits that quite possibly stimulated Harrison's hunger for further cultural knowledge. She also became aware of her longing to create an independent life for herself. Three years later, Harrison was encouraged by a girlhood friend to visit Chicago and learn about the new kindergarten system that was rapidly overtaking reform circles in the United States. Its exponents were not simply advocating the introduction of a pre-school program. The kindergarten movement was a comprehensive plan to develop the physical, mental, and moral nature of the child that gained wide support in the United States after the Civil War.

Harrison applied for admission to pioneer ALICE PUTNAM's kindergarten training school in Chicago. Accepted, Harrison began the thirty-six week course, which consisted of lectures on theory and method, classroom observation at Putnam's elite Loring School, and finally, student teaching in the kindergarten. Putnam also introduced Harrison to other kindergartners in the city, one of whom conducted a free kindergarten for poor children. (The term "kindergartner" meant both a teacher of kindergarten children and a trainer of kindergarten teachers.) In 1880, Harrison completed the kindergarten training course, receiving both a diploma and a certificate that entitled her to train kindergartners. Putnam invited her to return to the Loring School the following year as her paid assistant, and Harrison accepted.

Seeking further understanding of Fröbel's ideas, in 1881 Harrison traveled to St. Louis to observe Susan Blow, one of Fröbel's best interpreters in the United States. Harrison was so impressed by Blow's work that she returned to St. Louis in 1882 to train under her, completing the two-year training course in six months. At the same time she took private art lessons in the evenings with Halsey Ives, director of the St. Louis Art Museum. Impressed with Harrison's determination, Ives generously offered to aid her in developing her art skills so that she could better help children toward an appreciation of the beauty of proportion and balance, one of the bases of Fröbel's educational method.

After a short time in Iowa directing a public school kindergarten program, Harrison returned to Chicago to direct the kindergarten at Loring School, when her mentor Putnam left to begin a program elsewhere in the city. Before accepting the position, Harrison had negotiated with Stella Dyer Loring, the school's founder and principal, to take a leave of absence the second half of the school year and train in New York City with renowned kindergartners Maria Klaus Boelte and her husband, John Kraus.

Stimulated by the New York experience, Harrison sought ways to develop kindergartners as professional educators and, with Putnam, founded the Kindergarten Club in 1883. All twenty kindergartners in the city joined and Harrison served as president of the organization from 1883 to 1890. Harrison's course on the study of young children's instincts offered at the

club was so well received she repeated it for four years. Harrison now had to develop a method of reaching the mothers whose children were enrolled in the early kindergarten programs. To Harrison, following Fröbel's theories, mothers were integral to the equation. Her first attempt was in October 1884, when she invited Loring School mothers to attend a class on kindergarten theory and methods, hoping to interest them in "conscious" or "scientific motherhood." Having invited twenty-one women, she was disappointed when only two mothers attended the meeting. However, she continued the class with just two mothers and three young women attending.

In April 1885, RUMAH CROUSE, whose children were in the primary grades at Loring School, attended the mothers' class for the first time. Crouse, a member of Chicago's social elite, was impressed with Harrison's introduction to the concept of conscious motherhood and used her contacts and position to arrange a mothers' class in the parlor of the nearby Baptist church she attended. When Harrison arrived to conduct the class, there were two rooms full of women waiting to hear her speak. At the conclusion of the lecture, Crouse asked the women to join a mothers' class and pay for their instruction. Forty-five women promptly joined. This was the start of a successful partnership between Harrison and Crouse, lasting for more than a quarter century. Together they worked to further the idea of conscious motherhood in a variety of ways.

Beginning in 1886, Harrison received numerous invitations from around the city and, later, across the country, to speak on the kindergarten philosophy and system. As a result of Harrison's appeal, her classes began to attract hundreds of mothers and young women interested in teaching kindergarten. Her full schedule of speaking and teaching was exhausting and, in spring 1886, ill health forced Harrison to travel to Europe to recuperate. While there, she investigated kindergartens in Belgium and France. Rested and invigorated, she took up her kindergarten work with renewed enthusiasm on her return to Chicago. Besides her mothers' class, Harrison also taught a training class for teachers with the Loring School as the observation and practice site for trainees. By fall 1887, Harrison and her colleague Crouse had added teachers and soon moved the training classes to the new Art Institute building in downtown Chicago.

In fall 1889, Harrison and Crouse founded the Chicago Kindergarten Training School. The school offered both a teacher training course and mothers' classes. Dividing the work, Harrison, as president of the institution, designed the curriculum and taught courses, while Crouse, as business manager, dealt with all administrative matters. Over the years, as enrollments increased and programs expanded, the school underwent more changes of name and location, finally settling in Evanston, Illinois, a suburb just north of Chicago. In 1891 the school was incorporated as Chicago Kindergarten College (CKC) and, in 1912, it was renamed National Kindergarten College (NKC), to reflect that it was attracting students from all over the United States. By 1916 it became the National Kindergarten and Elementary College as its program enlarged to train elementary school teachers as well as kindergartners. (It is now called National-Louis University).

As Harrison's reputation grew, she was much in demand to

train kindergartners. During the first years of CKC, she traveled to Milwaukee one day a week to offer a class to two hundred public school teachers and another for three hundred mothers. Harrison was glad of opportunities to speak and teach beyond her school, feeling that it was her mission to share the kindergarten message with as many as she could. She also needed the fees she received for her school. Money was tight during its early years and Harrison's extra income kept the school going.

Harrison believed that teachers of small children, whether mothers or kindergartners, required more than mere training in child development. They should have a broad cultural knowledge so that they could provide a rich learning environment for children. She introduced the study of great literature in one of her mothers' classes; the lectures developed into a very successful "literary school" that was held for the next several years under the auspices of the CKC. A popular course in world literature was added to the curriculum of the college as a result of the literary school's success.

In June 1890, under the auspices of the United States government, Harrison traveled to Germany to see the kindergarten movement at its source. Accompanied by Crouse, Harrison visited several of Fröbel's students, now themselves kindergarten teachers who were extending his theories and adding refinements of their own. She met with Baroness von Marenholtz-Bülow—Fröbel's foremost disciple, who had written an influential volume on Fröbel's theory—for several weeks of productive discussion. As a result of her trip, Harrison began to view herself as an authority in her field.

Continuing her commitment to conscious motherhood, Harrison formalized her mothers' classes in 1890 by inaugurating a three-year course of lectures for mothers, with a diploma upon completion. The first class graduated in 1893.

In 1892 Harrison and other kindergartners founded the International Kindergarten Union (IKU). The group's immediate goal was to show the progress of the kindergarten movement at the World's Columbian Exposition to be held the following year in Chicago. The first official meeting of IKU occurred in July 1893 during the exposition. IKU linked kindergartners throughout the United States and, later, around the world. In 1903 the IKU formed a committee to define kindergarten theory and practice more clearly and to set standards for kindergarten training. Harrison and her colleagues Alice Putnam and Susan Blow were prominent members of the committee. The group also lobbied strongly for mandatory kindergartens in public schools throughout the United States. Continuing to look for ways to reach more mothers, Crouse suggested holding a Mothers' Convention in Chicago in 1894. Twelve hundred people attended this event in CKC Assembly Hall, coming from the East and West as well as the Midwest. Harrison was the featured speaker, and John Dewey, then a young University of Chicago professor interested in progressive education, gave a brief talk. Yearly conventions were held and, by 1897, the gathering became known as the National Congress of Mothers, a forerunner of the National Parent Teacher Association. Harrison had managed to bring along both organizations: mothers in the National Congress and educators in the IKU.

In the early 1900s, Harrison remained eager to study new methods and theories. In 1912, she went to Rome to spend five months with Maria Montessori, pioneer of progressive educational methods of teaching children with developmental disabilities. Montessori had been applying those methods to the teaching of very young children. Harrison attended the first classes given by Montessori for English-speaking teachers. When she returned, she supervised three experimental classes at NKC on Montessori techniques for different types of children. She also wrote a pamphlet, *The Montessori Method and the Kindergarten*, published by the U.S. Bureau of Education (1914) in which she described techniques she thought useful and criticized some with which she disagreed. Over the course of her career, Harrison authored other pamphlets and books on children's learning and kindergarten philosophy. The first and most successful, A *Study of Child Nature* (1890) became an influential textbook for kindergartners, going through fifty-two printings and translations into many languages.

Having suffered a heart attack a few years earlier, in 1919 Harrison was advised by her doctors to accept no more speaking engagements. In 1920, after nearly forty years of kindergarten work, Elizabeth Harrison resigned her presidency of the National Kindergarten and Elementary College. After her retirement, she moved to San Antonio, Texas, with her former student, colleague, and longtime companion Belle Woodson, seeking a more congenial climate. (From childhood, Harrison had suffered from chronic bronchitis and asthma.) During her retirement, Harrison wrote *The Unseen Side of Child Life* (1922); her autobiography, *Sketches Along Life's Road*, was published posthumously in 1930.

Harrison died of asthmatic and bronchial complications. Following funeral services in San Antonio, Harrison was buried in Davenport. As she reviewed her long career in her autobiography, Harrison gave an astute assessment of her significance to educational theory. "My own contribution," she wrote, "has been in the spreading of the ideal that true education is self-activity, and that this self-activity should begin in the pre-school age in the home, leading to all later creative work" (*Sketches*, 221–22). Through the school Harrison founded, she successfully interpreted to many student generations Fröbelian principles modified by her own insights. She also inspired countless mothers interested in guiding their children's intellectual and spiritual development from early childhood, encouraging teachers and mothers to be colleagues in the education of children.

Sources. Harrison's papers, including correspondence, unpublished writings, and her personal library, are in the Archives of National-Louis University, Evanston, Illinois. Her autobiography, *Sketches Along Life's Road* (1930), a brief biography by Agnes Snyder in *Dauntless Women in Childhood Education, 1856–1931* (1972), and Sandra F. Allen Branch, "Elizabeth Harrison and Her Contribution to the Kindergarten Movement in Chicago, 1880–1920" (Ph.D. diss., Loyola Univ. Chicago, 1992) give details on her life and work. Harrison published many books on her theory of child education, including *Some Silent Teachers* (1903), *Misunderstood Children* (1910), and *The Unseen Side of Child Life* (1922). She also wrote stories for children, including *In Storyland* (1895). *In the Story World, Best Legends for Boys and Girls* (1930) is a posthumous collection of her most popular children's stories. For a history of the school Harrison founded, see Janet Messenger, "The Story of National College of Education, 1886–1986," typed manuscript in the

National-Louis Univ. Archives, and Edna Dean Baker, *An Adventure in Higher Education* (1956). The Committee of Nineteen, *Pioneers of the Kindergarten in America* (1924), begins with a history of the kindergarten movement in America by Harrison. Elizabeth Dale Rose, *The Kindergarten Crusade: The Establishment of PreSchool Education in the United States* (1976), and Michael Shapiro, *Child's Garden: The Kindergarten Movement from Froebel to Dewey* (1983) provide a national context for Harrison's work; [n.a.], *History of the Kindergarten Movement in the Mid-Western States and in New York* (1938), provides a Chicago context for her work.

SANDRA F. BRANCH

HARSH, VIVIAN GORDON
May 27, 1890–August 17, 1960
LIBRARIAN, FOUNDER OF RESEARCH COLLECTION

A pioneering African American librarian and an early leader in the movement to preserve African American history, Vivian G. Harsh is best known as the founder of the Special Negro Collection, a research collection at the Chicago Public Library that grew into the largest repository of its kind in the Midwest. The collection is today called the Vivian G. Harsh Research Collection of Afro-American History and Literature.

Born in Chicago, Vivian Harsh was the first child and only daughter of Fenton W. and Maria L. (Drake) Harsh. The couple had one other child, Fenton W. (Pritt) Harsh Jr., a realtor and jazz musician. Her parents were both graduates of Fisk University; her mother was one of the first women to graduate from Fisk Normal School, earning her degree in 1878. Arriving in Chicago in the early 1880s, the couple entered the small and elite community of Chicago's "Old Settlers," the social circle of the city's first African American families.

Vivian Harsh grew up in the neighborhood that became the center of Chicago's pre–World War I black middle class. The family owned a home on the South Side. She attended Forrestville elementary school and graduated from Wendell Phillips High School in 1908, at a time when African American enrollment there was nearing 50 percent of the student body while the faculty remained almost entirely white. By December 1909, she obtained her first position with the Chicago Public Library, the only employer she would ever have. Beginning as a junior clerk at the system's Central Library, Harsh slowly rose through the clerical ranks. During World War I, she became active with the Chicago chapter of the Canteen Workers, which supported the black soldiers of the celebrated Eighth Regiment, Illinois National Guard, and was a prominent participant in their social functions. Although she was touted as a leader of exclusive social and club groups that typically featured couples, Harsh never married.

By 1921, she graduated from Simmons College Library School in Boston, and on February 26, 1924, she became the first African American appointed as a branch librarian for the Chicago Public Library. While serving as librarian for a series of small neighborhood branch libraries during the 1920s, Harsh threw her energies into the Chicago chapter of the Association for the Study of Negro Life and History, the organization funded in Chicago in 1915 by Carter G. Woodson. These two elements in Harsh's life began to merge in the late 1920s, when Dr. George Cleveland Hall, chief of staff at Provident Hospital and

another of the founders of the association, was appointed to the board of directors of the Chicago Public Library. Hall pressed the library to open a full-service branch in a South Side black community crowded with migrants arriving from the South.

Hall appealed to Chicago philanthropist and president of Sears, Roebuck and Company Julius Rosenwald, who agreed to donate the funds to purchase the site for the library, close to the location of the innovative housing complex (referred to as "The Rosenwald") that Rosenwald had financed for middle-class black Chicagoans. Hall died before the library was completed, but in 1931, while construction was still ongoing, the board of directors voted to name the branch library after Hall; Vivian G. Harsh was appointed its first head. She had just completed additional course work at the Graduate Library School of the University of Chicago.

Harsh's appointment proved to be controversial. In the summer of 1931, the Rosenwald Foundation granted her a traveling scholarship to tour African American collections in other cities, including New York Public Library's pathbreaking Schomburg Collection. Harsh returned from the trip determined to build a "Special Negro Collection" at the Hall Branch library and began acquiring books, pamphlets, clippings, and photographs from friends in the Association for the Study of Negro Life and History. By August 1931, Andrew J. Kolar, president of the library's board of directors, suggested her appointment was influenced by "politics" and questioned her ability and competence. Two months later, he charged that the books Harsh was "installing in the new Hall branch were likely to cause a race riot" (Kolar to Carl Roden, August and October 1931, Carl Roden Papers).

The new library was opened to the public on January 18, 1932, and immediately created a sensation in the surrounding community. The *Chicago Defender* ran a photo spread and headlined its story, "Crowd Jams Library on Opening Day." White newspapers marveled at the crowds, noting that at the new facility "nonfiction enjoys an unusual degree of popularity" ("Negroes Enjoy Non-Fiction Best"). Among its twenty thousand volumes were some three hundred that formed the nucleus of Harsh's collection of works on African American history and literature. Harsh also assembled a talented staff of black women professionals, headed by the pioneering children's librarian, CHARLEMAE ROLLINS.

Despite tight depression-era finances and bureaucratic opposition to the development of an African American history collection from the Chicago Public Library administration, Harsh persisted in expanding the collection. Donations from library patrons and a series of Rosenwald Foundation grants supported purchases; friends who traveled to other cities were encouraged to collect black history books, pamphlets, and brochures and add them to the resources at the George Cleveland Hall Branch.

In October 1933, Harsh launched a Book Review and Lecture Forum at the library, a semimonthly event designed to bring library patrons together with speakers on topics in black history, literature, and current events. The forum, which ran for the next twenty years, attracted an impressive array of speakers, including Richard Wright, Langston Hughes, Zora Neale Hurston, Arna Bontemps, Gwendolyn Brooks, Horace Cayton, William Attaway, Margaret Walker, St. Clair Drake, and Alain Locke. Many of the speakers also used the Special Negro Collection as a research site for their own writing. Richard Wright, Margaret Walker, and Horace Cayton all made extensive use of materials Harsh had collected.

By the late 1930s, the Hall Branch library had become a meeting place for young black writers, artists, and social scientists. Word of its holdings spread nationally; by the time of its seventh birthday in 1939, it was said to be known from "Wisconsin to Mississippi" ("Hall Library. Seven Years Old. Is Known from Wisconsin to Mississippi"). The *Chicago Defender* praised Harsh as the librarian who "has worked relentlessly toward supplying universal service on material concerning Race" ("Hall Branch Library Is Eight Years Old").

Harsh encouraged these writers to help build the Special Negro Collection. The Works Progress Administration's (WPA) Federal Writers Project authorized a study called "The Negro in Illinois" in 1936. More than one hundred researchers contributed to the project from 1936 to 1942; the library served as its unofficial headquarters. When the study was discontinued in 1942, Arna Bontemps turned over its research files to Harsh. Another WPA-funded study, a wide-ranging survey of African American history materials in Chicago-area libraries called the Chicago Afro-American Analytical Union Catalog, was also placed in the collection.

Langston Hughes, who had often used the collection when he was serving as director of the Skyloft Players at Chicago's Parkway Community House, donated typescripts and galley proofs of his autobiographical work, *The Big Sea*. He cited the library as one of the things he liked about Chicago, noting the excellent book collection and the charming librarians. In 1940, Richard Wright presented Harsh with an inscribed prepublication copy of *Native Son*, as well as manuscripts of some of the earlier research work he had done, and told a Hall Branch audience that the collection had enriched his knowledge of black experience.

The Hall Branch's fame reached its zenith during World War II. Library forums regularly drew more than one hundred participants, with prominent guest speakers. Programs to encourage political and civic awareness of black servicemen were especially stressed. One library series asked, "What Is the Negro Up Against?"; another outlined "A World View of Color." Harsh and Rollins publicized the library and its programs by writing reviews for the *Chicago Defender* and the *Chicago Bee*. They created bibliographies of history works for both children and adults, sponsored annual "Negro History Week" exhibits at the library, and helped organize the celebrated American Negro Exposition. Black history murals by such prominent artists as Charles White and Charles Davis were installed on the walls of the library. Harsh and Rollins also sought to introduce innovative programs for black women during World War II; hundreds of women participated in the library's Reading Guidance courses for parents.

By the 1940s, the Hall Branch library had taken its place among the constellation of black cultural, political, and intellectual institutions clustered in the South Side community then known as Bronzeville.

The Hall Branch staff considered Harsh a stern taskmaster and a detail-oriented supervisor. Behind her back they often called her "the Lieutenant," commented on the punctuality that characterized her neighborhood walks, and noted the very proper way she dressed at all times. High school students who studied at Hall in the 1930s and 1940s remembered the rigid rules she set for conduct in the library. In 1944, she moved from the home she had occupied all her life into an apartment in the Rosenwald houses. "The Rosenwald" was a center of black intellectual and cultural life, but Harsh evidently had few close friends and was viewed as a very private person.

Despite her intense involvement in the daily operation of the library, she remained active in a number of black history and civic organizations. Prominent nationally and locally in the Association for the Study of Negro Life and History, Harsh served on committees that organized its national conventions, directed its membership drives, and planned its programming. She also served on the board of Parkway Community House and the Young Women's Christian Association, was active in the local branch of the National Association for the Advancement of Colored People, and was a member of the Sixth Grace Presbyterian Church.

In the years immediately after World War II, Harsh organized forums on the problems of black workers, hosted conferences on independence movements in Africa, and worked with the black history radio series, "Destination Freedom." The DuSable History Club, led by Samuel Stratton, continued to bring students and local residents to the library to learn about African American history. By the 1950s, however, residential shifts in Chicago's black community, neighborhood deterioration, and the exhaustion of the South Side cultural flowering—often called the Chicago Renaissance—took their toll on the Hall Branch library. The committee that organized the Book Review and Lecture Forum ceased to function in 1954, and use of Harsh's Special Negro Collection declined.

After a bout with illness and depression, Harsh retired from the Chicago Public Library on November 10, 1958. Colleagues recalled that she found retirement difficult. She worked intermittently in the real estate office of her brother, Pritt, and occasionally visited Hall Branch library. To some of her closest colleagues, she complained that she was no longer able to accompany Pritt on summer vacations to Idlewild, the African American resort in Michigan where her parents had purchased a cottage in the 1920s. To others, she expressed despair over what she viewed as neglect of the Special Negro Collection.

On the morning of August 17, 1960, Harsh was found unconscious in her apartment and was taken to Provident Hospital, where she died. Her funeral was crowded with friends and former library patrons, and she was buried in historic Lincoln Cemetery. The *Chicago Defender* eulogized her as "the historian who never wrote" (Slaughter). Harsh did not live to see the revival of the Special Negro Collection, which gathered strength in the wake of the civil rights movements of the 1960s. In 1970, the Chicago Public Library renamed it the Vivian G. Harsh Research Collection of Afro-American History and Literature. By 1975, the collection was moved to the new Carter G. Woodson Regional Library, where a photograph of Harsh hangs adjacent to one of Woodson.

Vivian G. Harsh's work as a collector of African American

history sources places her alongside such better known black bibliophiles and collection builders as Arthur Schomburg and Jesse Moorland. Under difficult financial and administrative circumstances, she was able to institutionalize her collection and offer innovative programming in black history to both scholars and community residents. Above all, she was able to create a remarkable milieu that grew in the heart of Bronzeville and helped develop the work of many black scholars and writers.

Sources. The archives of the George Cleveland Hall Branch, CPL, are held at the Vivian G. Harsh Research Collection of Afro-American History and Literature at the Carter G. Woodson Regional Library, CPL. The archives include branch records, annual reports, programs, correspondence, newspaper clippings, and photographs. Other sources for the study of Harsh's life and work include the Doris Evans Saunders Papers, the Charlemae Hill Rollins Papers, and oral histories from former members of the Hall Branch library staff and the staff of Parkway Community House, all located in the Vivian G. Harsh Collection. Issues of *Chicago Public Library Staff News* and the Carl Roden Papers (CPL commissioner) are held at Spec. Coll., Harold Washington Library Center, as are oral interviews with Doris Evans Saunders, Nannie Pinckney, Joseph Rollins Jr., Doris Martin, Eileen Lawrence, and Susan Cayton Woodson. Information about Harsh's mother, Maria L. (Drake) Harsh, is found in Spec. Coll., Fisk Univ. Few documents authored by Harsh have survived, but an extensive vertical file compiled by her on African American subjects is included in the George Cleveland Hall Archives, as well as an excellent file of documents from the Association for the Study of African American Life and History. Biographical articles on Harsh have appeared in Jessie Carney Smith, ed., *Notable Black American Women* (1992) and *BWA*. The history of the Harsh Research Collection is traced in Donald Joyce, "Vivian G. Harsh Collection of Afro-American History and Literature, Chicago Public Library," *Library Quarterly*, Winter 1988. Among the many newspaper articles on Harsh and the Hall Branch library, two stand out: Roi Ottley, "Hall Library Becomes Negro Cultural Center," *CT*, February 21, 1954, and Adolph J. Slaughter, "The Historian Who Never Wrote: The Vivian G. Harsh Story," *Chicago Defender*, August 29, 1960. See also "Negroes Enjoy Non-Fiction Best," *Chicago Daily News*, April 12, 1932; "Hall Library. Seven Years Old. Is Known from Wisconsin to Mississippi," *Chicago Defender*, January 21, 1939; and "Hall Branch Library Is Eight Years Old," *Chicago Defender*, January 13, 1940.

MICHAEL L. FLUG

HARSHAW, RUTH HETZEL
October 30, 1889–January 18, 1968
RADIO BROADCASTER, EDUCATOR, AUTHOR

Ruth Harshaw, whose award-winning radio programs fostered a love of reading in hundreds of thousands of boys and girls, was born and raised on a farm near the small town of Almond, Wisconsin. One of three daughters and the youngest of the six children of Michael C. and Amanda (Messing) Hetzel, Florence Ruth Hetzel was always known by her middle name of Ruth. Hetzel attended a one-room school in the farming countryside but enjoyed the cultural enrichment of nearby Almond. While the small village of Almond was in a rural area, it had been established in 1852 by Hetzel's ancestors and other well-educated immigrants from the small German town of Eckartsweier, near Baden-Baden, including many neophyte Lutheran ministers and their young literate wives, who often befriended the Almond-area children. Though the Hetzel girl attended a

FIG. 49. *Ruth Harshaw broadcasting her children's book program.*

Methodist church, several of the wives took a special interest in her and fueled her enthusiasm for learning. Ruth Hetzel became an avid reader. One minister's wife, whom Harshaw recalled as having attended the Boston Conservatory of Music, gave her singing lessons and urged her to cultivate her fine voice.

When Hetzel reached high school age, she convinced her widowed father and older sister to live in Almond during the school term so that she could attend the public secondary school. Her graduation class consisted of five students in 1908, when she received a teaching certificate and prepared to teach school in the one-room school she had attended as a child while, at the same time, enrolling in Stevens Point Normal School. Her father did not believe in higher education for women, but Hetzel was persistent. At Stevens Point (later Wisconsin State College and now a branch of the University of Wisconsin), she studied pedagogy, elocution, and voice. Graduating from the two-year course in August 1913, she taught for a year in nearby Wausau.

During this period Hetzel met Myron Turner Harshaw, whom she married in 1917. Harshaw was the brother of one of Hetzel's normal school classmates. They became engaged after she graduated from Stevens Point. Hetzel was a talented teacher, and when the Wausau public school principal was asked to recommend one of his staff for a job in Winnetka, Illinois, he suggested Ruth Hetzel. She left Wisconsin for Winnetka, where she taught grade school for three years and, at the same time, continued her own education with voice lessons and courses at the University of Chicago.

Once more her efforts in the classroom were appreciated, and Winnetka's superintendent of schools recommended her for a job in the Willamette Valley outside Portland, Oregon. Hetzel left for Oregon in 1916 to help a group of parents start a progressive, private school. One year later she returned to Winnetka, where she became the principal of the Horace Mann Elementary School. On December 22 of that year she married Myron Harshaw. He had graduated from the University of Wisconsin and was a second lieutenant in the Army Air Force. Ruth Harshaw completed the school year in 1918, while her husband finished basic training. Lt. Harshaw was sent overseas in 1919 in the United States Army of Occupation and was discharged late that year. The couple settled in Winnetka permanently, and, in the 1920s, Myron Harshaw became a partner in an advertising agency. The Harshaws had four children: Martha Jane, Patricia Ruth, Hope Hathaway, and Myron Turner II.

Following the birth of her first child, Harshaw left classroom teaching and became a part-time supervisor of dramatics for the Winnetka Public Schools. Asked to help develop curriculum materials for an innovative educational program directed by the Superintendent of Schools, Carleton Washburn, Harshaw researched and wrote two children's books, *Council of the Gods* (1931), which wove Greek myths into one consecutive narrative, and *Reindeer of the Waves* (1934), a novel about Viking life.

Ruth Harshaw combined motherhood and educational consulting through the 1920s, a period of time when she brought the love of books and good literature to her own family as well as to the Winnetka schools. The Great Depression in the 1930s changed life for most Americans, the Harshaws included; Myron Harshaw's advertising agency lost income. When Ruth Harshaw was invited by Samuel Carson in 1933 to become director of the new Educational Services Bureau at Carson Pirie Scott & Company, one of Chicago's major department stores, she accepted. During the next sixteen years she developed innovative marketing programs for Carson's, including a monthly mail-order children's book club, Hobby Horse Book Foundation, in which books of her selection were advertised.

Harshaw soon became successful in developing new markets for children's literature. In the 1940s she was hired by the American Dental Association's Bureau of Public Relations to write fifteen-minute radio dramatizations of children's books. Distributed nationwide, these spots could be purchased for a usage fee as a public service to radio stations.

In the fall of 1946, Harshaw presented a new version of the fifteen-minute book dramatizations to Carson's, *The Hobby Horse Presents*, which ran from 1946 to 1949, Saturday mornings on station WMAQ. Highlighting not only Harshaw's knowledge of books, but also her well-trained, deep, and distinctive voice, the show developed an enthusiastic audience. This was a quasi-commercial enterprise, with thirty-five thousand copies of a newsletter, *Carson's Hobby Horse Review*, written by Ruth Harshaw, distributed monthly to the Chicago Public Schools. Readers learned about books, and Carson Pirie Scott & Company's image was carried into the homes of Chicago's public school families. When readers were asked to select their favorite books in 1946, twenty thousand votes were cast. In 1947 there were forty thousand.

During this period Harshaw gave hundreds of talks at school assemblies and book fairs, as well as lectures to Chicago-area librarians and the Parent Teacher Association (now National Parent Teacher Association) groups about how to bring books and children together. Dedicated to inspiring love of reading in children, in 1938 she created, with Dilla MacBean, director of the Division of Libraries of the Chicago Public Schools, an educational quiz show, *Battle of Books*. Every Friday two elementary schools brought teams of readers to vie with each other. The contestants were asked to identify titles and authors of children's books from questions sent in by school children. The program was broadcast weekly during school hours on WBEZ, the Chicago Board of Education radio station.

Boys and girls loved the *Battle*. Over the years they sent tens of thousands of book questions to the program. Harshaw sifted through them, choosing and editing those that were used on the air, always aiming to make them so intriguing that if a child had not read the book, she would want to do so. The winning team received a $37.50 gift certificate (a sum that would buy six to eight books) donated by Carson Pirie Scott to purchase books for its school library. The program continued until a few months before Harshaw's death in 1968.

On December 3, 1949, WMAQ-NBC in Chicago began to broadcast *The Hobby Horse Presents* as a public service under a new title, *Carnival of Books*. *Carnival* was a high-energy, fifteen-minute show that introduced students, parents, and teachers to current children's literature. Each weekly program featured a new book introduced by Harshaw, followed by an actor's reading of a tantalizing six-minute segment selected and edited by Harshaw. After the dramatized reading, Harshaw moderated an interview of the book's author by four young panelists, grade school students in Chicago-area schools. On April 8, 1951, NBC began network syndication of *Carnival of Books* in cooperation with the American Library Association. Now Harshaw's commanding voice reached across the country. The show was broadcast from coast to coast over fifty NBC affiliates and National Association of Educational Broadcasters' radio outlets. Publishers, eager to cooperate, sent authors to Chicago specifically to be on the program.

Originally *Carnival* was broadcast live from the Merchandise Mart in Chicago, but in the early 1950s Harshaw expanded its scope by recording interviews with authors and panels of local children in NBC studios on both the East and West Coasts. Armstrong Sperry, Eleanor Estes, Robert Heinlein, Theodor Geisel (Dr. Seuss), and Madeleine L'Engle were among the authors whom the show featured over the years. In 1956 Harshaw traveled to Europe to tape interviews with thirty authors in NBC studios in London, Paris, and Munich. The series *In Europe with Carnival of Books* included such famous writers as Astrid Lindgren of Stockholm, creator of the indomitable *Pippi Longstocking*, and Laurent de Brunhoff of Paris, author of the Babar books. These programs were broadcast from October 1956 through

April 1957. In 1965 she returned to London to tape a series of notable British authors, which was broadcast later that year.

In the fall of 1966, Harshaw made her final broadcast of *Carnival of Books*. In 1964, she had been stabbed in the throat by an intruder to her Northfield, Illinois, townhouse, where she lived alone, having been widowed earlier. The injury damaged her vocal cords, and it became increasingly difficult for her to project her voice while recording. With her resignation, the program, which was so clearly linked with her personality, voice, and insights, was canceled by NBC in Chicago. The series concluded on September 25, 1966, with guest author Marguerite Henry, with whom Harshaw had inaugurated the program twenty years earlier.

As a program that never condescended to children and consistently presented excellent authors of children's books in an engaging format, *Carnival of Books* set a high standard for children's broadcasting and won fourteen awards. In 1957 the Thomas Alva Edison Foundation named it "Best Children's Radio Program," an award given to encourage programming that showed goals and individuals that were worthwhile models for children. In 1963 the show received one of broadcasting's most prestigious honors, the Peabody Award, as an outstanding children's series.

Ruth Harshaw and *Carnival of Books* also received commendation from the Chicago Advertising Club in 1947 and 1955, the Association for Better Radio and Television in 1953 and 1955, and the National Association of Educational Broadcasters in 1957. Ruth Harshaw was honored by the Chicago Chapter of Theta Sigma Phi, Honorary Sorority for Women in Journalism.

Harshaw was active in her community as well as her profession, as a member of the Winnetka Historical Society, the Winnetka Women's Republican Club, and the Village Caucus. She served two terms as president of the Winnetka Women's Club and was a trustee of the Winnetka Public Library.

She died of breast cancer at the age of seventy-eight and was buried in the Harshaw plot in Stevens Point, Wisconsin. Her shows were so popular that the MacMillan Company published two volumes of *Battle of Books* sample questions: *What Book Is That?* (1948) by Ruth Harshaw and Dilla MacBean, and *In What Book?* (1970) by Harshaw and her daughter Hope Harshaw Evans. The quiz show format worked so well that schools and libraries began to adapt it for their own contests. As late as the 1990s schools and public libraries all over the United States continued to use Harshaw's format and to hold hard-fought *Battle of Books* events.

Sources. Harshaw's writings are cited above. More than one hundred *Carnival of Books* programs that aired between 1954 and 1956 are stored in the Recorded Sound Division, Library of Congress, Washington, D.C., on acetate discs. Only the January 8, 1956, broadcast has been transferred to preservation tapes. The rest are not available to researchers. Oral interviews with Hope Harshaw Evans, Patty Harshaw Boylston, and Jane Harshaw Clarke by Jamie Gilson provided helpful information. Useful articles include May Massee, "Making the 'Carnival of Books' Tick," *CT*, November 15, 1953, and Margaret Herguth, "Mrs. Harshaw Brings Children's Books to Life," *Winnetka Talk*, June 2, 1966. An obituary appeared in *Publisher's Weekly*, February 26, 1968.

JAMIE GILSON

HART, PEARL
April 7, 1890–March 22, 1975
LAWYER, CIVIL LIBERTIES ADVOCATE, GAY RIGHTS AND
SOCIAL ACTIVIST, LEGAL EDUCATOR

Pearl Hart, one of the founders of the National Lawyers Guild and an early fighter for the civil rights of gays and lesbians, was born Pearl Harchovsky in Traverse City, Michigan. Harchovsky was two years old when she arrived in Chicago with her parents, David and Sarah Harchovsky, and her four older sisters. She was the favorite of her father, Rabbi Harchovsky, who came to Chicago to supervise the slaughtering of animals for kosher meat establishments located in the Union Stockyards. Her mother came from a long line of distinguished rabbis. Harchovsky was educated in the Chicago public schools and in 1912, after graduation from high school, entered John Marshall Law School, attending classes in the evening. (At that time, a college degree was not a requirement for admission to law school.) She continued to live at home until the death of her parents, her mother in 1919 and her father in 1923. Family ties between the sisters remained close as Harchovsky became the bulwark of the family, handling any family business or legal problems or requests for extra money. Even after Harchovsky had her own home, she made it a practice to attend family Friday Sabbath meals, arriving with flowers and candy.

While in law school, she worked as a stenographer at the law offices of Pringle and Terwilliger and as a law clerk for Ferguson and Goodnow. Taking the name of Pearl Hart in 1914, she graduated from John Marshall Law School and gained admission to the bar.

Hart entered the field of law at a time when the legal profession and the courts were changing rapidly. The number of law school graduates began to increase dramatically over the next five years, and the Chicago court system emerged as a leader in the movement to reform the municipal court system and adapt it to the needs of an urban and industrial society. Illinois established the first Juvenile Court in 1899; specialized branches of the Municipal Court, Morals Court and Boys' Court, were created in 1913 and 1914, respectively. The Morals Court (later called the Women's Court) dealt with cases of child abandonment, bastardy, and child abuse. This court also dealt with women criminals such as prostitutes. The Boys' Court was created to deal with boys who were older than juveniles (more than ten years of age) and yet were not old enough to be treated as adults. A period of probation rather than punishment, with resulting rehabilitation, was an important part of the philosophy behind the creation of these different courts.

During the 1900s, women lawyers, including Hart, found both opportunities and career niches in this court system, which dealt primarily with women and children. Hart was an adult probation officer from 1915 to 1917 and became familiar with various branches of the Chicago Municipal Court.

Hart was closely tied both professionally and personally to a network of other activist women who turned their social policy concerns into professional careers. Through these interconnected networks, women like Hart effected social change for women, children, and those marginalized by society. In the first years of Hart's career, these legal networks included the Women's Law League and the local, state, and national wom-

FIG. 50. *Civil liberties and social justice activist Pearl Hart, one of the first women lawyers to teach at John Marshall Law School, Chicago.*

en's bar associations. Hart became president of the Women's Law League (1915–16), which included women law students and graduates of the various law schools in Chicago who were concerned with the welfare of women students and graduates. In 1917, Hart went into private legal practice, and she also supplemented her income by teaching. Hart's first teaching position was as a commercial law instructor at Carter Harrison High School from 1921 to 1922.

In 1925, Hart began to work with SOPHONISBA BRECKINRIDGE, prominent professor in the pioneering Chicago School of Civics and Philanthropy (later the University of Chicago's School of Social Service Administration). Breckinridge, a close colleague of progressive social reformers and one of the Hull-House women coalescing around JANE ADDAMS, was interested in reform of the court system and, specifically, with law and procedures pertaining to women and children. Breckinridge and other professional women of the era, including lawyers and physicians, worked with activist clubwomen to obtain the legislative changes so essential to carry out their political agenda. The Woman's City Club of Chicago (WCC) was such a women's coalition. Another was the Committee on Social Work in the Municipal Court—men and women social workers interested in reforming the system. The reformers shared the goal of enforcing the constitutional rights of women,

which were being ignored by the police department and judges. Hart observed the courts and worked with the Committee on Social Work and the WCC. She found that in the courts' efforts to take a strong stand against prostitution, women were being held pending examination by a health official for venereal disease. This was often done before they were officially charged, allowed to post bail, or seek legal counsel. Women merely walking alone, whom the police suspected of soliciting, would be rounded up by undercover vice squad officers. Many innocent, poor, and unsuspecting women were often among those coming before the court. Hart questioned whether prostitutes were more dangerous to the community than the threat to the rights of citizens posed by ordering medical examination of women before a finding of their guilt or innocence. Hart also believed women deserved adequate legal advice and thought a public defender in Morals Court on the payroll of the city or county would have greater official standing than a "mere volunteer" (Hart to Committee on Social Work, February 29, 1932, Breckinridge Papers)—the position in which she and other attorneys giving their time to protect women's rights found themselves.

It was during this time of women's rights activism and her first years in private law practice in the mid-1920s that Pearl Hart met Blossom Churan, the daughter of a lawyer who shared an office with Hart. She was ten years younger than Hart, a singer/actress with the Lyric Opera, who used the stage name of Patricia O'Bryan. To Hart, Blossom Churan was "the most beautiful woman she had ever seen" (quoted in Kuda, 29). After her father's death, Hart moved in with Blossom Churan and began a long-term relationship. She also invested money in two stage plays in which Churan performed.

In keeping with Hart's advocacy of full constitutional rights for women in the courts, she fought for women's political power in the postsuffrage era. While women had achieved the vote in 1920, they still contended with conservative cultural attitudes, legal disabilities, and a male-dominated political party system that excluded them from the seats of power. Women like Hart stretched the gender boundaries of what was acceptable political behavior for women. In 1928, Hart ran unsuccessfully for the position of associate judge of the Municipal Court.

Hart became one of the first public defenders in the now renamed Women's Court (1929). The *Chicago Daily Herald* recorded an example of her work in a case dealing with three black teenagers. In 1932, the Committee on Social Work in the Municipal Court had Hart report on women arrested and suspected of prostitution. Breckinridge and other leaders in the Committee on Social Work represented a variety of institutions that crossed racial, ethnic, and religious lines, including Harrison Dobbs, the University of Chicago; Father Frederick Siedenburg, Loyola University School of Social Work; and A. L. Foster, the Chicago Urban League. Again, Hart ran for the position of associate judge of Municipal Court, supported by Jane Addams and the Women's Bar Association of Illinois, which appointed a special campaign committee; nevertheless, she met with defeat. Women remained outside the system, attempting to reform it but not achieving the rank of judge, where they could influence the interpretation of the law.

Hart's career demonstrated a close connection between legal activism and social policy activism. She worked with reform and political coalitions and women's groups. She also constructed professional networks for women lawyers. Hart served as the president of the Women's Bar Association of Illinois (WBAI) in 1925 and on the board of directors from 1926 to 1927. In 1930, Hart extended her associations beyond Illinois to become involved with the National Association of Women Lawyers (NAWL) serving on the organizational committee for their annual convention held in Chicago (1930) and as Illinois state vice-president, a position she held from 1931 to 1932.

In 1934 Hart chaired the Woman's City Club's (WCC) Committee on Administration of Justice, which looked into the adult courts, police, sheriff, and states attorney's offices. By 1937, Hart was becoming an authority on women and the courts, conducting research on sex offenders for the WCC. Hart's work traced other national programs in their treatment of sex offenders, including those that placed all women's cases in one single court in order to provide continuity of action and to prevent lenient or arbitrary sentencing.

In a backward move, the Illinois Supreme Court ruled in the 1935 Susan Lattimore case that the original 1899 Juvenile Court legislation was unconstitutional. As a result, the courts criminalized children over the age of ten, placing them outside the scope of Juvenile Court and in contact with hardened criminals. As a juvenile public defender, Hart organized the WBAI Juvenile Court Committee in 1936 and was a special speaker for the WBAI, promoting legislation to raise the age of criminal responsibility from ten to seventeen years. Hart created the Citizens' Committee on the Juvenile Court (CCJC) in 1938.

The CCJC and the WBAI supported numerous pieces of successful legislation, including measures that allowed Illinois to qualify for Aid to Dependent Children under the Social Security Act in 1937. They secured personnel examinations for the Juvenile Detention Home intake department and worked with the Juvenile Court judge and the Cook County Board of Commissioners to improve the running of Juvenile Court. Improvements included merit exams for probation officers, a psychiatric unit for use by the court, and coordinated medical facilities to secure health and medical care for children who came before the court. The CCJC served as a watchdog over reformatory schools and outlined welfare policies that would improve the court's effectiveness in working with children and families.

In the 1930s, Hart also responded to the growth of racism in the United States and fascism in Europe. The economic and social dislocation caused by the worldwide Great Depression had produced extremes in the political arena. Some in the United States believed that repression or restriction of the activities of trade unions, civil rights' advocates, and immigrants ensured democracy. Hart disagreed; more than ever, she advocated a strong civil liberties approach, protecting the constitutional rights of all Americans. Hart was a founding member of the National Lawyers Guild (NLG) in 1937, one of a handful of men and women lawyers with immigrant or working-class backgrounds who were founders. Hart was its first national secretary. The NLG created a "progressive and racially integrated alternative to the American Bar Association" (*Encyclopedia of the American Left*, 504).

Around 1943, Hart's private life became more complicated. Her longtime partner, Blossom Churan, began an affair with Bertha Isaacs, a hematologist at Northwestern Hospital. Rather than separating from Churan, Hart invited the new woman into their home and into an arrangement the three maintained for twenty years. Hart's relationship with Churan and later with Isaacs was never discussed between Hart and her sisters. Hart effectively kept the two most important parts of her personal life separate from each other, except for the presence of her young niece, Tess Weiner, who often spent time at Hart's home. Weiner remembered on such holidays as Thanksgiving that if Hart was not with the family, she would send a turkey by taxi. Hart was described by Weiner as a large woman who was physically active, loved boxing, and was also known to have a gun collection, presumably taken away from gang members she had encountered in the court system. Thus, an important admonition for young Tess was never to go into Aunt Pearl's closet where the guns were kept. Hart also had a penchant for unusual cars, including a lavender Auburn that she owned as a young lawyer.

While Harchovsky family gatherings and Hart's personal household were kept separate, Hart was not totally secretive about her lifestyle. Both Churan and Isaacs accompanied Hart to social events connected with Hart's professional and political career. Besides supporting aspects of Churan's acting career, Hart owned a summer home with Churan in Holland, Michigan, called Windcrest.

Hart's leadership as a Chicago activist took additional turns. As cofounder of the George and Anne Portes Cancer Prevention Center, Hart joined with two other women in 1943 to open a one-night-a-week, all-volunteer clinic for early cancer detection in women. For thirty-two years, Hart contributed her services as secretary and general counsel to the center, helping it develop into one of the world's major medical examining facilities.

Hart's involvement with the National Lawyers Guild coincided with her early civil rights activism in Chicago. In 1944, the Citizens' Committee on the Juvenile Court asked for a report assessing the resources available for black children who came before the Juvenile Court. The CCJC was made up of a wide cross section of social reform groups that represented Catholics, Protestants, and Jews as well as representatives from the African American community such as the Urban League. The Woman's City Club representative to the CCJC was an African American woman, Ida Laws, who served in 1943. Leading social reformers, including Harrison Dobbs, Thomas Eliot at the School of Social Work at Northwestern University, Father Ralph Gallagher of Loyola University, and Sarah Schaar of Jewish Social Services worked with other concerned citizens to further their interest in Juvenile Court procedure and in Illinois institutions to which children were committed.

Three years later, in 1947, Hart spoke at a conference on civil rights at Hull-House. Hart became part of the executive board of the newly formed Civil Rights Congress (CRC) of Illinois in 1948 and its treasurer in 1949. The CRC sponsored a conference in 1949 at the Young Men's Christian Association in Chicago to discuss measures to end Jim Crow practices in housing. Hart acted as a trustee of the bail fund of the CRC.

Hart was appointed instructor of jurisprudence by John Marshall Law School in 1946, one of the few women to be named to a law school faculty. Her reputation had grown, but Hart was never elected to public office, although she made several attempts. Throughout the forties and fifties Hart served at the local, state, and national levels of the Progressive Party. In 1947, Hart ran for alderman on the Progressive Party ticket. The local Progressive Party in 1947 showed a strong third party challenge to the monopoly of the Democratic and Republican parties by sweeping numerous key areas. In addition, 65 percent of African American voters cast a straight Progressive Party ticket. While Hart took fourth place in her race for alderman, she received 181,896 votes. In 1948, Hart was a Progressive Party candidate for Municipal Court judge, and in 1951 Hart would again run for alderman. Hart continued to be active in the Progressive Party until 1952, serving in leadership roles as Illinois state vice-chairman, 1950–52, and on the national committee in 1950. While Hart supported Henry Wallace's bid for the presidency in 1948, she opposed his views on Korea in a 1950 letter to the *Sun Times* and urged the United States to work on a negotiated settlement.

Hart also began a period of intense legal work defending immigrants and radicals who were being investigated by the government for subversive activities. Beginning in the late 1940s, the Immigration Naturalization Service (INS) initiated deportation hearings against more than one hundred immigrants in the general anticommunist furor. Deportations and raids sweeping up immigrants increased to almost ten thousand by 1953 with the passage of the McCarran Act of 1950 and later the McCarran-Walter Act of 1952. Title I of the McCarran Act identified the U.S. Communist Party (CP) to be a clear and present danger to national security. CP membership per se was not a crime, but members were required to register. A Subversive Activities Control Board would decide which groups would be covered under these laws. The law barred members from federal jobs and passports, tightened espionage laws, and denied entrance to aliens who were Communist Party members or who had ever been associated with the CP. Title II mandated detention of likely spies, though they could appeal to a review board. The McCarran-Walter Act of 1952 refined the McCarran Act to include aliens suspected of CP affiliation and provision to deport them or, in the case of naturalized citizens, to revoke their citizenship. Hart's already liberal politics and her involvement with the NLG fueled her determination to defend numerous foreign-born aliens who were required to testify before the House UnAmerican Activities Committee (HUAC), and eventually were arrested, subject to long deportation proceedings. The INS held detainees without bail, often subjecting them to various kinds of harassment.

The experience of Katherine Hyndman, the first McCarran case in the Middle West, was typical of what immigrants faced during this period. She was a Yugoslavian who had lived most of her life in the United States and had been involved in CP-related labor activities in the thirties. She was arrested in 1949 and again in 1952, when she was jailed for almost a year and subject to deportation. During this period her bail was increased, and the stipulations for her parole were stiffened.

In a similar case in 1952, George Witkovich, a Chicago printer, was also arrested under the McCarran-Walter Act. Nationally, thirty-five hundred aliens were singled out for questioning; two were from Chicago, George Witkovich and James Keller, a machinist. "They refused to inform on what meetings they attended, what movies they saw, what newspapers they read, and other such questions" (*Daily Worker*, May 19, 1957, Hart Papers), citing their First Amendment rights and claiming that the requested information was not pertinent to the issue of deportation. Hart defended Keller and Witkovich.

The Witkovich case was appealed all the way to the U.S. Supreme Court. The Court agreed with Hart, making its ruling on May 19, 1957, that the attorney general was restricted to asking questions pertinent to the deportation question.

Hart's work with immigrants coincided with her involvement in the American Committee for the Protection of the Foreign Born (ACPFB). In 1947, she helped found the Mid-West Committee for the Protection of the Foreign Born (MCPFB). Hart served as its first chair from 1947 to 1951. She later was active at the national level, acting as one of five cochairs in 1948 and as vice-chair in 1949 and again in 1960. The ACPFB, founded in 1933 on the initiative of American Civil Liberties Union leader Roger Baldwin, specialized in the defense of radical aliens.

HUAC held hearings in Chicago on several occasions. In 1947, it subpoenaed seven editors of three foreign language newspapers in Chicago. Hart defended Vincent Andrulis, editor of a Lithuanian daily newspaper. In 1956, Ruth Heit, secretary for the MCPFB, was told to produce copies of all MCPFB documents and correspondence relating to revision or repeal of the McCarran-Walter Act, the Smith Act, and the Internal Security Law. Heit refused, on the advice of her counsel Pearl Hart, and HUAC never cited her for contempt.

HUAC continued to summon individuals well into the 1960s, targeting leaders involved with civil rights issues. Hart found herself defending Louis Diskin and Charles Wilson at 1965 HUAC hearings held in Chicago. The committee heard cooperating accusing witnesses in closed executive session. Congressman Edwin Willis of Louisiana, a major opponent of the Civil Rights Act of 1965, was chairman of the committee. A black woman, Lola Belle Holmes, testified for five hours about her activities as an FBI spy. She had worked for the Chicago Urban League. Hart pressed for a closed session to avoid derogatory publicity for the people that Holmes accused of being communists. Holmes stated she had joined the Communist Party in 1957 and then in 1963 testified against Illinois communist leader Claude Lightfoot. Holmes testified that Richard Criley, secretary for the Chicago Committee to Defend the Bill of Rights, was a Communist Party member. Criley organized student groups, peace organizations, and civil rights groups to protest these HUAC hearings. James Forman of the Student Nonviolent Coordinating Committee was one of the demonstrators.

Hart's McCarran-Walter Act cases included at least twenty-four defendants who were arrested for either political dissent and/or their nationalities. Those individuals who could not be deported because countries of origin refused to accept them were given supervisory parole. Deportees were put under house arrest, forbidden to travel beyond a fifty-mile radius, and compelled to submit to medical and psychiatric examinations and answer questions "deemed fit and proper" by the attorney general. Each violation was subject to a thousand dollar fine and a year in jail.

As a result of these continual violations of individuals' rights, Hart and others challenged HUAC and the McCarthy-like tactics that were being extended beyond immigrants to include those active in the emerging civil rights movement. Hart joined as a founding board member the Chicago Committee to Defend the Bill of Rights (CCDBR) in 1960. She acted as the CCDBR legal counsel and participated in rallies, lectures, and petitions to oppose the McCarran-Walter Act as well as other legislation and tactics that the government was using to thwart individual liberties. The CCDBR was part of a national movement, the American Committee to Defend the Bill of Rights (ACDBR), opposed to HUAC and other oppressive government actions. The ACDBR took regular steps to publicize HUAC's abuses by taking out full-page ads in major newspapers in order to build public support for the termination of HUAC. At the same time, the Chicago chapter of the NLG, at the urging of Hart and others, publicly opposed, in 1961, de facto segregation in the Chicago public schools and sought changes in credit laws that were particularly discriminatory toward minorities.

The last ten years of Hart's career were committed to securing gay and lesbian civil rights. In post–World War II America, homosexuals were dismissed from the federal government and discharged from the military at an increasing rate, the number reaching three thousand in 1960. In addition, gay bars were constantly subject to police raids, while thousands of homosexuals were arrested through entrapment. Out of both personal and professional interest, in 1965 Hart joined Bob Basker and Ira Jones and approached numerous people about organizing a Mattachine Society in Chicago, more than ten years after Harry Hay and several communists and leftists founded the first Mattachine Society in Los Angeles. Bob Basker was named president, and Hart addressed the first Chicago public meeting at the Midland Hotel on July 27, 1965.

Mattachine Midwest and its newsletter were the political arm of the gay community in its ongoing battle with the Chicago Police Department. In March 1969, Hart, drawing on her experience with other legally marginalized groups, addressed a Mattachine public meeting. Mattachine Midwest published her talk, "The Law and the Homosexual," in pamphlet form for mass distribution. Hart remained the Mattachine corporation counsel until her death.

Mattachine Midwest activist Jim Bradford remembered Hart as one who "exhorted us and supported us to fight police tactics and seek our own rights as human beings" (Bradford, 6). Indeed, that could have been the mantra of Pearl Hart's legal, professional, and personal life. Hart was considered the "Guardian Angel of Chicago's gay community" (Bradford, 1). Numerous other communities and countless individuals considered peripheral to mainstream America would have considered Hart their guardian angel.

Hart met author and poet Valerie Taylor in 1963 as they both worked with Mattachine. Taylor, who referred to Hart in "An Autobiographical Essay" written in 1991 as "the love of my life" (n.p.), moved around the corner from Hart while she was still living with Churan and Isaacs and willingly accepted the limitations of their unusual relationship. Taylor remained close to Hart until her death in 1975 and dedicated numerous amorous poems to her and their relationship. Meantime, Isaac and Hart had a difficult time during Churan's final illness (1965–69), and there was bitterness associated with the strain that this complicated relationship exacted from all of them.

As a champion of constitutional and human rights, Hart was honored by two large birthday celebrations by some five hundred people, first at her seventieth and later at her eightieth in 1970. Hart was greatly missed by those whose lives she touched after she died due to complications of cancer at age eighty-four at Northwestern Memorial Hospital. In 1992 Hart was posthumously inducted into the newly formed Chicago Gay & Lesbian Hall of Fame created by the City of Chicago's Commission on Human Relations.

Sources. The Pearl Hart Papers, CHS, cover mostly the events in her later career with some limited information about her family, early career as a lawyer in Municipal Court, and personal life. In addition, the CHS has the papers of the Citizens' Committee on the Juvenile Court; of the Chicago Police Department, which document Hart's political activities throughout the period after World War II; and the papers of Max Naimen, which include papers of the National Lawyers Guild and the Chicago Lawyers Guild. The CHS also has the papers of the Woman's City Club of Chicago, Chicago Municipal Court Judge Harry Olsen, Louise deKoven Bowen, and the Women's Bar Association of Illinois; these document Hart's work with Juvenile Court, Women's Court, and organizations associated with Municipal Court. Additional helpful collections are the Sophonisba Breckinridge Papers, UC Spec. Coll., and the Jane Addams Memorial Collection, UIC Spec. Coll. Both of these collections provide information about Hart's work in the various branches of Municipal Court. The Gerber-Hart Library, Chicago, named for Pearl Hart, contains a clipping file of Hart's activities and relationship with the gay and lesbian community in Chicago. In this collection are articles collected by Renee Hanover, including campaign literature published in 1928 and 1931. Also at Gerber-Hart Library is "An Autobiographical Essay by Valerie Taylor," in Tee A. Corinne, "A Resource Book," a typescript compiled September 24, 1991. Family history and Hart's relationship with her parents, sisters, and extended family come from an oral interview with Hart's niece, Tess Weiner, April 7, 1998. Tess Weiner made available a tape of her address given at Hart's memorial service, April 8, 1975. She also provided the project with a brief memoir, "How I Remember Pearl Hart," June 6, 1999. A biographical entry of Hart is in the Illinois Woman's Press Association's *Prominent Women in Illinois* (1932). Other biographical articles include one written by Marie Kuda, "Chicago's Gay and Lesbian History: From Prairie Settlement to World War II," *Outlines*, June 1994. Kuda was one of Hart's last students at John Marshall Law School and interviewed Hart's law colleague, Renee Hanover, as well as Hart's companion in her later years, Valerie Taylor. The John Marshall Law School alumni magazine, the *Briefcase*, April 1970, provides information about Hart's legal career as well as her teaching career. Some aspects of Hart's early legal career can be found in the *Women Lawyer's Journal* (1914–32) as well as contextual information regarding women lawyers in the Progressive Era. Jim Bradford pays tribute to Hart in "Pearl Hart Is Remembered on the Anniversary of Her Passing," *Chicago Gay Life*, March 19, 1976. Sources that contextualize the challenges of professional women after the passage of the Nineteenth Amendment include the work by Kristi Andersen, *After Suffrage: Women in Partisan and Electoral Politics before the New Deal* (1996). The post–World War II period, the cold war, and the activities of the McCarthy period are described in Richard Fried, *Nightmare in Red* (1990), and in *The Encyclopedia of the American Left* (1990), ed. Mari Jo Buhle, Paul Buhle, and Dan Georgakas.

BARBARA DOBSCHUETZ

HASKINS, SYLVIA SHAW JUDSON. *See* JUDSON HASKINS, SYLVIA SHAW

HEAP, JANE
November 1, 1883–June 16, 1964
EDITOR, WRITER, ARTIST

Jane Heap played an important role as coeditor of the journal *Little Review* (1914–29) and in the twentieth-century international avant-garde modernist movements in art and literature. Born in Topeka, Kansas, the daughter of George Heap, an immigrant from Cheshire, England, and Enna Heap, a Norwegian who descended from Lapps near the Arctic circle, Heap was the second of four children, three girls and a boy. A dreamy and sensitive child, Jane Heap often spent hours sketching from nature and writing poetry on the grounds of the Topeka State Insane Asylum, where her father worked as an engineer. After graduating from Topeka High School in 1901, Heap traveled to Chicago, where she studied at the Art Institute of Chicago from 1901 to 1905. Graduating in 1905 with thirteen Honorable Mentions for her work in figure drawing and composition, Heap traveled to Germany, where she studied tapestry and mural design briefly near Munich. Returning to Chicago, she worked as a teacher at the Lewis Institute (now the Illinois Institute of Technology), while taking night classes at the Art Institute from 1909 to 1911.

Heap soon gained attention as an artist in Chicago. In 1911 her work had been noticed in the *Sunday Tribune* with a favorable review from HARRIET MONROE, the editor of *Poetry: A Magazine of Verse*. She later had her paintings shown at the American Architecture Exhibit, the Municipal Art League, and the Artists Guild gallery. Heap gained enough attention to be featured in two articles in the *Topeka Capitol*, which reported on her success in Chicago and added that she did mural paintings in the home of two prominent midwest citizens and prepared murals for two public schools. Heap became a member of the Cordon Club, a Chicago club for professional women. The bylaws of the club described it as "an organization of women, formed for the purpose of establishing a common meeting ground for lovers of independence and self-expression" (*Cordon Club*, n.p.).

Heap also became a member of amateur theatrical companies, writing and acting in plays performed at the Lewis Institute. In 1912 Heap joined Maurice Browne's and ELLEN VAN VOLKENBURG's Little Theatre as both set designer and actor. She performed in the company's production of William Butler Yeats's *On Baile's Strand*.

It was an exciting time to be in the city—in the midst of what is now recognized as the "Chicago Renaissance," a literary and cultural movement that attracted young writers and artists who quoted Nietzsche and advocated cubism, psychoanalysis, free verse, and anything that broke with nineteenth-century conventions. One of the contributors to the transformation of the literary world was MARGARET ANDERSON, founder of the *Little Review*.

In 1916 Heap met Margaret Anderson in Chicago. Anderson, a beautiful and enthusiastic woman with a passion for literature and art, had left her middle-class family in Indiana in search of "an atmosphere in which . . . [she] could live and breathe" (*My Thirty Years' War*, 16). After a series of jobs, including working as a free-lance book reviewer for the *Literary Review of the Chicago Evening News*, Anderson founded the *Little Review* in March 1914. It published many Chicago-based writers, including Sherwood Anderson, Floyd Dell, Maxwell Bodenheim, EUNICE TIETJENS, and Ben Hecht, as well as the early works of T. S. Eliot, Hilda Doolittle, and Amy Lowell. Anderson also used the *Little Review* as a platform for radical political ideas, including anarchism, feminism, and tolerance of homosexuality. Her enthusiastic support of Emma Goldman cost her financial backing in the first year of the magazine.

Heap and Anderson met in the Fine Arts Building, where Browne's Little Theatre and the *Little Review* were both housed. The attraction for Anderson was immediate. She wrote in her autobiography that "here was my obsession—the special human being, the special point of view" (*My Thirty Years' War*, 107–108).

The two women were in many ways marked contrasts. Anderson was full of optimism and energy, Heap prone to depression and pessimism. Anderson was beautiful and feminine, attracting much male attention, whereas Heap was described by many contemporaries as "mannish." Heap was a cross-dresser by the time she met Anderson. She played male parts in various theatrical productions, and her favorite off-stage costume was a tuxedo with a long skirt.

Anderson was attracted by Heap's talent for conversation—the *Little Review* was to be a magazine based upon the latest conversation and debates on the new in art and literature. Impressed by Heap's background in art and theater, her acerbic wit and dry humor, Anderson convinced her to write for the *Little Review*. Initially reluctant, Heap soon had a profound impact on the *Little Review*. Her keen, sharp, and sometimes merciless critical columns entertained and frequently infuriated *Little Review* readers. Her first contributions were in the feature "And," a short series of comments reviewing current artistic events in Chicago. She then took on the role of editor in "Reader Critic" in which readers commented on the journal's articles and Heap responded. Heap signed most of her contributions simply "jh," creating a mystique that would follow her for the rest of her life. Under Heap's influence the covers of the magazine went from plain brown to bright colors with modern graphics.

In 1917 Anderson and Heap moved the *Little Review* to New York. During the next few years they published Djuna Barnes, Hart Crane, Mina Loy, Dorothy Richardson, and William Carlos Williams. Ezra Pound, based in London, became the journal's foreign editor and sent the two editors the work of Ford Madox Ford, Wyndham Lewis, and James Joyce. Anderson and Heap were the first to publish Joyce's novel *Ulysses*, which they serialized in the *Little Review* between 1918 and 1921. After several issues were confiscated and burned by the New York post office, the two women were tried for obscenity, found guilty, and fined one hundred dollars. *Ulysses* was not published in the United States again until the 1930s.

After the trial, Anderson and Heap left for Paris, where they became familiar figures in international bohemian circles during the interwar period. Their relationship came to an end when Anderson became involved with Belgian opera star Georgette Leblanc, leaving Heap with the primary responsibility for the *Little Review* from 1924 to 1929. The magazine became bolder and increasingly more avant-garde as Heap published articles on surrealism, constructivism, modern architecture, and "machine age" aesthetics. More interested in the visual arts than Anderson, Heap published reproductions of the works of Frank Stella, Fernand Léger, Joan Miró, and Constantin Brancusi. During the 1920s Heap traveled frequently between Paris and New York City, managing the Little Review Gallery, procuring foreign art for exhibitions, and staging ambitious projects such as the International Theater Exposition (1926) and the Machine Age Exposition (1927), both displays in New York City.

The year 1924 was a major turning point in Heap's life. She was introduced to the ideas of the philosophy of the Armenian mystic George Gurdjieff, an event that was to radically transform her views on both life and art. Gurdjieff taught that humans were "machines" that operated only by mechanical rote without any real consciousness of being. Complicated and opaque, "the Work," as it was called by Gurdjieff disciples, consisted of physical and mental exercises to awake the slumbering true essence of each individual. Heap studied at Gurdjieff's Institute for the Harmonious Development of Man in Fontainebleau, France, on and off during the 1920s. By the end of the decade she decided that art was only another buffer between human beings and spiritual awakening.

Reflecting these new views, Heap and Anderson together composed the last issue of the Little Review in 1929. It comprised a questionnaire that asked contributors such questions as "What do you consider your weakest characteristic?" and "What is your world view?" In her final editorial Heap wrote, "Self-expression is not enough; experiment is not enough; the recording of special moments is not enough. All the arts have broken faith or lost connection with their origin and function" (Little Review, Spring 1929, 5–6).

Under Gurdjieff's direction Heap moved in the late 1930s to London, where she taught his ideas to small numbers of followers. Revered as a teacher, she continued the groups during the blitz in World War II and escorted her pupils to France for meetings with Gurdjieff. She supported herself with help from her old Chicago friend Florence Reynolds and a shop called "The Rocking Horse," which collected and repaired toys from British country estates. She died in London from complications of diabetes and is buried in East Finchley, London.

The Little Review was one of the most influential literary journals of the early twentieth century. The scope of Jane Heap's contribution to the unique quality and bold radicalism of the magazine has been underestimated, in part due to Heap's own desire for a low profile during the Little Review years, compounded by her withdrawal from the arts after meeting Gurdjieff. The bright yet fleeting appearance that Jane Heap makes in the biographies, reminiscences, and memoirs of interwar European and American modernists only begins to suggest her influence in identifying and promoting modernist trends and artists.

Sources. The letters of Jane Heap are in the Little Review collection at the University of Wisconsin–Milwaukee and in the Florence Reynolds Collection at the University of Delaware. The pamphlet Cordon Club (n.d.) is in the Reynolds Collection. Some letters and other materials can be found in Holly Baggett, "Aloof from Natural Laws: Margaret C. Anderson and the Little Review: 1914–1929" (Ph.D. diss., Univ. of Delaware, 1992). Margaret Anderson's autobiographies, My Thirty Years' War (1930), The Fiery Fountains (1951), and Strange Necessity

(1969), give insights into Heap's elusive personality. The importance of Heap's career as an art critic is explored by Susan Noyes Platt, "Mysticism and the Machine Age: Jane Heap and the Little Review," Twenty/One, Fall 1989. Her role in the Gurdjieff following is briefly discussed in James Webb, The Harmonious Circle: The Lives and Work of G. I. Gurdjieff, P. D. Ouspensky and Their Followers (1987), and James Moore, Gurdjieff: The Anatomy of a Myth (1991). Heap's former student, A. L. Staveley, has written her reminiscences in Memories of Gurdjieff (1988). Jackson Bryer, "A Trial Track for Racers: Margaret C. Anderson and the Little Review" (Ph.D. diss., Univ. of Wisconsin—Milwaukee, 1964), is useful. A discussion of Heap's and Anderson's relationship, personal and professional, can be found in Jane Rule, Lesbian Images (1976); Jonathan Katz, Gay/Lesbian Almanac: A New Documentary History (1983); Steven Watson, Strange Bedfellows (1991); and Jayne Marek, Women Editing Modernism (1995). Jane Heap's obituary appeared in the NYT, June 23, 1964.

HOLLY A. BAGGETT

HEDGER, CAROLINE
January 12, 1868–July 10, 1951
PHYSICIAN, WRITER, HEALTH ADVOCATE FOR WOMEN
AND CHILDREN

Caroline Hedger was born in Braceville, Ohio, to John Richards and Maria Louise (Caskey) Hedger. She attended Willoughby High School and then went on to Berea College in Kentucky (1887–88) and Wellesley College (1889–90). Although very little information is available on Hedger's activities between her graduation from college and entry into medical school, she apparently trained and practiced as a nurse. In 1899 she received a medical degree from Northwestern University Woman's Medical School and began a private medical practice in Eau Claire, Wisconsin. Four years later, she moved to Chicago, where she received a second medical degree from Rush Medical College in 1904 and continued her practice in internal medicine until 1938. From 1912 until 1931, she had a medical office in the Heyworth Building in downtown Chicago.

Hedger's early career focused on the health needs of working-class immigrant families, particularly in Chicago's stockyards area. Her first two articles, published in Illinois Medical Journal (1905) and World's Work (1906), dealt with the unhealthy living conditions in that area—lack of natural light and fresh air in the homes, pollution, overcrowding, and poor nutrition. In addition, she described working conditions, which were appalling, with long hours, low wages, and unsanitary factories. The neighborhoods did not contribute anything more positive, with high rents and an overabundance of saloons. Hedger felt that these conditions taken together created an ideal environment for the spread of tuberculosis, which in turn led to unsafe standards for the food processed in the yards. She defended the residents of the area, stating that "one cannot blame these people for not keeping clean. . . . [A] living wage is not paid. The women are too busy fighting for a living to be able to do anything for their children, much less keep their homes in order" ("Asks a Nursery Law," Chicago Record-Herald). Her articles described the conditions reported by Upton Sinclair in his crusading novel, The Jungle, published in 1906. While other reformers were active in establishing day nurseries for the children of working mothers, Hedger called for a state law that would regulate nurseries, setting healthful standards of care.

In 1909 Hedger was director of a program to combat summer diarrhea in children, under the auspices of the United Charities, the Chicago Department of Health, and the Visiting Nurse Association. Data were collected by visiting health workers on such factors as nationality, type of milk fed, and number of cases in a ward; and these figures were correlated with the number of cases and resulting deaths. The end result was a plan for the education of mothers in child care, feeding, and cleanliness. That same year she was a member of the first American Conference on Prevention of Infant Mortality held in New Haven, Connecticut, under the auspices of the American Academy of Medicine. In 1911, she served on several committees for a Chicago Child Welfare Exhibit held at the Coliseum.

Hedger also concerned herself with the effect that long work hours and lack of education for women had on infant mortality rates. Excessive physical and nervous strain, no prenatal care, inability to breast-feed while working, and the impact of pregnancy on the ability to work all affected women and their chances of raising healthy children. In a talk to the Women's Trade Union League of Chicago (WTUL) on the "Toxin of Fatigue," she declared that "long hours of labor impaired the economic efficiency of women, destroyed their social relations and prevented them from attaining the crowning triumph of womanhood—home-making and child-bearing" ("Why Freak Styles?" *Chicago Record-Herald*). She advocated day nurseries and subsidies for mothers to enable them to stay home longer with their infants. In connection with these proposals, she served as one of several staff physicians for the WTUL. The goal of the WTUL in creating such a position was "to make the consultation of a good physician so inexpensive that a girl would go to her at the first sign of trouble and thus prevent what might be a serious and costly illness" (*Annual Report of the Women's Trade Union League of Chicago*, June 1915–June 1916).

In a 1912 investigation, done for the board of the University of Chicago Settlement, Hedger studied the correlation between developmental retardation in the children of the stockyards-area schools and various factors such as diet, health, ethnicity, home ownership, size of family, income, and age of starting school. She felt that all of these were not only important factors in the children's chances of getting a sound education, but also in their likelihood of becoming capable workers and citizens.

Hedger was a member of the Chicago Woman's Club from 1910 until the early 1940s, one of the professional women, such as physician and birth control advocate RACHELLE YARROS, who joined activist clubwomen in implementing a reform agenda to improve the health of women and children. In November 1914 the club received requests that she be sent to Belgium to assist with typhoid relief work there. The club formed the Belgian Typhoid Relief Expedition Fund, which raised money to cover her expenses. Physician Mary Lincoln, assistant professor of laboratory diagnosis at the University of Illinois College of Medicine and partner in the Lincoln-Gardner Laboratory, a clinical laboratory for physicians, contributed five thousand dollars' worth of typhoid vaccine to be used to conquer the epidemic. Hedger left Chicago for Belgium that month. Once there, in addition to her typhoid work, she organized the distribution of clothing to the needy.

After returning to Chicago in the late spring of 1915, Hedger gave talks on her experiences to the Woman's City Club, the Women's Trade Union League of Chicago, and the Chicago Woman's Club. She received a number of commendations for her relief work, including letters of thanks from the Rockefeller Foundation War Relief Commission and the burgomaster of the city of Antwerp. She also received a medal for her services from King Albert of Belgium.

In 1916 she was hired by JULIA LATHROP, head of the Children's Bureau of the U.S. Department of Labor, to visit rural districts and study the condition of mothers in those areas. Between 1917 and 1924 Hedger wrote a number of articles that dealt with the issue of the Americanization of immigrants. The Americanization movement was a reaction to the great influx of immigrants to this country in the early twentieth century. It was also influenced by a perception of a rise in radical activities after World War I. Hedger was inspired by sympathy for the immigrants and the need to prepare them for life in America rather than by a need to "protect" her country from dangerous foreigners and their ways. Through her medical work, particularly in the stockyards area, she had encountered many immigrant families who had experienced difficulty in making the transition to life in America. She served as head of the Americanization Committee that was formed in 1918 by the Woman's City Club. Under the committee's auspices she lectured on the teaching of English and child care practices to immigrants and traveled to New York to assist with Americanizing efforts there.

In her writings, she advocated the necessity of training teachers who could educate foreign-born students not only in the English language but also in the American standards of "civic righteousness, public health, and family life" (*Parent-Teacher Associations*, 1). There were a number of existing institutions that she felt would be helpful with the Americanization effort. Parent-teacher associations, which already had established connections with foreign-born parents, could teach them English along with child-care techniques. Kindergarten teachers would be ideal instructors of English as a second language through their role-playing techniques. Idiomatic English would be much more useful than book learning and could be taught through practical exercises such as cooking, child care, and shopping. In this way parents, especially mothers, would also learn the American way of life. She emphasized throughout her writing on Americanization, however, that immigrants should not be forced to give up their native languages and customs. Teachers should respect their students and appreciate what the immigrants could give to America by sharing their cultures. "Our national needs are a common language and the enlargement of community ideals. . . . The aim of the school must be wider than the ability to read and answer twenty questions for naturalization. It must include recreational, sanitary, and civic ideals, and these must be evolved from the historical and hero ideals of the nationalities in the school" ("Cost of Inadequate Night School," 106).

In addition, she felt that industries should look upon teaching their workers English not as a philanthropic act but rather as an investment. By doing so they could increase productivity and decrease the number of accidents caused by lack of understanding. She also saw through her work that a lack of English-speaking ability could affect immigrants' willingness to avail themselves of American medical facilities, particularly for their children. Along with the language barrier, other factors in this issue were a fear of unknown ways, a sense of isolation and helplessness, and unfamiliarity with modern medical practices. In addition to language classes, other suggested solutions were neighborhood clinics, tent hospitals, and tours of hospitals for the immigrants, conducted in their native languages. Her lack of writings on this subject after 1924 coincided with the increasing conservatism of the Americanization movement, with which she was uncomfortable.

In 1920, Hedger's work with women and children led to her association with the Elizabeth McCormick Memorial Fund (EMMF). She served as medical consultant for the EMMF for more than twenty years. The mission of the EMMF, founded in 1908 and incorporated in 1913, was "to study the condition of child life and to take such measures from time to time as may promise to promote the health, happiness and general welfare of children" (Branscombe, 1). The EMMF approached the study of child health from a holistic point of view, recognizing "the interdependence of the physical, mental, emotional, and environmental aspects of the life-process rather than consideration of any one of these as an isolated segment" (Branscombe, 3). This approach was clearly seen in Hedger's writings during this period.

Many of her articles focused on the health needs of children and the importance of intervention from schools and social agencies. She enumerated the interdependent factors of proper nutrition, the correct ratio between height and weight, a balanced amount of exercise and play, plenty of sleep, and appropriate medical treatment. She also urged the necessity of a child's being able to "grow a soul" ("Medical Inspection in the Schools," 316). Parents were encouraged to keep children's extracurricular activities to a manageable level and to make the family's social life compatible with the health of children. With proper upbringing children would become good citizens and workers and would in turn raise healthy families of their own. One methodology Hedger developed to encourage and guide parents in this area was the Parent's Score Card, which rated many aspects of child health and parenting techniques and allowed parents to score themselves on their behavior.

During the 1920s Hedger also gave several lectures and wrote articles promoting the concept of "positive health." This concept mirrored a shift in the emphasis of the EMMF's programs brought about by "the emerging new concept of health as a state of physical, mental and emotional well-being, not just as an absence of illness" (Branscombe, 10). A number of these articles and lectures were directed toward the nursing profession, particularly in the field of nurse training. Hedger exhorted the nursing schools to produce trainees who were examples of positive health themselves and who could be good role models for their patients. The same factors were important for adults as those she advocated for children: proper nutrition, plenty of sleep, attention to the height/weight ratio, exercise, and avocations outside of one's regular work. The idea of positive health gained new importance in Hedger's writing. Good health was not just something to strive for in order to attain personal satisfaction but was also one's social responsibility.

To promote her views on health, Hedger served on the board

of the American Child Hygiene Association in the 1920s. She also was a member of a number of organizations including the Chicago Medical Society, the Chicago Association of Infant Welfare, and the National Association of Infant Welfare.

In 1942, she retired as medical director of the Elizabeth McCormick Memorial Fund. She moved to a farm near LaPorte, Indiana, and then in the late 1940s, to Clinton, Connecticut. She died there from the results of arteriosclerosis and Parkinson's disease. She remained unmarried and childless throughout her life.

Throughout her career, Hedger's concerns, expressed in her writings and speeches, included the need for a holistic approach to medical treatment and an understanding of social issues that affected health; the necessity of social intervention in the health arena through legal, educational, and social welfare institutions; and the imperative of attention paid to the health and welfare of women and children, particularly in the working-classes. As she succinctly put it: "We are killing our own future citizens by the failure to have legal safeguards over their health and lives" ("Asks a Nursery Law").

Sources. Information on Hedger's work can be found in the publications and papers of the Chicago Woman's Club, Woman's City Club (Chicago), and Women's Trade Union League of Chicago, all at the CHS; a number of her articles are in the papers of the Elizabeth McCormick Memorial Fund, which are housed in the Chicago Community Trust collection, also at the CHS. A complete bibliography of her known works is available in the clipping files at the CHS. Hedger wrote more than thirty articles for the medical and social welfare literature, including "Cost of Inadequate Night School," *Addresses and Proceedings. National Education Association of the United States* (1917), and "Medical Inspection in the Schools, Its Techniques and Its Results," *Proceedings, National Conference of Social Work,* 1923. In addition, she wrote a number of small pamphlets for the Elizabeth McCormick Memorial Fund on child care, such as *The Well Baby Primer* (1919) and *The Well Child, Two to Six Years* (1926). In 1924 two pamphlets by Hedger were published by the U.S. Government Printing Office: *Milk and Health* and *Parent-Teacher Associations and Foreign-Born Women,* prepared for the Department of the Interior Bureau of Education. Martha Branscombe, *The Elizabeth McCormick Memorial Fund: The Story of Forty-five Years* (1954), is a history of the fund. Between 1910 and 1912 the *Chicago Record-Herald* published several articles on Hedger's concerns, including "Asks a Nursery Law to Safeguard Babies," January 14, 1910, and "Why Freak Styles: Women Too Busy," March 13, 1911. A brief biographical sketch is found in Chicago Medical Society, *History of Medicine and Surgery and Physicians and Surgeons of Chicago* (1922). An obituary appeared in the *CT* on July 13, 1951.

EMILY CLARK

HEFFERAN, HELEN MALEY
April 5, 1865–November 6, 1953
SCHOOL BOARD MEMBER, CLUBWOMAN, EDUCATOR

Helen Maley Hefferan was an independent, reform-minded member of the Chicago Board of Education for eighteen years in a period when machine politicians, middle-class reformers, and teachers battled for control of the Chicago schools. Labeled a "stormy petrel" (*Chicago Daily News,* November 8, 1953) by journalists, she earned a reputation for standing alone against the political corruption of the school system. Hefferan was born to Thomas E. and Sarah T. (Gibbons) Maley in Carlisle, Pennsylvania. At age three, she moved with her family to Chicago. She attended Key Elementary School and graduated from Austin High School in 1883. Two years later she completed the teacher training program at the Cook County Normal School, directed by Colonel Francis W. Parker. Parker was a pioneer of child-centered pedagogy, an innovator in the classroom, and a motivator of elementary school teachers. Apparently, Hefferan was an outstanding student of Parker's vision and techniques, for she was immediately hired at the Normal School as a training teacher. She taught there for seven years.

On June 8, 1892, Helen Maley married William Stephen Hefferan, a native of Chicago and a corporate lawyer. The couple had three children: William S. Jr., Thomas E., and Helen S. The Hefferans were active members of the Catholic Church. She was a member of the Illinois Catholic Women's Association and served as president for one term; she was also a trustee of Rosary College in River Forest, Illinois, a college for women run by the Sinsinawa Dominican sisters. Both Hefferans were also active in Democratic party politics.

Although her teaching career ended when she married, her involvement in public education did not. She gravitated toward the parent-teacher associations forming in Chicago and other urban areas, largely as a result of the kindergarten movement and its mother-training programs. Hefferan helped establish the Illinois Congress of Parents and Teachers in 1900 (later renamed the Illinois Parent Teacher Association [PTA]) and became its second president in 1902. She served four years in that position and remained on the board an additional eighteen years. Her pattern was to serve two-year terms on committees, changing to another committee after each term. She helped organize over one hundred parent-teacher groups across the state, tracked child labor legislation in the Illinois legislature, and promoted child hygiene in the schools. All her work was voluntary and at her own expense. During these years, she was awarded National and Illinois PTA life memberships.

Her links to the women's club movement were especially helpful to the Illinois PTA and later to her reform efforts in the Chicago public schools, since education was a primary concern of most women's clubs. She was active in the Chicago Woman's Club, the Woman's City Club, the Women's Democratic Club, and the Englewood Women's Club. Her skills as a parliamentarian and an organizer were evident to many, and she was often elected to executive leadership positions.

As a spokesperson of both the clubs and the PTA, Hefferan was drawn into the protracted struggle between the Chicago Teachers' Federation (CTF) and the Chicago Board of Education over the issue of the CTF's affiliation with organized labor. Since its organization in 1897, the elementary school teachers' union, led by MARGARET HALEY, had enjoyed the support of the Chicago Federation of Labor (CFL) in its battles for adequate pensions, salary increases, and better working conditions. The CTF joined the CFL in 1902, a partnership reinforced by Haley's personal friendship with CFL president John Fitzpatrick. Not all teachers were enamored with this alliance; many refused to join the CTF because of it. School board members were openly hostile. In 1915, Jacob Loeb persuaded his fellow board members to prohibit teachers from joining any organization associated with labor unions. Known as the Loeb

Rule, this action was a declaration of war against the CTF. However, Hefferan and other educational reformers sided with the teachers, objecting to the board's heavy-handed tactics. Court injunctions kept the Loeb Rule in check.

A year later, the board dismissed sixty-eight teachers, thirty-eight of whom were CTF members. All of the dismissed teachers had received excellent ratings and were given no explanation for their removal. Hefferan rallied supporters of the CTF on behalf of the dismissed teachers at a public meeting on July 17, 1916. She called upon middle-class civic organizations to back the teachers and urged the Illinois legislature to pass a tenure law for teachers. She then helped found the Public Education Association, an umbrella group representing twenty-eight civic organizations, which aimed to give trained educators greater autonomy in operating the schools.

In October 1916, the Illinois Supreme Court upheld the board's right to impose the Loeb Rule. The CTF had sustained a huge loss of membership and exhausted its reserve funds in the course of fighting the board. They had no choice but to compromise. A bill passed in the Illinois legislature in 1917 gave teachers tenure while granting the superintendent more power and a smaller, mayor-appointed board of education more control. The CTF then pulled out of the CFL and the board rehired the dismissed teachers.

Ironically, the board soon found it had a greater enemy in the mayor than in the teachers' union. Mayor William Thompson had no intention of liberating the board of education from political control and, with his allies, shamelessly turned the school system into a haven for patronage and graft. By 1923, after two terms as mayor, Thompson's blatant manipulation of the school system had made him so unpopular that he chose not to run for reelection. The Democratic mayoral candidate, William Dever, won, becoming the city's first Catholic mayor. Helen Maley Hefferan, known as a "public school Catholic" (Herrick, 235) because she enrolled her children in public rather than parochial schools, was one of eight new members Dever appointed to the school board. After Hefferan accepted Dever's appointment, she stepped down from her position as chair of the education committee of the Illinois League of Women Voters (ILWV). She continued on the ILWV's board of directors, a post she had held since the ILWV's founding in fall 1920.

When Hefferan became a school board member, the Chicago public school system had serious problems, including classroom overcrowding and poorly maintained school buildings, as well as entrenchment in the city's patronage system. One of the first actions of the new Dever-appointed board was to hire William McAndrews, an arrogant but highly qualified administrator, as superintendent of schools. McAndrews espoused greater efficiency, close supervision of teachers, extensive use of intelligence tests to track students, and the elimination of interference from politicians and teachers' unions alike.

Although Hefferan and McAndrews clashed on occasion, since each was too strong-willed to relinquish power easily to the other, Hefferan supported the new superintendent, as did Mayor Dever, who kept his hands off the schools. For McAndrews, efficiency entailed the end of teachers' councils and any role for teachers in determining education policy, goals that teachers had fought to achieve for several decades. He soon alienated himself from the CTF; Hefferan remained loyal to him and incurred the wrath of the teachers. In 1927, Mayor Dever reappointed her to the school board despite requests of the CFL to replace her. Dever's tenure as mayor was short-lived, however. In November 1927, he was defeated by former mayor William Thompson, who immediately began adding his cronies to the school board and launched an attack on Superintendent McAndrews that culminated in his dismissal in March 1928. Only Hefferan and one other board member voted in favor of re-hiring McAndrews.

Although Hefferan was heavily outnumbered on many other issues the board faced, she still exerted enormous influence through her membership on various board committees. Continuing the pattern she had followed in the first two decades of the century in her club work, she served on twenty-three different school board committees between 1923 and 1934. As one example of the influence she wielded, when she was head of the board's building construction committee in 1930, she was able to block all new construction until contractors purchased steel at lower prices.

In the early 1930s, Hefferan regained the affection of the teachers by coming to their support during the Great Depression, when they were being paid in scrip because the city was nearly bankrupt. In 1933, the board of education, now under the control of appointees of Mayor Edward Kelly, instituted emergency measures to give the teachers the back pay due them, but, at the same time, to reduce the budget severely. On July 12, 1933, in a secret session to which Hefferan was not invited, the board eliminated five million dollars from the annual budget, cut hundreds of teachers, and abolished the junior high schools, the junior college, and numerous programs for students with special needs. Hefferan immediately organized and led a protest of civic groups and teachers through a coalition known as the Citizens Schools Committee (CSC). The CSC sponsored a rally in Chicago Stadium on July 21 at which Hefferan was a featured speaker, but the protest had little effect. The board persevered and kept a tight rein on expenses during the rest of the 1930s. However, the teachers, including the new Chicago Teachers Union formed in 1937, publicly praised Hefferan as a true friend.

Hefferan continued to fight the Kelly machine when William Johnson was appointed superintendent in 1936. She alone voted against Johnson, who was eventually reprimanded by the National Association of Education and forced to resign in l946. In her view, Johnson was merely a puppet under the control of a politically oriented school board.

After serving for nearly two decades, Helen Maley Hefferan retired from the board in 1941. Following her husband's death, she moved in with her daughter and son-in-law in Hubbard Woods, Illinois, where she died after a long illness. Her funeral was conducted at Holy Name Cathedral in Chicago. Some months later, the Chicago Board of Education passed a resolution in her honor, noting, "She developed pronounced capacity for leadership and influence in her chosen field of enterprise—public school education. For it and to it she became a spokeswoman, often resolving differences, yet loving the thrill and spark of combat. She was highly respected by her contemporaries and associates for her devotion to teachers and pupils alike and for her diligence in the fulfillment of the high ideals which she professed" ("Resolution in Memoriam," 94).

Sources. Few, if any, personal papers of Hefferan are available in archival collections. *The Proceedings of the Chicago Board of Education* and the *Annual Reports of the Superintendent of Schools* are found in the Archives of the Board of Education in Chicago and provide a record of her board activities. Of particular interest is the "Resolution in Memoriam—Mrs. Helen Maley Hefferan" adopted at the July 28, 1954, regular meeting of the board of education. John Howatt's unpublished report, "Notes on the First One Hundred Years of Chicago School History," reviewing board history up to 1940, is available at CHS. The Citizens School Committee papers, also at CHS, provide some insight into Hefferan's involvement in that association. Hefferan is listed in *Who's Who in Chicago and Vicinity* (1941) together with her husband. She is mentioned frequently in Mary J. Herrick's *The Chicago Schools: A Social and Political History* (1971), the definitive history of public education in Chicago. Julia K. Wrigley's *Class Politics and the Public Schools: Chicago, 1900–1950* (1982), also refers to Hefferan in an excellent analysis of Chicago's educational politics. George S. Counts, *School and Society in Chicago* (1928), reviews the same battles but does not mention Hefferan by name. See also Lyman B. Burbank, "Chicago Public Schools and the Depression Years of 1928–1937," *Journal of Illinois State Historical Society*, Winter 1971; and Joan K. Smith, "The Thompson/Cermak School Board," *Vitae Scholastica*, vols. 3 and 4, 1984 and 1985. Lloyd Wendt, *Big Bill of Chicago* (1953), and Paul M. Green and Melvin G. Holli, eds., *The Mayors* (1987), are both helpful resources on the educational battles that Hefferan fought. Her obituary appeared in the *Chicago Daily News*, November 8, 1953.

PAUL H. HEIDEBRECHT

HENDERSON, ALICE CORBIN
April 16, 1881–July 18, 1949
EDITOR, POET, LITERARY CRITIC

Alice Corbin Henderson, associate editor of *Poetry: A Magazine of Verse*, played a critical role in the establishment of the magazine from 1912 to 1916. Born in St. Louis, Missouri, to Fillmore Mallory and Lula Hebe (Carradine) Corbin, Henderson was sent to Chicago in 1884 to live with her father's cousin, Alice Mallory Richardson, after the death of her mother of tuberculosis. In 1891, after her father's second marriage, Alice Corbin rejoined her family in Kansas and lived there until 1894, when she returned to Chicago.

She attended the University of Chicago at the urging of her high school English teacher, Harriet C. Brainard (see HARRIET MOODY), who later married poet William Vaughn Moody. In 1898, at the age of seventeen, Corbin published her first book of poetry, *Linnet Songs*, a chapbook of seventeen poems, and lived with Brainard for three years until tuberculosis forced her to move South, where Corbin attended Sophie Newcomb College in New Orleans for a year. New Orleans was the home of her mother's family, the Carradines. Corbin visited that summer with her mother's family in Ocean Springs and Biloxi, Mississippi, and worked as a book reviewer for the New Orleans *Times-Picayune*.

Returning to Chicago in 1903, Corbin wrote book reviews for the *Chicago Tribune* and *Evening Post*. She rented a study at the Academy of Fine Arts in 1904, where she met her future husband, William Penhallow Henderson, artist and teacher, later an architect, furniture designer, and builder. They married October 14, 1905, and Alice Oliver Henderson, their only child, was born January 27, 1907.

In 1908, Henderson, under her own name, Alice Corbin, published *Adam's Dream*, plays for children based on biblical stories, and *Anderson's Best Fairy Tales*, the latter illustrated with color lithographs by her husband. Using money earned from these books, the family traveled in Europe for fourteen months, from July 1910 to September 1911. Henderson published her second book of poetry, *The Spinning Woman of the Sky*, in 1912. In that same year, HARRIET MONROE asked her to be the first associate editor of *Poetry: A Magazine of Verse*, a journal which was to have a major influence in shaping modern poetry.

Both Harriet Monroe and Alice Corbin Henderson felt a fierce loyalty to *Poetry: A Magazine of Verse* and to the Chicago Renaissance and its writers. While on a trip east to visit publishers, Henderson wrote, "We've got a fresher point of view in Chicago, I believe" (October 10, 1915, *Poetry* magazine papers). Two years later the two women published an anthology, *The New Poetry*, to present that Chicago point of view, in contrast to Boston poet Amy Lowell's own anthology, *Some Imagist Poets: An Annual Anthology* (published 1915–17) and *Tendencies in Modern American Poetry* (1917), the latter critical of midwest poets.

Henderson and Monroe worked together to contact poets for submissions for the first issue. She and Monroe wrote to writers and told them to send in their poems. Henderson had formidable self-confidence in her own abilities as both a poet and critic. Henderson had met poet Ezra Pound on her earlier trip to Europe. Monroe appeared open and eager to learn from others, including Henderson and Pound, who served as *Poetry*'s foreign correspondent until 1917 and was responsible for bringing the work of T. S. Eliot and James Joyce to the journal.

While Monroe secured financial backing from Chicago's civic and social leaders, she relied on and praised Henderson in her role as "first reader" of submissions: "I could trust her to detect the keen note, the original style" (*A Poet's Life*, 286). Critic T. R. Pearce described her as Monroe's "coeditor" (*Alice Corbin Henderson*, 5). EUNICE TIETJENS, an assistant editor of *Poetry*, described Henderson's contribution in her own autobiography: "much of the attitude of the magazine towards the experimentation in new technique which was then beginning is due to her" (*The World At My Shoulder*, 24). Monroe relied strongly upon Henderson as an "assistant, critical foil, confidante, and 'sounding board'" (*A Poet's Life*, 286) and recalled her own "personal grief" at the "very serious loss to the magazine" when Henderson moved in 1916 to New Mexico, calling her an "indispensable member of *Poetry*'s staff" (318–19).

Yet Monroe did not publicly acknowledge the nature of the collaborative work that she and Henderson did in the early years of *Poetry*. In her autobiography, *A Poet's Life*, Monroe praised Henderson but minimized her major contribution to the modern poetry movement, making her almost invisible (Marek, *Illinois Writers Review*, 21). Monroe quoted from few letters from Henderson, none of her editorials, and did not discuss the differences between herself and Henderson, leaving the impression that Henderson's contributions were not particularly important. Following Ezra Pound's lead, critics portrayed Monroe

as an editor with provincial, bluestocking tastes, emphasizing instead Pound's control over the critical direction of *Poetry* and not that of the two women, Henderson and Monroe. Pound's reaction to Monroe was summed up in his 1913 comment, "You can't emasculate literature utterly" (*Selected Letters of Ezra Pound*, 18), suggesting that the female editor was attempting to control the male vitality of poetry. More recently, Ira B. Nadel, editor of Pound's letters to Henderson, described Monroe's "preoccupation with finances, editorial policy, and contributors" ("Introduction," xiv), implying her lack of concern with critical matters.

Supporters of Henderson have given her credit for the part she played in the editorial decisions of *Poetry*, but, in doing so, they have sometimes argued for her being more important than Monroe instead of looking at the nature of the women's collaboration. Witter Bynner, speaking in 1949, shortly before Henderson's death, asserted that Henderson was "co-founder" of *Poetry*; Bynner diminished the role of Monroe by relying upon a letter from Ezra Pound, who wrote: "Alice was my only comfort during that struggle [with Harriet Monroe]" (Bynner and La Farge, 42). Similarly, John Gould Fletcher noted in his 1937 autobiography, *Life is My Song*, "Without her [Henderson's] influence, Miss Monroe's paper might have been, I felt, narrower in its scope and less epoch-making in its effect" (p. 194).

Henderson certainly contributed her critical vision to *Poetry* through the eighty-five reviews and many editorials that she wrote. She also "discovered" several writers for *Poetry*, among them Sherwood Anderson, Edgar Lee Masters, and Carl Sandburg. She had a critical approach distinct from Monroe's. Her criteria had three major components: defining American poetry, judging what worked in contemporary poetry, and promoting criticism affirmed by current poetic techniques. In particular, in the magazine's pages she defended vers libre (free verse) with great enthusiasm.

In spite of Henderson's close working relationship with poet Ezra Pound, she did not perceive herself as an ally of Pound against Monroe. Her loyalty was to Monroe and to *Poetry*. She never lost sight of her goal to produce a better magazine. For example, she wrote Monroe that she was "utterly disgusted" that Pound had left *Poetry* to become the foreign correspondent for the *Little Review*: "Ezra has no sense of value," she wrote, adding it was "suicidal" to connect with the *Little Review* and that Pound was "a great idiot" (June 9, 1917, *Poetry* magazine papers).

In 1916, Henderson and her family moved to Santa Fe, where, suffering from tuberculosis, she entered a sanitarium. For several reasons, the collaboration between the two women gradually became more strained: Henderson's continuing criticism of Monroe's editorial decisions; the ongoing problem with finances that both women had; and the strains of maintaining a long-distance, working relationship between Chicago and New Mexico. Henderson continued to warn Monroe against poor style and lyrics, evidence of what she characterized as amateurism. She criticized the December 1917 issue as "not very exciting" (December 12, 1917, *Poetry* magazine papers), and she added that she had been dissatisfied with the quality of the work being published in the magazine for the last two years. In 1918, she suggested that Monroe was "surrounded by people who are willing to say the pleasant thing and the easy thing about *Poetry*, instead of the honest thing" (undated letter, *Poetry* magazine papers). In 1919, Monroe withheld a Henderson review in *Poetry*, and Henderson claimed she had been unjustly "accused of sullen backbiting" (October 13, 1919, *Poetry* magazine papers). Henderson's illness became worse in 1920 and "cut the stream of comment that had been emanating from Santa Fe since 1916" (Williams, 265).

The Monroe-Henderson collaboration came to an end in 1922 after a bitter disagreement over division of the royalties from the revised edition of *The New Poetry*. Financial security had always been a problem for both Henderson and Monroe. Monroe had struggled to keep *Poetry* going on the donations of Chicago civic leaders and to pay her contributors and editors. Henderson had been extensively involved in the preparation of the 1917 and 1923 editions of the anthology. Yet, Monroe wanted to reduce Henderson's share of the royalties from one-third to one-quarter for the revised edition. Henderson insisted Monroe adhere to the original agreement.

After a tense settlement, negotiated in part through lawyers and the publisher, Macmillan, Henderson's collaboration with Monroe ended in 1922 with her resignation as associate editor of *Poetry*. However, when it seemed that *Poetry* would fold in May 1932, before receiving a grant from Andrew Carnegie, Henderson agreed to write "reminiscences of 'Poetry,'" noting the irony of the existence of Chicago's Century of Progress Exposition at a time when *Poetry* was about to "close its doors" (May 24, 1931, *Poetry* magazine papers). Henderson noted a parallel between the dissolution of her collaboration with Monroe and the "confusion" and "de-civilization of society" (May 24, 1931, *Poetry* magazine papers) following World War I.

The metaphor of the world war captured the sense of desolation Henderson felt at the end of her ten-year collaboration with Monroe. Together, Henderson and Monroe had established *Poetry* and with it deeply influenced the modern poetry movement through the publication of free verse in the diverse works of T. S. Eliot, Ezra Pound, William Carlos Williams, and Wallace Stevens. In addition, the anthology, *The New Poetry* (1917), in its first introduction and subsequent editions (1923, 1932, 1936), continued to define modern poetry for at least fifteen years more through its use in college classes. Monroe proudly described the anthology in a 1922 letter as "the best collection of twentieth century verse" (Monroe to Estate of I. Rosenberg, Harriet Monroe Papers).

In New Mexico, Henderson continued to publish her own poetry. She also became active in work for civil rights for Native Americans, and the influence of Native American verse is present in her *Red Earth, Poems of New Mexico* (1920). The majority of poems in the book had been published earlier in *Poetry*. Henderson established the Poet's Round-up and the Writer's Edition, which published local writers and two of Henderson's own books. She published her poems under the name Alice Corbin. Her final book, *Brothers of Light*, illustrated by William Henderson, was published in 1937. William Henderson died in 1943. Alice Henderson died six years later at the age of sixty-eight of heart failure. Through her role as associate editor of *Poetry* and coeditor of the first two editions of *The New Poetry* (1917 and 1923), Alice Corbin Henderson contributed significantly to the Chicago Renaissance and influenced the shape of the modern poetry movement as critic and editor of *Poetry*.

Sources. The Alice Corbin Henderson Papers at the University of Texas–Austin contain correspondence, literary manuscripts, notes, and clippings, with most of the material dating from the 1920s and 1930s. The description of the collection has a biographical sketch. Letters from Alice Corbin Henderson are found in both the *Poetry* magazine papers and the Harriet Monroe Papers at UC Spec. Coll. Besides those mentioned above, Henderson's works include *The Turquoise Trail: An Anthology of New Mexico Poetry* (1928), *The Sun Turns West* (1933), and *A Child's Bouquet* (1935). The latter two were published by the Works Progress Administration Federal Writers Project in *Writer's Edition*; *New Mexico: A Guide to the Colorful State* (1940). Henderson published reviews and editorials in *Poetry*. For editorials, see "A Perfect Return," no. 1, 1913; "Poetic Prose and Vers Libre," no. 2, 1913; "Too Far from Paris," no. 4, 1914; "Lazy Criticism," no. 9, 1916; "Our Contemporaries," no. 3, 1914; "Our Contemporaries," no. 7, 1915; "Our Contemporaries," no. 8, 1916. Reviews include "Des Imagistes: An Anthology," no. 5, 1914; "Poetic Drama," no. 7, 1915; and "'Imagism' Secular and Esoteric," no. 11, 1918. A selection of her poetry is also included in all three editions of *The New Poetry*. Both Ellen Williams, *Harriet Monroe and the Poetry Renaissance* (1977), and Edith Wylie Miller, "Harriet Monroe: The Formative Years" (master's thesis, Stephen F. Austin State University, 1991), describe Henderson's editorial role in *Poetry*. Harriet Monroe, *A Poet's Life* (1938), and Eunice Tietjens, *The World at My Shoulder* (1938), also comment on Henderson's role. Jayne E. Marek's "'I Know Why I Say What I Do Say': Women Editors and Critics in the 'Little' Magazines, 1912–1933" (Ph.D. diss., Univ. of Wisconsin, 1991) devotes a chapter to the collaborative editorial practices of Monroe and Henderson and discusses the preparation of *The New Poetry*. For additional information on the anthology, see Craig S. Abbott, "Publishing the New Poetry: Harriet Monroe's Anthology," *Journal of Modern Literature*, March 1984. Marek discusses Henderson's articles in *Poetry* in "Alice Corbin Henderson, Harriet Monroe and *Poetry*'s Early Years," *Illinois Writers Review*, Winter 1988. Ira B. Nadel documents the extensive correspondence between Pound and Henderson in *The Letters of Ezra Pound to Alice Corbin Henderson* (1993). See also D. D. Paige, *Selected Letters of Ezra Pound* (1971). T. H. Pearce's monograph, *Alice Corbin Henderson* (1969), and "Alice Corbin: An Appreciation," ed. Witter Bynner and Oliver LaFarge, *New Mexico Quarterly Review*, vol. 19, 1949, provide biographical information.

JULIANN E. FLEENOR

HENROTIN, ELLEN MARTIN
July 6, 1847–June 29, 1922
SOCIAL AND LABOR REFORMER, CLUBWOMAN, REFORM WRITER

Ellen Martin Henrotin achieved reforms in labor, education, municipal suffrage, financial independence for women, and the eradication of vice in her leadership role in the women's club system. As a member of Chicago's upper class, she harnessed the energy and finances of her social and civic peers in Chicago, and then nationally and internationally, to improve working, educational, and financial conditions for women and children.

Ellen Martin was born in Portland, Maine, the first of six children, five daughters and one son, of Edward Byam and Sarah Ellen (Norris) Martin. When Ellen Martin was thirteen, her family inherited a house in London and another on the Isle of Wight. During their eight-year stay in London, she was educated in England, Paris, and Dresden and became fluent in French and German. In 1868 Ellen Martin's family moved to Chicago, and her father died within a year. The same year, she met Charles Henrotin, a cashier with the Merchants Loan and Trust Company. Charles Henrotin was born in 1843 and received his post–high school education in Belgium. The Henrotins married September 2, 1869, and had six children, three of whom, Adele (1874), Fortunee (1875), and Reginald (1878), died at birth or in infancy. Three children survived: Edward Clement (1871), Charles Martin (1876) and Norris Bates (1882). In 1876 Charles Henrotin succeeded his father as Belgian Consul, became the Turkish Consul in 1877, and in 1880 he founded the Chicago Stock Exchange, serving as its first president.

For nearly forty years, from the late 1870s to 1915, Ellen Henrotin's commitments and achievements in reform grew and expanded through the national women's club system, as the system itself grew and gained power. She received her early organizational, writing, and speaking experience in the Fortnightly, the Chicago Woman's Club (CWC), and the Friday Club. She joined the Fortnightly in 1874, the CWC in 1884, and helped found the Friday Club in 1887. While these organizations' primary focus was literary in the early years, she helped guide them toward reform. Her concept of the civic responsibilities of wealthy women was crystallized in a paper she gave in 1887 at Chicago's Fortnightly with her sister Kate Martin; it was published as *The Social Status of European and American Women*. They wrote about a new class of women coming forward, women who were "rich by courtesy" (p. 41) of the wealth of their husbands; and they emphasized the responsibility of those women to control the morals of society. Ellen Henrotin and other women reformers used the women's club system to advance their own moral views of financial independence for women, equal benefits and protection for poor women and children, and municipal suffrage for women.

While the Fortnightly and the Friday Club were primarily literary clubs, Henrotin and other women reformers developed the CWC into an umbrella organization from which several reform associations were founded. One of these was the Protective Agency for Women and Children, for which Henrotin served on the original governing board in 1886–87 and was treasurer in 1890. During Henrotin's tenure, the Protective Agency successfully filed court claims for wife abuse, desertion, and divorce; lobbied to raise the age of consent from ten years to fourteen years for young girls; and assisted young girls who had been seduced. Another spin-off organization from the CWC was the Kitchen-Garden Association, which Henrotin joined. Its purpose was to establish and support schools to train poor young women to be domestic servants and to educate them in modern and efficient housekeeping.

Henrotin expanded the public role of the CWC when she and other CWC members requested six months of women's educational congresses at the 1893 World's Columbian Exposition. As vice-president and acting director of the Woman's Branch of the World's Congress Auxiliary, she recruited four hundred CWC members and appointed twenty-six of them to chair thirty congresses. National and international women leaders spoke at congresses ranging from labor, government, education, suffrage, to the arts, medicine, household economics, public press, and religion.

In addition to her administrative tasks at the exposition, Henrotin gave speeches on financial independence for women at the Woman's Suffrage and Labor Congresses and at the Woman's Building. In "The Financial Independence of Women," Henrotin said that women were emerging from the home into the modern competitive labor market, making enormous sums of money and investing hundreds of millions of dollars in building and loan associations and real estate. She suggested that women had tremendous, not yet realized power, and should vote their own stock, become corporate directors, and learn to manage their own financial affairs. Her unique stance combined the concept of financial independence and responsibility for women and became a focus of her leadership of the General Federation of Women's Clubs and the Woman's Trade Union League.

In addition to women achieving power through control of their finances, Henrotin believed in the power of women's associations to accomplish reforms, a concept she crystallized in her role as acting director of the women's congresses. "Is there any abuse in the body politic to be reformed?" she asked. "At once a society is organized which conducts a propaganda, to arouse and educate public opinion on that subject.... It is the associate mind, the many hearts beating as one, that now move the world" (Henrotin, "World's Congress Auxiliary," 19, 20). She reinforced her beliefs about the power of women's association by helping to found several organizations at the 1893 women's congresses. These organizations included the National Household Economic Association, the National Council of Jewish Women, the National League of Roman Catholic Women, the International League of Lutheran Women, and the League of Superintendents of Manual Training Schools.

Her role as acting director of the 1893 women's congresses catapulted Henrotin to national fame and leadership. Her special gift as a leader was her ability to help women consolidate their own talents, energies, and finances to work collectively for reform. She spent the next fourteen years as president of some of the most powerful national and local women's reform organizations. From 1894 to 1898, she was president of the General Federation of Women's Clubs (GFWC). In agreement with the GFWC's motto "Unity in Diversity," she encouraged the formation of state federations, each of which would choose its own objective in sociology and civics. When she became president of the GFWC in 1894, it was comprised of 4 state federations, 350 individual clubs and 3 foreign clubs. By the end of her four-year tenure in 1898, there were 30 state federations and 595 independent clubs. During her presidency, the GFWC supported uniform state labor legislation, a request for a national health bureau, improvement of the state educational systems, the eight-hour working day for women, and women's business clubs committed to cooperation and self-support.

Henrotin's dedication to financial independence and responsibility for women was carried on in her presidency of the CWC (1903–1904), the Fortnightly (1904–1906), and the Women's Trade Union League (1904–1907). In 1904 at the CWC, Henrotin designed and chaired the conference "Women in Modern Industrialism," which presented papers on the economic and financial aspects of woman's status with resulting changes in her social and family relations. Again at this conference she spoke on the topic "Woman as Investor." With her friend and colleague, JANE ADDAMS, founder of Hull-House, she organized a discussion on "The Family and Financial Burdens Borne by Women." At the Fortnightly in 1905 Henrotin designed five round-table conferences on "What the World Is Doing," including topics on U.S. politics and industry.

Henrotin parlayed her local commitment to women's financial independence to a national influence in her presidency of the Women's Trade Union League from 1904 to 1907. She encouraged women to use collective bargaining "to secure a living wage, fair conditions, and in a word, the right to her share of her labor" (Henrotin, "Organizations for Women," 4). From her presidency of the GFWC to her presidency of the CWC, the Fortnightly, and the Women's Trade Union League, Henrotin drew together women socialites, trade union leaders, and workers to organize unions and lobby to legislate better working conditions. After these presidencies, Henrotin joined with Jane Addams to form a Chicago Industrial Exhibit in 1907 to show the work of women in industry. In 1910, she chaired a Citizens' Committee "Concerning Garment Workers' Strike," composed of influential social activists including Jane Addams, GRACE ABBOTT, Graham Taylor, and the Rev. Jenkin Lloyd Jones. The committee produced a report addressing the grievances of twenty-five thousand clothing employees, mainly immigrants, and the possible remedies through organization of labor and mediation with management.

Henrotin served as chair and honorary chair of several committees that lobbied unsuccessfully at the turn of the century for municipal suffrage for women. In 1909, she combined her commitment to women's fiscal power and responsibility with her support of women's municipal suffrage. Although Henrotin believed in suffrage for all women, she spoke on "The Need of a Ballot for Women with Property" at the Illinois State House of Representatives hearing on the Chicago Municipal Suffrage Bill, sponsored by the Illinois Equal Suffrage Association.

Henrotin continued her volunteerism by serving on the Board of Directors of the Park Ridge School for Girls in 1909, the Chicago Vice Commission in 1910, and the Amanda Smith Industrial School for Girls in 1916 (founded by AMANDA BERRY SMITH), all organizations devoted to helping disadvantaged girls and women. The Park Ridge School, a residence for 120 poor but not delinquent girls, gave them a public school education and trained them in household arts and gardening. Founded in 1877, the school was reorganized in 1906 by members of the CWC. Henrotin helped with finances, was honorary president of its board, and even had a garden named for her. She continued her work assisting abused girls and women as a representative of the General Federation of Women's Clubs for the Chicago Vice Commission in 1910 (one of two women out of thirty commissioners). The Commission studied prostitution in assignation houses and hotels, the relationship of saloons and prostitutes, and the efficiency of police in fighting prostitution and related crimes, and gave recommendations for methods of suppressing vice.

While an acknowledged leader in the national women's club system, Ellen Henrotin retained the traits and role of a society matron. She was praised in 1893 by Chicago's *Inter-Ocean* as a modern woman who could attend both to her home and public affairs. Many honors she received were awarded not only because of her reform contributions but courtesy of her husband's international prominence, including the Order of Chefakat in 1893 for her work at the World's Columbian Exposition, Officier de l'Académie by the French Republic in 1899, and medal of l'Ordre de Léopold in 1905 for her leadership at the 1904 St. Louis Exposition.

She fought her entire professional life for financial independence for women, but ironically became financially dependent on family and friends after her husband's death in 1914. Probate records revealed claims against the estate that far exceeded its assets. After administering Charles Henrotin's will and estate, she spent increased time with her son Edward in Cherry Plain, New York. Adoring friends approached her asking to "put a little sum in the Bank" for a woman of such "great importance in Civic and Social Matters . . . and association with every good progressive movement" (Nellie Butler Linn to Ellen Henrotin, April 29, 1914[?], papers of Maysie Henrotin). Henrotin died in her son's home in Cherry Plain in 1922 and was buried in Chicago's Rosehill Cemetery.

Henrotin's life was lived at the unique juncture of her role as a society matron and her commitment to reform. A close friend and member of the Fortnightly, summed up her finest traits in a memorial for the Fortnightly; Henrotin was "at once a great gentlewoman and a great commoner" ("The Fortnightly in Memoriam," papers of Maysie Henrotin).

Sources. The largest collection of materials about Ellen Henrotin is at the SL. This collection has two important reports from the Women's Branch of the World's Congress Auxiliary at the 1893 exposition, Henrotin's undated report, "The World's Congress Auxiliary of the World's Columbian Exposition," and more than twenty articles and speeches Ellen Henrotin wrote on reform. Two other significant collections are private: the papers of Maysie Henrotin (Glenwood, Pennsylvania) contain important genealogical materials, letters, and photographs; papers held by Phyllis Tholin (Evanston, Illinois) include documents from the 1893 World's Columbian Exposition. For information about the 1893 World's Columbian Exposition, the records of the Board of Lady Managers and especially Bertha Honoré Palmer's Papers, both at CHS, are helpful. Other notable collections are the President's Papers and issues of the *Cycle* and the *New Cycle* at the General Federation of Women's Clubs Archives in Washington, D.C. The *Minutes* of the Chicago Woman's Club are at the CHS, and the *Original Material for the Annals of the Chicago Woman's Club*, compiled by Henriette G. Frank and Amalie Jerome, vol. 1 (1876–1917), is at NL. Sources for the Fortnightly include *The Fortnightly of Chicago* by Muriel Beadle (1973) and the Fortnightly Papers at NL. The CHS also has the Agnes Nestor papers, with information about the Women's Trade Union League and the Suffrage Hearing in 1909, and the records of the Kitchen-Garden Association and the Protective Agency of Women and Children. The Jane Addams Papers at UIC Spec. Coll. contain records of organizations on whose boards both Addams and Henrotin participated. Henrotin reported on the Women's Trade Union League in "Organizations for Women," *Official Report, Woman's Trade Union League of America* (1905–1906). Henrotin and Kate Byam Martin wrote and published a paper, *The Social Status of European and American Women* (1887). Other sources include the report of the 1910 Vice Commission, *The Social Evil in Chicago* (1911); May Wright Sewall, ed., *The World's Congress of Representative Women* (1894); and a biography in *NAW* (1971).

ANN E. FELDMAN

HENRY, ALICE
March 21, 1857–February 14, 1943

JOURNALIST, SUFFRAGIST, LABOR REFORMER

Alice Henry was born in Melbourne, Victoria, Australia, when it was changing from a fledgling settlement to a prosperous city. The young girl grew to maturity along with the British colony. Her father, Charles Ferguson Henry, an accountant with Andrew and Walter Ferguson's importing firm, and her mother, Margaret Walker, a seamstress, had emigrated from Glasgow, Scotland, in 1852 as part of the gold rush and were married in the Congregational Church in Melbourne in June 1853. Alice Henry was their first surviving infant, followed by a younger brother, Alfred, in 1859. She was raised a Presbyterian but in adult life was more actively associated with Unitarianism. In later life Henry attributed her political idealism and commitment to her Scots ancestry and her youth spent in colonial Australia.

The gold discoveries at first brought increased population and a new prosperity to the colonies, but the impact of the American Civil War, which disrupted the cotton industry in England and closed the Ferguson importing firm, forced Charles Henry out of his job. He took the opportunity to try some farming and moved the family to a small section of land in a heavily forested area about fifty miles outside Melbourne. Like many pioneer settlers, they lived in a small bark hut with bare earth floors. Here the young Alice Henry lived without the restrictions imposed on girls in the city; she read boys' adventure stories and chased wild turkeys through the bush. The bush life was not a great success for her parents, however. Charles and Margaret Henry had always lived in the city and had no farming experience. After only three years, they moved back to their old Melbourne neighborhood and, for Alice Henry, to the greater confinements of city life.

Schooling began in earnest for nine-year-old Alice and seven-year-old Alfred. Their first lessons had been given to them by their mother, but now they were able to attend a local school and take advantage of the thriving cultural life. Already the colony had a university, an opera house, two daily newspapers, a museum, and a splendid library. At first the children had private tutoring with a governess. They "completed their primary schooling in a common school in North Melbourne" (Kirkby, 15), but since the colony did not yet have a state system of secondary schooling, Henry's secondary education was arranged privately, first with a tutor, then at an Educational Institute for Ladies run by the colony's former Inspector-General of schools, Richard Hale Budd, an enthusiast of the English public school system for boys. Budd established his girls' school along the same lines and was, therefore, a leader in providing Australian girls with the academic education they needed to attend university. Henry was one of his first pupils, at a time when women were just being allowed to sit for the university entrance but ten years before they were actually permitted to enroll. Like many young women at the time, she sat for the exams at the same time as her younger brother. Scottish families had a long tradition of valuing education for both their sons and their daughters, but in the colony it was often only when the boys were preparing to take an examination that the girls were given the same opportunity. In 1874, the year that Henry took the exam, 391 male stu-

dents and 67 female students took it. She was the only female candidate to pass with credit; now qualified to enter the university, Henry desired to study medicine at the University of Melbourne, but she was "denied university attendance because she was female" though "it is doubtful that her family's pecuniary circumstances would have enabled her to attend in any case" (Kirkby, 24).

Henry was faced not only with financial limitations; her mother suffered from breast cancer and died when Henry was nineteen. Unhappy teaching at Richard Hale Budd's college for governesses and privately, and having to carry the domestic responsibilities for her father and brother, Henry turned to writing.

From 1884 until her departure from the colony in 1905, Henry was a regular contributor to newspapers both in Australia and in England. Beginning with contributions to the Domestic Economy Column of the *Australasian*, a weekly newspaper, Henry first contributed "occasional articles, society reporting, and . . . recipes" (Kirkby, 25–26). She rapidly moved to writing on topics of social concern. She also wrote for Reverend Strong's reform paper, the *Australian Herald*. Her family had been a powerful influence on her politically. Imbued with a passionate commitment to democratic ideals and political debate from companionship with her father, influenced by the attitudes of her mother's circle of friends on women's capacity for physical and intellectual achievement, Henry now, in the early 1880s, involved herself in the burgeoning reform movement and the campaign for woman suffrage.

The first suffrage organizations were formed in the various Australian colonies at the time Henry was beginning her career as a journalist. By 1894, one state and the neighboring colony of New Zealand had granted women the vote, and when the new constitution for the Commonwealth of Australia was written at the end of the 1890s, woman suffrage (for white women) was granted federally. The campaign continued at the state level until final victory was won in 1908. Henry was an active campaigner. Her newspaper articles, however, could not reflect her political views because she was employed by the conservative press. She was forced, therefore, like so many other women journalists, to publish under a (usually male) pseudonym. Henry used A.L.F., her brother's initials. Nevertheless, she managed to build up a reputation as one of the most able women in the colony and as a courageous public speaker for social change. After twenty years, Henry felt keenly the lack of freedom and opportunity to pursue her talents and political commitments in Australia. She believed sisterhood was international; thus, in 1905 she left to try her luck overseas.

The Charity Organization Society, as well as Henry's close friend Catherine Helen Spence, contributed funds for Henry's travel overseas. Like Henry, Spence was a reformer, suffragist, and journalist. Since 1893, when Henry had introduced herself to Spence in Melbourne, the two women had developed a close friendship and professional alliance. Spence shared her knowledge of the opportunities for women in journalism and editing in the United States, and this information influenced Henry's decision to travel to the United States.

Henry first traveled to England in the summer of 1905 and remained there for six months, meeting the leaders of the more militant branch of the British suffrage movement, Christabel Pankhurst and Annie Kenney of the Women's Social and Political Union. Henry arrived in New York City with letters of introduction to Anna Garlin Spencer of the New York settlement house, Susan B. Anthony, JANE ADDAMS, and Chicago journalist and progressive Henry Demarest Lloyd and his family. One month after her arrival in the states in 1906, Henry attended the annual convention of the National American Woman Suffrage Association (NAWSA) in Baltimore, Maryland, where she spoke on the same platform as Susan B. Anthony, addressing the convention on Australian woman suffrage achievements. Addams invited Henry to come to Chicago.

For several months, Henry lived at Hull-House; it was there, in 1907, that she met MARGARET DREIER ROBINS, who invited her to become office secretary in the Chicago branch of the Women's Trade Union League (WTUL). Henry worked for the WTUL for the next twenty years, campaigning for woman suffrage, women's trade union organization, and most particularly, for industrial legislation limiting the hours and guaranteeing minimum wages to women workers. Her international connections and journalistic experience were valuable to the work of the WTUL. From 1908 to 1910, Henry was the editor for the Women's Department of the Chicago labor monthly, the *Union Labor Advocate*. During this time, the Women's Department of the Chicago labor monthly served as the official publication of the national WTUL. In 1910, to reach a larger and more socially diverse audience, the WTUL decided to publish its own journal, *Life and Labor*. The first issue appeared in January 1911 with Henry as editor. She remained editor until 1915, and the position brought her international recognition. *Life and Labor* was a major publication in its time and a brave effort at feminist publishing. Though it perished on the rock of financial insufficiency, it stands today as a source of invaluable insight into feminist labor reform and the work of the WTUL. Editing it was a high point in Henry's career as a journalist, but it was also a painful time for the clash it brought with WTUL president Margaret Dreier Robins, who provided much of the money to keep the journal afloat and who then exerted considerable pressure on the staff to do things her way. Henry advocated "vocational education to provide working-class women with skilled jobs and hence greater economic independence" (Kirkby, 119); Robins "had a more romanticized view of a woman's place" (p. 119), and "she perceived labor reform in moral and social terms which were at odds with . . . Henry's secular liberalism and moderate socialism" (p. 119).

All this time, Henry was actively campaigning for woman suffrage, urging American audiences to learn from the tactics employed by Australian and English women and get the organized labor movement on their side. She was thus in the vanguard of a new American approach to the suffrage struggle; she joined the Political Equality League of Self-Supporting Women in Chicago, which advocated the adoption of the more militant tactics of English suffragists. She was president of the West Side Equal Suffrage Association of Chicago and chair, with Emma Steghagen as vice-chair, of the Industrial Committee of the Illinois Equal Suffrage Association. Henry lectured at the Chicago Woman's Club and the Political Equality Union and was a member of the executive board of the Chicago WTUL, which

petitioned the Industrial Commission of Illinois and the Illinois General Assembly for an eight-hour day for women workers. In 1910, with other WTUL members, she was active on the picket line outside the Hart, Schaffner and Marx factories during the big strike of garment workers. Henry wrote constantly on the need for labor legislation; she advocated the involvement of the state as the third party in labor relations between employers and workers. She argued for the simultaneous union organization of women workers and was critical of male trade unionists who did not take women workers seriously.

In Chicago, Henry found employment that combined her feminist political ideals with her career aspirations. She enjoyed the greater opportunities for travel and the greater recognition she could receive, and she formed very close friendships with other women in the WTUL, including AGNES NESTOR; Emma Steghagen; ELISABETH CHRISTMAN, who described Henry as "a rare person and a beloved friend" (quoted in Kirkby, 224); MARY ANDERSON; Emma Pischel; Editha Phelps; and Isabel Newsham, who later helped Henry in her declining years in Melbourne. The WTUL provided an emotionally supportive atmosphere of female bonding, deliberately encouraging close friendships and good times to counteract conflicts across different class, ethnic, and generational backgrounds. Some of these friendships were sexual but apparently not for Henry. After Henry died, Mary Dreier wrote in the WTUL's *Life and Labor Bulletin* (the newsletter distributed after *Life and Labor* ended publication), "She was so completely selfless that her personal life was absorbed in her work and service for women who toil, and this had become her very existence" (quoted in Kirkby, 93). Henry never married. She worked closely with other Chicago reformers, including Louis and Alice Thacher Post, Paul Kellogg, and later Secretary of Labor Frances Perkins, who wrote to Isabel Newsham that Henry's work "was always not only an education to me but an inspiration" (quoted in Kirkby, 224). Henry admired Jane Addams greatly and was friends for many years with historian Mary Ritter Beard and Chicago realtor Frances Bird (who would be executor of her will). Her closest companion for her first ten years in Chicago was her fellow Australian and coeditor, Stella Franklin. Together they became good friends with William and LOLA MAVERICK LLOYD, at whose home in Winnetka, Illinois, they spent many weekends.

On resigning from the editorship of *Life and Labor* in March 1915, Alice Henry continued working for the WTUL as a lecturer; she wrote two books, *The Trade Union Woman* (1915) and *Women and the Labor Movement* (1923), today regarded as classic studies of labor history. From 1920 to 1923 she worked as a secretary of the WTUL's educational department, directing the WTUL's Training School for labor organizers in conjunction with the Young Women's Christian Association, the Chicago Federation of Labor, and the Chicago School of Civics and Philanthropy (now the School of Social Service Administration at the University of Chicago). This education program was the most successful of the WTUL's programs for social change.

Declining health and increasing age forced her retirement from the WTUL in 1924 and, after a world trip including a return visit to Australia, Henry lived in Chicago only another two years. In 1928 she moved to the warmth of California, and in 1933, in the midst of the Great Depression, she returned to Australia to live out her final years with more financial security and once again to be close to her brother. She died peacefully in her sleep in a Melbourne nursing home on St. Valentine's Day, one month short of her eighty-sixth birthday.

Alice Henry devoted her life to elevating the status of women. She lived according to her own aspirations and never lost sight of a collective identification with other women. Feminism and professionalism fueled her demands for change. She brought to her work in Chicago an understanding of the internationalism and interconnectedness of the woman suffrage and labor reform movements. She was an international feminist.

Sources. Alice Henry's papers are held in the National Library of Australia, Canberra, and in the Mitchell Library, Sydney, Australia, although they are sparse and contain very little of a personal nature. Her "Memoirs," in typescript, are available at several libraries in the U.S., including the CHS. Other valuable collections are the Margaret Dreier Robins Papers, Univ. of Florida; the official records of the National Women's Trade Union League, Library of Congress and SL; the Agnes Nestor Papers, CHS; the Chicago Women's Trade Union League Papers, UIC Spec. Coll.; and the Stella Franklin Papers, Mitchell Library, Sydney. The major biographical work is Diane Kirkby, *Alice Henry: The Power of Pen and Voice* (1991).

DIANE KIRKBY

HERRICK, GENEVIEVE FORBES
May 21, 1894–December 17, 1962
JOURNALIST, PUBLICIST, WRITER

Genevieve Forbes Herrick was one of the leading so-called "girl reporters" of the 1920s and 1930s, when the image of the reporter was at the height of its glamour. Her stories appeared regularly and prominently on the front pages of the *Chicago Tribune.*

One of three children, Genevieve Forbes was born in Chicago to Carolyn D. (Gee) Forbes and Frank G. Forbes, a salesman, later the owner of a tailor shop on Chicago's West Side. She graduated from Lake View (now Lakeview) High School and, in 1916, received an A.B. from Northwestern University, "where she was the first woman editor-in-chief of the *Daily Northwestern*" (Steiner and Gray, 9). The following year she received a master's degree in English from the University of Chicago.

After teaching high school in southern Illinois for one year, in 1918 Forbes returned to Chicago, where she became assistant to the exchange editor of the *Chicago Tribune.* She later attributed her opportunities in part to the fact that many male reporters were either serving in the war effort or were otherwise uninterested in low-status journalism jobs. In any case, she quickly climbed the *Tribune* hierarchy. She created a sensation in the fall of 1921 with a thirteen-part front page exposé of the United States immigration service. Forbes had posed as an Irish immigrant, traveling steerage class to New York, and her ensuing series effectively documented harassment and brutality by Ellis Island officials. Her articles spurred an official investigation by the U.S. House Committee on Immigration and Naturalization.

Forbes soon became known for crisp, lively articles on Chicago crime and criminals. While she was covering the Leopold and Loeb murder trial in 1924, she met her future husband, John Origen Herrick, another *Tribune* reporter who was also following the high-profile trial. Herrick was the son of a prominent Chicago doctor. They married that year. Genevieve Herrick's almost daily reportage on the trial managed to transform the various parties involved into fully developed characters worthy of a novel. At the same time, she guided her readers through the thicket of legal and psychiatric terminology used by both prosecution and defense. "In this case, the question was whether defense attorney Clarence Darrow would be able to persuade the judge that the confessed killers [privileged and well-educated] should not be sentenced to death on account of mitigating psychiatric 'factors'" (Steiner and Gray, 10).

Herrick was the first reporter to interview Al Capone after his 1930 release from prison. As had other career criminals she interviewed over the years, Capone tried to manipulate Herrick, but she was not intimidated. She also interviewed the wives and girlfriends of several of the most notorious denizens of Chicago's underworld. Unflappable and cool, Herrick let her subjects speak for themselves. Instead of moralizing or editorializing, she let her readers make their own judgments. Herrick, who criticized women for using "adjectives too freely" (quoted in La Rue, 20), followed the advice she gave others: "For a tingling style, use strong verbs" (p. 20).

Herrick covered a range of topics for the *Tribune* in the same ironic, modern, vernacular style she used for crime. Her forte seemed to be politics, both Chicago and national, as well as the intersection of politics with society. She took particular interest in the status and ambitions of women candidates and women officeholders. Herrick paid attention to women who refused to run as part of a woman's bloc. On the other hand, as Herrick noted, even these women recognized that their own success or lack thereof had a certain significance for and to women. For example, Herrick wrote a series of articles about RUTH HANNA McCORMICK, who was elected to a Chicago-area seat in the U.S. House of Representatives in 1928. Herrick admired the political savvy, intelligence, and toughness she found in women like McCormick. Herrick emphasized McCormick's disdain for the typical flowery clichés about women's responsibilities as housekeepers for Uncle Sam. Conversely, Herrick deftly applied her sense of irony in stories about incompetent female politicians. She let them skewer themselves through their own colorful, if not ridiculous quotes, just as she had with the gangster molls who had once talked to her so freely.

In 1930, the Herricks moved to Washington, D.C., where Herrick, known to her friends and to readers as "Geno," enjoyed being at the center of action and power while reporting for the Washington bureau of the *Tribune.* She covered a number of political events and was particularly adept in exposing the emerging evidence of government fraud, stupidity, and waste. Herrick, a genuinely friendly person able to socialize with diverse people, published a shrewd twelve-part sociological study on the struggle of newcomers to penetrate Washington's inner circle of power and status.

Herrick continued to write about women in politics. Several articles about conventions of the Republican and Democratic parties addressed whether the two parties either marginalized or included women. She also dealt with how women's organizations stood on various issues and how movements across the political spectrum treated women. In covering the National Woman's Party, which sponsored the original Equal Rights Amendment in 1923, for example, Herrick explained both the advantages and disadvantages of protective legislation for women, which critics of ERA feared would become unconstitutional, should the amendment pass. Her discussions of the movement to repeal the Eighteenth (Prohibition) Amendment noted that women's organizations on both sides of the fence claimed the "unanimous support of 'right-thinking women'" (Steiner and Gray, 12).

An attractive woman who dressed fashionably, Herrick regularly described the appearance and clothing of her subjects. These brief, passing references were not intended as routine fashion notes. Herrick once complained to some women reporters that "the woman's angle in journalism has become hopelessly enmeshed in silk and chiffon" (quoted in Steiner and Gray, 12). Her own writing instead made the point that women could manage to reject feminine ploys and dress plainly and efficiently. She also pointed out that women should not be dismissed, their intelligence underestimated, merely because they wore stereotypically pretty clothes.

Herrick enthusiastically covered Eleanor Roosevelt's press conferences during Franklin Delano Roosevelt's presidency. She approved of Eleanor Roosevelt's policy to keep her sessions off-limits to men as a way of giving women journalists "a new deal" at the same time Roosevelt generated some positive publicity for herself and for the president. The headline for Herrick's September 10, 1933, *Tribune* story declared the position of Herrick and her colleagues: "Girl Reporters Get New Status in Washington. Mrs. Roosevelt's Press Conferences Help the Women Scoop the News." Herrick and the others in the inner circle of the women's press corps in Washington came to form a congenial sorority. They socialized with each other and with the First Lady. Sometimes they even covered up some of her public relations gaffes.

Despite Herrick's popularity with readers and despite the fact that her approach to White House events was not unusual, Herrick's uncritical coverage of New Deal policies did not sit well with the *Tribune's* vehemently anti-Roosevelt publisher, Colonel Robert R. McCormick. Herrick left the *Tribune* in 1934 after McCormick criticized her as being too close to Eleanor Roosevelt. Herrick bitterly disputed McCormick's reproach and insisted that she was an individual as well as a reporter. At the same time she quit the weekly radio show on Washington social life and political gossip that she had been doing on the *Tribune*-owned station, WGN, for three years. Her husband John resigned his editorial position with the *Tribune* soon after and took a job with the U.S. Department of the Interior. Herrick grew closer to Eleanor Roosevelt after her resignation; they exchanged gifts, letters, and information. Herrick later wrote speeches and other materials for members of the Democratic administration.

Meanwhile, Herrick's resignation gave her the opportunity to try some other kinds of writing, including short stories. She published a handful of fictional pieces in magazines. Herrick wrote a column for the *New York Daily News* and for the North American Newspaper Alliance, a national syndication service. Her freelance articles, often about politics, appeared in several magazines, including *Collier's, Redbook,* and the *Independent Woman.* Between 1935 and 1942 she published a monthly column, "Women in the News," in *Country Gentleman.*

The *Tribune* frequently published accounts of her subsequent exploits. Nonetheless, she never attained the same degree of success and fame she had enjoyed as a reporter at the *Tribune.* More significantly, freelancing was not as profitable as Herrick had hoped; it did not pay as well as staff writing. Moreover, freed from the pressure of the deadline, Herrick found procrastination too easy. Compounding Herrick's post-resignation trauma and financial difficulties were significant health problems. In 1935, Herrick was seriously injured in a car accident while accompanying her friend ANNA ICKES on a tour of New Mexico. Ickes, wife of the Secretary of the Interior Harold Ickes, died in that accident. In 1938, Herrick was diagnosed with breast cancer. She did her best to ignore the cancer and hide her condition from others, but the surgery and radiation treatment left her anxious and permanently weakened.

Herrick also maintained a commitment to the cause of professional women. Herrick was a loyal and emotionally generous friend to several women writers. She was president of the Women's National Press Club from 1933 to 1935, helped found the Alliance of Business and Professional Women, and was active in Theta Sigma Phi, a journalism society.

Herrick was not involved in the feminist organizations of her day, and she generally accepted the notion of gender-specific spheres. "Women journalists will not write *the* war stories. To say so would be foolishly feministic" ("The Newspaper Woman Joins Up," 126), she stated in describing how World War II opened journalistic opportunities for women. While Herrick asserted that women reporters' sphere of coverage had broadened proportionately "as the arc of woman's sphere out in the world widened" ("Women in the News," April 1937, 50) she did not go so far as to claim that women reporters possessed authority, status, or skills equal to men's. But she understood the importance of taking women's issues seriously. Herrick explained in her April 1937 column for the *Country Gentlemen,* "Today, many a woman competent to write about anything she pleases, pleases to write about women" ("Women in the News," 50).

During World War II, Herrick undertook a number of government jobs writing public relations material for several agencies, including the U.S. Treasury Department, the Women's Army Corps (WAC), and the Office of War Information. After she completed a tour of WAC facilities in Europe in 1946 as a publicity consultant, Genevieve and John Herrick moved back to his family's summer home in Dorset, Vermont, where she resumed her freelance writing, and John tried a career in theater. The Herricks, who had no children, did not succeed there financially. She often was barely able to afford stamps for sending off her manuscripts. Always an intensely self-critical person, Herrick questioned her own talents and abilities. She berated herself when she felt she was not working hard enough and became "more deeply and depressingly convinced than ever" (quoted in Steiner and Gray, 14) that she wrote badly.

Through the 1950s, several newswriting textbooks, career counseling books and pamphlets, and public relations materials for the *Chicago Tribune*, where she published her best work, not only quoted her articles and her advice to would-be reporters, but also highlighted her accomplishments in a highly competitive field. For example, the *Matrix*, a publication for women journalists, and several textbooks quoted her suggestion that women write from a woman's viewpoint but with a man's pen point.

In 1951, the Herricks moved to New Mexico, where Herrick did public relations work and a little feature writing. John Herrick worked for a newspaper chain there until his death from lung cancer in 1955. Despite a second mastectomy in 1952, Genevieve Forbes Herrick died of cancer in Santa Fe, New Mexico, ten years later. An Episcopalian, she was buried in Arlington National Cemetery.

Ishbel Ross, a well-known front-page reporter for the *New York Herald Tribune*, succinctly summed up Herrick's career in her *Ladies of the Press:* "[Herrick's] talent was evident at once. She skyrocketed to fame in journalistic circles because of her clear and sparkling style, her vivid ways of finding the right phrase, her instinct for handling news" (p. 539). Ever modest, Herrick wrote in her diary that she was "mournful" (quoted in Steiner and Gray, 15, note 3) to read Ross's glowing description of her success. Nonetheless, while professional journalists today would not approve of the intimacy that emerged between Eleanor Roosevelt and the women who covered her, Herrick was a highly regarded model for the modern journalist. Herrick's intelligent accounts, untainted by sentimentality, pretension, or moralizing, were applauded by both her Chicago readers and her colleagues. She not only taught readers new ways to think about the emerging role of women in politics, she encouraged women journalists to see themselves and their work in new ways.

Sources. Genevieve Herrick's correspondence with Eleanor Roosevelt is in the Eleanor Roosevelt Papers at the Franklin D. Roosevelt Library, Hyde Park, New York. Herrick's articles include "Women in the News," *Country Gentlemen*, April 1937; "The Newspaper Woman Joins Up," in *Journalism in Wartime*, ed. Frank Luther Mott (1943). In addition to her newspaper and magazine articles, Genevieve and John Herrick published a fairly superficial biography, *The Life of William Jennings Bryan* (1925). Books referring to Herrick include Ishbel Ross, *Ladies of the Press* (1936); Lloyd Wendt, *Chicago Tribune: The Rise of a Great American Newspaper* (1979); Bess Furman, *Washington Byline: The Story of a Washington Hostess* (1937); John J. McPhaul, *Deadlines and Monkeyshines: The Fabled Work of Chicago Journalism* (1962); Marion Marzolf, *Up from the Footnote: A History of Women Journalists* (1977); and Maurine Beasley, *Eleanor Roosevelt and the Media: A Public Quest for Self-Fulfillment* (1987). Arlene La Rue, "Use Strong Verbs," *Matrix*, December 1933, discusses Herrick. A more complete account of Herrick is "Genevieve Forbes Herrick: A Front-Page Reporter 'Pleased to Write about Women,'" by Linda Steiner and Susanne Gray, *Journalism History*, Spring 1985.

LINDA STEINER

HERRICK, MARY JOSEPHINE
September 25, 1895–October 12, 1984
TEACHER, WRITER, UNION LEADER, CIVIL RIGHTS ACTIVIST

Mary Josephine Herrick's belief in grassroots democracy and self-reliance may be traced in part to her religious heritage. She was born to Horace Nelson and Mary Addie (Musick) Herrick in Eureka, Illinois, the third of five children. Mary Herrick's parents were staunch members of the Christian Church (Disciples of Christ), a liberal Protestant denomination that stressed egalitarianism and invited individual interpretation of the Bible. Horace Herrick and Mary Addie Musick met at Eureka College, Eureka, Illinois, a school founded by the Disciples of Christ. Herrick and Musick received B.A. degrees in 1886 and 1889, respectively. After completing additional degrees at Harvard University and Eureka, Horace Herrick taught mathematics and classical languages for several years at Eureka, and there he and Mary Addie Musick were married in 1890. The Herrick family moved to Chicago when Mary Herrick was two years old.

Young Mary Herrick learned about the critical problems of race and ethnicity in Chicago's public schools by closely observing her father's career, first as a high school teacher and later as an elementary school principal. From him she began to see the relationship between City Hall and the Chicago Board of Education and the role politics played in educational matters. As principal of Drummond Elementary School (1909–17), which was situated in a solidly Polish neighborhood, Horace Herrick learned Polish so that he could communicate with his students and their parents and interpret for them, if necessary, in the courts. He visited the homes of students and brought them to his own home on Saturdays. Above all, he attempted to convince immigrant parents of the importance of keeping their children in school. His example had a great impact on Mary Herrick's own sense of vocation and purpose. Later, as a teacher, she took an interest in her students inside and outside the classroom.

In 1912, Mary Herrick graduated first in her class at Chicago's Lake View (now Lakeview) High School. She received a B.A. degree from Northwestern University in 1916, majoring in English with minors in German, Latin, and Greek. An excellent student, she was elected to Phi Beta Kappa. Although she had great respect for a career in teaching, Mary Herrick was also awakened to social justice issues. She worked for the Young Women's Christian Association's (YWCA) campus division in Ohio and then returned to Chicago as the director of a church settlement on the city's West Side, sponsored by the First Methodist Church of Evanston and Northwestern University (1919–22).

In 1922 Herrick was hired to teach at her alma mater, Lake View High School, where she taught English. While at Lake View, Herrick joined the Federation of Women High School Teachers (FWHST). This move brought her in contact and sympathy with unionism in general, prompting her to join the Women's Trade Union League (WTUL) of Illinois, where she served as vice-president from 1926 to 1930.

Still vacillating in her career choice, in 1926 she quit classroom teaching and accepted a job with the YWCA, directing the Girl Reserves program in twenty-five Chicago high schools. Two years later, in 1928, she moved to the South Side, enrolled as a graduate student in the political science department at the University of Chicago, and took a teaching position in 1929 at Wendell Phillips High School. By the time Mary Herrick arrived, the Wendell Phillips building housed both segregated and overcrowded black junior high and senior high schools. Herrick also continued to participate in the Joint Committee on Public School Affairs, a group she had joined in 1926.

Mary Herrick soon developed friendships with two University of Chicago political science professors, Charles Merriam,

FIG. 51. *Educator and school reformer Mary Herrick speaks at the Labor Conference on Civil Rights; seated are Morris Bialis and David Feller.*

who was also an alderman from the Hyde Park neighborhood, and Paul Douglas, whose political career would eventually include terms as alderman, U.S. Congressman, and U.S. Senator. Douglas and Merriam were activist-academicians, deeply involved in both the theory and practice of American politics and government. Elected as reformers in opposition to Chicago-style patronage politics and the reigning political machine, they encouraged their students to do research about, and participate in, city politics. Her choice of research topic for her master's thesis, "Negro Employees of the Chicago Board of Education," demonstrated her understanding of the political and social context in which educational policy was made. Herrick's painstakingly gathered data on African Americans employed by the Chicago Board of Education identified the segregated employment patterns of Chicago's school system. Herrick explained the workings of the system, describing how political patronage, civil service, and socioeconomic forces contributed to the patterns of employee segregation. Herrick was granted the M.A. in 1931, early in the Great Depression. Herrick left Wendell Phillips in 1935 to become one of the original faculty members of the newly opened Jean Baptiste Pointe Du Sable High School, built on the South Side to house an all African American student body.

These were years of deep economic struggle, as Chicago and the nation dealt with the Great Depression. Chicago teachers retained their jobs but received substantial cuts in salary: from March 1930 to September 1934, teachers' pay was reduced by 11 percent. In addition, pay checks were often issued late, and frequently in the form of "scrip" bearing the words "Not Sufficient Funds," which creditors redeemed at only 70 percent of

face value. Herrick was responsible for the partial support of several family members since her widowed mother lived with her—as did her sister Grace and Grace's family—and was personally affected by these cuts.

In her capacity as chair of the Cook County Federation of Women's Clubs' education committee and as a member of the FWHST, Herrick was a strong voice, demanding that the Chicago Board of Education provide adequate teachers' salaries during this period. Keeping a careful watch on the school budget, Herrick challenged the school board's repeated claim that successive budget cuts were necessary to keep the schools open. Herrick contended that Chicago's schoolteachers were forced to make far more sacrifices than any other Chicago public employees during the depression and that Chicago teachers' pay cuts were greater than those of teachers in comparable urban systems. These "enforced loans" were the savings that kept the schools open in Chicago, not budgetary cuts, the board claimed.

In 1933, when the Chicago Board of Education voted drastic cuts in curriculum and services to schools, Herrick vowed to fight against City Hall/Board of Education collusion, which, she charged, favored bankers over school children. As the new president of the Federation of Women High School Teachers of Chicago, and also the group's liaison to the state legislature in Springfield, Herrick helped organize a mass rally of twenty-seven thousand teachers, parents, and concerned citizens held at the Chicago Stadium to protest the drastic curtailments. The same year, to wage this protest, Herrick helped organize a Save Our Schools (SOS) Committee, which soon became the Citizens Schools Committee (CSC).

Mary Herrick's role as a union leader grew in the 1930s, when she headed the Joint Board of Teachers Unions, a coalition that forged the Chicago Teachers Union in 1937. Two years later she became a board member of the Illinois State Federation of Teachers. Herrick already had a national profile among teachers, serving as vice-president of the American Federation of Teachers from 1935 to 1940.

Classroom teaching continued to be the central focus of Herrick's professional work. She set out to empower her students to work for social justice for themselves, their families, and the African American community. She set high academic standards and organized the classroom into small groups so that students could work cooperatively and democratically. Her curriculum included newspapers, research materials, and government reports that enabled students to evaluate current events locally and internationally. She promoted citizenship among her students and encouraged them to see their own social and political conditions in the context of world politics.

Herrick was concerned to develop relevant curriculum to teach students not only facts but also a method for learning about themselves, the institutions of government in a free society, and current issues at home and across the human experience internationally. As a teacher at Lake View High School, she had developed a core curriculum in English literature and social science. In 1929–30 she had worked as a research assistant for the Chicago Public School Advisory Committee to Study Civic Education, and in 1949, while still a classroom teacher at Du Sable High School, Herrick, working with the curriculum department of the Chicago Board of Education, transformed the traditional twelfth grade civics curriculum into an American social problems course. She was an officer and board member of the Chicago and Illinois Councils on Social Studies (1940–54).

During the post–World War II decades, Herrick accelerated her work in the field of race relations. Church and civic groups demanded greater cultural understanding among races, religions, and ethnicities as they attempted to make sense of a world that had almost been destroyed by deep-rooted racism, anti-Semitism, and ethnic hatreds. At home in the United States, returning African American veterans faced job and housing discrimination; their children continued to attend overcrowded, segregated schools in Chicago and elsewhere. Herrick became a member of the Illinois Human Relations Commission in 1946 and 1947. It had been created to deal with prejudice and discrimination. One of the institutions most resistant to change was the Chicago public school system. In 1950, when school Superintendent Herrold Hunt appointed Herrick to the position of Director of Human Relations for the Chicago Public Schools, the board of education rejected her nomination. Herrick continued to work for integration and improved race relations. She was a member of the Chicago Public Schools Staff Committee on Human Relations from 1950 to 1954.

In her own classroom Herrick implemented programs to facilitate conversation across the boundaries of race. She arranged for exchange visits at Du Sable High School with groups from all-white schools. Historian Sterling Stuckey, a student of Herrick, remembered a series of exchanges with Senn High School students. "For white and Black," he reflected, "it was our first meaningful contact across the color line" (transcript, "A Tribute to Mary J. Herrick"). Herrick gave students "the sense of the largeness of the world, the necessity to prepare oneself to be at home in it" (transcript, "A Tribute to Mary J. Herrick"). During these exchanges, students debated social issues and then visited over refreshments. Herrick regularly invited her students to her home for tea and encouraged them to borrow books from her library. John H. Johnson, president of Johnson Publishing Company, was one of those she invited. "She was the first white person who ever invited me to their home as a guest" (transcript, "A Tribute to Mary J. Herrick").

Herrick developed a strong mentor relationship with many of her students, including Harold Washington, the first African American mayor of Chicago (1983–87). Washington said that Herrick had stimulated more minds than any other teacher he had ever known. Among her former students were other prominent African Americans, including Alice Blair, a former deputy superintendent of the Chicago public schools, and businessman-author Dempsey Travis.

Herrick took a two-year leave of absence from her classroom responsibilities (1956–58) to be the Director of National Research for the American Federation of Teachers (AFT). She again served as AFT vice-president from 1958 to 1962.

Herrick's retirement from classroom teaching in 1961 began a new stage in her life as an educator. As assistant to the Dean of Students at Roosevelt University, Chicago, from 1961 to 1964, she counseled students. By this date the civil rights movement had turned the nation's attention to the race issues that Herrick and other activists had pioneered in addressing. President Lyndon B. Johnson's Great Society programs provided funds for community development and job training, both priorities in the struggle for equal rights and employment opportunities that Herrick had long regarded as a necessary foundation to combat prejudice and discrimination in the United States. Herrick was on the staff of three Vista Training groups (1964–65) under the National Federation of Settlements, and she participated in President Johnson's Conference on Education in 1965. That year she became a research assistant on the Havighurst-McCaul Project on Society and Education in Chicago at the University of Chicago (1965–68) and also studied community schools as a participant in the National Federation of Settlements' report on community organizations. The report had been prepared for Senator Paul Douglas's Commission on Urban Problems and was printed by the government and then published separately by the federation. During the next two years, Herrick worked on her major book, *Chicago Schools: A Political and Social History* (1971), considered by many to be the definitive study of the Chicago school system. Herrick traced the roots of the contemporary crisis in education to the ways in which corrupt politics had subverted the goals of education, but she did not let educational experts and the administrative bureaucracy off the hook in assessing reasons for failure.

At age seventy-six, Herrick turned her attention to the subject of aging. In 1972 she found a new challenge at Loop College (now Harold Washington College), one of the city colleges of Chicago, as a discussion group leader in the continuing education department. She led these discussion groups for older people for ten years, serving up heady sessions on social issues and on the history and politics of Chicago. With a federal Title

IV Grant for Training for Involvement of the Elderly in Community Service, Herrick designed a volunteer tutoring program at Loop College, where retired teachers tutored first-year students in math and writing skills. With a grant from the Illinois Council on the Humanities and the Chicago Community Trust (1978–79), Herrick directed volunteer programs for older citizens in Chicago's branch libraries. In the early 1980s Mary Herrick continued to teach Loop College classes to seniors on issues germane to aging. She was a member of the Mayor's Office for Senior Citizens Education Committee (1974–80), the Illinois State Council on Aging (1973–76, 1976–79), and the Chicago Advisory Council on Senior Citizens Safety Program (1977).

Herrick's health problems had become serious. Battling crippling arthritis and osteoporosis, she finished clearing home files and organizing archival materials and moved into an apartment on the residential floor of the Bowman Geriatric Center of Rush Presbyterian Hospital. That same year she attended her third and last White House Conference, this one on aging. She had attended the White House Conference on Youth in 1950 and the Conference on Children and Youth in 1960. Still, she continued to teach at Loop College until June 1983.

Early in 1984, friends from University Church planned a tribute to her. Former Du Sable students flocked to University Church Sunday afternoon, April 29, 1984, to honor their teacher. Music, laughter, and eloquent words from Mayor Harold Washington and others filled the gothic sanctuary. Deputy Superintendent of the Chicago Public Schools Alice Blair, who grew up in poverty on Chicago's South Side, said that Herrick "constantly made me believe that I was worthwhile, that I could achieve, and I could make a contribution not only to my family but to my race" (transcript, "A Tribute to Mary J. Herrick").

That day, from her wheelchair, Mary Herrick delivered her last civics lesson to a hushed audience. She died six months later at age eighty-nine. Following a service that celebrated her life, family and friends walked outside into University Church's memorial garden, where two nieces buried her ashes and planted a rose bush as the gathered group sang "Life Is a Gift."

Mary Herrick's awards were many, including one from the University of Chicago Alumni Association for Civic Service (1953) and, perhaps her favorite, from the Du Sable Alumni Association (1961). Herrick's most important book, *Chicago Schools: A Political and Social History*, relates her understanding of the common threads that linked schools to society, education to citizenship, individual rights to democratic community.

Sources. Mary Herrick's papers are in the Citizens Schools Committee records, CHS, and include personal papers and letters, journal articles, and radio speeches. The Young Women's Christian Association Papers, UIC Spec. Coll., have material on Herrick from 1926 to 1928. Herrick correspondence and files on continuing education, aging, and related subjects, are at Harold Washington College. Several uncataloged documents, including some of Herrick's lesson plans, can be found in the Department of Education Records, UC Spec. Coll. The Mary Herrick Collection at the Walter Reuther Library of Labor and Urban Affairs, Wayne State Univ., covers her American Federation of Teachers' activities. Materials on Herrick, sisters Helen and Grace, and brother George can be found at the Northwestern Univ. Archives. Tapes and transcripts of "A

Tribute to Mary J. Herrick," April 29, 1984, are at University Church in Chicago. Herrick's publications include "High School Education in Chicago," *School Review*, October 1934; *Education for Citizenship* (1935); *Government in Chicago* (1935); *Discipline, What for and How?* (1947); *Rise of Community Schools* (1967); and *Chicago Schools: A Political and Social History* (1971).

MAY SWEET LORD

HERSKOVITS, FRANCES SHAPIRO
October 21, 1897–May 4, 1972
ANTHROPOLOGIST, AUTHOR

Frances Shapiro Herskovits's contributions to the study of Africa and African American history came at a time when there was little scholarship on Africa in the United States. As chief collaborator, research associate, and coauthor with her husband Melville Jean Herskovits, she is considered by many Africanists to be one of the early leaders of African and African American studies in the United States. Their anthropological interests included music, art, economics, psychology, theory, and application of anthropology to practical affairs.

Frances Shapiro was born the youngest of three daughters to Max and Gertrude Shapiro in Minsk, Russia. She later emigrated to the United States with her family at the age of eight, living in New York City. She received her education there and as a young adult helped with her family's household expenses by working in a number of capacities, including as a legal secretary.

In the early 1920s, when New York was an important center of anthropological activity, Shapiro attended classes at the New School for Social Research and graduate seminars in anthropology at Columbia University. Her fellow students included Margaret Mead, Ruth Benedict, Elsie Clews Parsons, A. I. Hallowell, Malcolm Willey, and her future husband, Melville Jean Herskovits.

In 1923, the year Melville Herskovits received a Ph.D. from Columbia University under the guidance of Franz Boas, Frances Shapiro traveled to Italy to write a largely autobiographical "great American novel." During her stay she received word from Melville Herskovits to meet him in Paris, where he was studying as part of a grant from the National Research Council Board of Biological Science. As the family lore later described, Melville Herskovits was waiting there with a marriage license in hand and an "offer she could not refuse" (interview with Jean Herskovits). They married in Paris on July 12, 1924.

Throughout the rest of their married lives, Frances and Melville Herskovits were a professional team, and anthropology was their lifelong passion. Melville Herskovits remained a fellow of the National Research Council Board of Biological Science until 1926. They lived in New York City until 1927 in what Margaret Mead described later as an "attractive and bohemian apartment near Columbia" (quoted in Simpson, 3). He lectured at Columbia from 1924 to 1927, and in 1925 worked as an assistant professor of anthropology at Howard University.

The Herskovitses moved to Evanston, Illinois, in 1927, when he was appointed assistant professor of sociology at Northwestern University. Their early years at Northwestern were remembered as a hard time for them professionally. Funding for the study of Africans and African Americans was difficult to obtain, and they were the sole anthropologists working in an academically conservative environment.

Field research, conducted throughout their careers as anthropologists, contributed greatly to their ideas regarding African history and the African diaspora. Their first field study, sponsored by Franz Boas and accompanied by Morton Kahn, was conducted in South America in Dutch Guiana (now Surinam) in two phases, in 1928 and 1929. The fact that Frances Herskovits was an integral part of the team did not escape the attention of the media, and on her second trip to Dutch Guiana she was described in the June 16, 1929, *New York Times* as "probably . . . the first white woman to travel to the head of Surinam River." They divided the work, with Frances Herskovits responsible for obtaining data pertaining to women's work as well as information on various aspects of ritual, art, and other major activities. From this initial field research, Frances and Melville Herskovits coauthored two books, *Suriname [sic] Folk-lore* (1936) and *Rebel Destiny* (1971), as well as a number of articles. Commenting on their writing style, Margaret Mead noted that "*[Rebel Destiny]* was a magnificently written book, and showed no internal signs of such a unique form of authorship" (quoted in Simpson, 9).

Although their early African work had focused on the diaspora, their interests soon included Africa itself, and they became two of the first American anthropologists to conduct fieldwork there. In 1931, an initial grant from Elsie Clews Parsons, a prominent folklorist and their old classmate in New York City, financed a trip to Dahomey (now Benin). Further financial support was obtained with the assistance of Franz Boas. The research utilized their knowledge of French, Portuguese, and African languages. During this early work, as well as all the field research to follow, they made extensive use of the participant observation method. Although this expedition to West Africa was based in Dahomey, it included additional work in the Gold Coast (now Ghana) and Nigeria. From this study Frances Herskovits published two articles on Dahomean song poems and together they wrote *Dahomean Narrative* (1958). Although Frances Herskovits contributed greatly to *An Outline of Dahomean Religious Belief* (1933) and *Dahomey: An Ancient West African Kingdom* (1939) as well, she never accepted the title of coauthor unless she could declare that 50 percent of the work was hers.

In her introduction to *The New World Negro* (1966), written by Melville Herskovits and edited after his death by Frances Herskovits, she described how their field experience in Surinam had a profound influence on their thinking and findings. The Dahomean expedition had an equally strong impact on their ideas of and concepts around acculturation. Their interest in the African diaspora in the West continued with trips to Haiti (1934), Trinidad (1939), and Brazil (1942). The results of this research can be found in their many published articles and books, including their coauthored *Trinidad Village* (1947) and *Life in a Haitian Valley* (1937), written by Melville Herskovits.

Throughout their years at Northwestern University, Frances Herskovits's title remained colleague, research associate, and coauthor. Melville Herskovits became an associate professor in 1931, professor in 1935, and was the creator and first chairman of the Department of Anthropology in 1938. Frances Herskovits

was a key participant in seminars and assisted in the training of graduate students who were preparing for the field. According to their daughter, Jean Herskovits, the two cannot be discussed independently, and short of grading student papers, Frances Herskovits contributed to every aspect of their work.

Born in 1935, Jean Herskovits described domestic life as loving, happy, and cooperative. The evening meal was family time and conversation was stimulating. Frances Herskovits prioritized her daughter's well-being over their research, and Melville Herskovits supported that decision. He tried to arrange publication of Frances Herskovits's early novel, written in Italy. Unfortunately, the manuscript remained unpublished and was later burned by Frances Herskovits. Throughout their working lives he persistently insisted that she accept credit publicly for their work. Their daughter described her mother as intensely loyal, fiercely protective, and as the "mother tigress" (interview) who could be counted on to stand up for those she especially cared about, namely Melville and Jean Herskovits. During World War II, when Melville Herskovits commuted by train to Washington, D.C., to work for the government, Frances Herskovits managed to fill the void of his absences by continuing their lifework and by fulfilling the roles of both mother and father to their only daughter.

The Herskovitses' attention returned to Africa after World War II, with visits for field research in 1953, 1954, 1955, 1957, and 1962. In 1948 he was appointed director of the Program of African Studies at Northwestern, and later, in 1961, to the position of chair, the first of its kind in the United States. Through both his energy and hers, the Department of Anthropology and the Program of African Studies at Northwestern attained international recognition for outstanding scholarship.

Though they were secular in their Judaism, the Herskovitses were well aware of the effects anti-Semitism had on his professional career. Frances openly objected to what she perceived as the lack of recognition his work received due to anti-Semitic sentiments. She criticized the exclusion of Melville Herskovits's contribution to a Wenner-Gren Foundation Conference that resulted in the book *Anthropology Today*, edited by Alfred Kroeber. They both never doubted that he would have been welcomed for a tenured position by any of the Ivy League schools at the time, given his credentials, had it not been for anti-Semitism.

After Melville Herskovits's death in 1963, Frances Herskovits continued her work in African studies. In 1964 she assisted a young Nigerian researcher, Felicia Ekejiuba (Ph.D., Harvard), now on the faculty of the University of Nigeria, Nsukka, in her field research in Nigeria. After Herskovits's return to Evanston, she edited some previously unpublished work, including *Cultural Relativism: Perspectives in Cultural Pluralism*, published in 1972 soon after her death, with Frances Herskovits as editor and Melville Herskovits as author. She was particularly interested in African literature and studied the progress of modern African writing in English and French. From 1963 to 1966 she taught African literature at Northwestern in the Department of English and the Program of African Studies. She died of a heart attack in Evanston, Illinois, at the age of seventy-four.

The Herskovitses were a team whose life work cannot be discussed in singular terms. As their daughter, Jean Herskovits, described their collaborative research, "It was the work that mattered, rather than who received the credit" (interview). The shared effort was recognized in 1996 by the establishment of a Melville J. and Frances S. Herskovits Endowed Book Fund at Northwestern University. Their work continues to be pertinent. In 1998 Northwestern University Press republished *Dahomean Narrative* and the university mounted a major exhibit, *Living Tradition in Africa and the Americas: The World of Melville J. and Frances S. Herskovits.*

Sources. Frances and Melville Herskovits left behind many papers that document their work during a period of rapid growth of both anthropology and African studies. Professional and personal correspondence and manuscripts of publications make up the bulk of the papers that are part of the Africana collection in Northwestern University's library. The Herskovits Library of African Studies, named in his honor, is one of the most varied and comprehensive African collections in the United States. Frances Herskovits's articles, which include translated poems, are "Dahomean Songs," *Poetry*, 1934; "To Destiny: Warrior's Song: Poems from Dahomey," *Theater Arts Monthly*, May 1935. Much information was provided by Jean Herskovits, professor of history at State University of New York at Purchase, in an interview with Leslie Ashbaugh, December 27, 1995. One published biography, *Melville J. Herskovits* (1973) by George Eaton Simpson, briefly credits the contributions of Frances Herskovits. The relationship of wives of anthropologists to their husbands' scholarship and reputations is discussed in Groupe d'Étude et de Réflexion Théoriques sur les Recherches Universitaires et les Diplômes d'État, "Postface à quelque préfaces," *Cahiers d'études africaines*, vol. 17, 1977. The existence of anti-Semitism in academe is documented in Peter Novick, *That Noble Dream: The "Objectivity Question" and the American Historical Profession* (1988). Newspaper articles on Frances Herskovits include "Will Again Visit Negroes of Bush," *NYT*, June 16, 1929, and obituaries in the *NYT*, May 5, 1972, and the *Evanston Review*, May 11, 1972.

LESLIE ANN ASHBAUGH

HERSTEIN, LILLIAN
April 12, 1886–August 9, 1983

TEACHER, LABOR LEADER, POLITICAL ACTIVIST

Lillian Herstein, a Chicago school teacher best known for her social activism and service to the labor movement, was born in Chicago. Her parents emigrated from Russian-controlled Lithuania to the United States shortly after the American Civil War, following the common pattern of father coming first to work and then sending for his wife and child. Herstein was the youngest of six children, five of them born in the United States. Her father, Wolf Herstein, was sexton of one of the early synagogues in Chicago and proprietor of a Hebrew bookstore. The family supplemented his income by selling homemade wine and sweets for Jewish holidays. When Lillian Herstein was twelve, her father died from a heart attack and her mother took over his business to support the family.

All the Herstein children went to work at the age of fourteen to help support the family except Lillian. As the youngest child she was able to remain in school, and after graduating from Joseph Medill High School, she received financial aid from an uncle and two older brothers, which enabled her to attend Northwestern University, Evanston, Illinois, where she majored in Greek and Latin. She was one of only three Jewish students in residence at the time. During summer vacations she earned money working at Sears Roebuck Company. Following gradua-

tion she had a series of teaching jobs, first in 1908 at Franklin Grove, Illinois, where her teaching abilities were recognized by the president of the school board of this small-town school district. When she left, he wrote, "The board is sorry to lose Miss Herstein's services and have nothing but the best wishes for her. . . . She is particularly strong in English and history, and is the peer of any teacher we have had for the past twelve years as an instructor in German and Latin" (F. M. Banker, Letter of Recommendation, July 6, 1909, Herstein Papers). She then taught in Mt. Vernon, Indiana, where again, her teaching was appreciated. Herstein's goal, however, was to teach in a Chicago school. She left Mt. Vernon in spring 1911 to take a substitute teaching position at Lane Technical High School for Boys and then a full time job teaching English at Wendell Phillips High School. There she joined her first union, the High School Teachers Club. When the male teachers all subsequently resigned to form an exclusively male union, the women formed a Federation of Women High School Teachers. Herstein was always active in the affairs of her own union, the Federation of Women High School Teachers, beginning with her support of the sixty-eight teachers who were fired in 1916 for joining the union and who were out of work for a year before being restored to their jobs. Herstein changed jobs again to teach at Crane Technical High School on Chicago's West Side and from that position was promoted to teach English at Crane Junior College. She remained in the Chicago junior college system for the remainder of her teaching career. During summer vacations she worked for the Bureau of Personal Service, a legal aid service for poor Jewish immigrants.

Herstein had first become interested in the labor movement through the experiences of her older sister, Gusta, who worked as a sales clerk for the Mandel Brothers retail store and then for Marshall Field's department store. Gusta Herstein, who worked the traditional twelve hour day—with no opportunity to sit down even during a lull in business—became involved with the Chicago branch of the Women's Trade Union League (WTUL). She knew all the Chicago leaders. Lillian Herstein also joined the WTUL. The WTUL sent her to the Chicago Federation of Labor's (CFL) executive board to announce the classes the women's union was providing for workers. Herstein was elected to the CFL executive board, where she was the only woman member for the next twenty-five years. She developed a deep friendship with John Fitzpatrick, CFL president. From this association she began a lifetime of service to the labor movement as a teacher and speaker.

Under the presidency of AGNES NESTOR, the WTUL provided workers' classes in labor history, parliamentary law, and English. Herstein frequently taught WTUL night classes. She was first approached to help organize women workers in the International Ladies' Garment Workers' Union (ILGWU), but soon became a popular spokesperson for unions all over the state, including that of the miners in southern Illinois. During the 1919 steel strike she spoke on behalf of the union-organizing drive in Peoria, Joliet, and South Chicago, urging strikers' wives to bring their children with them to plead with scabs not to take their husbands' jobs and to discourage their husbands from engaging in violent resistance.

Herstein's WTUL involvement increased in the 1920s as she campaigned for child labor legislation in Indiana and Illinois. In

FIG. 52. *Labor leader Lillian Herstein, on the right, with immigrants' and children's rights advocate Grace Abbott; International Labor Organization, Geneva, Switzerland, 1939.*

1922 she represented the Chicago Federation of Labor at the state federation convention where she spoke strongly in support of a resolution to call a conference to consider amalgamating craft unions into industrial unions. She also joined the Women's International League for Peace and Freedom, founded by JANE ADDAMS, and attended an international convention in Mexico, where she introduced progressive Catholic Father Frederick J. Siedenburg, founder of the School of Social Work, Loyola University Chicago, as the main speaker.

Herstein's initial involvement with the CFL and the WTUL was at a time when labor organizing and trade union policy had an expansive, comprehensive approach including workers' education and third party politics. She represented the more progressive, Left forces in the unions affiliated with the American Federation of Labor (AFL), whose leadership following Samuel Gompers attempted to chart a centrist role for American skilled labor. In Chicago, John Fitzpatrick, president of the Chicago Federation of Labor, actively worked with progressives and socialists and, in 1919, ran for mayor of the city of Chicago on the Labor Party ticket. Lillian Herstein joined the Labor Party and in 1920 was part of a new coalition, the Farmer-Labor Party, of former members of the Progressive Party, trade unionists, and radical farmers' groups. That year Herstein addressed local unions and urged them to send delegates to the Farmer-Labor Party convention, where she served on the credentials committee. She ran on the new Farmer-Labor ticket for trustee of the Metropolitan Sanitary District and for State Superintendent of Education in 1922, but neither campaign was successful. Although her father had been a staunch Republican, based on his feelings for Abraham Lincoln and that party's role in ending slavery, Herstein had a strong affinity for the Socialist Party, in large part because of her labor experiences. Although she never

joined that party, she was a lifelong sympathizer, and its members were generally supportive of her. The Farmer-Labor Party drew little support from mainstream Chicago labor, with the exception of local unions from the Amalgamated Clothing Workers, the International Ladies' Garment Workers, and the Railroad Brotherhoods. In 1924 the struggling Farmer-Labor Party joined Robert La Follette's Progressive Party. Herstein was a major speaker for fund-raising events.

Herstein's WTUL work centered largely on the special education provided for working women. In the 1920s, the WTUL sponsored four women workers a year to attend their Chicago Trade Union College and enroll in classes on labor problems and trade unionism. Herstein supported those efforts teaching night classes in English and public speaking while still teaching a full schedule of courses in the Chicago junior college system. One of the trainees in the WTUL classes was Fania Cohn, who later became educational director of the ILGWU. Ultimately Herstein taught at the famous Bryn Mawr School for Women Workers in Industry founded by M. Carey Thomas, formerly dean and then president of Bryn Mawr. Scholarships, and in some cases missed wages, were provided to the women workers by the WTUL, and local college girls served as special tutors. During the third summer of the Chicago school's existence, Herstein taught students with language handicaps and, in 1934, she served as a director of the school.

Herstein continued to be active in the Progressive Party. In 1932, with the country in the throes of the Great Depression, Herstein supported Norman Thomas, the Socialist Party candidate for president, and ran for Congress from Illinois's 2nd District on the Progressive Party ticket, the coalition of Farmer-Labor Party and Progressives. Emily Taft Douglas headed Herstein's campaign committee. Herstein campaigned for unemployment insurance, old age pensions, full protection for bank depositors, and the abolition of war.

By 1936 the New Deal programs convinced Herstein to support President Franklin D. Roosevelt. She not only voted for him in 1936, she also directed the speakers bureau of labor's Non Partisan League, an organization formed to help Roosevelt win re-election. Herstein taught for two summers at the school for labor education at the University of Chicago sponsored by the Works Progress Administration. She met with Eleanor Roosevelt and others to plan the program. One of her outstanding pupils there was Hal Gibson, who later became a prominent leader of the Teamsters Union in St. Louis, Missouri.

During the 1930s Herstein battled to save the programs she had helped to initiate in the Chicago junior college system. Depression-era shortages hurt all levels of public education at the very time when Herstein believed the schools had to accept expanded civic responsibilities. Herstein used her connections to both the labor and the academic communities in Chicago to enrich the experiences of junior college students. The list of guest lecturers for 1935–36 included Rabbi Louis Mann, dynamic leader of Chicago Sinai Congregation; Professor James Taft Hatfield, Department of Economics, Northwestern University; KATHLEEN BLACKSHEAR and HELEN GARDNER, artists and professors of art and art history at the School of the Art Institute of Chicago; BERTHA JAQUES, etcher and lithographer; Glenn Dillard Gunn, Chicago Conservatory of Music; social scientists and professors Robert Redfield (husband of MARGARET PARK REDFIELD) and Louis Wirth of the University of Chicago; and anthropologist Melville J. Herskovits (husband of FRANCES HERSKOVITS) of Northwestern.

In 1937, Herstein was appointed a member of the U.S. delegation to the International Labor Organization (ILO) connected with the League of Nations. The U.S. government was allowed two delegates, one to represent business and one to represent labor. Bob Walt from the Painters Union was the union delegate, and Herstein was chosen to be one of his technical advisors on child labor legislation. While abroad, she also attended the international teachers convention in Paris.

During the 1930s, Herstein remained consistent in her principles; she did not conform entirely to either the CFL's "party line" or that espoused by Democratic Party politicians, even though she supported some aspects of both organizations. Herstein remained a progressive and agreed with some of the positions and unions affiliated with the Congress of Industrial Organizations (CIO). She liked the New Deal but resisted political party bossism. Herstein's long friendship with CFL President John Fitzpatrick was strained in 1938 when he refused to seat an appointee from the Evanston (Illinois) Teachers' Union on the CFL because the man had supported the American Newspaper Guild, which had joined the CIO. Herstein, who was assisting the Guild's organizing drive, went directly to William Green, president of the AFL, to try to get him to persuade Fitzpatrick to back down. Although they continued to differ about the value of the CIO, Fitzpatrick remained loyal to Herstein and supported her against Chicago Mayor Edward Kelly. Herstein opposed the mayor's continued pressure on teachers to buy tickets to a Democratic Party benefit. Although the proceeds were supposed to be used by the mayor to distribute food baskets to the poor, since

distribution was through his precinct organization, Herstein opposed "relief" based on the patronage system.

Herstein backed Fitzpatrick and the CFL when the new Chicago Teachers Union was formed in 1937. During the Great Depression, Chicago teachers were being paid in tax anticipation warrants, which they could cash for only three-quarters of their value. To gain greater solidarity and strength to combat such policies, a new union, the Chicago Teachers Union, was formed to unite the various existing unions. John Fitzpatrick praised "the militant Chicago women teachers who blazed the path for the new organization" (quoted in *Chicago Evening American*, October 29, 1937) and Herstein. A dispute developed over whether the new union should affiliate with the AFL or the new CIO. Herstein, in this case, supported the AFL because the city federation had supported their organizing efforts. (Also, at that time no city-wide CIO council was in existence.) She told the audience, "in the thirty years of our [teachers' union] affiliation with labor in all the vicissitudes through which the Chicago schools have gone . . . , we teachers have had the unwavering support of the Chicago Federation of Labor and the Illinois State Federation of labor" (*Chicago Evening American*, October 29, 1937).

Herstein also challenged the AFL's discriminatory policies toward African Americans. In 1940, Herstein attended the national AFL convention as a delegate of the CFL. Having assisted A. Philip Randolph in organizing the Chicago Brotherhood of Sleeping Car Porters by speaking at mass rallies in the 1920s and 1930s, she was prepared to support him at the convention in a battle to force the AFL's Brotherhood of Railway Clerks, a white-dominated union, to admit Blacks as full members, not auxiliary members with no voting rights. The issue, unfortunately, was referred to the AFL's Executive Board and never came up for discussion on the floor.

In 1942 the lectures established by Herstein for the junior colleges were abolished, ostensibly for budgetary reasons; but Hull-House director Charlotte Carr and academics from the University of Illinois, including Dean Thomas E. Benner, College of Education, questioned the motivation behind the move. Herstein was perceived as a socially minded liberal who told her students it was legitimate to ask questions and think critically about their society. As war hysteria and, later, cold war politics raised concerns about patriotism, it became increasingly difficult to maintain budgets for liberal arts programs that could be labeled unnecessary for basic education. Herstein was then appointed director of Defense Activities for the Chicago City Colleges but remained in that job only twelve days. Soon, however, her talents as organizer, educator, and labor leader would be called upon for the national war effort.

With America's entrance into World War II, Lillian Herstein was appointed the woman's consultant for the War Production Board. The board had nine vice-presidents, two of them from labor. Joe Keenan, the AFL vice-president, was responsible for her appointment to that position in 1942. Her job was to advise the board on child care and problems of absenteeism among women workers in war industries. She was sent to Los Angeles, California, where the Lockheed, Vega, Douglas, and North American plants and large shipyards all had women workers. Herstein worked with federal public housing personnel to help the women obtain decent housing, persuaded the corporations to provide in-plant food services, and attempted to have transportation to the plants improved. A major requirement for women workers was adequate child care. Congress had passed the Lanham Act that provided grants for child care to communities with war plants. Since there were traditional biases in many areas against public funding of child care, Herstein sometimes had to pressure communities to apply for these grants. She also fought to keep the mother's daily fee per child at fifty cents a day. By the end of the war, she was responsible for overseeing conditions of women workers in war industries on the entire West Coast.

Back in Chicago in 1945, Lillian Herstein continued to teach English in the Chicago junior colleges until her retirement in 1951. While she was still teaching, she "accepted a part-time job with the Jewish Labor Committee (JLC), which was organized about the time that Hitler . . . [rose to] power and had as its main activity rescuing Jewish and other labor leaders in Europe" (Herstein to Jennie, July 25, 1951, Herstein Papers). In retirement, Herstein worked full time for the JLC. The JLC fought discrimination in America, not only anti-Semitism, but racism as well, and spent money and lobbying efforts to pass "Fair Employment Practice legislation, [to work] for better housing, and [to promote] . . . equality in educational opportunity" (Herstein to Jennie, July 25, 1951). In the 1950s she considered problems facing minorities and racism against American Blacks the major injustice that had to be confronted. The JCL also opposed many of the restrictions of the McCarran Act passed in 1951 over the veto of President Harry S. Truman. Part of the anti-Left politics of the cold war, the act required the registration of communist and communist-front organizations.

In the 1950s Herstein became an advocate of programs in the schools designed to break down prejudice and discrimination. She worked with the Human Relations Committee of the Chicago Public Schools and participated frequently in conferences that focused on the concept of intercultural education, which she hoped would be integrated into the curriculum of the public schools on all levels from kindergarten through the junior college level. "Formerly our education often reflected the racial, religious and class prejudices that had crept into American thinking or else these subjects were avoided so that generations of American children grew up either with the prejudices of their elders or in complete ignorance of the problems involved in so diverse a population as we have in America," she wrote in an article for *Federation News*, September 3, 1951. The new curriculum made her hopeful. "Children will learn that there is nothing sacred or desirable in uniformity. They will learn . . . to enjoy diversity and to realize that the unity of America is enriched by the diversity of its population and not endangered" (September 3, 1951). In 1953 Herstein received the Thomas H. Wright Memorial Achievement Citation for her work in human relations, awarded by the Mayor's Commission on Human Relations.

She continued to teach classes for local unions, including an American history series for the Ladies Auxiliary of the Brotherhood of Sleeping Car Porters founded by HALENA WILSON. She wrote for the AFL-CIO *Federation News* and participated in local politics, campaigning for Adlai Stevenson at the national level and for anti-machine reformer Leon Despres for alderman. Despres was part of an independent political move-

ment eager to end the stranglehold that the patronage-ridden, status quo Democratic Party exerted on municipal politics in Chicago. In the 1960s, she opposed the labor movement's support of the Vietnam War.

At the end of her life Herstein was able to rethink her ideas about women and their dual role in society as breadwinners and homemakers. Reviewing *Woman at Work* (1951), the autobiography of labor leader MARY ANDERSON, Herstein was appreciative of the former U.S. Women's Bureau chief's understanding that women, like men, worked because they had to make a living. She also liked Anderson's realistic approach to the discrimination suffered by women from all groups of men, even men in the labor movement. Anderson, like Herstein, did not consider herself a feminist and refused to pursue sterile and unrealistic fights for women's rights. Herstein and Anderson were part of the generation of women trade unionists and social reformers who rejected the initial efforts to pass an Equal Rights Amendment (ERA) in the 1920s through 1940s. They feared that the hard-won protections for working women would be lost if the amendment were ratified. In the 1970s in a different context, however, Herstein supported the ERA.

Herstein never married and was always close to her family, living at times with a sister and niece. She died at age ninety-seven, after spending her final years in the Drexel Nursing Home, Chicago. There her last remaining sister had died before her.

Lillian Herstein's lifelong activism was broad in scope, and she worked with a wide spectrum of public figures, many of whom became her friends and honored her work with a testimonial dinner May 25, 1951, when she retired from teaching. Friends from the trade union movement, including MOLLIE LEVITAS and ELISABETH CHRISTMAN, reflected her commitment to women's rights as workers. Roger Baldwin, STELLA COUNSELBAUM, ANNETTA DIECKMANN, and Homer A. Jack were colleagues who shared Herstein's concern for improved human relations among all people. Mayor Martin Kennelley, Governor Adlai Stevenson, Congressional Representative Sidney R. Yates, and Socialist Party leader Norman Thomas were all listed as sponsors of the dinner to honor Herstein. Leon Despres chaired the event, which was attended by a wide array of people, including Senator Paul H. Douglas, who was the principal speaker; William A. Lee, president of the Chicago Federation of Labor; and Arthur J. Goldberg, who spoke on behalf of the CIO (and had been Lillian Herstein's student when he attended Crane Junior College on Chicago's West Side). As a champion of workers' rights, women's rights, and human rights, Lillian Herstein influenced the fields of education, labor reform, and trade unionism.

Sources. A transcript of a twelve-hour autobiographical interview of Lillian Herstein by Elizabeth Balanoff, January 15, 1971, is available in the Balanoff Oral History Collection, Center for New Deal Studies, Roosevelt Univ., Chicago. The interview is jointly owned by Roosevelt Univ. and the 20th Century Trade Union Woman Oral History Project at the Univ. of Michigan, Ann Arbor, Michigan. The Lillian Herstein Papers, CHS, include speeches, articles, clippings, and various published items of Herstein that relate to her teaching career and activities as a union leader with the Women's Trade Union League of Chicago. Articles by Herstein include "The Significance of the Southern School for Women

Workers in the Workers' Education Movement," *American Teacher*, January 1931. Articles about Herstein's activities in labor and education appear in *Chicago Evening American*, October 29, 1937; *Chicago Sun*, October 25, 1945; and *Chicago Daily News*, May 9, 1951, June 9, 1951, June 13, 1951, June 29, 1951. Lester E. Engelbrecht, "Lillian Herstein, Teacher and Activist," *Labor's Heritage*, April 1989, is based on an interview with Leon Despres.

ELIZABETH BALANOFF

HILL, ELIZABETH WEBB. *See* GARNETT BUTLER TALLEY, ISABELLA MAUDE

HILLMAN, BESSIE ABRAMOWITZ
May 15, 1889(?)–December 23, 1970
TRADE UNION ORGANIZER AND ACTIVIST

Bessie Abramowitz Hillman's career exemplified women's lifelong contributions to the American labor movement. She not only organized workers in the garment industry but also facilitated the entry of women into male-dominated unions.

She was born in Linoveh, a village outside of Grodno in Belarus (Belorussia), to Emanuel and Sarah (Rabinowitz) Abramowitz. The Abramowitzes named their fourth daughter Bas Sheva. Her father was a commission agent, and the family rented extra rooms to boarders. Eventually the Abramowitz family included eight girls and two boys, all educated at home by a private tutor. In 1905, to avoid being married off by a local marriage broker, fifteen-year-old Bas Sheva emigrated to the United States with two cousins. Renamed "Bessie" by an immigration official upon arrival, Abramowitz went immediately to Chicago to live with relatives who owned a boarding house.

Although she lived most of her life in New York, her early years in Chicago determined her life's work. She enrolled in night school at Hull-House and became a naturalized citizen in 1913. Like thousands of other young Eastern European Jewish immigrants, she quickly found work in the men's garment industry as a button sewer. One of the city's major employers, the clothing industry was notorious for its harsh working conditions. Abramowitz was paid the meager wage of two and one-half cents per coat, which amounted to three dollars for a sixty-hour week. When in 1908 her foreman deliberately altered the figures on her work sheet to reflect a lower rate per coat, Abramowitz organized a group of workers to protest to management. As a result of her activism she was fired and blacklisted. Forced to work outside of Chicago until the incident was forgotten, Abramowitz returned within the year and was employed under an assumed name at Hart, Schaffner and Marx (HSM), one of Chicago's largest men's clothing manufacturers.

On September 22, 1910, Hannah Shapiro, Bessie Abramowitz, and several other girls laid down their scissors, picked up their hats, and walked away from their jobs at HSM Shop Number 5 on Halsted Street, refusing to accept another wage reduction. This spontaneous protest amused male workers in the shop, who hesitated to join the young inexperienced women. Recounting the incident at a union convention years later, Abramowitz quipped, "It is not always the men who lead the women. It was a mighty hard struggle for those eight girls to pull out the men" (*Proceedings of the Thirteenth ACWA Convention*, 566). Thus began a four-month strike that eventually involved more than thirty-five thousand workers and crippled the entire industry.

The unorganized strikers desperately needed assistance, but the only union in the industry, the United Garment Workers (UGW), was reluctant to aid immigrant workers striking on an industry-wide basis. With nowhere to turn, the strikers appealed to JANE ADDAMS, who formed a committee of women from Hull-House and the Women's Trade Union League (WTUL) to work with the strikers. This coalition of women collaborated with the Chicago Federation of Labor, provided in excess of one hundred thousand dollars in relief aid, and helped distribute food and clothing to the strikers and their families. Under the direction of WTUL president, MARGARET DREIER ROBINS, the women strikers appealed to public sentiment throughout Chicago. WTUL leaders took young strikers into the homes of the wealthy and let them tell their stories. In early November, at a formal breakfast meeting at a restaurant, Abramowitz was one of twelve young women who "talked their hearts out" (WTUL, *Official Report of the Strike Committee*, 6), detailing a wide range of intolerable working conditions. Abramowitz revealed that, despite the Illinois Ten Hour Law, during rush periods she was forced to work twelve or thirteen hours without extra pay for overtime. Coupled with interviews of more than thirty strikers, these breakfast testimonies informed Chicagoans of exploitative conditions in the garment industry and prompted the establishment of a state Senate committee by Senator Johann Waage of Chicago to inquire into the strike.

In spite of these small successes, on February 2, at a meeting of the Strikers' Executive Committee at which UGW president Thomas Rickert and his organizers were present, the strike was called off without consulting the strikers or the other members of the Conference Committee in charge of the strike—representatives of WTUL, Chicago Federation of Labor, and the Garment Workers' Organization. Referring to the settlement as a "hunger bargain," Margaret Dreier Robins conceded to a reporter, "We are conquered, but we are not defeated" ("End of the Struggle," 88). Most workers involved in the strike gained nothing. Some were not even allowed to return to their jobs.

However, Abramowitz and the other eight thousand Hart, Schaffner and Marx employees returned to work with a guarantee of improved working conditions and a Board of Arbitration to address workers' grievances. This agreement between HSM and its employees provided the foundation for union contracts in the years to come. Abramowitz emerged from the strike with a reputation as a capable organizer. She also earned the nickname "Hatpin Bessie" for fearlessly prodding the rear ends of charging police horses with her hatpin.

In 1912 Abramowitz was one of four workers' deputies appointed to the UGW Trade Board that adjusted complaints and enforced decisions before they were appealed to the Board of Arbitration. In addition to her duties on the board, she served as the business agent for Chicago Vestmakers' Local 152 and worked as an organizer for the UGW in the years following the strike. During lunch hours in the years following the strike, Abramowitz, sometimes accompanied by Sidney Hillman, whom she had met during the HSM strike, went into the shops to explain the grievance system and encourage workers to join the union. An inspirational speaker, Abramowitz was especially effective among young Jewish women. Margaret Dreier Robins personally paid Abramowitz six dollars a week for her efforts.

By failing to provide adequate support for its members during the Chicago strike and later in New York and elsewhere, the UGW lost the support of progressive tailors, who accused the union of being inept at leadership and collective bargaining. Consequently, in 1914, more than one hundred New York delegates approached the UGW convention in Nashville intending to replace the union's conservative leaders. Representing more than half of the membership, the militant unionists were refused recognition, barred from the convention floor, and sent to the visitors' gallery. The recognized delegation from Chicago, including Bessie Abramowitz, led a battle supporting the excluded group. She addressed the convention and fought to gain the sympathy of the women delegates, who had been told by Margaret Daly, a member of the UGW's Executive Board, that the dissidents were "anarchists and Jews who were determined to capture and disrupt the union" (McCreesh, 198). Protesting their situation, the insurgents left and reconvened in nearby Duncan Hotel, declaring themselves the legal convention.

Successfully pushing to nominate Sidney Hillman as the new body's president, Abramowitz contacted him in New York, where he was serving as clerk for the International Ladies' Garment Workers' Union. She released Hillman from a secret engagement promise, wiring him: "[I] understand that personal pledges must cease when sister organization at stake. To become a martyr, I urge you to accept office" (October 13 or 14, 1914, Bessie Hillman Papers). Following some deliberation, Hillman accepted, and the Amalgamated Clothing Workers of America (ACWA) was born.

Bessie Abramowitz became the first female General Executive Board member of the new union in August 1915. Serving on the Credentials Committee, she continued to influence the union's national course of action while representing Chicago interests. Abramowitz was chosen secretary-treasurer of the ACWA's Chicago District Council Number 6. She also lobbied for the passage of an eight-hour-day labor law for women in Illinois.

In 1915 the ACWA led a strike of more than twenty thousand unorganized workers in the Chicago men's garment industry. Bessie Abramowitz once again played a significant part in the strike by heading the northwest district, one of four districts, each with its own headquarters, meeting hall, and relief committee. To avoid confrontation with the American Federation of Labor, to which UGW belonged, and with WTUL, which officially supported UGW, the garment workers turned to Hull-House once more for assistance. Although many individual WTUL members supported the strike, officially their leaders felt they had to dissociate themselves from Abramowitz. Her name was removed from their ballot as a delegate to the WTUL national convention. Later restored as a result of her protests, she received only a small number of votes from the members.

During the 1916 May Day parade, Bessie Abramowitz and Sidney Hillman publicly announced their engagement by linking arms and leading a contingent of clothing workers through Chicago. They were married two days later and proceeded to Rochester, New York, for the ACWA's second convention. The new Mrs. Hillman joined Dorothy Jacobs of Baltimore and Selma Goldblatt of Rochester in calling on the male leadership to address the situation of women within the union. They compelled their male colleagues to recognize that women comprised the majority of workers in the clothing industry and played a crucial role in the mass strike movement that had strengthened membership, and that the union could not survive without their cooperation. The convention approved a resolution that called for the establishment of separate women's locals, where women could discuss their special problems and new women members could learn more about the union. Working from within, the women shaped the union to provide a sense of family, offering educational and cultural programs to make the union experience both supportive and enriching.

To be closer to union headquarters, Bessie and Sidney Hillman moved to New York after their marriage, and she resigned from the ACWA General Executive Board. Her first daughter, Philoine, was born in November 1917 and her second daughter, Selma, in September 1921. She participated in ACWA picketing during a general lockout by clothing manufacturers in New York City in 1920–21. The lockout, which lasted five months, occurred when the ACWA rejected demands by the manufacturers for union concessions. Bessie Hillman returned to work as a full-time organizer in 1924, leaving the children in the care of a housekeeper in the family home in Lynbrook, Long Island. Taking time off only during the summer months, Hillman traveled to rural Pennsylvania, Connecticut, and upstate New York to organize shirt workers in sweatshops that had been moved from unionized metropolitan areas. Throughout the Great Depression years, the campaigns that Hillman orchestrated in these areas as well as in the South were extremely successful. Often an honored guest at local union functions throughout the country, Hillman was referred to as "Miss Bessie" by union members.

A leader in the ACWA's educational work, Hillman served as Education Director for the New York Laundry Workers Joint Board from 1937 to 1944. When World War II broke out, she became director of Amalgamated's War Activities Department, supervising a massive blood drive as well as savings bond sales and clothing and scrap collection drives. She served on the Advisory Board in the New York Office of Price Administration. As a member of the Child Welfare Committee of New York, Hillman helped open child care centers and recreational facilities for the children of war workers.

Both of the Hillmans protested zealously against the Holocaust. Their strong support of the war effort was in part a personal fight against the Nazi campaign to exterminate Jews. Bessie Hillman lost seventeen immediate relatives in the Holocaust, including one brother and two sisters. After the war Hillman traveled to Europe on a union-sponsored mission to examine the plight of displaced persons.

Hillman's activism and organizing work continued after World War II. Her involvement in union affairs culminated with her election in 1946 as ACWA vice-president, a position she held until her death. Politically active for the better part of her life, Hillman participated in the affairs of the American Labor Party during the 1940s and after the war affiliated with the Democratic Reform movement, working closely with Eleanor Roosevelt. In 1951 she was appointed a member of the newly formed U.S. Department of Defense Advisory Committee on Women in Armed Services. She represented American women's labor interests as a delegate to the United Nations' International Confederation of Free Trade Unions as well as during her work on the Committee for Protective Labor Legislation for President John F. Kennedy's Commission on the Status of Women. Concerned with paving the way for women of future generations, in a 1962 essay, "Gifted Women in the Trade Unions," Hillman encouraged women to assist with the labor movement. She also championed the causes of civil rights, education, and child welfare.

Hillman died in St. Vincent's Hospital in New York City at the age of eighty-one and was buried in the Westchester Cemetery Mausoleum in New York State. Her last words, "I'm only sorry to say good-by to my union" (interview with Philoine Fried), written on a slate to her daughter, indicate that for Bessie Abramowitz Hillman the union was more than a vehicle through which to accomplish her goals; it was her lifelong passion. For more than half a century, Abramowitz Hillman worked first to lay the foundations of the union and then to transform the nature of the ACWA from a union primarily concerned with immediate gains to an organization that demanded equity for workers both on and off the shop floor.

Sources. Bessie Abramowitz Hillman always spelled her maiden name "Abramovitz" or "Abramovitch," but it was anglicized by colleagues during her lifetime as Abramowitz. The Bessie Hillman Papers, contained within the Records of the Amalgamated Clothing Workers of America (ACWA), are at the Martin P. Catherwood Library, Cornell Univ., Ithaca, New York. This source consists of personal papers, press releases, speeches, documents, reports from her extensive committee service, and correspondence, including her letter to Sidney Hillman dated October 13 or 14, 1914, urging him to become president of ACWA. Included in this collection are the so-called "Red Books" or Hillman scrapbooks, which contain contemporary newspaper accounts concerning the union. Hillman's essay "Gifted Women in the Trade Unions" appears in Beverly Benner Cassara, ed., *American Women: The Changing Image* (1962). Karen Pastorello obtained information from Mrs. Hillman's daughter, Philoine Fried, in interviews between December 29, 1996, and March 20, 1997. Biographical entries for Hillman appear in Judith O'Sullivan and Rosemary Gallick, *Workers and Allies: Female Participation in the American Trade Union Movement, 1824–1976* (1975); *NCAB*, vol. 56 (1975); and Paula E. Hyman and Deborah Dash Moore, eds., *Jewish Women in America: An Historical Encyclopedia* (1997). Linda Kline wrote a play based on Hillman's life, "Hatpin Bessie," performed by the Laundry Workers Union, probably in the 1950s. Hillman's work is discussed in the following publications: *Proceedings of the Thirteenth ACWA Convention* (1904); Women's Trade Union League (WTUL), *Official Report of the Strike Committee* (1911); and WTUL, "The End of the Struggle," *Life and Labor*, March 1911. Bessie Abramowitz is discussed in Philip S. Foner, *Women and the American Labor Movement*, vol. 1 (1979), and in Carolyn Daniel McCreesh, *Women in the Campaign to Organize Garment Workers, 1880–1917* (1985). Hillman is mentioned in biographies of her husband: Matthew Josephson, *Sidney Hillman: Statesman of American Labor* (1952), and Steven Fraser, *Labor Will Rule: Sidney Hillman and the Rise of American Labor* (1991). Recent information on the 1910 strike is in Rebecca Sive-Tomashefsky, "Identifying a Lost Leader: Hannah Shapiro and the 1910 Chicago Garment Workers' Strike," *Signs*, Summer 1978; N. Sue Weiler, "Walkout: The Chicago Men's Garment Workers Strike, 1910–1911," *Chicago History*, Winter 1979–80; and N. Sue Weiler, "The Uprising in Chicago: The Men's Garment Workers Strike, 1910–1911," in *A Needle, a Bobbin, a Strike*, ed. Joan Jensen and Sue Davidson (1984). The Chicago Joint Board, Amalgamated Clothing Workers of America, *The Clothing Workers of Chicago, 1910–1922* (1922) discusses the strike and the founding of the ACWA.

KAREN PASTORELLO

N. SUE WEILER

HIMEBAUGH, SISTER M. CECILIA
(Edith Catherine Himebaugh)
May 18, 1892–June 5, 1977
TEACHER, LITURGIST, SCRIPTURE SCHOLAR, AUTHOR, SOCIAL JUSTICE ADVOCATE

Edith Catherine Himebaugh was born in Colorado Springs, Colorado. Her father, John Alexander Himebaugh, was born in Ohio in 1843. After the Civil War he walked and drove a team of oxen to Colorado to mine for gold. Eventually he settled in Colorado Springs. His first wife died at the birth of their third child. Himebaugh then married Georgia Eller Craig. She bore him two children, Edith Catherine and John Carl.

Edith Catherine Himebaugh's father was the proprietor of the Spaulding House hotel; the family lived there, and Georgia Himebaugh managed to provide a homey environment in spite of their unusual circumstances. However, she was not well, and she died when Edith was just thirteen. During her long illness the family's two youngest children, Edith and John Carl, became very close.

After her mother's death, Edith Himebaugh was sent to a Catholic boarding school, the Academy, in Canon City, Colorado. The school had been established by Bavarian-immigrant women religious of the Benedictine order, who had settled in Chicago as well. Although her father was a member of the Lutheran Reformed Church and had little use for Catholics, he wanted Edith to get an excellent education in a protected environment. Edith Himebaugh became a Catholic in 1907. Himebaugh wrote, "I fell in love with the [Benedictine] life long before I lost many of my prejudices against the [Catholic] religion" (quoted in "Sister Cecilia Himebaugh," 38). The interior spiritual Benedictine culture overrode the external anti-Catholic climate of early-twentieth-century Colorado and the political influence of the American Protective Association. Himebaugh graduated from the Academy with an academic diploma and a diploma in piano.

In 1911, Edith Himebaugh joined the Benedictine Community in Chicago. Her father disowned her, never again answering her letters, which she continued to write for a time. So painful was this rejection that for many years, as a professional educator and author, Edith Himebaugh refused to use her family name. Fortunately, her close relationship with her brother, Carl, who shared her interests in literature and music despite differences in religion, remained intact until his death at a young age.

Edith Himebaugh was given the name Sister Cecilia when she became a novice in 1912. She was very bright and continued her education, receiving a piano teacher's certificate, a B.A. from DePaul University, Chicago, in 1926, and a master's degree from Loyola University Chicago in 1931. Her thesis, "Theories Concerning Junior High School Curricula with their Practical Application to the Junior High Schools of Chicago," evidenced her early understanding of the importance of modernizing Catholic institutions of education and curriculum in order to adjust the core values of the religion to contemporary life.

Himebaugh returned to the Academy in Canon City, where she taught both music and academic subjects. Eventually she joined the faculty at the Benedictine-run St. Scholastica (Girls') High School in Chicago and became its principal from 1927 to 1932. Under her leadership, the Student Council, the Glee Club, and the school orchestra were organized. Two school publications were started: a newspaper, the *Raven*, and a yearbook, *The Scholastican*.

This was a time of growth and liturgical renewal for the Benedictine order in North America. The convent and chapel at St. Scholastica reflected this renewal in its religious art, its worship and liturgical conferences, and its commitment to expanded education for women religious. At the same time, Chicago Benedictine nuns, including Himebaugh, SISTER DOLORES SCHORSCH, and MOTHER IMELDA FISCHER and SISTER CELESTINE FISCHER became leaders in modern pedagogy and relevant curriculum for the teaching of religion to American-born Catholics. Himebaugh came to realize the necessity of bringing young people to understand religion as more than book learning or private devotion. Their faith must have an impact on them and on their world. This insight flowed from her Benedictine roots, with its commitment to community life and liturgical prayer and a foundation in Scripture that is to be lived out in all the daily circumstances of life. Female students began to study liturgy and its implications for social action, a new concept in curriculum development.

These experiences were not only formative for the students but also set in motion Himebaugh's greatest contribution to society, bringing Catholic social action to high school and college students through the Chicago Inter-Student Catholic Action movement (CISCA). Collaborating with Rev. Martin Carrabine, SJ, and following the lead of the greatest contemporary scholars and writers of the time, both in Europe and in the United States, Himebaugh shaped a program of study and action that allowed the lessons of the liturgy to bear upon the social problems of the day. CISCA brought together high school and college students to discuss weighty issues of race, economic justice, poverty, and war and peace. Meetings were held on Saturday mornings at a downtown hotel or meeting hall. The young men and women discussed Catholic action in all its aspects and put their words into practice. Himebaugh brought to these discussions issues of liturgical renewal before it had a name and challenged the young people to face racial problems before they knew they had them. Some became outstanding civil servants and had the lifetime opportunity to put into practice what they had learned. The Chicago church was known across the country for the quality of its social action program.

Writing in 1960 for the Benedictine Sisters community history, *Where There Was Need*, Himebaugh reflected on her efforts in 1935: "The mental nourishment youth had to assimilate in the 1960s consisted in a whole new world-view, both material and spiritual. Ciscans (members of CISCA) were encouraged to see themselves in a new way: not as isolated units of humanity, but as living and functioning cells in a world-wide organism, Christ's Mystical Body. This incarnational theology stated that all men were brothers, regardless of white or blue collars and the color of their skin. With this basic truth as a foundation, Ciscans were challenged to work out an existential orientation to all reality, so as to make God's dynamic truths relevant to their own lives and environment: cultural, economic, and social" (p. 151).

This vision was elaborated in the 1930s, a time of economic depression, social unrest, and political propaganda in Europe and the United States. "The youth of Chicago dedicated themselves . . . to establish not a Marxian paradise but a Christocracy, a world where Christ would reign" (*Where There Was Need*, 151), Himebaugh wrote, "for first and foremost, Catholic Action consists not in *doing things* but in *being Christ*: at home, in school, on the playing field and on dates" ("CISCA in Retrospect").

Himebaugh summed up her conception of CISCA: "By refusing to let teenagers dissipate their youthful energies in high-sounding crusades, by challenging them to think for themselves, and by developing their sense of responsibility, CISCA helped prepare thousands of Chicago high school and college graduates for mature Christian living" ("CISCA in Retrospect"). CISCA met every Saturday during the school year at a downtown location. It brought together hundreds of high school and college students for three hours of discussion, prayer, and action on the social issues of the times.

Himebaugh was an insatiable reader, especially in theology and Scripture. Since she was fluent in French, she was able to read all the new material coming out of the church in Belgium, where the liturgical renewal in the Catholic Church had its beginnings in the 1940s. Books and magazines were liberally underlined in red ink so that pertinent passages could be quickly identified. She shared her reading with her students and with Ciscans through her own writings.

As early as 1933 Himebaugh began writing for *Orate Fratres* and *Sponsa Regis*, two monthly publications from St. John's Abbey in Collegeville, Minnesota. In the beginning, these publications were considered "underground and subversive" ("Sister Cecilia Himebaugh," 39) for their progressive liturgical ideas. Himebaugh dealt with topics like the psalms and the liturgical seasons, always trying to make the pattern of life liturgical. Articles appeared periodically in these publications through 1958. Rev. Godfrey Diekmann, the editor of *Orate Frates*, in a letter written to Himebaugh in 1937, commented, "You have a happy faculty of making heavy thought palatable and pleasant reading, to make doctrine inspire action" (St. Scholastica Archives).

Throughout her years of teaching, administration, and organizing, Himebaugh wrote extensively for educational journals on liturgical practices and their potential impact on students' awareness of and involvement in the social issues of the day. She followed the lead of many of the great scholars of her day. To separate responsible social action from liturgical worship was simply unthinkable.

Her first book, *Companion to the Missal* (1954), interpreted the Mass for each Sunday and major feast so that the reader might understand the real significance of the celebration and its dynamic effect on life and choices and actions. It sold nineteen thousand copies in its first printing. In 1960, Himebaugh completed a second book, *The Psalms in Modern Life*, designed to bring the reader a greater love and appreciation for the psalmody.

During Himebaugh's years with CISCA, she and Carrabine published a number of pamphlets challenging the young people they were working with to pay attention to the world around them and to reach out in positive, Christ-like ways to those in need. Realizing that they had to catch the attention of the intended readers, they gave these works contemporary titles, using catch phrases like *The Parish Turns Red*.

A series of *Why* articles printed in leaflet form were introduced in the 1960s and were primarily scripture-oriented. Each gave in brief the origin and purpose of the various books of the Bible. Titles were self-revealing as a rule: *The Acts of the Apostle, Saint John's Gospel*; but there were also titles such as *Why Read the Old Testament?, Bible Discrepancies*, and one on Teilhard de Chardin, the great and often misunderstood Jesuit philosopher of the early twentieth century. In what appears to be an unpublished article on Chardin, Himebaugh observes: "He [Chardin] was so far ahead of his own time as to have furnished tomorrow's answers to today's problems, scientific as well as religious" (St. Scholastica Archives). One wonders how much of herself Himebaugh recognized in this description of the man she so admired.

Cecilia Himebaugh was a woman who made her home in Scripture, who celebrated it in liturgy, who taught and wrote about its ramifications for social thought and action. She, with many of the great liturgists and social activists of her time, men and women with whom she corresponded and traded ideas and insights, were perhaps ahead of their time. She both sought the advice of and contributed her own insights to Virgil Michel, OSB, founding editor of *Orate Fratres*; biblical scholars Father Carroll Stuhlmueller, Father Emeric Lawrence, Gerald Ellard, SJ, and Herbert van Zeller, OP; and liturgists Father Pius Parsch, Father Frederick McManus, and Father Martin Hellrigel. Among the more popular figures of the time were Dorothy Day, cofounder of the *Catholic Worker*, and Monsignor Fulton J. Sheen of television fame. Himebaugh contributed articles to the *Chicago Catholic Worker* in which she wrote about the battle being waged over the possession of the dispossessed by both capitalists and communists. She offered a third alternative, the way of Catholic liturgy and social action.

Most of Himebaugh's correspondence was with male scholars. The female scholar, especially in Scripture, was almost unheard of and, if visible, given little attention during Himebaugh's lifetime. Acknowledging this reality, Himebaugh refers to herself often as a "ghost writer," especially for Carrabine. "[During] 1935–43, I was acting as a ghost writer for . . . CISCA, for which I wrote the plans of such study courses as sought to implement our theories of a genuinely Christian social order" (quoted in "Sister Cecilia Himebaugh," 40).

One of the delights of her later years was her reconnection with her birth family. In 1955 she received a letter from a cousin, Raymond Himebaugh, who was trying to put together the genealogy of the Himebaugh family. This contact developed into a meaningful relationship with him and with his wife, Dorothy,

that went far beyond sharing family information. That it brought healing to a deep wound is evident by the fact that she was able, after so many years, to identify herself as Sister Cecilia Himebaugh.

Himebaugh's final years were spent in seclusion at St. Scholastica Monastery in Chicago. Her health had deteriorated to such a degree that she spent most of her time in bed. However, she remained the scholar, continuing to read and explore new ideas and the developing theology of Vatican II. Nor did she lose her sense of humor. When told that the Benedictine Community Chapter had voted to begin praying the Divine Office in English rather than Latin, a cause she had long supported, she commented that they realized at last that God knew English.

Cecilia Himebaugh died of heart-related complications at the age of eighty-five. She completed her sixty-six years of ministry to the church with the donation of her body to Loyola University Medical School. Her ashes are buried in the Benedictine Sisters community plot in Calvary Cemetery in Evanston, Illinois.

Cecilia Himebaugh played a significant role in the Catholic Church of Chicago, preparing the young people of the 1930s and 1940s to face the challenges and the opportunities of the Vatican II Council and beyond. She taught them to think, to pray, and to act and to have the courage of their convictions, as she so obviously had. She worked with young people as teacher, counselor and model of what it meant to "act justly, to love tenderly and to walk humbly with your God" (Micah 6:8).

Sources. Biographical materials, correspondence, and unpublished writings of Sister Cecilia Himebaugh are in the Archives of the Benedictine Sisters of Chicago, St. Scholastica Monastery, Chicago. These papers include an undated speech, "CISCA in Retrospect," and an unpublished article on Teilhard de Chardin. The archives have copies of the *St. Scholastica Priory Archives Newsletter* edited by Sister M. Vivian Ivantic, OSB, including the issue with the article "Sister Cecilia Himebaugh," October–November 1985. Himebaugh's writings include *Companion to the Missal for Sundays and Principal Feasts* (1954), *The Psalms in Modern Life* (1960), and the *Why* articles printed in leaflet form, *Acts of the Apostles, Saint John's Gospel, Why Read the Old Testament?, Bible Discrepancies, Jonah's Credibility Gap*, and *Teilhard de Chardin*, to name a few. Her articles appeared in the *Chicago Catholic Worker, Sponsa Regis, Orate Fratres*, and *Our Community*. For a history of the Chicago Benedictine Community, see Genevieve Harrison, *Where There Was Need* (1960).

MARY BENET MCKINNEY, OSB

HINMAN, MARY WOOD
February 14, 1878–July 4, 1952
DANCE TEACHER, FOLK DANCE SPECIALIST, LEADER IN
PAGEANTRY AND RECREATION

Mary Wood Hinman grew up in a musical family, first taught dance as a teenager, studied gymnastics and folk dancing in Europe, and returned to become a leader in Chicago education and recreation. Born in Ohio, Hinman began teaching neighbor children in her family's commodious home in the North Shore suburb of Kenilworth, Illinois, around 1894, apparently as a way of helping the family in a period of financial difficulty. She may have studied with Chicago dancing master Eugene Bournique and also with a Mr. Low, who called dances in Kenilworth during her childhood. By her own admission, however, she had little formal training for what was to become her life's work. In various schools, clubs, and hotels, Hinman expanded her folk and social dance classes into a successful business. In 1898 she coached the first Blackfriars Show at the University of Chicago, where she was already known for her popular coeducational classes.

Hinman developed as a teacher during the years when Melvin Ballou Gilbert taught hundreds of women "aesthetic calisthenics" (Odom, 65) at the Boston Normal School of Gymnastics, the Sargent School of Physical Education, and Harvard Summer School. Hinman may have come into contact with his methods through such Gilbert students teaching in Chicago as Elizabeth Burchenal, who held a position at the Women's Athletic Club between 1898 and 1902. By this time Hinman herself was well launched as a teacher, even though she, like Burchenal, was still only in her early twenties. Gilbert had not emphasized folk dancing as much as Hinman, Burchenal, and others soon would. These early folk dance specialists began to collect dances directly from human sources, drawing on the multicultural populations of cities such as Chicago and New York.

Around 1898 Hinman introduced dance at Hull-House, where JANE ADDAMS and her colleagues included the arts in their innovative program for the settlement and social integration of recent immigrants. Hull-House in the 1890s ran a day nursery, playground, gymnasium, and dispensary, and was the center for many kinds of classes and club meetings. As Addams explained, "In time we came to define a settlement as an institution attempting to learn from life itself" (quoted in Odom, 65–66). This perspective influenced the teaching practice of Hinman, whose academic education had ended with high school. Hinman both taught and learned at Hull-House, and her credo became "let us not *teach* as much as *share*" (Odom, 66).

In *I Came a Stranger: The Story of a Hull-House Girl*, HILDA SATT POLACHECK recalled, "The dancing class was in the charge of a beautiful, understanding woman . . . Mary Wood Hinman and we all loved her. She was always dressed in a gray accordion-pleated skirt, with a blouse of the same material, a red sash, and gray dancing shoes. She floated around that room like a graceful bird. We danced once a week in this carefree class, all winter. In June, the class closed for the summer with a gay cotillion, every bit as gay, if not as elaborate, as the ones staged today to introduce debutantes to society. No matter where the members of the dancing class came from, dingy hovels, overcrowded tenements, for that one night we were all living in a fairyland" (p. 77).

Reflecting on her work at Hull-House, Hinman wrote to physical education leader Luther Halsey Gulick in 1909, "The two most striking results were: first, the men gained the American attitude of respect for women, which they knew nothing of in their life in the other country; and second, they learned the value of self-respect" (quoted in Gulick, 75–76). She commented that the young people "gain healthy exercise, social intercourse in a pleasant setting and enough social technique to make them self-respecting. There seems to be no better, quicker, or surer way of obtaining our first hold on the young people we want most to bring off the street" (quoted in Gulick, 75–76). Noting that it was "astonishing to find how many young men and women were given better positions by their employers after attending class for a month or two," Hinman also observed that the children's classes "show immediate results in the new interest felt in the home life of their parents" (quoted in Gulick, 76–77). These views show how fully Hinman had absorbed the ethos of Hull-House.

Hinman's other mentor was John Dewey. She may have met Dewey at Hull-House, where he and his wife, educator Harriet Chipman Dewey, were both active; or she may have met him at the University of Chicago, where Dewey taught philosophy and education. In any case, soon after Hinman brought dance to Hull-House, and while she continued to supervise teaching in her vast network of classes throughout Chicago, she became involved in Dewey's experiments. She wrote, "I began this work in Professor Dewey's small school, called the 'Dewey School,' nine years ago [ca. 1900], and went with him into the University, now called the University of Chicago Elementary School" (quoted in Gulick, 79). Working in the context of Dewey's ideas about direct experience, problem solving, and the value of play in learning, Hinman developed a graded program of gymnastic, folk, and social dancing for kindergarten through high school, which took into account age, sex, motor and social skills, time available, and various types of indoor and outdoor spaces. After the University Elementary School merged with the Francis W. Parker School, Hinman worked at Parker from 1906 to 1919. There she taught the gifted future choreographer Doris Humphrey. Gulick's *The Healthful Art of Dancing* (1910) includes Hinman's twenty-one page letter reporting on Chicago activities, illustrated by photographs of school children dancing.

Around 1904, when Hinman was in her mid-twenties, she established the Hinman School of Gymnastic and Folk Dancing in Hyde Park, in order to prepare young women for a new vocation, teaching dance in the public schools and settlements. As she wrote in 1909, "Our well-educated young women, who come from cultured homes, are not satisfied to ornament the fireside, but long to be in touch with the life of to-day. We select girls who have a mental grasp of educational problems and are alive to the world as it is." She described the two-year program: "They do actual assisting every day at all the big classes, read books and write papers on how this work applies to the education of the child, also learning where each dance comes from, its history, what influences the different countries in their social life, etc., and each carries a class of her own in some settlement. They are trained to be good teachers, good organizers, an addition to any faculty, but they are not trained to be solo dancers and fancy dancers" (quoted in Gulick, 94–95). She noted proudly, "They can execute their work well, they know their technique, but first and foremost, they can teach simply and clearly, and keep uppermost in their minds the education of the child. It is the only school in the world of its kind. We cannot take all who apply" (quoted in Gulick, 94–95).

By 1917 the school's brochure outlined a broad curriculum of practical and theoretical study, including folk, English country, ballroom, and interpretative dancing; pantomime, ballet, and clogging; pedagogy with practice teaching; pageantry, including technical stage production; and "Books," a course on dance history, folk customs, the "new art" ("Outline of Class Work in the Normal Class," *Hinman School of Gymnastic and Folk Dancing*, n.p.), civic responsibility, and women's position in modern life. These courses reflected not only the ideals of Hull-House and the Dewey School but also the fact that beginning in 1906 Hinman traveled extensively. At a time when few American women studied abroad, Hinman believed in the necessity of experiencing dances in their original settings. From her teaching she earned enough to make a number of study trips to Europe. She first concentrated on Scandinavian dances, enrolling at the Royal College at Nääs, Sweden, from which she was graduated in 1907, and doing four months of fieldwork in the far north of that country. By 1912 she had spent several summers in Ireland and England, where she worked closely with William Kimber, the Oxfordshire bricklayer and Morris dancer, and with Cecil Sharp, who was reviving the traditional music and dances of England. Over the years, Hinman continued her practice of study in Russia, France, Sicily, Switzerland, Germany, Hungary, the Middle and Far East, and Central and South America. Her grand-niece, whom she took to see Hopi Indian ceremonies, recalled subsisting for a week with her on boiled eggs and canned pineapple: "Nothing daunted her. She would find a way to do it" (quoted in Odom, 68).

Although she was not a trained scholar, Hinman followed the procedure of learning dances thoroughly, taking detailed notes, and obtaining written music. She also collected costumes, photographs, and, when they became available, sound recordings. She applied what she learned not only in her own teaching but also in her work with the National Committee on Folk Dancing of the Playground Association of America (PAA), which was founded by Gulick and other leaders in 1906. In the "Festival of Play and Sport," the Playground Association's first congress, held in Chicago in June 1907, the local branch of the PAA sponsored exhibitions that featured folk dancing along with games and gymnastics, to international acclaim in the press. Hinman also demonstrated her work through many festivals and pageants, such as her staging of traditional dances for the Shakespeare Pageant given by the Drama League of Chicago in April 1912 at Lincoln Park. She helped to establish the United States branch of the English Folk-Dance Society and brought Cecil Sharp to teach in Chicago several times between 1915 and 1917.

Hinman produced hundreds of printed sheets of dance directions and music, which could be purchased for fifteen cents or ten for a dollar. Despite errors and imprecisions, many of the dances she described to assist teachers stand as a valuable record of the early collecting of folk dances. These materials led eventually to her five-volume series, *Gymnastic and Folk Dancing*, published by A. S. Barnes in several editions beginning in 1914. In these books she presented more than 250 dances through written descriptions, music, diagrams, stick figure drawings, and photographs. Ever practical, Hinman suggested which dances were suitable for different ages and situations. She often gave source and background information, and she peppered the pages of her books with inspiring quotations, fragments of poetry, and thoughts on teaching, such as "Don't talk! Do!" (Hinman, "To Teachers in Grade Schools," vol. 3, 5). "Every folk dance should have its history given as it is taught," she advised

teachers. "If the class is learning the 'Weaving Dance' tell the story of each step; the herding of the sheep, the shearing of the sheep, the washing of the wool, the weaving, the testing of the cloth, etc. . . . Connect every dance learned with one of the sister arts, if possible. Give it a literary, historical or geographical background and above all, enjoy and impart your joy in all that connects itself with the dance. Talk only one or one and a half minutes, and be quite sure what you say, in the mind of the students, is related to the dance they are learning. Suggest and stimulate, rather than teach" (Hinman, "The Necessity of Joy in the Teaching of Dancing," vol. 3, 105).

Hinman advocated what she called "dance building," or helping groups of students to make variations on a given traditional dance or dance style. Other types of dances were created by individuals for pageants or special occasions. Hinman published four original pageant dances by her young teaching associate Doris Humphrey, for example, including "Greek Sacrificial Dance," a gentle walking and running dance for three central girls and a chorus in tunics, set to music of Camille Saint-Saëns. Thus she enabled Humphrey to see herself not only as a teacher but also as a fledgling choreographer. Humphrey, her student through childhood at the Francis W. Parker School and a 1914 graduate of the Hinman School, wrote a fond recollection: "I had a wonderful teacher, and a wonderful teacher is one that you should cherish when you find one. This teacher not only had vision, but was interested in the whole field of dance. She used to go abroad and bring back whatever seemed to be of value as she was going on from year to year with her classes. She also had an individual interest in her students, and I was one she advised and encouraged" (quoted in Odom, 64). It was Hinman who suggested in 1917 that Humphrey go to California to study at the recently opened Denishawn School, the move that led to her career as a professional dancer. By 1917, 122 women had completed their studies at the Hinman School. Hinman employed or found work for many of them. She urged Lucy Duncan Hall, a 1911 graduate, to study with Émile Jacques-Dalcroze at Hellerau, Germany; after becoming the first American certified to teach his music teaching method based on movement, Hall introduced Dalcroze Eurhythmics at Parker and the Hinman School. Inspired by the innovative approaches to staging they saw while traveling together in Europe, Hinman and Hall mounted several pageants in the Chicago area, and they became involved in experimental productions and the training program of the Chicago Little Theatre.

During World War I, Hinman offered her services as a recreation leader for soldiers both at home and abroad through the Council of National Defense. After the war she worked for the U.S. government in Germany. Then, following the sudden death of her brother and the closing of her school, she had a severe nervous breakdown. During the late 1920s she resumed teaching, offering popular summer folk dance courses at the Utah Agricultural College in Logan. By 1930 she had moved to New York, where she helped to establish the Folk Festival Council. This private service organization sponsored dances, festivals, and performances involving some forty ethnic groups. Under its auspices Hinman created a course called "Dances of Many Peoples" and later "Folk Dances of Many Nations," given at the New School for Social Research beginning in 1932. Hinman also served on the board of the New School Young Dancers Series and continued to encourage Humphrey, urging her to film her modern dance works. In 1938 Hinman retired to Los Angeles, where she died fourteen years later. Her collection of folk costumes and related materials was given to the Center for the Study of Comparative Folklore and Mythology of the University of California, Los Angeles.

Hinman based her practice on the belief that the social and physical experience of dancing could enrich the lives of people of all ages, regardless of class and ethnic background. Her approach to teacher training redefined dance as a field offering women new opportunities in teaching, creative work, research, and community service.

Sources. Hinman's five-volume *Gymnastic and Folk Dancing* was published in several editions between 1914 and 1932. Mary Jane Hungerford wrote a tribute to Hinman, after her retirement, in *Educational Dance,* April 1939, and Virginia C. Anderson wrote her obituary for the folk dance publication *Viltis,* July 1953. Many key sources are gathered in the so-called "Swedish Book, Materials Relating to the Career of Mary Wood Hinman (ca. 1911–1917)," of the Doris Humphrey Collection (Dance Collection, New York Public Library). The Swedish Book materials include the brochure *Hinman School of Gymnastic and Folk Dancing* (1917) and other school brochures. Hinman's comments on her work at Hull-House were quoted in Luther H. Gulick, *The Healthful Art of Dancing* (1910). Two former students wrote about Hinman: Hilda Satt Polacheck, *I Came a Stranger: The Story of a Hull-House Girl* (1989), and Doris Humphrey, *New Dance, an Unfinished Autobiography,* which is the Spring 1966 issue of *Dance Perspectives.* A detailed recent account, from which this profile in part is drawn, is Selma Landen Odom, "Sharing the Dances of Many People: The Teaching Work of Mary Wood Hinman," *Proceedings Dance History Scholars,* Tenth Annual Conference, copyright 1987 by Selma Landen Odom and published by the Society of Dance History Scholars; used with permission. Most of the Odom biography has been pieced together from Hinman's writings, as corroborated by her colleague Patricia Parmelee and her two grand-nieces, Sarah Root Chapin and K. Elizabeth Morse, in letters and interviews with the author. Chapin and Morse were themselves involved in folk dancing and shared vivid memories of studying and traveling with Hinman. Linda Johnston Tomko considers Hinman in "Women, Artistic Dance Practices, and Social Change in the United States, 1890–1920" (Ph.D. diss., Univ. of California, Los Angeles, 1991). Tomko broadens her study in *Dancing Class: Gender, Ethnicity, and Social Divides in American Dance, 1890–1920* (1999).

SELMA LANDEN ODOM

HOGE, JANE CURRIE BLAIKIE
July 31, 1811–August 26, 1890
CIVIL WAR WORKER, EDUCATIONAL REFORMER

Jane Hoge, a volunteer public servant and champion of opportunity for women, was born in Philadelphia, Pennsylvania, the daughter of George Dundas and Mary (Monroe) Blaikie. Her father was an East India shipping merchant. Jane Blaikie was educated in Philadelphia at the Ladies Seminary operated by John Brewer, where she excelled in music. On June 2, 1831, she married Abraham Holmes (A. H.) Hoge of Pittsburgh, a merchant in the iron and nail business. Over the next twenty-two years, Jane Hoge bore thirteen children, eight of whom lived to adulthood. Little is known of her early married life in Pittsburgh. It

appears she was devoted primarily to raising her large family, but her public interest in women's and children's issues began when she served as secretary of the Pittsburgh Orphan Asylum.

In September 1848 the Hoges moved to Chicago, where A. H. Hoge became a partner in an iron works. He was subsequently involved in several different businesses and in the 1860s and 1870s was employed by the U.S. Assessors Office and the Internal Revenue Service in Chicago.

In the decade after the Hoges' move to Chicago, the city's population more than tripled, from nearly thirty thousand in 1850 to more than one hundred thousand by 1860; and the number of needy grew as well. In the 1840s and 1850s, relief organizations were founded by middle-class citizens to address the needs of increasing numbers of destitute women and children. Among the new agencies was the Chicago Home for the Friendless. Organized in March 1858 by Protestant church representatives to assist friendless women and children in finding suitable employment and permanent housing, the Home for the Friendless (now Family Care Services of Metropolitan Chicago) admitted women and children without regard to creed, color, or nationality. Jane Hoge was elected one of the charter members of the female board of managers. Another charter member was MARY LIVERMORE, and their work for the home marked the beginning of a long collaboration and friendship.

Board members were responsible not only for raising funds and setting policies; they were also deeply involved in the day-to-day operation of the home. These duties included rescuing women and children from the streets and bringing them to the home, a task that Hoge often performed. Hoge maintained an active interest in the home throughout her life, and at the time of her death she was still an honorary board member.

Hoge's executive ability was first recognized during her early work for the Home for the Friendless. While not personally wealthy, she was a remarkably successful fund-raiser. She foresaw the need for an industrial school at the home, labored hard to convert others to her point of view, and helped make the school a reality.

Following the outbreak of the Civil War, the Chicago (later called Northwestern) Branch of the United States Sanitary Commission was organized in the city in 1861 to assist the Medical Department of the Army with disease prevention and relief. Mary Livermore and Jane Hoge, whose two sons, Holmes and George, served in the Union Army, immediately became active with the commission. In December 1861 they, together with Ann P. (Hawes) Hosmer, organized a several-day benefit that raised $675 for the commission—a precursor to their later, large-scale fund-raising efforts.

In the spring of 1862, following reports of misappropriated supplies and substandard conditions in military hospitals, Mark Skinner and E. W. Blatchford, officers of the Northwestern Sanitary Commission, asked Hoge and Livermore to undertake an inspection tour of hospitals in St. Louis, Missouri, Mound City, Illinois, and Cairo, Illinois. This was the first of several tours taken on behalf of the commission. They set out in April 1862 and found things to be in order; their reports helped alleviate concern among civilians but also stressed the need for additional supplies.

In November 1862, Hoge served as a delegate to the Women's Council meeting in Washington, D.C., where she met President Lincoln at the White House. Returning from the meeting more committed than ever, Hoge and her friend Livermore were named associate managers of the Northwestern Sanitary Commission and began a thorough organization of the supply work. They wrote reports for the press, traveled extensively to organize new chapters throughout the states of the Old Northwest (now the Midwest), and visited existing chapters to improve morale and encourage their work. Hoge's numerous speeches to groups of both men and women in towns large and small, recounting at first hand the bravery, hardships, and needs of the soldiers at the front, were important tools in organizing the massive relief effort. Beginning in 1863, "the discouragement under which the Chicago branch had labored vanished" (Andreas, 318), due in large part to the enthusiasm and organizational skills Hoge and Livermore brought to the task.

Under Hoge and Livermore's direction, the work of the Northwestern Branch expanded to meet the ever increasing needs of the army in the Mississippi Valley. In the first half of 1863 Hoge made two inspection tours to Memphis and Vicksburg. She strongly believed that a woman's touch and skills were needed in military hospitals, and she worked hard to overcome the objections of many male surgeons to female nurses and hospital workers. One job of the sanitary commission was to recruit female hospital workers, and the growing acceptance of these workers was a point of pride for Hoge.

In June 1863, Hoge traveled to Vicksburg with a large shipment of supplies to visit her wounded son. While returning with him to Chicago, her steamer came under enemy fire, but she and her son escaped unharmed.

By late 1862 it was clear that the financial needs of the sanitary commission required larger, more dependable contributions. Hoge believed that one could not depend simply on people's goodwill to raise large sums of money but that a well-organized social event for the general public would tap previously untouched sources of income. Out of this insight came Hoge and Livermore's proposal for the first Chicago Sanitary Fair, an event that ran for two weeks in October 1863. Hoge noted that their proposal did not garner universal support, and that "some of our leading and patriotic men, who afterwards became the most assiduous helpers, gravely shook their heads, and prophesied failure to this quixotic scheme of womanly benevolence" (Hoge, *Boys in Blue*, 334). As managers of the fair, Hoge and Livermore oversaw an event that was planned largely by women and included a sales bazaar, dining area, entertainment, and a Manufacturers' Hall for the display of machinery. The Chicago Sanitary Fair netted nearly eighty thousand dollars, more than three times what was expected.

As the war began to wind down, the sanitary commission devoted more effort to the needs of returning injured soldiers and veterans' families. The commission office served as an information center, maintaining a Sanitary Hospital Directory, and also assisted sick and wounded soldiers in transit. Hoge served as corresponding secretary of the executive committee for the Second Chicago Sanitary Fair, which was to benefit both the sanitary commission and the Chicago Soldiers' Home. Although the fair did not open until May 30, 1865, after the surrender at Appo-mattox, soldiers in hospitals, returning veterans, and their families were still in need of assistance. This fair raised more than two hundred twenty thousand dollars.

Hoge recorded her wartime experiences in *The Boys in Blue; Or Heroes of the "Rank and File,"* published in 1867. About that time, she and her husband moved to Evanston, a suburb north of Chicago, where they remained until the mid-1870s, when they returned to the city. Hoge was recruited in 1871 by several Evanston women to serve as president of a women's educational association, organized to assist the newly formed Evanston College for Ladies, which named FRANCES E. WILLARD its first president.

Several features of the college, which opened in September 1871, appealed to Jane Hoge. The idea of women working for other women characterized her work with the Home for the Friendless, and a college for women, with an all-female board of trustees and female president, exemplified her belief that women were capable of improving their own lives and the lives of others. Hoge's executive ability and the reputation she earned through her work with the sanitary commission made her an ideal fund-raiser for the college.

Borrowing some of the ideas that made the sanitary fairs successful, Hoge suggested a woman's Fourth of July celebration, organized exclusively by women, to serve as a combined fund-raiser and cornerstone-laying ceremony for the new college. Billed as the "Pre-Emption of the Fourth of July in the interests of the girls of the North-west" ("Celebration under the Auspices," *Chicago Tribune*, July 5, 1871), the event attracted a crowd of over ten thousand celebrants. The day featured a parade, orations, bands, yacht races, baseball games, and military drills. More than thirty thousand dollars in pledges and receipts were collected.

The Evanston College for Ladies survived only two years before it was absorbed by Northwestern University in June 1873. During those two years, Hoge, as president of the Evanston Educational Association, was an ex-officio member of the college board, although she did not appear to have attended board meetings. The objectives of the educational association were to gather information on the latest educational methods, raise monies for the college, organize lectures and musical programs, help needy students, and provide programs to improve the "literary, intellectual and aesthetic character of the women of Evanston" (*Constitution and By-Laws*, 4).

Hoge, a lifelong Presbyterian, turned her attention next to the Woman's Presbyterian Board of Missions of the North-West, organized in December 1870. In 1872 she was elected to replace the original president, a position she held for the next thirteen years. Under her leadership the woman's board expanded from 70 auxiliaries in 8 states, to more than 1,430 auxiliaries in 11 states by 1885. The board-of-missions motto was "Woman's Work for Woman," with the focus being the Christianization of "heathen" women and the support of female missionaries. Members believed that by supporting the work of female missionaries they could Christianize more women, since females would have easier access to women in such places as harems, where men could not enter. Hoge fought a continuing battle to keep funds for foreign missions from decreasing or being diverted to domestic mission activities. Deafness finally forced her to step down from the presidency in 1885, and in recognition of her long service, she was named president emeritus.

Jane Hoge died at her home on the Near North Side of Chicago at age seventy-nine, only seven months after the death of her husband. Memorial services were held September 14, 1890, at the First Baptist Church of Evanston, where her son Holmes Hoge was a member; and at Church of the Covenant (Presbyterian) on September 28, 1890. She was buried at Graceland Cemetery.

Jane Hoge was devoted to causes that fell well within the bounds of acceptable female pursuits in the nineteenth century—church work, aiding poor families, and working for the war effort. Despite her unswerving faith in the power of women to effect change and her interest in female education, she was apparently not a supporter of woman suffrage. Hoge's remarkable executive ability was perhaps her most notable public talent. She was willing to take on what she saw as important causes. Combined with her ability to see the big picture was her genuine interest in the individual—the dying child at the Home for the Friendless, the injured soldier in the hospital, or the female college student in need of financial help. Her fund-raising skills demonstrated that women could bring not only moral authority to social issues but substantial financial resources as well. Hoge was able to initiate, organize, and carry through large-scale efforts for the causes she supported.

Sources. The CHS Library Clipping File contains a folder on Hoge, including an anonymous biographical sketch. Her work with the Evanston Educational Association is documented in records of the Evanston College for Ladies, including the *Constitution and By-Laws of the Women's Educational Association of Evanston* (1871), at the Northwestern Univ. Archives, Evanston, Illinois. See also "Celebrations under the Auspices of the Evanston College for Ladies," *CT*, July 5, 1871. Published annual reports and papers of the Chicago Home for the Friendless are at the CHS. Published annual reports of the Women's Presbyterian Board of Missions for the North-West are found at the CHS. These contain Hoge's annual meeting speeches and reports of executive board actions. Her book, *Boys in Blue; Or Heroes of the "Rank and File"* (1867) describes her work with the U.S. Sanitary Commission; further information on Hoge and the Sanitary Commission is found in Alfred T. Andreas, *History of Chicago*, vol. 2 (1885); Linus P. Brockett and Mary C. Vaughn, *Woman's Work in the Civil War* (1867); Sarah E. Henshaw, *Our Branch and Its Tributaries; Being a History of the Work of the Northwestern Sanitary Commission* (1868); Mary A. Livermore, *My Story of the War* (1887); and Mrs. John A. Logan, *The Part Taken by Women in American History* (1912). A biography appears in NAW (1971). Collected memorial tributes are published in *In Memoriam: Jane C. Hoge* (n.d.). Frances E. Willard's tribute appeared in *Woman's Journal*, September 1890.

PEGGY TUCK SINKO

HOLMES, LIZZIE MAY SWANK
1850–August 8, 1926
LABOR ACTIVIST, ANARCHIST, JOURNALIST

Lizzie Swank Holmes, early organizer of Chicago working women, member of the International Working Peoples' Association (IWPA), and a major contributor to *Alarm*, the leading anarchist paper in Chicago, was born Lizzie May Hunt. Her midwest family had a long tradition of radicalism and free thought that reached back to the American Revolution. Details of Lizzie Hunt's early life are lacking. She became a rural school teacher at fifteen and married her first husband at age seventeen, becoming Lizzie M. Swank. When her husband died five years later, she taught music to support herself and two small children.

Lizzie Swank was inspired by the drama of the Great Railroad Strike of 1877 that swept across the United States, virtually ending rail transport and erupting in episodes of violence. The strike ended when federal troops were called in, but Swank, like other working-class observers, experienced a sense of labor's potential power through solidarity. Swank moved to Chicago in the late 1870s to learn about the emerging labor movement. Although the small, dark-haired widow could not have known it at the time, Swank would find herself at the center of momentous events during the next decade.

In Chicago, Lizzie Swank continued to teach music, but she also took a succession of jobs between 1879 and 1881 as a seamstress, partly to supplement her small income from teaching and partly to acquaint herself with workplace conditions endured by women. She joined the fledgling Working Women's Union, founded in 1878 by such pioneer labor organizers as LUCY PARSONS, ALZINA PARSONS STEVENS, and ELIZABETH RODGERS. Conditions were grim in the sweatshops. Swank's labor organizing activity increased, and she became secretary of the union, strong in her opposition to low wages and the unjust treatment faced by women workers. The Working Women's Union joined the eight-hour day campaign that was just beginning. When, in 1879, the Chicago Eight-Hour League held a three-day festival culminating in a Fourth of July parade, the union had a pink float supporting labor organization for women.

Swank and her colleagues found it difficult to organize women in these years. Women suffered in silence because they believed that "no nice girl" (p. 408) would join a union, she wrote years later in a 1905 article, "Women Workers of Chicago." Lacking an understanding of their common cause, they looked upon wage labor as merely a temporary necessity prior to marriage. When in 1880 or 1881 Swank and her sister had found employment in a cloak and suit factory, they tried to organize with the other disgruntled needle-trade women. The women in their shop put together a list of grievances and signed it, presenting the paper to their boss. Then they stopped work. Only Lizzie Swank and her sister ignored the boss's threats and his demand that the women return to work. The strike lasted only three hours and cost Swank her job. Years later, Swank took pride in having encouraged what she believed to have been the first strike of women workers in Chicago history.

Swank returned to teaching music, partly because of her delicate health; but she still pursued union activities. When the Working Women's Union reorganized as Women's Assembly No. 1798 of the Knights of Labor in 1881, Swank was chosen as statistician, charged with the demanding task of investigating the wages and working conditions of Chicago's needle-trade women. That same year, Swank joined the Socialist Labor Party (SLP) and served as secretary of its Chicago branch. She was increasingly influenced, however, by Albert Parsons and the anarchism of the International Working People's Association (IWPA) and joined the American Group of the IWPA, the only English-language chapter in the Chicago area, during the winter of 1883–84. When Parsons began the IWPA's paper, *Alarm*, in October 1884, Lizzie Swank was made assistant editor.

Swank's shift from SLP to IWPA signified her disenchantment with electoral politics. SLP argued that social revolution would come through independent political action. Swank and the IWPA became convinced that electoral politics held no hope for the working class. She wrote in the *Alarm* in 1885 that for the working class, the election process offered no real choice. The voter "was offered a choice between two sets of men, of whom he knows nothing, nominated he does not know how, or why, or by whom, and actuated by one and the same principle—to get there" (quoted in Nelson, *Beyond the Martyrs*, 158). IWPA turned to labor organizing.

Living near Albert and Lucy Parsons on Chicago's Northwest Side, Swank emerged as a key member of the American Group, and she was chosen secretary in November 1885. That same month, she married William Holmes, an English-born member of the American Group who taught shorthand and elocution and lived in Geneva, Illinois, west of Chicago. Despite her marriage, she continued to use the name Lizzie M. Swank throughout her association with the IWPA. As the IWPA's labor militancy grew, so did her commitment to the movement. Her editorials and articles stressed the injustice of capitalism and the right of workers to defend themselves against economic oppression. In keeping with her growing anarchism, she also emphasized the inherent injustice of government. For example, her January 23, 1886, article in *Alarm*, "Abolition of Government," argued that government's sole function was "to protect private property—nothing else," and an editorial in *Alarm* that appeared on election day, November 14, 1885, derided elections as a "semi-annual farce." One month before the eventful May Day of 1886, Swank Holmes, in a style similar to that of other IWPA writers, offered apocalyptic warnings of coming revolution if workers did not receive the justice they deserved.

Swank Holmes's writings also expressed a feminism not usually represented in *Alarm*. She reviewed German socialist August Bebel's pioneering analysis, *Woman in the Past, Present and Future*, and in her contributions to the newspaper, debated whether or not socialist women should engage in the struggle for woman suffrage. Swank Homes argued that the ballot was not the cure for woman's problems, agreeing with Lucy Parsons and others who believed that the revolutionary workers' movement took priority and was, ultimately, the only way to improve conditions of women and men. Swank Holmes wrote that as long as women were economically oppressed, their conditions could never be improved by the meaningless right to select their capitalist oppressors. Pointing out that working men could vote, yet remained wage slaves, she dismissed the right to vote as a "delusion, a gorgeous bubble, pretty to look at but empty as air" (*Alarm*, November 14, 1885).

In the spring of 1886, Swank Holmes turned her attention to the growing eight-hour campaign. Agitation for the eight-hour work day, which had begun in Chicago in 1879, had gathered enormous support among workers, and organizing efforts in 1886 culminated in a march of eighty thousand workers down Chicago's major thoroughfare, Michigan Avenue, on May Day. The majority who marched were men, but Lizzie Swank

Holmes led hundreds of working women on their march. They marched through the garment district, some marchers stopping to encourage women to leave their sweatshops and join the parade. That same day anarchist August Spies addressed a strike meeting near the McCormick Reaper Works, where a protracted strike was ongoing. At the end of the shift, strikebreakers who had been hired by the McCormick company started to file out of the works, and the strikers and union supporters began to jeer them, calling them scabs. A police detail arrived, fired on the strikers, and then charged the crowd. At least two strikers were killed, five or six wounded, and others injured.

It was in this supercharged atmosphere that the call went out for a meeting the following day at Haymarket Square to protest police violence. The event, which took place in an alley off the square, was peaceful by all accounts, including that of Chicago's mayor, Carter Harrison, who had stopped by to assess the situation. He suggested that the police reserves called up for the event be sent home. Threatened by rain, the meeting was about to break up when the police arrived. A bomb exploded, chaos followed, and the police opened fire on the crowd. Seven police officers were killed and seventy others were injured. The bomb thrower was never identified, but the police department began a purge of the IWPA and named thirty-one men in its indictment; only eight were put on trial, including Albert Parsons, who had initially fled to William and Lizzie Holmes's house in Geneva. All the defendants were found guilty; one received a sentence of fifteen years, and the others were sentenced to death. Of those seven, one committed suicide and four, including Parsons, were hanged.

Lizzie Holmes had been at Zepf's Hall across from the Haymarket Square the night of the riot. She had experienced in a brief period of time both the exaltation of worker solidarity in the growth of support for the eight-hour day, and, within hours, the start of a period of repression as the authorities in Chicago pursued IWPA members and all those perceived as radicals dangerous to the state.

During the eighteen months between the arrests and the executions, she visited the imprisoned men twice each week. She was a member of the Amnesty Association that secured pardons for the three surviving but imprisoned Haymarket defendants in 1893. Swank Holmes contributed to Dyer D. Lum's revival of *Alarm* between 1887 and 1889, and she assisted Lucy Parsons in editing her anarchist periodical *Freedom* from 1890 to 1892 and in preparing a posthumous collection of Albert Parsons's writing.

The activist phase of Holmes's life was drawing to a close, however. She and her husband William both suffered periodically from poor health, and in the mid-1890s they moved to Colorado. They settled first in La Veta, where the recently pardoned Haymarket defendant Samuel Fielden was a neighbor, and then in Denver. There, Lizzie Holmes and her husband became involved in the short-lived Denver branch of the Labor Exchange, a cooperative scheme to finance businesses and exchange labor and products outside of the capitalist system. They edited the *Labor Exchange Guide* in 1897 and 1898, but the exchange and the paper collapsed early in 1898.

Lizzie Holmes's continuing impact on the labor and anarchist movements was based, to a large extent, on her voluminous writings. Throughout the 1890s, she contributed frequently on a wide variety of subjects to such anarchist periodicals as Moses Harman's *Lucifer* and Abe Isaak's *Free Society.* Many of her labor reform articles were syndicated across the country by the Associated Labor Press. In addition to articles, she wrote fictional sketches illustrating the follies of governmental authority and the oppression of the working classes. After 1900, the number of her articles began to decline, but Holmes still wrote for anarchist periodicals, and she contributed a series of short stories to the American Federation of Labor periodical, *American Federationist.*

Holmes's basic beliefs in the need to limit governmental power and provide economic justice to American workers never wavered. Her feminism also remained firm. Holmes's articles in *Lucifer* during the 1890s called upon women to free themselves from their double oppression by economic exploitation and male domination. Men had controlled women for so long, she argued in "Lucifer's Critics" (*Lucifer*, August 28, 1891), that neither gender was even conscious of the unequal distribution of power. In a tribute to "Mary Wollstonecraft" (*Lucifer*, April 30, 1903), she lauded women's rights advocates for fostering "the recognition of woman's rights to herself, to live her own life, to development, to a choice in the use of her powers in the world of industry, art, and learning." Holmes's only book-length work, *Hagar Lyndon; or, A Woman's Rebellion*, appeared as a serialized novel in twenty-two issues of *Lucifer* during 1893. The novel illustrated the evils of traditional marriage and assessed the opportunities for a woman to lead an independent life; Holmes ultimately concluded that the prospects for women's independence remained severely limited under existing social conditions.

In her writings after 1887, Holmes returned often to the events surrounding Haymarket, especially to the memory of her coworker and friend, Albert Parsons, whose legacy she worked to keep alive. She contributed almost annual November 11 tributes to the Haymarket martyrs commemorating the date of their execution in 1887, many of which appeared in the anarchist periodical *Free Society.* These memorial essays praised the virtues of the martyrs and called upon later generations to emulate their heroism. Holmes expressed her personal sense of loss and came back again and again to the meaning of the martyred men's deaths. She struggled with the question of whether their sacrifice had influenced the course of history, whether their principles had survived them. Holmes never resolved the question, and her Haymarket memorials alternated between hope and despair for the memory and ideal of her martyred comrades.

In later years, she and her husband moved to Farmington, New Mexico, and finally to Santa Fe, where she died. In her first article in *Alarm*, "The Great Question," which appeared on November 8, 1884, Holmes had argued that everyone must choose between supporting economic exploitation or supporting the rights of the workers to what they produce. Choosing the side of workers meant committing one's life to a noble cause; it was a way to make one's life worthwhile and face death with a clear conscience. This message captured the essence of Lizzie Holmes's importance. In the years after Haymarket, Holmes grew increasingly aware that the anarchist cause to which she had devoted herself was misunderstood and her own efforts often forgotten. Haymarket, however, remained a vivid inspiration

and call to commitment. Although her hopes dimmed, she never compromised her principles or expressed regret over the course of her life.

Sources. Only a few scattered letters from Lizzie Holmes exist. Particularly useful is her letter to Caro Lloyd Withington of July 8, 1909, because it provides a short synopsis of her career. This letter is part of the Henry Demarest Lloyd Papers, State Hist. Soc. of Wisconsin. The principle sources on Lizzie Holmes are the scores of articles she contributed to labor reform and anarchist periodicals. A good cross section of these, illustrating the variety of her interests over twenty years, can be found in *Alarm*, 1884–89; *Lucifer*, 1883–1907; and *Free Society*, 1897–1904. In "Personal Reminiscences of Albert R. Parsons," in Lucy Parsons, *Life of Albert R. Parsons* (1889), Holmes discusses her involvement with the International Working People's Association and the events surrounding the Haymarket bombing. The best source for Holmes's early labor organizing is her essay, "Women Workers of Chicago," *American Federationist*, August 1905. One of Holmes's Haymarket memorials, "Revolutionists," 1899, is reprinted in Dave Roediger and Franklin Rosemont, eds., *Haymarket Scrapbook* (1986). T. H. Bell contributed an obituary of Holmes to *The Road to Freedom*, September 1, 1926. Meredith Tax concentrates on Holmes's work with the Working Women's Union and the Woman's Assembly in *The Rising of the Women: Feminist Solidarity and Class Conflict, 1880–1917* (1980). Both Carolyn Ashbaugh's biography, *Lucy Parsons: American Revolutionary* (1976) and Paul Avrich's definitive narrative *The Haymarket Tragedy* (1984) discuss Holmes within the context of Haymarket; and both treat her relationship with Albert and Lucy Parsons. Bruce C. Nelson's *Beyond the Martyrs* (1988) is also helpful for understanding anarchist ideology and culture. Blaine McKinley analyzes Holmes's post-Haymarket writings in "'A Religion of the New Time': Anarchist Memorials to the Haymarket Martyrs," *Labor History*, Summer 1987; and in "Free Love and Domesticity: Lizzie M. Holmes, *Hagar Lyndon* (1893), and the Anarchist-Feminist Imagination," *Journal of American Culture*, Spring 1990.

BLAINE MCKINLEY

HOLT, NORA DOUGLAS
November 1883–January 25, 1974
MUSIC CRITIC, COMPOSER, RADIO PROGRAM HOST
AND PRODUCER

Nora Douglas was born in Missouri, although she considered herself a native of Kansas City, Kansas. She and her brother Lorenzo were the only children born to Calvin N. and Gracie (Brown) Douglas. Her father was a minister in the African Methodist Episcopal (AME) Church. A homemaker and educator, Gracie Douglas encouraged Nora to begin taking piano lessons at the age of four years. Her musical talents blossomed. By 1900, young Nora and her mother were residing at Western University, an AME school in Quindaro, Kansas, that, well into the first third of the twentieth century, provided a solid educational foundation for hundreds of African American families residing in the states of Kansas and Missouri. Nora Douglas's mother was one of the school's head administrators and a teacher of domestic economy. Douglas graduated with honors and was the class valedictorian. She also completed formal training at Kansas State College in 1915.

Her commitment to the uplifting of her race can be attributed to her early association with proud, educated, cultured African Americans; AME doctrine; and her parents' lifelong faithfulness to the church's mission. Rather than devoting her time and talents to the church as did her parents, she chose to uplift by using print, the most advanced medium of her day. Her only extended affiliation with any church prior to coming to Chicago was as organist for a number of years at the St. Augustine Episcopal Church in Kansas City, Missouri. While in Chicago, she was one of the favored lecturers on music at the Grace Presbyterian Church's monthly lyceum.

Douglas came to Chicago to study music at Chicago Musical College (CMC). Her enthusiasm for coming to CMC was undoubtedly ignited by her childhood music instructor, N. Clark Smith, who began his music training in Kansas City, Missouri, and completed it at CMC. As early as the 1890s, Chicago's institutions of higher education were welcoming black talent. Founded in 1867, CMC became part of Roosevelt University in the 1950s. Along with the American Conservatory, founded in 1886, the CMC welcomed African American musicians. One of CMC's distinguished protégés, Smith became an instructor of band and orchestra at Western University sometime after 1913. Holt credited Smith with taking her to her first concert to hear the Chicago Symphony Orchestra. One major source of Smith's impact on her was his devotion to Negro folk songs. Holt's classical training and often severe classical biases never hampered her adoration of and devotion to Negro spirituals and folk songs as representative forms of America's best music.

Douglas's talent as an artist was recognized early in her academic career. It preceded her to Chicago when William Henry Hackney's 1915 Second Annual All-Colored Composers Program at Orchestra Hall included her composition "Who Knows," which set to music the words of poet Paul Lawrence Dunbar. She was one of two women composers on the program.

Douglas is reported to have married at least three times before she left Kansas to pursue her degree at CMC. Some of her biographers speculate that she was married to Sky James, a musician, and later to Phillip Scoggins, a politician. She was reportedly next married to barber Bruce Jones for about one year. Speculation has it that Jones was the "Chicago husband" whom her fifth husband, Joseph Ray, in an attempt to obtain an annulment, asserted she had not properly divorced. She provided appropriate documentation in court to prove him wrong.

In 1917, Nora Douglas earned a bachelor's degree in music from CMC and accepted a marriage proposal from a very wealthy businessman who was twenty-three years her senior. George W. Holt, an investor in real estate and the major stockholder and treasurer of the Liberty Life Insurance Company, provided his bride with all the luxuries that life in Chicago's prosperous black community could offer. She was also able to pursue her education full time, earning a master's degree in music in 1918, perhaps the first African American in the United States to receive such a degree. She won the highest honors for her master's thesis, "a symphonic rhapsody of forty-two pages for an [sic] hundred piece orchestra" ("Lena James Holt Takes High Honors at Chicago Musical College," Chicago Defender, June 30, 1918), titled "Rhapsody on Negro Themes." She attributed her "musical success to the wonderful inspirative [sic] background her husband formed when he presented her an elegant residence at 4405 S. Prairie Avenue" ("Lena James Holt Takes High Honors at Chicago Musical College," Chicago Defender, June 30, 1918), fully decorated in New England style and with a Mason & Hamlin concert grand piano.

In November 1917, she began writing a music column in the Chicago Defender. Editor Robert S. Abbott, whom she praised for his "broad vision in seeing that music is one of the greatest refiners of the race" (Chicago Defender, January 1, 1921), contributed the space. Her column, initially entitled "The Opera" and later "News of the Music World," was the first music column to appear in an African American newspaper.

Home to a progressive, upwardly mobile African American community, Chicago was exceptionally fertile ground for Holt's writings. The Defender had a readership of more than one million, and Chicago was already acknowledged as a budding black musical mecca. Although she favored the opera and the symphony orchestra, she had a high regard for the music of the African American tradition. Her first column featured a description of the ambience of an opening night at the opera, painting a vivid picture for individuals in small hamlets in Mississippi as well as for Chicago opera lovers.

Holt had a flair for description but was also a tough critic. Whether her subject was white or black musicians performing in operas, orchestras, or recitals, she observed every aspect of their performance. She commented on the costuming, the presence or absence of musical training, etiquette, program protocols, voice coloration, inflections, diction, and the emotions of the performer. She noted if an artist appeared anxious or the performance fell short of her high standards. Holt frequently advised artists to obtain additional training to refine their talents or to restrict their musical endeavors to the genre in which their talent was more obvious. She was also very gracious and generous in bestowing praise on those artists she felt exhibited tremendous talent and prowess. Her column appeared regularly until the early 1920s and then sporadically until the final July 14, 1923, issue.

In general, Holt felt that Americans were less cultured than Europeans because they undervalued music. She felt that this lack provided Blacks who were willing to prepare themselves with an opportunity to excel on a world-class scale. She also characterized Chicago as suffering from "cultural aphasia" (Chicago Defender, December 8, 1917) until it presented Boston's Roland Hayes, a soon-to-be world-renowned tenor. His appearance at the South Park Methodist Episcopal Church caused Holt to proclaim a "Chicago Renaissance" (Chicago Defender, December 8, 1917). Her column announced every first and every progressive stride made by African Americans in the field of music. She annually posted national graduation announcements for individuals pursuing degrees and certificates in higher education in music. She championed the rights of musicians to be paid for their services, even by churches. She also issued the call, in her April 12, 1919, column, for a national organization of musicians with local chapters. She declared a "period of world reconstruction" (Chicago Defender, April 26, 1919) in which music by African Americans would transcend racial barriers and ultimately uplift the race.

Holt held the founding meeting for the Chicago Music Association at her home in the spring of 1919. She was elected its president, a position she held until 1922, when she refused nomination to the post. Her plans at that time were to pursue study in anthropology at Columbia University and travel to "Europe for extended study and research work" (*Chicago Defender*, April 15, 1922). She also hosted the March 12, 1919, founding meeting for the National Association of Negro Musicians (NANM) at her home. The organization's first national convention was held that year from July 29 to July 31 in Chicago. Holt was elected vice-president of the NANM and remained a member of its executive committee until 1922, when she resigned her post. The NANM's objective was to promote appreciation of traditional and contemporary music by African Americans, raise professional standards, and encourage the work of aspiring and seasoned musicians. In order to accomplish NANM's goals, Holt suggested the establishment of a scholarship fund; composer FLORENCE PRICE received an NANM scholarship in 1932.

Holt's views about music changed over time. Initially deriding jazz as "played by untutored, rampant horn tooters, reeking with reincarnate primitiveness" (*Chicago Defender*, October 1, 1922), she soon had a change of heart, classifying it as one of the musical forms, along with opera and symphony, that was making Chicago "mad with music" (*Chicago Defender*, November 18, 1922). Apparently her close association with such artists as Eubie Blake and J. Rosamond Johnson influenced her opinion. Nonetheless, she was quick to inform her readers that Blake often attended symphony orchestra performances.

In addition to her weekly column and leadership role with the NANM, she was a patron of a number of charitable organizations that included the Phyllis Wheatley Home. She was a frequent lecturer on musical topics. She developed papers and talks on such topics as "Music," "The Origin of Negro Music," "Musicianship," and "The New Era in Music." She was also a featured composer at Orchestra Hall in May 1922 when Chicago featured "A Night with the Negro."

In 1921 she founded and became the editor of *Music and Poetry*. Immediately popular, the magazine featured original musical scores by Holt and a number of her contemporaries and articles by some of the brightest and best musicians in America. To keep the magazine afloat, she received financial support from a number of women associated with such wealthy Chicago families as the Armours, Murphys, McCormicks, and Lobdells. Although the magazine was short-lived, it received numerous accolades in both the black and white press and could be found in the most elite black homes, as well as in the music library collections of universities and colleges around the world. By the time of its demise, Holt's energies had shifted.

There have been a number of assertions that Holt had a whirlwind romance with Joseph Luther Ray of Bethlehem, Pennsylvania. Secretary to Bethlehem Steel magnate Charles Schwab, Ray also owned the concessions contract for the steel firm. The July 28, 1923, *Defender* featured a front-page photo of Holt with an announcement of her wedding, identified as the social event of the year. Later accounts noted that Holt sported six carats of diamonds in each ear and also a black eye given to her by a Dr. Gordon Jackson, with whom she was allegedly having an affair. The marriage began to fall apart immediately upon Holt's and Ray's return from their honeymoon. He sued her for divorce and was willing to use any method available to degrade and demean her, alleging she had not properly divorced one of

her previous husbands. His verbal assaults were regularly published in the *Chicago Defender, The Light and Heebie Jeebies*, and the *InterState Tattler*. Holt withstood them all until February 6, 1927, when she wrote an extensive column for the *Chicago Defender* telling her side of the Holt/Ray conflict. Although it took until 1930 for the divorce decree to be issued, Holt emerged victorious, maintaining possession of jewelry, land, and her good name.

While her marriage to Ray was on the rocks, Holt began traveling to New York, meeting its black elite and making life-long friendships with such individuals as Carl Van Vechten. She earned a considerable reputation abroad as an entertainer, touring extensively in Europe (Paris, Monte Carlo, London, and Italy), Shanghai, and Japan. The *London Daily Express* referred to her as a "blond creole . . . [with] a presence and manner similar to Sophia [*sic*] Tucker" (Dannett, 147), but with a voice that was more outstanding and possessed greater range. In 1937, she returned to the United States only to discover that her books and manuscripts had been stolen. She quickly settled in California and, while there, reportedly taught in the California school system and was associated with a beauty salon.

In 1943, Holt returned to New York City to work at the *New York Amsterdam News* as its music editor, a post she held until 1956, although no music reviews appeared after 1952. Her first article appeared in January 1944. Shortly thereafter, the American Newspaper Guild admitted her into its ranks as the first African American member functioning with a union contract in the role of critic and music editor. In 1945, Virgil Thompson, music critic for the *New York Herald Tribune*, sponsored Holt as a member of the Music Critics Circle of New York. She was the first black member of this exclusive society.

From 1953 to 1963 Holt hosted her own radio program, *Nora Holt's Concert Showcase*, on New York's radio station WLIB. Her initial contact with this medium occurred in Chicago on October 27, 1922, when she accompanied soprano Maude Roberts George on the *Daily News* radio station. The program, *Hear America First*, was hosted by ANNE OBERN-DORFER.

In New York Holt became involved in a variety of music-related activities. Beginning in 1945 on radio station WNYC, Holt began staging an annual festival, *American Negro Artists*. She joined the *New York Courier* as its music critic in 1956; the dates of her tenure there are unclear. Holt continued her role as music critic and producer for *Concert Showcase* until she retired to Los Angeles, California, in 1964.

In 1966, she served as a member of the Communications Committee at the First World Festival of Negro Arts, which was held in Dakar, Senegal, in April. Her international travels apparently continued until 1973. She died in 1974 at ninety years of age.

Holt was a pioneer in the field of music appreciation among black audiences on a national scale. Her column served to educate African Americans about classical music and to encourage its study. She also encouraged music education as crucial to the fine-tuning of one's talents. Her credo was that "no race can rise higher than its culture" (Dannett, 149). She felt that the extensive training needed to become proficient in music would be the catalyst for the African American's progress. Holt believed that music was the great equalizer of the races. Although many of her detractors of the late twentieth century have found her adoration of classical music odious, they have had to admit that she also applauded the forms of music created by Blacks. She encouraged Blacks to become cultured in their musical tastes and to use that discernment to advance appreciation of their spirituals and folk songs. She did not allow her marital status to prevent her from pursuing a goal, and she encouraged both women and men to seek the highest education. Holt said that her life aim was to "serve the divine art of music and true musicians. All can aid and benefit if they keep their heart pure, their aims high, and their lives void of vanity. Only this type of musician will ever truly succeed" (*Chicago Defender*, October 17, 1921). Holt was able both to succeed and to provide the fertile ground on which other African American musicians could do likewise for generations to come.

Sources. This entry uses the 1900 U.S. Census birth date of November 1883 and Missouri as the birthplace for Nora Douglas; the entry in *BWA* uses 1885 and Kansas City, Kansas, as the birthplace. Her master's composition is described in "Lena James Holt Takes High Honors at Chicago Musical College," *Chicago Defender*, June 30, 1918. Nora Holt's column in the *Chicago Defender*, from November 17, 1917, through July 14, 1923, is an important source. She initially published her column under the byline Lena James Douglas but switched to Nora Douglas Holt. Her unpublished two-page biography of H. E. Hagan is in the Carl Van Vechten Papers, the Yale Collection of American Literature, Beinecke Rare Book and Manuscript Library, Yale Univ. An incomplete set of the first year of publication of *Music and Poetry*, January 21, 1921–October 21, 1921, is in the James W. Johnson Memorial Collection, the Yale Collection of American Literature, Beinecke Rare Book and Manuscript Library. Biographical sketches include G. L. Sylvia Dannett, "Nora Douglas Holt," in *Profiles of Negro Womanhood*, ed. G. L. Sylvia Dannett, vol. 2, *Twentieth Century* (1966); Bruce Kellner, "Nora Holt," in *The Harlem Renaissance: A Historical Dictionary for the Era*, ed. Bruce Kellner (1984); Eileen Southern, "Nora Holt," in *Biographical Dictionary of Afro-American and African Musicians*, ed. Eileen Southern (1982); Robert L. Johns, "Nora Holt," in *Notable Black American Women*, ed. Jessie Carney Smith (1992); Rawn Spearman, "Nora Douglas Holt," in *BWA*. See also Helen Walker-Hill, "Black Women Composers in Chicago: Then and Now," *Black Music Research Journal*, Spring 1992. Obituaries appear in *Black Perspective in Music*, Spring 1974, and *Los Angeles Times*, January 30, 1974.

DEBORAH C. UMRANI

HONIGBAUM, PESSIE HERSHFELD POMERANTZ. *See* POMERANTZ HONIGBAUM, PESSIE HERSHFELD

HOPKINS, JOSEPHINE EMMA CURTIS
September 2, 1849–April 8, 1925
FOUNDER OF AN ORGANIZED RELIGION, FEMINIST
THEOLOGIAN, TEACHER, WRITER

Emma Curtis Hopkins founded a nationwide ministry that organized New Thought in Chicago between 1886 and 1888 by mobilizing and empowering primarily women and some men who were also pioneers in this alternative religious tradition based on spiritual healing. She was the oldest of nine children born to Rufus and Lydia (Phillips) Curtis of Killingly, Connecticut. Emma Curtis attended the Congregational Church,

graduated from the local high school, and taught school prior to her marriage to George Irving Hopkins, a high school English teacher, on July 19, 1874. They had a son, John Carver, who was born June 8, 1875, and died in 1905. Hopkins and her husband were separated in the mid-1880s, when she devoted her life to spiritual healing and social activism; they divorced in 1900. Hopkins always spoke well of her husband. Yet, in the manner of some mystics, she believed she was married to God and her mission was more important than traditional matrimony.

The young Emma Curtis hoped to alleviate human suffering when she envisioned a children's hospital on a select portion of her parents' farm. In 1883, this vision was transformed when she heard Mary Baker Eddy speak of the spiritual healing of Christian Science as an alternative to medical treatment. She spoke of her childhood vision when she applied to Eddy for a space in her next class. She believed Eddy's method of silent healing worthy of exploration. Consequently, in December 1883, she traveled to Boston to take the one-week basic course of study with Eddy at the Massachusetts Metaphysical College; she graduated that month.

At Eddy's behest, Hopkins wrote for and then assumed an unpaid but full editorship of the *Christian Science Journal* on September 6, 1884. Sixteen months later, Hopkins was asked to resign her position and was excommunicated from the Christian Science Association by Eddy. The reasons were never formally disclosed; however, internal power struggles and sibling-type antagonism against Hopkins within Eddy's Christian Science Association seemed to be a factor in the discharge. Ideologically, Hopkins could not support some assumptions of Eddy's theology, especially the premise of malicious animal magnetism, which was supposed to be a form of evil influence projected mentally by one's enemies. Despite their differences, Hopkins never spoke ill of Eddy or her teaching.

"Sometime between 1885 and 1888 Hopkins shifted her visionary focus from the particular plan of her youth. The world became an extension of her parents' farm, and its inhabitants, the sick children. Her hospitals were lecture halls where she conveyed her message. New Thought emerged as the crucial therapy administered by minister-physicians who healed in silent communion through positive affirmation" (Harley, "Emma Curtis Hopkins," 144).

Historically, New Thought's antecedents were found in the work of noted eighteenth-century Swedish scientist Emanuel Swedenborg, who postulated that events in the supernatural realm correlated with phenomena in the finite world (the "as above—so below" principle). The Transcendentalists appropriated this idea and combined philosophical ideas from the sacred texts of the East. Phineas Parkhurst Quimby, of Belfast, Maine, sparked ideas about mental healing using a verbal process that linked the individual's spiritual nature with divine spirit. He was a healer, and one of his patients was Mary Baker Eddy. The intellectual and philosophical milieu from the 1860s onward provided this theoretical framework for the "mind cure" proponents who would meld bits and pieces of these ideas into a pragmatic organizational base. While New Thought had strong proponents in the East, it was in the Midwest that the concepts of metaphysical healing flourished and developed a democratic base.

Hopkins relocated in Chicago in early 1886 with the energetic Mary Plunkett, another excommunicant from Eddy's organization. That year they founded the Emma Curtis Hopkins College of Christian Science—using the term generically to indicate metaphysical healing. Hopkins served as the teacher and Plunkett performed the administrative duties as president. The first class to graduate from Hopkins College in June 1886 had thirty-seven students who formed an alumni group called the Hopkins Metaphysical Association (HMA). Ida Nichols founded and published *Christian Science*, the literary vehicle for the HMA. Among the first graduates were Helen Wilmans, newspaper journalist and founder of *Woman's World* magazine, and Mabel McCoy and Kate Bingham. McCoy and Bingham taught others who were instrumental in founding Divine Science, a metaphysical ministry based in Denver, Colorado. The far-reaching influence of this class earned for Hopkins the epithet "teacher of teachers" and upon this network she established her nationwide ministry.

By 1887, there were twenty-one Hopkins Associations stretched across the continent. The HMA network fostered the paradigm shift in thinking away from the allopathic school of medicine that presupposed a germ theory of sickness. Allopathic practitioners based medical care on the relief of acute symptoms in the physical body. Graduates of Hopkins College viewed the individual as an integration of mind, body, and spirit. This multidimensional approach to health provided one impetus for the growth of psychosomatic and holistic medical research in the twentieth century.

Celebrated for her charisma and oratorical power, Hopkins was a tall, slender, exquisitely groomed woman who wore large picture hats when she spoke to groups. Like Eddy, she taught her students that the Creative Principle (God) was the only reality and not an anthropomorphic deity. She denied evil, sickness, and death. She hypothesized that history consisted of three periods: the first, a patriarchal period ending with the birth of Jesus; the second, the period of Jesus's life and teachings, when the world would be prepared for the third and final era, the second coming of Christ. This second coming was not a physical resurrection but a spiritual advent that would change the world through application of divine healing methods symbolized by the feminine principle within the Trinity. Hopkins dedicated her entire Truth ministry to this feminine principle. By asserting the holiness of women through inclusion with divinity, she empowered women to seek pulpits of power and prestige that had previously been denied them in patriarchal culture.

In 1888, Hopkins dissolved the college and created the rigorously structured Christian Science Theological Seminary (CSTS). She purchased a large home to provide residential and seminary space. Following the model of Protestant seminaries, she designed the curriculum to prepare students specifically for the ministry. Such segments of the course as biblical hermeneutics were taught by specialists in that particular area. Everyone took the basic course in a classroom setting. However, because Hopkins believed her mission to be sacred and metaphysical healing, a spiritual profession, not a secular business, she personally taught the advanced healing course in "Theology and Practical Ministry" only to the most dedicated students.

The CSTS catalogue for 1893 demonstrated its universal ideals. The statement of purpose indicated that it was founded to compare the sacred scriptures of all religions and to show that miracles occur in them all; that there is a single divine judgment for all of humanity; and that the theology of the seminary teaches one to find prosperity, stamina, health, and spiritual protection. All ministers, teachers, home keepers, artisans, and lay people were invited to join in the daily services at the seminary at twelve noon or to commune silently.

Hopkins began writing spiritual healing texts prolifically, including *Class Lessons* (1888) and mystical texts such as *Drops of Gold* (1891), which contained specific daily affirmations for the year based on biblical passages of a mystical nature. She instituted weekly Bible lessons in *Christian Science* in 1888 and inaugurated weekly international Bible lessons in the Chicago *Inter-Ocean* newspaper that ran for almost nine years.

On January 10, 1889, the first class of twenty-two students graduated from Hopkins's CSTS. ELIZABETH HARBERT, writer of "A Woman's Kingdom," a major column for the *Inter-Ocean*, was astonished that twenty of the graduates were women. During her graduation address this noted suffragist and writer welcomed the group as public workers. Hopkins, as a creative catalyst, set the stage for radical innovations from her candidates for ordination. This was the first time in history that a woman assumed the authority of the head of a seminary, ordained women graduates as Christian ministers, and told them "the world is their church" (Harley, 100). Louisa Southworth, an officer of the National Woman Suffrage Association, felt privileged to be present at the "Ceremony of the New Era" (Harley, 122–23), the ordaining of women by a woman.

The CSTS's recently purchased large residence on the South Side of Chicago served as the central hub for its missionaries, who used discounted ministerial railroad passes to travel from Maine to California. Helen (Nellie) Van Anderson and Jane Yarnall took the lead in missionary activity. Van Anderson later founded the first long-term New Thought Center in Boston, Massachusetts, and Yarnall reorganized the branch in St. Louis, Missouri. Her student Frances Lord wrote *Christian Science Healing: Its Principles and Practices* (1888) and took this book back to her native England for dissemination there. The New Thought principle of prosperity originated in the work of Lord. Van Anderson authored *The Right Knock* (1889), which was a thinly veiled book about Hopkins and her movement for grand social and spiritual reform.

Responding to both sacred and secular causes within the social justice arena, Hopkins affiliated her graduates with the Illinois Woman's Alliance, a reform coalition representing twenty-five separate women's groups dedicated to protecting and bettering the lives of women and children, and encouraged HMA members to assist the Women's Federal Labor Union of Chicago with employment issues. Her alumni supported temperance as a spiritual norm through participation in the religiously affiliated King's Daughters Association. During the World's Columbian Exposition of 1893, the HMA supported other groups involved in the struggle for social justice by exhibiting with the egalitarian Queen Isabella Association instead of in the religion section.

By 1893, more than 350 students had completed the basic course at the CSTS and 111 had been ordained as ministers.

How many more were graduated is not known. Hopkins's enthusiastic ordinands ensured that New Thought would be a decided influence in American religion and become an exciting export to other nations. By 1895, yearning for the peace of solitary mysticism and sure of the secure foundation of New Thought in national and international circles, Hopkins believed her initial missionary quest successfully completed and closed the CSTS. Trusted lieutenants Fanny Harley and Annie Rix-Militz continued the Chicago work. Hopkins relocated to New York City that year.

Although she continued to write and teach, not much is known about Hopkins's later years until 1916, when, in her suite of rooms at the Warrington Hotel, she individually taught the avant-garde of art, literature, and drama, including Mabel Dodge Luhan, her twelve steps in mysticism. In 1918, Hopkins was voted honorary president of the International New Thought Alliance—a network of individuals and groups who supported religious and secular dimensions of New Thought. Because she believed her message more important than personal celebrity status, her work has been assimilated by others and her unique contributions have been veiled. Despite encroachment by men in New Thought, who took over the reins of institutional power in the early twentieth century, Hopkins's feminist theology survived, serving as a model for the twentieth century. Many late-twentieth-century New Thought and alternative religions support the feminist interpretations that Hopkins championed, such as the connection of Holy Spirit with the feminine aspect of God.

In 1923, ill with congestive heart failure, Hopkins left her suite at the Iroquois Hotel in New York City and returned to her childhood home in Connecticut. Two years later, she died at age seventy-five of chronic myocarditis at the farm of her sister, Estelle Darrow, in Killingly, Connecticut. She is buried in the Curtis family plot in Dayville Cemetery, Dayville, Connecticut.

Hopkins taught every founder of a significant New Thought ministry, including Ernest Holmes (Religious Science, Los Angeles), writer and poet Ella Wheeler Wilcox, and Selena Chamberlain. The Reverend Norman Vincent Peale, influenced by Holmes, spoke of the power contained in affirmative thinking. Hopkins's legacy can be traced to spiritual healing groups such as the Order of St. Luke, Episcopal Church, and her writings continue to be read.

Sources. Hopkins published frequently in *Christian Science* and the *Christian Metaphysician.* She also wrote for the Chicago newspaper *Inter-Ocean* from 1888 to 1897. Hopkins's books are still available through New Thought ministries and bookstores, including *Drops of Gold* (1891), *High Mysticism* (n.d.), *Resume* (n.d.), *Scientific Christian Mental Practice* (n.d.), and *Class Lessons* (1888). She is mentioned in Mabel Dodge Luhan, *New York Movers and Shakers,* vol. 3 of *Intimate Memories,* 3 vols. (1933). Writings about Hopkins contain significant errors, including the entry in *NAW* (1971), which has errors in birth and death dates, number of children in the Curtis family, and her sisters' names. Also, the entry supports her alleged (and erroneous) ownership of the *Christian Metaphysician.* She was a frequent contributor, but not an owner. The most up-to-date work on her is J. Gordon Melton, "Emma Curtis Hopkins: A Feminist of the 1880's and Mother of New Thought," in *Women's Leadership in Marginal Religions: Explorations Outside the Mainstream,* ed. Catherine Wessinger (1993). Two dissertations are

valuable: Gail M. Harley, "Emma Curtis Hopkins: 'Forgotten Founder' of New Thought" (Ph.D. diss., Florida State Univ., 1991), and Beryl E. Satter, "New Thought and the Era of Woman, 1875–1895" (Ph.D. diss., Yale Univ., 1992). See also Satter's publication, *Each Mind a Kingdom: American Women, Reform and the New Thought Movement, 1875–1920* (1999). A book by Gail M. Harley, with the same title as her dissertation, is forthcoming.

GAIL M. HARLEY

HUBBARD, MARY ANN MILLS
November 2, 1820–July 19, 1909
HOMEMAKER, CARETAKER

Mary Ann Hubbard's life as an early Chicago settler and a family caretaker shows the obligations of women in the years before modern medicine and housekeeping aids eased the burden of domestic work. In fulfilling her responsibilities, she provided support for male relations who were building success in the business community. Hubbard was the daughter of Ahira and Serena (Tucker) Hubbard, of colonial Massachusetts and Connecticut ancestry. Her older siblings, Henry G., Paulina, and Harriet, were born in Windsor, Vermont, where Ahira Hubbard was a highly educated merchant, a mathematician, and sometime surveyor. Financial reverses from the War of 1812 embargo and the paralyzing illness of Serena Hubbard's widowed mother at the Tucker home in Middleboro, Massachusetts, brought the Hubbards there to live as farmers for the next twenty years. Three more children were born at Middleboro—Mary Ann, usually called Ann by her family; Eliza; and Ellen Marie.

Ann and Eliza Hubbard were taught at home by their father and an older sister, but regular school hours were kept. One summer, a private school was available at the Congregational Church, and Ann Hubbard boarded part of one year at the local Pierce Academy for Young Men and Maidens. She gave up dolls at the age of eight, when she began to assist her mother with child care after the birth of her youngest sister. Thus began a life-long pattern of family caretaking that engaged Mary Ann Hubbard's talents. Hubbard described her sisters as beautiful and talented but saw herself as very large, very timid and sensitive, homely, stupid, and ungainly. A nephew credited her strong, un-self-centered religious faith for her ability to become a notably positive, cheerful adult.

The late 1820s began a period of major change for the Hubbard family. In 1827, two orphaned sons of Serena Hubbard's nephew joined the family. About the same time, Henry Hubbard, Ann's brother, joined the burgeoning movement to promising lands in the West, trying Utica, Indiana, and then Danville, Illinois. Ahira Hubbard visited his son in Danville in 1830, possibly to test the waters for a larger family migration. However, he there contracted malarial fever and ague, a disease unknown in New England, and was gone so long he was given up for dead before he finally reached home. He was not well for several years, and thoughts of a western move were abandoned.

By 1834, a lonesome Henry Hubbard had persuaded his sister Harriet to join him in the new town of Chicago, where he was now in business with his cousin Gurdon Saltonstall Hubbard, who had just left the declining fur trade in the region to engage in real estate speculation and the marketing of livestock. On March 25, 1835, Harriet Hubbard became the second wife of Richard J. Hamilton, a prominent Chicago lawyer and entrepreneur, and a widower with four children aged eight and under. At the same time, back in Middleboro, Ann Hubbard's sister Paulina Hubbard married Reland Tinkham and moved to Bangor, Maine, where she and her new baby soon died.

In 1836, with Ahira Hubbard's health improved, Ann Hubbard's two siblings already settled in Chicago urged further family migration. Thus the Middleboro Hubbards decided that "the prospect for the future seemed better" (Hubbard, *Family Memories*, 56) in the western boom town. To the family's regret, the two boys who had been part of the family for almost ten years remained behind at their legal guardian's insistence.

The day after their arrival in Chicago, Ann and Eliza Hubbard began school at FRANCES LANGDON WILLARD's private academy for girls. There Hubbard, who had firm religious and educational ideals, saw a dichotomy in the student body that she also observed in Chicago's society in general: the different lifestyles and attitudes of Chicagoans of southern and eastern origin. She regarded most southern girls as uneducated and eager to get into "society." In 1836, the zenith year of Chicago's speculative and easy credit era, they dressed extravagantly and lived for parties. To easterners like the Hubbards, "education seemed the one thing needful" (Hubbard, *Family Memories*, 69). Hubbard admired her mother for disdaining southern pretensions and for caring "not how hard she worked if she could have her family well-educated and with good manners and moral characters" (Hubbard, *Family Memories*, 69). Ann Hubbard realized that at sixteen she was considered by some Chicagoans as too old to be in school rather than society, yet she did not attend the parties. To her, it "would have been a severe trial . . . to have been obliged to be *grown up*. My ambition was to study and keep in school year after year" (Hubbard, *Family Memories*, 70).

Hubbard's scholarly ambition was thwarted at age seventeen when her sister, Harriet Hamilton, became ill after the death of her baby daughter, and then had a second girl. The Hamiltons, impoverished by the bad times of 1837, could no longer afford servants, so Ann Hubbard did housework, sewing, shopping, and, with her sister, divided continual care of the new baby, who died at eighteen months from an unknown illness. While Hubbard was still with the Hamiltons, her brother Henry married Julia Smith, daughter of Judge Theophilus W. Smith. Eliza Hubbard married next, to lawyer and real estate agent James Grant, and they moved to Iowa, near Davenport.

After Ann Hubbard had helped nurse Henry Hubbard through a near-fatal "congestive fever" he contracted while involved with the Illinois and Michigan Canal, her sister Eliza Grant in Iowa needed her help with an expected baby. Hubbard left Chicago for the rural, pioneer community of Rockingham in November 1839 and stayed nine months. James Grant had a prosperous farm and was an aspiring politician, with sufficient hired help to leave Hubbard and her lonely sister with time on their hands during his frequent absences. Hubbard read large histories, Shakespeare, and even Grant's law books, socialized, and sewed, but still felt homesick and uncomfortable with so little work to do.

When Ann Hubbard returned to Chicago, her mother was nursing chronically ill Harriet Hamilton, who now had an infant

son. Hubbard moved in with the Hamiltons so Serena Hubbard could join her husband in Lockport, where he was farming. As the ailing woman's lung problem grew worse, however, mother rejoined single daughter in caring for the invalid and the large Hamilton household. Hoping the Iowa climate would be better than Chicago's, Harriet Hamilton, her baby, Serena Hubbard, and a hired girl spent the summer of 1841 at the Grants' home. Ann Hubbard took over housekeeping for her father at Lockport, as well as supervising three Hamilton step-nieces, her own sister Ellen, and a niece of Richard Hamilton's. She remembered it as a summer of extreme drought, hard work, and toothache.

Against medical advice, a much-improved Harriet Hamilton returned to Chicago in the fall, anxious to reunite her family; she died, however, February 1842. In May of the same year, Eliza Grant also died. About the same time, Ahira Hubbard gave up the Lockport farm and thereafter maintained a home in Chicago. Around the time daughter Ann Hubbard, just twenty-three, married her wealthy first cousin Gurdon Hubbard, November 9, 1843, Ahira Hubbard became the businessman's bookkeeper. Gurdon Hubbard was eighteen years his new wife's senior, and a widower with a five-year-old son, Gurdon Jr.

Ann and Gurdon Hubbard had no children together, but they still brought up a family. In addition to Gurdon Jr., Margaret and Mary Clark, Gurdon's nieces, daughters of a widowed invalid sister, came to live with them sometime in the first decade of the marriage. About 1854 Alice Tinkham, a ten-year-old child of a later marriage of Reland Tinkham, who had first married Hubbard's sister Paulina, was sent to them by her again-widowed, dying father. Ahira Hubbard died of cholera in August 1849; his wife lived with the Gurdon Hubbards into the 1870s.

At the Gurdon Hubbard North Side home, dinner was always prepared in quantity for unexpected visitors, guests of the hospitable and well-connected businessman. Although Ann Hubbard remained retiring in nature, when her husband brought Abraham Lincoln and Orville H. Browning to visit in 1858, Browning found her "a more than usually spritely & vivacious and agreeable woman" (*Diary of Orville Hickman Browning*, 330). Ann Hubbard independently adhered to the Presbyterian Church. Her husband remained loyal to St. James' Episcopalian Church, which he helped found; sometimes his wife attended with him. The Hubbards' life included travel, even as far as California, and they, like many wealthy Chicagoans, had a summer place on Mackinac Island, in northern Michigan.

Gurdon Hubbard lost much of his wealth through business reverses and the Great Chicago Fire of 1871 but recouped enough to live with some comfort thereafter. In his last years, he was in very poor health and totally blind. His wife again became nurse and caretaker to make his last days comfortable until he died September 14, 1886.

After 1890, Ann Hubbard, with her companion Sarah Marsh, lived in the Marquette Building at Rush and Ohio streets. Her library was the gathering place for more than one generation of relatives, church workers, and others of various nationalities and social classes. The noon meal was still prepared in expectation of unexpected guests. Crippled with rheumatism, Hubbard nevertheless retained her inquiring mind. A

1909 Chicago Historical Society (CHS) memorial honoring her commented that "in her earlier life woman's activities were limited by custom, and in later years physical infirmities kept her in bonds" but marveled at her "almost masculine understanding and grasp of affairs generally" (CHS, *Annual Report*, 217–19). Among her quiet philanthropies, Hubbard, concerned with the importance of religion and education as tools for assimilating foreign-born immigrants to Chicago, built and equipped a mission chapel for Italian immigrants. After her death, Ann Hubbard still cared for people. Her will left her $113,000 estate to several individual women, most of them relatives; church causes; and the needy of Chicago. In 1914, a Bohemian Presbyterian church built with some of these funds was dedicated in her honor.

The story of (Mary) Ann Hubbard's life is inseparable from that of her close-knit family. As her life shows, single women could become almost itinerant, moving among various married siblings' and parents' homes to provide needed extra help. Married women provided the support systems for male city-builders and at the same time raised the next generation and provided assistance to these extended families. Ann Hubbard's life story also illustrates the powerful influence of family networking in western settlement and commercial development; one or two successful emigrants could be the catalysts for the rest of the family to move. Women gave up material comfort, ancestral territory, and, in many cases, a more healthful climate, in hopes of improving prospects for the future.

Sources. The chief source for the life of Mary Ann Hubbard is her own memoir, *Family Memories* (1912). Printed privately for family and friends, Hubbard's book sometimes neglects dates and sequences of events, but it is frank and insightful in its impressions of early Chicago, as well as in providing a description of one family's experience in the Great Chicago Fire. The only known letter in Hubbard's own hand is her note of November 7, 1907, in the E. W. Blatchford Collection, NL. In 1868, when the Hubbards celebrated their twenty-fifth wedding anniversary and his fiftieth year since coming to Chicago, they had guests sign a book, "Autographs of Friends–Chicago," now in the Gurdon Hubbard Collection, CHS, which contains signatures, place of nativity, and date of arrival in Chicago for many early Chicago settlers. Mary Ann Hubbard's "Scrapbook of Clippings Relating to Chicago, 1878–1897," CHS, illustrates her deep interest in early local history and has notices of the passing of friends and family. A similar scrapbook in the Gurdon Hubbard Collection, CHS, contains a great deal printed about and written by him, as well as obituary clippings for his wife and an undated item about the distribution of her estate. Manuscript letters addressed to, or which discuss, Ann Hubbard may be found in the NL Graff Collection and the CHS collections of Mrs. Harriet Louise Hubbard Hamilton, Richard Jones Hamilton, and Ahira Hubbard. She is mentioned in Theodore Calvin Pease and James G. Randall, eds., *The Diary of Orville Hickman Browning*, vol. 1 (1925). An obituary of Hubbard in the CHS *Annual Report 1909* adds information about her character and later life pursuits, as does Charles S. Holt, "Memorial Speech at Dedication Ceremonies of Hubbard Memorial Bohemian Presbyterian Church, January 13, 1914," Mary Ann Hubbard Collection, CHS. Carolyn McIlvaine, in her introduction to *The Autobiography of Gurdon Saltonstall Hubbard* (1911), briefly describes his marriage to Ann Hubbard as "ideal" and places them in early Chicago society with other city leaders. Caroline Kirkland, *Chicago Yesterdays* (1919), repeats some of Hubbard's memories of school days at Miss Willard's. Several sources are helpful in providing some of the dates and sequences that Hubbard's

reminiscence assumes readers would know: A. T. Andreas, *History of Cook County, Illinois* (1884); Chicago Genealogical Society, *Vital Records from Chicago Newspapers 1833–1848* (1971–); and U.S. Census Schedules 1850–1900.

WILLA G. CRAMTON

HUCK, WINNIFRED SPRAGUE MASON
September 14, 1882–August 24, 1936
CONGRESSWOMAN, JOURNALIST

Winnifred Mason Huck became the third woman elected to the U.S. Congress, succeeding her father, William Ernest "Capt. Billy" Mason, a Republican Party maverick who died in 1921 while serving as congressman-at-large from Illinois. Billy Mason had been a controversial figure. "Although a Republican, he bedeviled many in his party, including President [William] McKinley, by supporting independence for the Philippines, labor unions and women's suffrage" (Dean, 37). Winnifred Mason was the middle child and youngest daughter of Mason and Edith Julia (White) Mason, both of whom were children of pioneer settlers in Iowa. Her older siblings were Lewis, Ethel, and Ruth, and her younger brothers were William E. Jr., Roderick, and Lowell. By the time Winnifred Mason was born in Chicago, her father was already a well-established political figure, having served as a state representative from 1879 to 1880 and then as a state senator from 1883 to 1885. William Mason was elected to the U.S. Congress in 1887. The family lived in Washington, D.C., until 1891 and then returned again while Mason was serving in the U.S. Senate from 1897 to 1903. During her father's term as senator, Winnifred Mason attended Central High School, where she was described by the class president as "one of those mannish political women" (*Herald and Examiner*, November 13, 1922). While she was a high school student, she often accompanied her father to sessions of Congress.

Winnifred Mason met Robert Wardlow Huck, a fellow student at Central High, and they were married on June 29, 1904. The couple lived in Salida, Colorado, and later in Chicago. Robert Huck, who had trained as a civil engineer, initially had a difficult time finding steady employment. Later he became a steel executive. The couple had four children, Wallace, Donald, Edith, and Robert. Winnifred Huck was active in civic affairs and politics. Although she never found employment, the unsteady income from Robert Huck's engineering career propelled her to try her hand at freelance magazine writing.

In fall 1916, Winnifred Huck campaigned for her father, who had been out of office since 1903 and was running for a seat as congressman-at-large from Illinois. While kissing babies, she reminded their mothers that Billy Mason supported the national suffrage amendment. Victorious, Mason served as congressman-at-large from 1917 until June 1921, when he died suddenly in office. Almost immediately Winnifred Huck attempted to secure an appointment from Illinois Governor Lennington Small, a Republican, to complete her father's unexpired term. Small doubted whether he had the power to appoint a successor to a seat for a congressman-at-large. (Congressmen-at-large are elected by the voters of the whole state and not from a district. Such elections occur when a state is entitled to increased representation after a census but the state legislature has not redistricted. In Illinois, from 1910 through 1930, the state legislature ignored the need for reapportionment and voters elected two at-large congressmen regularly.) A resolution presented to the Illinois legislature to give Small the authority to make a temporary appointment to fill Mason's vacancy failed. During the following month, Huck personally asked for President Warren G. Harding's support and lobbied the Illinois congressional delegation. She claimed that Small wanted to appoint her in order to avoid the cost of a special election.

Governor Small, however, never made the appointment. Huck prepared to run in the contested April 1922 Illinois primary, hoping to win the Republican nomination in order to challenge the Democratic candidate in a special election November 7, 1922, for her father's unexpired seat. Should she win, she would serve the four remaining months of his term. Huck remained in the public eye, speaking before the Chicago Federation of Labor on Labor Day, alongside U.S. Senator Robert Marion La Follette of the Farmer-Labor Party, and "the Great Commoner" William Jennings Bryan, unsuccessful presidential nominee of the Democratic Party in 1896 and friend of the labor movement. In early November 1921, five months after her father's death, she further prepared for her intended career in politics by attending a school for citizenship offered by the League of Women Voters in New Haven, Connecticut. She published articles about the experience in the *Herald and Examiner*. Finally, on February 22, 1922, she filed a petition as candidate for congressman-at-large to complete her father's unexpired term in the 67th Congress as well as to be a candidate for a full term in the 68th Congress. She would run in the April 1922 primary for the Republican nomination for both the abbreviated [unexpired term] and for the 68th Congress [full term].

Huck ran a vigorous campaign, insisting that, despite an endorsement from Chicago's mayor, William "Big Bill" Hale Thompson, head of the city's Republican machine, she was independent. Thompson had supported Billy Mason's last two congressional campaigns. Huck sent out three thousand letters to local committeemen, received nine hundred endorsements, and was supported by the area's forty thousand schoolteachers because of her stated position that teachers were underpaid.

As a Chicagoan following in the footsteps of her father, she narrowly won nomination for a ballot position on the Republican ticket for his unexpired term with a surprisingly strong vote downstate. In a field of three candidates, she ran second both in the Chicago districts and downstate, but her scant two thousand vote margin suggested her strength was limited. At the same time, she lost the Republican nomination for the full term to Henry R. Rathbone, a lawyer from the exclusive North Shore suburb of Kenilworth.

Press coverage at the time of her primary victory emphasized that Huck was a mother and pictured her receiving the election news while preparing breakfast for her family. Her four children were still living at home and newspaper photographs showed her darning socks or playing the violin while her children accompanied her on various other musical instruments. It was reported that she planned to take her children along with her to Washington, because she thought the experience would be educational. It is not clear how much of this image was directed by Huck herself. While Huck believed that women should not run

on their differences from men, she stated that child-rearing provided a potential candidate with a liberal education; and she was not averse to using her image as a mother for political purposes. Huck did not fit the profile of the activist turned politician with deep roots in the suffrage movement or in women's organizations. Her closest ties were to the Republican Party and her father's network, yet she was not endorsed by the Illinois Republican Women's Club, which was divided by factionalism at the time.

Huck ran successfully in the special election November 7, 1922, for the remainder of the unexpired term of her father in the 67th Congress. She ran against Democratic candidate Allen D. Albert, a former writer and lecturer on social welfare and a political novice who listed his presidency of the International Association of Rotary Clubs from 1915 to 1916 in his campaign literature. "Sixteen women had run for Congress. . . . The only winner among them was Winnifred Mason Huck" (Young, 73). Sworn in on November 20, she had only four months to serve and determined she would ignore "the unwritten rule that new representatives should do nothing but 'look and listen.' She could not afford to waste time on custom" (Dean, 40). Her brief term of office was an active one and she followed the positions her father had taken, including calling for a peace treaty with the Central Powers in Europe, supporting a referendum on future declarations of war, and advocating adoption of the child labor amendment. Mason had also been in favor of independence for the Philippines and for Cuba, positions that had not endeared him with the Republican establishment. He also believed strongly in a free Irish republic. Huck followed these positions as well. Only her committee assignments—she was elected to the committees on Civil Service Reform, Woman Suffrage, and Expenditures in the Department of Commerce—differed from those held by her father.

High on her agenda was continuing Billy Mason's work for peace. She announced that she would propose a peace amendment in Congress, known as the "war plebiscite." Immediately following her election, Huck had introduced her ideas about a peace amendment in an Armistice Day address under the auspices of the Women's International League for Peace and Freedom, in Chicago. JANE ADDAMS presided at the meeting, which was denounced by some as a "gathering of pinks" (*Chicago Tribune*, November 12, 1922). "'I realize,' Huck said, 'that it is impossible to legislate a world peace, but my efforts in Congress will be devoted chiefly toward a constructive educational plan which, I believe, will show the folly of war'" ("War by Vote of People," *New York Times*, November 13, 1922, 3). Huck's office in Washington, D.C., became a clearing house for peace activists. She petitioned President Harding to release political prisoners in federal prisons, some of whom had been jailed for "treasonable and seditious utterances" (*Chicago Tribune*, December 11, 1922) during World War I. In a "No More War" meeting at New York City's Town Hall in December 1922, Huck advocated a war plebiscite and shared the platform with speakers who included the French socialist leader Jean Longuet and U.S. socialist Norman Thomas.

At the beginning of 1923, Congresswoman Huck proposed a resolution (H.J. Res. 423) requiring a referendum on future declarations of war, the "war plebiscite," arguing that the concentration of power in the hands of one man was the cause of most wars. Her bill would have empowered the president to tell all nations that the United States would not declare war, except by the direct vote of the people, against any country guaranteeing its people the same right. Countries that refused would be denied aid or credit by the United States. Huck claimed her plebiscite would make world peace easier to achieve. "I have been told that war cannot be prevented in that way—that other countries will resent our refusal to trade with them without such a stipulation," Huck stated; but, she continued, "We are in the lead today as a nation in a financial and moral way. It is the psychological time for us to provide a foundation for world peace" ("Plan for World Peace," *New York Times*, February 12, 1923, 2). She also called for an immediate peace treaty with the German-led Central Powers. She insisted that "Women are irrevocably opposed to war and never intend to rest until universal peace is established" (*Chicago Tribune*, January 17, 1923).

Huck was not, according to the *Chicago Tribune*, "an internationalist or an advocate of non-resistance" (January 17, 1923) but supported a strong army and navy until the plebiscite measure should make them unnecessary. To the disappointment of many women in the peace movement, Congresswoman Huck supported "the Ship Subsidy Bill, the only important legislation enacted in this session" (*NAW*, 232). Huck believed that the United States had to have an adequate Merchant Marine to become a leader in world commerce, and when it came time to count the votes, she marched next to Speaker of the House Joseph "Uncle Joe" Cannon, the powerful Congressman from Illinois and leader of the "Old Guard" Republicans. On the personal level, Huck was criticized for using her congressional privilege to appoint her son, Wallace, to the U.S. Naval Academy at Annapolis, Maryland. "She didn't raise her boy to be a soldier," reported the *New York Times*, "but it's going to be a long time before war is abolished, so Mrs. Winnifred Mason Huck sent . . . son Wallace off to be a sailor" (*New York Times*, July 24, 1923). Huck made the appointment before the expiration of her term in 1923.

Although she thought universal peace was the paramount issue, Huck worked for many other causes affecting women. She supported the Sheppard-Towner Federal Maternity and Infancy Act, which provided funds for maternal and child health clinics. She also worked for passage of the child labor amendment and uniform divorce laws. She supported the Equal Rights Amendment in 1923, although she favored exempting state laws that limited the hours and conditions under which women worked.

Shortly after Huck was sworn in on November 20, 1922, Republican Congressman James R. Mann, of Illinois, suddenly died. Huck arrived back in Chicago on the train bearing Mann's body and praised the former House minority leader for his conscientious work on behalf of his constituents. She was soon receiving letters urging her to run for his seat in the 2nd Congressional District. She was defeated in the primary on February 27, 1923, just days before her congressional term expired, running second in a field of six. The winner, Morton D. Hull, spent one hundred thousand dollars on the campaign and enjoyed the support of the Republican machine, to which he had contributed substantial sums. The *Chicago Tribune* observed that "the showing made by Mrs. Huck, who had virtually no organi-

zational backing, depending largely on the women vote, proved a complete surprise to the political prophets" (February 28, 1923). Winnifred Huck had been the third of three congresswomen to be defeated after only one term; the others were Jeannette Rankin (Republican from Montana) and Alice Robertson (Republican from Oklahoma). She had hoped to break the precedent, building on her earlier base of women voters, attracting additional support from business organizations for her work as a member of the Joint Waterway Legislative Committee, promoting Illinois's river and harbor development, and winning the loyalty of ex-servicemen for her prompt settlement of their claims and her support of the American Legion.

Immediately after her defeat, she appealed to women members of the state legislature to join her on the Political Council of the National Woman's Party to work for the election of more women to political office. She capitalized on her high visibility after she left Congress to continue to write and speak on a variety of issues, including world peace, more humane forms of execution (preferring chloroform or allowing suicide), and disability benefits for veterans.

The most spectacular of these endeavors was the way in which she went undercover to study the Ohio correctional system. "By arrangement with the governor, [Huck] was tried and convicted there, under an assumed name, for a petty theft" (*NAW*, 232). She spent almost a month in the woman's prison in Marysville. The night of her release, she dined in the governor's mansion, where she gave him her recommendations for prison reform. She then made her way east with the five dollars she had received on leaving prison, to discover what effect her jail time might have on employment opportunities. There was more work to be found in large cities than in small towns. Although a hotel in Pittsburgh, Pennsylvania, fired her from her job as a chambermaid after learning of her record, they offered her a job in the kitchen. She also obtained work in a factory in West Virginia. She published a syndicated series of articles about her experiences for the Newspaper Enterprise Association in the summer of 1925. The articles emphasized "the humanity of her fellow prisoners and the willingness of employers, in the prosperous '20's, to give an ex-convict a chance" (*NAW*, 232). In 1928 and 1929, Huck wrote for the Chicago *Evening Post* on the role of women's clubs in politics, contrasting the nonpartisan attitudes of the League of Women Voters and the National Federation of Women's Clubs with the Woman's City Club, which promoted women's involvement in partisan politics.

From 1931 until 1936, Winnifred Huck battled cancer, and she was bedridden for the last six months of her life. She died in Presbyterian Hospital, Chicago, three weeks before her fifty-fourth birthday, following an unsuccessful operation for idiopathic ulcerative colitis. She was a member of the Unitarian Church. Huck was cremated at Oak Woods Cemetery, Chicago.

Winnifred Huck was the first of many women who succeeded relatives in office. "Of the sixty-eight women who entered Congress between 1918 and 1963, thirty-one gained their seats in the first instance as relatives of the previous incumbent" (*NAW*, 232). However, it was often only through family connections that women could gain experience and make the contacts necessary for a life in politics, since they were handicapped by exclusion from meaningful positions in other networking forums. During her brief time in Congress, Winnifred Mason Huck was able to make a concrete proposal to abolish war, an issue of great importance to many of the Illinois women she represented.

Sources. Winnifred Huck's congressional experience is recorded officially in *Congressional Record*, 67 Congress, 4 Session; and in *Literary Digest*, November 25, 1922; *Equal Rights*, March 3, 1923; and her article, "What Happened to Me in Congress," *Woman's Home Companion*, July 1923. Information on her prison experience appeared in the *Chicago Evening Post*, July 7, 1925. Articles in the *NYT, CT,* Chicago *Herald and Examiner, Chicago Daily News, Chicago American,* and *Chicago Evening Post* contain material for the years 1920–36. Articles about Huck include Anna Steese Richardson, "What about the Ladies?" *Collier's,* September 27, 1924, and David Dean and Martha Dean, "Mama Went to Congress and Then to Jail," *American History Illustrated,* November 1977. Other biographical sources include *NAW* (1971) and Hope Chamberlin, *A Minority of Members: Women in the U.S. Congress* (1973). Louise M. Young, *In the Public Interest: The League of Women Voters, 1920–1970* (1989), covers some of the history of the few women who served in Congress during the 1920s.

KRISTIE MILLER

HULETT, ALTA MAY
June 4, 1854–March 26, 1877
LAWYER, WOMEN'S RIGHTS ACTIVIST

Alta Hulett was a woman of exceptional ability, drafting the law that opened professions to women and becoming the first woman lawyer admitted to the Illinois bar. Born on a farm in Rockton, outside of Rockford, Illinois, Hulett descended from a family of bright, daring, and successful men. She was the eldest child of Dr. Guy George Hulett, a man of many talents, described as a physician, a farmer, and a lawyer by varying accounts. She was the niece of McAllister Hulett, an early lawyer, described as a "brilliant legal practitioner" (Hubbard, n.p.) in LaSalle, Illinois. Hulett's paternal grandfather, Guy Hulett Sr., was a judge, physician, and editor in the LaSalle area and was well known as a "man of great energy, eccentricity, and originality of character" (Hubbard, n.p.). Hulett's father died in 1860, leaving his wife, Altie, and two daughters with only limited means. Hulett's mother took in borders to support the family, allowing Hulett to begin her education in the public schools. Though Hulett excelled in her schooling, she was required to leave school at the age of ten and work in a telegraph office in Rockton to help support the family. She learned the business so quickly that, despite her youth, she was appointed an operator. Financial circumstances improved for the family, and Hulett soon resumed her studies. In 1870, at the age of sixteen, she graduated from Rockford High School.

Hulett knew at this early age that she wanted to be a lawyer. Immediately after graduation, she began teaching school and studying law in the evenings on her own. Within a few months, Hulett formally initiated her legal studies in the law office of William B. Lathrop, JULIA LATHROP's father. Hulett studied with the clear intention of entering the legal profession despite the knowledge that at this time women were prohibited from admission to the Illinois bar. However, one year before Hulett commenced the study of law, Arabella Mansfield was admitted

to the Iowa bar, the first woman in the country to be admitted to the legal profession. Hulett also knew that in 1869 the Illinois Supreme Court had denied MYRA BRADWELL's application to the Illinois bar, and the case was on appeal to the United States Supreme Court.

Hulett was not deterred. She threw her energy into her studies and within a year successfully passed the bar examination. Hulett sent her certificate of qualification to Springfield, Illinois, and requested a license giving her the right to practice in state courts. The request was denied on the grounds that she was a woman. Hulett's hometown newspaper, the *Rockford Register,* sharply criticized the decision, characterizing it as arbitrary and arguing for equal treatment of the sexes. Since Bradwell's case was still on appeal, Hulett took an alternative approach to gain admittance to the Illinois bar, amending the state law that prohibited women from entering the legal profession. She enlisted the help of many brilliant legal minds, including her mentor William Lathrop and the Bradwells—both Myra and her lawyer husband James. Additionally, Hulett was assisted by Ada Kepley, who had also applied and been denied admission to the Illinois bar. Kepley, who had graduated from the (old) University of Chicago Law School in 1870, was assisted by her lawyer husband, Charles Kepley.

Hulett drafted a bill that prohibited any profession or occupation from discriminating on the basis of sex. She sent the bill to Thomas Turner, a state legislator from Freeport who supported the measure. She then began a campaign to secure its passage. Myra Bradwell published articles in support of the bill in her *Chicago Legal News,* and James Bradwell solicited support from his friends in the legislature. In November 1871, Turner introduced the bill in the Illinois House of Representatives, and John Early, state senator from Rockford, introduced the senate version into the Illinois Senate. On Saturday evening, November 25, Hulett debuted her lecture, "Justice vs. the Supreme Court" to an overflow crowd in Rockford's Brown Hall, which was filled to capacity; as many as four hundred people had to be turned away. Hulett respectfully criticized the Illinois Supreme Court's decision to bar women from the law. She asserted that Illinois statutes supported women's entrance into the legal profession and argued forcefully for the equality of the sexes. She expressed her dismay at the injustice of discrimination based on sex. Her audience approved Hulett's arguments, and the *Rockford Journal* described her as a new star in the lecture field.

Hulett lectured throughout northern Illinois, arguing the merits of the bill. ELLEN MARTIN, one of the early Illinois woman lawyers, later wrote that her colleague's lectures "met with a hearty response from the public" (quoted in "Admission of Women to the Bar," 79). Through continued perseverance, Hulett was able to argue her case directly to the legislators, impressing them with her earnestness and the justice of her arguments. When the bill came up for a final vote on March 22, 1872, it initially failed to receive enough votes for the constitutional majority required for passage; hastily, persuasive arguments were delivered by its supporters, and the house quickly moved to reconsider. The bill passed and the governor signed it the following day. The new law provided that no person should be excluded from any occupation, profession, or employment (except military) because of sex. But the legislators added that this act should not be interpreted to affect the eligibility of any person to an elective office, nor was it meant to require females to do street or roadwork or serve on juries. When Hulett was informed by telegram that her bill had become law, she exclaimed, "I shall never again know such happiness" (quoted in Lindvall, n.p.).

The battle for woman's suffrage continued for almost fifty years from the passage of Hulett's anti-sex-discrimination act in 1872. The subsequent postsuffrage legislative campaign in Illinois to seat women on juries was only successful in 1939. In retrospect, Hulett's campaign to open the legal profession to women, which took only one year, seemed to women's rights activists miraculous. Conservative legislators, however, were successful in increasing the requirement that applicants to the Illinois bar complete two additional years of legal study beyond the previous one-year requirement. Determined to fulfill these additional requirements, Hulett moved to Chicago and read law with Joseph Sleeper, attorney with the law firm Sleeper and Whiton. In 1873 she again applied to the Illinois Supreme Court for admission to the bar. Though she had previously taken and passed the bar examination with high honors, the court required her to retake the exam. Of the twenty-eight aspiring lawyers sitting for the exam that spring, Hulett passed at the head of her class, again with high honors. She was admitted to the Illinois bar on June 6, 1873, two days after her nineteenth birthday.

Hulett opened a LaSalle Street law office in downtown Chicago and earned high distinction almost immediately. She was admitted to the United States Court for the Northern District of Illinois, making her one of the first women admitted to the U.S. Court. While she was practicing, Charles D. Mosher, nineteenth-century biographer of Chicago lawyers, described Hulett as "alert, studious and energetic, she has met with almost uniform success in her legal practice. . . . she is an easy and fluent lecturer, concise and spirited in argument and forcible in delivery" ("Centennial Historical Albums of Biographies of the Chicago Bar," vol. 6, p. 49). Businessmen and women alike entrusted her with their legal affairs.

Though Hulett spent most of her time and energy on her law practice, she did engage in additional activities consistent with her ambitions and intellectual ability. She was appointed to the office of Notary Public, becoming one of the first women in Illinois to hold that position. Myra Bradwell had previously been denied that office on the basis of her sex. Hulett furthered her intellectual interests as a member of the Ladies Literary Society of Lawrence University, Appleton, Wisconsin. Most significantly, Hulett was also the corresponding secretary of the Philosophical Society of Chicago, an organization of leading men and women intellectuals in the city. The society was founded in 1873 as a forum to discuss issues of philosophy and theology. Most of the members were advocates of women's rights, but the society encouraged open discussions of a variety of viewpoints.

In her short and busy life, Hulett remained single. The *Chicago Tribune* reported that Hulett often said "she was not made to be married" ("Obituary Alta M. Hulett," March 28, 1877). Hulett's life was filled with close friendships from a circle of fellow lawyers and members of the Philosophical Society, including Ellen Martin and Mary Fredrika Perry, Charles B.

Waite, and A. J. Grover. Male lawyers Waite and Grover were known for their belief in the equality of the sexes and their radical and skeptical views of religion. Hulett was close with Grover and his family, living briefly with his mother.

Alta Hulett had a brief, but exceptional career; in four years of practice, she never lost a case before a jury. Tragically, in November 1876, she was diagnosed with pulmonary consumption and ordered by her doctor to give up law and move to California. Hulett was devastated at the notion that she would have to abandon her law practice and was concerned that if she left, her departure would be interpreted by some critics as evidence that women could not succeed in the legal profession. As the illness progressed, Hulett reluctantly moved with her mother, stepfather, and sister to San Francisco, and then to San Diego, California. She died a few months later and was buried in Mt. Hope Cemetery in San Diego.

Laura Hubbard, a member of the Philosophical Society, and Myra Bradwell emphasized how great the popular prejudice was against women entering the legal profession. Bradwell reported that one of the Illinois Supreme Court judges remarked, after Hulett was admitted to the bar, that while Hulett was qualified, if she were his daughter, he would disinherit her. Bradwell assessed, "Nothing save a blast from Gabriel's trumpet can dispel these lifetime prejudices" (*Chicago Legal News*, June 14, 1873, 453). Yet Ellen Martin believed that Hulett's short career had produced a favorable attitude in the public toward woman practitioners. At her death, the Chicago Bar Association passed a resolution praising Hulett's extraordinary ability; they acknowledged her right to practice law, and the resolution was unanimously adopted and placed in the four courthouses in Chicago, "a unique and unheard of honor" (McCulloch, "Alta M. Hulett," typescript, 9, Grace H. Harte Papers). Hulett's life and work left a legacy of accomplishment: she opened the legal profession to women and helped to change traditional patriarchal attitudes about women's role in society.

Sources. The Alta M. Hulett papers are at the CHS, including "Biographical Sketch of Alta Hulett" by Laura Hubbard (1881). The first biographical sketch of Hulett was written during her lifetime by Charles D. Mosher in the "Centennial Historical Albums of Biographies of the Chicago Bar," 6 vols., manuscripts, CHS; the Hulett sketch is in vol. 6. The Grace H. Harte Papers, Series III of the Mary Earhart Dillon Collection and the Catharine Waugh McCulloch Papers, Series IV of the Mary Earhart Dillon Collection, SL, have material on Hulett. The Dillon Collection is available on microfilm as part of the Women's Studies Manuscript Collection. Rockford Public Library has an unidentified news article, "Rockford's First Woman Lawyer," in the Rockfordania file. Newspaper accounts of Hulett's lecture, "Justice vs. the Supreme Court," were published in the *Rockford Gazette*, November 30, 1871; the *Rockford Journal*, December 2, 1871; and the *Rockford Register*, December 2, 1871. Myra Bradwell described the events of Hulett's bill becoming law in "Liberty of Pursuit Triumphant in Illinois," *Chicago Legal News*, March 23, 1872. Hulett's admission to the bar was reported in the *CT*, June 7, 1873, and subsequent objections to the event were reported by Bradwell in the *Chicago Legal News*, June 14, 1873. Elizabeth Cady Stanton, Susan B. Anthony, and Matilda Joslyn Gage, eds., *The History of Woman Suffrage*, vol. 3 (1876–85) also recount Hulett's work and the changes in the Illinois law. Elizabeth Boynton Harbert wrote an extensive tribute to Hulett in the Chicago *Inter-Ocean*, March 31, 1877. In 1887 Ellen Martin included Hulett in her article, "Admission of

Women to the Bar," *Chicago Law Times*, vol. 1, 1887. More recent accounts of Hulett's life are Hazel Hyde, "First Women Lawyers of Rockford," *Nuggets of History*, January–February 1966; Robert Lindvall, "Alta M. Hulett," *Nuggets of History*, Spring 1978; Meg Gorecki, "Legal Pioneers: Four of Illinois' First Women Lawyers," *Illinois Bar Journal*, October 1990; Charlotte Adelman, "A History of Women Lawyers in Illinois," *Illinois Bar Journal*, May 1986; Herman Kogan, "Myra Bradwell: Crusader at Law," *Chicago History*, Fall 1974. Hulett's obituary was reported in the *CT*, March 28, 1877.

GWEN HOERR MCNAMEE

HULING, CAROLINE ALDEN
April 2, 1856–March 10, 1941
JOURNALIST, EDITOR, AUTHOR, SUFFRAGIST

Caroline Alden Huling was one of nine children born to Edmund James and Anna (Spooner) Huling in Sarasota Springs, New York. Like her siblings, Huling followed in the footsteps of her journalist father, a newspaper publisher and editor. Her mother's family was also well known in New York literary and publishing circles, which included the poet Henry Wadsworth Longfellow. All nine Huling offspring became writers in the newspaper business.

Caroline Huling attended public school in Sarasota and was tutored privately in music and languages, anticipating a career in teaching. Instead, her parents' ill health pushed her in the direction of the family business, the *Saratoga Sentinel*. Comfortable with journalism, she began reporting for her father's paper at the age of twelve. As a young woman, Huling took on more responsibilities, becoming the associate editor, supervising the company's bookbindery, and assisting her father with his work as the Associated Press representative in the upstate New York town. In addition, Huling free-lanced for other papers in New York State. As Huling became increasingly involved in the day-to-day operations of the business, her father wanted her to be appointed a notary public so that she could produce affidavits of publication for the many legal advertisements they published. Notary publics were appointed by the governor of the state with the approval of the legislature. No woman had ever been appointed in New York State. Without consulting his daughter, Huling requested Governor Grover Cleveland (later president of the United States) to appoint her. Caroline Huling thus became the first woman notary public in New York State, benefiting, most likely, from her father's influence in political circles.

During this period, women in Saratoga Springs were engaged in temperance and suffrage reform. Huling's parents were part of the civic and moral reform circles, and Caroline Huling was a founding member—"one of the first to don the white ribbon" (Willard and Livermore, 402)—of the Woman's Christian Temperance Union's local chapter in 1874. She was secretary of the local woman suffrage society. When, in 1877, New York State women were eligible to vote in local school elections, the twenty-one-year-old Caroline Huling was a leader in the separate woman's caucus that selected two women candidates to run for the Saratoga Board of Education. Successfully elected, the two women uncovered information about kickbacks to male board members from local school vendors whose contracts were renewed annually. To the women, these kickbacks explained both why the men on the board served without salary for many

terms and why they were so hostile to the new female members. Huling's father, who publicized the chicanery in his paper, was "decidedly modern in his support of the woman suffrage cause" (C. A. Huling to Huling relative, October 9, 1940, Huling Papers). He actively participated in the group of allies who strategized with the women board members as they faced opposition to all of their initiatives. Huling's education in politics was to continue as she joined national circles of the woman suffrage movement during winters passed in Boston, where she worked with Lucy Stone and Julia Ward Howe. From Boston Huling regularly sent columns for the *Sentinel*.

After a decade in the family business and eager to pursue a career in journalism on her own, in 1884 Caroline Huling answered an advertisement for an editor of a stationers' trade journal, the *Western Stationer*, in Chicago. Signing her name "C. A. Huling," she obtained an interview and found, as she expected, that the company was disappointed that she was not a man. Huling convinced her interviewer that she knew a great deal about the work, as an associate editor of her father's paper, and she was hired for the position. Later she edited a dozen such trade journals.

Chicago also interested Huling because of the opportunities its growing women's political culture offered. A coalition of suffrage activists, clubwomen, and moral and political reformers supported the 1884 suffrage convention held in Chicago, which Huling attended. Her earlier suffrage and temperance work and her eastern connections helped her develop new midwest affiliations, and she found herself in a leadership role overnight. She was elected secretary of the Cook County Equal Suffrage Association and superintendent of press work for the Illinois Woman Suffrage Association.

Huling had misgivings about her public stances and believed her prominent place in temperance and suffrage work "militated against getting a big salaried position. Men in big business did not like women to be too prominent" (C. A. Huling to Huling relative October 9, 1940, Huling Papers), she later reflected. On the other hand, the network of women's organizations kept her busy and independent.

In 1885 she became a founding member of the Illinois Woman's Press Association (IWPA) along with temperance leader FRANCES E. WILLARD; suffragist ELIZABETH HARBERT; physician ALICE STOCKHAM, who was an early promoter of sex education and birth control; and editor and publisher of *Chicago Legal News* MYRA BRADWELL, who had been denied admittance to the Illinois bar because she was a woman. The IWPA was not designed initially to be a trade union or to include newspaper workers only, although it advocated the interests of women as writers. Only later did its bylaws define active members as those who were paid for their work. In the beginning IWPA included old and young women who rebelled against a male monopoly of well-paying occupations, limiting women's ability to support themselves or to serve as financial heads of their households. Members included physicians and lawyers as well as journalists, editors, publishers, and writers. Many had experimented with women-owned and women-oriented publishing companies and, in the case of Alice Stockham, a subscription book business for women. Career-minded, the original IWPA members found divergent ways to work in their chosen male-dominated fields. Huling, a member of IWPA for forty-seven years, held various official positions.

Huling's professional ambitions merged with her militancy in the struggle for woman suffrage when she determined to establish a suffrage journal in Chicago. This was not the first such venture. The suffrage movement in the Midwest had dreamed of having its own woman suffrage journal from 1869 when, right after the first suffrage convention in Chicago, MARY LIVERMORE began a short-lived paper, the *Agitator*. Elizabeth Harbert edited and published the *New Era* in 1885, which brought together temperance and suffrage issues. The paper folded within two years, and in October 1887, Caroline Huling launched *Justitia, A Court for the Unrepresented*. Huling had the minimal financial backing of a wealthy but erratic female donor. *Justitia*, the organ of the Illinois State Equal Suffrage Association, also advocated social purity and temperance reforms.

In March 1888, Huling was a delegate to the first International Council of Women, held in Washington, D.C., and, following it, the convention of the National Woman Suffrage Association (NWSA). As an officer of the Chicago suffrage organization as well as the Illinois state society, Huling socialized at various receptions and events. She was amazed at her good fortune to be in Washington at all, since she was "desperately hard up" for money (C. A. Huling to Huling relative, March 30, 1940, Huling Papers) and, by comparison with the other delegates, not well known. Excelling as an entrepreneur, Huling needed transportation to Washington; she contracted with the Baltimore and Ohio Railroad for a special car and advertised for women delegates to buy tickets to fill it. She took the latest issue of her paper to Washington with plans to get subscriptions at the convention. Huling managed to arrange accommodations in the capitol by accompanying a well-to-do but shy woman who wanted companionship while she attended the meetings. They shared a fine hotel suite and three meals per day for two weeks.

The idea for this first international council began with Elizabeth Cady Stanton, who helped interest the women in England and France in the idea of an international organization of women. The International Council of Women identified women as the chief protagonists of social justice in the new industrial age. Women, organized and educated, would work for human betterment. Susan B. Anthony's efforts made possible the formation of the International Council of Women in 1888. Representatives of fifty-three women's organizations from ten nations exchanged opinions on the important questions of the day as they related to women. The meeting was also a celebration commemorating the fortieth anniversary of the first women's rights convention at Seneca Falls, New York, and Stanton, as the woman who had called it together, was the featured speaker. The council, however, was not a suffrage organization; its list of goals did not include woman suffrage but emphasized women's battle to obtain equal wages for equal work. This focus on equal rights in the workplace typified Caroline Huling's generation of women's rights activists.

Huling remained in Washington, D.C., for the National Woman Suffrage Association convention. Along with Susan B. Anthony and Isabella Beecher Hooker, Huling was part of the NWSA committee presenting a memorial to the platform committee of the National Republican Party convention, also in the nation's capitol at the time. Huling covered the events for the Associated Press.

Back in Chicago, Huling worked hard to keep her suffrage journal, *Justitia*, alive. She believed that the distribution of the journal was being suppressed and discouraged by leaders in the women's movement, particularly Susan B. Anthony, who was opposed to the proliferation of small suffrage journals in the western and midwestern states. Instead, Anthony encouraged the small groups to cooperate on a large daily newspaper to serve the western part of the nation and build a more unified movement. Huling turned to Lucy Stone, head of the rival American Woman Suffrage Association, for advice about *Justitia* and national affiliation in the divided suffrage movement. Stone replied that it was quite natural for Anthony to back a central newspaper. About the question of affiliation, Stone counseled a wait-and-see approach, hinting that the old divisions were about to be healed. "The old causes of division have ceased," Stone wrote Huling, October 26, 1888. "We have no fear of Geo. Francis Main or Mrs. Woodhull and I have nothing against Susan's [Anthony's] present methods of work or against her and if we could all come together in a friendly spirit of trust and cooperation it would be best" (Huling Papers). For Huling, the decision whether to continue *Justitia* was made for her; without financial resources, the paper folded like the other Chicago-based woman suffrage papers that preceded it. Two years later, in 1890, the two organizations of the woman suffrage movement reunited in the National American Woman Suffrage Association.

In her participation at the NWSA convention in Washington, D.C., and the International Council, Huling expressed the two-pronged approach to women's advancement endorsed by more and more women. Not only was it necessary to work for the vote, but alongside this and as important, if not more immediately critical, was the battle for social and economic gains for women and children.

In addition to her suffrage work, as one of the leaders of the new Illinois Woman's Alliance (IWA), Huling advocated major legislation to combat women's economic plight. The immediate stimulus for the formation of the IWA was a series of articles, "City Slave Girls," published in the *Chicago Times* during the summer of 1888. These articles graphically detailed the dangerous conditions women and children endured as underpaid laborers in tenement sweatshops throughout the city. Almost spontaneously, groups of women representing different parts of the organized women's movement in Chicago reached out with the same idea of forging an alliance to combat the evils of the sweatshop. ELIZABETH MORGAN, of the Ladies' Federal Labor Union and the Chicago Trades and Labor Assembly, was an important figure who brought socialists and trade unionists to this new cross-class coalition that included Christians of all shades of orthodoxy, dress reformers, woman suffrage activists, spiritualists, temperance advocates, and clubwomen. The IWA's first coordinating committee consisted of CORINNE BROWN, representing the Ladies' Federal Labor Union; Caroline Huling of the Cook County Equal Suffrage Association; Annie H. White of the Woodlawn Reading Club; Elizabeth Morgan, representing the Chicago Trades and Labor Assembly; Jennie Howison of the Miriam Chapter of the Order of the Eastern Star; Dr. Harriet Fox of the Women's Physiological Society; Frances N. Owen of the Woodlawn Presbyterian Ladies' Aid; and Alva Perry of the South End Flower Mission. Huling served as president from 1888 to 1890.

With so varied a coalition, the group debated its approach. Should the IWA function as a charity, a service group, or a political bloc agitating for legislative changes? In May 1889, Huling argued that the IWA had been formed to change laws and win practical reforms rather than engage in philanthropic or service work. She believed that private charity groups did tasks that were the responsibility of the city or state. IWA would work to get at the causes of the evils instead of abating them.

In order to advance this political agenda, IWA members became experts in the affairs of municipal government, the public schools, the police courts, and state institutions. Members observed meetings and wrote critiques that exposed abuses. The campaign against sweatshops led to the IWA's support of child protection laws, including legislation to prohibit child labor and require school attendance. Huling presided over the IWA's fight to improve the state's compulsory education law. The women understood that sweatshops depended on child labor and flourished in urban centers, where thousands of children did not attend school. The IWA estimated that there were at least fifty thousand children between the ages of seven and fourteen in Chicago who did not attend school or work in legitimate businesses. These children were either working in sweatshops or wandering the streets. Further investigation by the IWA revealed that at least ten thousand children were homeless. One year after its formation, the IWA successfully sponsored a state compulsory education bill, which became law in May 1889. Not perfect, the new law provided for a twelve- to twenty-four-week school year for children from seven to fourteen years of age. The IWA reported that at least sixteen hundred more children were attending Chicago schools in 1890 than in 1889.

As a middle-class "working woman" (Huling to relatives, October 9, 1940) striving to develop her own independent career, Caroline Huling tapered off her work with IWA at the end of 1890, when she became involved in a club for working women and continued her own publishing and editing ventures. In addition, that year she became one of the organizers and the secretary of the Woman's Baking Company, created to provide a good investment opportunity for women's small savings and an avenue of employment for working-class women.

Huling's major career network was the Illinois Woman's Press Association. In 1890 Huling represented the IWPA at the National Editorial Association and was elected assistant recording secretary of that body. The IWPA functioned as a support system and network for women at a time when custom and law marginalized many career women and created a need for women to advance the cause of womanhood at the same time that they struggled to maintain individual careers. In the next ten years, she edited IWPA's journal, the *Stylus*, a periodical for professional writers, and also a related journal, *Latest Literature*. By 1896, Huling was running a Literary Bureau that critiqued the work of fledgling writers. From 1904 to 1911 she was the editor, owner, and publisher of the *Bookseller*, a trade journal containing information of interest for the publisher, jobber, and retail dealer, including book dealers, clubwomen, and libraries. It included book reviews as well as trade news.

Caroline Huling never married. She had a keen interest in the younger generation and in two publications addressed the new generation. *The Courage of Her Convictions* (1896), a first novel by Huling written at age forty, tells the story of a young woman who undergoes artificial insemination because she is disillusioned by the character of men and decides she wants a child of her own. By the end of the book, however, the daring young woman falls in love with a young male doctor who is really the father of the baby. She marries him, realizing that her child needs a father as well as a mother. Published by Charles H. Kerr, a publisher of socialist and radical authors, Huling's novel resembled the genre of utopian-type romances, authored by women, that were popular in the late nineteenth century. In this mode, Elizabeth Boynton Harbert's *Amore* (1894) conjured up a new kind of marriage based on the universal law of love that recognizes woman's intuition and spiritual guidance for the human race. Huling and Harbert, whose involvement in the Illinois woman suffrage movement began in the mid-1870s, saw women as different from men but in a new relationship of equality and cooperation with them, destined to bring about a new world of justice and moral perfection.

Huling's second book, *Letters of a Business Woman to Her Niece* (1906), deals with young women's choices in education and work and offers advice on finance and etiquette. Huling tells young women that a home is not complete without children. Although Huling never commented on her own choice not to marry, her activities, from this decade on, focused on her extended family. Founding the Midwest Chapter of Alden Kindred of America in 1912, for the descendants of John and Priscilla Alden, Huling spearheaded annual picnics in Lincoln Park and monthly dinner meetings. She edited the bulletin of the midwest chapter. She was chapter president from 1912 to 1914 and served as secretary and treasurer in later years. Huling's genealogical and patriotic interests increased, and she was active in the Daughters of the American Revolution, the Huguenot Society of Pennsylvania, the American Order of Patriots, and the American Institute of Genealogy.

Huling continued to edit various trade and technical journals well into her sixties, including a stint from 1920 to 1922 as the editor of *Social Progress*, the official publication of the Child Conservation League of America. Ten years later she returned to active participation in the IWPA, serving as editor of its 1932 publication *Prominent Women of Illinois*, a biographical compendium including many of her longtime colleagues and friends. Her final days were spent in a nursing home in Maywood, Illinois, where she died at eighty-four years of age and was buried alongside other midwestern family members in Oak Hill Cemetery, Downers Grove, Illinois. Both as a journalist and a worker for women's rights, Huling served in many leadership positions in the woman suffrage movement and in associations and enterprises created by women activists to achieve women's economic independence and advancement in the professions.

Sources. The Caroline Alden Huling Papers, UIC Spec. Coll., contain correspondence, speeches, manuscript notes for articles, photographs, and a copy of *Letters of a Business Woman to Her Niece* and other published works by Huling, as well as related correspondence, advertisements, and reviews. The Illinois Woman's Press Association Papers (IWPA) are at the CHS. Biographies of Huling can be found in Frances E. Willard and Mary A. Livermore, eds., *A Woman of the Century* (1893), and in *Prominent Women of Illinois* (1932), published by the IWPA. Her obituary appears in the *Saratogian*, Saratoga Springs, New York, March 12, 1941.

MARILYN SOLTIS

HUMPAL-ZEMAN, JOSEFA VERONIKA
January 9, 1870–April 23, 1906
JOURNALIST, WOMEN'S RIGHTS ACTIVIST, PUBLISHER

Josefa Veronika Humpal, founder of the Bohemian Women's Publishing Company as well as *Ženské Listy* (Women's journal), the first Bohemian women's newspaper written by women in the United States, was the eldest daughter of Josef Humpal, a farmer's son, and Anna Srnka, a coachman's daughter, in Sušice, Bohemia. Josef Humpal, outspoken Czech patriot and freethinker, had a minor position in the Austro-Hungarian government. He emigrated to the United States, arriving in New York on June 8, 1874, with his four-year-old daughter, Josefa, and his mother. One month later, Anna Humpal followed, bringing nine-year-old František and three-month-old Jaroslav. The family made its way to Chicago, joining the nearly forty-five thousand Bohemians already settled there, many of them escapees from military conscription and economic hardship in their homeland.

Humpal described the first Chicago school she attended as "Czech-English Freethinking." At the age of nine she transferred to public school. Then in 1881 Josef Humpal took the family back to Písek, Bohemia, for a European education. Josefa Humpal studied at the local high school. When her mother died in 1884, the family returned to the United States, settling just outside Chicago.

Josefa Humpal continued to study and read on her own. She joined Vlasta No. 19 of the Jednota Českých Dam (Union of Czech Women), the largest self-help insurance society for Czech women in the United States. Eager to be independent, she worked as a fabric cutter and, for a brief time, as an amateur actress in a Czech theater troupe. Very soon after her father's death in February 1887, Humpal met Robert Zeman, a Chicago teacher. They were married in June 1887 and moved to Cleveland, Ohio, where Robert Zeman worked as an editor. It was soon apparent to Humpal-Zeman that the marriage was a mistake. Because his new wife was a minor, Zeman took her small inheritance, saying he needed it to furnish their apartment. Eight months later, having seen no trace of the money or the furnishings, and troubled by his "unusual habits" (Humpal-Zeman, *Ženské Listy*, January 1, 1896, 218–19), Humpal-Zeman left him. On August 11, 1888, six months after leaving her husband, she bore a son, Benjamin, who lived just over a year. When the child died early in 1890, Humpal-Zeman felt "emotionally destroyed" (Humpal-Zeman, *Ženské Listy*, January 1, 1896, 218–19).

During this difficult period, Mary Ingersoll, a prominent Cleveland Presbyterian churchwoman and leader in the Woman's Christian Temperance movement, became Humpal-Zeman's patron, whom Humpal-Zeman described as "an angel

in the flesh" (*Ženské Listy*, January 1, 1896, 218–19). Humpal-Zeman later dedicated her book, *Amerika v pravém světle* (*America in Its True Light*), to "my second mother Mary Ingersoll" (Čapek, 201). Humpal-Zeman converted to Presbyterianism and embraced the temperance cause. Since she had been a freethinker, her conversion to Christianity was accompanied by deep personal turmoil. In 1890, on the advice of her mentor, she enrolled in the College for Women of the Western Reserve, where she studied English, Bible, psychology, history, ethics, geology, and German. She also threw herself into benevolent activities: visiting typhoid patients, teaching Sunday school, and organizing temperance chapters among Bohemian women. She wrote a constitution for the Bohemian Woman's Christian Temperance Union (WCTU) in Cleveland and traveled to Chicago to establish a second chapter among Bohemian women. Humpal-Zeman became known as a public speaker in both English and Czech, addressing local churches and women's organizations such as Sorosis. In 1892, Humpal-Zeman was elected vice-president of the college's Women's Christian Association and was awarded a six hundred dollar scholarship by the college.

Humpal-Zeman became a journalist in this period. She edited the student newspaper, *College Folio*, and supported herself in part by contributing articles to midwest Slavic journals, including *Nova Doba* (Omaha, Nebraska) and *Slavia* (Racine, Wisconsin), using the penname M. A. Kalinová. Reading about the writer George Sand, Humpal-Zeman jotted in her diary, "What a life—so much like mine! She too embodied her own life in her writings and I want to do the same" (college diary, 1890–92). Humpal-Zeman dreamed of starting a women's newspaper.

Before the World's Columbian Exposition of 1893 in Chicago, Humpal-Zeman corresponded with prominent American and Bohemian women, including the head of the Board of Lady Managers, BERTHA HONORÉ PALMER, Czech poet Eliška Krásnohorská, and Czech reformer and women's rights advocate Josefa Náprstek, about representation of Czech women at the exposition. She became secretary of the Bohemian Columbian Exposition Committee in 1892 and withdrew from college in May 1893 to help organize the Bohemian women's exhibit.

The exhibit included 307 books authored by Czech women and twenty pieces of needlework, a traditional symbol of Czech nationalism. Unfortunately, through a misunderstanding, the prized pieces of embroidery slated to remain on display with Palmer's Board of Lady Managers were put up for auction. The outraged local Czech press blamed Humpal-Zeman, accusing her of a lack of nationalism and of "poking her nose into things she cannot understand" (interview with Alena Zárasová). Although she managed to save the embroidery from the auction block, the local Bohemian press never forgot the incident.

The work on the exposition was a turning point in Josefa Humpal-Zeman's career as a writer, lecturer, and advocate of the advancement of women. At this event she met JANE ADDAMS and LUCY FLOWER, influential Chicago reformers. At the close of the exposition, Humpal-Zeman, with two friends from Bohemia who had worked on the women's exhibit, Karla Máchova and Anna Roeslova, traveled to California, where they

FIG. 53. *Josefa Humpal-Zeman edited and published a weekly Czech American women's newspaper printed in Chicago by the woman-owned and operated Bohemian Women's Publishing Company.*

FIG. 54. *Women printers at work, Bohemian Women's Publishing Company.*

FIG. 55. *Josefa Humpal-Zeman, left foreground, and other women printers at work in the Bohemian Women's Publishing Company, Chicago.*

visited many Bohemian settlements and met with like-minded women.

Upon her return to Chicago, Humpal-Zeman became a resident of Hull-House and enrolled at the University of Chicago. With Karla Máchova she started a Bohemian women's newspaper, *Ženské Listy*, one of the first Bohemian women's weeklies in the world. The masthead of *Ženské Listy*, "V osvětě zrodila se ženě svoboda!" (Through education is women's freedom born!), expressed Humpal-Zeman's philosophy. The first edition appeared June 15, 1894, with articles on women's education and achievements, including Hull-House activities; it featured Czech women in literature.

The paper was received enthusiastically by Bohemian women, but three free thinking Czech-language editors, leaders in the Bohemian community, campaigned against Humpal-Zeman's Christian message and her advocacy of women's rights. Antonín Geringer of the Chicago *Svornost*, Václav Šnajder of *Dennice Novověku*, a paper written by men for women, and Bartoš Bittner of Chicago's *Šotek* viewed this new women's paper as serious competition. She was attacked personally, caricatured in words and cartoons, and denounced as a hypocrite, unfit to be a journalist. In spite of this steady stream of attacks, Humpal-Zeman's newspaper thrived. Two years after establishing *Ženské Listy*, she was elected secretary of the Union of Slovenian Journalists, an entirely male association. The Bohemian Women's Publishing Company was established in 1900, with a total work force of fifty women.

In 1894, Humpal-Zeman was elected chair of Vlasta No. 19. The next year she arranged the organization's New Year's meeting at Thalia Hall, bringing together Czech women leaders and Hull-House friends. Here two thousand men and women heard speeches in Czech and English calling for women's advancement through education in the United States and in Europe. FLORENCE KELLEY encouraged the Bohemian women to contact Illinois legislators in support of the new factory inspection law. ELLEN HENROTIN advocated joining the federated club movement among women worldwide. Physician JULIA HOLMES SMITH recommended that Bohemian women use the services of women doctors in their community. Jane Addams spoke on the settlement idea and told the largely immigrant audience, "To me Hull House will be a disappointment if the impression exists that it belongs to one kind of people or nationality" ("All Meet as Sisters," *Chicago Tribune*).

Humpal-Zeman became more and more active in the Bohemian community. She joined a committee to help organize a Czech-American exhibit for the 1895 Ethnographic Exhibition in Prague that was spearheaded by her friends Vojta and Josefa Náprstek. Humpal-Zeman shared the Náprsteks' goal of bringing Western goods and ideas to the people of Prague. Meanwhile her home became a meeting place for Bohemian artists, musicians, professional men and women, artisans and laborers, and their wives and children.

As the personal attacks by Humpal-Zeman's male competitors continued, she became fearful that her association with *Ženské Listy* would lead to its demise. The April 13, 1901, issue of her paper announced Humpal-Zeman's departure with an emotional good-bye letter, praising her skill in sustaining the company through hardship and persecution. Exhausted, Humpal-

Zeman left Chicago and traveled to California before resettling in Prague.

In Europe Humpal-Zeman concentrated on writing and worked as a correspondent for the Chicago *Daily News*. She toured some thirty towns in Bohemia, Moravia, and Silesia, speaking about life in the United States and praising the American public school system for what she perceived as equality of opportunity for women. She also believed that American women exerted a dominant role in their homes and told Bohemians to emulate them. In Humpal-Zeman's mind, this female-dominated home was at the center of American political life. In 1903 she published a selection of these lectures, *Amerika v pravém světle (America in Its True Light)*. The book was well received in Bohemia, but was criticized for its misunderstanding of American social conditions. Humpal-Zeman's old rivals in the Czech-American press ignored the book and helped to prevent its publication in the United States.

Humpal-Zeman made a final trip to Chicago in November 1903 to help her sister Rose Čunat through a difficult pregnancy and birth. She feared getting caught up again in arguments with her critics and in the spring of 1904 returned to Prague, where she had taken a job as secretary of Ženské klub (Women's Club). With Josefa Náprstek's enthusiastic endorsement, she founded another women's newspaper, *Šťastný Domov (Happy Home)*. The first issue, October 1, 1904, contained articles about women reformers and American domesticity, including kitchen and bathroom floor plans. Humpal-Zeman made it clear she wanted no controversy and was simply publishing articles to help people have satisfying domestic lives.

During the last two years of her life, Humpal-Zeman wrote two novels in English: *My Crime* and *The Victim Triumphs: A Panorama of Modern Society* (1903) under the penname Josephine Zeman. In the latter novel the heroine is caught in society's double standard and triumphs over the hypocritical mores of traditional society with the help of a progressive woman.

On April 5, 1905, at the age of thirty-five, Josefa Humpal-Zeman suffered an apoplectic stroke. During the illness that followed, she continued to correspond with close friends, although she was barely able to speak or write. She died a year later and was buried in Prague's Olšany Cemetery, where a monument by the Czech sculptor Stanislav Sucharda was erected on her grave on March 25, 1907.

Like many immigrants, Josefa Humpal-Zeman was torn between two cultures. Her ardent advocacy of women's rights both in her native Bohemia and in the United States provoked strong negative responses; yet through her organizing and writing she brought together European and American women activists. Her role models were George Sand, Jane Addams, Josefa Náprstek—strong iconoclasts like herself. *Ženské Listy* remained in publication until 1976, changing owners, its name, and perspective over the years.

Sources. The Josefa Humpal-Zeman Papers, Náprstek Museum, Prague, Czech Republic, include correspondence, college diaries, photographs, notes for articles. Alena Zárasová, Charles University, Prague, translated excerpts from Humpal-Zeman's college diary and personal correspondence. The Scrapbook of the Bohemian Women's Publishing

Company (c. 1900), UIC Spec. Coll., contains photographs of employees and samples of print jobs. Women's College of the Western Reserve registrar records for Josefa Humpal-Zeman are found in the Case Western Reserve Univ. Archives. Josefa Humpal's birth certificate is on record at the County Archives, Plzeň Czech Republic. *Ženské Listy*, June 15, 1894, through 1976, is available in the Czechoslovak Heritage Museum, Oak Brook, Illinois. Julia E. Noblitt interviewed Alena Zárasová, Prague, Czech Republic, September 6, 1994. Alena Zárasová also wrote several informative letters to Noblitt on June 16, 1994; December 18, 1994; August 3, 1994; March 17, 1995. Articles and books by Josefa Humpal-Zeman include "The Bohemian People in Chicago," *Hull-House Maps and Papers* (1895); "Bohemia: A Stir of Its Social Conscience," *The Commons*, July 1904; *Amerika v pravém světle (America in Its True Light)* (1903); and in 1903 under the penname Josephine Zeman, *My Crime* and *The Victim's Triumph: A Panorama of Modern Society*. Jane Addams's comments at a meeting arranged by Humpal-Zemen appeared in "All Meet as Sisters," *CT*, January 2, 1895. Articles about Josefa Humpal-Zeman include many short biographical sketches published in *Ženské Listy* and *Šťastný Domov* in 1906, the year of her death; a short sketch in Jan Habenicht, *Dějiny Čechův Amerických (History of American Czechs)* (1910); mentions in Thomas Čapek, *The Čechs (Bohemians) in America* (1920). See also Maxine Seller, "Beyond the Stereotype: A New Look at the Immigrant Woman, 1880–1924," *Journal of Ethnic Studies*, Spring 1975; this article was written without the biographical information located in Prague. The most comprehensive work written about Humpal-Zeman is "Josefa Humpal-Zemanová," Alena Zárasová, postupová práce, Ústav Ethnologie a Folkloristiky (Faculty of Philosophy, Charles University, Prague), 1994–95.

JULIA E. NOBLITT

WITH ALENA ZÁRASOVÁ

HUNCKE, OLGA HARRIET
1884–1973
EDUCATOR, ARTIST, MUSICIAN, FUND-RAISER, COMMUNITY ACTIVIST

A public school teacher and fund-raiser for the Chinese Christian Union Church, Olga Huncke became so revered for her service that members of the Chinatown community established a scholarship fund in her name. She was affectionately referred to as "paw paw" (grandma). Parents named their children after her.

Huncke's father, Erich Wilhelm Huncke, emigrated from the Lippe region of Germany in the 1860s to establish a business in Chicago. He developed an extensive network of professional relationships in his real estate ventures and, as a result, gained great wealth. Huncke's mother, Mathilde Heidenheim, moved from Iowa to Chicago with her German immigrant parents, who also came to establish a business. Heidenheim worked in millinery factories when she was young to help her family recover financially from the Great Chicago Fire of 1871. Soon thereafter, she went on to pursue a career in music before her marriage.

Married in the early 1870s, Olga Huncke's parents had six children between 1875 and 1896. The family was economically stable but, in 1897, the Huncke marriage was officially dissolved. The reason for the dissolution was abusiveness on the part of Huncke's father, who regularly beat his eldest son and wife and had a string of extramarital affairs. Olga Huncke and her two younger siblings lived with their mother after the divorce.

Olga Huncke graduated from Lake View (now Lakeview) High School in 1904 and attended Chicago Normal School for teacher training—a common path for many young women. The eldest sibling at home, she probably had family responsibilities that involved taking care of her two younger siblings. Since the public school system did not require teachers to attend college, Huncke was able to complete teacher training and one year of student teaching in a timely fashion. In 1908, she was assigned to teach kindergarten at the newly established John C. Haines School in the neighborhood that was soon to become Chinatown.

When Huncke began teaching at Haines school, the surrounding neighborhood consisted of Croatian, German, and Italian immigrant families. Two years later, in 1910, the city's Chinese population moved south of central Chicago to housing units within the Haines school district. The move was a result of increased taxes that were intended to force out residents to make way for expansion in the downtown business district. Men who had come to the United States via California to make money to send back to their families in Toishan (now Taishan), China, a district in Canton (now Guangdong) province, were the most prevalent group. However, a Chinese mission established in 1900 to serve the needs of Toishanese women and children targeted women from laboring families who worked in Chicago's prostitution district. Once the Chinese population relocated in 1910, the Chinese Christian Union Church was established in the neighborhood and supported financially by the Chicago Council of Churches and a handful of wealthy Chinese entrepreneurs who had wives and children in Chicago. Membership in the church was relatively low. Both wealthy merchants and laboring families lived in the surrounding area.

When Huncke began to have Chinese children in her class at Haines school, the Chinese population was undergoing the traumas of relocation and scrutiny by the Immigration and Naturalization Service (INS). The Chinese Exclusion Act, enforced between 1882 and 1943, severely limited the category of Chinese who were allowed to come to the United States to merchants, their wives and children, students, and visitors. Chinese from the laboring class were no longer allowed entry into the United States. Wives and children could not join the laboring men who had come over to work before 1882. One result was the skewed sex ratio of Chinese communities; in Chicago in the 1920s, there were ten Chinese men for every Chinese woman. As the INS actively engaged in deporting illegal aliens, Chung Hua, a hierarchical, merchant-based entity, was the only organization that focused on helping Chinese families establish residency. The lack of outside support meant that the Toishanese immigrants became even more insular. As a result of these policies, Chinese did not become part of mainstream American society until long after other immigrant groups had assimilated.

During this period, Huncke's interaction with Chinese students was limited but, nonetheless, intense. The students attended school with a sense of seriousness. They brought to the classroom an acceptance of hierarchy and obedience to authority. It is difficult to determine the extent to which Huncke, thirty years old at the time, was aware of the outside pressures of relocation and the INS scrutiny. She was a relatively new teacher and also was taking classes in pottery and bookbinding at the Art Institute of Chicago. Working with students, she learned about their secluded lives.

By the 1920s, corruption and warfare between Chinese fraternal organizations (the Hip Sing and On Leong tongs) were

FIG. 56. *Olga Huncke, far left, attends a buffet in Chinatown, the community she served as a teacher and fund-raiser for the Chinese Christian Union Church.*

rampant. Huncke became devoted to protecting women and children, who often were the victims of growing frustration within the community. Huncke stormed into the homes of drunken husbands who, having lost a great deal of money gambling in the tong halls, were beating their wives. Evidently, her presence as a tall and broad-shouldered white woman was intimidating enough to stave off the abusive behavior. To engage her students in classroom activities, in 1917, Huncke developed a music program in which everyone was encouraged to participate: a Chinese Children's Rhythm Band. Huncke did not anticipate the children's strong enthusiasm for the band. Until she witnessed it, she did not know that the children would work better in groups than on their own. Once they were in the band, the children seemingly were transformed into natural performers. Parents and other teachers at Haines School were equally amazed by the children's performance. Under Huncke's direction, the Chinese Children's Rhythm Band performed a combination of European classical, traditional Chinese, and patriotic music. This included Antonin Dvořák's "Humoresque"; Franz Schubert's "Military March"; Gum Choy's "Animated Book with Yellow River Song," "Snake, Dragon, and Lobster," and "Chinese Finger Plays"; such Chinese folk songs as "Brother Rides the Dragon" and "Jasmine Soldier"; and the Kuomintang's "Chinese National Anthem."

Many Chinese Americans maintained an intense interest in events in China, specifically during the Sino-Japanese war, 1937–45, and the civil war between the Chinese Communist Party and the Chinese Nationalist force of the Kuomintang (KMT), 1945–49. Chinese-American organizations raised more than fifty-six million dollars to support the KMT, and Chi-

nese-American women participated in nationwide protests against U.S. sales of scrap iron to Japan. In the 1940s, Chinese who lived in the city paid a compulsory "fee" to support the Chinese Nationalist cause, a fee imposed by Chinese organizations that had banded together to raise funds for the KMT. There were many who were uninterested in politics and did not want to pay the fee. They moved out of the city and into the suburbs. Those with whom Huncke primarily interacted were strongly committed to Chinese nationalism.

Huncke's work with the children in the period between World War I and World War II coincided with changes in the American public's attitude toward China and Chinese Americans. The change was from widespread resentment against immigrant Chinese who were perceived as taking jobs from American workers to relief that the Chinese population was organized and vocal in its support of the U.S. government's support of the KMT as an anti-Communist, nationalist party on the Chinese mainland. In the 1930s, Pearl S. Buck had won two Pulitzer prizes for her fictionalized stories about China. In this atmosphere, the mass media became interested in such people as Huncke, who had first-hand experience with Chinese communities.

In 1943, Huncke organized the Chinese Children's Rhythm Band to perform in a program to commemorate the visit of Madame Chiang Kai-shek, wife of the KMT leader. The band's performance at the Chicago Stadium attracted a great deal of media attention and Huncke was featured. After Madame Chiang's visit, Huncke led the band to numerous other performances at schools and private clubs throughout greater Chicago to raise funds for China relief, including such varied institutions as the University of Chicago Laboratory Schools, the Municipal Art League of Chicago, Hinsdale China Relief, and the Chicago Woman's Club.

For forty years, Hunke commuted to Chinatown from the North Side of Chicago, where she lived with her mother and younger sister, until her mother died in 1938, and then with her sister. With the money she received from her father and younger brother, Huncke chose to travel to China. She designed a display on China for the Berlitz School of Languages for the opening of the United Nations building in New York.

After World War II, when Huncke retired from teaching, she did not stop working in Chinatown. She shifted the focus of her energies from Haines School to the Chinese Christian Union Church. Huncke favored the missionary efforts of the Protestant churches in Chinatown and voiced strong disapproval of the competition provided by St. Therese's Catholic Mission and School established in 1941. Perhaps because it was run by missionaries fluent in Cantonese, many Chinese families sent their children to St. Therese's school. Few, however, became Catholic. Huncke became involved in fund-raising for the Chinese Christian Union Church nursery school. She made crafts to sell at the church bazaar and sent out several hundred invitations to the bazaar to friends and associates.

Her relationships with her students were the mainstay of Huncke's experience in Chinatown. These relationships formed the basis of *The Green Ginger Jar* (1949), the first book by children's author CLARA JUDSON, in her series, "They Came From." Huncke inspired both Ruth Ann Koesun, whom she followed throughout her career as the first Amerasian ballerina in the American Ballet Theatre, and Robert Lawrence, who was the first African American astronaut. She also inspired a number of others—Victor Ing, a Cantonese immigrant who became a well-known Chicago artist; Jean Moy Joe, an actress and educator; teacher Walter Moy; architect Bing Jin; Ping Tom, who graduated from law school and became a civic leader in Chinatown; and chemist Arthur Toy.

In addition, Huncke inspired many Chinese American women, who for years were vastly underrepresented in Chinatown's "bachelor society," where older immigrant men were predominant. From the early 1900s until well into the 1960s, Huncke encouraged a number of women who had been her students, first, to become active in Chinatown civic affairs and second, to become first-rate homemakers. Huncke helped established a chapter of the Girl Scouts in Chinatown. Her support was important in the Chinese American context to improve conditions for the community. Also, she was focused on cultivating future generations to succeed in a predominately white, Anglo-Saxon, and Protestant context. By the time of her death—the result of complications from diabetes—and cremation in 1973, her female students and colleagues already had established a scholarship fund in her name.

Sources. The Olga Huncke Papers at the CHS include seven of Huncke's scrapbooks and other materials. Information about Huncke comes from interviews with her former students and colleagues and family members 1993–95. They include Leland Chinn, Celia Chung, Brian Huncke, Leslie Walter Huncke, Pauline and Randy Luke, Florence Tun, Gung Hsing Wang, and Eunice Tom Wong. Susan Lee Moy

verified historical facts on the development of Chicago's Chinatown. Huncke's personnel file at the Chicago Board of Education documents her career as a public school teacher. Information on Chinese Americans can be found in Betty L. Sung, *Mountain of Gold: The Story of the Chinese in America* (1967); Yuan Liang, *The Chinese Family in Chicago* (1951); Judy Yung, *Chinese Women of America* (1987); Yuan-li Wu, *The Economic Conditions of Chinese in America* (1980); Tin Chui Fan, *Chinese Residents in Chicago* (1925); Ruthanne Lum McCunn, *Chinese-American Portraits* (1988); and Susan Lee Moy's "The Chinese of Chicago: The First One Hundred Years," in *Ethnic Chicago*, ed. Melvin G. Holli and Peter d'A. Jones (1995).

PEGGY SPITZER CHRISTOFF

HURLEY, SISTER MARY AGATHA
(Eleanor Hurley)
September 3, 1826–May 5, 1902
EDUCATOR

In the thirty-five years that she lived and worked in Chicago, Sister Mary Agatha Hurley, herself an immigrant, established and supervised many of Chicago's Catholic parish schools, beginning with St. Aloysius School that opened on the city's Near West Side in 1867. She provided education over the years for thousands of girls, the majority of whom were the daughters of immigrant Catholic families.

Eleanor Hurley was born to Lawrence and Johanna (Ahern) Hurley in Cloyne Parish, Country Cork, Ireland. In 1835, her family immigrated to the United States, settling first in Lockport, New York, and then moving in 1842 to Dubuque, Iowa, on the Mississippi River, part of Iowa Territory. Already contemplating a life of religious vocation, Hurley determined she would enter the Sisters of Charity of the Blessed Virgin Mary (BVMs) after meeting members of the congregation, including Mary Frances Clarke, the leader of the band of five who had been brought to Dubuque in 1843 by Bishop Mathias Loras. Her parents resisted her choice, but, after more than a year, they were persuaded, and she took the name Sister Mary Agatha on January 23, 1845. The following January she made her first vows.

There is no information about Hurley's education, but she was soon a teaching sister with assignments in Dubuque, in Potosi, Wisconsin, and then in Dubuque again. That city was becoming a center of midwest Catholicism and in 1852 Hurley was appointed superior at St. Mary's Academy (later St. Raphael), the Dubuque Cathedral school. Three years later she was sent to open St. Ambrose School (later called St. Anthony) in Davenport, Iowa, and in 1861 she opened St. Agatha Academy in Iowa City, Iowa. From there, Hurley went to Muscatine, Iowa, where she supervised a system of three schools.

Hurley could have continued a long and productive career in the Catholic schools of Iowa, where it was hard to staff fully the schools BVMs already had opened; but the explosion of population in the immigrant neighborhoods of Chicago called for extraordinary efforts on the part of the Catholic Church and the religious congregations of teaching sisters. Other congregations, including the Irish Mercy Sisters and the German Daughters of Charity, had already established schools, orphanages, and hospitals in Chicago. Their efforts were significant but could not begin to satisfy the needs of Catholic immigrants who were coming to the United States in greater numbers in the decades after the American Civil War. A Belgian Jesuit, Father Arnold Damen, the founding pastor of Holy Family parish on Chicago's Near West Side—a rapidly developing region full of recent immigrants—had traveled in Muscatine and Dubuque, Iowa. There, while giving sermons as a visiting priest, he met many BVMs and recognized their talents. He envisioned a system of Catholic schools in Chicago radiating out from Holy Family Church that would educate from primary grades through university. In 1865, Jesuit brothers opened Holy Family School for boys. In the vicinity, Sacred Heart sisters operated a convent school or seminary for well-to-do girls, including those of the Protestant faith, but no facility for the daughters of the working class. The Iowa BVMs appeared to Damen a likely choice to found such a school in his Chicago parish. He petitioned Father Terence Donaghoe, spiritual director of the BVMs, to ask for a group of sisters to teach in his proposed parish schools. Donaghoe called Hurley to the new venture, and Father Philip Laurent, the pastor in Muscatine, concurred. "You could not make a better choice than Sister Mary Agatha for the new place and in a few years Chicago will speak for itself" (Coogan, vol. 1, 379).

Hurley and Sister Mary Veronica Dunphy arrived in Chicago August 6, 1867. Sisters Mary Angela Quigley, Cleophas Collins, Scholastica McLaughlin, Annunciation Hannon, Clotilda Walsh, Thomas Burke, and Zita Dunne arrived within a week. They all stayed with the family of James Doran, a flour and feed dealer, until the house Father Damen had rented on South Halsted Street was ready for them. Damen had already rented two buildings to serve as schools, a former chair factory on Maxwell Street and a store building on Eighteenth Street. The schools, named for two Jesuit saints, St. Aloysius and St. Stanislaus, had to be cleaned by the sisters before they could open. The sisters began their work during a Chicago heat wave, but in record time five hundred girls began school at St. Aloysius on August 19; a week later about two hundred girls started their education at St. Stanislaus. Hurley became so ill from working in the heat and drinking the contaminated Lake Michigan water that it was feared she was near death. She managed to direct the work of the sisters from her bed.

By September 12, there were seven hundred students at St. Aloysius, and Father Damen boasted, "If we had room, they would have 1,000" (Coogan, vol. 1, 382). Three more BVMs were sent from Iowa. Three years later, grades six through eight moved into a new school building. Later, other primary schools opened in sections of the parish: Guardian Angel (1874), St. Joseph (1878), and St. Agnes (1886). Records from 1876 show that students attended school eleven months of the year. Hurley directed all of these as well as St. Stanislaus. At its peak enrollment, St. Aloysius enrolled some twelve hundred girls. In 1896, the BVMs assumed responsibility for teaching the parish boys as well as the girls—in separate facilities. Altogether, at its apex, there were more than four thousand children in the schools of Holy Family parish.

Gradually the huge parish was divided. The northern end became Annunciation parish and Hurley opened a school there in 1871; in 1873, the area around St. Stanislaus became Sacred Heart parish and the school changed its name to Sacred Heart. With the divisions, the new pastors applied to Hurley for additional BVMs to teach in parish schools. There were never enough teaching sisters, but Hurley did open parish schools at St. Pius (1875), St. Bridget (1876), St. Charles Borromeo (1883), and St. Vincent de Paul (1883). Finally, in 1899, the southern end of Holy Family parish became Holy Guardian Angel parish, an Italian language parish. Since the largely Irish BVMs felt they were not equipped to teach there, they withdrew from that school.

In 1869 Sister Mary Frances Clarke—shrewd, devout, and reclusive—was elected superior general, replacing Father Donaghoe, who had died. Mother Clarke seldom left her home ten miles outside Dubuque but constantly corresponded with her congregation of sisters. Although Clarke had been called Mother since the BVM community was formed in Philadelphia in 1833 and had substantial responsibility, she had no real (legal or canonical) authority until after Donaghoe's death. She immediately moved to better situate the community legally in the state of Iowa and canonically in the wider church, accomplishing this goal by 1870. Clarke then turned to updating the community's Rule of 1845, a constitution under which they operated, which Father Donaghoe had given the sisters. Clarke looked to other members of the community for advice and assistance in governance. At this time in their history, the congregation was small enough that Clarke knew everyone, including Hurley. Valuing her advice, she delegated great authority to Hurley and made her a member of the congregation's council. Hurley regularly traveled to Dubuque for meetings. When Clarke died in 1887, Mary Gertrude Regan was elected superior. The youngest and smallest of the five original BVM sisters who had come to Dubuque in 1843 with Clarke, she continued to rely on Hurley.

Hurley's title, Sister Visitor, meant that she supervised BVM-run schools; she evaluated prospective school sites, negotiated with pastors, and transferred sisters within the Chicago area, which stretched as far as Elgin, Illinois, and Milwaukee, Wisconsin. Hurley opened schools in Milwaukee. In Chicago, she was called Mother Agatha, although she did not hold the official position in the order. She was given the title Mother out of respect for her work.

Hurley and the BVMs were part of Chicago's history. During the Great Chicago Fire of 1871, the BVMs escaped destruction from the flames as the fire shifted its course before it reached Holy Family parish. Less fortunate were the sisters and orphans who fled from St. Joseph's Asylum and the women religious from Good Shepherd Convent. Altogether Hurley welcomed about two hundred of these refugees to St. Aloysius School. The Holy Family parishioners, grateful that their wooden cottages as well as the great brick church had been spared, brought supplies. Old friends and neighbors in Dubuque sent more help.

By the time of the World's Columbian Exposition in Chicago in 1893, Catholic Chicago's progress in establishing a system of parish schools was substantial. The archdiocese mounted displays that included a Catholic educational exhibit. The BVM-run schools contributed examples of students' work for the exhibit. A chartered train took more than a thousand students enrolled in the Holy Family schools to the fairgrounds to celebrate Catholic Education Day, September 2, 1893. After the exposition, Holy Family parish, one of the largest parishes in the world, was one of the popular Chicago sights that Catholic dignitaries viewed. American cardinals and papal delegates attended Sunday Mass April 30, 1893, at Holy Family parish, along with Spanish dignitary Don Cristobal Colon de Toledo de la Cerda y Gente, the Duke of Veragua and Admiral of the Indies.

In 1894, the new BVM leader, Mother Mary Cecilia Dougherty, called a meeting of superiors of BVM schools and the teachers of the highest grade. Fifty-two schools were represented at the July meeting in Dubuque, Iowa. Hurley, who was superior at St. Aloysius, attended. The superiors convened separately from the classroom teachers. Both groups discussed methods, textbooks, and grading. Not all parochial schools were divided into grades, and each school was under the authority of the parish priest without regulation or supervision by the diocese. (The Archdiocese of Chicago did not have a superintendent of schools until 1916, when Archbishop George W. Mundelein appointed three—one each for English-, German-, and Polish-speaking parishes.) Local control had its good points, but the BVM sisters knew they could learn from others' experiences. Some parish priests left school arrangements up to the sister superior; presumably it was her area of expertise. Others wanted to direct the schools personally, following traditions in their countries of birth. An individual superior could not oppose the priest, but the head of a religious congregation could lay down rules for schools her sisters staffed and refuse to supply sisters unless the rules were followed.

The July 1894 Dubuque meeting resulted in a plan of action. All BVMs with five years or more of teaching experience were to embark on a three-year program to plan a course of study (curriculum) for grammar schools and academies. They were to submit courses worked out in their own schools with suggestions for teaching methods and lists of textbook evaluations. These course elaborations were due May 1, 1895. After two years of experimentation and revision, the combined version would be introduced into all of their schools for a five-year trial period. Agatha Hurley retired in 1896, however, before the new course of study was published.

On Christmas Day 1895, St. Aloysius Convent was vandalized. Chicago newspapers covered the incident the next day, reporting contradictory stories. There was agreement, however, that a hail of rocks and other missiles broke the windows, damaged the building, and terrorized the sisters. The incident was part of a long campaign of malicious mischief against the school premises, and police were sent to guard the convent. The *Chicago Tribune*, December 26, 1895, speculated that the attack was motivated not only by religious prejudice but in the hope that the desirable property—the site of the convent—would be put up for sale, which soon happened. The sisters moved to property across from Holy Family Church until a new St. Aloysius Convent was built in 1902 behind the church.

By 1896, many of the neighborhoods that were part of Holy Family parish had become commercial or industrial. In addition, new immigrant groups had moved into neighborhoods once heavily populated by Catholics. The satellite primary schools closed one by one. St. Aloysius Convent School for Girls remained at its location well after the area east of Halsted Street turned Jewish and registration dropped to about two hundred. Always forward-thinking, Agatha Hurley had already opened

Blessed Sacrament School in Lawndale, in 1896 still a suburb of Chicago (later annexed to the city). Blessed Sacrament was the last school Hurley opened. She lived in poor health in the new St. Aloysius Convent until her death at age seventy-six. Other BVMs had been taken back to the motherhouse in Dubuque when they were near death, but it had not seemed right to take Agatha Hurley away from Chicago. Her obituary in the Catholic newspaper, *New World*, commented, "Sister Mary Agatha was laid to rest in Calvary Cemetery, near the great city she loved so well and for whose children she had spent her noble, heroic life" (May 17, 1902).

When Patrick Augustine Feehan, archbishop of Chicago, celebrated Mass for Mary Agatha Hurley's Golden Jubilee December 13, 1894, there was standing room only in a church that seated thirteen hundred. Pope Leo XIII sent congratulations. Tens of thousands of children had been schooled in the institutions founded by Agatha Hurley and the BVM congregation. Her labors were integral to the growth of Catholicism in the Midwest.

Sources. The Sisters of Charity of the Blessed Virgin Mary Archives, Dubuque, Iowa, have Sister Mary Agatha Hurley's personal file. Other pertinent materials there include a handwritten diary (1894–96) by Sister Mary Crescentia Markey and typed annals of Sister Mary Pulcheria Maguire (1901–1906). The *Catholic Educational Exhibit*, a printed catalog, 1894, describes Holy Family parish school displays at the World's Columbian Exposition, 1893. Newspaper accounts of the St. Aloysius Convent vandalism are in the Chicago *Times-Herald*, December 26, 1895, and the *CT*, December 26, 1895. The following provide historical context: Jane Coogan, *The Price of Our Heritage: History of the Sisters of Charity of the Blessed Virgin Mary*, 2 vols. (1975, 1978); Mary Lambertina Doran, *In the Early Days* (1912); Thomas M. Mulkerins, *Holy Family Parish* (1923); Dominic Pacyga and Ellen Skerrett, *Chicago: City of Neighborhoods, Histories and Tours* (1986).

MARY A. HEALEY, BVM

HYMAN, LIBBIE HENRIETTA
December 6, 1888–August 3, 1969
ZOOLOGIST, WRITER, RESEARCHER

Libbie Hyman, acclaimed author of a six-volume synthesis and analysis of data on invertebrates, was born in Des Moines, Iowa, the third of four children and only daughter of Joseph and Sabina (Neumann) Hyman. Her parents were Jewish immigrants. Her father, a tailor who replaced his Russian name with Hyman, left Konin, in Russian Poland, at fourteen years of age and lived for several years in London. When he came to the United States, he opened a clothing business in Des Moines with a partner. Her mother migrated from Stettin, Germany, to Des Moines, where her brother lived. She married Joseph Hyman, who was twenty years older than she, in 1884.

Hyman grew up in Fort Dodge, Iowa, and recalled an unhappy home life "devoid of affection and consideration" ("Autobiography," 2). Her mother insisted that Hyman, because she was a girl, do housework, while her brothers were idle. The family was poor, but Hyman admired her father for educating himself. He collected a small library on various subjects and passed on to her his enjoyment of literature. She had an interest in nature from childhood, seeking wild flowers and learning their scientific names and taxonomic classifications.

FIG. 57. *Zoologist Libbie Hyman draws a specimen at a blackboard.*

She was valedictorian of her graduating class at Fort Dodge High School in 1905. Hyman passed the state examination for teachers for country schools but was too young to be given a position. She played piano, and her mother hoped she would become a music teacher. She continued her education with one year of postgraduate work at the high school, taking additional courses in German and science. Hyman then took a job at a Mother's Rolled Oats factory pasting labels on boxes. Mary Crawford, one of her high school teachers, shocked to find her at a factory, opened higher education to Hyman by arranging for a tuition scholarship at the University of Chicago, beginning in the fall 1906. Hyman supported herself by part-time jobs and continued to receive a tuition scholarship each year.

With a strong interest in science, Hyman began her studies in the botany department, where she perceived attempts to flunk her to be anti-Semitic. She switched to chemistry but did not like the quantitative procedures and finally majored in zoology, a field in which she was to spend the rest of her life. Hyman's course work with Professor Charles Manning Child, an expert on invertebrates, was a turning point in determining her specialization. After earning a B.A. degree in 1910, Phi Beta Kappa with honors in zoology, she continued in graduate work

under Child, receiving a Ph.D. in 1915. Her dissertation on regeneration in oligochaetes, a class of invertebrates, was published in 1916.

When Hyman's father died in 1907, her mother and brothers moved to Chicago, and she lived with them until she left the city in 1931. The family never encouraged her academic career, and fault-finding and scolding were her "daily portion" ("Autobiography," 5). In later years she viewed living at home after receiving the doctorate as the "great mistake" ("Autobiography," 5) of her life.

In 1915 Child appointed Hyman as his research assistant, and she contributed to his experimental work on the physiology of lower invertebrates, including planarians—the family of worms. Although she saw herself as a data collector rather than a researcher, between 1916 and 1932 she published forty-five analytical or research articles, most of them studies on invertebrate physiology, metabolism, taxonomy, and morphology. Child found Hyman's knowledge of chemistry especially useful, and in this area she made outstanding contributions to some of their joint studies.

In 1916 she underwent sinus surgery, which she felt impaired her health permanently. Over the years her looks changed as a result of the surgery, with some distortion of the nose and cheekbones. Hyman reported in her "Autobiography" in 1965, "I have never been really well since that time and have lived in a depressed state of mind" (p. 8). Her life was devoted to zoological work, with little time for socializing or nonprofessional involvements.

Although she did not care for teaching, she was interested in the research of graduate students. She helped foreign students write their theses. On a summer visit in 1923 to the marine station at Woods Hole, Massachusetts, she assisted a Japanese scholar, Taku Komai, in selecting and naming wildflower specimens that were deposited at Kyoto University.

During her years at the University of Chicago, Hyman wrote two outstanding laboratory manuals in vertebrate anatomy. As a laboratory assistant in graduate school, she was dissatisfied with the guidebook available for students and wrote her own, a *Laboratory Manual for Elementary Zoology*, published in 1919 by the University of Chicago Press. The book was so successful that the press published an expanded edition in 1929. The second guide, *Laboratory Manual for Comparative Vertebrate Anatomy*, published in 1922, was similarly successful and was revised as *Comparative Vertebrate Anatomy* in 1942.

The success of the laboratory manuals made possible a major change in Hyman's life. In the early 1930s, Professor Child was preparing for retirement. Hyman's mother died in 1929, and her brothers expected Hyman to keep house for them. To escape from the family situation, she decided to leave Chicago in 1931. Royalties from the laboratory manuals provided enough income to support her, and she chose not to have paid employment thereafter. She traveled for fifteen months in western Europe, where she visited the Naples Zoological Station, a famed research facility.

On her return she settled in New York City near the American Museum of Natural History (AMNH) to continue studying invertebrates; she began the work that would occupy her full time, the preparation of a multivolume treatise on invertebrates.

She had begun thinking about writing an advanced textbook in 1925 and had started the research in 1931 while still in Chicago. When she moved to New York, Hyman already had an excellent reputation among colleagues for her work in Chicago and was listed in *American Men of Science* in 1933 as a distinguished scientist. Initially she worked at her apartment, living near the museum in order to use its library, which she considered indispensable to her work. In 1937 she became an honorary research associate in the Department of Experimental Biology. This unpaid position gave her an office and a laboratory and continued access to the library.

Hyman became the only expert in the Western Hemisphere on Turbellarians, free-living—non-parasitic—flatworms. In 1938, President Franklin Roosevelt, with a naturalist from the Smithsonian Institution, collected aquatic specimens on an expedition in waters from California to Florida. The worms collected were sent to Hyman to identify and classify. The United States National Museum in Washington, D.C., had Hyman identify its flatworm specimens.

She did all of the work necessary to write the books, organizing information on invertebrates based on original sources in English and European languages, which she translated fluently. In addition to synthesis of data, she presented her views, which often differed from those of other experts. She prepared the laboratory slides needed. When the publisher declined to pay for illustrations essential for the books, Hyman learned to make accurate drawings. During several summers she collected specimens for drawings at the Marine Biological Laboratory in Woods Hole, Massachusetts, the AMNH Lerner Marine Laboratory in the Bahamas, and other marine stations.

The first volume of *The Invertebrates*, dealing with the smallest and simplest, was published in 1940. Hyman described the work as "essentially a compilation from the literature" (vol. I, preface), but later zoologists saw "incisive analysis, judicious evaluation, and masterly integration of information" (*Biology of the Turbellaria*, xi).

In 1941, Hyman experienced two happy events. Her alma mater, the University of Chicago, awarded her an honorary Sc.D. degree, the first of four honorary degrees that she would receive. She had always wished to live in the country, and she purchased a home in Millwood, New York, where she could indulge her love of flowers and gardening.

In 1943 she transferred to the Department of Invertebrates at AMNH, after the retirement of a chair who would not accept women or Jews. She published the second and third volumes of *The Invertebrates* in 1951; it dealt with worms, including flatworms, ribbon worms, and other varieties. The books were organized with higher levels of invertebrates covered in each succeeding volume.

In 1952, despite her pleasure with country living, she sold the house and moved to a hotel apartment in Manhattan. She felt that the commuting time to and from the museum and the days that she worked in the garden were detracting from work on the invertebrate manuscript and were slowing her progress. Hyman spent most of her time at the museum library, where she developed friendships with the librarians. She did little socializing with colleagues and was sometimes perceived as brusque and rude. She resented interruption except by scientists with information relevant to her research. At the same time, Hyman helped students who came to her office, often giving them cultures from her collection for their studies. During summers at marine laboratories, students found her enthusiastic, helpful, and relaxed. In the little time she allowed for leisure activities, Hyman attended concerts and played piano. She purchased art works that became a valuable small collection.

Hyman kept in close touch with scientists all over the world through memberships in several professional organizations. In 1953 she served as vice-president of the American Society of Zoologists and in 1959 was president of the Society of Systematic Zoology (SSZ). During her term at SSZ, she found that the society's journal, *Systematic Zoology*, was falling behind in its publishing schedule. In her direct manner Hyman traveled to the editor in New Haven, Connecticut, announced that she was taking over the work, took the manuscripts and other materials back to New York, and edited the journal until 1963.

In 1954 the National Academy of Sciences awarded Hyman the Daniel Giraud Elliot medal for her work on invertebrates. The president of the academy, Detlef Bronk, emphasized that she was the first woman to receive the award. It took the academy seven more years to elect Hyman to membership.

Volumes 3 and 4 of her treatise were published in 1955 and 1959, respectively. Her achievements received international recognition in 1960 when the Linnaean Society of London gave her its annual Gold Medal in Zoology for her work on invertebrates and for the manual on vertebrate anatomy, citing her as the world authority on Turbellarian worms. She was only the third American to receive the award since its establishment in 1888. By 1960 the two laboratory manuals had sold more than two hundred thousand copies, but she declined the publisher's request to revise the guide on vertebrate anatomy. She explained that she hated writing college textbooks and did not like vertebrates.

Hyman showed the first symptoms of Parkinson's Disease in 1956. She had begun losing strength about seven years earlier but continued an intense work schedule of twelve to fourteen hours daily at the museum. During her final years she was confined to a wheelchair and came to the museum each day with a nurse to do four to five hours of work at her desk. After completing the sixth volume of *The Invertebrates*, published in 1967, she was no longer able to continue the series, which she had projected to eight volumes. In retiring from the field, Hyman believed she had achieved the goal of stimulating the study of invertebrates. Throughout the years of work on the treatise, from 1934 to 1966, she also published some ninety research articles.

On April 6, 1969, the museum presented a Gold Medal Award for Distinguished Achievement in Science to Hyman and four other eminent scientists. The award statement cited Hyman's "prodigious treatise" as the "definitive work in its field" (AMNH Press Release April 6, 1969) and praised her assistance to students.

Three months later Hyman died. She left instructions that her body be used in medical science. She directed that no religious services be held. Hyman paid tribute to her professional home by bequeathing most of her estate and all future royalties from the sale of her books to the American Museum of Natural History.

Libbie Hyman found a resourceful solution to the limitations imposed on women in the scientific academic world during the first half of the twentieth century. Despite valuable contributions to scientific knowledge, she remained a research assistant for sixteen years. Income from the sales of her laboratory manuals enabled Hyman to choose an independent course of research and writing without seeking paid employment. The value of her publications, acknowledged by zoologists during her lifetime, has been sustained in the years since her death. A third edition of her manual on vertebrate anatomy was edited and published in 1979. Paul A. Meglitsch and Frederic R. Schram, in their 1991 *Invertebrate Anatomy*, cited Hyman's six volumes as the best invertebrate survey ever done by one author. Her work on invertebrates filled a need in zoological knowledge by assembling, organizing, and analyzing information from many disparate sources.

Sources. The Libbie Hyman collection at the American Museum of Natural History Department of Library Services Archives, New York, includes an eight-page typescript, "Autobiography of Libbie H. Hyman" [1965]; several press releases issued by the museum during the 1960s on Hyman's achievements and at her death; the "Last Will and Testament of Libbie H. Hyman," April 20, 1967, typescript, with accounts of the financial legacy left to the museum by Hyman; a brief typescript, "Libbie Hyman—Chronology"; and a few miscellaneous pieces of correspondence and museum documents about Hyman. A bibliography of her works, including the books described above and published articles, compiled by a member of the museum staff, William Emerson, is found in each of the following memorial publications, in which colleagues recall her achievements and her life: Richard E. Blackwelder, "in memoriam," *Worm Runners' Digest/Journal of Biological Psychology*, October 1970, and Horace W. Stunkard, "In Memoriam Libbie Henrietta Hyman, 1888–1969," in *Biology of the Turbellaria*, ed. Nathan W. Riser and M. Patricia Morse (1974). Accounts of her work written during her lifetime include Edna Yost, "Libbie Henrietta Hyman," *American Women of Science* (1944), and a report of an interview with Hyman, "Gold Medalist," *New Yorker*, August 20, 1960. The citation for the Linnean Gold Medal describes her achievements in *Proceedings of the Linnean Society of London*, July 7, 1961. A biography is published in *NAW* (1980). Judith Winston presents a biographical account, "Great Invertebrate Zoologists: Libbie Henrietta Hyman (1888–1969)," in *Division of Invertebrate Zoologists American Society of Zoologists Newsletter*, Fall 1991. Obituaries appear in the *NYT*, August 5, 1969; *Nature*, January 24, 1970; and *Transactions of the American Microscopical Society*, April 1970. Margaret W. Rossiter describes achievements of women scientists and the limitations they encountered because of gender in *Women Scientists in America: Struggles and Strategies to 1940* (1982) and *Women Scientists in America: Before Affirmative Action 1940–1972* (1995).

ADELE HAST

ICKES, ANNA WILMARTH THOMPSON
January 27, 1873–August 31, 1935
SOCIAL REFORMER, STATE LEGISLATOR

Anna Wilmarth Ickes and her husband, Harold LeClair Ickes, were leaders in the progressive reform movements in Illinois during the 1910s and 1920s. Like Raymond and MARGARET DREIER ROBINS and Medill and RUTH HANNA Mc-CORMICK—other progressive Chicagoans—the Ickeses as a couple created a synergy that neither would have been able to achieve alone. Anna Wilmarth was the reform-minded daughter of a reform-minded mother, MARY WILMARTH. She and her husband, Henry Martin Wilmarth, were descendants of seventeenth-century New England colonists. Henry Wilmarth came to Chicago at age nineteen and made considerable money from gas lighting fixtures and real estate investments before he died in 1885. Anna was the youngest of three daughters.

Anna Wilmarth attended South Division High School in Chicago. She finished her secondary education at Miss Hersey's School in Boston and a French boarding school in Paris. She enrolled at the newly founded University of Chicago in 1893, one of the first women students. There she met both James Westfall Thompson, a young instructor in the history department who would go on to become a noted scholar of the Middle Ages, and Harold LeClair Ickes, later a member of President Franklin D. Roosevelt's cabinet. Anna Wilmarth married Thompson in 1897 and a son, Wilmarth, was born in 1899. Anna Thompson's money enabled them to buy a large house, which Harold Ickes, who in 1903 was between jobs, was invited to share. Ickes felt increasingly uncomfortable in this unorthodox arrangement, because he had always been attracted to Anna Wilmarth; but she convinced him that she needed his protection from her husband. Ickes became an affectionate companion to her boy, who was somewhat neglected by his father. In 1909, Anna Thompson adopted a girl of about thirteen, Frances Shook, from the Chicago Home for the Friendless. Later that year, Anna Thompson, claiming James had made sexual overtures toward the girl, demanded and received a divorce. She did not wish to give the impression that she had divorced James Thompson for Harold Ickes, and the two did not wed until after James Thompson had remarried in 1910. Harold Ickes and Anna Thompson were married by their friend Raymond Robins on September 16, 1911. At the time of their wedding, Harold Ickes, now a lawyer, was the manager of the Chicago mayoral campaign of the Republican reform candidate Charles H. Merriam.

Anna Ickes was situated in the center of both the men's progressive reform network and the women's. Her mother, a trustee and financial contributor to Hull-House, was one of the leaders in women's political culture, an informal network that connected reform-minded clubwomen, settlement house residents, and working-class women to a broad social reform agenda. Before her marriage to Ickes, Anna and her mother had supported the garment workers' strike against Hart, Schaffner and Marx in 1910. Hull-House, the site of the founding of the Chicago Chapter of the Women's Trade Union League (WTUL), connected clubwomen of the middle class and upper class with trade union activists from the working class. Harold Ickes was the lawyer representing Hull-House and the Chicago WTUL during the strike, when strike-sympathizer ELLEN GATES STARR, of Hull-House and the WTUL, and other strikers were arrested by the Chicago police for disorderly conduct.

In 1912, the Robinses and the Ickeses supported Theodore Roosevelt's candidacy at the head of the Progressive or "Bull Moose" party. Mary Wilmarth, together with JANE ADDAMS, the founder of Hull-House, was delegate-at-large from Illinois to the Progressive National Convention in August.

Anna and Harold Ickes's son, Raymond Wilmarth, was born on June 23, 1912, the day after the Theodore Roosevelt insurgents had bolted the Republican convention in Chicago's Coliseum. After two miscarriages, Anna and Harold Ickes, wanting companionship for their son, adopted a boy two months younger than Raymond, whom they named Robert.

The Progressive Party, which had made some gains in 1912, lost heavily in the 1914 elections. In 1916, when Theodore Roosevelt declined the Progressive presidential nomination, Ickes joined the national campaign committee of Republican candidate Charles Evans Hughes.

During World War I, Anna Ickes, at home with the two small boys, industriously churned out socks and sweaters for soldiers, while finding time to head up a survey of industrial plants in the Chicago area and to teach patriotism as well as social hygiene along with other Chicago reformers, including Margaret Robins. Anna Ickes's son Wilmarth Thompson Ickes enlisted; her daughter, Frances Ickes, joined the Red Cross, and Harold Ickes served overseas in the administration of the YMCA.

After the war, and her mother's death in 1919, Anna Ickes became active again in a large number of clubs, including the Fortnightly, the Women's University Club, the League of Women Voters, the National Consumers' League, and the Chicago Woman's Club, of which she was elected president in 1925. The Ickes marriage, later described by Harold Ickes's biographer, was a tempestuous one, and the female solidarity she found among clubwomen may well have been emotionally satisfying as well as politically instructive. The *Chicago American* quoted her on October 29, 1925, as saying that women joined clubs "for the joy of learning to know and love other women."

Although Anna and Harold Ickes had rejoined the Republican Party after the Progressive Party disintegrated in 1916, they could not accept the nomination of Warren G. Harding in 1920. Instead, Anna Ickes campaigned for the Democratic candidates for president and vice-president, James M. Cox and Franklin Delano Roosevelt. In 1924, Republican Illinois Governor Lennington Small appointed Anna Ickes to fill a vacancy on the board of trustees of the University of Illinois, and she was elected in her own right later that year to a four-year term, serving until January 1929. She urged newly enfranchised women to educate themselves politically and stressed the importance of public schools and state universities. She also served on the boards of the Chicago Home for the Friendless and the Chicago Regional Planning Association, which was granted a charter by the Illinois General Assembly to undertake a comprehensive survey of resources and needs in a fifteen-county tristate area centered on Chicago.

Anna Ickes was described in the press at this time as a "picturesque" woman of the "fiery Spanish type," with her dark auburn hair and dark eyes. She was said to have a "good deal of the actress" about her, to know "the value of posture and creating impressions." Her "fighting jaw and firm upper lip" (*Chicago American*, November 7, 1924) were also noted.

Anna Ickes had begun to travel regularly to New Mexico for respite from asthma; in the early 1920s, she built a small adobe house near Coolidge, New Mexico, about twenty miles from Gallup within view of the Sangre de Cristo mountains. She developed an interest in the Navajo and Zuni tribes and the Pueblo people of the Rio Grande and became a member of the Indian Welfare Committee of the General Federation of Women's Clubs. Around 1922, she and her husband met John Collier, an activist for American Indians, and helped him found the American Indian Defense Fund.

In 1928, Anna Ickes, running as a Republican with Harold Ickes as her campaign manager, was elected to the Illinois General Assembly. He had managed a large number of unsuccessful campaigns in the previous thirty years and had begun to say that his wife was "the real politician in the family" (Watkins, 216); certainly she was better known in Illinois than her husband, who later achieved national recognition through his work in the Franklin Delano Roosevelt administration. That same election saw a number of wins for Chicago women, including Ruth Hanna McCormick, elected representative-at-large to the U.S. House of Representatives; Florence Fifer Bohrer, reelected state senator; LOTTIE O'NEILL and two other women, reelected to their second terms as representatives to the General Assembly; and FLORA CHENEY, who, along with Anna Ickes, was elected to her first term.

Anna Ickes represented the 7th District, the so-called "shoestring" district, which was composed of a fringe of territory on the north and northwest edges of Chicago; it was considered a hard district to win, according to the *Chicago Tribune*, because there were many political activists in the rapidly growing municipalities who considered themselves qualified for the job. Sometimes referred to as the "Outer Belt," her district extended around Chicago from Barrington in the north to Chicago Heights in the south, including almost all the country towns of the county encircling Chicago except those on the eastern shore. She was reelected in 1930, having supported important legislation for many of her towns, including aid in sewage disposal. In her second term, she introduced legislation for low-income housing in Chicago. Her diligence, energy, and grasp of the issues were praised by the Legislative Voters' League.

Ickes was elected to the Illinois Assembly again in 1932, although she also served on the national committee of the National Progressive League created by Senator George Norris of Nebraska for Republican support of Franklin Roosevelt; her husband headed the Western Independent Republican Committee backing the Democratic nominee. Her election was remarkable also because she steadfastly supported the continuation of Prohibition at a time when most candidates, including other women candidates, had abandoned the cause.

Issues of conflicting party politics faced her at this time. President Roosevelt named Harold Ickes Secretary of the Interior, a position he held until 1946. Anna Ickes insisted she would serve out her term and managed to strike a balance between competing political loyalties. As a Republican legislator, she introduced and supported a number of welfare bills, and Illinois was one of the first states to accept the Federal Rehabilitation Act.

More difficult to reconcile were the conflicting demands on her time. She did not entertain much in Washington, D.C., although she maintained the Wednesday afternoon "at home" custom among cabinet wives whenever she could. In July of 1933 she insisted that she did not plan to retire. "My heart and soul are in the work at Springfield. . . . I don't want to give it up"

(*Herald-Examiner*, July 10, 1933). Six months later, she was forced to admit that her life had become too complicated by the frequent commuting between Washington, D.C., and Springfield, Illinois. She announced that she wanted to spend more time in Washington because of her enthusiasm for the Roosevelt administration. Her term ended in January 1935, and she did not seek reelection. In May, she presided over a peace movement rally in Washington attended by two thousand supporters who had come to mark the twentieth anniversary of the Women's International League for Peace and Freedom.

Anna Ickes continued to pursue her interest in the American Indians of the Southwest, especially with regard to reforming the system of government boarding schools and curbing the distribution of alcohol. In 1933 she published a book, *Mesa Land: The History and Romance of the American Southwest*, based on ten years of travel and research, an account of the past and current life of the Navajo, Zuni, and Hopis.

Anna Ickes was returning from an expedition to Taos Pueblo north of Santa Fe on August 31, 1935, with two guests, GENEVIEVE HERRICK, a former *Chicago Tribune* reporter and Washington correspondent, and Ibrahim Seyfullah, a secretary at the Turkish Embassy, when her car went out of control on a wet road near Velarde, New Mexico, and overturned, killing Ickes and her driver. Her Episcopal funeral service in Chicago was attended by Eleanor Roosevelt and other prominent New Deal politicians, as well as by Anna Ickes's colleagues from the state legislature. She was buried in Memorial Park Cemetery, Skokie. A year later, on the anniversary of his mother's death, Wilmarth Thompson Ickes killed himself. Harold Ickes remarried in 1938 and lived until 1952.

Although she was praised posthumously in the *Herald-Examiner* on September 5, 1935, for "shoulder[ing] every concept of the duties of her sex to civilization" through her work for better housing and child welfare, Anna Ickes prided herself on support from labor groups and other male-dominated organizations. Like many women elected to office in the 1920s, she sought to be on an equal footing with men. "I've never been a feminist," she was quoted by the *Chicago Tribune* as saying on March 31, 1932. "The sex element just doesn't enter into state politics. Ability is all that counts, I think, and although there is a difference in men's and women's minds, it is only in approach. Ours are more detailed. That's from centuries of housework."

Sources. The Harold L. Ickes Papers in the Manuscript Reading Room at the Library of Congress contain family papers, including correspondence between Anna and James W. Thompson before her marriage to Harold Ickes. T. H. Watkins's massive biography of Harold L. Ickes, *Righteous Pilgrim* (1990), provides extensive material on Anna Ickes, mostly from the point of view of her relationship with her husband, as do Harold Ickes's *Autobiography of a Curmudgeon* (1943) and *The Secret Diary of Harold Ickes*, 3 vols. (1953–54). The *NYT, Chicago American, CT, Chicago Examiner, Chicago News*, and *Herald-Examiner* contain contemporary accounts of her political career covering the years 1917–35. She is listed in *NAW* (1971) as well as in *Biographical Cyclopedia of American Women*, vol. 3 (1928). Information on her legislative career can be found in the *Blue Book of the State of Illinois* (1929–30) and later issues, and in *Illinois Voter*, published by the League of Women Voters of Illinois.

KRISTIE MILLER

ITO, MIYOKO
April 1918–August 18, 1983
PAINTER

Miyoko Ito was a painter of abstract, highly structured works based on complex spatial arrangements of elements derived from still life, interior, and landscape references. Ito's quiet artistic vision was evident in her thoughtful articulation of planar forms, harmonious color, and delicate surfaces. The paintings, both intense and calm, reveal Ito's skillful use of visual elements.

Ito's father was a Japanese immigrant who came to the United States in 1904. Following his graduation with a degree in psychology from the University of California, Berkeley, in 1914, he returned to Nagoya, Japan, for an arranged marriage with a first cousin. She joined him in Berkeley in 1915, and the first of two daughters, Miyoko, was born in 1918. Ito's sister was born in 1920, during a period of relative prosperity in which the family lived in San Francisco. Ito's father worked for a Japanese steamship company and could afford a nurse for his small children. Although he was proficient in English, Japanese was spoken in the home. In 1923, while his wife was pregnant with their third child, Ito's father sent his family to Japan for what became a five-year residence. Shortly after their arrival, a son was stillborn.

Ito and her younger sister were raised in the provincial central area of Japan by their illiterate grandmother and their mother, a school teacher, who taught Ito to read at a very early age. Ito suffered a physically debilitating illness that she later characterized as a childhood nervous breakdown. Her inability to walk prevented her from participating in athletic competitions that were stressed in the schools during this period of Japanese expansion into the Pacific region; but her achievements in calligraphy, writing, and landscape painting were recognized by her teachers.

In 1928, the family returned to the United States to join Ito's father in Berkeley. In a move that he considered to be protective of his frail elder daughter, he placed Ito along with her sister in the first grade of a public school that had a predominant population of African American and Asian students. Ito received an excellent well-rounded grammar school education, followed by strong exposure to music and art in junior high school and high school. Later, she entered the University of California, Berkeley, to major in art and minor in English. In the art department, Ito worked with a number of instructors who favored abstraction over the regionalism of such popular American artists as Thomas Hart Benton and Grant Wood. Along with other Bay area watercolorists, she was drawn to European modernism. *Guernica* and other works by Picasso influenced Ito's use of form, and her paintings were thought to be quite advanced by graduate students and faculty. She was well supported by the faculty for her efforts to understand cubism and to incorporate structural components in her paintings. At that time, the University of California was segregated into ethnic constituencies. Ito was a member of a Japanese sorority, and her future husband, Harry Ichiyasu, a business major, was the president of the Japanese constituency of the senior class.

Following the start of World War II in 1941 and just prior to Ito's graduation from the University of California in 1942, Japanese American students were notified that they were to be sent to internment camps. On April 11, 1942, Ito married Ichiyasu in hopes that they would be sent to the same camp. Three months after their internment at Tanforan Assembly Center, San Bruno, California, Ito received her bachelor of arts diploma with a notification of graduation with high honors, a distinction that had particular meaning to her, because the faculty had supported her candidacy. While in the camp, Ito's husband gave her a questionnaire that the American Society of Friends (Quakers) was providing to encourage application to graduate institutions. Although she had to leave Ichiyasu behind in the camp, Ito gained permission to leave after securing a graduate scholarship to Smith College in 1943. In the art department at Smith College, she worked with instructors who were watercolorists, and she benefited from a remarkable visiting artist program that included Rufino Tamayo and other European painters. Her paintings were influenced by the clearly defined structural elements and loosely applied color of synthetic cubism, references that became the hallmark of her later work.

In 1944, Ito realized that the emphasis at Smith College on history and philosophy did not suit her need for studio practice. Although she wanted to return to Berkeley, Japanese American students were not allowed to matriculate at the school at that time, since government policy sought to keep all Japanese Americans away from the West Coast. She applied for and received a graduate tuition scholarship to the School of the Art Institute of Chicago (SAIC). Ito's husband was released from the camp at the end of the war in 1945 and joined her in Chicago. At SAIC, Ito studied with Margaret Artingstall and LAURA VAN PAPPELENDAM; she was influenced by the teaching and enthusiasm of KATHLEEN BLACKSHEAR, the well-known art historian who integrated work by primitive artists and artists from other cultures into her curriculum on surrealism. Ito attended summer sessions at Oxbow, an artist's retreat in Michigan, in 1948 and 1949 and produced watercolors that melded the structural abstraction of Hans Hofmann's forms with the surface delicacy and color of Pierre Bonnard.

Ito taught herself lithography in 1949 as a means to explore the range of tone in black and white images and to simplify form as a bridge from watercolor to oil paint. She bought a lithographic press and made works that were reductive abstractions with a clear focus on the interaction of color. The gradation of value in fields of color became the device that allowed planar forms to emerge and recede spatially in her later works. She attended night classes at SAIC, where she continued her study of color lithography with Max Kahn until pregnancy with her first child curtailed her use of that strenuous medium. At Kahn's suggestion she took an etching class with Vera Berdich, and she began to paint in oil after the birth of her daughter, Elissa, in 1949. Ito's first solo show was mounted in that year at the Palmer House Galleries in Chicago. The birth of her son, Alan, followed in 1950.

During the early years at home with her children, Ito painted a modest number of works in which she investigated semihard edge abstraction. Although she did not receive critical acclaim for these paintings, the visual vocabulary was pivotal to the development of her mature style. Her admiration for the paintings and drawings of Giorgio Morandi was evident in her

focus on form and in the rhythmic intensity of her structures. By the late 1950s Ito was painting about ten works a year that revealed her mature style, in which enigmatic spatial configurations were balanced with invented forms and subtle color. The geometric constructions and transparent planar projections of synthetic cubist works by Juan Gris and Georges Braque also provided references for Ito's paintings. Dry brushstrokes were pulled across the surface of the canvas to reiterate or emphasize elliptical shapes within organic abstractions. In 1961, Ito's work was included in a two-person exhibition at the Zabriskie Gallery in New York City. During the early 1960s, her paintings were exhibited in Chicago at the Superior Street Gallery. The gallery was supported in part by Joseph R. Shapiro, who later became the first president of the Museum of Contemporary Art, Chicago. Ito met with and exhibited her work annually with the Gaku Guild, a group of Japanese American artists that included Hide Sato, his wife Chiko Sato, and Natsuko Takashita.

In a painting titled *Step by Step* from 1962, Ito's characteristic horizontal brushstrokes were enclosed by delicate linear elements. The iconic structure—showing the relationship of form and meaning—was developed through a lengthy process of drawing in charcoal over a green painted ground, much like the approach used by sixteenth- and seventeenth-century Venetian and Spanish painters. Colors ranged from highly saturated warm hues to neutrals that were modulated tonally to create a subtle pulsation as the forms appeared to shimmer in space through light caught on the edges of the brushstrokes. Ito responded to the pop movement in the mid-1960s with an intensification of color from somber tones in earlier works to a brighter palette in which reds and oranges were balanced with greens and blues. Images shifted from interior references to forms that suggested topography. In many works, Ito used protruding tacks on the side of the stretcher frames to emphasize the fact that a painting could be considered an object, not just a surface, a consideration shared by a number of Chicago artists.

In 1973, Phyllis Kind became her gallery dealer in Chicago, and Ito had her first major one-person exhibition at the Phyllis Kind Gallery in that year. Her work was featured in a one-person exhibition at the Kornblee Gallery, New York City, in 1975. Ito received a residency at the MacDowell Colony in New Hampshire in 1977, and she was awarded a John Simon Guggenheim Memorial Fellowship in 1977. During the late 1970s and into the 1980s, Ito's paintings were shown along with works by a younger generation of Chicago artists known as the imagists. The group included Roger Brown, Ed Paschke, Gladys Nilsson, and Karl Wirsum. Works such as *Sea Changes* (1977) and *Habitat* (1979) were based on architectonic structures that were compared to works from the Heian period of Japanese art by painter Ray Yoshida. Open vistas of undulating color contrasted bordering devices, and whimsical curved lines punctuated the stable formal constructions. Ito's travel to Egypt, India, New Mexico, and Mexico influenced her responses to light and color. *Dream of a Dream* (1979) set a dynamic orthogonal projection into a stable elliptical space; modulated tones of red and blue evoked the hues of dusk and dawn. She received support from Don Baum, a Chicago artist, curator, and arts organizer at the Hyde Park Art Center, where her work was included in many group exhibitions of the Chicago imagists and was also shown among works by artists referred to as allusive abstractionists. When Phyllis Kind opened her New York Gallery in 1978, Ito was one of the first artists to be featured in a one-person exhibition.

Miyoko Ito was hospitalized twice in her later years, for a nervous breakdown and for chemotherapy to treat breast cancer. Despite her illnesses and periods of recuperation, Ito continued to paint exquisite works that balanced stable form with atmospheric color.

Her work was included in many exhibitions in Chicago, including twenty-two *Chicago and Vicinity* shows at the Art Institute of Chicago and *Chicago Imagist Art* at the Museum of Contemporary Art (1972). Other important exhibitions included the *1975 Biennial Exhibition: Contemporary American Art*, Whitney Museum of American Art, New York City; *Painting and Sculpture Today* at the Indianapolis Museum of Art, Indiana, (1976); and *Detroit and Chicago: Art of the 70's*, Detroit Institute of Arts (1978). Between 1976 and 1986, Ito's paintings were viewed in a number of university art museums and galleries in the Midwest and South. Other museum exhibitions included the John and Mable Ringling Museum in Sarasota, Florida (1959, 1960); the Illinois State Museum, Springfield (1976); the Phoenix Art Museum, Phoenix, Arizona; and the Newport Harbor Art Museum, Newport Beach, California (1977). Ito's paintings are exhibited in many public collections including Continental Bank in Amsterdam and Tokyo, and Atlantic Richfield in San Francisco. Museum collections include the Smithsonian Institution, Washington, D.C.; the San Francisco Museum of Art, California; the Illinois State Museum, Springfield; the Pennsylvania Academy of Fine Arts, Philadelphia; and the Art Institute of Chicago.

In 1980 the Renaissance Society at the University of Chicago mounted a major retrospective of Ito's work (1948–79) with a catalog and essay by the Chicago critic, Dennis Adrian. In her later years, Miyoko Ito shared rich relationships with a number of artists, writers, and composers with whom she corresponded. Although she had said that painting could reveal a "better self" (Artner, 1983, 19) than one might record in a diary, she considered giving it up for writing, a discussion that was doubted by her friends and family, who had long understood the intensity of her commitment to painting. Her son remembered his mother telling him, "I am nothing unless I am painting" (Artner, 1983, 19). She died of a heart attack at age sixty-five in Chicago. Her personal artistic vision, her beautifully designed notes and letters to friends, colleagues, and admirers, and her extraordinary visage in diaphanous fabrics added to the legendary status of one of Chicago's most influential and accomplished artists. An article on Ito's work and career that appeared in the *Chicago Tribune* on March 22, 1985, during a posthumous exhibit at the Phyllis Kind Gallery, described Ito: "She was, from first to last, a highly self-critical artist, always going deeper, pressing toward greater refinement" (Artner, 49).

Sources. A videotaped interview and transcript by Kate Horsfield, *Miyoko Ito, Profile*, vol. 4, no. 1, January 1984, are available through the Video Data Bank at the School of the Art Institute of Chicago. The Archives of American Art at the Smithsonian Museum have a microfilmed transcript of an interview with Chicago artist Don Baum. The Phyllis Kind Gallery, Chicago and New York, maintains a box of Ito's exhibition announcements, slides, reviews by art critics in journals and periodicals, exhibition catalogs, and biographical information. *Miyoko Ito: A Review* was published by the Renaissance Society, University of Chicago, in 1980, with an essay by Dennis Adrian that provides an overview of Ito's work, including biographical information and a bibliography. Ito's work is included in *Fantastic Images: Chicago Art since 1945* (1972) by Franz Schulze and in numerous catalogs that accompanied exhibitions at university galleries. Alan G. Artner's brief biography and description of her work appear in "Miyoko Ito Remembered: Daring, Demanding Master Who Will Be Missed," *CT*, August 28, 1983. Artner also wrote on her work in "Never-Shown Paintings Highlight Ito Display," *CT*, March 22, 1985.

SUSAN SENSEMANN

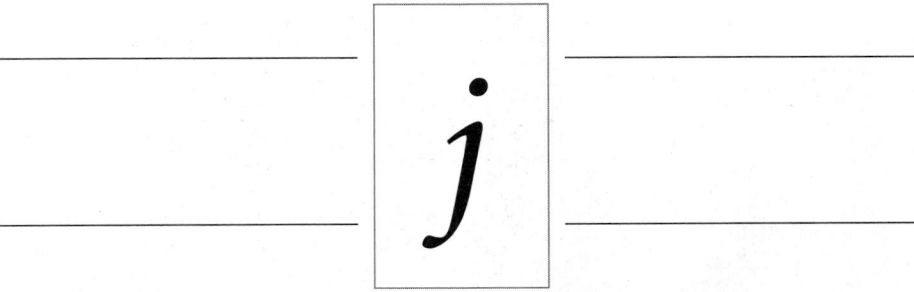

JACKSON, MAHALIA
October 26, 1911–January 27, 1972
GOSPEL SINGER, RECORDING ARTIST

Mahalia Jackson rose from singing in storefront churches on Chicago's South Side to become one of the world's most acclaimed gospel vocalists during her lifetime. Her style owed much to her deep personal faith and background in African American spiritual music. She refused to perform jazz or blues, always insisting that her voice remain an instrument of worship. "Blues are the songs of despair," she explained in her autobiography, "but gospel songs are the songs of hope. When you sing them you are delivered of your burden. . . . When you get through with the blues, you've got nothing to rest on" (Jackson with Wylie, 72). Through this commitment to her music, Jackson did more than any other artist to introduce gospel to American popular culture.

Jackson was born in New Orleans, the daughter of Charity Clark and Johnny Jackson. She had an older brother, William, and several half-siblings who lived with their mother. Her maternal grandfather, Paul Clark, was a Baptist minister who had been born into slavery on a Louisiana cotton plantation. Charity Clark had followed several of her siblings to New Orleans, where she was a domestic laborer. Johnny Jackson was also descended from a Louisiana slave family, and he earned his living as a dockworker, barber, and preacher. Charity Clark died when Mahalia Jackson was only five years old, and her father took her and her brother to live in New Orleans with their maternal aunt, Mahalia Paul, known to the family as Aunt Duke. In her new home, Jackson shared a close bond with her aunt's son Fred, a musician who introduced her to such jazz and blues artists as Ma Rainey, Bessie Smith, King Oliver, and Jelly Roll Morton. Jackson also continued to visit her father's family, which included several vaudeville entertainers. From an early age, this extended family instilled in her a love of music and a strong Baptist faith.

In the ten years she spent with Aunt Duke, Mahalia Jackson attended grade school, worked as a domestic laborer, and sang with the youth choir of the Mount Moriah Baptist Church. Although New Orleans was awash in music, a very clear line divided the sacred from the sinful. Aunt Duke was a strong disciplinarian who did not permit ragtime, dixieland jazz, or rhythm and blues in her household; but in the streets, there was no escaping the sounds that poured from homes, barrooms, and nightclubs. In particular, Mahalia Jackson favored the music of the Sanctified or Holiness Church next door to Aunt Duke's home. Congregants there used different instrumentation and a heavier beat, providing the young Jackson with an example of how to blend popular and religious styles in praising the Lord.

In late 1927, Jackson moved to Chicago to live with her aunt Hannah Robinson, another of her mother's sisters. The difference between her new home and New Orleans struck her immediately. As she recalled in her autobiography, "The South Side was a Negro city. It had Negro policemen and firemen and schoolteachers. There were Negro doctors and lawyers and aldermen" (Jackson with Wylie, 46). In this new world she hoped to become a nurse, but worked as a laundress and learned beauty culture to support herself. She soon found her niche in the Greater Salem Baptist Church. Jackson joined the Johnson Gospel Singers, a group that featured her pastor's three sons and gave Jackson her first professional experience. They performed at local churches and, as their reputation grew, at regional tent shows and Baptist conventions. After the Johnson Gospel Singers broke up in the mid-1930s, Jackson began a long association with Thomas A. Dorsey, a gospel composer, pianist, and Baptist minister. Dorsey had made a name for himself playing piano with blues singer Ma Rainey. The songs he wrote for Jackson combined the spirituality of traditional church hymns with the upbeat swing of urban African American music, creating the unique Chicago gospel sound.

In her early career, Jackson's style was considered undigni-

FIG. 58. *Gospel singer Mahalia Jackson at work in Chicago, 1954.*

In 1938 Jackson married Isaac Hockenhull, who had great hopes for her career. He encouraged her to take professional singing lessons and at one point convinced her to audition for a Chicago stage musical. Jackson's rendition of "Sometimes I Feel Like a Motherless Child" won her a leading role, but when she learned that her husband had landed a new job that same day, she abandoned the project. Since she considered herself a gospel singer, she had taken the role only to earn money. To make ends meet, she and Isaac made and sold cosmetics out of their kitchen, and Jackson opened a neighborhood beauty salon and floral shop. Her refusal to turn singing into a more lucrative profession, however, caused friction between them and contributed to their divorce in 1943. They had no children.

Jackson's career took off when she returned to recording after World War II. In 1946 she signed a contract with Bess Berman, who ran Apollo Records in New York. At this time, the recording industry reflected the racial segregation in American society. Labels marketed jazz and blues as "race records," targeting mostly urban black listeners. In signing Jackson, Berman was banking on gospel's ability to tap into the commercial audience that already existed for Apollo's blues releases. That breakthrough came a year later with Jackson's recording of "Move on up a Little Higher," which sold close to two million copies. Jackson had at last found a profitable outlet for her talents.

Back in Chicago her popularity received a considerable boost from interviewer Studs Terkel, who played her Apollo releases on his WENR radio program. Terkel exposed nonchurch audiences to Jackson's music, making possible the stunning sales of her records. With radio airplay, Jackson began to perform in larger venues. Her sellout 1950 appearance at Carnegie Hall ushered in gospel's golden age of commercial and critical success. Two years later she toured France, Denmark, and England before sickness forced her to return home. In 1957 and 1958 Jackson performed at the Newport Jazz Festival, bringing gospel to the nation's premiere jazz showcase. Though her audiences continued to grow, she refused offers from nightclubs or theaters that served liquor, at one point turning down twenty-five thousand dollars a week to appear in Las Vegas.

In 1953 Columbia Records wooed Jackson away from Apollo Records, with which she had disputed royalty distributions. A powerhouse in the recording industry, Columbia billed Jackson as "The World's Greatest Gospel Singer" and put great energy into promoting her. The publicity campaign included a weekly radio program on the CBS network, which debuted on September 26, 1954, with Studs Terkel as its writer. Despite critical praise, the program failed to attract a sponsor and folded after twenty weeks. Radio, like the recording industry, still catered to racially segregated markets, and network advertisers were reluctant to support a program featuring an African American so prominently. At the time of the radio program's demise, however, WBBM-TV in Chicago offered Jackson a weekly television show. Terkel again served as writer, sitting off-camera and asking Jackson questions about songs she performed live each week. Unfortunately, *The Mahalia Jackson Show* met the same fate as the radio program. Jackson found television confining anyway. She noted in her autobiography, "TV and I don't see eye to eye about time. . . . I'm used to singing in church where they don't stop me until the Lord comes. But the first thing they start telling me

fied by some black ministers and church elders. While everyone applauded her beautiful contralto voice, some northern Blacks objected to the theatricality of her performances. She shook, twisted, and rocked as she sang, sometimes kneeling and interjecting "Lord have mercy" and "yeah, yeah, yeah" into her lyrics. Contemporaries described her as a sensual performer who flirted with the men in her audiences and, in more jubilant songs, even lifted her robes a bit off the ground.

Although Jackson performed constantly, she was not able to earn a living from her singing during the Great Depression. She appeared mostly in church concerts organized to raise money for mortgage and heating bills. Jackson therefore supplemented her meager earnings with domestic and factory labor. In 1937 she cut her first record, *God's Gonna Separate the Wheat from the Tares,* on the Decca label. Decca was taking a chance in recording gospel, which had not yet found an audience outside of black churches. When the record failed to do much business, the label pressured Jackson to switch to the blues. She declined and did not record again for nine years.

when we get to a TV rehearsal is 'Look out! Watch your time!' and they start to cut the song down" (Jackson with Wylie, 108).

During the 1950s and 1960s Jackson also lent her voice to the civil rights movement. In 1956 the Rev. Ralph Abernathy asked her to perform in Alabama at a fund-raiser marking the anniversary of the Montgomery bus boycott. Jackson quickly agreed, and when asked about her fee, replied, "I don't charge the walking people" (Goreau, 219). In early 1957 she moved into a new home in a white neighborhood on Chicago's South Side. Verbal and physical harassment followed, culminating in bullets fired through her living room window. Jackson stood her ground, and the incident drew national attention. In a network television interview, she appeared on Edward R. Murrow's *Person to Person* to denounce housing discrimination.

Jackson soon became one of the civil rights movement's most ubiquitous supporters. In 1957 she appeared at the Lincoln Memorial in Washington, D.C., with several leading members of the Southern Christian Leadership Conference (SCLC). She sang "I Been 'Buked and I Been Scorned," which became her trademark performance at civil rights rallies. Six years later she returned to Washington to sing before Dr. Martin Luther King delivered his "I Have a Dream" speech. Other landmark performances for Jackson included singing in Constitution Hall in 1960, where the Daughters of the American Revolution had barred the black contralto Marian Anderson twenty-one years earlier. She also sang "The Star-Spangled Banner" at John F. Kennedy's inauguration and organized Chicago benefits for Martin Luther King and SCLC in 1963 and 1966. In the second of these, thousands attended a rally in Soldier Field to hear King call for an end to housing discrimination in Chicago.

The final years of Jackson's life were troubled. In 1964 she married Sigmund "Minters" Galloway, a jazz musician who pressured Jackson to advance his career and expand her repertoire beyond gospel music. Jackson resented his intrusions and his condescending attitude toward her untutored musical style. During their two-year marriage, she suffered from exhaustion, heart problems, and severe weight loss. The couple divorced in 1967 after a bitter and well-publicized trial. Despite such physical and emotional difficulties, she continued to tour, visiting Europe in 1969, Africa in 1970, and Japan and India in 1971. She became an unofficial goodwill ambassador for the United States, meeting with heads of state William Tubman, Indira Gandhi, and Emperor Hirohito. During a series of European concerts in 1971, Jackson fell ill and returned to Chicago. She died of heart failure in January 1972 in Evergreen Park, Illinois. Close to one hundred thousand people attended memorial services held in Chicago and New Orleans; she was buried in Providence Memorial Park in Metairie, a New Orleans suburb.

Jackson maintained a boundary between her sacred and secular worlds but never neglected one for the other. Ironically, her refusal to bow to commercial pressures brought her fame and fortune unprecedented for gospel artists. At the time of her death, she left an estate estimated at more than $1 million, having invested her earnings in several charitable and business enterprises. Despite such wealth, she lived simply, never wandering far from her family and religious roots in New Orleans and on Chicago's South Side.

Success did not come without costs. Constant touring—

much of it undertaken in years when legalized discrimination made travel especially difficult for black entertainers—led to health problems in her final years. Music critics and gospel historians agreed that her recordings with Columbia in the 1950s and 1960s lacked the drive and inspiration of her early Apollo work. Jackson's best work went unrecorded, performed before live audiences in the churches and tent shows of the 1930s and 1940s. Nevertheless, she was the performer most responsible for gospel's exposure to a popular and integrated audience. By singing in support of the civil rights movement, she helped reshape the world around her. At the time of Jackson's death, actor Harry Belafonte described her as "the single most powerful black woman in the United States, the woman-power for the grass roots. There was not a single field-hand, a single black worker, a single black intellectual who did not respond to her Civil Rights message" (Schwerin, 183). In that message, Jackson perfectly blended her spiritual and secular worlds.

Sources. Jackson's autobiography, written with Evan McLeod Wylie, *Movin' On Up* (1966) discusses her involvement in the civil rights movement and contains a select discography. Jackson wrote about her 1967 divorce in "Marital Bliss vs. Single Blessedness," *Ebony,* April 1968. Jackson is listed in Jesse Carney Smith, ed., *Notable Black American Women* (1992), *BWA,* and *NAW* (1980). Jules Schwerin, *Got to Tell It: Mahalia Jackson, Queen of Gospel* (1992) is a brief biography that contains an appendix of Jackson's recordings and radio programs. Laurraine Goreau, *Just Mahalia, Baby: The Mahalia Jackson Story* (1984, originally published 1975) is a detailed biography. For assessments of Jackson's music, see "Mahalia the Queen" in Tony Heilbut, *The Gospel Sound: Good News and Bad Times* (1975, originally published 1971), and "Mahalia Jackson" in Henry Pleasants, *The Great American Popular Singers* (1974). Ralph Ellison reviewed her music and appearances at the Newport Jazz Festival in *Saturday Review,* September 27, 1958. Joe Goldberg examined Jackson's experience in television in "When Mahalia Had Her Own TV Show," *Rolling Stone,* March 2, 1972. For obituaries, see *NYT,* January 28, 1972, and "Two Cities Pay Tribute to Mahalia Jackson," *Ebony,* April 1972. Columbia has reissued some of Jackson's music on compact disc, including *Gospels, Spirituals, and Hymns* (C2K-47083); *Silent Night* (CK-38304); and *Mahalia Jackson Sings America's Favorite Hymns* (CGK-30744).

TIMOTHY J. SHANNON

JACOBS-BOND, CARRIE
August 11, 1862–December 28, 1946
COMPOSER, LYRICIST, PERFORMER, MUSIC PUBLISHER

Carrie Jacobs was born into an upper-class Episcopalian family in Janesville, Wisconsin, to Hannibal Cyrus Jacobs, a physician, and Mary Emogene (Davis) Jacobs. An only child, she grew up at the fifteen-acre home of her grandfather, German H. Davis, who owned the Davis House hotel in Janesville.

Music was a strong and early influence. Jacobs's father played the flute, an uncle played the guitar, an aunt composed waltzes, and her grandmother Jacobs's first cousin, John Howard Payne, composed "Home Sweet Home." By age six she could play songs by ear. Her first public appearance came at age eight, when she repeated, without sheet music, a march performed by touring pianist Blind Tom at a recital at the Myers Opera House in Janesville. At age ten she began eight years of piano lessons with local teachers, though she never received formal instruction in harmony or composition.

FIG. 59. *Composer and publisher Carrie Jacobs-Bond with sheet music folio in her Chicago living room, 1902.*

A series of tragedies that punctuated Jacobs's life began with her father's sudden death in 1873, after a grain panic in the commodities market wiped out his fortune. Her grandfather sold his estate outside of town, and the family moved into his hotel downtown. Her mother remarried twice, first John Phelps Williams in 1871, then James Benjamin Miner in 1880, a union that gave Jacobs a half-brother, James.

At eighteen Jacobs wed Edward J. Smith. Their son, Frederick Jacobs Smith, was born in 1882. They divorced seven years later, and she soon married physician Frank Lewis Bond. The family moved to Iron River in northern Michigan, where Jacobs-Bond claimed she spent the happiest years of her life. To encourage her love of music, Frank Bond gave her a piano as a wedding present. She gave piano lessons, wrote songs, painted china, played organ in church, and often accompanied her husband on his rounds, bringing food and clothing for poor patients. This comfortable way of life ended abruptly when the area's economic mainstay, the iron mines, shut down, drastically reducing for the couple both their investments and income from patients.

Jacobs-Bond suggested she try selling some of her songs to make ends meet until her husband could establish a new practice in a different town. Overcoming her husband's initial reluctance, Jacobs-Bond launched a network of contacts that was to serve her throughout her career. She wrote to an editor at the *Chicago Herald,* who referred her to Amber Holden, a local socialite. He invited Jacobs-Bond to play piano for a meeting of Chicago's Bohemian Club, a group of poets and journalists, and introduced her to a Chicago publisher of children's songs.

The flush of this success was doused soon after Jacobs-Bond's return to Michigan, when her husband was playfully pushed in the snow by a young neighbor and died five days later of a ruptured spleen. Jacobs-Bond and her son moved to Janesville, then to Chicago in 1896. She took in students as boarders, moving eventually to a three-room flat that became the site of her publishing house, the Bond Shop. In 1898, she helped organize "30 Years of Freedom," a celebration of African American music, and assisted in arranging choral music for the five hundred black singers at the concert.

The poverty Jacobs-Bond endured for years left a lasting mark in both her personal nature and later business strategies. Bit by bit she sold most of her possessions—except her beloved piano—to supplement her meager income from selling hand-painted china. Her own impoverished circumstances fostered an empathy with people even worse off; she routinely let homeless strangers stay in one of her rooms in exchange for chores like shoveling snow or bringing in coal.

Jacobs-Bond felt that these acts of compassion gave her courage and a business philosophy of trusting everyone once, qualities evident as she made her way around Chicago pitching her work. Dressed in handmade clothes, she performed in stores in hopes the managers would order her music. Realizing she needed to create a demand for her music, Jacobs-Bond played and sang or recited her poetry in friends' homes for ten dollars a night and then added small public recitals as well. She did not particularly like performing, and she and critics acknowledged that her singing voice was pleasant but not magnificent.

Jacobs-Bond knew that if famous singers performed her work, she would glean greater publicity. She wrote to popular singers, but only those she felt would be sympathetic. The courtesy and consideration Jacobs-Bond extended in asking professionals for their patronage was returned. A former star of a Boston opera company, Jessie Bartlett Davis, gave Jacobs-Bond two hundred and fifty dollars, which, matched equally with Jacobs-Bond's savings, enabled the struggling songwriter to have seven songs published in 1901 by N. Nelson in Chicago. Two of these tunes, "I Love You Truly" and "Just a Wearyin' for You," became such big hits that eventually they were published separately.

During a tour around Iowa, Jacobs-Bond met Elbert Hubbard, a performer, artisan in the Arts and Crafts movement, and publisher, whose influence proved integral to advancing Jacobs-Bond's career. He publicized her work favorably in *The Philistine* magazine. He also agreed to pay for Jacobs-Bond to travel to New York if she gave a recital at his publishing house, the Roycroft Shop.

In 1904 Jacobs-Bond made her first vaudeville appearance at a theater in Chicago. It was an awful experience: suffering from stage fright and uncomfortable wearing heavy makeup, she was booed off the stage. Spurred by financial need, however, she would sign vaudeville contracts after World War I that paid one thousand dollars a week in New York.

Strongly encouraged by Hubbard to become her own publisher, Jacobs-Bond moved to a larger flat; the hall closet served as her first stockroom. Nelson, her printer, never billed her; he trusted that she would pay him when she could. She hired another musician/composer, Henry Sawyer, to write down her music; musical notation was a difficult task for her because of her lack of formal training and because she experienced recurring bouts of neuritis. Jacobs-Bond also called on her son, Frederick, to join her expanding business, overseeing the accounts, inventory, and delivery.

Despite unfailing support from friends and associates, Jacobs-Bond, heavily in debt, suffered a nervous breakdown. She owed Nelson alone fifteen hundred dollars. She checked herself into a sanitarium and told a woman friend there she had come to die. That woman contacted Walter H. Gale, husband of a childhood friend of Jacobs-Bond and a wealthy businessperson. He visited Jacobs-Bond at the sanitarium, reassuring her that every entrepreneur needed to borrow money when starting a business. He estimated her business to be worth nine thousand dollars and lent her fifteen hundred, becoming a silent partner in the Bond Shop.

The next day Jacobs-Bond left the sanitarium, paid Nelson, and doggedly plowed forward with her career. She rented a stockroom on Michigan Avenue, where her son loaded the sidecar of his motorcycle with five thousand copies of sheet music to deliver around town. The Bond Shop relocated to a five-room apartment in 1904, when net profits were one hundred and fifty dollars a month. Two years later the business grew into a seven-room space.

One success was overtaken by another in the ensuing years. She sang children's songs in the White House—"It ain't so much the doing, / As the way the thing is did"—to which President Theodore Roosevelt responded, "Mrs. Bond, you will never say truer words than these" (Jacobs-Bond, 127).

The crowning glory of Jacobs-Bond's career was the worldwide success of the song "When You Come to the End of a Perfect Day," published in 1910. For several years Jacobs-Bond traveled to California on the Santa Fe Railroad, stopping enroute to perform for families of railway workers. She stayed at the Holly-

wood Hotel, planning weekly concerts and performing monthly in exchange for room and board. During a drive with friends around Mount Rubidoux in Riverside, she found inspiration for the song's verses in a glorious sunset. From this expression of appreciation for nature and friendship evolved sixty different arrangements, fifty recordings, fan mail from around the world, and a fortune in revenue. This song "appeared at the right psychological moment, combining as it did the pathos and optimism of the era that came to an end with the Great War" (*NAW*, 195). Soldiers sang it, cartoonists parodied it, and a wild crowd of thousands bellowed it on Armistice Day (1918) in New York. A reporter wrote in 1924 that the song had sold more than five million copies and had been translated into more languages than any other. At the Chicagoland Music Festival in 1939, Jacobs-Bond witnessed one hundred thousand people singing "A Perfect Day" at Soldier Field.

Such a phenomenon required a move to larger business quarters. Jacobs-Bond moved to a winter home outside San Diego in 1911, then permanently to Hollywood in 1917. She wrote songs there while her son managed the business in Chicago until 1922, when Frederick, his family, and the Bond Shop moved to California. Three months later publisher Gustav Schirmer proposed that his Boston firm oversee publication and distribution of Jacobs-Bond's material, and Jacobs-Bond agreed. The Bond Shop in Hollywood continued as a retail outlet, while its owner composed songs.

Sadly, Jacobs-Bond's life never seemed to evade tragedy for long. A severe blow came in 1928 with the death of her son, who shot himself in a mountainside cabin. Friends in Michigan speculated that Frederick was torn between his wife and his mother. Jacobs-Bond entered a period of mourning and retirement for several years.

Eventually her irrepressible urge to write emerged. Her songs at first were melancholy, but gradually they came to reflect her contentment as a gracious woman tending her garden and spending quiet times with her dogs and friends. Her lifelong achievement won her several accolades, from radio stations celebrating her birthday to enrollment in the Songwriters Hall of Fame. An elementary public school in Chicago was named after her.

When Jacobs-Bond died in Hollywood of a heart attack, the *Chicago Tribune* called her "one of America's great song writers whose heart appeal compared with the songs of Stephen Foster" (December 29, 1946). Former U.S. President Herbert Hoover described her as a "beloved composer of . . . songs that express the loves and longings, sadness and gladness of all people everywhere. . . . She was America's gallant lady of song" (quoted in Finger, 32). A number of her songs have endured and are still familiar to listeners.

Sources. A few newspaper clippings and samples of Jacobs-Bond's sheet music and children's poetry are available at NL and the CHS. The Library of Congress in Washington, D.C., has an extensive collection of her music. The archives at the Rock County [Wisconsin] Hist. Soc. and the Iron County [Michigan] Hist. and Museum Soc., contain letters and clippings. Jacobs-Bond details her life from childhood to her early years in California in *The Roads to Melody* (1927); the book includes several photographs and excerpts of her poetry and songs. The meticulously researched Ph.D. dissertation by Susan Pearl Finger, "The Los Angeles Heritage: Four Women Composers, 1918–1939" (Univ. of California, Los Angeles, 1986), contains comments on the technical musical merits of Jacobs-Bond's work. Phyllis Roth Bruce's master's thesis, "From Rags to Roses: The Life and Works of Carrie Jacobs-Bond, an American Composer" (Wesleyan Univ., 1980), is an extensive biography. Biographical information also is found in Neil M. Clark, "Carrie Jacobs-Bond Has Written Her Life into Her Songs," *American Magazine*, January 1924 and *NAW* (1971). A listing of Jacobs-Bond's songs appears in a brief pamphlet by Edith Brown Kirkwood, *Carrie Jacobs-Bond and the Bond Shop* (1907). Articles about her appear in the *CT*, December 29, 1946, and October 27, 1966.

LAURA E. LARSON

JAQUES, BERTHA EVELYN CLAUSON
October 24, 1863–March 30, 1941
ETCHER, PRINTER, WRITER, LECTURER

Bertha Evelyn Clauson was born to John W. and Charlotta A. (Wild) Clauson of Covington, Ohio. Covington was a small, picturesque town of eight hundred families in the Stillwater River Valley at the time that her parents settled there. Its river scenes and landscapes may later have influenced Clauson's choice of subject matter in her work.

Clauson's education in Covington was basic and general. Besides reading and writing, she learned the fundamental arts of communication upon which she would rely heavily in her later years. In art, although she was basically self-taught, her talent and skills in drawing were strong enough that Clauson was able to secure a job as a magazine writer and illustrator in Cedar Rapids, Iowa, working from 1885 to 1889 and having her illustrations published by the Torch Press. While in Cedar Rapids, she met her future husband, William Kilbourne Jaques, a graduate of Cornell College, Mount Vernon, Iowa—located near Cedar Rapids.

Clauson married Jaques on Thanksgiving Day, November 28, 1889. He was a "medical doctor four years her senior, who had recently set up his practice in Chicago" (Agabiti, 3). The couple settled on the South Side in Chicago's Kenwood community. William Jaques became "a successful surgeon . . . [at one time] . . . serving simultaneously as city roentgenologist, chief of the antitoxin staff in the Chicago Health Department, and director of the municipal laboratory" (Agabiti, 3). Bertha Jaques began studying drawing under the tutelage of Caroline Wade at the School of the Art Institute of Chicago (SAIC) but soon withdrew as her attempts to start a family met with complications. Between 1889 and 1893, Jaques gave birth to three children, all of whom died in early infancy.

In the summer of 1893, Chicago was brimming with excitement in anticipation of the opening of the World's Columbian Exposition. When Bertha Jaques and her husband came to the exposition from their home just a few miles away, Jaques discovered the art of etching and determined it would be her profession. She viewed prints, including those of French artist Felix Braquemond; American artists James Abbott McNeill Whistler, J. Alden Weir, and Timothy Cole; English printmakers Seymour Haden, Frank Short, and William Strong; and Swedish artist Anders Zorn.

Etching was a young art form in the United States in 1893, although printmaking had been practiced for many years. Etching was a process of printmaking that involved covering the surface of a copper plate, carving lines in that surface through which acid would eat into the copper, then making prints with this plate. In contrast, printmaking involved wood blocks as opposed to metal plates, and the quality of the product was different in printmaking than in etching. As an art form, etching had at times been rather controversial both as to its value and its practicality. When approached about offering etching as an art form to be taught at SAIC, the director, William M. R. French, replied to Bertha Jaques that "etching was a reproductive process" rather than a creative process and "had no place in a school of painting" (quoted in Agabiti, n.p.).

Jaques's interest in the new art form was unabated, however, and her husband's desire to see her fill the void left by their deceased children inspired him to fashion from his surgical instruments and from dental equipment tools she could use for etching. At home, she studied two standard texts of the time: Philip Gilbert Hammerton, *Etching and Etchers*, and Maxime Lalanne, *A Treatise on Etching* (French edition 1866; translated by A. R. Koehler, 1880). The subject of her first etching, *Fine Arts Building* (1893), was one she returned to in 1900. Immediately she began to promote etching as a form of printmaking at the same time that she educated herself through imitation and trial and error. When a second-hand Hammersmith press became available, Jaques and her husband traveled to Milwaukee, Wisconsin, to purchase it. Between 1894 and 1905, Jaques experimented with etching techniques, using her homemade tools. She produced a group of early works including Chicago scenes such as *Fine Arts Building, West Front–Fine Arts Building* (c. 1900), *Buckingham Fountain–Chicago* (c. 1905), *Rainy Day* (1904), and *Field Museum by Moonlight* (1904). Her *Promenade* (1897) illustrates the Chicago lakefront, and her Chicago river views are "unidealized, the harsh almost brutal ugliness of the urban scene . . . presented forthrightly and turned into an intimate vignette of actual time and place" (de Vecsey, n.p.).

Jaques was also active in meeting other artists and developing relationships that lasted for years. One of her most important friendships was with Helen Hyde, a painter and printmaker from San Francisco. Hyde was known for her representations of children, most notably Asian children, while Jaques's work was primarily of natural and botanical subjects. Jaques sought out Hyde when she read an article about Hyde's colored etchings in *International Studio* in 1898. Jaques herself did not incorporate color into her etching and, in general, did not approve of color in etchings; Jaques wrote to Hyde to ask her opinion. Hyde replied that "she had very little to say about the matter theoretically, as her work was largely the result of an accident and her success unlooked for" (*Helen Hyde*, 7). This discussion was the beginning of a long and productive friendship for Bertha Jaques.

Helen Hyde, unlike Jaques, was a professionally trained artist. She began studying art at the age of twelve under the tutelage of Franz Richardt; this was followed by "a period in a San Francisco art school under Emil Carlsen, an impressionist, who, perhaps, helped in establishing . . . Hyde's broad method in water colors" (*Helen Hyde*, 11). She worked for a time at the Art Students' League in New York. After New York, Hyde went to Europe studying under Franz Skarbina in Berlin, and Raphael Collins and Albert Sterner in Paris. She studied in Japan under

Kano Tomonobu, "the ninth and last in the line of the great Kano school of painters" (*Helen Hyde*, 14).

When she learned from Jaques that the Chicago etcher printed her own work, Hyde was surprised and asked how (*Helen Hyde*, 8). Hyde hired someone to print her sketches, a common practice among artistic printers but not one of which Jaques wholly approved. According to Jaques, "The most satisfactory results are obtained when the artist does his own work, from the first drawing to the final print" (*Concerning Etchings*, 10).

Though the approach of the two artists was very different, they developed an appreciation for each other's work and felt a desire to learn and to exchange information. The two became lasting friends. Hyde, who had no children of her own, referred to her prints as her children, and Jaques enjoyed watching Hyde's "family" grow and become successful. Whenever one of her prints was bought, Hyde called it an adoption. "Just think," she wrote, "the children have had a lovely tea party in Paris and not one of them came home. Would you believe the French would like Japanese children so well?" (quoted in *Helen Hyde*, 8).

Eleven of Jaques's etchings appeared in the exhibition of Chicago Artists in the Art Institute in 1903. Sixteen impressions were purchased, eleven by BERTHA HONORÉ PALMER. "With that success . . . Jaques became the leading spirit in a group pioneering the art of etching in Chicago" ("A Leader Retires," 25).

In 1908, Jaques traveled to Japan to visit Hyde, who had gone there for six months but stayed three years. While in Japan, Jaques wrote extensively to her husband about everything she saw and everything she learned about Japanese culture. Upon her return from Japan, Jaques wrote "Red Letter Days in Japan, Being an Account of a Visit to Miss Helen Hyde of Tokyo, in Letters Written to Her Husband, Dr. W. K. Jaques," with prints of scenes and people she saw in Japan.

The trip to Japan gave Jaques a greater appreciation of Hyde's work, since she spent much of her time in Hyde's studio watching Hyde and her printer work. She studied the children she saw, knowing they were all potential subjects for Hyde, and she was inspired by Japanese botanical drawings to create some etchings of Japanese trees, bushes, and flowers.

Jaques had established a name for herself within the etching community, but she felt that etching needed an organization to bring a wider audience to the art. She and other local etchers, including Earl H. Reed, Otto J. Schneider, and Ralph M. Pearson, founded the Chicago Society of Etchers in 1909–10, and Jaques served as secretary-treasurer of the group for twenty-six years. The early membership included Helen Hyde, BEATRICE LEVY, Charles W. Dahlgreen, Charles B. Keeler, and Robert Roscovich.

Determined to educate a general public about etching, Jaques lectured and wrote for the nonspecialist. In 1912 she published the first edition of *Concerning Etchings*. Jaques carefully outlined the process of etching, the materials involved, and the methodologies followed by different artists. She described the process step by step, tool by tool. Heightening the appreciation and understanding of etching was her mission. In her dedication, she laid out the purpose of her pamphlet: "This is writ-

ten for those who are not familiar with etchings or how they are made, in the belief that understanding begets appreciation. Much of it is in direct answer to questions that have been asked many times" (*Concerning Etchings*, n.p.). While on vacation in the Lake Michigan resort town of South Haven, Michigan, in 1914, Jaques wrote "a small, personal record of a summer in the country" ("A Leader Retires," 25). Published in 1936, *A Country Quest* showed her "almost scientific eye for nature" (p. 25). Jaques combined an interest in architecture and cityscapes—some of her earliest works—with an interest in botany. She traveled extensively to Japan, Egypt, Italy, Holland, Sweden, and London, and her prints include street scenes and architectural studies from these sites. She noted nature as well. "Her cyanotypes are photo-realistic outlines of plants collected from her travels" (*Iowa Women Artists from the Permanent Collection*, catalog, Cedar Rapids Museum of Art, February 4–March 26, 1995).

In 1915, twenty prints by Bertha Jaques were included in the Panama-Pacific International Exposition, San Francisco, California. These featured themes from her European travels and included *Venice Fisherman, Palazzo Minelli*, Venice; *The Tangle*, Chioggia, Italy; *Rain on Thames*, London; and *The Columns*, Rome. Forty-one prints by Helen Hyde were also in the exhibition, including many from her Japanese themes.

Jaques became a popular lecturer on the subject of etching and etchers. Her standard lecture included a history of the art, biographies of prominent etchers, and a detailed description of the process itself. Combining the lecture with an actual demonstration of her craft, Jaques illustrated the process from start to finish, bringing out her tools and printing one plate for her audience. This performance was repeated for clubs and art associations in Illinois, Indiana, Iowa, South Carolina, Georgia, Ohio, Pennsylvania, and California.

After her friend Helen Hyde died in 1919, Jaques published *Helen Hyde and Her Work: An Appreciation* (1922), as a tribute. It was not until 1933, when Jaques met James Swann, that she found an art friendship to resemble the one she had shared with Hyde. She became Swann's mentor and "made initial inquiry to the Chicago Society of Etchers on behalf of Swann's associate membership" (Czestochowski, 27). Jaques encouraged him to go to New York City in 1937 and meet artists Ernest Roth, Gordon Grant, Charles S. White, and Frank Weitenkampf—all active with the Chicago Society of Etchers. One year later, Jaques "helped arrange with R. P. Tolman, . . . acting director of the National Collection of Fine Arts, for an exhibition of fifty works by Swann at the United States National Museum (Smithsonian Institution) in Washington, D.C." (Czestochowski, 28).

In a lecture she gave in 1935 (and subsequently published), Jaques captures the essence of etching as she discusses line. Entitled "The Beauty of Line," the lecture pinpoints line as the fundamental component of representation. She begins by saying, "Line, straight or curved, is the basic utterance of life" (p. 54). She goes on to describe line in its different forms and how sentiments are expressed by the different shapes and contortions of the line. "A vertical line expresses power, dignity, aspiration, grandeur, like a tree and an upright man. A horizontal line expresses repose, calmness, quietude, like a figure reclining. There is no haste or rush in a horizontal line. A slanting line suggests movement; it does not support itself and must go on or fall. A circle is complete harmony, continuity, in which there is no beginning and no end—a symbol of the universe" (p. 54). Jaques's philosophy of life and art was influenced by her embracing of Theosophy in 1922, a religion to which she adhered until her death.

Between 1937 and 1940, Jaques and James Swann visited the "Cedar Rapids–Mount Vernon area for lectures and print demonstrations. During that time Jaques made a number of gifts to Cornell College, including some works by Swann, who in 1937 succeeded Jaques as secretary-treasurer of the Chicago Society of Etchers" (Czestochowski, preface, n.p.).

In 1939, Jaques retired from her position as secretary of the Chicago Society of Etchers after twenty-seven years with the organization. That year Jaques finally had her first "one-man show" in Chicago, an exhibition of her etchings, aquatints, drypoints, and drypoints in color at the Albert Roullier Art Galleries, October 6–31, sponsored by the Chicago Society of Etchers. There were ninety-one prints, including *Jimson Weed*, a drypoint that was featured in the annual publication of the Chicago Society of Etchers in 1939. She continued to work on her etchings, but she no longer wrote or lectured on the art of etching. She died in 1941, leaving behind her a legacy of artistry and advocacy.

With Bertha E. Jaques's leadership, the Chicago Society of Etchers became a significant association nationally and was a catalyst for the founding of etching societies elsewhere. Interest in Bertha Jaques has been rekindled in the 1980s. Deborah Lovely, Lovely Fine Arts Incorporated, a gallery near the College of DuPage in Illinois, had an exhibition and prepared a catalog on the prints and drawings of Bertha E. Jaques in 1983.

Sources. Thomas Agabiti provided the source materials listed below. Printmaker James Swann, who was mentored by Bertha Jaques, left his collection of Jaques's prints to the Cedar Rapids Museum of Art. Jaques bequeathed to James Swann the contents of her studio, including a collection of prints and etching plates. Joseph S. Czestochowski has prepared "Bertha E. Jaques Catalogue Raisonné of the Published Prints" as "Appendix D" in *James Swann: In Quest of Printmaker with Presentation Prints of the Chicago Society of Etchers, Prairie Printmakers and the Woodcut Society* (1990). He writes: "This Checklist was derived from a handwritten ledger kept by Bertha E. Jaques from 1894 to 1939. The ledger together with an extensive collection of letters, diaries, lectures, and etchings were given to James Swann at the time of her death in 1941. These materials were subsequently given to the Cedar Rapids Museum of Art in 1984 by James Swann" (p. 157). Jaques wrote "Red Letter Days in Japan," typescript, 1908, Fine Arts Museums of San Francisco; *Concerning Etchings* (1912); *A Country Quest* (1936); *Helen Hyde and Her Work: An Appreciation* (1922); and "The Beauty of Line," *American Theosophist*, March 1936. (Originally Jaques presented "The Beauty of Line" as a lecture, October 27, 1935.) Printed catalogs include *Iowa Women Artists from the Permanent Collection*, catalog for an exhibition, February 4–March 26, 1995, Cedar Rapids Museum of Art; *Exhibition of Etchings—Aquatints—Drypoints and Drypoints in Color by Bertha E. Jaques* (1939); Phyllis Peet, *American Women of the Etching Revival*, catalog for an exhibition, February 9–May 9, 1988, High Museum of Art, Atlanta, Georgia. Biographical and exhibition information about Jaques is found in Thomas Agabiti, "Bertha Evelyn Clauson Jaques," unpublished notes; Raymond L. Wilson, *Index of American Print Exhibitions, 1882–1940* (1988); Esther de Vecsey, *Bertha E.*

Jaques (1863–1941) an American Printmaker: A Retrospective, April–May 1982 (1982); Doris Ostrander Dawdy, *Artists of the American West Volume II: A Biographical Dictionary* (1981); Virginia Hope Duncan, "Bertha E. Jaques," *Prints*, January 1933; Charles Holme, ed., *Modern Etchings, Mezzotints, and Drypoints* (1913); "The 'Little Mother' of the Etchers Society," *Sunday Record-Herald*, January 25, 1914; "A Leader Retires," *Art Digest*, October 1, 1937. Her obituary appeared in the *CT*, March 30, 1941, and in "Mrs. Jaques Dies," *Art Digest*, April 15, 1941.

SARAH M. HUNT

JARRELL, SISTER HELEN
October 28, 1879–February 24, 1951
NURSE, EDUCATOR, ADMINISTRATOR

Helen Jarrell dedicated her life, as a member of the Religious Hospitallers of St. Joseph, to the care of the sick. As a nurse and an administrator in nursing education, she was skilled in negotiating among diverse interests for common ground in professional work.

Jarrell was the fourth of nine children, four girls and five boys, born to James Paul and Catherine Jarrell. Both her parents were immigrants; her father came from Norfolk County in England, and her mother from County Armagh, Ireland. They established their home in the hamlet of Burnt Hills in Brewer's Mills Parish near Kingston, Ontario, Canada, where Helen Jarrell was born. James Paul Jarrell converted to Roman Catholicism, and the family members were devout in their religious practice. Jarrell completed her elementary school education at Leo Lake Primary School in Frontenac County, Ontario. She attended Notre Dame High School in Kingston but did not graduate. At nineteen she was working at the Rectory of St. Mary's Cathedral, Kingston, near the Hotel Dieu, a hospital established by the Religious Hospitallers of St. Joseph. While attending Midnight Mass on Christmas Eve 1898 with the hospitallers—members of a religious order involved in caring for the sick—Jarrell made a decision to join the community. She began her postulancy on August 15, 1899, and a few weeks before her twenty-second birthday, on October 8, 1901, she made her profession of vows. Two years later she earned a nursing diploma at the Hotel Dieu and began her lifework as a nurse hospitaller. She was the youngest of a group of seven hospitallers from Kingston who emigrated to the United States to establish St. Bernard Hospital in the Englewood neighborhood on Chicago's South Side. The sisters were responding to a request made, with the approval of Archbishop James E. Quigley, by Bernard J. Murray, S.J., for his growing St. Bernard parish. Thus began Jarrell's lifelong collaboration with members of the Society of Jesus (Jesuits).

From the moment of her arrival in Chicago, Jarrell's life was part of the development of Catholic institutions in the city. The sisters moved into a two-story residence that served as a convent and work area for the preparation of linens, bedding, and bandages for the new hospital. The sisters also solicited funds for the hospital door to door. One year after their arrival, a fire destroyed the convent and all the hospital supplies. All the sisters narrowly escaped.

Jarrell was asleep on the second floor when the fire awakened her. Risking the burning stairway and nearly overcome with smoke, she fell but managed to crawl down to safety.

Shortly after her escape, firemen rescued the two sisters still trapped on the second floor. The homeless sisters stayed with the Sisters of Loretto, who staffed the parish school, until a new house was moved to the site of the burned convent.

Despite the setback, the building of the hospital went forward. St. Bernard Hospital opened on November 21, 1905, and was busy from the first moment. The Religious Hospitallers immediately applied to the State of Illinois for a charter to establish a School of Nursing, which was granted on February 17, 1906. The first class of sixteen lay nurses and five sisters graduated from St. Bernard in June 1909.

Jarrell worked as an operating room nurse and supervisor of the operating room at St. Bernard from 1906 to 1916. Her move into more public leadership roles in Catholic health care began when she became a charter member of the Catholic Hospital Association (CHA), established in 1915. The CHA primarily served the need for communication among the religious orders of women who had established Catholic hospitals throughout the United States and Canada. Because of the canonical limitations on sisters' travel, which were incorporated into the constitutions of religious congregations, the CHA bylaws prohibited sisters from holding full-time office in the association. Although the executive board elected by the association was composed primarily of sisters until the bylaws were changed in 1965, the CHA was headed by a Jesuit priest. Jarrell was elected to the executive board in 1918 and continued to serve until her death in 1951.

The national movement for standardization of health care in hospitals included the qualifications of doctors and nurses. The Presbyterian Hospital School of Nursing in Chicago had been established in 1903, under founding director M. HELENA McMILLAN, just three years before the Hospitallers' School of Nursing. During the two preceding decades, a number of nursing schools had been established throughout the United States. These included the Illinois Training School for Nurses founded in Chicago in 1880; Provident Hospital's nursing school established in Chicago in 1891 to provide training for African American women, who were not accepted to other nursing schools because of race; a nursing school at Johns Hopkins Hospital, Baltimore, Maryland, opened in 1889; and the Frances Payne Bolten School of Nursing, founded in 1877 in Cleveland, Ohio. Nursing education was a major interest of the newly formed CHA. Jarrell became director of the School of Nursing at St. Bernard Hospital in 1916, the first year in which nurse graduates were included in the Loyola University commencement. A major challenge she faced was to incorporate into St. Bernard's program both the standard curriculum for schools of nursing published in 1917 by the National League of Nursing Education and later the recommendations for university standards in the Goldmark report of 1923. Her decisions influenced other Catholic schools of nursing because of her position within the CHA.

Jarrell had always been one to lead by example. Realizing that modern nursing required practitioners to acquire a strong academic foundation as well as hands-on experience, she returned to school to earn a bachelor's degree in nursing education at Loyola University Chicago. Receiving her degree in 1928, at age forty-nine, she then completed a master's degree in sociology at Loyola in 1931. Jarrell's professional responsibilities did not lessen while she continued her education. They increased, since in 1927 she represented St. Bernard in negotiating an educational affiliation agreement among six hospital schools of nursing and Loyola University and supervised the construction of a new school of nursing at St. Bernard, which was dedicated in 1928.

Patrick Mahan, S.J., Regent of the Loyola School of Medicine since 1918 and Director of Hospitals for the Archdiocese of Chicago since 1919, initiated the idea of educational affiliation as part of the continuing movement for standardization and improved quality in Catholic health care. Mahan, Jarrell, and Sister Lidwina, a Sister of Mercy, reported the results of the new agreement at the International Congress of Graduate Nurses meeting held in Milwaukee in 1927.

Jarrell worked closely with the Jesuit leaders of the CHA as well as with Jesuits at Loyola. Her tact and diplomacy were recognized as helpful in dealing with a delicate transition in CHA leadership between 1928 and 1931. She worked well with Alphonse Schwitalla, S.J., the new president of the CHA, and served as secretary during his term as president, which lasted until 1947. She chaired the CHA committee on nursing education and was elected the official delegate of the CHA to the International Congress of Nurses at Paris and International Catholic Federation of Nurses at Lourdes, France, in July 1933.

Jarrell's writings, seven articles published in *Hospital Progress*, related directly to her professional work. She was careful to respect tradition while tactfully advocating change. Catholics, in her view, must not do less than others in meeting professional standards. Jarrell's delight in and devotion to the Catholic tradition did not prevent her from learning the latest developments in the nursing profession from every source.

Her descriptions in "Problems in School Administration for the Educational Director" were drawn from her own experience: "the eternal conflict between the two functions of the hospital—service and education—is a constant nightmare to the educational director" (p. 41). Jarrell never led by compulsion and was "absolutely against anything that savors of it in our schools" (p. 44). Rather, Jarrell encouraged her colleagues and students to aspire toward excellence in education and the highest ideals of patient care.

Loyola administrators decided in 1935 to centralize the direction of the School of Nursing by creating an administrative board comprised of representatives of the hospital schools of nursing and by appointing a director from among them. T. H. Ahearn, S.J., Regent of the Loyola Medical School, recommended the appointment of Jarrell to Samuel K. Wilson, president of Loyola, as "the outstanding nun in Catholic nursing circles." She was intellectually capable and honest. Her renown would benefit Loyola because "she would lose no opportunity to let the entire Catholic group know that she was the Directress of a University School of Nursing" (Ahearn to Wilson, February 11, 1935, Wilson Papers). Wilson offered her the position in February 1935. She accepted the appointment, assuring her superiors that she would do her "best to have our Loyola School of Nursing second to none in the country" (Jarrell to Wilson, February 20, 1935, Wilson Papers). The new administrative system directed by Jarrell replaced the 1927 arrangement and lasted until 1947.

Jarrell established a curriculum that allowed nurses who completed hospital training to continue at Loyola in order to earn a Bachelor of Science degree in Nursing or Nursing Education. A Public Health Nursing program that began in 1937 had a separate director, Margaret Cleary, appointed in 1938 under the auspices of the medical school. Nursing courses at Loyola were under the purview of both the regent of the medical school and the dean of University College, the downtown campus for undergraduates.

Jarrell and the administrative board recommended in 1937 that the School of Nursing be made an autonomous unit of the university with its own faculty. Her proposal was not accepted, but in 1939 Jarrell became dean of the Loyola University School of Nursing in order to distinguish her position from that of the various directors of the affiliated hospital schools.

During World War II Jarrell helped to secure the nurses needed to establish the Loyola Base Hospital Unit 108. One hundred five nurses from the six affiliated units of the Loyola School of Nursing served in Unit 108, the largest U.S. Army Medical Corps group; they received a unit citation for meritorious service in the European Theater of Operations. Jarrell was appointed by the Federal Security Administrator to the advisory committee on the Nurse Cadet program administered by Lucille Petry, director of the Nurse Education Division of the U.S. Public Health Service. Loyola School of Nursing joined the cadet program in 1943.

Despite Jarrell's highly developed consensus building skills, her reluctance to use direct authority and the cumbersome Loyola administrative structure led to problems of accountability in administering the hospital school units. In 1945 Dr. Howard Egan recommended that administration of the nursing programs be consolidated at the Lewis Towers campus in downtown Chicago. He also recommended that Jarrell retain the title dean but be replaced in day-to-day administration. Gladys Kiniery, who had come to Loyola in 1947 as director of the Department of Public Health Nursing, assumed administration of all nursing programs. Under Jarrell's leadership the Loyola School of Nursing awarded 2,420 certificates of nursing to graduates of the six hospital units, 24 degrees of Bachelor of Science in Nursing, and 148 degrees of Bachelor of Science in Nursing Education.

Jarrell suffered a series of strokes in 1948 and retired from Loyola. In 1949 she retired as director of the School of Nursing at St. Bernard Hospital. The 1937 recommendation that the School of Nursing be an autonomous unit in the university with its own faculty was finally acted upon in 1948.

Jarrell joined a community of women whose spiritual life was characterized by "the holy liberty of the children of God" (*Jérôme Le Royer*, 69). Jarrell's professional achievements mark her as a woman who understood holy liberty as a willingness to respond to opportunities for leadership. She was described by her sisters as a tall woman, about five feet seven inches, with an olive complexion, graceful posture, and small expressive hands. She always dressed in a spotless, wrinkle-free habit that expressed her professionalism and self-confidence. Jarrell chose to become an American citizen. She died of a stroke at St. Anne's Infirmary in Techny, Illinois, and was buried at Mt. Olivet cemetery in Chicago.

Jarrell's leadership was exercised primarily in developing collaborative relationships among the congregations of women religious who provided health care and nursing education in Chicago and in the United States. In addition to her work in Chicago she contributed to the development of Catholic health care services internationally as a member of the executive board of the Catholic Hospital Association of the United States and Canada. She held an important place among the individual sisters and congregations of women religious who made many and varied contributions to civic and to church history.

Sources. Helen Jarrell's papers and the records of St. Bernard Hospital and Nursing School are at the Province Archives of the Religious Hospitallers of St. Joseph (RHSJ) in Kingston, Ontario, Canada. The Loyola Univ. Archives contain material on Jarrell among the papers of William Kane, S.J., and George L. Warth, S.J., and in the Office of the President Papers (Samuel Knox Wilson, S.J.). The Catholic Hospital Association Archives (now Catholic Health Association) in St. Louis, Missouri, were not open to researchers in 1996 but may become available in the future. *Hospital Progress*, the Journal of the Catholic Hospital Association, is available on microfilm. Jarrell published seven articles in *Hospital Progress*: "Casting the Nursing Curriculum Into an Educational Mold," October 1927; "Loyola University Nursing Curriculum," August 1928; "Problems in School Administration for the Educational Director," February 1931; "Results of State-Board Examinations in Pharmacology," September 1931; "Why Should We Answer Questionnaires?" October 1931; "The International Congress of Nurses," November 1933; "The Guidance Program: Statement Prepared by the Council on Nursing Education," October 1942. Information about Jarrell's work at Loyola appears in Linda J. White, "A History of the Formation of the Loyola University School of Nursing: 1917 to 1935" (master's thesis, Loyola Univ. Chicago, 1987), and Sally A. Bozenec, "The Development of Nursing Education at Loyola University of Chicago: 1913–1980" (Ph.D. diss., Loyola Univ. Chicago, 1991). Cecile Renault, RHSJ, Superior General, *Jérôme Le Royer de la Dauversière and the Religious Hospitallers of St. Joseph* (1975), describes the founding of the religious order. Christopher J. Kauffman, *Ministry and Meaning: A Religious History of Catholic Health Care in the United States* (1995) explains the Catholic context in which Jarrell worked.

PRUDENCE A. MOYLAN

JAVARAS, PARASKEVE VOULA
February 22, 1899–December 7, 1978
JOURNALIST, BUSINESSPERSON

Paraskeve Voula Javaras was born in the town of Valtetsi, Arcadia, Greece. Valtetsi is a small town in the center of the Peloponnesian peninsula in southern Greece; it had just over five hundred inhabitants in 1900. Javaras was the youngest of ten children (with only six surviving) born to George P. and Georgia (Bacoyiannis) Javaras. Her father was the county tax collector, and the family was financially comfortable until his untimely death in 1899 from pneumonia. The family's fortunes changed. The eldest son, Peter G. Javaras, emigrated to the United States and settled in Chicago in 1901, where he worked as a vegetable peddler. He did well, and in 1903 he sent money to Greece so that his brothers Paul and Alex could emigrate. They arrived that year and, after a brief visit with an uncle in New Orleans, Louisiana, settled in Chicago with their brother Peter.

In 1907 Peter Javaras traveled to Greece to find a bride and to visit his family. He did not marry, in fact remaining a bachelor until he died at age ninety-five; but he brought his widowed mother, Georgia, his sisters Evangeline and Paraskeve (Voula), his brother Basil, and seventeen other first cousins and assorted relatives to the United States. Since their ship had to undergo repairs in France, it took them well over a month to arrive in the New York port. By the time the twenty-two arrived in Chicago, they were entirely without funds but in excellent spirits, and walked, singing popular Greek songs, to the home of their uncle, who lived in the Greek colony located near Damen and Randolph streets on Chicago's West Side.

Voula, Evangeline, Basil, and Paul (who had arrived in 1903) attended school. Shortly after arriving in Chicago Voula was enrolled in the Socrates parochial school of Holy Trinity Church; she later attended McKinley High School. Alex went to work with Peter briefly; eventually Peter and Basil Javaras formed a wholesale vegetable business.

The brothers and sisters, with their mother, whom they called Ma'me, remained a close family whose personal and business ties were strong. When Voula and Evangeline Javaras graduated from high school, they went on to college. Voula Javaras attended the University of Illinois, which gave her "an unusual educational background for a young immigrant girl of that time" (Kopan, "Voula Javaras"). From a young age, she did the paper work for the produce business. When Paul Javaras, who had cut short his studies at the University of Chicago to fight in Greece in the first and second Balkan Wars (1912–13), returned in 1914 to Chicago and founded a Greek language magazine, *Nea Zoe* (*New Life*), Voula Javaras worked at her brother's printing shop and wrote articles in Greek and English for the magazine. Her articles were concerned with the problem of Greek immigrant adjustment in the New World. She continued to work for the magazine and the produce business until 1924, when Alex Javaras convinced the whole family to join him in his real estate company. Basil and Peter sold their vegetable business, and Paul Javaras and Sotirios Demopoulos, who worked with him at *New Life* and who had married Evangeline Javaras, sold the magazine business. Alex Javaras had done very well in real estate; he specialized in selling vacant commercial lots to Greek investors and building large retail and office buildings both for these investors and for the Javaras family.

When in 1924 her sister Evangeline died in childbirth, Voula Javaras's life changed dramatically. Now, in addition to helping her mother, Ma'me, care for the entire family, including her brothers and brother-in-law Demopoulos, and working at her brothers' real estate office, she and Ma'me proceeded to raise young Basil Demopoulos for the next six years.

In 1929 Paul Javaras and Voula Javaras founded the *Greek Press* newspaper. (It later merged with the Greek weekly newspaper, *Thessaloniki*, founded in 1913.) She wrote two columns for the paper in both Greek and English. One dealt with subjects and problems of interest to women, and the other dealt with the preparation of Greek foods. Her "social commentary column entitled 'PIPIDA' . . . ran for over twenty years" (Kopan, "Voula Javaras"). Her column "Oikodespina" on good housekeeping, "expressed novel ideas about the role of women in the Greek community some of which were considered 'radical' for the time" (Kopan, "Voula Javaras").

The Javaras family experienced serious economic problems along with the rest of the American people during the Great Depression. In 1931 Voula Javaras set up another business in a suburb of Chicago, Oak Park; it was a silk hosiery repair shop and employed from two to four women. This business kept the entire Javaras family off the relief rolls. By the late 1930s, Basil and Peter Javaras opened a florist shop, Oak Park Gardens Florist, and immediately began doing an excellent business. Voula Javaras also worked with them in the business for many years. At the same time, Basil bought and operated a small bowling business on Madison and Laramie streets in Chicago. In a short time, funds from Basil and Peter's businesses provided sufficient funds for Alex to start once again in real estate, in which he prospered.

The 1940s were very productive years for everyone; Voula Javaras was working at the *Greek Press* and at the Oak Park Gardens Florist shop. She was known in the Greek community as a capable and independent woman. The strength of her skills became apparent, however, in the 1950s, when Voula Javaras's mother died. In 1953, her brother Paul was afflicted with the beginning stages of Alzheimer's disease, and she cared for him and edited the *Greek Press* at the same time for the next three years. She continued to work weekends and do all of the books at the Oak Park Gardens Florist shop, which by now had grown into a large business. After her brother Paul died in 1956, she sold the newspaper; the following year her brother Basil died. His two sons—George B. and Paul B. Javaras—along with her other nephew, Basil Demopoulos, became even more important to Voula Javaras. In 1957, the garden shop and its land were sold to a builder.

Voula Javaras remained connected with her hometown of Valtetsi, Greece, and in 1958 she donated five thousand dollars to bring water lines to the town. For several hundred years the villagers relied on cisterns for some of their water, but had to bring drinking water on horseback from two kilometers away. Even though she was only seven years old when she left Valtetsi, she remained aware of the many hardships of the inhabitants. She shared, as well, a pride in her birthplace because it was there, on May 11, 1829, that the last major land battle of the Greek revolutionary war against the Turks took place.

When her brother Alex was diagnosed with prostate cancer in 1960, she helped to care for him until his death in 1961. From that year until 1978, Voula Javaras worked in her late brother's real estate office together with her nephew Paul B. Javaras.

Voula Javaras died at age seventy-nine. She was buried next to her brother Paul G. Javaras in Elmwood Cemetery, River Grove, Illinois.

Twenty years after her death, memorial services were held for Voula Javaras at the St. Spyridon Greek Orthodox Church, Palos Heights, Illinois, and in the Assumption Church, Valtetsi, Greece. Remembered as an "early feminist and writer" (Kopan, "Early Chicago Writer Remembered"), her life illustrates the ways in which some Greek immigrant women defied traditional boundaries of domesticity and entered the realms of business and public affairs. For immigrant Greeks—both men and women—the family remained paramount. Voula Javaras's life demonstrates the degree to which successful immigration in the United States required the concerted, focused efforts of the entire extended family. Educated and independent and devoted to the survival of her family, she adapted her considerable skills as a writer and woman of entrepreneurial talents to family business in ways that were considered innovative by her contemporaries.

Sources. Paul B. Javaras, Voula Javaras's nephew, brings his personal and family information to this biography. Javaras's articles include "The Greek Woman and Her Evolution" in [n.a.], *Forty Years of Greek Life in Chicago* (1937), written in Greek. Andrew T. Kopan has written two articles about Voula Javaras: "Voula Javaras: Early Chicago Feminist Remembered," *Greek Press*, November 22, 1998, and "Early Chicago Writer Remembered," *Greek American*, November 28, 1998.

PAUL B. JAVARAS

JOHNSON, VIOLETTE NEATLEY ANDERSON. *See* ANDERSON JOHNSON, VIOLETTE NEATLEY

JONES, MARY JANE RICHARDSON
October 28, 1819–January 2, 1910
EARLY SETTLER, UNDERGROUND RAILROAD CONDUCTOR, CLUBWOMAN

Mary Jane Richardson was born outside Memphis, Tennessee. It is quite possible that her mother, Diza, was a Caucasian. Her father, identified alternatively by the names Alfred and Elijah, was a free African American blacksmith. Nothing is known about Mary Richardson's early life in Tennessee until 1836, when the Richardson family relocated to Alton, Illinois, hoping to find better treatment for African Americans. In 1841, Richardson was engaged to John Jones, whom she had known in Memphis. Richardson and Jones were married in 1844. Their daughter, Lavinia, had been born the previous year.

In November 1844, John and Mary Jones filed for certificates of freedom from the clerk in Madison County Court. Under the Illinois Black Laws, all free African Americans were required to carry such a certificate, as well as to post a one thousand dollar bond, in order to reside in the state. A few months later, the family relocated to Chicago. They traveled by stage from Alton to Ottawa, and then by canal to Chicago. The trip took almost a week and was further postponed when the young family was stopped on suspicion of being fugitive slaves. When the Jones family arrived in Chicago in March 1845, they had only $3.50 in their coffers. Setting up housekeeping in a one-room cottage, John Jones pawned his watch to raise the money to buy two stoves—one for the cottage, and one for his new tailoring business. A local African American grocer extended them two dollars in credit.

In 1845, there were only 140 African Americans in a population of 12,000 in the fast-growing new commercial city. Chicago was becoming a transportation center linking the East with the Mississippi River Valley and the western regions of the country. The terminus for the western routes of the Underground Railroad, Chicago was so staunch in its antislavery sentiments that it had gained the reputation throughout the state as the "sink hole of abolition" (quoted in Drake and Cayton, 33). John and Mary Jones were quickly befriended by the city's most prominent abolitionists, including police detective Allan Pinkerton, physician Charles B. Dyer, and attorney Lemuel Covell

Paine Freer. Freer wrote all of the Joneses' correspondence in these early days, but the couple, who had been denied an education under the system of slavery in the South, soon learned the skills on their own. John Jones published articles in the most important abolitionist newspapers of the day. Mary Jones composed family letters to such national leaders as Frederick Douglass, who was a lifelong friend and a frequent visitor to the Jones home.

The Joneses' home, first at 218 Third Avenue and then at 43 Ray Street, immediately became an abolitionist meeting place. It was one of only two Underground Railroad terminals operated by African Americans in the city, the other being the Quinn African Methodist Episcopal (AME) Chapel, the oldest African American church in Chicago. Although John and Mary Jones had obtained their freedom papers, they nevertheless put themselves at tremendous jeopardy in their involvement in the Underground Railroad. According to the Fugitive Slave Law of 1793, harboring or preventing the arrest of a fugitive slave was a crime punishable by a five hundred dollar fine and possible enslavement for free Blacks. The Fugitive Slave Act of 1850 "denied the alleged fugitive a trial by jury and the right to summon witnesses or testify in court. Ownership was determined by a single affidavit of the person claiming the slave" (Gliozzo, 181). The Act of 1850 led to manhunts by mercenary slave catchers, many of whom were not beyond capturing and putting into slavery those who had never been slaves.

The abolitionist community responded to the new law with quick political action. The day after the law was passed, a group of Chicago citizens, calling themselves "the friends of freedom" (quoted in Blanchard, vol. 2, 298), chartered railway cars to transport to Canada every fugitive in Chicago and its environs. The mass exodus was supported by the city's affluent citizens, including John and Mary Jones. A few days later, Jones and her husband were among some three hundred African Americans who attended a mass meeting at the Quinn AME Chapel. John Jones was appointed to head a committee to present to the Chicago Common Council a formal resolution stating that the law was unconstitutional and that the African American community would fight with every means at its disposal—including violence, if necessary—to protect one another from bondage. A liberty association was formed at Quinn Chapel at the conclusion of the meeting. "Seven patrols of six persons each were assigned 'to keep an eye out for interlopers'" (*Black Metropolis*, 34)—slave catchers.

Throughout the 1850s and early 1860s, fugitive slaves flooded to Chicago, and the Jones family was said to have helped hundreds to safety in Canada. The Underground Railroad was at once an expensive financial venture and an intensely domestic endeavor. John and Mary Jones worked side by side as "conductors," providing food, shelter, clothing, money for transportation, and often bail and bond for the fugitives. John Jones was the premiere tailor for the city's white elite as well as a shrewd investor in real estate, and the Jones household was soon the most affluent African American family in the city. His wealth and business associations helped to hide, even while funding, his and Mary Jones's illegal abolitionist activities.

The financial success of the Joneses also allowed Mary Jones to lead an exclusively domestic life, a luxury offered to only a small minority of African American women at the time. Yet, while Jones's life resembled that of a respectable middle-class housewife, her household was far from typical. Many of her most basic domestic responsibilities were considered illegal under the Fugitive Slave Law. At one time, her home provided refuge to the most notorious fugitives of the day—the abolitionist John Brown and his band of followers. Brown was first brought to the Jones home by Frederick Douglass, who vouched for Brown's decency and requested overnight provisions. Mary Jones assented to the request, although, as she later remembered, she thought Brown "a little off on the slavery question" (quoted in Blanchard, vol. 2, 298). The next morning, while her husband was at work, Jones and Brown discussed Brown's proposed raids into Pennsylvania and Virginia over a cup of coffee. Jones doubted that "he could ever do what he wanted to do," and prophetically predicted that "somebody would have to give up his life before it was done" (quoted in Blanchard, vol. 2, 298). She and her husband had worked hard to establish themselves as model American citizens, and she strongly objected to Brown's violent militancy, especially as Brown would leave unprotected a large family if his plan failed. "How are you going to free them [the slaves]?" (p. 298), Jones wondered. After this first overnight visit, Brown became a frequent visitor to the Jones home, at one point ringing their bell in the early dawn asking for shelter for himself, his band of followers, and thirteen fugitive slaves from Kansas. Jones soon found herself housemother to a collection of the "roughest looking men" (quoted in Blanchard, vol. 2, 300) she had ever seen and commenced to feed them breakfast—an illegal act.

Like the wives of many antislavery speakers and organizers, Jones often was responsible for holding the family's household and abolitionist activities together as her husband traveled throughout the country coordinating railroad networks, participating in the convention movement, and rallying other free African Americans in the North. With Mary Jones's support, John Jones was able to lead an active civic life. He waged a twenty-year campaign against the Illinois Black Laws, and their repeal in 1865 was attributed to him. In 1871, he became the first African American to win an elected seat in the state of Illinois and served as Cook County Commissioner for the next four years; he was reelected in 1872 for a three-year term.

Mary Jones supported the early suffrage movement in Chicago, hosting in her home leading suffragists Susan B. Anthony, Carrie Chapman Catt, and Emma Chandler. It is possible that Jones first met Anthony and Elizabeth Cady Stanton when they came to Chicago in February 1869 to address the first woman suffrage convention held in the city.

In the late 1860s, Jones became increasingly active in voluntary church associations in the African American community. In 1861, John and Mary Jones were among the founders of the Olivet Baptist Church. In addition to prayer meetings, Bible study, and Sunday worship, Olivet housed a library of 128 volumes—the first library of its kind open to African Americans in Chicago. In 1878, a Choral Study Club was added, and in 1885, the Young People's Literary Society was formed. In 1871, Jones and three other women organized the Workers for the King, a quasi-religious group that offered aid to the growing African American poor in the city. By the 1890s, the Workers had more

than fifty members, and one of the third generation of Jones women—Mary Jones's granddaughter Theodora Lee—served as secretary.

In late 1878, John Jones was confined to his home with Bright's disease, and it is probable that his wife took responsibility for his constant care. He died in late May 1879, bequeathing to his wife an estate worth an estimated fifty-five thousand dollars. After she was widowed, Mary Jones, who had long been an established member of the "black 400" (as Chicago's African American social elite was then called), continued in a leadership role. She lent her wealth and prestige to the many social reform movements growing out of the response by affluent African Americans to the influx of rural poor migrants from the South.

In 1879, Mary Jones's home once again became a place of refuge—this time to Daniel Hale Williams, later famous for his contributions to open heart surgery. Williams was a struggling medical student when he lodged at the Jones home for a meager $3.75 a month. He was quickly accepted as one of the family in the Jones household, which included Mary Jones; her widowed daughter, Lavina Lee; her eight-year-old granddaughter, Theodora Lee; and her thirty-year-old adopted daughter, Raynie Petit. When Williams began his medical practice in 1883, Jones was among his first patients, signaling Williams as the premier African American doctor in the city. She was also among the first to contribute to Williams's work in the founding of Provident Hospital. Opened in 1890, the hospital was established as an interracial institution; however, in the segregated system of health care existing at the time, it served primarily the black community. Its nursing school was the first and only training available for African American women in Chicago hoping to enter the nursing profession.

The social elite, to which Jones belonged, carefully crafted itself as a model of exemplary cultivation and refinement for the "untutored masses" then beginning to arrive in the city. In the homes of the black upper class, elaborate salons featured lectures, recitals, and meetings of literary clubs open by invitation only to an exclusive list comprised of the city's African American elite. Perhaps the most prestigious of these gatherings was the Prudence Crandall Club, a literary society founded in 1887. The club, which often held its receptions at the home of Mary Jones, was dedicated to the self-education of its members, who studied art, literature, science, and philosophy. Crandall Club meetings were devoted to such topics as evolutionary theory. (In segregated Chicago, the Prudence Crandall Club's programs paralleled those of the white Chicago Philosophical Society, but there is no evidence that the two groups ever crossed paths.) The Prudence Crandall Club helped to preserve the abolitionist legacy of its members and, in a series of lectures the club sponsored in 1893, Frederick Douglass identified the early antislavery fighters of Chicago, including Mary and John Jones.

As the city's African American population continued to increase in the 1890s, so too did prejudice and racism in the white community. Chicago's African American abolitionists had always been staunch promoters of assimilation and integration. Yet, with the dismantling of the Reconstruction era's federally mandated attempts to provide citizenship to freedmen, the spread of Jim Crowism or racial discrimination, backed up by an increase in lynching and other acts of mob violence, made such goals virtually impossible. Chicago's African American leaders had already engaged in self-help and mutual aid. Such efforts grew in the 1890s with the maturation of the black community. African American women in Chicago engaged in club movement activities in response to community needs and in recognition of their own abilities to influence civic culture. One of the first such clubs in Chicago, the Tourgee Ladies' Club, was formed in the summer of 1893 under the leadership of Ida B. Wells (see IDA B. WELLS-BARNETT), who asked the more senior Mary Jones to "head the movement" as honorary chair because "it would lend prestige to have such a genteel, highbred old lady of the race . . . lead them" (*Crusade for Justice*, 121–22). The club was enormously popular and soon raised funds to prosecute a white police officer for the wrongful death of an African American man. The club, named Ida B. Wells Club in 1894, supported its namesake's antilynching crusade. In Chicago, it organized the first African American orchestra and established the first kindergarten for African American children who were denied entrance to the whites-only programs that existed. (At the time, kindergartens were not part of the public school system but were privately organized and often affiliated with settlement houses; these, too, were segregated.)

In 1896, Mary Jones became a member of the Phyllis Wheatley Women's Club. The club was among the first to address the increasing sexual exploitation of young African American women arriving in Chicago during the Great Migration of rural blacks from the South. Employment opportunities for unskilled African American women were even more restricted and low-paying than those available to unskilled white women. The agencies established to aid working girls, such as the Young Women's Christian Association, were generally placed in white or immigrant neighborhoods and were restricted because of segregationist policies to African Americans. The Phyllis Wheatley Home for Girls, first opened in 1908, provided new arrivals to Chicago with low-cost housing, employment counseling, and social facilities. African American clubwomen, like their white counterparts, feared that young women detached from their traditional communities and families would be prey to the prostitution trade. Myths about the sexuality of African American women, which were tied up with racist theories, gave African American clubwomen a heightened incentive to provide respectable housing and employment for young black women in the city. The Wheatley Home was entirely supported by African American women civic leaders, including Mary Jones. They identified themselves with the goal of lifting up the women of their race and, by 1914, lodged more than three hundred girls and found reputable employment for more than five hundred.

Mary Jones contributed generously to the Home for the Aged and the Infirm Colored People, founded in 1898. With her connections, Mary Jones arranged for Provident Hospital to supply free medicine to the home's residents, some of whom suffered from senility and blindness.

In 1899, the National Association of Colored Women (NACW) held its first biennial meeting in Chicago. To host the event, a number of Chicago's African American women's clubs, including the Phyllis Wheatley Women's Club and the Ida B. Wells Club (in both of which Jones was a member), formed the Women's Conference. The biennial took place at the historic Quinn Chapel—the venue where, close to fifty years earlier, Jones had also witnessed the organization of the black community to combat the Fugitive Slave Law. After the NACW meeting, the separate clubs in the Women's Conference merged to form the Illinois Federation of Colored Women's Clubs. Illinois was thereafter one of the first states to join the NACW. By that time, Jones was eighty-one years old and ready to hand over her mantle to the younger generation of African American women, including FANNIE BARRIER WILLIAMS, ELIZABETH DAVIS, and Ida B. Wells-Barnett.

Mary Richardson Jones died at the age of ninety-one. She is buried at Graceland Cemetery, Chicago, beside her husband, John Jones, and near fellow abolitionists Allan Pinkerton and Charles Dyer. Her grave, in poetic understatement, is simply marked, "Grandma Jonsie."

As social matriarch of the "black 400," Jones gave generously of her wealth to those African Americans who were most vulnerable to exploitation and abuse—the elderly of the Home for the Aged, the young women of the Phyllis Wheatley Home, and the fugitive slaves in her own home. Her life spanned a time in Chicago history during which a small enclave of African Americans grew in numbers and in strength to establish a thriving "Black Metropolis."

Sources. Jones Family Papers, CHS, include two informative letters by Theodora Lee Purnell, Mary Jones's granddaughter. A first-person memoir of Jones's Underground Railroad activities is included in Rufus Blanchard, *Discovery and Conquests of the Northwest with the History of Chicago*, 2 vols. (1900). The abridged memoir and a letter from Jones to Frederick Douglass is in Dorothy Sterling, ed., *We Are Your Sisters: Black Women in the Nineteenth Century* (1984). Carl G. Hodges and Helene L. Levene, *Illinois Negro History Makers* (1964), discuss the Joneses' Underground Railroad involvement. For an account of the Joneses in the context of early Chicago, see St. Clair Drake and Horace R. Cayton, *Black Metropolis: A Study of Negro Life in a Northern City* (revised edition 1993), and Allan H. Spear, *Black Chicago: The Making of a Negro Ghetto, 1890–1920* (1967). For an account of Mary and John Jones's early life in Chicago, see Arna Bontemps and Jack Conroy, *They Seek A City* (1945), and John Jones's obituary, *CT*, May 22, 1879. For Mary Jones's involvement in voluntary organizations, see St. Clair Drake, "Churches and Voluntary Associations in the Chicago Negro Community," Works Projects Administration, Chicago, Illinois, December 1940, typed copy in Hull House Association Records, UIC Spec. Coll. *Crusade for Justice: The Autobiography of Ida B. Wells-Barnett*, ed. Alfreda M. Duster (1970), discusses Jones's role as honorary head of the Tourgee Club. Although Jones is not mentioned in either source, both Elizabeth Lindsay Davis, *The Story of the Illinois Federation of the Colored Women's Clubs* (1922), and Anne Meis Knupfer, *Toward a Tenderer Humanity and a Nobler Womanhood: African American Women's Clubs in Turn-of-the-Century Chicago* (1996), are invaluable sources for understanding the various women's clubs to which Jones belonged. Helen Buckler, *Daniel Hale Williams: Negro Surgeon* (1968), provides a domestic view of Jones's life in her later years. Willard B. Gatewood, *Aristocrats of Color: The Black Elite, 1880–1920* (1990), discusses Chicago's "black 400." Charles A. Gliozzo, "John Jones: A Study of a Black Chicagoan," *Illinois Historical Journal*, Autumn 1987, and William Loren Katz, *Black People Who Made the Old West* (1992), provide information on the life of John Jones. Olivia Mahoney, "Black Abolitionists," *Chicago History*, Spring/Summer 1991, provides general context.

THERESA CORA DE LANGIS

JORDAN, MARIAN DRISCOLL
April 15, 1898–April 7, 1961

RADIO ACTRESS

In her guise as "Molly," the wise, tolerant, and eternally patient wife of "Fibber McGee," Marian Jordan became an icon of American popular culture. During the "golden age of radio" from the 1930s through the 1950s, she reached a larger audience, over a longer period of time, than did any other female entertainer.

Marian Driscoll was the youngest of thirteen children born to Daniel Driscoll, a Peoria, Illinois, coal miner, and his wife, Anna (Carroll) Driscoll. Musically gifted, Marian Driscoll attended Catholic grade school and high school before enrolling in the Runnels School of Music in Peoria to study piano, violin, and voice. She met her future husband, James Jordan, while both were singing in the choir at St. John's Catholic Church, Peoria, in 1915. They were married on August 13, 1918, just a few days before he was sent to France for military duty in World War I. They had two children, Kathryn, born in 1920, and James Carroll, born in 1923. Marian Jordan supported herself by giving piano lessons both during and after James Jordan's time in France. After practicing song and dance routines in Peoria clubs and church halls, the young couple embarked on a tour of midwest concert halls.

After three struggling years on the concert and vaudeville circuit, the Jordans successfully auditioned for a spot on radio station WIBO in Chicago. They began by performing their song and dance numbers but soon incorporated light banter and comedy routines in their repertory. In 1927, they moved to radio station WENR. Over the next four years, Chicago radio audiences heard the Jordans play in a number of radio series, including *Air Scouts*, a children's program, *Luke and Mirandi*, a farm show with comic relief, and *The Smith Family*, a domestic comedy serial focusing on an Irish policeman, his wife, and his daughter. Switching to station WMAQ in 1931, the Jordans starred in *Smackout*, a fifteen-minute daily program about a couple who ran a country general store that was always "smack out" of everything. The show inaugurated their long collaboration with writer Don Quinn, who later helped the Jordans create "Fibber" and "Molly."

The success of *Smackout*, and especially its popularity with Henrietta Johnson Louis, the daughter of Johnson Wax president Herbert Fisk Johnson, resulted in the creation of *The Johnson Wax Show with Fibber McGee and Molly*. The program debuted in Chicago on April 16, 1935. Despite a slow start in the ratings, it eventually earned a prime time slot Tuesdays on NBC's "Red" Network. (The "Red" network, a series of radio stations, was the forerunner of the National Broadcasting Corporation; the parallel "Blue" network was the forerunner of the American Broadcasting Company.) Within a few years, the program began to compete for top rating among radio comedy shows. By the 1940s, between one-quarter and one-third of American households regularly tuned in *Fibber McGee and Molly*. The Jordans' salary mushroomed from $250 to $3,500 per week in less than a decade.

Molly, Marian Jordan's character, was a judicious and delightful blend of loving tolerance and sharp dry humor, an exemplar of common sense and realism who clearly cherished her eccentric husband's hidden virtues while being all too aware of his indolence, delusions of grandeur, and frequent prevarications. Beneath the cheery humor and the lighthearted banter, Molly personified the strong and capable women who held together countless numbers of shaky families during the Great Depression and World War II. She was prototypically Irish American and midwestern, and her warm humanity touched a responsive chord in people.

Marian Jordan's well-developed gift for impersonation enabled her to double in several character roles on the show, including "Mrs. Bedelia Wearybottom," "Lady Vere-de-Vere," "Old Lady Cornelia Wheedledeck," "Geraldine," and "Teeny," the precocious moppet next door. The last characterization enabled Jordan to launch frontal assaults on Fibber's fantasies and pretensions, deflating them with a childlike honesty and realism. Teeny's endless questions ("Whatcha doin', huh mister, whatcha?"), oft-repeated phrases ("I betcha . . . I betcha"), and her frequent game of "What? Where? When? Why?" usually reduced Fibber to blustering frustration.

In September 1937, exhausted by overwork and the hectic pace of weekly broadcasts, personal appearances, and child rearing, Marian Jordan suffered an almost total breakdown. Ordered to undertake complete bed rest between broadcasts, she was eventually forced to leave the show entirely for eighteen months, spending much of that period in Sacred Heart Sanitarium in Milwaukee, Wisconsin. Her illness was kept secret from the public, while new characters were introduced to fill the void. The ruse kept the show alive, but its ratings dropped significantly. When she eventually returned to the program on April 18, 1939, the entire operation had moved to southern California in order to afford Marian a more healthy climate. Despite their physical relocation, the Jordans continued to suffuse their program with the same folksy, midwest ambience and to draw upon their personal experiences of life in America's heartland. The couple bought a ranch in Encino, California, which became their permanent home. Characteristically, the Jordans ignored the Hollywood social scene almost entirely, living a private, family-oriented existence, with Marian Jordan enjoying gardening, cooking, and collecting Dresden and Meissen figurines.

Buoyed by Marian Jordan's return, the show climbed steadily in the audience ratings, competing with Jack Benny, Bob Hope, and Edgar Bergen and Charlie McCarthy for the distinction of most popular radio comedy program. On several occasions, Fibber McGee and Molly reached more than 40 percent of the radio audience in their time slot. Throughout World War II, the programs aimed at keeping up the morale of both civilians and soldiers and at urging listeners to support the war effort through volunteer work and contributions to bond drives. The Jordans' popularity continued at a high level throughout the remainder of the decade. They also ventured into serious drama, starring in episodes of the highly regarded *Suspense* program. Moving to California facilitated the couple's venture into motion pictures, which included *This Way Please* (1937), *Look Who's Laughing* (1941), *Here We Go Again* (1942), *Heavenly Days* (1944), and *Is Everybody Listening?* (1947). Because their comedy relied so much on elements supplied by each listener's imagination, it did not translate well into communication media that were primarily visual in nature. The Jordans' popularity and reputation, like that of several other radio personalities, continued to rest primarily on their virtuosity at creating mental images out of sound and the spoken word. An effort by NBC to convert the show to television in 1949 ended ingloriously.

Declining ratings caused the Johnson Wax Company to end its sponsorship of the program on May 23, 1950. The Jordans picked up new sponsors in Pet Milk and Reynolds Aluminum and continued their half-hour format as "Fibber and Molly" until June 30, 1953, ending a run of 739 broadcasts. Between then and March 1956, they appeared in 578 more programs, in a five-day-a-week, fifteen-minute format. From 1957 through early 1961, they appeared on NBC's Weekend Monitor series, performing over three hundred five-part, five-minute vignettes each Saturday and Sunday. Between their debut in 1923 and their finale in 1961, Marian and Jim Jordan appeared on nearly seven thousand radio shows, including frequent guest appearances on other programs.

On Marian Jordan's fiftieth birthday, she and her husband received honorary Doctor of Law degrees from St. Joseph's College of Collegeville, Indiana, for their contributions to healthy entertainment and to society. In May 1950, Marian Jordan was named "Mother of the Year" by the Flowers by Wire division of Western Union. Stricken with ovarian cancer, Marian Jordan died in 1961 at her Encino home, with her husband and two children at her bedside.

Few radio entertainers inspired such deep and abiding affection in their legions of listeners as did Marian Jordan. According to a survey conducted by the Johnson Wax Company in the early 1970s, two-thirds of women under thirty years of age and 94 percent of women over that age retained fond memories of "Fibber McGee and Molly." Radio historian Arthur Frank Wertheim asserted that Marian Jordan, in her various roles, "was indispensable to the program's success" (*Radio Comedy*, 228). Writers Charles Strumpf and Tom Price titled their story of the McGees *Heavenly Days*, a tribute to Marian Jordan's most famous utterance.

Sources. The Peoria Hist. Soc.'s collection of the papers and memorabilia of Marian and Jim Jordan is housed in the Bradley Univ. Library in Peoria, Illinois. The Johnson Wax Company of Racine, Wisconsin, long-time sponsor of the *Fibber McGee and Molly Show,* has a small collection in its corporate archives of papers and memorabilia relating to their collaboration. The most comprehensive examination of the Jordans' career can be found in Charles Stumpf and Tom Price, *Heavenly Days!: The Story of Fibber McGee and Molly* (1987). The most cogent analysis of the couple's appeal and of Marian Jordan's personal contribution to their success is in Arthur Frank Wertheim, *Radio Comedy* (1979). John Dunning, in *Tune in Yesterday* (1976), places the Jordans within the context of radio's "golden days." For the most careful statistical analysis of the couple's standing in the radio listener rating system of the time, see J. Fred MacDonald, *Don't Touch That Dial: Radio Programming in American Life, 1920–1960* (1979). A doctoral dissertation in American Studies, "Six Radio Comedians: An Introduction and Investigative Analysis" (Univ. of New Mexico, 1977), written by Henry W. Tschopp, places Marian and Jim Jordan in the company of such radio comedic giants as Jack Benny, Fred Allen, and Edgar Bergen. Also useful are Fred Buxton and Bill Owen, *Radio's Golden Age: The Programs and Personalities* (1966); Jim Harmon, *The Great Radio Comedians,* (1970); and Ronald W. Lackmann, *Remember Radio* (1970).

JOHN D. BUENKER

JUDSON, CLARA INGRAM
May 4, 1879–May 24, 1960
CHILDREN'S AUTHOR, PUBLIC SPEAKER

Clara Ingram Judson, whose writing career began with a newspaper column and ended with the prestigious Laura Ingalls Wilder Award in children's literature, was born in Logansport, Indiana. Her parents, John Carl Ingram, a banker, and Mary (Colby) Ingram, had four children, of whom Clara was the eldest and the only girl. When Clara Ingram was six years old, the family moved to Indianapolis, where she attended public schools, graduating from Indianapolis (now Shortridge) High School in 1896 and from Girls' Classical School in 1898. For two years afterwards, she taught in a public school and Sunday schools.

In 1901, she married James McIntosh Judson, a Sinclair Refining Company official, in Richmond, Indiana. They had two daughters, Alice and Mary Jane. The Judsons moved to Chicago in 1914 and to Evanston, Illinois, in 1925. James Judson died in 1944.

Judson did not start writing seriously until she was in her thirties. As she convalesced from a long illness, she wrote down the bedtime stories she told her daughters as they were growing up and sent them to her former local newspaper, the Richmond (Indiana) *Item*, which accepted and published them in 1913 as "Bed Time Tales." The stories were an instant success, and six weeks later Judson was writing a daily column that was syndicated as a national newspaper feature by the *Indianapolis Star.* From 1913 to 1920, Judson produced two newspaper columns, "Read It to Me Now" and "Woodland Fairies," and served as the children's editor of the *Indianapolis Star.*

On an impulse, she sent a collection of her best stories to the publisher Rand McNally, where they were accepted and published as *Flower Fairies* in 1915. During the following years, at least seventy-eight more of her books were published by major companies, primarily Scribners, Houghton Mifflin, and Follett Publishing Company. Alice McGuire, editor of the *Bulletin of the Center for Children's Books* at the University of Chicago, noted in a memorial tribute in *Horn Book* that Judson never once received a rejection slip. Her publications included nineteen books making up the long-running "Mary Jane" series, in which the title character toured the United States, Canada, and Europe. Judson also contributed several fanciful short stories to children's periodicals, including *Child Life, St. Nicholas,* and *Youth's Companion.* At the time of her death, it was estimated that well over six million copies of her books had been sold.

Her activities during World War I initiated her career as a public speaker and gained her a reputation, mainly based on her lectures, as an authority on family finance. This patriotic work began when the United States Treasury Department sent her to several large high schools in Illinois to talk to students about the importance of war bonds. Soon thereafter she was lecturing to women's clubs, farm and home bureaus, state extension meetings, and adult education courses in colleges and universities all over the country about thrift, time and money budgets, and financial training for children. She published more than two thousand articles on these topics in various magazines, including *Ladies' Home Journal, Women's Home Companion, Banker's Life, Industrial Banker, Journal of Home Economics, Farmer's*

Life, Fruit Garden and Home, American Legion, Country Gentleman, and *Fire*—a magazine of the Chicago Fire Department.

In the early 1920s she wrote four brief books for adults on household budgeting and became a consultant to two banks. She had her own weekly radio program as one of the early women broadcasters in Chicago. Beginning in 1928, she entertained and educated radio listeners on aspects of child training, homemaking, and household economics.

She was a longtime member of Theta Sigma Phi, a national organization of women in communications, later called Women in Communications, Inc. (WICI). In 1948 she was a recipient of its Headline Award, the organization's highest honor, which recognizes recent national and/or international accomplishments in the communication industry, as well as consistent excellence. After her death, WICI established the Clara Ingram Judson Scholarship in her honor. Judson was also a member of the Illinois Woman's Press Association (IWPA) from 1915 until her death and served as its president from 1923 to 1925.

Long after the war ended, she continued to travel around the Midwest, delivering lectures and radio broadcasts. She came into contact with a great variety of people and grew to dislike the term "melting pot." As Judson explained, "It occurred to me that America isn't really a melting pot that reduces everything to a common mass. It's more like a tapestry with the charm and strength of many interwoven elements. And the charm and strength come from the differences, you know. Some people seem to want to be all alike, which would be simply deadly" (quoted in McGuire, *Horn Book,* 392).

As a result of her travels, instead of writing more fanciful tales and more of the "Mary Jane" series, she began writing about great Americans and about people of foreign backgrounds who made America great. These were her best books, by far. In the 1940s Judson began a series of books that dramatized the coming of immigrant families to America. These became known as the "They Came From" series and featured immigrants from Sweden, France, Scotland, Yugoslavia, and Ireland. The last two books in the series, *The Lost Violin* (1947) and *The Green Ginger Jar* (1949), depicted Bohemian and Chinese families, respectively, in Chicago.

In each of these books, she endeavored to show the immigrants as part of the "tapestry" of their new homeland. The newcomers' neighbors and how they received the newcomers were as important to her as the newcomers themselves. Judson took care to write her books with historically accurate detail and became well known for her thorough and diligent research. Her books were based on careful study, not only of written records, letters, and diaries, but also of the locales of her books. In *Library Journal,* she explained her approach: "In a hundred small ways I have made my stories accurate. Even the weather, when mentioned, is the weather of that day and place. Much of this, I well know, is not important to a young reader. But it is important to me to know that materially and spiritually these books are true. Writing fiction is pleasant work, but this unraveling of history has been a more rewarding experience" (August 1947, 1077).

In *Current Biography* (1948) Judson described the creed that guided her personally and professionally: "I feel so deeply that as we help children to understand our neighbors, we help

in understanding of world problems. Peace, real lasting peace, is a growth from the hearth and spreads to the neighborhood, the community, the town, the country and some day throughout the world, and our hope lies in the children" (p. 332).

In addition to writing about immigrant experiences, she began writing biographies of notable people in American history. She strove to infuse each biography with vitality and a spirit of adventure. Her thirty-eighth book but her first biography for young people was *Pioneer Girl* (1939), about FRANCES E. WILLARD, social reformer and organizer of the temperance movement, who also happened to be a founding member of the Illinois Woman's Press Association. Other early biographies were about men whose technology changed this country, such as *Boat Builder: The Story of Robert Fulton* (1940), *Railway Engineer: The Story of George Stephenson* (1941), and *Reaper Man: The Story of Cyrus Hall McCormick* (1948).

Later, she wrote biographies of political and social figures, including *Abraham Lincoln, Friend of the People* (1950), illustrated with photo reproductions of the Chicago Historical Society's Lincoln Diorama; *City Neighbor: The Story of Jane Addams* (1951), whom Judson knew personally; *George Washington, Leader of the People* (1951); *Thomas Jefferson, Champion of the People* (1952); *Mr. Justice Holmes* (1956); and *Andrew Carnegie,* published posthumously in 1964. By the end of her life, she had written biographies of seventeen Americans for a junior high school audience. She also rewrote three of the biographies for primary grades. Her biographies received plaudits and honors, one of them winning the Thomas Edison Award, two the Indiana Authors' Day Award, and three the Newbery Honor Book citations.

Judson's biographies received nearly unanimous praise from reviewers. For example, Polly Goodwin in the *Chicago Sunday Tribune* complimented *Abraham Lincoln:* "We all know his story, yet how fresh it seems in this excellent retelling for children so clearly and simply that a child of ten can understand it" (November 12, 1950). Louise Bechtel, in a *New York Herald Tribune* review on November 26, 1950, commended Judson's research: "The Judson story is written with deep feeling for Lincoln's various home countrysides based on travel in his footsteps over five states. It is also based on a thorough job of research in up-to-date Lincoln material." Many other reviewers praised her vivid writing and her painstaking research.

Judson's purpose in writing biographies was apparent to reviewers. Louise Bechtel's review of the biography of JANE ADDAMS noted, "Young people of today, anywhere in the world, who read a life of this great American, will have a deepened sense of American ideals and of our progress in democratic living. Miss Judson's brief biography, with easily read type, will appeal mostly to those of junior high age. It might also be useful in adult Americanization classes" (*New York Herald Tribune,* June 3, 1951).

Judson's friends described her as a kind, gracious, soft-spoken woman. She was small and, in her later years, youthful looking; her white hair surrounded a friendly face with bright blue eyes and a firm chin. In spite of the heart ailment she suffered for many years, she was the picture of health, vigor, and youth. In biographical accounts, she listed reading, fine needlework, travel, and gardening as her hobbies. Throughout her life, she was active in many local and statewide social and professional clubs, including the Chicago Authors' Club, Chicago Woman's Club, Evanston Country Club, Woman's City Club, and Evanston Woman's Club.

Judson died in her apartment in Evanston, Illinois. She was cremated, and her ashes were scattered at Memorial Park in Skokie, Illinois.

Four weeks after her death, she was posthumously honored with the Laura Ingalls Wilder Award, given by the American Library Association to an "author or illustrator whose books, published in the United States, have over a period of years made a substantial and lasting contribution to literature for children" (Livsey, "Presentation," 388). The award was begun in 1954. Laura Ingalls Wilder, author of the *Little House on the Prairie* series, received the first award, and Judson was its second recipient. In the acceptance speech she finished just days before her death, she wrote that her purpose in writing "was to show that life is more useful and rewarding when lived harmoniously with ourselves and those around us" ("Acceptance," 390), a theme she stressed throughout her work. In the final paragraph of her *St. Lawrence Seaway* (1959), a book she wrote at eighty years of age, she concluded, "The world can see that when countries work with one another, as have the United States of America and the Dominion of Canada in the creation of the seaway, further miracles are possible, miracles as great as men's dreams" (p. 160).

Judson's writing and lecturing embodied her faith in the United States, in its people, and in the family. An analysis of Judson's life and work was aptly provided by Alice McGuire in her memorial tribute to her. She noted that Judson, like Laura Ingalls Wilder, did a "peerless job in capturing the essence of American democracy for children," but Judson "assessed two other important facets of democracy—the character and ideals of key figures in our historical development and the cultural contributions of the varied strains which infuse the American people with strength and color" (p. 394).

In 1961 the Clara Ingram Judson Award was established by the Society of Midland Authors, an organization in which she served as director and treasurer. The award is given annually to the most outstanding book written for children by an author from the Midwest.

Sources. Judson's papers are included in the Kerlan Collection at the Univ. of Minnesota. Judson's article, "Writing Juveniles Isn't All Fun," which explains why and how she researched materials for her books, is found in *Library Journal*, August 1947. Both the CHS and the Evanston Hist. Soc. hold newspaper clippings concerning Judson. Comprehensive biographical sketches can be found in *Current Biography* (1948); Charlemae Rollins's "Clara Ingram Judson: Interpreter of America," *Elementary English*, December 1953; *Something about the Author*, vol. 38, 1985, containing a complete bibliography of Judson's books; and *Major Authors and Illustrators for Children and Young Adults* (1993). Polly Goodwin's review of *Abraham Lincoln, Friend of the People* was published in *Chicago Sunday Tribune*, November 12, 1950. Louise Bechtel's review of *Abraham Lincoln, Friend of the People* is found in *New York Herald Tribune Book Review*, November 26, 1950, and her review of *City Neighbor: The Story of Jane Addams* is in *New York Herald Tribune Book Review*, June 3, 1951. Alice Brooks McGuire's moving tribute, "Clara Ingram Judson," is found in *Horn Book Magazine*, October 1960, as are Rosemary Livsey's "The Laura Ingalls Wilder Award

Presentation" and Judson's acceptance speech, "Acceptance." Obituaries are in *CT*, May 25, 1960; *NYT*, May 25, 1960; *Publishers' Weekly*, June 13, 1960; and *Matrix*, March–April, 1961.

ANN D. CARLSON

JUDSON HASKINS, SYLVIA SHAW
June 30, 1897–September 1978
SCULPTOR

Sylvia Shaw, whose sculpture graces many private and public gardens, was a second generation Chicagoan born into a comfortable middle-class family, the middle daughter of three. Her father was the noted Chicago architect Howard Van Doren Shaw, who designed Chicago's Goodman Theater, Cliff Dwellers Club, Quadrangle Club, Fourth Presbyterian Church, and many other buildings. Her mother, Frances (Wells) Shaw, was a writer and poet and an early supporter of *Poetry* magazine.

In a family that valued creativity, Sylvia Shaw learned early that art was a deeply satisfying occupation. In the introduction to her book, *For Gardens and Other Places*, she referred to an evening from her childhood when she heard her father "chuckling to himself [as he worked at his drawing board designing houses,] 'to think that people pay me for doing this!'" ("Sculptor's Introduction," Judson Haskins Papers). Because she exhibited talent early, her father encouraged her to pursue art as a career.

Sylvia Shaw attended the Laboratory School of the University of Chicago and Westover School, Middlebury, Connecticut. Her first art instruction came from the well-known animal sculptor Anna Hyatt during the summer of 1915 in her Annisquam, Massachusetts, studio, where Shaw worked as an apprentice. She attended the School of the Art Institute of Chicago, studying under Czech-born Albin Polasek, whose public sculpture in Chicago included the Theodore Thomas Memorial *Spirit of Music* in Grant Park, the Thomas Garrigue Masaryk Memorial on the Midway, and a statue of Gotthold Ephraim Lessing in Washington Park. After graduation in 1919, Shaw worked in New York briefly and then went to Paris to study with Antoine Bourdelle, the famous French sculptor, at the Académie de la Grande Chaumière. She found Paris confusing and wrote her father in 1920 or 1921 that she wanted to keep her ideas "simple and uncomplicated by methods and things" (Judson Haskins Papers). She greatly admired sculptor Aristide Maillol's work and felt an affinity with the works of German expressionist sculptor Gerhard Marcks. The sculptured animals she saw on a trip to China with her father in 1917 were a direct inspiration to her.

When she returned to Chicago in 1921 to marry Clay Judson, an attorney, she continued her work on her own. Looking back in 1960, she said that hers was the generation of emancipated women who were expected to do some work, but she wondered whether the emancipation of wives was best for husbands. She commended her husband for being concerned and helpful.

Sylvia Shaw Judson's first studio was in the basement laundry of her apartment building. Later she worked in the top floor corridor of the nearby Newberry Library. By the time the children were born, Alice in 1922 and Clay Jr. in 1926, she earned enough by selling her sculpture to hire help for the children so that she could work in the afternoons.

In 1934 she created a work space for herself at Ragdale, the

Fig. 60. *Sculptor Sylvia Shaw Judson in her studio, 1953.*

summer home built by her father in 1897 on fifty acres of prairie land in suburban Lake Forest. Judson and her sisters inherited the estate in 1937 after their parents died, and all three chose to live there. The Judsons were given the Arts and Crafts style main house, which they winterized and occupied year-round after 1942. Living in the place she said she loved most, Sylvia Judson built her permanent studio in a wooded spot in the meadow overlooking the prairie.

Words such as "tranquil," "harmonious," and "quiet" were often used to describe Judson's sculpture. For her 1938 exhibition at the Art Institute of Chicago the catalog stated, "Her sculpture is distinguished for its simplicity of design, delicacy of feeling and unobtrusive architectural unity" (Judson Haskins Papers).

"Perhaps I was a Quaker sculptor before I was a Quaker. . . . Certain qualities that I have aimed for in my sculpture have an affinity with certain Quaker qualities," Judson wrote (Judson Haskins Papers). Although born and raised a Presbyterian, Judson became a Quaker when she was in her early fifties after years of preparation and study. About her beliefs she wrote that happiness came from doing a worthwhile job well and that she valued "just plain living" and took "pleasure in simple things" ("I Believe," Judson Haskins Papers). The Judsons established the first Quaker Meeting in Lake Forest in 1952.

Judson's earliest sculptures were made for private homes and gardens. She was a gardener herself and an ardent observer of nature. She compared her sculpture to the use of rocks in Japanese gardens as foils to nature and said, "What we look for in a garden is refreshment and peace and a sense of relationship to nature" ("Garden Sculpture," 45). She believed that sculp-

ture should be part of the architectural scheme and contribute to the mood of the garden. Her figurative work of animals and children was fresh and original and could be found often in gardens along Chicago's suburban North Shore. She found animals to sketch at Brookfield Zoo and used her own children, grandchildren, and those of friends as models. She portrayed her youthful subjects resting, sleeping, dancing, playing musical instruments, and holding pets.

Judson usually made her sculptures in plasticine, an oil-based clay. Her father gave her an enormous chest of this clay when she graduated from the Art Institute, and almost everything she did for the next sixty years was made from this reusable clay and was then cast in bronze, stone, or metal. Occasionally she carved directly in stone or made small figures from terracotta clay that could be fired in a kiln. She continued to work until the year of her death in 1978, keeping careful business records and handling all of the sales herself.

Judson's lead figure of a young boy holding a potted plant, called *The Gardener*, won the Art Institute of Chicago's Logan Prize in 1929 and years later graced John F. Kennedy's White House garden. The Art Institute of Chicago showed twenty of her works in 1938, Judson's first solo exhibition. Museum director Daniel Catton Rich described her garden pieces as "large and simple in feeling[,] . . . miles removed from much of the ornate 'statuary' that haunts our formal landscape" (quoted in Arden Gallery catalog, Judson Haskins Papers).

Other public places have her large bronzes. *Girl with Squirrel* (1932) is found at Kosciusko Park, Milwaukee, Wisconsin. A large fountain at Brookfield Zoo in Chicago (1954) features life-size animal skulls with horns. At the outdoor Ravinia Festival grounds in Chicago's northern suburbs are *Girl with Violin* (1955) and *Dancer* (1974). Two figures of children are in Lake Forest's Market Square, designed by her father in 1912. Other sculptures of children or animals are located at hospitals, schools, libraries, arboretums, parks, or zoos in Boston, Philadelphia, Toronto, and other cities. Her best-known work is the *Mary Dyer Monument* (1959), in which she portrayed the Quaker martyr in a pose of quiet meditation in front of the Massachusetts State House, facing Boston Common where she died. Copies are at Earlham College in Richmond, Indiana, and the Friends Center in Philadelphia.

Commissions for cemeteries and churches included a large granite Madonna figure for Queen of Heaven Cemetery, Hillside, Illinois. Just after her husband's death in 1960, Judson was commissioned to depict *Stations of the Cross* for the Church of the Sacred Heart in Winnetka, Illinois. The expressive bronze panels, installed in 1963, are executed in low relief.

Her many honors and awards include the Art Institute's 1929 Logan Prize, the Purchase Prize at the Philadelphia Museum's 1949 International Sculpture Show, the Milbrook Garden Club Medal in 1957, and an honorary Ph.D. from Lake Forest College in 1952. She had one-person exhibits at New York's Arden Gallery in 1940 and the Sculpture Center in 1957; she exhibited in group shows at Chicago's 1933–34 Century of Progress Exposition, the Milwaukee Art Institute, the Whitney Museum, and the Museum of Modern Art, where a New York critic judged her sculpture best in the show.

Judson often gave talks to groups; she wrote and spoke about her life and work to fellow members of the Scribblers and Friday clubs. The Scribblers were a group of friends, mostly from Lake Forest, who presented their own written work to each other at monthly meetings. The Friday Club, a women's group that remained active in the 1990s, held monthly programs. Judson also addressed garden clubs and Quaker organizations. She was president of the Chicago Public School Art Society (now called A.R.T.) from 1947 to 1950; vice-president of the Woman's Board of the Art Institute, 1953–54; clerk of the Lake Forest Friends Meeting, 1956–57; and a member of the Humanities Visiting Committee of the University of Chicago from 1962 to 1974. She was also a member and fellow of the National Sculpture Society and the National Academy of Design.

Sylvia Shaw Judson wrote two books that reflected her beliefs and presented her work. In a foreword to the 1982 edition of *The Quiet Eye* (published originally in 1954), her daughter Alice Judson Hayes (writing as Alice Ryerson) wrote that as a Quaker her mother "was much bothered by [The Friends'] official unconcern for art." Because she "believed sincerely that the visible outward form truly expresses the spirit within[,] . . . she applied this belief to her sculpture, to the way she lived and to the making of *The Quiet Eye.*" The book paired thirty-three works of art by artists of many cultures with quotations from some of the world's great thinkers for the purpose of giving the reader the experience of art. Her second book, *For Gardens and Other Places* (1968), was a pictorial record of more than sixty pieces of her work from 1932 to 1967.

Calling it her greatest challenge, Judson accepted an invitation in 1963 to teach sculpture for a five-month term at American University in Cairo. Sixty-five years old, she had never taught before, but she found it stimulating. Later she told an audience that the experience in Cairo so rejuvenated her that upon her return to Chicago, "when an old friend [Sidney Gatter Haskins] suggested that we be married, I said 'yes' with alacrity" ("Cairo" talk, Judson Haskins Papers).

Ten years later, at the monthly Lake Forest Quaker Meeting, Sylvia Judson heard the customary question, "What are you doing to simplify your life?" and concluded that she should give up the growing burdens of life at Ragdale and move to a Quaker retirement village in Pennsylvania called "Kendal," near her children, pieces of her sculpture, and other Quakers. She and Haskins continued to summer in Ragdale.

Sylvia Judson's only living child, poet and writer Alice Judson Hayes, formed the Ragdale Foundation in 1976 with her mother's blessing and turned the estate into a center where writers and artists and musicians would come to work.

Sylvia Judson returned to Ragdale in the summer of 1978, where she died at the age of eighty-one. She asked to be cremated and have her ashes scattered at Ragdale. Her name is also on the Shaw family grave in Graceland Cemetery alongside her husband Clay's.

Sylvia Shaw Judson thought of herself as a sculptor from the time she was seventeen. She became a devoted wife, mother, active member of the Society of Friends, and civic leader in the Chicago community. She developed her own distinctive art style and enjoyed recognition and wide success, selling nearly everything she produced. She recognized her own good fortune when she wrote that hers was not "a life calculated to produce an art of protest" (Introduction, *For Gardens and Other Places*), but added that she was always sensitive to the "anxieties" of her time.

Her sculptures continue to be appreciated. In 1994 a photograph of Judson's unsigned bronze figure of *Bird Girl* (1938) in a Savannah cemetery appeared on the cover of *Midnight in the Garden of Good and Evil* by John Berendt. After publication, her identity was discovered and subsequent printings will bear Sylvia Shaw Judson's name. A new cast of *Bird Girl* appears in the movie version of the book.

Sources. The Sylvia Shaw Judson Haskins Papers are at the CHS. Eleven boxes contain correspondence, sketches, drawings, notes, lists, her two books, a cassette of her Egyptian teaching lectures, copies of her speeches, travel journals, newspaper articles, and other memorabilia. The Archives of American Art at the Smithsonian Museum have microfilmed her papers and also possess her original business records. Microfilms are also at the Art Institute of Chicago library. Judson's books are described above. She wrote about the place of sculpture in gardens in "Garden Sculpture," *Bulletin of the Garden Club of America*, November 1960. Alice Judson Hayes, interviewed in 1994 by Mary Gray, is an inexhaustible source of information about her mother, the family, and Ragdale. Judson is listed in *Who Was Who in American Art* (1985), *Brookgreen Gardens* (1968), Charlotte Rubenstein's *Women Sculptors of America* (1988), and Gary Sandman's *Quaker Artists* (1992). The Ragdale Foundation in Lake Forest, Illinois, is open to visitors and has published booklets such as *Ragdale: A History and Guide* by Alice Hayes and Susan Moon (1990).

MARY LACKRITZ GRAY

KASSEL, MYRNA SIEGENDORF BORDELON
September 23, 1918–February 22, 1972
LABOR EDUCATOR

Myrna Siegendorf Bordelon Kassel's early life directed her toward a vocation combining education and trade union activism. She came of age with a "fantastic sweeping corps of intellectual activists in the 1940s" (Grossner interview transcript, 48) during "an incredible period when the labor movement was able to garner" (p. 48) resources and attract real talent. Myrna Siegendorf was born in Passaic, New Jersey, the daughter of Jewish immigrants Celia (Feinstein) Siegendorf, born in England, and Herman Siegendorf, from Austria. Her first memories were of the Polish and Slavic neighborhood where her father was a house painter and several other relatives were merchants. Three brothers died, one before her birth. When Myrna Siegendorf was ten years old, her mother was killed by a train as she walked on the main street of Passaic. Siegendorf went to live with her grandmother in Philadelphia, Pennsylvania, where the family lived above a millinery store and a chicken market. She remembered a "childhood [which] was very much involved with a kind of sense of the despair in people, the hopelessness in people as they wandered in and out of the stores" (interview transcript, 3).

When her grandmother died, Siegendorf returned to Passaic to live with her father and to attend Passaic High School. It was during the Great Depression, and she tutored children for fifty cents a week and sold hats at a relative's shop. A good student in high school, she joined the Latin and French clubs and participated in the debating team, where she first began to think about social problems. Her high school teachers encouraged her to compete for a scholarship to the New Jersey College for Women (in 1954 Douglass College and now part of Rutgers University) and helped her enroll in the National Youth Administration (NYA), a New Deal work-study program for high school and college students. Siegendorf received sixteen dollars a month for work at the college. With her scholarship and an ad-

ditional job as a waitress, she was able to attend college full time from 1935 to 1939.

Starting in her freshman year, Siegendorf attracted a number of influential mentors. Initially she concentrated on Latin and Greek studies. Then she became friends with professors Evelyn Clark and Miriam West, two women who were "lifelong companion[s]" (interview transcript, 6) and shared a house together. West, a communist, influenced Siegendorf's studies. The young woman began to focus on economics instead of languages. West and Clark "became in a sense mothers" (interview transcript, 6) to the young woman who had experienced the loss of her mother and grandmother; and they helped Siegendorf link her personal experience of poverty during the Great Depression with an economic and political explanation found in Marxism. She began to see "the absurd competition that [took] . . . place between the small merchant and the ghetto consumer" (interview transcript, 7).

The New Jersey College of Women was located in New Brunswick, New Jersey, where the Johnson and Johnson Company was the principal employer and, during the 1930s, laid off many workers. A group called the Workers Alliance was organizing in New Brunswick, and Siegendorf participated in its activities. At the same time she joined with hundreds of thousands of depression-era students in campus activism. Siegendorf was an organizer of the American Student Union (ASU), the merger of two groups—the communist-led National Student League and the Student League for Industrial Democracy—that "became the largest student activist organization in the nation's history, with some 20,000 members" (Cohen, 754). During her organizing days with the ASU, Siegendorf met students from many universities, heard speakers including socialists, communists, and pacifists. She was influenced by socialist Norman Thomas and Sherman Eddie, an organizer of southern sharecroppers. During the depths of the depression, her college economics club sent Siegendorf to New York City, "where the Socialist League for Industrial Democracy was running a summer program for kids" (interview transcript, 9). There she met Joel Seidman, the leader of the summer program for children, who eventually taught labor relations at the University of Chicago. The summer was "an extraordinary experience" (p. 9) for Siegendorf, who worked in the Bowery neighborhood of New York and saw the worst effects of the depression. She returned to college committed to the study of economics.

The following summer she was given a scholarship by the Quaker-affiliated American Friends Service Committee to work in their project with unemployed miners in the coal fields of western Pennsylvania. Siegendorf described it later as "a kind of VISTA or Peace Corps" (interview transcript, 10) program, and "one of the most important summers of my life" (p. 10). She had contact with working people, "working side by side" (p. 10).

By 1939, as she finished her last year in college, she began to reach out to groups in her own community and also assisted the Coal Workers Alliance. Since the New Deal relief programs were being cut back that year, many relief clients were without any aid. She and other women from her campus joined with other activists and gave leaflets to relief clients in downtown New Brunswick, encouraging them to organize for better conditions. Siegendorf was arrested with others in her group on the charge of littering. She graduated in 1939 from the New Jersey College for Women with a bachelor's degree and honors, with special distinction in economics. "During 1940 and 1941 [Siegendorf] was awarded the Vorhees Fellowship by the New Jersey College for Women for advanced study in the field of economics" (Myrna Bordelon Kassel, Resume, interview transcript, Appendix). It was rescinded when she was jailed. "It was quite a blow, but then through the help of Dr. West and others" (interview transcript, 13) Siegendorf was awarded a scholarship to the University of Wisconsin, West's alma mater. At the University of Wisconsin she received a master's degree from the School of Economics in 1941. John R. Commons, who was professor of economics at Wisconsin from 1904 to 1932, had been influential in the development of the Wisconsin approach to economics, making it one of the best places in the United States to study labor economics. Siegendorf wrote her master's thesis on J. D. H. Cole and the British trade union movement.

After completing her master's degree, Siegendorf "began to feel a strong desire to get back in the world again" (interview transcript, 14). She moved in 1941 to New York City, where she worked as education director of the New York Women's Trade Union League (WTUL). She left the position in 1942 because she felt the WTUL was peripheral to the trade union movement. She returned to Wisconsin to continue graduate work and became Professor Selig Perlman's graduate assistant. As his assistant she taught during three summers at the University of Wisconsin School for Workers, an extension service for training trade union leaders. Staff members taught in small towns all through Wisconsin, and Siegendorf was part of the traveling circuit.

Her teaching in the extension school gave her experience in working with trade union leaders, the people who were selected to be shop stewards and middle level union officials. She realized that the United States was "moving from a blue collar to a white collar society" (interview transcript, 16) and that "one of

the most important fields of trade union organization would be white collar workers" (p. 16). She became interested in "what was happening in the Montgomery Ward case" (interview transcript, 16) in Chicago. The workers there, organized into Local 20 of the United Retail, Wholesale and Department Store Employees, affiliated with the Congress of Industrial Organizations (CIO), had concluded their first contract with the company just before the outbreak of World War II. During wartime, Montgomery Ward hired young women in their mail order house division. They presented challenges for union organization, and Siegendorf was interested in new ways, largely social and educational, to reach them. When the contract was coming up for renewal in 1942–43, Siegendorf thought that it would be interesting to do her doctoral dissertation on the Montgomery Ward case and examine how the National Labor Relations Board was functioning during wartime. Not only did she study the Montgomery Ward workers who had joined Local 20 of the United Retail, Wholesale and Department Store Employees Union, but the union also hired her from 1943 to 1945 as its education and public relations director. Siegendorf worked with newly hired workers in Montgomery Ward's mail order house; most were young women and were called "the Babushka Bobby Sox Brigade, because they were very young . . . very inexperienced and they knew nothing about unions" (interview transcript, 19). Her first assignment was to bring together the older warehousemen and the newly hired mail order workers. Siegendorf also ran a storefront for the union. Located in an industrial neighborhood, it was a "dark, foreboding and unfriendly place" (interview transcript, 34). Innovative in her approach, Siegendorf boldly wrote to architect Frank Lloyd Wright, asking for advice about how she could transform the place into one more inviting and accessible for organizing young women. Wright introduced her to his colleague and ex-student, Molly Leninbraugh, who taught interior design at the School of the Art Institute of Chicago. Leninbraugh helped Siegendorf, and for a small fee, "[transformed] that storefront into something simple but really bright and beautiful in good taste" (interview transcript, 34).

Siegendorf edited a weekly mimeographed paper for the union, the *Spotlight*, supervised negotiation practice sessions, and organized a public relations campaign to gain community support, while the U.S. Army kept Montgomery Ward's open during the Local 20 strike in 1942–43, during World War II. She created a committee to support the union, cochaired by Edward Sparling, head of the Young Men's Christian Association (YMCA) Central College, Chicago, and other distinguished citizens.

A national CIO Community Services Committee was organized during Local 20's strike against Montgomery Ward in 1942–43. The United Retail, Wholesale and Department Store Employees Union asked which groups in local communities actually benefited from funds raised by Community Chests and other charitable organizations and asked how much money was allocated for striking workers, for example. In Chicago, the Chicago CIO Cook County Industrial Union Council organized a local Community Services Committee. Siegendorf, who had become a delegate from Local 20 to the Chicago CIO Cook County Industrial Union Council, became chair and then executive secretary of the local Community Services Committee.

In 1944 Siegendorf, representing the council, joined the advisory committee of Community Referral Service of Metro Chicago, a private agency supported by community funds under the auspices of the Welfare Council of Chicago. The service had been created to meet a steadily increasing number of requests for direction to social services coming from individuals and agencies in the community, including representatives of labor unions. In 1945, Siegendorf left Local 20 and joined the Cook County Industrial Union Council to develop a stronger relationship between social service organizations and labor in Chicago.

From the union side, Siegendorf developed a community services program that became a model for unions elsewhere. During the labor strikes of the 1940s and 1950s, Siegendorf was able to negotiate with city agencies for relief for strikers. She also involved agencies like the Salvation Army, which provided food and help in strike kitchens.

By the time Siegendorf completed her doctoral dissertation, "Montgomery Ward versus the Union: A Case Study in Industrial Conflict," and received a Ph.D. in 1946, she had traveled a long way, intellectually and in terms of her experiences, from the politics and trade unionism of the 1930s. She had opposed the influence of the Communist Party (CP) in the CIO-affiliated unions because she felt the CP had its own agenda and strategy and that it was not the same as the point of view of the American labor movement. She felt, however, that the most significant internal difficulty that unionism faced was not whether or not there were communists involved, but "just [the] sheer apathy" (interview transcript, 41) that existed. Traditional worker education did not work, she contended, and the trade unions needed a more dynamic, up-to-date form of leadership instruction "to train people for power, to assume power realistically and democratically" (interview transcript, 65).

In the 1940s, Siegendorf attempted to invigorate the way in which trade unions educated and developed new leadership. The old model of worker's education, which was "basically built around . . . authoritarian concepts of teaching" (interview transcript, 53), was "fifty years behind the times in terms of how we conducted the learning experience" (p. 54). She began working on a whole new concept of leadership training, which eventually resulted in the establishment of the National Training Laboratories. She began to train union counselors in how to lead discussions, relinquish the chairing of groups to the rank and file, and rotate the responsibility for leading groups among the members of the group. She began to use innovative teaching techniques but found that "nowhere in the labor movement was there any support" (interview transcript, 54) for what she was attempting to inaugurate. Instead, she felt her new methods were threatening. "The old union counselor training design was essentially to bring the expert in . . . and I was going to use the training situation as a crucible in which people in the group could actually structure the use of the resource person . . . [and] start developing along lines that were more relevant to themselves" (interview transcript, 55).

Her reason for attempting to revamp worker's education came out of her experience in integrating labor union representatives into the infrastructure of welfare and community agencies in Chicago. She had found that even when progressive agencies or groups such as the Metropolitan Housing and Planning Commission wanted labor participation, union representatives were not trained to interact effectively on boards and commissions. Siegendorf realized that in order for labor to participate in real rather than token ways, trade union representatives needed to be trained.

The social work community also understood the need for labor representatives and labor participation in its activities. In 1945 Myrna Siegendorf became a staff member of the Welfare Council's Labor-Welfare Project. "For the following five years, [Siegendorf] functioned as Liaison Officer between the Labor-Welfare Project of the Welfare Council and the Chicago Industrial Union Council" (Myrna Bordelon Kassel, Resume, interview transcript, Appendix). Labor representatives asked for money from the Community Fund to employ personnel competent to assist them in their welfare planning. Social agencies asked community service officers of the unions, a new kind of labor official Siegendorf believed was needed, to assist in setting up cooperative projects for workers. Under Siegendorf's leadership, by 1947 the Labor-Welfare Project was concentrating on the training of union counselors with classes in health and safety and in strike counseling for the unemployed. The unions seemed to be going in the direction Siegendorf had anticipated and advocated.

In 1946 Siegendorf attended a seminar on labor at the Jewish Theological Seminary in New York City, where she gave a talk. The general topic of the meeting was an exploration of the spiritual autobiography of labor leaders. Professor Liston Pope of Yale University, a noted sociologist of religion, was one of the organizers of the seminar. Its proceedings were published as *Autobiographies of Labor Leaders* and Siegendorf authored a chapter. It was at this meeting that she met Sam Bordelon, whom she married in 1948. In August of that year Sam Bordelon established Bordelons, a contemporary design studio specializing in custom furniture design and manufacture. It was located in the Hyde Park neighborhood in Chicago. Myrna Bordelon resigned her position with the Welfare Council of Chicago in 1950 to give her attention to Bordelons. It was a time of struggles within the leadership of the CIO. Anxieties about the kind of union counseling program she was directing converged with other tensions during a visit from the New York Community Services Committee of the CIO. Myrna Bordelon was pregnant with her first child, and after the meeting where her methods and approaches were questioned, she announced her resignation. She left "feeling very hurt and distraught" (interview transcript, 56), even though she had intended to leave to have her child. Her son, Jeffery, was born in 1950; a daughter, Amy, was born in 1951.

In 1955 Myrna and Sam Bordelon moved their business to the Near North Side. She served as president of the company from 1959, supervising the interior design program, purchasing, advertising, display, sales training, sales promotion, and general administration. With the establishment of a contract division that year, Bordelons enlarged its scope to include services to business, professional, commercial, and institutional clients. Little is known about Myrna Bordelon's personal life; by 1961 she had divorced Sam Bordelon and married Don Kassel, May 21, 1961. Bordelons went out of business in 1963. In 1964

Myrna Kassel went to work with the Illinois Department of Mental Health, serving first as assistant director of personnel services, then as assistant director of the professional services division. There she used her skills to set up training programs for workers and conferences for training agency personnel. She was soon promoted to director of the Illinois Labor Department Human Services Manpower Career Center, a position she held until her death. Myrna Kassel became ill with cancer and died at age fifty-four. Although she was not affiliated with any religious group, funeral services were held at the First Unitarian Church.

Myrna Siegendorf Bordelon Kassel was influenced by the world of poverty, unemployment, and family dislocation during the Great Depression that affected her own life and the lives of others who suffered the insecurity and deprivations of economic hardship. She was aided by mentors and teachers who saw in her the promise of intellectual achievement and encouraged her to focus on economic solutions to human problems. Determined to improve people's lives, she worked within organizations with the same goals. In the 1940s trade unions within the Congress of Industrial Organizations were organizing workers to improve their lives. In the 1960s, the hope for working-class people came from the Great Society programs run by the government and from community organization. In both eras, she was intent on helping people learn how to improve their lives, just as she had done. "It didn't occur to me that the program would not somehow carry on" (interview transcript, 65) she said about the trade union education work. "To me, education means development of leadership, to train people for power, to assume power realistically and democratically" (p. 66).

Sources. The oral interview of Myrna Siegendorf Bordelon Kassel by Isabel Grossner, December 11, 1970, with transcript, Balanoff Oral History Collection, Center for New Deal Studies, Roosevelt Univ., Chicago, is the most complete document about her life. The interview is jointly owned by Roosevelt Univ. and the 20th Century Trade Union Woman Oral History Project at the Univ. of Michigan, Ann Arbor, Michigan. An interview with Rayfield Mooty, Balanoff Oral History Collection, is also helpful. CHS has a file on Bordelons, the interior design and furniture company operated by Sam and Myrna Bordelon. Don Kassel was interviewed by N. Sue Weiler on August 3, 1993. Obituaries of Myrna Siegendorf Bordelon Kassel appeared in *Chicago Today*, February 25, 1972, and *CT*, February 22, 1972. See also Robert Cohen, "Student Movements—1930s," in *Encyclopedia of the American Left*, ed. Paul Buhle, Mari Jo Buhle, and Dan Georgakas (1992).

N. SUE WEILER

KAUPAS, MOTHER MARIA (Casimira Kaupas)
January 6, 1880–April 17, 1940
FOUNDER OF A RELIGIOUS ORDER

Mother Maria Kaupas, founder of the Sisters of St. Casimir in Chicago, the first Lithuanian American sisterhood in the United States, was born in the small village of Gudeliai, Lithuania, the fifth of eleven children. Her parents, Anufras Kaupas, a furniture maker, and Antanina (Glebauskas) Kaupas, a skilled weaver, had a family farm that provided the family with a work-filled but comfortable existence. Casimira Kaupas assisted her mother in all the household and farm chores and cared for her younger siblings.

Casimira Kaupas grew up in Russian-controlled Lithuania during a period of severe persecution and suppression of the Lithuanian language, culture, and religion by the czarist regime. This oppression spawned a nationalist movement that kindled the rebirth of the literary and cultural spirit of Lithuania. The Kaupas family belonged to a broad social class of farmers and peasants who participated in this movement for a free press and for religious freedom. Kaupas's father, an avid reader of literature, was one of the many book "smugglers" disseminating Lithuanian books printed in Prussia, hiding them on his farm and sharing them with his neighbors.

Though she received no formal education, Casimira Kaupas was taught to read by her older sister, Josephine. Her brother Anthony, a priest, had emigrated to the United States in 1892; when Casimira Kaupas was seventeen, he asked her to join him in Scranton, Pennsylvania, to assist him in his parish work as the rectory housekeeper. To prepare for this position, Kaupas assisted a rectory housekeeper in Ramygala, Lithuania. While there, a local dressmaker taught Kaupas to write so she could enroll in a school in nearby Panevėžys.

In 1897 Casimira Kaupas left for the United States, a voyage fraught with uncertainty, danger, and discomfort. Because she was too young to obtain a passport, her father's friends first smuggled her across the Prussian border, and at a German port city, she was placed on an American ship. After arriving at the New York port, she traveled to Scranton, Pennsylvania, and her brother's parish. At the turn of the century, the largest concentration of Lithuanians in the United States was in Pennsylvania. Mostly uneducated agricultural workers from an agrarian society, these immigrants found employment in Pennsylvania's coal mines and with the railroad companies.

Kaupas made few friends during her first four years, preferring to spend her time reading religious books. As a new immigrant, Kaupas found the United States to be "materialistic and superficial" (*The Founding of the Sisters of St. Casimir*, 17). She heard about the activities of a Lithuanian physician, Jonas Šliūpas, who worked in the Lithuanian community. Šliūpas, a prominent and charismatic Lithuanian American activist-founder of newspapers and immigrant organizations to promote Lithuanian culture and identity, was a free-thinker with socialist and anticlerical views in conflict with the Lithuanian Catholic clergy. Kaupas found Šliūpas's views antithetical to her own. She began to move in the direction of a religious vocation.

Kaupas first became attracted to women's religious life after seeing congregations of sisters dressed in their habits, something not possible in her homeland, where Catholic schools and religious orders had been banned by the Russians. After a visit to a Polish convent in Brooklyn, New York, she talked to her brother about becoming a nun. Homesick for her family, however, Kaupas returned to Lithuania in 1901; but she did not forget about convent life. She corresponded with a friend in Chicago who had entered a Polish convent and was teaching Lithuanian children in a parish school, an exciting prospect to Kaupus, who wrote her brother about her intentions to enter this convent. Instead, he encouraged her to found a congregation of Lithuanian sisters and prepare them to teach in Lithuanian parishes throughout the United States, an idea that Lithuanian American priests had been considering for several years. Kaupas readily accepted this suggestion since it fulfilled two of her goals: the pursuit of a religious life and the opportunity to teach and work for her own people. In 1902, to prepare for this work, since her formal education was very limited, her brother arranged for Kaupas to receive further education with the Sisters of Mercy of the Holy Cross in Ingenbohl, Switzerland. She studied there for three years.

Casimira Kaupas and two companions—Judith Dvaranauskas and Antoinette Unguraitis—came to the United States in 1905 to begin their training under the direction of Mother M. Cyril, superior general of the Sisters of the Immaculate Heart of Mary in Scranton, Pennsylvania. However, Kaupas's plan to found a Lithuanian congregation of sisters met with opposition from Bishop Shanahan of Harrisburg, Pennsylvania. Although the United States was considered a missionary territory by the Catholic Church and fertile ground for apostolic work in ethnic communities, distrust of "foreigners" by the predominantly Irish Catholic hierarchy was common. Bishop Shanahan wrote to Mother Cyril about the "cussedness of the Lithuanian people" who, he worried, "may put a stick of dynamite under the Convent and blow the Sisters into Kingdom Come" (*The Founding of the Sisters of St. Casimir*, 33). The tensions in the Lithuanian community were more complicated, however, than the simple division between more assimilated and English-speaking Irish Catholics and the newcomers speaking Lithuanian. By 1900 the Lithuanian community was split among traditionalists with loyalty to Roman Catholicism and deference to the clergy, including Polish clergy; nationalists who separated from the Poles; and secularists who were anticlerical and nationalistic. Antagonistic factions supporting or opposing the local pastor created tensions that periodically resulted in violence, including riots and the bombing of two rectories. In addition, increasing numbers of Lithuanian socialist supporters were developing fraternal organizations, local clubs, evening schools, and societies with strong antireligious attitudes.

Faced with these factions, the Lithuanian clergy in America adapted their programs and erected an extensive institutional structure to reassert the church's authority in the lives of the immigrants. Father Antanas Staniukynas, who arrived in the United States in 1904 and gradually assumed the role of informal bishop for the Lithuanian Catholic group, was a leading force in this adaptation process. Casimira Kaupas and the Sisters of St. Casimir were a critical element in the success of this plan to expand the religious infrastructure.

The Lithuanian clergy, increasingly more organized, persisted in their request for Catholic education taught in the Lithuanian language. In 1907 Rome finally authorized the founding of the Sisters of St. Casimir. The first school of the Sisters of St. Casimir, Holy Cross School, opened in 1908 in Mount Carmel, a small mining town in Pennsylvania, with Casimira Kaupas, now Sister Maria, in a leadership role. In two years the congregation had outgrown its quarters. After a lengthy search for a new motherhouse, Archbishop James E. Quigley of Chicago located a site in the Marquette Park area of Chicago. Father Antanas Staniukynas, the director of the congregation of the Sisters of St. Casimir in Pennyslvania, purchased the five-acre marshy plot in 1909. Chicago, in 1911, had overtaken Pennsylvania as the center of Lithuanian Catholic culture. There were eight established Lithuanian parishes in the city.

Lithuanian immigrants worked in the Union Stockyards, the world's largest slaughtering and meatpacking facility, and, by 1914, there were about fifty thousand Lithuanians living in the Bridgeport, Brighton Park, and Marquette Park neighborhoods. Maria Kaupas and four other Casimirite sisters moved into the newly built Chicago motherhouse in 1911 and took over the administration of the Lithuanian parochial schools and the training of teachers. The first school, All Saints, opened in 1911; in the same year St. Casimir Academy for Girls was established on the premises of the motherhouse. The girls studied the Lithuanian language, literature, history, folklore, and culture. Commercial and home economics courses were also offered.

In 1913 Kaupas was elected the first mother general of the order and held this office until her death in 1940. With scant prior administrative experience, she successfully administered several schools and two hospitals. She made difficult decisions about education, religious training, expansion of schools and other buildings, and finances. In 1931, twenty-five hundred pupils were enrolled in Chicago's Lithuanian schools, and there were sixty-two hundred students in the twenty-five Lithuanian parishes throughout the United States. They were all under Mother Maria's leadership. In addition, the congregation took charge of Holy Cross Hospital, which had been built in Chicago in 1928 by United Catholic Charities of America.

In 1920, when Lithuania first gained its independence from Russia, the bishops of Lithuania appealed to Mother Maria for help in revitalizing Lithuanian Catholic life by establishing a congregation of the Sisters of St. Casimir there. The Archbishop of Chicago, George Mundelein, had refused to send any of the Casimirite sisters because there was such demand for their work in the Lithuanian parishes in the United States. Appealing to Rome, the Lithuanian bishops were granted their request by Pope Benedict XV. Mother Maria, with four women religious, returned to Lithuania in 1920 and established a congregation at Pažaislis (Mount Peace), an ancient monastery that for centuries had been the home of Camaldolese monks. A decade later, in recognition of her achievements among Lithuanians at home and abroad, Mother Maria received Lithuania's highest decoration, the Order of the Grand Duke Gediminas.

Returning to the United States, Mother Kaupas spent a total of thirty-three years with the Sisters of St. Casimir, twenty-seven of them as the superior general. The use of her native language in the parochial schools she established was an important goal, since she saw language as the vehicle by which ethnic identity would be preserved. By the 1920s and 1930s it became increasingly difficult to maintain the primary use of the Lithuanian language in the schools. Many of the teaching sisters were born in the United States and saw themselves as Americans first, and their American-born students were speaking English at home and at school. Mother Maria persisted in encouraging the use of Lithuanian, writing to her congregation that it was "by word and example" (*Loving You, Community Circular Letters*, 121) that the students would learn to love and respect the Lithuanian Catholic Church and the customs and traditions of Lithuania.

Mother Kaupas employed the technique of writing lengthy letters to her congregation, thereby circulating her thoughts and advice throughout the community wherever they happened to be working and living beyond the walls of the central motherhouse. This method of communication was used by many sisterhoods in the United States. Her values, expressed in the community circular letters, were traditional ones: obedience, humility, acceptance, poverty, docility, patience, and endurance.

Mother Kaupas was first diagnosed with cancer in 1933. Just prior to her death on April 17, 1940, she placed her own illness in the context of her religious training and belief, turning her lengthy bouts with pain into an opportunity to atone for sins. She was buried on April 22 at St. Casimir Cemetery, Chicago. On May 23, 1993, Mother Maria Kaupas Day was celebrated in Chicago, with street signs honoring her in the Lithuanian neighborhood where she had established parochial schools to strengthen the Catholicism and ethnic identity of Lithuanian immigrants and their children.

Sources. The records of the Sisters of St. Casimir are found in the Congregational Archives, St. Casimir Motherhouse, Chicago, Illinois. Mother Kaupas's letters are published in *Loving You, Community Circular Letters of Mother Maria* (1980). See also Linda Strozdas S.S.C., "The Experience of Grace and Suffering in Selected Writings of Mother Maria Kaupas" (master's thesis, Loyola Univ. Chicago, 1983). The most complete histories of the Sisters of St. Casimir are Katherine Burton, *Lily and Sword and Crown* (1958), and *The Founding of the Sisters of St. Casimir* (1981); the latter includes many of Mother Maria's writings. For information on Lithuanian Americans, see two books by David Fainhauz: *Lithuanians in Multi-Ethnic Chicago until World War II* (1977) and *Lithuanians in the USA: Aspects of Ethnic Identity* (1991). See also Antanas J. van Reenan, *Lithuanian Diaspora: Königsberg to Chicago* (1990).

VITA LUTHMERS

KAWIN, IRENE
September 26, 1887–June 14, 1976
SOCIAL WORKER, PROBATION OFFICER, JUVENILE
CASEWORK SPECIALIST

Irene Kawin devoted her entire professional life to improving the lives of infants, children, youth, and families whose circumstances placed them outside the accepted social structure of their times. She was the elder of two daughters born to Nathan and Lottie (Goldstein) Kawin in Peoria, Illinois. The Kawins moved to Chicago during the girls' childhood and remained there for the rest of their lives. Both Irene and her sister, Ethel, selected lifelong careers in fields related to child and family welfare. Ethel Kawin, a child psychologist with the Institute for Juvenile Research, also taught at the University of Chicago and authored several books. Irene Kawin never married and lived near the university community for the rest of her life, sharing her Hyde Park living quarters at different times with her sister and her parents.

Kawin came of age at the turn of the century at a time of heightened awareness nationwide of the plight of the child living in poverty and in troubled circumstances. A rise in delinquency disturbed reformers who had come to believe that children and adolescents—heretofore placed with adult offenders—required a separate court system. A major initiative of reform-minded women in Chicago led to the founding in 1899 of the country's first Juvenile Court. Pressure and outspoken advocacy from a committee of prominent Chicago women with access to political and financial resources, including

LOUISE deKOVEN BOWEN, JANE ADDAMS, and JULIA LATHROP, hastened the establishment of the court. The juvenile court movement gained additional credibility and clout from support by professional women such as physicians SARAH HACKETT STEVENSON and JULIA HOLMES SMITH. Active advocacy also came from the Chicago Woman's Club, whose members campaigned for better detention conditions and special institutions for children. They were joined by the State Board of Public Charities, the Illinois Federation of Women's Clubs, the Chicago Bar Association, and the State Conference of Charities and Corrections.

The women reformers who advocated for the creation of Juvenile Court also participated as volunteers in the new system and, since the initial legislation did not provide funds, raised money to provide salaries for the court's first professional probation officers. Chicago Woman's Club members Julia Lathrop, Louise deKoven Bowen, LUCY FLOWER, Jane Addams, and HANNAH SOLOMON played an instrumental role in financing the probation officers of the court. By 1905, however, the legislature appropriated money for salaries, and the new court became one of the first welfare-related agencies to be run by professionally trained social workers.

In 1909, Irene Kawin graduated from the University of Chicago with two B.A. degrees—in philosophy and education—when opportunities for professional social workers were beginning to appear. After working briefly as a school teacher and as a social worker, Kawin began her career in 1913 as a Juvenile Court social worker, a position she held for five years. In 1918 she was appointed director of the Mothers' Pension division of the Chicago Juvenile Court. This division dealt with child dependency cases, which accounted for more than half of those heard by the court. A large percentage of those cases resulted from the death of or desertion by one or both parents. Other factors of parental "unfitness" that resulted in dependency, including drunkenness, immorality, illness, and insanity, also came before this court. Widowed and deserted mothers brought the majority of dependent cases to the court and frequently requested aid from public or private agencies. The Juvenile Court referred those families to private and public charities or, at times, sent children to training or industrial schools.

Kawin was named Deputy Chief Probation Officer of the Cook County Juvenile Court in 1927. She continued to focus on the disposition of children born to dependent, unmarried women. Sympathetic to the "terrible handicap under which the illegitimate child enters the world" ("The Illegitimate Child in the Juvenile Court," 1), Kawin thought the role of the court was to consider the situation of each child "as an individual problem" (p. 2). In many cases, illegitimacy was only one factor in the total situation; its relative importance to the other factors lessened with time when the mother raised her child as "merely a fatherless child" (p. 2). Those children, however, who required the services of the court in early infancy were Kawin's concern. Such children needed placement, if possible with relatives, in a boarding home, often in adoption. The complicated cases were those where the needs of the mother and the child had to be considered. Kawin was not convinced that every child should be put up for adoption. She acknowledged that many felt it was best always for the illegitimate child to be placed in adoption. Others believed that every effort should be made to keep mother and child together. Kawin asked, "Has the violation of our moral code—under who can know what stress?—deprived the mother forever of her right to that spiritual development which motherhood may bring?" ("The Illegitimate Child in the Juvenile Court," 4). She thought not. "In our work with unmarried mothers," Kawin counseled, "we must make it possible for them to make . . . decisions freely. The mother should not be coerced by relatives or others, nor persuaded, nor forced by economic considerations either to marry the father of her child, to keep the child, or to give it in adoption" (p. 4). Instead, Kawin advocated that the mother "should be given financial aid on the same basis she would receive it had her child been born in wedlock" (p. 4). This decision, Kawin contended, should not be made during a period of stress and insecurity. "We must make it possible for the new born babe to remain with its mother for a while at least" (p. 5) in order for her to realize what motherhood meant beyond the physical experience of pregnancy and delivery. Kawin advocated a list of rights or considerations for the single mother. She was entitled to decent shelter, wholesome food, and decent clothing, but "she must be expected to do as much as possible toward procuring these things for herself" (p. 7). She needed a happy, normal social life and had to be taught "how to find happiness in simple wholesome forms of recreation" (p. 7). Her educational development should not be neglected, and her "spiritual interests should be looked after as the interests of other young women in more fortunate circumstances . . . are cared for" (p. 7).

Kawin was critical of the lack of any coordinated community program in Chicago to deal with illegitimacy. This was a period of serious economic dislocation, the Great Depression years, and the welfare system—both private and public—was stretched beyond its capacities. Kawin suggested that there was a need for some agency or institution already dealing with the unmarried mother and her child to assume leadership. As a first step, she advocated establishing a nursery at the State Training School for Girls, Geneva, Illinois, where dozens of pregnant girls from all parts of the state were sent. Since the school lacked a facility for newborns, Kawin wrote, "when their babies arrive, either the girl must be released—in many cases, while she still needs institutional care—or her baby must be taken from her" ("The Illegitimate Child in the Juvenile Court," 8). In the Cook County Juvenile Court, where Kawin supervised the program, no young woman was asked to consent to the adoption of her baby while she was still within the walls of the institution, even though the court had to pay for the infant's board. Kawin looked to the political culture of maternalism, through the vehicle of women voting, for redress of the inadequacies that existed in the state system.

As Deputy Chief Probation Officer, Kawin advocated an enlightened approach that recognized the need for treatment for those on probation. Kawin realized that the average citizen, and even many judges, lawyers, and public officials, had a superficial idea of probation, visualizing it as giving the juvenile offender a second chance. This was a passive approach in which the probation officer basically observed and reported on the behavior of the offender. While social thinking on juvenile delinquency had

advanced to incorporate ideas about prevention, Kawin argued that prevention was not a substitute for treatment. "Even if Preventive agencies functioned with maximum effect, there would still be adults and children in the Courts, requiring effective treatment there" ("Modern Trends in Probation," 4). There were two ways to pursue treatment: the patient and family could voluntarily seek the help of the clinic; or, in the context of the court system itself, the child on probation could work with caseworkers who took a psychiatric approach. Some contended that Juvenile Court could not practice casework because it was essentially authoritarian, and psychiatric social work was non-authoritarian. Kawin contended in 1940 that modern social work had to accept the authoritarian setting in which those who worked in probation functioned. "Authority must be limited and clearly defined" ("Modern Trends in Probation," 5), she argued. "If properly applied, authority is not inconsistent with sympathetic understanding. A skillful case-worker can integrate modern case-work techniques into the authoritarian setting. Courts will become truly socialized only when the highest type of casework is an integral part of court procedure" (p. 5).

She recommended the creation of a state department of probation, to be run under a civil service administration, with a staff that would be required to have both experience and professional training in social work. "This department should serve in an advisory capacity to judges and probation officers throughout the State" (p. 5), she advised. She also advocated the "establishment of a merit system in Probation . . . requiring Judges to appoint as Probation Officers only those certified as eligible after a merit test conducted by the State" (p. 6).

Despite the strength of Kawin's qualifications, knowledge, and forcefulness, she was never named Chief Probation Officer, traditionally a position held by a man. If a system that valued gender more than qualifications rankled her, she endured without complaint at least until her final years of work, when her frustration with a burgeoning bureaucracy would become evident.

During the 1930s through 1960s, Helen Cannon and Helen Prochazka were Juvenile Court social workers under Kawin's supervision. Cannon recalled the tenuous status of all women employed in the legal system during this time. "Women attorneys were not respected in most courts at that time" (interview with Helen Cannon), Cannon reported. "However, most of the employees at the Juvenile Court were female assistant probation officers who were not respected. Few lawyers came to the Juvenile Court" (Cannon to Shirley Lundin, June 4, 1994). In the thirties, employees in Cook County also had to contend with depression-era scarce budgets.

Cannon and Prochazka both remembered Kawin as powerful yet pleasant; sympathetic yet objective; a clear-thinking, unflappable, and intelligent person who thrived in the intellectual atmosphere of the University of Chicago. Cannon and Prochazka spoke with respect and affection, describing Kawin as an imposing, well-groomed woman who could hold her own in the male-dominated court system. She required that all social workers in her division present case reports to a hearing committee for approval and supervision. It was an intimidating experience to give such a presentation, but Kawin offered support and encouragement.

As Deputy Chief Probation Officer, Kawin worked with women volunteers, continuing a tradition begun by reformers in the Progressive Era when the Juvenile Court system was first created. With professionalization of social work and increased use of paid probation workers, voluntarism was both criticized and diminished in importance. In her early years, Kawin had fully supported supplementary volunteer activities, writing letters between November 1935 and October 1940 to encourage and recognize the Mortar Board Project, a group of women who regularly provided enrichment activities for young wards of the court. However, in December 1969, she wrote a highly critical review of the book *Using Volunteers in Court Settings: A Manual for Volunteer Probation Programs* by Ivan H. Scheier and Leroy P. Goter. Refuting the book's claim that "volunteer services to the court setting began in the 1960s" ("Use of Volunteers in Probation," 67), she wrote, "This is inaccurate. Probation service began with volunteers; there has been a long struggle to convince the judiciary and the public that professional knowledge and casework techniques are essential in this field" (p. 67). Her adamant opposition to volunteers within a modern court setting reflected her lifelong struggle to professionalize and upgrade court services that originated with the volunteer "child saving" movement of the late nineteenth century.

Kawin's organizational and analytical acumen was solicited and respected by her colleagues in the court. In 1947, Judge Robert Jerome Dunne requested recommendations from her to improve the investigative division. Kawin's "professional integrity" (Kawin to Dunne, n.d., Kawin Papers) demanded she state that "this court as organized at present cannot serve dependent, neglected and delinquent children in Cook County effectively." She likened the Juvenile Court to an outmoded and badly abused 1913 model automobile. "We can repair it, oil it and adjust it . . . but we cannot" (Kawin to Dunne) make it perform really effectively. Referring to radical changes in casework philosophy and techniques over the preceding three decades, she prescribed smaller case loads, district reorganization, better training for personnel, and elimination of political appointees and senseless busy work.

Although Kawin continued to promote the intentional, skillful use of authoritarian techniques as an effective method in rehabilitating delinquents, in 1953 she questioned whether "drastic authority . . . [can] also serve to so rehabilitate the offender that he can be integrated into normal social life?" ("Therapeutic Uses of Authority," 4–5). Lambasting current, ineffective practices for rehabilitating delinquents and preventing juvenile delinquency, she recommended using authority appropriately in the context of a program "which focuses all effort on the rehabilitation of the delinquent" (p. 6). She criticized social workers and psychiatrists who deplored and avoided use of drastic authority entirely, "leaving it [instead] to the police, the courts" (p. 6).

When Kawin neared the end of her career, the Juvenile Court system (now called Family Court) had mushroomed. Her impatience with the bureaucracy grew evident. Kawin sarcastically and angrily protested having to sign caseworkers' time sheets, something she considered useless busy work and an obstacle to more important work. In 1960, she wrote to her supervisor, the Chief Probation Officer, "As a matter of my own professional integrity and in order to make clear that my standards are those of a professional probation officer, I wish to explain that my initials on a time sheet are not in any way vouching for its accuracy." She indicated that "there [were] many ways in which competent supervisors can know whether or not those they are supervising are performing honestly and satisfactorily" (Kawin to Edward J. Nerad, May 5, 1960, Kawin Papers). She defined the major role of the probation staff as service to clients and the community, not to bureaucratic red tape.

Kawin retired in 1962, but she continued to exert influence on the Juvenile Court system through speaking, writing, and critiquing books. In 1963, as a member of the Commission on Services for Children and Their Families, she helped prepare a report for an Illinois legislative committee. In her final years, she was confined to a wheelchair. Irene Kawin died at age eighty-eight. She is buried near her sister in Rosehill Cemetery, Chicago.

Irene Kawin dedicated her life to a social experiment that offered humane and intelligent treatment and service to children, youth, and families. Throughout her forty-nine years of service to the Cook County Juvenile Court, she demanded and prescribed sympathetic treatment for delinquent youth, both male and female, and their families. As early as 1933, she described the Juvenile Court as "the agency through which the state, as a loving parent, compensates for serious inadequacy in a child's natural home" ("The Illegitimate Child in the Juvenile Court," 1). Her defense of juvenile offenders, whether pregnant girls or delinquent boys, was matched only by her appeals to improve working conditions for probation officers and social workers through better training and reduced case load. The casework standards and methods she established were models for later systems. She gained stature in a male-dominated court system that measured achievement by gender through her professionalism in the female-intensive field of social work.

Sources. The Ethel and Irene Kawin Papers, UIC Spec. Coll., have correspondence, as well as Ethel Kawin's original manuscripts of articles, books, and papers presented at meetings, including "Modern Case Work in a Legal Setting," May 22, 1922; "The Illegitimate Child in the Juvenile Court," July 24, 1933; "Vitalizing Our Program of Parole," June 27, 1934; and "Modern Trends in Probation," April 25, 1940. Other unpublished reports include "Social Work as a Profession," November 1922. The Kawin Papers contain a book manuscript, "Therapeutic Use of Authority," dated September 1953. Her book review, "Use of Volunteers in Probation," of Ivan H. Scheier's and Leroy P. Goter's *Using Volunteers in Court Settings: A Manual for Volunteer Probation Programs*, appeared in *Federal Probation*, December 1969, and included her position on volunteerism. Shirley M. Lundin conducted two interviews: Helen Cannon was interviewed May 1994, with correspondence June 4, 1994; and Helen Prochazka was interviewed April 1994.

SHIRLEY M. LUNDIN

KELLEY, FLORENCE
September 12, 1859–February 17, 1932
SOCIAL REFORMER

Florence Kelley and her generation of white, middle-class, college-educated women reformers occupied an important turning point in American history during the Progressive Era between 1890 and 1920. Together they did much to shift the American

FIG. 61. *Social reformer Florence Kelley, Hull-House resident; appointed Chief Factory Inspector for Illinois in 1893 by Governor John Peter Altgeld.*

founding member of the Republican party, Radical Reconstructionist, and U.S. Congressman from Philadelphia from 1860 until his death in 1890, became her chief mentor, teaching her to read and instructing her in politics. Sarah Pugh, head of the Philadelphia Female Antislavery Society, a close friend of Lucretia Mott, and correspondent of British reformers such as Richard Cobden and John Bright, exemplified the ability of single women to devote their lives to reform causes. Kelley often visited her grandparents' home, where Sarah Pugh lived, and heard about the women's rights activism of Pugh and Mott. For her, Sarah Pugh became "conscience incarnate" (Sklar, *Florence Kelley*, 16).

During six mostly unschooled years before she entered Cornell University, Kelley systematically read her father's library, immersing herself in the fiction of Charles Dickens, William Makepeace Thackeray, Louisa May Alcott, and Horatio Alger; the poetry of William Shakespeare, John Milton, George Gordon Byron, and Oliver Goldsmith; the writings of James Madison; histories by George Bancroft, William Prescott, and Francis Parkman; and the moral and political philosophy of Ralph Waldo Emerson, Edward Channing, Edmund Burke, Thomas Carlyle, William Godwin, and Herbert Spencer.

Kelley's childhood was shaped as well by her mother's permanent depression—caused by the death of five of her eight children before they had reached the age of six. Two brothers but no sisters survived. Caroline Kelley developed a "settled, gentle melancholy" (Sklar, *Autobiography of Florence Kelley*, 30) that threatened to envelop her daughter so long as she lived at home.

At Cornell, Kelley studied history and social science, graduating in 1882. She spent her senior year in Washington, D.C., where she lived with her father and researched her honors essay in the Library of Congress. That essay, "On Some Changes in the Legal Status of the Child since Blackstone," was published in 1882 in the *International Review*. Facing a very limited set of opportunities after college, her application for graduate study having been rejected by the University of Pennsylvania on account of her sex, Kelley threw her energies into the New Century Working Women's Guild, an organization that fostered middle-class aid for self-supporting women. She helped found the guild, taught classes in history, and assembled the group's library.

Like higher education, the newly emerging field of social science served as another critical vehicle by which middle-class women expanded the space they occupied within American civic life between 1860 and 1890. Social science leveled the playing field on which women interacted with men in public life. It offered tools of analysis that enhanced women's ability to investigate economic and social change, speak for the welfare of society as a whole, devise policy initiatives, and oversee their implementation. Yet at the same time, social science also deepened women's gender identity in public life and attached their civic activism even more securely to gender-specific issues.

In the fall of 1882 Florence Kelley heralded the importance of women social scientists as molders of public policy. Her first writing after graduation, "Need Our Working Women Despair?" addressed an arresting ethical question. She answered it by recommending female-specific sociology as an antidote for

social contract from a Social Darwinist to a social interventionist basis. Social Darwinist views of the "survival of the fittest," derived from Charles Darwin's 1859 book, *Origin of Species*, promoted social policies that limited public responsibility for the welfare of poor people and wage-earning people in the 1870s and 1880s. Kelley and Progressive Era women reformers intervened in public life in ways that created new forms of governmental responsibility for working-class Americans. By creating minimum standards for working women and children, they provided a floor beneath which workers could not legally sink. Rejecting the notion that employers could impose whatever terms they wished on workers, they established the legal principle that society had an interest in regulating those terms.

Florence Kelley was born into a patrician Quaker and Unitarian family in Philadelphia, Pennsylvania, the daughter of William Darrah Kelley, a leading politician, and Caroline Bartram (Bonsall) Kelley, a descendant of John Bartram, the Quaker botanist. Kelley's rural residence and a childhood plagued by illness meant that she attended school only sporadically. Although her brief enrollment in Quaker schools introduced her to a wider reform world beyond her family and taught her mental discipline, most of her intellectual development occurred as part of her relationship with her father and her mother's aunt, Sarah Pugh. William Kelley, an abolitionist, despair. Together, college-trained women and wage-earning women could produce new knowledge capable of enhancing the lives of both. "In the field of sociology," she wrote, "there is brain work waiting for women which men cannot do" (Sklar, *Florence Kelley*, 69). The new "science of human relations" can only be complete "when accomplished by the whole human consciousness, i.e., by that two-fold nature, masculine and feminine, which expresses itself as a whole in human relations" (p. 70).

A dutiful daughter, in 1882 she accompanied her older brother when his doctor prescribed a winter of European travel to cure temporary blindness. In Europe she encountered M. Carey Thomas, a Cornell acquaintance, who had just completed a Ph.D. at the University of Zurich, the only European university that granted degrees to women. From 1883 to 1886 Kelley also studied there, initially accompanied by her mother and younger brother. Her focus on government and law brought her into contact with the vital group of Russian émigrés, and in 1884 she married Lazare Wischnewetzky, a Russian Jewish socialist medical student. The first of their three children, Nicholas, was born in July 1885.

Kelley also joined the German Social Democratic Party. Outlawed in Germany, the party maintained its European headquarters in Zurich, and Kelley met many of its leaders. Abandoning her pursuit of a postgraduate degree, she instead translated into English a classic work by Friedrich Engels, *The Conditions of the Working Class in England*, originally published in German in 1845. This project launched a close but troubled relationship with Engels that persisted until his death in 1895.

Kelley returned to the United States in the fall of 1886 with her husband and young son, taking up residence in New York City. Another child, Margaret, was born in 1886, and another son, John, in 1888. In New York she found it extremely difficult to continue the political commitments she had begun in Zurich. Her Philadelphia friend Rachel Foster Avery, then secretary of the National Woman Suffrage Association, financed the publication of her translation of Engel's *Condition* (the book listed Avery as the copyright holder), but Kelley's insistence on the importance of the writings of Marx and Engels led to her expulsion from the Socialist Labor Party in 1887. Party leaders resented Engel's preface to the *Condition*, which, at Kelley's urging, chastised the German-speaking majority of the party for its isolation from the American labor movement.

Forced to pursue a new path, Kelley returned to her interest in child labor. She quickly became known as a sharp critic of state bureaus of labor statistics for their inadequate attention to child labor, and she published articles on child labor in popular magazines. Her husband, meanwhile, never found his footing in the United States. His medical practice dwindled to nonexistence, and he began to beat his wife. At the end of 1891, Kelley fled with their children to Chicago, going first to the Woman's Temple headquarters of the Woman's Christian Temperance Union (WCTU). The Woman's Temple was a twelve-story office building and hotel constructed by the WCTU. The WCTU press had published her hard-hitting pamphlet, *Our Toiling Children* (1889); her editor there directed Kelley to Hull-House, the innovative social settlement founded by JANE ADDAMS

and ELLEN GATES STARR in 1889. "We were welcomed as though we had been invited," Kelley later wrote about her arrival at Hull-House. "We stayed" (Sklar, *Autobiography of Florence Kelley*, 77). There she lived happily and productively until 1899.

Chicago and the remarkable political culture of the city's women opened opportunities to Kelley that she had sought in vain in Philadelphia, Germany, and New York. Exploiting those opportunities to the fullest, she drew on the strength of three overlapping circles of politically active women. The core of her support lay in the community of women at Hull-House. This remarkable group helped her reconstruct her political identity within women's class-bridging activism and provided her with an economic and emotional alternative to married family life. Partly overlapping with this nucleus were women trade unionists. By drawing women and men trade unionists into the settlement community, she achieved the passage of pathbreaking legislation. Toward the end of her years in Chicago, she worked with the circle of middle-class and upper-middle-class women who supported Hull-House and labor reform.

Florence Kelley's productive life in Chicago began with her relationship with Jane Addams. JULIA LATHROP, another Hull-House resident, reported that Kelley and Addams "understood each other's powers" instantly and worked together in a "wonderfully effective way" (Addams, 77). Addams, with a deep and philosophical appreciation of the unity of life, was better able to construct a vehicle for expressing that unity in day-to-day living than she was capable of devising a diagram for charting the future. And Kelley, the politician with a thorough understanding of what the future should look like, was better able to invoke that future than to express it in her day-to-day existence. Addams taught Kelley how to live and have faith in an imperfect world, and Kelley taught Addams how to make demands on the future.

At Hull-House Kelley joined a community of college-educated women reformers who, like Addams and herself, sought work commensurate with their talents. Julia Lathrop, about twenty years later the first director of the U.S. Children's Bureau, had joined the settlement before Kelley. ALICE HAMILTON, who arrived in 1897, developed the field of industrial medicine. These four, with MARY ROZET SMITH, Jane Addams's life partner, became the settlement's main leaders. In addition to these women, Kelley forged close ties with Mary Kenney (see MARY KENNEY O'SULLIVAN), a trade union organizer affiliated with the settlement, who lived nearby with her mother.

Kelley exerted an immediate and dramatic influence on the generation of women reformers who clustered within the social settlement movement during the Progressive Era. Her understanding of the material basis of class conflict and her familiarity with American political institutions, combined with her spirited personality, placed her in the vanguard of a generation of reformers who sought to make American government more responsive to what they saw as the needs of working people. In this way they were critical components in the process by which American governments, state and national, shifted from liberal laissez-faire policies to positive regulatory programs.

Soon after her arrival in Chicago Kelley resumed the law

studies she had begun in Zurich, completing her degree at Northwestern University Law School in 1895. First, however, Addams helped Kelley place her children in the comfortable home of Henry Demarest Lloyd and Jessie Bross Lloyd in nearby Winnetka. Since her father had lost most of his money before his death in 1890, Kelley had to support herself and her children. Jane Addams aided Kelley's appointment as a special agent of the Illinois Bureau of Labor Statistics. In that capacity Kelley completed roughly one thousand forms by "sweaters victims" in the garment industry, first visiting them at work, then at home. Hearing of her reputation, Carroll Wright, head of the U.S. Department of Labor, hired her in the fall of 1892 to direct a cadre of "schedule men" who collected data from each house, tenement, and room in the 19th Ward, where Hull-House was located. With the help of other Hull-House residents, she used this data to compile pathbreaking occupational and nationality maps later printed in *Hull House Maps and Papers* (1895). Kelley and the other Hull-House residents, using only data about nationalities and wages in conjunction with residential information, created color-coded maps that displayed geographic patterns that told more than Wright's charts. Because the maps defined spatial relationships among human groups, they vividly depicted social and economic relationships: the concentration of certain ethnic groups in certain blocks; the relationship between poverty and race; the distances between the isolated brothel district and the rest of the ward; the very poor who lived in crowded, airless rooms in the rear of tenements and those with more resources in the front; and the omniscient observer and the observed. As an expression of the democratic relationship among Hull-House residents, *Hull House Maps and Papers* listed only "Residents of Hull House" as the volume's editors.

Kelley described the transformative effect of the Hull-House community on her personal life in a letter to her mother a few weeks after her arrival. "In the few weeks of my stay here I have won for the children and myself many and dear friends whose generous hospitality astonishes me. It is understood that I am to resume the maiden name and that the children are to have it" (Kelley to Caroline B. Kelley, Chicago, February 24, 1892, Nicholas Kelley Papers). By joining a community of women, she had achieved a new degree of personal autonomy.

Her forceful personality flourished at Hull-House. Jane Addams's nephew, who occasionally resided at the settlement, was awed by the way Kelley "hurled the spears of her thought with such apparent carelessness of what breasts they pierced" but nevertheless felt that she was "full of love" (Linn, 138). He thought her "the toughest customer in the reform riot, the finest rough-and-tumble fighter for the good life for others, that Hull House ever knew: Any weapon was a good weapon in her hand—evidence, argument, irony or invective" (p. 138).

In the spring of 1892, Kelley used Hull-House as a base to exert leadership within an anti-sweatshop campaign that had been launched in 1888 by the Illinois Woman's Alliance, a class-bridging coalition of women's organizations. One of the founders of the alliance, ELIZABETH MORGAN, British-born socialist and a leading member of the Chicago Trade and Labor Assembly, was already alienated from Mary Kenney and hence from Kelley. However, another alliance founder, CORINNE BROWN, daughter of a stair-maker, worked closely with Kelley.

For example, in 1892 she and Brown coauthored a report on the condition of the public schools of Chicago in which they denounced the board of education and the city council for their neglect of children in poor wards. That year the leadership of the anti-sweatshop movement passed from Morgan and the Illinois Woman's Alliance to Kelley and Hull-House. At mass meetings that attacked the sweatshop system, Kelley shared the podium with Mary Kenney, Henry Demarest Lloyd, and other Chicago notables such as Reverend Jenkin Lloyd Jones, minister at All Souls' Unitarian Church, the most liberal pulpit in Chicago, and with such young trade union organizers in the clothing industry as Abraham Bisno.

Campaigns against sweatshops were widespread in American cities in the 1890s. These efforts targeted "predatory management" and "parasitic manufacturers" (Sklar, "Two Political Cultures," 58), who paid such low wages to their workers as to require them to seek support from relief or charity, thereby indirectly providing employers with subsidies that enabled them to lower wages further. Supported by trade unions, these campaigns used a variety of strategies to shift work from tenement sweatshops to factories. In factories, union organizing could more easily succeed in improving working conditions and raising wages to levels necessary to sustain life.

Outcries raised by anti-sweatshop campaigns prompted government inquiries and, in 1893 after intense lobbying in Springfield by Hull-House residents and other well-known Chicago women, the passage of pathbreaking legislation drafted by Florence Kelley. That year Governor John Peter Altgeld appointed Kelley to a position the new statute created: Chief Factory Inspector of Illinois. Nowhere else in the Western world was a woman trusted to enforce the labor legislation of a city, let alone of a large industrial region the size of Illinois. With eleven deputies, five of whom were required to be women, and a budget of twenty-eight thousand dollars, for the next three years Kelley enforced the act's chief clauses. The act banned the labor of children under fourteen years of age; it regulated the labor of children age fourteen to sixteen; it outlawed the production of garments in tenements; it prohibited the employment of women and minors for more than eight hours a day; and it created a state office of factory inspection.

The statute's eight-hour clause made it the most advanced in the United States, equaled only by an eight-hour law for all workers in Australia. The limitation of hours, whether through statutes or union negotiations with employers, was the second most important goal of the labor movement between 1870 and 1910, the first being the recognition of the right of workers to form unions. Skilled workers had acquired the eight-hour day for themselves in many trades by the 1890s, but since women were not admitted to most skilled occupations, their hours remained long, often extending to twelve or even fourteen hours a day. In the late 1880s more than 85 percent of female wage earners were between the ages of fourteen and twenty-five and only about 5 percent were married. Excluded from access to skilled jobs and presumed to leave the paid labor force upon marriage, they were crowded into a few unskilled occupations, where they were easily replaced, and employers exploited them by requiring long hours and paying low wages. Statutes that limited women's hours limited this exploitation. Reduction of hours without reduction of wages was a challenge that Kelley's office met by promoting the formation of unions among affected women workers, thereby helping them negotiate better wages for the hours they worked.

The reduction of women's hours by statute had other beneficial effects; in many occupations it also reduced the hours of unskilled men, as was the case in garment-making sweatshops. In this and many other occupations, it proved impossible to keep men working longer than the legal limit of the working day for women. In this way, hours statutes drove sweatshops out of business, since their profits could only be achieved through long hours. In the United States more than in other industrializing nations, the union movement consisted, with few exceptions (miners chief among them), of skilled workers who shunned responsibility for the welfare of unskilled workers. Therefore, in the United States more than elsewhere, gender-specific reforms like Kelley's 1893 legislation—undertaken by women for women—also had the effect of aiding all unskilled workers, men as well as women and children. In the United States, where labor movements were not as strong as they were in other countries, gender-specific reforms accomplished goals that elsewhere were achieved under the auspices of class-specific efforts.

Kelley's first steps in enforcing Illinois's new law were smart: she located her office close to Hull-House, and she chose AL-ZINA PARSONS STEVENS as her chief assistant. Stevens had risen to national prominence in the Knights of Labor in Toledo in the 1880s and moved to Chicago to coedit the *Vanguard*, a weekly newspaper promoting economic and industrial reform. When Stevens joined Kelley's staff, she moved into Hull-House. Mary Kenney and Abraham Bisno also served as deputy inspectors.

In an era when courts nullified legislative attempts to intervene in the laissez-faire relationship between capital and labor, it was inevitable that Kelley's enforcement of this new eight-hour law would be challenged in the courts. In 1895 the Illinois Supreme Court found the eight-hour clause of the 1893 law unconstitutional because it violated women's right to contract their labor on any terms set by their employer. This setback made Kelley determined to change the power of state courts to overturn hours laws for women.

The high tide of Kelley's achievements between 1893 and 1896 ebbed quickly when Altgeld lost the election of 1896. His successor replaced her with a person who did not challenge the economic status quo, and she was unable to find work commensurate with her talents. German admirers came to her rescue. For fifty dollars a month she provided a leading German reform periodical with assessments of recent American social legislation. She also worked in the Crerar Library, a reference library specializing in economic, scientific, and medical topics.

Needing to reach beyond the limits of Hull-House activities, Kelley began to work more closely with ELLEN HENROTIN. Wife of a leading Chicago banker, Henrotin had supported Kelley's legislation in 1892 and spoke vigorously at a rally to defend the law in 1894, urging those in attendance to "agitate for shorter hours for women because it means in the end shorter hours for all workers, men and women" ("Hit at Sweat Shops"). Henrotin's organization in 1893 of thirty women's congresses at the World's Columbian Exposition catapulted her into the presidency of the General Federation of Women's Clubs (GFWC founded 1890) from 1894 to 1898. By 1897 the GFWC served as an umbrella organization for more than five hundred women's clubs, including the powerful Chicago Woman's Club. Fostering the creation of more than twenty state federations to coordinate those clubs, Henrotin moved the GFWC in progressive directions by establishing national committees on industrial working conditions and national health. In this way she directed the path of what was to become one of the largest grassroots organizations of American women beyond the minimal goals of good government and civil service reform to the more challenging issues of social inequalities and social justice.

Reflecting her growing awareness of the potential power of women's organizations as a vehicle for her social justice agenda, in 1897 Kelley began to work closely with Henrotin in organizing an Illinois Consumers' League. They built on the example of the New York Consumers' League, which had been founded in 1891 to channel consumers' consciousness toward political action on behalf of workers who made the goods that consumers purchased.

Kelley's work with Henrotin helped her make the biggest career step of her life when, in 1899, she agreed to serve as secretary of the newly formed National Consumers' League (NCL), a position she held until her death in 1932. With a salary of fifteen hundred dollars plus traveling and other expenses, the job offered financial stability and a chance to develop a more radical and more focused women's organization than the GFWC. This position took her to New York, where between 1899 and 1926 she lived at the Henry Street settlement, Lillian Wald's "nurses' settlement" on Manhattan's Lower East Side. Her children moved with her. Supported by aid from Mary Rozet Smith, Nicholas Kelley graduated from Harvard in 1905 and then from Harvard Law School. He remained in Manhattan and became his mother's closest adviser. In a blow that caused Kelley to spend the rest of the year in retirement in Maine, her daughter Margaret Kelley died of heart failure during her first week at Smith College in 1905. After this bereavement Kelley maintained a summer home on Penobscot Bay, Maine, where she retreated for periods of intense work with a secretary each summer. John Kelley never found a professional niche but remained close to his mother and joined her in Maine each summer.

Kelley made the National Consumers' League into the nation's leading promoter of protective legislation for women and children. Between 1900 and 1904 she built sixty-four local consumer leagues—one in nearly every large city outside the South. Through a demanding travel schedule, which meant that she spent one day on the road for every day she worked at her desk, Kelley maintained close contact with local leagues, urging them to implement the national organization's agenda and inspiring them to greater action within their states and municipalities.

Aiding the development of local leagues was the NCL's campaign to promote the adoption of the Consumers' White Label among local manufacturers. The national branch of the consumers' league had been formed in 1898 to coordinate the efforts of previously existing leagues in New York City, Brooklyn, Philadelphia, Boston, and Chicago, all of which had conducted campaigns against sweatshops. Kelley was a leader within this movement, and that year, at a convention of the locals called to coordinate their anti-sweatshop efforts, she proposed the creation of a consumers' label as a way of identifying goods made under fair conditions. Her proposal galvanized the convention into creating a national organization "for the express purpose of offering a Consumers' League Label" nationally, recognizing that local efforts against sweatshops could never succeed until all producers were "compelled to compete on a higher level" (Sklar, *Florence Kelley*, 309) and agreeing that the label could be a means of achieving that goal.

The NCL awarded its label to manufacturers who obeyed state factory laws, produced goods only on their own premises, did not require employees to work overtime, and did not employ children under sixteen years of age. In determining whether local factories qualified for the label, league members learned a great deal about local working conditions. Factories had to be inspected, and local leagues employed their own factory inspectors. Kelley became the league's national inspector. The inspectors prepared local groups for the next stage of league work—the promotion of state laws limiting the working day of women to ten hours. The NCL also promoted its agenda through alliances with mainstream women's organizations. Between 1900 and 1902, within the General Federation of Women's Clubs, Kelley chaired NCL's standing committee on the Industrial Problem as It Affects Women and Children, and in 1903 she chaired the child labor committees in both the National Congress of Mothers and the National American Woman Suffrage Association. In her 1905 book, *Some Ethical Gains through Legislation*, Kelley argued that for working children, women, and men, "the right to leisure is a human right in process of recognition as a statutory right" (p. 168).

In determining whether local factories qualified for the consumers' label, local league members had to educate themselves about local working conditions. They had to pose and answer questions new to middle-class women, though painfully familiar to union organizers: Did the manufacturer subcontract to home workers in tenements? Were children employed? Were state factory laws violated? Could workers live on their wages or were they forced to augment their pay with relief or charitable donations? How far below the standard set by the consumers' label were their own state laws? Even more technical questions arose when leagues came into contact with factory inspectors, bureaus of labor statistics, state legislatures, and courts. Should the state issue licenses for home workers? What was the relationship between illiteracy in child workers and the enforcement of effective child labor laws? Was their own state high or low on the NCL's ranked list showing the number of illiterate child workers in each? Should laws prohibit the labor of children at age fourteen or sixteen? Should exceptions be made for the children of widows? How energetically were state factory laws enforced? How could local factory standards be improved? These questions, recently quite alien to middle-class women, now held the interest of thousands of the most politically active among them. This was no small accomplishment. State leagues differed in the degree to which they worked with state officials, but wherever they existed they created new civic space in which women used their new knowledge and power to expand state responsibility for the welfare of women and children workers.

On the road steadily between 1900 and 1907, Kelley inspected workshops, awarded the label to qualified manufacturers, and strengthened local leagues. Her efforts were rewarded by the spectacular growth of NCL locals, both in number and location. The NCL's 1901 report mentioned thirty leagues in eleven states; by 1906 they numbered sixty-three in twenty states. The Massachusetts league described the effects of Kelley's leadership in 1903: "[She] can travel from one end of the Continent to the other without losing her hold upon local problems in State Leagues the farthest removed from her bodily presence, stirring our zeal and opening new fields for our activity by letters, which are prompt and full as if letter writing were the chief occupation of her day" ("Consumers' League of Massachusetts," NCL, *Fourth Annual Report*, 37–39). Mrs. Kelley, the report concluded, "gives us service which it is impossible to overestimate" (p. 39).

Flourishing local leagues sustained the national's existence, channeling money, ideas, and the support of other local groups into the national office. At the same time locals implemented the national agenda at the state level. Most league members were white, urban, northern, middle-class Protestants, but Jewish women held important positions of leadership. Catholic women became more visible after Cardinal James Gibbons of Baltimore consented to serve as vice-president of a Maryland league, and Bishop J. Regis Canevin of Pittsburgh encouraged members of that city's Ladies Catholic Benevolent Association to join. Two important reasons for the absence of black women from the NCL's membership and agenda were the league's focus on northern urban manufacturing and the residence of 90 percent of the nation's black population in the South in 1900, where they were employed primarily in agriculture. Nevertheless, in 1903 the Massachusetts league undertook a systematic effort "to enlist the wives of farmers through the Farmers' Institutes, Granges, etc." ("Consumers' League of Massachusetts," NCL *Fourth Annual Report*, 7).

Having accomplished the task of educating her constituency by 1907, Kelley implemented a second stage of league work. With the use of social science data, the NCL overcame legal obstacles to the passage of state laws limiting women's working hours. The overturning of Illinois's 1893 law by the Illinois Supreme Court in 1895 made Kelley determined to defend such laws before the U.S. Supreme Court. When an Oregon ten-hour law came before the court in 1907, she threw the resources of the NCL into its defense. This case, *Muller v. Oregon*, pitted the NCL and its Oregon branch against a laundry owner who disputed the state's authority to regulate working hours in nonhazardous occupations. For what became known as the "Brandeis Brief," Kelley's research director, Josephine Goldmark, gathered printed evidence from medical and other authorities (most of whom were British or European) to demonstrate that work days longer than ten hours were hazardous to the health of women. Goldmark obtained the services of her brother-in-law, Louis D. Brandeis, a leading Boston attorney, who successfully argued the case on sociological rather than legal grounds, using the evidence that Goldmark had compiled. Thus at the same time that this case cleared the way for state hours laws for women, it also established the court's recognition of sociological evidence, which, for example, in *Brown v. Board of Education of Topeka, Kansas*, in 1954 sustained the court's ruling against segregated schools.

In the years immediately following the *Muller* decision, inspired by Kelley's leadership, and supported by other groups, local consumer leagues gained the passage in twenty states of the first laws limiting women's working hours. Also responding to the decision, nineteen other states revised and expanded their laws governing women's working hours.

The Supreme Court's 1908 opinion tried to block the possibility of extending such protections to men by emphasizing women's special legal status (they did not possess the same contractual rights as men), and their physiological difference from men (their health affected the health of their future children). Nevertheless, in 1917 Kelley and the NCL again cooperated successfully with the Oregon league in arguing another case on sociological grounds before the U.S. Supreme Court, *Bunting v. Oregon*, in which the Court upheld the constitutionality of hours laws for men in nonhazardous occupations. Viewing laws for women as an entering wedge for improving conditions for all working people, Kelley achieved that goal in the progression from *Muller* to *Bunting*. In this as in other aspects of her work with the league, though nominally focused on gender, her reforms had class-wide effects.

As early as 1899 Florence Kelley had hoped "to include a requirement as to minimal wages" (Kelley, "Aims and Principles of the Consumers' League," 298) in the NCL's White Label. Australia and New Zealand had already organized wage boards as part of compulsory arbitration, but the path to an American equivalent did not seem clear until 1908, when she and other Consumers' League members attended the First International Conference of Consumers' Leagues, in Geneva, where they learned about the proposed British wage law, eventually passed in 1909, which implemented minimum wages for all workers in certain poorly paid occupations.

Almost immediately on her return Kelley established her leadership in what became an enormously successful campaign for minimum wage laws for women in the United States. In her campaign she denounced the large profits made in three industries: retail stores, sweatshop garment making, and textile manufacturers. "Low wages produce more poverty than all other causes together," she insisted, urging that "goods and profits are not ends in themselves to which human welfare may continue to be sacrificed" (Kelley, "Minimum Wage Boards," 303–14).

Kelley argued that minimum wages would raise the standards in women's employment by recognizing their need to support themselves. "So long as women's wages rest upon the assumption that every woman has a husband, father, brother, or lover contributing to her support, so long these sinister incidents of women's industrial employment (tuberculosis, insanity, vice) are inevitable." She urged that "society itself must build the floor beneath their feet" (Kelley, "Ten Years from Now," 978–81). Wage legislation "pierces to the heart the classic claim that industry is a purely private affair" (Sklar, "Two Political Cultures," 60). Kelley and the NCL were unaided in their efforts by their male-dominated equivalent, the American Association for Labor Legislation (AALL), which thought the wage campaign too radical. When Kelley appealed for aid in 1910 to AALL's execu-

tive director, John Andrews, he loftily replied: "I question very seriously the wisdom of injecting the minimum wage proposal into the legislative campaign of this year, because I do not believe our courts would at the present time uphold such legislation, and I am afraid it would seriously jeopardize the splendid progress now being made to establish maximum working hours" (Andrews to Eric Stern, New York, December 14, 1910, American Association for Labor Legislation Papers). Two years later the AALL still opposed wage legislation as premature.

Kelley and the NCL were able to move ahead with this pathbreaking legislation because they could mobilize grassroots support for it at local and state levels. The AALL had no local branches; instead, their power flowed from a network of male academic experts who advised politicians about legislation. If politicians were not ready to move, neither was the AALL. The NCL, by contrast, had in its sixty-four local branches enough political muscle to take the initiative and lead politicians where they otherwise would not have gone.

In 1912 Massachusetts passed the first minimum wage law for women, followed in 1913 by eight additional states: California, Colorado, Minnesota, Nebraska, Oregon, Utah, Washington, and Wisconsin. By 1919 fourteen states and the District of Columbia and Puerto Rico had enacted minimum wage statutes for women. The success of these laws informed the inclusion of a minimum wage for men and women in the Fair Labor Standards Act (FLSA) of 1938. In 1942, when the U.S. Supreme Court approved the constitutionality of the FLSA, the eight-hour day and the minimum wage become part of the social contract for most American workers. The class-bridging activism of middle-class women in the NCL forged the way with these fundamental reforms.

At Henry Street, Kelley continued to benefit from the same consolidation of female reform talents that had sustained her efforts at Hull-House in Chicago. For example, the creation of the U.S. Children's Bureau in 1911 sprang from her discussions with Lillian Wald. The Children's Bureau was the only governmental agency in any industrial society that was headed and run by women. Kelley thought that her most important contribution to social change was the passage in 1921 of the Sheppard-Towner Maternity and Infancy Protection Act, which first allocated federal funds to health care. She was instrumental in the creation of the coalition that backed the act's passage, the Women's Joint Congressional Committee, and in the coalition's successful campaign for the bill in Congress. Although limited to a program administered by the Children's Bureau to combat infant and maternal mortality, Kelley thought the Sheppard-Towner Act marked the beginning of a national health care program.

After this high point in 1921, however, the decade brought a series of reversals that threatened to undo most of her achievements. In 1923 the U.S. Supreme Court in *Adkins v. Children's Hospital* found the Washington, D.C., wage law for women unconstitutional. Although many state wage boards continued to function during the 1920s and 1930s, providing ample evidence of the benefits of the law, no new wage laws were passed. In 1926, Congress refused to allocate new funds for Sheppard-Towner programs, and the responsibility for maternal and infant health returned to the state and county level.

Just as important, by 1922 Kelley's strategy of using gender-specific legislation as a surrogate for class legislation had generated opposition from a new quarter—women who did not themselves benefit from gendered laws. The National Woman's Party (NWP), formed in 1916 through the charismatic leadership of Alice Paul and funded almost entirely by Alva Belmont, created a small coalition consisting primarily of professional women with some wage-earning women who worked in male-dominated occupations. Despite Kelley's strong objections about the damage they would do to gender-specific legislation, including the Sheppard-Towner Act, the NWP proposed an Equal Rights Amendment to the U.S. Constitution (ERA) in 1921. Although mainstream organizations such as the General Federation of Women's Clubs and the League of Women Voters continued to support gender-specific legislation, the NWP's proposed amendment undercut the momentum of such gendered strategies. In the 1920s most wage-earning women opposed the ERA because they stood to lose rather than benefit from it. By the 1970s, changes in working conditions and protective labor laws meant that most wage-earning women stood to benefit from the amendment and many more supported it.

Even more damaging than these reversals, however, were the right-wing attacks launched by hyper-patriots against Kelley and other women reformers during the "red scare" of the 1920s. *Woman Patriot* exemplified these attacks. Launched in 1916 and published twice a month, this newsletter was subtitled, before the enactment of the woman suffrage amendment, *Dedicated to the Defense of Womanhood, Motherhood, the Family and the State AGAINST Suffragism, Feminism and Socialism.* After 1920, the newsletter dropped its reference to suffrage but continued its virulent attacks on the social agenda of women reformers. "Shall Bolshevist-Feminists Secretly Govern America?" their headlines screamed, referring to the Sheppard-Towner Act. When the *Woman Patriot* referred to Kelley as "Mrs. Wischnewetzky" and called her "Moscow's chief conspirator" (November 1, 1921, 1), Kelley urged Addams to join her in a libel suit against them. Addams gently persuaded her to ignore the attacks. Kelley then wrote an impassioned series of autobiographical articles that established her lineage as an inheritor of American ideals and a dedicated promoter of American values.

Attacks on women reformers in the 1920s were in part generated by supporters of American military expansion in the aftermath of World War I, when Kelley and many other women reformers were actively promoting peace and disarmament. For example, the *Woman Patriot* characterized the support that women reformers were giving to disarmament as "an organized internationalist Bolshevist-Feminist plot to embarrass the Limitation of Armaments Conference" (Harper, website). Government employees joined the attack in 1924, when Lucia Maxwell of the Chemical Warfare Department of the Department of War issued a "Spider Web Chart" entitled "The Socialist-Pacifist Movement in America Is an Absolutely Fundamental and Integral Part of International Socialism." Depicting the connections between women's organizations and congressional lobbying for social legislation and for disarmament, the chart sought to characterize as "pacifist-socialist" most women's organizations in the United States, including the National Consumers' League, the League of Women Voters, the General Federation of Women's Clubs, the Woman's Christian Temperance Union, the National Congress of Mothers and Parent Teacher Association, the National Women's Trade Union League, the American Home Economics Association, the American Association of University Women, the National Council of Jewish Women, the Girls' Friendly Society, the Young Women's Christian Association, and the National Federation of Business and Professional Women.

Historians have not measured the effect of these attacks on the political agendas of women's organizations, but after these attacks the agendas of many women's organizations, for example that of the League of Women Voters, shifted from social justice to good government projects, from support for a Child Labor Amendment to the U.S. Constitution, and to advocacy for a city manager forms of governance. Such a shift was in keeping with the demise of the progressive movement after World War I, but that demise was hastened by the rise of "red scare" tactics in American political culture.

Florence Kelley did not live to see that many of her initiatives were incorporated into federal legislation in the 1930s. Faced with the collapse of the American economy in the Great Depression of 1929–39, policy makers drew heavily on the legacy of progressive reforms initiated between 1890 and 1920. Florence Kelley's legacy, including minimum wage and maximum hours legislation incorporated in the Fair Labor Standards Act of 1938, was strong enough to survive the reversals of the 1920s. In 1933, with the inauguration of Franklin Delano Roosevelt as president, Kelley's protégée, Frances Perkins, became the first woman to serve as a cabinet member. Reflecting the power of women's organizations in shaping a new social contract for American working people, Perkins was appointed Secretary of Labor.

Kelley's legacy reaches beyond any specific policies. U.S. Supreme Court Justice Felix Frankfurter said in 1953 that the nation owed Kelley an "enduring debt for the continuing process she so largely helped to initiate, by which social legislation is promoted and eventually gets on the statute books" (foreword to Goldmark, v). As Kelley shaped it during her long reform career between 1890 and 1930, that process relied heavily on women's organizations and their ability to act independently of the political status quo.

Sources. Florence Kelley's personal papers are at the New York Public Library. The National Consumer League Papers are located at the Library of Congress. Other related collections include the Jane Addams Papers at Swarthmore College, Swarthmore, Pennsylvania; the Nicholas Kelley Papers at the New York Public Library; the Lillian Wald Papers at the New York Public Library and at Columbia Univ.; the Consumers' League of Massachusetts Papers at SL; the American Association for Labor Legislation Papers, Cornell Univ.; and the Henry Demarest Lloyd Papers at the State Hist. Soc. of Wisconsin. Kelley's writings are voluminous. Her brief autobiography has been reprinted as *The Autobiography of Florence Kelley: Notes of Sixty Years*, ed. Kathryn Kish Sklar (1986). See also Kelley's book, *Some Ethical Gains through Legislation* (1905), as well as "Aims and Principles of the Consumers' League," *American Journal of Sociology*, November 1899; "Minimum Wage Boards," *American Journal of Sociology*, November 1911; "Ten Years from Now," *Survey*, March 26, 1910. See the National Consumers' League, "Consumers' League of Massachusetts," *Fourth Annual Report,*

1903. Kathryn Kish Sklar's essay, "Florence Kelley," from which this profile in part is drawn, is in *American National Biography*, edited by John A. Garraty and Mark C. Carnes, copyright 1999 by the American Council of Learned Societies. Reprinted by permission of Oxford University Press, Inc. For a most complete account of Kelley's life before 1900 and for a bibliography of her writings before 1900, see Sklar, *Florence Kelley and the Nation's Work: The Rise of Women's Political Culture, 1830–1900* (1995). On the eight-hour law, see "Hit at Sweat Shops," *CT*, April 23, 1894. For the National Consumers' League's minimum wage work, see Sklar, "Two Political Cultures in the Progressive Era: The National Consumers' League and the American Association for Labor Legislation," in *U.S. History as Women's History: New Feminist Essays*, ed. Linda K. Kerber et al. (1995). See also Nicholas Kelley, "Early Days at Hull House," *Social Service Review*, December 1954; Felix Frankfurter, foreword to Josephine Goldmark, *Impatient Crusader: Florence Kelley's Life Story* (1953); and Dorothy Rose Blumberg, "Dear 'Mr. Engels': Unpublished Letters, 1884–1894, of Florence Kelley (Wischnewetzky) to Friedrich Engels," *Labor History*, Spring 1964; Dorothy Rose Blumberg, *Florence Kelley: The Making of a Social Pioneer* (1966); and Louis Athey, "The Consumers' Leagues and Social Reform, 1890–1923" (Ph.D. diss., Univ. of Delaware, 1965). Jane Addams, *My Friend Julia Lathrop* (1935), and James Weber Linn, *Jane Addams: A Biography* (1938), discuss the relationship of Kelley and Addams. The red scare opposition to Kelley is in the *Woman Patriot*, November 1, 1921. For the correspondence between Kelley and Jane Addams regarding attacks on them, see Anissa Harper, "Pacifism vs. Patriotism in Women's Organizations in the 1920s: How Was the Debate Shaped by the Expansion of the American Military," in *Women and Social Movements in the United States, 1830–1930*, an Internet website edited by Kathryn Kish Sklar and Thomas Dublin, *http://womhist.binghamton.edu*. Obituaries are in *NYT* and the *Boston Evening Globe*, both February 18, 1932.

KATHRYN KISH SKLAR

KELLOGG TYLER, ALICE DeWOLF

December 27, 1862–February 14, 1900

PAINTER, ART INSTRUCTOR, ILLUSTRATOR

Alice Kellogg was the fifth of six daughters born to Dr. John Leonard and Harriet (Scott) Kellogg. In 1851, Dr. Kellogg, a homeopathic physician, moved his family west from Manlius, New York, settling in Englewood, a Chicago suburb. The Kelloggs were members of the Unitarian Church and were interested in Christian Science, Theosophy, and the ideas of Emmanuel Swedenborg, founder of Swedenborgianism. Alice Kellogg maintained a lifelong interest in metaphysical subjects. The family eventually moved to a seventy-acre farm south of the city in what is now the South Side suburb of Evergreen Park. Education was encouraged and the family read extensively; Emerson and Thoreau were among their favorites. Kate Starr Kellogg, Alice's older sister, had begun a career as a teacher and administrator with the Chicago public schools. As closest sister and confidant, she offered Alice Kellogg a role model of an independent career woman. In 1879, Kellogg enrolled in the new Academy of Fine Arts, established as the Chicago Academy of Design in 1866, where she made rapid progress. By the time the Academy became the Art Institute of Chicago in 1882, Kellogg had been awarded a scholarship and was appointed assistant instructor under Henry F. Spread, one of the academy's founders.

In 1880, Kellogg and a friend, Marie Koupal, along with a handful of other students, established the Bohemian Art Club, one of the first art associations for women in Chicago. Membership in the organization, named for Koupal's nationality, grew rapidly as the club became a much needed support system for serious women artists. The group met on Saturdays for discussions, to give criticisms of each other's work, and to sketch from live models. Each summer the group went off to camp to sketch for two weeks in the country. In 1883, the club held its first annual art exhibition at the Art Institute of Chicago.

At this time Kellogg became attracted to Arthur B. Davies from Utica, New York, one of her students at the Art Institute and later a nationally recognized painter. Their relationship developed as the two spent time together painting, sketching, and discussing their common interest in metaphysics.

By the mid-1880s, Kellogg had opened a studio in the Central Music Hall building with Ida C. Haskell, another artist and her best friend. During this period, Kellogg held private classes in the studio and out-of-doors and taught as well at the Art Institute. In 1887, Kellogg and Haskell resolved to study in Europe to advance their training in figure painting. In October of that year, they traveled to Paris, accompanied by Kellogg's sister Gertrude and Haskell's mother. Davies, unable to afford a European education, left Chicago to seek his fame and fortune in New York City.

The young women joined several other Bohemian Art Club members in Paris, including Pauline Dohn, Eva Webster, Anna Page Scott, and Nan Stanley. The group roomed together to defray expenses for rent and studios. Kellogg entered L'École Julian in Paris, studying under the masters Gustave Boulanger and Jules Lefebvre. She also attended classes at the studio of American teacher Charles Lasar. After only a year of study, she had a drawing accepted in the Paris Salon, the official exhibition of art annually sponsored by the French government. In the summer of 1888 Kellogg and several colleagues traveled to Rijsoord, Holland, to sketch and to tour art museums as a major part of their European education.

That fall, Kellogg and some of her friends moved to the Latin Quarter of Paris to be near to the Colarossi School, where she studied under the masters Gustave Courtois, Jean Rixens, and Pascal Dagnan-Bouveret.

Kellogg debated whether to enroll in a coeducational sketching class that employed nude models. She loved the freedom given the students in Paris but not the liberties taken by French men. She was surprised and disappointed at the harassment and lack of respect given women students. "These French men are not decent," she wrote to her family (letter to her mother, October 25, 1888).

Once settled in, however, she enjoyed herself tremendously at Colarossi's school. "One has the utmost liberty. . . . We go in the forenoon from eight to twelve, then home to a good lunch after which we go to the galleries, to interesting places about Paris, coming home to dinner at nearly six, then two hours of talking, reading, or writing [letters] when we again sally forth to the evening class. This is great fun!" (Kellogg to her family, November 2, 1888).

In 1889, Kellogg spent six weeks touring the museums of Italy and made a brief visit to Switzerland. Upon returning, she learned that another of her drawings had been accepted in the Paris Salon. At the same time, a portrait of her sister Gertrude,

Miss G.E.K., was accepted in the Fine Arts Pavilion at the Paris Universal Exposition. The 1889 Paris Exposition was the largest and most diverse world's fair to date. Although there were 572 works exhibited in the American fine arts section, Kellogg and Frederick Freer were the only Chicagoans represented at the fair. Other Americans who exhibited were William Merritt Chase, Elizabeth Jane Gardner, and John Singer Sargent. In the studio, Kellogg hired a model and quietly painted a picture of a mother and baby entitled *The Mother*.

In August 1889, Kellogg took a steamboat back to the United States, stopping in New York to see Davies. During their separation, the two artists had kept up their romance, sending each other letters and gifts. Several times Kellogg had written home that she and Davies were considering marriage.

Upon her return to Chicago, Kellogg opened a studio. While in Paris, she had acquired new techniques, including a knowledge of "frotte," a process of washing in a transparent layer of approximate colors and values, onto a clean canvas, in order to establish and evaluate the composition before proceeding with final application of the pigment. In addition she had begun to experiment with rendering her subjects in an outdoor setting, a style developed by the impressionists, as opposed to her earlier, more traditional, academic landscapes and indoor portraits. Building upon these new techniques, she continued her artwork in Chicago and saw demand for her compositions and portraits grow. At the time, Kellogg was planning to marry Davies and continue her career in New York. For reasons unknown, Davies abruptly ended the relationship, marrying another woman in 1892. Kellogg responded to the unexpected loss by increasing her workload, although she did not resume her teaching position at the Art Institute until 1892.

In 1890 Kellogg became associated with the social settlement at Hull-House, established by JANE ADDAMS and ELLEN GATES STARR in 1889. Already known for its advocacy and leadership of the arts and crafts movement in the city, Hull-House attracted artists, craftswomen, and craftsmen and was one of the significant art enclaves in late nineteenth-century Chicago. Jane Addams recalled Kellogg as the first among the Chicago artists who generously gave service to Hull-House. Kellogg began lecturing, teaching art, and exhibiting her work at Hull-House during the 1890s. She taught in the studio of Hull-House's Butler Gallery during the spring of 1892. Kellogg eventually developed close relationships with Jane Addams and with many Hull-House residents and associates.

In 1891, Kellogg drew national attention when her painting *The Mother* was accepted for exhibition by the Society of American Artists in New York. Soon thereafter, Kellogg was inducted as a member of this prestigious organization. She was the first Chicagoan and the only midwestern artist at the time to be admitted to the association. As a result, Kellogg was the featured artist in *Century Magazine*'s Series of American Artists in January 1893, and *The Mother* was illustrated on the cover.

The Bohemian Art Club was gaining influence. In 1888, the group's name was changed to the Palette Club to reflect the professionalism that it had attained. During the economic depression of the 1890s, paintings became difficult to sell. The Palette Club members decided to reduce the size of their paintings to make them more affordable to the public. This decision proved

a wise business move. Kellogg produced many paintings in small format throughout the 1890s. By 1893, membership in the Palette Club totaled more than seventy women, one-third of whom had studied abroad. Kellogg was elected president in 1891, 1892, and again in 1895.

The World's Columbian Exposition, held in Chicago in 1893, served as a vehicle for success for individual members of the Palette Club, as well as for the club as a whole. The all-male jury, established to select work to be exhibited in the Palace of Fine Arts, chose 520 painters and sculptors, 104 of whom were women. Of these women, eight were members of the Palette Club. Kellogg's painting, *The Mother*, and a drawing, *Intermezzo*, were included. The painting of Kellogg's sister Gertrude, *Miss G.E.K.*, was hung on the wall of the boardroom of the Woman's Building.

The Palette Club was also invited to decorate the Women's Department of the Illinois Building. A five-panel frieze was painted representing different accomplishments of women. Kellogg's mural, *Instruction*, occupied one of the panels. The Palette Club exhibited 125 works within the building, four of which were Kellogg's.

After the exposition, Kellogg continued painting in her studio, holding private classes, and teaching classes at the Art Institute and at Hull-House. In addition to the Palette Club and Society of American Artists, Kellogg was a member of the Cosmopolitan Art Club, the New York Watercolor Club, the Society of Western Artists, and the Chicago Art Association.

In spite of her full schedule, Kellogg had always planned to have a family. In 1894, she married Chicagoan Orno James Tyler, a self-taught artist, who worked as the secretary of Story and Clark Organ and Piano Company. Mutually devoted and supportive, theirs appears to have been a fulfilling and happy marriage.

During the 1890s, Kellogg Tyler painted portraits of many influential Chicagoans, several of whom were associated with Hull-House. Among them were Jane Addams; ELEANOR SMITH, Hull-House Music School director; Jenny Dow, Hull-House kindergarten teacher; MARY ROZET SMITH, and LYDIA COONLEY-WARD, Hull-House benefactors; and CORNELIA DE BEY, physician and Hull-House supporter. In 1897, Kellogg Tyler illustrated the book *Singing Verses for Children* by Lydia Avery Coonley [Lydia Coonley-Ward] and other Hull-House associates. The delicate drawings in this book revealed Kellogg Tyler's affection for and sensitivity to children.

The same year that the book was released, Kellogg Tyler had a miscarriage very late in pregnancy. By the end of 1898 her health began to deteriorate; she was dying of Bright's disease, a complication of diabetes. She was cared for by her physician, Dr. Cornelia De Bey, who lived with Kellogg Tyler's sister, Kate Starr Kellogg.

Suffering from pain, weakness, and recurring blindness, she produced very little artwork in her last year. Alice Kellogg Tyler died at age thirty-seven and was buried at Mt. Greenwood Cemetery in Chicago. Jane Addams wrote her eulogy and read it at the funeral.

A leader among women artists in Chicago during the late nineteenth century, Alice DeWolf Kellogg Tyler distinguished herself during her brief career as a teacher and artist. Noted

Chicago sculptor Lorado Taft, a friend and colleague, wrote a tribute on the first anniversary of her death in which he summed up her short but productive life: "Mrs. Tyler's art was distinctly up to date in the best sense of the term. . . . To me she seemed almost an ideal artist—the soul of art personified. In her frank, zestful love of her work, of nature, of life, there was something rare and exalted" (*Chicago Record*). Her work has recently come to the attention of art critics and patrons. In 1989, the Pennsylvania Academy of Fine Arts did a Paris 1889 exhibit, featuring American artists at the Parisian Universal Exposition. Interest in Alice Kellogg Tyler continues to grow as a result of this show, as she is reevaluated and her importance as an American artist identified.

Sources. Kellogg's letters to her family, 1887–89, are located in the Alice Kellogg Tyler Papers, Archives of American Art, Washington, D.C. Other letters and materials are located in the Jane Addams Memorial Collection, UIC Spec. Coll. Information about Kellogg can be found in Annette Blaugrund with Joanne W. Bowie, "Alice D. Kellogg: Letters from Paris, 1887–1889," *Archives of American Art Journal*, vol. 28, 1988, and Annette Blaugrund, *Paris 1889, American Artists at the Universal Exposition*, catalog for the exhibition (1989). Lorado Taft's tribute to Kellogg appeared in the *Chicago Record*, February 14, 1901. Kellogg's paintings are located at the Jane Addams' Hull-House Museum, UIC; at CHS; and in private collections.

JOANNE WIEMERS BOWIE

KERR, MAY WALDEN
September 3, 1865–1953
SOCIALIST, JOURNALIST, PAMPHLETEER

May Walden was born in Metamora, Illinois, the daughter of Theron and Elizabeth (Gribling) Walden. Her initiation as a social activist came at the age of sixteen. Driven by the desire to save her father, a disabled Civil War veteran who had taken to drink, she joined the ranks of the Woman's Christian Temperance Union (WCTU), perhaps the single most significant preparatory school for an entire generation of women activists. She entered the Illinois Industrial University at Champaign but moved with her family to Highlands, North Carolina, Elizabeth Gribling's ancestral home, in 1885.

Concerned that she not burden her hard-pressed parents and eager to strike out on her own, May Walden returned to Illinois not long afterwards. She briefly worked at the public library at Peoria but soon moved to Chicago and went to work in the U.S. Pension Office, where she had initially ventured in search of assistance for her beleaguered father. A co-worker at the pension office introduced her to Charles Kerr, who had founded Charles H. Kerr and Company in 1886, the publisher for the Chicago-based Western Unitarian Conference.

Kerr's wife had recently died, and he and May Walden began to share each other's company. They were married in Jenkin Lloyd Jones's Unitarian All Souls' Church on April 2, 1892. As members of All Souls', the Kerrs became part of an enlightened, reform-minded circle. May Walden Kerr by that time was already carrying their first child, Althea, who was born in November 1892. Eager to assist her husband, Walden Kerr continued working at the pension office and volunteered as a Sunday school teacher at All Souls'. The Kerrs moved to Glen Ellyn, a village west of Chicago, in 1893, and a second

daughter, Katharine, was born in 1894. (Althea died at the age of four.)

Charles Kerr began a monthly magazine, *New Occasions*, in June 1893. It provided a platform for the discussion of political and social questions. Promoted as a journal of social and industrial progress, it placed the Kerrs in contact with a broad spectrum of social critics and populist activists. Walden Kerr ventured into journalism with a monthly column of advice, "The Home," in the pages of *New Occasions*' successor, the *New Time*, beginning in March 1898.

In this period, the Kerrs were looking for solutions to the problems of inequality in industrial society but had not yet moved toward an embrace of socialism. Walden Kerr saw the possibility of reform in the application of rational action both in the public and the private spheres. Her column, "The Home," had been created "to emphasize the equal need of rational action in the life of each and every home" (March 1898). Her approach was reminiscent of writings of other women reformers such as ELIZABETH HARBERT, editor of the *New Era*, a short-lived woman suffrage and reform journal, or the essays of MARY LIVERMORE, whose article "Cooperative Womanhood in the State," in the *North American Review* (1891) postulated a new period of progress and harmony in which women and men would adopt more nurturing, harmonious, and rational or scientific solutions in both the public and private spheres. Women were key as they created bridges from the home to the larger community. Walden Kerr frequently wrote about the "new dawn" that would be inaugurated when the present social order had run its course. This new order would arrive "in the homes of those who are already awake to the criminal injustice of present social conditions, that the leaders of the future must be nurtured and trained" to redress. Such leaders must be prepared in a "home atmosphere of liberty, helpfulness and love" ("The Home," March 1898).

May Walden Kerr and Charles Kerr joined the socialist cause just prior to 1900, influenced, in part, by Algie M. Simons and his wife, MAY WOOD SIMONS, activists in the Chicago ranks of the Socialist Labor Party. The Simons's vigorous commitment to Marxian socialism had an immense impact on the Kerrs. The articulate analytical strength of Algie Simons's arguments among the small circle of left-leaning activists who had come to gather regularly at the Kerrs' Glen Ellyn home engendered an enthusiasm "that nearly set the house afire" ("How Come?" handwritten memoir, Kerr Papers). Years later, Walden Kerr recalled that she and her husband had "gone through the William Jennings Bryan campaign and sopped up a lot of crazy ideas that we had to give up to make way for Marxism" ("How Come?"). Chicago, at the turn of the century, was a major center of the socialist movement.

Strategically located at the heart of the nation's rail system, the city housed the national headquarters for a number of left-wing organizations and labor unions. The Kerr publishing venture soon came to attract a veritable who's who of the socialist movement's notables, and Charles and May Walden Kerr came to know many of them personally.

As much the activist as her husband, Walden Kerr's political development blossomed during those years. She made a series of insightful contributions to the expanding list of pamphlets,

The Pocket Books of Socialism, issued by Kerr and Company, by then a socialist cooperative publishing venture. She also contributed occasional articles to the socialist periodical press. As a speaker and polemicist for the broader movement and the Socialist Party, founded at Chicago in 1901, and a student of what she considered Marx's materialist view of history, her primary interest centered on the bases for the role and status of women, both in society at large and within the developing socialist movement. She readily linked the oppression of women to an economic basis; the emancipation of women, for her, could only take place under socialism. Speaking to America's working-class women, she argued that "the freedom that we crave, and which we must have, is economic freedom. We working people are all slaves, and women are in greater slavery than men, for we are slaves politically, economically and socially" ("Three Principles of Socialist Philosophy," 20–21). Her understanding of women's subordination came out of her critique of patriarchal marriage, which was based on a definition of women, juridically and politically, as the private property of men. "It is only in a state of society where woman is looked upon as private property of man," she wrote, "that such perversions of woman's nature can be found: the prostitute, the childless woman, and the worn-out, over-burdened mother" ("Three Principles," 22–23). Walden Kerr's Socialism and the Home (1901) assailed the bourgeois notion of "fashion" as a form of oppression imposed upon working women, noting that "as soon as a fashion is taken up by the lower classes, the upper classes change for something new" (p. 12). She called for an emancipation from the vagaries and demands of bourgeois fashion as well as from styles that kept a woman from moving freely and healthfully.

Believing that the "Cooperative Commonwealth" was just around the corner, Walden Kerr confidently proclaimed in 1901, "Socialism is not a theory, it is the next stage in the development of society" (Socialism and the Home, 30). To speed the arrival of the socialist epoch, which she believed would occur without violence, she wrote extensively for the socialist press in Chicago, contributing to the Worker's Call, the Chicago Socialist, the Chicago Daily Socialist, and the monthly Chicago-based Socialist Woman, an early socialist feminist magazine edited by her close associates Kiichi Kanecko and Josephine Conger Kanecko. An activist stump speaker and organizer for the Socialist Party of Illinois, she also volunteered as a soap box speaker on Chicago's street corners and as a poll watcher during some of the city's more hotly contested elections. During the spring and autumn of 1913, she embarked on two lengthy speaking tours for the Socialist Party, which took her to numerous small towns throughout southern and central Illinois.

May Walden Kerr and Charles Kerr were divorced in 1904. The underlying tensions and exact reasons for their estrangement remain unclear. In part the rift had to do with his absorption with the publishing house; it was a preoccupation that took the form of a near obsession at times. Readily willing to sacrifice every penny for the continued operation of the company, he expected his wife and daughter to follow suit and do without on occasion. That situation placed a strain on the relationship. In some ironic manner, meanwhile, the Kerrs' developing political and social critiques also took a toll. Both had developed analyses of marriage as a relationship based in property rights and the rel-

egated inferiority of women. In her memoir, Walden Kerr recounted how she and her husband received many of the Socialist Party's notables and numerous social activists in their Glen Ellyn home. The guests entertained Charles Kerr while she "sweated out in the kitchen preparing the meals" ("How Come?"). Whatever the specifics, clearly all was not well between them, and they both seemingly reached a point where their marriage was no longer tenable.

Their actual break came in the wake of the 1904 Socialist Party National Convention, held at Chicago's Brand Hall. During the opening day of that conference, May Walden Kerr was introduced to another socialist woman as "Mrs. Charles Kerr." The other woman responded that "it couldn't be"; that she "had just met 'Mrs. Kerr,' in Mr. Kerr's office" (M. W. Kerr, "Notes on C.H.K.'s Ancestry," handwritten memoir, Kerr Papers). The faux pas set off a minor scandal among the middle-class women at the convention. The word was out that Charles Kerr, indeed, was involved with another woman. Walden Kerr nevertheless maintained her composure and refused to allow her personal feelings to interfere with political principle. She went on to side with the same faction as her husband on a number of votes on key issues to the chagrin of some of the women present.

Charles Kerr took up permanent residence in Chicago following the divorce. May Walden Kerr received the house in Glen Ellyn and an agreement from Kerr to assist with daughter Katharine's support. The two, according to Walden Kerr's memoir, wept upon parting. She remained in the Chicago area through 1913, where she continued as an activist for the Illinois Socialist Party. A regular speaker and contributor to the party press, she also worked on such projects as the Political Refugee Defense League, a group that assisted exiles fleeing political repression in Mexico. Walden Kerr left Chicago for the last time in December 1913 to assist her ailing mother, then residing at Avon Park, Florida. She continued to speak out regularly on issues of social justice, peace, and socialism. She spent most of her remaining years in Florida, where she died in 1953.

May Walden Kerr played a significant role in the formative years of the pre–World War I socialist movement in Illinois. She made a name for herself within left-wing circles as a statewide Socialist Party organizer, polemicist, and voice for the rights of working-class women.

Sources. The primary source for materials on Walden Kerr is the May Walden Kerr Papers at NL, Chicago. These include the memoirs cited above. Her two most significant writings are the pamphlets, Woman and Socialism (1900) and Socialism and the Home (1901). For a sense of her early contributions as a columnist, see "The Home," New Time, March 1898 and April 1898. For her political outlook and social perceptions, see her "Three Principles of Socialist Philosophy," Worker's Call, October 26, 1901; "In North Carolina," Worker's Call, July 13, 1901; "Woman's Place in the Socialist Party," Chicago Socialist, April 26, 1902; "In the Shopping District," Chicago Socialist, August 11, 1906; "After Forty Years," Chicago Socialist, September 1, 1906; "Woman's Slavery," Socialist Woman, September 1907; "Co-operative Housekeeping," Daily Socialist (Chicago), October 30, 1907; "Organization Work for the Woman's Committee," Daily Socialist, August 8, 1908; "True Homes under Socialism," Socialist Woman, January 1908; "The Twentieth Century Is Woman's," Socialist Woman, February 1908; "How to Organize a Study Club," Socialist Woman, June 1908; "Socialist

Woman's Study Club," *Socialist Woman*, July 1908. See also Allen M. Ruff, *"We Called Each Other Comrade": Charles H. Kerr & Company, Radical Publishers* (1997). Mari Jo Buhle's book, *Women and American Socialism* (1986), is useful for the national historical context.

ALLEN M. RUFF

KINZIE, JULIETTE AUGUSTA MAGILL
September 11, 1806–September 15, 1870
EARLY SETTLER, NOVELIST, POPULAR HISTORIAN

The English social critic and writer of travel memoirs Harriet Martineau visited Chicago in 1836 and met Juliette and John H. Kinzie who, she said, "seem to have the art of making themselves as absolutely Indian in their sympathies and manners as the welfare of the savages among whom they lived required" (Martineau, 39). Martineau added, "They were the only persons I met with who, really knowing the Indians, had any regard for them" (p. 39). The Kinzies participated in the transition of Chicago from a fur-trading frontier settlement to a commercial boom town. Their fortunes rose and fell with the real estate fever that peaked in 1836 and reached rock bottom in 1837. Although they were able to reestablish themselves, they never regained the edge they had held as precommercial settlers anticipating the profits from real estate and commercial investment that would come their way. Positioned in this way, Juliette Kinzie became the historian of her husband's pioneer family and, in this role, claimed for them a place in Chicago history and myth to match the legends of railroad kings, steel mill barons, and department store magnates.

Juliette Augusta Magill, born in Middletown, Connecticut, to Arthur William and Frances (Wolcott) Magill, was descended on her maternal side from one of the oldest Connecticut families. Her father, Arthur Magill, was her mother's second husband and had worked as a cashier of a Middletown bank. In what would be a recurrent pattern in Juliette Magill's life, her father did not do well in business. "He left his post . . . under a cloud in 1820; thereafter he apparently lived in New York state, where his daughter may for a time have joined him" (Byrne, 337). The family's financial misfortunes took their toll on Juliette Magill's formal education. She briefly attended a New Haven boarding school at age fifteen and attended the Troy (New York) Female Seminary operated by Emma Willard; she left when her family ran out of money. Nonetheless, she was well educated, spoke French fluently, knew enough Latin to tutor her brothers in preparation of their college Latin requirements, and read Spanish and Italian. Her uncle, Dr. Alexander Wolcott Jr., a graduate of Yale College, had a hand in her education. Later on, in Chicago, when German immigration to the city had grown, she learned German as well.

In 1820 Dr. Wolcott took part in a government expedition supervised by Michigan Territorial Governor Lewis Cass; the group began in Detroit and traveled through the upper Great Lakes to the sources of the Mississippi River. Wolcott became an Indian agent in Chicago in August 1821 and witnessed the signing of a treaty with the Indians. Two years later he married Ellen Marion Kinzie, eldest daughter of John and Eleanor Kinzie, after she returned from her schooling at Mount Holyoke Seminary (now Mount Holyoke College). It was through her uncle that Juliette Magill met John Kinzie's son, John Harrison

FIG. 62. *Pioneer settler Juliette Augusta Magill Kinzie, author of* Wau-Bun: The "Early Day" in the North-West *(1856).*

Kinzie, in Boston, Massachusetts. John Harrison Kinzie, born in Canada and brought to Chicago as an infant by his fur trader father, had apprenticed to John Jacob Astor's American Fur Company. After five years with Astor, Kinzie Jr. was transferred from Mackinac Island—headquarters of the company—to Prairie du Chien, Wisconsin, where he learned the Winnebago language. He soon became knowledgeable in the Indian tribal dialects. This expertise attracted the attention of Cass, who appointed John Harrison Kinzie his private secretary in 1826. He was appointed agent to the upper bands of the Winnebagos in 1829; in that year Fort Winnebago (in the Wisconsin area of Michigan territory) was constructed.

Juliette Magill and John Harrison Kinzie were married August 9, 1830, at New Hartford, New York. The couple first traveled to Detroit, Michigan, and from there, married for just one month, Juliette Kinzie accompanied her new husband on a boat trip to Fort Winnebago, where they lived for three years. Her experiences at the fort and on visits to Chicago later became part of her narrative of early Illinois history, *Wau-Bun: The "Early*

Day" in the North-West, published in 1856. In 1832, almost at the end of their residence at Fort Winnebago, the Sauk War—Black Hawk War—was fought. The Winnebago Indians were punished by the federal government for their "complicity with the Sauks" (Baym, introduction to *Wau-Bun*, xiii). Juliette Kinzie's account in 1856 revealed that she found fault, in fact was "outrage[d] at the U.S. treatment of the Winnebagos" (p. xiii).

The Kinzies settled permanently in Chicago in 1834 in the midst of land speculation fever. John H. Kinzie was appointed the first president of the newly incorporated village. His father's home, the Old Kinzie Mansion, was a small cottage situated on the north side of the Chicago River opposite Fort Dearborn and near the village's yet undeveloped lake harbor. Juliette Kinzie later described the house as a "long, low building with a piazza extending along its front, a range of four or five rooms. A broad green space was enclosed between it and the river, and shaded by a row of Lombardy poplars" (Mayer and Wade, 10, fig. 1). A well-cultivated garden and various small buildings, including a dairy, a bake house, stables, and a lodging house, were part of the Kinzie domain. By 1837 Juliette and John Harrison Kinzie had moved into a large brick residence in the up-and-coming Near North neighborhood where many of the city's business elite resided. The couple had seven children, six sons and one daughter, Eleanor Lytle. Of the six sons, Alexander Wolcott, Julian Magill, and Francis William died in childhood.

John H. Kinzie had inherited land from his father; it was centrally located and soon became very valuable as town lots were platted and sold to local investors and capitalists from the East. Talk was in the air about canal and railroad construction to link Chicago, the Great Lakes, and the Mississippi River in one great transportation system. Local businessmen like Kinzie were situated to make enormous profits, but they were short of investment capital and, with trepidation, entered into business deals with entrepreneurs from the East. John H. Kinzie's real estate speculations included land outside Chicago.

In 1834 Chicago's boosters often gathered at the Old Kinzie Mansion, where John H. Kinzie played his fiddle. Before the first St. James Episcopal Church was built in 1837, the Kinzie house also served as the center of the small community of Episcopalians in Chicago. The first Episcopal service in Chicago was conducted in the Presbyterian Meeting-House, October 12, 1834, by the Reverend Palmer Dyer, who stayed at the Kinzie house. "Juliette Kinzie had been reared in 'the vigorous school of churchmanship for which Connecticut was famous,' and it was through her efforts that the Domestic and Foreign Missionary Society for the Episcopal Church sent a young Connecticut clergyman, the Reverend Isaac W. Hallam, and his wife and child, to Chicago" (Schultz, *The Church and the City*, 22). The optimistic mood brought on by the incredible rise in the value of real estate in the newly platted village inspired the vestry and Ladies' Sewing Society to raise funds to build Chicago's first brick church. Beginning in 1835, Juliette Kinzie and the other women conducted a series of bazaars, netting in all fifty-six hundred dollars. The Kinzie family donated two lots, and in July 1835, ground was broken for St. James Church in the midst of a vast tract of wild prairie on the edge of settlement. "This same location in less than fifteen years would become a teeming,

crowded commercial section, near huge warehouses and railroad tracks" (p. 26).

The congregation was made up of some of the city's leading businessmen, including William Butler Ogden, Walter Loomis Newberry, and Gurdon S. Hubbard. In the North Side neighborhood they began to build more substantial residences for themselves, and Ogden, a Democrat with strong political and economic connections to New York Democrats in the Andrew Jackson and Martin Van Buren administrations, was elected Chicago's first mayor in 1837. Whig John H. Kinzie had been Ogden's unsuccessful opponent. The political defeat must have been difficult for Kinzie and his wife. The location of cultural and political power in the young community had initially been in their hands. With the increase in new settlers, predominantly from New York State and New England, as well as substantial out-of-town investments in land and other enterprises by New York capitalist Arthur Bronson, an associate of Ogden, the balance was now leaning to the transplanted New York crowd. Ogden built a residence resembling a country estate. There he entertained political and literary guests, including Martin Van Buren, Daniel Webster, Samuel J. Tilden, William Cullen Bryant, Harriet Martineau, Fredrika Bremer, Margaret Fuller, Ralph Waldo Emerson, Wendell Phillips, and Charlotte Cushman. This list illustrates the connections with the East and the new frontier elite; it also suggests that the meteoric rise of Chicago held a kind of fascination for Americans interested in the West.

The congregants at St. James were riding high at the peak of an incredible real estate boom when they held their first service in the fully completed brick church on Easter Sunday, March 26, 1837. Not only had the women raised money, but close to fourteen thousand dollars were realized by the sale of church pews, the typical way most Protestant churches were funded in the nineteenth century. Families bought pews according to their status and wealth in the community, and pew maps, printed for the congregation, showed the family name, amount, and location of each sold or rented pew. These maps conformed to the ways in which residential neighborhoods divided into stately and wealthy residences on prime boulevards, more modest homes on lesser streets, and working-class shacks and multi-family dwellings in more congested, less desirable subdivisions, close to industrial or commercial sites. John Harrison and Juliette Kinzie moved their family into a large brick home in 1837 on the up-and-coming Near North Side where influential neighbors included Walter Loomis Newberry and his wife JULIA NEWBERRY. Gurdon S. Hubbard lived there with his first wife as well. (In 1843 the widowed Hubbard married his second cousin MARY ANN HUBBARD, and she became part of the active social life of the fashionable community.)

Economic instability with booms and busts in the business cycle were symptomatic of the expansion of capitalism and use of credit during the nineteenth century. A national bank panic and business depression in 1837 ended the demand for Chicago lots. Local men such as Kinzie immediately obtained new loans from the East; Kinzie used his Chicago property, now devalued, as collateral. While he and other local businessmen were initially bailed out by such loans, Kinzie and many others soon found themselves in a descending spiral. When the loans had to be repaid, many, including Kinzie, could not meet their creditors' demands. The Illinois legislature favored local debtors and passed an appraisal law which "stipulated that property sold at auction must reach a price representing two-thirds of the property's value as determined by local citizens" (Schultz, "The Businessman's Role," 59). This was an attempt by local debtors to retain some of their property until business conditions improved. Kinzie believed he had a chance to salvage "a small remnant for [his] young family," as he wrote to his creditor (p. 59). Unfortunately, his New York creditor sued him and the case, *Bronson v. Kinzie*, was argued before the U.S. Supreme Court. In 1842 the court found for the creditor. The majority decision offered by Chief Justice Roger Taney upheld the original business contract entered into by Kinzie and indicated that the appraisal law enacted by the Illinois legislature impaired Arthur Bronson's rights and was unconstitutional.

Juliette Kinzie, however, maintained her leadership in things social and religious. She taught the older children's Sunday school class and organized the first choir. Mary Ann Hubbard commented that although Kinzie would "start off singing in a most croaking unmusical voice . . . she played the piano well" (Hubbard, 62). Juliette Kinzie's husband was one of the managers of the Orphan Benevolent Association, while she and other St. James women actually did the day-to-day work of transforming a frame house into the Chicago Orphan Asylum in 1850, fund-raising by giving dinners and sponsoring a fair to raise money so that they could purchase a block of land on Chicago's South Side. St. James's women were joined by women benevolent workers from other churches in the city. Juliette Kinzie was on the board of lady managers, but the women's married status meant they could own no property. Thus a separate board of men trustees supervised the finances. Until the women's movement in post–Civil War Chicago lobbied for changes, benevolent women did not control the financial boards of charities and organizations, including parish vestries, although women's efforts were critical for both successful fund-raising and administrative expertise. In 1854 the women of St. James worked with their rector and established St. James Hospital, one of the few free hospitals in the city at the time.

In 1844 Juliette Kinzie anonymously authored her first local history, *Narrative of the Massacre at Chicago*, an account of the massacre of the garrison at Fort Dearborn during the War of 1812. Her account "has been the primary source of material on this event since Henry Brown paraphrased it in his *History of Illinois* later in 1844" (Byrne, 337). Her account also portrays her father-in-law, John Kinzie, as the "Father of Chicago" and gives the Kinzie family a "prominent role as progenitors of the city" (p. 337). It was "based on the oral narratives of her mother-in-law, Eleanor Kinzie, and her sister-in-law, Margaret Helm (Eleanor's daughter from an earlier marriage)" and it "effectively installed the Kinzie version of events at the very fountainhead of Illinois history" (Baym, introduction to *Wau-Bun*, xii). Literary critic Nina Baym writes that Eleanor Kinzie had "the idea of transforming family history into public history, and she summoned her daughter-in-law's literary skills for the job" (p. xii). In this rendering of the family's story, and in the chronicle Kinzie wrote and published in 1856, *Wau-Bun: The "Early Day" in the North-West*, the details of John Kinzie's life are sanitized. She does not write that he was a speculator and squatter who lost his property and was bankrupt in 1812, the year of the massacre. Nor does she speculate about why he had a reputation for trying to grab title to Indian lands just before treaties were made between the American government and the Indian tribes. Some of his contemporaries described him as a common horse thief. The most perplexing issue, however, was John Kinzie's role in the Fort Dearborn Massacre. The massacre occurred during the War of 1812 after the American general, William Hull, had surrendered his army as well as Detroit and the Michigan Territory to the British. Hull ordered the evacuation of Fort Dearborn and commanded that all extra arms and ammunition be destroyed. John Kinzie opposed this plan, but Commander Heald followed General Hull's orders and evacuated Fort Dearborn on August 15, 1812. Less than two miles from the fort, the sixty-eight Americans who had left the garrison were ambushed by some five hundred Indians. Fifty-three Americans were killed, including twenty-six soldiers, twelve militia, the Indian scout Captain William Wells, two women, and twelve children. John Kinzie, who remained neutral and accompanied the Fort Dearborn group, was not hurt. Nor did any harm come to his family, which had left separately and was aided by friendly Indians. Juliette Kinzie, who wrote the story almost fifty years after the event and without the use of primary documents, told the tale from the point of view of those who criticized the actions of the fort's top ranking officer, Commander Heald. "As a Kinzie, she was quite aware of the image which her father-in-law maintained in the days after the Massacre. The fact that he was not harmed when those with him were either wounded or killed did cause unasked and unanswered questions" (Williams, 47). As speculation about John Kinzie's role continued during the 1830s through 1850s, his daughter-in-law "took a defensive position" (Williams, 47).

Juliette Kinzie's *Wau-Bun* demonstrates her writing talents and reveals her familiarity with "travel accounts, massacre stories, captivity narratives, Indian folktales, landscape descriptives" (Baym, introduction to *Wau-Bun*, xiii). The entire chronicle is about the territory between Fort Winnebago and Chicago during its frontier period between the Indian wars of 1812 and 1832, before the rise of a commercial city. Written in a romantic and idealistic view of the past, Kinzie constructs a past in which her husband's father is a hero whose honorable treatment of the Indian tribes stands in contrast to that of entrepreneurial capitalists. The latter, she implies, care only for profits and have no respect for the land or its indigenous inhabitants. One of the outcomes of this viewpoint is that Kinzie is sympathetic to the culture and behavior of the Indian people; she points out that their cultural practices arise from religious belief, and she shows considerable respect for Indian spirituality. Unlike ELIZA CHAPPELL PORTER, whose missionary zeal brought her to the Midwest and Indian territory and who attempted to teach the tribes she encountered to read in order to convert them to Christianity, Kinzie does not pursue such goals. She sees her religious obligation in terms of simple Christian charity for those in need and respects the differences between them. Kinzie is able to maintain this sympathetic rendering of the Indians even though violence is often close to the surface or out in the open in her accounts. The inclusion of her mother-in-law's captivity story is an example of how Juliette Kinzie locates herself and her husband's family in the narrative of Chicago history. As a prepubescent girl, her mother-in-law, Eleanor Lytle Kinzie, was taken away by a Seneca Indian tribe. This story, just as almost all the accounts in the book, is told in such an upbeat manner that it becomes a story about mother love rather than violent abduction. Kinzie tells the reader the ten-year-old Eleanor has been captured to replace the lost child of the old queen. Kinzie does not deny that there has been violence in other captivity experiences and recounts the tale of a little boy who is kidnapped and dies. But Eleanor Lytle is treated well by the Indians, who, Kinzie shows, appreciate the love of parent and child. Eventually Eleanor Lytle is released to her own people. What the reader finds out through the variety of tales is that in the precommercial period, the American Indians were the Kinzies' biggest allies. The John Kinzie family is hurt by what happens later in Chicago when economic development and entrepreneurial schemes eclipse the former way of life.

Juliette Kinzie further distinguishes her husband's family from the booster elite in her discussion of how the Kinzies got their land. Acting for the family, Robert Kinzie, John Harrison's brother, took title in 1830 for the Kinzie Addition. Juliette Kinzie's view is that the family was buying the land not to speculate but to have a home, and she emphasizes "how moderate were, in fact the anticipations of most persons at that period" (Kinzie, *Wau-Bun*, 141). "The certificate [of land ownership] . . . described only a fractional quarter section of one hundred and two acres, instead of one hundred and sixty acres, the river and Lake Michigan cutting off fifty-eight acres on the southern and eastern lines of the quarter" (p. 141). Kinzie was allowed to select a complement of fifty-eight acres from any unappropriated land that suited the family. His mother suggested a cornfield at Wolf Point that "will always be valuable for cultivation—besides, as it faces down the main river, the situation will always be a convenient one" (p. 141). Juliette Kinzie records that Robert Kinzie laughed heartily at his mother because he felt he had "more than we shall ever want, or know what to do with" (p. 141) in the one hundred and two acres. Juliette Kinzie concludes the story by saying that he did not take his mother's advice and never claimed the fifty-eight additional acres to which the Kinzie family was rightfully entitled. Distinguishing the prespeculation era from what was to come next, she writes, "There was, I think, a very general impression that asking for our just rights in the case would have a very grasping, covetous, look. How much wiser five and twenty years have made us!" (p. 141).

Wau-Bun provides us with insight into the complex character of Juliette Kinzie. From her description of life at Fort Winnebago emerges the image of a newly wed, middle-class woman who is having an adventure with her daring, but always considerate, husband. She has a piano and rugs brought to their lodging at the fort, and in the midst of rude frontier conditions, Kinzie therefore establishes herself as a woman of refinement and cultivation. Later in the book the Kinzie family is portrayed as the antithesis of the greedy, rapacious, and aggressive eastern capitalists who arrive in Chicago not as homesteaders but to make money. By the 1850s, when Juliette Kinzie was writing *Wau-Bun*, she had reason to assess her experiences over the past twenty-five years. The frontier settlement was now a bustling city

with a population in 1850 of 30,000 and, ten years later, a population of more than 109,000. The Episcopalians who attended the original St. James Church built on two lots donated by the Kinzie family now worshipped in a recently built yellow Illinois stone Gothic church—more impressive than the first brick building. Her husband had been a member of the prestigious building committee that included William B. Ogden. The total cost of the new church was sixty thousand dollars, a good deal more than the fifteen thousand dollars it had cost to build and furnish the first one. J. H. Kinzie still retained his status in Chicago as an old settler. Juliette Kinzie's pen had created a family pedigree that could, perhaps, compensate or offset a middling economic situation.

With the coming of the Civil War, Juliette Kinzie's life changed drastically. Her daughter Eleanor Lytle (Nellie) married William Washington Gordon, a Southerner, in 1857 and moved to Savannah, Georgia. Her son John Harris was killed in the war, and two other sons, Arthur Magill and George Herbert, were imprisoned by the Confederate Army. The Kinzie men were patriots at a time when other sons of businessmen in Chicago were able to avoid military service by providing the cost of a substitute soldier. John Harrison Kinzie, whose political connections had led to a succession of positions including Collector of Tolls for the Illinois and Michigan Canal, Registrar of Public Lands, and Receiver of Public Moneys and Depositary, was appointed Paymaster in the Army in 1861 by President Abraham Lincoln. He held the office until the close of the war. J. H. Kinzie died suddenly in 1865 while on vacation, traveling east with his family.

Juliette Kinzie turned to her writing. In 1869 she published *Walter Ogilby*, a romantic novel based on scenes of her girlhood in Connecticut and New York. Her unpublished fiction includes a story, "The Captives," about Indians during and after the Revolutionary War; a novel set in 1827 about a Winnebago chieftain, persons of mixed blood, and two sisters who travel to Prairie du Chien; and an untitled story about the good works of several young ladies for the Dorcas Society, a religious benevolent association. *Mark Logan, the Bourgeois* (1887) was published posthumously; it is a fictional account of the material Kinzie had used in *Wau-Bun*.

In a fluke accident, Juliette Kinzie died at the age of sixty-four after taking morphine tablets delivered by mistake instead of the quinine that had been prescribed for her while she was on vacation at Amagansett, New York. She is buried in Graceland Cemetery, Chicago.

For Juliette Kinzie, a well-educated, literary woman, the frontier was an adventure she relished sharing with her husband and his family. Of course, she did not experience the hardships and alienation of women separated from their loved ones on the Great Plains, nor did she endure the backbreaking physical toil that was the lot of immigrant and working-class women. Hers was a journey cushioned by her husband's status and connections, if not outright wealth. Her piano was brought to Fort Winnebago in record time; she sketched scenes with her water colors and adorned her lodging with carpets and rugs. Yet she was not immune to the vagaries of economic conditions and the risks of childbirth, infant mortality, and ultimately, of the loss of a son to war. Through her writing she had considerable influence in the shaping of the legend of Chicago's beginnings, and she reminds us of the scope of women's cultural and literary activity in nineteenth-century America.

Sources. The CHS has a small collection of family letters written to Juliette Kinzie and manuscripts of fiction written by her, including the manuscript for *Mark Logan, the Young Bourgeois* (1887). There are Juliette Kinzie letters in the Gordon Family Papers at the Univ. of North Carolina Library, Chapel Hill, Southern Historical Collection. The letters in the Gordon Papers are on microfilm reels available at the CHS. Editions of *Wau-Bun, the "Early Day" in the North-West* (1856; with an introduction and notes by Reuben Gold Thwaites, 1901; edited and with notes and introduction by Eleanor Kinzie Gordon, 1901; with historical introduction by Milo Milton Quaife, 1932) are available in the Ayer and Wing collections at NL. The most recent edition of the book, published in 1992, includes an excellent introduction by Nina Baym. Works consulted include Alfred T. Andreas, *History of Chicago*, vols. 1 and 2 (1884); Mary Ann Hubbard, *Family Memories* (privately printed 1912); Harriet Martineau, "Chicago in 1836: Strange Early Days" *Annals of Chicago*, no. 9, 1876; Archibald J. Byrne, "Kinzie, Juliette Augusta Magill," in *NAW* (1971); Kenny J. Williams, *Prairie Voices: A Literary History of Chicago from the Frontier to 1893* (1980); Gladys Denny Shultz and Daisy Gordon Lawrence, *Lady from Savannah: The Life of Juliette Low* (1958); and Harold M. Mayer and Richard C. Wade, *Chicago: Growth of a Metropolis* (1969). Juliette Low, the founder of the Girl Scouts of America, was named for her grandmother, Juliette Kinzie. For a discussion of the early business development of Chicago and John Harrison Kinzie's real estate ventures, see Rima Lunin Schultz, "The Businessman's Role in Western Settlement: The Entrepreneurial Frontier, Chicago, 1833–1872" (Ph.D. diss., Boston Univ., 1985). For a discussion of Juliette Kinzie's involvement with St. James Episcopal Church, see Rima Lunin Schultz, *The Church and the City: A Social History of 150 Years at Saint James, Chicago* (1986).

RIMA LUNIN SCHULTZ

KOCH, HELEN LOIS
August 26, 1895–1977
CHILD DEVELOPMENTAL PSYCHOLOGIST, EDUCATOR

Helen Koch, a national figure in the field of developmental psychology, was born in Blue Island, Illinois, to Louis G. and Sophia (Uhlich) Koch, both of German ancestry. She had one sister. Little is known about her family and her early years. She earned a Ph.B. in 1918 and a Ph.D. in psychology in 1921 from the University of Chicago. She then became an instructor of educational psychology at the University of Texas, advancing quickly through the academic ranks to become associate professor in 1926 and full professor in 1928. Koch became the only graduate professor in education in 1929.

Koch's research at Texas compared intelligence and test performance of children from Caucasian, African American, and Hispanic backgrounds. Interested in child development, she participated in the foundation of a nursery school at the University of Texas. Koch was also one of twelve founders of Delta Kappa Gamma at the university, an honorary organization for women in teaching. She maintained ties to this society throughout her career, establishing a branch in Illinois and serving as the 1966–68 founding members' representative to the group's administrative board.

Koch's attachment to the University of Chicago continued, and between 1927 and 1930 she returned during the summers to teach classes there. She moved back to Chicago permanently in 1930 after accepting a position as associate professor in the University of Chicago's Department of Home Economics. She came to the home economics department one year after its head, KATHARINE BLUNT, had left to become president of Connecticut College. Blunt left an outstanding curriculum to train researchers and nutritionists, especially in relation to children's health. The doctoral program was also oriented toward Koch's interests in childhood development, forming the basis for the department's association with the University Cooperative Nursery School.

The nursery school was started in 1916 by mothers who were in the workforce during World War I. The educational possibilities and also the need for professional input led faculty from the departments of home economics and education to start projects in the nursery school. The benefits of this association were twofold: children and families received quality instruction and care, and members of the university gained an excellent site for research and training. In 1923, the nursery became officially aligned with the University of Chicago and was titled the University Cooperative Nursery School. The tie was a loose one; the university provided necessities like light and heat, and the school's program was guided by university staff. Soon after starting at the university, Koch became involved with the nursery school, and she joined the nursery's administrative board in 1931. The chair of home economics, LYDIA ROBERTS, was already working with the nursery school and a member of its board. Both Koch and Roberts served on the University Committee on Child Development. Koch worked closely with the nursery and with other faculty in home economics to shape programs focused on children's nutrition, education, psychosocial development, and welfare. In 1933 Koch became director of the nursery school. The next year, the nursery school board gave the Department of Home Economics the authority to supervise the school instead of having an advisory role. The move allowed the school to be used in observation and practice work in courses in child development and nutrition. Koch supervised all aspects: budget, selection of teachers, coordination of programs, and continuing research. The school provided research and training for many physicians and teachers from various institutions. Koch reported that it was possible that at least one visitor from a Chicago area institution was there observing the children and the program on any given day. In addition, the children and their parents benefited from increased knowledge of nutrition and new findings on emotional and intellectual advancement.

The University Cooperative Nursery School, unlike other nursery programs, struggled successfully through the Great Depression, although it suffered some reductions in its programs. The need for nursery schools was recognized when the Works Progress Administration (WPA) programs, introduced in the 1930s, made their establishment part of its goals. Nursery schools provided employment for teachers and child care for working parents and enhanced the health, nutrition, and mental ability of children whose families were devastated by the depression. The University Cooperative Nursery School was a model for nursery schools established by the WPA. Koch, as coordinator of the school, arranged programs on nutrition, social development, health, and parenting. She also employed twenty individuals through the WPA in her research for a child behavior study. Koch's courses and research at the University of Chicago were tied to her work at the nursery, including classes on nursery school methodology and early childhood development as well as research on child development. In 1938, the school became the University of Chicago Nursery School when the board gave the school and its buildings to the university. As part of the move, direction of the school was placed in the Committee on Child Development (later the Committee on Human Development), on which Koch served, instead of in the home economics department.

World War II again led women to work outside the home and increased the number of children in need of daytime child care and education. The University of Chicago Nursery School staff provided day and night school training courses for teachers in newly established nurseries. Koch was a major figure in arranging these programs and overseeing their progress as well as developing a workshop that consisted of nationally known speakers focusing on the negative effects of the war on aspects of child development. She served on the Mayor's Committee for Child Welfare in Metropolitan Chicago and one of its subcommittees, the War Nursery Committee, which supervised the "War Nurseries" (Dye, 187).

In February 1947, Koch became a member of the Department of Psychology while retaining her position in the Department of Home Economics. The next year, Koch left as coordinator of the nursery school so that she would have more time to pursue research on child behavioral and social development; but she continued to advise the nursery school. During 1948, Koch traveled with a team from the University of Chicago to Frankfurt, Würzburg, and Marburg/Lahn, Germany, to stimulate the development of university programs focusing on psychological factors in child development. As a result of this work, she served as visiting professor for the year 1954–55 at the universities in Frankfurt, Würzburg, and Marburg and returned in 1958 to Frankfurt for a semester to observe the relevant research programs.

While contributing to knowledge in developmental psychology through her work on child behavior, Koch also devoted herself to training students. She was an excellent academic mentor, "recognized for her care [and] attention" (interview with Neugarten) to students, acting as an adviser for more than fifty graduate students. She worked with students in both the home economics and psychology departments, even before she officially joined psychology in the late 1940s. Most of her Ph.D. students received degrees either in the Department of Psychology or from the Committee on Human Development, while her M.A. students worked in home economics or psychology, depending on their research.

When Koch retired in 1961, a group of her former graduate students published *Collected Papers in Child Psychology*. The book had eighteen of her articles, with a focus on sibling research, as well as a complete bibliography of her publications, including sixty articles spanning 1919 to 1960. Her research covered a broad range of topics in child development, such as family and sibling relations and behavioral characteristics. The students expressed their admiration and respect for her. "Fortunate . . . was the generation of students who studied with

Professor Koch from 1929 to 1960 at the University of Chicago. She was a teacher who learned along with the student, thereby creating the illusion that it was the student who led and she who followed. . . . In fellowship with her, the student felt . . . both dignified and honored. No greater gift could any teacher bestow upon a student" ("Foreword," n.p.).

After retirement, Koch continued her study on child development, focusing on sibling relations and twin relations. In 1950 she had been given permission by the Chicago Board of Education to use students from the Chicago public schools for her research. Her work for the next ten years involved children from Chicago, Evanston, and other local areas. In 1966 she published *Twins and Twin Relations*, which focused on the developmental and behavioral factors associated with twins. The book reported the results of a study that investigated the characteristics of ninety sets of twin children, compared to singletons. Physical development, mental and language abilities, and personality were among the traits studied.

Active in professional organizations throughout her career, Koch served as secretary-treasurer and then president of the Illinois Society for Consulting Psychology and was an officer in the Chicago Psychology Club and the Chicago Association for Child Study and Parent Education. She was a fellow of the American Psychological Association (APA) and a charter member and fellow of the Society for Research in Child Development, an organization for which she served as secretary in 1934 and president in 1937. In APA, Koch was active in the clinical section and in the developmental section and was president in 1961. In 1967, Koch was recognized for her contributions to developmental psychology in the field of child development and for her outstanding teaching by the APA developmental division, when she was the first recipient of its prestigious G. Stanley Hall award.

Koch never married. She had one married sister, Alice R. Langenbach, who lived in the Chicago area in Blue Island and with whom Koch remained close. While totally devoted to research and teaching, she pursued other interests in her leisure time. She was widely read in physics, philosophy of science, Egyptology, and other topics. A lover of music, Koch had a sizable record collection and attended the symphony for years. She also practiced gardening as a hobby at her home near the university.

Koch died at the age of eighty-two. She was an important researcher in the field of developmental psychology, with national and international influence. She contributed greatly to the knowledge and methodology associated with nursery and preschool education and care through work in Chicago, research, and most importantly her outreach with the nursery. Her research on child development and on sibling and twin relations is considered fundamental work in the area of human development.

Sources. The Helen L. Koch collection at UC Spec. Coll. has correspondence, manuscripts, lecture materials, copies of published biographical sketches, and the typed transcript of an interview with Koch, "The History of the Nursery School," by Ida B. De Pencier in August 1965. The interview is a rich source of information on the University of Chicago Nursery School and Koch's role. Bernice Neugarten provided helpful information in an interview with Stephanie Riger on June 20, 1995. For Koch's writings, see Helen L. Koch, *Collected Papers in Child*

Psychology, compiled by Walter Emmerich et al. (privately printed, n.d.); and Koch, *Twins and Twin Relations* (1966). Marie Dye, *History of the Department of Home Economics University of Chicago* (1962), describes Koch's career at the university.

HOLLY RICE

STEPHANIE RIGER

KOHN, ESTHER LOEB
January 12, 1875–September 1, 1965

CLUBWOMAN, SOCIAL WORKER, SOCIAL REFORMER

Esther Loeb Kohn's life of public service, which spanned more than half a century, illustrates the process by which the humanitarian work of volunteer women was transformed into the professional field of social work. The daughter of William and Emma (Mannheimer) Loeb, prosperous German Jews, she was born in Chicago's Near North Side neighborhood and lived there for many years. She was the oldest daughter and second oldest of seven children. Although a member of one of Chicago's most prominent Jewish families, Loeb learned about religious prejudice at an early age when, as a student in the Chicago public schools, she questioned her classmates about the meaning of "hell"—a concept for which there is no equivalent in the Jewish tradition. Introduced to the word in one of the Bible passages that were customarily read at the beginning of the school day, she found that her "innocent question was the opening of a gulf between [her] and [her] non-Jewish playmates" (Kohn, handwritten manuscript on immigration, n.d., 19, Kohn Papers). Much later in life, Esther Loeb not only strongly opposed the inclusion of religious teachings in the public schools, she objected to parochial schools because she believed these schools isolated immigrants from integration into American society.

At the age of fifteen Loeb ended her public school education and helped raise her brothers and sisters. Four years later, in 1894, she married Alfred Kohn, who had a Ph.D. in English and aspired to a career in medicine. Immediately after her marriage, Esther Kohn began studies at the University of Chicago, while her husband prepared for a medical degree. The couple left for an extended stay in Europe, where Alfred completed medical training in Germany and Esther studied at the University of Vienna and followed her interests in music with teachers in Munich and Paris.

The Kohns returned to Chicago, where Alfred Kohn, now a physician, pursued his career and took an interest in public health issues. In 1907, when he was appointed to the Chicago Board of Education, he supported the establishment of the first nutrition program for students in the public schools. Among his fellow board members were JANE ADDAMS and ANITA McCORMICK BLAINE, which placed him in the center of progressive reform circles. Esther Kohn had been raised in a family where the Jewish tradition of charity was strong. Like her husband, she believed in personal service and had a concern for civic betterment. In this milieu, Esther Kohn began to take courses at the new Chicago School of Civics and Philanthropy (CSCP), an outgrowth of settlement movement leader Graham Taylor's social work training courses. Run in 1908 as an independent training center, its faculty included JULIA LATHROP, SOPHONISBA BRECKINRIDGE, and EDITH ABBOTT—

all associated with Hull-House, the location for many of the courses. Kohn eventually completed the program and received a certificate from CSCP.

The Kohns' marriage was, by all accounts, a happy one. Alfred Kohn's sudden death in December 1909, at the age of thirty-seven, forced Kohn to begin life anew in her mid-thirties. For the next half century, Kohn lived off her deceased husband's estate while providing unpaid services to more than thirty organizations and to a multitude of charitable causes.

Encouraged by Jane Addams to continue her husband's nutrition work with the city's poor children, Kohn moved to Hull-House. During her thirty years of residency there, Kohn served as director of children's activities at Hull-House, organizing a recreation program, arranging to send hundreds of city children to rural camps each summer, and working to establish a trade school for girls who had to leave public schools in order to find employment. The trade school program was later adopted by the Chicago Public Schools. "It developed into the Vocational Guidance program and the Scholarship and Guidance Association, established in 1911" (Pfeffer, 748).

Kohn became a friend and then head of the Finance Committee of the Immigrants' Protective League, an agency located at Hull-House and directed by GRACE ABBOTT. "The League sought to ease the adjustment of newcomers to America; it established waiting rooms at railroad stations, where multi-lingual men and women helped recent arrivals find their relatives or friends" (Bryan and Davis, 124). To protect the newcomers against fraud, it investigated employment agencies, immigrant banks, and other services used by immigrants. While at Hull-House, Kohn also provided volunteer services to a number of Jewish organizations. From 1921 to 1941, she was board director, vice-president, and president of the Jewish Social Service Bureau. She also served as a board member of the Jewish Vocational Center and Employment Service, where she was instrumental in organizing a workshop for the handicapped at a time when little was being done for the physically handicapped. In 1929–30, she served as president of the Scholarship Association for Jewish Children.

Soon after arriving at Hull-House, Kohn found a major focus for her organizational skills in the campaign to end child labor. She noticed child labor in the neighborhood surrounding the settlement; children worked until so late at night completing piece work in their tenement apartments to supplement their families' low adult wages that they could not stay awake in school. In addition, thousands of children did not attend school, instead working sixty, seventy, or eighty hours a week in factories, sweatshops, or as bootblacks and newsboys.

In 1921, Kohn participated in lobbying efforts supported by the Hull-House community and its network of reformers to gain passage of the Sheppard-Towner Maternity and Infancy Act, which successfully provided a variety of services to improve the health of pregnant women, and of the Newton Bill, which provided national funding for research in maternal and child hygiene.

Opponents of child labor had worked for its eradication since the 1880s; by the 1920s the efforts to protect children centered on the ratification of the Child Labor Amendment that Congress had passed and sent to the states in 1924. In the same year the Child Welfare Committee of the Illinois League of Women Voters organized an Illinois Joint Committee to urge the ratification of the Child Labor Amendment. Thirty organizations were mobilized, but despite the pressure exerted, in 1925 the Illinois legislature did not ratify the amendment. In 1926 the Joint Committee was reorganized as the Illinois Child Labor Committee and included Anne Davis as chair, Esther Kohn, Grace Abbott, Sophonisba Breckinridge, AGNES NESTOR, and Edith Abbott. Kohn and Davis regularly met with state legislators in Springfield, Illinois, and attempted to keep up the pressure for ratification. As a member of the Illinois Child Labor Committee during the late 1920s and early 1930s, Kohn continued to work vigorously for ratification of the Federal Child Labor Amendment; it was never ratified by a sufficient number of states to become law. She also worked for establishment of a division for women and children in the Illinois Department of Labor; passage of the industrial home-work law, a minimum wage law for women and children; and enactment of the Child Health Act.

Kohn's interest in improving the lives of children earned her several committee appointments. In 1922, Judge Victor R. Arnold appointed Kohn to serve on a five-member committee to create a list of eligible persons for appointment to the probation staff of Chicago's Juvenile Court. In 1929, she was named to a committee to investigate reports of corporal punishment at the St. Charles (Illinois) School for Boys. Governor Henry Horner appointed Kohn in 1934 to the advisory board for enforcement and administration of the minimum wage law for women and children. In 1949, she was appointed by Governor Adlai E. Stevenson to serve on an advisory committee to the State Training School for Girls at Geneva, Illinois.

Kohn's many activities and interests, along with her aptitude for oral and written expression, increasingly involved her in politics. Believing that an educated public was crucial to the passage of legislation that would improve living conditions, Kohn worked tirelessly, in speeches made from the 1920s through the 1940s, to educate the public on such topics as hazardous occupations for children, the Workman's Compensation Law, child labor, child health, the medically indigent, child care for working women, maternity and prenatal care, the needs of the physically handicapped, and the needs of World War II draftees and their families. Kohn often suggested names of qualified women to serve on state and national committees. In 1932, she worked to promote the nomination of Grace Abbott for Secretary of Labor in the cabinet of Franklin Delano Roosevelt. Abbott, who had known Kohn during her days as director of the Immigrants' Protective League in Chicago, was chief of the U.S. Children's Bureau, a position she had held since 1921. She declined to be considered for Secretary of Labor and urged her supporters to push for the appointment of Frances Perkins.

In 1934, Kohn lobbied for the appointment of Anne Davis, HAZEL KYRK, and Mollie Ray Carroll to the commission for the enforcement and administration of the minimum wage law for women and children.

As a lay person, Kohn was influential in the professionalization of the field of social work. She was especially proud of having assisted, as a trustee, along with Edith Abbott and Sophonisba Breckinridge, in the 1920 merger of her alma mater, the School of Civics and Philanthropy, with the University of Chicago. It became the School of Social Service Administration (SSA), one of the first schools offering advanced degrees in the field at a United States university, a giant step toward making social work a respected profession. Yet, as the field of social work became increasingly professionalized and the reformer and volunteer were increasingly isolated from paid social workers, the value of the volunteer was downgraded. Kohn worked hard to bridge this widening gap and emphasized the value of volunteer services while demanding adequate training for professionals, particularly in the newly emerging field of medical social work in which Kohn was a pioneer.

In her September 1938 paper, "Functions of the Medical Social Worker," delivered to the Committee on Lay Participation of the American Association of Medical Social Workers, Illinois district, Kohn recommended that all social workers receive some medical training. She described the medical social worker as part of a team approach to the social aspects of patient care and recommended that all public maternity hospitals have a trained medical social worker on the staff to help physicians deal with problems that were both medical and social. Poignantly she wrote in that paper, "Of what value is the skill of a great surgeon when those he is treating are living on substandard budgets and are being deprived of specific allowances for diets or minimum allowances for food in order to satisfy a pressing landlord? Of what value is the skill of a psychiatrist to a man who fears that he will return to find his wife and children evicted from the home?" (p. 10, Kohn Papers).

As a volunteer, Kohn was a member of the Cook County Department of Welfare for twenty years and organized voluntary medical social work services at various Chicago hospitals. She also served on many boards and committees at Michael Reese Hospital, Cook County Hospital's School of Nursing, the Central Service for the Chronically Ill of Chicago's Institute of Medicine, and the University of Chicago Clinics. In 1942, Kohn developed a training course for volunteers at the Jewish Social Services Bureau to teach nonclinical social workers some of the basic techniques of interviewing utilized by mental health professionals.

Kohn's public service extended beyond local and state concerns to national and international affairs. Kohn attended the White House Conference on the Care of Dependent Children in 1909, and the White House Conference on Children in 1919 and again in 1929. Also in 1929, Kohn traveled with Jane Addams to Russia and to Geneva, Switzerland, as a delegate to the Permanent Conference of Private Organizations for the Protection of Immigrants. In 1931, Kohn served as a delegate to the National Conference on Social Work and the following year attended the International Conference on Social Work, Commission on the Immigrant, held in Frankfurt, Germany. In 1935, she was a delegate to the Pan American Child Welfare Conference in Mexico City.

With other members of the Hull-House coterie, Kohn embarked on a number of personal and semiofficial trips abroad to further the cause of improving living conditions for the world's peoples. These travels included a 1923 trip to Puerto Rico with Grace Abbott to survey child welfare problems there and to visit that country's Children's Bureau. Following World War I, she attended with Jane Addams, FLORENCE KELLEY, and ALICE HAMILTON the 1921 peace conference in Vienna held "under the auspices of the Women's International League for Peace and Freedom" (Pfeffer, 748). Accompanied by Julia Lathrop and members of the press, Kohn visited Russia in 1929 to witness the communist experiment there. "A confirmed pacifist" (Pfeffer, 748), in the 1930s Kohn "backed groups such as the Chicago Committee Against Rearming Europe, and she opposed peacetime conscription following World War II" (p. 748). She joined a number of "groups engaged in rescuing victims of Nazi tyranny, and later she was active in the Chicago Committee on Displaced Persons and the Jewish-American Joint Distribution Committee, organizations that helped displaced persons admitted to the United States" (Pfeffer, 748).

After Jane Addams died in 1935, Kohn became involved in the internal politics of Hull-House as the settlement sought to find a head resident to replace the revered Addams. She was a member of the committee chosen to work with the Hull-House board in making this choice. Kohn, a longtime resident, became disillusioned when board members ignored the advice and opinions of the residents; she left Hull-House in 1941 and, with a widowed sister, moved into an apartment.

Kohn remained active in volunteer service well into her eighties. She received many honors toward the end of her long life. In 1953, she was given the Illinois Welfare Association Award for distinguished service. In 1956, she was awarded a Citizen Fellowship at the Institute of Medicine of Chicago. Upon her retirement from the Immigrants' Service League (formerly the Immigrants' Protective League) in 1961, the organization named an annual award for service to the community in her honor. In 1964, Kohn was awarded the Jane Addams Memorial Medal in conjunction with the seventy-fifth anniversary of Hull-House. Esther Loeb Kohn died of bronchial pneumonia at the age of ninety and is buried at Mt. Maariv Cemetery in Chicago.

In her acceptance remarks upon receiving the Golden Age Hall of Fame Award in 1960, Kohn insisted that no one can accomplish things alone and cited the many politicians and lay people with whom she had worked over the years. Kohn served as an important liaison between the government and the public, using her intimate knowledge of issues to move public opinion into action and, reciprocally, representing the needs of the lay person at the government level.

Sources. The Esther Loeb Kohn Papers, UIC Spec. Coll., consist of more than three hundred folders, which, while providing incomplete information on her personal life, document her many years of public service. The papers include personal and official correspondence, 1896–1965, with Hull-House residents, public figures, and educators; an untitled, undated manuscript by Kohn on immigration and religious teaching in the public schools; agendas and minutes of the boards and service organizations to which Kohn belonged; speeches and articles written by and about Kohn and her husband; photographs of Kohn and other residents of Hull-House; information on the Illinois Committee on Child Welfare Legislation; the activities of various Jewish charities in Chicago; information on the immigration of European Jews to the United States and Palestine; attempts to promote the candidacy of Grace Abbott to the position of U.S. Secretary of Labor; material on peace organizations such as the Women's International League for Peace and Freedom; and the contributions of the Illinois and National

Leagues of Women Voters to child labor legislation. Dates of birth and death, names of Kohn's parents, cause of death and place of burial are taken from Kohn's death certificate, which was provided by the Cook County, Illinois, Office of Vital Statistics. Kohn's biography, Paula F. Pfeffer's "Esther Loeb Kohn," appears in *Jewish Women in America: An Historical Encyclopedia*, ed. Paula E. Hyman and Deborah Dash Moore, 2 vols. (1998). For information on Hull-House activities, see *100 Years at Hull-House*, ed. Mary Lynn McCree Bryan and Allen F. Davis (1990).

AMY SPRAGUE CHAMPEAU

KRAUSE, ALVINA E.
January 28, 1893–December 31, 1981
THEATER EDUCATOR, ACTING TEACHER, THEATRICAL PRODUCER AND DIRECTOR

Alvina Krause was a major figure in theater education. She taught in the School of Speech at Northwestern University from 1930 to 1963 and created the renowned four-year acting program there. Many of her students became prominent in theater and movies as actors, directors, critics, and teachers.

Alvina Krause was born in New Lisbon, Wisconsin, a small town about sixty miles northwest of Madison. Her father was Charles Frederick Krause, a dairy farmer who had emigrated from Germany in the 1860s. Her mother, Caroline (Tesch) Krause, was a third generation descendant of Bavarian immigrants. Alvina was the youngest of five children. Edward, born in 1870, Emma Marie, born in 1873, and Otelia, born in 1875, worked on the family farm. Johanna, born in 1883, took care of Alvina and later took a job at the local newspaper. In the local public school Krause read voraciously and knew from an early age that she wanted to be a teacher. In high school she participated in declamation contests in which students gave formal speeches or recitations. Her interest in drama was piqued when she read Henrik Ibsen's *A Doll's House*, and decided to read all of his plays to learn what he was saying about women and their society.

She graduated from high school in 1912 intent upon having a career. When a classmate proposed marriage, she laughed and responded that she planned to do things and have a career rather than get married. In 1914 she enrolled in the Cumnock School of Oratory at Northwestern, which later became the School of Speech, and completed the two-year diploma course in 1916. Upon graduation, she taught high school in Springfield, Missouri, from 1916 to 1919. One of her students there was Lucy McCammon, with whom she developed a close lifelong friendship. Krause then spent a year teaching in Fort Morgan, Colorado. She briefly attended the University of Wisconsin from 1922 to 1923, then returned to teaching in a high school in Seaside, Oregon, where her sister Johanna and brother Edward had moved. In Seaside, Krause taught from 1923 to 1928 and coached the girls' basketball team to a state championship. In 1928 she returned to Northwestern to complete a B.S. degree, which she received in 1929. She then accepted a position in the drama department of Hamline University in St. Paul, Minnesota. The following summer she brought a student production of a one-act farce to a drama competition at Northwestern. The group took first place after finishing last the previous year. The dean of the School of Speech at Northwestern took notice and offered Krause a job as a private instructor of voice and interpretation in the School of Speech. She was to remain at Northwestern for the rest of her formal teaching career.

When Krause began teaching, there were six other private instructors, all of whom were women, in addition to four regular instructors. Private instruction was a key part of the curriculum, providing students with individual instruction and coaching on voice improvement and textual interpretation at no extra cost. At the same time Krause continued her own studies and received an M.S. degree from the School of Speech in 1933. In the mid-1930s, private instruction was phased out because it was not cost-efficient. When Krause was informed that the program, and therefore her job, were to be eliminated, she pointed out that students would no longer have instruction in reading drama. She was asked to design a course to fill that void and was the only private instructor in the School of Speech to make the transition to regular faculty status. Krause offered her first regular course, Fundamentals of Speech, in 1934–35.

Krause continued to provide private instruction for which the university charged a separate fee. In 1936 she created a course, Creative Oral Interpretation, followed by another course in acting. These two classes were among the most popular courses in the department and became the core of Northwestern's famous drama program. In time, she taught all of the advanced acting courses in the curriculum. She had expanded the one-semester acting class to a full three-year course. She was chair of the Studio Theatre board and in 1938 was the first woman to direct a University Theatre play. In the early 1940s Krause was promoted to assistant professor of interpretation, guaranteeing her continuing presence at Northwestern. She was promoted to associate professor of dramatic production in 1957–58, the rank she held until her retirement in 1963. Krause was a small woman, just five feet two inches tall, and was described by one of her students as "a sparrow of a woman, lightly smiling, poised gently on her chair" (quoted in Fields, "Northwestern Theater Department," 50). However, she had quite an impact, as actor Richard Benjamin remembered: "She's a tiny woman . . . who has steel blue eyes that see into your skull. You can't hide" (quoted in Amory, "Trade Winds," 8).

Krause's teaching style grew out of her experiences as a private instructor. The program she designed began with the development of techniques in voice, movement, and interpretation. Then the focus moved to characterization and dramatization and finally to principles of style and the actor as communicator. Students were encouraged to study history, music, art, and literature to gain an understanding of the plays they would study. A.K., as she was known to her students, encouraged students to use their own experiences as material for characterization. Thus, she asked each to record in a journal any experiences or insights that would help in acting; she read these journals every week. Her classes were described as ever changing and intense. She was a coach to the actors on the stage, using her great knowledge of both the play and the student to help each understand the essence of the character, at the same time showing the process to the students in the audience. The technique varied: sometimes she acted along with her students and made small gestures they would incorporate into their roles; other times she might slap an actor to elicit the emotion she wanted.

She told one student who was about to begin teaching acting that she could not tell him what exercises to use. He would have to develop his own to match the mood of the moment. When discussing the "secret" of an actor's success, she replied, "Hard work" (Krause, "Forever Beginning," 3); but she also acknowledged a "sense of mystery of the metamorphosis" (p. 12) of the actor. Speaking of the source of the actor's creativity, she freely admitted, "I can not [sic] endow actors with it. I can only make them aware of the need" (Krause, "Forever Beginning," 12).

Although teaching consumed most of her energies, she also had an active career as producer and director. In 1945 she and her friend Lucy McCammon opened a summer repertory theater, the Playhouse, in Eagle's Mere, Pennsylvania, a mountain resort town. Krause believed that the ideal theater was a repertory theater in which a resident company would perform a variety of productions. The focus would be on the play rather than on the actor. Krause selected about twenty Northwestern drama students each summer to work at the Playhouse. After three years of financial failure, the theater became successful enough to be self-sufficient, and Krause was able to purchase a small hotel she called the Player's Lodge to house her students. The students not only had the opportunity of playing a variety of roles, they also were involved in every aspect of production from building sets to cooking. The Playhouse ran for nearly twenty years. Krause decided to retire from it in 1964, the year after her retirement from Northwestern. During that time she staged 180 productions, ranging from classical drama to nineteenth-century melodrama.

Krause retired from Northwestern in 1963 amid controversy. She had reached the university's mandatory retirement age of sixty-eight two years earlier, but had been allowed to keep teaching part-time as an Associate Professor Emeritus of Dramatic Production. In 1963 Northwestern officials decided to enforce the retirement rules and make Krause retire. The decision outraged students and graduates of the School of Speech, and 256 of them petitioned the university to allow her to keep teaching, stating, "Great teachers in any subject at any time are rare and Miss Krause is surely one of them" (quoted in Jack Peyrouse, "Alvina Krause Presentation," Doane College, May 25, 1970, typescript, Krause Faculty Biographical File). The petition included prominent names and brought national attention, as did a cocktail party in her support in New York City; but the university held fast and Krause was forced to retire. Just before retirement, her office was burglarized and all of her personal papers and class notes were stolen. The papers were never found and the theft remains unsolved. The year after her retirement, Krause was involved in another controversy. A group of students asked her to direct a production of Eugène Ionesco's *Rhinoceros* at the Northwestern Symposium, an annual intellectual seminar. The students acted without official approval, and, when Krause's acceptance was announced, symposium planners expressed opposition to the idea. They feared the controversy over her retirement might begin again and detract from the goals of the symposium. However, opposition to the play generated publicity, and approval was quickly granted. *Rhinoceros* was Krause's last production at Northwestern and was a triumphal exit for her.

After her retirement, Krause traveled across the country giving lectures and conducting workshops and master classes at colleges, universities, and even a few high schools. She also made several attempts to bring repertory theater to Chicago. In the summer of 1964 the owners of the Ivanhoe Restaurant on the city's North Side announced that Krause and John Van Meter would operate a repertory company at a theater to be built next to the restaurant. Unfortunately, the restaurant was mysteriously bombed later that summer, and the plans fell through. In the winter of 1966 Krause founded a repertory theater called Eagles Mere Associates at Harper Theatre in the Hyde Park neighborhood of Chicago. The reviews were lukewarm and the audiences were small, possibly because it was a harsh winter, and the group lasted only one season. She spent the years 1969 and 1970 in Santa Maria, California, where she was artist in residence and directed plays at the Pacific Conservatory of the Performing Arts at Allan Hancock College.

In 1971 she moved to Bloomsburg, Pennsylvania, to share a home with her friend Lucy McCammon, who had retired from her position as a physical education teacher at Bloomsburg State College. Although Krause had planned a quiet retirement, students began to seek her out and soon she was conducting informal acting classes in her home.

By 1977 the students had formed the Bloomsburg Theatre Ensemble (or BTE) and convinced Krause, then age eighty-four, to be its artistic director. The BTE developed into a professional repertory theater company, which not only trained its young actors and actresses but also provided theatrical education for local elementary and high schools.

Krause received many honors. She was granted an honorary Doctorate of Humane Letters from Doane College, Crete, Nebraska, in 1970, and an award from Bucknell University, Lewisburg, Pennsylvania, in 1979 for her arts achievements. Northwestern University honored her twice, in 1964 with an award of merit, and again in 1980 when she received the President's Medal for Distinguished Service. In 1974 the American College Theatre Festival presented her an award of excellence. In November 1980 a theater in New York City was named after her by the resident Meat and Potatoes Theatre Company. In the summer of 1981 the American Association of University Women named Krause Woman of the Year for Cultural Activities and gave her one of four Centenary awards.

On December 22, 1981, Krause went to New York City to attend a tribute by the Northwestern University Alumni Club of New York. However, when she arrived in New York, she felt ill and was too weak to attend. Upon her return to Bloomsburg she entered the local hospital, where she died of a heart attack. Memorial services were held on January 10, 1982, at the Wesley United Methodist Church in Bloomsburg, on January 15 at Annie May Swift Hall Auditorium at Northwestern, and on January 18 at the Alvina Krause Theatre in New York. Her remains were cremated and the ashes taken to New Lisbon, Wisconsin. On August 5, 1984, the Bloomsburg Theatre Ensemble dedicated an old movie palace it had purchased and renovated as the Alvina Krause Theatre, as a permanent tribute.

Alvina Krause once began a speech by saying, "Who am I? I am a teacher" ("Speech by Alvina Krause at Gala Dedication," 2). She was of a generation of women who had to choose between a family and a career. Having chosen a career, she devoted herself to it wholeheartedly. Although she had hobbies—gardening, literature, and music—her students and the theater were her life. She spent her spare time lecturing about the theater to various women's groups and schools. Her legacy is in the many students who achieved prominence in the theater and movies and thus exerted influence on the profession. Her students included Pulitzer Prize–winning critic Walter Kerr (whom she advised not to act); Obie (Off Broadway award by newspaper *Village Voice*) winner, director Gerald Freedman; and Academy Award winners Charlton Heston, Warren Beatty, Cloris Leachman, and nominee Patricia Neal, among others. Actor Tony Roberts attended Northwestern to study with Krause because drama coach Lee Strasberg called her the best acting teacher in the country. Her unusual approach, not devoted to any one system but combining improvisation with the Stanislavsky-based "method" and a careful reading of the play itself, lives on in the program she created at Northwestern, in the many acting teachers who studied with her, and in the continuing work of the actors she trained.

Sources. Alvina E. Krause Faculty Biographical File, Northwestern Univ. Archives, is an important source and includes the typescript, "Speech by Alvina Krause at the Gala Dedication of the Northwestern University Theatre and Interpretation Center," 1980. The Bloomsburg Theatre Ensemble has the rehearsal and production notes from her Pennsylvania theaters. Alvina Krause, "Forever Beginning," *Triquarterly*, Fall 1962, offers information on her teaching style. She is profiled in Helen Krich Jenoy and Linda Walsh Jenkins, eds., *Women in the American Theatre: Careers, Images, Movements* (1981), and in Alice M. Robinson, Vera Mowry Roberts, and Milly S. Barranger, eds., *Notable Women in the American Theatre: A Biographical Dictionary* (1989). Lynn Miller Rein, *Northwestern University School of Speech: A History* (1981), provides a biographical sketch of Krause and details her impact on the theater program. She is the subject of a Ph.D. dissertation, David Robert Press, "The Acting Teaching of Alvina Krause: Theory and Practice" (Carnegie-Mellon Univ., 1971). Useful articles include William H. Wegner, "Alvina Krause Revisited," *Educational Theatre Journal*, May 1977; Cleveland Amory, "Trade Winds," *Saturday Review of Literature*, July 26, 1969; and Beverly Fields, "Northwestern Theatre Department: No Trade School," *Chicago*, May 1954. Eva Mekler, *The New Generation of Acting Teachers* (1987), contains a brief description of her teaching by Bud Beyer, head of acting at Northwestern at that time. She is also the subject of several films, including *Alvina Krause: Class Notes 1976–1977*, a documentary by Jerry Holway; and *Acting: A Study of Life*, a series of short films introduced by actor Charlton Heston and produced by the University of South Dakota in 1971. Krause felt that the South Dakota films did not accurately capture her teaching style because she worked with students who were not familiar to her.

CATHLYN SCHALLHORN

KYRK, HAZEL
November 19, 1886–August 6, 1957
ECONOMIST, FAMILY AND CONSUMER SCIENTIST, EDUCATOR

Hazel Kyrk, one of the first American women to receive a doctorate in economics, was instrumental in defining and delineating the fields of family and consumption economics, served as adviser to government agencies, and spoke out on the economic disadvantages experienced by working women. She was born in Ashley, Ohio, the only child of Elmer and Jane (Benedict) Kyrk. She was of English ancestry on her mother's side. Her father's Scotch Irish family settled in Ohio in the early nineteenth century after migrating to the United States in the mid-1700s. David Kyrk, her paternal grandfather, built the family homestead in 1820. Her father hauled goods by wagon, while her mother, who died in 1889, was a homemaker. From her birth until she left Ashley in 1904, Kyrk lived in a small house on the Kyrk family homestead. She graduated from Ashley School in 1902. Soon after graduation, Kyrk began supporting herself by teaching at the Marlboro Township School, a one room school near her home.

At the age of eighteen, she enrolled at Ohio Wesleyan University in Delaware, Ohio, which she attended for two years. There, Kyrk supported herself by working for the family of economics professor Leon Carroll Marshall. Between 1906 and 1908, she taught at Ashley High School. Marshall joined the economics department at the University of Chicago in 1906, and Kyrk again worked for the family when she transferred to the University of Chicago in 1908. Kyrk completed a Ph.B. degree in economics from the University of Chicago in 1910, earning a Phi Beta Kappa key. Marshall would remain Kyrk's mentor, advising and assisting her as both student and professional economist.

Kyrk began Ph.D. study in economics at the University of Chicago in the autumn of 1910. From January to June 1911, she was economics instructor at Iowa State College, Ames, Iowa (now Iowa State University). She then worked during the 1911–12 academic year as an instructor in economics at Wellesley College, Wellesley, Massachusetts, where she taught three courses: "Elements of Economics," "Money and Banking," and "The Trust Problem." After completing another year of graduate work in economics at the University of Chicago, Kyrk was employed by Oberlin College, Oberlin, Ohio, in 1914 as an instructor in economics and was promoted to assistant professor in 1918. She took a leave of absence for 1918–19 to work on her dissertation but instead spent the year with the Allied Maritime Transport Council in London, England. The opportunity for Kyrk to travel to London and participate in service during World War I was the result of an invitation from her adviser at the University of Chicago, James Alfred Field. In her capacity as a statistician, Kyrk conducted economic research in London. Kyrk characterized the work of the council as being connected with the American commission for negotiating terms of peace.

Upon completion of the war work, Kyrk returned to her position at Oberlin College and completed her dissertation. She was awarded a Ph.D. degree in economics by the University of Chicago in 1920. The next year she received the first place award for her thesis, "The Consumer's Guidance of Economic Activity," from the clothing manufacturer Hart, Schaffner and Marx, in the firm's annual contest on economic essays. The monographs were judged by a committee of five economists, including two well-known and highly distinguished economists— J. B. Clark and Wesley C. Mitchell. The prize of one thousand dollars was equal to the amount Kyrk had earned per year as an instructor at Oberlin College. In 1923, as part of the prize, her thesis was published in revised form as a book titled A Theory of Consumption. Hazel Kyrk's published thesis drew on an interdisciplinary body of literature to shed light on such topics as how consumers choose what to purchase, the reasons producers might take advantage of consumers, and the need for state intervention to protect consumers.

"A study of consumption is in the main a study of human behavior" (Theory of Consumption, vii). With these words Hazel Kyrk perhaps laid the groundwork for a major field of inquiry in economics. The economic study of human behavior would not begin to gain widespread acceptance until the 1960s, when Nobel Laureates Theodore W. Schultz and Gary S. Becker, also University of Chicago economists, and others began to develop the field theoretically and methodologically. As a student at the University of Chicago, Becker had been exposed to the ideas of Margaret Reid, a student of Hazel Kyrk, on household production and consumption. Kyrk's thesis work laid the foundation for the development of the field of consumption economics (also referred to as consumer economics in some programs) in the area of family and consumer sciences (formerly known as home economics).

While at Oberlin, Kyrk was active in the Association of Collegiate Alumnae (called American Association of University Women after 1921), an organization founded in 1882 by MARION TALBOT for mutual support by college-educated women. Kyrk was elected president of the Oberlin group in 1920. In 1921, she left Oberlin, although she did not have another job. She asked Professor Marshall to help her find a position. Although she did not state the reason that she resigned, she hoped that Marshall had a male candidate to send to Oberlin. A letter in 1924 from a representative of the president of Oberlin, recommending Kyrk for a position at Cornell University, described her difficulties in teaching because of student reaction to a woman. She taught banking and transportation to classes of mostly male students. The writer contended that a man teaching the same material with the same methods would be considered totally satisfactory. Whatever her difficulties, Kyrk did not attribute them to college policy. In a letter in January 1922 to the president of the college, Kyrk praised Oberlin and counted herself as a member of its community.

After leaving Oberlin, Kyrk showed a lifelong interest in eliminating inequities for women that she saw in the workplace. She was involved briefly, in 1922, with the Women's Trade Union League of Philadelphia, an organization of middle-class and working-class women. During the summers 1922–25, she taught at the Bryn Mawr College Summer School for Women Workers in Industry. Working women studied humanism and political theory, including trade union development and Marxist thought.

She spent the year 1923–24 at Stanford University, Palo Alto, California, as an associate at the Food Research Institute. The result of that work was a monograph coauthored with the director of the institute, Joseph Stancliffe Davis, The American Baking Industry 1849–1923 as Shown in the Census Reports, published in 1925. She analyzed the growth of the industry, its economic and financial characteristics, and its personnel. During 1924–25 she was professor of economics at Iowa State College in Ames. In 1925, Kyrk began employment as an associate professor at the University of Chicago. She held appointments in both the Department of Economics and of Home Economics. The joint appointment was arranged by Field and Marshall with KATHARINE BLUNT, head of home economics.

At Chicago, Kyrk continued to focus on consumer economics within the framework of the family as an economic unit. She broadened the curriculum to span both home economics and economics in the area of family and consumption economics. She helped to define the field of family economics, as she clarified the role of the social and economic sciences in the field of home economics in the mid to late 1920s. She developed such courses as "The Family in the American Economy," "Consumers and the Market," and "Patterns and Standards of Consumption." Katharine Blunt had built an excellent graduate program in home economics, with a focus on nutrition, and Kyrk expanded the program to make the department outstanding in consumption and family economics. Kyrk became adviser and mentor to graduate students, mostly women, many of whom received Ph.D. degrees and went on to distinguished careers in teaching and research in family and consumption economics. In 1933 she published *Economic Problems of the Family*.

In addition to her teaching and academic research, Kyrk contributed to consumer economics through two areas outside academia: organizational work dealing with the status of working women, public speaking, and writing; and government employment. She became active in the Women's Trade Union League of Chicago, serving on the Exhibit Committee for the city's first Women's Industrial Exhibit, held in 1928. In 1932 she wrote, in the *American Federationist*, about the unsatisfactory work conditions of women household employees, the need for work standards and minimum wages, and the difficulty of organizing household workers in unions.

The Women's Division of the New York State Department of Labor hired Kyrk in 1937 to provide data for determining the minimum wage required for "girl" workers to ensure their maintenance and good health. Under a recent minimum-wage law, a state wage board would use Kyrk's statistics to set minimum pay in a variety of industries. Kyrk explained the consumer aspect of the budget that her staff would propose—a determination of the price of necessities, including food, clothing, and health safeguards, purchased by a woman worker.

The next year, Kyrk began part-time work with the federal government on consumer issues. In her article "The Government and the Consumer," published in the April 1935 *Journal of Home Economics*, she wrote about government responsibility to protect consumer interest rather than producer interest. She discussed New Deal agencies that dealt with consumer protection, including the Bureau of Home Economics. Four years later, she was appointed chief economist of the Bureau of Home Economics, where she spent the spring quarter of each academic year—April through June—between 1938 and 1941. At the bureau, she worked on a multi-volume Consumer Purchases Study and coauthored a number of volumes, including *Family Expenditures for Housing and Household Operation* (two volumes, coauthored with Day Monroe and others, in 1941).

In 1943 Kyrk was appointed head of the National Consumer Advisory Committee established for the Office of Price Administration (OPA). The committee, which met until 1946, assessed existing programs and proposed new rationing programs. Kyrk was concerned with protecting households from hardship due to price increases on scarce goods, especially lower-priced clothing and other small furnishings.

In 1945–46, when the U.S. Bureau of Labor Statistics decided to create an adequate budget for a family, Kyrk chaired the Technical Advisory Committee on Minimum Standard Budgets. The City Worker's Family Budget, formulated by the committee, "for many years was the most quoted yardstick of the economic welfare of families" (Dye, *History of the Department of Home Economics*, 185).

At the University of Chicago, while continuing her academic responsibilities, Kyrk also involved community members in discussions of consumer issues. In 1940, as an expert in housing issues, she organized a conference, Programs for Housing Improvement, at the Department of Home Economics with the cooperation of the Illinois League of Women Voters. Participants included academic home economists; U.S., state, and city officials; and realtors, architects, and engineers. In addition, Kyrk authored four government bulletins on housing and housing expenditures.

Kyrk remained single her entire life and maintained close ties to family. A teen-age daughter of one of Kyrk's cousins left Ashley, Ohio, to live in Chicago with Kyrk, who raised her as a "foster daughter" (*NAW*, 406). In her local community, she served on the board of the Consumer Cooperative in Hyde Park.

In 1941, sixteen years after her appointment as associate professor, she was promoted to full professor. Six years later, she was elected to the University Council, the legislative body for academic affairs. She was one of only six women who had served on the council to that date. Kyrk retired from the University of Chicago in 1952 and moved to Washington, D.C. In 1953, Ohio Wesleyan University awarded her a Doctor of Humane Letters degree for her work as teacher, researcher in home economics, and adviser to governmental agencies and private groups.

She revised and extended her 1933 publication *Economic Problems of the Family*, and it was published in 1953 as *The Family in the American Economy*. The book addressed many topics that have become central elements of the fields of labor economics and demographic economics. *The Family in the American Economy* was a study of the economic welfare of American families, "an analysis of their economic position in terms of incomes, prices and standards of living" (p. v). It dealt with the relationship between the economy and family economic welfare. The book was largely descriptive, rich with data, and representative of the type of economic analysis known as institutional economics. It was innovative in focusing on families in their income-generating roles, with attention to maximizing and maintaining the flow of income to the family. Important topics of concern included income distribution and poverty. The book also analyzed public policies designed to address income problems. The book introduced ideas or concepts still in use, such as the life cycle of the family and the family as a joint decision-making unit. Kyrk stressed that the family was the decision-making unit with respect to consumption, and it was the family rather than the individual that allocated resources to alternative uses. This idea was a main component in Becker's work. Foreshadowing approaches that would later develop into major areas of study, the book addressed several issues—women in the labor market, racial differences in family characteristics, and family structure—as key determinants of the economic position of the family.

Kyrk died in August 1957 of chronic heart disease at her summer home in West Dover, Vermont, and was buried in Ashley, Ohio. Her pioneering work in consumption and family economics has been influential in subsequent research. *A Theory of Consumption* was reprinted in 1976. *The Family in the American Economy* remained in use after her death and was reprinted in 1976 and 1980.

Sources. The Records of the Department of Economics at UC Spec. Coll. has correspondence between Kyrk and Leon Carroll Marshall and other papers on Kyrk's career at the university. Information on Kyrk's earlier appointments can be found in the Wellesley College Archives and Oberlin College Archives. The United Methodist Archives Center at Beeghly Library, Ohio Wesleyan University, has information on Kyrk in alumni files and in articles in *Ohio Wesleyan Magazine.* An interview by Helen Murray in January 1995 with Josephine Staab, who did her graduate work with Kyrk, provides information on Kyrk's accomplishments. In addition to Kyrk's publications cited above, her books in the Consumer Purchases Study series include *Family Housing and Facilities,* coauthored with Day Monroe and others (1940). Some of Kyrk's studies in consumer and family economics appear in the *Journal of Home Economics.* The work of the Technical Advisory Committee for the U.S. Bureau of Labor Statistics is reported in *Workers' Budgets in the United States: City Families and Single Persons, 1946 and 1947,* U.S. Department of Labor, Bureau of Labor Statistics, Bulletin No. 927 (1948). Biographies are found in *NAW* (1980) and in "Headliners in the Field of Home Economics," *Ohio Wesleyan Magazine,* June 1952. Margaret G. Reid, "Miss Hazel Kyrk," in Marie Dye, *History of the Department of Home Economics University of Chicago* (1972), evaluates Kyrk's contribution to the fields of consumption and family economics. Articles in the *Journal of Feminist Economics* mention Kyrk's contributions to the development of the fields of consumption and family economics: one example is Yun-Ae Yi, "Margaret G. Reid: Life and Achievements," vol. 2, 1996. Obituaries are in several newspapers, including *Chicago Daily News* and *NYT,* August 7, 1957; *CT* and *Washington Post,* August 8, 1957. For discussion of the position of women in economics and home economics prior to 1940, see Barbara Libby, "Women in Economics before 1940," in *Essays in Economic and Business History,* vol. 3, ed. Edwin J. Perkins (1984); and *Women of Value: Feminist Essays on the History of Women in Economics,* ed. Mary Ann Dimand, Robert W. Dimand, and Evelyn L. Forget (1955). Margaret I. Liston, *History of Family Economics Research: 1882–1962* (1993), traces the history of family economics research from 1862 to 1962.

ANDREA H. BELLER

D. E. KISS

l

LAMB, MARTHA JOANNA READE NASH
August 12, 1826–January 2, 1893

HISTORIAN, WRITER, CHARITY ORGANIZER

Martha Joanna Reade Nash Lamb's adult life and career spanned three periods, her years as a mathematics teacher prior to her marriage, her years as a married Chicago woman active in social and charitable causes, and her years as a single woman in New York, where she ultimately gained a considerable reputation as a historian and magazine editor. Bridging the second two careers was a brief period in which she produced children's stories and poems and one notable novel, *Spicy*.

Born in Plainfield, Massachusetts, Martha Nash was descended on her mother's side from French Huguenots and on her father's from a Mayflower settler. Her ancestry also connected her to the British novelist Charles Reade. Her mother Lucinda (Vinton) Nash died when Martha was very young. Martha Nash was the third of four children of Arvin and Lucy Nash; Arvin Nash had two more children with his second wife. Lamb maintained close contact throughout her life with her sister Maria Whitmarsh, whose daughter Mattie (Martha Polly) was her favorite niece.

As a child attending public school in Goshen, Massachusetts, Martha Nash flourished under the tutelage of a beloved teacher, Charles Burgess, who encouraged her in both mathematics and writing. Her interest in history was likewise spurred. Because her reading was carefully regulated by her father, she surreptitiously read *The Scottish Chiefs* by Sarah Porter. Her father's library contained no novels—a reflection of New England Puritan values. Although the undaunted Nash later tried her hand at a romantic novel, a departure from her strict background, she remained a devoted Presbyterian and churchgoer all her life.

Her excellence as a math student in 1844–45 at Williston Seminary in Easthampton, Massachusetts, which later excluded

women, followed by a year at Northampton High School, led to her first career as a math teacher. She first taught near her home, then in Newark, New Jersey, and finally in Maumee, Ohio, where she met Charles Lamb, whom some accounts describe as a furniture salesman, others a mechanic. She married Lamb on September 8, 1852. Martha Lamb wrote papers for the Ladies Literary Society in Maumee and, under a pen name, Emogene, wrote for the *Ladies Offering*, a Maumee publication. In Maumee, the Lambs became friends with Morrison Remick Waite and his wife. Waite's successful career as a lawyer led to his becoming Chief Justice of the United States Supreme Court in 1874, and he would introduce Martha Lamb to Washington society after her career as a historian had begun.

The Lambs stayed only briefly in Maumee, moving to Chicago in 1858. She was a good stepmother to Lamb's two daughters by a former marriage. She was one of the founders of the Home for the Friendless (1858) and the Half-Orphan Asylum. After the Civil War broke out in 1861, she threw herself into the war effort by acting as secretary for the Sanitary Fair of 1863, the first of several events held to raise money for wounded soldiers.

Lamb was an extremely industrious woman with high goals for herself and those around her. Her part in the war effort gave vent to her talents, ideals, and need for stimulation. She realized, as did MARY LIVERMORE, associate manager of the Northwestern Sanitary Fair of 1863, and other women leaders of the organized efforts to aid the war effort, that females were capable of running vast charitable structures that resembled businesses or governmental departments. Women's successes contradicted the perception of women's subordinate status; and in a letter to her sister Maria, Lamb implored her not to let her niece Mattie settle for being a milliner. Women, Lamb argued, should set higher goals for themselves.

Lamb apparently left Chicago for New York in 1867, depressed by the failure of her marriage (which ultimately ended in divorce), ill, and financially compromised upon her arrival. Her first literary efforts since before her marriage were obviously tied to her need to survive. She started by publishing children's literature, because there was a good market for it. These efforts, *Play School Stories for Little Folks* (1869), and *Aunt Mattie's Library* (1870), were undistinguished but sold well. Her novel *Spicy*, published in 1872, was one of the earliest accounts of the Great Chicago Fire by a novelist.

The narrator of the novel appears to reflect Lamb's character and interests. For Lamb, the Chicago years were an important formative time that provided female role models who helped nurture her own sense of worth; along with the impetus of financial need, they gave rise to her growth as a career woman.

The narrator in *Spicy* is a married woman who, in her husband's long absences during the Civil War, engages in multiple charitable activities in Chicago. The character Spicy is a younger sister/ward of the narrator, possibly modeled on Anna Lamb or Mattie's mother, Maria. The plot is zany but serves as a vehicle for telling some history and, more importantly, reflects the values and opinions of the narrator against the backdrop of the Civil War, the Sanitary Fair, the assassination of President Abraham Lincoln, and the Great Chicago Fire of 1871. The two characters in the novel find love letters in a rented house, where a mysterious ghost appears in the closet where the letters are found; the ghost later turns out to be the mentally ill wife to whom the letters have been addressed (and who conveniently perishes during the Great Chicago Fire). The writer of the letters later appears as a character and is freed by the wife's death to marry an old love, Ida, who happens to have masqueraded as a servant to Spicy and her sister/narrator. The persona presented by the narrator sounds much like the voice of Martha Lamb in her diaries—high-minded and stoically making the best of circumstances. There are revealing feminist observations, as when the narrator recounts that Spicy, although the valedictorian of her class at a New York boarding school, is not allowed to read her speech. The male teacher selected to read it for her ruins it with his monotonous speaking voice.

Women characters are strong and heroic in the novel. Spicy's husband, Fred, "learned what a woman could do and had done!" (*Spicy*, 167). There are also long passages commending Mrs. Vance, an activist who is perhaps a composite Chicago woman or singly modeled on JANE HOGE, a charter member of the Home for the Friendless, or Mary Livermore.

Martha Lamb then began her history of New York City. It was a project of many years. She interviewed people from old New York families, who, flattered at being included, provided her with social and other networking connections. Although she could afford to rent only a tiny apartment in Lower Manhattan, she was able to visit and converse with her subjects or their descendants, such as J. Carson Brevoort. She also enjoyed the opportunity of doing the job better than it had been done by her predecessors, more accurately and with more fairness to the original Dutch settlers. Lamb used "source materials which had been almost untouched by earlier historians of the city" (Kunitz and Haycraft, *Biographical Dictionary*, 447). *History of the City of New York: Its Origin, Rise, and Progress* appeared in two vol-

umes, the first in 1877 and the second in 1881. She had begun the city history in serial form in 1876. In later years Lamb would be best known for her history of New York.

During these early years in New York, Lamb not only worked on her history but turned out a study of Lyon Gardiner, of Gardiner's Island near Long Island, presented as a paper at the New York Historical Society. She wrote a regular serialized feature, "The Broken Pitcher," and other potbboiler serials, including "The Christmas Owl," and "The Christmas Basket," that were collected and published as books with the same titles in 1881 and 1882, respectively. She was also invited to write and produce an article on the Coast Survey (a U.S. government project on the East Coast), as well as *The Homes of America*, a large volume on distinguished American houses that contained 103 illustrations. In New York, Lamb enjoyed a busy social life and ever-growing acclaim for her accomplishments as a historian; this eventually led to her editorship in 1883 of the fledgling *Magazine of American History*, which she made popular and which was later sold to a company that she set up with her nephew. Seemingly indefatigable, she did most of the work for the magazine, and by 1892 had become a member of twenty-seven learned societies.

Lamb had been pursued by at least two men who wanted to marry her. Although she remained single, she had a life that was fulfilling both professionally and personally. Her later years included invitations to the Grover Cleveland White House (prompted by her old friend Justice Waite), an offer that was followed by an invitation to become the only female member of the American Historical Society later in 1886. At around this time, she also began an active correspondence with her niece Mattie, and she took the granddaughter of political leader Thurlow Weed to the December 1889 meeting of the American Historical Society. She complained at this time of her family's neglect and also about how exhausting her career had become. By 1890, she was seeking other editors for the magazine, even putting in a request to Theodore Roosevelt. She died of pneumonia in January 1893. In New York, she had been a member of the Madison Square Presbyterian Church, where her funeral service was held. Representatives from the Colonial Dames and the Huguenot Society attended, as did Phoebe A. Hanaford of New York's Sorosis, the first literary society established by women in the United States. Lamb is buried in Spring Grove Cemetery, Florence, Massachusetts, near relatives.

Sources. The two major repositories of Lamb's original papers, manuscripts, and letters are the New York Hist. Soc. and the Sophia Smith Collection at Smith College. The latter is the better source for personal letters and for information on the pre-Chicago period. The New York collection has the notes of Mary Persis Craft on Lamb chronology and genealogy. The New York collection contains nine manuscript boxes of Lamb's papers, including the original manuscript "History of the City of New York: Its Origin, Rise, and Progress," most of her professional correspondence concerning its publication, original manuscripts of her other published works, letters about her work as editor of the *Magazine of American History*, and a poster style bibliography of her writings. Works by Martha J. Lamb include *Play School Stories for Little Folks*, 4 vols. (1869); *Aunt Mattie's Library* (1870); *Spicy* (1872); *The Homes of America* (1879); "Lyon Gardiner, Founder of the Manor of Gardiner's Island, the First English Settlement within the State of New York," a paper read by the librarian of the New York Historical Society, November 1878; "The Broken Pitcher," published serially in the monthly *Andrew's Bazaar*, 1878–79; two booklets of light verse, *The Christmas Owl* (1881) and *The Christmas Basket* (1882); *History of the City of New York*, 2 vols. (1879, 1881); and *Memorial of Dr. J. D. Russ* (privately printed 1882). Articles include "The United States Coast Survey," *Harper's Magazine*, March 1879; "Formative Influences," *Forum*, March 1891. The most complete study of Lamb's life and career is Susan Elizabeth Lyman, *Lady Historian: Martha J. Lamb* (1969). Brief articles about Lamb appear in the following reference works: Lina Mainero and Langdon Lynne Faust, eds., *American Women Writers: A Critical Reference Guide from Colonial Times to the Present*, 4 vols. (1979–82); Stanley J. Kunitz and Howard Haycraft, eds., *A Biographical Dictionary of American Literature: American Authors 1600–1900* (1938). Her biography is in *NAW* (1971). The most extensive contemporary account is in *Godey's Lady's Book*, November 1887.

ELIZABETH Q. SULLIVAN

LATHAM, VIDA ANNETTE
February 4, 1866–January 17, 1958
DENTIST, PHYSICIAN, RESEARCHER

Vida Latham, who practiced both dentistry and medicine, believed that dentistry was part of medicine. She saw dentistry as part of the medical field of stomatology—the science of structure, function, and diseases of the mouth—to be studied by those preparing for careers in both fields. She was a leader in the Stomatological Section of the American Medical Association (AMA), which focused on research and on the relationship between medicine and dentistry.

Latham was born in Manchester, England, the youngest of ten children of John Latham, a physician, and Mary Ann (Whalley) Latham. She graduated from Norwich High School, studied at Ellerslie College in Manchester, then attended Cambridge University from 1883 to 1887. She worked with a dentist in London and embarked on a lifelong pursuit of clinical and research studies in dentistry, publishing her first article drawn from London work, "Reflex Pain Following the Extraction of a Tooth," in the *Dental Register* in 1888. That same year she also published a study on tooth anatomy, "The Forms and Origins of the Teeth," in the *Ohio Journal of Dental Science* and in a German journal. At the same time she was a graduate student at the University of London, where she received a Master of Science degree in 1889. Latham decided to study dentistry in the United States and enrolled at the University of Michigan. At the time a dental degree from Michigan was recognized in Great Britain as acceptable training, but this recognition was ended by the General Medical Council of Great Britain in 1892, the year that Latham graduated with a D.D.S. degree. Before graduation she gave presentations to the Students' Dental Society at Michigan on techniques for preparing histological specimens of teeth, published as an article, "Preparing Sections of Teeth for Histology and Bacteriology" in the *Dental Register* in 1891. While at Michigan, Latham, an organist and pianist, played the organ at the Methodist Episcopal Church in Ann Arbor.

In 1891 Latham published a discussion of the connection between medicine and dentistry, explaining that "medical men know too little of dentistry and the dentist too little of general medicine to be able to thoroughly examine cases and to treat them as is necessary" (quoted in Loevy and Kowitz, 12). The question of a proper dental curriculum was being discussed by American educators when Latham came to the United States. Some dental and medical educators believed that a student should receive an M.D. degree before attending dental school. Latham saw dentistry as a medical specialty, requiring the same basic science courses in anatomy, histology, embryology, and physiology. She criticized the focus of dental educators on manual skills in treatment rather than on science and treatment of disease. Since medical and dental studies were separated, a dentist should secure a medical degree. In 1892, Latham moved to Chicago, settling in the Rogers Park area, where she lived for the rest of her life. She immediately enrolled at Northwestern University Woman's Medical School (formerly the Woman's Medical College of Chicago, which became part of the university in 1892). During medical training and continuing until 1898, Latham supported herself by teaching dental pathology, histology, and bacteriology at the American Dental College, a proprietary school that later became part of Northwestern University. She became involved in the community when she was vice-president of the dental congress held as part of the World's Columbian Exposition of 1893.

While still a medical student, she gave a paper to the Section on Dental and Oral Surgery (renamed Stomatological Section in 1897) of the AMA at its annual meeting in Baltimore, Maryland, in 1895. Published in *JAMA* (*Journal of the American Medical Association*) in 1896 as "The Value of Differential Diagnosis in Dentistry," the study focused on pulp and periodontal problems. Within the paper she discussed the differences between medical and dental curricula, pointing out that the teaching of basic sciences in dentistry was inadequate. In future papers she repeatedly returned to the theme of the need for science in dentistry.

After receiving the M.D. degree in 1895, Latham joined the staffs at two institutions. At Northwestern, she became an assistant professor of pathology and director of the microscopical laboratories, where she immediately made improvements in procedures and standards. She also served as secretary of the medical staff, pathologist, and dental surgeon at Mary Thompson Hospital. With a busy schedule at a medical school and a hospital, Latham held office hours for her patients Thursday through Sunday. By 1897 she was in full-time practice in dentistry and medicine but kept an affiliation with the Northwestern laboratories for her research. She set up her practice with Dr. Bertha Estella Bush, a surgeon who had graduated from Woman's Medical College in 1889. The two women shared a residence and offices on Morse Avenue for the rest of their lives.

At Northwestern, Latham worked with Professor Eugene Talbot, a dental surgeon who, like her, had both medical and dental degrees, and who saw her as a colleague in research. During their collaboration, she also taught with Talbot for a time at Rush Medical College.

Latham had a special interest in the use of the microscope and a "remarkable knowledge of specimen preparation for microscopic study" (Loevy and Kowitz, 13). Latham's research papers often provided precise descriptions of the microscopic techniques that she used and procedures for preparing specimens for study. Concerned with the sharing of research among professionals, she served with two publications in microscopy. In 1895 she was associate editor of the *International Journal of Microscopy and Natural Science*. She later became editor of the *Illinois Microscopical Society Bulletin*. In 1895 she was vice-president of the American Microscopical Society. By 1905 Latham was elected a fellow of the Royal Microscopical Society of London for her work in the field. At the Illinois State Microscopical Society, she served as secretary and then president.

Since the dental profession focused on the mechanics of treatment rather than on research, Latham presented her studies through the medical route of the Stomatological Section of the AMA. At the section's annual meeting in 1901, she reviewed the research literature on the embryology and histology of dental pulp. In the publication that followed in *JAMA* in 1902, she described the microscopic stains used and included many illustrations, an unusual addition in contemporary research literature. Able to read European languages, Latham included foreign-language publications in her review. She believed that the omission of discussion of foreign literature in American journals impeded progress in dental research. In 1905 she became head of the Stomatological Section and spoke on scientific progress in the field.

Throughout her career, Latham supported women in dentistry. She was involved as teacher and researcher in the preparation of women for dentistry and medicine. In 1901, she included Dr. Martha Anderson, one of her medical students, in the dental research that Latham and Eugene Talbot were doing on the embryology of teeth. Anderson, like Latham, published reports on the microscopic study of teeth.

At a meeting of University of Michigan alumni, Latham spoke on the suitability of women for dentistry and published her views in 1901 in the article "The Profession of Dentistry for Women." Although she described marriage as "useful" and "pleasant" (p. 16), she believed that a woman had the need and the right to become self-supporting. For women who were able to deal with life-and-death situations, she recommended dentistry and medicine as a means of supporting themselves. She recognized that women's "position in the professional world is . . . difficult through the prejudice against their sex by both men and women" (p. 15); but she urged women who were self-confident to consider dentistry. While she realized that married women generally gave up their professions, she opened the possibility that they could continue to practice, depending on their skills, adaptability, and income. She denied the view of contemporaries that the study of science, including medicine and dentistry, made a woman "unfeminine or less womanly" (p. 18). She told women that "we do and must acquire self-reliance, firmness to stand alone, convictions of our own opinion" (p. 18).

For women already in dental or medical practice, Latham proposed career possibilities in research work. In a talk in 1906 to alumnae of the Women's Medical College of Pennsylvania, she described the importance of biology in medical studies and suggested research areas in both zoology and botany. She saw the economics of biology as a necessary field of research and gave several examples, among them studies on crop disease and crop rotation, food chemistry and adulteration, and diseases of working people exposed to harmful chemicals. She spoke at the same time about medical practice for women. Latham sug-

gested that women medical students focus on histology and physiology and prepare for general practice rather than surgery, because men physicians "and the public are against women being so strong-minded as to attempt that specialty" (Latham, "Suggestions in Special Lines of Research Work for Women," 731).

Latham interrupted her practice and research during World War I to work as a dentist for the U.S. Marine Corps in a volunteer service organized by American women's hospitals. She also headed a committee for sanitary inspection of military camps, to check on health conditions and medical facilities.

In 1921, she and eleven other women dentists, seeing a need for a women's professional group, founded the National Dental Sorority. It became, in 1928, the American Association of Women Dentists, an organization active into the 1990s.

As the field of dentistry developed, American Dental Association meetings included discussions of research, and Latham gave a presentation in microscopy as part of the scientific program at the annual meeting in Milwaukee, Wisconsin, in 1921. By 1925, medical researchers no longer saw a need to include dentistry as a study area, and the AMA discontinued its Stomatological Section. In 1930, at a meeting of the International Stomatological Association in Venice, Italy, she decried the AMA's action as "a blot upon the progress of medicine and dentistry in our country" ("Stomatology, Its History and Its Relationship to Medicine," 6) and asked dentists and physicians to work together to remedy the situation.

Latham gave few research presentations after 1930, but she continued to practice dentistry and medicine. She was on the staff of Edgewater Hospital in Chicago and of St. Francis Hospital in suburban Evanston, where she established a system of cottages for patients with contagious diseases. She remained active in professional organizations and in 1933 was elected president of the Woman's Medical Club of Chicago.

When Latham was ninety, Zonta, a club of professional women, named her "medical woman of the year" (*Chicago Tribune*, January 18, 1958). She died at the age of ninety-one, "one of Chicago's oldest practicing doctor-dentists" (*Chicago Sun-Times*, January 18, 1958).

Throughout her career, Latham was seen by colleagues as a prominent woman dentist. She made an important contribution to early dental research through presentations at scientific meetings and publications. She published more than fifty articles on clinical techniques and pathologies in dentistry, as well as case reports on conditions in the mouth. Although her view of the unity of dentistry and medicine did not persist, her focus on the importance of dental research was an influence in the later development of such research as an essential part of dentistry. In relating dentistry to medicine, she showed a broader vision of the field than did some of her contemporaries who defined dentistry as mechanical practice.

Sources. Several Latham articles are described above. In addition, her articles on women in dentistry and medicine include "The Profession of Dentistry for Women," *Dental Era*, vol. 4, 1905, and "Suggestions in Special Lines of Research Work for Women," vol. 12, 1906. *Woman's Medical School, Northwestern University (Woman's Medical College of Chicago) The Institution and Its Founders* (1896) has brief information on her education, employment, and publications. A detailed discussion of her views on the relationship of dentistry and medicine is found in her article, "Stomatology, Its History and Its Relationship to Medicine," *American Journal of Stomatology and Odontology*, October 1930. An article by Hannelore T. Loevy and Aletha Kowitz, "Health Science Pioneer: Vida A. Latham, DDS, MD," *Proceedings of the Institute of Medicine of Chicago*, vol. 44, 1991, describes her work and provides a selected listing of eighteen Latham articles. Rae Paul, "The Journal of Vida Latham (1866–1958)," *Illinois Dental Journal*, May 1976, gives a brief report on her clinical daybook. Obituaries appear in the *Chicago Sun-Times*, January 18, 1958; *CT*, January 18, 1958; and *Illinois Dental Journal*, vol. 27, 1958.

HANNELORE T. LOEVY

LATHROP, JULIA CLIFFORD
June 29, 1858–April 15, 1932
SOCIAL WORKER, SETTLEMENT RESIDENT, REFORMER

Julia Clifford Lathrop, the first chief of the federal Children's Bureau, was born in Rockford, Illinois. Her father, English-descended William Lathrop, immigrated to the prairie village in northern Illinois from western New York in 1851. A Republican and opponent of slavery, William Lathrop practiced law and eventually served in the Illinois legislature and the United States Congress. Lathrop's mother, Sarah Adeline (Potter) Lathrop, who also emigrated from New York, lived her commitment to women's education by graduating from Rockford Female Seminary in 1854 and remaining a lifelong proponent of woman suffrage.

As an eldest child, Lathrop helped to care for her younger siblings (one girl and three boys) and, despite that responsibility, finished high school and aspired to higher education. Following in her mother's footsteps, she first attended Rockford Female Seminary, but after only one year, she left to attend Vassar College, one of the nation's first women's colleges.

After earning her degree in 1880, Lathrop, like so many members of the first generation of college-educated women, returned to her family. She served as her father's secretary, read law in his office, and identified with the local Republican party; yet none of these promised her a career. Although the doors of higher education had swung open to women, the gates to professions, business, and electoral politics for the most part remained closed. Women like Lathrop, brimming with intelligence and ambition, had to clear new paths to independence and public authority, a challenge that her generation began to meet very effectively in 1889.

In that year, JANE ADDAMS and ELLEN GATES STARR opened Hull-House, one of the city's most important institutions of social reform and women's emancipation. Although their method was undefined in the beginning, Addams and Starr expected their social settlement to house young, middle-class women and men who wanted to exchange cultural and material resources with their working-class, mostly immigrant neighbors. In 1890, Lathrop joined the settlement venture, taking up residence at Hull-House.

Lathrop, from the beginning of her residency, displayed the settlement spirit. She flourished in serving the neighborhood and living in a community of peers. In fact, Lathrop, who never married, found communal living utterly satisfying. She seemed especially suited to this life by her lively sense of humor and

FIG. 63. *Hull-House resident Julia Clifford Lathrop, who became the first director of the federal Children's Bureau in 1912.*

what one resident called her "gift for friendship" (Abbott, "Julia Lathrop," 306). Indeed, throughout her career, Lathrop projected an empathy with other people that simultaneously made her approachable and gave her special authority. She could, according to one later observer, bring together disputing factions no one else had been able to reconcile.

She demonstrated these gifts very soon after coming to Hull-House. Working-class families suffering from a smallpox epidemic welcomed her as nurse and counselor, while older men in the neighborhood accepted her as leader of their philosophical discussion group, the Plato Club. In 1893, Lathrop began a long stint on the Illinois State Board of Charities to which reforming Governor John P. Altgeld appointed her. She intrepidly inspected all 102 county institutions for the sick, homeless, and insane and approached this investigative task in a pathbreaking way. According to Addams, Lathrop looked at those institutions from the standpoint of the inmates themselves. She usually found them wanting, of course, and began to advocate state rather than county institutions, with clients housed according to their age and particular disadvantage.

As a member of the Board of Charities (1893–1901, 1905–1909), Lathrop also deepened her commitment to civil service reform, a value she shared with her dear friend and Hull-House coresident, FLORENCE KELLEY. She believed that the county institutions were poorly run in part because the people directing them were political appointees rather than experts in public administration or in the treatment of disabled people. She advocated filling these positions on the basis of special knowledge and experience, a view she articulated first in her chapter in *Hull-House Maps and Papers* (1895). This opinion eventually triumphed, when in 1909 the state replaced its voluntary Board of Charities with a salaried Charities Commission to oversee Illinois's institutions for the sick, delinquent, and insane.

Lathrop broadened her commitment to expertise in the delivery of social services when she joined fellow Chicagoan and head resident of the Chicago Commons Settlement, Graham Taylor, in creating an institution for training those who provided social services. As early as 1903–1904, Taylor and Lathrop were offering a series of courses aimed at systematizing the investigation of potential clients by the city's charities. By 1907, they had won a five-year grant to add a research component to their initiative, and Lathrop hired on temporarily as director of research. In 1908, they officially chartered their enterprise as the Chicago School of Civics and Philanthropy. To run the research department, Lathrop shrewdly recruited political scientist SOPHONISBA BRECKINRIDGE, then at the University of Chicago, who, in turn, hired as her associate economist EDITH ABBOTT. Lathrop remained integral to the school until it joined the University of Chicago as its School of Social Service Administration in 1920.

Precisely because she helped to establish the curriculum and commitments of the Chicago School of Civics, Lathrop looked to it for research assistance and employee recruitment once she moved into a policymaking position in the federal government. In 1912, as a result of intense lobbying by settlement workers and the National Child Labor Committee, Congress created the Children's Bureau in the Department of Commerce and Labor. Jane Addams and her New York colleague, Lillian Wald, founder and head resident of the Henry Street settlement, believing they now had their main chance to move a woman into a position of official, national power, urged President William Howard Taft to appoint Julia Lathrop to head the new bureau. They believed that Lathrop's expertise in child welfare was particularly demonstrated by her participation with LUCY FLOWER in founding the Chicago Juvenile Court in 1899, her leadership on the subsequent Juvenile Court Committee, and in her investigation of conditions in the public schools of the Philippines. Taft agreed, and Lathrop became the first woman to head a federal government agency.

As Chief of the Children's Bureau from 1912 to 1921, Lathrop created a nearly all-female agency, which was instructed to investigate all aspects of children's lives in the United States. With very few resources in the early years, Lathrop inaugurated local studies of infant mortality and soon branched into maternal mortality, juvenile delinquency, child labor, and mothers' pensions, only a few of the areas her bureau studied. The young agency published not only the conclusions of these studies but also, at Lathrop's insistence, the most up-to-date advice on the

care of pregnant women, infants, babies, and children. These advice pamphlets became some of the best-selling publications of the Government Printing Office. The Children's Bureau thus participated in professionalizing motherhood, transforming it from a set of qualities presumed to be innate to a body of knowledge learned from experts in the fields of nutrition, medicine, child development, and home economics. Lathrop was so committed to the professionalization of motherhood, in fact, that she campaigned to have her alma mater, Vassar, add domestic science to its curriculum, which it did in 1924.

Perhaps the most important achievement of Lathrop's career was her drafting and winning passage of the Sheppard-Towner Maternity and Infancy Act. The Children's Bureau's studies of maternal and infant mortality revealed throughout the 1910s that the United States had some of the highest mortality rates in the industrialized world and that many of the deaths could have been prevented by better prenatal and infant care. Especially worried about the lack of information and care in rural areas, Lathrop used the opportunity of World War I to gain support for her plan to provide federal funds for educating women to care for themselves during pregnancy and their children after birth.

She declared April 6, 1918, the beginning of Children's Year, a period dedicated to improving the health of America's children. Americans were particularly receptive to the call, because military physicals had revealed widespread disabilities among American young men. The Children's Year crusade, running almost simultaneously with Lathrop's presidency of the National Conference of Social Work, popularized the Children's Bureau and organized the country's child welfare advocates under the bureau's leadership. They were then ready after the war to lobby Congress on behalf of Lathrop's program for maternal health education. When it passed in November 1921, the Sheppard-Towner Maternity and Infancy Act became the first piece of federal social welfare legislation in United States history.

Satisfied with her tenure as chief, Lathrop resigned from the Children's Bureau shortly before her bill passed but not before she had ensconced her hand-picked successor, GRACE ABBOTT, as the new chief of the Children's Bureau. A sister Hull-House resident, Abbott originally impressed Lathrop through her performance as the first director of Illinois's Immigrants' Protective League (IPL), which Lathrop helped to found in 1908. Lathrop had previously succeeded in bringing Abbott to Washington to administer the first federal child labor law in 1917 but lost her the next year when the Supreme Court judged the law unconstitutional. Once Abbott held the Children's Bureau's reins, Lathrop moved out of the residential hotel that had been her home in Washington and returned to Rockford, where she lived with her widowed sister, Anna Lathrop Case.

Retirement from the bureau, however, in no way represented a retreat from public life. Although Lathrop toyed with the idea of running for public office, she, like many women of her generation, ultimately opted for continued nonpartisan activism even after the victory of woman suffrage in 1920. In keeping with this decision, she served as president of the Illinois League of Women Voters from 1922 to 1924. In that capacity, she lobbied the state legislature to accept Sheppard-Towner funds and came to believe that, to be effective activists, women in the league had to begin to study state finances. In mid-decade, President Calvin Coolidge named her to a commission to investigate conditions on Ellis Island, and in 1925 the League of Nations appointed her as an assessor for the Child Welfare Committee of its Commission on the Welfare of Children and Young Persons. She served on that committee (a sort of international Children's Bureau, charged as it was with gathering information on children's lives the world over) for six years.

Julia Lathrop died in Rockford after a goiter operation in 1932. She was buried in Rockford's Greenwood Cemetery and mourned throughout the social work community that she had helped to create. In a eulogy published in the *Social Service Review*, Edith Abbott capsulized Lathrop's achievements: "To the end of her life she saw visions and dreamed dreams that she tried to make part of the world in which she lived" (Abbott, "Julia Lathrop," 306). Lathrop had, in fact, helped to build many of the engines that powered the twentieth-century United States. An expanded civil service, juvenile courts, mothers' pensions, immigrant protection programs, the profession of social work, and federally funded social services, all of which were contested and modified throughout the century, continued to define the American state and its politics.

Sources. Julia Lathrop's personal papers are at Rockford College, and much of her correspondence is in the Grace and Edith Abbott Papers, UC Spec. Coll., as well as in the Children's Bureau Records, National Archives, Washington, D.C. *The Jane Addams Papers on Microfilm*, ed. Mary Lynn McCree Bryan (1984), also contain correspondence with and about Lathrop as well as Hull-House Records that document her role in that institution. Julia Lathrop's ideas can be traced in part through her own publications. She contributed an essay to the pathbreaking social scientific study written by "Residents of Hull-House," *Hull-House Maps and Papers* (1895), and later wrote *Suggestions for Visitors to County Poorhouses and to Other Public Charitable Institutions* (1905). She produced an important and original introduction to Sophonisba Breckinridge's and Edith Abbott's *The Delinquent Child and the Home* (1912); another, titled "Standards of Child Welfare," for James Bossard, ed., *Child Welfare* (1921); and an essay, "The Background of the Juvenile Court in Illinois," for Jane Addams et al., *The Child, The Clinic and The Court* (1927). In addition, she delivered many addresses before professional and voluntary organizations, wrote for popular magazines, and compiled reports on the Children's Bureau 1913–21. The only book-length biography is Jane Addams, *My Friend, Julia Lathrop* (1935). Other sources include Edith Abbott, "Julia Lathrop and the Public Social Services," and Jane Addams, "A Great Public Servant, Julia Lathrop," *Social Service Review*, June 1932. Further information can be gleaned from Edith Abbott, "The Hull House of Jane Addams," *Social Service Review*, September 1952; James Weber Linn, *Jane Addams, A Biography* (1935); and *NAW* (1971). Especially on Lathrop's years as chief of the Children's Bureau, see Robyn Muncy, *Creating a Female Dominion in American Reform, 1890–1935* (1991).

ROBYN MUNCY

LAUDYN, STEFANIA (Laudyn-Chrzanowska)
January 2, 1872–February 28, 1942
JOURNALIST, AUTHOR, SOCIAL ACTIVIST

Stefania Laudyn, longtime editor of the Polish Women's Alliance newspaper, *Głos Polek (Polish Women's Voice)*, was born in Rochaczów, near Mohylew, Bielorus. Her father, Franciszek Borowski, was a landholder and Mohylew high school teacher.

Her mother's maiden name was Laska. At the time, Poland had ceased to exist as a state, and Stefania Borowska was raised under Russian rule. Her intense Polish patriotism was shaped by her early experiences of Russian oppression, particularly in the aftermath of the failed Polish uprising of 1863. As a schoolgirl, she felt the effects of enforced Russification, aimed at undermining Roman Catholicism, the Polish language, and ultimately Polish identity. She was especially influenced and inspired by a personal acquaintance with the Korsak sisters, Kamilla and Adela, exiled insurrectionists who returned to Mohylew from Siberia when Borowska was a young girl. Her vocal proclamation of her Polishness led to conflicts with officials and with her parents, who were concerned about their daughter's welfare under Russian rule. Her first husband, Kazimierz Laudyn, brought her to Moscow and into contact with Russian intellectuals. Laudyn later recalled that it was through these contacts and her studies as a free listener at Moscow University that her "internal 'I' matured" (*Głos Polek*, August 2–16, 1917).

Laudyn had already published two plays, *Zmarnowane życie* (The Wasted Life) (1895) and *Bez słońca* (Without the Sun) (1903), when in 1904 she began writing anonymously to a St. Petersburg newspaper, arguing in favor of Polish political rights. To her surprise, these letters, signed simply "A Polish Woman," attracted much attention and admiration among Polish intellectuals and activists, including renowned novelist Eliza Orzeszkowa, who was even suspected of being their author. The letters were collected in *Kwestja polska i inne: Listy polityczne "Polki"* (The Polish Question and Other Matters: Political Letters by "A Polish Woman") (1908), which was burned by Russian censors. Laudyn soon became a frequent contributor to Moscow and Kraków newspapers.

Laudyn was a proponent of pan-Slavism, which called for the unity of all Slavic peoples for their common interests. Although the movement was widely accused of submerging all Slavs under Russian cultural and political hegemony, Laudyn herself always argued passionately for the Polish cause. Although she hoped for Polish independence, she was also convinced by her own experience that Russians and Poles could cooperate on terms of mutual respect, no matter what the political structure. Like many Polish positivists, she concentrated her efforts on improving education and political and cultural awareness among her fellow Poles and on easing restrictions imposed by Moscow. She even addressed an open letter to Leo Tolstoy, calling for his response to Russian and Prussian oppression of Poles and prompting a public reply.

In 1907 Laudyn founded Moscow's Polish Women's Alliance (Związek Kobiet Polskich) for the purpose of educating Polish workers in that city. At the same time, hoping to unite Polish women in all three partitioned areas, Laudyn lobbied throughout Russian and Galician Poland for the creation of a League of Slavic Women (Liga Kobiet Słowiańskich). In Prague she received the discouraging news that the Austro-Hungarian government had denied the organization's petition to exist, ruling that since women in Austria had no political rights, a political league could not be established. She returned to Moscow to find her husband dangerously ill. When he died, she was "free to choose [her] path in life, unfettered and secure" (*Głos Polek*, March 30, 1944).

Searching for the place where she could work most freely, Laudyn decided to emigrate to the United States in order to do national work within the immigrant community, particularly because, as she described it, "I had established a certain contact through the [Polish American] press in order to arrange the matter" (*Głos Polek*, March 30, 1944). That contact was Adam Chrzanowski, a Chicago law student and former foundry worker thirteen years her junior. They had struck up a correspondence after Chrzanowski placed an open letter in the European and immigrant press, inviting other students to write to him regarding Polish political issues. He and Laudyn became engaged through the mail, without having met each other. Polish American newspapers reported on their courtship in July 1909, claiming that Chrzanowski had misrepresented himself to his fiancée. According to the press, his letters had actually been written by a medical student friend because Chrzanowski himself was barely literate. This friend allegedly confessed to reporters because he was worried about the legality of what he had done, especially after Laudyn sent Chrzanowski five hundred rubles and set sail for America with marriage in mind. Chicago's satirical *Bicz Boży*, on August 1, 1909, thinly disguising the parties' names, ridiculed "Chrzan" as a village yokel and called "Longinówna" "material too manhandled for a wife, because she is a divorcee!" Whatever the circumstances, Laudyn landed in New York around June 1909, and on April 24, 1910, married Adam Chrzanowski, who had already legally changed his middle name from "Mikołaj" to "Laudyn." His wife continued to sign her work alternately "Stefania Laudyn" and "Stefania Laudyn-Chrzanowska." Chrzanowski's naturalization papers, issued shortly after their marriage, indicated that Laudyn may have left an eighteen-year-old son behind in Russia, but she never mentioned this child in any of her published writings.

Any scandal seemed to have been forgotten, however, when in November 1910 Stefania Laudyn took over the editorship of the Polish Women's Alliance newspaper, *Głos Polek*. The Polish Women's Alliance, or Związek Polek w Ameryce (ZPA) had been formed in Chicago, in 1898, by Polish-born STEFANIA CHMIELIŃSKA and TEOFILA SAMOLIŃSKA, in response to the failure of other Polish immigrant organizations to grant full membership rights to women. The ZPA was not the first or only Polish immigrant women's organization, but it was the most long lasting and defended Polish national ideals and the rights of women. *Głos Polek*, established in 1902, had been reduced since 1903 to a monthly page in Chicago's *Dziennik Narodowy*. Under Laudyn's editorship the paper was once again published independently, as it remained in the 1990s, and reached readers far beyond the sizeable ZPA membership. In addition to local chapter news, the weekly *Głos Polek* included poetry and short fiction but paid special attention to reports of international events of interest to women and to Poles. The paper ran a column, "From the Women's Movement," reported sympathetically on American labor activities, and featured frequent articles by Polish feminists such as Maria Konopnicka and Eliza Orzeszkowa.

Besides her work for the ZPA, Laudyn was a busy organizer. In 1911 she was among the cofounders and the first treasurer of the Society of Polish Writers and Journalists (Towarzystwo Literatów i Dziennikarzy Polskich), based in Chicago, which lasted until 1914. She was also a proponent of the Polish Alma Mater, a system of schools for immigrants based on a Polish nationalist model.

Although the ZPA had at first praised Laudyn glowingly, calling her a "Pole through and through," (*Głos Polek*, November 17, 1910), relations soon became strained between the organization and its editor, who left *Głos Polek* in 1912. As Laudyn reported it, she was dismissed. ZPA officials, however, claimed that Laudyn had resigned because she was unhappy with their decisions, particularly with the executive board's insistence on maintaining final control over the newspaper editorship. They accused Laudyn of putting her own ideological goals, especially her work for the Polish Society of Writers and Journalists and for the Polish Alma Mater, above ZPA interests. "We don't know where and when Mrs. Laudyn completed her university studies," *Głos Polek* editorialized on June 1, 1912, "but we do know that the 12,000 Polish women organized by our Alliance have so much strength of spirit and love for the fatherland that these 'poorly educated' women have built an organization here the likes of which the 'so very enlightened' Mrs. Laudyn never imagined even in the old country." By 1913, the ZPA was calling the avowedly Roman Catholic Laudyn not only a Moscow-sympathizer, but a member of the Russian Orthodox church. The conflicts were evidently smoothed out, however, because Laudyn resumed the editorship of *Głos Polek* in 1914. When she resigned four years later, she put the blame on poor health, not professional differences, and continued to contribute articles and advertisements to the paper for several more years.

Laudyn's many articles on political and social issues appeared frequently not only in *Głos Polek* but in such other Polish American newspapers as Chicago's *Dziennik Związkowy*, *Gazeta Polska w Chicago*, and the World War I era English-language *Free Poland*. She wrote about such matters as the Polish American parochial school system, the influence of women on Polish immigrant life, the sexual exploitation of immigrant girls, domestic abuse and the need for abstinence from alcohol, literary depictions of women in Polish literature, and the official relationship of Polonia—the Polish community in America—to the reborn Poland. She also wrote several patriotic plays, including *Majowy cud* (The May Miracle) (1917); *Września*, based on a series of school strikes in Prussian Poland (1907; reprinted 1917); *Matka* (Mother) (date unknown); and *Obrazek z Powstania Stycznego* (A Picture from the January Uprising) (date unknown). Laudyn's collection of short stories, *Galerja obrazów z krainy dolara* (A Gallery of Pictures from the Land of the Dollar), published around 1920, drawn from Polish immigrant life in Chicago, confronts problems of unemployment, class conflict, Americanization, and women's autonomy. But of her many books, only one has been translated into English, the anti-Semitic *A World Problem: Jews—Poland—Humanity* (1920). Though she was progressive in so many other ways, Laudyn, in the name of patriotism, blamed many of Poland's political and social problems on its Jewish population.

From 1914 on, Laudyn appears to have divided her time between Chicago and Indiana Harbor, Indiana, where her husband established a law practice. In 1922 she returned to the newly independent Poland, but she came back to the United

States between 1924 and 1927 to edit New York's *Kuryer Narodowy*. Eventually she resettled in the Polish mountain resort of Zakopane, where Adam Chrzanowski operated the elegant Bristol Hotel. Continuing the work she had begun more than twenty years before, Laudyn organized the Society of Slavic Women (Towarzystwo Kobiet Słowiańskich), made up of women from Bulgaria, Czechoslovakia, Poland, and Yugoslavia, and in 1929 was elected vice-president at its first congress, held in Prague. In February 1942, while Adam Chrzanowski was interned by the Nazis, Laudyn, long in frail health, died in Zakopane. She is buried there.

Laudyn's name is all but forgotten, even among scholars of immigration; but her voice was certainly heard by tens of thousands of Polish immigrants, particularly immigrant women, during American Polonia's formative years. When her husband ran for an Indiana Harbor judicial seat in 1918, he ran as Adam Laudyn-Chrzanowski, making strategic public use of his wife's well-known name. On the other hand, when *Głos Polek* received news of Stefania Laudyn's death, it was able to publish only the most general sketch of her life and work and had to ask readers for more specific information about her. Laudyn was a very vocal participant in the vital, heated debates in the Polish American immigrant community over the meaning and perpetuation of Polishness both in America and in the partitioned homeland. In particular, Laudyn was among a handful of immigrant women who tried to shape a discourse of Polishness that recognized women's contributions, linked women's issues with Polish national aspirations on both sides of the ocean, and acquainted a largely working-class female readership with the aims of world feminism.

Sources. In addition to her several plays, her collection of short stories, and various political tracts, *Głos Polek*, available on microfilm, not only contains much of Laudyn's writing but also reflects her orientation on women's rights, Polish independence, immigrant conditions, and many other issues. *Sprawa polska w Ameryce Północnej* (The Polish Question in North America) (1912), published by the Towarzystwo Literatów i Dziennikarzy Polskich, contains an introduction by Laudyn in addition to her article, "Kobieta wobec przyszłości" (Women Facing the Future). Several of Laudyn's own articles contain information about her early life in Europe, including the *Głos Polek* series "Nasze 'wczoraj'—a nasze 'dziś'" (Our Yesterday and Our Today), August 2–September 6, 1917, and the posthumously published "Idzie nowa era—era ducha" (A New Era of the Spirit Is Coming) (*Głos Polek*, March 30, 1944). One of the few sources for specific biographical information is a February 18, 1949, article on Laudyn in Chicago's *Dziennik Związkowy*. Information in English about Stefania Laudyn is very limited. Thaddeus Radzilowski's "Immigrant Nationalism and Feminism: *Głos Polek* and the Polish Women's Alliance in America, 1898–1917," *Review Journal of Philosophy and Social Science*, vol. 2, 1977, discusses the impact of *Głos Polek* under her editorship. Readers of Polish will find a handful of publications useful. The three-volume Polish-language history of the ZPA, *Historia Związku Polek w Ameryce* (1938–81), is only marginally helpful. Laudyn receives passing mention in a number of other historical works, including Stanisław Osada's *Prasa i publicystyka polska w Ameryce* (The Polish Press and Journalism in America) (1930). Her first play, *Zmarnowane życie* (A Wasted Life) (1895), is reviewed at length in Piotr Chmielowski, *Nasza literatura dramatyczna*, vol. 2 (1898).

KAREN M. MAJEWSKI

LAUGHLIN, CLARA ELIZABETH
August 3, 1873–March 3, 1941

EDITOR, JOURNALIST, AUTHOR, CLUBWOMAN, TRAVEL EXPERT

Clara Laughlin was the eldest child of well-to-do New Yorker Elizabeth Wylie (Abbott) Laughlin and immigrant Samuel Wilson Laughlin of Belfast, Ireland. Laughlin's thematically organized 1934 autobiography, *Traveling through Life*, recalled her father as "a fine *raconteur*" whose "veneration for Shakespeare" introduced her to theater, and her strict mother also as a natural "storyteller" (pp. 7, 29, 3).

A year after Laughlin's birth in New York City, her family moved, to save money, to Milwaukee, Wisconsin, where her brother William was born, then to Chicago in 1878, where Abbott and Alice were born. The Laughlins often visited family in New York, traveling on railroads that employed two uncles and the fathers of several childhood friends. Her first trip to Europe took place when her mother went for treatment for gout in 1879. Laughlin attributed her acceptance of cultural differences to her enthusiasm for the foods she tasted abroad. Pilgrimages to long-imagined scenes in her mother's tales from British and French royal history established a lifelong habit of associating places with dramatic stories. Historical characters were Laughlin's early familiars, and she made up stories for friends while walking to the house where they received informal schooling, then to Lincoln School. Before her graduation from North Division High School in 1890, Laughlin had met one of the *Chicago Tribune*'s early women reporters, ELIA PEATTIE, published a story in *Waverly Magazine*, and won the senior essay contest.

Samuel Laughlin's risky business ventures meant financial insecurity and usually pinched circumstances after the 1881 birth of their last, retarded child, Alice, who required constant attention until she died in 1905. When Clara Laughlin's father died of pleurisy in 1891, the family's resources were "practically nil" (*Traveling through Life*, 55). Laughlin's mother took in boarders. Her older brother left school to go to work, and Laughlin found a job through her active involvement in Presbyterian church activities and the acquaintance of nearby seminary students. Laughlin began work in 1892 as literary editor and writer for the *Interior*, published by Cyrus McCormick and considered by the *London Times* to be America's "ablest religious weekly" (quoted in *Traveling through Life*, 58). She continued to hold this position until 1911.

At the *Interior*, besides reviewing "Lighter Literature," Laughlin edited columns of regional church news, family life, and both children's and adult poetry and fiction. She used her editorial contacts to publish her own work elsewhere for additional money. The earliest of her essays about reviewing and editing, sometimes poking fun at her own practices, were published by periodical editors she met on annual *Interior* trips to Boston and New York. Her first book publications—*The Golden Year* (1898) and *Riley Love-Lyrics* (1899)—compiled poems by James Whitcomb Riley, from whom she had brashly solicited "twenty-five dollars' worth of your very best poetry" (quoted in *Life*, 63) for the *Interior*. When Riley died in 1916, she described their friendship for the September *Ladies' Home Journal* and in *Reminiscences of James Whitcomb Riley*.

By 1898 she was able to afford a Pine Grove Avenue home looking out on Lake Michigan. She lived her adult years in the Lincoln Park area near her mother, her older brother and business partner, and her ultimate traveling companions, Nannie and Betty Laughlin, the two daughters of her younger brother, who died in 1917. Although a self-declared "domestic being" (quoted in *Life*, 88) who acknowledged several engagements, she never married, identifying her happiness with her work.

The next books Laughlin wrote established her primary genres. *Stories of Authors' Loves* (1902) was a series of biographies, and she wrote many more. She remained well known for *The Evolution of a Girl's Ideal* (1902), the first of eight sentimental, didactic novellas that Chicago's Fleming H. Revell Company published as gift books. These included one named for Jean François Millet's painting *The Gleaners* (1911), which typified small-town domestic settings and focused on women's development of personal wisdom, often inspired by art works. The first of Laughlin's many works of personal and social advice, *Miladi* (1903), explicitly declared her characteristic "home-world" (p. 33) concerns with domestic affairs. These and most of Laughlin's books included material she had previously published in the *Delineator*, *Scribner's*, *Harper's Bazaar*, *McClure's*, *Ladies' Home Journal*, *Good Housekeeping*, and other national periodicals.

Advances for editing *The Complete Hostess*, *The Complete Dressmaker*, and *The Complete Home* (1906–1907) broke Laughlin's economic reliance on periodicals. Through Riley she had met some friends who offered her a retreat in Mississippi, where she wrote her first full novel, *Felicity* (1907). Felicity Fergus's lonely fame as an actress, always traveling, played against her desire for companionship and "an abiding place" (p. 111), expressed Laughlin's own idealistic beliefs in the importance of both professional service and domestic intimacy for human fulfillment. *Felicity*'s sympathetic depiction of theater people, in an age when they were considered generally unrespectable, insured Laughlin's welcome in theaters nationwide. She counted Frances Starr and Ada Dwyer Russell as friends and often traveled with Mabel Taliaferro, beginning with a 1908 summer trip West. For a wartime benefit, Laughlin was Sarah Bernhardt's Chicago companion and announced her Illinois Theater performance. Theatrical interests framed some of Laughlin's advice to young women in *Ladies' Home Journal* and *Good Housekeeping* and contributed to her two years' research on John Wilkes Booth and his associates in the Ford's Theater plot, leading to *The Death of Lincoln* (1908) for publisher S. S. McClure.

She began reviewing manuscripts for McClure in 1906, the year his famous muckraking magazine *McClure's* lost Ida Tarbell and gained Willa Cather. Laughlin's association with S. S. McClure reinforced a journalistic interest in social welfare initiated by an 1890s report on a visit to Jane Addams's Hull-House and an 1895 review of Frederick Wine's influential *Punishment and Reform*, followed by a three-year investigation begun in 1910 for a *Pearson's Magazine* series that led to *The Work-a-Day Girl* in 1913. Combining personal stories with social documentation and feminist critique to trace the problems of "wayward girls" back to the conditions of working-class women, and urg-

ing readers to support minimum-wage laws and practice personal neighborliness instead of large-scale public charity, this excellent 1913 study capped Laughlin's period of fictional realism and documentary writing about Chicago.

Her six years of Chicago writing had begun in 1907 with the first of five *McClure's* short stories (1907–11) that examined working-class strikes, ethnic relations, child labor, and family economics. They drew dialect and incidents from the Maxwell Street neighbors and Irish American family with whom her friend, photographer Elizabeth Brownell, lived. Laughlin incorporated these "Mary Casey stories" into her best novel on contemporary life, *"Just Folks"* (1910), about a young probation officer who rejects Hull-House residency to live with an Irish American family. Beth Tully wrestles with conflicts between upper-class condescension and cross-class neighboring among her diverse acquaintances, between her fiancé's legalism and her own compassion, between romance and career. Director David Belasco commissioned Laughlin to turn the "Mary Casey stories" into a vehicle for her friend Ada Dwyer Russell but never staged the play. MARGARET ANDERSON remembered Laughlin reading it to her and characterized it as sentimental in Anderson's *My Thirty Years' War* (1930). Laughlin's other 19th Ward novel on similar themes, *The Penny Philanthropist* (1911), became a Wholesome Film for which she wrote the screenplay and did Chicago production work in 1916. Working-class issues, along with Laughlin's other interests, were packed into an ungainly 1911 novel, *Children of To-Morrow*.

In 1911 Laughlin resigned her editorship at the *Interior* (renamed the *Continent* in 1910), eventually recommending as her successor Margaret Anderson. In her 1930 memoirs, Anderson credited Laughlin with providing reviewing jobs that enabled Anderson's move to Chicago to found the *Little Review*; but she dismissed Laughlin's journalism as conventional hackwork.

Between 1911 and 1914, Laughlin traveled in Europe four times, nearly half a year each time, with her actress friends and family members. She was shaken by the experience of being in Paris at the beginning of World War I. Later decorated as a Chevalier of the Legion of Honor for promoting Americans' support of the French and their wartime allies, Laughlin helped found Chicago's English-Speaking Union, Italy-America Society, and Friends of France; and she was a member of the Women's Executive Committee of the Alliance Française. After the United States entered the war, she wrote "Over There" articles for the *American*, which also serialized her martial biography, *Foch the Man* (1918). *The Heart of Her Highness* (1917) embodied an interpretation of evolving Western ideals and European conflicts in an excellent historical novel about the fifteenth century's Mary of Burgundy.

Laughlin exercised leadership in many Chicago clubs during the six years between her 1914 and 1921 European trips. Having rented a study in the Fine Arts Building, which housed numerous organizations and artists, she regularly poured tea at the Little Room meetings there. She had been on the Little Room's executive committee in 1902–1903, and she later named that "fellowship" the one "wherein I felt least strange" (*Life*, 179) during her reentry from France. After the male-only

Cliff Dwellers refused her request for a women's auxiliary, Laughlin became founding president of the Cordon Club for professional women in 1915.

Although Zona Gale reported Laughlin's inclusion on a National Woman's Party committee, she did not do explicitly political writing, and her closest fictional counterpart, Eleanor Atwell, voiced "heretical [views] about women's rights" in Laughlin's 1918 novel, *The Keys of Heaven*. Eleanor explained, "I think we've always had about as many [rights] as we truly desired, and when we were in bondage it was not to men's conscious tyranny so much as to our own notions of expediency" (pp. 180–81). Eleanor's views on woman's nature resembled those of the National Woman's Party more than those of the social feminists of the Progressive Era, who advocated legislation to protect women. The latter had argued for women's right to vote on the basis of female differences (including qualities of nurture, caretaking, and moral reasoning), while the former viewed women as being like men, capable of doing their "full share of the world's work" (p. 181).

Keys of Heaven's singularly autobiographical heroine, Eleanor Atwell, reenacted Laughlin's last European trip before World War I and foreshadowed the career as travel director into which her first postwar trip propelled her. She returned from Europe in 1921 to nurse her recently invalided mother, with whom she shared a new Lincoln Park West apartment until Elizabeth Laughlin's death in 1936. Laughlin gave travel talks at the Fine Arts Building and wrote a Travel Study Course as a series of letters in 1922. Her first guidebook—*So You're Going to Paris!*—was an instant success in 1924. Swamped by requests for travel advice when she returned from an Italian trip that year, Laughlin opened Clara Laughlin Travel Service in the Fine Arts Building. She believed herself to be the first woman to run a U.S. travel agency and the first person to broadcast radio talks on travel, on WMAZ beginning in 1925. Her travel services were incorporated at a New York office in 1925 and experienced their best business year in 1930. A Los Angeles office opened in 1931 and a Paris office in 1932.

Meanwhile Laughlin published *So You're Going To* guides for Italy (1925), England (1926), and France (1927); for Italy, Switzerland, and the Tyrol (1928); for Rome (1928), Germany and Austria (1930), Spain (1931), Ireland and Scotland (1932), the Mediterranean (1935), and Scandinavia (1937)—several in multiple editions. From 1924 until 1933, she managed an extended European trip every year—several alone, one with *Chicago Tribune* journalist FANNY BUTCHER, and her last six with her two young nieces. She wrote two children's travel guides, *Where It All Comes True in France* and *Scandinavia*, both published in 1929. She consulted on tourism with the soon-to-be-deposed king of Spain in 1930, began publishing a monthly "*So You're Going*" *News* in 1931, became a fellow of the American Geographical Society in 1932, and made a presentation on the Black Forest village at Chicago's 1933 Century of Progress Exposition.

After 1933, however, Laughlin refocused her attention on the United States. In 1935 she pursued her historical interests as vice-president of the American History Society, which published genealogies and local histories. She wrote a 1938 book of generic travel advice, *So You're Going to Travel*, and *So You're*

Going books on *Visiting New York City* (1939), *Seeing New England* and *Going South* (1940). She died in Chicago and was buried in the Laughlin family plot at Graceland Cemetery.

Laughlin's work combined her interests in dramatic stories, travel, and commercial success. She contributed most to Chicago as a regional editor and church publicist beginning in the 1890s, as a journalist writing about working-class life and as a social novelist during the Progressive Era, as a clubwoman and friend of France during World War I, and finally as a businesswoman and travel expert. Nationally, the *New York Times* reviewed twenty-five of the forty-six fiction and non-fiction books she wrote. Her travel books were widely and favorably reviewed; they provided the focus for obituaries in *Time Magazine* for March 17, 1941, and elsewhere. Clara Laughlin's writing was commercially targeted to particular audiences, usually conversational in tone and idealistic in sentiment, and typically explicit in drawing morals from often touching incidents. Although committed to individualism in social welfare, she consistently urged tolerance and enthusiasm toward cultural differences.

Sources. Eight boxes and eight volumes of personal and business correspondence, radio travel talks and *So You're Going* newsletters, and reviews and clippings on her publications are included in the Clara Elizabeth Laughlin Papers 1903–41, in the Sophia Smith Collection at Smith College. Both the Little Room and Alice Gerstenberg Papers at NL contain minor references to her. Besides her autobiography, *Traveling through Life* (1939) and other works mentioned above, Laughlin's books include Revell's gift books *Divided: The Story of a Poem* (1904), *When Joy Begins* (1905), *The Lady in Gray* (1908), *Everybody's Lonesome* (1910), *When My Ship Comes Home* (1915), and *Jeanne-Marie's Triumph* (1922), and two wartime books on France, *Everybody's Birthright: A Vision of Jeanne d'Arc* (1914) and *The Martyred Towns of France* (1919). Her columns for *Interior (Continent)* lack bylines, but many Laughlin articles and short stories in national periodicals are indexed in *The Reader's Guide to Periodical Literature*. *The Work-a-Day Girl* (1913) was reprinted in 1974. Of her books, about one a year was reviewed nationally after 1907, often in *Atlantic, Bookman, Literary Digest, Nation*, and *Outlook*, besides *NYT*. Margaret Anderson's dismissive characterization of Laughlin in *My Thirty Years' War* (1930) was adopted by Dale Kramer, *Chicago Renaissance* (1966). Bernard Duffey, *Chicago Renaissance in American Letters* (1956), mentions her only briefly. "*Just Folks*" received serious interpretation in Sidney Bremer, "Lost Continuities," *Soundings* 64 (1981), and is discussed in Babette Inglehart's "Illinois Women and Their Fiction" in Robert Bray, ed., *A Reader's Guide to Illinois Literature* (1985).

SIDNEY H. BREMER

LAVOIE-HERZ, DJANE (Djane Hearst)
October 7, 1889–March 2, 1982
PIANIST, TEACHER, SALON HOSTESS

Djane (pronounced Dianne) Lavoie was born in Ottawa to French Canadian parents and first studied music at the Sacred Heart Convent. She studied piano in Montreal with Alfred Laliberté, a disciple of modernist Alexander Scriabin, and at age sixteen, she went to the Royal Academy of Music in London, England. In 1909 she left to study in Paris, with the support of Lady Laurier, the wife of the Canadian prime minister. That year, she met Scriabin in Berlin and subsequently spent two years attached to his circle in Brussels. Her experience with Scriabin, a noted figure in the transition to modernism and an ardent

Theosophist, converted her to this mystical movement. Also, for some years she studied with pianist Arthur Schnabel, spending the winters in Berlin and the summers in the Austrian Tyrol.

In 1912 in Toronto, Djane Lavoie married Siegfried Herz, a writer who had come to Canada from Germany in 1907 and worked for Nordheimer, a Canadian piano manufacturer and music publisher in Toronto. The couple took the name Lavoie-Herz at their marriage. They had one son, Tristan, born on January 10, 1914. Djane Lavoie-Herz gave acclaimed recitals in Ottawa, Montreal, and elsewhere, including two recitals in New York in late 1915. Her repertoire was devoted in particular to works of Franz Liszt, Johannes Brahms, and Scriabin. She also taught music, and in 1916–17, several of her students gave solo recitals in Toronto. An accident to her hand around 1918 made the continuation of her concert career impossible, and she devoted more time to teaching.

In 1919 the Lavoie-Herz family moved to Chicago. Djane Lavoie-Herz taught privately, and Siegfried Lavoie-Herz was a representative for the Arthur Judson concert management agency. His work offered the Lavoie-Herzes opportunities to get to know many top artists. She became well known as an outstanding teacher, especially after her nineteen-year-old student, Gitta Gradova, gave a warmly received debut recital in New York in 1923. Two students of Lavoie-Herz became noted composers: RUTH CRAWFORD SEEGER and Vivian Fine.

Lavoie-Herz's teaching style was open and encompassed much more than a one-hour-per-week lesson. "Students are permitted to listen to all lessons, and they may ask questions; there is no following of the clock, and after lessons they discuss music, books or other interesting subjects," reported Evelyn French in 1923 in "Around the Chicago Studios" (p. 562). During the early to mid-1920s, Lavoie-Herz was particularly interested in Theosophy and Eastern mysticism in general. Theosophy was a widespread spiritual movement that was founded in the United States in the 1870s but enjoyed a worldwide following; it hoped to spread the ideas of Eastern religions in the West to counter the influence of Christianity. Djane Lavoie-Herz frequently suggested books for her students to read, especially *Isis Unveiled*, the first book by Helene Blavatsky, the most prominent leader of the Theosophical movement. Lavoie-Herz influenced others besides her students to take a serious interest in Theosophy, most notably composer Dane Rudhyar, who visited Chicago in 1925 and 1928 and commented on Lavoie-Herz's extensive library on occultism and Theosophy.

However, Lavoie-Herz's interest in Theosophy did not last. Later she noted in the margins of her copy of *Isis Unveiled* that Blavatsky was a charlatan. Her intellectual interests turned toward other philosophers, notably Friedrich Nietzsche, on whose work *Thus Spake Zarathustra* Lavoie-Herz's husband organized summer seminars. Participants included some of Lavoie-Herz's students as well as professors from the University of Chicago.

Lavoie-Herz's charismatic presence and the atmosphere of her studio drew followers. Her students remembered her striking appearance: "She was a small, thin person with short, straight black hair and bangs, and while teaching, wore long, brightly colored velvet or velour robes. Quite exotic" (correspondence, Ann Besser Scott to Lynn Hooker, July 14, 1995).

She filled her apartment-studio with oriental, medieval, and Renaissance art, as well as contemporary art and some works of her own.

There were very few opportunities to hear new music performed in Chicago during the 1920s, especially experimental music. In addition to being a studio and informal library, the Lavoie-Herz home also became a salon for avant-garde music. Alfred Frankenstein, who was an undergraduate at the University of Chicago in the 1920s and later became the music and art critic for the San Francisco *Chronicle*, recalled the importance of this salon: "New music activity [in Chicago] was largely confined to small groups like that of Djane Hertz [*sic*] and her circle. . . . Madame Hertz had a salon, and every now and then Ruth [Crawford] and I would go there for performances of new music by composers" (Mead, "conversation," 320). As Vivian Fine said in a 1978 interview, the Herz home was "a kind of Mecca for visiting contemporary musicians" and a place where "the six-and-a-half people interested in" (quoted in Tick, *Ruth Crawford Seeger*, 48) avant-garde music in Chicago could gather.

Lavoie-Herz's salon, a gathering place for such luminaries as composers Henry Cowell, Edgard Varèse, and Dane Rudhyar, filled a void in Chicago's relatively conservative, Eurocentric musical life, which was oriented particularly toward Germany at this time. This salon gave young aspiring composers like Ruth Crawford and Vivian Fine a space to grow, exposure to ideas — musical and otherwise — of more experienced modernist musicians, and a place to try out some of their own work. Gitta Gradova incorporated some of Crawford's piano pieces into her recital programs because of their connection through Lavoie-Herz. Ruth Crawford dedicated her "Piano Preludes" of 1924–28 to her; and composer Dane Rudhyar, who also frequented her studio, dedicated "Moments," his set of fifteen tone poems for piano of 1924–26, to her.

By 1929 Lavoie-Herz's husband had anglicized his name to Hearst, and in late 1931, when the family moved from Chicago to New York City, Djane followed suit. Some of her students, Vivian Fine and Albert Hirsh, for example, followed her from Chicago to New York. The New York studio was even more active as a meeting place than that in Chicago; according to her son, "At one moment you would see Jascha Heifetz and Isaac Stern playing the violin together and then Fritz Busch, the conductor, would be playing [piano] fourhands with [virtuoso pianist] Artur Rubinstein, and so on" (letter from Tristan Hearst to Lynn Hooker, November 12, 1995). There is little record of Djane Hearst's activities in New York, however. She taught privately in New York at least through 1958.

In New York, Hearst became interested in rational philosophy and psychoanalysis as well as the views of thinkers Bertrand Russell and Erich Fromm and such psychologists and psychiatrists as Harold Lasswell and Karen Horney. She wrote two unpublished plays that took psychoanalysis as their subject matter: "Compassionate Retaliation: The Brennian Family" (1959) and "The Gordian Knot" (1963). She spent time each summer in Europe, teaching seminars at Sils-Maria in Austria. A few years before World War II, her son built a cabin for her at her small estate, San Sebastien, outside Santa Fe, New Mexico, and she held seminars there each summer. Hearst and her husband promoted these seminars together and helped her top students begin their concert careers. Eventually, they retired to San Sebastien. Siegfried Hearst died in Santa Fe in 1965.

Tristan Hearst moved to Sydney, Australia, in 1947. Sometime after her husband's death, when Djane Hearst was no longer able to live on her own, her son convinced her to move to Sydney to be near him. Djane Hearst died in Sydney at ninety-two years of age.

Pianist Djane Lavoie-Herz's teaching studio/salon was a focal point for avant-garde music in Chicago in the 1920s, at a time when there were few venues for young composers in the city. Her studio served as a meeting place for composers and performers traveling through Chicago as well as for her own students. She gave a sound technical foundation to her students, but at least as important, she inspired them to reach for a spiritual ideal in music making, in keeping with her philosophy.

Sources. Djane Lavoie-Herz's papers, including clippings of concert reviews, a passport, and other items, are in the possession of her son, Tristan Hearst, of Sydney, Australia. Tristan Hearst also provided information to Lynn Hooker by telephone interview September 14, 1995, and by letter November 12, 1995. Other sources include correspondence with Albert Hirsh and Ann Besser Scott, former students of Lavoie-Herz. Rita Mead's interview with Alfred Frankenstein, one of the attendees at the Lavoie-Herz salon in Chicago, is published as "A Conversation with Alfred Frankenstein about Henry Cowell's *New Music,*" in *A Celebration of American Music*, ed. Richard Crawford, R. Allen Lott, and Carol J. Oja (1990). A contemporary report about Lavoie-Herz's Chicago studio, written by Evelyn M. French, appears in "Around the Chicago Studios," *Musical Leader*, vol. 46, 1923. In addition, Judith Tick's works on Ruth Crawford contain substantial portions on Lavoie-Herz, concentrating on her impact on Crawford but also reflecting on her role in the Chicago intellectual and music scene. These works are "Ruth Crawford's 'Spiritual Concept,'" *Journal of the American Musicological Society*, vol. 44, 1991; "Ruth Crawford—Modernist Pioneer," introductory essay to Ruth Crawford's *Music for Small Orchestra (1926)* and *Suite No. 2 for Four Strings and Piano (1929)*, ed. Judith Tick and Wayne Schneider, in the series, Recent Researches in American Music, vol. 19: Music of the United States of America, vol. 1 (1993); and *Ruth Crawford Seeger: A Composer's Search for American Music* (1997).

LYNN M. HOOKER

LEE, ROSE HUM
August 20, 1904–March 25, 1964
SOCIOLOGIST, AUTHOR

Rose Hum Lee, professor and later head of the sociology department at Roosevelt University in Chicago, was the first Chinese American woman to chair an academic department at an American university. She was born in Butte, Montana, to Hum Wah-Lung and Hum Lin Fong, the second daughter and second of seven children. After a series of jobs as ranch hand, miner, and laundry worker, Hum Wah-Lung had his own business in Butte in 1900. He married Hum Lin Fong, a mail-order bride. After he died, when Rose Hum was still a child, Hum Lin Fong took over the business. Less traditional than some of her relatives and other immigrant Chinese, she encouraged her children to study rather than to provide immediate family support.

After graduating from Butte High School in 1921, Rose Hum married Ku Young Lee. In the late 1920s, the couple moved to China, where they remained through a decade that was marked by civil war between the Chinese Communist Party

and Chiang Kai-shek's Kuomintang Nationalist Party (KMT). There, Rose Hum Lee worked for the Canton Raw Silk Testing Bureau (1931–36), the National City Bank of New York (1936–38), the Municipal Telephone Exchange (1937–38), and the Sun Life Assurance Company (1937–38).

Lee participated actively in the efforts of the KMT government to resist the Japanese invasion of China and to deal with the aftermath. Lee was in Canton during eighteen months of concentrated bombing by the Japanese in 1937–38 and worked with the Emergency Committee for Relief of Refugees, the Red Cross Chinese Women's War Relief Association, and the Overseas Relief Unit to help evacuate refugees, equip hospital units, and make arrangements for war orphans. In 1938, Lee was a radio receptor of enemy broadcasts from Tokyo.

In 1938 Lee returned to the United States with her daughter Elaine, a war orphan she adopted in China. Nothing more is known about her husband. She supported herself and her daughter as a writer and lecturer. Lee planned to use the earnings to finance her education. Although her more traditional relatives objected, her mother continued to encourage Lee, providing a home for Elaine while Lee was a student. During this period she spent time in Pittsburgh, where in 1942 she earned a B.S. degree in social work from Carnegie Institute of Technology. Lee earned money by contributing articles to *Girls Today* and *Child Life*. She also wrote two children's plays, *Shoes for Shoe Street* (1944) and *Little Lee Bo-Bo: Detective for Chinatown*. *Little Lee Bo-Bo* deals with the reactions of first-generation Chinese children in Los Angeles in 1912 to the customs and ideas of their parents and grandparents.

After completing her work at Carnegie, Lee began graduate school at the University of Chicago, where she earned a master's degree in 1943. She began lecturing for the Adult Education Council in 1942 and continued to do so through 1962. In 1944 she lectured for Rotary International and the United China Relief Speakers Bureau. She addressed human rights and women's roles in China and spoke about Chinese in America. In 1944, in recognition of this work to promote international understanding and for her work in China, she was awarded an Honorary Doctorate of Humane Letters by the Illinois College of Law. The next year she began teaching at Chicago's Roosevelt College (now Roosevelt University) and, at the same time, her play, *Little Lee Bo-Bo*, was produced at the Goodman Theater. The play was published by Children's Theater Press in 1947.

In 1945, Edward Sparling, the first president of Roosevelt University, appointed her to the sociology department, the first women of Chinese descent to hold such a position in a U.S. university. She continued to study for a doctorate, teach and lecture, and in 1947 was awarded the Ph.D. in sociology from the University of Chicago.

As a sociologist and as an individual, Lee recognized the dynamics of prejudice and discrimination. "I was a woman; I was in a man's field, and I was Chinese. That meant three strikes against me. . . . The fact that I was able to overcome these barriers is a tremendous encouragement to others, particularly women who belong to minority groups" ("College's 'First' Lady").

Rose Hum Lee lived in Hyde Park with her second husband, Glenn Ginn, a Chinese American attorney, whom she married in 1951. She was a pacifist and a Quaker, deeply committed to racial and religious harmony. She was a member of the education committee of the Chicago Commission on Human Relations and the Chicago branch of the National Conference of Christian and Jews. In addition, she chaired the Scholarship Fund East-West Association and served as a board member of the Hyde Park Kenwood Community Conference and the Kenwood-Ellis Community Center and became a member of the International Society for the Study of Race Relations. In 1955–56, when the Kenwood-Oakland neighborhood was experiencing racial and demographic changes, she participated in a resurvey of the North Kenwood–Oakland community in conjunction with the Kenwood-Ellis Community Center. She studied juvenile delinquency, truancy, and crime. For her efforts, in 1959 B'nai B'rith, a Jewish fraternal organization, presented her with a Woman of Achievement Award.

During the 1950s Lee traveled to Europe and Asia. In 1958 she led a tour of social workers, teachers, and students to the Ninth International Conference of Social Workers in Tokyo. The group also visited and studied the social welfare problems of ten countries. Continuing to teach at Roosevelt, she was appointed acting head of the sociology department and in 1956 became the chair.

Sociologist Stanford Lyman stated that "for over twenty years she was the only American sociologist studying the Chinese in America" ("In Memoriam," 127–28). She began her research in Chinese communities of which she was a part and received research grants to study others. Her approach was based on natural histories of urban communities in the tradition of Robert Park and colleagues from the Chicago school of sociology at the University of Chicago. For her 1947 doctoral dissertation, "The Growth and Decline of Chinese Communities in the Rocky Mountain Region," Lee examined the social and economic factors affecting these communities. Her essay, "Social Institutions of a Rocky Mountain Chinatown," published in *Social Forces* in 1948, reflected the Chinatown in which she grew up in Butte, Montana. In 1949 she received a grant from the Social Science Research Council to study recent Chinese immigrants in the San Francisco–Oakland area. Rose Hum Lee's most famous essay, "The Decline of Chinatowns in the United States," first published in 1949, has been reprinted in numerous anthologies on racial and ethnic minorities.

In 1955 Lee published her first book, *The City: Urbanism and Urbanization in Major World Regions*, a Chicago-oriented text. Lee's intellectual debt to the Chicago school is evident in her portrayal of the cycles of conflict, competition, and accommodation that characterize ethnic communities.

Rose Hum Lee's most important work, *The Chinese in the United States of America*, was published in 1960. Here, she brings together and analyzes her previous research in an overview of Chinese American relations: demographic trends, Chinatowns, culture, economic institutions, tongs (secret societies), family life, and religion. Throughout the book Lee emphasizes the variety of Chinese behavior and assimilation patterns. She also portrays the effects of immigration on women and the sexual double standard inherent in Chinese culture. She concludes that Chinese should strive for assimilation into American culture. She ends her book with a plea to American-born Chinese to resist the pressure of the old Chinese norms, values, and attitudes and a plea to other Americans that, as "acculturation, assimilation and integration form a two-way process," they must help by thinking of newcomers as fellow citizens. "Only thus can true integration be achieved and made effective in America" (p. 430).

Lee reveals the source of her belief in the benefits of assimilation in an autobiographical anecdote in *The Chinese in the United States of America*, describing the commitment to education of a widow with seven children, over objections from immigrant Chinese relatives. When one daughter gets a teaching position at a local university, escaping the clutches of the relatives, they falsely accuse the university of being communist. Time does not heal the relationship.

Consonant with both her work for the KMT in the 1930s and with cold war liberalism, Lee was fiercely anti-communist. Before her book was published, Lee indicated, in a letter to Roosevelt University President Edward Sparling and his wife, Marion, that she and Ginn were being approached by Chinese who they believed were working undercover for the communist Chinese government. She said the two were pressed to devote their professional skills to the communist cause, threatening blackmail. Lee believed newspaper stories about Chinese drug rings in the United States sending money to China. She also believed that the threat of infiltration by Asian students was serious enough to warrant the monitoring of the background and activities of all Asian students.

Lee moved to Phoenix, Arizona, in 1961 to join her husband. She taught at Phoenix College. Her research in Arizona focused on migrant laborers and the legal status of American Indian children. The latter interest drew upon her earlier life. In a research proposal to Roosevelt University in 1961, she observed that she had seldom known the Indians who lived in Montana. She pointed to parallels between Indian and Chinese communities and worked to improve the lives of racial and ethnic minorities.

Lee's enduring affection for and loyalty to Roosevelt University was revealed in her correspondence: "The faculty [at Phoenix College] is like ours at Roosevelt, and it is the only vocal group in the community sponsoring freedom of speech, interracial and interfaith relations, academic freedom, etc." (Lee to Sparling, November 19, 1962, Roosevelt University Archives). Rose Hum Lee died of a brain embolism on March 25, 1964, in Phoenix.

Rose Hum Lee published studies in urban sociology and Chinese immigration for more than twenty years. She actively promoted assimilation and interracialism, which she viewed as important principles of American society.

Sources. Rose Hum Lee's file at the Roosevelt Univ. Library Archives, Spec. Coll., provides basic information on her career. Helena Lopata, interviewed by Jean Peterman October 30, 1995, described Lee's work in the sociology department and issues of concern for her safety. Rose Hum Lee's works, in addition to those cited above, include "The Decline of Chinatowns in the United States," *American Journal of Sociology*, March 1949; *The City: Urbanism and Urbanization in Major World Regions* (1955); and *The Chinese in the United States of America* (1960). Her work is described in Terri Phillips, "Rose Hum Lee," *Women in Sociology: A Bio-Bibliographical Sourcebook*, ed. Mary Jo Deegan (1991).

She is a subject in *NAW* (1980). An article in the *Chicago Sun-Times*, "College's 'First' Lady," April 10, 1950, presents her discussion of discrimination. A lengthy obituary, "In Memoriam," appears in the *American Sociological Review*, February 1965, and each of her books is reviewed there (June 1955 and February 1961).

JEAN PAULSON PETERMAN

LEMBERG, ROSA EMILIA CLAY
August 31, 1875–October 1959
ACTRESS, SINGER, DRAMA AND CHOIR DIRECTOR, MUSICIAN, TEACHER

Rosa Clay, a "black Finn," was born in Omaruru, South West Africa (Namibia after 1990). In the course of her life, she became a popular performer in the activities sponsored by the Chicago Finnish socialist organization that preserved Finnish culture. She was the illegitimate daughter of Feroza Sabina Hazara, an Arab African, and British colonial official Charles Wiljam Clay. Acknowledging Rosa Emilia as his daughter, Clay placed the three-year-old girl with a missionary family, the Weikkolins, at the Ondangua, Ovamboland, Lutheran Mission and School in northern South West Africa until she was nine years old. Then he permitted the Weikkolins to take her to Finland to be educated in Finnish schools, including a teachers' seminary.

In Finland, Rosa Clay did well in her studies and was admitted to Sortavala Teachers Seminary, where she became a resident student. She graduated in 1898 as a certified teacher. She had demonstrated considerable musical talent, including perfect pitch and a magnificent voice.

Growing up as the rare African in Finland, Clay attracted much attention, discrimination, and racist ridicule. School children followed and harassed her verbally. She encountered similar treatment from both children and adults during her first teaching job in 1899–1900 in Mustinlahti, near Kuopio, in south central Finland.

After a miserable year, Clay returned to Helsinki to apply for a teaching position in the African Mission. However, her experiences with Lutheran Christians had made her doubt the strength of her own Christian beliefs and question the purpose of missionary activity. To strengthen those Christian beliefs, she took a position as governess for four daughters of a highly regarded theologian. Clay was well accepted by the parishioners, whose choir director she became. However, when the theologian allegedly impregnated the household's maid, Clay's faith was further undermined. She decided not to return to Africa as a missionary but instead to remain in Finland as an elementary school teacher, a position she held for three years.

In her third year Clay became engaged to a Russian doctor who was conducting research in Finland. One week before the planned wedding, in a deranged state caused by testing the drugs he was researching, the doctor shot himself fatally. Realizing in her sorrow that she could not stay in Finland, and having determined that she would not return to Africa, Clay decided to go to America in hopes of finding greater acceptance as a person of mixed race.

Although her motivation for emigrating was unusual, in age and marital status Clay was typical of Finns who left the country between 1901 and 1920; three-quarters of those emigrants were unmarried, and two-thirds of them were between the ages of sixteen and thirty. In June 1904, twenty-nine-year-old Rosa Clay arrived in New York City, alone, without friends or relatives, knowing no English, and with very little money. With the help of the Christian Women's Aid to Immigrants Committee, she obtained a domestic position with a family whose Finnish cook introduced her to the group activities of New York City Finns. Initially the Finns looked askance at her, wondering what a black person was doing in their midst. However, her excellent Finnish, far better than that of many in the group, won her speedy acceptance. This welcome was her introduction to American Finn Hall activity, with which she remained associated for fifty years. Whether Finnish halls were based upon an affirmation of Lutheranism and temperance or on socialism—the key ideologies that competed for Finnish American loyalties—these organizations reinforced and kept alive Finnish culture. The socialist halls' activities included committee meetings and local Marxist-oriented conferences and programs as well as classes in Finnish for the children. Events routinely included gym classes; amateur choir, band, and orchestra practices; and evening programs, amateur plays, musical dramas, and full public dances. The evening programs followed a pattern that included an ideological speech; solos, orchestra, band, or choir performances; poems and story recitations; a one-act play; and, finally, a public dance. The amateur play and program evenings had two purposes—socializing for the immigrant Finns and fund-raising for the organization. Dramatic events were advertised via playbills in the Finnish socialist newspaper *Työmies* [Workingman], the largest of more than 350 Finnish papers and periodicals; *Työmies* continued to exist into the 1990s. It also publicized the concerts and evening programs and listed the participants.

Clay obtained a vestmakers' job in a Finnish men's tailoring shop, where she encountered ideas about socialism. The socialist tradition among American Finns developed in the 1890s, fed by immigrants fleeing tsarist Russification programs. (Finland had become a Russian duchy in 1809.) New York Finns formed the Imatra Society, one of the two workers' associations after which later Finnish socialist groups were patterned. The Finnish Socialist Federation, founded in 1906, "grew by 1913 to 260 chapters with 13,000 members throughout the nation" (Karni, 228). In the tailoring shop where Clay worked, her fellow workers embraced socialist ideas and Clay learned from them. In 1905, she joined the New York Finnish socialist local. For fifty years she continued to be a member of groups with a socialist-labor orientation.

Clay quickly became involved in the musical and drama activities of the New York Finnish socialist local. She performed many major roles in plays, especially musicals, and soon was chosen director of the choir. In about 1907, at a choir practice, Clay met Lauri Lemberg (born 1887), who had emigrated in 1903 from Finland to Maynard, Massachusetts, where he worked as a drama director. When she met him, he had recently moved to New York City. They married several months after meeting. In 1900 nearly half of all Finns in the United States lived in Michigan or Minnesota. The Lembergs' next relocation took them into the heart of this community. In June 1908, Lauri Lemberg moved to the mining town of Ironwood,

Michigan, to become the drama director for the new Palace Hall. His wife followed in a few months. Their daughter, Irja Liedes, was born on December 19, 1908. In early 1909, Lauri Lemberg moved to Astoria, Oregon, a community with a significant Finnish population employed in salmon fishing; there he became drama director of the Astoria Finnish Socialist Association's Drama Club. Again, his wife and daughter followed in a few months. Their son, Kalervo Rexford, known all his life as Orvo, was born January 10, 1910.

Rosa Lemberg's years in Astoria from 1909 to 1913 were taken up with childrearing and with participation in many plays, concerts, and program events. She became well known in the Northwest as a skilled actress and especially as a singer with a magnificent voice. The marriage came to an end, for reasons unknown, early in 1910. Shortly after marrying, Rosa Lemberg had begun to regret her decision but, because she was pregnant, remained with Lauri Lemberg. He did not wish to have children and was particularly disappointed that their first child was a girl. After their divorce, Rosa Lemberg assumed full responsibility for raising the children.

After several years in various locations in Washington State as a summer school teacher for Finnish children and as a drama and choir director, Lemberg moved to Butte, Montana. Her job as the well-paid drama director of the Butte Finnish Workers Club, which was linked to the Industrial Workers of the World (IWW), was terminated when the club's hall was closed in a court case against an IWW member for antiwar activities during World War I. Lemberg worked for several months as the sole night chambermaid for a thirty-six-bed hotel. She received a letter from the cultural chair of the Chicago Finnish Socialist local asking if she was interested in coming to Chicago to be the drama and choir director for the Imperial Hall on north Halsted Street. Early in the 1920s, Lemberg came with her children to Chicago, a city that was the site of the "infamous [post–World War I] mass trial of IWW leaders" (Karni, 228) that included five Finns.

Lemberg's Imperial Hall participation included several assignments, among them teaching children Finnish. She was also involved for many years in entertainment activity, directing and acting in plays, leading the women's choir, performing as a singer, and reciting poems at programs. Her first two appearances at Imperial Hall were in 1921, when she sang at a fund-raising program for the Agitation Committee on February 5 and recited a poem at the International Women's Day evening on February 21.

Serving for a few years after 1921 as the Hall's drama director, Lemberg made a major contribution as an actor and singer in full-length plays and musicals. Her first drama appearance was in the musical *Hungarian Gypsies* in October 1921. Between 1921 and 1940, Lemberg had major roles in at least fourteen amateur plays.

Rosa Lemberg's greatest love, however, was music. In March 1922, she gave her first voice concert. In addition to Lemberg's four solos, son Orvo played a violin solo and daughter Irja danced to fill out the program. Between 1931 and 1952, Lemberg appeared in twenty-eight concerts with the Kipinä Choir, which she most likely had organized, and with other choirs or singers. She was a frequent solo or duet singer, poem

reciter or storyteller in fund-raising or ideological programs. Between 1921 and 1948, thirty such appearances were itemized in Finnish newspapers.

Having taken on the responsibility of raising two children, Lemberg found her small income from paid drama or choir direction inadequate to meet daily needs. As she had since coming to the United States, she supplemented whatever payment she received from Hall activities with the income earned through teaching piano, sewing, cooking in boarding houses or cafes, and working in domestic service or as a janitor. Despite financial problems, she provided dancing and music lessons for her children. In their teens they were active in Imperial Hall entertainment. Orvo became a skilled violinist and dancer; Irja, a dancer, also acted in a few plays, once with her mother. Orvo and Irja toured Cleveland, Detroit, and Waukegan in a song-and-dance program and once in a play written by their father. Rosa Lemberg's dream was that when the children completed high school, the three of them would tour America and perhaps even go to Finland with a music, song, and dance program. However, shortly after her graduation, Irja married and left Chicago. Orvo also married in his teens but stayed in Chicago and was active in Imperial Hall entertainment and as violin soloist and accompanist as late as 1929.

Rosalia, a somewhat romanticized life story of Rosa Lemberg, was written by Arvo Lindewall, a fellow Imperial Hall musician, in full (though unacknowledged) collaboration with Lemberg. The book was published in 1942 and made use of pseudonyms, described unnamed places, and omitted dates. Lemberg feared the impact on her children of revealing that she had been born black in Africa. She felt this concern despite being fully accepted among American Finns because of her magnificent talent, her quiet dignified demeanor, and her gentle and skilled choir and drama directing activities. She brought honor and distinction to socialist and worker-oriented Finn Hall activity.

Although "the level of organized activities remained high in the interwar period" (Hoglund, 369) in consumer cooperatives that cut costs by eliminating intermediaries, both Lutheran/temperance and socialist associations struggled during the Great Depression. Fund-raising became increasingly important as membership decreased due to the near elimination of Finnish immigration after World War I, internal divisions, and the assimilation of Finns into American society and culture. By 1930, "almost 90 percent of all Finnish immigrants who were 10 or older could speak English" (Hoglund, 369). These trends accelerated in the 1940s. The anticommunism of the 1950s further undercut socialist-oriented organizations.

In 1956, now eighty-one years old and in failing health, Lemberg was taken by her daughter and son to the Finnish Rest Home in Covington, Michigan. Here she diligently studied the missionary tracts given her, sang hymns with other residents, and received communion. During all her years in America, as far as is known, Lemberg took no part in Finnish Lutheran Church activity, except during her final days.

In 1959, at the age of eighty-four, Rosa Lemberg died; she was buried in Covington Cemetery. She dedicated her life to her children and to continuing participation in, and direction of, dramatic and musical entertainment activities of the Finnish socialist or progressive working-class organizations for the preservation of the cultural heritage of immigrant Finns. She brought pleasure to their lives and raised operating funds for liberal, worker-oriented organizations in various Finnish communities in the East, West, and Midwest. She is remembered as a talented and skilled actress and as a magnificent singer.

Sources. Finnish newspapers, replete with playbills and program content listings, as well as books, magazines, and personal correspondence, all at the Immigration History Research Center of the Univ. of Minnesota, serve as major reference sources. The first sixty years of Rosa Lemberg's life are told in *Rosalia* (1942), written by an Imperial Hall musical colleague, Arvo Lindewall, with full collaboration of Lemberg; twenty pages about her days at the African Finnish Mission and her first days in Finland are by Lemberg herself. A key to the pseudonyms, unnamed American towns, and missing dates is provided in Eva H. Erickson, *The Rosa Lemberg Story* (1993). Background information on Finns in the United States and on Finnish socialist activity, respectively, is found in A. William Hoglund, "Finns," in *Harvard Encyclopedia of American Ethnic Groups*, ed. Stephan Thernstrom (1980), and Michael Karni, "Finnish Americans," in *Encyclopedia of the American Left*, ed. Paul Buhle, Mari Jo Buhle, and Dan Georgakas (1992).

EVA H. ERICKSON

LESLIE, AMY (Lillie West Brown Buck)
October 11, 1855–July 3, 1939
DRAMA CRITIC, JOURNALIST, SINGER

Amy Leslie enjoyed remarkable success as drama critic for the Chicago *Daily News* from 1890 until her retirement in 1930. Writer Ben Hecht included her among "the finest group of drama critics I have ever seen" (Hecht, 13). Her reviews and feature articles on theater averaged two to three a week, making Leslie a prolific critic.

Born in West Burlington, Iowa, and christened Lillie West, she was the eldest of five children—two daughters and three sons—of Albert and Kate Content (Webb) West. Her father, a newspaper editor first in Indiana and later in Iowa, in 1845 co-founded the St. Joseph Valley *Register* with Schuyler Colfax. In 1849, Albert West and William Bausman founded the Lafayette *Journal.* Her mother was also a writer and a friend of many well-known women, including women's rights advocates Elizabeth Cady Stanton and Susan B. Anthony. Little is known of Lillie West's early schooling, although records indicate she attended Sacred Heart Academy in St. Joseph, Missouri, and Saint Mary's Academy in Notre Dame, Indiana. Although educated at Catholic schools, West remained a Protestant throughout her life. While at St. Mary's, West studied vocal music and domestic economy as well as math, history, science, writing, and elocution. Graduating in 1874, she received honors from the music department. After additional training at the Chicago Conservatory of Music, Lillie West became a popular singer with the Grayman Comic Opera Company, which toured in the East during the 1870s and 1880s. Her fame as a light opera singer was secured with her New York City debut as Fiametta in *La Mascotta* in May 1881. At about this time, she married Harry Brown, a fellow performer, and for a few years they toured the United States and Canada with the Norcross, Grau, and other companies. This was the heyday of comic and sentimental opera.

In 1889, their only child, Francis Albert, died of diphtheria at the age of four. Though her husband continued to tour, Lillie West retired from the stage and settled in Chicago with her mother, who encouraged her to seek a career in journalism. Her contributions to the Chicago *Daily News* column, "What One Woman Thinks," drew the attention of the managing editor, H. Ten Eyck White. In 1890 he engaged her to write drama criticism, a position she maintained for forty years. She chose the pen name Amy Leslie and became one of the most respected of all Chicago drama critics. Not long after her career as a drama critic was established, Leslie and Brown were divorced.

Leslie also did regular reporting and feature writing for the *Daily News.* In 1893 she was the paper's special correspondent to the World's Columbian Exposition. Her reports of this event became the basis of her first book, *Amy Leslie at the Fair* (1893). In April 1898, during the Spanish-American War, she visited Camp Tanner in Springfield, Illinois, to report on the activities of soldiers waiting to move out to join other forces in Cuba. Over the years her features included weekly columns titled "Plays for Next Week," "Echoes from Mimic Land," "Notes on Amusements," "At the Sunday Theaters," and "Plays and Players." During June, July, August, and early September of 1900, the "Plays and Players" columns were submitted from Paris and London. In addition to dramatic criticism, throughout her career Leslie also wrote reviews of opera, concerts, and vaudeville performances in and around Chicago. In 1900, Leslie wrote a playlet entitled *Lone Amy, the Sherman House Orphan*, which was published privately by Eugene Byfield, the son of the owner of the Sherman House, where Leslie lived for many years.

Leslie's intimate knowledge of the theater and her friendships with many of the major stars of the day gave her reviews a personal resonance that was missing from the reviews of other drama critics. She counted among her close friends numerous actors, including Richard Mansfield and his wife Beatrice Cameron, Julia Marlowe, E. H. Sothern, Nat Godwin, Ellen Terry, Minnie Maddern Fiske, William Gillette, and Lillian Russell, of whom lively and personal accounts appear in Leslie's second book, *Some Players* (1899).

While not hesitant to talk of the romantic involvements of her friends, and certainly acquainted with many handsome and eligible men, Leslie seldom revealed her own romantic attachments. It was rumored that she was in love with George Ade, a young reporter (later famous as a humorist and playwright) who worked in the same newspaper office. Her reviews of William Gillette were suggestively sensual. For example, her February 11, 1911, review in the *Daily News* referred to his "sympathetic and smoldering" eyes, "his slim, untaught physique," and "his white lover-like vigor . . . and expressive firmness." It is not known whether a romantic relationship ever existed between the two. From 1895 to 1897, Leslie and a much younger Stephen Crane, the novelist and poet, were romantically involved in a relationship that ended in a legal dispute. On January 3, 1898, she sued Crane for money he had allegedly borrowed and never repaid.

In 1901, Leslie's second marriage made front-page headlines in Chicago, when she eloped with Frank Buck, then a bell captain at the Virginia Hotel where Leslie lived at the time. Leslie was forty-five, and Buck gave his age to the marriage clerk as twenty-three; however, the birthdate in a published biography

FIG. 64. *Amy Leslie, drama critic for the* Chicago Daily News *for four decades, talks with pioneer film director D. W. Griffith in 1922.*

made Buck only seventeen at the time of the marriage. Despite the age difference, they remained together for sixteen years.

Amy Leslie's reputation as a knowledgeable and fair critic continued to grow in Chicago and New York, where, while reviewing productions, she was often introduced to audiences along with other visiting dignitaries. To Leslie, encouragement was part of a critic's job, and she devoted many columns to praising American actors and plays. She often deplored in print the critical trend of praising performers and plays from Europe while decrying the lack of good American plays and actors. This practice, she felt, led many American performers to flee to Europe to make a living. In *Some Players* (1899) she wrote, "To begrudge encouragement to American actors is falsest of all affectations. It is a nation that ought to produce signal artists for the stage. Not one master of tragedy, not a sole man who can move all people to laughter or tears, or one woman who shall be queen among actresses, but plenty of them, witty men and soulful women and melodious singers, the country ought to be aflame with them: all they want is bringing out and culture" (p. 333). Again in her review in the *Daily News*, June 10, 1907, she wrote, "All the good plays, all the fine, virile characters of the stage today are American."

Leslie's reviews gave Chicago audiences a penetrating and colorful picture of Chicago theater at a time when melodrama and romanticism were giving way to realism as the dominant mode of production. Leslie often revealed conflicting attitudes in her writing. For instance, she exhibited an ambivalence toward the changing styles of acting, admiring the "old style" and, at the same time, praising "scientific acting," which called for intense study combined with inspiration on the part of the actor. She admired several theatrical innovations in acting, dialogue, character development, and scenic elements, as well as experi-

ments with form and content. Her harshest criticism fell upon playwrights and actors who introduced subject matter and acting techniques she considered unsuitable for the stage. Leslie's discomfort with Henrick Ibsen's realism was illustrated by her belief that "there [was] a vast difference between truth and realism" (*Daily News*, November 6, 1908). Her *Daily News* review distinguished between the former and the latter: "The Ibsen idea of truth is only its absolute denial, for truth is lovely and full of sun and glory. Realism is physical, material and might as well be kept in the dark where it can breed better thoughts than itself. Ibsen is not a truth teller at all."

Changes in society also affected the views expressed in Leslie's reviews. The new feminist movement and the new status of women in business, education, and the professions, as well as the dissemination of Sigmund Freud's theories of sexuality, led to the emergence of an important character in drama—the "new woman." As a "new woman" herself—educated, financially independent, and working in a male-dominated profession—Leslie often revealed her determination to deal with topics of special concern to women as depicted in the popular plays of the day. In her comments on the double standard, divorce, new-found independence, poverty, eugenics, and working conditions for children and young girls, Leslie championed a freer, more egalitarian lifestyle for women. For instance, her reviews of Stanley Houghton's *Hindle Wakes*, Charles Klein's *The Lion and the Mouse*, and George H. Broadhurst's *Bought and Paid For*, among others, clearly revealed Leslie's sympathies with women fighting against injustice and oppression. In her review of *Hindle Wakes*, she called Fanny Hawthorne "a bold, saner factory girl" who set forth "a side of sex responsibility which has never before been suggested. . . .

She [was] broad, new, [and] impudently courageous" (*Daily News*, February 8, 1913).

As an early woman critic holding a prestigious position with a major newspaper, Leslie was a model for other women with similar ambitions. Her retirement in 1930 prompted letters of tribute from well-known personalities around the country, including George Ade; George M. Cohan, actor, playwright, and producer; David Belasco, producer; and Sophie Tucker, actress. Nine years later, Amy Leslie died in her home at the Parkway Hotel in Chicago. According to her wishes, she was cremated and her ashes cast into Lake Michigan.

Writing during a time when "the woman question" was a topic of daily conversation, Amy Leslie was a transitional figure—a woman entering a new field while trying to maintain her image as a "respectable" woman. Her writing style was partly that of the woman writer of sentimental novels of the nineteenth century—descriptive, subjective and emotional—and partly that of the "new" twentieth-century woman—vigorous and hardhitting, in the manner of the new, more realistic drama then being written by Ibsen and George Bernard Shaw. Her style was described as ornate and girlishly enthusiastic by men such as Ben Hecht and George Ade, a judgment based on selected reviews. Taken overall, her style was also cutting, direct, and to the point. Her career was summed up in the words of her friend and coworker, George Ade, who wrote in the *Daily News*, August 28, 1930, that "she approached the theater with a generous, open, and catholic mind."

Sources. In addition to those titles cited above, Leslie's works include thousands of articles and reviews in the Chicago *Daily News*. Articles about Leslie include Joseph Katz, "Some Light on the Stephen Crane–Amy Leslie Affair," *Mad River Review*, Winter 1964–65, and Ben Hecht, "Wistfully Yours," *Theater Arts*, July 1952. She is mentioned in Charles H. Dennis, *Victor Lawson: His Time and His Work* (1935); Vincent Starrett, *Born in a Bookshop* (1965); Alson J. Smith, *Chicago's Left Bank* (1953); and Frank Buck and Ferrin Fraser, *All in a Lifetime* (1941). Biographies of Leslie are found in *NAW* (1971); *The Oxford Companion to the American Theater* (1984); and *Notable Women in the American Theater* (1989).

ALMA J. BENNETT

LEVITAS, MOLLIE SYBIL M.
May 1885–January 19, 1984
TRADE UNION LEADER, LABOR ORGANIZER

Mollie Levitas, who played a pivotal role in the Chicago women's labor movement, was born in Russian Latvia and emigrated from Riga with her mother, father Abraham, older sister Sarah, and older brother Michael to Chicago in 1887. The Levitas family settled on the city's Near West Side, an area dominated by Russian-Polish Jews, many of whom fled increasing victimization under Russian rule in their homelands during the 1880s. By 1900, approximately fifty-two thousand eastern European Jews had settled in Chicago in a small area roughly bounded by Canal and Damen streets, Polk Street, and Sixteenth Street. Levitas's mother bore three more children in Chicago—Goldie in 1887, Max in 1889, and Walter in 1892. When she died, Abraham Levitas, left widowed with six children, worked various day labor jobs and peddled goods to help support his family.

Levitas and her younger siblings attended school, while her older sister and brother worked to bring income into the household. Mollie attended two years of high school and completed her business training at Bryant and Stratton Business College. By 1910, she was a stenographer in a printing office located on Clark Street. She also briefly worked for Carrier Engineering Company in Chicago's commercial district, where her father worked. She later recalled that her father talked about labor issues among his peers at Carrier and that her sister Sarah had married a man active in the socialist movement in the city. She felt she had been imbued at an early age with the rights of labor and the rewards that collective action brings to the common worker.

In 1926, a friend and active Chicago labor leader, LILLIAN HERSTEIN, informed Levitas that an opening for a secretary to President John Fitzpatrick and Secretary Edward Nockels existed at the Chicago Federation of Labor (CFL). Levitas decided to leave Carrier and take the federation job. She stayed for thirty years and through her position became intimately involved in the city's rapidly expanding trade union movement. Levitas's work at the CFL required considerable commitment to the union cause and often placed her in positions of authority that bore witness to her remarkable intelligence, tact, loyalty, and organizational skills.

The CFL was a small organization when Levitas joined the staff. She, Fitzpatrick, Nockels, and the engineer for the infant labor radio station, WCFL, staffed a loft space shared by the *Federation News*, the CFL's house organ, and the Illinois State Federation of Labor. Levitas handled considerable correspondence for Nockels in a battle to keep WCFL on the air, despite federal and local pressure to limit the station's band and transmission power. Perched on the end of Navy Pier, the WCFL studio absorbed a lion's share of the CFL's operating budget. Throughout the 1930s, the CFL staff had to accept reduced salaries to keep the radio station solvent, a situation rectified only when Levitas asked for restoration to the earlier level.

Described in the *Federation News* as President Fitzpatrick's "good right hand" (January 12, 1957, 3), Levitas served as the glue to a talented but disparate group of Chicago labor leaders. She worked closely with Ed Nockels in the fight to keep WCFL in operation, single-handedly responding to voluminous correspondence. She maintained contact with imprisoned union members and compiled many organizational files by acting as recording secretary to weekly CFL Executive Board meetings. Levitas regularly used vacation time to attend American Federation of Labor (AFL) annual conferences as a delegate from the CFL and to pursue her interests in the women's and office workers' labor movements. The CFL was more receptive to women's organizing than the national AFL. John Fitzpatrick had a major role in establishing a women's department in the *Union Labor Advocate*, the national AFL's official journal.

Through her participation in the CFL and the Chicago Women's Trade Union League (WTUL) and as a working woman, Levitas felt compelled to bring office workers, increasingly female as the twentieth century progressed, the protection and benefits that organization could provide. The Stenographers, Typists, Bookkeepers, and Assistants Union Local No. 20074 (STB&A), chartered directly under the AFL, began recruitment in 1935. Although strongly supported by the CFL's Fitzpatrick, the STB&A had its charter revoked by him in 1937 because some of its members defied his authority and honored a Congress of Industrial Organizations' (CIO) picket line at the National Tea Company. The AFL did not recognize the strike. The company's office employees were organized under the AFL and the rest of the employees belonged to the CIO. The picket dilemma typified the intense rivalry that existed between the AFL and the CIO, a competition rooted in AFL concern about communist sympathies among CIO members.

Levitas, who remained loyal to the CFL, began immediately to help reconstruct the office employees' union. In May 1937, eighty former STB&A members were invited to join the newly chartered Office Employees Union (OEU) Local No. 20732. By 1942, the AFL granted the office workers a national council charter, a step that recognized the union's growth and Levitas's personal labors. The OEU reached international status in 1945. Throughout the early years of organizing the OEU, Levitas played an integral role as CFL delegate, organizer, committee member, and officer. Her connections at the CFL greatly benefited the immature OEU and gave Levitas the political leverage necessary to convince other AFL-affiliated unions to organize their office staffs. Levitas wrote numerous letters and articles for the *Federation News* supporting the right of office workers to organize.

While she dove headlong into the role of union activist, Levitas carried increased responsibilities at her job at the CFL. The effort to command the resources of organized labor before, during, and after World War II placed the CFL's leadership increasingly out of the office and inattentive to the union's daily affairs. Competent and conscientious, Levitas became the de facto CFL secretary, fulfilling the duties of the office without recognition in increased salary or even the mantle of office. The AFL and the CFL remained trade-oriented male organizations despite the changing composition of their membership and the female talent in their midst.

Levitas served as vice-president for the OEU from 1936 to 1942 and as president from 1943 to 1944. She pursued the union's recognition by the AFL and petitioned strongly for an international charter. Throughout her tenure as an active force in the OEU, Levitas worked behind the scenes, cajoling prominent labor leaders to honor their union principles and extend the benefits they received to their largely female office staffs. She was actively involved, primarily through correspondence and a subtle form of harassment, in organizing the office staffs of union offices and more stridently throughout the Cuneo Press strike and the Polish National Alliance legal dispute.

Levitas's public involvement with the Chicago labor movement reached full throttle in the 1950s. While she held office in the OEU and maintained her employment at the CFL, she also succeeded longtime Women's Trade Union League President AGNES NESTOR after her death in 1948. The WTUL disbanded nationwide in 1955. Levitas also participated, in her "spare time" (*Federation News*, February 16, 1957), in the Histadrut, a Zionist organization; the Independent Voters of Illinois; and the American Civil Liberties Union.

Levitas's personal and professional relationships strongly illustrated her sense of purpose, her feminism, and her remarkable talents. She shared the admiration and affection of some of the most influential people in the Chicago labor movement: John Fitzpatrick, Ed Nockels, Lillian Herstein, and Agnes

Nestor. With Fitzpatrick and Nockels, Levitas enjoyed a warm and mutually respected relationship. She clearly admired the struggles and sacrifices these men made to gain the right to organize. "The men who started the labor movement were men who sacrificed a great deal," she said in a 1970 interview (p. 54). At her retirement dinner from the CFL, Levitas welcomed more than four hundred friends and peers to the Bismark Hotel and brought memories of her friendships with Agnes Nestor and Elizabeth O'Grady of the Chicago Women's Trade Union League, and with Victor Olander, Tom Mooney, and John Fitzpatrick from the CFL and the AFL. Levitas maintained contact with her good friend Lillian Herstein throughout her life. Upon Levitas's retirement from the CFL in 1957, she and Herstein embarked on a three-month world tour, the one vacation Levitas took that did not involve a labor conference.

Levitas immersed herself in the Chicago labor movement although she never sought the kind of public recognition that her friends and peers achieved. She apparently enjoyed good health and remained active in labor organizations and affiliated associations well into her seventies. The last official post she maintained was president of the Chicago WTUL. She died following surgery.

Sources. The primary sources regarding Levitas's public activities are in the Chicago Federation of Labor Papers at the CHS, particularly the John Fitzpatrick Papers, which include some of the Office Employee Union Papers. Another significant source is an interview, conducted July 24 and 27, 1970, when Levitas was eighty-five years old, by Elizabeth Balanoff. The transcript is available in the Balanoff Oral History Collection, Center for New Deal Studies, Roosevelt Univ., Chicago. Levitas also wrote for the *Federation News*, on microfilm at the CHS but not indexed. The Federal Census for Chicago for 1900 and 1910 provides some family background and confirms her birth year and age at immigration. City directory research provides early employment history. Sources on the Chicago Women's Trade Union League and the Chicago Federation of Labor ignore Levitas or place her in a footnote; they include Colette A. Hyman, "The Chicago Women's Trade Union League: Labor Organizing and Female Institution Building, 1904–1924" (master's thesis, Univ. of Minnesota, 1982); Nancy S. Dye, *As Equals and as Sisters: Feminism, the Labor Movement, and the Women's Trade Union League of New York* (1980); John H. Keiser, "John Fitzpatrick and Progressive Unionism, 1915–1925" (Ph.D. diss., Northwestern Univ., 1965); and Elizabeth Payne, *Reform, Labor and Feminism* (1988).

MAUREEN CARROLL GILLIGAN

LEVY, BEATRICE STEINFELT
April 3, 1892–July 19, 1974
PAINTER, ETCHER

Painter and printmaker Beatrice Levy exhibited extensively in Chicago between 1917 and 1945, with works included in the annual Art Institute of Chicago (AIC) *Chicago and Vicinity* exhibitions (1917–35) and the annual AIC *American Artists* exhibitions (1919–45). Levy's father, Samuel Levy, had emigrated to Kansas from Germany in the late 1800s and had studied at the University of Kansas at Lawrence. After completing his degree, he moved to Chicago. Through acquaintances in Kentucky he met his wife, Sarah Steinfelt, and they were married at Temple Adas Israel in Louisville, Kentucky, on June 25, 1890. The Levys settled in Chicago, where their only child, Beatrice, was born.

Little is known about the family except that Samuel Levy worked as a traveling salesman during Beatrice Levy's entire childhood.

While in grammar school Beatrice Levy demonstrated artistic aptitude, and her parents enrolled her in Saturday classes at the School of the Art Institute of Chicago (SAIC). Beatrice Levy also studied at the religious school of Temple Isaiah, a reform synagogue progressive in its approach toward the religious education of females. She was confirmed there on May 30, 1906. Levy continued to take art classes at SAIC after grammar school while she attended Wendell Phillips High School. Graduating in 1910, Levy promptly enrolled in SAIC as a full-time student. There she studied under American painter Ralph Clarkson.

In 1913 the *International Exhibition of Modern Art* (the Armory Show) opened at the Art Institute of Chicago as the *Post-Impressionist Exhibition* and created controversy and excitement among artists and the general public. For Beatrice Levy, seeing works for the first time by European artists Henri Matisse, Pablo Picasso, Paul Cezanne, and Paul Gauguin, and by Americans Edward Hopper, George Bellows, and John Sloan became formative for her development as a painter. Levy was serving as the secretary of the Art Students League. In contrast to the opinion of most of her fellow students, who staged a mock trial of Henri Matisse on April 16, 1913, the closing day of the exhibit, she became one of the show's most ardent advocates. William M. R. French, AIC's director, who had been encouraged by trustees Charles T. Hutchinson, George F. Porter, and Arthur T. Aldis to bring the New York show to the Art Institute, was not in Chicago during the exhibition, having made plans to be on the West Coast; Newton H. Carpenter, AIC's business secretary, was actually in charge and had interceded when art students, after finding Matisse guilty, were prepared to burn him in effigy. Carpenter persuaded them to burn copies of Matisse paintings instead. With a few like-minded students, Levy formed a coalition in support of the modernists; they voiced their appreciation of the exhibit to the administration.

After the exhibit, art student Levy experimented with abstraction but continued to produce representational works as well. During the summers between semesters at SAIC, she lived in Kentucky with her mother's parents. There she sketched and painted scenes of rural life, returning later for subsequent visits and, as a mature artist, to these early visual experiences.

Immediately after graduation from SAIC in spring 1914, she set out for Provincetown, Massachusetts, to study with Charles W. Hawthorne for the summer. Accepted as a student of the Bohemian-born etcher Vojtech Preissig, who had emigrated to New York from Prague in 1911 and was teaching at the Art Students League in New York, Levy moved from oil painting to studying modern etching. Preissig brought to New York a modern revival of color etching that had begun in Prague. Levy became expert in this technique. While still Preissig's student, she exhibited her etchings at AIC and, the next year, one of her etchings was exhibited in the Panama-Pacific International Exposition, held in San Francisco. Levy's etching, *Song of Summer*, a nude bent in a conventional attitude at the edge of a pool in which is reflected its inverted image, won honorable mention. As the youngest artist to receive such an award at the 1915 show, she benefited from immediate attention and interest in her

work. By 1918 she had three color etchings in an AIC exhibition and one at the Arts Club's show of locals. She also had become a member of the Chicago Society of Etchers, contributing her prints to the society's traveling exhibits in such American cities as New York and Philadelphia.

Levy was also experimenting with portrait painting. In 1919 two of her portraits, *Agnes* and *Mrs. Lazard*, were selected by the Chicago Society of Artists for their annual exhibition at AIC. Two of her prints were donated to the permanent print collection at AIC by the Chicago Society of Etchers. A show at the Art Institute of Milwaukee in May 1923 featured a collection of etchings and prints by Levy, including *Provincetown*, *Central Park Nocturne*, *Edge of the Desert*, and *Songs of Summer*. That same year she received the Robert Rice Jenkins Prize at AIC. Levy had a one-person show of prints at the Goupil gallery in New York, and she held her first one-person show of paintings at the AIC at the invitation of Robert B. Harshe, director of AIC from 1921 to 1938.

Even more than abstractionism, which she ultimately did not pursue until late in life, Levy was intrigued with the idea of "art for art's sake." In the 1920s she joined with other rebels in forming a society that believed in no particular school or movement. Included in this group were Gerrit Sinclair, Ramon Shiva, Carol Hoeckner, and Agnes Potter, among others. Russian painter Nicholas Roerich named them the Cor Ardens (burning center) Society on one of his visits to Chicago. He hoped the small group of rebels would be a nucleus of something international, a new hope for art. Roerich selected one of Levy's most popular prints, *St. Francis of Assisi*, a color aquatint, to show in his gallery in New York City.

Levy exhibited a large group of her color etchings in Philadelphia in 1924 at the Print Club. She had succeeded in obtaining unusual color combinations in her etchings through painstaking experiments with technique. One reviewer described how her prints resembled watercolor in the smoothness and lack of inkiness. Several were of religious subjects, for example, *I Will Lift Mine Eyes unto the Mountains*, and *St. Francis' Sermon to the Birds*; yet these Christian themes were not exact reproductions and had the feel of Japanese prints, thereby expressing Levy's revisioning of antique themes in modern and culturally universal terms. Included in this show were landscapes of the Canadian Rockies near Banff, a scene of Provincetown houses, a composition called *The Pines*, and one titled *The Edge of the Desert*.

In Chicago Levy became an active member of the Chicago Society of Artists (CSA), which she joined in 1928, the year CSA awarded her a gold medal for her prints, and of the Chicago Society of Etchers. In later years she served as a president of the CSA.

Levy, who never married, maintained her base in Chicago, living and working in one of the Fifty-seventh Street artists' colony studios. She drew inspiration for her work from her extensive travels. Over her lifetime Beatrice Levy painted and etched figures and scenes of Kentucky, including one of her most famous oil paintings, *A Kentucky Road*. She painted scenes of Corisca, Mexico, the Basque countryside, California, and New York, including urban and rural compositions as well as many portraits. Levy remarked that subject matter usually was her starting point. Although she traveled throughout Europe, Africa, and Mexico, her work reflected the expression of her own time and place. "Inasmuch as the work of an artist, if it be sincere, is an expression of his time and country so my work, because I am an American and a Chicagoan must have something in it of the quality of America and Chicago," she wrote in *Art of Today, Chicago 1933* (Jacobson, 90).

Levy's prints were published in *Fine Prints of the Year* (1933) and her works were included in the Century of Progress exhibitions of 1933 and 1934 held at AIC. The Great Depression, however, reorganized the structure of the art community in Chicago and other American cities. The Works Progress Administration (WPA) Federal Arts Project (FAP), created in 1935 to help remove artists from the dole, employed artists who could demonstrate a sufficient level of poverty. Beatrice Levy supervised the Easel Painting Division for the WPA/FAP in 1936 and ran the WPA Art Project Gallery in Chicago.

At the end of the thirties, Levy continued to show in Chicago and elsewhere. Her etchings appeared in an exhibition of prints in Sweden in 1937, her prints in *Fifty Years of American Painting* exhibit held at AIC in 1939–40. After World War II, Levy's prints were shown in the National Academy's *American Drawings* shows in 1945, 1946, and 1947. It was during 1947 that Levy preserved an important piece of Chicago's art history by making an etching of the Fifty-seventh Street artists' colony before it was razed. She watched the demolition of the building that had housed her studio and the studios of countless other Chicago artists.

In 1950 Levy moved to La Jolla, California. Here she spent the last twenty-four years of her life, continuing to paint, etch, and to exhibit her work both in California and abroad. In 1955 she exhibited watercolors at the La Jolla Art Center, and later that same year she had a one-person show of prints and watercolors at the center. After years of experimentation, she had begun to work consistently in a nonobjective style during her California residence. A reviewer described her art in this period as "characterized by restrained and muted symbols, by an engaging and subtle perspective into the sometimes commonplace, sometimes crucial events of contemporary life, by a fresh and inventive use of textural phrasing and color rhyming, by a technical mastery over her medium and lastly, by a strong personal conviction of the value of her art" ("New One-Man Series Opens at Center"). The eight prints and five watercolors in the show had all been the products of the post-1950 California period. Another review identified the persistent representational elements in the group of abstractions, commenting that "Beatrice S. Levy's nature tends toward moderation, carefully avoiding all extremes" (Kietzmann). Continuing to experiment, Levy introduced a wealth of textures in her 1950s works, produced by a combination of collage and print techniques. Levy also exhibited in 1955 with another southern California artist, Elsie Donaldson, at the Mezzanine Gallery in San Diego. Included was Levy's print, *Mutative*, that had won an award in the San Diego Art Guild's annual watercolor and graphic arts show. It was her response to the fear of the post-Hiroshima world that radioactive dust might cause mutations in human, animal, and plant life, which she expressed through the use of hieroglyphs.

Levy taught at the La Jolla Museum of Arts and Crafts from 1961 to 1962. In 1963–64, in her last international exhibition, Levy's works were shown in Yokohama, Japan, as part of a cross-cultural art exchange. Yokohama was San Diego's "sister city." In an ironic twist, Levy exhibited ceramics rather than prints in the Yokohama show, the former a relatively new medium for her; she had received acclaim for prints that were known for their Japanese quality, recalling centuries-old wood-block prints.

Levy continued to produce art until her death. Her works are included in the Art Institute of Chicago Print Collection, the permanent collections of the Smithsonian Institute, the Los Angeles County Museum of Art, the Library of Congress, and the Bibliothèque Nationale, Paris.

Levy played an important role in Chicago's art community at the time of the controversial Armory Show in 1913 when, as a young woman art student, she championed the cause of the avant-garde and adopted an eclectic and experimental approach in her own development as an artist. Known for her consistent commitment to the technical as well as the conceptual in printmaking, she enlarged her repertoire in the printer's craft every decade of her life as an artist.

Sources. Beatrice S. Levy Scrapbooks, Archives of American Art, Smithsonian Institution, Washington, D.C., are available on microfilm. The collection contains biographical materials including letters, newspaper clippings, printed material, photographs, and artwork. The Art Institute of Chicago's Print Department has the following Levy etchings in its permanent collection: *In Orchestra Hall* (1930), *St. Francis of Assisi* (n.d.), *I Will Lift Mine Eyes unto the Mountains* (1918). A short autobiographical statement by Levy is included in J. Z. Jacobson, ed., *Art of Today, Chicago 1933* (1933). C. J. Bulliet, "Artists of Chicago Past and Present," *Chicago Daily News*, August 8, 1936, is biographical. Levy is discussed in Louise Yochim's *Role and Impact: The History of the Chicago Society of Artists* (1979). Reviews of her work can be found in "New One-Man Series Opens at Center," *La Jolla Light*, November 24, 1955; Dr. Armin Kietzmann, "Art by Levy: Both Intuitive and Intellectual," *San Diego Union*, November 20, 1955; Naomi Baker, "The Art Circle," San Diego *Evening Tribune*, July 2, 1955; "An Artist in the Basque Provinces," *Christian Science Monitor*, July 11, 1928; C. H. Bonte, "Beatrice Levy's Color Etchings," *Philadelphia Inquirer*, October 19, 1924.

BENJAMIN J. KLEINMAN

LILLIE, FRANCES CRANE
August 30, 1869–February 2, 1958
SOCIALIST, SOCIAL REFORMER, PHYSICIAN

Frances Crane was born in Chicago, one of nine children of Richard Teller and Mary (Prentice) Crane. The Crane family was a prominent business family in the city. Richard T. Crane, who arrived in Chicago from the East in 1855, had begun his own company, the Crane Bell and Brass Foundry, shortly thereafter; he transformed the company from its modest beginnings into one of the city's leading manufacturers, the Crane Elevator Company. Unlike many wealthy women of the late nineteenth century, Frances Crane not only attended a university, she studied at Woman's Medical College of Chicago, graduating in 1892, just before it became affiliated with Northwestern University. Dr. MARIE MERGLER was one of her teachers. Crane graduated with honors in gynecology and planned to go into obstetrics and gynecology to deliver babies in the slums of Chicago. By 1890 she had already met JANE ADDAMS and ELLEN GATES STARR, and that year, while still attending college, she joined the governing board of the Protective Agency for Women and Children. The agency, begun under the auspices of the Chicago Women's Club (became Chicago Woman's Club in 1895), provided women with legal assistance in their battles in the municipal court regarding domestic abuse, divorce, and child custody matters.

Participating in the work of the Protective Agency brought Crane into contact with many of those women who, over the next three decades, would lead the women's social and political reform movements in the city, women such as ELLEN HENROTIN, ADA SWEET, JULIA HOLMES SMITH, and CORINNE BROWN. Pressured by her family, who worried about the dangers of her work and insisted she take her brother along as an escort (he carried a revolver strapped to his waist outside his coat), she was persuaded to try ophthalmology. She began graduate studies at the University of Chicago with this career plan in mind, taking courses in science. In 1893 she hung out a brass plate, Frances Crane, M.D., on the front door of her father's new mansion on Michigan Avenue. Her attempt to practice medicine, however, was unsuccessful, and she then worked briefly at the Chicago Polyclinic, in the ear and eye division. At the university, she met her future husband, University of Chicago professor of biology and zoology Frank R. Lillie. When she took a summer course at Woods Hole, the university's outdoor biology laboratory in Massachusetts, she had more opportunity to develop a friendship with Lillie, who also supervised that facility. Back in Chicago after Woods Hole, Frances Crane continued to take courses, studying with Jacques Loeb, who taught and did research in the field of physiological optics. During this period Crane and Lillie corresponded, and their letters contained discussions on women's rights and suffrage, the study of science, and ideas about womanhood and manhood. Crane also described her interest in the immigrant and working-class sections of Chicago and her earliest reflections about her personal need to experience religion more fully than was possible in the Protestant churches of her class.

Frances Crane and Frank Lillie were married in June 1895; their family eventually included seven children. Five children, three of whom were adopted, lived to adulthood; two died shortly after birth. Frances Crane Lillie's first pregnancy ended in a stillbirth; desperate over this loss, she persuaded her husband that they should adopt a child, a son, Albert. She decided to give up any idea of becoming a practicing physician and in 1898 attempted a second pregnancy, successfully giving birth to a daughter, Katherine Crane. Settling in a home near the University of Chicago, Frances Lillie began a period of intense devotion to her children and adopted another child, Ralph Aiken, in 1901. He was about two years old when the Lillies brought him home from the Chicago Children's Home, and they changed his name to Ethan when he was three. These adoptions were unusual for this period, when orphans generally were placed in institutions rather than in private adoptive homes. Even more unusual was the adoption of a child beyond the age of infancy.

During this period of maternity and motherhood, Frances Lillie absorbed ideas about domesticity and childrearing from the Arts and Crafts movement that had gained considerable popularity among a stratum of elite women and men in the United States. Eager to develop the proper environment for her family according to the movement's guidelines, Lillie hired Allen B. and Irving K. Pond, who had one of the leading Arts and Crafts–influenced firms in Chicago, to build a new home. The Ponds had designed new Hull-House buildings and were part of the group of intellectuals, artists, reformers, and artisans engaged in arts and crafts activities centered at the settlement. Frances Lillie was pregnant for a fourth time in 1906. She successfully gave birth to daughter Mary Prentice on September 27, 1906, in Boston, after the family had spent the summer at Woods Hole. She adopted a blind child, Karl, while he was still a baby, and had yet another pregnancy in 1909. This time the infant, a girl they named Alice, died at three months. Her interest in children extended beyond her own family. In 1907 the day nursery she funded at Hull-House became the Mary Crane Nursery, named after her mother.

Her involvement with the day nursery was purely financial. Frances Lillie envisioned a community where she and her children could live for extended periods with the children of the poor. Whether as a result of her sense of noblesse oblige and guilt—she had been deeply burdened by the knowledge of her family's manufacturing plant where boys and girls worked in substandard conditions—or out of her mystical religious ideas tied to a social gospel message, Frances Lillie hoped to establish a place where class differences were abolished. In 1907 Frances and Frank Lillie purchased Buffalo Creek Farm in Wheeling, Illinois; there he did studies in cattle embryology and she organized a colony where she resettled working-class Chicago families of widows with children. Eventually nine or ten families at a time stayed until their children reached age sixteen. Each family received a small cash income, according to how many children were being supported. A school was inaugurated for the children, and the farm colony was renamed Childerley.

Around 1914, Frances Crane Lillie emerged from her home and the circle of her children to play an active role in promoting the causes of children and working women. She did so within a group of women she already knew and with whom she had previously worked and in the context of personal concerns that were more than two and a half decades old. In February 1915, for example, she was included in the list of activist women asked to participate in a meeting to protest the plans of the Cook County Board to eliminate the bureaus of public welfare and children's summer outings.

Frances Lillie's greatest participation in Chicago affairs, however, came over the issue of the rights of workers, especially working women. Her activities in this area brought her into conflict with others of her social status, for she appeared to have adopted a highly individualist approach that made her look for an avenue other than middle-class women's organizations through which to reform society. Although she worked with many middle-class women reformers, she seemed to have distrusted their abilities to work truly for the benefit of other classes in society. Frances Lillie worked instead largely outside organized women's groups, and in 1915, she even joined the Socialist

Party. She believed that the poorer classes of society had to join together in order to protect themselves, and society in general, from rich people. As she specifically stated in a letter to a Dr. Cattell, written December 27, 1915, the poor had "to protect society from us" (Crane-Lillie Family Papers).

In pursuit of her objective of fighting for the rights of working women, Frances Crane Lillie joined several other middle-class women in late 1915 in picketing to show support for the city's striking garment workers. This action was a protest against the ability of Chicago's business owners to use the police against striking workers. When Chicago's clothing manufacturers persuaded the police to limit picketing by the strikers, middle-class women marched the picket lines carrying signs that said they were picketing for those driven off the picketing line. That December Crane Lillie was arrested while picketing. Her arrest generated much newspaper coverage of her actions, including a long article about her and other striking women written by Carl Sandburg. Her arrest also gave her the opportunity and a public forum for airing her ideas about the democratic rights of workers. She declared the general strike to be the most important weapon of democracy. She also justified her decision to join the Socialist Party because of the collusion she believed existed between business and government to use the organized police power of the state against workers. The notoriety her picketing and arrest generated for the garment workers earned her a letter of heartfelt thanks from Sidney Hillman, head of the Amalgamated Clothing Workers.

Frances Crane Lillie's ideas and actions in support of striking workers not surprisingly brought her into conflict with her brothers, who had inherited the family business. In early 1919 she wrote to her brother Richard T. Crane Jr., urging him to allow his workers to unionize and arguing that unionization was needed in a democracy. He rejected her ideas. Later that year, newspapers reported that Crane Lillie was supporting the seven thousand workers striking against the Crane Company, despite the fact that she herself was a large stockholder in the company. In a letter to American Federation of Labor organizer John Kikulski, cited in the *Chicago Examiner*, August 14, 1919, she justified her support for the strikers, saying that the Crane family was receiving huge amounts of money each year from the work of other people without giving society a corresponding return. The same newspaper article quoted her brother Charles, who, despite being a bit of a family rebel himself, dismissed her activities by saying that she belonged to the Hull-House group of sociologists who were radical.

Lillie was an individualist in the way in which she attempted to formulate her own agenda for resolving the ills of society. She drafted an undated open letter to the president (Woodrow Wilson was in office) in which she drew together her concerns for women, children, and workers by asking him to support the eight-hour day, pure food laws, and public nurseries for working mothers inside public schools. In 1918, she reiterated these ideas in "A Platform (tentative) for the Women of Illinois." Twenty-five years later she continued to advocate similar ideas. She wrote to the head of the Crane Company, telling him that working men and women were entitled to spend more time with their children than they were currently allowed by American industry.

Frances Crane Lillie's search for a philosophy within which to live and work led her in several directions. In 1919, she declared herself a member of the newly formed Labor Party in Chicago. In 1920, she embraced Roman Catholicism. Perhaps in this last, she was following the example of her friend Ellen Gates Starr, who, in 1917, had declared herself a socialist because she was above all a Christian. Starr and Lillie had deliberated on the connection of Christianity and socialism from the late 1890s at the beginning of their friendship. Both women sought a resolution of their personal need for authentic devotional experience and their belief that as individuals they had to commit themselves to a life that followed the social gospel of Jesus Christ. Both raised as Protestants, they traveled first to membership in the Episcopal Church, where a social gospel theology combined Catholic worship with social action. Discouraged by the lack of progress of Episcopalians and their church institutions to go beyond rhetoric in support of the working class, Lillie and Starr left that denomination and converted to Roman Catholicism.

In addition to engaging in various social causes and protests, Frances Crane Lillie used her personal fortune to found or support a number of social institutions that recalled her concerns for children. Among these institutions were the Mary Crane Nursery, the University of Chicago Nursery School, and the experimental Dewey School. The Woods Hole Summer School of Science, dedicated to the study of marine biology, received her constant support. Crane Lillie also contributed monetarily to women's causes in the city, for instance to settlement house resident Ellen Gates Starr and to AGNES NESTOR when she ran for a seat in the Illinois legislature in 1928.

Frances Crane Lillie's radicalism did not end after World War I. In the immediate postwar years she put up more than thirty thousand dollars in bail money for radicals detained during the Palmer Raids (1919–20), when President Woodrow Wilson's attorney general, A. Mitchell Palmer, overreacted to postwar radicalism by using private spies to conduct a series of raids on private homes and labor headquarters suspected of harboring communist agitators. Nearly three thousand persons were rounded up; ultimately a few hundred were deported. Most of those arrested in no way endangered the country. She worked with Robert M. Lovett, professor of English, University of Chicago, to set up a fund for political prisoners.

She continued to pursue social justice issues as a practicing Roman Catholic. She contributed her estate, Childerley, to the Catholic Archdiocese of Chicago, and it became a home for widows and children.

As an older woman, Frances Crane Lillie reflected on the difficulties she had encountered when, as a student of medicine in the early 1890s, she had experienced ambivalence concerning a career as a physician. It was at this time that she first met Jane Addams and Ellen Gates Starr. "Even now I cannot understand why I did not drop the study of medicine and go to live with them forever, such was my enthusiasm, but I did not" (Barrows, "God and My Mother," 46). She completed her studies but found that her upper-class life, even before her decision to marry and become a mother, interfered with her desire to meld religious fervor to pursue social justice with her professional training. Instead, as an ally of working men and women, she became an ardent supporter of social justice causes and a champion of the rights of the working class and of radicals.

Sources. The Crane-Lillie Family Papers at the CHS contain accounts of her strike activities; correspondence, including letters to Marie Mergler; a typed manuscript, "The Story of My Life," by Frances Crane Lillie, n.d.; and a newspaper clippings scrapbook of the 1915 strike in which Frances Lillie was a participant. Also in the Crane-Lillie Family Papers, Mary Prentice Lillie Barrows, "God and My Mother," typescript, 1977, is a useful source. Her correspondence with Starr is in Ellen Gates Starr Papers, Sophia Smith Collection, Smith College, Northampton, Massachusetts. The 1890 *Annual Report* of the Protective Agency for Women and Children is at the CHS.

MAUREEN A. FLANAGAN

LIN, MARGARET HIE DING
March 17, 1888–June 30, 1973
PHYSICIAN, COMMUNITY ACTIVIST

One of the first medical students to come to Chicago from China, Margaret Lin became a legendary figure in Chicago's Chinatown. She practiced medicine both in China and Chicago. She grew up in the province of Fujian, northeast of Canton (now Guangdong province), from which many of the early Chinese immigrants to the United States came. Lin's family may have been more receptive to Western culture than most early immigrants. Lin's father, Mik Sing Lin, became a Christian minister. He and his wife, Ciong Ung, lived near Fuzhou College, an institution founded by Western missionaries. As an educated man, he was part of an elite group in China.

Little else is known about Margaret Lin's childhood or family, not even whether she had any siblings. Friends of hers report that she had a nephew who lived in the United States. Given the confusion in Chinese family lineage—many Chinese created false birth records to indicate that clan members and friends in China had been born in the United States (referred to as the "paper sons" phenomenon)—it is not clear that Lin's nephew was even a blood relative. All that is known for certain is that after graduation from Fuzhou College in 1907, Margaret Lin came to the United States to attend medical school. She had a preceptor—a mentor—in Minnesota before she began formal academic training at the medical school of the University of Illinois. She was one of the first immigrant Chinese women to study at a medical school in the United States.

As a woman, Margaret Lin faced particular difficulties entering the United States. Students such as Lin were exempt from restrictions imposed by the Chinese Exclusion Act, enforced between 1882 and 1943, which severely limited the category of Chinese who were allowed to come to the United States and included only merchants, their wives and children, students, and visitors. Nonetheless, females still were subjected to intense interrogation and detained from two weeks to several months at the point of entry on Angel Island in the San Francisco Bay. Legend has it that Margaret Lin dressed in male attire in order to disguise her gender. Although this story cannot be confirmed, it was not an uncommon practice.

Sun Yat-sen, founder of the Nationalist Party in China, visited Chicago the year that Lin began medical school. His impassioned appeals for support to establish a modern form of government in China inspired many overseas Chinese, including Lin. Sun Yat-sen himself had studied medicine in Hawaii, and many Chinese parents held him up as a role model for their children. Lin also regarded him in this light. Her choice of a career in medicine and her association with other Chinese in Chicago made Lin well known in her community.

One problem Lin faced in these early years was finding a

FIG. 65. *Dr. Margaret Hie Ding Lin attended medical school at the University of Illinois between 1910 and 1915.*

suitable place to live. While getting housing was difficult for most Chinese students, it was particularly hard for Lin because she was a woman. She could not stay with male students who lived near the University of Chicago, nor was she welcome in the immigrant Chinese bachelor society. Furthermore, white landlords were in the process of increasing rents to force Chinese out of the city to make way for expansion of the central business district. Between 1910 and 1911, Chinese immigrants who had moved to Chicago from California in the 1870s were forced to relocate into the filthiest section of the city. In the end, YOKELUND WONG FOIN and her husband Chin Foin, a wealthy Chinese merchant, offered Lin a place to live in their home. Lin was the first female student of Foin's acquaintance and, probably because they were the same age, they became lifelong friends. After her formal medical training was completed in 1915, she interned for one year at the Mary Thompson Hospital of Chicago for Women and Children.

At the conclusion of the internship, Lin's mother asked her to return to China. Demonstrating her filial piety, Lin left for China and did not come back for twenty-three years. Her prolonged absence meant that she missed many of the changes that Chinese Americans experienced between 1917 and 1940. She had no connections with the Chinese Benevolent Society, the largest social service organization for Chinese in the United States. During the time that Lin was in China, the Chinese Benevolent Society was most active in providing medical service to Chinatown residents. She did not develop professional relationships with other medical professionals in the United States, who would have been her colleagues had she remained. On the other hand, by returning to China, Lin escaped the intense racial discrimination that Chinese encountered in Chicago and throughout the United States. While she actively practiced medicine in China, Chinese in the United States were not allowed to become licensed doctors and were barred from joining professional medical societies.

Once back in Fuzhou, Lin embarked on an exceptional and intense career. She began as a medical supervisor at the Fujian Industrial School and Orphanage (1917–18) and became active in helping to establish Fujian General Hospital. Despite male domination in the Chinese world, she served as president of the hospital. She had ample opportunity to pursue many branches of medicine. At the beginning of her career, Lin specialized in obstetrics and pediatrics. After she established Fujian General Hospital, she became head surgeon for the hospital. She was also one of the editors of the prestigious *China Medical Journal*.

Her experience in China contrasted sharply with that of Chinese who remained in the United States. In the 1920s and 1930s, even many second-generation Chinese Americans with professional degrees could not find work. Many Chinese Americans, whose career mobility was obstructed in the United States, went to China to give service during the Chinese civil war in the late 1920s and 1930s. For example, ROSE HUM LEE, who became a noted sociologist and department head at Roosevelt University of Chicago, served in China. Draconian American immigration regulations continued to bar the entry of Chinese women into the United States. Between 1924 and 1930, no Chinese women were allowed to enter the United

States; and between 1931 and 1941, only sixty women per year were admitted.

When Lin returned to Chicago in 1941, she was qualified to serve as an assistant in surgery at the medical center of the University of Illinois, then located at Navy Pier. She told friends in the United States that she decided to return because of the poor physical conditions in China under which she was required to work. The field of medicine in the United States had changed in twenty-five years, and Lin's age and experience did not fit the criteria of what was needed in Chicago. The position of assistant in surgery allowed Lin to pursue her professional interest without the pressure of competing for top status. After living in Chicago for three years, she became a staff member of the Illinois Department of Public Welfare. Lin continued to develop a public service career. Ironically, the Chinatown community that had once snubbed her when she was a student came to regard her as a heroine.

Sometime later, Lin set up a medical practice in Chinatown. Although many Chinese Americans had moved into the suburbs, especially in the 1950s when jobs were easier to obtain, they still returned to Chinatown on weekends to shop, socialize, and attend to their health needs. Lin worked in Chinatown on weekends. During the week, she attended patients at the Cook County Tuberculosis Hospital in Oak Forest, Illinois.

She was not part of either the 1950s wave of successful immigrant Chinese professionals nor the older generation of Cantonese immigrants who first came to the United States. Lin's generation was a transitional one whose women had severe problems adjusting to the country. Lin was never formally certified to practice medicine in Illinois, yet she was admired by the Chinatown community that successfully nominated her in 1964 to be inducted into the Senior Citizens Hall of Fame in Chicago for her community service. The larger Chicago community, on the other hand, never recognized her contributions in such fields as geriatric medicine, in which she worked at Oak Forest Hospital.

Margaret Lin was a larger-than-life figure in Chicago's Chinatown. Her reputation may have been enhanced by her service on the executive committee of the International Anti-opium Society or by the story that she was related to Lin Zexu (Lin Tse-hsu), the Manchu official who rebelled against the British for selling opium. She dressed flamboyantly and wore large hats, and she had an outgoing personality. When she died at eighty-three years of age at Oak Forest Hospital, where she had lived for many years in the New Nurses Apartments, she was buried in the Chinese section at Rosehill Cemetery. She had provided an important service as a physician both in the Chinese community and in hospitals outside Chinatown.

Sources. Information about Lin comes from interviews with her friends and patients, 1993–95. They include Reverend and Mrs. Peter W. Fu, Therese O'Young, Gung Hsing Wang, and Gladys Chen Wong. The Univ. of Illinois Library of the Health Sciences has information about Lin's career as a student and faculty member. Susan Lee Moy verified historical facts on the development of Chicago's Chinatown. Information on Chinese Americans can be found in Tin Chiu Fan's *Chinese Residents in Chicago* (1925); Yuan Liang's *The Chinese Family in Chicago* (1951); Betty L. Sung's *Mountain of Gold: The Story of the Chinese in America* (1967); Yuan-Li Wu's *Economic Conditions of Chinese* in America (1980); Judy Yung's *Chinese Women of America* (1987); Ruthanne Lum McCunn's *Chinese American Portraits* (1988); Roger Daniel's *Asian America* (1988); Suchen Chan's "The Exclusion of Chinese Women, 1870–1943," in *Chinese America: History and Perspectives* (1994); Susan Lee Moy's "The Chinese of Chicago: The First One Hundred Years," in *Ethnic Chicago*, ed. Melvin G. Holli and Peter d'A. Jones (4th edition, 1995); and in Lisa See's *On Gold Mountain* (1995).

PEGGY SPITZER CHRISTOFF

LIVERMORE, MARY ASHTON RICE
December 19, 1820–May 23, 1905
CIVIL WAR WORKER, LECTURER, TEMPERANCE AND WOMEN'S RIGHTS REFORMER

Bostonian Mary Livermore became a Union heroine in Chicago, working for the Northwestern Sanitary Commission during the Civil War. She drew upon this fame and her network of coworkers for thirty years as a reformer and as one of the most successful public lecturers of her day. The fourth child of Timothy and Zebiah Vose Glover (Ashton) Rice, she was their first to survive infancy; she had two younger sisters. Her father was a Calvinistic Baptist, holding twice-daily religious services and requiring his children to read the entire Bible each year. Although Timothy Rice was a veteran of the War of 1812 and had family connections in Boston, he supported his family as a laborer. Zebiah Rice, the daughter of an English sea captain, taught her daughters to admire Ann Hasseltine Judson, an early missionary to India. While Mary Rice saw herself as the protector of weaker and poorer children, she also feared being a burden to her parents and felt their relative poverty.

Mary Rice was a large, vigorous child and a brilliant student. In adolescence, her impressive homework prompted a teacher to charge her with plagiarism, which she disproved by composing an essay on the spot. She grew up in Boston, except for two years in western New York in the 1830s while Timothy Rice tried farming. Graduating as a prize-winning scholar at age fourteen from Boston's Hancock Grammar School, Mary Rice served a brief apprenticeship to a dressmaker before her parents sent her to the Charlestown Female Seminary. After two years she taught Latin and French while continuing to study Greek for another year.

Mary Rice experienced a religious crisis during her adolescence. At fourteen she was converted and joined the First Baptist Church of Boston. After several years attempting to convert her invalid younger sister, Mary was inconsolable when Rachel died unconverted. Her conviction of her sister's damnation led to a revulsion against religion and a permanent rejection of orthodox Christianity. Alienated from home, she worked for several years as a governess on a Virginia plantation, coming to know slavery firsthand. Her access to her elite employers' household and extensive library provided valuable social and intellectual experience.

Mary Rice returned to Massachusetts around 1842 and took charge of a private secondary school in Duxbury. An abolitionist, she subscribed to the antislavery newspaper the *Liberator*. She became an active worker in the Washingtonian temperance movement; she organized children, edited a juvenile temperance paper, and published a book of songs and stories, *The Children's Army* (1844). In Duxbury, Mary Rice was converted to

Universalism by clergyman Daniel Parker Livermore. The Universalist rejection of hell and emphasis on a forgiving God offered her a return to faith.

She married Livermore against her father's wishes on May 6, 1845; they were married for fifty-four years. Between 1845 and 1857, she followed him to pastorates in Fall River, Massachusetts; Stafford, Connecticut; Malden and Weymouth, Massachusetts; and Auburn, New York. Her three daughters, Mary Eliza (1848), Henrietta White (1851), and Marcia Elizabeth (1854) were born during this period; her firstborn died at age five. Daniel Livermore shared his wife's commitment to temperance; he resigned his pastorate at Stafford, Connecticut, rather than modify his temperance views. During this period, Mary Livermore published regularly in religious and women's publications and occasionally in general-interest magazines. *Thirty Years too Late*, a prize-winning temperance story published by the Washingtonians, a temperance organization, around 1848, had an international circulation and was republished in Boston in 1878.

Daniel Livermore persuaded his wife to join abolitionists moving to Kansas in 1857, but the plan was abandoned when, en route, their youngest daughter Lizzie developed "a most hopeless and mysterious illness" (Livermore, *My Life*, 455). By 1873, Lizzie was a permanent invalid. The Livermores lived in Chicago from 1857 until 1869. Daniel Livermore bought the Universalist weekly newspaper, *New Covenant*, publishing it with his wife's help until 1869. Mary Livermore's name appeared below his on the editorial page, and many articles were signed by her.

Chicago, growing at the rate of about twenty thousand people per year in the 1860s, needed social services. Robustly healthy and a prodigious worker, Mary Livermore soon emerged as a philanthropic leader. She was a mainstay of the Universalist Church of the Redeemer, and in 1858 she joined with JANE HOGE and other prominent Chicagoans to found the Home for the Friendless, serving on its board until 1869. Although the officers were men, the board of women directors did all the work, providing help to women and children applicants. Mary Livermore also cofounded the Home for Aged Women (1861) and the Hospital for Women and Children (1863).

Mary Livermore's initial fame resulted from her Civil War work as an organizer, fund-raiser, and executive for the Chicago (later Northwestern) branch of the United States Sanitary Commission (USSC), a government-sanctioned organization of civilians created by elite northern men in the fall of 1861 to aid Union soldiers. The USSC took over control of women's voluntary work in soldiers' aid societies, superseding the leadership of the Women's Central Association of Relief, which had initiated civilian volunteer efforts in April 1861. As with prewar charities, most of the commission's workers were women, while its officers were men. However, USSC's dependence on women as producers, leaders, and nurses in the long national emergency gave northern women like Mary Livermore new leverage. As "associate managers" of USSC branches, women learned how to run mass organizations and how to inspire other women to join a national cause.

In Chicago, Livermore hired household help and volunteered for the duration of the war. She and her friend Hoge raised money for the commission through a festival in December 1861. Their report on their tour of army hospitals in the spring of 1862 led to appointments by Sanitary Commission head Dr. Henry Bellows as associate members of the commission. During the national Woman's Council meeting in Washington, D.C., in November 1862, they were authorized by Dorothea L. Dix, superintendent of women nurses, to recruit nurses in the West. In December, they succeeded ELIZA PORTER as the Northwestern commission's associate managers.

Livermore and Hoge transformed the Northwestern Commission branch into the "first in importance in the list of our auxiliaries at the West" (Newberry, 111), creating a reliable supply system via local aid societies throughout a largely rural, frontier region. They accomplished this system by a massive letter-writing campaign (120 letters a day), followed often by personal visits and public speaking. Livermore was also writer and publicist for the commission, turning out circulars, monthly bulletins, and news articles. The women's tasks were complicated by the existence of such rival organizations as the Christian Commission and by unfounded accusations that the Sanitary Commission was incompetent or dishonest. Nevertheless, about three thousand aid societies contributed to the Northwestern Sanitary Commission, many organized directly by Livermore and Hoge.

In 1862 and 1863 Livermore made extensive tours of federal encampments to deliver supplies, evaluate needs, and publicize conditions. In battlefront hospitals, ministering to suffering and dying soldiers, she gained both authority as an organizer and new respect for "the lowest tier of human beings" (Livermore, *My Story of the War*, 178). Responding with Hoge to an emergency call for vegetables and fruits to save Grant's army at Vicksburg from scurvy early in 1863, Livermore's tour of hospitals from Illinois to Tennessee prompted her to propose a major fund-raising fair to restore depleted resources. The male commissioners greeted the suggestion skeptically. Livermore and Hoge convened four hundred women from all over the Northwest to plan the event and canvassed the East for donations. Their network of aid societies donated enormous quantities of goods, and the fair became a national event, lasting two weeks in October and netting more than eighty thousand dollars. The prototype of later Sanitary Commission fairs, it offered both entertainment and opportunities for public patriotism. The women's leadership was widely publicized; Mary Livermore and Jane Hoge became "household words throughout the country" (Henshaw, 94).

By 1865, Livermore was persuaded that women's help was needed in governing the country, as it had been in winning the war. In March 1867 she spoke out for woman suffrage in the *New Covenant* and offered her services to Susan B. Anthony. She also worked with her husband to increase opportunities for Universalist women ministers. In June 1868, inspired by New York's Sorosis, the first formal women's club in the United States, Mary Livermore joined former Sanitary Commission worker Elizabeth J. Loomis and editor M. L. Rayne to form a Women's Association, later the Chicago Sorosis. Livermore took leadership in one faction of the group, with longtime neighbor and friend, MYRA BRADWELL, and KATE NEWELL DOGGETT, both fellow war workers.

Livermore organized Chicago's first woman suffrage convention in February 1869, featuring suffragists Anthony, Elizabeth Cady Stanton, Lucy Stone, and Anna Dickinson, along with local clergymen and judges. The Chicago convention outdrew Anthony and Stanton's convention in New York several months later and resulted in the founding of the Illinois Woman Suffrage Association. A spin-off committee, lobbying the Illinois legislature for women's rights, helped to get Myra Bradwell's married women's property bill passed in March. Stanton praised Livermore as the West's Susan B. Anthony.

Livermore established a suffrage newspaper, the *Agitator*, in March 1869, and Daniel Livermore sold the *New Covenant* in May to help her. Livermore drew upon suffragists Kate Doggett, Kate Boynton (see ELIZABETH BOYNTON HARBERT), CATHARINE WAITE, and male suffragists, including Unitarian minister Robert Collyer and Catherine Waite's husband Judge C. B. Waite.

Livermore's second suffrage convention, held in Chicago in September, was a battleground; Stanton and Anthony of New York and Lucy Stone of New England vied for leadership of the national woman suffrage movement. Livermore chose the Boston wing and used her influence to bring Illinois into Stone's American Woman Suffrage Association (AWSA). She sold the *Agitator* to Stone that fall, agreeing to edit it in Boston as the *Woman's Journal* for two years.

Mary Livermore maintained her Chicago connections after her move in 1870 to Massachusetts. She worked with Doggett and Bradwell in the Association for the Advancement of Women (AAW) and in AWSA. In 1871, helping Hoge raise funds for the Evanston College for Ladies, Livermore met and befriended FRANCES E. WILLARD, nearly twenty years her junior. Livermore supported Willard's decision to make a career of temperance work in 1874 and became her lifelong ally in the Woman's Christian Temperance Union (WCTU), both as president of the Massachusetts WCTU from 1875 to 1885 and as a popular temperance speaker.

Livermore left full-time woman suffrage work when her editorship of *Woman's Journal* ended in 1872, though she served as AWSA president 1875–78. For the rest of her life Livermore was an active member of women's organizations such as WCTU, the New England Woman's Club, and the Boston Women's Education and Industrial Union; she served as the first president of AAW in 1873–74. She also worked with both men and women in a wide variety of causes, from the cooperative housekeeping movement (which advocated communal cooking arrangements to free women for other work) and prison reform to spiritualism (the American Psychic Society) and various veteran's aid groups. She was attracted to socialism, which she viewed as "applied Christianity" (Livermore, *New Nation*, June 6, 1891) and, prompted by Nationalist supporter Frances Willard, joined the short-lived Nationalist movement led by Edward Bellamy to advocate the cooperative socialist system dramatized in his popular novel *Looking Backward* (1888); she also supported the Society of Christian Socialists. Her socialist views did not prevent her from supporting the Republican party, and though unable to vote she was twice elected a delegate from Melrose to the Republican state convention.

Though Livermore worked for many organizations and

causes after the Civil War, she was not a full-time reformer like Willard and Susan B. Anthony; she neither founded an important organization nor created new strategies and arguments to further her goals. Her role instead was to popularize ideas she shared with a national network of women reformers about the importance of women's organizing to secure their own rights to citizenship, education, and employment and to protect the interests of other women and children. Her principal work for twenty-five years after 1872 was lecturing to general audiences, most often in former Union states, on topics of public interest, booked by the leading agent of the day, James Redpath's Lyceum Bureau. Livermore was among the early women to make a commercial success of public lecturing. Initially, audiences came to see a Civil War heroine, but she continued to draw bookings for decades on the grounds of her reputation as a speaker. Responding to requests, she usually lectured about women—their history, their rights, their duties, their future—though she was careful not to urge reforms upon listeners unless invited. Her most popular topic was "What Shall We Do with Our Daughters?" and she proposed equal education and "careful moral culture" (Livermore, *My Life*, 492) for women. She averaged 150 lectures a year for a decade and continued lecturing well into her seventies, consistently promoting wider opportunities for women and a maternalist vision of a morally progressive future. Henry Blackwell, widower of Lucy Stone and lifelong reformer, claimed about Livermore that "no man or woman of her generation addressed audiences so numerous, on topics so varied and inspiring" and that she "molded the thoughts of millions" (Blackwell, 82). She also reached out to a general audience in her two popular autobiographies, *My Story of the War* (1887) and *The Story of My Life* (1897), and in articles she wrote for national magazines.

Daniel Livermore died in 1899; committed to women's equality, he had been his wife's chief supporter. She died in 1905 of heart disease after a brief illness, and her ashes were buried in Wyoming Cemetery, Melrose, Massachusetts.

Mary Livermore's long career as a public speaker, built upon her Chicago experience and western connections, demonstrated that a woman's patriotic work could win a hearing on national issues. Livermore mounted the public platform as a middle-aged woman to argue the importance of expanding women's participation in American public life, and because she was famous for wartime national service, she reached a middle-class audience that rejected women identified principally as reformers. Ironically, Livermore's fame dwindled after her death for the same reason she was effective during her lifetime—she did not leave behind an organization or single reform with which she was principally identified. Nevertheless, in Gilded Age America she commanded popular attention on the grounds of pioneering public service and good sense, and her career enabled other women to claim authority in public forums.

Sources. The major archival collections for a study of Livermore include the Mary A. Livermore Collection, Princeton Univ.; the Kate Fields Collection, the Boston Public Library; the National American Woman Suffrage Papers, the Library of Congress. Livermore published two autobiographical works: *My Story of the War* (1887) and *The Story of My Life* (1897). She also wrote *The Two Families* (1848), *Christmas Child*

(1859), *Pen Pictures: Or Sketches from Domestic Life* (1862), *What Shall We Do with Our Daughters?* (1883), and articles in *Arena*, December 1889, August 1892; *North American Review*, January and December 1890, September 1891, February 1896; *New Nation*, June 6, 1891; as well as other periodicals. There are biographical entries on Livermore in *NAW* (1971) and Frances E. Willard and Mary A. Livermore, eds., *A Woman of the Century* (1893). Contemporary views of Livermore appear in Mrs. E. R. Hanson, *Our Women Workers* (1882); Mrs. Sarah E. Henshaw, *Our Branch and Its Tributaries: Being a History of the Work of the Northwestern Sanitary Commission* (1883); Phebe A. Hanaford, *Daughters of America* (1882); L. P. Brockett and Mary C. Vaughan, *Woman's Work in the Civil War* (1867); John S. Newberry, *The U.S. Sanitary Commission in the Valley of the Mississippi* (1871); Elizabeth Cady Stanton et al., *History of Woman Suffrage*, vols. 2 and 3 (1881–[1922]); Lillian Whiting, *Women Who Have Ennobled Life* (1915); Henry McCormick, *The Women of Illinois* (1913); Sarah Bolton, *Lives of Girls Who Became Famous* (1914); and Henry Blackwell, editorial, *Woman's Journal*, May 27, 1905. Mary Livermore is one of the women analyzed in Blanche Glassman Hersh, *The Slavery of Sex* (1978); Livermore's views on cooperative housekeeping are discussed in one chapter of Dolores Hayden, *The Grand Domestic Revolution* (1981). Livermore as part of a Chicago network of women is treated in Lana Ruegamer, "'The Paradise of Exceptional Women': Chicago Women Reformers, 1863–1893" (Ph.D. diss., Indiana Univ., 1982).

LANA RUEGAMER

LIVSHIS, ANNA MINDLIN (Annie)
March 25, 1864–April 1, 1953
FEMINIST ANARCHIST, TRADE UNIONIST, HOMESTEADER

Anna (Annie) Livshis was born Chana Mindlin in Smadumna, Vitebsk Gobernia, Russia (now Belarus). She was the third child and first daughter of Joshua and Sarah Esther (Swerdlov) Mindlin's eight children, six of whom were boys. Her younger sister, Yetta, protested that Smadumna (familiarly, Samedumka) was not even a shtetl (village) but only an inn, a *kretchme*, at a crossroads. On the south side of the Dvina River, between Vitebsk and Polotsk, the inn and farm around it formed the Mindlin "homestead." Since Jews were prohibited from owning land, the homestead was rented from two gentile maiden sisters.

The Mindlins' was a poor Orthodox Jewish household, in which Sarah Mindlin ran the inn while Joshua Mindlin studied Torah and prayed. Annie Mindlin recalled both her father and paternal grandfather as prudent and temperate men. When talk of emigrating to America engaged the family, Mindlin's grandfather, like many Orthodox Jews, was skeptical of emigration to a land where secularization could undermine religious faith. Later he made the hazardous journey to Jerusalem to merit, on his death, the right of burial on the Mount of Olives.

Education was only for Mindlin's brothers—Michael David, Harris, Max, Henry, Albert, and Nathan—who were sent to *cheyder* (elementary Hebrew school); Annie Mindlin learned her alphabet informally from a brother. Later Mindlin and her sister learned to read English comfortably, although they could hardly write.

Annie Mindlin's mother was remembered as a strong-minded woman who died from overwork. She and her eldest child, Michael David, were buried in the Old Country and Michael David's wife and children emigrated to England. The Mindlins, like all Russian Jews, suffered long and bitter perse-

FIG. 66. *Anarchist, factory worker, and homesteader Anna Mindlin Livshis, seated in the front row, on the left, by her father, Joshua Mindlin.*

cution under the czars. The remaining Mindlin offspring set out one by one for the New World.

The Mindlins' emigration to America began with Harris Mindlin in the early 1880s, when pogroms, anti-Semitic attacks, and destruction of the Jewish communities threatened to annihilate Russian Jewry. Annie Mindlin arrived in New York in April 1886, a watershed year in American labor history. Her brother, Harris Mindlin, had already become part of New York's radical intelligentsia; and he and his friend, Israel Kopeloff, the articulate anarchist spokesman and follower of Johann Most, fired Annie Mindlin's imagination with the concept of a free society where no person could exploit another. Excited by the prospect of a transformed society, she joined her brother and others who formed the group Pioneers of Liberty. It was the first Jewish anarchist group organized in the United States and was officially established on November 11, 1887, to coincide with the infamous day of execution of the Haymarket martyrs in Chicago, Illinois. The Pioneers of Liberty had been influenced by the Haymarket bombing on May 4, 1886, and the subsequent trial and execution of four of the anarchists. The Jewish anarchists believed that a terrible miscarriage of justice had occurred and joined with other radicals and labor unionists in the United States to protest the state's violence.

Like thousands of other immigrants, Annie Mindlin went to work sewing in a sweatshop in New York City. Women's wages in sweatshops averaged three to six dollars for a work week of sixty to eighty hours. The exploitation of the sweatshop and the misery of tenement life, though anticipated, were more than Mindlin could bear, and after two months she prepared for a radical change in her life that would still enable her to help her family. With other members of the Mindlin family,

Annie Mindlin came to believe that the American frontier held the key to their future. In this view she was following the lead of her uncle, Chaim Mindlin, a follower of the *Am Olam* (Eternal people) movement. Chaim Mindlin was a product of the European *Haskalah* (Jewish enlightenment) that promoted Hebrew education along with modern secular studies. He was influenced also by *Am Olam*, with its goal of the physical emancipation and spiritual renewal of the Jewish people through farming and communal life. In the United States, the Homestead Act of 1862 promised a quarter section (160 acres) of unbroken government land to any immigrant over the age of twenty-one who had filed a "Declaration of Intention" to become a citizen of the United States, who would live on the land, and who would cultivate ten acres in the first six months. Jewish immigrants, single persons, and occasionally family groups established agricultural colonies in a number of states through this program.

In Kansas alone, seven colonies were established between 1883 and 1886. In one of these, the Lasker Colony, Chaim Mindlin and his growing family comprised more than a third of the original complement of thirty settlers. The colony was named for Eduard Lasker, German liberal politician and author, who had died in the early 1880s in the United States. Annie Mindlin prepared to leave New York and its sweatshops and filed her "Declaration of Intention" on June 7, 1886, signing the document with a bold X. The trunk that accompanied her from Samedumka with bedding, a few utensils, and clothing she had sewn herself was readied for the trip to western Kansas; and a one-way ticket was purchased with hard-earned dollars.

Annie Mindlin found out that land in the Lasker Colony did not come under the Homestead Act but under the terms of the

Osage Trust and Diminished Reserve Lands Act of Congress May 28, 1880, which made additional land in Kansas available for homesteading. This land, however, was obtainable only by purchase, and the Lasker colonists proved their claims by buying land on the installment plan at $1.25 per acre, proceeds placed to the credit of the Osage tribe at 5 percent annual interest. Payments plus interest were deposited with the U.S. Land Office, and the quarter-section homestead was paid off in three or four installments in as many years.

The hot summer of 1886 foreshadowed years of drought ahead for the arid plains, and Mindlin's heart sank as the train chugged across miles of dusty farmland sprouting meager crops. When the train pulled up near Lasker, however, a marvelous sight greeted her eyes. There were flowers everywhere. Her *chevre* (group) had tenderly placed wildflowers in glasses of water in the ground to welcome their newest member.

The following month, on August 5, 1886, Annie Mindlin proved to the satisfaction of the Ford County Land Office in Garden City, Kansas, that she was a genuine homesteader. She lived in her own sod house on the land, had one plow, bedding, and a trunk, and she had already planted nine acres in corn and one acre in garden. Chaim Mindlin and his sons had helped her quickly fulfill all of the conditions.

The Livshis brothers, Jacob and Moses, were among Annie Mindlin's first friends at the colony, and it was Moses who built her little sod house. Before many months had passed Annie Mindlin was betrothed to Jacob (Jake) Livshis. She was twenty-three and Jake twenty-six when they were married by the Justice of the Peace in nearby Dodge City, Kansas, November 7, 1887. Their Jewish religious wedding ceremony came later, with Uncle Chaim Mindlin officiating in the sod-house synagogue at Lasker. The Ford City *Boomer* reported that "a sumptuous repast was served at the home of Moses Livshis and there were [*sic*] lots of enjoyment" (October 7, 1891).

In 1888, when farming proved impractical, Annie and Jake Livshis took factory jobs in Chicago, the former as a finisher, the latter as a cloakmaker. Immediately recognizing the same exploitative conditions in Chicago sweatshops that Annie Livshis had endured in New York, the two began to organize workers in the needle trades. With the help of a young lawyer, Peter Sissman, and several other activists, they succeeded, in spite of great opposition, in organizing the workers, striving to give some dignity and meaning to the chaos of their lives. The resulting Cloak Makers' Union, founded in Chicago in 1890, was the first formal Jewish trade union in the city, with Peter Sissman as secretary and Jacob Livshis as the first treasurer. Annie and Jake Livshis also found time to form a political study group.

Later, in 1890, as prospects for farming improved, the couple returned to the Lasker Colony. Their *chevre* gathered repeatedly in the soddy used as a meeting house, to hear with their own ears all that Annie and Jake Livshis had learned and experienced in Chicago. In time two children were born while the Livshises lived on the homestead, Peter in March 1894, and Annie in April 1897. Peter was born totally deaf and he was, in addition, asthmatic. Annie was sickly from birth and was still a young child when she died in Chicago.

By 1898, the drought-ravaged land had destroyed their dreams of a viable community in Lasker. The Livshises pulled up their stakes and moved permanently to Chicago. In addition to the economic problems they had encountered, it had been difficult to find special education facilities for Peter and medical help for their daughter. They hoped to obtain the needed support for their children in Chicago.

Before the century was over, all seven Kansas colonies had been dissolved, although a few individual farmers remained. The Mindlin and Livshis families maintained their goals of human liberation and the brotherhood of man. From the Lasker *chevre* they brought with them to Chicago their vision of social justice, making it part of their urban experience.

Chicago beckoned like a lamp to Annie and Jake Livshis. At the turn of the century, the anarchist movement was perhaps stronger in Chicago than in any other city in the United States. Anarchist groups and publications flourished and, in this milieu, the Livshises became known. On their return to Chicago, the Livshises founded the David Edelstadt Group, named in memory of the radical poet whose death in 1892 at the age of twenty-six shocked the entire anarchist community. Edelstadt almost lost his life in a pogrom in the Ukraine before emigrating to the United States, where he became an editor of the Yiddish language anarchist newspaper the *Fraye Arbeter Shtime* (Free Voice of Labor) before his death from tuberculosis. Groups named for Edelstadt sprang up in several American cities, where Yiddish-speaking immigrants like the Livshises found in his poetry the most profound expression of their yearnings.

Meanwhile, the emigration of the European Mindlins continued until the youngest, Nathan Mindlin, arrived in New York in 1900. By then a widower, Joshua Mindlin, Annie Mindlin Livshis's father and the patriarch of the family, followed his seven children to New York City where his widowed sister, Dvora, kept house. They lived on the Lower East Side where Joshua Mindlin attended the Henry Street Synagogue.

In Chicago, Jake Livshis became a cigar maker and was a member of the cigar makers' pioneer union. In time he became a cigar manufacturer. Later Annie and Jake Livshis opened a dry goods store. Whether in their first Chicago flats or eventually in their house at 2038 Potomac Avenue in the Wicker Park neighborhood, their home quickly became a center for anarchists in Chicago. Rudolph Rocker, the eminent British anarchist editor and writer, visited there on his North American tour in 1913. Emma Goldman stayed with the Livshises, whether alone or with Alexander Berkman, when the two had speaking engagements in Chicago. The Livshis home was her unofficial and sometimes clandestine residence. Goldman's periodical, *Mother Earth*, regularly reported the activities of the groups in which Annie Livshis was involved. Renowned intellectuals of the time, anarchist or socialist, were recipients of Annie Livshis's interest and hospitality. Sadakichi Hartmann, anarchist and dramatist, gave a reading of his play *Mohammed* at a gathering in the Livshis home in 1906. Abraham Cahan, editor of the *Jewish Daily Forward*, and Michael Zametkin, both prominent socialists, were her guests.

The most cherished member of the group that gathered in the Livshis home was Voltairine de Cleyre, "one of the most prolific anarchist writers of her time" (Georgakas, "Voltairine de Cleyre," *Encyclopedia of the American Left*, 187). Delicate in health, and in temperament the opposite of the flamboyant

Emma Goldman, de Cleyre required repose to write poetry and prepare her speeches for the anarchist cause. Constant activity in the house in Wicker Park made her retreat to her little room under the third floor eaves. In addition to the Livshis family and de Cleyre, there were boarders, all relatives. Annie Livshis's brother Albert Mindlin, his wife, Lena, their infant son, Victor, and their bachelor cousin, Barnett Mindlin, son of Uncle Chaim, who also had homesteaded at Lasker, all lived together in this urban commune. Tranquility was at a premium, especially when the rakish anarchist, Ben Reitman, was around. LUCY PARSONS, widow of the martyred anarchist Albert Parsons, was a close friend.

Voltairine de Cleyre stayed with the Livshises when she came to Chicago to speak at annual memorials for the Haymarket martyrs. During the last nineteen months of her life, until her death in 1912, she made her home with them. Annie Livshis saw to her burial at Waldheim Cemetery (now Forest Home Cemetery), Forest Park, Illinois, at the foot of the Haymarket Martyrs monument, and privately published a pamphlet, *In Memoriam: Voltairine de Cleyre* (1912), to raise money for the publication of her works.

Annie Livshis's ambition that her son Peter be educated was fulfilled when she arranged his admission to an out-of-district program for deaf children at Moose Elementary School, a public school in Chicago. Later Peter graduated from Tuley High School, Chicago, and tried courses at the University of Chicago, but the lecture method proved too difficult. He took up the printing trade. Both in correspondence and in person, Voltairine de Cleyre took an active interest in his education. She encouraged his academic ambitions, urging him to study hard and develop his literary talents. This encouragement was augmented by his friendship with two cousins close to him in age, Will and Albert Parsons Lewin, the sons of Annie Livshis's sister, Yetta Mindlin Lewin.

Before Jake Livshis's untimely death of a cerebral hemorrhage in 1925, Annie Livshis made her home with her son, Peter, and his wife, Inez Barcus, both for reasons of economy and in order to help them as the hearing member of the family. Peter had met Inez at the Deaf Club. Annie Livshis continued the work she had done with her husband. When she reached the age of eighty, a dinner was held in her honor. Boris Yelensky, the venerable anarchist journalist, in an article in the *Fraye Arbeter Shtime*, hailed her as "a perfect role model for the younger generation because of her lifetime of devotion to the cause of free thought and free labor" (March 28, 1947). Peter Livshis printed his own speech for the occasion; it was read by another person at the dinner and began, "Mother, Mother." It was a testimonial to the mother who had given him her devotion and her idealism.

In 1950, Annie, Peter, and Inez Livshis moved to Arvada, Colorado, where the climate would be better for Peter's asthma. Annie Livshis outlived her husband Jake by almost thirty years and died of old age at eighty-nine years. At her request, her body was cremated.

All her life, Annie Mindlin Livshis stayed true to the political vision that nourished her spirit. Whether or not society was ready, she and those who shared her vision continued to work for the rights of labor. The movement in which she participated had an impact on the Eight-Hour Association, the Industrial Workers of the World (the Wobblies), as well as the Free Society. Her home and the values she espoused and lived each day provided the space and nutriment that supported leaders whose outspoken ideas placed them on the margins of society, sometimes in personal danger.

Sources. Annie and Peter Livshis Papers are at the Labadie Collection, University of Michigan. The Kansas Heritage Center, Dodge City, has numerous local records substantiating the lives of the Livshis and Mindlin families and other pioneer members of the Lasker Colony. Federal and local census materials are at NL. The *Fraye Arbeter Shtime* is on microfilm, Labadie Collection, University of Michigan. In her autobiography, *Living My Life* (1931), Emma Goldman makes several references to the Livshis family. Paul Avrich writes extensively of Annie, Jake, and Peter in his biography, *An American Anarchist: The Life of Voltairine de Cleyre* (1978). In *Anarchist Portraits* (1988), Paul Avrich writes of the Pioneers of Liberty. In *The London Years* (1956), Rudolph Rocker writes of his meeting at the Livshis home. Irving Howe, *World of Our Fathers: The Journey of the East European Jews to America and the Life They Found and Made* (1976) is an invaluable resource on immigrant life in New York City in the 1880s. Gerald Sorin, *The Prophetic Minority: American Jewish Immigrant Radicals, 1880–1920* (1985) writes of *Am Olam* and David Edelstadt. And see Mari Jo Buhle, Paul Buhle, and Dan Georgakas, eds., *Encyclopedia of the American Left* (1990, rev. ed. 1998).

ANN LEWIN DIAMENT

LLOYD, LOLA MAVERICK
November 24, 1875–July 25, 1944
PEACE ACTIVIST, SUFFRAGIST, WORLD GOVERNMENT ADVOCATE

Lola Maverick Lloyd was born in Castroville, Texas, near San Antonio. According to tradition and legend, her paternal grandfather, Samuel Augustus Maverick, did not brand his roaming cattle; subsequently unbranded cattle became known as "mavericks," and the word came to describe idiosyncratic, nonconformist, and aggressive action. Her father, George Madison Maverick, was educated at the universities of North Carolina and Virginia. In 1872 he and Mary Elizabeth Vance, a Texas woman, were married. The couple had six children, with Lola Maverick the second oldest. They were raised on the family ranch outside of Castroville and in St. Louis, Missouri.

Lola Maverick attended a day school, the Mary Institute, in St. Louis, where she developed an interest in both mathematics and art. In 1893 she enrolled in Smith College, Northampton, Massachusetts. In 1896 she visited Lillian Wald's Henry Street Settlement in New York City and planned on a career in settlement work. Instead, after graduation, she returned to her family's home in Texas, where she spent the next five years in what she called "restless" activity without any specific duties. Still interested in a career, she returned to Smith in 1901 to teach mathematics and also to study archeology and architecture. During the summer of 1902 she joined Smith friends in Skonnet, Rhode Island, where she met William Bross Lloyd, a Harvard Law School graduate and the eldest son of Henry Demarest Lloyd and Jessie Bross Lloyd of Chicago. They were married on November 1, 1902.

Maverick married into a family that supported women in

public and political life. Henry Demarest Lloyd was famous for his social reform work and his writings. Jessie Bross Lloyd, a philanthropist, was the daughter of William Bross, a former lieutenant governor of Illinois and part owner of the *Chicago Tribune*. After they were married, Lola and William Lloyd settled at the "Wayside," the Lloyd family home in Winnetka, Illinois. The "Wayside" was a focal point for Chicago reformers, including JANE ADDAMS and FLORENCE KELLEY, whose two children lived there while their mother worked at Hull-House. The Lloyd family and the circle of reformers who visited introduced Lola Lloyd to the political life of both Winnetka and Chicago. In 1905, she and her husband joined the Socialist Party. In 1911 she helped organize the Woman's Club of Winnetka. She also attended lectures and meetings in Chicago, sponsored by groups such as the Chicago Woman's Club, and the Commonwealth Club and by Hull-House. Between 1904 and 1913, Lola Lloyd gave birth to four children, William Bross Lloyd Jr., Mary, Georgia, and Jessie. By 1913, the Lloyd marriage had broken down, and the couple divorced in March 1916. She wrote to her sister Augusta, wife of Florence Kelley's son Nicholas, that to "get through with matrimony for life" (letter to Augusta Kelley, July 12, 1915, Nicholas Kelley Papers), she had new calling cards printed up. They read "Lola Maverick Lloyd."

During 1913 and 1914, Lloyd's public life was chiefly devoted to the woman suffrage movement and support of Alice Paul's National Woman's Party. On the evening of November 20, 1914, Lloyd's political life entered a new phase when she heard the Hungarian feminist pacifist Rosika Schwimmer speak at the Chicago College Club on the war in Europe and call for an immediate armistice. For the next five years, Lloyd dedicated her public life to the peace movement, working with the Chicago Federation of Peace Forces, which was reorganized in January 1915 as the Emergency Peace Federation, and the Woman's Peace Party (WPP). She was a founding member of WPP in Washington, D.C., in January 1915. The location of the headquarters of the WPP in Chicago allowed Lloyd to participate in the WPP's work to promote mediation efforts to end the European war. At the same time, Lloyd entered an important political relationship with Schwimmer, providing her with financial support and promoting her ideas to Lloyd's wide circle of contacts. Whenever possible, Lloyd attempted to promote Schwimmer's call for immediate peace. Peace agitation had become, Lloyd wrote her mother, a duty.

In April 1915, while the war progressed, Lloyd was one of forty-seven American women who traveled to the International Congress of Women at The Hague, joining European women who agreed that international disputes should be settled by pacific means and that parliamentary franchise should be extended to women. The women delegates carried no portfolio of their individual governments. Instead they came as representatives of local women's organizations. Lloyd participated as an official delegate from the WPP affiliate of the Woman's Club of Winnetka and performed the duties of assistant to Rosika Schwimmer. Lloyd and Schwimmer wrote two important resolutions that were presented to the International Congress of Women: a call for an immediate armistice and a plan of action for mediation efforts. The second, but not the first, was ac-

cepted, in part because other resolutions for mediation had been drafted and were supported by participants. At the congress, members elected two delegations to go to the capitals of Europe and present their resolutions to heads of state; Schwimmer was elected to visit the Scandinavian capitals, and Lloyd attended as her assistant and companion. Lloyd also joined the delegation led by Jane Addams during their visit to Berlin. After rejoining Schwimmer in Copenhagen and traveling to Christiania (now Oslo), Norway, Lloyd left the delegation and sailed for New York on June 5, 1915. Upon arriving in the United States, Lloyd gave speeches to women's organizations about the work of the congress. She also continued to provide financial support to Schwimmer, who was revisiting state officials in Europe. She promoted the work of the women's peace movement to her network of friends in the reform, socialist, and labor communities.

Lola Lloyd was an important contact in the peace movement for other American women before the United States entered the war. In late 1915, Lloyd worked daily at the Chicago peace office directing a newspaper campaign and attending to other WPP business as the organization unsuccessfully pressed its cause to get President Wilson to endorse a continuous mediation plan.

When Detroit automobile magnate Henry Ford planned an expedition to Europe to convene an unofficial conference that would bring about an end to the war, Lloyd worked in New York on arrangements for the voyage. Ford, impressed with her work, asked her to join the peace expedition as a delegate.

Traveling with her brother Lewis, her three oldest children, and a nursemaid, Lloyd joined fifty-five other delegates on the Ford Peace Ship, the Oscar II, which sailed for Europe on December 4, 1915. Because of her commitment to Schwimmer and her friendship with reformer Louis Lochner, both of whom worked closely with Ford on the expedition, Lloyd became part of what was known as the "inner circle." The platform they drew up pledged support for the expedition, endorsed a policy of international disarmament, and declared opposition to military preparedness in the United States. Disunity among the inner circle resulted from a debate over the preparedness resolution and Ford's sudden departure four days after the group arrived in Europe. Lloyd was appointed by Ford to a Committee of Seven to carry on the work of the expedition, which culminated in a meeting of peace delegates from neutral countries at The Hague Neutral Conference for Continuous Mediation.

After the conference, Lloyd returned to the United States and worked with the Chicago WPP on a peace exhibit for the Panama Pacific Medal Winners Exposition held in Chicago in March 1916. Lloyd also supported an unsuccessful attempt of New York women to build a constituency for an International Disarmament League. Instead, most peace and mediation advocates, including Lloyd, supported the formation of the American Neutral Conference Committee (ANCC), which sought to impress Wilson with the strength of the country's promediation sentiments. When the United States severed diplomatic ties with Germany on February 3, 1917, the ANCC became the Emergency Peace Federation. Working in Chicago and watching American involvement in war grow nearer in February, Lloyd wrote in her diary, "This world is all insane" (February 26,

1917, Schwimmer-Lloyd Collection). In late March and early April, she joined members of the Emergency Peace Federation in Washington, D.C., and returned afterwards to Illinois, writing in her diary that Congress had "passed the declaration of war. . . . My brain is paralyzed" (April 9, 1917).

After the United States entered the war, Lloyd worked with the Woman's Peace Party, urging its members to give as little cooperation to the war effort as possible, a stance that placed her in the minority. Lloyd also worked with new peace organizations, including the American Liberty Defense League and the First American Conference for Democracy and Terms of Peace, which eventually became the People's Council of America, a pacifist-socialist organization. Although public sentiment toward pacifists was hostile and many of the organizations to which she belonged held infrequent meetings or disbanded because of government restrictions or harassment, Lloyd remained committed to antiwar work throughout 1917 and 1918. During this period she wrote two pamphlets that received a favorable response from a number of peace advocates with whom she worked. The first, a two-page pamphlet, *For a People's Peace*, called for a peace conference to be composed of popularly elected representatives from all the nations at war. The second, *A New Application of Democracy*, extended her ideas on elected peace commissioners.

In addition to working in peace organizations, Lloyd often provided financial or other material support to the cause. In 1917, when she perceived that the Woman's Peace Party was growing weak, she rented an office in Chicago to provide a place for both peace and suffrage efforts. After World War I, she continued work with the Woman's Peace Party, which was transformed into the Woman's International League for Peace and Freedom (WILPF) in 1919; and she began to work on the unpopular cause of amnesty for war protesters and resisters. As a vice-president and a member of the executive board of WILPF, Lloyd remained active in the organization for the rest of her life. She also returned to active suffrage work, which she had put on hold during the war. After the passage of the Nineteenth Amendment in 1920, she supported Alice Paul's National Woman's Party in its campaign for an Equal Rights Amendment.

Celebrations for peace and suffrage were followed by a Red Scare, a period during which the country was fearful of communist and socialist influences. Lloyd's work and affiliations earned her a place on the War Department's "spider web" chart published in 1923; it purported to show a conspiracy involving pacifist, progressive, and women's organizations. Lloyd was also targeted by the government for surveillance because of her former marriage to William Lloyd, who helped found the American Communist Party in 1919.

Lloyd believed that women "are sorely needed in all places in public power. . . . By taking ourselves seriously and demanding all our human rights we create the only just basis for the international commonwealth for the future" ("Feminist Attack," 333–34). Toward this end, during the 1920s and 1930s Lloyd held positions on the international relations board and the committee on world government of the WILPF. In 1935 she proposed to the WILPF a People's Mandate to government to take joint action for peace by reduction of arms and peaceful settlement of ongoing conflict. The WILPF adopted the mandate and made it the major work of national sections of the next year. Two years later she cofounded and chaired an international Campaign for World Government. She also served for fifteen years as a board member of the Women's Peace Union, which supported and promoted a constitutional amendment outlawing war. She continued to work with Rosika Schwimmer, promoting the idea for a federation of countries that was democratic and not military.

Active until the end of her life, Lloyd died of pancreatic and liver cancer at sixty-eight years of age and was buried in San Antonio, Texas. A memorial service was held for her on August 4, 1944, in Chicago. Speakers included Reverend Alva Tompkins; Alice Paul; Charles F. Weller of World Fellowship, Inc., of Conway, New Hampshire; Rosika Schwimmer; Norman Thomas; and her daughter JESSIE LLOYD O'CONNOR. Lloyd dedicated her public life to helping the causes of woman suffrage, peace, and world government by doing the day-to-day organizing, distributing leaflets, organizing meetings, giving financial support, and creating supportive networks with women and men. Like other suffragists, after 1920 Lloyd followed several directions to achieve equality of women. While supporting an Equal Rights Amendment, she focused her efforts on movements to promote peace, including the outlawry of war by federal amendment and the establishment of a world government. A leader in peace organizations during the last twenty-five years of her life, Lloyd was internationally known for her work.

Sources. Lloyd kept detailed diaries from the time she entered Smith College until her death, recording both her activities and her personal feelings about public events. Lloyd also carried on an extensive correspondence with family, friends, and prominent individuals. These materials, copies of her writings, notes she took during meetings, and peace and suffrage literature are a part of the Schwimmer-Lloyd Collection at the New York Public Library. Also in the collection are two privately published pamphlets by Lloyd, *For a People's Peace* (1917) and *A New Application of Democracy* (1918). Additional Lloyd correspondence is in the Nicholas Kelley Papers at the New York Public Library and in the Florence Kelley Papers at Columbia University's Rare Book and Manuscript Library, New York. A brief typescript autobiography written in 1938 and materials on peace and world government are at the Sophia Smith Collection, Smith College. The Woman's Peace Party Papers and the Ford Peace Expedition Papers, both located in the Swarthmore College Library, contain letters to and from Lloyd. She combined her views on peace and women's rights in "Feminist Attack," *Equal Rights*, November 17, 1934. Published works on Lola Maverick Lloyd include Janet Stevenson's "Lola Maverick Lloyd: 'I Must Do Something for Peace,'" *Chicago History*, Spring 1980. Nancy L. Roberts, *American Peace Writers, Editors, and Periodicals: A Dictionary* (1991), contains a biography of Lloyd. The following studies provide background information for Lloyd's peace activities: Marie Louise Degan, *The History of the Woman's Peace Party* (1939, reprinted 1972); Jane Addams et al., *Women at The Hague: The International Congress of Women and Its Results* (1972); Barbara Kraft, *The Peace Ship: Henry Ford's Pacifist Adventure in the First World War* (1978); Harriet Hyman Alonso, *The Woman's Peace Union and the Outlawry of War, 1921–1942* (1989); and Alonso, *Peace as a Woman's Issue: A History of the U.S. Movement for World Peace and Women's Rights* (1993).

MELANIE GUSTAFSON

LOW, MINNIE F.
November 9, 1867–May 28, 1922

SOCIAL REFORMER, SETTLEMENT WORKER, SOCIAL WORKER

Minnie Low was a leader among the Chicago women who worked in social reform and social service between 1890 and 1920. Low was born in New York City, the second child of six in a Jewish family. Her parents' names, occupations, and country of birth are unknown. When she was ten years old, the family moved to Chicago, where she finished elementary school. She attended South Division High School for less than a year and left school because she was in poor health.

Low's first recorded job was as HANNAH SOLOMON's secretary, when Solomon was organizing the Jewish Women's Congress for the Parliament of Religions at the World's Columbian Exposition in 1893. Low may have been working with Solomon as early as 1891. At that time Solomon began to send correspondence about the congress to women throughout the country. Under Solomon's leadership, the Jewish Women's Congress formed a permanent organization, the National Council of Jewish Women (NCJW).

Low had entered volunteer social welfare work by 1893 as well, when she cofounded the Maxwell Street Settlement near Jefferson Street. This West Side social settlement served a Jewish community composed primarily of immigrants from eastern Europe, especially Russia and Poland. Although many Jewish residents of the neighborhood participated in Hull-House activities, Low believed that Jewish settlement workers could best serve immigrant Jewish communities.

The initial meetings to organize the settlement were held at Hull-House, headed by JANE ADDAMS. Addams's enduring relationship to Low began in the "winter of 1893 and 1894 when [they] . . . met often to consider the many problems arising out of mass feeding for 'soup kitchens'" (Addams, 1). The economic depression during the Chicago World's Columbian Exposition of 1893 galvanized reformers, including Low, to organize against brutal conditions facing the poor, whose lives contrasted with the glamour and promise displayed at the exposition.

In 1897 Hannah Solomon and other members of the Chicago section of NCJW established a Bureau of Associated Charities in the 7th Ward of Chicago. The name was soon changed to the Bureau of Personal Service (BPS), independent of the NCJW. Low became the paid executive director and Solomon chaired the volunteer board. Low served with the organization for the rest of her life. Although nominally nonsectarian, in practice the BPS served mostly Jewish cases and sent non-Jewish clients to another branch of Associated Charities. Under Low's leadership, BPS set up a workroom to serve Jewish women, arranged for legal aid, established a summer playground in a local park, and created the Helen Day Nursery where working mothers could leave their children. Seeking to improve living conditions, the BPS took part in a study of tenement conditions and supported improved housing laws.

Also in 1897, Low joined Solomon and others to found the Women's Loan Association (WLA), which required its clients to submit a loan application and the signatures of two persons in business. After a short investigation, the loan decision was made. Low headed the group making these investigations and decisions, and she was involved in fund-raising. Most of the loans

went to Jewish immigrants, often to help them set up or maintain small businesses. Low made "spirited efforts to secure a loan fund to be used during the seasons of unemployment; to curb the extortion practices so often [used] by the immigrant banks; [and] to prevent the exploitation of newly arrived immigrants by those who had come to the United States a little earlier" (Addams, 1). Although men could apply for loans and financially support the organization, women conducted its business and made the decisions.

The BPS and the WLA emphasized women helping women. The two groups helped persons in need, usually Jews, by promoting self-sufficiency. Both were opposed to charity and to emotionally distant interactions. Low used the technique that she called "Friendly Visiting" (Bogen, 320), particularly for the services of BPS. A friendly visitor, a woman, helped members of a family to achieve goals not by giving direct money gifts but by providing advice, assistance, and information. This approach, stressing help offered by a member of a community to another member, was similar to that called "scientific tzedakah [philanthropy]" ("Minnie Low and Scientific Tzedakah"). Although Low wanted philanthropy to be more "scientific" and "to foster the eventual economic independence . . . of its recipients" ("Minnie Low and Scientific Tzedakah"), she emphasized the importance of Jewish and female participation more than this "scientific" approach did.

Low often sought the support of Julius Rosenwald, the Chicago philanthropist and founder of Sears Roebuck and Company, to fund her activities. They shared a similar commitment to Jewish social services. For many years Rosenwald gave her money each month to care for the cases she brought to his attention or sent cases to her along with the money to aid them. Low's work for Rosenwald entailed a description of the problem, a suggestion for the amount of money needed, and follow-up reports. Minnie Jacobs Berlin assisted Low in this work. Low belonged to a committee that managed a fund donated by Julius Rosenwald to establish a country club for social workers.

The formation of the Juvenile Court in Chicago in 1899 was one of the major achievements of the Progressive Era, and Low played an important role in it. Judge Julian Mack; LOUISE deKOVEN BOWEN, a Chicago philanthropist and Hull-House leader; JULIA LATHROP, also from Hull-House; and LUCY FLOWER, another leader in Chicago's social reform circles and women's clubs, joined forces to establish the Juvenile Court Committee in 1900. This committee paid the salary of some probation officers and maintained a detention home for children awaiting trial. The BPS provided funds for three probation officers' salaries. Low and Minnie Jacobs Berlin became two of the early probation officers for the Juvenile Court, focusing on the needs of Jewish children.

A separate but related group, including Low, Mack, and the social worker Hastings Hart, formed the Juvenile Protective Association (JPA). When the Juvenile Court Committee's functions were taken over by Cook County in 1907, the JPA absorbed many of the volunteers and citizens who had worked previously for the committee. Hannah Solomon and Sara Hart—like Low, active in social reform and philanthropy—played important roles on the original committee and the JPA, although Low's work was full-time, paid, professional employment while the

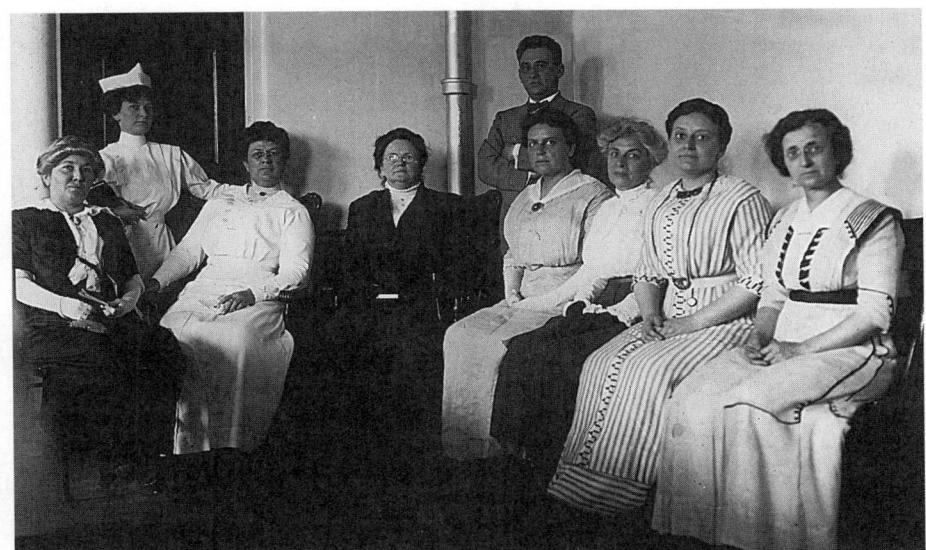

Fig. 67. *Social worker Minnie F. Low, first woman on the far right, was a probation officer for the Chicago Police Department, 1913.*

other women's work was a volunteer activity in addition to their married lives.

At the same time that she was dealing with the problems of juveniles in the city, Low was concerned with the abduction of young women—especially naive and confused immigrant girls—into prostitution. Low joined the struggle to combat this white slave traffic, collecting information and then securing and enforcing legislation designed to control and abolish this activity. A few years before the U.S. Congress approved a white slave traffic law in 1910, Illinois passed an act against pandering. Because of this action, Chicago "[made] a determined businesslike fight against the procuring of girls. . . . [Low's] gallant efforts in behalf of these unhappy victims never faltered and only her fellow workers [could] know how difficult and complicated the situation often became" (Addams, 2).

In addition to her social service work, Low was active in professional conferences and published several important papers. She attended social work conferences where she sometimes was the only Jewish participant. In 1911, at the National Conference of Charities and Correction, she presented "Discussion" on "The Present Status of Family Desertion and Non-Support Laws," published in the organization's *Proceedings*. The following year, the *Proceedings* of the same conference included an abstract of her paper, "Co-operation between Courts and Voluntary Public Agencies." In 1920, she spoke at the National Conference of Social Work (formerly the National Conference of Charities and Correction); her paper, "The Wider Use of Registration," appeared in the *Proceedings*. Low's expertise on Russian Jews was reflected in her discussion of philanthropy, "Chicago," in *The Russian Jew in the United States*, edited by Charles Bernheimer in 1905.

On the national level of professional organizations, she was elected president of the National Conference of Jewish Charities in 1914, a post she held for two years. Low also served on a number of social welfare advisory boards. She was on the board

of directors of the Home for Jewish Friendless, where BPS placed thirteen-to-sixteen-year-old girls as part of a program for dealing with "juvenile delinquency . . . among girls" (Bogen, 291) by finding them satisfactory homes and providing each girl with a woman mentor. She was a member of the board of the Jewish Home Finding Society, which helped widows with dependent children and was also an adoption agency. Continuing her leadership in Jewish social services, she founded the Central Bureau of Jewish Charities, which became the Research Bureau of the Jewish Charities of Chicago.

Although Low was part of a Jewish women's network in Chicago that included powerful and wealthy married women, she never married and was self-supporting. Low regretted her unmarried state and lack of children. She wrote to Julius Rosenwald, "Every woman feels the need of love and protection, and if she be normally constituted she has the innate maternal instinct which cannot be substituted by anything else on earth" (Rosenwald Papers, August 17, 1913). On another occasion, Low wrote Rosenwald that she felt like a failure because she had never advanced beyond her work as superintendent of the BPS. She felt that if she had been wealthy, he would have supported her work in more important ways and shared more of his responsibilities with her.

In 1921, the BPS, a member of the umbrella organization Associated Jewish Charities, was discontinued. BPS and another agency, the Relief Department, were duplicating efforts. Both organizations were "concerned with the problem of family case work" (Karpf, 37–38), but BPS dealt with social or legal problems, while the Relief Department handled financial assistance. The two agencies were merged into a new organization, the Jewish Social Service Bureau (JSSB), a case work agency. Low was asked to become the superintendent of JSSB for six months, but she declined, giving poor health as the reason. The direction of change was away from the social service of women that Low had developed. The director of the newly formed JSSB of Chicago, Maurice Karpf, deemed the old system inefficient and unprofessional. He established bureaucratic policies and emphasized social work as a formal profession. Low became associate director of the Research Bureau of the Associated Jewish Charities.

After a seven-month illness, Low died in Chicago at Michael Reese Hospital at the age of fifty-four. She was buried at Oak Woods Cemetery in Chicago.

Low was a major leader in Jewish social services and family work. She struggled with personal problems arising from ill-health, limited finances, her status as a working woman, and loneliness and conquered these problems through her public work for immigrant families and the poor. At Low's memorial service, Jane Addams honored her life, exclaiming, "May the social workers of Chicago be able to maintain the standards set by her, one of the most illustrious of their pioneers!" (Addams, 3).

Sources. Several files on Minnie Low and on the Bureau of Personal Service are in the Julius Rosenwald Papers at UC Spec. Coll. These outline her relationship to Rosenwald and some of her professional views. A few letters discuss her loneliness and emotional dependence on friends. There is also material on Low in the National Association of Jewish Social Workers Papers housed at the American Jewish Hist. Soc., Waltham, Massachusetts. Jane Addams's typescript eulogy to Minnie Low, "Tribute to Minnie Low, post May 29, 1922," is in the Swarthmore College Peace Collection, Jane Addams Papers. Minnie Low's writings deal with professional social work issues and the special needs of Jewish women and social services. In addition to the publications cited above, a summary of a speech by Low is found in "Maryland Discussion of Widows' Pensions," *Survey*, December 13, 1913. Hannah G. Solomon's autobiography, *Fabric of My Life* (1946), and collected writings in *A Sheaf of Leaves* (1911) provide information on projects in which Low participated and played major roles, although Low is rarely mentioned by name. Julius Rosenwald's biography, M. R. Werner, *Julius Rosenwald: The Life of a Practical Humanitarian* (1939), mentions Low and discusses many of these projects. Louise deKoven Bowen writes about the Juvenile Court Committee and the court's work, although Low is rarely mentioned, in *Growing Up with a City* (1926). Sara L. Hart, in *The Pleasure Is Mine: An Autobiography* (1947), discusses several issues close to Minnie Low but dismisses Low for interpersonal reasons. Brief biographical information on Low is found in *History of the Jews of Chicago*, ed. Herman Meites (1924, reprinted 1990); the newspaper article "Minnie Low and Scientific Tzedakah," *Forward*, November 21, 1997, and her obituary in *CT*, May 29, 1922. Shelly Tenenbaum's entry, "Minnie Low," in *Jewish Women in America: An Historical Encyclopedia*, ed. Paula Hyman and Deborah Dash Moore (1998), is an excellent overview of Low's life and work. Tenenbaum's *A Credit to Their Community: Jewish Loan Societies, 1880–1945* (1993) includes some discussion of the Women's Loan Association. A helpful account of Jewish social welfare with several discussions of Low is found in Boris D. Bogen, *Jewish Philanthropy: An Exposition of Principles and Methods of Jewish Social Service in the United States* (1917). The series of organizational changes affecting Low and Chicago's Jewish social services is found in Maurice J. Karpf's *A Social Audit of a Social Service Agency: The Jewish Aid Society and the Jewish Social Service Bureau of Chicago 1919–1925* [1926].

MARY JO DEEGAN

LUNDE, LAURA HUGHES
November 13, 1886–January 16, 1966
CIVIC LEADER, REFORMER

Laura Hughes Lunde, who spent her adult life working to improve government, education, and health care in Chicago, was born in Toronto, Canada, the daughter of James L. and Adelia

(Marean) Hughes, called Ada. James Hughes was head of the Toronto public elementary school system for nearly forty years. Ada Marean, who was one of the first kindergarten teachers trained in the United States in the Froebelian method, was recruited by Hughes to work with him to establish the first private and, subsequently, the first public kindergartens in Canada. After the death of his first wife, James Hughes married his colleague, Ada Marean. Now Ada Hughes, she continued to supervise kindergartens and train teachers for some twelve to fourteen years as an unpaid volunteer, since James Hughes did not believe that both he and his wife should be on the public payroll.

Laura Hughes was reared in a household that included a younger brother, who was subsequently killed in World War I, and two older half sisters, children of her father and his first wife. It was an intellectually stimulating environment. Educators from around the English-speaking world were entertained in their home. An aunt, whose husband was head of the local teachers college, lived nearby, and there were frequent interchanges between the two families. Hughes's parents encouraged her intellectual development; she learned to read at age four, apparently the result of her parents' interest in testing a pilot program of the latest preschool education methods. When Hughes graduated from high school at age fifteen, too young for college, she was sent to New York City for kindergarten teacher training under Madame Kraus-Boelte, who was a student of the German educator Friedrich Fröbel (also Froebel). Kraus-Boelte had taught Laura Hughes's mother, Ada. Laura Hughes finished the program but was too young to teach. She stayed in New York City and studied singing.

Hughes's interest in civic and reform causes was also influenced by her parents' activities. Her father was a major supporter of a sanitarium for tubercular children and developed an outdoor class they could attend. Ada Hughes and her friends discussed the poor working conditions in Toronto's textile mills, stimulating Laura Hughes's interest in and sympathy for workers' conditions. Laura Hughes assumed a false identity and worked briefly in the mills so that she could learn firsthand about conditions. She reported to the local trade unions council and to the newspapers about her experiences and what she found. Again emulating her mother, Hughes became an active suffragist. At age seventeen she became a life member of the National American Woman Suffrage Association (NAWSA) when her father made a fifty-dollar donation in her name. In the years immediately preceding United States involvement in World War I, Laura Hughes attended woman suffrage rallies in the United States.

It was, however, through her involvement in the peace movement that Laura Hughes found her way to Chicago. In 1915 Hughes attended the International Congress of Women at The Hague, the Netherlands, where she heard JANE ADDAMS deliver the presidential address. Women from twelve countries drew up resolutions that embodied a number of the statements later included in President Woodrow Wilson's Fourteen Points. Hughes met Addams, who from 1915 to 1929 was the national head of the Women's International League for Peace and Freedom. Following the International Congress of Women, Hughes spoke at a peace meeting in Chicago, where she met her future husband, Erling H. Lunde, a mechanical engineer who had attended the University of Chicago and the

Armour Institute (later the Illinois Institute of Technology). Hughes and Lunde became engaged in August 1915 and planned to marry the following December. Lunde, however, was a conscientious objector (CO) to war, and when he resisted the draft, he was sent to a CO camp. During this period, Hughes resided with her future father-in-law in Edison Park (now part of Chicago). Hughes and Lunde were married in December 1917 and purchased a home in Edison Park, where they lived the rest of their married lives. Lunde became a successful machine tool salesman and factory owner. They had two sons, who were born in 1919 and 1920.

Once her sons were old enough to attend school, Laura Hughes Lunde renewed her interest in reform movements. When discussing the suffrage movement in later years, Lunde explained she was among "those women who wanted the vote because they believed it would enable them to improve the laws, particularly those laws which governed women and children" ("The Illinois Women's Conference on Legislation," 1). After 1920, Lunde joined other women suffragists who established the Illinois League of Women Voters (ILWV). They believed that women "needed wide understanding of the law-making process; they needed greater knowledge of existing laws and their weaknesses; and finally, they needed to organize with a view to gaining support for the enactment of changes in the laws" ("The Illinois Women's Conference on Legislation," 1). Lunde became secretary of the Illinois Women's Conference on Legislation, a coalition of women's organizations (including the ILWV) established in 1924 to research and pool information about legislation of interest to member organizations. Lunde remained secretary, a volunteer position, for more than thirty years. Included among the conference's early special committees were those devoted to education and election reform, public health, and jury duty for women. Since 1920, Laura Lunde and the ILWV had advocated the inclusion of women in juries. Their exclusion from jury duty was one of the pieces of unfinished business in an agenda that advanced the equal status of women. Illinois women achieved the right to participate as jurors in 1939. That year Lunde became the first woman to serve as a "foreman" on a federal grand jury in Illinois.

Lunde became chair of the Illinois League of Women Voter's Department of Education in 1930, a position she held for the next ten years. Lunde led the campaign to modernize the outdated system of public education in the state. "Picture to yourself our 9,691 one-room schools with an average of only four pupils per school" she wrote in the ILWV publication *The Illinois Voter* in October 1933. "Each tiny school [is] managed entirely by three lay board members, who are elected through political preferment, just as they were a hundred years ago, who know little of education beyond what they received forty or fifty years ago" (p. 1). She acknowledged that there were some "enlightened districts" (p. 1) in the state, which were large enough to have trained educators and modern approaches to education, but she said that the vast majority of the 47,109 local board members were unable to guide their small, old-fashioned schools in the direction of "adequate up-to-date education" (p. 1).

When Lunde looked at the Chicago public school system she found inefficiency and political corruption. "Ten absolutely inexperienced men [the board of education] have nearly wrecked one of the better educational systems in this country," she concluded. "They have attacked everything which had been put in the schools to fit the children to live in our complicated civilization. They did this in the name of economy" (p. 1). Lunde tied the problems of education to the structure of the school system itself, which she believed had to go through a wholesale reorganization, consolidating small units into larger and effective administrative ones. She pointed out the lack of appropriate funding by the state and the need to equalize the distribution of resources and provide an adequate standard of education for all students. The immediate crisis of education in Illinois was due in large part to the effects of the Great Depression, but Lunde feared further cuts in spending. She warned that any progress in education depended on expanded funding and could only occur if there was major reform of the antiquated tax systems.

Lunde was one of the leaders in calling for a redress of the imbalance of education facilities in Illinois where, she wrote in March 1936, "We do not provide equal educational opportunity for all our children. We have some splendid schools . . . and we have some schools so backward that they would have been a disgrace a hundred years ago" ("The Corner Stone for Better Education," 3). Commenting on a statewide report that called for a state school board with sufficient authority to give leadership and advise the Illinois General Assembly on needed school legislation, Lunde reminded members of the Illinois league that their state was one of the five states in the nation that lacked such a nonpartisan, statewide structure. To keep such a board out of the hands of the politicians, Lunde contended its members should receive no salary and give no contracts; it was to be, "in other words, a board which receives no material compensation for its services" ("The Corner Stone for Better Education," 3). Lunde believed that "the selfish politician will never serve on such a board" (p. 3).

After thorough study of the school problem, Lunde and the ILWV lobbied for the creation of units for school taxation and administration large enough for economy and efficiency. They supported sufficient state aid to equalize educational opportunity and supplement local support of schools from property taxes. They advocated establishing a state board of education and school boards that functioned as policy-forming bodies only. Professional superintendents should be hired to administer school districts and report to boards of education. School administrative officials at state and county levels should be appointed not elected. Redundant county offices should be eliminated. Public schools should provide free textbooks; public librarians should be certified. To improve teaching, Lunde and the league supported higher standards for the selection of teachers, tenure that assured academic freedom, and retirement plans.

In 1933, Lunde was among the founders of the ad hoc Citizens' Save Our Schools Committee (SOS), a group created to protest depression-era plans of the Chicago Board of Education to eliminate the city colleges, reduce the number of kindergarten classes, and cut a variety of programs in the city's elementary and secondary schools. In 1934, SOS was chartered and renamed the Citizens Schools Committee (CSC). In the next several years, CSC devoted its efforts to separating the public school system from partisan politician influence. "The CSC campaigned for the appointment of teachers and other personnel on the basis of merit rather than political favor especially in 1937 after it was revealed that school superintendent William H. Johnson had manipulated the results of the principal's examination to enable those candidates with political connections to pass" (Citizens Schools Committee collection description, CSC records). Lunde served on CSC's board until 1940. Among the leaders of CSC was MARY HERRICK, a leader in the Chicago Teachers' Union.

In the field of public health, Lunde renewed her interest in tuberculosis. After learning about the poor conditions that existed in Chicago's Municipal Tuberculosis Sanitarium in the 1930s, Lunde became an organizer and served for many years as cochair of the Illinois Committee for the Eradication of Tuberculosis. This group played a major role in obtaining increased state funding for tuberculosis (TB) research and free sanitarium care for TB patients in the years immediately following World War II. In 1947 the legislature created the Illinois Advisory Hospital Council to advise the Illinois Department of Public Health on hospital administration, new construction, and in development of minimum standards for the delivery of hospital services. Lunde was a member of the council from its inception until her death. In 1955 Chicago Mayor Martin J. Kennelly appointed Lunde chair of a committee designated to develop a plan to modernize the city's Department of Health.

Many of Lunde's reform initiatives drew her into the field of electoral politics. Here, as in the area of education, Lunde realized that machine politics corrupted the process. She became aware of the potential for clean or honest elections if voting machines were used and other safeguards were put into effect. She realized how "far behind the times" ("History of the Voting Machine Movement in Chicago," 2) Illinois was because its voters still used paper ballots. In 1934, after seeing a demonstration of a voting machine, Lunde initiated an effort by the Woman's City Club of Chicago—for which she was chair of the municipal citizenship committee—and the Illinois Federation of Women's Clubs to demonstrate voting machines widely throughout the state. The success of that effort led to the creation of the Illinois Joint Committee for Voting Machines, a coalition that ultimately included more than twenty-five civic-minded groups. In 1941, with Lunde as its legislative chair and self-financed lobbyist, the Joint Committee succeeded in obtaining passage of key enabling legislation by the General Assembly. Improvements in the legislation were passed in 1943; and in 1946, Chicago voters approved voting machines in a referendum.

Illinois and Chicago were notorious for corrupt machine politics. Even with the advent of voting machines, election fraud continued as corrupt precinct election judges who owed allegiance to corrupt precinct captains, ward committeemen, and political bosses controlled the election process at the local polling centers. To combat this kind of fraud, Lunde was a leader in the Joint Civic Committee on Elections, a coalition of civic and reform-minded groups. Beginning in the early 1940s, this committee recruited, trained, and assigned thousands of volunteer poll watchers, concentrating them in the more suspicious precincts. This army of good government volunteers observed the way in which the politically appointed precinct judges administered local polling centers. When the volunteers saw fraudulent practices, they reported them. Lunde, a driving force behind this effort, was a frequent poll watcher in precincts where the worst voting fraud had taken place in the past.

Lunde toured the state with her message of the importance of honest elections. She was a guest lecturer for twenty-three years at Illinois Girls State, an annual event sponsored by the American Legion Auxiliary, which brought together three to four hundred junior high school girls to study city, county, and state government in Illinois. From the 1930s, Lunde also taught immigrants about the electoral process for the Citizenship Council of Metropolitan Chicago. During this decade, Lunde used radio broadcasts to educate the public on various issues and gave talks frequently on WCFL, the station of the Chicago Federation of Labor. "Tidying Up Illinois School Districts," "The Public Speaks," and "What Price Education" were some of the titles of her radio broadcasts.

In 1952, the murder of a West Side ward committeeman aroused public indignation when the link between organized crime and machine politics became public. City hall was implicated. With the support of 126 civic organizations, the Chicago Association of Commerce and Industry formed a Committee of Nineteen—civic leaders, including Lunde, to identify the shortcomings of city government and make recommendations for change. In its final report, the committee made nine recommendations. Basic to any changes in Chicago municipal government was the degree to which the city's governing council controlled its own destiny. As of 1952, Chicago council members and the citizens of Chicago could not legislate charter revisions without going through the state legislature. All other cities in Illinois were empowered by the General Assembly to choose one of three types of city government by referendum. Chicago had to secure a new charter through passage by the General Assembly and then ratification by a majority of Chicago voters at an election. The Committee of Nineteen called for the state legislature to pass a "home rule amendment granting broad powers of self-government to municipalities, including the power to call a charter convention or commission to draft a charter subject *only* to approval at a local referendum." Such an amendment "would benefit not only Chicago but all the cities and villages in the State" (*The Nine Needs of Chicago*, 3). The Committee of Nineteen asked, "Why should busy legislators spend valuable time considering minute details of Chicago's, Peoria's and East St. Louis' many problems?" (pp. 3–4). The committee called for state district reapportionment so that population representation disparities in Chicago's legislative districts could be corrected. It also cited the need for judicial reform, extension and improvement of the civil service system, and the reform of election laws with provisions for better enforcement. Citizens of Greater Chicago (CGC) was established before the end of 1952 to implement the recommendations of the Committee of Nineteen. Lunde remained on the CGC board, focusing on election law reform, home rule, and civil service recommendations.

During her lifetime, Laura Hughes Lunde received many awards, including one in 1955 from the Illinois Public Health Association; in 1962, she received the National Municipal League's Distinguished Citizen Award. The House of Representatives of the Illinois General Assembly honored her with

House Resolution No. 256, adopted June 30, 1965, for her civic and charitable endeavors. Contemporaries saw a personal side of Lunde as well. She always had her knitting bag with her, in her later years making sweaters and socks for her grandchildren. She kept a substantial garden, baked cookies almost every week, often giving them to friends and associates. "I tell people I am a homemaker who chooses good government instead of playing bridge," she claimed, "because it's more fun" ("Biographical Data: Laura Hughes Lunde").

Laura Lunde died at Swedish Covenant Hospital, Chicago, at age seventy-nine, after a brief illness. "By almost any standard of judgment Mrs. Laura Hughes Lunde ranked as one of Chicago's most useful citizens" (January 21, 1966), the *Chicago Daily News* commented. "Although she never held public office herself," the article continued, "she made good government and civic betterment her lifelong concern. . . . Her death closes a career of service as a volunteer matched by few persons who make government service their profession." Following her death, the head of the Executive Committee, National Municipal League, described Lunde as a "hellcat with fangs" in dealing with illegal activity at the polls, and said, "Our best information about affairs at Chicago have [*sic*] been coming to us for years in her pungent language and we shall miss her tart contributions to the discussions at our conventions" (Richard S. Childs to Erling H. Lunde, January 27, 1966, Laura Hughes Lunde Papers). In 1974, the Citizens of Greater Chicago, the Illinois Women's Conference on legislation and the Illinois Civic Exchange contributed funds in her memory to endow the Laura Hughes Lunde Resource room at the Ebinger School, the neighborhood public school that her children attended and where she had been active in the Parent Teacher Association.

Sources. The Laura Hughes Lunde Papers, UIC Spec. Coll., include references to her work with Citizens of Greater Chicago, election reform, public health, and her support of various state constitutional amendments. The Erling and Laura Hughes Lunde Papers, CHS, include the 1963 typescript, "Biographical Data: Laura Hughes Lunde" and information on her activism. Also at the CHS are the Citizens Schools Committee records. Conrad Sulzer Regional Library, CPL, has clippings from local newspapers that document aspects of Lunde's life and work. An oral interview by Roberta Kay Sweetow of Anne S. Lunde, Laura's granddaughter, August 19, 1994, provides personal insights into the family's history. Articles by Lunde published in the Illinois League of Women Voter *Illinois Voter* include "Our Phantom Children," January 1939; "Education 1833 to 1933," October 1933; "Looking Ahead in Education," June 1934; "A 1935 Challenge to Citizens," January 1935; "The Corner Stone for Better Education," March 1936. Lunde wrote "The Illinois Women's Conference on Legislation," *Public Aid in Illinois*, February 1952. Her unpublished typescript, "History of the Voting Machine Movement in Chicago" is in the Erling and Laura Lunde Papers, CHS. An important committee report to which Lunde contributed is *The Nine Needs of Chicago*, September 1952, a pamphlet printed by the Citizens of Greater Chicago. It is the final report of the Committee of Nineteen. Articles about reforming Chicago that mention Lunde's work include John Kay Adams, "Reforming Chicago: Slow but Not Hopeless," *Harper's Magazine*, June 1958, and "Chicago Finally Gets Het [*sic*] Up," *Life*, March 3, 1952. See also "City Reform Proposal Includes Salary Tax," *Chicago Sun-Times*, September 10, 1952; "Here's Lineup against Mob," *Chicago Daily News*, February 13, 1952.

CARLYN LOVGREN WHITEHAND

LUNDEEN, EVELYN C.
February 15, 1900–January 29, 1963
NURSE, RESEARCHER, WRITER, EDUCATOR

Evelyn Lundeen's pioneering nursing techniques for treating premature babies resulted in a significant decline in the death rate of these infants and made her a nationally recognized authority on perinatal nursing care. Lundeen was born of Scandinavian parents in Rockford, Illinois. Her mother died when Lundeen was three, and she and her sister went to live with their grandparents in California. Not until their father remarried did the sisters return to Rock Island, Illinois, to live with him. Lundeen graduated from Augustana College in Rock Island before entering the School of Nursing at Lutheran Hospital in Moline, Illinois, where she graduated in 1922. Her work there was so outstanding that it drew the attention of famed Chicago pediatrician Julius Hess, who asked her in 1924 to become the first nursing supervisor of the new premature infant station at Sarah Morris Children's Hospital, a post she held for thirty-eight years.

Sarah Morris Children's Hospital was the pediatric division of Chicago's Michael Reese Hospital. One of the first children's hospitals in Chicago, it was largely the brainchild of Isaac Abt, a physician who was eventually labeled "the father of pediatrics" in Chicago. After Edward Morris, a Chicago meat packer, approached Abt in 1910 about establishing a children's hospital as a memorial to his mother, Abt toured Europe studying hospitals in preparation for the building of Sarah Morris. There he learned that isolation in order to prevent cross-infection was the most important aspect of the care of hospitalized children. In order to save money, he suggested Sarah Morris affiliate with Michael Reese but insisted that the children's hospital be housed in its own building. A separate building, he argued, was the only way to cope properly with the needs of sick children. The Sarah Morris Children's Hospital was opened in 1913 — replete with a children's playroom and a milk laboratory with sophisticated pasteurizing equipment, since milk was not required by law to be pasteurized in Chicago until 1916 — with Abt at the helm.

When Lundeen came to work at Sarah Morris in 1924, its new premature infant station was the largest in the country. That year 1,054 babies died in Chicago because of complications from premature birth. This represented almost 25 percent of the total deaths of children under one year of age that year. It had been only four years since so-called birth accidents exceeded diarrhea as by far the largest single cause of infant death in the city. The medical community was still congratulating itself on the dramatic lowering of diarrheal deaths, and not much attention was being paid to the plight of premature infants. Premature babies were deemed not worth saving because their lives were too tenuous. Upon her arrival at Sarah Morris, however, Lundeen was undaunted. Over the next few years she developed techniques that resulted in a 20 percent drop in the death rate among premature infants. In the first three years of her tenure, 45 percent of the premature babies hospitalized at Sarah Morris survived. During her years at Sarah Morris, the struggle to save premature babies became an increasingly important one. As Lundeen and Hess noted, the birth rate had dropped so dramatically between 1930 and 1940 that "preserving infant life and . . . giving all possible assistance toward the development of healthy minds and bodies" (*Premature Infant*, v) took on new meaning.

Lundeen ran the premature station at Sarah Morris with singular authority. One doctor recalled many years later that Lundeen was "very strict and didn't allow many doctors in there at all. . . . You had to be a special privileged character to get in to see a premature baby" (Gordon, 93). The few doctors whom Lundeen did allow to visit the station were ordered to wash their hands thoroughly upon entering.

Asepsis was, in fact, a mainstay of Lundeen's technique—"as vital a part of the nursery routine as breath is to the individual" ("Newer Trends," 9), she wrote. Her program for the improved care of premature babies included the scrubbing of hands before touching a baby, no contact whatever among infants, the sterilization of any item that came into contact with a baby, the separation of diapering and feeding areas, and the complete isolation of any sick baby. On hand washing she was particularly fanatic, insisting that all persons in the station scrub their hands and arms up to the elbow each and every time they entered the station, cared for, fed, or diapered a baby, or touched anything in the nursery other than a baby. Even after the discovery of antibiotics she refused to let her guard down, writing, "Morbidity is always potential mortality. Antibiotics must not be allowed to replace aseptic nursing technic" ("Prematures Present Special Problem," 61). Prevention of an infection, she argued, was a far greater achievement than the ability to cure it.

Lundeen believed that what, how, when, and how much to feed premature infants was key to their survival. She avoided feeding them immediately after birth because, she discovered, they were usually too weak to swallow, and aspiration pneumonia often resulted. Instead, she offered them food twelve to forty-eight hours after birth and in the interval injected a salt solution directly into their thighs twice a day to prevent dehydration. She devised this precursor to intravenous fluids in conjunction with her longtime collaborator Hess, a former student of Abt's. She also decreased the total caloric intake of premature babies in order to reduce vomiting and diarrhea, counteracting the tendency to overfeed them in an attempt to fatten them up quickly.

Just the mechanics of feeding premature babies were problematic. They were so weak, some could not even suck. Lundeen devised several feeding methods. Nurses either fed premature babies laboriously by medicine dropper—the system Lundeen preferred—or, if absolutely necessary, by gavage—a stomach tube. Only when babies were demonstrably strong were they fed directly via breast or bottle.

Breast milk, Lundeen insisted, was "paramount" ("Feeding the Premature Baby," 599) to the survival of premature infants. As late as 1954 Lundeen insisted that breast milk be the exclusive food of every premature baby in her care, at least until they weighed four pounds. She did everything possible to encourage the mothers of premature infants to breast-feed. Nurses visited these women in their homes while their babies were still hospitalized, teaching them how to express their milk manually. Mothers learned to express milk four or five times each day and to bring the milk to the premature station daily. The purpose of this exercise was three-fold. First, and most importantly, it supplied their babies with human milk. Second, it gave nurses an opportunity to discuss infant care with each mother and to assess—and if necessary work with the mother on improving—the conditions in the home in preparation for the baby's arrival. It also let Lundeen know whether or not an infant's mother kept up her milk supply. If she did not, Lundeen had to devise a safe artificial feeding regimen before the baby was discharged. All premature babies cared for at Sarah Morris continued to receive follow-up care from a visiting nurse after they were discharged.

If mothers did not supply their babies with milk, Lundeen still fed them breast milk until they reached the desired weight. An entire wing of Sarah Morris was devoted to wet nurses' living quarters. There, wet nurses breast-fed their own babies during the day and awoke every four hours at night to express milk into sterile bottles for the use of premature babies. In later years, after Sarah Morris had abandoned the employment of wet nurses, Lundeen asked mothers in the postpartum unit who had had a healthy delivery to share their excess breast milk. She also came to depend on the Chicago Board of Health Mothers' Breast Milk Station for human milk. The Breast Milk Station, where about forty nursing mothers came daily to express their milk for five cents an ounce, was opened by the Board of Health in 1938. It remained open for the next twenty-three years. Breast Milk Station milk was provided free to any premature or sick baby in the city. Lundeen requested milk from the station daily.

Lundeen was a researcher. She also taught the proper care of premature babies to nursing students. She assisted physicians in the development of improved incubators and heated beds, which were vital to her work because the bodies of premature babies were too small and immature to regulate body heat. Lundeen, however, never relied heavily on technological innovation in her quest to save premature babies. "Simplicity is emphasized in all procedures" ("Prematures Present Special Problems," 65), she wrote. If hospitals did not have access to the latest incubators or heated beds, Lundeen recommended they use an improvised heated crib or, in an emergency, a cardboard box with hot bricks, heated sandbags, or hot water bottles. Lundeen also experimented constantly with feeding techniques and food formulas. One room at the premature station was her laboratory, where she worked at developing a formula for premature babies. By 1954 Lundeen's premature infant station was expanded and completely refurbished to her specifications. The new unit represented two decades of Lundeen's hard-won knowledge and included an admitting room; a doctors' scrub room; a large room for the care of new admissions; another room for "graduates," babies weighing 1,800 grams (almost 4 pounds or more); an isolation room for babies with infectious diseases; a nurses' station where all three nursery rooms could be clearly seen; a formula room; treatment rooms where mothers could also breast-feed their babies; a linen room; a utility room; and a nurses' lounge.

Lundeen never married. She died in Chicago—at Michael Reese Hospital, where she lived in the hospital nursing home— of a chronic heart ailment. As a nurse, Lundeen carved an important niche for herself. In the medical text on care of the premature infant that she coauthored with Hess, the nurse was said to be at least as important as the doctor. "Since it is our conviction that untiring, unremitting care has no substitute in the care of the premature infant," they wrote, "we have deemed it essential to give equal prominence to the role of the nurse" (*Premature Infant*, vi). Her work was so successful that doctors and nurses from all over the country and personnel from the U.S. Children's Bureau traveled routinely to Sarah Morris to study her methods. In the medical world, where physicians customarily claimed credit for newly acquired knowledge and technological innovation, Lundeen was the acknowledged national authority on the care of premature infants.

Sources. Evelyn Lundeen published articles in *The American Journal of Nursing, Nursing World, The Modern Hospital,* and *Hospitals* throughout her career. These articles include "Feeding the Premature Baby," *American Journal of Nursing* 39 (1939); "Prematures Present Special Problems: Basic Factors in Nursing Care," *Modern Hospital,* April 1945; and "Newer Trends in the Care of Premature Infants," *Nursing World,* May 1959. She was the coauthor of two books, *The Premature Infant: Its Medical and Nursing Care* with Julius H. Hess (1941, 2nd ed. 1948), and *Care of the Premature Infant* with Ralph H. Kundstadter (1958). Her work is discussed in Sarah Gordon, ed., *All Our Lives: A Centennial History of Michael Reese Hospital and Medical Center 1881–1981* (1981) and in Vernon Bullough and Lilli Stenz, eds., *American Nursing: A Biographical Dictionary,* vol. 3 (forthcoming). An article about her life and work appeared in *Neonatal Network,* February 1986. The Michael Reese Hospital Papers, which contain several folders on Lundeen's work and some information on Sarah Morris Children's Hospital, are at the Chicago Jewish Archives of Spertus College in Chicago.

JACQUELINE H. WOLF

LYONS, BERTHA GLORIA
February 20, 1896–October 3, 1982
FOUNDER OF EDUCATIONAL ORGANIZATION FOR CHILDREN, MONOLOGIST, PERFORMER, TEACHER

Lyons, founder of the Juvenile Welfare Association (JWA), an organization that provided cultural and educational services for underprivileged children, was born at the Welfare Island City Hospital in New York. On May 31, 1896, she was admitted to the New York Foundling Hospital. Lyons was placed in the home of William and Alice Lyons McCartney on September 21, 1898, in Indiana. Alice McCartney's mother, Bridget Lyons, actually initiated proceedings to adopt the little girl, but Alice and William McCartney legally signed the placement papers. As a child, Bertha Lyons maintained a close relationship with both Bridget Lyons and Alice McCartney.

Soon after the McCartneys took Bertha Lyons into their home, Alice McCartney gave birth to the first of their six children. The McCartneys had four girls and two boys in addition to Lyons. The McCartneys later discovered that they had not legally adopted Lyons; she was legally placed in their care only as a foster child. When Lyons learned the truth, she was deeply disappointed. The McCartneys moved from Indiana to Grand Rapids, Michigan, where William McCartney became the owner of a wholesale candy and paper warehouse.

Bertha Lyons demonstrated her artistic talent early in life. She was awarded first place in an oral interpretation contest in Grand Rapids around 1912. From Michigan, the family moved to Waterloo, Iowa, where Lyons enrolled in the Ross Conservatory of Music. After graduating from the Ross Conservatory in June 1914, majoring in theory of dramatic art, Lyons taught drama to young children at a Waterloo elementary school and gave private lessons. She also took education courses at Iowa State Teachers College in Cedar Falls, Iowa. Lyons then accepted a sales position at the Leonard Fowler Advertising Agency. Lyons learned valuable sales skills that undoubtedly aided her subsequent fund-raising efforts for the JWA. Lyons never stopped pursuing her real passion, drama and arts. She studied under actor and director Elias Day as well as Donald Robertson.

In the late 1910s, Lyons obtained a position with the Western Lyceum Bureau, performing monologues as well as booking talent for the midwest circuit. In the early twentieth century, public entertainment usually consisted of live performances of plays, poems, or music. Monologue recitation was popular and played an important role in middle-class culture. In addition to performing with the Western Lyceum Bureau, Lyons edited an entertainment newspaper in Waterloo.

Lyons decided to continue her career in a city with a burgeoning artistic community. Many young people, including Lyons, were drawn to the emerging theater scene in Chicago. In 1919, she and a friend, Margaret Madigan, moved to Chicago, where Lyons opened her own studio. She taught drama, speech, and social deportment. Shortly thereafter, Lyons began incorporating drama in her work with children in orphanages, most likely prompted by her own status as a foundling. This period was one of heightened consciousness shared by the reform community about the treatment of orphans and dependent children. Chicago's Juvenile Court, founded in 1899 and the first to be established in the United States, was among the most important innovations in the care and protection of the city's children.

In 1921, Lyons founded the Juvenile Welfare Association and, with the assistance of Victor Arnold, judge of the Juvenile Court, incorporated the JWA as a nonprofit agency in 1923. Lyons published a short-lived magazine, the *Children's Educator,* in 1924 to assist fund-raising efforts for the JWA.

JWA's purpose was to provide enrichment and self-help courses for children living in orphanages and charitable institutions. Convinced that children in such agencies needed supplementary courses to help develop their natural abilities, JWA staff offered a wide range of cultural and social education, including programs on dance, drama, and music. JWA's instructors also gave lessons in self-development and social and business deportment. Included were courses that trained children and adolescents in business tactics and salesmanship; they were taught how to secure and hold positions so that when they left their homes or the institutions in which they had lived, they were able to be self-sustaining, confident, and secure in a variety of social and business settings. Charm and etiquette instruction gave children confidence to enter social settings that might otherwise seem intimidating. Because the association augmented the programs of orphanages and other charitable institutions, Lyons maintained that the JWA provided educational training, not charity.

Offering its services throughout Chicago, the nonsectarian JWA worked with institutions regardless of their religious affiliation, including Catholic, Protestant, and Jewish agencies. Lyons and the other instructors conducted classes at many institutions, including the Catholic Social Center, Bohemian Old Peoples Home and Orphan Asylum, Chicago Boys Club, DePaul Settlement House, Marks Nathan Jewish Orphans Home, St. Patrick's High School, and Uhlich Evangelical Lutheran Orphan Asylum. The JWA provided their services to these institutions at no charge. The dance and music instruction offered by JWA also benefited some institutions financially. Some agencies or schools used the instruction to develop theatrical performances and raised money through admission fees.

Lyons conducted most of the fund-raising for the JWA. Private contributions and membership fees sustained the association financially. Lyons raised funds through mail and telephone solicitations to large corporations as well as individuals. Contributors included Ford Motor Company, Jewel Food Stores, Walgreen Drug Stores, and General Electric. Lyons developed creative solicitation correspondence adapted to the season or specific situation. Lyons's selling techniques were persuasive and her personal rapport with many contributors high so that during the Great Depression in the 1930s several individuals continued to contribute to the JWA. Lyons touched many individuals. A letter from a contributor stated, "I offer this small token of my esteem & love. May your star always shine & may I be priviledged [sic] to behold it" (Albert Kudracheff to Bertha Lyons, 1941?, JWA records).

Lyons developed a close relationship with many individuals associated with the institutions at which she taught drama and self-improvement. She had close friendships with many women religious who were staff and faculty members at St. Patrick's High School, where Lyons and the association worked until the school closed in 1970. Many women continued their friendship by corresponding with Lyons after leaving Chicago. She also affected the children she taught. Occasionally, a child ran away from an orphanage and came to Lyons's home because of deep affection for her. Since she devoted herself so deeply to the objectives of the association, her personal life often intertwined with her professional life. Lyons never married.

Despite the praise many individuals heaped on Lyons and the JWA, neither remained untouched by criticism. The nature of social work changed rapidly after World War I, and by the mid-twentieth century the professionalization of the field affected many agencies unwilling to conform to the standards and intrusions of professional social work organizations. In Chicago, the Chicago Council of Social Agencies (later the Welfare Council of Metropolitan Chicago), created in part to promote professionalism and coordination of social service activities, also evaluated agencies in order to determine their ability to meet certain general standards of service. A poor evaluation could hurt the capacity of an agency to raise funds. In 1924 the Council evaluated the JWA, indicating that Lyons's talent and enthusiasm were a major source of the agency's effectiveness. Beginning in 1929, however, the Council criticized JWA's programs and questioned the value of providing poor children with cultural enrichments rather than basic necessities. During the Great Depression, many social workers considered survival the paramount concern. Lyons's philosophy was not in agreement with that held by the Council of Social Agencies. Lyons advocated preparing children for a future where they would no longer require public assistance. She believed they needed education so that they could fit into the world of the middle class.

In the 1940s, the Welfare Council of Metropolitan Chicago questioned the fund-raising techniques employed by the JWA and considered it inappropriate for an independent agency to raise funds for instruction at various other not-for-profit institutions. The Welfare Council argued that these institutions should provide all educational and cultural programs internally. In 1945, the executive director of Marks Nathan Jewish Orphans Home ended its nearly twenty-five year relationship with JWA under pressure from the board of directors. The board's decision was based on the Welfare Council's lack of endorsement for JWA. The executive director of Marks Nathan adamantly maintained that the lessons taught by Lyons and her teachers were invaluable. He felt the teachers were well trained.

By 1947, criticism of Bertha Lyons and JWA came from two directions. Internally, Lyons and certain members of the JWA's board of directors disputed who controlled the association's finances and programs. Externally, the Welfare Council's opposition to Lyons and the JWA program damaged the JWA's reputation in the philanthropic and business communities. The dual criticism led to an investigation of the association by the Chicago Police Department in 1947, revealing that JWA's charter had lapsed and that the association had been operating without a charter for the previous three years.

The internal strife culminated in the resignation of many of JWA's directors. In 1950, the association reorganized and named a new board of directors. Lyons remained with the organization, but she continued to experience opposition from professional social workers. Despite the earlier controversy, however, the JWA successfully continued its program and instructed children in a variety of institutions.

Lyons retired from the JWA in the 1970s due to failing health. She died at the age of eighty-six. Her funeral was held at St. Michael Redemptorist Church, and she was buried in Memorial Park Cemetery, Skokie, Illinois.

Bertha Gloria Lyons dedicated her life to the cultural and social education of dependent and underprivileged children and adolescents living in orphanages and other institutions. Her agency provided teachers for schools, settlement houses, and community centers so that courses in self-help and self-improvement, in vocational guidance, and in the arts were available to children from a variety of backgrounds. She brought her interest in drama and the arts to her unique contribution to social service. The Juvenile Welfare Association, founded and managed for nearly fifty years by Lyons, still exists.

Sources. The records of the Juvenile Welfare Association (JWA) are located in Spec. Coll. and Preservation Division, Harold Washington Library Center, CPL. The collection contains information from 1924 to the 1960s. Personal information on Lyons is sparse, but the records are rich for information about the JWA's programs and internal organization. In addition, the papers of the Welfare Council of Metropolitan Chicago (formerly the Chicago Council of Social Agencies), CHS, provide a small amount of information on the JWA. Interviews with Helen Wegner, Bertha Lyons's sister, and Susanne Mansfield, current director of JWA and a friend of Lyons, were conducted by Eileen Ford in 1997.

EILEEN M. FORD

MacLEAN, ANNIE MARION
1870?–May 1, 1934

SOCIOLOGIST, RESEARCHER, EDUCATOR

Annie MacLean, a pioneer in the field of sociology whose primary research and writing focused upon women in the labor force, was born at St. Peters Bay on Prince Edward Island, Canada, and raised in Nova Scotia. She was the daughter of Reverend John and Christina (MacDonald) MacLean. Very little is known about MacLean's early years.

After obtaining A.B. (1893) and A.M. (1894) degrees from Acadia College, Nova Scotia, the latter with first-class honors in philosophy and modern languages, MacLean immigrated to the United States, coming to the University of Chicago, where she was granted a Ph.M. in 1897, the first woman to earn that degree in sociology at Chicago. Her thesis, "Factory Legislation for Women in the United States," began for her a lifelong interest in the conditions of working women. In it she made many progressive recommendations, including a minimum wage for women and the appointment of women factory inspectors. MacLean published three articles in the *American Journal of Sociology* on factory legislation for women and research about department store saleswomen.

MacLean was the second woman to earn a Ph.D. in sociology (1900) from Chicago; her dissertation dealt with "The Acadian Element in the Population of Nova Scotia." While at the university, MacLean was greatly influenced by three professors: Albion Small, Charles Henderson, and George Herbert Mead. Small served on MacLean's master's and doctoral committees, and MacLean modeled herself on his values by dedicating herself to applied sociology. Henderson advised her on one of her research projects, and Mead, who trained several women scholars at Chicago, including EDITH ABBOTT, was influential through his support of women's academic advancement. In addition, all three were concerned with research topics central to MacLean's interests, such as economic issues and urban life.

However, male faculty support of women students was limited. Although MacLean, an outstanding sociology student, far surpassed the productivity of her male peers in graduate school, she was never hired as a full-time faculty member in the department as were former male students. Rather, she remained on the margins of the discipline in the Home Study Division, which an early sociologist, Everett C. Hughes, remembered as "always a step-child: . . . the pay was low and there were no benefits . . . just cheap piece work" (quoted in Fish, "Annie Marion MacLean," 47).

After brief teaching assignments at Royal Victoria College in Montreal, Canada, (1900–1901) and John B. Stetson College (1901–1903), MacLean was a professor of sociology at Adelphi College from 1906 to 1916 and at the National Training School of the Young Women's Christian Association (YWCA) from 1903 to 1916, both in New York City. The latter was a graduate facility for YWCA workers. She also held less prestigious jobs in sociology, including one at the Women's Educational and Industrial Union, which operated the graduate program at Simmons College in Boston. From 1903 until shortly before her death in 1934 she was an assistant professor of sociology at the University of Chicago in the Home Study, later the Extension, Division that was responsible for correspondence courses at the university. Here she was part of a community of women teachers and researchers, including Edith Abbott and SOPHONISBA BRECKINRIDGE. Like so many of her generation of women careerists, MacLean did not marry. When asked whether she was to be addressed as Professor, Dr., Mrs., or Miss, she wrote rather flippantly, "since Mrs. . . . is a title that I have been able to avoid only by exercise of the most subtle diplomacy it is a point of honor with me to object to its use in connection with myself" (quoted in Fish, "Annie Marion MacLean," 48).

MacLean enjoyed teaching, especially during the last years of her life when health problems (probably arthritis) otherwise severely limited her. Her repertoire of courses included ones on rural life, social technology, and modern immigration. Because she was never a bona fide member of the sociology department at Chicago, she seldom taught the core courses for majors but rather gave the service courses for nonmajors, often older students. MacLean wrote personal letters to her students and extended her interest in them beyond the more formal academic aspects of her career. During twenty years of correspondence teaching, MacLean taught 799 students in forty-seven states and Hawaii and nine foreign countries.

MacLean was also an enthusiastic researcher and outstanding methodologist who was more advanced than the male sociologists of that era. She utilized both the social survey and the social worlds techniques. In the latter, the researcher attempts to portray life as experienced by participants in a particular group or setting. Her work is representative of the early urban behavior research at the University of Chicago. To gather data on the working conditions of women, she engaged extensively in a variety of short-term participant observer experiences, including those of hop picker, sweatshop worker, sales clerk, and striker. While in Oregon to pick hops, MacLean remembered "pillowless strawbeds . . . not conductive to sleep, especially with the rain coming in. . . . I opened an umbrella and finally slept, only to dream of icebergs" (MacLean, *Wage-Earning Women*, 105). MacLean also clerked in two Chicago department stores during the holiday season to investigate whether overtime compensation was given.

While on picket duty during a strike in a factory, MacLean observed—and reported in her article "On Picket Duty"—that although employers could deal with a conflict with men, they treated women as though they were misbehaving children. MacLean's employment in a tenement sweatshop pointed to the need for some kind of collective action, since hours were unregulated and many families, including small children, worked very long hours.

Like other Chicago women social investigators of this era, MacLean placed great emphasis upon humanitarian concerns and social reform and fused the ideals of research and service in her focus upon the social worlds of women. MacLean's growing stature as a researcher on women in industry climaxed during 1907–1908, when the national board of the YWCA formed a sociological investigation committee directed by her to study the typical conditions of women in representative occupations in the United States. Out of this research came a major work, *Wage-Earning Women* (1910), which drew upon her participatory research and the massive data collected by a staff of twenty-nine women. About four hundred establishments employing 135,000 women in more than a score of cities were studied. This research was the first national study of industrial life undertaken by a body of college women commissioned by a religious organization. She used the women's sociology network in Chicago to hire the staff. This extensive project elicited a wealth of information and advocated many measures, including regular investigations by both public and private agencies.

Both *Wage-Earning Women* and Edith Abbott's *Women in Industry* provided inestimable data regarding the position of women in industry and their discriminatory treatment by employers. Intended for a more general audience, MacLean's *Women Workers and Society* (1916) amplified and expanded upon such themes as industrial conflicts, developed in *Wage-Earning Women*. MacLean wrote favorably of the Women's Trade Union League (WTUL), a cross-class alliance concerned with such issues as the eight-hour day. MacLean strongly supported trade unions at a time when such advocacy was seen as radical. To her, they represented a rational theory of betterment in which the employee, not the employer, was the active force.

MacLean's strong interest in immigration culminated in the publication of *Modern Immigration* (1925) and *Our Neighbors* (1922), a folksy, popular work. Although *Modern Immigration*, modeled after the scholarly documents series compiled by Edith Abbott and Sophonisba Breckinridge, illustrated the desirability of the assimilation process, the implicit assumption was that white Anglo-Saxon Protestants were especially desirable immigrants, a view that Abbott and Breckinridge did not share. While male sociologists at Chicago studied primarily eastern Europeans, MacLean focused upon large-scale global immigration in the 1920s, including that from such countries as Australia, Canada, and Brazil.

Some Problems of Reconstruction (1921), while not representing a major focus of her research, discussed problems needing attention in the United States after World War I, including labor reforms to benefit women. This period of bitter political unrest witnessed a "Red Scare" that vilified many female sociologists and social activists, including JANE ADDAMS and GRACE ABBOTT. *Some Problems of Reconstruction*, along with *Women Workers and Society*, was part of a social science series in which MacLean maintained that "a democracy that does not give enlarged opportunity to its women workers is only an autocracy below the surface, and merits oblivion" (*Reconstruction*, 62). While many Chicago sociologists addressed the theme of democracy, MacLean was among the first to criticize its ineffectiveness.

MacLean also published *Cheero* (1928), which contained whimsical fragments from the story of an illness, and *Mary Ann's Malady* (1916), a satire. Both appear to be about her own search for a cure for arthritis. She published innumerable articles in the *American Journal of Sociology, Survey, Forum,* and *Scribners* on such topics as her own research and her experiences in teaching correspondence courses. MacLean's writing style was straightforward and eminently readable. A puckish sense of humor kept her writing from taking on a preaching tone.

MacLean's writings, added to those of Abbott and Breckinridge, contained rich insights into questions relating to women and work and into a host of social problems that still concern sociologists, such as poverty and unfair labor practices. MacLean wrote insightfully about women's place within the work force. She felt that women were gradually realizing the power of united effort and coming to see that trade unionism stood for equal suffrage. She scoffed at the idea that women worked for pin money, insisting, "Self-support is the driving force for the young girl" (*Wage-Earning Women*, 177). Shrewdly she observed that while strength was not always a factor, it had been a potent argument in keeping women from entering occupations traditionally requiring strength. The young age at which women entered the workforce and their short working careers exacerbated their exclusion from male-dominated work.

During MacLean's later professional life, women were her most important colleagues. She favored suffrage and was a member of several women's organizations in New York City, including the Intercollegiate Suffrage Society and the Woman's Political Union. She also belonged to the WTUL and the Association of Collegiate Alumnae (later the American Association of University Women), a support group for women college graduates. For her many contributions she was awarded an honorary doctorate by Acadia College in 1923.

MacLean died at home in Pasadena, California. A passionate and competent teacher, MacLean concerned herself with the lives as well as the academic progress of students. Her research focused on women as vibrant and dynamic, not passive, beings.

Sources. In addition to the books cited above, the following articles by MacLean provide various glimpses into her teaching and research worlds: "Twenty Years of Sociology by Correspondence," *American Journal of Sociology*, January 1923; and "On Picket Duty," *Forum*, December 1923. MacLean's obituary in the *American Journal of Sociology*, July 1934, is useful, as is a biography of her by Virginia Kemp Fish, in *American Women Writers*, vol. 3, ed. Lina Mainiero (1981). The biography of MacLean in Mary Jo Deegan, ed., *Women in Sociology: A Bio-Bibliographical Sourcebook* (1992), provides an extensive bibliography of materials by and about MacLean. Virginia Kemp Fish, "Annie Marion MacLean: A Neglected Part of the Chicago School," *Journal of the History of Sociology*, Spring 1981, places MacLean and her work within the context of the early days of American sociology at the University of Chicago.

VIRGINIA KEMP FISH

MALEK, LEONA ALFORD KRAG (Prudence Penny, Jean Prescott Adams)
1878–March 20, 1951

JOURNALIST, HOME ECONOMICS SPECIALIST, CLUBWOMAN
Leona Alford was born and raised in Chicago where she lived all her life. Her parents, Albert and Mary Ann (Parsons) Alford, were both of English descent. Her father served in the Civil War and later became a Chicago businessman and writer. Her mother's ancestors were Puritans who settled in Springfield, Massachusetts, in 1650.

Alford studied at the Lewis Institute (later Illinois Institute of Technology), a technological and vocational training school, which offered classes in home economics. She graduated from Chicago Teachers College. She also attended the Zeigfield School in Dramatic Art and Music and studied voice with a private instructor at Kimball Hall. Initially Alford taught in the Chicago public school system. Later, she opened the Jackson School of Reading, a private cultural studio.

In 1902, Alford married Franz Kilsen Krag, a marine engineer and an officer in the Danish navy. After their marriage, the couple toured northern Europe together on an extensive trip. On their return, Leona Krag devoted herself to full time homemaking and motherhood. After the death of her young daughter, Laurine Marion, Krag returned to teaching. At the same time she began a career in writing, publishing many magazine articles on the new field of home economics. Her ideas came from her experiences as a homemaker and her training at the Lewis Institute, one of the pioneer institutions in training

women in domestic science or home economics. Krag became a successful freelance writer, publishing in many popular magazines, including the *Ladies' Home Journal*, *National Women's Magazine*, *People's Home Journal*, *Modern Priscilla*, and *Southern Women's Magazine*. She became an editor of several trade magazines and in this capacity met many advertising executives who represented major companies. Krag worked for the advertising executive whose client was Armour and Company, a leading Chicago meat-packing company that did national and international business. In 1914 Krag was asked to direct a new food economics department at Armour. She created recipes for Armour and acted as liaison between the company and housewives who wrote letters with questions about food preparation. During World War I, food shortages created the need for new food conservation methods, and Krag responded by producing recipes that were nutritious, tasty, and economical. She established herself nationwide as an expert in food economy.

It was during her tenure with Armour and Company that Krag took the pseudonym Jean Prescott Adams. This use of a female persona to educate the public about new products was an effective marketing device in the 1920s and 1930s; for example, home economist Ethel Kemper was "Virginia Page" of Sears, Roebuck, headquartered in Chicago, and was the company's domestic science editor. As Adams, Krag authored a popular pamphlet, *The Business of Being a Housewife: A Manual to Promote Household Efficiency and Economy*, printed in 1917 by Armour and Company. Reflecting trends in home economics and "the burgeoning twentieth-century consumer society" (Stage and Vincenti, 275), Krag as Jean Prescott Adams affirmed that "the knowledge of housewifery . . . [had] been systemized into an exact science" (*The Business of Being a Housewife*, 2) and that the goal of her pamphlet was to offer "practical ideas regarding food preparation and recipes, with tested methods of promoting household efficiency and economy not generally treated in books on cookery" (p. 2). The manual addressed such issues as table service, serving meals without a maid, and how to keep a family budget; and, since this was a vehicle for commercial advertising as well, it included recipes for the preparation of Armour and Company's products. Krag remained at Armour and Company for eight years, then resigned to accept the position of president and business manager of the Illinois Women's Athletic Club in Chicago.

In 1925 Leona Krag married again. Her husband, Alois W. Malek, was a businessman from Oak Park, Illinois. The same year she began writing as Prudence Penny for the *Herald and Examiner*, a Chicago daily newspaper. She wrote the daily home economics column, edited the woman's page and, as Jean Prescott Adams, wrote a column on home decoration, serving as editor of this section of the *Herald and Examiner* as well. It was as Prudence Penny, however, that she became popular. The Prudence Penny column appeared daily, but on Wednesdays it appeared in an expanded two-page layout titled "The Woman in the Home." Although many of her columns and articles were on traditional home economics topics such as cooking and cleaning, Leona Malek also addressed other women's issues. Columns such as "Prudence Penny Tells Mothers to Share Thrills of Play with Their Children: Let 'Em Mess Up Your Hair," and "Prudence Penny Tells Housewives They Mustn't Let Their

Work Bury Them" were not uncommon. She also wrote on marriage and beauty in "That Hope Chest and What Should Go into It" and "Hints Regarding Artistic Use of Rouge Powder." Her columns often included letters from housewives and Malek's responses. This space was also used to offer pamphlets for housewives such as *Budget Plan* and *Vegetable Buying for Two*. In her Prudence Penny column Malek invited her readers to attend her lectures on home economics, which were held at Chicago's Balaban and Katz Theater, and to listen to her weekly radio program broadcast on Chicago's station KYW. She continued to serve her two million strong Prudence Penny readership until 1932.

Malek was one of a growing number of professional women who generally fit the rubric of woman journalist. They often specialized in areas targeted for a female audience, and some were trained in the new field of home economics. Knowledge of homemaking, nutrition, child rearing, fashion, and decoration, when used in combination with communication skills, launched a variety of professional roles including jobs in the print media, advertising, public relations, and radio broadcasting. In 1922 Malek joined one of the oldest organizations in Illinois for women in communication, the Illinois Woman's Press Association (IWPA). Established in 1885 as a western branch of the National Association of Women Journalists, its local founders included JULIA HOLMES SMITH, FRANCES E. WILLARD, and CAROLINE HULING. From its inception IWPA members promoted the advancement and equality of women as professional writers. By the 1920s, the organization's members were focused on expanding the opportunities of women in the related fields of communication. Malek was elected president of IWPA in 1929, a position she held until 1935. Her discovery of the power of radio was generously taught and passed on to IWPA members. Among her first initiatives was her appointment of a radio committee to arrange air time for the association's members. Malek's own positive experiences with radio programming encouraged her to give IWPA members the opportunity to publicize their work. She remained committed to this endeavor, and four years after her appointment of the radio committee, IWPA members had appeared on more than two hundred weekly Saturday afternoon programs on such Chicago stations as WMAQ, WGN, and WCFL.

Another of Malek's early efforts as IWPA president was the creation of a committee to promote the association's participation in the Century of Progress Exposition, the world's fair that opened in Chicago in 1933. In preparation for the event, the IWPA held a "Gala World's Fair Dinner" in May 1931 to honor organizers of the Century of Progress and plan for ways to ensure that women writers would be represented at the exposition. During the Century of Progress the IWPA committee organized a party for women writers who were visiting from all over the world.

During her six years as president of the IWPA, Malek instituted several programs designed for the advancement of her colleagues, including the Author's Jubilee and Book Fair established in 1929 as a forum for the sale of members' books. She secured a booth for the IWPA at the Chicago *Herald and Examiner*'s food show in 1930, which resulted in extensive publicity for the works of IWPA members. She guided the association

through the production of the book *Prominent Women of Illinois* (1932), the sale of which benefited the organization as well as those members who were paid to write the individual biographies included in the publication. During the early years of the Great Depression, IWPA created the Swan Fund from which interest-free loans were made to IWPA members. In response to the economic disaster, Malek also declared that initiation fees would be waived to encourage more women writers to join the association. IWPA coordinated an authors' reception and book shower in 1934 for the Chicago Public Library (CPL). More than five thousand books were donated to the CPL during the event by IWPA members and their friends. In 1935, she resigned the presidency of the IWPA and was voted honorary vice-president. IWP celebrated its golden anniversary that year with a formal banquet and program at the Lake Shore Drive Hotel, commemorating the work of the founding members, only one of whom was alive and attended—Caroline Huling. Speakers that evening included HARRIET MONROE. Twenty-five IWPA members dressed in historically authentic costumes took part in a pageant, "When Black Velvet Took the Place of Royal Purple," created and produced by MINNA SCHMIDT.

The golden anniversary benefit and other IWPA activities resembled the kind of events typical of women's clubs in the 1930s to which Malek belonged. She was a member of the Order of the Eastern Star, the National Women's Republican Club, the Klio Association, the Daughters of the American Revolution (DAR), and the Cook County Federation of Women's Clubs. She was one of the founders of the Abigail Adams Group, a unit of the DAR that met in the evenings so that those members who worked during the day could take part in club activities. Throughout her career Malek lectured nationwide, offering talks on a variety of home economics topics, including "Putting the Home on a Business Basis," "Feeding the Family for Health, Happiness and Success," and "How to Make Your Dreams Come True." Malek's club and lecture work were substantial components of her career. After her tenure as IWPA president, she continued to write articles, lecture, and take part in club activities. She died at age seventy-three.

Malek's white, Anglo-Saxon, Protestant background and her membership in the DAR testified to her interest in traditional values. However, her active professional career reflected her support of the education and advancement of women. She saw housewifery as a legitimate occupation essential to the well-being of the family and, although unpaid, important enough to warrant scientific study and improvement. One of the major concerns of the Progressive Era was better efficiency and management in business, and Malek, a product of her time, sought ways for housewives to be better organized and to use scientific processes and expertise. Her advocacy was not intended to support the notion that women's work should be relegated entirely to the domestic sphere (to which her own career as a professional journalist attested), but rather to legitimize housework as a worthy occupation that could be less time-consuming if organizational and scientific methods were applied. Although she was not the first woman to broadcast her ideas over radio airwaves, and she was not the first to study home economics, Leona Alford Malek was an early disseminator of domestic science ideas to a broad female audience.

Sources. The Illinois Woman's Press Association records, CHS, establish Leona Alford Malek's participation in the organization and reflect its activities from the 1920s. CHS has issues of the IWPA newsletter *Pen Points.* Jean Prescott Adams's *The Business of Being a Housewife: A Manual to Promote Household Efficiency and Economy* (1917) was written by Malek using one of her two pseudonyms. Under her second and more famous pseudonym, Prudence Penny, Malek's columns were printed in the Chicago newspaper *Herald and Examiner,* 1925 through 1932, and are on microfilm, available at CHS. A biography of Malek is found in Donna Duesel De La Torriente, *So We All Can Be Heard: An History of the Illinois Woman's Press Association 1885–1987* (1987), published by the Illinois Woman's Press Association. Sarah Stage and Virginia B. Vicenti, eds., *Rethinking Home Economics: Women and the History of a Profession* (1997), provides historical context. Two eulogies are Preston Bradley, *Down Memory Lane: A Tribute to Leona Alford Malek* (1951), and Maude I. G. Oliver, "Services for Leona Malek," *Pen Points,* April 1951.

JOANNE MURRAY GROSSMAN

MALONEY, ELIZABETH

November 19, 1880–October 26, 1921

WAITRESS, UNION ORGANIZER, SUFFRAGE ADVOCATE

Elizabeth Maloney, labor leader and lobbyist for hours legislation, was born in Joliet, Illinois. Her father, William Maloney, was Irish by birth, and her mother, Margaret Krok, was born and raised in Joliet. Little is known about her girlhood, but by 1902, when she was twenty-two, Maloney was settled in Chicago and working as a waitress. She never married or had children, instead devoting her life to a range of labor and women's issues.

Turn-of-the-century Chicago was a propitious place for Maloney. Maloney arrived in Chicago with thousands of other single, unmarried young women, the first such generation to set up independent households. For these women, restaurants held a multi-layered meaning. Many could not afford to rent apartments with kitchens, requiring that they find meals elsewhere. Many found employment at the same places they found meals. Restaurants provided both work and a place for socializing. Chicago was also boiling with women's labor activism. Women in several trades, including teaching, textiles and needlework, as well as restaurant work, were beginning to organize for collective action.

As a waitress, Maloney recognized the inequity in the restaurant trades. Waitresses typically worked up to fourteen hours a day, seven days a week, often for less than a dollar a day. Sickness was frequent, resulting from the long hours in humid conditions and poor food provided to waitresses; but because of their low wages, few could afford either time away from work or professional health care. Many waitresses relied on tips from customers, a practice Maloney feared coerced women to tolerate indecent behavior from male patrons.

Maloney felt a direct affinity with all waitresses. MARGARET DREIER ROBINS of the Women's Trade Union League (WTUL) later recalled, "I remember so well how hard and unremitting was the labor of those women and girls in restaurants and hotels, as waitresses, or cooks, dishwashers or helpers in the kitchen. This was especially true of those young girls, many times mere children from ten to twelve years old, working in the poorer sections of our city, in the cheaper restaurants and coffee houses. Their long hours, often lasting until after midnight, and the wretched conditions of their work weighed heavily on the heart and mind of Elizabeth [Maloney]" (quoted in Dreier, 9).

In 1902, Maloney and two dozen other waitresses formed Local 484, which soon had fifteen hundred members. The union quickly won a series of victories, reducing hours to ten a day, six days a week, while raising wages two dollars a week at more than one hundred union shops around the city. Maloney left waitressing to devote her full attention to union work. Local 484 affiliated with the Hotel and Restaurant Employees' International Alliance and the American Federation of Labor. Maloney served Local 484 as financial secretary and the International Alliance as vice-president. Local 484 also affiliated with the National WTUL, and Maloney served on the boards of both the National WTUL and the Chicago chapter.

What Maloney had won for waitresses she wanted to share with all workers. Although unions often won shorter days for their workers, women, who were less likely to belong to a union, often labored from twelve to fourteen hours a day. The Waitresses' Union led the drive for legislation limiting the hours that women could work for wages, and Maloney lobbied regularly in Springfield, Illinois. When the Waitresses' Union drafted new legislation for a ten-hour law in 1909, Maloney testified before a state senate committee in March.

Maloney's testimony must have seemed out of place, as the 1909 legislation did not cover restaurant workers. But the 1909 law fit within a well-crafted legal strategy designed to culminate in hours legislation for all workers. Illinois had adopted a law limiting women to eight hours of work a day in 1893, but a unanimous state supreme court struck down the eight-hour law in 1895, holding it a violation of a woman's individual right to contract for longer hours. Maloney and her supporters needed a series of laws that would not only pass the legislature but would also survive constitutional challenges.

Waitresses knew well that workers needed the protection of hours legislation. Passage of a law that both limited hours and satisfied the court was of supreme importance, even if its scope excluded waitresses. The 1909 law differed from the earlier statute in that it limited hours to ten instead of eight; it applied to all factories and laundries, while the 1893 law applied only to clothing manufacture; and it explicitly tied hours legislation to women's health, safety, and morals, while the earlier law had not. Each of these changes addressed grounds on which the court had struck down the 1893 law.

The 1909 law was approved by the legislative and executive branches; when the challenge to the law was heard by the supreme court, Maloney attended oral arguments. The legal strategy focused attention on the physical hardship of long hours of labor. In this, Maloney and her associates borrowed from the strategy employed in *Muller v Oregon* (1908), in which the U.S. Supreme Court upheld hours legislation for women. The strategy was useful because it created the basis for expanding the scope of occupations with limited hours; once the court accepted a link between hours legislation and the health, safety, and morals of factory workers, other types of workers could argue for the same protection.

Formulating their position in this way put the waitresses in an odd position, however, as the strategy played upon centuries-old stereotypes of women as the weaker sex, even though the objective was to aid women who were radically redefining their social and economic roles in society. Yet the women themselves saw no inconsistency, focusing instead on the long-range goal of worker protection. Consequently, Assistant Attorney General Fred H. Hand "almost drew applause from the women," according to one journalist, with his argument that "the right to live and perpetuate the race; [and] the duty to bring forth children endowed with health and strength, with time to care for, educate and rear them, justified the legislature in curtailing the right to contract as to women" (WTUL of Chicago Scrapbook, leaf 6).

Passage of the 1909 law was only the beginning for Maloney. For days after passage, Maloney and Margaret Dreier Robins stood on street corners proclaiming the news to working women. Maloney dedicated herself to a new drive for expanded hours legislation. In 1911, 1913, and 1915, she testified at the state capitol, arguing in 1911 to expand the scope of the ten-hour law to include women working in hotels, restaurants, telegraph and telephone companies, public utilities, entertainment, and public institutions. While she was unable during her lifetime to secure a reduction of hours to eight, Maloney set the foundation for successful hours legislation drives during the 1930s.

In addition to legislative testimony, Maloney became an active union organizer. Maloney started with the other culinary trades, helping to organize cooks and waiters in the wake of the 1909 hours law. In May 1913 she spoke to a rally of department store clerks who were then trying to form a union. Observers noted that Maloney did not mince words, and crowds cheered her for her forthright, charismatic style. She spoke regularly at WTUL of Chicago functions, sharing the podium in 1913 with John Mitchell and in 1915 with Mother Jones. Her address to the WTUL of Chicago's Tenth Annual Dinner in July 1913, entitled "Legislation and Its Relation to Organization," stressed the need to buttress legislative initiatives with constituent unity. Appointed the WTUL of Chicago delegate to the Illinois State Federation of Labor in 1912 and 1913, she joined Emma Steghagen and AGNES NESTOR, other permanent union organizers, in presenting a "plea for the eight hour day"; an observer noted that the three women had "more real enthusiasm for the cause than any half dozen men combined" (WTUL of Chicago Scrapbook, leaf 6).

Her organizing work culminated in the Henrici strike of 1914. In concert with cooks, waiters, bakers, and other unionized workers, the Waitresses' Union targeted thirty-five members of the Restaurant Keepers Association (RKA) who had refused to recognize their workers' unions. To conserve funds, the unions planned to make an example of just one member of the RKA; further, they decided against calling workers out but instead planned informational pickets and a call for patrons to eat elsewhere. The unions also announced plans to put "dry petitions" (anti-liquor local referendums) on the ballot during the next election and to seek Chicago Health Department inspections of targeted restaurants as pressure tactics against recalcitrant owners, moves that would not tax the unions' resources. On the eve of the strike, Chicago newspapers openly wondered which of the thirty-five RKA members would fall victim to the strike.

On February 6, 1914, the waitresses gathered outside Henrici's Restaurant in downtown Chicago. Maloney, then business agent of the Waitresses' Union, joined with eight other women in distributing leaflets and asking patrons not to eat there. The next day she left the picketing to others in order to begin making the rounds of the other thirty-four non-picketed RKA members, looking for weak links. Maloney also coordinated support from other unions, including grocery delivery drivers, butchers, and brewers. Before long, she also had to organize bail and legal help for picketers who had been arrested.

Police harassment of the strike began almost immediately. The pickets began each day just before lunch; by noon, the police would have arrested many. By early afternoon, Maloney was usually able to arrange for their release, but by then the lunch trade was over. Henrici hired plainclothes detectives, termed gunmen by the waitresses, who were deputized by the police. These gunmen followed Henrici staff to and from work; those suspected of being union members were summarily fired. On February 8, Maloney joined with officers of the Chicago Federation of Labor in a meeting with police officials in an effort to find an acceptable means of picketing, but the police were adamant. Days later, police announced plans to arrest Maloney herself on charges of conspiring to hurt a business through boycott, a crime under state law. Although the bluff was never carried out, it succeeded in making evident police hostility to the strike.

The waitresses' spirits remained strong, but in the face of such swift, unreasonable, and harsh resistance, the strike was broken. Within thirty days, there were 139 arrests; bail alone totaled more than $170,000. Many of those arrested complained of police brutality, and one suffered a dislocated shoulder. The coup de grace came in the form of a court-ordered injunction that forbade all picketing, not because of the behavior of the picketers, who had been trained in peaceful procedures, but because the crowds they attracted caused a disturbance. "According to this decision," Maloney later noted, "there is no way we could have done peaceful picketing . . . except in a desert" ("The Henrici Strike," 203).

Hours legislation continued to take up much of Maloney's time. From 1918 to 1919, Maloney served on the Committee on Social and Industrial Reconstruction of the National WTUL, which advocated expanding the scope of hours legislation as part of postwar economic policy. Also in 1918, Maloney was appointed by Governor Frank O. Lowden to the Illinois Industrial Survey to study the need for additional hours legislation. The following year, the survey released its report, urging an eight hour day for all women.

Maloney's work for hours legislation taught her two lessons, and she devoted energy to these causes. The first was the value of union membership. The second was suffrage. According to one observer, Maloney's success with the ten hour law "was a striking revelation of what women may accomplish and to what extent they are able to mix in the political affairs of state" (WTUL Scrapbook, leaf 29). Because Maloney saw that women's political power was severely limited by their inability to vote, she helped found, in October 1913, the Wage Earners Suffrage League, bringing four hundred waitresses to that organization.

Maloney's health began to fail in 1920. In February she was diagnosed with breast cancer. Surgery the next month did little to stop the disease. Nonetheless, she remained active in the Waitresses' Union and WTUL until her death at age forty-one. She was buried at Mt. Carmel Cemetery in Chicago.

In fitting tribute, her funeral featured many of the most prominent women speakers of the time, including JANE ADDAMS and ELLEN GATES STARR of Hull-House, ALICE HENRY of the WTUL, Agnes Nestor of the International Glove Workers' Union, and Margaret Dreier Robins. At a time when few people gave any thought to the women who served them in restaurants, Elizabeth Maloney made significant strides in the battle to make waitressing "a real trade by which any girl might be proud to earn her living" (quoted in Franklin, 36).

Sources. The Women's Trade Union League of Chicago Papers, including the Scrapbook, at UIC Spec. Coll., contain many newspaper clippings that refer to Maloney's work. The CHS also has several useful papers, mostly printed programs to annual dinners and pamphlets written in support of hours legislation. The case law of hours legislation includes *Ritchie v People* (1895); *Ritchie & Co. v Wayman* (1910); *People v Elerding*, 254 Ill 579 (1912); and *People v City of Chicago*, 256 Ill 558 (1912). Despite Maloney's highly visible role in the fight for hours legislation, her public record appears limited to quotes in the newspapers, particularly during the Henrici strike. Maloney's comments to the City Club of Chicago are transcribed in "The Henrici Strike," *City Club Bulletin*, June 13, 1914. Contemporary writings about Maloney include S. M. Franklin, "Elizabeth Maloney and the High Calling of the Waitress," *Life & Labor*, February 1913; Esther Taber, "Women in Unions: Through Trade Union Organization Waitresses Have Secured Marked Improvements in Conditions," *American Federationist*, December 1905; and Ellen Gates Starr, "Efforts to Standardize Chicago Restaurants—The Henrici Strike," *Survey*, May 23, 1914. Especially useful studies include Joanne Meyerowitz, *Women Adrift: Independent Wage Earners in Chicago, 1880–1930* (1988), and Dorothy Sue Cobble, *Dishing It Out: Waitresses and Their Unions in the Twentieth Century* (1991). Also useful is Mary E. Dreier, *Margaret Dreier Robins: Her Life, Letters, and Work* (1950).

DAVID MORRISON

MARCY, MARY EDNA TOBIAS
1877–December 8, 1922
SOCIALIST ACTIVIST, EDITOR, WRITER

Eugene Victor Debs, the most notable leader of the socialist movement in the United States during the first two decades of the twentieth century, referred to Mary Edna Marcy as "the brainiest woman in the socialist movement" (Carney, 10). Marcy was one of the inner circle that comprised the staff of the *International Socialist Review (ISR)*, the radical socialist monthly published in Chicago by Charles H. Kerr & Company. She wrote articles, editorials, pamphlets, and books that reached an untold number of socialist adherents during that heyday of American socialism. A central figure among the left-wingers who gravitated to the Kerr Company, she served both the publishing house and the socialist cause until her premature death in 1922.

Born in Belleville, Illinois, near East St. Louis, Mary Edna Tobias lost her parents at an early age. The eldest of three children, she taught herself stenography and went to work as a clerical while attending high school in order to support her siblings,

Inez and Roscoe. She was fired from her job as a stenographer for wearing a William Jennings Bryan button during the presidential campaign of 1896. Attorney Clarence Darrow heard of her situation and secured a position for her as a secretary to the University of Chicago's president, William Rainey Harper, who was known for his concern for impoverished students. Taking advantage of free tuition, she studied advanced courses in philosophy and English literature and became a student of educator John Dewey.

She married Leslie H. Marcy in 1901. Leaving Chicago with her husband, she went to work as a secretary for the treasurer of a major Kansas City meat-packing firm. Three years in that position provided the information and insights that resulted in her "Letters of a Pork Packer's Stenographer," a scathing exposé of the "Beef Trust" that ran serially in the *ISR* between August 1904 and January 1905. The series led to Marcy's subpoena to appear before a Chicago grand jury investigating the beef trust. It also won the author instant notoriety within left circles.

Marcy briefly worked for the Associated Charities of Kansas City but quickly found herself at odds with that body's procedures. Her fictionalized *Out of the Dump* (1909), initially serialized in the *ISR*, depicted the harsh living conditions, unemployment, and family upheaval experienced by those more in need of concrete assistance than lectures on morality.

Returning to Chicago, Marcy joined the staff of the *International Socialist Review* as an assistant editor in 1908. From that period until the magazine's suppression by the federal authorities during World War I, barely a month went by without a contribution from her. Her writing style and political acumen as associate editor and columnist helped increase the popularity of the monthly among movement rank and file activists as subscriptions increased from six thousand in 1908 to forty thousand by 1911.

Her tireless and energetic pen found a broad following and proved influential in movement debates spanning a wide array of issues for more than a decade. At the time that Marcy joined the staff of the *ISR*, the socialist movement had already become polarized. A more conservative right wing wedded to reformist electoral politics and to the exclusive craft unionism of the American Federation of Labor (AFL) found itself at odds with a left wing committed to mass-based industrial unionism, direct action, and "revolutionary" socialism. Mary Marcy supported the movement's left wing as critic, commentator, and editorialist. Her unwavering partisanship won her both avid supporters and the enmity of numerous conservative detractors.

Marcy held a fundamental conviction in the power of the written word. She was convinced that the teachings of Marx had to be made more accessible if the socialist movement were to make any headway. Devoted to socialist education and instruction in the fundamentals of Marxism, Marcy contributed numerous didactic pieces to the *ISR*. The most notable, her *Shop Talks on Economics*, "an attempt to say, in the language of working men and women, the things Marx says in his own books" (p. 1), initially appeared in serial installments during 1911. Published in pamphlet form that year, this classic primer in Marxian economics went through numerous editions and subsequently found its way into Japanese, Chinese, Finnish, Romanian, French, Italian, and Greek translations. More than two million copies of *Shop Talks* had circulated by the time of Marcy's death in 1922.

She found time to write on every question of significance to the socialist cause despite a heavy administrative load as secretary of the Kerr Company and managing editor of the *ISR* after 1911. In support of industrial unionism, the recruitment of all workers in an industry regardless of skill, she wrote articles on technological changes in various industries that illustrated the erosion of the skilled trades, the base of AFL support. She provided coverage and publicity for the major strikes of the prewar era, such as the Lawrence Mill Workers' Strike of 1912. She wrote on the situation of working farmers.

Rarely concerned with reform measures, she voiced limited concern for the "woman question" and wrote virtually nothing on behalf of the struggle for female suffrage. Some of her writings, however, did focus on the plight of working-class women. For example, Kerr, in 1918, brought out a pamphlet on the status of women as men's property, *Women as Sex Vendors*, by Mary Marcy and her brother, Roscoe Tobias. Marcy also penned a short play on social and sexual relations, published in 1921, *A Free Union: A One Act Comedy of Free Love*, an examination of the "new woman" of the early twentieth century.

Marcy consistently spoke out against imperialism and war as the consequence of international capitalist competition. She remained adamantly opposed to U.S. intervention in the Mexican revolution and argued that American workers had no business fighting their fellow workers in Mexico for corporate interests. Her world changed irrevocably with the coming of World War I. Her attention for the next four years became fixed on the war in Europe and its revolutionary potential. Appalled by the support of European socialist parties for the war, she went on to champion calls for mass action and a general strike against war as the only possible way to prevent U.S. entry.

By the time of the U.S. entry into the war in April 1917, the idea of a general strike to bring down the government and its war machine had become a central theme of Marcy's writings. She also became convinced that the war would create new possibilities for the overthrow of capitalism and the establishment of socialism. American entry was accompanied by harsh state repression aimed at all opponents of the war. The entire circle of Kerr associates, relentless in their antiwar stance, came under surveillance. Federal censors suppressed the *ISR* in February 1918 by barring it from the mail. Federal authorities raided and ransacked the Marcys' home in the Chicago suburb of Bowmanvill.

Seemingly as irrepressible as ever, despite the accompanying stress and difficulties of the war period, Marcy continued her left-wing educational work. In addition to numerous columns and editorials in the *ISR* and its short-lived successor, the *Labor Scrapbook*, she produced a diverse number of longer pamphlets and several book-length works between 1916 and 1921, including *How the Farmer Can Get His* (1916), *Stories of the Cave People* (1917), *Industrial Autocracy* (1919), *The Right to Strike* (1920), and *Open the Factories* (1920). She also composed the text for an illustrated collection of children's stories and poems, *Rhymes of the Jungle Folk* (1922).

Marcy joined the radical labor union, the Industrial Workers of the World (IWW), also known as the "Wobblies," in 1918. She had already become quite active in political defense work

for IWW members following the arrest of several tiers of the organization's leadership in September 1917. Her support of the IWW, in tandem with its unyielding opposition to World War I, brought her and Leslie Marcy under close scrutiny of federal, state, and local authorities. Both Mary and Leslie Marcy remained under regular government surveillance in the period 1918–21.

Among those apprehended in the national roundup of IWW leaders in September 1917 was the *ISR*'s illustrator, poet Ralph Chaplin, and its associate editor, William D. "Big Bill" Haywood. Indicted and arraigned within weeks on more than ten thousand separate charges, 113 Wobblies, among them the two Kerr associates, sat in Cook County jail awaiting a mass trial that finally got underway on April 1, 1918. Found guilty on all counts by a highly prejudiced court in an inflamed political environment, the defendants were sent to Leavenworth Penitentiary. Chaplin and Haywood each received twenty-year sentences. The work of the Marcys in defense campaigns for the Wobblies and other radicals brought them under further scrutiny by the authorities. Undeterred, they managed to procure enough security by putting up their own individual property and cash to help obtain Haywood's release on a thirty thousand dollar bond, pending appeal, in August 1919. Haywood again faced arrest in the "Red Scare" raids at the beginning of 1920. The IWW leader dropped out of sight and subsequently made his way to the Soviet Union. With his failure to appear, of course, he forfeited his bond. The loss of that bail wreaked havoc on the personal lives of his longtime associates at the Kerr company, including the Marcys, who forfeited their Bowmanvill home when Haywood jumped bail.

Haywood's flight took an exceptionally heavy personal toll on Mary Marcy. They had a close, intimate relationship, and his departure came at a time when the broad movement she so selflessly served, attacked from outside and fractured within, had reached an extreme state of disarray. She continued her writing, pouring out pamphlets and essays. She had become physically and emotionally drained, however, by the events of the war period and its aftermath. Her marriage to Leslie Marcy had become strained as well; they divorced. She could no longer draw strength, by 1921 or 1922, from those glimmerings of revolutionary potential that had fueled her confidence but a few years earlier. Mary Marcy committed suicide in December 1922 by swallowing rat poison.

With the passing of Mary Marcy, the movement for radical change in the United States lost one of its most significant voices. There is no question that she made an indelible mark on the political terrain of the American left, but she did so from behind the scenes as editor, columnist, and pamphleteer.

Sources. Material on Mary Marcy is limited. Scant material about her exists in the May Walden Kerr Collection, NL. The National Archives and Records Administration, Washington, D.C., Record Group 65, FBI Investigative Case Files, and Record Group 165, Military Intelligence Division, both indexed, trace some of her activity during the war period. Her writings appear in the *International Socialist Review*, 1900–18. An anthology of Marcy's writings exists: Frederick Giffen, ed., *The Tongue of Angels: The Mary Marcy Reader* (1989). For her antiwar writings, see Franklin Rosemont, ed., *You Have No Country! Workers' Struggle against War* (1984). The standard biographical work is Jack Carney's

Mary Marcy (1923). See also Allen M. Ruff, *"We Called Each Other Comrade": Charles H. Kerr & Company, Radical Publishers* (1997); and Allen Ruff, "International Socialist Review," in *Encyclopedia of the American Left,* ed. Mari Jo Buhle, Paul Buhle, and Dan Georgakis (1990). Sally M. Miller provided information that appeared in her essay "Mary Marcy" in *Race, Ethnicity and Gender in Early Twentieth Century American Socialism,* ed. Miller (1996).

ALLEN M. RUFF

MARTIN, ELLEN ANNETTE
January 16, 1847–April 27, 1916
LAWYER, SUFFRAGIST

A pioneering lawyer who successfully voted in 1891, Ellen Annette Martin was born to Abram and Mary Eliza (Burnham) Martin in Kiantone, New York. She had two brothers, Willis E. and George Burnham Martin. A well-known attorney, her father gave his family detailed accounts of his cases and arguments, helping and inspiring Ellen Martin in her study of law. Martin was educated first at Randolph Academy (later renamed Jamestown Academy) and then graduated from Clinton Liberal Institution in 1865. At some point during her education in the East, she was a classmate of Mary Fredrika Perry. The two developed a lasting friendship. Perry was the daughter of Caroline B. Vance and stepdaughter of Hallack Joseph Vance of New Jersey. Ellen Martin boarded with the Vance family in New Jersey; later in the 1870s, after law school, she lived with the Vances in Lombard, Illinois, where they had relocated. Martin never married but stayed close to the Vance family her whole life.

Martin began her study of law in 1871 with the firm of Cook and Lockwood in Chautauqua County, New York. In 1873, she entered the University of Michigan law school with Mary Fredrika Perry. Both had been denied admission to Harvard University's law school. Harvard's policy of not allowing young men and women use of the law library at the same time was the excuse given for denying the women admission. Martin wrote, sardonically, "It was not considered fair to admit to the Law School without giving privileges of the library. I believe the authorities have not yet found any way to get around or over this mountain of difficulty" (*Chicago Law Times,* 1886).

Ellen Martin graduated and was admitted to the Michigan bar in 1875. She then moved to Chicago to join Perry. On January 7, 1876, she became the third woman lawyer admitted to the Illinois bar following Perry, September 1875, and ALTA HULETT, June 1873. Martin and Perry then formed one of the first women law partnerships in the country; the two women opened a law office in Chicago's downtown commercial district and specialized in real estate law. They lived in Lombard with the Vance family.

During their first years of practice, both Martin and Perry conducted pro bono legal work for indigent women. Perry earned a reputation for her dedication to the poor, braving severe weather conditions to bring warm clothing to those in need as well as donating her legal services. Overwork and a brutally cold winter weakened Perry, who contracted pneumonia and died on June 3, 1883.

Feeling the loss deeply, Martin kept the sign "Perry & Martin" outside her office until 1915 when she retired. Martin blamed Perry's death on the extra work done for the poor and

vowed to limit her charity to monetary contributions and never again to provide free legal services. Martin never doubted women's intellectual abilities for law, but after Perry's death she took the unpopular position among women lawyers that practicing law was more taxing physically for women than men, unless women were in excellent physical condition. She also endorsed Victorian gynecological theories about the relationship of the brain or intellect and women's reproductive organs, accepting that diseases of the latter had a peculiarly female relationship to the nervous system. Many women lawyers argued against such biological determinism, citing its use by men to keep women outside the profession.

On the other hand, Ellen Martin was dedicated to helping young women lawyers and advocated female admission to law schools. In 1888, Martin became a member of the Equity Club, the first American organization of women lawyers. Founded by Letitia Burlingame and six other women law students at the University of Michigan on October 6, 1886, the club developed a community of support reaching out beyond the university. In Chicago, Martin mentored Zetta Strawn, who studied law in her office in the 1890s and then went on to Northwestern University law school.

Ellen Martin was a militant advocate of women's political equality, believing that the Fourteenth and Fifteenth Amendments to the United States Constitution extended full citizenship to women, including the franchise. Suffragists arguing from this legal position, including Susan B. Anthony, considered it unnecessary to pass any further suffrage amendment and, acting upon this interpretation, took direct action and attempted to cast votes. This stage of suffrage agitation, known as the "New Departure," had advocates throughout the nation. Ellen Martin attempted to vote in 1891 in the town of Lombard, having developed a similar legal argument based on the wording of the town charter, which did not include the word "male" but stated that all citizens age twenty-one and over were entitled to vote. Arriving at the polling place with law books and a voluminous legal brief, she demanded to be allowed to vote. If the judges denied her the right, she was prepared to have the election adjourned so that she could read her brief and obtain a hearing on the spot. Allowed to cast her vote, Martin then gathered up fourteen other women, including Caroline Vance and Carrie Towne, Fredrika Perry's mother and sister, respectively, and brought them back to the polling place where they also voted.

Male voters expressed their outrage that women were allowed to vote, and the town magistrates passed provisions ensuring that women would not attempt to vote in the forthcoming general elections. At the same time in Illinois, the general assembly passed the school suffrage bill (1891) allowing women to vote for school boards and the trustees of the University of Illinois. This piece of legislation, however, reflected the mounting pressure of the organized woman suffrage movement and the argument that women had a special role in the education of children, not the equal-rights interpretation under the Constitution implied in the direct action of Ellen Martin.

Martin's approach to suffrage and the advancement of women in law made her an appropriate candidate to join the ranks of the Queen Isabella Association, a group of women physicians, educators, and lawyers interested in having a sculpture of Queen Isabella of Spain commissioned for the World's Columbian Exposition in 1893. Queen Isabella, almost forgotten in the rush to commemorate Christopher Columbus, had made his voyage possible, contended the association's members. The Isabellas challenged the Board of Lady Managers, a woman's auxiliary put in place by the male leaders of the Columbian Exposition. The Isabellas hoped women's political struggle for equal rights and suffrage would be featured in the proposed Woman's Building; not finding support for their position from the lady managers and having their request for space to hold their own exhibit on the exposition grounds denied, the Isabellas erected a club house and hall two blocks away. Ellen Martin was made vice-president of the board of directors and chair of the legal department and organized a meeting of women lawyers that was held August 3–5, 1893. Fourteen prominent women attorneys spoke on a variety of topics, including Martin on "The Myra Bradwell Case in Illinois." (MYRA BRADWELL was the first woman in Illinois to apply for a license to practice law.) At the close of the Columbian Exposition in September 1893, the lawyers' department of the Queen Isabella Association formed the National League of Women Lawyers to promote the interests of women in the practical work of the legal profession.

In 1894, Martin joined her law colleague (and Isabella member) CATHARINE WAUGH McCULLOCH and thirteen other members of the Chicago Woman's Club in founding the Chicago Political Equality League. A suffrage organization, the league paid dues to the Illinois Equal Suffrage Association, an affiliate of the National American Woman Suffrage Association. Martin was on the league board for twelve years, corresponding secretary for four, and chair of the suffrage committee for seven years. She retired at age sixty-seven in 1914 after the league had successfully campaigned for passage of the "Illinois Law" or Presidential Suffrage Bill in 1913, which gave Illinois women the vote for presidential electors and virtually all local offices—county, town, municipal, and village.

In 1915, after forty years in private practice, Martin closed the firm of Perry & Martin. She and Carrie Towne sold their property in Lombard, Illinois, and Martin returned to Chautauqua County, New York. She died at sixty-nine years of age at the home of her sister-in-law Tella Evans Martin in Jamestown, New York.

Sources. Archives on the Queen Isabella Association and some of their journals, chronicling Ellen Martin's involvement, as well as yearbooks of the Chicago Political Equality League, are at the CHS. Archives on Ellen Martin are kept at the Lombard Hist. Soc., Lombard, Illinois. Ellen Martin's papers are in the Bentley Hist. Library, Univ. of Michigan, Ann Arbor, Michigan. Articles by Martin include "Admission of Women to the Bar," *Chicago Law Times*, vol. 1, 1886; "Letter to the Equity Club," May 25, 1888, in *Women Lawyers and the Origins of Professional Identity in America: The Letters of the Equity Club, 1887 to 1890* (1993), ed. Virginia Drachman; "The Women Voters at Lombard," *Chicago Legal News*, vol. 23, 1891; "M. Fredrika Perry," *Chicago Legal News*, vol. 15, 1883. Martin is discussed in John P. Downs and Fenwick Y. Hedley, *History of Chautauqua County and Its People* (1875); Ada M. Bittenbender, "Woman in Law," *Chicago Law Times*, vol. 2, 1887; Lelia J. Robinson, "Women Lawyers in the United States," *Green Bag*, vol. 2, 1890; James B. Bradwell, "Women Lawyers of Illinois," *Chicago Legal News*, vol. 32, 1900; and Karen Berger Morello, *The Invisible Bar: The Woman Lawyer in America 1638 to the Present* (1986). Martin's direct-action vote is chronicled in "The Ladies of Lombard," *Daily Inter-Ocean*, April 11, 1891, and "Women and Municipal Suffrage," *Chicago Legal News*, vol. 23, 1891. The founding of the National League of Women Lawyers is noted in the *American Lawyer*, vol. 1, 1893. Jeanne Madeline Weimann, *The Fair Women* (1981), has a discussion of the Queen Isabella Society.

GWEN HOERR McNAMEE

MARTIN, ROBERTA EVELYN (Lubirda Winston)
February 14, 1906–January 13, 1969
GOSPEL MUSIC INNOVATOR, CONTRALTO, COMPOSER, PUBLISHER, SINGING GROUP AND CHOIR ORGANIZER

A major innovator of African American gospel music, Roberta Evelyn Martin was born Lubirda Winston in Helena, a small town near the Mississippi River in southeastern Arkansas. Her mother, Annaliza (Clopton) Winston, bore eight children between 1878 and 1915, the last five fathered by her second husband, William B. Winston. Lubirda was the next to the last of Annaliza Winston's children.

Lubirda Winston came from southern middle-class parentage. She performed chores and led a tomboy's life on the family farm and in the grocery store owned by William Winston. Her formal education began at the nearby private Inter-State Academy. At age six, she began taking piano lessons from an older half-brother's wife and played the piano in her Sunday school.

Part of the Black Diaspora of 1914–18, Annaliza Winston and two children moved first to Cairo, Illinois, when Lubirda was eight, and then to Chicago when she was ten. William Winston joined the family about six years later; he supported the family by running a business and working for the city of Chicago hauling refuse. During a serious illness when she was fifteen, Lubirda became more involved with gospel music. It may have been the severity of this illness that delayed her entry to Wendell Phillips High School until she was sixteen. There she studied piano with Mildred Bryant Jones. The Winstons lived in the Black Belt of Chicago, in an area that was part of a larger community changing in composition from white to black. The more established African Americans of Chicago blamed the Black Belt's deterioration, as well as their troubled relations with Whites and other urban problems, on the new black immigrants.

On November 28, 1928, Lubirda Winston married William Martin, who had migrated to Chicago in 1923. The Martins had no children and separated within one year. William Martin sued for divorce in 1939, and the divorce was granted March 19, 1943.

In 1932, while continuing her studies to become a concert pianist, Martin began her career as a performer of gospel music as the pianist for the newly organized Junior Gospel Choir at Ebenezer Baptist Church, an old-line black Chicago congregation. The Rev. J. H. L. Smith, recently arrived in Chicago from Birmingham, Alabama, had encouraged the Ebenezer congregation to replace its traditional European worship music with the old-time music of southern black folk. This was a major departure. The world's first gospel choir, a senior, adult chorus of more than one hundred voices, debuted at Ebenezer in January 1932, with Theodore R. Frye as director and Thomas A. Dorsey as pianist. That same year, Dorsey and Frye recruited Roberta Martin to become the pianist of the newly established Ebenezer Junior Gospel Chorus (also known as the Young People's Choir) and the first gospel choir organized at Pilgrim Baptist Church.

In the thirties, Chicago was the center of the new gospel music industry. The earliest forms of this music had emerged in late-nineteenth- and early-twentieth-century Pentecostal and sanctified churches of the South. Gospel spread and flourished throughout black America by way of migration and cultural assimilation and as a means to provide witness to the sanctifying power of the Word of God. Believers submitted themselves to the lifelong process and lifestyle of sanctification, an internal, psychological cleansing that included eschewing evil thoughts and deeds and that resulted from studying and obediently practicing the truths recorded in the Scriptures. Music historians consider Roberta Martin to be one of the most distinguished "children" of the "father" of black gospel music, Thomas Andrew Dorsey; both of them were committed to the marriage of tradition and innovation.

In 1933, the Bertha Wise Singers from Georgia visited Ebenezer. Wise played piano and sang along with her male quartet. Before the year was out, Martin adopted the Wise gospel piano style. Also in 1933, Martin and Frye, with the help of Dorsey, organized the Martin-Frye Singers (also known as the Martin-Frye Quartet), a group of male vocalists Martin chose from the youthful talent pool of her church choirs, establishing a preference for young talent that would endure throughout her career. Martin sang along with and provided piano accompaniment to the group. Martin renamed the group the Roberta Martin Singers after ending her relationship with Frye in the mid-1930s. While still together with Frye, Martin became the director of the choirs of the Englewood community's Shiloh Baptist church, pastored by L. W. Hale, the husband of her sister Beatrice Hall.

In the 1930s and 1940s, the Roberta Martin Singers gained focus while undergoing name and personnel changes. In an era dominated by either male or female gospel groups, Martin's groups were sexually integrated. From the late 1930s to 1940, an older performer, Sallie Martin (no relation), became the group's first female singer besides Roberta Martin, and the group was known as the Martin and Martin Singers. In the mid-1940s, the youthful Bessie Folk and Delois Barrett Campbell joined. Martin stirred controversy by inducing singers to leave other groups to join her. As the group gained prominence, it played to both large and small churches in the highly segregated black communities of Chicago. From New Year's Eve until June each year, the group traveled the gospel highway, the circuit of churches and auditoriums Martin had helped to develop. Initially, they traveled by car, buying their own groceries rather than eating in segregated restaurants in order to cope with not merely the depressed national economy but also segregationist Jim Crow laws. By the late forties, the group drew such large crowds when they appeared in Chicago that they held their anniversaries in the Armory and the Coliseum.

Gospel, this new and evolving musical form, was controversial throughout Roberta Martin's life and remained so through the 1990s. Many early-twentieth-century church pastors and congregations rejected the newer gospel music. Some conser-

vative believers continued to suspect at the end of the century that not the Holy Spirit but some rather unholy spirits rode the syncopated rhythms and beats borrowed from secular black music. Also, some believers regretted or decried the paucity of doctrine in the lyrics of gospel music, in comparison with the lyrics of the hymns. This controversy reflected cultural and class differences, including education and regional origins, among the members of African American churches. Unlike many other gospel performers, Martin refused to secularize the performance of gospel music. She never viewed herself as an entertainer; she refused to appear where her name could be displayed on a marquee or where tickets were sold.

Martin developed a refined style of gospel singing and piano playing. With her group, Martin moved beyond the vocal traditions of early gospel, preferring the well-modulated voice over the "encumbered, raspy" (Boyer, 749) voice; she harmonized female high and second sopranos and alto with male first and second tenors and high baritone instead of depending on the low bass voice. Martin preferred the "aggressive rather than passive lead" (Boyer, 749) voice, supported by a background vocal response of humming rather than repetitions of the lead lyrics. The overall effect of her voicing was to create a uniquely mellow and smooth harmonic sound. This voicing was performed in the context of African American oral traditions captured in the "Baptist moan . . . ; the [Thomas A.] Dorsey bounce, the sanctified churches' syncopation, and a smidgen of semiclassical pretension" (Heilbut, quoted in William-Jones, "Roberta Martin: Spirit of an Era," 255). The moan evolved from the vocalized yet veiled complaints of African slaves. Dorsey's bounce captured the danceable rhythms of black music—with emphasis on the second and fourth beats of duple rhythms—that can be traced to West African cultures. One of Martin's innovations was to create the first all-star gospel ensemble in which each singer functioned as soloist and stylist as well as support. Martin influenced gospel piano style as well as singing. Her style was "marked more by nuance and refinement than virtuosity and flamboyance" (Boyer, 749). Her harmonic innovations included developing subtler chord progressions or substitution chords.

In August 1947, Roberta Martin met business owner and music salesperson James Austin, the father of one of her pianists, Lucy Smith Collier. (Austin's first wife, who died in 1927, was Viola Smith, the daughter of Pentecostal minister LUCY MADDEN SMITH.) Martin and Austin married four months later on December 31, 1947. James Austin was supportive of Martin's creative lifestyle, not interfering with the spontaneity of her creativity and the privacy she sought in order to compose. In 1948 the couple adopted a son, Leonard (also known as Sonny). Soon after the formation of this new family, Martin stopped traveling the gospel highway. Instead, she limited herself to composing, arranging, and managing her business and to recording with the group.

In 1939, Martin had opened the Roberta Martin Studio of Music, one of several publishing houses in Chicago's Black Belt, to publish gospel music composed by herself and others. She wisely maintained her own publishing rights to the songs the Roberta Martin Singers recorded, and she negotiated significant general advances on her royalties. Since Martin's publications were limited to the repertoire of the Roberta Martin singers, her song sheets were also a principle method of promoting and advertising her singing group. Managed first by Anna Winston and then by Leona Price, the business prospered until the era of xerography. After their marriage, Austin managed the financial operation of the studio, along with writing and arranging music, while Price managed the mail order and sales department. Price and Austin carried on the business after Martin's death.

From 1956 to 1968, Martin served as music director for her home congregation, Mount Pisgah Baptist Church. One of her crowning achievements was to direct, in 1960, a thousand-voice choir for the National Baptist Convention at Chicago's Coliseum, for which she also arranged the featured song delivered by Delois Barrett Campbell, "Grace Is Sufficient" by James Cleveland.

Roberta Martin was highly respected for her work in the recording industry. She received six gold records for selling one million or more copies of a song or album. Martin recorded with Savoy Records from 1958 until her death. Under her own name and with Fay Brown, Roberta Martin composed more than one hundred gospel songs, including her first gospel composition, "Try Jesus, He Satisfies" (1943), "God Is Still on the Throne" (1959), "No Other Help I Know" (1961), "Let It Be" (1959), and "Teach Me Lord" (1963). Martin published 280 songs during her lifetime, 51 of which she composed. She arranged 259 of these songs. Concerned about the work of others, Martin published the work of many composers, including Anna Shepherd, whose "Only a Look" became Martin's theme song and most famous publication.

Martin was a complex personality. Charismatic, charming, and intelligent, Martin, who stood 5' 5" or 5' 6," dressed and furnished her home with taste and in a fashion that reflected her success and status in the black middle class. She owned a considerable wardrobe, drove Cadillacs, and lived in comfortable homes. She was seen as a paragon of Christian generosity. Singers and musicians emphasize Martin's beauty and her winning smile, as well as her commitment to Christian values. Leona Price believed her to be introverted and "a meek and humble and fully dedicated Christian woman" (quoted in Williams-Jones and Reagon, "Conversations," 290) with a "tremendous wit and extremely subtle humor" (p. 295).

Roberta Martin died at Mercy Medical Center, following an anguishing three-year bout with cervical cancer, for which she resisted treatment, medication, and surgery. At the time of her death, Roberta Martin was living in the South Shore community of Chicago. More than fifty thousand African Americans viewed her body January 18, 1969, at Mount Pisgah Baptist Church in Chicago. She was buried in Burr Oak Cemetery in Alsip, Illinois, surrounded by the graves of her parents and siblings. Friends formed the Roberta Martin Benevolent Society to continue Martin's charitable work. As part of his mourning, James Austin composed and arranged "Soldier of the Cross Well Done" to capture the significance of Martin's commitment to Christianity.

For more than thirty years, Martin distinguished herself as a contralto, pianist, composer, arranger, publisher, distributor, organizer, director, and teacher of gospel groups and choirs. Many well-known gospel singers apprenticed with her. Moreover, she founded and operated the largest gospel music publishing house in Chicago, and she left what gospel historian Clayton L. Hannah calls "a portfolio of unduplicated gospel music" (quoted in Williams-Jones, "Roberta Martin," 255). Her work contributed to the development of the Chicago School of Gospel, created during the golden age of gospel music, 1945–60. In 1981, the Smithsonian Institution sponsored a conference honoring Martin by exploring her musical legacy.

Sources. Roberta Martin's birth date is differently reported. Two documents, her Wendell Phillips High School transcript and her 1928 marriage license, indicate 1906 as the year of birth. Horace Clarence Boyer's biography of Martin in *BWA* gives 1907 as the year; a Ph.D. dissertation by Irene V. Jackson, "Afro-American Gospel Music and Its Social Setting with Special Attention to Roberta Martin" (Wesleyan Univ., 1974), says she was born February 12, 1912, but does not provide documentation. Anthony Heilbut, *The Gospel Sound* (1985), is useful. Bernice Johnson Reagon, ed., *We'll Understand It Better By and By* (1992), includes Portia K. Maultsby, "The Impact of Gospel Music on the Secular Music Industry"; Anthony Heilbut, "If I Fail, You Tell The World I Tried"; Pearl Williams-Jones, "Roberta Martin: Spirit of an Era"; Horace Clarence Boyer, "Roberta Martin: Innovator of Modern Gospel"; and Pearl Williams-Jones and Bernice Johnson Reagon, "Conversations: Roberta Martin Singers Roundtable." Also useful are Bernice Johnson Reagon and Linn Shapiro, *The Roberta Martin Singers: The Legacy and the Music* (1982), and Paul Oliver, Max Harrison, and William Bolcom, *The New Grove: Gospel, Blues and Jazz (with Spirituals and Ragtime)* (1986). The 1981 Smithsonian Institution conference included a colloquium and a reconstruction concert series with Pearl Williams-Jones directing performers who had worked with Martin. The three concerts took place February 6, 7, and 8, 1981, in the Baird Auditorium of the Museum of Natural History of the Smithsonian, Washington, D.C. See Bernice Johnson Reagon, ed., *Black American Culture and Scholarship: Contemporary Issues* (1985), a collection of papers presented at Smithsonian Institution conferences. Recordings include *The Unforgettable Voice of Roberta Martin* (Savoy MG 14221), *What a Friend We Have in Jesus* (Apollo 238), *The Best of the Roberta Martin Singers* (Savoy SGL 7018), *From Out of Nowhere: The Roberta Martin Singers "Live"* (Savoy MG 14066), *God Is Still on the Throne* (Savoy 14031), and *The Original Roberta Martin Singers: Here This Sunday* (Kenwood 480).

PHILIP M. ROYSTER

MARTINEZ, MARIA DIAZ
October 31, 1952–October 8, 1990
SOCIAL WORKER, FOUNDING MEMBER OF SOCIAL SERVICE
AGENCY AND GRASS ROOTS ORGANIZATION

Maria Diaz Martinez worked toward the improvement of people's lives, both on a collective and an individual level, through various organizations, including Mujeres Latinas en Acción (Latin Women in Action), the first Latina women's agency in Chicago. Known to everyone as Maruca, Diaz was born in South Chicago. She was the firstborn of her mother Carmen Sanchez's second marriage, to Alejo Silva Diaz. Carmen Sanchez came to Chicago from Detroit via Montana; born in Mexico City, Alejo Silva Diaz arrived in Chicago from Oakland, California. Maria Diaz had older half siblings Marie, Shirley, Rudolph, and Angie; younger siblings Alicia and Anthony; and a younger half brother from her mother's third marriage, Celestino.

Mexicans began arriving in Chicago in the early twentieth century and came in increasing numbers after the 1920s.

Through the 1950s, South Chicago was a regular port of entry for Mexicans who then settled in Chicago; Gary, Indiana; and Indiana Harbor, Indiana. In 1955, the Diaz family moved to Chicago's Near West Side, in the vicinity of Hull-House, the settlement house formerly run by JANE ADDAMS. At that time the neighborhood was primarily Italian but also housed a large population of Scandinavian, German, Jewish, and Mexican people. In the early 1960s, however, eleven of the thirteen Hull-House buildings were razed to make space for the new public university, the University of Illinois at Chicago Circle (now the University of Illinois at Chicago); the work of the Hull-House social service agency was dispersed to various locations in the city. Many of the established families were forced to relocate; Diaz and her family moved to neighboring Pilsen, a Mexican enclave southwest of downtown Chicago.

Her experiences in various neighborhoods, hospitals, and schools awakened Maria Diaz to social consciousness and action. Born with bronchitis, she suffered from asthma and respiratory problems. By age six, she had already had a first operation, which improved her breathing but did not stop her chronic asthma attacks. During her hospital stays, she noticed the different treatment accorded Latinos compared to Anglos and the disadvantage of Spanish-speaking patients in the absence of interpreters. Diaz questioned these differences and remained unconvinced by her parents' explanation that the difference in treatment occurred because the Anglos had insurance.

Diaz's longing for social justice was augmented by having to attend Spaulding, a school for children with mental and physical handicaps. Her asthma was so severe that she could not attend public schools. She felt isolated and angry. She fought with the teachers because she felt the school's services were based on the parents' ability to pay the expensive tuition rather than

teachers' and administrators' desire to help the children. She felt the children deserved better care and attention from both teachers and parents.

Diaz's ordeals at hospitals also led her father to prohibit her and her siblings from learning Spanish. He reasoned that with English as their primary language, they would not have difficulties in school and would also be able to defend themselves at every level. Having labored in the farming, railroad, and mining industries, he believed that being a person of color and speaking with an accent were great handicaps in the United States. In Pilsen, the children were already experiencing name-calling from their Czechoslovakian, Polish, and Italian neighbors. In 1964 Diaz's parents were divorced. Her mother and the children moved from Pilsen west into Little Village. Although by the 1980s Little Village was another center of Mexican population, the Diaz family moved into what was then an entirely non-Latino neighborhood and were not welcomed by their neighbors. The children were rejected by business owners, and other forms of racism were apparent.

Diaz became a rebellious child. She had been very close to her father and found it difficult to cope with his absence after the divorce. She resented the treatment she experienced as a Mexican child with asthma. An angry child, she was frustrated at not being able to be as active as other children. After receiving constant calls from schools and visits from truant officers, her mother enrolled Diaz at St. Pius Catholic School, hoping she would become more disciplined. However, Diaz left after a heated fight with the nuns and did not return. She dropped out of school by eighth grade. Diaz rebelled against authority. Because her mother worked two or three jobs regularly to provide for the family, Diaz and her siblings were left to care for themselves. Without parental supervision, the children joined street gangs; Diaz became a member of the Spartanettes. She also ran away from home several times.

At age fifteen, Diaz became pregnant and was forced to marry the child's father, whose last name was Martinez. Her in-laws did not want the marriage, nor did she. At her parents' insistence, Diaz reluctantly married on February 14, 1968, at the height of U.S. involvement in Vietnam. Her husband was drafted into the U.S. Army shortly after their wedding, and Maria Martinez took advantage of her freedom, renouncing her responsibility as a mother. Around the same time, her sister Alicia also had a daughter and quit school to find a night job at a factory to support the child. Martinez, on the other hand, still spent a lot of time with her friends while Alicia cared for both her own child and Martinez's son, Danny.

During one of his leaves, Martinez's husband decided that Martinez should not continue this behavior and took her to live with him in Virginia where he was stationed. While in Virginia, Martinez attempted to organize the other mothers and house-wives living at the base. In her view, they were not given enough family time, the women had no venues for self-improvement, and the children were not receiving a good education. Although some women showed signs of support, the men on the base were opposed to her thinking, and nothing developed from her efforts. Martinez was miserable in Virginia. It was very difficult to be separated from her family, especially when her husband became abusive.

Her mother and siblings intervened, and despite her husband's objection, Martinez moved back to Chicago and into her mother's house around 1971. When her husband left the service, he pursued her, promising that he had changed and wishing to be close to Danny and a second son, born in Virginia, named Alejo, after her father. Although she preferred to separate, Martinez thought it was more important for her sons to enjoy their father. In 1972 Martinez had her third boy, whom she named José. She left her husband before José's first birthday and moved in with her mother for a short time. Then, through public assistance, employment, and help from her family, she moved into her own apartment. Martinez worked for stores, banks, laundromats, and a taffy apple company.

Around 1972, Martinez was diagnosed with cervical cancer, yet she remained an energetic and active woman, volunteering at different agencies and enrolling herself in school. During the many ordeals with her husband, Martinez began socializing with a group of people who were involved with a new education system in Pilsen.

Called the University without Walls, the school was an outpost of Northeastern Illinois University. It allowed Mexican Americans who had not completed their education to continue their studies. Martinez knew of the school through Maria Mangual, a close friend and a founding member of Mujeres Latinas en Acción. Martinez began to read voraciously on a wide range of subjects: social upheavals, the history of immigration in Pilsen, the parallels between older immigrants and more recent ones, the connections and similarities between racial groups, Jane Addams and the social service movement, Mexican history and culture. Although she was battling cancer, raising three boys, and had only an eighth grade education, she entered the University without Walls and obtained a bachelor's degree in social work.

Knowing that her children would be well cared for by her mother and sister, Martinez became more active in the Chicano movement. In the 1960s, Mexican Americans reclaimed the disparaging term Chicano and organized around a wide range of issues as migrant farm workers, disfranchised urban dwellers, workers without necessary immigration documents, and Spanish-speakers in an English-speaking country. She was a close friend of activist Rudy Lozano and admired his strength and commitment toward the Mexican community in Chicago. Both she and her sister Alicia Amador remained active in Lozano's political career as an aldermanic candidate until he was murdered in 1983.

During this time, Martinez also joined organizations and volunteered with the budding Mujeres Latinas en Acción. Martinez is remembered as a founding member of this agency, along with a core group that included Maria Mangual, Gwen Stern, and Hilda Frontani. The women realized the strong need for a women's agency after they attended a women's leadership conference in South Bend, Indiana. Because existing agencies provided services for men and boys only, Maria Mangual and Hilda Frontani decided to begin holding conferences that would respond to women's needs. From their efforts, in conjunction with other women who supported and volunteered, the idea to establish an agency arose.

It was extremely difficult to establish Mujeres Latinas. Representatives of male-dominated community organizations accused them of divisiveness, church personnel claimed they encouraged women to divorce their husbands, and many neighborhood women were indifferent. Eventually El Centro de la Causa, a youth organization in Pilsen, offered use of a rectory. Mujeres Latinas organizers shoveled out trash left behind by drug dealers and heroin addicts, cleaned up, debated what services and programs were needed, and opened in 1973. They were accused of competing as women against other organizations for scarce funds. They began to receive hate mail. They were called bra-burners, men-haters, communists, lesbians. Many received threats, and some were physically beaten. Six months after the agency opened, their building was torched. Though the fire broke the spirits of many of the women, a core of approximately ten members maintained the vision and began anew. They moved the agency to another location that began as a drop-in center for runaway girls and offered various classes and workshops.

In 1974 Martinez began volunteering at Mujeres Latinas. When she received a bachelor's degree in social work, she became its first paid staff member. Since Mujeres Latinas still had no funding, another agency, Latino Youth, offered to fund Martinez to work at Mujeres Latinas with girls attending Benito Juarez High School. She worked as a crisis intervener, counselor, and receptionist. Martinez also did outreach around the neighborhood and the parks where teens hung out to stop the girls from getting involved in gangs, drugs, or prostitution. For the board members, this task sometimes entailed becoming a foster parent for the girls. An effective peer counselor, Martinez "put a face on the agency" (interview with Maria Mangual). She gave young girls jobs at the agency, and with the jobs, responsibility.

Because Mujeres Latinas was unique, its founders knew little about obtaining funds, organizing conferences, or convincing other women of the need to take control of their lives. They were an amalgamation from all walks of life: housewives, college students, and socialists. Some had organizational experience, many did not. They joined the executive boards of other organizations in order to learn the many aspects of running an agency. They went to such agencies as Latino Youth and Pilsen Mental Health; however their participation was not always welcome, and initially they were treated condescendingly by the men who ran various agencies.

Mujeres Latinas grew from nothing to a strong force in the community. Because they had no funding, they had sparse furniture and no phone. Martinez always kept a cup on her desk into which people dropped dimes so that she could use the pay phone to call clients and procure references and resources. Initially, Mujeres Latinas offered GED (General Education Development Tests for high school equivalency) and English language classes, had a food cooperative, gave workshops, and opened during the evenings as a drop-in center. By 2000, it was preparing to move into a new, expanded building and offered seven programs for women and men, girls and boys, around domestic violence, Latina leadership, sexual assault counseling, parent support, and child care.

In 1976, Martinez enrolled at Roosevelt University, where she received a master's degree in social work. While in school, Martinez left Mujeres Latinas, but she returned as an executive board member in 1978. Besides Mujeres Latinas, Martinez also worked for United Way in downtown Chicago, where she was a proposals analyst, deciding which agencies would receive funding. She sought to educate funders to distribute funds more equally among the various neighborhoods, dispelling stereotypes and challenging the fear and negativity attributed to African American and Mexican neighborhoods. She also worked at the Chicago Area Project (CAP), founded in 1925 to improve treatment of juvenile offenders and low-income people at the community level. Martinez later worked for the Illinois Migrants Council, where she traveled to Hoopston, Illinois, and investigated the conditions of the workers there. She advocated for insurance, better pay, increased rights, and a better education system. Just before she died, she was about to begin working at the Mexican American Legal Defense and Education Fund. Throughout her life and career, Martinez never stopped being part of the Mexican community. Although she worked downtown and moved in 1987 to the suburb of Oak Park, she remained very active in Pilsen and with Mexican people.

Martinez initially had overcome the cervical cancer, but in time the cancer returned. She battled through it on her own, not wanting to burden others. Her family noticed that she was very ill at times, but Martinez claimed that her fatigue was due to a flu or other sickness. After medical treatments or surgery she returned to work rather than resting at home. On October 6, 1990, she drove herself to the emergency room at West Suburban Hospital in Oak Park, though she was in terrible pain. Within two days she was placed on a respirator. Knowing that, with her prognosis, she would not want to continue living, her family decided to cut off all life support.

Martinez is buried at St. Mary's Cemetery. Her wake was held in Pilsen, and Alderman Jesús García, a close friend, gave the eulogy. Many people walked the long procession to the cemetery along with her, feeling both the loss of a friend and a great loss to the community. Her friends and fellow activists noted that she never forgot where she came from, nor did she let her degrees and jobs redefine who she was. They recalled her infectious laugh, her strength and force of will to continue despite all obstacles. She was a woman who knew very little fear and confronted gang members loitering outside her home as well as corporate executives downtown. Throughout her life, she strove to provide guidance, comfort, and advice to others. She lobbied among her neighbors to work together to improve the appearance and conditions of the community in Little Village. She made an issue of the acrid racism she faced in Oak Park. She raised her voice and she sought opportunities for herself and others. She strove throughout her life for social justice. In 1998 Mujeres Latinas en Acción, the organization she helped found, instituted the Maria "Maruca" Martinez Community Service Award.

Sources. For biographical information, Martha Espinoza interviewed Maria Martinez's sister Alicia Amador, as well as Linda Coronado, Lupe Lozano, Maria Mangual, and Virginia Martinez. Additional information about Mujeres Latinas en Acción came from a video, *Maria Mangual* (n.d.). The video and Mujeres Latinas records are kept within the agency itself. Information on the Chicago Area Project is available at CHS. Information on Mexican Americans is found in Jorge Casuso and Eduardo Camacho, "Latino Chicago," in *Ethnic Chicago: A Multicultural Portrait*, ed. Melvin G. Holli and Peter d'A. Jones (4th ed., 1995); Carlos E. Cortés, "Mexicans," in *Harvard Encyclopedia of American Ethnic Groups*, ed. Stephan Thernstrom (1980); Louise Año Nuevo Kerr, "The Chicano Experience in Chicago: 1920–1970 (Ph.D. diss., Univ. of Illinois at Chicago Circle, 1976); and "Mexican Chicago: Chicano Assimilation Aborted, 1939–1954," in *The Ethnic Frontier: Essays in the History of Group Survival in Chicago and the Midwest*, ed. Melvin G. Holli and Peter d'A. Jones (1977). Glen E. Holt and Dominic A. Pacyga, *Chicago: A Historical Guide to the Neighborhoods, the Loop and South Side* (1979), is helpful.

MARTHA ELENA ESPINOZA

MAYER, MARIA GOEPPERT
June 28, 1906–February 20, 1972
THEORETICAL PHYSICIST

Maria Goeppert Mayer received the Nobel Prize in physics in 1963 for her work on the shell model of the nucleus, which she did while at the University of Chicago's Institute for Nuclear Studies (INS) and Argonne National Laboratory. Mayer was the third woman in history to win the prize in a science category, the second after Marie Curie to be awarded the laureate in physics. Her husband, Joseph Mayer, had a faculty appointment at the University of Chicago in chemistry. Mayer made her most important scientific contributions in the years from 1946 to 1959 in association with the INS and Argonne Laboratory, although, as a result of academic conventions at the time that prohibited husbands and wives from both having faculty appointments at the same institution, she never held a full-time paid position.

Goeppert was born in Kattowicz, Germany (now Poland), the only child of Friedrich and Maria (Wolff) Goeppert. In 1910 her father assumed the post of professor of pediatrics at Georgia Augusta University in Göttingen, and Goeppert spent most of her youth in the old university town. Her mother had been a

FIG. 69. *Maria Goeppert Mayer, awarded the Nobel Prize in physics in 1963, at her desk at the University of Chicago.*

teacher before her marriage, and Goeppert was actively encouraged by her father to look beyond the confines of a typical woman's career and to develop her scientific curiosity. Goeppert remembered her father preparing special glasses for her at age seven so she might watch an eclipse of the sun; they took science walks together, collected fossils, and she learned the nomenclature of plants and trees. Maria Goeppert attended the *Höhere Töchterschule* until 1921, when she entered the *Frauenstudium*, a private school established by a group of suffragists to prepare young women for university entrance examinations. Her father played a central role in Goeppert's decision to take a degree in mathematics at Göttingen University, which she entered in 1924.

Although Goeppert began in mathematics at Göttingen, she subsequently switched to physics and took her degree under the mathematical physicist Max Born. She developed a close scientific relationship with both Born and experimental physicist James Franck. Born and Franck together set the scene for Mayer's entire scientific career. Her early work reflected Born's emphasis on the use of abstract mathematical theory to interpret nature; over time, her work came more to follow Franck's approach in its shift away from mathematical formalism toward physical intuition and more reliance on experimental results. With the exception of one semester spent at Cambridge University, Goeppert's entire education was acquired in Göttingen.

Her 1930 doctoral dissertation outlined a theory of double-photon emission or absorption in atoms, based on P. A. M. Dirac's quantum mechanical theory of radiation and matter. Physicist Eugene Wigner later referred to her dissertation as "a masterpiece of clarity and concreteness" (*Physics Today*, 77).

While working on her degree at Göttingen, Goeppert met and married Joseph Edward Mayer, an American chemist who had taken a Ph.D. degree at the University of California, Berkeley, and was in Göttingen on a Rockefeller International Education Board Fellowship for 1929–30. After their marriage in January 1930, Mayer completed her doctoral degree, and she and her husband moved to Baltimore, Maryland, where Joseph Mayer took up a position in the chemistry department at Johns Hopkins University.

Although Mayer was more skilled in the new field of quantum mechanics than anyone else at Johns Hopkins, she had no regular academic appointment for the nine years she and her husband were there. She taught occasional courses in the physics and chemistry departments and collaborated with her husband and the theoretical chemical physicist Karl F. Herzfeld. Most of her research during the years 1930 to 1939 was therefore in the fields of chemical physics and physical chemistry. While she explored more classical topics with Herzfeld, Mayer's work with Joseph Mayer centered on the application of quantum mechanics to chemistry. These collaborations exposed Mayer to the use of experimental data in the development of theory and taught her how to apply mathematical talents to specific physical problems.

In 1938 Mayer began work with Alfred Lee Sklar (a student of Herzfeld) on the quantum mechanical determination of the structure of benzene, one of the first calculations of energy levels for a complex molecule from strictly theoretical principles. This work was further detailed in 1939, when Sklar collaborated with Hertha Sponer, Lothar Nordheim, and Edward Teller on a systematic analysis of the benzene spectrum. This became the method most commonly used, and Mayer was generally regarded, between 1939 and 1949, as a specialist in the analysis of the spectra of complex systems.

The Mayers' two children were both born in Baltimore, Maria Ann (known as Marianne) in 1933 and Peter Conrad in 1938. Mayer became an American citizen the year her daughter was born. Mayer took her responsibilities as a parent seriously, and although she tried to emulate her father in not restricting her children's natural inclinations, she also worried about the amount of time she spent away from them. Although they had limited means, the Mayers always had part-time household help and a series of European-born nannies.

In 1939 Joseph Mayer's contract at Johns Hopkins was not renewed. Joseph Mayer was immediately offered a position in chemistry at Columbia University, and in 1939 the Mayers moved north, purchasing a house in Leonia, New Jersey, near several colleagues from the university. The following year the textbook the Mayers had written in collaboration, *Statistical Mechanics* (1940), appeared, representing the work they had done in the 1930s. The book made Joseph Mayer's reputation as a theoretical chemist, although it had very little impact on Maria Mayer's career. It seems to have been commonly and erroneously assumed that her role was strictly clerical.

Maria Mayer was not offered an appointment in physics, but her lack of an official position at Columbia did not in any way prevent her involvement in research. Prompted by conversations with physicist Enrico Fermi, she calculated an accurate prediction of the chemical behaviors of a number of elements beyond uranium that had not yet been discovered. In addition to research work at Columbia, she began teaching mathematics and science, in 1942, at Sarah Lawrence College, her first regular paid position.

After the outbreak of World War II, Mayer was asked to join Harold Urey's group, the Substitute Alloy Materials Laboratory (SAM), which was devoted to solving the problem of isotope separation for the American nuclear weapons project, the Manhattan Project. Mayer worked on several projects, including photochemical separation, chemical separation, and an analysis of the structure of uranium hexafluoride (UF_6) from measurements of its spectrum. Joseph Mayer did not work on the Manhattan Project; because of his work at the Naval Ordinance Laboratory in Aberdeen, Maryland, throughout most of the war he was home in New Jersey only one day a week. As a result of this separation and security restrictions on discussions of her work, Mayer was working for the first time without her husband's intellectual and emotional support. Later she regarded this period as the beginning of her career as an independent professional scientist.

In 1946 both Mayers were invited to join the University of Chicago, which had been the center of a very lively scientific community during the war. In 1946 the university formed three interdisciplinary scientific institutes as a way of bringing together on a permanent basis many of the participants in the Manhattan Project. Mayer and her husband were both offered positions in the Institute for Nuclear Studies. Other members included Fermi, Urey, Willard Libby, Leo Szilard, and Edward Teller. Mayer was appointed voluntary associate professor of physics because of unwritten anti-nepotism rules. In this capacity she participated as a full member of the physics department, teaching, directing graduate students, serving on various committees, and, eventually, voting at meetings.

In addition to the INS, the University of Chicago was also home to Argonne National Laboratory. Robert G. Sachs, her former student at Johns Hopkins, offered Mayer a research position there. She subsequently worked half-time as senior physicist at Argonne and half-time as a member of the INS. With the assistance of her colleagues, she began for the first time to pay serious attention to questions of nuclear physics. Although her approach to the subject was not systematic, she learned much from the discussions going on around her, and this arrangement proved to be an advantage for Mayer in the long run. Unburdened by the conventional notions of the nucleus shared by her colleagues, she was able to bring an alternative view to bear on problems of nuclear structure.

In 1945 the common understanding of nuclear structure was based on George Gamow's and Niels Bohr's assumption that the nucleus behaves like a liquid drop in which individual neutrons and protons cannot be distinguished. Early in 1947, however, Mayer came across clear experimental evidence suggesting that the nucleus consists of individual particles occupying different energy levels or shells. She found that isotopes with particular "magic numbers" of neutrons or protons were unusually abundant in nature and therefore must be unusually stable. The liquid drop model could not account for this phenomenon. Although Mayer could find no satisfactory theoretical explanation for the particular numbers of nucleons in stable isotopes, she published a summary of all the evidence leading to the conclusion that nucleons (neutrons and protons) occupy discrete energy levels in the nucleus.

Since 1933 nuclear physicists had recognized the existence of the magic numbers but could not explain them. Mayer persisted in looking for a way to account for the magic numbers, and sometime early in 1949 she solved the problem with the help of a suggestion made by Fermi. Mayer realized that nucleon energy levels are modified by the interaction between the spin and the orbital angular momentum of the nucleon, an effect called spin-orbit coupling. It is a strong effect for nucleons and, when this is taken into account, the magic numbers can be explained readily. Mayer first published a brief account of her theory in June 1949 and a more complete description followed the next year.

Mayer's nuclear shell model quickly gained wide acceptance. It had great value to experimentalists, because it could account for many of the newly measured properties of atomic nuclei. The same model was proposed simultaneously and independently in Germany by Otto Haxel, Hans Jensen, and Hans Suess. Mayer subsequently wrote, with Jensen, the primary text on the shell model, *Elementary Theory of Nuclear Shell Structure* (1955). The following year Maria Mayer was elected to the prestigious National Academy of Sciences.

Mayer was involved in various political activities throughout her career and was known for her positions of balance and moderation. Unlike most of the scientific refugees who came to the United States in the 1930s to escape Nazi persecution, she came voluntarily. She became active in an organization formed to give aid to displaced German scientists in the 1930s. She was also active in 1945 and 1946 in the scientists' campaign against military control of nuclear research and energy.

By the late 1950s the Mayers found that much of the early excitement of working at Chicago had dwindled. Fermi had died in 1954, and Urey and Teller had both moved on. The University of Chicago finally offered Mayer a salary for the first time in 1959. Nevertheless, when the Mayers were both offered full-time paid professorships at a new graduate research program established as part of the University of California, they left Chicago and moved to La Jolla in 1960. Shortly after they arrived in California in 1960, Maria Mayer suffered a stroke. Although she continued to work, and particularly to teach, she never fully regained her health, and her scientific contributions after she relocated to La Jolla were minimal. In 1963 she and Jensen equally shared the Nobel Prize in physics for their work on the nuclear shell model. Maria Mayer died in 1972 of heart failure after having been in poor health for a number of years.

Mayer's scientific output, though not of great quantity, was unusually consistent in quality. Her contributions to atomic physics and chemistry early in her career have not been generally recognized, yet it is remarkable that so many of these mathematically derived theories have retained their physical validity. Mayer's theories in almost all of her early work have served as a solid theoretical base for later development. Her later work, the nuclear shell model, while no longer viewed as valid for all nuclei, still dominates any study of nuclear structure and systematics. A series of lectures was established in her name at the University of California, San Diego, in 1974. The Maria Goeppert Mayer Award is given each year by the American Physics Society to recognize the achievements of women physicists.

Sources. The Maria Goeppert Mayer Papers are in the Spec. Coll. of the Mandeville Library at the Univ. of California, San Diego, as are the Joseph Mayer Papers. Mayer's papers include several hundred letters she wrote to her mother in Germany during the 1930s, describing her reactions to her new home and providing a good picture of the Mayers' daily lives. Among Mayer's scientific publications not cited above, those of particular note include "Über Elementarakte mit zwei Quantensprüngen" (Fundamental processes with two quantum transitions), *Annalen der Physik*, vol. 9, 1931; "Double Beta-Disintegration," *Physical Review*, vol. 48, 1935; (with Alfred L. Sklar) "Calculations of the Lower Excited Levels of Benzene," *Journal of Chemical Physics*, vol. 6, 1938; "Rare-Earth and Transuranic Elements," *Physical Review*, vol. 60, 1941; "On Closed in Nuclei," *Physical Review*, vol. 74, 1948; "Nuclear Configurations in the Spin-Orbit Coupling Model," *Physical Review*, vol. 78, 1950. Mayer's own most complete account of her scientific work can be found in her Nobel address, "The Shell Model," *Nobel Lectures: Physics* (1972). Maria Mayer, "The Shell Model," a less technical discussion of her discovery, appears in *Science*, September 4, 1974. Robert Sachs has written two biographical memoirs, "Maria Goeppert Mayer," National Academy of Sciences, *Biographical Memoirs* (1979), and "Maria Goeppert Mayer," in *Remembering the University of Chicago: Teachers, Scientists, and Scholars,* ed. Edward Shils (1991). The first includes a complete bibliography of Mayer's published work, while the second includes more detail about Mayer's Chicago years. The most complete general account of Mayer's life is Joan Dash, *A Life of One's Own: Three Gifted Women and the Men They Married* (1973). Appraisals of Mayer's work by her peers may be found in Eugene Wigner, "Maria Goeppert Mayer," *Physics Today*, May 1972, and Harold Urey, "Maria Goeppert Mayer (1906–1972)," *American Philosophical Society Yearbook 1972* (1973). For a detailed analysis of Mayer's scientific work, see Karen E. Johnson, "Maria Goeppert Mayer," *Dictionary of Scientific Biography, Supplement II* (1990).

KAREN E. JOHNSON

McCLAIN, LEANITA
October 2, 1951–May 28, 1984
JOURNALIST

Leanita McClain joined the staff of the *Chicago Tribune* newspaper in 1973. She became the first African American member of the editorial board in 1982 and its second black staff columnist, making her the highest ranking African American woman in the *Tribune's* then 137-year history. During the early 1980s, McClain was the most promising African American journalist on the national scene and regularly in demand as a speaker at universities, journalism association meetings, and television broadcasts. She epitomized professionalism and journalistic commitment to her craft by consistently striving for a balanced portrayal in her persistent coverage of Chicago's volatile racial and political climate. National attention was focused on McClain's candid and controversial assessments of Chicago's well-publicized racial polarities, especially during the candidacy and tenure of Chicago's first black mayor, Harold Washington.

Ironically, although she won wide acclaim and numerous honors, McClain was often ostracized by a contingency of both black and white readers, who saw her writings as biased. Black readers were often agitated over what some of them viewed as McClain's lack of cultural allegiance, and white readers, by contrast, resented McClain's frank and revealing commentary about the true nature of racial and political relationships in Chicago. In addition to her eloquent rhetorical style and deft journalistic skills, McClain had the advantage of being a native Chicagoan who knew, firsthand, its history of racial problems.

Leanita McClain was the youngest of three daughters born in Chicago to Elizabeth, a homemaker, and Lloyd McClain, a factory worker. She was raised in a South Side housing project, named for the pioneer African American female journalist IDA B. WELLS-BARNETT. McClain attended Chicago's Doolittle Elementary School, Lucy Flower High School for girls, and Chicago State University. McClain's sisters became public school teachers, but McClain shifted her focus to writing and earned a full scholarship to the Medill School of Journalism at Northwestern University, Evanston, Illinois.

McClain had always been a high achiever, and her history of scholarly excellence continued through graduate study at Northwestern; in 1973, just prior to graduation, she was rewarded with an internship at the *Chicago Tribune*. Following graduation, the *Tribune* offered her a full-time position as general assignment reporter. Success, acceptance, and promotions followed rapidly. In less than two years, she advanced to the copy desk, where her accomplishments earned her a fine reputation and more challenging opportunities, first at the picture desk and later in the "Perspective" department. While at the *Tribune*, McClain met and married fellow black journalist Clarence Page in 1974. The marriage ended in divorce in 1982.

McClain scaled the *Tribune's* journalistic ladder rapidly. She adhered to her youthful pattern of achievement, confronted each new challenge with enthusiasm, and received continued accolades and promotions. In barely ten years she moved through the ranks of assistant and then full "Perspective" section editor, occasional and then weekly columnist, editorial board, and twice-weekly columnist. McClain presented her commentary in a fresh, young, journalistic voice that conveyed her disappointment in America's rampant social ills, but by contrast, articulated the hopes of many readers who felt that there could be a better and stronger America. The strident tones and rhetorical style of her columns caught the public's attention, and McClain quickly garnered a captive audience both within the confines of the media as well as the population at large.

In addition to her successful career at the *Tribune*, McClain had won, by the time she was thirty-two, honors, recognition, and awards from many professional organizations. In 1982 she won the Peter Lisagor Award for Exemplary Journalism from the Headline Club (the Chicago chapter of Sigma Delta Chi, the national journalism honorary fraternity). In 1983 she received the "top award for commentary" (Page, *A Foot in Each World*, 3) by the Chicago Association for Black Journalists and the Kizzy Award for outstanding black women role models in Chicago. That same year she participated in ABC television's *Nightline* talk show to discuss the state of black America since the 1963 "March on Washington," staged by hundreds of thousands of civil rights advocates. In March 1984, she was selected as one of the ten most outstanding working women in America by *Glamour* magazine.

McClain first catapulted into national prominence in 1980 when *Newsweek* published her essay, "The Middle-Class Black's Burden" on the "My Turn" opinion page. Based upon her seven-year career as a journalist, McClain candidly stated her case as an increasingly agitated and isolated member of the new emerging population of black baby boomer professionals, who often defined their dual and complex racial existence as living between two worlds. McClain wrote: "I run a gauntlet between two worlds, and I am cursed and blessed by both; I can also be used by both. If I am a token in my downtown office, so am I at my cousin's church tea. I assuage white guilt. I disprove black inadequacy and prove to my parent's generation that their patience was indeed a virtue. . . . I have a foot in each world, but I cannot fool myself about either. I can see the transparent deceptions of some whites and the bitter hopelessness of some blacks. I know how tenuous my grip on one way of life is, and how strangling the grip of the other way of life can be" (p. 21).

McClain personalized her own racial dilemma as a microcosm of the larger population of African American professionals who grappled with the cultural disparity of their own educational and economic affluence against the backdrop of poverty and illiteracy stifling the lives of their families, friends, and neighbors. The sensitivity McClain displayed in exposing the rupture in America's race relations was also a personal source of anguish for her. Though visibly African American, McClain acknowledged her "off-white trappings" (Campbell, 69)—light skin, green eyes, freckles, and sandy hair emanating from her mixed African American, American Indian, and European ancestry. She had struggled long with the problem of personal identity and the ever-looming inequality of being Black in America; both were unresolved at the time of her death.

Her essays revealed a journalist who was as concerned with Chicago's pervasive air of crime and punishment, the state of education, and home and family issues as with her more familiar focus on race and politics. She wrote articles like the October 1981 cover story in *Chicago* magazine, "Can Our Schools Be Saved?" and others in the *Chicago Tribune*: "The CHA [Chicago Housing Authority], My Alma Mater" and "Pathetic State of Chicago Schools." But it was her focus on race and politics that stirred up a national controversy, when, in 1983, she unveiled a forthright portrait of Chicago's race relations and how they impacted the political scene.

McClain wrote numerous articles about the political landscape in Chicago, but her columns took on a new fervor as she became infused with the intensity of Chicago's politics during Harold Washington's campaign for mayor. Though Chicago had always been a political hotbed, and McClain had addressed many of its most volatile issues in *Tribune* columns like "A Corner-Tavern Fight in the Council" and "Media Ignorance is Showing," the candidacy of its first African American mayor stirred up new levels of racial animosity and public sparring. Just after Harold Washington won his first election, she published her personal retrospective account of the climate of the Washington campaign in the July 24, 1983, edition of the *Washington Post*; the editors titled her essay: "How Chicago Taught Me to

Hate Whites." Reaction to the national exposure given to McClain's professional tensions and personal anguish was local and national, immediate and volatile.

McClain saw the campaign as a "race war" and said so in her article. She admitted to the overwhelming sense of betrayal she felt when white colleagues with whom she had socialized and formed friendships, along with a "horrified white Chicago," seemed to resent Washington's primary victory and ultimate election to the office of mayor. The persistent reference to African Americans as "the blacks," a reference that, to McClain, permeated the environment and identified her, along with her entire cultural group, as "just another nigger," sent her into an emotional tailspin and prompted her to write the article. McClain's despair was evident in her words: "*The* blacks. It is the article that offends. The words are held out like a foul-smelling sock transported two-fingered at the end of an outstretched arm to the hamper while the nose is pinched shut." She closed the article by admitting that she no longer held any hope for a cultural melting pot. "This affair has cemented my journalist's acquired cynicism, robbing me of most of my innate black hope for true integration."

Reprisals were swift. McClain and the *Tribune* were inundated with telephone calls from angry readers. A majority bloc of the Chicago City Council censured McClain and demanded an apology to its Chicago constituency. Chicago radio personality John Madigan devoted several radio commentaries to denouncing McClain's article and recommended her termination from the *Tribune*. Hate mail filled three cardboard boxes. By contrast, however, there were those who understood McClain's sense of betrayal and supported her pointed commentary; once again, she was the voice of the unheard masses of black Americans who, like McClain, felt mounting frustration at the bitter racial animosities expressed in the aftermath of the Washington election. Ultimately, for McClain, the turmoil was unbearable. Less than a year later, on May 28, 1984, she committed suicide by taking an overdose of the drugs prescribed for her sporadic depression. She was eulogized at Zion Temple Missionary Baptist Church on Chicago's South Side and buried in Burr Oak Cemetery in Alsip, Illinois.

The professional stresses of playing the dual role she depicted in her article, "The Middle-Class Black's Burden," coupled with her ongoing bouts of personal depression, were finally overwhelming. Although McClain had occasionally sought professional counseling for her mounting sense of frustration at the futility of expending energy to improve race relations in Chicago, as well as her personal identity crises, she ultimately fell victim to the ongoing tensions of her life, which included the death of her four-year-old nephew, DeLaurence. McClain spoke publicly about the stresses assailing her life and specifically cited the pressure of being a role model: "Being the first black editor of Perspective, . . . I knew that if I did not succeed, there probably never would be another black editor at the *Tribune*" (Locke, *Chicago Defender*, May 31, 1984).

With a specific focus on McClain's suicide, *Washington Post* columnist Kevin Klose conducted an investigation of the pressures confronting black professionals in white America. He interviewed African American Harvard psychiatrist Alvin Poussaint, who commented on the multiple stresses confronting

McClain and noted that both the racial and cultural isolation she faced were unique to the new vanguard of black professionals. In addition to the strain posed by the racial animosity directed at her by a hostile white readership, McClain also faced an intraracial cultural struggle from the African American community, predicated upon her light skin tone. Dr. Poussaint assessed the duality of her dilemma when he noted the criticism she faced from black people who perceived her success as based as much on skin color as ability, contrasted with whites who saw her as biased because of her blackness. Klose summarized his investigative findings in the *Post* article: "These racial pioneers may possess special reservoirs of eloquence, as did McClain. But they must withstand enormous strains of isolation that whites seldom encounter in achieving similar success" ("Tormented Black Rising Star").

Despite the emotional turmoil of her life, McClain made significant contributions. As an editorial writer for the *Chicago Tribune*, she used her journalistic talents to speak for a new audience of young black professionals and working class people who were disturbed at the state of race relations in Chicago. Additionally, she spoke for whites who felt that the continued emphasis on race in Chicago politics was often at the expense of other equally critical public concerns. On a different level, McClain's suicide brought to national attention the severe toll exacted by racial polarization, especially on a new generation of future leaders in America, and a psychological profile of the danger signs. At McClain's death, the Chicago City Council, which had earlier censured her, voted unanimously to pass a resolution eulogizing her. The Reverend George Riddick, vice-president of Chicago's Operation Push organization, remembered McClain as "one of the most gifted and versatile artists in her field" (Locke, 22).

Sources. McClain's published articles include "How Chicago Taught Me to Hate Whites," *Washington Post*, July 24, 1983; "Can Our Schools Be Saved?" *Chicago*, October 1981; and "The Middle-Class Black's Burden," *Newsweek*, October 31, 1980. A collection of her articles, *A Foot in Each World: Essays and Articles* (1986), was edited by Clarence Page. McClain is listed in *BWA*. Obituaries can be found in the *CT*, May 30, 1984; *Time* magazine, June 11, 1984; and *Newsweek* magazine, June 11, 1984. Articles about her include Bebe Moore Campbell, "To Be Black, Gifted, and Alone," *Savvy*, December 1984; Kevin Klose, "Tormented Black Rising Star, Dead by Her Own Hand," *Washington Post*, August 5, 1984; "The Inside Story on Leanita McClain," *Chicago Defender*, August 2, 1984; Theophilus Green, "Psychotherapist's Corner: Regarding Stress and Suicide," *Chicago Defender*, July 7, 1984; A. S. Doc Young, "The Death of a Journalist," *Los Angeles Sentinel*, June 14, 1984; M. Jean Terrell and Johnnie C. Cravens Jr., "Letters to the Editor," *Chicago Defender*, June 11, 1984; "Chicago Journalist Takes Life," *Los Angeles Sentinel*, June 11, 1984; Karin E. English, "Insight: Anger and Leanita McClain," *Chicago Defender*, June 5, 1984; Henry Locke, "Mourn Death of Noted Journalist," and Chinta Strausberg, "Say McClain's Despondency Led to Apparent Suicide," both in *Chicago Defender*, May 31, 1984. "Bibliography on Leanita McClain" is included in John Ponciano's *Journeys: A Project That Looks at the Life of Leanita McClain as a Metaphor of Success for Minorities* (1993).

B. J. BOLDEN

McCORMICK, EDITH ROCKEFELLER
August 31, 1872–August 25, 1932

PHILANTHROPIST, SOCIETY LEADER, JUNGIAN ANALYST

Born into one of the wealthiest families in the world and judged the richest woman in the United States during the 1920s, Edith Rockefeller McCormick was the top society leader in Chicago in the early 1900s. She was born in Cleveland, Ohio, the second daughter of John Davison Rockefeller, founder and owner of Standard Oil Company, and Laura Celestia (Spelman) Rockefeller, a school teacher, abolitionist, and supporter of the Woman's Christian Temperance Union and Baptist missionary work. The Rockefeller family moved to New York City when Edith was a young teenager. As a child and young woman, she loved intellectual pursuits: reading books, studying languages, and playing the cello. She was raised a Baptist as her parents wished. Shielded from public exposure, she was educated by private tutors until she attended Rye Academy, a girls' boarding school in New York.

On November 26, 1895, Edith Rockefeller married one of her brothers' schoolmates, Harold McCormick, son of wealthy Chicago business leader Cyrus H. McCormick, inventor of the reaper, and NETTIE FOWLER McCORMICK. Harold McCormick went to work for his father's company, and the couple moved to Council Bluffs, Iowa, where he was to train in the business by managing a branch. After spending two years in Iowa, the McCormicks returned to Chicago, moving into a forty-one room mansion on the Gold Coast, an elite neighborhood on the city's Near North Side. The mansion was a gift from Edith McCormick's father, and she decorated it lavishly, displaying rare pieces of furniture and accessories throughout. She was a connoisseur of fine jewelry, art, rugs, and antiques, and a collector of rare books. The substantial work involved in the upkeep of the mansion required a staff of at least twenty servants.

The McCormicks had five children: John D. Rockefeller (1897–1901), who died at age four from scarlet fever; Harold Fowler McCormick (1898–1973); Muriel (1902–59); Mathilde (1905–47); and Edith, born in 1903, who died before her first birthday. As a memorial to their son John, the McCormicks founded the John McCormick Institute for Infectious Diseases in Chicago in 1903. Under the institute's auspices, a cure for scarlet fever was eventually discovered. Edith McCormick was vitally involved with the development of the institute, assisting with its architectural planning.

From her mansion with its sumptuous furnishings and priceless collections, Edith Rockefeller McCormick reigned as the queen of Chicago society in the early 1900s, taking over the role from BERTHA HONORÉ PALMER, who preferred by that time to be at her home in Newport, Rhode Island, and then in Florida. There was no competition for McCormick; she was by far the wealthiest woman in Chicago. She had the etiquette and poise of royalty, traits that qualified her as the first lady of the city. McCormick enjoyed entertaining guests from upper-class society, often including members of royal families. At her dinner parties, place cards were set out with guests' names written in gold; the menus were in French. Her dining room could seat two hundred guests. She enforced only one house rule: she did not serve alcohol in her home because she had made a pledge to her father on her wedding day that she would not do so.

McCormick was easily able to fill the role of philanthropist expected of Chicago's social leaders, giving large sums of money and great amounts of time to many social and cultural causes. One of McCormick's earliest ventures into philanthropy was her support of Chicago's Juvenile Court system, established in 1899. Legislation authorized the appointment of juvenile probation officers as an arm of the Juvenile Court, but had not allotted funds to pay them. McCormick stepped forward to help fund the work of the probation officers.

In 1909, she began her support of the Art Institute of Chicago. That year the Art Institute's board founded Friends of American Art, a women's auxiliary that would provide funds for the yearly acquisition of works by American artists. Edith McCormick became a charter member of the group, making generous contributions over the years and lending pieces from her personal art collection for display at the Art Institute.

Much of her energy during the first two decades of the twentieth century, however, was focused on bringing opera to Chicago. Both she and her husband were avid opera fans; and in 1909, along with other wealthy Chicago and New York opera lovers, they founded the Grand Opera Company, Chicago's first. Although Harold McCormick became the president of the board of the Grand Opera Company, Chicagoans agreed that Edith McCormick was the real force behind the company's popularity and growth. After a year of preparation and fund-raising, the Chicago opera company opened its first season with *Aida* in November 1910. Deeply involved from the beginning in furthering the company's cultural mission to make opera popular with a wide audience of Chicagoans, McCormick encouraged the presentation of foreign operas in English and the search for operas written by Americans and with American themes. She underwrote many translation projects and American composers' works during the 1910s.

McCormick also contributed to the spectacle of Chicago's opera scene. Whenever McCormick, the grande dame of Chicago society, attended the opera, it became common knowledge, and the shows were sold out. Her legendary pre-opera dinners were highlighted in the society columns of Chicago's newspapers. A stickler for schedules, her dinners were timed to the second so that she and her guests, chauffeured in her plum-colored Rolls Royce, would be in their seats well before the opening curtain. Once seated in her box, she focused solely on the performance, making it clear that opera engaged the intellect and artistic sense. She also made it possible for people who could not otherwise afford opera to attend, inviting them as dinner guests, who would, of course, be accompanying her and her more wealthy guests to the performances.

The opera company, initially a financial and critical success, was in trouble by the 1913–14 season. Reorganized in 1915 under new management as the Chicago Opera Association, it was now directed by a board made up exclusively of Chicagoans and virtually dominated by Edith and Harold McCormick, its chief financial backers. The association, which lasted until 1922, continued to present exciting opera to Chicago. The McCormicks were influential in bringing such rising prima donnas as MARY GARDEN and ROSA RAISA to perform regularly. Even though Edith McCormick was living abroad in Europe for most of the Chicago Opera Association's life, she was, nevertheless, very much involved in decision making about its direction and the choice of its leadership.

McCormick's eight-year stay in Europe was precipitated by a severe depression in 1912. As a young woman she had experienced what was then diagnosed as hysteria (anorexia nervosa)— a general weakness, exhaustion, lack of appetite, and consequent weight loss. She was successfully treated by the renowned neurologist S. Weir Mitchell. In her late thirties her emotional turmoil reappeared, and after a stay at a health spa in New York, she contacted Swiss psychoanalyst Carl Jung, who agreed to come to New York to consult with both Edith McCormick and her husband about their emotional conditions. Following a brief stay, Jung urged McCormick to travel to Zurich to be treated there. McCormick left Chicago in April 1913 for Switzerland, accompanied by her son Fowler and her daughter Muriel. Her husband and their daughter Mathilde joined them later that year. The trip was originally planned for two months; however, she remained until 1921.

Edith McCormick underwent an extended analysis with Jung, benefiting both emotionally and intellectually from crucial insights Jung gained during this period as he developed his psychological system. She studied his method intensely, becoming a Jungian analyst in the late 1910s, with a full-time practice of more than fifty patients. At the same time, she pursued other intellectual interests, with private tutorials in philosophy and voluminous reading in comparative religion, archaeology, and psychology. Already fluent in French, German, and several other languages, she now began to study Sanskrit.

Edith and Harold McCormick's relationship to Jung went far beyond that of analysands to analyst. They encouraged and supported the development of Jungian psychology by forming the Psychological Club in 1916 in Zurich, purchasing and outfitting a building for lectures and meetings and where Jung's visiting students and colleagues could board. The club became a gathering place for Jungians, leading to the establishment of professional relationships among an international network of analysts. In order to disseminate Jung's ideas to a larger audience, Edith McCormick paid for his writings to be translated into English. The McCormicks' financial and personal contributions were indispensable during this early period in the promotion of Jungian psychology.

In addition to her support of Jung's work, Edith McCormick became a patron for several artists, including opera composer Ermanno Wolf-Ferrari and novelist James Joyce. Edith McCormick returned to Chicago in 1921. By that time, her marriage, which had been shaky for much of the 1910s, was over, and she obtained a divorce on grounds of desertion in December of that year. Harold McCormick had gone back to Chicago in 1918 to resume his responsibilities with International Harvester. In his wife's absence, he had begun a widely publicized affair with Polish opera singer Ganna Walska; subsequently he married her. Yet Edith McCormick and her husband remained friends until her death.

McCormick, back in Chicago, established a flourishing psychoanalytic practice, which attracted socialites from many areas of the United States. She dreamed of founding a psychoanalytic center at Villa Turicum, her Lake Forest mansion, which she had built in 1912 before she left for Zurich. While studying with Jung, McCormick had become acquainted with a fellow student, Edwin W. Krenn, a Swiss landscape architect. He returned to Chicago with her to help prepare Villa Turicum by designing and overseeing landscaping of the site, but McCormick's dream of a psychoanalytic center was never realized. McCormick and Krenn stayed close friends until she died. They spent much time together dining and attending cultural events, Krenn accompanying McCormick to the theater and the opera.

In 1923 McCormick and Krenn became business partners, together with Ernest A. Dato, a Swiss friend of Krenn who had lived in Chicago for many years and who was employed by International Harvester. The three partners launched a real estate firm with more than five million dollars worth of Standard Oil securities that McCormick placed in a trust fund to underwrite the venture. The company's goal was to provide affordable housing for working-class people. The firm acquired land parcels in the city and surrounding northern and western suburbs, building reasonably priced houses that sold quickly. It also bought up apartment buildings and offered low-rent apartments. By mid-decade the firm of Krenn and Dato was highly successful, becoming one of the nation's largest subdividers, with subsidiary corporations that managed property and provided engineering consultants.

In other efforts to benefit the larger Chicago community beyond her own class, McCormick donated several hundred acres in Riverside, Illinois, to establish the Chicago Zoological Gardens in 1922. Three years later, she helped fund the Woman's World's Fair in Chicago to celebrate women's achievements and acquaint them with the variety of careers that were opening up to them. The fair was held annually for four years, and McCormick continued to support it financially and serve on the fair's board of directors.

By 1926 the country's economic climate was changing from boom to bust, anticipating the Great Depression during the 1930s. Many real estate firms were in serious trouble, Krenn and Dato among them. Even McCormick's infusions of cash and securities were not sufficient to offset the firm's losses, and Krenn and Dato continued to lose money into the 1930s. Because of the deepening economic depression, homeowners in the firm's many subdivisions could not make their rent and mortgage payments. Understanding their deep financial distress, McCormick allowed the firm's tenants and homeowners to continue to live in their apartments and homes even though they could not afford to keep up payments. At the same time, she continued to maintain her lavish lifestyle, acquiring more costly art and antique furnishings, ignoring the economic belt-tightening measures necessary to save her real estate firm. By June 1932, she had lost so much of her wealth that her father and her brother, John D. Rockefeller Jr., became worried that her losses would begin to affect the entire Rockefeller fortune. They insisted that she move out of her Gold Coast mansion and into a hotel to save money, and they put her on a strict allowance to curtail her spending on art and antiques. By this time, Edith McCormick was ill and bedridden. In 1930 she had undergone surgery on a malignant tumor, but physicians were unable to remove all of it. She died of liver cancer just days before her sixtieth birthday. At her side were her three children, reunited with her after many years of alienation; her ex-husband Harold; and her dear friend

Edwin Krenn, invited by the family to be present in her last hours. After a funeral service in her mansion, she was buried in Chicago's Graceland Cemetery in the McCormick family plot near her husband's grave.

At the time of McCormick's death, many bills remained unpaid. Her treasured collections of art, furniture, and jewelry were auctioned off to raise money to settle her estate. Everything was undersold in the depressed market following the 1929 stock market crash and the deepening economic decline of the Great Depression. Her suburban estate, Villa Turicum, was offered to the city of Lake Forest, Illinois, as a gift; but the city refused it. McCormick had hoped that both of her mansions would be turned into museums after her death, but they sold for very little and were eventually torn down. It took nineteen years for attorneys, accountants, and trust supervisors to settle her estate, once valued at forty to fifty million dollars. In 1951 her estate still owed one and a half million dollars.

Although much of her wealth was depleted by the time of her death, Edith Rockefeller McCormick's position as the reigning queen of Chicago society for the first third of the twentieth century was indisputable. She maintained, throughout the period, an extravagant way of life that provided society columnists a steady stream of stories with which they could dazzle readers. By the end of her life, when the nation was in the depths of economic depression, such a display of wealth was becoming inappropriate. As one of her friends, author Arthur Meeker wrote, assessing her life a generation after she died, "Mrs. McCormick's death marked the end of an era. No one again could afford to live as she has lived—nor perhaps, even if they could, would they have wanted to" (quoted in "This Was 1000 Lake Shore Dr."). Yet McCormick had an intellectual side that was as intriguing as her wealth and far less appreciated. As a valued colleague of one of the century's leading psychologists; a serious student of languages, comparative religions, and philosophy; and a lover of the arts who immersed herself in many facets of artistic production in order to enrich Chicago's cultural life, Edith Rockefeller McCormick enthusiastically participated in many of the most important intellectual and cultural currents of her time.

Sources. Information on Edith Rockefeller McCormick can be found in the McCormick Family Papers, State Hist. Soc. of Wisconsin Library, Madison, Wisconsin. Some of her correspondence is located in the John D. Rockefeller Papers, Rockefeller Archive Center, Pocantico, New York. A biographical file on Edith McCormick at CHS contains numerous newspaper articles, particularly those reporting on her death and her estate. For a description of her life style, see "This Was 1000 Lake Shore Dr.—Before High Rises," *CT*, September 19, 1965. Clarice Stasz, *The Rockefeller Women* (1995), is the most recent and extensive writing on McCormick. Stephen Birmingham, *The Grandes Dames* (1982), contains a chapter on McCormick. For information on McCormick's involvement in the Chicago Opera scene, see Ronald L. Davis, *Opera in Chicago* (1966). Kristie Miller, "Yesterday's City," *Chicago History,* Summer 1995, describes McCormick's involvement with the Woman's World Fair. There is an entry on McCormick in *NAW* (1971).

CYNTHIA L. BEARDSLEY

McCORMICK, NETTIE FOWLER
February 8, 1835–July 5, 1923
BUSINESSWOMAN, PHILANTHROPIST

Nettie Fowler McCormick was a prominent member of the Chicago elite. Her wealth and social status were based on the prosperous McCormick Reaper Works, one of the city's leading industries. Infused with an evangelical Protestant morality that governed her conduct of both business and religious affairs, she became one of Chicago's leading philanthropists, contributing more than eight million dollars to religious and educational causes.

Nancy Maria Fowler (called Nettie) was born in Brownsville, New York, the second child and only daughter of Melzar and Clarissa (Spicer) Fowler. Melzar Fowler, a well-established merchant, was killed in an accident soon after the birth of his daughter, leaving his wife in charge of his business interests as well as responsible for Nettie and her brother, Eldridge. Seven years later, Clarissa Fowler also died, leaving her two children in the care of their grandmother, Maria Fowler, in Clayton, New York, and that of Maria Fowler's son-in-law, Eldridge Merick. Merick, who owned substantial shipping interests on the upper St. Lawrence River, was able to provide for his mother-in-law and her two orphaned grandchildren.

The Merick family encouraged Nettie Fowler's participation in the Methodist Episcopal Church and directed her toward academic pursuits. Between 1850 and 1855, Fowler attended three seminaries: the Falley Seminary, Fulton, New York, and the Troy Female Seminary directed by Emma Willard—both for women; and the Genesee Wesleyan Seminary, Lima, New York, a coeducational institution. Fowler did not graduate from any of these institutions, but she took advantage of the increased educational opportunities available to American women in the antebellum period. At Lima, for example, she was able to take her courses at a nearby coeducational college. She studied French, rhetoric, logic, natural philosophy, electricity, chemistry, music, and oil painting. After Genessee Wesleyan, Fowler taught for several months in the public school she had attended in Clayton.

In these formative years, Fowler kept a personal diary in which she meditated on her spiritual condition and regularly examined her conduct with regard to the religious responsibility she believed she had to fulfill toward the larger society. In one entry she wrote, "Another week is added to my life. Am I one week better? Am I better prepared to enter upon eternal life than one week ago?" (quoted in Burgess, 9). She actively participated in church and mission society work. Moving away from Methodism and toward the Presbyterianism she ultimately embraced, hers was a disciplined and self-critical religious practice based on an unquestioned acceptance of a Calvinistic divine providence.

At age twenty-one, Nettie Fowler visited a cousin in Chicago, Illinois. During her stay she was introduced to Cyrus Hall McCormick, the inventor of the reaper and owner of the growing McCormick Reaper Works, one of the largest manufacturing plants in the pre–Civil War city. Cyrus McCormick, an "Old-School" Presbyterian from Virginia, was driven by a Calvinist work ethic. Unmarried and twenty-six years Nettie Fowler's senior, he was attracted to her gentility, her Calvinism, and her keen business sense. On January 26, 1858, taking time between two reaper patent litigations, Cyrus McCormick and Nettie Fowler were married. McCormick's business was expanding in the United States and in Europe, but the reaper king faced patent challenges by many of his competitors. His competitors' assertions probably heightened the feeling he had of being under attack; a Southerner, he fought the growing anti-slavery sentiment among Chicago Presbyterians. He was a Democrat, with strong convictions about the states' rights arguments of the southern branch of the party, but he worked with leading capitalists in Chicago whose pro-free-soil sentiments had thrust them into the ranks of the new Republican Party. When Cyrus McCormick became the sole owner of the Presbyterian magazine the *Interior*, using it to promote his conservative brand of Presbyterianism after the Civil War, Nettie McCormick had a hand in the editing.

Nettie Fowler McCormick quickly assumed the domestic and social responsibilities of the wife of a member of the Chicago elite who was an opinionated and conservative man with discordant views. The McCormicks maintained a home in Chicago, but because of Cyrus McCormick's domestic and foreign business interests and his involvement in national politics, the family frequently spent months and even years living in New York City, Washington, D.C., and Europe. In a fifteen-year period, Nettie and Cyrus McCormick had seven children—Cyrus II, Mary Virginia, Robert, Anita, Alice, Harold Fowler, and Stanley. Robert and Alice died in early childhood. Motherhood presented McCormick with conflicts over her responsibilities to the children and to her husband, who, with increasing age, required her constant involvement in his business affairs. She approached motherhood seriously, promoting the moral discipline of her children and the ideal of a "well-regulated family" (Roderick, 70), concepts that reflected her understanding of the social order, with the importance of individual responsibility and self-restraint as its foundation. Their wealth enabled the McCormicks to employ private tutors and enroll their children in private schools. Yet Nettie McCormick maintained close supervision and often regretted the time she spent away from them.

During the early years of her marriage, Nettie McCormick added to her concerns the burdens of supporting her husband's unsuccessful attempts to win election to public office. In 1860, Cyrus McCormick ran unsuccessfully in the Democratic primary in Chicago for mayor. Four years later he ran for U.S. Congress and again lost. The McCormicks spent the next seven years with their children in New York City, enjoying the social companionship of other Southerners who had settled in the North before the outbreak of the war or had come at its close. Nettie McCormick participated with other women in fund-raising by the New York Ladies' Southern Relief Society to alleviate the needs of women and children of the South. By 1865 and the death of her son Robert, she was praying to be a better mother; yet her involvement in her husband's business affairs increased from her early years of serving as his private secretary. She had acquired a clear understanding of the details and overall management of his business.

Nettie McCormick's involvement in business decisions increased in the aftermath of the Chicago Fire of 1871; the McCormick Reaper plant was destroyed in the blaze. When confronted with the smoldering ruins, Nettie McCormick urged her

FIG. 70. *Businesswoman and philanthropist Nettie McCormick inspired husband Cyrus H. McCormick to rebuild the McCormick Reaper Works after the Great Chicago Fire of 1871 destroyed the original plant.*

despondent husband to rebuild and modernize the business. In her journal "she wrote that Cyrus chided her for 'urging him on with whip and spur,' and told her that he 'makes the decision now to go on . . . principally under my [Nettie's] influence'" (Burgess, 23). Harold McCormick was born in 1873, after the fire, and Nettie McCormick's journal revealed the complications of her life. "Tonight I am so tired—children's lessons to see to for the tutor tomorrow—Baby to nurse—buildings to look after—architects to see—some letters to write. Well after all this is done the flesh is indeed weary" (quoted in Roderick, 103).

As Cyrus McCormick grew older, Nettie McCormick assumed more business responsibilities. She mediated between the uncompromising McCormick and his lawyers, buyers, and competitors. Particularly difficult was an ongoing conflict among Cyrus McCormick and his two younger brothers, Robert Hall and Leander. Nettie McCormick advantageously negotiated the formation of the McCormick Harvesting Machine Company by selling one quarter of the company stock to the two brothers while retaining the other three quarters of the business. Nettie McCormick responded to new conditions in business and social life in her later years. Beginning in 1878 when Cyrus McCormick became ill during a business trip to Paris, France, Nettie McCormick assumed more business authority. She was completely knowledgeable of the operation of the McCormick Harvesting Machine Company, discussing company business with the English Lord Chancellor, corresponding directly with the firm's European lawyer, and advising her eldest son, Cyrus H. McCormick Jr., who was still at Princeton University. He entered the company in 1879 and, after the death of his father in 1884, became president. Nettie McCormick remained an important adviser on business matters to her son Cyrus and con-

tinued to have a role in company policy. She was the chief stockholder and corresponded with lawyers, financial agents, and advisers, including J. Pierpont Morgan, George W. Perkins, Cyrus Bentley, Edward A. Ackerman, and Charles Deering. She participated in the discussions leading to the formation of the International Harvester Company in 1902. Five companies were involved: McCormick Harvesting Machine, Deering, Warder, Bushnell & Glessner, the Plano Company, and the Milwaukee Harvester Company. Nettie McCormick joined her sons in these negotiations and brought her brother Eldridge Fowler with her. "Acceptance was not easy for Nettie McCormick; as the negotiations were approaching conclusion she held up decisions for perhaps four days, while she weighed all the details" (Roderick, 226).

Even after the consolidation, Nettie McCormick continued to have ideas about how the company should be run. Her grandson Fowler McCormick credited his grandmother with having "advanced positions on labor and management in the company" (quoted in Roderick, 234), which led to the establishment of a pension system, one of the earliest in the country; a plan for workmen's compensation two years before any law in the United States had been passed; and a system of profit sharing for employees. She never forgot the "awful episode in 1886 . . . all arising from the unwisdom" (quoted in Roderick, 234–35) of a middle management decision, she contended. The strike at the McCormick Reaper plant in Chicago in 1886 had resulted in bloodshed and, within a few days, the famous Haymarket incident.

The McCormicks were active in several Presbyterian churches in Chicago; in her later years, Nettie McCormick was a member of Fourth Presbyterian Church. Nettie and Cyrus McCormick supported city missions, including the Young

Men's and Young Women's Christian Associations, the Pacific Garden Mission, the Woman's Christian Temperance Union, the Chicago Bible Work, and the Moody Bible Institute. For thirty-four years Nettie McCormick served as vice-president of the Presbyterian Board of Missions of the Northwest, a women's missionary society that financed more than seven hundred church workers for foreign missions. Locally, Cyrus McCormick focused on the Presbyterian Seminary of the Northwest (later McCormick Theological Seminary). He donated an initial one hundred thousand dollars in 1859, hoping that the institution would serve as a bulwark against liberal theology within the denomination and promoting "Old School" theology. While he was alive, Nettie McCormick supported her husband's ideals; after his death in 1884, she seemed to let go of her husband's old battle with theological liberalism and became tolerant of the inroads liberal theology was making at the seminary. She continued to provide substantial funding.

In other respects she retained her conservative approach to charitable giving. According to Nettie McCormick, every individual needed to discipline any tendencies toward wastefulness, frivolity, and laziness with frugality, dedication, and industry. She subjected her own life to this type of control and expected that any individuals or institutions worthy of her charity would evidence these same virtues. To this end, Nettie McCormick maintained a highly personal style of philanthropy. She kept detailed records filled with directives for the distribution of large sums of money as well as used clothing, food, heating coal, and even hat racks. She wasted nothing, and her support was given only after consultation and scrutiny to insure its proper use. A constant stream of visitors, including civic leaders, ministers, and missionaries, passed through her doors, and their requests were evaluated according to her standards. "Her total donations to Hull House reflected her preference for personal rather than institutional giving to the poor. Over the years she gave Hull House only $2,085. She feared that unwise gifts to the poor would discredit her on judgment day. Because 'what we have is lent to us as a trust,' careful judgment and selection had to be exercised at all times in making donations" (Burgess, 51).

With the death of Cyrus McCormick, Nettie McCormick managed both the business and his estate, which was estimated at nearly ten million dollars. Between 1884 and 1889 she donated $475,000 to organizations that had been sanctioned by her husband—Presbyterian churches, church-related colleges, and the McCormick Theological Seminary. In the last thirty-four years of her life she broadened her philanthropy to include a wide variety of individuals, educational institutions, churches, youth activities, orphanages, hospitals, and war relief agencies. She donated large sums to the Shantung (now Shandong) Christian University, Tsinan (now Jinan), China; the University of Nanking (now Nanjing), China; and the North China Union University, Peking (now Beijing)—all associated with the American Presbyterian Mission Board.

"Between 1890 and 1923, . . . Nettie McCormick donated approximately eight million dollars to educational institutions, churches, youth activities, orphanages, hospitals, disaster and war relief agencies and countless individuals" (Burgess, 41). She believed in making education available, especially because she perceived that literacy was connected to the spread of Chris-

tianity—a concern she maintained all her life. Private American schools and colleges received $3,652,580. "She was particularly concerned with the inadequate educational facilities in the rural Midwest, the frontier regions of the West, and the highlands and other backward areas of the South" (Burgess, 45). She gave $647,625 to mission fields throughout the world, much of it primarily for education.

Nettie McCormick's philanthropy and particularly her commitment to education provided the means to further her own social principles and religious ideals. McCormick became increasingly deaf throughout her life, and most of her conversations were assisted with a horn to facilitate her hearing. Yet her obvious social authority and her determination to insure the proper use of McCormick money in the business world and in philanthropy were not deterred by this difficulty. As her hearing deteriorated, McCormick abruptly ended conversations by simply removing her horn, thereby ending a discussion and leaving her own opinions unchallenged.

In 1916, a year after celebrating her eightieth birthday, Nettie McCormick left her Chicago residence and moved to House-in-the-Woods, a country home in Lake Forest, Illinois. She withdrew from most business involvements but continued to travel and to maintain her voluminous correspondence. She also actively endorsed political reform efforts in both parties. In 1911, she supported the Republican mayoral reform candidate, Charles Merriam; in 1914 she supported settlement leader MARY McDOWELL's candidacy for the Cook County Board of Commissioners. On the national level, she continued her husband's long-term allegiance to the Democratic Party and supported Woodrow Wilson in 1916. Her daughter, philanthropist ANITA McCORMICK BLAINE, was a major force in the progressive education reform movement of the late nineteenth and early twentieth centuries; Blaine also advocated social reforms and peace initiatives worldwide. Mother and daughter maintained a close relationship. It is conceivable that Anita Blaine's politics were influential in Nettie McCormick's later years.

In June 1923, at the age of eighty-eight, Nettie McCormick developed mild pneumonia that doctors were unable to cure. She died soon after at her Lake Forest Home. After a funeral service at the Fourth Presbyterian Church, she was buried at Graceland Cemetery, Chicago.

Nettie McCormick did not plan to upset the ideal of a Victorian patriarchal marriage, nor did she consciously move away from the ideal of Christian motherhood. In her marriage to a wealthy captain of industry twenty-six years her senior, her skills and intellectual capacities became vital to the future of her family's business. She crossed the boundary between domesticity and the world of commerce, becoming a knowledgeable and influential figure in the McCormick Harvesting Machine Company and, later, in the formation of International Harvester Company. She remained a devout Christian, earnestly engaged in proving that she could be a just steward and a person whose good judgment was reflected in her charitable acts.

Sources. Nettie Fowler McCormick Papers, the McCormick Manuscript Collection, State Hist. Soc. of Wisconsin, Madison, are in 451 boxes that include correspondence, legal documents, volumes of diaries, memoranda, and scrapbooks. In addition, the papers contain letters, genealogies, recollections, and interviews relating to her collected by the Nettie Fowler McCormick Biographical Association. The clippings file, CHS, has material on Nettie and Cyrus H. McCormick, including obituaries. Biographies of Nettie McCormick include Stella Virginia Roderick, *Nettie Fowler McCormick* (1956); Charles O. Burgess, *Nettie Fowler McCormick: Profile of a Philanthropist* (1962); and an entry in *NAW* (1971). Thekla Ellen Caldwell, "Women, Men, and Revival: The Third Awakening in Chicago" (Ph.D. diss., Univ. of Illinois at Chicago, 1991), discusses Nettie McCormick's evangelism and philanthropy.

THEKLA ELLEN CALDWELL

McCORMICK, RUTH HANNA
March 27, 1880–December 31, 1944
POLITICIAN, CONGRESSWOMAN, SUFFRAGIST

Ruth Hanna McCormick, suffragist and politician, encouraged women to participate in the unpopular field of politics. She remarked that "women mouth the phrase 'going into politics' as if it were either dangerous or corrupt. Yet women cannot separate politics from civic life and expect to advance that civic life" (quoted in *Chicago Tribune*, March 19, 1928).

Ruth Hanna was the last child born to Marcus (Mark) Alonzo and Charlotte "Gussie" Augusta (Rhodes) Hanna in Cleveland, Ohio. Her two siblings were Daniel and Mabel. Mark Hanna, a United States senator and one of the most successful political bosses in American political history, was a businessman descended from a Scotch-Irish family with a Quaker religious tradition.

Ruth Hanna studied at Hathaway-Brown School in Cleveland, Ohio, and in 1897 briefly attended Masters School in Dobbs Ferry, New York, and Miss Porter's School in Farmington, Connecticut. Students liked her and she enjoyed her classes, yet she never excelled.

Politics rather than academic study intrigued Ruth Hanna. When she was sixteen, her father successfully managed Republican William McKinley's 1896 presidential race against Democrat William Jennings Bryan. Since Mark Hanna conducted most of his affairs at home, Charlotte Hanna hosted the business and political dinners and was known as a shrewd observer. Ruth Hanna also participated, accompanying her father on the presidential campaign trail. She liked to say that she was her father's political legacy. Under her father's tutelage, she met politicians, witnessed senatorial debates, and absorbed information about the ins and outs of legislative procedure. She attended McKinley's presidential inauguration with her father.

After graduating from Miss Porter's School, she became her father's personal secretary at which time, she said, "[her] education began in earnest" (Miller, 21). In the early 1900s, Hanna worked actively in the Welfare Department of the National Civic Federation, of which her father was president. An expansion of the Chicago Civic Federation, the national group and its subsidiaries encouraged communication between employers and employees at a time when industrial labor conflict was acute.

Hanna made her social debut in 1901. She married (Joseph) Medill McCormick, the grandson of *Chicago Tribune* publisher Joseph Medill, on June 10, 1903. Medill McCormick was the son of diplomat Robert Sanderson McCormick, a nephew of reaper-king Cyrus H. McCormick. The couple resided in Chicago, where Medill McCormick had gone to work on the *Tribune* after graduating from Yale University in 1900. The McCormicks had three children: Katherine Augusta (born 1912); Medill, known as Johnny (1916); and Ruth Elizabeth (1921).

Mark Hanna died in 1904, but his daughter continued her interest in politics, a concern she shared with her husband. The young couple became part of the reform movement, whose political expression was the Progressive Party. Interested in "improving social and economic conditions in Chicago . . . for a time they lived at the University of Chicago Settlement" (NAW, 293). They had been encouraged to live in the settlement by their friends Bill and Anne Hard, journalists with connections to reform causes. The McCormicks lived at the settlement under assumed names. With other residents, they studied living conditions of the settlement's poor and working-class neighbors and used this data to advocate legislation to protect workers, especially women and children. However, "the McCormicks came to understand that they could do little in such an atmosphere" (Miller, 39–40) to make significant changes in the system.

Ruth McCormick turned to organizing women to enter the civic sphere en masse and to upgrade politics and public policy even before suffrage was achieved. On January 6, 1910, seventy-five women assembled in the tea room at the Marshall Field department store to hear a talk by McCormick's husband on civic righteousness; after the talk, a Committee of Ten was formed to plan for future political action. They were clubwomen, activists, and social reformers, including McCormick, MARY WILMARTH, HANNAH SOLOMON, Harriet Park Thomas, LYDIA COONLEY-WARD, MARY McDOWELL, and RACHELLE YARROS. Determined to improve the quality of municipal life in Chicago, the committee launched the Woman's City Club of Chicago, with Wilmarth serving as the first president. Civic-minded and interested in reforming government itself—getting rid of the spoils system—the Woman's City Club soon was in the forefront of public policy discussions and legislative initiatives. Women organized by wards analyzed candidates' records and views, making recommendations that influenced elections.

Along with her work in the Woman's City Club, Ruth McCormick supported the Women's Trade Union League (WTUL), a cross-class alliance of working-class and middle- and upper-class women engaged in educational work, lobbying for labor legislation—including the minimum wage and advocacy of labor unions for women workers. In support of her interest in the protection of women workers and the elimination of child labor, McCormick lobbied for the establishment of the U.S. Children's Bureau and the Women's Bureau of the U.S. Department of Labor. She campaigned for the minimum wage; and as a lobbyist for the Illinois Consumers' League, in 1915 she encouraged state legislators to support a child labor bill. At the time, one out of four children between the ages of ten and fourteen was employed.

Ruth and Medill McCormick supported Theodore Roosevelt's candidacy for president in 1912 on the Bull Moose (Progressive) Party ticket. She had broken with her father's Republican path, noting that joining the Illinois Progressive Party was "respectable but not fashionable" (Miller, 55). Supporters of the Roosevelt campaign encouraged women's involvement in poli-

FIG. 71. *Congresswoman Ruth Hanna McCormick speaks in Chicago, 1930, the year she ran unsuccessfully for a seat in the U.S. Senate.*

FIG. 72. *Congresswoman Ruth Hanna McCormick, standing next to Jane Addams and Illinois governor Louis L. Emmerson, c. 1930.*

tics. Women activists believed that the Progressive Party gave them the best chance of achieving the goals of labor reform legislation, child labor laws, pure food and drug regulation, and woman suffrage. McCormick was appointed chair of the Chicago Committee of 100, a branch of the Progressive Party. Although Theodore Roosevelt lost the election, the successful efforts of Progressive Party workers to organize women in Illinois were a factor in the passage of the Illinois Equal Suffrage Act in 1913, which gave Illinois women the right to vote in municipal and presidential elections.

In 1912, Medill McCormick was elected to the Illinois House of Representatives. Pregnant with her first child, Ruth McCormick worked for suffrage and in her husband's campaign. Although Medill McCormick was victorious, the Progressive Party's presidential defeat had repercussions for the National American Woman Suffrage Association (NAWSA), and woman suffrage leaders debated what strategy to pursue to achieve suffrage in all the states through the federal or Anthony amendment. Although nearly a million women were able to vote by 1912, Woodrow Wilson's election and the election of Southern Democrats to the Congress were not favorable for the success of a federal amendment. Soon after Woodrow Wilson was inaugurated, Alice Paul became head of NAWSA's Congressional Committee, bringing a new, controversial militancy to NAWSA. Paul also created the Congressional Union for Woman Suffrage (after 1916 the National Woman's Party); although it was a separate organization from the Congressional Committee, Paul's leadership blurred this distinction and caused tensions among NAWSA's leaders. They relieved Paul of the chair and replaced her with Ruth McCormick, who was considered by many a dynamic suffrage leader and an excellent choice to run this crucial arm of the suffrage movement. Other committee members viewed McCormick as a "society woman" (Miller, 85) who was too identified with partisan (Republican Party) politics. McCormick "soon embroiled NAWSA in a new conflict" (Young, 20) when the Congressional Committee "drafted a new constitutional amendment seeking to herald a shift of focus of suffrage activity to the state level" (p. 20). The Shafroth-McCormick (later Shafroth-Palmer) Amendment that NAWSA "placed before Congress on March 2, 1914" was "conceived as a political counter to objections that a simple federal suffrage amendment would be an invasion of states' rights. . . . [It] would have required any state to hold a referendum on woman suffrage whenever 8 percent of its legal voters so petitioned" (NAW, 294). Shafroth-Palmer met with opposition from within segments of the suffrage movement, and the 1915 NAWSA convention voted to withdraw support for it. McCormick, whose leadership had been rejected, resigned and turned her attentions to her husband's political career and "recruiting women into the Republican party" (Young, 20).

Almost immediately after his election in 1912, the couple had eyed a congressional seat for Medill McCormick and began to plan his successful 1916 campaign. Serving one term in the House of Representatives, McCormick next ran for the U.S. Senate and was elected in 1918. During this period Ruth McCormick continued to advocate women's participation in the Republican Party. Her organizational skills and efforts were noticed, and in 1920, Ruth McCormick chaired the first woman's executive committee of the Republican National Committee. She described the appointment as her "preparation for going into . . . politics on [her] own account[,] . . . [her] first official service with the Party" (Miller, 113). McCormick urged women to join a major political party rather than a nonpartisan association or a separate woman's political organization. She supported ideas of men and women working together in political parties with women "on equal footing with men" (Miller, 125). She made progress toward this goal as one of eight women selected for the Republican National Committee's executive board. McCormick served from 1919 until 1924, when she became the first elected Republican national committeewoman from Illinois. As a committeewoman, she lobbied for women's equal participation in the Republican Party's councils.

Ruth McCormick's family felt the reverberations from both her and Medill's political activities. Although she believed that she spent a great deal of time with her children, they felt her absences and vied for her attention. Family tensions mounted when Medill McCormick was defeated in the 1924 Republican primary for U.S. Senate. He had already suffered from bouts with depression and had a problem with alcohol abuse that predated his entry into politics. He had consulted experts, including psychiatrist Carl Jung, who treated him for manic depression. On February 26, 1925, Medill McCormick died suddenly in Washington, D.C. Obituaries in the New York Times and Chicago Tribune attributed his death to myocarditis, calling it an "acute dilation of the heart" (New York Times, February 26, 1925). Family members speculate that he died from an overdose of barbiturates. "When Ruth [McCormick] arrived at Medill's hotel room, she opened his trunk and found it contained several empty vials. She believed this was his way of letting her know what he'd done; he knew no one else would be able to open the trunk . . ." (Miller, 151). After her husband's funeral, McCormick withdrew to her farm in Illinois.

In April 1928, Ruth McCormick won the Republican nomination for one of two congressman-at-large seats from Illinois by a two-to-one margin. Congressmen-at-large were elected statewide rather than from a single district because the state legislature had not yet reapportioned its congressional districts to adjust to a new census count. The two at-large seats had existed in Illinois since 1910; they were discontinued after 1930 when reapportionment finally took place. McCormick campaigned for agricultural subsidies, Prohibition law enforcement, and the proposed treaty (later called the Kellogg-Briand Peace Pact) to outlaw war. McCormick's position on peace, however, did not put her in the camp of Women's International League for Peace and Freedom leaders such as JANE ADDAMS. McCormick believed "in military preparedness and adequate national defense" and was "not in favor of the United States' entrance into the World Court 'because it [was] a part of the League of Nations'" (Illinois Voter, April 1930, 6), which she opposed as well. Her position on Prohibition was complicated by her personal experiences; while she thought that Prohibition was a mistake, she supported its enforcement since it was still on the books as law. She ran a vigorous campaign, writing letters and shaking the hands of the people.

Ruth McCormick received 1,711,651 votes and won with a 400,000-vote plurality. Although she credited women for her victory, she insisted that she represented all people. She was featured on the April 23, 1928, *Time* magazine cover, one of the few female politicians to receive such attention until the early 1960s. In Illinois, however, there were divisions among Republican women, perhaps the result of Ruth McCormick's approach to the whole concept of separate women's organizations. She consistently advised women to "integrate" into the male-dominated political structure. Yet she gained power from the support she garnered from the statewide women's Republican clubs. These had been organized by McCormick and numbered several thousand members, "a following which some contemporary observers felt constituted almost a personal political machine" (*NAW*, 294). In 1929, McCormick was challenged by fellow Republican and longtime rival LOTTIE O'NEILL, the first woman state representative in Illinois. O'Neill had hoped to be appointed chair of the education committee of the Illinois House. When the appointment did not happen, O'Neill blamed McCormick, who, she believed, influenced the decision against her. McCormick publicly stated that she regretted that O'Neill had not been appointed because she would have filled the position ably. O'Neill soon resigned as vice-president of the Illinois Federation of Republican Women in objection to McCormick's bossism. The feud between the two women continued to have repercussions when, in the general election for the U.S. Senate seat from Illinois, McCormick was opposed not only by the Democratic candidate, James Hamilton Lewis, but also by Lottie O'Neill, who ran as an Independent candidate supported by the Illinois Anti-Saloon League. Lewis ran on a ticket that called for state control of Prohibition, which amounted to repeal. McCormick's position generally agreed with O'Neill's on liquor, and so the pro-Prohibitionists were split.

McCormick was defeated in 1930; her pro-Prohibition stand, her gender, and the absence of a campaign manager contributed to the defeat. The liquor question, however, was not the crucial one. The general climate of economic crisis—widespread unemployment and financial failures following the stock market crash of 1929—was the backdrop for Lottie O'Neill's critique of McCormick as a wealthy spendthrift who carried on an exorbitant primary campaign in the midst of hardship. During the campaign, Senator Gerald P. Nye's Select Committee to Investigate Contributions and Expenses of Senatorial Candidates investigated McCormick's primary campaign expenses of more than seventy-five thousand dollars, creating unfavorable publicity. Perhaps more than the other factors, the rejection of President Herbert Hoover's policies and the voters' hope for change by selecting Democrats explain her defeat. McCormick ran in a year "that saw Republicans lose fifty-three House and eight Senate seats" (*Women in Congress*, 156).

After the election, McCormick focused on business affairs. She had bought the Rockford, Illinois, *Daily Republic* in 1928 and, in 1930, she merged it with the *Morning Star and Register Gazette*. That year she also purchased a radio station. She already owned and managed Rock River Farm, a 2,200-acre dairy farm near Byron, Illinois; and she had inherited investments and property from her husband's estate. McCormick proved to be an adept businesswoman.

On March 9, 1932, Ruth McCormick married Albert Gallatin Simms, whom she had met while they both served in Congress. They moved to Albuquerque, New Mexico, where McCormick started the Sandia School and helped establish the Allied Arts Extension. She developed a 250,000-acre cattle and sheep ranch at Trinchera, Colorado. In June 1938, McCormick's son Johnny was killed while photographing a lightning storm. She endowed the Fountain Valley School for Boys, Colorado Springs, Colorado, in his memory.

McCormick resumed an active role in politics as cochair with J. Russell Sprague, the Long Island, New York, Republican leader, of the 1939 Thomas E. Dewey preconvention campaign for the Republican nomination for president. Unsuccessful in obtaining Dewey's nomination, after the Republican convention she initially supported Wendell Willkie. McCormick "later denounced him for his support of military aid to Great Britain" (*Women in Congress*, 156). She served on the Republican National Committee in 1944 and that year backed Dewey in his unsuccessful campaign for president.

McCormick died in her sleep at Chicago's Billings Hospital following an operation for pancreatitis. She was buried in Fairview Cemetery, Albuquerque, New Mexico.

Ruth Hanna McCormick grew up in a politically connected household where she was given many opportunities by her father and his peers to learn the art of politics. While Hanna's "wealth and name . . . opened doors for her," which "at that time . . . were closed to most women" (Shey), McCormick had a natural talent for politics and an interest in forging a path for women in government as the equals of men.

Sources. The Hanna-McCormick Family Papers are located in the Manuscript Division, Library of Congress. Kristie Miller, granddaughter of McCormick, holds McCormick family papers and provided information for this entry. The most complete biography of McCormick is Kristie Miller, *Ruth Hanna McCormick: A Life in Politics, 1880–1944* (1992). McCormick's biography is in *NAW* (1971). Newspaper articles of interest include "Ruth McCormick Campaigns Like a Man," *CT*, March 19, 1928; "Seniority Rule Halts Ambition of Mrs. O'Neill" and "Ruth McCormick Denies Charges by Mrs. Lottie O'Neill," *CT*, February 1, 1929; Arthur Evans, "Mrs. McCormick Gibes at Foe's Gloom Picture," *CT*, October 30, 1930; and three articles by Genevieve Forbes Herrick: "Women Fewer, but No Longer in Minor Roles," *CT*, June 11, 1928; "Women Get Small Comfort Out of Share in Platform," *CT*, June 15, 1928; "Women at Big Conventions to Ask Real Work," *CT*, June 5, 1932. Books providing useful background include William T. Hutchinson, *Lowden of Illinois* (1957); Nancy Woloch, *Women and the American Experience* (1984); Dorothy M. Brown, *Setting a Course: American Women in the 1920s* (1987); Louise Young, *In the Public Interest: The League of Women Voters, 1920–1970* (1989); *Women in Congress, 1917–1990* (U.S. Government Printing Office, 1991); and Dorothy Schneider and Carl J. Schneider, *American Women in the Progressive Era, 1900–1920* (1993). Helpful articles include Emily Newell Blair, "Women at the Convention," *Current History*, October 1920; Ida C. Clarke, "A Woman in the White House," *Century Magazine*, March 1927; Charles A. Selden, "The Father Complex of Alice Roosevelt Longworth and Ruth Hanna McCormick," *Ladies' Home Journal*, March 1927; and William G. Shepherd, "Mark Another Hanna," *Colliers*, March 15, 1930. Obituaries appeared in the *NYT*, January 1, 1945, and the *CT*, January 1, 1945. For a recent discussion, see Sarah J. Shey, "The McCormicks, Ruth and Medill," *Philadelphia Inquirer*, November 22, 1999.

SARAH JEAN SHEY

McCREA, ANNETTE E. MAXSON
July 16, 1858–September 20, 1928
LANDSCAPE ARCHITECT

Annette E. McCrea created the attractive grounds surrounding many railroad stations, part of her design work for six major railroad companies. With railroads new to the commissioning of professional landscapers, McCrea promoted the importance of employing landscape architects to ensure beautiful station grounds. Her work also included landscape plans for homes, parks, roadways, and state institutions in Wisconsin and upper Michigan.

Annette Maxson, daughter of Levi S. and Cordelia (Shoole) Maxson, was born in Cooperstown, New York. The family included three sisters, Lilla, Pamella, and Dora, and a brother, Charles. About 1866 their father was shot accidentally and died, leaving the mother to care for the five children.

Annette Maxson married J. Franklin McCrea, a nursery owner. They had two daughters: Dorothy, born in Norwich, New York, in 1876, and Euena, born in 1880 in Detroit, where Franklin McCrea owned J. Frank McCrea and Company, the largest nursery business in the area. Annette McCrea's brother moved to Michigan in 1877 to work for his brother-in-law.

Because of Frank McCrea's poor health, the family moved frequently until his death of heart failure in Denver, Colorado, in 1892. He was buried in Kalamazoo, Michigan, where Charles Maxson lived.

At that time Annette McCrea embarked on her professional life in Kalamazoo, running her husband's nursery and landscape gardening business. Her first commission was for a prominent Kalamazoo resident, Frank Henderson. She began this work early in the development of landscape architecture as a profession, when few women were in the business. Beatrix Farrand, the only woman among eleven charter members of the American Society of Landscape Architects in 1899, had opened a practice in Manhattan in 1897. Aware of the small number of women landscape architects, McCrea supported the addition of landscape gardening to the course of study at agricultural colleges to provide training in the profession for women.

In the late 1890s, she and her daughters moved to Chicago. She sought an appointment as consulting landscape architect for Lincoln Park in June 1899 and was hired in January 1900. By late February the horticulture committee and the park commissioners approved her plans for trees and shrubbery for Lincoln and Chicago Avenue parks. In April, the commissioners asked her to plant shrubs and other plants in the park at Astor and Goethe Streets. She had some sort of dispute with her immediate supervisor, the superintendent of the park, over the use of a horse and buggy, and was dismissed. Later explanations gave political differences as an explanation for her dismissal.

Nevertheless, her schedule was full. She had commissions in Marquette, Michigan, from the board of education and in other cities in upper Michigan. Besides private work, she had orders to draw landscaping plans for two city parks, a lake shore boulevard, and the grounds at a normal school, state prison, and mental hospital.

She obtained positions as consulting landscape architect with several railroad companies—Chicago, Milwaukee, and St. Paul; Chicago and Northwestern; Chicago, Burlington and Quincy; Illinois Central; Chicago and Alton; Southern Pacific; and others. Railroad companies were developing depot parks to provide an attractive landscape of plantings for travelers using the trains.

McCrea started her work for the Milwaukee Road in 1902 in typical fashion, touring the route between Milwaukee and La Crosse, Wisconsin, with officials in a railroad business car. At a cost of ten thousand dollars, the company put McCrea in charge of "beautifying the garden spots around its depots in Wisconsin" (*Milwaukee Sentinel*, May 15, 1902). When the Milwaukee Road opened a new station at Wausau, Wisconsin, that same year, McCrea prepared a plan to lay out five acres attractively after spending several days studying the terrain. She felt that the spaciousness would allow her to display her artistry.

Around 1900 she became head of the Committee on Railroad Grounds of the American Park and Outdoor Art Association (APOAA), an organization of landscapers. In 1904, APOAA and the American League for Civic Improvement merged to form the American Civic Association, an organization dedicated to promoting improvement in the appearance of cities, villages, and neighborhoods; preserving the landscape and developing it; and advancing outdoor art. McCrea continued to be active as vice-president of the Department of Railroad Improvements.

For the next few years, she sent a survey to the presidents of about 125 railroads, asking for information on work done by their companies or planned for the near future to improve the surroundings of their stations. She reported the results in a series of articles in the *Railroad Gazette*. In her report on May 13, 1904, "Railroad Station Improvement," McCrea expressed pride in an almost universal development of station parks. She took the opportunity to stress the importance of employing a landscape architect to get utilitarian and beautiful results. McCrea explained that station improvement was "in a state of evolution" and that "not until recently have the services of experienced landscape architects been considered necessary" (p. 357). She also saw building planning and selection of paint colors as part of the work of the landscaper.

McCrea described the work being done by specific railroad companies. Sections of her report in June 1904 at the convention of the APOAA in St. Louis appeared in the *Railroad Gazette* on September 23, 1904. She praised the parks of the Chicago and Northwestern and the Chicago, Milwaukee and St. Paul railroads, which were "made as artistic as money and the skill of the landscape architect can make them without sacrificing needed space for the requirements of the business" (p. 373). McCrea reported that the Milwaukee Road had improved parks at 275 stations in two and one-half years. She acknowledged the efforts of the Chicago and Alton in starting improvements when other railroads were retrenching. The thoroughness and good taste of its officers entitled the company "to the approval of the America Park and Outdoor Art Association" (p. 373), she stated.

Although McCrea did not name the landscaper for the designs described in her articles and convention reports, she had done much of the work. In 1904 she worked for the Chicago and Alton. The Illinois Central hired her in 1905 to plant grass, shrubs, and flowers at its main stations. Before beginning the work, she and the chief landscape gardener visited the Illinois Central stations in a railway business car.

She carried the work of railway landscaping to Chautauquans in 1904; a summary in the *Chautauquan* took a practical approach: "The advantages and economy of planting hardy trees, shrubs, and vines, which grow more beautiful with each succeeding year, and require no transplanting, are rapidly leading to the extermination of the monotonous, inartistic, and expensive greenhouse planting" (p. 368), she said.

The 1907 survey, which she wrote during her employment at the Office of the Landscape Architect, Chicago, Milwaukee and St. Paul Railway Company, described retrenchment by many railroads. In her report to the American Civic Association's annual meeting at Providence, Rhode Island, she was consoled by the knowledge that completed work would not be totally undone. She further contended that village improvements sprang from station park landscaping, which became the core for community improvements such as plantings on high school land and courthouse grounds.

McCrea was involved in such community work, although she did not reveal her commissions in the convention reports. In 1907 she designed a large park near the Chicago, Milwaukee and St. Paul station in Tomahawk, Wisconsin. Thirteen warehouses, on land belonging to the railroad, were transported to the suburbs, with a donation of eight hundred dollars from Tomahawk residents, and the park laid out in the area. In addition, the railroads sold a supply of shrubs at cost, and McCrea participated in designing and planning home gardens. She also planned a drive for the Bradley Company with views of nearby lakes and the Wisconsin River.

Railroad work declined as the federal Interstate Commerce Commission, with powers granted by Congress in the Mann-Elkins Act (1910), denied rate increases. McCrea complained in 1911 that ICC decisions had stopped railroad improvements and her income. Nevertheless, she remained outspoken in her criticism of station decoration done by unqualified workers rather than landscapers. J. Horace McFarland, president of the American Civic Association, told about her successes in dealing with railroad officers. "I remember that a most capable railroad station improver—Mrs. Annette E. McCrea, who has done great things for the Chicago and Northwestern—discussed with the president of one of the eastern railroads the crude, glaring and unreasonably ugly manner in which his stations were painted. He listened with reasonable impatience, because Mrs. McCrea is a lady, and finally burst out with, 'After all, Mrs. McCrea, it is a question of taste, isn't it?' To this, quick as a flash, Mrs. McCrea replied: 'yes, Mr. President; it is a question of taste—of good taste or of bad taste!' . . . There was no defense left to the apologist for mixing orange and brown before the eyes of the defenseless millions who had to use his steel highway" (*American City*, 441).

She continued to be active in the American Civic Association and became a member of the executive board in 1908. With fewer railroad commissions, McCrea turned her attention to opportunities for civic improvement. She gave talks on community landscaping needs and sometimes received commissions for the work she had recommended. In February 1910, in two talks arranged by the Civic Beauty Committee of the Green Bay (Wisconsin) Business Men's Association, she urged city officials to establish a park commission and provide more public playgrounds. Children in seventh grade and above came with their teachers to hear McCrea's lecture on school gardens and grounds, "Civic Beauty and Cleanliness." The mayor and town council were invited to attend. She used lantern slides to show beautiful streets, parks, and gardens. Her first commissions in the area came in May 1911, as she placed two thousand shrubs in St. James Park in Green Bay and developed plans for Riverside Park in nearby De Pere. Five years later she planned the station grounds in De Pere for the Chicago and Northwestern. In 1915 she became a member of the Chicago Woman's Club, initially serving on the art and literature committee.

McCrea sometimes used her professional talks to focus on her views on women's rights. In 1916, when she was planting shrubbery and laying out flower beds and driveways at the state reformatory near the De Pere–Green Bay Road, she spoke to the De Pere Woman's Club about woman suffrage. Although she had been asked to discuss city improvement, she devoted most of the talk to the suffrage issue, urging Wisconsin women to support the suffrage amendment. She explained, "Child labor states and brewery states never permit women to have a voice in state policy: so the only hope of suffrage is through a federal amendment to the constitution" (quoted in *De Pere News*, May 25, 1916).

McCrea supervised the planting of a row of elm trees on each side of a concrete highway between Green Bay and De Pere. The beautification project was planned by the City Beautiful committees of both the Green Bay and the De Pere Woman's Clubs. Planting started in 1916, and work continued until the boulevard was dedicated as a memorial to World War I veterans in 1920.

She moved to De Pere in 1917 with her daughter and son-in-law, Euena and John Larimer. She worked with private clients on home landscaping, including work on the Frank and Emily Murphy estate in Allouez, near De Pere, completed in 1922. In 1924, she returned to the Chicago area, moving with the Larimers to north suburban Evanston. The *Green Bay Gazette* summed up her impact in Wisconsin. Her advent "marked the evolution of the art of home beautifying. The aesthetic in arrangement of grounds and gardens had largely been sacrificed to the practical and Mrs. McCrea introduced the fact that a combination of the two could be accomplished. . . . Scores of beautiful homes . . . are due entirely to her art and ingenuity" (October 7, 1924). Her final move, also with her daughter and son-in-law, was to Minneapolis about 1927.

She died the next year of myocarditis—inflammation of the heart's muscular tissue. After a funeral at St. Luke's Episcopal Church in Kalamazoo, she was buried next to her husband at Mountain Home Cemetery. Considered a noted landscape artist in the Midwest, McCrea, because of her designs, civic activity, and ability to promote landscape architecture in the railroad trade press, brought prestige and recognition to the profession during its growth early in the twentieth century.

Sources. Information on McCrea's family came from the papers of her daughter, Dorothy Mead Jacobson, held by Barbara J. Neal. McCrea's reports, "Railroad Station Improvement," were published in the *Railroad Gazette* between 1904 and 1908. Her article, "Railroad Station Improvement," appeared in the *Chautauquan*, June 1904. McCrea, Andrew Wright Crawford, and C. L. Ackiss published a pamphlet for the American Civic Association, *Railroad Improvements* (1905), which included the responses to her survey of railroads on landscape work. J. Horace McFarland described McCrea's forthright discussion of landscaping in "How to Improve Railroad Stations and Their Surroundings," *American City*, November 1913. Articles on McCrea in Wisconsin newspapers included "Will Beautify Its Stations," *Milwaukee Sentinel*, May 15, 1902, and a discussion of her talk on woman suffrage in the *De Pere News*, May 25, 1916. John Gruber discussed McCrea in "Woman Landscape Architect Promotes Station Parks," *Mid-Continent Railway Gazette*, January–February 1983. Obituaries appeared in "Annette M'Crea, 70, Noted Artist, Dies," *Kalamazoo Gazette*, September 21, 1928; "Annette M'Crea, Pioneer Garden Architect, Dies," *CT* and *NYT*, September 22, 1928; and *De Pere, Journal-Democrat*, September 27, 1928. For an overview of the work of women landscape architects, including that of McCrea, see Frances Copley Seavey, "Women in Business: XIV—Women in Horticulture," *Chicago Record-Herald*, September 22, 1901.

JOHN E. GRUBER

McCULLOCH, CATHARINE GOUGER WAUGH
June 4, 1862–April 20, 1945
LAWYER, SUFFRAGIST, POLITICAL ACTIVIST

Catharine Waugh McCulloch, the attorney and activist who helped lead the campaign for equal suffrage in Illinois, was born in Ransomville, New York. In 1867, her parents—Abraham Miller and Susan (Gouger) Waugh—moved the family to a farm in New Milford, Illinois. There Catharine Waugh and her younger brother, Edwin, attended the village school and joined in the youth activities of the Congregational Church. Foreshadowing her strong adult friendships with Reverend Anna Howard Shaw and ELLA SEASS STEWART, Waugh had many close girlfriends in the village. To her mother's dismay, these relationships led Catharine into fist fights with local boys who teased the girls. She delighted in being a tomboy, fighting, climbing trees, and wading in the river.

The Waugh family supported woman suffrage, but when Catharine Waugh tried to share this view with her schoolmates, the boys laughed. The ten-year-old then vowed never to marry and to devote herself to a career in law. Like the fathers of many first generation college women, Abraham Waugh encouraged his daughter to study and prepare for a profession. In practicing law, Catharine Waugh would also fulfill ambitions her father had previously abandoned for himself.

In 1878, Catharine entered Rockford (Illinois) Female Seminary (now Rockford College). She was guided and encouraged through school by JANE ADDAMS, who became a lifelong friend. At Rockford, "Kittie" was known for her intelligence, graduating first in her class, as well as for her sense of fun and love of music. The class prophecy predicted that her beauty—petite frame, dark hair, and "the most smiling brown eyes in the world" (*Rockford Seminary Annual*, n.p., reel 13, McCulloch Papers)—would attract many men, but they would be disappointed, as law came first for Waugh.

After graduating in 1882, Waugh stayed in Rockford and read law in the offices of Marshall and Taggart. In 1885, she entered Union College of Law (later Northwestern University's law school) in Chicago. Waugh faced a difficult transition to law school, made easier by the support of the only other woman in her class, CATHARINE WAITE. Until the women proved themselves, the men pelted them with spitballs during recitations. The one exception, Frank Hathorn McCulloch, not only ranked first in the class, but supported equal suffrage, and Waugh later told the *Boston Globe*, "he never smelled of alcohol or tobacco" (August 11, 1913). For five years he pursued Waugh, but committed to her career and to her vow of celibacy, she refused all of his proposals.

Waugh was admitted to the Illinois bar in 1886. Despite her qualifications, she could not obtain a position in Chicago. Male attorneys told her to go home and take in sewing, or said that she appeared to lack the stamina for law. Two lawyers offered her clerkships in exchange for sexual favors. Disgusted, Waugh returned to Rockford in 1887 and opened her own practice. During these trying times, Waugh received support from letters exchanged with members of the Equity Club, the first association of women lawyers in the country. As a law student, Waugh had been instrumental in the establishment of this organization.

While in Rockford, Waugh continued her studies at Rockford Seminary, and "in 1888, having written a thesis on 'Woman's Wages,' was awarded both a B.A. and an M.A. degree" (*NAW*, 459). Her thesis demonstrated the importance of minimum wage standards and reflected her emerging concern for economic as well as political equality for women. Many of Waugh's first clients were women beset by problems related to their lack of legal status: wage discrimination, divorce, probate, child custody, abuse. She wrote to the Equity Club that her usual client was "a poor woman who cannot afford to pay anything. I call that a free dispensary case and rejoice that I had an opportunity to learn some new point there" (Drachman, 174). These cases propelled Catharine Waugh into a leading role in the women's movement and made her one of the foremost advocates of woman suffrage in Illinois. A passion to redress the inequities women experienced brought her and Frank McCulloch together. Even before their marriage, this passion cast her as a public crusader for women's rights. Her earliest publications reflected the nineteenth-century view that women needed the ballot to protect themselves from abuse and discrimination.

Waugh felt a special sympathy for clients who had been seduced and abandoned by men who refused to support the children of these unions. Under state law an attorney could do little for these women. She tried in vain to find homes where the mothers could work and raise their babies. The citizens of Rockford, including her parents, criticized Waugh's involvement with "fallen" women. Only Frank McCulloch encouraged the mission. Waugh began to believe that a married woman, with a supportive husband, could accomplish as much for women as a single woman, whose activities and associations always provoked questions, and she finally agreed to marry McCulloch.

The McCulloch union lasted almost fifty-five years and was by all accounts a happy partnership; but it began in acrimony. Her parents did not like the groom, and his mother objected to the Waughs' Irish ancestry. Only twenty somber guests gathered on May 30, 1890, to witness the marriage. The bride's close friend, Reverend Anna Howard Shaw, conducted the ceremony. The two met through suffrage work, and four years later Shaw became president of the National American Woman Suffrage Association (NAWSA) in which McCulloch would serve

FIG. 73. *Lawyer and suffragist Catharine Waugh McCulloch, first woman Justice of the Peace in Evanston, Illinois, a suburb of Chicago.*

as an officer. The McCullochs honeymooned in South Dakota, where the bride was already scheduled to speak on behalf of woman suffrage.

The couple returned to Chicago and opened a law partnership. In 1891, their first child, Hugh Waugh, was born. Three more children were born (Hathorn Waugh, 1899, Catharine Waugh, 1901, and Frank Waugh, 1905). McCulloch continued her suffrage advocacy and her law practice. She had begun chairing the Legislative Committee of the Illinois Equal Suffrage Association (IESA) in 1890 and continued in that position for the next twenty-two years. In Illinois, there was not enough support for a constitutional amendment on woman suffrage, so McCulloch devised an alternative strategy. Under "statutory suffrage" women would be allowed to vote for president and in all other elections not constitutionally limited to men. McCulloch's bill was introduced in 1893 and every year thereafter. "In support of the bill [in 1893] she road on a whistle-stop train with Jane Addams, making speeches from Chicago to Springfield on the importance of women's suffrage" (Harrigan, 30).

As the family grew, the McCullochs moved from their first apartment in Chicago to a much larger home in Evanston, Illinois. For several years while her children were small, McCulloch also cared for her invalid mother. In order to pay for household help to assist her in caring for her extended family, McCulloch continued to practice law. Yet, at the same time, she felt she should be at home. Though aware that this ideal was clearly impossible for many women, McCulloch's autobiography stated her belief that a woman's most important job was motherhood. McCulloch's *Mr. Lex* (1899), a fictionalized account of some women's legal disabilities, led to legislation she drafted that guaranteed mothers the same rights as fathers in custody cases.

In 1905, McCulloch wrote the bill that strengthened rape laws and raised the age of consent in Illinois. Her play, *Bridget's Sisters*, produced in 1911, brought attention to a woman's need for greater protection from an abusive or alcoholic husband. Her writings led to public speaking engagements, and by 1908 McCulloch was addressing international audiences. That year, she traveled to Amsterdam, the Netherlands, with Anna Howard Shaw and Ella Seass Stewart as a NAWSA delegate to the International Suffrage Alliance convention. McCulloch's reform causes included temperance, moral purity, child welfare, labor reform, the ordination of women, and peace. To her, they all stemmed from a woman's restricted citizenship. A tireless campaign for equal suffrage became her way of redressing all the problems of women.

The central dilemma in her own life became how to balance the children's needs with her own career ambitions and reform objectives. She solved this problem between 1907 and 1913 by serving as Justice of the Peace in Evanston. McCulloch was one of the first, if not the first, women in the country to hold a judicial post. In campaigning for the office, McCulloch stressed that, as the mother of small children, she needed to be at home and thus would always be available to perform the duties of a justice. Twice an all-male electorate gave her a wide margin of victory.

McCulloch carefully disassociated herself from the most militant suffragists and disavowed their tactics of picketing and subjecting themselves to arrest. McCulloch maintained that women could only advance through proper legal channels and confined her own activities to lobbying, writing, and speechmaking. Her concern with proper and legal behavior stemmed from her belief that women had a special mission to purify and perfect politics.

As Progressive Era governments exhibited greater interest in the issues of municipal housekeeping—pure food and water, moral reform, public health, education—suffragists claimed they needed women's traditional expertise in these areas. The rationale for equal suffrage changed from how the ballot could help women to how voting women could help the community. Catharine McCulloch was in the forefront of this transition and was particularly effective in discussing a mother's contribution to civilization.

In 1912, IESA elected GRACE WILBUR TROUT president. McCulloch resigned from the organization because she felt Trout's tactics were too passive and accommodating. Trout's supporters considered McCulloch too radical. After McCulloch's resignation from IESA, she traveled from New York to Oregon speaking in favor of votes for women. The IESA, however, once again asked the lawmakers to extend presidential and municipal suffrage to Illinois women, reintroducing the same bill McCulloch had written and first brought to the General Assembly in 1893. Ironically, within one year of Trout's ascendancy to IESA leadership, the General Assembly finally passed the suffrage bill. Trout and her followers attributed this victory to a series of new political strategies they adopted, including sending motor cars of suffrage supporters to the state capital with much fanfare and publicity. Antisuffragists charged that McCulloch was "the guy who put the ill in Illinois" (*Boston Globe*, August 11, 1913).

McCulloch expanded her professional activities, becoming legal adviser to the Woman's Christian Temperance Union (WCTU), headquartered in Chicago. "In 1913, McCulloch was appointed as Law Dean at the Illinois College of Law (now known as DePaul University College of Law)" (Harrigan, 31). From 1916 to 1920, she served as president of the Women's Bar Association of Illinois. In 1917, she became the first woman master in chancery of the Cook County Superior Court, serving until 1925. With Frank McCulloch, she wrote *A Manual of the Law of Will Contests in Illinois* (1929). In 1940, recognizing her fifty years of superior service, the Illinois Bar Association honored Catharine McCulloch by naming her senior counselor. She evaluated her accomplishments on her own terms. McCulloch told the *Chicago Record-Herald* that she was proudest of proving that it was possible "to be at one and the same time a good lawyer, a good justice of the peace, a good housekeeper, and a most devoted mother" (November 28, 1909).

McCulloch argued that women differed from men. They were more chaste, sober, intelligent, and peaceful. They thus had special interests and values that should be represented in the government. As early as 1889, McCulloch had written in the *Farmer's Voice*, "Woman, the last and most perfect of her Creator's handiwork, stands at the top of the ascending scale," and as mothers, women bear responsibility for the future of civilization. Years later, in a 1912 issue of the *Glencoe Record*, McCulloch questioned whether any had a greater "stake in government" than a mother who was selflessly devoted to securing her children's happiness.

For McCulloch a woman's responsibility did not end with enfranchisement. It also included seeking office and serving the public good. In 1894, she led the successful campaign to elect LUCY FLOWER as the first woman trustee of the University of Illinois. Two years later, the Prohibition Party nominated Mc-

Culloch for state's attorney. For many years she identified herself as an independent, but after 1912 she became a Wilsonian Democrat. She explained this choice in a 1916 campaign speech, saying, "My place is with those who are robbed, who are poor, who are hungry, who have no advantages" ("Draft Speech," reel 14, McCulloch Papers). That year, the Democrats selected McCulloch as a presidential elector, one of the first women in the nation to be so honored. In the early 1920s, the members of the Illinois Women's Democratic Club chose McCulloch as their first president.

After ratification of the Nineteenth Amendment giving women the right to vote, McCulloch chaired the League of Women Voters committee on uniform laws. She continued her involvement with the WCTU, Rockford College, the American Civil Liberties Union, the Chicago Commons social settlement, and the Women's International League for Peace and Freedom. With her children grown and equal suffrage achieved, McCulloch took more time for travel, sometimes with her husband, other times alone. She made several trips to Europe and South America, adding to her lifelong study of the legal conditions of women. McCulloch maintained her practice with her husband and sons until her death at age eighty-two. After a two-week cancer-related illness, Catharine McCulloch died at Evanston Hospital. She was buried at Graceland Cemetery in Chicago.

As a woman of the nineteenth century who achieved eminence in the twentieth century, Catharine Waugh McCulloch struck a complicated balance in her life. She traveled independently and chose her own reform endeavors, while devoting herself to her husband and marriage. She mothered four children as she established a pioneering legal career. A confident and assertive activist on behalf of the causes she supported, McCulloch rejected militant tactics in favor of legally grounded appeals. She received wholehearted support from men in her private life but faced scorn and contempt from many of those she encountered in the public arena. Because of these complexities, Catharine McCulloch could see, and persuasively argue, that women needed the protection of their government and that they had essential talents to offer in return. Her own exhaustive efforts helped to win fundamental rights of citizenship for the women of Illinois and the nation.

Sources. The Catharine Gouger Waugh McCulloch Papers, SL, include personal and professional correspondence, legal documents, book drafts, speeches, and scrapbooks. Also, 281 files of McCulloch's suffrage papers, correspondence, and publications are included in the Mary Earhart Dillon Collection, SL. Both the McCulloch Papers and the Dillon Collection are available on microfilm. Articles on McCulloch's work and views include her essay in *Farmer's Voice*, June 22, 1889; "Equal Suffrage Talk by Mrs. M'Culloch," *Glencoe Record*, June 1, 1912; and "Author of Suffrage Bill," *Boston Globe*, August 11, 1913. McCulloch's work in establishing the Equity Club is detailed in Virginia G. Drachman, *Women Lawyers and the Origins of Professional Identity in America: The Letters of the Equity Club, 1887 to 1890* (1993). The volume includes circular letters written to Equity members by McCulloch. McCulloch's biography is in *NAW* (1971). See also Maria A. Harrigan, "Catherine [*sic*] McCulloch," *CBA Record*, vol. 12, 1998.

MARY LINEHAN

McDOWELL, MARY ELIZA
November 30, 1854–October 14, 1936
SOCIAL REFORMER, SETTLEMENT DIRECTOR, PUBLIC
WELFARE COMMISSIONER

Mary Eliza McDowell was born in Cincinnati, Ohio, the eldest of six children—two daughters and four sons—of Malcolm and Jane (Gordon) McDowell. Her maternal grandfather was an early steamboat builder. Her father worked for the first railroad to enter Cincinnati and stayed on to manufacture sheet iron. During the Civil War, Malcolm McDowell served on the staff of his brother, Brigadier-General Irvin McDowell, while his wife and children remained in the spacious house on the banks of the Ohio River built in the 1830s by her maternal grandfather, Archibald Gordon. Mary McDowell's earliest memories were of Irish and German working-class neighbors, her mother's charitable work for Union soldiers and their families, and her father's ardent commitment to the abolition of slavery and his admiration for President Lincoln. She attended public school until her early teens, when she switched to a private girls' school in the more exclusive neighborhood of Walnut Hills. Although her mother was a graduate of Wesleyan Female College in Cincinnati, Mary McDowell chose not to continue her formal education, a decision she later regretted. She was fully satisfied, however, with her decision at age eleven to follow her father into a modest Methodist chapel which emphasized good works.

In 1870 Malcolm McDowell moved his family to Chicago, where he continued to manufacture iron and steel, retiring from the McDowell Steel Company in the mid-1890s. The family first lived on the Near North Side of the city, then in Ravenswood, and in the early 1880s they moved to Evanston, a suburb north of Chicago. Father and daughter were active in Methodist churches, he as a class meeting leader and she as a successful Sunday school teacher. In the aftermath of the 1871 fire, she helped her Methodist pastor distribute food and clothing to refugees. In December 1878 she heard FRANCES E. WILLARD, corresponding secretary of the Woman's Christian Temperance Union (WCTU), address a group of young women in Chicago. Impressed by Willard and the temperance work of the WCTU branches, McDowell joined. She organized young women in Illinois and other states and by 1887 was the national director of this work. She was also interested in the new kindergarten movement and, with WCTU approval, spent the academic year of 1889–90 studying at ELIZABETH HARRISON's Chicago Kindergarten Training School. Upon completion of that course, she worked as a kindergarten teacher in New York City while also supervising the WCTU's kindergartens.

McDowell returned to Chicago in 1891 to become the kindergarten teacher at Hull-House, the social settlement directed by JANE ADDAMS. The settlement philosophy appealed to her as an effective way to apply her religious principles, and Addams, who was only six years younger, would become her closest friend and confidant. In addition to running the kindergarten, McDowell started a club for mothers of the children in her classes, and this group blossomed into the Hull-House Woman's Club early in 1892. Her own mother's illness necessitated her return to Evanston in 1893. However, she made frequent trips to Hull-House and to the Northwestern University Settlement, whose founders were Evanston friends. She read

FIG. 74. *Mary E. McDowell and Jane Addams marched together for peace, Chicago, 1917.*

widely during her time at home, almost certainly the works of Washington Gladden and Richard T. Ely on social Christianity, and discussed contemporary issues with her father and his friends. The violent Chicago railroad strike in 1894 prompted her to go to the town of Pullman to talk with Rev. William Carwardine, a supporter of the strikers and their trade union. Unbeknownst to McDowell, some students and faculty members at the new University of Chicago had formed a Christian Union and had sent a few students to live in the vicinity of the stockyards and meatpacking plants on the southwest side of Chicago in 1893. The following year they decided to expand their effort and asked Jane Addams to recommend a director. She suggested McDowell, who accepted and moved in September 1894 to a small flat in Back of the Yards, as that industrial neighborhood was called.

The University of Chicago Settlement was McDowell's base of operation until she relinquished active direction in 1923, the year she became Chicago's Commissioner of Public Welfare. Although the settlement was loyally supported by the university community, it was not funded by that institution. McDowell and her board of directors raised the money to purchase two lots on Gross Avenue (later renamed McDowell Avenue) for settlement expansion. A ten-thousand-dollar combined gymnasium and auditorium was constructed in 1899, and in 1905 a three-story settlement building valued at twenty-five thousand dollars was completed. The latter contained a parlor, dining facilities, library, office, and meeting rooms on the first floor plus quarters for seventeen residents above. Expansion of the settlement house program kept pace. Starting with a kindergarten and day nursery, mothers' club, and activities for boys and girls, residents and volunteers added musical, dramatic, and athletic groups, classes in arts and crafts for children, and English and citizenship for foreign-born adults. McDowell's efforts to find outdoor play space gave rise to vacation schools in Chicago and spurred the development of inner-city neighborhood parks like Davis Square and Sherman Park in Back of the Yards.

McDowell helped launch the Chicago Federation of Settlements (1894), a forerunner of the 1911 National Federation of Settlements over which she presided in 1914–15. She spoke frequently about settlement work to women's organizations, religious groups, and professional associations, always emphasizing, "It is not the works of a settlement that define it, it is the attitude of the mind . . . enthusiasm for humanity, for democracy, that tells in the *living with*, not for, people" (McDowell, "Social Settlements," 6).

Over the years, Irish and German neighbors in the University of Chicago settlement gave way to Bohemians, Poles, Lithuanians, Slavs, and, by the 1920s, some Mexicans. Long hours of arduous, repetitive work for low wages were the norm for many of her neighbors, and McDowell sought to address these injustices through trade unionism and legislation. She gave strong support to Michael Donnelly, head of the Amalgamated Meat Cutters and Butcher Workmen, who began organizing Chicago packinghouse workers in 1901. She encouraged females in the can-labeling division to start a woman's local that included African Americans, and McDowell represented that local at the 1903 American Federation of Labor convention in Boston. There she joined with others in founding the Women's Trade Union League (WTUL); she launched a Chicago branch of the league early in 1904 and served as its president until 1907. She drew MARY ANDERSON and AGNES NESTOR, among others, into trade union activity, and she worked closely with MARGARET DREIER ROBINS, president of the local league after 1907 and later the national WTUL. During the bitterly contested packinghouse strike of 1904, McDowell spoke and wrote in support of the union and interpreted its grievances to the broader community. When it was clear that the meatpackers would not yield to union demands, McDowell, Addams, and neighborhood physician CORNELIA DE BEY met with and convinced the packers to take back the strikers with their union intact.

The need for better information about working women and children prompted McDowell, SOPHONISBA BRECKINRIDGE, and EDITH ABBOTT, all of them associated with the newly created Chicago School of Civics and Philanthropy (after 1920 the School of Social Service Administration, University of Chicago), to ask President Theodore Roosevelt for a federal investigation. He agreed only after they marshaled support from the labor movement and women's organizations. The 1907–1909 Bureau of Labor study resulted in the multi-volume *Report on Conditions of Woman and Child Wage-Earners in the*

United States (1910–13). Drawing on this information, McDowell joined scores of other progressives in lobbying for state legislation to restrict the hours of work for women and children and to establish minimum wages for women in industry. As a member of President Woodrow Wilson's Committee on Women in Industry, she saw to it that these laws were observed in the defense industries during World War I. McDowell also helped secure in 1920 a Women's Bureau within the Department of Labor and the appointment of Mary Anderson as its first director.

When McDowell moved to Back of the Yards in 1894, Chicago was disposing of garbage, trash, and street sweepings in noxious open dumps, one of which was in her vicinity. Children played there, and adults combed the dump for useful castoffs. She first organized a Civic Improvement Association, which pleaded with city officials but accomplished little. She then informed other areas of Chicago about sanitary problems in Back of the Yards and contrasted Chicago waste disposal policies with those in other American cities. ETHEL STURGES DUMMER, a leading Chicago philanthropist, financed a trip McDowell made in the summer of 1911 to European cities to study their procedures. Upon her return, she put together a coalition of supporters drawn from the male City Club and Citizens' Association, the University of Chicago faculty, Chicago Woman's Club, and the new Woman's City Club. The supporters demanded that Chicago improve its methods of collecting trash and garbage and build either incinerators or reduction plants to dispose of wastes. Politicians showed little interest until Chicago women secured municipal suffrage in 1913. Then Mayor Carter Harrison appointed a City Waste Commission of which McDowell was a member and promised money to hire sanitary engineers to devise a solution. Chicago followed the commission's recommendations and the open dumps were finally phased out. As president of the Woman's City Club in 1915–16, McDowell campaigned for the bond issue that funded Chicago's new sanitary policy.

McDowell's commitment to woman suffrage dated back to her WCTU affiliation. She worked with the Illinois Equal Suffrage Association and in the 1912 presidential election with the Progressive Party, because its platform supported woman suffrage as well as many social and economic reforms she had long championed. The following year the Illinois legislature passed a law permitting women to vote in local and national contests. In the fall of 1914 Mary McDowell and HARRIET VITTUM, director of Northwestern University Settlement and an unsuccessful aldermanic candidate in the spring of that year, ran on the Progressive Party ticket for seats on the Cook County Board of Commissioners. A last-minute judicial ruling held that women could run for county offices but could not vote in county elections. McDowell and Vittum each received about half as many male votes as the successful Democrats. They probably would have won, had the nearly two hundred thousand registered women been allowed to participate.

McDowell held appointive office from 1923 to 1927 in the administration of a reform Democratic mayor, William E. Dever. As Commissioner of Public Welfare, she revitalized the moribund department by reopening a lodging house for homeless men and adding to it an employment and social service office. Her department's Bureau of Research published studies of the elderly poor and housing conditions for Chicago's newest arrivals, Mexican immigrants and African Americans from the South. To publicize the need for low-income housing, she sponsored a conference in 1926 and persuaded Dever to appoint the city's first Housing Commission. Her visibility in city government gave her an opportunity to promote interracial contacts in the aftermath of the 1919 riot. McDowell had strong ties to black women's clubs, had invited black speakers to the settlement, and was active in both the National Association for the Advancement of Colored People and the Chicago Urban League. In the 1920s she pushed for the integration of Chicago's women's clubs and was one of the sponsors of the 1927 *Negro in Art Exhibition* that showcased black artists, writers, and musicians.

Mary McDowell lived on at the settlement until she suffered a paralytic stroke shortly before her death in 1936. She was buried in Rosehill Cemetery in Chicago. A memorial service at the University of Chicago Settlement paid tribute to her warm personality, rapport with immigrants and African Americans, staunch support of wage earners, and her significant impact on public policy in Chicago.

Sources. The Mary McDowell/University of Chicago Settlement Papers at the CHS contain extensive settlement records and incomplete material on McDowell, including some correspondence, drafts of speeches, and a brief, unfinished autobiography. The Woman's Christian Temperance Union's newspaper, *Union Signal*, carried occasional dispatches about her activities during the 1880s. She wrote more than five dozen articles appearing in the *Commons* (including "Social Settlements," vol. 5, 1900), the *Survey*, and many other journals and magazines. Caroline M. Hill compiled essays by McDowell and her associates in *Mary McDowell and Municipal Housekeeping* (1938). Howard E. Wilson expanded a University of Chicago master's thesis into *Mary McDowell, Neighbor* (1928). For her role in the settlement movement, see Lea D. Taylor, "The Social Settlement and Civic Responsibility—the Life Work of Mary McDowell and Graham Taylor," *Social Service Review*, March 1954; Allen F. Davis, *Spearheads for Reform* (1967); and Mina Carson, *Settlement Folk* (1990). For her ties to the Women's Trade Union League, see Agnes Nestor, *Woman's Labor Leader* (1954); Mary Anderson, *Woman at Work* (1951); and Elizabeth Payne, *Reform, Labor, and Feminism* (1988). For Chicago's Back of the Yards neighborhood, see Louise Carroll Wade, *Chicago's Pride: The Stockyards, Packingtown, and Environs in the Nineteenth Century* (1987), and James R. Barrett, *Work and Community in the Jungle: Chicago's Packinghouse Workers, 1894–1922* (1987). See also *NAW* (1971), and *American National Biography*, ed. John A. Garraty and Mark C. Carnes (1999).

LOUISE CARROLL WADE

McGRATH, SISTER ALBERTUS MAGNUS
(Marion Cecily McGrath)
January 4, 1911–October 8, 1978
PROFESSOR, HISTORIAN, FEMINIST

Marion Cecily McGrath, professor of history, feminist, and author of *What a Modern Catholic Believes about Women*, was born on Chicago's South Side, the last of seven children and the fourth of four daughters of Michael George and Nora (Keane) McGrath. Her parents were born in different towns of County Waterford, Ireland. They emigrated to the United States and met in Chicago, where they were married in 1892. Before her marriage, Nora Keane was employed as a cook for a well-to-do family. Michael McGrath worked as a salesman, providing a modest living for his large family.

Marion McGrath attended first Visitation and then St. Basil Grade School, skipping grades three and six, an early indication of her lively intelligence. She was twelve years old when she entered Visitation High School in 1923. She enrolled at Rosary College (became Dominican University in 1997) in River Forest, Illinois, in 1927 and graduated with a B.A. degree in 1931. Her areas of interest and concentration were history, English, Latin, and mathematics.

The Sinsinawa Dominican nuns exerted a profound influence on McGrath. From first grade through college she had been taught by these well-educated women, and it did not come as a surprise to her family and friends when McGrath decided to enter the Sinsinawa Dominican Congregation. Mother Emily Power and Mother Samuel Coughlin, the first two elected leaders of the congregation, placed a heavy emphasis on study and on excellence in teaching. Sinsinawa Dominicans taught at every level in schools throughout the United States. Sought by pastors trying to respond to the educational needs of the fast-growing immigrant church, they served in parish schools; the sisters also established educational institutions of their own, including Rosary College, founded in 1922 for Catholic women in the Chicago area.

After graduating from Rosary College, McGrath entered the Dominican novitiate at Sinsinawa, Wisconsin, taking the name Sister Albertus Magnus at the suggestion of the novice mistress who must have recognized in McGrath an independent spirit of inquiry. McGrath easily identified with her namesake, the thirteenth-century Dominican scientist and educator.

Sister Albertus Magnus first taught at Edgewood High School and at Edgewood College, Sinsinawa Dominican-sponsored educational institutions in Madison, Wisconsin. While continuing to teach history, English, Latin, and mathematics in the high school, and history and sociology at the college, she was asked by her religious superiors to enroll in the history department of the University of Wisconsin in 1937 for advanced study. In their emphasis on doctoral studies and in their choice of secular universities, the Sinsinawa Dominicans were forerunners in what would become more common among American sisterhoods only after Vatican Council II (1962–65). By 1947, twenty-seven Sinsinawa Dominican sisters had earned Ph.D. degrees and 184 had earned M.A. degrees from outstanding universities both in the United States and abroad, including Oxford University, England; the University of Fribourg, Switzerland; Yale and Columbia universities.

In Madison and at the university, Sister Albertus Magnus found herself in a milieu of progressive and reformist thinking and New Deal politics. As a lifelong Democrat, McGrath breathed easily in this atmosphere. Her research focused, however, not on American history or politics, but on modern Europe. She earned an M.A. in 1942, writing her thesis on Great Britain and the Weimar Republic; for her doctorate in history and English, completed in 1947, she wrote on the nineteenth-century Anglo-Catholic movement.

In 1946, McGrath joined the history department at Rosary College, River Forest, Illinois. Seventy-three Sinsinawa Dominicans had faculty appointments at the college; others staffed the all-girls Trinity High School in the same village. McGrath became part of an extensive educational network of women re-

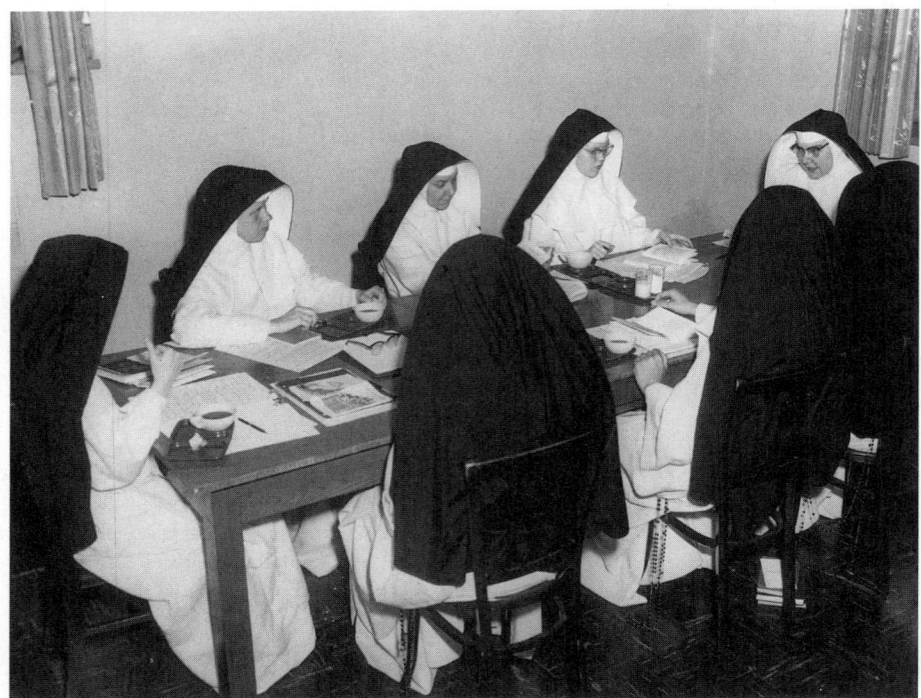

Fig. 75. *Sister Albertus Magnus McGrath, at far right wearing glasses, and student sisters, Rosary College (now Dominican University), c. 1960.*

ligious who supported and mentored one another. At the same time her appetite for learning was not sated; during summer sessions she studied in Fribourg, Switzerland, where Rosary College ran a junior-year-abroad program in conjunction with the university, and at Columbia and Harvard universities. The financing of such study among Sinsinawa Dominicans was possible because of simple living arrangements in convents and the combination of part-time study with teaching assignments. Any earnings from teaching not absorbed by their modest living needs were sent back to the motherhouse and placed in a common fund.

In 1965–66 Sister Albertus Magnus McGrath was granted a research fellowship at Yale Divinity School, where she studied the apostolate of women after the Industrial Revolution. Her interest in the history of women in Christianity paralleled the new research in women's history by secular scholars and the emergence of the women's movement. McGrath gave the keynote address at the national convention of Kappa Gamma Pi (Catholic women's graduate honor society), held in Chicago June 30–July 2, 1967. The convention theme, "Catholic Women Leaders—Genesis and Exodus," was the right context for McGrath's address, "Emphasis on Excellence, with Love and Anger." Here McGrath introduced, for the first time, ideas later fully developed in her book, *What a Modern Catholic Believes about Women* (1972). McGrath exhorted her audience to direct their energies toward civic and intellectual problems in the United States at the highest levels and to reject associations that were intellectually mediocre and morally shoddy. During this period McGrath continued to teach; her students selected her for Rosary's Excellence-in-Teaching Award in 1969.

McGrath's consciousness of discrimination against women predated the second wave of feminism of the late 1960s and early 1970s. A convergence of factors in the 1960s served to deepen her convictions and her determination to speak out for justice for women in church and society. The Second Vatican Council (1962–65) was one factor. Called by Pope John Paul XXIII, the council redefined the church in relation to its own members, to the world, and to other churches and religions. It precipitated a renewal of revolutionary proportions in every aspect of church thought and practice: liturgy, ministry, the exercise of authority, the role of the laity, and the understanding of religious life. Pope John Paul XXIII's encyclical *Pacem in Terris* recognized the changing role of women. He identified as one of the signs of the times women's determination to claim in both domestic and public life the rights and duties that befit human dignity.

The council was taking place at the same moment that the civil rights movement and the women's liberation movement were gaining momentum in the United States. Sister Albertus Magnus welcomed and helped popularize and disseminate the ideas unleashed by these three intersecting forces. Going further than the church fathers at the Second Vatican Council, she turned a critical eye on the institutional structures of the church as they affected women's struggle for self-determination. In a 1974 interview in *St. Anthony's Messenger*—"Are Women Oppressed in the Church?"—McGrath answered with a resounding "Yes"; and she did not hesitate to call herself a propagandist whose energy was often directed to challenging oppressive male structures in the church.

Based on solid historical research, *What a Modern Catholic*

Believes about Women had a powerful impact on women religious and laywomen alike. McGrath reveals the contempt with which women have often been treated in clerical circles despite declarations by the hierarchy of the equality of women and men as children of God. Jesus claimed women as friends and called them to be disciples, but she reminded her readers that the institutional church gradually eliminated women from official service as the organization and structure came to resemble that of the Roman Empire. In the book's final chapter, "Women as 'Niggers' of the Church," McGrath characterizes the Catholic Church as "over-protective of women on the one hand, and, on the other, as the land of the perpetual putdown of the feminine" (p. 100). McGrath used the derogatory term "nigger" to underline that damaging stereotypes kept both black persons and women of every race subordinate and servile. McGrath challenges the ban on the ordination of women, argues persuasively for a change in the tradition, and although not optimistic about how long such transformation would take, positions women to be "instruments of the Spirit to hasten this development in the direction of justice and love" (p. 115).

Already a popular speaker, after the publication of her book McGrath was sought after by sisters' councils and councils of Catholic women throughout the United States. Sisters' councils were formed after Vatican II to bring together women religious from various United States congregations to discuss adaptations of their ministries and community life and their changing conception of themselves as women and as religious. The mood of the times was one of excitement, discovery, growth, of courage, eloquence, and vision. Women religious were ready, but change was also painful, confusing, and conflictual. Sister Albertus Magnus played an important role in the dialogue among religious during this period of profound self-examination, serving as a trusted and inspiring role model. She also communicated to laywomen what was occurring among women religious.

On the national level, McGrath became an advocate for equal educational opportunities for women. Long aware of the inequities women experienced in higher education, she participated in 1971 in a month-long institute sponsored by the United States Office of Education. In *ex-CHANGE*, a Sinsinawa Dominican magazine, she publicized the information she had absorbed. In this way she linked her readers with the larger movement to strengthen federal support of higher education and equal opportunity for women. Although an ardent feminist, McGrath was valued by the Archdiocese of Chicago for her passion for justice and her objectivity. She served on the Chicago Archdiocesan Board of Conciliation and Arbitration in the 1970s, playing a leadership role within this body that considered parish disputes ranging from financial and personnel issues to theological and liturgical ones.

McGrath was an early member of the National Assembly of Women Religious (later the National Assembly of Religious Women—including both nuns and laywomen). In 1974 McGrath participated in discussions at Rosary College on the ordination of women in the Catholic Church that were initiated by Mary B. Lynch. McGrath attended the Women's Ordination Conference in 1976 and, by this date, was seen as a leading voice for Catholic women. Chicago Catholic Women, a feminist organization, selected McGrath to chair a meeting of the women in Chicago for the purpose of gathering testimony to be transmitted to the National Call to Action. This position placed McGrath in the center of a supercharged, emotional debate within the church, since the Call to Action was a nationwide assembly of Catholics called by the bishops in the United States and charged with the responsibility of hearing from all sectors of American Catholicism.

McGrath, a member of the National Organization of Women (NOW) and an ardent proponent of the Equal Rights Amendment (ERA), went public—rare for religious women—with a pro-ERA advertisement in the *Chicago Sun-Times* that featured her photograph accompanied by the quote, "Sometimes I think Illinois seems almost past praying for when it comes to equality for women" (McGrath Papers, Sinsinawa Dominican Archives). Catholic laywoman Susan Catania—mother of seven daughters, lawyer, and member of the Illinois General Assembly from 1973 to 1983—was the principal sponsor of the ERA. After McGrath's death, Catania, chair of the Illinois Commission on the Status of Women, wrote to her colleague on the commission and president of Rosary College, Sister Candida Lund, that "the best way for us to honor her [McGrath] is to carry on with her crusade for equal rights for women in the Church and for the women's movement in general" (Catania to Lund, October 23, 1978, Rosary College Archives).

World peace was another social and political issue that engaged Sr. Albertus Magnus's dedicated attention; she was a member of the Catholic Association for International Peace. In 1958, she was invited to participate in a symposium sponsored by the ecumenical Church Peace Union, entering with evident delight into the wide-ranging discussion of foreign policy and world affairs.

In the last two years of her life, Sister Albertus Magnus began to show signs of what would later be diagnosed as chronic hydrocephalus. She fell on several occasions and developed a fear of falling. She spent much of the time from 1976 to 1978 at St. Dominic Villa, the Sinsinawa Dominican nursing care facility located in Dubuque, Iowa. She died at the nearby Mercy Health Center after a fall. She is buried at the cemetery at Sinsinawa Mound, Wisconsin.

The Eightieth Illinois General Assembly passed a resolution in memory of Sister Albertus Magnus McGrath on November 28, 1978, recognizing her work for the ERA and for women's rights in the church. McGrath exercised a profound influence on successive generations of students during her thirty-year tenure at Rosary College. She challenged her women students, especially, to use their intelligence to its fullest capacity and to use their hearts, daring, and instinct to transform unjust social structures.

Sources. The Sister Albertus Magnus McGrath Papers are in the Sinsinawa Dominican Archives, Sinsinawa, Wisconsin, and in the Rosary College Archives, River Forest, Illinois. At Sinsinawa, papers include correspondence, photographs, her writings, articles about her, reviews of her book, her lectures, and notes. There is also a Personal File with information on her family, mission assignments, obituary, and death certificate. A file at Rosary College Archives contains correspondence, press releases, faculty briefs, contracts, information on the Scholarship Fund set up in her honor, and the tributes delivered at her Memorial Mass Service. Works by Sister Albertus Magnus McGrath include "Great Britain and the Weimar Republic" (master's thesis, Univ. of Wisconsin, 1942); "The History of the Anglo-Catholic Movement 1850–1875" (Ph.D. diss., Univ. of Wisconsin, 1946); *What a Modern Catholic Believes about Women* (1972), reprinted as *Women and the Church* (1976). An interview with her conducted by Jack Wintz, O.F.M., appears in the February 1974 issue of the *St. Anthony Messenger*.

KAYE ASHE, OP

McILVAINE, CAROLINE MARGARET
November 4, 1868–November 26, 1945
LIBRARIAN, MUSEUM CURATOR

Caroline McIlvaine, a promoter of Chicago and midwest history and a leader in museum management, was born in Chicago to John Slaymaker and Laura Jane (Hinds) McIlvaine. Her father's ancestors came to Delaware from Ireland in 1719. Her first maternal American ancestor came from England to Salem, Massachusetts, in 1637. Her parents met and married in Dixon, Illinois, where her father attended college and her mother was a schoolteacher. Her father was in the wholesale grocery business. She had one sibling, a sister, Mabel, younger by three years, who was her close friend and colleague throughout her life. She spent her childhood in Chicago with summers in Dixon, Illinois, visiting her maternal grandparents.

Business matters took the family to Minneapolis for two years, where McIlvaine attended high school; she graduated upon their return to Chicago. Soon thereafter, in 1889, John McIlvaine died at age forty-six, leaving only a small financial inheritance to his wife and daughters. With a high school education and language instruction from private tutors, McIlvaine followed her mother's example and become a teacher, serving at the Ogden School in Chicago for three years. She remained unmarried, living with her mother and sister.

In 1891, when both Caroline and Mabel McIlvaine decided upon library careers, they sought employment at the Newberry Library, which had been established four years earlier. Seeking further education, Caroline McIlvaine attended classes at the University of Chicago Extension Program. She worked in all of the library's departments, annotated the collection of Bibles, and in 1896 became head cataloger and director of an Index of Genealogy.

Caroline McIlvaine left the Newberry Library in December 1901 for greater responsibilities at the Chicago Historical Society (CHS). The society had dismissed its secretary/librarian and separated the two functions; Caroline McIlvaine was appointed librarian. The secretary was in charge of the building, books, and matters pertaining to the collection. The librarian's duties were to classify and catalog the library and work under the secretary's direction. From 1906, when the secretary was removed from office, to 1921, when another was installed, McIlvaine performed both jobs as librarian and acting secretary. In practice, she functioned as director; during her tenure no officer held the title of director and the nominal head was the president, a trustee. Involved in all aspects of operations, she cultivated donors, negotiated acquisitions and publications agreements, supervised the maintenance staff, contracted for building repairs, and acted as promotional spokesperson.

McIlvaine promoted the visualization of history through field trips and experienced an extraordinary example in 1906, when the society received a most unusual living bequest. Ossian Guthrie, a longtime resident of Chicago, bequeathed to the city, through CHS, his knowledge of the city's early history and the arrival of Father Marquette. To deliver this living bequest, Guthrie led an expedition for McIlvaine, two trustees, and a photographer. His guided tour through the woods traced Marquette's 1673–75 path from central Chicago to the southwest region. McIlvaine later initiated field trips to historic sites in Illinois as museum education programs. In July 1926 she arranged a trip for twenty-five American and five French children and a group of historical writers to the Pacific Coast for the Columbia River Historical Expedition.

McIlvaine popularized history by interpreting events with personal stories. She recorded interviews with early Chicagoans who founded the CHS in 1856 and with survivors of the Great Fire of 1871. In 1911 she brought Texas resident Emily Beaubien LeBeau to Chicago for interviews. LeBeau was the daughter of Mark Beaubien, one of Chicago's first settlers, and was the last living person who knew Chicago as it was in 1829.

McIlvaine's eye for valuable historical material led her to acquire collections of manuscripts, maps, documents, and correspondence concerning French explorations, Indian treaties, records of early Chicago real estate and railroads, military papers, as well as artworks and artifacts. In 1912 she purchased from Charles H. Conover the most complete collection extant of Lewis and Clark literature. The highlight of her curatorial career was the acquisition and management of Charles F. Gunther's collection. Gunther, a candy manufacturer, CHS trustee, and longtime friend of McIlvaine's family, died in 1920, and his family offered his unusual collection, valued at three hundred thousand dollars, to the CHS for one hundred fifty thousand dollars. McIlvaine understood that this collection would propel the Chicago Historical Society into the ranks of major American historical museums. The eclectic collection included antiquities such as Assyrian cuneiform tablets, soldiers' uniforms from the Revolutionary and Civil Wars, memorabilia from Presidents Washington and Lincoln, prints illustrating American history, manuscripts, books, and maps. In 1925 she sold foreign items in the Gunther collection at a New York art auction house to raise funds to purchase the Americana, thus refining the scope of the CHS and retaining materials that placed local history in a national context.

She concerned herself with civic issues involving the erection and maintenance of monuments and the preservation of historic buildings, such as the Water Tower. In 1918 she worked with the Chicago Plan Commission to determine which historic sites in Chicago were important enough to be marked. She organized events, including monument dedications and anniversary commemorations, to attract new members and press coverage. She recruited descendants of Chicago's founders and business leaders for fund-raising. HARRIET PULLMAN, widow of the railroad car magnate George Pullman, supported McIlvaine's Sunday afternoon concerts and suppers for soldiers and sailors during World War I.

In the late nineteenth and early twentieth centuries, major American cities absorbed waves of European immigrants. Responding to the resulting cultural changes, McIlvaine believed

Fig. 76. *Chicago Historical Society museum curator and librarian Caroline McIlvaine, center, with Thomas Dent and others, Chicago, 1912.*

that museums could help educate both native-born and immigrant Americans. She transformed the CHS from a special collections library to a lively museum providing popular education. Speaking at a December 1923 meeting of the Historical Section of the American Association of Museums, she noted, "While historical societies may have been storage houses in the past, they are becoming storage batteries of Americanism. . . . The ultimate object of every American historical society is the making of better Americans" ("The Function of Historical Museums," 4). At the same time that she was seeking to enlarge CHS membership, McIlvaine had to carry out a restrictive policy set by the society's officers. In 1925 the president instructed her to refuse membership to Dr. A. G. Fairfax because he was an African American.

McIlvaine included publications in her educational program, serving as editor of the *Chicago Historical Society Bulletin*, published between 1922 and 1926, and supervising publication of studies on Chicago history. McIlvaine's articles and speeches were printed in historical and popular publications; a number of her lectures and reports, such as *Cahokia Mound Park* (1922), became published pamphlets.

Throughout her years at CHS, McIlvaine was an advocate for recognition of women's achievements and education of girls. One of her early projects was documentation of Chicago as it existed before the 1871 Fire. When she sent out requests for portraits and views of streetscapes, she found that the many responses rarely included women's portraits. She tried with little success to remedy that situation in the museum collections. In 1909, she recognized that few women were visiting the museum and established special programs to encourage membership and enliven programming. She organized the Women's Auxiliary of

the CHS in 1920 to raise one hundred fifty thousand dollars to purchase the Gunther collection, then approached Illinois women's clubs in 1922 to donate funds to publish women's histories from the Civil War and pioneer times derived from material in that collection. In April 1924 she established a girl's week to help girls be better citizens by heralding history's important women and gave a talk to a thousand young women employed by Marshall Field's department store.

In the 1920s and earlier, McIlvaine initiated methods of development and public programming that were new in museum management. Understanding the impact of radio for reaching new audiences, she gave broadcasts concerning services the society could offer to the citizens of Chicago and asking for their support. In 1925 JUDITH WALLER, general manager at WMAQ, the radio station owned by the *Chicago Daily News*, offered to broadcast talks on CHS and on Chicago history. McIlvaine's resulting broadcast about the Great Chicago Fire in 1871 was accompanied by a "Radio Photologue" in the *Chicago Daily News* on October 10, 1925, so that listeners could view photographs of sites she described. In the vanguard of what later was termed "outreach," McIlvaine organized special tours with docent/interpreters for subscribers to Polish newspapers, promoted the museum by advertising in streetcars, and displayed objects from the collection at Orchestra Hall and in downtown stores and office buildings. She proposed using CHS passes as incentives that teachers could distribute to students and printing postcards showing objects from the museum's collection as fund-raising and promotional tools.

Along with contemporaries in museum education, she developed children's programs, such as Saturday morning visits for public school children, to bring creative discovery to textbook learning. She believed that children from immigrant laborer families would help their parents in the "Americanization" adjustment to a new urban culture by sharing what they learned at the museum about America's rural past. In 1925 she established a Junior Auxiliary for CHS members' children. She prepared lectures, entertainment, and special exhibits for them.

McIlvaine was a leader in an emerging museum management profession. When the American Association of Museums (AAM) held its second annual meeting in Chicago in 1907, McIlvaine hosted a session at the CHS. She became an individual member in 1909. The CHS joined in 1917. When women in museums were most often benefactors, not staff, and at a time when curators at historical museums were stereotyped as "retired clergymen and broken down school teachers" ("The Function of Historical Museums," 3), she established a level of professionalism in presenting history in visual formats. She advocated national standardization of museum practice and "scientific" collection strategies during an era when historical museums were often repositories of relics and curiosities haphazardly collected by hobbyists. McIlvaine hosted study visits to her institution for colleagues and attended annual meetings of the AAM and groups such as the Mississippi Valley Historical Association. She absorbed the latest ideas in museum administration from visionary curators. Her progressive ideas found support and respect among peers working in museums around the country. In the 1920s the AAM's bimonthly journal *Museum Work* often described collections and current programming at CHS. McIlvaine delivered papers at several AAM annual meetings, adding her perspective to current topics and participating in roundtables such as the "Training of Museum Workers" (1918). She was active in AAM, serving on four committees between 1923 and 1925: Historical Societies, the Use of Cultural Material, Ethics, and School-Museum Relations. Two of her papers were included in the 1928 A *Bibliography of Museums and Museum Work*.

From 1919 to 1924 she was editor of the history section of *Museum Work*, which provided her a forum for reporting programs at the CHS and commenting on activities at other museums. McIlvaine organized meetings of librarians and museum professionals and suggested they coordinate local history preservation and education by making photographic surveys of historic districts.

McIlvaine's diverse projects in public programming, with an emphasis on education, had to be approved by the society's Executive Committee of trustees. In the 1920s she appeared to be in conflict with male trustees, who did not support her expansive views, excluded her in departmental restructuring, and questioned her collection of delinquent accounts. On October 21, 1926, she resigned, stating that she was unhappy with her salary and working conditions. In her resignation letter, McIlvaine stated that she had been working "an average of ten hours a day, summer as well as winter" and had been given "evasive reasons . . . for failure to grant salary advance due two years ago and for which I was compelled to ask repeatedly without result" (CHS General Administration correspondence). In using education as a focus for determining museum policies and programs, McIlvaine was pioneering a change in museum functions. Although existing records do not fully explain the reasons

for her departure, she may have been moving faster than the board of trustees would accept in developing new goals for the society's library and collections. At a special Executive Committee meeting called to discuss her resignation, an honorary stipend of twenty-five hundred dollars was granted as a mark of esteem for her quarter century of service.

Little documentation remains from McIlvaine's next nineteen years. After her departure from the CHS, she made her living as a lecturer and writer. Her promotional brochure, in which she called herself the "former Director of the Chicago Historical Society" (McIlvaine Papers), listed a repertoire of twenty lantern lectures on "Chicago's Background Seen through the Eyes of Early Settlers" along with enthusiastic testimonials. In 1927 Judith Waller again engaged McIlvaine to broadcast a series of talks on notable Chicagoans, directed to the city's primary schools. McIlvaine wrote a column, "Historical Spots in and around Chicago," in the *Chicago Daily News* during August and September of 1927. She tried unsuccessfully to get another commission in 1929 at the same newspaper and in 1931 at the *Chicago Tribune*. As historical advisor to Paul Gilbert and Charles Lee Bryson, the authors of *Chicago and Its Makers,* an illustrated eleven-hundred-page volume published in 1929, she largely determined the book's content and wrote the preface. She planned a book about Chicago's historical street names and places and wrote a history of H.O. Stone real estate investment company. She died in Chicago at age seventy-seven of arteriosclerosis and was buried in the family plot at Rosehill Cemetery.

McIlvaine's life was dedicated to making history real for all people. She played an important role in the growth and structuring of the Chicago Historical Society. During the quarter-century when she managed the CHS, she changed both the function of the institution and the nature of its collections. She developed an active public program to provide education to Chicago's residents. She replaced storage of antiquarian objects with a collection policy to acquire materials relevant to Chicago history. Policies of the CHS regarding expansion of programs, acquisitions, and exhibits that were put into place by Caroline McIlvaine have continued to the present.

Sources. The Caroline McIlvaine Papers at the NL include materials for her years of employment there as well as correspondence dating 1927 to 1943. General Administration files at NL contain pay records and Librarian William Poole's correspondence on McIlvaine's employment. The CHS holds materials relating to McIlvaine: manuscript papers include a biographical summary by Mabel McIlvaine Baker and typescript copies of McIlvaine's speeches and radio broadcast scripts. The collection has her articles in the *Chicago Daily News* in 1927, her published pamphlets, and books for which she wrote historical introductions. For her years at CHS, records in the CHS Archives, including correspondence, Annual Librarian's Reports to the Trustees written by McIlvaine, and Board of Trustees Minutes, show her wide-ranging responsibilities and achievements. McIlvaine's article, "The Function of Historical Museums," appeared in the *Chicago Historical Society Bulletin* in October 1924. Articles by McIlvaine in *Museum Work, Including the Proceedings of the American Association of Museums,* 1907–27, indicate the breadth of her activities. *The Biographical Cyclopaedia of American Women,* vol. 2 (1925), provides basic biographical information on Caroline McIlvaine. McIlvaine's contributions are mentioned in two published histories of the CHS, Paul M. Angle's *The Chicago Historical Society, 1856–1956, An Unconventional Chronicle* (1956) and

Robert L. Brubaker's "The Development of an Urban Research Center: The Chicago Historical Society's Library" in *Chicago History*, Spring 1978. McIlvaine's place on the national scene as a woman in the museum profession can be interpreted from articles on contemporary issues published in *Museum Work*, 1920–27. The American Association of Museums, *Women's Changing Role in Museums Conference Proceedings* (1986), and *Gender Perspectives, Essays on Women in Museums* by Jane R. Glaser and Artemis A. Zenetou (1994) provide additional background on women in the profession.

VICTORIA KASUBA MATRANGA

McKINLEY, ADA SOPHIA DENNISON
June 26, 1868–August 25, 1952
SETTLEMENT FOUNDER, SOCIAL WELFARE ACTIVIST,
EDUCATOR, MISSIONARY, CIVIC LEADER

Ada Sophia Dennison McKinley, a dedicated social welfare pioneer, was one of a group of African American women who created settlements, missions, and social centers in the first two decades of the twentieth century. Most of these institutions were short-lived, but South Side Settlement House, founded by McKinley in 1918–19, survived and, through the 1990s called Ada S. McKinley Community Services, Inc., continued to exist at the beginning of the twenty-first century. McKinley devoted her life's work to creating and implementing community programs that addressed a variety of Chicago's complex family and social needs. The results of her efforts were of crucial significance to thousands and were of particular benefit to the city's South Side communities during World War I and World War II and decades of heavy migration and settlement of African Americans from the South. McKinley's settlement was founded solely through the financial support of the African American community and was fully staffed by African Americans.

Ada Sophia Dennison was born in Galveston, Texas, the first child of Joseph and Alice (Thompson) Dennison. The earliest years of her childhood were during the Reconstruction Era (1866–77), when most of the South was under the occupation of federal troops following the passage of the Military Reconstruction Acts. Troops were sent to Texas after the state's refusal to ratify the Thirteenth and Fourteenth Amendments (passed in 1865 and 1868, respectively) to the United States Constitution at the close of the Civil War. Ada Dennison's only known sibling, brother Octavius, was born in 1871. The family moved to Corpus Christi, Texas, where Joseph Dennison was employed as a hotel waiter and Alice Dennison as a laundress. Both children attended elementary school there. Ada Dennison later graduated from Prairie View College, in Waller County, and from Tillotson Missionary College, San Antonio, Texas.

As a young woman, Ada Dennison made her home in Austin, Texas, while pursuing a teaching career. She met William Buchanan McKinley there. He was a dentist from Tennessee. Ada Dennison and William McKinley were married in 1887. The couple had three children. Tragedy occurred when several cities in Texas experienced a diphtheria epidemic that also took the lives of McKinley's three children.

The McKinleys moved to Chicago before 1900 and established residence on Thirty-seventh Street and Dearborn in the Black Belt on Chicago's South Side. In 1907, a fourth child, William Rogers Robert McKinley, was born. The family lived

FIG. 77. *Social reformer and settlement leader Ada S. McKinley founded the South Side Settlement House (now Ada S. McKinley Community Services) in 1918–19.*

for a brief time on Forrest Avenue before eventually residing at McKinley's settlement house on Wabash Avenue.

The period 1914 to 1919 presented opportunities for African Americans both in the industrial cities of the North and in the federal military. The cessation of foreign immigration during the war and the quota restrictions on new immigrants after 1919 created demands for industrial workers that Blacks filled. African Americans were promised new opportunities and, with a move North, rejected the South's Jim Crow segregationism and violence. Hundreds of thousands of southern Blacks migrated North. Concurrently, African Americans joined the U.S. armed services and participated in World War I; they trained and served, however, in segregated units. At the end of the war, with the return of black and white soldiers, many African Americans in the South and the North suffered brutal and fatal assaults by anti-black, racist organizations. The African American community in Chicago responded to the emerging crisis, as black soldiers required places to stay prior to going overseas and, after their return, adjustment to postwar life in an increasingly hostile Jim Crow environment. In 1918, Ada McKinley volunteered to serve as a hostess to black soldiers at War Camp Community Services, a government project organized by the Chicago Urban League's T. Arnold Hill. War Camp Community Services was established in the partially run-down, twelve-room, three-story

Keeley mansion on South Wabash. There, in 1919, McKinley organized the Soldiers and Sailors Club, a recreational program for soldiers and their friends. Her long friendship with IRENE McCOY GAINES, later a president of the National Association of Colored Women, began when Gaines served as a department head in the War Camp Community Services. After the war, in response to the large influx of southern Blacks and returning soldiers, McKinley began to furnish and locate shelter, jobs, and food for displaced families. As news of McKinley's assistance spread, many appeared on her doorstep seeking help. In a short time she achieved a reputation as a woman of extraordinary abilities.

Crowded conditions caused by inadequate housing, segregation, and competition for jobs at a time of transition from war production to a peace economy created additional strains that fueled conflicts among ethnic and racial groups in the city. On July 27, 1919, a race riot erupted in Chicago; at the time, Lake Michigan beaches in Chicago were segregated and when, by accident, an African American youth swam into a whites-only area, he was stoned to death. White assaults on Blacks followed his drowning at the Twenty-ninth Street Beach. The ensuing riots received national attention. Working to relieve race tension and disharmony, Ada McKinley bravely linked arms with friends JANE ADDAMS, MARY McDOWELL, and HARRIET VITTUM. The four women—all associated with settlement houses and community activism—courageously walked through hordes of angry mobs in a salient demonstration of peace and unity. Rioters were startled when they observed the ladies undauntedly sitting in a neighborhood restaurant, breaking the color line and enjoying the camaraderie of each other's company. The severe turmoil and violence lasted four days, leaving thirty-eight citizens dead, more than five hundred injured, and thousands homeless. McKinley helped soothe tensions by assisting the Chicago Commission on Race Relations with plans to restore order to the city and organize job placement programs. She arranged for a work pay station at her settlement facility. Harriet Vittum became a friend of McKinley's; the two gave public lectures together.

After the close of the war, government financial support was withdrawn from War Camp Community Services. McKinley's programs, however, had come to play a vital part in the community's survival. As heavy southern migration continued, housing conditions and poverty gave rise to serious public health problems, and the numbers of unemployed mounted. McKinley vowed to continue her services. Assisted by Jesse Binga, an affluent banker and realtor in the Black Metropolis, and Mary E. McDowell, director of the University of Chicago Settlement House, McKinley made plans to keep the facility open. Using a small remnant of War Services funds, McKinley continued to labor in the community, launching a major fund-raising pageant. The event, which was directed by New York's Ada Crogman, took place at Chicago's Auditorium Theater, with many well-known performers participating. The pageant held promise of realizing a sizable sum to provide a solid foundation for the settlement house. It was well supported by many of Chicago's prominent citizens, but McKinley was disappointed when the settlement received only twelve hundred dollars of the more than five thousand dollars raised by the campaign. Additionally,

it had taken substantial monetary investment to host the pageant. Almost completely without financial support, McKinley managed to maintain the building, while developing new programs. She named her revitalized establishment South Side Community Services. On December 8, 1924, McKinley incorporated South Side Community Services, with herself and supporters Jesse Binga, John R. Marshall, William H. Scott, and M. Blount Jones comprising its small board. In 1926, she renamed the facility South Side Settlement House, simultaneously serving as the organization's president, head resident, teacher, and office worker. Later, Harriet Vittum served on McKinley's board.

During the late 1920s and 1930s, the South Side Settlement House eagerly responded to many needs of the rapidly expanding community. McKinley initiated numerous programs that relieved human suffering by focusing on economic and cultural values. She gained the support and involvement of community residents, clubs, sororities, and organizations. Local, state, and national politicians backed her programs. Relying primarily on a few volunteers, limited financial support, and a small salaried staff, McKinley's settlement house had, by 1927, provided supportive social services to more than twenty-five thousand people.

McKinley was an active member of the Social Workers Round Table, an organization comprised of forty-seven members who met regularly at the South Side Settlement House to plan and provide educational seminars. Several of Chicago's foremost social workers were affiliated. Included among them were representatives from United Charities, Chicago Visiting Nurse Association, the Urban League, and Illinois Children's Home and Aid. In addition, McKinley sponsored an infant welfare station that addressed the health care and nurture of approximately four hundred children who visited the nursery monthly. She also provided literacy programs for adults, along with crafts and trades training. In order to furnish adequate recreation programs for community youth, she established Camp Fire Girls clubs and Boy and Girl Scout troops at the settlement. Corneal A. Davis, later an influential Illinois state representative, assisted with Boy Scout Troop No. 545, which held every scout rank available. Davis served as the city's first African American scoutmaster. McKinley's son, William, a member of Davis's troop, later headed the settlement's Young Republican Club. William McKinley also served as the settlement's director of Chicago Leisure Time Services, a recreational program.

The South Side Settlement House provided space where new groups were formed and later continued to meet, including the Giles Post of the American Legion. Several clubs, guilds, political, labor, and entrepreneurial organizations formed and met regularly on its premises. In addition, two periodicals, the *Colored Embalmer* and the *American Life Magazine*, were published at the facility.

The settlement house was nonpartisan in its political philosophy, and McKinley believed that good citizenship was critical for a prosperous community. She was an early supporter of the League of Women Voters of Chicago and one of the organizers of the Douglas branch of the League, an all-black chapter. The Douglas branch frequently met at the South Side Settlement House. McKinley also shared a longtime friendship with many politicians, particularly William L. Dawson, who was, at one time, the committeeman of the predominantly black 2nd Ward and also a U.S. congressman. McKinley's civic interest and involvement led to her formation of a neighborhood club comprised of community residents. The club promoted civic awareness, providing a voice for the community in addressing local problems and in combating political inertia. McKinley also operated the South Side Settlement House without affiliation with any particular religious denomination. She was a member of several churches of different denominations and a founder of a King's Daughters Lodge. McKinley and others met regularly at the settlement for prayer and discussion of the community's spiritual needs.

During the mid-1930s and early 1940s, McKinley managed the South Side Settlement House with support from the federal Works Progress Administration (WPA—renamed Work Projects Administration in 1939), a New Deal program initiated in the depths of the Great Depression in the United States. WPA funds financed courses that taught such skills as painting, sewing, cooking, pottery, and ceramics, encouraging industrial and self-employment opportunities and the manufacture of products that could be sold to supplement family income.

As a tribute to its founder, on April 1, 1949, the South Side Settlement House was renamed Ada S. McKinley Community House by its board of directors. Retired as head of the settlement house, McKinley continued to serve as a mentor to graduate students of social work. During that decade, the Illinois Institute of Technology (IIT), whose campus was near the settlement, began a community renovation project. The settlement house's deteriorating structure on South Wabash Avenue was targeted for demolition. IIT faculty members and wives joined Clara S. Langston, friend and president of the settlement's Women's Guild, in raising funds to construct a new building. The cornerstone was dedicated on August 24, 1952, and eighty-four-year-old Ada McKinley gave a speech in honor of the occasion. Placement of the stone seemed to symbolize fulfillment of McKinley's long and difficult mission. That evening she suffered a cerebral hemorrhage that took her life the following morning at Provident Hospital, Chicago.

Ada McKinley's career as a social worker emerged out of her genuine love for humanity and her belief in the dignity of families and communities. While eloquently soft-spoken and simple in attire, she was persuasive and a capable educator. She possessed personal strength and stamina, enduring sweltering summers and winters in the poorly heated old settlement house building. Frequently she donated her own money to those in need, worked without salary, and often fed others, ignoring her own needs. Ada S. McKinley Community Services, Inc., remains one of America's largest and most diverse social service organizations.

Sources. Ada S. McKinley Community Services, Inc., Chicago, has a limited number of brochures, legal documents, and writings of interest to researchers. The Federal Writers' Project Records, Illinois State Hist. Library, Springfield, contain several boxes with a small number of folders reporting on Ada S. McKinley and the South Side Settlement House in the 1930s, including Hortense Bratton, "Settlement Houses and Community Clubs in the Colored Districts of Chicago," with information on McKinley and the settlement; and J. Prior, "South Side Settle-

ment House," which describes Works Progress Administration classes held at McKinley's settlement. The Washington Intercollegiate Club of Chicago published *1927 Intercollegian Wonder Book, or, 1779—The Negro in Chicago—1927*, vol. 1, ed. Frederic H. Robb (1927), which included several references to Ada S. McKinley and the South Side Settlement House. The Chicago Commission on Race Relations, *The Negro in Chicago: A Study on Race Relations and a Race Riot* (1922), mentions McKinley's work related to the 1919 riot and its aftermath and contains an illustration of the original South Side Settlement House building. Jack Mabley, "Child Care Center Looted, Asks Your Support," *American*, August 2, 1966, provides a small amount of background on McKinley and references to some of her actions during Chicago's 1919 riot. See St. Clair Drake and Horace R. Cayton, *Black Metropolis: A Study of Negro Life in a Northern City* (1945, reprinted 1962, 1970, 1993) for historical context. Elisabeth Lasch-Quinn, *Black Neighbors: Race and the Limits of Reform in the American Settlement House Movement, 1890–1945* (1993), writes about the race attitudes of the white settlement house movement in Chicago but fails to mention either Fannie Emanuel and her settlement, established in 1908 in Chicago, or Ada S. McKinley and the South Side Settlement House. Obituaries are "Stroke Kills Civic Leader after Cornerstone Laying," "Chicago Woman, 84, Was Center Founder," *Chicago Defender*, September 6, 1952, and Madelon Golden, "S. Side Loses an Old Friend and Benefactor," *Chicago Sun-Times*, October 8, 1952.

CATHERYN ELAINE LAMPKIN

McMILLAN, M. HELENA
October 23, 1868–January 28, 1970
NURSE, NURSING EDUCATION REFORMER, DIRECTOR OF NURSING SCHOOLS

The motivating force behind M. Helena McMillan's long career in nursing education and administration, which included founding two nurse training schools, was her belief that nurses' education took precedence over hospital labor needs. This view was as radical when she retired in 1938 as it had been when she started her career.

McMillan, of Scottish ancestry, was born in Montreal, Canada, to David and Maria McMillan and was reared as a Methodist. She was educated in private schools before entering Montreal's McGill University. Women had been allowed to enter McGill only since 1884 and were educated apart from the male students. Although women students were harassed by the young men at the school, such hostility did not prevent McMillan from attaining a Bachelor of Arts degree in 1891.

McMillan wanted to pursue a medical career, but her father opposed her choice. In September 1892 McMillan entered the Illinois Training School for Nurses (ITS) in Chicago. Her sister lived in Chicago, and McMillan had frequently stayed with her. McMillan, like her fellow students, had just twenty-eight days off during her twenty-five-month training, attending lectures in the evening after twelve hours of work on the wards. Nursing students, not graduate nurses, provided almost all nursing care for the hospitals associated with the school, which for ITS were Cook County and Presbyterian hospitals. The use of students as the primary source of nursing care was accepted practice in nurse training schools at that time. Upon completion of training in October 1894, McMillan was described in the class record as having a fair amount of practical skill.

The limitations of her skills in practical nursing did not hinder McMillan. As a nurse with a bachelor's degree she pursued a career in nursing administration and education. Her first position took her back to Canada. For the next two years McMillan was lady superintendent of Kingston General Hospital in Ontario. While there she joined, in 1895, the newly founded American Society of Superintendents of Training Schools for Nurses, which later became the National League of Nursing Education. The following year, McMillan was a member of the committee that worked to establish the Victorian Order of Nurses, the Canadian version of England's Queen Victoria Jubilee Institute for Nurses, an organization of visiting nurses.

In 1897, McMillan returned to the United States and became superintendent of nurses, matron of the hospital, and first director of the school of nursing at the new Lakeside Hospital in Cleveland, Ohio. Her diverse appointments meant that she had to find both a dietitian and a housekeeper, as well as graduate nurses and students. McMillan devised an advanced nursing school program. Student nurses worked just eight hours a day and were not given the stipend that was customary, since payment would classify them as workers rather than students. McMillan herself gave weekly classes on practical nursing. A few months later, in April 1898, this strong beginning was strained by the Spanish-American War. Graduate nurses were moved by patriotic fervor and left for the front, leaving junior students to care for the returning soldiers, sick with typhoid, dysentery, malaria, and pneumonia, the most lethal enemies in nineteenth-century warfare.

McMillan continued her strong professional commitment while at Lakeside. She helped found and became the first president of the Graduate Nurses' Association of Cleveland, and in 1899 she became a founding member and councilor of the International Council of Nurses, established to promote professional self-government. In 1901, McMillan was appointed to the board of directors of the Cleveland Visiting Nurses' Association. McMillan left Lakeside in the fall of 1902 to gain postgraduate experience in public health nursing. She spent the next few months working at Lillian Wald's Henry Street settlement in New York, which provided visiting nurses' service for the poor.

McMillan returned to Chicago in January 1903 to become superintendent of nurses and founding director of Presbyterian Hospital's new school of nursing. Within a year McMillan had to open a nurse training school, find women aspiring to be nurses, and hire a corps of graduate nurses willing to work without salary as postgraduate students until the new students gained enough expertise. She had no typewriter, no secretary, and no office and wrote hundreds of letters, by hand, from her bedroom. The new nurses' residence, two houses near the hospital, was not quite ready in late March when McMillan moved in. Fifty years later, McMillan still remembered eating in the kitchen, with her plate on her lap, during those early days.

McMillan was described as a quiet, cultured woman, poised and dignified. She was slightly built. A former student remembered that McMillan chided her for not being large enough for a nurse, yet, according to the student, McMillan herself was only slightly taller and not as heavy as she was.

In spite of the necessity of rapidly providing a nursing service, McMillan opened Presbyterian Hospital Training School as one of the most progressive nursing schools in the world. Prospective students had to be high school graduates, with pref-

erence given to applicants with one or more years of college education. Tuition was charged—twenty-five dollars for the first six months—to emphasize the school's educational mission; and, as McMillan had insisted at Lakeside, students worked only eight hours a day. The first twelve students, from Wisconsin, Ohio, Montana, Minnesota, as well as Illinois, arrived in April 1903.

The three-and-one-half-year course began with a six-month period of preliminary training, during which the students did not enter the hospital. The six-month introduction was an innovation in nursing education. In 1905, Presbyterian was one of just six nursing schools in the United States that gave such a course. A further educational change was affiliation of the School of Nursing with Rush Medical College. The faculty of Rush and the hospital were jointly responsible for all educational matters, and students used the laboratories, classrooms, and library of the medical college. In 1907, Presbyterian was one of the first nursing schools in the country to offer a course in pharmacy. McMillan was also innovative in practical matters; students' caps were simple to make and launder, unlike the stiff, complicated, ornamental headgear worn in other institutions.

McMillan's concern for the education and welfare of student nurses was the focus of her papers published in the *American Journal of Nursing* between 1902 and 1922. Concerning the role of hospitals in nursing education, she wrote in July 1906, "They are tying us down, binding us and grinding out whatever aspirations we may have to make the best and most of our schools. To accomplish anything we must be free" ("Affiliation of Training Schools," 712). In 1907, McMillan discussed the results of her survey of twenty-three schools of nursing concerning the health of student nurses. Many students were reported ill with typhoid, tuberculosis, or other infectious diseases, and sixteen had died during their training. McMillan charged that physical exhaustion, combined with exposure to disease, contributed to the students' morbidity and mortality and called for a reduction in student hours. In May 1922, McMillan still complained that students were physically overworked, fulfilling a hospital rather than an academic need, without being allowed time to study. She wrote: "The public does not fail to expect an educated graduate nurse, but so far has troubled little to provide conditions for that education" ("What Nurses Need to Know," 612).

Professional organizations provided another public forum for McMillan to promote nursing education, and within these she played a leadership role. As a member of the American Society of Superintendents of Training Schools, she was among those who worked to establish a course in nursing administration and education at Teachers' College, Columbia University, in 1899; she was later a member of the Committee on Hospital Economics that guided these courses during their early years. She was a member of the board of the American Nurses' Association and president of the Illinois State Nurses' Association (ISNA) five times between 1905 and 1920. Within the ISNA, McMillan chaired a University Relations Committee that was largely responsible for the development of courses for graduate nurses at the University of Chicago. As ISNA President, McMillan was active for several years in promoting the Illinois Nurse Practice Act during its stormy passage through the state legislature; it was finally made into law in 1907. During this time, she was influential in keeping Adda Eldridge, ISNA's Springfield lobbyist, out of jail, when she was unable to pay her large hotel bill. McMillan raised the money, using her connections with physicians, staff, and possibly even the patients at Presbyterian Hospital. The Nurse Practice Act allowed qualified nurses to become registered by the state. McMillan's concern that her nurses be credited for their education had led her, in 1906, to apply successfully for permission for them to take the New York State licensure examination, if they wished.

In 1912, McMillan helped draw up the constitution and by-laws of the new First District of the Illinois State Nurses' Association, representing Cook, DuPage, and Kane counties. McMillan enrolled as a Red Cross Nurse in 1912 and later became a member of the state and national committees of the American Red Cross. The American Nurses' Association was affiliated with the Red Cross, pledging to provide nurses if needed in an emergency. McMillan remained an active member of the National League of Nursing Education, serving on its board as well as holding the offices of second vice-president, secretary, and treasurer, and serving on many committees. She was also president of the Illinois League of Nursing Education for five terms. In 1917, McMillan was a member of the Committee on Nursing Education that formulated a standard curriculum for nursing schools, an early attempt to upgrade and standardize nursing education.

At Presbyterian, McMillan continued as educator and administrator. In 1911, she proposed to the women's board that a campaign for a million dollar endowment for the school be started, allowing graduate nurses to be hired to relieve student nurses of some hospital chores. A campaign was started, but by the nurses, not the women's board, which had responded with "kindly laughter" (McMillan, "Some Remembrances," 6). In 1917, with American entry into World War I looming, McMillan responded to the directives of the National Council of Defense by admitting a large class of sixty-four students. This student increase was fortuitous for the hospital administration during the 1919 influenza pandemic, when about six nurses were incapacitated by the disease every day. McMillan also supported the cause of rank for army nurses, concerned with the welfare of both nurses and soldiers. The excitement of woman suffrage came to Presbyterian when the vice-president of the Illinois Suffrage Association visited in September 1920 and taught the students how to mark their ballots. In 1930, McMillan was a member of the Committee on Unemployment organized by the First District of the Illinois State Nurses' Association.

The American Nurses Association honored McMillan in 1936 with the Walter Burns Saunders Memorial Medal for her excellent service to nursing. In October 1938 she retired from Presbyterian. She went to live with her brother and his wife in Evanston, Illinois, north of Chicago, but continued to attend various Presbyterian Hospital meetings. She later moved to Boulder, Colorado, to be near her sister-in-law. Although McMillan had become very hard-of-hearing, she continued to show an interest in the school at Presbyterian Hospital, attending the meetings of a nearby Presbyterian graduate organization. In 1953 she traveled to Chicago to be an honored guest at the school's fiftieth anniversary celebration. During that visit, a for-

mer student attempted to support the eighty-four year old McMillan by holding her arm, but McMillan quickly pulled away. The would-be assistant noted that McMillan's reaction was typical; she had always cherished her independence. McMillan died in a nursing home at 101 years of age.

McMillan's determined, energetic defense of nurses' health, education, and practice during the profession's formative years left a national legacy. At her retirement, in October 1938, the *American Journal of Nursing* editors wrote in "M. Helena McMillan" that she had been "associated with practically every progressive movement in nursing" (p. 1,164). Her obituary in the *Alumnae News and Views* of March 19, 1970, stated, "Her unselfish devotion to high standards of nursing was of inestimable national value" (p. 2).

Sources. Details of the history of Presbyterian Hospital's Nursing School, including McMillan's reports and a few of her papers, are at Rush-Presbyterian-St. Luke's Medical Center Archives in Chicago. These include "Some Remembrances" that McMillan wrote for a 1953 Presbyterian Hospital pamphlet, *Fiftieth Anniversary of the School of Nursing of Presbyterian Hospital, Chicago;* a letter from her describing the school's early uniforms; and an unpublished history of the school by Nella C. Den Herder, "History Highlights of the School of Nursing of the Presbyterian Hospital of the City of Chicago, 1903–1953." UIC Spec. Coll. contains the records of the Illinois Training School. Several early histories contain references to McMillan; most useful are Ruth Johnson's *School of Nursing, Presbyterian Hospital, 1903–1956* (1959) and Mary Dunwiddie's *A History of the Illinois State Nurses' Association, 1901–1935* (1937). McMillan published articles between 1902 and 1922 in the *Annual Report, American Society of Superintendents of Training Schools for Nurses,* and in the *American Journal of Nursing.* Her articles in the *American Journal of Nursing* include "The Affiliation of Training Schools," July 1906; "The Physical Effect of the Three Years' Course," July 1907; and "What Nurses Need to Know about Food and Dietetics," May 1922. Her biography is included in Vern L. Bullough, Olga M. Church, and Alice P. Stein, eds., *American Nursing: A Biographical Dictionary,* vol. 1 (1988), and in "M. Helena McMillan," *American Journal of Nursing,* October 1938. An obituary appears in *Alumnae News and Views,* March 19, 1970.

BRIGID LUSK

McRAE, EDNA LOUISE
June 15, 1901–June 7, 1990
BALLET DANCER, CHOREOGRAPHER

Edna Louise McRae was born in Chicago, the daughter of William M. ("Big Mac") and Marie L. McRae. Edna McRae had an older sister, Elma M., and a brother, Malcolm Al. "Big Mac" McRae, who began as a foreman of construction at the McCormick Reaper Works, Chicago, in 1885, had a thirty-seven year career with the company. Edna McRae attended Beaubien School on Chicago's Northwest Side and became interested in dance when she attended Carl Schurz High School. The story is told that while she was in high school, McRae had three pupils whom she taught dance in her living room, as her mother played accompaniment on the piano.

Beginning in 1915, McRae and her sister Elma, who had excelled in sports and dance while in high school, participated in recitals and performances in Chicago. As a high school senior in March 1918, Edna McRae danced four solos as part of "Comfort Kit Entertainment," a program given at the Calathusian

Club of Norwood Park, Illinois, to aid World War I soldiers and sailors by raising money for the Norwood Park Red Cross. Also that year, she began to dance with the famous Pavley-Oukrainsky Ballet. One of the performances was at the Blackstone Theater, Chicago, where she danced in the *Ballet Romantique.*

After graduating from high school in 1918, McRae attended the Chicago Normal School of Physical Education (CNSPE), where Pavley and Oukrainsky taught. M. Andreas Pavley, of Dutch and Russian parents, had been the partner of the famous Russian ballerina Anna Pavlova. M. Serge Oukrainsky, born in Odessa, Russia, first appeared in Paris as St. John in *Salome,* and he also had been Anna Pavlova's partner in many of her dances and had designed a number of her costumes and choreographed some of her ballets.

McRae was active at CNSPE, serving as captain of her hockey team, coming in second in the running broad jump event at track, and playing third base on the baseball team. The two years she spent in the program at CNSPE were a happy time for McRae; her teachers and classmates commented in her yearbook that they loved to watch her dance. While attending CNSPE, McRae taught for two years at Francis W. Parker School, the private elementary and secondary school on Chicago's North Side founded by ANITA McCORMICK BLAINE and known for its educational innovations. McRae graduated from CNSPE in 1920. From 1920 to 1922, she was a member of the Parker faculty, teaching in the Physical Training Department and supervising playgrounds. Her sister Elma, who became a physical education teacher at Carl Schurz High School, also continued her involvement with the dance world and was appointed ballet mistress with the Chicago Opera Company in 1921. In the 1920s and 1930s, Edna McRae continued to study dance. Her teachers in Chicago included Madeline B. Hazlitt, Marie Landry, Adolph Bolm, and Vecheslav Swoboda as well as Pavley and Oukrainsky. During summers she studied in New York with Michael Folkine and Chester Hale; in London with Nicolas Legat, Tamara Karsavina, Phyllis Bedells, Lydia Sokolova, and Laurent Novikoff; in Paris, her teachers included Matilda Kechessinkaya, Olga Preobragenskaya, Vera Trefilova, and Lubov Egorova. The European dance world had a formative influence on McRae, who recalled that "when at last she saw [Anna] Pavlova dance, she was entranced with the unforgettable beauty of her art, and she realized that that beauty had been made attainable through a knowledge of the science of movement itself" (Turbyfill, 24). She rejected the notion that ballet could only come out of Europe, however. Although "for generations people in this country [America] were apparently unaware of their bodies" (Turbyfill, 24), McRae "determined that . . . [dance] should be practiced with dignity and native self-assurance in America—even in Chicago" (p. 24). McRae "attribute[d] her success to what she describe[d] as a unique background. This included advanced studies in music, anatomy, kinesiology, teaching methods, and the Dalcroze system of relating movement to music" (Terry, 52). McRae's training was eclectic, from European-trained dancers, including émigré ballerinas from the Russian Imperial Ballet in Paris, to John Bubbles, of Buck and Bubbles fame, with whom she studied tap dancing in the United States.

McRae performed at the Eighth Street Theater, Chicago, on April 24, 1922. She spent two nine-week terms at the Rocky Mountain Dancing Camp (Perry Mansfield's camp) in Steamboat Springs, Colorado, where the principal "consider[ed] her to be one of the best American teachers . . . [she had] ever seen[,] . . . thorough in her work as a teacher, splendid in her leadership of girls, and excellent in her own technique" (Portia Mansfield Swett letter, n.d., Barzel Dance Collection). McRae had herself graduated from the Rocky Mountain Dancing Camp before her stint as a teacher.

In 1923, Adolph Bolm was hired to direct the ballet corps of the Chicago Opera. McRae had studied with Bolm, and he asked her to assist him in the project. After two seasons, however, his contract with the opera was not renewed. During the time Bolm was teaching in Chicago and directing his dance company, the Adolph Bolm Ballet, McRae danced frequently with them, including performances at the Apollo Theatre, the Eighth Street Theater, and at the Kenneth Sawyer Goodman Memorial Theatre. She also danced with Allied Arts and with the Pavley-Oukrainsky Ballet. At the same time, McRae taught at the Pavley-Oukrainsky and Adolph Bolm schools in Chicago. In 1925, McRae opened her own school of dance. She also formed a ballet company and with her dancers performed frequently in Chicago. In 1926, she and Marie Peterson danced the *Reverie* by Frédéric Chopin; McRae also had a solo role in the *Valse Caprice* by Anton Rubinstein. The Edna McRae Dancers performed at her alma mater, Carl Schurz High School, and her repertoire included *Scarf Dance* by Charles-François Gounod, *Tarantelle* by Gioacchino Rossini, and *Polish Mazurka* by Léo Delibes.

Edna McRae's ballet students performed for the 1933 and 1934 Century of Progress Exposition, Chicago, appearing on the stage of the Enchanted Island Children's Theatre. They did *Sleeping Princess,* a ballet in one act with music by Peter Ilyich Tchaikovsky. McRae formed the Fine Arts Ballet Company in 1933 as a training ground for young dancers. The group first appeared at the Century of Progress Exposition. They also performed with the Peoria Symphony Orchestra, the Marshall Field Choral Society, at the Civic Opera House, and before the Lake View Musical Society, Chicago. McRae also choreographed ballets for the Chicago Park District Opera groups, the Chicago Concert and Opera Guild, the Society of Polish Artists, and the Germania Theater. For example, in June 1944, the Chicago Concert and Opera Guild presented the *Tales of Hoffman* by Jacques Offenbach, and McRae was the choreographer. By the 1930s and 1940s, McRae's ballet school in the Fine Arts Building was well known. Not only did she attract many generations of students, but "her studio . . . became one of the places where traveling ballet companies took classes while they were in Chicago" (*Chicago Tribune,* June 11, 1990). Students remembered her as a perfectionist who "really worked people very, very hard" (*Chicago Tribune,* June 11, 1990). A former student recalled that "after your lesson, she used to write notes on the blackboard, and you'd have to copy them down in . . . [your] notebook. It was all in French. And you had to practice. If it was clear you didn't practice, you were in trouble" (*Chicago Tribune,* June 11, 1990). Marilyn Miglin, successful cosmetics entrepreneur, took classes from McRae as a teenager. "'One day in class I made a great error,' she said. 'Miss McRae stopped the class and they all stared at me'" (quoted in Zorn, 2). When asked by McRae why she had made the mistake, Miglin told her ballet teacher that she was sorry. McRae retorted, "No you're not. . . . If you were sorry, you wouldn't have done it" (p. 2).

In terms of the history of dance education in the United States, McRae's influence on future generations of dance instructors was significant. She believed that all children should have ballet training to help them with their other activities. She thought they should not start until they reached eight or nine years of age. Her students differed widely in professional accomplishment and talent, but those who went on to teach locally—whether they ever attained even regional professional careers or not—gave credit to McRae for instilling a point of view and for upholding a model of strict pedagogical standards for the dance instructor. McRae felt that "the most important function of a dance teacher, other than being technically correct, is to direct each pupil separately. 'No two are alike. Each needs to be guided into what she or he does best'" (Terry, 52–53). One of McRae's more famous pupils was Carol Laraia (later Carol Lawrence). Lawrence, who became a Broadway star, began taking dance lessons from McRae at age thirteen. Jules Walton, who died in 1985 at age eighty-four, studied with McRae in 1925, the year he introduced the Charleston, the 1920s dance craze, to Chicago. Walton and his wife, Joanne Boenke, the other half of Jules and Joanne, became one of Chicago's popular dance teams in the field of ballroom dancing. Later, after retiring from dancing, he taught dance classes at community centers and schools. Patricia Klekovic, who became director of the children's ballet program at the Ruth Page Foundation School of Dance, Chicago, also studied with McRae. "After graduating from St. Procopius High School in Chicago's Pilsen neighborhood on the Near West Side in 1954, Klekovic studied full time with McRae for a year, taking 25 classes a week" (Kassner, 64). Eighteen years later, when Klekovic began her children's program, she asked McRae to advise her. Orrin Kayan, another student of McRae and a Chicago ballet dancer for whom Ruth Page created several ballets, performed with a number of companies, including the Chicago Ballet, the Lyric Opera of Chicago, and the Chicago Opera Ballet. He became a teacher with Ruth Page Foundation School of Dance, Chicago, and the Academy of Dance and Movement, Oak Park, Illinois. Ruth Lowe, director of children for the *Nutcracker* performances at the Arie Crown Theater in the 1990s, studied with McRae as a child; in the early 1970s, Lowe assisted McRae when the latter was the associate director in charge of children for the annual *Nutcracker* production at Arie Crown. Sherrie Sommerfeld, a dance instructor in community center and park department programs in the Chicago area, studied with McRae. Sommerfeld, who was sixteen when she first danced professionally, came back to Chicago when she was in her twenties and found her lifework as a teacher "after numerous conversations with McRae" (Leopold, 18). Sommerfeld and others like her were part of a network of instructors in dance who introduced a broad public to the world of the dance, popularizing the art and creating the audience necessary for future appreciation of the art form.

Although Edna McRae traveled to Europe frequently and performed in different cities in the United States, she was mainly active in Chicago, where she continued to operate a studio in the Fine Arts Building on Michigan Avenue in the downtown area. In February 1954, McRae was the ballet mistress for the Lyric Opera of Chicago, which presented *Don Giovanni*. Renaming her dance company the Fine Arts Ballet Company, she directed the group in March 1954 in the *Capriccio Espagnole, Op. 34*, by Nicolai Rimsky-Korsakov. That year her school was still offering a "thorough training in classical ballet. . . . In addition, classes in tap dancing and character, or national, dancing . . . [were] given to provide the balance of a well-developed background of the various dance forms." The school produced "fine and accomplished dancers for the theatrical and teaching professions, as well as developing an appreciation and intelligent understanding of the art in those who are interested from an educational and cultural point of view" (McRae to Mr. Rim Soo Young, June 30, 1954, Barzel Dance Collection). In 1961, a survey of ballet teaching in the United States was sponsored by the Ford Foundation as a part of its continuing study of the artist and the institutions in this country. The survey was conducted by choreographer George Balanchine, and Edna McRae's school was selected as one of the sites for personal visits by experienced dancers. Balanchine sent principal dancer Melissa Hayden to visit McRae and observe some classes. McRae continued to teach in the Fine Arts Building until 1963, when she and Keith Allison announced the opening of the Edna McRae and Keith Allison School of Dance not far from McRae's original location.

On August 1, 1964, Edna McRae retired from the new studio. Both she and her sister, Elma McRae, who had been a physical education teacher for forty-five years at Carl Schurz High School, moved to the Georgian, a retirement residence in Evanston, Illinois. Elma McRae died of cancer on August 1, 1968.

For Edna McRae, retirement meant the beginning of another career as a guest teacher with Robert Joffrey, director of the Joffrey Ballet, and others. In 1965, she became the assistant director in charge of the children of the McCormick Place and Opera House *Nutcracker* production sponsored by the *Chicago Tribune* company. That year she also supervised the original Joffrey Ballet Apprentice Program in New York City. From 1965 to 1970, she was the director of the City Center Joffrey Ballet's Summer Scholarship Training Program, which was sponsored by the Pacific Northwest Ballet Association at Pacific Lutheran University south of Tacoma, Washington. In March 1968 she traveled to St. Louis, Missouri, to be a guest teacher with Stanley Herbertt, a former pupil, who was artistic director of the St. Louis Civic Ballet. That same year she was interviewed by dance critic Walter Terry for the *Saturday Review*. Terry described her as the "Grande Dame of Chicago's Ballet Mistresses" (May 11, 1968). He characterized her as "racy, sometimes bawdy, learned, eager ('I get mad but I'm never bored'), and wholly dedicated." In the interview McRae said, "If I were younger, I'd be studying modern jazz. . . . I love all that rhythm stuff."

During the next few years McRae traveled almost constantly. Between February 11 and March 12, 1969, she traveled to Memphis and Nashville, Tennessee; to Atlanta, Georgia; Tampa, Boca Raton, and Ft. Lauderdale, Florida; and to New York City. Her trips involved a heavy work schedule in which she conducted seminars on dance for teachers and advanced students. On April 14, 1969, she spent two weeks in Tacoma, Washington, where she screened candidates for the New York City Center Joffrey Ballet's Summer Scholarship Training Program. That summer she was a member of the dance department faculty at Juilliard School, New York. McRae maintained this pace until April 11, 1974, when she suffered a serious, nearly fatal heart attack. She was scheduled to go to Knoxville, Tennessee, that summer, but her brother wrote to Irma O'Fallon, School of Ballet Arts in Knoxville, that his sister would probably experience a long, slow recovery. By November, however, McRae was able to travel to Chicago.

McRae traveled to Chicago that year to receive the first of several honors, the Cliff Dwellers Award of Merit for distinguished service to the arts in Chicago. Fellow recipients were Mrs. Glen Lloyd, chair of the Ravinia Festival Association; Richard Hunt, sculptor; and Henry Mazer, associate conductor of the Chicago Symphony Orchestra. The award had been established in 1968 to honor men and women who made significant contributions to the cultural life of the city. In 1986, Richard Ellis and his wife, Christine DuBoulay, owners of the Ellis-DuBoulay School of Ballet, established the Edna McRae Scholarship Program. They hoped to be able to raise enough money to award scholarships for students annually. Edna McRae received the 1987 Ruth Page Award for lifetime service to dance from the Chicago Dance Coalition, and in 1990 she was inducted into the Carl Schurz Hall of Fame.

Edna McRae died at age eighty-eight. A memorial service was held June 23, 1990, at the Newberry Library, Chicago. Edna McRae had a nontraditional start in the dance, beginning her study of ballet when she was already in high school. She entered the world of dance at a time of rapid change when the politics of revolutionary Russia and the conditions of war-torn Europe provided motivation for many highly trained dancers to emigrate to the United States and to England. By the 1920s, as McRae took advantage of the availability of great teachers in her own country and overseas, a new interest in classical ballet took hold in the United States. McRae's career spanned this period and her major contribution to dance was the result of her talents as a teacher not only of young students but of professional dancers and dance educators.

Sources. Edna McRae's papers are part of the Barzel Dance Collection, NL, and include correspondence, clippings, and photographs. Mark Turbyfill, "Ballet—American Version: Edna McRae Has Put a New Word into the Dance Vocabulary of Chicago," *Dance Magazine,* March 1930, identifies McRae as an innovative dance educator. Walter Terry, "World of Dance," *Saturday Review,* May 11, 1968, describes her career. Other useful articles about McRae's students and the world of dance in Chicago include Richard Christiansen, "She Keeps Her Eye on Beautiful Dancing," *Sunday CT,* January 15, 1995; Pam Kassner, "Ballet Teacher Understands Pirouettes and Kids' Faux Pas," *CT,* September 14, 1994; Michael Kates, "Orrin Kayan, 57; Danced with Top Ballet Companies," *CT,* February 13, 1993; Wendy Leopold, "Dance Teacher Stays in Step with Students," *CT,* October 18, 1989; Kenan Heise, "Jules Walton, 84; Chicagoan Danced His Way to Fame with Wife, Joanne," *CT,* December 11, 1985; Eric Zorn, "Devilishly Good Tribute Paid to a Ballet Legend," *CT,* October 28, 1985. Obituaries appeared in *CT,* June 11, 1990; *NYT,* June 13, 1990; and the *Los Angeles Times,* June 13, 1990.

WINIFRED O. WHELAN

McWHINNIE, MARY ALICE
August 10, 1922–March 17, 1980
BIOLOGIST, ANTARCTIC EXPLORER, ENVIRONMENTALIST, EDUCATOR

DePaul University biologist Mary Alice McWhinnie became the first woman scientist to join the ongoing U.S. Antarctic research program as part of a team of scientists aboard the USNS *Eltanin* in 1962. The breakthrough opened the door for other women scientists, and the honor was one among many firsts for McWhinnie. She was the first woman to chair the biology department at DePaul (1966–68) and the first woman to direct an Antarctic research team (1974). The team wintered at McMurdo Station, a U.S. naval station on Ross Island facing the South Pacific Ocean. She also did research at the Palmer Station, on the Antarctic Peninsula, where the biological laboratory was named the Mary Alice McWhinnie Marine Biology Center soon after her death.

McWhinnie did pioneering research in the areas of cell regeneration and invertebrate molting cycles, the cycles by which crustaceans such as the crayfish and lobster shed one shell, grow larger, and generate a new shell. She made eleven trips to the Antarctic, where her trailblazing research on the shrimp-like krill established it as a vital link in the Antarctic food chain.

McWhinnie was born in the Chicago suburb of Elmhurst, Illinois. Her father, David Anthony McWhinnie, came from a Massachusetts family of Scottish and Irish fishermen. He was a scholarly man who had some college and learned Greek and Latin on his own. Her mother, Ruth Margaret (Brann) McWhinnie, came from an Irish family. She was orphaned as a child and grew up in Chicago, where she was reared by two aunts. Ruth Brann completed high school and most likely met David McWhinnie on a visit he made to Chicago. They married in 1917 and moved briefly to Harrisburg, Pennsylvania, where their first child, Ruth, was born. They moved back to Illinois and settled in Elmhurst, where their other four children were born: Vivina, David, Mary Alice, and Dolores.

David McWhinnie Sr. instilled a lifelong love of animals in his children. He had a horse and beagles for small-game hunting in the woods and farmlands that surrounded Elmhurst, a country town that rapidly urbanized after World War II. He worked at odd jobs and delivered milk and coal. Jobs dropped off during the 1930s depression, and the McWhinnie home burnt down in 1939, adding to the family's financial hardships. The family moved that year to an apartment in Cicero, a suburb bordering Chicago. The move to nearby Oak Park in 1940 was permanent. The family joined Ascension Roman Catholic Church in Oak Park, and throughout her life Mary Alice McWhinnie attended Sunday mass there whenever she was in Chicago.

In 1940 McWhinnie graduated from Lucy Flower High School in Chicago and decided to follow her brother David to DePaul University. Her love of animals and the financial aid available through work-study programs in the sciences sparked her decision to major in biology. She graduated in 1944 and earned an M.S. degree in biology at DePaul in 1946. She completed her Ph.D. at Northwestern University, Evanston, Illinois, in 1952. In her doctoral thesis, "The Effect of Colchincine on Reconstitutional Development in Dugesia Dorotocephala," she identified the source of cell regeneration in planaria, a genus of

FIG. 78. *Biologist Mary Alice McWhinnie, who made her last trip to the Antarctic in 1978–79.*

worms. She taught at DePaul part-time while working on her Ph.D. and joined the faculty after completing the degree. At the time, only a handful of American women scientists held full-time professorships at coeducational universities.

McWhinnie's sister, endocrinologist Dolores McWhinnie, came to DePaul to study biology in 1951. She earned a Ph.D. from Marquette University, Milwaukee, Wisconsin, before returning to DePaul as a faculty member in 1965. The sisters had laboratories on adjacent floors of the university's science building. They both had apartments near campus and spent weekends with their mother in Oak Park, a much needed respite for Mary Alice McWhinnie, who never married and who devoted herself to her family and to science.

Mary Alice McWhinnie frequently worked eighteen-hour days teaching and doing research in her laboratory at DePaul, a superhuman schedule that she fueled with an intense sense of mission, "working on twenty cups of coffee and four packs of cigarettes a day" (interview with Dolores McWhinnie). She taught a variety of biology classes at the university, where students called her the "White Princess" because she always wore her lab coat. The trim, energetic McWhinnie was a whirlwind of ideas and information in class. Students thought of her as tough and

imposing, but she was never too busy to give individual help, and she lavished encouragement on those who showed a commitment to science.

McWhinnie's laboratory was filled with experiments relating to crustacea such as lobsters and crayfish. She continued to study their life cycles and biochemistry after 1962, when she started her research in the Antarctic. Her focus on krill was an extension of this earlier work.

The United States and eleven other nations initiated a cooperative Antarctic research program in 1957. The National Science Foundation coordinated the U.S. program. Scientists submitted proposals to join the research teams that worked aboard vessels and at stations operated by the U.S. Navy. McWhinnie submitted her first proposal in 1959, but her arrival aboard the *Eltanin* three years later was hard won. "Approval of my project preceded by years approval of my person," she noted in a 1963 *Chicago Tribune* article.

U.S. Navy officials were dismayed to learn, after the National Science Foundation had accepted her promising Antarctic research proposal, that Dr. M. A. McWhinnie was a woman. The government had consistently offered the excuse that "lack of suitable facilities" (Chipman, 110) made it impossible to accept women into the research program. She successfully convinced naval officials that bed and bath requirements for women scientists could be met in the Antarctic, and she agreed to travel with a female associate, a former student who served as her laboratory assistant on that trip.

McWhinnie recognized the krill and other Antarctic sea life as an important potential food source that could not be transplanted. Her 1962–63 research aboard the *Eltanin* established that krill required freezing temperatures to survive. McWhinnie's research approach combined observation of living sea life with study of tissue samples. That approach, rare in the 1960s, furthered the now commonplace marriage of physiology and biochemistry to environmental ecology.

She followed up the research on temperature responses of krill with studies of how metabolism and hormones function in freezing temperatures. Over the years, she sketched out the fundamentals of the life cycle, distribution, and biochemistry of krill.

McWhinnie reported on these findings and on her research at DePaul in some fifty articles published in scientific journals. On August 25, 1963, the *Chicago Tribune* published her entertaining account of her first Antarctic adventure. The lengthy letters she wrote home from her voyages provide a fascinating and candid account of the human side of science conducted in one of the harshest environments on earth. The letters often read like journals, covering several weeks aboard ship and the six-month Antarctic winter, when staff at the research stations were physically cut off from the outside world.

McWhinnie spent seven research seasons aboard the *Eltanin* between 1962 and 1972. The ship could travel only during Antarctic summer, from early October through January. Her shipboard letters make light of Thanksgiving dinner eaten in half-hour shifts, improvised Christmas presents, and "pickled krill," a recipe she invented when a batch died en route from sea to laboratory. She wrote satirical and impatient descriptions of pompous scientists and petty personality conflicts that ate up the energy and morale of the research teams.

McWhinnie arrived at McMurdo for her term as station scientific leader in January 1974. She was accompanied by Sister Mary Odile Cahoon, a friend and biologist making her first trip to the Antarctic. The last mail pickup left on February 22. There would be only one air drop of mail and no deliveries of "freshies" (fresh fruit, vegetables, or milk) until September when she left. Ham radio afforded the only communication with the outside world. Antarctic winter officially started on April 24 at 1:45 P.M. when the sun set, not to rise again until August. Together, McWhinnie and Cahoon made history as the first women to winter in Antarctica.

They joined 128 men at McMurdo—other scientists, support personnel, and a naval force. The station was a self-sufficient village of interlinked administrative, research, and living facilities, including the National Science Foundation building that the staff called the "Chalet." They referred to ham radio messages as "hamgrams."

Humor battled the numbing toll that isolation, darkness, and cold took on the human psyche. Windchill temperatures typically hovered at eighty degrees below zero. No one was allowed to venture out alone, and blizzards confined everyone indoors. McWhinnie and other biologists wore their parkas and gloves even in the laboratory, where freezing temperatures maintained a homelike environment for krill.

The 1974 winter was successful from a research standpoint but blighted for McWhinnie by the death in May of the young biology laboratory manager at McMurdo. He froze when a truck he was driving veered off the road. She traveled to Nevada for his memorial service in September, when his body could finally be brought home.

McWhinnie spent subsequent Antarctic summers at Palmer Station. She served on numerous scientific panels and committees, including the Polar Research Board of the National Academy of Sciences, the Advisory Committee for Research and the Ocean Sciences Committee of the National Science Foundation, and the Ocean Affairs Committee of the Department of State.

McWhinnie attained an international reputation in marine biology with her Antarctic research. She was the world's authority on krill, and research has continued to build upon her scientific findings. Several nations pursue her prophetic vision of the krill as a food source and the Antarctic seas as a breadbasket, though more than twenty years later, the krill still has defied efforts to process it: it becomes salty and inedible when frozen.

While McWhinnie recognized the potential of the Antarctic for helping humanity, she also saw the disastrous potential for exploitation as well. McWhinnie was among the first scientists to warn against the environmental hazards of overfishing the oceans and using the oceans as a dumping ground for wastes.

McWhinnie died of lung cancer at Hinsdale Hospital, Hinsdale, Illinois. Dozens of graduate students from around the country had joined McWhinnie's Antarctic research teams, testament to her influence as an educator. Her successful battle with naval officials, which won her a place on the USNS *Eltanin*, overturned the long-standing resistance to the participation of women scientists in the polar research programs. Her breakthrough reflected her continuing determination to raise the status of women scientists. "She would not tolerate any sort of glass ceiling. She broke them in the university, she broke them in Washington, and she broke them in the Antarctic" (interview), Dolores McWhinnie said.

Sources. A collection of McWhinnie's letters to friends and family from Antarctica as well as copies of articles she published in technical journals can be found at the DePaul Univ. Library, Spec. Coll., Chicago, Illinois. Extensive details about McWhinnie's personal life and career are provided by oral interviews of September 1993 with Father John Robert Cortelyou, Chancellor Emeritus of DePaul Univ. and a lifelong friend; Emma Rose (Dolly) Dieter, Assistant Director for Marine Operations of the National Science Foundation and a former student of McWhinnie; and Dolores McWhinnie, Mary Alice McWhinnie's sister. Descriptions of Mary Alice McWhinnie's Antarctic experiences and research are included in two books: *Women on the Ice: A History of Women in the Far South* by Elizabeth Chipman (1986) and *The New Explorers: Women in Antarctica* by Barbara Land (1981). See also Raymond Dieter, "Mary Alice McWhinnie: First Woman to Winter Over in Antarctica," *Arctic Medical Research*, vol. 53, supplement 2 (*Proceedings of the International College of Circumpolar Health*), 1994. Detailed obituaries appeared in *Polar Biology*, Spring 1982; *Antarctic Journal*, June 1980; and the *CT*, March 19, 1980. *CT* ran numerous other articles about her: October 14, 1962; August 25, 1963; September 29, 1966; July 19, 1970; December 24, 1971; February 27, 1971; and February 3, 1974.

Aʙɪɢᴀɪʟ M. Fᴏᴇʀsᴛɴᴇʀ

MENTSCHIKOFF, SOIA
April 2, 1915–June 18, 1984
Aᴛᴛᴏʀɴᴇʏ, ʟᴇɢᴀʟ sᴄʜᴏʟᴀʀ, ᴇᴅᴜᴄᴀᴛᴏʀ

Soia Mentschikoff forged new methods of studying legal institutions, and her work had a permanent impact in the field of commercial law. The first woman to become a partner at a major New York City law firm, the first woman appointed to the law school faculty at both Harvard and the University of Chicago and, with her appointment as dean of the University of Miami Law School, the second woman to head an American law school, Mentschikoff always sought to be recognized as an outstanding lawyer and scholar in her own right.

Soia Mentschikoff was born in Moscow, Russia, the daughter of American citizens Eugenia A. (Ossipov) Mentschikoff and Roman S. Mentschikoff, who was working in Russia at the time of Soia's birth. In 1917, Soia Mentschikoff's family returned to New York City, where she grew up on the Upper West Side. Though no one in her family practiced law, Mentschikoff knew early that she wanted to be a lawyer and, at the age of ten, predicted, "I will be a lawyer and a public speaker" (Allegato, "Law School Dean Retiring").

In 1934, Mentschikoff graduated from New York City's Hunter College, where she wrote for the school newspaper and was president of the student government and captain of the basketball team. Later that year, she enrolled in Columbia University Law School. The professor for her first year contracts course was Karl Nickerson Llewellyn, a prominent legal scholar and an expert in contract law and commercial law. In 1937 Llewellyn undertook the enormous project of drafting the Uniform Commercial Code, the most comprehensive codification of national commercial law ever compiled. This project became Mentschikoff's as well. During her first year as a law student, Mentschikoff established a working rapport with Llewellyn, and in her second year of law school, she became Llewellyn's research assistant. When Mentschikoff graduated from Columbia Law School in 1937 and passed the New York state bar examination, very few law firms were hiring women as practicing attorneys. Mentschikoff managed to land a job as an associate with a New York firm, Scandrett, Tuttle & Chalaire, where she specialized in the relatively new field of labor relations. In 1944, Mentschikoff was the first woman to become a partner at a major Wall Street law firm, Spence, Hotchkiss, Parker & Duryee.

Concurrently, she also worked with Llewellyn in drafting the Uniform Commercial Code. The code was a piece of national legislation conceived by two national legal organizations, the National Conference of Commissioners on Uniform State Laws and the American Law Institute, to integrate, modernize and simplify laws across the country governing commercial transactions. In 1942 Llewellyn became chief reporter (editor and a principal author) and Mentschikoff assistant chief reporter for the code. Llewellyn and Mentschikoff wrote the initial drafts for more than half of the sections of the code, and every section was at some point revised or totally redrafted by one or both of them. Mentschikoff was reporter (principal author) on the investment instruments article of the code and associate reporter on the sales article.

In 1946, Erwin Griswold, dean of Harvard Law School, impressed with Mentschikoff's work on the code, asked her to come to Harvard Law School as a visiting professor. Mentschikoff accepted the appointment, thus becoming the first woman on the faculty of Harvard Law School—four years before women were admitted as students. That same year she and Llewellyn married. Mentschikoff continued to use her maiden name professionally, unusual for a woman at the time. The couple never had children of their own but unofficially adopted Mentschikoff's two nieces, Eugenia and Alexandria.

Mentschikoff and Llewellyn continued to work together on the drafting of the Uniform Commercial Code, and by 1949, a draft was completed. Mentschikoff traveled around the country during the next two years, lobbying for acceptance of the Uniform Commercial Code and seeking input and comments from relevant trade groups, organizations, legislators, industry counsels, and other interested parties. Work on the code continued for more than fifteen years, until it was adopted during the 1950s and 1960s by the District of Columbia and by every state except Louisiana.

In 1950, while Mentschikoff and Llewellyn were attending a conference on the code sponsored by the University of Chicago, the law school's dean, Edward Levi, asked Llewellyn to join the University of Chicago Law School faculty. Reportedly, Llewellyn asked Levi whether he meant "me or we" (Dunlop, "Soia Mentschikoff Makes Strong Case"). Teaching offers were extended to both Llewellyn and Mentschikoff, who became the first woman faculty member of the University of Chicago Law School in 1951. Llewellyn joined the faculty as a professor of law. Because of the University of Chicago Law School's anti-nepotism rule, Mentschikoff was made a "professorial lecturer" (Bruck, 36) with voting privileges who was technically on the chancellor's staff. Mentschikoff retained the professorial lecturer title for eleven years before being named professor of law, with tenure, after Llewellyn's death in 1962.

While at Chicago, Mentschikoff participated in several comprehensive long-term research projects of a type never before undertaken by law school faculty. In 1953, using a Ford Foundation grant, the University of Chicago established the Law and Behavioral Science Research Program to apply the techniques of behavioral science research to the study and understanding of legal institutions. Mentschikoff was heavily involved in two projects: the characteristics and performance of arbitration and the nature and operation of the jury system.

The Arbitration Project, headed by Mentschikoff, conducted a long-term study of commercial arbitration. The study included an extensive survey of hundreds of trade associations with regard to their use of commercial arbitration, and it examined more than five hundred arbitration cases heard by the American Arbitration Association. The project also conducted an empirical experiment in which more than fifty experimental arbitration panels were assembled, each of which heard the same case. This application of behavioral science methods of experimentation was a novel method of studying legal institutions. Mentschikoff published a lengthy article in the *Columbia Law Review* in 1961, describing the Arbitration Project's findings.

Mentschikoff was also involved in the Jury Project, which studied the nature and operation of the American jury system. She and her colleagues were interested in methods of jury selection, including the effect of interrogation of the panel and of challenges to individual jurors, a comparison of jury verdicts with decisions made by the judge, the deliberative process jurors used to reach verdicts, and the costs of the jury system. This was probably the first time these questions were examined systematically, and all continue to be of central importance to trial attorneys.

In 1967, in addition to her position at the University of Chicago, Mentschikoff began teaching as a Distinguished Visiting Professor at the University of Miami School of Law, in Coral Gables, Florida. In 1972, Mentschikoff became one of the first two women to be appointed a trustee of the Rand Corporation, the Santa Monica research organization. In 1973, she was the first woman elected president of the Association of American Law Schools. The same year she was asked to become dean of the University of Miami School of Law. With her appointment at the University of Miami, Mentschikoff became only the second woman to head a nationally accredited American law school. Mentschikoff said that she accepted the appointment because she wanted to create a nationally recognized law school in the South and to try out new ideas for legal education.

Mentschikoff's eight-year tenure as dean of University of Miami's law school was widely credited with raising the law school from a position of relative academic obscurity to one of national prominence. She improved the quality and rigor of the curriculum, built a new library as well as a new classroom building, and founded the Center for Law and Economics, which brought in visiting professors from other law schools to teach seminars. Not everyone at Miami was enamored of Mentschikoff's forceful and sometimes autocratic style of management, however. She was known at the law school as the "Czarina" and alternatively as "the Russian Bear" in deference to her Russian heritage and sometimes fearsome demeanor.

While dean at Miami, Mentschikoff maintained her involvement in various activities in the legal community outside academia. Mentschikoff continued to be called upon to interpret the application of the Uniform Commercial Code in real-world commercial disputes, and her interest and involvement in alternative dispute resolution continued throughout her career. In 1980, President Jimmy Carter appointed Mentschikoff to the Panel of Arbitrators of the International Centre for the Settlement of Investment Disputes, an agency of the World Bank. In 1967, 1971, and 1975, Mentschikoff's name appeared on a variety of lists presented to the president, recommending that she be considered for nomination to the United States Supreme Court. Mentschikoff indicated that if asked, she would accept the appointment if she considered the next candidate to be asked "inferior" to her. But she made it clear that she would be interested in the appointment only if it were offered because she was a good lawyer, not because she was a woman. Mentschikoff in no way considered herself a feminist, because she believed that male bias was a barrier that could be overcome easily when one was first rate. In an interview for a profile in the *American Lawyer* in 1982, Mentschikoff said that she was against affirmative action programs for two reasons: "First, I don't like single-dimensional thinking. You're a woman, but . . . you have all sorts of other characteristics. Second, a great many people who believe in affirmative action really don't believe that women are as good as men: that's why they'll hire any goddamned woman that comes down the pike. I think it's insulting" (Bruck, 37).

Mentschikoff retired as dean of the University of Miami School of Law in 1982. The May–September 1983 issue of the *University of Miami Law Review* was dedicated to Mentschikoff and included articles by Miami law faculty honoring her contributions to the development of American commercial law. United States Supreme Court Chief Justice Warren E. Burger introduced the special issue with his own tribute to Mentschikoff. He said that she was "far ahead of most of her contemporaries for more than three decades" in that "she pressed the importance of arbitration, mediation, and negotiation as alternatives to litigation" ("Tribute," n.p.). After her retirement from academic life, Mentschikoff was active as a public speaker, a consultant, and an expert witness in commercial litigation.

Soia Mentschikoff died of cancer at her home in Coral Gables, Florida. Funeral services were held on June 21, 1984, at Sts. Peter and Paul Russian Orthodox Church on Chicago's South Side, followed by burial in Chicago. A memorial service was held in Coral Gables, Florida, on June 29, 1984.

While Mentschikoff's importance was often cited as stemming from her history of being the first woman to hold various important positions in the legal world, Mentschikoff saw herself as a lawyer who made contributions to legal scholarship and practice that were important in their own right. She did not view herself as a trailblazer for other women. Rather, she wanted her contributions to be evaluated apart from the issue of gender. Indeed, the Uniform Commercial Code stands as an enduring and functioning legacy of her legal scholarship.

Sources. The major source of Mentschikoff's professional materials is the Soia Mentschikoff Papers, U.C. Spec. Coll. The collection includes professional correspondence, memoranda to and from Dean Edward Levi and other members of the UC law faculty regarding research projects, drafts and texts of papers, speeches, book manuscripts, research files, study and course materials, selected student papers, and other materials. The Office of Law Alumni and Development at the Univ. of Miami School of Law maintains a collection of newspaper articles and other materials regarding Mentschikoff. Included among these materials is the text of an address, "Soia's Way: Toiling in the Common Law Tradition," delivered at a memorial service held for Mentschikoff on June 29, 1984, by Professor Irwin P. Stotzky of University of Miami School of Law. Mentschikoff's books include *Unification of Private International Law,* with Nicholas Katzenbach (1961); *Commercial Transactions, Cases and Materials* (1970); and *The Theory and Craft of American Law—Elements,* with Irwin P. Stotzky (1981). Her articles include "Commercial Arbitration," *Columbia Law Review,* vol. 61, 1961, and other articles in scholarly journals. Mention of Mentschikoff is made in William Twining, *Karl Llewellyn and the Realist Movement* (1973), in connection with the research, drafting, and promulgation of the Uniform Commercial Code by Llewellyn, Mentschikoff, and others. Several profiles of Mentschikoff appeared in journals and newspapers during her lifetime, including Beth Dunlop, "Soia Mentschikoff Makes Strong Case for UM Law School," *Miami Herald,* March 12, 1978; Rose Allegato, "Law School Dean Retiring after String of Firsts," *Miami Herald,* October 19, 1979; C. Bruck, "The First Woman Everything," *American Lawyer,* October 1982; Marilyn A. Moore, "Retiring Law Dean Leaves a Legend in U-M's Time," *Miami News,* January 28, 1982. *University of Miami Law Review,* May–September 1983, was dedicated to Mentschikoff. An obituary by George Volsky, "Soia Mentschikoff, Professor and Ex-Law Dean, Dies at 69," appeared in *NYT* June 19, 1984.

ELIZABETH L. INGLEHART

MERGLER, MARIE JOSEPHA
May 18, 1851–May 17, 1901
GYNECOLOGIC SURGEON, PROFESSOR, ADMINISTRATOR

Marie Josepha Mergler, who practiced and taught medicine, served as dean of the Woman's Medical School of Northwestern University and as head physician and surgeon of the Mary Thompson Hospital in Chicago. She was born in Mainstockheim, near Würzburg in Bavaria, Germany. She was the youngest of the three children, all daughters, of Francis R. and Henriette (Rittershausen) Mergler. Her father was a physician, and her mother came from a German family that traced its roots to the sixteenth century. The family moved to the United States in 1853 and settled in Wheeling, Illinois, where Dr. Mergler was the only physician in the area.

Most of Marie Mergler's early education came at home from her parents. She gradually became interested in her father's work, and he increasingly called upon her for assistance. This early home atmosphere and experience eventually led her to choose medicine for her own career.

Her formal education began at the Cook County Normal School, from which she graduated in 1869. The school had been established two years earlier, and Mergler and her sister, Ernestine, were members of the first graduating class. Mergler then entered the New York State Normal School in Oswego, graduating from its classical course in 1872.

That year Marie Mergler moved to the town of Englewood (annexed by Chicago in 1889), southeast of Chicago, and spent the next four years as a teacher and assistant principal at Englewood High School. These activities, however, did not provide her with the intellectual challenge and satisfaction she was seeking in a career. She turned to medicine in the fall of 1876 and entered the Woman's Hospital Medical College in Chicago, which became the Woman's Medical College in 1879.

Life for a woman medical student then, even at a medical school limited to women, was not always pleasant or productive. In their middle year, Mergler and her classmates first attended clinical lectures at the Cook County Hospital. Here one of their professors greeted his class the first morning with a statement that he would begin when the women left.

One of the teachers at the college who did not believe in women doctors did not provide them with a proper surgical education. However, after five seniors, Mergler among them, took the surgical examination for Cook County Hospital and did badly, the teacher reversed his attitude and gave the next classes a much better grounding.

Mergler graduated in 1879 as valedictorian of her class. A few days later Mergler took the test for appointment as intern at the Cook County Insane Asylum at Dunning. She finished first but did not receive the appointment. Later, when a colleague commiserated with Mergler over the Dunning episode, she asserted that this was the best thing that could have happened to her, since she then decided to go to Switzerland to obtain postgraduate experience in clinical medicine and pathology at Zurich. This experience proved of considerable value throughout her career.

In 1881 Mergler started a general practice but gradually became more and more interested in gynecology and obstetrics, focusing on surgery. By the middle 1880s she had limited her practice to these specialties.

She developed her skill as a teacher serving in 1879–80 as assistant to Dr. William Maynard, professor of materia medica at the Woman's Medical College, and teaching histology. In 1882 Mergler became professor of materia medica at Woman's Medical College. That same year Mergler was appointed an attending physician at Cook County Hospital, the second woman to hold such a position; SARAH HACKETT STEVENSON had been the first. She also taught as a medical lecturer at the Illinois Training School for Nurses in 1883–84. From 1885 to 1899 she served as secretary of the faculty at the Woman's Medical College, which became the Northwestern University Woman's Medical School in 1892. In 1890, upon the death of Dr. William H. Byford, Mergler succeeded him as professor of gynecology. In 1895 her teaching skills led to her appointment as professor of gynecology at the Post-Graduate Medical School in Chicago, a position she held until her death.

She began early to write for medical publications and to speak at professional meetings. In 1879, Mergler prepared microscopical specimens and made camera lucida drawings for a paper on tubercular meningitis by Professor Charles W. Earle. In 1886 she spoke on "Progress in Gynecology" at the annual meeting of the Illinois State Medical Society (ISMS). This thorough paper, published the same year in the transactions of the society, surveyed the foreign literature and expressed the results in tables and text. She emphasized the need to prevent the spread of infection by handling tissues as gently and as little as possible.

In 1888 she again addressed the ISMS, this time on the subject of salpingitis—an inflammation of the fallopian tubes that was becoming of considerable interest to gynecologists. In the resulting publication in the society's transactions that year, as elsewhere in her writings, Mergler stressed the importance of avoiding infection. She described her diagnostic and operative procedures in considerable detail. Her growing skill in these two areas of medicine gradually raised her stature not only in the eyes of her patients but also among her professional colleagues, who began to seek her advice.

Mergler presented another detailed paper in 1892, this dealing with abdominal section. Two years later, at the annual meeting of the ISMS, she reviewed fifty-three consecutive cases of fibroid tumors of the uterus from the college's gynecologic clinic, where she was in charge. This study thoroughly reviewed the European literature and gave detailed accounts of her own cases.

To help her students, Mergler produced in 1893 A Guide to the Study of Gynecology. This manual had alternate blank pages for students to use as a notebook for class and later in their professional work. Mergler wrote a few more medical articles as well as several on the history of the college.

Dr. MARY HARRIS THOMPSON, head physician and surgeon at her own Chicago Hospital for Women and Children (renamed Mary Thompson Hospital) died suddenly in 1895, and a search began for her successor. Mergler, receiving the unanimous support of the Chicago Gynecological Society and the support of a large majority of the medical profession in the city, served in this important position until 1897, when Dr. LUCY WAITE, who had been appointed head surgeon and medical superintendent in 1895, returned from two years of study in Europe.

When Issac Newton Danforth, dean of the Northwestern University Woman's Medical School, retired from that position in 1899, Mergler was named his successor. She retained this position until her death two years later.

Mergler had another side to her personality beyond her administrative, operative, and teaching skills. Her role as counselor to many students and physicians was often mentioned by colleagues. This counseling took place at the medical school, in various hospitals and clinics, but particularly at her home. The three homes Mergler had at different times in Chicago meant much to her as places of retreat and renewal and as comfortable locations for reading her favorite poets and fiction writers, many of them in the original German. Mergler did not marry.

Because of health problems, at the turn of the century Mergler made several visits to southern California. She died in Los Angeles of pernicious anemia. Her will left three thousand dollars to the University of Chicago, the interest from which is still used for scholarships for women in physiology. At a memorial service at the Union Park Congregational Church in Chicago on May 26, 1901, her colleagues spoke of Mergler's many contributions. I. N. Danforth recalled her poise and iron will, which aided her throughout her career. He went on to state, "Her untimely death is due to the fact that she was literally and absolutely worn out with hard work, and the nervous wear and tear of responsibilities which brought with them honors indeed, but honors which cost more than they were worth" (Danforth, 293). With little known about the treatment of pernicious anemia, Danforth, eulogizing Mergler, attributed her death to overwork.

Marie Josepha Mergler supported opening the medical profession to women in the areas of education, teaching, and administration, as well as in hospitals and societies. Her skills as a diagnostician and operative surgeon achieved for her an international reputation. At the time of her death, professional peers considered her one of the outstanding women in American medicine and without equal among European women surgeons.

Sources. Mergler's publications include "History of the Northwestern University Woman's Medical School," in *Woman's Medical School Northwestern University* (published by H. G. Cutler, 1896). William K. Beatty's "Marie J. Mergler: Surgeon and Friend," *Proceedings of the Institute of Medicine of Chicago,* July–September 1983, lists Mergler's publications and summarizes their content. Accounts of Mergler's life appear in two articles by colleagues who spoke at her memorial service: Eliza H. Root, "Dr. Marie J. Mergler as Woman and Physician," and I. N. Danforth, "Marie Josepha Mergler, M.D.," both in *Woman's Medical Journal,* August 1901. Obituaries are in *Chicago Medical Recorder,* July 1901, and *CT,* May 22, 1901. Useful material is also found in F. M. Sperry, comp., *A Group of Distinguished Physicians and Surgeons of Chicago* (1904); Howard A. Kelly and Walter L. Burrage, *Dictionary of American Medical Biography* (1928); and *NAW* (1971).

WILLIAM K. BEATTY

MERRILL, IRIS BARBARA
August 24, 1934–March 26, 1983
LABOR ORGANIZER AND LEADER, WOMEN'S AND
CIVIL RIGHTS ACTIVIST

From her identity as a black trade union woman, Barbara Merrill's activities radiated like the spokes of a wheel. She helped found a union for public employees in Chicago and national organizations for both women and African American trade unionists. She served as regional coordinator for a national campaign against J.P. Stevens and served and participated in numerous civil rights, women's rights, and labor organizations.

Merrill came from a middle-class black family on the South Side of Chicago. Both her father, Jackson Merrill, born in Cortland, Alabama, and her mother, Lula Mae (Childress) Merrill, born in Oklahoma City, Oklahoma, had migrated as children to the city where their families settled in the Grand Boulevard section of Chicago's "Black Metropolis." They married directly out of high school in 1931. Jackson Merrill started college and joined the army, where he served as a master sergeant in the 33rd Division. After World War II, he attended night classes at DePaul University, Chicago, where in 1953 he earned a Ph.B. degree in social work with honors. He worked with the Department of Welfare of the City of Chicago (merged with the Cook County Department of Public Aid in 1958). Merrill's mother was first a homemaker, then later worked for the federal government. During Merrill's life, her mother had several serious illnesses, including several bouts with cancer from the 1930s on and many hospital stays. As a child and adult, Merrill was particularly close to her mother.

Merrill's parents separated when she was eight years old. She and her older sister, Rena Jeannette, lived primarily with her mother's family, though she also remained close to her father. Her maternal grandparents were influential. William Smith Childress was a proud, strict, warm, intelligent man who worked

as a bellhop. He took the young Barbara to hear speeches on union organizing and radical causes at Washington ("Bughouse") Square, the free speech park on Chicago's North Side. Her grandmother, Georgetta Childress, who was part Cherokee, part Caucasian, and part African American, was also a strong soul. When William Childress died unexpectedly in 1954, "Dearie" (as Merrill called her grandmother) learned to drive and took classes to earn a certificate as a licensed practical nurse. Merrill, her mother, and grandparents all lived together on the South Side, finally buying a two-flat house together in 1954. "For three women, and three black women, [getting a mortgage] . . . was really difficult back in those days, but First Federal [Savings and Loan] did give us a mortgage" (Balanoff interview with Merrill, 17).

Merrill graduated from the newly integrating Englewood High School in 1951 with the goal of becoming a math teacher. According to Merrill, she married directly out of high school, but the marriage dissolved after the birth of Merrill's first child and her husband's return from the military in Korea. Merrill had been attending the University of Illinois at Navy Pier during her pregnancy, but once a single mother, she left college to support her daughter, Camille Denise.

After a few unsatisfactory jobs in retail and the federal government, Merrill took a clerical position at the Cook County Department of Public Aid in a different area from her father. Her mother and grandmother helped care for her daughter and later for her "adopted" daughter, her sister's daughter Rosalind. Starting out at a West Side office, Merrill was shocked by how different the culture was from the South Side and arranged to be transferred to another office. The West Side was populated by the most recent migrants from the South, whose lack of skills and formal education frustrated their dreams of economic opportunity. Unlike the South Side black community, where long-standing black-owned commercial, cultural, and social institutions mediated the poverty and dislocation of new migrants, the West Side was undeveloped. By the early 1960s, Merrill was promoted to financial clerk at the Department of Public Aid's North Side office—the first African American to hold such a position in that office. After completing the six-month probation period, Merrill joined a union, Local 73 of the Building Services Employees International Union/General Services Employees Union (GSEU). Although the state of Illinois did not recognize collective bargaining for public employees, the unions were affiliated closely with the Democratic Party, and labor peace was maintained through arranged contracts or even more informal agreements, called "sweetheart contracts" (Bellush, 93).

Merrill had been excited to join the union; she had been influenced by her grandfather's belief in unions as a way to gain equality. Her excitement quickly turned to disappointment. After one union meeting in 1965, she met with five or six union members also frustrated with the union and with working conditions among public aid workers. Union officers undemocratically ran the local and spent more time explaining management's side than supporting workers' concerns. Merrill and the other dissidents—primarily caseworkers who had recently graduated from the University of Chicago—formed an independent group to study labor history and plan strategy to reform the local. They were influenced by the national and local civil rights movement, which in Chicago centered around education and real estate practices, and by New Left work in Freedom Schools in the South and poor white communities in the North. Concurrently, the "Great Society" of President Lyndon B. Johnson had expanded the number of welfare recipients without increasing the budget to administer aid. Despite increased demands, workers' salaries had been frozen. Moreover, public aid administrators treated workers paternalistically and arbitrarily disciplined them. Job dissatisfaction ran high: many caseworkers felt they pushed more paper than directly helped clients, and clerical workers were deluged with paperwork.

The core group began building an opposition faction, talking individually to coworkers at lunch or in their homes. Merrill was particularly adept at garnering the support of clerical workers. As their organization coalesced, the opposition faction held small protests on the job directed at a particular problem or to demonstrate its burgeoning strength. For example, when paychecks once were late, Merrill gave an impromptu workshop on budgeting.

On May 11, 1966, the Independent Union of Public Aid Employees (IUPAE) was born when thousands walked off their jobs in support of nearly four hundred workers who had been suspended after a one-hour work stoppage. The opposition union joined the Coordinating Council of Community Organizations (CCCO). The union linked many of its goals to the concerns of welfare recipients and distributed "A Manifesto for a More Humane Welfare System." Major unions, civil rights organizations, churches, and welfare rights groups supported the striking public aid workers. After two weeks, Mayor Richard J. Daley finally stepped in behind the scenes, his usual practice in labor negotiations, and told his allies on the Cook County Board to settle the strike.

For Merrill and others, what began as an attempt to democratize their union became a fight to gain recognition for an independent union, reform the welfare system, and, in its broadest implications, force the state to address collective bargaining rights for public employees. Federal employees had been given that right by President John F. Kennedy in 1962. In December 1966 public aid employees voted for the IUPAE to be their representative rather than GSEU Local 73, went out on a difficult seven-week strike to gain a contract in May of the following year, and slowly established themselves. They were known throughout the state as a tough, tight union. In 1967 Merrill help found a national organization of public aid workers, the National Social Service Employees Union.

From the beginning of her career as a public employee, Merrill had despised the condescending and arbitrary practices of supervisors. She defended herself and coworkers who were wrongly treated. In both public and private life, Merrill was seen as a leader; in her family, she was the strong, steady one to whom people would turn. She carried herself with an air of authority and self-confidence, yet could be warm. She was an articulate, opinionated speaker, but prudently chose when to speak. She took on work—some say too much—and always followed through. Though she was not charismatic and did not care to promote herself, she mentored many young women new to the workforce and trade unionism, bringing them to union and social activities, passing on her leadership qualities.

Despite her large base of support, Merrill initially shied from holding office in the union. She found an affinity for organizing and preferred to stay closest to the workers as a union steward. When the vice-president for IUPAE clerical workers died suddenly, Merrill took on the job. She held that office for five years and then served as president of the IUPAE from 1970 to 1972, a position she did not find satisfying. When the IUPAE merged with the American Federation of State, County, and Municipal Employees (AFSCME) in 1973, Merrill moved to its district office. At that time she left the County Department of Public Aid, where she had reached the level of supervisor of the financial control unit.

Merrill had been a leader in organizing public employees; now she became a leader in the new agenda developed by women trade unionists with the formation of the Coalition of Labor Union Women (CLUW). Union women, influenced by the women's movement, wanted to join the fight for the Equal Rights Amendment (ERA) as trade unionists and sought more power and recognition within their unions as women. (Heretofore, union women and their supporters typically had opposed the ERA, viewing it as a threat to hard-won protective legislation for women.) CLUW emerged after a meeting of eight female union leaders who convened in Chicago in 1973. Cofounders Addie Wyatt of the Amalgamated Meatcutters Union and Clara Day of the Teamsters immediately invited Merrill to join the organizing activities. In mid-1973, Merrill was one of the coordinators of the Midwest Conference of Union Women, a prototype of the national organization. Two hundred women from eighteen states, representing twenty national unions, participated in the regional conference. A year later, Merrill helped coordinate the founding national conference in which thirty-five hundred union women from across the nation converged on Chicago. Only two thousand had been expected.

Merrill relished the heady days of the founding conference. Having started a union from the ground up, she leapt into the demands of organizing this new organization. She served as one of the three state conveners for Illinois and as first president of the Chicago Chapter of CLUW from 1975 to 1977. The chapter ran a speakers bureau, conducted educational classes, including one on parliamentary procedure conducted by Merrill; it organized nonunion women, supported striking workers, lobbied for passage of the Equal Rights Amendment, and held demonstrations for a full employment bill. The chapter supported establishing an International Women's Day. Chicago CLUW worked to obtain maternity leave for working women and adequate day care. Issues of occupational safety and affirmative action were also major concerns. Merrill's willingness to take on all tasks, her dignity and demeanor, and her studied use of laughter helped solidify the Chicago chapter and alleviate the tensions that arose between radical women in CLUW and more mainstream and reform members. As a state convener, Merrill traveled throughout Illinois, working with union women interested in setting up local CLUW chapters. She also took on more visible roles, testifying at Congressional hearings on sex and race discrimination in 1974, speaking on television and radio shows, and teaching classes for union women. After three years as CLUW president, she left and served through the 1970s as state vice-president, parliamentary officer of the Chicago chapter, and as a member of the CLUW national executive board. CLUW had expanded Merrill's involvement in unionism from the world of public employees to nationwide trade union women from almost every trade.

As she learned about other workers' struggles through her CLUW activities, she concluded that the nonunion South was the key to a strong labor movement. When the opportunity came to help black and white Southern textile workers win recognition and a contract from the textile giant, she joined the campaign. In 1977 she became regional coordinator of the J.P. Stevens boycott for the American Clothing Workers of America, which merged during the course of the campaign with the Textile Workers of America to become the Amalgamated Clothing and Textile Workers Union (ACTWU). (In 1996 the union became UNITE—Union of Needle Trades, Industrial, and Textile Employees—after ACTWU merged with the International Ladies' Garment Workers' Union.) The union employed a novel approach called the corporate campaign. This strategy depends upon the public's not only boycotting goods, but also putting pressure on the corporation's board members and business allies. Merrill coordinated the activities of the unions, religious groups, and others who were sympathetic to the workers' plight. As in all of Merrill's jobs, she put herself totally into the work, though she felt hampered by the lack of autonomy. Merrill's understanding of labor struggles broadened further when she met leaders of COSATU, the coalition of South African unions. The two groups supported each others' struggles—against apartheid in South Africa and anti-unionism in the United States. When J.P. Stevens and the union settled in 1981, Merrill moved on.

While working with the American Clothing Workers, Merrill was diagnosed with cancer but continued to work in the women's, trade union, and civil rights movements. In 1980, while in remission, Merrill traveled to China with a group of nine female trade unionists at the invitation of Chinese trade unionists. It was one of the high points of her life. Merrill was appalled by working conditions in the textile factories, literally getting sick at one. As a matter of principle, she bought few souvenirs in the country out of concern for the working conditions under which they were produced.

Merrill organized, mobilized, and worked until she was physically unable to continue. She staffed the 1981 Midwest Labor Coalition for Jobs, which led organizing efforts in Chicago for the historic Solidarity Day March of two hundred thousand unionists on the nation's capitol on August 31, 1981. She also staffed the labor office for the first Chicago mayoral campaign of Harold Washington in 1982–83. Since the Chicago Federation of Labor did not support Washington, she and Harold Rogers of the Cook County Teachers Union went directly to sympathetic unions to build support and garner contributions. Washington was elected the first African American mayor of Chicago.

Barbara Merrill was not known by her birth name, Iris; she quipped that no one leading illegal strikes could have such a pretty name. She had been a teacher as well as an organizer. She taught Sunday School at St. Edmund's (Episcopal) Church, where she was a member along with her mother and grandmother. She also taught labor history, collective bargaining,

parliamentary procedure, and union negotiating to women workers' schools in the Midwest.

Her work with CLUW linked her to many feminist organizations, including the Labor Committee of the Illinois Commission on the Status of Women. She represented Illinois as one of the fifty-four elected delegates at the International Women's Decade Conference held in Houston, Texas, in 1977. She also served on the boards of the Illinois Women's Agenda and Women Employed. She did not identify herself as a feminist, viewing most feminist organizations as too middle class; but she participated in women's groups where she could speak up for the working class. On the other hand, she took part in labor and civil rights organizations as an African American woman.

Civil rights were an integral part of Merrill's life—even as a child—though she did not take any leadership roles. Her earliest childhood recollection was of how she and her sister attempted to integrate a bus in Oklahoma City, Oklahoma, where they were staying with their grandparents. As a young adult visiting her aunt in Washington, D.C., she and the family integrated a neighborhood in the city and one of the public beaches. Merrill joined open housing and other civil rights marches in Chicago and traveled to Murfreesboro, Tennessee, and Cairo, Illinois. She did not join the schools for nonviolent action run by James Bevel in Chicago, however, since she was not prepared to tolerate the kind of abuse typically heaped on nonviolent protesters.

Merrill also helped found the Black Labor Leaders of Chicago, a precursor to both CLUW and the Coalition of Black Trade Unionists. The founding members were African American officers in a number of Chicago unions who wanted to advocate for more black leadership in the local unions. In addition, they organized union contributions to the rebuilding of Chicago's West Side after the riots following the assassination of Martin Luther King Jr. in 1968, and they worked with the local office of the Southern Christian Leadership Conference. Merrill participated in the A. Phillip Randolph Institute, a mainstream American Federation of Labor-Congress of Industrial Organizations (AFL-CIO) organization for African Americans; the activist, politically progressive Coalition of Black Trade Unionists; the National Association for the Advancement of Colored People (NAACP); and the Chicago Black United Fund, made up of automatic employee paycheck contributions to African American community organizations. From her alliances with other unionists, she worked with the Jewish Labor Committee, Labor Committee on Public Utilities, and the Conference on Religion and Labor.

In 1973 Merrill received the Albert Yeatman Award from the Coalition of Black Trade Unionists (CBTU) as one of the fifteen outstanding black women in organized labor; in 1975 she was one of ten labor union women honored by Jesse Jackson's Operation PUSH. Additionally, Merrill received the Martin Luther King Jr. Social Justice Award and the FLORENCE CRILEY Award from the Chicago Chapter of CLUW. Merrill died of cancer at the age of forty-nine. Her funeral was held at St. Edmund's Church. Since her death, both CLUW and CBTU have named awards in her memory.

Merrill identified herself as a trade union woman in civil rights organizations, as a black woman in trade union settings, and as a black trade unionist in women's rights settings. Commenting about being a black woman, she said, "We are the two most well-defined minorities of this nation and have endured suffering equal to none" (quoted in Heise, "Iris Merrill"). While she saw the trade union movement as a place to gain equality, she knew the struggle. She believed in giving women the basic skills to take their full places and assume their equal rights with male trade unionists in the labor union movement.

Merrill never gained the national fame bestowed upon some of her union sisters; her reserved style better fit local leadership roles. That role was her preference. National leaders could count on her to take on whatever job needed to be done—mobilize people, clarify problems, articulate the issues, seek solutions, and confront the adversary. Always rising to the needs and challenges of the particular movement, Barbara Merrill was an indefatigable warrior for women's, civil, and workers' rights.

Sources. Elizabeth Balanoff's interview of Iris Barbara Merrill, September 20, 1978, in the Balanoff Oral History Project, Center for New Deal Studies, Roosevelt Univ., Chicago, is the best source of personal information. The interview is jointly owned by Roosevelt Univ. and the 20th Century Trade Union Woman Oral History Project at the Univ. of Michigan, Ann Arbor, Michigan, where the Merrill transcript was copyrighted in 1978. Additional information came from interviews by Lisa Oppenheim in 1996 and 1997 with Merrill's daughter Camille Denise Nichols, her son-in-law William Burns, Heather Booth, Brownwen Zwirner, Harold Rogers, Allen Kaplan, and Barbara Jones. The following sources also provide insight into Merrill's activities: Sheli A. Lulkin Papers, Marie Fese Papers, and International Women's Year Coordinating Committee records, all at UIC Spec. Coll.; Midwest Academy Papers and Raymond M. Hilliard Papers, CHS; Mayor Harold Washington Papers, Harold Washingtion Library Center, Spec. Coll., CPL. Merrill gave testimony before the United States Commission on Civil Rights, *Hearing Held in Chicago, Illinois*, vol. 1: Testimony, June 17–19, 1974. Articles in the *Chicago Sun-Times, CT, Chicago Defender, Common Sense* (newspaper of the Independent Union of Public Aid Employees), *Bread & Roses* (Chicago Chapter of CLUW newsletter) are useful. An interview with Merrill appears in Adade Mitchell Wheeler, *The Roads They Made: Women in Illinois History* (1977). Published books and articles relevant to Merrill's life and times include Alan B. Anderson and George W. Pickering, *Confronting the Color Line: The Broken Promise of the Civil Rights Movement in Chicago* (1986); Diane Balser, *Sisterhood and Solidarity* (1987); Jewel Belush and Bernard Belush, *Victor Gotbaum and District Council 37* (1984); Russell K. Schutt, *Organization in a Changing Environment: Unionization of Welfare Employees* (1986); Jean McKelvey, "Document: Cook County Commissioners' Fact Finding Board Report on Collective Bargaining and County Public Aid Employees," *Industrial and Labor Relations Review*, April 1967; Arnold Weber, "Paradise Lost; or Whatever Happened to the Chicago Social Workers," *Industrial and Labor Relations Review*, April 22, 1969; David L. Carlton, "J.P. Stevens and Co.," in *Encyclopedia of Southern Culture*, ed. Charles Reagan Wilson and William Ferris (1989); Jack D. Douglas, "Urban Politics and Public Employee Unions," in *Public Employee Unions: A Study of the Crisis in Public Sector Labor Relations*, ed. A. Lawrence Chickering (1976); Allen Kaplan, "The Social Activist," in Philip L. Quaglieri, *America's Labor Leaders* (1989). See also the newspaper *New Left Notes*. Obituaries of Merrill include Kenan Heise, "Iris Merrill; Helped Found 3 Labor Groups," *CT*, March 30, 1983; Omawale-Ketu Oladuwa, "Funeral Services for Iris Barbara," *Chicago Defender*, March 30, 1983; and *Chicago Sun-Times*, March 31, 1983.

LISA OPPENHEIM

MEYER, LUCY JANE RIDER
September 9, 1849–March 16, 1922
DEACONESS TRAINING SCHOOL FOUNDER, EDUCATOR,
SOCIAL REFORMER, CHURCHWOMAN

Lucy Rider Meyer, founder of the Chicago Training School for City, Home and Foreign Missions of the Methodist Episcopal Church (MEC), was born in northwestern Vermont. Her father, Richard Rider, was a farmer who could trace his family to the pilgrims of Plymouth Bay Colony. Jane (Child) Rider, Richard Rider's second wife, was descended from Massachusetts Puritans. Lucy was Jane Rider's first child and was followed by sons Eben and Ellsworth. Richard Rider had six children by a previous marriage.

Rider's childhood was generally a happy one, in which books and reading played a prominent role. During her teen years, Rider committed herself to a life of Christian service.

Rider's early schooling took her from a rural schoolhouse to nearby Weybridge. She then attended her brother Norman's select school in Addison and a school in Middlebury, finally graduating in 1867 from Upham Theological Seminary (later New Hampton Institute), a secondary school in Fairfax, Vermont.

Following teaching experiences in a nearby high school and a Quaker freedmen's school in Greensborough, North Carolina, Rider was able to enter Oberlin College as a junior due to her private reading and study. By then, Oberlin had lost some of its earlier social reform ideals, but Rider continued to develop a social conscience there. She enrolled in the College, rather than the Ladies Course, and excelled in science. She graduated in 1872 with a Bachelor of Arts degree. In 1880, Oberlin awarded her an honorary Master of Arts degree.

While at Oberlin, Rider fell in love with a fellow student who was preparing to go to India as a medical missionary. Planning to marry and accompany him, she entered the Women's Medical College in Philadelphia in 1872. Little is known of the man with whom Rider had planned to spend her future in India. His death from cholera in 1874 changed the direction of her life and sent her back to Vermont to recover from the loss. Caring for her aging parents and her teenage brother Ellsworth in the family home, Rider taught a boys' Bible class in a nearby Sunday school. She was a gifted teacher, and the quizzes, lessons, and music she developed for her class were published in Sunday school periodicals. Soon, she was lecturing on the newly developed Chautauqua circuit.

Following her father's death in July 1876, Rider took a position as "lady principal" at Troy Annual Conference Academy, a Methodist institution in Poultney, Vermont. She assumed lifelong responsibility for her mother and brother Ellsworth. She continued to write for Sunday school periodicals, preparing in one year more than four thousand questions on the Bible and related topics. While at Poultney, she wrote her first book, *The Fairy Land of Chemistry*, continuing her interest in science.

After a year of teaching, she attended the Boston School of Technology (later Massachusetts Institute of Technology) for one year, preparing to teach chemistry. She spent a few months at the Cook County Normal School in Englewood, Illinois, on the outskirts of Chicago, studying teaching methods. In September 1879, she became professor of chemistry at McKendree College, a Methodist higher education institution in Lebanon,

Illinois. She spent weekends traveling, teaching, and lecturing at Sunday school conventions. In 1880, she resigned her position at McKendree to accept the position of field secretary of the Illinois State Sunday School Association. Her assignment was to raise the standards of Sunday school instruction. In 1883, she published a book on children's meetings that remained in print until the mid-1920s.

Rider's contemporaries remarked on her plain, sometimes careless dress, without rouge or ruffles. She had presence rather than beauty, with striking grey eyes and soft brown hair. She was tall and confident in her bearing. When she smiled, she was radiant; when she talked and lectured, she sparkled and glowed. Her persuasive speaking and writing style, honed during her Sunday School Association years, would help her to excite others about her growing vision of educating women for Christian mission.

Rider's four years with the Sunday School Association put her in contact with religious educators from across the nation and nourished her vision. She taught Bible and music at revivalist Dwight L. Moody's School for Girls in Northfield, Massachusetts, during the winter of 1884–85. While there, she composed music and wrote hymns, a practice she continued throughout her life. She left that position to marry Josiah Shelly Meyer, a Chicago businessman, on May 21, 1885, at the home of her distant cousin in Arlington Heights, Illinois. Their only child, a son named Shelly, was born September 5, 1887. His birth marked the beginning of Meyer's chronic ill health.

The marriage began a lifelong partnership that combined her vision, personal magnetism, and writing, teaching, and speaking skills with his business and money-handling capabilities. He gave a practical foundation to her dream, sharing both her zeal for a training school for Christian workers and a commitment to a life of Christian service. On October 20, 1885, they opened the Chicago Training School in a rented building with four resident students. A year later, they bought a building on Chicago's Near North Side to house the school.

Meyer took inspiration from a German pastor, Theodore Fliedner, and the deaconess system he established in 1833, training and deploying working-class German women as nurses and teachers. Kaiserwerth, the institution he founded, with its schools, orphanages, asylums, and hospitals, inspired European and then American churches to consider this type of ministry for women.

Meyer wanted to train women for missionary activities and work among the urban poor as well as prepare them for overseas missionary work. In a two-year program, students studied Bible, hygiene, citizenship, and social and family relations; and they heard lectures on the theory of domestic industry, kindergarten work, temperance, and practical medical knowledge. The Meyers taught Bible and church history. Visiting social workers, doctors, nurses, and kindergarten teachers taught the students, who attended classes, did the housework, and visited in the slums of Chicago as part of their training.

In the final decades of the nineteenth century, Chicago was undergoing massive industrialization and was teeming with immigrants from the European countryside and American farms. Poverty, disease, and an early death awaited many of Chicago's poorest residents. At the same time, urbanization brought diminishing roles for single women in rural and small town America. Such women were attracted to Meyer's Training School, which offered an education and useful work to do.

Meyer completed her medical education and received an M.D. from the Woman's Medical College (later part of Northwestern University) in 1887. Although she apparently never practiced medicine, Meyer included an emphasis on ministering to the health need of the community that the Training School students served. Anticipating the summer of 1887, when the Training School would be vacant, Meyer invited students of the school to live there in what she called a Deaconess Home. Eight women responded, and in that first summer they made 2,751 home visits, gathered children into Sunday school, and visited sick and dying residents of Chicago's tenements.

By the second year of the Deaconess Home, the women living there recognized themselves as deaconesses, consecrated to Christian service and vowing to remain single. They adopted a simple black uniform with long sleeves, floor-length skirt, and a high collar; the stiff black bonnet they wore had white streamers that tied under the chin. The uniform gave them protection and recognition as they moved through the city slums and also symbolized the sisterhood and equality of the wearers. Meyer designed the costume and wore it until 1908, when she was ordered by the Methodist Episcopal General Conference (MEC) to remove it because she was married.

At the end of the third year of the Training School's existence, twenty-four graduates were serving as missionaries in Asia, Africa, and South and Central America. Twenty-seven were home missionaries posted throughout the United States. The latter were among those entering the Deaconess Home in Chicago, for which preparation through study at the Training School was now required. Eventually, deaconesses were not only visiting among the poor of the city but were working as evangelists, nurses, church secretaries, teachers, writers, housekeepers, prison workers, bookkeepers, and superintendents of hospitals, homes, and schools. In payment they received board and room, laundry service, and a uniform, plus a monthly allowance of eight dollars.

Meyer had added trained nurses to the ranks of city visitors, because disease was endemic to slum dwellers. In further response to the need for health care for the poor, Wesley Hospital was chartered in 1890 as an affiliated institution of the Training School. Shelly Meyer served as superintendent, and the deaconesses performed many duties there, joining nurses and doctors in the first Methodist hospital in the Midwest.

On the basis of the recommendation of the Rock River Annual Conference and in affirmation of Meyer's work, the 1888 MEC established the deaconess as a church office. Meyer wanted this recognition, seeing it as a validation of deaconess work. For the remainder of her active years, Meyer was to struggle with the MEC's Women's Home Missionary Society for control of the deaconess movement. This conflict caused Meyer continuing anguish. She conceived of deaconess as an office equal in status to that of male clergy, and she believed that having it under the supervision of an all-woman organization would reduce that status. At the same time, she contended with those who resisted the movement because they suspected that the office of deaconess was a stepping stone to ordaining women preachers.

Throughout her active life, Meyer wrote and edited the newsletters of the training school and deaconess home, the *Message* and the *Deaconess Advocate*. She also authored numerous articles and books to advance her causes and to educate the public. In 1889, she published *Deaconesses and Their Work: Biblical, Early Church, European, American*, a book on the history of deaconesses and the founding of the Chicago Training School and Chicago Deaconess Home. In 1895, she published a *Shorter Bible*, omitting parts she deemed of interest only to scholars, rearranging material, and using modern language. In 1900, *Deaconess Stories* was published. In 1903, *Mary North*, a novel about the dangers faced by a poor girl alone in a large city, appeared. Continuing her lifelong interest in science, Meyer completed an unpublished manuscript on radium in 1916, claiming that civilization would be revolutionized when it learned to use radium. She was also a tireless correspondent, writing and receiving letters from all over the world, as she sought support for her Training School.

In 1895, the Training School outgrew its quarters and moved to Chicago's South Side, to property given by Norman Wait Harris, founder of Harris Trust and Savings Bank and a leading philanthropist. The highest enrollment in the Training School was in 1910, when 256 were registered and 84 were in the graduating class. Harris Hall Chapel, built with a fifty thousand dollar gift, opened that year.

The Gustavus Swift Library, gift of the wealthy owner of a meatpacking firm, was enlarged. Two more buildings were added, the gift of Cordelia Monnett, another supporter of Meyer's enterprise. However, after the peak year of 1910, enrollment in the Training School began to decline, and financial problems, always vexing, became more acute with each passing year. A key cause of the decline in enrollment was that other occupations and professions more attractive to women were opening during the second decade of the twentieth century. Even the admission of men to the Training School in 1914 did not stop the decline.

Besides enrollment and financial problems, conflict surfaced between Meyer and her husband over the course of study at the Training School. The Meyers differed intensely over the direction Bible study and teaching were taking. Shelly Meyer was a biblical literalist who believed that declining enrollment was due to innovations in biblical interpretations, too much emphasis on social studies, and loss of an earlier simplicity in educational approach. Lucy Rider Meyer embraced the most current ideas in biblical criticism and in solutions to social problems and was committed to a search for truth, no matter where it led. She was a modernist, delighting in freedom of thought and new ideas for herself and her students. He was a fundamentalist who felt threatened by science and liberal thinking.

Frustrated and worried by the crisis in enrollment and finances at the school, their own disagreements, and the state of her health, the Meyers relinquished control of the Training School in January 1918. At that time, the school had seven buildings and property worth half a million dollars. Its principal for more than thirty-two years, Lucy Rider Meyer had never received a salary. She remained president emeritus of the institution until her death.

In 1919, she traveled throughout the western United States to observe and celebrate Methodist deaconess work, welcomed wherever she went as the "Archbishop of Deaconesses." Meyer continued to write almost until her death of heart disease, complicated by Bright's disease and an inflammatory condition of the nerves. She was buried in Oak Woods Cemetery, Chicago.

Together, Meyer and graduates of the Training School began forty different health, educational, and social service institutions, some of which continued in operation through the end of the twentieth century. She was a writer and a promoter who used the power of her pen and her personality to build an enduring legacy of care for the bodies and souls of women and children in Chicago and around the world. Faced with both the effects of urbanization in Chicago and the resulting poverty and dislocation of single women from farms and small towns, Meyer presented women with an opportunity for education, Christian service, and ministry sanctioned by the church. Before social work and nursing were established as female professions, she offered women a strong identity as deaconesses and the chance for meaningful lives outside of marriage and family.

Sources. In 1925 Josiah Shelly Meyer prepared an unpublished manuscript of recollections about the Training School, "Modern Miracles," a copy of which is in the archives of the Garrett-Evangelical Theological Seminary (GETS), Evanston, Illinois. Photographs, papers, personal correspondence, and memorabilia related to the Training School are also in the GETS archives. Meyer's key writings, including *Deaconesses and Their Work: Biblical, Early Church, European, American* (1889), provide information on the Training School, the deaconess movement, and her struggles with church politics. *Message* and *Deaconess Advocate*, published and edited by Meyer for the Training School and the Deaconess Home, are on microfiche at GETS. Elizabeth Holding, *A Satisfying Life* (1900), gives an early view of deaconess life by one of the first Methodist deaconesses. Christian Golder's *History of the Deaconess Movement* (1903) is a comprehensive look at the deaconess movement until that time, including Meyer's contributions. The only biography of Meyer is *High Adventure* (1928) by Deaconess Isabelle Horton. Elizabeth Meredith Lee wrote a history of the deaconess movement, *As Among the Methodists: Deaconesses Yesterday, Today, and Tomorrow* (1963). Mary Agnes Theresa Dougherty, "The Methodist Deaconess, 1885–1918: A Study on Religious Feminism" (Ph.D. diss., Univ. of California, Davis, 1979), has extensive treatment of Meyer. Catherine M. Prelinger and Rosemary S. Keller, "The Function of Female Bonding," in *Women in New Worlds: Historical Perspectives on Wesleyan Tradition*, vol. 2 (1982), finds deaconesses' strength in their sisterhood. Additional articles by Keller are "Belle Harris Bennett and Lucy Rider Meyer," in *Something More Than Human: Biographies of Leaders in American Methodist Higher Education*, ed. Charles E. Cole (1986), and "Creating a Sphere for Women: The Methodist Episcopal Church, 1869–1906," in *Perspectives on American Methodism*, ed. Russell E. Richey, Kenneth E. Rowe, and Jean Miller Schmidt (1993). See Carolyn De Swarte Gifford's introduction in *The American Deaconess Movement in the Early Twentieth Century* (1987) for a brief history of the deaconess movement in Methodism. Journals of the Rock River Methodist Annual Conference and of the Methodist Episcopal General Conferences, found at GETS, carry reports on the activities of the Training School and deaconesses.

CAROLYN HENNINGER OEHLER

MILLER, EMILY CLARK HUNTINGTON
October 22, 1833–November 2, 1913
WRITER, EDUCATOR, TEMPERANCE WORKER

Emily Clark Huntington was born in Brooklyn, Connecticut, the second of five children and second daughter of Thomas Huntington and his second wife, Paulina (Clark) Huntington. Thomas Huntington also had five children by a previous marriage to Elizabeth Colfax, who died in 1830. Emily Huntington's grandfather was Jedediah Huntington, a Revolutionary War hero, prominent Connecticut businessman, and politician. She was raised in a staunch Christian environment. Her father, a physician by profession, was also an ordained minister.

Emily Huntington attended public school and a local academy in her hometown. During her childhood, Huntington developed two lifelong interests. The first was gardening, a passion that was a recurring image in her written work. The other interest was writing itself. She began writing poetry and prose as a young schoolgirl and fostered that avocation as a member of her college's literary club. She entered Oberlin College in Ohio in 1854, earning her bachelor's degree in literature in 1857 and staying on as a teacher for a brief period after graduation. While there, she met John Edwin Miller of Greentown, Ohio, a graduate of Oberlin's Theological Seminary and a professor of classics. They were married on September 5, 1860. They had three sons, Harry Huntington (born 1861), Frederick Clark (1863), and George Alfred (1868). A daughter, Emily Louisa (1865), died in infancy. During the early years of their marriage, the Millers moved frequently, as John Miller took several teaching and administrative posts around the Midwest.

In 1868, John Miller left the teaching profession and became copublisher of the *Little Corporal*, a children's literary magazine founded during the Civil War by Alfred Sewell and based in Chicago. The couple moved to Evanston, Illinois, finally settling long enough to establish a home and providing Emily Huntington Miller a place from which to build her own career. She became associate editor of *Little Corporal* and, in 1871, took over as editor. She was a frequent contributor to the magazine throughout its existence and even after it was absorbed by Scribner's publishers into its more popular competitor, *St. Nicholas*, in 1875. To the *Little Corporal* audience, Miller was best known for her serial stories, including *The House That Johnny Rented* (1865), *The Bear's Den* (1867), *Camp Bruce* (1867), *The Royal Road to Fortune* (1868), and many others. The stories were moral tales, instructing in the principles of obedience, temperance, education, and "all that is good and true," as the magazine's motto promised. In addition to the serials, she contributed a number of poems, short stories, word puzzles, and letters from the editor to *Little Corporal*'s young readership. Miller's association with *Little Corporal* launched her career as a writer of national renown. Some of her serials were published as books in England, beginning with *The Bear's Den* in 1878.

In addition to the writing world, Miller turned her attention to other segments of society as well. She became an active participant in the First Methodist Episcopal Church in Evanston, where her husband was superintendent of the Sunday school. She was engaged in both foreign and local missionary efforts. Some of her works reflected her missionary zeal. *The Parish at Fair Haven* is the best known example. It is the fictional account of a midwest parish that becomes indifferent to the plight of those "heathens" beyond the comfortable walls of the church; it offers a stern warning about church members' complacency toward the nonbeliever. Miller was also active in various Methodist women's organizations. In 1871, a group of Methodist women, including Miller, founded the Evanston College for Ladies, which merged with Northwestern University in 1872. As a result of this union, Miller was elected trustee and was the first woman member of the board's executive committee.

For Miller and her cofounders, this merger with Northwestern thrust them into a tumultuous period in which their convictions regarding the education of young women were challenged and scrutinized. There was a great deal of debate as to whether governance of the women students should be kept separate or integrated with the governance of male students. Miller saw this new union as an important opportunity for women. In a speech years later, she compared the schooling of boys and girls together to maintaining a garden of different varieties of flowers, indicating that both "draw upon the same sources for a widely differing life" (*Chautauqua Assembly Herald*, August 3, 1882). However, many of her cofounders disagreed; one of them was FRANCES E. WILLARD, then dean of the women's college. This disagreement caused Miller to break philosophically with some of these founders and to support the university's efforts toward integration. This issue led to the resignation of Frances Willard as dean in June 1874.

The same year, Miller's brother-in-law, Lewis Miller, coestablished the Chautauqua Institution. What began as a Sunday school movement evolved into a major religious, educational, and social force in the American Protestant community. Emily Miller embarked on the first of what were to become annual journeys, sometimes with John Miller and occasionally alone, to the Chautauqua Lake retreat center in western New York. In addition to the yearly trips east, both Millers continued the work of Chautauqua in Evanston and its environs, John as organizer of local Sunday school retreats and Emily as a lecturer and member of the local Chautauqua literary club. Emily Miller gave a lecture at the first national assembly in New York.

At the first Chautauqua gathering in 1874, Miller served as secretary in the call for a national women's temperance organization, which met for the first time later that fall as the National Woman's Christian Temperance Union (WCTU). At the WCTU's twentieth anniversary, Miller recollected what an opportune moment the Chautauqua gathering had provided, bringing together Christians from all over the country and giving prestige to the movement as well as providing a future rallying center. Miller's other commitments prevented her from becoming involved in the national leadership of the WCTU, but she remained a supporter of the cause and became a regular contributor to the WCTU's publications and a member of its youth committee. Women's programming became an increasingly important part of the annual Chautauqua meetings, and in 1882 Miller was given responsibility for coordinating all women's activities. In 1889, Miller was elected the first president of the Chautauqua Women's Club, a post she retained until 1895.

While Miller flourished in their Evanston world, her husband did not thrive as well. After the dissolution of *Little Corporal*, he continued in the publishing business and then took a sales position with an iron merchant that required frequent travel around the Midwest and kept him away from Evanston and his family for greater stretches of time than his prior duties had required. Concerned about the lack of influence he had in his own family members' lives, particularly in the upbringing of his sons, John Miller eventually sought a job that demanded less travel. In 1878 he accepted a position with the St. Paul Harvester Works in St. Paul, Minnesota. The departure from Evanston seemed to be much easier for husband than wife, and he regretted taking Miller away from the environment in which she had achieved such success. Nonetheless the family moved and remained in St. Paul together until John Miller's death in 1882. While living there, Miller continued to pursue her writing career, publishing mostly articles, children's stories, and verse; and she maintained her associations with Northwestern, Chautauqua, and the Methodist Church.

In 1889 Miller returned to Evanston and once again made the Chicago suburb her home. She was appointed dean of the Women's College and assistant professor of English at Northwestern in 1891, positions that she held for nearly ten years. By this time, Miller's career and reputation were firmly established. She wished to focus more energy on her writing and in June 1897, shortly after publication of the poetry collection *From Avalon*, left the deanship to write. She returned as dean for a brief period in 1900, filling the position left open by the death of her successor. Two years later, she left Northwestern altogether and turned her efforts fully to writing.

In the first decade of the twentieth century, Miller continued to take part in temperance activities, church work, and education, mostly as a writer and lecturer. Once again she moved away from Evanston, spending her last years in Minnesota, where her youngest son lived with his family, and at a summer residence in New Jersey. She made a final trip to Evanston in 1909 to receive an honorary doctorate of literature from Northwestern University. She died of heart disease in Northfield, Minnesota, in 1913, while living with her brother, a retired professor from Carleton College.

During her life, Miller published many volumes of fiction and poetry. More than a hundred of her verses were set to music, some in hymns and some in children's songs. She also published articles and fiction in a number of journals, including the *Atlantic*, *Harper's*, *Saturday Evening Post*, *Scribner's*, and *Ladies Home Journal*. A well-known author, Emily Huntington Miller was a household name. Her life embodied the emergence during the mid-nineteenth century of an independent, well-educated, and public woman whose work and vision of the world were driven by strong evangelical beliefs about an individual's moral obligation to society. That obligation, for Miller, meant extending the Christian home beyond the family and into the public sphere. All the paths she pursued sprang from this calling to expand that realm.

Sources. What remains of Miller's papers is scattered and, for the most part, uncataloged. Some of her personal papers are collected at the Minnesota Hist. Soc., including family letters, photographs, and manuscript notes. Both the Northwestern Univ. archives and the Evanston Hist. Soc. have files on her. For background on the Huntington genealogy, Elijah B. Huntington's *The Huntington Family in America* was useful, though the book was published in 1863, when Miller was about thirty, and thus only partially covered her generation. *NAW* (1971), *NCAB*, vol. 10 (1909); Frances E. Willard and Mary A. Livermore, eds., *A Woman of the Century* (1893); Mark Edward Lender, *Dictionary of American Temperance Biography: From Temperance Reform to Alcohol Research, the 1600s to the 1980s*, provided good groundwork on Miller. She was mentioned briefly in several histories of Northwestern and Evanston, including Robert D. Sheppard and Harvey B. Hurd's *History of Northwestern University and Evanston* (1906), and Frances E. Willard, *A Classic Town: The Story of Evanston by an "Old Timer,"* Frances E. Willard (1891). For information on Miller's involvement in the temperance movement and the Woman's Christian Temperance Union (WCTU), Willard's *Woman and Temperance: Or, the Work and Workers of the Woman's Christian Temperance Union* (1883) was useful. Alfreda Locke Irwin's *Chautauqua Women's Club History 1889–1989* (1989) and articles from the *Chautauqua Assembly Herald* provided information about her work there. An obituary appeared in *Oberlin Alumni Magazine*, March 1914.

MEGAN MURRAY CUSICK

MIRABELLA, ROSAMOND LIBONATI
August 24, 1885–January 16, 1985
CLUBWOMAN, TEACHER, COMMUNITY ACTIVIST

Nearly a century old when she died, Rosamond Mirabella (called Rosa) remained throughout her life a clubwoman. While the Italian Woman's Club provided Mirabella with organizational and leadership experience, her work spanned a range of activities including the care of young people in her local community and beautification and redevelopment projects. Her love of country and compatriots, both in the United States and in her parent's homeland, Italy, propelled her to take on civic tasks and emergency relief initiatives during World War II and in its aftermath.

One of six children of Ernesto and Flora (Pellettieri) Libonati, Rosamond Libonati was born in Chicago and was raised in the Italian community at Clark and Polk streets. Both of her parents were Italian immigrants, from south central Italy, just north of the Gulf of Taranto. Ernesto Libonati was born in the province of Potenza, Flora Libonati in the province of Matera. The Italian communities in Chicago retained provincial affiliations, and first generation children like Rosa Libonati defined themselves accordingly. Northern Italian immigrants tended to remain segregated from southern Italians even after they immigrated to the United States. Rosa Libonati considered her family "Neapolitan" and was proud of her maternal grandparents, the Pellettieris, who were Neapolitans and had settled on the Near North Side in the early 1870s, among immigrants from Genoa and Naples. In his homeland, Libonati's maternal grandfather, Louis Pellettieri, had been a prison warden under the Bourbon regime, a job he apparently disliked. Grandfather Pellettieri brought three young boys with him when he arrived in Chicago in 1870. Family legend held that their families in Naples had entrusted them to his care: the boys worked for him and he cared for them as if they were part of his "family" until they were "Americanized" and ready to be on their own. This informal and often abusive system of contract labor among Italian and other immigrant groups was reportedly carried on in an honorable manner in the Pellettieri household. Pellettieri returned to Italy the following year to bring the rest of his family to Chicago. While he was gone the house in which he lived burned down in the Great Chicago Fire of 1871. Returning to Chicago, the family moved to a new apartment. The three "wards" of the family gave their wages to Pellettieri, who managed the household finances.

Rosa Libonati's childhood was filled with memorable events that underscored her relationship to her Old World Italian heritage and to the kin- and village-based identity reformulated in the New World. She later wrote about "trips to the [World's Columbian Exposition of 1893] . . . with mother and Grandma . . . [to] visit one of the three ships, replicas of those that brought Columbus to America" and "mother's concern for fear of an accident to grandma's stumbling" (handwritten family history, 3). The next year, 1894, the first religious *festa*, "the feast of the Madonna" (oral interview transcript, May 23, 1980, 28, Mirabella Papers), was held in Melrose Park, a suburb sixteen miles from Chicago's downtown, at the time still countrified with farmlike open lots owned by Italians, including members of the Pellietieri family. Her mother's family had helped purchase the statue of Our Lady of Mount Carmel, their village's patron saint, which had been fabricated in Italy. "The growth and development of the feast of Our Lady of Mount Carmel . . . attracted increased numbers of Italians and eventually saw Melrose Park become identified as the quintessential Italian suburb in the Chicago area" (Candeloro, 234).

Later in life, Rosa Mirabella (Libonati) remembered the *festa* as an event run by a "society of women . . . congregazione . . . made [up] of seven Italian women" (oral interview transcript, May 23, 1980, 26). Sunday, the day of the *festa*, the participants would take big baskets of food, which had been prepared all day Saturday, and travel via the Chicago and Northwestern Railroad to Melrose Park, gathering on Aunt Emmanuella DeStefano's land. The Libonatis and Pellettieris had lunch in the DeStefano farmhouse. The crowds of people ate outside; a procession would take form, with about eight men carrying the statue of the Madonna on their shoulders. Rosa Mirabella remembered the congregation of women leading the procession through Melrose Park. After 1905, when the newly built Our Lady Of Mount Carmel Church was completed, everyone would go to the church and celebrate the mass. The DeStefanos had donated money for the land and the church built upon it.

Rosa Libonati lived with her family and other relatives in a four-story building that had "four and five family flats on each floor" (oral interview transcript, May 23, 1980, 19). Her uncle, Emilio DeStefano, managed an Italian bakery housed in the basement of the building. On the first floor was a saloon with a restaurant, either owned or managed by Rosa Libonati's father, and on the next floor were flats. Holidays were celebrated among the extended family; Rosa Libonati's father was also a musician who played for the family's parties. Eventually he played music in a small Italian orchestra in halls and restaurants.

Rosa Libonati attended a kindergarten about two blocks from her family's flat on Polk Street in Chicago, and she gradu-

ated from the elementary school in 1900. She later wrote, "Our mother was a [disciplinarian] and very ambitious for her children" (handwritten family history, 2). She graduated from South Division High School in 1904 and from the Froebel Kindergarten College in 1906. At the time the kindergarten pioneer ALICE PUTNAM was still supervising teacher training. Trained for work with kindergarten and primary grades, Libonati "taught in the public schools as a substitute . . . [but] did not take the exam for certification to teach public school" (handwritten family history, 15). She also worked in the Bohemian kindergarten, one of Chicago's first established kindergarten programs and one of the largest in the city. It served the Near West Side Bohemian immigrant community and was not far from Libonati's Italian neighborhood.

Rosa Libonati married Sicilian Salvatore "Toto" Mirabella July 30, 1910. They had met two years earlier at a club social and eventually overcame the biases their families shared against the match; Sicilians and Neapolitans were wary of each other. Mirabella, born in Termini Immersee, Sicily, May 17, 1884, was a physician. He graduated from the University of Illinois College of Medicine in 1907. The newlyweds moved to the Near West Side Italian neighborhood, "the settlement of Toscani, where many worked at the McCormick Reaper plant, a few miles southwest of the Loop at 24th and Oakley Avenue" (Candeloro, 232). Salvatore Mirabella became the physician for the Tuscan (Toscano) Mutual Aid Society. Eventually he became the physician for several of the Italian self-help societies. The Mirabellas had one daughter, Josephine, born April 23, 1912. They lived in an apartment that also housed Dr. Mirabella's office.

The Libonatis and the Mirabellas were ardent American patriots in the Italian American community during World War I and World War II. Rosa Mirabella's brother Michael Libonati had graduated from the University of Michigan School of Law. He ran for associate judge of the Municipal Court before he gave up his law practice and joined the U.S. Army to fight in World War I. He died in France. Another brother, Elliodor Libonati, who had studied at the University of Chicago from 1910 to 1914, where he played baseball, was a supply sergeant in the U.S. Army stationed in San Antonio, Texas, in October 1917. From there he was shipped overseas. Also a lawyer, after the war he became active in the American Legion's Americanization work. Between the wars, Libonati became an outspoken anticommunist and antifascist.

When Rosa Mirabella's daughter, Josephine, was ten, Mirabella began teaching occasionally in the Chicago public schools as a substitute teacher. She also began taking classes at the University of Chicago where, from 1923 to 1929, she studied French, English, and Italian. She joined L'Alliance Française de Chicago, a French language and travel society affiliated with the University of Chicago and Northwestern University.

Rosa Mirabella had belonged to neighborhood clubs in her teenage years, but little is known about this early period. As the wife of a prominent Italian physician, and proud of her aristocratic heritage—"the Libonati's saw themselves as aristocracy" (interview with Florence Scala, December 15, 1998)—Mirabella was one of the founding members of the Chicago Italian

Woman's Club, whose first meeting was held at the Palmer House hotel in downtown Chicago in 1927. She served as the club's second president. In addition to serving the various social needs of Italian Americans and Italian immigrants, the organization participated in the Melrose Park *festa*. As with other women's clubs, involvement with the Chicago Italian Woman's Club provided opportunities for learning organizational, leadership, and networking skills. Mirabella studied parliamentary procedure so that she could lead the club effectively. She was a member of the Native Daughters of Illinois, an Italian American club, from at least 1926, when she began a term as secretary-treasurer. Her club work continued to be significant. The Italian Women's Club became affiliated with the Illinois Federation of Women's Clubs (IFWC). Mirabella became an activist in the IFWC and served at different times as director, vice-president, and historian. Locally, Mirabella was one of the founders of the Pickard School Parent Teacher Association, a grammar school where she had worked as a substitute teacher.

With the improvement in the family's economic status, the Mirabellas moved to a new and larger apartment in the same neighborhood in 1928. Dr. Mirabella again had one of his medical offices in the apartment where "the dining room with its long window bench plus the dining room chairs, served as a waiting room while we dined in our roomy kitchen except on holidays" (handwritten family history, 8). As the wife of a physician, Rosa Mirabella was responsible for furnishing the new home and, on occasions when her husband was absent, for dealing with patients.

In fall 1930, Rosa, Salvatore, and Josephine Mirabella, as well as a family friend, Clara Gurney, Rosa's schoolmate from childhood, booked passage on a boat destined for Naples. In Naples, they began a three-month European tour. The trip was costly, particularly for the depression years. The Mirabellas also made subsequent trips to Europe.

The Mirabellas were well connected socially in the Italian American community of Chicago. Rosa Mirabella was a Republican, and she expressed little tolerance for the Italian American socialists of the 1930s who held meetings just down the block from her home. Salvatore and Rosa Mirabella were once invited to a concert of classical music at the Casino Club as guests of Harold Fowler McCormick, son of Cyrus McCormick, the reaper manufacturer and patron of the opera. In July 1933, when Italian aviator Italo Balbo's squadron of planes completed their transatlantic flight, landing in Lake Michigan as part of Century of Progress Exposition activities, the Mirabellas were among the invited guests for the High Mass celebrated at the Holy Name Cathedral to welcome the Italian hero. They had attended the opening of the Italian Pavilion at the Century of Progress that same year.

Mirabella appreciated art and history. She was a member of the Municipal Art League of Chicago and later joined Friends of American Writers, a group of women who encouraged interest in American literature. Throughout her life she took courses in art and art history. From 1937 to 1940, she served as state chair of the IFWC art department.

Rosa Mirabella's interest in constructing a positive image of Italian immigrants was part of her motivation for stewardship in her community. She also had a great deal of family pride. As

early as 1927, when the Chicago *Herald and Examiner* mentioned "Louis Pellettieri, grandfather of the Libonati brothers who practice law here" (October 17, 1927), her family's involvement with the history of Italians in Chicago gave Mirabella a sense of pride and a determination to let Americans know about Italian Americans who did not fit mafia stereotypes. On May 7, 1938, her mother, Flora (Flower) Libonati, was featured in a *Chicago American* story, "Chicago Sons and Daughters Honor Mother Tomorrow." A huge photograph showed Flora Libonati in her home, and she was quoted as saying, "It's great to be a mother—[when] your children don't forget you." Later, Mirabella participated in activities sponsored by the Cultural Affairs Committee of the Joint Civic Committee of Italian Americans. Her most visible display of Italian American civic responsibility was her involvement that began in the 1930s with the women's auxiliary of St. Frances Cabrini Hospital in the Near West Side neighborhood. The hospital, founded in 1917, was supported by fund-raising efforts of local Italian American women. Membership drives, fund-raising benefits, and hands-on work, including the collection of linens and supplies for the hospital, were undertaken with Mirabella's leadership. Salvatore Mirabella was the chief surgeon at St. Frances Cabrini Hospital.

During World War II, the Mirabella family retained contact with Salvatore's relatives and friends in Italy, including his cousin Dr. Filippe Mirabella in Rome. They sent numerous packages to relatives who sustained damage during the war. There was never a question of loyalty to the United States, however. At home in Chicago, Rosa Mirabella was appointed head of women's activities for the women's division of the Chicago Commission of Civilian Defense. The various civilian defense activities included blackouts and air-raid drills during the war years. Rosa Mirabella also purchased more than two hundred dollars in war bonds.

After the war, Mirabella continued her activities with the hospital auxiliary and the women's clubs. The clubwomen were looking at postwar problems. In a 1947 report to the Illinois Federation of Women's Clubs, she wrote, "Public welfare is an important part of the national program, as homemakers, club women have felt a great responsibility for the increased juvenile delinquency. In Illinois the First District is foremost in the State for its outstanding work in human rehabilitation and this past year has been no exception since $50,000 has been expended for the underprivileged" (Mirabella Papers). In 1949, Mirabella was president of the women's auxiliary of St. Frances Cabrini Hospital. In that year Rosa Mirabella was finally "elected" (Margaret N. White, letter to R. Mirabella, March 1, 1949, Mirabella Papers) to membership in the Chicago Woman's Club, the prestigious organization established in 1876 and, during the Progressive Era, a source of reform agendas for American-born, well-to-do, predominantly Protestant women.

Rosa Mirabella's eclectic activism also included community improvement. She served as regional vice-president of the Central Cermak Community Council and as chair of its Community Improvement Committee. Such work included pressuring landlords to comply with requests for covering trash cans and requesting that the city keep streets cleared in winter. She also served as regional vice-president of the Heart of Chicago Community Council, which served the western half of the city's 21st Ward. In 1959 the group attempted to prevent International Harvester from shutting down its McCormick Works, which were crucial to the healthy economy of the community. The group requested that instead International Harvester consider selling its property to the city. In 1962 the company decided to sell to the city a strip of land on Blue Island Avenue between Leavitt and Oakley. The McCormick Works were eventually sold to Santa Fe Railroad. Rosa Mirabella was apparently behind the Community Council's sponsorship of the 1962 Youth Festival, part of an effort to address juvenile delinquency. Mirabella was congratulated by Mayor Richard J. Daley when she was selected for the Senior Citizens Hall of Fame in 1962.

Salvatore Mirabella had grown ill and spent a period of convalescence from surgery in Havana, Cuba. He died of a heart ailment on January 8, 1962.

Rosa Mirabella continued to work with community groups interested in economic development and the maintenance of good public schools. As vice-president of the Heart of Chicago Community Council, she submitted a statement to the Chicago Board of Education's budget hearing, December 18, 1963, in support of the Pickard, Whittier, and Cooper elementary schools and Harrison High School. "This community is a melting pot of families of various nationalities and creeds, living together as neighbors and earnestly striving to give their children a better education" ("Statement," December 18, 1963, n.p., Mirabella Papers), she wrote. Her immigrant Italian family had sent Mirabella and her brothers to Chicago public schools, not to the Catholic parochial system. She, in turn, had educated her daughter in the neighborhood public schools and a private, but not Catholic, college, the University of Chicago. While proud of her Italian heritage, and nominally interested in the Catholic parish in her neighborhood, Mirabella believed in the importance of public education. "Community efforts are focused on the preservation and betterment of our entire area," she explained to the board of education. "We are therefore sincerely interested in the present educational system employed in our locale" ("Statement," December 18, 1963, n.p., Mirabella Papers).

In 1966 the mayor invited Rosa Mirabella to join an official beautification committee. Already in her eighties, Mirabella continued to give philanthropic donations and demonstrate concern for her community. By 1969, however, when she had been identified as "one of the grand dames of the Illinois Federation of Women's Clubs," she was slowing down and was "absent for the first time in the 40-year history of the [Italian Women's Club] ball" (Powers, "Mini-Skirted Corps a Hit Again in Show"). She continued to correspond with numerous friends and associates, and her Christmas list in 1978 and 1979 remained extensive. She responded to countless requests for contributions. Always the community loyalist, she continued in her nineties to make generous contributions to the Gads Hill Center, the settlement house on the Lower West Side that continued to serve the diverse population that made up Pilsen, Little Village, and Heart of Chicago. She died seven months shy of her hundredth birthday. Her funeral mass was held at St. Michael's Church, and she was buried at Mt. Carmel Cemetery in Chicago.

Sources. The Rosamond Mirabella Papers, UIC Spec. Coll., include an oral interview with Mirabella; letters, photos, newspaper articles, and other miscellaneous papers; and Mirabella's undated handwritten family history, written on her husband's blank prescription forms. Roland Libonati Papers, CHS, have little about Rosamond Mirabella but do provide family information. Newspaper articles with information about the Pelletieris, Libonatis, and Mirabella include "Louis Pellettieri, Grandfather of the Libonati Brothers," *Herald and Examiner*, October 17, 1927; "Chicago Sons and Daughters Honor Mother Tomorrow," *Chicago American*, May 7, 1938; Irene Powers, "Mini-Skirted Corps a Hit Again in Show," *CT*, January 11, 1969. A biography of Mirabella is in Giovanni Schiavo, ed., *Italian-American Who's Who: A Biographical Dictionary of Italian-American Leaders* (1966–67). Dominic Candeloro, "Chicago's Italians: A Survey of the Ethnic Factor, 1850–1990," in *Ethnic Chicago: A Multicultural Portrait*, ed. Melvin Holli and Peter d'A. Jones (1995) is helpful. See also Humbert Nelli, *The Italians in Chicago: A Study in Ethnic Mobility* (1970). An interview with Florence Scala was conducted December 15, 1998. Mauda Bregoli-Russo, Department of Romance Languages, UIC, translated letters and writings, from the Italian, in the Mirabella Papers, UIC. Laura Magnavite, research assistant for the Historical Encyclopedia of Chicago Women Project 1993–95, contributed research for this entry.

ERIC R. SMITH

MONHOLLAND, MOTHER MARY FRANCIS De SALES (Mary Monholland)
1816–December 8, 1888
ADMINISTRATOR, FOUNDER OF HOSPITALS AND SCHOOLS, RELIGIOUS LEADER

Mary Monholland was born in Armagh, Ireland, the eldest child of Patrick and Mary (Maher) Monholland. She had three brothers, Charles, Bernard, and John. When she was an adolescent, her father moved the family to New York City, but her mother died prior to emigration. Mary assumed care of the younger children and household duties and continued even after her father remarried. She attended a private academy to learn bookkeeping and arithmetic in addition to grammar and Christian doctrine. Her father owned a prosperous wholesale grocery store, and he depended on his daughter to assist him in keeping ledgers and bookkeeping. Because of this reliance on her in both family and business matters, Mary Monholland's father opposed her decision to pursue a religious vocation. She put her plans in abeyance but did not renounce them. Eventually, the younger children became more independent, and thirty-year-old Monholland decided it was "now or never" (O'Connor, 16), time to live the life to which she felt God called her.

Mary Monholland first worked with the Sisters of Charity in their New York City orphan asylum. From her confessor, Bishop William Quarter, she learned of the work of the Sisters of Mercy, a new order to be founded in Chicago. He encouraged Monholland to join. She and two young sodality women trained by the Sisters of Charity traveled to Chicago by stage and ship. When the group was aboard, in full view of Milwaukee Harbor, a huge wave swept the boat deck of passengers. Mary Monholland was rescued and carried to shore by William Butler Ogden, in 1837 the first mayor of Chicago. In a hired vehicle she and her companions rode the rest of the way to Chicago, arriving in the city November 27, 1846. Bishop Quarter and MOTHER MARY AGATHA O'BRIEN welcomed them.

FIG. 79. *Mother Mary Francis De Sales Monholland bought the property for the first Mercy Hospital in 1849; by 1892 (pictured here) it had become a major medical institution in Chicago.*

Mary Monholland began her novitiate April 10, 1847, taking the religious name Sister Mary Francis De Sales Monholland. From the beginning, because of her maturity, experience, and financial acumen, Monholland held positions of trust and responsibility in the religious community. Still a novice, on February 27, 1847, Monholland signed the original charter from the State of Illinois incorporating St. Xavier Academy, the school run by the Mercy sisters. At a time when married women in Illinois struggled with legal disabilities that prohibited them from owning property, Monholland and her coreligionists were able to create a corporation through which they held property. St. Xavier Academy began operations ten years before Chicago erected its first public high school.

At first Monholland taught mathematics and bookkeeping. Later she served as director of St. Xavier from 1853 to 1867. Monholland, along with other sisters in the convent, gave up their daily hour of recreation to teach women reading, writing, and catechism in night classes. She read both questions and answers and the women learned by listening to the words.

Although she was educated and soon assumed a leadership role in the congregation, Monholland took on the daily tasks of cleaning the fireplaces in the classrooms and bringing in the kindling, considering herself more "used to hard work" (O'Connor, 27). Physical labor was difficult for Monholland, who limped noticeably, since one leg was shorter than the other. Also, she suffered severe pain in her jaw and facial disfigurement, the result of a botched tooth extraction. Contemporaries remarked that her looks were transformed by the twinkle in her eyes and her encouraging disposition.

Early in her convent life, Monholland stocked a chest with medicines and surgical instruments to perform minor operations and to splint sprains and breaks for the sisters and the students. Gradually, she discontinued these duties when doctors

friendly to the sisters arrived and took charge. In the meantime, she had saved the community hundreds of dollars.

During Mother O'Brien's absence from the community from April to August 1849, Sister Monholland became acting superior. Having only recently completed her own training for the sisterhood, Monholland took charge during a difficult period. She organized her community to nurse the victims of the cholera epidemic raging in the city and to take responsibility for the children whose parents had perished. The first orphans were waifs she picked up in the streets of Chicago. The Mercy sisters housed the girls in a rented house, and the boys were cared for temporarily in the residence of one of the priests from the cathedral. The orphan asylum, which opened February 13, 1852, was constructed in back of the first building the Mercys used as a hospital. Monholland signed the state incorporation papers for the asylum on June 21, 1852. Over the years, she was unfairly criticized by some of the clergy for not doing more for the orphans, but the Cook County supervisors did not contribute a penny to support the orphanage, and the sisters had limited operating funds. Fees from St. Xavier and some individual donations and an occasional fund-raising fair provided meager support. The building remained unsanitary, with no room to segregate the contagious. As an additional complication, at times the sisters had to house destitute or inebriated parents of the children.

As the Mercy sisters expanded their work, they proceeded to purchase property and establish new charitable and educational institutions in Chicago. Their plans and interests clashed with those of the male hierarchy of the diocese. Both Bishop James Oliver Van de Velde and later Bishop Anthony O'Regan opposed religious women holding title to properties and real estate. This was not the first clash of the sisters' interests with those of the administrators of the diocese. The conflict may be attributed to the fact that three of the first four bishops of Chicago were Irish and could have been influenced by a tradition in Irish law that did not allow religious women living in community to own land outright. Land inherited or purchased by women religious had to be returned to male kindred after the death of an abbess. When Bishop William Quarter died intestate in 1848, Bishop Van de Velde objected when the administrator, Father Walter Quarter, honoring his brother's wishes, transferred seventeen acres lying along the shore of Lake Michigan and three lots in downtown Chicago to the Mercy order. Fortunately, farsighted and tenacious Monholland persuaded Mother O'Brien to resist pressure from the bishop and to retain the property deeds, saying this was the "only property the sisters owned and it rightfully belonged to them" (O'Connor, 79).

Sister Monholland, displaying an astute business sense and real estate acumen, made two significant property purchases on behalf of her community. In 1849 she bought a green, stagnant swamp on the corner of Van Buren and Wabash, persuading Mother O'Brien that it could be purchased cheaply, filled in, and then used as the site of the new Mercy hospital. Monholland supervised the draining and filling of the swamp and construction of the building. Officially the hospital opened on October 16, 1853, but celebrations were marred by a property dispute with Bishop Van de Velde, who had returned from Rome and claimed the hospital property belonged to the Diocese of Chicago, not the Mercys. He insisted that the deed be so recorded but promised to transfer ownership back to the Mercy order when the hospital became self-supporting. The transfer never took place and Monholland "shed bitter tears" (O'Connor, 42–43). To the sisters this loss seemed very unfair because the hospital was supported by income from St. Xavier Academy.

In 1853, Monholland again made an independent real estate deal for her community. She purchased fifty acres of unbroken prairie at Forty-ninth Street and Cottage Grove Avenue for ten thousand dollars. Monholland envisaged raising vegetables, livestock, and chickens on the farm to provide milk, butter, eggs, and meat for both the sisters and the orphans. She was also convinced it could be used as a retreat for the sisters and eventually would be worth its weight in gold, and "the saving of the community" (O'Connor, 73). She was proved right, as sales of parcels of this land after the Chicago Fire of 1871 rescued the sisters from debt or ruin on a number of occasions.

In 1854, Monholland supervised construction of St. Agatha Academy on property at Twenty-sixth Street and Calumet Avenue; she negotiated with the contractor to put up the building with his own money, and she repaid him over time. Construction of St. Agatha was underway when the sisters were called to nurse victims of a cholera epidemic in Chicago. Despite Monholland's devoted efforts, four of the Mercy sisters, including Mother O'Brien, contracted the disease and died the same day.

Monholland was elected superior of the Sisters of Mercy in 1858 and was elected two more times, serving from 1858 to 1867. There was strong sentiment to have her appointed for life. In 1858, Mother Monholland established the Magdalen Asylum for women with unwanted pregnancies or who recently had been released from jail. It gave these women in transition a safe temporary home and a private place to readjust to society. A year later the Mercy sisters, busy with other demands, gave the home to the Sisters of the Good Shepherd. Mother Monholland ne-

gotiated an exchange of the three downtown lots bequeathed by Bishop Quarter for others so that both a new convent and an addition to St. Xavier Academy could be built. The actual construction had to wait until the end of the Civil War.

The Sisters of Mercy received requests for sisters to staff schools in other cities in Illinois. Not all of these efforts were successful. Yet, Mother Monholland was criticized when she withdrew her sisters from Galena, Illinois, in 1858. In 1859, she sent a colony of sisters to found a school in Ottawa, Illinois. In Chicago, she opened a boarding house and employment office for women in the rear of the Mercy convent, calling it a House of Providence. Both St. Xavier and St. Agatha were flourishing. Fees earned from their operation continued to support the orphan asylum and Mercy Hospital. Mercy had recently affiliated with Chicago Medical College, which provided medical training to students at Northwestern University. Mercy became the primary teaching hospital in the city.

When the Civil War erupted, the only trained nurses available to the North or South were Catholic and Protestant sisters, and the Sisters of Mercy were one of the twelve orders of Catholic nuns who responded to calls for help. Their effort was an "important morale builder and the women bandaged, gave medicine, washed, cooked, sang, wrote letters, [read], prayed and washed sweat from the brows of the dying boys" (Brooks, 53–55). The Sisters of Mercy were more experienced nurses than most others because they had learned their nursing skills working under Florence Nightingale in the Crimean War. They were valued for their patience, self-denial, and charity.

Colonel James A. Mulligan, the organizer of the Chicago Irish Brigade and a friend of Mother Monholland, asked her to send Mercy sisters to nurse his men stationed at Lexington, Missouri. Camp sanitation was poor and the men suffered terribly from the cold, drafts, measles, smallpox, and pneumonia. On September 3, 1861, Mother Monholland led five sisters to Lexington by way of St. Louis and Jefferson City, Missouri. The sisters made two attempts on the steamboat *Sioux City* to navigate the Missouri River. They were finally turned back when the boat was ambushed from both sides of the river by heavy Confederate fire. When the sisters arrived back at Jefferson City, the authorities begged them to take charge of the hospital there. Mother Monholland gave permission, settled the sisters into their hospital duties, and then returned to her duties in Chicago. To assist the nuns in Missouri, she dispatched a group of thirty lay women she had organized. In addition, she sent two more sisters, provisions, encouraging letters, and contributions. She managed one more visit herself that fall.

In April 1862, the authorities closed the hospital at Jefferson City, Missouri, and the Mercy sisters intended to return to their prewar duties in Chicago. On their trip home, the sisters stopped in St. Louis, Missouri, where members of the U.S. Sanitary Commission asked them to take charge of the hospital ship *Empress*, about to leave for the Shiloh battlefield. The battle had ended, but many of the wounded were still lying on the battlefield or in tents awaiting transportation to hospitals farther north. For five weeks the sisters nursed the men as they were shifted from Pittsburgh Landing (Battle of Shiloh), Tennessee, to Louisville, Kentucky; St. Louis, Missouri; and Keokuk, Iowa. The sisters did not return to Chicago until May 1862.

In 1863, Mother Monholland again directed her sisters in nursing the Chicago victims of typhoid and smallpox. Mercy Hospital was overwhelmed by the number of sick and dying. In the same year she supervised extensive maintenance at both St. Xavier and the hospital in an effort to prevent future epidemics and flooding. City lots were filled in and the ground level raised; foundations of stone were built; the water supply was improved and distributed through logs bored at various heights.

All this effort must have seemed fruitless in 1864, when Mother Monholland received word from Bishop James Duggan that he had put the Mercy Hospital property up for sale and she had two days to move her patients. On a boiling hot day in July 1864, Mother Monholland used wagons to move one hundred hospital patients to St. Agatha Academy. She laid them on stretchers and propped them up on pillows but allowed no one except herself to touch the dying, and she ended the day carrying a dying girl to her room. That evening, Mother Monholland, who had not eaten all day and was worn out from exhaustion, had to be rescued from complete collapse by another sister. In the meantime, the sixty-five St. Agatha boarders had been hastily moved to overcrowded St. Xavier.

In 1864, Camp Douglas, a prison holding Confederate soldiers located on Chicago's South Side, became the focus of charges of neglect and food shortages. Mother Monholland was asked by a civic committee to investigate conditions in the camp and to distribute two wagon loads of supplies to the prisoners. Although she was reluctant to interfere, when she was refused entrance by Colonel Benjamin J. Sweet, the camp superintendent, she secured an entry permit from Chicago mayor Francis C. Sherman. She conducted a group of sisters into the wards to minister to the prisoners. When she needed additional supplies and provisions and was turned down by the U.S. War Department, she wrote directly to President Abraham Lincoln. He replied with an open letter ordering the military hospital in Washington, D.C., to supply the needed provisions and "charge the purchases to the War Department" (Condon, 3). Busy as she was, Mother Monholland visited the camp regularly, bringing food and bathing and nursing the captives. Both living conditions and morale improved greatly.

Mother Monholland, undaunted by earlier trials, opened a parochial school in St. James parish. In 1865 she added a third story to the original St. Xavier and adjoining it she erected a new brick building, at a cost of thirty-two thousand dollars, to accommodate the influx of students from St. Agatha.

Under Monholland's careful management, the Mercy order in 1867 was debt free and had money in the bank for future improvements. Monholland, who had finished her third term as superior, was made assistant to the new superior and appointed to manage Mercy hospital. Unfortunately, friction developed within the community and Monholland was removed a year later. In 1869 she offered to assist Mother Mary Borromeo Johnson, a close friend and nurse-companion from Civil War days, in new Mercy enterprises in Iowa. Monholland built a convent and school in De Witt, Iowa, but one important Chicago project still remained for her. She returned long enough to superintend the construction of a new Mercy Hospital on the Twenty-sixth and Calumet site; the cornerstone was laid on July 25, 1869.

Monholland moved from De Witt, Iowa, to Independence, Iowa, in 1869, where she founded a seminary for girls and a free school. She served variously as superior, teacher, counselor, and financier from 1869 to 1882. She regularly visited the sick in addition to all her other duties, "walking miles over the prairie to find them" (O'Connor, 137–38). There was no hospital in the state of Iowa at that time. When the citizens of Davenport, Iowa, asked Mother Johnson to establish a hospital there for the insane and sick poor, Mother Monholland urged her to accept the challenge. Monholland then commuted frequently from Independence to Davenport to help in the construction of the hospital, often traveling all night.

Monholland moved to Davenport, Iowa, in 1882, after the death of Mother Borromeo Johnson. She reluctantly allowed herself to be named superior of the Davenport community when Bishop John McMullen ordered her to serve. She was elected superior twice and at the time of her death was serving as assistant. During her tenure in Davenport, Mother Monholland founded St. John's and added an addition to St. Elizabeth's, hospitals for men and women, respectively, with mental illness.

At the end of her life, Monholland's illness was brief, but her previous suffering had been intense and of long duration. Always she suffered terrible headaches and frequent hemorrhages. After her death, the sisters found, in addition to the shortened, shriveled leg and a painful jaw condition caused by decayed bone splinters working their way to the surface, a dreadful "imperfectly healed wound on her hip" (O'Connor, 157). The sisters also found marks on her body made by a cilice or an iron chain, which she wore in penance. None of these physical infirmities prevented Monholland from performing her duties, and there was no slackening of her determination or discipline. She continued to oversee the construction of a school until one week before her death and did not break down until her daily prayers were completed. She said her last farewells and died at age seventy-two. She is buried in Davenport, Iowa.

Considered by many to be the guiding spirit of the Chicago Sisters of Mercy, "the power behind the throne[,] . . . the unusual success of the Order of Mercy in Chicago was largely due to [Monholland's] zeal and energy" (O'Connor, 135). She held positions of leadership and trust; and she preferred to keep the Sisters of Mercy in Chicago despite many demands for nuns from the rest of Illinois. At a time when few women had opportunities for education or a profession, let alone leadership roles, she rose from immigrant status to combine a religious vocation with nursing, the administration of schools and hospitals, and the supervision of the finances and property of her community.

Sources. The Archives of the Sisters of Mercy, Chicago, hold the majority of records for the Sisters of Mercy and Mother Francis De Sales Monholland. Useful secondary sources include Alfred Theodore Andreas, *History of Chicago*, 3 vols. (1885); Austin Carroll, *Leaves from the Annals of the Sisters of Mercy* (1889); Isidore O'Connor, *Life of Mary Monholland* (1894); Gabriel O'Brien, *Reminiscences of Seventy Years* (1916); Mary Fidelis Convey, "Mother Agatha O'Brien and the Pioneers" (master's thesis, Loyola Univ. at Chicago, 1929); Ellen Ryan Jolly, *Nuns of the Battlefield* (1929); Mary Eulalia, *Sisters of Mercy in the United States* (1929); Stewart M. Brooks, *Civil War Medicine* (1966); Madeline Woods, *Serving God and Humanity in Chicago, 100 Years* (1946); Mary Kerin, *The Relief of Suffering Humanity: A Centennial History of Mercy Hospital* (1969); Kathleen Healy, *Frances Warde: Amer-*

ican *Founder of the Sisters of Mercy* (1973); Joy Clough, *In Service to Chicago: The History of Mercy Hospital* (1979); Kathleen Healy, *Sources of American Spirituality: Sisters of Mercy* (1992); Brigid Condon, *From Obscurity to Distinction* (1993); Gilbert Markus, ed., *The Radical Tradition* (1993); and Mary Denis Maher, *To Bind Up the Wounds: Catholic Sister Nurses in the U.S. Civil War* (1989).

ANN LEONARD

MONROE, HARRIET
December 23, 1860–September 26, 1936
EDITOR, CRITIC, POET, JOURNALIST

Harriet Monroe was founding editor and publisher of *Poetry: A Magazine of Verse*. In that role, she profoundly influenced the Chicago literary renaissance of the early twentieth century and the shape of modern poetry. A pioneer woman entrepreneur, she led and energized literary activity in that important period of history.

Harriet Monroe was born in Chicago to attorney Henry Stanton and Martha (Mitchell) Monroe. Of their seven children, three daughters and one son survived beyond infancy. Harriet Monroe was the second daughter.

Although Harriet Monroe was born into affluence, her father's career took a downturn in the 1880s and he had to declare bankruptcy. Monroe remembered that her father withheld business topics from the family. She described her mother as "very unbookish" (*A Poet's Life*, 8) and disinterested in events outside the home, often ruling the quarrelsome household with strictness. Further, Monroe's "all-powerful" (p. 28) sister Dora Louise—older by three years—dominated her as they were growing up. In this restrictive environment, Monroe suffered an "overwrought nervous condition" (p. 34), perhaps triggered by the suicide of a classmate, that manifested itself in uncontrollable, bewildering feelings. After a period of lassitude that confined Monroe to her bed for several months when she was sixteen, she later concluded that she had become "sex inhibited . . . shut up . . . in an impenetrable shell of self-consciousness" (p. 35). This revelation suggests that her inability ever to form a romantic relationship prevented her from experiencing the conventional role of wife and mother and enabled her instead to reserve a passion for the pursuit of her career.

Still convalescing from frail health—the first of several episodes—Monroe enrolled at Georgetown Visitation Convent, Washington, D.C., in September 1877. The seventeen-year-old Protestant newcomer spent the next two years at this austere Catholic boarding school, where she managed to penetrate literature and languages more deeply than the typical finishing school curriculum would have allowed. Two nuns were influential; one taught her Latin and German—Monroe was the only student of these languages—and Sister Paulina, a "modern mystic" (*A Poet's Life*, 48) was "the only great inspirational teacher" (p. 49) she ever had and was "ahead of her time" (p. 49) in the way she encouraged Monroe's study of literature and interest in writing. Although she briefly considered a career in acting or the law, upon graduation from Visitation, Monroe returned to a dutiful life in her parents' home in Chicago. For most of the 1880s she remained there, making fitful starts toward a career in journalism as an art critic. In 1888 she moved to New York as an occasional arts correspondent to the *Chicago Tribune*.

As she would throughout her life, Monroe energetically cultivated a network of influential acquaintances there. She remained active in the artistic and literary life of New York, and she acquired an appreciation for modern art. In late 1889, she returned to Chicago.

Her interest in poetry remained strong; back in Chicago, Monroe composed "Cantata" to commemorate the dedication of the Adler and Sullivan Auditorium in December 1889, and she continued work on *Valeria*, a drama in verse that she would self-publish in 1892. She took leave from a position as drama and art critic for the *Chicago Tribune* in 1890 when she impulsively embarked with friends on her first trip to Europe, where she became acquainted with European literati. Shortly after her return to the United States six weeks later, Monroe was forced to resign her *Chicago Tribune* position after its management learned that her younger sister, Lucy, was employed at a rival newspaper.

From the beginning, Monroe felt a "consecration" (*A Poet's Life*, 55) to a high destiny. Professing to forego "ordinary human happiness for the shining bauble of 'immortal fame,' " (p. 55), she held herself to strict standards.

Convinced that poetry was undervalued as an art form, Monroe prevailed upon a planning committee to commission her to write an ode to open the World's Columbian Exposition of 1893. After minor surgery in 1891 impeded her ability to work because she had been "permitted to leave [her] bed and return to work too soon" (*A Poet's Life*, 118), Monroe suffered "two years of nervous prostration" (p. 118) that became "a tempestuous voyage to discovery" (*A Poet's Life*, 119). Still she doggedly continued composition of "The Columbian Ode."

Meanwhile, committee member James Ellsworth, a prominent industrialist, attempted to jettison Monroe's ode in favor of one by the more established poet James Greenleaf Whittier. When Ellsworth recommended paying Monroe her commission but excluding her ode from the ceremony, Monroe fought back. With the unabashed confidence that characterized much of her career, she delivered the completed ode to the committee and argued successfully that the committee should honor the original bargain. She prevailed; a live choral performance of five thousand voices presented "The Columbian Ode" at the exposition's ceremony. Further, because the New York *World* published the ode without her permission, Monroe subsequently sued the newspaper and won, therein setting an important precedent for the rights of authors to control their unpublished works whether copyrighted or not. She won a judgment of five thousand dollars. From a literary point of view, however, "The Columbian Ode," as critic Anna Massa commented, "was not good at all" ("The 'Columbian Ode' and *Poetry, A Magazine of Verse*," 59) and "[Monroe's] modest talent" (p. 61) was less important than her zeal to make the ode a prominent part of the World's Fair ceremonies.

In such poems as "The Hotel," "At the Prado," "The Turbine," and "A Power-plant," Monroe's choice of topics showed the influence of extensive travel, art criticism, and twentieth-century industrialization. Despite her choice of contemporary subjects, a curious dissonance between the modern topic and archaic tropes sometimes emerges, even though Monroe consciously abandoned Victorian conventions for experimentation with new verse forms and meter. There is general critical agreement that her role in shaping other poets was of more value than were her own efforts at writing poetry.

When her younger sister, Lucy, married and moved from Chicago, Monroe resumed writing art criticism for the *Chicago Tribune* and published more than two hundred articles during the years 1909 to 1914. She kept the Chicago reader apprised of numerous exhibits at the Art Institute of Chicago and addressed philosophical questions in such articles as "What Is Art? A Variety of Answers." Her other employment consisted largely of freelance journalism for Chicago newspapers, teaching English at a girls' school, and publishing articles and poems in periodicals including *Atlantic Monthly, Century Magazine,* and the *Fortnightly Review.* Her income remained meager, as it had been for several decades.

By 1911, in her fifty-first year, Monroe resolved to change what she considered the lamentable position of poetry in American culture. Again observing that all arts except poetry had the support of institutional funding or endowments, she envisioned founding a journal dedicated to poetry. Critic Ellen Williams characterizes this period of American poetry as "empty of interesting poets" (*Harriet Monroe and the Poetry Renaissance,* 3). Few publishers considered poetry seriously, and what little was published was used as filler in popular magazines. Yet, buoyed by her entrepreneurial spirit, Monroe held to her vision. Encouraged by arts patron Hobart Chatfield-Taylor, for much of this year Monroe solicited wealthy and influential members of the business, literary, and social world, primarily of Chicago. She succeeded in securing one hundred pledges of fifty dollars a year for the next five years from guarantors who included KATE BUCKINGHAM, also a patron of the Art Institute; BERTHA HONORÉ PALMER, wife of the hotel magnate; EDITH ROCKEFELLER McCORMICK, wife of Harold McCormick, son of wealthy manufacturer Cyrus H. McCormick; and Augusta Rosenwald, wife of Julius Rosenwald, head of Sears, Roebuck. This financial guarantee enabled Monroe to found the first American journal devoted exclusively to poetry and covered operating expenses, including payment to contributors, for a half decade. The first issue of *Poetry: A Magazine of Verse* was published the following year, 1912.

In her resolve to publish only the finest poetry, Monroe familiarized herself with contemporary poetry by perusing current periodicals and books. Simultaneously she canvassed a list of poets that included Vachel Lindsay, Amy Lowell, Ezra Pound, Edwin Arlington Robinson, Louis Untermeyer, and Helen Hay Whitney and invited them to submit poetry for the proposed magazine, promising to include classical poetry of excellence but giving preference to modern topics. As Jayne E. Marek observes, "She stressed the importance of newly envisioned work written in a modern idiom" (*Women Editing Modernism,* 42).

Poetry gained international prestige when Monroe named renegade poet Ezra Pound as foreign correspondent. The two had never met, but publisher Elkin Mathews introduced her to Pound's work during a European trip in 1910. Upon her return to the United States, Monroe wrote the expatriate poet about her plans for a magazine and invited him to send a group of poems. Thus began a correspondence between the two that invigorated the early stages of *Poetry*'s existence. It was a trade-off: she bene-

fited from Pound's contacts with European writers, while he found a vehicle through which to transmit to an American audience the poetry he was promoting. Their relationship began with a unity of purpose, but Pound soon took on the role of pedagogue, highly critical of what he considered Monroe's provincial midwest attitude.

Monroe steadfastly tolerated Pound's abuse of her and of *Poetry*'s readers, but reacting to Pound's rudeness, in October 1913 Monroe commented, "We are obeying your orders—but I confess it would be with more pleasure if they had been uttered a bit more suavely" (Monroe to Pound, October 13, 1913, *Poetry* Magazine Papers). Despite Pound's criticism, "Monroe's editorials reveal that she was neither prudish nor timid, as she has been accused of being, but a persistent spokesperson for innovation and expertise in modern poetic art, as well as a defender of those whose work was a bit too 'modern' for her readers' tastes" (Marek, *Women Editing Modernism,* 29).

Still, Pound's influence in the early years of 1912 to 1916 energized the controversy over modern verse. His connections with such poets as W. B. Yeats, T. S. Eliot, and Rabindranath Tagore helped establish the credibility of *Poetry.*

Yet much of the magazine's success is due to the critical judgment of Monroe's coeditor ALICE HENDERSON, who served in that role from 1912 until 1916, when she moved to New Mexico because of ill health. In marked contrast to the condescending one-way directives of Pound, Monroe and Henderson engaged in a critical give and take that demonstrated "an instance of cooperative work in a literary world dominated by men" (Marek, "'I Know Why I Say What I Do Say,'" 44). Further, their commentaries reinforced *Poetry*'s role as an editorial force that helped establish modernism. "Henderson's contributions to *Poetry,* both critical and editorial, rest in large part on her ability—and willingness—to criticize contemporary writing. She did not hesitate to make sharp comments about Monroe's choices for the magazine if she thought *Poetry* was not serving the art well" (Marek, *Women Editing Modernism,* 32). The two women enjoyed a healthy working relationship until estrangement over a disagreement about division of royalties for their coedited anthology *The New Poetry.*

Henderson's departure to New Mexico left Monroe overworked and shorthanded, particularly because she had recently committed to collecting material for the anthology. Compounding the situation was the constant challenge of meeting expenses, not the least of which were payments to contributors. Her office staff changed frequently during this time. Writers Helen Hoyt, Marion Strobel, EUNICE TIETJENS, and EDITH WYATT all held editorial or advisory positions, but no one matched Henderson for her critical acumen.

Monroe's editorial influence reached audiences more widely through the anthology *The New Poetry* than through *Poetry* magazine. The book's editions—1917, 1923, 1932, and 1936—presented experimental poetry to a broad audience, most notably for schools. A spate of competing anthologies and books of criticism reached the market during these years, and when Louis Untermeyer's *Modern American Poetry: An Introduction* surpassed sales of *The New Poetry,* Monroe complained that her publisher's advertising department was shirking its responsibility in marketing her book.

Credited with moving poetry from its nineteenth-century artifice into modernism, including such radical varieties as imagism and vers libre, Monroe used *Poetry* to publish (sometimes for the first time) the work of Hilda Doolittle, T. S. Eliot, D. H. Lawrence, Vachel Lindsay, Amy Lowell, Ezra Pound, Edwin Arlington Robinson, Carl Sandburg, Wallace Stevens, Rabindranath Tagore, Sara Teasdale, William Carlos Williams, William Butler Yeats, and others. Monroe prided herself on having an open door policy that transcended national boundaries; and she published poetry of integrity, whatever its school, in her magazine. Longtime colleague Eunice Tietjens characterized Monroe's interaction with poets as being direct, sometimes cruelly blunt, but always fair. The work of Monroe's friends held no advantage over that of strangers or hostile acquaintances in being selected for publication.

In establishing *Poetry* as more than a regional journal by publishing works of national and international poets, and by introducing literary modernism to America, Monroe brought recognition to Chicago as a center of poetic ferment. Tietjens declared that with the founding of the magazine, "Chicago became . . . the functional center, the fountain-head, of the art of poetry in this country, indeed in the English-speaking world" (*World at My Shoulder*, 21). Writer Vincent Starrett commented that her "pre-eminent part in the Chicago renascence . . . can scarcely be exaggerated" (*Born in a Bookshop*, 180–81). While others left the city for the East or West Coast or for Europe, Monroe led the movement in the Midwest and made Chicago a center for poets to visit. At the same time, she included reviews of works of Chicago's women writers, believing such public recognition to be essential for their inclusion in Chicago's artistic scene. These included Edith Wyatt, Alice C. Henderson, MARY ALDIS, ALICE GERSTENBERG, Eunice Tietjens, and Marion Strobel.

Monroe created a poets' haven in the offices of *Poetry*, giving her a grounding she had never felt before: "I had never been the actual mistress of any home which had sheltered me, but this little kingdom was mine, and I rather enjoyed dispensing its fleeting hospitalities" (*A Poet's Life*, 317). Aspiring poets as well as established ones turned up for encouragement and conversation at her office, first in a mansion renovated for use as office space on Chicago's Near North Side, and later in another building in the vicinity. A nearby Italian restaurant functioned as an informal salon during the first decade of *Poetry* magazine's existence.

Although all her siblings married, Monroe remained single and lived an independent life. In 1882, she quoted a friend's remark to her: "Don't you remember the other night, when I said I should enjoy being the wife of a famous man, you said you would rather be a famous woman?" (diary, Monroe Papers).

Tietjens characterized Monroe, petite in size, as "a little dynamo of determination" (*World at My Shoulder*, 31). Early photographs show her with thick brown hair pulled away from her comely face in a bun. Later her hair gleams with streaks of silver, and she wears thin wire spectacles. Always, her expression is grave, congruent with the seriousness of purpose that typified her personality.

During her lifetime, Monroe traveled widely, despite her limited financial resources. In addition to European travel, which included a year in 1897, she sojourned in the western United States

in 1901, made two trips to the Orient, and toured Mexico extensively in 1933. In 1936, she traveled to the International Association of Poets, Playwrights, Editors, Essayists, and Novelists Conference in Buenos Aires. On a side trip to view the ruins at Machu Picchu, the altitude proved too thin for the septuagenarian adventurer, and Harriet Monroe died suddenly of a cerebral hemorrhage in September 1936. Her remains are buried in a cemetery located on an extinct volcano in Arequipa, Peru.

Despite hostility to female entrepreneurship, Harriet Monroe founded and nurtured a prestigious magazine that endures even today. Compelled to be a canny business person, an artful manager of people, and an incisive critic, she succeeded in each role. She was a central figure in the evolution of modern poetry. Through her recognition of new talent and her acceptance of unorthodox prosody, her magazine has had a lasting effect on the shape and significance of poetry in America. Critic Ellen Williams summarizes, "It was her hope and her faith that *Poetry* had ushered in a great era of poetry, and that faith was justified" (*Harriet Monroe and the Poetry Renaissance*, 294). Marek concludes, "Monroe's insistence upon giving place to many kinds of new work helped provide the basis for the range of experimentation and accomplishment that characterizes early twentieth-century poetry" (*Women Editing Modernism*, 59).

Sources. The Harriet Monroe Papers and the *Poetry* Magazine Papers are collected at UC Spec. Coll. Harriet Monroe's body of work includes *Valeria and Other Poems* 1891, the biography *John Wellborn Root* (1896), *The Passing Show: Five Modern Plays in Verse* (1903), *You and I* (1914), *The New Poetry* (with Alice Corbin Henderson) (1917, 1923, 1932), *Poets and Their Art* (1926 and 1932), *Chosen Poems* (1935), and criticism, most notably in issues of *Poetry*. Her posthumously published autobiography, *A Poet's Life: Seventy Years in a Changing World* (1938), presents significant happenings in her life. Daniel J. Cahill, *Harriet Monroe* (1973), concisely chronicles her life. Ellen Williams, *Harriet Monroe and the Poetry Renaissance: The First Ten Years of Poetry, 1912–22* (1977) focuses on the early years of *Poetry* magazine. Enlightening chapters or passages are found in Mary Colum, *Life and the Dream* (1947); Bernard Duffey, *The Chicago Renaissance in American Letters: A Critical History* (1944); Harry Hansen, *Midwest Portraits: A Book of Memories and Friendships* (1923); Dale Kramer, *Chicago Renaissance: The Literary Life in the Midwest 1900–1930* (1966); Jayne E. Marek, *Women Editing Modernism: "Little" Magazines and Literary History* (1995); Henry Regnery, *Creative Chicago: From the Chap-Book to the University* (1993); Alson Jesse Smith, *Chicago's Left Bank* (1953); Vincent Starrett, *Born in a Bookshop: Chapters from the Chicago Renascence* (1965); Eunice Tietjens, *World at My Shoulder* (1938); Steven Watson, *Strange Bedfellows* (1991); and Jeanne Madeline Weimann's *The Fair Women* (1981). Articles include Geoffrey Johnson's "Little Captain of the Ragged, the Mad Army of Poets," *Chicago Reader*, September 6, 1985; Anna Massa, "'The Columbian Ode' and *Poetry, A Magazine of Verse*: Harriet Monroe's Entrepreneurial Triumphs," *Journal of American Studies*, vol. 20, 1986; Kenny J. Williams, "An Invisible Partnership and an Unlikely Relationship: William Stanley Braithwaite and Harriet Monroe," *Callaloo: An Afro-American and African Journal of Arts and Letters*, vol. 10, 1987; and Jayne E. Marek, "Alice Corbin Henderson, Harriet Monroe, and *Poetry*'s Early Years," *Illinois Writers Review*, vol. 7, Winter 1988. See also Marek, "'I Know Why I Say What I Do Say': Women Editors and Critics in the 'Little' Magazines, 1912–1933" (Ph.D. diss., Univ. of Wisconsin–Madison, 1991). A biography of Monroe appears in *NAW* (1971).

LYNN MILLER

MONTAY, SISTER MARY INNOCENTA
(Mary Montay)
January 10, 1906–January 20, 1976
EDUCATOR, COLLEGE FOUNDER, SCHOLAR

Mary Montay was born in Green Bay, Wisconsin, the only child of Albert and Anna (Starzynski) Montay. Her father, a French Canadian, died when Montay was one month old, and her mother, Milwaukee-born of Polish descent, died when Mary was sixteen.

Montay attended Grant Elementary School and St. Michael School in Wausau, Wisconsin. Her secondary school years began in 1922 at Wausau Public High School and, after she entered religious life on July 22, 1922, continued at Good Counsel High School, Chicago, where she graduated in 1924. A self-reliant child and young woman, Montay was an independent thinker, intellectually precocious, a talented writer mature beyond her age, a self-professed "book worm" who, as a Wausau high school student, "read while walking" (interview).

Montay arrived in Chicago during a period of expansion in Catholic education. After World War I, Polish Catholics in Chicago outnumbered both German and Irish Catholics for the first time. Polish immigrants demanded a Catholic education for their children and challenged the resources of the Felicians, a Polish religious order, to provide sufficient teachers and physical facilities. The Felician congregation members had to develop programs to train new sister teachers at the same time that they had to staff the new Catholic schools being founded to address the needs of the growing Catholic population.

Chicago Felicians provided for the children of Polish Catholic immigrants. Benedictines, originally from Bavaria, developed schools in Chicago for the children of German-speaking immigrants, and in a parallel manner, the predominantly Irish Sisters of Mercy and Sisters of Charity of the Blessed Virgin Mary (BVMs) staffed schools for the children of Irish immigrants. The teaching orders remained separate from each other, developing independent school systems. The arrival in 1915 of Cardinal George W. Mundelein, archbishop of Chicago, heralded changes in the diocesan approach to education. Mundelein instituted a plan in 1916 for the reorganization of Catholic schools. Teaching sisters, including the Felicians, the Mercys, and the BVMs, were challenged to meet new standards for teacher training as Cardinal Mundelein attempted to overcome the ethnic boundaries that characterized the structure of Chicago Catholicism. Instead of having each school operate as a separate entity, Mundelein established goals for a unified Catholic school system that would have a uniform curriculum, similar teaching methods, and common textbooks. It took time to overcome the traditional patterns. Despite strained relations between Mundelein and Polish Catholics over control and priorities of their local parish churches and clergy, the Felicians worked enthusiastically in the reorganized school community, taking several leadership positions. Montay's student days and early teaching years corresponded to the period of the order's growth, when numbers and missions were increasing. The Mother of Good Counsel Provincial Convent buildings were erected in 1925 on a thirty-three acre tract of land on Chicago's Northwest Side.

Montay taught at St. John of God, an elementary school, from 1926 to 1935 and later at Good Counsel High School from 1938 to 1947. As was common for women religious during the 1920s, Montay's college course work was taken during summer breaks and concurrently with her teaching assignments. Beginning in 1915, college-type courses for Felicians were taught within the Mother of Good Counsel Convent by faculty that the archdiocese supplied. From 1927 to 1954, Felicians were prepared to teach in a special extension program run by Loyola University Chicago. A few Felicians, including Mary Innocenta Montay, had the opportunity to attend the Catholic Sisters College, Washington, D.C. There Montay received a B.A. degree in 1937. Such programs as the Catholic Sisters College took the place of regular college attendance and gave teaching sisters basic skills during summer months so that they could return to classroom teaching during the school year.

Montay's graduate work was undertaken during the 1930s through the early 1950s at Catholic University of America, Washington, D.C., where in 1938 she earned an M.A. degree and, in 1953, a Ph.D. Her dissertation, "The History of Catholic Secondary Education in Chicago," until that time the only thorough study ever done of the system, was published by the university the same year.

From 1947 on, Montay's teaching and administrative duties were concentrated at the college level. Her stature within the order greatly increased as she took on more challenging offices in the province, including professor of education, college administrator, and provincial leader. Montay had a key role in developing the order's modern mission of providing a liberal arts education for women religious. The idea of a college for the Felician community had been in the planning stages since Montay was a young student. In anticipation of founding a liberal arts college, the Felicians had filed incorporation papers with the state of Illinois in 1926. In the 1940s and early 1950s, religious leaders looked critically at the way in which sisters were educated. The heavy demands on religious orders to staff Catholic schools with their burgeoning enrollments meant that many young sisters taught from ten to fifteen years before they were able to finish a B.A. degree. "Sisters had been accustomed to on-the-job training: they had been teaching for years on a combination of goodwill, self-education, tutorial supervision, and holy obedience" (Weaver, 79–80). The new sister formation movement sought to change this system and integrate intellectual and professional development with spiritual and religious training before a sister began a career in teaching. The change meant expanding opportunities for higher education. College programs were in demand, and the Felicians returned to the dormant Illinois state charter to make it active. Felician College opened in 1953 with sixty-one students. Montay's insistence on a sound liberal arts curriculum, high academic standards, and a strong library reflected her conviction that Felicians should be broadly rather than narrowly educated. This was the direction of the sister formation movement as well.

Montay's service to the college went beyond leadership in its foundation. It included her appointments to teaching and administrative posts, including professor of education, director of junior studies, dean of studies, and finally, president of the board of trustees of Felician College. She became provincial superior of the order on January 1, 1963, serving until March 1975, when her health failed. During her service as provincial superior in the 1960s and 1970s, several important and innovative projects were undertaken. Along with managing the growth of the college, she supported the foundation of the Felician Library Service Project, the brainchild of Sister Chrysantha Rudnik, who designed and supervised the unique training program in library education for teachers in the Felician Schools. The program established professionally organized and staffed libraries in each of the fifty-five Felician schools.

Despite these accomplishments, the 1960s and 1970s were years of mixed blessings. The times blunted accomplishments that might have been made under Montay's able administration. The 1960s and 1970s were years of turmoil for the Roman Catholic Church, when adjustments to the Second Vatican Council were often made with difficulty. The Felician order, along with other Catholic orders, declined in membership.

Montay's authority stemmed from a composed and reverent demeanor. Measuring about five foot three inches in height, she had dark eyes and a medium frame. Contemporaries recall a consistently controlled and friendly individual, one who was demonstrative in her teaching style, but was never undignified.

Mary Innocenta Montay died at age seventy at Resurrection Hospital, Chicago, from complications due to lifelong diabetes and vascular disorders. The immediate cause was cerebral thrombosis and arteriosclerosis following surgery. She lay in a coma for one week before she died. She is buried at St. Adalbert's Cemetery, Niles, Illinois.

Mary Innocenta Montay's accomplishment was recognized posthumously in December 1987 when the Felician College Board of Trustees voted unanimously to bestow an honor on the founder and rename the college Montay College. Montay was a gifted individual, a scholar of depth and precision, a hard worker, and an effective classroom teacher with broad interests. As an innovator in the education of sister teachers, she encouraged educational breadth beyond traditional expectations for convent learning. An exemplar in Marian devotion and Catholic practice, Montay advised toleration toward faiths other than Catholicism decades before the pronouncements of the Second Vatican Council. This outlook identified Montay's "global vision" (interview).

Sources. The Collected Papers of Sister Mary Innocenta Montay, Felician Sisters Archives, Chicago, Illinois, contain biographical materials including Montay's "Hail Mary. My King. Thoughts from Novitiate," 1925–27 (typed and bound 1941), and "The Spiral Notebook," handwritten notes, n.d. Mary Montay, *The History of Catholic Secondary Education in the Archdiocese of Chicago* (1953), is her published dissertation from Catholic Univ. of America. An interview was conducted by Margaret W. Norton with Chrysantha Rudnik, January 21, 1995. Useful published materials include [anonymous], *Fifty Years: A Memoir on the Fiftieth Anniversary of the Mother of Good Counsel Province of the Congregations of the Sisters of St. Felix [Felicians]* (1960), and the February 1976 issues of *Contact: Newsletter of the Chicago Mother of Good Counsel Province* and *Felician College Quest.* Context is provided by Joseph Hohn Parot, *Polish Catholics in Chicago, 1850–1920* (1981); George V. Fornero, "The Expansion and Decline of Enrollment and Faculties of Secondary Schools in the Archdiocese of Chicago, 1955–1980" (Ph.D. diss., Loyola Univ. Chicago, 1990); and Mary Jo Weaver, *New Catholic Women: A Contemporary Challenge to Traditional Religious Authority* (1986).

MARGARET W. NORTON

MOODY, HARRIET CONVERSE TILDEN BRAINARD

March 18, 1857–February 22, 1932

PATRON OF THE ARTS, CATERER, RESTAURATEUR, TEACHER

Harriet Converse Moody stands as a model of fin-de-siècle female independence. An entrepreneur, *salonière* (salon organizer), and friend of the arts, she is representative of many women of her era who pursued complex, multifaceted careers. Moody's name became a byword in the Chicago restaurant business and beyond; more important to her own self-fulfillment, she took a position of understated leadership in the Chicago literary renaissance and the *Poetry* magazine circle.

Harriet Converse Tilden was born in Parkman, Ohio, the first of three children and the only girl. At about age eleven, she moved with her family to Chicago, where her father, William Mason Tilden, made a prosperous career as a livestock broker. Her mother, Harriet Converse, was devoted to learning and to the gracious management of her home. According to a biographer, Harriet Tilden was a tomboy and the object of her father's "excessive idolatry" (Dunbar, 18). Despite early resistance to parental authority, she greatly admired her abolitionist parents.

Harriet Tilden was educated at the Howland School, a Quaker institution, in Union Springs, New York. She went on, despite her father's objections, to Cornell University, Ithaca, New York, where she graduated in 1876 with a degree in English literature. At Cornell, she lived at the home of Hiram Corson, professor of English, who became her mentor and introduced her to spiritualism. In autumn 1876 Harriet Tilden, over her parents' objections, enrolled at the Women's Medical College in Philadelphia. After a year she returned to Chicago for her social debut, her parents having agreed that she would then resume her studies. Instead, she remained in Chicago to marry a bright, troubled young lawyer named Edwin Brainard, despite parental opposition. The marriage was not a success. When the Brainards were divorced sometime in the 1880s, Harriet Tilden returned her one hundred thousand dollar marriage settlement. After the death of her father, she assumed financial responsibility for her invalid mother and began her business career.

In 1889 Tilden became a schoolteacher in Chicago. She made a lifelong friend of her student ALICE HENDERSON, later associate editor of *Poetry* magazine. Tilden's first venture in publishing was the Windtryst Press, set up in her home to print her students' work.

Teaching, however, could not support a large home and a mother accustomed to luxury. At the suggestion of a friend, she experimented in 1889 with a gingerbread recipe for the tea room at Marshall Field's department store. Chicken salad soon followed, and her Home Delicacy Association (HDA) began its work in the basement of her home. The business moved to the top floor of her new house in the Hyde Park neighborhood, and, later, to its own building. Tilden was from the outset determined to cook homestyle food of the highest quality, regarding this work as a moral responsibility. The HDA sought to honor the modern home by providing proper sustenance, lovingly prepared for ceremonial dining. Although Tilden marketed her restaurant and catering services to the privileged classes, she also wrote *Delineator Institute* booklets and advertising brochures di-

Fig. 80. *Businesswoman and patron of artists and poets Harriet Moody, seated on the floor in the front row, next to woman with flag on the right, surrounded by employees and friends, ran a catering service.*

rected to middle-class and working-class readers. Soon the HDA had become a Chicago institution whose products were sold at Marshall Field and Company, at the Field Museum of Natural History cafeteria, at the tearoom of the Chicago Little Theatre, and at clubs and corporations. Tilden also stocked the dining cars of many rail lines that passed through the city. She maintained a branch at Selfridge's in London and a restaurant, Le Petit Gourmet, on Chicago's North Michigan Avenue. For at least a decade, then, Tilden maintained two careers. She continued to teach while she managed the HDA, her mother's household, and her own.

In 1892 Harriet Tilden began graduate school in the Department of English at the University of Chicago. In 1899 she was introduced to the poet William Vaughn Moody, a professor of English at the university. They soon became good friends, sharing a devotion to poetry and spiritualism. Beautiful, forceful, and energetic, Tilden embodied an ideal of femininity current at the turn of the century. Eleven years her junior, Will Moody was intensely romantic and eager for experience. For several years they were lovers. Although Will Moody pressed his suit, they put off marriage. Her mother objected to the match, and the couple's correspondence suggests that Tilden herself did not wish to remarry.

On May 7, 1909, they did marry, however, at a time of sharp decline in Will Moody's health. After he died of brain cancer in 1910, Harriet Moody devoted herself completely to poetry and the HDA, partly because she wished to advance her husband's reputation and manage his literary estate, and partly because she had to support herself. Her subsequent promotions of the arts cannot be adequately explained by her devotion to Will,

however. She was beginning to conceive of her work for the arts and for the palate as a unified whole.

Moody joined *Poetry* magazine as one of its original one hundred financial backers. Before the first issue came out, a Boston journal threatened to use the same title, and editor HARRIET MONROE had to rush the first number into print in October 1912. As she had few important poems and only fourteen pages of text, "Mrs. William Vaughn Moody came to the rescue, as in various later emergencies she so often did, by permitting us the first printing of her dead husband's poem 'I Am the Woman'" (Monroe, 285). Ironically, the poem celebrates not Harriet Moody's talent or mind but her primitive feminine essence, eulogized in florid mythopoetic language of the kind *Poetry* would soon repudiate.

In her own life Moody was unconstrained by this narrow conception of femininity. She gave financial help and advice to an astonishing array of literary, visual, and musical artists, including material sustenance in the form of room and board at her large home on the Near South Side. She arrived in her chauffeur-driven car at Union Station to welcome new artists. Her legendary, unconventional dinner parties were held in her drawing room, where she sat in a settee suspended from the ceiling, so that her feet did not touch the floor. This arrangement was necessary because of a serious ankle injury in 1901 that left her with a permanent limp. Each guest was seated in an easy chair and served at an individual table. The food was the best HDA could provide, and the ambience encouraged good conversation. A brilliant conversationalist, Moody responded quickly to intelligence and humor. Her evenings ran late, and her guests left with richly provisioned hampers of food and other gifts.

Moody established a series of poetry readings, which she called Les Petits Jeux Floraux. These began late in 1920 at Le Petit Gourmet on Sunday evenings; refreshments were served. She handled the publicity and charged one dollar for admission, giving the total to the artist. Moody's friendships with poets and her connections in the art world guaranteed good attendance. Robert Frost, Vachel Lindsay, Carl Sandburg, and Padraic Colum came yearly; other readers included Maxwell Bodenheim, Countee Cullen, Alfred Kreymborg, Percy MacKaye, Edna St. Vincent Millay, Amy Lowell, Harriet Monroe, Ridgely Torrence, and Margery Swett.

Moody also arranged readings at the University of Chicago, Northwestern University, and other universities, including Cornell, where she served from 1912 to 1922 as the only female trustee. Her doors were open to visiting artists in her apartment in Greenwich Village, New York City; her farm in West Cummington, Massachusetts; and a summer retreat at Mackinac Island, Michigan. Thus, she had a moveable salon. At a time when artists' colonies were hardly known and public and foundation grants not available, she provided the means for artistic work, apparently without regard to nationality, ethnicity, or race. Unlike other philanthropists, she earned her money largely to give it away. She was, as her biographer Olivia Dunbar put it, almost irrationally unselfish.

Moody had a genius for networking and sound critical judgment, enabling her to advance a friend's career. Edwin Arlington Robinson asked her to forward "Eros Turanos" to Harriet Monroe for publication in *Poetry*, suggesting that her endorsement might encourage acceptance. Vachel Lindsay had almost filial relations with Moody, bringing her his poetry. The two supported the antilynching campaign current in the United States to end violence against African Americans in the South. She wrote letters of introduction for young Robert Frost to a number of universities and clubs, as she did for many others. She handled the details of Frost's itinerary and put him up at her Chicago home.

In her relations with Rabindranath Tagore, later a Nobel Laureate, Moody approached an ideal of friendship. Among the earliest to promote the Indian writer's work in this country, she invited Tagore to visit in 1912. The two discovered a strong affinity of beliefs. Her faith in Will Moody's constant presence corresponded to Tagore's faith. His otherworldliness appealed to her because, although Moody was successful in her business, she disliked the realm of commerce.

Because Moody's gift was, as Percy MacKaye put it, "native to air, not to ink" (*Letters to Harriet*, 9), she left few documents that revealed introspection. She left no written sign that she thought of herself as a feminist. Moody's sexual freedom—she lived for years with Will Moody while refusing to marry him—stood out in sharp contrast to her HDA work of catering to weddings and to being cited as an expert on marriage etiquette in the *Ladies' Home Journal*.

Some, mostly men, used her as a mirror. Her quick artistic sympathy, her clear-sightedness and wit encouraged creative interaction. Some, like Vachel Lindsay, Hart Crane, and the youthful Richard Eberhart, depended on her for inspiration.

Indeed, she was thought by some to be more interested in men than in women. Yet she surrounded herself with women. Alice Corbin and University of Chicago professor MARTHA

CROW lived with her. Many of her senior HDA employees were female; Le Petit Gourmet was managed and staffed by women. As a Cornell trustee, she devoted herself to women's concerns. And she raised funds for scientist Marie Curie's research.

In 1929 the HDA folded due to financial troubles. She wrote sometime in 1929 to her friend Elizabeth Wallace, "I think it would be well for me to take to the lecture platform, advising all women to keep out of business. . . . This seems for the moment to be the curtain on my own life" (quoted in Dunbar, 253). Yet she added that she wanted to live "indefinitely" (p. 253).

In her last three years she eked out a living teaching deaf women to cook. She also planned a cookbook combining her recipes with essays by poet friends, but the book came out without the essays. It succeeded, but not on a large enough scale to insure her comfort. A young woman admirer gave her a yearly income and an anonymous former student bought her house and asked her to remain, which she did until she died of bronchial asthma in 1932.

The modernist movement was a creation of an international community sustained by the work of women like Harriet Moody, Harriet Monroe, MARGARET ANDERSON, Winifred Ellerman, Sylvia Beach, and Caresse Crosby—a few representative publishers, editors, and patrons—as well as by writers. A powerful creator of words, of cookery, of the ambience language and food together can produce, Harriet Moody made art happen.

Sources. The primary source of material is the Harriet Brainard Moody Papers, UC Spec. Coll. The collection includes personal correspondence, business correspondence and documents, newspaper and magazine articles, photographs and advertising materials, unpublished manuscripts, and Moody's secretary Edith Kellogg's unpublished writings and scrapbooks. Unpublished manuscripts and correspondence are also in the William Vaughn Moody Papers, UC Spec. Coll. William Vaughn Moody's letters to Moody are in the Huntington Library, San Marino, California. Harriet Moody's letters to Houghton Mifflin Co. are in the Houghton Library, Harvard Univ. For a biographical memoir, see Olivia Howard Dunbar, *A House in Chicago* (1947). Additional information on Moody can be found in William Vaughn Moody, *Letters to Harriet*, ed. Percy MacKaye (1935); Harriet Monroe, *A Poet's Life: Seventy Years in a Changing World* (1938); Martin Halpern, *William Vaughn Moody* (1964); Maurice F. Browne, *Estranging Dawn: The Life and Works of William Vaughn Moody* (1973). A discussion of Moody's career, from which this profile in part is drawn, is Susan Albertine, "Cakes and Poetry: The Career of Harriet Moody," in *A Living of Words: American Women in Print Culture*, ed. Susan Albertine, copyright © 1995 by The University of Tennessee Press, used by permission. Brief mention of Moody can be found in biographies and published correspondence of a number of writers; see, for example, Eleanor Ruggles, *The West-Going Heart: A Life of Vachel Lindsay* (1959); Arnold Grade, ed., *Family Letters of Robert and Elinor Frost* (1972); Lawrance Thompson, *Robert Frost: The Years of Triumph, 1915–1938* (1970); and in Dale Kramer, *Chicago Renaissance: The Literary Life of the Midwest, 1900–1930* (1966).

SUSAN ALBERTINE

MOORE GARBE, RUTH
April 3, 1908–January 2, 1989
JOURNALIST, AUTHOR, COMMUNITY ACTIVIST

Ruth Moore, professional journalist and writer of science books for the general reader, was the older of two children born to William Dunn and Ethel (Sledd) Moore in St. Louis, Missouri.

Her mother devoted all of her energy to her family and the management of her home. Her father, a lawyer, judge, and justice of the peace, encouraged Ruth and her brother Norman to explore civic and political interests. The two siblings remained close throughout their lives.

As a teenager, Ruth Moore engaged in sports at school and at her family's vacation cottage in southern Illinois during the summer months. There she and her brother spent the days playing golf and tennis and swimming. At Cleveland High School in St. Louis, Moore was a member of the student council; she was elected to the honor society, took part in the debate team, and maintained an A average.

After high school, Moore registered for law school at Washington University, St. Louis, only to be dissuaded by her father and the dean of the law school, who was her father's friend. The men argued that law was not a good field for women. Instead, Moore majored in political science at Washington University, where she was Phi Beta Kappa and president of the university chapter of the League of Women Voters. Moore received an A.B. degree in 1929 and an M.A. from Washington University in 1930.

Moore's first job after graduation was as executive secretary for the League of Women Voters of Missouri. She handled their publicity and, as a result, developed a close relationship with various newspapers, in the process realizing her attraction to journalism. Moore's career as a cub reporter began in the early 1930s at the St. Louis Star-Times. She wrote a series of articles called "A Woman's Guide to the Missouri Legislature." She was well suited for this assignment because her previous work with the League of Women Voters had given her familiarity with the state legislature. Her work on the series increased her interest in political and civic affairs. Moore wrote for the Star-Times for more than seven years.

In Chicago, meanwhile, Marshall Field had just bought the old Chicago Sun newspaper. When Field heard that an editor from the Star-Times (Ruth Moore's former editor) had recently retired, Field hired him to help reorganize his new acquisition. An opportunity opened up for Ruth Moore when her former editor recruited her to work for him and she accepted a staff position as a Washington, D.C., bureau correspondent for the Chicago Sun in 1943. She covered the Washington political scene, including the White House and several government departments. The Sun merged with the Times in 1948 to become the Sun-Times. In 1950, when the Sun-Times Washington bureau staff was cut back, Moore moved to Chicago and began to cover city planning and urban design. She became well known for her writing on architectural preservation, science, urban renewal, city planning, and other community matters. In addition, as a result of opportunities that came from her experiences in journalism, she also began writing popular science books.

In the early 1950s, Moore's career in writing popular science books was launched by chance when she overheard a University of Chicago professor comment, "We're [i.e., scientists are] rewriting the theory of evolution" (preface to Man, Time and Fossils). He was referring to the use of carbon 14 to date prehistoric fossils. Moore had a keen ear for a good story and followed up this offhand remark by an interview with Nobel Prize recipient Willard F. Libby, a chemist at the University of Chicago.

Moore's subsequent article for the Sun-Times on the discovery of carbon 14—a radioactive isotope of carbon—caught the eye of the editor-in-chief of Alfred Knopf publishers, and she was asked to expand the newspaper story into a book. Man, Time and Fossils: The Story of Evolution was published in 1953. Her second book, Charles Darwin: A Great Life in Brief, a short biography of the scientist responsible for the theory of evolution, was published in 1955 and focused on the voyage of the H.M.S. Beagle, the conflicts experienced by Darwin after he proposed his theory, and its final acceptance by the scientific community. The year that Charles Darwin was published, Man, Time and Fossils received the top award from the Friends of Literature and was the American Library Association's notable book choice. Eventually, Man, Time and Fossils was translated and published in seven languages. MacMurray College in Jacksonville, Illinois, awarded Moore an honorary doctorate of literature in recognition of her best-selling history of the theory of evolution. In 1955 Moore also published The Earth We Live On: The Story of Geological Discovery, which traced the history of the earth's evolution by exploring the science of geology.

Moore was made science editor of the Sun-Times in 1959, a position she held until 1967. Moore wrote about new developments in science in special features and in news stories. She also covered new developments in anthropology through book reviews. She wrote several Sun-Times articles on the centennial of the publication of Darwin's Origin of Species (1859). Moore continued to write popular science books, publishing Coil of Life: The Story of Great Discoveries in the Life Sciences (1961), about the discovery of DNA; Evolution (1962), exploring Darwin's theory and its meaning for human life; and Niels Bohr: The Man, His Science and the World They Changed (1966), a biography of the founder of quantum mechanics.

The Bohr biography included discussions of the political and social aspects of the discovery of atomic structure and the subsequent development of the atomic bomb. During the course of U.S. efforts to develop the first atomic bomb, Bohr tried to persuade President Franklin D. Roosevelt and other world leaders to share their knowledge of atomic energy. To Moore, Bohr was a scientist who "stepped outside the . . . realm of science to set a direction toward peace and survival and away from what could be annihilation" (preface to Niels Bohr).

As a journalist and editor in a world where change was rapid, Moore pursued the possibilities and problems inherent in new technology. In addition to her science writing, however, she also began to cover urban affairs in the 1950s, examining issues related to transportation, housing renewal, neighborhood economic redevelopment, and the preservation of natural resources, including Chicago's lakefront. Moore covered the political struggles in the 1950s surrounding urban renewal and public housing on Chicago's South Side, including Woodlawn, Hyde Park, and Kenwood. She received an award from the American Association of Planning Officials in 1960 for her 1959 series on urban renewal in seven American cities.

In 1967 Ruth Moore married Raymond Garbe, a prominent architect and partner in the firm of Schmidt, Garden and Erikson. She had previously shown a personal interest in architecture and urban planning that was steadily nurtured by her close relationship with her brother, Norman Moore, an architect.

Moore reported on the issue of landmark preservation, covering the battles that developed between preservationists and commercial developers in Chicago. She published articles about the significance of Chicago architecture in the *Sun-Times* and in the local magazines *Midwest* and *Chicago*. Her articles on the Garrick and the Auditorium theaters, both the work of renowned architect Louis Sullivan and slated for destruction in the 1960s, educated readers about Chicago's architectural heritage. In a *Sun-Times* article, "The Stencils," November 19, 1967, Moore described as outstanding achievements Sullivan's original stencils, which were uncovered in the process of restoring the theaters.

During the 1960s Moore also explored the political conflicts embedded in urban planning initiatives. She covered the controversial Crosstown Expressway proposal, an attempt by city government and urban planners to connect two existing expressways—one on the Northwest Side of Chicago and the other on the Southwest Side—via a western corridor that would run through residential neighborhoods. Opponents of the plan complained about the destruction of houses; proponents lobbied for the relief of traffic congestion. The Crosstown Expressway was never constructed. Moore's newspaper reports informed the public of the complicated politics involved in the debate. In 1970 the Metropolitan Housing and Planning Council, a private citizens' group advocating professional urban policy based on people's needs rather than on vested interests and political agendas, gave Ruth Moore the Champion Fighter for a Better Chicago Award. It was an acknowledgment of her numerous articles on urban policy issues. She also received awards from the National Municipal League.

In the early 1970s Moore again turned to popular science, collaborating with Sherwood L. Washburn, a University of Chicago professor and scientist. They coauthored *Ape into Man* (1973; reissued in 1980 as *Ape into Human*). Washburn applauded Moore's talent at rendering accessible to the general reader the specialized knowledge of science.

Following Moore's retirement from the *Sun-Times* in 1971, Mayor Richard J. Daley appointed her to the Chicago Historical and Architectural Landmarks Commission. She served as a commissioner from 1974 to 1986. As chair of the Prairie Avenue Historic District Committee, she played an important role in the rehabilitation of the once fashionable, historically significant neighborhood. Moore was president of the Chicago Architectural Foundation from 1978 to 1980. Her efforts to save historic buildings won her the title of Chicago Preservationist of the Year in 1981. She was made an honorary member of the Chicago chapter of the American Institute of Architects (AIA).

Moore and her husband Raymond Garbe donated one hundred fifty thousand dollars to the Art Institute of Chicago for the purchase of American art. In 1986, Moore and her brother established the Ruth and Norman Moore Professorship in Architecture at Washington University, St. Louis, Missouri. The following year, Moore and her husband endowed a professorship in urban studies at Harvard University.

Ruth Moore and Raymond Garbe moved to San Francisco, California, in 1985. After her husband died on October 1, 1988, Moore lived with her brother Norman Moore in San Francisco. She died there at age eighty of a stroke believed to have been caused by the chemotherapy treatments she was undergoing for cancer.

As a writer of popular science books, Ruth Moore made scientific discoveries understandable to a general reading public. In her newspaper reporting and feature stories, she revealed the multilayered aspects of urban development, exploring the ins and outs of zoning, urban renewal, and historic preservation. As a Chicagoan, she pursued a second career as a community activist and preservationist.

Sources. Ruth Moore Papers, CHS, include correspondence, newspaper and magazine clippings, memorandums, reports, and informational flyers documenting her professional and personal interest in science, urban affairs, and architecture. Norman G. Moore provided written information in March 1995 and January 1997 about his sister Ruth's childhood and family life. Ruth Moore's major works include *Charles Darwin: A Great Life in Brief* (1955); *The Earth We Live On: The Story of Geological Discovery* (1955); *The Coil of Life: The Story of Great Discoveries in the Life Sciences* (1961); *Evolution* (1962); *Man, Time and Fossils: The Story of Evolution* (1963); *Niels Bohr: The Man, His Science and the World They Changed* (1966); and *Ape into Man*, coauthored with Sherwood L. Wasburn (1973). Obituaries include Kenan Heise, "Ruth Moore Garbe, 80, Author and Ex-Reporter," *CT*, January 5, 1989; "Ruth Moore, 80, Dies; Wrote about Science," *NYT*, January 5, 1989; and "Ruth Moore Garbe; Author, Ex-Reporter for *Star-Times*," the *Post-Dispatch*, January 6, 1989.

MARCIA J. PRADZINSKI

MORGAN, ANNA
February 24, 1851–August 27, 1936
MONOLOGIST, TEACHER OF DRAMATICS AND SPEECH

Anna Morgan, dramatic reader, teacher, and leading figure in Chicago's turn-of-the-century cultural arts community, was born near Auburn, New York. She was the eldest of five children born to Allen Denison and Mary Jane (Thornton) Morgan. Her father, a well-to-do gentleman farmer, served one year (1860–61) in the New York legislature. Anna Morgan was first schooled in Auburn. The family survived the financial panic of 1873, but when her father died in 1876, her mother moved the family to Chicago. There they settled in an affluent neighborhood amidst the city's civic leaders and just down the street from Abraham Lincoln's widow. Morgan's sister taught art to affluent Chicagoans, using her society connections to build classes in cultural refinement, a pattern Morgan would later follow herself.

At a friend's suggestion Morgan decided upon a career as a monologist. She first studied elocution at the Hershey School of Music in 1877, and three years later she debuted in a school recital performing "a little Scotch [*sic*] dialect selection called 'Charlie Machree'" (*My Chicago*, 15). Her career quickly blossomed. She first performed in and around Chicago, presenting such dramatic monologues as "How the Old Horse Won the Bet" and "How Ruby Played." In 1882, she returned to Auburn to perform and then toured as far west as Kansas, Nebraska, and Missouri. Morgan's big break came in 1883 when she convinced Mrs. Scott Siddons, a leading English actress then visiting Chicago, to include her as part of Siddons's program. Morgan's success established her reputation and enabled her to present more widely. She toured for the Redpath Lyceum Bureau and performed in New York City, Boston, and various midwest cities, blending popular homespun monologues with selections from William Shakespeare, Friedrich Schiller, Robert Browning, and Christina Rossetti. She sought a more relaxed, naturalistic style of performance than was generally used at the time and won recognition for her interpretations and portrayals. Her approach to oral interpretation became the basis for her teaching.

In 1884 the newly built Chicago Opera House's manager established an affiliated school, the Chicago Opera House Conservatory (later the Chicago Conservatory), and invited Morgan to join the faculty to teach dramatics. She continued to perform occasionally but concentrated her efforts on teaching elocution and speech, which became her life's work. Her students primarily prepared monologues for recital presentation for family, friends, and invited guests. Morgan also began to direct them in small production plays. Though intended as recitals, Morgan nonetheless often selected plays unknown to American audiences and thereby introduced the latest works of leading European playwrights. Her students gave the American premieres of Henrik Ibsen's *The Master Builder* (1895), Maurice Maeterlinck's one-act *The Intruder* (1897), William Butler Yeats's *The Land of Heart's Desire* (1898), and, though centuries old, Carlo Goldoni's classic, *The Fan* (1898), in a translation Morgan commissioned from her friend, Chicago author Henry Blake Fuller. Morgan was also the first American to stage George Bernard Shaw's *Candida* (1899). By chance, Shaw's copatriot and friend, theater critic William Archer, happened to be in Chicago at the time, saw all four performances, and recommended Morgan's work to Shaw. When Morgan traveled next to Europe, she visited with Shaw, who granted her special permission to produce his plays. In 1902, she presented the American premiere of Shaw's *Caesar and Cleopatra*, which reportedly shocked Shaw because of its all-woman cast. Morgan also later presented Maurice Maeterlinck's *The Blue Bird* and John Millington Synge's *The Shadow of the Glen*; she created some controversy when she staged Shakespeare's *Hamlet* with an all-woman cast in 1903. Beginning in 1894, her productions ignored elaborate scenery in favor of simple draperies, thereby placing greater focus on the actors' work. This simple staging was consistent with the leading ideas of the day in experimental theater.

In 1898 Morgan felt confident enough in her reputation to resign from the conservatory and open the Anna Morgan Studios on the eighth floor of Chicago's Fine Arts Building. Designed by architect Irving K. Pond, Morgan's eight-room suite included a large conservatory with a small stage at one end and a completely equipped gymnasium. Though largely intended for women, men could also participate. Morgan designed her program to promote not only expressive skill, but health, physical grace, and mental well-being. She and her staff later added classes in voice, public reading, pantomime, "deportment," stagecraft, dramatic literature, and French. Early on, her stated goals stressed cultivation of social skills and refinement; in later years, she placed greater emphasis on teaching dramatic literature and on developing professional performers and teachers. The studio's motto remained, "Art is a constant source of power."

Morgan's training techniques emphasized her own approach to the Delsarte Method, which preached that emotion could best be expressed through physical positioning and gesture. Morgan learned François Delsarte's system from the playwright/visionary Steele MacKaye—who had studied with Delsarte—but modified it according to her own beliefs, largely drawn from her experience as a dramatic reader. In 1890 she wrote a book, *An Hour With Delsarte*, in which she described her methods. In brief, Morgan placed faith in Delsarte's ideas regarding physical control and expressiveness but also promoted a more believable and naturalistic style of acting and behavior.

Much of Anna Morgan's clientele came from Chicago's affluent families. Some probably viewed her studio as a finishing school, a place to train children in the social graces. Others found that training there prepared them for careers in the arts. Chicago playwright ALICE GERSTENBERG studied at the studio as a child and later turned from writing novels to playwriting, when Morgan commissioned her to write a series of one-act plays for student presentation. Among the many who went on to acting careers were Sarah Truax (a member of Otis Skinner's company), and Walker Whiteside (star of Israel Zangwill's *The Melting Pot*). Others built careers as dramatic readers. Costumer and author Lucy Barton also studied with Morgan, as did Marjorie Benton Cooke, author of *Bambi*.

Morgan's studio in the Fine Arts Building also attracted distinguished theater artists on visits to Chicago. Some came to sit and watch the students work. These included the actors Richard Mansfield, Henry Irving, Ellen Terry, Maxine Elliott, and Joseph Jefferson III. Ever the businesswoman, Morgan cited their praise in studio brochures alongside quotes from newspaper reviews of her work as a performer. She also often included a photograph of herself with Bernard Shaw as his implicit endorsement of her work. When in the 1910s Chicago became home to numerous little theaters, Morgan took credit for being the first of the group. While it is true that she did present a number of important premieres, hers was essentially a school, with no long-standing commitment to art theater work. Credit more properly belongs to LAURA DAINTY PELHAM for her theater work at Chicago's Hull-House settlement.

True to its name, the Fine Arts Building housed a collection of Chicago artists and craftspeople. Tenants of the building's upper floors socialized together, forming a community that met daily for high tea and regularly entertained visitors. Resident artists included Chicago's leading newspaper cartoonist, John T. McCutcheon, the writer George Ade, sculptor Lorado Taft, painter Ralph Clarkson, and a host of others. For the most part, the residents represented the city's genteel arts traditions, though, in the 1910s, Maurice Browne's and ELLEN VAN VOLKENBURG's influential Chicago Little Theatre was also housed in the Fine Arts Building. This group's get-togethers often took place in Morgan's studio, with Morgan serving as salon hostess.

Personally, Morgan was an attractive, charismatic woman. She was tall, with dark hair and eyes, proud of being "lady-like" yet strong, independent, and accomplished. She never married. Though by professional necessity she was skilled at self-promotion, Morgan successfully cultivated a reputation for gentility that allied her with Chicago's cultural and civic elite.

Morgan also became active in Chicago's club world. She was one of a few female members of the Press and Whitechapel Clubs. She later joined the Antiquarian, Chicago Woman's, and Cordon Clubs. Most significantly, Morgan helped found the Little Room in the early 1890s, a group composed of many Fine Arts Building residents and their friends. Other members included architects Irving K. Pond and Allen B. Pond and Howard Van Doren Shaw; critic I. K. Friedman; sculptor BESSIE POTTER VONNOH; writers Henry Blake Fuller, Hamlin Garland, ELIA PEATTIE, EDITH WYATT, and Hobart C. Chatfield-Taylor; playwrights MARY ALDIS and Alice Gerstenberg; social reformer JANE ADDAMS; and HARRIET MONROE, founder of *Poetry* magazine. It was an informal group, a pleasant mix of artists and society, which proved quite influential in shaping Chicago's art world.

Morgan ran her studio until retiring in about 1925. Other studios sprang up in Chicago, most notably that of Grace Hickox, but Morgan remained competitive. She cemented her connections with Chicago's affluent and artistic communities and assumed a posture of prominence and success. In her autobiography, *My Chicago* (1918), Morgan made a special effort to catalogue appreciatively the city's civic and cultural leaders, tacitly placing herself in their midst. In 1908 she purchased a home north of Chicago, in fashionable Ravinia, which she dubbed "Eastgate." There she lived with her sister and carefully kept a register of her many distinguished guests. When her sister died in 1918, Morgan moved back to the city, where she died thirteen years later at the age of eighty-five. Morgan was buried in Chicago's Graceland Cemetery.

In retrospect, Morgan proved a vital force in the establishment and legitimization of art theater in fin-de-siècle Chicago. Though she aligned herself with Chicago's conservative gentry, Morgan still introduced the latest experimental works of Shaw, Maeterlinck, Synge, Ibsen, and others to her students and audiences, thereby helping to lay the groundwork for the establishment of art theater in Chicago. The long success of the Anna Morgan Studios and the consequent success and respect of her students attest to Morgan's profound legacy as a teacher. She repeatedly declined offers to teach elsewhere, including overseas. Morgan's ability to create and maintain circles of artistic and affluent friends had much to do with the establishment of Chicago's burgeoning art theater community of the 1910s.

Sources. The Anna Morgan Papers are at CHS and include Morgan's scrapbooks, Eastgate guest registry, and correspondence. There is also mention of Morgan in the Alice Gerstenberg Papers, CHS, and the Little Room Papers, NL. Morgan's autobiography, *My Chicago* (1918), is a valuable resource, though largely anecdotal, and occasionally inaccurate with regard to dates. Morgan also wrote *The Art of Speech and Deportment* (1909), *Selected Readings* (1909), and edited a volume of tributes to her friend, *Henry B. Fuller* (1929). See Fuller's "The Upward Movement in Chicago," *Atlantic Monthly*, October 1897, for an insider's look at Chicago's cultural growth during this era. Joyce L. C. Sozen examines Morgan's life and work in detail in "Anna Morgan: Reader, Teacher, and Director" (Ph.D. diss., Univ. of Illinois-Urbana, 1961). Sozen accepts Morgan's claim in *My Chicago* to being the first of the group of little theaters in Chicago, but Stuart J. Hecht, "Hull-House Theatre: An Analytical and Evaluative History" (Ph.D. diss., Northwestern Univ., 1983), argues that the credit more properly belongs to Laura Dainty Pelham for theater work at Chicago's Hull-House settlement. Other works to consult on the Little Room group include Perry Duis, *Chicago: Creating New Traditions* (1976), and Bernard Duffey, *The*

Chicago Renaissance in American Letters (1954). Morgan's obituary is in the *CT*, August 28, 1936.

STUART J. HECHT

MORGAN, ELIZABETH CHAMBERS
June 16, 1850–February 11, 1944
SOCIALIST, TRADE UNIONIST, REFORMER

Elizabeth Chambers Morgan earned her reputation as a radical. She combined the roles of mother and homemaker with those of labor organizer, social reformer, and socialist agitator. Coming from a poor, working-class background, this rugged and wiry woman became a leading figure in the struggle to protect working women and children against the ravages of late-nineteenth-century capitalism.

Born in Birmingham, England, Elizabeth Chambers was one of ten children of Thomas and Sarah (Maybury) Chambers, who were unskilled factory workers. With little formal education, Elizabeth Chambers became a mill hand at age eleven, working ten to sixteen hours a day. At age seventeen, she married Thomas J. Morgan, a Birmingham machinist, on January 26, 1868. Their joint earnings provided a bare subsistence.

After suffering the anguish of a stillbirth, and captivated by news of abundant job opportunities in the United States, the Morgans immigrated to Chicago in 1869. While her husband worked as a brass finisher, Elizabeth Morgan cared for their two small children (Thomas S. and Annie), performed household work, and managed the family's finances. The Panic of 1873 not only economically devastated the Morgans but also provided the catalyst for their conversion to socialism. Elizabeth and Thomas Morgan became partners in a spirited defense of workers' rights.

Embracing the socialist tenet of class struggle, Elizabeth Morgan became a charter member, in 1874, of the Sovereigns of Industry, a cooperative society, and served as its secretary. When this society declined, she collaborated with other Chicago socialist women in the organization of a labor union that affiliated with the Knights of Labor in 1881 as Local Assembly 1789. The assembly demanded equal pay for equal work, opposed child labor, and supported enfranchisement of women and African Americans. The group drew membership from a variety of female wage earners as well as a significant number of housewives. Elizabeth Morgan held the local's top leadership post of master workman and later served as the local's delegate to the Chicago Trade and Labor Assembly, a citywide association of trade unions.

From 1888 to 1895 Elizabeth Morgan became the leading female figure in the Chicago labor movement. A growing number of women worked for low wages in gender-segregated jobs, lacked political power, and encountered public opposition to unionization. Children were also employed in wretched conditions. Elizabeth Morgan mobilized a coalition of women who addressed these issues, combining trade unionism and political action.

Following a series of ideological disputes between socialist, conservative, and anarchist factions that decimated Local Assembly 1789, Morgan spearheaded a successful drive to form the Ladies' Federal Labor Union No. 2703 in June 1888. Chartered by the American Federation of Labor and incorporated in the state of Illinois, the new organization brought together dressmakers, confectionery workers, typists, bookbinders, music teachers, clerks, and others. In the local Morgan was organizer, delegate to the Chicago Trade and Labor Assembly, and secretary. Spurred by Morgan, the union helped form twenty-three separate American Federation of Labor (AFL)-chartered craft unions by 1892. This local became an important collective voice for working women in Chicago and "the most important organization of women workers affiliated to the early A.F. of L." (Foner, *History of the Labor Movement*, 190).

In the summer of 1888, the *Chicago Times* ran a series of articles revealing the horrendous conditions endured by female garment employees in city factories and workshops. Responding to the exposé, Morgan forged a united front of female socialists, settlement house workers, and trade unionists that founded the Illinois Woman's Alliance in the fall of 1888 to wage a major campaign for investigation of factory conditions and for compulsory education legislation. In its proclaimed mission to "prevent the moral, mental, and physical degradation of women and children . . . [employed] as wage workers" (quoted in Scharnau, 342), the Alliance sought the collaboration of other labor organizations and women's groups. The Alliance won the support of a number of middle-class women's groups interested in suffrage, literature, art, medicine, religion, and temperance. This cross-class coalition drew support from labor leaders FLORENCE KELLEY, CORINNE BROWN, Mary Kenney (see MARY KENNEY O'SULLIVAN), and Fanny Kavanaugh, and from organizations ranging from the Cook County Suffrage Association to the South End Flower Mission. Morgan became an influential figure, serving on the Alliance executive committee and chairing the delegation from the Chicago Trade and Labor Assembly.

Operating under the slogan, "Justice to Children, Loyalty to Women," Illinois Woman's Alliance and Ladies' Federal Labor Union members, under Elizabeth Morgan's leadership, recorded a number of achievements relating to the protection of women and children. Estimating that fifty thousand children, aged seven to fourteen, worked in sweatshops or roamed city streets, Alliance and union members successfully lobbied the Illinois General Assembly in 1889 to lower the mandatory school entrance age from eight to seven and extend the minimum required attendance period from twelve weeks to sixteen weeks each year. Alliance activists also convinced the Chicago Board of Education to appoint more truant officers, including three women, and to appoint an Alliance woman to the board. The board also agreed to construct new schools. At the same time the Alliance sponsored a clothing drive for school children from poor families.

Chairing the Alliance's Committee on Child Labor, Morgan persuaded the city council to authorize the health commissioner to appoint five women as factory inspectors in July 1889. When the inspectors met resistance from employers, Morgan coordinated the drive for a new local ordinance in 1890, prohibiting the factory employment of children under fourteen and increasing fines for violators. This Chicago ordinance became the model for the first general child labor law passed by the state of Illinois. However, both the local ordinance and the state law were weakened by exemption provisions and enforcement problems.

The Alliance's most memorable accomplishment was enactment by the Illinois General Assembly of the Factory and Workshop Inspection Act (also known as the Sweatshop Act) in June 1893. The impetus for this legislation began in the late summer of 1891 when Elizabeth Morgan headed a committee of the Chicago Trade and Labor Assembly that investigated the city's clothing industry sweatshops. Morgan's report, *The New Slavery: Investigation into the Sweating System as Applied to the Manufacture of Wearing Apparel* (1891), graphically depicted the misery of women and children employed by Chicago's clothing manufacturers in filthy, crowded tenement rooms for ten to fourteen hours daily at pitifully low wages. Morgan led tours for the press and public officials through the city's sweatshop districts and testified before various local, state, and national committees. An awakened public snapped up the ten thousand copies of the report printed by the Trade Assembly. The 1893 Sweatshop Act set sanitary standards, prohibited the employment of children under fourteen in any manufacturing enterprises, limited working hours of females to eight, and increased the enforcement powers of factory inspectors. This legislation was a personal triumph for Elizabeth Morgan and a testimony to the staunch support of trade unions, Hull-House residents—especially Florence Kelley—women's organizations, and John P. Altgeld, the state's liberal governor. Despite an 1895 Illinois Supreme Court decision overturning the eight-hour clause and despite defects in the measure itself, the landmark act reduced the number of child laborers and created healthier and safer workplaces.

In revealing the exploitation of women and children, Elizabeth Morgan operated from a dual power base, presiding over several Alliance and Trade Assembly committees. She made effective use of on-site investigations and statistical documentation in presentations before public bodies and in the press. A Chicago Trade and Labor Assembly committee she headed investigated convict labor at the Joliet, Illinois, penitentiary and found that the convicts suffered from long hours, low wages, and excessive work. Morgan chaired a committee of the Illinois Woman's Alliance that convinced the Chicago City Council to appropriate twenty-five thousand dollars for free public baths. She also investigated conditions at a number of public institutions. At the county poorhouse, asylum, and hospital, the Alliance cited overcrowding, poor nutrition, and resident abuse. At local police stations, the Alliance found prostitutes subjected to verbal harassment, trial irregularities, and large fines. An Alliance study of conditions of school teachers found summary dismissals, overcrowded classes, and the withholding of pay.

The 1894 convention of the American Federation of Labor recognized Elizabeth Morgan's vigorous defense of women and children with a standing ovation. As the only female delegate in attendance, Morgan represented the now-famous Ladies' Federal Labor Union Number 2703. She offered three resolutions that the convention approved. The first cited factory employment as detrimental to the moral, intellectual, and physical development of children and called for the enactment and enforcement of state compulsory education laws. The second urged states to enact the eight-hour workday for women and children in manufacturing establishments. The third advocated state action to abolish the sweating system and tenement house manufacturing. Nominated for the post of first vice-president, Elizabeth Morgan lost to incumbent P. J. McGuire by a margin of 1,865 to 226, "a vote for those days large enough to reflect credit equally upon the woman for whom it was cast and on the men who cast it" (Henry, 54). No woman had ever aspired to such a high AFL office.

By this time Elizabeth Morgan had already resigned her position with the Illinois Woman's Alliance. Tensions had arisen within the Alliance between labor delegates like Morgan who supported paid city inspectors, strikes, and militant political action to correct inequities, and the middle-class delegates who espoused charity work, considered strikes too confrontational, and relied on voluntary and philanthropic activities to better society. The Panic of 1893 and the Pullman Strike of 1894 deepened the class rift. Subsequent internal conflicts resulted in the disintegration of the once powerful Illinois Woman's Alliance. Morgan's attempt, in the fall of 1894, to fashion a new working-class-only coalition to succeed the Alliance failed when a schism occurred between pure-and-simple trade unionists and socialists.

Elizabeth Morgan now turned her energies to a new collaborative venture. Thomas J. Morgan began attending the Chicago College of Law in 1893. In 1895 he graduated and passed the bar examination. Elizabeth Morgan studied law with her husband and managed his law office, serving as secretary, bookkeeper, and notary. The Morgans saw the legal profession not as an avenue to monetary success but as a way to protect the interests of labor and contend for the principles of socialism. After nearly twenty years of a law practice dedicated to defending wage earners, the Morgans, now in their sixties, decided to retire in California. The train on which the San Diego-bound Morgans and their daughter Annie and her children were traveling crashed at Williams, Arizona, on December 10, 1912. Thomas J. Morgan was killed, but Elizabeth and the others escaped serious injury. She settled in the countryside near San Diego, where she resided for thirty-one years, apparently disengaged from labor activities. She died at the age of ninety-three.

Elizabeth Morgan's public career displayed an extraordinary level of militance and involvement. Her confrontational style combined impassioned utterances in print and in speech with statistical documentation. She also possessed strategic, organizational, and coalition-building talents. Her advocacy on behalf of the working class was fused with feminism and concern for children. Her radical socialist vision required organizing along both economic and political lines and she persistently struggled to create a new society based on justice and equity.

Sources. The Thomas J. Morgan Collection, Illinois Hist. Survey, Univ. of Illinois at Urbana-Champaign, provides some information on Elizabeth Morgan, mostly from newspaper clippings that she had arranged chronologically. A few references to the work of Elizabeth Morgan can also be found in the Henry D. Lloyd Papers at the State Hist. Soc. of Wisconsin in Madison and in the Samuel Gompers's Letterbooks in the Library of Congress. Profiles of Elizabeth Morgan appear in Ralph Scharnau, "Elizabeth Morgan, Crusader for Labor Reform," *Labor History*, Summer 1973, and Ellen M. Ritter, "Elizabeth Morgan: Pioneer Female Labor Agitator," *Central States Speech Journal*, Fall 1971. Shorter sketches of Morgan can be found in Meredith Tax, *The Rising of the Women: Feminist Solidarity and Class Conflict, 1880–1917* (1980); Alice Henry, *Women and the Labor Movement* (1923); Philip S. Foner,

History of the Labor Movement in the United States, vol. 2: *From the Founding of the American Federation of Labor to the Emergence of American Imperialism* (1955), and *Women and the American Labor Movement: From the First Trade Unions to the Present* (1982); Barbara Mayer Wertheimer, *We Were There: The Story of Working Women in America* (1977); and Mari Jo Buhle, Paul Buhle, and Dan Georgakas, eds., *Encyclopedia of the American Left* (1990).

RALPH SCHARNAU

MURAKAMI, CHIYO KASHIWAGI
July 29, 1917–September 25, 1990
LABORATORY MANAGER, MEDICAL TECHNOLOGIST

Chiyo Kashiwagi, a Nisei (second generation Japanese American), earned a B.A. degree in biochemistry and was hired for her first job in a Chicago laboratory while interned in a War Relocation camp during World War II. She later participated in research on infectious mononucleosis.

Kashiwagi was born in Hayward, California, the eldest of six children of Frank Kashiwagi and his second wife, Tatsu (Furusawa) Kashiwagi. Chiyo Kashiwagi's father emigrated to the United States from Yokohama, Japan, in 1896 to work. When his first wife died in 1915 in the United States, the three children by that marriage were sent to Japan to be raised by grandparents. Frank Kashiwagi's family in Japan arranged for a second marriage, to Tatsu Furusawa, from a family in the Yokohama area. Although the families in Japan had some dealings with each other, Tatsu Furusawa arrived in the United States in 1916 a picture bride, for she and Frank had not met before. Frank Kashiwagi was a foreman on the three-thousand-acre Meek Estate in Hayward, which was planted with fruit trees and other crops.

Chiyo Kashiwagi began her formal education at San Lorenzo Grade School in Hayward in 1924. When the Meek Estate began to be divided up and sold, the Kashiwagi family moved to Knights Landing, California. In 1932 the family moved to Woodland, California, where Frank became an independent farmer. Kashiwagi attended Woodland High School and graduated as valedictorian of her class in 1936.

Kashiwagi's parents felt that it was important for their daughters to be educated, and she started her postsecondary education in 1936 at the University of California, Berkeley, with a premedical major. Tuberculosis forced her into a sanitarium for a time, but she returned to Berkeley.

In December 1941, the United States declared war on Japan following the bombing of the U.S. Pacific naval fleet at Pearl Harbor, Hawaii. Tensions and fears escalated on the West Coast of the United States, the culmination of a long history of antagonism toward Japanese Americans, exemplified by the denial of naturalization to persons of Japanese heritage under the Naturalization Act of 1790, which limited citizenship to free white persons. With Japan now an enemy, the situation became explosive, as rumors of collusion and sabotage multiplied. President Franklin D. Roosevelt signed Executive Order 9066 on February 19, 1942, giving the War Department the right to designate military areas from which any person could be barred. This order paved the way for the evacuation and internment of 120,000 Japanese and Japanese Americans residing in California, Arizona, Oregon, and Washington. Two types of camps were created. Justice Department camps confined some 7,000 persons considered most dangerous to the United States. War Relocation camps imprisoned more than 110,000 persons, two-thirds of them American citizens, in ten isolated areas in California, Arizona, Colorado, Utah, Wyoming, Arkansas, and Idaho. The Kashiwagi family was temporarily confined at an assembly center in Merced, California, from May 1942 until their internment in September 1942, along with 7,000 others, at Camp Amache near Granada, Colorado. In the nearby town of Lamar, signs declaring "Japs Not Wanted Here" (Girdner and Loftis, 218) were posted.

Amache, described by an internee as Colorado's newest city, was one mile square and fenced in with barbed wire. The camp contained 360 barracks, each housing six families. Every family was given one room, sparsely furnished with army cots, mattresses, a stove, a bucket, and a broom. One element of camp life that proved especially difficult for the internees was the communal mess hall. Meals were eaten cafeteria style, at long tables, making impossible the traditional family meal.

While interned at Amache, Chiyo Kashiwagi graduated in absentia from the University of California, Berkeley, with a B.A. degree in biochemistry in May 1942. She remained in the camp until spring of 1943, working in the laboratory of the hospital on the grounds. Beginning in early 1943, the government allowed persons to leave camp to join the military, to complete a college education, or to secure employment, preferably in the Midwest. Many Japanese Americans resettled in Chicago, where workers were needed. Kashiwagi applied for a job as a laboratory technician at Mount Sinai Hospital, Chicago, and Dr. Israel Davidsohn wrote to her offering the position. She asked for a temporary leave of one month from camp, which was approved, and moved to Chicago in March 1943. She found housing in a room rented from a Mexican American family. The move was changed to an indefinite leave as of April 1943.

Four of Kashiwagi's siblings were also able to leave camp. Her sister June completed a nursing program in Galveston, Texas. Her brothers Robert, George, and Thomas went into the U.S. Army and served in Europe. The Kashiwagi family exemplified the contradictions caused by the internment of Japanese American families. Parents and younger siblings were left prisoners in camp, while their children and brothers and sisters were serving in the U.S. military.

Kashiwagi began her career in science working for Davidsohn, director of the Department of Pathology, on blood bank research. In 1946 Kashiwagi was certified as a medical technologist by the American Society of Clinical Pathologists. She was third author with Davidsohn and Dr. Kurt Stern of four research articles. Their work on a test for the detection of infectious mononucleosis, "The Differential Test for Infectious Mononucleosis," was first published in 1949 in the *Abraham Levinson Anniversary Volume Studies in Pediatrics and Medical History*. The article supported the effectiveness of the serologic test under discussion. In another article with the same title in *American Journal of Clinical Pathology* (1951), the authors recommended a simplified serologic test for detecting infectious mononucleosis. Their next publication on the subject, "Antisheep Agglutinins in Infectious Mononucleosis: Experimental Investigations," appeared the same year in the *Military Surgeon*. Kashiwagi did laboratory work with Davidsohn and Stern on

blood typing by Rh factor, described in "Mass Blood Grouping and Rh Typing, a Tentative Plan" and published in the *American Journal of Clinical Pathology* in 1951.

At Mount Sinai Hospital Kashiwagi met her husband, Tadao Murakami, who was working as a morgue attendant. Although they had been in the same internment camp, they had never met. They were married on August 7, 1946. Gregory, the first child of Chiyo and Tadao Murakami, was born in 1951; he was followed by Clifford in 1956 and Barbara in 1958.

In 1953 the Murakamis moved to Melrose Park, a western suburb of Chicago, where they could afford a larger home, though not without some difficulty. The builder of the home they wanted to buy was reluctant to sell to Japanese Americans in a predominantly Italian and German community. A friend of Tadao Murakami bought the home in his own name, then sold it to the Murakamis. The family never experienced any hostility from their neighbors.

Chiyo Murakami began in 1959 to take night calls at the laboratory at Westlake Community Hospital in Melrose Park; she started full-time work in the laboratory there in 1963, serving first as chief technologist and then as laboratory manager until her retirement in 1987. She was responsible for the laboratory budget and supervised the heads of several sections. Dr. Shakuntala Rajagopal, Director of Laboratories since 1970, who worked closely with Murakami for fourteen years, said that despite her research background, her patient orientation made her give "150 percent to patient care" (Rajagopal interview). On more than one occasion, she was honored as the outstanding hospital worker for that year, based on a vote of the staff.

The Murakamis were nonpracticing Buddhists. After the family moved to Melrose Park, a neighbor invited Chiyo and Tadao Murakami to St. Paul's Lutheran Church in Melrose Park. Christianity made sense to them; after attending services for a time, they were welcomed by the community and were baptized in March 1956.

Murakami's two hobbies were her garden, which always flourished, especially her roses, and her art work. She drew murals on the living room wall, and from time to time would paint over them and create new artistic pieces.

Murakami died of breast cancer at home at the age of seventy-three. She was cremated, and her ashes were placed at Elm Lawn Cemetery in Elmhurst, Illinois.

The year Murakami died, the U.S. government began issuing entitlement checks of twenty thousand dollars to every surviving Japanese American internee, the result of a long-fought redress movement that began in the 1970s. On November 25, 1978, the first Day of Remembrance, more than two thousand Japanese Americans and their friends reenacted the evacuation experience in a public manner in Seattle, Washington. Murakami herself was not active in the movement, but like every other Japanese American who had been interned, her life had been dramatically altered by the experience.

Chiyo Murakami exemplifies the tenacious spirit of a woman who would not be deterred by adverse circumstances. Despite her early illness and the unjust treatment meted out by the U.S. government, Murakami completed her education, eventually having a productive career in the health sciences. Her story provides a glimpse into one of the most egregious violations of civil rights in U.S. history. At the same time, ironically, the war effort benefited females, including Japanese American women, by opening career opportunities to them.

Sources. Articles on Murakami's research are described above. Information on her experience in internment camp is in the files of the War Relocation Authority at the National Archives and Records Administration, Washington, D.C. Further information came from interviews by Ann M. Harrington with Tadao Murakami on June 11 and June 26, 1995; son Gregory Murakami, August 25, 1995; daughter Barbara Polowinczak, June 11 and June 27, 1995; brother Robert Kashiwagi, June 23 and 25, 1995; sister June Yokote, June 23, 1995; and physician coworker Shakuntala Rajagopal, July 11, 1995. The *CT* published an obituary on September 28, 1990. The internment of Japanese Americans during World War II is discussed in the following studies: Audrie Girdner and Anne Foltes, *The Great Betrayal: The Evacuation of the Japanese-Americans during World War II* (1960); Roger Daniels, *Asian America: Chinese and Japanese in the United States since 1850* (1988); and Ronald Takaki, *Strangers from a Different Shore: A History of Asian Americans* (1989).

ANN M. HARRINGTON

MURPHY, MOTHER EVELYN
(Katherine Murphy)
September 16, 1881–September 9, 1955
EDUCATOR, ADMINISTRATOR, RELIGIOUS LEADER

Katherine Murphy pioneered two international study programs for women students and served as a college dean and president. Later she served as the mother general of the Sinsinawa Dominican Congregation, a religious community made up of more than fifteen hundred Catholic women religious.

Murphy was born in Kewanee, Illinois, the first child of John and Mary Ann (McDonough) Murphy. In 1887 her mother died, leaving the care of three young children to her husband. John Murphy, a coal miner, was unable to manage such a task and sought assistance from his family. Agnes Murphy, the second eldest child and only four years of age, was sent to live with relatives in St. Paul, Minnesota. John Murphy, daughter Katherine, and infant son John moved in with his brother and sister-in-law in Kewanee. That arrangement, however, was brief.

While living with her aunt and uncle, Katherine Murphy attended school sporadically. Rose O'Brien, a respected Kewanee public school teacher, observed the consequence of the child's frequent absences. She reported to Katherine (McDonough) O'Connor, Katherine Murphy's maternal aunt, that she saw the little girl sitting in the corner of a classroom wearing a dunce hat on her head. O'Connor and her husband, Martin, both avid proponents of education, convinced John Murphy to let them rear his daughter. The O'Connors immediately transferred Katherine Murphy to Visitation, Kewanee's parochial grade school.

The example of Fidelia Delaney, a Dominican sister at Visitation, inspired Katherine Murphy to enter the predominantly Irish American community of Dominican sisters. She was admitted into the novitiate of the Congregation of the Most Holy Rosary, Sinsinawa, Wisconsin, on August 4, 1899. According to the practice of religious orders at the time, she chose a new name, Sister Mary Evelyn. As a member of the Sinsinawa Dominican Congregation, Sister Evelyn Murphy dedicated her life to prayer, study, and the educational ministry of the Catholic Church. This vowed lifestyle afforded her the opportunity to exert significant influence upon the education of the young, particularly the higher education of young women.

Sister Murphy spent her first missions or teaching assignments in Iowa from 1901 to 1905 and then in Washington, D.C., from 1905 to 1918—at St. Dominic's School for eight years and then as superior for five at the Academy of the Sacred Heart. While teaching in Washington, D.C., she also studied at the Catholic University of America in order to complete the B.A. degree requirements for St. Clara College, Sinsinawa, Wisconsin. In the summer of 1918, the mother general of the Sinsinawa Dominicans, Mother Samuel Coughlin, asked Sister Murphy and three other sisters to embark on a difficult assignment. In 1917, the Sinsinawa Dominican Congregation had received an offer from the Master General of the Dominican Order to purchase property in Fribourg, Switzerland, and to administer a house of studies for women students. Reverend Joachim Berthier, founder of the Institut de Hautes Études, had organized a special study program for women of various countries who were enrolled at the University of Fribourg. The institute provided additional courses, tutors, and housing for the young students. The Sinsinawa community found the offer to own and operate the Institut de Hautes Études and its residency, Villa des Fougères, very attractive for two reasons. For several decades, the Sinsinawan Dominican sisters had traveled to various countries in Europe for postgraduate education. A convent and school in the Swiss university town would provide both educational opportunities and a home base for them while studying in Europe. The congregation planned to transfer its college, St. Clara, from Sinsinawa, Wisconsin, to River Forest, Illinois. The college, renamed Rosary College (later Dominican University), would also benefit from this European connection. Sisters Mary George and Grace James traveled to Fribourg in 1917 to investigate the matter. Sister George had extensive knowledge of languages, and Sister James knew German and had business skills. It was a difficult first year; the purchase of the villa by the order placed an additional heavy burden on the limited financial resources of the Sinsinawan Dominican congregation, which, in the United States, was building a new college campus in River Forest. In summer 1918, however, Sister George died. She had suffered from bouts of illness during the year. On September 18, 1918, Sister Murphy and her three colleagues arrived, having crossed the waters of the Atlantic in wartime to develop the new enterprise.

Sister Evelyn Murphy began her new assignment as directress of the Institut de Haute Études and prioress or superior of the new convent during the last months of World War I. Though war, postwar conditions, and influenza epidemics militated against the new venture, Murphy and her companions managed to open the institute by December 1918. One of the initial hopes for the Fribourg mission was to conduct two schools of study—one for religious training and the other for training in social work. The latter was designed to prepare students to apply Catholic social teachings to the societal needs of the twentieth century. This school was discontinued in 1924, however, because of financial difficulties and its small enrollment. Despite this disappointment, Murphy turned her energies toward a new project in the United States.

Fig. 81. *Mother Evelyn Murphy lifts the first clod of dirt at the groundbreaking for the Fine Arts Building, Rosary College (now Dominican University), May 31, 1950.*

In 1924, Murphy participated in the inception of the Rosary College Plan for Undergraduate Foreign Study, a junior year of international study directed and sponsored by the college but attended also by women from other colleges or universities in the United States. Beginning in fall 1925, two junior year women enrolled—one from Rosary College, the other from Trinity College, Washington, D.C. The program was "a European extension of Rosary College" (quoted in McCarty, 459). Students took courses both in the international University of Fribourg and in the Institut de Hautes Études and received college credit. Emphasis was placed on French language study. The program afforded many young women the cultural and educational advantages of living and learning abroad from 1925 until 1978, with the exception of the period from the outbreak of World War II until 1947.

Sister Murphy began her doctoral studies at the University of Fribourg in 1925. At the same time, she continued to contribute to the educational and religious life of the Institut de Hautes Études. In 1928, she completed the Ph.D. degree, writing her dissertation on "Blessed Clara Gambacorta," a fourteenth-century Italian Dominican woman religious. She was the first to translate the letters of this medieval saint into English, informing the English reading public about Gambacorta's life and work.

After spending a decade in Switzerland, Sister Evelyn Murphy returned to the United States to assume administrative responsibilities at Rosary College. She served as dean of the college from 1928 to 1937 and was appointed college president and prioress of Rosary Convent in 1937. During Murphy's fifteen years in administration, the institution increased its enrollment

and gained recognition as a women's college. Its students came from throughout the United States, Canada, and Latin America. The majority, however, were Catholic Chicagoans, the daughters of Irish, German, Italian, and eastern European immigrants. By 1931, a small number of Asian American and African American women attended Rosary and also a few students who were not Catholic.

In the 1930s, the college's liberal arts tradition, with its emphasis on academic rigor and social activism, exposed women students to lectures by notable scholars, including Hugh S. Taylor, professor of chemistry, Princeton University; Sir Herbert Ames, first treasurer of the League of Nations; Catholic editors Maisie Ward Sheed and Michael Williams; Jacques Maritain, French Catholic philosopher; and Dorothy Day and Peter Maurin of the Catholic Worker movement, a radical lay organization with social justice goals that stressed the individual's responsibility to reform society. Combining literary goals and the spirit of social action, Sister Murphy, while dean of the college, became the director of Rosary Sodality, reorganizing it and supporting its monthly publication, *Speculum Justitiae*. The monthly gave accounts of sodality activities and other aspects of school life, drawing students into the infrastructure of Catholic social action by modeling personal acts.

The idealism of the Rosary students was also ignited by their introduction to the philosophy of the Catholic Evidence Guild, first developed among English Catholics by Maisie Ward Sheed, who lectured to Rosary students and faculty in 1934 on the Catholic literary revival and modern trends in Catholic literature. After her formal presentation, she spoke informally to a small group of students about the Catholic Evidence Guild. Sheed's experience as a member of a religious minority in Anglican England resonated with American Catholic women, many of whom were the daughters of recent immigrants. It took courage to make public one's religious convictions in a cultural climate that still harbored anti-Catholic prejudice—true in England and in the United States. Sheed described how a small group of English Catholics "defied the convention of reticence that had been developed by their co-religionists" (Egan, "Editorial," *Rosary College Eagle*, April 1935, 180) and matched their doctrines with communists and freethinkers. They began to participate in "street-preaching."

Sheed told the Rosary students about the Reverend Stephen Leven of Oklahoma, who with other priests in his diocese was doing guild work. Father Leven came to Rosary College some weeks later. "He broke, for many of us, the wall of complacent self-satisfaction and smugness, characteristic of the average Catholic College student, and aroused us to the possibility contained in the command, 'Go ye therefore, and teach all nations,'" wrote the *Rosary College Eagle* editor in April 1935. The Rosary Evidence Guild was formed, and Father Reynold Hillenbrand, liturgical and social reformer in the Archdiocese of Chicago, gave instructions to the young women preparing for street preaching. Hillenbrand, who had completed his doctoral studies in 1931 and then spent time in Europe, where he was influenced by the efforts of Canon Joseph Cardijn "to reclaim disaffected workers for Christianity" (Avella, 33), had been deeply affected by the human tragedies he saw in Chicago's streets during the Great Depression of the 1930s. Hillenbrand saw personal mission as an answer to the social disorder caused by poverty and unemployment, and he advocated a social activism grounded in Catholic values. As a result of Hillenbrand's training, four Rosary College students traveled in July 1935 to southwestern Oklahoma, where they worked with local guild leaders and stood on street corners in small towns to preach the gospel. Groups of students continued to participate in guild activities in Oklahoma in subsequent years.

During Murphy's deanship and in the heady milieu of Catholic social action, Rosary College sponsored the first regional conference of the Catholic Association for International Peace (CAIP) on November 20, 1936; it featured an address by Eleanor Roosevelt and was attended by student representatives from the University of Notre Dame and St. Mary's College, South Bend, Indiana; Mundelein and St. Xavier colleges, Chicago; and Rosary College.

At the same time that the college encouraged the involvement of its students in social action, it also extended educational goals beyond its traditional community. In October 1934, in the depths of the Great Depression, Rosary College inaugurated "Education for Leisure," a free adult education program open to adults of all backgrounds and faiths. During the first year of the program, more than five hundred adults attended noncredit courses taught by Rosary College faculty in contemporary literature, English composition, conversational French or German, music, art, history, and government. One course dealt with the background and development of the New Deal.

While the 1930s were a period of diminished economic resources and growing international conflict, for Rosary College it was a time of development. Sister Evelyn Murphy, having initiated international study programs for college women, was active in national associations of higher learning—both Catholic and non-Catholic. In 1935 she was appointed to the Committee on the Financing of Catholic Colleges of the Department of Colleges, the National Catholic Education Association. She was one of eight sister administrators chosen from the entire country. The Sinsinawa Dominicans recognized her skill in administration, and in 1943, having served as president of Rosary College for six years, she was elected to the congregation's General Council. She advised and assisted Mother Samuel Coughlin in the administration of the religious community, which numbered more than fifteen hundred Catholic women religious, and its ministerial commitments. As a council member, she employed her European experience and fluency in Italian for the benefit of Rosary College. In 1941, steel magnate Myron Taylor donated his villa in Florence, Italy, to the Vatican, deeding it with the stipulation that it be used for educational purposes under the direction of the Sinsinawa Dominicans. This gift was the culmination of a long correspondence Taylor had with Sister Catherine Wall of the Rosary College art department, and after Wall's death with Mother Samuel Coughlin, about a foreign center for the study of art. From 1946 to 1947, Sister Murphy, representing the Sinsinawa Dominican Congregation, negotiated with the Roman authorities over the details of the transfer of ownership of Taylor's Villa Schifanoia to the Vatican. She returned to Sinsinawa in October 1947 at the conclusion of the negotiations. In October 1948, Pius XII Institute at the Villa Schifanoia opened for the study of music and the fine arts. Rosary College granted graduate students in this program the Master of Fine Arts degree and provided undergraduate and graduate women the opportunity for international study.

In 1949, the Sinsinawa Dominican General Chapter elected Sister Evelyn Murphy mother general of the congregation. During her six years in office, Mother Murphy directed the founding of twenty new schools throughout the United States. She approved the construction of Edgewood Campus School, Madison, Wisconsin, designed as a teacher training laboratory for the congregation's Edgewood College education program. Mother Murphy continued the congregation's historic commitment to the higher education of Sinsinawa Dominican sisters. During her term of office, sisters attended Catholic universities as well as many state universities (Wisconsin, Illinois, Michigan, Minnesota, Iowa, Wyoming) and private schools, including Northwestern University, the University of Chicago, Columbia University, the Juilliard School of Music, and the School of the Art Institute of Chicago.

As Mother General of a nationally known religious congregation, Mother Murphy addressed the first National Congress of Religious in the United States in 1952. In 1954, she presented a paper, "What Religious Communities of Teachers Expect of Diocesan Superintendents," to the National Catholic Education Association. She was, however, in failing health. Doctors at the Mayo Clinic, Rochester, Minnesota, had diagnosed Murphy with lymphosarcoma in 1951. In the next four years she endured numerous operations and cancer treatments. She died at St. Dominic Villa, Dubuque, Iowa, at age seventy-four.

For more than fifty-five years, Mother Evelyn Murphy was dedicated to the teaching mission of her congregation, beginning as a teacher of Latin, French, and English. At a time when relatively few women achieved careers in higher education or obtained advanced degrees, Murphy—a coal miner's daughter—expanded opportunities for international and national graduate and undergraduate education for women. In the 1920s she told a Rosary College student who was enrolled in the program at Fribourg, "To be educated is to be made whole" (quoted in "She Chose to Stand," *Rosary College Eagle*, Winter 1955, 11).

Sources. Mother Evelyn Murphy Papers, Sinsinawa Dominican Archives, Sinsinawa, Wisconsin, provide the details of her life and work. The archives also have the records of the Sinsinawa Dominican Sisters' ministry in the Chicago area, in the United States, and in Europe and South America. Issues of the *Rosary College Eagle* and *Annals*, a publication of the Rosary Convent, River Forest, Illinois, both available at the Sinsinawa Dominican Archives, reveal the rich intellectual and religious opportunities for college women. Particularly useful were the following issues of *Rosary College Eagle*: July 1930, February 1932, November 1934, February and April 1935, November 1936, April 1937, November 1938, and Winter 1955. Eva McCarty, *The Sinsinawa Dominicans: Outlines of Twentieth Century Development 1901–1949* (1952); Alice O'Rourke, *Let Us Set Out: Sinsinawa Dominicans, 1849–1985* (1986); and Steven M. Avella, *This Confident Church: Catholic Leadership and Life in Chicago, 1940–1965* (1992) provide historical context.

JANET WELSH

MYHRMAN, OTHELIA MÖRK
July 9, 1858–May 22, 1936
COMMUNITY LEADER, REFORMER, DIRECTOR OF
EMPLOYMENT BUREAU

Swedish American community activist Josefina Ottiliana Mörk, the seventh of Peter and Brita Maria (Nanfelt) Mörk's nine children, was born in Finspång, Sweden. Her father was a blacksmith. Planning to become a teacher, she studied under educator Anders Berg, advocate of modern, progressive methods and father of prominent Swedish educator and reformer Fridtjuv Berg. Her father's poor economic situation prevented her from pursuing a teaching career. As a result of diminished economic prospects in Sweden, her older siblings had migrated to the United States in search of work. Two sisters, Sofia and Charlotta, returned to Sweden for a visit in 1875. Ottiliana Mörk, working as a teacher's aid, decided that she, too, could find a more lucrative position in the United States and returned with them to Chicago. Now calling herself "Othelia," an Americanized version of her name, Mörk found work as a domestic servant as had so many other young Swedish women. Often living as roomers in boarding houses, they and other foreign-born single women were among the first group of unattached women inhabiting the fast-growing industrial cities in the United States. Among women reformers there was great concern for the working and living conditions of these young women workers, who were often exploited by their employers and even by some of their own countrymen who were interested in profiting from the

funneling of cheap labor to different industries and occupations. Experiencing the difficulties firsthand, Mörk joined with other Swedish immigrants in Chicago to improve the working conditions of Swedish domestics.

Othelia Mörk and her two sisters sent tickets to their mother, sister, and two brothers, who left Sweden in 1880 after the death of their father. The Mörk family was part of the great migration of Swedes to Chicago, whose Swedish population rose from nearly thirteen thousand in 1880 to forty-three thousand in 1890.

In 1883, at the age of twenty-six, Othelia Mörk married Gustaf Myhrman, a Swedish immigrant who was a talented woodworker. They remained childless. Othelia Myhrman ended her domestic employment and became active in the growing Swedish American community. During the 1890s, she and her husband were active in the International Order of Good Templars (IOGT), a temperance organization that was popular in Sweden and among Swedish immigrants in the United States.

The IOGT was to the political left of the American temperance organizations that focused upon urban saloons and on reforming immigrant workers' individual behavior. In contrast, the Swedish IOGT lodges placed the temperance problem in the context of larger economic and social issues, welcoming a free exchange of ideas on a variety of worker-related subjects, including socialism, unemployment, and oppression of the lower classes. The Myhrmans participated in these open, well-attended discussions, and Othelia Myhrman earned a reputation as a lecturer on temperance in Chicago and throughout the Midwest. In the 1890s, she represented Swedish lodges at International Grand Lodge meetings in Edinburgh, Zurich, and Boston, taking the more radical side of the issues, as instructed by the Swedish Templars, who disliked the conservatism of their American counterparts.

In 1890, Gustaf Myhrman was one of the founders of the Independent Order of Vikings, a Swedish men's fraternal lodge. When in December 1893 one of their members was shot and killed by two policemen without apparent provocation, Othelia and Gustaf Myhrman joined other Swedish American leaders in defense of Swedes. They formed the Swedish National Association (SNA) early in 1894 to protect Swedish Americans. SNA kept the issue before the public, and the city of Chicago prosecuted the two policemen who, in a precedent-setting verdict, were found guilty and sentenced to several years in prison.

Tensions in Chicago ran high, in part because of the severe economic depression that gripped the city by 1894. Beginning in the East in 1893, the depression's effects had been delayed in Chicago where the World's Columbian Exposition continued to sustain local employment. By 1894 the collapse of the American economy, with the concomitant layoff of hundreds of thousands of industrial workers and the reduction of wages for many others, resulted in the worst, most protracted depression the country had experienced. Workers needed assistance, and the SNA established the Swedish Free Employment Bureau in downtown Chicago. Othelia Myhrman was put in charge. She was an able administrator, and her bureau processed nearly one hundred persons every day, attempting to find jobs for Swedes in a shrinking labor market. Myhrman sought positions for

FIG. 82. *Club president Othelia Mörk Myhrman stands behind guest of honor Jane Addams, just awarded the Nobel Peace Prize, at the American Daughters of Sweden luncheon, 1932; seated, left to right, are C. Lundquist, consul of Sweden, Jane Addams, and Mrs. Charles Rasberg. Standing, left to right, are G. E. L. Johnson, Othelia Myhrman, and Olaf Bernts, Consul of Norway.*

Swedish workers in factories, hotels, private homes, and stores, but the most common placements were for general laborers and domestic servants. In order to continue the employment bureau's work, Myhrman organized fund-raising events, including such festivals as the traditional Swedish midsummer celebrations. Myhrman's booming voice, tall and commanding presence, keen organizational skills, and her habit of smoking cigarillos made a lasting impression, since few married Swedish women of her generation held such prominent public positions in the community. She was respected because her public work was organized benevolence, in keeping with the ideal role constructed for women.

Under Myhrman's leadership, the SNA maintained the employment bureau for eighteen years, finding employment for nearly one hundred thousand persons. When the bureau closed in 1912, Myhrman opened her own agency, calling it the Swedish National Employment Bureau, which she ran independently from the SNA. Myhrman promoted Swedish cultural activities in Chicago, devoting her last decade to the American Daughters of Sweden (ADS), which she helped establish on January 19, 1926; she served as president for ten years. ADS encouraged interest in Swedish culture and history, and especially the interests of Swedish American women. In 1931, the ADS endowed a scholarship fund at the University of Chicago for young women of Swedish descent who studied Swedish literature. The ADS later expanded to provide scholarships for students at Augustana College in Rock Island and North Park College, Chicago (later North Park University). Under Myhrman's leadership, ADS sponsored numerous cultural programs: a 1929 concert at the Civic Opera House,

cosponsored by the Swedish Glee Club featuring the Swedish tenor Folke Anderson, the first time that a foreign group used the auditorium; and Swedish Day participation at the Century of Progress Exposition in 1934 and 1935. In 1932, the ADS gave a luncheon to honor JANE ADDAMS, just awarded the Nobel Peace Prize. ADS also hosted visits by Crown Princess Louise of Sweden; Dr. Ann Wicksell, the Swedish representative to the League of Nations; and Anna Lena Elgstrom, Sweden's foremost woman literary critic.

Through the ADS, Myhrman also continued her assistance to needy Swedish immigrants and made donations to causes that helped the unemployed. On Myhrman's seventy-fifth birthday in July 1934, the ADS held a dinner in her honor. (In reality, this was her seventy-sixth birthday, but at some point during her career, she subtracted one year from her age.) She spent her last Christmas with ADS members, who gave her a monetary gift on behalf of the group. In January 1936, Myhrman herself organized a tenth anniversary celebration of the group's foundation. She attended her last ADS meeting on April 14, 1936, and although she did not preside, she was reelected to the position of president. She died in her Chicago home of stomach cancer, two months before her seventy-eighth birthday.

At the time of her death, Swedish newspapers hailed Othelia Myhrman as Chicago's best-known Swede. She was a proponent of Swedish culture and benevolent activities. In 1929 Myhrman was awarded the Vasa Medal of Honor by the king of Sweden for her work among Chicago Swedes.

Sources. Manuscript collections at the Swedish American Archives of Greater Chicago (SAA), located at North Park University, include papers from the Swedish National Association, the International Order of Good Templars, and most notably, the American Daughters of Sweden. Personal recollections were provided by Elin Burgeson Schunk in a letter to Anita R. Olson, May 9, 1994. Birth records for Josefina Ottiliana Mörk are found in *Risinge Parish Birth Records*, and her Swedish family information is located in *Risinge Parish Clerical Survey*, both found in the Provincial Archives of Vadstena, Sweden. The family's emigration records are found in *Göteborg Passenger Lists* (1875) and *Index of Emigrants from Östergötland 1851–1974* (Central Bureau of Statistics, Stockholm, Sweden). Information on Myhrman's teacher is found in *Svenska Män och Kvinnor I* (1942). Entries for Othelia Myhrman are included in Ernest W. Olson, ed., *History of Swedes in Illinois* (1908), and Ernest W. Olson, ed., *The Swedish Element in Illinois: Survey of the Past Seven Decades* (1917). Both can be found at the CHS, as can *Runrist-ningar: Independent Order of Vikings, 1890–1915* (1915) and newspaper articles "Free Swedish Employment Bureau," *CT*, January 20, 1896, and "Mrs. Myhrman, Swedish Leader, Is Dead at 76," *Chicago Sunday Tribune*, May 24, 1936. Myhrman's obituary in the Swedish American press, found in SAA, is "Et långt, verksamt liv för svenskheten är nu avslutat," *Svenska-Amerikaneren Tribunen*, May 28, 1936. For further information about the Swedish immigrant community in Chicago, see Ulf Beijbom, *Swedes in Chicago: A Demographic and Social Study of the 1846–1880 Immigration* (1971), and Anita R. Olson, "Swedish Chicago: The Extension and Transformation of an Urban Immigrant Community, 1880–1920" (Ph.D. diss., Northwestern Univ., 1990).

ANITA OLSON GUSTAFSON

n

NANCREDE, EDITH de
December 14, 1877–May 31, 1936
SETTLEMENT WORKER, THEATER DIRECTOR, DANCE
AND ART TEACHER

Edith de Nancrede, one of four daughters, was born in Philadelphia, Pennsylvania, to Charles Beylard Guerard and Alice Howard (Dunnington) de Nancrede. Her father, a prominent surgeon, moved the family to Ann Arbor, Michigan, in the early 1890s, when he took an appointment as professor of surgery at the University of Michigan. He later became dean of the medical school.

A student of the visual arts, for two years in the mid-1890s Edith de Nancrede studied painting in Rome, where she lived with her uncle, the Reverend Harry de Nancrede, rector of the American Episcopal Church. When she returned to the United States, she moved to Chicago to continue studying at the School of the Art Institute of Chicago (SAIC). While studying at SAIC she discovered Hull-House, where she began to volunteer. Founded by JANE ADDAMS and ELLEN GATES STARR in 1889, the social settlement was staffed by female and male reformers who had moved into an immigrant and working-class neighborhood to ameliorate the working and living conditions of Chicago's Near West Side. Central to its mission was a belief in the importance of cross-class and cross-cultural communication; with members of different groups placed in proximity to one another, new forms of democratic sociability could be developed.

By the time Nancrede arrived in 1897, Hull-House had expanded to four buildings—a physical complex that reflected the settlement's growing mission. Included were an art gallery, a coffeehouse and gymnasium, a children's nursery and kindergarten, as well as an additional floor built onto the original building to accommodate an increasing resident membership.

Initially working as a volunteer in 1897, Nancrede moved into one of Hull-House's newly renovated single rooms when her application for residency was accepted in 1898. She earned money for her room and board by teaching art at several North Shore private schools and later the University School for Girls, maintaining a balance of paid employment and volunteer settlement work until the end of her life. Nancrede's first responsibilities at Hull-House were to initiate programs for the Boys' Club, sharing the task of supervising 120 youngsters with several fellow residents. Such flexible groupings of young people—social clubs—were the central method by which Hull-House worked to build a relationship with its neighborhood. At times appealing to the civilizing function of art, at other times appealing to its role in forging community, Hull-House workers often organized artistic activities for these clubs—drawing, singing, painting, reading, and acting. From these initial endeavors, combined with the ingenuity of residents such as Nancrede, was born a far-ranging network of clubs integrating the arts and settlement sociability.

Though her training had been as a visual artist, Nancrede discovered that she preferred "to make pictures for the stage" ("Rites for Miss De Nancrede, Famed Hull House Worker," unidentified newspaper clipping, Jane Addams Memorial Collection [JAMC] Small Manuscripts Collection). Participating as an actress in several productions of the Hull-House Dramatic Association, she encouraged the Boys' Club members to begin an extensive program of theatrical productions soon after becoming involved with them. Serving as director, Nancrede staged diverse productions, including *Wat Tyler* (1902), *Julius Caesar* (1903), *Queen Esther* (1903), *William Tell* (1904), *A Midsummer Night's Dream* (1904), and *Le Bourgeois Gentilhomme* (1905). These productions made use of drama and other arts to achieve a variety of social and ideological aims—to encourage group cooperation, to acquaint young people with the works of high culture, to elicit children's interest and imagination through selected stories, to teach proper elocution and bodily comportment, and to draw on the boys' immigrant culture for theatrical inspiration. Nancrede's interdisciplinary artistic skills were vital to the success of these efforts; in addition to directing, she usually staged the choreography, created costumes, and designed and painted the scenery. Eventually the club's name was changed to the Hull-House Junior Dramatic Association, and later the Marionette Club.

The plays attracted a diverse audience, including people from the surrounding neighborhood, Hull-House financial supporters, and established theater critics, who learned to understand and articulate the underlying social function of this amateur theater group. In later years she identified "the almost unique power a dramatic club has of holding a group of people together from childhood, through adolescence, and into maturity" (Nancrede, "Dramatic Work at Hull House," 276).

Nancrede remained committed to the use of theater as a means of creating and maintaining social relationships and community. She distinguished her dramatics groups, whose members stayed together from childhood until young adulthood, from Hull-House's "more transient social groups" ("Dramatic Work at Hull House," 276), which did not have the power of drama to unite them. "It is the 'art' side that holds them when they grow older," she wrote Jane Addams. "No matter how good a time I give them socially, they would drift apart after they are grown up but for the plays" (Nancrede to Addams, August 13, 1931, JAMC).

Nancrede's artistic practice functioned at Hull-House not only as a means of creating internal group cohesion and expression but also as a way of facilitating communication and cooperation among the various activities and programs of the settlement. Maintaining that departmental isolation violated the settlement ideal, Addams, in the first issue of the *Hull-House Bulletin,* called for programming that integrated the settlement groups. One solution was the formation by the dramatics supervisor, Walter Pietsch, of the Hull-House Dramatic Association (later the Hull-House Players)—a troupe of the "best" actors selected from all of the young people's clubs and classes. Nancrede's approach was to create artistic and performance genres that drew from the skills of several disciplines, requiring students and members of each of these classes to work together.

An example of the interdisciplinary approach was the Hull-House production, directed by Edith de Nancrede, of *The Trolls' Holiday* in May 1905. Written by HARRIET MONROE—a short-term resident and Chicago poet, set to music by ELEANOR SMITH, and with a set designed by ENELLA BENEDICT and constructed in the Hull-House shops, the production elicited the cooperation of the settlement's art school, music school, shops, dramatic clubs, and the movement and gymnastic classes of MARY HINMAN and ROSE MARIE GYLES. Such collaborations, prompted initially by social ideals, also generated innovative aesthetic forms. The Hull-House Christmas Program, a prominent and well-attended settlement tradition, gained new life when Enella Benedict, Eleanor Smith, and Edith de Nancrede introduced the Christmas Tableaux—a performance form incorporating music, song, image, and narration to stage biblical stories. Later, they produced a series of Hull-House Cantatas that added mime and movement to the tableau structure, continuing to develop an interdisciplinary practice that was at once socially and artistically innovative.

Eventually, Nancrede and devoted youth from the neighborhood formed a network of social clubs that had dramatics as their central unifying theme. Each of these groups was mixed in gender and ethnicity, reflecting Hull-House's general move away from single sex and single nationality formations of community. Instead, age served as the principle of organization: six or more groups totaling 240 children ranging in age from four to thirty years. While the division by age originally evolved from practical concerns, new clubs often developed to accommodate older children's younger siblings. The age hierarchy also reflected an art-based theory of child development. Following prevalent developmental theories that defined the differing needs of children, youth, and adolescents, the activities and play curriculum of each group increased in complexity and sophistication as the participants grew older. Meanwhile, members of the older groups served as role models for the younger ones.

Nancrede's practice was to keep a group together as the participants matured, starting a new club with each emergent set of younger siblings and neighborhood children. These groups performed a range of productions—fairy stories, classics, Hull-House Cantatas, and contemporary plays such as George Bernard Shaw's *Arms and the Man* or Israel Zangwill's *The Melting Pot.* When Hull-House dance instructor Mary Hinman left the settlement, Nancrede took over dance and movement courses as well, incorporating folk dancing and rhythmic instruction into the activities of her social clubs and extending her own interdisciplinary repertoire as an artist and teacher.

After the death in 1924 of LAURA DAINTY PELHAM, director of the Hull-House Players, two of Nancrede's clubs combined into the Hull-House Actors Guild, emerging in the public eye as Hull-House's new prominent theater troupe.

Garnering a reputation within social service circles, Edith de Nancrede expressed her artistic philosophy and dramatic method in a number of venues—including Yale University's 1927 Drama Conference, the 1930 Midwest Conference on the Emotional Life of the Child, and her 1928 article in *Playground,* a social service magazine. In 1929, Nancrede and Gertrude Smith, of the Hull-House Music School, collaborated in writing a book of songs and dances especially designed for children, *Mother Goose Dances.*

While acknowledging that Hull-House produced professional performers such as Vincenzo Celli, a lead dancer at La Scala opera house in Milan, Nancrede wrote of her new methods "that it is impossible to judge of the results only [by] those who make a profession of some form of art" (Nancrede to Addams, August 13, 1931). Rather, she emphasized the impact aesthetic education had on other aspects of neighbors' lives—offering intellectual stimulus to young people who left school as well as increasing their motivation to return to night school. She also suggested that the arts and drama taught youths how to "move with grace and ease" ("Dramatic Work at Hull House," 277) and offered training in the "use of the voice, of pronunciation and diction" (p. 277). More often, however, she emphasized the arts as a tool in awakening the imaginative life of young people. Invoking Hull-House's interdisciplinary aesthetic program, she promoted the all-round artistic development of a young person, paralleling Friedrich Fröbel's (also Froebel) and John Dewey's theories on the importance of educating the whole child. Arguing, however, that "imitation destroys the power to create" ("Creative Possibilities of Art for Children," 309), she maintained that such an artistic plan should proceed as much as possible "through the medium of the child's own creative impulse" ("Creative Possibilities," 306) rather than from a rigid, prescribed curriculum. Nancrede also emphasized creative art's role as an emotional release for the young—noting its power of "freeing people from inhibitions and repressions" ("Creative Possibilities," 311). Stating that the "most outstanding and most diligent pupils are the so-called 'bad' children" (p. 307) and, furthermore, that "the boys enjoy the plays most intensely" (p. 307), she explained that this success and enthusiasm were because such children had "less opportunity for this emotional outlet in their daily lives" (p. 307). Finally, citing the longevity of her many social clubs, Nancrede emphasized the power of drama in creating and sustaining a group's feeling of cohesion and community. Admitting that the development of such enduring groups did need "continuity in direction" ("Dramatic Work at Hull House," 277), she said that such a requirement was not difficult for the settlement.

The groups were run in a democratic fashion; Nancrede found plays she thought fitted the club's interests and abilities, but the actors had the final word on whether to accept her choice. Chicago drama critic James O'Donnell Bennett wrote that Nancrede believed in the "amazing rightness" of the boys' "taste in choosing plays for performance" ("Music and Drama"). Nancrede's presence was influential, but she led by encouraging the actors to form their own interpretations of the characters they played. In addition, the dramatic groups were self-supporting and self-sufficient, selling tickets for their performances.

Edith de Nancrede exemplifies the impact a single individual could have on the lives of so many Hull-House residents and neighbors. Even in the daily world of residential living, Nancrede's presence contributed to the emotional bonds of friendship and mutual support that maintained the settlement, prompting other residents to organize birthday parties and celebrations that solidified the esprit de corps of the group of hardworking reformers. A woman who, as journalist and Hull-House resident Francis Hackett recalled, was "skilled in vanishing from the successes she contrived" ("Hull-House—A Souvenir," 275), Nancrede focused her energies on local efforts in the Hull-House community. When she died—one year after Jane Addams and in the midst of rehearsing *The Three Musketeers*—young people from her clubs acted as pallbearers and delivered the eulogy, conveying to an assembled audience of notable Chicagoans that "to us, she is Hull-House" (Clippings, "Notes for Eulogy," JAMC Small Manuscript Collection). They had relied on her to be a "counselor all the time" and to "live, play, and rejoice with us" (Clippings, "Notes for Eulogy") on a daily basis.

Sources. Documents relating to Edith de Nancrede's life, including newspaper clippings, can be found in the Jane Addams Memorial Collection and the Small Manuscripts Collection, UIC Spec. Coll. Most references to her work will be found in the "Theatre at Hull-House" categories of the collection and throughout the *Hull-House Bulletin* and *Hull-House Yearbook* from 1902 to 1933. Her own statements about Hull-House and the arts were published in her articles, "Dramatic Work at Hull House," *Playground*, August 1928, and "Creative Possibilities of Art for Children," *The Child's Emotions. Proceedings of the Mid-West Conference on Character Development, February, 1930* (1930). With Gertrude Smith, Nancrede wrote *Mother Goose Dances* (1940). The most complete documentation of her work can be found in Stuart Joel Hecht, "Hull-House Theatre: An Analytical and Evaluative History" (Ph.D. diss., Northwestern Univ., 1983). See also James O'Donnell Bennett, "Music and Drama," *Chicago Record-Herald*, March 6, 1906, and Francis Hackett, "Hull-House—A Souvenir," *Survey*, June 1, 1925.

SHANNON JACKSON

NATKIN, ESTHER WEINSHENKER
March 4, 1877–1928
COMMUNITY ORGANIZER, CLUBWOMAN

Esther Weinshenker Natkin, an advocate for Chicago's Eastern European Jewish immigrant community and a founding director of the Chicago Hebrew Institute, was born in Moghilev, Russia. One of fourteen children of Tobias and Elka (Markman) Weinshenker, and among their ten children who immigrated to the United States, Esther Weinshenker came to Chicago with her family in 1887. Tobias Weinshenker worked briefly in the Chicago stockyards before he found employment in a mattress company, ultimately saving enough money to open his own business. He eventually achieved considerable financial success and was well known in Chicago as a Hebrew scholar and generous sponsor of other Russian Jews seeking entrance to the United States. His philanthropic reach extended to scholarship funds, Zionist organizations, and a variety of Jewish communal organizations, including those serving orphans, the elderly, and the impoverished immigrant Near West Side community. Tobias and Elka Weinshenker created a traditional Jewish home that was considered a hub of Chicago's intellectual Zionist community and the frequent destination for visiting Jewish dignitaries. Esther Weinshenker's energetic style and volunteer work in the public arena both emerged from and enhanced her family's commitment to the Zionist ideal—the dream that the Jewish people would one day reclaim a homeland.

Esther Weinshenker attended Chicago public schools and graduated from business college. Engaged throughout her adult life in informal study, she was an avid reader and autodidact, whose wit, logic, and self-confidence were admired by contemporaries. In 1903, she was elected to the board of directors of the National Council of Jewish Women's (NCJW) Chicago section. Among the leaders of this primarily German-Jewish organization were HANNAH SOLOMON and SADIE AMERICAN, who were active in the Reform branch of Judaism and participants in the broader women's political culture of Chicago during the Progressive Era. Weinshenker's election to the board of the Chicago section signified her talent to lead, even within a group whose membership and mission were different from her Orthodox Jewish religious affiliation and Eastern European background.

Her work with the Chicago NCJW brought her into the arena of reform; her philanthropy and affiliation with charitable endeavors focused her attention on the plight of recent Jewish immigrants. Interested in the welfare of the Eastern European immigrants on the city's Near West Side, Weinshenker collaborated with Julian Mack, MINNIE LOW, and other community leaders who were organizing the Juvenile Protective Association (JPA) in 1904. They, along with a network of Hull-House women, Chicago Woman's Club members, and other community leaders from various ethnic groups, as well as professionals from the legal system and the schools, were concerned about the alarming incidence of juvenile crime in poor and immigrant neighborhoods. Julian W. Mack, a judge of the children's court, and Minnie Low, a probation officer and social worker, were leaders in Jewish communal affairs as well as reformers of the juvenile court system. JPA, a small organization at its start, by 1907 had combined its prevention work with the Juvenile Court Committee, an association initiated to support the earliest efforts to establish and implement the new juvenile court system in Chicago from 1899. The enlarged JPA had the support of LOUISE deKOVEN BOWEN and other community leaders, and its twenty-two officers met at Hull-House weekly with their executive committee to discuss conditions influencing the lives of children and adolescents.

Soon after she began her work with the JPA, Weinshenker wrote her first strong defense of the growing Eastern European Jewish population on Chicago's Near West Side, attempting to correct the negative image of the immigrant community held by its harshest critics, many of whom were members of the city's upper-class and middle-class German Jewish community. Having arrived in Chicago in the mid-nineteenth century, prior to the massive waves of immigration of Eastern European Jews in the 1880s, 1890s, and 1900s, German Jews often brought professional and mercantile skills, substantial savings, and family connections that assured their prosperity and successful assimilation in America. Many became alarmed by the prospect of needing to provide financial support for the growing numbers of impoverished Eastern European immigrants. Among the German Jews were individuals who felt embarrassed by the possibility of being associated with the newcomers and who feared identification in the public eye with the Old World appearance, Yiddish language, and Orthodox religious practices of the Eastern Europeans. Conversely, the immigrants from Russia scarcely recognized the Reform religious practice of the German Jews and deeply resented the patronizing attitude that permeated the relief efforts of the more established community. Weinshenker spoke forthrightly about the hostility between the two communities, writing across the cultural gap in an impassioned letter in which she decried the harsh critic who "places all Russian immigrants in the category of beggars . . . who have never tasted of a decent meal until tasting of the hand of charity" ("A Jewish Center in Chicago," *Reform Advocate*). The *Reform Advocate* was the newspaper popular among Chicago's German Jews. In its pages, Weinshenker described the tradition of education and refined culture that many Eastern European immigrants brought to America, and she attempted to dislodge the notion that they all arrived as paupers. She challenged the city's German Jews not only to recognize the poverty and hardships facing the new immigrants but to value as well their rich heritage and determination to succeed in America. In an eloquent description of the proposed permanent home for the Chicago Hebrew Institute, she envisioned the variety of benefits a social and educational center would extend to the diverse, lively community on the Near West Side.

On September 17, 1905, she married Isidor (Isadore) Natkin, with whom she had one son, Herzl Weinshenker

Natkin. The couple shared many interests, particularly Zionism, and Natkin enjoyed her husband's support for her extensive involvement in the community.

Two years later, she was named to the advisory committee of the Chicago Hebrew Institute (CHI), encouraged by one of its founders, Nathan Kaplan, to lend her talents to the multidimensional Near West Side social center that she had so eloquently advocated. The CHI, first housed in 1903 in rented quarters near Maxwell Street's immigrant district, moved to a more substantial building in 1907.

In April 1907, Natkin refined her position on the relationship of the two Jewish communities in an address she delivered at Chicago Sinai Congregation, the leading Reform temple in Chicago, to an audience of predominantly German Jewish women, most of whom were members of the NCJW. Her lecture, "The Philanthropic Activities of the West Side" (later known as the Near West Side), detailed in chronological order the many social institutions that Eastern European Jews had successfully organized and financed through their own steady, though necessarily small, contributions. She repeatedly emphasized the commitment within the traditional community, particularly among its women, to assess and support its own needs independent of outside charity societies. One by one she listed Near West Side agencies—among them a shelter for homeless immigrants, food pantries, schools, a home for the aged, an orphanage, and the Women's (interest free) Loan Association—all the result of the "collection boxes receiving mostly nickels and smaller coins" (*Jewish Star*, April 13, 1907) from the poor but devoted families in her community. In her ability to confront and dispel the conventional stereotype of immigrants as passive beggars draining the resources of the city and the established Jewish communal societies, Natkin shifted the focus from the immigrants' disabilities to a celebration of their collective resources. This theme continued to appear in Natkin's speeches and writings.

Natkin's 1907 NCJW speech at Chicago Sinai Congregation typified the talent and insight she brought to public life. Her compassion for the ordinary people of the Near West Side neighborhood, her in-depth knowledge of the community's organizational life, and her determination to portray and defend her community to its worst critics revealed her energetic style of participation in community affairs. She understood that her speech, delivered at a time when Eastern European Jewish immigration to this country was high, defended a growing immigrant population that her audience undoubtedly feared and resented. She proudly recounted traditional religious and cultural practices to an audience of German Jewish women who heard in her speech, perhaps for the first time, a rich account of the immigrant community's internal resources and financial independence.

Esther Natkin committed her most intensive leadership endeavors to the Chicago Hebrew Institute. She served on the CHI's board of directors for ten years beginning in 1905. In 1910 she helped organize the Institute Woman's Club, the female auxiliary responsible for raising funds to support a piano school, provide religious festivities for the children, and, in 1913, organize the CHI's response to Christian missionary efforts among Jewish children on the Near West Side. Natkin served as secretary and president of the Institute Woman's Club board for five years, beginning in 1913. In that capacity she helped to develop the rich variety of CHI's social events, including plays, chaperoned dances, and Jewish holiday celebrations. She was also a member and secretary of the Institute Players' Club, a performing group that presented fully staged theater productions, sponsored music and drama classes, and raised scholarship funds for students.

Natkin also organized the early efforts among women in Chicago in support of Zionist causes. She served as president and treasurer of the Clara de Hirsch Gate, Chicago's young women's society associated with the Knights of Zion. During the group's meeting on October 25, 1913, Henrietta Szold, the founder of Hadassah in 1912, introduced Chicago's Zionist women to her organization's dual mission: promoting the Jewish education of Jewish women and providing material support to public health nurses in Palestine. Soon the Hadassah organization would focus on building a hospital in Palestine. Natkin helped reorganize the women of the Clara de Hirsch Gate as the Clara de Hirsch Chapter of Hadassah, and by December 1913, she received a letter from Szold congratulating her on the Chicago chapter's membership growth.

Despite criticism from those who felt little sympathy for her pioneering Zionist endeavors, Natkin remained a respected civic leader who participated in a broad variety of Jewish organizations. In 1913, for example, she joined forces with the Anti Stage-Jew Vigilance Committee, an eclectic group of Chicago Jewry including Jacob M. Loeb, who served on the Chicago Board of Education; Ernest Freund, a professor of jurisprudence and public law interested in immigration; and Hannah G. Solomon, past president of the NCJC and board member of the Associated Jewish Charities and the Illinois Federation of Women's Clubs. They organized to protest stereotypical portrayals of Jews in Chicago's professional theater.

Natkin considered the volunteer work of women essential to the life and development of the CHI and other community institutions. She credited the broad vision, energy, and political voice of women with improved social welfare institutions. She also understood that club work offered women the opportunity to leave the confines of home in order to learn together, organize collectively, and enhance their position in the public domain. She wrote that "organized womanhood bonded together to protest against [the] mental slavery in which women were held until recent years. Posterity will point to the club woman as the Emancipator of her sex" (handwritten ms., n.t., n.d., n.p., Natkin Papers). She considered the club a training ground, the school and bureau of information for women's advancement and heightened competence in life beyond the domestic realm.

In the 1920s, Natkin's contribution to the Jewish community was acknowledged. Her extensive work with the American Jewish Congress culminated in her election as a Chicago delegate to the national convention in 1923. Of the forty candidates running as delegates from Chicago, Esther Natkin was one of five women nominated.

Her husband, Isadore Natkin, died on September 17, 1923. Natkin continued her work and remained a strong defender of the Near West Side Jewish community. She continued her involvement with the Chicago Hebrew Institute, which had by 1922 outgrown its initial mission. As immigration waned and the community achieved more middle-class status, CHI became one of the most influential social centers and acquired a new name, the Jewish People's Institute. Ironically, the rapid success of the first generation of immigrants and their children brought the Jewish community another set of problems. Natkin was aware of the pitfalls of social mobility. In 1923, she criticized those Eastern European immigrants who succeeded financially and were able to move out of the old neighborhood. With characteristic insight and frankness, she underscored the social and financial achievements of her community while simultaneously voicing its collective resentment toward Eastern European immigrants who had managed to do well in the world but "instead of paying back to the community in some small measure what it has done for them . . . forget their heritage" ("In Defense of the 'West Side'").

In 1928, following a sudden and brief illness, Esther Natkin died at the age of fifty-one. In her memory, the women of the Lawndale Junior Hadassah unanimously voted to rename their chapter Esther Natkin Junior Hadassah of Lawndale.

Esther Natkin had an impressive career as a volunteer activist and communal leader in Chicago's Jewish community. As one of the first women in Chicago to promote Zionist causes, she launched her lifelong commitment to American Zionism when, as a young woman, she affiliated with the national Federation of American Zionists and the local Order of the Knights of Zion. As a Russian immigrant and activist in the Near West Side community and concurrently a respected member of the preeminent German Jewish women's organization, the National Council of Jewish Women, Natkin stood in two worlds. Capable of walking between the two communities, Natkin forged a style of leadership that managed to maintain close emotional and pragmatic connections within her own community while building networks of influence and friendship with German Jews.

Sources. Esther Natkin's papers—letters, unpublished writings, and newspaper articles—are in the Chicago Jewish Archives, Asher Library, Spertus Institute of Jewish Studies. Issues of the *Chicago Hebrew Institute Observer*, which record much of Natkin's contribution to the organization, are at the CHS. Among Natkin's published articles are "A Jewish Center in Chicago," *Reform Advocate*, April 8, 1905, and "In Defense of the 'West Side,'" *Chicago Jewish Chronicle*, July 13, 1923. Natkin's speech to the Chicago section of the Council of Jewish Women is reported in "Chicago Section—Council of Jewish Women," *Jewish Star*, April 13, 1907. Esther Natkin is mentioned in Hyman L. Meites, ed., *History of the Jews of Chicago* (1924, reprinted 1990), and Philip P. Bregstone, *Chicago and Its Jews: A Cultural History* (1933).

KATHI M. LIEB

NELSON ROLLINS, IDA GRAY
March 4, 1867–May 3, 1953
DENTIST

In 1895, Ida Gray Nelson was the first African American woman to establish a dental practice in Chicago. Very little is known of her childhood and family, and she never explained the career choice she made despite prejudice against both Blacks and professional women. According to her report in 1910 to the alumni office at the University of Michigan, she was born in Clarksville, Tennessee, the daughter of Jennie Gray John. Ten years later, she wrote that her birth year was 1870 and her birthplace Cincinnati, Ohio.

She graduated from high school in Cincinnati, then entered Ann Arbor College (Ann Arbor, Michigan), receiving a B.S. degree in 1887. Gray found a mentor in Dr. Jonathan Taft, the founding dean at the dental school of the University of Michigan, who had a practice in Cincinnati. Taft encouraged women to become dentists and in 1859 had hired an apprentice, Lucy Hobbs, who became the first woman in the world to complete academic dental training, at the Ohio College of Dentistry in 1866. Gray later reported that she had become interested in dentistry as a career and had worked for Taft.

She entered the University of Michigan Dental School in 1887, with Taft recorded as her preceptor. When Gray completed training in 1890, she had the dual distinction of being the first African American woman graduate of the school and the first black woman in the country to receive a D.D.S. degree. She joined more than 1,330 women dentists in the United States.

Gray returned to Cincinnati, where she practiced general dentistry. She seemed to have a pleasing manner with patients. A newspaper editor, writing about Gray, said, "Her blushing, winning ways makes [sic] you feel like finding an extra tooth anyway to allow her to pull" (quoted in Salem, 211). She believed that children liked "motherly dentists" and that women avoided dentistry as a profession because of "their horror of hurting patients by extraction" ("Lady Dentist," 40).

In 1895 she married James Sanford Nelson, an attorney and accountant. He would later serve as captain and quartermaster in the Chicago Black Illinois Army unit called the "Famed Eighth Regiment" and fight in the Spanish-American War (Driskell, 11).

Ida and James Nelson moved to Chicago, where she established a general dental practice in the South Side area known as the Black Belt. She later opened a second office on the South Side and had a racially mixed practice. This area had been settled almost entirely by African Americans who had come from the South in order to find work in Chicago following the Civil War.

She was one of a small number of black dentists in Chicago. The first African American dentist, James H. Smith, father of composer FLORENCE PRICE, came just before the Great Fire of 1871. In 1890, only one other black dentist, Charles Edwin Bentley, had a practice in Chicago. Even as other African American dental professionals opened offices, Ida Nelson remained the only black woman dentist. Nelson came to Chicago at a time when some women, both African American and white, were breaking away from stereotypic female roles to enter male-dominated professions.

Pleased to see other women move into the profession, Nelson became mentor to one of her patients, Olive M. Henderson, who, inspired by Nelson, entered dental school. Henderson started a practice in 1912, the second African American woman dentist in Chicago.

James Nelson died in 1926. Three years later, Ida Nelson married William A. Rollins and made her professional name Ida Nelson Rollins, D.D.S. He died in 1938. She had no children in either marriage.

Further information is not available on Nelson Rollins's personal and professional life or on possible community or organizational involvements. She continued to live in Chicago until her death at the age of eighty-seven. She was buried in Lincoln Cemetery, Blue Island, Illinois. Her contemporaries, aware of her achievement, placed on her gravestone the words, "Dr. Ida Gray Nelson Rollins, First Negro Woman Dentist in America" (quoted in Salem, 211).

Sources. The records of Ann Arbor College are at the Univ. of Michigan Library. Biographical information on Nelson Rollins is found in Charles C. Kelsey, "Ida Gray, Class of 1890," *School of Dentistry Alumni Bulletin,* University of Michigan, 1977–78; Vivian Ovelton Sammons, "Ida Gray Nelson," *Blacks in Science and Medicine* (1990); and Dorothy C. Salem, ed., "Ida Gray," *African American Women: A Biographical Dictionary* (1993). Nelson Rollins is mentioned in "Lady Dentist," *Ebony,* no. 10, 1946. For background information on black dentists in Chicago, see Claude Evans Driskell, *Chicago Black Dental Professionals 1850–1983 [sic]* (1982).

ALETHA A. KOWITZ

NESTOR, AGNES
June 24, 1880–December 28, 1948
TRADE UNION ORGANIZER, POLITICAL ACTIVIST

Agnes Nestor was a founder and officer of the International Glove Workers' Union of America and president of the Chicago Women's Trade Union League for three decades. She made significant contributions to the lives of working women in Chicago, Illinois, and the nation through union organizing, lobbying for protective labor legislation for women and children, and serving on state and national advisory bodies.

Nestor was born in Grand Rapids, Michigan, to Thomas and Anna (McEwen) Nestor. She was their third child and second daughter. Her mother had been born in upstate New York and her father in Maryland. The Nestors were Roman Catholics who identified strongly with their Irish heritage. Nestor attended both public and parochial grammar schools, but not continuously, as her health was often poor. In Grand Rapids, her father worked as a machinist, later owned a grocery store, and was elected alderman for two terms, then city marshall. Thomas Nestor served as assistant city treasurer but was defeated when he ran for sheriff. Out of political office and without his store, he could not find work at his craft during the depression of the 1890s. Searching for greater opportunity, he moved his family to Chicago in 1897.

This move ended Agnes Nestor's schooling at the eighth grade, and she began her life as a working woman. When they arrived in Chicago, Nestor, aged seventeen, and her older sister, Mary, went to work to help out the family. The family settled on the North Side of Chicago, and the young women found jobs near home at the Eisendrath Glove Company. Nestor was proud of her skill as a glove maker, and this ability became the basis of her trade union philosophy. She championed craft unions, not industry-wide ones.

During her twentieth year Nestor kept a diary that revealed the tenor of her daily life as a Chicago working girl. Nestor had a close circle of friends and loved the theater and shopping. Her work was exhausting, but the young women socialized and

FIG. 83. *Agnes Nestor, president of the Chicago Women's Trade Union League for three decades.*

the next year they formed Local No. 2 under Nestor's leadership. Nestor saw separate locals as necessary not only because women and men did different jobs but also because in mixed locals men dominated the leadership positions and decision-making. Although she worked in many organizations with men, Nestor believed that women's voices and influence could prevail only in their own institutions.

In 1902 Nestor was a delegate from Local No. 2 to the founding convention of the International Glove Workers' Union of America (IGWU). Because of her talents as an organizer and negotiator, she became one of the few women in national leadership of the trade union. She was third vice-president and a member of the executive board of the IGWU from 1903 to 1906; secretary-treasurer, a paid, full-time position, 1906–13; and president from 1913 to 1916. Thereafter, she remained vice-president until 1939. The union brought improvements for all glove workers through higher piece rates, the abolition of extra charges for power and needles, and special rates for overtime work. Nestor believed that the higher overtime rates were particularly important, as they virtually abolished overly long hours that destroyed women's health. Nestor's own health was weakened by overwork, and she suffered periodically from physical breakdowns.

Nestor thought all working women deserved a decent standard of living and respect as workers. Achieving these goals depended on equal pay for equal work for women and men, a living wage for an eight-hour day, and leisure for education and enjoyment. This vision led her to the Women's Trade Union League (WTUL), founded in 1903 to bring trade union women and allies from the middle and upper classes together to promote trade union organization among women workers. Early WTUL members included leading settlement house head residents JANE ADDAMS and MARY McDOWELL as well as trade unionists MARY KENNEY O'SULLIVAN and Leonora O'Reilly. Nestor joined the Chicago branch in its first year, 1904. She was elected to the executive board of the national WTUL in 1906 and became the first president of the Chicago branch from the ranks of the working class in 1913, following the presidencies of McDowell and social reformer MARGARET DREIER ROBINS. Nestor retained both positions until her death. With WTUL and union responsibilities, she gave up working as a glove maker in 1906.

Nestor organized working women in many localities and industries, including garment makers, clerks, and hospital workers. In Chicago in 1911, Nestor aided Margaret Dreier Robins, then president of the Chicago WTUL, and union organizers Sidney Hillman and Bessie Abramowitz (see BESSIE ABRAMOWITZ HILLMAN), in leading the first large strike of garment workers. The resulting contract with the firm of Hart, Schaffner and Marx became the basis for union-employer bargaining in the industry.

Nestor also became a champion of legislation to help working women. She campaigned for woman suffrage in Illinois from 1909 to 1913 to advance the cause of working women. In her article, "The Working Girl's Need for Suffrage," Nestor explained that working women needed the ballot to make full use of their citizenship and to improve their conditions of work, securing proper laws for their health and safety. "A new spirit for

helped each other produce their quotas. They worked at least ten hours a day for piece rates. They also had to pay for the power for their machines and any needles that broke. The women often protested against wage cuts and unfair policies by going on strike. By 1898 Agnes Nestor was leading those strikes and, by 1901, along with some men glove makers, seeking to organize a union.

Agnes Nestor's militancy was not simply a reaction to the loss of a comfortable childhood but was grounded in her parents' experiences and beliefs. Anna Nestor's health was ruined by child labor; by age ten she was orphaned and working in a cotton textile mill. Thomas Nestor was a member of the Knights of Labor and a machinist's union. He was on strike several times during the year his daughter kept her diary. Both parents encouraged and supported Nestor's activities, and she credited her father with helping her to understand parliamentary procedure.

Chicago's glove makers formed Glove Makers Local No. 1 in 1901 after a successful strike during which Nestor led the women operators. The latter wanted their local, however, and work and an added sense of power to bring about justice will come to every woman through full enfranchisement" (quoted in Mason, 188). In 1909 she joined other Chicago union women lobbying the Illinois state legislature to limit working hours for women to eight hours a day. Despite strenuous opposition from manufacturers, the lobbyists succeeded in getting a compromise ten-hour law for women factory workers.

Two years later, lobbyists were able to broaden the law's coverage to women in mercantile and service work. Nestor's reputation for being politically very shrewd arose from this successful lobbying effort, but the shorter hours movement lost momentum thereafter. Nestor and her Chicago League allies never gave up lobbying in each session of the state legislature until an eight-hour law for women passed in 1937.

One of the most important goals of the WTUL was the education of the woman worker in two related ways: teaching women to be activists in the work place and teaching women English. The Chicago WTUL had inaugurated English classes for immigrant women workers in 1908. These were taught by volunteers from the Chicago Federation of Teachers. After the garment strikes from 1909 to 1911, the league heightened its efforts to teach women English in their own homes. When Agnes Nestor became president of the Chicago branch, the labor situation called for more trained women organizers. Working with the national WTUL, whose headquarters had been moved permanently to Chicago, Nestor established a new Training School for Women Organizers in 1914, dividing the student's time between class time and fieldwork. There were two students enrolled for the first year and they attended courses on trade union organizing, industrial organization, labor history, public speaking, bookkeeping, and writing. Agnes Nestor and MARY ANDERSON directed their fieldwork, which consisted of participating in union meetings and learning from union leaders about the process of grievances, strikes, initiating new members, and negotiating with employers. The school was the first full-time labor school in the United States. As head of the Chicago Federation of Labor's Committee for its Chicago Trade Union College, Nestor expanded this program to men as well as women.

Nestor's interest in public school education led to her first appointment to a national advisory body; in 1909 she served on a committee of the American Federation of Labor (AFL) to consider the place of vocational education in the public schools. Like other AFL leaders, Nestor rejected the German system of separate vocational and liberal education, because she believed that it led to rigid class distinctions. Locally, in 1913, the Commercial Club of Chicago, an association of leading manufacturers and businessmen, proposed that the Chicago Board of Education implement a program whereby 90 percent of the city's children after the eighth grade would study only vocational subjects. Agnes Nestor opposed the plan, explaining that it would deny "all opportunity for cultural development" (quoted in Payne, 85). In 1914 President Woodrow Wilson named her to the federal Commission on Vocational Education that shaped the Smith-Hughes Act of 1917, providing the first federal aid to vocational education. Nestor countered conservatives on the commission who sought to exclude women from industry and assured that the act included support for women's education in fields other than domestic science.

Nestor's effectiveness in dealing with politicians and the general public was enhanced by her physical appearance, which conformed to the popular image of the working woman as a young, and hence unthreatening, girl. She was five feet tall, slim, blue-eyed, and fair. An admiring article by Octavia Roberts in *American Magazine* in 1912 described her as "a gray-eyed sweet faced little working girl," after the thirty-one-year-old labor leader had successfully countered lobbying by Illinois Manufacturers Association and the Chamber of Commerce in the state legislature. Nestor was quite aware of how her appearance belied her competence and allowed this image to go uncontested.

Nestor never married, but she left no record of the reasons for her choice. Her diary, autobiography, and correspondence revealed little of her emotions or motivation. She lived with her parents and siblings until the former died and then continued to make a home with her sister Mary, who was her best friend, and her younger brother, Owen. Their Irish Catholic heritage supported celibacy as an option, and all remained single. Nestor had made many women friends in her work, including ELISABETH CHRISTMAN, Margaret Dreier Robins, Mary McDowell, ELIZABETH MALONEY, and Mary Anderson, but her family was most important to her. Upon her death, a close family friend wrote to her sister and brother, "Agnes led an exemplary Christian life, her God and you two were her genuine loves" (Edward Flanigan, December 29, 1948, 2).

As a Roman Catholic, Agnes Nestor also worked on labor issues through church-affiliated groups. She was chair of the Committee on Women in Industry of the National Council of Catholic Women and vice-president of the Catholic Conference on Industrial Problems. In Chicago she encouraged the founding of the De Paul Day Nursery and Social Center in 1915 to provide day care for children of working mothers and arranged the donation of a suitable building to the Daughters of Charity, who staffed the service. In recognition of her achievements for working women and because her life was "animated by the highest Christian idealism" ("Agnes Nestor" Candidates for the Degree of Laws, *Commencement Program*, 18), Nestor was awarded an honorary degree of doctor of laws by Loyola University Chicago in 1929.

Unlike many women reformers who were from middle-class Protestant and Republican backgrounds, Nestor's working-class Irish Catholic parents bequeathed to her a loyalty to the Democratic Party. She refused to join other reformers supporting Republican Theodore Roosevelt as the Progressive Party candidate for president in 1912. She explained in her autobiography that she "was not so sure the Progressives would protest against industrial conditions" (*Woman's Labor Leader*, 135). As one of the few women who was a national-level union official and a loyal Democrat, Nestor was appointed to governmental advisory boards whenever the Democrats were in power.

During World War I, when the government encouraged women to take new jobs in industry, Nestor was called to Washington and served on several commissions to coordinate the war effort, most notably as the only woman on a seven-member advisory council to the Secretary of Labor to establish the wartime labor boards that structured labor-management relations. After the war, she worked to create the Women's Bureau in the Department of Labor in 1920 and to appoint as its head Mary Anderson, longtime WTUL activist whose position on women's issues reflected Nestor's. The Bureau took the lead in investigating and encouraging women's participation in the paid labor force.

Since 1910 Samuel Gompers, president of the AFL, had been forming alliances with anti-socialist elements in the labor community. Nestor's connections with moderate Roman Catholic labor leaders made her a useful ally, and Gompers enlisted Nestor in this campaign during the war, appointing her to the 1918 American labor mission to England and France. This group attempted to rally the noncommunist international labor movement on the basis of President Wilson's program for postwar peace. Nestor had working meetings with heads of state and European labor leaders and also enjoyed sightseeing and visits to American troops in France.

At the end of the war Nestor returned to Chicago and continued her work organizing, lobbying, and educating. When the city's leading glove manufacturers joined the open shop campaign and abrogated union contracts, Nestor formed a Cooperative Glove Association of Chicago among workers in the trade. She headed the cooperative from 1921 to 1925, but it could not compete successfully with older firms and failed. Nestor was assistant director of the Bryn Mawr Summer School for Women Workers in 1922 and 1923. She even entered politics in support of the eight-hour law for women workers. In 1928 she ran unsuccessfully in the Democratic primary for the state legislature against an incumbent who refused to support the protective law.

Nestor's activities continued to be shaped by the views of women, labor, and society she had formed in her youth. She opposed the National Woman's Party and the Equal Rights Amendment (ERA) introduced in 1923 because of the threat she believed they posed to protective legislation for working women. Her craft-union philosophy and her ties to the AFL leadership led Nestor to resist Sidney Hillman's call for the glove makers to join the Amalgamated Clothing Workers of America in the breakaway Congress of Industrial Organizations (CIO) in 1937. Although a majority of the International Glove Workers' Union (IGWU) voted to join the Amalgamated and her friend Elisabeth Christman sided with the majority, Nestor balked. She contributed to the bitter fight between the AFL and the CIO by forming a dual union, the IGWU-AFL, that had strength in the Midwest.

During the depression of the 1930s, when the Democrats were once more in power, Nestor was again active in governmental bodies. She helped write and enforce codes for the glovemaking industry for the National Recovery Administration and served on many state and local commissions dealing with unemployment. Nestor also took a wider role in city affairs, serving on the Chicago Recreation Commission (1934), the Advisory Committee of the Chicago Planning Commission (1939), and the Board of Trustees of Chicago's Century of Progress Exposition (1933–34).

In the 1940s, as her health deteriorated, Nestor concentrated on writing and education. As director of research and education for the IGWU-AFL, she wrote a *Brief History of the International Glove Workers' Union of America* in 1942. In 1944 she taught at the Institute on Industry sponsored by the National Council of Catholic Women and the Social Action Department of the National Catholic Welfare Conference. She also wrote an autobiography, published in 1954 as *Woman's Labor Leader*. In 1946, Nestor was diagnosed with rheumatic fever, and she had surgery in 1948. After a three-month illness, she died in Chicago and was buried in Mt. Carmel Cemetery.

Agnes Nestor was honored in her lifetime for her achievements for women, working people, and the union movement. Her successful public life was a model of what women could accomplish in the early twentieth century—if they remained single and childless. She supported equality for women in both the civic and economic realms, but, as was common then, she believed these ends necessitated special legislation protecting women as well as women's self-organization.

Sources. Agnes Nestor's papers, including her diary, correspondence to her, and a small number of letters by her, are at the CHS. A letter in the papers from Edward L. Flanigan to Mary and Owen Nestor, December 29, 1948, describes Nestor's personality and praises her work. Other correspondence is scattered in various collections of papers of the Women's Trade Union League. These have been microfilmed as the *Papers of the Women's Trade Union League and Its Principal Leaders* (1981) and are available at the CHS. The *Guide* to the microfilm edition has an excellent biographical note on Nestor, including an extensive bibliography. *The Program of the Fifty-Ninth Annual Commencement of Loyola University of Chicago June 12, 1929* (1929), at the Loyola Univ. of Chicago Archives, includes a description of her achievements. Nestor's autobiography, *Woman's Labor Leader* (1954), is an important source but must be checked for accuracy against earlier documents. Nestor says her father was born in County Galway, Ireland, but her siblings' birth certificates and the manuscript of the 1900 U.S. census list his birthplace as Maryland. Nestor occasionally wrote articles for trade union and social service publications; most useful for her life and ideas is "The Experiences of a Pioneer Woman Trade Unionist," *American Federationist*, March 1929. Nestor's public image during her early years is revealed in Octavia Roberts, "Agnes Nestor," *American Magazine*, vol. 73, 1912, and Stella Franklin, "Agnes Nestor of the Glove Workers: A Leader in the Women's Movement," *Life and Labor*, vol. 3, 1913. Elizabeth Anne Payne's *Reform, Labor and Feminism: Margaret Dreier Robins and the Women's Trade Union League* (1988) situates Nestor in Chicago's social reform movement. The most recent scholarly interpretation is Karen M. Mason's profile of Nestor as one of four successful women of the early twentieth century in "Testing the Boundaries: Women, Politics, and Gender Roles in Chicago, 1890–1930" (Ph.D. diss., Univ. of Michigan, 1991). Nestor is also discussed in *NAW* (1971).

SUSAN E. HIRSCH

NEWBERRY, JULIA BUTLER CLAPP

May 12, 1818–December 9, 1885

EARLY SETTLER

Born in Oxford, Chenango County, New York, a seat of much wealth, refinement, and learning, Julia Butler Clapp was the daughter of James Clapp, one of the county's most respected lawyers and a man of broad culture. On her mother's side, she could trace her ancestry to the titled Dolbeare family, whose coat-of-arms she was later proud to display. Julia Clapp's grandfather Benjamin Butler, a wealthy landowner and also a man of much cultivation, spared no expense to give her mother, Julia Hyde Butler, the best education obtainable. Physically beautiful and socially graceful, Julia Hyde Butler Clapp died in 1832 when her daughter was only fourteen.

In the same year, James Clapp served as trustee of the Oxford Academy, the local preparatory school, and was instrumental in introducing a "female department" with a woman instructor. As a result, his daughter Julia Clapp enrolled in the 1833–34 terms at the Academy. There she became a member of the "Sigourney Circle" whose purpose was "improvement in the intellectual and moral life" and whose activities included "discussions, reading aloud, making experiments, dissecting chickens' eyes, etc." (*Oxford Academy Centennial*, 40). The women also published a newspaper, the *School Mirror*, "filled with original effusions . . . gentle hints on conduct and manners, poetic efforts, etc. Its motto was, 'Discretion shall preserve thee'" (*Oxford Academy Centennial*, 40).

Julia Clapp also enjoyed the social life, the lectures, and the concerts in Utica, New York, where she paid extended visits to her aunt Mary Dolbeare Butler, who had married the wealthy entrepreneur-landowner Nicholas Devereux. Clapp always regarded "Aunt Devereux" as a surrogate mother and her household in Utica as a second home.

Little is known of Walter Loomis Newberry's courtship of Julia Clapp, because the Chicago Fire of 1871 destroyed the family's personal correspondence. Newberry was often in Utica or its vicinity either to visit his family in nearby Sangerfield and Waterville, or to conduct business with Arthur Bronson, a New York land developer with whom he was associated in Chicago. Writing to Bronson from Waterville, near Utica, on November 6, 1842, Newberry referred obliquely to his coming marriage: "I am necessarily called away from Chicago by very particular business . . . P.S. Please address me at Utica" (November 6, 1842, Arthur Bronson Papers). Fourteen years Julia Clapp's senior and already an established force in the development of Chicago, Newberry offered her personal and social opportunities unavailable to her in Oxford. She, on the other hand, brought to the marriage a lively wit and intelligence, combined with well-developed social skills that Newberry had had little opportunity to cultivate. They were married in Oxford November 22, 1842, and Newberry promptly went off to New York City on business, leaving Julia Newberry in Utica for several months. Her Aunt Devereux was apprehensive about the wrenching move to Chicago, especially when she observed Julia Newberry's low spirits and Walter Newberry's possessiveness: "He will take good care of Julia and provide her with every comfort but he must have her completely identified with himself" (Mary B. Devereux to Cornelia B. Pierrepont, June 3, 1843, Devereux-Kernan Papers).

When Julia Newberry finally arrived in Chicago later in 1843, the city built on a swamp must have seemed particularly unwholesome to her. Pregnant with her first child, she had undoubtedly been forewarned of the "bilious fevers" provoked by the change in climate from her upland home to the "unbroken, champaign country of the west and along the lakes" (*History of Chenango County*, 49). Julia Newberry herself described her coming to Chicago as "plunging into the Wilderness far away from home and family" (letter to E. W. Blatchford, June 22, 1878, Newberry Papers), and she soon must have realized that in the wilderness a coat-of-arms and an academy education counted for less than driving ambition and unremitting labor.

Julia Newberry's sister, Mary Clapp, was with her for the birth of her first son, Walter Butler Newberry, in October 1843, and cared for her during the ten weeks Julia Newberry was bedridden with fever. By New Year 1844 Newberry was performing the social duties expected of the wife of an important man, receiving calls from guests who came by various means—carriage, horseback, and on foot—and entertaining the governors of Illinois and Massachusetts at dinner on venison and turkey. Meanwhile, the muddy streets of the city were swarming with less prestigious guests—hundreds of cattle and pigs on their way to eastern markets.

Social life in Chicago was hectic; entertaining four hundred guests at a single party was not uncommon, with six or seven gentlemen to every lady. Charades and "tableaux vivants" were typical activities, but Newberry would have appreciated more time to herself: "In Oxford people are content to live quietly for a month at a time but here there is no such thing. A few days of quiet and the inquiry is What next? Must we stagnate? Can't we do this or that, and so something is under way the whole time" (letter to Elizabeth Butler, March 14, 1844, Devereux-Kernan Papers). Acutely conscious of her own talents, Newberry was chagrined to find herself excluded from certain all-male social events: "Mr. Newberry has gone to celebrate the landing of the Pilgrim Fathers. . . . I think it a great shame we, poor women, are left out of all public dinners and merry makings—I am sure we have as much wit and can make as good speeches and toasts as any of them" (letter to Elizabeth Butler, December 22, 1848, Newberry Papers). For women's organizations she had little patience, dismissing the activities of "The Daughters of New England" as simply making Johnny cakes and darning stockings. She remained aloof from the sewing society at St. James Episcopal Church, where the Newberrys were members, "because certain venerable old dames are always to be found at it—they discuss the affairs of the town and keep all the young married ladies in order" (letter to Elizabeth Butler, December 22, 1848, Newberry Papers).

Concerning their marriage, Julia Newberry describes her husband as "more lively and talkative," but "always full of business" and at home "only in the evening" (letter to Elizabeth Butler, March 14, 1844, Newberry Papers). These remarks suggest that she missed the companionship of her family. She was instrumental in bringing both her brothers James and Nicholas to Chicago where Walter Newberry helped them in their careers. Julia Newberry's sister Mary described Newberry as "the most kind and attentive husband I ever saw" during his wife's illness, and several relatives mention his spoiling his children (Mary Clapp to Elizabeth Butler, November 19, 1843, Devereux-Kernan Papers). But the prevailing opinion of the New York relatives, like Hannah Devereux Kernan, was that Newberry was distant and preoccupied: "Mr. N. was reserved and did not exert himself to be agreeable" (letter to Elizabeth Butler, September 26, 1846, Devereux-Kernan Papers).

Death was almost a constant presence within the Newberry-Clapp families during the first ten years of Julia's married life. In order to escape the unhealthy Chicago climate and to receive the aid and comfort of her family, Julia frequently made the difficult trip via the Great Lakes to Oxford and Utica with her children. Her first-born son died on August 17, 1844; he was eleven months old. When her sister Mary died in January 5, 1845, after a visit to Chicago, Julia was deprived of a much-loved companion and nurse, and Julia was alone when her daughter Mary Louisa was born August 12, 1845. Julia Newberry's second son, James Clapp Newberry, born some time in 1846–47, died at age three on March 26, 1850, during a visit to Utica; he is buried in Oxford. Julia Newberry recalled later that, after two sons had died, her husband suggested they move near her family in Utica because "the Western climate & life in a new country" (letter to E. W. Blatchford, July 25, 1876, Newberry Papers) did not agree with her and her children, and he actually bought property on Chancellor Square in Utica near the house of her Aunt Devereux. When he explained a year later that such a move would cause a decline in their fortunes, Julia Newberry agreed to remain in Chicago.

In 1850 Julia Newberry lost a third son, Walter Pierrepont, at the age of five months. A fourth unnamed son, perhaps born prematurely, was buried in 1851. Aunt Devereux wrote to Julia Newberry's father in January 1852: "The severe losses she [Julia] meets with in her children requires great strength of body and mind, fortified by religious principles to endure" (Devereux-Kernan Papers). On December 28, 1853, the Newberrys' fifth and last child, Julia Rosa, was born.

Walter Newberry's health began to decline at the beginning of the 1860s, and he was advised to avoid Chicago winters for the warmer climate of Europe. Julia Newberry relished the amenities of life on the Continent—the interesting old cities with their paved streets, the wealth of art and culture. Soon the Newberry home on the North Side was filled with European *objets d'art*, and Julia Newberry's invitation lists gave preference to those guests who had traveled in Europe. To equip them for life in Europe, Julia Newberry saw to it that her daughters were educated in foreign languages, and Mary was accordingly schooled abroad. Aunt Devereux reported that she had received "a very pleasant letter from Mary Newberry," who was then sixteen: "She is leaving School, they contemplate a visit into Germany and up the Rhine during this month and talk of spending the next winter in Florence. Mary will from this time remain with her Mother, otherwise she would be in danger of losing her English as she never hears it when separated from her" (letter to Elizabeth Butler, Devereux-Kernan Papers). A year later daughter Julia was placed in a *pensionat* in Geneva while the rest of the family traveled on the Continent. As a consequence of this early and prolonged exposure, both girls were proficient in French and German. Mary continued her education for two years in the fashionable Miss Haines's school in New York, which offered instruction in both French and English, and Julia also was briefly enrolled in the same school.

While on his way to join his family in Nice, Walter Newberry died on November 6, 1868, aboard ship. At the time of her husband's death, it is likely that Julia Newberry did not possess any private resources, her father having left the bulk of his estate to her three brothers at his death in January 1854. Walter Newberry's will provided that his entire estate, both real and personal property valued at about three million dollars, be put in trust for his two surviving children, Mary and Julia, with the provision that after their deaths without lawful issue and the death of his wife, half of the estate should be distributed to his collateral rel-

atives and the other half used to found a free public library. His wife, Julia, provided she relinquished her dower rights, was to receive ten thousand dollars a year. Publicity given the will humiliated Julia Newberry, who felt entitled to at least half of the property. As advised by Mark Skinner, executor of the estate, Julia Newberry renounced the will, then sued for and was awarded her dower rights—a life interest in one-third of the real estate. In addition, she was given absolute possession of one-third of her husband's personal property—around three hundred thousand dollars. These awards, which gave her an annual income of about three times the size of the annuity bequeathed her by her husband, reduced the capital of the estate, complicated its administration, and created resentment on the part of her daughters and even Mark Skinner himself.

Although Julia Newberry was never completely reconciled to the terms of the will, she participated actively in decisions affecting the administration of the estate. She protected her own interests with a staff of male assistants: an agent who worked with the trustees to collect her income, an attorney who represented her in all legal matters concerning the estate, and a butler who managed her personal affairs. When there was a particularly difficult question that had to be settled, she called upon her cousin Hannah's husband, U.S. Senator Francis Kernan (1875–81), for his personal assistance. The policy she advocated concerning the estate, with the concurrence of the trustees, was to convert the undeveloped land—much of it in Wisconsin—into cash that could then be invested in securities. From the beginning, Julia Newberry was informed of all activity in the estate, and she looked back with pride on "this noble property that we have watched over and guarded so long and well together" (Julia Newberry to E. W. Blatchford, April 16, 1876, Newberry Papers). Though she had left Chicago in 1870 for Europe, she contributed to the city's renewal after the fire of 1871 by rebuilding the profitable Newberry Block: "we all worked for Chicago—for the rebuilding of homes and churches—the restoration of society" (Julia Newberry to E. W. Blatchford, May 20, 1878, Newberry Papers). She also continued her contributions to the charitable activities of St. James Church where she paid for and retained a pew until the end of her life. She was considering "plans for the benefit and improvement of Chicago when time and strength permitted, and things of value to be given which my acquaintance with the old institutions and libraries of Europe had brought into my possession" (Julia Newberry to E. W. Blatchford, August 8, 1877, Newberry Papers) but, wearied and discouraged, she never returned to Chicago to execute her plans.

From August 1870 to April 1876, Julia Newberry was preoccupied with the health of her daughters as they searched for better climates and cures in various European resorts. The life of Mary, who also suffered from the tuberculosis that killed her father, ended first; she succumbed to a massive hemorrhage in Pau in the French Pyrenees on February 18, 1874. After Mary's death, Julia Newberry and her surviving daughter were forced by the precarious state of Julia Rosa's health to give up plans to live permanently in the United States. Julia Rosa found that traveling provided a necessary distraction from her grief over her sister's death, and accordingly they once more toured the spas of Europe, finding some relief in the dull routine at Bad Schwalbach. From there they went briefly to Paris, where Julia New-berry had taken a house, and then decided to spend the winter in Egypt. Unfortunately, they left Egypt's warm climate prematurely to spend Easter in Rome, and Julia Rosa took cold and died of a throat infection there on April 4, 1876. Now, left completely alone, Julia Newberry withdrew to her home in Paris.

A series of legal actions intensely embarrassing to Julia Newberry began immediately after Julia Rosa's death and ended shortly before Julia Newberry's own death nine years later. Although Julia Newberry was named sole heir to her daughter's estate of one hundred ten thousand dollars the will stipulated that before receiving the bequest, she had to devise a will of her own in which she bequeathed whatever remained of her daughter's property to a "charitable institution for women in said City of Chicago as she may select" (Julia Rosa Newberry, Last Will and Testament, Newberry Papers). Julia Newberry balked at the provision and renounced the will, which made it null and void. Then, after Julia Rosa was declared to have died intestate, Julia Newberry claimed and received the estate as sole heir and next of kin. Despite the decision of the Probate Court in her favor in July 1879, Julia Newberry had to endure the further humiliation of two suits by different charitable institutions, one in 1880 and another in 1883–84. Not until 1885 did the Supreme Court confirm the decision of 1879.

The most serious of the legal actions involved the demand by Newberry's collateral heirs, upon the death of Julia Rosa, to have their half of the estate distributed to them. Such distribution would have violated the clause of Newberry's will in which he clearly stipulated that distribution could not be made until after his wife's death. Despite the ruling of the Supreme Court against distribution in 1878, litigation continued until 1883, when the final plea for distribution was disallowed; the estate remained intact. As Julia Newberry wrote to the trustees: "The decision of Judge Tuley gives promise of more *Rest & Tranquility* in the affairs of the estate than we have had for some time past" (letter to E. W. Blatchford, September 24, 1883, Newberry Papers).

With no further reason to return to Chicago, Julia Newberry spent the last two years of her life in regal exile in Europe, where she felt at home in aristocratic circles. For summer visits to her family in New York, she had built a summer home on property purchased from her brother Benjamin in Lake Luzerne, New York. A stained glass window in the reception room contained the Dolbeare coat-of-arms.

Instinctively an aristocrat herself, Julia Newberry lived by an old-fashioned principle of noblesse oblige toward her immediate family retainers, who rewarded her with their loyalty. Even after the Newberry home had burned down in the Great Fire of 1871, Julia Newberry continued to provide employment for her old gardener, Tristan, who kept the vacant grounds planted with trees and flowers. William H. Bradley, one of the estate's trustees, commended the loyalty of Enos Johnson, who, having been employed originally by Walter Newberry, continued to serve as Julia Newberry's agent: "It is pleasant to see the devotion of old servants to those who have been kind to them" (W. H. Bradley to Julia Newberry, May 4, 1885, Newberry Library Trustees' Correspondence). Her former housekeeper Ernestine Theiss was among the few who met the train bringing her body

back to Chicago for burial in Graceland Cemetery. All those who had served Julia Newberry were remembered with sizable bequests in her will.

With Julia Newberry's death, the Walter Newberry estate was distributed, one half to the collateral relatives and one half for the construction of a free public library. For having preserved the estate until it doubled in value, Julia Newberry felt she was entitled to a monument in the Newberry Library "with inscription stating how and when I died" (Julia Butler Newberry Will).

Among her charitable bequests were those to St. James Episcopal Church in Chicago, where a stained glass window was erected in her memory, and to St. Paul's Episcopal Church in Oxford, where a brass lectern and silver communion service remember her. The American churches in Paris and Rome also contain memorials for her and her daughter Julia Rosa. Among the most touching of her bequests are the souvenirs of "my Julia" to many of her titled friends. The bulk of her estate, which amounted to close to five hundred thousand dollars, she bequeathed to her brothers James and Nicholas. In her will she provided her own epitaph: "My life has been devoted to my family and friends and to works of charity" (Julia Butler Newberry Will).

Sources. The major manuscript collections for a life of Julia Butler Clapp Newberry are the Walter L. Newberry Papers and the New-berry/Clapp Correspondence, both at the NL. Additional information on the early life of Julia Newberry is found in the Devereux-Kernan Papers, Division of Rare and Manuscript Coll., Cornell Univ. Library. The wills of James Clapp Sr., James Clapp Jr., and Julia Newberry provide useful information. Julia Butler Newberry's will is at the Warren County Clerk's Office, Lake George, New York. Newberry Library Trustees' Correspondence, 1868–85, contains useful details about the lives of the Newberry women. Probate Records and court documents are found in these files. The Arthur Bronson papers, with correspondence from Walter Newberry, are at CHS. See O. H. Curtis, ed., *Oxford Academy Centennial, June 28, 29, 1894* (1895) for information on Julia Clapp's school years. Hiram C. Clark, *History of Chenango County* (1850), discusses the changes in geography and weather that Julia Newberry encountered in her move to Chicago.

JOAN G. SCHROETER

NEWBURY, MOLLIE NETCHER
April 15, 1867–December 12, 1954
BUSINESSWOMAN

Mollie Netcher Newbury was the only women to control one of the great State Street department stores in Chicago's major downtown retail area. She was, according to the *Chicago Tribune,* "one of Chicago's most famous business women" (December 14, 1954). For forty years she exercised full control over the Boston Store, whose low prices and wide variety of services appealed chiefly to lower-middle-class customers.

Mollie Alpiner was born and raised in Chicago, the daughter of Morris and Ernestine (Solomon) Alpiner. Her Austrian-born father was a cigar maker and tobacconist. Nothing is known of her education. At the age of sixteen she went to work as a clerk at the predecessor to the Boston Store, C.W. & E. Pardridge. There she met Charles Netcher, a manager at Pardridge. Born in Buffalo, New York, in 1852, he first worked "as a cash boy and bundle wrapper for Edward and C.W.

FIG. 84. *Department store chief Mollie Netcher Newbury rebuilt her Boston Store in downtown Chicago, 1915.*

recalled. "I just nodded my head" (p. 35). They were married on July 2, 1891.

On the surface, Mollie Netcher lived the typical life of a wealthy Chicago matron in an elegant home on Drexel Boulevard. She raised four children and devoted herself to her husband and his business. They rarely appeared in society. Inside the marriage, however, Mollie Netcher maintained her strong interest in business affairs. As she told a newspaper reporter soon after her husband's sudden death from appendicitis in 1904, "We talked business just as other people talk love" (Clarke, "Steps from Her Home to Manage Business"). The Netchers "planned to double the size" (Corwin, 35) of the Boston Store. After her husband's death, Mollie Netcher took over the six-story Boston Store, enlarging it first in 1907, again in 1912, and finally, in 1915, commissioning the architecture firm of Holabird and Roche to design an expanded store. It was finished in 1917, had "seventeen stories and contained twenty acres of floor space at State and Madison" (Corwin, 36), the heart of the downtown Chicago shopping district.

The Boston Store, with nearly four thousand employees, housed a candy factory and a cigar factory; ice cream was made on the fifteenth floor and baked goods on several floors. Advertising as the world's tallest retail establishment, it offered a full line of merchandise and provided a wide variety of services, including a toy department and a children's playroom staffed with attendants, a barber shop, a Western Union office, a post office, and a postal savings bank. It was billed as "America's Greatest Family Store." Mollie Netcher maintained a strict cash-only policy while her upscale competitors offered charge accounts. The Boston Store also published an extensive mail order catalog into the early 1920s, chiefly of women's clothing. All evidence suggests that the store was managed directly by Mollie Netcher herself, although her son, Charles Netcher Jr., played an active role in the business from the early 1920s until his death in 1931. She worked long hours, even when her children were young, reviewing all the store's large financial details. According to a 1904 *Chicago Tribune* article, "Unlike other businesswomen, Mollie went home at noon for a midday dinner with her children and spent another hour on correspondence and personal matters. After an hour of rest, she would change her gown and receive business callers. Later, she returned to her office and stayed until the store closed" (quoted in Corwin, 36).

Mollie Netcher described her business practices as building upon her husband's good example. She defended the unfashionable cash-only policy and boasted that the store paid cash to all its suppliers. She wrote in 1919, "We don't have people getting angry at us because there is some mistake in the bill. And we don't have to hire any collectors, for the reason that we *have* no outstanding bills" ("What I Know about Running a Business," 170). Sales clerks were motivated by small salaries and generous commissions, and the store provided a variety of fringe benefits for its employees, including lunchrooms, classrooms for instruction, billiards and magazine rooms, and full-sized tennis courts on the roof. "Mollie [Netcher] caused a stir in 1916 by providing a summer resort where employees could rent cottages cheaply on a ten-acre estate in Lake Beulah, Wisconsin" (Corwin, 36).

On July 13, 1913, Mollie Netcher surprised her friends by

Pardridge" (Corwin, 34) before they moved west with their business to the fast-growing new commercial center on Lake Michigan. They took Netcher with them and established a dry-goods store in 1869. Chicago's soaring population and economic growth was only temporarily affected by the Great Chicago Fire in 1871, which destroyed Pardridge's entire dry-goods inventory. Illustrating his entrepreneurial skill, Netcher suggested that they relocate on the South Side of the city in an inexpensive building and sell their merchandise then en route by rail to Chicago. It was a great idea; and soon Netcher was manager of the store, working long hours and eventually purchasing larger and larger interests in the company until he owned it and renamed it the Boston Store. Mollie Alpiner first met Netcher in 1890, when she had already worked at the Boston Store for seven years and was the store's chief underwear buyer. In her memory, the meeting was a dramatic event. "One day I was called to Mr. Netcher's office. I was dismayed since my only thought was that I was being called in to be dismissed. Even when he seemed kind, and asked if he might drive me home in his carriage with its spanking team, I told myself 'He's only trying to fire me in the easiest way'" (quoted in Corwin, 34–35). That same day, after riding home in Netcher's carriage, the department store owner asked Mollie Alpiner, who considered herself "plain in appearance" (p. 35), if she would marry him. "I was flabbergasted," she marrying Solomon (later known as Saul) Neuberger while on a visit to Portland, Oregon. Neuberger was a Chicago paint salesman, described sometimes as Netcher's childhood sweetheart. Although he kept an office at the Boston Store, Neuberger played no role in its management or in any other business. Mollie Netcher's granddaughter Mollie Netcher Bragno commented, "Grandmother was a matriarch. It was difficult for her second husband, being married to a woman of her strength and drive. He turned to collecting stamps" (quoted in Corwin, 40). The Neubergers explained that they changed their name to Newbury in the early 1920s "because it was easier to spell" (*Chicago Tribune*, February 2, 1950). When Saul Newbury died in 1950, he was deemed the city's leading philatelist.

For many years Mollie Netcher Newbury, who always used the names of both husbands, was generally regarded as a successful department store operator, although the Boston Store's sales peaked in 1922. Years later she was criticized for adhering too long to the policies set by her first husband, particularly his insistence on cash-only payment. The Boston Store became rather old-fashioned, no longer aggressive in its merchandising, but it survived the Great Depression in the 1930s and returned to profitability in 1941. Sales increased modestly after the mid-1930s but remained far below the levels of the early 1920s. During the 1930s, the store advertised itself as Netcher's Boston Store and it was often referred to as "Netcher's." Its well-publicized annual sale, called "Netcher Day," was discontinued at the beginning of World War II.

Mollie Netcher Newbury never used her own given name in the store's advertising and she was virtually unknown to the public. She was almost eighty when in 1946 she sold both the business and the real estate lots upon which it was built for a reported fourteen million dollars. The new owners were unsuccessful despite heavy spending for improvements; they closed the New Boston Store two years later, converting the building to offices while renting street-level space for retail use.

Mollie Netcher Newbury's retirement years were troubled by prolonged litigation regarding her management of Charles Netcher's estate and its chief asset, the Boston Store. She died in Chicago and was buried in the Netcher family plot at Rosehill Cemetery.

Two years after her death Cook County Superior Court ruled in favor of the Netcher estate and found that she had mismanaged the property between 1904 and 1923, when she rejected an opportunity to sell it for nineteen million dollars. Netcher's will had provided, somewhat ambiguously, for the sale of the store and creation of a trust fund for their children. Although Mollie Netcher Newbury was once considered an outstanding businesswoman, her entire estate was consumed to pay the judgment won by the Netcher estate.

Sources. Clipping files on Mollie Netcher Newbury and the Boston Store and a "Prospectus" for the New Boston Store of Chicago, Inc., 1946, can be found at the CHS. The "Prospectus" is a good financial summary. The Netcher Estate Files in the Cook County Circuit Court Archives (Case No. 52S6219) provide a very detailed financial record of the Boston Store. The best summary is a seventy-five-page report (May 16, 1956) by Llewellyn A. Wescott, the Master in Chancery. The transcript of testimony runs to more than thirty-two hundred pages. Her theory and practice of business are detailed in Mollie Netcher Neuberger,

"What I Know about Running a Business," *American Magazine*, June 1919. The *CT* published lengthy obituaries for Charles Netcher (June 21, 1904) and Mollie Netcher Newbury (December 14, 1954), as well as a brief notice for Saul Newbury (February 2, 1950). Grace R. Clarke, "Steps from Her Home to Manage Business," *CT*, July 10, 1904, and Margaret Corwin, "Mollie Netcher Newbury: The Merchant Princess," *Chicago History*, Spring 1977, are useful. William Leach, *Land of Desire: Merchants, Power, and the Rise of a New American Culture* (1993), and Joseph Siry, *Carson Pirie Scott: Louis Sullivan and the Chicago Department Store* (1987), provide context.

PATRICK J. FURLONG

NICE, MARGARET MORSE
December 6, 1883–June 26, 1974
ORNITHOLOGIST, CONSERVATIONIST

Margaret Morse Nice was an internationally known ornithologist, a pioneer in research on the song sparrow. She developed the technique of using color bands on individual birds for long-term study of a specific bird population. She was born in Amherst, Massachusetts. Her parents were Anson Daniel Morse, a history professor at Amherst College, and Margaret Duncan (Ely) Morse. She was the fourth born of seven children, the second of three daughters. Like her mother, Margaret Morse attended Mount Holyoke College, South Hadley, Massachusetts, where she studied languages—French, Italian, German, Latin—and natural sciences. After a trip to Europe with her grandmother, she graduated in 1906 with a B.A. degree. She then did graduate work in biology at Clark University in Worcester, Massachusetts, from 1907 to 1909, planning to get both M.A. and Ph.D. degrees; she did not complete the requirements.

In 1909 Margaret Morse married Leonard Blaine Nice, also a graduate student at Clark, who received a Ph.D. in physiology in 1911. The couple lived briefly in Boston, where Blaine Nice was an instructor at Harvard Medical School. In June 1910, based on her graduate research, Margaret Nice published her first paper in ornithology, "The Food of the Bobwhite," in the *Journal of Economic Entomology*. In 1913 the Nices moved to Norman, Oklahoma, where Leonard became professor of physiology at the University of Oklahoma.

Margaret Nice had five children, all daughters. Constance was born in 1910, Marjorie in 1912, Barbara in 1915, Eleanor in 1918 (died ten years later), and Janice in 1923. Doing research was a necessity to Nice. While she was at home with her young children, she developed an interest in child psychology, particularly language development. In 1915 her study of "The Development of a Child's Vocabulary in Relation to Environment" was published in *Pedagogical Seminary*. She analyzed the vocabularies of her daughter Constance and other children at ages eighteen months, three, and four years. In 1926, with this paper as a thesis, Clark University granted Nice a Master of Arts in psychology dated 1915. She continued to keep records of her children's language development and published seventeen papers on the subject between 1915 and 1933.

It was also in Oklahoma, in 1919, that Nice fought her first major conservationist battle. Hunting season on the mourning dove was due to open on August 2. It was widely assumed that the dove's nesting season was over by then. With a packed sup-

FIG. 85. *Ornithologist and conservationist Margaret Morse Nice, flanked by two of her daughters, Janice, left, and Constance.*

per and their baby daughter in tow, the Nices located doves on nest in August. A week later they found three more, evidence to prove that the doves indeed were still nesting even in September. She sent a protest letter to Oklahoma City and Norman newspapers titled "Doves Must Not Be Shot in August." She also notified the Oklahoma Game Department and the United States Biological Survey. She won the battle and hunting season was delayed.

Margaret's daughters and her husband became involved in her passion for birds and often assisted her on research outings. Blaine Nice was very supportive of his wife's interests and her serious research. During their years in Oklahoma, they often went bird-watching together, and the husband and wife team wrote a short journal of bird-watching, *The Birds of Oklahoma*, published in 1927.

In 1928 the family moved to Columbus, Ohio, where Blaine Nice became a professor on the faculty of Ohio State University Medical Center. It was here that Margaret found a home she loved and where she did the most important fieldwork of her career.

In the river valley overlooking the Olentangy River, Nice conducted long-term research on the song sparrow. Her home

faced what she described as a "wild, neglected piece of flood plain," which she named "'Interpont,' that is, 'Between the Bridges'" [*Research Is a Passion with Me*, 89–90]. Nice began banding song sparrows and then meticulously recording their daily habits.

Nice pursued research on the song sparrow almost without interruption during her time in Columbus. She pioneered a field of study that allowed the researcher to study the life history of individual birds by using color-coded bands for identification. Irish ornithologist J. P. Burkitt had used this technique in studies of robins in 1924, and Nice made important further developments, banding large numbers of birds. With great patience and focus, she observed particular song sparrows and was able to follow their lives from a slight distance, learning about their relations to other sparrows in their groups, examining their rates of fertility, and gaining other new information. Her census-taking and scrupulously kept tables and charts enabled her to continue writing about the song sparrow many years after the observation and research had been completed.

Nice was a bird lover as well as a scholar on bird behavior, and her love of birds led her to keep several in the house. In his biography of Nice, Milton Trautman recalled difficulty concentrating on dinner conversation at her home as birds flew in and out of the dining room, even stopping to land on his dinner plate.

While in Columbus, Nice began attending meetings of various ornithological societies, including the American Ornithologists' Union (AOU) and the Wilson Ornithological Society. Here she met leaders in the field and presented her work. However, Nice was snubbed by the local Wheaton Ornithological Club of Columbus because she was a woman. She was accepted for membership in the AOU in 1931, the fifth woman to become a member.

During this time Nice began writing reviews of foreign ornithological studies, drawing on her command of several languages. These reviews were published in *Bird-Banding* magazine and were the beginning of Nice's long association with the journal. She became its associate editor in June 1935 and continued writing reviews for the magazine until 1971.

In 1936 Blaine Nice became professor of medicine at the University of Chicago. It pained Margaret Nice to leave the life and research projects she had built in Columbus. Upon moving to the Hyde Park neighborhood, Nice's life changed drastically. Living in the city, she could no longer spend her days in the field observing and identifying birds as intimately as she was able to do at Interpont. Still, she discovered the forest preserves in and around Chicago. She greatly enjoyed these visits as well as trips to the Morton Arboretum and the Indiana Dunes. She continued to write and publish during her years in Chicago. Her findings on the sparrow, *Studies in the Life History of the Song Sparrow*, were published by the New York Linnaean Society in two well-received volumes in 1937 and 1943, respectively. In 1939 she published *Watcher at the Nest*, a nontechnical report for the general reader on her research, with drawings by the noted illustrator-ornithologist Roger Tory Peterson. She also continued her involvement with national ornithological organizations and became active in Chicago's ornithological community. In 1937

Nice was made a fellow of the AOU, and in 1940 the organization awarded her the Brewster Award for her work on the song sparrow. She was the first woman president of the Wilson Ornithological Society (1938–39), president of the Chicago Ornithological Society from 1940 to 1942, and a director of the Illinois Audubon Society.

Nice visited Jackson Park regularly, and in 1949 she found the nest of a red-eyed vireo there; she published "Red-Eyed Vireo in Jackson Park" in the *Bulletin of the Illinois Audubon Society* in 1950. Two years later she published her records of breeding birds in Jackson Park. Nice was also interested in the birds in Lincoln Park and was called upon to complete a study of bird migration there. It was published in 1950 as *William Dreuth's Study of Bird Migration in Lincoln Park, Chicago,* attributed to Charles T. Clark and Margaret Morse Nice. Dreuth had accumulated thirty-six notebooks of data that he donated to the Chicago Academy of Sciences in 1946. Dreuth had collected the data from the 5.5 acres in and around Waveland Avenue and Lake Michigan, which had been set aside as a bird sanctuary. The data were considered important but were not in publishable form. The academy asked Clark to "summarize and tabulate the records for publication" and asked Nice to "bring the work into final form for publication" ("Foreword," 3). Nice's report provided information on "changes in bird life in Lincoln Park" ("Introduction," 5) during the previous half century, enhancing sections about breeding birds and changes in status.

Even with her involvement in the Lincoln Park study and census-taking in Jackson Park, Nice repeatedly lamented the lack of suitable space and birds. In a letter to her daughter Marjorie, she complained that "a great city is no proper home for me. We had no birds around our home but English sparrows. . . . Most of my work was desk work" (quoted in Trautman, "In Memoriam," 436). Her "desk work" consisted of writing up her song sparrow research, and writing and editing the many articles and reviews that she published throughout her life. During her years in Chicago, Nice wrote seventy-nine articles and five books.

Because Jackson Park was so close to her home and she visited it so often, Nice became concerned about the building and the city expansion that were threatening the wildlife in Jackson Park. One incident of destruction ignited her ire. An important hedge that protected the park from city dirt and noise was being destroyed. On March 19, 1949, she wrote to Chicago Mayor Martin Kennelly to "protest against this wanton destruction of our city's beauty. We sincerely hope that this deplorable policy will be reversed at once" (Correspondence, Nice Papers).

Conservation had always been important to Nice, and she sought to educate others on its importance. She spoke to groups, talked on the radio, and entered some publicized battles in Oklahoma, Indiana, and California. In her later years, Nice's correspondence included the condemnation of the unrestricted use of pesticides and the misuse of wildlife refuges. She wrote letters to magazines, newspapers, senators, and conservationists about the proposed taking over of the Wichita Mountain's Wildlife Refuge by the U.S. Army. Her paper, "Wichita Mountains Wildlife Refuge in Peril," was published in *Nature Magazine,* June/July 1955. A successful battle was also waged with the

U.S. Army to deter it from taking over an enclave of woods in Jackson Park for officers' quarters. Nice's efforts also helped preserve Dinosaur National Monument, redwood trees in California, and sections of the Indiana Dunes. She admitted defeat, however, in her struggles against the "wholesale poisoning of the world with death-dealing pesticides" (*Research Is a Passion with Me,* 261).

The modest success of her personal account of research on the song sparrow, *Watcher at the Nest,* fostered Nice's desire to write for a general audience. Nice also drew the illustrations for some of her papers as well as for an article by her daughter Constance Nice, "Bird Babes of Delta Marsh," *Nature Magazine* in 1954. Her drawings also appeared in her book *Development of Behavior in Precocial Birds,* published in 1962 by the Linnaean Society, and in her second autobiography, *Research Is a Passion with Me.* The latter was published posthumously in 1979 by a Canadian women's ornithological group named after Nice, the Margaret Morse Nice Ornithological Club, founded in 1952 because the Toronto Ornithological Club excluded women.

Because many male ornithologists were reluctant to admit women into their midst and into their organizations—especially women with no formal training—Margaret Nice sought support from other women with similar interests. Largely through correspondence, Nice became a member of a group of women ornithologists. Her contacts with women ornithologists were part of her larger correspondence on birds and research on birds with colleagues throughout the world.

Through her support network of other women ornithologists, Nice traded information and advice. The most well-known of these friendships was that with Althea Sherman, a woman almost thirty years Nice's senior. Nice grew increasingly frustrated with the domestic demands placed on her. Although she loved her family very much, she found the responsibility of running a household cumbersome. Throughout her life she was annoyed at being viewed by male ornithologists as a housewife, insisting, "I am *not* a housewife, I am a *trained zoologist*" (quoted in Trautman, "In Memoriam," 440). Sherman's letters to Nice encouraged her work and sympathized with her frustration at having to maintain a household, raise a family, and pursue her work. Sherman wrote, "Like you I rebel against spending time on menial tasks" (Bonta, *Women in the Field,* 183). Nice and Sherman corresponded for eleven years but had the opportunity to meet face-to-face only twice, in 1922 in Chicago and in 1931 in Detroit. Nice also had a strong connection with Amelia Rudolph Laskey, who had begun ornithological work nine years after Nice. Their correspondence, begun in the late 1930s and continuing for the rest of their lives, provides "the best record that exists of the network women in ornithology had established from the 1940s until the early 1970s" (Bonta, *Women in the Field,* 185).

A prolific writer, reviewer, and editor, Nice continued to write about ornithology, review the work of colleagues, and edit periodicals until just before her death in 1974. She published about 250 articles in scientific periodicals and gave a count of 3,313 reviews. Among her publications were several articles in German.

Nice's honors included a Doctor of Science degree from Mount Holyoke College in 1956 and from Elmira College

(Elmira, New York) in 1962. The Wilson Ornithological Club created the Margaret Morse Nice grant for self-trained researchers. A song sparrow subspecies, *Melospiza melodia niceae*, was named for her. She was elected to honorary membership in the British Ornithological Union as well as in ornithological societies in Finland, Germany, the Netherlands, and Switzerland. She was also a corresponding member of the Hungarian Institute for Ornithology.

Margaret Morse Nice became ill in her later years, suffering from eye ailments and a condition misdiagnosed as a heart problem. She died in 1974 at the age of ninety from arteriosclerosis. Her husband had died just a few months earlier. She was buried in the plot of the Nice family in New Marshfield Cemetery, Athens County, Ohio.

In a letter dated January 30, 1952, and addressed to the Margaret Morse Nice Ornithological Club at its founding, Nice described the philosophy that guided her research: "The study of nature is a limitless field, the most fascinating pursuit in the world. . . . We must *see clearly, record fully and accurately*, and *try to understand*. . . . We should try to open the eyes of the unseeing to the beauty and wonder of nature" (*Research Is a Passion*, 268). Nice's sparrow studies brought her international acclaim in ornithology. Her research served as the basis for bird population studies, which became important in American ornithology. Many ornithologists consider Nice the founder of the movement to observe the life history of individual birds.

Sources. The Margaret Morse Nice Papers, which contain professional and personal papers and correspondence, are at the Division of Rare and Manuscript Collections, Cornell Univ. Library. The Mount Holyoke College Archives have reports from Nice to the *Mount Holyoke Alumnae Quarterly* and for a class letter in 1938; newspaper clippings; and a typescript obituary-biography, "Margaret Morse Nice, Ornithologist," by her brother, Edward S. Morse, July 18, 1974. "A Partial Bibliography of Margaret Morse Nice," a typescript list of her publications from 1910 to 1965 compiled by Milton B. Trautman in September 1976, is at the Museum of Zoology of the Museum of Biological Diversity, Ohio State Univ., Columbus, Ohio. In addition to the works discussed above, Nice's important publications include the first report on her song-sparrow studies, which appeared in German as "Zur Naturgeschichte des Singhammers," *Journal für Ornithologie*, October 1933 and January 1934; and "The Theory of Territorialism and Its Development" in *Fifty Years' Progress of American Ornithology, 1883–1933* (1933) for the American Ornithologists Union. Morse's *Research Is a Passion with Me* (1979) is valuable for information on her life and work. Milton B. Trautman, "In Memoriam: Margaret Morse Nice," *Auk*, July 1977, is a detailed biography with discussion of her achievements. Marcia Myers Bonta, in "Margaret Morse Nice: Ethologist of the Song Sparrow," *Women in the Field: America's Pioneering Women Naturalists* (1991), places Nice's biography in the context of women ornithologists. Other useful biographical studies are Pnina G. Abir-Am and Dorinda Outram, eds., *Uneasy Careers and Intimate Lives: Women in Science 1789–1979* (1987), which includes a discussion of Nice; and Marcia Bonta, "Song Sparrow Lady: Margaret Morse Nice and Her Passion for Research," *Birder's World*, August 1993. Nice's biography appears in *NAW* (1980). For an appraisal of her work as pioneering, see Erwin Stresemann, *Ornithology: From Aristotle to the Present* (1975). Margaret W. Rossiter provides a brief discussion of Nice's career within the context of the lives of women in science in *Women Scientists in America: Struggles and Strategies to 1940* (1982).

JILL S. POLLACK

NICHOLES, ANNA E.
May 2, 1865–July 20, 1917
SOCIAL REFORMER, SETTLEMENT LEADER, SUFFRAGIST, CIVIL SERVICE COMMISSIONER

Anna Nicholes, the first woman appointed to the Cook County Civil Service Board and one of the leading organizers of Chicago's influential progressive women's reform coalition, was born in Englewood, Illinois (later annexed to Chicago), to Ira and Eleanor (Hall) Nicholes. A sister, Sarah Grace, was born ten years later. Ira Nicholes was a successful Chicago lawyer, well-known for his activism in religious, civic, and community organizations.

Anna Nicholes graduated from Englewood High School in 1882 and went to Rockford Female Seminary (name changed to Rockford College in 1892), Rockford, Illinois, graduating in 1886. Her sister graduated from Wellesley College in 1894. Ira Nicholes died in 1881, before his daughters entered college. His estate, however, left the Nicholes women free of financial worry and provided ample financial support for the sisters' philanthropic careers.

Little is known about Nicholes's life from 1886 to 1899, when both sisters began to reside at the Neighborhood Settlement House, on Chicago's Southwest Side. Neighborhood House was established in 1897 by Harriet Van Der Vaart, clubwoman and later a Consumer's League activist. It grew out of the efforts of the young people of the Universalist Church of Englewood to found a kindergarten in 1896. The Nicholes sisters joined Van Der Vaart and her husband to become permanent, unpaid residents responsible for the leadership of all social, educational, and cultural activities.

Like many college-educated women who were seeking constructive use of their educational training, Nicholes and her sister Grace found career opportunities through settlement work, women's clubs, and socially active organizations. The Nicholes sisters joined another Rockford Female Seminary graduate, JANE ADDAMS, in the Federation of Chicago Settlements. Settlement activities led to leadership by the Nicholes sisters of the Englewood Women's Club (1899–1913) and Neighborhood House Women's Club (1899–1913). In 1901, Anna Nicholes was elected president of the Federation of Chicago Settlements. Settlement work brought confrontation with the realities of neighborhood working-class life and, for many middle-class women reformers, contact with young women workers, some of whom had already embraced ideas of trade unionism and advocated reform of workplace conditions.

Nicholes's advocacy of labor reform legislation and trade union organization began when she joined the Federation of Settlements. She identified problems inherent in women's work—low pay, poor and unsafe conditions, and long hours, in a 1904 article, "Woman and Trade Unions," which appeared in the *Commons*. Many defined women workers as only temporary and as secondary contributors to family incomes, thus justifying their lower wages. Nicholes strongly argued that statistics proved otherwise: women workers between 1890 and 1900 had increased by two million. Women were permanently staying in the work force and therefore needed to "agitate, educate and organize" ("Women and Trade Unions," 273) if they were going to get wages, conditions, and hours that resembled a living wage. In addition, because they worked at a lower pay scale, women were considered a threat to job security by male workers and were generally ignored by trade unions organizers.

Nicholes's article announced the formation of the Women's Trade Union League (WTUL), a new union for women, first organized in Boston. The WTUL had a unique philosophy of bringing women union workers together with educated middle-class women, known as allies. By 1904, a branch of the WTUL had been organized in Chicago with offices in Hull-House. Jane Addams and other Hull-House residents were on the governing board. Anna Nicholes served as secretary from 1904 to 1907, and as part of her work with the WTUL, assumed the editorship of the Women's Department in the *Union Labor Advocate*, a monthly magazine that was the official organ of the Chicago Federation of Labor (CFL), an affiliation of various Chicago labor unions.

Male-dominated trade unions often met in rooms located in taverns, but the WTUL's meeting place — Hull-House — served as a safer and socially acceptable alternative for young immigrant women workers. This successful strategy presented unions in an acceptable light to working women and their families. In addition, Hull-House became a place of mediation between working-class and middle-class women. They could build a cross-class coalition that would be effective in labor negotiations, support of strikes, and the establishment of new unions.

Middle-class women, Anna Nicholes wrote in "The Club Woman and the Union Girl" in the *Union Labor Advocate*, November 1905, became aware of the needs and issues of working women and the necessities of labor legislation for women and children through their involvement in the WTUL. As editor of the Women's Department, Nicholes educated and informed union members of legislative measures pertaining to a shorter work day and safer conditions. She wrote about the necessity for a whole community to be involved in the labor issues of women and children. Nicholes urged government investigations into the working conditions of women in order to inform and protect workers and to dispel the notion that the nation's social ills were caused by women's increased presence in the workforce. Nicholes remained as the WTUL contributor to the CFL paper until 1908, when the organization hired a professional journalist, ALICE HENRY, as editor of the Women's Department. In 1911, the WTUL began to publish its own journal, *Life and Labor*.

By 1910, Anna Nicholes was beginning to be recognized as one of Chicago's women leaders. Through her work with the WTUL, Neighborhood House and the women's clubs, Nicholes emerged as an experienced organizer and spokesperson for reform ideology and programs. The Woman's City Club of Chicago (WCC) appointed Anna Nicholes its first superintendent; she was responsible for directing the club's office and functioning as its spokeswoman. The organization, founded in 1910, coordinated a variety of women's political reform efforts. Employing the gendered language dubbed "municipal housekeeping," the WCC announced an interest in "the maintenance of good government, and the ennobling of that larger home of all — the city" (Flanagan, 1032). Differing from the businessmen who were members of the male City Club of Chicago (and frequently were the husbands of WCC members), the WCC

was open "to cross class alliances" (Flanagan, 1050) similar to those of the WTUL. The WCC supported solutions to municipal problems that attempted to address workers and capitalists in the city.

The men and women of the sex-separated city clubs shared a concern for civil service reform to rid city government of patronage politics and corruption. Both the Woman's City Club and the men's City Club entered into the controversial election of the Cook County Board chairman in 1912. They joined together to support Alexander McCormick, the reform candidate of both the Progressive and the Republican parties. McCormick (no relation to the more famous Chicago McCormicks) opposed the Democratic Party machine incumbent, Peter Bartzen. While national attention was on the Progressive Party of Theodore Roosevelt and Jane Addams's endorsement of him at the national convention in Chicago in the summer of 1912, all of Chicago was glued to the Chicago-style political campaign between McCormick and Bartzen.

Anna Nicholes and a number of women from various women's groups publicly charged that Bartzen packed the county government payroll with excessive numbers of political appointees. Many of these appointees were unnecessary or unqualified and jeopardized the lives of poor men, women, and children who made use of services at the county hospital, the Juvenile Court and detention home, and Oak Forest Infirmary (poorhouse) for the elderly and mentally ill. McCormick charged that Bartzen's padding of the county payroll with unnecessary employees was costing the county in excess of a million dollars. The *Inter-Ocean*, a leading Chicago paper, reported in the fall of 1912 that, through the efforts of Anna Nicholes and the Woman's City Club and other women's clubs of Chicago, ten thousand women mobilized to fight against Bartzen's reelection.

McCormick won and fulfilled his campaign promise to appoint a woman associated with the Progressive Party to a county position in place of a current Democratic politician by choosing his political ally, Anna Nicholes, as the first woman to serve on the County Civil Service Board. The Merit law of 1895 allowed the county board president to remove any civil service board commissioner for "neglect of duty, incompetency or malfeasance" ("Tatge and Greer Ousted"). Taking the opportunity to rid the civil service board of the corruption that Progressives charged to the previous board president and his appointees, McCormick quickly dismissed two of Bartzen's commissioners and appointed Anna Nicholes to one of the vacated positions. On the day she was sworn into office, the former commissioners challenged her appointment in court and refused to vacate their office in the county building. Nicholes was escorted to the county building by LOUISE deKOVEN BOWEN, the Woman's City Club president, and a number of bodyguards.

As the controversy over the appointment died down, Nicholes and the other Cook County Civil Service commissioners began to expose many problems within the system. They introduced stricter county hiring procedures that produced savings and a greater degree of equity. These measures included such things as scheduling regular civil service exams, prohibiting employees from being on more than one public payroll, and shortening the length of vacation time from thirty days to two weeks.

During Nicholes's tenure as board commissioner, she hosted events for women county employees. The first of these gatherings was held in July 1913 at Hull-House. Jane Addams and Alexander McCormick were the featured speakers. The gatherings that Nicholes hosted resembled those conducted by the WTUL. Nicholes wanted to make certain that women were kept abreast of their rights as county employees with respect to job security and knew that their jobs would be free of partisan politics.

Believing women were best suited for "community housekeeping" (*Inter-Ocean*, June 29, 1913) and should seek civil service careers, McCormick, in his speeches, echoed the language of the Woman's City Club. Nicholes, as McCormick's appointee, hired women and encouraged them to take the tests for assistant county attorney, relief work, and county medical positions. This support led to the first appointment of a woman to head the Tuberculosis Hospital at Dunning in 1913.

Nicholes's tenure on the civil service commission lasted for only two years. A Democrat was elected to the Cook County Board presidency in late 1914, and Nicholes resigned in 1915. It is uncertain whether the efforts of Nicholes and others at reforming county government were received favorably by the majority of Cook County citizens in the 1914 election. Indeed, many from the immigrant communities resented these middle-class progressive women and men and considered them to be meddling in their affairs in order to exert social control.

Anna Nicholes returned to settlement work in 1915. Two years later, illness forced her to move to Traverse City, Michigan, and she died there from a stroke. She was buried in Chicago.

Nicholes's career demonstrated the settlement philosophy of commitment to community service through living side by side with the poor in Englewood. As a woman of the Progressive Era, Nicholes's settlement experience and networking placed her as a leader in the public sphere of local politics. There she linked Chicago women from a variety of organizations and ethnic and social classes, enabling them to act directly in Chicago politics.

This sophisticated participation in the Chicago political system opened the door for her appointment to the all-male arena of county government and legitimized women's active engagement in future Chicago municipal housekeeping projects.

Sources. Biographical information for Anna E. Nicholes can be found in the following manuscript collections: Jane Addams Memorial Collection (JAMC), UIC Spec. Coll.; the Chicago Woman's Club, the Englewood Woman's Club, the Illinois Federation of Women's Clubs, the Illinois Equal Suffrage Association, the Woman's City Club of Chicago, CHS. JAMC materials include references to Anna Nicholes in the minutes from the Chicago Homes Association, the Woman's City Club, and the Federation of Chicago Settlements in which Addams and Nicholes participated. UIC Spec. Coll. also holds scrapbooks of the Chicago branch of the Women's Trade Union League (WTUL). The most detailed information about Nicholes's appointment to the Cook Country Merit Board is found in the six scrapbooks of Alexander A. McCormick, NL Spec. Coll. Nicholes published articles in *Commons*, including "Women and Trade Unions," June 9, 1904, and in *Union Labor Advocate*. The following news articles are important for information about her political activities: "Women Wage War against Bartzen," *Inter-Ocean*, October 29, 1912; "McCormick Promises to Appoint Woman," *Journal*, February 25, 1913; "Tatge and Greer Ousted," *Journal*, February 25, 1913; "First Woman on Merit Board," *American*, February 27, 1913; "New Merit Board Ousts Chief Aid," *CT*, March 5, 1913; "Doctors Must Work," *Record Herald*, March 4, 1913; "Bars Politics from County Employees," *Chicago Daily News*, March 5, 1913; "Cuts County Job Vacations," *Journal*, March 11, 1913; "Civil Service Law Praised by Women," *Inter-Ocean*, July 26, 1913; "Women Victors in County Test," *Chicago Examiner*, June 3, 1913; "Women's Involvement in Civil Service," *Inter-Ocean*, June 29, 1913. Articles that provide background and interpretative information about the Woman's City Club, the WTUL, and the settlement movement are Maureen A. Flanagan, "Gender and Urban Political Reform: The City Club and the Woman's City Club of Chicago in the Progressive Era," *American Historical Review*, October 1990; Collette A. Hyman, "Labor Organizing and Female Institution-Building: The Chicago Women's Trade Union League, 1904–24," in *Women, Work and Protest: A Century of US Women's Labor History*, ed. Ruth Milkman (1985).

BARBARA DOBSCHUETZ

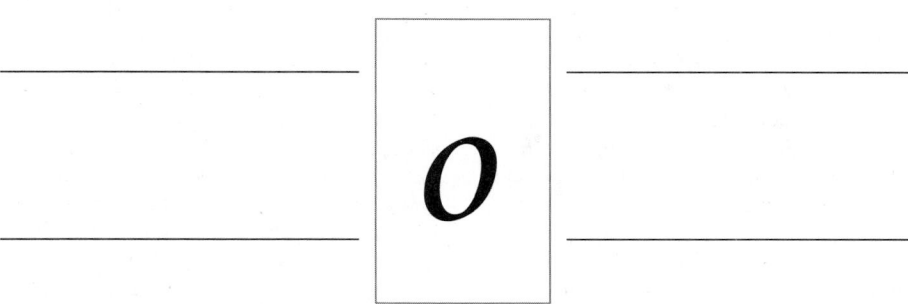

OBERNDORFER, ANNE SHAW FAULKNER
September 26, 1877–April 1, 1948
MUSIC EDUCATOR, WRITER, LECTURER

Anne Shaw Faulkner Oberndorfer, known both locally and nationally for her writings and lectures on music, dedicated her career to a view of music as "one of the greatest forces in our everyday lives" (*Ladies' Home Journal*, November 1919, 37). Anne Faulkner's father, Samuel Faulkner, was born in Nova Scotia and was drawn to Chicago in 1851 by business prospects. He soon became a partner in Wells and Faulkner, one of the most well-known wholesale grocery houses in Chicago. Faulkner married Cornelia E. Smith in 1857. The couple had eleven children during their sixty-one year marriage, ten of whom were daughters; three of the children—a son and two daughters—died during childhood.

A strong Presbyterian family, the Faulkner household placed primary emphasis on community and church involvement. Samuel Faulkner was a trustee in the village of Hyde Park and a member of the village board. In addition, he held a long-term position as elder in the First Presbyterian Church. Education was highly valued as well, and it played a prominent role in the sisters' lives. Anne Faulkner attended the Kenwood Institute, the Chicago Conservatory of Music, and the Caruthers Normal School of Music. Her oldest sister, Elizabeth Faulkner, founded the Faulkner School for Girls in 1909. Her sister Georgene Faulkner was children's editor of the *Chicago Tribune* 1911–19.

Anne Faulkner's early efforts as a music educator came in response to requests from friends and acquaintances. In 1897, at the behest of a group of fellow South Side Chicagoans attending Chicago Symphony Orchestra concerts, Faulkner began offering weekly classes—usually scheduled the day before each concert's dress rehearsal—designed to enhance appreciation of the music through study and discussion of the upcoming musical program. Initially a small endeavor, Faulkner's classes evolved into the first program classes in connection with the Chicago Symphony Orchestra. Although never officially affiliated with the symphony itself, they nevertheless became extremely popular and fashionable preconcert events.

On February 12, 1913, Anne Shaw Faulkner married Marx A. Oberndorfer, a concert pianist who would later become a conductor with the Chicago Grand Opera Company and the music director of the Civic Music Association of Chicago. They had one daughter, Elizabeth Anne, born on November 10, 1913. The Oberndorfers' union was a profitable musical partnership, and their shared vision of the importance of music education and their high visibility in the Chicago music scene propelled a number of joint endeavors. Continuing the program classes Anne Oberndorfer had begun, the pair offered music lectures targeting the community at large, often corresponding to specific concerts. In 1916, for example, the Oberndorfers gave a series of lectures on Wagner in conjunction with the Chicago Civic Opera season and performed a similar function at Ravinia Park, north of Chicago, in the 1920s. Even the pair's social events were coupled with music education; in 1929, the *Herald and Examiner* newspaper reported that the Oberndorfers followed a dinner party with a stereopticon version of Richard Wagner's operas.

Augmenting her community lectures were Oberndorfer's publications, through which she disseminated her views on music's position in the community. Her textbook, *What We Hear in Music*, published by the Victor Talking Machine Company in 1913, was one of the first books for music appreciation used in the public schools. She geared the textbook toward music education for high school and college students, music clubs, and home study, a reflection of her hopes of making music a necessary part of a larger educational experience accessible to all. As its thirteen reprintings in eleven years indicated, *What We Hear in Music* enjoyed immense popularity. Oberndorfer also collected and published music for specific occasions and uses, including *Music in the Home* (1916), *Americanization Songs*

(1917), *General Federation Song Book* (1921), *Best Hymns for Sunday School*, (1923), and *Noels* (1932).

Oberndorfer not only believed that music should play a role in people's education but also was convinced that music had power both to affect individuals' lives and to impact their views and beliefs profoundly. From 1920 to 1926 Oberndorfer headed the music division of the General Federation of Women's Clubs. As the coordinating body for women's clubs throughout the United States, the federation proposed to unite women from disparate backgrounds through various means. The fine arts provided one way, in their view, for women, whether rich or poor, urban or rural, conservative or radical, to realize that what they shared was far deeper than what separated them. Oberndorfer's strong background in music education, her popular textbook, and her numerous other publications made her one of the best-known music educators to hold this position.

Oberndorfer's publications during her tenure with the federation reflected various aspects of the debates over music that took place in the first decades of the twentieth century. At a time when technology was making rapid dissemination of music increasingly possible, defining and promoting a specifically "American" music was a particular concern of many of the nation's cultural leaders. Responses to the issue took many forms. Preservation of "indigenous" traditions—American Indian, Appalachian, "Negro," and lumberjack, among others—was one reaction, illustrated strikingly by her 1919 article in the *Ladies' Home Journal*, "We Need a Universal Language." According to Oberndorfer, the amalgamation of foreigners in America should be extended to music and composition; not only should all folk songs be sung in English, but composers should also assimilate music from other countries into the music from America. Oberndorfer's song compilations, which attempted to consolidate music from these seemingly diffuse traditions, further underscored this belief. If put to the task of defining what was "American," Oberndorfer wrote, music had the potential to become the "universal language" ("We Need a Universal Language," 37) the country so desperately needed.

In addition to preserving and promoting multifarious musical traditions, another of Oberndorfer's imperatives was music's propriety; as a particularly powerful art, music should promote and correct morals, values, and virtuous action. As the motto of the federation's music division—"To Make Good Music Popular, and Popular Music Good"—suggested, debates over the merits of popular music, especially jazz, figured prominently in the 1920s. Although the discussion surrounding jazz music was widespread, some of the loudest voices came from white people—some who owned or managed publications, some who were musicians, critics, and educators—all of whom saw jazz as transforming both white and black culture. Many prominent women's groups and magazines were strenuously opposed to jazz, citing its encouragement of dancing and other "lascivious" behavior as the primary problem. Oberndorfer's 1921 article in *Ladies' Home Journal*, which proposed to answer the question, "Does Jazz Put the Sin in Syncopation?" was a striking example of this perspective. Basing her argument on medical studies claiming to document atrophy of brain cells seen in persons who were influenced by the use of syncopation, Oberndorfer concluded that jazz disorganized order and encouraged flaunting of conventions. Oberndorfer presented numerous public lectures on jazz, discussing theories of its origins in sixteenth-century Peru or the path toward insane asylums and penitentiaries down which its listeners would inevitably be led.

Alongside her tenure with the General Federation of Women's Clubs, Oberndorfer held several other positions in the 1920s. In 1922–23, she was the music editor for *Child Life Magazine*, serving in the same position for *Better Homes and Gardens* from 1923 to 1924. After leaving her position with the General Federation of Women's Clubs, Oberndorfer continued her educational projects and publications. In an attempt to continue promoting an Americanized body of music, she and her husband published *The New American Songbook* in 1933 for use by family, school, community, and club. Like many collections of its time, the songbook contained music from a wide variety of sources, ranging from French Creoles and southwestern Hispanics to American hymns and the songs of Stephen Foster.

In addition to their joint publications, the Oberndorfers embarked on a new series of program classes in connection with the Chicago Symphony Orchestra's season in 1929, the first of which was entitled, "What Orchestral Music Can Mean to You." That same year they also turned to the radio as another way of making music accessible to a large number of people, becoming involved in a series of music memory contests supported by the Chicago Symphony Orchestra. With the symphony orchestra playing musical excerpts to accompany her, Oberndorfer broadcast weekly lectures discussing the contest material, and the outlines of her talks were published in the *Chicago Daily News*. On three Friday evening broadcasts a month, Anne and Marx Oberndorfer played twenty musical selections, while contestants at home wrote down the name of each piece, its composer, period, and nationality. The *Daily News* awarded prizes for the best set of answers. The Oberndorfers additionally became pioneers in the area of radio opera broadcast, publishing a series of opera librettos for radio performance in 1939.

After a lengthy illness, Oberndorfer died in Chicago. Her unwavering belief in music's importance as a national resource and her work to carry out her ideals made her nationally prominent as a music educator, lecturer, and critic. Her commitment to the public in all aspects of her career, from Chicago Symphony Program classes to service in the General Federation of Women's Clubs, played an important role in bringing music into the lives of many.

Sources. Information about Oberndorfer's family is found under the names of Samuel Faulkner, Elizabeth Faulkner, and Georgene Faulkner at the CHS. Mentions of Oberndorfer's activity are scattered throughout Chicago newspapers, particularly the *Sun-Times*, the *CT*, and the *Chicago Examiner*. Many of her writings can be found in the *Ladies' Home Journal*, including Anne Shaw Faulkner, "We Need a Universal Language," November 1919, as well as in publications of the General Federation of Women's Clubs. Karen Blair's *The Torchbearers: Women and Their Arts Associations in America* (1994) provides valuable information about women's arts organizations during Oberndorfer's lifetime, and Kathy J. Ogren's *The Jazz Revolution* (1989) provides context for Oberndorfer's attitude toward jazz music.

JENNIFER MORE

O'BRIEN, MOTHER MARY AGATHA
(Margaret O'Brien)
September 22, 1822–July 8, 1854
EDUCATOR, SOCIAL SERVICE PROVIDER

Margaret O'Brien was born in Graigue (across the River Barrow from Carlow), County Carlow, Ireland. She was one of seventeen children born to Esther (Costello) O'Brien and John O'Brien, a cooper. Margaret O'Brien was educated by the Presentation nuns in Carlow but followed the example of her older sister and entered the Carlow Sisters of Mercy as a lay sister (a nun without a dowry) in May 1843. She worked in the kitchen until later that year, when she and six others emigrated to Pittsburgh, the first foundation of Mercy Sisters in the United States.

In Ireland, during the nineteenth century and much of the twentieth, it was customary and necessary for young women who chose religious life to contribute a sizable dowry that helped support them in the communities in which they would live. These women became choir sisters and were engaged largely in teaching or nursing. Women who came from working-class families and could not provide a dowry became lay sisters and carried out those tasks necessary to maintaining a well-ordered convent, such as cooking, cleaning, and gardening. They were generally not as well educated as choir sisters; but, in individual instances and as Ireland's national school system developed, lay sisters were usually literate and often quite well-educated, as was Sister Agatha O'Brien.

In November 1843 she was one of seven selected to journey out to Pittsburgh. The invitation came from the Irish-born bishop of Pittsburgh, Michael O'Connor, who subsequently accompanied the small group from Dublin to New York City. On the long voyage Bishop O'Connor became better acquainted with his traveling companions and was particularly impressed with the youngest, Margaret O'Brien. In February 1844, when she received the name of "Sister Mary Agatha" and the Mercy habit, she did so as a choir sister. Several years after her death, Bishop O'Connor, who remembered her as a woman "capable of ruling a nation," said he did not want to be deprived of her services "because her father happened to be a poor man in Ireland" (Carroll, 245). Sister Agatha's talents and education were to be used to the fullest in a country where the need was immense. Over time many young Irish women of little means would emigrate to America to become teaching or nursing professionals in an array of religious orders, an opportunity not available to them at home.

When Bishop O'Connor and the Mercy Sisters from Carlow arrived in New York on their way to Pittsburgh in 1843, they were met by Father William J. Quarter, an Irish priest who had recently been chosen as the first bishop of the newly created Chicago Diocese. Already considering his future needs, he remarked to Mother Frances Warde, superior of the group, that he would like to bring Mercy Sisters to Chicago once he was settled. Bishops were attracted to the Mercy Order for several reasons. This group was not cloistered, and its foundress, Mother Catherine McAuley, and its members had distinguished themselves in Ireland by undertaking a wide range of charitable activities. In addition to the nuns' adaptability, each foundation was independent; there was no central motherhouse or outside religious superior, other than the local bishop.

In 1846, Bishop Quarter succeeded in bringing five women religious from Pittsburgh (where that foundation had grown from seven to thirty-eight members) to Chicago, a frontier town of fewer than twenty thousand people. The Catholic population, for the most part, was made up of Irish and German immigrants. Poor and uneducated, they found jobs at public works construction sites, where their muscle and sweat built a network of canals and railroads. They were forced to eat and sleep near where they worked, and they lived in ramshackle and unsanitary shacks, often called "rookeries" or "shanties." For these afflicted newcomers, as well as for the thousands of victims of the potato famine in Ireland who would soon arrive, this young band of Mercy pioneers spent themselves. Within eight years, four of them would be dead.

Mother Agatha, superior and eldest of the group, was only twenty-four when she arrived in Chicago in 1846. Of medium height, with brown eyes and an olive complexion, she was an energetic woman with an "animated manner" and a "robust constitution" (Carroll, 245–46). Well-acquainted with poverty and its unreasonable demands, she was not disheartened when she entered the one-story frame structure near the lakefront that temporarily served as a convent for the Mercy sisters. Although Mother Agatha later described it as "incapable of accommodating more than two or three persons comfortably" (Mother Agatha letter, December 4, 1847), it served as the first convent for more than a year. During that time Mother Agatha and her companions overlooked innumerable inconveniences and overcame harsh adversities while educating the young, especially the children of Irish exiles, and visiting the sick.

Almost immediately the Sisters of Mercy opened three schools: St. Mary's (girls), St. Joseph's (boys), and St. Francis Xavier Female Academy, which provided post-grammar school education. It was largely through the academy's tuition, paid by both the Catholic and Protestant families of its students, that the nuns supported themselves, their schools, and their charities. In 1847, when Mother Agatha requested funds for an orphanage from the president of the Society for the Propagation of the Faith at Lyons, France, she remarked, "Ladies do not usually bring a dowry to Convents in this country, and hence we are obliged to keep a pay school to enable us to live" (Mother Agatha letter, December 4, 1847). Through regular donations from the Propagation of the Faith—Bishop Quarter received four thousand dollars following Mother Agatha's and his request in 1847, for example—and other fund-raising activities conducted primarily by bishops and priests, the Mercy Sisters sometimes received additional aid for the diocesan institutions they staffed. For day-to-day affairs, however, they depended on themselves and generous friends and neighbors. Farmers who brought produce to a marketplace located next to the city's jail supplied the nuns with food to distribute among prisoners and the poor.

The Mercy Sisters' good works resulted in immediate success. Other young women joined them, and their number increased from five to eleven within the first year. In November 1847 they moved into a much larger brick convent, adjacent to the cathedral on Wabash Avenue, which Bishop Quarter had built for them; it also housed St. Xavier Academy. Once in their new quarters, the nuns first opened a night school for adults who wanted to learn how to read and write and later an employment office and boarding house for working women. They had become Chicago's first visiting nurses, and they had also created a kind of social settlement.

By 1851 Chicago's Mercy Sisters, then forty-four strong, were operating two orphan asylums, three Sunday schools, and a forerunner of Mercy Hospital in addition to two free schools and an academy. They had also opened a branch house in 1848 in Galena, Illinois, where the sisters taught school and operated an orphanage. These years of growth, however, also brought unexpected deaths and disappointments. Sister Gertrude McGuire, who had accompanied Mother Agatha from Pittsburgh, died of tuberculosis in Galena, and the Mercy Sisters' great friend and supporter Bishop Quarter died suddenly that same year. His successor, Bishop James Van de Velde, caused Mother Agatha untold suffering.

Trouble began shortly after Bishop Van de Velde's arrival in Chicago, when he challenged the nuns' right to hold property in common. He specifically questioned seventeen acres of lakeshore property promised to them by Bishop Quarter and given to them by Father Walter Quarter, who was appointed administrator of the Chicago Diocese immediately following his brother's death. When Bishop Van de Velde asked for the deed to the property, twenty-six-year-old Mother Agatha refused to hand it over and appealed to Bishop Michael O'Connor and Mother Frances Warde for support.

In April 1849 Bishop O'Connor recalled Mother Agatha to Pittsburgh. Determined to protect the interests of the Mercy Sisters, she had offered to withdraw them from Chicago if their property rights were not honored. Bishop Van de Velde, eager to resolve the dispute, also traveled to Pittsburgh. In the end, Mother Agatha's action was upheld; there was proof that the Archbishop of Baltimore, who had jurisdiction over the Chicago Diocese, had approved the transaction between Father Quarter and Mother Agatha. It was, however, a Pyrrhic victory. Mother Agatha, drained and disillusioned, was reluctant to return to Chicago, although she eventually did so some four months later following pleas from the Chicago community. Two years after her death, in 1856, a docile Mercy superior followed Bishop Anthony O'Regan's directive and exchanged the deed to the valuable lakeshore property for those to the convent and grounds on Wabash Avenue. O'Regan also required the nuns to pay off a four thousand dollar promissory note, in installments, at 6 percent interest.

When Mother Agatha returned to Chicago in August 1849, she and her community did not shy away from real estate ventures. Almost immediately they rented a building to house children orphaned by that summer's cholera epidemic. During Mother Agatha's absence, MOTHER MARY FRANCIS MONHOLLAND, who was both acting superior and bursar, purchased a swampy, undeveloped area in the city; it was filled and subsequently became the site of the first Mercy Hospital and Orphan Asylum (incorporated in 1852) owned by the sisters. Mother Agatha, ever ready to expand the Mercy network but resolved to avoid confusion over deeds, bought fifty acres in a suburb south of Chicago in 1852 and a strip of land on the outskirts of the city in 1853. Here, on this country property adjacent to Chicago, she planned to open a second academy and a rest house for the sisters.

Mother Agatha's plan came to fruition, but she lived only to see the beginnings of what people began calling "the big brick house on the prairie" (Carroll, 268). During the intensely hot summer of 1854, cholera again raged in Chicago. It was a terrifying disease that killed with unusual speed; individuals who seemed healthy one morning could be dead the next. Nevertheless, the sisters went where they were needed, setting aside all other duties to nurse the sick and dying. Because of the ferocity of the epidemic, they organized bands of lay women to assist them with their rounds of mercy. Following a full day of nursing on July 7, Mother Agatha became ill; she died the next day at the age of thirty-two. By July 11, three more nuns had also become cholera victims. They were among the 1,424 Chicagoans who succumbed to a disease that no one yet understood.

When the Mercy Sisters' second academy opened in December 1854, it bore the name of St. Agatha. The community wished to honor its founder, the young woman from Carlow who they believed "succeeded by her zeal and wisdom in diffusing extensively the blessings" (*Metropolitan Catholic Almanac*, 285) of their order. Unfortunately, so little of what she and other women religious accomplished is known because so much was taken for granted and rarely celebrated in a church governed by men. The sisters themselves, encouraged by a spirituality that emphasized humility and detachment, often covered their tracks. They believed that their good works, underpinning the dramatic gains in Chicago's Catholic population, would be recognized in the hereafter by an all-knowing God. The contributions of the Sisters of Mercy and other Catholic nuns stand very well alongside those of Chicago's more famous Protestant or secular women. Catharine Beecher, pioneer educator and nineteenth-century women's rights advocate, realized, with envy, that Catholic women religious had "posts of competence, usefulness, and honor" (*The True Remedy*, 51) not yet achieved by American Protestant women.

Sources. A small collection of Mother Agatha's letters remain, and they can be read at the Sisters of Mercy Archives, Regional Community of Chicago. The letters include her letter to the President of the Society for Propagation of the Faith at Lyon, December 4, 1847. Most of these letters are quoted in full or in part in two important sources: Mother Mary Austin Carroll, *Leaves from the Annals of the Sisters of Mercy in Four Volumes*, vol. 3: *Containing Sketches of the Order in Newfoundland and the United States* (1889), and Sister Mary Fidelis Convey, "Mother Agatha O'Brien and the Pioneers" (master's thesis, Loyola Univ., 1929). Overviews of the work of Mercy Sisters in Chicago during the early years include: A Sister of the Community, "The Sisters of Mercy: Chicago's Pioneer Nurses and Teachers, 1846–1921," *Illinois Catholic Historical Review*, April 1921; chapter 3 in Sister Mary Eulalia Herron, *The Sisters of Mercy in the United States, 1843–1928* (1929); and chapters 9 and 10 in Kathleen Healy, *Frances Warde: American Founder of the Sisters of Mercy* (1973). The obituary for "Mother Mary Agatha (Margaret O'Brien)" appears in *The Metropolitan Catholic Almanac and Laity's Directory, for the Year of Our Lord 1855*. Excellent studies of nineteenth-century Irish nuns are Caitriona Clear, *Nuns in Nineteenth-Century Ireland* (1988), and Mary Peckham Magray, *The Transforming Power of the Nuns: Women, Religion, and Cultural Change in Ireland, 1750–1900* (1998). Suellen Hoy explains why so many Irish women emigrated in "The Journey Out: The Recruitment and Emigration of Irish Religious Women to the United States, 1812–1914," *Journal of Women's History*, Winter 1995. Deirdre Mageean describes the role of pioneer nuns in

"Catholic Sisterhoods and the Immigrant Church," in Donna Gabaccia, *Seeking Common Ground: Multidisciplinary Studies of Immigrant Women in the United States* (1992). On Mercy Hospital, see Sister Joy Clough, *In Service to Chicago: The History of Mercy Hospital* (1979). On the education of Chicago's immigrant population, see Gilbert J. Garraghan, S.J., *The Catholic Church in Chicago, 1673–1871* (1921); James W. Sanders, *The Education of an Urban Minority: Catholics in Chicago, 1833–1965* (1977); and Timothy Walch, "Catholic Education in Chicago: The Formative Years, 1840–1890," *Chicago History*, Summer 1978. For Catharine E. Beecher's views of the Catholic Church and nuns, see especially *An Address to the Protestant Clergy of the United States* (1846) and *The True Remedy for the Wrongs of Woman* (1851).

SUELLEN HOY

OCCOMY, MARITA BONNER. *See* BONNER OCCOMY, MARITA

O'CONNOR, JESSIE LLOYD
February 14, 1904–December 24, 1988
LABOR JOURNALIST, PEACE ACTIVIST

Jessie Lloyd O'Connor, who devoted her life to documenting the lives of others less fortunate than herself, was born in Chicago. She was the first child of William Bross Lloyd, an attorney known as the "millionaire socialist" ("More Power to Galoshes, Girls," unspecified newspaper clipping, February 17, 1921, Jessie Lloyd O'Connor Papers), part of whose wealth was based upon a controlling interest in the *Chicago Tribune*, and LOLA MAVERICK LLOYD, an ardent peace activist who came from a wealthy Texas cattle family. Her paternal grandfather, Henry Demarest Lloyd, was a well-known nineteenth-century reformer and the author of several social critiques, most notably *Wealth against Commonwealth* (1894). In 1906, Jessie Lloyd's parents moved their growing family—another daughter, Mary, was born in 1904 followed by a son, William Jr., two years later—to the affluent Chicago suburb of Winnetka.

There, Jessie Lloyd attended local private and public schools, played the violin and field hockey, excelled at her studies, and wrestled with the consequences of her self-acknowledged shyness. Summers were spent visiting Texas relatives and sailing along the Massachusetts coast. As Jessie Lloyd later remembered in her 1988 memoir *Harvey and Jessie: A Couple of Radicals*, "Our wealth gave us a great deal of freedom" (p. 60). Her parents' political activities added a somewhat unusual element to the typical childhood in such a well-to-do family. Household visitors included the socialist Ella Reeve Bloor and the radical journalist John Reed. Her father joined the Socialist Party in 1906, and in 1914 her mother became involved in peace work and was a founding member of the Women's Peace Party in 1915.

That same year, Lola Maverick Lloyd took her three oldest children (another daughter, Georgia had been born in 1913) with her to Europe on Henry Ford's highly publicized Peace Ship. Jessie Lloyd was only eleven, but the significance of this attempt to bring peace to a continent at war was not lost on the precocious child. She had started reading the work of the radical feminist Charlotte Perkins Gilman a year earlier. More than seventy years later, Jessie Lloyd recalled the horror of war when she wrote that "nothing could have prepared me for what I saw. The great long trains of Red Cross cars and the wounded men

stunned me" (*Harvey and Jessie,* 73). The influence of her mother and her own vivid introduction to the human costs of war shaped Jessie Lloyd's lifelong pacifism.

Her feelings regarding marriage were also formed during this period, as her parents entered into divorce proceedings in 1916. In an unpublished autobiography, "The Contumacious Couple," Jessie Lloyd wrote that the ingredients for a successful marriage "would be frankness from the beginning, and of course the ability to endure frankness, and a sense of humor, and the elimination of jealousy" (pp. 99–100). During her teenage years, Jessie Lloyd knew only that her father was dissatisfied with the custody arrangements that allowed paternal visits only every third Saturday and six weeks during the summer. Despite her father's frequent outbursts and her mother's increased devotion to her peace work, Jessie Lloyd spent her high school years involved with the Camp Fire Girls and worked on her high school newspaper, the *New Trier News*, serving as associate editor during her senior year. She graduated from high school in 1921 and entered Smith College, one of the nation's elite women's colleges, from which her mother had graduated in 1897.

At Smith, the already politically astute seventeen-year-old was initially disappointed to find that "there was a good deal of talk about family backgrounds, about weekends, clothes, and of course, professors and classes" ("The Contumacious Couple," 151). Nonetheless, she threw herself into the rich academic life there, majoring in economics. She was also active in a variety of extracurricular activities, most of which, with the exception of playing second violin in the Smith College orchestra and two years of field hockey, were journalism related. She was a member of the Smith College Press Board, an assistant news editor for the *Smith College Weekly*, and she was invited to join the staff of the exclusive and satirical student publication, *The Campus Cat*. In 1925, Jessie Lloyd graduated magna cum laude during a commencement filled with even more ceremony than usual, as the college marked its fiftieth anniversary.

Upon graduation, she and her sister Mary left for Europe. Generous family allowances and her mother's wide circle of European contacts formed through her decade of peace work eased the way for the young Lloyd women. After traveling through Portugal, Greece, and Italy, they settled in Paris for a prolonged sojourn of cafe-sitting and sight-seeing. But within a few months, Jessie Lloyd grew bored and was soon swept up into the economic turmoil so rampant in Europe during the interwar period. In the spring of 1926, she traveled to London with her uncle John Bartram Kelley, a freelance journalist based in Paris who had been called to London to report on the nationwide general strike. Disturbed as much by the conditions under which workers labored and lived as by the inaccurate reports printed in the mainstream press, Jessie Lloyd resolved what would be her life's work. She later recalled that "at college friends would ask me if I believed in the class struggle. 'I don't believe in it,' I said, 'I see it'" ("The Contumacious Couple," 196). She would spend the next sixty years not only seeing the class struggle but sympathetically reporting on it.

After several months of working as a stringer—paid by the article—for both the *London Daily Herald* and her family newspaper, the *Chicago Tribune*, Jessie Lloyd considered returning to America and pursuing her career as a journalist. But before she did, she decided to visit the Soviet Union and stayed for more than a year, reporting on advances in Russian life brought on by the revolution as she saw it. In late 1928, a now much more experienced and much less shy Jessie Lloyd returned to America, determined to continue her work as a reporter of the class struggle.

By the summer of 1929, she was in New York City, working for the left-wing news bureau, the Federated Press (FP). Founded in 1919, the FP provided coverage of labor actions and political disputes often not picked up by the mainstream press. Given her desire to report such events and the fact that her family allowance meant she did not need to be paid for her services, Jessie Lloyd was an ideal reporter for the cash-strapped news agency. Jessie Lloyd also met the young labor journalist Harvey O'Connor.

With working-class parents who struggled to keep their son in school, O'Connor grew up in Tacoma, Washington. After finishing high school, he took the only job he could find—in the logging camps of Washington State, where the brutal conditions of labor provided fertile ground for labor organizing, much of it done by the radical Industrial Workers of the World. After taking part in the 1919 Seattle General Strike, he moved on to newspaper work, primarily for left-wing or labor-oriented presses. By 1929, Harvey O'Connor had moved east to work for the FP as their Eastern Bureau chief and was in the process of ending his first marriage. Despite their vastly different class backgrounds, Jessie Lloyd and Harvey O'Connor soon became "friends who adore[d] each other's work for a common cause" ("The Contumacious Couple," 296); they eventually married in June 1930.

For her first major assignment, the FP sent Jessie Lloyd to Gastonia, North Carolina, to cover the ongoing and increasingly violent strike of white southern textile workers. During the late summer and early fall of 1929, she sent back vivid dispatches, detailing the police assaults, the questionable legal charges levied against union leaders, and the continued dignity of workers faced with grinding poverty and exploitative work conditions. She used the same simple yet strong prose to report on another violent strike—this time of coal miners—in Harlan County, Kentucky, during the fall of 1931.

By that time, Jessie Lloyd and Harvey O'Connor had moved to Pittsburgh to open up a local FP office in that city, headquarters of the United States Steel Corporation and a notoriously anti-union area. A year later, in August 1932, the O'Connors spent several months in the Soviet Union, assisting fellow American and radical journalist Anna Louise Strong in establishing a pro-communist English language newspaper, the *Moscow Daily News*. They returned to the United States just as the New Deal got under way and turned their journalistic talents to covering the growing demands of American organized labor. Now writing under the byline of Jessie Lloyd O'Connor, the journalist made headlines of her own in 1935 for speaking out during a United States Steel Corporation shareholders' meeting. As the owner of twenty shares, Lloyd O'Connor made a motion that the company recognize national trade unions. None of the other three hundred shareholders would second that motion. Although Lloyd O'Connor's demands were brushed aside, they were reported in newspapers around the country. That same year Harvey O'Connor published his second book, *Steel Dictator*, in

which he acknowledged Jessie Lloyd's invaluable contributions in the research and editing of this exposé of the steel industry.

In 1937 the O'Connors moved to Chicago, where Harvey O'Connor set up the People's Press, an offshoot of the FP. Seeking to be part of a community, the couple moved into the famed settlement, Hull-House. Jessie Lloyd was involved in a myriad of reform activities and organizations, including the Metropolitan Housing and Planning Council, for which she made a film documenting the substandard housing of her Chicago neighbors. Many of her activities focused on women, for example, the League of Women Shoppers, a consumer action group; the Stop and Go Light Mothers, who sought traffic lights for busy city streets; as well as the more traditional League of Women Voters. Still a devout pacifist, she remained active throughout the 1930s in the Women's International League for Peace and Freedom, Spanish Civil War Refugee Relief, and the League against War and Fascism, as the world headed once again toward another world war.

In the midst of all this activity, the O'Connors decided to start a family. In 1942 they adopted an eighteen-month-old boy named Stephen and a year later adopted eleven-month-old Kathleen. As Lloyd O'Connor later recalled, "Mothering two small children was as demanding as anything I have ever done" (*Harvey and Jessie*, 208). At the same time, she readily admitted that, given her inherited wealth, "unlike most women, I almost always had [hired] help" (p. 208). In 1945 the family moved to Fort Worth, Texas, where Harvey O'Connor had taken a job as publicity director for the Oil Workers' International Union. Originally dismayed to leave Chicago, Lloyd O'Connor soon threw herself into social activism in her new home as well as into visits with her Texas relations, the Mavericks. Three years later, the O'Connors made what turned out to be their last move. In 1948, Lloyd O'Connor bought a large house, along with guest cottage and barn, in Little Compton on the Rhode Island shore. There, by the sea, usually surrounded by numerous house guests, the O'Connors spent the rest of their lives.

As she later wrote, however, "The peacefulness of Little Compton could not shut out the problems of the rest of the world" (*Harvey and Jessie*, 213). The anti-communist hysteria of the late 1940s and early 1950s impacted the O'Connors as it did all American radicals. Twice during the 1950s, Harvey O'Connor was called to testify before federal commissions in hopes he would incriminate himself and others as communists. This he refused to do; instead, both O'Connors continued to speak out against what they saw as government persecution. They also used Jessie Lloyd's inherited wealth to finance the legal battles of many other activists during the witch-hunts of the 1950s. Still an ardent pacifist, Lloyd O'Connor was one of the earliest to denounce military intervention, first by France, then the United States, in Vietnam. She later wrote that "Vietnam grabbed my heart the way Spain did in the thirties" (*Harvey and Jessie*, 218). She continued publicly to protest the Vietnam war until its bitter end in 1975.

In the midst of the political repression and growing world militarism so abhorred by the O'Connors and their cohorts, they made their Little Compton home a refuge for fellow social justice workers looking for a few days of rest. On any given night, more than a dozen house guests shared good food and good talk, followed by folk dancing in the living room, a favorite pastime of Lloyd O'Connor's. According to the civil rights activist Anne Braden, the yearly visits she and her husband, Carl, made to Little Compton "were probably what enabled us to stay in the social-justice movement, and we were only two of many who went there to recharge tired batteries" ("A Couple of Radicals," 57).

In the 1980s, the O'Connors spent their final years speaking out against the economic policies of the Reagan administration and coming to terms with their own growing frailties. Harvey O'Connor spent most of his last few years crippled by arthritis and died in 1987. Despite near total blindness, until her death in 1988 Jessie Lloyd O'Connor continued to send off fiery letters to the editor protesting various outrages against humanity, as she had done for six decades. Early in her career as a journalist, she "wanted to help people see the waste of human possibilities that grinding poverty creates, and make them want to do something about it" ("The Contumacious Couple," 295). Born to considerable wealth, the heiress to the *Chicago Tribune* fortune well understood the power of the written word. For more than sixty years, she used that power to help those less fortunate than herself.

Sources. The Jessie Lloyd O'Connor Papers are at the Sophia Smith Collection, Smith College, Northampton, Massachusetts. These papers include correspondence, articles both by and about the O'Connors, pamphlets, drafts of unpublished work, photographs, and memorabilia. Within the papers can be found the unpublished manuscript, "The Contumacious Couple: Memoirs of Harvey and Jessie O'Connor" (1985), a more than six-hundred-page joint autobiography of both O'Connors. Additional correspondence and information can be found in the Schwimmer-Lloyd Collection, New York Public Library; the Harvey O'Connor Papers, Wayne State Univ. and Brown Univ.; the Henry Demarest Lloyd Papers, Wisconsin State Hist. Soc. Library; and the Federated Press Collection, Columbia Univ. Susan M. Bowler coauthored a joint autobiography of the O'Connors, *Harvey and Jessie: A Couple of Radicals* (1988). A review of that book by Anne Braden, "A Couple of Radicals," *Monthly Review*, February 1989, is useful for gaining a sense of both O'Connors in their later years.

KATHLEEN BANKS NUTTER

O'HANLON, SISTER MARY ELLEN
(Catherine O'Hanlon)
November 5, 1882–August 25, 1961
BIOLOGIST, SOCIAL ACTIVIST

Catherine O'Hanlon, the fifth of the seven children of James Joseph and Ellen Frances (Sullivan) O'Hanlon, was born on a farm in Johnson County, Iowa, near Iowa City. Three grandparents—her father's mother and the parents of her mother, Ellen—were born in Ireland. Catherine O'Hanlon's father was a contractor and bridge builder. As a member of a Catholic family in rural Iowa, Catherine O'Hanlon was twelve years old before she received her first Holy Communion. "We children from the public schools—this meant one-room country schools—for most of us—spent the days during a six-week period (the lenten season to be exact) just studying the Baltimore Catechism—the girls at St. Agatha Seminary and the boys at St. Patrick's parish school for boys. We recited it to each other, and, periodically, to some one of the good BVM (Sisters of Charity of the Blessed Vir-

gin Mary) sisters, who found time to hear us" ("Three Careers," 87–88). Catherine and the other Catholic children attended public school during the day and in the afternoons received their religious instruction. Her instructor, Father John O'Farrell, had been educated and ordained in Ireland.

After completing her eighth grade education in the Johnson County district school in 1895, O'Hanlon attended St. Agatha Seminary, a Catholic girls' private school run by the BVMs. "Sister Mary Hortense BVM, the principal teacher, might well have been called a one-room teacher because she taught nearly all of the 'solid subjects' to about sixteen of us at various levels of the secondary program" ("Three Careers," 89). Sister Mary Hortense was the first woman religious to take a degree from the University of Iowa and had a great influence on O'Hanlon, who called her "a liberally educated woman" who prepared her students for "future study and the independent solution of life's problems" ("Three Careers," 89).

O'Hanlon began her teaching career at St. Agnes Seminary, Iowa City. Then, after a summer session studying physics, algebra, and education methods at the University of Iowa in 1907, she passed the state exam and began teaching eighth grade in Coon Rapids, Iowa. The next summer she studied at the University of Iowa again, taking courses in Shakespeare, the teaching of English, and American biography. She left Coon Rapids in April 1908 to take a position in the Des Moines, Iowa, public schools.

O'Hanlon thought about a religious vocation during this period. In Coon Rapids, she was one of five close friends—four were schoolteachers and one an ex-teacher—who were contemplating entering a religious order. Of the five, three including O'Hanlon became nuns. For a Catholic, Des Moines offered an opportunity to attend daily Mass and to enjoy other religious advantages not available in a small country town like Coon Rapids. She realized that "it was one thing to be fully convinced of a religious vocation and still another to settle upon the exact religious institute in which [her] life was to be dedicated" ("Three Careers," 10). She knew the BVMs, but after visiting her sister Genevieve, a student at the Sinsinawan Dominican-run St. Clara Academy, Sinsinawa, Wisconsin, she was immediately attracted to the Sinsinawa Dominican order and joined in August 1912, receiving her religious name of Sister Mary Ellen O'Hanlon. Before taking her permanent religious vows, postulant Sister Ellen O'Hanlon taught in a Catholic girls' academy in Bloomington, Illinois. "Living as the postulants did—much closer to the sisters of the [Sinsinawan Dominican] community than we would have had we remained in the motherhouse—also had its advantages" ("Three Careers," 31), O'Hanlon contended. It was a small community in Bloomington. Besides her teaching duties, she had chores and she had her community life.

St. Clara College (distinct from the Academy but also run by the Sinsinawa Dominicans) was about to organize a course in home economics. In the process of expanding and developing their college, the Dominicans began to train members of their congregation to serve as faculty members. O'Hanlon was selected to prepare to teach in the home economics course. She discovered she had little aptitude for the subject, but her course work in plant science revealed a natural talent for science. After her profession of vows in 1913, she took a summer course in textiles at the University of Wisconsin, Madison, that included studying the chemistry and biology of textile fibers. In the fall, O'Hanlon continued her St. Clara College work in home economics and received a B.S. degree in 1917. At St. Clara, she was taught by Sarah L. Doubt, then very near completion of her Ph.D. in plant physiology at the University of Chicago. The summer that she graduated, O'Hanlon entered the graduate school at the University of Wisconsin, receiving an M.S. in botany in 1919. Her master's thesis, "The Germination of the Spores of *Conocephalum conicum*," was published in the *American Journal of Botany* in 1920. At the 1921 annual convention of the American Association for the Advancement of Science (AAAS), of which she was a member, O'Hanlon heard William Bateson, the English biologist who had published an English translation of Gregor Mendel's classic papers, speak on orthogenesis (organic evolution). Bateson and other speakers in the symposium on organic evolution were of special interest to O'Hanlon as she prepared to attend the 1922 AAAS meeting at Harvard University. That year the convention's focus was on the centenary of the birth of two great scientists—Gregor Mendel and Louis Pasteur. O'Hanlon was drawn to orthogenesis. Bateson had stated that "the manner in which evolution operated was most probably something which man was never supposed to know" (quoted in "Three Careers," 139). Orthogenesis theorized that the variation of organisms in successive generations takes place in some predestined direction and results in progressive evolutionary trends independent of external factors. O'Hanlon saw in this theory a way to reconcile her science work with her religious convictions. Meeting Bateson so early in her career was critical to her development, "not just for the opportunity of seeing the outstanding neo-Mendelian of the time but also for having [her] own private convictions upheld by this kind of championship" ("Three Careers," 140).

In September 1922, St. Clara College relocated to a new campus in River Forest, Illinois, a western suburb of Chicago, and changed its name to Rosary College (later Dominican University). O'Hanlon studied the taxonomy of seed plants and the history of biology at Notre Dame University during the summer of 1922 in preparation for her role as chair of the new department of botany at Rosary College. Father Julius A. Nieuwland, a priest-scientist versed in philosophy, theology, and plant chemistry, was her mentor there. Nieuwland provided facilities for field work in taxonomy. She did research in the Michigan sand dunes and the immediate Indiana-Michigan area, including the sphagnum bogs near Michigan City, Indiana. Father Nieuwland was editor of the *American Midland Naturalist*, and O'Hanlon contributed a few short articles to the periodical while he was its editor.

O'Hanlon continued her education in May 1923 as a doctoral candidate at the University of Chicago, working with C. J. Chamberlain and W. J. G. Land. Chamberlain was familiar with sister students and had been the major professor for two nuns. O'Hanlon received a scholarship and managed to fulfill residence requirements and her course work through ingenuity in the use of summer sessions and by doing independent research in the biological laboratory at Rosary College. When she had to make botanical collections, wearing her Dominican

habit and sandals, "rain or shine" she drove an "old horse hitched to a phaeton" ("Three Careers," 144) through the countryside, forest preserves, and sand dunes. All the while she fulfilled her responsibilities to the Dominican congregation of which she was part, and as a member of the Rosary faculty. She received a Ph.D. in 1925, *magna cum laude*, and her doctoral dissertation, "Germination of Spores and Early Stages in the Development of the Gametophyte of *Marchantia polymorpha*," was published in 1926 in the *Botanical Gazette*, a University of Chicago journal.

O'Hanlon presented her first scientific paper at an AAAS meeting at the University of Pennsylvania in the winter of 1926. Her second presentation was in 1928 in New York City. While in New York she participated in the formation of a new group, later called the Catholic Round Table of Science, founded to encourage Catholic scientists and teachers of science to attend national meetings and pursue scientific research. Prime movers of the Catholic Round Table included Reverend Anselm M. Keefe, a botanist from St. Norbert College, West De Pere, Wisconsin; the Right Reverend Monsignor John M. Cooper, an anthropologist from Catholic University; and Hugh S. Taylor of Princeton University. The Catholic Round Table flourished through 1948. Later the Albertus Magnus Guild had a similar purpose.

O'Hanlon was given a year-long sabbatical leave in 1934–35, which she took in Europe. Sailing from New York City in fall 1934, she spent several days in Paris before traveling by train to Fribourg, Switzerland, where the Sinsinawan Dominicans ran the Institut de Hautes Études and the Villa des Fougères, their residence. The Rosary College Junior Year Abroad Program, established in 1925 by MOTHER EVELYN MURPHY and others from the Rosary faculty, was based in Fribourg. O'Hanlon, eager to affiliate with the university community, met with Professor Uhrsprung, head of botany and professor of plant physiology at the University of Fribourg. Fortuitously, he had the September 1934 issue of the *Botanical Gazette* that included the latest article published by O'Hanlon, "Comparative Morphology of *Dumortiera hirsuta*." She became a guest of the university, attending classes in natural science and lectures in philosophy and sociology. Similar privileges were extended to O'Hanlon at the universities in Bern and Zurich. While in Europe she visited Amsterdam, the Netherlands, attending the 7th International Congress of Botanists, September 1935, where she met Neil E. Stevens, a plant pathologist who soon after was made head of the department of botany at the University of Illinois. O'Hanlon considered him "one of [her] best professional neighbors" ("Three Careers," 188).

During her sabbatical year abroad, O'Hanlon experienced what might be termed a political awakening. Europeans were eager to engage O'Hanlon in discussions comparing their countries with life in America. In Amsterdam she was asked what she liked and disliked about Europe and she gave an answer "which proved to be quite rash" ("Three Careers," 204). She "had the temerity to say that [she] did not like the caste system in European countries—their distinctions between the peasantry and the upper classes" (p. 204). She had scarcely finished her sentence when a European asked a question that "completely floored [her]: 'What of the Negro in America?'" (p. 204). "Up to that time," O'Hanlon later wrote, "I had lived my life with relatively little experience which otherwise might have awakened me to the realities that I had not faced" (p. 204). Ironically, soon after her return to the United States she heard about race prejudice at a prestigious women's college. At the same time, Father John T. Gillard, chaplain for the Oblate Sisters of Providence, Baltimore, Maryland, negotiated for several Oblate sisters to enter Rosary College as students. These women broke the color line at Rosary. The Oblates were one of three congregations of African American women religious. In the next few years, O'Hanlon began to move away from her research science approach and concentration on plant physiology toward the direction of human relations, in which she attempted to use an enlightened, scientific approach to human differences to combat racism and prejudice. For O'Hanlon, this development was in keeping with her efforts to combine scientific fact with Catholic principles.

O'Hanlon wrote two college texts, *Biology: A Study of the Principles of Life for the College Student* (1937), coauthored with U. A. Hauber, professor of biology, St. Ambrose College, Davenport, Iowa; and *Fundamentals of Plant Science* (1941). A review of *Biology* in the Catholic publication *Orate Fratres*, October 1937, considered it "[a] first-class textbook in natural science which frankly includes God in its final explanation of the physical cosmos" and thought it deserved "widespread adoption, especially among Catholic colleges" (quoted in reviews summary by F.S. Crofts & Co., n.p., O'Hanlon Papers). Her field research had taken her to Wisconsin, Illinois, Michigan, Indiana, Canada, Washington State, Oregon, California, Utah, Colorado, Wyoming, Ohio, Kentucky, Washington, D.C., and even the Swiss Alps. She was active in the Cowles Botanical Society of Chicago and was made president of the society during the winter of 1944. The society had a program of speakers for its monthly meetings. In this context, O'Hanlon met Percy Julian, a chemist of considerable prominence known for his work in syntheses for steroid hormone-based drugs including cortisone. O'Hanlon already knew Julian's wife, Anna, who had been active in brotherhood or human rights meetings at Rosary College. Not only did Percy Julian speak to the Cowles Botanical Society meeting April 18, 1944, at the Chicago Academy of Sciences, but he also gave lectures to the Rosary College faculty and student assembly on different subjects, including his first lecture, an analysis of the concept, "Negro Inferiority in American Thought." Her work with the Julians, who were soon to battle discrimination when they moved into a home they purchased in the then white suburb of Oak Park, Illinois (located next door to the similarly all-white suburb of River Forest), brought O'Hanlon into the rising civil rights movement. For more than a decade prior to her retirement as a college professor, O'Hanlon's personal interests steadily increased in the sociological rather than the biological aspects of her endeavors.

O'Hanlon had published "Genetics and Human Traits," in *Thought*, December 1943, establishing that scientific study and human relations "very pertinently join hands" ("Three Careers," 218). She was asked to speak on this topic at DePaul University, Chicago, to graduate students from many allied science and medical fields. In developing her February 1945 talk for the DePaul seminar, she had the nucleus for what was published in 1946 in a pamphlet as *Racial Myths*. It was widely distributed, and O'Hanlon also continued to present her talk to groups at

Loyola University Chicago, Friendship House, the Catholic Interracial Council of Chicago, the Shiel School of Social Studies in Chicago, and elsewhere. She was a risk taker as she was teaching a new self-criticism about white people's racism in the pre–*Brown v. Board of Education of Topeka* days. The Supreme Court had not yet found separate not to be equal, and the majority of white Americans resisted attempts at desegregation and the dismantling of Jim Crowism.

Advanced in her thinking for her time, O'Hanlon nonetheless examined her own beliefs and challenged her own biases. Percy Julian wrote her in summer 1946, after *Racial Myths* was published, "If I had any comment to make . . . it would be the hope that in another hundred years Sister Mary Ellen would write less apologetically about the question of inter-marriage. It is hardly enough for one of the Catholic faith to leave this question resting largely upon the statement that 'negroes do not wish it any more than white.' That is an emphasis upon the schism between the races rather than upon the fundamental principle of mutual respect" (quoted in "Three Careers," 219). "Of course," he wrote O'Hanlon, "you had all of these inferences in your discussion, but I think this is a question which as the years go by we are going to have to be even more blunt about than you were. If two people of like tastes, similar ideals, mutual respect and love wish to marry, it is time that the Catholic Church should say 'God Bless them'" (p. 219). O'Hanlon said that "Dr. Julian was right" (p. 220), and she saw her relationship with Julian as part of a further awakening in her becoming "fully Catholic" (p. 220). She wrote "Color, Caprice, and Circumstance," in *Today*, December 1, 1947, in an attempt to pursue the concept of what a true Catholic should believe about race. Her acceptance of interracial marriage among Catholics in 1947 was unusual; this was a time when twenty-nine states in the United States had laws against interracial marriage. She wanted to do something about the taunt, "Would you want your sister to marry a Negro?" which was used, she believed, to dodge the real issue of racism.

After *Racial Myths* was published, Father Edmund J. Goebel, superintendent of the Catholic Schools of the Archdiocese of Milwaukee, Wisconsin, appointed O'Hanlon a consultant to his Intercultural Committee. O'Hanlon led seminars in Milwaukee for teachers, mostly priests and sisters, during 1947 and 1948. In 1947, O'Hanlon and another activist for racial justice at Rosary, sociologist Sister Mary Henry Gibbs, traveled together in the South visiting Dominican institutes, including Pure Heart of Mary Convent, Mobile, Alabama. They met with young African American women at Tuskegee Institute and encouraged them to enter religious orders. On their way, they were learning firsthand about race relations in the South. Back in the Midwest, O'Hanlon continued to speak out against racism to Catholic groups, including the Grand Rapids, Michigan, Diocesan Council of the National Council of Catholic Women, and the Marywood Lecture Series, Marywood Academy, Grand Rapids. She counseled at the interracial summer school at Marathon, Wisconsin, in the summer of 1949, and she did a radio broadcast with Father Daniel Cantwell, chaplain of the Catholic Labor Alliance and assistant chaplain of the Catholic Interracial Council of Chicago. O'Hanlon's broadcast was sponsored by the National Council of Catholic Men. In 1950, O'Hanlon wrote *The Heresy of Race*.

Sister Mary Henry Gibbs introduced O'Hanlon to STELLA COUNSELBAUM, who was internationally known for her work in human relations. Counselbaum, who worked with the Chicago office of the National Conference of Christians and Jews (NCCJ) and the city of Chicago's Commission on Human Relations, invited O'Hanlon to address the Midwest Educators' Committee on Discrimination in Higher Education in November 1952. The conference, sponsored by the Anti-Defamation League, a Jewish organization dedicated to fighting anti-Semitism and racism, had delegates from the Midwest Regional Committee on Discrimination in Higher Education and the Committee on Discrimination in Higher Education of the American Council on Education. O'Hanlon's speech demanded that educators strive to eradicate all "of the noxious weeds of injustice which are strangling the very essence of human brotherhood" ("Three Careers," 237). Acknowledging that this goal was a big order, she said that "if higher education is to function fully in meeting it, all subject matter which is presented and discussed in our classrooms must be purged of all bias, bigotry, and belligerence" (p. 237). She called for a critical look at the textbooks and other materials used in teaching. "For too long our textbooks have reeked with half-truths, distorted views and, most of all, conspicuous lacunae, all of which contribute to, and confirm the ignorance about facts which every student should know" (p. 237).

O'Hanlon's speaking engagements to promote interracial justice continued until January 1954, when she entered the infirmary St. Dominic Villa, Dubuque, Iowa, as a patient. The next seven years she continued to serve her community, spending intervals of time at the infirmary until she became too weak from anemia and arthritis to leave her bed. She died at the age of seventy-eight.

Mary Ellen O'Hanlon broke new ground as a woman religious, biologist, and social activist. She was a leader in Catholic social action for interracial justice, one of the architects of the intellectual framework that guided college students, workers, and Catholic groups toward the civil rights agenda of the 1950s and 1960s.

Sources. The Mary Ellen O'Hanlon Papers are in the Sinsinawa Dominican Archives, Sinsinawa, Wisconsin, and include correspondence; papers written on racial and human rights issues, science and education, and specifically, on biology and plant physiology. O'Hanlon's unpublished autobiography, "Three Careers: Highlights and Overtones," was edited and typed by Sister Benvenuta Bras in 1994. Copies are available in the archives. Bras also wrote an introduction and conclusion to the autobiography. O'Hanlon's published works include *Biology: A Study of the Principles of Life for the College Student,* coauthor U. A. Hauber (1937); *Fundamentals of Plant Science* (1941); *Racial Myths* (1946); and *The Heresy of Race* (1950). She also published sixty-six journal articles on justice, racism, science, and education, including "The Germination of the Spores of the *Conocephalum conicum,*" *American Journal of Botany,* December 1920, published under the name of Sister M. Ellen; "Germination of Spores and Early Stages in Development of Gametophyte of *Marchantia polymorpha,*" *Botanical Gazette,* October 1926; and "Color, Caprice, and Circumstance," *Today,* December 1, 1947.

RIMA LUNIN SCHULTZ
BENVENUTA BRAS, OP

O'NEILL, LOTTIE HOLMAN
November 7, 1878–February 17, 1967
STATE LEGISLATOR, POLITICIAN, CHILDREN'S AND WOMEN'S RIGHTS ADVOCATE

Lottie Holman was born in Barry, Illinois, the daughter of Thomas and Mary (Robbins) Holman. Her maternal grandparents were Southerners who moved north after their lands and lifestyle had been destroyed in the Civil War. Mary Robbins and Thomas Holman were married in Hannibal, Missouri, on October 31, 1877.

In 1893, Mary Holman, deserted by her husband, took her four-year-old son Elmer and her daughter, Lottie, then fifteen years old, to Duluth, Minnesota, to live near friends and relatives. Lottie Holman attended public school, while her mother worked at a hotel. After Holman's graduation from school in 1895, her mother moved her small family to Chicago, where her daughter had greater opportunity for a successful career. After attending the Bryant Stratton Business College, Chicago, Holman became a private secretary to George Holt, president of the American Lumber Company in Chicago. There Holman met her future husband, William J. (Tommy) O'Neill, a buyer for a floor manufacturer. O'Neill was a native of Ireland who had been reared in Australia.

Married in 1904, the O'Neills lived on the South Side of Chicago, where they had two sons, Elmer H. (born 1905) and William J. Jr. (born 1906). In 1908 the family moved to Downers Grove, Illinois, in DuPage County. There they owned and operated a flooring materials business. While Lottie O'Neill worked in the business, her mother came to live with them to care for the boys and manage the household. Mary Holman made her home with the O'Neills until her death in 1955.

The O'Neills were active in the community, working with youth groups; the Parent Teacher Association; and church, political, and community service organizations. Lottie O'Neill joined the newly organized League of Women Voters following the ratification of the Nineteenth Amendment, which in 1920 gave women the vote. Tommy O'Neill, a naturalized citizen, had vowed he would not vote until his wife and all American women had the right to vote.

On January 7, 1922, the DuPage County Republican Woman's Club was organized. Its goal was to elect a DuPage County woman state representative for the 41st Illinois House District. The primarily rural legislative district at the time included all of DuPage and Will counties.

After several attempts to get other women who were community leaders to run for office, Lottie O'Neill, Downers Grove Township chair of the DuPage Republican Woman's Club board, agreed to run. She was acknowledged as a competent, hard worker who had the strength to stand up for her convictions. She filed her nominating petitions shortly before the deadline on the final filing day; her name was last on the Republican primary ballot of eleven (ten men) who sought the two nominations for the November general election. The 1870 state constitution provided for the election of three members of the House of Representatives from each state district. This feature gave the Illinois house representation from both the majority and minority parties, since each party could have only two candidates listed on the ballot. Under a cumulative voting system, voters cast ballots for one, two, or three candidates of their choice. If the voter marked the ballot for only one candidate, three votes were automatically cast; marking for two gave each candidate one and one-half votes, and marking for three gave each one vote. O'Neill's campaign workers urged her supporters to "bullet ballot"—give her three votes by only marking their ballot for one candidate. In the primary, April 11, 1922, O'Neill led the ticket with twice as many votes as the next highest nominee.

Tommy O'Neill was his wife's mentor, campaign manager, and confidant. He helped write her speeches and directed her campaign strategies. When the ballots were counted on November 7, 1922 (O'Neill's forty-fourth birthday), she was the first woman elected to the Illinois state legislature and the first DuPage resident to serve the 41st District in eight years.

Thousands of Illinois women went to Springfield, Illinois, the state capital, for Lottie O'Neill's inauguration on January 3, 1923. They came to celebrate the victory of having a woman in the state legislature. Two days of ceremonies and events marked the occasion to salute the "Lady from DuPage," as O'Neill was frequently described. State newspapers gave extensive coverage to the events, covering her maiden speech, describing her dark blue business suit and matching hat, and commenting on her gracious demeanor. She had the honor of seconding the nomination of State Representative David Shanahan for speaker of the Illinois House of Representatives.

JULIA LATHROP, president of the League of Women Voters of Illinois, presided at the evening banquet and warned the senators and representatives "that this is far more than a junket trip, for the women know very well what they are doing" (Forbes, "Mrs. O'Neill Is Inducted Amid Women's Cheers"). As the celebration continued, O'Neill reminded her audience that prior to the election she was given little chance of winning. Addressing this skepticism, she said, "To the men of this district who said the time was not right for a woman to run, I desire to express a tiny 'I told you so,' and to the women who worked so hard, a fervent, 'Thank you'" (Forbes).

An immediate problem for the former all-male legislature was the need for a woman's lounge on the third floor of the state capitol, where the two legislative bodies met. The only woman's lounge was on the second floor, and O'Neill demanded a third-floor lounge. She did not want to waste time going to another floor while the House of Representatives held major discussions and votes. A third floor secretarial office was converted into a woman's lounge. Affectionately known as "Lottie's Potty" (quoted in Dunham and Wandschneider, 112), it was eventually remodeled to meet the needs of increasing numbers of women legislators.

O'Neill served on state legislative committees concerned with her interests in education, charities and corrections, civil service, efficiency and economy, and industrial affairs and on a joint legislative-public commission to visit charitable institutions. At the first meeting of one of her assigned committees, the chairman asked O'Neill to take minutes. She responded that although she was a secretary, she was an equal official on the committee. She refused to take the minutes.

Three O'Neill-sponsored bills became law in her first term. "These bills included an appropriation of two hundred thousand dollars for the excess cost of education of crippled children;

the amendment of the descent property act to provide for the widow's receiving one-third of the real estate of her deceased husband in place of the dower right to a share in the income of his real estate during her lifetime; and a bill forbidding the purchase or sale of certain wild flowers which [were] in danger of extinction" (*Bulletin of the Illinois League of Women Voters,* July–August 1923, 1).

O'Neill became a member of the Illinois State Educational Commission, which initiated a movement to reform the funding of education. The commission was instrumental in the creation of a state board of education and also influenced the state legislature to study school finance, including the financial organization of rural schools and the educational revenue system of Illinois.

On July 4, 1925, Tommy O'Neill died at home of a heart attack. Expressions of sympathy and accolades honored the man who had encouraged his wife to enter the political arena. The older son, a student at the University of Illinois, left his studies and returned home to manage the family business. His brother continued his studies at Knox College, Galesburg, Illinois. With the help of friends and political supporters, O'Neill continued her service in the state legislature for more than three decades.

In 1928, O'Neill and RUTH HANNA McCORMICK, a prominent political figure who was the Congressman-at-large from Illinois, found themselves in different factions within the Illinois Republican Party. Ruth McCormick, daughter of Mark Hanna, a U.S. Senator and influential Republican Party leader, was the widow of Joseph Medill McCormick, the son of *Chicago Tribune* owner Robert S. McCormick. Joseph Medill McCormick had served as a U.S. Congressman and as a U.S. Senator before his death in 1925. Lottie O'Neill's and Ruth McCormick's disagreement went beyond differences over internal party affairs. It was also a clash of women who were from different backgrounds, who inhabited different spheres of influence. In 1929, after Ruth McCormick's election to the U.S. Congress, O'Neill hoped to be appointed chair of the Committee on Education of the Illinois House of Representatives. The appointment never happened and O'Neill blamed McCormick, who was a powerful force in the state Republican Party. O'Neill resigned as vice-president of the Illinois Federation of Republican Women and vowed to fight Ruth McCormick's anticipated candidacy in the 1930 race for the U.S. Senate seat held by Charles Deneen. Deneen had defeated Joseph Medill McCormick in 1924.

Against her advisers' counsel, O'Neill sought and lost a bid to unseat Illinois Senator Richard Barr in the 1930 Illinois primary. Following this defeat, O'Neill determined to oppose Ruth McCormick, winner of the Republican primary for a U.S. Senate seat, and J. Hamilton Lewis, the Democratic candidate. O'Neill ran as an Independent. One of the major issues in the 1930 race was the proposed repeal of the Eighteenth (Prohibition) Amendment. O'Neill, a strong prohibitionist, was supported by the Illinois Anti-Saloon League. Both women lost in the November election.

Out of office for the first time in eight years, Lottie O'Neill immediately began a campaign to regain her Illinois house seat in 1932. America had fallen into the deepest depression in the country's history. O'Neill developed strategies she felt would help Illinois face unemployment and financial disaster. Despite the Democratic Party landslide at all levels of government, O'Neill was victorious. For the next eighteen years, she was one of Illinois's busiest and most productive legislators.

O'Neill had campaigned for the eight-hour workday for women from her earliest days as a legislator; on July 1, 1938, her longtime goal was achieved when that provision became law in Illinois. She continued to cosponsor the woman jury bill to permit women to serve on Illinois juries. The woman jury law, which had been declared unconstitutional in 1931 by the Illinois Supreme Court, became law July 1, 1939. Other bills cosponsored by O'Neill in the 1930s addressed depression-era welfare needs, including replacement of the state sales tax—considered regressive—with a state property tax.

Most of the laws enacted in the 1940s pertained to wartime needs. O'Neill served on several key committees: education, elections, appropriations, executive revenue, and waterways. Illinois played a major role in the nation's war efforts in industry, agriculture, and oil production. The Joliet Arsenal, located in O'Neill's district, was important. The state also was home to numerous military installations, including the Great Lakes Naval Training Center, Fort Sheridan, Camp Grant, Camp Butler, Camp Ellis, Glenview Naval Air Station, and Scott and Chanute airfields. O'Neill supported new laws that enabled the state's Civil Defense committees and councils to protect residents from possible enemy attack during World War II.

O'Neill's interest in education continued. Her initiatives reflected her desire to address the demands of a growing urban society rather than the agrarian society of earlier decades. Among her initiatives was a 1941 law that set a nine-month school year with twenty school days required per month. She also supported a law that made it illegal for a school board to dismiss a woman teacher because she was married. She sponsored a bill enacting a program of state aid to families caring for foster children. O'Neill and fellow State Representative Charles Clabaugh cosponsored a bill in 1946 that created the Illinois School Problems Commission to deal with the many revisions of the state education system brought about by post–World War II needs. The commission, composed of both legislators and citizens at large, continued to guide and reform the Illinois public school system until 1987, when it was disbanded.

Illinois State Senator Richard Barr retired in 1950. Vying for his seat, Lottie O'Neill defeated James Barr, handpicked successor and nephew of the state senator, in the primary, although the men in her party had opposed her. O'Neill went on to win election to the state senate, where she chaired the public welfare committee, was vice-chair of the education committee, and served as a member of the civil service and industrial affairs committees.

In 1958, at the age of seventy-nine, O'Neill faced a serious challenge to her senate seat when Harris Fawell, a twenty-nine-year-old attorney from Naperville, ran against her in the Republican primary campaign with the theme, "Youth vs. Age." The *Downers Grove Reporter* endorsed O'Neill, contending that she was as active and capable as she had been throughout her long career. O'Neill won by only a thousand votes in a race in which almost forty thousand votes were cast.

During her later years in office, O'Neill became increasingly conservative and often criticized members of her own political party, accusing them of surrendering party principles to expediency. She strongly opposed U.S. participation in the United Nations and in 1950 urged that the United Nations flag be banned from public buildings. In an interview in the 1950s, O'Neill explained her reluctance to spend additional dollars. "I've lived on a budget for many years in my own home. I am reluctant to put in the frills when we cannot afford them" (Moore, "Lottie Holman O'Neill").

O'Neill retired in 1963 at the age of eighty-four. At this time she was the dean of all women legislators in the United States. While she ended her elected service to Illinois, she remained active in politics and women's groups until shortly before her death. O'Neill died at her Downers Grove home and is buried in Oak Crest Memorial Park, Downers Grove.

O'Neill was considered a liberal when she entered the legislature in 1923, when the automobile was replacing the horse and buggy. By the time she retired in 1963, her views were more conservative, and the nation had launched its first manned space flight. Robert P. Howard, retired legislative correspondent for the *Chicago Tribune*, recalled O'Neill as "very conservative, but influential. If there was something she wanted, she'd get in there and battle for it" (Root, "Proposed Statue of Pike Native"). In 1976, the legislature recognized O'Neill by placing a bronze statue of her in the rotunda of the state capitol, the first woman to be so honored. One of her many hats hangs on the wall in the Downers Grove Park District Museum.

Sources. The Downers Grove Historical Society has copies of the *Downers Grove Reporter* and other local history sources pertinent to O'Neill's life and political career. Lottie Holman O'Neill, "After One Session in the Legislature," *Bulletin of the Illinois League of Women Voters*, July–August 1923, provides insights. Lottie O'Neill's legislative record and political activism can be traced through issues of the *Bulletin of the Illinois League of Women Voters*, 1923–63 (title varies with *Illinois League of Women Voters Bulletin*). Legislative information can be found in Louis L. Emmerson, ed., *Blue Book of the State of Illinois* (1923–24); subsequent editions from the Secretary of State's Office, titled *Illinois Blue Book*; and in newspapers, including the *CT*. Relevant articles include Genevieve Forbes, "Mrs. O'Neill Is Inducted amid Women's Cheers," *CT*, January 4, 1923; Jean Moore, "Lottie Holman O'Neill: A Pioneer in Politics," the *Daily Journal*, Wheaton, Illinois, March 6, 1983; Deana Root, "Proposed Statue of Pike Native," *Downers Grove Reporter*, Spring 1975. Jean Moore and Hiawatha Bray, *DuPage at 150 and Those Who Shaped Our World* (1989); David E. Maas and Charles W. Weber, eds., *A Bicentennial View: DuPage Discovery 1776–1976* (1976); Montrew Dunham and Pauline Wandschneider, *Downers Grove 1832–1982* (1982); and Kristie Miller, *Ruth Hanna McCormick: A Life in Politics, 1880–1944* (1992) provide context. Obituaries of O'Neill appeared February 18, 1967, in the *CT* and *NYT*.

JEAN MOORE

ORMES, ZELDA JACKSON (Jackie)
August 1, 1917–December 26, 1985
JOURNALIST, CARTOONIST, ARTIST

Zelda Jackson "Jackie" Ormes was the first African American woman to have a nationally syndicated comic strip, and her *Torchy Brown in Dixie to Harlem* pioneered by featuring an African American woman as its heroine. Zelda Jackson was born the second daughter of William W. and Mary R. Jackson in Pittsburgh, Pennsylvania. Her father was an artist. In 1920, when Jackson was six, her father died in an automobile accident. Her

FIG. 86. *Cartoonist and journalist Jackie Ormes holds layouts of her cartoon columns.*

mother remarried, and she and her sister, Delores, moved to Monongahela, just outside of Pittsburgh. It was a quiet, spacious community. Jackson liked Monongahela but wanted to move on. "I thought the world would be a pretty nice place to go chop up," she told journalist David Jackson. "I was ready for it, honey" (*Reader*, 18).

Jackson drew and wrote essays and poems through her high school years. Already writing a regular column for the school paper, she wrote a letter to Robert Van, publisher of the *Pittsburgh Courier*, Pittsburgh's only African American newspaper, but with a circulation and influence among African Americans nationwide. Van wrote back, and Jackson's professional career began. A boxing match was her first assignment. Because she was still in high school, she was escorted to her first match by the *Courier's* sports editor, Chuck Washington. "Sportswriters were sitting around the edges," she reminisced with David Jackson. "They were getting splattered with sweat. . . . It was nasty, and I was enjoying it" (p. 18). By the time she graduated from high school, where she was editor-in-chief and art director of the school yearbook, Jackson had become a seasoned reporter of boxing.

Around 1936 Jackson went to work for the *Courier* as an editor and feature writer, enjoying the freedom of being able to find stories to write. Later that year she married Earl C. Ormes, an accountant, and they moved to his hometown, Salem, Ohio. Ormes stopped writing during this period, and she attended and graduated from Salem Ohio Business College. After graduation, finding few outlets for her artistic talents, she grew restless. While a feature writer for the *Courier*, she had studied art in Pittsburgh and had contributed occasional drawings, eventually developing a comic strip called *Torchy Brown in Dixie to Harlem*, which debuted in the *Courier* on May 1, 1937. Ormes also introduced her pen name, Jackie Ormes, taken from her family name and her married name.

The strip was about a young African American woman from the South who settled in New York City's Harlem, intending to become an entertainer. *Torchy Brown* was a lot like her creator, an independent African American female. Torchy left the South with hopes and ambitions of success in the North. Ormes made Torchy a reflection of the experiences of African Americans in the United States. She dealt with the realities of life and prejudices against both women and African Americans. Ormes even made Torchy look different from the standard cartoon heroine of the day. She had a sexy, curvaceous body that attracted male as well as female readers to the *Courier* comic section. Torchy was smart, independent, and aware of the limitations others put on her sex and race. Ormes allowed her to live and experience the day-to-day struggle of African Americans. There had been comic strips about white female characters by white women cartoonists, starting with Rose O'Neill's Kewpies in 1909, Nell Brinkley's *Brinkley Girls* in the 1920s, and Ethel Hays's *Flapper Fanny*. Closer in time to Jackie Ormes's creation, Martha Orr's *Mary Worth* and Dale Messick's *Brenda Starr, Reporter* showed stereotypic feminine leading women. Ormes's *Torchy Brown* deviated from this model by showing a woman who was strong, independent, and more like the male-drawn comic strips of the times. Jackie Ormes's creation, however, did not fit into the model of other black-drawn comics of the era. "There were two other strips at the Courier when I got there," Ormes recalled. "One was called *Sonny Boy*. It was a family-related thing full of typical kids' mishaps . . . always end[ing] on the fourth frame with a splash or a bang" (*Reader*, 24). She remembered the other strip about a man named Holloway, always "raggedy as a batch of sauerkraut" (p. 24). Ormes's character was unique in terms of projecting a new kind of womanhood for the comics as well as a new type of African American depicted in the popular medium. She accomplished this characterization at a time when *Amos 'n'*

Andy, a stereotypical view of African Americans, was the major popular radio (and then television) program heard by white and black Americans.

Setting *Torchy* among the thousands of African Americans who moved to major northern urban centers to seek better jobs and living conditions told a story more in keeping with what the *Pittsburgh Courier*'s news articles revealed. Harlem, New York, in the thirties caught the imagination of African American migrants. It became synonymous with all that was best in the African American population. The *Pittsburgh Courier* used its national circulation to influence millions of African Americans to move beyond the boundaries of their cities. It strove to stimulate migration from the South to the North and to define issues and tactics for fighting discrimination. It acted as a voice for African Americans. *Torchy* and the *Courier* complemented one another well.

Torchy ran daily in the *Courier* and its fourteen syndicated papers. In 1943, Ormes and her husband moved to Chicago, where he worked for Supreme Life Insurance Company of America, the oldest African American owned business in the North at that time. He also managed one of Chicago's premier African American hotels, the Sutherland. Ormes was hired as general assignment reporter by the *Chicago Defender*, Chicago's major black newspaper. She reported on racial tensions at the Great Lakes Naval Training Center, court cases, and other straight news stories. While working at the *Defender*, she also took classes at the Art Institute of Chicago.

Ormes started her second daily cartoon, *Candy*, in the *Chicago Defender* in the mid-1940s. *Candy* was a smart and observant maid. Ormes's third cartoon, *Patty Jo 'n' Ginger*, continued her commentary on the issues of the times—sexism, racial inequality, and politics. *Patty Jo 'n' Ginger* were sisters who observed and commented on the adult world around them. With *Candy* and *Patty Jo 'n' Ginger*, Ormes addressed issues ranging from the continuing practice of segregation in the military during World War II to nuclear weapons in the 1950s. Her cartoons were some of the first to deal with sexism, women's rights, and sexual harassment of women in the workplace.

During the 1940s and 1950s Ormes became active in several community organizations in Chicago. She was a board member and president of the Urbanaides, a women's support and fund-raising group for the Chicago Urban League. She was also active in the South Side Art Center, Windy City Press Club, Chicago Negro Chamber of Commerce, American Newspaper Guild, and March of Dimes. She served as a board member at the DuSable Museum of African American History and Art.

The *Patty Jo 'n' Ginger* comic strip in 1948 led to America's first African American character doll, Patty Jo. Ormes created the doll; by 1950 it was being manufactured by the Terri Lee Company of Lincoln, Nebraska, and sold in department stores. As with the creation of her comic strip characters, Ormes not only invented the first black character doll to be sold to both white and black markets, she developed an up-and-coming, modern doll whose sixty-five-dollar wardrobe made her a "far cry from 'the dolly with a hole in her stocking'" ("New Queen of Dolldom," n.p.) relegated to cabin and cornfield or from the stereotypical mammy. Later, Ormes decided that Patty Jo needed a brother,

and she created "Benji." With this project began Ormes's fascination with dolls, which led her to become an active member of Guys'n'Dolls Funtastique Doll Club of America.

Torchy returned to the *Pittsburgh Courier* in a color feature, *Torchy Brown's Heartbeat*, on Sunday from 1950 through 1955. When John Sengstacke, owner of the *Defender*, bought the *Courier* in 1955, the comic section was taken from the newspaper. Ormes offered *Torchy* and *Patty Jo 'n' Ginger* to the *Chicago Tribune*, but when she found that seven people would be engaged in producing each cartoon, she withdrew her offer, uncomfortable with a system so different from her prior experience of total artistic and technical responsibility.

In the 1960s, Ormes focused her artistic talents on personal expression. She created art in all forms, from portraits to murals, until rheumatoid arthritis ended her artistic career in the late 1960s. Ormes's husband died in 1978. She continued to live in Chicago and remained active in community organizations until her death from a massive stroke.

Through her long career as a journalist and an artist, Zelda "Jackie" Ormes had the ability to create images and communicate ideas through the stroke of a pen. As an African American cartoonist, she used this power to show accurate and positive images of the African American community. From *Torchy Brown* to *Patty Jo 'n' Ginger*, Ormes's characters reflected the reality of the African American community, while the majority of cartoons dealt with fantasy and superheroes with amazing abilities. Ormes lived her philosophy of life "that you don't wait for someone to encourage you to do things. . . . If you want to do it, then do it" (Delores Towles, Ormes's sister, quoted in *Chicago Tribune*, January 3, 1986).

Sources. Ormes's cartoon strips *Torchy Brown in Dixie to Harlem* (a daily strip, 1937–40), *Patty Jo 'n' Ginger* (a daily in the feature section, 1946–65), and *Torchy Brown's Heartbeat* (a weekly color feature on Sunday, 1950–55) appeared in the *Pittsburgh Courier*. *Candy* appeared daily in the *Chicago Defender* in the mid-1940s. Ormes was listed in Joan Potter, *African American Firsts* (1994); *BWA*; Lynn Moody Igoe, *250 Years of Afro-American Art, an Annotated Bibliography* (1981); *In Black and White* (1980); and *Who's Who among Black Americans, 1977–1978* (1978). She was discussed in "New Queen of Dolldom," *Ebony*, January 1948; "Black Cartoonists," *Ebony Man*, October 1991; and "Torchy Brown Will Be Big Hit in Courier," *Pittsburgh Courier*, August 12, 1950. She was interviewed by David Jackson, in "The Amazing Adventures of Jackie Ormes," *Reader*, August 16, 1985. Ormes's obituary appeared in *CT*, January 3, 1986; *Chicago Defender*, January 4, 1986; and *Jet*, January 20, 1986.

DENISE M. ENGLISH

O'SULLIVAN, MARY KENNEY
January 8, 1864–January 18, 1943
TRADE UNIONIST, WOMAN SUFFRAGE ADVOCATE,
FACTORY INSPECTOR

Born in Hannibal, Missouri, the daughter of Irish immigrants Michael Kenney, a railroad machinist, and Mary (Kelley) Kenney, a former railroad cook, Mary Kenney started work at the age of fourteen. Twenty-five years later, she became a cofounder of the Women's Trade Union League, an organization dedicated to bringing wage-earning women like herself into viable trade unions. After more than two decades of wage work, Kenney

FIG. 87. *Settlement resident and women's trade union leader Mary Kenney O'Sullivan, on left, stands with Mary E. McDowell, head resident of the University of Chicago Settlement and advocate of labor reform.*

O'Sullivan knew firsthand "the necessity of organization" (Kenney, "Organization of Working Women," 871).

As the youngest of four children, and the only child still at home, fourteen-year-old Mary Kenney had to support herself and her recently widowed and chronically ill mother. She briefly worked as a dressmaker's apprentice before finding work in a Hannibal bookbindery. Working eleven hours a day, six days a week for a weekly wage of two dollars, Kenney "was given a chance to learn every branch of the trade done by women" (autobiography, 16). Like so many traditional crafts that underwent mechanization in the nineteenth century, bookbinding employed a gendered division of labor, and Kenney's experience was typical of that of most women who entered such crafts. Limited to the less skilled and poorer paid end of production, Kenney nonetheless excelled at her work and was made a bindery forewoman at the age of nineteen. When the firm moved to Keokuk, Iowa, Mary Kenney and her mother moved as well, living there for five years before the bindery closed down for good.

As did so many young Americans during the nineteenth century, Kenney decided to move to the area's largest city, hoping that more steady work could be found there. In 1888 she and her mother moved to Chicago, where the two lived for the next six years.

Within a few days of her arrival in Chicago, Mary Kenney found work at the J. M. W. Jones bindery, earning seven dollars a week. Kenney soon grew frustrated with conditions at the Jones bindery. Although she had secured a raise of one dollar a week, the long hours and wage differential between men and women increasingly irked her. When asked to cover for a male coworker out sick, she willingly took on the man's more skilled task and demanded the same wage. The company refused and Kenney became "convinced that workers must organize" (autobiography, 34).

As a self-supporting woman, skilled at her trade, Kenney came to realize that the only way she and other women like her could ever hope to earn a decent wage and shorter hours was through organization. Kenney became a "tramp" bindery worker, moving from job to job, staying just long enough to speak with the other women bindery workers about the need for a trade union and, if necessary, report the often inadequate and unsanitary facilities to the Chicago Board of Health. With the assistance of the Chicago Trade and Labor Assembly, Kenney held a meeting, and the "Women's Bookbinding Union No. 1 was born" (autobiography, 44).

In Chicago, the fledgling women's bookbinding union and its organizer were fortunate to be part of a vibrant labor community. Still, the position of women in trade unions at this time was ambiguous at best. Most trade union activity in this period, particularly as carried out by the American Federation of Labor, founded in 1886, focused on improving wages and work conditions for skilled male workers. Women, if they worked at all, were expected only to work before marriage for "pin money." The reality was far from the social ideal, as millions of women entered the industrial work force at the end of the nineteenth century, and increasing numbers of them realized their need for union protection.

Further complicating the issue of trade unionism for working-class women was the lack of an appropriate meeting place. In a day when many trade union meetings were held above the local saloon, a place that respectable women would not enter, Mary Kenney later remembered that finding "a meeting place was one of our hardest problems" (autobiography, 44). This dilemma was soon solved by a timely dinner invitation from JANE ADDAMS, cofounder of Chicago's Hull-House. Initially, Mary Kenney was somewhat skeptical that someone of Addams's economic and social class could truly be interested in the cause of working men and women. Addams soon won the young bookbinder over with an offer of a meeting place and the money needed to print the meeting notices.

Hull-House, opened by Addams and ELLEN GATES STARR in 1889, soon became Kenney's base of operations and her home; for by 1890 Kenney and her mother had joined a dozen or so other residents in a cooperative boarding arrangement named the "Jane Club" after their sponsor Addams. While Kenney also found time to attend classes at Hull-House, her primary focus continued to be labor organizing. In addition to expanding the Women's Bookbinding Union, she assisted in the organization of women garment workers and retail clerks. While living and working at Hull-House in 1892, she came to the attention of American Federation of Labor (AFL) president Samuel Gompers, who offered Kenney a full-time position as the first AFL woman organizer. Leaving her mother and her home in Chicago would be difficult, but Kenney accepted the challenge.

Even more challenging was the organizing work that Mary Kenney set out to do. Although she spent weeks on the road, organizing women garment makers in Troy and Albany, New York, and shoemakers in Massachusetts, Kenney found her efforts frustrating. In attempting to bring women workers into trade unionism, she simultaneously confronted the resistance of male trade unionists and the hesitancy of women wage earners to overstep the gender constraints of their day. Only in Boston, where she spent several weeks during the summer of 1892, did Kenney have much success as the AFL woman organizer. Like Chicago, there was an active labor community, which assisted her efforts. With an introduction from Jane Addams, Kenney made important contacts with the residents of Denison House, a settlement in Boston's South End that provided Kenney with the same sort of base that Hull-House had given her in Chicago. Two years later, Kenney would make Boston her home. During that summer of 1892, she met her future husband, John O'Sullivan. Known as Jack, O'Sullivan was a labor news reporter for the *Boston Globe*, a longtime organizer for the AFL, and a close friend of AFL president Gompers.

Meeting O'Sullivan was likely a highpoint in an otherwise frustrating period in Kenney's career as a labor organizer. By fall 1892, the AFL executive council decided it was no longer cost effective to pay a woman organizer, and Kenney came back to Chicago. She resumed labor organizing in that city and aided fellow Hull-House resident FLORENCE KELLEY as she worked to have the legislature approve the Illinois Factory Inspection Act of 1893. The Factory Act sought to establish protective legislation for women and children wage earners in the garment trades. Kenney helped collect data to support the legislation and lobbied state politicians. After the Factory Act became law, Kenney served briefly as a deputy factory inspector for the state of Illinois.

Like many other Chicagoans, Kenney was involved with the World's Columbian Exposition of 1893. As the only working-class woman and labor organizer to speak before the World's Congress of Representative Women, which was held as part of the exposition, Kenney relied upon her recent experience as AFL woman organizer. She told her audience, "To say that it is difficult to organize women is not saying the half of it. . . . If our mothers would teach us self-reliance and independence, that it is our duty to depend wholly upon ourselves, we should then learn the necessity of organization" ("The Organization of Working Women," 871).

Even after her return to Boston and her marriage in the fall of 1894, Mary Kenney O'Sullivan continued her efforts to organize other women like herself. Jack O'Sullivan fully supported his wife's union activities, often opting to be the O'Sullivan who stayed home with their growing family when Kenney O'Sullivan went out to yet another meeting, yet another strike.

Together, the O'Sullivans were active in the Boston Central Labor Union, holding various offices, leading meetings and, most importantly, organizing workers, both men and women, into trade unions. The last few years of the nineteenth century were busy and for the most part, happy ones for Kenney O'Sullivan. She continued her association with Denison House, organized silk mill workers, rubber apparel workers, and garment workers, and gave birth to four children, one of whom died in infancy. In 1895, Kenney expanded her contacts with the middle-class social reform movement in Boston through her increased involvement with the Women's Educational and Industrial Union when she organized the Union for Industrial Progress (UIP). The UIP sponsored speakers on topics related to labor and assisted in labor organizing in Boston and nearby towns. As in Chicago, Kenney O'Sullivan continued to try to bring together the female-dominated social reform movement and the predominately male labor movement in her quest to bring trade unionism to as many wage-earning women as possible.

This productive period of her life was tragically altered in September of 1902, when Jack O'Sullivan stepped off the wrong side of a street car and was killed instantly. Grief-stricken and left a widow with three young children, all under the age of four, Kenney O'Sullivan received the support of the communities of which she was a part. She wrote on labor issues for the *Boston Globe* and, through a wealthy friend, earned additional income as a rental agent for the Lawrence Minot Real Estate Company. Without the support of her husband, however, it was difficult for the young mother to continue organizing workers as she had done for more than a decade, though Kenney O'Sullivan still felt passionately about the need for unions, especially for women. In 1903, while the AFL annual convention met in Boston, she joined with other trade unionists and settlement house workers in organizing the Women's Trade Union League (WTUL). For the next nine years, Kenney O'Sullivan was a driving force in the WTUL.

Designed as a cross-class alliance of wage-earning women and middle-class and upper-class women, the WTUL dedicated itself to organization, education, and protective labor legislation. Within a year of the WTUL's founding, branch leagues opened in New York, Boston, and Chicago. Kenney O'Sullivan was an officer in both the national WTUL, headquartered in Chicago, and in the Boston branch, assisting in the Fall River, Massachusetts, textile strike of twenty-five thousand workers in 1904–1905 and the much smaller strike of Boston carpet makers in 1910. The WTUL also joined the struggle for woman suffrage, encouraging a much greater participation of wage-earning women in that movement. While the WTUL had some successes in its early years, its achievements were limited. One limitation was, despite Kenney O'Sullivan's numerous personal appeals to her old friend Samuel Gompers, the refusal of the AFL to formally recognize the WTUL. Other complications were the frequently tense relations between wage-earning women and their middle-class and upper-class allies, especially in Boston. Nonetheless, Kenney O'Sullivan devoted much of her time and energy into making the WTUL an effective vehicle for the organization of wage-earning women.

Kenney O'Sullivan, however, had her limits. In 1912 she resigned from the WTUL over its handling of the massive strike of textile workers in Lawrence, Massachusetts. She publicly condemned the role of the AFL as well, claiming that it was the much more radical Industrial Workers of the World (IWW) who best understood the needs of the unskilled, primarily immigrant textile workers of Lawrence. When the AFL refused to support the strike, in large part because of the presence of the IWW, the WTUL followed its lead, and in response, Kenney O'Sullivan resigned in protest from "the organization she had helped create" (Nutter, *American National Biography*).

After more than twenty years as a labor organizer, Kenney O'Sullivan did not turn her back on the interests of labor. She also still needed to support herself and her children. In 1914, at the age of fifty, Kenney O'Sullivan, with four other women, became a factory inspector for the newly created Massachusetts State Board of Labor and Industries. For the next twenty years, she inspected work places across the state, still trying to improve the conditions of labor for women and men wage earners. In her later years, she became involved in a growing peace movement and was a delegate to the 1926 Women's Peace Conference, held that year in her ancestral homeland, Ireland. Mary Kenney O'Sullivan's death, due to heart disease, came at the age of seventy-nine. As a wage earner for more than six decades, she fully appreciated the "necessity of organization" (Nutter, "The 'Necessity of Organization'") and devoted much of her adult life to assisting others in meeting that need.

Sources. The Mary Kenney O'Sullivan Papers, including her unpublished autobiography, c. 1930, are held by SL. There too can be found the papers of the National Women's Trade Union League. The text of Mary Kenney's speech, "The Organization of Working Women," can be found in *World's Congress of Representative Women* (1893). A detailed discussion of Kenney O'Sullivan's years in Chicago is in Meredith Tax, *The Rising of the Women: Feminist Solidarity and Class Conflict* (1980). For a general overview of Mary Kenney O'Sullivan, see Kathleen Banks Nutter, "Organizing Women during the Progressive Era: Mary Kenney O'Sullivan and the Labor Movement," *Labor's Heritage*, Winter 1997; *American National Biography*, ed. John A. Garraty and Mark C. Carnes (1999). See also Nutter's dissertation, "'The Necessity of Organization': Mary Kenney O'Sullivan, the American Federation of Labor, and the Boston Women's Trade Union League, 1892–1919" (Ph.D. diss., Univ. of Massachusetts at Amherst, 1998). Mary Kenney O'Sullivan's obituary appeared in the *Boston Globe*, January 19, 1943.

KATHLEEN BANKS NUTTER

OUILMETTE, ARCHANGE CHEVALLIER
1781(?)–November 25, 1840
EARLY SETTLER, LANDOWNER, FUR-TRADE PARTICIPANT

Archange Chevallier Ouilmette, one of Chicago's earliest recorded inhabitants, was a member of the French Indian fur-trading community. Ouilmette lived in the settlement before it became an incorporated town in 1833. The record of her life is incomplete, but what is known about her provides a look at the role of American Indian women in the early community at Chicago.

Archange Chevallier was born at Sugar Creek, Michigan, to Pierese Chevallier, a French fur trader, and his Potawatomi wife, Chopa. In 1796 or 1797 she married Antoine Ouilmette, a French Canadian fur trader who came to Chicago in 1790. They were married at Gross Point, an area named after a point of land that juts out into Lake Michigan in present-day Evanston, Illinois. Gross Point was a minor trading post and a settlement of métis—people of mixed Native American and French heritage. Potawatomi villages were located throughout the region.

Archange Ouilmette's marriage to a fur trader was a relationship similar to that of her mother and father. Marriages of European men and Native American or métis women were brought about by the circumstances of the fur trade. When the French and Indians began to trade in the late 1600s, American Indian women played a major role in the success of the venture. Women like Archange Ouilmette acted as intermediaries between tribal groups and Europeans, interpreting both language and cultural traditions. These women of the Great Lakes region also possessed skills needed for the fur trade. They knew the wooded terrain, could set trap lines and dress hides, and were accustomed to carrying heavy loads on hunting expeditions. The customs of early trading communities such as the one located at Chicago were patterned after local Indian ways of life.

Alliances between European men and Indian or métis women were not purely economic. They found in each other good companions, and such marriages often lasted a lifetime, as in the case of the Ouilmettes. Despite the French Canadian influences in her life, Ouilmette maintained strong ties to the Potawatomi community.

Archange and Antoine Ouilmette had eight children, four boys and four girls. They were Louis, Joseph, Michael (also referred to as Mitchell), Francis, Elizabeth, Archange, Josette, and Sophia. Four were born between 1808 and 1817, and the other four probably were born before 1808.

By 1803, when soldiers arrived to build Fort Dearborn, Antoine and Archange Ouilmette were living in a cabin on the north side of the Chicago River, across the river from the site of the fort. Another French Indian family and a French trader were living in the same vicinity as the Ouilmettes. Early Chicago was a sparsely populated community of traders employed largely by the American Fur Company. These traders were heavily dependent upon the Potawatomi for furs. Ouilmette's husband was involved in a number of occupations over the years. As a fur trader, he worked first for the American Fur Company and later for John Kinzie, a Britisher at Chicago who was in the trade. As a farmer, Antoine Ouilmette supplied livestock and cordwood to Fort Dearborn. His chief means of employment as a guide was, perhaps, shared with Archange Ouilmette. Together they may have transported travelers and their cargo across the portage connecting the Chicago and Des Plaines Rivers.

During the War of 1812, the Potawatomi, who sided with the British, attacked the men, women, and children fleeing Fort Dearborn for safety in Detroit. Only a few residents remained behind, including Archange Ouilmette and her sister, Mrs. Bisson. JULIETTE AUGUSTA MAGILL KINZIE, who wrote in *Wau-Bun* about life in Chicago at the time, told a story of how these two women saved the lives of two remaining Fort Dearborn residents. Margaret Helm, wife of Lieutenant Linai T. Helm, was hidden under a large feather bed in Archange Ouilmette's house. Ouilmette's sister sat on the bed with her sewing while the Potawatomi searched the house. When a non-commissioned officer climbed into the Ouilmette house through a window, Ouilmette dressed him as a French trader, a disguise he used to escape. Because of familial ties with the Potawatomi tribe, Archange Ouilmette and her family were not harmed. They remained in Chicago during the interim period between the burning of the first fort by the Indians in 1812 and the construction of the second fort in 1816.

Around 1825, nearly half of the inhabitants of the Chicago area were French or French Indian. Besides the Ouilmettes, French Indian families included those of Jean Baptiste Beaubien and François LaFramboise. Ouilmette and her family moved north from Chicago to the area that is now Wilmette about 1829. In the U.S. treaty with the Chippewa, Ottawa, and Potawatomi Indians concluded at Prairie du Chien, then in Michigan Territory, on July 29, 1829, Archange Ouilmette was granted 1,280 acres, "two sections for herself and her children, on Lake Michigan, south of and adjoining the northern boundary of the cession herein made by the Indians aforesaid to the United States" (Kappler, 298), located in present-day Wilmette and Evanston. The reason for the land grant was not recorded. The family was probably granted land that it was already occupying. In the 1830s, the Ouilmette cabin, one of the few residences in the area, served as an informal stopping place for visitors to the region. The family operated a large farm, raising vegetables and cattle.

On April 4, 1833, Antoine Ouilmette and family signed a petition to secure a priest for the French families of Roman Catholic faith who were living in Cook County. Also that same year, the Potawatomi, Chippewa, and Ottawa ceded to the United States their lands east of the Mississippi not already ceded in the 1829 treaty. Antoine Ouilmette and several Ouilmette children were among those awarded cash in the treaty.

In the late 1830s the Ouilmette family was involved in a legal dispute with Joseph Fountain of Evanston over the alleged theft of timber from the Ouilmette property; they lost the court case. Soon after, in 1838, Ouilmette and her family left their home and moved to Council Bluffs, Iowa, where other Potawatomi had gone after the treaties of 1829 and 1833. Ouilmette died there two years later. After her death, several of her children, including daughters Archange and Josette, petitioned the U.S. government to sell her land, saying that with one exception they were all living with the Potawatomi at Council Bluffs and had no intention of moving back. The land was sold in 1845, except for one small portion, which was retained by son Joseph Ouilmette and sold at a later date.

Archange Ouilmette's life demonstrated the role of métis women in the Chicago area before Europeans had made a major impact upon the region. Although the introduction of the fur trade began a cultural and physical transformation, the Potawatomi still dominated the area. Men of European descent in the community worked for the American Fur Company at middle- and lower-level positions, eking out a subsistence level existence, which was very much dependent upon the local Indians, both men and women. Ouilmette's decision to marry one of these traders was not an unusual one for the time. The details of her biography reveal the impact of U.S. government action through treaty and removal of Native Americans, as non-Indians moved into the area.

Sources. Much of the published information on Ouilmette cannot be independently substantiated. George D. Bushnell's *Wilmette: A History* (1976, revised editions 1984, 1997) gives a general overview of her life. Archange Ouilmette's year of birth is uncertain, possibly 1764, 1781, or 1782. The year 1764 is used in many published sources, including Bushnell's history, but there does not appear to be any supporting documentation for this date. A "Mission Register" from a Catholic mission at Council Bluffs, Iowa, dated August 15, 1838, in the Council Bluffs Register at the Jesuit Missouri Province Archives, St. Louis, Missouri, indicates that Ouilmette's birth year was either 1781 or 1782. The birth dates of Ouilmette's four youngest children between 1808 and 1817 support the later birth year; if born in 1864, Ouilmette would have been between forty-four and fifty-three years of age when the four children were born. Jacqueline Peterson's article "'Wild' Chicago: The Formation and Destruction of a Multiracial Community on the Midwestern Frontier, 1816–1837," in Melvin G. Holli and Peter d'A. Jones's collection of essays, *The Ethnic Frontier: Essays in the History of Group Survival in Chicago and the Midwest* (1977), presents an excellent portrayal of early Chicago and mentions the Ouilmettes as one of the French Indian families in the area. Frank Grover's monograph, *Antoine Ouilmette* (1908), focuses on Antoine Ouilmette but also provides some details of Archange Ouilmette's life. Mrs. John H. Kinzie (Juliette M. Kinzie), *Wau-Bun: The "Early Day" in the North-West* (1856), gives an account of the early Chicago settlement. Milo M. Quaife's history of early Chicago, *Checagou: From Indian Wigwam to Modern City 1673–1835* (1933), provides a general background to the era. Sylvia Van Kirk's study of Canadian Indian women in the fur trade, *"Many Tender Ties": Women in Fur-Trade Society in Western Canada, 1670–1870* (1980), while not about the Great Lakes area, is an in-depth study of women's experiences and influence in the fur trade. Two additional useful sources are "Treaty with the Chippewa, Etc., 1829," *Indian Affairs: Laws and Treaties*, ed. Charles J. Kappler (1903), and Helen Hornbeck Tanner, ed., *Atlas of Great Lakes Indian History* (1987).

KATHY L. HUSSEY-ARNTSON

OWENS, FRANCES JOHNSTON (Genie)
May 4, 1843–December 30, 1903
TEACHER, AUTHOR, PUBLISHER, CLUBWOMAN

Always known as Genie, Frances Johnston Owens, author and publisher of a nationally successful cookbook, was born to William Strong Johnston and Fannie (Dickerman) Johnston in Sidney, New York. She was the second youngest child of twelve. When Genie Johnston was ten years old, the family left Sidney to stay with relatives in New York, Pennsylvania, and Ohio, before settling on a farm near Preston, Pennsylvania, in 1854. Three years later, the Johnston family moved to Clyde, Ohio. Johnston began her career in education at age fourteen, teaching in a one-room schoolhouse in the Tuttle Hill district of Sandusky County, Ohio. At this time, Johnston began writing a daily journal that she kept for most of her life. In March 1858, the family moved to Chicago, where Johnston enrolled in the Chicago Normal School for Teachers, finishing second in her class. After graduating in 1860, she taught for four years at the Foster School in Chicago and then served as principal of the school for another four years.

Chicago in the 1860s was a tumultuous and exciting place for a young woman, and Johnston became active in religious and social reform organizations. To support the Union cause during the Civil War, she joined a ladies' aid society and the United States Christian Commission, founded by religious leader Dwight L. Moody in 1861 to focus on soldiers' needs. Johnston volunteered at the Northwestern Sanitary Fairs of 1863 and 1865, sponsored by both the Northwestern Sanitary Commission and the Christian Commission. She taught Sunday school at a Baptist mission school and worked with Moody at the Young Men's Christian Association. An ardent supporter of temperance, she joined the Independent Order of Good Templars in 1863. Johnston also pursued her talent as an amateur musician, taking voice lessons, singing, and playing the organ at churches to earn extra money. She was a member of the Chicago Harmonic Union and sang at Chicago's funeral observances for President Abraham Lincoln in 1865.

On October 8, 1864, while visiting relatives in Clyde, Ohio, Genie Johnston married William Lawson Hathaway Owens, a newspaper printer from Maysville, Kentucky. She worried that the marriage would take away her independence, writing in her diary that "women have to do the work, raise the children by the half dozen and . . . be scolded by her [sic] husband, the father of those same children. Men are awfully exacting" (April 1, 1864). Owens could not have known at the time just how prescient her worries were. The couple had five children: May, Amy, Guy, Roy, and Fay, nicknamed Ivy.

The Owens family lost everything in the Great Chicago Fire of 1871, which started just a few blocks from their home. They moved to Vermillion, South Dakota, then part of the Dakota Territory, in the summer of 1872. William Owens had been offered a job at the *Clay County Register,* a newspaper founded to promote the political campaign of a Republican candidate for Congress. Genie Owens helped her husband, writing and editing parts of the paper. She wrote a fashion column under the guise of a New York correspondent, culling information from monthly fashion magazines. To supplement the family's income, Owens also taught singing and grammar at the county school, sold musical instruments, played the organ at the church, served as superintendent of the Baptist Sunday school, and ran a lending library.

Conditions were difficult in Vermillion, and the family faced many hardships, including shoddy housing, blizzards, and crop-destroying locusts. Since there was no doctor in the town, Owens used her home medical kit to diagnose and treat her family's ailments. William Owens contributed to the family's difficulties, often disappearing for weeks at a time. Genie Owens humorously advertised his absence in the newspaper on February 20, 1873, noting: "Strayed or stolen, the editor of the *Register.* This is to notify all parties harboring the same, that this office, under present management, pays no debts of his contracting. In fact, it can hardly pay its own." A fire destroyed the newspaper building in 1875. While William Owens returned to Chicago to find printing work, Genie Owens kept the newspaper running with the help of an office boy. After they found a buyer, she took her children to Chicago, where they joined her husband in 1877.

In response to her husband's unpredictable income and behavior over the next four years, Genie Owens began to compile all of her recipes and home remedies into a cookbook to help support her family. The first edition of the *Mrs. Owens's Cook Book and Useful Household Hints,* dedicated to "those untiring workers who, with true nobility, add to the responsibilities of wives and mothers the perplexing cares of housekeeping," was published in 1881. In it Owens stressed the economical management of the household and included instructions for cleaning, preparing, and cooking all kinds of foods from soups to beaver, as well as directions for curing common physical ailments. A final section gave instructions for household chores like setting tables and cleaning mattresses. In keeping with her dedication to temperance, Owens did not include any recipes that used alcohol. Five more editions followed between 1882 and 1903. Owens sold more than one hundred thousand copies of her book through subscription and hired agents across the country to promote it. In 1884, Owens and her husband founded the Owens Publishing Company and took over the publication of the cookbook, adding illustrations, a farmer's department, a lumberman's guide, and recipes sent in from readers across the country. Owens also wrote several columns on cooking and household hints for the *Chicago Times* in 1886 and 1887 and contributed to a collection of recipes published in 1895 by New York cooking school teacher Juliet Corson.

Her marriage began to fall apart in August 1881, when William Owens suffered what the family called a "sunstroke." Owens struggled to support the family on her own, because her husband never recovered mentally. He believed he was wealthy, incurred large debts, and forced Genie Owens to hire a conservator to help her. William Owens deserted the family several times between 1881 and 1886, when he finally left for good. Owens divorced her husband in absentia on June 18, 1888, in a Chicago court, describing his irrational behavior and claiming that William Owens was infatuated with another woman. Although courts were beginning to question the indissolubility of marriage and to reconsider assumptions about the family, it was still difficult for a woman to divorce her husband in the United States during the 1880s. By court order, William Owens took two of their children, Roy and Ivy, back to his home in Kentucky with the understanding that they would be returned to Chicago in six months. When he did not comply, Genie Owens and her daughter, May, went to Kentucky to kidnap the children, a recovery that involved "a long search, tramps of miles across the fields, midnight ferries, a chance freight train" (*World,* March 5, 1899).

After the divorce, Genie Owens moved to Woodlawn, a community on the South Side of Chicago, and became involved in a number of writing and publishing activities. She was one of forty-seven founders of the Illinois Woman's Press Association (IWPA) and was elected treasurer in 1888, a position she held for sixteen years. As a delegate to the Illinois group, Owens attended the National Editorial Association convention in St. Paul, Minnesota, in 1891, and Portland, Oregon, in 1899, as well as the annual meeting of the International League of Press Clubs in San Francisco in 1892. During the early 1890s, she had a department in the *Chef,* the publication of the French Cooks Association, and edited the *Journal of Industrial Education,* a monthly magazine devoted to manual training, kindergarten, and business (later called the *New England Kitchen Magazine*). Owens joined the editorial staff of the *Woodlawn Observer* in the late 1890s and contributed to many newspapers and magazines.

In her participation with the IWPA, Owens was part of a growing reform culture among women who saw the necessity to obtain greater economic independence through paid employment. The IWPA attempted to further the careers of women as professional writers, editors, and publishers. Owens also joined other women reformers in the fight for better working conditions for females employed in factories and sweatshops. Owens, representing the Woodlawn Woman's Club, joined the Illinois Woman's Alliance (IWA), a coalition of women's clubs, trade unions, and religious societies dedicated to the improvement of working conditions for women and children. Formed after a series of articles detailing sweatshop conditions appeared in the *Chicago Times* in 1888, the IWA worked for protective legislation for women and children.

Working toward the goal of economic independence for women, Owens was the auditor for the Woman's Baking Company, run and operated by women in the 1890s. Traditional female occupations were being reevaluated in terms of women's rights and ideas of economic independence. As a cookbook writer and columnist commenting on work in the home, Owens had an appreciation of appropriately performed domestic work. She was a charter member of the Columbian Association of Housekeepers, formed in 1891 from the Household Committee of the World's Fair Congress. The association believed that homemakers and their servants should approach tasks done in the home with scientific knowledge of the economic values of various foods and fuels, and with information about plumbing, drainage, and other sanitary aspects. Later she served as treasurer of the National Household Economic Association.

Owens's work was cut short tragically when she and her daughter, Amy, died in the fire at the Iroquois Theater on December 30, 1903. The blaze, which started onstage during a matinee performance of *Mr. Bluebeard*, killed at least 602 people, mostly women and children, in about ten minutes, due to locked and unfinished exits, trampling, asphyxiation, and panic. The Iroquois Theater Fire, in a building which management claimed was absolutely fireproof, was the second largest disaster in Chicago history, killing 352 more people than the Great Chicago Fire did in 1871. Owens's death in a fire marked the ironic end to a long string of fires that had threatened her physical and financial security, beginning in 1844 when her family home had burned down. Without modern firefighting equipment, fire was a constant threat in nineteenth-century America, killing people and destroying property before anyone could react. Fire played a big role in Owens's life, often forcing her to move her family and start over, as she did when her family moved to South Dakota after the Great Chicago Fire. Ironically, just after the fifth fire destroyed the upper stories of her house in 1899, a newspaper article stated, "she is now an experienced phoenix and will no doubt rise again with renewed effort" (*World*, March 5, 1899). As a witness to her work, the Illinois Woman's Press Association devoted most of its January 1904 issue of the *Stylus* to the memory of Owens and founded the Frances Owens Memorial Association to care for poor women writers when they became old and infirm. She was buried in Graceland Cemetery in Chicago.

Like the phoenix to which she was compared, Owens often rose up from the destruction of her home or marriage using her strong will, resourcefulness, and determination to succeed. Her son Roy once asked his mother how she had managed to cope with all of the struggles in her life, and she responded by saying, "First: I resolved to live a day at a time and not to carry over today's troubles to tomorrow. In other words, live in the eternal now. Second: I taught myself to be able to lie down on the couch and instantly fall fast asleep and awaken in about fifteen minutes thoroughly refreshed. Third: I always went to a concert, entertainment, lecture or theater every chance I had" (quoted in Lundin, 3). With like resolve, Owens drew upon her strength and expertise as a wife, mother, and housekeeper to overcome whatever challenge she faced, whether it was rebuilding the family home, supporting her family, writing a successful cookbook, running a publishing company, or working toward social reform.

Sources. CHS holds six volumes of Genie Owens's diaries. The journals provide daily accounts of life in Chicago in the years 1861, 1863–65, and 1869. Owens describes historical events and provides detailed information about entertainment, living conditions, and social life. Some notes about her later diaries, taken by her son Roy Owens, for a meeting of the Woodlawn Hist. Soc. in 1939, are held in Spec. Coll., the Bessie Coleman branch of the CPL. The Univ. of California, Santa Barbara, has her book *Mrs. Owens's Cook Book and Useful Household Hints* of 1894. *The Clay County Register* is available on microfilm at the Clay County Hist. Soc. in Vermillion, South Dakota. Contemporary accounts of her life story in newspapers include the Maysville, Kentucky, *Sunday Morning Call*, June 17, 1893, and the *Chicago Telegram*, September 14, 1895. *World* (New York City), March 5, 1899, has a story about Owens, "Woman Publisher Not Beaten by Five Successive Fires." A typescript, "Presentation," written by Rhonda Lundin in 1996 and in her possession, provides a brief biography of Owens. Owens is listed in the genealogy *Owens Family of Virginia and Kentucky* (1991), written by her great-grandson, David H. Owens. Her obituary appears in *Woodlawn Observer*, January 8, 1904, and in *Stylus*, January 1904, the publication of the Illinois Woman's Press Association.

RHONDA LUNDIN

O'YOUNG, MANSIE YOKWAI CHUNG
October 30, 1901–February 13, 1976
INSURANCE UNDERWRITER, BUSINESS OWNER, COMMUNITY ACTIVIST, ART COLLECTOR, CLUBWOMAN

Mansie Yokwai Chung O'Young had a multi-faceted career, consistently grounded in community service in Chicago's Chinatown. O'Young worked as an insurance underwriter, a part owner of one of the oldest businesses in Chinatown, and a leader of numerous Chinatown community organizations.

Mansie Chung was born in Oakland, California, in 1901, twenty years after the enactment of the Chinese Exclusion Acts. Beginning in 1882 and extending until 1943, the American government passed a series of laws specifying that the only Chinese people allowed into the United States were merchants and their families, students, and visitors. Mansie Chung's parents fit the allowable categories for a California Chinese couple. Her father Git Chung was born in Hoiping (now Kaiping) in southern China in 1859 and came to California as a merchant in the late nineteenth century. Born in California, Chung's mother, May Tom, was just twenty years old when she married Git Chung, who was forty-two. Between 1901 and 1915, she bore seven children, the eldest of whom was Mansie. By the time Mansie Chung was born, her father owned his own life insurance company and was an elder in the local Presbyterian church.

FIG. 88. *Left to right: Frances Moy Chung, Mansie O'Young, and Helen Wong Jean, members of the China-town unit of the American Women's Volunteer Service, which operated a hospitality center for Chinese American servicemen in Chicago from 1943 to 1945.*

Her father was a major influence in Mansie Chung's life, encouraging her to pursue higher education. She was among the first Asian American women to graduate from the University of California, Berkeley, College of Commerce in 1924. Although her father supported her psychologically, Chung paid for her own education and was motivated to graduate one year early.

Mansie Chung carried on her father's line of work in Chicago. In 1925 Git Chung sold his insurance company to Sun Life Insurance Company of Canada and was managing a branch office in Oakland. The following year, father and daughter traveled to Chicago so that Git Chung could establish Mansie Chung as the Chinese agent for the Sun Life branch office in the midwest city. Some fifty Chinese families, largely from the Toishan (now Taishan) area in southern China, lived in the vicinity of Chicago's Chinatown. Most were having difficulty maintaining a steady source of income.

Mansie Chung overcame several challenges as she developed the insurance business among Chicago's Chinese. Chinese families generally were afraid to buy life insurance for fear that the very act would bring forth an untimely death. In California, life insurance had overcome traditional resistance because it met the needs of complex family situations there. However, in Chicago, families provided for themselves because they were well-defined and close-knit. In addition to encouraging them to accept the concept of life insurance, Mansie Chung had to convince the Chinatown community that they could do business with a woman, since her professional ambitions were considered odd. Mansie Chung's success was due largely to her identity as a member of a southern Chinese family and to Git Chung's connections with clansmen. She served as a notary public when she first came to Chicago and notarized documents for one of the earliest families in Chinatown, headed by Moy Dung Hoy. He had come from the same village as Mansie Chung's father, who probably introduced her to Moy. This connection helped her gain acceptance in the Chinese merchant community. Later in her career she joined the Chinese Benevolent Society as its first female member under the Chung family name.

Through formal correspondence, Git Chung's cousin introduced Mansie Chung to his roommate, Henry Au Yeung. In 1928, they married; later the Au Yeung was changed to O'Young. Henry Au Yeung was an immigrant merchant from the Toishan (now Taishan) village who sold supplies to Chinese laundries. He maintained strong ties to his family in China, bringing over nephews and other family members. His merchant status allowed him to travel easily between the United States and China. In Chicago, the O'Youngs bought their first home in the Roger's Park neighborhood.

Despite the initial hesitancy on the part of Chinese customers, Mansie and Henry O'Young developed life insurance into a viable business. In Chinatown, however, he sold the insurance and she did the bookkeeping. This presentation was replicated when the couple bought the Hong Kong Noodle Company, one of the oldest businesses in Chinatown. He was in charge of the marketing—developing all of the professional connections—and she was in charge of payroll. This division of labor did not offend Chinese American customers' notions of proper gender roles, and Mansie O'Young also preferred the detail-oriented aspects of the business. A granddaughter remembers her perfectly manicured red nails clicking across the beads of the Chinese abacus as she tallied accounts. Her husband made the contacts in Chinatown and sold the insurance policies, while Mansie O'Young acquired the official credentials. In 1935, she became the first Chinese American woman to become chartered as a life underwriter. Eventually, she was accepted by her male peers and was considered to be the stronger business partner.

In the 1930s, Mansie O'Young was regarded by those in Chinatown as a true pioneer because she had obtained a college degree from a prestigious university and subsequently pursued a career in business. Yet despite her education and business acumen, O'Young faced discrimination. American banks in Chicago and elsewhere generally would not do business with Chinese clients. Thus, she had to deal with banks in Chinatown even though she lived elsewhere, and the Sun Life office where she worked was in the central business district in Chicago.

In the early 1930s, she adopted her first child, Agnes, through an agency in California. Shortly thereafter, her mother and father died. After their deaths, O'Young began to travel regularly to China. She eventually adopted another child from China, Herbert, her husband's nephew. Continuing her business, O'Young hired a nanny to care for the children.

In her travels, O'Young collected a vast array of Chinese art and sculpture. In Chicago she became friends with another admirer of Chinese art, OLGA HUNCKE—an American from a German immigrant family—who taught at Haines Elementary School in Chinatown. Both O'Young and Huncke lived on the North Side of Chicago, commuted daily to Chinatown, and contributed to, but did not attend, the Chinese Christian Union Church. In contrast to Huncke, who had already defined her role in Chinatown as a friend and advocate of the Chinese and had become deeply involved in the personal lives of many Chinatown families, O'Young still had not found a place.

By the 1950s O'Young was part of a cadre of well-educated Chinese Americans who collectively were interested in asserting their rights as American citizens and also in upholding Chinese cultural values. She served as the treasurer of the Chinese Association of Civic Affairs, the primary civic organization of Chinatown, and as president of the Chinese Women's Club. The women's club, whose members included such professionals as Dr. MARGARET LIN, focused on local issues but also worked in cooperation with national groups like the American Red Cross.

O'Young also achieved recognition beyond the borders of Chinatown. Over the years she and her husband cultivated the friendships of many of Chicago's political, business, and social leaders, including Mayor Richard J. Daley. The O'Youngs attended many high-profile social functions with other city leaders. Mansie O'Young's art collection grew and, on display in her luxury apartment on the North Side, her Chinese sculpture and art became a Chicago treasure. Inviting the news media to visit and view her collection, O'Young furthered her relationship with the broader Chicago community. Mansie O'Young died of cancer at the age of seventy-five, six months after her husband's death, also of cancer. She is buried at Rosehill Cemetery.

Sources. The Olga Huncke papers at the CHS provided several pieces of information on O'Young's career and community service. Further information about O'Young came from interviews with her friends and family 1993–95. They include Theresa O'Young, a niece who knew her very well throughout her life and cared for her and her husband when she was ill; Gung Hsing Wang, a real estate developer and community activist in Chinatown; Celia Chung and Pauline Luke, community activists; Ping Tom, business owner and community leader; and Mansie Jean O'Leary, a granddaughter. Susan Lee Moy verified historical facts on the development of Chicago's Chinatown. Information on Chinese Americans can be found in Tin Chiu Fan's *Chinese Residents in Chicago* (1925); Yuan Liang's *The Chinese Family in Chicago* (1951); Betty L. Sung's *Mountain of Gold: The Story of the Chinese in America* (1967); Yuan-li Wu's *The Economic Conditions of Chinese in America* (1980); Judy Yung's *Chinese Women of America* (1987); Ruthanne Lum McCunn's *Chinese American Portraits* (1988); Roger Daniels's *Asian America* (1988); Suchen Chan's "The Exclusion of Chinese Women, 1870–1943," in the Chinese Hist. Soc. of America's *Chinese America: History and Perspectives* (1994); Susan Lee Moy's "The Chinese of Chicago: The First One Hundred Years," in *Ethnic Chicago,* ed. Melvin G. Holli and Peter d'A. Jones (1995); and Lisa See's *On Gold Mountain* (1995).

PEGGY SPITZER CHRISTOFF

PALERMO, LUCY MARY RUSSO
October 17, 1885–December 9, 1979
POLITICAL ACTIVIST, POLITICIAN, SOCIAL SERVICE WORKER,
CLUBWOMAN

According to her daughter, lawyer Julia Martoccio, Lucy Russo Palermo became the first woman of Italian descent to be elected to a major political office in the United States. Palermo was elected to serve as a Cook County Commissioner from 1934 to 1938, a position that allowed her the opportunity to serve the interests of the indigent and infirm during the depths of the Great Depression. A lifelong social and political activist, Lucy Russo was born to Leonardo and Theresa Russo in Roseland, Illinois, a village southwest of Chicago later incorporated in the metropolis. Immigrants from Laurensana, Italy, a small town near Naples, Lucy Russo's parents arrived in the Chicago area in the early 1880s. Lucy was one of six children. When Lucy Russo was young, the family moved to the predominantly Italian immigrant community in the Taylor and Halsted Street neighborhood. Leonardo Russo operated a saloon near Polk and Des Plaines Streets on Chicago's Near West Side.

At seventeen, Lucy Russo married Eugene Palermo, who had immigrated to Chicago from Calabria, Italy. The couple wed on June 14, 1903, in the Guardian Angel Roman Catholic Church. Eugene Palermo had not yet become a naturalized citizen. American law at the time followed the common-law practice of coverture, according to which women, once they married, assumed the legal status of their husbands. As a consequence of her marriage, Lucy Russo Palermo lost her U.S. citizenship.

Eugene Palermo established a horse and buggy business that years later grew into a livery rental company with a fleet of Pierce-Arrow cruising cars. The cars were rented primarily to service funerals. The Palermos had five children: Rose, Amiel, Julia, Eugene Jr., and Albert. Despite her busy household, Palermo participated with other Italian American women in fund-raising activities to support Francis Xavier Cabrini Hospital, a facility in the Italian Near West Side neighborhood that was founded by Mother Francis Xavier Cabrini during one of her missionary visits to the United States. Lucy Palermo organized the Italian Aid Society in 1926 and acted as supervisor of social services for the organization. The group focused on aiding residents of the Oak Forest Institution for the Aged and Infirm (later the Oak Forest Infirmary and Tuberculosis Sanitarium), which Palermo began visiting in 1922. She continued to devote her time to the home for twenty-five years. The women in the society brought the patients weekly dinners and worked to improve the conditions of the institution, which was notoriously overcrowded.

Throughout her years in Chicago, Palermo was deeply involved in a wide variety of social service efforts and local women's clubs. Founder and president of the Columbus Club, an Italian American women's organization affiliated with the Illinois Federation of Women's Clubs (IFWC), Palermo later became president of the Italian Aid Federated Clubs, an organization that she had founded in 1926; it was made up of representatives of Italian women's clubs in the city. In 1936 the federation, with offices on Chicago's Near West Side, increased its membership from the original twelve clubs to five hundred. She was also a vice-president of the Chicago and Cook County Federation of Women's Organizations, with which the Italian Aid Federated Clubs were affiliated. Palermo sat on the board of directors of the Italian Youth Recreation League, was president of the Illinois Free Emergency Ambulance Service, and sponsored her own softball team, the Lucy Palermos, in 1934, the year that she ran for public office for the first time. That year she served as one of the honorary hostesses at Chicago's Century of Progress Exposition. In that capacity she had the opportunity to meet First Lady Eleanor Roosevelt.

In 1934, as the economic conditions of the nation worsened and the politics of Franklin Delano Roosevelt and the New Deal coalition were in the ascendancy, Lucy Palermo ran for the Cook County Board of Commissioners. She entered the race as an independent Democrat candidate, but after the death of Democratic Party candidate Joseph M. Fitzgerald, she won the endorsement of the party and Fitzgerald's spot on the Democratic ticket. Her advertisements announced that she was "the Friend of the Poor" and listed her achievements in area clubs and social service work. Palermo won the election, becoming one of three women on the thirteen-member board, all of them Democrats. Independent in her views, Palermo was a forceful personality on the county board, taking her direction from inner convictions rather than from the party leadership or more experienced commissioners. Her conflicts with the other women commissioners were a source of interest to the news media.

Palermo used her position on the Cook County Board to continue to advance a social service agenda for the needy of Chicago that she had worked for as a volunteer activist and clubwoman. In February 1937, Palermo encouraged the board to hire an efficiency expert to examine operations at the Cook County Hospital and to assist the commissioners in overseeing the Oak Forest Infirmary and Tuberculosis Sanitarium. She served on the hospital's blood bank committee, established in Chicago in March 1937 and one of the first of its kind in the United States. As part of her duties, she also served as vice-president of the Court Committee of the Juvenile Home and chaired the Cook County Public Welfare Committee. As a commissioner she was also involved with the Cook County Hospital and the Cook County Hospital Nurses' Home. She worked to establish Camp Palermo, on Archer Avenue, a summer recreation center for school children. In keeping with her longtime commitment to upgrading the quality of life of senior citizens, Palermo was a leading voice in favor of establishing old age pensions in Illinois. She influenced the writing of the successful legislation introduced in the Illinois legislature on January 10, 1935, by Democratic State Senator A. J. Prigano.

At the same time that the nation faced economic depression at home, many Americans began to respond to the growing tension in Europe and impending world war. Palermo joined the pro-Fascist antiwar group, "We the Mothers Mobilize for America, Inc.," prior to America's entrance into World War II and served as its vice-president. Palermo had shown an independent attitude toward her fellow Democrats before, so it was not unusual for her to break with New Deal Democrats who supported the pro-ally stance of President Roosevelt. First generation Americans had to deal with loyalties at home and abroad, and until the United States entered the war, local groups divided over European events. Yet "We the Mothers" was an extremist group whose attacks on other Americans went beyond the issue of isolationism. Led by the openly anti-Semitic Lyrl Clark Van Hyning, the members of the group feared sending their sons overseas into battle and worried that this action would leave the continental United States without adequate manpower for self-defense. "We the Mothers" was the largest isolationist mother's organization active during World War II. It was incorporated as a tax-exempt organization in February 1941 by Van Hyning, Lucy Palermo, and Grace Keefe. That same month, the Chicago chapter of "We the Mothers" gained national attention by joining with other women from across the country in a mass

demonstration in Washington, D.C., led by ELIZABETH DILLING. Dilling, a Nazi sympathizer and member of "We the Mothers," led the Washington mobilization to protest President Franklin D. Roosevelt's Lend-Lease plan, which had been signed into law on March 11, 1941. Although the United States was still neutral, Roosevelt asked Congress to provide military aid to foreign countries whose defense he judged vital to the United States. To show their opposition, "We the Mothers" wore traditional black mourning dresses and veils as they staged a sit-in on the White House steps. Locally, "We the Mothers" held weekly meetings in members' homes to organize their many antiwar activities, including lobbying, letter writing, and publication of the virulently anti-Semitic *Women's Voice*.

Palermo maintained her membership in "We the Mothers" after the United States entered the war in December 1941, but she no longer fully supported the isolationist position of the group. Palermo told interviewers that "now that we are in it, I am in favor of doing everything possible to go along with the government in the prosecution of the war" (Mueller, "Question 2 More 'We Mothers'"). Palermo demonstrated this commitment with her work for the Ogden Park Auxiliary of the American Red Cross.

In 1942, Palermo and other leaders of "We the Mothers" were investigated for sedition against the United States by the Federal Bureau of Investigation (FBI). In addition to investigation of individuals, organizations such as "We the Mothers" were being examined to determine whether or not they were the source of antiwar propaganda. On April 30, 1942, Palermo appeared before a federal grand jury. By January 4, 1943, however, "We the Mothers" was no longer under suspicion. It remains unclear why the charges against the movement were dropped. Palermo claimed she escaped examination as an individual due to the fact that her sons were serving in the U.S. military, but similar circumstances did not free others involved with antiwar groups.

Palermo's son Amiel, a physician with the 31st Infantry, was held captive for two years by Japanese forces in the Philippines before returning home. Palermo founded the Bataan War Prisoners Relief of Illinois, which worked to ease the conditions of American prisoners of war who were survivors of the infamous death march to prison camps in the Philippine Islands and also others in Japanese camps. In a letter dated August 6, 1945, ironically the day the first atomic bomb was dropped on the Japanese city of Hiroshima, Palermo encouraged U.S. citizens to address protests to the State and War departments in Washington, D.C., to demand *"protection* for each and every prisoner" of war ("Dear Friend," Bataan War Prisoners Relief of Illinois, August 6, 1945, Palermo's papers).

Palermo and her husband moved to Tucson, Arizona, in the early 1950s, and Palermo again involved herself in politics. She opened an antique store in Tucson after her husband died in 1953, and she founded the Tucson Property Owners Protective Association (POPA), which helped to preserve Tucson's historic City Hall from demolition. Palermo served as a board member of POPA, as chair of its fact-finding committee, and as the publisher of the *Pima County Women's Crusader*, the organization's bulletin. Palermo published the bulletin from her home for twenty years.

A lifelong Democrat despite her work with the extreme Right during World War II, Palermo also was president of the Italian American division of the Democratic National Committee. She sat on the executive and organizing committees of the Pima County Democratic Central Committee and worked to rally support for Democratic candidates, including John F. Kennedy and Lyndon B. Johnson. During her years in Tucson, Palermo was a member of the Order of the Sons of Italy in America, Old Pueblo Lodge #2349. She also sold her own brand of beauty cream called "Eternal Youth."

In 1971, at age eighty-six, Palermo tried again to gain political office, running for the Pima County Board of Supervisors, District 4. Announcing that she would serve only one term, Palermo said, "I just want to have enough time to clean up this place and to have someone for an understudy to continue my investigations" (quoted in Christina Collins, "Great-Grandmother Vows to Clean Up Pima County," unidentified newspaper clipping, December 2, 1971, Palermo's papers). She told voters, "I'm going to put myself into this campaign and I won't stop until I'm laid in that coffin" (quoted in Collins). Palermo campaigned by distributing pamphlets she had written using her one-finger typing method. She mimeographed copies at home, just as she had printed issues of her *Women's Crusader*. She lost the election but continued her interest in government.

Palermo died at age ninety-four from complications after a heart attack. She is buried at the Holy Hope Cemetery, Tucson. Although she held office only from 1934 to 1938, she remained active in politics for the rest of her life. On September 18, 1994, Palermo was honored posthumously for her life of public achievement by the Women's Division of the Joint Civic Committee of Italian Americans. She was one of the committee's first four Impresa Award recipients.

Sources. Copies of personal papers belonging to Lucy Russo Palermo are located in the Italian Cultural Center Library, Stone Park, Illinois. This article also draws on interviews in 1995 by Lisa Boehm with Julia Palermo Martoccio, daughter of Lucy Palermo. Records pertaining to Cook County Hospital are held by CHS, including records of meetings attended by Palermo and documents pertaining to the establishment of the Cook County Hospital blood bank. Information regarding Palermo can also be found in most contemporary Chicago newspapers, especially the *CT*. Glen Jeansonne's *Women of the Far Right: The Mother's Movement and World War II* (1996) provides background information on "We the Mothers of America" and briefly mentions Palermo's contributions to the organization. Henry Hoke, *It's a Secret* (1946) follows the course of the grand jury sedition investigations of "We the Mothers" but makes no mention of Palermo. See William A. Mueller, "Question 2 More 'We Mothers,'" *Chicago Daily Times*, April 29, 1942, and "Two More Heard in Grand Jury's Sedition Probe," *CT*, April 30, 1942.

LISA KRISSOFF BOEHM

PALMER, BERTHA HONORÉ
May 22, 1849–May 5, 1918

PHILANTHROPIST, CLUBWOMAN, ART COLLECTOR

Bertha Honoré Palmer achieved national prominence as president of the Board of Lady Managers during the 1893 World's Columbian Exposition. An adventurous purchaser of art, she donated her significant collection of French impressionist paintings to the Art Institute of Chicago (AIC).

FIG. 89. *Society leader and art patron Bertha Honoré Palmer in 1900.*

Bertha Honoré was born in Louisville, Kentucky, the second of six children and the first of two daughters of Henry Hamilton and Eliza Jane (Carr) Honoré. The Honorés ran a cutlery and hardware importing business in Louisville and had a family estate in Bowling Green, Kentucky. In 1855, when Bertha Honoré was six, Henry Honoré moved his family to Chicago, where he invested in real estate. The family lived in Union Square on Chicago's West Side, then a fashionable neighborhood settled by Kentuckians. The Honorés attended the First Christian Church.

During the Civil War, the Honorés comforted Confederate prisoners at Camp Douglas in Chicago with food and clothing, motivated by Christian charity and ties to the South. They supported the Northwestern Sanitary fairs, held in 1863 and 1865, to raise money for supplies to aid wounded and ill Union soldiers. Bertha Honoré's parents raised her with a sense of noblesse oblige.

Bertha Honoré attended St. Xavier Academy and then Dearborn Seminary, in Chicago. After the Civil War, she attended Visitation Convent, a finishing school run by Catholic nuns in the fashionable Georgetown neighborhood of Washington, D.C. She graduated with honors in 1867 and returned to Chicago, where she made her social debut, entering her parents' milieu. The circle included Potter Palmer, whom Bertha Honoré first met in 1862, when she was thirteen and he was thirty-six.

Potter Palmer had come to Chicago from New York in 1852 to pursue a career as a dry-goods merchant. He soon became a leading retailer by establishing an innovative credit system for his customers. Twelve years later he sold his store to Levi Leiter and Marshall Field, then turned his business acumen to real estate development. Worth seven million dollars by 1865, Palmer created a new retail center in downtown Chicago anchored by his luxurious Palmer House Hotel.

Bertha Honoré and Potter Palmer were married in July 1870 at the Honoré home. The Palmer House hotel was completed just days before the Great Chicago Fire of October 8 and 9, 1871. The fire destroyed almost all of downtown Chicago, including the hotel and most of Potter Palmer's other commercial properties. The Palmers and the city recovered rapidly. Their first son, Honoré, was born in 1874, the year the family moved into the rebuilt Palmer House. Their second and last child, Potter Jr., was born the following year.

In 1882, architects Henry Ives Cobb and Charles S. Frost built a castle-like mansion for the Palmers on a lot occupying half a city block on Chicago's North Side. Again, the Palmers were ahead of the crowd: the location was unusual and relatively undeveloped with most of Chicago's wealthy elite living on the South Side in the Prairie Avenue neighborhood. Completed in 1885, the mansion included a red-velvet-paneled ballroom where the Palmers displayed their impressive art collection. With home, family, and fortune established by the mid-1880s, Bertha Palmer was poised to join other wealthy Chicago women in literary and cultural clubs that were both social and philanthropic in their aims.

From the 1870s on, women's clubs provided upper-class and middle-class women with opportunities to participate in public life. The clubs' programs were traditionally feminine, however, and women directed their attentions to decorative and literary arts and the needs of other women, the elderly, and children. Societies of Decorative Arts (SDA) provided women with career opportunities through the sale of decorative objects made in the home. SDA clubwomen combined self-help initiatives with theories of cultural uplift taken from the writings of Englishman John Ruskin. American women visiting Philadelphia in 1876 to tour the Centennial Exposition were inspired by beautiful handcrafted needlework from the South Kensington Museum, London.

The Chicago Society of Decorative Art (CSDA) was organized in 1877 as an offshoot of the New York Society. Bertha Palmer served on the CSDA board from 1878 to 1884 (except for 1882) and briefly chaired its embroidery and sales committees. CSDA members increasingly were more interested in cultural patronage than in providing employment for needy women. The CSDA eventually abandoned philanthropy to concentrate solely on raising standards of taste in the decorative arts.

CSDA members pursued a relationship with the Art Institute of Chicago (AIC) and began to set aside money for the purchase of decorative art objects to be donated to AIC. They were encouraged by the director and trustees of AIC. CSDA reorganized in 1888, becoming the Antiquarian Society of the Art Institute. Palmer, a prime mover in the new focus on acquiring decorative art for the museum, was particularly interested in strengthening the AIC's holdings of medieval tapestries and achieved this goal through her participation in the Antiquarian Society. In this way Palmer and other women of her class negotiated a close relationship and influence with fine arts museums, institutions whose leadership was exclusively composed of wealthy men.

Bertha Palmer was also a leader in the Fortnightly of Chicago, a literary club whose members studied music, literature, and the fine arts. Many of the members were also active Antiquarians. Palmer joined in 1880 and was president in 1901. She was also active in the Chicago Woman's Club from 1888 and served on its reform committee beginning in 1891. These memberships placed Palmer at the heart of late-nineteenth-century women's culture, preparing her for the leading role she took in managing the participation of women in the World's Columbian Exposition in 1893.

Her role as a society leader complemented the qualities she brought to the fair. Marriage to Potter Palmer had ensured her access to the city's elite; her younger sister Ida's marriage in 1874 to Frederick Dent Grant, son of President Ulysses S. Grant, connected her to a national elite. Palmer's charity balls, held annually from 1887, were major events in the social calendar of the upper class. Guests paid an expensive admission fee.

In 1890, Palmer's social position made her a favorite choice to be appointed president of the Board of Lady Managers of the World's Columbian Exposition. Although Palmer had wide recognition and many supporters, she was a controversial choice among different groups of women. The Queen Isabella Association, largely professional women and suffragists, protested both Palmer's leadership and the idea of separating women's achievements from men's. Initially, Phoebe Couzins, who served as secretary of the board, represented the Isabella position. Couzins was ousted in 1891 through a complex series of political maneuverings. This move left the board with no opposition to Palmer's more conservative leadership. Other external opposition to Palmer came from several African American groups whose demands for black representation on the board had been ignored. FANNIE BARRIER WILLIAMS, the choice of many African Americans, was well known to several prominent white women associated with the exposition. Palmer's Board of Lady Managers was national, and she had to mediate the conflicting opinions and interests of women from the South and the North. Her decision to exclude black women from leadership reflected the nation's increasing adherence to segregation.

The Board of Lady Managers was charged with responsibility for the Woman's Building and its exhibits and programs. Designed by young Boston architect Sophia Hayden, whose plan was chosen in a national competition, the building housed decorative art objects from forty-seven nations. Palmer's personal diplomacy with noblewomen in Austria, England, and France facilitated obtaining the pieces. Palmer commissioned American painters Mary Cassatt and Mary Fairchild MacMonnies to paint two murals for the walls of the large exhibition hall in the Woman's Building. Smaller panels by women artists Amanda Brewster Sewell, Lucia Fairchild, Lydia Emmet, and Rosina Emmet Sherwood appeared in the hall with Cassatt's *Modern Woman* and MacMonnies's *Primitive Woman*.

In her remarks delivered at the dedication ceremonies of the World's Columbian Exposition on October 21, 1892, Palmer made clear that she saw the Woman's Building and its displays as an opportunity to demonstrate women's capabilities and accomplishments in order to advance their economic status. "Without touching upon politics, suffrage, or other irrelevant issues," she argued, "this unique organization of women for women will devote itself to the promotion of their [women's] material interests . . . favor women's industrial equality, and her receiving just compensation for services rendered" (*Addresses and Reports of Mrs. Potter Palmer*, 116).

Prominent fair visitors to Chicago in 1893 were invited to see the Palmers' private art collection at their mansion. Bertha and Potter Palmer were early art collectors in post-fire Chicago; Potter's involvement with the Inter-State Industrial Expositions held in Chicago beginning in 1873 put the Palmers in contact with SARA HALLOWELL and Chicago's leading art collectors, including Marshall Field, Martin A. Ryerson, and Charles L. Hutchinson. Hallowell was a friend of the American expatriate painter Mary Cassatt and the influential Parisian art dealer Paul Durand-Ruel. Bertha Palmer was so impressed by Hallowell's expertise that she lobbied, though unsuccessfully, for Hallowell's appointment as the director of art at the World's Columbian Exposition.

While Palmer was publicly engaged with the Antiquarians and as president of the Lady Managers, she was privately building a collection of contemporary French and American art, including paintings by George Inness, Claude Monet, Pierre Auguste Renoir, Camille Pissarro, and Pierre Puvis de Chavannes. Bertha Palmer, rather than Potter Palmer, generally receives credit for the progressiveness of the collection. At one time she owned as many as ninety works by Monet, the majority of which were painted in the 1890s, when Bertha Palmer was most active as a collector. "Without doubt, she was the first private collector to recognize the significance of Monet's serial paintings," concluded art historian Richard R. Brettell (p. 19).

A number of the Palmers' paintings were included in the loan exhibition at the Columbian Exposition in 1893, but the impressionist paintings were rarely loaned for public exhibitions, remaining on display in Bertha Palmer's private gallery at home. The impressionist collection was essentially complete by 1893.

Bertha Palmer was proud of her city and the private art collection she and her husband had amassed. She was also aware that Chicago revealed dramatic contradictions of poverty and wealth. Visitors to the Columbian Exposition also viewed the living conditions of working people and the poor in the industrial city, contrasting these scenes with those of the White City, so named because of the white façade of the fair. In 1893–94 a national financial panic was followed by a severe depression with high unemployment among factory and industrial workers. The contradictions between the White City and the neighborhoods where working class and poor families struggled to survive were brought into dramatic relief by English journalist and re-

former William T. Stead in his book, *If Christ Came to Chicago* (1894). Inspired by Stead, Turlington W. Harvey, lumberman and supporter of religious evangelist Dwight L. Moody, invited a group of distinguished reformers, businessmen, and religious leaders, including Bertha Palmer, JANE ADDAMS, Graham Taylor, Lyman J. Gage, ELLEN HENROTIN, and Rabbi Emil G. Hirsch, to plan the scope of work to be undertaken by a new organization, the Civic Federation. They began a campaign to eliminate vice in the city and, more immediately, to aid the unemployed and their families. Palmer agreed to serve as first vice-president, Lyman J. Gage, president.

Bertha Palmer, on behalf of the Civic Federation, directly appealed to George M. Pullman during the Pullman strike in 1894 and asked him to take a more conciliatory attitude toward his workers. His refusal to heed what she believed to be his civic duty contributed to her disillusion with the Civic Federation and its approach to industrial conflict.

After 1896, Bertha Palmer, the undisputed queen of Chicago society, successfully entered the social scene in exclusive Newport, Rhode Island. Her popularity mounted with the marriage in 1899 of her niece Julia Grant to Russian nobleman Prince Michel Cantacuzene. Not long after, President William McKinley named Palmer as a commissioner to the Paris Exposition of 1900, the only woman from the United States to serve on that board. She then used her influence to obtain Jane Addams's appointment as a member of the Jury of International Awards at the Paris Exposition.

Potter Palmer died in 1902, and in his name Bertha Palmer established a medal and cash award for American art at the Art Institute of Chicago's annual exhibition. After her husband's death, Palmer spent much of her time in Europe, at Hampden House in London or at her Paris residence. Less and less involved with Chicago, in 1910 she purchased property near Sarasota, Florida, where she built a house, The Oaks, at Osprey. She also acquired property near Tampa. Palmer ranched and farmed on a large scale. She had large tracts cleared for the cultivation of citrus fruit, bred cattle, and was part of the early development of the west coast of Florida.

Bertha Palmer died of breast cancer at The Oaks; she was sixty-nine. She is buried at Graceland Cemetery, Chicago, in the Palmer family's neoclassical mausoleum.

Bertha Honoré Palmer is best remembered as one of Chicago's most prominent social luminaries and for her bequest of paintings to the Art Institute of Chicago. Less known is her advocacy of improved conditions for American workers, especially equal opportunity for women in professional fields and trades. She also had business acumen. Art historian Richard R. Brettell considers Bertha Palmer "as much a dealer as she was a collector. . . . She bought and sold pictures at a profit, often after short periods, very much as she and her husband bought and sold real estate" (p. 19). In addition, in the twenty years between her husband's death and her own, she increased the family fortune by more than 100 percent. As a collector of decorative art and an advocate for the introduction of this category of artwork into the arena of the museum, Palmer and her female colleagues transformed the definition of fine art. As a clubwoman with international fame, she contributed to a redefinition of upper-class women's social roles.

Sources. Bertha Honoré Palmer and Potter Palmer Papers are at the CHS and include material concerning her management of the Palmer estate following her husband's death. The Sarasota County (Florida) Historical Commission has Bertha Palmer papers. Additional letters are at the Ryerson Library, the Art Institute of Chicago. Papers of the Antiquarian Society, the Friends of American Art, and the Potter Palmer [Art] Collection are in the Art Institute of Chicago's archives. Papers of the Chicago Woman's Club, the Chicago Society of Decorative Art, and the Board of Lady Managers of the World's Columbian Exposition are at CHS. Palmer's speeches are published in *Addresses and Reports of Mrs. Potter Palmer* (1894). Ishbell Ross's 1960 *Silhouette in Diamonds: The Life of Mrs. Potter Palmer* is a popular biography. See also *NAW* (1971). Aline Saarinen, *The Proud Possessors* (1958), and Richard R. Brettell, "Monet's Haystacks Reconsidered," *Art Institute of Chicago Museum Studies,* Fall 1984, provide information on Palmer's art collection. Margo M. Hobbs, "Bertha Palmer's Philanthropy in the Arts" (master's thesis, School of the Art Institute of Chicago, 1992), discusses Palmer's involvement with the Chicago Society of Decorative Art and her art collection. Jeanne Madeleine Weimann, *The Fair Women* (1981), contains an account of Palmer's participation in the 1893 World's Columbian Exposition. See Anna Massa, "Black Women in the 'White City,'" *Phylon,* Winter 1965, for an in-depth discussion of unsuccessful attempts by African Americans to participate with the Board of Lady Managers. Judy Sund, "Columbus and Columbia in Chicago, 1893: Man of Genius Meets Generic Woman," *Art Bulletin,* September 1993, is useful. Two books by Kathleen D. McCarthy are pertinent: *Noblesse Oblige: Charity and Cultural Philanthropy in Chicago, 1849–1929* (1982) and *Women's Culture: American Philanthropy and Art, 1830–1930* (1991).

MARGO HOBBS THOMPSON

PALMER, PAULINE LENNARDS
1867–August 15, 1938
ARTIST, LECTURER

One of the best-known and most prolific woman artists of her era, Pauline Palmer was an active member and pioneering woman officer of many artist's organizations. Indeed, during her lifetime, she was second in reputation as an American impressionist to Mary Cassatt. Although an active painter and artistic leader in Chicago for thirty years, she painted in each of the areas where she resided or visited, and her portraits, landscapes, and genre pieces are found throughout the country.

Pauline Lennards was born in McHenry, Illinois, to German parents who had fled the revolutions of 1848. Both her merchant father, Nicholas Lennards, and her mother, Franciska (Spangemacher) Lennards, spoke German in the home. She had at least two siblings and remained close to her sister Marie. The Lennards are recorded as looking favorably on the arts, and when the young Pauline Lennards showed an interest and some ability in drawing, they hired a private teacher to develop her talent. After completing her elementary education in McHenry and Harvard, Illinois, she was sent to a convent school in Milwaukee at the age of thirteen, where her interest in art continued.

When she graduated from high school, the young artist moved to Chicago and began teaching in the public schools in the city. She married Dr. Albert Elwood Palmer on May 21, 1891.

After taking classes as a part-time student at the School of the Art Institute of Chicago and having work exhibited at the World's Columbian Exposition in 1893, Pauline Palmer studied full time with William Merritt Chase, who commuted from New York City. Her work was exhibited as part of the *Art Students League* exhibitions in 1896 and 1897. She also presented her work throughout the United States and was accepted in exhibitions in Cincinnati in 1896, Omaha in 1898, and Philadelphia in 1899. This last was at the Pennsylvania Academy, and she was to exhibit there in thirteen different annual exhibitions.

In spite of these early successes, Chase suggested further study, and she spent a large part of the next three years in France, studying painting at both the Académie Colarossi, under Gustav Courtois; the Académie de la Grande Chaumière, with Lucien Simon; and, during 1900–1902, at the École des Beaux-Arts with René Prinet. She also worked closely with, and was befriended by, the American expatriate painter Richard E. Miller, returning to Europe to paint with him in later years. Palmer was already in her early thirties when she reached Paris, but she undertook the same kind of dedicated studio life as the younger students, competing for and winning prizes at each of the schools she attended. She also sent her work back to the United States, exhibiting at the Pan-American Exposition in Buffalo in 1901 and in Chicago, exhibiting in one or more shows at the Art Institute of Chicago every year from 1896 through the rest of her life, except for 1934. The artist continued her relationship with the Parisian art scene for some years, exhibiting at the Paris Salon from 1903–1906 and again in 1911; she also exhibited in Naples in the latter year.

Before returning to Paris and traveling to Spain during the summer of 1903, Palmer served as a juror for the *American Watercolors* exhibition of 1902, a service she was to perform again in 1904; it was the beginning of a long career of service as a juror and officer of many artist's organizations. Also in 1904, the painter won her first prize outside Chicago and Paris when she was awarded a bronze medal at the Universal Exposition in St. Louis.

Palmer set up her portraiture practice in Chicago, moving into the highly desirable Tree Studios on the Near North Side. She was in the fortunate position of being a successful painter whose family income enabled her to travel widely. Her commissions increased dramatically after the opera star Ernestine Schumann-Heink invited her to New Jersey to paint portraits of her children. While keeping up an active exhibition schedule and winning prizes and recognition both in Chicago and increasingly around the country, Palmer was able to revisit France several times and to make extended trips to Germany, Austria, and Italy. In 1907 alone, she won three major prizes associated with the Art Institute.

The years between 1910 and 1920 were a period of intense activity for the artist, with the Palmers spending part of several winters in Charleston, where Albert Palmer had family and friends, and where the painter completed her figure studies, street scenes, and landscapes. She had her first one-person show, appropriately enough, at the Art Institute of Chicago, from March 24 to April 8, 1913, where her sixty-eight impressionist-style portraits, genre scenes, and landscapes were much more appreciated than the work of the diverse modernists represented at the Armory Show that was exhibited for most of the same time. In addition, Pauline Palmer was elected to a three-year term as president of the Chicago Society of Artists in 1918, the first woman to be accorded that honor. Palmer received many other honors in these years as her reputation began to grow, and her work routinely garnered prizes in the exhibitions she entered.

Starting in 1915, the Palmers began to spend at least part of each summer in Provincetown, Massachusetts, where they had a home and where she arranged for a studio that she maintained for the rest of her life. She became a close associate of Charles W. Hawthorne, the dean of the Provincetown summer art colony, and played an increasingly active part in the life of that community. She became known as "The Painter Lady" in Provincetown, where she painted and befriended many of the Portuguese fisherman's families. Their children were often the subjects of both her genre and her figural paintings. She used the opportunity of painting the children to buy them gifts, equipping some of the boys with cowboy outfits in which to paint them. She worked in oil, watercolor, and pastel, with greater attention to smaller works during the summer. Upon the death of her husband in 1920, Palmer spent more of her time in Provincetown, with fewer trips abroad.

Her civic and organizational activities increased, and she won one or more awards and prizes almost every year through that decade. Most of her artistic life centered around the two poles of Chicago and Provincetown, and she came to have substantial authority in both professional artists' organizations and civic bodies dedicated to the arts. She served as president of the AIC Alumni Association; as a director of the Arts Club of Chicago, the Chicago Drama League, and the Chicago branch of the MacDowell Society; and she was a member of another dozen organizations.

Her skills as a portraitist were always in high demand, though she evidenced less interest in that form in the later half of her career. Legal, business, and academic figures—the men who ran Chicago and belonged to its clubs—were painted as solid and impressive forms, with sufficient visible brushstroke and blending of color to maintain her link with the impressionism of her youth. Changes in fashion put her kind of painting on the defensive in artistic circles, but her popularity never waned among the core of her wealthy clients. Palmer apparently also developed a fledgling business, noted in some accounts. Pauline Palmer, Inc., either demonstrated or taught "scientific" exercises for the face, but nothing much is known about the matter.

Accompanied by her most intimate friend, her sister Marie, Palmer undertook a major trip to England and Scandinavia in the summer of 1938, during which she caught pneumonia. She suffered for ten days before dying on August 15 of that year. She had purchased a pile of scarves in Scotland for the children she enjoyed in Provincetown, and her sister made a final trip the following summer to present them on her behalf. Palmer left funds for the Art Institute of Chicago to offer an annual prize in her name at the *Chicago and Vicinity* shows. She was honored with two memorial exhibitions in her adopted city in 1939, at the Art Institute and the Union League Club. In 1984, the Lakeview Museum of Arts and Sciences in Peoria, Illinois, mounted an exhibition of her works, *Pauline Palmer: American Impressionist.*

As a leading American exponent of the impressionism that had already gone out of favor in France by the time she studied there, and with subjects chosen from portraiture of the well-to-do and well-connected to pleasing landscape and picturesque genre scenes, Pauline Palmer appealed to a conservative taste in American society. Yet, as a tireless proponent of artist's organizations and professionalism, she managed to serve as a progressive member of the artistic community. Through the offices she held in those organizations, she served as a forward-looking role model for professional women who followed her in establishing full-fledged artistic careers.

Sources. There has been very little research on the life and work of Pauline Palmer, with much of the known information contained in obituaries, brief entries in exhibition catalogs, and listings of artist organizations to which she belonged. The major sources are the catalogs of the various exhibitions in which her work appeared over the years of her career; "Woman Heads Artists Society in Chicago," *Fort Dearborn Magazine*, 1920; C. J. Bulliet, *Artists of Chicago: Past and Present* (1936); her obituaries in the *McHenry Plaindealer*, the *Chicago Evening American*, and the *Chicago Daily News*, all in 1938; the retrospective catalog published by the Woman's Club of Evanston in 1939; and "Chicago's 'Painter Lady,'" a brief appreciation by Paul Schulze, chair of the Art Committee of the Union League Club, published in the *Bulletin of the Union League Club*, September 1, 1939. Fred W. Soady's essay, "A Brief History of the Artist," is in *Pauline Palmer: American Impressionist* (1984), published by the Lakeview Museum of Arts and Sciences.

DAVID M. SOKOL

PARKER, BERTHA MORRIS
February 7, 1890–November 14, 1980
SCIENCE EDUCATOR, AUTHOR

Bertha Parker, who taught science at the University of Chicago Laboratory Schools for almost forty years and authored nearly three hundred publications about science education, was born in Rochester, Illinois. Her parents, Homer Darius Parker, a pharmacist, and Margaret Elizabeth (Lawrence) Parker, had four daughters. Bertha Parker's older sisters were Anna and Edith, and her younger sister was Margaret. Of the four, only Anna married; Edith Putnam Parker became a geography professor at the University of Chicago, and Margaret Terrell Parker taught geography at Wellesley College.

Parker attended high school in Springfield, Illinois, and was a student at Oberlin College for one year (1908–1909) and at Columbia University's summer school (1909) in New York. After teaching in the elementary schools in Springfield from 1909 to 1912, she earned an S.B. degree in 1914 from the University of Chicago, graduating Phi Beta Kappa. Following graduation, she returned to Springfield to teach science at Lawrence Junior High School for two years. In the fall of 1916, she began teaching at the University of Chicago Laboratory Schools in the Lower School (then called the University Elementary School) and began work on an S.M. degree, which she received in 1923 at the University of Chicago. She majored in botany as an undergraduate and in her graduate studies.

Parker taught at the University of Chicago Laboratory Schools from 1916 to 1955. During those thirty-nine years, she was a science teacher at the Lower School and served as chair of the science department from 1940 to 1955. During World War II, when it was difficult to get and keep science teachers, she also taught in the high school. In addition to her elementary and secondary school teaching, she was an instructor in science at the Colorado State College of Education in the summer of 1935

Fig. 90. *Science educator Bertha Morris Parker at a party with friends in 1962. Pictured in back row are Lenore John, Laura Oftedal, Sally Fenwick, and Ida DePencier; middle row, Jessie Carter, Bertha Parker, and Alice Fleckenger; in front, Illa Podendorf.*

and taught courses for science teachers during summers through the University of Chicago's School of Education.

Parker's goal was to make science come alive and be meaningful to her students. Her teaching methods were imaginative and exciting. She believed that the purpose of science education was "to build up a fund of rationalized experiences which will make for a more intelligent attitude toward various aspects of one's material environment, and to give some acquaintance with the scientific method of attacking a problem" (*Introductory Course in Science*, 1). A former student tells of a typical end of class where fifth graders lining up at the door were each given a paper clip and asked to put it into a nearly full beaker of water as Parker went down the line. As more and more paper clips were added, and the water bulged above the top of the beaker, Parker pointed out that the topic of the next class would be the principle of surface tension.

In her teaching, Parker made use of activities like experimenting, reading, constructing objects such as toys, observing materials and phenomena, participating in field trips, drawing, making plasticine models, planting gardens, and caring for plants and animals. She discussed these methods in *Introductory*

Course in Science in the Intermediate Grades (1931) as well as in other writings, so that science teachers could use her methods. Her discussion of planting and caring for gardens was typical in its thoroughness and meticulousness. Since many urban children had never had experiences with planting and plant growth, it was an appropriate method of instruction for the study of botany. As for plot size, Parker suggested that pairs of children tend plots that were six feet square. She saw that small plots involved each child in a greater variety of activities and gave each an increased sense of responsibility for the plot.

Along with her creative teaching methods, Parker focused on the teaching of "units" of instruction. Henry Clinton Morrison, superintendent of the Laboratory Schools from 1919 to 1928, first implemented the practice of teaching units in the early 1920s and outlined it in his classic *The Practice of Teaching in the Secondary Schools* (1924). The unit emphasized the student's mastery of understanding, not ingestion and recall of facts. Since units of nature study or applied science did not exist, Parker began developing these for her classes. In time, she had dozens of prepared units, which she eventually published.

During the 1930s, Parker put much time and energy into

professional activities. She served on committees of numerous science education organizations. Beginning in 1933, she chaired the elementary school section of the Central Association of Science and Mathematics Teachers. Moving to the national level, she edited *Science News Notes*, the publication of the National Council on Elementary Science, from 1934 to 1938, and served as president of the organization in 1935. From 1938 until 1945, she was an associate editor of *Science Education*, a publication of the National Association for Research in Science Teaching.

Parker also contributed articles to various professional journals. Between 1930 and 1935, she wrote many short articles for *Normal Instructor and Primary Plans* (later the *Instructor*). All looked at some aspect of teaching applied science, such as "Organization in a Science Unit" (September 1930) or "Motor Activities in a Science Course" (October 1930).

In addition to editing science education journals and writing articles, Parker spoke at many conferences and served as consultant for various organizations during the 1930s. Her energy seemed boundless. Along with teaching, she presented papers at the National Education Association Science Section, the American Science Teaching Association, and the National Association on Research in Science Teaching in a three-month period from December 1937 to February 1938. During the same decade, Parker served as education adviser to the National Dairy Council, science advisor to the Columbia School of the Air, and consultant to the Rosenwald Fund.

One group of professional publications by Parker is noteworthy. During 1932 and 1933, Parker wrote six adult education brochures that were published by the American Council on Education and the Subcommittee on Political Education of the American Political Science Association. All but one were thirty-two pages long, and taken together, they made up the Achievements of Civilization series. Titles included *The Story of Writing*, *Telling Time throughout the Centuries*, *Our Calendar*. These were popular, and fifty thousand copies of each title were printed. While writing these brochures, Parker found that she could write thirty-two pages on a topic quickly, and she eventually used this format for many of her books for children.

Later in her life, Parker claimed she was encouraged to write by Charles Judd, professor of education at the University of Chicago, who asked her to write science books to fill a void. She was, however, well aware of that need. In an article she wrote for the *Elementary School Journal*, September 1937, in which she discussed the important role of reading in science education, Parker lamented that there was not nearly enough science reading material for children. At that time, textbooks on specific topics crowded information into a few pages, thereby producing dense but limited coverage. She called for simple material that would elaborate on topics covered in the science textbook and that was attractively presented in order to motivate children to spend some of their leisure time on science.

With the help of Dr. Judd, who provided a full-time secretary from the School of Education to assist her, Parker went on to create such material. Many of her books were appealingly small (6 ½ by 8 ½ inches), thin (rarely longer than thirty-six pages), lavishly illustrated (usually two or three illustrations per page that wrapped around small blocks of text), inexpensive

(typically thirty-two cents for those produced before World War II, and ranging between one and two dollars after the war through the 1960s), and focused on a single subject. Inside, readers found a simply written but not condescending text. More than eighty of these inviting books were published between 1941 and 1966 by Row, Peterson and Company, Evanston, Illinois, and became known as the Basic Science Education Series. The books in the series were called Unitexts, since each dealt with a single subject.

Of the eighty titles in this series, most were written for the nine- to eleven-year-old, but some were for the five-year-old and others for the fifteen-year-old. A sampling of books includes meteorology (*Ask the Weatherman*, 1941), botany (*Dependent Plants*, 1944), paleontology (*Life through the Ages*, 1942), physical geography (*The Earth's Changing Surface*, 1942), chemistry (*What Things Are Made Of*, 1944), zoology (*Animals of the Seashore*, 1942), and the environment (*Saving Our Wildlife*, 1944). Nearly every book was reviewed for accuracy by an expert in the field or by an agency, such as the United States Weather Bureau. Parker wrote twenty-four of these Unitexts during 1941, many of them undoubtedly stemming from the science units she taught to her students. She continued producing these books for the next twenty-five years at an average of six annually. In addition, she revised a majority of the books so that nearly all of the titles published during the 1940s were redone in the late 1950s and early 1960s. In total, Parker wrote or revised more than 130 books.

Before Parker retired from the Laboratory Schools in 1955, she became a research associate at Chicago's Field Museum of Natural History, an affiliation she kept until her death. At her retirement, she gave the Laboratory Schools a 16 millimeter projector and funds to buy some film strips for use in the science department. Parker also returned to writing more substantial science books for children. Parker served as consultant for Ida DePencier's *How the Sun Helps Us* (1959).

Parker's major contribution, aside from her dedication to teaching, was as author of full-length science books for young people. Early in her career, she wrote two books, *The Book of Plants* (1925) and *The Book of Electricity* (1928). Two of her best-known science books for children are *The Golden Treasury of Natural History* (1952, revised 1968) and *The Golden Book of Science* (1956, revised 1963). Her books have been translated into nearly thirty languages. After serving as the editor of the 1959 *Golden Book Encyclopedia*, Parker wrote several books for Golden Press. Her best-known titles include *Wonders of Science* (1963), *The 50 States* (1965), and *Science and Us* (1969). Parker wrote her last book, *Rocks and Minerals*, in 1974 at the age of eighty-four.

In physical appearance, Parker, called Bee by her friends and coworkers, was relatively short, between five feet two inches and five feet four inches, and was somewhat heavy set. Her dark hair turned gray, and friends recall that there often seemed to be out-of-control wisps encircling her head. Although she listed her religious preference as Methodist on forms, her friends do not remember her as an active church member. Friends and acquaintances have described Bertha Parker as an energetic, generous, no-nonsense person who spoke her mind. Throughout her life, Parker was an avid reader, especially of science and natural history.

Parker lived in her apartment in Hyde Park near the University of Chicago and the Laboratory Schools until the beginning of November 1980, when she began experiencing digestive troubles. She died a short time later at age ninety. Services were held in Glen Ellyn, Illinois, and she was buried in Rochester, Illinois.

Bertha Parker was an outstanding and dedicated educator. She wanted children not just to ingest scientific facts but also to understand science and regard it as an important part of their lives. Understanding that teachers needed science materials that allowed learning to be experiential as well as abstract, she developed appropriate curricula and was a leader in disseminating her methodology through professional educational societies.

Sources. Material from Bertha Parker's file, UC Laboratory Schools, provided biographical and career information. An oral interview was conducted on October 7, 1944, by Ann D. Carlson with Ida DePencier, former University of Chicago Laboratory Schools teacher and good friend of Bertha Parker. Parker's professional articles include "Air Pressure: An Intermediate Grade Unit in Science," *Science Education,* December 1934; "Guidance in Reading in Elementary Science," *Recent Trends in Reading. Proceedings of the Conference on Reading Held at the University of Chicago,* vol. 1 (1939); "Magnets: An Intermediate Grade Unit in Science," *School Science and Math,* January 1933; "Motor Activities in a Science Course," *Normal Instructor and Primary Plans,* October 1930; "Reading in an Intermediate Grade Science Program," *Elementary School Journal,* September 1937; "Science Exercise," *School Science and Math,* May 1935; "Suggestions for a Unit on Thermometers," *School Science and Math,* June 1935. Her teaching methods and explanation and samples of science units are best described in her book *Introductory Course in Science in the Intermediate Grades* (1931). A detailed chronology of dates and a listing of her books can be found in *Contemporary Authors,* vol. 5, ed. Barbara Harte and Carolyn Riley (1963), and vol. 102, ed. Frances C. Lochner (1981). Ida B. DePencier, *The History of the Laboratory Schools: The University of Chicago, 1896–1965* (1967) provides context for Parker's teaching career.

ANN D. CARLSON

FIG. 91. *Revolutionary Lucy Parsons, Chicago, 1915.*

PARSONS, LUCY E.
March 1853–March 7, 1942

SEAMSTRESS, REVOLUTIONARY, LABOR ORGANIZER, JOURNALIST

According to Carolyn Ashbaugh, whose full-length biography, *Lucy Parsons: American Revolutionary* (1976), remains the standard work, there are few documented facts and many conflicting stories about Lucy Parsons's origins, including those recounted by the subject herself. Lucy Parsons identified herself as Native American and Chicana, Ashbaugh contends, "in an effort to cover up her black heritage" (p. 268). Alfredo Mirande and Evangelina Enriquez, in *La Chicana: The Mexican-American Woman* (1979), argue for acceptance of Parsons's self-identification. They contend that Ashbaugh, "acknowledging that 'little is known of Lucy's origins' . . . delve[s] into [her] psyche, suggesting that her Mexican identity was but an excuse [*sic*] in self-denial" (p. 91). In 1976, Ashbaugh, aware of the controversy her conclusions about Lucy Parsons's identity had provoked, spoke with Katharine Parsons Russell, who told her that "although the Parsons family denied publicly that Lucy was black, . . . the family privately" acknowledged "her black ancestry" (Ashbaugh, 267, note 4). Lucy Parsons lived her entire life as a woman of color, in a society where the construction of a racial identity had increasing importance and racism prevailed. Throughout her life, Lucy Parsons championed the rights of the oppressed and the enslaved and in words and deeds spoke out forcefully against racism and for equality. People of color—Chicanas, Native Americans, African Americans, Hispanics—identify with her struggle and feel a kinship with this revolutionary woman. Until there is conclusive evidence, it seems appropriate to call her a woman of color who sought the liberation of all peoples oppressed by racism.

Even Lucy Parsons's name remains in question. Lulu Parsons and Lucy Ella Parsons are two versions found in the record. Her family name may have been Gathings, from the Gathings family that owned slaves in Waco, Texas, but this theory is based on speculation by Ashbaugh rather than any documentation. On the other hand, Ashbaugh writes, "Henry and Marie del Gather (whom [*sic*] Lucy claimed were her uncle and mother, respectively) and John Waller (the civilized Creek Indian who was supposedly her father) are probably fictitious" (p. 268). To complicate matters, Lucy Parsons gave different maiden names on the birth certificates of her son and her daughter—Carter on the former and Hull on the latter—and "provided Gonzales [*sic*] as her maiden name to the *Dictionary of American Biography* for its account of Albert Parsons. On Lucy's death certificate her parents are listed as Pedro Diaz and Marie Gonzales [*sic*]" (p. 268).

Beyond this serious confusion, little is known about Lucy E. Parsons's childhood in Waco, Texas. There is no documentation to prove that she was born into slavery in Texas, but during the Reconstruction era, she most likely witnessed the "atrocities of the Ku Klux Klan in the South. Among the crimes committed by the Klan in or near Waco were the castration of a black boy in January, 1867; the murder of an eight year old black girl by rape in July, 1867; and the murder of a black man in the Waco Public Square in February, 1868" (Ashbaugh, 14). She met Albert Richard Parsons, who was white and the descendant of New England Puritans. Orphaned, he had traveled to Texas where his eldest brother William Henry Parsons, who was twenty years his senior, was an attorney and journalist. Albert Parsons, at the age of nineteen, was the founding editor in Waco of a Radical Republican weekly paper, the *Spectator,* from 1867 to 1868. Although he and his brother William had fought for the Confederacy during the Civil War, both switched sides, and Albert Parsons advocated civil rights for black freedmen after the war. Albert Parsons and his brother William both went into politics, joining the Radical Republicans and participating in the Reconstruction struggle in Texas. Albert Parsons was threatened with lynching when he attempted to register black voters in Waco. He became "a traveling correspondent and subscription agent" (Avrich, 10) for the *Houston Telegraph,* a newspaper published by his brother William, and it was during a long trip through northwestern Texas in 1869 that he first met his future wife. Albert Parsons's autobiography describes Lucy as a "charming young Spanish Indian maiden" (Avrich, 11). She was living on her uncle's ranch in Johnson County, according to Parsons, and three years later he returned to marry her. Ashbaugh doubts whether Lucy and Albert Parsons were ever formally married, since "laws against miscegenation would have prevented that" (p. 14). However, "both bride and groom maintained that they were married in Austin [Texas] in 1872, as does William Parsons, who insists that the wedding was 'a matter of public record in that city,' adding that Lucy's claim to Spanish and Indian ancestry was 'never questioned'" (Avrich, 12). No marriage license has been found, however. In the world of Reconstruction America, where terrible violence against people of color was an everyday occurrence, the construction of identity takes on a quality quite different from today's world. The couple, who were "deeply and passionately in love" and "remained devoted to each other" (Avrich, 12), moved to Chicago in 1873, leaving behind the heightened violence of the Ku Klux Klan in Texas.

The Parsons' arrival in the northern industrial city coincided with nationwide economic depression and labor agitation. The depression in 1873 deepened as "cities like Chicago recorded a rising number of deaths from starvation . . . homeless men and women wandered the streets . . . lining up daily before the soup kitchens established in working-class neighborhoods . . . [until] by 1877, according to some accounts, the number of unemployed had risen to nearly three million—in a nation of forty-five million people" (Avrich, 16). "As many as fifteen million"

struggled to survive "at the poverty level" (Avrich, 16). A militant labor movement emerged in this period of hunger parades and mass meetings, and American-born and foreign-born leaders debated strategies and ideologies to combat the power of the capitalist class. In Chicago, in particular, events had been building toward a confrontation between labor and capital. Enormous dislocation of working-class families, caused by the Great Chicago Fire of 1871, preceded the depression in 1873. Discontent with the way in which the wealthy managers of the Chicago Relief and Aid Society, including George Pullman and Marshall Field, handled the disbursement of funds to the needy provoked a response. By December 1873, Chicago witnessed a series of demonstrations by the unemployed, including marches through the streets, mass meetings, and demands on local government to relieve the plight of the poor and homeless. The Chicago Relief and Aid Society itself was targeted by the desperate protesters. On December 21, 1873, the "labor organizations in the city arranged a mass meeting in which some five thousand persons took part" (Avrich, 17); reflecting the diversity of the city's population, "speeches were delivered in five languages" (p. 17). From this mass meeting a committee was formed to present demands to the municipal government. The city council did nothing and the mayor called upon the Chicago and Relief Aid to distribute "part of the fund that had been collected for victims of the 1871 fire" (p. 17). Ten thousand workers and unemployed assembled in front of the Chicago Relief and Aid Society offices demanding that the unemployed be given adequate relief promptly. Other marches by socialists and trade unionists had become more frequent.

In Chicago, the Parsons lived in poor working-class German neighborhoods, where workers labored in "basement sweatshops" (Ashbaugh, 16), families lived in crowded quarters, and the infant mortality rate was the highest in the city. "Albert Parsons worked as a printer and joined Typographical Union No. 16 in 1874" (Ashbaugh, 16). In March 1876, Parsons "attended a meeting of the Social Democratic Working Men's [*sic*] Party of North America" (Avrich, 20), where he heard Peter McGuire outline "the program of his party, which called for the abolition of capitalism and its replacement by a socialist commonwealth" (Avrich, 20). McGuire asked those interested in forming an English section of the party to meet with him at the end of the meeting, and Parsons, together with George A. Schilling and Thomas J. Morgan, "future stalwarts in the Chicago labor movement" (Avrich, 20), came forward. This step launched Parsons's career as a labor organizer who expounded the evils of capitalism and the virtues of a socialist system.

The Chicago English group of the Workingmen's Party met regularly at the home of Lucy and Albert Parsons. Lucy Parsons and her husband read the works of Karl Marx and German socialist Ferdinand Lassalle. Those who followed Lassalle favored a political approach to social change, whereas the Marxists advocated organizing trade unions and achieving change through economic organization and action. The Workingmen's Party in Chicago attempted to include both positions, a compromise accepted by Albert Parsons. Parsons, in addition to becoming a member of Typographical Union No. 16, was also one of the founders of Local 400, the first local assembly of the Knights of Labor in Chicago.

In the summer of 1877, with the economy still not recovered from the depression that had begun in 1873, the country faced a nationwide railroad strike that began in the East and moved westward. Not only did railroad workers stop rail transport, but sympathetic trade unionists in other crafts also walked off their jobs. By July 25, 1877, there was a virtual general strike that reached all the way to the Pacific. The strike continued for two weeks. "For the first time federal troops had to be called out during peacetime to suppress a domestic disturbance" (Avrich, 26). Albert Parsons emerged as a leading figure during the strike days in Chicago. He spoke on July 23, 1877, to a crowd of thousands, imploring workers to use the legislative process, not violence. Both he and the Workingmen's Party received substantial attention in the local press, and Parsons was blamed for the riots that accompanied the walkouts of different craft unions in Chicago. As the striking continued, crowds of workers assembled for meetings. Women as well as men participated in the struggles between workers and police. There were reports of women's participation in a skirmish between police and workers that took place at the Halsted Street viaduct and then again at the German workers' Turner Hall. Articles in newspapers characterized these women as "enraged female rioters . . . the unsexed mob of female incendiaries . . . the Amazonian army" (Tax, 40). On July 25, 1877, a violent confrontation occurred between police officers and "strikers who, a thousand strong, had been heckling a group of scabs" (Avrich, 32) that was brought in to replace striking workers at the McCormick Reaper Works. Two workers were killed by the police and many were beaten. Business and industrial interests in the city were alarmed by the continuation of organized protest, striking, and mounting violence. "Meanwhile additional forces were arriving in the city . . . by July 26, 1877" (Avrich, 33), and the following day the strike was broken. At its annual convention in December 1877, the Workingmen's Party changed its name to the Socialistic Labor Party of North America (SLP); during the next two years the SLP engaged in political campaigns and won a number of state and municipal elections.

The events of 1877 began the Parsonses' journey from democratic socialism to anarchism. During the strike, Albert Parsons, who had achieved considerable notoriety, was fired from his typesetting job. When he sought other positions in his craft, he realized he had been blacklisted. Lucy Parsons opened a dress shop and proceeded to support them. Albert Parsons remained on the blacklist for several years; during that time, he took orders for his wife's shop. In 1878, Lucy Parsons, who had begun to meet other women in the socialist and labor movements, joined with ALZINA PARSONS STEVENS, LIZZIE HOLMES, and ELIZABETH RODGERS to organize Working Women's Union No. 1 (WWU). The organization, at the time the only women's union in the city, had almost one thousand members, including women in trades—domestic servants and seamstresses, who made up the majority of the city's wage earners—and homemakers, the latter predominating. Stevens was the first president and she obtained financial help from the powerful Chicago Typographical Union to organize women into a separate union. Parsons and the others visited workplaces to talk to women and encourage them to organize, and they handed out leaflets. The WWU platform advocated teaching school children to honor labor, suffrage for women, and equal pay for equal work for women. The WWU joined the eight hour day campaign that was just beginning in Chicago. Albert Parsons was also engaged in the eight hour day campaign.

Lucy Parsons wrote articles for the *Socialist*, the SLP's newspaper, from 1878 until the paper ceased publication in 1879. Her poem, "A Parody," printed in the December 7, 1878, edition of the *Socialist*, described her despair over the continued economic depression and the circumstances that pitted workers against the unemployed in the struggle for survival. She defended Civil War veterans who petitioned the government for financial assistance and criticized the newspapers for their negative statements about the former soldiers. She began to criticize the way in which the powerful state engaged soldiers, many from the working class, with patriotic rhetoric. Since the men were no longer needed as soldiers, the government was not interested in providing them with the means to a livelihood. In another article, Parsons wrote about women workers, illustrating the exploitative attitudes prevalent toward domestic workers. While Lucy and Albert Parsons continued to support the more militant labor unions, they also began to believe that workers had to arm themselves in protection against police and military assaults. Such workers' groups, often organized in groups along ethnic lines and known variously as the *Lehr-und-Wehr Verein* (Education and defense society), Bohemian Sharpshooters, Jaeger Verein, and Irish Labor Guards, alarmed businessmen and industrialists. In 1879, the Illinois legislature passed a law—upheld by the Illinois Supreme Court—banning all paramilitary groups. The question of self-defense was divisive in the SLP, and some groups continued to maintain self-defense societies underground.

On September 14, 1879, Lucy Parsons gave birth to her son, Albert Richard. She continued to write and to speak out for the WWU. In the factional struggles that racked the socialist movement from 1879 to 1881, Lucy Parsons became a speaker for the most militant faction. Lucy and Albert Parsons had initially tried to bring about change through legislative means; Albert had run for political office unsuccessfully from 1877 to 1882—three times for alderman, two times for state assemblyman, and once each for sheriff and county clerk. While there had been some notable electoral victories for SLP candidates, by 1880 many in the SLP, including Albert and Lucy Parsons, questioned whether political activity had any value for the working class. Lucy and Albert Parsons were among the forty-four SLP delegates in attendance at the Greenback–Labor Party nominating convention in Chicago in the summer of 1880. They advocated inserting a socialist program into the Greenback-Labor platform, but were not successful. The Greenback Party, organized after the financial crisis of 1873, had become the Greenback–Labor Party in 1878 when some labor plans had been introduced into its platforms.

Between 1880 and 1883 there was a major shift in the direction and ideology of the SLP. Those in the SLP—including Lucy and Albert Parsons—who were disaffected by corruption and the lack of success of political tactics after 1880 were also disturbed by the increase in state-sponsored violence against labor militancy. The ideas of European revolutionaries like Johann Most, who immigrated to the United States in 1882, and

American social revolutionaries who were forming clubs from 1880, attracted the radical wing of the SLP, which embraced Most's ardent endorsement of direct action. "These social revolutionary clubs formed the embryo of a revolutionary anarchist movement in America. In Chicago [Albert] Parsons was one of the first to affiliate himself with the new organization" (Avrich, 51). He had turned to direct action, calling for strikes, boycotts, union organization and, when necessary, revolutionary action, believing that "no meaningful reform could be obtained within the framework of the capitalist system" (p. 51). Lucy Parsons, whose second child, a daughter, Lulu Eda, was born in 1881, had moved in the same ideological direction and would write extensively on the use of direct action in the class struggle. "Her whole being, said Albert, was 'wrapped up in the progress of the social revolution'" (p. 117).

When Albert Parsons attended a major social revolutionary congress held in Pittsburgh, Pennsylvania, in October 1883, his and Lucy Parsons's transformation was complete. Albert Parsons and August Spies, who acted as secretary of the congress, brought a devotion to the cause of trade unionism—"the Chicago idea" (Avrich, 73)—to the meeting and countered the extreme anarchism of other delegates. "For the midwesterners the union was more than a vehicle of class struggle. It was, as [Albert] Parsons described it, 'an autonomous commune in the process of incubation,' the 'embryonic group of the future "free society"'" (Avrich, 73). The Pittsburgh congress gave birth to the International Working People's Association (IWPA), which grew from 1883 to the Haymarket explosion of 1886. In Chicago, the new journal for the group, the *Alarm*, was edited by Albert Parsons; Lucy Parsons became one of its writers. She was influenced by Johann Most's call to "'propaganda by the deed,' acts of individualism terrorism" (Ashbaugh, 56). She "argued that a dynamite bomb set off in Westminster Abbey [England] would be 'a shot fired in the center of civilization, whose echoes are heard around the world'" (Ashbaugh, 56). Throughout the 1880s, Albert Parsons earned only eight dollars a week as editor of the *Alarm*. Lucy Parsons continued to run a small ladies' tailor shop, for which she did the sewing and her husband solicited business.

The winter of 1883–84 had been one of the most severe in Chicago memory. An economic depression, not as severe as the one ten years earlier but serious enough—left many unemployed and homeless. Many died of hunger and exposure. Lucy Parsons's article, "To Tramps," published on the front page of the first issue of *Alarm* and later reprinted by the IWPA and distributed as a pamphlet, reflected her intense anger at the society that permitted such injustices. Lucy and Albert Parsons had come to believe "that the wage slaves of 1884 were no better off than the chattel slaves of 1860, and they believed that wage slavery would be defeated in the same way chattel slavery had been defeated. This time, however, a new force was introduced into the configuration: dynamite" (Ashbaugh, 55). Lucy Parsons and other anarchists saw dynamite as a countervailing force to use against state sanctioned violence. If anything, Lucy Parsons was more committed to propaganda by the deed than was Albert, as a result of "all the oppression which . . . [she] suffered for her dark skin and her womanhood" (p. 55).

In part, the adoption of an ideology of propaganda by the deed was a response to the situation in Chicago. A report of the Citizens' Association in Chicago told "of 'the wretched condition of the tenements into which thousands of workingmen are huddled, the wholesale violation of all rules . . . [of] safety . . . the neglect of all laws of health . . . the unwholesome character of their food'" (Avrich, 79–80) and made it clear that workers and the poor lived in unspeakable conditions. At the same time, the clash between labor and capital in the form of strikes, demonstrations, and boycotts became more and more frequent. The IWPA in Chicago and nationwide achieved its greatest strength from the fall of 1885 to the spring of 1886, with "five thousand members" and "three times as many sympathizers and supporters" (Avrich, 83). Chicago was the center of IWPA affiliation.

In this milieu, Lucy Parsons and other women participated in the growing American membership of the IWPA in Chicago, which also included immigrants. The group had Wednesday and Sunday meetings and engaged in many public activities. The American Group sent speakers on the lecture circuit, arranged street parades with placards and banners, and, to raise funds for the *Alarm*, they sponsored picnics, dances, and other entertainments. On April 28, 1885, Lucy Parsons and Lizzie Swank Holmes were at the head of the anarchists' march on the new Board of Trade building. That spring there had been a series of strikes among quarrymen of Lemont, Lockport, and Joliet, Illinois. On May 4, 1885, militia had opened fire on a group of unarmed strikers in Lemont, killing at least two and wounding others. Men and women bystanders were clubbed and bayoneted in the streets. Termed a "massacre" by the anarchists, the Lemont incident was reported by Albert Parsons in the May 5, 1885, *Alarm*. Lucy Parsons achieved notoriety when on May 7, 1885, the *Chicago Tribune* reported her as having stated, "Let every dirty, lousy tramp arm himself with a revolver or knife, and lay in wait on the steps of the palaces of the rich and stab or shoot the owners as they come out. Let us kill them without mercy, and let it be a war of extermination and without pity. Let us devastate the avenues where the wealthy live as Sheridan devastated the beautiful valley of the Shenandoah" (Avrich, 91). In the meantime, the radical labor unions had broken away from the Chicago Trades Assembly, which they deemed too reformist, and established the Central Labor Union. The Central Labor Union contended that there could be no reconciliation or arbitration between capital and labor.

Chicago's two labor coalitions had separate Labor Day celebrations September 6 and 7, 1885. At the former, the moderate Trades Assembly had Mayor Carter Harrison as featured speaker; at the latter, anarchists marched through downtown Chicago, and first in line was a contingent of women (including Lucy Parsons) "in decorated wagons, which bore the slogans: 'Down with Government, God and Gold' and 'Our Civilization: The Bullet and Policeman's Club'" (Avrich, 93). Albert Parsons delivered an impassioned speech addressing a crowd that was estimated to have reached several thousand. On Thanksgiving Day 1885, Lucy Parsons led a march of poor people down Prairie Avenue, the heart of the neighborhood of Chicago's wealthiest capitalists, where Marshall Field and George Pullman had built their stately mansions. Lucy Parsons's brigade rang the doorbells. Such events were part of the "counterculture" (Avrich, 131–49) of the anarchist movement.

"What took place in Chicago on May 4, 1886, was the culmination of passions and prejudices that had been accumulating for several years" (Avrich, 181). The nationwide crusade for the eight hour day, an intense struggle by the American labor movement, even garnered support from the IWPA in Chicago. Albert Parsons had supported the eight hour day movement in the late 1870s, turned against it as a reform that would be irrelevant ultimately to the workers, and again, in 1886, embraced it, realizing how deeply committed workers were and how opposed were employers. On May 1, 1886, "more than 300,000 workers stopped work in 13,000 establishments throughout the country. In Chicago . . . 40,000 went out on strike" (Avrich, 186). Demonstrations and meetings occurred in all parts of Chicago on May Day; one of the most impressive was one organized by the IWPA and Central Labor Union. Lucy and Albert Parsons, accompanied by their two children, "led 80,000 workers up Michigan Avenue, singing and marching arm in arm" (Avrich, 186). The prominence of anarchists in the labor movement troubled Chicago's establishment, yet May 1 passed without any rioting or disorder. On May 3, however, a bloody encounter occurred between strikers and police at the McCormick Reaper Works. The company had a long history of labor disputes. The year before, the company "had been forced by a strike to restore a 15 percent wage cut in what has been described as 'the bitterest' labor-management struggle in the company's history'" (Avrich, 188). Cyrus H. McCormick Jr. had told the press, "The right to hire any man, white or black, union or non-union, Protestant or Catholic, is something I will not surrender" (Avrich, 188).

Following the May 3 clash, a meeting at Haymarket Square was called for May 4. That day a large crowd of two to three thousand people gathered. Albert Parsons, who was attending a meeting of the American Group in the offices of *Alarm*, was called on to speak and did so after August Spies. Mayor Carter Harrison, who had been notified earlier in the day of the planned Haymarket meeting, had joined the crowd and was in the audience when Spies spoke. Parsons, with his wife Lucy and others from the American Group, arrived at Haymarket while Spies was still speaking. Parsons was introduced as the next speaker, and given the general sentiment of the moment, he was "surprisingly temperate" (Avrich, 202) and "concluded by declaring that the only hope of the workers lay in socialism. . . . He called on his listeners to make every effort to secure the eight-hour day, to defend their rights and liberties, and above all 'to combine, to unite, for in union there is strength!'" (Avrich, 202–203). Mayor Harrison was convinced of the harmless character of the meeting and decided to leave after Parsons concluded his speech. He told Captain John Bonfield, the police officer in charge of the nearby Desplaines Street station, that the meeting was quiet and probably would not require any intervention or additional personnel.

Parsons introduced the last speaker, Samuel Fielden, who spoke for about ten minutes; suddenly the weather changed and it looked like rain. People began to leave and Albert Parsons called out that the meeting should adjourn to Zepf's Hall, a tavern half a block north. Someone announced that another group was at Zepf's, so Fielden announced he would finish in a few minutes and then the crowd should go home. Bonfield led 180 police in an attempt to break up what had been a peaceable and orderly meeting, one that was almost over. Moments later, after the arrival of Bonfield and the police, a bomb exploded, sparking a police riot. Eight policemen died as a result of the bombing and the crossfire among police. In the disorder that followed the bomb explosion, an undetermined number of demonstrators lost their lives. The authorities never did determine the identity of the person who threw the bomb. Eight anarchists were tried and received guilty verdicts for conspiracy to murder policeman Mathias Degan, who died at Haymarket. Four defendants—August Spies, Albert Parsons, George Engel, and Adolph Fischer—were executed by hanging. A fifth condemned anarchist, Louis Lingg, committed suicide in jail; Oscar Neebe, Samuel Fielden, and Michael Schwab remained in jail until released in 1893 by Illinois governor John Peter Altgeld. His "pardon message acknowledged the injustice of the trial" (Roediger, 297).

Lucy Parsons was arrested three times on May 5, 1886. Police arrested August Spies and Michael Schwab early that morning. Initially she was arrested at the *Alarm* office; police released her in hopes that she would lead them to Albert. They arrested her a second time when she was with her children in a friend's apartment. Released, she was arrested a third time that evening and then released again later that night. She immediately sent out circulars to all IWPA sections telling them about the Haymarket and related events and asking them for donations to defend the Chicago comrades.

The trial of the Haymarket eight was conspicuously biased against the defendants; witnesses testified that Parsons, Fischer, Schwab, Engel, Lingg, and Neebe were at the scene when the bomb was thrown. In reality, only Spies and Fielden were at the scene, and neither of them threw the bomb. The atmosphere surrounding the trial was supercharged; the prosecution put anarchist ideas on trial and introduced inflammatory articles that had been written by the defendants for *Alarm*, *Arbeiter-Zeitung*, and *Vorbote*. Lucy Parsons's "To Tramps" was introduced by the prosecution as People's Exhibit No. 18. On August 20, 1886, the verdict was announced after the jury had deliberated for three hours. When the sentencing was over, Lucy Parsons pledged to tell the American people that a miscarriage of justice had been done. She and her children had been evicted from their apartment because they did not have rent money. Soon her son was sent to stay with friends in Waukesha, Wisconsin, and her daughter with friends in another state. Lucy Parsons immediately began a seven-week tour to gain support and raise funds to appeal the case. "With the execution set for December 3, the defense committee worked feverishly for a stay of execution and a new trial" (Ashbaugh, 105). Parsons traveled to the East and spoke to Knights of Labor Assemblies, to IWPA locals, and to other socialist, anarchist, and labor gatherings. In March 1887, Lucy Parsons again traveled east to raise money for the defense since the case had gone to the Illinois Supreme Court. The appeal was unsuccessful.

Immediately after Albert Parsons's death, Parsons published his *Anarchism: Its Philosophy and Scientific Basis* (1887), written while he was in prison awaiting execution. She did so not only as an organizing tool but from economic necessity. Lucy Parsons also received financial support from the Chicago Pioneer Benefit and Aid Association, established to help the families of the Haymarket martyrs. The society loaned Parsons $593 to expedite her publishing project and set up a fund to give all the Haymarket widows $8 a week and a few additional dollars for each child. (The fund continued to give money to the families for eight years.) On October 13, 1889, Lula Eda, Lucy Parsons's eight-year-old daughter, died of a disease of the lymph glands. This condition may have been brought on by the scarlet fever that she had in 1886.

Parsons regarded her writing and public speaking as a continuation of the work that her comrades could not finish. As early as 1888, Parsons saw herself as a movement historian. Writing in *Alarm* September 22, 1888, she stated that "future generations will prize every detail in the history of these fast-moving years; the movement toward a higher civilization needs a correct presentation of facts[,] and the veil of prejudice, which an unrelenting ruling class has woven about the events of the past two years, must be torn aside before it shapes into tradition" (p. 2). She wrote about the movement in *Freedom: A Revolutionary Communist-Anarchist Monthly*, edited by Lizzie Swank Holmes and Parsons. The first issue, November 11, 1890, included excepts from a lecture, "Communism: Its Historical Development," delivered by Parsons at the reopening of the American Group's weekly IWPA meeting. Parsons described the evolution of communism and concluded with a brief history of the International Working People's Association, identifying Albert Parsons, August Spies, and Johann Most as the leaders of this new movement. Lucy Parsons published the autobiographies of Albert Parsons and August Spies in serialized form in the magazine *Freedom*, from December 1890 to May 1891, in hopes of preserving the legacy of the Haymarket martyrs.

Lucy Parsons began to write about race issues in a January 1891 article in *Freedom*. She commended the Colored Farmers' Alliance of Florida for its strong call for land ownership, arguing that land is not property but belongs to those who live on it and improve it. "Are the 'ignorant' negroes to teach 'intelligent' white people a lesson in basic principles?'" (p. 3) she asked rhetorically. Writing about Southern lynchings in April 1892, she compared these atrocities to reports of pogroms against Jews in Russia. Parsons called for Blacks to organize a revolution around the "spirit of martyrdom" ("Southern Lynchings," *Freedom*, April 1892, 2). She acknowledged that many might die but argued that this was the only way social change would occur. Lucy Parsons's analysis of racism in American society came from her identification with the oppressed and marginalized, not from a position as a race woman who proclaimed that her own liberation was tied to the liberation of her race, as did IDA B. WELLS-BARNETT. (Wells-Barnett was an anti-lynching crusader who, by 1893, was living in Chicago and writing passionately against the brutalities and injustices experienced by Blacks in the South.) In other articles Parsons advocated that the poor reject charity and take what was rightfully theirs as producers; she criticized Socialist Party leaders, in particular Thomas J. Morgan, who advocated on behalf of skilled labor at the expense of unskilled labor; she noted the growing disparity between rich and poor.

Lucy Parsons opposed the Spanish-American War in 1898, calling it a war of imperialism and discouraging young men from enlisting. Her public antiwar campaign occurred at a time when she opposed her own son's enlistment in the army. Albert Parsons Jr. had also taken an interest in religion, attending church services and becoming involved in the Spiritualist movement. Parsons determined that he was mentally ill and decided to have him committed to the Illinois Northern Hospital for the Insane, appearing in court on July 27, 1899, to testify to his insanity. The court accepted Lucy Parsons's reasoning, declared him insane, and issued a warrant for his arrest; he was admitted to the hospital on July 31, 1899. Although one of the hospital doctors who examined Albert Jr. found him to be normal physically and mentally, after his admission he deteriorated. Harassed by patients and hospital personnel because of his parents' political activities, he remained uncooperative and was put in confinement and in restraints. He remained at Illinois Northern for the next twenty years, until his death from tuberculosis on August 15, 1919. Lucy Parsons was criticized by associates in the radical movement, including Emma Goldman, for what was perceived as mistreatment of her son. Goldman felt that Parsons had driven Albert Jr. "into the army and then had him put in a lunatic asylum" (Ashbaugh, 208). Ashbaugh concludes that "there must have been a long history of conflict between Lucy and Albert Jr., most of it unknown due to Lucy's refusal to discuss her private life. What remains is that she committed him to the mental institution. She had put her political commitments first and had attempted to make . . . [him] a part of her larger political vision" (Ashbaugh, 208).

In the years after Haymarket the anarchist ideas of the Pittsburgh Manifesto and the IWPA lost popularity and the movement splintered. Lucy Parsons's dominant interest was in maintaining a press where the ideas of revolutionary socialism and the legacy of the Chicago anarchists could be kept alive. Beyond this action, as she wrote, "There [was] no way of building up a movement, strengthening it and keeping it intact, except by a press, at least weeklies, if dailies are impossible" ("The Importance of a Press," *Liberator*, April 14, 1906, 2). Parsons continued to participate in the counterculture of the movement and worked hard to represent the Haymarket tradition. The *Alarm* continued to be produced during the Haymarket trial and appeal and after the execution of the Haymarket defendants. Dyer D. Lum continued as editor; Lucy Parsons disagreed with his policies, believing that his views on anarchism did not represent the political position of the American Group of the IWPA. He had moved to New York and had taken the newspaper with him. From 1890 to 1892, Lucy Parsons published and edited *Freedom: A Revolutionary Communist-Anarchist Monthly*, personally raising money to keep it alive so that she could continue to define the meaning of Haymarket. Her articles on the horrors of lynching and on women's oppression were always written in the context of the philosophy of revolutionary socialism. Next Parsons wrote the Chicago column for *Free Society*, edited by Abe Isaak and published from 1897 to 1904 in San Francisco, Chicago, and New York. After the assassination of President William McKinley in September 1901 by the anarchist Leon Czolgosz, the Chicago police destroyed the *Free Society* press and arrested members of the *Free Society* publishing group, but not Parsons, who had been interviewed by a reporter and had said, "Nothing could be worse for the cause of anarchism. What is the use to strike individuals? That is not true anarchy. Another ruler rises to take his place and no good is accomplished" (Ashbaugh, 211). By 1905, Parsons had begun to edit the *Liberator*. It lasted one year. In that time Parsons wrote about industrial unionism and argued for the relevance of the philosophy of anarchism for the working-class struggle. As she had in the past, Parsons included speeches and writings of her husband and historical overviews of the labor movement that supported the Haymarket tradition.

In 1905, Lucy Parsons, together with labor leaders Mother Jones and Bill Haywood and socialist Eugene Victor Debs, took part in the founding convention of the Industrial Workers of the World (IWW) in Chicago. Jones was the first woman and Parsons the second to join the IWW. Parsons came to the convention as, in her words, "the representative of the most oppressed of humanity, child laborers and prostitutes—'my sisters whom I can see in the night when I go out in Chicago'" (Ashbaugh, 217). She addressed the convention after speeches were delivered by Debs, socialist Daniel DeLeon, and others. Parsons "called for a program of 'revolutionary socialism' that would usher in a society in which 'the land shall belong to the landless, the tools to the toilers, and the product to the producers'" (Avrich, 452). In contrast to her earlier writings, in which she justified the need to use violence in opposition to an intransigent capitalist class, Parsons now stressed that when the workers decide to take what is rightfully theirs, there will be no need for armed violence. She advocated the use of the general strike where workers, instead of walking off their jobs and then starving, would take possession of the property needed for production.

Parsons was the only woman to speak at the IWW's founding convention in 1905. Her words pointed to the lack of women's participation and, spontaneously, the leaders called for Mother Jones to speak. She was absent from the hall at the time of the belated invitation and did not appear at the podium. Parsons, however, was not interested in what she understood as the bourgeois woman suffrage movement. Although she admired Susan B. Anthony and even printed in *Liberator*, November 5, 1905, the report on industrial conditions of working women done by the Chicago Woman's Club, she maintained her earliest position on the subject—that equal rights for women would happen only when revolutionary socialism established the new society. When Susan B. Anthony died March 12, 1906, Parsons editorialized, "It is unnecessary for us to agree with her in the field of reform which she mapped out for herself. . . . We can at any rate admire the sterling qualities of the woman herself" (*Liberator*, March 18, 1906, 2). Parsons wrote, "If the economic question had been a factor in American life at the beginning of Miss Anthony's career, she might have devoted her life to that cause, for she was a progressive thinker" (p. 2), a statement revealing far more about Parsons's lack of experience with or understanding of the woman suffrage movement than about the nature of Anthony's contribution. Writing in an earlier edition of her paper, Parsons took an optimistic view of the progress of the "new woman," stating, "I know of no activity from which woman is debarred because of her sex" (*Liberator*, September 3, 1905, 3).

At the same time that women activists decried the slow progress in the workplace and the lack of change in the political sphere, Parsons saw the American woman as having made enormous strides. "In America, woman competes with man not only in the factory but in the store, the office, the classroom, in jurisprudence, in medics, in positions of public trust. Woman is fast becoming the ruling sex. Whether that ever will extend to political power only time can tell" (*Liberator*, September 3, 1905, 3). To a large extent this question of whether or not women would obtain the vote was an academic one for Parsons, who never changed her attitude toward electoral politics once she and Albert Parsons abandoned it after 1880 as a viable strategy for workers. Parsons was much more concerned about what role working women would take in the struggle between labor and capital. Using an argument employed by traditional trade union men, Parsons claimed that "woman is allowing herself to be used to reduce the standard of life by working for lower wages than those demanded by men" (p. 3). Nor did Parsons join the newly formed Women's Trade Union League, affiliated with the American Federation of Labor, an organization she and other revolutionary socialists deplored.

In 1910, Lucy Parsons reprinted *The Famous Speeches of the Eight Chicago Anarchists in Court* and added pamphlets by Emma Goldman and Alexander Berkman, works of Peter Kropotkin, and her own "Principles of Anarchism." Parsons met William Z. Foster, an IWW member who later was president of the Communist Party, United States of America, and who founded the Syndicalist League of North America. "Participation in the labor movement presented revolutionaries with a paradox" (Barrett, "Dual Unionism," 200). Unions were organizations that were reformist rather than radical by nature. They worked to improve workers' conditions within the system. It was difficult for revolutionaries to function within unions, but these organizations were where the organized working class was concentrated. Foster's syndicalism was "an alternative to dual unionism," and he argued "that the mainstream unions could indeed be radicalized but only through long-term agitation by a 'militant minority' within the regular trade union organizations. Foster and his group developed their critique of dual unionism first within the IWW and then through a series of organizations they formed between 1911 and 1920" (Barrett, "Dual Unionism," 201). Lucy Parsons supported Foster's efforts and gave lectures across the country in support of syndicalism; but by 1914 the league, which had never achieved a mass following, had dissolved.

The political climate had changed since the 1880s, and Lucy Parsons had difficulty connecting with the next generation of activists. Her absorption in the history and martyrdom of her husband had kept her motivated; but it failed to create new alliances and contributed to a stereotyping of her as the widow from a bygone era, no longer relevant. When events brought workers into the streets, however, Lucy Parsons continued to participate in and support actions that dramatized the plight of marginalized workers, the unemployed, the homeless, and the hungry. The winter of 1915 was a difficult one for many workers who lost jobs when factories closed because the war in Europe had drastically cut the foreign market for American goods. In Chicago the unemployed marched in the streets. Lucy Parsons had resumed editing and publishing the *Liberator* and reported on the conditions of the working class. On January 17, 1915, Parsons was one of many speakers at a meeting of the unemployed at a local assembly hall not far from the Hull-House settlement. The hall was crowded to capacity, and there were banners "held aloft here and there in the crowd," some bearing the word 'Hunger' in huge letters . . . others decorated with the Lord's Prayer, with 'Give us this day our daily bread' typed out conspicuously" ("Police Club Unemployed"). Parsons was reported to have told the crowd, "'As long as you accept charity, capitalists will not give you work!'" ("Police Club Unemployed"). Following the speeches, the crowd began to form a procession outside the hall but was immediately accosted by mounted and foot police officers who had rushed to the neighborhood of Hull-House. Women and men marchers were indiscriminately knocked down as the police used their clubs; twenty-two of the marchers were arrested, seven of them women, including Lucy Parsons.

The social reformers at Hull-House came to the defense of Lucy Parsons, who was portrayed by the authorities as a dangerous woman who had incited the crowd to violence and encouraged them to attack the police. MARY WILMARTH provided bail for eight of the group—including Parsons—who had been arrested and charged with rioting, unlawful assemblage, and parading without a permit. JANE ADDAMS and SOPHONISBA BRECKINRIDGE helped secure jury trials for the defendants; Addams arranged for attorneys, and Addams, Breckinridge, and birth control advocate RACHELLE YARROS, also associated with Hull-House, testified in behalf of Lucy Parsons and the other defendants on January 28, 1915. Breckinridge told the press, "Mrs. Parsons said nothing that would start a riot. . . . She merely explained that labor is different from other commodities; that if it isn't sold one day, it cannot be held in stock and sold the next" ("Hunger Marchers Face Trial").

The defense argued that the courts had invalidated the Chicago city ordinance that gave the police chief the right to license street parades and won the case. The police chief then obtained a ruling from the city's corporation counsel that gave the head of the police department discretionary powers to issue parade permits. The protesters and their supporters planned their next demonstration; as ELLEN GATES STARR of Hull-House told reporters, "The unemployed would not ask for a permit from police" since "they have a court decision to justify them now" (Ashbaugh, 242). When a meeting to discuss whether or not to march was held at Hull-House January 31, Jane Addams admonished the crowd to be content with the victory they had won in the courts. "Lucy Parsons stood at the door shouting to the people, 'Come on! March! March!'" (Ashbaugh, 242) and "600 people marched through the rain and slush determined to test their court victory for the free use of the streets" (p. 242). As a result of Lucy Parsons's leadership, joined by the anarchists of Chicago's West Side, many interests from the liberal and reform community focused on the unemployment crisis. The Chicago Federation of Labor (CFL), the Socialist Party, and Hull-House called a mass demonstration for February 12, 1915, Abraham Lincoln's birthday. Jane Addams and Lucy Parsons worked together to plan the event, and Parsons was appointed to the arrangements committee with John Fitzpatrick, head of the CFL, and others. This was not a sign, however, that Parsons had joined what she perceived to be the nonrevolutionary reformist labor and political movements.

She continued to campaign wherever the most marginalized workers were fighting for their rights: in the summer of 1916 with striking iron miners at the Mesabi Range, Minnesota; in support of Tom Mooney, the union organizer who was sentenced to death for a bomb explosion that killed ten people during a Preparedness Day parade in San Francisco, California, July 16, 1916; in 1917 in support of Cassius Cook, arrested for his antiwar work as secretary of the League of Humanity (Parsons's house was used as collateral to cover the last seven thousand dollars of his bond). Passage of the Espionage Act in 1917 and the Sedition Act in 1918 during wartime put all radicals at risk of prison, or of deportation if they were not born in the United States or were not naturalized citizens. Antiradical hysteria made all antiwar and radical labor activities dangerous. The U.S. Postal Service denied hundreds of radical publications access to the mails; among the suppressed publications was the *Liberator*. Bill Haywood and one hundred other IWW members were tried in 1918 on conspiracy charges and all of the men were convicted and sentenced to prison. The entire executive committee of the Socialist Party was indicted under the Espionage Act but never brought to trial. Eugene Victor Debs was convicted for an antiwar speech made in Canton, Ohio, and was sent to the federal penitentiary. Emma Goldman and Alexander Berkman were deported to Russia on December 21, 1919.

At the same time that the government pursued the imprisonment or deportation of those deemed subversive, culminating in the Palmer Raids of the 1920s led by U.S. Attorney General Mitchell Palmer, revolutionaries gained ground worldwide with the seizure of power in Russia by the Bolsheviks on November 7, 1917. In 1921, the Workers' Party of America, which became the Communist Party, USA (CP), was formed. Lucy Parsons and other anarchists had to decide whether or not Bolshevism in the Soviet Union was the implementation of their vision or even the initial stage of what would lead to a socialist society. Lucy Parsons shared William Z. Foster's enthusiasm for communism. She saw the Communist Party as "the legitimate successor to prior radical movements" (Ashbaugh, 251) and found that the CP "adopted the history of the Haymarket Affair and the Eight Hour Movement as its history" (p. 251). In 1927, Parsons attended the second annual convention of the International Labor Defense (ILD), a coalition founded by CP members in 1925; she was elected vice-chair of the convention and a member of its National Committee, which included Elizabeth Gurley Flynn and Ella Reeve Bloor.

Forty-four years after her appearance in the 1886 May Day parade in Chicago, she spoke again on May 1, 1930, to a crowd of thousands. The stock market had crashed six months before, and working people were beginning to feel the impact of unemployment. By 1934, she was depressed about the possibilities for revolutionary change: "I have nothing worthwhile to write about. We radicals get together in our little groups, talk to each other, and go home. The Roosevelt wind has blown the radical movement to Hell!" (Ashbaugh, 256). She realized that anarchism was a dead issue in the United States, and she saw in the rise of Adolph Hitler in Germany a tremendous threat to world radicalism. She continued to travel and lecture in the 1930s, although she was losing her sight. In Chicago, young radicals came to see her, for she "had become a legend in her own time and a folk hero of Communist Party youth" (Ashbaugh, 260). Even the Chicago newspapers that had regarded her as a threat to society published articles about her in 1936, the fiftieth anniversary of the Haymarket police riot. The next year, Parsons spoke in Chicago on the fiftieth anniversary of the execution of her husband, November 11, 1937, "concluding, 'Oh, Misery, I have drunk thy cup of sorrow to its dregs, but I am still a rebel'" (Ashbaugh, 260). That year International Publishers, the Communist Party press, published *Labor Agitator: The Story of Albert R. Parsons* by Alan Calmer. Alexander Trachtenberg, head of International Publishers, persuaded Lucy Parsons to join the CP in 1939. She continued to be active, and one of her last public appearances was to speak to strikers at International Harvester, successor to the McCormick Reaper Works, where police brutality in 1886 had prompted the Haymarket protest meeting. She made comparisons and spoke about how police and employer brutality were realities still. On March 7, 1942, there was a fire in the small house on Chicago's North Side where Lucy Parsons lived with George Markstall, her longtime partner, who died trying to save her. The fire had started in the wood-burning stove. When her friends arrived at her house the next day to retrieve her personal books—close to three thousand volumes—and papers, they could find only a few badly damaged books. The rest of the collection and her papers were gone. Neither the FBI nor the Red Squad accepted responsibility for their disappearance. She was cremated and her ashes were buried at the monument for the Haymarket martyrs, Forest Home Cemetery, Forest Park, Illinois.

Lucy Parsons was twenty when she arrived in Chicago in 1873. She had already witnessed what racism and injustice meant for people of color in her native state of Texas. She propelled herself into the labor movement at a time when workers had embryonic organizations and little standing in the law courts or with the public. The early years of organizing trade unions for working women and men, and, with her husband, Albert Parsons, of attempting change through participation in the political system, convinced her that the class struggle was central to workers' liberation; she contended that workers could obtain justice only when they took the means of production into their own hands and that no establishment would transfer power peacefully because it was voted out of office. Although Parsons entered into coalitions with groups and organizations that did not subscribe completely to her revolutionary program, she held fast to her anarchist vision of a worker's commonwealth. She refused to allow the passage of time to erase the memory of her husband and fought valiantly to narrate his life and the history of anarchism so that in losing the battle to save his life, she could win the ultimate victory of constructing the popular version of the events of Haymarket. In this effort she achieved a measure of success.

Sources. The Labadie Collection at the Univ. of Michigan, Ann Arbor, contains letters of Lucy Parsons and other important anarchists involved in the Haymarket case; UIC Spec. Coll. has the Ben L. Reitman Papers, which include letters from Lucy Parsons. CHS has a rich collection of Haymarket materials. NL has a good selection from the radical press. The State Hist. Soc. of Wisconsin, Madison, has the papers of Albert R. Parsons. Lucy Parsons's articles are in *Socialist* (1878–79), *Alarm* (1884–89), *Freedom: An Anarchist-Communist Monthly* (1890–92),

Firebrand (1895–97), *Free Society* (1897–1904), and *Liberator* (1905–1906, 1915–17); they are the major source for her theoretical positions as well as for reports on movement activities, the culture of the anarchist community, and her interpretation of events and people in politics, reform, and the labor movement more generally. Her publications include the following works that she edited: *The Life of Albert R. Parsons, with Brief History of the Labor Movement in America* (1889); *Altgeld's Reasons for Pardoning Fielden, Schwab and Nebbe* (1915); and *The Famous Speeches of the Eight Chicago Anarchists in Court* (1910, reprinted 1969, 1994). See "Hunger Marchers Face Trial in Chicago Today," *Republican* [Springfield, Missouri], January 28, 1915, and "Police Club Unemployed in Riot at Hull-House," New York *World*, January 18, 1915, for a discussion of her protest activity with the unemployed. Books that are useful include Carolyn Ashbaugh, *Lucy Parsons: American Revolutionary* (1976); Paul Avrich, *The Haymarket Tragedy* (1984); Meredith Tax, *The Rising of the Women: Feminist Solidarity and Class Conflict, 1880–1917* (1980); Bruce Nelson, *Beyond the Martyrs: A Social History of Chicago's Anarchists, 1870–1900* (1988). Helpful are articles by James R. Barrett, "Dual Unionism" and "Syndicalist League of North America"; David Roediger, "Haymarket Incident"; and Paul Buhle, "Socialist Labor Party," all in *Encyclopedia of the American Left*, ed. Mari Jo Buhle, Paul Buhle, and Dan Georgakas (1992). Biographies of Lucy Parsons have to deal with the identity question. Ashbaugh's position has already been described. Alfredo Mirande and Evangelina Enriquez, *La Chicana: The Mexican-American Woman* (1979) consider her a Chicana. Robin D. G. Kelley, "Lucy Parsons (1853–1942)," in *BWA*, says Parsons was of African, Indian, and Mexican ancestry. ·

RIMA LUNIN SCHULTZ
AMY C. SCHNEIDHORST

PAYNE, VIRGINIA
June 19, 1908–February 9, 1977
ACTRESS, UNION ORGANIZER

Virginia Payne, pioneering radio entertainer, was best known for her role as radio's *Ma Perkins*. Broadcast from Chicago from 1933 through 1947, *Ma Perkins* attracted millions of listeners, most of them women. Although years younger than the character of Ma, Payne won the part when she was in her early twenties. Offstage she dedicated many hours to answering mail that poured in from her listening audience, giving advice and consoling thousands of women and men during the depression era and World War II. Active in labor organizing, Payne helped form a local union in Chicago for radio actors and actresses. In 1959 she was elected the first woman president of a national entertainment union.

The eldest of three children in a Roman Catholic family, Payne was born in Cincinnati, Ohio, to John Louis Payne, a general family physician and a professor at a medical college, and Anne (Brophy) Payne, a woman with an appreciation for fine poetry and literature. Payne's brother, John Hilliard Payne, became a surgeon. Her sister, Adele (Payne) Hollem, became director of Home Service for the Red Cross.

Although many members of the family chose medical careers, medicine did not appeal to Payne. She shared instead her mother's love of literature. As a toddler, she recited bits of poetry. At five she began to study acting and soon performed in recitals at church and at parent-teacher meetings. Neighborhood children gathered at the Payne household to read for parts in a play written and directed by the young Virginia Payne. She charged admission to the performances and donated the proceeds to various causes, such as care of stray cats or the Red Cross. At the age of thirteen, Payne enrolled in the Schuster-Martin School of Drama in Cincinnati, where one of her classmates was Tyrone Power, who was a famous movie star from the 1930s through the 1950s. At Schuster-Martin her teachers immediately recognized her talent.

Following high school she attended the University of Cincinnati, continued with her drama studies, and appeared in summer stock. In college she helped an African American organization, the University Players, present two musical comedies. She received a bachelor's degree at the University of Cincinnati, and in 1932 she earned a master's degree in English literature.

Payne began working at WLW radio in Cincinnati during high school. She starred as *Honey Adams,* a singing southern heroine, played an American Indian in *Little Scarface,* and the lead in an early mystery series, *The Step on the Stairs*. It was at WLW that *Ma Perkins* first aired in 1933. Ma was characterized as a widow who struggled to raise her three children while operating her late husband's lumber yard. Nearly five hundred other actresses, some from Hollywood and New York, auditioned for the lead part. Hidden from view, only the voices of the auditioning women were heard. Payne's voice was perfect for the part.

Within six months the program went to the network and the show moved to Chicago with three of the original cast members, including Payne. She made the trip accompanied by her father, who helped her find a hotel on the Near North Side. Shortly after, she moved to an apartment in that area. *Ma Perkins* debuted in Chicago on December 4, 1933. The show was broadcast for thirteen years from the Merchandise Mart, which, when built in 1929, was the world's largest building filled with wholesale showrooms and offices. Payne said of the Mart, "The place was enormous; at first I used to arrive early so I'd have time to get lost" (quoted in Westin, 232).

The fifteen-minute shows required daily five-hour rehearsals. Payne did three recordings of *Ma Perkins* a day, and the program aired on both NBC's Red and Blue networks (a rare occurrence) five days a week. At first the soap opera attracted only 2 percent of radio ratings and was dubbed a "washboard weeper" (quoted in Westin, 232). A new writing staff improved the ratings to 12 percent within a few years. *Ma Perkins* became one of the highest rated daytime shows on radio.

The hard times of the Great Depression drew many Americans to radio, where for a short time each day men and women escaped the harsh realities of life while listening to this newly popular entertainment. According to Payne, Ma was like other women of the thirties. She had strong community ties, believed in prayer, and had hope for the future. Payne said, "Ma . . . was a tolerant, understanding woman; she was slow to judge. This was very admirable to fans. She was always counseling, 'Wait till the facts are in'" (quoted in Westin, 235).

Proctor and Gamble's Oxydol sponsored the program, and Ma was called "Oxydol's Champion Saleswoman." The popular show, featured on more than thirty-two local NBC affiliates, was heard by an estimated five million women. The program maintained first place ratings for many of the years that it aired. Some of the shows were taped and sent to Hawaii, Canada, and

throughout Europe, where they could be heard on 228 other stations. Ma had quite a following. Despite her hectic schedule, Payne spent hours answering much of the fan mail that arrived at the rate of about a thousand letters a week. Payne received many practical and oftentimes handmade gifts and was inundated with cards, especially on Mother's Day.

Considered the capital of daytime radio serials in the 1930s and the 1940s, Chicago became home to many favorite soap operas. Actors and actresses played parts on other shows as well as their own, and Payne was no exception. In addition to *Ma Perkins,* she took on roles in *First Nighter, Grand Hotel, U.S. Steel Hour, Cavalcade of America, Eternal Light,* and *Today's Children*. She also appeared in *Lonely Women,* which ran for a season in 1942. The show had an all-woman cast with dramas that reflected the hardships of women during wartime. Payne costarred in radio dramas with Claude Rains, Freddie Bartholomew, Tyrone Power, Leo G. Carroll, and Orson Welles before they became movie stars. With the interchanging of roles, the cast of *Ma Perkins* and other programs shared daily experiences with one another and became close-knit on radio and in life.

Due to Payne's youthful appearance, the network hid her real identity until the 1950s. While she received billing on *Ma Perkins,* her name was not used in conjunction with the character of Ma. Periodically Payne would be written out of the script to take short trips either to make personal appearances or for pleasure. She made personal appearances in an older woman's costume consisting of a gray wig, granny glasses, low-heeled orthopedic shoes, and a plain dress. People came by the busloads to see Ma when she appeared in Des Moines, Iowa, and other places. On stage, Payne stood far enough from the crowd to hide her age. She also appeared in costume for fan magazines and gift photographs given out by sponsors.

When she was not appearing before her fans, Virginia Payne talked to fellow workers and encouraged them to become union members of the Chicago local of the American Federation of Radio Artists (AFRA) that she helped organize in August 1937. As AFRA's Chicago membership chair, Payne recruited the first four hundred performers to the new union. Over the years, she held many union positions, including local president and national vice-president. Credited with being one of the people responsible for the union's success, Payne took an active part in negotiations and in merger talks that led to radio and television actors' coming together in a joint union, the American Federation of Television and Radio Artists (AFTRA). Elected national president of AFTRA in 1959, Payne became the first woman to serve as president of a national entertainment union. She retained that position until 1961. In 1962, she won AFTRA's George Heller Memorial Gold Card Award, and in 1975, AFTRA named her Woman of the Year.

Virginia Payne loved music. She had attended the Conservatory of Music in Cincinnati, where she had sung and played the piano. An accomplished pianist, she studied at the Chicago Conservatory of Music from 1940 to 1946. In addition to her musical activities, Payne became sorority president of Omega Upsilon from 1932 to 1934; lectured at Northwestern University in 1940 and 1941; was chairwoman of Stage for Action, Inc., a theatrical group that stimulated interest in political and social problems through interpretive plays; and served as secretary of the Independent Citizens' Committee of the Arts, Science and Professions, an organization supporting world security. Active in the war effort during World War II, Payne chaired several organizations, including the Midwest Camp and Hospital Committee, the National Entertainment Industries Council, and the Midwest United Theatrical War Activities. In 1946 she won awards from the United States Treasury Department, the United States Navy, and the American Red Cross for war services.

In 1942, *Ma Perkins* was sold to CBS, and in 1947, the show moved to New York. It aired on the East Coast until November 25, 1960, when the show ended with its 7,065th broadcast. Payne never missed a performance during the twenty-seven years the show aired; once, after breaking her ankle, she performed on crutches. At the time of the show's end, Payne was the highest paid daytime actress and made up to fifty thousand dollars a year.

The show ended, but Payne's career did not. In the 1950s she performed in summer stock as Lola in *Come Back Little Sheba* and as Amanda in *The Glass Menagerie*. Payne departed from her motherly radio image in 1960 when she toured the country doing theater performances in *Carousel* and *Oklahoma!* In 1964, she made her Broadway musical debut in *Fade Out–Fade In*, which starred comedian Carol Burnett. Wishing to be recognized for her current merits, she asked that announcers and interviewers not reveal her identity as *Ma Perkins* until the end of the credits.

Although she moved to New York, Payne preferred the simple life of her summer home by the ocean in Ogunquit, Maine, where she became part of the community's life, cooking suppers for friends, attending church functions, and becoming an unofficial adoptee of a local Perkins family. Payne collected oil paintings and antiques and grew roses. Two varieties of roses were named for her by rose growers, one "Virginia Payne" and the other "Ma Perkins."

Payne worked until two months before her death. She performed for the last time in December 1976 in a stage production of *Oliver* at her hometown. She died in Cincinnati, Ohio. She was inducted into the Radio Hall of Fame in 1988.

Never married, Payne was surrounded by friends who praised her kindness, gentleness, and intelligence. Throughout her life, Virginia Payne's real-life persona was like that of Ma Perkins's radio image, a down-to-earth woman who saw the good in people. Payne's characterization of Ma helped many Americans during the tough times of the 1930s and 1940s by being a voice of comfort over the airwaves. "If Roosevelt was the father figure of the thirties," Payne once said, "then Ma Perkins was the mother figure" (quoted in Westin, 235).

Sources. Although all articles written on Virginia Payne state her birth year as 1910, June 19, 1908, is listed on her records at the New York AFTRA office. In the Westin book, Payne said that she began performing in *Ma Perkins* at the age of nineteen, placing her birth date in 1914. A 1919 picture of Payne with her family in *TV Radio Mirror* shows her as definitely more than five years old. When she died in 1977, one obituary gave her age as 66 while another gave 67, putting her birth date at 1910 or 1911. This biography keeps the date recorded at the American Federation of Television and Radio Artists (AFTRA). Virginia Payne's narrative, "Virginia Payne's Story," in Jeane Westin's *Making Do: How*

Women Survived the '30s (1976) provides the best insight into Payne's personality, her portrayal of Ma Perkins, and the years she spent in Chicago. Information from the New York office of AFTRA and a telephone interview by Marilyn Perry with Payne's fellow New York union member Martha Greenhouse on February 10, 1995, were helpful in establishing correct dates and titles for Payne's union activities. Additional information can be found in Frances Kish, "Cincinnati's Ma Perkins," *TV Radio Mirror*, April 1957; Bernard Stengren, "Network's Ma, Union's Big Sister," *NYT*, September 20, 1959; and William Ramsey, "Hoi Polloi and 'Soap Opera': A Defense," *Bulletin of the Historical and Philosophical Society of Ohio: Cincinnati*, October 1962. Obituaries appeared in *NYT*, February 12, 1977, and the *Cincinnati Post*, February 11, 1977.

MARILYN ELIZABETH PERRY

PEATTIE, ELIA AMANDA WILKINSON
January 15, 1862–July 12, 1935
JOURNALIST, SHORT STORY WRITER, NOVELIST, CHILDREN'S AUTHOR, CLUBWOMAN

According to the *Chicago Tribune*, Elia Wilkinson Peattie became, in 1884, the first woman to work as a reporter for the newspaper and was its influential book-page editor for two decades. A prolific writer of books for adults and children, a leading clubwoman and literary hostess, she raised herself and her family of writers well above the limited circumstances of her childhood. Her father, Frederick Wilkinson, was an English immigrant who attended the University of Michigan, graduated from Kalamazoo (Michigan) Law School, went West to seek gold at Pike's Peak, and gained election to Colorado's territorial legislature. He married Amanda Marie Cahill and was serving the Union when she bore Elia Amanda Wilkinson in Kalamazoo in 1862. Frederick Wilkinson returned shell-shocked. He began traveling as a collection attorney for wholesale merchants. Although suffering from nervous spasms, Amanda Wilkinson managed household, livestock, and garden alone, and she raised a family that eventually included five daughters; two sons died. As Elia Peattie recalled in her private memoirs, "The Star Wagon," her father's penchant for starting grandiose, unaffordable projects— especially houses—resulted in poverty and toil for the family.

After the Great Chicago Fire of 1871, Elia Wilkinson stayed at the home of her namesake aunt, Elia Cahill Walker, wife of James Walker. The Walkers' aristocratic home contrasted with the Wilkinsons' ugly new duplex. Elia Wilkinson attended Brown School with her sisters until she left during seventh grade to set type in her father's print shop and help her mother keep house—just as Amanda Wilkinson had left school to help her own mother, and Peattie's daughter later would leave during high school to help her. Describing herself as precocious and ambitious, Peattie recorded in her memoirs the cultural and social impoverishment she endured. Her father's tight domestic economies precluded books and city amusements. He failed to keep up payments on Elia's piano and elocution lessons. He objected to her dancing at the church-related youth parties where, in 1877, she met twenty-year-old Robert Burns Peattie, a reporter for the Western News Company.

Robert Peattie wooed her with books, flowers, and theater trips, with the arts and sociability, away from her dreary life in Windsor Park, the remote, undeveloped South Chicago suburb where the Wilkinsons lived. She tried to write, but the sphere of domesticity and her "father's nervous complainings" ("Star Wagon," 45) left her too weary. In November 1882 Elia Wilkinson collapsed from nervous paralysis and prostration; on doctor's orders, she was taken into the city to recuperate. In 1883 she published her first poem, "Ode to Neptune," in the *Chicago Times* and, ending a six-year engagement, married Robert Peattie.

The Peatties soon began writing stories together, Elia dictating to Robert as she sewed and rocked the baby. Thus began her life of juggling career and family. The Peatties had four children: Edward Cahill (born 1884), Barbara (1885), Roderick (1891), and Donald Culross (1898). Donald Peattie, in his own memoirs, recalled growing up in "a house where . . . the peck of my mother's typewriter sounded from . . . early until late" (*Road of a Naturalist*, 116). Although extended professional travel made arrangements for child care difficult, she continued to write and sell stories. In 1884, Peattie began reporting on art and society for the *Chicago Tribune*. Although she disliked the social "snubs" she risked, she treasured friendships with artists like Lorado Taft, interviews with actress Ellen Terry and activist Emma Goldman, and assignments to report on western resorts. She later lauded "The Artistic Side of Chicago" in an *Atlantic Monthly* essay (December 1899). Peattie began magazine writing with an 1887 story for the *Youth's Companion*. Eventually she published more than eighty stories in national periodicals that included *Cosmopolitan, Atlantic Monthly, Harper's* and its *Bazaar* and *Weekly*, and *Saint Nicholas*, helping to support a growing family.

The Peatties relocated to Omaha, Nebraska, in 1888, when the *World-Herald* offered two salaries, editorial responsibilities for Robert, and wide-ranging, signed columns for Elia. Soon thereafter she won nine hundred dollars from the *Detroit Free Press* for a melodramatic Chicago novel. *The Judge*, published in 1891, catches its heroine between a fiancé accused of murder and a guilty father with whom her relationship has erotic undertones; their country isolation is contrasted to the warmth of a working-class Chicago neighborhood. In 1890, Peattie published *A Journey through Wonderland* about her Alaskan trip commissioned by the Northern Pacific Railroad—for which she had to leave sick children in Chicago.

Political reporting in Omaha led Peattie into the Populist Party and friendships with William Jennings Bryan and Hamlin Garland. Peattie was intrigued by Bryan's ideas and proud that she and the *World-Herald* helped expose the hardships caused by railroad monopolies and eastern capitalists. When a political pamphlet she coauthored, *The American Peasant*, became part of Bryan's platform, he dubbed Peattie "the first Bryan man" ("Star Wagon," 102). Her short story, "Jim Lancy's Waterloo," was distributed in a campaign against the railroads. Epitomizing Peattie's theme of weak men whose ambitions increase women's domestic burdens, it was the most famous of her stories in *A Mountain Woman* (1896).

During eight years in Omaha, Nebraska, Peattie began lecturing and met student Willa Cather at a University of Nebraska engagement. Peattie traveled increasingly, often with her children. She helped organize women's clubs throughout the state, promoting their cross-class contacts for urban women and cultural enrichment for isolated ranch women. As president of the Omaha Woman's Club, she shared the stage with Susan B. Anthony at the General Federation of Women's Clubs' 1894 Philadelphia convention. The Peatties helped found the organized charities and a day nursery, but Robert's physical deterioration after pneumonia in 1890 and recuperative trips constrained her ability to maintain an Omaha household.

Peattie had returned to Chicago on visits before she moved her family back in 1896. She read three papers at the 1893 World's Columbian Exposition, where she met the fair's chief "lady manager" BERTHA HONORÉ PALMER and poet HARRIET MONROE. In revised editions of *The Story of America* (1889), Peattie celebrated Chicago's exposition. She herself was celebrated for *A Mountain Woman* at a Chicago reception attended by local writer Madeline Yale Wynne, novelist Henry Blake Fuller, columnist George Ade, sculptor Bessie Potter (see BESSIE POTTER VONNOH), and portraitist Ralph Clarkson. In 1898, they and dramatist ANNA MORGAN formed the Little Room, a salon in the Fine Arts Building that eventually included nearly all of Chicago's residential novelists, along with many artists and other occupants of studios in the building.

While her husband worked on the *Chronicle*, Peattie freelanced for the *Daily News* and collected her ghost stories into *The Shape of Fear* (1898). In 1899, she wrote a hundred fictional sketches for the *Chicago Tribune* to pay to renovate the Wilkinsons' old Windsor Park home for her own family. Her by-lined book reviews as the *Tribune*'s literary editor from 1901 until 1917 benefited her family economically but cost her artistically. She read some ten books a week; her husband estimated her *Tribune* reviews at five thousand total columns, many discussing Chicago writers—most favorably EDITH WYATT, Margaret Potter, Robert Herrick, CLARA LAUGHLIN, Maude Radford Warren, Harriet Monroe, and JANE ADDAMS. "It was the eternal reading and reviewing of books . . . that destroyed my originality and ate up my vitality," Peattie believed, "but the bills were paid, the children educated" ("Star Wagon," 307). She also promoted a *Tribune* experiment of publishing daily poems, written by various authors, which she collected into *Poems You Ought to Know* and *To Comfort You* (1903). She published no further books, however, until 1911.

Meanwhile, the Peatties' Sunday brunches in the book-filled "old house home" ("Star Wagon," 250) welcomed members of the Little Room literary club, extended family members, and Chicago authors, as well as Chicago journalists, including Peattie's best man, Eugene Field; longtime friends Lorado Taft, Hamlin Garland, and Willa Cather; poet Edgar Lee Masters; and novelists Zona Gale and Ellen Glasgow. These "gatherings were famous, and to be invited was the final literary accolade" (*Chicago Tribune*, March 15, 1964), recalled FANNY BUTCHER, Peattie's *Tribune* assistant.

Peattie's literary lectures took her to women's clubs and annually to Hull-House. She joined the exclusive Fortnightly and Chicago Woman's Club and became president of the Windsor Park Woman's Club, a delegate to the 1902 Los Angeles convention of the General Federation of Women's Clubs, and a founder and president of the Cordon Club for professional women, participating actively in such groups until she left Chicago after World War I. In *The Book of the Fine Arts Building* (1911), she applauded the downtown location that many women's organizations shared with artists' studios. Contributing to Chicago's little theater movement, too, she wrote a one-act opera, *The Love of a Caliban* (1898), a prelude to three medieval fantasies she published between 1901 and 1903.

Although both her literary taste and her own style were fairly conventional, Elia Peattie wrote a pseudonymous working-class poetic monologue, "The Milliner," for MARGARET ANDERSON's *Little Review* (1914). Her book reviews, however, harshly criticized the more naturalistic realism of Mary Wilkins Freeman and Theodore Dreiser and promoted the expression of human ideals in the context of social realism by such writers as William Dean Howells and Edith Wyatt. In addition to profiling Jane Addams as a practical idealist in *Harper's Bazaar* (October 1904, July 1907), she reviewed Addams's work repeatedly, calling her a "little sister to the world" (*Chicago Tribune*, November 12, 1910) in one review. In the process of conceptualizing social service as an extension of women's "maternal" role in an April 24, 1909, review, Peattie developed a broader feminist perspective. She persistently urged women's intellectual development, independence, and work. She both promoted women's comradeship with men and criticized romantic feminine self-sacrifice.

Peattie expressed her feminist views fully in her 1914 suffrage novel. *The Precipice* reflects critically on Peattie's childhood home life when its young heroine leaves an isolated country town, tyrannical father, and docile mother for Chicago. Praised in the *New York Times Book Review* (February 22, 1914) and elsewhere, the novel's "gallery of women" ranges from an isolated and overweening intellectual to a wifely scientist working on behalf of her husband's career, from a selfish flirt to a singer who relinquishes career for family. Its heroine, Kate Barrington, is partly modeled on Katherine Ostrander, a social worker living with the Peatties. Kate insists on a marriage that gives her scope to continue as one of the "Addams Breed," a "Sister of the World" (*Precipice*, 103, 225), although the novel criticizes both the Hull-House and University of Chicago communities as too removed from the "civic family" (p. 182) Kate serves.

Peattie's literary success became uneven after 1908. Her adult publications in national periodicals ended in 1911. After *The Precipice* she concentrated on girls' books. Having had an earlier success with *Ickery Ann* (1899), she now brought out *Edda and the Oak* (1911), a four-novel *Azalea* series (1912–15), *Lotta Embury's Career* (1915), *Sarah Brewster's Relatives* (1916), and *The Newcomers* (1917). The teenage heroines of the last three dramatize Peattie's feminist values of work and social cooperation within the family setting that her published childhood memoir *Painted Windows* (1918) also sentimentalizes.

Peattie's husband assumed a position on the *New York Tribune* in 1917. She joined him a year later, after scripting a parade on women's history in *Times and Manners* (1918), a Chicago Woman's Club wartime benefit pageant. Although chronically ill, Elia Peattie continued to write *New York Tribune* reviews until 1920 and joined the National Poetry Society and City Club. She made few friends, however, in a city where "there are no neighbors" ("Star Wagon," 312).

The "neighboring" Peattie so valued she found again in Tryon, North Carolina, where she and her husband retired in 1920. Her mother lived with the couple until she died in 1922.

Writing only poetry and plays now, Peattie published *The Wander Weed, and Seven Other Little Theater Plays* (1923). She lectured on topics ranging from clubs to the arts at the Lanier Club (now Tryon's Lanier Library). She served this local woman's club regularly as an officer and as a representative to state and national meetings. She read her own poetry and published *Songs from a Southern Garden* (1930). *The Great Delusion* was published in 1932, two years after her husband's death. Elia Peattie died of heart disease in Vermont and was buried in Tryon at Markham Cemetery.

Although born in an era when the word "ambitious was a credit to a man and a shame to a woman" (*Precipice*, 137), Elia Wilkinson Peattie became a groundbreaking professional journalist. She developed a nonconventional domesticity that combined her career with her husband's. She raised herself out of poverty and her children into intellectual achievement. Roderick and Donald became writers, and Donald married another writer; Edward became an engineer; Barbara wrote poetry and bore three sons before she died at age thirty. While commercial considerations dominated Peattie's literary life, her best fiction—*A Mountain Woman* and *The Precipice*—draws deeply on gender issues. Her complex feminism also enriched her contributions to the women's club movement and to the social life of Chicago's artistic and literary establishment.

Sources. The Henry Blake Fuller Papers and other collections at NL contain some of her correspondence, as do the papers of Donald Culross Peattie at the University of California, Santa Barbara, which include Robert Peattie's letter listing her publications. Donald Peattie wrote about his mother in *The Road of a Naturalist* (1941). Along with her husband's manuscript, "The Story of R. B. P." (1929), her own 1929 manuscript memoirs "The Star Wagon" and "Barbara" as well as letters to Kate Cleary are privately held by her grandson Mark Peattie. The contents of "The Star Wagon" are well reported in Joan Falcone, "The Bonds of Sisterhood in Chicago Women Writers: The Voice of Elia Wilkinson Peattie" (Ph.D. diss., Illinois State Univ., 1992), which also transcribes some letters and poems held by Mark Peattie. Besides those mentioned above, Peattie's published books include *With Script and Staff* (1891), *Our Chosen Land* (1896), *The Pictorial Story of America* (1896), *Pippins and Cheese* (1897), *The Edge of Things* (1903), and *The Angel with a Broom* (1915). Peattie's early achievements received contemporary notice in Frances E. Willard and Mary A. Livermore, eds., *American Women: Fifteen Hundred Biographies* (1897). *Mountain Woman, The Shape of Fear,* and *The Precipice* were reviewed in *Nation, Atlantic, NYT, Critic,* and *Bookman.* Retrospectively, Peattie was briefly characterized by journalists Burton Rascoe, *Before I Forget* (1937); Charles Collins, *Critics and Reviewers* (1942); and Fanny Butcher, "Books and Writers in an Earlier Day," *CT,* March 15, 1964. See also Bernard Duffey, *Chicago Renaissance in American Letters* (1956), and Babette Inglehart, "Illinois Women and Their Fiction," in *A Reader's Guide to Illinois Literature,* ed. Robert Bray, (1985). Her life and work were recently recovered in Sidney Bremer, "Lost Continuities: Alternative Urban Visions in Chicago Novels, 1890–1915," *Soundings: An Interdisciplinary Journal,* vol. 64, 1981, and further discussed in Bremer's "Willa Cather's Lost Chicago Sisters," in *Women Writers and the City,* ed. Susan Squier (1984), and Bremer's *Urban Intersections: Meetings of Life and Literature in United States Cities* (1992). *The Precipice* was reprinted in 1992 with a critical introduction by Bremer.

SIDNEY H. BREMER
JOAN STEVENSON FALCONE

PEBWORTH, MARY MARJORIE MULL
August 19, 1911–April 3, 1967
POLITICAL ACTIVIST, LEGISLATOR

Marjorie Pebworth was a woman a generation ahead of her time. While most middle-class, white women in the 1950s and 1960s concentrated their efforts on homemaking, Pebworth was working outside the home in paid and volunteer positions. Her years of volunteer work while raising two sons prepared her to become one of seven women to serve in the 1965 session of the Illinois General Assembly.

Mary Marjorie Mull was the eldest child of Donald and Mary (Hester) Mull of Homer, Indiana. She was six when, in 1917, her mother died while giving birth to a son. Marjorie Mull, her sister Martha, and her brother Fred were sent to live separately with relatives. Although Donald Mull remarried, he never took his children back to live with him. Marjorie Mull lived with her aunt, Eulalie Mull, who was a home economics teacher as well as a representative for a stove manufacturer. Marjorie Mull learned at an early age that women were not confined to stereotypical roles of housewife and mother. Mull enrolled at Indiana University to study psychology and journalism and soon became active on the university's newspaper. In 1932 she received an A.B. degree. While at Indiana she met Robert Pebworth, editor of the newspaper. The two were married on September 23, 1934.

The couple lived in Shelbyville, Indiana, where Marjorie Pebworth took a job as a high school librarian and then as a clerk with the Indiana State Teachers License Bureau. She worked as secretary-librarian for the Indiana Legislative Reference Bureau, where she developed her budding interest in politics.

In 1937 the Pebworths moved to Riverdale, Illinois, where their two sons, first Robert (called Robin) and then Donald, were born. Husband Robert Pebworth was a public relations executive with Sears, Roebuck and Company. The Pebworths joined St. Clement's Episcopal Church in Harvey, Illinois, where "Margie," as she was called, worked on various committees. During World War II, Pebworth and her sons moved back to Indiana to be near family. After the war, the family moved back to Riverdale and resumed their involvement with St. Clement's.

In postwar suburban Riverdale, as in many other suburban communities near metropolitan areas with large minority populations, a small number of community leaders began to advocate social policies to counteract the patterns of segregated housing, education, and employment that reflected society's deep-seated racism and discrimination against African Americans. Marjorie Pebworth's father, Donald Mull, held strong beliefs about racial equality, and, although his daughter did not reside in his household in her adolescence, she had been influenced by her family's ideas about racial tolerance. Having grown up in the 1920s in an Indiana where the Ku Klux Klan was public and active, Pebworth had seen the ugly side of racism. A logical outcome of her interest in politics and in fair play for all citizens was Pebworth's commitment to local groups in her community who were engaged in efforts to improve human relations and ensure that all Americans had the rights and freedoms of full citizenship. She joined the Department of Social Relations in St. Clement's Church and selected the Christian citizenship group, which worked on such issues as open housing. Pebworth also served on the board of Benton House, a neighborhood settlement house affiliated with the Episcopal Diocese of Chicago. She took her sons along to various meetings and was able to demonstrate to them her ideas of social justice, equality, and compassion.

Increasingly the contradiction of the existence of segregation in a society founded on the principles of equality and freedom for all challenged religious leaders and their congregations as well as elected officials and community leaders. Pebworth was part of the lay leadership within the Episcopal Church in the United States advocating that clergy and laity participate in movements for social change and involve themselves in lobbying for particular legislation to implement their beliefs on issues of social justice, civil rights, and civil liberties. While there had always been an urban ministry to the poor in American cities, by the late 1950s and early 1960s the direction taken by clergy and laity was in the arena of direct political action. In a new departure, religious groups brought pressure on government to enact fair housing and fair employment practices. These groups acknowledged the systemic or institutional racism of society that created barriers to the advancement of Blacks regardless of personal character, education, or skills. In the field of social justice and governmental reform, Pebworth also worked with church groups to abolish the death penalty. She encouraged Episcopal clergy to urge their parishioners to vote for more governmental spending for mental hospitals and education.

The suburban area in which the Pebworth family resided experienced racial change as middle-class Blacks sought better housing. The schools were one of the first institutions in these communities to deal with the tensions that emerged as the new families moved in. In 1958 Pebworth was the first woman elected to the Thornton Township High School and Junior College Board. As a member of this board, she was instrumental in getting the first black teacher hired in the Thornton district, demonstrating her belief that social change begins at home in small, significant steps.

During the 1950s, as Pebworth worked on social issues through her church and on education issues as a local elected official, she joined the League of Women Voters (LWV) and began her steady rise in its leadership. In 1954 and 1956 Pebworth was editor of the *Illinois Voter's Handbook*, a know-your-state government publication of the league. From 1958 to 1961 she was the legislative chair of the LWV. Pebworth said that her job title was "a lady-like word for lobbyist" ("Wife Becomes Legislator," 22). It was Pebworth's job to report on the activities of the Illinois General Assembly in Springfield to league members around the state. Her reports contained analysis, intellect, humor, and practicality, as she urged league members to contact their elected officials regarding issues of interest to the league.

By 1959 Pebworth was one of three vice-presidents of the League of Women Voters of Illinois (LWVI). In 1961 she was elected president, leading active local league organizations in all major Illinois cities, suburbs, and rural areas and a total membership of nearly ten thousand statewide. As LWVI president, Pebworth directed the work of the state board and local leagues. Through her column in the *Illinois Voter*, Pebworth urged members to participate in their government and implement the league agenda. A top priority of that agenda in 1961 was the need for a new constitution for the state of Illinois. Such a revision could only occur when a majority of the legislators called a constitutional convention. Pebworth led the campaign for a constitutional convention ("ConCon") to study and revise the state constitution that had been written in 1870 and had never been revised, despite major changes in population, industrial development, communications, and types of property in Illinois. Unlike the federal constitution, Illinois's constitution was not flexible and was almost impossible to amend. The LWVI and other organizations had worked throughout the 1940s but were unable to get a resolution for a constitutional convention through the Illinois legislature. The Gateway Amendment passed in 1950 improved the ability to amend the constitution but did not solve the basic problems with the document. In 1959 league members committed themselves to work for a constitutional convention as a long-term goal. The LWVI began a major push and lobbied legislators to support a constitutional convention. The league hoped to get the vote on a convention by the 1968 election, so that a new constitution could be drawn up and voted on by 1970, the hundredth anniversary of the existing document.

With the end of her presidency in the spring of 1961, Pebworth made plans to return to more personal interests. She ran for and won a second term on the Thornton District School Board, helped organized a local Tri-City Human Relations Council, and agreed to be vice-president of her golf group. Late in 1963 the Episcopal Bishop of Chicago, Gerald Francis Burrill, appointed Pebworth to the church's official Commission on Race Relations for the Chicago diocese. The commission hoped to play an important and moderating role in the improvement of race and social relations in Chicago and the suburbs at a time when strong views and extreme feelings were being expressed by many factions. Political events in the state, however, sent Pebworth in a new direction.

State legislative politics in Illinois were in turmoil. Historically, Illinois ranked among the worst states in its record on the reapportionment of legislative districts. Prior to 1954 there was no legal provision to compel revision of legislative boundaries when population changes had occurred. In 1954 an amendment was passed requiring that the Illinois state legislature be redistricted every ten years, based on population changes. Yet ten years later in 1964, the commission established to carry out the terms of the 1954 amendment failed to agree to terms for redistricting, forcing a statewide at-large election. The situation put all 177 state legislative seats up for election. As each party examined its incumbents and supporters for potential candidates, a third group sponsored by the Better Business Association and Independent Voters of Illinois considered putting forth an independent slate of candidates and asked Pebworth to run. She declined this invitation, but when the regular Republican Party approached her, she accepted its offer to run as one of 118 Republican candidates on what would become known as the orange or bed-sheet ballot, so named because of the large size needed to accommodate the number of candidates listed.

With her husband acting as campaign manager and chauffeur, Pebworth contacted her numerous friends and volunteer contacts across the state. Many women sponsored coffees—

small group meetings hosted by neighbors in their homes— where Pebworth and candidates answered questions about their positions on various topics. Pebworth concentrated her campaign in the Chicago metropolitan area, running on a platform dedicated to better government, judicial reform, and better education. As the campaign leading to a November 1964 election sorted itself out, Pebworth was one of about sixty-five candidates from both parties to be identified by the editorial board of the *Chicago Daily News* as "Blue Ribbon" (Editorial Page, October 15, 1964), that is, deserving of support from voters in both parties.

The orange bed-sheet ballot listed more than three hundred names for the 177 assembly seats up for election. On Election Day, November 3, 1964, long lines of voters waited to cast their votes. When the polls closed, the ballots had to be hand counted. The process of cross voting, selecting candidates from both parties instead of voting a straight ticket, made the count even more tedious and painstakingly slow. The unofficial results were not available until December 4, 1964. The official result was announced on January 5, 1965, the day after the legislature convened. Voters elected 118 Democrats and 59 Republicans. Pebworth placed seventh on the latter list with more than two million votes. Pebworth was flabbergasted that she had won and had received so many votes.

January 6, 1965, marked the opening day of the seventy-fourth session of the Illinois General Assembly. Pebworth joined seventy-three other new house members (more newcomers than in any other previous session) in the first day's ceremonies, which were attended by many families and friends who came to watch the proceedings. The seven women state legislators— ESTHER SAPERSTEIN, Marjorie Pebworth, Frances Dawson, Brooks McCormick, Mary K. Meany, Dorah Grow, and Eugenia S. Chapman—wore corsages presented by the LWVI to celebrate their election.

During the early days of January 1965, Pebworth visited many of the state offices in Springfield that she had frequented as a political activist. Many state employees expressed their delight at seeing her return as an elected official. "Welcome home, that's how I feel," Pebworth exclaimed. "I'm home. I've been down here lobbying for the League [of Women Voters] many times, but I never dreamed, I'd be down here as a voting member one day" ("Women Blossom in Legislature").

When the House organized itself, Pebworth was given her first three choices in committee assignments: education; election; and public aid, health, and safety. When Pebworth learned she had replaced a five-term Republican woman on the public aid committee, she realized how important her election results had been in determining committee assignments. Pebworth was also chosen secretary of the Republican Caucus.

Pebworth had long worked through her church and other avenues to gather support to abolish the death sentence. As a freshman legislator, she cosponsored a House bill to abolish capital punishment in Illinois. In March 1965, Pebworth quietly waited her turn to make her maiden speech on the floor of the House amidst a wild legislative scene; one legislator waved a revolver; another sounded a police siren. Finally, after many dozens of speeches, the Democratic Speaker of the House recognized Pebworth, saying, "May I say we've kept the best for last" (Hanson). In her remarks, Pebworth said, "If our creator can afford to worry about the sparrow, I think we can afford to worry about human lives" (Hanson). The bill passed in the House that day and later in the Senate, becoming law and abolishing the death penalty in Illinois. (It was later reinstated.)

As a first term representative, Pebworth was respected for her practicality and for doing her homework. Bills from the Education Committee calling for increased funding for junior colleges as well as for elementary and high schools often passed largely due to Pebworth's persistence in lobbying her fellow legislators. In October 1965, Illinois Governor Otto Kerner signed a bill sponsored by Pebworth to create a commission to study the Illinois Constitution, with the possibility of calling a constitutional convention. In the summer of 1965 Democratic Governor Otto Kerner named Pebworth to two separate state commissions. She was selected as one of two Republicans to serve on the Commission on the Organization of the General Assembly, tremendous recognition for a first-term legislator. She was also appointed one of six public members to the Constitutional Study Commission and was subsequently voted chair by the committee. The *Chicago Tribune* described Pebworth as an authority on the state constitution and said that Pebworth's being named chair of the commission during her first year was a "rare honor" ("State Rep. Marjorie Pebworth Dies").

By 1966 it was clear that, although Pebworth was a hardworking, conscientious legislator, she was not part of the inner circle of Republican politicians. Four Republican township committeemen decided not to slate Pebworth for reelection. They were angry that she had introduced a bill to bar racial discrimination in housing. Knowing she had the support of major party leaders, Pebworth decided to run for reelection as an independent Republican candidate in the June 24, 1966, primary in which four other candidates were running. She staged a practical campaign, shaking hands in supermarkets, speaking at coffees, and going door-to-door with her platform, which included the need for fair housing legislation in Illinois. As a member of the Tri-City Council on Human Relations, Pebworth aimed her housing argument at homeowners rather than realtors. Her belief was that because people cannot choose their neighbors, and realtors are basically agents for the sellers, some form of legislation was needed to ensure that individuals who could afford housing were free to choose where they wanted to live. Although a state fair housing law was never achieved, Governor Kerner did issue an open occupancy order in July 1966; it called for revocation or suspension of licenses of brokers who listed any property that the owners did not want sold or rented to Blacks or minority religious groups.

Prior to the June primary, the Better Business Association and various newspapers, angry with the 6th District (Pebworth's legislative district) committeemen who opposed Pebworth, supported her reelection. At that time voters in Illinois were allowed to cast a total of three votes (called cumulative voting) for Illinois House candidates. A voter could cast one vote for each of three candidates, one and a half votes for each of two candidates or all three votes—"bullet" vote—for one candidate. In a preelection editorial, the *Chicago Daily News* urged voters to cast all three of their votes for Pebworth, saying, "She has an outstanding record for good government," and "the township committeemen need to be reminded that the party still belongs to the people" (June 9, 1966).

Pebworth won the primary and the coveted first spot on the ballot for the general election in November; she was reelected by more than seventy-five thousand votes. Eager to get the referendum to call an Illinois Constitutional Convention placed on the November 1968 ballot, Pebworth headed back to Springfield full of her usual vim and vigor and with a renewed sense of confidence that she was the people's choice. This would be the fulfillment of her efforts to reform state government, which had begun in the 1950s with her work on the state League of Women Voters.

In February 1967, Pebworth was told she had a form of diabetes that could be controlled through diet and medication but that she was otherwise well. On March 1, 1967, the report of the Constitutional Study Commission was delivered to the governor and to the Illinois General Assembly. The commission recommended that the question calling for a Constitutional Convention be put on the November 1968 ballot. On April 3, 1967, newspapers reported that Marjorie Pebworth had died in her sleep of what was reported to be natural causes. There was an immediate outpouring of disbelief and grief. Pebworth's minister, the Reverend Thomas J. Brady, recalls that he received a call from Springfield wanting to reserve fifty seats in the first rows for the funeral mass. Brady politely told the caller that St. Clement's did not hold many more than that number and that Springfield people were welcome to listen to the mass in the basement of the church. After a simple mass, Pebworth was buried in Lixton, Indiana.

The *Thornton Trumpeter* wrote that Pebworth's proudest governmental appointment was as chair of the Constitutional Study Commission, the result of a devotion to updating the Illinois Constitution that began when she was a member of the League of Women Voters. She was so linked to this project that the Constitutional Convention was dedicated to her in 1970, the referendum having been placed on the ballot and approved in 1968 in her name.

Pebworth was a woman of strong convictions. She worked to better the schools in her south suburban community. She fostered equality and social justice through her volunteer work. Pebworth developed her expertise in government through her work with the League of Women Voters of Illinois. Even when she first arrived in the Illinois General Assembly, she was not regarded as a novice legislator because of her record as a citizen activist for governmental reform and for social justice and education issues. She immediately began work to improve government as she saw it. She was persistent and practical, knowing how to get things done. Yet, in her obituary on April 4, 1967, the *Chicago Daily News* wrote, "It may be that Mrs. Pebworth's greatest service to Illinois was her recent exemplary campaign for reelection. Because of her support of open occupancy bills, the regular Republican organization in her district tried to deny her renomination last year. . . . Pebworth decided to go it alone. Her strength and character will be missed in the Legislature and a Republican Party not overburdened with leaders of the caliber of Marjorie Pebworth."

Sources. Debbie and Donald Pebworth provided background about Pebworth's personal and family life in a March 1994 interview with Adele M. Dalesandro-Haug, who also conducted an interview with

Father Thomas J. Brady, April 13, 1994. League material can be found in LWVI archives, which are held in UIC Spec. Coll. The Archives of the Episcopal Diocese of Chicago, Chicago, have records of the Christian Citizenship Committee. The article, "Wife Becomes Legislator: Mrs. Pebworth Already 'Seasoned' as New Illinois Legislator," *Indiana Alumni Magazine*, May 1965, gives a biographical description of Pebworth. Information about Pebworth's legislative career is in newspaper reports, including "Women Blossom in Legislature," *Chicago Daily News*, January 12, 1965; Henry Hanson, "State Senate to Vote Curb on Death Penalty: Canfield," *Chicago Daily News*, March 3, 1965; and an editorial, "The Daily News Today Recommends," *Chicago Daily News*, June 9, 1966. Many area newspapers carried obituaries, including "State Rep. Marjorie Pebworth Dies," *CT*, April 4, 1967; "GOP Legislator: Mrs. Pebworth's Funeral Friday," *Chicago Daily News*, April 4, 1967; and a eulogy by state representative John Henry Kleine in the *Illinois Voter*, May–June, 1967. Pebworth is listed in the *Illinois Blue Books* for 1964–65 and 1966–67. Issues of the *Illinois Voter* of the League of Women Voters of Illinois are helpful.

ADELE M. DALESANDRO-HAUG

PELHAM, LAURA DAINTY
August 30, 1849–February 22, 1924
DIRECTOR, ACTRESS, THEATER PRODUCER, CLUBWOMAN

Laura Dainty Pelham, director of Chicago's Hull-House Players, was born Laura Mount in Southwick, Massachusetts, the daughter of physician Charles T. Mount and his wife Maria (Perkins) Mount. Little is known about Laura Mount's early family life, though in 1861 her widowed mother married Charles D. Crafts of Deerfield, Massachusetts, a jeweler and dentist. Mount was educated in the district school. Her family relocated to Tuscola, Illinois, in 1866. In 1870 she married Albert H. Dainty, a Chicago salesman, from whom she was separated three years later. They had one daughter, Louise.

Laura Dainty was already performing dramatic readings prior to her marriage and started a professional career in 1871. She toured the Chautauqua circuit as a dramatic reader, winning acclaim for her renditions of humorous stories such as "How the Old Horse Won the Bet," "A Naughty Little Girl's Views of Life in a Hotel," "Tom's Little Star," and "The Dead Doll." By 1879 she was a featured performer for Redpath Lyceum Bureau. Her performances in the Midwest, Massachusetts, and Rhode Island received praise from newspaper reviewers "as well as from the distinguished moral arbiters Wendell Phillips and Edward Everett Hale" (Hecht, "Hull-House Theatre," 106). The Redpath agency's publicity credited Laura Dainty's success to her "indomitable will, hard labor, inflexible determination"; and it described her as "petite in figure with dark hair, a bright face, a winning smile, and an easy, graceful presence" (Redpath Lyceum Bureau, *Laura Dainty*, 1). She was a "self-made artiste" (*Laura Dainty*, 1) who achieved success without the financial assistance of others.

Dainty began to act in plays around 1875. She first earned theatrical recognition as the title character in Dion Boucicault's melodrama, *Kathleen Mavourneen*; but her greatest success came about 1884 when she played the character Sincerity Weeks in Morgan Bates and Elwyn Barron's melodrama, *A Mountain Pink*. An astute businesswoman, Dainty formed her own company of *A Mountain Pink* and toured the play for

FIG. 92. *Laura Dainty Pelham founded and directed the Hull-House Players.*

several years. Dainty specialized in playing the role of the "soubrette," the secondary, often comedic woman servant, and took great pride in her ability to create screams that were "piercing and bloodcurdling" (Hecht, "Hull-House Theatre," 106). Though acting in plays, Laura Dainty maintained her career as a stage reader; ANNA MORGAN remembered Dainty as one of Chicago's leading readers of the 1880s. In 1892, Dainty married Fred Pelham, with whom she ran the Chicago office of the Redpath Lyceum Bureau.

Although a popular performer and administrator of dramatic performances, it was at Hull-House that Laura Dainty Pelham made her major contribution to theater history in the United States. She was drawn to JANE ADDAMS and the community at Hull-House because of the settlement's social goals as well as the opportunity to innovate in theater. At Hull-House, under Jane Addams's leadership, drama was introduced for its value as art and its potential as an outlet for social expression. As early as 1893, one of the social clubs produced Oliver Goldsmith's *She Stoops to Conquer*. With the subsequent growth in theatrical activity, Hull-House appointed a member of its resident staff, Hervey White, to supervise dramatics. In 1897 Walter Pietsch replaced White. Pietsch brought expertise, having studied theater while a student at Cornell University. He selected the best performers from the various social clubs to create the Hull-House Dramatic Association.

It is not clear when Laura Dainty Pelham first came to Hull-House. She corresponded with cofounder Jane Addams in 1897, and by April 1899 she was vice-president of the Hull-House Woman's Club. Pelham's interests and concerns had never been limited to art. In 1879, when on tour, she regularly used her free time to visit prisons and asylums to perform readings for the inmates. Perhaps Pelham's personal and professional struggles made her empathetic to those without means. The Hull-House Woman's Club, composed of neighborhood women, provided a forum for lectures and discussions on domestic issues, child care, and the advancement of women. It appealed to Pelham's interests in both suffrage and social reform. Pelham was elected to a four-year term as club president in 1900 and she remained a Woman's Club member the rest of her life.

Walter Pietsch left Hull-House in 1899. Resident George Twose tried unsuccessfully to succeed him. Disorder led Addams to call for the group's reorganization in 1900, and Laura Dainty Pelham was chosen as director. With the death of her husband the same year, Laura Pelham's ties to the Chicago office of the Redpath Lyceum ended, and she was able to take on new responsibilities. It is reasonable to speculate that Addams sought out Pelham, who had experience in theatrical activity and also shared with the Hull-House group a common purpose in the social goals of the settlement. Addams recognized the influential power of theater but decried popular melodramas, arguing that they presented impossible role models that distracted local youths from addressing the real issues of their own lives. Addams encouraged dramatics at Hull-House to develop a more useful theatrical alternative.

Pelham restructured the Hull-House Dramatic Association into an ensemble of fourteen. Drawn from the surrounding tenement communities, company members were amateurs who worked at regular jobs during the day and rehearsed at night. For a time Pelham herself maintained an outside business, Laura Dainty Pelham Amusements, with offices in the Tribune Building. By 1906 she had moved into a Hull-House apartment. By becoming a Hull-House resident, Pelham showed a growing commitment to and involvement in its work.

The revamped Hull-House Dramatic Association opened on December 10, 1900, with Pelham's familiar and proven melodrama, *The Mountain Pink*. Although Addams disliked melodrama, Pelham insisted; the production generated both neighborhood interest and much-needed funds. Following the advice of the renowned American actor Joseph Jefferson III, who was visiting Hull-House, Pelham chose to direct a series of melodramas and light comedies in the next few years in order to refine the ensemble's acting technique. In 1905–1906 Pelham judged the company ready to attempt George Bernard Shaw's

You Never Can Tell and also staged the American premiere of Henrik Ibsen's *The Pillars of Society*.

Jane Addams's social reform goals no doubt motivated Pelham's later innovative play selection. Such naturalist plays were largely unknown to American audiences. Inspired by Émile Zola's call-to-arms that art should serve as a scientific laboratory for the investigation of social ills, naturalist plays used lifelike settings to portray tales centered on the injustices of modern life. Naturalism appealed to Addams for, unlike melodrama, it presented life as it actually was, including depictions of social injustice and tenement life that Hull-House sought to cure.

It is unclear if it was Pelham or Addams who first suggested the use of naturalism at Hull-House, but Pelham certainly embraced the form, directing the group (in 1910 the Hull-House Players) in a series of naturalist works and encouraging their use of what was also a new, more lifelike acting style in simple realistic settings. This chapter in the company's work culminated in the 1911 American premiere of Englishman John Galsworthy's *Justice*, a play already credited with inspiring Winston Churchill to sponsor prison reform in Britain. Theodore Roosevelt, on a visit to Chicago, was impressed with the Hull-House Players' production, and Jane Addams recalled that he had not heard of Galsworthy before seeing *Justice* but was so impressed that he purchased every Galsworthy book he could find to read during his train ride back to New York. When Galsworthy visited Hull-House in 1912, he met with the Players, discussed their work on *Justice*, and invited them to stage the American premiere of his play *The Pigeon*.

National and international celebrities visited Hull-House to see the social experiment, which benefited the theater group. Some came as theatergoers; others came to see a group of immigrants perform avant-garde drama with unexpected proficiency. Local theater critics James O'Donnell Bennett and Percy Hammond reviewed the productions, often praising the Hull-House Players' development, though admittedly from a sociological rather than an aesthetic perspective. The free use of the Hull-House 230-seat proscenium stage enabled the Players to experiment without the need for commercial success. Ironically, given Addams's ideals, the Players appealed less and less to neighboring immigrant tastes and instead found an audience among the settlement's affluent supporters. The Hull-House Players' work also influenced local theater practice. Maurice Browne, who began his Little Theatre in Chicago almost a decade after the Players' first experiments, praised the Hull-House productions in his theater reviews, and late in life wrote, "Mrs. Pelham, not I, was the true founder of 'the American Little Theatre Movement'" (*Too Late to Lament*, 128).

In 1911 Pelham shifted the Players' focus toward the emerging Irish drama. She directed the Chicago premieres of Lady Augusta Gregory's *The Rising of the Moon*, John Masefield's *The Tragedy of Nan*, and John Millington Synge's *Riders to the Sea*. When Ireland's Abbey Players visited Chicago in 1912, the Hull-House actors attended the opening performance and sent roses to Lady Gregory. She had heard of the Players and, in turn, came to Hull-House and attended performances of her plays staged by the Players. The two acting companies became friends. At one point they collaborated on a performance of *The*

Rising of the Moon, with two Hull-House actors starting the piece and two Irish players finishing it. At the end of the Abbey Players' stay in Chicago, they invited the Hull-House Players to visit Ireland.

Eager to visit Ireland, Pelham accelerated the Players' schedule in order to raise sufficient funds for the trip. She scheduled eight plays in eight months, including a week of repertory at Chicago's Fine Arts Building, sponsored by the Chicago Theatre Society. For the first time the Players met with scalding reviews from Chicago theater critics. James Bennett expressed outrage that the amateur company members should be paid to perform at a major Chicago theater, blaming the fund-raising effort on "some wild project the players have of going to Dublin to act at the Abbey Theater" (quoted in Hecht, "Hull-House Theatre," 131), and describing himself and others as "Frankensteins" who "unwittingly cooperated in the creation of a being that now is released to plague the public" ("Hull-House Theatre," 131–32). Pelham wrote to Bennett to defend the Players, explaining that the Chicago Theatre Society set the ticket prices and that "all of the club but two are wage earners" ("Hull-House Theatre," 132) and hence needed this method of raising money. Nonetheless, Chicago critics stopped reviewing the Players' shows.

Upon returning to America from their trip abroad, the Hull-House Players were rocked by dissension. With Pelham still overseas, several members tried to take over the group. Still feeling the critics' sting, they attacked Pelham's stage direction as uninspired and dated and argued that they deserved more up-to-date leadership. Pelham returned before the mutineers could open a show and, with Jane Addams's backing, reasserted her authority. However, the rebellion resulted in the breakup of the ensemble, with eight of the fourteen members leaving. Pelham moved quickly to find replacements.

From 1914 until Pelham's death in February 1924, the Hull-House Players included a core of actors with additional performers used as needed. Though the new company remained successful, it lacked the proficiency shown by the earlier ensemble. In 1924 company member Maurice J. Cooney replaced Pelham as director.

Pelham died of Bright's Disease, a degenerative disorder of the kidneys. On May 24, 1925, the Laura Dainty Pelham cottage was dedicated at the Bowen Country Club, the Hull-House summer residence and camp situated north of Waukegan on the banks of Lake Michigan.

Laura Dainty Pelham made her mark directing the Hull-House Players, which was a fitting venue for one who fought to build her own career and who consistently balanced her theatrical work with the impulse to help others. She came out of the nineteenth century as a self-made woman, a successful performer and businesswoman, well schooled in popular, commercial fare while attaining a goodly measure of respectability. At Hull-House Pelham discarded old stage practices, instead experimenting with new dramatic forms and stagings. The plays of Ibsen, Galsworthy, and Shaw not only served the settlement's mission; they also represented the latest avant-garde trends. Pelham's artistic work thereby inadvertently anticipated radical changes in American theater. The Hull-House Players can be credited, as America's first "little theatre," with initiating a movement that reestablished non-commercial theater nationwide

during the first third of the twentieth century. Perhaps Pelham's artistry did grow dated, but despite her schooling in nineteenth-century theater practice and experience in melodramas, she could recognize and promote groundbreaking drama and the new stagecraft.

Sources. Genealogical information on Laura Dainty Pelham and her family is in the Deerfield, Massachusetts, Memorial Library, and in the records of the Congregational Church, Southwick Public Library, Southwick, Massachusetts. For the Hull-House years see the Hull-House Association Papers, Jane Addams Memorial Collection, UIC Spec. Coll., especially issues of the *Hull-House Yearbook* and the *Hull-House Bulletin*; and Jane Addams Papers, Swarthmore College Peace Collection, Swarthmore, Pennsylvania. The Eric Hjorth Collection, UIC Spec. Coll., contains some personal information on Pelham, including copies of her obituary and a Redpath Lyceum Bureau brochure, *Laura Dainty: Humorous and Dramatic Recitations: Season 1879–80.* Chautauqua Collection, Univ. of Iowa, has a lyceum brochure. Scrapbooks of the Chicago branch of the Women's Trade Union League, UIC Spec. Coll., contain information on Pelham's activities. Pelham's own account of her work with the Hull-House Players, "The Story of the Hull-House Players," *Drama Magazine*, May 1916, provides an anecdotal history but ignores the 1912 actors' revolt. Contemporary writing on Pelham and the Players includes Elsie Weil, "The Hull-House Players," *Theatre Magazine*, September 1913; Albert Phelps, "How the Hull-House Players Fought Their Way to Success," *Theatre Magazine*, November 1914. See Anna Morgan, *My Chicago* (1918), for a description of Pelham's career as a reader. Maurice Browne, *Too Late to Lament: An Autobiography* (1956), describes her influence on the Little Theatre movement. A comprehensive account of the Hull-House Players and Pelham, including bibliography and lists of dramatic reviews, is Stuart J. Hecht, "Hull-House Theatre: An Analytical and Evaluative History, 1889–1982" (Ph.D. diss., Northwestern Univ., 1983). See also Hecht, "Social and Artistic Integration: The Emergence of Hull-House Theatre," *Theatre Journal*, May 1982; J. Dennis Rich, "Art Theatre at Hull-House," in *Women in American Theatre*, ed. Helen Krich Chinoy and Linda Walsh Jenkins (1981). An obituary for Pelham is in the *CT*, February 23, 1924.

STUART J. HECHT

WITH LAUREN BUFFERD

PERKINS, LUCY FITCH
July 12, 1865–March 18, 1937
ARTIST, CHILDREN'S AUTHOR, SOCIAL REFORMER

Lucy Fitch Perkins was best known for the series of twenty-eight books she wrote that used the fictional adventures of twins to teach children an appreciation for the customs and cultures of other countries. With sales of more than two million copies, the books made Perkins one of the best-selling children's authors of her day.

Lucy Fitch was born in Maples, Indiana, to a family that honored the values of charity, thrift, hard work, temperance, independence, and obedience to God handed down by its Puritan ancestors. The second of five daughters born to Appleton Howe and Elizabeth (Bennett) Fitch, she was known as "the warrior of the family" (*Eve among the Puritans*, 5) according to her biographer, Eleanor Ellis Perkins. Quick to act on her feelings, she was always ready to protest any injustice on behalf of herself or others.

Fitch's mother grew up in Stowe, Vermont, and had been a teacher. Her father graduated from Amherst College in Amherst, Massachusetts; became a school principal in Chicago; taught

FIG. 93. *Lucy Fitch Perkins, author of the famous twins books, reads to neighborhood children.*

high school in Peoria, Illinois; served in the Union Army during the Civil War; and returned to help run the family farm in Hopkinton, Massachusetts, before moving his family to Maples, Indiana. There he helped his uncle set up a barrel-stave factory. The factory burned when Lucy Fitch was eight years old, and she was sent, along with her mother and three sisters, back to Hopkinton for three years while her father stayed to rebuild. By 1875, the family was reunited in Maples, but within a few years they left to open a woodworking factory in Kalamazoo, Michigan, seeking better financial and educational opportunities.

Until they moved to Kalamazoo, the Fitch girls had been educated primarily at home by their parents; but Lucy Fitch had attended school in Hopkinton in 1873. Elizabeth Fitch had read her children works by Charles Dickens and Sir Walter Scott, as well as Harriet Beecher Stowe's *Uncle Tom's Cabin*. Appleton Fitch shared his knowledge of Greek and Latin and read to his daughters from the *Iliad* and the *Odyssey*, John Milton's *Paradise Lost*, Thomas Bulfinch's *Bulfinch's Mythology*, and Alfred Tennyson's *Idylls of the King*. Although they worried that they were neglecting their daughters' education, the girls thrived on this intellectual diet. Lucy Fitch, especially, profited from the fact that her parents' lives were so demanding, because it left her time to dream, to sketch, to observe, and to imagine.

Fitch's interest in art was apparent early and was supported by her family. She received her first public recognition as an artist at age sixteen, when some of her drawings appeared in the *Kalamazoo Gazette*. Her talent captured the attention of a respected aunt who urged the family to send Lucy Fitch to art school. It was agreed, after some misgivings, to send her to the Museum of Fine Arts School, Boston, after her graduation from the Kalamazoo high school in 1883. She ranked first academically in her high school class.

The years from 1883 until she graduated in 1886 were very important in laying the groundwork for her future life. Fitch

met her future husband, Dwight Heald Perkins, in Boston. He was studying architecture at the Massachusetts Institute of Technology. The road to marriage was not entirely smooth, as Fitch and Perkins had religious differences: the former was a strict Congregationalist, the latter a member of the liberal All Souls (Unitarian) Church. Perkins was a close friend of All Souls' minister and social reformer Jenkin Lloyd Jones, a supporter of JANE ADDAMS and the social settlement movement in Chicago. Fitch began work at the Louis Prang Educational Company, where she did illustrations for educational materials. Fitch also began doing freelance work for *Young Folks Magazine*.

In 1887, Walter Scott Perry, who had observed her work at Prang, asked Fitch to come to Brooklyn, New York, and assist him in his new job as director of Pratt Institute, a recently established school of manual arts and engineering. She spent the next four years teaching there, while Dwight Perkins took an architectural position in the Chicago architecture firm of Burnham & Root.

Lucy Fitch left Brooklyn in 1891 to join Perkins in Chicago, where they were married on August 18, 1891, and began to attend Jenkins' All Souls Church together. Dwight Perkins included an art studio in their house on Chicago's Near South Side that he designed as a wedding present, even though Lucy Perkins did not intend to pursue her career after their marriage. Lucy Perkins returned to work with the Chicago office of the Prang company in 1893 to supplement the family's income during the national economic depression that hit Chicago badly after the World's Columbian Exposition closed. The same year she gave birth to her first child, Eleanor Ellis. Additionally, her husband Dwight Perkins became seriously ill.

Lucy Perkins spent the next ten years publishing illustrations, teaching and lecturing, and even painting murals for public buildings, including panels of King Arthur and Ivanhoe for the walls of a public school. By 1904, Dwight Perkins's career had rebounded. He designed a new home and moved the family to Evanston, a suburb north of Chicago. Lucy Perkins had found her work too rewarding to stop. She continued to focus on art, creating murals for the dining room of the Old Chicago Beach Hotel and the interior of a home in Hubbard Woods in north suburban Winnetka, as well as a decoration above the mantel for her own home. She also edited and illustrated several books for young children. Perkins gave birth to her second and last child, Lawrence Bradford, in 1908.

Perkins's talents for writing and art came together after 1911 when she created *The Dutch Twins* and began her noteworthy series. A gift of photographs of Dutch life had inspired her to draw little Dutch figures and tell stories about them to her four-year-old son, when one afternoon, a publishing friend, Edwin O. Grover, arrived early for dinner. He picked up the drawings from the floor and urged her to turn the stories and illustrations into a book.

Perkins spent the next twenty-five years of her life writing and illustrating one and sometimes two books a year about twin children. The books taught eight to ten-year-old readers about the lives, customs, and cultures of children around the world in the format of stories filled with adventure, mystery, and humor. The Houghton Mifflin Company eventually published twenty-six twins books by Perkins. The *Dutch Twins* was followed by the *Japanese Twins*, the *Irish Twins*, and the *Indian Twins*.

When asked where she derived the inspiration for the twins series, Perkins recalled both a trip to Ellis Island and an experience she had at a Chicago public school while working for the Prang company. "I remember visiting a school which was attended by children of twenty-seven different nationalities. There were, naturally, antagonisms and racial prejudices, which manifested themselves in such names as 'sheeny,' 'nigger,' and 'dagoes'" (Perkins letter to Laderman, December 26, 1931, Perkins Papers), she recalled. Perkins thought the school symbolized the country as a whole, "where different nationalities [were] trying to live together without understanding each other's backgrounds" (letter to Laderman), and she conceived of books that would encourage a sympathetic interest and understanding among people of their differences. She hoped her books would contribute to wiping "out racial boundary lines" (letter to Laderman). Perkins eventually expanded the series to include twins from American history because she felt that it was equally important for the foreign-born to understand something of their adopted culture.

Although she had not visited all of the countries she wrote about, Perkins was a meticulous researcher and made a point of talking to someone who had grown up in each country to get a child's viewpoint. Franklin S. Hoyt, her publisher, praised her thoroughness. "Keenly sensitive to any suggestion of inaccuracy in her books, she left no stone unturned to verify every fact and description before a manuscript left her hands" (Memorial Service, typescript, April 4, 1937, Perkins Papers).

Perkins felt her training as an artist gave her a sensitivity to detail that was an advantage in writing for children. When asked how to learn to write for children, she often answered, "Learn to draw" (*Eve among the Puritans*, 228). One of her gifts was the ability to see things from a child's perspective. She read every-

thing she wrote to her "Poison Squad," a group of neighborhood children she organized to give their reactions to her books while she was revising and editing them.

Perkins treasured her privacy and balanced her private life with membership in the League of Women Voters, the Chicago Woman's Club, and the Midland Authors Club. Her sensitivity to people's feelings enhanced her writing but also limited her emotional stamina. When the two-millionth copy of her twins series was published in October 1935, Carl B. Roden of the Chicago Public Library presented her with a specially bound copy at a ceremony in her honor. Although her publishers wanted to throw a large party for her in New York, Perkins insisted on a small ceremony in Chicago, inviting only her family, her first poison squad, and Louise Ayars Garnett, a close friend and writing colleague.

Perkins died of coronary thrombosis in Pasadena, California, where she and her husband owned a second home. Her ashes were interred at Chicago's Graceland Cemetery. Her last book, *The Dutch Twins and Little Brother*, written with her daughter, Eleanor Ellis Perkins, was published posthumously in 1938. More than 250 people gathered at the Lincolnwood School in Evanston to pay tribute to Perkins after her death. The setting for the service was particularly meaningful because her architect husband had designed the school and Perkins had created the school's mural.

Lucy Fitch Perkins believed in the necessity of mutual respect and understanding among people of different nationalities if there was to be peace on the planet. She was convinced that tolerance and respect for others could be taught to children through literature that captured their imaginations and engaged their sympathies.

Sources. Lucy Fitch Perkins Papers, Evanston Hist. Soc., are an important collection. The principal published source on Perkins is Eleanor Ellis Perkins, *Eve among the Puritans: A Biography of Lucy Fitch Perkins* (1956). See also Stanley J. Kunitz and Howard Haycraft, eds., *The Junior Book of Authors* (1934); NAW (1971); and Diane Telgen, ed., *Something about the Author*, vol. 72 (1993).

PAMELA TODD

PETERSON, ANNA J.
June 27, 1870–July 19, 1952

COMMERCIAL HOME ECONOMIST, RADIO PERSONALITY

Johanna Josephine Murphy was born in Manchester, New Hampshire. To family and close friends she was always known as "Anna J," but to Chicagoans during the 1920s and 1930s, it was "Mrs. Peterson" that became a household name. As the popular director of the Home Service Department for the Peoples Gas Light and Coke Co. (Peoples Gas), she earned a following that included an enormous audience who listened to her daily radio cooking show, thousands who attended her cooking classes and demonstrations, and hordes of housewives who relied on her published recipes and cookbooks.

Anna Murphy was the eldest of nine children born to Irish immigrants who settled in New England during the 1850s in the wake of Ireland's potato famine. The names of her parents are not known and little is known about them, except that her mother was Catholic and her father likely worked in one of the area's many textile mills. Anna Murphy later acknowledged that her education began at home and that she learned about women from her female-dominated family. Indeed, the six Murphy children who survived to adulthood were all girls.

Anna Murphy moved to Boston in 1887, at age seventeen. She may have attended the Boston Cooking School during Fanny Farmer's tenure there in the 1890s. She likely supported herself cooking for restaurants and boarding houses, eventually running her own boarding house in the vicinity of Haverill, Massachusetts.

In 1900 Anna Murphy gave birth to her only child, a daughter named Dorothy. She married Adolph F. Peterson during this decade but the match was a bad one and around 1910, determined to make a fresh start, Peterson left her husband. Arriving in Chicago with her young daughter, Anna J. Peterson presented herself as a "widow" and within a few years established herself as a freelance demonstrator of cooking and household techniques.

Peterson made a name for herself demonstrating a variety of domestic products to Chicago's female consumers in the years before and after World War I. She pitched toys at Marshall Field's department store, cooking ingredients and recipes for Corn Products Refining Company, and an assortment of foodstuffs—from baking powder to breakfast cereals—at grocery stores throughout the city. So impressive were Peterson's skills as an engaging and effective demonstrator that a colleague recounted with awe her ability to sell English tea to Irish immigrants. Comfortable in front of crowds, Peterson came across to her audiences as wise but not intimidating and well prepared but not rehearsed. A natural teacher and performer known for her quick wit and extemporaneous public speaking skills, she was a middle-aged matron who exuded maternal confidence and competence.

New sources of power and light began transforming life in America's homes and kitchens during the years between the two world wars. In contrast to the homes run by their nineteenth-century mothers, housewives of the 1920s and 1930s employed mechanical servants powered by gas and electricity. An explosion in the production of stoves, refrigerators, water heaters, and washing machines helped transform the way domestic work was done, and by whom. By 1930, most nonrural Americans lived in electrified dwellings and more than half of all households, especially those in metropolitan areas like Chicago, were cooking with gas.

The rise of the home economics profession paralleled this transformation of household labor in the servantless home. Home economists encouraged the American housewife to see housewifery as less of a drudge and more of an expression of her personality and devotion to her family. Self-taught home economists like Peterson, along with a growing number of college-educated women credentialed in the field, gave voice to this new domestic outlook through their work in both the public and private sectors. Home economists working in utility-sponsored home service departments played a vital role in boosting the sales of gas and electric products while also promoting do-it-yourself housewifery.

When Anna J. Peterson was appointed director of the newly established Home Service Department at Peoples Gas in March 1922, she was nearly fifty-two years old. Her immediate responsibilities included supervising a staff of four women who answered queries from the public and establishing a demonstration kitchen at the company's downtown headquarters. Within her first month on the job, Peterson was teaching a cooking course for young women employees of the gas company; by the end of the year, she was offering a full series of classes to the public. Her starting salary was a generous three hundred dollars per month.

From its inception the Home Service Department was committed to enhancing public relations and broadening its audience. Within her first months at Peoples Gas, Peterson oversaw the debut of a motorized model kitchen on wheels that traveled about the city offering cooking instruction and household advice to women in neighborhoods far from downtown Chicago. In December of 1922, she began broadcasting short cooking demonstrations from radio station KYW. These fifteen-minute daily *Table Talks*, likely the first cooking programs broadcast in America, featured simple and easy-to-follow recipes and advice—from baking an angel food cake to preparing low-cost meals for high-cost times. Peterson's radio following grew rapidly, and by 1924 the *Chicago Evening American* began printing a transcript of her popular daily broadcasts, along with featured recipes.

With homemakers clamoring for a cookbook that articulated her "easy ways of wholesome inexpensive cooking" (p. 5), Peoples Gas published *Mrs. Peterson's Simplified Cooking* in 1924. Borrowing from her "treasured store" (p. 5) of recipes, Peterson offered a basic recipe in each branch of cooking and supplied variations for an assortment of delicious, easily prepared dishes. The "secret" (p. 9) of her approach to planning a meal revolved around an understanding of the basic food groups and the importance of preparing a well-balanced meal. She informed her readers about the value of vitamins, then a "newly discovered substance" (p. 10), to health and growth and decreed vegetables to be the most important part of dinner. Although she advised readers that a salad a day would keep the doctor away, she was quick to admit that the key to a successful dinner was a good dessert. Five of the book's seventeen chapters are devoted to dessert recipes, including a special one entitled "For My Kiddies." Proclaiming pie "the great American dessert" (p. 159), she offered basic tips on making and rolling crusts as well as more than twenty different pie recipes, from apple to rhubarb raisin. Extolling the virtues of freshly baked cookies, she declared "a cookie jar filled with crisp, delicious cookies" (p. 19) to be an asset in every pantry. Make all these cookies, she urged, and your boy "will brag all his life about the cookies mother used to make" (p. 191).

Peoples Gas was quick to capitalize on its popular Home Service Department and its star personality. Construction of a five-hundred-seat auditorium in the basement of company headquarters at Adams Street and Michigan Avenue was completed in 1923 to accommodate the growing crowds who attended Peterson's classes and demonstrations. Her private office was even equipped with special remote broadcasting equipment so that she could greet her "radio pals" (*Peoples Gas Club News*, July 15, 1924) without leaving the Home Service Department.

Consumer demand for neighborhood-based services

prompted Peoples Gas to open eight branch stores between 1923 and 1926. Home service was integral to the mission and function of these neighborhood stores, which featured spacious auditoriums designed for cooking classes and demonstrations alongside bill-paying centers and appliances for sale. From these middle-class retailing districts Peterson and her staff extended the reach of the Home Service Department even further into the community, offering programs to Chicago's economically, ethnically, and racially diverse population. She acknowledged the Urban League, assorted community and settlement houses, and "Polish, Italian, and Colored Mothers' Clubs" in the company's 1927 yearbook, noting that among the foreign born, instruction in cooking and home-making is "distinctly a contribution to Americanization" (p. 19).

Under Peterson's direction, the Home Service Department grew to include twenty-two women, and it offered something for everyone: from camp cooking classes for men in the evening to a special series of Saturday programs designed to teach children how to cook and entertain. The radio broadcasts she pioneered in 1922 became so popular that programming was quickly expanded. Her daily *Table Talks* were soon carried by two stations, and she took a series of certificate cooking classes, originally held at the Peoples Gas auditorium, to the airwaves in 1923. Peterson willingly shared her microphone with others in her department. An evening show hosted by one of her assistants accommodated listeners who were busy during the day; another hosted a radio cooking club for girls and boys during the summer months. She encouraged women on her staff, many of them college-educated home economists, to develop their own areas of expertise and to present programs that ranged from how to pack the perfect picnic basket to early childhood development and children's literature.

Peterson's fans were given plenty of opportunity to meet and greet the robust and spectacled Irish grandmother whose cheery and lilting voice they knew so well. Described as a "gracious and charming hostess" (*Peoples Gas Club News*, April 15, 1932), she presided over countless holiday parties, teas, and branch store openings. An engaging and effective spokeswoman for Peoples Gas, she traveled to trade shows and business conventions, often speaking to predominantly male audiences. As she approached her sixties, Peterson routinely worked ten to twelve-hour days while also making public appearances in the evenings and on Saturdays. The value Peoples Gas ascribed to its star employee was reflected in her salary, which tripled in seven years. By 1930 she was earning $10,000 per year, more than four times the median family income. It was an impressive wage for any American.

During the Great Depression Anna Peterson and the Home Service Department helped consumers stretch their household budgets, offering courses and programs devoted to economical menus, sewing, laundry, canning, and making do with less. As Peterson celebrated her twelfth anniversary on the air in 1934, Peoples Gas took stock of her accomplishments. They credited the sixty-four year-old with distributing thirty million recipe and menu lesson sheets, receiving letters from 360,000 radio listeners, responding to 350,000 telephone calls for advice, and lecturing to more than one million people.

Anna Peterson built a country home outside of Elgin, Illi-

nois, in the mid-1920s and equipped it with the latest gas-powered conveniences. There, with the help of a gardener and housekeeper, she finally had the chance to enjoy many of the homemaking pleasures she had been promoting for years. An avid needlewoman, she stitched her way to work on the commuter train and furnished her house with antique chairs adorned with her own needlepoint designs. Around 1936 she suffered a bout with arthritis and was unable to work for three years. Peoples Gas kept her on the payroll as an adviser to the Home Service Department and continued to pay her a stipend until she officially retired in 1939 at the age of sixty-nine. Her second cookbook, *Delectable Dinners*, was also published that year. A compilation of complete meals, Peterson and her coauthor, Nena Badenoch, offered cooks an array of pre-planned dinner menus featuring four or more courses. All 143 menus centered around the meat course and preparation times for each menu were noted.

Peterson enjoyed gardening and the company of her three granddaughters and pet Airedale during her retirement years in the 1940s. She died at age eighty-one and was buried at St. Joseph Cemetery in River Grove, Illinois.

A single working mother, Anna J. Peterson coupled performance skills with sound domestic advice to become Chicago's most celebrated housewife. A self-made woman who came into her own at a grandmotherly age, she tailored her nineteenth-century ethos and expertise to meet the needs of a changing domestic order in the twentieth century.

Sources. The Peoples Gas Light and Coke Company (Peoples Gas), now known as Peoples Energy Corporation, maintained a library and historical archives throughout most of the twentieth century. Since the closing of the company's library in 1995, the Office of Public Relations inherited some, but not all, of the historical corporate records from the era when Anna J. Peterson served as head of the Home Service Department (1922–39). The company's in-house publications, *Peoples Gas Club News* (for employees), *Peoples Gas Gazette* (for customers), and the *Yearbook*, were especially useful in reconstructing the history of the department. Articles written by Peterson that appeared in the *American Gas Journal* shed light on her role as an industry spokesperson. For a contemporary account of Anna Peterson's early radio days, see colleague Nena Badenoch's article, "Meet Our Radio Mother," which appeared in a 1925 issue of *Radio Age*. Anna J. Peterson's granddaughters Virginia Sayad, Carita Klevickis, and Judy Snow shared their sense of family history and memories about their grandmother with Terry J. Fife. Peterson's two published cookbooks, *Simplified Cooking* (1924) and *Delectable Dinners* (1939), are essential reading and offer much insight into her philosophies about cooking and meal planning. Carolyn M. Goldstein, "Mediating Consumption: Home Economics and American Consumers, 1900–1940" (Ph.D. diss., Univ. of Delaware, 1994), features an entire chapter on the role of home economists in light and power companies. A revised version of Goldstein's chapter appeared as an article, "From Service to Sales: Home Economics in Light and Power, 1920–1940," in a special issue of *Technology and Culture*, January 1997, devoted to gender analysis and the history of technology. The work of Ruth Schwartz Cowan, especially her 1983 book, *More Work for Mother*, provides vital context about the history of housework. On the history of eating, cooking, and Fanny Farmer, see Laura Shapiro, *Perfection Salad: Women and Cooking at the Turn of the Century* (1986). Harvey Levenstein, *Revolution at the Table* (1988), also provides instructive background on the changing American diet over time.

TERRY J. FIFE

PETRAKIS, STELLA CHRISTOULAKIS
May 8, 1888–May 7, 1979

PHILANTHROPIST, ACTIVIST, CIVIC LEADER, CLUBWOMAN

Stella Christoulakis, the daughter of Charalambos and Irene (Katsandreakis) Christoulakis, a teacher at the local Greek gymnasium (high school), was born in the "village of Nipos not far from Rethymnon [Réthímnon] in Central Crete" (Petrakis, *Stelmark: A Family Recollection,* 16), then part of the Ottoman Empire. Because three previous children had died in infancy, her parents dedicated their daughter to St. Stylianus, patron saint of infants, and she was christened Styliané (Stella). She attended school in her native town, and as the daughter of a teacher, she received an education beyond what was ordinarily available for girls at the time. Stella Christoulakis married Mark E. Petrakis, an aspiring seminarian, on February 10, 1908, in the Cathedral of [Réthímnon], Crete. Her uncle, Bishop Dionysios, who had arranged the marriage, performed the wedding ceremony.

Men entering the priesthood of the Greek Orthodox Church were permitted to marry prior to, but not after, ordination. One week after the wedding ceremony, Mark Petrakis was ordained by Bishop Dionysios and was assigned to parishes in Crete. During that period, Stella Petrakis, now a *presbytera* or elder/first mother—a title given to the wives of Greek Orthodox priests—"became involved with aid and relief to the fleeing Greek refugees from Asia Minor, who were being uprooted from their ancestral homeland by the Turks" (Kopan, "Stella Petrakis"). Petrakis continued this relief work for many years, even after coming to America. It was her first experience with philanthropy, an endeavor she would ardently pursue her entire lifetime. While in Crete, Petrakis had four children, two boys and two girls. Another boy and girl were born later, after the family immigrated to the United States.

In May 1916, responding to a call from Cretan immigrants working in the copper mines of Utah, the young presbytera accompanied her husband and four children to the United States, where Mark Petrakis organized the Greek Orthodox parish of Assumption Church in Price, Utah. The Petrakis family was greeted enthusiastically "by a multitude of almost 1,000 miners who had come from towns as far as 100 miles away to greet them with a celebratory thunder of gunshots fired into the air" (Petrakis, "Memories," 20).

While her husband ministered to the spiritual needs of his new parishioners, Stella Petrakis, one of the few married women in the community, attended to the physical needs of the adolescent boys and bachelors in the mining camps, especially in the area of sanitation. She organized the few women into a local women's aid society to provide the miners with some of the comforts and moral influences of home life, sorely lacking in the rough mining community. With the outbreak of World War I, Petrakis organized her first American Red Cross unit for women of the parish. They made bandages for the armed forces and Petrakis sold government Liberty Bonds, forging a patriotic identification for the Greek immigrant community. Petrakis continued to work with the Red Cross for the rest of her life, organizing units in all the Greek parishes in which her husband served. She also founded local women's charitable groups in St. Paul Church, Savannah, Georgia (1919–21), and St. Nicholas

FIG. 94. *Presbytera Stella Petrakis with her husband, Reverend Mark E. Petrakis, a Greek Orthodox priest, immigrated to America in 1916.*

Church, St. Louis, Missouri (1921–23), where the *Elpis Philoptochos* (Friends of the Poor) Society still exists.

In 1923, Mark Petrakis was assigned to the parish of Saints Constantine and Helen Church in the Woodlawn neighborhood on Chicago's South Side. Stella Petrakis fully committed herself to serve her constituents and the broader community. She founded the St. Helen's Philoptochos Society. In 1924 Petrakis and GEORGIA POOLEY established chapters of this society in Chicago. In the 1930s, the two women worked together to transform it into a national organization that became one of the largest philanthropic societies in America. Stella Petrakis also founded the Koraes School Mothers Club, which focused on the needs of the parish parochial school; *Aghia Paraskevé* (the Young Ladies Hellenic Society); the St. Constantine Red Cross Unit; and the Amalthea chapter of the Cretan Women in Chicago. "In addition to her involvement with these parish organizations, she found time to teach Sunday School, organize cultural and patriotic events, conduct relief drives for refugees and earthquake victims, provide succor and immediate help for destitute families, [and] give counsel to those in need" (Kopan, "Stella Petrakis").

Better educated than most other Greek immigrant women, Petrakis was prepared to organize and lead these societies. Also, she was an early feminist, occupying a rare and dangerous position in the patriarchal Greek community where she championed the right of immigrant women to education and equality. At the meetings of the ladies' groups she organized, she would often be found reading from Greek or American newspapers to the assembled women, including stories of family life. They were delighted to hear news about the world outside their restricted lives in their immigrant homes. Interested in the larger community, Petrakis participated in volunteer work outside the Greek community, serving in hospital auxiliaries, religious interfaith groups, and women's networks. She was closely affiliated with Woodlawn and Jackson Park hospitals.

Stella Petrakis sometimes incurred the displeasure of her husband who, as a priest in the Greek American community, needed a dutiful wife whose views and conduct were above reproach and in conformity with the prevailing patriarchal beliefs concerning the status of women. Her son Harry Petrakis, novelist and chronicler of the Greek community, described the tension between his father and mother because of her fierce spirit of independence in *Stelmark: A Family Recollection* (1970). Presbytera Petrakis did not compromise her strongly held principles in conflicts with her husband. Standing less than five feet tall, her long black hair in a bun, she made a dramatic figure.

Her son remembered how "in an effort to supplement her family's sparse finances as well as make her contribution to the war effort" (Petrakis, "Memories," 21), when World War II began, Stella Petrakis went to work in a factory that had been converted to war production. Taking the night shift and working on the assembly line manufacturing bullets, she returned to her family in the morning, changing her clothes and beginning a new day's homemaking without stopping to sleep. Her shop foreman discharged her for falling asleep at work too many times.

During World War II, she volunteered with the Greek War Relief Association, providing food for the thousands of starving people living in German-occupied Greece. She also sold U.S. Defense bonds and was a founder and leader of the Greek-American Star Mothers; this organization prepared and sent food and gift parcels with letters to Greek American servicemen. She was cited for her patriotic efforts by President Harry S. Truman, and King Paul of Greece awarded her the Gold Cross of King George I.

Petrakis continued to look after the poor and hungry in the parish, bringing them baskets of food or soliciting assistance for them. Although a devoted parent, she never allowed parenthood to interfere with her dedication to service. Being "the wife of a poor parish priest, [she] was forever scraping and scrimping to provide for her children . . . never . . . [going] to a beauty shop. . . . Her dresses were purchased for utilitarian value. She wore them until they wore out, heedless of any innovation in the world of fashion" (Petrakis, "Memories," 21). When her husband died in 1951 at the age of sixty-six, Petrakis was left with few financial resources but continued to contribute to her family, her church, and her community.

Alternatively referred to as the Greek community's JANE ADDAMS and the Eleanor Roosevelt of the Greek community in America, she was widely recognized for her efforts. Many acknowledged her philanthropic activities, including religious and civic leaders in Greece and in the United States. The American Red Cross recognized Petrakis in 1962 for her sixty years of service to the organization. In 1974 Archbishop Iakovos, primate of the Greek Orthodox Church in America, presented the St. Paul Medal to Petrakis.

When she died in a nursing home where she had been confined because of failing health, she was mourned by the entire community. Her son wrote, "As [she] blazed a trail for so many women in her life, so in death she was again a pioneer." Her body was "allowed to lie in state in our church [Saints Constantine and Helen Church, Palos Hills, Illinois]," an honor usually reserved "only to priests, bishops, and the most distinguished laymen" (Petrakis, "Memories," 22). Hundreds of people walked by her coffin to pay their respects. Her funeral was held on May 11, 1979; interment was at Evergreen Cemetery, Chicago.

Presbytera Petrakis's benevolent work anticipated the activities of organized agencies and modern social service professionals. Patriarch Athenagoras, world leader of the Orthodox Christian Church, acknowledged her long career in philanthropy as a "unique act of unselfish love" (quoted in Kopan, "Stella Petrakis"). She was a commanding figure and worked for the improvement of the status of immigrant Greek women and their families.

Sources. Harry Mark Petrakis, son of Stella Petrakis, has written extensively about his mother in *Stelmark: A Family Recollection* (1970); *Petrakis Reflections: A Writer's Life, A Writer's Work* (1983); "Two Ends of the Table," *U.S. Catholic and Jubilee*, August 1970; "Memories: Reflections on the Lives and Deaths of Two Mothers," *Chicago Tribune Magazine*, May 14, 1995. Andrew T. Kopan interviewed Stella Petrakis October 10, 1967; he wrote her obituary, "Stella Petrakis, 1888–1979: Lifetime of Service to the Greek Community," *Greek Star*, June 14, 1979. Information about Petrakis and other early Greek immigrants can be found in Kopan, *Education and Greek Immigrants in Chicago, 1892–1973: A Study in Ethnic Survival* (1990).

ANDREW T. KOPAN
ALICE ORPHANOS KOPAN

PEURALA, ALICE MELICKIAN
March 29, 1928–June 19, 1986
TRADE UNIONIST, CIVIL RIGHTS ACTIVIST

Alice Melickian Peurala, president of Local 65 of the United Steelworkers of America (USWA) and the first woman to rise to an important leadership role in a steelworkers local in the United States, was born in St. Louis, Missouri. Her parents were Armenian immigrants whose lives were disrupted by the Balkan War. As a result of the Soviet Union's support of Armenia against Turkish aggression, the Melickian family was sympathetic to the Soviet cause. Melickian's father, Setrak, helped organize a steelworkers local at a St. Louis foundry and taught his four children—two daughters and two sons—that "the only protection for workers is [through] their unions" (Richards).

Alice Melickian attended St. Louis public schools and began working in the eighth grade, when she became a cashier in a movie theater. Her first job was followed by a string of jobs in "little two by four factories" (Peurala interview transcript, 6). In one factory, Melickian made soles for shoes; and she described her job as unpleasant, perhaps harmful, explaining that various shoe parts were soaked in "different solutions. Your hands would get messy and the solutions would smell terrible. I used to think in later years it was probably dangerous to your health" (Peurala interview transcript, 6).

After completing high school, Melickian worked as a cashier in a St. Louis clothing store. She joined the Retail, Wholesale Department Store Employees Union, served on a negotiating committee, and became involved in organizing new members for the union. She was also on the board of the Labor Health Institute, a program providing free health care for union members, paid for by employers' contributions of 5 percent of their payroll and staffed by doctors from various hospitals and private practices in the city who provided professional services one day a week. The St. Louis local of the Retail, Wholesale Union encouraged Peurala to play an active role in union business. She attended labor schools and wrote articles for the union paper. Melickian believed that union officials in the Retail, Wholesale Union were "extremely unusual people" who "practiced a great deal of democracy" and were not "threatened by people that they organized . . . into the union" (Peurala interview transcript, 10). Melickian found a nexus between the behavior of several union officials, Harold Gibbons and Dick Kavener in particular, and their ideological beliefs. Both men were socialists who devoted themselves entirely to the needs of the labor movement; Melickian later described them as individuals who never lost touch with the workers whom they represented.

During the 1940s, Melickian joined the Congress of Racial Equality (CORE), an organization committed to nonviolent direct action to end racial discrimination that was founded in Chicago in 1942. One of the major campaigns of CORE was to integrate public facilities, including lunchrooms, public accommodations, and transportation. Melickian participated in CORE sit-ins at department store lunch counters in St. Louis, experiencing more resistance from the waitresses and store management than from the general public.

Melickian moved to Chicago in 1950 with a friend, civil rights activist and labor organizer Bernice Fisher, who worked with Bayard Rustin, one of the founders of CORE. Fisher was an organizer for the Retail, Wholesale Department Store Employees Union and left St. Louis first, finding a place to live. Melickian joined her in Chicago, where they both continued organizing women in clothing stores for the Retail, Wholesale Union. Melickian found women workers receptive to unionization but had to contend with management's efforts to interfere with the process by unfairly influencing their workers against voting for a union and finding ways to derail the process on technicalities. Management argued that all the stores in a chain were operated under centralized management and personnel offices and therefore all the shops had to vote at the same time to establish the union. This opposition made Melickian's work more difficult. Additionally, York Women's Apparel, the department store where Melickian was a salesperson in the hosiery department, fired her. Melickian and the union's lawyer, Francis Heisler, challenged her firing and management's assertion that personnel hiring was centralized, the basis for the ruling that all units of the chain store had to be organized and vote at the same

time for union recognition. Melickian took the initiative to apply for a job at a different store in the department chain to test her suspicion that hiring was not centralized. She was hired by the store manager without having to go through the central office and provided Heisler with evidence to contradict management's arguments. The National Labor Relations Board (NLRB) determined that Melickian should be reinstated in her job, with the condition that she establish her competency as a salesperson. She had been fired for incompetence and inefficiency. NLRB also agreed that each store in the chain was an independent voting unit. The union election was held, and the store in which Melickian had done substantial organizing voted for a union shop. In the other store, the employees, who had been individually "courted" through informal socializing with management, voted not to join. Had management's assertion of centralized hiring prevailed, the workers voting "yes" would have been cancelled out by the workers in the second store in the chain. It was a small victory and illustrated the kinds of management tactics with which labor organizers contended regularly.

Melickian next worked at Chicago's Stewart Warner plant, where she was a member of the rank and file organizing committee that workers formed to bring the International Union of Electrical Workers (IUE), a union competing with the old United Electrical, Radio and Machine Workers of America (UE), to the shop that was presently represented by the International Brotherhood of Electrical Workers (IBEW). The IUE was a union that came into being after the parent Congress of Industrial Organizations (CIO) had expelled the UE, one of its original union affiliates. According to Melickian, the IUE was interested in organizing some of the plants that had been "disenfranchised" because they had been with the UE. From the mid-1930s through the 1950s, workers' struggles were not only against management but were part of an internal battle for control of unionism in the United States. The CIO, formed during the depths of the Great Depression, initially brought a new and Left-oriented leadership to the labor movement. The UE was one of the unions that prospered during the height of CIO organizing activity. As cold war anti-radicalism began to dominate politics and labor in the aftermath of World War II, and with the passage of the conservative Taft-Hartley Act in 1947, labor unions, especially those affiliated with the CIO, were put on the defensive. Taft-Hartley required union officers to take oaths swearing they were not communists; injunctions against strikes were reinstituted; and the act gave courts the power to fine unions for alleged violations. The anticommunist provision meant that "any union with an elected or appointed Communist officer could not use the NLRB to gain certification as a collective bargaining unit even if the majority of workers voted for it and that any certified union that did not meet the act's provisions could be decertified" (*Encyclopedia of the American Left*, 767). Taft-Hartley provisions, which included establishing a sixty-day cooling off period when strikes could not be declared, outlawing mass picketing, and providing for the suing of labor unions for unfair labor practices, created an anti-union environment. Under assault, the CIO became divided and "between November 1949 and August 1950, the CIO kicked out ten unions [including the UE]. . . . The combined membership of these unions came to nearly a million workers" (*Encyclopedia of the American Left*, 769).

Management at Stewart Warner, allegedly acting on an anonymous tip, accused Melickian of being a Communist Party organizer; she denied the accusation and willingly signed an affidavit to that effect. Not satisfied, the company insisted that she take a lie detector test which, on principle, she refused. Subsequently fired, Melickian never learned the source of the tip or the names of her accusers or the basis for the charge against her. She conjectured that the genesis of the charge may have been her previous association with Armenian organizations sympathetic to a Soviet Armenia. It could also have emanated from her attendance at the Progressive Party Convention in 1948 that nominated Henry Wallace for president. In the context of the anticommunist sentiment of cold war America, however, such accusations were not uncommon as employers tried to rid themselves of strong labor organizers.

Melickian lived on unemployment compensation and a small amount of financial support from friends until she found work in another clothing store. She was soon identified for her past union activities and terminated. She next worked at Leaf Brands candy factory, where she performed backbreaking labor, filling boxes with candy ten pieces at a time. Workers were paid according to the number of boxes they packed. Women who had been there for fifteen years "were permanently hunch backed" (Peurala interview transcript, 22) because of the way in which they had to bend over to reach the candies and pack them into the boxes. Ironically, the candy factory was an organized shop. Melickian also worked at the Jays Potato Chip factory, a non-union plant with terrible working conditions. Jays recognized the threat she posed as a potential organizer and fired her. Both factories sensitized an already empathetic worker to the physical and mental hazards of certain workplace conditions.

Melickian had been in Chicago only three years but had accumulated a wealth of experience, including an understanding of how women in particular were victimized by cheap wages and poor working conditions. Raised in a home where socialism was admired, Melickian now had opportunities to formulate her own socialist philosophy. Through her union activities and membership in CORE she met socialists who greatly impressed her for their advocacy of trade unionism and civil rights.

In 1953 Melickian found employment at the United States Steel Corporation's South Works plant as a metallurgical observer, a quality-testing job then common for women. It was a fateful move for the young woman with a work history of union agitation and repeated terminations. At U.S. Steel she would impact both labor and management in ways no one could predict. U.S. Steel was a dramatic change for Melickian; she found it "very interesting" and also a "challenge" (Peurala interview transcript, 25). Most significant was the fact that her previous jobs were in typically female trades. Although women were aggressively recruited into heavy industry during World War II, by the 1950s the number of female workers had declined dramatically in such stereotypical male bastions as the steel industry. A number of men believed women did not belong in the mill, but Melickian found "most of the men on the whole were ok" (Peurala interview transcript, 25). She established comfortable relationships with her bosses, some of whom she called "marvelous"

(p. 26). Her wage was also superior to any she had previously earned. She joined the USWA, but she was not active initially. A year after she began her job at U.S. Steel, Alice Melickian married a man named Peurala, an ex-seaman who had been blacklisted because of internal union problems. He became a carpenter, and she met him in Chicago through mutual friends. They had a daughter, Jami, and by the time Jami was a year old, they had separated and then divorced. Alice Peurala returned "to the mill weeks after giving birth, in part because she learned that an involuntary pregnancy layoff was not covered by state unemployment benefits" (Richards). She then faced the problems that challenged single women who raised children on their own. She worked the swing shift, managing to find baby-sitters for her daughter. Eventually she found a retired high school teacher who lived in Hyde Park to care for her daughter. "[Myra] really thought of Jami eventually as her granddaughter. They were very close, so that really helped. Myra's home became Jami's second home" (Peurala interview transcript, 27).

By the late 1950s, along with her work shift and child care responsibilities, Peurala had become involved in the steelworkers local, attending meetings but remaining marginally involved. The circumstances changed when, in 1967, U.S. Steel denied Alice Peurala a promotion because of sex. "When I was hired as a metallurgical observer . . . they told me it was a good job for women. . . . I began to see many of the men I had trained get promoted to better jobs while the women went nowhere. Then I got mad" (quoted in Sheppard). Invoking the 1964 Civil Rights Act, Peurala filed a sex discrimination complaint with the Equal Employment Opportunity Commission. The commission investigated Peurala's complaint and, two years later in 1969, found probable cause. When U.S. Steel refused to reverse itself, Peurala sued the company for sex discrimination. Though she was frustrated by the government's inability to provide an attorney for her and nearly lost on a technicality, Peurala somehow persevered. U.S. Steel eventually entered into a settlement wherein it agreed to assign the next job opening as a product tester to Peurala. However, the company breached this agreement and Peurala returned to court; the company was forced in 1974 to place Peurala in the contested job.

Peurala began her serious involvement with the Steelworkers Union, Local 65, in 1969, because she was "dissatisfied . . . [that] . . . [the union] had not helped her in her fight for equal status with men" (Sheppard). This was a period of crisis and transformation in American society. The anti–Vietnam War movement and the social movements for liberation among African Americans, American Indians, Latinos, and women challenged the way in which institutions in society, including public and private sector establishments, were run by white men. The situation was the same for the labor unions, and Peurala became involved with women and men interested in gaining greater representation for minorities, including women, in the leadership of the unions. The movement toward union democracy coincided with efforts by the women's movement to obtain jobs in areas heretofore prohibited to women. In 1970 Peurala ran unsuccessfully for recording secretary of the local. She received more than five hundred votes to her opponent's eleven hundred. For a first try, it was a decent showing, especially since there was no encouragement for women's participation in union politics. She lost a second bid for the same job and, in 1973, ran for another union position, losing by only seven votes. She became associated with Ed Sadlowski and his group of Local 65 activist-reformers, who were "talking about union democracy and the rank and file running the union" (Peurala interview transcript, 38).

At the same time that Peurala was working within her local for expanded rank and file involvement, she attended the founding conference of the Coalition of Labor Union Women (CLUW) in Chicago in 1974, where thirty-five hundred women converged from all over the nation. Union women, influenced by the women's movement, wanted to join the fight as trade unionists to add the Equal Rights Amendment (ERA) to the U.S. Constitution. (For decades, the labor movement had opposed the ERA on the grounds that it would dismantle protective legislation for women.) They also sought more power and recognition within their unions as women. The Chicago chapter of CLUW ran a speakers bureau and conducted educational classes; it organized non-union women, supported striking workers, lobbied for passage of the ERA in Illinois, and held demonstrations for a full employment bill. Peurala was never an official member of CLUW and after its founding conference attended meetings infrequently. She had become involved with the No-Strike Agreement fight in the steel industry, which consumed a great deal of her time. Yet she participated in demonstrations for abortion rights during this period. Issues of occupational safety and affirmative action, major concerns of CLUW activists, were also the kinds of issues with which Peurala was involved at U.S. Steel's South Works.

After Peurala was made a product tester in 1974, her experiences at the South Works plant expanded. Her job took her through the ten divisions of Local 65, where she interacted with hundreds of other workers. In 1976 she won a seat on the local's grievance committee, and there she developed a reputation as a fighter for the rights of all workers. Old-time workers told James Balanoff, a union official, "'Jim, that gal is the best griever we ever had'" (quoted in Richards). While she was concerned with protecting and defending the rights of all union members, Peurala was aware that women workers had even more problems. She began meeting with other women in Local 65, and they pressured the executive board and union president to appoint a women's committee. Peurala wanted to have plant management recognize the committee as an official committee of the union, but in 1977 this demand was rejected. Two years later, Peurala ran successfully for president of Local 65 and became the only woman in the nation to head a basic-steel unit. She was defeated for reelection in 1982 "by a more moderate candidate supported by union leaders in Pittsburgh" (Warren), but in 1985 she regained the presidency. She felt that her victory occurred because workers were angry with the "big cuts in wages and benefits" (Warren) without commensurate preservation of jobs or investment in the industry. These had been promised by management when workers had agreed to concessions during contract negotiations. South Works employed seventy-five hundred workers in 1979 but fewer than one thousand in 1985. She had fought hard for workers' rights and women's rights at a time when changes in the structure of steel production and the choices made by American industrialists to "adapt" to the chal-

lenge resulted in the destruction of tens of thousands of jobs. One year after her reelection as president of Local 65, Alice Peurala died at age fifty-eight of cancer.

Early in her life Alice Peurala believed it was not necessary to pass ERA; she had argued that with such an amendment women might lose the protective legislation hard won by generations of labor women. She realized, through her own experiences, that "provisions of the so-called protective laws were used against [her]" (Peurala interview transcript, 43), and she came to conclude that "equality of opportunity on the job" (p. 44) was crucial, as was having an effective union willing to stop "the harassment that still exist[ed] for women . . . by male bosses" (p. 44). In her efforts to expand the rights of workers, Alice Peurala had done much to improve the conditions of labor women and had taken on conservative forces both within trade unionism and in society at large.

Sources. Elizabeth Balanoff's interview of Alice Melickian Peurala, September 30, 1977, Balanoff Oral History Collection, Center for New Deal Studies, Roosevelt Univ., is an essential document. Nathaniel Sheppard Jr., "Woman in Steel: Drive for Equality," *NYT*, June 18, 1979, is helpful. Three obituaries are *NYT*, June 23, 1986; Cindy Richards, "Alice Peurala, 58; Headed Steelworkers Local at South Works," *Chicago Sun-Times*, June 21, 1986; James Warren, "Alice Peurala, 58, Steelunion Leader," *CT*, June 21, 1986. Contextual information is found in David Bensman and Roberta Lynch, *Rusted Dreams: Hard Times in a Steel Community* (1987); Milton Derber, *Labor in Illinois: The Affluent Years, 1945–1980* (1989); and Paul Buhle, Mari Jo Buhle, and Dan Georgakas, eds., *Encyclopedia of the American Left* (1992).

MAUREEN L. GILL

PHILLIPS, IRNA
July 1, 1901–December 22, 1973
RADIO AND TELEVISION WRITER

Irna Phillips, creator and writer of soap operas for more than forty years, was born in Chicago, the youngest of William S. and Betty (Buxbaum) Phillips's ten children. Her parents, German Jews who had come to Chicago in the late nineteenth century, owned and operated a small dry-goods and grocery store, above which the family lived. William Phillips died when his daughter was only eight years old, leaving Betty Phillips to raise her large family alone. Irna Phillips later recalled a lonely, "introspective, ugly-duckling childhood," in which she was a "plain, sickly, silent child" who lived in "a world of books and make-believe" (*McCall's*, 116, 117).

Phillips attended public schools in Chicago and later enrolled at Northwestern University (1918–19) before transferring to the University of Illinois (1919–22), where she pursued a major in drama and dreamed of becoming an actress. Her dreams were shattered when, at auditions for a play, the drama coach informed her that, although talented, she had "neither the looks nor the stature to achieve professional success" (*McCall's*, 116). Persuaded by her mother to go into teaching, she graduated with a B.S. in education and taught speech and drama at a junior college in Fulton, Missouri, before enrolling at the University of Wisconsin–Madison (1924) to do graduate work in journalism. From 1925 to 1929, Phillips again taught speech at a junior college in Dayton, Ohio.

Unsatisfied with her teaching career, Phillips still longed to become an actress. At age twenty-eight on a tour of the broadcasting studio of Chicago radio station WGN, when she found herself mistaken for an aspiring actress, she readily auditioned for a radio part. Her reading of Eugene Field's poem "The Bowleg Boy" so impressed the director that the station offered her an unpaid acting job, which she refused. Later, however, she accepted a summer of unpaid work at another station before WGN offered her fifty dollars a week to write and perform in what was to be a "family serial," slated to air for ten minutes daily, five days a week. Phillips created a story line based in part on her own experiences. Called *Painted Dreams*, the serial was broadcast on WGN from 1929 to 1931, with Phillips as both writer and performer. The show revolved around the life and struggles of widowed Mother Monahan, her daughter Irene, and their neighbors.

Although *Painted Dreams* did not achieve immediate success and was unable to attract a permanent sponsor on WGN, it set a precedent as the first daytime radio serial that specifically targeted women as its audience. Phillips tried to convince WGN to sell the show to network radio, but the Chicago station was uninterested. Phillips then brought suit against WGN, claiming that the show was her creation, and, therefore, hers to sell. The court did not agree and ruled that the show belonged to the radio station. Determined to bring the show to a national audience, Phillips simply changed the title and character names and moved the show to the National Broadcasting Company (NBC) where, as *Today's Children*, a drama about the daily life of Mother Moran and her daughter Eileen, it ran from 1932 to 1938.

The instincts that propelled Phillips to move her show to network radio served her well. By 1938, when she decided to pull *Today's Children* off the air, despite the protests of sponsors and fans, because she believed that her characters had "run through all possible logical situations" (*Time*, June 10, 1940), it had become the most popular daytime serial on radio. In addition, Phillips had created two other soap operas during the previous year: *The Road of Life* and *The Guiding Light*, both of which enjoyed immense success, especially the latter, which continues in the 1990s in its television format.

Phillips wrote many more successful radio serials in the following years, including *Woman in White* (1938); *The Right to Happiness* (1939); *Lonely Women* (1942), soon retitled *The "New" Today's Children*; and *The Brighter Day* (1948). Attributing her remarkable success to her ability to observe the world around her, Phillips proclaimed, "I am a reporter, a fascinated observer of life, not a novelist or a teller of tales. All my stories are taken from my own experiences and those of people I have known" (*McCalls*, 117). *Woman in White*, featuring nurse Karen Adams, was dedicated to the nurses who had, in Phillips' words, "fought so hard to extend my mother's life" (*McCalls*, 117) during her final illness. Phillips created the character of Dr. John Rutledge, the inspiring pastor in *The Guiding Light*, in honor of a minister she had known in Chicago.

By 1943, Phillips had five dramas on the air and was earning two hundred fifty thousand dollars a year as one of the highest paid writers in radio. Employing six assistant writers, she continued to write daily scenes for many of the serials, acting out each character's part as she dictated dialogue to her secretary.

Despite such professional and financial success, Phillips's personal life changed little. From childhood until Betty Phillips's death in 1938 at age eighty, Irna Phillips shared a room with her mother. And while she "weathered several unhappy love affairs" (*McCall's*, 117) over the years, she never married. At the age of forty, wanting a family of her own, she adopted an infant son, Thomas Dirk Phillips, and less than two years later, a daughter, Katherine Louise Phillips. She maintained close friendships with Rose Cooperman, her secretary of more than twenty years, and Procter & Gamble executive Bill Ramsey and his wife, Olivia.

Unlike many other radio soap opera writers in the 1950s, Phillips made the transition to television quite easily, earning the praise of some as "the single most important influence in television soaps" (*The Soaps*, 46). Although she moved many of her radio dramas to television, including *The Guiding Light* and *The Brighter Day*, she also developed others specifically for the new medium, among them *As the World Turns* (1956), the first half-hour television soap. Other television credits included *The Road of Life* (1954), *Another World* (1964), *Days of Our Lives* (1965), and *Love Is a Many Splendored Thing* (1967). In addition, she served as a consultant for *Peyton Place* (1964), the first successful prime-time soap opera on television.

Radio and television scholars have credited Irna Phillips, along with Frank and Anne Hummert and Elaine Carrington, with inventing the soap opera. Phillips's contributions to the genre focused on the content of her dramas rather than on their structure or production style. With the creation of characters such as the Reverend John Rutledge, nurse Karen Adams, and Dr. Jim Brent of *The Road of Life*, Phillips brought professional occupations, especially those centered around the field of medicine, to daytime dramas, establishing a lasting trend. She also introduced the concept of the "crossover," the use of a primary character in one soap as a secondary character in another. She made amnesia respectable as a plot technique.

The stories that Phillips wrote typically moved slowly in comparison to those of other soap operas. Such was the case with *As the World Turns*, which was described as a "non-story story" (*Soap World*, 105). In the early years, an entire episode of this show often revolved around a single discussion between the lead characters, Chris and Nancy Hughes. In all of her dramas, Phillips concentrated on the psychological development of her characters, building stories on "the built-in life and death melodrama of their working lives" (*Soap World*, 20).

Despite the emphasis on professionals in her soaps, Phillips always built her dramas around family life. Most of her female characters longed for marriage and motherhood rather than careers. This view was consonant with the soap opera genre, which strengthened and stabilized the traditional homemaker role. As Phillips said in a magazine interview, reflecting on one of her most popular characters, Nancy Hughes: "She finds her happiness within her home and herself, and she believes that this is woman's true function." Phillips continued, "Truly, all our lives are serial stories, and the marriage ceremony outlines the plot for (women) at the altar: 'For better, for worse, for richer, for poorer, in sickness, and in health. . . .' This is the basic story line of every daytime serial, and a blueprint of every woman's life" (*McCall's*, 268). Aware that her own life as a single, highly paid professional woman was very different from this blueprint, she felt the contradictions between her story and the ideal of womanhood that she espoused. She maintained that she shared with other women the "experiences of love and failure and fear of the unknown—and the undemanding, uncritical, requited love that children alone can bring" (*McCall's*, 117). Phillips was disdainful of the new wave of feminism in the 1960s and 1970s, believing instead in "strong men and helpful women" (*Chicago Daily News*, January 12–13, 1974). She was convinced that the millions of women who followed her soap operas felt as she did.

Although Phillips insisted on upholding traditional roles for women, she was willing to brave controversy when it came to matters of race. In 1965, civil rights groups such as the Congress of Racial Equality (CORE) campaigned to break the color barrier on soap operas and applauded Phillips for publicly declaring her unhappiness with sponsor Procter & Gamble's unwillingness to consider African American characters in dramas they produced. Two years later, Phillips developed *Love Is a Many Splendored Thing*, a soap that featured an interracial romance between an Asian woman and a white man. The network that ran the drama asked that the controversial story line be discontinued, whereupon Phillips immediately left the show.

Phillips was unable to convince her sponsors to support racial integration, but in most areas she wielded an enormous amount of power for a woman who never produced her own creations. Her dramas were popular and, thus, financial successes; as long as they remained so, most sponsors left her in charge of the daily proceedings of the show. Phillips, however, had forged a reputation as someone who was extremely difficult to work with, often firing actors or writers on the spot for changing her scripts only slightly. On soaps such as *Another World* and *As the World Turns*, Phillips was said to have created a tense atmosphere by the use of such techniques. In addition, Phillips's creative independence caused tensions. When her characterization of an independent woman in *As the World Turns* cast a shadow on the leading man's perfect image, not only were the television viewers taken aback, but the drop in ratings resulted in Procter & Gamble's firing her in mid-1973. This was a blow to Phillips, and she became depressed. She suffered a heart attack and died in December 1973.

Feared by some, Phillips was respected by many for her contributions to the world of soap operas. Indeed, Phillips's influence on the world of soaps extended beyond her own creations. Many of her assistant writers went on to develop their own dramas, among them Agnes Nixon, creator of *One Life to Live* and *All My Children*, and William J. Bell, who, along with Lee Phillip Bell, created *The Young and the Restless*. In 1970, Phillips helped her daughter, Katherine, launch her own soap, the short-lived *A World Apart*, which revolved around the life of a soap opera writer and her adopted children. While Phillips influenced many within the world of soap operas, perhaps her most enduring legacy is the millions of people who tune in to watch her creations still broadcast decades after Phillips first created them.

Sources. Irna Phillips's papers, including original scripts for radio and television dramas, correspondence, and other related materials, are available at the State Hist. Soc. of Wisconsin, Madison, Wisconsin.

Phillips provides an account of her life and writing career in "Every Woman's Life Is a Soap Opera," Irna Phillips as told to Helen Markel, *McCall's*, March 1965. For other articles based on interviews with Phillips, see: "Life as Soap Opera: The Story of Irna," *Chicago Daily News*, January 12–13, 1974; "Script Queen," *Time*, June 10, 1940; and "Writing On: Irna Phillips Mends with Tradition," *Broadcasting*, November 6, 1972. Several histories of soap operas address the role Phillips played in the development of the genre, including: Peter Buckman, *All for Love* (1984); Muriel Cantor and Suzanne Pingree, *The Soap Opera* (1983); Madeleine Edmondson and David Rounds, *From Mary Noble to Mary Hartman* (1976) and *The Soaps* (1973); and Robert LaGuardia, *Soap World* (1983). A biography appears in *NAW* (1980).

AYESHA SHARIFF

PIERCE, BESSIE LOUISE
April 20, 1888–October 3, 1974
HISTORIAN

Bessie Louise Pierce, one of America's pioneer academic urban historians, was known primarily for her four volumes on Chicago, which comprise the first scholarly history of a major American city. She was born in Caro, Michigan, the eldest of the two daughters of Clifton and Minnie (Pierson) Pierce. In 1889, her father, a salesman, moved the family to Waverly, Iowa, where he established a thriving dry-goods business and joined civic organizations and the local Episcopal church. As Bessie Pierce later recounted, she and her sister, Anne "did all the things girls do in small towns, danced, played cards, read a lot" (Haas, *Chicago Daily News*). After graduation from Waverly High School in 1905, she enrolled at the State University of Iowa.

The diminutive Bessie Louise Pierce might have settled down to married life in a small midwest town, but, on several occasions throughout her career, she was willing to sacrifice security for advancement despite risk of failure. This approach would be a lesson she would repeat to later generations of students. Her initial inspiration came from her father's sister, Della M. Pierce, one of the first woman physicians in Michigan. The Kalamazoo doctor had become well-known in that state at the turn of the century for her work in breaking down the public's fears of hospitals, which were often perceived as places of death rather than healing.

Inspired to pursue a profession, Bessie Pierce graduated from the State University of Iowa in 1910 and began teaching in the high school at Sanborn, and later Mason City, Iowa. Few teachers at that time even had bachelor's degrees, but she was determined to advance herself. In 1913 she entered the graduate program of the University of Chicago, spending summers in Chicago after each school year in Iowa had concluded. She completed an M.A. degree in 1918. Meanwhile, in 1916, she had joined the staff of the University of Iowa's high school in Iowa City, with an affiliate status in the university history department as an instructor specializing in teacher training.

Arthur M. Schlesinger Sr., who had recently arrived to teach in Iowa and was already known for his pioneering work in American social history, especially the roles of women and cities, asked Pierce to be his first graduate student. She gave up her high school position, working as his graduate assistant and babysitter to support herself while taking classes. She completed a Ph.D. in 1923 and immediately became an assistant professor in

Fig. 95. *Historian Bessie Louise Pierce stands next to colleagues John Hope Franklin and W. T. Hutchinson at a dinner for Hutchinson, March 9, 1970.*

gious, but temporary, position at Chicago, but also changing her field of research. She agonized over the decision for a month, seeking the advice of friends and colleagues across the country before finally accepting Merriam's offer. She arrived in the city in the fall of 1929—"with the stock market crash" (Duis's conversations with Pierce), as she later remarked. She came at a time when many of the first generation of women at the university were retiring, and few were arriving to take their places. During the career that followed, Pierce had only one female colleague in the history department, Frances Gillespie, who died in 1950.

It was clear from the beginning that Bessie Pierce wanted to be more than a glorified research assistant to the university's famed sociologists and political scientists. Her History of Chicago Project was destined to take on a life of its own. She quickly assembled a staff of graduate students. Her researchers numbered as many as a dozen as the Great Depression deepened and young academics found no other opportunities. A few of them came from Harvard University, where her mentor Arthur Schlesinger Sr. had moved in 1925. Determined to lift her history of Chicago above the level of popular, but often inaccurate, booster histories, she directed an exhaustive canvass of primary resources. Her staff pored through everything from manuscript records and letters to court cases and newspapers. They soon began filling filing cabinets with notes taken by hand on half-sheets of cheap paper. Then, under her supervision, they wrote detailed reports about each narrow subject area. She insisted that her staff members check and recheck each other's work for accuracy. In the meantime, she divided her time between writing, seeking foundation support, and teaching a variety of courses in the history department. She also managed to finish *Citizens Organizations and the Civic Training of Youth* (1933), the last of her works on education. This book studied the influence of organizations as diverse as the American Legion, American Peace Society, and the Red Cross on schools after World War I. Dispassionately describing only their ideas and tactics, she avoided passing judgment on their motives.

The first fruits of the History of Chicago Project also appeared in 1933, when she published *As Others See Chicago*, an edited collection of travelers' accounts that enjoyed brisk sales during the centennial Century of Progress year. Her lengthy chapter introductions contained the seeds of a planned multivolume study. Some readers were no doubt shocked that the documents themselves were often critical of the city, demonstrating her determination to tell the whole story, not just what boosters wanted to hear.

It took four more years to complete the first volume of *A History of Chicago*, subtitled *The Beginning of a City, 1673–1848*. Research in the pioneer period involved using scattered sources to piece together a narrative. The thoroughness of her work was obvious in the extensive footnotes establishing the book's foundation in archival materials and in the fact that its 455 pages covered only the years through 1848. That date, which saw the introduction of plank roads, the telegraph, and the railroad, was an obvious turning point in the city's history. Volume 1 was the first scholarly history of a major American city, and its publication may be regarded as the beginning of the field of urban history. Three years later, she published the second volume, subtitled

the Iowa history department, where she taught courses in teacher education and American history. Three years later she published her dissertation as *Public Opinion and the Teaching of History*, a study of how popular political movements impacted what children learned in textbooks. She advanced to the rank of associate professor and gained a wider reputation as president of the National Council for the Social Studies.

In 1929 she published her second book, *Civic Attitudes in American School Textbooks*. This work analyzed the way 389 social studies textbooks portrayed historical events and how they helped shape the attitudes of children toward government. The book assured promotion to full professor at Iowa, but Bessie Pierce once more had to choose between security and the quest for distinction. In April 1929, a letter arrived from Professor Charles Merriam of the University of Chicago, her former teacher. He offered her a three-year staff appointment in social sciences. Pierce's work would involve assembling historical information for the university's pioneering investigations in urban studies. Although the appointment carried the title associate professor, Merriam warned that she could not consider it a permanent position. This condition meant—at the age of forty-one—not only giving up tenure at Iowa for a more presti-

From Town to City, 1848–1871, which took the story through the Great Chicago Fire.

In both volumes, she attempted to blend a sense of gradual chronological development with a chapter organization that was basically topical. Pierce careful subdivided the story into sections dealing with society, politics, government, religious and humanitarian work, and culture. Compared with most history books of their time, the volumes contained a large amount of social history, discussing for the first time in print stories of the poor, women, immigrants, and African Americans in an objective, detailed manner. Each succeeding volume, however, demonstrated Pierce's belief that economic factors played an increasingly important role in the city's story. This strong emphasis on commerce, industry, and labor is common among historians who reflected the depression era in which they worked. Her third volume, subtitled *The Rise of a Modern City, 1871–1893* and published only in 1957, covered the years from the Great Chicago Fire to the 1893 World's Columbian Exposition and devoted 40 percent of its 513 pages to an exhaustive discussion of economic and labor topics.

The beginning of World War II brought an unanticipated interruption in Pierce's work. Many of her assistants and colleagues joined the military, leaving the remaining members of the department with heavier teaching loads, while research grant support largely disappeared. She became active in Hyde Park Democratic Party politics, working to elect antimachine alderman and friend Paul Douglas, the future senator. As a war bond campaign warden she went door to door persuading her Hyde Park neighbors to buy defense bonds. Reaching the rank of full professor in 1943, she took an academic detour three years later when she was asked by several midwest railroads to provide expert testimony in a struggle over who would take over the routes of the bankrupt Chicago and Alton Railroad. She was hired to deflate the claim by the Santa Fe railway that, because it had been responsible for Chicago's growth, it should gain direct access to St. Louis. Her testimony in the case proved crucial, and she used the railroads' money to hire additional researchers to compile detailed economic data on Chicago's growth.

The railroad case proved to be one of several distractions that drew her away for a time from the completion of her third volume on Chicago. Her teaching load now included seminars and lecture courses on American urban history, some of the first such courses taught anywhere. She remained active in the American Historical Association, which continued to draw upon her previous work on the social and political influences on textbooks. She also embarked on a college textbook project that she never completed. Her retirement from the University of Chicago history department in 1953 finally provided enough time to complete her third volume.

Accolades and praise followed her retirement, including an honorary doctorate from Northwestern University in 1954, but her later years were not as productive as her earlier ones. Much of her time was spent helping her sister, whose health was declining. Anne Pierce had become a professional concert singer, later retiring to teach music from 1926 to 1955 at the University of Iowa. The sisters, neither of whom married, divided their time between homes in Iowa City and Chicago.

By the late 1950s, the History of Chicago Project notes filled some 120 filing cabinet drawers, over half of them for the 1893–1915 period. Foundation support guaranteed a continuing staff of assistants in cramped office space in the east tower of the University of Chicago's Harper Library. The sheer volume of information that Pierce had accumulated on the city at the turn of the century completely overwhelmed her detailed and narrative approach to the subject. It became increasingly difficult for her to sort out critical facts from the unimportant. By the 1960s, the fashions of the profession had also changed. When Bessie Pierce began her project, it had been considered innovative even to mention women and ethnic groups. Later historians were not only more willing to expand the interpretation of the sources, they also placed a much greater emphasis on social history than those of Pierce's generation.

Bessie Louise Pierce never completed the fourth volume of her work. Declining health forced her to leave Chicago in the early 1970s. She died at the age of eighty-six in Iowa City, Iowa, where she is buried. Her three books on the history of education and four volumes on Chicago continue to enjoy a reputation for accuracy and excellence, while the story of her career remains a testament to her determination to risk security in pursuit of advancement.

Sources. Bessie Louise Pierce Papers are found in Spec. Coll., UC. These contain her personal correspondence, material related to her association with UC, and the History of Chicago Project papers, including research assistants' reports. History of Chicago research notes are at the CHS. Perry R. Duis used information from recollections of conversations with Bessie Pierce from January 1966 through August 1968, when he was her research assistant. Biographical information based on an interview with Pierce was found in Joseph Haas, "Bessie Pierce Loves Chicago," *Chicago Daily News*, March 25, 1967. See also Perry R. Duis, "Bessie Louise Pierce: Symbol and Scholar," *Chicago History*, Fall 1976.

PERRY R. DUIS

PLATT, IDA
September 29, 1863–death date unknown
LAWYER

In 1894 Ida Platt became the first African American woman to earn an Illinois law license. Overcoming tremendous obstacles, Platt maintained a legal career that spanned more than three decades. Born in Chicago, she came from a long line of free, financially successful African Americans. Her paternal grandfather, Benjamin Platt, owned and operated a lumber mill and a tannery in New York in the early nineteenth century. Her father, Jacob Platt, was a bright, ambitious, self-educated man who established his own lumber business in Penn Yan, New York. In 1840 he married Amelia B. Matthews, a native of Philadelphia, Pennsylvania. The couple initially lived in New York, where they had five children who survived infancy.

In 1852 the Platts moved to Chicago, where they had three more children, the youngest of whom was Ida. In 1876 Platt's father suffered a stroke and was forced to retire. While his only son, Jacob Jr., continued to run his father's lumber business, Jacob Platt Sr. ensured that all his daughters graduated from high school and assisted them in their occupational pursuits. When he died in 1888, Platt's father left his family a considerable estate estimated at between fifty and one hundred thousand dollars. Both white and black newspapers reported that he was one of the most respected black businessmen in the area.

Ida Platt, an extraordinarily bright and talented child, was accepted by the white community in which she lived. She attended Central High School, a Chicago public school attended by black and white students in the pre-1920 era, when segregated schools were not the practice or policy of the Chicago Board of Education. At Central High School she became proficient in German and French and graduated with honors at age sixteen. After graduation she initially chose to study music with the acclaimed Madame Eugenie de Roode Rice, a white immigrant from Holland. In 1883, though she was a gifted pianist, Platt decided to enter the business world and began working for Holger de Roode, Madame Rice's brother and general manager of the western branch of the Clinton Fire Insurance Company. Platt was de Roode's secretary, stenographer, and the head of the insurance company's claims department.

Throughout Platt's life she remained close to her family and near the white community. Two years after her father died, Platt, her mother, and five of her six siblings moved from their residence on Chicago's West Side to a home on the South Side of the city. Platt's sister, Ellen Dale Platt, who had wed William C. Phillips in 1881, moved to a home nearby. The Phillipses had three children, but only one, Ida Hope Phillips, lived to adulthood. Over the next six years the Platt family moved two more times, establishing their main residence in 1896 on South Wabash Street, where they stayed for the next decade. Although all of their residences were located on Chicago's South Side, where the majority of the city's black population lived, the Platts chose locations where the percentage of African Americans was small. The home where the Platts settled was located on a broad avenue boasting big, beautiful homes owned by middle-class and upper-class Blacks. Wabash was a street in between, positioned on the eastern edge of the city's main black residential community and on the western edge of a wealthy white community.

After working for nine years in the insurance business, Platt decided to become a lawyer. She believed that the profession was open to her even though no black woman had been admitted to the Illinois bar. The first African American licensed to practice law in Illinois was Lloyd G. Wheeler, who was admitted in 1869 shortly after the passage of the Fourteenth Amendment. Though MYRA BRADWELL, a white woman who had also applied for admission to the Illinois bar in 1869, was denied a license because of her gender, ALTA HULETT opened the state bar to women when she was admitted in 1873.

Despite the fact that African American men were allowed to enter the legal profession four years before white women were, the number of African American men admitted to practice law in Illinois increased at a slow rate. When Platt was awarded her license in 1894, more women had already been admitted to the bar than African Americans. By 1896, just two years later, there were more than twice as many women lawyers (seventy) as African American lawyers (thirty-three). Platt remained the sole African American woman lawyer in the state until 1920.

Growing prejudice and volatile race and gender relations largely accounted for the slow rise in the number of African

American male lawyers and the absence of an increase in the number of African American women lawyers during these years. While race relations in Chicago after the Civil War were relatively relaxed, tensions heightened significantly after Reconstruction ended in 1877, when many African Americans migrated to Chicago to escape the increasing violence and oppression in the South. Though initially some white legislators in the city responded positively to these new residents, passing laws to desegregate the public schools and enacting a state Civil Rights Act in 1885 that was strengthened in 1897, social attitudes soon began to change. As the number of African Americans rose dramatically throughout the first decades of the twentieth century, many white residents exhibited increased hostility toward all African Americans. These attitudes manifested themselves in social restrictions that dictated where Blacks could live, work, or go to school. Restrictions on African American women were even more cumbersome. It was in this context that Ida Platt sought entry to the bar and then practiced law.

Though Platt entered the legal world quietly, her admission to the bar made national news. Platt began taking evening courses at the Chicago College of Law in 1892 while she was working during the day as a stenographer in the law office of Jesse Cox, a well-established and respected white Chicago attorney who specialized in patent law. The following year, Platt opened her own office as a general stenographer and law reporter while she completed her studies. In 1894, at the age of thirty-one, Platt graduated from law school, one of two women, both of whom ranked at the top in their class. Platt was immediately admitted to the Illinois bar. As reported in the *Chicago Legal News*, one of the Illinois Supreme Court Justices who signed Platt's license acknowledged the significance of the occasion by remarking, "We have done today what we have never done before—admitted a colored woman to the bar; and it may now truly be said that persons are admitted to the Illinois bar without regard to race, sex or color" (1894, 352). The *Chicago Legal News*, founded, edited, and published by Myra Bradwell until her death in 1894 and then by her husband lawyer and ex-judge James Bradwell, went on to welcome Platt into the profession praising her intellect, her temperament, and her talents. Though a preeminent white legal journal, the *American Law Review*, focused on Platt's appearance and speculated that she could pass as white without detection, African American newspapers cited Platt's admission as a living refutation of the argument that persons of color (and particularly women of color) could not learn.

Platt began her career practicing law in the office of Joseph Washington Errant, a white Chicago attorney. Errant, a high school classmate of Platt admitted to the bar in 1886, married Derexa Morey, a physician, two years later and spent all of his career supporting progressive social justice and legal reform movements. While working with Errant in their office in downtown Chicago, Platt earned a reputation as a proficient lawyer concentrating on probate and real estate law. She developed a large clientele of foreigners, due in part to her fluency in German and French. Platt did not follow Errant in his reform work, however. Instead, Platt spent her time practicing law, teaching shorthand and typing in the evenings at a Chicago high school, and supporting her family as they endured a series of hardships. In 1894

Ida Platt's sister Maria died. Three years later, brother Jacob died and William Phillips, Ellen's husband, was diagnosed with tuberculosis. William moved into the Chicago Home for Incurables, and Ellen and her children moved back home with her mother and remaining sisters. In 1902 Platt's mother died. At that point she left Errant's law office; from 1903 through 1905, Ida Platt then worked at home, listing no business address in the Chicago city or law directories.

Platt began to make significant changes in 1906. First, she opened her own law office on Van Buren Street in Chicago, where she practiced law until 1910. Next, Platt began to move the family residence further away from the area that was referred to as Chicago's Black Belt. The first move was in 1907 to a home several blocks east of Wabash, across the dividing line between the black and white neighborhoods. The second move occurred in 1909, when the Platt family moved to the prestigious, and mostly white, Hyde Park community. The family at this time consisted of Platt's sisters Amelia, Mary, and Ellen, Ellen's children, and Richard T. Greener, a close relative of Platt's mother whom the girls regarded as their brother.

The move to Hyde Park occurred in the midst of escalating racial tensions over housing issues throughout Chicago's South Side. During this time the number of southern black men and women arriving in Chicago was increasing significantly, with most of these new migrants settling in the already overcrowded Black Belt. In response, many upper-class and middle-class Blacks moved into neighboring white communities. The community Platt chose, Hyde Park, reacted negatively to the influx of black residents. In 1908 many of the white residents created the Hyde Park Improvement Protective Club with the goal of keeping the community white. Through rhetoric, force, and violence they were mostly successful in their efforts; but the Platts remained.

The remainder of Platt's career existed outside of public attention. In 1911, when Platt's former colleague Joseph Errant suffered a severe stroke and was forced to retire, Platt closed her Van Buren office. She continued to list herself as a lawyer at her home address in Hyde Park but maintained no other business address. The following year, when Errant moved with his family to California, Platt opened an office in the North American Building on prestigious State Street in downtown Chicago, where many white lawyers and businessmen had their offices. Platt continued to practice law without joining any legal or professional organizations, distant from any black or white women's movements and outside the attention of the press. Platt lived and worked in such anonymity that when VIOLETTE ANDERSON was admitted to the bar in 1920, she was hailed as the first black woman lawyer admitted to the Illinois bar. Platt's achievement twenty-six years earlier was forgotten, and her continued work as a black woman lawyer practicing in Chicago was overlooked.

The belief that Anderson was the first woman of color admitted to the Illinois bar advanced by the *Chicago Legal News* and by Anderson herself was made possible because of Platt's own actions. Isolating herself from the black male legal community and abstaining from any organized work for the race, Platt did not outwardly claim a black identity. Platt continued to live in a white neighborhood, and she associated with white businessmen in her work. In 1923, while maintaining her private practice, Platt joined with Benjamin Rosenthal and several other prominent white businessmen in Chicago and became an officer in the Republic Realty Mortgage Corporation for one year. Rosenthal, who was president of Importers' and Manufacturers' Millinery Company and was a principal with the wholesale millinery company Stummer, Rosenthal & Eckstein, had been an associate of Joseph Errant and maintained an office in the same building as Platt. The chairman of the board of Republic Realty was Gordon Strong, a patent lawyer with degrees from Harvard and Columbian University (now George Washington University, Washington, D.C.). Other members of the board, all wealthy white businessmen in Chicago, included John Cuneo and Charles Wrigley. The officers for the corporation included Rosenthal as president and Ida Platt as secretary.

There is some evidence that sometime after both Platt's father and mother died, she may have changed her racial designation from "colored" to white. In the census of 1910, Platt and her sisters Amelia and Mary and their relative Richard T. Greener were all listed as "white." While the race designation of a census must be considered with skepticism—often the census takers did not ask the family about race but merely indicated the race based on the enumerator's observation—the 1910 designation was a change from the racial status recorded in the census for the prior years, which listed the whole Platt family as "mulatto" in 1870 and 1880, and as "black" in 1900. It is conceivable that Platt "passed" as white. As a descendant of wealthy free Blacks from the Northeast who had been treated with respect by much of the white community for most of her life, Platt believed she was entitled to the privileges of whiteness. Further, Platt's skin color was very light and her other physical characteristics resembled white European features. Though courts throughout the country were using "blood" over appearance as the determining factor in deciding legal racial status, physical appearance, education, and economic position were often factors that determined a person's social racial status.

Further evidence that Platt had changed her racial identification to white occurred in 1922 when Richard T. Greener died. Greener was a close relative of Platt's mother and had come to live with Platt and her sisters sixteen years earlier after an extraordinary career as an intellectual and a diplomat. Greener was a member of the group that W. E. B. Du Bois dubbed the "talented tenth" ("The Talented Tenth," 34); in 1898, after an academic career that included political advocacy for the advancement of the race, Greener accepted an appointment as the American consul to Vladivostok, Russia, a position he held for eight years. Despite Greener's extraordinary career and public recognition as a black scholar and diplomat, on his death certificate Platt listed Greener's "color or race" as white. She also listed her sister Mary, who died the following year, as white. By changing the racial designation of her family members, Platt created evidence to support and maintain her own identity as white.

While Platt's identification of Greener as "white" went against Greener's self-definition, Platt acted in a manner she believed consistent with Greener's philosophy. An advocate of American liberalism, Greener celebrated individual autonomy and freedom of opportunity throughout his career. Although an ardent supporter of black civil rights and a strong supporter of women's rights, Greener prized individualism above almost all else.

In 1925, Ida Platt became a member of the Women's Bar Association of Illinois (WBAI). This was the first known professional organization that Platt joined. Established in 1914, the WBAI was an activist organization whose goal was to advance women's rights and support women's position within the profession. There are no extant records discussing the membership requirements or restrictions of the association, but the focus of the WBAI clearly followed the agenda of white women lawyers and reformers advancing the rights and protection of women without any agenda to advance racial equality. Platt maintained her membership in the WBAI at least through 1927.

In 1928, at age sixty-five, Ida Platt disappeared from the city and legal directories in Chicago. Her one surviving sister, Amelia, age seventy-seven, continued to live in Chicago, and for the first time in their lives, Ida and Amelia did not live together. When Amelia died in 1934, the *Chicago Defender's* obituary indicated that her known living relatives were a niece, Mrs. [sic] Phillips, address unknown, and a sister, "Mrs. Ida Burke," living in England. It is possible that the *Defender* was in error, but it is also possible that sometime in her sixties or seventies, Ida Platt married and moved to England.

As black men and women earned their way into the legal profession, breaking down barriers against their entrance and advancement, black women faced even further obstacles. Though wealthy and talented, Ida Platt was subject to the racist and sexist practices of the legal profession and society. As the only black woman lawyer in Chicago for most of her career, Platt was left isolated to develop her own strategies and form her own path within the profession. In 1927 African American lawyer Edith Sampson, examining the careers of black women, wrote, "Are Our Women Holding Their Own" for the *Intercollegian Wonder Book,* and aptly described Platt as an "ambitious and brave individual" (p. 79). Platt had found a way to avert some of the race obstacles she faced and maintain a law practice for more than thirty years.

Sources. The papers of the Women's Bar Association of Illinois are at the CHS. The Platt family history was pieced together from the U.S. Census for the years 1860, 1870, 1880, 1900, 1910, 1920, and 1930—the 1890 census information on the Platts did not survive; *Chicago City Directories,* 1894–1907; *Lakeside Chicago City Directories,* 1860–88, microfilm, NL; the *W. B. Sullivan's Chicago Law Directories;* and the death certificates of William C. Phillips, March 22, 1917; Amelia B. Platt, April 2, 1902; Richard T. Greener, May 2, 1922; Mary J. Platt, December 31, 1923; and Amelia Platt, October 22, 1934, all issued by the State of Illinois Department of Health, Division of Vital Statistics. The burial records for the family plot of Jacob Platt, which include an affidavit by Ida Platt dated May 23, 1924, Graceland Cemetery, Chicago, also contain important information on the Platt family history. Platt's position as an officer in the Republic Realty Mortgage Corporation is documented in the annual reports of the company filed with the Office of the Secretary of State, Corporation Department, Springfield, Illinois, and is listed in the *Chicago City Directory* (1923) and the *Chicago Legal Directory* (1923). Information on Platt's father and grandfather is found in "Obituary, Jacob F. Platt," *Inter-Ocean,* February 18, 1888, and "Jacob F. Platt Dead," *Chicago Herald,* February 18, 1888. Amelia

Platt's obituary, "Retired Librarian Dies at Age of 83," appears in the *Chicago Defender,* October 27, 1934. Additional biographical information on Platt, including her law school career and bar admission, is in James Bradwell, "Women Lawyers of Illinois," *Chicago Legal News,* vol. 32, 1900; M. A. Majors, *Noted Negro Women: Their Triumphs and Activities* (1893, reprint 1986); James B. Bradwell, "The Colored Bar of Chicago," *Chicago Legal News,* vol. 29, 1896; [n.a.], "Chicago College of Law," *Chicago Legal News,* vol. 26, 1894; [n.a.], "The Legal World Moves," *Chicago Legal News,* vol. 30, 1897; [n.a.], "Colored Members of the Chicago Bar," *American Law Review,* vol. 30, 1896; [n.a.], "We Envy Each Other," *Raleigh Gazette,* August 14, 1897; [n.a.], "The Colored Bar of Chicago," the *Freeman,* November 7, 1896. The best source for Richard T. Greener is Allison Blakely, "Richard T. Greener and the 'Talented Tenth's' Dilemma," *Journal of Negro History,* October 1974. Numerous articles by and on Greener appear in several black newspapers, including Greener, "The White Problem," *Freeman,* September 1, 1894; "Hon. Richard T. Greener," *Freeman,* September 5, 1896; and "St. Mark's Lyceum Presents Hon. R. T. Greener," *Chicago Defender,* July 13, 1918. Obituaries for Greener are "R. T. Greener, Ex-Consul, Dies," *Chicago Defender,* May 13, 1922; "Prof. Rich. T. Greener Dead," *Cleveland Gazette,* May 20, 1922; "Richard T. Greener Died May 9 [sic] in Chicago," the *New York Age,* May 20, 1922; and "Rites for Prof. R. T. Greener," *Chicago Daily News,* May 4, 1922. Information on Holger de Roode, Joseph Errant, Gordon Strong, John Cuneo, and Charles Wrigley can be found in John W. Leonard, *The Book of Chicagoans* (1905, 1917, 1926, 1931, 1936), and in Leonard's *Who's Who in Chicago and Illinois* (1945). Information on Jesse Cox is in A. N. Waterman, *Historical Review of Chicago and Cook County and Selected Biography* (1908); on Errant, "Obituary, Joseph E. Errant," *Chicago Legal News,* vol. 47, 1915; and "Obituary," *Chicago Daily Journal,* July 2, 1915. Information on Benjamin Rosenthal is in Hyman L. Meites, ed., *History of the Jews of Chicago* (1924, reprint 1990). The article establishing that Errant and Rosenthal served on the Chicago Public School Board together is [n.a.], "Dedication of the Myra Bradwell School," *Chicago Legal News,* vol. 27, 1895. See Edith Sampson, "Are Our Women Holding Their Own," *1927 Intercollegian Wonder Book, or, 1779—The Negro in Chicago—1927,* vol. 1, ed. Frederic H. Robb (1927); [n.a.], "Miss Violette N. Anderson," *Chicago Legal News,* vol. 52, 1920; and Wendy Brown, "Violette N. Anderson," *BWA* (1993). Two excellent sources on race relations and racial housing patterns in Chicago are Allan H. Spear, *Black Chicago: The Making of a Negro Ghetto 1890–1920* (1967), and James R. Grossman, *Land of Hope: Chicago, Black Southerners, and the Great Migration* (1989). Cheryl Harris, "Whiteness as Property," *Harvard Law Review,* vol. 106, 1993, is a study of social and legal racial construction around the turn of the century. See also W. E. B. Du Bois, "The Talented Tenth," in Booker T. Washington, *The Negro Problem* (1903). Lawrence Wright, "One Drop of Blood," the *New Yorker,* July 25, 1994, offers an interesting history of racial determinations and the U.S. Census. Some general information on women lawyers' fight to enter the legal profession can be found in Lelia Robinson, "Women Lawyers in the United States," *Green Bag,* vol. 2, 1890; D. Kelly Weisberg, "Barred from the Bar: Women and Legal Education in the United States 1870–1890," *Journal of Legal Education,* vol. 28, 1977; Karen Berger Morello, *The Invisible Bar: The Woman Lawyer in America, 1638 to Present* (1986); Cynthia Fuchs Epstein, *Women in Law* (1981, reprint 1993); Virginia Drachman, *Sisters in Law: Women Lawyers in Modern American History* (1998); and Gwen Hoerr McNamee, ed., *Bar None: 125 Years of Women Lawyers in Illinois* (1998). The only significant source on African American women lawyers is J. Clay Smith Jr., ed., *Rebels in Law: Voices in the History of Black Women Lawyers* (1998).

GWEN HOERR MCNAMEE

POLACHECK, HILDA SATT
October 12, 1882–May 18, 1967
WRITER, SOCIAL ACTIVIST, CLUBWOMAN

Hilda Polacheck was born Hinda Satt in Wloclawek, Poland, a community located in the Pale of Settlement, the area to which Jews were confined; during the late nineteenth century, the area was under the control of the tsarist Russian government. She was the eighth of twelve children of Dena Miriam (Faltz) Satt, a housewife, and Louis Satt, a tombstone carver. Her parents were members of a well-established Jewish community. Only six of the twelve children survived to come to America in 1892. Although Satt's family was relatively prosperous in Poland, her parents emigrated to Chicago to avoid military service in the Russian army for their three sons.

During the first year in Chicago, the family settled in the Jewish immigrant neighborhood near Hull-House on the city's Near West Side. The older children enrolled in the area's Jewish Training School, an institution established by wealthy German Jews to educate the new arrivals from eastern Europe. The school clerk Americanized Hinda's name to Hilda. The Satt family visited the World's Columbian Exposition held in Chicago in 1893, and its buildings, exhibits, and entertainments left a lasting impression on young Hilda, then eleven years old.

The sudden death of Hilda Satt's father on March 4, 1894, plunged the family into poverty. Her mother did not speak English and had never worked outside the home. Satt, who had just started fifth grade, and her older sister, Rose, left school to work in a knitting factory. Their meager wages supplemented the bare subsistence their mother earned peddling foodstuffs from door to door. Even worse than the physical poverty was the deadly monotony of daily drudgery that continued until Hilda Satt reached the age of eighteen. That year she discovered Hull-House and met JANE ADDAMS.

Hilda Satt had attended a Hull-House Christmas party with a playmate several years earlier, but she did not become aware of what the settlement had to offer until 1900. Addams introduced her to the Hull-House Labor Museum, where Satt learned to spin and weave. The museum, established in 1900, was an effort by Hull-House residents to restore immigrants' pride and confidence in their traditional arts and crafts and to teach their children, by example, their cultural history and heritage. Satt learned to spin and weave cloth and demonstrated these traditional skills to many Hull-House visitors and friends. She soon branched out into other activities: classes in English literature, dancing, lectures, plays, political meetings, and social clubs. Thinking about Hull-House and the many interesting events she attended there made her workdays bearable.

At Jane Addams's suggestion, Satt enrolled in a Hull-House English composition class, for which she composed what she later described as her first piece of writing. Her teacher, a University of Chicago instructor, was impressed with her effort and arranged for a scholarship so that Hilda Satt could enroll at the university as an unclassified student for the spring quarter in 1904. It was Satt's first formal education since fifth grade. The money she would have earned during this period was provided her family by a loan from a Hull-House benefactor.

After a stimulating quarter at the University of Chicago, Satt began to work at Hull-House, answering the door and escorting visitors around the settlement complex that, by 1905, numbered eleven buildings and that, two years later, had its full complement of thirteen edifices. Hull-House had become a prime tourist attraction in Chicago, and "toting" visitors was a steady assignment. When students in an English language class requested that it be continued during the summer, Satt volunteered to teach the course, although she had no training as a teacher.

Begun as an experiment, the class succeeded admirably, using the Declaration of Independence as a text, followed by a manual on naturalization. As the students learned English, they also learned how to apply for citizenship. Satt attached great importance to becoming an American citizen and learning English. She believed these were the preconditions to a fuller, richer life. In the fall, when the regular volunteers returned, Satt decided to apply for office jobs in Chicago firms. After several unsatisfactory experiences, she went to work for A. C. McClurg & Company, a publishing firm that also ran a wholesale and retail book business, the largest bookstore at that time in Chicago. At last she found congenial employment.

Satt's evenings were still spent at Hull-House, acting in plays; meeting notable visitors such as Prince Peter Kropotkin, the Russian anarchist; and enjoying the company of other young people. In addition, she began attending theater and concerts. When her employer asked her to supplant a sick fellow worker, Satt refused and quit her job. She then took a temporary position as assistant superintendent of the Marks Nathan Orphan Home, followed by a similar post at the Deborah Boys' Club.

A friend, Sidney Teller, superintendent of the boys' club, edited a little magazine called the *Butterfly* to which Satt began to contribute articles in 1909. One, "The Old Woman and the New World," described the plight of mature immigrant women torn from familiar Old World surroundings and forced to adjust to crowded, noisy, unsanitary New World conditions in which they felt isolated and alone. In this essay, Satt was undoubtedly describing her widowed mother.

In 1911 Satt published two articles in the *Sentinel*, a Chicago Jewish newspaper. In April 1911, two one-act plays—*The Kind Lady* and *Case No. 29,129*—written by Satt, were performed at the Chicago Hebrew Institute. The plays were directed by Louis Alter, who worked with theater groups at Hull-House. When *Case No. 29,129* was performed again in Milwaukee, Wisconsin, the *Milwaukee Leader* announced: "Play Slams Out Home Run in War against Tenement Homes" (May 29, 1912).

In the spring of 1911, Jane Addams proposed that Satt dramatize a novel, *The Walking Delegate*, by Hull-House resident Leroy Scott. Its theme was the corruption of a trade union official. Satt's play, conceived as a neighborhood drama, was to be produced by the Hull-House Players, an ensemble of amateur actors directed by LAURA DAINTY PELHAM. The players rehearsed at night and held regular jobs during the day. Satt required some free time to write the play, and she also needed employment. Addams suggested that Satt take a summer job waiting on tables at the Forward Movement Park, a camp in Saugatuck, Michigan, run under the auspices of the Methodist Episcopal

Church, which furnished "vacations for deaf, crippled, and blind children, cared for in groups" (quoted in Polacheck, 221, note 4). Addams added, "You would get your food and lodging for . . . [waiting on tables], and it would only take an hour of your time at each meal. You could write the rest of the time" (quoted in Polacheck, 111). During her stay in Saugatuck, Satt became engaged to a young Milwaukee businessman and socialist, William Polacheck, whom she had met through Sidney Teller.

After much revision, Satt's play was produced by the Hull-House players April 10–27, 1912. On April 17, Satt and Polacheck were married, attending the play in the evening. Addams hosted a wedding reception in the Hull-House Coffee House after the performance.

As well as encouraging Hilda Polacheck's playwriting, Jane Addams introduced her to the woman suffrage movement. At Addams's suggestion, Polacheck campaigned for woman's suffrage, handing out leaflets and participating in demonstrations. Despite the fact that she taught others about the process of naturalization, Polacheck had not yet applied for citizenship, feeling it was meaningless if she could not vote. With her marriage to an American citizen, however, she automatically became a citizen under the Naturalization Law of 1907. Prior to the Cable Act of 1922, married women had no citizenship of their own but assumed the citizenship of their husbands; women born in the United States lost their citizenship when they married men of foreign citizenship.

The Polachecks soon moved to Milwaukee, where Hilda Polacheck wrote theater reviews for the *Milwaukee Leader*, a socialist newspaper. She received no pay for her columns. Eventually, her outspoken criticism antagonized local theater owners. In Milwaukee she was also active in local organizations, including the National Council of Jewish Women and the Abraham Lincoln House, a settlement modeled on Hull-House.

The birth of her first child, Charles Lessing, in 1914 did not limit Polacheck's activities, but the outbreak of World War I did. Supporting the ideas put forward in 1915 by Jane Addams and a group of women who met in Washington, D.C., and organized the Woman's Peace Party, Polacheck was dismayed when the climate of public opinion turned against war protesters and pacifists. Outspoken pacifists were arrested and imprisoned. In Milwaukee, where the population was predominantly of German extraction, "people stopped talking to old friends" (Polacheck, 143), and "every organization with which [she] had affiliated since . . . coming to [the city] cooperated with the war effort" (p. 144). Polacheck promised her husband she "would not say anything in public that might endanger [her] freedom" (p. 144) while her three small children needed her. Meanwhile she stopped going to meetings and resigned from every organization that supported the war. A second child, daughter Dena Julia, was born in 1916; two years later, a second son, Demarest Lloyd, was born, and in 1923, daughter Jessie.

At the close of World War I, Polacheck joined the militant National Woman's Party (NWP) and redoubled her efforts to obtain suffrage for women. When the NWP "'Prison Special' train traveled across the country to arouse public opinion by having women speak who had been jailed for suffrage activities" (Polacheck, xviii), visiting Milwaukee in March 1919, Polacheck housed a visiting NWP activist, Mrs. W. D. Ascough of Detroit,

in her home. Polacheck was sure "that Miss Addams did not approve" (Polacheck, xvii) of the militant NWP. Polacheck was in charge of providing Milwaukee newspapers with appropriate material and photographs when the Nineteenth Amendment became law in August 1919. "Later in the 1920s when labor and radical feminists split over the issue of equal rights versus protective labor legislation, [Polacheck] resigned from her position as a local officer of the Woman's party, consistent with her labor sympathies" (Polacheck, xviii).

Physically, Hilda Polacheck was short and stocky, about five feet tall. Not a beauty, she had plain strong features; her brown eyes were always animated, her smile and hearty laugh infectious. In her youth she had abundant black hair, which she bobbed in the 1920s. In later years, it became completely gray.

Her political beliefs, nurtured in the labor strife of Chicago's garment trades, were always left-leaning. She voted for the first time in 1920 for Eugene V. Debs, candidate for president on the Socialist Party ticket, who was then in prison for his opposition to World War I. In the 1920s, Polacheck became an organizer of a local peace society, which became the Wisconsin branch of the Women's International League for Peace and Freedom (WILPF). She resumed her involvement with the National Council of Jewish Women and took an active role in the Milwaukee Open Forum, a lecture series featuring notable speakers, including English philosopher and pacifist Bertrand Russell and American author James Weldon Johnson. When Margaret Sanger spoke on birth control, Polacheck advocated the founding of birth control clinics, and she called for "a federal law sanctioning birth control" (quoted in Polacheck, 184).

Polacheck's busy and active life was shattered in December 1927, when her husband died, leaving her with four children ranging in age from four to fourteen. Times were bad for business enterprises and, with the onset of the Great Depression, she made a valiant, but unsuccessful, attempt to operate her husband's business. After going through bankruptcy in 1930, she moved to Chicago, where friends helped her find work as a manager of apartment houses that were put in receivership because landlords could not pay taxes and maintain property. The family, who lived in the current building managed by Polacheck, moved frequently as the apartment houses managed were sold and new ones required management.

Around 1936, Polacheck rented a building near the University of Chicago campus. Her plan was to open a restaurant on the first floor and to house students in apartments above. When the restaurant did not prosper, the building was turned into a student cooperative with Polacheck as cook. Here she was surrounded by radical students who greatly admired her. A year or so later, she was hired by the Federal Emergency Administration of Public Works to select tenants for the Jane Addams Housing Project, where she worked until January 1938.

Hilda Polacheck then found employment as a writer with the Illinois Writers' Project of the Works Progress Administration (renamed Work Projects Administration in 1939), where she continued to work through the early 1940s. Her unpublished writing, now among the project's papers in the Library of Congress, Washington, D.C., includes pieces on Hull-House, immigrant life, and folktales. Polacheck also wrote a number of one-act plays now in the Illinois State Historical Library, Springfield, Illinois.

During World War II, when the Federal Writers' Project ended, Polacheck supervised a clothing collection center for Russian war relief. Throughout these various jobs she somehow managed to educate her children, making sure that they attended concerts and theater performances, which she believed were an important part of their education. Her children found part-time and full-time jobs as they continued their education with the aid of scholarships and loans.

At age sixty-three and with the support of her children, Hilda Polacheck was able to retire from work at the end of World War II. She assisted in the raising of her sixteen grandchildren. At the same time she continued to take an active interest in social questions and politics. She remained an active member of WILPF and participated in various local political campaigns. About 1953, she spent the winter in New Jersey at the home of her daughter Dena Julia Epstein. It was here that she wrote her autobiography. Commercial publishers contacted at the time rejected her manuscript, saying, "Who wants to read about an obscure woman like you? Write about Jane Addams. We might be interested in that" (Polacheck, 179). Undaunted, she made several attempts to rewrite her manuscript but finally gave up in disappointment.

In July 1962, Polacheck attended an international meeting of the WILPF in Asilomar, California. Sharing a room with a delegate from Poland, she recalled, to her pleasant surprise, enough Polish to converse with her, even though she had not spoken the language for more than fifty years. The following year, in August 1963, Polacheck accompanied two granddaughters to the civil rights march in Washington, D.C., where she heard Martin Luther King Jr. deliver his "I Have a Dream" speech. She endured the discomfort of an overnight bus ride to the Capitol to be present at what she regarded as a most historic occasion.

Hilda Polacheck died of a stroke at age eighty-five in Chicago at the home of her daughter Jessie. She was cremated. In 1989, in time for the Hull-House centennial, Hilda Polacheck's autobiography, *I Came a Stranger: The Story of a Hull-House Girl*, was published by the University of Illinois Press. Her daughter, Dena J. Polacheck Epstein, edited the manuscript her mother had written many years earlier, reconstructing it "from the loose sheets and revisions found" (Polacheck, ix) among her mother's papers. Epstein writes, "Although she probably did not know it, her [Hilda Polacheck's] story is the only known description of Hull-House written by a woman from the neighborhood" (Polacheck, 179).

Sources. The Hilda Satt Polacheck Papers are at UIC Spec. Coll. Her autobiography, *I Came a Stranger: The Story of a Hull-House Girl* (1989), ed. Dena J. Polacheck Epstein, is essential. It contains an appendix with a detailed bibliographic essay on the writings of Hilda Polacheck, including published articles, plays, and materials archived in the Federal Writers' Project, Illinois State Historical Library, Springfield, and the Folklore Project, Work Projects Administration (WPA) Federal Writers' Project, Manuscript Division, Library of Congress. Other useful sources are Mary Lynn McCree Bryan and Allen F. Davis, eds., *100 Years at Hull-House* (1990); Jane Addams, *Forty Years at Hull-House* (1935); and Elsie F. Weil, "The Hull-House Players," *Theater Magazine*, September 1913.

DENA J. POLACHECK EPSTEIN

POMERANTZ HONIGBAUM, PESSIE HERSHFELD

May 20, 1900–August 8, 1978

POET

A member of the first generation of published Yiddish women poets in America, Pessie Hershfeld Pomerantz was born into the shtetl (village) culture of eastern Europe. She spent her childhood in the town of Kammenobrod in the Ukraine. Her father, Harry (Zvi Hirsh) Hershfeld, was an engraver by trade, while her mother, Clara (Chaya) (Zimring) Hershfeld, was a homemaker. Pessie Hershfeld's parents observed most Jewish traditions, but her brother and sisters were active participants in secular political movements, particularly socialist activities. Her older brother, Sam, a dedicated communist, lived much of his adult life in Czechoslovakia.

Hershfeld, the youngest member of her family, immigrated to the United States in 1913 with her parents, two sisters, and a brother. They joined two siblings already in the country. An older sister, Fannie, had already settled in Chicago and had opened a china shop with her husband. Members of the Pomerantz family worked there. Pessie worked at the shop as a salesgirl from the early 1920s until her marriage in 1928.

Pessie Hershfeld's first published poem appeared in 1918 in the magazine *Der Groyser Kundes* (The big stick). She quickly established a national reputation, both for the quality of her poetry and because she was one of very few Jewish woman poets. Her first book, *Kareln* (Beads), was published in 1926 and earned favorable reviews in newspapers in and outside of Chicago. She and other Yiddish writers published in anthologies, held readings, invited lecturers, and supported institutions that were mainstays of Chicago's Jewish community. Hershfeld quickly became a visible and active presence on the Jewish literary scene.

Hershfeld's writing came out of a self-conscious literary movement, *Di Yunge* (The young generation), among young Jewish immigrants. *Di Yunge* was an international movement of Yiddish authors and critics. It marked Yiddish poetry's first serious forays into modernism, and particularly into modernism's concern with individual expression. Hershfeld herself was deeply influenced by Walt Whitman, especially his use of pastoral imagery and his emphasis on personal emotions. As a prolific member of *Di Yunge*, she applied stylistic and linguistic innovations to descriptions of women's traditional roles as wives and mothers.

Chicago authors who, like Hershfeld, considered themselves part of the movement *Di Yunge*, called themselves *Yung Chicago*. The name expressed allegiances with *Di Yunge* while emphasizing the situation of these writers—describing what they saw and felt in Chicago, far from the culture of New York City.

Indeed, *Yung Chicago* was deeply embedded in Chicago's Jewish institutions, its members forming only one segment of an active Jewish intelligentsia. During most of Hershfeld's childhood and young adulthood, Jewish communities in the Lawndale and Garfield Park neighborhoods seemed nearly self-contained, supporting Yiddish language theaters, stores, reading circles, publishing houses, and a number of synagogues. These West Side neighborhoods contained the highest concentration of Jews in the city of Chicago for much of the 1920s and 1930s.

Bookstores, restaurants, community centers, and newspapers all served as centers for lively debate and cultural exchanges. Debates often focused on the risks and benefits of American culture. Members of *Yung Chicago*, in addition to providing a supportive audience for each others' work, played vital roles in these debates. Their readings, lectures, and publications all implicitly argued that modern life and literary trends ought to be brought into Yiddish culture. The group was influential enough that its activities were followed closely by the *Chicago Jewish Courier*, the dominant Yiddish daily paper. Pessie Hershfeld's poetry reflected personal themes, but these themes were written as part of a self-consciously public movement.

On June 3, 1928, she married Israel Chaim Pomerantz, a Yiddish teacher and eventually director of Yiddish schooling in the Sholem Aleichem Folk Institute in Chicago. Jewish immigrants from eastern European centers carried to the United States their Yiddish mother tongue with its rich literary tradition. They established secular Yiddish schools, which their children attended part-time after public school hours to study Yiddish language and literature, Jewish history, and Jewish culture. After brief stays in Detroit, Michigan, and in Mishawaka, Indiana, where Chaim Pomerantz taught in Yiddish schools, they worked for a short time on a communal farm in South Haven, Michigan, and then returned to Chicago. A daughter, Clare (Chaikey), was born on November 26, 1928, and a second daughter, Fradle, on March 31, 1933.

Pomerantz wove writing into her work as a wife and mother. The year of her marriage she published seven poems in a national anthology, *Yiddishe Dichterins Antologie* (Yiddish women poets anthology), under her maiden name. She published a collected volume, *Geklibene Lider* (Selected poems), in 1931 and a third book of new poetry in 1939, *Roiter Toi* (Red dew). She also continued to publish in journals and to do public readings.

As part of a young generation of Yiddish poets, Pomerantz broke with past traditions of explicitly political or moralistic poetry. Pomerantz's poetry was deeply personal, often taking the form of love poems or celebrations of her motherhood. In the poem "Pregnancy" ("Shvangershaft"), written in 1932 or 1933 she wrote, "I am the field that carries in my self your seed. / Your love is breath, rain, wind, and sun. / I would be quickly corrupted without your love, / As is the pregnant field with no rain or sun. / It grows in me and streams in me your seed / And fills me with belief in the harvest / And like the field—I dream about the harvest, / Of a successful harvest and of golden grain" (translated by Tal, 12–13). As "Pregnancy" suggests, Pomerantz consistently used images from the natural world. She wrote in "Colorado Mountains," published in 1957, "Most ancient, mystical splendor / Enwooded / Peaks of mountains— / I feel myself / In your gigantic presence / Helpless, mothy and stilled" (translation in Cooperman, 410–11).

While Pomerantz was primarily concerned with artistic expression and the revitalization of Yiddish poetry, some critics focused on her identity as a woman. Her work was often compared to the work of other women poets rather than to that of the male poets with whom she worked closest. The critic Abraham Bik, reviewing *Roiter Toi* in the *Yiddish Courier*, complimented Pomerantz on being better than most women poets. "In *Roiter*

Toi there is none of this easy melancholy, the effusion (of sentiment), and the cult of the image that one finds in Rokhl [Rachel] Korn and that is characteristic of our women's poetry in general." Another review of the same book described how men were moved when a woman published her feelings in poetry and compared Pomerantz to the Greek woman poet Sappho.

In spite of critical focus on her as a woman poet, much of her professional life, and a good deal of personal satisfaction, came from working within an almost entirely male world. Such well-known Yiddish writers as Chaim Grade and H. Leivick were frequent guests and personal friends. She was especially involved in the literary work of Shlomo Schwartz and Mattes Deitch, both prolific writers in Yiddish and English. Pomerantz, Deitch, and Schwartz were particularly close; they critiqued drafts of each other's writings, exchanged anecdotes about their personal lives, and encouraged each other always to continue writing. Even when Pomerantz, Deitch, and Schwartz found themselves living far apart, they maintained a lively correspondence punctuated by visits.

Pomerantz became an important link in an international network of Yiddish writers. Her home served as a home-away-from-home for dozens of visiting scholars. She hosted and organized informal meetings, served as a catalyst for discussion groups and reading circles, and maintained a voluminous correspondence with other writers and poets. The network she helped to sustain was a wellspring of support and encouragement for Yiddish literati.

Pomerantz's work in maintaining the network of Yiddish writers grew particularly important as authors and artists found themselves spread across the country. In 1940 the Pomerantz family left Chicago, moving first to Cincinnati and then to New York, so that Chaim Pomerantz could maintain steady employment with the Manischewitz Company. Pessie and Chaim Pomerantz became more observant than they had been and joined synagogues, while they continued to work for Yiddish culture and language. In Cincinnati, the couple started a Yiddish reading circle within a community that had previously only focused on Zionism and promotion of Hebrew. In the late 1950s the couple returned to Chicago.

The Holocaust, World War II, and Joseph Stalin's purge of Yiddish writers in the early 1950s weighed heavily on Pomerantz. Her poems became more despondent and far more serious. Bik's review of *Roiter Toi* in 1940 noted that much of the book was filled with social concerns, that the contemporary world became a catalyst for her writing. The creation of the State of Israel in 1948 was a watershed for her, and Israel's land and scenery gradually assumed central roles in her work. She had long been an outspoken Zionist and a member of the Zionist women's organization Pioneer Women. Once Israel won independence, Pomerantz began a series of visits to the country. Her daughter Fradle's emigration there strengthened Pomerantz's ties to Israel. Her final book, *Fun Ale Meine Lider* (Of all my poems) was published in 1969 in Haifa. It contained numerous references to Israel landscapes and Zionist activists, interspersed with poems set in America.

Chaim Pomerantz died in December 1962, soon after the couple's return to Chicago. Pessie Pomerantz remarried on December 15, 1965. Moishe (Morris) Honigbaum, her second husband, was an old family friend and a vocal promoter of Yiddish culture. When she joined him in Miami, soon after the marriage, her home there became a center of Yiddish activity. She remained in Miami until her death. She was buried in the Jewish National Workers Alliance Cemetery at Waldheim, in Forest Park, Illinois.

Pessie Hershfeld Pomerantz challenged traditional Jewish practices that reserved intellectual legitimacy for men. Working in Chicago for much of her professional life, she maintained its status as a source of Jewish culture. She worked tirelessly to promote the Yiddish language and Yiddish culture wherever she lived, not only writing in Yiddish but also opening her home to Yiddish activists and artists.

Pomerantz established a reputation as an important poet and vital force within the Yiddish literary community. Her poems were frequently reprinted in anthologies during her life, and many were set to music. She became especially well known for the dense style and nuanced emotions contained in her poetry. After her death, she became the subject of critical reviews in both Yiddish and English. An essay on her writings appeared in 1989 in the Israeli monthly *Yiddish-Velt*, and her poems are taught in courses in Jewish studies at Bar-Ilan University in Israel.

Sources. Pessie Hershfeld Pomerantz's name in English appears in several spellings, including Bessie Hershfield, Pessie Hershfeld-Pomerantz, and Pessie Pomerantz-Honigbaum. Her letters and manuscripts, in Yiddish, are in the possession of her daughter, Clare Pomerantz Greenberg, who also provided information in an interview with Tracey Deutsch, October 2, 1995. Pomerantz's poems have been collected in *Kareln* (1926), *Geklibene Lider* (1931), *Roiter Toi* (1939), *Reges fun Genod: Geklibene Lider* (1957), and *Fun Ale Meine Lider* (1969). Five of her poems were translated into English in Jeheil Cooperman and Sarah Cooperman, eds., *America in Yiddish Poetry* (1967). She is mentioned in Philip Bregstone's *Chicago and Its Jews* (1933) and Sol Liptzin's *A History of Yiddish Literature* (1972). She is also discussed in a paper by Aviva Tal, "Three Yiddish Women Poets: Roots and Relationships: A View of Three Poets, Geographically Remote yet Spiritually Connected," typescript, 1995, Bar-Ilan University, Ramat Gan, Israel. Much of the information on Pomerantz is in Yiddish-language publications. She was frequently reviewed in Chicago's *Jewish Courier*. See, for example, *Daily Jewish Courier*, October 15, 1926, and Abraham Bik, "Dichter Un Verk: Pessie Hershfeld-Pomerantz, 'Roiter Toi,'" *Yiddish Courier*, August 14, 1940, translated by Judith Nysenholc. A brief biography of Pomerantz's young adulthood appears in E. Korman's *Yiddishe Dichterins Antologie* (Yiddish women poets anthology) (1928).

TRACEY DEUTSCH

POOLEY, GEORGIA BITZIS
1849–June 1, 1945
CIVIC AND CHARITY LEADER, ORGANIZER OF BENEVOLENT SOCIETIES, CLUBWOMAN

Georgia Bitzis was born in Corfu, an island off the west coast of Greece in the Ionian Sea, the third child of seven (five girls and two boys), of Alexander and Isabella Bitzis. As the daughter of an established, wealthy mercantile family, Bitzis was educated at the town's academy, where she became proficient in her native Greek along with Italian, French, and English. At the time, it was not a common practice for a Greek woman to attend formal

FIG. 96. *Greek immigrant Georgia Bitzis Pooley, a leader in the newly developing Greek American community in Chicago, 1885.*

school. Her education reflected the wealth and social position of the family.

In 1884, Georgia Bitzis married Captain Peter Pooley (Panagoitis Poulis), who had returned from Chicago to his native Corfu seeking a bride. Captain Pooley, who had visited Chicago several times by way of the port of New Orleans and the Mississippi River, had engaged in a cargo transportation business on Lake Michigan. Impressed with the economic opportunities of this growing midwest city, he returned to Corfu to recruit others to immigrate. As the head of a prosperous Corfiote family with five daughters, Alexander Bitzis was concerned that each would marry within the proper station of the family and with appropriate dowries. Apparently, Captain Pooley, with his international mercantile experience, satisfied these requirements, and Bitzis's daughter was promptly betrothed to him.

Arriving in Chicago in 1885 with her husband, the thirty-six year old Georgia Pooley became the first Greek woman immigrant of whom there is any record. Joining the miniscule Greek community of Chicago, which then numbered fewer than a thousand young men and boys, the Pooleys made their home in the city's center near the wholesale produce market—where the first "Greektown" evolved. Later, they moved to the vicinity of the Annunciation Greek Orthodox Cathedral on the city's Near North Side. About 1902 the Pooleys bought a home in the neighborhood, and Captain Pooley operated his confectionery business next door.

In 1886, the Pooleys started their family. They had seven children, all born in Chicago over a fifteen-year span. The first two children, Adele (1886) and Christos (1887), died before the others were born. Elizabeth was born in 1888, Harry in 1890, Catherine in 1894, Alexander in 1896, and, finally, Mary in 1899, when Georgia Pooley was fifty years old.

One of Georgia Pooley's early concerns was to respond to the urgent needs of the fledgling immigrant Greek community. Since Greek immigration to the United States was almost exclusively a male phenomenon, most residents in Chicago were young bachelors, many of them food peddlers, who lived together in non-family groups of from ten to twenty persons, often sharing sleeping accommodations in rental facilities above stables. From Pooley's perspective, they lived without the care and restraints of family life and the nurture and moral influence of mothers and sisters.

Appalled at the unsanitary living conditions and the low level of social morality, Georgia Pooley reacted by immediately organizing a Greek voluntary society with mature Greek men who were married to non-Greek women, mostly Italian and Irish, and who could assist in improving and uplifting the lives of these young Greek men.

Pooley was convinced that religious values reinforced family life and raised the moral standards of the community. She persuaded the more mature family men among the earliest Greek settlers to consider establishing a church for Greek Orthodox worship services. Due to the small number of Greek immigrants in the city, Pooley encouraged the elders to join forces with their coreligionists, the Orthodox Slavs—Russians and Serbians—to form the Greco-Slavonic Brotherhood in 1885. In organizing this first benevolent society of its kind in Chicago, Pooley believed that the brotherhood would not only serve the spiritual and moral needs of these immigrants but would assist them in the social and economic aspects of their struggles in a new society. Rented facilities were established on Chicago's Near North Side; and itinerant Greek-speaking Russian and Serbian Orthodox priests, some from distant areas, performed Divine Liturgy for the nascent Orthodox Christian community in Chicago. These clergymen also visited the homes of immigrants and administered the sacraments of marriage and baptism.

In 1891, several hundred immigrants from the Greek province of Laconia who were unwilling to be part of the Pan-Slavism movement of the Russian Orthodox Church in America broke away from the Greco-Slavonic Brotherhood. They created their own group, the Lycurgus Society, named after the lawgiver of ancient Sparta. It became the catalyst for the founding in 1892 of the first Greek Orthodox Church, the Annunciation, which held services in rented quarters until 1897, when it was replaced by Holy Trinity, in the 1990s the oldest Greek Orthodox church in the city in continuous existence.

During her long life, Georgia Pooley served as a significant and spirited role model for Greek immigrant women, who began arriving in Chicago after 1910. This influx of Greek women was the result of increased immigration of young Greek men to America, many of them coming directly to Chicago, which already had an established Greek community. The peak year of Greek immigration was 1907, when 36,580 men arrived in the United States. The following decade, 1911 to 1920, 184,201 more arrived, a larger number than in any decade before or after. By 1910, the Chicago school census counted 1,448 Greeks under the age of twenty-one living in the city.

The unmarried Greek men requested that relatives in Greece arrange marriages for them. This process resulted in the picture-bride phenomenon, according to which marriages were for the most part arranged without the usual dowry required in Greece. Eager to dispose of their marriageable daughters at such a "bargain," relatives quickly shipped them off to America. The women arriving in Chicago had little or no formal education but wanted to rear their families in the religion and ethnic tradition of their homeland.

Despite her duties as a mother, Pooley continued to exercise leadership in the Greek community, concentrating on the social and economic needs of immigrant families. Her association with JANE ADDAMS of Hull-House led her to persuade Greek American families living in the emerging Greektown community near the settlement to use its facilities. Greek American involvement at Hull-House was perhaps the most extensive of any ethnic group at that time, in part because of Hull-House's proximity to Greektown. Also influential was Jane Addams's ceaseless dedication to creating in Hull-House a climate that nurtured the cultural values and aspirations of the Greeks, making the settlement a veritable second home. In fact, the Greeks began to think of it as their own institution, often trying to keep other ethnic groups from using its facilities. Jane Addams, who was intimately involved with Greek activities at the settlement house, recognized this tendency and saw to it that the facilities remained open to all.

There is some evidence that Georgia Pooley was a founding member of the first organized Greek women's organization in Chicago, which was formed at Hull-House in 1909. Known as the Philoptochos Society of Greek Women (Friends of the Poor), this club looked after the needs of indigent Greek families. It served as a prototype of the National Ladies Philoptochos Society, which was formally organized in 1931 in New York City by the Greek Orthodox Archdiocese of North and South America. During the Great Depression of the 1930s, Pooley joined her younger Chicago colleague STELLA PETRAKIS, one of the most active women in Greek charities, in organizing chapters throughout the city. The National Ladies Philoptochos Society became one of the largest Greek American women's philanthropic organizations in the United States. In addition to its charitable activities, the society's other goal was to provide a social and educational outlet for Greek immigrant women. Twice-monthly meetings were held, providing lessons in English, civics, and "European-style" dances.

Georgia Pooley continued her efforts to protect and advance children and youth. Well educated herself, she was cognizant of the advantages of schooling. Under the tutelage of Jane Addams, Pooley promoted the formation in 1908 of the Hellenic League for the Molding of Young Men at Hull-House. It was something of a para-military organization, the boys being instructed in military drill and training by former noncommissioned officers of the Greek army. Its main objective, however, was the moral development of its members. In this respect, it was the forerunner of the later youth groups that were established in Chicago's Greek community.

Georgia Pooley was probably instrumental in organizing the first educational center for Greek children, but because she operated in an intensely patriarchal society, she has not been given credit for this effort. Greek male immigrants frowned on women who were actively engaged outside the home. Yet as a member of the Society of Family Leaders that she had helped organize, Pooley is believed to have assisted in the founding of the first Greek day school in Chicago between 1905 and 1906. Since most Greek immigrants considered themselves to be in America temporarily, its purpose was to teach their children Greek language and culture along with the Orthodox Christian faith which, they assumed, they would need when their families returned to Greece. Many of the immigrants did return to their homeland as soon as they secured sufficient funds. The school did not survive, however, but served as a forerunner for the first permanent Greek day school, the Socrates School. It was established in 1908 and is still in existence. Socrates School was followed by other day schools, making Chicago the leading Greek educational center in the nation until it was surpassed by New York shortly after World War II.

When Greece was invaded by the Axis powers during World War II, Georgia Pooley helped organize the Greek War Relief Association and led successful fund-raising campaigns to secure money to aid the starving and homeless victims of the Nazi occupation of Greece. Thus, for most of her life, until her death in 1945 at the age of ninety-six, Georgia Pooley continued her charitable work for the Greek Orthodox community of Chicago. She died in Chicago and is buried in Elmwood Cemetery, near the Greek Orthodox Chapel of the Holy Transfiguration, River Grove, Illinois.

A well-educated, multilingual activist and philanthropist, Georgia Pooley played a significant leadership role in Chicago's Greek American community by initiating diverse ethnic institutions and organizations that helped meet the needs of young immigrant men, women, and children. In the context of the patriarchal Greek subculture of that era, this kind of spirited involvement and independent leadership was unusual for a Greek immigrant woman who was married and had the responsibilities of a large family. Her work played an important early role in the growth of a strong Greek culture and in the establishment of a social support system for Greek immigrants.

Sources. Written information on Georgia Pooley is sketchy and inferential. Limited reference to her is found in the Hull-House Association Papers, UIC Spec. Coll. There is mention of Pooley in several newspaper articles: *CT*, February 15 and 21, 1897; *Chicago Daily Journal*, April 22, 1924; and *Greek Star*, April 9, 1937. References are also found in a number of books about the early Greek community in Chicago, written mostly in Greek: Spyridon A. Kotakis, *E Hellenes en Ameriki* (The Greeks in America) (1906); Seraphim A. Canoutas, *Hellenism in America or the History of the Greeks in America* (1918); and Basil T. Zoustis, *The Greeks*

in America and Their Activities (1954). For an understanding of the conditions in which Pooley undertook her humanitarian endeavors, see Residents of Hull-House, *Hull-House Maps and Papers: A Presentation of Nationalities and Wages in a Congested District of Chicago, Together with Comments and Essays on Problems Growing Out of the Social Conditions* (1895); Edith Abbott, *Immigration: Selected Documents and Case Reports* (1924); and Grace Abbott, "A Study of the Greeks in Chicago," *American Journal of Sociology*, November 1909. For information regarding the role of women in the Greek community, see Constance Callinicos, *American Aphrodite: Becoming Female in Greek America* (1990). Later works are Andrew T. Kopan, *Education and Greek Immigrants in Chicago 1892–1973: A Study in Ethnic Survival* (1990), and Andrew T. Kopan, "Greek Survival in Chicago," in Melvin G. Holli and Peter d'A. Jones, eds., *Ethnic Chicago: A Multicultural Portrait* (1995).

ANDREW T. KOPAN

ALICE ORPHANOS KOPAN

PORTER, ELIZA EMILY CHAPPELL
November 5, 1807–January 1, 1888
EDUCATOR, MISSIONARY, RELIEF WORKER

Eliza Chappell Porter established numerous schools, including one of the first in Chicago, and ministered to thousands of the sick and dying during the Civil War. A descendant of Huguenots and Pilgrims, Chappell was born at Geneseo in western New York, the seventh of eight children and the youngest of three daughters. Her mother, Elizabeth Kneeland, was the daughter of a physician; her father, Robert Chappell, was a lieutenant in the American Revolutionary War who died when Chappell was four years old and left his widow and eight children in poverty. Chappell spent several years of her childhood in Franklin, New York, in the home of relatives. At the age of twelve, she returned to her own home, where she helped her mother and attended school. Chappell was very pious, as was her mother, and she read theological works with great interest. She became a member of her mother's Presbyterian church, unlike most of her siblings, who became Methodists. After a year of schooling in Rochester, New York, she returned to Geneseo where, at the age of sixteen, she began to teach in a local school while assisting her mother in the care of her deceased sister's four children.

Chappell was short, slight, and in frail health. During these years she was often ill, and a pattern of overwork followed by lengthy periods of recuperation was established. During her long periods of inactivity, she tried to discern what God wanted of her, and, on one occasion after reading her Bible, she came to the conclusion that she should teach children and bring the Christian message to them. This was a profound religious experience for her, and she entered into church services and her work as a teacher with a renewed sense of purpose and enthusiasm. She took charge of a small school in Rochester, New York, where she participated in the Second Great Awakening revivals of 1828 and continued her religious reading. She also learned all she could about the recently introduced infant school system, bringing the Pestalozzian model, initiated in New York City by Joanna Graham Bethune, to Rochester. Johann Pestalozzi was a Swiss educator whose ideas on early childhood education influenced educators worldwide in the nineteenth century. Bethune's purpose, more narrow than that of Pestalozzi, was to provide religiously oriented teaching to poor children.

In 1831, shortly after the death of her mother, Chappell was invited to go to Mackinac, Michigan, to teach the Robert Stuart children. Stuart was the resident partner of John Jacob Astor's fur company in the frontier outpost of Mackinac Island. Despite her fragile health, Chappell undertook the journey and the job. At Mackinac she taught some fifty-five students at the mission school; started another school at St. Ignace on the mainland, which was attended by more than twenty pupils; and taught Sunday school.

The work soon overwhelmed her strength, and she returned to Geneseo to recuperate with relatives. As she recovered, she began to travel around New York to teacher-training institutions, where she described the great need for teachers on the frontier. Shortly after her return to Mackinac, more teachers arrived. Chappell moved on to Chicago in 1833, where she started Chicago's first school. Because her school was partially supported by money from the public school fund, Chappell is considered the first Chicago public schoolteacher. The number of students soon grew too large, and she relocated to rooms in the First Presbyterian Church building, one of the few roomy structures in the small and crude settlement. Chappell expanded her work to include the education of young women from rural areas who boarded with her, in effect establishing the first teacher-training institution in Chicago. She also found time to organize activities within the church, to visit the sick and bereaved, and to travel to neighboring settlements to give Christian instruction and help her fledgling teachers start their new schools.

Once again her health failed her, and in 1835 she had to relinquish responsibility for her school. When Chappell recovered, she became engaged to Jeremiah Porter, a young Presbyterian minister from Hadley, Massachusetts, and a member of the American Home Mission Society, whom she had met at the Stuart home on Mackinac. Jeremiah Porter had traveled on to Sault Sainte Marie, and from there he had moved to Chicago in 1833 with the United States troops sent to fight in the Black Hawk War. In Chicago he established the First Presbyterian Church. Although most of their friends and family thought it was foolish and irresponsible of them to marry since she was so obviously unfit for the arduous life of a missionary's wife, they were married in Rochester, New York, on June 15, 1835. The young couple returned to Chicago, but in the next few years moved to Peoria and then Farmington, Illinois, and, in 1840, to Green Bay, Wisconsin, where Jeremiah Porter served as pastor.

Although the Porters lost three children to death in infancy, they raised six children during their eighteen years in Green Bay. Porter lived the life of a loving mother and pastor's wife. She offered hospitality to numerous guests and boarders, often young teachers and relatives. The Porter home was a stop on the Underground Railroad, the last stop for fleeing African American slaves before they crossed by boat from Green Bay into Canada. In addition to all this, Porter continued her practice of establishing schools. She encouraged the founding of schools in Green Bay, starting one herself with more than one hundred students. Here she taught along with other teachers, including her husband, who taught Latin and mathematics. She also organized a Sunday school several miles outside of Green Bay.

In 1858 the Porters moved back to Chicago, where Jeremiah

Porter became pastor of a mission church. Within a short time the Porters lost two more of their children to typhus, the oldest girl, Charlotte (1843–59), and the youngest boy, Robert (1851–59). Four of the Porter's nine children survived: James W. (1838–1934), Edwards W. (1841–1928), Henry D. (1845–1916), and Mary H. (1847–1929).

The outbreak of the Civil War brought great changes to the family. The eldest son, James, enlisted in the Union Army, and Jeremiah Porter was appointed chaplain to an army unit. Later in the war, the youngest son, Henry, also joined up. Because of her abhorrence of slavery, Porter supported the war vigorously. She became a field agent of the United States Sanitary Commission's branch in Chicago, the Northwestern Sanitary Commission. She frequently worked with another woman, Mary A. Bickerdyke. As a field agent, Porter traveled with supplies and distributed them to soldiers in town and field hospitals. When she arrived at these hospitals, sometimes within sound of a battle, Porter helped in caring for the sick, wounded, and dying; prepared the dead for burial; and wrote to soldiers' families, often under unimaginable conditions. Despite her disapproval of the Confederacy, she was devoted in her care of southern soldiers as well. She assisted at hospitals and brought nurses and supplies to many places, among them Mound City and Cairo, Illinois; Chattanooga and Savannah, Tennessee; Kingston and Marietta, Georgia; Huntsville, Alabama; and Vicksburg and Corinth, Mississippi. She spent ten months cooking for the seriously ill in a convalescent camp in Memphis, Tennessee, where her husband was chaplain, and helped spread the idea of separate diet kitchens for the sick. Later in the war, she and her husband went to Savannah, Georgia, where she worked in the hospitals; she continued to work in the South through the end of the war. The Porters even accompanied and distributed supplies during the Mexican campaign after the Civil War.

True to her lifelong pattern, she was instrumental in the establishment of schools, one in Memphis for freedmen who came to the city in 1863 after the passage of the Emancipation Proclamation, and one in Texas during the Mexican campaign. Porter also took up the cause of permitting Union soldiers to recuperate in the more healthful climate and less crowded hospitals of the North or in their own homes. On one occasion, she and her husband met with President Lincoln in Washington to persuade him to allow debilitated soldiers to be sent North.

In 1866 the Porters moved to Prairie du Chien, Wisconsin, where Jeremiah Porter became pastor to a Congregational church. Within two years their daughter Mary finished her studies to become a foreign missionary and departed for China, as did their son Henry after his marriage four years later. Eliza and Jeremiah Porter then left for Brownsville, Texas, where Porter took charge of the school, teaching and securing more teachers, while her husband took up the work of pastor and acted as chaplain to the troops at Fort Brown. In 1870 Jeremiah Porter received a commission as an army chaplain and he continued in that capacity until his retirement in 1882. The Porters spent the next twelve years in a succession of western army camps. Wherever Porter found herself, she started a school and taught in it herself, as well as doing what she could to relieve the poor and needy. Porter, now in her late sixties, relinquished her responsibilities, especially during the hottest summer and the coldest winter months, and lived with some of her many friends in the Midwest, especially in Chicago and in Beloit, Wisconsin.

When Jeremiah Porter's health made it impossible for him to continue his duties as army chaplain, the Porters moved first to California and then retired to the home of their son Edwards in Detroit, Michigan. Eliza Porter remained active, visiting the sick, writing letters, and visiting friends. The Porters spent the coldest winter months of these years with friends in Texas, California, and Florida. In these places Eliza Porter established several Sunday schools and a kindergarten. The Porters celebrated their golden wedding anniversary in Detroit in 1885.

Eliza Porter became ill with pneumonia on Christmas Day 1887 in Santa Barbara, California. She died a week later, with her husband, daughter, and friends beside her. The funeral service was held in Chicago, and Porter was buried in Rosehill Cemetery. An elementary school in Chicago, Eliza Chappell School, is named in her honor.

Sustained and motivated by her religious convictions and undeterred by her physical condition, Eliza Chappell Porter brought education to the frontier as one of the first generation of female school teachers. Operating in the world of female benevolence that typified Protestant womanhood in the nineteenth century, Eliza Porter became an effective leader during the Civil War in the nursing and charity efforts of Union women.

Sources. The principal source for Eliza Chappell Porter's life is the book written by her daughter, which includes Porter's journals and letters: Mary H. Porter, *Eliza Chappell Porter: A Memoir* (1892). Other sources include Alfred T. Andreas, *History of Chicago* (1884); *NAW* (1980); and Mary Ann O'Ryan, "A Tale of Two Women: Life in the Old Northwest, 1830–1835," *Transactions of the Illinois State Historical Society*, 1989.

MARY ANN O'RYAN

PORTER, JULIA FOSTER
August 22, 1846–August 23, 1936
HOSPITAL FOUNDER, PHILANTHROPIST, ADMINISTRATOR

Julia Foster was born into one of Chicago's early settler families of prominence. Her father, John Herbert Foster, a physician and surgeon, moved from his native New Hampshire to Morgan County, Illinois, in 1832 to invest in land and to practice medicine. In 1835, he moved to Chicago to oversee the estate of his brother, who, in 1830, had purchased some of the original town lots of Chicago. This property became the source of the family's considerable wealth, and Foster soon gave up the practice of medicine to manage his real estate and other business investments. In 1840, Foster married Nancy Smith, also of New Hampshire. Julia was their third child. She had two sisters, Clara and Adele, and two brothers, John Herbert Foster Jr. and William, who died at nine months. Two other siblings died in early infancy.

Little is known about Julia Foster's childhood. Her parents were active in Unitarianism and belonged to Unity Church on the city's North Side. The family was part of Chicago's civic and business elite, and John Foster supported charitable and cultural institutions, including the Chicago Historical Society, the Humane Society, and the Half-Orphan Asylum. He also served on both the Chicago and state boards of education. When Julia Foster was thirteen, the Fosters moved to Clark and Belden,

then a wooded area at the north end of Lincoln Park. That year she won a Foster medal, given to grammar school students displaying outstanding merit. Her father had established the award fund in 1857 with a grant of one thousand dollars to the Chicago Board of Education.

In 1866, at the age of twenty, Julia Foster married the Reverend Edward Clark Porter, an Episcopal priest who had graduated from Yale University in 1858 and had then studied for a year at Andover (Massachusetts) Theological Seminary. He taught in schools across the Midwest and received a master's degree from Yale in 1861. That year he came to Chicago to teach metaphysics and English literature at Chicago High School. Three years later he was appointed a deacon at St. James (Episcopal) Church, Chicago, and then, a month before his marriage to Julia Foster, he was ordained a priest in September 1866.

In 1867, the Porters moved to Racine, Wisconsin, where Edward Porter was appointed rector of St. Luke's Church. Their sons were born in Racine, Maurice Foster Porter in 1868 and James Foster Porter in 1871. A popular rector, Porter and his congregation worked hard to complete a new church building begun several years earlier. In 1871, he and a group of parishioners founded St. Luke's Hospital, Racine's first private hospital. Initially located in a small house, St. Luke's began with four beds and offered free medical care to all needy patients.

Edward Porter's health began to fail, and in 1873 the family traveled through Europe for a year with the hope that his health would improve. The Porters visited Trier and Coblenz, Germany, and Brussels, Belgium. Julia Porter understood French, had an interest in Belgian lace, and wrote letters to her sister Adele that demonstrated her culture and education.

The next few years were traumatic and tragic for Julia Porter. First, in 1874, her father died of a head injury after a freak carriage accident. Then, despite the trip abroad, her husband's health continued to decline and he was forced to resign his rectorship at St. Luke's in early 1875. One year later, after four years of illness and suffering, he died of acute appendicitis at age thirty-six. Three months after her husband's death, Julia Porter, who had an inheritance from her father, acquired city lots in Racine that she donated for the permanent site of St. Luke's Hospital. She also furnished four beds in the Porter ward of the hospital and contributed financial support to the hospital for many years.

The widowed Porter and her two sons returned to Chicago in 1876 and joined the household of Julia's widowed mother. Five years later, the Foster-Porter household moved to Fullerton Avenue, near Julia Porter's sister, Adele. Julia Porter became involved in benevolent work and became a member of the Board of Lady Managers of the Chicago Nursery and Half-Orphan Asylum, an organization that assisted homeless and orphaned children. Her father had been a director.

In 1881, Porter's son Maurice died at age thirteen of acute rheumatism. After his death, Porter went into deep mourning for the rest of her life, dressing in black floor-length shirtwaists buttoned to her neck. Already shy and aloof, she became more and more reclusive, except for regular church attendance and her benevolent work with the Maurice F. Porter Memorial Hospital (now Children's Memorial Hospital) that she founded in 1882, in memory of her son. The hospital's mission was to provide free medical care to children between the ages of three and thirteen. Children with contagious diseases were not accepted nor were those with incurable or chronic conditions unless the medical staff foresaw permanent benefit from hospitalization. The hospital did not discriminate based on race, creed, or ability to pay.

Maurice F. Porter Memorial Hospital was located at Belden and Halsted streets, just a few blocks from the Porter home, on property her father had inherited in 1832 and deeded to Julia Foster Porter and her sisters. In addition, John Foster had left more than half his real property to his three daughters, making them wealthy women. Using part of her inheritance, Julia Foster Porter spent thirteen thousand dollars to remodel a small three-story residence as the first location of the children's hospital. She furnished it with eight beds and placed Truman W. Miller, a surgeon and the doctor who had attended her father and son in their last illnesses, in charge. "He remained associated with the hospital as doctor in charge and president of the small medical staff, until his death in 1900" (Greenwood, 448). Porter hired a matron and two assistants, thus beginning a long line of female matrons/superintendents that lasted for sixty years.

Almost immediately Porter began planning a larger facility. In 1883, she purchased nearby property for eight thousand dollars, and, three years later, a three-story, twenty-two-bed hospital was built at Fullerton Avenue. In its first ten years, the hospital cared for 232 patients. During that time, Julia Porter was not merely a benefactor but actually ran the hospital herself. Hers was the spirit that animated the place; the doctors were volunteers who worked part-time providing medical care but not administrating the staff. Porter hired the matrons and their assistants, but they most likely followed Porter's directions. The first matron was not a nurse and remained for only two years; subsequent matrons were trained as nurses, and the hospital went through a succession of them during its first twelve years.

Porter was also intimately involved in the day-to-day activities of the hospital, referred to by Chicagoans as "Mrs. Porter's hospital" (McCausland, 14). She probably visited daily, admitted and tended to patients, purchased supplies and medicine, hired and fired all staff, and did whatever was necessary to sustain the hospital. That Porter played such a large personal role in the early years of the hospital was not unusual. Many of Chicago's charitable institutions began with female volunteers who were extremely dedicated and personally involved in every aspect of management, including nursing, which in the late nineteenth century was just beginning to achieve a level of professionalization. Sewing, cooking, fund-raising, and purchasing of supplies were conventional activities undertaken by benevolent women who were inspired by their churches' understanding of what it meant to be a good Christian and by the moral literature of the period. At the same time, the women were increasingly aware of the social problems associated with the rapid growth of cities during the middle of the nineteenth century.

Julia Porter, in control of her considerable inheritance, personally provided for the hospital's operating expenses, amounting annually to two or three thousand dollars. Rather than give a fixed amount each year, Porter reviewed and controlled expenditures and paid only those she knew had been incurred. She was penurious and refused to allow expenses she thought unnecessary. At one point, for example, she was hesitant to purchase additional linens and washcloths, believing that patients could share one washcloth that would be rinsed out between baths.

Porter believed that medical treatment alone was not enough to care for or cure children. She stressed the need to consider the whole child and viewed social services to children as a necessary supplement to their medical treatment. She made sure patients had books, art, education, and entertainment. Her use of play as therapy became a hallmark of the later Children's Memorial Hospital.

After the hospital's first ten years, Porter's role in its day-to-day management began to decline. She was in her late forties and not as robust as she had been. Moreover, the hospital had changed. The number of patients began to increase dramatically. In 1892, the hospital admitted almost a third of the number admitted over the entire previous ten years. The medical staff had increased to six, though still part-time. At the same time, pediatrics finally had gained recognition as a separate medical field, prompting greater interest in the hospital from the medical community and the public. As a result, the hospital could no longer be viewed from Julia Porter's viewpoint as the "large house" (Greenwood, 449) for sick children. It was an expanding, more complex medical institution and Porter needed to share its management. In 1892, Julia Porter invited nine prominent women, including LOUISE deKOVEN BOWEN, to act as an advisory board of managers and assist her with the hospital. It was a working board that set the hospital routines, purchased supplies, controlled the budget, and tended to patients. Over the next two years, however, the board became increasingly concerned that the hospital's secluded location and Porter's "extreme modesty" (McCausland, 25) in promoting the hospital to a broader benevolent public was holding back its development.

To achieve wider recognition and financial support, the hospital was incorporated in 1894. An all-male board of directors was created, but its only responsibility was to appoint a board of lady managers. The lady managers were in charge of managing the hospital and appointing and defining the duties of the medical staff. Porter was an ex-officio member of the board of directors and a member of the board of lady managers. Many other charitable institutions, including the Half-Orphan Asylum, also had inactive male and active female boards, based on a belief that a male board was needed to lend legal and financial respectability to the institution.

The hospital prospered. Admissions increased; a kindergarten and nursing school were started and the age limit for patients was expanded from three to thirteen to two to fourteen years. During the same time, Julia Porter's active involvement declined even further. In 1896, she funded a six thousand dollar addition that enlarged the hospital to a fifty-bed capacity. She also stepped down as president of the board of lady managers, becoming honorary president. That same year, the hospital dropped Memorial from its name and became the Maurice F. Porter Free Hospital for Children. A year later, in 1898, Porter donated the hospital building and land to the board of directors. She still continued to pay the hospital's annual operating expenses and members of her family remained on the board.

Along with her hospital activities, Julia Porter adopted two girls, Charlotte and Frances, in response to a solicitation in an Episcopal journal for homes for orphans. In 1901, after the death of her mother, Julia Porter and her two adopted daughters moved to Lakeside (later Hubbard Woods, in the northern suburb of Winnetka). Julia Porter's son, James, an architect, had built two adjacent homes on a bluff overlooking Lake Michigan. One, a summer home, was remodeled as a permanent home for Porter and her daughters.

In 1903, the hospital directors and managers wrote Porter, asking for a final gift of seventy-five thousand dollars to endow a new building. The existing facility was aging, and the two boards believed that Chicago needed a more modern, better equipped children's hospital. They also suggested that its name be changed to Children's Memorial Hospital because they believed that Maurice F. Porter Free Hospital suggested a private, rather than a public, hospital and inhibited donations from the public. Julia Porter agreed. In 1908, the Maurice F. Porter Pavilion was built across from the existing hospital on Fullerton Avenue. The pavilion was razed in 1963 to make room for new research and other hospital facilities.

With her final gift in 1903, twenty-one years after the hospital was created, Julia Porter's long involvement ended. She spent the rest of her life in Lakeside, attending Christ Church, Winnetka, and occasionally traveling to her son's vacation home on Great Spruce Head Island, Maine. Those who met her during this time remember her as beautiful, religious, and reserved. Her grandchildren found her reticence and mourning attire daunting; they did, however, credit her with setting high standards of conduct for her son, their father, and instilling "truth, honesty, and fulfillment of promises" (Eliot Porter, 50) as the guiding principles of his life.

Julia Foster Porter died at home at age ninety. She had suffered from arteriosclerosis for several years and ultimately died of pneumonia and circulatory failure. She was not buried in the Foster family plot in Rosehill Cemetery. Instead, she was cremated, and her ashes were spread at Graceland Cemetery, Chicago.

Julia Porter's grief over the loss of her son Maurice was profound. Benevolent activity had been carefully inculcated in her at an early age through Christian doctrine and the examples of her parents' extensive involvement in civic and cultural affairs. The direction she took, however, in establishing a children's hospital, was a bold move for a woman of her era at a time when the field of pediatrics was largely undeveloped. Yet Porter was well aware of the severe health and social problems many children faced during the 1870s and 1880s in Chicago. Poverty and disease were widespread and childhood mortality rates were high. Chicago's lack of a hospital devoted exclusively to children was widely discussed and criticized. Porter's initiative is an example of how women's benevolence became linked with innovation and reform in the decades of the Civil War and its aftermath. Bolstered by successful charity endeavors, women realized they could play an expanded role outside the home.

Porter, like other benevolent women of her generation, created new structures that became the foundation of modern social welfare and philanthropic institutions.

Sources. Julia Foster Papers are privately held by Stephen Porter, Bellefonte, Pennsylvania, including two of his great-grandmother's letters, photographs, and other materials relating to Porter family history. Printed materials relating to the early operation of the Maurice F. Porter Memorial Hospital, including annual reports, are at the CHS. The most complete account of Julia Foster Porter and the hospital is found in Clare McCausland, *An Element of Love: A History of the Children's Memorial Hospital of Chicago, Illinois* (1981). Ronald D. Greenwood, "A Children's Hospital In Chicago 1882–1904," *Illinois Medical Journal*, November 1974, is helpful. For more about the Porter family, see two books by Eliot Porter, *Summer Island: Penobscot Country* (1966) and *Eliot Porter* (1987). Background on medicine in Chicago and charity can be found in Thomas Neville Bonner, *Medicine in Chicago 1850–1950: A Chapter in the Social and Scientific Development of a City* (1991), and Kathleen D. McCarthy, *Noblesse Oblige: Charity and Cultural Philanthropy in Chicago, 1849–1929* (1982).

PIPER WENTZ ROTHSCHILD

PRESCOTT, ANNABEL CAREY
February 13, 1894–July 29, 1982
EDUCATOR, CIVIL RIGHTS ADVOCATE

In a world of circumscribed roles and circumscribed thought for women and African Americans, Annabel Carey Prescott stands out as a creative, politically astute champion of quality education for the children of Chicago's public schools. Born in Athens, Georgia, to Archibald J. and Elizabeth (Davis) Carey, Annabel Carey came to Chicago with her family in 1898, when her father, the child of ex-slaves, was called to serve as pastor of Quinn Chapel, the city's largest African Methodist Episcopal (AME) Church. The Careys became one of the most prestigious old-settler black families of Chicago with Archibald Carey's rise to bishop in the AME church. Annabel Carey's brother, Archibald J. Carey Jr., a lawyer, was elected twice to the Chicago City Council. The Careys were leaders in the black community during the first and again during the second great migration of rural Blacks from the South.

Annabel Carey attended public schools in Chicago, Doolittle Elementary and Wendell Phillips High School. She graduated from the University of Chicago in 1916 and received an M.A. in education from DePaul University. In 1922 she began her teaching career at Doolittle Elementary. Two years later she married Patrick Benjamin Prescott, who had come from New Orleans to Chicago in 1910. Prescott had been transferred from the U.S. Postal Service in New Orleans to a position in Chicago, where he also worked as a newspaperman, writing the "Grist Mill" column for the *Whip* newspaper. The Prescotts were part of the professional class in an era when that was exceptional for Blacks; both had fathers with successful professional careers and involvement in Republican party politics. Annabel Prescott continued to teach, and Patrick Prescott entered John Marshall Law School. After graduation, Prescott's first law partner was Joseph Bibb, editor and publisher of the *Whip*. In 1927 Mayor William Hale Thompson appointed Prescott assistant corporation counsel. Annabel Prescott's father, Archibald Carey, "exercised considerable power in Republican circles" (Gosnell, 98). Although he was not a politician, he had used his influence from a prestigious pulpit in the black community to get out the vote for Thompson.

Annabel Prescott first taught French and Spanish and then served as dean of girls at Wendell Phillips High School. In 1935 she became assistant principal of DuSable High School. Although the Prescotts were highly educated professionals with their careers in place and their social position in the black community assured, they lived in an era in which possibilities for black Americans were severely limited and based upon an ability to assimilate—to look, act, and talk like the majority culture. Even within the black community itself, there were class distinctions based on color prejudice. Actress-singer and community leader Etta Moten Barnett related how, in the 1930s, "light-skinned blacks had a better time of it" (interview with Barnett). Light-skinned blacks, in Chicago, in the early and mid-twentieth century, were privileged if they behaved "correctly." Prescott was taught to behave in a genteel fashion for just this reason, so she could assimilate. Nevertheless, she was not to let this situation muzzle her commitments. There were numerous sororities, bridge clubs, and dances for middle-class Blacks who distinguished themselves from lower-class Blacks by avoiding cheap taverns and rhythm and blues music. Annabel Prescott had light skin and European features. "She might have been considered a 'white acting' person," Barnett recalled, "but in reality she had a way that showed empathy with all people" (interview).

Prescott was arbitrarily transferred from DuSable without notice on the first day of the 1943 school year. She left an all-black school in a mixed neighborhood (Grand Boulevard) of upwardly mobile as well as poor people to be assistant principal at Medill High School on Chicago's West Side. Prescott taught there until the school's consolidation with McKinley High School in 1948, when she was made assistant principal in charge of the new freshman-sophomore Cregier Branch of Crane Technical High School.

Annabel Prescott's father, Archibald Carey, had been part of the black leadership in Chicago during the first wave of migration from the South. Carey and other educated "old settlers" worried about the racial tensions that were emerging with poor, uneducated, southern Blacks arriving in great numbers. With the second wave of migration, Annabel Prescott found herself in a challenging position. Her husband was a municipal judge appointed by Republican Governor Dwight H. Green. She had enjoyed a career in the public schools without controversy. Now she found herself on the West Side, no longer sheltered by her social circles. In addition, Patrick Prescott died of a heart attack in 1945 after a physical breakdown that forced him to leave his position as the midwest chair of the Republican National Committee in 1944.

As assistant principal, part of Prescott's mandate was to deal with rising racial tension in the school and neighboring communities surrounding the newly constructed Cregier Branch of Crane Technical High School. It had an enrollment of African American, Italian, and Mexican students from the racially changing nearby neighborhoods. In addition to poverty, the West Side was experiencing serious racial tension as the second wave of black migrants from the South settled there. The other ethnic groups attending Cregier came from neighborhoods resisting integration. Schoolteachers and administrators faced the possibility of fights, if not of all-out race riots. Prescott determined that racial tension in the community could be overcome and behaviors changed. Through long hours of intervention, she was able to make the initial transition a peaceful one.

Prescott was, at this time, part of an educational reform movement in the Chicago public school system and advocated using the schools to teach democracy. Prescott saw Cregier as a potential model for breaking down the wall of misunderstanding and discrimination that so effectively made Chicago a segregated city and the United States a land of discrimination against nonwhite people. She brought to her job a sensitivity to the cultures of immigrants and rural migrants. African American migrants came north to escape the rejection in employment, housing, and public accommodations they experienced in the South. "As integrated schools turn all black," she later explained, "through white flight, black children feel that same rejection, and their resentment turns into an 'I dare you to teach me anything' attitude" (Prescott, "A Program," 137). Mexican immigrants, Prescott found, had similar experiences. She condemned the practice of passively permitting this "undemocratic, prejudicial state of affairs (ghettoization of schools) to be acted out without a challenge" ("A Program," 126) from the educational system.

Prescott regarded Cregier as a school with a mission to show the world that segregation could be untaught in public education. She enlisted all the resources she could muster to reduce white flight from Cregier, encouraging teachers to feel a special commitment to breaking down the hostility toward the system felt by immigrant and black children. She developed and conducted in-service workshops on educating children from nonwhite immigrant cultures. Teachers were given pep talks about the value of their work. In 1951 she asked for and obtained assistance from the University of Chicago so that she could hold community workshops on reducing prejudice. That year and the following she took a leave of absence and began graduate work at Columbia University in the field of intergroup relations, obtaining a master's degree. On her return, the Cregier Branch was selected as a pilot school in intergroup relations.

Reform-minded Superintendent of Schools Herold Hunt advocated the kinds of programs Prescott initiated. To aid her work and that of others in the system, he convinced the Chicago Board of Education to make it harder to get permissive transfers, commonly used by white parents to pull their children out of integrating schools. Prescott advocated pay incentives for teachers at "tough" schools. Failing to get them, she obtained "recognition" incentives for teachers. Prescott unsuccessfully worked to get rezoning of gerrymandered school attendance boundaries that had been configured to preserve segregation. Prescott argued the benefits of the Cregier program and tried to sell the idea of integration to local community groups. The temporary stabilization of Cregier was a significant achievement in cooperative effort. The cooperative mode was her style of democratic leadership. Prescott became a key person in Superintendent Hunt's administration, serving as a member of the Currriculum Council. She also was a member of Hunt's seminar group working on the preparation of a human relations manual for the use of all school board employees. Prescott served on the Education Committee of the Mayor's Commission on Human Relations and was an advisory member of the Executive Committee of the Women's Council on Fair Education Practices. She worked closely with the National Conference of Christians and Jews, with the Anti-Defamation League, and with the Urban League in helping coordinate their educational programs with that of the public schools.

Superintendent Hunt came under an intense redbaiting attack from the old guard and those forces that benefited from segregation and the patronage system of the schools. Labeled a communist by the *Chicago Tribune* because he had attended Columbia University, which was identified as communist-led, Hunt was on his way out by 1953. That year Prescott began a doctoral program at Columbia University with Hunt's encouragement. Based on her work at Cregier, she was offered a yearlong fellowship in intergroup relations at Columbia University's School of Education. There she worked with Martin P. Chworowsky. Her experience and research propelled her into the forefront of human relations activity, and she was asked to speak or lead discussions at workshops held at National Teachers College (now National-Louis University), Evanston, Illinois; the University of Illinois; and the University of Minnesota. She was codirector of the Northwestern University Summer Workshop in Human Relations in the 1950s.

In 1954 Prescott received the Thomas Wright Award from the Chicago Commission on Human Relations for her pilot program in human relations at Cregier High School. She completed her Ph.D. degree in 1956, writing her dissertation on the work she had undertaken at Cregier, "A Program in Inter-Group Relations for the Cregier High School in Chicago." Herold Hunt's successor, Benjamin Willis, appointed Prescott teacher in charge of the Committee on Human Relations of the Chicago Public Schools. Benjamin Willis was leading the fight to save segregated schools in Chicago. Appointed by the mayor with help from segregationist aldermen, he wanted Prescott, like her mentor Herold Hunt, out. He took away her staff and her budget. However, he could not get her removed. She fought on.

In 1956 Prescott was awarded the Distinguished Citizen citation by the University of Chicago Alumni Association. In February of 1956 the *Chicago Herald American* featured her as "Woman of the Week." Two years later Prescott was the recipient of the Teacher Achievement Award presented by the Mid-West Division of B'nai B'rith Women. That same year she received the Phi Delta Kappa Award for human rights work. One year later, her retirement party was hosted by leading organizations involved in interracial justice: the American Jewish Committee, Anti-Defamation League of B'nai B'rith, Chicago Committee on Human Relations, Chicago Urban League, Citizens School Committee, Illinois Committee on Human Relations, and the National Conference of Christians and Jews.

In her later years Prescott continued to support human relations and social justice projects, serving on the board of the Edwin Markham Community Center and working with the Beacon Neighborhood Settlement House. She was appointed to the Illinois Board of Junior Colleges in 1965, chaired the human rights committee of the Girl Scouts of Chicago, and was a member of the United Church Women of Greater Chicago. She quietly supported the school boycott of the 1960s, which pushed to oust Benjamin Willis from his job and which was aimed at integrating the schools, an action Willis ardently opposed. She held her tongue when asked to condemn radical black youth. Annabel Carey Prescott died at age eighty-eight and was buried at Lincoln Cemetery, Chicago.

Prescott attempted to implement the highest values of democracy and public education at a time when many professional educators and politicians were unwilling to go against the prevailing prejudice in society. Valuing students from all backgrounds, Prescott began the work of desegregation in the hearts and minds of Chicagoans and midwesterners.

Sources. The Patrick B. and Annabel Carey Prescott papers are available at the CHS. The Archibald J. Carey Sr. and Jr. papers are also at the CHS and provide background for the life of Annabel Carey Prescott. Biographical information on Prescott is found in an unpublished obituary at the Unity Funeral Parlor, Chicago. Jon F. Rice interviewed Lucille Boysaw—who worked with Prescott—on July 11, 1994, and Etta Moten Barnett on August 15, 1994. Prescott's "A Program in Inter-Group Relations for the Cregier High School in Chicago" (Ph.D. diss., Columbia Univ., 1956) clarifies her motives in creating the human relations program at Cregier and later at the Chicago Board of Education. Mary Herrick's *The Chicago Schools: A Social and Political History* (1971) provides useful context for Prescott's work. Harold F. Gosnell, *Negro Politicians: The Rise of Negro Politics in Chicago* (1953), is helpful for information about the Careys.

JON RICE

PRICE, DOROTHY
November 12, 1899–November 17, 1980
ENDOCRINOLOGIST, ZOOLOGIST

Dorothy Price was a pioneer researcher in neuroendocrinology, the zoological field dealing with the physiology of interaction between endocrines—hormones—and the central nervous system. Her research in 1930 on the feedback mechanism between the pituitary gland and male hormones established physiological principles that led to the development of contraceptive pills. She later did important research on fetal sex differentiation, continuing her focus on the study of reproductive endocrinology.

Price was born in Aurora, Illinois, and attended the University of Chicago, majoring in zoology. She received a B.S. degree *cum laude* at the end of 1922 and immediately embarked on graduate study. Little is known about her family and early life. In the summer of 1923, while at her family's summer home, she "made a decision" that, according to Price, "shaped my future scientific career" ("Feedback Control," 220). Because of family financial difficulties, she decided to seek a job instead of returning to graduate school.

Frank R. Lillie, chairman of the zoological department and a researcher on fetal sex differentiation, offered Price a position as a technician and assistant in a "developing research program of studies on sex" ("Feedback Control," 220). She did not return to graduate studies for several years. Instead, she became involved in groundbreaking research in what would become the field of neuroendocrinology. In 1923 she quickly became an assistant to Professor Carl Moore, with whom she had studied embryology. Moore was doing research on endocrines in reproductive physiology. Beginning as a histological technician and an assistant in hormone research on animals, Price "gradually became a research partner . . . with whom Moore discussed his research problems and results" ("Feedback Control," 221). She read research papers that he planned to publish and suggested corrections.

In the 1920s Price found herself in the midst of exciting research on the physiology of reproduction, as scientists made new findings on sex hormones—estrogens, progestins, and androgens. Most science researchers were men, and Price was aware of being treated unequally because she was a woman. Her salary and work status were below her responsibilities. She perceived Moore as "a male chauvinist" and felt that "he did not realize the depth of his prejudice." Her experience showed her that "women (with the possible exception of a few including me on *some* occasions) were not really to be considered scientifically equal to men" ("Feedback Control," 221).

As Moore's research assistant, she worked with him in 1929 and 1930 on experiments in which they injected hormones into animals. They found that injections of male hormones, which added hormones to those produced by reproductive glands, had harmful effects on testicular weight, but they could not interpret the results. Price explained how she found the answer. "After dinner . . . I sat down at my desk and thought! . . . Then, quite suddenly a plausible explanation occurred to me" ("Feedback Control," 228). Scientists knew that the anterior pituitary gland controlled sex hormone secretion. She concluded that the pituitary would cease to release gonadotropic hormone if blood levels of hormone were increased. This theory, explaining how levels of hormones in the blood are physiologically controlled, came to be known as the Moore-Price negative feedback system or Moore-Price Law. In later years, she described her elation, declaring, "On that night in May 1930 I had my first taste of the joy of scientific discovery." The next morning, when she gave Moore her solution to the "riddle," he thought about it and "soon he began to consider it a brilliant idea" ("Feedback Control," 230). Price and Moore published their findings in two articles, "The Question of Sex Hormone Antagonisms" (1930) and "Gonad Hormone Functions, and the Reciprocal Influence between Gonads and Hypophysis with Its Bearing on the Problem of Sex Hormone Antagonism" (1932). Price reported that she and Moore, from their research on male animals, "were the first to propose a reciprocal relationship between the gonads and the pituitary . . . and to visualize how a feedback must be operating to control hormone levels in the blood and effect cyclic events in females" ("Feedback Control," 235). Others then developed the research on females. The principle of a feedback mechanism between the anterior pituitary and the ovary was important in the development of contraceptive pills that use estrogen to suppress ovulation. The pills first became available in the United States by prescription in 1960.

Price went on to other research in endocrinology and the physiology of reproduction. She completed the Ph.D. degree in zoology in 1935 with dissertation research on androgens and the development of the prostate gland. Remaining at the University of Chicago in the Department of Zoology, Price was appointed a research associate and stayed at that rank for twelve years, despite her experience and accomplishments. In 1947 she became an assistant professor and was promoted to associate professor three years later. She did not become a full professor until 1958.

Dorothy Price did not marry and remained close to family members. In 1940, and perhaps earlier, she was living in the University of Chicago's Hyde Park neighborhood with her mother, Anna A. Price, and her niece, Eleanor Burton, whose mother was Price's sister. A lover of music, Price collected folk and recorder music and played the recorder.

From the 1940s on, she moved into new areas of endocrinology. In 1944 she coauthored a report with Evelina Ortiz, "The Relation of Age to Reactivity in the Reproductive System of the Rat." She later became involved in research on fetal sex differentiation and secretions of fetal gonads. Her coresearchers in this work were Evelina Ortiz at the University of Puerto Rico and Johanna Zaaijer at the University of Leiden in The Netherlands. They published a number of papers in a relationship that she considered a "long-term, long-distance collaboration between Chicago, Leiden, and Puerto Rico" (quoted in Foreman, 544).

In addition to her work as a researcher, Price was active in publishing in zoology. From 1958 to 1969 she was a department editor at *Encyclopaedia Britannica*. She served on the editorial board of the periodical *Physiological Zoology* beginning in 1956 and of the *Journal of General and Comparative Endocrinology* between 1961 and 1969. Her professional memberships included the American Society of Zoologists, the Association for the Study of Internal Secretions, and the Endocrine Society.

She retired as Professor Emeritus in 1965 and was a visiting professor the following year at Johns Hopkins University. She served as visiting research professor at the University of Leiden and the University of Puerto Rico. Price continued to do research with Ortiz and Zaaijer at Leiden, where she had an appointment as Boerhaave Professor for the academic year 1967–68. In 1967 she was awarded the Medal of Honor for Distinguished Service to the University of Leiden. Four years later, her alma mater gave her the University of Chicago Professional Achievement Award for Alumni. In the course of her career, Price published about seventy research papers. She continued to do research full time almost to the end of her life. She died in Leiden at eighty-one years of age.

During her lifetime, Price received widespread recognition for her work on the negative feedback theory and for her "pioneer studies on embryonic sexual differentiation" (press release, December 1980). An early researcher in the field of neuroendocrinology, Dorothy Price found an important principle that would be used by the next generation of scientists in successful research for the production of oral contraceptives.

Sources. Information on Dorothy Price's research career appears in the handwritten *curriculum vitae*, "Dorothy Price," November 1, 1940, and in a press release on Price, "For Release: Immediate, The University of Chicago," typescript, December 3, 1980, both in the Archival Biographical File, UC Spec. Coll. Price provides detailed discussion of her research in her chapter, "Feedback Control of Gonadal and Hypophyseal Hormones: Evolution of the Concept," in *Pioneers in Neuroendocrinology*, ed. Joseph Meites, Bernard T. Donovan, and Samuel M. McCann (1975). Her research articles include Carl R. Moore and Dorothy Price, "The Question of Sex Hormone Antagonism," *Proceed-*

ings of the Society for Experimental Biology and Medicine, vol. 28, 1930; Moore and Price, "Gonad Hormone Functions, and the Reciprocal Influence between Gonads and Hypophysis with Its Bearing on the Problem of Sex Hormone Antagonism," *American Journal of Anatomy*, vol. 50, 1932; and Dorothy Price, Evelina Ortiz, and Johanna J. P. Zaaijer, "Organ Culture Studies of Hormone Secretion in Endocrine Glands of Fetal Guinea Pigs: III. The Relation of Testicular Hormone to Sex Differentiation of the Reproductive Ducts," *Anatomical Record*, January 1967. Price and H. Guy Williams-Ashman have a chapter, "The Accessory Reproductive Glands of Mammals," in *Sex and Internal Secretions*, ed. W. C. Young (1961). Her work on negative feedback is discussed in Darhl Foreman, "The Concept of Negative Feedback—Moore and Price," *Endocrinology*, August 1992. Price is listed in *American Men of Science* (1967). For discussion of the Moore-Price Law as a breakthrough in research on the contraceptive pill, see S. R. M. Reynolds, "Letters," in *Science*, March 17, 1967, and S. R. M. Reynolds, Carl G. Hartman, "Letters," *Science*, June 16, 1967. An obituary appears in *CT*, November 21, 1980.

ADELE HAST

PRICE, FLORENCE BEATRICE SMITH
April 9, 1888–June 3, 1953
COMPOSER, PIANIST, ORGANIST

An African American composer of classical music, Florence Smith Price received international recognition for her works. Born in Little Rock, Arkansas, she was the second daughter and third child of James H. and Florence Irene (Gulliver) Smith. Her father was a dentist. He later owned a dental office in Chicago, wrote novels, and painted in oils. A talented soprano and pianist, Florence Gulliver was an elementary school music teacher in her home town of Indianapolis, Indiana. Through her mother's classical influence and personal teachings, Florence Smith became productive in the field of music at an early age. When she was four, Smith made her first public appearance. At the age of eleven, she published her first musical composition, and at sixteen, she was paid for one of her compositions.

Florence Smith attended a black segregated elementary school in Little Rock, where Charlotte Stephens, a black teacher who had studied at Oberlin College and had training in music, was her teacher. In 1902 she graduated as valedictorian from Capitol High School in Little Rock. Subsequently, she was accepted at the New England Conservatory of Music in Boston, Massachusetts, where her nationality was listed as Mexican and her hometown as Pueblo, Mexico, presumably to disguise her racial identity. While at the conservatory, Florence Smith performed in two programs as a pianist and as an organist. She graduated in 1906 with a diploma that qualified her as an organ soloist and piano teacher. From 1906 to 1912 she held teaching positions at three different schools: Arkadelphia Academy in Cotton Plant, Arkansas; Shorter College in North Little Rock, Arkansas; and Clark University in Atlanta, Georgia, where she was head of the music department. In September 1912 she married Thomas J. Price, an attorney in Little Rock.

During the first fifteen years of their marriage, Florence Smith Price and her husband had three children—a boy named Tommy, who died in infancy, and two girls, Florence Louise and Edith. In memory of her son, Price set to music the words of Julia Johnson Davis's poem "To My Little Son." Along with her re-

FIG. 97. *Florence Beatrice Smith Price, musician and composer of symphonies, concertos, and choral works.*

sponsibilities as a wife and mother, Price gave private lessons in both organ and piano.

Racial problems continually affected Price's life. While she resided in Little Rock, she applied for membership to the Arkansas Music Teachers Association and was denied because of her race. Lynchings and other racial incidents prompted the Prices to move to Chicago in 1926, where they initially lived with Estelle Bonds, a well-known organist and music teacher. Leaving the South during this period of racial strife provided Florence Price with the opportunity to expand her musical career in a city where black people had excelled in classical music.

In the first decades of the twentieth century, African American male composers achieved public fame for their works. In Chicago from 1914 to 1916 there were annual "All Colored Composer's Concerts," usually held at Orchestra Hall. At these concerts black women and men performed as soloists, violinists, pianists, and accompanists, and the compositions of black male composers were featured.

In 1925 and 1927 Price won recognition for her own compositions, "Memories of Dixieland" and "In the Land of Cotton," respectively, in a contest sponsored by the black magazine *Opportunity*. Then, in 1928, Price's piano piece, *At the Cotton*

Gin, was awarded a prize by the publisher G. Schirmer; the composition was submitted by her husband without her knowledge. By this time she was making plans with another publisher to issue some teaching pieces for piano. She also wrote musical jingles for radio commercials.

During the decade of the 1930s, Florence Price's public career soared. In 1931, she received an honorable mention in the Rodman Wanamaker Foundation competition. A year later, she won two Wanamaker awards: $500 for her "Symphony in E Minor," which later became her most prominent symphonic composition, and $250 for a piano sonata. The third part of the award was won by one of Florence Price's black female students, MARGARET BONDS, daughter of Estelle Bonds, for her song "The Sea Ghost." After winning both the Wanamaker Award and the National Association of Negro Musicians' Scholarship in 1932, Price was noticed by Frederick Stock, the Chicago Symphony Orchestra conductor, who featured Price's "Symphony in E Minor" at Orchestra Hall in June 1933. It was the first time that a black woman's composition was performed by a prominent American symphony orchestra. That summer, Stock conducted Price's symphony again at the Century of Progress Exposition, where Price performed her own works in a program that featured her music.

A year later, at the commencement exercise for the Chicago Musical College, Price performed her piano composition "Concerto in D Minor." During the same year, Price's "Concerto in F Minor" was performed by the Women's Symphony Orchestra of Chicago in Grant Park with Margaret Bonds as piano soloist. In the 1930s British conductor Sir John Barbirolli requested that Florence Price compose music for strings that reflected the style of black American spirituals. She accepted the challenge and Barbirolli conducted the musical piece, which was a suite, in Manchester, England.

By 1940 Florence Price was a member of the American Society of Composers, Authors, and Publishers (ASCAP). Joining this organization made her larger works accessible in manuscript form. She further disseminated her works by permitting such artists as Marian Anderson to perform her spiritual arrangement My Soul's Been Anchored in de Lord. In November 1940, the Works Progress Administration Symphony Orchestra in Detroit, Michigan, performed Price's "Symphony No. 3 in C Minor."

During this period Price pursued graduate studies at the Chicago Musical College, Chicago Teachers College, University of Chicago, and the American Conservatory of Music in Chicago. In 1942 her husband passed away, and Price continued to compose music and to perform.

Her music, numbering more than five hundred works, ranged from teaching pieces to complex symphonic works. Price wrote some of her own lyrics, such as "Resignation," while other works were developed for particular poems. Her musical piece Songs to A Dark Virgin (1941) is set to the poem of the same title by Langston Hughes. She dedicated this work to her daughter Florence Louise. In 1937, Carl Fischer published Price's Song for Snow for mixed chorus with piano accompaniment. Elizabeth Coatsworth had written and published the lyrics in 1934.

Florence Price's music belonged to a school of black nationalist composers who were born before 1900. These composers, most of whom were men, were known for using musical styles that were characteristic of their own black folk expression. In some compositions Price reflected the spirit and rhythm of black music, using it imaginatively to structure folk expression in a classical framework. She was the first composer to use juba rhythms in a symphony. Juba, an African-derived antebellum slave folk dance, featured foot tapping, hand clapping, and thigh slapping to different rhythms. Price used this style in the third movement of her "Symphony in E Minor" (1931) and in a piece called "Silk Hat and Walking Cane" from Dances in the Canebrakes (1953).

My Soul's Been Anchored in de Lord is recognized as her most famous spiritual; she initially arranged it for voice and piano when it was published in 1937 by Gamble Hinged Music Company. Her arrangements were recorded by singers Marian Anderson and Leontyne Price. Price's use of varied rhythms and rich harmony is found also in a selection of Two Traditional Negro Spirituals, "I am Bound for the Kingdom" and "I'm Workin' on my Buildin'," published in 1949 by Handy Brothers Music Company.

One of her most famous works, classified as piano etudes (study pieces) because the individual pieces were written originally for solo piano, stands out as black folk music. This collection of short pieces, entitled Three Little Negro Dances, includes "Hoe Cake," "Rabbit Foot," and "Ticklin' Toes." All three pieces are lively and fast, but their basic structural features are distinctly different. In "Ticklin' Toes," Price incorporated juba rhythms. Price also arranged these pieces for two pianos. Published originally in 1933, these pieces were later arranged again by the publisher for band music in standard and symphonic form. The United States Marine Band and New York Symphonic Band have played these works.

Florence Price continued to use her training and skills as an organist. A member of the Chicago Club of Women Organists, she maintained an active position in work known then as theater organ, which covered such areas as radio broadcasting and church organ work. A friend, Helen Westbrook, who worked as a staff organist for radio station WGN in Chicago, used Price's material in her programs. Price also belonged to the National Association for American Composers and Conductors and the Musicians Club for Women.

In the spring of 1953, Price was planning to travel to Europe to perform. In that same year, however, after a short illness, she died of a stroke at St. Luke's Hospital in Chicago. Her funeral was held at Grace Presbyterian Church and she was buried at Lincoln Cemetery.

In December 1954 some of her works were performed in Europe at the University of Grenoble, France. Eleven years after her death, a Chicago elementary school was named in her honor, and at the dedication ceremony Florence Price's "Violin Concerto No. 2" was played.

Florence Price was a prolific composer of classical music for concert performance. She left a legacy as one of the first and most outstanding African American female composers of the black nationalist school of classical music.

Sources. Florence Price Papers and Musical Scores are located at the Spec. Coll. Dept. of the Univ. of Arkansas Libraries in Fayetteville,

Arkansas. The collection includes published and unpublished works, personal letters from the 1930s to the 1950s to and from Florence Price's colleagues and acquaintants, diary entries in the late 1940s, and programs of concerts of her works. Scores of Price's compositions are found in *Music of Florence Beatrice Price*, series 1, ed. Calvert Johnson (Fayetteville, Arkansas: ClarNan Editions, 1993). Some of her works are listed in *Black Music in the Harlem Renaissance* (1990); Mildred Denby Green, *Black Women Composers: A Genesis* (1983), which also discusses her work; and Ora Williams, *American Black Women in the Arts and Social Sciences: A Bibliographic Survey* (1973). Brief sketches of Florence Price's life and work can be found in *BWA*; *Baker's Biographical Dictionary of Musicians* (1992); *ASCAP Biographical Dictionary* (1980); *NAW* (1980); Raoul Abdul, *Blacks in Classical Music* (1977); and *History of the Musicians Club of Women* (1975), a self-published handbook available at CHS. Detailed information about her life and work appear in Rae Linda Brown, "William Grant Still, Florence Price, and William Dawson: Echoes of the Harlem Renaissance," in *Black Music in the Harlem Renaissance* (1990); Rae Brown's "Selected Orchestral Music of Florence B. Price (1888–1953): In the Context of Her Life and Work" (Ph.D. diss., Yale Univ.,1987); Mildred Derby Green's thesis, "A Study of the Lives and Works of Five Black Women Composers in America" (Ph.D. diss., Univ. of Oklahoma, 1975); and Barbara Garvey Jackson, "Florence Price, Composer," *Black Perspective in Music*, Spring 1977. Obituaries can be found in *Etude* (August 1953); *Musical America* (July 1953); *Musical Courier* (July 1953); and the *Chicago Defender* (June 1953). Cambria Records of Lomita, California, issued eight of Florence Price's works on *Black Diamonds: Althea Waites Plays Music by African-African Composers* (1993) as well as *Cotton Dance for Piano, Dances in the Canebrakes for Piano* (1953), *The Old Boatman for Piano* (1932), *Sonata in E for Piano* (1932), and *Dark Virgin CD 1037*.

GLORIA YVONNE

PRINZ, TOBEY SILBERT SCHEIN
November 3, 1911–June 26, 1984
TEACHER, UNION LEADER, COMMUNITY ACTIVIST

Tobey Silbert Schein Prinz, Chicago neighborhood activist, was the daughter of Abraham and Mollie Silbert, Lithuanian Jewish immigrants, who came to the United States in 1903. Silbert's father, a suitcase maker who was active in labor union politics, and her mother, a homemaker, had four daughters, Mae, Frieda, Tobey, and Zelda. Although her father practiced no religion, he attended the Jewish People's Institute (later the Chicago Hebrew Institute) in the Near West Side neighborhood where the family resided. There he earned an eighth-grade certificate. While Tobey Silbert's mother attended a synagogue and centered her interests on home and children, her father believed in trade unionism and focused his interests on world politics.

Even though the family moved often, mostly on the Near West Side and eventually to the Northwest Side, Silbert thrived, establishing varied friendships, excelling in academics and in athletics, particularly swimming, field, and track. Through the Jewish People's Institute, she belonged to the Girl Scouts and the Helping Girls, where she spent time each week bathing children in the institute's day nursery. Her duties at home, even when she was just ten or eleven years old, included accompanying her crippled mother to a free clinic. There they endured long waits and callous treatment from medical personnel who made no effort to listen to or communicate with patients, some of whom had language difficulties. Silbert became angry at this disrespectful treatment and later recalled that such incidents fu-

eled in her a lifelong desire for fair play in the treatment of people.

Silbert finished high school in three years and entered Chicago Normal School (later Chicago State University) with a major in physical education. After receiving a teaching certificate in 1931, she enrolled at Northwestern University, Evanston. She planned to become a social worker or a physiotherapist. The country was in the throes of the Great Depression and she needed to get a job. She continued at Northwestern part-time and, with her habitual energy and commitment, rose at 6 A.M. to attend classes in Evanston, then traveled to Garfield Park on Chicago's West Side, where she worked as a playground teacher until 9 P.M. She returned home by 10 P.M. to eat and do homework. A weekend job helped supplement her income. She joined the Playground Teachers' Union.

Graduating in 1934 from Northwestern with a B.A. degree, she first worked as a substitute teacher. Two years later she was assigned to a school to teach physical education. She joined the Elementary School Union, one of many unions representing various groups of Chicago teachers. At the time, the unions seemed unable to improve teaching conditions or pay. Silbert began to work with other union members who shared her interest in strengthening workers' organizations.

In 1936 Silbert took a vacation that proved fateful. Traveling alone to western Canada and staying in the resort town of Lake Louise, Banff, she met some people who were recruiting volunteers to fight on the side of the Loyalists in the Civil War in Spain. Prior to this chance meeting, "[she] didn't even know there was a war in Spain" (Prinz interview transcript, 1983, 10). Impressed with their message, she began to involve herself with world affairs. Back in Chicago she met socialists and communists who were involved in teachers' union activities and who supported the anti-Franco workers' militias in Spain. Silbert was asked to organize a teachers' committee for medical aid to Spain (Teachers' Committee Against War & Fascism) and to coordinate house parties and rallies for fund-raising efforts. In 1937 she accompanied a friend to a workers' meeting and joined the Communist Party (CP), which she felt shared her own commitment to create economic security and social justice for all people and which encouraged activism locally and internationally. CP membership in the United States reached sixty-five thousand in the mid-1930s, and the party "attained a very wide following in many sections of American life. Providing national, regional and local leadership of many important industrial unions as well as liberal, student, and cultural organizations, Communists and 'fellow travelers' served as a dynamic wedge of radicalism within the dominant New Deal liberalism" (*Encyclopedia of the American Left*, 151) of the Great Depression era.

During the depression, the Chicago schools were cutting back on music, art, and physical education instruction and eliminating kindergarten programs. It was a difficult time; and Silbert, who mostly taught the children of the poor, "could put [her] hand on poverty" (Prinz interview transcript, 16). She and other public school teachers were paid with scrip, a substitute for currency that was frequently not accepted by landlords and shop owners. When accepted, scrip was often discounted. Silbert, then twenty-five years old, was elected secretary of her union. She was actively involved in 1936–37 in the movement to consolidate the power of organized teachers; she encouraged the merger of the various American Federation of Teachers (AFT) locals in Chicago as they came together to form the Chicago Teachers Union (CTU), becoming Local #1 of the AFT. On October 28, 1937, Tobey Silbert was one of twenty-two signatories of the CTU charter.

Silbert's political views were strengthened in 1939 when, with war looming, she sailed for Europe, spending a month in the Soviet Union, and then visiting family members in Poland for almost two months. In the Soviet Union, Silbert was part of a tour group that included a number of Chicago teachers and three students from Antioch College. In a side trip to Poland, where she traveled on her own, she met her uncles, aunts, and cousins. Anti-Semitism was high, the economy was in poor shape, and for Silbert it was a "horrible experience" (Prinz interview transcript, 13). Heartbroken to see her relatives struggling to survive, frightened for their future, she left as much of her clothing and money as she could. She traveled to Switzerland, where she reconnected with the tour. Only three members of Silbert's family in Poland survived the war.

From Switzerland, Silbert and her companions traveled to France, where they were able to make contact with a "French organization that . . . [provided] food and medicine for the children of the [Loyalist] Spanish refugees" (Prinz interview transcript, 14). As Americans, they had an entrée to this camp through one of the tour members, an Antioch College student whose father was a minister active in the Spanish campaign. They traveled in southern France in the delivery trucks bringing food and other supplies to the camps, obtaining "permission from every [town] mayor" (Prinz interview transcript, 14) to enter the local camp. Silbert observed that the French who were participating in the effort to aid the Spanish refugee camps frequently were communists. At the same time, she was dismayed at the neutrality of the western European democracies and the United States and their refusal to intervene on behalf of the Spanish anti-fascist Loyalists. When she returned home, she worked to raise money to send an ambulance to the area. (Chicago social worker and journalist THYRA EDWARDS also organized pro-Loyalist activities to raise funds to purchase an ambulance.) During World War II Silbert attended an international conference in Mexico City, Mexico, where she met some of the Spanish refugees who were living there.

Tobey Silbert married Lester Schein in 1943. They had two sons, Howard, born in 1944, and Frederick, born in 1948. The family lived in the Rogers Park neighborhood of Chicago, and Tobey Schein continued her activism. "She was always in motion and she never stopped" (interview) recalled her son, Howard Schein. She continued to teach and was active in the Progressive Party campaign in 1948 to elect Henry Wallace president of the United States. Wallace was supported by many in the American Left, including the CP. It was an important election: the regular Democrats supported Harry S. Truman, and the Republican Party endorsed Thomas E. Dewey. By the time Truman was elected, the wave of anti-communism later personified by Senator Joseph McCarthy dominated politics. Conservatives sought to purge the government, labor unions, and American society at large of alleged communists and communist sympathizers. The imposition of loyalty oaths, the pas-

sage of anti-communist provisions in labor legislation (the Taft-Hartley Act in 1949), and the proceedings of the House Un-American Activities Committee were manifestations of the postwar political climate. Tobey Schein believed that a Wallace victory would have moved the country "in an entirely different direction" (Prinz interview transcript, 19). The Wallace supporters had failed to reach the trade union movement and mobilize large masses of workers. Wallace's campaign opposed the cold war with its massive military rearmament, including the proliferation of nuclear weapons.

By the 1950s, signing a loyalty oath stating that you were not presently a member of the CP, nor had you ever been a member, had become a standard aspect of hiring contracts for public school teachers, faculty at state and city universities, and for all federal and state government employees. A pragmatist, Tobey Schein signed a loyalty oath but continued her membership in the CP. She did not identify herself publicly, however, and never discussed her party membership with her children. Schein established the ad hoc Committee on Community Relations within the Chicago Teachers Union as well as the Concerned Rank & File Teachers, groups geared toward giving power to working people. She also supported efforts to overturn the death sentence ordered in the spy case of CP members Julius and Ethel Rosenberg, whom she felt had been unjustly convicted of passing atomic secrets to the Soviet Union. Schein participated in the coalition of peace and CP groups that worked for international acceptance of the Stockholm Peace Appeal aimed at stopping nuclear war. Schein worked with other activists in her local Parent Teacher Association (PTA) to reject the national organization's proposed endorsement of a universal military draft in peacetime. In the context of McCarthy-era cold war politics, it was courageous to oppose a universal military draft. Schein worked with ESTHER SAPERSTEIN, who was one of the leaders of the PTA. They developed tactics and strategies, working with the Illinois PTA and their local chapter.

It was typical of Schein to participate in local, national, and international issues simultaneously. At the same time that she worried about the proliferation of nuclear weapons and argued for the integration of Chicago's public schools, Schein found herself involved in a skirmish in her own neighborhood. Rogers Park had a public beach fronting Lake Michigan, and in 1954 when Schein took her boys on one of their trips to the lake, she found the beach fenced in. The land had been designated for condominium development. Schein began what came to be known as the "beach fights." Becoming one of the early founders of the Rogers Park Community Council (RPCC), she and other community activists in 1954 gathered thirty thousand signatures that were presented to Mayor Richard J. Daley demanding that the city of Chicago buy land along Lake Michigan and preserve it for public use. RPCC's efforts resulted in the Chicago City Council's floating a bond issue to buy seven parcels of Rogers Park lakefront, extending from the Loyola University campus to Howard Street, the northern boundary between Chicago and Evanston, Illinois. The Rogers Park lakefront is virtually the only section on Chicago's North Side without high rises. She had "a deep and abiding faith in people. When issues [were] made clear to them, they respond[ed]" (quoted in Koehler). Later she remarked that she received the most satisfaction when she saw children playing in the lakefront parks she had helped save.

In 1960 Tobey Schein divorced her husband. Schein had to balance home life and public life. She gave her son Frederick considerable independence. "My mother did her thing and I did mine" (interview), he recalled, including her involvement with the CP, which he said he knew nothing about when he was a child. Son Howard felt "her public life kept her from having a totally successful private life" and that she "was still pounding pavement and . . . knock[ing] on doors long after she should have been sitting in a chair planning strategy but having others . . . carry it out" (interview). She was a coalition builder, an exceptional, experienced organizer who worked among people and cared about them but needed to be involved in the day-to-day strategies and activities of any group with which she was involved.

Schein continued to teach swimming and girls' physical education. She helped children overcome fears and develop self-confidence by teaching regular swimming classes and by producing and directing dance shows, gymnastic exhibitions, and water ballets. Schein dealt with many children who were suffering unnecessarily from preventable diseases and physical conditions resulting from their families' lack of adequate health care and substandard living conditions stemming from poverty and racism; and she became increasingly sensitive to and concerned with the problems of racism that existed in the public schools and in Chicago neighborhoods. By the 1950s, housing and school segregation had worsened. In the 1940s and 1950s, "and especially the fifteen years following the conclusion of World War II" (Hirsch, 4) there was a renewal of massive black migration to Chicago but no change in patterns of segregation. Expansion of the black population on Chicago's South and West sides occurred, but opposition to any integration of all-white neighborhoods persisted. African American children were forced to attend increasingly overcrowded, antiquated, and poorly funded public schools. Members of the Chicago Teachers Union, including Schein, realized they could not do their jobs without major improvements in the conditions of the families of the children they taught. Schein worked within the CTU to have its members endorse a housing resolution calling for reforms and an open housing policy in the city. It was sent to the Chicago City Council and Mayor Richard J. Daley, but nothing came of the resolution.

At the same time, Schein worked to encourage her union to advocate the integration of the public schools in Chicago. By the late 1950s and early 1960s, the use of temporary trailers called "Willis Wagons"—for Superintendent of Schools Benjamin J. Willis—"*the* symbol of racial recalcitrance" (Reed, 199), was a glaring example of separate and unequal educational facilities and the failure of the political system to deal appropriately and with justice and fairness to African Americans. Willis had introduced the temporary classrooms as a way to accommodate the overflow of black students without changing racial and neighborhood attendance boundaries. Schein worked through the CTU to fight the underlying racism and challenge the segregation that created social problems in the schools, and she became a leader in the Teachers Committee for Integrated Schools in the 1960s. Schein believed the riots of the 1960s and the terrible racial conflict that they reflected could have been avoided had there been a decent fair housing act in the 1940s and appropriate integration of neighborhoods and schools.

Tobey Schein marched in the 1963 March on Washington, D.C., joining hundreds of thousands of Americans in a protest against discrimination and racism; she heard Martin Luther King Jr. give his famous "I Have A Dream" speech and returned to Chicago even more convinced of the need for change. She had also become a part of the antiwar movement, protesting the U.S. government's undeclared war in Vietnam. In 1966, Schein married Morton Prinz, who supported her community and peace work.

The Rogers Park area was rapidly changing in the late 1960s and early 1970s. People from the rural South and immigrants who could not afford to buy property and were unable to afford huge rent increases needed help to organize for better conditions. Unfortunately, the newcomers had arrived in Chicago at the same time that urban problems had reached crisis proportions. At the same time, the administration of President Richard Nixon continued the undeclared war in Vietnam and began to dismantle the gains made under President Lyndon B. Johnson in community projects to fight poverty and to reduce unemployment. High unemployment, escalating costs of fuel, food, and housing and the loss of industrial jobs had placed neighborhoods like Uptown and Rogers Park at risk. Schein became a leader in local coalitions focused on rent control, unemployment, and inflation. She worked with a wide range of social justice activists from religious groups, community organizations, and local political caucuses. After her work with the Rogers Park Community Council to save the Rogers Park lakefront, Prinz became interested in the problems of inflation, unemployment, and hunger in the Rogers Park and Uptown neighborhoods. The Rogers Park Committee Against Inflation and Unemployment (RPCAUI) was organized in 1973. That year, Prinz joined nineteen other RPCAUI delegates in a rally in Washington, D.C., where activists from over the country demanded jobs for the nation's unemployed, whose numbers were on the rise. RPCAUI continued to meet and the group was energized when a nun from the Roman Catholic Sisters of Charity of the Blessed Virgin Mary (BVM) community, Katherine McHugh, a former director of the Howard Area Community Center, spoke about hunger and opened the group's eyes to the seriousness of the situation. RPCAUI members soon realized that many of the problems with which they were dealing were related to tenant issues. By 1978 the group evolved into the Rogers Park Tenants Committee (RPTC). Tobey Prinz initially ran the office on a volunteer basis. RPTC became the leading tenants' organization in Chicago and in 1976 joined with several other community groups in the city to form the Coalition Against Rent Exploitation (CARE), which campaigned for rent control. CARE forced Mayor Daley to appoint a blue ribbon commission to study the need for rent control, which, much to the dismay of the activists, was headed by real estate developer Harry Chaddick. The commission concluded that rent control was unnecessary; agitation for control of rising rents continued, however. A group of aldermen attempted unsuccessfully to pass an ordinance to create a fair rent commission.

Prinz also fought for other tenants' rights legislation at the city and state level and against real estate industry attempts to undo local protenant protections. The Rogers Park Tenant Committee, which educated people about their rights as renters and provided job counseling, legal assistance, and health information, also pushed adoption by the city council of a Tenants Bill of Rights. Prinz led the fight to restrict condominium conversions throughout Chicago. In all of these endeavors Prinz was fighting for the rights of low and moderate income working people to decent housing and good schools for their children. She battled, too, for a broad government-sponsored safety net of full employment, an adequate minimum wage, social insurance, and health care for all members of society.

In 1976, Prinz retired from teaching full-time but continued her community work, increasingly ignoring her own health. By 1979 Prinz also started motivating political progressives to run for office in the 49th Ward. She met David Orr, a professor at Mundelein College (now part of Loyola University Chicago), during a 1975 political campaign. After working with him on tenants' problems and ward issues, she encouraged him to make a successful bid for alderman in 1979, helping organize his campaign. She also assisted Sister Patricia Crowley, a Benedictine sister, then working with the Howard Area Community Center, which provided day care, employment counseling, youth services, and community organizing for the neighborhood. Prinz introduced Crowley to the influential groups in the ward and helped with fund-raising.

In 1983, Prinz toured model schools in Cuba and came home angrier than ever about the treatment accorded the children of the urban poor in the United States. As a member of Educators for Social Responsibility, she worked to elect Harold Washington, an African American politician who challenged the regular Democratic Party candidate in his successful run for mayor of Chicago. She held candidate dinner parties and coffees, helped raise funds, and knocked on doors, campaigning for Washington's election.

After the election, family members hoped Prinz might slow down since diagnosis showed that she had a hole in the septum of her heart. Instead she continued knocking on doors and became a founding member of the Chicago Metropolitan Tenants Organization and a board member of the National Tenants Union, where she tried to provide help for poor people shut out of affordable housing. On June 14, 1984, having just returned from a National Tenants Union conference in Detroit, Michigan, she suffered a heart attack. She died soon after in St. Francis Hospital, Evanston, Illinois. She was buried in Forest Home Cemetery, Forest Park, Illinois, in the area reserved for members and leaders of the American Communist Party. A lifelong party member, Prinz had served on the Illinois District Communist Party as well as the Illinois State Committee.

As her friend, classmate, and coworker Johanna Goldberg put it, "Everybody liked Tobey—Communist or not. Even when she made mistakes, people knew she was a genuine person who would never double-cross you in any way" (interview). Prinz was eulogized by Mayor Harold Washington for her efforts on behalf of tenants rights, peace, and the nuclear freeze movement. "'The Tobey Prinzes of the world don't come around very often,' he said. He described . . . Prinz as a woman who was able to combine a global view with a personal view in her activism" (obituary, *Sunday Star*). In honor of Prinz, the Rogers Park Tenants Committee (later the Rogers Park Community Action Network) created the Tobey Prinz Award honoring one or two people a year for exceptional community service. By 1986, two years after Prinz's death, the first Chicago Landlord-Tenants Bill, which protected the rights of both property owners and renters, and for which she had worked so hard, was passed. According to Cook County Clerk David Orr, then alderman from the 49th Ward and sponsor of the bill, "Tobey had more to do with its passage than anyone else" (interview). Honoring her long commitment to the education of children, the Howard Area Community Center placed a memorial plaque honoring Prinz at the entrance of their day care center. Tobey Prinz had a radical vision of a just society where human rights were more important than private property and private gain, and where peace rather than war prevailed around the world. Understanding of how far human beings were from reaching these goals did not lessen her belief or diminish her energy in working every day for the smallest improvement in the direction of their achievement.

Sources. Interviews were conducted by Mary Cannon with Mark Almberg, Gertrude Berger, Evangeline Swan, and Johanna Goldberg on February 11, 1995; with Charlotte Koch, February 28, 1995; with Sister Patricia Crowley, OSB, April 8, 1995; with Mae Welleck, April 8, 1995; with Frederick Schein, April 26, 1995; with Howard Schein, May 1, 1995; with David Orr, May 2, 1995; with Alice Robbin, July 28, 1995. Alice Robbin interviewed Tobey Prinz in 1983 and the tapes of this interview and a transcript were used for this biography. Articles in community newspapers the *Sunday Star* and the *Rogers Park News* were consulted, including Robert Koehler, "Activist Tobey Prinz's Long Involvement," *Rogers Park News*, March 26, 1980. Paul Buhle, Mari Jo Buhle, and Dan Georgakas, eds., *Encyclopedia of the American Left* (1992); Arnold R. Hirsch, *Making the Second Ghetto: Race and Housing in Chicago 1940–1960* (1983); and Christopher Robert Reed, *The Chicago NAACP and the Rise of Black Professional Leadership, 1910–1966* (1997), were helpful. Obituaries appeared in the *Sunday Star*, July 1, 1984, and the *Chicago Sun-Times*, June 28, 1984.

MARY CANNON

PUCIŃSKA, STANISLAWA-LIDIA JĘDRZEJOWSKA
1896–October 25, 1984
ACTRESS, THEATER DIRECTOR

Lidia Pucińska acted in and directed numerous plays and musicals in Chicago and from 1933 to 1984 hosted the popular radio program the *Sunshine Hour*. She was born Stanislawa-Lidia Jędrzejowska in Kraków, Poland, daughter of Władysław and Rozalia (Rozia) (Biskupowna) Jędrzejowski. Jędrzejowska's father had been a restaurant owner and prominent businessman in Kraków. He was a descendant of Poland's *stara szlachta* or old nobility, and his family was titled in the early seventeenth century as a reward for patriotic service. Rozalia Biskupowna came from Makowa, a rural town, and her widowed father, Józef Biskup, as a young man had fought against the Muscovites. Biskup sent his three daughters and two sons to schools in Kraków. After completing her education, Rozia Biskupowna received a portion of her father's land holdings.

Rozia Biskupowna and Władysław Jędrzejowski met in Kraków, where they married. They had two daughters, Aniela-Kazimiera and Stanislawa-Lidia. The older daughter was pensive and quiet, the younger outgoing. The girls spent summers in Makowa with aunts. Here Lidia Jędrzejowska enjoyed the bonfires and songs and dances of the countryside. In the evenings, the young people listened to their maternal grandfather's war reminiscences.

In 1907, Jędrzejowska's father died. Her older sister was sent to Vienna. Jędrzejowska spent approximately a year in Makowa and then was sent to Kraków, where she attended Konarski School. During this time her mother and older sister left for the United States, where the status of family property in Texas had to be resolved. In Kraków, Jędrzejowska joined a drama circle called the Star, *Gwiazda*. She studied drama under Marian Hoffman Marski and continued to be influenced throughout her career by the latter's approach to acting with its emphasis on voice and diction.

Jędrzejowska married Michael Puciński when she was sixteen. The couple immigrated to Chicago, where Lidia Pucińska's family was already residing. Soon after her arrival, her mother returned to Poland. Pucińska embarked on an acting career, traveling to Detroit, Michigan, New York, and other U.S. cities where Polish immigrants had established thriving cultural, religious, and social institutions, including ethnic-based theaters. In 1910 there were approximately 1,664,000 Polish American immigrants and their children living in the United States. In Chicago, 210,000 Polish Americans made up the "Polonia" or Polish enclave, which was clustered in several ethnic neighborhoods. By 1930, the population of Polish American immigrants and their children in the United States had climbed to 3,342,000, and the population of Chicago's Polonia had reached 401,000. The first three decades of the twentieth century were a time when immigrants from Poland integrated into American society and culture and also maintained the language and cultural traditions of their homeland. Polish American theater productions, and later radio programs broadcast in Polish, were important sources of education, acculturation, and identity formation. Lidia Pucińska played a significant role in the preservation of Polish culture in the United States.

Between 1910 and 1929, theatrical productions in Polish enjoyed tremendous success. Often theatergoers stood in lines several city blocks long waiting to purchase tickets. Chicago had fourteen Polish theaters between 1916 and 1918. During World War I, theaters bolstered patriotic sentiment and served as places to raise funds for the war cause. Pucińska was active in recruiting and fund-raising efforts. During World War I she helped recruit the "Blue Army," an expeditionary force of Polish immigrants from the United States that fought alongside Allied troops.

Pucińska had three children, Halina Lidia (later Pawlowski-Pawl), Wieslaw (Wesley in English), and Roman, who later served as a United States congressman and a Chicago alderman. Little is known about her personal life during these years. She remained in the United States and visited Poland only once, in 1927, after receiving word that her mother was seriously ill. She returned to the United States as the nation began to experience the first traumatic waves of business failure, the stock market crash, and the beginning of the Great Depression. Around this time, Pucińska was divorced. She was an exceedingly independent soul. A divorced actress with three children was hardly the norm in the early 1930s, especially among immigrant groups. Her personal crisis paralleled the decline of the theatrical world. By 1929, most Chicago Polish American theaters had closed their doors, with a final performance at the popular Logan Square Theater. From 1929 to 1939, single performances took place in Polish American theaters in the United States, but little, if any, organized theater existed. With the decline of permanent theaters, Pucińska began in 1933 to organize theater productions and also shifted her attention to a new medium, radio. She began airing her *Sunshine Hour-Godzina Słoneczna* program on WEDC, a local station that carried Polish language programs. *Godzina Słoneczna* was exclusively in Polish and aired on weekdays in midmorning. It was aimed at an audience of women and retired persons. The programming consisted of Polonia news, commentary on cultural and theatrical events, literary readings, music, practical household and childrearing tips, and current events in Poland. The themes and literary readings were patriotic. Pucińska's gentle and homespun style endeared her to several generations of listeners. She signed off asking her audience to remember to feed Chicago's sparrows.

In 1933, Pucińska married "her knight in golden armor riding on a white stallion" (*Golden Jubilee of Her Artistic and Civic Work*, 12), Stefan Rutkowski. In the 1930s and 1940s, Pucińska-Rutkowska was known in Chicago's Polonia as an actress and director of serious and musical theater. Although there were no permanent theater groups or theaters, series of performances were presented at local auditoriums in schools and churches, including Holy Trinity Church and Lane Technical High School.

As events in Europe in the late 1930s once again placed Poland on the defensive, Pucińska used theatrical events and her daily radio program as vehicles for raising money for the war cause, both for Poland and the United States. In the 1940s, her promotion of war bond sales helped finance the purchase of an entire squadron of B-51 fighter planes, a B-29 super bomber, which was appropriately named Chicago's Polonia, and a troop of heavy weapons carriers. Her radio programs sold war books worth millions of dollars during World War II. President Harry S. Truman sent personal thanks.

Pucińska was also active in local institution-building for the Polish American community. As a founding member of the Illinois division of the Polish American Congress organized in 1944, she organized many benefit performances to raise money for the division and was also instrumental in getting funds to purchase the first Polish American Congress building on Division Street. In 1947, she collaborated with Bolesław Wolski, who directed the Polonez Choir. The resulting operas and operettas in Polish enjoyed great popularity. She also raised money for Polish Relief, including funds for typewriters in braille for blind children. These efforts continued into the 1950s when dissidents in a postwar, Soviet Union–controlled Poland suffered severe political and economic punishments. She headed a committee of the Polish National Alliance that supplied packages to political prisoners who were released in 1956.

Throughout her life Pucińska received many awards and acknowledgments of her work from fraternal societies, veterans groups, and community and charitable organizations in the United States, Europe, and Poland, including, on October 9, 1963, the Immigrant's Service League Distinguished Achievement Award. A coalition of community groups organized a "Golden Jubilee of Her Artistic and Civic Work" on October 20, 1963.

On March 19, 1971, she was named Woman of the Year by the Polish-American Scholarship Fund. In 1972, for her patriotic programs denouncing the communist regime in Poland, she received the Polish Restituta award from Polish officials exiled in London. In 1974, she was chosen as Polish Mother of the Year. On April 29, 1978, the Restore Ellis Island Committee gave her the Ellis Island Award honoring her achievements in radio. In 1979, she received the Heritage Award from the Polish American Congress for her benefit performances each year at Christmas time for disabled Polish Army veterans. On November 19, 1980, during a WEDC radio broadcast, she received the Polish National Alliance Hundredth Anniversary Medal for her work in promoting Polish language and culture.

Lidia Pucińska acted in, wrote, translated, directed, and produced theatrical pieces throughout her long life. She retained her radio program, the *Sunshine Hour,* until three weeks before her death. She served as president of the Polish Artist Guild through 1984. Until her death, she lived close to the "heart of the old Polonia" on Ashland Avenue, near Milwaukee, Ashland, and Division, the *trójkąt*—three corners. Lidia Pucińska died at the age of eighty-eight. A Roman Catholic mass was held at Holy Trinity Church, and both English and Polish language print media covered the event.

Lidia Pucińska nurtured and represented theater and the cultural benefits of theater in Chicago's Polonia. According to recollections of family and friends, she put on her plays as she ran her household, with authority. Her theatrical career throughout her long life influenced several generations of Polish-born and American-born Poles in Chicago.

Sources. The booklet *Golden Jubilee of Her Artistic and Civic Work* (October 20, 1963) was printed for the commemorative event with the same name by a coalition of community groups that included the Polish American Congress, the Polish National Alliance (PNA), the Polish Women's Alliance, and the Polish Roman Catholic Union. Another celebratory booklet, *Lidia Pucińska—Woman of the Year—1971,* was printed by the Polish American Scholarship Fund, 1971. The archives for the Polish language press are found at the Polish Museum library housed at the Polish Roman Catholic Union building in Chicago. The *Dziennik Chicagoski* (Polish daily) ceased publication in the early 1980s. The *Dziennik Związkowy* (Alliance daily) is still published by the PNA, which has headquarters in Chicago. In addition to a newspaper archive, the PNA library has a collection of historical information on Polonia's cultural and theatrical events, community leaders, and other influential personalities. The Związek Polek (Polish Women's Alliance, PWA) still publishes a monthly, *Głos Polek (Polish Women's Voice).* The archives for the latter are found at PWA headquarters in Chicago. In addition, the PWA library has information on notable Polonia women. Awards, letters from presidents, and coverage of Pucińska's funeral in the English-language press were prompted by the political status of her son, Roman Pucinski. Informative newspaper articles in the Polish-language press are found in *Dziennik Związkowy,* May 21, 1974, May 2, 1978, October 29, 1984; and *Głos Polek,* November 15, 1984; and in the English-language press, *Chicago Daily News,* May 7, 1974; *Chicago Sun-Times,*

March 22, 1971, October 25, 1984; *Intelligencer,* May 6, 1974; and *NYT,* April 30, 1978.

EMMA A. KOWALENKO

PULLMAN, HARRIET AMELIA SANGER
April 18, 1842–March 28, 1921
SOCIALITE, PHILANTHROPIST

Harriet Sanger Pullman, wife of sleeping car magnate George M. Pullman, was a leader of Chicago's social elite. With her daughters and husband she supported programs designed to help single working-class women—the so-called "women adrift" (Meyerowitz) in the urban environment—find uplifting recreational activities. She was born in Chicago, the only daughter of James Young and Mary Catherine (McKibben) Sanger. James Sanger was a Chicago pioneer and building contractor whose projects included construction of railroads in Illinois, Missouri, and California. As a result, Harriet Sanger attended schools in Chicago; St. Louis, Missouri; and Sacramento, California, depending on where her father's construction projects were based. She finished her formal education in 1860 in San Francisco at an Episcopal school run by nuns of that denomination; she soon returned to Chicago.

During the Civil War, Sanger did volunteer work in support of wounded Union soldiers. In 1862, accompanied by Mary Logan, wife of Major General John A. Logan, Harriet Sanger visited hospitals in Memphis, Tennessee, passing out delicacies and providing companionship to the wounded soldiers. When Sanger and Logan were ordered north, Sanger returned to Chicago and became one of the numerous women volunteers whose work on behalf of Union soldiers was coordinated through the Northwestern Sanitary Commission directed by MARY LIVERMORE and JANE HOGE. Mary Logan later wrote that Harriet Sanger was beautiful, charming, and had scores of admirers. She was a somewhat stout, dark-haired, energetic beauty.

According to Pullman family tradition, Harriet Sanger met George Pullman in 1867 at a party celebrating the completion of the Pullman Palace Car Company's first hotel railroad car. She was then twenty-five years old. After a brief but intense courtship, Harriet Sanger married George Pullman on June 13, 1867, at 11:30 P.M., at the bedside of Sanger's father, who was seriously ill with pneumonia and died two weeks later. Over the next eight years Harriet and George Pullman had four children: Florence, born August 11, 1868; Harriet, born September 17, 1869; and twin boys, George Jr., and Walter Sanger, born June 25, 1875.

After their marriage the Pullmans lived in a succession of homes just south of downtown Chicago. In their home at Sixteenth and Michigan Avenue, the Pullmans were beyond the area affected by the Great Chicago Fire of 1871. Harriet Pullman wrote in her diary that October 8, 1871, was "a lovely quiet Sunday" and that "at midnight [we] were awakened by the Great Fire" (Miller, 144). George Pullman went immediately to his office downtown and was able to transport everything of value to their residence by freight car over the Illinois Central tracks before the office at Randolph and Lake streets was consumed by fire early the next morning. After the fire, Pullman and her husband were involved in relief efforts to provide housing, food, and clothing to those who had lost everything. "George [Pullman] served as chairman of the relief committee in October 1871 before becoming treasurer of the Chicago Relief and Aid Society, a position he continued to hold until 1873" (Leyendecker, 109).

The Pullmans moved into a newly completed residence located in the fashionable Prairie Avenue neighborhood on January 13, 1876. Prairie Avenue was the home of many prominent business owners, meat packers, and manufacturers, including the families of Marshall Field and Philip Armour. The Pullmans participated fully in the social and cultural life of Chicago and often entertained in their home, a palatial mansion of massive brownstone surrounded by large gardens and containing a bowling alley, billiard room, a music room with a pipe organ, and a small theater.

Harriet and George Pullman shared the belief that they had a responsibility to provide leadership in the shaping of Chicago's social order—George through his business affairs and Harriet through society affairs and participation in cultural activities. Cultural events at the Prairie Avenue mansion included plays, musicals, lectures, French classes, dance classes, and receptions for visiting dignitaries, musicians, and actors. The Pullmans contributed funds to the newly organized Chicago Symphony Orchestra directed by Theodore Thomas. They competed with others of their social class to set the tone of cultural life and dominate the social scene; Harriet Pullman and her clique vied for a dominant role during the opera season in 1886, and a local newspaper published news of her rivalry with Nannie Field.

At home Harriet Pullman directed the upbringing of the couple's four children according to Victorian standards, which included dancing lessons for daughters Florence and Harriet by the time they were eight and seven years old, respectively. The family attended the Second Presbyterian Church not far from their Prairie Avenue dwelling; it was the faith in which Harriet Pullman had been raised.

Like other upper-class families, the Pullmans owned a summer residence, a mansion they named Fairlawn, in Elberon, New Jersey. They also acquired one of the islands in the Thousand Island region of New York state, which they named Pullman Island. Here they built several cabins. The Pullmans entertained frequently at each of their homes. George and Harriet Pullman also spent considerable time away from each other between George Pullman's business trips and Harriet Pullman's extended visits to doctors, health spas, temperate climates, and friends. Pullman's letters to her husband convey complaints about her health and regret at being away from the family.

In 1880, George Pullman bought four thousand acres of land in the Lake Calumet area south of Chicago for an expansion of the Pullman Palace Car Company and the creation of a planned community for workers. In addition to housing for employees, the town of Pullman eventually included shops, a library, bank, meeting hall, church, and the lavish Florence Hotel. The sale of alcohol was forbidden, except at the Florence Hotel, which was frequented by visitors to the town and Pullman's managers, not factory workers. George Pullman contended that his goal was to provide for the welfare of his workers; his paternalism and concern for implanting middle-class values and a work ethic that would benefit his company were noted later by critics.

Harriet Pullman extended her role as cultural arbiter from Chicago to Pullman. She arranged for classes in German, French, Shakespeare, painting, drama, and dancing for the benefit of Pullman employees and their families. She also established a ladies' charitable union and a whist club. Both Harriet and George believed that the creation of Pullman was a major economic and cultural accomplishment; they enjoyed entertaining family, potential customers, and visitors there.

Harriet Pullman had similar ideas to those implemented by the Pullman-planned community when she attempted to provide a wholesome, suitable environment for women workers through the formation of the Wildwood Club in 1891. Harriet Pullman, like many middle- and upper-middle-class women of the late nineteenth century, worried about the moral well-being of young, independent women who came to Chicago and other cities and lived far from the influence of family. These unmarried women were potentially disruptive of the moral order of society. The Wildwood Club was one of numerous experiments at the time organized by affluent women to provide wholesome leisure activities for self-supporting girls. Harriet Pullman herself was not directly involved with managing the club. Her daughters were board members of Wildwood; the first meeting of the club was held at the Prairie Avenue mansion. There were three kinds of members: regular, associate, and honorary. The first category was for self-supporting girls over the age of sixteen, who paid what were considered reasonable dues; the second were young women who pledged to carry on the work of the club (and functioned as supervisors). The last category was of wealthy women patrons who paid ten dollars annually to aid the cause. The plan was to have the working women or regular members be in the majority, but the officers of the club for 1891–92 were the associates or supervisors and included some of the wealthiest matrons and young ladies of the city's elite. The associates were described as "women of means and leisure" who "have chosen this practical method of lending a helping hand to those of their sisters who are courageously helping themselves. In order to save money needed in paying the running expenses, the ladies [associates] do all the work themselves, except the heavier part of it" (unidentified clipping, "Wildwood Club Where Young Women Eat, Drink, and Are Merry," Wildwood clipping file).

Initially, George Pullman offered one of the family properties, Wildwood Place, a few miles south of Pullman, to the club to provide a vacation residence. For a modest cost, working girls could spend a week away from the city pursuing wholesome, supervised, Christian activities, including visits to Pullman, Illinois, and attendance at a concert by the Pullman Band. During the first summer at Wildwood the clubhouse was open for eleven weeks and 44 associates and 163 regular members attended. Every morning began with prayer and Bible study, prayers were said before meals, and the Sabbath was observed. This first project was so successful that the Wildwood Club located space for a lunchroom and library in downtown Chicago, where working girls could enjoy leisure time in an uplifting environment for the modest membership cost of twenty-five cents a month. It was so successful that it soon moved to larger quarters downtown. Enthusiasts saw the club as a way to bridge the gap between rich and poor and to aid self-supporting women in an atmosphere that respected them rather than demeaned them by resembling alms giving. One of the associates remarked, "It is not in any sense a charitable organization . . . [since] even at the low rates charged, it has been entirely self-supporting" (unidentified newspaper clipping, "Wildwood Club Where Young Women Eat, Drink, and Are Merry"). The second year, a supervised vacation home was provided by the Henry Demarest Lloyd family of Winnetka, Illinois.

On June 7, 1892, "little Harriet" married Francis J. (Frank) Carolan, son of a San Francisco hardware merchant. The ceremony took place at the Prairie Avenue mansion. Originally, an extravagant reception for two thousand guests was planned; however, George Pullman's mother, Emily, had died only a few weeks before, so the festivities were toned down. Nevertheless, the wedding was "rich and sumptuous in every detail" (Leyendecker, 212). The following year Harriet and George Pullman reached the height of their influence, participating in the World's Columbian Exposition as two of Chicago's most influential citizens. Pullman was chosen as a lady patroness of the exposition's ball. As part of the exposition, frequent trains and trolleys connected the fairgrounds with the town of Pullman, and during the summer of 1893 the model town for workers attracted ten thousand foreign visitors. Within a few months, however, the cultural and economic world the Pullmans had created would come crashing down.

During the 1890s the U.S. economy experienced a prolonged depression, although the Pullman Company initially continued to prosper. Toward the end of 1893, George Pullman cut the wages of his factory workers without reducing the rents and utility rates for the residences in his town. In May 1894, the workers began what eventually became an internationally publicized bitter strike. To support the strikers, members of the American Railway Union refused to handle Pullman cars. George Pullman eventually won the strike by persuading President Grover Cleveland to send in federal troops so that railroad transportation could resume. Pullman's reputation as a leading citizen, however, had been tarnished. He was perceived increasingly as an autocratic and ruthless industrialist. The strike split the city of Chicago into two warring camps. According to JANE ADDAMS, the strike dramatically revealed the inequalities of class that had always existed beneath the veneer of the so-called benevolent company town. Socialite BERTHA HONORÉ PALMER, a member of a committee of distinguished citizens selected to convince Pullman to take a more reasonable stance with his workers, was disgusted by the industrialist's arrogance.

For Harriet Pullman, the strike put an additional strain on their marriage. George and Harriet Pullman were often apart during and after the strike. In a letter to George written in December 1895, Harriet Pullman referred to his "horrible business cares" (quoted in Miller, 153) and let him know "how deeply . . . [she was] sympathizing with [him] in these troubled times" (p. 153).

Their oldest daughter, Florence, had met and fallen in love with Frank O. Lowden, later an Illinois congressional representative and then governor of the state. Initially, George Pullman withheld his consent for their marriage, but by late 1895 he relented. Although Harriet Pullman was absent from Chicago during February and March 1896, she was busy planning the wedding and ordering furnishings for Florence's new home. She was especially concerned about linen for house and table. In a letter to her husband, Harriet Pullman wrote that she wanted the linen to be "nice and properly embroidered and those sort of things more than any other, speak to the taste and refinement of the lady of the house and should be *the very best*" (Miller, 153). The wedding took place on April 29, 1896, and was a lavish affair at the Pullman mansion, with a reception for one thousand guests.

Less than eighteen months later, on October 19, 1897, George Pullman died of a massive heart attack. According to the terms of his will, Harriet Pullman and her daughters were to receive substantial inheritances; the twin sons were awarded only small yearly allowances. The twins, Walter Sanger and George Jr., were a terrible disappointment to their parents, unsuccessful in school and both having problems with alcohol abuse. Their father's bequest to them was meant as a rebuke. Harriet Pullman, however, renounced the terms of her husband's will in order to provide more income to her sons. Instead, she insisted on her dower right (one third interest) in the Pullman estate, as permitted by law, and in this way was able to increase her share, allowing her to provide more income to her sons. Although she did not approve of their lifestyle or their eventual choice of marriage partners, Harriet Pullman continued to pay her sons' debts. George Jr. died in 1901 at the age of twenty-six and Walter Sanger died four years later. At the time of George Pullman's death, his estate was worth an estimated $7,600,000. Harriet Pullman developed a business acumen and attention to detail that enabled her to increase the value of the Pullman estate to more than eighteen million dollars.

Harriet Pullman maintained her life as a socialite and philanthropist after a period of mourning for her husband. She served on the board of the Mary Thompson Hospital for Women and Children, Chicago, and gave St. Luke (Episcopal) Hospital a gift of five hundred thousand dollars. She provided scholarships for young music students for study abroad and she supported the Pullman Library until it was taken over by the Chicago Public Library, becoming the George M. Pullman Branch. Harriet Pullman divided her time between Chicago and Elberon, New Jersey (summers), and Washington, D.C. (winters). While in Washington, she lived in a mansion she had built during the late 1890s. Here, she and widowed Chicago neighbor (and former social rival) Nannie Field helped preside over Washington society. Pullman sold her Washington, D.C., home in 1913 and thereafter spent much of the winter at the Raymond Hotel, Pasadena, California. She continued to host parties and receptions at the Prairie Avenue mansion, including one during the Republican National Convention in June 1920. Pullman was among the last of the old Chicago families to maintain a residence there, as did FRANCES GLESSNER, and the mansions of the Pullmans and Glessners were regarded as two of the last outposts of old Chicago society.

Harriet Pullman died of pneumonia in Pasadena, California, at age eighty-two. At her bedside were her daughter Florence and son-in-law, Frank Lowden, and their four children. The funeral was held at the Prairie Avenue mansion and Pullman was buried beside her husband at Graceland Cemetery,

Chicago. Pullman's funeral was the last function held at the Prairie Avenue mansion; shortly after, it was torn down.

Harriet Pullman had a reputation among many of her peers for generosity and gracious hospitality; others saw her as competitive and cliquish. She lived through the industrial strife that broke out into open warfare when federal troops were called in to end the strike of railway workers trying to defend the rights of her husband's Pullman Palace Car Company employees. Workers challenged the Pullman model town and its paternalism, and George Pullman had to relinquish his ownership, thereby separating his company from the planned community so important to him and Harriet Pullman. Within her own home Harriet Pullman faced disappointments with her sons and the early death of her husband. There is no evidence to suggest that she understood the seriousness of the Pullman strike and related labor unrest. She maintained the lifestyle and values of a noblesse oblige philosophy, asserting the leadership and authority of her class.

Sources. Clippings and articles relating to Harriet Sanger Pullman available at the CHS are in the Harriet Sanger Pullman clipping file, the Wildwood Club clipping file, and the Wildwood Club miscellaneous pamphlets file. Florence Lowden Miller, "The Pullmans of Prairie Avenue: A Domestic Portrait from Letters and Diaries," *Chicago History,* Spring 1971, is useful. Other books consulted include Liston Edgington Leyendecker, *Palace Car Prince: A Biography of George Mortimer Pullman* (1992); James Gilbert, *Perfect Cities: Chicago's Utopias of 1893* (1991); and Joanne J. Meyerowitz, *Women Adrift: Independent Wage Earners in Chicago 1880–1930* (1991).

JEAN PAULSON PETERMAN

PURVIN, JENNIE FRANKLIN
August 23, 1873–November 1, 1958
COMMUNAL VOLUNTEER, CLUBWOMAN, CIVIC REFORMER, ART GALLERY MANAGER

Jennie Franklin Purvin was one of Chicago's diligent female activists and one of only a few Chicago Jewish women to take an active interest in civic as well as Jewish communal work. In the midst of Progressive Era reform, Purvin brought her energies to bear upon the shape of Chicago's geography and culture and saw it bend to her will. Active in civic, educational, and Jewish concerns, she was best known for her successful campaign to create public bathing beaches and facilities along the shores of Lake Michigan.

Jennie Franklin's mother, Hannah Mayer, was born and educated in Chicago, the daughter of German-Jewish immigrants who came to Chicago in the 1840s. Her father, Henry B. Franklin, emigrated from Germany in 1867 and became a cigar manufacturer in Chicago. She had one sister and three brothers. Two of her brothers eventually took over their father's cigar business, while the third served as a rabbi in northern California.

Jennie Franklin's interests as a young girl foreshadowed some of her future concerns as a community activist. She fought with her parents to be given swimming lessons. Applying the same patient persistence that would characterize her future battles with Chicago's municipal authorities, she eventually won her point. At the time, as she would later recall, it was not considered seemly for a girl to swim. When, as a teenager, her swim-

ming won some admiration, she noted that it was "probably because so few young ladies swim" (diaries, July 15, 1890).

While still an adolescent, Jennie Franklin displayed an energy and interest in associational life that later grew into an intense involvement in Chicago's civic, Jewish, and women's organizations. In high school, she took an active role in the Literary Society at Chicago Sinai Congregation, the Reform Jewish congregation that her maternal grandfather had helped to found. After high school, she became one of the active organizers and the recording secretary of "the Philomathians," a society of young men and women who gathered to "promote mental development" ("Constitution and By-Laws," typescript Minute Book, Purvin Collection). Jennie Franklin graduated from Chicago's North Division High School in 1891. Her plans to attend the University of Michigan were put aside when her father became ill and she stayed home to assist him with the cigar business. She never received a college degree but pursued further study through extension classes at the University of Chicago.

In 1899, she married Moses L. Purvin, who worked for a Chicago business concern. Jennie Purvin's communal activism as an adult began with her interest in the education of her two daughters, Nata and Janet. In 1907, she founded the Oakland Parent Teacher Association and served as its president until 1914. As Purvin widened her civic interests during this period beyond her children's schooling, she connected with an expanding circle of middle- and upper-class Chicago female activists whose work in women's clubs was moving, as she later described it, from "desultory giving to conducting civic projects" ("Address of Mrs. M. L. Purvin at the 25th Anniversary Meeting of the Scholarship Association for Jewish Children," 1938, Purvin Collection).

Purvin further pursued her interests in education when she was appointed in 1911 to Chicago's Bureau of Employment Supervision for Boys and Girls. The purpose of this committee was to encourage children to stay in school rather than go to work. Poverty, however, proved to be a much more powerful factor than well-intentioned guidance in determining the destiny of so many children. In 1912, Purvin convinced Chicago Women's Aid, a Jewish women's organization that she served as president, to take on the support of a Vocational Guidance Bureau, which became the Children's Scholarship League, to gather scholarship funds to help keep poor children in school. Purvin gained the support of Women's Aid by hiring Ethel Kawin to serve as a special adviser to any Jewish children who came to the bureau for help. In 1913, the Jewish side of the Children's Scholarship League separated to become the Committee on Scholarships for Jewish Children, with Jennie Purvin as its first president.

Purvin sustained an active involvement with the Chicago women's club movement as the organizer and first president of a branch of the elite Woman's City Club in Chicago's 3rd Ward and as an active member and officer of the Illinois Federation of Women's Clubs (IFWC). Chicago's leading progressive reformers ran the Woman's City Club, including LOUISE deKOVEN BOWEN, MARY WILMARTH, and ANNA NICHOLES. They combined expertise in areas of social policy and city government with an astute sense of the political climate. Purvin also pursued social policy issues with a pragmatic participation in politics. Her interests focused on the core issues that defined the agenda of most of Chicago's upper-class women's associations in reforms related to the education and lives of children. Although Purvin was chair of the Civics Department of the IFWC in 1913 when limited suffrage was won for women in Illinois, she was not outspoken as a suffragist. Yet, she understood the possibility of advancing the educational welfare of Chicago's children through political means. Her introduction to city politics came with her involvement as head of the Women's Independent Commission for the unsuccessful reform mayoral candidate Charles E. Merriam. The entire progressive reform coalition, with its tentacles reaching into the women's clubs, the settlement movement, and university social scientists, came together to support University of Chicago political science professor Merriam.

As her political and organizational connections continued to expand, so did her interests and involvements. During World War I she organized and directed the Women's Clubs Division of the War Savings Program in Chicago and also helped organize the Jewish Welfare Board of Chicago, which focused on the needs of Jewish soldiers. In the years after World War I, as president of the Chicago section of the National Council of Jewish Women (1920–22) and the sisterhood of Chicago Sinai Congregation (1925–27), she led the Jewish women's organizations that represented the most affluent and acculturated elements of Chicago's Jewish population. She also arranged for the establishment and maintenance of a fund that would offer financial support to students from Cincinnati's Hebrew Union College who came to study in Chicago during their summer recess.

The movement with which she was most prominently associated was the effort to turn the shore of Lake Michigan into an asset to the city of Chicago rather than a dumping ground for its refuse. Purvin's initial efforts were prompted after a lesser fight in 1911 that gained the support of Mayor Carter Harrison for the creation of a usable beach for neighborhood children at the foot of Thirty-ninth Street. When Purvin brought her daughters to that site, she realized that all of Chicago's children would benefit from access to clean beaches. Under the auspices of the Woman's City Club, she initiated a Bathing Beach Committee in 1911 and went to work to convince the municipal authorities to create a series of beaches on Chicago's lakefront. Purvin and her colleagues from the Woman's City Club first made a thorough study of the Chicago lakeshore. They then entered upon a sustained campaign to convince city, state, and national authorities to obtain the necessary rights of way from the Illinois Central Railroad, clear the required land, hire lifeguards, and build changing rooms, lavatories, and showers. An extensive and systematic lobbying effort of many years finally prodded the city's politicians into directing the money and resources necessary toward transforming the city's neglected lakeshore into an accessible and beautiful public park. From the beaches, Purvin extended her concern for Chicago's public recreational facilities, taking an interest in all aspects of the city's parks, from comfort stations to playgrounds to statuary.

Purvin's energy and success in civic affairs made her an influential player in Chicago city politics. Political figures sought her favor, but having gained much insight into the workings of politics, she dispensed it carefully. In 1923 William E. Dever

was running as a reformer for mayor of Chicago and was supported by progressives, including the Woman's City Club infrastructure and important national figures like MARY McDOWELL, JULIA LATHROP, Raymond Robins, and Graham Taylor. When Dever asked Purvin for her support, she was impressed with his receptiveness to ideas about recreation but withheld her endorsement until she could be convinced that those who would serve as the "power behind the Mayor" (Purvin to Martin J. ObBrien [sic], March 9, 1923) would be worthy of her support in the fight "against drunkenness [sic] vice and crime" (March 9, 1923). Apparently satisfied, Purvin accepted the role of city chair of the Women's Independent Committee to elect William E. Dever. After Dever's victory, Purvin hoped to secure an appointment to Chicago's Board of Education. Purvin had powerful supporters, and an announcement of her impending appointment even appeared in the Chicago press. In the end, to Purvin's great disappointment, the seats that Dever apparently designated for women went to Grace Temple, past president of the Chicago Woman's Club, and HELEN HEFFERAN, prominent Catholic clubwomen. A Jew also was appointed to the board, Edgar N. Greenebaum, a banker and leader in Jewish community affairs.

Though this experience dampened her political aspirations, Purvin carried on her multifarious community involvements with continued energy. In 1933, after the election of the machine-based Democrat Edward Kelly as mayor, Jennie Purvin again hoped for an appointment to the Board of Education. Instead of this much desired appointment, she was offered a position on the board of directors of the Chicago Public Library. Purvin accepted this compromise with some reluctance, but characteristically, she embraced her new role in advancing the library's interests with great enthusiasm. In this and other capacities, Purvin was often called upon as a public speaker. She also was a regular contributor to Chicago's Jewish publications and to other periodicals.

Membership in the acculturated Jewish community associated with Chicago Sinai Congregation offered Purvin access to Chicago's circle of elite women. Yet Purvin's leading role in many of Chicago's elite women's organizations was not a measure of her wealth or her social connections. She took no pride in fashion, and, though supportive of philanthropy, her own contributions to worthy causes rarely exceeded five dollars. Whatever status and recognition she attained came as a result of her energy, persistence, and effectiveness.

When Purvin realized, in the midst of the Great Depression, that she was not going to win appointment to the Board of Education, she turned her attention to more pragmatic pursuits. In 1933, at the age of sixty, Purvin entered into a relationship with Chicago's Mandel Brothers Department Store, becoming involved in the creation of a number of enterprises there that would occupy the rest of her working life. She approached the store with the suggestion that it sponsor a central meeting place for the clubwomen of Chicago. The Club Women's Bureau under the supervision of Jennie Purvin offered an information center, meeting facilities, programs, and services for the city's women's clubs.

Like the Club Women's Bureau, which attracted many affluent women to the sales floors of Mandel Brothers, Purvin's further activities at the store, while formulated to advance the community's interests, also served the business interests of Mandel Brothers. In 1937, Purvin organized an art exhibition space at Mandel Brothers, which, for the next twenty years, served as a showcase for the work of young and unknown as well as established Chicago-based artists.

In 1938, Purvin organized a Camp Advisory Bureau intended to provide parents with helpful information and advice about potential summer camps for their children. In Purvin's extensive tours to gather information about the camps, she also served as a sales representative of Mandel Brothers, attempting to secure contracts to provide the clothing and supplies that camps required their campers to purchase. Both these services were meant to increase Mandel Brothers business, yet artists, art associations, camp directors, and parents all attested to their appreciation of what they viewed as vital community institutions. Purvin maintained her public role on the Library Board and at Mandel Brothers until her retirement in 1955. She died in Chicago at age eighty-five.

During her lifetime Jennie Purvin was known as the "mother" of Chicago's bathing beaches. Much of the impact of her career, however, was not recorded in books but in the experience of so many who lived richer lives because Jennie Purvin fought to create a community that would truly promote the education, health, enjoyment, and involvement of its citizens.

Sources. Most information about Jennie Franklin Purvin is found in the Jennie Franklin Purvin Collection at the American Jewish Archives, Cincinnati, Ohio. This collection contains extensive material documenting Purvin's professional, family, and personal life, including her diaries and letters. Other relevant manuscript collections include Chicago Woman's Aid, UIC Spec. Coll.; the National Council of Jewish Women, 1898–1968, CHS; and the Woman's City Club of Chicago, 1916–66, CHS. One pamphlet, published by the American Jewish Archives, has been written about Purvin's life: Neil Kominsky, *Jennie Franklin Purvin, a Study in Womanpower* (1968). A version of Kominsky's profile, with a few additional comments, appears in Jacob Rader Marcus, *The American Jewish Woman: A Documentary History* (1981).

KARLA GOLDMAN

PUTNAM, ALICE HARVEY WHITING
January 18, 1841–January 19, 1919
EDUCATOR, KINDERGARTNER

Alice Harvey Whiting was born in Chicago, the third and youngest daughter of a Connecticut-born couple, William Loring and Mary (Starr) Whiting. Her father was a grain broker and founding member of the Chicago Board of Trade (1848). Alice Whiting was taught at home by her mother and sister and later attended the private Dearborn Seminary, a school for young women founded in 1854. In 1868 she married Joseph Putnam and left the Episcopal Church, in which she had been raised, to join the New Jerusalem Church, a Swedenborgian church. Putnam, who had come to Chicago from Maine as a young man, built up a real estate business that provided a comfortable living for the family. By 1871 the Putnams had two daughters, Charlotte and Alice. Another daughter, Helen, was born soon after, and a son, Henry Sibley, some years later. The Putnams were part of a circle of Chicago intellectuals interested in the latest theories of science, education, and religion; the circle included

many members of the small, but influential, New Jerusalem Church. In this milieu Alice Putnam became acquainted with the latest educational theories from Europe and read the *Kindergarten Messenger*, a journal advocating the educational approaches of German theorist Friedrich Fröbel (also Froebel).

In 1874, Alice Putnam responded to a letter in the *Kindergarten Messenger* by Bostonian educational reformer Elizabeth Peabody, an enthusiastic promoter of kindergartens, by opening in her parlor one of the first kindergartens in Chicago. She also began a parents' study group that read and discussed the works of Froebel. Froebel's romantic, spiritual view of childhood and motherhood was enthusiastically adopted by American women who saw in his ideas a vindication of the importance of mothers and women teachers in the lives of young children. Froebel held the idealistic view that children possessed within themselves the germ of all future development. He believed that early education should draw out and strengthen through children's own activity their latent sense of the unity of all things. His underlying idealist philosophy complemented Swedenborgian concepts of the unity of the material and spiritual world current in Putnam's thinking at the time.

Froebel, in order to translate his new theories about the nature of the child to practical educational methods, invented carefully planned teaching materials called "gifts" and "occupations" for mothers and teachers to introduce to children. The "gifts" were blocks of varied geometric shapes; the "occupations" were such handwork as paper folding and weaving. Carefully sequenced activities based on the gifts and occupations, along with songs, games, stories, and nature study, provided the basis for the nineteenth-century American kindergarten curriculum.

Alice Putnam studied Froebel's ideas with the major American proponents of his educational system, which had been introduced into the United States in the 1850s and 1860s. She first traveled to Columbus, Ohio, taking her oldest daughter with her, to study with Anna J. Ogden. Later she studied with the most famous proponents of Froebel's views in this country, Susan Blow in St. Louis, Missouri, and then Maria Kraus-Boelte in New York City. In 1880, Putnam attended progressive educator Francis W. Parker's summer school for teachers on Martha's Vineyard, Massachusetts, and was inspired by the realization that Froebel's ideas could be carried beyond the kindergarten into elementary education.

Putnam's Froebel study group for parents evolved into a training class for prospective kindergarten teachers as well as mothers. ELIZABETH HARRISON, who later founded the Chicago Kindergarten College (later National-Louis University), was an early member of the class. Enrolling in 1879, Harrison completed a year-long program in which she observed the three existing kindergartens in the city, attended lectures and "handwork" classes in Putnam's home, and student-taught under Putnam's supervision.

In 1880, along with members of her original study group, Putnam founded the Chicago Froebel Association as a vehicle for spreading the gospel of Froebel and as a school for kindergarten teachers. For a number of years Putnam did most of the teaching in the Chicago Froebel Association Training School. Until 1894, classes were held in the lecture room of the New

Jerusalem Church; from 1894 to 1902 classes were held at Hull-House. By the time of Putnam's retirement in 1910, the association had trained eight hundred kindergarten teachers. The Chicago Froebel Association also supported similar organizations in other cities; by 1893, its graduates were training other kindergarten teachers through kindergarten associations in Minnesota, Wisconsin, and Illinois.

Further support for kindergartens and kindergarten teachers was provided by the Chicago Kindergarten Club, founded by Putnam and Elizabeth Harrison in 1883. Composed of teachers, the club met every Saturday for five years and subsequently at monthly intervals, providing continuing education, working for the establishment of kindergartens in churches and settlement houses, and supporting the connections between kindergartens and the public schools. The dramatic growth of kindergartens in Chicago was reflected in the growth of the kindergarten club. In 1880 its membership was twenty, all the kindergartners (both teachers of kindergarten children and trainers of kindergarten teachers) in the city. Almost twenty years later, the club included representatives from sixty-nine private kindergartens, thirty-four kindergartens in social settlements, four in missions, and eighty-seven in public schools in the Chicago area. A substantial number of teachers in these kindergartens were products of Putnam's classes.

After studying with Francis Parker in Martha's Vineyard, Putnam recognized his strengths and in 1882 advocated his appointment as principal of Cook County Normal School. Shortly thereafter she moved with her family to a house near the school in suburban Englewood so that her daughters could attend the model elementary school and the training school for teachers. Parker invited her to supervise the model school's kindergarten and to teach twice-weekly classes on kindergarten methods to prospective elementary teachers. Putnam's teaching influenced the attitude of many new teachers toward the idea of the kindergarten and made them a force in support of public school kindergarten programs. At the time, compulsory attendance in school was required only for children between the ages of eight and fourteen years. There was resistance to committing public funds for kindergarten programs or the education of kindergarten teachers.

From 1883 to 1888, Putnam continued her work at Cook County Normal, in addition to her Froebel Association classes, without pay, since Parker was never able to convince the county to accept her as a member of the faculty. She was also a member of the circle of normal school faculty and other progressive educators who met regularly at Parker's home.

When Hull-House completed its Children's Building in 1894, JANE ADDAMS proposed that Putnam move her training class for kindergarten teachers there. In exchange for the use of a room and of the gymnasium for the training class, a member of the Froebel Association assumed the expenses of the Hull-House Kindergarten, already in operation. The association continued at Hull-House as an independent entity, but closely linked with the settlement's philosophy and activities, until 1902, when classes were moved to downtown Chicago. At Hull-House, senior students were encouraged to lead children's clubs and involve themselves in activities that would expose them to children beyond kindergarten age. Putnam still

taught theory and practice of kindergarten, but course work had expanded beyond Froebelian theory and handwork, with the new subjects of vocal music, drawing, physical culture, and psychology, each taught by a specialist. Special lecturers addressed the class on such topics as psychology, hygiene, and history of education.

Putnam was a regular participant in the discussions of progressive education that took place at Hull-House. Jane Addams deeply respected her scholarship and her "absolute devotion to children, and unfailing interest in their affairs" (quoted in Newall, 214). She said of Putnam, "She always insisted that, though we had twenty-six nationalities in our kindergarten, all the little children were surprisingly like those in the other groups with which she came in contact" (quoted in Newall, 214). This perceived similarity among children gave Putnam a sense of optimism that it was possible to solve problems associated with immigration through education.

In Chicago, the expansion of the kindergarten followed a pattern that was common across the country. Kindergartens began as private ventures for middle-class children, were taken up by settlement houses and other charitable agencies working with the poor and immigrants, and were finally incorporated into the public school system. A step in the process of gaining public school support was the provision by public schools of space for privately funded kindergartens. Under the auspices of the Chicago Froebel Association, the first of these kindergartens in Chicago opened in 1886 in the Brennan School in the Stockyards District; it was taught by an association graduate, Elsie Payne, with a paid assistant. Putnam took an intense interest in this venture and often visited and advised the teachers, making the trip to the school "down the 'Archey Road' in slow street cars" (Newall, 211). By 1892, nine formerly funded kindergartens were housed in public schools and the public school system assumed their full support. In 1899, the Chicago Public Schools incorporated kindergartens as a standard part of the school program.

Putnam's organizational work in support of the spread of kindergartens included her activities in the Chicago Woman's Club, the International Kindergarten Union (of which she was president in 1901), and the Kindergarten Section of the National Education Association. She presented many addresses and reports to those organizations. From 1906 to 1916, she taught two courses in the correspondence department of the University of Chicago, "The Training of Children (A Course for Mothers)" and "An Introduction to Kindergarten Theory and Practice."

Putnam's career spanned an era in the history of the kindergarten when the initially doctrinaire acceptance of Froebel's idealistic view of children and rigid set of methods gave way to a more empirically based, scientific approach to child psychology. For a time, both of the major kindergarten organizations—the International Kindergarten Union and the Kindergarten Department of the National Education Association—were sharply divided by conflict between the advocates of these two approaches. Susan Blow, the most doctrinaire of the followers of Froebel, regarded Putnam as a radical, saying in a letter in 1893, "There are some like Mrs. Putnam and Miss [Anna] Bryan of Chicago who think every new thing true" (quoted in Shapiro,

155). Putnam's willingness to modify strict Froebelian practice and particularly her openness to the ideas of G. Stanley Hall, Blow's arch-rival for the mind of kindergarten leaders, rankled the Froebelian. Hall, a pioneering psychologist at Clark University, criticized Froebel's method because it was not based on empirical observation of children's actual behavior and development, noting, for example, that the "gifts" and "occupations" were too small to be manipulated comfortably by young children. Putnam attended Hall's summer sessions at Clark University. When Hall undertook to investigate the thinking of kindergarten children by means of a questionnaire, he asked Putnam and Anna Bryan, head of the kindergarten department at Chicago's Armour Institute, to compose the questions.

Putnam resisted categorization, however. Though always open to new ideas in child psychology, she remained true, she believed, to the spirit of Froebel, holding to his principle of balance as a central idea that should be illustrated for children in construction, art, games, and dance. She introduced some of his occupations to her student teachers to demonstrate how he thought the child mind was revealed through manual arts, but she did not recommend their use with children. "I could have a kindergarten in a meadow with a group of children and only the flowers, grasses, earth, and my own two hands. Let the children lead you, and you will not go far astray. Study them, and let their actions serve as your guide" (quoted in Newall, 218).

Putnam spent the last few years of her life with her grown children, who had scattered to other cities. She continued to visit Chicago and died of nephritis on one such return in 1919. She was buried in Oak Woods Cemetery and a memorial service was held at the Francis W. Parker School.

Putnam's career illustrates important characteristics of the kindergarten movement, which opened up numerous opportunities for women, but unlike public education in this era, allowed for individual enterprise. A married woman from an affluent family could find a place in it, because the lines between charity and volunteerism, as opposed to paid employment, were still blurred. In this respect, as in its missionary fervor and its decidedly feminine cast, the movement resembles more closely the social settlement movement, with its support from women's clubs and wealthy individual women, than the school system of which it soon became a part. In addition, the association of motherhood with early childhood education both legitimated Putnam's participation and was a source of financial and political support, as wealthy and politically influential clubwomen joined the kindergarten movement.

Sources. Most of Alice Putnam's published work was taken from addresses presented to the International Kindergarten Union or the Kindergarten Section of the National Education Association (NEA). An exception, however, is an article, "The Use of Kindergarten Material in Primary Schools," in *The Kindergarten and the School by Four Active Workers* (1884). Addresses published in the *NEA Journal of Proceedings and Addresses* include "Shall Reading and Writing Be Taught in the Kindergarten?" 1893, and "Work and Play in the Kindergarten," 1901. Addresses published in the *Kindergarten Review* include a report on the planning of the International Kindergarten Union Conference, 1898, and "Froebel's Suggestions on Fostering Language," 1902–1903. The best source on Putnam's life is the article by her student Bertha Payne Newell, "Alice Putnam, 1848–1919," in a volume authorized by the International Kindergarten Union, *Pioneers of the Kindergarten in America* (1924). Another biographical source is Mary Jean Miller, "Account of the Chicago Kindergarten Club," *Kindergarten Magazine*, November 1897. Three more recent works place Putnam in the context of the kindergarten movement: Evelyn Weber, *The Kindergarten: Its Encounter with Educational Thought in America* (1969); Elizabeth Ross, *The Kindergarten Crusade: The Establishment of Preschool Education in America* (1976); and Michael Shapiro, *Child's Garden: The Kindergarten Movement from Froebel to Dewey* (1983). Putnam is included in *NAW* (1971).

NANCY STEWART GREEN

r

RAISA, ROSA BURSCHSTEIN
May 30, 1893–September 28, 1963

OPERATIC SOPRANO, VOICE TEACHER, SUPPORTER OF OPERA

Recognized as influential in efforts to establish a presence for opera in Chicago, Rosa Raisa (born Rose Burschstein) was born in Bialystok, a Russian sector of partitioned Poland. The youngest of three children, she was raised by her father, Herschel Burschstein, who worked as a trading contractor. Her mother died before she turned six. Her father remarried, and thereafter Burschstein spent a substantial amount of time caring for the child of her cousins, Dr. Paulo and Mrs. Wigdorchik, who also lived in Bialystok. Heavily persecuted for their Jewish faith, Burschstein and the Wigdorchiks felt the political climate grow increasingly more oppressive following the turn of the century. After surviving a bloody anti-Semitic pogrom that swept through the town in 1907, she and her cousins fled to the island of Capri.

Until this time, Burschstein's vocal training had consisted only of informal lessons provided by a family friend, Bertha Yuchnovetskaia, who taught her songs and gave her firm encouragement. Her professional instruction began when she arrived on Capri. Due to the influence and patronage of a wealthy Neapolitan family named Ascarelli that befriended Paulo Wigdorchik, Burschstein secured an audition at the Pietro-in-Maiella Conservatory in Naples, Italy. The conservatory accepted her immediately with a scholarship, and she became a student of the famous voice teacher Barbara Marchisio. Under Marchisio's tutelage from 1908 through 1912, Burschstein developed a flawless vocal technique, first studying the coloratura roles of Vincenzo Bellini, Gioacchino Rossini, and Gaetano Donizetti, and then taking on more dramatic parts from Giuseppe Verdi's and Giacomo Puccini's operas.

After Rose Burschstein graduated from the conservatory in 1912, Marchisio escorted her to Milan, Italy, where she auditioned for Cleofonte Campanini, world renowned maestro and musical director of the Chicago Grand Opera Company. The conductor and his wife, the famous soprano Eva Tetrazzini, instantly recognized her talent. After convincing her to change her name from Rose Burschstein to Rosa Raisa, Campanini arranged for her operatic debut as Leonora in Verdi's *Oberto, Conti di San Bonifacio* in Parma, Italy, on September 6, 1913. The audience enthusiastically responded to this performance, part of the centennial celebration of Verdi's birth, and Raisa received her first favorable public notice. In October of that year, she and Campanini traveled to Philadelphia, Pennsylvania, where she made her American debut as Queen Isabella in Alberto Franchetti's *Cristoforo Colombo*. Campanini then brought her to Chicago and introduced her to the city with which she was to have a lifelong association. Indeed, Raisa's career was so closely tied to the vicissitudes of Chicago's early opera companies that the events of the next thirty-five years of her life cannot be outlined without also taking into account the narrative of opera in Chicago.

Opera represented an extremely popular form of entertainment among Chicago audiences. From 1850 on, traveling troupes from New York and other cities presented many laudable productions of the most recent operatic compositions. Although these traveling companies brought superlative performances to Chicago, demand for a resident organization grew dramatically following the founding of the Chicago Symphony Orchestra in 1891. As a result, financier Harold McCormick established the Chicago Grand Opera Company in 1909. Raisa became a welcome member of this troupe, and on November 29, 1913, she made her critically acclaimed Chicago debut as Verdi's Aida. She remained with this company for the remainder of the 1913–14 season, singing the roles of Mimi in Puccini's *La Bohème*, Santuzza in Pietro Mascagni's *Cavalleria Rusticana*, and Isabella in *Cristoforo Colombo*. At the conclusion of this season, the company, suffering from severe financial difficulties, resolved to disband for at least the coming year.

FIG. 98. *Opera star Rosa Raisa rehearsing with the Chicago Opera Association.*

During this time, Raisa, like other singers associated with the Chicago company, traveled abroad, performing extensively on stages throughout Europe and South America. In 1914, she made her debut in Covent Garden, London, England, singing opposite Enrico Caruso in *Aida* and appearing on this same stage in productions of Arrigo Boito's *Mefistofele* and Wolfgang Amadeus Mozart's *Le Nozze di Figaro*. From there she traveled to Paris's Theatre des Champs-Élysées, where she sang in Verdi's *Un Ballo in Maschera*, and then to Rome's Teatro al Costanzi for Riccardo Zandonai's *Francesca da Rimini* and Verdi's *Aida*. During these years Raisa established an international reputation as one of the world's finest dramatic sopranos. Consequently, in January 1916, while singing at the Teatro Colon in Buenos Aires, she received invitations to join both the Metropolitan Opera Company in New York City and the newly reorganized Chicago Opera Association. Grateful to Campanini, who was still musical director in Chicago, Raisa made her decision to return to the more familiar stage rather than move to New York. In the fall of 1916, Raisa rejoined the Chicago company for what would be the first of sixteen consecutive seasons with this group.

During this same year, a promising baritone from Verona, Giacomo Rimini, made his debut in Chicago. He and Raisa began to appear together in performances of *Aida*, *Andrea Chenier*, and *Falstaff*. The two became virtually inseparable, and on November 20, 1919, they were married in St. Joseph, Michigan.

Between 1915 and 1921, the Chicago Opera Association gathered together a roster of singers including Claudia Muzio, Edith Mason, Tito Ruffo, Lucien Muratore, and Amelita Galli-Curci who, together with Raisa and Rimini, made this opera company one of the finest and most well respected in the world. Despite its resounding success, however, the association confronted some serious difficulties beginning in the 1920s. The trouble began when Cleofonte Campanini died in December 1919, and shortly thereafter both the artistic and executive directors resigned. Rather than hiring two people to fill these jobs, Harold McCormick announced that MARY GARDEN, the world-renowned soprano, would take on both positions as well as continue as prima donna. Her duties, however, proved far too arduous for one person, and the company fell almost immediately into dire financial straits. Consequently, at the conclusion of this season the Chicago Opera Association reorganized as the Chicago Civic Opera. Under the leadership of Samuel Insull as president and Giorgio Polacco as musical director, this company prospered from 1922 to 1932.

Although Chicago was Raisa's home base, she did not limit her activities exclusively to this city, nor did she restrict herself to the operatic stage. Among her many engagements were vocal recitals presented in Chicago, New York, and other cities throughout the United States. Oftentimes, she and Rimini concertized together, and they frequently donated the proceeds of their performances to Jewish orphanages. Raisa also traveled regularly through North America on annual three-month tours with the Chicago Opera Association and the Chicago Civic Opera. Raisa's engagements included seven South American and Mexican seasons.

One of the most exciting aspects of Raisa's career was her ongoing participation in American and world premieres of important operatic works. She appeared, for instance, in the first

American performances of Pietro Mascagni's *Isabeau* (1917), Italo Montemezzi's *La Nave* (1919), and Ottorino Respighi's *La Fiamma* (1935). She displayed her support of the opera-in-English movement, popular during the first half of the twentieth century, by starring in the premiere of W. Franke Harling's *A Light from St. Agnes* (1925). Far more significant than all these debuts, however, were two of her performances at the Teatro alla Scala in Milan, Italy: in 1924 she sang the part of Asteria in the long-awaited first production of Boito's *Nerone*, and two years later, Giacomo Puccini chose her to be his first Turandot.

While her participation in these Italian premiers situated Raisa partially in the nineteenth-century tradition of operatic production in which composers knew the voices for which they wrote, many of her other activities indicated that she was very much an artist of the twentieth century. She was among the earliest group of opera singers, for example, to preserve their voices on long-playing records; she made five groups of recordings from 1917 to 1933 for four labels (Pathe, Vocalion, Brunswick, and Voce del Padrone). Among the works she recorded were selections from *Aida*, *Mefistofele*, *I Vespri Siciliani*, *Il Trovatore*, *La Gioconda*, and *Andrea Chenier*. In addition to making these recordings, Raisa actively participated in the burgeoning life of live opera radio broadcasts. On November 13, 1922, the Chicago Opera Company became the first to perform an operatic work in its entirety over the radio on Chicago station KYW. The opera was Verdi's *Aida*, and Raisa sang the title role.

Raisa and Rimini became parents on July 7, 1931, to their only child, Rosa Giulietta. Shortly thereafter, in 1932, the Chicago Civic Opera disbanded, and the family went to Italy, where they remained until the fall of 1933. At this time, Chicago became home to a resident company, the Chicago Grand Opera Company, which, in 1935, changed its name to the Chicago City Opera Company. Raisa and Rimini sang with these groups until 1936, when they retired from the operatic stage to devote themselves full time to parenting.

The two artists remained active in the Chicago musical world following their retirement. Raisa emerged once, but only briefly, to sing the part of Leah in the American debut of Lodovico Rocca's *Il Dibuc* in Detroit, Michigan. She and Rimini focused their energy on establishing the Raisa-Rimini vocal studio, where they gave singing lessons. Through this studio, they formed an experimental chamber-opera group with the intention of creating more opportunities for young American singers to perform in public. Raisa and Rimini both became involved in their students' futures and regularly took the most promising among them to Italy for intensive training. Unfortunately, they were forced to shut down both the studio and opera company in the mid-1940s due to financial difficulties and World War II. Raisa then opened her own studio in the Fine Arts Building in downtown Chicago, where she taught many students through the 1950s who went on to sing at the Metropolitan and other major opera houses throughout the world. In addition to teaching, Raisa maintained an active role in the Chicago opera scene; she advised the organizers of the Lyric theatre, which became the city's longest lasting opera company, the Lyric Opera of Chicago.

Giacomo Rimini died on March 6, 1952. Several years later, Raisa moved to Pacific Palisades, California, where her daughter lived with her family. She traveled extensively during her later years to Italy and back to Chicago for Lyric Opera performances, but she spent the largest part of her time caring for her grandchildren. Raisa died in her home in Pacific Palisades following a long illness and was buried at Holy Cross Cemetery.

Rosa Raisa's brilliant soprano voice captured the attention of opera audiences in Chicago and around the world for nearly thirty-five years. Throughout her extensive career, her performances commanded overwhelming praise from both her musical peers and the press, and she is remembered for her musical talent as well as her deep commitment to Chicago's opera companies.

Sources. A microfilm reel of newspaper clippings, reviews, photographs, and programs pertaining to Raisa's work between 1922 and 1925 is located in the Music Division, New York Public Library. Several magazine and journal articles contain information on Raisa's life and career. The most thorough is Ruth Duskin Feldman, "Queen Mother of Opera," *Chicago*, October 1956. Others include Mary Jane Matz, "First Ladies of Puccini Premieres: Rosa Raisa," *Opera News*, March 4, 1961; "This Golden Voice Is Chicago's Own," *Opera Topics*, May 1931; and "Persecution in Russia Drove Rosa Raisa to Vocal Career," *Musical America*, December 2, 1916. Biographical entries on Raisa are found in *The New Grove Dictionary of Music and Musicians* (1992), *Dizionario critico-biografico dei cantanti con discografia operistica* (1964), and the *International Dictionary of Opera* (1990). Further information on Raisa is located in books and encyclopedias dealing specifically with Jewish history, including *The Universal Jewish Encyclopedia* (1969), *Great Jews in Music* (1986), *Famous Musicians of Jewish Origin* (1949), and Philip B. Bregstone, *Chicago and Its Jews: A Cultural History* (1933).

HILARY PORISS

REDFIELD, MARGARET PARK
December 6, 1898–February 6, 1977
ANTHROPOLOGIST

Margaret Park Redfield contributed to anthropology both as an independent researcher and in collaboration with her husband. She was born Margaret Lucy Park in Lansing, Michigan, the third of four children. Her father, Robert Park, was one of the principal founders of modern sociology at the University of Chicago; her mother, Clara Cahill, was a gifted artist who had studied art in Cincinnati and New York. Robert Park had begun his graduate studies in philosophy at Harvard and continued in Berlin, Germany, at the time Margaret was born. His young family then accompanied Park to Strasbourg and Heidelberg, where he received his doctorate in philosophy in 1903. While her older brother and sister returned to the United States with their maternal grandparents toward the end of Park's stay in Germany, Margaret Park remained with her parents as they tramped the Black Forest, where Robert Park studied the German peasant.

Margaret Park's childhood and early adolescence were spent in Wollaston, Massachusetts, where the family lived while Park completed his doctoral dissertation at Harvard. After graduation, Park served as press agent and director of public relations for Tuskegee Institute, Booker T. Washington's school in Alabama, visiting his wife and children during the summers and on holidays. Margaret Park's mother, interested in political and social reform, participated on the Massachusetts commission to create a widow's pension law.

Margaret Park graduated from Quincy High School, Wollaston, Massachusetts, where educator Francis Parker first initiated programs based on his theories of progressive education. In 1916, after her freshman year at Wellesley College, Margaret Park moved with her family to Chicago, enrolling at the University of Chicago. Her father had joined the sociology department at the University of Chicago in 1914. Margaret Park majored in Russian studies. Her mother's interest in Russian history and philosophy predated her marriage and later was shared by Park's father. The four years from 1916 to 1920, when Margaret Park completed her bachelor of philosophy degree, paralleled the revolutionary period in Russian history and the foundation of the new soviet system. She studied with Samuel Harper, professor of Russian languages and institutions, who was appointed by President Woodrow Wilson to a U.S. commission to Russia in 1917. Harper had collected information on the Russian peasant for the University of Chicago research project on peasant peoples conducted by Professors W. I. Thomas and Robert Park. Margaret Park planned to accompany Harper to Russia on one of his research missions so that she could study the effects of the revolutionary changes in Russia on the peasantry. By 1919, the year the trip was to take place, the situation in Russia was deemed too hazardous and Harper abandoned his plans. Margaret Park's classmate and close friend—soon to be her husband—Robert Redfield warned her about visiting Russia.

Margaret Park and Robert Redfield were married on June 14, 1920, after her graduation. She worked as a research assistant for her father, while Redfield, whose main field of study in college was biology, worked in his father's law practice. At this time Robert Park had begun to enrich his sociology research approach with new theories and techniques from anthropology and social psychology. Influential in the thinking of his group was William Graham Sumner's *Folkways* (1906). Armed with a copy of *Folkways* and supported by a stipend from Robert Park, the Redfields traveled to Mexico to assess its possibilities for sociological and anthropological field research. They decided that Mexico, where little anthropological research had been conducted, offered extensive resources as a culture from which to compare the extensively studied Native American cultures.

Margaret and Robert Redfield returned from Mexico in 1923. Robert Redfield began formal graduate studies at the University of Chicago in the Department of Sociology and Anthropology in 1924. Their first child, Lisa, was born that year, and a second, Robert III, "Tito," in 1926. The Redfields returned to Mexico and settled in the small mountain community of Tepoztlan, Morelos, where Robert Redfield began his dissertation research.

Margaret Redfield proved an invaluable collaborator on the Tepoztlan research, as she was successful in gaining the trust of the women of the village in order to assemble information on the birth customs of the Tepoztecos. From this information she published "A Child Is Born in Tepoztlan" in 1928 in *Mexican Folkways*. Margaret Redfield explained how childbirth customs in Tepoztlan were a combination of elements of practical utility and magic. In 1929 she published a longer article from her Tepoztlan research in the *Journal of American Folklore*, "Notes on the Cookery of Tepoztlan, Morelos." This article on the food habits of the community assesses the presence of Aztec and Spanish elements in food preparation and its relation to the calendric cycle of the festivals, a central aspect of village life. In addition to birth and food customs, Margaret Redfield recorded the *corridos*, local songs that constituted a source of news in the semiliterate community. The transcription and interpretation of these songs were vital to the Tepoztlan study, since they provided clues to the nature of the place of the village in the continuum of development from traditional rural to urban culture.

In 1930 Robert Redfield published his dissertation as *Tepoztlan, A Mexican Village: A Study of Folk Life.* In it he traces the effects on the small mountain village of modernizing elements emanating from Mexico City, some fifty miles away. *Tepoztlan* defined the "folk society" as a new topic of anthropological study. The Redfields' publications describe how cultural change takes place, examining how the older culture influences elements of the new to produce cultural forms that are distinct and original.

In 1932 the Redfields began field work in Yucatan. Robert Redfield had been appointed research associate with the Carnegie Institute of Washington, D.C., early in 1930, and Carnegie sponsored his new research to compare four communities in Yucatan, beginning with a small bush community and progressing to the larger village of Dzitas, the town of Chan Kom, and the city of Merida. From 1932 to 1935 the Redfields focused on Chan Kom and Dzitas. In "The Folk Literature of a Yucatecan Town" (1935), Margaret Redfield analyzes a collection of oral stories gathered in Dzitas during the winter of 1933. Just as she had with the *corridos* in Tepoztlan, Margaret Redfield studied the content rather than the formal aspects of the stories to illuminate the process of cultural change taking place on the Yucatan peninsula. She viewed the stories from the standpoint of the folk society in order to understand their social function and to discover why particular oral literatures survived while others disappeared.

A third child, Joanna, was born in 1930 and a fourth, James, in 1935. Robert Redfield was in Yucatan in early 1930 and 1931 without Margaret and the family. In 1932–33, Margaret was present in Yucatan to help with field work in Dzitas and Chan Kom. The Redfield family was in Agua Escondida, Guatemala, in 1937 and again between 1939 and 1940. Tragedy struck the family when their twelve-year-old son, Tito, was killed in a sledding accident in 1938 in Illinois between these trips to Central America.

In either 1937 or 1939, Margaret Park Redfield wrote "Antonia," an unpublished account of the life story of the mestizo cook/laundress employed by the Redfields at some point during their field work in Merida, Yucatan. Antonia is about thirty-eight years old, wears the traditional costume of *huipil* and skirt, and is of the "self-respecting lower class" (p. 1), although as a child she had "seen better days" (p. 1). Park Redfield writes that she decided to record Antonia's story because it would help anthropologists gain a clearer picture of the customs and culture of a typical urban dweller of the region. In addition, she explains how Antonia's story resulted from a relationship of confidence and friendship that grew up between the two women, close in age and experience as mothers but of very different backgrounds. The descriptions of Antonia's childhood, her first and second troubled marriages, and the web of relationships existing between Antonia and her sister's families are interspersed with vignettes concerning birth and child-rearing customs that are a blend of folk custom and modern medicine.

Antonia's story was gleaned while both women worked side by side in the Redfield kitchen. The cook was viewed not simply as an informant but as an equal, at least as far as gender experiences were concerned. This empathy helped Park Redfield gain an intimate and honest view of her friend's experiences. Preserving the voice of an urban working class woman, "Antonia" is an unpublished but valuable contribution to anthropological literature.

In the 1940s Margaret Redfield began to study the American family. Her father's close colleague and collaborator at the University of Chicago, Ernest W. Burgess, viewed changes in the contemporary American family as dynamic and creative. Others, such as Pitirim A. Sorokin, identified the changes observed in the American family in the 1940s as unstable and destructive. Margaret Redfield pointed out in 1946 in "The American Family: Consensus and Freedom" that "a tendency to instability does not necessarily mean complete disintegration" (p. 176). In a world of weakened community life, where individuals faced many choices based on values largely determined by commercial sources, "consensus" or stable values were vitally important. These values, Margaret Redfield contended, came from consistent and shared family rituals and other forms of cultural organization that united members of the family to one another and to society at large. Anticipating Robert Redfield's questioning of whether social science objectivity was either possible or entirely desirable, which he expressed in his 1953 work *The Primitive World and Its Transformations*, Margaret Redfield critiqued the goal of scientific objectivity.

Margaret Redfield began to work with Fei Hsiao-tung, a former student of her father, who applied the principles of the Chicago sociologists to his work on a Chinese province. Margaret Redfield assisted Fei with the revision of his first book, *Earthbound China: A Study of Rural Economy in Yunnan*, republished in the United States in 1945. Fei verbally translated most of the work into English while she transcribed it. Fei encouraged the Redfields to come to China. The trip planned for 1944 was postponed until the fall of 1948 due to political unrest in China; it was then cut short as the communists took over Peiping in January 1949. The Redfields slowly returned to the United States that winter and the following spring, when Robert Redfield delivered a planned series of lectures at Wolfgang Goethe University in Frankfurt am Main, Germany. Margaret Redfield's interest in China continued, and in 1953 she edited the second of Fei Hsiao-tung's books, *China's Gentry: Essays in Urban-Rural Relations*, while her husband wrote the book's introduction.

In the spring of 1955, Robert Redfield became seriously ill with the first symptoms of lymphatic leukemia, a disease that took his life five years later. After her husband's death, Margaret Redfield worked with Everett C. Hughs and others to edit her husband's papers; the first volume, *Human Nature and the Study of Society*, appeared in 1962 and the second, *The Social Uses of Social Science*, in 1963. She also worked with Charles Leslie, who prepared the entry on Robert Redfield for the *Inter-*

national Encyclopedia of the Social Sciences, and with Winifred Raushenbush, her father's former student, who wrote *Robert E. Park: Biography of a Sociologist* (1979). Margaret Redfield died in 1977 at the age of seventy-eight.

Margaret Park Redfield exemplified a new generation of college-educated women who began to bridge the gap between professional and family life. In the 1880s and 1890s, college-trained women such as JANE ADDAMS generally had to forego marriage and children if they wanted to put their education to professional use. By the time Margaret Park Redfield married in the early 1920s, young women with college degrees began experimenting with ways to have both. Although it was still unusual and difficult, Margaret Park Redfield blended family responsibilities and professional pursuits in ways that helped her own and her husband's work flourish. After her husband's death, she continued strong professional relationships. Her work is of interest because of the contributions she made to anthropology, her exploration of the ways in which the Mexican communities she studied bridged folk belief and modern ideas of health and hygiene in the raising of children and the treatment of disease, her focus on the social function of oral "literatures" in modernizing societies, and her examination of the dynamics of a working class Mexican laundress's life before such a subject and approach were common. It is useful to evaluate her life and works in terms of the historical problems of how women have articulated the multiple roles their lives require.

Sources. The Margaret Park Redfield Papers are at UC Spec. Coll. and include personal correspondence, material related to her work with Fei Hsiao-tung, some written field material, and a reprint of "Notes on the Cookery of Tepoztlan, Morelos." Correspondence is also in the Robert Redfield Papers, UC Spec. Coll., as are copies and/or manuscripts of her major anthropological writings. See also the Samuel Northrup Harper Papers, UC Spec. Coll. For further biographical information about Margaret Redfield, an oral interview with James Redfield was conducted by Jean Kadel on March 27, 1995. Margaret Redfield wrote "A Child Is Born in Tepoztlan," *Mexican Folkways*, April–June 1928; "Notes on the Cookery of Tepoztlan, Morelos," *Journal of American Folklore*, April–June 1929; "The Folk Literature of a Yucatecan Town," *Contributions in American Archaeology*, Carnegie Institute of Washington, D.C., June 1935; "The American Family: Consensus and Freedom," *American Journal of Sociology*, November 1946. She coauthored, with Robert Redfield, *Disease and Its Treatment in Dzitas, Yucatan*, *Contributions to American Anthropology and History*, no. 32, Carnegie Institute of Washington, D.C., publication no. 523, June 1940. Two biographies of Margaret Park Redfield's father give some insights into her early life: Fred H. Matthews, *Quest for an American Sociology: Robert E. Park and the Chicago School* (1977), and Winifred Raushenbush, *Robert E. Park: Biography of a Sociologist* (1979).

JEAN KADEL

REED, MYRTLE
September 27, 1874–August 17, 1911
NOVELIST, COOKBOOK EDITOR

Myrtle Reed, one of the more popular novelists of her day, was born in Norwood Park, then a suburb of Chicago. Her mother, Elizabeth (Armstrong) Reed, born in Maine, was a scholar of Greek and Hebrew and wrote books on the Bible, Hinduism, Buddhism, and Persian literature. Myrtle Reed's father, Hiram Von Reed, had been a preacher for the Disciples of Christ in Harvard, Illinois. He established a literary magazine in Chicago called the *Western Monthly*. Myrtle Reed had two older brothers, Earl Howell Reed, a founder and president of the Chicago Society of Etchers, and Charles B. Reed, a Chicago surgeon and obstetrician. Both were published writers. In such a family it was not surprising that Reed's parents assumed she would become a writer. Her name was chosen because her father thought it would look good in print. Her first publication, when she was about ten years old, was a story in a juvenile magazine, *The Acorn*.

Myrtle Reed had dark brown hair and eyes and a pleasant face, accented by dark eyebrows. She was overweight even as a child and did not participate in the usual games and sports, choosing instead books and conversations with adults. She learned eventually to anticipate and even to initiate jokes about her size.

Myrtle Reed attended public schools in Chicago, graduating in 1893 from West Division High School, where her years were marked by good grades. Following her graduation from high school, she suffered from emotional problems, blamed on overwork, which precluded further formal education. She continued to read widely, expressing a preference for Thomas Carlyle and Ralph Waldo Emerson but including science and medicine, fiction, humor, fantasy, poetry, and the occult. Her first signed story appeared in *Munsey's* in February 1896. The next year she published twenty-three signed magazine articles. Reed's first novel, *Love Letters of a Musician*, written in about five days of feverish activity, was rejected by several publishers before being accepted by Putnam's for publication in 1899. It consists of a series of fictional letters telling the romantic story of a young musician and the bride the letters won for him.

An immediate success, *Love Letters* was followed in 1900 by *Later Love Letters of a Musician*. Both novels are filled with idealism, romantic imagery, and poetic descriptions of nature. By October 1902, *Love Letters* was in its twelfth printing and *Later Love Letters* in its seventh. Publishers began to solicit Reed for her manuscripts, but she remained loyal to Putnam's, which had been the first publisher to give her a chance.

In 1901 she published *The Spinster Book*, a series of humorous essays on gender relationships that contrasts sharply with her two previous books. Her comments were often satirical, with many negative references to men. Many of the generalizations about helpless females and insensitive males, though tinged with humor, echoed the conventional stereotypes of that time. *Lavender and Old Lace*, which was to become her most popular novel, appeared in 1902. In it she told the story of a middle-aged woman who waited faithfully for more than thirty years for her seafaring lover and was at last united with him through death. Two themes predominate in this romance: one, woman's need for and dependence on love; the other, woman's steadfastness and strength of character even in the face of her lover's unfaithfulness. These themes were to be repeated in different ways through all of her fiction.

Myrtle Reed's work was characterized by a romantic imagination, high moral tone, and facility of language. With the exception of her one historical novel, *The Shadow of Victory*, a tale of the Fort Dearborn Massacre, none were set in Chicago. Most are devoid of any detail that would place them geographically other than on a sea coast or in the country. Reed was a member of Chicago's literary club, the Little Room, from 1906 until her death. That she spurned the emerging movement toward literary realism was probably due to her intrinsic idealism and her commitment to promoting traditional moral values.

With the income from her writing, Reed purchased a two-flat building on Chicago's North Side, and until 1906 she lived there with her parents in an apartment that she dubbed "Quality Coop." There she assumed responsibility for the housekeeping, and, under the pseudonym "Olive Green," began a series of cookbooks that subsequently grew to ten volumes. The cookbooks were written with both thoroughness and humor, as were numerous housekeeping articles published under the name Katherine LaFarge Norton.

During her high school years, Reed had edited the West Division High School paper, the *Voice*, and in that capacity had entered into a correspondence with James Sydney McCullough, a young man who held a similar position at a Toronto school. A romance developed and continued through the mail for about six years. Then, after a brief face-to-face meeting in New York, McCullough moved to Chicago and established himself in the real estate business. The couple were quietly married in October 1906, at Benton Harbor, Michigan. The elopement and marriage ceremony were written into her next novel, *Flower of the Dusk* (1908).

The McCulloughs moved into "Paradise Flat," an apartment on Chicago's North Side in a building they had built previous to their marriage. Reed continued to write. Novels, magazine articles, poems, cookbooks, and biographical sketches appeared regularly under her name or one of her pen names, some of which she chose not to reveal. Her pattern for work on the novels was to withdraw from society for a time. During these writing periods her maid ran the household and protected her from all intrusion. Sometimes Reed went out of town to a hotel or resort, where she wrote a novel in four to six weeks. She began a novel with an idea for the title. Then she designed a rough outline of the plot and characters, wrote the last chapter, and finally the central part. The novels were heavily sprinkled with her own philosophy and moral reflections.

The completion of a novel was usually celebrated with some sort of social occasion at "Paradise Flat," and then Reed and her husband might go on a fishing trip. She frequently affirmed that the highest calling of any woman was to be wife and homemaker, yet her writing enabled her to contribute substantially to the financial support of herself and her husband and to support her parents as well. Most of her heroines gave up their careers for marriage, but Reed was neither willing nor able to do that. McCullough encouraged and praised her work, though he urged her to keep to a more disciplined work schedule.

Unfortunately, the marriage failed to live up to Reed's high ideals. McCullough began drinking heavily and was often absent on business trips. Reed had a history of emotional problems. Under the stress of her writing schedule, she resorted to the barbiturate Veronal to relieve chronic insomnia. She continued to present her marriage to her friends and family as ideally happy, but a few weeks before her death, she shared her unhappiness and disappointment with her mother. Although the last year of her life was marked by severe depression, she published two cookbooks, a novel, *The Master of the Vineyard*, and her only book of poetry, *Sonnets to a Lover*, dedicated to her husband. In addition she completed her last novel, *A Weaver of Dream*, and began work on another. Her later books became more somber as she examined love triangles and suicide and defined love as service, sacrifice, and self-denial. In *Master of the Vineyard* she seems to present her own marital unhappiness and unequivocally rejects divorce as a solution.

On August 16, 1911, Reed planned a special celebration of the fifth anniversary of their engagement. McCullough forgot the occasion, arriving at home after midnight, and left the following morning for a business trip without saying good-bye. Myrtle Reed died that day after an overdose of Veronal, leaving her maid the following note: "Dear Annie—I am leaving you a check for $1,000 for your true and faithful service during four years. If my husband had been as good and kind to me and as considerate as you, I would not be going where I am now" (*Chicago Record-Herald*, August 19–21, 1911). A coroner's inquest declared her to have been insane at the time. Based on her instructions, funeral services were held in an Episcopal chapel, and her body was cremated. Reed's estate was valued at $80,000, and she was earning about $25,000 annually in royalties. Her will, dated December 1908, left the entire estate in trust to her parents and, after their deaths, to McCullough as beneficiary.

Although Myrtle Reed never attained the literary heights to which she aspired, she did achieve a large measure of recognition and popularity in her own time. When she died at the age of thirty-six, she left thirty-one books, six of which were edited and published posthumously. *Lavender and Old Lace* passed its fortieth printing in late 1911, and a dramatic version was published by Rose Warner in 1938. In 1916 twenty of her books were still being advertised by Putnam's under the heading "Over one million copies sold." One of the posthumous books, *A Woman's Career* (1914), expresses her bitterness at the dual demands of housekeeping and career, demands not experienced by men. Never a suffragist, she felt gender inequalities deeply and saved her more sarcastic humor for them: "Women climb Parnassus to the jangle of pots and pans, further hampered by corsets, french heels, nursing bottles, and men who, like Kipling's Vampire, cannot understand" (*A Woman's Career*, 49). Yet she maintained a vision of hope for women's achievements: "If we accept no handicaps save those of nature, we shall ascend to our destined heights, and take our places in such a manor as we may deserve" (*A Woman's Career*, 56).

Sources. Myrtle Reed's will and probate file can be found in the archives of the Circuit Court of Chicago. A six-page letter to Richard Carpenter (January 26, 1898) that includes some of her early theories about writing is in the Richard Carpenter Papers, CHS. A letter to Allen Pond is in the Little Room collection, NL. Reed's works include eleven cookbooks; eleven novels, including one historical novel, *The Shadow of Victory* (1903), and one humorous novel, *At the Sign of the Jack O'Lantern* (1905); one book of children's songs (with Eva Cruzen Hart), *Pickaback Songs* (1903); two books of short biographies; one book of poetry; six books of essays, short stories, and sayings, including two that are distinctly humorous and satirical; and numerous contributions to periodicals of the day. Other sources include introductions by Mary B. Powell in *The Myrtle Reed Year Book* (1911) and *Happy Women* (1913); and a pamphlet, *Myrtle Reed* (1911), which includes "Myrtle Reed as Her Friends Know Her" and "Why Myrtle Reed's Books Are Popular" by

Ethel S. Colson and Norma B. Carson, respectively, both reprints from *Book News Monthly*, January 1911. The Chicago newspapers *CT, Daily Journal*, and *Record-Herald* carried extensive articles August 18–21, 1911, and the *Record-Herald* Sunday Supplement for October 20, 1911, included "The Myrtle Reed I Knew" by Virginia Fair. *NAW* (1971) includes an entry for Reed.

PHYLLIS ECKARDT THOLIN

REIS, NANNIE ASCHENHEIM
December 28, 1871–October 14, 1940
CLUBWOMAN, NEWSPAPER COLUMNIST, COMMUNAL LEADER

Nannie Aschenheim Reis participated in an array of social and cultural projects and dedicated herself to the proposition that women's ideas and women's energies were vital to Chicago, America, and the world. Born to Adolph and Zerlina (Cohn) Aschenheim in Dresden, Germany, she immigrated to Chicago with her family in 1883. She remained a Chicagoan the rest of her life and dedicated herself to making the city work as a community. A firm believer in the principle that women should organize themselves for the betterment of society, she was active in a variety of clubs designed to help immigrants assimilate to the new world, aid strangers stranded in uncomfortable circumstances, assist the blind, and tap the political energies of women in general. As the women's clubs columnist with the English language Jewish newspaper the *Reform Advocate* for almost three decades, she was one of the most visible and articulate figures in a movement that saw women as essential actors in bettering society.

Developing proficiency in English soon after her arrival in Chicago, Aschenheim retained her fluency in German. She read avidly and was familiar with the literature of both of her chief languages. Throughout her career as a writer and community activist, she asserted that literature was important for the sense of history and the sense of moral empowerment it could give. She saw intellectual exercise as linked to social and political activity. The more women and men read and reflected on great ideas, the more likely they were to work toward specific communal goals. As she put it in a *Reform Advocate* column May 1, 1915, "Let then the club who has graduated from Rousseau, Rosetti [*sic*] and Ruskin, and from 'School extension' or 'Social service' devote itself to creating and spreading an honest, intelligent public opinion."

In 1895, she married Ignace J. Reis, a Chicago chiropodist. The couple had two children. Ralph, the older of the two, became an obstetrician and gynecologist in Chicago, while Herbert died in late childhood following an accident.

Nannie Reis was deeply involved with Reform Judaism. She was president of the Temple Israel Ladies Society from 1904 to 1906 and then president of the B'nai Sholom Temple Israel Ladies Society from 1906 to 1911 after the two congregations merged. In addition, she came to know Rabbi Emil G. Hirsch of Chicago Sinai Congregation and Hirsch's son-in-law Gerson Levi, the eventual rabbi of B'nai Sholom Temple Israel congregation. The two rabbis were publisher and assistant publisher, respectively, of the *Reform Advocate* (the *Advocate* after 1937), and through her association with them, Reis became a contributor in 1910. After a second article, "A Survey of the Jewish Women's Clubs," on May 31, 1913, she began to write regularly, eventually contributing a column, "In the World of Jewish Womankind," which first appeared on December 19, 1914. She continued writing the column until her death, although it was renamed "This, Our Day" some time in the late 1930s.

At the same time that she commented on the activities of clubwomen, Reis gained her chief renown as a club member and community activist. In 1910, she cofounded with HANNAH SOLOMON and Mrs. M. A. Weinberg the Conference of Jewish Women's Organizations, an association of representatives of more than eighty different Jewish clubs in the Chicago area. An earlier organization of Jewish women's groups, the Conference of Jewish Women, had disbanded in 1900. She saw the organization as a vehicle for bringing together the energies of women active in a variety of different associations, and she praised it for breaking down barriers between people in the city. Writing about the role of clubs and organized womanhood, Reis stated that club life "vitalizes for local purposes, for home use, so to speak, not only energy of all women who are interested in the same objects and ideals but brings into play all the varied courses of thought and action, all the varying starting points and aims that will act and re-act on all they encounter. It is this variety that endows the Conference [of Jewish Women's Organizations] with its greatest power" ("A Survey of the Jewish Women's Clubs," *Reform Advocate*, May 31, 1913). As an immigrant, Reis was deeply involved with the Traveler's Aid Society, serving as recording secretary from 1914 to 1933 and as a board member from 1914 until her death in 1940, when her son Ralph succeeded to her position.

Reis's first piece in the *Reform Advocate* appeared on May 21, 1910, and established the thoughtful, critical, and elegantly humorous tone she retained throughout her writing career. Calling the article "The Woman and the Club," Reis made broad use of the two meanings of the word "club," the one a stick used in prehistoric times to force women into submission and the other a form of organization that allowed women to take an important place in society. She proposed that women in clubs were not only capable of making important contributions to the social debate but that their combined strength in clubs would make them impossible to ignore. She considered the club a central means by which modern woman could have her say in a world that habitually discounted women's thinking.

Reis was a founder of the Women of Rotary, for whom she served as founding vice-president (1921–22), president (1923–24), and advisory board member from 1924 until her death. Her contributions to Rotary functions ranged from the book discussions she led to the clever fund-raising ideas she devised.

Reis was involved with the National Council of Jewish Women for much of her life. About a decade younger than Hannah Solomon, SADIE AMERICAN, and the other women who founded the organization in 1893, Reis saw it as one of the most enduring institutions for harnessing women's political power. She reported on the activities of the council regularly from 1915 through 1940 and was herself active in it. She eventually became president of the Chicago branch from 1922 to 1926, and she took pride in seeing the council as something that she and her contemporaries had inherited, strengthened, and passed on to their daughters. As she wrote in her March 22, 1935, column

for the *Reform Advocate*, "the National Council of Jewish Women is continuing to perpetuate itself by arousing the living interest of the young women of Jewry still retaining the time-worn and time-tried loyalty of the envisioned generation of the founder [Hannah Solomon] herself and that equally sturdy one in between these two."

Reis's activism extended beyond the Jewish world to include a wide variety of cultural and social issues. In that same spirit, she was active in a number of service organizations. She was a founding board member of the Illinois League of Women Voters (1922–24); she served on the boards of B'nai B'rith Women's Auxiliary and Maimonides Hospital (later Mount Sinai Hospital); and she was active in the United Order of True Sisters, the Blind Service Association, and the Chicago Round Table of Christians and Jews. She also led a number of book discussion groups across the city. One group on the South Side lasted for about twenty-five years and boasted eighteen loyal members.

With her love of literature and her fluency in two languages, Reis was a natural to try her hand at translation as a means of opening up communication between two worlds. She often led discussions of books written in other languages, and friends reported that she attempted to translate book-length works on two or three occasions. In her capacity as a club member, she would occasionally serve as translator for German speakers, something she did most famously on March 5, 1931, for Albert Einstein, when he gave an address on pacifism at Chicago's Union Station.

While the topics of Reis's columns changed to reflect the times in which she wrote, her subjects remained consistent. Throughout her years as a writer, she condemned racial and ethnic hatred and praised America as a place that could accommodate differences. In an article on August 16, 1919, she condemned the Chicago race riots; on December 26, 1925, she critiqued immigrant education efforts; and on May 3, 1935, she condemned fascism and Bolshevism as anti-democratic. Shocked by the rise to power of Adolph Hitler in her homeland, Germany, she took the opportunity to praise an America that permitted strangers to assimilate to its mores and that asked its women to lead the way. In one of her final columns for the *Advocate*, published March 10, 1939, she wrote about the need for Jewish women's groups to help train German refugees in American social practices. Women, she argued, were the real bulwarks of American society. She wrote, "In American life it is the woman who determines the social standing of the family. . . . Her family's social standing is determined by the sort of gentility she can stamp upon the family."

Following the death of her husband in 1938, Reis moved in with her son and daughter-in-law. She continued her writing and club activities until weeks before her death from what was diagnosed as a cerebral hemorrhage. Rabbi Charles Shulman of the North Shore Congregation Israel, Glencoe, Illinois, delivered her eulogy, and she was buried in Mt. Isaiah Israel Cemetery in Chicago.

In the course of her life, Nannie Reis crossed a number of borders and worked to open communication between the different worlds she knew firsthand. Born in Germany and yet fully at home in America, she translated not only German for English speakers but also described what it meant to come to a new country for those who had always been here. As a woman excluded from formal political participation for much of her adult life, she helped other women find alternate ways to shape society. At the same time, she celebrated the power of women before an audience that included men. She sought to understand immigrants and outsiders and she sought to give voice to the women of her community. She used her considerable gifts as a writer and her service as a clubwoman to those ends.

Sources. Reform Advocate (*Advocate* after 1937) contains Nannie Aschenheim Reis's column as it appeared from 1910 to 1940. Her essay "The Modern Esther" appeared in the January–March 1928 issue of *Jewish Woman.* The fullest published account of her life appears in a lengthy obituary from the *Advocate,* October 18, 1940. A good supplement to that article is Rabbi Charles Shulman's eulogy for her in the Charles Shulman Papers, the American Jewish Archives, Cincinnati, Ohio. In addition, a copy of a memorial prepared at her death is on file in the Chicago Jewish Archives, the Spertus Institute of Jewish Studies, Chicago. Her name appears frequently in the papers of the Conference of Jewish Women and the National Council of Jewish Women, available at the Chicago Jewish Archives; in the Women of Rotary Papers at Rotary International, Chicago, Illinois; in the Illinois Traveler's Aid Society Papers and the Jane Addams Papers, UIC Spec. Coll.; and the Illinois League of Women Voters papers at CHS. Reis is mentioned in H. L. Meites, *History of the Jews of Chicago* (1924, reprint 1990); Faith Rogow, *Gone to Another Meeting: The National Council of Jewish Women, 1893–1993* (1993); and the *Chicago Chronicle: Jewish Pioneers Issue,* undated, in the *Reform Advocate* file at the Chicago Jewish Archives.

JOE KRAUS

RICE, HARRIET ALLEYNE
January 14, 1866–May 24, 1958
PHYSICIAN, SETTLEMENT WORKER

Harriet Rice was born in Newport, Rhode Island, the daughter of African American parents, George Addison Rice, a steamer steward, and Lucinda (Webster) Rice. Her father, born in Maryland, prospered sufficiently for the family to own its own home. Aspiring to self-employment, he at one point opened a restaurant, but the business failed and he returned to work for the steamer lines.

The third daughter and fourth surviving child, Rice attended Rogers High School, Newport's integrated public secondary institution. An excellent student, her achievements merited her receiving the first prize for Greek at her graduation exercises, but because the terms of the seventy-five dollar prize required that it go to a male pupil, she was denied it. A man in New York, learning of the unfair treatment, sent her, care of the school principal, a check for the prize amount.

Harriet Rice was the first daughter and the second child in her family to attend college. She entered as a freshman at Wellesley College in the fall of 1883. She was the first African American to graduate from Wellesley.

At Wellesley, as Rice would later describe it, she was among "the 'creme de la creme' of American Womanhood" ("Our Fiftieth Reunion," 5). The president of Wellesley during Rice's years there was Alice Freeman, graduate of the University of Michigan, who provided guidance to many undergraduates. Over the years, Freeman took a particular interest in supporting the ambitions of young African American women. Freeman encouraged Rice, who later recalled the president's pleasing smile.

Early in her senior year, Rice experienced a serious fall that forced her to return to Newport to recuperate. Although she graduated in 1887 with her class, her recovery was only partial. The nature of her condition is not known.

In September 1888 she enrolled as a medical student at the University of Michigan, three years after the university had graduated its first African American female physician. Rice's much older brother George, who enrolled in medical school in Europe when she was only four, had preceded her in the profession. Rice completed her first year, but she became very ill the following summer due to the lingering effects of her accident. Dropping out of medical school, she underwent two operations the following autumn.

By September 1890 she had recovered sufficiently to enroll in the M.D. degree program at the Woman's Medical College of the New York Infirmary for Women and Children. After earning an M.D. in 1891, Rice interned the following year in Boston at the prestigious New England Hospital for Women and Children.

Rice had chosen a field in which women were making great strides. Although in 1870 there were only 544 trained women doctors, by 1900 the number would burgeon to 7,382, as additional colleges for women were founded and coeducational medical schools enrolled women. Rice was therefore in the second generation of women doctors, a generation that, unlike the pioneering first generation, expected to join the ranks of male physicians as equals. She was also in the second generation of African American women doctors. The first African American woman completed her medical degree in 1858; by 1896, there were 115 African American women with medical degrees.

Harriet Rice spent the following year doing postgraduate work in Philadelphia at one of two women's hospitals there. By fall of 1893, she had resettled in Chicago and taken up residence at Hull-House, the settlement house cofounded by JANE ADDAMS and ELLEN GATES STARR.

Two women Rice had known in the East had recently moved to Chicago: BERTHA VAN HOOSEN, who had been the resident physician at New England Hospital for Women while Rice was there and who was now struggling to establish her own Chicago practice; and the now married Alice Freeman Palmer, who came to Chicago in 1892 to serve part-time as the first dean of women at the University of Chicago. Palmer favored educated women's involvement in urban life through the work of settlement houses and may have put Rice in touch with Jane Addams.

Rice arrived in Chicago at age twenty-seven with impressive credentials. As late as 1904, only half of the graduates of medical schools had received any postgraduate training. Nevertheless, like the other approximately two hundred women doctors in the city, she faced enormous hurdles. Male doctors refused to let women physicians send their patients to the hospitals they controlled. Furthermore, white physicians refused to let black physicians refer cases to white hospitals, and white patients were horrified by the idea of being treated by a black doctor.

At Hull-House, Rice first worked with another woman doctor at the settlement's new medical dispensary and clinic. Its clients were the immigrant and nonimmigrant working poor and the destitute poor. Almost all, if not all, of them were eastern and southern European, that is, white. Blacks made up 1.3 percent of the population of Chicago in 1890, and most lived on Chicago's South Side. After Rice's first year at the clinic, she declined to continue working there. Rice's refusal to work with the neighborhood people troubled Jane Addams. "She makes . . . us indignant by her utter refusal to do anything for the sick neighbors even when they are friends of the House," Addams wrote close friend and Hull-House supporter MARY ROZET SMITH. Declaring herself "constantly perplexed," Addams concluded that Rice did not have "the settlement spirit" (Addams to M. R. Smith, February 3, 1895, Jane Addams Collection, Swarthmore College Peace Collection).

White immigrants to Chicago in these years were, like white persons native to Chicago, often racist in their views of African Americans. Rice would have encountered such racism among her patients at the clinic, but she also did not wish to treat poor people even of her own race. She declined to work with poor African Americans at Provident Hospital, the only hospital in the city that welcomed black and white patients and worked with black and white physicians. In January of 1895, when Rice was unemployed, Hull-House resident JULIA LATHROP planned to urge Rice to consider employment at Provident but expected Rice to refuse.

Rice had spent more than eight years in college, medical school, and doing postgraduate work, training alongside white women. The logical next step was to open a private practice. However, almost all African American female doctors who met with any success in these years practiced medicine among African American poor and/or taught at black medical schools to train others for that purpose. For Rice, whose upwardly mobile family believed in integration, such a career suggested failure.

Instead of affiliation with Provident, Rice worked in the Hull-House branch of the Chicago Public Library. Jane Addams arranged for her to receive a fellowship from Mary Rozet Smith for her library work, but the twenty-five dollar monthly stipend plus whatever she earned as physician for the Hull-House residents was not enough to cover her room and board at Hull-House.

Eventually Jane Addams devised a compromise that appealed to Rice. From June 1895 through June 1896, Rice ran the dispensary, which Hull-House had been planning to close because of ongoing debt, and conducted her first downtown part-time private practice, sharing an office with Edythe Fyffe, Effa V. Davis, and SARAH HACKETT STEVENSON, all of whom also taught at the Northwestern University Woman's Medical School. The arrangement lasted only a year. The Hull-House Dispensary closed permanently in the summer of 1896, as did Rice's shared office space downtown.

Though Rice remained at Hull-House and socialized with the residents, she was never a "resident" in the official sense. Rather, she was an independent resident, one of a handful of individuals, including JOSEFA HUMPAL-ZEMAN, who lived at or near Hull-House and were part of the life of the settlement but did not choose to be admitted by vote to resident membership and its associated responsibilities.

In 1896, Rice undertook a project for the Illinois Board of Charities, on which Julia Lathrop served as a member. This work resulted in her first publication, "Tabulations of Records of Cook County Institutions with Notes."

Later in 1897, Rice was hired to be resident physician, and only doctor, of the Chicago Maternity Hospital and Training School for Nursery Maids, a modest new establishment. To her Wellesley classmates, she reported that she was "Medical Superintendent" (Rice File, Alumnae Files, Wellesley College Archives). By 1898 the hospital closed.

In the spring of 1899, Rice became seriously ill and was forced to return home to Newport for surgery. She remained away from Hull-House and Chicago until 1901, when she returned briefly to work in the Hull-House branch of the Chicago Bureau of Charities office, doing relief work. Two years later, after her mother died, she returned again, this time to live in a Hull-House building. At Hull-House, she knew she could rely on a welcome and could count on Mary Rozet Smith, Julia Lathrop, and Jane Addams to help her find a way to earn a living.

In 1904, Rice was the Hull-House cashier. It was to be her last position there. For some reason not recorded, she left the settlement and Chicago that same year. Decades later, in a Christmas letter written to Addams, Rice alluded to her departure from Hull-House, hoping for reconciliation with Addams and Smith.

Little is known of Rice between 1904 and 1910, when she found a job in Boston as an assistant in a pathology laboratory at the Boston Dispensary. After two years, she returned to live in Newport with her sister Sophie at her family home, where she may have practiced medicine. In 1906 she was active in the Providence, Rhode Island, chapter of the Society of the Companions of the Holy Cross, an Episcopal lay sisterhood of college-educated, reform-minded women such as Vida Scudder and Ellen Gates Starr.

When World War I broke out in Europe, Rice, now forty-nine years old, took a decisive step: she volunteered to serve as a medical intern in France. Assigned to a hospital in Poitiers, she threw herself into the work. Her Wellesley classmates collected fifty dollars at their 1917 reunion for Rice to distribute in her war work. Receiving the cabled funds, she wrote back, thanking them, "No one living can make francs go farther than I can!" (*Fortieth Anniversary Record*, 47). Later she recalled that she spent "three and a half happy years" in France, caring for "wounded men [who were] shedding their blood and winning their souls' safety" ("Biographical Record," 1935).

The years in France offered her not only the opportunity she had longed for to practice medicine with dignity; they also brought her, for the first and only time, personal honor and public recognition. In July 1919, in Washington, D.C., the Prince de Béarn, chargé d'affaires of the French embassy, awarded her, on behalf of the French government, the bronze medal of Reconnaissance Française for her "immense services" and for "her devotion and ability in caring for the French wounded" ("Dr. Harriet Rice, 92, Native of Newport") from January 1915 to October 1918.

After the war, Rice settled again in Newport. When her sister died in 1925, she took a position at St. Mary's School, Germantown, Pennsylvania. She informed her Wellesley class-mates of her sister's death. "Her passing has meant for me the breaking up of an old homestead, and now I am a lonely wan-derer on the face of the earth, without friends, without home, or settled employment of any kind" (*Fortieth Anniversary Record*, 47). Bleakly, she concluded, at age sixty-one, that she was "looking forward without hope, and backward only, with re-gret" (p. 47).

By 1933, Rice was working in a laboratory at Columbia University Medical Center in New York City. When the eco-nomic depression worsened that spring, she learned she would be laid off and suspected her gender made her a likely target. Now sixty-seven years old, she wrote to Mary Rozet Smith for help: "This is a man's world and they won't let a woman get far-ther than they can help—or hinder" (Rice to Smith, June 12, 1933, Jane Addams Memorial Collection, UIC Special Col-lections). She hated, as she put it, to "beg for work" but she felt she had no choice; she even hinted in her letter that she was close to suicide. In the end, Rice stayed at Columbia through at least 1935.

In that year, Harriet Rice received a survey from her Welles-ley College class that posed a series of questions to each alumna about her life and accomplishments. Most of the questions did not apply to the unmarried Rice. She answered only one: "Have you any handicap, physical or other, which has been a deter-mining factor in your activity?" ("Biographical Record," 1935). "Yes!" Rice wrote in bold, emphatic letters in the space allotted for a reply: "I'm colored which is worse than any crime in this *God blessed Christian* country!" ("Biographical Record").

Rice lived on for many years, all the while looking forward to death. She died in 1958 in Worcester, Massachusetts, at age ninety-two, and was buried with an Episcopal service in New-port in the section of the city's common burial ground to which African Americans, including her own family, were restricted. If her medical career was not all that she had hoped it would be, her preparation for it was a remarkable accomplishment in itself.

Sources. There is a small amount of biographical information in collec-tions in the Wellesley College Archives, including the *Fortieth Anniver-sary Record* for the class of 1887, June 1927, the "Biographical Record," 1935, and "Our Fiftieth Reunion," *Alumnae Magazine*, 1937. Between January 15, 1895, and July 19, 1901, Jane Addams wrote six letters to Mary Rozet Smith that mention Harriet Rice; Rice wrote Addams and Smith in 1928 and 1933, respectively. The letters can be found in the Jane Addams Collection, Swarthmore College Peace Collection, Swarthmore, Pennsylvania, or the Jane Addams Memorial Collection, UIC Spec. Coll.; on microfilm, Mary Lynn McCree Bryan, ed., *The Jane Addams Papers* (1985); and indexed in *The Jane Addams Papers: A Comprehensive Guide* (1996), also edited by Bryan. Rice published "The New Year's Quest," *Wellesley Verse, 1875–1925*, ed. Martha Hale Shackford (1925), and "Tabulations of Records of Cook County Institu-tions with Notes," Illinois Board of Charities *Annual Report* (1897). Robyn Muncy, *Creating a Female Dominion, 1890–1935* (1991), dis-cusses Rice during her years at Hull-House. An obituary, "Dr. Harriet Rice, 92, Native of Newport," appears in the *Newport Daily News*, May 27, 1958.

LOUISE W. KNIGHT

RICH, ADENA MILLER
October 12, 1888–March 10, 1967
SETTLEMENT WORKER, SOCIAL WORKER, DIRECTOR OF IMMIGRANT AID AGENCY

Adena Miller, who was born in Erie, Pennsylvania, was a lead-ing social worker, social reformer, and the successor to JANE ADDAMS as head resident of Hull-House in her adopted city of Chicago. Her father, Thomas C. Miller, was a practicing attor-ney in Erie, and her mother, Emma (Lewis) Miller, was a home-maker and Sunday school teacher. Adena Miller, the second of three children, had a younger brother, Thomas Miller Jr., and an older brother, Blaine.

Miller's parents were able to trace their ancestors back through several generations in America. Her parents' house, in which she was born, was, by legend, built by her grandfather, who had joined the stream of nineteenth-century westward-bound migrants. Miller grew up hearing stories about the ex-ploits of her Revolutionary War ancestors and her mothers' four brothers, who had fought for the Union in the American Civil War. Later in life Miller recalled that her family was close and her childhood happy. She and her family attended the local Presbyterian church and she was a pupil at the Sunday school in which her mother taught.

After graduating from Erie High School, Adena Miller at-tended Oberlin College, Oberlin, Ohio, where she studied sociology, economics, and ethics; she graduated with an A.B. degree in 1911. In the unconventional and questioning atmo-sphere of Oberlin, she developed a keen interest in social ser-vice and public welfare, which she pursued at graduate school. She continued her studies at the Chicago School of Civics and Philanthropy (after 1920 the University of Chicago's School of Social Service Administration) and the New York School of So-cial Work. At the Chicago School of Civics and Philanthropy she came under the guiding influence of EDITH ABBOTT (later dean of the School of Social Service Administration), who encouraged her to devote herself to social work, which she did upon graduation.

In 1912, Adena Miller began work as supervisor of visitors for the Immigrants' Protective League (IPL) in Chicago. The IPL was formed by social reformers and residents of Hull-House in 1908 in order to help immigrants adjust to their adopted country. Under GRACE ABBOTT's direction, the IPL gave ad-vice to immigrants on finding employment, obtaining medical care, and procuring loans. It also helped immigrants attain citi-zenship, investigated cases of exploitation, and offered adult ed-ucation classes.

In addition to her full-time paid employment, Adena Miller began to volunteer at settlement houses in Chicago. For a short time she was a volunteer at both the Eli Bates Home and Henry Booth House, and in 1915 she began her association with Hull-House, where she ran various social and educational clubs and organized dances for the largely immigrant population in the neighborhood. She was supervisor of fieldwork for the Chicago School of Civics and Philanthropy between 1914 and 1916. In 1916–17 she went to Cincinnati, Ohio, to work as civic director of the Woman's City Club.

Back in Chicago at Hull-House, Adena Miller met Kenneth Rich, a stockbroker at the Chicago Board of Trade who taught arithmetic at the settlement's boys' club. The couple were married in Pennsylvania on May 29, 1917. From 1914 to 1926, she and her husband, first separately and then as a married couple, lived intermittently at Hull-House, and they were permanent residents between 1926 and 1935. The couple had no children. Without children, Adena Miller Rich was able to devote her time to her career as a social worker. Subsequently, she was director of the Girls' Protective Bureau, a wartime agency, in 1918–19; a lecturer of courses in civics to women's clubs in 1920–21; and a director of surveys for the Chicago Community Trust in 1921–22.

Adena Miller Rich became director of the Immigrants' Protective League (IPL) in 1926 and worked with the University of Chicago's School of Social Service Administration (SSA) in investigating the living conditions of Chicago's immigrants. This research collaboration produced extensive studies on various ethnic groups. Besides running the IPL, Rich wrote pamphlets that called for the extension of nonquota status to families of American citizens under the provisions of the 1921 and 1924 immigration acts.

Rich continued to direct some of her participation in reform agendas to issues related to women's political activity. She was executive vice-president of the Illinois League of Women Voters between 1923 and 1926. The league emerged at the moment when it was clear that the two million-member National American Woman Suffrage Association (NAWSA) was about to be successful in 1920 with the passage of the Nineteenth Amendment. A large flank of NAWSA feared the loss of women's solidarity and believed that "women had to be trained for their political role" (Young, 36). The new organization, "firmly nonpartisan" (p. 36), met in Chicago in February 1920 for its Victory Convention. A number of nationally known reformers, including JULIA LATHROP, returned to their roots in Chicago and turned to League of Women Voters work with serious commitment.

During the 1920s, Rich participated in the developing professionalization of social work and was a member of the board of directors of the Chicago chapter of the American Association of Social Workers. She also served on local committees having to do with criminal justice and the courts, including the Citizens' Jail Committee of Cook County and the Citizens' Committee on Social Service in municipal courts. During this period Rich published reports on a variety of issues, including the condition of women offenders in Cook County jails, U.S. immigration policy, and parental care in Chicago.

From 1926 to 1935, Rich acted as secretary to Jane Addams, founder of Hull-House. The two women developed a close personal relationship and Rich became Addams's choice to succeed her as head resident of Hull-House. After the death of Addams in 1935, Rich was selected by the Hull-House Association's Board of Trustees to succeed Addams as head resident. She continued to direct the IPL and, like Addams, refused a salary for the position.

Rich took over the post of head resident at a difficult time for the Hull-House settlement. With the founder and guiding light no longer on the scene, the direction of the settlement seemed in doubt. Falling income due to the Great Depression and loss of funds that Addams personally had raised led the trustees to seek economies and run the settlement on a more businesslike footing. Rich, however, wanted to continue the traditional programs, put more emphasis on immigration work, and keep the informal neighborhood atmosphere of the settlement. During her time as head resident, Rich gained the respect of the other residents but constantly clashed with the Board of Trustees. The board, under the direction of LOUISE deKOVEN BOWEN, repeatedly sought control over the running of Hull-House. Rich was informed that she would have no authority to distribute Hull-House funds and that the board rather than residents would have greater responsibility for settlement programs. The board also believed that Rich should resign from her position as director of the IPL and devote her time exclusively to Hull-House. Ultimately, she refused to become a full-time salaried worker at Hull-House, and in March 1937 she resigned as head resident of the settlement.

After her resignation from Hull-House, Rich continued as director of the IPL. When the United States entered World War II in 1941, Rich contributed directly to the war effort, serving as state chair outside Cook County for the Women's Division of the Illinois War Finance Committee. In 1942, she initiated a drive to purchase defense savings bonds in Chicago.

After World War II, Rich devoted her time to the work of the IPL. The IPL, often fighting against government regulation, helped to reunite families separated due to wartime disruption; it also assisted in the evacuation of refugees to the United States. During this period, Rich contributed to many social service journals, carried out numerous studies and surveys on immigration issues, and lectured on immigration at the University of Chicago. Many of her published writings and public lectures highlighted the benefits to immigrants, and to American society in general, of their obtaining American citizenship; she also discussed the need for the government to remove restrictions on achieving citizenship. Rich was heavily involved in the day-to-day running of the IPL. She was described by her coworkers as a woman of "loyalty, integrity, [and] wisdom" (Mrs. Hyman M. Atlas letter to Richard C. Stevenson, April 15, 1955, Rich Papers), someone it was "a privilege and an inspiration to know" (Jane Dich letter to Adena Miller Rich, April 19, 1955, Rich Papers).

Rich retired from the ILP in February 1954. She and her husband then relocated to a farm in La Crosse, Indiana. From there she carried on her active work as a trustee of Oberlin College. She and her husband, however, spent most of their time reading, writing letters, receiving visitors, and taking trips to the countryside. Kenneth Rich died on July 1, 1962, at the age of seventy-two. In the last years of her life, Rich moved back to the Chicago area. In 1963 she became a member of the restoration committee for the Jane Addams Memorial Fund, which sought to preserve the Hull-House buildings when plans were announced to build a Chicago campus of the University of Illinois in the neighborhood. The committee was successful in preserving and restoring the original Hull-House mansion. Rich died at age seventy-eight in a Presbyterian residential home in Evanston, Illinois, after a six-week illness. She is buried in Fairview Cemetery, Erie, Pennsylvania.

With exceptional energy and commitment, Adena Miller Rich was able to contribute to a multitude of social and civic organizations. Looking back in the mid-1960s on her life, however, she said it was her work with the IPL that made her most proud. As director of the IPL, she helped immigrants in Chicago adjust to their new homeland, overcome discrimination, and, through her writing and speeches, made state and national legislators aware of immigrant problems. She said, "I like to defend people who need it, defenseless people who need someone to champion them" (Adena Miller Rich interview).

Sources. The Adena Miller Rich Papers and the Immigrants' Protective League Records are housed at UIC Spec. Coll. Both contain personal letters, newspaper clippings, and copies of some of her writings. Correspondence between Rich and her friends is found in the correspondence folder, January 1928–April 1967, Eveline Belden Paulson Papers; and in the Adena Miller Rich letters folder, Jane Addams Memorial Collection, both at UIC Spec. Coll. Correspondence between Rich and Jane Addams is in *The Jane Addams Papers* (Microfilm Edition, 1985). The CHS has pamphlets written by Rich and the papers of the Illinois League of Women Voters. A fascinating interview by an unknown interviewer of Adena Miller Rich, no date but certainly toward the end of her life, is deposited at UIC Spec. Coll. For background, see Louise Young, *In the Public Interest: The League of Women Voters, 1920–1970* (1989).

JOHN F. LYONS

RICHMOND, CORA LINN VICTORIA SCOTT HATCH DANIELS TAPPAN

April 21, 1840–January 2, 1923

MINISTER AND TRANCE MEDIUM, LECTURER, AUTHOR, SOCIAL ACTIVIST

An attractive and charismatic speaker, Cora Scott Richmond, Spiritualist minister, was known for delivering spontaneous lectures and poems on topics chosen by audiences. These discourses, delivered while the speaker was in a trance, were believed to be messages from the spirit world. Richmond's spirit controls included an impressive cast of national figures—Andrew Jackson, Benjamin Rush, William Ellery Channing, and Abraham Lincoln; but most frequently Richmond said that the spirit speaking through her was either Adin Augustus Ballou (the son of Adin Ballou, founder of the Christian socialist commune known as Hopedale) or a young half-Native American woman named Ouina. Among her followers, Richmond was especially beloved for her gifts of spirit-name poems. Controlled by Ouina, Richmond would describe someone's character in a brief impromptu poem and name the person with a word or phrase summing up the individual's essential spiritual qualities. Richmond's own spirit name was "Water Lily." She had a seventy-one-year career of almost constant religious and professional activity; forty-seven of those years were spent in Chicago, where she was pastor of the First Society of Spiritualists before founding the Church of the Soul.

Cora Scott was born near Cuba, New York, one of four children in a farming family with a philosophical turn. Her parents, David and Lodensy (Butterfield) Scott, were admirers of Adin Ballou's Hopedale, an intentional, voluntary community based on principles of activism and cooperation known as Practical Christianity. Shortly after the inaugural event of modern Spiritualism, when in 1848 the young Fox sisters of Hydesville, New York, claimed to have established contact with the spirit world through a code of knocks or raps, the Scotts moved, in 1851, to

rural Wisconsin to help create a community modeled on Hopedale. Soon thereafter Cora Scott began falling into trances and practicing "automatic writing," delivering written spirit messages while in an unconscious state. Eventually she began to deliver spoken messages and to work as a healer, all while in a trance state, converting her family to Spiritualism in the process. She began her public career as a speaker with her father as her manager in Lake Mills, Wisconsin, at age eleven; she quit school at age twelve.

Her father died in 1854, the same year that Cora Scott accepted her first regular job as lecturer for a Spiritualist society in Buffalo, New York, where she remained for two years. On August 7, 1856, in Attica, New York, she married Dr. Benjamin Franklin Hatch, nearly forty years her senior. Hatch was a "magnetic" physician, a healer who employed hypnotism and based his practice on esoteric theories of the supposed electromagnetic properties of various personality types. Making New York City her center of operations, Cora Scott Hatch toured major cities of the East with her husband as her manager. In mid-1858, just as she had begun to acquire a reputation and to publish her discourses, she left Hatch and eventually sued him for divorce, accusing him of abuse, financial misconduct, and sexual irregularities. He responded in 1859 by writing *Spiritualists' Iniquities Unmasked, and the Hatch Divorce Case* and drew the divorce process out for almost seven years.

In the meantime, Cora Hatch toured the Midwest with her brother, Edwin T. Scott, working intermittently in Boston and New York. Her friends among New York and Boston Spiritualists at this time were largely abolitionists. Significant numbers of them appear to have been working with the Underground Railroad, helping fugitive slaves escape to sympathizers in northern states or to Canada. In 1863 twenty-two-year-old Henry James, later known as a great fiction writer, went to hear Hatch in Boston. Critics now believe he based the character Verena Tarrant of *The Bostonians* on Cora Hatch.

In late 1865, she moved to Washington, D.C., and, on December 8, 1865, married Colonel Nathan W. Daniels. Daniels had led African American Union troops from Louisiana during the Civil War and subsequently worked as the New Orleans correspondent for the *National Anti-Slavery Standard* under the name "Viator." Cora Daniels was friendly with Sojourner Truth, black abolitionist and women's rights activist, then living in Washington, D.C. During this period African American churches in Washington, D.C., "welcomed the white medium . . . in their pulpits, something no white evangelical church ever did" (Braude, 29). The Danielses spent most of the next year and a half lobbying in Washington and lecturing on behalf of the freedmen; they were particularly interested in seeing that ex-slaves in Louisiana were able to acquire their own land. In late 1867 Colonel Daniels and their one-year-old daughter, Rosebud, died of yellow fever in New Orleans, and Cora Daniels returned to Washington, D.C., to join the Spiritualist civil rights lobby there.

Cora Daniels was married again in 1869, this time to Colonel Samuel F. Tappan, a journalist turned social activist who had been one of the Free-Soil Party founders of the state of Kansas. After the Civil War he was a member of the Indian Peace Commission and turned his energies to fighting the military-driven U.S. Indian policies of the era. About the time of this marriage, Tappan adopted a Cheyenne girl who was one of three orphans captured by U.S. soldiers after the November 1865 massacre of Sand Creek, Colorado; she later died at a girls' school in New York. In 1869 the Tappans attended a suffrage convention in Boston, along with their friends Spiritualists Andrew and Mary (Robinson) Davis. In 1871 Cora Tappan published *Hesperia*, allegorical poems about Astraea, the goddess of justice, and her struggles with "Llamia, the serpent of policy" (n.p.), who is the mother of slavery; she used verse more specifically to argue against genocidal offensives directed at Native Americans. That same year she was invited to be a regular speaker at Lyric Hall, New York City. Publicity statements about the appointment make the New York Spiritualist Society's intentions clear: its members believed that having Tappan in their pulpit would secure a more positive image for women as participants in the public sphere.

Although Cora Tappan continued to achieve success as a Spiritualist minister, once again she experienced personal problems. In 1873 she replied to rumors in the press that she had left her husband with the disclaimer that she had gone abroad for health reasons. Carrying letters of introduction from Robert Dale Owen, she went on the Spiritualist lecture circuit in London, northern England, and Scotland from 1873 to 1875, enjoying appreciative audiences among believers and other reformers. In 1876 Cora Tappan filed for divorce in Chicago, claiming that Tappan had deserted her in October 1872. Waiving his right to appear in court, Samuel Tappan allowed Cora Tappan's account of the failed marriage to stand uncontested.

By the age of thirty-six Cora Tappan had lost her parents (her mother had died shortly after her marriage to Tappan in 1869), a husband, and her only child, and had been married three times and divorced twice. She had published two major works and had completed her first tour abroad. The turning point of her life occurred in 1876 when, after being awarded a divorce, she settled in Chicago, where she enjoyed a period of relative personal and financial stability. She was hired as the pastor of the First Society of Spiritualists in Chicago, and on October 12, 1876, she married William Richmond, descendant of a pioneer Chicago family. She remained in this pulpit for twenty years, until in 1896 she founded the Church of the Soul, also in Chicago. Cora Richmond's yearly calendar always included trips to Spiritualist summer camp meetings, especially in Lilydale, New York; Camp Brady, Ohio; and Onset, Massachusetts. She made extended visits to San Francisco and Washington, D.C., and traveled abroad to England in 1880, 1898, and 1907, and to France and Holland in 1907.

Despite the relative calm, the scandal attendant upon her marital history and controversial political stances continued to plague her throughout her Chicago years. Unlike her more infamous Spiritualist colleague, suffragist Victoria Woodhull, labeled by the press as "Mrs. Satan" for her forthright statements about the desirability of sexual freedom, Richmond was not a self-proclaimed supporter of social attitudes loosely termed "free love"; but her four marriages caused her to be perceived as such. *Religio-Philosophical Journal* editor John C. Bundy had never quite believed that Richmond's lectures were the products of spirit control; when Richmond defended other Spiritualists crit-

icized by Bundy, he was provoked to begin a lengthy campaign against her. He stopped publishing her work and began to criticize Richmond in public. No doubt his articles and letters had some effect upon her congregation. Shortly afterward the Richmonds went to England for six months. When they returned to Chicago in January 1881, almost five hundred people came to hear Cora Richmond speak.

Part of what troubled Bundy about Richmond proved to be one of her greatest contributions to Spiritualism, her "soul teachings." In the first two decades of her work in Chicago, Richmond taught private classes at her home. Also, at the office of the Spiritualist newspaper, the *Progressive Thinker*, she worked with smaller groups or individuals to articulate a theory of Spiritualism that accounted for the relationship between spirit and soul and explained progressive stages of the soul's fulfillment. The soul teachings provided an elaborate metaphysics, detailing angelic hierarchies and messianic cycles of history and weaving together mythological elements from many religions. Her detractors derided these teachings as "reincarnation" and assumed that they represented a pernicious and self-justifying rationalization of immoral behavior. However, Richmond's followers of more than twenty years felt that she had charged their lives with meaning and made Spiritualism more acceptable by presenting it in the context of a historically grounded narrative of human progress from the Universalist religion. Most importantly, she had given them a comprehensive mapping of the spiritual world that rendered believable the frequently repeated Spiritualist assertion that the immaterial aspect of the individual lives on after physical death.

Conservative Spiritualists sometimes recoiled from the movement's generally radical stances and insisted that the home circle or private seance was the proper locus of Spiritualist activities. Richmond, however, concurred with the majority of Spiritualists in treating the imperatives of the religious and the political as inextricably bound together.

In Chicago history, Richmond is primarily remembered for her role in the Haymarket incident. In May 1886, a series of violent interchanges between locked-out McCormick Reaper Works operatives and armed Pinkerton guards concluded with a worker meeting in Haymarket Square. A bomb exploded just as the police arrived, resulting in the deaths of seven police officers. Although a clear link between the bomb and the anarchist leaders of the local Eight Hour Day movement—Albert Parsons, August Spies, Adolph Fischer, George Engel, Louis Lingg, Michael Schwab, Samuel Fielden, and Oscar Neebe—was never established, they were convicted in part because their paper, the *Alarm*, had issued a "Revenge Circular" advising workers to arm and defend themselves after Pinkerton security guards killed four strikers at McCormick. In November 1886, Richmond went to Springfield, Illinois, as a representative of the Amnesty Association, presented signed petitions of support, and, under the inspiration of her spirit guides, pleaded with Governor Richard J. Oglesby to save the lives of the anarchist leaders. She had the support of her congregation in this action. Later she engaged in debates surrounding the Washington, D.C., march of Coxey's Army of unemployed in 1894 and the more general question of child labor, going so far as to meet with industrial workers in person. By 1901 her political reputation was such that a hostile writer for the Chicago paper *Star of the Magi* speculated on whether Richmond's newest spirit guide would be Leon Czolgosz, the assassin of President William McKinley.

The National Spiritualists Association (NSA), which first met in Chicago in September 1893 and which Richmond helped to found, also issued statements deploring the expanding power of capital and supporting the rights of the working class. In addition to this array of political stances, Spiritualists traditionally pointed to the dialogical relationship between Spiritualism and the women's rights movement, since their dual emergence in 1848 in western New York State was understood as a connection with divine significance. Predictably, at the first NSA convention, Richmond took the occasion in an opening address to reflect on that auspicious moment when "the spirit world chose little girls to" deliver the world from materialism and "theological bondage" (*Proceedings*, 1893, 9–10). In subsequent meetings she would take her male colleagues to task for using masculine generics unself-consciously, and she delighted audiences by insisting with self-directed humor that "women are always more successful when they have their own way" (*Proceedings*, 1896, 98). Eventually she served four terms as vice-president of NSA, and in October 1893 she delivered an address representing Spiritualism at the World's Parliament of Religions in Chicago.

In the mid-1890s, shortly after she received her twentieth annual call to be the First Society of Spiritualist's regular speaker, the Society moved to a more centrally located meeting place and resolved to make itself more accessible to a general audience. As part of this transition, Richmond made soul teachings explicitly part of her public work, and very soon afterward she founded the Church of the Soul, which superseded the First Society and eventually moved to the Masonic Temple. When her duties for NSA kept her away during the late 1890s, she ordained a group of longtime followers, in particular Sarah J. Ashton, to lead the church in her absence.

In the early twentieth century she continued to use the insights of Spiritualism in an ongoing commentary on public affairs. Richmond became involved in the Illinois and Wisconsin State Spiritualist Associations and was elected secretary of the Morris Pratt Institute, a Spiritualist school in Whitewater, Wisconsin. In 1907 she was chosen to represent the Morris Pratt Institute at the International Peace Congress held at The Hague in the Netherlands. After her husband, William Richmond, died on March 14, 1909, she continued working, writing two more major works during the World War I period, *Psychosophy* (1915) and *My Experiences while Out of My Body and My Return after Many Days* (1923). She died at home at age eighty-three. Her ashes were scattered in Graceland Cemetery, Chicago.

Richmond's life's work, best summarized in an early lecture given under spirit control, remained consistent with the Hopedale commune's emphasis on lived religion. She argued that it was better to embody one's religion, a state defined as love, than to have faith or hope. The latter began with the premise of a distance between the self and its revered principles, thus making religion into an intellectual exercise bordering on "idolatry" or the worship of an abstraction outside the self. Her lifelong concern was to balance an insistence on the primacy of spiritual life with the understanding that Spiritualism could only fight materialism by being a vibrant, politically engaged public religion.

Sources. Harrison D. Barrett, ed. and comp., *Life Work of Cora L. V. Richmond* (1895) gives a highly selective and favorable view of Richmond; probably based on her scrapbook, it includes laudatory letters from fans and lifelong friends and appears to have been written jointly by Barrett, Cora Richmond herself, and William Richmond. The John C. Bundy Papers, UIC Spec. Coll., contain fifteen volumes of letters that mention her frequently. Representative works by Richmond include *A Discourse on Faith, Hope, and Love* (1858), *Hesperia* (1871), *Ouina's Canoe and Christmas Offering* (1882), and *The Soul: Its Nature, Relations, and Expressions in Human Embodiments* (1887). *Psychosophy* (1915) is the functional equivalent of a sermon collection, giving a six-part summation of the soul teachings. See the published *Proceedings* of the annual conventions of the National Spiritualists Association of the United States of America, 1893–98, for addresses by Richmond. No comprehensive account of Richmond's life and activities exists. An overall understanding of her life and work may be gained only by following her progress in newspaper sources, including *Banner of Light*, the longest running American Spiritualist newspaper of the nineteenth century. Chicago's *Religio-Philosophical Journal* and *Progressive Thinker* give her significant coverage. Helpful studies include Ann Braude, *Radical Spirits: Spiritualism and Women's Rights in Nineteenth-Century America* (1990), which offers revealing glimpses of Richmond's life in political context. Two articles—Joseph Jablonski, "Spirit's Progress: Radical Mediums in the Haymarket Era," in *Haymarket Scrapbook*, ed. David Roediger and Franklin Rosemont (1986), and Howard Kerr, "'The Young Prophetess': Memories of Spiritualism and Intimations of Occult Consciousness in Henry James's *The Bostonians*," in *Mediums, and Spirit-Rappers, and Roaring Radicals: Spiritualism in American Literature*, ed. Howard Kerr (1972)—provide sharply focused discussions.

HESTER L. FUREY

RICKERT, EDITH
July 11, 1871–May 23, 1938
MEDIEVALIST, UNIVERSITY PROFESSOR, WRITER

Edith Rickert, an editor and scholar of medieval literature, was born in Canal Dover, Ohio. Named Martha Edith, she was the eldest child of Francis E. and Josephine (Newburgh) Rickert. She had three surviving younger siblings—Frances Edna, Ethel, and Margaret, who became a professor of art history, specializing in the Middle Ages as well. (Another sister died at age three and a brother at eighteen months.) Her maternal grandparents were Methodists, but Rickert's mother raised her daughter an Episcopalian. Details from her life—her grandmother's spinning wheel, her favorite stories from the children's annual *Chatterbox*, her mother's failing health and weakening constitution under the burden of household responsibilities—all made their way into the pages of her published fiction and her unpublished typescripts.

After attending North Division High School in Chicago, Rickert was awarded a full scholarship to Vassar College, graduating with honors in 1891. Rickert's interest in creative writing emerged during her college years, and she won a prize for the best short story by an American undergraduate awarded by the journal *Kate Field's Washington*. Rickert's parents were continually concerned for her material needs at Vassar, sending clothes (often sewn by her mother), food, and occasional money when they could. Rickert's father worried that his daughter did not come from as wealthy a family as other girls at Vassar. Rickert herself was concerned that her parents were working too hard

FIG. 99. *Chaucer scholar Edith Rickert at her desk with manuscripts.*

in her absence, her father in a chemists store and her mother at home with the "babies." Her parents lived both in Chicago and its surrounding suburbs at various times. Their movements appeared largely the effect of financial concerns. Long hours of housekeeping and a poor diet weakened her mother, who died sometime between 1891 and 1893.

Directly following her Vassar graduation, Rickert returned to help support her family and raise her sisters by working in Chicago-area schools as a teacher. She taught English at Lyons Township High School in Cook County from 1891 to 1894. She began graduate studies at the University of Chicago in 1894 while supporting herself by teaching at Hyde Park High School in Chicago from 1894 to 1896. In the summer of 1896 Rickert spent her first year abroad, chiefly in England, and developed an interest in research that would keep her returning to Europe. Rickert spent the final years of her graduate education (1898–99) working to complete a Ph.D. degree while teaching at Vassar, as an instructor of English, a position that she held until 1900. She earned a doctorate *magna cum laude* in English letters and philology in 1899, the same year she was elected to Phi Beta Kappa. Rickert was the first woman (and second individual) to be awarded a Ph.D. in English letters and philology with that academic honor at the University of Chicago. For her dissertation she produced an edition of the fourteenth-century romance *Emaré*, which was eventually published by the Early English Text Society in 1908.

She remained at Vassar following her graduation from the University of Chicago, but she gave up the security of a faculty position in 1900 to live independently in England and write fiction, which she did for nine years. Five of her six published novels date from this period abroad: *Out of the Cypress Swamp* (1902), *The Reaper* (1904, 1925), *Folly* (1906), *The Golden Hawk* (1907), and *The Beggar in the Heart* (1909). Her best-known novel, *Severn Woods* (1930), published in Britain as *Olwen Growing*, was produced some twenty years later, when Rickert sought to return to fiction writing and earlier material after finishing her academic research projects.

While her life in England centered around writing and research, she spent almost all of her free time with the other women who lived in her boardinghouse, attending lectures at the Ethical Society or Philological Society, concerts, galleries, and theater, and traveling about England. These women even formed an unofficial "society" that held its meetings over tea and after dinner: "the order of Ancient Spinsters." Their motto was "single we stand, united we fall." A brief knighting ceremony conferred membership on each new "mistress" of the society. Eventually Rickert moved into a small flat with one of these women, Kate Platt, then a medical student in London. Soon Rickert's sister Ethel joined them. At some point during her nine-year stay, Rickert, her sister, and Platt moved out of London to Edenbridge, Kent, to a small cottage called Tibbles Green. Rickert and Platt remained lifelong friends.

While working on her five novels, Rickert supported herself by selling stories to British and American magazines, writing general interest stories about England for Chicago newspapers, selling her photographs that she developed herself, copying manuscripts, and doing other research tasks for American professors. But she also managed to carry out scholarly work of her own, some of which can be seen in the translations produced during this period, including *Marie de France: Seven of Her Lays Done into English* (1901), *The Babees' Book: Medieval Manners for the Young Done into Modern English from Dr. Furnivall's Texts* (1908, 1966), *Ancient English Christmas Carols, 1400–1700* (1910, 1914, 1925, 1966), *Early English Romances in Verse: Romance of Friendship* (1908, 1966), and *Early English Romances in Verse: Romances of Love* (1908, 1966).

Rickert returned to the United States in 1909 because the failing economy made it more difficult to sell her work. She joined the editorial staff of publisher D.C. Heath in Boston from 1909 to 1910 and the *Ladies Home Journal* in Philadelphia from 1911 to 1914. During this period she coedited, with Jessie Paton, an edition of selected contemporary *American Lyrics* (1912) for which she wrote the introductory essay and in which she reprinted the poems of some friends—Katherine Lee Bates and John Burroughs.

In 1914 Rickert moved back to Chicago. She began working for the Commercial Club, a civic-oriented businessmen's association, in their campaign for the first federal support of vocational education in public high schools. Rickert focused on that part of the legislation dealing with vocational programs for women students. At the same time she began teaching on a part-time basis as an assistant in the Department of English at the University of Chicago. Rickert taught not only Geoffrey Chaucer's writings but also contemporary British and American literature, modern subjects that "were not [at the time] in very good repute" (Millet, 9). It was significant for her major Chaucer research that Rickert renewed her acquaintance with Professor John Matthews Manly, whom she had first met while finishing her dissertation in 1899. Manly had joined the University of Chicago faculty as chair of the English department while Rickert was teaching at Vassar. Although she was not his student, Rickert seems to have gotten good advice at the very end of her doctoral work and some much needed encouragement to continue seriously in her scholarly pursuits.

In 1918 Manly invited Rickert to join the Cryptographic Section of Military Intelligence for the War Department in Washington, D.C., which he was heading. Along with other scholars, Rickert worked to break the German code.

After the war Rickert and Manly returned to the English department, and they coauthored bibliographies and study outlines, *Contemporary British Literature* (1921) and *Contemporary American Literature* (1922, rev. ed. 1940), as well as writing manuals, *The Writing of English* (1919) and *The Writer's Index of Good Form and Good English* (1923), which were well-used textbooks. In the 1920s Rickert had attempted to develop a "scientific" method of analyzing modern literary style that grew out of her War Department experience. Many of Rickert's essays, such as "Political Propaganda and Satire in *A Midsummer's Night's Dream*" (1923) and "A New Interpretation of the *Parlement of Foules*" (1920), indulge in the quasi-scientific method of historical identification. Literature was treated as a cipher and had only to be read for its encryption of specific historical content behind the screen of fiction. This kind of pursuit was often described as "literary detective work," a term that clearly romanticized the historicist effort. Rickert published *New Methods for the Study of Literature* in 1927, which was a further exploration of the scientific method of analyzing modern literary style that grew out of her experience in the War Department.

Rickert continued to write all her life and eventually published more than fifty short stories and three children's books: *The Bojabi Tree* (1923), *The Blacksmith and the Blackbirds* (1928), and *The Greedy Goroo* (1929), besides her many scholarly and pedagogical publications.

Rickert was made an associate professor at the University of Chicago in 1924, rather late in her scholarly career. Many of her academic publications predate her university appointment. When Rickert and two other women faculty members were promoted to full professorships in 1930, only eight of the university's two hundred full professors were women. Rickert was well liked by her students and was remembered by many of them for both aid and encouragement in their work.

The eleven years she spent as an official faculty member of the university before retiring from teaching in 1935 when she reached the mandatory retirement age do not, however, adequately reflect her intellectual involvements and accomplishments. Rickert is best known for her collaboration with Manly on the eight-volume *Text of the Canterbury Tales, Studies on the Basis of All Known Manuscripts* (1940). In their editing of Chaucer, Manly and Rickert brought to the task the "scientific" impulse that their war experiences with cryptography had triggered. The project marked a watershed in the editing of Chaucer's most important work. Manly and Rickert attempted to edit the *Canterbury Tales* by recension, a process of critical text revision that excluded subjectivity in editing and sought to find the prototype of all the manuscripts that survived.

For the *Canterbury Tales* project Rickert spent every winter and spring quarter from 1926 to 1936 in England collecting photostats and bibliographic information on all known Chaucer manuscripts. These photostats represented, at the time, the most extensive collection of Chaucer materials under one roof in the world. The "Chaucer Laboratory" on the fourth floor of Wieboldt Hall made the University of Chicago famous with *Canterbury Tales* scholars. On the way to completing the edition of the *Canterbury Tales*, Rickert compiled enough primary materials to fill a large volume of background material on Chaucer's world. Eventually her students, Martin M. Crow and Clair C. Olson, published her research and notes in *Chaucer's World* in 1948.

Rickert's six-month journeys to the libraries of England ended when, in March 1936, she had a heart attack that eventually proved fatal. Bedridden for most of the rest of her life, she continued to proofread, write, and organize her scholarly work as best she could. She died in her home on May 23, 1938, after suffering a severe stroke. She was cremated and her ashes buried at Oak Woods Cemetery, Chicago.

While Rickert was remembered fondly by her students, her work remains somewhat slighted by the academic profession. A full-scale reading of the archival materials of the *Canterbury Tales* project needs to be carried out, as does a detailed account of Rickert's participation in the project. Neglect of her contributions was evident when, in 1939, John Matthews Manly received the Sir Israel Gollancz Medal from the British Academy for Manly and Rickert's edition of Chaucer. Although Rickert's coauthorship was mentioned, she was not formally recognized by the British Academy. Again, in 1942, when Manly posthumously received the Haskins Medal from the Medieval Academy of America, Rickert was not mentioned.

The legacy of Manly and Rickert's intellectual efforts remains impressive, if not as important as it once seemed. Their efforts must be understood historically, in terms of the kind of editorial knowledge available to them and the fashions of literary criticism and research of their day. The project they took on was huge, its scope daunting. Many of the reviews of the project take into account its somewhat hasty publication. Rickert had already died and Manly was in failing health when the text was brought to press (perhaps prematurely) in 1940. Manly and Rickert concluded that no exclusive ancestor to all the known *Canterbury Tales* manuscripts could be retrieved. But even if the Manly and Rickert text could not fulfill the intended goal of recovering an archetype from all the known Chaucer manuscripts, as they acknowledged, the project did put together more information about Chaucer's texts and his life than had ever been gathered before. The four final volumes recording the corpus of variants, though by no means easy to use, place the information in all eighty-two manuscripts and two Caxton prints in any student's hands. The *Chaucer Life Records* was eventually published in 1966, also by Crow and Olson, from notes and papers collected by Rickert and Lilian Redstone (one of her colleagues in England); this is, perhaps, Edith Rickert's most impressive and important gift to Chaucerians.

Sources. Edith Rickert's private papers are found in UC Spec. Coll. These include family, personal, and professional correspondence, notebooks, journals, manuscripts of unpublished novels and stories, manuscripts and offprints of stories, poems, and essays. Also included are biographical clippings, memorabilia, and photographs. Information about Rickert is also found in the John M. Manly Papers and Records, the Department of English, UC Spec. Coll. Rickert's extensive published works are mentioned above, including novels, children's books, pedagogical publications, translations, and scholarly publications. An entry on Rickert is in *NAW* (1971). See also Fred B. Millett, *Edith Rickert: A Memoir* (1944).

ELIZABETH SCALA

RICO, ANGELINA MORENO
October 2, 1898–June 23, 1984
CULTURAL ACTIVIST

By organizing Mexican cultural events, Angelina Moreno Rico both introduced Mexican culture to non-Mexican audiences in Chicago and motivated Mexican youths toward educational and cultural advancement at a time when Mexicans were disparaged as immigrants in the United States. Organizing Mexican Christmas celebrations and folk dance programs was a way of contesting that disparagement. Rico was born in Mexico City. Her mother, Francisca Moreno, had Angelina Moreno and nine other children before her husband died. Although Francisca Moreno married again, it was Angelina Moreno's eldest brother Guillermo who provided for the family and encouraged Angelina Moreno to pursue an education. Moreno was able to attend college in Mexico City for two years before she married. Guillermo Moreno pushed his sister to learn English and Japanese; however, thinking that she would never use either language, she refused. Instead, she left school and, on October 10, 1919, married Trinidad Rico (later José T. Rico), her childhood sweetheart, despite her family's concern that he was poor and uneducated. At the time, she was employed at Casa Cumbre, a very elegant and exclusive shop where, because of her fine skill in sewing, Rico worked solely on bridal gowns.

After the Mexican Revolution of 1910, jobs were scarce not only in Mexico City but in many other parts of the country. José T. Rico had been a chauffeur for upper-class Mexicans in Mexico City and, later, an automobile mechanic. He left for the United States in 1926, following his dream. Like other male migrants, he told his wife to wait one year for him to establish himself before following with their three sons, George, Angelo, and Manuel, who at the time were ages four, three, and two, respectively. Like other female migrants, Angelina Rico followed her husband. Because her friends claimed a gringa would steal her husband, Rico boarded a train with her children only three months after her husband left. The Ricos were part of the first major wave of mass migration to Chicago in the twentieth century and arrived during the peak years of this movement. Strong recruitment efforts on the part of U.S. companies resulted in the rapid rise of Mexican immigration beginning in 1916 and reaching its peak in the late 1920s.

Despite problems resulting from her lack of English, Rico nonetheless took the train to Chicago and reconnected with José Rico. The Ricos' first year in Chicago was full of hardship. They rented an apartment on the Near West Side, where they stayed until 1956. They began, however, with no furniture. Their youngest son, Manuel, caught rheumatic fever and died because they knew nothing about the disease and had poor access to health care. In 1929, Rico gave birth to a fourth son and also named him Manuel. She had several miscarriages but gave birth to her last child, Elena, in 1931. A few years later Elena survived rheumatic fever. Recognizing the symptoms, they were able to rush her to La Rabida Sanatorium for Children, where Elena stayed for two years.

Education became a major goal for the Ricos. Facing such daily difficulties as shopping without a knowledge of English, Rico enrolled herself and José Rico in night school at Crane High School, where they completed elementary courses, high school, and several college courses. Rico also took charge of her children's education. Blocked by poverty from learning piano as a child, Rico ensured that all her children received a musical education. Although she had begun working at Marshall Field and Company, the downtown department store, as a seamstress, her husband did not want her to work. She stretched each dollar her husband earned by doing such things as washing their laundry by hand rather than sending it out. Thus she paid for George and Angelo to take music and voice lessons. Her dedication paid off; three of Rico's children became professional musicians, and the whole family participated in the cultural activities that came to be associated with the Rico name.

The Ricos became active in the community through Firman House, a settlement house connected with St. Mark's Church. Firman House went into operation in November 1938 on the Near West Side, west of Hull-House. Firman was a settlement affiliated with the Presbyterian church. It provided services primarily to Mexicans, because the Italians and African Americans in the area already had functioning community organizations. It offered classes in sewing, art, drama, handicrafts, carpentry, and music; it also housed a library. Although activities were mainly centered around the church, the staff hoped to expand later into social services.

José Rico, who had been skeptical in Mexico about the Catholic religion, became Presbyterian after his arrival in Chicago and, after much effort, convinced Angelina Rico to join him. Both Angelina and José Rico became active in local organizations. In 1944, José Rico joined the board of directors of the Mexican Civic Committee, which tackled problems of high infant mortality, lack of educational opportunities, rising delinquency, poor housing, and substandard health conditions. Recognizing that second-generation Mexican youth felt no connection to either the United States or Mexico and that they felt lost in the complexity of the city, the Mexican Civic Committee implemented various programs for youths and adults in order to help them better adjust to the city. One such program included the first Mexican Boy Scout Troop, headed by José Rico, which began in March 1944. Angelina Rico was a member of the Mother's Club and, at one point, president.

Angelina Rico noticed that many youths were ashamed of calling themselves Mexican, an estrangement undoubtedly fed by negative stereotypes of Mexicans in advertisements, government propaganda, and film. Many youths denied they were Mexican, passed as Italians, and refused to learn Spanish. Rico attempted to combat this attitude by instilling pride in youth as well as by teaching other nationalities about Mexican culture. Using her sons' musical talents, Angelina Rico began performing traditional folk songs from Mexico. Because they had no sheet music, she sang *Posadas* (traditional Christmas songs), to her son George, and he wrote the music. They sang during Christmas in Chicago-area churches.

The Museum of Science and Industry began a program called "Christmas around the World" in 1942, inviting the various ethnic groups in Chicago to perform songs from their native countries. Each group began by performing one song, but as audiences grew over the years, the time expanded to one hour per group. Recommended to the museum by a friend of George Rico who worked there, Rico and her family began performing the *Posadas* at the museum in 1946; they continued for twenty-five years.

Posadas are part of the religious tradition in Mexico. They trace Mary and Joseph's pilgrimage through Bethlehem as they search for lodging. Because the celebration at the Museum of Science and Industry was meant to be more secular, the Ricos could not delve into the religious aspects; but they did perform the cultural games and dances that accompany the *Posadas*. They divided their performance into three parts: a procession in search of shelter; hymns sung to baby Jesus; and a celebration, or fiesta, with *piñatas* and such folk dances as "El Jarabe Tapatío," "La Bamba," and "El Jarabe de la Botella."

The Ricos' performance became a very popular show among the museum's audiences, eventually reaching five hour-long performances in one day. Part of the "Christmas around the World" celebration at the Museum of Science and Industry included Christmas tree decorating. The family made little *piñatas* of eggshells to use as tree ornaments; weeks in advance, José Rico made the larger *piñatas* for each of the five shows. The women made their own costumes as well. Angelina and Elena Rico, who trimmed the tree in the rotunda, carried the displays of ornaments, costumes, and other decorations by bus to the museum.

In 1949, the eldest son, George Rico, decided that they should perform year-round. He established the Chicago Fiesta Guild, the first Mexican folkloric dance group in Chicago, to bring Mexican culture to both non-Mexican audiences and to his own family. He and his brothers had married non-Mexican women, and like his mother, he felt it was important for them and the children to learn the Spanish language and culture. Preparations and performances for the "Christmas around the World" were always a family affair, involving nieces, nephews, wives, and children. Other youths from the community joined the Chicago Fiesta Guild as well. The guild performed at Northwestern University, Hull-House, Pan-American parades, and other civic celebrations around Chicago.

Rico had a total of nineteen operations during her life. She had heart problems, goiter, hemorrhoids, and an appendectomy, among many other physical problems. Doctors studied her body throughout her life, and Rico was willing to let students continue after her death. Both she and her husband donated their bodies to science. She died at eighty-five years of age.

Rico loved music and gave that gift to her children and to the people of Chicago. She endured hardships but pushed both herself and her husband to overcome communication, economic, and cultural barriers. Rico pushed her children as well. It was through her encouragement that they began the "Christmas around the World" performances at the Museum of Science and Industry and later formed the Chicago Fiesta Guild. She was a simple woman, a migrant like other Mexicans in the early decades of the twentieth century, but her energy and motivation inspired Mexican youths. Rico invited everyone to learn about Mexican culture and actively encouraged Mexican young people to speak their native language and be proud of their culture. The Chicago Fiesta Guild, her family's contribution to Chicago, promoted community cohesion and provided a basis on which other organizations could be built. Rico and her family challenged prevailing attitudes toward Mexicans and their culture.

Sources. Interviews with Elena Rico provided most information about Angelina Moreno Rico's life. CHS contains information regarding the Chicago Fiesta Guild scattered throughout the Welfare Council Papers but primarily in Boxes 88 and 373. Information on Mexican Americans is found in Louise Año Nuevo Kerr, "The Chicano Experience in Chicago: 1920–1970 (Ph.D. diss., Univ. of Illinois at Chicago Circle, 1976); Jorge Casuso and Eduardo Camacho, "Latino Chicago," in *Ethnic Chicago: A Multicultural Portrait*, ed. Melvin G. Holli and Peter d'A. Jones (4th ed., 1995); and Carlos E. Cortés, "Mexicans," in *Harvard Encyclopedia of American Ethnic Groups*, ed. Stephan Thernstrom (1980).

MARTHA ELENA ESPINOZA

RIPERTON, MINNIE JULIA
November 8, 1947–July 12, 1979
VOCALIST, SONG WRITER, PRODUCER, WOMEN'S
HEALTH ADVOCATE

Minnie Riperton, "the brave coloratura soprano of popular music" (Pruter, 107), is best remembered for her incredible musical ability and melodic voice that spanned more than five octaves. The youngest of Daniel and Thelma (Matthews) Riperton's eight children, Minnie Riperton was born at the family home on Chicago's South Side before her mother could be taken to a hospital. Daniel Riperton, a native of Houstonville, Kentucky, was a Pullman porter. Thelma Riperton graduated from Rust College in Mississippi, majoring in English, but after migrating to Chicago could find work only as a cleaning woman. She devoted the bulk of her time to her family and the church.

Musical talent seemed to run in the family. Young Minnie Riperton received an early exposure to jazz, soul, gospel, and classical music from her parents, brothers, and sisters, all of whom either sang or played a musical instrument. Recognizing her daughter's natural talent, Thelma Riperton enrolled ten-year-old Minnie Riperton at the Abraham Lincoln Center, a local community center that offered classes in dance, voice, drama, and the visual arts to African American children and adults from Chicago's South Side.

While enrolled at the Abraham Lincoln Center, Riperton began nine and a half years of private lessons with renowned voice instructor Marion Jeffery, who took an immediate liking to her. Minnie Riperton's exceptional progress under Jeffery's tutelage earned her the offer of a place with Chicago's prestigious Junior Lyric Opera. Although she had long aspired to become a professional opera singer, Riperton turned down this opportunity because of a growing interest in more popular styles of music, such as rhythm and blues and rock 'n' roll. As a professional singer, however, she consistently incorporated her early operatic training into her vocal style. During these years, Riperton attended Oakwood and later John Fisk Elementary School, and she graduated from Hyde Park High School.

In 1965, Chicago was still a major hub for the recording and promotion of black music. Its famed "record row" along South Michigan Avenue was home to such renowned record companies and distribution houses as Decca, Brunswick, Constellation, and One-derful, as well as Vee Jay and Chess, two names that became synonymous with soul music in Chicago. Vee Jay was the country's largest black-owned record company prior to the founding of Motown Records by Berry Gordy in Detroit. Chicago's record companies and distributors, along with such radio stations as WVON and entertainment venues like the Regal Theater, helped shape the careers of many artists, including Jerry Butler, Curtis Mayfield, Otis Clay, Tyrone Davis, the Dells, and the Chi-Lites, as they parlayed local renown into national acclaim.

Riperton joined this world in 1963 at age fifteen. Raynard Miner and Rose Miller, who discovered her performing in the Hyde Park High School a cappella choir, recruited her to sing with a group called the Gems, a local version of the "girl groups" popular in the 1960s. Miner, the musical director, and Miller, the manager of the Gems, were impressed with Minnie's sweet voice and felt she would be the perfect complement to the five-member group. The Gems's introduction to the recording industry was as in-house backup singers for some of Chess Records's most popular acts, including the Dells, Muddy Waters, and Ramsey Lewis.

Although the Gems stopped recording together after three years and four recordings, Chess Records continued to promote Riperton as a solo performer both in the studio and on the Chicago club circuit. Her 1966 release, *Lonely Girl*, was recorded under the name Andrea Davis at the company's insistence, because it was believed to have more commercial appeal than her given name.

Minnie Riperton was in constant demand by local producers in need of backup vocalists and received much of her early exposure from her recording of TV and radio commercial jingles, an avenue that later proved quite lucrative. At the same time, she worked as a receptionist/secretary at Chess, where Billy Davis, specialist in artists and repertoire, took her under his wing and trained her in many aspects of the record business.

In 1967, Chess Records cast Riperton as a lead vocalist of the Rotary Connection, the only rock 'n' roll band ever signed by the company. Of the Connection's seven members, Riperton and fellow vocalist Sidney Barnes were the only African Americans, and Riperton the only female for most of the group's time together. The Rotary Connection was a product of the so-called "psychedelic era" in music that began in the late 1960s. They performed at numerous major music festivals, opening for such rock superstars as Janis Joplin, Jefferson Airplane, Led Zeppelin, and the Rolling Stones. Chess Records's inexperience in promoting groups like the Connection, the members' resulting frustration, and the turmoil caused by the sale of Chess to GRT Records led to the group's eventual dissolution, three years and six long-playing records (LPs) later. Despite the group's limited commercial success, Riperton's experience with the Connection brought her one step closer to perfecting the vocal style that would later become her trademark: the use of her multifaceted voice to recreate the sounds of instruments as she moved effortlessly from one octave to another.

Minnie Riperton married Richard (Dick) Rudolph in 1967 after a brief but intense courtship. They met while she was performing with the Rotary Connection at a night club he managed in Chicago called the Kinetic Playground. Their marriage united them creatively as well as spiritually. Together they wrote and produced most of the songs Riperton recorded during the latter part of her career, including four hit LPs.

In 1970, Riperton continued her solo career with the release of *Come to My Garden* (GRT Records, 1970), an LP produced by Charles Stepney. Stepney, who possessed extraordinary talent and received considerable acclaim as an arranger and producer, collaborated with Riperton's husband to compose material for the album, which also featured pianist Ramsey Lewis. Unfortunately, due to limited distribution and air play, sales of *Come to My Garden* were disappointing. By the 1990s, it would be considered a collector's item and one of the best remaining examples of Riperton's remarkable vocal range.

In 1971, Riperton and her husband decided to leave Chicago in order to explore other creative options. An unfortunate eviction attempt by a North Side apartment manager opposed to renting to interracial couples quelled any doubts they might have had about uprooting their young family. Having won the resulting court case, they headed for New York with their son, Marc (born 1968). Their stay was brief, however. Riperton's distaste for the climate, as well as a string of encounters with record company executives who wanted to categorize her style and pigeonhole her sound, led them to Gainesville, Florida, where Riperton gave birth to her second child, Maya, in 1973. She continued to write songs with her husband, who had taken a job teaching school.

Though Riperton remained out of the public eye for nearly three years, she had acquired a small following through her work with the Rotary Connection and *Come to My Garden*. By 1973, tapes of her voice were circulating among record industry executives in Los Angeles; Epic Records successfully signed Riperton to her first major recording contract. Leary of repeating her

New York experience, she agreed to sign with Epic only if the company conceded complete creative control, which at that time was highly coveted but rarely obtained by most artists, especially if they were black and/or female. Riperton later commented that racism in the music industry was much more pervasive than sexism and that it was the industry's biggest problem.

Upon relocating to Los Angeles in 1973, Riperton divided her time between studio session work at Epic and writing songs with her husband for her impending first Epic release. Epic initially paired Riperton with producer Quincy Jones, whose hit single, "If I Ever Lose This Heaven," featured her and singer/song writer Leon Ware. Riperton also recorded and toured with Roberta Flack and with Freddie Hubbard and the Crusaders, while anxiously anticipating her own album. In 1973 she met Stevie Wonder in Chicago, where he expressed an interest in working with her, impressed by her in the Rotary Connection's rendition of his song "This Town."

Finally, in 1974, Epic Records released Riperton's *Perfect Angel* LP. Coproduced by Stevie Wonder, it featured two songs written by him, including the title track. The rest of the songs were cowritten by Riperton and her husband. Although the first three singles released from the album did not do well commercially, the fourth single, "Lovin' You," was an enormous success, reaching the number one position on the national record charts early in 1975 with impressive positions on British and Japanese charts. "Lovin' You," the song for which she is best remembered, made Riperton a star. After *Perfect Angel*, Riperton released her second LP on the Epic label, *Adventures in Paradise*, employing such impressive personnel as Joe Sample, Tom Scott, and Larry Carlton. This LP added to Minnie's reputation as a singer of sultry, soul-stirring ballads.

The recording sessions and personal appearances came to an abrupt halt just before Easter of 1976, when Riperton was diagnosed with breast cancer. A mastectomy followed, along with chemotherapy. Riperton's bout with cancer remained unpublicized for several months. That summer she was named Female Artist of the Year in the R&B/Pop (Rhythm & Blues/Pop) category by *Ebony Magazine* and received the accompanying Ebony Music Award during a nationally televised presentation, one of the few times she was seen in public so soon after her operation.

In the fall of 1976, during a television appearance on the *Tonight Show*, Riperton openly discussed her mastectomy. Although her announcement was unplanned, she was aware of the potential positive impact it might have on women's lives, since the public was not widely educated about breast cancer at the time.

Riperton's initial prognosis was grim, and she was told by her doctors that she only had six months to live. Always the optimist, her positive outlook helped extend her life beyond expectations. Her efforts to educate women about the prevention and early detection of breast cancer gained momentum with her appointment as the American Cancer Society's National Education Chairman. She traveled extensively on the society's behalf. In April 1977, President Jimmy Carter presented Riperton with the American Cancer Society Courage Award, the organization's highest honor.

Riperton released her third and final LP for Epic Records in May of 1977, *Stay in Love: A Romantic Fantasy Set to Music*. Although she found her role as cowriter and coproducer creatively rewarding, she decided to change management as well as record companies in order to propel her career into its next phase. By the summer of 1978, she had signed a 2.5 million dollar, three-album recording contract with Capitol Records. The album, simply entitled *Minnie*, was released in April 1979. Although her condition changed suddenly, she finished the album despite pain and discomfort. She was able to make a few public appearances to help promote the album, but her health faded rapidly.

Minnie Riperton, the pretty, petite songbird, died in her husband's arms at a Los Angeles hospital. "Memory Lane," the first single released from the *Minnie* LP, was still climbing the charts. Memorial services were held in both Los Angeles and Chicago.

The title of her first hit solo LP, *Perfect Angel*, became her signature, describing not only the impeccable quality of her voice but also the very endearing qualities identified in her by friends and colleagues. In the last years of her life, Riperton appeared before numerous audiences, not just to sing but also to impart important messages to women about the prevention and early detection of breast cancer.

Sources. Information on Riperton's musical career is available through the Center for Black Music Research at Columbia College in Chicago. The American Cancer Society archives in Atlanta and Los Angeles maintain files on the work she did on their behalf. Interviews by Leticia McCollum during 1993 with relatives and others who knew Riperton provided information. Minnie Riperton is the subject of numerous newspaper and magazine articles published between 1974 and 1980 in *Ebony, Jet, Rolling Stone, Soul, Goldmine*, the *Chicago Defender*, and the *Chicago Sun-Times*. She is also featured in *Chicago Soul* by Robert Pruter (1992), the *Penguin Encyclopedia of Popular Music* (1989), Joe Whitburn's *Top R&B Singles* (1988), and the *Billboard Book of Top 40 Hits* (1983).

LETICIA Y. MCCOLLUM

ROBERTS, LYDIA JANE
June 30, 1879–May 28, 1965
NUTRITIONIST, EDUCATOR, COMMUNITY REFORMER

Lydia Roberts was an expert on the importance of good nutrition, especially for children's health. Through her research and the development of practical programs based on her findings, she was able to improve the living conditions of children by educating families and assisting entire communities. She was born in Hope Township, Michigan, to Warren and Mary (McKibbin) Roberts. Her father was a carpenter and they lived in Martin, Michigan, a small farming area where Roberts and her two older sisters and younger brother spent their childhood.

At the age of twenty, Lydia Roberts completed a one-year course at Mount Pleasant Normal School in Mount Pleasant, Michigan (now Central Michigan University). At this early age, Roberts "was officially launched on the teaching career she was to follow" (Bing, 3). In 1909, after she had taught in Michigan, Montana, and Virginia, Mount Pleasant Normal School gave Roberts a life certificate, allowing her to teach at any elementary school in Michigan. She then taught at an elementary school in Dillon, Montana, and also worked in the normal school there (later Western Montana College) "as a critic teacher" (Bing, 4).

FIG. 100. *Lydia J. Roberts, on the right, head of the Department of Home Economics, University of Chicago, receiving the 1938 Borden Award.*

In 1915, Roberts enrolled as an undergraduate at the University of Chicago, where she was granted advanced standing as a result of her teaching experience. Roberts majored in home economics. Her desire was to learn how to feed children and help them lead healthy lives. Roberts's exposure to children, through her teaching experience and summer employment at a Montana children's institution, created in her an interest in learning about the correlation between diet and health. Roberts received a B.S. degree in 1917 with Phi Beta Kappa honors. However, Roberts's educational pursuits did not stop there. KATHARINE BLUNT, a biochemist and chair of the department, encouraged Lydia Roberts to pursue an M.S. degree in home economics. Her master's thesis, "A Malnutrition Clinic as a University Problem in Applied Nutrition," was based on her work on child nutrition at a free dispensary at Rush Medical College, arranged by Blunt. Roberts received her degree in 1918 and was made an assistant professor in the department the following year. For the next decade, Roberts and her students continued to work on malnutrition problems in children, publishing their findings in articles and in several bulletins for the U.S. Children's Bureau.

In 1928, Lydia Roberts received a Ph.D. degree in home economics and was promoted to associate professor. She presented her book, *Nutrition Work with Children*, as her disserta-

tion. The book had been completed in 1926 and published in 1927. A revised edition of her book was published in 1935. Lydia Roberts's book "constituted a pioneer effort in a new phase of nutrition service" (p. viii). The purpose of her book was to provide better information to college and university students on how to improve children's health. Roberts recognized all aspects of the development of the child, including physical, mental, social, and emotional factors. Through her book, she wanted to provide a basic understanding of nutrition and all the problems that malnutrition could bring to an individual. Themes such as causes of malnutrition, assurance of good nutrition, and nutrition programs in schools and communities were the primary focuses of her publication.

The content of her book was the result of many studies that she conducted along with her students. Roberts offered a course in nutrition, in which her students learned about the problems of malnutrition in childhood development. Her students did the laboratory work for many of her studies. She believed in letting her students participate and get hands-on experience. At the same time, Roberts expected her students to work efficiently and to their full potential. "She had a way of bringing out the best in her students and . . . they adored her" (Bing, 6). Her students' names appeared in her publications as collaborators. Roberts trained more than one hundred students for M.S. degrees and more than fifteen for Ph.D. degrees. Many of her students went on to distinguished careers as teachers and researchers.

Never married, Roberts was close to students, associates, and family. She lived with her sister Lillian, who worked at a university office, and shared a cottage in Indiana with her friend and colleague, Evelyn Halliday.

In her dissertation, Roberts studied the nutritional causes of malnutrition—an inadequate breakfast and lunch, low and inadequate intake of foods, too little milk, among many others; however, Roberts took a step further and also studied the underlying causes of malnutrition. Roberts recognized that poor health and malnutrition were society's problems. As part of her work, she desired to attack the problem from its roots. Roberts identified poverty and lack of knowledge of good nutrition as the main underlying causes of malnutrition. She wanted to create consciousness of nutrition in parents, and she taught them how to improve the nutrition of their children.

In 1929, Blunt became president of Connecticut College for Women. The next year, after much consideration and referrals, Lydia Roberts replaced Blunt as chair of the department. Her coworkers believed that she was the most qualified person to take the position. At the same time Roberts was promoted to full professor. She became head of a department with a strong graduate program in home economics and a record of outstanding research. Under her leadership, both the quantity and the scope of research increased in the various areas of home economics.

As head of the home economics department, Roberts was involved with the nursery school, which had been formed in 1916 by mothers and wives of university faculty for the care of their children. She advised them on matters of nutrition pertaining to children's lunches and was a member of the board of directors for many years. The nursery school served as a laboratory for the research of Roberts's students as she developed undergraduate and graduate courses on nutrition. She worked with HELEN KOCH, who came to the university in 1930 and became director of the nursery school two years later.

Roberts was very active in her field and joined many committees and organizations, including the American Dietetic Association, American Home Economics Association, and the American Institute of Nutrition. In 1929 she was appointed to the White House Conference on Child Health and Protection, where she was active on the Committee on Nutrition as well as other committees. As a member of the Council on Foods and Nutrition of the American Medical Association between 1934 and 1948, Roberts introduced in 1940 her views in favor of "addition of selected vitamins and minerals to selected foods" (Bing, 9). That year Roberts became a member of the federal Food and Nutrition Board of the National Research Council. It was a rule not to allow anyone over sixty to join the board, but because Lydia Roberts never reported her age for *American Men of Science*, her age was not known. However, Roberts was unaware of the policy when she joined. Later the policy was changed, and older and renowned nutritionists were able to join the board.

The head of the Food and Nutrition Board appointed Roberts head of a committee whose task was to decide on the labeling of foods for special dietary purposes. Roberts and her committee were given one day to report their advice on dietary standards. Roberts took this assignment seriously and successfully presented the committee's advice to the board. As a result, Roberts was assigned to be chair of a committee that was to determine daily dietary "allowances"; the use of the word "allowances in place of requirements was . . . her terminology" (Bing, 10). Roberts presented her theories on daily dietary allowances and they were accepted. Wanting to have full assurance of her theories, Roberts consulted other experts on nutrition. In 1941, with their advice and her expertise, she developed the first report of recommended dietary allowances.

Roberts's ability to communicate with people at different levels allowed her to reach them through her many publications on various aspects of nutrition. During her career, she published more than seventy-five articles, which included research done with her students, approaches to teaching nutrition, and materials on nutrition for lay readers. She also developed five bulletins for U.S. government agencies between 1927 and 1947. In addition to her involvement in committees and research, Roberts conducted workshops for secondary and college educators on public health, nutrition, child development, and family relations.

In 1944, Roberts received a visit from the chancellor at the University of Puerto Rico. Roberts had conducted workshops on nutrition education and a nutrition survey for the United States Department of Agriculture on the island. The chancellor asked her to become part of the faculty. He came at an opportune time because Roberts would soon be forced to retire due to her age. By then, Roberts was "one of the leading nutritionists of the United States" (Dye, 93), and her work on nutrition had become a foundation for future programs and research. Roberts accepted the offer and moved that year to Puerto Rico. For the next two years, she returned from time to time to Chicago, which she still considered her residence, but by 1946 she called Puerto Rico her home.

Through her work in Puerto Rico, she was able to study the living conditions of families at different socioeconomic levels. The results of her studies were published in 1949 in her book *Patterns of Living in Puerto Rican Families*, written with colleague Rosa L. Stefani. Based on her study, the Department of Home Economics at the University of Puerto Rico revised the curriculum to include the customs and habits of the Puerto Rican people. As a result of her work, the Department of Home Economics was strengthened and "grew in stature" (Dye, 173). Head of the department between 1946 and 1952, she trained other members of the home economics faculty in the teaching of nutrition.

While Roberts was working in the home economics department at the University of Puerto Rico, she helped in the improvement of the general economy of the island through industrialization programs that created jobs, thereby improving the living standard of families in urban areas. The programs of industrialization had not yet reached the poor isolated rural areas of the island. This need was the opportunity that Roberts had been waiting for; she described it as a "pipedream . . . [she] had long had" (Roberts, *The Dona Elena Project*, v). Roberts desired to turn more of her theories and plans into action.

Roberts's dream entailed choosing an isolated rural community of about one hundred families and conducting a study of their living conditions. After the study, Roberts wanted to create a plan that would help them to improve their nutrition as well as their standard of living. The Puerto Rico Nutrition Committee supported Roberts's proposal to work with a community. With the cooperation of the Department of Health and the Department of Home Economics of the University of Puerto Rico, all the staff and services required for the project were obtained.

In order to choose the right community for the project, staff members visited different villages. Many of the villages had connecting roads, but others had to be reached by jeep or on foot. After traveling to different communities, Roberts selected Doña Elena Alto, a community located in a mountainous area and dedicated to the cultivation of tobacco. She made weekly visits to the community to explain the project and persuade the residents to participate. During the visits, Roberts and the residents discussed the problems that the community faced and possible solutions. The people of Doña Elena welcomed the project and agreed to cooperate, and community workers became part of the project.

The Doña Elena project began in 1956 and lasted five years. As Roberts studied current living conditions, she was fully convinced that the project would be a "human demonstration that nutrition makes a difference in the growth, physical status, and health of the people" (*Dona Elena Project*, 4). Roberts's initial focus centered the project on school and children. Within a year it was evident that the community needed improvement, not only in its nutritional education but also in the betterment of roads, water, electricity, and housing. Roberts knew that the socioeconomic status of families largely determined the nutrition and health of the children. Therefore she decided to work on the betterment of living conditions that were the underlying causes of malnutrition among their children.

The reforms in the Doña Elena project were initiated by having a couple move into the community and become a living example of what the community was being taught. Children had three meals a day at school, where the food served met recommended daily dietary allowances, and families began to see a difference in the health of their children. The attitude of the people changed, and they started participating more in the betterment of their community. Families began to improve their homes, to plant gardens, and to clean their surroundings. They became optimistic about their future.

At the beginning of the program children who were in fifth and sixth grade had the bodies of second and third graders. Many had calcium and other nutritional deficiencies. The majority of the families did not have adequate cooking utensils and kitchens. New houses needed to be built, and decent sleeping conditions had to be provided. Most of the families did not have latrines, making their surroundings dirty and unhealthy.

By the end of the fifth year, the program was successful in improving the growth and nutrition of the children. Families reported their most apparent improvement in diet. They were consuming more milk and protein, and their breakfast consisted of cereal, milk, and eggs. The housing facilities greatly improved, and 41 percent of the families had new houses. All of the families had new kitchens and latrines. Electricity and water were made available for everyone, and a road connecting two neighboring communities was built. Funding for these improvements initially came from the Puerto Rican government and later from the Department of Health.

The project was described in Roberts's book, *The Dona [sic] Elena Project: A Better Living Program in an Isolated Rural Community*, published by the University of Puerto Rico in 1963. Roberts was able to measure the success of her project by the accomplishments in the community. "The change in the attitudes and spirit of the community" was so great that the hopelessness turned into optimism that could "be felt though [it could not] be measured" (p. 13). By 1965, about thirty communities had developed similar programs, and their living conditions were improving.

Lydia Roberts died in Rio Piedras, Puerto Rico. She was found unconscious at her desk, where she had been working on a college textbook on nutrition for the Caribbean area. She was taken to the hospital, where she died two hours later due to a ruptured aneurysm of the aorta. Roberts was buried in Martin, Michigan, on May 31, 1965.

The lives of many individuals and entire communities improved as a result of Roberts's drive to turn her work in nutrition into community action. In the Puerto Rican years, her work had an international impact through surveys she conducted for the World Health Organization and other groups in several countries, including Uganda, East Africa, Jamaica, and Costa Rica. Roberts's basic study, *Nutrition Work with Children*, considered by colleagues "one of the masterpieces of the literature on nutrition" (Bing, 6) continued to be used, with revised editions in 1954 and 1978.

Sources. Roberts's books are cited above. Ethel Austin Martin rewrote *Nutrition Work with Children* for third and fourth editions in 1954 and 1978 under the title *Roberts' Nutrition Work with Children*. A list of Roberts's publications is in Ethel Austin Martin, "The Life Works of Lydia J. Roberts," *Journal of the American Dietetic Association*, vol. 49,

1966. Martin also wrote a biography of Roberts, "Lydia Jane Roberts, June 30, 1879–May 28, 1965," in *Journal of the American Dietetic Association*, vol. 46, August 1965. Franklin C. Bing, "Lydia Jane Roberts—A Biographical Sketch," *Journal of Nutrition*, vol. 93, 1967, provides a detailed description of Roberts's career. Another biographical profile of Roberts is in *NAW* (1980). *The History of the Laboratory Schools* (1967) by Ida B. DePencier gives a brief description of Roberts's involvement in the University Cooperative Nursery School. Marie Dye's *History of the Department of Home Economics, University of Chicago* (1972) includes information on Roberts's work in the Department of Home Economics.

GERALDINE FRANCO

ROBERTSON, INA LAW
July 27, 1867–March 6, 1916
FOUNDER OF HOUSING FOR WOMEN, PHILANTHROPIST

Ina Robertson was the younger of two daughters born to Robert Martin and Nancy Robertson, early settlers in the Pacific Northwest. Her father (called Martin Robertson), of Scottish descent, was born in South Carolina in 1830; his family moved West to Ohio in 1832 to live in an area free from the practice of slavery, then later moved to Iowa. At age twenty-two, Martin Robertson traveled to Oregon and lived in several locations, logging, mining for gold, and then farming. In 1861, he married Nancy McMeekin. After several years of farming, the couple moved to the town of Buena Vista, where Martin Robertson became a wheat merchant and where Ina Robertson was born. In 1874, the family moved to Albany, Oregon, where better schooling opportunities existed for Ina and her sister, Lillian. The family was United Presbyterian; Martin Robertson was a church elder, and Ina joined the church at the age of twelve.

Ina and Lillian Robertson were educated in public schools in Albany and also, briefly, in Halsey, Oregon. At age fifteen, Ina began teaching school in Millersburg, Oregon, while continuing her own studies; when she was eighteen she started teaching full-time. After a few years she resumed her own education, attending Albany College (now Lewis and Clark College) and graduating with a B.S. degree in 1889. Ina Robertson's interests in teaching and in United Presbyterian missionary activities were combined after college graduation, when she became the first woman teacher and principal of Waitsburg Academy, a United Presbyterian Home Mission School in Waitsburg, Washington. On a fund-raising trip east, Robertson met James Law and his sister, Eleanor Law, wealthy United Presbyterians in New York State. The Laws were greatly impressed with Robertson and began to contribute money to Waitsburg Academy.

In 1895, Robertson moved to Chicago to attend graduate school at the newly founded University of Chicago. She studied English literature and French language in the graduate school for two quarters in 1896, then transferred to the divinity school, where she took courses in church history. She ventured often into the downtown commercial district, where she met young women who were working in the city's big department stores. Her conversations with saleswomen led Robertson to begin thinking about ways to make the transition from rural home life to urban business life safer and happier for these "women adrift" (Meyerowitz, *Women Adrift*), many of whom had come to the city from small midwest towns and were without friends or relatives in Chicago.

Around this time, Robertson came into a sizable fortune. James Law designated her, along with his sister, Eleanor Law, trustees of his estate. The two women were to oversee expenditures for philanthropic causes. In addition, James Law intended that Robertson would care for his elderly sister after his death. Out of respect for James Law, Robertson took Law as her middle name and was known from then on as Ina Law Robertson. She left the divinity school in 1897, returning in the summer of 1903 and autumn of 1904. James Law died in 1899, leaving his property jointly to his sister and Robertson. The two women lived together in Hyde Park near the University of Chicago.

In their first philanthropic efforts, Ina Robertson and Eleanor Law donated twelve thousand dollars to the United Presbyterian Church's Mission College in India and took over the operating expenses of the *Midland,* a midwest religious newspaper. By appealing for financial contributions through *Midland,* the women secured funding for enterprises such as a low-cost boarding house for miners in Spokane, Washington.

Robertson quickly assumed the leadership role in these philanthropic activities. In 1898 she began to address the housing needs of Chicago's working women by opening a low-cost boardinghouse intended to be a safe haven from the dangers of urban life. Originally called the Eleanor Hotel, both in honor of Eleanor Law and because "Eleanor" means "light" in Greek, this first building provided room and board to twenty-eight young women. The boardinghouse was established on the premise that "the business girl desired living conditions on just as self-respecting a basis as any business man would wish," recognizing also "the necessity of companionship and of homelike surroundings for the girl isolated in a great city" (Veeder, 1).

The Eleanor Hotel soon filled to capacity. Within a few years, Robertson moved the enterprise into a building large enough to house eighty-one women and changed its name to the Eleanor Club, which, she felt, evoked a social, communal atmosphere far better than the impersonal term "hotel." Robertson opened a second Eleanor Club in 1905 and four more over the next nine years. She was constantly searching for new properties suitable for conversion into clubs, often moving established clubs into larger premises. By 1916, the clubs accommodated six hundred women.

The self-governing housing clubs provided each resident with her own single or shared bedroom and a host of communal spaces: parlors, reading rooms, sewing rooms, laundry facilities, and dining rooms large enough to seat all residents at once. While the majority of women living in the Eleanor Clubs, especially in the early years, were office and store workers, any "self-supporting girl of good character" (G. Coulter, 25), was eligible to join. Students, too, were welcomed, especially those working their way through school. There was no age or wage limit, but the "young girl on the low wage" (G. Coulter, 25) was always the first consideration, for Robertson believed that limited wage "exposed her in a peculiar manner to life's hardships and temptations" (Robertson, "Home for Chicago Working Women," 78). Married and divorced women were not viewed as potential residents.

By carefully managing funds, the clubs were expected to be self-supporting, as were the women who lived in them. Robertson was so adamant that no charity be involved in the provision of Eleanor Club housing and that the clubs be nondenominational that she refused the persistent overtures of the United Presbyterian Church to sponsor Eleanor Club work. Over this issue, Robertson left the United Presbyterian Church altogether and joined instead the Presbyterian Church in Chicago.

In some ways, Robertson's low-cost accommodations for working women were nothing new. In New York by the 1850s, a Working Women's Home housed some five hundred residents dormitory-style in converted tenements, while a Ladies Christian Association established a boardinghouse in 1858. The idea spread rapidly in the second half of the nineteenth century, becoming firmly associated with the Young Women's Christian Association (YWCA). The number of such boardinghouses began to decline in Chicago in the 1890s, as furnished rooms and rooming houses, often accommodating both men and women under the same roof, proliferated. Areas just to the north, west, and south of the downtown district became known as furnished room districts, where residents took their meals at cheap restaurants and cafeterias or cooked on gas plates in their own rooms. In contrast, the single-sex, supervised Eleanor Clubs were located safely beyond the furnished room districts, in established middle-class neighborhoods like Robertson's own Hyde Park. The buildings were large mansions, apartment houses, or old hotels, made over into genteel boardinghouses. When funds permitted, two Eleanor Clubs built for the purpose were constructed in 1914 and 1916. By 1914, Chicago had thirty-one boarding houses that were organized, the majority of them associated with church groups such as the YWCA. Robertson was one of the city's few independent providers of housing for young women on the boardinghouse plan.

Settlement houses, such as JANE ADDAMS's Hull-House, were conspicuously located in immigrant neighborhoods. Robertson perceived her work to be distinctly different from that of Jane Addams, noting in her diary on October 13, 1906, "had meeting with Miss Jane Addams by appointment at Hull House. Talked over location of factory girls and plans for greater cooperation of all engaged in housing Chicago working girls." Robertson clearly saw her Eleanor Clubs, located in middle-class neighborhoods, as serving women of a different class from those helped through Hull-House.

Robertson's service to women working in offices and stores, rather than factories, also included providing a facility downtown where a working woman could rest or read and enjoy "the privilege of making herself a cup of tea . . . after the rush and fret of the day" (*Eleanor Record,* May 1918, 7). Such a place, the Central Eleanor Club, opened in 1908, then moved twice to larger quarters. By 1920, Central Eleanor boasted a membership of twenty-four hundred and shared almost an entire floor in the Stevens Building downtown with the offices of the Eleanor Association, which governed the entire Eleanor operation. Central Eleanor hosted "evening classes, Sunday afternoon At Homes, dramatic entertainments, and community effort of every sort" (Veeder, 5). In 1916 alone, the Central Eleanor tea room served fifty-eight thousand persons, while more than two thousand young women attended classes in gymnastics, folk-dancing, dramatics, millinery, and English.

Robertson established Eleanor banking facilities; a magazine, the *Eleanor Record,* written by and for Eleanor Club members; the Eleanor League for younger girls aged twelve to sixteen; and a neighborhood social center, located in one of the residential Eleanor Clubs. In addition, hundreds of young women from the city were able to enjoy summer holidays at the Eleanor Camp at Lake Geneva, Wisconsin. Robertson's work brought together, at least in social situations and spaces, women whose work differed in status, ranging from store seamstresses and office filing clerks to personnel directors and shop owners. Ina Robertson often spoke at women's clubs on the work of the Eleanor Association and met with employers of women, especially department store officials, to discuss and promote Eleanor Club housing. In addition to employing large numbers of potential Eleanor Club members, Chicago's downtown department stores, particularly Marshall Field and Company, were used by Robertson for business purposes. Robertson purchased club furnishings at Field. Eleanor Association committees, as well as various Chicago Woman's Club and Chicago Woman's City Club committees with which Robertson was involved, frequently held their meetings in the restaurants of these grand department stores. Robertson instituted close ties between the Eleanor Clubs and the Chicago Woman's City Club, serving on its housing committee. She was also active in the Philanthropy Department of the Chicago Woman's Club, the Social Hygiene Committee of the YWCA, and the Juvenile Protective Association.

A deeply religious woman, Robertson frequently attended and also spoke before missionary meetings. She brought Christianity directly to the Eleanor Clubs by ensuring that a weekly Sunday service was held at each one. She presided over one of these services every Sunday. While Eleanor enterprises were open "to women of all faiths or of none" (G. Coulter, 38), Christian teaching was a central principle of the Eleanor Association work, and "Christian courtesy and helpfulness" (Robertson, "Home for Chicago Working Women," 80) the Eleanor ideal. Robertson also led the Young Ladies' Bible Class of the Woodlawn Presbyterian Church and founded a Diakonia class for deaconesses-in-training.

Robertson never married. She was very sociable, often dining out or having friends to her home for meals. One of these friends was sociologist ANNIE MacLEAN, author of several articles and books on working women and the conditions of their employment. MacLean pointed to the Eleanor Clubs as an example of housing young working women at low cost without loss of self-respect.

Robertson died in Chicago, at forty-eight years of age, of complications following a hysterectomy. Funeral services were held at the Woodlawn Presbyterian Church, Chicago, followed by burial at Mount Hope Cemetery in south Chicago. MARY McDOWELL, head of the University of Chicago settlement and Progressive reformer, described Robertson as a "citizen-philanthropist" with a "well-developed civic consciousness that included within itself a recognition of the social and industrial problems pressing upon every wage-earning girl" (*Eleanor Record*, April 1916, 16).

On March 8, 1916, the *Chicago Daily Tribune* ran an editorial, "Miss Robertson, Home Maker." Robertson's business, the *Tribune* stated, "was to make the transition of women from home life into business easier and less dangerous. She was really a home maker on a grand scale." Indeed, Robertson's work fo-

cused on securing, furnishing, and running facilities that could only be described in terms of the home. The safe, homelike nature of the Eleanor Clubs masked the role they played in facilitating the shift from home life to business life for young women, many of whom had come from the country to seek work in the city. As demand for single-sex, supervised Christian housing began to fade, however, the residential Eleanor Clubs, which had operated at full capacity with waiting lists in the 1910s and early 1920s, gradually closed down. The legacy of Robertson's work lives on in one remaining Chicago dormitory, now called the Eleanor Residence for Working Women and Students, built for the Eleanor Association in 1956.

Sources. The Eleanor Residence for Working Women and Students in Chicago retains a vast amount of documentation pertaining to Robertson and the clubs from 1898 to the present. Items include Ina Robertson's diary covering the period August 20, 1906–December 11, 1911, and some correspondence and personal mementos. Other materials include data cards kept on the members of the Central Eleanor Club, single and bound copies of the *Eleanor Record*, pamphlets and postcards advertising the housing clubs and their rates, numerous interior and exterior photographs of the clubs and of Camp Eleanor, and scrapbooks of photographs and ephemera. Records of Robertson's education are held by the College Archives at Lewis and Clark College, Portland, Oregon; the UC Registrar's Office; and the UC Archives. Robertson described the clubs in "Home for Chicago Working Women: Hotel Eleanor Aids Girls Who Must Earn Living at Low Wage," *Women's Welfare*, November 1905. A useful pamphlet by Jessie Veeder, *The Eleanor Association: Organization and Policy* (June 1920), describes the history of the various Eleanor enterprises. The Eleanor Residence also has copies of the most informative, though hagiographic, source on Robertson's life, a memoir written in 1922 by Dr. John M. Coulter, *The Power of an Ideal: The Story of the Life and Work of Ina Law Robertson, 1867–1916, Founder and First President of The Eleanor Association*, privately printed in 1977. Robertson appears in Fred Nutting's newspaper articles, "Old Time Albany," published in the *Albany Democrat-Herald* in the 1930s and compiled in *Linn County, Oregon Pioneer Settlers* by Nina Williamson (1982). The Eleanor Clubs are described by contemporaries in Grace A. Coulter, "The Eleanor Clubs in Chicago," *Forbes Magazine*, April 20, 1918, and Annie Marion MacLean, *Wage-Earning Women* (1910) and *Women Workers and Society* (1916). Lisa M. Fine provides information and analysis of the lives of Eleanor Club residents in *The Souls of the Skyscraper: Female Clerical Workers in Chicago, 1870–1930* (1990) and "Between Two Worlds: Business Women in a Chicago Boarding House 1900–1930," *Journal of Social History*, Spring 1986. This profile is drawn, in part, from biographical information in Jeanne Catherine Lawrence, "Chicago's Eleanor Clubs: Housing Working Women in the Early Twentieth Century," in *People, Power, Places: Perspectives in Vernacular Architecture, VIII*, ed. Annmarie Adams and Sally McMurray, copyright 2000 by The University of Tennessee Press; used by permission. For an excellent study of the wider population of Chicago women working and living apart from the homes of family, relatives, and employers, see Joanne Meyerowitz, *Women Adrift: Independent Wage Earners in Chicago, 1880–1930* (1988). Meyerowitz's "Sexual Geography and Gender Economy: The Furnished Room Districts of Chicago, 1890–1930," *Gender & History*, Autumn 1990, discusses housing in particular. On housing for working women, see also Elizabeth Cromley, "Apartments and Collective Life in Nineteenth-Century New York," in *New Households: New Housing*, ed. Karen A. Franck and Sherry Ahrentzen (1989), and Nina Mjagkij and Margaret Spratt, eds., *Men and Women Adrift: The YMCA and the YWCA in the City* (1997).

JEANNE CATHERINE LAWRENCE

ROBINS, MARGARET DREIER
September 6, 1868–February 21, 1945
LABOR REFORMER, SOCIAL REFORMER

Margaret Dreier Robins, this country's leading exponent of the rights of unskilled working women during the Progressive Era, was brilliantly prepared for a career in social reform by her German émigré parents. Theodor Dreier, who had made a fortune importing iron, and Dorothea Dreier, an active volunteer in charities in Brooklyn, New York, emphasized the piety of their German Evangelical Church while also providing their five children with the educational and artistic stimulation afforded by living in nineteenth-century Brooklyn. Few American families would produce four daughters noted for such achievement and social innovation. As the eldest and her father's favorite, Margaret was the pacesetter. Dorothea Dreier (1870–1923) broke with the impressionist school to paint workers realistically. Mary Dreier (1875–1963) modeled her career on Margaret's in labor, suffrage, and peace organizations. Katherine Dreier (1877–1952) exhibited her *Blue Bowl* in the famous 1913 Armory Show and subsequently founded Société Anonyme to promote modern art. Throughout their lives, each sister stirred the others' imagination but also offered a safe haven, as all four sought self-consciously adventurous lives. A fourth sibling, Edward, led a more conventional life, focusing on his family and his career as a stockbroker.

Margaret Dreier's childhood and youth were afflicted with no major pains or losses. She was a student at George Brackett's private school in Brooklyn Heights, graduating in 1885. At age nineteen, she launched her career as a volunteer when she joined the Women's Auxiliary at Brooklyn Hospital. Her father was a trustee of the hospital. For the next fifteen years, the hospital remained her primary civic concern. She served as the auxiliary's treasurer and as the hospital's (volunteer) dietitian. "Volunteer women wielded considerable authority through hospital auxiliaries ranging from providing funds and supplies to supervising student nurses" (Payne, 22). She also "became a member of the State Charities Aid Association's city visiting committee for institutions for the insane, where she benefited from the guidance of the welfare leader Homer Folks" (Davis, 179). She expanded her intellectual horizons by studying history and philosophy informally with Brooklyn minister Richard Salter Storrs, of Brooklyn's Church of the Pilgrims, and by taking lessons in rhetoric and composition with journalist Lucia Gilbert Runkle, a former writer for the *New York Tribune*. It was probably through these two mentors that she came in contact with Josephine Shaw Lowell, the woman whose life inspired Dreier to envision herself as a social reformer.

To others, Dreier's life appeared satisfying and full of meaningful activity, but she would recall the years of her twenties and early thirties as marked by indecision, turmoil, and illness. Headaches that defied diagnosis "by her early twenties . . . had become incapacitating" (Payne, 15). She had lost her direction in late adolescence. Then, in the space of a few months—between December 1904, when she joined the New York Women's Trade Union League (WTUL), and June 1905, when she married Raymond Robins—she regained her equilibrium.

Her path to the WTUL had been set when Josephine Shaw Lowell recruited her for the Woman's Municipal League (WML), New York's first women's civic organization. As head of the WML's legislative committee, Dreier began investigating the relationship between organized prostitution and the city's employment agencies. She recruited Frances A. Kellor to investigate the city's employment agencies, an investigation that led to Kellor's publication *Out of Work* (1905), an exceptionally thorough and scholarly piece of muckraking. Kellor's research provided the documentation for a bill to regulate agencies written by Dreier's committee and passed into law in 1904. It was Dreier's first legislative effort, but her organizing and lobbying triumph brought her into the public eye and into the mainstream of women's civic reform in New York. Indeed, her work with the WML played a significant role in building sentiment that led to "white slave" legislation in New York and ultimately to the federal Mann Act (White Slave Traffic Act) in 1910, which prohibited interstate transportation of women for immoral purposes.

Dreier and Kellor founded the New York Association for Household Research in the spring of 1904 to continue their work on behalf of prostitutes, but Dreier's interests quickly expanded. Dreier's efforts with the WML and the Household Research Association had grown out of her concern to protect women she thought vulnerable as workers—job seekers, domestics, and immigrants—from becoming trapped into prostitution. Her efforts against prostitution led directly to identifying with the labor movement. For her, the exploitation of an individual's sexuality and the exploitation of her labor were identical: both turned elemental aspects of human expressiveness into commodities.

Leadership of the WML's legislative committee and work with the Association for Household Research foreshadowed Dreier's role in the WTUL. Founded in 1903, the National Women's Trade Union League (NWTUL) forged an alliance between working women and their middle-class allies to organize women into trade unions and to educate the public on labor concerns. Dreier joined the New York branch of the WTUL in December 1904 and was immediately elected treasurer. She became its leader in title the following March. Until she joined, the WTUL was little more than a paper organization. She breathed life into the organization by recruiting working women like Rose Schneiderman and by supporting strikes in which women were involved. At the same time, her social connections opened the purses of upper-middle-class sympathizers and, along with her own financial resources, enabled the WTUL to become a pivotal player in women's organizations concerned with working women. The meeting of Dreier and the WTUL was a fortuitous one: for her, the WTUL was an empty but inviting stage in need of her vast energies; for the organization, Dreier was a person who could bring the association to life.

Dreier met Raymond Robins (1874–1954) the month after she became president of the New York WTUL; they were married two months later, on June 21, 1905. A lawyer and an ordained minister in both the Methodist and Congregational churches, Robins had made a modest fortune in the Alaska gold rush and then settled in Chicago in 1901. A card-carrying member of the Western Federation of Miners, he had worked in the Colorado lead mines before studying law. He also was the principal negotiator for the United Mine Workers during the great anthracite coal strike in 1902. He was head of the Northwestern University Settlement in Chicago when Dreier met him. Her meteoric courtship and marriage stunned her family—she had always said she would never marry—but the conjunction of finding both her life's work and her partner meant that she would always look back to the spring of 1905 as the time when her life assumed the direction it was meant to have, to the time when she had never felt younger.

Margaret Dreier Robins settled with her new husband in a cold-water, third-floor flat in an immigrant neighborhood on Chicago's West Side. From this home located about a mile north of Hull-House, the Robinses presided for the next seventeen years over a whirlwind of reform activities centered on but not limited to Chicago. Having promised each other "unhampered freedom" to work for "the growing good of the world" (quoted in Payne, 31), the couple saw themselves as a team working through different channels for the same goals. Margaret Dreier Robins maintained her own arena of activity in labor, suffrage, and civic organizations. However, she clearly benefited, especially in the early years of her marriage, from her husband's respected standing in civic and labor circles. Through Raymond Robins's labor and civic connections as well as her own association with Hull-House reformers, Dreier Robins met and began to work with the exciting group of reformers committed to changing the shape of Chicago's public life. Through the Chicago WTUL, over which she presided from 1907 to 1913, she forged an effective alliance with such Chicago trade union women as ELISABETH CHRISTMAN, MARY ANDERSON, AGNES NESTOR, MARGARET HALEY, ELIZABETH MALONEY, and BESSIE ABRAMOWITZ HILLMAN. From 1908 to 1917, she was a member of the executive board of the Chicago Federation of Labor and a trusted friend of its president, John Fitzpatrick. These ties, in addition to those with Hull-House reformers, meant that Dreier Robins was uniquely positioned to have a critical voice in the emerging national discussion concerning women workers.

That voice was substantially amplified when she became president of the NWTUL. From 1907 to 1922, the years of the league's most effective work, Dreier Robins presided over the NWTUL's efforts to carve out a home for working women in the nation's labor institutions. She exhorted the organization to follow simultaneously its three main goals, which she saw as compatible and mutually supportive: organizing women into trade unions; educating the public on issues concerning working women; and seeking protective legislation, especially regarding minimum wages and maximum hours.

When Dreier Robins married, she expected to have children. For several years after her marriage, she tried but failed to conceive the child she desperately wanted. Nurturing and affectionate, her husband "congratulated his wife on the League's success, writing her that the organization 'is one of your children that *you* raised from feeble infancy into maturity and power'" (Payne, 34). Indeed, she enjoyed a role akin to a surrogate mother with several young trade unionists, especially Elisabeth Christman and Agnes Nestor. Later in the 1920s, she virtually adopted Lisa von Borowsky, the young German woman who came to work for her in Florida. Margaret Dreier Robins's great-

est contribution to the league was mentoring younger women. She had a genius for recognizing talent among young trade union women, and she scouted eagerly for able young women her organization might groom for leadership. She would be most vividly remembered in inspirational terms. An old friend, for example, wrote the recently retired league president that a mutual friend had commented that Dreier Robins had "more power to quicken young women than any person she had ever known" (Payne, 142).

Under her direction the WTUL founded *Life and Labor*, a journal that Dreier Robins initially edited and that focused on women's issues. She was also the one primarily responsible for establishing the Training School for Women Workers, the league's heroic effort to train women workers for leadership in its labor organizations. As president of the NWTUL during the garment workers' strikes of 1909–11 in New York, Philadelphia, and Chicago, Dreier Robins shaped the organization into this country's most effective agency for supporting the rights of working women. During the Hart, Schaffner and Marx strike in 1910–11, for example, the Chicago WTUL under her direction raised more than seventy thousand dollars for the strikers. She secured legal counsel, marched in picket lines, organized relief, and worked tirelessly to inform the public on the conditions of the workers.

Margaret Dreier Robins played a critical role in creating and refining the arbitration machinery at Hart, Schaffner and Marx after the strike. The procedures established for addressing grievances secured a measure of self-government for workers, eventually established the preferential shop, and later became a landmark in labor history. It was the achievement she treasured most in her social reform career, but her victory also signaled the fragile ties between the WTUL and the American Federation of Labor (AFL). With a commitment to organizing workers around traditional trade divisions, the AFL showed little interest in organizing women, or, for that matter, unskilled workers of either sex. This tension came to a head in 1914 when the Hart, Schaffner and Marx workers belonging to the AFL's United Garment Workers joined the New York workers to form the Amalgamated Clothing Workers Union. The AFL and its leader, Samuel Gompers, held Margaret Dreier Robins and the WTUL responsible for this insurgency. On one level, they were correct. Sidney Hillman, leader of the Amalgamated, and Robins spoke the same language and shared the same goals for a labor organization. Gompers correctly understood that Robins and the WTUL had helped pave the way for the creation of the Amalgamated, described by Hillman as concerned with "ultimate aims" and "social service" (Payne, 94). Robins and Gompers as well as the WTUL and the AFL increasingly distrusted each other after 1914.

Like the careers of most activists of her generation, Robins's social reform career cut a broad swath. Her first public action as president of the Chicago WTUL was to lead "a protest parade of some twenty thousand working men and women through Chicago" (Davis, 180) in May 1907, when "'Big Bill' Haywood and two other labor leaders were arrested, forcibly transferred from Colorado to Idaho, and placed on trial for the murder of a former governor of Idaho (a charge of which they were eventually cleared)" (Davis, 180). She described her work in labor as recasting the American Revolution in industrial terms. Likewise, she saw women's suffrage as furthering democratic values. Although she criticized suffragists who failed to identify with the interests of labor, she "served on the Leslie Woman Suffrage Commission, a national lobbying group for the amendment. . . . Robins saw the woman's movement and the labor struggle as twin expressions of the same goals, but although she wanted suffragists to join with the labor movement, the alliance never took place. In the end, branches of the league formed their own separate organizations to further the cause of suffrage" (Payne, 144–45), including the Chicago WTUL.

Briefly around 1910–11, Robins flirted with the idea of helping to organize a labor party in the United States but ultimately concluded that such an effort was untenable. She supported William Jennings Bryan in 1908 but became an ardent member of the Progressive Party in 1912, campaigning for Charles Evans Hughes in 1916. She drafted Warren G. Harding's speech on social welfare, which was delivered during the presidential campaign in 1920 and in which he called for legislation providing medical care for infants and pregnant mothers. Its basic ideas were implemented in the Sheppard-Towner Act (1921).

Margaret Dreier Robins resigned from the presidency of the NWTUL in 1922 intending to focus on the International Federation of Working Women, an organization largely of her creation. Because of contrasting emphases between American and European labor circles, however, Robins resigned in 1923. The following year, she and her husband moved permanently to Chinsequt, a two-thousand acre plantation near Brooksville, Florida. There they hoped to develop new "breeds and seeds" (Payne, 155) to combat the poverty of the area. She applauded the efforts of the WTUL in the South and in 1937 became the chair of its committee on Southern work.

She witnessed the ebb tide of reform activity with anxiety and alarm, finding it difficult to accommodate herself to the reversals of the 1920s and 1930s. She had opposed this country's entry into World War I, and her anti-militarism helped earn her a central place in the War Department's famous "spider-web" of 1924. Furthermore, she opposed those women who favored the Equal Rights Amendment, calling them individualistic feminists. Neither did she support many of the new departures of the New Deal, although she was enthusiastic about the Tennessee Valley Authority and most of the provisions of the Social Security Administration. Faced with public humiliation surrounding the disappearance in 1932 of her husband for several months—he had amnesia—she never completely regained the sure-footedness that had characterized her reform career.

Margaret Dreier Robins died of pernicious anemia and heart failure and was buried under her favorite oak tree at Chinsequt Hill. Deeply religious, Robins always saw her work as an expression of her faith. Originally German Evangelical, she later became a Congregationalist. To be sure, she had enjoyed certain tangible successes in her social reform career, but her real contribution lay in two areas infused with spiritual meaning for women at the time. She breathed life into and lovingly tended the organization that enabled thousands of women of all classes to work for labor, when that privilege was reserved mainly for skilled men. She inspired dozens of young women to recast their visions of the future. They accordingly credited her with profound transformations in their lives, as when Bessie Hillman wrote on hearing of Margaret Dreier Robins's death, "She made me what I am today" (Payne, 95).

Sources. Margaret Dreier Robins Papers are at the Univ. of Florida Library, Gainesville, Florida. Also see the Raymond Robins Papers, Wisconsin State Hist. Soc., Madison, Wisconsin. Other important manuscript collections include Papers of the National Women's Trade Union League, Library of Congress, as well as the Mary Elisabeth Dreier Papers, SL. Mary E. Dreier, *Margaret Dreier Robins: Her Life, Letters and Work* (1950) contains the best published source of Margaret Robins's writing, including her most important speeches and letters. The National Women's Trade Union League's journal, *Life and Labor*, vols. 1–12, contain her speeches and several of her editorials. For the origins of the league, see Allen F. Davis, "The Women's Trade Union League: Origins and Organization," *Labor History*, vol. 5, 1964. For Robins's work with the league, see Gladys Boone, *The Women's Trade Union Leagues in Great Britain and the United States of America* (1942), and Mary Anderson as told to Mary N. Winslow, *Woman at Work: The Autobiography of Mary Anderson* (1951). See Robin Miller Jacoby, "The British and American Women's Trade Union League, 1890–1923" (Ph.D. diss., Harvard Univ., 1977), for an excellent analysis of Robins's ideological perspective in comparison to the British. Allen F. Davis, "Margaret Dreier Robins," *NAW* (1971), is a fine summary of her public activities. Elizabeth Anne Payne, *Reform, Labor and Feminism: Margaret Dreier Robins and the Women's Trade Union League* (1988), focuses on the relationship between Robins's life and leadership and the institutional shape of the league, especially the Chicago branch of the Women's Trade Union League and the Chicago context of the national league. See also Elizabeth A. Payne Moore, "'Life and Labor': Margaret Dreier Robins and the Women's Trade Union League" (Ph.D. diss., Univ. of Illinois at Chicago, 1981). For accounts of Raymond Robins's career, see William A. Williams, "Raymond Robins and Russian-American Relations, 1917–1938" (Ph.D. diss., Univ. of Wisconsin, 1951), and Allen F. Davis, "Raymond Robins: The Settlement Worker as Municipal Reformer," *Social Service Review*, June 1959.

ELIZABETH ANNE PAYNE

ROBINSON, INCREASE (Josephine Dorothea Reichmann Robinson)
April 2, 1890–1981
PAINTER, GALLERY OWNER, ARTS ADMINISTRATOR

Josephine Dorothea Reichmann was the third child of Hyde Park business owner Frederick J. Reichmann, who made his fortune in rails and freight, and the talented watercolorist Josephine (Lemos) Reichmann. Josephine Dorothea Reichmann was born to a family with a rich artistic legacy. Her maternal great-grandfather, Baron Eustace Wyszynski, fled Poland in 1830 after participating in the Polish insurrection against Russia. In North America, he fought Seminole Indians in Florida and mapped the adjacent lands of Canada and the United States. Moving to New York, Wyszynski designed miniatures for Tiffany and Company. In 1865 he came to Chicago, where he received a commission to paint a miniature of Peter B. Van Beuren through which he met Van Beuren's daughter, Johanna, whom he later wed.

The younger daughter, Josephine Dorothea was tutored by her mother in art at an early age. She graduated from Hyde Park High School, where she was class vice-president. She attended Wellesley College, Wellesley, Massachusetts; the University of

Chicago; and the School of the Art Institute of Chicago. Among her art teachers were John Norton, Ernest Thurn, and Hans Hofman. She then transferred to the University of California, where she studied art, returning to Chicago around 1913 to marry a college sweetheart, Baron Philip Increase Robinson. By the 1920s he had died, at which time she legally became Increase Robinson to end confusion between her and her mother, both active Chicago artists who shared the same name. Little is known of her personal life; apparently she married again.

During the 1920s she and her parents were active in Chicago's art scene. Her father was a founding member of the Arts Club of Chicago and represented it on the Illinois Academy of Fine Arts, a group that sought to establish an art gallery in the Illinois State Museum. The Illinois Academy of Fine Arts sponsored the first competitive state art show; both Robinson and her mother exhibited in the state's second show. In the 1920s and 1930s, Increase Robinson had one-artist shows at the Chicago Cordon Club and Chicago Woman's Aid Club. In addition, between 1927 and 1935, she exhibited six times in Art Institute of Chicago (AIC) *Chicago and Vicinity* shows as well as in other AIC shows, including *A Century of Progress Exhibition of Paintings and Sculpture*, 1933; the Pennsylvania Academy of Fine Arts; and elsewhere throughout traveling exhibitions. She was also active in arts organizations. She was a member of the Chicago Society of Artists (CSA) and served as its secretary and president several times between 1928 and 1938. Through the CSA she solidified her knowledge of contemporary art and honed her critical skills.

During the 1920s Robinson opened the first of several art galleries while she continued to exhibit her own work. With Katharine Kuh in 1929 she opened the Increase Robinson Studio Gallery in Michigan Square in the Diana Court Building. The gallery offered painting classes and provided exhibits of such midwest artists as Aaron Bohrod and Grant Wood. Such special shows as *A Flower Show by Chicago Artists* called for individual interpretation on a subtle or bold design. Kuh and Robinson "were profoundly influential in widening the scope of artistic vision and in developing a keen sense of appreciation for contemporary trends in art in Chicago and elsewhere" (Yochim, 42).

In 1933, when she was discussing her artistic contribution to society, Robinson said, "Every canvas has been merely an experiment in space composition, born of a desire to express something that has caught and held my attention" (Jacobson, 111). What interested her most was "composition based upon the movement and rhythm that always exists in nature but . . . is not perceived by the average spectator. The intense consciousness of this, the love of organizing forms through line, planes and color, and the attempt to satisfy myself with a three-dimensional design on a flat surface . . . will keep me experimenting forever" (Jacobson, 111).

Being either an artist or a gallery owner was difficult during the Great Depression. "Of the nation's major cities, Chicago was one of the hardest hit, and had one of the worst records for relief," according to historian David Shannon (quoted in Mavigliano and Lawson, xvii). As part of its economic recovery program, President Franklin D. Roosevelt's administration undertook several initiatives to aid artists. Thus, "for the first time the government actually became a patron of the arts. It provided three meals per day, a place to execute works, and encouraged individuals to produce the best that were distributed to government institutions, hospitals, and schools for all to view and enjoy" (Yochim, 8).

The first federal initiative, in 1933, was the Public Works of Art Project (PWAP), which commissioned art for public buildings. Two separate programs evolved out of it. One, in the Treasury Department, established the Section of Painting and Sculpture to hire "the best available professional nonrelief artists to decorate public buildings" (Mavigliano and Lawson, xix). In 1935, President Roosevelt created by executive order the Works Progress Administration (WPA; after 1939 the Works Projects Administration), one of whose activities was the Federal Art Project (FAP). The FAP hired artists on the basis of need more than skills, qualifications, or reputation. Overall, the FAP "set forth on a national objective to put thousands (90 percent relief and 10 percent nonrelief) of unemployed artists to work" (Mavigliano and Lawson, xxi).

Robinson's reputation as a gallery owner and a practicing artist brought her membership on the committee that advised PWAP Region Ten administrator Walter Brewster, whom she replaced in 1934. When the project ended in April of that year, more than three thousand artists had brought works of art to schools, libraries, community centers, government, and public buildings across the nation. In 1935 she undertook consulting responsibilities for states in midwest Region Ten and, in October, was appointed director of the Illinois Arts Project (IAP), one of the largest FAP programs.

Supporters and detractors alike noted her intensity. She was later described by artist Aaron Bohrod as "a forbidding New England WASP [white, Anglo-Saxon Protestant] type. . . . She was tall, handsome, dignified, austere and somewhat unbending" (quoted in Mavigliano and Lawson, 23). Friend and artist Andrene Kaufman viewed Robinson as "one of the finest executives I have ever known: a good artist; had excellent taste in art and in the works of other artists; had understanding of people; a really outstanding person; strong organizing force for both PWAP and WPA" (quoted in Mavigliano and Lawson, 23).

The IAP (1935–43) was one of four cultural projects supporting art in the fields of theater, music, writing, and art. When the theater project was dropped, the remaining three were merged into the WPA Art Programming from 1939 to 1942. Among the twelve divisions that artists contributed were murals, sculpture, creative home planning, posters, scenic designing, posters, and photographs. The *Index of American Design* (IAD) cataloged unique ethnic cultural works from rural communities. Through the IAP initiative, the public could attend gallery tours and lectures or take classes in ceramics, stained glass, or painting.

Robinson oversaw the twelve artistic divisions of the IAP. The artwork was displayed in public community buildings, federal art galleries, and such newly developed community art centers as the South Shore Art Center in Chicago. Private exhibitions such as the Marshall Field exhibit held at his store displayed art works for the public to examine. The FAP's traveling exhibits received staff, art materials, and vehicles to move art activities about the countryside. Children were offered free art classes, lectures, and workshops.

From the start, the 9 to 1 proportion of relief to nonrelief—need versus skill as the criterion for selecting the artist—was problematic; indeed, the government-mandated proportion was adjusted from time to time. Artists took a "pauper's oath" (Mavigliano and Lawson, 34) after meeting professional and state relief requirements. Candidates underwent periodic review to remain eligible. Under Robinson's directorship, the Illinois ratios sometimes reached 4 to 1 or 3 to 1.

Large cities such as Chicago accounted for the largest number of artists being subsidized. Among the Chicago artists supported by the IAP were GERTRUDE ABERCROMBIE, MACENA BARTON, FRITZI BROD, FRANCES FOY, BEATRICE LEVY, ETHEL SPEARS, FRANCES STRAIN, and LAURA VAN PAPPELENDAM.

Robinson's tenure as director was marked by major problems with staff and artists that led eventually to her replacement. The first related to aesthetics. Robinson vigorously promoted the notion that "American artists [should] look to his [sic] own environment for subjects worthy of his consideration, to make a lively record of life of our own time and place" (quoted in Mavigliano and Lawson, 24). The preferred style, the "American Scene" (p. 24), called for representational art work, depicting rural or urban landscapes or interpretative paintings based on issues of social significance. The rule was "no nudes, no dives, and no social propaganda" (Mavigliano and Lawson, 24). Many Chicago artists felt limited by this directive and found Robinson provincial.

A second difficulty arose over shared authority and the preparation of the *Index of American Design Manual*. The IAD, which was added to the IAP's list of projects, "put artists to work making watercolors or photographing ceramics, costumes, coverlets, embroideries, furniture, glass, pewter, silver, textiles, toys, wood carvings, and 'other things which were made in America between 1620 and 1900'" (Mavigliano and Lawson, 26). Implementation varied by region. In the Atlantic area, industrial arts were highlighted. The IAP focused on documenting the cultural traits of unique ethnic cultures found in small communities throughout the region. Hildegarde Crosby Melzer (referred to as Crosby), head of the Illinois IAD, and Robinson had "strained relations" (Mavigliano and Lawson, 30), as a result of which Robinson sought to replace Crosby with Marshall Smith, a close friend and confidant from the PWAP, even though the latter's administration of the Poster Division had not been good. To justify the replacement, Robinson questioned Crosby's fiscal management. An investigation by the Washington, D.C., office vindicated Crosby.

The final question arose in conjunction with Robinson's relationship with the Chicago Artists Union, a national organization of sixteen locals and thirteen hundred members by the mid-1930s. Some Artist Union members were socialists and chafed at the content restrictions on IAP art. Both they and the less radical majority of members were concerned about conditions of work as artists in the program. They sought a role in decision making and evaluation of the artists who were hired. They argued, according to scholars George J. Mavigliano and Richard A. Lawson, that "Robinson had been interpreting FAP guidelines by substituting her own notions of quality rather than by accepting the program for what it was—relief for artists in need" (Mavigliano and Lawson, 33). The Artist's Union obtained statistical reports from other regions on the number and type of artists employed and the programs implemented in these regions. They were able to prove that Region Ten did not employ appropriate numbers of needy eligible artists and instead favored known artists.

The investigation of the array of Artists Union's charges against Robinson resulted in her being replaced as director on March 1, 1938. According to Mavigliano and Lawson, she was found to have run the IAP "like a factory rather than as a creative relief-works program," to have failed at labor relations, not to have facilitated IAP efforts outside Chicago, and to have administered poorly by virtue of "play[ing] favorites" (Mavigliano and Lawson, 44). She continued to work with the FAP for a year.

Robinson ceased to be active in Chicago after 1938, and little is known about her after that date. In the 1940s, she painted a history of Corpus Christi, Texas.

Robinson's contribution to Chicago lay in her own work as an artist and her promotion of the work of other artists through her galleries and arts administration. As part of the federal government's support for artists in the 1930s, she served as a prime contributor to public art programs operating in Chicago and throughout the Midwest.

Sources. The microfilmed Increase Robinson Papers at the Ryerson Library, Art Institute of Chicago, provide photographs of and information about family members. Other sources relating to Robinson's public art administrative posts are on microfilm from the Archives of American Art in Detroit; pertinent rolls are DC 61, DC 73, DC 74, and DC 75. For discussion of the Federal Art Project (FAP), consult Maureen A. McKenna, *After the Great Crash: New Deal Art in Illinois* (1983), and George J. Mavigliano and Richard A. Lawson, *The Federal Art Project in Illinois, 1935–1943* (1990). The latter study has an exceptional bibliography and a chapter on Robinson's term at the Illinois Arts Project. Robinson's art work and administration of the FAP are well covered in Louise Yochim's *Role and Impact: The Chicago Society of Artists* (1979). J. Z. Jacobson, ed., *Art of Today, Chicago 1933* (1932), quotes Robinson in discussing her work, includes a painting, and provides a biographical sketch.

PATRICIA A. NIKOLITCH

RODGERS, ELIZABETH FLYNN
August 25, 1847–August 27, 1939
LABOR LEADER, FOUNDER AND LEADER OF A COOPERATIVE INSURANCE SOCIETY

Elizabeth Flynn Rodgers, first female Master Workman of the Knights of Labor and High Chief Ranger of the Women's Catholic Order of Foresters, was born in Woodford, Galway County, Ireland. Her parents, Robert and Bridget (Campbell) Flynn, emigrated to London, Ontario, when Elizabeth was five years old. In Ontario, Rodgers received her education and met her future husband, George Rodgers, an iron molder.

As a young couple, the Rodgerses became involved in labor activities and, as a result, were frequently blacklisted and compelled to relocate "all over this western country" (Levine, 331). Rodgers later recalled the sacrifices involved in those years, including having to take in boarders and needing to sell their furniture each time they moved. Thus, as a young woman, Rodgers was forced to balance her desire for domestic tranquility and stability with her commitment to the labor movement.

During the early 1870s, Rodgers and her family finally settled down in Chicago's working-class Irish Near West Side. Here Rodgers pioneered in the organization of women workers by assisting in the creation of the city's first union of women household workers in the depression years of the mid-1870s. The task of recruiting domestic servants and seamstresses, who made up the majority of the city's female wage earners, proved difficult. As LIZZIE MAY SWANK HOLMES, a coworker of Rodgers, remembered, "the idea that working women had 'a cause' was new and . . . scarcely to be entertained by these women. . . . They might be induced to attend a meeting or two, and even be delighted there, but joining a union—that was a different thing" (Holmes, 508–509). Rodgers presided over the union, which consisted almost exclusively of non-wage-earning housekeepers, such as Mrs. George Schilling, wife of the Chicago labor leader. The union included LUCY PARSONS, wife of the anarchist Albert Parsons, who publicized abuses in factories and sweatshops. The members discussed industrial conditions with employers and employees, and organized educational meetings in public halls or in private homes.

By the mid-1880s, with the rise of the Noble and Holy Order of the Knights of Labor, trade unionism in Chicago, as elsewhere, was booming; Rodgers stood at its forefront. The Knights of Labor, the nation's first labor organization to include women workers on a large scale (and the last one to accept housekeepers as full-fledged members), provided fertile ground for Rodgers's social activism. From 1880 to 1887 she served as a delegate to the State Trades' Assembly of Illinois and worked as a judge in the organization's district court. In September 1881 she led one of the Knights' first all-women assemblies, and, in August 1886, Rodgers was elected the first female Master Workman of District Assembly No. 24, whose jurisdiction extended over most of Chicago. A month later, she acquired nationwide prominence as a delegate to the Knights of Labor's national convention in Richmond, Virginia. When Rodgers brought her two-week-old daughter to the proceedings, the assembled representatives, "as a mark of their appreciation of this infant's early devotion to the cause" (Andrews and Bliss, 127), presented the child with a silver cup and her mother with a gold watch.

This incident, publicized nationally by the press, revealed Rodgers's determination to combine social and domestic commitments. Her emergence as a prominent labor leader as well as a temperance crusader went side by side with raising ten children. (She bore twelve children; ten survived.) Rodgers and other female Knights considered their domestic roles compatible with efforts at reforming the workplace and society. Working-class reformers like Rodgers utilized ideals associated with the familial realm, such as cooperation and the right to a dignified and comfortable life, to forge a critique of a competitive capitalist ethic and economy. Like many nineteenth-century women, Rodgers upheld a notion of sex-based separate spheres, but she wanted to apply what she considered women's unique abilities beyond the home.

Rodgers's next major venue for social reform signaled both continuities with and sharp breaks from her days in the Knights. After the rapid decline of the Knights of Labor in the wake of the 1886 Haymarket affair, with Rodgers's Chicago local suspended in 1890, she directed her efforts at establishing a women's life insurance cooperative. In 1891, the death of a mother of six children in Chicago's Holy Family parish prompted Rodgers and others to demand the creation of a women's auxiliary to the male-only Catholic Order of Foresters, a fraternal insurance society founded in the early 1880s. When their request was denied, Rodgers, along with thirty-seven other women in the church, formed a new organization, the Women's Catholic Order of Foresters (WCOF), in July 1891. (The name "Forester" derived from Masonic traditions, especially the Robin Hood legend, and did not indicate any relation to the industry of forestry.) Under Rodgers's leadership, the cooperative expanded in 1894 into a statewide, then nationwide, insurance society led and run by women. Its membership expanded from five hundred to more than two thousand within the first year and by 1898 included more than sixteen thousand beneficiaries. The number of associated local cooperatives, or courts, organized in specific Catholic parishes, rose from 39 in 1895 to 250 three years later. At the WCOF's first convention in 1894, Rodgers was elected High Chief Ranger, a position she retained until 1908.

Rodgers's activities in the WCOF revealed her energetic leadership and her continued devotion to a mutualist ethic. During her years as leader of the WCOF, Rodgers created a vast, centralized network of courts all across the Midwest and East. Although each court drew its members from its own parish and elected its own Chief Ranger, it had to obtain a charter from the central organization. Members also sent their monthly premiums directly to the executive office, which, in turn, issued death benefits. In 1897 alone, Rodgers initiated 250 courts, traveling more than twenty-five thousand miles to do so. That year she spent 215 working days in the central office, attended 25 board meetings, and responded to almost two thousand pieces of correspondence. A strong faith in the beneficial purpose of the organization informed her activism. She regarded the order as a kind of school where mothers could bring "their daughters and female relatives, training them to more intelligent, parliamentary and practical business transactions" (Rodgers, *Women's Catholic Forester*, May 25, 1897, 4). Above all, Rodgers considered the WCOF a successful vehicle for achieving societal unity. Not only did the WCOF work toward "breaking down the barriers of selfishness," but it also, in her view, managed to assimilate and weld together "various European nationalities" (Rodgers, *Women's Catholic Forester*, May 25, 1897, 4). Yet, at least during the years of her leadership, the WCOF remained largely an organization of Irish-Americans, interspersed by an occasional Polish and some German members.

Within the Irish community, however, Rodgers's ideal of cooperation squared with the order's activities, which concerned not only collecting and issuing money but also fostering a culture of mutual support, charity, and entertainment. One court, for example, held a fund-raiser for an ill sister whose house had been mortgaged. In exchange for receiving benefits from fifty-two masses, members of another court collected money for a new altar. Piano or vocal solos often opened a business meeting, and social activities, such as playing cards, concluded them.

Moving from Master Workman to High Chief Ranger marked change as well as continuity in Rodgers's outlook. At the turn of the century, when the unionization of working women experienced a brief revival, Rodgers appeared to have turned her back on organized labor. In 1902, for example, Chicago's Allied Printing Trades Council complained to Rodgers that her order printed its journal at a nonunion shop. Presiding over the expanding bureaucracy of the Foresters, she also came to assume the role of watchful supervisor; thus, in her 1900 report, she complained about the tardiness of the order's clerks and admonished them to put in full working days. Rodgers, however, did not completely abandon her sensitivity to matters of class. Addressing the WCOF's 1898 convention, she advised those "versed in the classics" that "they are no better material than the most illiterate among us" (*Women's Catholic Forester*, May 15, 1898). Yet, a few years later, Rodgers was criticized for setting up enrollment fees prohibitive for low-income initiates: "money is spent very freely in the order for large salaries," a court's representative complained, but "if this is a working women's order, let it work for the better condition of its members" (*Women's Catholic Forester*, April 14, 1902, 6).

Complaints about high salaries—Rodgers's pay was high for the era at two thousand dollars annually—formed part of a mounting challenge to what many considered her authoritarian leadership. At the 1898 convention, for instance, a dispute erupted over the selection of officers to the executive. When St. Agnes Court asserted its right to choose its own officers, Rodgers, with the aid of the Chicago police, quickly expelled the local, only to see it reinstated over her veto at the next convention. Similarly, her honorary appointment as High Chief Ranger for life raised the ire of democratic-minded court members, such as MARGARET HALEY, then a local court officer and later a leader of the Chicago Teachers Federation. Although Haley's denunciation of Rodgers as "an autocrat" who dominated via "gag rule" (Haley, 30) may have been an exaggeration, Rodgers did have a low tolerance for dissent and expelled Haley from the Foresters. When, in response, Haley sued the order, Rodgers asserted in her 1898 report that the Foresters were the only ones to decide what rules and measures they would take, so long as Rodgers was High Chief Ranger. In patronizing fashion, Rodgers tended to brush off internal criticism as that of misguided friends. In 1908, after several unsuccessful attempts—one in 1904 led by teacher's union leader CATHARINE GOGGIN—Rodgers's opponents succeeded in ousting her from office. Although the details of these events remain unclear, a court injunction filed by Rodgers against the order reveals that she did not voluntarily resign from office.

Little is known about the last one-third of Rodgers's life. She continued to reside on Chicago's Near West Side for almost three decades, until 1936, when she moved in with her daughter, Elizabeth (Rodgers) McLogan, in Wauwatosa, Wisconsin. It was there, two days after her ninety-second birthday, that Rodgers died of a stroke. Her funeral was held at St. Agnes Church in Chicago, and she was buried in Mount Olivet Cemetery.

Elizabeth Rodgers exemplified women's importance in furthering a social reform of mutualism and cooperation. She conceived of her public agenda and her leadership style in maternalist terms, embracing a working-class version of female domesticity that encouraged women to act as social housekeepers. As High Chief Ranger she was benevolent but authoritarian, the latter probably contributing to the somewhat early end of

her career. Rodgers's legacy is most evident in the continued health of the Women's Foresters. Renamed the National Catholic Society of Foresters, it has retained its headquarters in the Chicago area and a membership in the 1990s of nearly sixty thousand.

Sources. The records of Rodgers's life are sporadic, since neither a published monograph nor collected papers exist. Documents on her later work as insurance leader can be found at the headquarters of the National Catholic Society of Foresters in Mount Prospect, Illinois. The *National Catholic Forester*, Late Summer 1989, and the organization's centennial brochure, *One Hundred Years of Excellence* (1991), both at the National Catholic Society of Foresters Archives in Chicago, provide a good overview of Rodgers's years with the Foresters. The Society preserved some issues of the order's journal, the *Women's Catholic Forester*, which contain her annual reports as High Chief Ranger and statistical information on the organization's membership and finances. Miscellaneous records of Women's Catholic Order of Foresters board meetings and some letters to Rodgers provide a glimpse of her leadership style and of the order's activities in general. For basic coverage of her childhood and her years in Ontario, see the *Detroit Labor Leaf*, December 29, 1886. Rodgers's first trade union activities in the 1870s Chicago are briefly described by Lizzie M. Swank Holmes, "Women Workers of Chicago," *American Federationist*, August 1905. For an excellent analysis of Rodgers's years with the Knights of Labor, see Susan Levine, "Labor's True Women: Domesticity and Equal Rights in the Knights of Labor," *Journal of American History*, September 1983. Two earlier publications also refer to her role in the labor movement of the 1880s: Frances E. Willard, *Glimpses of Fifty Years* (1889), and John B. Andrews and W. D. P. Bliss, *History of Women in Trade Unions*, vol. 10 of *Report on Conditions of Women and Child Wage-Earners in the United States* (Government Printing Office, 1911). A good biography appears in *NAW* (1980). For a highly critical view of Rodgers, see Margaret A. Haley, *Battleground: The Autobiography of Margaret A. Haley*, ed. Robert L. Reid (1982).

GEORG LEIDENBERGER

ROLLINS, CHARLEMAE HILL
June 20, 1897–February 2, 1979
CHILDREN'S LIBRARIAN, AUTHOR, EDUCATOR

As an African American librarian, Charlemae Rollins worked for the creation of well-written children's literature free of racial and ethnic distortion. She played a critical role in changing the image of the African American in children's literature. She was born in Holly Springs, Mississippi, to Allen G. and Birdie (Tucker) Hill. Her parents married June 10, 1896, in Louise, Mississippi. Her mother was a school teacher in Yazoo, Mississippi, before marriage and graduated from Rust College in Holly Springs in 1901. Her father, son of the local doctor, owned a farm in Silver Creek, Mississippi. Charlemae Hill was the oldest of five children.

The family migrated to the Oklahoma Territory in 1904 in the wake of the effects of family illness and the Mississippi floods of 1903. The Oklahoma Indian Territory was home to an indigenous population of Indians, Mexicans, and whites, but few African Americans. The family settled in the little town of Beggs. Allen Hill tried the mercantile business but eventually went back to his first love, farming. After Oklahoma Territory became a state in 1907, the Hill family was soon joined by other black families. Charlemae Hill's father and others built Pleasant Hill

School, which she attended until she was thirteen years old. Her mother taught there occasionally to supplement the family income.

Since there was no high school for black children, Hill was sent to black secondary schools in St. Louis, Missouri, and Holly Springs, Mississippi. She graduated from high school at Western University, a black boarding school in Quindaro, Kansas, in 1916. She returned to Beggs, got a teaching certificate, and taught there for a short while, then studied at Howard University in Washington, D.C., in 1917. She returned to Oklahoma to marry Joseph Walter Rollins on April 8, 1918, and remained there while her husband was stationed in France during World War I. After his return in 1919, the couple migrated to Chicago. Except for a short sojourn in Oklahoma awaiting the birth of her son, Joseph W. Rollins Jr., in 1920, Charlemae Rollins lived the rest of her life in Chicago. Joseph W. Rollins's entire working career was spent as a government meat inspector.

In 1926 Charlemae Rollins began her career in library work as a junior library assistant at the Hardin Square Branch of the Chicago Public Library, serving a multi-ethnic population with no visible African Americans. Rollins credited her love of books to her grandmother, a freed slave who inherited the library of her former master. Rollins spent several years at Hardin Square and decided to stay in the library field. The Chicago Public Library provided funds for her training, and she attended summer sessions at Columbia University School of Library Science (1932) and the University of Chicago (1934–36).

Rollins became the first children's librarian at the George Cleveland Hall Branch library in 1932 and remained in that position until her retirement thirty-one years later. Hall Branch was the first library established for the diverse and growing African American community residing in the Black Belt on the South Side of Chicago. George Cleveland Hall, chief of staff at Provident Hospital, was appointed to the board of directors of the Chicago Public Library in 1927. Hall and VIVIAN HARSH, Chicago Public Library's first black librarian, had pushed for a library to serve the needs of the growing black community. Hall died before the library was completed, and the Chicago Public Library Board named it in his honor. Hall Branch opened its doors on January 18, 1932, with Vivian G. Harsh as head librarian.

Throughout the 1930s Rollins performed the ordinary duties of a librarian and made extraordinary efforts on behalf of children. She did reference work, had a regular storytelling hour, prepared book reviews, made book selections, and ran workshops for both parents and teachers. As a member of the book selection committee of the Children's Department of the Chicago Public Library, she played a pivotal role in educating her colleagues on the detrimental effects to children in the African American community of ethnic and racial misrepresentation.

From her earliest years as a librarian, Rollins agitated against racism in children's books. She asserted that "an important part of our job in the community has been the evaluation of books on the Negro written for children" ("Library Work with Negroes," 93). She wrote letters of protest against the 1931 publication of LUCY FITCH PERKINS's The Pickaninny Twins. She succeeded in having Elvira Garner's Ezekiel pulled from the

Chicago Public Library's selection list in 1937, because the black child, Ezekiel, was portrayed offensively as a pickaninny, that is, an unkempt and uneducable black child. Sensitive to the need for new literature, she worked with writers. During the Great Depression, when the Works Progress Administration developed the Illinois Writers Project, authors working on The Negro in Illinois project met at Hall and sought Rollins's advice and encouragement.

Wishing to establish criteria for literature about African Americans, Rollins wrote to 150 white and African American high school principals, asking for descriptions of books they used that dealt with race. The indifference of educators—only two principals replied—showed her the need for a guide for teachers. At the request of the National Council of Teachers of English (NCTE), she worked for several years on We Build Together: A Reader's Guide to Negro Life and Literature for Elementary and High School Use, published in 1941 and revised in 1948 and 1967. The pamphlet was a bibliography of acceptable depictions of minorities in children's books. Rollins asserted in its preface that "whether books are written for Negro children or about them for other children, the objective should be the same. They should interpret life. They should help young people to live together with tolerance and to understand each other better." In 1941 she joined the advisory committee of the University of Chicago's Bulletin of the Center for Children's Books and remained an adviser until 1977.

Because of her work on We Build Together, she was invited as the luncheon speaker at the 1941 convention of the NCTE held in Atlanta, Georgia. Governor Eugene Talmadge's memo to Georgia schools threatening to dismiss any teachers who ate with Blacks caused the NCTE to cancel the luncheon, although Rollins attended the conference. Rollins objected to this experience with Jim Crow as well as to segregation on trains and in southern hotels, and in 1945 the NCTE resolved not to meet in cities where all members could not participate in all functions and activities. Rollins waged a similar campaign within the American Library Association (ALA) in 1944, charging that ALA condoned segregation by scheduling meetings at hotels that barred African Americans.

Rollins began writing books in an effort to bridge the gap between teachers and libraries. She often had students come into the library to do assignments on black history, only to find that no books on their topics existed. She organized the children in library clubs to encourage them to learn more about their identity. At the same time she repeatedly wrote to publishers seeking information on black culture. She collected newspaper and magazine articles and clippings about African Americans.

Vivian G. Harsh and Charlemae Hill Rollins worked together closely, and Harsh allowed Rollins great latitude in her quest for better reading materials for black children and the black community. In 1942, staff members at Hall Branch library and William Johnson, superintendent of the Chicago Board of Education, collaborated on a research project to choose available materials for the preparation of black history courses to be included in the regular school curriculum. Rollins and Harsh started a Reading Guidance Clinic for parents. Mothers met regularly at the library to discuss books and relevant reading materials for the children. Rollins conducted story hour for the children at Provident Hospital in the Dermatology Clinic for a number of years. To foster greater racial consciousness, she instituted "Appreciation Hours" at Hall Library, where teachers were invited to bring their classes to hear stories of African American achievements. She invited black writers, poets, and artists to give lectures.

Rollins traveled and lectured widely in an effort to bridge the gap between black reality and fiction. During a 1944 writers' conference, Rollins's closing address admonished the public "to let the Negro child be allowed to see himself portrayed as an honored and respected member of the children of literature and not merely as Little Black Sambo" (McCarthy, "Annual Writers Conference"). In 1946, she joined the staff at Roosevelt University in Chicago, teaching "Children's Literature," which became a required course for education majors in 1955. She taught there until her retirement from the university in 1960. During these years she conducted workshops and summer session classes at colleges throughout the United States, including the University of Chicago; Rosary College (later Dominican University) in River Forest, Illinois; Fisk University, Nashville, Tennessee; and Morgan State University in Baltimore, Maryland. In the 1950s Rollins became a leader in professional groups, promoting good children's literature. She was head of the Children's Section of the Illinois Library Association and served as president of the Children's Services Division of the ALA from 1957 to 1958, becoming the first black librarian to lead the division. In 1956–57 she chaired the Newbery-Caldecott Awards Committee of ALA, which selected the best children's books published each year.

Rollins retired from the Chicago Public Library on August 23, 1963. Retirement allowed her to write full-time, creating the type of books she had sought for black children. She published *Christmas Gif', an Anthology of Christmas Poems, Songs and Stories Written by and about Negroes* (1963); *They Showed the Way: Forty American Negro Leaders* (1964); *Famous American Negro Poets* (1965); *Famous Negro Entertainers of Stage, Screen, and TV* (1967); and *Black Troubadour Langston Hughes* (1970). Her realistic portrayals in the biographical volumes provided role models to black children.

Rollins's work earned her many honors and awards, including the 1970 Constance Lindsey Skinner Award given by the Women's National Book Association for her contribution to books and to American culture through books. Among the other awards she received were the American Brotherhood Award of the National Conference of Christians and Jews, 1952; Library Letter Award of the American Library Association, 1953; Children's Reading Round Table Award, 1963; and the Coretta Scott King Award, 1971, for her book on Langston Hughes. Columbia College in Chicago gave Rollins an honorary doctorate in humane letters in 1974.

Charlemae Hill Rollins died of pneumonia complications at Michael Reese Hospital in Chicago. She was buried at Burr Oak Cemetery in Alsip, Illinois.

Rollins spent more than thirty years as a children's librarian in a branch of the Chicago Public Library system, and she garnered international fame for her efforts in the field of children's services. She concentrated her energies on battling a negative stereotypic image of black men and women portrayed in the pages of American literature. She promoted and supported library programs to raise the literary quality of children's fiction and to add realistic minority representation to their books. In 1980, the Charlemae Hill Rollins Colloquium, a biennial symposium, was initiated by North Carolina Central University's School of Library and Information Sciences, dedicated to improving library services to all children. Eleven years later, her achievements were commemorated by the founding of the Charlemae Hill Rollins Foundation, which works for an honest portrayal of African Americans in literature, especially that for children.

Sources. The Charlemae Hill Rollins Papers and the Archives of the George Cleveland Hall branch of the CPL are held at the Vivian G. Harsh Research Collection of Afro-American History and Literature, Carter G. Woodson Regional Library, CPL. The Rollins Papers include her published articles and Birdie Hill's memoir, "Silver Creek" (typescript, n.d.), on Hill family life in Mississippi and Oklahoma. The Hall archives contain correspondence, branch records, interviews, newspaper clippings and photographs. Rollins discusses books on African Americans for children in her article, "Library Work with Negroes," *Illinois Libraries*, February 1943. Newspaper discussions of Rollins's work include Dorsey McCarthy, "Annual Writers Conference Closing Session," *Chicago Sun Book Week*, August 6, 1944. Biographical information on Rollins appears in *BWA*; Jessie Carney Smith, ed., *Notable Black American Women* (1992); and the clipping files of the CPL. Materials on Charlemae Hill Rollins are also housed at the School of Library and Information Sciences at North Carolina Central Univ. in Durham and in the Spec. Coll. Dept. of the Fisk Univ. Library.

BEVERLY A. COOK

ROLLINS, IDA GRAY NELSON. *See* NELSON ROLLINS, IDA GRAY

ROULLIER, ALICE

1883–December 19, 1963

GALLERY OWNER, ARTS ADMINISTRATOR, ART PATRON

Alice Roullier, a cofounder of the Arts Club of Chicago with RUE CARPENTER, was born in New York City to Albert and Adele (Ratti) Roullier. Her father, a native of Paris, France, was an expert on French art and a print dealer who collected rare prints. Alice Roullier received her primary and secondary education at private schools—Miss Berry's, New York City, and St. Matthew's, Painesville, Ohio—but her major education was at the side of her father, with whom she worked from an early age. The Roullier family came to Chicago around 1900, and Albert Roullier worked with Frederick Keppel & Company. Roullier built a large business in the Middle West and began Albert Roullier Galleries. He had an unusual knowledge of the history of prints and advised Chicago's art patrons on purchases for their collections. Alice Roullier assisted her father in his galleries, often writing the text for catalogs.

Albert Roullier's expertise was continually solicited by the Department of Prints of the Art Institute of Chicago (AIC); not only did he influence AIC's collections directly by working as a paid consultant with museum personnel, he also shaped the museum's collections in his role as dealer to the major AIC patrons whose prints later became part of the museum holdings. Albert Roullier and his family continued to visit friends and rel-

FIG. 101. *Drawing of Arts Club cofounder Alice Roullier by Pavel Tchelitchew, 1935.*

and American modern art. Roullier headed the Exhibitions Committee from 1918 until 1941. During these years the Arts Club introduced Chicago not only to postimpressionist art but also to the new in many cultural forms, including the works of composer Aaron Copland, poet Archibald MacLeish, writer Gertrude Stein, and dancer Martha Graham. Although interested in American and European work, both Roullier and Carpenter shared a special passion for France and French culture.

Initially, the Arts Club found gallery space in the Fine Arts Building on Michigan Avenue, the same building where the Albert Roullier Galleries were located, and where Alice Roullier spent much of her time. In 1918 the Arts Club moved south to a larger and more accessible gallery on Michigan Avenue. The Arts Club moved twice during Roullier's tenure as head of the Exhibitions Committee—in 1924, to the Wrigley Building, and in 1936, to different quarters in the same building—and she was intimately involved with these site changes.

The early history of the Arts Club is marked by a succession of exhibits that introduced Chicagoans to artists whose works were already making history in New York and Paris. In 1919, there was a group exhibition that included work by Gaston Lachaise and Joseph Stella and in 1920, an exhibition of paintings and drawings by Leon Bakst and a one-artist exhibition of work by Foujita. Alice Roullier's influence was critical in shaping these exhibits that gave the Arts Club its avant-garde image. She was soon to make even greater inroads for modernist works in the mainstream art world at AIC, as she stepped into the space vacated there by her father's death.

A major change in Alice Roullier's life occurred in 1920, when Albert Roullier died at age sixty-two, having become a life member of AIC and, shortly before his death, having been decorated *Officier de l'Instruction Publique* by the French Ministry of Fine Arts. Continuing her work with both the Arts Club and the Albert Roullier Galleries, Alice Roullier established with her mother the Albert Roullier Memorial Print Collection in 1921. More prints were to be added later. In the 1990s AIC lists more than seven hundred works of art that were either acquired from or were donated by the Roulliers.

The year the Roulliers established the memorial print collection, the Arts Club rented gallery space from AIC, and Alice Roullier and Rue Carpenter brought Arts Club exhibitions to the prestigious institution. In 1922, 1923, and 1924, the Arts Club displayed paintings and stage designs by Nathalie Goncharova, paintings by Walt Kuhn, and sculpture by Ellie Nadelman. Roullier organized the first American showing of work by Picasso in 1923 and assembled Georges Braque's first solo show in 1924. In 1925, the club exhibited paintings by Marc Chagall. In 1926, a Henri Matisse retrospective and an exhibition of work by Yasuo Kuniyoshi were organized, and in 1927, paintings by Marsden Hartley and drawings by Picasso were shown. In the 1930s, Roullier coordinated the only major exhibition of work by Chaim Soutine during the artist's lifetime. Roullier also assisted the acquisition of several important works of art for the Art Institute of Chicago through the Arts Club. These include sculpture *Brother and Sister* by Auguste Rodin, drawings by Alfeo Faggi and Odilon Redon, drawings and lithography by Walt Kuhn, and Constantin Brancusi's famous sculpture *Golden Bird*.

Surrealist Marcel Duchamp became a close correspondent

atives in France and to buy artwork for the galleries in Chicago. These trips became the basis of Alice Roullier's expertise and contacts; expanding beyond prints, Alice Roullier became intrigued with post-impressionist painting and sculpture.

Her connections with contemporary European artists, the AIC's directors and staff, and the world of Chicago art patrons, as well as her knowledge of the French language and of the new art forms afforded Alice Roullier a strategic position from which to create a positive reception of postimpressionist art in this rather conservative midwest city. Beginning in 1913, when AIC's *Post-Impressionist Exhibition* (the name given to the Armory Show when it came to Chicago) created havoc in the local art world with a majority of artists, teachers, and patrons who rejected the new forms, there were individuals interested in opening Chicago's eyes to the works of Henri Matisse, Pablo Picasso, Georges Braque, Marcel Duchamp, and Constantin Brancusi. Alice Roullier became a leading figure in the introduction of the postimpressionists to Chicago. She was a member of the early group of cofounders of the Arts Club in 1916. By 1918 Alice Roullier, who was head of the Exhibitions Committee, and Rue Carpenter, who became the second president and replaced Mrs. Robert McGann, ran the Arts Club, which was dedicated to curating ground-breaking exhibitions of European after Roullier met him in 1927, when he traveled to Chicago to mount an exhibition of work by Brancusi at the Arts Club. She became his friend as well as a business contact. Roullier introduced Duchamp to Chicago collectors and helped him to sell his multiples and to find buyers for his Brancusi sculpture.

In addition to her work with the Arts Club, Roullier was appointed governing member by the Board of Trustees of AIC in 1931. In the 1930s she served on the boards of the Renaissance Society of the University of Chicago and the Chicago Public School Art Society.

The destruction of World War II to people and art collections did not disconnect Alice Roullier from the other country that she loved. After the war Roullier lived in Paris for more than a year in the 1950s and was awarded the *Chevalier Legion d'Honneur, Officier d'Instruction Publique* for her promotion of French art in America.

In 1953 the seventy-year-old Roullier closed Albert Roullier Galleries by merging with Findlay Galleries in Chicago. Strapped for money, she asked her friend Duchamp to help her find a dealer for a work by Joseph Stella that she owned. Duchamp said he knew of no one who wanted her Stella and suggested she contact galleries in New York. Little is known of Alice Roullier's last ten years. She had donated much of her own collection of paintings and sculpture to AIC and found herself with few financial resources. Her generosity to AIC continued into the early 1950s. Her donations from the 1920s through the 1950s included work by Braque, E. Gordon Craig, Paul Cezanne, Honoré Daumier, Hermine David, Paul Gauguin, Jean Louis Géricault, Fantin Latour, Marie Laurencin, Aristide Maillol, Edouard Manet, Matisse, Picasso, Auguste Renoir, and Paul Signac. She appeared to have taken over her father's love of art and passion for new forms without his business acumen, and, in 1963 this formidable champion of the avant-garde died alone and impoverished in Barrington, Illinois. The legacy of Roullier and her family remains for the public to enjoy in the collections of the AIC and in the activities of the Arts Club, which, after her death, established the Friends of Alice Roullier Fund to purchase new acquisitions.

Sources. Personal letters from artists, family photographs and papers related to Arts Club exhibitions and activities are found at the NL, which holds the Arts Club of Chicago Archives and Alice Roullier Papers. Business letters from the 1920s to the 1950s pertaining to Roullier's donations and the activities of the Arts Club of Chicago are located in the Art Institute of Chicago Archives. Her portrait by Pavel Tchelitchew is at the Art Institute of Chicago's Department of Prints and Drawings, drawings of Roullier by Goncharova and Mikhail Larionov at the theater department of the Museum of Modern Art in New York. The Arts Club of Chicago published three books, *The Arts Club of Chicago: Drawings 1916/1966* (1966); *The Arts Club of Chicago, Portrait of an Era: Rue Winterbotham Carpenter and The Arts Club of Chicago, 1916–1931* (1986); and *The Arts Club of Chicago: Seventy-fifth Anniversary Exhibition, The Arts Club of Chicago, May 11–June 26, 1992* (1992), which document its history and describe Roullier's involvement and influence. The newspaper article "Fine Print Memorial Founded at Museum," in the *Chicago Evening Post,* January 10, 1922, gave a description of the foundation and value of the Albert Roullier Memorial Print Collection. *New Art Examiner,* March 1974, published a lengthy article about Roullier, "Duchamp Letters Found," by Jane Allen and Derek Guthrie.

COLLEEN BECKER

RUDOLPH, ANNE
January 24, 1907–February 3, 1988
DANCER, ATHLETE, ACTRESS, MOVEMENT EDUCATOR, HEALER

Anne Rudolph, internationally acclaimed dancer, was born in Hoboken, New Jersey, the second of three children and the only daughter of Fred and Henriette (Klein) Rudolph. German residents at the time of their marriage, the Rudolphs, at the insistence of Henriette, traveled to the United States for their honeymoon and were so taken with the "New World" (interview with Zohara Schuster) that they decided to stay. Fred Rudolph found employment with a railroad company.

From childhood, Anne Rudolph exhibited a "tremendous craving for movement"; she "had an innate sense of order and rhythm" (interview with Rudolph) and a fervent love of dance. At age six she danced to the melodies of the street musicians in Hoboken. In her parents' milieu, the reputation of dancers and the theatrical world of the time was, however, unsavory at best; and Rudolph's mother, a strict Lutheran, forbade any dance performances by her daughter in public. Her mother did, however, encourage an interest in gymnastics. Undaunted, Anne Rudolph "danced in secret" and "decided to be the 'best dancer on the block'" (interview with Rudolph). Although she was not allowed to attend a school of dance, she was able to look at pictures of dancers and practice their moves.

At the onset of World War I, a rise in American nationalism led to displays of extremely xenophobic behavior toward Germans and German Americans. Anne Rudolph's heritage made her the target of neighborhood bullies who chased "the German" down the street. Years later, when she won her first competitive race as a runner and was asked who taught her to run so fast, she replied, "Fear" (O'Connor, n.p.). At age thirteen she was introduced to team sports but ultimately found them unsatisfying. She longed instead for something she could do that did not require special equipment.

In 1921, Henriette Rudolph became ill and returned with her family to her birthplace, Bad Oeynhausen, Germany, a renowned spa town where Anne Rudolph was first exposed to the benefits of the therapeutic movement popular in Germany at the time. She became aware of the relationship between physical well-being or health and proper exercise, posture, and knowledge of how the body works. Her education and experiences in Bad Oeynhausen set in motion what would become a many-faceted career.

Rudolph was tutored privately during her early years in Germany. In an effort to redirect her daughter, Henriette Rudolph encouraged athletics. A naturally tenacious and driven child, Anne Rudolph excelled in the broad and high jumps, seventy-five-meter run, and gymnastics. She also trained in fencing, discus, and shot put. She began training for the Olympics but never participated in the games. Unbeknownst to her family, she continued to dream of life on the stage and believed that, as a dancer, she would need a superbly trained body. She felt that athletics provided the perfect vehicle to that end.

Rudolph convinced her parents to allow her to attend the Elisabeth Estas School of Body Movement in Cologne, Germany, from which her mother extracted a promise that her daughter would never receive a single dance lesson. Simultaneously, Rudolph enrolled at the University of Cologne in a program that combined academics and athletics.

Rudolph's passion for performance could not be contained, however. At age sixteen she staged naturalistic dances in the mountains above her home. "One [dance], taking place at nightfall, involved a procession of torchbearers snaking up the mountains near her home. The patterns of their moving lights could be seen for miles around" (O'Connor, n.p.). She secretly danced in public until the fateful day when her mother discovered that her missing draperies had been used by her daughter as a costume. In defense, Anne Rudolph misquoted a passage in the Bible, adding her own interpretation, "And King David danced naked before his people" (O'Connor, n.p.) and won her mother's long withheld permission to perform. The quote, combined with the cultural significance of performing in a Shakespearean work, softened her mother's stance and led to Anne Rudolph's official stage debut at the Cologne Schauspielhaus as a shepherd boy in *As You Like It*.

At this time the liberation of the art of dance from the rigidity of late-nineteenth-century ballet into the artistic expressiveness of modern dance was well underway. Isadora Duncan, whom Anne Rudolph felt "related to in spirit" (interview with Rudolph), blazed across European stages. Mary Wigman, the German dancer, brought artistically expressed social commentary and the passions of her innermost self to the stage. After years of technical confinement, dance as a powerful form of self-expression was coming into its own. It was within this context that the vivacious beauty Anne Rudolph stepped on the stage for the first time. Within the next six years, "the American" (Adler, 1), as Rudolph was known in Germany, had more than 350 engagements that encompassed dance, pantomime, and theater in European cities, including Berlin, Hanover, Vienna, Paris, and Brussels.

Anne Rudolph's popularity soared. She auditioned for and won a part with one of Germany's top filmmakers; choreographed an opera for her ailing music teacher; and, on a moment's notice, filled in for a notable dancer at a theater's afternoon tea, completely improvising her solo dance and costume and winning rave reviews. Additionally, she was asked to audition for both Mary Wigman and Sally Rand, the "fan dancer"; she rejected their requests to join them because she was so intent on developing her own unique style.

Although already well known as a stage performer, Rudolph was drawn to the physical education or "body motion" movement in Germany, which was based on a combination of dance, gymnastics, exercise, and philosophy. Following the suggestion of a noted German physician who had encouraged her to turn her talents in the direction of therapeutic movement, she opened her own school of rhythmic body gymnastics in Bad Oeynhausen in 1927.

In 1934 Rudolph came to the United States. Initially her intention was to visit for three months. She broke a signed contract for a cross-country European tour and left her fiancé behind. She had one brother, Hans, who lived in the United States. While performing at the Cameo Salon in Chicago, Anne Rudolph met Howard Bartfield, a dentist. He fell in love with the free-spirited dancer the first time he watched her perform. The couple eloped within the year but kept their marriage secret for several years, until Anne Rudolph traveled back to Germany personally to end her engagement.

In 1934 Anne Rudolph visited Hull-House, an institution with which her work would later become affiliated, and met JANE ADDAMS in the last year of the great settlement movement leader's life. Also in 1934 Rudolph opened the Anne Rudolph School of Modern Body Education and Dance in downtown Chicago. The school's goals were "to modernize the archaic form of body education still taught today which is unfit for modern times. To promote the finest form of body activity there is, and to encourage the dance as an art form" (Johnson, 9). The broader vision of the school was that "fine body development is not the privilege of a chosen few, but belongs to the whole world" (p. 9).

In keeping with these goals, Anne Rudolph's classes were open to people from all walks of life, from professionals to lay people, and to children as well as adults. Classes were held in body education and dance, and specialized sessions were available for people with spinal problems as well as for infants and children with handicaps. The only prerequisite was that the student "have a body" (Epstein, n.p.). Anne Rudolph's altruism and generosity assured that tuition fees were kept to a minimum and often voided altogether. When she held classes in nearby Grant Park, she encouraged passersby to join in and experience the power of motion for health, beauty, and joy.

As an accomplished dancer, Rudolph continued to perform impressive solo concerts at the Goodman and Civic theaters in Chicago throughout the 1930s and 1940s. She also danced with students who were members of her Motion Choir—people who worked ordinary jobs by day but came together in the evenings as performers to demonstrate the power and beauty of self-applied movement. In 1951 she danced in a retrospective concert with Ruth St. Denis held at New Trier High School Auditorium, Winnetka, Illinois.

Rudolph employed the term "Anrudics" for a time to describe her work, but later she dropped it because she felt it sounded too mechanical. She also lectured on the benefits of conscious movement. In 1958 she spoke on the power of motion in a talk given at Roosevelt University's Rudolph Ganz Hall. She argued that body motion had a functional and creative place in society, both for individuals and groups, and for uses that were therapeutic as well as aesthetic.

In the 1950s a physician friend asked Rudolph to use her body movement work therapeutically with a young patient. The experience led to Rudolph's work as a volunteer at Cook County and Michael Reese hospitals. She worked with children with such afflictions as polio and cerebral palsy as well as other physically debilitating handicaps. She was often asked to work with patients for whom other professionals held little hope. Many times her dedication and insistent but good-natured prodding brought results that others deemed miraculous.

From 1939 Anne Rudolph's school had a Michigan Avenue location; by the 1950s escalating rent made prohibitive her policy of never turning away a student who lacked the tuition. The school closed. Although Anne Rudolph and her husband now had an opportunity to travel together, an activity that they greatly enjoyed, it was also a problematic time for her. With the exception of a trip to California, she all but dropped from public attention during the 1960s. It was not until November 1967 that she returned to her teaching career. A dedicated student helped raise the funds to build her a studio, and she resumed her teaching career at the new Beacon Street Hull-House in Chicago's Uptown neighborhood. (The original Hull-House complex had been torn down in 1963, save for the original Hull mansion and the dining hall, when the University of Illinois at Chicago moved from its Navy Pier location to its new campus.)

During the 1970s, Anne Rudolph's fascination with the human body and the way it moved continued to grow, and her work evolved. In articles she wrote for the *Evergreen Gazette*, an independent weekly published in Chicago's Lake View neighborhood, she urged people to listen to their bodies, to cease their neglect of physical fitness, and to see body consciousness as the road to greater health. She believed that body education was the human being's closest friend. She stressed the power and importance of the interrelationship of body and mind long before that view became fashionable in contemporary American popular culture. Often she urged seriously debilitated students, such as those recovering from surgery, to "think" a movement even when the body was unable or unwilling to physically perform it.

Rudolph conducted several group classes each week at Hull-House and gave private and semi-private lessons in her North Side apartment. Once again, her classes attracted both able-bodied students and those with a wide range of special needs. She focused on the spine and spinal ailments, which she believed came from the disjunction of the human form and the urban, cement environment. Body education was to counteract premature decay, to reinforce the systems of the body, to heal and preserve impaired and deteriorating muscles and tissues, to improve the efficiency, harmony, and strength of interdependent body parts, and to encourage self-reliance. She often used a hands-on approach with her students so they could experience the feeling of a correctly aligned spine and limbs, but she insisted that each student must learn to be "alert and vigilant at all times" (Rudolph, "Moving with Anne Rudolph," 2) and, ultimately, do the work independently.

In 1979, Anne Rudolph was dealt a devastating blow by the death of her husband. Several years later she was approached by Isadora Guggenheim, a young local dancer, with a request to collaborate on a concert. The result was the 1982 presentation of *Palimpsest*, performed at Chicago's MoMing Dance and Arts Center. It was her first public performance in nearly twenty years and provided the necessary "injection" (Adler, 9) to bring the heartbroken performer back to life.

On the occasion of her eightieth birthday in January 1987, friends, family, and students of Anne Rudolph came together at the Brown Bear Cafe on Devon Avenue in Chicago's Roger's Park neighborhood for a joyous celebration of her life and work. Shortly thereafter, Anne Rudolph's brother, George, who had been living with her, died. Forlorn over his loss and that of her husband Howard, she spent much of the summer of 1987 traveling throughout Europe. When she returned, her spirits were high but her health was failing, and she was unable to continue her previously rigorous teaching schedule. She died at home the following winter. Although cancerous cells had been detected, she died peacefully of an aneurysm. Her final words, "Straighten me out" (interview with Schuster), bespoke a lifetime of fully living her vocation. Her brother, Hans, released her ashes, together with those of their brother George and those of her husband, Howard, into Lake Michigan at Montrose Harbor, Chicago, for one final, free-spirited dance. Although she gained international recognition as a dancer and performer, Anne Rudolph's greatest legacy was as an innovative teacher and theoretician of the science of movement, and as a practitioner whose therapeutic approaches were innovative and reached a wide variety of adults and children.

Sources. Interviews were conducted by Lisa Klare with Muriel Aronson, June 1997; Jill Lending, January 8, 1998; and Zohara Schuster (formerly known as Teena Sweet and Teena Schuster), January 23, 1998. Lisa Klare interviewed Anne Rudolph in 1985. Anne Rudolph's occasional columns in the *Evergreen Gazette* included "Moving with Anne Rudolph: Women Dream the Impossible Dream," February 4, 1975. Mary Ann Johnson, "An Historical Overview of Anne Rudolph's Life," Slide Program, A Tribute to Anne Rudolph, the University of Illinois at Chicago, May 20, 1990, typed transcript, provided information about Rudolph's school. Useful articles include Sean O'Connor, "Anne Rudolph: Dancer, Teacher, Healer Extraordinaire!" unidentified newspaper clipping; Leslie Adler, "Encore: At 75 Dancer to Perform after 20 Years off Stage," *Skyline*, January 21, 1982; Charles Epstein, "Anne Rudolph's Reflections," *Evergreen Gazette*, October 26, 1976; and Sandra Pesmen, "For and about Women," *Chicago Daily News*, April 24, 1969.

LISA KLARE

SALAVA, BOŽENA

November 12, 1867–December 16, 1960

MISSIONARY, TEACHER

Božena Salava, a Congregationalist missionary who lived and worked among her fellow Czechs at the Bethlehem Church and community center in the Pilsen district of Chicago from 1885 to 1924, was born near Podebrady, Bohemia, within the Austro-Hungarian Empire. Her father traced his lineage to a member of the Waldensian brethren, a medieval heretical group that emphasized poverty, simplicity, and moral rigor. Both parents were members of the Protestant Reformed Church, into which Božena was received at age thirteen. At age seventeen, in 1885, Salava emigrated with her parents and four siblings to Chicago.

The Czechs were the first Slavs to reach the United States in significant numbers, with 350,000 arrivals between 1848 and 1914. They emigrated from Bohemia, Moravia, and Czech Silesia, but because the majority came from Bohemia, they were called "Bohemians" before World War I. The Salavas were typical of Czech newcomers, who usually migrated in family groups, were skilled laborers, and had literacy rates as high as 97 percent. Chicago was the most popular destination of Czech migration to urban areas, with 41,000 first and second generation Czechs by 1890. The Pilsen district, southwest of Chicago's commercial district, reached its height as a center of Czech settlement in 1895. Thus, when the Salavas arrived, they entered a rich institutional ethnic subculture in Chicago, which by 1918 boasted ninety-one benevolent societies, 125 building and loan associations with $15,000,000 in assets and 30,000 members, fifteen fraternal orders, numerous gymnastic societies (Sokols), and four daily newspapers.

Božena Salava worked within a competitive orbit of ideological and religious cleavages that divided this vital Czech subculture in Chicago. During her thirty-five years of missionary labor in the Chicago area, she witnessed the operation of eleven Bohemian Roman Catholic parishes and schools, eighteen Freethinker afternoon or weekend schools, fourteen Protestant churches and missions, and a Socialist Workingman's School. The Czechs were nominal Catholics in their homeland, but many were indifferent to the Catholic faith. Their national consciousness was linked to a tradition of dissent that memorialized the reformer Jan Hus, who was executed as a heretic in 1415. Czechs remembered the defeat of their Protestant forebears at the hands of the German Catholic Hapsburgs during the Thirty Years' War.

In the United States, Czechs presented grave organizational difficulties for the Catholic Church, as irreligion thrived in their Freethinker societies. American Protestants noted Czech anti-clericalism and sought to evangelize and Americanize the Slav newcomers through missionary outreach funded by an array of denominational home missionary societies. Within this context, Salava labored for the Congregationalists at the Bethlehem Church in Pilsen. In spite of efforts at evangelization, through the years of Salava's missionary labors, Czechs in America remained fewer than 2 percent Protestant.

Upon her arrival in the United States, Salava was already well versed in the Bible. In 1885, she began teaching in Pilsen at a Sunday school of three hundred children run by the Congregationalist storefront mission. From the expanding mission, Bethlehem Church was established on March 30, 1888, under the pastorate of the Rev. Edwin A. Adams. While Adams had lived in Bohemia and knew the language and culture of the Czech community, he did not, according to Salava, associate too intimately with people of Pilsen. Salava worked closely with Mrs. Adams and her two daughters at several extra-ecclesial programs that soon developed around the church. With the financial support of the Chicago Congregational Missionary Board, Bethlehem Chapel was built at a cost of thirty-five thousand dollars and dedicated on May 4, 1890.

After two years of Sunday school teaching at the mission between 1885 and 1887, Salava, supported by the Illinois Woman's

Home Missionary Union of the Congregationalist Church, entered the Bethlehem Missionary Training School in Cleveland for two years. Salava returned to Chicago during the summers, when she lived with her parents and continued to teach at the Sunday school in Pilsen. The training school in Cleveland emphasized Bible studies to prepare Czech missionaries to work in the Congregational Church. In Cleveland, Salava experienced a deep disappointment at the tragic death of a Czech minister to whom she was engaged. Salava remained unmarried her entire life.

Salava's autobiographical reflections, written in 1924, concerning her commitment to Christ and religious work among her people, emphasized her detachment from worldly goods and a Christocentric world view. "Never attracted by the allurements of the world, I had gladly accepted the offer to devote my life to missionary work. . . . Christ was my model for all my teaching and all other work which was before me to do. He was my way. To Him I went" (quoted in Bond, 123, 126). This semi-monastic sensibility echoed the piety of her Waldensian ancestors as well as that of other young evangelical women whose labors went unnoticed by institutional church leaders.

Upon her return to Chicago in June 1889, Salava took charge of the Bohemian Primary Sabbath School and the Mothers' Prayer Meeting at Bethlehem Church. In addition, she worked at the Industrial (Sewing) School, visited the parents of the Sunday school children and members of the church, and played the organ at the Bohemian religious services. The music and crafts she taught reflected a commitment to preserve the cultural heritage of her homeland as well as to cultivate an evangelical faith among children and women. Annual reports of the Illinois Home Missionary Society made frequent reference to Salava's contribution to the expanding mission field at Bethlehem, where she made more home visits than any of her colleagues, averaging nearly one hundred visits a month. Salava made monthly reports to the Illinois Woman's Home Missionary Union, which continued to support her in Chicago.

Salava's responsibilities grew as she took over work left by others or initiated her own programs. In 1891, she began *Besídka*, an after-school program for children that consisted of devotional singing, storytelling, and games. She often substituted for the minister at prayer meetings or at Sunday evening Bohemian services. In 1907, when the Adams family left Bethlehem, she became the director of the Industrial School and also supervised women from Moody Bible Institute who volunteered at Bethlehem's various institutional activities. During Salava's long tenure at Bethlehem, when the church found itself without a pastor four times, she stepped in to take charge. She gave sermons in Bohemian at the Mothers Sewing Club. Salava's role extended to fund-raising for her patrons, the Illinois Woman's Home Missionary Union. She became a de facto pastor to the Bohemian-speaking women and children in the church.

Salava was aware of her pastoral abilities and in her autobiographical reflections recounted an interesting episode in which she nearly left Bethlehem to go to seminary. At an Illinois State Conference of the Congregationalist Church in 1894 or 1895, she gave a presentation on Congregationalist work among the Bohemians. A woman pastor present noted her ability as a speaker and offered to pay her expenses to seminary. Salava declined the offer since "all the children at Bethlehem and the promise to Dr. A[dams] to be his helper was before me" (quoted in Bond, 129). The woman wrote to Adams, who questioned Salava about her decision. Salava answered vaguely, stating, "If my service is needed here, here I stay." She recorded ambiguously that Adams told her "not to trouble myself about this anymore for he himself would answer the letter. Thus I lost an opportunity to have a title and be a Reverend" (quoted in Bond, 129–30).

In spite of Salava's consistent presence at Bethlehem, her salary never approached that of the pastor. During Salava's uninterrupted tenure at Bethlehem, the pastorate changed hands five times. Her annual salary in 1904 was $400 compared to Adams's $2,100; in 1917 her annual salary was $600 compared to the Czech pastor's salary of $1,500. In September 1914, the Chicago City Missionary Society recognized the twenty-fifth anniversary of Salava's work at Bethlehem with a twenty-five dollar gift. In May 1916, the same society allocated fifty dollars to decorate and improve her room. Of that grant, seventeen dollars would go toward installing a bathroom for the women working at Bethlehem, if they could secure sufficient additional funding.

Although laboring within an institution with the professed goal of "Americanization," which in this context meant inculcating an evangelical faith as well as cultivating American patriotism and civic commitments, Salava actively participated in Czech national festivals, including the commemoration on July 6, 1915, of the five-hundredth anniversary of Jan Hus's death. Preparations for this anniversary occupied both the Freethinkers and Bohemian Protestants throughout the United States. Bohemian Protestant pastors from all over the United States met at Bethlehem Church in Chicago in 1914 to plan for the gala events. Chicago's Freethinkers called for Czech families to decorate their homes with flags and photos of Hus and for businesses to close on July 6 to allow employees to attend functions held downtown in honor of the national hero. The evening following the anniversary, the United Bohemian Protestants sponsored their own celebration, replete with Bible readings, a procession of children in national garb, and a chorus made up of choirs from several Bohemian Protestant Churches. Chicago's *Denni Hlasatel*, a Czech newspaper, singled out Salava for the care with which she trained the children who sang chorales with words by Hus and the Bohemian National Anthem.

Demographic shifts in Pilsen, whose immigrant character was disappearing by 1920 as Czechs migrated to such western suburbs as Cicero and Berwyn, forced the Bethlehem Church and community center to adapt. As Czech residents moved westward out of Pilsen, and as the second generation began to outnumber foreign-born Czechs, both Bethlehem and Salava adjusted. The former evangelistic and missionary thrust took on a greater social character, which placed a higher value on the importance of recreational and social services, as Social Gospel ideas permeated conceptions of urban ministry in American mainline denominations between 1900 and 1920. The playground, kindergarten, and recreational activities took on enhanced importance, and by 1920 Salava noted how her workload with children and mothers grew beyond her capacities. In 1920, *Denni Hlasatel* recorded that the Bethlehem Sunday School alone had produced more than ten thousand graduates during the previous thirty years, many of whom were prominent members of the community. In 1921, Bethlehem reorganized its plant, restructuring the church auditorium into a large gymnasium and installing facilities that converted the church into a community center.

Salava's health failed in the early 1920s during this transitional period. The all-male board of directors of the Chicago City Missionary Society discussed its responsibility to Salava in consideration of her decades of service. The directors formed a committee to take up the matter with the State Board of Ministerial Relief, but thereafter their records did not mention Salava again. After an accident in 1924 in which she broke her arm, Salava chose to leave Bethlehem.

She then moved out of Pilsen and took up residence with her niece, M. (Klapka) Dušek, an organist at a local Presbyterian church. Salava never worked for the institutional church again, although she continued to visit Protestant churches for the rest of her life. In 1939, Salava moved with Dušek's family to San Angelo, Texas. During her last years in Texas, Salava maintained a vibrant faith, continued to visit Protestant churches in San Angelo, and developed close bonds with her niece's two sons. Salava died at ninety-three years of age. Her body was returned to Chicago, where she was buried at the Bohemian National Cemetery.

In Salava's work at Bethlehem, she was important as the most stable and consistent presence at an institution that grew from humble beginnings into a significant place in the Pilsen neighborhood. Furthermore, she oversaw and adapted to Bethlehem's changing role from an evangelical and Americanizing mission into an institution for social and recreational services. When Eleanor Margaret Bond, a divinity student at the Chicago Theological Seminary, wrote her study of Bethlehem in 1940, she interviewed Salava and found her an "unassuming person" who "radiates enthusiasm" (Bond, 33). Salava was particularly proud of her role as a Bible teacher for children who, as adults, became active church members in American Protestant churches throughout Chicago.

Sources. Mrs. Henry E. Dušek (M. Klapka) provided information in an interview with Peter D'Agostino on April 5, 1995. Central for a biographical reconstruction of Salava is Eleanor Margaret Bond, "Factors in the Shift from the Evangelistic Approach to the Educational and Recreational Approach in the Program of the Bethlehem Community Center" (master's thesis, Chicago Theological Seminary, 1940). Its appendixes include annual reports on Bethlehem, Salava's reflections on Rev. Adams, and her autobiographical recollections. Salava's obituary is "Miss Salaza [*sic*], 93, Angelo; Illinois Rites," *San Angelo Standard Times*, December 16, 1960. The Illinois Home Missionary Society's *Annual Reports* and the typescript Records of the Chicago City Missionary Society (which became the Chicago Congregational Missionary and Extension Society in 1919) can be found at the Chicago Theological Seminary. Translations of such Czech newspapers as *Denni Hlasatel* are in the Chicago Foreign Language Press Survey, UC Spec. Coll. Helpful on Czech immigration are Jakub Horak, "Assimilation of Czechs in Chicago" (Ph.D. diss., Univ. of Chicago, 1920); Daniel D. Droba, ed., *Czech and Slovak Leaders in Metropolitan Chicago* (1934); Thomas Capek, *The Czechs (Bohemians) in America* (1920); Joseph Chada, *The Czechs in the United States* (1981); Karen Johnson Freeze, "Czechs," in *Harvard Encyclopedia of American Ethnic Groups*, ed. Stephan Thernstrom (1980).

PETER R. D'AGOSTINO

SAMOLIŃSKA, TEOFILA CWIKLIŃSKA
April 22, 1848–December 1, 1913
CLUBWOMAN, PLAYWRIGHT, POET

Teofila Cwiklińska Samolińska was a pioneer leader in Polish American organizations. She was born in Poznania, a province of the German partition of Poland. Little is known about her background. She grew up in a Roman Catholic family concerned about education but apparently not deeply religious. Her schooling included attendance for a period at an academic high school; her subsequent skill in written Polish indicated not only talent but training. At a time when a large majority of Poles consisted of peasants, her urban upbringing prepared her more effectively for an adulthood spent in America's cities.

The nineteenth century was a time of turmoil in divided Poland. Increasingly, urban intellectuals propagated nationalism among the townspeople and peasants. Teofila Cwiklińska was born in a revolutionary era in which Poles under German occupation struggled unsuccessfully to liberate their homeland. In 1863, when she was only fifteen, another revolt broke out in the neighboring Russian partition and was crushed brutally by the army of the Russian tsar. Perhaps this example of unsuccessful resistance and continuing suppression of nationalist aspirations prompted Cwiklińska both to pursue her own destiny and further the cause of independence in a more favorable environment.

Dark-haired and with pleasant, regular features, Cwiklińska married John (Jan) Samoliński in 1866. They emigrated to America that year. John Samoliński was a fitting mate, both in his generous temperament and intelligence and as a veteran of the 1863 uprising against the Russians. The young couple likely landed in New York but soon settled for a time in Cincinnati. As a skilled machinist, he entered the post–Civil War United States at an opportune time. America was booming, and he could market his mechanical skills to good advantage. His successful employment proved advantageous to Teofila Samolińska as well. With her husband earning a good wage, she was more free from economic pressures than were most Slavic immigrant women. Patriarchal Polish society ideally saw women as homemakers, and she conformed in this respect by not entering the labor market. The couple had no children. Thus Samolińska had the time, financial resources, and apparently the support of her husband to enter areas of life unusual for Polish women. Her patriotic sentiments undergirded and directed her activity.

In 1870, Teofila Samolińska sent a poem to John Barzynski, editor of *Orzeł Polski* (The Polish eagle), the second Polish newspaper published in the United States. The work encompassed several themes that characterized her life: "Still your complaints, still your groans / Free Poles in this free land / But who can forget the condemned's agony / Our brothers, who perish in the conquerors' 'paradise.'" One element was gratitude to America for opening its doors to Poles fleeing tyranny; another expressed a deep love for the land of her birth, along with a desire for its political resurrection. Poetry, often with patriotic themes, became one of her favorite modes of written expression.

By 1872 the couple moved to Chicago, which became their permanent home. In a pattern characteristic of Polish immigrants, they lived at a half dozen addresses across the years, but always on Chicago's South Side in St. Adalbert's parish (commonly called *Wojciechowo*, the ethnic neighborhood of St. Adalbert's). Once again her husband worked as a machinist, now at the McCormick Harvesting Machine Company plant.

Teofila Samolińska enlarged her public activity to include an interest in amateur theater. Ethnic communities nourished theatrical productions, utilizing the literature and language of the homeland. These entertainments were popular with fraternal benefit societies, other ethnic associations, and Roman Catholic parishes. Not only were theatrical productions successful in raising funds for the societies; they also entertained, uplifted, and nurtured Polish nationalism.

Samolińska performed frequently in these productions. Gifted not only with dramatic talent but also with a pleasant soprano voice, her leading roles often included singing. She acted in *Karpaccy Górale* (The Carpathian mountaineers), *Chłopcy Arystokratów* (The peasant aristocrats), and several other works. Plays were staged inexpensively and frequently, and many of the actors were from the working class.

To the young actress, drama had an additional function, one that reflected her interest in social improvement. In an era when the Roman Catholic Church frowned on dancing on Saturday evening, Samolińska saw plays as a desirable alternative to the saloon. Not an advocate of temperance, she, like most Polish women, accepted the male saloon culture, although she viewed it with some disdain.

Samolińska went beyond acting. She translated the American play *Two Sisters* into Polish, demonstrating an impressive grasp of her adopted language. By the 1880s, she developed a reputation as a playwright. Samolińska's play *Trzy Flory* (The three flowers) won a prize in 1880 in Warsaw. In this period she wrote and produced *Emancypacja Kobiet* (The emancipation of women), a comedic melodrama that satirized the dictatorship of men and spoke to her lifelong interest in equality. She complemented her interest in drama with a pioneering effort to found a Polish library in 1882. The 1908 formation of the Friends of Drama Society (*Tow. Miłosników Sceny*), the first Polish amateur acting group under professional direction, drew her ardent support, as did the opening of the first Polish playhouse—the Kościuszko Theater in Chicago—in 1911.

Her vision of poetry and theater went beyond Polish traditional folk arts; she brought her devotion to Polish high culture to fraternal organizations. One of the two earliest Polish mutual aid organizations in America was the Polish Commune (*Gmina Polska*), founded in 1864 almost simultaneously with the St. Stanislaus Kostka Society (*Tow. Św. Stanisława Kostka*), both in Chicago. Though overwhelmingly Catholic in membership, the commune was less overtly religious and more liberal in attitude. Samolińska became an ardent supporter of the commune, which sponsored ethnic events. Cultural presentations urged the acquisition of the ancestral high culture; by 1873, the commune's dramatic circle presented five plays annually. Although her husband was a member, she and other women were excluded from official membership, a common fraternal practice up through 1900. She continued to participate, however, and even corresponded with Agaton Giller, a noted patriot in exile in Switzerland.

An ardent Polish nationalist, Giller sought to mobilize the growing Polish presence in America on behalf of homeland in-

dependence. By 1879, he and Samolińska corresponded about Giller's desire to establish a Polish fraternal federation in the United States. In 1880, the Polish National Alliance (*Związek Narodowy Polski*) (PNA) was founded. Headquartered in Chicago, it became the leading force in Polonian nationalism. While most of the credit for the PNA went to men, Samolińska eventually became known as the mother of the alliance. The PNA followed Polonian tradition in barring women from membership. Perhaps because she maintained cordial ties with the leaders, Samolińska did not become publicly bitter, but the exclusion drove her interest in other directions.

In 1886, Samolińska's support of public roles for females in organizations, especially in the theater, sparked a controversy in the ethnic press. Samolińska had the self-confidence to pursue her radical ideas about women, and she drew attention to herself. That year she became a member of Pennies for Poland (*Grosz Polski*), an ephemeral organization that addressed both homeland nationalism (contributing money to buy land from Germans for Polish farmers in the German partition) and more local interests (a shelter for single girls). Unique at this time, the association admitted both men and women. Men held the top posts, however, and, after a few months, the society split on gender lines over both authority and lack of action on the shelter, the latter a particular concern of the female members.

By early 1887 Samolińska served as a secretary of a committee to set up a society for women. She held the organizational meeting in her home for what became the Central Association of Polish Women, *Centralne Towarzystwo Polek* (CAPW), and was elected its first president. Essentially a fraternal type of organization, it advocated mutual aid, patriotism, and culture—all typical goals of ethnic fraternal groups. More reflective of traditional feminine concerns, the CAPW also promoted charity toward women, children, and the elderly. This combination of nationalism, mutual insurance, and social concern came to define the future orientation of Polonian female activists. Under her long-term leadership, the CAPW took a broad public role, appearing in patriotic events and parades. But despite its title, the CAPW remained a single society, never expanding into a federation in the pattern of the PNA.

The impetus to expand female organizations may have been undercut for a time by the simultaneous development that attracted Samolińska and younger Chicago female activists: the appearance of the first American Falcon organization. Modeled on the Czech society of the same name, the Falcons (*Sokół*) combined physical culture with nationalism and began in Austrian Poland in 1881. A middle-class movement there, it first replicated itself in the United States in Chicago, the capital of Polish America, in 1887. Among the founders was John Samoliński, whose longstanding support of his wife's public activity may have been expressed in the structure of the new organization, the first durable group to accept women along with men. She promptly joined what, as in the old country, became a disproportionately middle-class group. At the beginning women comprised one-third of the membership. While the proportion of men grew, women remained barred from officer status. By 1897 Samolińska, STEPHANIA CHMIELIŃSKA, Gabriela Laudon, and Maria Rokosz, all activists in the movement, complained to the governing board. They protested their absence of voting privileges and other grievances and requested "full equality," in the phrase of Samolińska. The board listened politely but refused on the grounds that women could not be trained as soldiers, an emerging dimension of what became an increasingly military society of young patriots.

The outcome of the confrontation had important personal and public consequences. Samolińska subsequently urged the other complainants to join her in an expansion of the CAPW. Apparently a clash of personalities and ambition followed, and since the others were unwilling to accept Samolińska's leadership, they left the CAPW and formed the Polish Women's Alliance (*Związek Polek*) in 1898. All became officers in what emerged as the first Polish fraternal-type federation for women and subsequently the major vehicle for feminist concerns within the ethnic community. Samolińska remained active in the CAPW, which persisted as a prestigious but decreasingly influential independent organization, until it dissolved after World War II.

Samolińska's political and patriotic efforts insured her prominence in Polonia, while her literary productions and flair for the theater gave her an artistic recognition unparalleled for Polonian women in her day. She was a significant figure, a rare combination of patriot, thinker, and artist. Her death at age sixty-five in Chicago was marked by numerous obituaries in both religious and secular journals, and in 1988 by a prominent marker in St. Adalbert's Polish cemetery. She will be remembered as an outstanding Polish American public woman of the nineteenth century, whose pioneering efforts in artistic and nationalistic endeavors opened doors to later female activists.

Sources. The manuscripts of Teofila Samolińska were deposited at Alliance College in Cambridge Springs, Pennsylvania, but were destroyed in a fire in 1931. Chicago newspapers of her era, especially *Dziennik Chicagoski*, *Naród Polski* and *Zgoda*—all of Chicago—have occasional items on her activities. These and other newspapers that may contain items on her are held at the Polish Museum of America in Chicago and at the Center for Research Libraries and the Immigration History Research Center at the University of Minnesota. Her poem appeared in *Orzeł Polski* on February 22, 1870. A useful background work for Chicago and national Polonia, without specific reference to her, is Victor Greene, *For God and Country: The Rise of Polish and Lithuanian Ethnic Consciousness in America, 1860–1910* (1975). A fine general interpretation of American Polish history is John Bukowczyk, *And My Children Did Not Know Me: A History of the Polish Americans* (1987). Scholarly references in English are in Donald Pienkos, *PNA: A Centennial History* (1984). For material on the origins of the Falcons, see his *One Hundred Years Young: A History of the Polish Falcons of America, 1887–1987* (1987). A description of Samolińska's early organizational activity appears in William J. Galush, "Purity and Power: Chicago Polonian Feminists, 1880–1914," *Polish American Studies*, Spring 1990. Material by ethnic writers includes a brief biography by Joseph Wytrywal in the commemorative pamphlet "Teofila Samolińska, 1848–1913" (1988), available at the Polish Museum of America, as well as Rev. Francis Bolek, *Who's Who in Polish America* (1970, reprint of 1943 edition). Scholarly works in Polish with occasional references to her include Emil Orzechowski, *Teatr polonijny w stanach zjednoczonych* (Polish theater in the United States) (1989). There are no scholarly studies of Teofila Samolińska, but she appears in a variety of ethnic works. The most extensive biographies are by Arthur Waldo. One is a privately published pamphlet entitled "Teofila Samolińska Matka Związku Narodowego Polskiego w Ameryce" (Teofila Samolińska: The mother of the

Polish National Alliance) (1980). See also his *Pierwsza sokolica Teofila Samolińska (The First Falconette: Theophila Samolinski)* (1975), and his *Sokolstwo przednia straz narodu: dzieje idei i organizacji w Ameryce (Falcons, The Advance Guard of the Nation: A History of Their Conception and Organizations in America)* (1953). Maria Sakowska (Sakowski) discusses her in a memoir, "Z Minionej Przeszłości Słów Kilka o Poetce i Literatce Teofili Samolińskiej," *Kalendarz Związkowy* (Alliance almanac) (1946). References to Samolińska's role in the formation of the Polish National Alliance appear also in Stanislaus Osada, *Historia Związku Narodowego Polskiego* (A history of the Polish National Alliance) (1905, 1957); Jadwiga Karłowiczowa, *Historia Związku Polek w Ameryce* (A history of the Polish Women's Alliance) (1938); and Karol Wachtl, *Polonja w Ameryce* (Polonia in America) (1944). Recent press references include *Dziennik Związkowy* (Polish daily news), July 8–9, 1988; July 27, 1988; September 27, 1988; *Nowy Dziennik* (New daily), August 30, 1988; *Sokół Polski* (Polish falcon), June 1, 1988. Obituaries may be found in *Dziennik Związkowy*, December 2, 1913, and *Dziennik Chicagoski*, December 3, 1913. Examples of her controversial writing are in *Wiarus* (Veteran), May 27, 1886; June 17, 1886.

WILLIAM J. GALUSH

SAMPSON, EDITH SPURLOCK
October 13, 1901–October 8, 1979
LAWYER, CIVIL RIGHTS AND INTERNATIONAL HUMAN RIGHTS ADVOCATE, JUDGE

Edith Spurlock was one of eight children born to Louis and Elizabeth (McGruder) Spurlock in Pittsburgh, Pennsylvania. Her parents had no formal education, but they passed on to their children the value of education. The family owned its own home. Spurlock's father worked in a dry cleaning business and held outside jobs to help make ends meet. Her mother worked from home as a seamstress. As an adult, Spurlock described her family as being poor but never knowing it. "We had a good home. We wore hand-me-down clothes, and we all worked. To supplement family income my mother made buckram hat frames. I worked in a fish market; the other children worked too. We ate regularly, slept in clean beds and went to Sunday school and church" (quoted in Ratcliff, 27). As an adult, Spurlock learned from a family member that her grandparents on both sides of her family were free, not slaves.

Education was always important to Spurlock; she attended public elementary schools in Pittsburgh and graduated from Peabody High School. Following graduation from high school, she sought a teaching job. When she could not get one, a Sunday school teacher helped her obtain a job at Associated Charities. Through this connection with a social service organization, she was later able to attend the New York School of Social Work. When she was twenty years old she married Rufus Sampson, a field agent for Tuskegee Institute in Alabama. The couple moved to Chicago, where she stayed home the first two years of her marriage, helping raise her sister's two small children after her sister's death.

Sampson then returned to school, attending the School of Social Service Administration at the University of Chicago. She worked at the Young Women's Christian Association (YWCA) and the Illinois Children's Home and Aid Society and began taking classes in the night division of John Marshall Law School. She received an LL.B. degree in 1925 but failed to pass the bar examination on her first try. She attributed her failure to having

FIG. 102. *Edith Sampson, lawyer, judge, U.S. delegate to the United Nations, speaking at the U.N., 1955.*

been overconfident. She then enrolled in the Loyola University School of Law, Chicago, and in 1927 became the first woman to receive an LL.M. degree from that institution. That same year she passed the Illinois bar examination.

In 1934 Sampson was admitted to practice before the U.S. Supreme Court, one of the first African American women to be admitted. Sampson was proud of her educational accomplishments; she often offered herself as an example of how one can achieve a dream when one is willing to work hard for it. She saw the legal profession as finally opening up to women, and she believed that women had much to offer the profession, writing that "the law needs women who will bring a trained and active intelligence to bear upon the many and difficult problems of justice in modern human relations" ("Legal Profession Followed by Nation's Best Known Socialites").

As her career began to flourish, her marriage failed. She was divorced in 1934 but continued to use the name Sampson professionally. The same year she married Joseph E. Clayton Jr., a noted black Chicago criminal attorney. The couple began a joint practice on the city's South Side, the heart of Chicago's black community. She practiced law while working as probation officer and juvenile referee in Family Court of Cook County. In

1947 Sampson was the first black woman named an assistant state's attorney for Cook County. Sampson was widowed in 1956 when Clayton, at the age of fifty-one, died suddenly. Sampson and her husband had no children. She never remarried, but she remained close to her siblings and their children. Two of her nephews followed in her legal footsteps, becoming lawyers and later judges.

Regardless of her job title, Sampson remained a social worker at heart, advocating for the rights of children and families, emphasizing the importance of a family foundation for society, and stressing the role of black women in that society. In later years, she urged black mothers to educate their children for positions that would become available with integration.

In 1949, through her involvement with the National Council of Negro Women (NCNW), in which she served as the chairwoman of its executive committee, Sampson made her first trip abroad. She served as the NCNW's representative to the World Town Hall of the Air, an outgrowth of the popular radio program America's Town Meeting of the Air, which was produced by the University of Chicago. Against the backdrop of postwar Europe, the trip to more than twenty European, Asian, and Middle Eastern countries brought together black and white participants and cultural and labor leaders from organizations across the United States, who took part in public debates on current political topics with leading figures in each locale.

The trip changed Sampson's life and the focus of her life's work. It also thrust her into the public spotlight. "After visiting and talking with people of other countries, I knew that I could never make my law practice my primary business of life; I would have to devote myself to the course of world brotherhood and world peace," she wrote ("I Like America," 3–8). Her personality, skills, and ability to express her views and to get along with many different types of people made her a popular program participant. When the organization was made permanent as the World Town Hall Seminar, Sampson was elected president. She lectured in Germany, Austria, and in the Scandinavian countries.

In this period of heightened tensions between the countries of the Western bloc, with the United States in a leadership role, and the countries of the Eastern bloc and the Soviet Union, Sampson had to deal with the rhetoric and the realities of cold war politics. In this supercharged political environment, the treatment of Blacks in the United States became part of global politics as the communist bloc nations pointed out the contradictions and deep social injustices that existed in the United States. American Blacks found themselves caught up in this global discussion. W. E. B. Du Bois increasingly found himself identifying with the aims and programs of socialist and communist countries outside the United States and spoke out against the hypocrisy of his native land. Sampson, as she traveled the globe, began to see herself not just as a "Negro" but as an American. She became quite patriotic about the American way of life and was convinced that the country's core values could help it overcome its racial and social flaws. She was often challenged by those—particularly leaders from the Soviet Union—who highlighted America's Jim Crow segregation laws and other politics of social inequity toward African Americans. After seeing firsthand the economic and social conditions under which many people in the world lived, Sampson responded to a heckler in India, "I would rather be a Negro in America than a citizen in any other land" (Ratcliff, 28).

In 1950 Sampson was appointed by President Harry S. Truman as an alternate to the American delegation at the United Nations (UN). She was the first African American representative to this international body. She was reappointed in 1952. She also served as a member-at-large of the U.S. Commission for the United Nations Educational, Scientific, and Cultural Organization (UNESCO) early in the Dwight David Eisenhower presidential administration. Sampson's UN appointment triggered criticism among some Blacks and Whites who said she was being used to offset Soviet propaganda that attacked U.S. racial politics practiced at home. Her response was that, while things were bad in America for black people, they were not as bad as the Soviets would like to picture. Some African Americans disagreed. In an article in the *Crisis*, the journal of the National Association for the Advancement of Colored People (NAACP), Sampson was criticized for painting an unrealistically positive picture of the situation of black Americans.

Those who thought the appointment was just race relations window dressing were in for a surprise when Sampson used her appointment to voice her opinions on a variety of matters, from apartheid in South Africa and European colonial practices in Africa to human rights around the world. She served on the Committee of Three—the Social, Humanitarian and Cultural Committee—along with Eleanor Roosevelt. Sampson saw the world globally and looked for those things that connected human beings rather than what separated them. She constantly related international issues to domestic issues, particularly to matters of race. When speaking against South Africa's apartheid policies, she talked about discrimination against black Americans in her own country.

During her years with the United Nations, between 1951 and 1958, she traveled and lectured extensively in Europe and the Middle East as a proponent of democracy and the American way of life. In 1951 and 1952 she served as guest lecturer in Europe for the U.S. State Department, talking about the status of Blacks in America. She became a popular and frequently sought after speaker to conferences and groups around the world. In 1961 and 1962 she was one of eighteen Americans appointed a member of the United States Citizens Committee on the North Atlantic Treaty Organization (NATO). In 1964 she was a member of the Advisory Committee on Private Enterprise in Foreign Aid.

Overlapping her international interests, Sampson's professional life in Chicago changed when, in 1955, she was named assistant corporation counsel for the city of Chicago, a post she held until she was appointed a judge of the Domestic Relations Court in 1962. Later in 1962, Sampson made history when she was elected associate judge of the Municipal Court of Chicago, the first black woman elected to the bench in Illinois. She was a lifelong Democrat, but her nomination by the Democratic Party of Chicago, supported by Mayor Richard J. Daley, placed her at odds with U.S. Congressman William L. Dawson. An African American political leader in Chicago, he opposed her appointment, saying, "Her behavior around white folks was not creditable" (Travis, 301).

During the race for judge, critics tried to use Sampson's vast international experience against her as an example of her being disconnected from local issues; but she reminded people of her early years working in the city's court system as a lawyer, probation officer, and juvenile court referee. Sampson said she never expected to become a judge, but she saw it as an opportunity to demonstrate that an African American could be part of mainstream American life. She hoped also to be an inspiration for young women who might enter the legal profession after seeing her success. In 1964 and 1970, she was elected associate judge of the Circuit Court of Cook County. In 1971 and 1976, she was elected judge of the Circuit Court of Cook County, a post she held until she retired in 1978.

Sampson's judicial work covered a variety of cases ranging from traffic violations to landlord-tenant disputes and family domestic matters. About 75 percent of the people who came before her in court were black and poor. "This is their Supreme Court," she said. "Since they have not money for appeal, they either get justice here or not at all" (quoted in Ratcliff, 27). Sampson's personality permeated her style on the bench. She was known for her humanity, a sharp sense of humor, and a blunt way of talking in a voice husky from years of smoking. She was quick to offer personal advice along with a penalty. In Marriage Court, in an effort to make the wedding ceremony more meaningful, she found volunteers from the courthouse to serve as translators during the ceremonies of non-English-speaking couples, saying that her international experience made her sensitive to language difficulties.

Sampson had her critics. In the mid-1960s, she angered tenants and landlords over the way she handled cases. In one instance, after she threatened to evict a group of striking renters, a tenant group called for her suspension, contending she did not respect poor people. The disputing parties later reached an agreement, and the eviction notice was dismissed. She also faced criticism from some sectors of the black community. Like many older prominent African Americans, she was criticized by young black social activists for being too slow in demanding change for black people in American society.

Sampson stood her ground, reiterating her belief in America's ideals and opportunities. She criticized young people who were impatient and who seemed "bent on ripping the fabric of the nation to shreds" (Ratcliff, 28). She believed in moderation and preparation; "Don't tear down the old homestead until you have a clear idea of what you'll build in its place" (p. 28), she counseled.

In 1976, the Chicago Bar Association, which had once noted her exemplary work, criticized her performance, finding her "Not Recommended" for reelection and citing as reasons for rejecting her candidacy her "age and condition of health" and questioning "the adequacy of [her] . . . legal knowledge, legal ability and judicial temperament" (Kenneth C. Prince to Edith S. Sampson, September 22, 1976, Sampson Papers). The Chicago Council of Lawyers also found Sampson not qualified for retention and stated that she had been "assigned to marriage court where her functions are largely limited to performing marriage ceremonies. Prior to that assignment, she had a variety of judicial posts . . . including a number of years handling eviction matters" ("Evaluation of Circuit Judges Seeking Retention in

November 1976 Elections," typescript, 13, Sampson Papers). The Chicago Council of Lawyers went on to say that lawyers were "virtually unanimous in regarding her as without the requisite legal ability and judicial temperament to be a Circuit Judge, repeatedly describing her as arbitrary, opinionated and without knowledge of the law" (p. 13). Sampson ran for reelection without the endorsements and won. She retired in 1978 at age seventy-seven. It is difficult to account for the harsh judgments leveled against her by attorneys in Chicago. She was past the age when many retire and would live for only one more year.

Sampson received many awards, including an honorary degree and a distinguished alumni award from John Marshall Law School and an Award of Merit from the Cook County Bar Association. She served as a trustee for Roosevelt University from 1957 to 1977. She belonged to several bar associations, including the Women's Bar Association of Illinois and the National Association of Women Lawyers. Sampson died at Northwestern Memorial Hospital after several months of declining health.

Throughout her professional life Edith Sampson had to deal with controversy when she broke new ground as a woman and as an African American. While supporters lauded her as conducting her court with justice from the heart, her detractors disparaged her for lack of interest in the law. Over the years a major concern about which she wrote and lectured was the preparation and encouragement of Blacks to enter the mainstream of American life. She upheld the goal of an integrated society and world—a view that lost popularity in the 1970s. When Edith Sampson graduated from John Marshall Law School in 1925, she received a special commendation from Dean Edward T. Lee. She had attended the night school division of John Marshall and worked during the day as a probation officer for the Cook County Juvenile Court—thereby experiencing social mobility as an individual African American while observing the hard lot of the majority of Blacks whose lives of poverty and racial discrimination on Chicago's South Side changed very slowly, if at all. Her experience convinced her that there was opportunity in American society if a person took responsibility and became educated. When asked while on tour in India "whether Negroes have equal rights in America" (Kramer, 16), she answered "no." While she remained dissatisfied with the status of Blacks, Sampson believed that of all the places in the world where discrimination existed, it was in America, "under a democracy" that there was "freedom and opportunity to *better* existing conditions" (p. 16).

Sources. Edith Spurlock Sampson Papers, SL, are largely about her activities as a judge, especially her election campaigns, and about her other professional and volunteer work; but there is little about her personal life or work as a lawyer. Judith Grove Harris, Cambridge, Massachusetts, contributed substantially to this biography by researching the Sampson Papers at the SL and providing the Historical Encyclopedia of Chicago Women Project with copies of relevant materials and a written summary. Articles by Sampson include "Equal Opportunity-Equal Responsibility: These are Two Sides of the Same Single Coin," *Vital Speeches of the Day*, June 1957; "Show the East How the Freedom Revolution Works: Industrial Civilizations Are Built from the Bottom Up," *Vital Speeches of the Day*, February 15, 1951; "Legal Profession Followed by Nation's Best Known Socialites," *Chicago Defender*, May 4, 1935; "I Like America," *Negro Digest*, December 1950; "Law Day—

Every Day," *Trial Judges Journal*, April 1968. Biographical sketches on Sampson can be found in Jessie Carney Smith, ed., *Notable Black American Women* (1992); *BWA*; and *Current Biography* (1950). Additional articles on Sampson include J. D. Ratcliff, "Justice from the Heart," *Christian Herald*, November 1967; Dale Kramer, "America's Newest Diplomat," *New Republic*, January 22, 1951. See also Dempsey J. Travis, *An Autobiography of Black Politics* (1987).

WILMA JEAN EMANUEL RANDLE

SAPERSTEIN, ESTHER RICHMAN
October 22, 1901–May 17, 1988
LEGISLATOR, WOMEN'S RIGHTS ADVOCATE, MENTAL HEALTH ACTIVIST

Esther Richman Saperstein was born on Chicago's Near West Side to Jewish immigrant parents. Her father, Ellis Richman, immigrated to the United States with his family from Russia. At age fifteen, her mother, Mary Dresser, came to the United States, alone, from Dobczyne, a small village near Crakow, Poland. Richman's father died when she was only a year old, and her mother went to work. As a result, Richman spent the early part of her childhood in the home of her paternal grandparents, Aaron Joseph and Molly Richman.

Although she grew up surrounded by the love of her grandparents and four uncles, Saperstein later was to say that she missed her mother tremendously and often felt insecure. This insecurity was alleviated somewhat when she started school, as she loved learning. She spent hours reading history, literature, biographies, and fairy tales. She also developed a passion for music.

When Richman was about nine, her mother remarried, and Richman went to live with her mother and stepfather, Albert Lipshitz. The family lived in a predominantly Jewish area above the restaurant that they owned. Unlike her paternal grandparents who, as Orthodox Jews, had insisted on Richman's receiving a Jewish education, her mother and stepfather were not involved in the synagogue but rather focused their energies on their work, Richman, and the two children they had together.

Richman graduated from high school in 1919 and began taking classes at the University of Chicago. Three years later, Richman married her boyfriend of two years, Abraham (Abe) Saperstein. Born in Bialystok, Poland, then under the control of the Russian government, he had come to the United States as a young man with his parents, two sisters, and one brother. After graduating from high school, he went into the hotel business. When he met Richman, Abe Saperstein owned the Division Street Hotel and Bathhouse with his brother and his father.

Saperstein did not work outside the home during the early years of her marriage, when her family moved to the Rogers Park neighborhood on Chicago's North Side. For a brief six-month period during the Great Depression, she would do some phone soliciting for a real estate office. Instead she focused on her son Sidney, born June 11, 1923, and daughter Natalie, born September 4, 1927. She took classes at Northwestern University when her children were young and began to participate in community organizations.

Saperstein's first foray into politics came shortly after her daughter was born in 1927, when she went door to door encouraging women to vote. However, it was not until the early

1930s when she joined the Parent Teacher Association (PTA) that she began to take on leadership roles. When Saperstein joined the PTA, local PTAs could not take action without the approval of the organization's state board. Saperstein organized the Chicago region as an autonomous organization so that it could act more quickly. She served as the Chicago region PTA's first president from 1947 to 1951. During her tenure as president, Saperstein helped start the Lighted Schoolhouse Program that used school buildings after class hours for adult and children's activities.

Saperstein's involvement with the PTA led to invitations to join various city committees and boards of directors. She became president of the Montefiore Special School for Delinquent Boys, a school for juveniles who were unable to adapt to the schoolroom and needed both physical and psychiatric care. She joined the board of Little City, a residential community for retarded children who could not live at home. She helped found and served as the second president of Chicago's City of Hope, an organization dedicated to improving medical care and medical research. She was also involved with the Chicago Area Project, which tried to combat juvenile delinquency through community efforts, and the Juvenile Protective Association, which lobbied for laws to protect children from abuse.

By the 1950s, Saperstein had become active in local politics. As the chair of a local political group on the North Side, she actively supported Richard J. Daley in his successful 1954 campaign for mayor. Her efforts on Daley's behalf led him to appoint her to the Welfare Council of Metropolitan Chicago, the Human Relations Council, and the All Chicago Women's Committee.

In 1955, at the age of fifty-three, Saperstein made her first bid for elective office. At the request of community leaders, she ran as an Independent for the office of alderman of the 49th Ward. Although Saperstein's husband did not share her fondness for politics and rarely discussed political issues, he supported her bid for elective office. She lost the election, but she found that she loved campaigning.

In 1956, impressed with Saperstein's campaign the year before, Democratic Party regulars asked her to run for state representative in the Eighth District. This time her bid for office was successful, and in January 1957, she became one of only a handful of women serving in the Illinois House of Representatives. Saperstein served as a state representative for five consecutive terms, from 1957 to 1967, when she was asked by her committeeman and Mayor Daley to run for a new seat in the Illinois Senate. She won easily, becoming the first female Democratic senator in the Illinois Senate's 149-year history. She served in the Illinois Senate from January 1967 to June 1975, when she gave up her senate seat to become a full-time Chicago alderman. Throughout her political career, Saperstein was a staunch supporter of the Democratic Party, calling her choice in a party a way of life and saying that she "believed that the Democratic Party believed in people" (Esther Saperstein Memoir, vol. 1, 84).

Recognizing the barriers to female legislators and adopting the maxim that for a woman to be successful in politics "she must look like a woman, think like a man, and work like a dog" (Carroll, "2 Achieve Government Status for Womankind"),

Saperstein threw herself into her activities, frequently working through lunch and sleeping on average only five to six hours a night. As a state representative, and later as a state senator, Saperstein focused her legislative efforts in the areas relating to children, mental health, and women's rights, often coalescing bipartisan support for the bills she supported.

One of her early successes came in 1959 when she sponsored a bill that required health examinations for children in the first, fifth, and ninth grades. She was also instrumental in securing the passage of a bill providing free health exams for indigent children.

Shortly after these bills were passed in 1959, Saperstein's husband died, and she found herself in a financial bind. As a representative, Saperstein made five to six thousand dollars a year. While this salary was sufficient to support a home in both Chicago and Springfield while her husband was alive, it became sadly inadequate after he died. Saperstein brought her problem to Mayor Daley. Because of her work in the areas of health and education, Daley appointed her as the liaison between the Chicago Board of Health and the Board of Education, a position paying thirty-five hundred dollars a year. As liaison, Saperstein was able to organize the health examinations program and later a program that provided free polio shots to Chicago children.

In 1957, the Illinois Mental Health Commission was created, and Saperstein was appointed its first secretary. She later became chair of the commission. Through the commission, Saperstein was instrumental in the enactment of many laws that improved conditions for the residents of state mental hospitals and nursing homes. Saperstein was not always popular on the commission; she felt that in order to reform the state's mental health code there needed to be publicity about the problems. Commission members tried twice to remove Saperstein as chair. Despite this opposition, she was successful in securing passage of a package of reforms to improve conditions and aftercare treatment for Illinois's mental health patients. Saperstein remained a member of the Mental Health Commission until her death.

Throughout her political career, Saperstein worked to pass legislation to improve the lives of women. In 1963, she joined with Republican Frances Dawson and Democrat Lillian Piotrowski to introduce a bill to create an Illinois Commission on the Status of Women to study the inequities facing women, particularly in the work force. Saperstein, Dawson, and Piotrowski were the only women members of the Illinois House of Representatives. With passage of the bill, Saperstein was appointed head of the commission.

The first Illinois Commission on the Status of Women was disbanded in 1965 after it made a report of its findings to the General Assembly. Since the General Assembly failed to authorize funding for a second commission or for any of the commission's recommended programs, Governor Otto Kerner appointed his own commission. However, the Kerner commission was not given any state funds, and members had to raise their own funds from grants, or from their own pockets, in order to pay for the commission's expenses.

In 1967, as a new senator, Saperstein attempted to reestablish a Commission on the Status of Women with funding from the General Assembly. When the General Assembly again failed to provide funds, Saperstein took up the battle. She launched a filibuster that resulted in a compromise on funding for the commission.

Saperstein used the Commission on the Status of Women as a springboard for introducing and supporting legislation designed to bring equality to women. Her efforts reflected progress made at this level on the national front. After the National Commission on the Status of Women documented the inequalities existing between men and women, Congress passed the 1963 Equal Pay Act and the Civil Rights Act of 1964, which prohibited sex discrimination in employment.

Unfortunately, Saperstein's efforts in Illinois were not as successful as those taking place in Washington, D.C. Beginning in 1963, Saperstein repeatedly introduced bills requiring pay equality for men and women and the repeal of the Eight Hour Day law, which effectively prevented female workers from working more than eight hours a day. Each time, her bills failed to pass. Refusing to give up, Saperstein introduced the bills in each new session. Her efforts led Lerner newspapers to call her a "modern-day champion of women's rights" ("Champion of Women's Rights"). The objectives of the bills were not accomplished until after Saperstein left the General Assembly.

In 1969, Saperstein introduced and secured passage of the first grant-in-aid bill to provide for day-care centers. This bill provided for matching funds for proprietary day-care centers for working mothers. Highest priority was given to caring for the children of mothers trying to keep off public assistance rolls by seeking employment or job training. In Illinois, 134 centers were funded to provide this service for seven thousand children. Saperstein continued to work for day care.

In March 1972, the U.S. Congress passed the Equal Rights Amendment (ERA), and attention turned to the states for ratification. In April 1972, identical ERA ratification bills were introduced in the Illinois houses with Saperstein as sponsor in the senate. Each bill had a majority of members of each house listed as cosponsors. Still, both bills failed to pass. In February 1973, identical bills were again introduced in both houses. After the 1972 vote, a new house rule had been adopted that required that constitutional amendments pass only upon the affirmative vote of three-fifths of the members rather than by a majority vote. Once again, neither bill passed.

Saperstein cosponsored another ERA bill in 1974 but was forced to move for a postponement of the bill when it became apparent that it would not pass. The president of the senate had ruled that an extra majority of three-fifths would be required to pass the bill. Again, the bill failed. Despite having an equal rights provision in its state constitution, Illinois was the only northern state to fail to ratify the ERA.

Saperstein received a number of accolades and awards during her years in the General Assembly. Among the most noteworthy was being named Mrs. Mental Health in 1962 by the Research Foundation for the Mentally Ill and Woman of the Year in 1974 by the Women's Share in Public Service. She also received the 1973 Annual Leadership for Freedom Award from the Woman's Scholarship Association of Roosevelt University for her efforts in the areas of mental health, education, and women's rights.

In 1974, at age seventy-two, Saperstein announced she was leaving the Illinois Senate and resigning from the Chicago Board of Health to run for a seat on the Chicago City Council from the 49th Ward. Saperstein won the election and became the third female alderman to sit on the Chicago City Council. During her tenure on the council, Saperstein continued her efforts on behalf of women and children. She supported early childhood intervention programs, worked to improve the public schools in the Rogers Park area, and cosponsored a council resolution urging the General Assembly to approve ERA. She sat on the Committee of Police, Firemen and Schools; the Health Committee; and the Finance Committee. She planned to run for a second term but fell in February 1979, just before the primary, and withdrew from the election.

Saperstein traveled extensively in her later years, visiting the South Pacific, the Middle East, and Europe. She met with politicians and community leaders in the countries that she visited to discuss local politics and global issues. During a 1972 trip to Europe, she was given a private audience with Pope Paul VI, who commended her on her work on behalf of children and in the area of education.

Saperstein remained active in community affairs and continued to seek new challenges up to her death. Always she sought to learn. Shortly before her death, she discussed her love for learning with an interviewer, saying, "Everything about education, everything about learning has been a source of great pleasure, I even like it now. It's the greatest experience in life I think" (Memoirs, vol. 1, 34).

Saperstein died at the age of eighty-six and was buried at Westlake Cemetery, Chicago. She had devoted nearly half a century to public service, and her first priority was her community, children, and the mentally ill.

Sources. Esther Richman Saperstein's papers are at UIC Spec. Coll. The collection contains her general papers, letters, campaign materials, copies of newspaper articles, and other memorabilia. Saperstein was interviewed for an oral history as part of the Illinois General Assembly Oral History Program. The oral history is contained in a two-volume set, *Esther Saperstein Memoir* (1987). Saperstein's role in the battle to pass ERA in Illinois is discussed in Adade Mitchell Wheeler and Marlene Stein Wortman, *The Roads They Made: Women in Illinois History* (1977). Articles about Saperstein include "Champion of Women's Rights," *Rogers Park-Edgewood News*, May 7, 1967; and Margaret Carroll, "2 Achieve Government Status for Womankind," *Today*, July 19, 1973.

DEBRA L. STETTER

SAUCEDO, MARIA del JESUS
April 23, 1954–November 12, 1981
COMMUNITY ACTIVIST, POET, THEATER PERFORMER, TEACHER, REVOLUTIONARY

Born in Monterrey, Mexico, Maria Saucedo grew up in the United States during the rising fervor of the Chicano (Mexican American) movement of the 1960s and 1970s. She fought for the rights of oppressed people; for the working class; for quality education, including bilingual education; and for pride in Mexican culture and heritage.

Daughter of Juan and Maria (Reynosa) Saucedo, she was the eldest of eight surviving children and originally a twin; however, her sister did not survive. Her other siblings were Juanita, Silvia,

Juan Jr., José, Fernando, Alicia, and Teresa. The Saucedos also adopted a nephew named Marco Antonio. Saucedo's parents met and married in Monterrey, and in 1955 her father migrated to the United States to find work. Mexican immigrants with permanent visas increased significantly during this time; nearly two hundred seventy-five thousand Mexican immigrants arrived legally in the United States in the 1950s. Holding permanent resident status, Juan Saucedo served in the army shortly after arriving. His wife and three children waited until 1959 to join him.

The family settled in Pilsen, a growing Mexican neighborhood that would later become a primary locus of Mexican population, and they moved from apartment to apartment within Pilsen. Their constant moving allowed Saucedo, who always surrounded herself with people, to observe her neighbors' lives and experiences. Everyone remembers "Chuchis," as Saucedo was called, for her humor, wit, and curiosity. From childhood, Saucedo was a strong-willed and outspoken person who commented on her family's and other people's conditions.

The family faced difficulties common to Mexican immigrants. Chicanos held low-paying jobs, and many lacked adequate English-language skills. As a result, they often did not receive necessary services or were poorly treated at hospitals and other public service agencies. With relatively few registered voters and little wealth, Chicano neighborhoods had poor public services and schools. The Immigration and Naturalization Service (INS) routinely arrested immigrants found without proper documents. Saucedo and others came to see these problems as structural, systemic, and shared by non-Chicano working-class and poor people. Thus, she believed, fundamental change was required to solve her community's problems.

Besides Saucedo's social awareness, a great impetus for her development as an activist was her mother's activism. Maria Reynosa first learned to communicate for the welfare of herself and her family; she then focused on the community. In 1962 she began helping pregnant mothers who had no knowledge of the English language to claim insurance rights and receive proper care in hospitals. Reynosa and Saucedo attended strikes, rallies, and solidarity marches in Pilsen, and they followed the Chicano movement throughout the country. They supported the efforts of Cesar Chavez, Dolores Huerta, and other leaders of the United Farm Workers Union (UFWU) in organizing farm workers in California and New Mexico. Although they were strong advocates of the Chicano movement, the Saucedos did not limit themselves to this cause. They marched with civil rights leader Martin Luther King Jr. to integrate neighborhoods in the Chicago area and rallied against the United States involvement in Guatemala and El Salvador.

In 1973 Maria Saucedo began studying at Northeastern Illinois University (NIU), where she majored in early childhood education and graduated with honors in 1975. For the Saucedos, school in the United States had been an early challenge, since the Catholic school they attended did not teach in English but in Polish, because Pilsen at the time had predominantly Polish residents. However, Saucedo was a bright student and advanced rapidly. As a child, she had begun first grade at age four; she entered college as a sophomore rather than a freshman.

When Saucedo began attending NIU, the university did not have a large Latino population. Saucedo pushed the school to recruit more Latino/Chicano students and faculty; she developed recruitment methods herself. Saucedo, Mariestela Carabez, Elvira Carrizales, and Alma Alvarado together founded the Chicano Student Union (CSU) in 1974. Prior to the establishment of the CSU, the Union for Puerto Rican Students (UPRS) was the only Latino organization existing at NIU. Saucedo and other Chicanos objected to UPRS's efforts to subsume Mexican American students under the UPRS. CSU founders wanted their own identity and "a piece of the pie" (interview with Santos Rivera), but not, they insisted, the Puerto Rican students' piece. They were not being divisive as the UPRS charged but rather were demanding expanded resources for Latinos/Chicanos. Saucedo wrote the CSU constitution and served as the organization's first chairperson. The CSU strove to unify and organize the Chicano/Latino student body at NIU, to "create awareness of identity, culture, history, and to develop a political consciousness for the progress of Third World People" (CSU Constitution).

Through CSU, Saucedo began the Noche de Familia, an event that encouraged interaction between students, parents, and professors on campus. With donations from local businesses, students and parents prepared food served at the event, which featured live music and entertainment. Saucedo emphasized student and parent involvement; because many of the students were or had been involved in gangs, the experience was new, different, and necessary. Saucedo also led the attempt to recruit Chicano professors to teach Chicano history, Latino sociology, and bilingual education.

Saucedo was a prolific writer. During her time at NIU, Saucedo founded and edited *Contra la Pared* (Against the wall), a newsletter that addressed Chicano issues. A metaphor for their political situation, the name alludes to a Spanish saying, "entre la espada y la pared" or "between a rock and a hard place," having nowhere to turn. Saucedo wrote articles about INS raids of places where Latinos were employed, mass deportations, and Chicano history in the United States.

Throughout her years in school, Saucedo remained active within Pilsen. Her fellow activists and friends described her as an intellectual totally in contact with less educated members of the community. Saucedo became involved with Compañia Trucha, a street theater housed at Casa Aztlán. Previously a settlement house called Howell House, Casa Aztlán was a grass roots organization and the center of the Chicano movement in Chicago in the 1970s. Many Chicano youths felt they needed a center where they could organize, discuss issues in the community, and provide medical, educational, and civic activities. At Casa Aztlán, Compañia Trucha developed as a street theater group and performed throughout Chicago. Street theater was a prevalent form of activism during the 1970s. Compañia Trucha itself was styled after Teatro Campesino, which came out of Cesar Chavez's UFWU and was headed by Luis Valdes. In essence, these were political theater groups. Both street and political theater drew upon a long tradition of religious theater in Mexico and other Latin American countries. In Chicago itself in the 1940s, ANGELINA RICO choreographed such cultural performances.

Saucedo and her husband Filberto Ramírez formed Compañia Trucha's core leadership, along with Hector and Maria

Gamboa and Antonio and Ricardo Zavala. They produced theater that dramatized significant events extracted from the lives of Mexican people in Chicago. For example, INS officers—the dreaded *migra*—harassed Mexicans, demanding to see documentation papers both on the street and in places of employment. The actors also addressed issues regarding the quality of education, poor medical attention, and the condition of the working class in the United States, among other themes. Their performances were satiric and biting but also educational. Compañia Trucha aimed to teach people in the audience—many illiterate and uneducated—about their rights.

As a tool of protest, Compañia Trucha demonstrated at Rush Presbyterian St. Luke's Hospital in 1976. There an employee was fired after seventeen years of service for talking to patients and Latino medical students about a patient's right to informed consent, that is, the right to be fully informed about treatment options and to agree or decline to be treated. Around the country, public hospitals were being challenged for allegedly sterilizing Latinas and other low-income patients without their knowledge and consent. A support committee called for rehiring the employee and also for hiring more Latino staff and interpreters. Spanish-speaking janitors were being asked to translate, a task that was outside their job description and for which they were neither trained nor paid. The members of Compañia Trucha supported the committee's sit-in demonstration and held performances alleging poor treatment of Latinos. Twenty-three protesters were arrested; four, including Saucedo, chose to represent themselves in court. Ultimately, charges against all twenty-three were dropped.

Saucedo met her husband, Filberto Ramírez, while working with Compañia Trucha. They married in June 1977 on a day when they were scheduled to perform at the Daley Center, where they could obtain a civil marriage ceremony. They had one son, Albizu Emiliano. The name Albizu was for Albizu Campos, the Puerto Rican independence leader imprisoned in 1950; Emiliano was for Emiliano Zapata, a leader in Mexico's revolution of 1910–20, who fought for land rights and land redistribution among agrarian workers. Saucedo also admired Cesar Chavez, Cuban revolutionary Ernesto "Che" Guevara, and Mao Ze Dong, leader of the People's Republic of China. Like them, she gave herself completely to her cause. Saucedo assigned full custody rights of Albizu to her mother in case anything should happen to herself and her husband. To those who did not understand her reasons, she would respond, "I can stay home and take care of my child, but if I only take care of my child, I cannot take care of the rest of my children" (interview with Saucedo family).

Influenced by Saucedo and Gamboa, Compañia Trucha addressed women's issues. Both in their plays and in discussion with other theater groups, Saucedo emphasized that it was important to be unified in the struggle for rights but not to relegate women to supportive roles or limit them to the virgin/whore stereotype. She argued that women's portrayals must reflect their actual roles as leaders in their communities and that women's issues needed to be addressed rather than swallowed up in the bigger struggle. At the same time, Saucedo did not call herself a feminist. She did not see the Latino male as the primary problem for Latinas. Because Latino males were oppressed themselves, she believed in a unified struggle involving both men and women.

With Compañia Trucha and other youth from Casa Aztlán, Saucedo traveled to Iowa, California, Texas, New Mexico, Mexico City, and several other places to lend support to other groups and perform with the theater. During protests, Saucedo often played her guitar and sang *corridos* (traditional protest songs). She wrote songs in support of each cause and used her poetry to vent her frustration. Her poetry not only documents her life but also reflects the struggles and hardships Chicanos endured. One such poem emerged during a demonstration, which lasted several days, in favor of bilingual education. A portion of the poem reads, "Tengo hambre / no he comido / siento el estómago vacio / este pinche sistema / me está robando el corazon / me está robando el grito" (Maria Reynosa Papers) (I am hungry / I haven't eaten / I feel my stomach empty / this fucking system / robs me of my heart / robs me of my voice).

The three things that Saucedo valued most were family, her people, and education. She saw education not only as a method of self-improvement but also as the key toward the improvement of living conditions for Mexican people. She not only became an educator but took action in the building of the Benito Juarez High School in Pilsen. Even during the 1970s, overcrowding in schools was already an issue. Once the Board of Education approved the building of a new high school, the community appointed a committee to push for the school to be built in Pilsen. Saucedo, her sisters, and her mother were involved in this effort. Community activists lobbied for Mexican-style architecture. Many issues remained unresolved in spite of the struggle for the Benito Juarez school: the board built a school that was too small, and it assigned a principal even though the Pilsen community wished to select the principal.

After graduating from Northeastern Illinois University in 1975, Saucedo taught at Kosciusko Elementary School and later at Pickard School. Shortly before her death, she was fired from Pickard for refusing to implement a new policy whereby teachers had to ask students to show a green immigration card proving that they were legally in the United States. Saucedo believed all children had a right to receive an education regardless of immigration status.

Among her projects, Saucedo cofounded the Mexican Teacher's Organization (MTO) around the same time she began teaching. Not only was it difficult for newly arrived immigrant children to attend school, but bilingual education was also under attack. The MTO's goals were to improve the quality of education of Latino children and to encourage more Latinos to become educators. For Saucedo, language was a strong tie to both culture and identity. At the time, Saucedo was attending DePaul University; she was studying for a master's degree in reading with a bilingual component.

On November 12, 1981, Maria Saucedo died in a fire. Although most who knew her prefer to think it was an accident, almost all conclude that the fire was most likely due to arson. Fire Department officials first claimed it was arson and then, without an official investigation, declared the cause to be the electrical system. Family members were forced to jump from their third-story apartment. Her son and husband survived but suffered severe injuries. Saucedo, who was eight months pregnant, also jumped, but she fell head first. She died instantly. Whether or not her death was accidental, its circumstances—arson, aging and easily flammable housing stock, and inadequate fire services—were not unique. Following her death, her activist friends formed the Maria Saucedo Fire Committee to push for better equipment, service, and code enforcement. True to Saucedo's commitment not to take some other group's "piece of the pie" for her community's benefit, the committee rejected a "cherry picker" for removing people from upper stories of burning buildings when they learned it had been taken from the African American community.

The day of her wake, a throng of people who had known and loved Saucedo gathered at Casa Aztlán and marched through the neighborhood to her home, ending their pilgrimage at the funeral home. A crowd of perhaps three hundred marched in the streets, carrying a banner imprinted with her name and the words "Revolutionary, Teacher, Mother." The crowd read her poetry and told stories. After the wake her body was sent to Monterrey, Mexico, where she is buried. In 1986, Harrison High School was renamed the Maria Saucedo Scholastic Academy in her honor.

Maria Saucedo dedicated herself to challenging class and racial/ethnic inequality. She used her socialist beliefs, her love for her people, her struggle against injustices, and her wit and humor to make people aware of their rights, to instill pride in Mexican culture, and to create another level of consciousness for future generations. An obituary identified Maria Saucedo as a leader who had dedicated herself to the liberation of all people who suffered from oppression.

Sources. Maria Reynosa has a large amount of information, including photographs, video documentation taken at Saucedo's wake, and her collection of poetry. Laura Paz also holds newspaper clippings on Saucedo's death, including an obituary taken from an unnamed and undated newspaper article. Martha Espinoza conducted extensive interviews with Saucedo's parents, Maria Reynosa and Juan Saucedo; sisters Juanita and Teresa; and brothers Juan, José, and Fernando; as well as friends and coworkers Maria Gamboa, Isaura Gonzales, Laura Paz, Victoria Perez, and Santos Rivera. Juanita Saucedo provided a video taken of the tenth anniversary of the naming of the Maria Saucedo Scholastic Academy. Information about the fatal fire is from *El Heraldo de Chicago*, December 3, 1981, and *La Raza*, December 2–8, 1981. The "Chicano Student Union Constitution" (n.d.) is available at Northeastern Illinois Univ. in the Chimexla Student Union archives. Information on Mexican Americans is found in Jorge Casuso and Eduardo Camacho, "Latino Chicago," in *Ethnic Chicago: A Multicultural Portrait*, ed. Melvin G. Holli and Peter d'A. Jones (4th ed., 1995); Carlos E. Cortés, "Mexicans," in *Harvard Encyclopedia of American Ethnic Groups*, ed. Stephan Thernstrom (1980); and Louise Año Nuevo Kerr, "The Chicano Experience in Chicago: 1920–1970 (Ph.D. diss., Univ. of Illinois at Chicago Circle, 1976).

MARTHA ELENA ESPINOZA

SCHMIDT, MINNA MOSCHEROSCH
March 18, 1866–December 8, 1961
COSTUMER, ENTREPRENEUR

Minna Moscherosch Schmidt owned the largest costume rental business in early twentieth-century Chicago and was an authority on the history of clothing. Through the study of women's fashions she documented the lives of women in world history and in the story of Chicago.

Minna Moscherosch was born near Stuttgart, Germany, in the small town of Sindelfingen, the eldest of Wilhem and Friedericke (Leonhardt) Moscherosch's seventeen children. Her creative talents were evident when, as a young girl, she made outfits for her dolls, assisted and encouraged by her grandmother. For several generations the Moscherosch family were skilled artisans in crafts related to the manufacture of clothes, including military uniforms, shoes, and gloves. By age thirteen Minna Moscherosch advanced from making wardrobes for her dolls to sewing garments for her younger brothers and sisters.

After graduating from the public *Volksschule* (primary school) at age fourteen, Moscherosch worked first as a nursemaid in Stuttgart and, two years later, as a governess in Frankfurt. Opportunities in higher education were rare for women in the nineteenth century, especially for those from families of meagre circumstances. Always interested in expanding her education, however, she attended a sewing school while in Stuttgart and obtained the skills that were to serve as the basis of her costume business. While in Frankfurt, she studied dance and physical training in the evenings.

In 1886, at age twenty, Moscherosch emigrated to the United States, hoping to escape the tyranny of the rigid class system prevalent in Europe. She answered an advertisement in a local paper for a job in America: "Wanted: a healthy young girl who can teach two boys the German language, wait on an invalid lady (85 years old), do the sewing for the family; Wages, $3.00 a week" (Schmidt, *400 Outstanding Women*, 515–16).

Moscherosch saved enough money to pay steerage passage and arrived in Chicago in December 1886. The following year, her childhood sweetheart, Julius Schmidt, came to join her. They were married on October 5, 1887, and had two sons, Edwin (born 1889) and Helmut (born 1894).

The Schmidts settled in a German neighborhood on Chicago's North Side. Julius Schmidt, who had taught Latin in Sindelfingen, did not continue in the teaching profession but opened a neighborhood tavern. The Schmidts lived in an apartment above the tavern. Difficult financial circumstances during the depression of 1893 prompted Minna Schmidt to find employment. Calling upon her previous studies in dance and physical training, Schmidt coached plays and taught dance, also performing as a solo danseuse. She eventually opened a school of dance, the Locust Studio, with classes in physical training, dance, costume, and make-up for pupils ranging in age from six to sixty.

In addition to teaching dance, Schmidt's work in the Locust Studio included staging her own amateur pageants and plays, based on her translations of German fairy tales. Since rental prices were high, Schmidt began to sew costumes for these productions. Hearing of her talents, the Swabian Women's Society, a German social club, offered Schmidt her first commission to costume a play. Soon her proficiency in constructing period costumes with an attention to detail attracted the notice of other clubs and schools, and Schmidt's part-time vocation turned into a full-time career.

In the days before radio and television, amateur and professional theatricals filled the need for stories and entertainment.

FIG. 103. *Costume designer Minna Schmidt displays her creations in 1930.*

Cities like Chicago, with large and diverse immigrant populations, had the added dimension of folk and ethnic theater productions associated with social and fraternal clubs, church groups, and schools. In this environment, Schmidt's entrepreneurship succeeded. Her costume business, run from the Schmidt household, eventually expanded to include Julius Schmidt as bookkeeper and secretary, son Edwin as make-up specialist and producer of plays, and son Helmut as manager of the art and rental departments. It was not until 1915, however, that Schmidt purchased property on the North Side to build the two-story Schmidt Costume and Wig Shop.

By the mid-1920s, the Schmidt Costume and Wig Shop was the largest costume rental house in Chicago, and by the end of the decade, it was a million dollar enterprise. Half of the shop's customers consisted of clubs, schools, and churches; the other half were private clients renting or purchasing costumes for fancy dress balls and parties. By the end of the 1930s, sixty thousand costumes were rented annually. During these peak business years, Schmidt also pursued other civic and professional activities. In 1921, Schmidt organized the Costumer's Association of Chicago.

Also in 1921, Schmidt enrolled in the evening program at the Kent College of Law. In preparation for admission, she had first completed preparatory school. Schmidt graduated from

Kent with a Bachelor of Law degree in 1924, followed in 1929 by a Master of Law degree. Her thesis, "Ancient Laws and Customs and the Evolution of the Status of Women," reflected her growing interest in the role of women in history. There is no record that she was admitted to the Illinois bar or practiced law, although she planned to use her legal knowledge to benefit the interests of women and those in need.

Parallel to her interests in business and law, Schmidt was becoming an able historian of fashion and clothing. She had always been a stickler for historical accuracy and detail. Since there were few books on costume history at the turn of the century, Schmidt studied the Bible and general history books for references to clothing styles. She traveled to Europe and the Near East visiting museums and collecting examples of indigenous dress and ornament. She also gathered whatever material was available on the subject of costume, eventually acquiring one of the largest libraries on the subject in the United States. In museums, Schmidt visited those collections that displayed clothing, particularly the doll exhibitions. Inspired, she adopted the tradition of using dolls to convey fashion eras and planned to create a series of wax doll figurines as a memorial to the achievements of women. This goal originated when Schmidt visited the Woman's Building at the World's Columbian Exposition of 1893.

Schmidt portrayed women who she believed were "representatives of true womanhood," (Corwin, 233) from all walks of life. Her figurines were of women who had been mothers, wives, sisters, and daughters, and who had served their communities either professionally or through social work, philanthropy, or charity.

The first series of figurines she created, *3000 Years of Fashion*, represented 120 historical and literary figures from the biblical Eve to the prevailing flapper styles of 1924. The sixteen-inch figurines were initially modeled in clay. A plaster cast of the model was then fashioned and wax poured into the mold. Hair was inserted into the still-warm wax; the face was finely chiseled and then painted with oil paints. Each figure was based on information Schmidt gleaned from historial and literary sources, with the goal of representing the actual historical person as accurately as possible.

Interested in creating some lasting memorial for her adopted city, in 1923 Schmidt devised a plan to create a record of important women in Chicago's history. Schmidt left the selection of subjects to the Chicago Historical Society (CHS). She soon discovered there were few portraits or memorials to Chicago women. It became necessary, therefore, to retrieve Chicago women from obscurity. Among the women selected for *Figurines of Historic Chicago Women* were JULIETTE AUGUSTA MAGILL KINZIE, MARY LIVERMORE, BERTHA HONORÉ PALMER, SARAH HACKETT STEVENSON, and ELLA FLAGG YOUNG. Since many of the descendants of these women and others selected were active CHS members, Schmidt was able to collect biographical information, portraits, and swatches of fabric from clothing worn by the historical subjects. These artifacts were used to create the figurines. On March 23, 1924, Schmidt donated the series of seventy-two wax figurines to the CHS at a special presentation.

On April 8, 1927, Schmidt opened the Chicago Schmidt

College of Scientific Costuming in her store to provide a course of study for the research and construction of costume. Lectures on period costume were offered by Schmidt, and instructions on historical hair styles and headdress were given by Emily Lundgren, an employee of the Schmidt Costume and Wig Shop. Helmut Schmidt taught character make-up and Edwin Schmidt a course on Shakespearean dress. Minna Schmidt's costume library was open to the students, as were the workrooms of the shop. Each student was required to construct a period costume using one of the sixteen-inch figurines developed by Schmidt.

Schmidt created a set of 129 figurines for the Illinois State Historical Society in 1929, representing women who had played an important role in the history of the state. Biographies of the women were compiled by Georgia L. Osborne in *Brief Biographies of the Figurines on Display in the Illinois State Historical Library* (1932).

In 1929 Schmidt was asked by the University of Chicago to conduct a workshop in the study and construction of historical and stage costumes, a first for American universities. After a successful workshop, the university established a program to train students in professional costuming. Schmidt was asked to teach, holding the position of lecturer in the Department of Home Economics until 1937. She was a special lecturer in the School of Speech, Northwestern University, for the 1936–37 academic year.

Schmidt's *400 Outstanding Women of the World*, displayed at the 1933 Century of Progress Exposition, Chicago, was her most extensive exhibition. Her figurines represented women in the history of forty-six countries. Schmidt had asked representatives of the countries to list their four or five outstanding women and to provide biographical information and portraits. She recommended that the selections be of women (deceased) from all levels of society, chosen on the basis of their merit and morality. Emphasis was to be placed on the mothers of great men, reflecting Schmidt's conception of the true mission of women. Schmidt compiled illustrations of the four hundred figurines with the biographies of the subjects for a book with the same title as the exhibit. She also included in this volume her own family's history and an autobiographical essay.

Minna Schmidt became a wealthy woman. Self-made, she built herself an eighteen-room mansion in Evanston, Illinois, "but preferred to spend her time in the little apartment above her costume shop" (Corwin, 235). She was generous, providing for the education of seventeen brothers, sisters, nephews, and cousins. She financed a hospital for women and children in her native Sindelfingen. Her Evanston mansion was eventually donated to Northwestern University.

In 1944, Schmidt retired from the costume business. She sold the building and relocated to a space at Holy Family Academy, a Roman Catholic school in Chicago, where she continued to make figurines. A special room was constructed for the display of a thousand dolls she had made over the course of her career. Minna Schmidt died at the age of ninety-five and lived the last five years of her life at St. Mary's Hospital, Chicago. She was buried in Wunder's Cemetery, Chicago.

Minna Schmidt carved out new fields of endeavor and enterprise. Utilizing her Old World artisan skills, she adapted to the New World. She worked first in her ethnic community, out of her household and with her family, and eventually developed her specialty into an "art," exhibited widely, and a "science," taught at the University of Chicago and other places. Her interest in demonstrating the achievements of womanhood led to the rescue from obscurity of women who figured prominently in Chicago, Illinois, and world history.

Sources. The CHS has a collection of clippings, brochures, and pamphlets about Minna Schmidt, including a typescript copy of the speeches offered in tribute to Schmidt by her colleagues December 29, 1936, at Thorne Hall, Northwestern Univ. Registrar Exhibition Files, CHS, have the correspondence for the Society's *Figurines of Historic Chicago Women*; the figurines are stored at CHS. Miscellaneous biographical information on Schmidt is in the Vertical Files, the Illinois State Hist. Library, Springfield. Schmidt donated her 129 figurines of Illinois women to the Illinois State Hist. Library; they can be found today in the Illinois State Museum, Springfield, in the Minna Schmidt Dolls, Decorative Arts Collection. The museum has a collection of black and white photographs of the dolls taken by Betty Madden; several are included in Madden's *Art, Crafts, and Architecture in Early Illinois* (1974). See also Georgia L. Osborne, comp., *Brief Biographies of the Figurines on Display in the Illinois State Historical Library* (1932). Schmidt's *400 Outstanding Women of the World and Costumology of Their Time* (1933) is a compilation of biographies of the women whose likenesses she created for the Century of Progress Exposition; the book also includes autobiographical information and material on Schmidt's business endeavors. Short biographies of Schmidt are in *The Biographical Cyclopaedia of American Women*, vol. 2 (1925); Agnes Geneva Gilman and Gertrude Marcelle Gilman, *Who's Who in Illinois: Women-Makers of History* (1927); and Paul Gilbert and Charles Lee Bryson, *Chicago and Its Makers* (1929). *Fifty Years of Public Service in Costumology in America* (1936) is a commemorative program from the event honoring Schmidt at Thorne Hall, Northwestern Univ., December 29, 1936, and includes photographs of her costume designs. Margaret Corwin, "Minna Schmidt: Businesswoman, Feminist, and Fairy Godmother to Chicago," *Chicago History*, Winter 1978–79, is an extensive article on Schmidt, containing an informative bibliography.

GAYLE STREGE

SCHORSCH, SISTER DOLORES (Alma Frances Schorsch)
June 16, 1896–June 17, 1984
EDUCATOR, LECTURER, AUTHOR

Sister Dolores Schorsch radically transformed the way in which hundreds of thousands of children in Catholic schools were given religious instruction. Introducing modern pedagogical theory and experimenting with a variety of educational materials, including films and workbooks, Schorsch encouraged Catholic educators to abandon the rote methods of the past.

Alma Frances Schorsch was born in Morris, Illinois. Her father, Anton Schorsch, born in 1852, owned and operated a tannery in Austria-Hungary until 1894. He married Maria Czagany (born 1863), and they had seven children while still living in Europe. When Anton Schorsch lost his business, the family migrated to America, settling in Morris. Alma was the first child born in the United States. Four more children followed.

The family lived in extreme poverty with the older children doing what they could to put food on the table. Devout Catholics, the children found ways to pay their way through St. Agnes Elementary School. After graduating from the local public high school, where she completed four years of study in three years, and attending the Illinois State Normal School, Schorsch began her teaching career at age seventeen, first in Morris, in a one-room country school, then in the Norwood Park area of Chicago. She immediately set her sights on professional development, enrolling at DePaul University in Chicago. Between 1915 and 1922, industrious, goal-oriented Schorsch earned three degrees from DePaul University: A.B., 1920 (science and mathematics); A.M., 1921 (education and philosophy); B.S., 1922 (chemistry and biology). During this time she also began teaching as an instructor at DePaul and earned a certificate in advanced piano from Saint Scholastica Academy in Chicago.

Schorsch became acquainted with the Benedictine Sisters of Chicago through her piano teacher, Sister Amelia Buscher. Schorsch joined the Benedictines on February 12, 1922, and received the name Dolores. This was a significant period intellectually and spiritually for the Chicago Benedictines. Immigrating first to Pennsylvania in 1852, the Benedictine sisters arrived in Chicago in 1861 and began furnishing the German Catholic immigrant community of the city with Catholic elementary schools and charitable societies. With MOTHER IMELDA FISCHER, the new prioress of the Chicago Benedictines in 1921, the order began a period of leadership as a center for Benedictine liturgical revival with the development of art, music, and ritual at St. Scholastica Academy and Convent. Schorsch experienced her religious formation in this heady environment.

Well educated in secular and religious subjects, Schorsch soon found herself propelled beyond Chicago as she and other women religious were dispersed to meet the educational and religious needs of an expanding Catholic population in the United States. This work involved teaching pedagogy to women religious, creating new elementary and secondary schools, and creating materials appropriate for teachers and students in this burgeoning Catholic system. Her first assignment as a Benedictine was to teach at the Academy of Saint Scholastica in Canon City, Colorado. Her experience in teaching and her advanced work at the university level qualified her to conduct courses at the high school and college level for members of the religious congregation who had not yet completed their education. Schorsch wrote her own textbooks and had them approved by faculty at DePaul University. Her students received credit through the Catholic University of America, Washington, D.C., and DePaul University.

Schorsch was a teacher of teachers. Her basic philosophy of education was as simple as it was profound. Students were not simply to be taught; they were to be actively involved in their learning. It was this philosophy that motivated her to develop new and creative teaching techniques, to speak and to lecture to thousands of educators throughout the country, and to teach classes in education at both college and graduate level. Schorsch was appointed an instructor at DePaul University in 1921.

Schorsch's most noteworthy contribution to the educational field was a course in religion for elementary schools that she coauthored with her brother, Alexander Schorsch, Congregation of the Mission (Vincentians), dean of the Graduate School of DePaul University. In 1930 they began their collaboration on a new approach to teaching religion in Catholic elementary schools. Three years later the Archdiocese of Chicago officially adopted the *Jesu-Maria Course in Religion* for grades one through eight, with guidebooks for teachers and student workbooks for the children. From 1934 to 1938, Sister Dolores and teaching assistants used the new, experimental materials in classrooms.

The Schorsches' series literally revolutionized the way religion was taught in the Catholic elementary schools in the Archdiocese of Chicago and in many other places throughout the country and the world. Father Schorsch was the theologian exploring all theological and philosophical issues; Dolores Schorsch was the methodologist and did most of the writing and all of the editing. They broke away from the catechetical method of question and answer, developing an integrated unit presentation, with devices for assimilation and recitation that encouraged mastery of content and restatement of the material in the child's own words. Attractive materials and the game technique for drill made religion classes interesting and stimulating to the child.

Each grade level had a teacher guidebook and a student workbook. The guidebooks provided informational material in the form of exploration, presentation, and assimilation questions for character formation; lists of key words and phrases as they occurred in the student workbook; and correlated poems, picture lists, and hymns. The student workbook had informational material in the form of activities, games, poems, quotations, and pertinent doctrine. The program gave both students and teachers a new, creative, and interactive way to learn their religious traditions. In addition, the curriculum provided for an expansion of students' vocabulary; training in writing and speaking; and development of an appreciation for literature, art, and music.

Hundreds wrote in support of the new curriculum. The Reverend David Gildea, Superintendent of Catholic Schools in Syracuse, New York, found in the new approach "a welcome departure from the old ways of imparting instruction" (letter to Sister Dolores Schorsch, 1934). Joseph P. Donovan was grateful that "at last the problem of instructing the young in their religion, rather training them in their religion as far as the school is concerned, has been solved not only in principle but also in application" (Joseph P. Donovan, CM, Kenrick Seminary, Webster Grove, Missouri, letter to Sister Dolores Schorsch, 1934).

Others found the new curriculum demanding. "Because it required deeper preparation on the part of teachers, much initial resistance to the method had to be overcome," noted the "Nomination Application W. Clement Stone Endow A Dream Award" (Benedictine Sisters Archives). More highly trained than many of the Benedictine sisters, Schorsch had to deal with some amount of resistance to her new program, which was revolutionary and innovative in religious education.

The Schorsches did frequent updates based on feedback from teachers and their own observations. Beginning in 1935, the authors crisscrossed the country giving demonstrations at workshops and institutes while continuing their regularly scheduled classes at DePaul. They wrote articles for various educational journals. Both kept up a steady correspondence with authors of catechetical works and leading exponents of catechetical thinking in Europe and the United States. Well-known theologians were consulted and new concepts explored in depth.

During many of these same years—1928–42, 1944–49, and 1951–68—Schorsch also served as Supervisor of Schools for the Benedictine Sisters of Chicago. This responsibility kept her in close contact with a large pool of elementary school teachers and students and assisted in the constant updating of the series. Active in the Chicago Archdiocesan Supervisors' Association, she served as president for two years.

As supervisor, her concerns went far beyond the teaching of religion. Schorsch enrolled some of the community schools in the "Open Court" method of teaching reading. She issued a monthly newsletter in which she offered methods of teaching, practical aids, testing programs, programs for poor readers, vocabulary skills, and student achievement measurements. She checked the physical facilities of all the schools and made recommendations for improvements. Her bulletins contained lengthy notes on reading skills and suggestions for seatwork, guidance, lesson plans, and report cards. She monitored the progress of the teachers and offered assistance where it was needed.

Besides the Archdiocese of Chicago, the course was used in many dioceses of the United States. By 1938 the books were being used by two hundred thousand children, and the dioceses of Chicago, Seattle, Helena, Des Moines, and Peoria had adopted the course. Usage spread as catechists in London, the British West Indies, New Zealand, Australia, and Canada also used it; the course was adopted for use among Chinese Catholics and translated into the Chinese languages. The books were sold as cheaply as possible, workbooks for twenty-five cents and guidebooks for fifty cents. Royalties were one cent a book. These books were in use from 1934 to 1959. An advocate of using modern communication methods to teach traditional themes, Schorsch wrote the narrative for the Catholic version of *The Life of Christ in Art* (c. 1955), which was produced by Coronet Films. Sister Dolores also pioneered the use of film strips on religious subjects for the classroom, writing the scripts for *Early History of the Church* (1961), a series of eight filmstrips produced by Encyclopaedia Britannica Films, Incorporated.

Beginning in 1935 and continuing through 1957, Schorsch moved about the country at the request of dioceses, religious communities, and colleges, presenting lectures and classes on methods and materials. Back in Chicago, Schorsch was principal of St. Scholastica High School from 1942 to 1944.

Schorsch was a prolific writer. With her brother she produced a series of thirteen pamphlets on methods and techniques for the teaching of religion. Most of these were published in 1938 and 1939, with some updating done in 1949. Schorsch wrote articles for a variety of periodicals, among them the *Journal of Religious Instruction, Catholic Educator,* and *Family Digest.*

Always eager to increase her knowledge and skills, Schorsch earned an Ed.D. in education and philosophy from Loyola University Chicago in 1953 with a dissertation on "John Dewey's Philosophy of Education in Relation to Inquiry as Method and Process." While she respected Dewey, she did not agree with all of his positions. Schorsch continued to teach at DePaul University and was a member of the faculty until 1969.

In 1957, shortly before her brother died, Dolores and Alexander wrote and published *Our Lord and Our Lady,* an accomplishment that was dear to their hearts. Alexander Schorsch died August 10, 1957. His death was a severe blow to Schorsch. She lost not only a beloved brother but one who had been her mentor and her coworker for most of her life.

Schorsch promoted interfaith understanding and was chair of the Northeast Council of Interfaith Ministry for ten years. This group included Christians and Jews. In later years she served at the Howard Community Center on Chicago's North Side, actively engaged in interfaith dialogues with Jewish and Protestant groups. In 1980, at age eighty-four, Sister Dolores was volunteering at the Chicago Public Library's Legler branch, in the heart of a needy slum neighborhood, and ironically, not very far from the site where the original Chicago Benedictine sisters had ministered to newly arrived German immigrants.

Four years later Sister Dolores Schorsch died of cancer. She is buried at All Saints Cemetery, Des Plaines, Illinois. At her funeral at St. Scholastica Monastery, Jane Reilly, OSB (Order of St. Benedictine), her trusted friend and confidant, memorialized her in these words: "We all know Sister Dolores's twofold synthesis: raise the level of aspiration and recognize the power of positive thinking. What did it mean for her, particularly in her last months? It meant knowing who she was: a Schorsch, a Benedictine, a scholar, a woman of the church."

Sources. Materials on Dolores Schorsch, including letters, are in the Archives of the Benedictine Sisters of Chicago, St. Scholastica Monastery, Chicago, Illinois. A full list of Schorsch's publications includes the pamphlet series written by Dolores and Alexander Schorsch and many titles of mimeographed materials prepared by the sister and brother team for use by teachers. Schorsch coauthored with Alexander P. Schorsch, *A Course in Religion for Elementary Schools,* the DePaul Course in Religion (1934–42); *Jesu-Maria Course in Religion* (1954–63); and *Our Lord and Our Lady* (1957). Her writings include *Receiving Jesus and the Holy Spirit* (1955), *Jesus the Christ Child* (1934), *Jesus the Redeemer* (1934), *Jesus the Good Shepherd* (1934), *Jesus the High Priest* (1934), *Jesus the Life* (1934), *Jesus the King* (1935), *Jesus the Head of the Church* (1936), and *Jesus the Son of God Made Man* (1937). Her film narrative and scripts are described above.

MARY BENET MCKINNEY, OSB

SCHÜTZE, EVA LAWRENCE WATSON. *See* WATSON SCHÜTZE, EVA LAWRENCE

SEEGER, RUTH CRAWFORD
July 3, 1901–November 18, 1953
COMPOSER, TRANSCRIBER, AND ARRANGER OF AMERICAN TRADITIONAL MUSIC

Ruth Crawford Seeger had two important careers in American music: the first as a modernist composer active in the 1920s and 1930s, and the second as a folk music scholar, arranger, and editor. Seeger's coming-of-age as an American musician occurred in the heady avant-garde culture of 1920s Chicago, where she and other writers, poets, musicians, and artists forged new cultural idioms.

Ruth Crawford's early childhood was shaped by the Methodist Church. Her father, Clark Crawford, was a Methodist minister, and her mother, Clara (Graves) Crawford, was the daughter of a Methodist minister. Crawford was the second of two children; her brother, Carl, was born in 1895. Methodist ministers and their families moved every few years. Born in East Liverpool, Ohio, Crawford moved with her family to Akron in 1902; to St. Louis in 1904; to Muncie, Indiana, in 1906; to Blufton, Indiana, in 1910; and to Jacksonville, Florida, in 1912. She regarded Muncie as the most important home-base of her childhood.

Given this nomadic existence, her early music training was spotty, although Clara Crawford played the piano and found teachers for her daughter in each new place. After Clark Crawford's death in 1914, the family remained in Jacksonville, and for the first time Ruth Crawford had consistent training from serious teachers at the School for Musical Art, first with its director, Bertha Foster, and then with the Norwegian pianist, Madame Valborg Collett. After graduating from Duval High School in 1918, Crawford worked as a junior piano teacher for Foster's school. In September 1921, she moved to Chicago to enroll in a teacher training program at the American Conservatory of Music. Her mother had attended Northwestern University and encouraged Crawford to return to what she called one of the "advanced" cities of the world for what was supposed to be a one-year stay.

One year stretched into nine, for Crawford found her voice as a composer in the Chicago of the 1920s, a city that enjoyed an opulent musical life, perhaps second in the United States only to New York's. She learned the old and the new simultaneously by attending performances at MARY GARDEN's Chicago Civic Opera and at the Chicago Symphony Orchestra, which offered many premieres of both American and European compositions and had a wider, more varied repertory than that of any other major orchestra in the period. Crawford had much catching up to do, hearing Beethoven symphonies and Stravinsky's early ballets for the first time. At the American Conservatory of Music, she discovered her interest in theory and her gift for composition with her primary teachers, the composer, Adolph Weidig, and the music educator, Louise Robyn. In 1924 Crawford composed her first important composition, "Kaleidoscopic Changes—Theme and Variations with a Fugue," to complete bachelor's degree requirements. A master's degree followed in 1927, as did a Weidig gold medal in composition in 1928. Crawford joined the junior faculty of the conservatory, teaching theory as well as piano; she also taught harmony and theory at Elmhurst College.

Chicago proved decisive in other ways as well. In 1924 Crawford began to study piano with DJANE LAVOIE-HERZ, a French Canadian musician whose reputation was based mainly on her exposure to Scriabin and his circle in Brussels. Lavoie-Herz introduced Crawford to the piano music of Scriabin and to esoteric philosophy, including Theosophy and Chinese mysticism. The Herz home was a mecca for Chicago intellectuals and contemporary musicians, particularly those interested in avant-garde ideas and styles. There Crawford met two important figures, the French composer Dane Rudhyar and the American ultra-modern composer Henry Cowell. By 1926 Crawford had joined the board of Cowell's New Music Society, and Herz's prize pupil, Gitta Gradova, had played the second of Crawford's "Five Preludes for Piano" (1924–25) in a New York recital, winning a favorable review. That same year Crawford composed

"Music for Small Orchestra," probably inspired by programs of the same title organized by Eric De Lamarter for Chicago Allied Arts, a collaborative music and dance project.

Crawford also became active in the few small new-music groups that were established in Chicago in the late 1920s, among them the Pro Musica Society, established in 1927, and the Chicago chapter of the International Society for Contemporary Music, established in 1928. The latter's inaugural concert included her Sonata for Violin and Piano, a premiere that was a highlight of her early career.

When Alfred Frankenstein (who would later become a prominent arts critic) introduced Crawford to Carl Sandburg, she found both a friend and a mentor in the famous poet. In 1927 she contributed four arrangements to Sandburg's collection *The American Songbag*, which is regarded as a landmark in the discovery and dissemination of American folk songs. Crawford later referred to this experience as crucial for her own interest in traditional music. Sandburg as poet influenced her just as deeply. She used his poems as texts for almost all of her vocal compositions, including a set of "Five Songs for Mezzo Soprano and Piano" (1929).

The music Crawford wrote in Chicago between 1924 and 1929 drew on a rich synthesis of diverse influences, including not only Sandburg, but also Henry David Thoreau, Walt Whitman, the Theosophist Helena Blavatsky, and the Chinese philosopher Lao-Tse. Her approach to post-tonal idioms took as its starting point Scriabin's harmonies, Rudhyar's intuitive methods, and Carl Ruggles's dissonant counterpoint. In 1928 Henry Cowell published her second set of *Preludes for Piano*. Another early professional milestone was the premiere of the Sonata for Violin and Piano (1926) at the Copland-Sessions concert series in New York in 1927.

After the death of her mother, who had moved to Chicago in 1924 to be with her daughter, Crawford decided to leave Chicago. A summer at the MacDowell Colony in New Hampshire was followed by a year in New York, which Crawford spent studying dissonant counterpoint with Charles Seeger. Cowell had arranged both the work with Seeger and her free lodgings at the home of one of his patrons, Blanche Walton. The year's work with Seeger proved a major turning point in Crawford's musical development. She developed Seeger's methods of dissonant counterpoint into what she regarded as a distinctive medium of modern dissonant music, and her style shifted away from its dense harmonic focus to radical heterophony. "Four Diaphonic Suites" for solo or duo instruments (1930–31); a "Piano Study in Mixed Accents" (1930); "Three Songs on Poems by Carl Sandburg" (1930–32); and her most famous piece, the String Quartet 1931, were written in this new language.

Some of this music was composed in various places in Europe, rather than in New York, for in 1930 Crawford won a Guggenheim Fellowship in composition—the first woman to be so honored and the only one for the next fifteen years. She spent several months in Berlin but did not meet the city's most famous teacher, Arnold Schoenberg. Her letters from 1930 to 1931 revealed both her disappointment at the rise of neoclassicism and her own partisan attitudes toward dissonant music, which she regarded as an American competitor to Schoenberg's twelve-tone method.

Returning to New York in November 1931, Crawford lived with and then married Charles Seeger in the summer of 1932. The Great Depression changed her prospects and her own artistic priorities. How could contemporary classical music contribute to solutions to the problems of the day and be made socially relevant? She and Seeger found potential solutions in the radical Left, and Ruth Crawford Seeger essayed "proletarian" music, producing two songs on radical texts, "Chinaman! Laundryman!" and "Sacco, Vanzetti" in 1932. Both were performed at conventional modern music concerts and at the first American Workers' Music Olympiad, a festival of radical socialist and communist music groups. These songs, along with the orchestral *ostinati* she wrote for the "Three Songs on Poems by Carl Sandburg" were the last original compositions that Ruth Crawford Seeger wrote in her modern dissonant style until 1952.

When Charles Seeger took a job as the music adviser for Franklin D. Roosevelt's Resettlement Administration in 1936, the family, which by that time included two small children, Mike (born 1933) and Peggy (born 1935), moved to Washington. Exposure to indigenous traditions in the South, as well as the rising interest in American identity so characteristic of the depression period, changed the Seegers into New Deal urban folk song revivalists, who recast modernist aspirations into new oppositional forms. The more they discovered the beauty and vitality of the folk song, the more they saw its values in opposition to conventional tonal classical music, and the more actively they proselytized for its dissemination and recognition among the educated musical establishment. In 1936–37 Ruth Crawford Seeger composed twenty-two arrangements of American folk tunes for piano, nineteen of which were published posthumously. She introduced them with a statement about the kinship between contemporary and archaic musical expression and the importance of training children in their own national musical heritage.

Ruth Crawford Seeger's subsequent collaborations with the collectors John and Alan Lomax proved decisive for the kind of work that would occupy her for the rest of her life. For their anthology, *Our Singing Country* (1941), she transcribed hundreds of field recordings that the Lomaxes had collected on extensive field trips and then donated to the Archive of American Folk Song at the Library of Congress. (The archive became Ruth Crawford Seeger's unofficial workplace.) She and her husband also contributed arrangements for the Lomaxes' next anthology, *Folk Song USA* (1946). This effort laid the groundwork for Ruth Crawford Seeger's innovative work in the use of American folk song in music education, which came to fruition in the now classic *American Folk Songs for Children* (1948), *Animal Folk Songs for Children* (1950), and *American Folk Songs for Christmas* (1953). The written materials in these books, in which the practical wisdom of a teacher is combined with the insights of a composer, have endeared them to generations of professional musicians as well as to amateurs. A profound understanding of oral tradition shapes the fresh and vital piano accompaniments in these books, enhancing their pedagogical value.

Ruth Crawford Seeger had two more children by 1943 (Barbara, born 1937, and Penny, born 1943), and she helped support the family by teaching piano in the suburbs of Maryland and running music programs in a number of private schools in the area, beginning with the Silver Spring Cooperative Nursery School in 1941.

At the time of her death from intestinal cancer in Chevy Chase, Maryland, Ruth Crawford Seeger was known primarily for her work in folk music. Her reputation expanded slowly in the 1980s and 1990s through a process of recognition of her historical position as a pioneering figure in early American modernism and as one of the major female composers of the century. Performances and recordings of the String Quartet 1931 proved particularly crucial for the resurgence of interest in her music that began in the 1970s and continued as the historical record of the American experimental tradition was documented and its legacy better appreciated.

Sources. Manuscripts of scores and personal papers are held in the Music Division of the Library of Congress, which has made musical works available on microfilm. Recent CDs devoted exclusively to Crawford Seeger's work are: *Ruth Crawford: American Masters Series.* CD CRI 658 (1993) (remastering of LP recordings from the archive of Composers' Recordings Inc.); *Ruth Crawford Seeger: American Visionary,* CD Musical Heritage Society, 513493M (1993); and *Ruth Crawford Seeger — Portrait.* CD Deutsche Grammophone 449–925–2 (1997). *Five Songs on Sandburg Poems* is published by C. F. Peters. *Music for Small Orchestra* (1926 — recorded on *Premiere Performances* CD Delos 1012) and *Suite No. II for Four Strings and Piano* (1929 — recorded in *Pulse: Works for Percussion and Strings,* The New Music Consort, *Recorded Anthology of American Music,* New World Records 319, 1984), edited by Judith Tick and Wayne Schneider, are published together as volume 1 of the series Music of the United States of America (1993). Performances of the String Quartet 1931 are available by the Arditi String Quartet, Gramavision R 215 79440. *American Folksongs for Children* (1948) remained in print in the 1990s. *Animal Folksongs for Children* was reissued through the Shoe String Press, Hamden, Connecticut (1993). Mike and Peggy Seeger recorded the songs in both books on compact discs (CDs) with the same title, available from Rounder Records. Further information about Ruth Crawford Seeger's life and work can be found in Matilda Gaume's biography, *Ruth Crawford Seeger: Memories, Memoirs, Music* (1986) and her essay in *Women Making Music: The Western Art Tradition 1150–1950* (1986); and Judith Tick's biography, *Ruth Crawford Seeger: A Composer's Search for American Music* (1997). Important analytic studies include Joseph Straus, *The Music of Ruth Crawford Seeger* (1995); David Nicholls, *Experimental Music 1890–1940* (1990); Mark Nelson, "In Pursuit of Charles Seeger's Heterophonic Ideal: Three Palindromic Works by Ruth Crawford," *Musical Quarterly,* 1986; Judith Tick, "Dissonant Counterpoint Revisited: The First Movement of Ruth Crawford's *String Quartet 1931,*" in A *Celebration of Words and Music in Honor of H. Wiley Hitchcock,* ed. Richard Crawford, R. Allen Lott, and Carol J. Oja (1990); and Judith Tick, "Ruth Crawford's 'Spiritual Concept': The Sound Ideals of an Early American Modernist," *Journal of the American Musicological Society,* Summer 1991.

JUDITH TICK

SEYMOUR, FLORA WARREN SMITH
January 24, 1888–December 5, 1948

LAWYER, GOVERNMENT OFFICIAL, AUTHOR, CLUBWOMAN

Flora Warren Seymour, lawyer and author of many books and articles about American Indians, applied her legal expertise and political activism in defense of an Indian policy that "would turn all Indians into individual land owners and break up traditional tribal relations" (Prucha, 231), a policy advocated by many

FIG. 104. *Flora Seymour standing in front of a United States Indian Service vehicle.*

the Board of Indian Commissioners, a watchdog organization established by executive order in 1869. The Board of Commissioners consisted of ten individuals noted for their philanthropic and intellectual interests and abilities, who served without financial compensation. The duties of the board were to advise the Interior Secretary and the Commissioner of Indian Affairs regarding Indian policy, to oversee the disbursement of funds appropriated by Congress and distributed by the Indian Service, and to supervise the appointment of Indian Service personnel. Seymour was the only woman appointed to the board in its sixty-three year history.

According to her own calculations, Seymour visited more than two hundred Indian reservations during her tenure on the board and wrote numerous reports on health, legal, economic, religious, and educational conditions in Indian country. No romantic with respect to Indian cultures, Seymour believed that the forces of "progress" and "civilization" were inexorable; she was an impassioned advocate of the assimilation or "Americanization" of the Indian, a position she retained throughout her career as author and political activist. Against paternalism of any form, Seymour maintained that "Indians should be treated as human beings, not as museum pieces or as perpetual dependents" (*Current Biography*, 754).

Despite the declared independence of the Board of Indian Commissioners, its emphasis on assimilation was perfectly compatible with U.S. Indian policy, which was committed to the allotment of lands held by the tribes and the suppression of indigenous religions, cultural practices, and aboriginal languages, all in the supposed interest of promoting the eventual citizenship of the American Indian. The assimilationist view was not supported by most Native Americans. Soon after Seymour's appointment to the Board of Indian Commissioners, a reform movement led by John Collier, former secretary of the American Indian Defense Association, began to push for sweeping changes in U.S. Indian policy. Collier and other reformers criticized the BIA's management of Indian affairs and called for a governmental survey of conditions in Indian country. The outcome of the study was the Merriam Report. It documented appalling conditions on the reservations, advocated support for the cultural practices of tribal communities, and suggested that assimilation, the dominant Indian policy of the last century, was not working.

In response to the growing pressure for reform, President Franklin D. Roosevelt disbanded the Board of Indian Commissioners in 1933 and appointed John Collier his new commissioner of the Bureau of Indian Affairs. Collier's Indian policy, sometimes called the Indian New Deal, was based on self-determination rather than assimilation, a position still officially advocated by the BIA. While Collier was criticized by some Indian groups for his paternalistic administration of BIA programs, he correctly recognized the central importance of cultural continuity within the Indian community, a factor that well-meaning assimilationists like Seymour consistently ignored. The driving force behind Seymour's activities on the Board of Indian Commissioners was her belief in the importance of full citizenship for the American Indian, and citizenship remained one of her consuming passions.

After the Board of Indian Commissioners was disbanded, Seymour continued to argue against the Indian New Deal. She

Americans of European ancestry for most of the nineteenth century and the first decades of the twentieth.

Born in Cleveland, Ohio, to Charles Payne and Eleanor De Forest (Potter) Smith, Flora Smith later moved with her family to Colorado Springs, Colorado, where her parents were employed in the printing business. After graduating from high school, Smith attended George Washington University, Washington, D.C., where she received a B.A. degree. For the next six years she worked for the legal department of the United States Indian Service, now called the Bureau of Indian Affairs (BIA). This experience stimulated Smith's interest in the law. In 1915, she earned an LL.B. degree from the Washington College of Law, was admitted to the District of Columbia Bar, and married fellow law student George Steele Seymour. The following year the couple moved to Chicago, where Flora Seymour received an LL.M. degree from Chicago-Kent College of Law and was admitted to the Illinois Bar Association.

Between 1919 and 1922, Seymour argued cases for the Indian Service before the U.S. Supreme Court; she was one of the first women lawyers to be admitted to the Supreme Court Bar. In 1922, President Warren G. Harding appointed Seymour to believed that Collier's policies would promote geographical and cultural segregation and result in the perpetual wardship of the American Indian. An articulate speaker and lecturer, Seymour addressed Chicago clubs, societies, churches, and schools on American Indian history and U.S. Indian policy. Her numerous articles on public policy and Indian life were informed by her assimilationist views.

In addition to Seymour's lifelong interest in contemporary Indian affairs, she also developed an interest in the historical interactions between native and white people. An indefatigable author, she published some twenty books, despite the fact that she often had to convince prospective publishers of the market for historical works about Indians. Ironically, Seymour, who was often chastised by political opponents for her hard-edged pragmatism about Indian affairs, was just as often characterized by reviewers as a romantic idealist, despite the fact that she argued in print for less sentimentality and more historical accuracy in works about the American Indian. As Seymour herself put it, "I seem to have the misfortune to be considered by my conservative friends as a wild-eyed radical, while my radical friends look upon me as a hidebound conservative. For this I blame my parents, who told me when I was a child to listen to both sides and make up my own mind about things" (quoted in *Current Biography*, 755).

Critical opinion about her work was often divided. For example, while John G. Neihardt, poet and author of *Black Elk Speaks*, considered her best-known book, *The Story of the Red Man* (1929), to be a history of Native Americans that was encompassing as well as accurate, her political opponent, John Collier, claimed it exhibited "unconscious race prejudice" (review, *New York Herald Tribune*, September 29, 1929). Other Seymour books widely read and reviewed were *Lords of the Valley: Sir William Johnson and His Mohawk Brothers* (1930), *Women of Trail and Wigwam* (1930), and *Indian Agents of the Old Frontier* (1941).

Although Seymour's own literary ventures were confined to journalism and history, she was deeply interested in books of all kinds. In 1919, Seymour and her husband George founded an international literary organization called the Order of the Bookfellows, which operated out of the Seymour home in Chicago's Hyde Park neighborhood. Bookfellows considered itself a democratic organization; its only requirement for membership was a love of books. Nonetheless, many well-known literary figures were among the club's members; they included Van Wyck Brooks, Dorothy Canfield Fisher, Hamlin Garland, Ellen Glasgow, John G. Neihardt, Conrad Richter, Edwin Arlington Robinson, Carl Sandburg, Sara Teasdale, and Carl Van Doren.

Committed to reading, writing, and "bookly fellowship," Bookfellows produced a monthly literary magazine of fiction, poetry, and essays called the *Step Ladder*, which was edited for thirty years by Flora Seymour. Mandated to found libraries that would promote reading in a society that was rapidly developing alternative means of entertainment, education, and communication, the organization prided itself on its position against commercialism.

A devoted daughter and lifelong reader, Seymour had a longstanding dream of founding a library in honor of her mother. After her mother's death in 1925, Seymour and her sib-lings donated their mother's private library and family home in Colorado Springs to the Bookfellows Foundation for use as the Eleanor De Forest Smith Memorial Library. Despite years of planning and fund-raising, the Colorado library never came to fruition. Next Seymour made plans to build a similar library in Cass County, Michigan, some three hours east of Chicago. The nucleus of the proposed library was to include Smith's two thousand volume collection and five thousand books donated by the members of Bookfellows. HARRIET MONROE of *Poetry* magazine and members of the Chicago Poetry Circle, of which Flora Seymour was a member, attended the 1932 groundbreaking ceremony. The rustic retreat finally opened to Bookfellows members in the late 1930s but never solidified as a working library. The outbreak of World War II prevented further development plans.

A dedicated clubwoman, Seymour was actively involved in local and national organizations such as the Women's Bar Association, the Illinois Bar Association, and the Suffrage Amendment Alliance. In addition, she served as vice-president of the Women's Chamber of Commerce in Chicago, president of the Bureau of Volunteer Social Services, recording secretary for the National Federation of College Women, corresponding secretary of the Illinois Woman's Press Association, and dean of the Chicago-Kent chapter of Kappa Beta Pi.

George Seymour died on June 21, 1945, after a prolonged illness. Seymour herself died three years later. A childless couple, the Seymours left most of their worldly possessions to the Bookfellows. A few years after Flora Seymour's death, trustees of the Bookfellows donated the organization's five thousand volumes and most of its assets to Knox College, Galesburg, Illinois, and the collection is housed in the Knox College Library. The Bookfellows Room, an elegant reading room dedicated to the memory of Bookfellows' founders, is all that remains of Seymour's desire to leave a memorial to her mother.

In her writing about American Indians, Seymour worked to avoid romanticism and sentimentality on the one side and rancor and dismissal on the other. While some of the views expressed in her books and articles may strike current readers as wrongheaded, if not ethnocentric, Seymour seems to have genuinely believed that cultural assimilation was in the best interests of all Native Americans. She wrote about the Indian past and worked actively for an Indian future from the point of view of her values, using her many political and civic connections to further the agenda in which she so deeply believed. Never a one-issue woman, Seymour also maintained a lifelong interest in literature as well as in the social and political affairs of Chicago and Illinois.

Sources. The papers of George Steele Seymour and Flora Warren Seymour, Knox College Library, include diaries, scrapbooks, correspondence with family, friends, publishers, authors, and political figures, newspaper clippings, and Seymour family records. The papers of Hamlin Garland, Knox College Library, include correspondence with Flora Seymour. Seymour's numerous articles on public policy and Indian life include "Our Indian Land Policy," *Journal of Land and Public Utility Economics*, January 1926; "New Trails for the Indian Woman," *Women's Press*, June 1930; "Red Man and White," *Religious Education*, February 1931; "Cooperative Shamanism," *Journal of Clinical Medicine*, 1935; and "Thunder over the South West," *Saturday Evening Post*, April 1939.

Her books include *Lords of the Valley: Sir William Johnson and His Mohawk Brothers* (1930), *Women of Trail and Wigwam* (1930), and *Indian Agents of the Old Frontier* (1941). See *Current Biography* (1942) for a short entry on Seymour. Other books consulted include Francis Paul Prucha, *Indian Policy in the United States: Historical Essays* (1981); and Vine Deloria Jr., *American Indian Policy in the Twentieth Century* (1985).

ELIZABETH BLAIR

SHARNOVA, SONIA
May 2, 1896–December 3, 1988
OPERA SINGER, VOICE TEACHER

Sonia Sharnova, contralto with the Chicago Civic Opera Company, was born Ethel Shapiro in Chicago to Joseph Shapiro, a furniture mover, and Leah (Berg) Shapiro. Her parents were Russian Jews who encouraged the musical aspirations of their five children. Ethel Shapiro's brother, David, was a professional violinist with the San Francisco Symphony Orchestra; her older brother, Irving, a noted urologist with Michael Reese Hospital, was an amateur violinist in the Businessman's Orchestra of Chicago; sister Sophie was an amateur singer; and Miriam, the youngest sibling, was a great lover of the musical arts.

Ethel Shapiro studied both voice and piano as a child; in her youth she began singing in the choir at Temple Emmanuel on Chicago's West Side. She also attended performances of the Chicago Opera Company and was intrigued with such stars as ROSA RAISA and MARY GARDEN. She was "fascinated with the dramatic as well as the musical possibilities in opera" (Andries, "North Shore Arts"). She was encouraged to pursue vocal studies in Europe, which her aunt, Sonia Roberg, subsidized. Roberg helped raise Shapiro and her siblings after the death of her mother. Out of affection and gratitude for her help, Shapiro took her aunt's first name for her stage name, and changed Shapiro to what she felt was the more exotic, Russian-sounding name of Sharnova.

From 1925 until 1927, Sonia Sharnova studied and sang professionally in France, Italy, and Germany. While in Europe she married Lester J. Luechauer, a singer. Sharnova studied with Jean de Reszke in Nice, France, where she made her professional debut in 1925. While in the south of France, she sang with Reynaldo Hahn in Cannes and for assorted dignitaries and members of royalty. Following de Reszke's advice, Sharnova went to Milan, Italy, that same year, where, at the Carcano Theatre she sang the role of Aszucena in Giuseppe Verdi's *Il Trovatore*. Performances in Italy during this time included more productions of *Il Trovatore* and a two-month engagement at Livorno. Unfortunately, her much desired engagement with Arturo Toscanini at La Scala fell through. She left for Germany.

Later Sharnova recalled that the Italians were very covetous of roles in the Italian houses, and what seemed to her at the time to be a misfortune was in actuality a great blessing. In Berlin she discovered Richard Wagner, and she later said, "A whole world opened up to me" (quoted in Andries). While in Germany, Sharnova learned some of the composer's mezzo-soprano roles and many German lieder. However, with the rise of anti-Semitism and stormy political conditions in Germany in the late 1920s, Sharnova decided to return home. Her husband, who

was not Jewish, did not feel the urgency to leave, and the couple separated. Their divorce became final in 1930.

Upon her return to America in 1929, Sharnova became a member of the German Opera Company of New York, with which she toured the United States in 1930. She joined the Chicago Civic Opera Company in October 1930 and made her Chicago debut on November 29 of that year as Ulrica in Verdi's *Ballo in Maschera*. During her early years with this company, Sharnova sang opposite many other famous prima donnas, including Rosa Raisa, internationally known Lotte Lehmann, Maria Jeritza, and Kirsten Flagstad. Sharnova's principal roles during the early 1930s included Ulrica; Ortrud in Wagner's *Lohengrin* and Magdalena in *Die Meistersinger*; La Cieca in Amilcare Ponchielli's *La Gioconda*; Herodias in Richard Strauss's *Salome* opposite Maria Jeritza; and Amneris in Verdi's *Aida* opposite Rosa Raisa. On December 2, 1935, Sharnova was part of the American premiere of Ottorino Respighi's *La Fiamma*, in which she sang the role of Agnese.

Throughout her career, Sonia Sharnova made contributions to Chicago's Jewish community. She gave many recitals that featured Jewish folk music and sang at Chicago Sinai Congregation, a liberal Reform congregation known for its liturgical music.

On May 15, 1936, Sharnova married I. T. Feingold, president of the Chicago-based furniture manufacturing company J. L. Chase. Sharnova was introduced to Feingold by his daughter, Henrietta Chase, who was also a gifted Chicago opera singer and whom Sharnova had met earlier in New York.

Sharnova's remaining seasons with the Chicago Civic Opera included the role of Fricka (opposite Flagstad's Brünnhilde in Wagner's *Die Walküre*); Herodias in *Salome*; Katrinka in Friedrich Smetana's *The Bartered Bride*; the witch in Engelbert Humperdinck's *Hänsel und Gretel*; and Dame Quickly in Verdi's *Falstaff*. Although in her publicity advertisements Sharnova was celebrated as a great Wagnerian contralto, her Wagnerian roles with the Civic Opera, unfortunately, were few. She sang the roles of Waltraute in *Götterdämmerung*, Erda in *Die Walküre*, and Brangäne in *Tristan und Isolde* with the German Grand Opera Company of New York. In the late 1930s, Sharnova appeared a few times on the recital stage singing primarily German lieder to great acclaim.

Sharnova's voice was described by *Chicago Daily News* critic Eugene Stinson as "dark and brilliant" ("Music Views") and by *Chicago American* critic Herman Devries as "rich and powerful" ("Music in Review"). She was also praised for her intelligence and expressiveness as a singer. Sharnova's voice has been compared with that of Jessye Norman.

In 1941, Sharnova's final season, she appeared with the Chicago Civic Opera in *Lohengrin* and *Falstaff*. After her retirement from the stage, she devoted her time and talent to teaching voice students and enjoying her family. She was delighted to have a ready-made family when she married Feingold and was as devoted to them as they were to her. She and Feingold were happily married until his premature death of cancer in 1943. A consummate hostess, Sharnova loved to prepare dinner parties and entertain. She counted among her intimate friends many noted Chicagoans in the music and business worlds.

As a dedicated teacher, Sharnova was the first president of the Chicago Chapter of the National Association of Teachers of

Singing and she served one term as president of the Society of American Musicians. From 1974 to 1976, Sharnova was the forty-seventh president of the Musicians Club of Women in Chicago and an honorary member of Sigma Alpha Iota, the international sorority of women musicians. In addition to teaching and serving as chair of the voice department at Chicago Conservatory College (now Roosevelt University School of Music), Sharnova maintained a private studio in the Fine Arts Building in downtown Chicago, where she taught only the most serious students. Later she taught such students in her home. Among her students were Ardis Krainik, who became artistic director of the Lyric Opera of Chicago; and Edith Lang, who went on to establish her professional operatic career in Hamburg, Germany.

Sharnova taught her students how vocal production felt internally and what the student was doing physically to produce sound, an approach that has been defined as mechanistic. Always possessing a keen ear, Sharnova was able to deduce vocal problems and remedy them by means of demonstration and repetition. She championed a natural, unhindered style of vocal production. After the Chicago Conservatory closed in 1979, Sharnova continued to have a private studio in her home.

Her ninetieth birthday, May 2, 1986, was designated Sonia Sharnova Day by Mayor Harold Washington. Although she was hospitalized briefly at this time for surgery, Sharnova managed to serenade the nurses in her room with selections from *Il Trovatore*. For her age and health, her voice was still strong and sure of tone, though she confessed that if she sang too long, she became dizzy. In 1987, Sharnova was featured on Chicago's WGN News. This brief special report highlighted not only her career on the operatic stage but her tenacious commitment to teaching voice, which she sustained until her death the following year.

Sources. Sonia Sharnova's nephew, Arthur Segil, holds a small but interesting collection of mementos, including news clippings, letters, photographs, and programs. Interviews were conducted by Timothy Flynn in August 1996 with Sonia Sharnova's two surviving relatives, Arthur Segil, and her step-daughter, Thelma Feldman; and with a former student, Ian Geller, in September 1997. Articles about Sharnova include Dorothy Andries, "North Shore Arts," *Wilmette Life* and other Pioneer Press newspapers, May 4, 1972; Herman Devries, "Music in Review," *Chicago American*, May 8, 1939; Eugene Stinson, "Music Views: Singing," *Chicago Daily News*, May 8, 1939; and Cecil Smith, "Sonia Sharnova Puts Individual Touch in Songs," *Chicago Daily Tribune*, May 8, 1939. Information about Sharnova appears in K. J. Kutsch, Leo Riemens, and K. G. Saur, *Grosses Sängerlexikon: Ergänzungsband* (1991); Ronald L. Davis, *Opera in Chicago* (1966); and Ruth Klauber Friedman, *History of the Musicians Club of Women, Formerly Amateur Musical Club, Chicago, Illinois* (1975), available at CHS. An obituary appeared in the *CT*, December 5, 1988.

TIMOTHY S. FLYNN

SHARP, KATHARINE LUCINDA
May 21, 1865–June 1, 1914
LIBRARIAN, LIBRARY EDUCATOR

Katharine Lucinda Sharp, founder of the first formal school of education for librarians in the Midwest, was born in Elgin, Illinois. Her parents were John William Sharp, a commission merchant and businessman originally from Arkport, New York, and Phebe Thompson, from Dundee, Illinois. Katharine Sharp's maternal grandfather, Thomas Hinckley Thompson, was an early settler in Dundee and a county commissioner. Her brother died when he was only one or two years old, and her mother died at age thirty-three, when Katharine Sharp was seven. Sharp was raised primarily by her mother's family, since her father lived in Oakland, California, from 1874 through 1879. When he returned to Chicago, he married Charlotte Nicholson in 1880 and lived in Maywood, Illinois. Sharp's half-brother, Robert Nicholson Sharp, of whom she grew quite fond, was born in 1881.

Sharp was educated at the progressive Elgin Academy from 1872 to 1880, except for one year spent at the Oakland (California) High School, 1878–79. She received a diploma from the academy in 1880 and enrolled at the Women's College of Northwestern University in September 1881. Here she gained a strong background in languages and literature. She was active in various campus social and literary organizations and on the editorial board of the college annual, as well as vice-president of the class of 1885. As a first-year student, Sharp was a charter member and secretary of the Upsilon chapter of Kappa Kappa Gamma sorority, founded in 1882, a group primarily interested in literary activities. Sharp received a Bachelor of Philosophy degree in June 1885 with honors in general, Latin, and special scholarship. When a Phi Beta Kappa chapter was established on the Northwestern campus in 1899, members from prior classes were elected, including Sharp. She received a Master of Philosophy degree from Northwestern in 1889.

Following completion of her undergraduate education, Sharp returned to the Elgin Academy as a teacher in Latin, French, and German, remaining there from 1886 through 1887. She then became the assistant librarian of the new Scoville Institute in 1888 (later the Oak Park [Illinois] Public Library). Wishing to obtain further professional education, Sharp traveled East in the fall of 1890 and entered the second class of the pioneering New York State Library School in Albany, headed by Melvil Dewey, founder of the first school of library economy (now library science) in 1887. She was described by Dewey as "so easily first" (Grotzinger, *Power and Dignity*, 37) in a class of distinguished students. Dewey remained her mentor throughout her career. He provided the impetus for a network of colleagues that included Sharp and a number of librarians who attended school during that first decade of formal library education. After two years of study at Albany, Sharp received a Bachelor of Library Science degree in 1892. In the summer of 1891, she had organized the Adams Memorial Library in Wheaton, Illinois, and during the next summer, she set up the public library at Xenia, Ohio.

On behalf of the New York State Library School, Sharp was selected to coordinate and administer the Comparative Library Exhibit for the World's Columbian Exposition of 1893 in Chicago. The exhibit contained samples, models, and photographs of library furniture, architecture, forms, appliances, equipment, and examples of library administrative procedures. Sharp also presented a paper, "The University Extension Movement in America," delivered at the University Extension Congress in conjunction with the exposition in July 1893.

In January 1893, Sharp was appointed librarian and head of the department of library economy at the new Armour Institute of Technology in Chicago. President Frank W. Gunsaulus, who respected books and libraries, had asked Melvil Dewey for his recommendation of the best man in America to head the new library and department. Dewey responded that "the best man in America is a woman and she's in the next room" (Grotzinger, *Power and Dignity*, 60), thus recommending Sharp for the position. The new library school, which opened in September 1893, was only the fourth such program in the United States and the first formal school of education for librarians in the Midwest.

Sharp modeled the curriculum after Dewey's Albany school and set high standards with a required entrance examination. She used the institute library as a laboratory for training assistants as well as for organizing apprentice training in libraries throughout the community. Students were able to gain practical experience by establishing libraries in schools, Sunday schools, and settlement houses such as the Northwestern University Settlement. Sharp brought in outside lecturers as well as providing extension programs at the Cleveland Public Library in December 1896 and in Geneva, Illinois, in January 1897. Between fall 1893 and spring 1897, fifty-nine librarians matriculated at Armour Institute's library economy department. The one year of instruction in three terms could be supplemented by a second year; however, many of the students moved into full-time library work after their first year because of the demand for their services.

During this time, Sharp also directed a summer school for the Wisconsin Library Association in 1895 and 1896 and lectured on library economy for the University of Chicago in 1896. In 1897, Sharp received two offers to move her school, one to the University of Wisconsin and another to the University of Illinois. Illinois president Andrew Draper, who had been the state superintendent of public instruction in New York, was a friend of Melvil Dewey, and once again Dewey recommended Sharp. Because the Illinois position offered Sharp a chance to head both the university library and the library school, she moved the Armour program to Urbana-Champaign in September 1897 with the cooperation of the Armour Institute. Sharp became professor of library economy, head librarian, and director of the Illinois State Library School (later the Graduate School of Library and Information Science). Through developing systematic procedures for book selection and acquisitions and by modernizing operational methods, Sharp built a strong collection and staff at the university library, setting the stage for the large research library at the University of Illinois in the 1990s. During her ten years at Illinois, her staff grew from three to fifteen and the number of volumes increased from 37,000 to 96,000.

Sharp promoted library development and extension throughout the state of Illinois. Her school served as an informal bureau providing information on request. She wrote *Illinois Libraries* (1906–1908), a five-volume history of all libraries in the state, for which she earned a master's degree in library science from the New York State Library School in 1906.

Sharp was committed to the value of formal preparation to help promote the acceptance of librarianship as an important new professional opportunity for young women. She established a full degree program and sought to increase the value of the education by raising the admission requirement to two years of college work followed by two years of library courses, to result in the

Bachelor of Library Science degree. In 1903, the entrance requirements were raised to three years of college. Although she advocated for a graduate degree in library science, especially at the 1901 meeting of the Association of Collegiate Alumnae, this development did not occur until after she had left the school.

Sharp had an almost missionary zeal toward librarianship and considered it one of the most compelling forces in society, second only to the church in its ability to do good. She encouraged her students to hold high ideals and had much influence on the young women with whom she came in contact. She was a strong role model for many of them, including Margaret Mann and Isadore Mudge, who became well known in the library profession. Harriet Howe, a student and later colleague of Sharp, wrote about her "criticalness, concentration, accuracy, judgment, adaptability, professional knowledge, and forcefulness" (Howe, 171). Sharp was among the first librarians to realize that professional networks were essential. She was in constant written and verbal communication with former students and other library leaders. She wrote extensive letters of recommendation for employment, recommended salaries, and was a mentor to many graduates who wrote to her from their jobs for guidance and advice.

Much of Sharp's networking was done within the many professional associations in which she was active. These included the American Library Association, where she served on the Council from 1895 to 1905 and as vice-president in 1898 and 1907; the Illinois Library Association, where she served as president in 1903; and the Chicago Library Club. She attended the Second International Conference of Librarians in London in 1897. She was a member of the Bibliographic Society of America and was selected as a fellow of the American Library Institute in 1906. She was also national president of the Kappa Kappa Gamma sorority 1894–96. Even with her many professional and sorority leadership commitments, she found time to be active within the University of Illinois community and the local Episcopal church.

By 1907, the physical and emotional strain of her demanding professional duties began to take a toll on Sharp's health. Ever since a bout with typhoid fever in 1896 while she was creating the Armour Institute's library program, she had had periods of ill health from which she never fully recovered. Finally in January 1906, she took a leave of absence from her position at the University of Illinois library. Her ill health was compounded by personal losses: in 1905 her father died, followed in 1906 by her brother, the last member of her immediate family. Exhausted and grieving, Sharp went to stay with Melvil Dewey and his family at their home on Lake Placid, New York, to recuperate, as she had done on many previous occasions. She returned to her job at Illinois in May only to face increased pressure from her administrative duties as director of the University Library, which kept her from devoting as much attention and time as she wished to give to her real passion, the library school. The tensions created by the dual positions she held compelled her to resign from the university in September 1907. In recognition of her service, the university awarded her an honorary Master of Arts degree.

After her resignation, Sharp returned to Lake Placid to live with the Deweys, who had become her second family. Sharp, who never married, found a congenial home with her longtime mentor, his wife, Anne, and their children. The Deweys had founded the Lake Placid Club, a private resort owned by shareholders who built vacation homes on land Dewey had purchased. Sharp appreciated the scenic beauty of the area, the peaceful atmosphere of the community, and the friendship of the Deweys, and she became a shareholder and vice-president of the club, handling a variety of administrative duties.

Although many of her friends expected her to go on with her professional library career, Sharp became vitally involved in directing the activities of the Lake Placid Club, which grew rapidly over the second decade of the twentieth century, developing into a cultural center and conference site. Her work with the club was tragically cut short when she was seriously injured in an automobile accident in the Adirondack Mountains in May 1914, shortly after her forty-ninth birthday. She died a few days later in Saranac Lake, New York, of a massive brain concussion. After a special memorial service at Lake Placid, she was buried in the family plot at the Dundee, Illinois, cemetery. Her former colleagues in the University of Illinois Senate recognized her in a memorial. Later, a bronze bas-relief portrait by sculptor Lorado Taft, located in the University of Illinois Graduate School of Library and Information Science, perpetuated her memory; it was given by her former students and dedicated March 12, 1922, by the library school alumni association. The inscription sums up her contributions: "Nobility of character and grace of person were united with intellectual vigor and scholarly attainments. She inspired her students and associates with sound standards of librarianship and ideals of service." Her legacy lives on; in 1995 the students at the University of Illinois Graduate School of Library and Information Science named a new electronic journal of student papers the *Katharine Sharp Review*, in honor of the founder of their school.

Sources. The Univ. of Illinois, Urbana-Champaign Library holds a collection of Katharine L. Sharp Papers. Additional Sharp material can be found in the Melvil Dewey Papers, Columbia University. Writings by Sharp include: "The A.L.A. Library Exhibit at the World's Fair," *Library Journal*, August 1893; "The University Extension Movement in America," *University Extension World*, September 1893; "The Department of Library Science of Armour Institute, Chicago," *Library Journal*, May 1894; "Librarianship as a Profession," *Public Libraries*, January 1898; and *Illinois Libraries* (1906–08). Laurel Grotzinger's biography, *The Power and the Dignity: Librarianship and Katharine Sharp* (1966), contains citations for all of Sharp's writings. Grotzinger has also written many articles and biographical entries on Sharp, as well as essays on the development of the profession of librarianship and women's role in it, including: "The Proto-Feminist Librarian at the Turn of the Century: Two Studies," *Journal of Library History*, July 1975; "Women Who 'Spoke for Themselves,'" *College & Research Libraries*, May 1978; "Remarkable Beginnings: The First Half Century of the Graduate School of Library and Information Science," in *Ideals and Standards: The History of the University of Illinois Graduate School of Library and Information Science, 1893–1993*, ed. Walter C. Allen and Robert F. Delzell (1993); and "Invisible, Indestructible Network: Women and the Diffusion of Librarianship at the Turn of the Century," in *Women's Work: Vision and Change in Librarianship*, ed. Laurel Grotzinger, James V. Carmichael Jr., and Mary Niles Maack (1994). See also Harriet E. Howe, "Katharine Lucinda Sharp," in *Pioneering Leaders in Librarianship*, ed. Emily Miller Danton (1953). For further background reading, see Joan Passet,

"Entering the Professions: Women Library Educators and the Placement of Female Students, 1887–1912," *History of Education Quarterly*, Summer 1991.

MARGARET MYERS

SHAW, ANNIE CORNELIA
September 16, 1852–August 31, 1887
ARTIST

Annie Cornelia Shaw's life as an artist was short but prolific. A catalog of her posthumous exhibit at the Art Institute of Chicago the year of her death listed 270 oil paintings. Shaw was born in Troy, New York, the second daughter of Dr. S. W. and Lois M. Shaw. The family moved to Illinois where, by the age of twelve, Annie Shaw had already evidenced a talent for art, submitting a pencil drawing to the art division of the 1864 Illinois State Fair that won a silver medal.

Shaw was fortunate to be in Chicago where opportunities for art education were developing in the 1860s. Although the nation was engaged in the Civil War, citizens starved for works of beauty and culture flocked to expositions and fairs to purchase art as well as more basic commodities. Chicago's growth as a commercial entrepôt made it an important art market that attracted artists trained in Europe and the eastern states. Such an individual, Henry Chapman Ford, a landscape artist originally from Livonia, New York, relocated to Chicago during the Civil War. At age sixteen, Shaw began to study with Ford at the Chicago Academy of Design. Begun in 1866 and incorporated March 16, 1869, the academy had an impressive art faculty that included Ford; sculptor Leonard Wells Volk; James F. Gookins, a painter of historical and mythological scenes, who was American-born but trained in Munich; the German-born and German-trained portrait painter C. F. Schwerdt, who arrived in Chicago in 1869; and transplanted Bostonian portraitist George P. A. Healy. What classes Shaw took is unknown. The academy offered "'Life,' 'Antique,' and 'Rudimentary' drawing" (Andreas, vol. 2, 558), and, in the first years, when she was a student, there was no tuition; but monthly dues of one dollar were collected from each artist member. It was 1868, the same year that Shaw began formal classes with the Chicago Academy, when the Pennsylvania Academy of Fine Arts opened its life classes to women. (Cooper Union in New York began admitting women art students in 1860.)

Shaw was primarily interested in painting landscapes. She exhibited her *View on the Des Plaines* in 1873 at the second annual Chicago Inter-State Industrial Exposition, run by Chicago artists and business owners and hosted in a large exposition building on the lakefront. The galleries displayed oil and watercolor paintings, engravings, statuary, and bronzes. Private galleries, art associations, and fairs in pre–museum era Chicago proliferated as the rising fortunes of Chicago business owners made private art collection affordable and desirable. In this expansive market, local artists' works were in demand. Shaw exhibited at the Inter-State Industrial Expositions in 1875, 1881, 1882, and 1883.

Annie Shaw's first studio was established in 1874 in Chicago. Although female artists were in the minority and did not achieve the dominant place in the art world that their male counterparts inhabited, they formed a significant minority of students, teachers, and practitioners. CORNELIA FASSETT entered her portraits and paintings in the Chicago Academy of Design's exhibitions, having been admitted as an associate member in 1874. The following year Annie Shaw was elected an associate member of the Chicago Academy of Design and four years later was elected to full status as an academician.

The Centennial Exposition held in Philadelphia in 1876 provided an opportunity for women artists to display their work in a national setting. Shaw's painting *An Illinois Prairie* was exhibited there. That same year the Chicago *Inter-Ocean* noted that Shaw's painting *Summer Afternoon* was featured in the window of Jansen, McClurg & Co.'s bookstore. The small painting, referred to as a "little gem," was described as "the strongest and most expressive picture that has yet come from the easel of this rising young artist" (February 19, 1876). The scene was a western prairie with men haying. "The excellence . . . consists," the review continued, "in the vigorous and generous manner with which [Shaw] has used her colors."

Shaw's works were exhibited regularly in Chicago and eastern U.S. cities. She exhibited with the National Academy of Design in New York City (1878, 1880, 1883, 1884). At the Pennsylvania Academy of Fine Arts (1880, 1881, 1883), *After the Shower*, *In the Clearing*, and *The Oak* were shown. Some of her frequently exhibited works in this period include *On the Calumet*; *Willow Island, Keene Valley, New York*; *In the Rye Field*; *Close of a Summer Day*; *Ebb-Tide on the Coast of Maine*; *Head of a Jersey Bull*. In addition to her landscape work, she became known for painting animals. Distinguishing herself from artists of the period who specialized in domestic genre painting, Shaw followed the model of the landscape artist and took summer excursions to Mackinac Island in Michigan, the Adirondacks, and the coast of Maine. Shaw's work was executed primarily in oil, although she worked in watercolor and tried her hand at etching as well.

A reporter with the *Boston Evening Transcript* discussed, in February 1885, Shaw's painting of several old willow trees in a crowded swamp. The painting, then being exhibited at Doll and Richards' Gallery, was deemed startling, daring, and bold. The article noted that Shaw, in seeking a rich tone, gave up "purity" and "delicacy." Pure and delicate were adjectives regularly associated with the work of women artists, and Shaw appeared to have departed from the feminine model as defined by the art convention of the times. She was in a position to study and absorb the work of major American artists, having opened a studio in New York City in 1881 and one in Boston from 1884 to 1885. Shaw's use of a rapid brushstroke and work *en plein air*—in the open air—echo the impressionistic style with which she may have become familiar in Boston, since it was the first city in America to embrace impressionism. Conceived in France during the last third of the nineteenth century, impressionism used short brush strokes of vivid color to recreate the impression of light on objects. The titles of many of Shaw's works indicate an interest in the atmospheric effects of light, color, and shadow akin to that of the impressionists: *Fading Light*, *Nature's Coloring*, *Rich Tints of October*, *Hazy Morning*, *A Hazy Afternoon*, *Sunset on the Marshes*, *August on the Marsh Lands*, and twenty-two *Cloud Studies*. Although knowledge of Shaw's life is scant, a *Catalog of Paintings, Studies and Sketches of Annie C. Shaw*,

published posthumously, provides a clear vision of her productivity. The catalog was printed in conjunction with a special exhibition of her work on December 15, 1887, at the Art Institute of Chicago. One of the purposes of the exhibition was to dispose of the paintings of the recently departed young artist, hence all of the approximately three hundred pieces, including 270 paintings, were for sale. The catalog noted that "Miss Shaw's last works" were painted "in the fall of 1886." The prices in the catalog range from $5 to $800, and the subjects vary from studies of the heads of cows to interior views of her studios, both in New York and Boston, to a vast range of landscapes in many sections of the United States east of the Mississippi River. Several years after the exhibition, the Art Institute of Chicago acquired two of the works, *Bull and Sheep* and *Russet Years*, but later deaccessioned them. She was elected an honorary member of the Art Institute of Chicago in 1886 and was also an honorary member of the Bohemian Club of Chicago.

Shaw executed very few portraits—the usual bread and butter of an artist's oeuvre. *The Pet* and *My Uncle* are two paintings whose titles indicate they may be portraits. Another subject supposedly common in the work of women, flower painting, is absent in the listing of Shaw's work. Mary Cassatt, the most famous American woman impressionist, used women and children as subject matter very frequently, but Shaw did not. Cassatt's world was comprised of sisters, nieces, and nephews who provided the artist with sitters and scenes familiar to her. Since we do not know enough about Shaw's family situation, it is unclear whether she was uninvolved with people, or like Claude Monet, preferred marshes, fields in harvest, landscape, and the effect of light. Ahead of her time, Shaw was painting in the impressionistic mode in America within eight to ten years after the first works of impressionism appeared in Paris in 1874.

Shaw was one of the few women to obtain full status in the prestigious Chicago Academy of Design—on equal footing with her male colleagues. When she exhibited with the New York Etching Club at the National Academy of Design in New York in 1882, she was one of two women whose work was included. Her etchings were displayed in the company of work by such established and well-recognized artists as James A. McNeill Whistler, A. F. Bellows, Jean Baptiste Camille Corot, Samuel Colman, and F. S. Church. In 1909, Shaw's work was exhibited posthumously with the Boston Art Club.

Until more information comes to light about Shaw, it is difficult to analyze her work in the context of her very brief life. Her extensive oeuvre and her choice of subject matter tell much about her ability to persevere in a conservative country that did not support art as a general rule, especially the art of women. It is not known how Shaw supported herself, moving with seeming relative ease from city to city and establishing studios wherever she went. She was courageous in her decision to embrace the new style of impressionism when very few artists—male or female—were doing so, especially in the United States.

Sources. Works by Shaw are at the CHS and the Western Reserve Hist. Soc. *Sunday Stroll*, an oil on canvas painting, was exhibited at Raymond Agler Fine Arts, North Andover, Massachusetts, in 1994. Du Mouchelles Art Galleries Co. of Detroit, Michigan, sold *Cows in Meadow* in 1991. Several of her other paintings are in private collections. *Catalog of Paintings, Studies and Sketches of Annie C. Shaw* (1887) and the Chicago Academy of Design Papers are at the Ryerson Library, Art Institute of Chicago. The Chicago newspaper *Inter-Ocean* reported on her progress on February 19, 1876. Two sources for biographical information about Shaw are "Art Notes," *Graphic: An Illustrated Weekly Newspaper* [Chicago], February 6, 1892, and Charlotte Streifer Rubinstein, *American Women Artists: From Early Indian Times to the Present* (1982). Information about the Chicago art scene and the Chicago Academy of Design can be found in Alfred T. Andreas, *History of Chicago*, vols. 2 and 3 (1884); Esther Sparks, "A Biographical Dictionary of Painters and Sculptors in Illinois 1808–1945," (Ph.D. diss., Northwestern Univ., 1971); and Ralph Clarkson, "Chicago Painters," *Graphic: An Illustrated Weekly Newspaper*, February 6, 1892. See also Jim Collins, *Women Artists in America: Eighteenth Century to the Present* (1973), and Whitney Chadwick, *Women, Art, and Society* (1990, 1991).

MARIANNE BERGER WOODS

SIKES, MADELEINE WALLIN
October 12, 1868–1955
CLUBWOMAN, SETTLEMENT HOUSE RESIDENT, ACTIVIST FOR PUBLIC EDUCATION

Madeleine Wallin was born in St. Peter, Minnesota, the only child of Alfred and Ellen Gray (Keyes) Wallin. Her mother was a native of Elgin, Illinois. Wallin was raised in Fargo, North Dakota, where her father practiced law and, aside from four years at Smith College, she lived her entire life in the Middle West.

Wallin received an excellent advanced education. After graduating as valedictorian from Elgin Academy in 1887, she returned home to spend a year as a typist and stenographer in her father's law firm. In 1888 she resumed her studies, journeying east to Smith College in Northampton, Massachusetts. She returned to the Midwest two years later to finish her undergraduate education at the University of Minnesota, graduating with a degree in literature in 1892. Wallin then studied at the University of Chicago, where she earned an M.A. in history in 1894. She went to Smith College, where she had accepted a post teaching history. She taught for two years at Smith, returning again to Chicago in 1896.

Wallin belonged to that generation of middle-class white women who straddled the line, often uncomfortably, but nonetheless resolutely, between duties to marriage and family and the desire for education, accomplishment, and an independent self. While at the University of Minnesota she had contemplated a career in journalism, writing for the *Ariel*, the student newspaper, and serving on the paper's board during her senior year as the only woman member. Going to Chicago to do graduate studies, however, shifted the course of her life. In Chicago she met the man she would marry, George Cushing Sikes, a journalist and municipal reformer whom Graham Taylor later referred to as a true civic patriot. It was there also that she was introduced to the settlement house movement. Both occurrences profoundly influenced the remainder of her life. During her two years at the University of Chicago, Wallin worked on the philanthropic committee of the University's Christian Union. This group established the University of Chicago Settlement on the city's South Side, and during her time at the university Wallin worked at the settlement. Deeply impressed with the new social movement, she delivered talks on social settlements as a new philanthropy; these were printed in the Fargo, North Dakota, newspaper, the *Commonwealth*, July 22, 1895. She also spent time at Chicago's most famous settlement house, Hull-House. There she lived for a time after she returned to Chicago in 1896; she held her wedding reception at Hull-House in February 1897. Afterwards, she and George Sikes resided there for a period of time following their marriage. She never forgot the lessons in civic participation that she learned in her young adult association with the settlements.

Her decision to marry Sikes was not made without much contemplation and struggle. Letters that she and George Sikes exchanged during their courtship and early years of marriage, and letters to her father, indicate clearly that Madeleine Wallin Sikes was torn between fulfilling the ideal that it was a woman's duty to devote herself full-time to the personal orbit of family and home and her own desire to contribute directly to the life and well-being of the broader society. The birth of her son Alfred Wallin in 1898 and her daughter Eleanor in 1903 consumed much of her attention in the first years of her marriage. Gradually, however, Sikes resolved most of her qualms about dividing her life between the personal and the public, and she reinserted herself into the public life of the city.

Thus, at the turn of the century, Sikes became part of the women's municipal reform movements that spread across the country as part of a national progressive reform movement. She spent much of the rest of her life working through women's organizations in Chicago to reform the city's system of public education, to enact compulsory education laws, to obtain woman suffrage, and to outlaw child labor. Toward the end of her life she engaged in the debate over universal health care in the United States.

Sikes's engagement in municipal work after her marriage began in 1899 when she joined the Chicago branch of the Association of Collegiate Alumnae (ACA, later the American Association of University Women—AAUW). Sikes's parents had instilled in her a profound belief in the value of education. They had supported her desires to obtain university degrees far beyond what the vast majority of women achieved in the late nineteenth century. As a woman activist in the twentieth century, Sikes translated her belief in education into a lifelong crusade to improve public education and to bring its benefits to all children. In 1900, she chaired the Chicago ACA's committee studying education legislation, compulsory education, and child labor, working with LUCY FLOWER and JULIA LATHROP. The following year the good-government reform group, the Civic Federation, asked her to serve on a Citizen's Committee to study the problems of public education. From that moment, Sikes moved steadily into public affairs. Sikes became part of a coalition of women's clubs and organizations organized to support child labor and compulsory education laws that included CORNELIA DE BEY, ELLEN HENROTIN, and Harriet M. Van der Vaart, as well as Lathrop and Flower. The recently formed Congress of Illinois Mothers, the Federation of Women's Clubs, and the Association of Collegiate Women participated in a major conference held in Chicago in April 1902— seven years before the first White House Conference on Children—to set an agenda to improve the conditions of children and prevent juvenile delinquency. Julia Lathrop spoke on the problem of the boy, FLORENCE KELLEY discussed child labor, and Madeleine Wallin Sikes commented on compulsory education. That year Sikes wrote a widely distributed pamphlet on child labor legislation for the National Consumers' League.

In order to educate herself better on the subject, Sikes used the research skills she learned while in college to collect and compile statistics and reports on child labor and education laws. She corresponded with women across the country who were doing similar work, and she spread her message as a tireless speaker before local and national women's organizations. She coauthored with Josephine Goldmark the *Child Labor Legislation Handbook*, also printed and distributed by the National Consumers' League. In 1905, Sikes chaired the Committee on Education of the League of Cook County Clubs. Speaking to the Woman's Club of the First Congregational Church in 1907, Sikes recommended the establishment of industrial schools. She became a member of the Committee of the Department of Backward, Truant and Delinquent Children, associated with the National Conference of Charities and Corrections.

Sikes joined the Woman's City Club of Chicago when it was founded in 1910 and participated in the reformist culture of women's clubs at the neighborhood, citywide, state, and national levels. That same year she urged fellow members of the Austin Woman's Club to work for suffrage; Sikes served as president of the club in 1912. She was a member of the Chicago Settlement League, and she belonged to the Illinois Federation of Women's Clubs and the League of Cook County Clubs; both organizations were dedicated to coordinating the work of the hundreds of women's clubs that were bringing women more directly into municipal work to reform existing social, economic, and political conditions in Chicago.

Sikes believed that all college-educated women, with the knowledge and skills they had acquired in their education, owed it to society to play an active role in civic affairs. She also believed that in order to have this role, activist women had to use their female organizations as the means to participate more fully in municipal affairs. In 1905, while serving as chair of the education legislation committee for the national ACA, she developed a plan for bringing together the work of all local branches into a national effort to effect education reform. Her plan was to coordinate all local branches to train their members to campaign actively for federal education legislation and to monitor closely all state legislation and the activities of local school boards. Working in the Chicago branch, Sikes kept the city's residents apprised of the activities of the Chicago City Council and the Board of Education. A strong supporter of ELLA FLAGG YOUNG, the controversial superintendent of Chicago's public schools from 1903 to 1915, Sikes, as a member of the Chicago ACA, opposed Young's resignation as superintendent and tried to find a solution to the impasse between the reform-minded professional Young and the council politicians and mayor responsible for the superintendent's appointment and budget.

Sikes's dedication to education brought her into other areas of civic work. Although she came rather slowly, in comparison to other activist Chicago women, to believe in woman suffrage, beginning in 1909 she worked actively for suffrage; she had come to realize that little could be accomplished in true municipal reform without the power of the ballot. She was especially anxious to secure municipal suffrage as the most efficacious way for women to implement their proposed education programs. As part of her new recognition of the need for extensive political activity, Sikes also recognized that reform could not be secured in one problem area without reforming other problems simultaneously. From her position on the ACA committee on education legislation she worked with other activist Chicago women, including JANE ADDAMS, MARGARET DREIER ROBINS, AGNES NESTOR, and ANNA NICHOLES, to coordinate Chicago women's efforts to secure new state legislation regulating education, working conditions for women, child labor, and woman suffrage, among other measures.

Once the legislature gave Illinois women the vote in local and federal elections in 1913, Sikes continued to support municipal efforts and candidates for reform, although she never seemed to have engaged directly in political party affairs. In 1914 she served as chair of the 33rd Ward women's Civic League and was a member of the Women's Nonpartisan Sanitary District Campaign Committee. In 1919 she belonged to the Woman's Campaign Committee for Charles Merriam's unsuccessful mayoral campaign. Merriam, a political scientist and University of Chicago professor, was a leading progressive municipal reformer. In 1920, she headed the Chicago Woman's Club subcommittee to study the issue of municipal home rule as part of the club's participation in the effort to write a new state constitution.

Keeping within her focus on women's organizations and women's political efforts, Sikes joined the Illinois League of Women Voters after it was organized in 1920. Within the organization she continued to speak to women's organizations in Chicago and Cook County, especially about the problems of the Chicago public schools. This concern led her to serve on the Council and Executive Committee of the Cook County League of Women Voters from 1928 to 1931. On February 13, 1933, she contributed a guest editorial to the *Chicago Daily News* in which she scoffed at the dearly held notion in Chicago's business community that the public schools should be run by businessmen. She labeled businessmen more of a problem than an asset to schools and declared that "no amount spent on buildings and equity, or operation compares with the importance of the instructional service. The teacher and the pupils make the school." In her later years, Sikes decreased her public activities but retained her ties to women's organizations and continued to speak out for the need for women and society as a whole to work to better the human condition. Following the death of her husband, she moved to San Antonio, Texas. Sometime in the early 1950s Sikes became interested in the new British national health system. She wrote in defense of a universal health insurance system and countered the American Medical Association's objections to a plan for the United States. Sikes thought that access to health care should be every person's right.

Madeleine Wallin Sikes was an active, tireless, and influential political activist. She worked in the early twentieth-century women's clubs of Chicago to promote reform of government and to encourage an educated citizenry to participate in civic matters and in the exercise of the franchise. Her work for the public schools and for legislation to protect women and children in the workplace was based on an expanded conception of government's responsibility for the safety and welfare of its citizens, a concept she shared with the leading progressive reformers in Chicago.

Sources. The Madeleine Wallin Sikes Papers are at the CHS. Included in this collection is correspondence with her parents and her husband, as well as miscellaneous other correspondence; reports and accounts of her activities within the various women's organizations; copies of speeches and papers. There is also a smaller Wallin Collection at UC Spec. Coll. Mention of her activities with the Illinois League of Women Voters can be found in that group's papers at the CHS. Karen M. Mason, "Testing the Boundaries: Women, Politics, and Gender Roles in Chicago, 1890–1930" (Ph.D. diss., Univ. of Michigan, 1991), examines Sikes as one of four case studies of activist Chicago women. Steven J. Diner, *A City and Its Universities: Public Policy in Chicago, 1892–1919* (1980), includes Madeleine Wallin Sikes as one of the leading women reformers in Chicago between 1890 and 1920.

MAUREEN A. FLANAGAN

SIMONS, MAY WOOD
1873(?)–December 3, 1948
SOCIAL REFORMER, WRITER, TEACHER

During a public career that spanned nearly half a century, catapulting her from a one-room Wisconsin schoolhouse to the University of Chicago and Northwestern University and ranging from membership in the Socialist Party to the League of Women Voters, May Wood Simons remained dedicated to the ideals of sexual equality and social justice. Along the way, she developed nationally acclaimed programs for the Americanization of immigrants and the political education of women, taught economics in high school and college, and published several notable works.

Eleanor May Wood was born in Baraboo, Wisconsin, the youngest of seven children of Philip Avery and Anna (Crook) Wood. Her father, the son of English immigrants, was a bookkeeper in a local woolen mill, while her mother was descended from colonial American stock. Both had moved to Wisconsin from Delaware County, New York, in 1866. After graduating from Baraboo High School in 1891, May Wood taught school in rural North Freedom, Wisconsin, until 1893, when she enrolled in Northwestern University, Evanston, Illinois, with the goal of becoming a medical missionary. A "B" student and the first Northwestern pledge to Pi Beta Phi, an exclusive social sorority, Wood struggled financially and intellectually in her new environment. She found herself in conflict over the theory of evolution and the fundamentalist Presbyterian teachings of her youth. When her two brothers-in-law, members of Northwestern's theology faculty, engaged in a bitter and protracted dispute over translation of the Gospel of John, May Wood withdrew from college in 1895. Returning to Wisconsin that summer, she taught mathematics and history at Baraboo High School before marrying her high school sweetheart, Algie Martin Simons, on June 15, 1897. The two had maintained close contact since graduation; he had introduced her to readings in history, economics, and sociology that helped her to shake her philosophical moorings and to awaken in her a devotion to socialism and feminism.

The young couple moved to Evanston, Illinois, where May Simons served as a volunteer for United Charities. She also volunteered at the University of Chicago Settlement. She and her husband soon joined the Socialist Labor Party (SLP), determined to wage "a fierce rebellion against the conditions that made people come begging for a pittance" (May Wood Simons, quoted in Huston, 32). When Algie Simons became editor of *Workers' Call*, the SLP weekly, in 1899, May Simons contributed numerous educational and feminist pieces, including translations of articles written by German revisionist socialists. She helped organize a Socialist Women's Society in Chicago that pressed for woman suffrage, equal pay for equal work, and opportunities for women outside the home. Within a few years, May Simons was widely recognized as one of U.S. socialism's foremost champions of equal rights and woman suffrage.

In 1899, May Simons published her most famous work, *Woman and the Social Problem*, a pamphlet written to inform the American woman of "her economic condition, the effects of capitalistic industry upon her and the changes that socialism would make in her position" (reprinted in *Flawed Liberation*, 186). Simons argued that modern industrial capitalism had made working-class women "dependents of wage slaves" (p. 190) and turned their homes into sweatshops where even little children "work from daylight until far into the night for a starvation wage" (p. 192). Proclaiming that "it is to socialism alone that the home life must look for the rescue and purification" (p. 192), May Simons urged women to take an "active part in this proletarian movement" (p. 196) and "to unite with laboring men in the struggle for economic freedom" (p. 196).

The couple's brief career with *Workers' Call* ended in December 1899 after a fierce battle between Algie Simons and SLP leader Daniel De Leon over whether or not to cooperate with the newly formed Social Democratic Party of Eugene V. Debs and Victor L. Berger. In the same year, the accidental death of their eighteen-month-old son, Laurence, who swallowed a lethal dose of poison found in the medicine cabinet at the home of friends, devastated the young parents and caused them to adopt a highly protective attitude toward their daughter, Miriam Eleanor, who was born in 1900. Until Miriam's 1925 marriage to Gerald Leuck, all three kept in almost constant contact, writing warm, effusive, daily letters to one another on those rare occasions of separation. For several decades, May Simons did a remarkable job of balancing social activism and family involvement, at considerable sacrifice of self. In 1899, grief-stricken May Wood and Algie Simons recuperated during a European sojourn on funds raised by fellow settlement workers, including JANE ADDAMS and MARY McDOWELL. While in Europe, they established lasting relationships with several luminaries of the Socialist International, the organization founded by Karl Marx to promote a proletarian comradeship that transcended national boundaries.

When the couple returned to Chicago in mid-1900, Algie Simons became editor of the *Internationalist Socialist Review* until 1906, and he edited the *Chicago Daily Socialist* until 1910. May Simons contributed to both newspapers several articles dealing with such topics as the concentration of wealth and industry, the rise of labor, democracy and education, and art and socialism. Her work increasingly focused on the role of women in society and in the socialist movement, and on the function of the educational system in a capitalist society. She also criticized the effects of school segregation in an essay entitled "Education in the South," published in the *American Journal of Sociology* in November 1904. In 1905, May Simons received a Ph.B. degree in economics, with honors, from the University of Chicago. She taught economics-related subjects at socialist-oriented Ruskin University in suburban Glen Ellyn, Illinois, as well as at the Socialist Party's Chicago School for Workers. In 1906, she ran unsuccessfully for the office of Illinois State Superintendent of Schools. During that same decade, she was a frequent contributor to *Appeal to Reason, Vanguard, Wilshire's Magazine,* and *Technical World,* where she concentrated ever more directly on women's issues. From 1907 to 1910, May Simons served as associate editor of the *Chicago Daily Socialist.*

Increasingly involved in the fledgling Socialist Party of America, she became a lecturer for its Lyceum Bureau and Intercollegiate Socialist Society, a delegate to its national party conventions in 1908 and 1910, and a member of its National Committee. She played a key role in the formation and operation of both the Woman's National Committee (WNC), to which she was elected in 1908, and the publication the *Socialist (Progressive) Woman* in 1907. She wrote several articles on women's issues and on the school system for the latter and was chosen head of the WNC.

In her writings and speeches, May Simons increasingly stressed the inseparability of woman suffrage and socialism, siding with those socialists who refused to cooperate with bourgeois suffrage associations. She insisted that the vote was merely the means by which men and women together could effect the triumph of the cooperative commonwealth. "You cannot wipe away the class struggle among women," she stated in 1910, "and say it is just a beautiful sisterhood" (quoted in Kreuter and Kreuter, "May Wood Simons," 48). That same year, May Simons was a delegate to the International Socialist Congress in Copenhagen, Denmark, where she also attended the International Socialist Women's Conference, and functioned as secretary to the American delegation. Returning to Chicago, she received a master's degree in economics at Northwestern University, winning the prestigious Harris Prize in economics in 1910 and publishing an article, "The Scope of Economic Study," in the *Progressive Journal of Education.*

In August 1910, Algie Simons was forced to resign as editor of the *Chicago Daily Socialist* and began a three-year hiatus in Girard, Kansas, accompanied by his wife and daughter. There the Simonses coedited the *Coming Nation,* a literary and artistic supplement to the widely circulated socialist newspaper *Appeal to Reason.* May Simons contributed frequent articles to *Coming Nation,* many of them urging adoption of school reforms pioneered by Maria Montessori. She ran for Crawford County Superintendent of Schools in 1912, losing by a mere one hundred votes. As a delegate to the Socialist National Party Convention in 1912, May Simons delivered her report to the WNC, stressing the importance of vocational education. Although she had studied the subject extensively and was careful to insist that the "first duty of a housewife is to her children, husband and home" (Kreuter and Kreuter, *An American Dissenter,* 36), male delegates rejected the report as "meddling" (p. 36) in

an area beyond the legitimate province of the WNC. Early in 1913, persistent financial and subscription problems convinced the publisher of the *Coming Nation* to transfer its editorial offices to Chicago, permitting the couple to end their Kansas "exile." When publication was suspended indefinitely later that year, May Simons reluctantly sustained the family by working on another socialist periodical, the *Party Builder.*

In June 1913, the Simonses were summoned to Milwaukee, where Algie Simons was appointed associate editor of the *Leader,* the newspaper run by Victor Berger, head of the Wisconsin Social Democratic Party. May Simons taught high school history and civics classes, began work on a doctorate at Northwestern University, wrote articles on equal rights and woman suffrage for the WNC, and chaired the party's National Education Committee. However, the party's indifference toward women's issues so frustrated May Simons that she resigned from the WNC in late 1914; she took no further part in national level socialist activities.

The outbreak of World War I in Europe ignited a titanic struggle between the heavily German American antiwar majority of the American Socialist Party and an influential minority who favored United States involvement on the side of Great Britain and France. Both Simonses dissented from the national party's antiwar declaration on disarmament and world peace and were incensed by the *Leader*'s open defense of German actions and policies. May Simons was especially horrified by the pro-German reaction of many of her students to the sinking of the *Lusitania* and by the *Leader*'s editorial justification of the attack. Her husband resigned his associate editorship of the newspaper in 1917 over the war issue and was appointed head of the literature bureau of the Wisconsin Loyalty Legion. Equally concerned over the sizable opposition in Wisconsin—a state settled by many German immigrants proud of their heritage—to American entry in the war, May Simons became chair of the Americanization Committee of the Milwaukee County Council of Defense, an organization dedicated to mandatory use of the English language and to fostering "a united intelligent citizenship" (Korman, 173). Under her leadership, the committee pursued its interrelated goals through the public schools, as well as by night school courses designed to acculturate adult immigrants. It also established Americanization classes in several of the city's factories and in ethnic homes, boarding houses, and churches. In November 1918, May Simons helped organize a Milwaukee conference on Americanization that stressed methods for acculturating industrial workers. She also taught Americanization and citizenship courses through the extension division of the University of Wisconsin. In May 1919, she organized an Americanization pageant in which 613 newcomers went through the naturalization process. Still staunchly prolabor and socialist, May Simons refused to equate loyalty and patriotism with repressive economic and political policies. As the business leaders of the Americanization Committee increasingly utilized the body as a mechanism for the indoctrination and subordination of industrial workers by 1920, she denounced other board members as "a group of extreme reactionaries" and told them "to go whistle" (Korman, 191).

Unable to pursue equal rights and social justice any further through either the Socialist Party or the Americanization movement, May Simons turned her considerable energies toward educating her newly enfranchised sisters for intelligent and effective citizenship. She joined the fledgling League of Women Voters (LWV) and quickly rose to a position of leadership in the nonpartisan organization that was an outgrowth of the successful woman suffrage movement. In 1920, May Wood Simons wrote the *Wisconsin Citizen's Handbook,* an eighty-page primer widely distributed by the state LWV and used extensively in junior and senior high schools. The *Handbook* emphasized the workings of government at various levels and discussed in an objective manner such controversial issues as municipal ownership of utilities. She also functioned as chair of the league's citizenship program, conducting classes organized around the theme that the "power to vote is not a privilege, but an office" (undated, unspecified newspaper clipping, probably *Milwaukee Journal,* 1920, Simons Papers). She was a moving force in the organization of two-day citizenship schools, co-sponsored by the LWV and the University of Wisconsin extension, in which she lectured regularly on municipal government. Reflecting her growing movement toward conventional respectability, May Wood Simons and her daughter joined the Episcopal church in 1921.

When her husband joined a Chicago engineering firm as a personnel management expert, May Wood Simons moved to Evanston and became personnel manager for Montgomery Ward. After only six months, she left to become a reader in the Northwestern University economics department, where she graded papers, tutored, and directed the reading programs of undergraduate students. She also assumed leadership of the citizenship training program of the Illinois League of Women Voters in 1922; represented the state organization at the summer session on politics and government given by the national LWV and Columbia University, New York City; and organized citizenship classes for women voters in conjunction with Northwestern and Loyola universities, and the universities of Chicago and Illinois. In 1926, she published an article on the bicameral legislative systems of Illinois and Wisconsin in the *Illinois Law Review.* After receiving a doctorate in economics from Northwestern University in 1930, she was appointed part-time instructor, tutoring and grading papers until her retirement in 1944. For the February 1931 issue of *Current History,* May Simons collaborated with her daughter Miriam (now Miriam Leuck) in writing "The Changing American Home." In a cruel twist of fate, the family was devastated by the death of two-year-old Elizabeth, Miriam's only child, a loss that sent the grandparents on another grief-inspired trip to Europe. In 1945, May Simons published *Everyday Problems in Economics,* a textbook written from the consumer's perspective and designed for use in high school, college, and correspondence courses.

Following May Simons's retirement from Northwestern, she and her husband moved with their daughter and son-in-law to New York City, where they lived until 1948. In that year, the Simonses and Leucks relocated to Martinsville, West Virginia, where May Wood Simons died. Her body was cremated and the ashes eventually scattered on the grave of her infant son in Baraboo, Wisconsin, when her husband made his last trip to Chicago in June 1949.

May Wood Simons was a significant figure in the socialist movement and in the League of Women Voters, although she is perhaps most remembered for her role in the Americanization movement during World War I. Throughout her various career changes, she remained passionately committed to sexual equality and social justice. Her pursuit of those ideals through the medium of the Socialist Party was eventually frustrated due to the sexism of her male comrades and to her own position on American entry into World War I. Her attempt to reconcile her values in the movement to Americanize immigrants foundered because she was unwilling to promote patriotism at the expense of social justice and equal rights. Eventually, May Simons realized some measure of ideological resolution in her sustained activities for the League of Women Voters. That work was probably her most lasting achievement, but it was also a metamorphosis made possible only by her eventual acceptance of a socioeconomic system that socialists believed incapable of promoting true social justice.

Sources. The State Historical Society of Wisconsin (SHSW) is the repository for the papers of Algie Martin and May Wood Simons. The papers include correspondence, newspaper clippings, writings, memorabilia, and May Wood Simons's diary. The Simonses destroyed many records of their socialist years during the 1940s. Material relating to the couple can be found in the papers of Daniel De Leon, Richard T. Ely, Morris Hillquit, Henry Demarest Lloyd, and the Loyalty Legion, also at the SHSW, as well as in the papers of the Milwaukee Socialist Democratic Party, Milwaukee County Hist. Soc., and the Socialist Party Collection at Duke Univ. Library. Important are May Wood Simons's publications, especially the pamphlets *Women and the Social Problem* (1899), *Wisconsin Citizen's Handbook* (1920), and *Everyday Problems in Economics* (1945). Her articles in socialist newspapers and journals such as the *Chicago Daily Socialist, International Socialist Review, Socialist (Progressive) Woman,* and *Appeal to Reason* are in the SHSW. See Kent Kreuter and Gretchen Kreuter, *An American Dissenter: The Life of Algie Martin Simons, 1870–1950* (1969), and the Kreuters' "May Wood Simons: Party Theorist" in Sally M. Miller, ed., *Flawed Liberation: Socialism and Feminism* (1981). A reprint of May Wood Simons's *Women and the Social Problem* is an appendix to *Flawed Liberation.* The socialist years are detailed in Robert Stuart Huston, "A. M. Simons and the American Socialist Movement" (Ph.D. diss., Univ. of Wisconsin–Madison, 1965). Her involvement in the Americanization movement is analyzed in Gerd Korman, *Industrialization, Immigrants and Americanizers: The View from Milwaukee, 1866–1921* (1967).

JOHN D. BUENKER

SKENANDORE, AMY LEICHER
October 15, 1914–June 28, 1990
DIRECTOR OF SOCIAL SERVICE CENTER

Amy Leicher Skenandore, the first Native American director of Chicago's St. Augustine's Indian Center, was born in Red Springs, Wisconsin, to Fred and Aidis (Quinney) Leicher. She was a member of the Stockbridge-Mahican group, Christian American Indians from eastern New York State, who settled in a mission village in Stockbridge, Massachusetts, around 1738, following devastating wars and disease. Through her mother, Amy Leicher was a great-granddaughter of John W. Quinney, a Mahican Indian Baptist preacher, who in 1828 led a group of Stockbridge to Wisconsin, where he was elected grand sachem of the tribe in 1852 and later helped the Stockbridge negotiate a treaty giving them the townships of Bartelme and Red Springs in Shawano County, Wisconsin.

Amy Leicher grew up near the Stockbridge lands on her family's farm just outside Morgan, Wisconsin. At nine years of age, she left her parent's farm to live with her father's sister and her husband, Maude and Frank Morgan, while attending school in Winneconne, Wisconsin. She returned to her parents' home during her high school years and, while helping them with the farm work, also taught Sunday school in Morgan. At this time, Amy Leicher developed a lifelong interest in sports and athletics under the influence of her father, who coached local sports teams.

In 1933, Leicher married Benjamin Ninham, a member of the Oneida tribe, and moved with him to the Oneida reservation in Wisconsin. Together they had fourteen children between 1933 and 1950; ten survived into adulthood. Benjamin Ninham died in the early 1950s.

She later married Norbert Skenandore of the Oneida tribe. Because of the scarcity of work on the Oneida reservation, they moved to St. Ignace, Michigan, where Norbert Skenandore worked on construction of the Mackinac Bridge. Amy Skenandore gave birth to a son, John, in 1955. By 1957, Norbert Skenandore was again looking for work and better pay, and the family moved to Chicago in 1958.

Years later, Amy Skenandore recalled that she reacted to Chicago's size and confusion by secluding herself in the family's small apartment; "I made myself sick because I didn't like it" (interview with Skenandore). Such experiences later gave her an empathetic understanding for the problems other Indians encountered in making a transition to city life.

Through her daughter, Joyce Ninham, who had been living in the city for several years, Skenandore made contact with the American Indian Center, established in the early 1950s by Native Americans in the city to provide recreational and social assistance programs for Chicago's growing number of Indians. Center staff helped her get a job at a local bindery, where Skenandore worked for two years. In 1958, her daughter introduced her to Father Peter J. Powell, an Episcopalian priest who was working with local groups interested in Indian affairs in the city. She credited Father Powell with helping her to take pride in her Indian heritage, helping her understand "what an Indian is" (interview with Skenandore).

Skenandore arrived in Chicago at a time when its Native American community was growing rapidly, as thousands came to the city on their own and through the federal government's voluntary Relocation Program under the Bureau of Indian Affairs. Indians were encouraged to move from reservations to urban areas, where they might find employment. Five cities, including Chicago, were designated centers for relocation. In making such a move, a Native American gave up treaty benefits received on the reservation. Because many of the relocatees faced poverty, homelessness, and loneliness in the city, in 1962 Father Powell, through the Episcopal Diocese of Chicago, founded St. Augustine's Center for American Indians, in the Uptown neighborhood of Chicago, to deal with relocation problems.

With the opening of St. Augustine's, Skenandore became a volunteer staff member, later moving into a paid staff position in charge of food and clothing distribution. Skenandore was elected the first president of the Father Philip Deloria Guild, a religious organization of women from many Indian tribes, named in honor of a venerated Sioux priest and based at St. Augustine's. Guild members created mass vestments that featured sacred symbols of their respective tribes, used in the center's chapel. Skenandore was president of the guild from 1962 until 1972. For Skenandore, participation in the Episcopal church through St. Augustine's was an especially important part of her life.

From the beginning of her association with St. Augustine's, Skenandore acted as an informal counselor for center clients who sought her assistance. Her aptitude for counseling was soon recognized. In 1965, when the center received a grant from the federal War on Poverty program, the first such award to an urban Indian center, Skenandore was given training and became an assistant intake worker.

When Father Powell resigned as director of St. Augustine's in 1972, citing the need to place the leadership of the center in Native American hands, Skenandore became the director of the center. Skenandore's long association with the center, her "leadership and administrative abilities, mingled with her wisdom and warmth, made her the natural choice" (Powell, 2) to lead the center, which by this time was the largest Native American casework agency in the nation, serving approximately twelve hundred families from more than sixty tribes.

Skenandore's leadership of the center reflected the centrality of Indian identity to St. Augustine's program. She saw St. Augustine's counseling work as rooted in a Native American emphasis on the sharing of talents and skills as well as on material aid. All three of the center's caseworkers were Native Americans. Skenandore explained in a *Chicago Daily News* interview, "Our people relate better to Indian counselors. . . . With a white counselor they are likely to clam up. When they have personal problems they will talk to another Indian" (Eulenberg).

Amy Skenandore expanded St. Augustine's programming by establishing the Boujou Neejee (Chippewa for "Welcome Friends") Center for alcohol treatment, offering counseling, meals, and emergency medical help to those in need. Concerned that some Indian children raised in the city did not know about their heritage, she offered them cultural programs and also increased St. Augustine's counseling services for youth. Recognizing a malnutrition problem among St. Augustine's clientele, Skenandore started a food distribution program at the center. She made sure her counselors brought to this program an understanding of Indian eating patterns, noting that attempts to force unfamiliar foods upon Indian clients would be self-defeating. Continuing her lifelong interest in athletics, Skenandore sponsored basketball and bowling teams at St. Augustine's.

Amy Skenandore retired as director of St. Augustine's on December 31, 1980. In October 1982, she was named by the Episcopal Bishop and Diocese of Chicago as the year's honored woman for her outstanding leadership. Even in retirement, she remained active as an informal advisor for midwest programs for Native Americans. Skenandore died at seventy-four years of age and was buried in Holy Apostles Cemetery in Oneida, Wisconsin.

Skenandore's leadership at St. Augustine's reflected an ability to link her sense of Native American identity and cultural heritage with an understanding of the challenges that faced Native Americans moving into a city. In the programs she initiated, Amy Skenandore laid the foundation for ongoing services at St. Augustine's. The Boujou Neejee Center remained in the 1990s a major program. The youth counseling services that Skenandore established became the Indian Child Welfare Program, important at the center. Father Powell summarized the extent of Skenandore's contribution: "That St. Augustine's Center possesses a national reputation as being the most stable Native American casework agency in the nation is the direct outgrowth of her leadership" (Powell, 3).

Sources. Amy Skenandore spoke about her life in an interview done by Peggy Desjarlait in the Chicago American Indian Oral History Project, June 21, 1984, #003, The Newberry Library and NAES (Native American Educational Services) College Library, Chicago, Illinois. Her work at St. Augustine's is described in Father Peter Powell, "Amy Leicher Skenandore," typescript, n.d., St. Augustine's Center. Further discussion of the center appears in Edward H. Eulenberg, "Indians Reach Out to Help Each Other," *Chicago Daily News,* October 27, 1975. Background information on the Stockbridge-Mahican Indians appears in T. J. Brasser, "Mahican," in *Northeast,* ed. Bruce G. Trigger (1978), vol. 15 of *Handbook of North American Indians,* ed. William C. Sturtevant (1978–96).

GRANT P. ARNDT

SLAGLE, ELEANOR CLARKE
October 13, 1871–September 18, 1942
OCCUPATIONAL THERAPY EDUCATOR

Eleanor Clarke Slagle was a nationally recognized leader of occupational therapy for almost thirty years, serving as the first director of the pioneering Henry B. Favill School of Occupations (1915–20). She was one of the founding members in 1917 of the National Society for the Promotion of Occupational Therapy, later renamed the American Occupational Therapy Association. Described as the "Jane Addams of occupational therapy" (Cromwell, 647) (see JANE ADDAMS), she followed the Hull-House example of using ethical service combined with the authority of social science in her pioneering efforts to develop a humane treatment of the mentally and physically handicapped.

Eleanor Clarke was born in Hobart, New York, the younger child and only daughter of William John and Emmaline J. (Davenport) Clarke. She was named Ella May and later took Eleanor as her name. Clarke's father, a cooper or barrel maker, became an officer during the Civil War and later sheriff of Delaware County. Her brother, John Davenport Clarke, served for several terms as a U.S. congressional representative from New York. Details about Eleanor Clarke's childhood and early life are scant. Her parents divorced and she lived with her father. Eleanor Clarke attended Claverack College, a four-year Methodist school in Claverack, New York, for at least one term and married Robert E. Slagle of Chicago, probably in 1894. Information about him is sketchy; he was a railroad ticket agent and later a district superintendent with offices in Union Station. The circumstances of their marriage and divorce after 1900 remain a mystery.

There is no information about the years between her marriage and her first experiences in 1908 as a social work student except for a brief few sentences where she identified "a period of years of interest" she had "in the unfair social attitude toward the dependency of mentally and physically handicapped" (curriculum vitae of Eleanor Clarke Slagle, n.d., n.p., Illinois Occupational Therapy Association Archives). This interest led to her search for more formal education in the newly developing field of social work. Slagle was one of a group of reform women who were encouraged by Hull-House resident JULIA LATHROP, head of the Illinois State Board of Charities from 1893 to 1901 and a board member from 1905 to 1909, to take an active interest in the way in which the 102 county institutions in Illinois were being run. On one such inspection, Slagle was moved by the deplorable treatment of the mentally insane at the Kankakee State Hospital. She met a woman incarcerated there who was trying desperately to knit a shirt out of the threads of her unraveled undershirt with two straightened-out hair pins. When asked if this was a shirt for her child, the woman's face lit up and she explained she had four children. Slagle could not accept the neglect and lack of any meaningful activities for residents of institutions who were, to use a later term, being warehoused. Such experiences were later identified by Slagle as catalytic in pushing her in a new direction, not only personally in her own career development but as an innovator of a whole new field of therapy.

In 1908, in her late thirties, Eleanor Clarke Slagle enrolled as a student in the new Chicago School of Civics and Philanthropy (CSCP), then located at the Hull-House settlement. Graham Taylor, of Chicago Commons settlement, headed the new school. Dr. Adolph Meyer was influential in bringing his ideas about mental illness and the treatment of mental patients in institutions to Taylor and Julia Lathrop, who also taught at CSCP. Meyer, a psychiatrist who had worked in hospitals for the insane in Massachusetts and New York, was now at the Kankakee State Hospital in Illinois. He had begun to use occupational therapy—manual and mental—to rehabilitate and reeducate the mentally ill. He believed that mental illness caused disorganization of a patient's moral and daily living habits. Meyer used occupational therapy to restore organization to a patient's most basic living and moral habits.

Lathrop was inspired by Meyer's work to develop a special course for CSCP to educate attendants of mental patients so that they could substitute "the educational for the custodial idea" (Loomis and Wade, 2) in the daily care of patients. Slagle was encouraged by Lathrop and Addams to take Lathrop's special course. The CSCP course taught that "the humblest sort of occupation or labor" could be used to rehabilitate and reeducate patients to become "more intelligent and reasonable" (CSCP Summer Course, 2, Graham Taylor Papers). It emphasized hands-on training combined with courses in social science. Slagle formed her vision for working with mentally and physically handicapped patients during the two summer sessions she attended at Hull-House. She would use this experience as a model for training therapists elsewhere.

After completing her summer studies in 1911, Slagle spent six months observing programs in hospitals in Michigan and New York. In both the state hospital in Newberry, Michigan, and the facility in Central Islip, Long Island, Slagle organized training programs to disseminate the new occupational methods she had only recently absorbed in Chicago. Her work at State Hospital, Central Islip, was funded by the Sage Foundation through the efforts of Mary Richmond, a leading figure in the development of casework and research in the new field of social work. At the same time, Slagle continued to return to Hull-House where she participated as a faculty member in the summer course. When Adolph Meyer became the first director of Phipps Clinic at Johns Hopkins Hospital, Baltimore, Maryland, he invited Slagle to join him there to create and direct the new department of occupational training.

As director of occupational therapy at Phipps from 1912 to 1914, Slagle incorporated both Lathrop's and Meyer's ideas of habit and moral training into a system "designed to train regressed and deteriorated mental patients in 'decent' bodily and social habits" (Loomis and Wade, 5). She introduced a twenty-four-hour schedule of activities, which were supervised by attendants. Included in Slagle's program were activities that incorporated games, organized play and recreation, and handwork.

Slagle returned to Chicago in 1915 after she was recruited by the Illinois Society for Mental Hygiene to direct a program to train persons who would run community workshops and departments of occupational therapy. LOUISE deKOVEN BOWEN and the Hull-House women had connections with NETTIE FOWLER McCORMICK and her daughter ANITA McCORMICK BLAINE, wealthy women committed to funding the Illinois Society for Mental Hygiene, an organization dedicated to reform of the state's treatment of the mentally ill. Thus Slagle was positioned to work with a unique group of innovative professionals and activists interested in the social problems associated with mass industrial society: in the slum, the sweatshop, the asylum and other places of incarceration where inmates with so-called incurable mental and physical maladies were virtually passed over as worthless creatures. The society had begun workshops around 1909 because they were unable to find a sufficient number of jobs for their clients with mental illness who had the capacity to be employed. Staff members examined follow-up data on these clients and concluded that workshops were very productive. Slagle began her work for the society, becoming the director of what was later named the Henry B. Favill School of Occupations to memorialize the first vice-president of the society. The school, located at Hull-House, ran a five-month program that included course work in physiological, psychological, and sociological theory; practical experience in state institutions; and principles of administration, management, and organization. Slagle referred to the use of occupational therapy as "the experiment," in a letter to her colleague in the field, Dr. William Dunton, and indicated that she thought the popularity of occupational therapy was "conclusive proof that it . . . [was] one of the best ways of handling the Mental Hygiene question" (November 12, 1915, American Occupational Therapy Association Archives).

From 1915 to 1920, at the same time that she directed the Favill school, Slagle also taught seminars at Hull-House, took summer courses in educational psychology at Columbia University (1916), and conducted an eight-week seminar in occupational work at the Bedford Reformatory Social Hygiene Laboratory in Bedford, New York. In these years Slagle increasingly thought about the worthiness of a professional organization for the field of occupational therapy. In 1917 she was one of the participants at a conference in Clifton Springs, New York, that launched the National Society for the Promotion of Occupational Therapy (NSPOT). Others attending included William Dunton, Isabel G. Newton, Thomas B. Kidner, and George Edward Barton. Slagle served NSPOT as vice-president in 1917 and 1919, secretary in 1918, and president in 1920. NSPOT was renamed the American Occupational Therapy Association (AOTA) in 1923, the year Slagle was appointed its first paid executive secretary, a position she held until 1937.

Through her work with NSPOT, and as a result of her consultations with mental hospitals in New York, Michigan, Maryland, and Illinois, Slagle had a national reputation by 1917. That year Governor Frank Lowden of Illinois appointed Slagle as the general superintendent for occupational therapy for the Illinois Department of Public Welfare, including supervision of the occupational therapy programs for the entire state hospital system. She merged the Favill program with her work as superintendent and thereby created a natural outlet for the practical training of Favill students. In addition, the state hospital attendants were offered an opportunity to enhance their skills through additional course work in new methods in mental health science offered by Favill. During this period, Slagle broadened the application of occupational therapy beyond the mentally handicapped to include those with physical handicaps, soldiers who needed rehabilitation, children with learning disabilities, and inmates of prisons and reform schools.

World War I created a new area of work for occupational therapists; injured and shell-shocked soldiers needed therapy before they successfully could return to civilian life. In the summer of 1917, Slagle studied the effective uses of occupational therapy with returning soldiers. She toured Canadian military hospitals as a guest of National Society for the Promotion of Occupational Therapy member Thomas B. Kidner, vocational secretary of the Canadian Military Commission. The Canadian visit proved valuable when, in 1918, the Chicago Red Cross chapter asked Slagle to train volunteers in occupational therapy techniques. Slagle supervised the six-week occupational therapy course to meet the urgent needs of returning soldiers.

After success with the Red Cross course, Slagle and her colleague William Dunton approached the American Armed Services, presenting their methods and the evidence for occupational therapy's positive impact on the rehabilitation of soldiers. Slagle had to overcome the initial negative reaction; some thought occupational therapy too experimental from a medical point of view or too radical because women therapists would be recruited to work with military personnel. Slagle persisted and eventually persuaded the U.S. Surgeon General's office to appoint her as a consultant to the army charged with training "reconstruction aides" (*Then—and Now*, 7). In a whirlwind six-months, Slagle toured some twenty military hospitals and oversaw the training of four thousand therapists. With Slagle's leadership, occupational therapy salvaged thousands of soldiers from despondency and despair. Her work raised consciousness within the medical community of the value of occupational therapy and led to new methods of training and higher standards for the profession.

Slagle had suffered a serious bout with influenza and pneumonia in the spring of 1919. Her mother had been ill since 1917 and died in 1920. At the same time the Henry B. Favill School of Occupations had run into operating problems. Close colleague William Dunton observed in 1921 in the *Maryland Psychiatric Quarterly* that Favill's existence was tied to Slagle's leadership. He regretted that "no one felt it his or her duty to combat the influences which were apparently bent upon the destruction of the School" (quoted in Loomis, "The Henry B. Favill School of Occupations and Eleanor Slagle," 36). Slagle, meanwhile, was recruited for a new position; her work as superintendent of occupational therapy for the Illinois Department of Public Welfare had been so successful that in 1922 she was appointed director of occupational therapy for the New York State Department of Mental Hygiene.

Slagle continued to base her training of therapists and her work with patients on the theory of habit training she had perfected at the Favill school. Expanding these concepts to include new areas of application, Slagle encouraged research and from 1924 sponsored annual institutes for her hospital staff to improve therapists' skills. Her institutes brought professionals in the field together so they could present seminars on new research and treatment. The popularity of the institutes grew; other hospital systems developed similar institutes, often calling on Slagle as a featured speaker.

At the same time that she developed her New York State activities, she worked hard in organizing and developing the American Occupational Therapy Association as its executive secretary. She was a leader in the formulation of the association's "theoretical beliefs, [and] the design of its treatment and education programs" (Cromwell, 646). In the mid-1930s, Slagle responded to requests from many physicians and hospitals that AOTA deal with standards for the training of occupational therapists. Minimal standards and guidelines for the accreditation of occupational therapy programs were developed with assistance from the American Medical Association (AMA). AOTA was able to provide standards for programs in independent schools, training courses given in connection with collegiate work, and postgraduate courses offered for students specializing in mental hospital practice, orthopedic practice, or in curative workshop activities with orthopedic, arthritic, or other cases. The diversity of programs reflected the transformation and professionalization of the field. In addition, Slagle worked with the AMA to develop registration of qualified workers in the field; a plan for a national registration system for occupational therapists was approved by the AOTA membership in 1930, and the first directory of names was available the following year.

Slagle's leadership of AOTA ended with her retirement as executive secretary of the organization in 1937. Eleanor Roosevelt was the featured speaker at a banquet given in her honor. Her colleague of many years, Adolph Meyer, also praised her contributions. The AOTA membership provided her with a gift of two thousand dollars, which helped her purchase a home in Philipse Manor, near Tarrytown, New York.

For the next five years, Slagle continued her work as director of occupational therapy for the New York State Hospital Commission until her death of a coronary thrombosis. Funeral services were held in Christ Episcopal Church, Philipse Manor,

September 21, 1942, and Slagle was buried at Locust Hill Cemetery, Hobart, New York.

Eleanor Clarke Slagle was one of the pioneering career women who carved out new professions to address the needs of an industrial United States. Hull-House brought together activists and theoreticians eager to set social policy, lobby for constructive legislation, and disseminate discoveries of new methods of caring for the diverse needs of the population. At Hull-House Eleanor Slagle found like-minded and receptive women and men eager to envision a more humane and productive approach for the education and rehabilitation of mentally ill patients in hospitals and asylums. Chicago and its extensive reform network provided Slagle with the opportunity and connections to forge a new direction for the care of people with mental and physical disabilities and, in terms of her own career aspirations, to become a leader in the new field of occupational therapy. As a testimony to Slagle's influence, AOTA established a lectureship in her name in 1954. Thirty-five years after her death, Slagle's contributions remained "the essential basis for the theory and practice of occupational therapy" (Cromwell, 646).

Sources. The papers of Eleanor Clarke Slagle are held in the archives of the American Occupational Therapy Association (AOTA), Rockville, Maryland, and in the Illinois Occupational Therapy Association Archives, UIC Library of Health Sciences. These collections include correspondence, Slagle's articles and speeches, newspaper clippings, and other memorabilia. Information on the early years of the Chicago School of Civics and Philanthropy can be found in the Graham Taylor Papers, NL. Slagle's biography is in *NAW* (1971). Useful articles about the beginnings of the field of occupational therapy and Slagle's leadership include Florence S. Cromwell, "Eleanor Clarke Slagle, the Leader, the Woman," *American Journal of Occupational Therapy,* November–December 1977; Barbara Loomis, "The Henry B. Favill School of Occupations and Eleanor Clarke Slagle," *American Journal of Occupational Therapy,* January 1992. Barbara Loomis and Beatrice D. Wade, *Occupational Therapy Beginnings: Hull House, the Henry B. Favill School of Occupations and Eleanor Clarke Slagle,* a pamphlet produced by the Illinois Occupational Therapy Association (1973), is useful. See also American Occupational Therapy Association, *Then—and Now 1917–1967: 50th Anniversary* (1967).

BARBARA DOBSCHUETZ

SLYE, MAUD

February 8, 1869–September 17, 1954

SCIENTIST, RESEARCHER, POET

At a time when the field of biological research in human diseases was in its infancy, Maud Slye pursued her innovative ideas about the relationship of heredity and cancer as a largely self-taught scientist without either a Ph.D. or an M.D. degree. Slye spent thirty-six years researching the connection between cancer and heredity, meticulously tracing the occurrence of the disease through 108 generations of mice.

Born in Minneapolis, Minnesota, Slye was the middle child of James Alvin and Florence Alden (Wheeler) Slye and had an older sister and a younger brother. Her father was a lawyer and a writer. Her parents both wrote poetry, as did Slye herself. The family was not well off, especially after her father's death when

Slye was ten. By then they had moved to Iowa, where Slye's grandparents lived, and then to St. Paul, Minnesota.

In 1895, Slye attended the University of Chicago as an undergraduate student. To support herself, she became secretary to William Rainey Harper, president of the university. After three years of intense work and study, Slye suffered what was described as a nervous breakdown. She left the university to recuperate with relatives in Massachusetts. There she studied at the Woods Hole Marine Biological Laboratory, later entering Brown University and completing her bachelor's degree in 1899. An excellent student, Slye was elected to both Phi Beta Kappa and Sigma Xi, the honor society in science. Between 1899 and 1905, she taught psychology and pedagogy at the Rhode Island State Normal School (later Rhode Island College) in Providence, becoming interested in genetics during that time. In 1908, one of Slye's teachers at Woods Hole, Charles Otis Whitman, invited her to come back to the University of Chicago as his research assistant in the biology department, which he had just been asked to head. In the basement of the zoology building, Slye began the work to which she was to devote her life. What started as a project on an apparently inherited nervous disorder exhibited by a strain of mice known as waltzing mice soon evolved into a study of cancer, using mice because they were physiologically similar to humans. While other researchers were interested in heredity as a factor in mouse cancer, Slye was the first to develop a comprehensive program of "controlled breeding experiments" (Slye, "Relation of Heredity to Cancer," 535) to study the genetics of cancer to establish inheritability. Slye worked with descendants of three strains of mice. She trapped the first group in a farm building, received the second from an academic researcher, and purchased the third strain, Japanese waltzing mice, in a pet shop.

Since the mice experiments were Slye's own project, she financed the work almost completely. Barely surviving on her small university fellowship, Slye sometimes went hungry or got by on a meager diet in order to feed her test animals. She worked tirelessly, seven days a week, keeping the cages scrupulously clean; boiling and filtering drinking water; conducting an autopsy on every mouse at death; collecting tissue samples; and maintaining detailed cage, autopsy, and genealogical records. Her dedication and painstaking attention to detail garnered support. When the Sprague Memorial Institute for medical research was established at the University of Chicago in 1911, Slye was asked to join the staff. This position meant a salary and a large laboratory. More important for Slye's scientific credibility, the highly respected director of the institute, H. Gideon Wells, agreed to verify her tissue samples. A well-to-do pathologist, Harriet Holmes, volunteered to be an unpaid laboratory assistant after she visited Slye's laboratory and became familiar with the promising work. Holmes prepared tissue samples and collaborated on research papers.

After Slye's appointment to the Sprague Memorial Institute, her work began to be recognized. On May 5, 1913, she presented a research paper, "The Incidence and Inheritability of Spontaneous Cancer in Mice," at a meeting of the American Society for Cancer Research, citing inherited susceptibility, not contagion, as the transmission source. She also concluded that irritation had to be present as a factor in the production of can-

cer. In 1914 Slye mounted an exhibit on her research at the Sixty-Fourth Annual Session of the American Medical Association and was awarded a gold medal for the best scientific exhibit at the meeting. In 1915 she received the Ricketts Prize of the University of Chicago for her research. The university made her director of its Cancer Laboratory in 1919 and promoted her from instructor to assistant professor in pathology in 1922. That same year she was awarded a gold medal by the American Radiological Society for her work.

By 1926, when Slye became an associate professor, she was known well enough to evoke strong reactions from colleagues who disagreed with her. Cancer research at that time was a volatile field with sharply divided factions arguing for everything from germs to toxins to vitamin deficiencies as the cause of the disease. Slye's studies ruled out many of these possibilities to the sometimes vitriolic dismay of their proponents. She held that "an external factor acting with internal factors upon a susceptible soil is probably the cause of cancer," that "the genetic difference between cancer susceptibility and cancer insusceptibility involves one gene," and that "cancer susceptibility behaves like a recessive" Mendelian trait (Slye, "Relation of Heredity to Cancer," 582). In the nineteenth century, Gregor Mendel had established that dominant and recessive traits result from the interaction of genes inherited in pairs.

Among Slye's most vocal opponents were Clarence Cook Little, a researcher at Harvard University and developer of inbred mice, who cast some doubt on her understanding of Mendel, and Francis Carter Wood, the influential editor of the *Journal of Cancer Research*, who did not think her results with mice were fully applicable to humans. Slye spoke out at a meeting of the American Society for the Control of Cancer in the mid-twenties about the need to collect human cancer statistics, a point she made again and again throughout her career. This claim and her remarks on inherited susceptibility to cancer engendered strong responses both pro and con. Some of her colleagues were impressed enough to suggest recommending her for a Nobel Prize, but a Chicago physician accused her of doing "a cruel, dastardly and unscientific thing in broadcasting to the world that cancer is hereditary" (G. W. Boot to Maud Slye, February 12, 1926, Slye Papers). On the whole, the association members seemed to agree with the latter assessment and in a white paper muted her conclusions. Slye's perception of her critics was that her research was being questioned because of controversy over the cause of cancer and because she was a woman in a male-dominated field.

Soon after, Slye delivered an invited lecture to the Columbus Academy of Medicine in Ohio and received a similar mixed reaction. In a letter of support from a physician came the news that another researcher had accused her of unprofessional behavior. Slye pursued the matter until the source of the remark was discovered. The trail led to Francis Carter Wood. Although Slye got a retraction and an apology, this incident was to have a lasting effect on her reputation. As late as 1940, a university memo argued against support of her work, stating, among other things, that "she has antagonized a number of workers in her immediate field" (Presidents' Papers 1950–55).

In 1933 Slye exhibited at the Century of Progress Exposition "the most complete genealogical tables ever assembled" (Press

Release, April 10, 1933, Archival Biographical Files). She delineated her cancer research on mice.

In contrast to the constructed focus of science, Slye was also a poet, writing more than a thousand poems in her lifetime. In 1934 her first book of poems, *Songs and Solace*, was published by the Stratford Company in Boston. A second volume, *I in the Wind: Symphony No. 1 and Minor Songs*, also published by the Stratford Company, appeared in 1936. She described her poetry as dealing with nature, love, and life. In "At Night My Laboratory Stands," she poeticized her love for scientific work: "At night my laboratory stands / Sheltered in dark, all its wide work of day / Silenced for rest. On both its sides / Flanked by still space, it looms alone, / The sky above it and the dark around, / O all my heart is there! / I watch it standing in the night / And silent dark — / There is a light that gleams above its brow / Like a high crown, that brings me benediction; / Let there be light above it and within!" (*I in the Wind*, 403).

That same year, Slye went to Europe on a combined lecture tour and vacation, the first vacation since she had begun her research. She spoke at the International Congress for the Control of Cancer in Brussels and gave talks to scientists and physicians in Amsterdam, Berlin, Paris, and London. A small group of European scientists disputed her conclusions, while others dubbed her the "American Curie" (McCoy, *Cancer Lady*, 171). By 1936, based on other research on the genetics of cancer, Slye modified her long-held view that cancer could be traced to one gene. She propounded a more complex theory about "the relation of inherited susceptibility to the type, the site, and the date of occurrence of cancer" (manuscript, Archival Biographical Files) and stated that she could predict what kind of cancer would occur in what organ based on genealogical records. Slye always asserted that cancer could "be bred out of a family by the right selective mating" (Slye, "Studies in the Nature and Inheritability of Cancer," 75) and was able to do so in mice after several generations of controlled breeding. Both of these views overstated the case, but they helped to establish the importance of family history in the diagnosis of cancer.

In 1937 Slye was awarded an honorary doctorate by her alma mater Brown University. She was active in professional organizations, serving in the 1940s as vice-president of the Chicago Institute of Medicine and as a member of the Association for Cancer Research and the American Association for the Advancement of Science. As the Great Depression and World War II drew funds away from cancer research, Slye had to fight for support. Approaching mandatory retirement made the fight difficult, and she began once again to use her own funds to carry on the work. Cashing in her life insurance policy, she paid the salaries of a janitor and the animal caretakers. In 1939, she was asked to phase out her animal studies and let her subjects die off. The last years of Slye's long career involved negotiations with the university for space and time to consolidate her data. Long-standing criticism of her theory and other approaches to cancer research had diminished the importance of Slye's work in the eyes of colleagues and administrators at the University of Chicago. Her earliest supporters gone, she had no one to advocate for her project. Slye did everything she could to maintain the project intact, including taking her story to the public via press interviews. She was allowed to remain in the university-owned apartment, across from her laboratory, where she had lived for many years without paying rent. She shared the residence with her unmarried sister, Katherine, who had been a Chicago school teacher, and with her laboratory assistant, Edith Farrer. Slye retired as emeritus professor in 1945.

Like her sister, Slye never married. She devoted herself to research and poetry and gardened in her leisure time. As a younger woman, she had played the piano and the cello and loved sailing. After retirement, she continued to fight for her beliefs. In 1949, as head of the Chicago Council of Arts, Sciences, and Professions, she defended that group against accusations of communist infiltration that were leveled when it held a peace rally to protest against the North Atlantic Pact, the first peacetime alliance formed by the United States with European nations. American participation in the pact under which an army was created for the North Atlantic Treaty Organization — NATO — was based on fear of Soviet power and Russian communism. Slye died in Chicago after a heart attack and was buried in Oak Woods Cemetery, not far from the university.

In more than thirty-five years of research, Slye published forty-two papers on her studies and established high standards in the care of laboratory animals. She was recognized in her lifetime for "epochal" (Jaffee, 129) work in comprehensive, well-organized studies that drew scientists from all over the world to her laboratory. Her findings have been supplanted by later studies, but Maud Slye was an important early researcher on genetic factors in cancer development.

Sources. In employment records, Slye gave 1879 as her birth year, but the 1880 census and her graduation from Marshalltown High School in Iowa in 1886 indicate 1869. Most of the available information on Maud Slye exists in the UC Spec. Coll. The Maud Slye papers contain enlightening professional correspondence, including an acerbic letter from G. W. Boot and letters related to the Francis Carter Wood incident. Cage records, genealogical charts, and autopsy reports on the laboratory mice are also part of this collection. Memoranda and letters collected in the Presidents' Papers 1950–55, UC Spec. Coll., demonstrate the university's dwindling support of Slye's work after 1938, due to funding problems, as well as Slye's reluctance to give up her research. Her published articles include "Studies in the Nature of Inheritability of Cancer," *University Record*, January 1926, and "The Relation of Heredity to Cancer Occurrence as Shown in Strain 73," *American Journal of Cancer*, July 1933. Many of Slye's articles appeared in *American Journal of Cancer* and *Journal of Cancer Research* from 1913 into the 1940s. Her published poetry is described above. The Maud Slye Archival Biographical Collection, UC Spec. Coll., contains the only book-length biography of Slye, which focuses on her scientific work: J. J. McCoy's manuscript *The Mouse Lady* (1976), published one year later as *The Cancer Lady: Maud Slye and Her Heredity Studies*. Also in the biographical collection are newspaper articles about Slye's scientific and poetic works, including Guy Forshey's "Dr. Maud Slye: The Woman Who Raises Mice," *St. Louis Post-Dispatch*, September 17, 1925, as well as obituaries in the *CT* and *NYT* on September 18, 1954. UC press releases in the Archival Biographical Files provide colorful information about Slye's life and work. The entry for Slye in *NAW* (1980) details the sources that support a birthdate in 1869. Bernard Jaffee describes her research in "Cancer," *Outposts of Science* (1935).

BROOKE BERGAN

SMITH, AMANDA JANE BERRY
January 23, 1837–February 25, 1915

EVANGELIST, MISSIONARY, TEMPERANCE REFORMER

Amanda Berry Smith, an internationally famous Holiness evangelist and missionary, and founder of a privately funded orphanage for African American children, was born on a farm in Long Green, Maryland, about twenty miles north of Baltimore. Smith was the second oldest child and the first daughter in a family of thirteen children. Her parents, Samuel and Miriam (Matthews) Berry, were slaves on neighboring farms. Her father managed to save enough money to buy his and his family's freedom by making brooms and selling them in Baltimore's busy market. As free people, the Berrys moved to Pennsylvania and settled in York County, where their home became a station on the Underground Railroad.

Barred from school by racial restrictions, the Berry children were taught to read at home by their parents. At thirteen, Amanda went to work as a live-in maid. When she was seventeen, she married Calvin Devine and moved with him to Columbia in neighboring Lancaster County. Their first child died in infancy. Their second, a girl named Mazie, survived. In 1856, Amanda had a conversion experience and became a Christian while praying in the basement of a Quaker family for whom she worked as a maid. Soon afterward she said she had a vision during which God called her to preach. Two years after the Civil War broke out, her husband joined the Union army and never returned from the South.

She moved to Philadelphia, where she met and married James Smith, an African Methodist Episcopal (AME) choir director, deacon, and aspiring minister fifteen years older than she. Hoping for a contented life as an AME minister's wife, Amanda Berry Smith moved with her new husband and daughter to New York. She went to work as a washerwoman and her husband as a waiter and coachman. Marital discord developed when James Smith admitted that he had pretended that he planned to become a minister so that she would agree to marry him. His primary goal was to become a part of New York's emerging black elite. He and Amanda Berry Smith worked hard to earn money to pay dues in various lodges and to buy clothes to wear to social functions, but for the next four years her disappointment turned to despair as she gave birth to three more children, all of whom died in infancy. As tension grew between her and James Smith, she and her daughter Mazie eked out a living washing and ironing in their damp basement apartment. Her husband lived in Brooklyn, where he found a lucrative position as a driver.

As her problems mounted, Smith embraced the ideas of the post-war Holiness movement led by a group of Methodist preachers in the Philadelphia–New York area. One Sunday she attended Greene Street Methodist Church where John Inskip, one of the founders of the newly formed National Holiness Camp Meeting Association, preached a sermon on sanctification. Since her conversion experience, Smith had remained dissatisfied with her spiritual life, especially with what she called her "difficult" disposition and conflicts with her husband. Adherents of Holiness doctrine as taught by Phoebe Palmer and other pioneers of the nineteenth-century Holiness Revival believed that after conversion the Christian needed a "second blessing" during which God imparted the "grace" to endure trouble and completed the change of heart necessary for a holy life. While listening to Inskip preach, Smith experienced the "second blessing" she described as heart purity and immediately began telling fellow AME church members and neighbors, "The Lord has sanctified my soul" (*Autobiography*, 79). She then withdrew from the clubs she and her husband had joined.

When her husband died in 1869, she quit her trade as washerwoman and began to preach full-time, first in local AME churches, then among both black and white congregations throughout the Northeast. In the summers, vast crowds of mostly white camp meeting followers heard her stirring testimonies and moving contralto singing voice. She gained special notice at the Ocean Grove Camp Meeting in New Jersey, where Woman's Christian Temperance Union (WCTU) leaders often shared the platform with Holiness preachers.

In 1875 she joined the WCTU's Brooklyn chapter as a white ribbon member, the pioneers whom the WCTU credited with having founded the organization. In 1878 Mary Coffin Johnson, president of the Brooklyn WCTU, invited her to the Keswick Convention, an annual gathering of Holiness leaders in England. After a successful speaking tour in Europe, Smith left for India, where she spent two years preaching at open air meetings on the streets of Calcutta and Bombay and resting in the Himalaya mountains before returning to England. She then went to West Africa, where she lived and worked in Liberia as an itinerant missionary from 1881 to 1889. In 1890, when she returned to the United States, she came as a major figure in temperance and evangelical circles.

In October 1892, she accepted an invitation to preach a ten-day revival at Chicago's South Park Avenue Church. In November she sealed an agreement with a Chicago businessman to publish her autobiography. By winter she moved to Chicago, where she finished her book. After a speaking tour in England for the British WCTU, she began the work of establishing an orphan home and industrial school for African American children in Harvey, Illinois, the new temperance town south of Chicago, founded by Dwight L. Moody and lumber magnate Turlington W. Harvey.

In December 1895, she bought two lots and a building in the Academy Addition to Harvey, a newly incorporated section adjacent to the town's industrial area. In January 1896 she launched a three-year speaking campaign that took her from coast to coast raising funds to pay off the mortgage. By March 1899, she had amassed five thousand dollars to make the final payment. On June 18, 1899, the Amanda Smith Orphanage and Industrial Home for Abandoned and Destitute Colored Children officially opened, debt-free, with an interracial group of ministers and civic leaders presiding over its inaugural celebration. Crossing racial and denominational barriers, the Smith home attracted visitors to Harvey and helped boost the town's reputation.

For eight years, Smith managed the home, published its newsletter, the *Helper,* and continued to attract huge congregations at camp meetings and revivals. She bought sixteen adjacent lots and built a cottage. Cook County Juvenile Court and child welfare agencies referred children to the home but provided no financial support. She relied on proceeds from her autobiography, which sold for one dollar a copy, profits from the sale of *Helper*, funds collected from her speaking tours, and other contributions from supporters. She tried unsuccessfully to establish a twenty thousand dollar endowment fund to sustain the work.

In the November 1907 issue of the *Helper*, she defined her goal as "rescu[ing] destitute, needy children, especially those of colored parentage," provid[ing] them with "care, education and industrial training" (p. 2), and ultimately finding them suitable, permanent homes. Smith's educational philosophy was that "the highest end of education is not learning but character." She said it would be "better to not know how to read and be true in action rather than to be learned in all sciences and in all languages" (p. 2).

The children initially attended the local school, but she later employed a teacher and took part in their religious training. In keeping with the self-help philosophy popular at the turn of the century, she believed that children should learn to be "self-reliant and self-helpful even from childhood" and "self-supporting at the earliest possible age [because] all honest work is honorable" (*Helper*, November 1907, 2). They grew their own vegetables, and she helped them raise chickens and pigs. In publicity for the school she noted that some of the children trained at the home were "now employed in household work" (p. 2).

By June 1903, the Smith home accommodated thirty-one children and had taken care of sixty-five. As the number increased and operating expenses mounted, funds needed to maintain a stable support staff or pay for fuel and other necessities quickly dried up. African American clubwomen in the Chicago area provided consistent, but inadequate, help. Author and speaker Hallie Q. Brown, crusading journalist and civil rights leader IDA B. WELLS-BARNETT, and temperance advocate Lucy Thurman attempted to raise money for the home, but their efforts fell far short. Wells-Barnett tried to persuade AME leaders to sustain the home, but these efforts also failed.

By 1905 the institution teetered on the brink of financial disaster. In October, Charles Virden, the newly appointed state agent for the visitation of children, reported that the Smith home was in considerable debt and the children poorly supervised because Smith was often absent on fund-raising missions. When there, he claimed she spent most of her time in her room due to her age. Despite these reportedly poor conditions, state officials allowed the home to continue operating, mainly because, as Virden explained, it was the only important institution in Illinois that took care of black children.

In 1906, Smith relinquished legal control to an interracial trustee board made up of local business and religious leaders, headed by J. A. Burhans—a Chicago attorney, real estate broker, and Methodist church leader. After the new administration took over, the State Board of Public Charities gave the home a satisfactory rating, issued a certificate, and approved its new charter. Smith remained as a trustee founder and manager but turned over all property rights to the new board, whose officers immediately mortgaged the two primary lots and main building for one thousand dollars.

Despite mounting pressures, Smith's fund-raising ability declined along with her health. On November 15, 1912, frail and exhausted, at age seventy-five, she gave up her duties at the

home and moved to Sebring, Florida, where she lived the last three years of her life in a lakeside cottage built for her by wealthy Ohio manufacturer George Sebring, the town's founder. Sebring supported her until she died of cerebral thrombosis. He returned her body to Chicago by train for a funeral at Chicago's Quinn Chapel AME church, where she had been a member. She was buried in Homewood Cemetery, Homewood, Illinois.

In April 1915, the Smith home became the Amanda Smith Industrial School for Girls. Adah M. Waters, a graduate of Cheney Training School for Colored Teachers, became superintendent. Waters made plans to reconstruct the school. Julius Rosenwald, head of Sears-Roebuck Corporation, made two modest donations, none substantial enough for necessary repairs and renovations. On November 21, 1918, faulty electrical wiring sparked a blaze that destroyed the main building. Two children died in the fire. The Children's Home and Aid Society found homes for the survivors, and creditors claimed the property for commercial use.

Despite Smith's international reputation as preacher and reform leader, the institution she founded crumbled under a mounting weight of debt and neglect. Nevertheless, Smith's forty-five years of ministry left a bridge between black and white Holiness leaders. As a champion of racial and gender equality, she helped develop a legacy of interracial cooperation among social and religious reformers that endured on an informal basis until the mid-1920s. Smith's contemporaries considered her "one of the most powerful evangelists and effective missionaries of the nineteenth century" (Dayton, 96).

Sources. Information on Amanda Smith's life and the Amanda Smith Industrial Home include the Julius Rosenwald Papers, UC Spec. Coll., and the *Chicago Defender*, 1890–1915. The major source of information is Amanda Smith, *An Autobiography: The Story of the Lord's Dealings with Mrs. Amanda Smith* (1893). A condensed version of it appeared the year after her death: M. H. Cadbury, *The Life of Amanda Smith: "The African Sibyl, the Christian Saint"* (1916). Another condensation was E. Harvey, ed., *Amanda Smith: The King's Daughter* (n.d.). Major excerpts from her autobiography appear in Bert James Loewenberg and Ruth Bogin, eds., *Black Women in Nineteenth-Century American Life: Their Words, Their Thoughts, Their Feelings* (1976). Many of her letters to friends and to the public are reprinted in Christian newspapers, the most extensive collection being found in the *Christian Standard and Home Journal*, a publication of the National Holiness Association. The United Methodist Archives at Drew Univ. in Madison, New Jersey, has a full collection of these volumes. Her letters and accounts of her testimonies and preaching also appear in other Holiness publications available at Drew, such as *Guide to Holiness, Christian Recorder*, and *Ocean Grove Record*. Copies of her newsletter, the *Helper*, are available in the Booker T. Washington Papers at the Library of Congress and in the Moorland-Spingarn Room in Founders Library, Howard Univ. For a full biography, see Adrienne M. Israel, *Amanda Berry Smith: From Washerwoman to Evangelist* (1998). Marshall W. Taylor, *The Life, Travels, and Helpers of Mrs. Amanda Smith* (1886), is an account of her work in Liberia. See also *BWA* and Nancy A. Hardesty, "Amanda Berry Smith: 'A Downright, Outright Christian,'" in *Spirituality and Social Responsibility: The Vocational Vision of United Methodist Women*, ed. Rosemary Keller (1993). Smith is mentioned in a number of studies on the Holiness movement and women in ministry, including Nancy A. Hardesty's *Great Women of Faith: The Strength and Influence of Christian Women* (1980) and *Women Called to Witness*

(1984); Sylvia M. Jacobs, "Afro-American Missionaries Confront the African Way of Life," *Women in Africa and the African Diaspora* (1987); Sylvia M. Jacobs and Paul R. Dekar, eds., *Black Americans and the Missionary Movement in Africa* (1982); and Jacobs, "Three Afro-American Women: Missionaries in Africa, 1882–1904," in *Women in New Worlds: Historical Perspectives on the Wesleyan Tradition*, ed. Hilah F. Thomas, Rosemary Skinner Keller, and Louis L. Queen, vol. 2 (1982). Smith's work in Africa is mentioned by Walter L. Williams in *Black Americans and the Evangelization of Africa, 1877–1900* (1982). Williams credits her with initiating Methodist mission work among Africans in the interior of Liberia. Background on some figures in the Holiness movement, including Smith, can be found in Donald Dayton, *Discovering an Evangelical Heritage* (1976). The Woman's Christian Temperance Union library in Evanston, Illinois, has volumes of the WCTU publication, the *Union Signal,* which contain significant records of Smith's work with the WCTU. Discussion of her orphanage work appears in David C. Bartlett and Larry A. McClellan, "The Final Ministry of Amanda Berry Smith: An Orphanage in Harvey, Illinois, 1895–1918," *Illinois Heritage,* Winter 1998.

ADRIENNE M. ISRAEL

SMITH, ELEANOR SOPHIA
June 15, 1858–June 30, 1942
COMPOSER, MUSIC EDUCATOR, AUTHOR, FOUNDER OF
MUSIC SCHOOL

Eleanor Smith, a prolific composer of vocal music and a pioneer in the field of music education in America, was described by JANE ADDAMS as "one of the three creative geniuses at Hull-House" (quoted in "Eleanor Smith, Once Hull House 'Genius', Is Dead"). The second of seven children, Smith was born in Atlanta, Illinois, to Willard Newton and Matilda (Jasperson) Smith. Her father was a close friend of Abraham Lincoln and served as one of the original team of Lincoln campaigners in southern Illinois.

Smith's musical abilities in childhood and adolescence were largely self-taught. During her childhood she displayed a remarkable ear, duplicating melodies and harmonies at the piano with great accuracy. She taught herself to play the piano and began formal musical training only when she was eighteen years old, at which time she started voice and composition lessons. Troubled with very poor vision and a possibility of blindness, Smith was sometimes forced to use her eyes for only a brief period each day. Her musical drive was so strong, however, that she would often use whatever time she could to work on the composition at hand.

In the 1880s, Smith moved to Berlin, Germany, a center for music education, to study voice with Julius Hey and composition with Moritz Moszkowski. During her three years there she met and became friends with a young woman, Amalie Hannig, who was a piano instructor at the Klindworth Conservatory. Smith and Hannig not only shared a love for music, they shared similar pedagogical philosophies as well. Both women emphasized the need for strong technical training for musicians. They believed this training should focus on physical facility as well as mental aptitude and that both of these should be brought to life through "emotional feeling and expressiveness" ("Eleanor Smith's Brief Autobiography," 1). Smith wrote in her unpublished autobiography: "We were quite sure that all these must be cultivated in childhood by intelligent teachers. Moreover, as

FIG. 105. *On the left, founder of the Hull-House Music School, Eleanor Smith with philanthropist Mary Rozet Smith, longtime friend of Jane Addams.*

music must be beautiful, its disciples should early be given the best music possible" (p. 1). Smith and Hannig would later have the opportunity to put this philosophy into practice, when they became colleagues at Hull-House.

In autumn 1890, Smith arrived in Chicago. Soon after, she visited Hull-House, a social settlement that had been founded by Jane Addams and ELLEN GATES STARR in September 1889. Soon after her initial visit, Smith began teaching music at the settlement to children and adults from the surrounding neighborhood. At the time, the Hull-House neighborhood was composed primarily of European immigrants. Irish, Germans, Bohemians, Italians, and Russian and Polish Jews predominated. Amalie Hannig joined the Hull-House staff as a piano teacher a short time later.

Courses in singing, ear training, and reading and writing of music were taught by Smith in the Hull-House reception room, which had an upright piano. Children who displayed exceptional aptitude were also given piano lessons. Music courses were offered from October to June. In later years, summer instruction was added. Fees were, in Smith's words, "negligible" ("Eleanor Smith's Brief Autobiography," 2), and sometimes sheet music was furnished at no charge. Although the facilities were at times inadequate and the students often came from impoverished families, Smith did not scrimp when it came to applying the philosophical ideals she had formed during her own training. From the beginning, she was an exacting teacher who held her students to the highest musical standards. She employed instructional materials of the highest caliber, and all music students were expected to study beyond their chosen instruments; singers studied piano and instrumentalists studied voice.

Smith's strong philosophical convictions, coupled with her energy and devotion to the Hull-House music program, attracted enough students to establish the Hull-House Music School in 1893, the first settlement music school in the country. The music school was financed in large part by MARY ROZET SMITH (no relation to Eleanor Smith), a wealthy benefactor of Hull-House. In 1895, the music school was moved onto the fourth floor of the newly opened Smith building—referred to as the Children's House, which had been built with money donated by Mary Rozet Smith's family. The school remained there until 1903, when it moved one last time to six rooms overlooking the quadrangle. One of these rooms served as a music library. In 1897 Eleanor Smith moved into Hull-House, becoming a full-time resident. By 1924 she had moved into the home of Mary Rozet Smith, where she lived until shortly after Mary Smith's death in 1934. Records indicate that Eleanor Smith moved back to Hull-House and remained a resident there until her retirement in 1936.

Within the first few years of her association with Hull-House, Smith initiated one of the settlement's most enduring and popular traditions, the annual Christmas concert, which featured a series of tableaux or "Living Pictures" ("Eleanor Smith's Brief Autobiography," 4), static reenactments presented simultaneously with musical performances. The music included traditional seasonal pieces and original compositions by Smith and other Hull-House residents. The first concerts were strictly musical offerings; later, tableaux designed in the manner of such Renaissance artists as Fra Angelico and Sandro Botticelli were added. Smith and her staff conducted research to coordinate appropriate music with each tableau. The staging of these tableaux was created by the Hull-House dramatics students under the direction of EDITH de NANCREDE, while the costumes were designed and executed by Hull-House Art School director ENELLA BENEDICT and her students. For many neighborhood residents the annual Christmas concert-and-tableaux presentation at Hull-House was the high point of the year. Every holiday season, Bowen Hall was packed to capacity with neighbors eagerly awaiting the unveiling of the first dramatic and colorful tableau.

The annual Christmas concert was only one of the many programs initiated by Smith and presented by the students of the music school. Under Smith's direction, the Hull-House Music School grew into a significant artistic force in Chicago, featuring regular choral, orchestral, and chamber music performances as well as solo voice and instrumental recitals. Smith composed an extraordinary amount of music for the school, including vocal solos, shorter choral works, and operettas, which she frequently referred to as cantatas. Competent in-

structors were brought in to teach. A number of students went on to have careers in music, while many more developed a lifelong appreciation for music. Art Hodes, the renowned jazz pianist, recalled his early music training with Smith at Hull-House in a 1963 *Down Beat* article: "One week I'd be in the soprano section, the next, alto, and so on. Switch you around so you never got set, but they knew what they were doing . . . and today how I thank her [Smith]. She developed my hearing; she made it possible for me to hear (at least) three parts to a tune. These were dedicated sisters; it couldn't have been the money. The singing class was free, and the piano lesson was two-bits" (p. 39).

Smith's strong views on music pedagogy were compatible with contemporary trends in education. In 1897, Francis W. Parker of the Chicago Normal School for teachers put Smith in charge of the Department of Vocal Music. In 1902, Smith began similar associations with John Dewey, a leading educational philosopher, who invited her to teach music to aspiring teachers at the University of Chicago's School of Education and to assist him in revising curriculum for music education. In addition, her pedagogical and philosophical ideals found expression through courses she taught at the Froebel Kindergarten College and the Chicago Kindergarten College.

Smith also joined the effort to introduce music into the Chicago public schools and became a leader in that movement with the publication in 1898 of her first textbook series, *The Modern Music Series*. A collaborative venture with Robert Foresman, this series brought to music instruction the somewhat controversial "new education" (Birge, 154) movement, which focused on understanding the nature of the child and incorporating these insights into educational methods. A musical manifestation of this movement was the so-called "song method" (p. 152) of teaching, a process whereby students learned the elements and skills for reading music from songs. This method was radically different from the traditional "sight-singing" (p. 153) method in which students relied on drilling and memorizing single musical elements at a time.

The Modern Music Series incorporated the song method as its educational premise, and Smith, serving as editor of the series, used many of her own songs as teaching tools in the books. Hailed as the standard-bearer for a new age in music education, the series was enormously popular and spawned a number of other textbook series that adopted similar pedagogical ideas. Smith's second series, *The Eleanor Smith Music Series*, was published in 1908.

In 1915, in celebration of its twenty-fifth anniversary, Hull-House published the *Hull-House Songs*, five pieces with music composed by Eleanor Smith. These songs expressed Hull-House's support of various social issues and included the "Suffrage Song," "The Land of the Noonday Night" about unsafe conditions in the mines, and "The Shadow Child" with words by Chicago poet HARRIET MONROE, which reflected the agonies of child labor.

In 1936, Smith retired from the Hull-House Music School for health reasons. Her sister, Gertrude, an accomplished pianist who also taught music at the settlement, took over as director of the school. Eleanor Smith's remaining years were spent at a relative's farm in Midland, Michigan. There she died of pneumonia, contracted after a fall that broke her hip. She was cremated and her ashes were placed in a family plot near Annapolis, Maryland. At the time of her death, the music school that she had founded some fifty years before boasted an enrollment of approximately three hundred adults and children. Several months after Smith's death, during a memorial service held in her honor at Hull-House, two of the rooms in which she taught were named the Eleanor Smith Rooms.

Smith's prodigious musical output was a mirror of her life, reflecting her multifaceted career as a composer, voice teacher, choral conductor, opera coach, pianist, and music educator. Through her work at Hull-House over more than forty years, she inspired thousands of young people and adults in classes and music productions. She sought the highest standards in her own art and expected the same level of achievement from her students and colleagues. Her ideals were reflected in all facets of her career, and her impact on American music education, through her work with progressive educators John Dewey and Francis W. Parker, was far-reaching.

Sources. The Eleanor and Gertrude Smith Papers (including published compositions and unpublished manuscripts as well as programs from Hull-House Music School events) are in UIC Spec. Coll. Her unpublished operettas include "A Fable in Flowers" (composed 1918), "The Troll's Holiday" (composed 1905), "The Merman's Bride" (composed 1928), and "The Golden Asp" (possibly unfinished). Also in the collection is "Service to Honor the Memory of Eleanor Smith, Founder of Hull-House Music School," October 3, 1942, a useful source of biographical data. Alma Birmingham's Papers at UIC Spec. Coll. include a copy of "Eleanor Smith's Brief Autobiography," typescript, 1938–42. Information comes from Pamela Elrod's Ph.D. dissertation in progress, "Music at Hull-House: An Overview of Choral Music Events from 1893 to 1942 and a Study of the Life and Works of Eleanor Smith, Founder of the Hull-House Music School" (Univ. of Illinois at Urbana-Champaign). Smith's great-great nephew, Richard Shipps, provided family information in an interview with Pamela Elrod on November 6, 1995. In addition to the textbooks and songbooks mentioned above, Eleanor Smith wrote *Songs for Little Children* (1887), *Song Pictures: Poems* (1891), *Twelve Songs for Twelve Boys* (1896), *Singing Verses for Children* with Lydia Avery Coonley-Ward (1897), *The Beginner's Book of Vocal Music* (1898), *Songs of Life and Nature* (1898), *A First Book in Vocal Music* (1891), *Second Book in Vocal Music* with C. E. Richard Mueller (1898), *The Alternate Third Book of Vocal Music* (1898), *A Third Book in Vocal Music* (1899), *A Handbook for the Teaching of Vocal Music in the Schools* (1900), *A Primer of Vocal Music* (1900), *Singing Verses for Children* (1900), *A Third Book in Vocal Music* with C. E. Richard Mueller (1901), *The Alternate Third Book of Vocal Music* (1903), *The Common School Book of Vocal Music* (1904), *The Fourth Book of Vocal Music* (1905), *The High School Book of Vocal Music* (1905), *The Eleanor Smith Music Course* (1908), *The Eleanor Smith Music Course Manual* (1909), *Songs of a Little Child's Day* (1910), *The Special Third Book of Vocal Music* (1910), *The Eleanor Smith Music Primer* (1911), *Songs of a Little Child's Day* (1915), *The Children's Hymnal* with Charles H. Farnsworth and C. A. Fullerton (1918), *Song Devices and Jingles* (1920). Edward Bailey Birge's *History of Public School Music in the United States* (1928) provides information on Smith's role in music education as well as insight into pedagogical trends of the late nineteenth and early twentieth centuries. See also Art Hodes, "Sittin' In," *Down Beat*, August 1, 1963. An obituary, "Eleanor Smith, Once Hull House 'Genius', Is Dead," is in *Chicago Sun*, July 1, 1942.

PAMELA G. ELROD

SMITH, JULIA HOLMES ABBOT
December 23, 1838–November 10, 1930
PHYSICIAN, SUFFRAGIST, CLUBWOMAN

Born to antebellum luxury and ease in Savannah, Georgia, Julia Holmes Smith was the first child of Margaret Manning (Turner) Holmes and Willis Holmes, a prosperous cotton broker and commission merchant. She was raised in a large Presbyterian household that included four brothers—Willis, Enoch, Manley, and George; her aunt, Charlotte Turner; her grandmother, Abigail (McNeil) Turner; and many personal slaves. Margaret Holmes, who suffered miscarriages, stillbirths, and the deaths of two children, turned the management of the home and education of the children over to her severe but fair-minded sister, Charlotte.

Willis Holmes moved his family and business to New Orleans in 1847. In the four-storied row house and on the inland plantations where the family spent the summers to escape the dreaded yellow fever, Julia Holmes competed strenuously with her brothers. They coasted down the carpeted staircase on heavy silver trays, rode horseback, watched hog butchering, and studied Latin, Greek, algebra, calculus, and the classics with their aunt and tutors in the third-floor classroom.

Julia Holmes followed her brothers North for further education and graduated in 1856 from the Abbot Collegiate Institute for Young Ladies in New York City. During her three years there, she received an education equal to that of the boys and preparation for the unlikely time that she might become dependent on her own resources.

Although Julia Holmes went back to New Orleans for her debut, the center of her world remained in New York with Waldo Abbot, the nephew of the principal of her school. The two were married February 7, 1860, in New Orleans and returned North on the eve of the Civil War. During the next four years, the young couple often lived from hand to mouth because of Abbot's frail health, a series of failed business ventures, and Willis Holmes's wartime financial ruin. The Abbots' daughter, Margaret, born in December 1860, lived only eight months. Their son, Willis John, was born in 1863.

In June 1864, after receiving the news of Willis Holmes's death in March, Julia Holmes gave premature birth to another daughter, Elizabeth, in Key West, Florida, where Waldo Abbot had been sent as United States District Attorney. In July Waldo Abbot died of yellow fever, leaving his wife near death with yellow fever and a breast abscess. Julia Abbot, her infant daughter, and her sixteen-month-old son, returned on the warship *Huntsville* to Connecticut and her husband's family. Baby Elizabeth died within months, and by 1866, Julia Abbot, wishing to earn her own living, left Willis with his grandfather in New Haven and returned with her mother to New Orleans. There, Julia Holmes Abbot became a drama writer for the *New Orleans Picayune*.

Uncomfortable in the postwar south, Smith soon returned North to study the new Peabody-Froebel kindergarten method in Boston before opening her own kindergarten in New Haven. In 1872, she married Sabin Smith, a merchant twenty years her senior, with grown children, including two daughters. The family moved to Boston where, in 1873, their only daughter, Helen Page Smith, was born.

FIG. 106. *Physician Julia Holmes Smith marching for woman suffrage, 1913.*

Encouraged by Dr. Mercy Jackson, who treated her after Helen's birth, and Sabin Smith, who gladly paid her tuition, Julia Holmes Smith entered Boston University Medical School in 1873. When her husband was transferred to Pelham, New York, in 1875, Julia Smith studied there with a private doctor and treated medical problems of women textile workers without charge.

In 1876, the Smiths and their family, which included at least one of his daughters, moved to Chicago, where Sabin Smith managed a dry-goods store. Julia Smith, already acquainted with Chicago women through the Association for the Advancement of Women, founded by clubwomen in 1872 to improve economic, educational, and social conditions for women, immediately joined the fashionable Fortnightly and the Chicago Women's Club (later Chicago Woman's Club). She completed her medical education at the Chicago Homeopathic College in March 1877.

Julia Holmes Smith practiced homeopathic family medicine in Chicago for the next forty years. Homeopathy was a system of medicine developed in the early nineteenth century, partly in reaction to what its practitioners saw as excessive bloodletting and dosing with drugs done by allopathic doctors. Homeopathic physicians treated diseases by the administration to patients of minute doses of drugs and other remedies known to produce similar disease symptoms in healthy persons. Homeopathy also encouraged a commonsense lifestyle that included

fresh air, exercise, and comfortable clothing. From her home in the early morning and late afternoon, and in her nearby downtown office at midday, she treated women, children, and adolescent girls of the wealthier classes, the group who preferred homeopathic to allopathic medicine.

In the early 1880s Dr. Smith founded a clinic for poor women at Dwight Moody's Chicago Avenue Church. Believing, however, that the poor should be trained to help themselves, she became a lecturer (1886–1907) and director (1886–1920) at the Illinois Training School for Nurses, founded in 1880 to train working women for a profession and to supply trained nurses to the poor. Smith was a professor, then dean, of the National (Homeopathic) Medical College from 1897 to 1903 and was consulting physician from 1904 to 1907 at the Frances Willard Temperance Hospital, founded in 1880 to treat patients with non-alcoholic drugs.

Through this practice, her leadership in local, state, and national homeopathic medical societies, and articles for homeopathic journals, Smith established a solid local and national reputation as an authority on the diseases and lifestyles of women and children. She contributed to the section on gynecology in *Dr. Hugo Arndt's System of Medicine, Based upon the Law of Homeopathy* (1886) and published a series of articles in the *New York Ledger* in the 1890s on "Common Sense for Mothers and Nurses."

Smith's active club life provided her with the contacts necessary to advance her medical career as well as her reformist philosophy. As president of the Chicago Women's Club in 1879–81 and 1883–84, Smith led the club into municipal reform and presided over the biennial meeting of the Association for the Advancement of Women in Chicago in 1883. She served on Julia Ward Howe's Woman's Committee at the World's Industrial and Cotton Centennial Exposition in New Orleans in 1884–85 as Special Commissioner for the Northwest.

Smith never lost her interest in literary pursuits. In 1885–86, she and other Chicago women journalists organized the Illinois Woman's Press Association. Their model was the National Woman's Press Association founded at the New Orleans exposition, when women journalists found it difficult to get publicity for the women's events.

Julia Holmes Smith represented a broad spectrum of women's interests at the 1893 World's Columbian Exposition. In 1889, she and other prosuffrage professionals organized the Queen Isabella Association, a group opposed to the separate display of women's work. When the Isabellas lost this argument to their rival organization, the Board of Lady Managers and their government-funded Woman's Building, Smith associated herself with the Illinois Women's Exposition Board and the Illinois Training School for Nurses, planning a model hospital and emergency clinic for women and children at the exposition. This exhibit had a building of its own, where the model hospital showed an up-to-date operating room, diet kitchen, office and reception room, a section of a child's ward and woman's ward, and a private room for patients. Drs. Smith, SARAH HACKETT STEVENSON, and Marie Reasner recruited volunteer women homeopathic, allopathic, and eclectic doctors and nurses to staff the clinic, which treated more than three thousand patients during the exposition.

Julia Holmes Smith also served on the committee planning the Congress of Representative Women, one of the many congresses held in conjunction with the Columbian Exposition, a highly publicized meeting that brought women from all over the world together to discuss social, political, religious, and economic issues. Smith read leading American woman physician Dr. Mary Putnam Jacobi's paper on "Women in Science" and led the discussion that followed. Smith was the only woman on the committee that organized the Homeopathic Physicians and Surgeons Congress and was head of the Woman's Committee of the same congress. Criticized by ELLEN HENROTIN, vice-president of the Women's Auxiliary of the World's Congress Auxiliary, for having few women on the homeopathic panels, Smith replied that no woman not a doctor could understand the strong opposition of men and the pull of home life that women in medicine faced.

Smith, converted to woman suffrage in the 1870s by William Lloyd Garrison, worked for municipal suffrage in 1886. In June 1894, the first year that women could vote in a state election for school officials, the Illinois State Suffrage Association convinced the state Democratic Party at its convention to nominate a woman for trustee of the University of Illinois. When the first choice, CATHARINE McCULLOCH, declined to run, Dr. Julia Holmes Smith became the candidate. In this campaign, where fashionable women voted alongside their servants, the women candidates received much publicity. Although the Democrats lost to the Republicans, Dr. Smith was appointed in January 1895 by Governor John Peter Altgeld to fill the unexpired term of a male trustee who died; she thus became the first woman trustee of the University of Illinois, taking office a month before the Republican winner, LUCY FLOWER. Smith remained a trustee until 1897, serving as a member of the Instruction and Finance committee and chair of the Student's Welfare Committee.

In 1900 Smith suffered a series of personal and professional losses that left her in low spirits. Her beloved daughter, Helen Page Smith, who had managed her household during the preceding decade while Smith worked to support her invalid husband and aging mother, married Hyde (Hiram) Wallace Perce in December and moved into her own home. In an election marked by apathy of women voters, Smith was defeated for the second term for trustee of the University of Illinois. Her pessimism spilled over to her medical practice, and she declared that 999 of 1,000 women were not fit for the responsibility of motherhood.

Never one for extended self-pity, however, Smith redoubled her efforts for woman suffrage, organizing the Women's Democratic League, and serving as an officer of local and state suffrage societies. In 1901, she convinced many conservative members of the General Federation of Women's Clubs to support an ultimately successful bill that gave women equal powers, rights, and duties in the guardianship of minor children. In 1920, at age eighty-one, she tearfully rejoiced in the passage of the Nineteenth Amendment, proud of her own efforts in the struggle.

Smith continued to practice medicine after her husband's death in November 1906. She retired at age seventy-eight in 1917 but remained active in many professional, literary, and medical societies and devoted to her family. Her grandchildren,

who called her "Docti," admired the fiercely independent, mischievous spirit inside the lilac-scented, always feminine exterior of lace-trimmed dresses, brimless bonnets, white gloves, and kid shoes.

Julia Holmes Abbot Smith died at ninety-one in the North Shore Nursing Home in Winnetka of myocarditis and senility of two years duration. Her memorial service was at her daughter's home in Oak Park, and she was cremated at Graceland Cemetery in Chicago.

Smith once denigrated her professional and reform achievements as slight. Her contemporaries, whose lives were changed and empowered by her actions, thought differently. They saw her as a rare woman who successfully combined home life with social and professional obligations and who inspired others never to give up when faced with adversity.

Sources. Personal material on Julia Holmes Smith in the possession of her great-grandson, Hyde Perce, of New Canaan, Connecticut, includes remembrances by Smith's granddaughter, Doris Perce, newspaper clippings and articles by Smith, her obituary and that of her son; Turner family genealogical records; and correspondence between Doris Perce and relatives. The Catharine Waugh McCulloch Papers in the Mary Dillon Collection at SL include important material about Smith's activities in the Illinois Woman's Suffrage Association and a number of personal letters. The Julia Ward Howe Papers, SL; the Abbot Memorial Collection, Bowdoin College, Brunswick, Maine; and the Elizabeth Boynton Harbert Papers, Huntington Library, San Marino, California, all contain material about Smith. Several Chicago archives hold material on Smith, including CHS, John Crerar, UC Library, and Spec. Coll. UIC. Articles and papers by Smith include "The Higher Education of Woman from a Physical Standpoint: Section of Sanitary Science. A Paper Read before the American Institute of Homeopathy at Atlantic City, June 1899," *Syracuse Clinic,* September 1899; "Commonsense for Mothers and Nurses: A Series of Articles," *New York Ledger,* 1890–91; sections on gynecology in all three volumes of H. R. Arndt, ed., *System of Medicine, Based upon the Law of Homeopathy* (1886). There are short biographies in *History of Medicine and Surgery and Physicians and Surgeons of Chicago* (1922); Sarah Hobson, "Dr. Julia Holmes Smith: The Glory of Service," *Medical Woman's Journal,* vol. 31, 1924; and *Prominent Women of Illinois, 1885–1932* (1932).

JULIA WOOD KRAMER

SMITH, LUCY MADDEN
January 14, 1875–June 18, 1952
PASTOR, EVANGELIST, RADIO PREACHER, FAITH HEALER

Lucy Madden Smith profoundly shaped the African American religious culture of Chicago. Within a few years of migrating to the city, Smith organized a roving congregation into an established church—the first woman in Chicago ever to do so—and built two churches from the ground up. By the 1950s, her congregation, the All Nations Pentecostal Church, was a highly influential, racially integrated church with a membership of five thousand people.

One of six children, Lucy Madden was born on a plantation in Oglethorpe County, Georgia. As a child she faced the deprivations common to most African American families in the postbellum rural South. The one-room log cabin where she lived with her mother and siblings contained a few furnishings, a fireplace made of two stones, and an open roof loft in which the children slept. Though Madden never knew her father, she re-

FIG. 107. *Pentecostalist minister and faith healer Lucy Madden Smith at Langley Avenue All Nations Pentecostal Church, late 1920s.*

membered her mother as affectionate and kind. Their food was meager—usually syrup and gravy, with meat several times each week eaten from a tin pan. Having attended school only four months of the year as mandated for black children in Georgia, Madden had a negligible formal education. Yet she not only learned to read later in life, she also made numerous business transactions concerning her two churches and radio program, often signing her name with a small "x."

In 1896 Lucy Madden married William Smith, the man whose name she carried for the rest of her life. Two years after the marriage she bore the first of their nine children. After farming in rural Georgia for an additional fourteen years, the Smith family then moved to Athens, Georgia, where William Smith abandoned the family. Lucy Smith struggled alone in Athens for a year to support her children before relocating in 1909 to Atlanta, where she found work as a seamstress. Following the pattern set by thousands of African Americans, who went first to urban centers in the South and then to northern enclaves to find greater economic opportunities, Smith soon moved with her children to Chicago, arriving by train in the spring of 1910. A reconciliation with William Smith in Chicago lasted a number of years and produced two children but was ultimately unsuccessful.

The African American population of Chicago had grown to a considerable 44,103 by 1910, up from just 14,271 two decades

earlier. The large increase was beginning to tax the scant resources of the city's black community, but many churches and civic organizations attempted to meet the needs of the growing population. One such institution, which Lucy Smith joined upon her arrival in Chicago, was Olivet Baptist Church, which, with nearly fifteen thousand members by the mid-1920s, would soon claim to have the largest membership of all Baptist churches anywhere. Staying only briefly, Smith affiliated with Olivet to become acclimated to the urban North, as well as for the varied programs of material outreach offered there. Dissatisfied with Olivet and with Ebenezer, another influential Baptist church with which she briefly associated, Lucy Smith left the Baptist faith altogether in 1914 to join Stone Church, a white Pentecostal assembly. At Stone Church, Smith underwent a series of experiences that redirected her life and led to the formation of the church of All Nations.

Like a number of black women of the nineteenth century who underwent conversion experiences—AMANDA BERRY SMITH, Jerena Lee, Rebecca Cox Jackson, Zilpha Elaw, and Julia Foote—Lucy Smith received her "call" in dramatic fashion. She recalled, "Oh how the voice of the Lord did speak to me" (*Pamphlet of the Glorious Church*, 3). It was clear to Smith from the outset that her primary spiritual service would eventually be "divine healing" (Strong, 395), but after two years of contemplation, she expressed her desire to start a church to three women who met regularly with her for prayer. This small group made up the core of what began as a tent mission and later became the five-thousand-member All Nations Pentecostal Church.

The beginning years were difficult for Smith and her band of "Saints." In Pentecostal parlance, Saints had experienced baptism with the Holy Spirit, shown by speaking in tongues. With little money and no permanent home, the mission church moved about constantly to various points on the South Side for nearly a decade. Along with a number of outdoor tents, All Nations occupied the Star Theater, a Masonic Hall, and the Pekin Theater. On December 19, 1926, however, Lucy Smith led her growing church on a "Saints march" (*Pamphlet of the Glorious Church*, 6) from her home to its new permanent location, which she called the Langley Avenue All Nations Pentecostal Church. Cut into a single stone placed outside the church was a quote from the Bible: "My house shall be called a house of prayer for all nations" (quoted in Herbert Smith, 9).

At Langley Avenue Lucy Smith became known as the "preacher to the disinherited class" (Herbert Smith, 7). In contrast to the luminous white facade of the church, the area surrounding it was blighted, deteriorating, and desperately poor. The Federal Slum Clearance Committee had determined that the entire area needed demolition. Many of the homes were virtually uninhabitable despite the often exorbitant rents charged by absentee property owners. In time, many of the area residents who attended All Nations Pentecostal for spiritual succor also leaned upon the church's resources for material help. Lucy Smith responded with a systematic program of social outreach, using her influence and the auspices of All Nations for social service to the community. When the Great Depression reached its severest levels in Chicago, Smith was feeding and clothing thousands from her own congregation and from other parts of the city.

"Elder Lucy Smith," as she was called, was also a pioneer in black gospel radio. Her spirited "Glorious Church of The Air" (*Pamphlet of the Glorious Church*, cover) was first broadcast in 1933 over station WSLC and later on WIND, WFLC, and WGES. The popular services earned her fame as the "world's greatest Radio Pastor" (*Pamphlet of the Glorious Church*, cover), while bridging gaps between secular and sacred, middle and lower class, black and white persons. Often giving exposure to young artists like MAHALIA JACKSON, Lucy Smith's radio broadcast maintained its undisputed rule over the airwaves of migration-era Chicago.

When Lucy Smith started her radio broadcast, it gave exposure to her ministry of charity and social service. She was the first in Chicago to mix gospel programming with appeals to radio listeners for material goods to be given to the poor. Area businesses responded by donating food that Smith and a staff of volunteer workers distributed to hundreds who lined up for meals almost daily.

The broadcast, however, drew the sharpest attention to Lucy Smith's ministry of healing. Tall in stature and weighing more than three hundred pounds, Smith considered herself primarily a "faith healer." Word of her gift spread swiftly throughout the city, drawing large crowds to All Nations in search of her touch. Some too poor to afford medical attention, others simply distrustful of traditional medicine, a wide spectrum of Chicago's citizens embraced Lucy Smith and looked to her for care and for cures. Though Smith never accepted money for the use of her gift, she nevertheless published a number of testimonials given by those claiming to have benefited from her touch. Foreshadowing the practices of later twentieth-century faith healers, Smith stored canes and crutches that had been abandoned by their former users in the basement of All Nations Pentecostal Church, calling this the "trophy room" (quoted in Herbert Smith, 10). Smith maintained that she healed close to two hundred thousand people in her lifetime.

The popularity of Smith's church and broadcasts was largely responsible for bringing the concept of "divine healing" into the mainstream among African Americans in Chicago. As a consequence, All Nations church grew to defy the standard typology of Pentecostal lower-class churches and challenged the primacy of mainline black Baptist and Methodist congregations. Smith's church reached a level of acclaim and influence not achieved by churches like hers. Her crowning achievement was the second home of the All Nations church built on Oakwood Boulevard on the South Side, where she and her congregation moved on May 28, 1939. The large modern building solidified Smith's status as one of the most important and influential ministers in Chicago. Joining her at the ground breaking for the new structure were alderman William Dawson; Chicago businesswoman Marjorie Stewart Joyner, one of the founders of MARY EVANS's Cosmopolitan Community Church; and Adam Patterson, a representative for Mayor Edward J. Kelly. All Nations at Oakwood Boulevard had become sizable, prosperous, progressive, and well organized. True to Smith's strongly held belief in interracialism, All Nations was the only decidedly interracial congregation on the South Side. Smith was known to proclaim that "this is not a colored church. . . . We don't make no difference between colors here" (quoted in Herbert Smith, 13, 19).

All Nations counted among its membership a number of native Whites, Filipinos, Swedes, Poles, Italians, and Native Americans. Lucy Smith defied the racial particularism prevalent in most Chicago black and white churches at the time. From a premise steeped in biblical theology and egalitarian philosophy, Smith insisted on a congregation made up of "All Nations."

In addition to dismantling racial barriers, Lucy Smith tackled class divisions among Chicago's black churches. Smith garnered the scorn of those who were uncomfortable with women in positions of ecclesiastical authority. Some took issue with her "down home manner" and unsophisticated speech. Nevertheless, Blacks of the upper and middle classes were just as likely to attend one of Smith's midnight healing services as Chicago's poorer residents. A number of Chicago's most prominent citizens and church leaders held Lucy Smith in high regard. After taking up residence at Oakwood Boulevard, Smith engaged in a fair amount of exchange with Chicago's black ministers. Junius C. Austin, pastor of Pilgrim Baptist Church, visited All Nations frequently. He gave the eulogy for Lucy Smith's son, William, one of six children who preceded her in death. Mary G. Evans had a close relationship with Smith. The father and son duo, Archibald J. Carey Sr. and Jr. of the African Methodist Episcopal denomination, as well as the redoubtable "Father" Clarence Cobb of First Church of Deliverance, Rev. Louis Bodie of Greater Harvest Baptist, and Joseph M. Evans of Metropolitan Community, were all close friends and frequent guests of Lucy Smith. Attesting to her good fellowship with most of Chicago's black clerics, Smith reported, "I been to mighty near all de churches. Dem few I ain't been to—it's because I been busy, not because they haven't asked me. They all recognize me. Most of the preachers has been here too" (quoted in Herbert Smith, 18). The church's motto seemed to express Smith's central aim for All Nations and the black religious community at large: A Friendly Church in the Heart of a Friendly Community.

Lucy Smith died in her home following a brief illness. Sixty thousand people made their way to view the body at the A. A. Raynor Chapel on Cottage Grove Avenue. A reported fifty thousand lined the streets to watch the seventy-five-car processional travel to Lincoln Cemetery. The surviving children of Lucy Smith—John, Henry, and Ardella—received more than four thousand letters of condolence, including messages from the governor of the state, the mayor of the city, and a core of African American ministers and civic leaders. Elder Lucy Smith significantly shaped the African American religious culture of Chicago, set the standard for live gospel broadcasting, and agitated for racial and class unity in Chicago's religious and civic life. In the process, she challenged the accepted boundaries for black women of faith in the public sphere.

Sources. The papers of Lucy Madden Smith are in the Lucy Smith Collier Papers, held in the Vivian G. Harsh Research Collection of Afro-American History and Literature at the Carter G. Woodson Regional Library, CPL. The Collier collection includes Smith's unpublished autobiography, testimonials of healings, brochures and correspondence from All Nations Pentecostal Church, newspaper clippings, and a large number of photographs of Smith, her family and congregation, and her funeral. The papers contain a pamphlet advertising Smith's church and radio program, A *Pamphlet of the Glorious Church of the Air* (1936). Also included are transcribed interviews by Wallace Best with Smith's granddaughter, Lucy Smith Collier ("Little Lucy"), on November 5 and December 2, 1996. Apart from Smith's personal papers, the best sources of information on her life and work appear in two theses: Herbert Morrison Smith (no relation to Lucy Smith), "Three Negro Preachers in Chicago: A Study in Religious Leadership" (Ph.D. diss., Univ. of Chicago, 1935) contains the only known full interview of the evangelist; Samuel M. Strong, "Social Types in the Negro Community of Chicago: An Example of the Social Type Method" (Ph.D. diss., Univ. of Chicago, 1940) includes a version of Smith's autobiography with the title, "The Biography of L.S.: From Farm to Pulpit." Information on All Nations Pentecostal Church is in the "Illinois Writer's Project" materials at Carter G. Woodson Library. The *Chicago Defender* covered the life of Elder Smith and activities at All Nations in the 1930s and 1940s. Sherry Sherrod DuPree, *Biographical Dictionary of African-American Holiness-Pentecostals, 1880–1990* (1989) has an entry on Smith. For discussion of Elder Lucy Smith at various levels of detail, see St. Clair Drake and Horace Cayton, *Black Metropolis: A Study of Negro Life in a Northern City* (1945); Allan Spear, *Black Chicago: The Making of a Negro Ghetto* (1967); Eric Foner, *America's Black Past: A Reader in Afro-American History* (1970); and Milton C. Sernett, *Bound for the Promised Land: African American Religion and the Great Migration* (1997). Obituaries appeared in *Chicago Defender*, June 21, 1952; *Chicago Herald American*, June 25, 1952; and in a press release, "Famed Chicago Radio Pastor, Elder Lucy Smith, Dies," June 25, 1952, Claude Barnett Papers, CHS.

WALLACE BEST

SMITH, MARY ROZET
December 23, 1868–February 22, 1934
PHILANTHROPIST

The only daughter of Charles Mather and Sarah (Rozet) Smith, Mary Rozet Smith was born in a house on Walton Place built by her father before the Great Chicago Fire of 1871. It was one of the few structures in the Near North Side neighborhood that did not burn in the conflagration and was a visible link between the old settlers of the antebellum era and the industrial city of the Progressive Era. Mary Rozet Smith had two brothers, Charles Frederick and Francis Drexel. Her father came to Chicago in 1850 from Ogdensburg, New York. He first worked for the Illinois Central Railroad and then, in 1873, became president of the Bradner-Smith Paper Company, a business founded by his cousin. "Her mother was a Philadelphia woman of 'position'" (Linn, 147). Mary Smith attended the Kirkland School, where ELLEN GATES STARR taught before cofounding Hull-House. Accompanied by her mother and father, Smith traveled abroad extensively during her adolescent years.

In 1890 Mary Smith found herself without any practical work and, seemingly, lacking any particular passion or goals for her future. She had not attended college, which was not that unusual for a wealthy young woman in the late 1880s and early 1890s. Her friend Jennie Dow had begun to teach the kindergarten class at Hull-House, and Mary Smith "drifted to the House in the course of its first year, to see whether there was anything she could do there" (Linn, 147). "From that day until she died, forty-three years later," James Linn, nephew and biographer of JANE ADDAMS writes, "the interests of the House remained the center of her own interests, and the friendship of Mary Smith soon became and always remained the highest and clearest note in the music of Jane Addams's personal life" (Linn, 147).

Eight years younger than Addams, Mary Smith's sweetness and physical loveliness were mentioned by Hull-House participants and friends of Addams, and Addams herself writes of her as "A girl, both tall and fair to see, / (To look at her gives one a thrill)" (Linn, 289) in a poem written in 1895 about the woman who, by then, had become her partner. Since Addams instructed her nephew James Linn to destroy her personal correspondence with Smith, a not uncommon decision made by women in same-sex relationships, there is little direct evidence about the nature of the relationship she and Smith shared. Linn found in her papers after she died the unfinished draft of Addams's poem to Mary Smith. The poem goes on to recount how at first Addams only thought about Mary Smith's skills and how she might fit into the Hull-House program. "You see, I had forgotten love, / And only thought of Hull-House then" (quoted in Linn, 289). She explains further, "That is the way with women folks / When they attempt the things of men" (p. 290) and tells us she "was blind and deaf those years / To all save one absorbing care, / And did not guess what now I know—/ Delivering love was sitting there!" (p. 290).

The nature of the romantic friendship between Jane Addams and Mary Rozet Smith remains unknowable in its specific details. Leila J. Rupp's *A Desired Past: A Short History of Same-Sex Love in America* (1999) sums up the difficulty in correctly describing relationships as "lesbian" or even "homosexual" in the case of "individuals who desired or loved or engaged in sexual activities with others of the same sex unless they lived at a time when those categories had been named and claimed" (p. 8). Instead, Rupp uses the term "same-sex love and sexuality" to describe "a wide variety of desires and emotions and behaviors throughout American history" (p. 8). Addams and Smith began their relationship in the late nineteenth century and had been raised by parents in Victorian America at a time when it was acceptable for young women friends to travel together, to share beds, to have deep friendships with sentimental correspondence, and to show a level of physical affection and tenderness strange to later generations. By 1920 such activity would have been thought of as obsessive, perhaps deviant. The precise moment of the change has been debated among historians. Chicago literary bohemians MARGARET ANDERSON and JANE HEAP had in the 1910s defended homosexuality in their magazine *Little Review* and proceeded to live as a lesbian couple. It is quite probable that most women of the late Victorian era would not have recognized any similarity between their same-sex romantic friendships and the erotic, sexually charged relationship shared by Anderson and Heap. Lillian Faderman writes about the "Boston marriage," a term "used in late nineteenth-century New England to describe a long-term monogamous relationship between two otherwise unmarried women" (Faderman, 190) and concludes that "whether these unions sometimes or often included sex we will never know, but we do know that these women spent their lives primarily with other women, they gave to other women the bulk of their energy and attention, and they formed powerful emotional ties with other women" (p. 190). There simply is not enough evidence in this instance to accept or reject Faderman's notion that "if their personalities could be projected to our times, it is probable that they would see themselves as 'women-identified-women,' i.e., what we would call lesbians, regardless of the level of their sexual interests" (p. 190).

Smith continued to live with her parents and never moved into Hull-House. Her devotion to her parents and extended family was lifelong; with the passage of years, she became involved with the details of Jane Addams's family just as Addams showed her affection and devotion to Smith family needs. Even a superficial reading of the hundreds of extant letters written by Addams and Smith to each other and also to each other's respective families reveals how intertwined the two women's lives became. Jane Addams's schedule included writing, lecturing, and months of travel each year. Smith made certain that nephews and nieces received birthday greetings and Christmas presents; in later years the two women visited grandnephews and grandnieces with Smith frequently making the arrangements. The Smith family included Jane Addams in their circle of intimates and endorsed her projects enthusiastically. When Sarah Smith died in 1903, Mary Smith donated an organ to Hull-House in her mother's memory. Smith's father donated money to Hull-House, including the money for the Children's Building, subsequently named the Smith Building after him. Sarah Porter Smith, Charles Mather Smith's older sister, also lived in the family home in Chicago. She was a benefactor of Hull-House, especially of the Jane Club.

Of the six women who were closest to Jane Addams—Ellen Gates Starr, JULIA LATHROP, FLORENCE KELLEY, LOUISE deKOVEN BOWEN, ALICE HAMILTON, and Mary Rozet Smith—Smith's role in Hull-House affairs is the hardest to define. All of them cared about Hull-House programs and initiatives; all of them were devoted to Jane Addams. The five other women all had careers, including Bowen, who was a career volunteer, in which they were recognized for their expertise apart from Hull-House and Jane Addams. Mary Rozet Smith's consummate interest was in sustaining the efforts of her friend, Jane Addams; her devotion and assistance both financially and emotionally to Addams has been recognized as her major contribution.

The preponderance of funding for Hull-House came from three sources. Initially, Jane Addams used her own inheritance. In the mid-1890s Mary Rozet Smith "began to pay [Addams's] bills, and soon thereafter her close friend, Louise deKoven Bowen, provided for the settlement's needs" (Sklar, 95). Mary Smith made her first large contribution to the general expenses of the settlement in May 1895, when she paid $328 for paving and for building a wall in the yard. Sklar tells us that "Mary Smith's gift had more in common with Addams's own than with those of other Hull House [sic] benefactors. Smith's contribution . . . represented the beginnings of a sea change in Addams's financial burden" (p. 101). Smith contributed $116,395 to the settlement between 1906 and 1934. Contributions were not systematically recorded before 1906, but Sklar estimates from Smith's correspondence with Addams "that her annual donations reached about the same scale between 1895 and 1906" (p. 104). Other major contributors included Bowen and HELEN CULVER, niece and beneficiary of the man who built Hull-House in 1856. Culver owned the land around Hull-House. She donated that parcel and "some adjacent lots, worth a total of $76,800. In 1920 Culver gave Hull-House its largest

single gift—a $250,000 endowment, one-quarter of the income of which was to be reinvested until the total amounted to $300,000" (Sklar, 106).

Mary Rozet Smith and Louise deKoven Bowen gave Addams financial support on a regular basis and were involved in the daily activities of Hull-House. Bowen contributed a total of $542,282 over a period of thirty-four years. She became treasurer of Hull-House in 1907, a position she held until after Addams's death. Sklar has called Bowen "the power behind Addams's throne" (p. 107).

Both James Linn and Kathryn Kish Sklar identify a singular element in the financial role played by Mary Rozet Smith. In absolute figures her contribution was not nearly as large as Culver's or Bowen's. Instead, it was her generosity and unconditional support of Addams's work in combination with her role as uncritical and loving confidant that was so significant. Addams was able to open up to Smith and share her fears and anxieties about financial and other matters. Linn writes that in the early years, it was Mary Rozet Smith's "constant overcoming of deficits here and there, small but apparently unsurmountable, that literally kept the work going, or at any rate kept Jane Addams from black discouragement" (Linn, 147–48).

Smith was known for her participation in Hull-House activities and as the person who helped out where she was needed, especially in the music school and with the nursery and groups of young children. She was responsible for many of the social clubs in which neighborhood residents participated. She knew the different children who lived in the neighborhood and came to the settlement. Her focus on the clubs and classes for children was in line with Jane Addams's concerns. The earliest activities of Hull-House were clubs and classes for children; the kindergarten, nursery, studio, and music school were the first additions to the initial activities. Addams saw Hull-House as a place in the neighborhood where immigrants and their children could learn to understand each other; parents and children were often unable to communicate because of the strong assimilative forces that shaped the first generation born in the United States. Addams, Kelley, Bowen, Hamilton, and others investigated conditions in which children lived and advocated numerous changes in law to strengthen education, protect children, and provide for structures of prevention and rehabilitation for troubled youth. Mary Rozet Smith implicitly supported all of these initiatives through her funding of Hull-House itself as a central place for research and policy-making on children's issues. She did not, however, undertake sociological studies or write scholarly reports. She was remembered instead for her warmth and personal engagement in the lives of children who came through the doors of Hull-House.

Jane Addams traveled extensively in her lifetime; when possible, Mary Smith accompanied her. When she was unable to accompany Addams, the correspondence between the two of them was liberally interspersed with a sense of homesickness and longing for each other. Jane Addams traveled to Europe in 1900 to attend the Paris Exposition as a member of the Jury of International Awards. It was an exciting time for Addams, and she wrote back letters filled with reports on interesting people she had met and exhibits she had viewed. Throughout, however, a persistent theme recurs: finding a way to have Mary

Smith meet her in Europe as soon as possible. For Addams, enjoyment of a wonderful play or an opera was enhanced enormously by having Mary Smith at her side. When Mary Rozet Smith was absent because of her family obligations, Addams suffered. "I got so [depressed] yesterday that I brought your picture down from the studio and have it this minute over my mantle—from which I got a surprising comfort. I do wish you were back" Addams wrote Smith in April 1898 (Addams to Mary Rozet Smith, April 1898, Swarthmore College Peace Collection). On another occasion when they were apart, Addams wrote, "I think of you long and often, always with love and yearning—it is only a week from today when I shall be back. Bless you darling" (Addams to Mary Rozet Smith, June 20, 1909, Swarthmore College Peace Collection). Jane Addams's niece Marcet Haldeman-Julius realized that Mary Rozet Smith completed Jane Addams and brought to the surface all that was most sensitive and considerate in the famous woman's inner being.

Having worried about Jane Addams's illnesses for so long, it was a shock when the younger woman, Mary Rozet Smith, died one year before her dearest friend. In early February, Jane Addams suffered a heart attack but recovered. Later that month Mary Rozet Smith died of pneumonia in her home in Chicago. Addams was so grief-stricken that friends and family worried whether she would be able to survive the emotional loss. Letters of condolence poured in and illustrated the degree to which Addams's allies, friends, and relatives had understood the depth of her relationship with Smith. One communication was particularly poignant. Ellen Gates Starr wrote to her old friend, "I have always—at any rate for a great many years—been thankful that Mary came to supply what you needed. At all events, I thank God that I never was envious of her in any vulgar or ignoble way. One could't [sic] be of anyone so noble and generous and in every way fair-minded as she, and so humble" (Starr to Addams, April 12, 1935, Ellen Gates Starr Letters). Ellen Starr had desired to have that special place in Jane Addams's life, but such a relationship did not evolve. The two founders of Hull-House had grown apart for many reasons, one of which undeniably was the place in her heart Jane Addams found for Mary Rozet Smith.

Mary Rozet Smith's financial support of Hull-House came at a crucial time in the life of the institution. Her fidelity to Addams's vision gave the head resident of Hull-House the freedom to take risks and empowered her to bring together a group of bright, inventive, and committed social reformers and then to allow these women to experiment and to innovate.

Sources. There are twelve folders in the Mary Rozet Smith Papers, Jane Addams Memorial Collection, UIC Spec. Coll. There are letters in the Swarthmore College Peace Collection and in the Ellen Gates Starr Letters, Sophia Smith Collection, Smith College, Northampton, Massachusetts. For a complete listing of the Smith-Addams correspondence, see Mary Lynn McCree Bryan, ed., *The Jane Addams Papers: A Comprehensive Guide* (1996). James Weber Linn, *Jane Addams: A Biography* (1935), contains an excellent chapter, "Six Women," that includes an insightful analysis of his Aunt Jane's relationship with Mary Rozet Smith. See also Marcet Haldeman-Julius, *Jane Addams as I Knew Her* (1936). Kathryn Kish Sklar's "Who Funded Hull House?" in *Lady Bountiful Revisited: Women, Philanthropy, and Power*, ed. Kathleen D. McCarthy (1990), is a thorough exploration of the financial activities of the leading supporters of Hull-House. Books on the topic of same-sex friendship in Victorian America include Lillian Faderman, *Surpassing the Love of Men: Romantic Friendship and Love between Women from the Renaissance to the Present* (1981); Leila J. Rupp, *A Desired Past: A Short History of Same-Sex Love in America* (1999); and John D'Emilio and Estelle B. Freedman, *Intimate Matters: A History of Sexuality in America* 1997).

RIMA LUNIN SCHULTZ

SOLOMON, HANNAH GREENEBAUM
January 14, 1858–December 7, 1942
FOUNDER AND PRESIDENT OF NATIONAL ORGANIZATION, SOCIAL ACTIVIST, CIVIC REFORMER, CLUBWOMAN

As founder and president of the National Council of Jewish Women, Hannah Greenebaum Solomon was prominent in the American Jewish community and renowned internationally. In addition she moved into leadership positions in the larger Chicago community through her organizational work in progressive social and civic reform.

Hannah Greenebaum was born in Chicago, one of ten children of Michael and Sarah (Spiegel) Greenebaum, immigrants from Germany. She had three older and two younger sisters and four younger brothers. Her father, trained as a tinsmith, came in 1845 from Eppelsheim, a German village in the Rhenish Palatinate. After living in New York City for a year, he moved to Chicago, thinking the climate might be better. By 1852, his entire family—parents and seven siblings—had come to Chicago. Sarah Spiegel, Michael Greenebaum's cousin, and her family emigrated to New York in 1848 from Abendheim, Germany. Michael and Sarah Greenebaum were married in Chicago in 1852. He had begun work as a salesman in a hardware business; after their marriage, he became "a prosperous hardware merchant" (*Fabric of My Life*, 21). Michael Greenebaum was one of the founders, in 1861, of the first Reform synagogue in Chicago, Sinai Congregation. Hannah Greenebaum would be a lifelong member of Sinai Congregation and would engage in social action, influenced by the attitude of Rabbi Emil G. Hirsch, a progressive reformer.

Greenebaum first attended private school at Reform Temple Zion, where she studied Hebrew and German; she then moved to a public school, Skinner Grammar School. In 1871 she entered West Division High School, just before the Great Fire. The Greenebaum home was far enough away not to be burned, and the family gave shelter to persons whose homes had been destroyed. Two years later, when her parents gave her a choice of completing her schooling in Germany or with tutors at home, she chose to focus on piano study. She took lessons from Carl Wolfsohn, who was also teaching Fannie Bloomfield, later the great pianist FANNIE BLOOMFIELD ZEISLER. Greenebaum practiced three hours each day and performed often in public student recitals.

A lover of music all her life, Greenebaum joined the Beethoven Society, a choral group formed by Wolfsohn in 1873 that presented public concerts. In 1877 she became a member of the first board of the Zion Literary Society, founded by her father as a social and cultural group engaged in lectures, music, and other educational programs, and that prepared a newspaper for which she was assistant editor. She remained active until 1892, when the group disbanded.

FIG. 108. *Hannah Greenebaum Solomon, founder of the National Council of Jewish Women in 1893.*

Although her life was focused on her own family and on activities among upper-class and upper-middle-class members of the German Jewish community, Hannah Greenebaum had an opportunity to meet non-Jewish women of the same classes in the larger Chicago community. When the Chicago Women's Club (CWC) was formed in 1876 (it became Chicago Woman's Club in 1895), some members were friends of Hannah Greenebaum and her sister Henriette. The next year, club members considered inviting the Greenebaum sisters to become members but were concerned that "the presence of women of a different faith might prevent frank and open discussion of certain important issues" (*Fabric of My Life*, 42). A member of the club therefore came to the Greenebaum home to meet the candidates without telling the reason for the visit. Shortly afterward, the sisters became the first Jewish women elected to membership.

On May 14, 1879, she married Henry Solomon, successful in the sale of men's clothing, whom she had met at the Zion Literary Society. It was the beginning of a long and happy relationship; he died in 1913. Her first child, Henry (who died in 1899), was born in 1880, followed by Helen in 1882 and Frank in 1888.

For about a decade, while her children were young, she devoted her time to running the household and raising her children. She pursued self-education, reading a great deal and studying astronomy with a neighbor. Music continued to be an important pleasure; a weekly gathering of amateur musicians at Solomon's home brought performances of classical music. She gave her children their first piano lessons.

Solomon remained involved in the Chicago Women's Club. In 1891, as a member of the Philosophy and Science Department of the club, she presented "Review of Spinoza's Theologico-Politicus" based on her reading of Spinoza in German. The following year, the program committee asked her to talk about religion, the first time for this subject. Solomon drew upon her Jewish identity for the paper, "Our Debt to Judaism." She gave a history of the development of Judaism, which to her meant the Judaic religion, in the context of the story of the Jewish people, discussing Jewish thought as the root of Christian and Muslim ethics. Solomon contended that "the whole world owe[d] a greater debt to Judaism than [was] often acknowledged" (p. 21). That same year she again gave a talk at the Chicago Women's Club, "Italian Women," which focused on a topic on which she would speak again—legal restrictions on women and the need for "equal rights of both sexes" (p. 36).

At this time she was already involved in a major project for the World's Columbian Exposition, which was to open in Chicago in 1893. ELLEN HENROTIN, who was vice-president of the Board of Lady Managers (with BERTHA HONORÉ PALMER as president), asked Hannah Solomon to call together Jewish women under the Woman's Branch of the World's Congress Auxiliary. Since Solomon defined being Jewish in purely religious terms, she believed that Jewish women belonged in the Parliament of Religions, one of the important assemblies of the exposition. She became a member of the women's board of the parliament and in that capacity chaired the committee to arrange a Jewish Women's Congress, called by Henrotin and Palmer a "Congress of Jewish Church" (letter of Palmer and Henrotin to Solomon, January 30, 1894). Ellen Henrotin, a member of Chicago's upper class, knew Hannah Solomon through the Chicago Women's Club and other social and cultural activities that were part of the life of their class. Solomon's acceptance of this invitation brought her into an important activity in the non-Jewish world based on her Jewish identity. In 1891 she began work on two of the major tasks involved in organizing a Jewish Women's Congress—developing a program and inviting Jewish women to participate. She felt it was necessary to involve women throughout the country and wrote to rabbis in larger communities and cities for the names of women leaders in their congregations. As a result, Solomon herself wrote letters about the congress to ninety women. She appointed a committee, mainly women members of Sinai and a few from other cities, to work with her. By 1892, she and the committee members had written some two thousand letters to women all over the country. She asked them to set up committees to select delegates to the congress. From the outset, she explained, a goal of the Jewish Women's Congress would be to establish a permanent organization. At the congress, ninety-three women came as representatives of Jewish women in twenty-nine cities. Solomon considered these women authorized to consider plans for a new organization.

By March 1893, Solomon had commissioned two Jewish women speakers, Henrietta Szold and Josephine Lazarus, for the general program of the parliament and was commissioning additional talks for the Jewish Women's Congress. The men arranging a Jewish congress invited Solomon to a planning meeting to talk about cooperation with the women's group. She explained that the plans of the women were already well in process but that they would join the men if the women participated in the program. After consideration, the men presented her with a program without Szold's and Lazarus's names and refused to add any women speakers. Solomon responded sharply: "Under these circumstances we do not care to cooperate with you, and I request that the fact of our presence at this meeting be expunged from the records" (*Fabric of My Life*, 83).

She and her committee developed, as the Jewish Women's Congress, a four-day program of speakers and discussion. Some papers dealt with Judaism, Jewish religion, and women's role in the synagogue. In addition, Solomon went beyond religious themes to deal with secular social and political issues. Julia Richman discussed women wage-earners, especially immigrants. In the session "How Can Nations Be Influenced to Protest or Even to Interfere in Cases of Persecution?" discussants included Emil Hirsch and Christian reformer Reverend Jenkin Lloyd Jones. The congress was well attended, with audiences often too large for the hall. The highlight of the final day was SADIE AMERICAN's enthusiastic speech, "Organization," in which she proposed a national organization of Jewish women. Solomon selected American, a member of the Jewish Women's Committee, to present the proposal and plan for the organization, which took the name National Council of Jewish Women (NCJW). Solomon's decision to allow Sadie American to propose the organization was to have repercussions in later years in disputes over who founded NCJW. At the congress, the assembly adopted goals for NCJW that focused on religious education for Jewish women. The women would work in the fields of religion, philanthropy, and education. They would study principles of Judaism as well as Jewish history and customs. Further, they would work to improve Sabbath schools. They would also become involved in social reform. Through the NCJW (in its early years also called the Council of Jewish Women), Hannah Solomon brought women into a realm dominated by men—the study of religion and concern for religious education. Solomon was elected president and Sadie American became corresponding secretary. Under Solomon's leadership, NCJW developed sections throughout the country. By 1896, fifty cities had branches with a total of four thousand members; by the third triennial convention, held in 1902 in Baltimore, NCJW had some seven thousand members.

During her years of leadership in NCJW, Hannah Solomon continued to do social service in the community. In December 1893, the Chicago Women's Club opened an emergency workroom to provide jobs for women who had been employed at the World's Columbian Exposition. Solomon, a member of the CWC board, took charge once a week and made new contacts in the Chicago Jewish community. She found that about one-third of the women were Russian Jews. They spoke Yiddish, a language that Solomon, in her German Jewish surroundings, had hardly ever heard. Visiting the homes of the Russian Jewish women, Solomon became aware of the needs of these immigrant families. As a result of this experience, Solomon obtained funding from the Chicago section of NCJW to set up a nonsectarian Bureau of Associated Charities in the 7th Ward in 1897. The group soon became the Bureau of Personal Service, which received Jewish clients from another branch of Associated Charities and sent non-Jewish cases to them. Solomon chaired the bureau, which was set up independently of NCJW, with MINNIE LOW as executive director. The organization provided legal aid, reviewed applications for loans, and organized a workroom for Jewish women, modeled on the one run by CWC. The neighborhood near Hull-House had a large Jewish population, and Solomon worked with JANE ADDAMS to provide services to the residents; the bureau reviewed and approved requests for coal received by Hull-House. The Bureau of Personal Service participated in a study of tenements and worked for better housing laws, opened a summer playground in a neighborhood park, and built a day nursery that was run by Solomon's daughter for children of working mothers.

Through her work in the Bureau of Personal Service and her knowledge of the efforts of the Chicago Woman's Club on behalf of children in the city jail, Solomon became involved in efforts to reform the court system. When, through the leadership of LUCY FLOWER and JULIA LATHROP, a Cook County Juvenile Court was established by the state legislature in 1899, no provision was made for probation officers. Solomon joined the Juvenile Court Committee, which raised money for the salaries of probation workers. The Bureau of Personal Service eventually funded three salaries.

As organizations of Jewish women broadened their civic and philanthropic activities, Solomon saw a need for these groups to work together to avoid duplication of services. In 1895 she joined with LIZZIE BARBE, her cousin and lifetime friend, and others to form the first Conference of Jewish Women, twenty-six groups that coordinated their activities. The conference remained active until 1900, when a new organization, the Associated Jewish Charities (AJC), was formed; it included both men's and women's charity groups. Solomon became the sole woman trustee of AJC, representing the women's societies. She continued to manage the Bureau of Personal Services until 1910, when it became part of Associated Jewish Charities.

Once the National Council of Jewish Women became established, Solomon saw the importance of connection with other women's groups. In 1894, NCJW under Hannah Solomon became a member of the National Council of Women, which included many groups in the United States and which belonged to the International Council of Women (ICW). Elizabeth Cady Stanton, a founder of the National Woman Suffrage Association in 1869, had joined with others in 1888 to organize the ICW to support social reform activities and woman suffrage. When NCJW took part in 1895 in the convention of the National Council of Women in Washington, D.C., Hannah Solomon and FRANCES E. WILLARD ran a program, with each of them chairing half of the meeting. Here, Solomon met leaders of other national women's organizations, including Susan B. Anthony, president of the National American Woman

Suffrage Association, with whom she developed a lifetime friendship. In 1899 the National Council of Women elected Solomon treasurer.

Because of its philanthropic work, NCJW was also invited to join the General Federation of Women's Clubs (organized in 1890); but NCJW refused because it saw itself as a religious group. However, when the federation started to organize state branches in 1894, state Councils of Jewish Women became interested. Solomon was involved in organizing an Illinois State Federation of Women's Clubs and served as a vice-president. She went to the General Federation meeting in Louisville, Kentucky, in 1896 as delegate from both the Illinois Federation and the NCJW.

Solomon took every opportunity to spread information about the work of NCJW. When Emil Hirsch asked her to take the pulpit in his absence and address the Sinai congregation on February 14, 1897—the first such invitation to a Jewish woman at Sinai—she gave a talk, "Council of Jewish Women: Its Work and Possibilities." Six months earlier, in the *Reform Advocate*, May 9, 1896, Hirsch had published an editorial, "Signs of the Times," describing the importance of the NCJW in fostering Judaic religion. He noted that men, recognizing the effectiveness of the organization, now wished to join, but that the restriction to women was "for the time being the indispensable condition of successful work." Solomon spoke about the strength of women's organizations and the goals of NCJW to foster religious education and to do social welfare work to help the poor.

Operating from a secure family base, Solomon involved her husband and children in her work for NCJW. Since she was speaking at Sinai without benefit of amplification, she instructed her children to sit in the balcony and let her know, by shaking their heads, whether she could be heard. Her daughter, Helen Levy, recalling the experience many years later, told of how she traveled with Solomon, who was invited because of her renown in NCJW, when she gave talks in synagogues in other cities. Solomon was a petite woman—four feet six inches in height, who stood on a footstool when she spoke at a podium. When Solomon sat in the rabbis' chairs, her feet did not touch the ground, but, according to Levy, Solomon's words carried strength both in volume and in content.

In June 1904 she combined work for the International Council of Women and the National Council of Jewish Women on an extended European trip. Since her family went with her, the journey took on personal as well as organizational aspects. She attended the ICW meeting in Berlin as an American delegate and also met with Jewish women in several European cities to encourage them to establish sections of National Council. In London, she spoke at the Jewish Study Society, a women's group that had been founded in 1899. When she met with women in Paris, she distributed a French translation of the NCJW constitution as well as a file of the organization's reports, and the recipients became interested in creating a similar group. In Germany she spoke before a men's committee of the B'nai B'rith lodge. She talked about NCJW to a group of German women who represented several organizations and gave them copies of the council's constitution in German. In the years that followed, German women organized sections of the Council of Jewish Women.

Because Solomon was fluent in both French and German, she served at the International Council of Women as interpreter for Susan B. Anthony, also a delegate from the United States. Solomon's knowledge of languages placed her on the nominating committee, which she chaired. The ICW, with delegates from all over the world, covered such issues as woman suffrage and women's political equality, racial rights, and white slavery. In an interview in Germany with a Chicago *Daily News* correspondent, Solomon reported that the two dominant matters discussed were the need for woman suffrage and the importance of coeducation.

Although she did not become active in promoting woman suffrage beyond her work for ICW, Solomon believed that women needed the vote to have the fullest influence on legislation to gain equal rights for women. She thought that the women's congresses at the World's Columbian Exposition had "converted a surprising number of people, men included, to the point where suffrage actually became fashionable!" (*Fabric of My Life*, 109). In June 1916 she would be one of some five thousand in the woman suffrage parade on Michigan Avenue in Chicago, organized by GRACE WILBUR TROUT.

While she was in Germany, Solomon learned that the Democratic Party in Cook County had nominated her to run for the office of Trustee of the University of Illinois, although she was not a part of the party's machine politics. She was amused by what she perceived as a token nomination, since she believed that Republicans outnumbered Democrats; she was defeated. In her only other foray into local politics, she again ran for the same office in 1916 but was not elected.

Solomon's involvement in ICW was a reflection of her views on the role and status of women. She called herself a "confirmed woman's-rights-er" (*Fabric of My Life*, 48), but her perceptions of such rights were a mix of traditional and progressive approaches. For Solomon, the most desired role for a woman was as wife and mother. She contended, "There is no higher or holier duty, nor one more to be coveted than guardian of home, mother and protector of children, the companion and friend of husband" ("Women as Breadwinners," 65). She did not believe that a woman attained freedom by not marrying and working to support herself and insisted that "life offers no freedom equal to that of a married woman" ("Women as Breadwinners," 61). At the same time, she knew that many women would not be able to marry and would have to work outside the home, and she spoke out strongly against discrimination in the workplace. In a talk to a men's group, Chicago Beefsteak Club, in January 1896, she challenged the belief that women were weaker than men and should be restricted to certain occupations or education, explaining, "Women in schools and colleges, in universities and the few professions open to them have proven the fallacy of every argument against higher education for women on the score of physical weakness" ("Women as Breadwinners," 62). She insisted that women should have "fullest freedom to compete with men in every line for which they have talent" ("Women as Breadwinners," 67). In discussing work conditions, she held a progressive view: wealthy women should "in public agitate for and secure shorter hours for all, demand equal pay for equal work, a fair field and no favors to man or woman." They should "not buy a garment that had not given living wage to every one that handled it" ("Women as Breadwinners," 67).

Until 1905, Hannah Solomon was reelected president of the National Council of Jewish Women at each triennial meeting, and she focused her efforts on the goals of the organization. By 1905, the organization was well established and was giving greater focus to philanthropic and social reform activities with less stress on the religious educational goals so important to Solomon at the outset. When she declined the presidency, the council board elected her honorary president, a title and role that she kept for the rest of her life, except for one brief period— 1908–11—when she resigned because of a disagreement over NCJW policy. The organization had raised annual dues in 1905 from one to two dollars to demonstrate an increased philanthropic focus. The Cleveland Section refused payment and was told in 1908 that it would be expelled. Solomon was appointed to head an arbitration committee, which canceled the expulsion. When the executive board, led by Sadie American and the president, overrode the committee's decision, Solomon refused election as honorary president until the next triennial convention.

She continued to serve NCJW on committees and boards and attended the triennial meetings but was ready by 1905 to free time to move into leadership in a community organization. Five years earlier, in her report to the NCJW triennial convention in 1900, she had complained that the president and secretary had too much work and that women had a responsibility to their duties in organizations other than NCJW.

During her presidency, Hannah Solomon worked closely with the corresponding secretary, Sadie American, but over the years between 1900 and 1910, their relationship, both personal and professional, was marred by disagreements and ill feelings. At first, they seemed to work well together. In 1895, Solomon gave "the greatest praise" to American "for the faithful, able performance of her duties . . . and her unselfish labor" ("Report of the National President," *First Annual Report,* 3–4). In planning for the NCJW convention in 1900, Solomon asked American for her opinion on program papers, arrangements, and any other items that she thought it important to consider. Solomon again praised American in her official talk prepared for the 1900 national convention, reporting that "her exceptional ability, . . . her devotion to the cause, have been the greatest power in whatever measure of success we have achieved" ("Address of the President," *Proceedings,* 22). American, in her official report to the 1900 convention, bestowed similar encomiums on Solomon. "To our President, I wish here to express, both in my official and personal capacity, my deep appreciation of her wisdom, kindness and helpfulness in managing the affairs of the Council. . . . It will perhaps never be known to any but those closely associated with her, with what open-minded justice, with what clear thought, with what self-sacrificing zeal she has wrought for the Council all these years" ("Report of the Corresponding Secretary," *Proceedings,* 94).

During the proceedings at the 1900 meeting, however, a conflict arose involving Sadie American and several members of the board that revealed tensions between her and Solomon. A recent talk at Sinai by American supporting the congregants' observance of the Sabbath on Sunday had been given newspaper publicity, and some NCJW officers accused her of giving the opinion as a representative of National Council. Although Solomon practiced Sunday Sabbath, she did not discuss the matter at NCJW meetings. In an unhappy letter to Solomon after the meeting, American responded to a letter that she had received from Solomon. According to American, Solomon had criticized her behavior, accusing American of trying to dominate Solomon and describing American's manner as impossible. American related how Solomon secretly supported another woman for corresponding secretary and brought in a slate of candidates who were all Sinai Temple members. Sadie American, a single middle-class woman who worked outside the home—receiving pay for teaching at the Sinai Sunday school— was not a member of Hannah Solomon's social community of Jewish upper-class married women. American felt that Solomon took an unwarranted liberty in talking to American's mother about how to train her. Nevertheless, both were reelected and continued to work together, although conflict continued. American moved to New York City in 1901, where immigrant aid— especially at Ellis Island—the project most important to her, "became Council's primary focus" (Rogow, 118), increasing her power. She was sometimes "accused of making important decisions on her own rather than consulting the board" (Rogow, 118).

When the NCJW board selected Solomon as delegate to the ICW meeting in 1904, American wished to go. Solomon opposed American's participation, but put the matter to a vote, ready to veto the proposal in case of a tie. The board gave a positive vote and provided five hundred dollars for American's expenses. In 1905 she was elected executive secretary of NCJW, the first member of the staff to receive a salary.

By 1908, when the board overturned the decision of Solomon's arbitration committee, her break with American was almost complete. Solomon believed that American wished her to resign as honorary president. The final break came in 1910 when Sadie American attempted to have the executive board recognize her and Hannah Solomon as cofounders of NCJW. In a letter to Carrie Wolf, a member of Solomon's planning committee for the World's Columbian Exposition, asking for her recollections of the founding of the organization, Solomon summarized her sense of class, her views on Sadie American, her continuing disagreement with American on NCJW policies, and her dismay at being accused of taking credit falsely. She justified her position, stating, "Sadie was only a casual acquaintance of mine, socially secluded, and unknown in Organizations. I had the purpose and plan of forming a National Organization before she came into our meetings. . . . In the beginning she . . . helped me to carry out my plans. . . . Had I not known that I was the Founder I should have denied it long ago. . . . I totally differ with Sadie as to the entire National policy and work as at present conducted. . . . I cannot allow the implication that I wore honors for years to which I was not entitled by my thought and work" (February 4, 1910).

When Solomon gave up the presidency of NCJW in 1905, the Reform Department at the Chicago Woman's Club was about to investigate and reorganize the Illinois Industrial School for Girls in Evanston, Illinois—a residential school for girls who needed a home—and Solomon joined the investigation committee. She soon became a member of the board of the school and then president in 1906. The school needed funds to provide adequate care to the children and to obtain a building in good condition. In January 1907, a new board was established that included Jane Addams and Ellen Henrotin. Solomon served as president until 1909, then continued to be an active board member. The CWC provided some money, including income from a legacy, and the board raised the rest. Solomon and the board had a new school built, a group of cottages, on land owned by CWC in Park Ridge, Illinois, and renamed it the Park Ridge School for Girls. The first cottage at the entrance was named after Hannah Solomon. She lobbied successfully at the state legislature to raise the allowance of public funds from ten dollars to fifteen dollars for every girl at a public institution. In later years, Solomon reported, "No project ever affected me more deeply" (*Fabric of My Life*, 151).

Solomon remained involved in the International Council of Women. When the organization held a meeting in Toronto, Canada, in 1909, and delegates visited Chicago, Solomon headed the committee that arranged events for the visitors, with Jane Addams as honorary chair.

In 1910, Solomon and other women concerned with city management organized the Woman's City Club to deal with civic affairs. Solomon took the office of vice-president. She immediately became head of the Committee on City Waste; MARY McDOWELL and HARRIET VITTUM were members of the committee. They investigated Chicago procedures for dealing with garbage and reported on problems such as polluted water and uncovered garbage trucks. Solomon realized how little the women knew about the subject when she arranged to inspect a city dump and came carrying a parasol and wearing a long white lace gown, her usual evening dress.

At the same time, Solomon continued to work on social reform issues through the Chicago Woman's Club. When the club formed a Committee on City Ordinances in 1911, she became vice-chair, later serving as head of the group. The goal was to educate Chicagoans about city laws and government. The committee selected ordinances and had them published in newspapers in English and other languages, making the information available to immigrants. In 1916, under Solomon's leadership, the committee published a booklet, *Ordinances of the City of Chicago*, with laws arranged alphabetically by topic. The pamphlet was designed for use by school children; according to Solomon, the school superintendent requested thousands of copies.

Pursuing her interest in law enforcement, Solomon became chair of the CWC Committee on Motion Pictures. The women helped write a movie censorship law that was passed by the legislature in 1907 and upheld two years later by the state supreme court. The law prohibited public showings, including movies, stage plays, and advertising, that displayed "vice, crime, degradation of women and defiance of laws" (*Fabric of My Life*, 170), and Solomon believed that such censorship was necessary for "decency" (p. 170). In her usual method of seeking increased power by coalescing various groups, she brought together delegates from women's organizations interested in taking similar action and formed the Joint Committee on Motion Pictures. The CWC committee aided the legally provided censor in the Police Department and was upheld in court controversies over censorship.

In 1916, Hannah Solomon took a brief step into national politics by supporting the reelection of President Woodrow Wilson. She served on the local committee of the Woman's National Democratic Committee and attended the inauguration of Wilson in Washington, D.C. Although her support was based on Wilson's promise of peace, when the United States entered World War I, Solomon led women's participation in the war effort. She met with members of the Chicago National Council of Jewish Women to discuss their involvement but ultimately concentrated her efforts on the work of the State Council of Defense. As head of the Ward Leaders' Committee of the Chicago unit in 1917, she led a survey in the city's wards to determine the most useful work that needed to be done. Once again, she dealt with immigrant women, bringing them information on food conservation, enlisting their service, aiding them on matters regarding their sons overseas in the military, and helping with other essentials.

Beginning in the 1920s, Solomon reduced her active leadership work and did a great deal of traveling all over the world, mostly with young women relatives and friends. She continued to attend NCJW triennial conferences and was often the celebrated speaker. In 1917 the NCJW had established the Hannah G. Solomon Scholarship Fund from which an annual award was made. Solomon chose to give the scholarship to women entering social service, partly because she perceived a great need for professional social workers. At a Jewish International Conference in London in June 1927, she attended meetings of the Jewish Association for the Protection of Girls and Women and the Union of Jewish Women, descendant of the Jewish Study Society that Solomon had visited in 1904. At Solomon's seventieth birthday, the Sinai Temple Sisterhood, an activist women's group, commemorated her concern for peace by establishing the Hannah G. Solomon Peace Fund, which gave prizes to children in the religious school who wrote the best essays about peace. She gave the awards and delivered a talk each year.

For the Century of Progress Exposition in Chicago in 1933, Governor Henry Horner appointed her a hostess in the Illinois State House. At the fair, the Chicago Woman's Club presented lectures on the progress women had made, and Solomon spoke on the topic "Woman in Organization." That same year an International Congress of Women was held in Chicago, sponsored by the U.S. National Council of Women, and the exhibits included a recording by Solomon about the origin, goals, and development of NCJW.

When Solomon reached her seventies, the National Council of Jewish Women observed her birthdays with special celebrations. For her seventieth, in 1933, the Chicago section of council invited the national president and Jane Addams as special guests and speakers at a birthday luncheon. For her seventy-ninth birthday, an international radio broadcast brought Solomon greetings from women in the United States, Canada, and European countries. Solomon also spoke. To celebrate her eightieth birthday, two hundred sections of NCJW met throughout January, many convening simultaneously.

Solomon remained active, attending her final NCJW triennial convention in 1941. She completed her autobiography, *Fabric of My Life,* during her last year of life and awarded the Hannah G. Solomon Peace Fund at Sinai Temple just two weeks before her death. She died at the age of eighty-four and was buried in Graceland Cemetery in Chicago.

Hannah Solomon understood the importance of the National Council of Jewish Women that she founded in 1893. One hundred years later, its national membership totaled some ninety thousand women, and it is still a thriving organization in the year 2000. She always was involved in council to some degree; as she explained, "The firm thread of the National Council of Jewish Women runs unbroken through the fabric of my life" (*Fabric of My Life,* 205). She moved Jewish women into the realm of religious education and philanthropy on a national scale and then became an effective progressive reformer in the larger non-Jewish community, serving as a leader in secular organizations seeking civic and social change.

Sources. The Hannah Greenebaum Solomon Papers at the Library of Congress contain writings and speeches of Solomon; correspondence, including Solomon's letter to Carrie Wolf, February 4, 1910, and letters of Sadie American to Solomon; biographical information; and organizational material, much of it dealing with her founding of the National Council of Jewish Women (NCJW). Sadie American's comments on her relationship with Solomon are found in her undated letter to Hannah Solomon [1900]; a transcription was made by Julia Wood Kramer and is held by Ann E. Feldman. Records of the NCJW national office also are at the Library of Congress. The Hannah Solomon Collection in the American Jewish Archives, Cincinnati, Ohio, has "Interview with Mrs. Philip Angel of Charleston, W. Va. by Gerald Kane," April 20, 1970; this typescript of an interview with Solomon's granddaughter, Frances Levy Angel, provides biographical information. Materials in a scrapbook in the collection at American Jewish Archives include a letter from Bertha Palmer and Ellen Henrotin to Solomon, January 30, 1894; Emil J. Hirsch's "Editorial: Signs of the Times," *Reform Advocate,* May 9, 1896; and an unidentified clipping about Solomon's campaign for University of Illinois trustee, October 1916. The CHS holds materials from the NCJW Chicago Section, with information on Solomon as well as her travel diaries from 1917 to 1927. Julia Wood Kramer discusses Solomon's work for the Parliament of Religions in "'Paradise Was Not Perfect without Woman': World's Fair Women of 1893 and the Founding of the National Council of Jewish Women," a paper given at a meeting of the Chicago Jewish Hist. Soc., April 18, 1993. Hannah Solomon's autobiography, *Fabric of My Life* (1946), provides detailed information on her personal and organizational life. Solomon's *A Sheaf of Leaves* (privately printed, 1911) contains articles she wrote, some based on speeches, including "Our Debt to Judaism," 1892; "Italian Women," 1892; "Women as Breadwinners," 1896; "Council of Jewish Women; Its Work and Possibilities," 1897; and "Addresses as President of the Council of Jewish Women, 1893–1905." For Solomon's early reports as NCJW president, see "Report of the National President," *National Council of Jewish Women: First Annual Report, 1894–1895* (1895) and "Address of the President," *Proceedings of the Council of Jewish Women,* Second Triennial Convention (1900); the 1900 *Proceedings* include Sadie American's "Report of the Corresponding Secretary." Recent biographical sketches of Solomon are Beth Wenger's "Hannah Greenebaum Solomon (1858–1942)," in *Jewish Women in America: An Historical Encyclopedia,* ed. Paula E. Hyman and Deborah Dash Moore (1998), and Gerald Soren's essay in *American National Biography,* ed. John A. Garraty and Mark C. Carnes (1999). Two histories of NCJW from different perspectives discuss Solomon's impact: Ellen Sue Levi Elwell, "The Founding and Early Programs of the National Council of Jewish

Women: Study and Practice as Jewish Women's Religious Expression" (Ph.D. diss., Indiana Univ., 1982), and Faith Rogow, *Gone to Another Meeting: The National Council of Jewish Women, 1893–1993* (1993).

ADELE HAST

SPEARS, ETHEL GRACE
October 5, 1902–August 2, 1974
ARTIST, DESIGNER, EDUCATOR

As an artist, designer, and teacher, Ethel Spears brought an extraordinary vision to her humorous and highly detailed depictions of everyday life. The youngest of five daughters, Spears was born and raised in Chicago. Her mother, Mathilda A. (Carlson) Spears, was born in Minnesota. Her father, Charles Albert Spears, an engineer, was born in Aurora, Illinois.

Ethel Spears grew up in the Chicago neighborhood of Beverly and resided there well into adulthood. There is little known documentation about her childhood or early adolescent years. Spears made brief mention in a letter of having taken art classes at the School of the Art Institute of Chicago (SAIC) as a child, but no known formal verification of these studies exists. At the age of seventeen, Spears enrolled at SAIC in the Department of Design in 1920. Recognition of Spears as an artist of merit followed almost immediately, when she was just an undergraduate, with the commissioning of two murals for the Art Institute of Chicago's (AIC) tearoom. After earning a three-year certificate in design in 1923, Spears continued her studies at SAIC in the Department of Drawing, Painting, and Illustration. Among her teachers was John Norton, who challenged Spears "to paint the life of her immediate surroundings" (Williams, "Press Release," January 9, 1933, Spears Papers). Many of the titles of Spears's watercolors, such as *The Cafeteria, Maxwell Street,* and *Thirty-third Street, Next to the Tracks,* reveal how literally Spears embraced Norton's challenge. Bringing a new perspective to familiar scenes known by fellow classmates and Chicagoans, Spears gave new meaning to the word immediate. These watercolors and similar works were exhibited by Spears in Annual Exhibitions at the Art Institute beginning in 1926 and continuing sporadically for the next three decades.

Working as a monitor in Norton's class also enabled Spears to meet KATHLEEN BLACKSHEAR, who studied with Norton in 1926. The two women influenced each other artistically, were members of the Chicago Society of Artists, and frequently showed their artwork in the same exhibitions. Although it is unknown when Spears and Blackshear began their relationship, it is known that they later devoted their lives to one another as life partners.

Spears supplemented her studies at SAIC by taking classes in New York State during her summer and winter semester breaks. In 1924, Spears studied with the abstract sculptor Alexander Archipenko at his summer school in Woodstock and, in 1925, at his winter school in New York City. Spears also took classes at the Art Students' League of New York from 1925 to 1927, where she studied lithography with Charles Locke.

Following graduation from SAIC in 1927, Spears made New York City her home. In addition to attending classes in printing design at New York University, Spears spent the next four years working as a freelance artist, designer, and illustrator. Among her sundry projects were textile and batik designs, the

FIG. 109. *Artist Ethel Spears holds one of her paintings.*

printing and design of greeting cards, the design of a lamp shade that was printed and presented by the Park Avenue Gallery, and the illustration of a set of ten children's story books, published by Harold Rugg of Columbia University. In 1928, Spears gained national recognition in the *New Yorker* magazine for an exhibition of her paintings at the Weyhe Gallery in New York. Described by critic Murdock Pemberton as "a bright newcomer from Chicago" ("The Art Galleries," 60), Spears was applauded for her fresh perspective on "Americana" and for bringing relief to art suffering from "high hat" (p. 60) and Parisian influence.

Spears spent the summer of 1930 in France. In the fall, she returned to Chicago and began actively to exhibit her artwork. Spears and her humorous approach to art received favorable critical attention from both the *Chicago Tribune* critic and chief proponent of Josephine Logan's Sanity in Art movement, Eleanor Jewett, and from C. J. Bulliet, critic for the *Chicago Daily News* and the modern art movement's chief spokesperson. According to Jewett, Spears's works were "full of color and crowded with amusing natural incidents" (quoted from Jewett, *Chicago Daily Tribune*, May 21, 1931), while Bulliet referred to

Spears in his review of her work in a Chicago Women's Salon Show as "one of our better humorists" ("Around the Galleries"). The admiration of Spears by both critics continued for many years.

In 1930, Spears began teaching on Saturdays in a nonfaculty position in the Junior School at SAIC under its then current director Matilda Vanderpoel—a position that, according to Spears's personal records, she kept for the next five years. In 1931, Spears resumed her studies at SAIC with courses in still life painting and lithography. For the Century of Progress Exposition in 1933, Spears completed colored illustrations for the official guidebook for the fair and made a series of small dioramas for the social science building demonstrating the difference between life in the 1930s and that of one hundred years earlier. Another set of dioramas made by Spears was used in a housing exhibit.

From December 1933 to May 1934, Spears worked for the Federal Treasury Department's Public Works of Art Project in Illinois, Wisconsin, and Minnesota under the direction of regional chairman Walter S. Brewster. While employed by this program, Spears won a competition to paint a mural for the Hartford, Wisconsin, post office. She also completed, among other projects, two murals for the Oakton School in Evanston, Illinois, and thirty to forty large tempera paintings that were made available by the Treasury Department for display in public buildings throughout the United States.

Spears was subsequently hired to work for the Federal Art Project of the Works Progress Administration (WPA) in the mural and easel painting divisions in 1935. For the next seven years, under the direction of Chicago gallery owner INCREASE ROBINSON, assistant to the national director, Spears completed numerous easel paintings that were distributed nationally and approximately twenty additional murals for field houses, hospitals, libraries, recreation centers, and schools in Illinois. Two such murals were painted on canvas for the now-razed Lowell Elementary School in Oak Park, Illinois, in 1937. Titled *Children in Park, Winter and Summer*, these murals contrasted the two seasons by juxtaposing images of children in their appropriate apparel playing games against outdoor settings depicting the appearance of nature in each season.

After World War II began, Spears and other WPA painters were asked to produce large pictorial charts for training courses in the armed forces. One such series of charts was used for training soldiers in camouflage techniques, demonstrating the defensive strategy of blending fully into one's immediate surroundings. To convey this information, these charts explained how animals are camouflaged in their natural habitats by showing, for example, the white fur of the polar bear and the patterns in the giraffe's skin. There is a similarity between these charts and wall text panels showing the relationship between modern art and patterns in nature. Such wall text panels were later exhibited by Katharine Kuh in the Art Institute's Gallery of Art Interpretation in order to help viewers understand and accept modern art. Spears and the other WPA painters had collectively set a precedent.

In 1943, when the WPA came to an end, Spears was hired as a faculty member in the Department of Drawing and Painting at SAIC. Former student and teacher Barbara Aubin remembered Spears and fellow faculty member, Kathleen Blackshear, as "special teachers who cared about their students—so much that they shared their own art making experience with us. Who else would work along with us on joint projects in their own home/studios and ours?" (quoted in Tormollan, 13). Influenced by Blackshear, Spears also took her students to the Field Museum of Natural History and to other locations throughout Chicago. In addition, Spears shared Blackshear's interest in non-Western art. Spears's later artwork appeared to some critics to have been influenced by Blackshear. In response to an exhibition of Spears's and Blackshear's work at the Cromer and Quint Galleries in 1954 in Chicago, for example, critic Copeland C. Burg noted that Spears had "changed her style, deriving from Miss Blackshear" ("Art and Artists"). Offering a second opinion on the same exhibition, however, was *Chicago Sun-Times* critic, Frank Holland, who placed Spears's later artwork in the continuum of her previous works. To do so, Holland directed the viewer's attention to how Spears "effectively combine[d] design, realism and humor in her distinctive works" ("Momentum Show in June").

The depth of Spears's distinctive contribution to SAIC is evidenced in the vast changes that took place under her leadership. During the eighteen years she devoted to teaching at the school, Spears was responsible for establishing two new departments, one in serigraphy in 1948 and the other in enameling in 1953. Overcrowded conditions and poor ventilation in the enameling studios are probably to blame for Spears's development of lead poisoning, a condition about which she began seeking information in 1954 and which was formally diagnosed in 1955. Spears subsequently sought treatment and protective measures for herself, the students, and other faculty. In 1961, however, the school's insurance company denied further coverage for Spears's treatment, claiming that she showed no current evidence of lead poisoning. This refusal and the continuation of unsafe working conditions at the school prompted Spears to retire. Two years short of the twenty years of teaching required for a full pension, Spears appealed to the Art Institute's board of trustees through her attorney. The board ultimately awarded Spears a partial pension and later, in response to Spears's letter of protest, sent her an additional two hundred dollars.

Upon retiring in 1961, Spears accompanied Kathleen Blackshear to Blackshear's hometown of Navasota, Texas, where Spears continued to lecture and exhibit her artwork and to teach art classes out of her studio. Spears's health continued to deteriorate. The lead poisoning affected her teeth and brain. Although Spears remained very active, she became thin and confused. The confusion became permanent following Spears's and Blackshear's 1970 trip to Chicago in order to sell Spears's childhood home and to transfer its contents to their home in Navasota. Spears's sister, Lilly, who was very ill at that time, returned with them to Navasota accompanied by a nurse. In Navasota, Lilly resided at the Sweetbriar Home until her death on September 15, 1971. When Spears's disorientation eventually led to her wandering from her Navasota home, she was admitted to the Grimes Memorial Convalescent Home, where she died. She was buried in Oakland Cemetery in Navasota, next to her sister Lilly. A third plot was reserved for Blackshear. An oak tree Blackshear planted graced a fourth plot.

Sources. Ethel Spears's papers are at the Archives of American Art, Smithsonian Institution, including *Chicago Daily News* critic and gallery owner Marguerite B. Williams's press release of January 9, 1933. Additional information was obtained from the Department of Archives and the Ryerson Library at the Art Institute of Chicago and from Jane Terrell, wife of William J. Terrell Sr., executor of the Spears estate. See also Murdock Pemberton, "The Art Galleries," *New Yorker*, September 22, 1928; Eleanor Jewett, *Chicago Daily Tribune*, May 21, 1931; C. J. Bulliet, "Around the Galleries," *Chicago Daily News*, November 5, 1938; Copeland C. Burg, "Art and Artists: Chicagoans' New Work on View," *Chicago Herald-American*, February 13, 1954; Frank Holland, "Momentum Show in June," *Chicago Sun-Times*, February 28, 1954. Further information is available in Louise Dunn Yochim, *Role and Impact: The Chicago Society of Artists* (1979); Patricia Trenton, ed., *Independent Spirits: Women Painters of the American West, 1890–1945* (1995); and Carole Tormollan, *A Tribute to Kathleen Blackshear* (1990).

CAROLE TORMOLLAN

SPECTOR, BERTHA KAPLAN
October 9, 1896–March 26, 1938
BACTERIOLOGIST, PROTOZOOLOGIST

Bertha Kaplan Spector, whose investigative work in the field of amebic dysentery helped control an epidemic in Chicago in 1933, was born in the village of Kobrin in the Pale of Settlement, an area in tsarist Russia designated for Jews. She was the fifth of nine children and the third of four daughters of Rose (Hausman) Kaplan and Samuel Kaplan, a dairy farmer and peddler. In 1905, Bertha Kaplan's family joined the masses of Russian Jewish immigrants who came to America looking for better economic opportunities and religious tolerance. Her family settled on Chicago's Near West Side, as did many recent Jewish arrivals. Bertha Kaplan's father took a job delivering coal, and her mother, along with two daughters, continued the family enterprise of making and selling cheese and butter.

Financial circumstances required the Kaplan children to end their formal education at the minimum age mandated by law in order to take full-time employment. When Bertha Kaplan reached the age of sixteen, a high school staff member prevailed on Ethel Kawin, a guidance counselor, to find a part-time job for a "bright young lady who was going to leave school in order to help support her family" (quoted in interview with Avron Spector). In assisting Bertha Kaplan to complete high school, Kawin helped to change her future course.

Bertha Kaplan received a B.S. degree from the University of Chicago in 1916. She was one of approximately 440 women in science who received baccalaureate degrees in the United States before 1920.

Her first position after graduation took her to Harvard University for two years as a research assistant in Bussey Institute, its graduate school of applied biology. During World War I, laboratory scientists were needed to diagnose diseases contracted by servicemen; there were shortages of qualified male workers in many sectors of government. In 1917 women became eligible for the first time to take the entrance examination for bacteriology positions in government service. As a result, Kaplan joined the war effort in 1918, moving to the base hospital laboratory at Fort Riley, Kansas, where she became a member of the first group of women employed by the government as bacteriologists. It may have been her experience at Fort Riley that sparked Bertha Kaplan's interest in studying bacteriology.

In 1919, Kaplan returned to the University of Chicago, earning an M.S. degree in hygiene and bacteriology two years later. She also became a member of the American Society of Bacteriologists, an association whose prewar female membership comprised less than 1 percent of its total. After the war, the society opened its doors to women, boasting a female membership of roughly 20 percent in the year that Bertha Kaplan joined. During her career, she also joined the American Society of Parasitologists and the American Public Health Association.

From 1921 to 1923, she worked as a bacteriologist at the U.S. Veterans Hospital in Chicago. Kaplan then moved to Cook County Hospital, where she remained until 1926. There she did her first original research, which resulted in several published articles on gynecological bacterial infections.

In 1926, Kaplan became an instructor of bacteriology and parasitology in the medical school of the University of Illinois and directed her attention to research on amebic dysentery and its protozoan source. The field she chose was relatively new. Protozoa and bacteria had gained wide attention as potential pathogens only a few decades earlier, with medicine's acceptance of the germ theory, that is, that microorganisms could cause disease. Amebic dysentery, long thought to be a disease of tropical climates, claimed notice when it accompanied servicemen returning home from the war. Interest was further heightened when later studies showed that the incidence of amebic dysentery in servicemen stationed in the United States during the war was approximately the same as the incidence in soldiers returning from foreign lands. It became clear that amebic dysentery was not only a tropical disease but also a significant factor in the United States.

Over the next few years, she published articles on several studies of amebic dysentery in collaboration with C. S. Wiliamson, M.D., head of internal medicine at the University of Illinois, and J. C. Geiger, M.D., of the Chicago Department of Health and the Hooper Foundation of Medical Research at the University of California. She contributed to a chapter, "The Advance against Amebic Dysentery" in the treatise *Chemistry in Medicine* (1928). She also published research on chronic ulcerative colitis.

In 1928, the University of Illinois awarded Kaplan the Beaumont Prize for her research on diseases of the gastrointestinal tract. That same year, she spent time at the Institut für Schiff und Tropen Krankheiten (Institute for Tropical Diseases) in Hamburg, Germany, seeking to gain expertise on amebic dysentery. Prior to the first World War, the scientific community in the United States had high regard for German institutions for their research and laboratory techniques.

Kaplan returned to her position with the University of Illinois for an eight-month commitment beginning in January 1929. On March 8, 1929, she married Morris Spector, the brother of one of her friends. Spector shared his wife's interest in science. He combined a degree from Illinois Institute of Technology in Chicago with studies in the law, graduating in 1927 from John Marshall Law School. While he struggled to survive in his foundling law firm during the depths of the depression, Bertha Spector's income was the family's main support. At the

end of June 1929, with the consent of Williamson, she left the University of Illinois and became a research associate at the Douglas Smith Foundation of the University of Chicago's medical school. When the University of Illinois refused to pay her salary for the remaining two months of her contract, she sued, unsuccessfully, for the sum; the court ruled that it had no jurisdiction in the case.

Bertha Kaplan Spector had two children: Rosa Leah (Rosalie), born August 23, 1930, and Avron Newton, born September 1, 1933. At the University of Chicago, she received a Ph.D. in hygiene and bacteriology in 1931 for her study of diagnostic methods for amebic dysentery and other infections caused by *Entamoeba histolytica*. Her work had been recognized in January 1930 in an article in the *American Hebrew* about Jewish women scientists. In the years that followed, she further concentrated her research efforts on the study of the pathogenic protozoan *Entamoeba histolytica*.

In 1933, Bertha Spector's research on amebic dysentery proved its great value. Eight and a half million people visited the City of Chicago for the Century of Progress Exposition, creating unusual crowding. After many of the guests had returned to their homes around the nation, reports of cases of amebic dysentery began to trickle into the Chicago Department of Health. Eventually, more than fourteen hundred cases of the disease, including ninety-eight deaths, were reported, making the outbreak the only known large-scale epidemic of amebic dysentery until that time. A significant number of the fatalities was attributed to physicians' unfamiliarity with the disease, which had resulted in misdiagnosis. Unsanitary conditions at two large hotels were found to be the source of the outbreak. During the investigation, authoritative research on amebic dysentery by Bertha Spector and her colleagues was translated from the pages of medical journals into practical application; lives were saved as a result of improved standards of hygiene as well as instruction to physicians on the prompt and accurate diagnosis and treatment of the disease.

Taking guidance from her own research, she lunched only on hard-boiled eggs and boiled water during her investigative work, remaining healthy while many of her coworkers contracted the disease. She brought her knowledge home from work as well. When utility pipes were repaired on the street where her family lived and she feared that drinking water would be contaminated, she "admonish[ed] her family to 'boil the water!'" (Sales, 1296).

After the epidemic, Spector continued her research on amebic dysentery in the dual roles of research associate at the University of Chicago and her new position as associate protozoologist for the U.S. Public Health Service beginning in 1934. Spector's research confirmed the reliability of rapid sand water filtration to remove *Entamoeba histolytica* from water, thereby safeguarding the public from future epidemics of amebic dysentery. She examined the pathogenic ameba in various states of growth, which resulted in a better understanding of the importance of good hygiene. In 1937, she read an article before the Laboratory Section of the American Public Health Association that reported the results of her study of amebiasis in Chicago during the three years following the 1933 epidemic.

Spector continued as a research associate for the remainder

of her career, earning the high regard of her colleagues at the University of Chicago as a diagnostician. Research associates, who generally held doctorates, worked as part of a team, often with public or private funding from such institutions as the Douglas Smith Foundation. Major universities welcomed women with doctorates as research associates because they were highly qualified scientists who worked for low pay and had little opportunity for advancement to faculty status.

Spector's research on *Entamoeba histolytica* for the U.S. Public Health Service took Spector and her children to Albuquerque, New Mexico, during the summers of 1936 and 1937. She studied the incidence of infection by the protozoan among different cultural groups, especially Latin Americans and Native Americans. Spector observed a high incidence of *Entamoeba histolytica* infection, but without a correspondingly high number of cases of amebic dysentery. The article in which she published her findings, "Studies of Acute Diarrheal Diseases," noted this and other questions for further study—research in which Spector would not participate. In 1935, she had diagnosed herself with Hodgkin's Disease, which greatly debilitated her over the following two years and led to her death in 1938. Spector was buried at Waldheim Cemetery in Chicago, near her mother and other members of Kehilas Jacob Anshe Drohitzin, a congregation near her place of birth in Russia.

Bertha Kaplan Spector's short life was a long journey from the Russian village of Kobrin, where she learned cheesemaking, to the laboratories of the University of Chicago, where she conducted studies that helped safeguard the public from disease. Her research contributed to improved standards of hygiene, a better understanding of amebic dysentery and its causes, and prevention of future epidemics of the disease.

Sources. Spector published the following journal articles on her research, as well as more than a dozen others, from 1925 until 1939; all of them are referenced in *Index Medicus*: with C. S. Williamson and J. C. Geiger, "Amebic Dysentery in Chicago: Preliminary Report of Survey of Food Handlers Following Small Outbreak," *Journal of the American Medical Association* (*JAMA*), March 26, 1927; with M. H. Streicher, "Chronic Ulcerative Colitis," *JAMA*, January 4, 1930; "Comparative Study of Cultural and Immunological Methods of Diagnosing Infections with *Endameba* [sic] *Histolytica*," *Journal of Preventive Medicine*, March 1932; with J. R. Baylis and O. Gullans, "Effectiveness of Filtration in Removing from Water, and of Chlorine in Killing, Causative Organism of Amoebic Dysentery," *Public Health Reports*, July 6, 1934; "Amebiasis in Chicago, December 1933 to June 1936," *American Journal of Public Health*, July 1937; with A. V. Hardy, "Studies of Acute Diarrheal Diseases: Parasitological Observations," *Public Health Reports*, June 23, 1939. She coauthored with J. C. Geiger and C. S. Williamson, "The Advance against Amoebic Dysentery," in *Chemistry in Medicine: A Cooperative Treatise Intended to Give Examples of Progress Made in Medicine with the Aid of Chemistry*, ed. Julius Stieglitz (1928). Details of the Century of Progress Exposition epidemic can be found in the U.S. Treasury Department Public Health Service National Institute of Health Bulletin No. 166, *Epidemic Amebic Dysentery: The Chicago Outbreak of 1933* (March 1936), which uses Spector's laboratory research. Her research is cited in Morris Goldberg, "Women in the Realm of Science," *American Hebrew*, January 3, 1930. Biographical information is contained in John Simons, ed., *Who's Who in American Jewry*, vol. 3 (1938–39). Spector's salary at UIC is reported in the *Thirty-Fourth Report of the Board of Trustees of the University of Illinois* (1926–28) and *Thirty-Fifth Report* (1928–30). A biographical essay on Spector by Charlene Kanter Sales is in Paula E. Hyman and Deborah Dash Moore, eds., *Jewish Women in America: An Historical Encyclopedia* (1997). Additional information came from interviews by Charlene Kanter Sales with Rosalie Minsk (daughter), November 1996 and July 1999; Avron Spector (son), July 1999; and, as cited in *Jewish Women in America*, Dr. Joseph B. Kirsner, UC Medical Center, November 1996. Obituaries appeared March 27, 1938, in *CT* and *NYT*. For contextual information, see Irving Cutler, *The Jews of Chicago* (1996); Arthur Hertzberg, *The Jews in America: Four Centuries of an Uneasy Encounter—A History* (1989); Margaret W. Rossiter, *Women Scientists in America: Struggles and Strategies to 1940* (1982); Thomas Neville Bonner, *Medicine in Chicago, 1850–1950* (1957); and Thomas Wakefield Goodspeed, *The History of the University of Chicago* (1916).

CHARLENE KANTER SALES

SPONLAND, SISTER INGEBORG
March 25, 1860–December 3, 1951
DEACONESS, HOSPITAL ADMINISTRATOR

Ingeborg Sponland came to America to visit and stayed the rest of her life, which she devoted to service and ministry to people in need. Born in Hevne, Norway, the third of five children and eldest daughter of Johannes and Magnhild Lee Sponland, her father fished and her mother ran the home and family farm. Although Ingeborg was named for her maternal grandmother, her paternal grandmother, who lived with the family until her death when Ingeborg was twelve, had a strong influence on the young woman's developing spirituality, which was evident from an early age. The distance from the family home on the Norwegian coast to both school and church required that the children board with local families in order to attend classes. After six weeks of daily lessons in preparation for confirmation, the rite of membership in the Lutheran church, Ingeborg ranked highest among the girls in her class of 120 confirmands. When she was fourteen, she heard the pastor read a report at church of the activities of the Oslo Deaconess Home and later recalled that "the thought came to me: 'There is the work that shall be mine'" (Sponland, 9).

Lutheran deaconess ministry was a nineteenth-century revival of an early Christian model of women's service. It grew out of the Pietist movement on the European continent and its attendant emphasis on social activism. The resulting development of institutions of care required caregivers to meet especially the needs of women and children in early industrial societies, and deaconesses provided that service. The female diaconate became an acceptable outlet for unmarried and committed Christian women. Though all were trained as nurses, deaconess ministry was not limited to nursing nor synonymous with it.

In the spring of 1881, Sponland arrived at the Lovisenberg Deaconess Institute in Oslo, where she began training. That fall she was sent to the county hospital in Fredrikstad, where she learned practical nursing, returning to Oslo to complete her training in early 1884. Her first assignment was at a government hospital in Oslo, where she served for three years before moving to the Bergen city hospital for two years. In 1889 she became supervisor of nursing at the Stavanger city hospital, her first position as an administrator. At Stavanger, which she called "more than a hospital" (Sponland, 27), she worked with delinquents or "street girls" (p. 27), the aged and poor, sailors, the insane, and women and men detained in the workhouse. On September 13, 1886, Sponland was consecrated as a deaconess, making a voluntary commitment to what she considered her life calling of service to God.

In 1891 Sponland requested a year's leave to travel to America, where her siblings had emigrated. She planned to accompany her visiting parents back to Norway, but instead she remained in the United States. From New York City, where she met Sister Elizabeth Fedde at the Brooklyn Deaconess Motherhouse, she traveled to Minneapolis, Minnesota, and to North Dakota. While visiting, she was asked to serve as sister superior of the Deaconess Home and Hospital in Minneapolis, which Fedde had founded in 1888. During the thirteen years Sponland had oversight of the Minneapolis hospital, she helped establish seven other hospitals in Grand Forks, Hillsboro, Fargo, and Grafton, North Dakota; and in Crookston, Fergus Falls, and Austin, Minnesota; and she sent deaconesses to work in adjunct agencies such as children's and what were then called "old people's" homes. As hospital administrator, Sponland was responsible for teaching and training the deaconesses, whose number increased from six in 1891 to thirty-eight in 1897.

During those years Minneapolis experienced prolonged epidemics of both typhoid fever and tuberculosis, the "white plague" (Sponland, 49–50). As the needs of the community it served increased, Sponland pressed the hospital board for a larger facility. The board would neither agree with her assessment nor accept her subsequent resignation, based on failing health, in 1903. After a year of waiting for promised changes, she again resigned and in 1904 moved with her brother to Thief River Falls, Minnesota, to homestead. She remained there the required fourteen months to prove her claim, despite offers from both the Brooklyn and Chicago motherhouses.

By 1906, her health regained, Sponland was ready to return to the deaconess ministry and agreed to serve as sister superior of the Norwegian Lutheran Home and Hospital in Chicago. Her first impression on arriving in the city was that she was "a stranger in a strange city, in surroundings far different from what I had expected—wondering just how I happened to be there" (Sponland, 59), especially when she first saw the hospital, "the lone little building . . . in the midst of the swampland" (p. 59) at the corner of Haddon Avenue and Leavitt Street.

Sponland served as administrator of the hospital for thirty years. She participated in reorganization of the medical staff and oversaw expansion of the deaconess roster, which reached a peak of sixty-five in 1920. She recognized in Chicago, as she had in Minneapolis, that physical expansion of the building was essential to the growth of services. Together with hospital rector Rev. H. B. Kildahl, Sponland fought for a new wing as well as for more deaconesses, and in 1910 a new hundred-bed hospital was dedicated. A significant contribution toward the new hospital and future work had been made by the Ladies Auxiliary, which Sponland had organized in 1908.

A petite woman of stern appearance, probably largely due to the traditional heavy dark garb and starched cap that deaconesses wore, Sponland frequently met resistance to her efforts. Criticism and opposition came from various fronts, whether students who did not understand the servant nature of

deaconess work or pastors, some of whom "even worked against us" (Sponland, 61), or other critics who felt a Norwegian Lutheran hospital should treat only Norwegians, or only Lutherans, but not the Jewish patients who lived in the West Town neighborhood where the hospital was located. Finances were a perpetual problem, since patients were treated regardless of their ability to pay. Despite "the constant drain on our treasury" (Sponland, 70), Sponland remained grateful that the hospital board "never called on us to cut down our grocery bills" (p. 70). The sixty-five thousand dollar debt incurred by the new building was paid in full by 1917.

As the neighborhood around the hospital changed, new needs were identified and new programs introduced. In 1911 a kindergarten was opened and soon after that a day nursery, classes for mothers, and Sunday school for children. Uplift of and assistance to immigrants were important parts of deaconess outreach. Sponland, who called the diaconate "a ministry of mercy" (Sponland, xi), believed the whole purpose of her work was service given for the welfare of others. Her life's lament was that there were always far more needs than there were deaconesses to serve.

Even without adequate staff, Sponland's tenure was one of remarkable expansion of both facilities and services. World War I raised issues about hospital standards, and Sponland believed it essential that her hospital pass accreditation, no matter what that required. Some of the deaconesses were sent to train as pharmacists. By 1924 another building project added to the hospital a west wing and separate areas for surgery, pathology, and obstetrics, as well as 216 more patient beds. In 1926 a school of nursing was established, separate from the deaconess training school. By 1926, Sponland was again ready to retire.

Her request to resign was denied by the hospital board, which instead granted her a year's leave of absence. Having long held a "secret hope" (Sponland, 82) to travel to foreign mission sites, Sponland left for China in the fall of 1926. Her party reached Shanghai in early October and remained in China for more than six months, experiencing sometimes dangerous conditions as they visited mission sites. They continued on to Egypt and Palestine before traveling through Europe on their way to Norway, which Sponland had left thirty-six years earlier. She returned to Chicago and her position as mother superior of the hospital in the fall of 1927 with "new vision and encouragement" (Sponland, 142). At the General Convention of the Women's Missionary Federation of the Norwegian Lutheran Church in America in 1928, Sponland was awarded a gold medal from the King of Norway in recognition of her work on behalf of Norwegian "newcomers" (Sponland, 143) to the United States.

In 1931, Sponland's dream was fulfilled when a deaconess home and training school opened in Chicago. Funds for the building and its furnishings had been raised by the Women's Missionary Federation, a group for which Sponland held a special fondness. Not only was the federation a dynamic force in the church due to its remarkable fund-raising on behalf of the Chicago Lutheran Deaconess Home and Hospital, but it provided valuable opportunities for service through programs educating and unifying women. Sponland liked to report what a pastor once remarked to her, "You women *do* the business, while we discuss it" (Sponland, 149).

In 1936 Sponland retired and lived the remaining fifteen years of her life in her beloved Deaconess Home, where in 1938, with failing eyesight, she dictated her autobiography, *My Reasonable Service*. It remains a primary chronicle of Lutheran deaconess work in America. She died at age ninety-one and was buried at Mt. Olive Cemetery, the final resting place for many of Chicago's Norwegian Americans.

The Chicago Lutheran Deaconess Home and Hospital was sold in the early 1960s to St. Mary of Nazareth Hospital, and many of the deaconesses moved from the city to Lutheran General Hospital in suburban Park Ridge, of which Chicago Lutheran Deaconess had been the mother hospital. The original building, constructed and expanded under Ingeborg Sponland's administration, no longer stands.

At the fiftieth anniversary of the Chicago Lutheran Deaconess Home and Hospital in 1947, a nameless admirer said of Sponland, "Sister Ingeborg has breathed her spirit into every brick of the institution" (Ronning, 19). The work of the deaconesses she supervised paralleled many of the activities of religious women in Protestant and Catholic traditions, whose leadership in the development of social service institutions was especially significant in the period of immigration, when private benevolence provided the greatest share of assistance to those in need. Remembered as a woman of deeds and known for her strong will and insistence on progress and excellence, Ingeborg Sponland's legacy extends beyond her obvious accomplishments as a hospital administrator to the example she set through her selfless devotion to God and tireless service to those in need.

Sources. The primary document of record is Sister Ingeborg Sponland's autobiography, *My Reasonable Service*, published in 1938. Fiftieth anniversary booklets for the Lutheran Deaconess Home and Hospital in both Minneapolis and Chicago cite Sponland's book extensively to report the history of the formative periods in which she served each institution. Other historians, whether of Lutheran deaconesses or of Lutheran women with a Norwegian heritage, are equally reliant on her account. See N. N. Ronning, *Fiftieth Anniversary of the Lutheran Deaconess Home and Hospital, 1897–1947* (1947); Frederick S. Weiser, *Love's Response: A Story of Lutheran Deaconesses in America* (1962); DeAne Lagerquist, *From Our Mothers' Arms: A History of Women in the American Lutheran Church* (1987); and Jeannine E. Olson, *One Ministry, Many Roles: Deacons and Deaconesses through the Centuries* (1992).

MARY TODD

STAHLE, NORMA K.
March 19, 1891–April 2, 1950

INTERIOR DESIGNER, ART ORGANIZATION ADMINISTRATOR

From 1922 until 1938, Norma Stahle was chief fund-raiser and administrator for the Association of Arts and Industries, an organization founded to establish a school of industrial art in Chicago. In this position, she was responsible for bringing to Chicago the noted Bauhaus teacher and designer László Moholy-Nagy and for cofounding the New Bauhaus in Chicago, which had a year of luminous life from 1937 to 1938. According to design historian Lloyd Engelbrecht, Stahle "worked effectively behind the scenes to bring modern design to Chicago" (interview with Engelbrecht). In this work, she was heir to efforts begun by Prairie School architects, but the creative energy and innovative spirit that enabled those efforts to thrive at the turn of the century had dissipated by the time Stahle arrived in Chicago.

Little is known of Stahle's life prior to the establishment of the Association of Arts and Industries (AAI). Stahle was born in the small central Ohio town of Crestline, a railroad center established in 1853. She was one of three children born to Edwin S. and Emma (DeBolt) Stahle, a Pennsylvania native who died in 1895 when Norma was only four. A brother, Edwin M. Stahle, was born in 1889 while his parents were living in Texas; her sister, Lura, died two years after Emma Stahle.

Stahle's paternal grandparents were one of Crestline's founding families; Jacob Augustus Stahle and Rebecca (Moser) Stahle had come to Crestline from Berks County in central Pennsylvania. Jacob Stahle, whose family was Methodist and Republican, served two terms as Crestline's mayor. Norma Stahle's father, Edwin, was the youngest of Jacob and Rebecca Stahle's eleven children. As a young man he headed to Texas, where he initially worked as a telegraph operator and later as an auditor for the railroads. At the time of his death in 1924, he was in the oil leasing business in Camden, Arkansas, a small city in the southwestern part of the state.

Norma Stahle may have spent part of her childhood in her grandparents' hometown, perhaps living with her numerous maiden aunts and unmarried uncles after her mother's death. Her brother Edwin spent his early years in Crestline. In 1904, her father Edwin Stahle married again but had no more children; the following year Norma's brother rejoined their father in St. Louis, Missouri, where he attended college. Norma Stahle may have moved there, too. Though he worked as a telegraph operator, brother Edwin also was a writer who had several stories published in places like *Collier's* and the *Chicago Daily News*, where he won a major writing competition. A recurrent illness and a serious automobile accident led to his death in 1925 at age thirty-six. At that time he was living in Chicago; two of Edwin and Norma Stahle's aunts lived in the city at the time.

Norma Stahle had creative inclinations and so she, too, arrived in Chicago. In 1921, she listed herself as an artist with a studio in the Fine Arts Building, once a vibrant center for creative artists. By the time Stahle moved in, however, its role as stimulating incubator was over, though it was likely still a place where a newcomer might connect with Chicago's artistic community.

In 1922, Stahle was named to the board of the American Society of Arts and Industries. When the Association of Arts and Industries was established in 1922, an interest in the alliance between artists and industrialists had extended both to several Chicago manufacturers and to the Art Institute of Chicago. Newspaper articles at the time pointed out that manufacturing centers in Europe abounded with schools of design. Further, raw materials from the United States were being sent abroad to be turned into manufactured goods that were then imported back into cities like Chicago.

From the founding of AAI in 1922 until shortly before the New Bauhaus school was established in 1937, William Nelson Pelouze served as AAI president and provided office space. Though his social and business connections were essential to the association, Stahle's contributions have been characterized as "even more important than [those of] Pelouze" (Engelbrecht, "The Association of Arts and Industries," 41) and her voice was likely the most important one.

A photograph taken when Stahle was around fifty years old shows her to be somewhat austere but attractive. Some found her "withdrawn and elusive" (Engelbrecht, "The Association of Arts and Industries," 314). These qualities, however, were offset by others, "such as energy, persistence, and a sense for organizing and running things. On a number of occasions she displayed a sophisticated understanding of the issues involved in design and design education" (Engelbrecht, "The Association of Arts and Industries," 315).

It is likely that she worked part-time for Pelouze, perhaps as a designer, for there is no record that any of the $350,000 the association raised was spent on expenses, including a salary for Stahle, until after the New Bauhaus opened. Stahle may have come to regard her project to bring about the establishment of a school of industrial design as her most creative undertaking. The association's brief but distinguished history is best interpreted in the context of its time. Chicago was one of the world's most bustling cities; its rigorous industries produced both manufacturing materials and consumer goods, then flung them out across the land through a vast transportation network. Chicago's extraordinary economy had provided many with the leisure to pursue good works; Pelouze and other members of the association board were among them. There was, however, a lack of good design. The projected school would correct this deficiency and place Chicago on the map for its industrial design the way it had made itself a reputation as a capital of modern architecture years earlier.

In the fall of 1924, art critic Lena McCauley claimed, "Chicago is strategically situated, as the second city of the nation, [and] audaciously extending its art collections and educational opportunities is the art center of the nation" (*Chicago Evening Post Magazine of the Art World*, October 7, 1924). Her colleague C. J. Bulliet, whose advocacy of modern art won him a national reputation, wrote an editorial titled "What You Can Do for Art." In it he commented, "You add a tax to your purchase price because manufacturers in the United States do not realize that we must have school to train American art students and craftsmen to be designers" (*Chicago Evening Post*, October 7, 1924), a point Norma Stahle continually made on behalf of the association. An article in a following issue, December 9, 1924, reported that the head of the Illinois Federation of Women's Clubs, a group that represented twenty thousand women, had pledged its support for a school of industrial art. Stahle's efforts were more than likely behind that support.

The association's extensive coverage in newspapers and professional publications indicated that Stahle was an effective publicist. The round of AAI-sponsored activities demonstrated that she saw its role as nationally significant, yet she was also adept at holding amusements for Chicago socialites, including an arts ball in 1925 that attracted the crème of Chicago's cultural and social life. Reports of the association's activities abounded with names of Chicago's heralded designers. Sculptor Alfonso Iannelli, who briefly directed an industrial art program at the Art Institute of Chicago (AIC), served on several committees and panels; so did Marion Hickman Gheen, one of

Chicago's most prominent interior designers. Painter Oliver Dennett Grover was a long-time board member; popular sculptor Lorado Taft was also a member at one time. Multi-talented designer (automobiles as well as buildings) Henry K. Holsman was on the board throughout the association's existence, as was Frank Milhening, head of a substantial jewelry manufacturing firm. Officers of the Universal Portland Cement Company, the John Deere Company, the Kohler Company in Wisconsin, Montgomery Ward, R.R. Donnelley, and the Continental Bank served at one time or another. Directors of the AIC and the Chicago Association of Commerce also served. Stahle, however, provided the continuity and played an active role in promoting the acceptance of modern design. Knowledgeable about modernism, in the 1930s, for example, she corresponded with architect Frank Lloyd Wright, discussing significant design issues of the day.

Throughout the 1920s, the association concentrated on establishing an industrial arts program at the AIC and raised more than $350,000 with major contributions from Julius Rosenwald of Sears, Roebuck and from the General Education Fund in New York, a precursor to the Rockefeller Foundation. The industrial arts program at AIC was formally established in 1928; however, mutual dissatisfaction characterized the relationship between the AAI and the AIC. The conflict came down to whether students should learn primarily through drawing or through working with materials and machines.

In 1936, AIC and AAI severed their relationship. AIC returned $131,500 to AAI, and with this money Stahle endeavored to establish the sort of school envisioned fifteen years earlier. Now, however, she had to do it without Pelouze, who had resigned from the AAI. Replacing him was E. H. Powell, a former Sears official who had become president of the Encyclopaedia Britannica Company. Several other officers and board members remained the same, but Stahle had managed to expand it to include not only Walter Kohler but also Walter Paepcke, who was at the time building the Container Corporation of America into one of the nation's most prominent design-oriented firms. Though they gave their names, they apparently did not commit funds sufficient to continue the association's efforts.

Stahle must have surmised that the educational program of the German Bauhaus was more what she had in mind for a design school in Chicago, because in May 1937 she wrote to Bauhaus founder Walter Gropius, inquiring about his interest in coming to Chicago. He had recently joined the Harvard University faculty and declined, but he suggested his close collaborator László Moholy-Nagy. Stahle cabled Moholy in London, England, and two months later he was in Chicago; late in August the New Bauhaus was announced in the press from Illinois to England. Stahle told the *Chicago Daily News*, August 23, 1937, "It is our aim to establish a school of design that will meet the needs of industry and reintegrate the artists into the life of the nation. . . . It is especially fitting that the central west should be the locale of this great school of design." Coincidentally, a group of Chicago architects was courting another Bauhaus figure, Ludwig Mies van der Rohe, who would eventually head the architecture program at the Illinois Institute of Technology (IIT).

The New Bauhaus American School of Design opened in September in the former Marshall Field home on Prairie Avenue. Lloyd Engelbrecht wrote, "Few individual school years in the entire history of American education have received as much attention as the sole year of operation of the New Bauhaus" (Engelbrecht, "The Association of Arts and Industries," 273). A young faculty member, Henry Holmes Smith, later said, "What took place was a rare and essentially non repeatable educational experience: a creative interaction between student and teacher which was crucial to the artistic growth of the teacher as well as the students" (quoted in Engelbrecht, "The Association of Arts and Industries," 281). Though credit must go to Moholy and the faculty he assembled on the run, Moholy initially acknowledged Stahle's contribution. "In fifteen years of quiet and persistent work she broke the ground and prepared the understanding for the idea of Bauhaus education in this country" (quoted in Engelbrecht, "The Association of Arts and Industries," 281), he wrote in a March 1938 article that appeared in *Shelter*, then a leading design magazine.

Before the year was through, however, Stahle and Moholy were involved in a bitter dispute that ended the school's only year. Students were in revolt, the AAI was out of funds, and its board was divided. Moholy survived with support from Walter Paepcke, who made it possible for him to open a school of his own. This evolved into the Institute of Design, which eventually moved to IIT, along with Mies's school of architecture.

In 1939, Stahle joined Marshall Field & Company, perhaps through its eminent display director Arthur Fraser, who had participated in at least one AAI program. Nothing more was heard from her until a brief death notice appeared in the *Chicago Tribune* eleven years later. Norma Stahle died suddenly in her home of a heart ailment. A relative, Edith S. Locke, wife of Burt T. Locke, a retired druggist in Chicago's Kenwood neighborhood, made arrangements for her body to be cremated at Graceland Cemetery in Chicago.

Norma K. Stahle helped establish the New Bauhaus, a design school she felt Chicago needed; but her catalytic role was soon forgotten. She was, with a small group of design-conscious professionals and members of the business community, aware of the extraordinary opportunity Chicago's location provided for a marriage of commerce and art; and she dedicated herself to bringing that union into being.

Sources. Much of the information about Norma Stahle is in Lloyd C. Engelbrecht, "The Association of Arts and Industries: Background and Origins of the Bauhaus Movement in America" (Ph.D. diss., Univ. of Chicago, 1973) and the Institute of Design Archive, UIC Spec. Coll. Engelbrecht also provided information in an interview with Connie Heaton Goddard on March 12, 1999. Facts on the Stahle family are available in genealogy sources, including the Ohio Surname Index, and *A Centennial Biographical History of Crawford County, Ohio* (1902). Stahle family obituaries appeared in the weekly *Crestline Advocate*, November 13, 1924, and August 6, 1925, available through the Crestline Public Library. Death certificates for Edwin Mitchell Stahle and Norma K. Stahle are on file with the Department of Vital Statistics, Cook County, Illinois. Stahle wrote a small number of letters to Frank Lloyd Wright, which are in the Frank Lloyd Wright Archives, Frank Lloyd Wright Foundation, Scottsdale, Arizona. Articles in the *Chicago Evening Post Magazine of the Art World* (on microfilm at the Art Institute of Chicago and listed in the *Index to Art Periodicals*, commonly called the Ryerson Index) are useful. Another valuable source is James Sloan Allan, *The Romance of Commerce and Culture in Chicago* (1983),

on Walter and Elizabeth Paepcke and the Container Corporation. Engelbrecht's chapter "Modernism and Design in Chicago," in *The Old Guard and the Avant-Garde: Modernism in Chicago, 1910–1940*, ed. Sue Ann Prince (1990), should also be consulted. See also Engelbrecht, "László Moholy-Nagy in Chicago," in *Moholy's New Vision*, ed. Terry Suhre, catalog of exhibit, Illinois State Museum, Springfield, 1989–90.

CONNIE HEATON GODDARD

STANISIA, SISTER MARY (Monica Kurk, née Kurkowski)
May 4, 1878–January 28, 1967
PAINTER, EDUCATOR

Sister Mary Stanisia lived in two worlds. In the convent she obeyed strict communal guidelines and took a vow of poverty. As an artist, she competed in a secular world and produced portraits of well-known politicians and religious leaders alongside her religious murals.

Sister Mary Stanisia was born Monica Kurkowski in Chicago to Francis and Katherine Kurkowski, immigrants from German-partitioned Poland. As a young girl she observed her father, a woodcarver, work with tools to create objects of usefulness and beauty. The family changed its name to "Kurk" at some point. They lived in the Polish parish of St. Stanislaus, and Monica Kurk attended the Catholic parish elementary school and the Academy of Our Lady. At an early age she was sent to Europe to study with Polish-born religious artist Count Thaddeus von Zukotynski and was introduced to the art of mural painting depicting religious and mythological subjects.

Kurk's religious devotion became clear to her when she was a young girl. "It was while coming from the Communion Table when a small girl," she later recalled, "that I silently dedicated my life to God's service" (Kendall, "Lives of Great People"). When she returned from Europe in 1893, she decided to enter a religious convent and, "leaving a comfortable home, affectionate parents, brothers and sisters" (Kendall, "Lives of Great People"), she began the process of preparing for a religious life, serving as a novice from 1896 to 1899 at the motherhouse of the School Sisters of Notre Dame in Milwaukee, Wisconsin, and entering the order permanently in March 1899 at St. Mary's, Michigan City, Indiana.

With the religious name of Sister Mary Stanisia, she continued to paint throughout this period of religious preparation. "My desire was," she later reflected, "to spread devotion to Him through my art; to praise, honor and serve Him and to add happiness to all His people" (Kendall, "Lives of Great People"). Disappointed friends had predicted that Stanisia would withdraw from the artistic development she had nourished in Europe, but she navigated her spiritual path contemporaneously with an intense devotion to the art of painting. Her earliest known painting, *The Sacred Heart of Jesus* (1899), already revealed her abilities.

Sister Mary Stanisia continued to develop spiritually and as an artist when she was sent to teach in academies run by the School Sisters of Notre Dame. She taught art in the high school and gave private lessons while in residence at Our Lady of Lourdes, Marinette, Wisconsin, from the fall of 1899 to the fall of 1905, when she began to teach art in St. Mary's Academy, Prairie du Chien, Wisconsin. Two years later she arrived in Chicago and began to teach at the Academy of Our Lady, Longwood. Here she

FIG. 110. *Mayor Edward J. Kelly shakes artist Sister Mary Stanisia's hand, 1934.*

set up her own art studio and began a productive period of individual growth as an artist and great activity as a teacher of art. She founded the fine arts program there, becoming its first director in February 1907. She was given a large studio on the second floor, which boasted a ceiling high enough to permit the completion of murals before they were shipped to permanent locations.

Intent on learning more, she studied at the School of the Art Institute of Chicago (SAIC) from 1916 to 1919, which gave her one of the finest, though more conservative, educations in art in the country. There she studied portrait painting with Leopold Seyffert, mural painting with John Norton, landscape painting with Frank Peyraud, sculpture with Albin Polasek, and a subject in which she excelled, academic figure painting with Wellington Reynolds. She exhibited in all of the student annual shows, and a full-length portrait, *Her Great Grandmother's Wedding Gown,* was illustrated in the 1917–18 SAIC catalog. She graduated with a Bachelor of Fine Art degree (B.F.A.) and received an honorable mention for especially commendable work in life and portrait painting. Mary Stanisia continued to study painting. From 1915 to 1922 she was the pupil of acclaimed portraitist Robert Clarkson in Chicago. She spent a summer studying painting with Charles W. Hawthorne in Provincetown, Massachusetts. In 1922 she received a Bachelor of Philosophy degree from DePaul University, Chicago.

Zukotynski's training seems to have afforded Stanisia skills to model in the manner of proto-Renaissance artists—in the manner of an icon—but with a concern for sculptural form and for the feeling of true flesh. In her 1899 painting, she utilized a technique much closer to that of Italian primitives than the prevailing American taste for nineteenth-century academic painting, or for that matter, European modernism. By the time she left SAIC and her studies with Clarkson and Hawthorne, her style had changed dramatically. *Two Friends* (c. 1921), a nonreligious subject, documents this shift well. Stanisia's palette and technique are livelier; the brushstrokes breathe. This intimate, psychological study of two figures seated in an interior recalls comparable

works by Berthe Morisot, Edgar Degas, or Mary Cassatt. Although shown at rest, the figures tremble with a freshness and an emotional intensity new to her work. This quality, along with an objective yet probing attitude about portraiture, would later serve her finest portraits and religious subjects well, largely due to her studies with Hawthorne, Seyffert, and Reynolds.

In 1921, Stanisia was commissioned to paint the central panel for an altar piece at St. Hyacinth Church, Chicago, possibly her earliest surviving large-scale work. The work followed a composition by Zukotynski, which also hangs in St. Hyacinth Church, offering a rare opportunity to compare the master with the student.

By 1924, Sister Mary Stanisia received commissions from individuals and congregations, including a six-and-a-half-foot by twelve-foot mural for St. Paul's Cathedral, Minnesota. Her greatest success occurred in 1926 when she exhibited four canvases at the Eucharistic Congress in Chicago. Aimed toward the revitalization and promotion of Catholic eucharistic art, the exhibition provided a specific and appreciative audience, and Stanisia quickly attracted commissions.

Sister Mary Stanisia continued to live and work at the Academy of Our Lady, Longwood, but after 1926, preoccupied with commissions, she rarely taught classes in conjunction with the school. She enjoyed the freedom of conducting private classes in her studio and frequently counseled pupils individually. For a time, Stanisia was so busy with her projects that often she was found sleeping in her studio. Eventually she slept there regularly, an activity that scandalized the rest of the faculty.

Between 1926 and 1930, she completed an estimated fifty murals, portraits, and devotional subjects, including a highly acclaimed Stations of the Cross cycle (c. 1926) for St. Margaret of Scotland Church on Chicago's South Side. At this time, Sister Stanisia attracted critical and somewhat sensational attention from Chicago art critics. Many writers, charmed by the apparent novelty of a nun artist, demonstrated a lack of knowledge of the breadth of learning among men and women religious in the modern world. Pro-modernist critic C. J. Bulliet marveled at "a painter of unusually fine talent developing in the sheltered circles of nun" ("Artists of Chicago, No. 56"). Many failed to realize that for centuries women religious had been scholars who, unburdened by the expectations of traditional female roles, were able to concentrate on intense study of many subjects. Conservative critic Eleanor Jewett claimed that "terrifyingly little [religious art is being] done in the church today" ("Nun Portrays Exquisite Face"). Only a few years later the journal *Liturgical Arts* dispelled this notion. Yet even Catholic publications such as *Novena Notes*, which reported that Stanisia's paintings had saved suicidal souls and even converted the occasional atheist, saw her as a novelty.

In 1929 Sister Mary Stanisia founded the Department of Art at Mt. Mary College, Milwaukee, Wisconsin, one of the institutions of higher learning run by the School Sisters of Notre Dame. She continued to direct the art program at Longwood as well as the one in Milwaukee. In 1930 she founded the Art Guild of Chicago, whose gallery was housed at Longwood. Among the many purposes of the guild was the promotion of unknown artists and the furthering of their education. The guild also established a permanent gallery and held annual exhibitions of work by its members. It showed the work of artists whose limited means excluded them from exhibition opportunities.

Stanisia's own work flourished in the 1930s. In 1930–31 her work was included in the University of Chicago Renaissance Society's *Exhibition and Festival of Religious Art.* She won a silver medal at the Warsaw, Poland, World's Fair (1932) for a painting. Her portraits of Chicago Mayor Edward Kelly and Illinois Governor Henry Horner were unveiled during the Century of Progress Exposition in 1934. The following year, a one-woman show at the Davis Store, Evanston, Illinois, was a triumph; there Stanisia's secular subjects hung adjacent to her more popular religious paintings. In keeping with her vow of poverty, any prize money or commission received for her artworks was given back to her religious community.

Stanisia's lifelong preference for human models, selected after much contemplation, joined her to a tradition of painters of religious subjects such as Rembrandt van Rijn or Michelangelo da Caravaggio, who selected ordinary persons to represent Old and New Testament figures. Unlike those artists, however, Stanisia does not seem to have depicted herself as a participant in or observer of the events she was painting. Writers frequently commented on Stanisia's use of models from her own parish and from the South Side of Chicago. A notable example was her search for the ideal model to represent St. Martin de Porres, who was being considered for canonization by the Church in 1937. Stanisia interviewed approximately twelve African American men from the South Side of Chicago before choosing a man who "was known for his piety" (Lane) and fit her conception of a saintly being. She used a Longwood student as the model for the young Christ after a year-long search. Five hundred girls were interviewed before one "with all the qualities and attributes of the true Madonna type" (Long, "Nun's Painting Is Known as a Mystic Valentine") was chosen for the celebrated canvas *Ecce Ancilla Domini*. The ideal model for St. Therese was chosen for her "almost incredible resemblance" (Long, "Painting of St. Therese by Nun Called the Story of a 'Rose'") to the saint; like the others, it submitted to the transformation of anonymity and beautification.

Sister Mary Stanisia painted portraits of Cardinal Mundelein, Pope Pius XI, and Cardinal Stritch, as well as famous Illinois politicians. She did Mundelein's portrait twice and became a friend. Pope Pius XI's portrait was done from photographs. She also painted sports hero Knute Rockne, who posed for her.

Although primarily a painter of religious subjects, Stanisia said few things about the genre and its relevance to her calling. In the 1940s, however, Stanisia began a series of American "Madonnas," portraying an ideal of Catholic motherhood. These were probably a response to Pope Pius XI's encyclicals on social responsibility and marriage. This was as close as she came to intertwining religious and social issues with her art in an explicit manner.

In response to many of her most involved religious compositions, writers were frequently proud to herald Stanisia as a genius nun and a specifically American artist. One writer for the *New World*, a Catholic newspaper published in Chicago, described her Stations of the Cross cycle at St. Margaret of Scotland Church as "[painted] with more drama and divine love than ever before in the history of Catholic art. . . . [They are] the only original painted Stations of the Cross in this city" (Long, "Stations of the Cross"). Other depictions of the life cycle of Christ were judged "for the most part, copies of the European ecclesiastical painters" (Long, "Stations of the Cross"). Stanisia's work is not explicitly based on the religious work of the Old Masters. An Americanization of figure types and themes, comparable to a kind of glamorous Hollywood actor image, began to emerge quite early in her work and remained throughout her career. Examples are her Madonnas and a *Flight into Egypt*. Whether she was conscious of it or not, Stanisia seems to have been part of a growing consciousness in the United States of a purely American Catholic art, one that began to define its own set of parameters and iconography. One indication of the interest in art and specifically religious painting among women religious was the number of nuns who signed the Art Institute's ledger book for permission to take their easels into the galleries and copy paintings.

In 1928 Stanisia was commissioned to paint an image for publishing companies wishing to distribute thousands of copies throughout the world. The genre of her image, *Sacred Heart of Jesus,* is comparable to the American Protestant artist Warner Sallman's *Head of Christ* (1940), although the latter's image is estimated to have been reproduced five hundred million times between 1940 and 1984.

Stanisia lived the last years of her life at the Notre Dame Infirmary in Elm Grove, Wisconsin. She died at age eighty-eight, having lived nearly all of her life in Chicago. She is buried at the School Sisters of Notre Dame Cemetery, Elm Grove, Wisconsin.

Stanisia turned down a French artist's invitation to Paris to accept religious and portrait commissions saying, "I am a Religious, having dedicated my life to the service of our Divine Lord and here in this peaceful convent [in Chicago] I shall remain until He calls me to my heavenly home" (Kendall, "Writer Finds Tranquility in Gifted Nun's Studio"). In this seemingly constrained environment, Sister Mary Stanisia remained unbound by the social limitations and traditional expectations of the roles of women in community, family, and work.

Sources. The Leon T. Walkowicz Collection, Loyola University Chicago Archives, has materials related to the career and life of Sister Stanisia. Additional Stanisia materials are at the Archives of the Provincial House, Chicago Province of the School Sisters of Notre Dame, Berwyn, Illinois, including an undated clipping, Veva Elton Kendall, "Lives of Great People: Sister Mary Stanisia," reprinted from *Catholic Women Magazine.* Archives at the Polish Museum of America, Chicago, and the Academy of Our Lady, Chicago, also have items on Stanisia. See also the Archives of the Art Institute of Chicago. Stanisia's panel at St. Hyacinth Church, Chicago, now hangs in the sacristy of the church. Her Stations of the Cross are in St. Margaret of Scotland Church, Chicago. Several art critics wrote useful articles, including Clarence J. Bulliet, "Artists of Chicago, No. 56—Sister Mary Stanisia," *Chicago Daily News,* March 14, 1936; Veva Elton Kendall, "Writer Finds Tranquility in a Gifted Nun's Studio," *New World,* June 7, 1940; R. A. Lennon, "Nun Commissioned to Paint Cardinal," *Chicago Evening Post,* December 16, 1924; F. E. Blankenship, "Cathedral to Get Nun's Art," *Chicago Daily Journal,* July 11, 1928; Eleanor Jewett, "Nun Portrays Exquisite Face of Christ Child," *CT,* August 19, 1928; Margaret Weilert, "Convent Artist Does Mural for Cathedral," *Chicago Evening Post,* July 17, 1928; Clem Lane, "Catholics Seek Sainthood for Peruvian Negro," *Chicago Tribune,* March 19, 1937. A series of seven articles by Hersur Long in the *New World,* beginning with "Stations of the Cross," January 13, 1928, offer important discussion of the reception and planning of specific paintings by Stanisia. Long's articles include "Nun's Painting Is Known as a Mystic Valentine," February 24, 1928, and "Painting of St. Therese by Nun Called the Story of a 'Rose,'" March 9, 1928. For a history of the School Sisters of Notre Dame, see Dympna Flynn, *Mother Caroline and the School Sisters of Notre Dame in North America* (1928). John Dillenberger's *A Theology of Artistic Sensibilities: The Visual Arts and the Church* (1986) is a valuable study on the changing relationship between art and the church.

ROBERT COZZOLINO

FIG. 111. *Portrait of Eliza Allen Starr, Christian art scholar and poet, painted by George Peter A. Healey, 1861.*

STARR, ELIZA ALLEN

August 29, 1824–September 7, 1901

ART TEACHER, CRITIC OF RELIGIOUS ART, POET

Eliza Allen Starr lived a pious life devoted to exposing others to the beauty and the spiritual meaning of Christian art. She was born in Deerfield, Massachusetts, the daughter of Oliver and Lovina (Allen) Starr, both of whom were descendants of the early white settlers of New England. Her father was a farmer and dyer, a skill that her mother also had. Both parents encouraged their four children, of whom their daughter Eliza Ann was the second born, to appreciate the natural beauty of their Connecticut River Valley home and to record that beauty through poetry, painting, and embroidery.

Eliza Starr attended the local grammar school and studied painting with Caroline Negus, who later in life established herself as a respected painter of miniatures. In 1837, Starr entered Deerfield Academy, where her interests in art were further encouraged. She continued her training in art. In 1845 she moved to Boston to study again with Caroline Negus, who had moved to that city upon her marriage to the historian Richard Hildreth.

The summer of 1845 was a momentous one for Starr. In June 1845, in the company of the Hildreths, she attended a sermon given by Unitarian minister Theodore Parker. Influenced by the transcendentalists as well as by the growing social reform movement of his day, Parker was known for thought-provoking sermons that questioned the place of men and women in the rapidly industrializing society in which they lived. For Starr, though raised a Unitarian, Parker's sermon was a personally shattering moment, which sent her on a religious quest for most of the next decade. She later remembered that "as sentence after sentence came from the lips of the renown [*sic*] preacher, first a tremor, then an actual chill came over me, as with smoothly flowing language, but irresistible logic, I found him demolishing every foundation-stone of my religious faith, and even hope" (quoted in McGovern, 34). A month later, in July 1845, Starr was further shaken by the death of her fifteen-year-old brother, Oliver. Though she soon embarked on a career of teaching art, she continued her religious quest, suffering from poor health all the while.

Seeking a more favorable climate than that of Boston, Starr taught briefly in Brooklyn, New York, before moving to Philadelphia in 1848. There, for the first time, she "came into contact with educated Catholics" (quoted in McGovern, 35), especially her cousin George Allen, a Catholic convert and professor of Latin and Greek at the University of Pennsylvania. Still, Starr remained unsure of just what was to be her "authorized faith" (quoted in McGovern, p. 35). She began writing poetry, and at the same time she continued her teaching career, at one point working as a tutor on a Natchez, Mississippi, plantation from 1851 to 1853. In 1853 she was employed as a drawing teacher in a boarding school in Brooklyn and later taught in Philadelphia. Throughout this period she corresponded with Francis Kenrick, a Catholic bishop from Philadelphia, later archbishop of Baltimore, and a friend of Starr's cousin George Allen. She returned to Boston, moving ever closer to a decision regarding her religious quandary. Finally, on December 23, 1854, Eliza Starr was baptized a Catholic. Her journey to the Catholic faith had not been an easy one. As she later recalled, "after nine years of mental struggle the Roman Catholic Church rose before me as an authorized teacher of divine truth, the depository of Christian traditions" (quoted in McGovern, 36).

Starr continued her correspondence with Archbishop Kenrick, who dissuaded the recent convert from joining a religious order, mainly because of her frail health. Instead, he urged her to continue her teaching and her writing as a way of meeting her religious vocation. In 1856 Starr moved to Chicago, a city perhaps more hospitable to Catholics than Boston, the old Puritan city that in her lifetime was the center of her former faith, Unitarianism. Yet another reason for Starr's permanent relocation to the Midwest was the opportunity to be closer to her brother Caleb—father of ELLEN GATES STARR—who had settled his family on a farm in Durand, Illinois. Eliza Starr would spend much time on her brother's farm and would be an important figure in her young niece's long and impressive life.

In Chicago, Starr soon established herself as a popular and respected teacher of art, her approach based upon the advice of her mentor Caroline Negus Hildreth not to copy but rather to draw from life. In 1863 she finally had a studio of her own, when wealthy friends and well-connected prelates provided her with a home on the Near North Side that she called St. Joseph's Cottage. When her home was destroyed in the Great Fire of 1871, Starr lived for a time at St. Mary's Academy, the women's school attached to the University of Notre Dame. There, working with the Sisters of the Holy Cross, Starr helped organize St. Mary's art department and was first encouraged not just to teach art but to teach about art as well. Her lecture course on the history and spiritual meanings of religious art was given further inspiration when, in 1875, on a trip paid for by her friends, she traveled to Europe. There she gathered materials for future lectures as well as for her two-volume book, *Pilgrims and Shrines* (1885).

While her 1885 publication is generally seen as her most enduring work, it was the 1867 appearance of her first book of poetry that gave her the name by which she remains known. When George Allen collected and edited a volume of Starr's poems, he claimed to forget that her given middle name was Ann and instead published her work under the name Eliza Allen Starr. As that was her mother's family name and the middle name of both her sister and her surviving brother, Starr apparently accepted this name change and used it the rest of her life. Yet another volume of poetry, including those poems published earlier, appeared in 1887 in *Songs of a Lifetime*.

It was, however, as a critic of religious art that Eliza Allen Starr remained most recognized. In 1877, with the help of wealthy friends, her St. Joseph's Cottage rebuilt with a new auditorium on the second floor, Starr returned to Chicago and was soon giving weekly lectures to both Catholic and non-Catholic women, making use of slides and photographs obtained during her European trip. Starr was among the first lecturers in the United States to make substantial use of photographs and slides in presentations. She planned both day and evening classes so that teachers and persons who worked during the day could attend. In 1889, JANE ADDAMS and Starr's niece Ellen Gates Starr opened Hull-House, and it was Aunt Eliza who lectured on Florentine art during the settlement's first year. Later in the 1890s Starr was one of the originators of the Catholic Summer and Winter School movement, bringing her "Art Literature" lecture series to Catholic adult students throughout the Midwest.

Although well-trained in the techniques of art, Starr sought to use her lectures as a way of giving Catholics a better appreciation of their artistic heritage, at the same time providing non-Catholics with a firmer sense of the spiritual meanings of religious art. It was in this same spirit that she sought to play a leading role in the Chicago World's Columbian Exposition of 1893, hoping to ensure a place within the fair for Catholic women by publicizing the importance of Queen Isabella.

The Columbian Exposition was to mark the four hundredth anniversary of Columbus's "discovery" of the New World. In 1889, as plans for the fair got under way, a group of Chicago women including Starr formed the Queen Isabella Association in honor of the devoutly Catholic monarch of Spain who supported Columbus in his attempts to find a western water route to Asia in the 1490s. The association had two main goals. First, they wanted to erect a statue of Isabella that would be on the fairgrounds; and second, they wished to erect a Woman's Pavilion as part of the exposition itself. The president of the association was FRANCES DICKINSON, a Chicago ophthalmologist, cousin of Susan B. Anthony and, like most of the association members, an ardent suffragist. Starr was chosen vice-president and did her part by publishing a book, *Isabella of Castile* (1889), extolling the virtues and the significance of the association's namesake.

Unfortunately, the Isabella Association was almost immediately immersed in controversy, competing for the status of "official" women's fair committee with another group known as the Women's Auxiliary. Despite the efforts of its leaders, and while the statue of Isabella was commissioned and sculpted by Harriet Hosmer, the association lost its bid to be the official women's committee and resorted to erecting its own building a few blocks from the fairgrounds. Although much of the controversy stemmed from personal rivalries between the two groups, some objected to the Isabella Association on the grounds that the Catholic queen had been personally responsible for the Spanish Inquisition as well as the decimation of the Carib Indians encountered by Columbus in his forays into what is now the Caribbean. This was not the Isabella that Starr chose to portray in her *Isabella of Castile* (1889). Rather, Starr emphasized the queen's devout Catholicism, her patriotism in a troubled time, and her bravery in supporting Columbus when few others did. According to Starr, Isabella deserved to be honored because the "sounding line of her womanly instinct, guided by the experiences of an extraordinary reign, had fathomed the sublime resources of Columbus and his motives, and no dastardly maligner could uncrown him for Isabella" (*Isabella of Castile*, 101). Nor could anyone uncrown Isabella in the eyes of Eliza Allen Starr.

The 1893 Exposition gave American Catholics an opportunity to assert their long history of influence on the North American continent. When in 1892 Chicago Catholics began publishing the *New World*, Eliza Allen Starr's byline appeared on the front page with her lead story, "The Fair and Its Meaning: An Assertion of the Claims of Columbus and Isabella to the Esteem of the Nations." The New World had Catholic beginnings.

Starr received a much more cordial reception at the Catholic Congress held in conjunction with the Columbian Exposition in early September 1893. As the only woman to speak before the Catholic Congress, Starr took the occasion to remind her audience of the special contribution of women artists throughout the centuries. She also offered encouragement to contemporary American Catholic women, especially those interested in the arts. "Do not tell me that the atmosphere of your native land is chilling to devotion. Make your own atmosphere; make it by frequenting the sacraments, by living lives of loving devotion to the saints, by a frequent observance of, and attendance upon, all festivals . . . and—glory of glories to a true Christian painter or sculptor—you will live and speak to them from the altar-piece and altar-niche" (*The World's Columbian Catholic Congresses and Educational Exhibit*, vol. 2, 82). In effect, Starr was asking other women Catholics to do no less than she had done for her faith.

Always seeking as wide an audience as possible, Starr published several articles and books during the last decades of the nineteenth century. Here, too, her goals remained the same as in her lecture series—to share with Catholics the glory of their art and to make non-Catholics more aware of the religious significance rather than the aesthetic qualities of Christian art. Having found what she saw as her true home in the Catholic church, Starr devoted her considerable talents as a writer and art critic to sharing her pious appreciation of religious art. For her efforts, she was recognized by Catholics both outside and within the Church hierarchy. In 1885 Starr was the first woman to receive Notre Dame University's Laetare Medal, and in 1893 the aforementioned Catholic Congress at the World's Columbian Exposition presented her with a medal, both awards in recognition of her services to the Church as an interpreter of religious art. Perhaps her most treasured award was the papal medallion she received in 1900 upon the publication of *The Three Archangels and the Guardian Angel in Art* (1899), the last book she published.

By the beginning of the twentieth century, the increasingly frail Eliza Allen Starr spent more and more of her time at her brother Caleb's farm, nursed by her family, including her niece Ellen Gates Starr. Twenty-five years after her aunt's death in 1901, the niece would recall the profound influence Eliza Allen Starr had on her own journey from Unitarianism to Catholicism. "To my aunt's poems and other writings, and of course, chiefly to her prayers, throughout her loving life on earth, and I am sure in paradise, I owe, more than to any other one source, except God's grace, my ultimate, long-delayed conversion" (*Bypath into the Great Roadway*, 6).

Eliza Allen Starr died at her brother's farm just a few days after her seventy-seventh birthday. She was buried in Chicago's Calvary Cemetery, wearing the habit of a Dominican nun. In death, she was remembered as "beautiful in her youth, and she did not lose that charm in age," and as a "Catholic of the Catholics," who spent her life "crucified to her pen" (*Springfield Daily Republican*, September 28, 1901). Such dramatic imagery was fitting for a woman who defied many of the conventions of nineteenth-century Protestant America. Her early conversion to Catholicism occurred at a time when American culture was permeated with anti-Catholic sentiment. As a single woman who lived a life independent of any male relative, Starr's career in art and literature was sustained mainly outside the academy and, as a result of her idiosyncratic path as a Catholic convert, outside the dominant institutions of late nineteenth-century woman's political culture. She was a role model to the first generation of college-trained women, and especially to her niece, Ellen Gates Starr, exhibiting individualism and a connectedness and consciousness of Western culture's long tradition of women intellectuals.

Sources. Eliza Allen Starr's papers are found at the Archives of the Congregation of the Sisters of the Holy Cross, St. Mary's, Notre Dame, Indiana; the Univ. of Notre Dame Archives, Notre Dame, Indiana; and as part of the Ellen Gates Starr papers, Sophia Smith Collection, Smith College, Northampton, Massachusetts. In addition to her published work discussed above, Eliza Allen Starr also published *Patron Saints* (1st series, 1871; 2nd series, 1881), *Christian Art in Our Own Age* (1891), *Three Keys to the Camera Della Segnatura of the Vatican* (1895), and *The Seven Dolors of the Blessed Virgin Mary* (1898). She also published numerous articles in the *Catholic Mirror, Catholic World, Freeman's Journal*, and *London Monthly*. The full text of Starr's Catholic Congress speech can be found in *The World's Columbian Catholic Congresses and Educational Exhibit*, 2 vols. (1893, reprinted 1978). Her article, "The Fair and Its Meaning: An Assertion of the Claim of Columbus and Isabella to the Esteem of the Nations," appeared in the *New World*, October 10, 1892. Regarding Starr's influence on her niece, see Ellen Gates Starr, *A Bypath into the Great Roadway* (1926, reprinted from the *Catholic World*, May–June 1924). Additional biographical information can be found in Annette S. Driscoll, *Literary Convert Women* (1928); James J. McGovern, ed., *The Life and Letters of Eliza Allen Starr* (1905); and *NAW* (1971). Her obituary appeared in the *CT*, September 9, 1901, and a memorial article in the *Springfield Daily Republican*, September 28, 1901.

KATHLEEN BANKS NUTTER

STARR, ELLEN GATES
March 19, 1859–February 10, 1940
SETTLEMENT LEADER, LABOR ACTIVIST, SOCIAL REFORMER

Ellen Gates Starr was born in Laona, Illinois, the second daughter and third of four children of Caleb Allen Starr, farmer and businessman, and Susan Gates (Childs) Starr, homemaker. The Starrs, both of Deerfield, Massachusetts, were married in 1848 and moved to their farm, Spring Park, near Laona, Illinois, in 1855. In 1877 Caleb Starr sold the farm and moved the family to the neighboring town of Durand, Illinois, where he bought a pharmacy and lived out the remainder of his life. Starr's father, through his grange activity, which emphasized democracy and community action, and her aunt ELIZA ALLEN STARR, through her writings on European religious art and her conversion from Unitarianism to Catholicism, influenced Starr's early social, political, and religious development.

In 1877, with the assistance of her aunt Eliza Starr's personal contacts and moral support, Starr enrolled at the Rockford

FIG. 112. *Ellen Gates Starr, cofounder of Hull-House, Christian Socialist, and trade union ally.*

FIG. 113. *Ellen Gates Starr, center, and Cora Stein, far right, with unidentified woman, in Police Court; they were arrested in March 1914 for disturbing the peace during a garment workers' strike in Chicago.*

Female Seminary, Rockford, Illinois. At Rockford, Starr was exposed to the works of Charles Dickens, George Eliot, Thomas Carlyle, and John Ruskin. This literature, especially the works of Ruskin, had a major impact on her developing artistic, social, and political philosophies. Her father could finance only Ellen Starr's first year at Rockford, and in the fall of 1878 she left to become a teacher at a country school in Mount Morris, Illinois. A year later she began teaching at the prestigious Miss Kirkland's School for Girls in Chicago.

While at Rockford, Starr met JANE ADDAMS. Twelve years later the two friends founded Hull-House, the Chicago settlement. Both women experienced periods of restlessness while at college. They continued their friendship after Ellen Starr left school, through a correspondence that detailed their self-doubts about their futures and their concerns about living lives that lacked purpose and direction. Addams had confided to

her friend her periods of deep depression, her doubts about a career, and her early observations of the inequalities in the lives of the rich and the poor. Starr had written Addams her wish that they "do some work together. I believe," Starr wrote, "we should work well" (November 28, 1885, Starr Papers). By 1888 Starr had taught at Miss Kirkland's for almost nine years and had not found her calling in life; Addams was about to travel to Europe for a second time. The two friends traveled together, strengthening their relationship and making more specific their plans to "live among the poor in the hopes that some good might come of it" (Bosch, "The Life of Ellen Gates Starr," 35). Addams recalled that Starr embraced the idea with "vigor and enthusiasm" (*Forty Years at Hull-House*, 87). On her part, Addams visited Toynbee Hall, the pioneering social settlement situated in an East London slum, while Starr went back to Italy to visit places of religious and aesthetic value. "Starr, more than Addams, decided to become a settlement worker as a means of applying her religious beliefs to some positive deed" (Bosch, "The Life of Ellen Gates Starr," 49).

Addams and Starr began their work at Hull-House with a statement of purpose that outlined a general design. The new settlement was to "provide a center for higher civic and social life, to initiate and maintain educational and philanthropic enterprises and to investigate and improve the condition in the industrial districts of Chicago" (Addams, *Forty Years at Hull-House*, 112). Hull-House opened its doors to its immigrant neighbors in September 1889.

The first successful endeavors of Hull-House were Starr's reading parties and art exhibits, which evolved into formal educational programs and the establishment of the Butler Art Gallery, built in 1891. In these programs and in the creation of an environment in which art could be appreciated by the people of the neighborhood, Starr was implementing ideas about art's spiritual and civilizing qualities shared by many reformers of her generation. Starr and Addams, along with the founders of the Arts and Crafts movement in Chicago, believed that the dehumanizing elements of industrialism harmed individuals and jeopardized the collective spirit of a people. For democracy to flourish in industrial America, there had to be a resurgence of ethical behavior, a sense of responsibility among different classes and groups. Art was capable of elevating the goals of a society and, on the individual level, of developing the democratic spirit. From these ideas it naturally flowed that Starr, combining her artistic and educational interests, formed the Chicago Public School Art Society in 1894 for the purpose of placing works of art in classrooms to improve the decor and to educate and inspire the children. At Starr's recommendation, schoolroom walls were painted in cheerful colors to draw the interest of children back into the room itself. Once this change was accomplished, works of art were placed in the rooms and adjacent hallways depicting nature scenes, man-made structures, and portraits of prominent Americans, such as Abraham Lincoln. Starr served as the society's first president until 1897.

Starr connected the arts and crafts to the fight for improved conditions for workers in society. Believing with other reformers that industrialization had alienated workers from their skills and crafts, she promoted the return of dignity to the worker with a revival of crafts. Starr helped form the Chicago Society of Arts and Crafts in spring 1897 and believed that handicrafts should be taught to laborers to give them a renewed sense of purpose and pride in craftsmanship as well as a greater understanding of the industrial process. Handicrafts and the Hull-House Labor Museum thus became integral components of the settlement.

Taking her own lessons to heart, Starr left Chicago in 1897 to learn bookbinding from T. J. Cobden-Sanderson in London. She returned to Chicago in 1898 and opened the Hull-House bookbindery. This endeavor, however, attracted only a few students. Starr realized that training interested persons in traditional crafts was not a solution to the systemic problem of lost craftsmanship in an industrialized society. In the years to come, Starr, to her despair, also realized that her own craft of bookbinding was producing a product that only the rich could afford.

Hull-House provided Starr with a forum from which to launch both her artistic interests and her growing labor concerns. Starr's exposure to the working-class neighborhood surrounding Hull-House and to the philosophies of John Ruskin and William Morris influenced her involvement in Chicago's labor struggles. She moved beyond the arts and crafts approach, however, and became involved with unionism and the weapon of the strike as a way to achieve justice for laborers. Starr astutely summed up the ideal conditions for the laborer or artist as being "perfect freedom from pressure of personal necessity, combined with a wholesome degree of obligation to the service of others, beautiful surroundings, health and joy" ("Art and Labor," *Hull-House Maps and Papers*, 167). To achieve the minimum standards of life, liberty, and the pursuit of happiness, Starr took to the picket lines and joined workers in their struggles for better wages, shorter hours, and safe working conditions. Starr, a quiet, petite, frail woman who was not hesitant to stand firm against injustice, participated in labor strikes from 1896 to 1915. She collected milk funds to feed strikers' children, housed union members, picketed (for which she was often arrested), and wrote articles to promote public support and sympathy for the strikers.

Early on, Hull-House became identified as sympathetic to the unions, as it sponsored meetings for all types of workers. Hull-House served as the meeting place for the shirtmakers, organized in 1891, and the cloakmakers, organized in 1892. Residents like FLORENCE KELLEY were influential in helping pass labor legislation, such as Illinois's first Factory Inspection Act in July 1893, as well as child labor legislation. Starr's first known participation in Chicago's labor movement came with the garment workers' strike of 1896. The clothing cutters and tailors protested against their low wages and poor working conditions. Starr and other Hull-House residents took up collections to help feed the workers and their families.

After 1896 she became more concerned with women workers. Her approach to the problems of industrial evils, the persistence of inequality, and the exploitation of wage laborers (especially women and children) by a capitalist class began to depart from that employed by Addams and other Hull-House residents. Philosophically, Starr turned to identification with the oppressed workers and a change in the ownership of property; she worked for a socialist solution. Addams, concerned with the relationship of the classes to each other in the context of the American capitalist system, promoted the expansion of the role of the state in the amelioration of abusive industrial conditions, the protection of women and children, and the use of political democracy to reconcile differences. The two women also experienced a shift in their personal relationship. There were many reasons why they grew apart. Probably the most important was the friendship that emerged between MARY ROZET SMITH and Addams. Smith's involvement with Hull-House from the 1890s was an immediate and significant competition to Starr's closeness with Addams. Smith soon came to be Addams's most important personal confidant and friend. Addams and Starr also diverged as "living among the poor caused Starr to become more militant in her thoughts and actions and launched her into labor activities and into the Socialist Party in the following decades. Yet, the one change that neither of the two women had expected was the shift in their own relationship. The love and admiration that they shared for each other on the eve of the opening of Hull House [*sic*] vanished by 1900" (Bosch, "The

Life of Ellen Gates Starr," 38). In 1904 Starr helped establish Chicago's branch of the Women's Trade Union League (WTUL). She worked with close associates such as Mary Kenney (see MARY KENNEY O'SULLIVAN). While Starr joined women strikers, Jane Addams often recoiled from personal involvement in strikes. Starr accused Addams of "retreating to her study to write whenever a crisis occurred" (Davis, *Spearheads*, 106). ALICE HAMILTON, physician and longtime Hull-House resident, admitted that she would "picket only in the evening, when she was least likely to be arrested" (Davis, *American Heroine*, 111). Starr's aggressive actions aided the cause of the workers in several strikes between 1910 and 1917. The first was the garment workers' strike of 1910, "when Annie Shapiro, the daughter of a Russian immigrant, and sixteen other women walked out on their jobs at Hart, Schaffner and Marx, Chicago's largest manufacturer of men's clothing" (Bosch, "The Life of Ellen Gates Starr," 93). "Within weeks 10 percent of Chicago's working population had gone on strike in support of the striking women" (p. 94) and the WTUL "was quick to offer support and set up strike committees, which Starr joined" (p. 94). Starr's reports to the strike committee and their publication in local newspapers helped gain public support among the middle classes.

In 1914, risking negative public opinion directed toward Hull-House, Starr supported the striking Henrici Restaurant waitresses, which landed her in jail with a charge of disorderly conduct. "Starr's actions jeopardized contributions to Hull House [*sic*] from Chicago's upper echelon, who feared and resented her growing militancy" (Bosch, "The Life of Ellen Gates Starr," 97). Starr's subsequent trial served as a means by which she exposed the plight of the workers to the public and publicized the experiences of the female strikers both on the picket line and in jail. AGNES NESTOR, then president of the Chicago WTUL, stated, "She is positively fearless. Whenever the cause of justice and the right of free speech and personal liberty is at stake, Miss Starr is always in the foreground of the battle" ("Miss Starr Free," Starr Papers). Starr was acquitted and it was "a hilarious moment in the court-room when the officer who had arrested her declared that 'she had attacked him with violence' and had 'tried to frighten him from the discharge of his duty'" (quoted in Bosch, "The Life of Ellen Gates Starr," 100).

Starr became an honorary member of the Amalgamated Clothing Workers of America after supporting their 1915 strike for improved wages. In conferring this honor on Starr in a private letter, Sidney Hillman, the Amalgamated president, described her as "one of the best little soldiers in the fight" (Hillman to Starr, December 22, 1915, Starr Papers). Starr campaigned against low wages, long hours, and unsafe working conditions, especially for women. Defending the actions of strikers, she declared in her *New Republic* article, "'Cheap Clothes and Nasty,'" that "if one must starve, there are compensations in starving in a fight for freedom that are not to be found in starving for an employer" (pp. 218–19). This was for Starr a difficult strike in which to engage, since the Hillman union had seceded from the American Federation of Labor (AFL)-affiliated United Garment Workers in 1914. The Amalgamated, under the leadership of Hillman and BESSIE ABRAMOWITZ HILLMAN, was more radical and confrontational; neither the WTUL nor the AFL supported the 1915 strike. Starr stood her ground, but

as with other direct actions in which she engaged, she disagreed with many of the Hull-House residents.

Starr's labor activities led to her participation in Chicago's Socialist Party from 1911 to 1928. Explaining why she joined the Socialist Party, Starr wrote in 1916 that "Socialism only, so far as I could find out, offered any effectual method to put down the mighty from their seats and to exalt the humble and meek" ("Why I Became a Socialist," 1916, Starr Papers). In 1916 she ran on the Socialist ticket for alderman of the 19th Ward. Realizing that as a woman and as a Socialist she had little chance of winning, Starr used the opportunity to raise public awareness of society's ills. She explained that she was a Socialist because she was a Christian.

Starr condemned society for its lack of Christian values, believing that it was impossible to carry out the teachings of Christ under the existing capitalist system. She believed that the Christian religion taught that all men were brothers and that none should profit at the expense of others. Starr lost the aldermanic campaign, but did not give up her fight. She began to present lectures to religious groups throughout the Chicago area, emphasizing the need to reform American society and to return to a Christian way of life. Speaking to the Bible Study Department of the Hinsdale Woman's Club, in Hinsdale, Illinois, Starr argued that people had to apply the laws of Christ to the conditions of the times, and "if we cannot, as Christians we must admit that there is something wrong with our age and its conditions, not with His laws; and we must try to find out what, and how to remedy it" ("The Teachings of Christ on Industrial Order, Work, Wages, Hours and the Common Welfare," Starr Papers).

While fighting against the injustices of urban society, Starr simultaneously searched for a religion that would satisfy her intellectually, spiritually, and aesthetically. Starr came from a Unitarian background, but her aunt Eliza Starr, a Catholic convert herself, served as a role model. Starr was exposed to the aesthetic and spiritual appeal of Catholicism from her aunt's art, writings, and speeches on conversion. When Starr first began her religious quest to satisfy her spiritual craving she turned to Jane Addams for advice. Addams, though, was of little comfort, telling Starr that they should no longer discuss religion since they did not hold the same beliefs. Their divergent religious views created a rift in their friendship that would later be compounded by disagreements over the running of Hull-House and Starr's labor activism.

Filling the void left by Addams was Oberlin College mathematics professor Charles Wager, Starr's confidant of forty years. Wager supported Starr's every endeavor, including her religious seeking. In her quest, Starr drifted from Unitarianism to Episcopalianism, bonding with others in religious uncertainty, including Vida Scudder and FRANCES LILLIE. Starr joined the Episcopalian woman's lay order, the Society of the Companions of the Holy Cross (SCHC); Scudder was an influential member of the society. Under the guidance of Father James O. Huntington, Episcopal priest and founder in 1882 of the Order of the Holy Cross, a brotherhood devoted to an incarnational theology and a social gospel practice, Starr sought to reconcile her need for certainty in personal belief and her desire to work for social justice in the world. Huntington, who was also close to Scudder and the SCHC, remained in the Episcopal Church. Starr was drawn to Scudder, Huntington, and other Episcopalians who embraced a social gospel message and called for a reordering of society. What continued to depress Ellen Starr was the failure of the social gospel message to ignite a radical transformation inside the church. When Starr returned from the SCHC summer conference in 1909, she felt the gap between the words that were spoken at the highest levels of ecclesiastical institutions and the conditions of the poor. Attending services with other Episcopalians became increasingly difficult as she felt surrounded by privilege and pretension. She had written earlier, "The Ancient Egyptian priests had one religion for themselves and another for the people, and how like them we often are" ("Chicago's Hull-House," Report on the Address by Ellen Starr, 1895). Starr began to attend Catholic parish churches in the Hull-House neighborhood as her identification with the poor intensified. Now she decided to look closely at what Roman Catholicism might offer her. Even though the leadership of the Roman Catholic Church did not always advocate social reforms that Starr had accepted and supported, she believed that Catholicism with its rituals and masses would provide her with the structure and aestheticism her soul was seeking. Ultimately Starr concluded that she had been a "Catholic at heart" (Starr to Wager, March 3, 1920, Starr Papers) for quite a time. While her conversion aroused mixed reactions from friends, family, and coworkers, Starr had finally attained inner peace and harmony about her faith.

Starr's later years were ones of decreasing public involvement and increasing physical infirmities. In 1929, she was operated on for a spinal abscess. The operation left her paralyzed. With Hull-House residents unable to care for her, Starr moved into the Convent of the Holy Child in Suffern, New York. Here she spent her final years browsing through old letters, reading, painting, and corresponding with friends and family. She was able to rethink her relationship with Jane Addams before Addams's death; Addams, too, had begun the process of repairing the damage to their friendship. Ellen Starr died at age eighty.

Ellen Gates Starr contributed her talent and vision to the experiment of Hull-House. She translated her ideals of social justice and the importance of aesthetics in the lives of the lowly as well as the privileged into the programs and organizations of Chicago's Arts and Crafts and labor movements. Her commitment to take direct action against social injustice came out of her acceptance of the truth of Christianity's gospel message. "Though her outward appearance was one of assurance and confidence, her inward being was filled with religious turmoil. These two sides of Starr played against each other, culminating in her extreme drive to cure social ills while simultaneously fulfilling her Christian ideals" (Bosch, "The Life of Ellen Gates Starr," 4).

Sources. Ellen Gates Starr Papers are in the Sophia Smith Collection, Smith College, Northampton, Massachusetts, and include extensive notes by her niece Josephine Starr. Additional information regarding Starr can be found in the Jane Addams Papers, Swarthmore College Peace Collection, Swarthmore College, and the Charles Henry Adams Wager Papers, Spec. Coll., Oberlin College Library, Oberlin, Ohio, as well as in the American Federation of Labor Records: The Samuel Gompers Era, the Anita McCormick Blaine Papers, and the Henry Demarest Lloyd Papers, all of which are at the State Hist. Soc. of Wiscon-

sin, Madison. See "Chicago's Hull-House," Report on the Address by Ellen Starr, 1895, Hull-House Scrapbook, 3, Jane Addams Memorial Collection, UIC Spec. Coll. The Crane-Lillie Family Papers, CHS, contain correspondence between Lillie and Ellen Starr on topics of religion, conversion to Catholicism, Socialism, and labor in Chicago. The most noteworthy articles written by Starr include "Hull House Bookbindery," *Commons,* June 1900; "The Renaissance of Handicraft," *International Socialist Review,* February 1902; "Efforts to Standardize Chicago Restaurants—The Henrici Strike," *Survey,* May 1914; "'Cheap Clothes and Nasty,'" *New Republic,* January 1916; "The Chicago Clothing Strike," *New Review,* March 1916; "A Bypath into the Great Roadway," *Catholic World,* May and June 1924; "A Few Trials of a Happy Convert," the *Abbey Chronicle,* March 1929. Other pertinent sources are Jane Addams, *Twenty Years at Hull-House* (1910); Addams, *Forty Years at Hull-House: Being "Twenty Years at Hull-House" and "The Second Twenty Years at Hull-House"* (1935); Addams, "Art Work Done by Hull House," *Forum,* July 1895; Residents of Hull-House, *Hull House Maps and Papers* (1895); Vida Dutton Scudder, *On Journey* (1937). Notable secondary works are Allen F. Davis, *Spearheads for Reform: The Social Settlements and the Progressive Movement* (1967); Allen F. Davis, *American Heroine: The Life and Legend of Jane Addams* (1973); and Eileen Boris, *Art and Labor: Ruskin, Morris, and the Craftsman Ideal in America* (1986). Studies of interest include Jennifer Lynne Bosch, "The Life of Ellen Gates Starr, 1859–1940" (Ph.D. diss., Miami Univ. of Ohio, 1990); Elizabeth Palmer Carrell, "Reflections in a Mirror: The Progressive Woman and the Settlement Experience" (Ph.D. diss., Univ. of Texas at Austin, 1981); Polly H. Ullrich, "Women in the Arts and Crafts Movement of Chicago:1877–1915" (master's thesis, School of the Art Institute of Chicago, 1994). Jennifer L. Bosch's essay, "Ellen Gates Starr," from which this profile in part is drawn, is in *American National Biography,* edited by John A. Garraty and Mark C. Carnes, copyright 1999 by the American Council of Learned Societies; reprinted by permission of Oxford University Press, Inc. See also Jennifer L. Bosch, "Ellen Gates Starr; Hull House Labor Activist," in *Culture, Gender, Race and U.S. Labor History,* ed. Ronald C. Kent (1993). A recent book focuses on religion and the Hull-House women: Eleanor J. Stebner, *The Women of Hull House: A Study of Spirituality, Vocation, and Friendship* (1997). Obituaries appear in *NYT* and *CT,* February 11, 1940.

JENNIFER L. BOSCH

STEVENS, ALZINA ANN PARSONS
May 27, 1849–June 3, 1900
PRINTER, LABOR REFORMER, JOURNALIST, SETTLEMENT WORKER

Alzina Parsons Stevens won historical recognition for her association with Hull-House, where she helped to establish the Juvenile Court of Cook County and served as its first probation officer. Unlike the settlement's other early residents, Stevens came to that stage of her life with a remarkable history as a working-class activist. Out of her own experience in the workforce, she became a pioneer of organizing women into the labor movement, and to Hull-House she brought a long tradition of labor reform in Chicago and the nation.

Born in Parsonsfield, Maine, the youngest child of Enoch Parsons, a farmer and carpenter, and Louisa (Page) Parsons, Alzina Parsons attended high school in the mill town of Somersworth, New Hampshire, where her father moved the family when he gave up farming sometime before 1860. Her lifetime of self-supporting work began with a job in a textile mill after her father's death in 1864. Describing that work later in life for *John Swinton's Paper* (October 31, 1886), she called it a "grind" that threatened "to stunt [her] brain and narrow [her] life," but in New England other occupations open to women "were overcrowded and underpaid."

Chicago held the promise of more varied employment. About 1871, Alzina Parsons left New England for Chicago, in the company of a sister and brother-in-law, to learn a trade. After a year of knocking on doors, she was hired to learn the printer's craft in a small, nonunion book and job firm. She first came to public attention as president of Working Women's Union No. 1 at its founding in 1878. How she acquired her political education and leadership skills remains a mystery, though opportunities existed in both New England and Chicago. She had also married a Mr. Stevens in 1876 or 1877, and another mystery surrounds his identity and the fate of this marriage.

The goal of the Working Women's Union (WWU), the brainchild of the Chicago Council of Trades and Labor Unions and the Socialist Labor Party, was to organize "the unorganized masses" of women into affiliation with trade unions. Alzina Parsons Stevens obtained financial help from the powerful Chicago Typographical Union for this purpose. During a bitter printers' strike in the summer of 1879, the WWU probably influenced women who quit their jobs as bookbinders rather than cross the men's picket lines. The union's floats and banners became a notable feature of the city's labor parades. A proving ground for many of Chicago's most important women in the labor movement, WWU leaders also included ELIZABETH RODGERS, ELIZABETH MORGAN, and LIZZIE HOLMES.

In speeches to the union, Alzina Stevens presented a well-developed argument about woman's right to work and used it to counter tendencies in the labor movement that would reduce competition for jobs by driving women from the labor force. She insisted that the days of female dependency were done, that women were obliged to support themselves, and that their right to work equaled men's. Moreover, she asserted, the strength of the working class would be measured by men's acceptance of these new circumstances and their solidarity with women. Stevens herself obtained membership in the Chicago Typographical Union in 1879 when the union offered an amnesty program for nonunion printers, many of them women like Stevens who had found work only in nonunion shops.

Stevens moved to Toledo, Ohio, apparently without her husband, by April 1881, when she presented the traveling card of a journeyman printer to the city's typographical union. In the scanty records of her life that remain, she never explained this move. In Toledo, Stevens followed a career path familiar to male printers: she became a journalist. She worked first for H. H. Hardesty, publisher of local histories and atlases, where, in addition to proofreading and copyediting, she wrote a *Military History of Ohio*. She began to write for the labor press, notably for *John Swinton's Paper*, and her typographical union membership changed to an honorary one by 1888. In 1890, she was writing for the Democratic daily, the *Toledo Bee*.

Through this transition, Stevens remained active in the labor movement. She joined the Noble Order of the Knights of Labor, through a trade assembly for printers, in 1883, soon after the Knights permitted women to join; seven years later she headed the district assembly of the Knights in northwestern

Ohio. From a patchy record, certain themes of her work in this decade emerge. Her male colleagues trusted her judgment. She served, for example, on a committee to foster cooperation between Toledo's Knights and its Federation of Labor, and she lobbied at the state capital for labor legislation.

Her power also reflected her leadership among wage-earning women whose interest in the Knights climbed despite an exodus of men into craft unions. Stevens led the Joan of Arc Assembly, one of Toledo's two assemblies for women, and organized women in surrounding towns. Knights Master Workman Terence Powderly deemed her an authority on women's working conditions, and in 1890 the national assembly offered her the position, vacated by Leonora Barry, of General Investigator of Women's Work, which Stevens declined.

She also began to explore possible alliances between wage-earning women and the organized women's movement. It was she who introduced delegates from the Woman's Christian Temperance Union to the national meetings of the Knights of Labor, and she attended at least one annual meeting of the Ohio Woman Suffrage Association to make a pitch for the needs of working women.

Stevens also emerged as a strong advocate of political action by labor to offset the power of economic concentration. Writing in support of Henry George's candidacy for mayor of New York City in 1886, she opined that for the first time she regretted her disfranchisement. Here was an opportunity to vote "class against class," she wrote in *John Swinton's Paper* (October 31, 1886). Over the next few years, she modified her stance to favor alliances rather than confrontation between the working class and trust-busting reformers. Stevens pressed the Knights of Labor to join discussions leading to formation of the People's Party; and after the party's founding convention at St. Louis in 1892, she accepted an offer to coedit a weekly Populist newspaper, the *Vanguard*, published in Chicago.

Stevens returned to Chicago with an additional assignment from Terence Powderly: to represent the Knights of Labor on the Women's Labor Committee of the World's Congress Auxiliary, the body charged with planning labor meetings at the World's Columbian Exposition. Through this committee she met women in the city's new alliance of socialists, clubwomen, and settlement house workers; she joined forces with JANE ADDAMS and JULIA LATHROP of Hull-House, CORINNE BROWN of the Illinois Woman's Alliance, and Julia Dow Harvey of the Chicago Woman's Club. Her standing among them was soon evident when the head of the Congress Auxiliary rejected the committee's proposed program in favor of one deemed by the Women's Labor Committee too neutral to interest the laboring classes; Stevens led the committee to resign in protest. Although Stevens took part in the Exposition's Congress of Representative Women, at a meeting on women's trade unions with Corinne Brown, FLORENCE KELLEY, and Susan B. Anthony, she remained skeptical about the Exposition's "false atmosphere, in which we are trying to keep truths carefully covered out of sight and sound," as she wrote in the *Vanguard* (May 27, 1893).

The *Vanguard* completed its partisan mission to promote Populist candidates in the 1892 election and became, instead, a local paper promoting reforms. Stevens had returned to

Chicago during a campaign against the city's sweatshops, instigated by her old ally Elizabeth Morgan. Until her newspaper fell victim to a bank's failure and collapsed, Stevens covered the campaign and helped to coordinate lobbying in Springfield for passage of the Factory and Workshop Inspection Act in 1893. Under the terms of the new law, Governor John P. Altgeld appointed Stevens to be assistant factory inspector under Florence Kelley. She served until 1897. From their office at Hull-House, the inspectors monitored sanitary conditions in sweatshops, enforced the law's provisions limiting child labor and the hours of women's labor, and lobbied for additional legislation to protect children.

Proximity to Hull-House brought her into its programs, though she continued for some time to live with her sister's family. Hull-House provided her with full-time work for her last years. The list of her duties is varied and suggests her willingness to pitch in where help was needed, but she continued to experiment with ways to resist the exploitation of wage-earning women and children. She built unions in women's trades and led them to confront the citywide labor movement for recognition. She headed the Dorcas Federal Labor Union and worked with the Council of Women's Trade Unions of Chicago, both based at the settlement. She also presided over the Hull-House Women's Club. She is best known, however, for pursuing legal protection for children through better compulsory education laws and creation of the Juvenile Court of Cook County and for improvising a model for the work of juvenile probation officers. She became the court's first probation officer in 1899.

On August 16, 1888, the *Journal of United Labor* of the Knights of Labor described Stevens's life as "an epitome of the labor movement in this country during the last 20 years." Five years later *Woman of the Century* revised the thought: "an epitome of woman's work in the labor movement" (p. 684) in the same years. Always self-supporting, Stevens defied the odds against women's occupational mobility in her generation as she moved from unskilled factory labor to a skilled craft, then from craft to profession, and from the labor movement into full-time reform work. Through the eighties, she was optimistic that her experience might prevail and transform not only women's work but also the working class. Most of what can be learned about her life comes from autobiographical journalism addressed to working women, urging them to acquire skills, work in organized trades, and limit the power of their bosses. She expected working-class men, in turn, to recognize their need for "a companion in arms" rather than "a sick nurse, or a fireside companion." "The labor question can never be settled, *never*, without [women's] intelligent and hearty co-operation," she wrote in *John Swinton's Paper* on February 21, 1886.

Working conditions worsened, however; the segregation of men's and women's work increased, and craft unions failed to match the promise of the Knights of Labor as vehicles for women's economic power. Discouraged, but without abandoning hope for working-class solidarity, Stevens allied herself with middle-class reformers to gain protective legislation, and women were the vanguard of those reformers.

Stevens died of diabetes at Hull-House at fifty-one years of age. Her cremated remains were buried at Graceland Cemetery.

Sources. The only substantial body of Alzina Parsons Stevens correspondence survives in the Terence V. Powderly Papers, Catholic Univ. of America. A few of her letters are in the Henry Demarest Lloyd Papers, State Hist. Soc. of Wisconsin. Stevens began to write for *John Swinton's Paper* in 1885. Her *Military History of Ohio* appeared as a chapter of publisher H. H. Hardesty's local histories by 1884, before its publication as a book in 1887. A nearly complete run of the *Vanguard* is in the State Hist. Soc. of Wisconsin. In addition to annual reports on their factory inspections, Stevens and Florence Kelley coauthored the essay on wage-earning children in Residents of Hull-House, *Hull-House Maps and Papers* (1895); her investigations informed "The Tenement House Curse: Some Chicago Tenement Houses," *Arena*, April 1894, and "Child Slavery in America: The Child, the Factory and the State," *Arena*, June 1894. She also wrote "Life in a Social Settlement—Hull-House, Chicago," *Self-Culture*, March 1899. Two biographical sketches appeared in her lifetime, in the newspaper, *Journal of United Labor*, August 16, 1888, and in Frances E. Willard and Mary A. Livermore, eds., *A Woman of the Century* (1893). An entry appears in *NAW* (1971). Ann D. Gordon's essay, "Alzina Ann Parsons Stevens," from which this profile in part is drawn, is in *American National Biography*, edited by John A. Garraty and Mark C. Carnes, copyright 1999 by the American Council of Learned Societies. Reprinted by permission of Oxford University Press, Inc. For her family's history, see Henry Parsons, *Parsons Family. Descendants of Cornet Joseph Parsons* (1920), though Alzina and her siblings are not traced in this work. Meetings of the Working Women's Union were covered by the *Socialist* (Chicago) and the *CT*. Also useful are manuscript records of the Chicago Typographical Union, CHS. Important recollections are found in Lizzie Swank Holmes, "Women Workers of Chicago," *American Federationist*, August 1905, and "The Days of Our Infancy: A Reminiscence," *Progressive Woman*, August 1911. Cautious use can be made of "Work of the Sex," *Chicago Times*, September 2, 1894, purporting to be written from interviews with Stevens and other activists. Brief but insightful comments on her life are in Florence Kelley, "Industrial Democracy: Women in the Trade Unions," *Outlook*, December 15, 1906. Useful references to her early activism in the city are found in Carolyn Ashbaugh, *Lucy Parsons* (1976), and Mari Jo Buhle, *Women and American Socialism* (1981). Stevens crosses the pages of most major works on Chicago reformers in the late nineteenth century, notably Ray Ginger, *Altgeld's America* (1958); Dorothy R. Blumberg, *Florence Kelley* (1966); Meredith Tax, *The Rising of the Women* (1980); and Kathryn Kish Sklar, *Florence Kelley and the Nation's Work* (1995). Obituaries appeared in the *CT*, *Toledo Bee*, and *NYT*, all on June 4, 1900.

ANN D. GORDON

STEVENSON, SARAH HACKETT

February 2, 1841–August 14, 1909
PHYSICIAN, SOCIAL ACTIVIST

Born in Buffalo Grove (now Polo), in Ogle County, Illinois, Sarah Hackett Stevenson was one of seven children and the younger of two daughters. Her mother, Sarah T. Hackett, daughter of Captain Simon Hackett, was born into a prominent Philadelphia family. Her father, John D. Stevenson, was the eldest son of Ann (Davis) and Charles Stevenson, one of the earliest settlers of Ogle County. Charles Stevenson emigrated from County Donegal, Ireland, in 1798 and bought land in Ogle County. John Stevenson opened a store in his log cabin and later began farming and set up a sawmill business.

Sarah Hackett Stevenson attended Mount Carroll Seminary in Illinois and State Normal College in Bloomington, Illinois. She graduated as a teacher in 1863 and taught for four years in public schools in Bloomington, Mount Morris, and Sterling, where she was the principal. She then pursued an interest in scientific writing by studying anatomy and physiology at the Woman's Hospital Medical College in Chicago and the South Kensington Science School in London. While in England, Stevenson stayed with the philanthropist Emily Faithfull, who later visited her in Chicago.

After Stevenson's return to Illinois, she prepared to reenter the Woman's Hospital Medical College to complete medical education. Unfortunately, her timing was inauspicious. Stevenson received a telegram just as she was leaving home, in 1871, with the news that Chicago was in ashes. She collected necessities from neighbors and her own home and shipped a carload the next day to victims of the fire. The Woman's Hospital Medical College had burned to the ground. A new hospital and college were speedily opened, although the college was housed in a barn. Stevenson graduated with highest honors in 1874.

Stevenson traveled to Europe again for postgraduate study before starting practice. She visited several hospitals in London and Dublin and studied under scientists Thomas Huxley and Charles Darwin. Stevenson's first book, *Boys and Girls in Biology*, a high school textbook based on Huxley's lectures, was published in 1875. While Stevenson was in Europe, Illinois Governor John Beveridge appointed her a delegate to the First Sanitary Conference in Vienna. Sanitarians sought to identify and eliminate environmental conditions that caused health problems.

Returning to Chicago in 1875, Stevenson started her medical career. She served from 1875 to 1880 as physiology chair at the Woman's Hospital Medical College (in 1879 renamed the Woman's Medical College) and was elected to membership in the Illinois State Medical Society. Also in 1875, Stevenson was appointed head of the society's committee on progress in physiology. In 1876, she was made an alternate delegate to the American Medical Association's (AMA) convention in Philadelphia. The delegate was unable to attend and Stevenson took his place, thus becoming the first woman member. Just five years earlier, a motion to admit women had been tabled after rancorous debate. Stevenson continued to be active within the AMA. She served as delegate for three more conventions, in 1878 chaired an AMA special committee for advancing physical sciences, and gave a paper the following year on the sympathetic nervous system. Although Stevenson was accepted, the AMA did not formally admit women until 1915.

The next few years were busy ones. In 1877, Stevenson was elected to membership in the prestigious Fortnightly, a women's social and literary club. In the summer of 1880, a small group of socially prominent, civic-minded women, including Stevenson, planned a training school for nurses. When the resultant Illinois Training School opened in 1881, Stevenson was on the board of directors, chair of the hospital committee, and a member of the faculty. That year she joined the Woman's Christian Temperance Union (WCTU) and was appointed the first superintendent of the WCTU's department of hygiene, responsible for publicizing the deleterious effects of alcohol. When the Frances E. Willard National Temperance Hospital was opened in Chicago in 1886, Stevenson became president of the medical staff.

Through the 1880s and 1890s, the scope of Stevenson's activities and responsibilities widened. She developed a busy private practice. Emily Faithfull described Stevenson as "a leading physician in Chicago, with a large and increasing practice, often called upon to drive out into the country in the middle of the night through the frost and snow" (*Three Visits to America*, p. 112). In 1881, Stevenson became the first woman appointed to the staff of Cook County Hospital. She was an attending physician at the Chicago Hospital for Women and Children (renamed the Mary Thompson Hospital in 1895; see MARY HARRIS THOMPSON). She was a consultant to Bellevue Hospital in Batavia, Illinois, and Provident Hospital, in Chicago, established to provide medical training and services to African Americans. From 1880 to 1894, Stevenson served as professor of obstetrics at the Woman's Medical College. In 1894, two years after the Woman's Medical College became the Northwestern University Woman's Medical School, she became an associate professor of obstetrics, medical ethics, and the history of medicine at Northwestern.

She helped to found the Home for Incurables and the Chicago Maternity Hospital and was a director of the Children's Aid Society. Involved in professional organizations, Stevenson was a member of the Chicago Medical and the Chicago Medical-Surgical societies, was admitted in Brussels to the International Society of Obstetricians and Gynecologists, and served as vice-president in a Pan-American Medical Congress in Washington, D.C.

The issue of free public baths claimed Stevenson's energies, and she worked for their establishment. As a member of the Municipal Order League of Chicago, she complained in 1892 that Chicago had 22,400 square miles of water at its shores and no public baths except for public lavatories in saloons. Through her efforts, Chicago established free baths on the lakeshore. In 1893, Governor John P. Altgeld appointed Stevenson to the Illinois State Board of Health as the first woman member.

During the 1880s and 1890s, Stevenson continued to write. Her textbook on biology for school use was selling well. In 1881 she published *The Physiology of Women*, which was republished in two later editions. In this book she expressed a concern for women's rights, writing, "If a woman has an inalienable right in this world" it is the right to become a mother "in accordance with her own desires" (quoted in Morantz-Sanchez, 220). Stevenson's scholarly articles in medical journals included an important paper in the *Chicago Medical Recorder* in 1894, "A Study of the Placenta Previa; Especially the Causes of Hemorrhage," which showed her knowledge of American and European medical literature. In 1899, Stevenson undertook to be a staff correspondent for the *Chicago Record* newspaper. She cabled daily reports about the meeting of the International Council of Women, held that year in London.

As a clubwoman and a physician, Stevenson was actively involved in Chicago's World's Columbian Exposition of 1893. Stevenson was cochair, along with JULIA HOLMES SMITH, of the Medical and Surgery Congress and vice-president of the World's Congress of Medico-Climatology at the exposition. Stevenson also presented a paper, "Chicago Women," in which she discussed the work women did as domestic servants, factory workers, teachers, and homemakers. When Stevenson realized that no women physicians would be working at the exposition, in spite of an earlier promise by exposition authorities to place women doctors on staff, she and three other women approached the Illinois Woman's Exposition Board. They were given six thousand dollars to build and maintain a working model hospital to showcase the work of women pharmacists, physicians, and nurses. Stevenson served as chief of staff, and they treated more than three thousand patients. Stevenson was then president of the Chicago Women's Club (later Chicago Woman's Club), an influential group of activists in social reform and a sponsor of the work of women physicians and nurses at the exposition. She also was a member of the Queen Isabella Association, formed to increase women's visibility at the exposition by displaying their achievements with those of men. Many members of the association, including Stevenson, were supporters of woman suffrage.

Stevenson responded to the distress caused by the depression of 1893. In December 1893, the Chicago Women's Club formed an emergency association that Stevenson chaired. Enough money was raised to finance a system of paid work for women in need. That same year, at Stevenson's behest, the club established a lodging house near Hull-House for poor women and their children, where Stevenson herself lived for a time. In 1914, the house was named after Stevenson. She was also a member of the Chicago Civic Federation, formed to help those impoverished by the depression.

Stevenson's concern with the welfare and rights of women was evident during her presidency of the Chicago Women's Club. In 1893 she asked the influential BERTHA HONORÉ PALMER to appeal to Chicago's mayor regarding the placement of women on the Board of Education and gave her names of suitable candidates. Hearing nothing, Stevenson wrote again three weeks later. In that letter she also asked if Palmer knew whether a male physician intended to appoint a woman to his staff, explaining that women demanded to be treated by women physicians. The Chicago Women's Club established a committee to secure appointments of women physicians in institutions that cared for women and children.

In late 1894, "a negro woman, educated, cultivated, and refined" (*Chicago Tribune*, May 12, 1901), was proposed for membership in the Chicago Women's Club. A storm of protest arose from the women until Stevenson gave an impassioned speech in favor of her admission. The motion was tabled and Stevenson was away when the matter was next discussed, but she sent a telegram: "Justice is eternal, expediency is temporal. Be just and fear not" (Frank and Jerome, 145). The club accepted the proposed member, resolving that no woman could be excluded from membership because of race.

Stevenson was tall and striking in appearance. As a young woman she was reported to be quite attractive. A quarter of a century later, her face was described as strong, with clear-cut features set off and softened by almost snow-white hair. As she reached her early sixties, Stevenson slowed her pace, and by 1901, her medical work consisted mainly of consultations. In 1903, Stevenson became the first president of the newly formed Chicago Medical Women's Club. That same year, she suffered a stroke and retired from all professional work. At a reception for fifteen hundred people given in her honor three years later, Stevenson announced her complete retirement from active life. Her favorite nephew, Charles H. Stevenson, had suddenly died a short while before, and she was very distressed. A nominal Methodist for most of her life, after her nephew's death, Stevenson became a Catholic and in 1906 moved into St. Elizabeth's Hospital, where she resided until her death. She gave much of her money and property to the Sisters of Mercy at the hospital in return for her care. She was buried at St. Boniface Cemetery, Chicago.

Stevenson was acknowledged by her contemporaries as a leader in gaining recognition for the needs and abilities of women. Eight years before her death, the *Chicago Tribune* wrote: "She has done much to make the way easier for women who have had less of force, ability and tact than has she" (May 12, 1901). Fellow doctors called her an outstanding physician and one who improved the medical care of women. Her contributions as a physician supported the argument for women's admission to the profession, while her activism resulted in new social welfare programs for women and children.

Sources. Stevenson's paper at the World's Columbian Exposition, "Chicago Women," is published in Mary Kavanaugh Oldham Eagle, ed., *The Congress of Women Held in the Woman's Building, World's Columbian Exposition, Chicago, U.S.A., 1893* (1895). Documents concerning Stevenson are found among the records of the Chicago Woman's Club and the World's Columbian Exposition, located in the CHS. Information on Stevenson's family is found in *Portrait and Biographical Album of Ogle County, Illinois* (1886). Three articles describing Stevenson, including a detailed obituary, are in the CT: November 11, 1894; May 12, 1901; and August 15, 1909. Books containing information about her include Emily Faithfull, *Three Visits to America* (1884); F. M. Sperry, *Distinguished Physicians and Surgeons of Chicago* (1904); Henriette G. Frank and Amalie H. Jerome, *Annals of the Chicago Woman's Club, 1876–1916* (1916); *History of Medicine and Surgery and Physicians and Surgeons of Chicago* (1922); and Jeanne M. Weiman, *The Fair Women* (1981). William K. Beatty wrote a detailed although unreferenced biographical article, "Sarah Hackett Stevenson — Concerned Practitioner and Social Activist," *Proceedings of the Institute of Medicine of Chicago*, July 1982. NAW (1971) contains a biographical entry on Stevenson. A statement on Stevenson's conversion to Catholicism appears in Josephine Byrne Sullivan's "A Brilliant Coterie of Women," *New World*, September 11, 1909. For background information on women physicians in the late nineteenth century, see Regina Markell Morantz-Sanchez, *Sympathy and Science: Women Physicians in American Medicine* (1985).

BRIGID LUSK

STEWART, ELLA JANE SEASS
February 22, 1871–January 31, 1945
SUFFRAGE LEADER, TEMPERANCE REFORMER, BANKER, CLUBWOMAN

Ella Seass Stewart was a leader in the woman suffrage movement in Illinois, serving for many years as president of the Illinois Equal Suffrage Association (IESA) and working throughout her lifetime for the advancement of women's rights. Born Elvira Jane Seass in Arthur, Illinois, she was the second daughter in a family of six born to F. Levi and Elizabeth (Powell) Seass. Her father, a successful farmer who owned 536 acres in Moultrie County and was also a businessman and local politician, was largely a self-taught man who made sure his children acquired an excellent education. Elizabeth Seass was known as a woman of taste and intelligence.

While little is known of Seass's early life on the farm, she attended high school in Decatur, Illinois, and at age sixteen en-

FIG. 114. *From left to right, suffragists Mrs. Fred Lorenz, Ella Seass Stewart, and Bertha Seass, about to depart for Washington, D.C., rally.*

tered Eureka College, Eureka, Illinois. Early on she showed an interest in women's issues, choosing "Woman's Sphere" as the topic for her senior address. She completed an A.B. degree in 1890 and married a classmate, Oliver Wayne Stewart, several months later on August 20. She continued with her education, completing another A.B. at the University of Michigan in 1892 and, the following year, an A.M. degree at Eureka. Both Stewarts remained loyal to Eureka College, and Ella Stewart served as their first female trustee, a position she held for many years.

Her marriage to Oliver Stewart proved to be a lasting one and mutually beneficial. He served for a time as a minister of the Disciples of Christ church, of which Ella Stewart was a member, but most of his life's work revolved around the temperance issue. He held numerous leadership positions in a variety of prohibition organizations. Oliver Stewart also believed in rights for women. Early in their marriage, Stewart accompanied her husband on one of his many lecture tours, and she was often asked to speak on women's rights. It was at this time that she honed the oratorical skills for which she would become widely known.

While Stewart supported temperance, her primary interest was women's rights, including the right to vote. Upon hearing Susan B. Anthony speak at the University of Michigan in early 1894, Stewart decided to dedicate her life to the cause of woman suffrage. The Stewarts had no children and devoted themselves

fully to their respective reform interests. They moved to Chicago in 1900, making travel easier and gaining access to people, organizations, and resources not available in rural Illinois.

Like many other women in nineteenth-century America, Stewart's initial organizational involvement came through the Woman's Christian Temperance Union (WCTU). By the time she was twenty-three, she was already a district president of the Illinois WCTU and, from 1898 to 1908, she was both a director of the National WCTU franchise department and a leading lecturer and publicist for them. She also served as a vice-president of the Illinois WCTU but declined the presidency in order to focus more fully on woman suffrage.

To this end Stewart joined the IESA and soon gained positions of leadership, serving as the organization's vice-president from 1902 to 1905 and as president from 1906 to 1911. She was one of the youngest state presidents in the country. These were crucial years for the suffrage movement in Illinois, and Stewart helped build the IESA into a strong and respected organization. She worked closely with her friend and ally, CATHARINE Mc-CULLOCH, who served as the organization's strategist, legal adviser, and legislative superintendent. Stewart's talents were in the field of organizational and financial development. She had a knack for putting the right person in the right job and spent much of her time during these years organizing new suffrage groups across the state. Financially she put the IESA on firm footing, both with the subscription booklets she developed that allowed for more systematic giving and with her personal fundraising efforts and impassioned speeches that brought in a great deal of money. She established a permanent office in Chicago with this additional funding, enabling the organization to run more efficiently. Stewart also initiated a series of pamphlets on woman suffrage topics, written by various experts, which were printed and sold at cost to numerous school and suffrage organizations both in Illinois and across the country.

Although there were no major suffrage victories during her tenure in office, she did much to publicize the need for votes for women. The chartered suffrage trains that took women to their state conventions, and later the automobile tours, which Stewart, Catharine Waugh McCulloch, and GRACE WILBUR TROUT used so effectively, helped spread the message both to rural women and to state legislators. While president, Stewart started a suffrage oratory contest for college students. She was so impressed with one of the contestants, Harriet Grimm, that she raised funds to pay Grimm to be a professional organizer for the IESA and thus brought a talented young woman into the suffrage fold.

Efforts by Chicago reformers to revise the municipal charter offered suffrage advocates an opportunity to include municipal suffrage for women as part of the new document. IESA leaders were interested in influencing the charter reform process, although as women they could not do so directly as delegates to the charter convention. In 1906, male delegates to the Chicago charter convention completed writing a municipal charter that attempted to express the progressive reform agenda of the era, combining both social and structural changes for city government. By Christmas 1906 the delegates still had to consider several controversial issues, including whether or not the proposed new charter should grant municipal suffrage to women. Since women did not have representation among the delegates, the IESA asked Raymond Robins to lead the fight for suffrage inclusion. When it became clear that the delegates refused to place municipal suffrage for women in the new charter, an attempt was made to ask the convention instead to submit to the state legislature, along with the charter, a separate bill for female municipal suffrage in Chicago. Woman suffrage advocates hoped the delegates would agree to send along the separate suffrage bill, which also had to be passed by the legislature and then ratified by the Chicago voters. IESA and other suffrage groups strategized that when the voters ratified the new charter, they would also vote for municipal suffrage for women.

Stewart and Catharine McCulloch had developed strategies to force the issue of municipal suffrage for women into the political arena of the state legislature where any proposed new charter had to be approved before it was sent back to Chicago voters for ratification. Stewart and McCulloch sent a questionnaire to all candidates for public office, asking their opinion on woman suffrage and then publishing the answers in a booklet that they distributed to newspapers and women's groups across the state. Unfortunately, the charter convention delegates refused to send a separate municipal suffrage bill to the legislature. In addition, state legislators made further changes in the proposed charter, substantially weakening its already compromised

reform thrust. When it appeared on the ballot for Chicago voters' ratification, women suffragists and men and women social reformers worked to defeat it.

Stewart and McCulloch believed that some good had been accomplished in their unsuccessful campaign to have municipal suffrage for women included. They found that politicians who were now "on the record" as favoring woman suffrage stood by their word when it came to a vote later on. Even though the municipal charter did not pass, the work of the IESA converted more people to the woman suffrage cause and provided additional women with lobbying and organizational skills. Stewart recommended these strategies to the National American Woman Suffrage Association (NAWSA).

In late 1908, there was an attempt to revive the charter movement, and this time IESA leaders were allowed to argue their case directly for municipal suffrage for women. Once again, even though a number of women did appear before the charter convention, the majority of delegates refused to include municipal suffrage for women in the new charter. (Ironically, municipal suffrage would be granted to women by the state legislature in 1913, but charter reform failed in 1909 and again in 1914–15.)

By 1911 Stewart had been IESA president for five years and had introduced new organizational methods with success; she hoped to do more, including expansion of IESA's base of members by allowing a category of non-dues-paying members. Stewart's leadership was challenged, however, by more conservative women led by Grace Wilbur Trout. Trout hoped to gain control of the IESA and blocked any initiatives Stewart supported. Discouraged by the divisiveness of the movement and worn out by her many years of hard work, Stewart left the presidency in 1911. When Trout assumed the presidency in early 1912, both Stewart and McCulloch found their strategies denounced and themselves distanced from the new leadership. Trout was controversial; many felt she was more interested in personal glory than in the cause itself. Others felt she represented "upper-class interests" (Buechler, 176) among women, a charge that had been leveled against Trout when she was president of the Chicago Political Equality League from 1910 to 1912. Stewart was disheartened by Trout's election and angered when the IESA refused to appoint her and McCulloch as delegates to the NAWSA 1913 convention, although both were slated to speak at the national meeting.

In 1913, the presidential and municipal woman suffrage bill, "known as the 'Illinois Law' and the Presidential Suffrage Bill . . . modeled on previous Illinois suffrage bills that had granted the vote for offices not designated by the state constitution . . . permitted women to vote for all national offices and virtually all municipal, county, town, and village offices" (Buechler, 178), and was virtually the same legislation for which Stewart and McCulloch had fought so long. Trout, however, credited her new methods instituted since 1912 for this Illinois limited suffrage victory. In Trout's accounts, Stewart and all the work and effort of building up the IESA, lobbying, and developing a strong suffrage base across the state received scant notice.

Stewart, while disappointed in the turn of events, was thrilled at this suffrage victory. Immediately she began getting the women of Illinois out to vote, traveling for weeks in summer 1913 in the southern part of the state. There she created civic clubs to involve women in local politics. When Trout refused to press forward to bring about complete suffrage for Illinois women, Stewart became a charter member of Catharine McCulloch's Suffrage Amendment Alliance, serving on its state central committee. Many of the most prominent and progressive women reform leaders in Illinois, including SOPHONISBA BRECKINRIDGE, EDITH ABBOTT, and ELLEN HENROTIN, joined Stewart and McCulloch.

Internal politics and dissension also plagued NAWSA in the 1910s. Stewart had assumed leadership roles in the national movement, serving as an auditor, recording secretary, and second vice-president of NAWSA. There were NAWSA leaders who hoped Stewart would gain the presidency of the organization. Although this never happened, Stewart traveled extensively in the United States and abroad for NAWSA, spoke before committees of Congress, and addressed the organization's annual conventions. As members of the NAWSA board, Stewart and McCulloch were concerned about the growing eastern orientation of the organization. At the 1911 convention, realizing that the eastern faction had control, Stewart and McCulloch both chose to move on to new arenas rather than stay and fight.

Stewart, McCulloch, and others, including JANE ADDAMS, responded by creating the Mississippi Valley Equal Suffrage Conference, which held yearly conventions from 1912 through 1917 for women suffragists in the Midwest, West, and South to address their particular needs. Stewart organized the Mississippi Valley Equal Suffrage Conference convention in 1913 in St. Louis, Missouri.

After 1911, suffrage leaders called upon Stewart to help mediate conflicts between suffrage organizations and state WCTU organizations. At times these conflicts concerned personality clashes, but more often they revolved around the question of who would lead the suffrage campaign in a state—the WCTU or the state suffrage society. Suffrage organizations feared having the WCTU take a leading role, believing that the WCTU's open support would further arouse the fear and opposition to suffrage of the liquor interests. Stewart's own background in the WCTU and her husband's prominence in the prohibition movement made her an appropriate mediator, acceptable to both sides. Yet her primary allegiance was always woman suffrage and the successful passage of state and federal laws.

Stewart's political activism did not end when both the suffrage and prohibition amendments to the constitution were ratified in 1920 and 1919, respectively. During the 1920s she urged women to use their vote and supported the government's efforts to enforce prohibition effectively. Her work with the Chicago Woman's Club and the Woman's City Club of Chicago also made her aware of the plight of wage-earning women. Through the Chicago Woman's Club's joint committee of labor and clubwomen—the Reform Department Committee on the Improved Status of Women and Children, Stewart and others worked to improve the economic, legal, and social status of women and children. Later Stewart chaired the Chicago Woman's Club's industrial welfare committee. As a clubwoman she supported cross-class alliances with working women, beginning with female department store clerks. She supported female school teachers' demands for higher wages. Stewart believed in equal pay for equal work and supported women's access to employ-

ment, both professional and otherwise, in fields traditionally seen as men's domain.

Acting upon these beliefs, Stewart herself accepted full-time paid employment for the first time in 1927, when she was fifty-six years old, in banking, a field rarely open to women. She became director of the Women's Department of the University State Bank in Hyde Park, the neighborhood where the University of Chicago was located and in which she and her husband made their home. Stewart asserted that many of women's problems at the time were financial in nature, and she hoped to help married and single women budget their incomes wisely. She instituted a series of lectures for women on financial matters that were highly successful. Stewart became a leader of the Chicago Women Bankers Association.

Stewart left banking in 1930; she served two years as corresponding secretary of the Chicago Woman's Club. Club members unsuccessfully urged her to run for ward alderman. The last years of Stewart's life are more obscure. She did take a cruise around the world after her husband's death in 1937, and in typical style, gave a series of lectures about it on her return. Stewart died in Berea, Kentucky, where she was spending the winter, and services were held in Chicago.

Ella Seass Stewart's life was spent almost entirely in the cause of woman suffrage and the advancement of women's rights. As a businesswoman she advocated for women's equality in the work place and encouraged women's financial autonomy.

Sources. The Ella Seass Stewart Papers, deposited at SL, are an invaluable source. They are microfilmed as part of the Mary Earhart Dillon Collection and contain scrapbooks with newspaper clippings on Stewart, letters from fellow suffrage workers, professional flyers concerning her lecturing, and copies of her various suffrage speeches and pamphlets. The papers of her friend and colleague, Catharine Waugh McCulloch, are in the same collection. Ella Stewart's many articles, which deal with women's history and women's issues, especially woman suffrage, include "The Proper Education of Women," *Union Signal,* August 29, 1901; "Some Ancient New Women," *Arena,* November 1901; "The Symbol Versus the Fact," *Union Signal,* June 30, 1904; "Some Reasons Why Women Should Have the Ballot," *Christian Century,* November 24, 1904; "The New Ballot and Illinois Women," *Christian Century,* January 8, 1914; "Woman Suffrage and the Liquor Traffic," *Annals of the American Academy of Political and Social Science,* November 1914; "American Homes," *National Education Association Proceedings and Addresses* (1919); and "Noblesse Oblige," *Chicago's Woman's Club Bulletin,* 1919. Stewart also wrote widely for various Chicago newspapers and prohibition papers, especially the *National Enquirer.* For information on Stewart and her family, see Stewart Seass, *Our Family at Woodmanse* (1979). A good source of information on the Illinois woman suffrage campaign is Steven M. Buechler, *The Transformation of the Woman Suffrage Movement: The Case of Illinois, 1850–1920* (1986). Gertrude May Beldon, "A History of the Woman Suffrage Movement in Illinois" (master's thesis, UC, 1913), contains a brief interview with Stewart. An insightful look at the problems within the Illinois Equal Suffrage Association can be found in Adade Mitchell Wheeler, "Conflict in the Illinois Woman Suffrage Movement of 1913," *Journal of the Illinois State Historical Society,* Summer 1983. Information on Stewart's involvement in the National American Woman Suffrage Association (NAWSA) can be found in Ida Husted Harper, *The History of Woman Suffrage,* vols. 5 and 6 (1922). Her problems with NAWSA are chronicled in Paul E. Fuller, *Laura Clay and the Woman's Rights Movement* (1975).

BARBARA A. SPRINGER-SELIG

STIGLER, ELISA
March 11, 1914–November 14, 1973
DANCER, DANCE TEACHER, CHOREOGRAPHER, DANCE
EDUCATION THEORIST

Elisa Stigler was born in Manchester, England, the second of two daughters of Saul and Anna (Simon) Stigler. The Stiglers were of eastern European Jewish heritage. Her father died when Stigler was five years old. Stigler's earliest childhood years were spent in Newark, New Jersey, to which the family had emigrated. In the 1920s, Elisa Stigler moved to Chicago with her mother and her older sister, Rae. There Anna Stigler struggled to keep the family together financially and to provide Elisa Stigler with professional dance instruction.

During the 1920s, Stigler studied at the Glickman School of Music under ballet teacher EDNA McRAE, "to whom she was devoted all of her life" (Barzel, n.p.). Stigler remained a close friend of McRae, whom she considered her mentor in the field of dance. During summers in the late 1920s and early 1930s, Stigler traveled to New York and California to study ballet with Michel Fokine and flamenco and Spanish dance and choreography with Angel Cansino, Eduardo Cansino, Ernesto Lecuona, and Julio Zabaleta. The Cansinos were members of a large extended Spanish gypsy clan introduced to the United States by a wealthy art patron who sponsored them. Angel Cansino was the uncle and teacher of the accomplished flamenco dancer Margarita Cansino, who later became film actress Rita Hayworth. Using a notation format, Angel Cansino documented ethnographic dance of provincial Spain with percussion accompaniment, hand cymbals, and castanets. Stigler collected many pages of dance and castanet notation transcribed for her by the Cansinos, and she collaborated with Angel Cansino. Among their well-known choreographed pieces are *Andalucia, Bulerias, Jota, La Tana, La Feria,* and *Zambra.*

In the early 1940s, Elisa Stigler taught ballet, tap, and Spanish dance at a number of Chicago educational institutions, including the Chicago Musical College. Some of her ballet classes were taught with Edna McRae, her former teacher. By the mid-1940s, Stigler was recognized nationally as a specialist in Spanish dance and ethnographic character dance. She had mastered the complexities of Spanish castanet playing and was an authority on a large variety of Spanish regional ethnographic rhythms, heel work, and cultural dance. Stigler performed Spanish dance for business concerns, special events, and educational institutions. On September 9, 10, and 11, 1943, she was in charge of judging the dance groups representing various nations that appeared at Chicago's first Victory Garden Harvest Festival at Soldier Field.

As a dance teacher, Stigler welcomed and included African American pupils in her classes from the 1940s, a time when most educational institutions were segregated in the United States. Stigler continued to teach dance at the Chicago Musical College but offered classes at Chicago-area high schools, community centers, and colleges during the 1950s, including classes at Farragut High School (1950–54), Sullivan High School (1953–54), Rogers Park Community Center (1950–54), and Rosary College (1953–54). In 1954, when Chicago Musical College became affiliated with Roosevelt University, Stigler became head of the dance department.

During the early 1950s Stigler organized several dance teacher institutes. She served as an officer and principal for the convention and summer session of the Chicago National Association of Dancing Masters Incorporated. She developed peer instruction and led master classes in ballet and Spanish dance. Her reputation for leading peer instructional workshops grew; she was one of the organizers of a dance institute for more than seven hundred participants in Dallas, Texas, in 1959. Annual workshops taught by Stigler were in demand by advanced dance students as well as colleagues. One such workshop, held in January 1960 at the Boone Recreational Center, Boone, Iowa, was cotaught by Stigler and modern jazz specialist Gus Giordano.

Stigler made public appearances and offered lecture demonstrations such as the January 1959 Goodman Theatre presentation, *Ethnic Dance: The Spirit of Spanish Ballet,* which explored the more famous national dances of Spain and showed how they evolved from native rhythms. While head of the dance department at Roosevelt University, Stigler directed ballet and character dance presentations for a Chicago Musical College Dance Recital in June 1961; they were held at the Rudolph Ganz Recital Hall and showcased the accomplishments of sixty-three advanced students. A 1963 class demonstration in Rudolph Ganz Recital Hall included performances by two child dancers who would become professional artists, ballet dancer Michael Bjerknes and Spanish dancer Libby Komaiko. Directing nine of her advanced ballet and Spanish dance students in a lecture demonstration held in March 1964 at the Wieboldt Department Store, downtown Chicago, Stigler offered a performance of Spanish and American dances as part of the preview of the 1964 New York World's Fair. She directed a ballet performance of students from the Chicago Musical College at the Christ Unity Temple Drama and Music Festival in Chicago in 1966. During the summer of 1971, Elisa Stigler, as artistic director, collaborated with Jack Slater of the Peoria Civic Ballet Company, Peoria, Illinois, and arranged variations from the classical Russian repertoire, such as the *Lilac Fairy* from Petipa's *Sleeping Beauty.*

Stigler served as an officer of the Chicago National Association of Dancing Masters for more than thirty years. The association arranged for great dancers to give master classes for teachers from all over the United States who were members of National Association of Dance Masters (formerly Dancing Masters). Stigler brought such artists as Muriel Stuart, Robert Joffrey, Yurek Lazovsky, Bill Viscount-Martin, Johnny Mattison, Louis DaPron, Gus Giordano, and Donald Sawyer to conventions of the association. In this way she raised the standards of dance art in the United States.

Stigler was guest artistic director for the regional Florida Ballet Theatre Company under director Frank Rey; she ran a workshop for the company and continued to have a close friendship and professional relationship with Rey. "Through her expertise," Rey said about studying in Chicago with Stigler, "I learned not just to see dance but to see it through the reflection of history. Her training in the classroom and the theatre gave me the background necessary to empathize" ("Guest Columnist") with the great dancers of the past and present. "Everything in dance became exciting because she was. To analyze the classics and the various interpretations became our daily necessity" ("Guest

Columnist"), Rey recalled. "At night we would see the great dance companies, meet the dancers who were all her friends, and talk about the dance: its past—its present—and its future" ("Guest Columnist"). She continued to be active as an officer and peer instructor through July 1973, only a few months before her death. Among her more well-known professional colleagues at the Chicago Association of Dance Masters were the great jazz dancer Gus Giordano, leading ballet dancer and teacher Richard Arve, modern dancer Paul Haakon, and world-renowned ballet company director Robert Joffrey.

Elisa Stigler was a dedicated teacher who focused on efforts to advance the professional dance careers of her students, particularly those destined for lifetime professional work as performing artists. One of her more famous students was John Kriza, formerly of Berwyn, Illinois, who studied with Stigler for many years. He became one of the leading dancers of the American Ballet Theatre and had a distinguished international reputation during the mid-1950s and 1960s. Kriza remained Stigler's friend and colleague. They continued to be close associates during the late 1960s, when John Kriza held the position of dance teacher at Hull-House Association, Chicago. Kitty LaPointe, who owned, operated, managed, and taught dance classes at La-Pointe School of Ballet, Chicago, was a student of Elisa Stigler. The school was widely respected in the dance community for approximately twenty years from the late 1950s to the early 1970s. Michael Bjerknes, a ballet student since early childhood, danced with the National Ballet into the late 1990s; Libby Komaiko, the founder and artistic director of Ensemble Español, a Spanish dance company in residence at Northeastern Illinois University, Chicago, since 1976, was a ballet and Spanish dance student of Elisa Stigler from age nine until Stigler's death in 1973. Stigler provided this student with her earliest technical training, which included castanet playing and complex heel work. Stigler's personal friendship and peer relationship with José Greco helped several of her Spanish dance students to obtain scholarships to study in his master classes at the Northwood Institute, West Baden, Indiana. Stigler also worked with other members of the José Greco troupe, offering master classes that included Pascual Olivera, touring artist of international reputation. Although Elisa Stigler never married, her devoted admirer was the portrait photographer Ernest Martin (Martin E. Friedmann), who produced many studio portraits of Stigler that showed her as a striking woman of unusual, exotic beauty. Her photographs have been displayed in the studios and businesses of many of her colleagues, including Kling's Dance Footwear, whose founding owner, Sam Kling, was a close friend.

During her last years, Stigler suffered a number of serious personal tragedies. The first was a near fatal pedestrian automobile accident that caused her to be hospitalized for months. Stigler also struggled with breast cancer for approximately four years prior to her death. She continued, however, to teach, work, and lecture during those years. She died at age fifty-nine. She is buried at Jewish Waldheim Cemetery, Forest Park, Illinois.

Elisa Stigler's impact on the local and national dance community was pronounced, and she took on an original leadership role as organizer of professional dance teacher workshops and seminars. She introduced many prominent performing artists and dance company directors as peer instructors at the various seminars and conventions at which she served as teacher and principal. Her extensive research in the area of ethnographic music and dance, specifically Spanish dance and Far East Asian dance, expanded on the base of information she found when she entered the field. Her life as a dancer and dance researcher was her entire life. Her large and extended coterie of devoted friends shared her love of dance. Among them was Ann Barzel, dance writer and critic. Others who respected her work and memorialized her contribution to the professional dance world included José Greco, Paul Haakon, the Cansino family, Robert Joffrey, and Frank Rey.

Sources. Elisa Stigler Papers, Midwest Dance Collection, NL, has thirteen pages of dance sheet notations arranged by Stigler and Angel Cansino; correspondence; programs and announcements; and clippings, including Frank Rey, "Guest Columnist," an unidentified clipping. Elisa Stigler's *Curriculum Vitae* is on file at Chicago Musical College, Roosevelt Univ. An interview was conducted by Jackie Rosenstein Turlow with Ann Barzel, August 6, 1996. Ann Barzel, *Elisa Stigler* (1995), was written for the Elisa Stigler Memorial Collection at the Ruth Page Center, Chicago, and is useful. In addition to her professional dance notation manuscripts at NL, Stigler's dance literature and memorabilia collection is in the Elisa Stigler Memorial Collection at the Ruth Page Center; dance books and collectibles of the Stigler collection are also held at the Harold Washington Library Center, CPL. Stigler produced a record, *Spanish Dance Class* (1967), for the Idento Record Company. She authored a book, *Castanet Techniques* (c. 1960), and wrote "Basic Technique (Spanish Dance), Beginner Technique (Spanish Dance)," the *Training School*, July 1973. William Como, "On the Boards: A Series on Dancers and Choreographers in Showbusiness," *Dance Magazine*, June 1969, is useful. Stigler's obituary appeared in *Chicago Today*, November 14, 1973.

JOANNE PERRAULT
JACKIE ROSENSTEIN TURLOW

STOCKHAM, ALICE BUNKER
November 8, 1833–December 2, 1912
PHYSICIAN, SEXUAL REFORMER, AUTHOR, PUBLISHER

Alice Bunker Stockham, an internationally famous expert on women's health and sexuality, was born in Cardington, Ohio, one of seven children of Slocum and Mathilda (Wood) Bunker. When she was three years old, her family moved to rural Michigan, where Alice spent her childhood. Her parents were Quakers who embraced Thomsonian medicine and then hydropathy, alternative healing practices that were popular among reform-minded antebellum Americans. Thomsonianism was based on a belief in cold as the single cause of disease, to be treated by herbal medicines. Hydropathy used a water cure—both internal and external—for illness. The parents' beliefs perhaps explain why Alice Bunker developed an early and abiding interest in health and healing. While still a child, she showed nursing skills and often attended those who were sick.

As a teenager Alice Bunker worked as a school teacher and studied at Olivet College in Olivet, Michigan. One evening she attended a woman suffrage lecture, where she met Emma R. Coe, a pioneering woman lawyer, who encouraged her to study medicine. Despite some family opposition, Alice determined to follow Coe's advice. At the age of twenty Alice enrolled at the Eclectic Medical College of Cincinnati. Eclecticism, a popular medical sect that had absorbed Thomsonianism, accepted conventional science in medicine but rejected treatment by drugs and bleeding and used herbal medicines. She received her medical degree in 1854. In Cincinnati she met fellow medical student Gabriel H. Stockham. They were married on August 11, 1857. The couple had two children, William and Cora.

Alice Stockham spent the twenty-three years after her marriage practicing medicine in Kansas, Indiana, and Chicago. She specialized in the treatment of women and children. In 1880, Stockham completed a course of study at the Chicago Homeopathic College. Homeopathy stressed clinical treatment of illness through minute doses of drugs that would bring on the symptoms of the disease in a healthy person as well as a close relationship between doctor and patient for precise diagnosis. The following year she traveled to Sweden, Finland, Russia, and Germany, where she studied new educational methods.

In 1883, Stockham published her first book, *Tokology: A Book for Every Woman*, a manual on women's health and pregnancy. *Tokology* was an immediate hit. By 1891 it had sold 160,000 copies. By 1897 it was on its forty-fifth edition and was becoming the standard work on women's health, sexuality, pregnancy, and childbirth for literate Americans.

Stockham's *Tokology* presented straightforward discussions of the physiology of human reproduction. Using clear and unsensational language, Stockham described "the reproductive apparatus," menstruation, "conception," the stages of pregnancy, childbirth, postpartum diseases, and the care of infants, as well as "diseases of women" (pp. ix–xiv) and menopause. *Tokology* was equally notable for its bold stand on sexual politics. Stockham denounced the sexual double standard or the idea that "sexual union is a *necessity* to man, while it is not to woman" (p. 152). In her view, men who believed that sexual intercourse was necessary for male health subjected their wives to excessive sexual intercourse. Women who were raised to equate womanly modesty with sexual ignorance found themselves loathing the sexual demands of their husbands.

Stockham argued that warped ideas about male and female sexuality poisoned marriage. A changed attitude on the part of both partners could transform sexual intercourse from a horror to a communion. Stockham wrote that it was not sexual intercourse per se but frequent, loveless, and involuntary sex that was damaging to women. The solution was to raise young men and women with a single high moral standard of sexuality. Once married, the couple was to *"take time for the act, have it entirely mutual from first to last"* (*Tokology*, 156); the result, Stockham promised, would be that "the demand will not come so frequently" (*Tokology*, 156), and women's hatred for their husbands would be replaced with love. Most importantly, married couples were to observe absolute chastity during pregnancy. Stockham promised that this control would produce children in whom "a life of purity and self-control will be natural" (*Tokology*, 160).

Tokology was praised by diverse women, from suffrage and temperance leader MARY LIVERMORE to sex radical Mary Gove Nichols. Translations were published in German, French, Finnish, and Swedish. The book so impressed Russian author Leo Tolstoy that he arranged to have it translated into Russian. His preface to the Russian edition noted the radicalism of Stock-

ham's writings for late Victorian culture. "This book is one of those rare books which does not deal with what everybody talks about and nobody needs, but about what nobody talks about and everybody needs to know," Tolstoy wrote, adding that the book "immediately transports the reader into a new world of living human activity" (translation by Robert Edwards, "Tolstoy and Alice B. Stockham," 105).

After *Tokology*, Stockham continued to explore a wide range of alternative approaches to health, education, and character development. Her interests were eugenic in nature; she hoped to discover the combination of physical and mental disciplines that would produce moral and intellectual men and women who would then have spiritually and physically superior offspring. She adopted the educational ideas of the German philosopher Friedrich Fröbel (also Froebel), who believed that specially designed children's games could instill in children the divine attributes of maternal love. She embraced François Delsarte's philosophy of theater and performance, which claimed that the practice of certain physical poses insured that elevated gesture became habitual.

Perhaps the ideas that most engaged her were those promoted by turn-of-the-century New Thought healers. The basic premise of New Thought was that one's thoughts had the power to shape reality. Illness was caused by negative thoughts, New Thought leaders argued; therefore the focused "affirmation" of positive thoughts could restore health. Stockham's first exposure to New Thought was in 1886, when she and her close friend Lida Hood Talbot enrolled in a course on New Thought healing offered by a charismatic teacher, EMMA CURTIS HOPKINS. Stockham also embraced the ideas of Warren Felt Evans, another influential early New Thought author. By 1887 Stockham was participating in New Thought or "mental science" conventions and writing on mental healing for the Chicago New Thought press. She promoted and practiced New Thought healing for the remainder of her life.

Given Stockham's long involvement with health and alternative healing, it was perhaps inevitable that she would investigate mental healing, but Stockham had more personal reasons to turn to New Thought. For many years, everything Stockham ate caused her intense pain. Doctors diagnosed her illness as peritonitis, enteritis, colitis, or appendicitis, but could prescribe no cure. Stockham tried to avoid the pain by limiting her diet. As she described years later, the pain "recurred so severely as to make life almost intolerable" ("Non-Resistance as a Healing Power," 38). Stockham believed that the teachings of Hopkins and Evans brought her relief from this condition.

In 1887, Stockham started a publishing house, Alice B. Stockham & Company, later the Stockham Publishing Company. The company published *Tokology*; the works of British sex radicals Edward Carpenter and Havelock Ellis; the writings of Warren Felt Evans and other New Thought authors; and a variety of radical books on health, sexuality, and education. By 1893 Stockham's company was employing a dozen clerks and bringing in several thousand dollars a month. She had given up medical practice to devote full time to publishing. Stockham recruited women to act as door-to-door book agents for *Tokology*. She cast her publishing work as a form of womanly philanthropy. Her contemporaries agreed. The Woman's Christian Temperance Union (WCTU) paper *Union Signal* praised Stockham for "set[ting] up business on a purely 'woman's basis,' viz.: A book for every woman, written by a woman, published by a woman, canvassed almost exclusively by women, and bought by women" (quoted in Stockham, *Koradine Letters*, n.p.).

In 1890, Stockham moved to Evanston, a suburb of Chicago. Her home was designed for her by the eminent architects Frederick Bauman and J. K. Cady. She lived there with her daughter Cora, her nieces Cora Dean and Edith Dean, and three servants. (Her husband did not move with her to Evanston. His fate is unknown.) Her home served as something of a community center. There Stockham held girls' club meetings, public addresses by local literary celebrities, and language lessons. Stockham also hosted lavish entertainments that were reported in the Evanston press. The town of Evanston viewed her as one of its leading citizens. Officials named the street and park she lived on Stockham Place and Stockham Park in her honor.

In the early 1890s Stockham became involved in a wide range of reform activities. She supported woman suffrage and social purity, a sex-reform movement that promoted for both men and women a single moral standard of sexual behavior based on sexual control. A founding member of the Illinois Woman's Press Association, she represented the group in Washington, D.C., at the 1891 meeting of the National Council of Women of the United States, which was led by its first president, FRANCES E. WILLARD. Stockham promoted the kindergarten movement and successfully petitioned to have *slojd*, a Swedish handicraft system, taught in the Chicago public schools. Stockham was a prolific author during these years. In 1893, she and Lida Hood Talbot wrote *Koradine Letters*, an epistolary novel concerned with a young girl's "development . . . in body, mind and spirit" (back page). In 1894, she published a health manual for girls, *Creative Life*. Two years later she published *Karezza: Ethics of Marriage*, supporting motionless sexual intercourse without orgasm as a way to enhance personal character and marital love. The goal of "Karezza" was not to enhance pleasure but to master and spiritualize sexual or creative energy so that it could be drawn upon to enhance the intellectual abilities of both husband and wife. "In the Karezza relation the creative principle becomes active in both husband and wife . . . [and] ideas of great moment are conceived," Stockham explained (*Karezza*, 99). At a time when conservative and radical men alike were insisting that women could contribute to society only by more fully following their sexual and reproductive instincts, Stockham insisted that women as well as men were capable of transmuting sexual energy into intellectual strength.

She continued to travel as well. In 1891, she took a trip around the world, visiting India, China, Japan, and a number of Pacific islands.

By the mid-1890s, Stockham's fame was international. Tolstoy promoted her work in Russia. She was a friend of the Baroness Alexandra Gripenburg of Finland, a famous parliamentarian and newspaper publisher and leader of the woman's movement in Finland. British sex radical and socialist Edward Carpenter was Stockham's friend and professional admirer; later

editions of his *Love's Coming-of-Age* included excerpts from Stockham's *Karezza*. In return Stockham published his writings and cited him in her own works. By the mid-1890s British newspapers called Stockham "Dr. Alice, whom everybody loves" (quoted in Stockham, *Koradine Letters*, back page). Her works received wide praise, ranging from that in the WCTU *Union Signal* to the "weekly Anarchist-Freethought Journal," *Lucifer* (Sears, 64).

In 1897, Stockham established a New Thought school, the Vrilia Heights Metaphysical School, in Williams Bay, Wisconsin. In 1903, she wrote her opus, *The Lover's World*, a guide to all phases of life with an emphasis on love, marriage, and childbirth. Drawing upon the New Thought claim that "affirmations" could shape reality, *The Lover's World* provided affirmations to further the acceptance of one's sexual instincts: "I am not a child of evil; I am not begotten in sin; . . . all my inheritance is from the union of wisdom and love . . . ; thus that which gives a sign of this union—the sexual instinct—is good and not evil. . . . I welcome it as the insignia of life" (p. 68).

Stockham's activism, publications, business savvy, and society pleasures made her seem modern and exciting. The Chicago *Inter-Ocean* dubbed her the "original 'new woman' of the West" (May 21, 1905). Her career came to an abrupt halt in 1905, when she was seventy-two. That year, one of her pamphlets, *The Wedding Night*, came to the attention of the Society for Suppression of Vice. Just three years earlier, sex reformer IDA CRADDOCK had been prosecuted and hounded to suicide in New York City by the society's representative, Anthony Comstock. Stockham was arrested and indicted for "sending improper matter through the mails" ("Holds New Woman for Advice on Love"). She engaged attorney Clarence Darrow for her defense. Stockham had a great deal of support from local women but was found guilty. She was fined two hundred fifty dollars and her books on sexuality were banned. Neither the Alice B. Stockham Publishing Company nor Stockham's previous writings on sexuality survived the ruling. Only four years after the court case, attorney and free-speech activist Theodore Schroeder noted that Stockham's writings and any others similar to them were nowhere to be found.

After the trial Stockham moved to Alhambra, California, with her daughter. She continued to practice mental healing and to write occasional articles for the New Thought press, but her career as a proponent of women's health and sexuality effectively ended. She died at age seventy-nine at her home in Alhambra. The *New York Times* praised her work in "social purity, woman suffrage and social reform" and called her "one of the pioneers of the eugenic movement" (December 4, 1912). City officials in Evanston, Illinois, her home during her most active decade, did not join in the acclaim. The year of her death they changed the name of Stockham Place and Stockham Park to Burnham Place and Burnham Park.

Stockham was active during a period of transition from Victorian to modern views of gender and sexuality. Her ideas about sexuality enabled women to claim sexual passion but not to the end of enhancing sexual pleasure within marriage. Stockham lauded sexual passion in women because many late Victorians believed that sexual passion fueled intellectual achievement.

She argued that women and men were not only equally sexual but equally able to control or direct their sexuality to intellectual ends. This was the message lost when her books were banned at the start of the twentieth century.

Sources. In addition to the works mentioned above, Stockham's writings include *For Boys* (1887), *John and Mary in the Home* (n.d.), and *Tolstoi: A Man of Peace* (1900). Her articles include "Non-Resistance as a Healing Power," *Nautilus*, January 1910. A short biography of Stockham appears in Frances E. Willard and Mary A. Livermore, eds., *A Woman of the Century* (1893), and in Robert Edwards, "Tolstoy and Alice B. Stockham: The Influence of 'Tokology' on *The Kreutzer Sonata*," *Tolstoy Studies Journal* 4 (1993). Obituaries in *NYT*, and the *Evanston Press*, both on December 14, 1912, provide further biographical information. Stockham's writings on sexuality are discussed in Hal D. Sears, *The Sex Radicals: Free Love in High Victorian America* (1977); Taylor Stoehr, *Free Love in America: A Documentary History* (1979); and John D'Emilio and Estelle B. Freedman, *Intimate Matters: A History of Sexuality in America* (1988). Scattered references to Stockham can be found in *Truth* and *Christian Science* magazines, 1886–88, the *Evanston Press*, 1890–94, the Illinois Woman's Press Association Yearbooks, 1890–95, and *Mind* magazine, 1897–1905. Stockham's indictment for mailing *The Wedding Night* is described in "Holds New Woman for Advice on Love," Chicago *Inter-Ocean*, May 21, 1905. Analysis of Stockham's career and intellectual outlook, from which this profile in part is drawn, is in Beryl Satter, *Each Mind a Kingdom: American Women, Sexual Purity, and the New Thought Movement, 1875–1920*, copyright © 1999 The Regents of the University of California, used by permission of the University of California Press.

BERYL SATTER

STRAIN BIESEL, FRANCES
November 11, 1898–December 10, 1962
PAINTER, PRINTMAKER, GALLERY ADMINISTRATOR, CURATOR

Although Frances Strain was trained as an artist and produced art throughout her adult life, she was equally important in the actions she took to bring the work of other artists to the attention of the public. As one of the founding members of several important progressive exhibition groups (Chicago No-Jury Society of Artists and 10 Artists of Chicago) in the 1920s, and as exhibition director of the Renaissance Society at the University of Chicago from 1941 to 1962, Strain worked aggressively to bring modern art to the Chicago public.

Born in Chicago to James C. Strain, an Irishman involved in Cook County politics, and a Danish immigrant mother, Strain had three older half-siblings. Two of them were brothers, one of whom died before Frances Strain was born; the second died shortly thereafter. She had one younger sister, Virginia. Her father died in 1907, leaving her mother emotionally withdrawn and without a livelihood. Strain's half-sister, Helen Gertrude (called Dedie), who was about twenty years older than Frances, took over financial support of the family. She was a successful businesswoman who became an executive with Automatic Electric Company. The family lived first on the Near West Side, moving later to Hyde Park, where Frances Strain lived most of the rest of her life. Strain attended a small private school on the Near West Side of Chicago through high school. According to the progressive Chicago art critic C. J. Bulliet and others, she knew from childhood that she wanted to paint, although she had never met an artist. In the *Chicago Daily News*, March 21, 1936,

Bulliet described her first awed encounter with an artist, when she was a student at the School of the Art Institute and saw Adam Emory Albright (father of the twin painters Ivan and Malvin Albright); it was a major event in her young life.

During World War I, Strain entered the School of the Art Institute of Chicago (SAIC), where she studied with George Bellows and Randall Davey, New York urban realists associated with the Ashcan School, each of whom had a short teaching stint at SAIC during the 1919–20 academic year. They emphasized sincerity and personal expression over the technical mastery and figure drawing stressed in the conservative pedagogy of SAIC, attracting many of the more progressive students to their classes. Along with a group of students that included her future husband, Fred Biesel, Strain was invited to join Davey in Santa Fe, New Mexico, for the summer. There she met a number of artists, including John Sloan, one of the most important of the Ashcan School painters and president of the Society of Independent Artists (SIA) in New York, with whom she and Biesel returned to New York at the end of the summer. The couple lived and worked with Sloan for more than a year, returning to Santa Fe with him the following summer. With Sloan as teacher, the students extended their understanding of the Bellows-Davey philosophy of freedom of expression and met artists and writers such as John Butler Yeats, Walter Pach, Robert Henri, Walt Kuhn, and Marsden Hartley, most of whom were actively involved with the SIA. Biesel and Strain maintained a lifelong relationship with Sloan. Many of the connections forged in New York were significant when Strain began to organize exhibitions. Although the couple returned to Santa Fe almost every summer during the 1920s, by 1922 they had established themselves in Chicago, eventually renting a small studio in the South Shore neighborhood, doing commercial work as well as fine art, and becoming important figures in the progressive artistic community of Chicago.

Often excluded from the juried annual exhibitions at the Art Institute, the more modernist or progressive artists in Chicago began to seek alternative venues for exhibiting their work beginning as early as the late nineteen-tens. Strain exhibited with a group of independent, primarily New York artists called the introspectives in their single Chicago exhibition, held at the Arts Club in May 1921. She next participated in the 1922 *Salon des Refusés*, an exhibition of paintings rejected from the *American Annual* at the Art Institute, which represented the large-scale beginning of the "no-jury" mentality in Chicago. This exhibition, which came to be known as the Refuses, was the first in a series of artist-generated shows characterized by an egalitarian attitude eschewing juries and prizes. Along with Biesel's father, Charles, an artist who had established himself on the East Coast as a marine painter before moving to Chicago in the teens, and a number of other progressive local artists, Strain and Biesel were founding members of the Chicago No-Jury Society of Artists, a group dedicated explicitly to the principle that any artist who wished to exhibit could do so. Like the SIA, exhibitions were hung alphabetically and were distinguished by their tolerance and openness. Strain served as an officer or director of the society for many years and, with Biesel, served as a liaison with the New York Independents, successfully encouraging them to participate in the Chicago exhibitions, lending the No-Jury shows a national flavor.

After several years of living together without legal sanction, in 1926 Strain and Biesel married, according to the wishes of Charles Biesel. Strain continued to use her birth name professionally. In 1928, the Biesels traveled to Europe with their artist-friends Vin and Hazel Hannell and FRANCES FOY and her husband, Gustaf Dalstrom. In the same year, they purchased property in Furnessville, Indiana, near the Indiana Dunes, that was to become a refuge and summer home, a place to enjoy nature and family for the rest of their lives. On October 25, 1930, their only child, son Garnett, was born.

By this time, Strain had established herself as a professional artist, exhibiting in progressive Chicago venues such as IN-CREASE ROBINSON's Studio Gallery; with the Chicago Society of Artists, the oldest artists' group in the city, where she was awarded a gold medal for her *Still Life* in 1929; and with the No-Jury Society. She had one-person shows at the Romany Club in 1929 and at Chicago Woman's Aid in 1931. She exhibited at the Museum of New Mexico in 1920, with the SIA in New York as early as 1921, and in group shows at the Newark Museum (1927) and the Whitney Museum (1933). In 1928, she and Biesel, the Dalstroms, Vin Hannell, Emil Armin, Émile Grumieaux, George Josimovich, Charles Biesel, and sculptor TEN-NESSEE ANDERSON (replaced after her death in late 1929 by Jean Crawford Adams) formed 10 Artists of Chicago. The work of these artists was characterized by their intellectual commitment to modernist ideas and their stylistic moderation, an attitude that could be termed "moderate modernism." They held annual exhibitions in which each member contributed several works, occasionally holding a second exhibition in the Chicago area. They also exhibited in Madison, Wisconsin, and in New York. Although an integral part of 10 Artists, Strain maintained her strong connection to No-Jury and continued to exhibit in a variety of Chicago and national venues during the 1930s and 1940s. Between 1923 and 1944, she participated in ten of the prestigious juried exhibitions at the Art Institute of Chicago: *Artists of Chicago and Vicinity* (1923, 1931, 1933, 1939, 1940, 1944), *Watercolor* (1927, 1936, 1944), and *American Artists* (1941).

Strain worked in a range of styles, from the Ashcan School–derived *Cabaret* (c. 1926) reminiscent of Sloan's urban scenes, to the luxuriant, thickly painted *Still Life with Teapot* (1924), in which luscious colors and rich impasto dominate. *The Visitor (Portrait of Emil Armin)* and *The Conversation*, a portrait of Vin Hannell, Fred Biesel, and Gus Dalstrom, both from the late 1920s, exhibit the same rich surface texture and sumptuous color. In paintings from the 1930s such as *52nd and Dorchester* (c. 1929), she experimented with the kind of urban scene typical of the regionalists, emphasizing the peaceful small-town qualities of her Hyde Park neighborhood rather than the bustle of the skyscraper-dominated Loop downtown area. She even experimented with a kind of Chicago-derived surrealism. In *Life and Death in New Orleans* (1938), Strain depicts a solitary woman standing among the large monuments in a graveyard, looking directly out at the viewer in a way that suggests familiarity with the work of her Hyde Park neighbor, GERTRUDE ABERCROMBIE.

Like most of her contemporaries, Strain participated in the federal government–supported art projects of the 1930s, such as the Works Progress Administration (WPA). In 1935, Fred Biesel was appointed to an administrative position in the Illinois Art Project, holding the post of state director from 1941 until the project's end in 1943; although there were rules about participation by more than one member of a married couple, Strain is listed as a participant in the easel division.

By the late 1930s, Strain had become an active volunteer at the Renaissance Society, a gallery founded in 1915 at the University of Chicago for the purpose of mounting innovative exhibits as well as administering programs to educate the public about the arts in general. The mission of the Renaissance Society included supporting musical, literary, and performance events as well as visual art. Strain became exhibition director in 1941, holding the position until her death in 1962. Under her direction the Renaissance Society became a preeminent site for exhibitions in the Chicago area in the 1940s and 1950s, second only to the Art Institute. Strain's experience in organizing exhibitions in the 1920s and 1930s for the No-Jury Society and 10 Artists prepared her to arrange shows, and her relationships with artists and administrators in other cities provided her with the kinds of affiliations that made it possible for her to bring first-rate and innovative exhibitions to the city.

The exhibition of John Sloan's work (*John Sloan: Contemporary Work in Painting*) in the 1941–42 season was undoubtedly a result of her friendship with the artist. It was accompanied by Chicago artist Aaron Bohrod's gallery talk on the artist. In the 1944–45 season, *A Retrospective Exhibition of Etchings by John Sloan* brought the artist himself to Chicago to speak on "The Independence of the Artist." Strain's personal connections were important in realizing her vision of what the Renaissance Society should achieve. Dorothy Miller, a curator at the Museum of Modern Art in New York City, and a close friend and professional associate, helped Strain with loans and suggestions. Miller was married to Holger ("Eddie") Cahill, a friend of Fred Biesel, who served as national director of the Federal Art Project. In the mid-1940s, George Thorp, state director of the Illinois Art Project preceding Fred Biesel, was assistant director of the American Federation of the Arts (AFA), an organization on which Strain depended for traveling exhibitions. These relationships were never one-sided, however; Strain introduced Miller to Chicago artists, whom the latter included in New York exhibitions, and she originated shows that the AFA circulated. One of these shows became the annual *Contemporary Art for Young Collectors*, held for the first time in 1946 as *Pictures up to $20.00*. For this AFA event, Strain gathered the work of European and American artists, replenishing the exhibition as work was sold. By the mid-1950s, the show featured work ranging from that of local artists, including Abercrombie, Foy, and Dalstrom, to internationally known artists such as Marc Chagall, Käthe Kollwitz, and Pablo Picasso. The first of these exhibitions/sales was so successful (107 works sold) that the AFA sponsored a traveling version, with a top price of one hundred dollars. Strain's desire to make fine art available to the public at moderate prices resulted in the establishment of a number of collections. The *Young Collectors* show was one of the most popular events of the season and continued through the late 1980s.

In her role as the Renaissance Society's exhibition director, she showed the same commitment to artists of Chicago that she did to artists who worked elsewhere. Exhibitions of modern American art included Chicagoans. The society sponsored annual shows of artist-members beginning in 1948, offering exhibition opportunities to many local artists.

At the Renaissance Society, Strain almost single-handedly administered the gallery, organized and installed exhibitions (as many as nine a year), did publicity and fund-raising, and related to the board and the University of Chicago's art department faculty, aided by volunteers and a secretary, the only other paid staff member. She professionalized the organization, planning the calendar of events well in advance for the first time in the society's history. She insisted, however, on having her summers off, spending them in Furnessville painting and relaxing with her family, which included, in addition to her husband (until his death in 1954) and son, her sisters and nephews and assorted pets.

The art she produced in the last two decades of her life consisted of landscapes and flower paintings, many in watercolor. Despite her limited time, she was enormously productive. In 1960, she had four one-person exhibitions: at the Chicago Public Library; the Cliff Dwellers Club in Chicago; the Little Gallery, Park Forest, Illinois; and the Culver Military Academy gallery in northern Indiana. In 1961, she received a citation from the Chicago Chapter of the Artist's Equity Association, paying tribute to her role as a supporter and promoter of living artists.

After her death, she was honored with an exhibition at the Renaissance Society in 1963, a worthy memorial to a woman who brought art into the lives of so many Chicagoans. She was included in the exhibition, *The 'New Woman' in Chicago, 1910–1945*, at the Rockford College (Illinois) Art gallery in 1993.

Strain's artistic work was recognized and praised by her contemporaries during her lifetime, and a number of fine examples are in museums and private collections. At the same time she took on administrative and leadership roles in a variety of artists' organizations, in the WPA, and at the Renaissance Society. Strain provided generations of Chicagoans with access to the art of other local artists as well as that of national, international, and historical figures whose works might not have been seen in Chicago without her vision and dedication.

Sources. Strain's papers are part of the Biesel Family Papers, Archives of American Art, Smithsonian Institution. They include correspondence, much relating to the Renaissance Society. The papers include typescript biographies, newspaper clippings relating both to exhibitions in which Strain participated and to exhibitions of the No-Jury Society and 10 Artists, exhibition catalogs, scrapbooks with photographs of art work, and the texts of several lectures that Strain delivered. Garnett Biesel, Strain's son, provided valuable biographical and family information in an interview with Susan S. Weininger on May 28, 1995. A statement of Strain's artistic philosophy and a reproduction of *Crowd* are included in J. Z. Jacobson's *Art of Today: Chicago, 1933* (1932). A short entry is included in Esther Sparks, "A Biographical Dictionary of Painters and Sculptors in Illinois, 1808–1945" (Ph.D. diss., Northwestern Univ., 1971). She is mentioned in Louise Dunn Yochim, *Role and Impact: The Chicago Society of Artists* (1979). Her role and that of her husband, Fred Biesel, in the development of independent artists' organizations in Chicago are treated in Paul Kruty, "Declarations of Independents: Chicago's Alternative Art Groups of the 1920s," in *The Old Guard and the Avant-Garde*, ed. Sue Ann Prince (1990). Strain's work is discussed

in the catalog essay by Susan S. Weininger for the exhibition, *The 'New Woman' in Chicago, 1910–1945* (1993). The history of the Renaissance Society, along with very useful documentation of exhibitions and events, is found in *A History of the Renaissance Society: The First Seventy-Five Years*, ed. Joseph Scanlan (1993).

SUSAN S. WEININGER

SUNDAY, HELEN AMELIA THOMPSON
June 25, 1868–February 20, 1957
EVANGELIST

Helen Amelia Thompson Sunday, known to her contemporaries as "Ma" Sunday, was a shaper of mass evangelism technique and a leader of American Protestant fundamentalism for more than twenty years. She was born in the Chicago suburb of Dundee, the second of five children of William and Ellen (Binnie) Thompson. Her mother came to the United States from Scotland as a child. The Thompsons moved to Chicago when Helen was nine months old. William Thompson manufactured ice cream in the city but retained property in Dundee, where Helen (or Nell as her family called her) spent part of her childhood.

When Thompson was twelve, her Sunday school teacher asked her if she wanted to belong to Jesus. Thompson instantly agreed and many years later reflected, "From the very hour my Sunday School teacher led me to Christ, I have felt His unseen presence. Helping me through many trials, He has been my source of strength and comfort. He has never failed me" (Overmyer, 8–9). On Easter 1880, she joined Jefferson Park Presbyterian Church. By age eighteen she was superintendent of the intermediate department of the Sunday school, leader of the young people's Christian Endeavor Society, and a member of the choir. Around this time she graduated from high school and took courses at a business college.

Helen Thompson met Billy Sunday during a meeting of the Christian Endeavor Society. He was a poor, good-natured, sensitive young man, almost six years her senior, a rookie on the Chicago White Stockings baseball team. In November 1886, he was "born again," making a public confession of Jesus as his personal savior after listening to a street-corner evangelism service in Chicago. Sunday had begun attending Jefferson Presbyterian because of Helen Thompson and later joked, "She was a Presbyterian, so I am Presbyterian. If she had been a Catholic, I would have been a Catholic—because I was hot on the trail of Nell" (McLoughlin, 6). He was persistent in his wooing, and Thompson began to warm to him, despite her father's objections to the rowdy reputation of ballplayers. Sunday asked Thompson to marry him on New Year's Day 1888, and she agreed. Her mother approved of Sunday's Christian witness—he spoke at churches and Young Men's Christian Association (YMCA) clubs in cities his team visited—and encouraged the couple. Her father finally agreed to the marriage in June. Helen "Nell" Thompson and Billy Sunday were married in Thompson's home on September 9, 1888.

At first Billy Sunday followed the life of a ballplayer and Nell Sunday traveled with him. After a few months in Pittsburgh, they rented an apartment in Chicago. In January 1890, their daughter, Helen Edith, was born, and Nell Sunday no longer traveled with her husband. In the winter of 1890, Billy Sunday

FIG. 115. *A successful team, Helen Thompson Sunday organized the religious crusades and revivals of her husband, Billy Sunday.*

twentieth century, Nell Sunday alternated between spending time with her husband, as he held revivals in small towns throughout the Midwest, and with their growing family. Their second child, George Marquis, was born in 1892; William Ashley Jr. in 1901; and their last child, Paul Thompson, in 1907. Billy Sunday's popularity as an evangelist grew enormously, and he attracted large crowds for his preaching as well as much media attention. It became clear to him that he needed an organizer for his evangelistic campaign, and he began to ask Nell Sunday to take charge of the business side of the meetings. She finally gave in to his pleas for help, despite the considerable reluctance she felt about leaving her children for long stretches of time. The children were in the care of a trusted housekeeper, Nora Lynn, hired in 1910.

By the second decade of the twentieth century, Billy Sunday had acquired a national reputation. He was the star, the magnet of publicity; Nell Sunday was the administrator and the troubleshooter. They began to lead longer campaigns in large cities, culminating in New York in 1917 and Chicago in 1918. For each series of meetings the staff, working under Nell Sunday's close supervision, organized church support; held satellite meetings for youth, women, and other groups; arranged for the wooden temporary hall, called a "tabernacle," where the meetings were held; and took care of thousands of other chores in a campaign. This staff, which grew to about twenty-six at its peak, was called one of the most efficient and businesslike in America. Helen Sunday had brunette hair, dark eyes, and was about five feet, seven inches tall. A reporter wrote in 1913, "Mrs. Sunday is a homely woman in the truest sense of the old English word. Plain of face, comfortable of figure and characterized by a sympathetic smile and the kindest eyes in the world, her whole personality breathes quiet efficiency" (Frankenberg, 179). The Sundays were not innovators. They took the methodology with which they were familiar and reduced it to a system to organize the largest communities quickly for weeks of dramatic meetings.

Nell Sunday further refined the system, supervised their growing staff, and handled difficult problems of personnel and scheduling, including mix-ups when the leadership of Chicago had to be persuaded to change a scheduled date so that New York City could be accommodated. Nell Sunday, one of Billy Sunday's biographers wrote, "was hardheaded and hardworking, and she demanded as much from every member of the party as she gave herself. She could always be counted on to help out in any task, and she expected unquestioned obedience to her orders when she required some help. . . . They were all glad that she kept a more businesslike eye on the complex enterprise than her husband, but, while they gave obedience to her, they gave their affection to him" (McLoughlin, 77, 78). Although some of Sunday's evangelistic team called her "Ma," as Sunday himself did, most referred to her respectfully as "Mrs. Sunday." In 1915, when leftist journalist John Reed disregarded her orders not to interview her husband, he felt the rough side of Nell Sunday's tongue. "There was a rustle of skirts behind us and the nervous voice of Mrs. Sunday snapped, 'You villains! Didn't I tell you you couldn't see Billy? What have they been doing Billy—pumping you?' She went over to him, pulled up the covers, lifted his head, and turned over the pillow for him. 'Not a pump,' laughed Billy, 'they're just good-natured human beings

decided to leave baseball for a career in Christian evangelism. He joined the staff of the Chicago YMCA in March 1891.

The Sundays were part of the evolving conservative Protestant culture that would become known as fundamentalism in the early decades of the twentieth century. For fundamentalists, sin was personal and so was salvation; the most important decision of a person's life was to accept Jesus Christ as Savior, to enter into a personal relationship with Jesus through prayer and obedience to his Word in the Bible, on which the believer could rely absolutely. Believers were to testify to their faith and lead others to Christ, as Nell Sunday had been led by her Sunday school teacher. Along with many other Americans, the Sundays viewed with alarm tendencies in modern society such as liberal theological interpretations of the Bible. The Sundays were also unmoved by the Social Gospel movement, putting their reforming efforts into the national prohibition movement, among other efforts.

As Billy Sunday built an evangelistic ministry during the last decade of the nineteenth century and the first decade of the come to shake hands with me'" (Reed, 12). She also managed her husband, preserving his energies, guarding his time, and providing emotional encouragement. Billy Sunday himself acknowledged, "No man in this world ever owed more to his wife than I do. I doubt if anyone ever owed as much" (Nix, 264).

After the 1918 Chicago campaign, the Sundays started to hold campaigns in smaller cities before decreasing crowds. The crusading zeal found in such pre–World War I movements as the progressive movement, the prohibition movement, and the evangelistic campaigns of the Sundays and others seemed to go into sharp decline. Critics claimed that the time of mass evangelism was over, although they generally failed to notice that evangelistic campaigns continued to flourish in rural communities and among Protestant fundamentalists and Pentecostal congregations through the 1920s, 1930s, and 1940s. One of the reasons for the dwindling crowds at the Sundays' campaigns was that their reputation was tarnished by the wealth they acquired from the "love offerings" of their meetings, a standard practice of evangelists of the period.

At this time, personal problems became prominent in their lives. Their sons George and William both went through public divorces after exposure of marital infidelities. The death of their daughter Helen from pneumonia in 1932 was followed by George's apparent suicide in 1933. Nell Sunday believed the death of daughter Helen, always a loving support to her parents, affected her husband's health. He died in 1935 during a visit to Chicago.

"I was sixty-seven years old when Billy died and here I was starting kindergarten in a new life" (quoted in Overmyer, 15). Thus Sunday described her new career as speaker, fund-raiser, and national symbol of the fundamentalist movement. Never at a loss for speaking engagements, at the age of eighty-two she was still averaging six or seven appearances a month. Sunday served frequently as a board member of the Winona Lake (Indiana) Christian Assembly, probably the most influential of dozens of campgrounds around the country where conservative Christians could come for Bible study and preaching amid holiday surroundings. She was also a president of this assembly. When Youth for Christ (YFC) began holding its annual business meetings and conferences at Winona in 1944, Sunday became involved. The YFC officers—young men who included the soon to be famous evangelist Billy Graham—were prominent in the next generation of evangelical leaders. Sunday influenced most of them. She was also a formidable fund-raiser, spearheading drives for a variety of institutions. In recognition of Sunday's diverse skills, Bob Jones University, one of the citadels of fundamentalism, awarded her an honorary Doctorate of Divinity degree in 1940.

In Sunday's later years sorrows counterpointed her successes. Her remaining children died before her (William in 1938, Paul in 1944). Sunday's health began to deteriorate. She had a heart attack in 1948 and underwent cataract surgery on both eyes in 1954, but in each case she quickly returned to her responsibilities and was rarely at rest. Sunday wrote to a friend on April 11, 1950, "I'll be going home to Winona in a few days. Haven't been there since November—no one there only a dirty house so I'm not terribly anxious to get there" (Box 2, Ephemera of William Sunday).

When Nell Sunday was diagnosed with lung cancer in January 1957, she matter-of-factly informed friends of her impending demise and serenely accepted death a month later. Both of her funeral services, as she had wished, were partly evangelistic. The first was in Winona Lake, and the second was held, as Billy Sunday's had been, in the Moody Memorial Church, Chicago. She was buried with him and three of their children in Forest Home Cemetery, in Forest Park, Illinois, near her parents' graves. Helen Sunday's managerial talents and leadership were essential parts of her husband's evangelistic campaigns, which, in turn, were a significant influence on forming American fundamentalist culture. After his death, she continued as a symbol and leader of that culture.

Sources. The Papers of William Ashley and Helen Amelia Sunday are at the library of Grace College and Theological Seminary in Winona Lake, Indiana. Additional materials by and about the Sundays can be found in Ephemera of William Ashley Sunday in the Archives of the Billy Graham Center of Wheaton College in Wheaton, Illinois. A true expression of Sunday's voice can be found in *Ma Sunday Still Speaks* (1957), a transcript of her comments to John Marcus Hart about her life. Lee Thomas's *The Billy Sunday Story: The Life and Times of William Ashley Sunday, an Authorized Biography* (1961) is sprinkled throughout with quotes from the interviews he had with Helen Sunday. She was also the direct source for much of her personal data and opinions as found in William McLoughlin, *Billy Sunday Was His Real Name* (1955). The only book devoted to Helen Sunday is *Remarkable "Ma" Sunday, The Story of a Wonderful Life* (1957) by her friend Opal Cording Overmyer. All Billy Sunday biographies give significant attention to Helen Sunday. The two best are the most recent: Lyle Dorsett, *Billy Sunday and the Redemption of Urban America* (1991), is the most insightful biography on the Sundays' partnership and Helen Sunday's contribution to their joint work. See Roger Bruns, *Preacher: Billy Sunday and Big-Time American Evangelism* (1992), for a perceptive but less sympathetic view of the impact of Billy Sunday's (and to a lesser extent Helen Sunday's) work. See also Theodore Thomas Frankenberg, *The Spectacular Career of Billy Sunday, Famous Baseball Evangelist* (1913). John Reed wrote a contemporary account of Billy Sunday's evangelism team and Sunday's audience, "Back of Billy Sunday," in *Metropolitan New York*, May 1915. Preston Lamont Nix, "A Critical Analysis of the Organizational Methodology in Selected Evangelistic Campaigns of William Ashley (Billy) Sunday" (Ph.D. diss., Southwestern Baptist Theological Seminary, 1992), is the most detailed description of the system Helen Sunday refined and administered, although her contribution is explicitly dealt with only briefly.

ROBERT D. SHUSTER

SUNDSTROM, EBBA
February 26, 1896–January 5, 1963
CONDUCTOR, VIOLINIST

"By striving toward the highest standards of musicianship and character, surely the truly gifted and deserving young woman will find her niche in the orchestral world," wrote Ebba Sundstrom in a 1941 article entitled "Women as Conductors" (p. 757). Her recommendation was meant as a guide to young, aspiring musicians, but it could easily be interpreted as a description of her own career.

Ebba Sundstrom—concert violinist, teacher, and cofounder, concertmaster, and conductor of the Woman's Symphony Orchestra of Chicago (WSOC)—was born in Lindsborg,

Kansas, to Swedish Lutherans Carl Richard and Mathilda (Sandell) Sundstrom. She had one known sibling, a sister, whose married name was Mrs. Herbert W. Pendleton. Other than that, little is known about her early family life.

The biography of Ebba Sundstrom that appears in the program books of the Woman's Symphony Orchestra of Chicago describes her as "entirely a product of American musical training." American musical education was undergoing a patriotic renaissance after decades during which study in Europe was considered the only way a young musician could have any hope of a professional career. This new focus on quality American conservatory education opened the doors to many women who previously might not have been in a position, socially or financially, to study abroad.

Sundstrom began studying the violin at age seven, several years after starting piano lessons. She continued her education at Bethany College in Lindsborg, Kansas; Monmouth College in Monmouth, Illinois; and at the Minneapolis School of Music in Minneapolis, Minnesota. She received a Bachelor of Music degree from the Minneapolis Conservatory in 1917. Sundstrom also attended the Mozarteum in Salzburg, Austria, her one nod to de rigueur European musical education. At the Bush Conservatory in Chicago, she studied with Richard Czerwonky, head of the violin department and organizer of both the Bush Conservatory Symphony and the Woman's Symphony Orchestra.

It is uncertain what brought Sundstrom to Chicago—her desire to further her career in a larger city or her interest in attending and teaching at the Bush Conservatory. In any case, she arrived in Chicago shortly after she took her degree from the Minneapolis Conservatory in 1917 and stayed for the rest of her life. Sundstrom became an instructor of violin at Bush Conservatory in 1918, a post she held for fourteen years.

On September 4, 1920, Sundstrom was married in Minneapolis to Dr. Victor Theodore Nylander, a dentist and teacher of dentistry at the University of Minnesota. Nylander subsequently established his practice in Chicago and taught at the medical school at the University of Illinois. They had one son, Reinhold Fredrik Nylander, whose date of birth is unknown; he was a college student and a violist in the North Park College orchestra under his mother's baton in 1948–50.

Sundstrom began her performing career as a concert violinist. Her first Chicago performance on record was a Musicians Club of Women concert on March 31, 1919. She made her professional violin performance debut in Chicago at age twenty-five in 1921. Other than a few performances with the Musicians Club of Women and the Bush Conservatory of Music, she did not perform often on violin until the founding of the Woman's Symphony Orchestra of Chicago, although her program biography listed among her accomplishments solo performances with the Minneapolis and the Oklahoma City Symphony Orchestras.

Ebba Sundstrom was best known, as both violinist and conductor, for her work with the Woman's Symphony Orchestra of Chicago. The lack of performance opportunities, particularly in orchestras, for such highly talented, highly trained women as Sundstrom was widespread; it led, eventually, to the founding of nearly thirty professional and semiprofessional women's orches-

tras nationwide in the 1920s and 1930s. Part of the first wave of these orchestras, the WSOC was founded in 1925 in order to give "standard programs in which women could play" (WSOC program notes). Founder Marion Ochsner had tried unsuccessfully to start such an orchestra as early as 1920, but her efforts did not succeed until she joined forces with Richard Czerwonky and six Chicago women musicians, one of whom was Sundstrom. Their concert programs included primarily the standard orchestral repertoire, a necessity for any orchestra trying to prove worthiness of the "professional" label. The WSOC, however, was also committed to presenting the works of women composers, especially those from the Chicago area, such as CARRIE JACOBS-BOND, ELEANOR FREER, and FLORENCE PRICE. In 1934, support for the WSOC became an activity of the National Federation of Music Clubs.

The WSOC was dedicated to the vision of an entirely female orchestra. When possible, female soloists were featured. The orchestra was made up of about sixty players, a few of whom were men who played "essential" instruments for which no women performers could be found. Male players were listed in concert programs with first initials and last names instead of full names, as was the format for the women members. Czerwonky, Sundstrom's teacher, the orchestra's first conductor, and later, in 1930–31, president of the WSOC, led the orchestra in six programs at the Goodman Theater between 1926 and 1927 with the understanding that he would hold his job only "until a woman conductor might be found" (WSOC program notes). The final concert of the WSOC's first full season in 1926–27 featured a woman as guest conductor: Ethel Leginska, who had made a name for herself internationally as the conductor of the all-male Boston Philharmonic Orchestra and as a guest conductor with such orchestras as the New York Philharmonic, the Los Angeles Philharmonic, and the Berlin Philharmonic. Leginska was engaged for the second season, 1927–28, with Sundstrom, then the orchestra's concertmaster, as her assistant.

As assistant conductor, Sundstrom directed the opening concert of the orchestra's third season (1928–29), its first performance at the Eighth Street Theater, for which she received rave reviews. Leginska conducted three more concerts, all at Orchestra Hall. Sundstrom was hired as the permanent conductor for the following season and continued in this role until 1939.

Although the Woman's Symphony Orchestra of Chicago was one of a number of all-women orchestras in the country at the time, it was unique in several ways. At the time of its founding, it was the only fully professional orchestra of its kind. All members were paid, and most were members of the musician's union. It was also the first and only full-sized symphony orchestra for many years to feature a woman as its principal conductor.

Thus Sundstrom was the first woman in the country to hold a position as permanent conductor of a professional orchestra. Under Sundstrom's baton, the Woman's Symphony Orchestra appeared in eight seasons of regular concert series and tours, performances at the Century of Progress Exposition in Chicago in 1933 and 1934, and at the Grant Park Festival. The orchestra also performed a number of student soloist and benefit concerts for the Hull-House Music School.

The *History of the Musicians Club of Women* refers to Ebba Sundstrom as "the first woman conductor of a major symphony orchestra in this country" (p. 169). The ensemble was acclaimed as "The World's Greatest Women's Orchestra" in a concert program for a 1936 performance with the Lyric Male Chorus at the Auditorium Theater and was nationally known, thanks to a series of radio broadcasts in the 1930s (WSOC program notes). In addition to her directorship of the WSOC, Sundstrom also appeared as guest conductor with the Oklahoma City Symphony and twice with the Philadelphia Civic Orchestra, under the auspices of the Works Progress Administration's Federal Music Project.

Sundstrom took a leave of absence from the WSOC in its twelfth season, 1937–38, during which time Erno Rapee took the helm as guest conductor. Sundstrom never returned. Later reports suggested that she was asked to step down. After years of quarreling and backbiting between Sundstrom and the orchestra's board of directors, crowned by a deficit of thirty-five hundred dollars, Sundstrom departed under a cloud. GLADYS WELGE was named conductor in the orchestra's thirteenth season, 1938–39, but only for the first two concerts, after which Izler Solomon, later the conductor of the Indianapolis Symphony Orchestra, was appointed conductor. Welge, an orchestra member since 1925 and Sundstrom's assistant conductor since 1930, also departed. The Woman's Symphony Orchestra struggled through several more years with a number of conductors until gradually the performance opportunities and the funding began to dry up; it was dissolved in 1945. Most of the women's orchestras disappeared within a few years after the end of World War II. They had served their purpose; women were slowly being accepted into the professional orchestras that were formerly entirely male.

Following her tenure with the WSOC, Sundstrom remained active as a musician and most particularly as a teacher. She became director of her own chamber orchestra. Additionally, she held the position of professor of violin and director of the orchestra at North Park College from the fall of 1936 until 1951. By 1941 she was also on the faculty of Chicago's Cosmopolitan School of Music.

In addition to her extensive professional activities, Sundstrom was a member of the Lake View Musical Society, the Society of American Musicians (for which she served as a board member), the Chicago Artists' Association, and Mu Phi Music fraternity. She was also a member of the Chicago Musicians Club of Women from 1919 until her death in 1963 and served frequently in a variety of administrative positions. She became one of the organization's directors in 1929–30 and was later elected president, a post she held from 1934 to 1935. The Musicians Club of Women credited Sundstrom with the establishment of the Farwell awards in 1954. These awards, which continue to be given annually by the Musicians Club of Women, were created from a fund established under the will of Ava W. Farwell, a deceased club member. Sundstrom chaired the first Farwell awards committee, which established the format and rules governing the annual contests. In Ava Farwell's words, the awards were to "aid poor, worthy persons in obtaining a musical education, such persons to be selected and nominated by the Board of Directors of the Musicians Club of Women of Chicago" (Friedman, 35).

Unlike other officers of the Musicians Club of Women, who were financial donors or trustees of numerous organizations and institutions, Sundstrom's charitable contributions lay in her service as a musician. Sundstrom died in 1963 in Evanston, Illinois, one year after the death of her husband. One of the first women musicians to achieve professional status, Sundstrom helped open the door to women of subsequent generations who chose to make music their professional career. She presented a professional image, noting her achievements and awards rather than social activities or details of family life. In a rare autobiographical comment in her "Women as Conductors" article, she referred briefly to her "personal experiences . . . [as] a struggle and an up-hill path" (p. 757).

Sources. Other than Sundstrom's obituary in the *CT*, January 6, 1963, and records from Bush Conservatory and from North Park College, nearly all available information about Ebba Sundstrom is in archives about women orchestral musicians. By far the greatest repository of such information is the Helen Kotas archive at the CHS, which has a nearly complete run of programs of the Woman's Symphony Orchestra of Chicago (WSOC). The archive also includes a few newspaper clippings of concert reviews and a handful of programs for concerts in which Sundstrom conducted an ensemble other than the WSOC. The CHS also holds the Musicians Club of Women archives, which include annual membership lists and some concert programs for club events. The Alma Birmingham Papers at UIC Spec. Coll. feature a haphazardly arranged and documented scrapbook containing a great number of concert reviews. The NL is useful for periodicals, such as *Étude*, and *Who Is Who in Music 1941*, where Sundstrom's article, "Women as Conductors," appeared in 1941. Sundstrom is mentioned briefly in Christine Ammer, *Unsung: A History of Women in American Music* (1980), and Carol Neuls-Bates, "Women's Orchestras in the United States, 1925–45," in *Women in Music*, ed. Jane Bowers and Judith Tick (1986). See also Ruth Klauber Friedman, *History of the Musicians Club of Women* (1975).

ANNA-LISE PASCH

SUZUKI, IMAYO SUZUKI
March 18, 1900–May 17, 1979
RELIGIOUS LEADER, MISSIONARY

Imayo Suzuki, an Issei (first-generation Japanese American) woman, devoted her life to a religious mission for the Japanese American community in Chicago. She became the first official head minister of Tenrikyo in Chicago, a religion growing rapidly in Japan and abroad.

Imayo Suzuki was born in Hiroshima, Japan, the second of four children and the first of two daughters of Riemon and Hamayo (Suzuki) Suzuki. Her father was a wealthy landowner in Shinjo village and her mother a homemaker. The household had several servants. Because of her father's affluence and liberal attitude toward women's education, Suzuki attended school beyond grammar school level and became an elementary school teacher, one of the most privileged jobs open to women in Japan.

When she was eighteen years old, Suzuki married her cousin, Teiji Suzuki. Her husband's father, a successful business owner who had gone deeply in debt, moved with his wife to Portland, Oregon. They soon were successful in farming and called their son to take over the farm in 1918. Imayo Suzuki came to Portland to join her husband the next year, and her husband's parents returned to Japan. The Suzukis ran the farm together. They had three children, Louise (her Japanese name, Sadako) born in 1921, Helen (Toshiko) in 1923, and David (Masao) in 1930.

Suzuki first encountered Tenrikyo in 1927 at a church in Portland. Tenrikyo is the largest of the modern, popular religions that developed in mid-nineteenth century Japan. The religion is distinctive in its songs and ritual dances, with hand gestures that portray the teaching of God, and in its emphasis on pilgrimage to the city of Tenri, Nara, Japan. The church headquarters and its sacred site are at Tenri, along with other institutions of the religion including a university and hospitals. Tenrikyo came into existence in 1838 when Miki Nakayama, a housewife in Yamato (present-day Nara Prefecture), proclaimed herself the shrine of the God of Tenrikyo. Worshipped first as a goddess for safe childbirth, Nakayama soon began to heal the sick and reach out to the poor, preaching universal brotherhood and joyous life, the core teachings of Tenrikyo. Popular with commoners, especially peasants, but criticized by the government and Buddhist and Shinto groups, by the late 1880s Tenrikyo gained official recognition, and its missionaries began to open churches in Japan and later in Korea and China. Reflecting the flux of Japanese immigrants around the turn of the century, the first Tenrikyo church in the United States was established in San Francisco in 1927. By 1941 forty-two churches had opened on the West Coast, where the Japanese American population was concentrated.

Although the Suzukis began attending the Tenrikyo church in 1927, Imayo Suzuki's real commitment came in 1935. While visiting her parents in Hiroshima, Suzuki contracted spinal meningitis, which was diagnosed as incurable and untreatable. She was taken to the Tenrikyo church headquarters in Nara in a coma, where her illness was reportedly cured with no residual effects. Suzuki immediately joined the six-month missionary training course at the headquarter church to become fully initiated into the religion. After she returned to Portland, her husband also took the same training course in 1939, officially joining the religion.

With the enforcement of Japanese American evacuation in 1942 during World War II, 110,000 persons of Japanese descent were forced to move to relocation camps, and the growth of Tenrikyo in the United States temporarily stopped. The Suzuki family was taken to an assembly center in Portland and moved to the Minidoka relocation camp in Idaho, where they met other Tenrikyo members. Although they could not perform full services without adequate room and equipment in the camp, the Suzukis and other Tenrikyo followers continued to meet and pray together, reminding themselves of the importance of the joyous life that Tenrikyo teachings emphasized.

The Suzukis lost their property in Portland. In 1945, when the war ended, Imayo and Teiji Suzuki and their youngest son, David, came to Chicago, following their two daughters, who had moved to the city two years earlier for educational and vocational purposes. Beginning in June 1942, some camp residents were able to move to cities that were not on the West Coast. During and after World War II—from March 1943 through 1950—about thirty thousand Japanese Americans came to Chicago. Although almost half of them went back to the West Coast by 1960, nearly fifteen thousand persons of Japanese origin remained in Chicago. A few Japanese American institutions, including Buddhist temples and Christian churches, had existed in Chicago prior to the war, but modern religions such as Tenrikyo were not yet well established in the Midwest.

While working as a seamstress in Chicago, Imayo Suzuki joined with other relocated followers to spread Tenrikyo teachings. Since she did not speak much English, she looked for Japanese whom she could serve. In a manner similar to that in which the nineteenth-century Tenrikyo founder had spread the religion among Japanese peasants suffering famine and economic hardship, Suzuki visited hospitals and nursing homes to pray for the sick and old. She dressed in humble clothing, traveled extensively throughout the city, sometimes meeting rejection, but always willing to talk and pray with people. Refusing to ride, Suzuki walked wherever she went and was described by friends as a missionary who went on foot.

Many Japanese immigrants in Chicago found in the religion a means to preserve their community and culture while assimilating in other ways into the dominant culture. Most Issei resettlers felt helpless in the new environment and lacked facility in English. They welcomed Suzuki, who preached about Tenrikyo in Japanese. Some Japanese Americans, however, were prejudiced against the modern popular religion because the Japanese media often negatively portrayed its ritual dances and hand gestures.

For Tenrikyo followers, making a pilgrimage to the headquarter church in Tenri City, Japan, was one of the most important services. In 1950, when Imayo Suzuki made her pilgrimage and took a Head Minister Qualification course in Tenri City, her zeal and contribution to Tenrikyo were highly praised and the *shinbashira* (the head of the church) granted her permission to open the first official church in Chicago. Suzuki established the West Chicago Church on South Sawyer Avenue on August 25, 1950.

In 1956, Suzuki's husband finished his Head Minister Qualification course in Tenri City and was appointed head minister of the West Chicago Church. Although Tenrikyo doctrine emphasizes equality between men and women, and the religion has had many female ministers, men, often husbands, have conventionally taken over the position of a head minister when a church becomes well established. While the head minister is not only an administrator but also performs and instructs the ritual rites, women often maintain charismatic roles in Tenrikyo churches even after they hand the position over to men. Imayo Suzuki continued walking around the city to preach and pray for the sick and poor after her husband became head minister.

The West Chicago Church moved twice in 1957, first to Bell Street and then to North Clark Street. That same year, Suzuki's friends opened two more Tenrikyo churches in Chicago, the Illinois Church and Chicago Church, and Suzuki's West Chicago Church was renamed the Midwest Church.

In 1960 she was asked by the head of Tenrikyo mission headquarters in Japan to go to Washington, D.C., to help establish a Tenrikyo church there. "I was surprised when she accepted the request because she didn't know anyone in D.C. and she didn't even speak much English" (interview, June 1994), her son David recalled. Imayo Suzuki went back and forth to Washington, D.C., for a few years in order to spread Tenrikyo teachings and pray for the sick. Her missionary effort was later continued by other Tenrikyo members, and the Capitol Tenrikyo Church was established in 1975 as a branch of the Tenrikyo Midwest Church.

Imayo Suzuki became ill with lung cancer in early 1979 and died that year. Her funeral was held at the Tenrikyo Midwest Church. Tenrikyo officials recognized her devotion and contribution, which resulted in the opening of four churches in the United States, by keeping part of her ashes at the Tenrikyo Honjima Church, the church of the Tenrikyo Midwest Church in Japan; the rest were placed at Montrose Cemetery in Chicago. The Tenrikyo religion, which Suzuki introduced to so many Japanese immigrants in Chicago and Washington, D.C., provided them with a space to preserve their community and helped them survive in a foreign environment. The religion also formed a bridge for generations with different cultural experiences, as evidenced by Suzuki's son and daughter-in-law, both Nisei, who carry on the work of the Tenrikyo church that Suzuki established.

Sources. Much of the information on Imayo Suzuki and Tenrikyo churches in Chicago was based on interviews with David and Helen Suzuki, Imayo Suzuki's children, June 1994. Though not totally accurate on Suzuki's involvement with Tenrikyo, *50 Years of the Past: History of the Tenrikyo Mission Headquarters in America, 1934–1984* (Tenrikyo Mission Headquarters in America, 1984), kept at the West Chicago Tenrikyo Church, provides a history of Tenrikyo churches in Chicago as well as in the United States. Tenrikyo history and teachings are explained in literature published by Tenrikyo institutions, such as *Tenrikyo: A Pilgrimage Faith: The Structure and Meanings of a Modern Japanese Religion* (1982); *Tenrikyo: Teachings for the Joyous Life: Articles Printed in the Japan Times Prior to the 90th Anniversary of the Foundress* (Tenrikyo Overseas Mission Department, 1976); and *The Doctrine of Tenrikyo* (Headquarters of Tenrikyo Church, 1970). Suzuki is mentioned in the only comprehensive histories of Japanese Americans in Chicago: Ryoichi Fujii, *Chicago Nikkeijinshi* (History of Japanese Americans in Chicago) (1968); and Kazuo Ito, *Chicago Nikkei Hyakunenshi* (The one hundred years of Japanese Americans in Chicago) (1986). Masako Osako's "Japanese-Americans: Melting into the All-American Pot?" in *Ethnic Chicago*, ed. Peter d'A. Jones and Melvin G. Holli (1995), provides a general history of Japanese Americans in Chicago but does not mention religious life.

HIROMI MIZUNO

SWEET, ADA CELESTE
February 23, 1852–September 17, 1928
PENSION AGENT, SOCIAL REFORMER

Ada Celeste Sweet was born in Stockbridge, Wisconsin, the oldest of five children of Benjamin Jeffrey and Lovisa (Denslow) Sweet, both natives of upstate New York. Her father, who left his Wisconsin law practice to become a Union officer in the Civil War, lost the use of his right arm in 1862 in the battle of Perryville, Kentucky. Because of this disability, he served in the Veteran Reserve Corps and in 1864 took command of the military prison at Camp Douglas in Chicago. Ada, who attended St. Xavier Academy, run by the Sisters of Mercy, lived for a brief time at the camp. There her father achieved fame when he thwarted a planned attack on the camp by Confederate agents and sympathizers. His heroism won for him the rank of Brigadier General in 1865.

After the war, General Sweet brought his family to a farm in Lombard, about twenty miles west of Chicago, and opened a law practice. The Sweet family joined the local First Church of Christ. At about age fifteen, Ada became her father's assistant. She began by working in his law office as a copyist and later served as his chief clerk when he became United States Pension Agent for the Northern District of Illinois (1869) and then federal Supervisor of Internal Revenue for the State of Illinois (1871). She joined her father in Washington, D.C., in 1872, following his appointment as First Deputy Commissioner of Internal Revenue. Two years later, on January 1, 1874, he died of acute pneumonia at the age of forty-two and left a wife and five children without financial support. His youngest son, Benjamin, was only three; his oldest daughter, Ada, was then twenty-two.

Despite her youth, Ada Sweet assumed the care of her family, a responsibility that increased markedly four years later when her mother died. Ada's youngest sister, Winifred Sweet Black, who became a journalist (recognized widely by her pen name "Annie Laurie"), was brought up by Ada, eleven years her senior. In 1936, near the end of life, Black continued to believe that her sister was "the most interesting woman I ever knew" (Black, 36). "A beauty" to behold, according to Winifred Black, Ada was "tall and slender, exceedingly graceful" with "a smile that was like the sunrise on a June morning"; she was also "witty, highly intelligent, and . . . like nobody on earth" (Black, 36).

In 1874, following her father's unexpected death, Sweet felt the weight of her family's needs and did what she had to do to secure General Sweet's old job, United States pension agent in Chicago. Besides being a soldier's daughter, she believed herself fully qualified for the position. Three years later, when Illinois's four pension agencies were consolidated in the Chicago office, she stated that because of her past experience she was "intimately and practically acquainted with every part, down to the minutest detail, of the work of a Pension Office" (Sweet letter, May 10, 1877, National Archives). However, she was not yet wise to the ways of pension politics.

Sweet's first two years initiated her as nothing else had to the ways of work and politics in the Gilded Age. After a rough start as pension agent, involving a congressional investigation of the circumstances under which the previous incumbent transferred the agency to her, she learned quickly and well. Despite the rough-and-tumble nature of employment in one of the federal government's largest and politically sensitive bureaucracies, Sweet remained pension agent until 1885, during three Republican administrations, in what she proudly described as "the first position as disbursing officer ever given to a woman by the government of the United States" (Willard and Livermore, 702).

Since Sweet apparently left no diaries and few letters, it is difficult to know how she performed as pension agent. She stated in 1884 that she ran the office "on a strictly business basis, in no case appointing clerks for political reasons" (Rayne, 101).

She also said that she employed large numbers of women, especially those who had families to support, and placed them in good jobs. Each year she disbursed several million dollars. When her terms of office expired in 1878 and 1882, she successfully won reappointment despite attempts to replace her with veterans. Many politically prominent Illinoisans wrote on Sweet's behalf, mentioning her father's gallant Civil War service and the dependency of his young family, but they also spoke of her competence, devotion to duty, promptness, and "efforts to always do the right thing" (letter of support, March 8, 1882, National Archives).

Sweet's tenure as U.S. pension agent ended on September 30, 1885, following the 1884 election of a Democratic administration. However, she refused to be forced out of office by General John C. Black, the new commissioner of pensions, who contended that Sweet had kept the names of five hundred deceased pensioners on the books. By appealing directly to President Grover Cleveland, who had run on a civil service reform platform, she corrected the inaccurate charges and bought herself some time. Then, on September 5, 1885, once she had secured a management position in the New York branch of A. H. Andrews & Company, a Chicago-based furniture manufacturer, Sweet submitted her letter of resignation.

Sweet spent only a short time in New York. She returned to Chicago in 1886, following a trip to Europe, and became literary editor of the *Chicago Tribune* for almost two years. Here she unwittingly initiated the journalistic career of her sister, Winifred, by publishing a series of letters describing Winifred's misadventures as a budding actress in New York City and on tour. The enthusiastic response prompted Winifred to leave the theater and become a reporter on William Randolph Hearst's *San Francisco Examiner*.

Ada Sweet left full-time newspaper work in 1888, when she opened a claims office in the Commercial Bank Building on Dearborn Street. Until 1905 she continued her career as a private pension agent, conducting day-to-day affairs under the motto, "Despatch is the Soul of Business" (Sweet to Benjamin J. Harrison, March [n.d.] 1889, National Archives). At least once, in 1889, she attempted to regain the government position that she had held for eleven years; she was unsuccessful.

Sweet never married. Shortly after resigning in 1885, she publicly denied rumors that she had secretly wed. In a September 21 letter to the *Chicago Tribune*, she admitted being engaged only to business with "no time for matrimonial projects." She occasionally resided with friends but lived mostly with a brother or sister. In 1895 she and her brother rented a "simple and comfortable" apartment in Lake View, about three miles north of downtown. They still had their father's sword collection and "a library of 2,000 or 3,000 volumes" but, according to Sweet, they did not own "a single piece of upholstered furniture to invite moths and dust" (*Times Herald*, June 9, 1895). Sometime in the early 1900s, Sweet moved to Dearborn Street, where for a while she was closer to her claims office and where she remained until retiring to San Francisco in 1915.

Until she died in 1928, Sweet lived a full and purposeful life. Well-known in Chicago, she used her influence to improve local living conditions. In the fall of 1890, she presented the first police ambulance to the city, having raised money from friends and acquaintances to build and equip it. In early 1892, Sweet founded and served as first president of the Municipal Order League of Chicago, a society formed to clean up the city and ensure its healthfulness. Eager anticipation of the World's Columbian Exposition encouraged Chicagoans to support this effort.

Boosters and reformers alike wanted their city attractive and healthy for out-of-town visitors. Modeling the Municipal Order League after the Ladies' Health Protective Association in New York City, Sweet enlisted several neighborhood street-cleaning aid societies and, at a mass meeting in Central Music Hall on March 27, 1892, declared war on street cleaning by private contractors, who were ineffective and politically protected. On July 20, 1892, five days after the Chicago City Council passed an ordinance creating a new Department of Street Cleaning headed by a superintendent, the *Inter-Ocean* congratulated the league and Sweet, the organization's "prime mover."

The July 1892 ordinance did not completely abolish the contract system, but it was a major step in that direction. It also sought to deal with the difficult problem of garbage disposal, authorizing several new municipal incinerators. After visiting an incinerator, Sweet had stated publicly that Chicago should cremate its garbage and street sweepings. She, like other reformers in the 1890s, considered the burning of wastes at extremely high temperatures to be efficient, sanitary, scientific, and, therefore, the perfect disposal method. Chicagoans now believed that visitors to the exposition would find their city clean and orderly. Sweet told Elizabeth Cady Stanton, America's foremost woman's rights advocate, that public opinion in Chicago for a clean city was very strong.

Yet, despite fear that millions of summer visitors might provoke an outbreak of cholera or typhoid, Sweet and her colleagues could not sustain their success. She complained in August 1892 and subsequently that city inspectors were inattentive to areas outside the central business district. Several influential property owners eventually prevented the construction of incinerators in their neighborhoods. Such backslides disappointed league members and prompted them to direct more attention to a related reform, free public baths. Although Sweet fell short of demanding the ballot for women, she believed that sanitary improvements would occur only when citizens elected individuals who opposed the contract system and politically appointed inspectors. At the end of 1892, she told the Chicago Women's Club (changed to Chicago Woman's Club in October 1895) that she took pride in her municipal housekeeping, especially the City Council's seventy-five thousand dollar appropriation for incinerators, and in the start of the public bath system.

Sweet became a member of the Chicago Women's Club sometime in the late 1880s and stayed involved even while president of the Municipal Order League. Club minutes show that she regularly reported on the League's work and tried to entice club members to join it as well. In November 1892 Sweet was among the large majority of members who urged that the Columbian Exposition be kept open on Sundays; a year later, during the winter of the 1893 depression, she offered a resolution, which carried, begging owners and managers of dry-goods and department stores to retain as many young women employees as possible. In 1894 the six hundred members of the Chicago Women's Club elected Sweet president.

Under her leadership, the club's Protective Agency campaigned successfully for prison reforms affecting women and children. Police stations started hiring night matrons. The Women's Club also succeeded in having women and juveniles sent to stations separate from those handling men, and the chief of police began appointing club members to a Woman's Advisory Board to oversee the quarters of women, young people, and matrons. Finally, the chief matron obtained a place on the Police Trial Board to hear cases in which women brought charges of abuse against policemen.

Sweet's interest in local reform did not end in 1895, when she left the presidency of the Chicago Women's Club. In 1900–1901, as a columnist for the Hearst *Chicago American*, she advocated creating more public beaches along Lake Michigan, rebuilding dilapidated residences near the business district, and eliminating reeking smokestacks and chimneys. Sweet also urged prohibiting partisan appointments to state charities boards and opening more comfortable and convenient social clubs for Chicago's working young people.

A woman of many interests and talents, Sweet did not limit herself to her claims business. Besides contributing to newspapers and magazines, she became dean of the College of Women at Ruskin University in Glen Ellyn, Illinois, in 1903. A socialist institution founded in Ruskin, Tennessee, it offered courses in cooking, housekeeping, and domestic science to its female students. Sweet remained involved in this enterprise until it closed in 1905, the same year in which she ended her career as pension agent. From then until she retired in 1914, she was an editorial writer for the *Chicago Journal* (1906–1908) and the *National Civic Federation Review* (1909–10), and then manager of the newly organized Woman's Department in the Chicago office of the Equitable Life Assurance Society (1911–14). There she sold insurance to career women like herself.

Sweet was sixty-three years old when she joined her sister in San Francisco. Both served as directors of the San Francisco branch of the League of American Pen Women, and Sweet worked for a short time as an editorial writer for the *Santa Rosa Republican*. After a long illness, she died in a private sanitarium at the age of seventy-six.

On February 20, 1895, at a meeting of the Chicago Women's Club, Ada Sweet paraphrased Shakespeare's *Twelfth Night*, remarking "that some [women] were born great, some achieved greatness, and others had greatness thrust upon them" ("Minutes"). Indeed she belonged in the last category. At a very young age, she was forced by unfortunate circumstances to be strong and independent; one courageous step led to others, until she learned to take the lead. She became one of Chicago's earliest and most respected businesswomen and reformers, one who not only provided for herself and her siblings but also made Chicago a more liveable place.

Sources. Ada C. Sweet is an important but elusive figure. She appears to have left no unpublished papers or diaries. Material on Sweet's life can be found in public documents: Congressional Serials, U.S. House of Representatives, Committee on Reform in Civil Service, Summer 1876; Appointment Papers, Illinois Pension Agency, National Archives and Records Administration; as well as in "Minutes" of the Chicago Women's Club at the CHS. Biographical sketches exist in nineteenth-century sources: Mrs. M. L. Rayne, *What Can a Woman Do: Or, Her Position in the Business and Literary World* (1884); Eva Munson Smith, *Woman in Sacred Song* (1885); Frances E. Willard and Mary A. Livermore, *A Woman of the Century* (1893); and *Portrait and Biographical Record of Cook and DuPage Counties, Illinois* (1894). A personal description by her sister is in Winifred Black, "Rambles through My Memories," *Good Housekeeping*, February 1936. Not to be overlooked is an array of newspaper accounts in the *CT*, *Times Herald*, *Inter-Ocean*, *Chicago Journal*, and *Woman's Journal*. A few secondary sources mention Sweet. These include Bessie Louise Pierce, *A History of Chicago: The Rise of a Modern City, 1871–1893*, vol. 3 (1957), and Jeanne Madeline Weimann, *The Fair Women* (1982). In *Chasing Dirt: The American Pursuit of Cleanliness* (1995), Suellen Hoy devotes a section to Sweet's municipal housekeeping efforts. On the importance of municipal housekeeping, see Hoy, "'Municipal Housekeeping': The Role of Women in Improving Urban Sanitation Practices, 1880–1917," in *Pollution and Reform in American Cities, 1870–1930*, ed. Martin V. Melosi (1980); and Maureen Flanagan, "Gender and Urban Political Reform: The City Club and the Woman's City Club of Chicago in the Progressive Era," *American Historical Review*, October 1990. Two books are essential to understanding federal government work in the nineteenth century and the importance of the U.S. Pension Bureau in aiding Union veterans and their dependents: Cindy Sondik Aron, *Ladies and Gentlemen of the Civil Service: Middle-Class Workers in Victorian America* (1987), and Theda Skocpol, *Protecting Soldiers and Mothers: The Political Origins of Social Policy in the United States* (1992).

SUELLEN HOY

TALBOT, MARION
July 31, 1858–October 20, 1948
EDUCATIONAL REFORMER, UNIVERSITY ADMINISTRATOR,
HOME ECONOMIST

Marion Talbot, dean of women and guardian of women's interests at the University of Chicago (UC) during the school's first three decades, was born in Thurn, Switzerland, to American parents on a prolonged European tour. She was the eldest of six children—two of whom died in infancy—with a sister and two brothers. Her father, Israel Tisdale Talbot, was the dean of Boston University's School of Medicine. Her mother, Emily (Fairbanks) Talbot, had taught in Baltimore before she met her husband. Talbot attended Chauncy Hall School, a private boys' school that accepted a small number of girl students. Her mother, frustrated by the lack of college preparatory institutions for girls, led in the establishment of such an academy, the Boston Latin School for Girls.

Propelled by activist parents, Marion Talbot entered what became a lifelong connection with academia. She received an A.B. degree from Boston University in 1880 and an A.M. from the same institution in 1882. By 1888 she had earned an S.B. from Massachusetts Institute of Technology (MIT), where she worked under Ellen Richards, a central figure in the home economics movement that attempted to transform household management into a social science. Richards focused on sanitary or domestic science, an aspect of home economics that dealt with both family and community welfare. Sanitary science included the study of public health problems in an industrialized city as well as the use of scientific principles in running the household. In 1887 she and Talbot edited *Home Sanitation: A Manual for Housekeepers.*

During her years of graduate study, Talbot and other young women searched for ways to use their education to serve their communities. At her mother's suggestion, Talbot called a meeting in 1881 at MIT, where college-educated women might to-

gether consider their options. As a result, in January 1882, sixty-five women approved a constitution for the Association of Collegiate Alumnae, whose object was to organize alumnae of various institutions so that they could both support each other and lobby on behalf of women who entered academic institutions after them. Marion Talbot served the organization, which after 1921 became the American Association of University Women, first as secretary (1881–95), then as president (1895–97), and finally as an honorary member.

Despite the association and Richards's influence, Talbot's early post-degree years were somewhat undirected. She traveled abroad; lectured on home sanitation at Lasell Seminary (later Lasell College) in Auburndale, Massachusetts, between 1888 and 1891; and she instructed students in domestic science at Wellesley College in Massachusetts from 1890 to 1892. Talbot found herself an educated woman who had no vocation beyond the interest in sanitary science that she had developed in graduate study at MIT.

Meanwhile, events transpired that extended Talbot's geographical as well as intellectual reach. When Alice Freeman Palmer, former president of Wellesley College, accepted the position of dean of graduate women at the new University of Chicago in 1892, she named Marion Talbot as her assistant, and Talbot became dean of undergraduate women and assistant professor of sanitary science. Palmer, whose husband was a philosophy professor at Harvard, spent only three months each year in Chicago, but her commitments in Boston made even this limited stay a hardship. After three years Palmer withdrew, and Marion Talbot, as an associate professor, became the dean of women for the entire university. Talbot supervised all activities, both academic and social, involving women.

Talbot used her administrative experience in her research. In 1894, she and Ellen Richards wrote *Food as a Factor in Student Life,* a study of diet at the residences of women students. In

The Education of Women (1910), Talbot analyzed educational reactions to women's changing roles in society.

In her autobiography, *More than Lore*, and in many speeches, Talbot described a friend's present of a piece of Plymouth Rock upon her departure from Boston in 1892. This anecdote demonstrated the challenge that the Midwest and the new university represented for Talbot, who dated her New England heritage from 1636. Nonetheless, she transferred her geographical allegiance to the Midwest. Except for summers at a family home in Holderness, New Hampshire, Talbot resided in Chicago for the rest of her life.

Because of her family ties and university position, Talbot was included in Chicago's social scene and was soon a member of such elite organizations as the literary Fortnightly and the Chicago Woman's Club, which had a social reform orientation and an interest in education. One motive for Talbot's long-standing involvement in the city's women's organizations was to secure the financial and material aid of wealthy women for her students. When female students were housed temporarily in the Hotel Beatrice, Talbot solicited, through these groups, the cooperation of their members in furnishing the women's residences. In 1934 she deeded her perpetual membership in the Chicago Woman's Club to the university in order to keep institutional ties between the university and a group that was an important source of community interest and revenue.

One result of public interest in university women was scrutiny of their behavior. Talbot was determined that no lapses of female decorum give the administration an excuse to terminate women's welcome at UC. She fostered a way of house life in which women lived in separate halls and governed themselves under the supervision of a faculty member. She herself was the resident head of Green Hall, her home until she retired from the university. To preserve this democratic system of house life, Talbot opposed sororities and secret societies. The women's living arrangements were so admired by the university administration that eventually the house system was adopted for men's residence halls.

Talbot's interest in all aspects of women students' lives made her an autocrat to some observers, but she saw herself as "an old-time knight who draws his lance to defend a lady (in my case more than one!) and risking [*sic*] a mortal wound for the cause!" (Talbot to Harper, December 20, 1901, Presidents' Papers). Sometimes her lance was aimed at her own students. In one case that became a legal battle when Talbot accused student Esther Mercy of bad character based on evidence that included bill collectors' visits and expensive gifts from men. Mercy sued Talbot for one hundred thousand dollars. The Cook County Circuit Court awarded her twenty-five hundred dollars, but in 1912 the First District Appellate Court overturned the decision. Talbot saw that women's reputations were the foundation of their academic rights, and she set and enforced a strict code of behavior. She compromised, for example, when she allowed women to dance at parties held in their halls, because she believed a ban on dancing proposed by some faculty members would send students to music halls in the city. Talbot's construction of her job as the protector of young women who wanted a university education was acceptable to most of the students under her charge. The women's exemplary behavior freed them to pursue their ac-

ademic interests under the intense scrutiny of university administrators and critics of coeducation.

Shortly after the turn of the century, the number of women in higher education exploded and sparked a trend toward retrenchment in coeducational policies. At UC, the proportion of women undergraduates grew from 24 percent in 1892–93 to 52 percent in 1901–1902. Concerned about feminization of the university, President Harper in 1902 enacted a policy of academic gender segregation in the freshman and sophomore Junior College; the administration claimed that young men and women learned better apart. Marion Talbot adamantly registered her dissent from the policy and documented that the young women learned well in the integrated system and often collected more honors than their male classmates. Talbot was concerned that the public would not understand the policy and would believe that women were disruptive or academically inferior to men. The policy failed for structural reasons. Because the university charter prescribed equal opportunities for men and women, the segregated system had to offer men and women parallel classes. This duplication often was impossible. During the next decade the attempt at segregation faded, while the increasing proportion of men quelled fears that the university would become a female institution.

While preoccupied with the immediate challenge of guiding the integration of women into the university, Talbot sidelined her own academic interests. Because of an early shortage of funds, Harper placed Marion Talbot's courses on sanitation under the Department of Sociology with the understanding that a new department would be formed when money permitted. In 1904, when the Department of Household Administration was opened, Talbot was pleased but cautious; in the context of the Junior College segregation debate, she was concerned that graduate women might be sequestered in a female department. Instead, she envisioned a department that would attract both male and female students and would be as rigorous as the established social sciences. The new social science would investigate aspects of domestic life from boiling water to waste disposal and isolate the principles that made these activities more efficient. This project required a broad background; boiling water took the student into the field of chemistry, while analyzing waste disposal meant discussing municipal government. Thus, courses would be taught by chemists, political scientists, and economists. She believed that if women understood the scientific principles that are central to housekeeping, they could influence many aspects of modern industrial life, from wage laws to sanitation ordinances.

Talbot employed as her assistant SOPHONISBA BRECK-INRIDGE, who received a Ph.D. degree in political science in 1901 and a law degree in 1904, both from UC. Breckinridge taught in the Department of Household Administration until 1920. They collaborated on research, coauthoring *The Modern Household* in 1912, which argued that a woman needed to be educated to administer the complex institution that the home had become.

Since Talbot believed that most women students would become homemakers, she saw the need for educating them both to administer their homes and to become involved in social reform work in the community. As part of the students' education, in 1904 Talbot founded and led the Woman's Union, which brought to campus important women in the community who spoke on reform matters. Students volunteered at the University of Chicago Settlement, run by MARY McDOWELL, and at Hull-House, led by JANE ADDAMS.

In her position as dean, Talbot was concerned with the practice of racial segregation both within and outside the university. In 1907, when an African American student wished to live with white students in a women's residence hall, Talbot assigned Breckinridge to handle the matter, but the university policy for segregated housing remained in force. Talbot took a public stand on racial segregation when, in 1915, she wrote a letter to the *Chicago Herald* defending the decision of the principal of Wendell Phillips High School to allow an integrated dance and break the precedent of holding social activities for Euro-American and African American students on separate nights. Talbot was surprised by the hate mail that she received and wished to withdraw from the limelight. Although she did not like the treatment of African Americans, her energy was focused on women.

In the early 1900s, women came to hold power as consumers, and home economists saw that the vote could be used to extend household administration. In 1909 Talbot joined a group of women who addressed the Illinois House of Representatives. Her speech, "The Ballot for the Householder," advocated woman suffrage so that women could control the conditions of their work and become mothers fit to make citizens of their male children. Her views on suffrage grew from her theory of the household as a social unit from which women participated in community and political life.

Throughout her career, Talbot carried her teachings on sanitary science to women outside the academy. From June 1903 to May 1904, she conducted a section, "Home Economics," in the magazine *House Beautiful*. She wrote many of the articles and also engaged Breckinridge, Richards, and other colleagues to write on various aspects of home management and family life. A decade later, she brought the duality of home management and social reform to the general reader in her chapter, "Household Management," in *The Woman Citizen and the Home*. She pointed out that the home was "no longer an independent unit, but . . . a factor in the community life" (p. 3013). In buying clothing, the homemaker had to think of her "responsibility for the employment of children in the textile or knitting mills . . . and for the excessive fatigue from unduly long hours of girls in shops" (p. 3047). Talbot repeated the lesson she taught her students, that the homemaker needed to become involved in activities that would contribute to the "well-being of both home and community" (p. 3075).

She involved her students in community life during World War I. In April 1917 she established new courses on social service in wartime, conservation and production of food, and first aid. She urged women students "to support all agencies for social welfare . . . and to see to it that children be kept in school and the child labor laws not be broken down under the guise of the country's needs" (*More than Lore*, 206). For her own war service, Talbot provided information to the federal Department of Agriculture on food preservation.

Gradually, the household administration aspect of home economics lost the intellectual vigor of its early years. At some colleges where domestic science had become a popular topic, the subject was not characterized by the academic rigor and political activism charted by Talbot and other founders of the movement. At the University of Chicago, President Harper had seemed to grasp the potential importance of household administration; however, his successor, Harry Pratt Judson, supported the department because he believed that women were innately homemakers—in the traditional sense—and he was glad to see them separated into a "female" department. Despite such administrative diffidence, under Talbot's approach the university produced a generation of academically influential home economists. However, the Department of Household Administration did not survive Marion Talbot. In 1924, the year before her retirement, Household Administration was combined with the Department of Home Economics in the School of Education; the department, headed by KATHARINE BLUNT, had a strong graduate and research program to train professional home economists. The expanded home economics department was moved to the College of Arts, Literature and Science. The School of Social Service Administration, established in 1920, assumed some of the household administration course work.

In 1924, while her department was being disbanded, Talbot complained about discrimination against women faculty members in hiring and salary decisions and in slow promotions. As a result, the board of trustees promoted three women to full professor, Sophonisba Breckinridge, EDITH ABBOTT, and Katharine Blunt. Upon Talbot's retirement, no one succeeded her as dean of women. Her function was divided among women academics and administrators organized into a Women's University Council.

Intellectually active in retirement, she spent parts of the 1927–28 and 1931–32 academic years in Turkey as acting president and then president of Constantinople College for Women. In 1931 she and Lois Rosenberry published *The History of the American Association of University Women 1881–1931*, the organization she had helped found. Cornell College in Mount Vernon, Iowa, and Boston University in Massachusetts, her alma mater, had awarded Talbot LL.D. degrees in 1904 and 1924 respectively, and Tulane University, New Orleans, Louisiana, did so in 1935.

The friendship between Talbot and Breckinridge transcended their professional relations. They traveled together and summered at Talbot's cottage in Holderness. In 1941, the year before Breckinridge retired, Talbot added $1,125 to the Sophonisba Breckinridge Fellowship of the School of Social Service Administration "as a memorial of my rare friendship with her extending from the time of her matriculation in 1894 two years after I became a member of the faculty to the present." Talbot went on to summarize their life work. "During all these years we have devoted all our time and strength to the service of the University, helping each other by counsel and encouragement to put to the best possible use our rather wide social experience, our acknowledged scholarship in our respective fields, and our unusual administrative experience" (Talbot to the Comptroller, December 28, 1941, Talbot Papers).

Throughout her retirement years, Talbot maintained her

connection with the University of Chicago. In 1944 she wrote an open letter to Robert Maynard Hutchins in the *University of Chicago Magazine*, castigating the university's president for focusing the institution's endeavors on money-making and crass forms of enrichment. She remarked, "While writing thus frankly, I realize that I was put out of commission a good many years ago and have given you a grand opportunity to indulge in your pastime of wisecracking. I may be outmoded but I have not yet joined the seemingly popular group of rubber stampers, and I remember and cherish your exhortation that university training has the power and duty to make the use of the mind its highest aim" (p. 20).

Marion Talbot died at age ninety of chronic myocarditis and was buried in Chicago at Oak Woods Cemetery. A Unitarian by upbringing, Talbot hoped for a community of believers bound by lives of faith, not creeds. In a note found after she was buried, Talbot asked Breckinridge to see that her ashes were interred in the family plot with only a prayer and stated, "My hope is that I may live through my influence. I have no desire for any other kind of immortality" (n.d., Talbot Papers).

For thirty-three years she kept vigil over the course of women's education at the University of Chicago and oversaw the integration of female scholars into the academic community as students and faculty. While she fought for female students' rights and monitored their needs, she pursued the interests inspired by her own college and graduate training. Never marrying, Talbot worked to transform household management into a means by which homemakers could move beyond the home to influence politics and public issues.

Sources. The Marion Talbot Papers, personal and professional, are at UC Spec. Coll., where the Presidents' Papers 1889–1925 include her administrative correspondence. In addition to her books, mentioned above, Talbot revised *Home Sanitation* as *House Sanitation: A Manual for Housekeepers* (1912). Her major discussion, "Household Management," appeared in *The Woman Citizen and the Home* (1914), the twelfth and final volume of *The Woman Citizen's Library*, edited by Shailer Mathews. Besides her writings for the popular press, she published articles in such professional periodicals as the *American Journal of Sociology*. She published her autobiography, *More than Lore: Reminiscences of Marion Talbot* in 1936. Her "Open Letter to President R. M. Hutchins," critical of the university, appeared in *University of Chicago Magazine*, April 1944. A biographical essay appears in *NAW* (1971). Histories of women's education mention Talbot in different contexts. Rosalind Rosenberg's *Beyond Separate Spheres: Intellectual Roots of Modern Feminism* (1982) treats Talbot in the context of how university women defined sex differences. Barbara Miller Solomon's *In the Company of Educated Women: A History of Women and Higher Education in America* (1985) charts a generational history of college women and mentions Talbot both as a pioneer and as an influence on later generations of college women. In *Gender and Higher Education in the Progressive Era* (1990), Lynn D. Gordon uses the University of Chicago from 1892 to 1920 as the site of one of her case studies of Progressive Era student life and affords Marion Talbot a central role. Ellen Fitzgerald's *Endless Crusade: Women Social Scientists and Progressive Reform* (1990) places Talbot's achievements in the context of social science education. Alexandra Gillen, "From *Esprit de Corps* to *Joie de Vivre*," *Chicago History*, vol. 21, 1992, focuses on Talbot's role in the development of a woman's culture at the University of Chicago.

ALEXANDRA GILLEN

TALLEY, ISABELLA MAUDE GARNETT BUTLER. *See* GARNETT BUTLER TALLEY, ISABELLA MAUDE

TAYLOR, LEA DEMAREST
June 24, 1883–December 3, 1975
SETTLEMENT HOUSE HEAD RESIDENT, SOCIAL REFORMER

Lea Demarest Taylor, Chicago Commons Settlement House resident and director, devoted her life to numerous social reform issues, including race relations, housing, labor, and poverty. As the daughter of Graham Taylor, Chicago Commons founder and head resident from 1894 to 1921, she grew up at the settlement house in which the Taylor family lived. Following her father's example, she worked to make the settlement house movement a force for urban reform, particularly during the 1920s and 1930s. Unlike her father, she participated in the development of federally funded social welfare during the Great Depression and World War II years. Besides her family, her mentors and friends included JANE ADDAMS, HARRIET VITTUM, JULIA LATHROP, and MARY McDOWELL.

Married in 1873, Graham and Leah (Demarest) Taylor, the parents of Lea Demarest Taylor, represented a long line of ministers who had served the conservative Dutch Reformed Church in the eastern United States. Graham Taylor spent the seven years of his first pastorate in Hopewell Junction, New York, where daughter Helen Demarest (1876) and son Graham Romeyn Taylor (1880) were born. In 1880 he accepted the ministry of the Fourth Congregational Church of Hartford, Connecticut, where he greatly expanded his interest in and knowledge of urban working-class living conditions. The Taylor family circle became complete in Hartford with the birth of Lea Demarest (1883) and Katharine (1888).

Hoping to act upon the social welfare experience he had gained in Hartford, Graham Taylor accepted a professorship at the Congregational church's Chicago Theological Seminary in 1892. Inspired by the achievements of Jane Addams's Hull-House, he located a suitable building for his own settlement house on Chicago's Near Northwest Side, in a crowded port-of-entry neighborhood. The Chicago Commons Settlement opened in 1894. One year later, the entire Taylor family was residing there; Lea Taylor was then eleven years old.

At Chicago Commons the Taylors and the resident staff shared housekeeping, meals, and the hopeful excitement of the young settlement house movement. The visitors who streamed into the settlement from the neighborhood and the wider world acquainted Lea Taylor with rich and poor, native and immigrant, radical and conservative. Taylor played with the kindergarten children, helped with household chores, and attended the notable basement forum discussions in which leading thinkers of the day exercised the free speech denied them elsewhere. As the first resident settlement family in Chicago, the Taylors caused concern about their children's safety, voiced by many including Jane Addams, especially the threat of contagious disease. Lea Taylor later reflected on the role her mother played in this period. "My mother must have had many inner anxieties about our health, the unpredictable experiences we were having, and the financial outlook for the family and the settlement. No matter . . . she was always calm, always practical,

FIG. 116. *Lea Demarest Taylor, head resident at Chicago Commons Settlement and a civic leader concerned with housing and equal opportunity.*

and always aware of the need of the family for as normal a life as she could provide" (*Lea Demarest Taylor*, 20). The Taylors were the only family to remain completely in settlement house residence until their children reached adulthood.

Lea Taylor's education began inauspiciously at several Chicago public grammar schools that, in her opinion, taught her very little. When Lewis Institute (now Illinois Institute of Technology) opened, she enrolled and learned a great deal. Still she remained largely involved in what was happening at the settlement and did not join much in after-school social life. In 1899 the Chicago Commons Board of Directors formally elected her as a resident of Chicago Commons, in recognition of her "faithfulness, . . . sweetness of spirit, and . . . quiet doing of . . . duty" (*Lea Demarest Taylor*, 27–28). Residency required sharing household responsibilities and paying a weekly fee.

During these early years at Chicago Commons, Lea Taylor encountered issues of social welfare reform that she would take up as lifelong causes. She watched the Commons bring playgrounds to crowded nearby schools, and she felt a kinship to a bright African American student in her grammar school class. She witnessed her father's developing philosophy of Christian social reform during the Progressive Era, his method of practical community service, and his growing influence as national leader in the progressive reform movement. Graham Taylor informed the family members of his daily work and sought their counsel when making decisions that would affect them. Lea Taylor's mother devoted herself to support of her husband's work, taking responsibility for the family's welfare at home as well as participating in women's activities in the Congregational

church. Her mother's patience and steadfastness impressed Lea Taylor deeply. Yet it was the close relationship she and her siblings had with their father that ultimately shaped their professional lives in the fields of education, social welfare, and reform. The Taylors were bereft of Leah Demarest Taylor's motherly presence when she died of a lingering illness in 1918, but they continued to remain close throughout their own lives.

Matriculating at Vassar College in 1900, Lea Taylor continued her social group work activities with local children and also helped organize a club for dormitory maids. She graduated in 1904 and was elected to Phi Beta Kappa. Plunging immediately into the full range of the Commons work, she never pursued a graduate degree in social work. Looking back at her early yet varied social work experience, she explained, "This was my graduate education" (*Lea Demarest Taylor*, 34).

Also in 1900, Lea Taylor took over the work of her father's former secretary. She carried out his voluminous correspondence, managed his office at the Chicago School of Civics and Philanthropy, and handled Chicago Commons paperwork. With resident staff and neighborhood representatives, she served on the Chicago Commons Council, the settlement's fledgling democratic structure. As a staff member, she administered girls' work, particularly a club for working girls. She started a forum to train youth workers from other settlements. Out of this work grew her lifelong leadership in the organization of Chicago settlement houses, beginning with the Chicago Federation of Settlements (originally Association of Neighborhood Workers) and including such national supporting organizations as the National Federation of Settlements, the American Association of Social Workers (later the National Association of Social Workers), and the National Council of Social Workers. She promoted these organizations to further professional development and to create a powerful lobby for social welfare reform.

After 1910, Taylor began making careful studies of neighborhood problems, such as unemployment or malnutrition, and presented the data to skeptical legislators and reluctant philanthropists. She supported the striking workers in the 1910–11 garment workers strike and worked with such labor leaders as AGNES NESTOR, Mary McDowell, and MARGARET DREIER ROBINS in the Women's Trade Union League to improve women's working conditions and wages. Taylor helped prepare the 1913 study *Young Working Girls*, published by the National Federation of Settlements. She gave lifelong active support to labor issues.

In 1917 Lea Taylor was officially designated assistant head resident of Chicago Commons, responsible for administering the settlement and working closely with the board of directors. Challenged by U.S. entry into World War I, Chicago Commons served as headquarters for the local draft board. Taylor volunteered her services as draft board secretary and used the opportunity to collect an enormous amount of previously unavailable information about the local community, data that would inform her postwar work on issues of unemployment, health, and housing. When the Chicago Race Riot of 1919 erupted after the armistice, she studied the underlying causes through her brother Graham Romeyn Taylor, who was appointed by the governor of Illinois to the study commission that prepared the report *The Negro in Chicago*. Race relations continued as one of Taylor's primary concerns. During these busy years Taylor undertook the first of her trips abroad, attending international social work conferences and making visits to settlement houses throughout Europe to gather information and ideas.

The 1920s and 1930s were productive years for Lea Taylor. In 1921 she was elected head resident by the Chicago Commons board of directors, an acknowledgment in title of what she had been doing in effect for several years. Although retired, her father remained highly involved in Chicago Commons and in numerous progressive issues across the country. In 1934 Chicago Commons celebrated its fortieth anniversary. In *Chicago Commons through 40 Years*, Lea Taylor wrote movingly of how the Commons had tried to serve as advocate, forum, and example for its neighbors, even as the deepening depression made this task more difficult. Taylor had proved capable not just of leading Chicago Commons with its constant demand for revenue and staffing: she also provided quiet, principled leadership in the most critical issues facing Chicago and the nation: employment, race relations, child welfare, and housing.

Taylor pursued these issues primarily through her work in professional and social welfare associations: Chicago Federation of Settlements (president 1924–37); National Federation of Settlements (executive committee 1928, president 1930–34); Chicago Council of Social Agencies (delegate, board of directors, vice-president); National Council of Social Workers (division chair, executive committee); American Association of Social Workers (national council, vice-president). Taylor encouraged the Chicago Federation of Settlements to provide training and roundtables to settlement workers; nationally she

collaborated with the National Association for Study of Group Work. The Chicago Council of Social Agencies (predecessor of the Welfare Council of Metropolitan Chicago) prepared the way for Chicago's joint fund-raising methods. Taylor was a contributor to the Chicago Federation of Settlements study *The Financing of Social Agencies* (1924). When the Great Depression squeezed social welfare agencies, she suggested they look beyond private philanthropy to government funding. For example, she worked closely with the Works Progress Administration (WPA) in Chicago to employ WPA workers in settlement houses and to administer federal funds through the Chicago Council of Social Agencies. With Winifred Salisbury and Harriet E. Vittum, Taylor produced the study *The Administration and Activities of Chicago Settlements*. Taylor's articles, "Social Settlements" in the *Social Work Yearbook* (1934) and "The Future of Social Settlements" in *Social Action* (February 15, 1939) analyzed the philosophical and practical contributions settlements made to democratic life rather than the growing emphasis, within the field of social work, on individually oriented psychiatric casework. During this period Taylor also extended her professional involvement at the international level, attending several International Federation of Settlements conferences as well as visiting overseas settlement houses.

Chicago Commons's neighbors, mostly unskilled laborers, experienced unemployment for years before the 1929 stock market crash. Taylor (and other settlement workers with their ears to the ground) conducted neighborhood studies on unemployment and initiated a Conference on Unemployment in 1928. Taylor helped organize a Workers Committee on Unemployment based at Chicago Commons, which carried out demonstrations and confronted government officials. In 1931 Lea Taylor contributed to the National Federation of Settlements *Case Studies of Unemployment*, an attempt to alert the country to the situation via a moving description of the suffering endured by the unemployed and their families. Taylor also authored "Decent Standards of Relief" in the *Survey*, May 15, 1932, which roused social workers to demand adequate government funding levels. In Washington, D.C., she joined the National Federation of Settlements to lobby on Capitol Hill for labor legislation, and in Chicago she continued her work with the Women's Trade Union League. Her high profile produced numerous appointments to public policy-making bodies: the Illinois Governor's Unemployment Commission (1930); chair, the Cotton Dress Industry Wage Board (1931); the WPA Commission in Chicago; chair, Illinois Department of Labor Minimum Wage Division's Commission on Industrial Standards (1933); Cook County Consumer's Council (1934); WPA Chicago Leisure Time Services Project (1935–39); chair, WPA Personnel Standards and Jobs Analysis Commission (1937). A number of these commissions produced lengthy reports or oversaw programs affecting unemployment, working conditions and wages, and relief efforts.

The 1920s and 1930s saw widespread racial tension and discrimination, and Lea Taylor faced a number of challenges to her belief in racial equality. In 1929 the Chicago (and National) Federation of Settlements found that their African American members had been refused services at Chicago's Edgewater Beach Hotel; a similar situation arose at the 1934 National Council of Social Workers convention in Kansas City. The national organizations were unable to achieve accommodation and moved elsewhere. In Chicago, Taylor provided support as a board member of the Wendell Phillips settlement and promoted the Hayes School Social Center, both located on the West Side, an area of the city in which southern black migrants had sought housing. Under her leadership, Chicago Commons countered local white neighbors' opposition in order to offer integrated camping and club activities for all ages. To achieve citywide changes she joined activist Homer Jack's volunteer organization, the Council Against Discrimination.

Closely related to Lea Taylor's work in race relations was her long association with housing issues. The Commons had always collected data on neighborhood housing conditions and tried to encourage city code enforcement. As a member of the Woman's City Club board of directors, Taylor brought her experience in housing problems to a group with citywide impact when she served on the Housing and Zoning Committee. In 1934 she became the first woman to be appointed to the Metropolitan Housing and Planning Council, a group that would greatly influence the pattern of urban development for the next half century. When federal funds made public housing possible in the 1930s, Taylor advocated an open housing policy and resident support services. In 1937 she was appointed to the Chicago Housing Authority's Tenant Selection Committee and steadily supported those issues.

Providing adequate recreational facilities in a crowded urban environment had always been a concern of Chicago Commons, and Taylor continued her work in this area at the city level. In 1926 reform Mayor William Dever appointed her to the Chicago Recreation Commission, and a few years later the Chicago Board of Education selected her to serve on the Advisory Council on Schools and the Prevention of Juvenile Delinquency. Rising unemployment in the late 1920s meant more youths on the streets, even as the Great Depression shrank resources at schools and parks. Taylor's article "Cultural and Recreational Needs of the Average Citizen" (*Social Work*, October 1928), examined popular culture's destructive effects on the well-being of young people and family life. As a member of the Chicago Recreation Commission's Committee on Wider Use of the Schools, Taylor lobbied steadily, with some success, for schools to remain open after classes for sports and group activities. Many of her hopes for a comprehensive recreation program were realized when the Chicago Recreation Commission collaborated with the WPA City Wide Recreation Project in 1937.

In spite of Graham Taylor's ministry and professorship within the Congregational church, Chicago Commons always remained nonsectarian. The Taylors practiced a devout but quiet faith that consistently undergirded their work and lives. In 1933 Lea Taylor linked her faith to her social welfare concerns through the Congregational church's Council for Social Action and, soon after, the Congregation and Christian Conference of the Illinois Commission on Social Relations. Taylor worked to magnify the church's message on social welfare and civil rights issues, both to church members and to the nation as a whole.

When World War II began, Lea Taylor and the Chicago Commons had gained strength from two decades of struggle. Besides insuring that the Commons continued to offer services needed by the community in wartime, Taylor accepted (reluctantly) a civil defense post and served on the citywide Civil De-

fense Child Care Committee. She persisted with her Congregational church work and wrote "The Home Front," *Church Woman*, November 1940, to sustain members' faith and work. With "Building the Basis for Democratic Living," *Chicago Union Teacher*, December 1940, and "Hazards to Children," *Chicago Union Teacher*, June 1943, Taylor reminded educators that hunger and unemployment would thwart children's growth as good citizens. Chicago Commons celebrated its fiftieth anniversary in 1944, under war's shadow but without its founder. Graham Taylor had died in 1938, confident in the knowledge that his daughter had carried his work forward in her quiet, steadfast, effective way. As soon as the war ended in 1945, Lea Taylor foresaw that urban renewal and expressway construction would claim the Chicago Commons neighborhood. She encouraged the Commons to begin dialogue with Emerson House Settlement one mile to the west, and in 1948 a merger was forged that would eventually encompass a number of settlement houses throughout Chicago. With the Commons future now bright, she looked forward to retirement.

Characteristically, Lea Taylor had also prepared for the social changes that World War II brought to the neighborhood, city, and nation. In particular, she supported the Commons board of directors as it reaffirmed its policy of a racially integrated staff and activities open to all, in spite of strong opposition from local white residents. The extreme postwar housing shortage tempted unscrupulous absentee landlords to subdivide and overcrowd apartment buildings. They charged exorbitant rent to African Americans closed out of the white housing market. Taylor patiently worked both to enforce city building codes and to build racial tolerance toward the new tenants. When irate whites torched apartments housing African Americans, Taylor sat on the Cook County Coroner's jury that determined arson in the case, and she arranged for police to protect remaining African American residents. To further civil rights in the city as a whole, she joined Earl B. Dickerson's Council for Social Legislation (1940). Besides her other committees and boards, Taylor was appointed to the Metropolitan Housing and Planning Council's Committee on Race Relations (1946) and the Chicago Commission on Human Relations (1948, as Housing Committee chair), and she helped to organize a conference on civil rights and social welfare (1949). As Chicago's racial strife worsened, Taylor served on the Citizens Committee to Fight Slums (1950), the Chicago Recreation Commission's Committee on Housing (1946–57), and the Council Against Discrimination. She continued work on the Metropolitan Housing and Planning Commission until her eighty-fourth year. Concurrently, Taylor supported racial equality and civil rights through the numerous professional memberships and through the Congregational church's Council for Social Action (Committee on Minority Groups). In "My Faith and My Neighbors," *Christian Century*, May 7, 1952, Taylor recounted how steadfast faith and patient perseverance could remove mountains of prejudice through quiet example and careful listening.

Taylor persistently worked to expand school social centers for after-school recreation. In 1941 the Chicago Recreation Commission's Committee on Wider Use of the Schools saw four schools open for evening activities; ten years later Lea Taylor watched Illinois Governor Adlai Stevenson sign the Lighted

School House Bill into law. In 1948 Taylor worked to promote better human relations through the Save Our Schools Intercultural Relations Program.

After war had lowered unemployment, peacetime led to economic and social dislocations, all duly noted by Lea Taylor through Chicago Commons's careful data gathering. Taylor now focused on improving the use of volunteers by social welfare agencies, and she served on the Council of Social Agencies Committee to Determine Eligibility to Use Volunteer Bureaus (1942). Peacetime also made possible lengthy travel to Europe in 1951 and 1952.

In 1954, having spent most of her seventy years in settlement house leadership, Lea Taylor celebrated Chicago Commons's sixtieth anniversary and assumed the title Head Resident Emeritus. In tribute to her life's work, the Welfare Council of Metropolitan Chicago held an honorary program, with a special exhibit at the Chicago Public Library. Taylor nevertheless remained on the Commons board of directors, while the reorganized Chicago Commons Association continued at Emerson House under the capable leadership of director William Brueckner. The Chicago Commons Settlement building was sold to another social service agency, and Lea Taylor moved to Highland Park, Illinois, a suburb north of Chicago. The same year Taylor wrote "The Social Settlement and Civic Responsibility: The Life Work of Mary McDowell and Graham Taylor," *Social Service Review*, March 1954, a thoughtful retrospective; in "The Sense of Belonging," *Unity*, March–April 1955, she further described the unique contribution settlement houses could make to community life.

By the 1970s, settlement houses had metamorphosed into a new kind of social service agency, staffed by professional social workers trained to practice casework and largely supported by federal poverty program money. Community organizer Saul Alinsky had widely introduced his brand of confrontational activism, and many settlement workers had turned away from Graham Taylor's method of reasoned discussion. In 1962, the Welfare Council of Metropolitan Chicago's Chicago Housing Authority Advisory Committee on Health and Welfare had been disbanded, because the city of Chicago refused to acknowledge that public housing tenants needed the array of social services long advocated by Lea Taylor. Yet Taylor's own style of patient advocacy and practical collaboration still made her welcome where social welfare policy was created: the Chicago Recreation Commission's Committee on Public Housing (1961); the Metropolitan Housing and Planning Council (honorary board member, 1969); and many local and national professional associations. After settling in Highland Park's woodsy Ravinia neighborhood, Taylor quickly joined with civil rights and social welfare activists there—the League of Women Voters, the Highland Park Committee on Human Relations, and a B'nai B'rith special human relations project—and she enthusiastically entered the civil rights struggles of the 1960s and 1970s. Twenty-five years after the Great Depression had ended, she could castigate Illinois legislators for cutting welfare allowances. At the age of seventy-seven she traveled with family members to Europe, still seeking knowledge about the settlement house movement with which she had grown up.

During her lifetime Lea Taylor's quiet, selfless leadership brought her many awards. Among these were the 1948 Chicago Commission on Human Relations Award, the 1953 Rockford College Jane Addams Award for Distinguished Service, the 1954 Illinois Welfare Association Award for Meritorious Service, the 1960 National Federation of Settlements Distinguished Achievements Award, and the 1965 Hull House Achievement Award. Taylor was named lifetime honorary president of the National Federation of Settlements, honorary director of the Chicago Commons Association, and honorary board member of the Metropolitan Housing and Planning Council (1967).

Lea Taylor had never married nor had a family, but she maintained a lifelong closeness to her three siblings and their families through regular correspondence, frequent visits, and shared travel and vacations. During her last year of life she moved to her parents' home state of New Jersey. She died there near her family at the age of ninety-two.

The effect of Lea Demarest Taylor's life and work upon the social and physical fabric of Chicago is difficult to assess, for she stood for many years in the shadow of her more famous, more vocal father. Yet her work touched critical social welfare and civil rights reform issues in Chicago, with subtle persistence, consistency, and a concreteness rarely seen in reformers. Through the Progressive Era, the isolationist, conservative 1920s, the New Deal, the Eisenhower years, and the War on Poverty, she continued to listen to her neighbors and to promote humane living conditions for all. If her quiet, steadfast voice was not followed, it was certainly respected. Wrote a colleague: "It is you [Lea Taylor] who sets the standard for us all" (D. Ruble to Lea Taylor, January 31, 1974, Lea D. Taylor Papers).

Sources. Researchers will find the bulk of Lea Demarest Taylor's personal papers at CHS. They comprise more than two dozen boxes of correspondence, organizational papers, speeches, and other writings. Mostly the papers reflect Taylor's membership in organizations that focused on issues of unemployment, civil rights, child welfare, social work education, housing, health, and recreation. A separate collection of Chicago Commons Papers at CHS richly documents Lea Taylor's relationship to the Commons board, staff, and community as well as to other organizations and to her father. A second collection of Lea D. Taylor Papers is found at UIC Spec. Coll. These materials include minutes and other organizational items relating to the Chicago Federation of Settlements (later the Chicago Federation of Settlements and Neighborhood Centers) as well as some of Lea Taylor's own speeches and writings. A few items of correspondence involving Lea D. Taylor may be found in the Jane Addams Memorial Collection, UIC Spec. Coll. Some correspondence involving her father and siblings is located in the Graham Taylor Papers at the NL. An autobiographical tape recording of Lea D. Taylor was transcribed in 1969 by the Training Center of the National Federation of Settlements, Chicago, under the direction of Arthur Hillman. The transcription was published under the title *Lea Demarest Taylor: Her Life and Work between 1883 and 1968*; University Library, UIC has a bound copy. Graham Taylor's autobiography, *Pioneering on Social Frontiers* (1930) provides few candid glimpses of the Taylor family, although its detailed narrative is lively. See also his *Chicago Commons through Forty Years* (1934). Louise C. Wade, *Graham Taylor: Pioneer for Social Justice* (1964), gives a more complete and objective view but assigns Lea Taylor a minor part. No complete history of Chicago's reform movements in labor, civil rights, or social welfare could omit Lea Taylor. Those works that focus on the settlement movement itself during her leadership include Louise C. Wade, "The Heritage from Chicago's Early Settlement Houses," *Journal of the Illinois State Historical Society*, Winter 1967, which places the Commons within Chicago's flourishing settlement community through pioneering reform days, repressive 1920s, lean depression years, and confrontational 1960s. Allen F. Davis, *Spearheads for Reform: The Social Settlements and the Progressive Movement, 1899–1904* (1964), and Mina Carlson, *Settlement Folk: Social Thought and the American Settlement Movement* (1990), expand to a national viewpoint and show how Taylor and her colleagues struggled to influence national policy. Judith Ann Trolander, *Settlement Houses and the Great Depression* (1975), focuses on the 1930s to analyze how settlement leaders such as Lea Taylor were challenged by the development of community chest funding. Another work by Trolander, *Professionalism and Social Change: From the Settlement House Movement to Neighborhood Centers, 1886 to the Present* (1987), carries the analysis forward with an examination of confrontational community organizing and interracial relationships during the War on Poverty years. Elizabeth Lasch-Quinn, in *Black Neighbors: Race and the Limits of Reform in the American Settlement House Movement, 1890–1945* (1993), provides a look at the history of settlements in the African American communities of the United States and their relationship to white, nonsectarian settlements and professional organizations. Finally, the failure of Chicago settlements to uphold and practice racial integration from earliest days is scathingly pictured in *The Slum and the Ghetto* by Thomas Lee Philpott (1991) and is also discussed in Arnold R. Hirsch's *Making the Second Ghetto: Race and Housing in Chicago, 1940–1960* (1983). See also "Commons' Lea Taylor Honored," *Welfare Briefs*, Fall 1954; "Chicago Honors Lea Taylor," *Social Service Review*, March 1955; and Ray Gibbons, "Three Decades of Social Witness," *Social Action*, December 1968.

JEANIE F. CHILD

THECLA, JULIA
February 28, 1896–June 29, 1973
ARTIST

Julia Thecla Connell was born in Delavan, Illinois. Her mother, Julia Anne (Fitzpatrick) Connell, was Irish, and her father, James Gleason Connell, was Scottish. Connell was the youngest of their four daughters; she had one younger brother. She dropped the use of her surname sometime in the 1920s and took to using her middle name.

Thecla enjoyed weaving a field of mystery about herself and often told friends contradictory stories, making it difficult to determine what was correct. Thecla at times claimed to have a great-grandfather who was an Eskimo, but there is no supporting evidence. She told one person that the name Thecla was given to her by a devout cousin, who as a nun became Sister Thecla. She told another that it was her paternal aunt and godmother who was the nun. She told both that she had always liked the stories associated with Thecla, an early Christian saint and martyr who miraculously escaped many perils.

Thecla learned to read and write at the age of three and also began to display her artistic talents, making crayon drawings and clay animals. She told a story that one day a peddler came through town with terra-cotta figurines and that she had been inspired by a figure of Buddha and decided to make one from the clay of a nearby cave. Thecla was a shy child but reportedly liked the attention that her creativity brought her. She won first prize in drawing at age twelve in Tazewell County, Illinois. Thecla took her first art lesson at fifteen, paying her own way with money she had earned at a part-time office job.

Thecla graduated from Delavan High School in 1913, then studied at Illinois State Normal University, Normal, for the summer. For a time she taught first through seventh grades in a Tazewell County rural school. In the 1920s the nation was going through many changes; women became more independent and a new generation of feminists asserted influence and carved identities that rebelled against the maternalist image of the pre–World War I woman reformer and suffragist. The flapper became the symbol of that decade and of freedom from traditional women's roles. Thecla took advantage of this shift in attitudes and moved to Chicago around this time. She found an art community experimenting with new forms of expression. Thecla began to pursue her love of art and enrolled in classes at the School of the Art Institute of Chicago. She listed among her professors LAURA VAN PAPPELENDAM, who was a member of the Chicago Society of Artists, a group that Thecla later joined. Julia Thecla told a friend and fellow artist that her teachers argued that she must consider the whole human figure first and let it develop slowly, but she refused, saying, "I always drew the eyes and eyelashes first!" (Parker Panttila, "Julia Thecla," in McKenna, 32–33). Thecla interrupted her schooling to work, attending art school overall for about two years. She also took traditional college courses, mostly in poetry. Poetry was a private passion for Thecla over the years. She so valued her privacy that she chose not to publish her poetry, explaining, "In painting you can often disguise what you mean, but not in poetry" (Ford, "Artist Thecla Reluctantly Tells Her life"). The only poem Thecla allowed to be published appeared in the *Chicago Daily News* as part of an article by art critic C. J. Bulliet.

Julia Thecla supported herself at times as an industrial artist in factory design and decoration work, by doing secretarial and clerical work, and by art restoration. Her skill in crafting finely detailed paintings was credited to the small detail work she did in art restoration. C. J. Bulliet said that she had a rare mind for an art restorer, for she was able to create beautiful things on her own when she picked up a paintbrush. Thecla was raised Catholic in a home where religion was not questioned. After spending two years restoring a series of religious works, her adult mind first began to explore the discrepancies she saw, and in later years she considered herself an atheist.

Thecla's career as a painter began with her first exhibit in 1931 in the Art Institute's International Watercolor Exhibition. In the following years Thecla's paintings were frequently included in these exhibitions. In 1932 Thecla's work was part of Chicago's first outdoor art fair in Grant Park. The country was in the midst of the Great Depression, and overall sales were not high; but the artists enjoyed the camaraderie as well as the opportunity to be outdoors. Thecla was also represented in the exhibition at the Art Institute of Chicago held in conjunction with the World's Fair of 1934. The Albert Roullier Galleries exhibited Thecla's work in her first one-artist exhibition in 1937. Other galleries at which her work was shown included the Findlay Galleries, Katharine Kuh Gallery, and Mandel Brothers Gallery, all of Chicago, and the David Porter Gallery, Washington, D.C. Thecla's work was shown nationwide beginning with the Museum of Modern Art, New York City, in 1943. Other exhibitors included the Newark Museum, Newark, New Jersey; the Metropolitan Museum of Art, New York City; Philbrook Art Center, Tulsa, Oklahoma; Carnegie Institute, Pittsburgh, Pennsylvania; the University of Illinois, Urbana, Illinois; Norfolk Museum, Norfolk, Virginia; and the San Francisco Museum of Art, San Francisco, California.

The Federal Art Project of the Works Progress Administration (FAP/WPA) began in August 1935 under President Franklin Delano Roosevelt's social and economic reforms. The FAP marked the beginning of the government's involvement as a patron of the arts. As the country was in the midst of the Great Depression, art was a luxury that most could not afford. That left artists who were already accustomed to small incomes with next to nothing. This program guaranteed them money every month, providing some of them with a new experience: being paid for their art. Along with the income they were guaranteed an audience for their work. Artwork created through the project made its way to public schools, hospitals and other government buildings. During 1936 alone, more than six thousand institutions received art through the project.

Artists worked on a salary and were placed into divisions based on the type of work they did. Thecla was employed by the WPA from 1938 through 1942 in the easel division, although typically she laid her canvas on a horizontal surface and worked directly over it. According to friends she was pleased to have the freedom to paint full-time while receiving checks, and she even used models during this period. Maureen McKenna speculates that in her work for the WPA, Thecla tamed down her images so as to be more acceptable to the administration, but she nonetheless retained her use of fantasy images.

In her 1984 catalog of Thecla's work, author Maureen A. McKenna included essays by some of Thecla's contemporaries. Their musings about Julia Thecla offered insight into her personal life. Thecla was described as a very private person who would not even tell friends such facts as her real last name. However, she was also thought of as fun to be with, warm, sensitive, loyal, and spontaneous. Art curator and gallery owner Katharine Kuh was the only Chicago gallery owner who consistently showed modern art such as Thecla's. Thecla's appearance made an impression on those around her, as many friends remembered specific outfits she liked to wear. Kuh remembered Thecla as having an unusual style of dress, and wearing "layers of ungainly clothes" (Kuh, "Tea with Julia," in McKenna, 28). David Porter, Chicago painter and sculptor, remembered her wearing "tiny vests, quilted skirts with tight waistbands and flaring hems, and high button shoes" (Porter, "A Valentine for Julia," in McKenna, 29) or "suitlike but very feminine combinations such as a velvet skirt embroidered in tiny flowers with a puff sleeved bolero jacket. She wore doll-like shoes with a strap across the instep and milk-toned silk stockings" (Porter in McKenna, 32). Thecla was also fond of wearing a hat, whether it was a flat brimmed straw hat or a felt hat tied with a ribbon under the chin. The combined effect of her outfits and her five-foot frame gave an undeniably delicate, feminine look that was often described as childlike. Kuh guessed that the layering of clothes served to protect Thecla from the world and protect the privacy she cherished. Thecla's art was her way of reaching out to the world, but she did not like to discuss her work or the inspiration behind it. While Julia Thecla was remembered as a very private, quiet person, she was also very social and told former *Chicago Tribune* reporter Phyllis Ford-Choyke in 1943 that she did not work as much as she should because she liked to go to parties.

For many years Julia Thecla lived and worked in a little studio on Chicago's Near North Side. Those who were invited to visit described it as sparsely furnished, barren, like a nun's cell. Many remembered the unusual wooden desk with many cubbyholes that she used as storage for her art supplies. She used ornate Victorian coffee cups to serve a guest tea or whiskey. Thecla was known to keep unusual pets—a chicken, rabbits, cats and pigeons—that she kept on the windowsill.

In June 1969 Thecla was forced to move from her longtime residence due to renovation, and in the ensuing move her poems were lost. Thecla told Ford-Choyke during a visit that she felt she had made a great mistake by not finding a new place to live when she was told that her studio was to be torn down. She described her method for handling problems: "I used to curl up and go to sleep hoping when I woke up they'd have disappeared. This one didn't" (quoted in Ford-Choyke, "On Julia Thecla," in McKenna, 36). Finding herself without a home, Thecla spent some time with a sister, then was forced to move into a public welfare home. Thecla was moved to several other publicly funded facilities in the next two years. In early 1971 she was moved to the Sacred Heart Home of Chicago, which was to be her last residence. She was disturbed not to have her own belongings and said she was unable to paint, although several friends who learned of her situation sent her supplies or monetary donations. There were contrasting reports on whether her eyesight was failing at this time.

Critics have described Thecla's work as jewel-like, mystical, enchanted, and having a Victorian flavor. Thecla almost exclusively uses the female image, and frequently herself, as the subject of her work. The faces she paints are often close-up, dominating the painting, showing an unfocused stare. Thecla repeatedly creates an image of a subject who is quite alone and seemingly introspective. The subjects in her work, often a young girl or a girlish woman, seem unaware of the viewer. Critics have speculated that Thecla saw herself as a young girl, but based upon how she is remembered by friends, that is how the world saw her too.

A 1994 exhibit at the Illinois Art Gallery, *The "New Woman" in Chicago, 1910–1945: Paintings from Illinois Collections* included Thecla's work. Curator Susan S. Weininger notices that many paintings in this exhibit, including Thecla's, have an inward focus. She attributes this focus to the marginalization of the woman artist, who would tend to see the world differently and therefore not be interested in modeling her work on the male standard.

In Thecla's early work, small details abound. McKenna writes, of *Self Portrait* (1936), "The composition is so full it seems ready to spill out beyond its confining edges" (McKenna, 3). This work and those similar to it contrast with Thecla's surrealist paintings, such as *Hand at Red Door* (1941), which features a floating hand reaching toward a door in an open landscape. Thecla was very interested in astronomy and enjoyed combining fantasy images with space exploration. Flying horses, erupting volcanoes, and creatures half-animal and half-human can be found in Thecla's later work. Thecla was known to be a sensitive, self-absorbed, yet independent person. In her painting, as McKenna says, Thecla was able to use her vivid imagination in self-examination and self-expression.

Sources. Papers concerning Julia Thecla's life and work may be found in the Archives of the Art Institute of Chicago. The Harold Washington Library Center, CPL, has a collection of articles published about Thecla on file in its Artists Collection. The most comprehensive work on Thecla is Maureen A. McKenna, *Julia Thecla,* Catalog of Exhibition, Illinois State Museum, Springfield, November 11, 1984–February 17, 1985 (n.d.). Included are reminiscences by Katharine Kuh, David Porter, Parker Panttila, and Phyllis Ford-Choyke. Other useful articles are Phyllis Ford, "Artist Thecla Reluctantly Tells Her Life," *CT,* December 12, 1943; C. J. Bulliet, "Julia Thecla's Rich Fantasy Pervades Her New Paintings," *Chicago Daily News,* May 19, 1945; Bulliet, "Artists of Chicago: Past and Present, Julia Thecla," *Chicago Daily News,* November 23, 1935; and Edith Weigle, "Her Canvases Are Enchanted Worlds," *Chicago Sunday Tribune,* August 21, 1960. Susan S. Weininger, *The "New Woman" in Chicago, 1910–1945: Paintings from Illinois Collections* (1993), discusses Thecla and other women artists of her generation.

ERICA L. HOLM

THOMAS, ROSE FAY
September 4, 1852–April 19, 1929
AUTHOR, CLUBWOMAN, ANIMAL RIGHTS ACTIVIST

Rose Fay Thomas, organizer and founder of the National Federation of Women's Musical Clubs and the Chicago Anti-Cruelty Society, was born in St. Alban's, Vermont, the eighth of nine children. Her father, the Reverend Charles Fay, was an Episcopal clergyman. Both sides of her family were said to be musical. Fay's mother died when she was four. Several years later, she was sent to Cambridge, Massachusetts, to live with her older sister, Melusina Fay Peirce, who was an important influence on Rose Fay's sense of women's potential in the arts. Peirce, an avowed feminist and pioneer in the woman's movement, wrote a book, *Cooperative Housekeeping,* and a novel, *New York: A Symphonic Study;* founded a woman's orchestra; and worked to preserve Fraunces Tavern in New York City and Poe Cottage in the Bronx. Fay's brother, Charles Norman Fay, was an entrepreneur with business interests in New York and Chicago. Fay's sister, Amy, was a concert pianist, writer, teacher, and music clubwoman, whose letters from Europe were gathered into an important nineteenth-century book on music, *Music Study in Germany.*

Sometime after August 1877, Charles Norman Fay moved to Chicago to secure his business there. By the next year, Rose Fay and her sisters Amy and Lilly left Boston and joined him in Chicago. The Fays became part of a bustling arts community literally rebuilding itself after the loss of theaters, opera houses, music stores, schools, and music halls in the Great Fire of 1871. Despite the devastation of the fire, Chicagoans were eager not only to attend concerts but also to give concerts. Men and women joined music clubs and choral societies in order to learn and perform great choral standards. Clubs such as the Germania Männerchor, the Apollo Club, and the Beethoven Society, with memberships numbering in the hundreds, arranged recitals and gave concerts. Women with more professional ambitions, however, were limited to teaching positions, infrequent opportunities on the opera stage, or amateur performance, since it was not until the 1950s that women began to perform with any frequency in mixed-sex orchestras. Rose Fay found another alternative for women. This was the sex-segregated Amateur Musical Club that eventually served to support women in their musical as well as professional aspirations.

The all-female Amateur Musical Club, launched in the early 1870s by four women who started out studying piano quartets together, quickly grew into an organization of female pianists and singers with high aspirations. The early purposes of the club were both educational and social, providing opportunities to learn a wide range of masterworks through piano arrangements and broadening members' knowledge through meetings with other "bright and music-loving women" (Thomas, *Musicians Club,* 1). Soon numbering twenty to thirty women, the music club moved out of private parlors and into the public space of meeting rooms in downtown Chicago. Rose Fay, a pianist, performed at least twice and she served as secretary, treasurer, librarian, and from 1891 to 1893 as the club's second president.

Piano distributors and manufacturers such as Julius Bauer and Co., W. W. Kimball Company, A. Reed and Sons, and Lyon and Healy contributed meeting areas, excellent pianos, and printed programs for the music club. The membership jumped to four hundred, then to six hundred, with the addition of associate members who were not performers but constituted a paying audience. Rose Fay observed in her history of the club that this membership expansion changed forever its originally intimate nature but enlarged its possibilities and influence in several important ways. Mediocre performers felt pressure to improve to please a large and critical audience. Students aspired to become candidates for membership, and teachers were able to display their own pedagogical abilities through the performances of their finest students. What made Chicago's Amateur Musical Club so successful, she contended, was a membership that shared responsibilities ranging from training chamber performers and coaching singers to arranging programs and selecting music.

On May 7, 1890, Rose Fay became the second wife of the famous orchestra conductor Theodore Thomas. Thomas was a tireless promoter of classical music and traveled with small orchestras throughout the eastern and midwestern United States. As conductor of major orchestras in Boston, New York, Cincinnati, and Chicago, he considered himself an educator and organizer on a grand scale. He introduced classical music to many people across America through immense outdoor festivals, orchestral concerts, and concerts at the 1893 World's Columbian Exposition in Chicago. In an article in *Outlook Magazine* in 1910, Charles Fay chronicled how he invited Theodore Thomas and his orchestra to leave New York and move to Chicago—a move that eventually resulted in the orchestra's becoming the Chicago Symphony.

The Thomases had no children of their own. Theodore Thomas had four children from a previous marriage, Franz, Hector, Marion, and Minna, and Fay Thomas wrote briefly about the sons in her *Memoirs of Theodore Thomas* (1911). Thomas's marriage thrust her into a much more public role than before. As Mrs. Hamilton Mott described her in the August 1895 *Ladies Home Journal,* "As president [of the Amateur Musical Club of Chicago] and as the wife of Theodore Thomas, Mrs. Thomas is able to wield a great influence in the proper development and cultivation of music in Chicago, and she wields her power wisely" (p. 2).

Thomas had the idea of convening all women's music clubs in America at Chicago's World's Columbian Exposition of 1893. In her "Address of Welcome" to the representatives of thirty-four clubs attending that National Convention of Women's Amateur Musical Clubs on June 21, 1893, Thomas explained that she believed the value of amateur clubs was not in improvement of performance at the keyboard or in vocal techniques, "but in the deeper and broader culture it gives to the mind and heart—the power to think and feel with the mighty creators and their noble interpreters" (*National Convention*, 4). Thomas set up two days of short recitals and reading of reports of each club's activities, since she believed that much was to be gained from measuring and comparing accomplishments and performances. With Thomas as head of the Committee on Representation of Women's Amateur Musical Clubs, the Board of Lady Managers at the exposition hoped to demonstrate "the actual standard of musical culture amongst the best class of American women in all parts of the country, . . . to stimulate the formation of such clubs . . . [and] to give a national recognition to this department of woman's educational work, which has hitherto been overlooked" (*National Convention*, 2).

In 1894, Thomas and her husband purchased land in the White Mountains in Bethlehem, New Hampshire, hoping to escape from the summer dampness of Chicago to a place in the woods. Two years later, they built a small cottage and named their retreat *Felsengarten* (Cliffside Garden) because of the many outcroppings of large rocks. In *Our Mountain Garden*, published in 1904, Thomas described in detail how she planted large naturalized gardens and learned step-by-step to work with the soil and vegetation of that mountainous region. Thomas wrote of her love of observing animals in their natural setting and her distaste for the harm that humans often bring to them.

To discuss her concerns for the many animals in need of protection and shelter during Chicago's brutal winters, Thomas hosted a meeting at her home on January 19, 1899. Mrs. Frank Allport, Mrs. Roswell Mason, Mrs. Frank Gilbert, and Dr. John G. Shortall of the Illinois Humane Society decided with Thomas to form a new organization to aid mistreated and homeless animals. Although the Illinois Humane Society already existed, Thomas and her committee were not satisfied with that organization's offer to allow women only nonvoting membership. The new Anti-Cruelty Society of Chicago, with women as full members, met on March 7, 1899, electing Rose Thomas, the "founder and guiding spirit of the fledgling organization, President" (*History of the Anti-Cruelty Society*, 1).

Theodore Thomas died on January 4, 1905, and Thomas spent the next few years gathering letters, programs, and old magazine articles in order to document his long career. Her book, *Memoirs of Theodore Thomas*, published in 1911, was recognized at the time as a significant addition to his 1904 book, *Theodore Thomas, a Musical Autobiography*. It not only stands as a concert-by-concert accounting of the conductor's struggles to bring to a wide American public a growing repertoire of classical music, it also illuminates the conflicts encountered in the attempt to raise classical music onto a dignified and lofty pedestal. Although her husband was widely known to be strict, brusque, and irritable, she was able to record his affectionate and caring behavior as well as his deep disappointments.

In 1912, Thomas left Chicago for New York, where she stayed first with Theodore Thomas's son Hector and his family, then lived with her brother Charles. She continued to attend concerts and entertain a few musician friends, such as Ignace Paderewski and his family, when they visited New York.

As they grew older, Thomas, her brother Charles, and her sister Amy returned to New England. Rose Thomas died in Cambridge, Massachusetts, of acute endocarditis. She was buried in the family plot in Mount Auburn Cemetery near Boston.

Thomas was an organizer and clubwoman at a time when Chicago was rebuilding its musical community after the Great Fire of 1871. Her work helped to define a public space for women's music-making not only in Chicago but throughout the United States. Although many women's clubs of the late nineteenth century were the domain of middle-class and upper-middle-class women, the Amateur Musical Club in Chicago and its sister clubs elsewhere drew members from "many different circles of society" (Thomas, *Musicians Club*, 8) since professional and amateur musicians came together to further their artistic and organizational talents. Rose Fay Thomas appreciated the democratic make-up, observing that the "millionaire's daughter [was] placed side by side with the obscure music teacher" and the one who could "produce the sweetest music" (Thomas, *Musicians Club*, 8) was most valued. The club provided a place where women congregated in public and pursued goals that they defined for themselves, not only displaying their talents but also enabling them to pursue professional careers in music.

Sources. Music Club papers at the CHS include programs, published and unpublished pamphlets, meeting notes, and treasurers' reports under the current name Musicians Club of Women and the earlier name Amateur Musical Club of Chicago. The papers include Thomas's pamphlet, *Musicians Club of Women—Formerly the Amateur Musical Club* (1890), and the program, *National Convention of Women's Amateur Musical Clubs* (1893). The NL houses the Theodore Thomas Collection, which includes a section entitled "Women's Music" as part of Fay Thomas's "Official Report of the Bureau of Music, World's Columbian Exposition, Chicago, 1893." Thomas's works, in addition to those mentioned above, include "Women's Amateur Musical Clubs," *Music*, June 1901; "A New Hampshire Garden," *World To-Day*, June 1905; and "The Chicago Orchestral Institution," *World To-Day*, October 1905. Details about Thomas's work for the Amateur Musical Club can be found in Ruth Klauber Friedman's *History of the Musicians Club of Women formerly Amateur Musical Club, Chicago, Illinois* (1975), available at the CHS. Fay family information is detailed in the *Fay Genealogy: John Fay of Marlborough and His Descendants* by Orlin P. Fay (1898) at NL. The Fay family and Chicago musical life in the nineteenth century are discussed in Alfred T. Andreas, *History of Chicago from the Earliest Period to the Present Time*, vol. 2 (1885); W. S. B. Matthews, *A Hundred Years of Music in America* (1889); George P. Upton, "Music in Chicago," *New England Magazine*, December 1892; Mrs. Hamilton Mott, "Mrs. Theodore Thomas," *Ladies' Home Journal*, August 1895; Bessie Louise Pierce, *A History of Chicago*, vol. 3 (1957); and S. Margaret McCarthy, "Amy Fay: The American Years," *American Music*, Spring 1985. Roswell C. McCrea, *The Humane Movement: A Descriptive Survey* (1910), and Louis John Covotsos et al., *The Illinois Humane Society 1869 to 1979* (1981), provide an overview of the humane movement in America and Illinois. The pamphlet, *The History of the Anti-Cruelty Society* (1989), is available at the Chicago Anti-Cruelty Society. In *The Clubwoman as*

Feminist: True Womanhood Redefined, 1868–1914 (1980) and *The Torchbearers: Women and their Amateur Arts Associations in America, 1890–1930* (1994), Karen Blair documents the work of Thomas and of women's music clubs and evaluates their contributions to American life.

JOAN BENTLEY HOFFMAN

THOMPSON, MARY HARRIS
April 15, 1829–May 21, 1895
PHYSICIAN, SURGEON, FOUNDER OF HOSPITAL AND MEDICAL COLLEGE

When Mary Thompson entered the medical profession, she encountered restrictions that denied hospital care to sick women and prevented women from obtaining medical education. Unwilling to accept these limitations, Thompson responded by founding a hospital for women and children and working to establish a women's medical college.

She was born in New York State near the town of Fort Ann, the second child of Col. John Harris and Calista (Corbin) Thompson. Both parents had been born in the state. Her father was part owner of an iron mine. She began her education at a local school, where she studied mathematics and Latin on her own. Thompson then moved on to a Methodist school, Troy Conference Academy, located in West Poultney, Vermont. She finished her basic education at Fort Edward Collegiate Institute in Fort Edward, New York. While attending both institutions, she contributed to the cost of her schooling because her father was experiencing financial difficulties. Beginning at fifteen years of age, she taught at the schools where she was enrolled as well as at nearby public schools. Always an independent student, she taught herself anatomy, physiology, chemistry, and astronomy and then taught the first two subjects to her students.

Seeking laboratory experience in anatomy and physiology to improve her teaching, in 1860 Thompson registered at New England Female Medical College (NEFMC) in Boston to study these subjects. As a result of this training, she chose to prepare for a career in medicine. Like other women's medical schools, NEFMC had been established because women were not admitted to existing medical colleges. Although founders of women's medical colleges were concerned that the standards for instruction might not equal those of male institutions because of inadequate facilities and a lack of experienced faculty members, most women's medical colleges set high standards for their students. NEFMC, however, had an inferior course of study. Established as a medical college in 1856 after being a school of midwifery for eight years, it had an inadequately small faculty and insufficient clinical facilities. Dr. Marie Zakrzewski, who had come from the New York Infirmary for Women and Children (NYIWC) in 1859 to become a professor of obstetrics at NEFMC, left three years later when she was unable to raise the standards. Thompson, while a student at NEFMC, spent one year in an internship at NYIWC, perhaps encouraged by Zakrzewski to go there for clinical training. The New York infirmary, founded by physicians Emily and Elizabeth Blackwell, gave Thompson hospital experience. At the same time she supplemented the practical training by attending clinical lectures at Bellevue Hospital in Manhattan. In 1863 NEFMC awarded her the M.D. degree.

As soon as she graduated in July 1863, Thompson moved to Chicago rather than establish herself in a city she knew—New York, Boston, and Philadelphia—where she would be competing with other women physicians. She saw an opportunity to practice medicine in Chicago, a young and growing city, chartered just thirty years earlier.

Thompson found an immediate need for her medical services, treating Civil War veterans and their families who sought employment in Chicago. She worked with Dr. William G. Dyas and Miranda Dyas, his wife, in the Northwestern Sanitary Commission, the United States Sanitary Commission's Chicago branch, run by associate managers MARY LIVERMORE and JANE HOGE. The commission was a civilian organization that assisted the Union Army's medical department with treatment, supplies, and disease prevention. As the Civil War drew to a close, widows and children of Union soldiers, as well as injured soldiers with wives and children, came to Chicago; many lived in poverty. Mary Thompson realized that Chicago needed a hospital for women and children. The city had three hospitals, one of which did not accept women patients. She enlisted the aid of Rev. William R. Ryder, who formed a hospital association of philanthropists to raise funds. On May 8, 1865, Thompson opened the Chicago Hospital for Women and Children (CHWC). A small facility with fourteen beds, a dispensary, and a pharmacy, the hospital was modeled by Thompson on the New York Infirmary for Women and Children. She became chief surgeon and physician and head of the staff and remained in those positions as long as she lived. She called herself Mary Harris Thompson, adding her paternal grandmother's maiden name because other Mary Thompsons were receiving her mail.

The goals of the hospital were to provide inpatient treatment and outpatient dispensary care for poor women and children. During the first year, about two hundred patients were treated in the hospital and more than five hundred at the dispensary. Hospital fees were five dollars per week, but only one patient gave full payment; dispensary service was free. By July 1869, the facilities were inadequate, and the hospital moved to new quarters with sixteen beds and a larger dispensary.

From her early months in Chicago, Thompson felt the need for further medical training. She was twice refused admission by Rush Medical College because she was a woman. Dr. William H. Byford, professor of obstetrics and diseases of women and children at Chicago Medical College, supported medical education for women and arranged for the enrollment of Thompson and two other women during the 1869–70 academic session. Since Thompson was already a physician, Chicago Medical granted her an M.D. degree *ad eundem*—for a graduate of another institution—in 1870. That year, Chicago Medical College, as an independent institution, agreed to provide medical training to students at Northwestern University as its medical department. When Chicago Medical refused to register the other women for the next year because of complaints by male students that some clinical work and lecture material were omitted with women in the class, Thompson realized that women needed a medical school in Chicago. Although Chicago's Hahnemann Homeopathic College became coeducational in 1869, no allopathic medical training was available for women. She and Byford founded Woman's Hospital Medical College, and classes started in 1870 with a faculty of nine physicians, includ-

FIG. 117. *Mary Thompson Hospital, pictured here in 1909, was named for physician Mary Harris Thompson, who founded Chicago's first women's medical college and hospital for women and children.*

ing Thompson, Byford, and Dyas. Thompson saw in the affiliation with her hospital an opportunity for women who studied medicine to have hands-on instruction and experience. She held the position of professor of clinical obstetrics and hygiene—preventive medicine—in the medical college from 1870 to 1877. Seventeen students enrolled immediately. During the school's first year, classes were held in the hospital, and space for an anatomy laboratory was found in the loft of an old building. After a successful session with three graduates, the school moved to its own quarters near the hospital in October 1871. Four days later, the Great Chicago Fire destroyed the buildings of the college and the hospital as well as the homes and offices of most of the faculty.

When the fire started, Thompson dismissed the patients able to walk. She moved three patients to a home temporarily and then to a safe place outside the city. The college and hospital staffs kept both institutions going. The hospital reopened for burned and sick patients in a private home on Adams Street. During this emergency, Thompson and her staff treated both male and female patients, the only time that men were admitted to the woman's hospital. The college continued classes in an Adams Street residence a few blocks from the hospital.

Thompson traveled to Boston and New York to seek funds to support the hospital. In 1873, the Relief and Aid Society of Chicago gave twenty-five thousand dollars for a new hospital, with the understanding that free treatment would be given twenty-five patients each year. A house was purchased and ren-

ovated and enlarged for the hospital, and a building on the grounds became the medical college. The dispensary, closed since the fire, reopened that year.

The new building gave Thompson the opportunity to realize one of her goals for the hospital, to provide training for women to become nurses. Because of limited space and few beds, nursing education was not possible in the early years of the hospital, but in 1874 Thompson began directing a nursing school within the hospital. The school grew with the hospital, and Thompson taught large numbers of women who graduated as nurses. For Thompson, the nursing school not only allowed her to set standards and supervise the educational process, it also gave training to women in another professional area of medicine.

In 1877 the medical college separated from the hospital, becoming Woman's Medical College in 1879. After the reorganization, Thompson declined to continue on the school's faculty, devoting her full efforts to the hospital. There she took the title of clinical professor of obstetrics and gynecology. When the college became the Northwestern University Woman's Medical School in 1892, Thompson joined its faculty in the 1891–92 academic year as a clinical professor of gynecology at the Hospital for Women and Children.

Thompson's private practice as an abdominal and pelvic surgeon was part of her hospital work. For years she was the sole woman performing major surgery in Chicago. She was well known locally and nationally, and her work was respected by medical colleagues. By her example, she helped open up opportunities for other women through her own achievements as surgeon and physician. Thompson invented an abdominal needle that was used by surgeons and developed other surgical instruments. Under her direction, the use of the Chicago Hospital for Women and Children outgrew its capacity, and by 1884 the facility needed overhauling. Thompson designed a new eighty-bed building, which opened in 1885.

During the years 1879–93, Thompson gave papers on her clinical and surgical work at professional meetings and published eight articles in several medical journals. In the article, "Cases of Ovariotomy," published in June 1879, she described her use of Joseph Lister's antiseptic method, using carbolic acid to clean the operating room. Lister had introduced antiseptic surgery some twelve years earlier in Great Britain. His method was widely adopted by about 1880, when Thompson was already using Lister's procedures as a way to lessen postsurgical infection. Aware of the importance of Lister's techniques, she stressed that the "three successive cases terminated in perfect recovery, and illustrate the value of Lister's antiseptic method of operating" (p. 600). In 1884, her article on the removal of large ovarian cysts, "Two Interesting Cases of Ovariotomy," in the *American Journal of Obstetrics and Diseases of Women and Children*, again described her use of antiseptic methods; the ceiling, floor, and walls of the operating arena were washed with a carbolic solution, and the patient and nurses were ordered to have pre-operative baths. Thompson also presented two clinical reports at Illinois State Medical Society meetings in 1889 and 1893 that were published in the transactions of the society in the same years.

Although Thompson focused her time on management of the Chicago Hospital for Women and Children and on medical practice, she also accepted professional positions not given earlier to women physicians. After ten years of practice, she was admitted in 1873 to the Chicago Medical Society. In 1881, the organization made her its vice-president, the first woman to become an officer. The American Medical Association (AMA) voted her a member in 1886, when she gave a paper in St. Louis, Missouri, at the yearly meeting. (In 1876 SARAH HACKETT STEVENSON had been accepted as the first woman member of the AMA.) Thompson's paper, "Why Diseases of Children Should Be Made a Special Study," was the first presented by a woman to the Section on Diseases of Children, and the members of the section chose her as its chair at that meeting. In October of the same year, the *Journal of the American Medical Association* published the paper. At a time when children were viewed as small adults, Thompson pointed out that treatments used for adults were not suitable with children. She explained the need for a pediatric specialty; children were still growing and were often unable to describe their symptoms.

Beyond her work as a surgeon and physician, Thompson was concerned about the daily lives of her patients. They saw her as a friend to whom they could come for advice and assistance. Her care for poor patients included personal needs—food and housing. These relationships, as part of the medical work to which she devoted most of her time, may have had a place in her limited social life. Thompson never married. Her colleague, Dr. Nicholas Senn, described her appearance and character. Her eyes "were sentinels, black diamonds, refulgent with kindness, energy, enthusiasm and determination." She had "raven black

hair" and a "classical handsome face" ("Memorial of Dr. Mary Harris Thompson," 149). Shortly before her death at sixty-six years of age, she wrote a letter to a friend describing how hard she was working; Thompson commented "that if there was another life, . . . she would go on working there" ("Memorial of Dr. Mary Harris Thompson," 148). Thompson suffered a cerebral hemorrhage and died a few days later. She was buried in the Fort Ann village cemetery on the Thompson family grounds.

Thompson was a supporter of suffrage for women, and described as "a woman's rights woman" (*Chicago Medical Recorder*, July 1895, 59) by a contemporary, Dr. John Bartlett; but she put her greatest efforts into medicine. As she explained, she "was always too busy utilizing the opportunities for work . . . to spend time in preaching the gospel of the rights of her sex" (quoted in *Chicago Medical Recorder*, July 1895, 59). She made professional opportunities in medicine available to women through her involvement in two institutions that she helped found—a hospital where women had clinical training and practiced medicine and a woman's medical college. In 1895, after Thompson's death, the board of managers of CHWC changed the name to the Mary Thompson Hospital of Chicago for Women and Children. Ten years later, in memory of her accomplishments, the hospital board gave the Art Institute of Chicago a bust of Thompson that they had commissioned from sculptor Daniel Chester French. Mary Thompson's hospital continued to serve women and children until it closed in 1988.

Sources. Six of Thompson's eight publications focus on gynecological and obstetrical cases. Among her articles are the following: in the *Chicago Medical Journal and Examiner*, "Two Cases of Placenta Praevia," March 1879, and "Cases of Ovariotomy," June 1879; "A Case of Prolonged Gestation and Unusual Labor," *Medical and Surgical Reporter*, May 1881; and "Three Cases of Probable Pelvic Lymphorrhea," *American Journal of Obstetrics and Diseases of Women and Children*, vol. 17, 1884. Articles appearing in the *Transactions of the Illinois State Medical Society* are "Salpingitis, Its Diagnosis and Treatment," vol. 39, 1889, and "A Unique Case of Typhoid, with Several Relapses," vol. 43, 1893. Numerous biographical essays have been published during the twentieth century. The *Biographical Cyclopedia of American Women*, vol. 2 (1925), places Thompson's life within the frame of restrictions placed on women who wished to train to be physicians in the antebellum years. For an overview of her career, see Emilia J. Giryotas, "Dr. Mary Harris Thompson—Founder Women and Children's Hospital, Chicago," *Journal of the American Medical Women's Association*, vol. 5, 1950; NAW (1971); and Adele Hast, "Mary Harris Thompson," in *American National Biography*, ed. John A. Garraty and Mark C. Carnes (1999). William K. Beatty, in "Mary Harris Thompson—Pioneer Surgeon and Hospital Founder," *Proceedings of the Institute of Medicine in Chicago*, vol. 34, 1981, summarizes her published articles. Helga Ruud's account of the college and its students, "Woman's Medical College of Chicago," in *History of Medical Practice in Illinois*, vol. 2, ed. David J. Davis (1955), includes a brief biography of Thompson. Lucy Waite, "Mary Harris Thompson," in *A Group of Distinguished Physicians and Surgeons of Chicago*, comp. F. M. Sperry (1904), focuses on the history of the Chicago Hospital for Women and Children. The *Catalogue of the Northwestern University, at Evanston, Illinois, for the Academic Year, 1870–'71* (1871) has Thompson's ad eundem M.D. degree award. *Northwestern University. Catalogue. 1891–92* [n.d.], which includes faculty at its Woman's Medical School, lists Mary H. Thompson as Clinical Professor of Gynecology at the Hospital for Women and Children. Both catalogues are at Northwestern Univ. Archives. Obituaries include "Death of a Noted Woman Physician," *CT*, May 22, 1895, with incorrect burial information, and "Society Proceedings. The Chicago Medical Society," June 3, 1895, in *Chicago Medical Recorder*, January–June 1895. Tributes to Thompson are found in a booklet published by the board of managers of the hospital, *In Memoriam Mary Harris Thompson* (1896) and, on the occasion of the presentation of the bust of Thompson to the Art Institute, in "A Memorial of Dr. Mary Harris Thompson," *Chicago Medical Recorder*, February 15, 1905. Regina Markell Morantz-Sanchez, *Sympathy and Science: Women Physicians in American Medicine* (1985) is useful for historical context. For discussion of Lister's methods, see Paul Starr, *The Social Transformation of American Medicine* (1982).

ADELE HAST

THORNE, NARCISSA NIBLACK
May 2, 1882–June 25, 1966
CREATOR OF MINIATURE ROOMS, CLUBWOMAN

Narcissa Niblack was born in Vincennes, Indiana, to William Caldwell and Frances (Herr) Niblack. Her mother was from a milling family in Virginia. Her father was from Salem, Massachusetts, and a descendant of Mayflower passengers. As a child, Narcissa Niblack and her family moved to Chicago, where her father started a law practice. They lived in the Hyde Park area near the University of Chicago. Little is known about her siblings, but Niblack had at least one sister, Lydia, and remembered her mother's grieving over another child, a brother, who died before she was born.

Narcissa Niblack was educated at home by a governess until she was eleven. She then attended public school for a few years and completed her formal education at nearby Kenwood Institute, a finishing school. Although she often made light of her education, this type of rearing was common for girls from wealthy families at the turn of the century. Niblack was a shy, quiet person, but among high society's arbiters of taste, she was often complimented for her good looks and fashionable appearance.

On May 29, 1901, Narcissa Niblack married her childhood sweetheart, James Ward Thorne of Chicago, the son of George R. and Ellen M. (Cobb) Thorne. George Thorne was cofounder with A. Montgomery Ward of Montgomery Ward and Co. His son, James, became a director and vice-president of the company and worked alongside his three brothers. Narcissa and James Thorne had two children, Ward Thorne (born 1902) and Niblack Thorne (born 1905). The Thornes kept two homes, one in Lake Forest, Illinois, and the other on Lake Shore Drive in Chicago.

As was common for the time and for a woman of her prominence, Thorne took up many social causes, including fundraising for hospitals as well as the Art Institute of Chicago (AIC) and the Chicago Historical Society. In addition, Thorne was an active member of the Women's Exchange, a group formed to give women part-time work outside the home. She saw an opportunity for the women to sell more than just baked goods and took an active role in making the Exchange a place where women could use their needlework skills to make money.

Thorne is best known for the miniature rooms she created in the style of upper-class homes of England, France, and the United States in various periods. This love of miniatures stemmed from her childhood. At that time, her love of tiny things was encouraged by an uncle, Rear Admiral Albert P.

Niblack, who sent her souvenirs from his U.S. Navy tours abroad. After James Thorne retired in 1926 at age fifty-three, the couple traveled extensively, and Narcissa Thorne's childhood interest in collecting miniatures matured. During her travels she started collecting miniatures she found in antique shops throughout Europe. Many of these items came from once wealthy families who, because of political changes throughout Europe after World War I, sold many of their possessions to make ends meet. In an attempt to display these miniature masterpieces, Thorne built boxes ranging from two to three feet long by eighteen to twenty inches deep. In her quest to decorate these "rooms," Thorne also found materials in dime stores and resale shops in the United States.

The early 1900s were a time when museums added full-scale period rooms to their collections. The Rockefeller family also undertook the restoration of the town of Williamsburg, Virginia, with roots in the colonial past. It was also fashionable for wealthy individuals to redecorate their homes in the style of prior eras. Thorne saw an opportunity to introduce the public to interior design and decoration through the exhibition of her rooms, which dated to the time between 1600 and 1940. For years Thorne had her studio at the Women's Exchange on North Michigan Avenue. In 1960, when the exchange closed, Thorne established her studio in an apartment on North Michigan Avenue. She often worked seven days a week on her miniature rooms.

During the Great Depression, Thorne saw an opportunity to employ a few of the highly skilled crafts workers looking for employment. She also hired members of the Needlework and Textile Guild of Chicago to make tiny carpets and tapestry. A Danish American cabinet maker, a Swedish American artisan, a German American sculptor, Marshall Field's window designer, and a well-known Chicago architect all worked for Thorne in creating her rooms. In addition, her husband, an amateur photographer and woodworker, lent his assistance.

The first rooms were designed around antique miniatures. Her crafts workers created additional pieces according to Thorne's specifications. In addition, Thorne was imaginative in her substitution of common objects for those not available. For example she used silver Liberty dimes as tureen bottoms, a penny as a tray for a copper tea set, and earrings for wall sconces. She read widely and made every attempt to educate herself on period furnishing and styles. She had an eye for detail that resulted in a realistic depiction of the rooms. Unlike doll houses, the miniature rooms Thorne created to educate the public in interior design and decoration very rarely contain figures. In addition, doll houses are usually built larger. The miniature rooms were built to a scale of one-twelfth of the original and helped to set the standard for miniature room creation.

There are conflicting reports as to when Thorne's work debuted. Thorne is said to have exhibited several miniature rooms for the benefit of Children's Memorial Hospital, Chicago, in the early 1930s. Thorne exhibited thirty American and European miniature rooms at a 1932 private reception at the Chicago Historical Society. The reception was held to raise money for the Architectural Students' League.

The general public first had its opportunity to see Thorne's work at the 1933–34 Century of Progress Exposition, where hundreds of thousands of visitors viewed the miniature rooms. Representing three years of hard work, Thorne's miniature rooms were shown in their own building. In 1937, her miniature rooms were displayed at the AIC. Two years later they were exhibited at the Golden Gate International Exposition in San Francisco, California, and in 1940 at the New York World's Fair.

Thorne's work impressed not only "common folk" but also royalty. When the British royal family visited the AIC and saw Thorne's miniature rooms in 1936, Thorne was asked to make a library modeled after a room in Windsor Castle to be given to the Queen Mother the following year during Edward VIII's coronation. Though the coronation never took place, the Thornes went to Britain to present the room, and it was placed in the Victoria and Albert Museum.

Rooms of famous European homes were the subject of Thorne's second set of thirty-one rooms, completed in 1937. They were donated to the Art Institute of Chicago in 1942, for which Thorne was named an AIC benefactor. A third set of thirty-seven American rooms was completed that year. It took four weeks to install the third set of rooms when they were displayed at the Carnegie Institute, Pittsburgh, Pennsylvania. There were many objects and much of the detail work was done with tweezers. The rooms were also featured at fairs in Baltimore, Maryland; Boston, Massachusetts; St. Louis, Missouri; and Washington, D.C. The third set was also donated to the AIC. A permanent gallery for the rooms was established at the AIC in 1954. Thorne established a fund for their care.

The Thorne Miniature Rooms require a great deal of attention. The silver, copper, and brass, for example, need regular polishing. Cotton swabs are used to dust and tiny paintbrushes to sweep. Replacing the tiny artificial flowers in the floral arrangements requires delicate work with tweezers. Items moved because of vibration caused by the museum's air conditioning, for example, need straightening. A catalog of room layouts helps assure that items are correctly relocated after cleaning.

In 1945 Thorne was invited to be a member of the Decorative Arts committee at the AIC. In 1959 Thorne was named Honorary Curator of Decorative Arts by the AIC board of trustees. She received much acclaim for her work and was the subject of many newspaper and magazine articles across the country.

Thorne inherited an estate worth more than two million dollars from her husband when he died in 1946. Independently wealthy, Thorne continued to devote herself to her miniature artistry and her charitable causes. When it became too difficult to find skilled crafts workers to assist her in authentic period miniature reproductions, Thorne made dioramas and shadowboxes for family and friends. Thorne never received money for her artwork, and there is no record of how much she actually spent on her creations.

Thorne donated sixteen restored English, Spanish, and French rooms to the Phoenix Art Museum in Phoenix, Arizona, a memorial to her daughter-in-law Marie Gaetge Thorne, Niblack Thorne's deceased wife. Originally created in the 1930s, these rooms were owned at one time by International Business Machines (IBM), which sent them on tour around the country. There are also displays of Thorne's rooms in the Dulin Gallery

of Art in Knoxville, Tennessee, and in the Herron Museum of Indianapolis, Indiana.

Thorne also created some miniature rooms for Children's Memorial and Presbyterian–St. Luke's hospitals in Chicago. Two of the rooms are still on display in the lobby of Children's Memorial Hospital. In 1962 Thorne gave Presbyterian–St. Luke's Hospital a series of miniature rooms for display in the children's ward. In 1963 thirty additional rooms were sold for charity through the Russell Button Gallery. In poor health, Thorne closed the last of her studios and donated remaining items to charity in March 1966.

Narcissa Thorne died in Chicago of heart problems at the age of eighty-four. Memorial services were held in Westminster Chapel of the Fourth Presbyterian Church on Chicago's Near North Side, close to Thorne's home. She was buried in Rosehill Cemetery.

The Thorne rooms continue to attract visitors. In the 1970s the rooms were valued at around seventy-five hundred dollars each, and they have appreciated in value since that time. Thorne's generosity to the Art Institute of Chicago extended beyond the rooms themselves. She donated her unique collection of nineteenth-century color-plate books to the Department of Prints and Drawings. In addition, Thorne gave her working collection of books on interiors, furniture, and decorative arts to the Art Institute's Ryerson Library.

Sources. The James Ward Thorne file, CHS, contains numerous newspaper and magazine clippings regarding Narcissa Niblack Thorne and her miniature room work. Narcissa Niblack Thorne Papers are at the Art Institute of Chicago archives, including many of Thorne's scrapbooks and other documentation on the Thorne rooms. This collection includes biographical notes and an unpublished essay, "The Miniature Rooms of Mrs. James Ward Thorne," author unknown, edited by Althea H. Huber. Bruce Hatton Boyer, "Creating the Thorne Rooms," in *Miniature Rooms, the Thorne Rooms at the Art Institute of Chicago,* ed. Susan F. Rossen (1983), is a thorough discussion of Thorne's life and work. Suzanne M. Thorne, "Miniature Rooms," *Arizona Highways,* November 1972, is useful.

SUSEN TARAS

TIETJENS, EUNICE HAMMOND
July 29, 1884–September 6, 1944
POET, EDITOR, JOURNALIST, CRITIC

Eunice Tietjens, member of the editorial board of *Poetry: A Magazine of Verse,* played a key part in the Chicago literary renaissance and the modernist literary movement through her roles of editor, poet, and critic. Born in Chicago, the eldest of four children and the first of three daughters of William A. and Idea (Strong) Hammond, Eunice Hammond lived most of her childhood in nearby Evanston, Illinois. Her life changed when her father, a banker, drowned on New Year's Day 1897. After the death of her father, her mother, an artist, took the children to live in Geneva, Switzerland, where six years later, in 1904, the nineteen-year-old Eunice Hammond met and married Paul Tietjens, an American composer who collaborated with R. Frank Baum on the musical version of *The Wizard of Oz.* They separated in 1909, and the marriage ended in divorce in December 1914. One daughter, Janet, survived that marriage; another child, Idea, died. Leaving her husband and living on her own apparently spurred her poetic "birth," both in her own poetry and in the birth of a great new publication.

Tietjens joined editor HARRIET MONROE and *Poetry* magazine in 1913, about a year after the magazine began publication. She began as an office girl and moved to business manager, eventually becoming assistant and then associate editor. Later, Tietjens recalled that she had been hired because she had had a poem or two accepted in *Poetry*. From 1913 to 1917, she worked closely with Monroe and associate editor ALICE HENDERSON. She believed in the importance of *Poetry* as "the fountainhead of the art of poetry in this country, indeed in the English speaking world" (*The World at My Shoulder*, 21). Chicago, she maintained, was a major center of a "new vitality" and Chicago writers the focal point. For Tietjens, *Poetry* was the center of this creativity, "the clearing house, the mother in Israel, and the magnet which held it all together" (*The World at My Shoulder*, 22).

In 1914, Tietjens's mother took her to Asia to visit her sister, Louise, an Episcopalian missionary in China. At the time, Tietjens was economically dependent upon her family, and the trip was proposed by her family after they had successfully censored a poem by Tietjens, which had been due to be published in an anthology. However, the trip was a fortunate one, since it was there that Tietjens discovered Asian philosophy and verse. "I saw China . . . in its strong original essence," she remembered later, praising the Chinese for their humor, which was "rich and varied in their poetry and present in their daily life" ("The World at My Shoulder," ms, Newberry Library, 84–85). Tietjens was so influenced by the trip that on her return to Chicago, she began to wear Japanese-style dress. More important, it was Japanese poetry that influenced her own work. She liked the conciseness, the concentration upon image rather than abstract words, and the possibility of using image in her confessional poetry. Consequently, she, like poet Ezra Pound, incorporated aspects of Japanese poetry into her own verse.

By November 1916, Tietjens was living alone with her daughter, Janet, supporting herself with her salary from *Poetry* and in part by writing magazine serials, including a fifty-thousand-word serial potboiler entitled "My Jean" in five installments. By the time she left *Poetry* in 1917 to become a World War I foreign correspondent in Paris for the *Chicago Daily News*, she had become assistant editor of *Poetry*. A photograph of her in her war correspondent's military uniform reveals a woman with a long face with straight brows, large dark eyes, full lips, and two wings of hair with a part in the middle.

Returning to Chicago in 1918, she rejoined the magazine and was listed as associate editor for the January 7, 1918, issue, replacing Alice Corbin Henderson, who had moved to New Mexico for her health. The editorial direction of *Poetry* had originally been defined by Monroe and Henderson. Tietjens's letters to Monroe do not contain a dialogue with her over aesthetic or quality questions, as did the letters between Monroe and Henderson. Instead, Tietjens's letters to Monroe convey the sense of a relationship of a daughter to a mother. Nevertheless, as associate editor, Tietjens contributed to the literary milieu that introduced such international writers as T. S. Eliot, Ezra Pound, Wallace Stevens, and William Carlos Williams in the pages of *Poetry*. Even Tietjens's disapproval of Ezra Pound was based not on a disagreement over poetics, but on what she perceived was his lack of loyalty to Monroe. She disliked the tone of his letters to Monroe and characterized him as "part charlatan" (*The World at My Shoulder*, 22).

Tietjens was affected by her experience on the magazine and later wrote in her autobiography, *The World at My Shoulder* (1938), about the spiritual quality of the experience. She felt a camaraderie with other women in publishing. Earlier, in 1914, when she herself was struggling financially, she had helped MARGARET ANDERSON and JANE HEAP establish *The Little Review* by pawning her diamond engagement ring.

Tietjens's first book, *Profiles from China* (1917), went through three printings. Tietjens also published frequently in the *Dial, Literary Digest, Century*, and *Poetry*. A selection of her work was published in *The New Poetry*, the 1917 anthology edited by Monroe and Henderson, which for many years defined the poetry of the modernist literary movement. Her work was also included in the 1936 edition.

Tietjens's poetry was well received by readers and critics. Biographer W. N. S. Love describes her poetry as "expressions of the intricate progress of her soul through the experiences of living into spiritual and mental experience" ("Eunice Tietjens," 6). Perhaps because of its honesty, Tietjens's poetry was popular. Love claims, "Scarcely an anthology of contemporary poetry appeared for two decades that did not include some of her work" (p. 5).

Her poetic themes include her own struggle with social roles for women. Tietjens developed a strong female voice based on emotional responses and strong sensory details. Her poetry was frequently confessional and conveyed the emotional turmoil of her life. In the poem, "A Plaint of Complexity," published in *Body and Raiment* in 1919, Tietjens wrote of her different selves and described herself as independent and lonely.

Tietjens's ideas about gender often contradicted accepted concepts. She accepted the prevailing view that women were "different" from men, more emotional (and thus more confessional), but she also maintained that they were more sexual than commonly believed. Her belief contrasted with the dominant one in the early twentieth century that women were driven by spiritual and moral needs, not physical ones.

Attempts to express her sexuality in her poetry early met with the disapproval of her family, who forbade the publication of a poem, "Two Flames," which was to have appeared in 1914 in a poetry anthology under one of Tietjens's pseudonyms, Eloise Briton. The poem apparently describes Tietjens's relationship with a New York physician, in whose divorce Tietjens had been named a correspondent. Tietjens had to wait until 1929 to publish the poem in *Leaves in Windy Weather* under the title "From the Mountains." Perhaps thinking of this poem, she asserted that "a woman must write . . . , but she must, on pain of social ostracism, write only a certain kind of story, a certain established form of verse" ("Women and the Art of Today"). For Tietjens, it was the female writer's emotions that made her able to abandon old poetic forms and themes for new ones.

After her second marriage in 1920 to Cloyd Head, who was active in community and academic theater, she worked on *Poetry* at least until 1938; however, she was not actively involved with its day-to-day editorial decisions after she and Head moved to Europe and North Africa. The couple lived in Europe and Tunisia, and they traveled to the island of Moorea. They turned this experience into a play, *Arabesque,* produced unsuccessfully on Broadway in 1925.

As a critic and journalist, Tietjens was concerned with defining what was seen as the "new" poetry. Tietjens became a lecturer in Asian poetry in the English department at the University of Miami, Miami, Florida, from 1933 to 1935, while Cloyd Head was a member of the speech department. Tietjens lectured in poetry at the University of Miami, compiling from these lectures a book-length unpublished manuscript, "How Poetry Is Written." In the 1940s, Cloyd Head, former director of the Miami Players, became business manager for the Kenneth Sawyer Goodman Memorial Theater in Chicago, a job he had first held in 1927.

For Tietjens, in harmony with the Japanese poets she studied, the chief characteristics of poetry were a heightened mood and condensation. She believed that poetry should be written while under the influence of passion. Emotion was the genesis of poetry, and the poet was not to be detached.

While she believed that emotion was the beginning of poetry, Tietjens claimed that gender was irrelevant. Neither did she conceptualize in her poetry the economic and social constraints she experienced because of her gender. She believed that the sex of the poet was irrelevant and, instead, agreed with William Butler Yeats that all poetry was written from the "antiself" ("How Poetry Is Written," ms, Newberry Library), which contemplated what was lacking in the external self.

Critics agree that her best poetry appears in *Profiles from China* (1917) and *Body and Raiment* (1919), both published before her second marriage in 1920. After 1929, she published mainly children's travel books but continued to think of herself as a poet. She was dictating verses of an epic poem on her deathbed. She died in 1944 in Evanston of intestinal cancer.

Through her role at *Poetry* and through her correspondence with and support of other poets in the Chicago literary renaissance, Tietjens contributed vitally to the growth and eventual dominance of the modern poetry movement. She was one of those writers and editors who made significant, if unheralded, contributions to the milieu that produced the poets now seen as the major modern poets. She also brought the new poetry to the public's attention through her many newspaper articles and her thoughtful lectures on the subject at the University of Miami, solidifying the importance of modern poetry in the public mind. She was one of those who worked to establish the eminence and dominance of the modern poetry movement.

Sources. The Eunice Tietjens Papers at NL, Chicago, contain three thousand items, including extensive correspondence with Sara Teasdale and Harriet Monroe (the latter from the original Monroe collection at the Univ. of Chicago), and manuscripts, including "The World at My Shoulder," "How Poetry Is Written," and an outline for a detective story. In addition to the works mentioned above, which include her 1938 autobiography, *The World at My Shoulder,* Tietjens wrote *Japan, Korea, and Formosa,* ed. Burton Holmes (1924); *Profiles from Home* (1925); *Boy of the Desert* (1928); *Poetry of the Orient,* ed. Tietjens (1928); *The Romance of Antar,* trans. by Tietjens (1929); *China,* with L. S. Hammond, ed. Burton Holmes (1930); *The Jaw-Breaker's Alphabet,* with Janet Tietjens (1930); *Boy of the South Seas* (1931); *Manga Reva, the Forgotten Island,* with R. L. Eskridge (1931); *The Gingerbread Boy* (1932); and *An Adventure in Friendship,* ed. Tietjens (1941). Her articles on poetry and other writing include "Women and the Art of Today," *San Francisco Bul-*

letin, September 18, 1915. Critical studies of Tietjens include W. N. S. Love's "Eunice Tietjens: A Biographical and Critical Study" (Ph.D. diss., Univ. of Maryland, 1960), which draws upon interviews with family members and friends, although Love is circumspect on details of Tietjens's life. Her life and work are briefly described by Sidney H. Bremer in *American Women Writers* (1982). Bremer notes that Tietjens wrote under these pseudonyms: E. H., Eloise Briton, Guy Trevor MacKenzie, and Frances Trevor. Also, see *NAW* (1971); *Bookman,* August 1925, April 1929; *Masses,* August 1917; *New York Herald Tribune Books,* October 6, 1929; *NYT,* October 19, 1919; *Poetry,* September 1917, October 1917, February 1920, July 1925, September 1938, and November 1944; *Saturday Review,* October 7, 1944.

JULIANN E. FLEENOR

TORREY, MABEL LANDRUM
June 23, 1886–April 1, 1974
SCULPTOR, TEACHER

For more than fifty years, Mabel Landrum Torrey sculpted traditional portraits of ideal and real children in a consistently skillful and charming manner. She was able to maintain her nineteenth-century ideals in the face of newer and newer ones primarily because she shared and reinforced them daily with other unrepentant classicists. She and her husband, Fred M. Torrey, lived and worked at the Midway Studios of Lorado Taft, dean of Chicago sculpture.

Mabel Landrum was born in Sterling, Colorado, the daughter of Judge and Mrs. J. W. Landrum, Colorado pioneers. Her earliest ambition was to be a painter, but that was adjusted for her when a college instructor admired a bust she had modeled and announced, "You are a sculptor!" (Hamlin, ix). Upon graduating from Colorado State College of Education at Greeley with this newfound ambition, Landrum taught in a grade school in her native town until she earned sufficient funds to begin studying sculpture at the School of the Art Institute of Chicago (SAIC) in 1911.

The SAIC facility, the oldest and most distinguished art school in Chicago, maintained a curriculum based firmly on Renaissance standards. The memory of the dazzling successes such ideals had produced at the World's Columbian Exposition of 1893 kept classical training firmly entrenched in Chicago and was a magnet pulling in students from throughout the rural Midwest. The women who constituted the overwhelming majority of the student body were instilled with a reverence for past masters and instructed to emulate their techniques. In the sculpture program this approach meant diligent training until one could manipulate clay into idealized human forms that conveyed abstract concepts, or as Fred Torrey would explain to his biographer decades later, "It takes a lot of caressing of the clay before one makes a living thing of it" (Hamlin, 172).

While Landrum was a student, the legendary Armory Show opened in Chicago in March 1913 after dramatically introducing twentieth-century art to New York. The show's sculptural works emphasized sheer mass rather than meaning and clean, machine-like finishes at odds with hand-worked ones. Stern lectures from their faculty kept Chicago students immune to the new concepts, and thus Landrum completed her training in 1916 solidly ingrained with classical ideals and methods. That year she also married Fred Torrey, a native of West Virginia and fellow sculpture student.

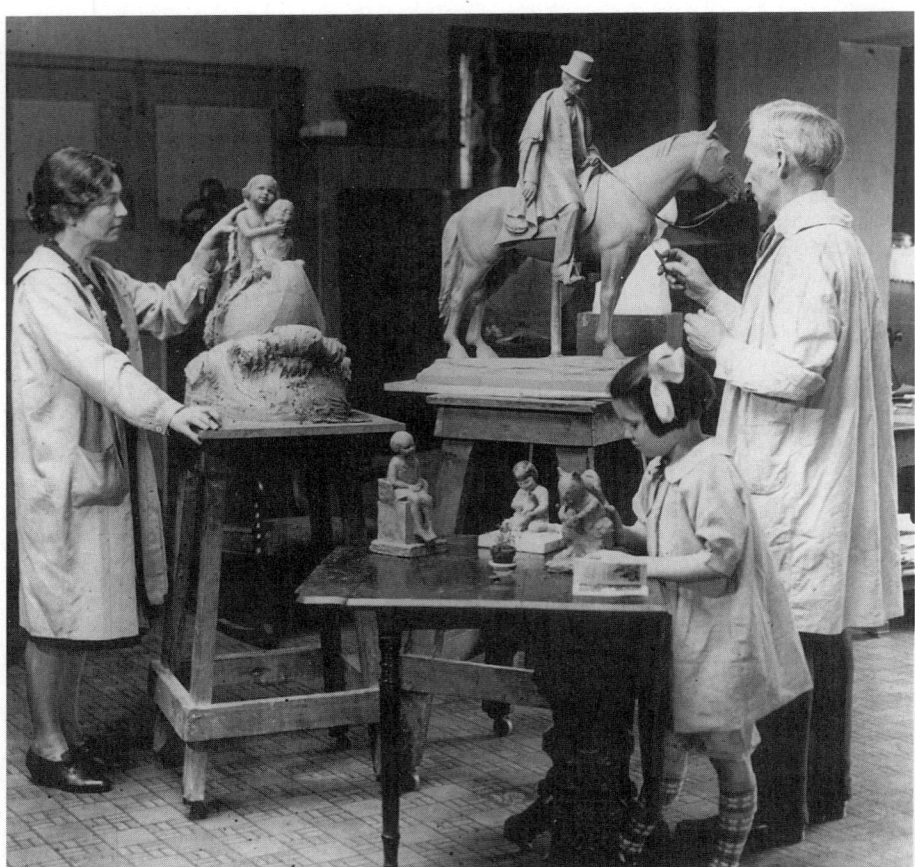

FIG. 118. *Sculptor Mabel Torrey with her husband and daughter, 1928.*

The couple immediately took up residence in Midway Studios, where in 1906 Lorado Taft had created an atelier in the manner of an Italian Renaissance artist's workshop around a brick barn offered to him by the University of Chicago. He selected both aspiring and accomplished artists to join him until he led what was believed to be the largest aggregation of its kind anywhere. A central, roofed court reserved for meals and group functions was dominated by Taft's full-sized model of five female figures arranged to symbolize the Great Lakes. The Torreys' living quarters had an interior window looking down from the rafters and over the head of the *Lake Superior* figure. In 1920 their only child, Elizabeth, known as Betty Jane, was born, and she grew up entirely within this heady environment. Betty Jane showed an early talent for sculpture, but she eventually chose photography as her art form.

Success of a moderate sort was immediate for Mabel Torrey. Her models were exhibited regularly in the Art Institute's *Chicago and Vicinity* shows from her student years through 1928. While teaching clay modeling at Francis Parker School, a progressive Chicago private school, she created her first major commission, *Wynken, Blynken and Nod Fountain.* This five-by-eight-foot marble work was dedicated in 1919 in Washington Park, Denver, Colorado, her native state. It commemorated the children's poet Eugene Field. Torrey's training had prepared her to approach the

nineteen-ton block of stone with confidence. That year Torrey also created what proved to be her most popular work, *Robin Song*, an eleven-inch statuette of a child enthralled with something she is hearing. Over the years four thousand copies in plaster or porcelain were sold; purchasers invariably said the work reminded them of their children or grandchildren. Betty Jane was the model that permitted Torrey to acquire a feel for the physiognomy of a child at any age. Torrey used this experience most skillfully in *Stanley*, a life-sized memorial plaque commissioned in 1928 for a Cincinnati hospital. Two of Torrey's most popular smaller works dated from 1938 to 1940. They were *Jerry*, an eight-inch head of a mischievous boy that was purchased by artists more often than any other Torrey design, and *The Morning Kiss*, a silhouette relief of a mother and child.

Torrey was never one of the associated artists with the Midway Studios. That distinction was entirely her husband's. Visitors of all kinds could be found in the studios at any given time, and Torrey appeared to have always been ready to encourage any interest in her husband's architectural reliefs and numerous renderings of Abraham Lincoln. Nonetheless, Torrey's growing collection of statuettes of children elicited considerable comment from visitors. A sufficiently steady number of commissions sustained both Torreys throughout the Great Depression and World War II. They also maintained active lecture schedules, employing slides as soon as the technology was available.

The Torreys maintained their spaces at the Midway Studios until the colony was dissolved in 1947 on the death of Taft's widow. The University of Chicago reclaimed the properties and turned them over to academic uses. (The complex has since been restored and declared a Chicago landmark.) The Torreys then acquired a home-studio in the neighborhood, but in 1957 they succumbed to their daughter's entreaties to join her family in Iowa. The move was particularly rewarding for Torrey, now almost seventy, for in Des Moines she met Ruth and C. Edward Christians, art porcelain makers who were seeking works suited to reproduction by their methods. Fifty years after creating the first piece, Torrey was able to turn her collection of statuettes into a commercial success.

Torrey's last major sculpture was begun in response to a request from the Christians to develop a grouping based on a famous Matthew Brady photograph of Abraham Lincoln showing a book to his son, Tad. Fred Torrey provided one more of his many portraits of the president, while Mabel Torrey crafted the image of Lincoln's son. The model came to the attention of a committee seeking a sculpture of Lincoln for the grounds of the Iowa statehouse. The bronze *Lincoln and Tad* was dedicated on November 19, 1961. It was one of the very few works on which the Torreys actually collaborated. Fred Torrey died in July 1967, and eighteen months later a book tracing the two sculptors' combined yet separate careers was published. By then Torrey was living in a retirement home in Ames, Iowa, where she died at the age of eighty-seven after a long illness.

Mabel Torrey maintained a continuously productive artistic career in a milieu where her husband's career was expected to take precedence. Her sculptures were always engaging and executed with skill, but they were nonetheless sentimental pieces, and history deems them dated. Lorado Taft, in his *History of American Sculpture*, proclaimed her "happy fountain" (p. 584), the *Wynken, Blynken and Nod*, her most important work. Torrey herself would have added the *Stanley* relief and *Morning Kiss*.

Sources. Gladys Hamlin Papers, Spec. Coll., Iowa State Univ. Library, includes photographs of Mabel Torrey's works. Hamlin, a member of the art faculty at Iowa State Univ., prepared a photographic study of the works of the Torreys, *The Sculpture of Fred and Mabel Torrey* (1969). This volume provides the most extensive information available of Mabel Torrey's life. Originals of the book's photographs are with Hamlin's papers in the Iowa State Univ. library. Articles in the files of the Des Moines (Iowa) *Register* and *Tribune* October 10, 1958, July 7, 1967, May 14, 1969, add a few details. *The Annual Exhibition Record of the Art Institute of Chicago 1888–1950* (1990) lists Torrey's works that were exhibited in the Art Institute's *Chicago and Vicinity* shows. Her work is mentioned in Lorado Taft, *The History of American Sculpture* (1930). Sue Ann Prince, ed., *The Old Guard and the Avant-Garde: Modernism in Chicago, 1910–1940* (1990), deals with Lorado Taft's career, the Armory Show, and education at the School of the Art Institute of Chicago. Sources dealing with life at the Midway Studios include Ada Bartlett Taft, *Lorado Taft Sculptor and Citizen* (1946), and Ruth Helming Mose, "Midway Studio," *American Magazine of Art*, August 1928. See Commission on Chicago Landmarks, *Lorado Taft Midway Studios* (1992), for a clear picture of the physical arrangements of the studios.

MARY ALICE MOLLOY

TOWLE, CHARLOTTE HELEN
November 17, 1896–October 1, 1966
EDUCATOR IN SOCIAL WORK, AUTHOR

Charlotte Towle was an educator in social work at the University of Chicago School of Social Service Administration from 1932 until her retirement in 1962. She was appointed by Dean EDITH ABBOTT to teach psychiatric social work. Her career resulted in teaching and writings that facilitated the expansion of case work theory, which produced changes in methods of education as well as actual casework practice. Towle's 1945 publication *Common Human Needs: An Interpretation for Staff in Public Assistance Agencies* outlined the basics of human behavior in interaction with governmental assistance programs. The book has become a classic in social work literature.

Towle's family lived in Butte, Montana, where she was born. Her father, Herman Augustus Towle, was a jeweler, who as a young man went west to seek his fortune. He returned to Indiana to marry Emily Kelsey and they moved to Butte. Charlotte Towle was born between two sisters, Mildred and Elise; they had a younger brother, John. Herman Towle's jewelry business prospered. The Towle's midwestern propriety and middle-class status removed them from the raucous life of Butte's copper mining community, but growing up with exposure to the wide-open, egalitarian ethic of the frontier made a strong impression on Charlotte Towle.

Emily Towle disliked Butte and turned her attention to her children. She filled their house with books and maintained a keen interest in social issues. During frequent discussions about politics and social welfare, she introduced Charlotte Towle to the work of JANE ADDAMS, JULIA LATHROP, and GRACE ABBOTT. Towle's mother tried to relocate the family, which resulted in two year-long childhood forays into communities very different from Butte. Emily Towle could not convince her husband to move to either southern California or Mishawaka, Indiana, after a lengthy residence in each locale, however, and Charlotte Towle learned early about the differences between life in predictable, respectable communities and life on the frontier.

Towle attended public schools in Butte and Mishawaka, graduating from Butte High School in 1915. Herman Towle expected his daughters to be able to support themselves, and while they were in high school he enrolled them in Butte Business College. Towle knew that she wanted to become a writer and convinced her father that she and her sister Mildred should go to college. They went to Virginia College, a small women's institution in Roanoke, for a year, until Towle transferred to Goucher College, Baltimore, Maryland.

Goucher's commitment to educate young women for domestic loyalty and social cooperation was not lost on Towle. In 1917, as America entered World War I, Towle, along with her classmates, participated in Baltimore's contribution to the war effort. The college prided itself on preparing its students for the hardships of war and added a series of emergency preparedness classes to its curriculum, including courses in the principles of administering relief. Here Towle received her first formal instruction in social work. During her junior year, Towle involved herself in two community volunteer projects, one with the Prisoner's Aid Association and the other with the American Red Cross.

Fig. 119. *Charlotte Towle taught social work at the School of Social Service Administration, University of Chicago; here at play with Jeremy Eppel, aged nearly 7 months, in 1955.*

Intent on becoming a social worker after graduating from Goucher in 1919, Towle took a job with the Baltimore office of the Red Cross. Her first placement was in Denver, Colorado. Six months later she was sent to Thermopolis, Wyoming, where she worked with tuberculosis rehabilitation cases. She learned on the job and looked upon these early positions, prior to her professional training, as doing her best with limited resources. In 1921, the Veterans Bureau in San Francisco hired her to process discharged servicemen's claims, but before long she was traveling in California, teaching others to take patients' social histories. Towle thrived in each setting and, by 1925, was director of psychiatric social service in the Veterans Bureau Hospital, American Lake, Washington. In spite of her success, she grew frustrated with the apsychological approach to case management that governed her interactions with clients. She became increasingly aware that she needed more professional training. She knew of advances in the field of psychiatry from colleagues and wanted to return to graduate school. Towle was accepted at the New York School of Social Work (later the Columbia School of Social Work) and received a twelve hundred dollar Commonwealth Fellowship from the philanthropic Commonwealth Fund.

The New York School exposed Towle to the social sciences as well as to the teachings of psychiatry and psychoanalysis. She trained at the Bureau of Child Guidance, where she worked closely with the "mother of the child guidance movement" (*New York Times*, June 27, 1980), psychoanalyst Marion Kenworthy.

Towle emerged concerned with the role of social workers as they interacted with psychiatric theory. She did not see social workers functioning as junior psychiatrists, and it was here that she began a career-long struggle to define a unique role for her profession using psychiatric and social science theory as a basis for practice. Towle's Commonwealth Fellowship supported her through only nine months of advanced study, and she left the New York School with no formal degree. While the lack of completion of a formal social work degree was not unusual for the time, the absence of an advanced degree would add to Towle's financial worries as she grew older and remained in an academic setting.

In the summer of 1926, Towle moved to Philadelphia, Pennsylvania, to work with adoptions and foster placements as the director of the home finding department of the Children's Aid Society. She lectured at the Pennsylvania School of Social Work and started to publish in social work journals. In Philadelphia, she worked closely with Virginia Robinson and Jessie Taft, the founders of the functionalist school of social work, which was based on the teachings of psychoanalyst Otto Rank. Robinson and Taft worked hard to develop a theoretical approach to case management that redefined and limited agency and worker involvement with clients. Towle was schooled in the more classical psychoanalytically based diagnostic school, and her exposure to the Philadelphia functionalists helped her, several years later, to speak with firsthand knowledge in the national debate that determined the role of psychoanalytic theory in social work practice. In 1928, Towle came back to New York to become a staff supervisor at the Institute for Child Guidance, a job which she kept for the next four years. While there, she served as a field placement teacher for students at the New York School and Smith College School of Social Work.

In 1932, Dean Edith Abbott of the University of Chicago School of Social Service Administration (SSA) offered Towle a position on the faculty. By the time she left New York, her reputation reached far beyond the East Coast due largely to her presence at professional meetings and her frequent publications. Towle's varied experiences and eclectic outlook appealed to Abbott's desire to expand the scope of the SSA curriculum.

Her acceptance of the Chicago faculty position reflected Towle's pioneering spirit. SSA enjoyed a national reputation as a center for social policy studies, stemming from close affiliations with Jane Addams and Hull-House and Grace Abbott's work at the U.S. Children's Bureau. But psychiatric training at SSA was in its infancy, reflecting Dean Edith Abbott's belief that improvements for the poor came from using quantifiable research methods to establish life-changing social policy rather than from addressing individual psychiatric problems. Dean Abbott warily recognized the growing importance of psychiatry. She welcomed Towle's balanced knowledge of both social science and psychiatry and Towle's desire to limit the latter's role in social work practice. Towle's Chicago mission was to open new territory in case work education. For the next fifteen years, she taught a heavy course load, supervised students at the Institute for Juvenile Research, delivered papers at national conferences, and published scores of articles dealing with philosophical issues affecting social work practice, the role of the social work professional, and educational issues relevant to social work training. Her first book, *Social Case Records from Psychiatric Clinics*, was published in 1941.

In the winter of 1939, Towle decided to complete her unfinished graduate degree in social work at SSA. Although she had continued to move up the university appointment ladder, she felt a need for academic credentials, fueled in large part by a wish to improve her earning capacity. Her studies with Edith Abbott exposed her at close range to SSA's rigorous curriculum, including many social policy courses. It was during this period that she solidified her identity as an educator and evolved a core set of teachings grounded in the social sciences, law, medicine, and the arts.

Towle wrote *Common Human Needs*, her most important publication, shortly after the end of World War II. In 1944 she had gone to Washington, D.C., to produce a manual for Bureau of Public Assistance supervisors. Her assignment was to help public assistance workers understand the psychological impact on a client of being economically dependent on a governmental agency. She wrote of a person's right to receive public assistance and of governmental responsibility in providing aid. These were powerful ideas at a time when few looked kindly on those receiving public funds. *Common Human Needs* went to press in the summer of 1945 and met with instant success. However, in spite of critical acclaim, the book caused enormous controversy.

In 1947, the Commission on Governmental Efficiency and Economy, a civic-minded group in Baltimore seeking to expose governmental waste in the administration of welfare, cited the book as evidence that the Bureau of Public Assistance was teaching its workers to foster dependency among clients. As evidence they cited a sentence in *Common Human Needs* that read, "Social security and public assistance are a basic essential for attainment of the socialized state envisaged in democratic ideology, a way of life which so far has been realized only in slight measure" (p. 57). The committee focused largely on the words "socialized state," which Towle meant in a psychological sense rather than a political one. Towle's words were regarded as scandalously left leaning and were picked up by wire services, resulting in news stories all over the country. Towle, who had returned to teaching in Chicago, was stunned by her sudden notoriety. Throughout the ensuing controversy, she was never asked by the press to explicate her views.

Oscar Ewing, Federal Security Administrator under President Harry S. Truman, was also responsible for the Bureau of Public Assistance, which made him ultimately accountable for the publication of *Common Human Needs*. Truman had asked Ewing to develop a ten-year plan for expanding health care systems. The American Medical Association (AMA) feared his plans would lead to "socialized medicine." Part of their ammunition against him was the critical sentence on the "socialized state" in *Common Human Needs*, which at the height of the McCarthy era, was viewed as un-American and evidence of creeping socialism. The president of the AMA called for Ewing to disavow before Congress his support for the principles expressed in *Common Human Needs*. Ewing replied with an angry statement to the AMA, but at the same time sent an order to the Government Printing Office to destroy existing copies of the book as well as the plates from which it was printed. The social work community quickly mobilized, resulting in a flood of letters to congressmen and President Truman, condemning Ewing's actions. The book was quickly republished by the American Association of Social Workers. Its classic description of the psychological impact of dependence on governmental assistance is still used in social work training. The book has had twenty-three printings in English, and more than eighty thousand copies have been sold. A revised edition was published in 1987. Translations into ten different languages have been published.

Towle published *The Learner in Education for the Professions* in 1954. She continued to serve on many Chicago and national committees, and she was adviser to the Mental Health Division of the U.S. Public Health Service. In 1954, she was invited to spend a sabbatical year at the London School of Economics to help organize a new English casework curriculum. She applied to the Fulbright Foundation for funding and informally received notice that Fulbright committees on both sides of the Atlantic had approved her application. Formal approval was denied when the Department of State refused to grant her a passport because of her alleged support for groups that were considered communist fronts as well as her signature on a letter to President Dwight David Eisenhower asking him to grant clemency for Julius and Ethel Rosenberg, who were about to be executed as spies. After much delay and more national publicity, Towle received a Fulbright fellowship and her passport. She spent 1955 in London attempting to launch a standard social work curriculum that was to be funded by the Carnegie Endowment. When she returned to Chicago she resumed her teaching responsibilities, worked on American curriculum reform, and introduced a new course on the teaching of social work. Because of failing health, she retired from teaching in 1962.

During Towle's final years on the SSA faculty, she received several honorary degrees and the prestigious Flora Lasker Social Work Award. In 1964, with continuing financial concerns, Towle accepted a position on the staff of Chicago's Scholarship and Guidance Association, where she worked for two years supervising students during their fieldwork and serving as a consultant. In September 1966, as she was preparing for two seminars to be delivered later in the fall, she died of a massive stroke during a vacation in Jackson, New Hampshire.

Charlotte Towle contributed significantly to the definition of the profession of social work. Her deep understanding of the complex issues that develop between those on governmental assistance and those in a helping role has provided generations of social workers with a solid foundation for their interventions. In no place is this contribution seen more clearly than in *Common Human Needs*, for it reflects an integration of the various strains of Towle's experience. Towle's acceptance of the limits of social workers' ability to change the lives of those with whom they worked provided the basis for important research that was done at SSA throughout the 1950s.

Towle enjoyed a position in a national network of social work women that dominated the profession until well into the 1950s. She enjoyed close relationships with many colleagues who, like herself, devoted their lives to their work, lived in long-term relationships with close friends, and sought to lessen human suffering. Her extensive contributions on the education of learners in social work have been recognized in the literature of the training of all professionals. Interviews with her former students tell of her great influence in the formation of their professional identities. Towle expanded the educational mission of social work in the "Chicago School," changed the nature of that training, and through her students influenced casework practice and education throughout much of the world.

Sources. The Charlotte Towle Papers, UC Spec. Coll., include her articles, information about her professional work, and considerable correspondence. Towle's extensive articles and books are available in social work journals from 1926 to 1965. Information on *Common Human Needs* can be found in the National Archives and Records Administration, Record Group 47, Suitland, Maryland, and at the Harry S. Truman Library, Independence, Missouri. Wendy Beth Posner, "Charlotte Towle: A Biography" (Ph.D. diss., Univ. of Chicago, 1986), has a complete bibliography of Towle's published works. Towle is listed in *NAW* (1980) and *The Encyclopedia of Social Work* (1977). For an updated review of the controversy around *Common Human Needs: An Interpretation for Staff in Public Assistance Agencies*, see Wendy Posner, "*Common Human Needs*: A Story from the Prehistory of Government by Special Interest," *Social Service Review*, June 1995.

WENDY BETH POSNER

TROUT, GRACE WILBUR
c. 1864–October 21, 1955
SUFFRAGIST, POLITICAL LEADER, ORATOR, CLUBWOMAN
Suffragist and community leader, possessing great skill both on the lecture platform and in politics, Grace Wilbur Trout was born in Maquoketa, Iowa, to Thomas and Anne (Belden)

Wilbur. Wilbur received a public school education in Maquoketa, supplemented by private instruction in languages, literature, and dramatic art. On January 5, 1886, Wilbur married George William Trout (1862–1949), also from Maquoketa. They had four sons: Thomas Wilbur, Philip Wilbur, Ralph Belden, and John Vernon. They later adopted a nephew, George William Sackett. George William Trout was a hardware merchant in Maquoketa for fifteen years until 1893, when he moved to Chicago, continuing in the hardware business. By 1896 his firm was George W. Trout and Company. In 1915 Trout changed his company into a merchandise and real estate brokerage, and around 1919 he became engaged in the oil business.

In the early 1900s, Grace Wilbur Trout became an active clubwoman, first in Chicago, and then in Oak Park, when the Trouts moved to the near western suburb in 1904. Like many upper-middle-class women of her time, Trout joined a number of clubs, including the West End Woman's Club, the Nineteenth Century Woman's Club of Oak Park, the Illinois Woman's Press Association, and the Chicago Chapter of the Daughters of the American Revolution. She served as president of the Ladies' Auxiliary of the Ashland Club of Chicago and of the Woman's Auxiliary of the Oak Park Club. She joined the Chicago Woman's Club in 1901 and the Chicago Political Equality League (CPEL) in 1903. During this period Trout also pursued an interest in women and Mormonism, the result of which was her 1896 novel, *A Mormon's Wife*.

Trout's emergence as a state suffrage leader in the second decade of the twentieth century illustrated the shift that took place within the ranks of the suffrage movement's leadership across the United States. Upper-middle-class, educated, socially conservative women embraced the campaign for women's political rights and gained preeminence in the movement. As a result, social activists like CATHARINE McCULLOCH, many of them middle-class and working-class women who had fought for suffrage for decades, lost the ability to shape the campaign. Trout's leadership, eloquence, and political and organizational skills were most fully engaged and demonstrated in her work for woman suffrage from 1910 to 1920. Her first active participation in suffrage work began when she was elected president of the Chicago Political Equality League in May 1910. Under her administration, the CPEL enlarged its focus to include constructing and staffing a parade float, undertaking an automobile tour, and completing a successful membership drive. These endeavors enhanced the group's visibility and presented people in Chicago and the surrounding area with the demand for women's political rights.

The CPEL entered the first suffrage float in Chicago's annual Sane Fourth Parade, held on July 4, 1910, after some hesitation on the part of the men's committee over whether such an innovation should be allowed. The CPEL was given permission, and after contributions were raised for its construction, mostly from among Trout's friends and neighbors in Oak Park, the float received more cheers from the crowd than any other entry in the parade, with the exception of the Union Civil War Veterans. A *Chicago Tribune* reporter, however, wondered how much of the cheering emanated from the crowd's sympathy for suffrage and how much from the sight of pretty young women on the float.

A week later, on July 11, 1910, the first Suffrage Automobile Tour in Illinois began, lasting five days. The entourage, led

FIG. 120. *Grace Wilbur Trout behind the wheel of her automobile in a parade for woman suffrage.*

by Trout, included Catharine Waugh McCulloch, legislative chair of the Illinois Equal Suffrage Association (IESA) and vice-president of the National American Woman Suffrage Association (NAWSA); ELLA SEASS STEWART, the state president of the IESA; and S. Grace Nicholes, corresponding secretary of the IESA. An Oak Park neighbor of Trout's donated the use of his expensive touring cars and his chauffeur for the project. At each stop Trout spoke first, outlining the idea of woman suffrage, and then introduced the other speakers, who addressed specific issues surrounding women's need for the vote. Setting a grueling pace for themselves (sixteen towns within forty miles of Chicago in five days), the women gathered crowds on street corners and at train stations, held up traffic, and used a megaphone in order to be heard. They waded through deep mud and drove through rain storms to meet their scheduled appointments. When there were no suffrage groups to welcome them, they organized the local women.

In contrast to McCulloch's confrontational style and militant strategies, one of Trout's strengths as a leader was her ability to use persuasion and diplomacy to win over opponents and hesitant supporters alike. She approached them as friends and colleagues, as uninformed and well-intentioned people who only needed gentle prodding and suggestion on the question of suffrage. Trout also accepted support for the cause from individuals not traditionally associated with the progressive women's reform agenda. For example, in 1913 Trout accepted the assistance of William Randolph Hearst, antilabor editor of the *Chicago Examiner*, despite the opposition of prolabor suffragists. McCulloch, a seasoned political lobbyist and good debater, clashed with Trout over philosophy as well as political methods.

McCulloch perceived suffrage as a tool women should use to improve their low social status. As part of the new wave of suffragists, Trout viewed the ballot as an end in itself, a natural right due to women because of their humanity. Trout's conciliatory approach allowed her to maintain good relations with the press and with her political opponents. During the automobile speaking tour, the *Chicago Tribune* assigned two reporters to travel with Trout in her car. Local newspapers also featured front page stories about the women's endeavors. Trout reported that their success encouraged similar automobile suffrage campaigns in other parts of the state by IESA members. Trout also maintained a generous attitude toward her political rivals. After one suffrage victory in Illinois, when asked if "her enemies" (opponents to suffrage) should be invited to the victory celebration, Trout replied, "We have no enemies" (Wheeler, 112).

During Trout's two-and-a-half-year tenure as CPEL president, the league was transformed into a more active, visible political organization. Dissatisfied with the CPEL's slow growth, Trout initiated a vigorous membership campaign in the summer of 1910, and by that fall the roll had increased from 143 to 388. By 1912 the CPEL had nearly one thousand members. Along with its size, the league also expanded its activities; in May 1911 it designated three areas of political work, known as the Legislative, Study, and Propaganda Sections of the CPEL. Each section met once every month, in addition to the regular monthly CPEL meetings, and each offered a course of lectures, often followed by discussion, on a particular topic pertaining to women and their social status.

In addition to her Chicago political work, Trout became a state board member of the IESA in October 1910. Her leadership and energy at the local CPEL level helped her to be elected president of the IESA on October 2, 1912, an office she held until 1920, with a one-year hiatus 1915–16. Although Trout initially did not want or seek the office and desired to retire from public life, she changed her mind after one of her sons encouraged her. Tragically, this young man died just three weeks after Trout's election to the presidency. In response to her loss, Trout dedicated her IESA work to his memory.

As IESA President, Trout decided to launch a statewide campaign to pass a bill in the Illinois state legislature granting women the right of presidential and municipal suffrage. Dismayed by previous campaigns at the legislature in Springfield, where suffragists were ignored and treated disrespectfully, Trout was determined to make the issue of woman suffrage a serious and respected issue. She decided to extend her collegial, persuasive style to the legislative fight. Her strategy also included embracing a nonpartisan approach to gain support for the suffrage bill, systematically learning about each legislator and foiling attempts to derail the bill in committee. Although many longtime suffragists were skeptical, and McCulloch openly showed opposition, Trout's practical strategy paid off: the Presidential and Municipal Suffrage Bill was brought up for final vote on June 11, 1913, and passed. On that morning, Trout remained alert to last-minute, antisuffrage political maneuverings. Realizing that a vote to defeat could be taken quickly if any legislators supporting the bill left the chamber, and that the doorkeeper, who opposed suffrage, would illegally admit antisuffrage lobbyists onto the floor if left unobserved, Trout stationed herself at the chamber door and successfully kept lobbyists out and suffrage supporters in until the vote was taken. For the first time in any state east of the Mississippi River, women won the right to limited suffrage.

Trout spent 1913–15 successfully defending the new suffrage law from attempts by opponents to declare it unconstitutional under the Illinois Constitution or to repeal it through further legislation. She also worked to gather more support for the law in Illinois and to push for federal suffrage. In addition to her legislative work, from 1912 to 1915 she raised forty-four thousand dollars for the Illinois suffrage cause. Her hard work took a toll on her, however, and in 1915 she declined to stand for reelection to the IESA. Declaring that she needed rest, Trout spent the winter of 1915–16 at her Florida home. She was reelected to the post in 1916. In that same year, the IESA, dissatisfied with the limited Illinois suffrage law, decided to propose legislation for a new Illinois Constitution that would grant full woman suffrage. Trout fought for the Constitutional Convention Resolution in the Illinois legislature and saw it passed before the 1916 session ended.

During this same period Trout was beginning to be recognized in suffrage circles at the national level. Known for her speaking ability, Trout was invited to make suffrage speeches in the summer of 1914 at fifty Chautauquas in nine states. In 1915 suffragists across the country encouraged her to accept a nomination for president of the NAWSA; however, Trout did not allow her name to be considered. A year later Trout was called upon by the NAWSA to organize a suffrage parade and demonstration in Chicago while the National Republican Convention was in session. At that June 7, 1916, event, known afterwards as the "rainy day suffrage parade," five thousand women marched through pouring rain for more than a mile down Michigan Avenue to the Coliseum convention site, arriving, drenched, just as Trout and three other NAWSA representatives concluded their suffrage plank appeal to the Platform Committee. The Republican delegates placed a suffrage plank in their platform. In 1917 Carrie Chapman Catt (president of the NAWSA) asked Trout to come to Washington, D.C., to work on the Federal Suffrage Amendment. During that time Trout met with President Woodrow Wilson to gain his support for the amendment. Finally, in 1919, she was called back to Washington by the NAWSA to work on the final push for passage of the suffrage amendment.

Trout was still president of the IESA in 1920 when the Nineteenth Amendment to the United States Constitution was ratified by the states. She closed her suffrage career in September 1920 when the IESA declared its work finished and formed the Illinois League of Women Voters.

In 1921 Trout moved permanently to Jacksonville, Florida, where she and her husband owned a vacation home. She did not retire from active community service, however; she joined numerous clubs and societies. Trout was also an honorary member of the General Federation of Women's Clubs. In addition to club work, she served as president of the Jacksonville City Planning Advisory Board beginning in 1928; she was reelected to the board every year until 1943, when she was named president emeritus. In 1928 the Jacksonville American Legion awarded Trout a medal of honor as the most public-spirited Jacksonville citizen. Trout died of pneumonia at the age of ninety-one and was buried in Evergreen Cemetery in Jacksonville.

Trout's tenure as president of IESA provided the Illinois suffrage movement with a strong leader who was able to communicate effectively to a vast audience using modern mass media techniques. Furthermore, her public speaking skill and political acumen were crucial in the 1913 suffrage victory in Illinois. As an upper-middle-class, relatively socially conservative woman, Trout exemplified the new, and last, wave of suffragists who came into prominence before 1920 and the Nineteenth Amendment. She was a decisive, effective leader at a turning point in Illinois, and suffrage, history.

Sources. The best description of Trout's suffrage work in Chicago and Illinois appears in a paper Trout wrote and presented at the annual meeting of the Illinois State Hist. Soc. on May 14, 1920; it was published as "Side Lights on Illinois Suffrage History," *Transactions of the Illinois State Historical Society for the Year 1920* (1920). A good analysis of the 1913 Illinois suffrage campaign and Trout's role in it is Adade Mitchell Wheeler's article, "Conflict in the Illinois Woman Suffrage Movement of 1913," *Journal of the Illinois State Historical Society*, Summer 1983. Steven M. Buechler includes information about Trout's suffrage leadership in *The Transformation of the Woman Suffrage Movement: The Case of Illinois 1850–1920* (1986). *CT* articles on Trout include "Here Come the Motoring Militant Suffragettes," July 10, 1910; "'Holds Up' Train for Votes," July 12, 1910; "Vote Pilgrims Still Militant," July 13, 1910; "Women on Suffrage Tour Gain Pledge of Support," July 14, 1910; "Crowd Leaves as Women Talk," July 15, 1910; "Suffrage Tour Ends in Triumph," July 16, 1910. The Oak Park newspaper *Oak Leaves* published "Grace Wilbur Trout," November 4, 1916. A biography of Trout appears in *NCAB* (1927).

RACHEL E. BOHLMANN

TRUE, CORINNE KNIGHT
November 1, 1861–April 3, 1961

RELIGIOUS LEADER

Corinne Knight True, a key figure in the establishment of the Bahā'ī Faith in the United States, was born in Kentucky during the Civil War, the eldest child of Moses Greene and Martha Thomas (Duerson) Knight. Skillful real estate investments in Chicago downtown property made Moses Knight prosperous, but when the Great Chicago Fire of 1871 swept the city, followed by the 1873 depression, Knight had to sell all his Kentucky property and move his family to Chicago to preserve his investments. Financial success enabled Knight to send his daughter to Miss Mary Baldwin's finishing school in Virginia. A few months after graduation, on November 24, 1882, Corinne Knight eloped, marrying Moses Adams True, the son of a next-door neighbor. Moses Knight opposed his daughter's marriage; and the resulting bitter divide between father and daughter, who formerly had been close, lasted ten years.

The Trues had eight children in rapid succession: Harriet Merrill (1883–92), Lawrence Knight (1885–1906), Charles Gilbert Davis (1886–1912), Edna Miriam (1888–1988), Arna Corinne (1890–1975), twins Katherine (1893–1963) and Kenneth (1893–1901), and Nathanael (1896–99). The family was close and prosperous; they hired a cook and sent the children to private school. The loss of four of the children before adulthood produced a series of successive blows that severely tested True and turned her thinking toward religion. After Harriet fell down the stone basement stairs and died at age nine, Corinne and Moses True drew away from mainline Protestantism to some newly developed approaches to religion: the Unity School of Christianity, then Christian Science, then Divine Science. When the baby of the family, Nathanael, died from complications following diphtheria, True deepened her religious search. Through a friend she encountered the Bahā'ī Faith late in 1899 and accepted it within a few months. In contrast, her husband was very sympathetic to Bahā'ī beliefs but never formally joined.

When True became a Bahā'ī, the American Bahā'ī community numbered fifteen hundred to two thousand and was five years old. The Bahā'ī religion began in 1863, when an Iranian noble named Mīrzā Ḥusayn-'Alī (1817–92), known as Bahā'u'llāh, founded a religion based on such principles as the oneness of God, the spiritual unity of the world's religions, the oneness of humanity, independent individual search for truth, and the equality of the sexes. A practical religion, it quickly spread beyond Iran and attracted Jews, Christians, Zoroastrians, and Buddhists as well as Muslims. When Bahā'u'll āh died, his son 'Abdu'l-Bahā (1844–1921) became head of the faith.

It is not known what attracted True to the Bahā'ī Faith, though its universal nature and inclusiveness were probably factors. She immediately became one of Chicago's most active Bahā'īs. When, in May 1901, the Chicago Bahā'īs elected an all-male governing body to run the community and a women's Auxiliary Board to assist, True became corresponding secretary of the latter. In March 1902 True delivered a talk at the Chicago Bahā'ī Sunday program titled "Fundamental Points of Behaism [*sic*]." Its contents indicate that True's understanding of the Bahā'ī Faith was as good as that of any of the other Chicago Bahā'īs at the time.

True wrote to 'Abdu'l-Bahā about the exclusion of women from the Chicago Bahā'ī governing body on February 25, 1902, noting that "many" felt it should be a "mixed board" because "women in America stand so conspicuously for all that is highest & best in every department" (Stockman, "Women in the Chicago Bahā'ī Community," 23). In his response 'Abdu'l-Bahā stated that while "in the sight of God, the conduct of women is the same as that of men" and there was "no difference" between the sexes, nevertheless the "House of Justice" had to consist only of men and that the "reason will presently appear, even as the sun at midday" ("Women in the Chicago Bahā'ī Community," 25).

True accepted 'Abdu'l-Bahā's ruling—which also affirmed the equality of the sexes—and poured her energy into the Chicago Bahā'ī women's organization, which 'Abdu'l-Bahā highly praised. For the next eight years Chicago had two parallel Bahā'ī organizations, one confined to men, the other to women. True served as president or secretary of the women's body at different times. By 1903 she had been instrumental in establishing the first Bahā'ī communities in Michigan—in Muskegon and Fruitport—near her family's summer residence. She also traveled to Wisconsin to speak about the Bahā'ī Faith.

In 1903 the Chicago Bahā'īs heard about the construction of the world's first Bahā'ī House of Worship, in what is today Turkmenistan (formerly Turkistan). They wrote to 'Abdu'l-Bahā asking for permission to build a temple of their own. 'Abdu'l-Bahā not only sent them two supportive letters in response, he wrote True and encouraged her to get involved in the effort. She was surprised, since until that time she had not been interested.

In spite of 'Abdu'l-Bahā's encouragement, nothing was done for several years. On August 5, 1906, True's oldest son, Lawrence, drowned during a sailing race on Lake Huron. The young man had just finished college and was about to get married. True reevaluated her own life as a result and decided to redirect her energy to the construction of the temple. She went to Akka, Palestine, to meet 'Abdu'l-Bahā, spending six days with him in late February 1907. He gave True detailed instructions about building a Bahā'ī House of Worship in America. When three prominent Chicago men arrived a few weeks later, 'Abdu'l-Bahā told them to work with True, that all his instructions for the Chicago Bahā'īs had been given to her.

Returning to Chicago in the spring of 1907, True began searching the area for potential building sites, especially those on the lake shore. The House of Spirituality (the Chicago Bahā'ī governing body) named her treasurer of the temple work. Since the project grew to an international effort, she wrote hundreds of letters to Bahā'īs and Bahā'ī communities around the world. 'Abdu'l-Bahā wrote to True and the House of Spirituality, encouraging them to work together and resolving any friction that arose between them. In late November 1907 the House of Spirituality hosted an informal convention of representatives of various Bahā'ī communities from around North America to build support for the temple. True did much of the planning for the convention, which was largely held at her home in Chicago.

In mid-March 1908 True found a site at the corner of Linden Avenue and Sheridan Road in Wilmette, Illinois. A newly excavated drainage canal bounded the site on one side and Lake Michigan on another; the plot also possessed some elevation.

The site's natural advantages, however, were offset by its distance from downtown Chicago on public transportation. In spite of this problem and the resulting opposition from some Chicago Bahá'ís, the House of Spirituality purchased the site on April 9, 1908.

True believed the choice of a site necessitated the establishment of a formal, national organization, for the building would be a national, not a local, House of Worship. She wrote 'Abdu'l-Bahá, proposing that the American Bahá'ís create a national organization. In late August 1908 he replied that he was pleased with her plan, which called for the national coordinating body to be chosen by delegates selected by the various local Bahá'í communities across the United States and Canada. He added that women should be included.

The first convention of the Bahai [sic] Temple Unity was held in March 1909 in Chicago, with several sessions held at the True home. The convention formally approved the Wilmette site for the House of Worship and elected nine Bahá'ís to serve on the executive board of the Bahai Temple Unity. Three were women, including Corinne True, who was chosen as the board's financial secretary. Thus she continued the role she had played for the temple on behalf of the Chicago Bahá'ís.

True's devotion to the temple project became her chief solace as another round of tragedies befell her. In mid-December 1909, Moses True died suddenly of a massive heart attack at the age of fifty-two. The following summer her sole surviving son, Charles, contracted tuberculosis, succumbing in April 1912. He died the night before 'Abdu'l-Bahá arrived in Wilmette to dedicate the temple site. True attended the dedication in spite of her grief. Before the ceremony 'Abdu'l-Bahá spent some minutes offering her consolation in private.

During 'Abdu'l-Bahá's visit to Chicago in 1912, he definitively removed all restrictions on the service of women in local Bahá'í institutions. True was one of the first group of three women to be elected to the nine-member Chicago House of Spirituality that year. One unexpected result of True's local and national duties was that she no longer had time to devote to Bahá'í women's activities. Across North America such bodies largely disappeared after 1912, once women were elected to local Bahá'í governing bodies.

Throughout the 1910s True was simultaneously a member of the Chicago and national Bahá'í coordinating bodies and served as financial secretary of the temple project. She traveled to Hawaii and California to lecture about the Bahá'í Faith. In 1919 True made a second pilgrimage to Akka, Palestine, visiting with 'Abdu'l-Bahá in November of that year. She attended the Bahai Temple Unity convention in 1920, which formally approved a design for the House of Worship. The Wilmette temple was a unique blend of Eastern and Western architectural elements. Its pillars were reminiscent of minarets, and it was decorated with Middle Eastern designs, though it was composed of ornamental concrete and Portland cement over structural steel. Like all Bahá'í temples, it had nine sides, a dome, and surrounding formal gardens.

On November 29, 1921, 'Abdu'l-Bahá died peacefully at age seventy-seven. The True home was plunged into intense grief, for True, like other prominent Bahá'ís, had developed a very close and special relationship with 'Abdu'l-Bahá. True played a pivotal role in consoling the Bahá'ís, whose morale was severely affected by the crisis.

'Abdu'l-Bahá had appointed his grandson Shoghi Effendi as his successor and Guardian of the Bahá'í Faith. True had already met Shoghi Effendi on her 1919 pilgrimage and had corresponded with him; thus she was in an excellent position to rally the Bahá'ís behind him. In early 1922, Shoghi Effendi invited a group of about fifteen prominent Bahá'ís from around the world to come to Haifa to consult with him about the future development of the faith. True was one of four members of the Bahai Temple Unity Executive board who were invited.

Over the next few years the Bahai Temple Unity Executive Board, under Shoghi Effendi's direction, evolved into a new body, the National Spiritual Assembly of the Bahá'ís of the United States and Canada. Internationally uniform guidelines for conducting Bahá'í elections and carrying out Bahá'í administrative activities were created. True wished to devote her time exclusively to the temple, a task that was the National Spiritual Assembly's most important responsibility. She no longer served on the American Bahá'í coordinating body after 1923 but continued to be appointed financial secretary of the temple project through 1927. Subsequently she served on various national committees, especially those related to the temple project. In 1930, True moved to Wilmette from Chicago to be closer to the House of Worship, which was then partially built.

True went on several more pilgrimages to meet with Shoghi Effendi during the 1920s and 1930s. Her last meeting with him was in Haifa in 1952, when she was ninety-one years old. She also made lecture tours of western Europe in 1947 and 1950 in order to assist the new Bahá'í communities there. In her later years True's reputation grew, and American Bahá'ís came to refer to her as "the mother of the Temple" and as "Mother True." On February 29, 1952, Shoghi Effendi appointed Corinne True a Hand of the Cause of God, a special spiritual status within the Bahá'í community that included no administrative authority but conveyed prestige and the privilege to counsel and advise Bahá'ís and their administrative institutions. Of the nineteen Hands then living, four were women.

On May 2, 1953, True was one of several Hands attending the dedication of the Bahá'í House of Worship in Wilmette. She was thus able to see the completion of the building to which she had devoted so much of her life. In April 1957—when True was ninety-five—Shoghi Effendi appointed her as his official representative to attend the first election of the National Spiritual Assembly of the Bahá'ís of the Greater Antilles in the Caribbean. It was True's last trip outside the United States. Her failing health prevented further travel.

On November 4, 1957, Shoghi Effendi died suddenly. The Hands of the Cause assumed collective control of the Bahá'í Faith until the Universal House of Justice could be elected. Because of her frail health, True was the only Hand unable to travel to Israel for the annual conclaves of the Hands. Nevertheless they kept her informed of their decisions and asked her to sign notarized affidavits of assent supporting all important statements on which they had unanimously agreed.

Corinne True died peacefully in her Wilmette home five

months into her hundredth year. She is remembered by the American Bahá'ís for her courage, faith, devotion, and persistence; historically she is one of the most prominent half dozen American Bahá'í women.

Sources. The National Bahá'í Archives, Wilmette, Illinois, possesses a collection, the Corinne True Family Papers, but it is not yet organized and available to researchers. Correspondence to or from True may also be found in that archives' Thornton Chase Papers, House of Spirituality Records, Albert R. Windust Papers, and several other collections. Most of the originals of True's letters from 'Abdu'l-Bahá are in the National Bahá'í Archives; some were published in ['Abdu'l-Bahá], *Tablets of Abdul-Baha Abbas* [*sic*]. Many of True's letters to 'Abdu'l-Bahá are in the International Bahá'í Archives in Haifa, Israel. A short summary of parts of True's life was published by Bruce Whitmore as "Mother of the Temple: The Story of Hand of the Cause of God Corinne Knight True," in *Bahá'í News*, January 1976. Nathan Rutstein's biography *Corinne True: Faithful Handmaid of 'Abdu'l-Bahá* (1987) provides far more detail but is a popular work that includes the author's guesses about True's thoughts and feelings and must be used with caution. Robert H. Stockman's "Women in the Chicago Bahá'í Community, 1900–1912," in *World Order*, Winter 1993–94, provides details of True's involvement in Chicago Bahá'í women's activities. Stockman's *Bahá'í Faith in America*, vol. two: *Early Expansion, 1900–1912* (1995), describes her role in the temple project, including her first pilgrimage to meet 'Abdu'l-Bahá.

ROBERT H. STOCKMAN

TUCKER, B. FAIN
April 7, 1899–September 26, 1970
LAWYER, JUDGE

B. Fain Tucker was the second woman judge of the Circuit Court of Cook County, elected thirty years after MARY BARTELME's initial pathbreaking victory. She was born in Greencastle, Indiana, the daughter of William W. and Bertha M. (Clark) Tucker. Her father was a physician and surgeon with a rural medical practice that he conducted in the tradition of several generations of his English ancestors. Bertha Fain Tucker was one of four children; she had two older brothers, Cassell and Glenn, and a sister, Mary. As an adult she was known as B. Fain Tucker.

Tucker learned about medicine when she accompanied her father as he drove his horse and carriage to the neighboring farmhouses. After graduation from the local high school in 1916, Tucker attended DePauw University in Greencastle, Indiana. There she majored in political science, developed her writing skills as woman's editor of the students' daily newspaper, and earned an A.B. degree. She was elected to Phi Beta Kappa and to Theta Sigma Phi, a women's national journalism honorary society.

In 1920, Tucker entered the University of Chicago Law School, where she was one of two or three women in a class of ninety. She graduated with her J.D. degree cum laude in 1923 and began work as a law clerk for a Chicago firm. She was admitted to the Illinois bar in 1925. Tucker started in practice with the law firm of Good, Childs, Bobb & Wescott, but she started her own practice in 1927. In the 1920s, most law firms refused to employ women as practicing lawyers. Of necessity, women attorneys became sole practitioners, as Tucker had, or formed

FIG. 121. *Newly elected Judge B. Fain Tucker, being helped into her robes by Judge Elmer J. Schnackenberg, Chicago, December 1, 1953.*

partnerships with other women. Some women gained admittance to major law firms as stenographers or secretaries, or taught law as part of civics in the public school system, while others did legal research for business corporations and banks.

Tucker's law practice initially dealt with corporations, trusts, estates, and administrative law. Her interests, however, extended to other fields, especially law cases related to medicine and to domestic relations. In addition to having her own practice from 1939 to 1943, Tucker became a special lecturer on family law to undergraduates at the University of Chicago.

Initially, women lawyers were prohibited from joining the bar associations to which male lawyers belonged, and even after women were grudgingly admitted, they had minimal opportunities for committee chairmanships. In reaction, in 1914 women lawyers established the Women's Bar Association of Illinois (WBAI). Its objectives were not only to promote opportunities for women in the field of law but also to enhance the voice of women lawyers on issues of concern to women. These included the right of women to serve on juries (finally achieved in Illinois in 1939); the appointment of women to public offices — especially dealing with children and the needy; and the enactment of protective labor legislation for women and children.

Tucker's early professional extracurricular activities included serving in various capacities on the WBAI board; and in 1941, Tucker became its president. Through the Women's Bar Association, Tucker developed close friendships with HELEN CIRESE, who became the Justice of the Peace in Oak Park, Illinois, and DOROTHEA BLENDER, who became vice-president of Commerce Clearing House, publisher of topical books on different fields of law. During World War II, Tucker served on the executive committee of the Cook County War Finance Committee and Defense Bond Organization. Aware of the country's lack of readiness at the start of the war, Tucker later advocated universal military training in a 1948 article for the *Women Lawyers Journal*.

In 1943, when the draft for the war was decimating the male staffs of law firms, Tucker became associated with the Chicago law firm of Pope & Ballard, serving for three years as assistant to Ernest S. Ballard, counsel in labor relations to leading industries in the country. She developed expertise in labor law and wrote the textbook, *Guide to the National Labor Relations Act* (1947).

Tucker researched and wrote on medico-legal issues, including artificial insemination and narcotics, publishing an early treatise on the former in the 1947 spring issue of *Women Lawyers Journal* and the latter in the 1952 spring issue of the same journal. She served in 1952 on a special WBAI narcotics committee. Tucker also researched the role of blood type in the law and lectured on the topic to women lawyers and doctors at joint professional committee meetings of the WBAI and the National Association of Women Lawyers (NAWL). In the 1950s, she was chair of the medico-legal committee of NAWL and served on the board of Women's and Children's Hospital.

During these same years, Tucker continued her civic involvements, giving legal advice as well as financial support to the Council of Christians and Jews; the Metropolitan Business and Professional Women's Club; and the DePauw University Alumni Association, of which she served a term as president. Tucker was an active member of the Episcopal Church and served on the National Layman's Committee of the National Churches of Christ of the United States of America. She respected all faiths and chose her friends without reference to their religion.

Tucker regularly participated in politics as a matter of conscience. In 1950, she was defeated as a candidate for judge of the municipal court. In 1953, the WBAI urged the Democratic and Republican parties to slate women as candidates for judgeships. Women candidates had been routinely rejected by the two parties. Only one woman, Mary Bartelme, had been elected judge in Illinois, in 1923, and she had retired from the bench in 1933. The Cook County Republican Committee in 1953, responding to the urging of the WBAI under the presidency of Mary A. Johnson, asked Tucker to run for judge of the Circuit Court of Cook County. She was endorsed by the Chicago Bar Association. The Republican Party also realized that the chance of getting another Republican judge elected in Democratic-dominated Cook County could probably be enhanced by the candidacy of a woman.

Members of the nonpartisan Women's Bar Association vigorously supported her regardless of their individual political affiliations, not only because she was the first woman to be nominated for such a long time, but because she was held in great esteem by the members and was deemed highly qualified by all bar associations. Members of other nonpartisan organizations, including the Parent Teacher Association (PTA) and the Chicago Federation of Women's Clubs, campaigned for Tucker. Her supporters functioned through a Committee to Elect B. Fain Tucker Judge, which was committed to working long hours with a minimal budget for her election. The chair of the committee was Marie Palumbo, a trial lawyer. Supporters included Juvenile Protective Association leader JESSIE BINFORD and Northwestern University Settlement head resident HARRIET VITTUM. Vittum and Binford had been part of the women's reform movement that had elected Mary Bartelme to a judgeship thirty years earlier. The three major Chicago newspapers endorsed Tucker. A new era for women in law began in 1953 when Tucker was installed as judge of the Circuit Court of Cook County.

Tucker had hoped she would be assigned to the Juvenile Court following in the tradition of Judge Bartelme. Instead, Tucker's first judicial assignment was to the Criminal Court of Cook County. "It was an open secret that her associates thought she would crack under the strain and prove that being a judge was exclusively a man's job" (p. 33), the *Chicago Sunday Tribune* reported May 8, 1955. Tucker realized that when she was assigned to the Criminal Court "it was thought I would not be able to take it" (quoted in Wright, "Woman Judge Proves Able: Wins Plaudits").

After serving on the Criminal Court bench, Judge Tucker was reelected in 1957 and assigned to the Common Law Division, where she presided over jury and non-jury trials relating to individual and business contracts, personal injury suits, and economic torts. Thereafter, she was sent to the Divorce Division and ultimately to the Chancery Division, involving equity jurisdiction, special remedies, trusts, and specific performance of real estate transactions. In 1961, Tucker was chosen by her nineteen fellow judges (all male) as the first woman chief judge of the Circuit Court of Cook County.

In the opinion of her friends, Judge Tucker preferred the Chancery Division because of its resemblance to the English court system of which she was especially knowledgeable. During summer court recesses she regularly visited the Inns of Court in London, and she enjoyed browsing in the old book shops of the city, where she bought books related to legal topics for her friends. Her personal library in her Chicago apartment, which she shared with her longtime friend Ruth Skinner, held floor-to-ceiling bookshelves jammed with volumes, many about English jurists, lawyers, and law cases—current, historical, and fictional. Tucker was not only an outstanding legal scholar; she was also an authority on mystery novels.

Judge Tucker was known for her thoughtfulness; her friends and their children were always remembered on birthdays and special occasions. She established the tradition of cooking and hosting an annual dinner at her home for the board of the WBAI in remembrance of its role in her election as judge. Tucker dressed conservatively in stylish clothes, and her auburn hair, blue eyes, and regular features gave her a pleasing appearance. It was her wit and warmth, however, that endeared her to people.

During her lifetime, Tucker received many awards, including the Woman of Distinction (1954) from the Women's Advertising Club of Chicago, the Achievement Award from the Chicago and Northern District Association of Colored Women (1954), and the Distinguished Service Award (1958) from Phi Beta Kappa. She was chosen one of nine women of achievement in 1959 by the Women's Board of the LaRabida Sanitarium.

In July 1970, at the age of seventy-one, Judge Tucker announced she would retire at the end of the year. She planned to continue studying the law, but she believed a younger woman should replace her on the bench. Just two months later, Tucker died in her home of natural causes. Services were held at the Cathedral of St. James (Episcopal), Chicago, and she was buried in Forest Hill Cemetery, Greencastle, Indiana.

B. Fain Tucker was a dedicated, learned lawyer and jurist; she demonstrated to the politicians and the public that women could serve the judiciary with distinction. After her years on the bench, both political parties and voters continued to select women lawyers, and they served with distinction. John S. Boyle, chief judge of the Circuit Court at the time of Tucker's death, said Tucker "was a great judge. . . . She proved that women can be great judges" (quoted in "Circuit Court Judge B. Fain Tucker Dies at 71").

Sources. The B. Fain Tucker Papers, DePauw Archives, DePauw Univ., Greencastle, Indiana, include articles, clippings, and the "Memorial Resolution," typescript, prepared by the Women's Bar Association of Illinois. Tucker's books are *What Every Serviceman's Dependents Should Know* (1942) and *Guide to the National Labor Relations Act* (1947). Her articles published in *Women Lawyers Journal* are "Equal Pay for Equal Work," Spring 1945; "Legal Problems of Artificial Insemination," Spring 1947; "Universal Military Training," Winter 1948; and "Legislative Aspects of the Narcotic Problem," Spring 1952. Articles about Tucker include Jeanette Oats, "Woman on Bench: B. Fain Tucker Sworn In," *Christian Science Monitor*, November 30, 1953; Gladys Erickson, "Fain Tucker Takes Oath," *Chicago American*, November 30, 1953; Norma Lee Browning, "Judge Tucker Teams a Legal Mind and Woman's Perception," *Chicago Daily Tribune*, October 2, 1955; George Wright, "Woman Judge Proves Able: Wins Plaudits," *Chicago Sunday Tribune*, May 8, 1955; W. H. Lynch, "Judge Tucker Blazes Trail," *Chicago American*, September 7, 1954. Obituaries appear September 27, 1970, in *CT* and *Chicago Today.* Also see "Circuit Court Judge B. Fain Tucker Dies at 71," *Chicago Sun-Times*, September 27, 1970.

THELMA BROOK SIMON

TUCKER, BEATRICE EDNA
October 4, 1897–June 12, 1984
OBSTETRICIAN, HOME BIRTH ADVOCATE, HEAD OF
MATERNITY CENTER

From 1932 until 1973, Dr. Beatrice Tucker was the director of the Chicago Maternity Center, whose physicians delivered babies in the home rather than at a hospital. She was an only child, born in Carbondale, Pennsylvania. Her mother, Nellie (Courtright) Tucker, had taught in a one-room country school for eight years before marriage. Her father, Evan Thomas Tucker, was from a Welsh coal-mining family. He came to America at the age of seventeen, also paying the way for his parents and eight siblings. When Beatrice Tucker was born, he was twenty-three and owned his own grocery store. Shortly afterward he

learned medicine from correspondence courses and books, and he began to practice without a license, often working with licensed physicians. He was financially successful, but he was in constant trouble with medical authorities and the law. The family traveled through the northern United States and Canada when Beatrice Tucker was a child, sometimes changing their surname to elude lawyers or the police.

In part, Beatrice Tucker's choices to become a medical doctor and to remain unmarried were the result of contradictions and tensions she experienced in her family's home. While Evan Tucker eventually became licensed as an optometrist and developed a flourishing practice in southern Illinois, Tucker spent her childhood and adolescence confused about her father: his illegal medical practices were both exciting and embarrassing. She was also confused about her mother's acceptance of her father's personal behavior, including gambling and at least one extramarital union resulting in the birth of a child. Later she reflected, "I was never married. I was dedicated to my work. And I never found anybody I loved; but I also wonder if I didn't want to subject myself to the suffering that I know my mother went through. And after my father, I was hungry for respectability, for status" (quoted in Berkow, 180).

Yet her parents also provided encouragement and love, anticipating that their daughter would have all the educational benefits and opportunities that had been unavailable to a poor Welsh immigrant and a schoolteacher. Tucker explained how influential her father had been in her becoming a doctor. "I always thought I'd be a doctor. My father kept talking about it all the time" (quoted in Berkow, 179). When she was a child, he had taken her on medical rounds. His love and acceptance of her was profound: "I adored my father," she recalled, "and he loved me, thought I was perfect" (quoted in Berkow, 179), but Tucker credited her mother with providing her discipline and keeping her "on a level key" (quoted in Berkow, 180). It was her mother, a fundamentalist Christian with strong moral values, who strengthened her resolve to finish medical school. Disturbed about her father's behavior, she left Rush Medical School twice rather than take money from him. The first time she quit, she went to a Chicago steel mill as a chemist for six months. Her mother, whom Tucker called "one of God's chosen people" (quoted in Berkow, 180) came to town and told her to go back to medical school both for herself and for humanitarian reasons.

Tucker attended grammar school in Bridgewater, Maine, and Syracuse, New York. She went to Bradley Polytechnic Institute (now Bradley University) in Peoria, Illinois, for high school and the first two years of college. She finished her college education at the University of Chicago and received a B.S. degree in 1918. In 1922 she graduated from Rush Medical School in Chicago. She did her internship at north suburban Evanston Hospital in 1921–22.

For the next seven years she tried several areas of medical practice. Between 1922 and 1926 she worked in public health at infant welfare clinics and for the city of Chicago at the Women's Venereal Disease Clinic and the Morals Court and Women's Department of the jail. She spent the next three years in Evanston as the assistant of Dr. Mary McEwen, a general surgeon.

In 1929 Tucker decided to enter the field of obstetrics and became a resident at the University of Chicago Lying-In Hospital. She obtained the appointment by applying during an absence of the chief of staff, Dr. Joseph Bolivar De Lee, who did not want women doctors on his service. When he made a disparaging comment about her, she went to his office and told him, "You shouldn't have talked like that. You don't know what I can do . . . and until you do, I think you should not make any remarks in front of anybody" (quoted in Berkow, 170–71). After this confrontation, De Lee became Tucker's most important teacher and mentor, despite his views about women doctors and despite Tucker's own conflicted feelings about De Lee because of his misogynist attitudes.

De Lee was the founder of the Chicago Lying-In Hospital and the Maxwell Street Dispensary, which became the Chicago Maternity Center in 1932. He founded the dispensary in 1895 to provide quality medical maternity care and home deliveries for poor women and as a teaching center for medical students, at a time when most babies were born at home, many delivered without medical assistance, and maternal and infant mortality rates were high. Started in two rooms, by 1910 the center occupied an entire building on Maxwell Street. The neighborhood, just southwest of the downtown area, was the home of recently arrived Jewish immigrants and the site of the open-air Maxwell Street market. The neighborhood, poor, rough, and overcrowded, was known as the "Bloody Twentieth" (de Kruif, 85) ward.

At De Lee's urging, Tucker became medical director of the Chicago Maternity Center in 1932 with Dr. Harry Benaron as codirector. Tucker was responsible for operation of prenatal and other clinics at the center, the home delivery service, and staff and professional administration. She herself was an active practitioner, delivering babies and training medical students and obstetrical residents. Under Tucker's direction, center staff taught about four hundred medical students each year from Chicago schools, as well as physicians who came from other states and countries. Her teaching went beyond the center's home delivery responsibilities and included lectures at medical societies in Illinois, Indiana, and Iowa on management of labor and delivery.

By the time Tucker became medical director, the center had ended its affiliation with the University of Chicago, which was no longer willing to continue funding it during the depression, and had begun to operate independently. The center made arrangements with other hospitals to provide backup service if a woman or child needed hospital care, and Tucker joined the staffs at these institutions. She was head of the Department of Obstetrics and Gynecology at Women's and Children's Hospital of Chicago 1933–39, then held the same position at Chicago Memorial Hospital 1939–46. When the center affiliated with Chicago Wesley Memorial Hospital in 1946, Tucker became a senior attending obstetrician and gynecologist there. In 1933 Tucker also became a member of the faculty at Northwestern University Medical School, where she rose to the rank of associate professor in 1946, emeritus in 1962.

Totally absorbed in her work, Tucker lived in a basement room in the Maternity Center building. Writing about the center in 1938, Paul de Kruif, in *The Fight for Life*, described

Tucker as "a woman of the future . . . a bundle of contradictions, hating poverty and death and glorying in this poverty that makes her death-fight an adventure" (pp. 89–90). The death fight in which she and the maternity center were engaged went far beyond the problems and confines of Maxwell Street. Childbirth at the time was dangerous for women. The national maternal death rate in the 1930s was 1 per 175. The center's record at the time was less than 1 death per 1,200 births. Tucker described the conditions under which many of these deliveries took place: "In the 1930s we'd deliver babies in rooms with dirt floors, no toilets and no electricity. We'd work by candlelight" ("Birth on the Kitchen Table," 58).

Before the discovery and development of antibiotics during and immediately following World War II, one of the major causes of maternal death was puerperal (childbed) fever. The center's insistence on absolute cleanliness surrounding the mother, coupled with the home setting, where the mother was not exposed to external sources of contagion, was part of the reason for the center's success. Another reason for success was Tucker's philosophy on procedures: "childbirth must march to its outcome with the very least possible scientific (and so often dangerous) meddling." Tucker declared, "We sit and wait" (de Kruif, 106).

Tucker believed that childbirth, as a natural process, should be interfered with only in the small percentage of cases where there was truly some difficulty. She maintained this view all her life, despite changing fashions in childbirth management and the medical profession's promises of easier and safer birth through modern science. In a 1948 article, "What Price Painless Childbirth?" in the *Ladies Home Journal*, Tucker wrote, "95 per cent of all babies born would be born successfully under Nature's care. In fact, if we take two groups of 100,000 women each in labor, and give drugs and anesthetics to one group and not to the other, we shall find that a higher number of complications arise in the group to which pain relief has been given" (p. 36).

In addition to her work for the maternity center during these years, she maintained a private practice with Harry Benaron, which they opened in 1932 at an office on Michigan Avenue. Although she never married, in the late forties Tucker adopted two sons. Evan Thomas Tucker II, named for her father, was delivered by Tucker. Her partner Benaron delivered her younger son, Peter Courtright Tucker. After the adoptions, she moved from the clinic to her own home.

Tucker understood the importance of having her innovative work in obstetrics reach the medical and basic science communities as well as the general public. She embarked on several projects with other clinicians and scientists at Northwestern University Medical School and Chicago Wesley Memorial Hospital to link her clinical findings with other information about infant and maternal mortality and child development. With her colleagues she published twenty-five articles in medical and research journals between 1934 and 1971 on clinical aspects of birthing, maternal mortality, and other obstetrical topics. Harry Benaron was coauthor for some of the studies, which appeared in the *American Journal of Obstetrics and Gynecology* and other clinical journals.

By the late 1960s and early 1970s there was a movement away from reliance on medical intervention during childbirth on the part of many young middle-class women, and Tucker was providing inspiration and support. In a 1973 interview in the *Chicago Daily News*, Tucker said, "I believe in home obstetrics. I think a woman has the right to choose where she wants to have her baby" (March 15, 1973). At this time she was also working to legalize abortion and to support birth control. She testified at the state legislature in Springfield, Illinois, for a law legalizing abortion. "I can't see why a man and woman should live in bondage because of a biological accident," Tucker said (*Daily News*, November 15, 1973).

In 1973 Tucker retired as head of the Chicago Maternity Center. Lake Forest College (Lake Forest, Illinois) recognized her achievements by awarding her an honorary Doctor of Science degree. In November of that year the center, affiliated with Northwestern University Medical School since 1965, ended home delivery service when the university moved the center to its new women's hospital.

Tucker continued in private practice, delivering babies at home. In 1975, when Harry Benaron died, she felt she had become too old for the work and closed the practice. At retirement she was a striking woman, almost six feet tall, with a head of short gray hair and a voice that registered delight. Her hobby was watercolor painting, and she produced many paintings of Maxwell Street scenes. Despite her painting, when she attempted complete retirement, she found it boring and went to work for the Chicago Board of Health as a prenatal and family planning clinician at West Side Health Center. She died at age eighty-six in Illinois Masonic Hospital in Chicago.

The home birth movement that was so important to Tucker has continued. In her later years she was looked to as a leader and mentor by natural childbirth advocates and in the home birth movement that emerged in the 1960s and 1970s. Dr. Mayer Eisenstein, one of Tucker's last students, who follows the medical principles he learned from Tucker, described her achievement: "Under her supervision . . . over 100,000 babies [were] delivered at home with a safety record unsurpassed" (p. 8).

Sources. The Chicago Lying-In Dispensary and Chicago Maternity Center Records (1895–1973), located at the Northwestern Memorial Hospital Archives, contain material on Tucker, including a typescript "Biography Beatrice Edna Tucker, M.D." (April 27, 1973). Her medical articles are listed in *Quarterly Cumulative Index Medicus* (1930–56), which became *Current List of Medical Literature* (1960–66), then *Cumulated Index Medicus* (1960–66), and is in the 1990s *Medline* database. Tucker wrote the article, "What Price Painless Childbirth?" for the *Ladies Home Journal* in June 1948. Her early work at the Chicago Maternity Center is described at length in Paul de Kruif's *The Fight for Life* (1938). A documentary film based on the book, also titled *The Fight for Life*, was made in 1939, but actors, all men, were used to portray the doctors at the center. Although Tucker was medical director of the center at the time, she is listed in the movie's credits only as a "Special Consultant." Extensive footage from this film was used in the 1974 documentary, *The Chicago Maternity Center Story*, made by Kartemquin Films in Chicago, which relates the unsuccessful struggle to keep the center open and contains a long section showing Tucker delivering a baby at home. Ira Berkow's *Maxwell Street: Survival in a Bazaar* (1977), contains a chapter about Tucker; the interview on which the chapter is based is in the Ira Berkow Papers at UIC Spec. Coll. An article on the home birth movement, "Birth on the Kitchen Table," in the August 18,

1972, issue of *Life* magazine, focuses on Tucker and the Chicago Maternity Center. Articles about Tucker in Chicago area newspapers and magazines include the *CT*, August 1, 1965, November 21, 1971, January 11, 1979, September 26, 1982, and June 15, 1984; the *Chicago Sun-Times*, October 31, 1973; and the *Chicago Daily News*, November 15, 1973. Mayer Eisenstein, in *The Home Court Advantage* (1988), describes Tucker's home birth principles.

SARA ANDREW SKOLNIK

TUITE, SISTER MARJORIE
October 15, 1922–June 28, 1986
POLITICAL ACTIVIST, EDUCATOR, COMMUNITY ORGANIZER

Sister Marjorie Tuite, an activist in the civil rights, peace, and women's movements, was born in New York City, the only child of Benjamin and Matilde (Fergerson) Tuite. Tuite attributed her gifts of humor and "tough love" to her Irish father, who was high school educated with vocational training. From her Norwegian-born mother she learned of the needs of neighbors and gained a vision of the world that went far beyond New York City. As Tuite recalled, "Between them they gave me a sense of compassion for the lives of others, a willingness to laugh at myself, and . . . a sense of courage and independence to move in the ways I must. . . . Most of all, they taught me to dream" (*Probe*, November/December 1986).

After completing high school, Marjorie Tuite entered the order of Dominican Sisters of St. Mary of the Springs, based in Columbus, Ohio, and received the name Sister Marie Veritas. Reflecting on Tuite's religious name, theologian Rosemary Radford Ruether wrote: "Veritas suited her as a religious name. Truth seeking defined her life; not just truth in theory, but truthful living, truth put into practice" (*Probe*, September/October 1986).

Tuite earned B.A. and M.A. degrees in English from Fordham University in New York City in 1949 and 1960, respectively. In addition, Tuite received an M.A. in Religious Education in 1967 from Manhattanville College in Purchase, New York, and completed doctoral courses for a Doctor of Ministry degree from St. Mary of the Lake Seminary in Chicago in the late 1970s.

From 1949 to 1967 Tuite worked in elementary and high schools in New York City and surrounding areas, serving for a significant time as a teacher and administrator for schools in Harlem. These experiences created a new awareness of the racism and economic exploitation that existed within the United States. Considering these years, Tuite commented, "I love teaching. . . . It was exciting because you were close to the neighborhood, close to the people, and close to a reality—the struggle of poor people to make it" (*Probe*, September/October 1986).

Tuite's life was greatly influenced by the Roman Catholic Church's Second Vatican Council (1961–65), with its emphasis on collegiality and social justice. In response to the Vatican's call to renew religious communities, many U.S. women's orders democratized their structures and diversified their works. It was at this time that Tuite changed her religious name from Marie Veritas back to Marjorie, the name given at her baptism.

Tuite was sent by her religious community to Chicago in 1967 and served as archdiocesan director of religious education.

After one year with the archdiocese, Tuite joined the staff of the National Urban Training Center, an ecumenical agency located on the West Side that did training, primarily with African Americans who were organizers, for the civil rights movement. Tuite described her decision to leave the archdiocesan office and begin work with the National Urban Training Center in these words, "One day I took a ride by myself on the el in Chicago and I went to the South side. There I saw Black people, like I saw in Harlem; and I saw the poor, struggling. When I went back to the religious education office, it was totally white. We were responding to white suburban people with the new Vatican II message. I couldn't stand it; it was against my integrity, so I quit. In those days, it was a first for women in religious congregations to quit" (*Probe*, November/December 1986).

Tuite served as director of women's training and field education for the National Urban Training Center from 1968 to 1972 and then became the coordinator and administrator in 1973. Tuite credited her time with the National Urban Training Center and her participation in the civil rights movement as key to her understanding of other struggles such as the antiwar movement, the feminist movement, and efforts to end U.S. intervention in Central America and the Caribbean. Tuite often emphasized that an individual could not touch the heart of any liberation movement the way she had done with black people and not begin to examine her own life.

Tuite also defined her time with the National Urban Training Center as critical to the development of the approach to community organizing that was to mark the workshops and educational seminars she gave throughout her life. Working with colleague and friend Sam Easley, a founding member of the Black Consortium and a member of the initial board for the Black Strategy Center in Chicago, they conducted workshops across the country on social analysis and leadership training, urging participants to confront systemic injustices and create effective strategies for racial justice and social change.

Tuite joined the faculty at the Jesuit School of Theology in Chicago in 1973, where she taught social justice courses and supervised students' field experiences, until the school closed in 1981. Tuite opposed the closing because she thought that it was due, at least in part, to the active, strong, and vocal women students pursuing equal participation in the institutional Roman Catholic Church.

During these years, Tuite taught in summer sessions of major universities both in the United States and Canada, always emphasizing the need to make connections among forms of oppression and to think globally and act locally for the sake of justice. For Tuite, racism, sexism, and classism were human rights violations that needed to be addressed. Her commitment was to enable people—especially women—to understand how political systems of church and state work and to strategize with others to bring about social change.

From September 1982 until the time of her death, Tuite served as national coordinator for the National Assembly of Religious Women (NARW), a Catholic feminist social justice ministry that she helped to found in 1968. NARW, based in Chicago, was the first of many Catholic feminist groups that emerged after Vatican II. Founded originally to provide a national and public voice for women in religious congregations,

NARW opened its membership in 1983 to all Catholic women. Tuite played a central role in NARW from its beginning, serving on the planning committee for the first national conference in 1970 and as national chair for the social justice committee. During this time she served as coordinator of the Ecumenical Citizen Action for Church Women United, a national ecumenical women's organization committed to peace and justice.

As a strong advocate of women's rights in church and society, Tuite's positions often brought her into sharp conflict with the Roman Catholic Church hierarchy. She was vocal on such rights as the ordination of women to the priesthood and the right of women in religious communities to run for political office. In 1984 Tuite was one of the signers of the *New York Times* advertisement calling for dialogue on the issue of abortion; she was subsequently threatened with expulsion from her religious congregation by the Vatican. Like others, Tuite signed the ad to protest New York Cardinal John O'Connor's attack on Democratic vice-presidential candidate Geraldine Ferraro's position on freedom of choice. This action did much to raise people's awareness about issues related to freedom of conscience, authority, and choice within the Catholic tradition. The signing of the *New York Times* ad was just one of the ways Tuite fought the hierarchical policies of her church that "deny dialogue as a possibility and demand submission as a sacrament" (*Probe*, April/May 1987).

During the 1980s, Marjorie Tuite turned her attention increasingly to issues related to Central America, actively opposing U.S. covert operations and all other destabilization activities against Nicaragua and other countries of Central America and the Caribbean. Speaking at a press conference of sixty national religious, labor, civil, and human rights leaders in Washington, D.C., in March 1983, Tuite stated, "I believe that there is no justification—political or moral—for the policy that the United States government is pursuing against the Nicaraguan government and its people" (*Probe*, March/April 1983). As a leading voice of opposition to U.S. intervention, Tuite was invited to attend the first meeting of the Women's Continental Coalition against Intervention in March 1982. One of the purposes of this coalition was to bring together women from diverse organizations to work together for peace. That same year Tuite founded the North American Women's Coalition to Stop U.S. Intervention in Central America and the Caribbean. She was also one of the founding members of the Religious Task Force on Central America both in Chicago and nationally.

Tuite made more than fifteen trips to Central America, often leading women's groups on fact-finding delegations. In November 1984 she served as a delegate to the First Congress on Human Rights in El Salvador. She was a member of Reverend Jesse Jackson's delegation to Central America during the 1984 presidential campaign. In December 1984 she was one of the key organizers of the peace pilgrimage to Honduras to raise awareness about the U.S. military installations being established in that country. Approximately one hundred fifty women of faith from the United States and Canada participated in this peace pilgrimage. In 1985 Tuite served as a delegate for both Church Women United and the National Council of Churches to the International Conference against Intervention in Central America held in Portugal. When Nicaraguan Foreign Minister and Maryknoll priest Miguel D'Escoto initiated a hunger strike to protest U.S. intervention in his country, Tuite traveled to Managua to demonstrate solidarity and to join his fast. For Tuite, fasting was "a religious act, but certainly not apart from the political task" (*Probe*, August/September 1985).

Marjorie Tuite consistently used her numerous forums to work for the defeat of congressional bills that would send millions of dollars in aid to the forces fighting to overthrow the legitimate Sandinista government in Nicaragua. She also participated in demonstrations and acts of civil disobedience. In March 1986, Tuite visited Nicaragua for the last time to participate in International Women's Day and to meet with Costa Rican women working for peace in Central America.

Tuite was the recipient of many awards throughout her lifetime. In 1978, she received the U.S. Catholic award for her leadership in furthering the cause of women in the church and the Catholic Committee Urban Ministry Award for her commitment to social justice. In 1985 she became the tenth recipient of the Boise Idaho Peace Quilt for outstanding work for peace; that year she also received the Mary Rhodes Award from the Sisters of Loretto Community for her contribution to peace and justice. With each of these awards Tuite reiterated her understanding that to raise up any one person was to honor the movement, or as she expressed it when receiving the Peace Quilt, "It is not one individual, it is the collective" (*Probe*, November/December 1986).

Tuite was a founding member of numerous organizations. Besides those previously mentioned, she helped to found Call to Action, an organization of Catholics working for justice in the spirit of Vatican II; the National Farm Worker Ministry; NETWORK, an independent Catholic women's lobbying group; the Religious Network for Equality for Women; and the Women's Ordination Conference. At the time of her death, Tuite was serving on the boards of nine national peace and antipoverty organizations.

Marjorie Tuite died from cancer at Mount Sinai Hospital in New York City. Funeral services were held on July 3, 1986, at Manhattan's St. Vincent Ferrer Catholic Church, where Tuite had served as high school principal in the late 1950s and early 1960s. In addition, memorial services were held across the country in Columbus, Ohio; Chicago, Illinois; Los Angeles, California; Washington, D.C.; Rochester, New York; Louisville, Kentucky; and other places.

Marjorie Tuite repeatedly expressed the wish that her ashes be buried in Nicaragua to rest alongside the heroes and martyrs of the revolution and with the people she had come to love so dearly. At Tuite's funeral service, Nora Astorga, Nicaragua's ambassador to the United Nations, spoke of Tuite's solidarity, strength, and steadfastness. "When I think of Margie, I can only say that women, children and men in Nicaragua have a special place for her in their hearts. She understood us, she had faith in us. . . . She loved us back as we loved her" (*National Catholic Reporter*, July 18, 1986). In March 1987, "Reveranda Margie," as she was hailed in Nicaragua, was welcomed home, and on March 9, 1987, Marjorie Tuite's ashes were buried in ceremony in Managua, Nicaragua.

Tuite wanted to be remembered as a woman of revolutionary integrity. She frequently stated that she lived by a justice that she would never see. In reflecting on her own life, Tuite stated,

"As I look back on my own journey and struggle . . . the deep commitment to justice began in my parent's walkup apartment on Manhattan's East Side. . . . It is a journey concretized in a tall, shy young woman crossing the bridge at Selma during the civil rights movement; it found its greatest hope in the people of Central America and their revolution. Deep within is the knowing that I have stayed in the struggle in spite of the long loneliness" (*Probe*, November/December 1986). Marjorie Tuite consistently urged others to listen to people and to be faithful to the struggle. Those affected by her life and words continue to carry on this commitment to peace with justice.

Sources. Marjorie Tuite's papers, including her writings, reflections, and correspondence, are at the Gannon Center for Women and Leadership, Loyola Univ. Chicago. Many of Tuite's presentations have been transcribed and reprinted in *Probe*, the bimonthly publication of the National Assembly of Religious Women. Marjorie Tuite's life is the subject of a video and study guide entitled *Marjorie Tuite—Presente!* She has also been a part of many video presentations, including *Changing Habits* and *Mobilizing for Systemic, Legislative and Community Change: Seeking Economic Justice for Women*. These videotapes are available from the Gannon Center for Women and Leadership. An obituary by Karl Johnson, "Dominican Sister Leaves Long Legacy of Commitment," appears in *National Catholic Reporter*, July 18, 1986.

JUDY VAUGHAN

TUNNICLIFF, RUTH
May 1, 1876–September 22, 1946
PHYSICIAN, BACTERIOLOGIST, IMMUNOLOGIST

One of the earliest female graduates from Rush Medical College, Ruth Tunnicliff pursued an illustrious career as a research scientist at Chicago's John McCormick Institute for Infectious Diseases, now known as the Hektoen Institute. Tunnicliff's work, highly respected by her peers, focused on bacteriology and immunology. Her parents, Damon G. and Sarah A. (Bacon) Tunnicliff, lived in Macomb, Illinois, and had three daughters, Helen, Sarah, and Ruth. Helen Tunnicliff, later Catterall, graduated from Vassar College, Poughkeepsie, New York, in 1889, took some courses at the University of Chicago, and practiced as a lawyer in Boston. Sarah Tunnicliff also attended Vassar, graduating in 1892, and took courses at the University of Chicago. In 1918 Sarah Tunnicliff was a member of the U.S. Fuel Administration and worked to alleviate the coal shortage in Chicago during World War I. Ruth Tunnicliff graduated from Vassar College with an A.B. degree in 1896 and embarked on a medical career.

Like her sisters, Tunnicliff took courses at the University of Chicago, spending two years there from 1898 to 1900. Tunnicliff then entered Northwestern University, where she stayed until 1902, when the university closed its women's medical school. The board of trustees of Rush Medical College voted to allow women to enter as third and fourth year students, and Tunnicliff was one of eleven women admitted. In 1903, Tunnicliff graduated with an M.D. degree, along with eight other women and about two hundred and fifty men. She then commenced a long association with the McCormick Institute for Infectious Diseases.

The institute was known until 1918 as the Memorial Institute for Infectious Diseases. It was founded in 1902 through the philanthropy of Harold F. and EDITH ROCKEFELLER Mc-

CORMICK in memory of their son, John Rockefeller Mc-Cormick, who had died of scarlet fever. Renowned pathologist Ludvig Hektoen was director.

In 1903 Tunnicliff joined the institute as an intern and researcher. Initially, the institute's physicians were involved in the care of patients admitted to a small scarlet fever hospital operated by Presbyterian Hospital of Chicago. Later, in 1913, the Annie W. Durand Hospital was built, through which Tunnicliff had access to patients. Tunnicliff was primarily concerned with bacteriology, particularly streptococci, immunology, and scarlet fever research. During her thirty-seven years at the institute, Tunnicliff wrote more than seventy articles. Most of the articles were published in the *Journal of Infectious Diseases*, but some research studies also appeared in *JAMA (Journal of the American Medical Association)* and other medical and dental journals. Opsonization and phagocytosis—protective cellular mechanisms in an immune response—were described in several of Tunnicliff's papers. Using animals, Tunnicliff experimented with immunizations, using streptococci killed by heat. Tunnicliff also isolated and classified several hitherto unknown streptococci. She explored the anti-infectious qualities of infants' blood and examined human colostrum and milk for the presence of antibodies. Tunnicliff and Hektoen, during the mid-1920s, were particularly excited about her experiments using serum from goats that were immune to measles. Hektoen advised Tunnicliff at that time to direct all her efforts to that research, which he considered preliminary to the development of measles immunization.

Throughout these years, Ludvig Hektoen was a friend, mentor, and collaborator with Tunnicliff. Their esteem for each other's professional judgment was evident in their correspondence. Following publication of a paper concerning the discovery of a type of streptococcus, Hektoen wrote to her that he was proud of her and he considered it a "splendid piece of work" (June 8, 1925, Hektoen Papers). Tunnicliff described her work to him in detail and he responded in kind. She was very dissatisfied with one of Hektoen's papers and returned it with many corrections, but closed on a friendly note, commenting that "the weather is perfect anyway" (July 21, 1932, Hektoen Papers). Hektoen quickly replied with thanks for her corrections.

Tunnicliff attracted the attention of ALICE HAMILTON, another eminent physician who worked at the McCormick Institute during its early years. In her autobiography, Hamilton described Tunnicliff as an outstanding bacteriologist who had achieved "brilliant" (p. 97) success in her field. Hamilton then asserted that although Tunnicliff had attained the respect of her colleagues and contributed through conferences and professional associations, she could not aspire to a senior medical school appointment because she was a woman. Hamilton illustrated this situation by describing a visit she and Tunnicliff had made to the head of a medical school pathology department. He received Tunnicliff with respect and they discussed their mutual scientific interests. The head had told the two women that the chair of bacteriology was vacant and discussed the qualifications of various candidates with Tunnicliff. Hamilton asserted that Tunnicliff, an outstanding bacteriologist, would almost certainly have been appointed if she had been a man, but as a woman she was not considered for the post.

During the summer of 1918, Tunnicliff spent three months at Camp Meade in Maryland, where she studied the bacteriology of measles that occurred in conjunction with influenza. That same year, Tunnicliff volunteered her services as a contract surgeon for the U.S. Army.

For several summers, Tunnicliff volunteered at Hull-House, JANE ADDAMS's settlement house. The mission at Hull-House was to help Chicago's diverse immigrant population adjust to American life. In 1919, Tunnicliff wrote that she lived at Hull-House for two months each year. Many people volunteered their expertise at Hull-House in this way when the regular resident staff took their vacations. In 1929, Tunnicliff's name was included in a list of Hull-House residents who had lived there for six consecutive months or more and had taken part in house activities.

In addition to Hull-House, Tunnicliff spent some weeks during each summer with her sister Sarah and her mother at their farm, Upland Meadows, near Bristol, New Hampshire. Gardening was one of her hobbies. In 1932 she complained in a letter to Hektoen that although the cool weather was most enjoyable, the radishes refused to grow. Tunnicliff also liked to collect berries around their farm. Her other interests included sketching, reading, and listening to music.

Active in professional organizations related to her research interests, Tunnicliff became president of the Chicago Pathological Society and in 1939 was made president of the Society of Illinois Bacteriologists. She was a member of several other professional societies, including the American Medical Association, the American Association of Pathologists and Bacteriologists, the Society of Immunologists, and the Chicago Medical Society. Tunnicliff also joined the Chicago Arts Club and the Woman's City Club. She declared herself an Episcopalian and politically was an independent voter.

During the early years of the 1930s, at the time of the Great Depression, financial difficulties surfaced at the research institute. Edith McCormick was dying of cancer, and her financial affairs were being managed by others. In July 1932, Hektoen found it necessary to write to Tunnicliff in New Hampshire, telling her with great concern that he was unable to pay her salary that month. Tunnicliff assured him that she would survive; her mother paid for the groceries and her cousin paid for the gasoline. She commiserated with Hektoen on his financial problems.

Possibly because of these financial difficulties, Tunnicliff took a position in 1935 as a bacteriological researcher for the Foundation for Dental Research of the Chicago College of Dental Surgery, part of the School of Dentistry of Loyola University. Through an anonymous donor, the foundation was established in the summer of 1935 and Ludvig Hektoen appointed as scientific advisor. At the foundation, she was considered a nationally outstanding bacteriologist. Tunnicliff focused her research on dental bacteria. She examined bacteria found in the gums and in the pulp of intact and carious teeth and studied the role of streptococcus viridans in the production of dental caries. Tunnicliff continued to work in the laboratories of the McCormick Institute, which were located next door to the dental school, and her professional association with the McCormick Institute was maintained. Papers published during this period stated her affiliation with both the institute and the dental foundation. Her lively correspondence with Hektoen, covering professional and social concerns, continued. In 1937 Tunnicliff told him that the streptococcus associated with dental caries grew daily "more perplex and interesting." In that same typewritten letter she told Hektoen that she was learning how to type and found it "entertaining" (April 18, 1937, Hektoen Papers). Her correspondence with Hektoen indicated that the two families were close. Tunnicliff was invited to the Hektoen home, and later letters expressed her concern about Mrs. Hektoen's declining health. Tunnicliff's letters frequently closed with best wishes to Hektoen from her mother and sister.

In 1940, Tunnicliff sustained an embolic stroke that affected her speech and precipitated her retirement. Later, she wrote that the stroke fortuitously coincided with her retirement plans. She had lived for many years on Chicago's South Side. Between 1940 and 1944 she and her sister moved to Lake Shore Drive and continued to spend their summers in New Hampshire. In a 1944 letter to Hektoen and his wife, Tunnicliff told them that she felt much stronger than she had during the previous year, and she thought her handwriting had improved. The following year her handwriting appeared to have greatly deteriorated. In 1946 she noted that her speech was much improved, but her hands were swollen with arthritis. She died that year of heart disease in her Chicago home. Tunnicliff's obituary in the *Vassar Alumnae Magazine* noted her distinguished career in pathology and bacteriology, but warmly described her "delightful and lovable personality," calling her "dear little Ruth."

In the years following her death, Tunnicliff's work remained highly regarded by her peers. In a 1951 obituary for Ludvig Hektoen, physician Morris Fishbein, longtime editor of *JAMA*, praised Hektoen's influence on young men who were noted in research, medical education, and pathology. Tunnicliff's name was included among these men. In 1965, an article by Fishbein on twentieth-century medicine in Chicago included Tunnicliff's work on the isolation and classification of a great variety of streptococci among the notable accomplishments of Chicago's physicians. One of the few women engaged in medical research during the early years of the century, Tunnicliff's achievements were noteworthy. As a respected scientist within the medical community, she collaborated with some of the foremost physicians in her field.

Sources. The Univ. of Chicago maintains the papers of Ludvig Hektoen, 1920–46. These include Hektoen's correspondence with Tunnicliff. The Vassar College Library has reprints of her articles and several entries for the Vassar *Alumnae Association Bulletin* written by Tunnicliff. A brief biography with a photograph is in the Chicago Medical Society's *History of Medicine and Surgery and Physicians and Surgeons of Chicago* (1922). Rush-Presbyterian-St. Luke's Medical Center Archives, in Chicago, have some biographical data. Alice Hamilton, in her autobiography *Exploring the Dangerous Trades* (1943), describes the career limitations faced by Tunnicliff because she was a woman. An obituary appears in *Vassar Alumnae Magazine*, March 1947, held at Spec. Coll., Vassar College Library.

BRIGID LUSK

TYLER, ALICE DeWOLF KELLOG. *See* KELLOGG TYLER, ALICE DeWOLF

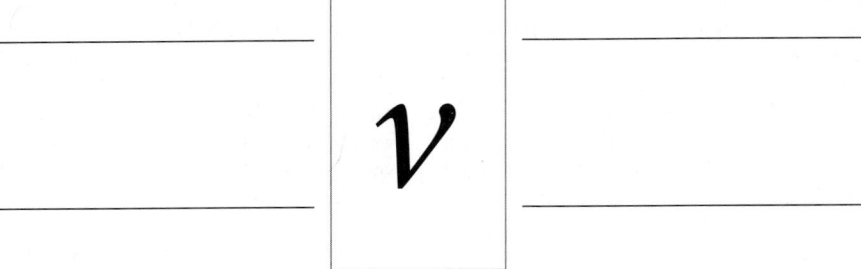

VAN der VRIES, BERNICE TABER
February 14, 1890–September 2, 1986

LEGISLATOR, POLITICAL ACTIVIST

Bernice Taber Van der Vries won election to the Illinois General Assembly in 1932 and was reelected ten times. Independent, gutsy, scrupulously honest, and indefatigable, she fought to make city manager government available to Illinois cities and to humanize and revise the state's mental health laws. She served as a model for women at a time when there were very few women representatives in the state legislature or in other elective offices.

Bernice Taber was born in Holton, Kansas, the first of two daughters of Otto Gaius and Ella May (Thomas) Taber. Her father, a bank teller, land manager, and business owner, was also active and outspoken in government affairs. Otto Taber was a member of the board of county commissioners and an unsuccessful candidate for the Kansas legislature. Bernice Taber "characterized him as 'an outspoken champion' who voiced his opinions loudly when he believed he was right. 'He fought for [good city government] . . . that's where I learned to fight'" (Haynes, 4). Taber's mother, noted for her organizational skills, worked to establish a library and hospital in Holton and founded a women's society at the local Presbyterian church. Taber spoke admiringly of her paternal grandmother, Elizabeth Parks Taber, a Kansas suffragist, and her maternal grandmother, who chose to work in the office of her husband, the elected country treasurer, rather than stay at home and do housework. The family's political activity was part of the reform spirit of Progressive Era Kansas. Bernice Taber recalled that when she was nine years of age, temperance reformer Carry Nation visited Holton. She heard Robert La Follette Sr. and William Jennings Bryan—each a spokesperson for the rights of common people—speak at the local Chautauqua grounds.

In the fall of 1907, Taber entered the University of Kansas at Lawrence, where she studied for the next two years and met her future husband, John Van der Vries, a mathematics professor fifteen years her senior. At her fiancé's suggestion, Taber spent her junior year attending Barnard College, New York. After their marriage in June 1910, the couple lived on the campus of the University of Kansas, where their only child, John N. Jr., was born in 1916. In 1918 John Van der Vries left academia to work with the U.S. Chamber of Commerce. The young family, after a brief stay in Washington, D.C., moved to Chicago, and then, in 1924, settled in Winnetka, Illinois.

As a result of persistent health problems, including rheumatoid arthritis, Bernice Van der Vries undertook long walks that her physician had prescribed. A Winnetka neighbor, observing that Van der Vries had time to walk in the neighborhood, recruited her as a voter registration block captain for the local League of Women Voters. Van der Vries, tall, handsome and articulate, brought a strong commitment and a sense of purpose to each organization with which she identified. She became president of the fourteen hundred member nonpartisan Winnetka League of Women Voters (later the League of Women Voters of Winnetka), 1927–29, and she also worked on the state board of the league. A member of Christ (Episcopal) Church, Winnetka, she was elected head of the women's auxiliary in 1931. After more than ten years of work to revise the canons of the Diocese of Chicago—the governing body of the Episcopal Church in northern Illinois—clergy and laity at the diocesan convention voted to allow women to serve on church vestries. Van der Vries became the first woman elected to serve on the vestry of Christ Church.

With her extensive work in community organizations, Van der Vries was asked to run for the Winnetka City Council in 1931. She hesitated because she was the driver in the family; she felt her husband needed her assistance, as she regularly chauffeured him over the large territory he covered in his work with the Chamber of Commerce. However, with the support her husband gave to her in this and every race for office, Van der

Vries ran successfully for a seat on the seven-person Winnetka City Council in 1931 and 1933. There she chaired the health committee and formed a close working relationship with the local health officer. She oversaw a program that enforced health standards in stores selling dairy products, and she improved and expanded the local program of vaccination of children. Her interest in health issues and her strategy of establishing close and effective working relationships repeated itself over and over again in her legislative career.

The opportunity for Van der Vries to run for a seat in the Illinois General Assembly came in 1934, when the Republican incumbent, ANNA ICKES, chose not to run for reelection after her husband, Harold Ickes, was appointed to the cabinet of President Franklin D. Roosevelt. Van der Vries threw herself wholeheartedly into an intense eleven-person Republican primary contest for the sprawling 7th District, which included 375,000 people in 104 Cook County municipalities and five Chicago wards. A political novice, she filed her nominating petitions at the last minute to assure herself, she thought, of the conspicuous last name position on the ballot. However, when the ballots came out, there were two names listed after hers. She overcame such tricks and indifference and hostility from many, including a publisher who threw her out of the Paddock Publications office because he did not want any women in office. Van der Vries came in first, ahead of the ten men on the ballot.

In 1935, at a time when women could not yet sit on juries in Illinois, in the midst of the worst depression the country had ever experienced, and during a period of popularity for Roosevelt's New Deal programs, Van der Vries became one of two women in the 153-member body and was a Republican in a Democrat-controlled legislature. Inexperienced but not naive, she disregarded the suggestion of her colleagues that the only two women legislators (she and Representative LOTTIE O'NEILL) sit together. Van der Vries chose to sit with a group of aggressive legislators who gave her advice and support that she put to immediate use. She was active and conscientious, introducing much legislation, including many bills on behalf of the 104 municipalities she represented. She sometimes received three hundred letters a day, and she answered all the mail—with the notable exception of letters addressed to Mr. Van der Vries, which went into the wastebasket unopened. When she ran in 1936, she won reelection easily, but her life changed when her husband died suddenly that year. Van der Vries's son was in college, and trips home from Springfield brought her to an empty house.

Van der Vries's four years in the Winnetka City Council and her legislative work on behalf of municipalities were valuable experience on which to draw when she became chair of the committee on municipalities in 1941, the first woman to chair a standing committee in the Illinois General Assembly. She also served for many years on an important intergovernmental body, the Council of State Governments, and was elected chair of this national body in 1948. Van der Vries introduced bills on many health issues, including care of epileptics, care of the mentally retarded, and licensing of practical nurses and nursing homes. She looked back on state funding of the Illinois Children's Hospital School for severely handicapped children as the pride of her legislative career. She was vitally concerned with education

and introduced special education bills for those with vision problems as well as for those with hearing impairment and physical disabilities.

Van der Vries saw government as housekeeping on a large scale and called on women to participate; she encouraged political parties to include women in the party structure. She checked on the housekeeping of government facilities and was appalled by what she saw and learned at the state's mental hospitals. Van der Vries succeeded in replacing the 1893 Lunacy Act, which identified the mentally ill as "lunatics" and "idiots," with the 1951 Mental Health Code. She established a bipartisan approach and worked closely with a Democratic colleague, Samuel Shapiro, who shared her interest in the mentally ill. Van der Vries took the lead when the Republicans were in power, and her Democratic colleague did the same when the Democrats were in control. Recognizing their respective strengths, she spoke to the social side of the issue and her Democratic colleague spoke to the legal aspects. The 1951 Mental Health Code established a Department of Mental Health, provided for voluntary commitment, and required patients to be treated humanely in the state's mental hospitals.

In 1951 she was finally able to see the passage of a measure she had supported for many years, the Illinois City Manager Act. The act enabled Illinois cities, with the exception of Chicago, to elect the city manager form of government. When the size of her district approached one million constituents, the largest state legislative district in the United States, a legislative reapportionment act was passed. She had strongly supported reapportionment for many years; when it was finally in place in 1956, Van der Vries chose to end her career as a state legislator.

Van der Vries stood up for those issues in which she believed, regardless of the popularity of an issue. In her early days in the legislature, when few legislators attacked the Ku Klux Klan by name, she spoke effectively for a desegregation education bill that the Klan opposed. She commented that she had always hoped to have the opportunity to speak out against the Klan, since she had seen its members lynch innocent people in Kansas.

When Van der Vries entered office, she served notice that she would not take part in the patronage system. She stood up against antivivisectionists who picketed her house, bombarded her with letters, and even issued death threats for her support of the use of animals for university research. She crossed party lines to support a call for a state constitutional convention. In 1937, when the Illinois General Assembly passed a bill making display of the American flag and recitation of the oath of allegiance mandatory in every school room, Van der Vries voted "no," contending that such legislation was foolish. However, later in the red-baiting era of Senator Joseph McCarthy and the House Un-American Activities Committee, she voted for a teachers' oath of allegiance, reasoning that if the legislators and attorneys were required to take such an oath, teachers could be also. She spoke out against requiring teachers to take additional oaths affirming that they were not communists, however, suggesting on the floor that bills requiring endless loyalty actions by the teachers would leave teachers without time to teach. She voted in favor of increases in legislators' salaries, saying she thought she should earn at least as much as the cleaning women in her area, and she defended lobbyists for the enlightenment they brought to pending legislation. Although she spoke out repeatedly for the rights of women, she voted against the Equal Pay for Women Bill in 1943, reasoning that it would require repeal of protective legislation for women. Van der Vries cast one of two votes against a fifty dollar World War II veterans' bonus, saying that it was too little to do much good for an individual and that the money would be better spent on educational benefits for veterans.

Regardless of the issue, Van der Vries's constituents knew where she stood. She wrote weekly columns for the local paper, *Winnetka Talk*. More than twenty of these columns were printed in 1939 alone. She spoke at dozens of meetings and traveled up and down the 7th District from Glencoe to Chicago Heights.

When she chose not to run for reelection in 1956, she worked first for the Crippled Children's Society and then accepted an appointment by the governor to the board of the financially troubled Chicago Transit Authority (CTA). (As a leader in the Illinois General Assembly in 1945, she had helped pass legislation that created the CTA.) While on the CTA board, she visited the CTA business offices each day and rode the CTA trains with a small notebook in hand in which she noted problems, major and minor, including discourtesy of personnel, unheated trains, unexplained delays, or unclean cars. When she lobbied the General Assembly for funds for the CTA, she was warmly greeted by her former colleagues.

Van der Vries served on the Illinois Council of Defense and Illinois War Council (1941–47), was a trustee of the Hull-House Association (1948), and a member of the board of governors of the American Red Cross (1953).

In 1977, at age eighty-seven, Van der Vries joined a group of women urging state representative James McCourt to support the Equal Rights Amendment (ERA). Several of the women spoke, giving their reasons for support of ERA and attempting to obtain a declaration of intent from McCourt. Finally, Van der Vries stood up. She held several three-by-five cards on which she had written pertinent quotations. With a trembling hand but a firm voice, she read a quotation from a 33rd District legislator who had referred to women on the floor of the General Assembly as "brainless, braless broads" (Gerson, "Notes," n.p.). "I am offended, sir" ("Notes"), said this dignified, intelligent woman who had spent most of her life working for decency and justice in government.

Van der Vries died at age ninety-six. She is remembered as a concerned citizen and as one of Illinois's "pioneer" women legislators.

Sources. An eleven-volume Scrap Book Diary, 1934–56, compiled by Van der Vries to document her legislative career, is at CHS. *Bernice T. Van der Vries Memoir*, 3 vols. (1980) is an oral history that recounts Van der Vries's life and legislative career and is part of the Illinois General Assembly's Oral History Project. Dona Gerson and Maxine H. Lange, "Notes," February 14, 1995, is a brief transcript account of a meeting in 1977 with state representative James McCourt, in which Van der Vries took part. Judith A. Haynes, "Portrait of a Woman Legislator: Bernice T. Van der Vries" (master's thesis, Sangamon State Univ., 1984), is useful. An obituary is in the *CT*, September 4, 1986.

DONA P. GERSON

VAN HOOSEN, BERTHA
March 26, 1863–June 7, 1952

PHYSICIAN, SURGEON, ACTIVIST FOR MEDICAL WOMEN

Bertha Van Hoosen practiced medicine during a transitional period in the history of women in medicine, when women's medical practice and education were shifting from sex-segregated to coeducational institutions. Van Hoosen, by personal example and through organizational activities, helped integrate women doctors into the male medical establishment.

Born in Stony Brook, Michigan, she was the second of two daughters of Joshua and Sarah Ann (Taylor) Van Hoosen. Sarah Van Hoosen was the granddaughter of Rev. Lemuel Taylor, one of Michigan's earliest pioneers and a founder of Stony Creek. She was educated in the school established by her family and went on to teach in a nearby district school. Joshua Van Hoosen, the son of Joshua Van Hoosen Sr., a Dutch immigrant, and his American-born wife Malinda Hunter, was born in Canada in 1830. In 1836, the Van Hoosen family moved to Stony Creek. At the age of twenty-two, Joshua Van Hoosen left to seek gold in California. He returned in 1857 with enough gold to buy a house and marry Sarah Taylor. Later he purchased the original Taylor homestead and farm.

Sarah and Joshua Van Hoosen believed strongly in the importance of educating their two daughters and expected them to attend college and to follow their mother's example by entering the most common profession for educated women, teaching. At considerable inconvenience and expense, they sent their girls first to a local one-room schoolhouse and then to the Rochester Academy in nearby Rochester, Michigan. After three years at the Rochester school, Bertha Van Hoosen, like her sister Alice Van Hoosen before her, lived in a boardinghouse in Pontiac, Michigan, and attended Pontiac High School. After graduation, she followed in her sister's footsteps and entered the University of Michigan's Literary Department in 1880. Her sister had already graduated and was working as a teacher. In her third year of college, Bertha Van Hoosen decided not to enter the teaching profession but to pursue a medical career. Van Hoosen's exposure to female medical students at the university strongly influenced her change of plans. She had not previously heard of women physicians and became curious when she learned that two young women living across the street were studying medicine. "The fact that these girls were 'hen-medics' did not deter me . . . from making their acquaintance," she wrote, adding, "Their enthusiasm for their work fired my imagination" (Van Hoosen, *Petticoat Surgeon*, 52–53).

Van Hoosen's parents were not at all pleased with her decision, refused to help finance something they opposed, and begged her to "teach school, or better still, come home" (*Petticoat Surgeon*, 56). Displaying the feistiness and independence that characterized her life, Van Hoosen vowed to earn her own money. She delayed entry into medical school, spent a year in St. Louis with her friend Dr. Mary McLean, and earned money by teaching calisthenics and physiology at a grammar and high school. She entered the University of Michigan Medical School in the fall of 1885 but could only support herself for one year. In the summer of 1886, she worked as a nurse at the Woman's Hospital in Detroit, Michigan, and spent the next year teaching mathematics at the Saginaw, Michigan, school where her sister taught. Toward the end of that year, Van Hoosen applied for and was awarded a position as a demonstrator of anatomy at the medical school. Her salary of fifty dollars per month enabled her to complete her medical education. She received the M.D. degree in 1888.

Feeling insufficiently competent to begin an independent medical practice, Van Hoosen embarked on a series of medical residencies. She worked at the Woman's Hospital in Detroit, the Michigan Asylum for the Insane in Kalamazoo, and at the New England Hospital for Women and Children in Boston, Massachusetts. In 1892, Van Hoosen opened her own practice in Chicago. Despite assistance from Chicago physician Rachel Hickey-Carr, who secured Van Hoosen a position as emergency physician at the dedication of the 1893 World's Columbian Exposition, it took her some time to develop a clientele. In a letter to her parents she admitted, "Patients do not bother me much but as long as my money holds out my courage does not flag" (April 10, 1893, Van Hoosen Papers). Van Hoosen did not rely on courage alone. She applied for and received a position as instructor in anatomy at the Northwestern University Woman's Medical School. Though unsalaried, the position occupied Van Hoosen with medical work and allowed her to meet other women doctors. Van Hoosen was encouraged and inspired by the success her colleagues enjoyed. "There is no way to estimate," she wrote, "the stimulation that a woman derives from her acquaintance with women who have achieved success" ("Petticoat Surgeon," unpublished ms, 2, 321, Van Hoosen Papers). After only one year, Van Hoosen had established a busy medical practice concentrating on the obstetric and general medical care of women. At the request of Dr. SARAH HACKETT STEVENSON, professor of obstetrics at the Woman's Medical School, Van Hoosen was promoted to clinical assistant in obstetrics. Her new duties included teaching a course in embryology.

In addition to private practice and teaching, Van Hoosen studied surgery under the direction of prominent Chicago surgeon Byron Robinson. Van Hoosen's favorite medical specialty was obstetrics, not surgery. She knew, however, that most male physicians did not regard obstetrics with much respect. In order to gain respect from all doctors, she believed she had to excel in a field men would value. "[Once] I had gained recognition as a surgeon," she wrote, "then I could turn my attention to obstetrics. Entering obstetrics through a surgical door, I could work in the birth room with skill and distinction" (Petticoat Surgeon, 129). In 1895, after two years with Robinson, Van Hoosen began operating independently. The Chicago Hospital for Women and Children, run by and for women, was the only institution willing to allow her to operate. In 1896 she became head of the obstetrical department of this hospital. In addition to improving the routine care of obstetric patients, she concentrated on the surgical repair of obstetric complications and rapidly acquired a reputation as an excellent surgeon. In 1899, Van Hoosen joined the surgical staff at Provident Hospital, a biracial hospital that provided service and training to African Americans. She brought many white patients to Provident and thus contributed to the hospital's success. In 1901, Van Hoosen became professor and head of gynecology at the Northwestern University Woman's Medical School, when the position opened follow-

ing the death of Dr. MARIE MERGLER. Unfortunately, nine months later Northwestern University closed the Woman's Medical School. Although this closing cost most female faculty members their academic careers, Van Hoosen went on to achieve considerable academic success.

Almost immediately after the closing, Van Hoosen, with the support of William E. Quine, dean of the College of Physicians and Surgeons (later the University of Illinois College of Medicine), overcame considerable faculty opposition and became the school's second female faculty member and its professor of clinical gynecology. She was initially given hospital privileges at West Side Hospital, which was next to the college and accepted patients of college faculty members; but within a year she was stopped from bringing hospitalized patients to the college's amphitheater by medical staff who would not accept a woman surgeon. Van Hoosen then set up a small charity hospital in a vacant store across the street. She brought patients from her hospital to the college's hospital clinic for surgical treatment. Van Hoosen ran her hospital for three years, at a personal cost of fifteen thousand dollars, until she was again accepted as a member of the hospital staff. Despite efforts by opponents to impede her progress, Van Hoosen remained with the College of Physicians and Surgeons for eight years.

During this time she began experimenting with the use of scopolamine-morphine anesthesia. By 1908, she had used the drug successfully in about two thousand surgical cases. She published a book and some articles based on her studies and became a vocal advocate for the use of scopolamine-morphine in births because the drug did not interfere with the physiological process of labor. In 1914–15, when women began arguing for their right to choose scopolomine-morphine anesthesia, or "twilight sleep," during childbirth, Van Hoosen was one of their main medical proponents. She became a prominent member of the National Twilight Sleep Association, an organization led by active feminists who aimed to inform women about "painless childbirth" and to convince doctors to use "twilight sleep."

In 1913, the Civil Service Board of Chicago announced that it would, for the first time, hold competitive examinations for positions on the gynecological staff of Cook County Hospital. Van Hoosen took the exam, received the highest grade, and became the first woman to serve as chief of the gynecological staff of Cook County Hospital. In 1918, Van Hoosen reached the height of her academic success with an appointment as head and professor of obstetrics at Loyola University in Chicago, a coeducational medical school. When the American Medical Association (AMA) gave Loyola's medical school an excellent rating and suggested that a man be made head of obstetrics, the dean supported Van Hoosen.

Van Hoosen carried her concerns for the health of women into community involvement. She served the Women's Trade Union League of Chicago as a staff physician, treating members under the auspices of the Health Committee. As a member of the Chicago Woman's Club, she also gave lectures on sexual anatomy and sex education to audiences of club women, mothers and children, working girls, and high school girls.

Although Van Hoosen had a very successful career, in her efforts to advance herself she often encountered substantial opposition and obstacles. The opposition she faced, including faculty protests to her appointment at the College of Physicians, the Chicago Gynecological and Obstetrical Society's refusal to admit women, the refusal of *JAMA (Journal of the American Medical Association)* to advertise her book on scopolamine-morphine anesthesia and its rejection of every article she submitted for publication, together with a profound sense of isolation she felt while attending AMA meetings, led her to believe that women needed to organize, to join forces, in order to succeed.

In 1915, in conjunction with the fiftieth anniversary of the Chicago Hospital for Women and Children (renamed the Mary Thompson Hospital for Women and Children; see MARY HARRIS THOMPSON), she gathered together a group of like-minded women, and they established the Medical Women's National Association (MWNA), later renamed the American Medical Women's Association. Van Hoosen became the first president of the organization. During her presidency and throughout her life she worked tirelessly to foster the progress of medical women and to combat discrimination. Among the MWNA committees she initiated was the Committee on Opportunities for Medical Women, which annually reported on internships available for women in hospitals across the nation and corresponded with hospitals that did not admit women in an effort to increase women's opportunities.

In addition to her organizational efforts to advance the cause of medical women, Van Hoosen also did much to promote the success of women practitioners by serving as a "circuit surgeon" ("Petticoat Surgeon," unpublished ms, 2, 291). She recognized that, in a small town, a woman doctor who referred surgical cases to another doctor, usually a man, tacitly acknowledged his superiority and consequently risked losing her patients to this doctor. To avoid such risk, Van Hoosen traveled to small towns near Chicago and in Michigan to perform surgery for her female colleagues. Van Hoosen was also highly cognizant of her position as a role model and dedicated herself to training women as surgeons. During the course of her career, she trained twenty women surgeons and strove to instill the highest standards in her students, whom she proudly and affectionately referred to as her "surgical daughters" (*Petticoat Surgeon*, 216).

Though Bertha Van Hoosen never married, she enjoyed a warm and loving family life. She maintained a close and supportive relationship with her parents, who, despite their early objections to her choice of career, took pride in their daughter's achievements. Her main source of love and support, however, was her sister Alice Van Hoosen, who eventually entered medical school at the University of Michigan but dropped out in her junior year and married Joseph Comstock Jones. After the birth of their daughter, Sarah, the Joneses moved to Chicago. They bought a house and occupied the top two floors. Bertha Van Hoosen used the basement for both living quarters and office space. After Joseph Jones's death four years later, the Van Hoosen sisters continued living together. Van Hoosen saw her sister's help and support as vital to her professional success. Bertha Van Hoosen helped raise Sarah Van Hoosen Jones as if she were her own child and took pride in the accomplishments of her niece, who obtained a Ph.D. in animal genetics from the University of Wisconsin in 1921 and returned to Stony Creek to manage the family farm.

Bertha Van Hoosen visited Stony Creek frequently. She suffered a stroke there in October 1951. She never fully recovered and died in a convalescent home in Romeo, Michigan.

Bertha Van Hoosen worked to overcome discrimination against women in medical practice through several professional strategies. In her own career, she successfully entered the male-dominated field of surgery and gained prestigious positions in previously male institutions. She also became a mentor and teacher for women who wished to practice surgery. Further, seeing a need for medical women to organize in order to maintain a place for women in medicine, she helped establish MWNA and promoted its activities. She was both a successful surgeon and obstetrician and a leader in medical women's struggle to achieve equality in their profession.

Sources. The Bertha Van Hoosen Papers, housed in the Bentley Hist. Library at the Univ. of Michigan, contain unpublished manuscript versions of her autobiography, *Petticoat Surgeon* (1947), which is the most important source of information about her life and career. The Bentley collection also includes letters from Van Hoosen to her family. The Univ. Archives at UIC Spec. Coll. maintain a small collection of Van Hoosen's papers, including correspondence between Van Hoosen and her "surgical daughters." The institutional records of the College of Physicians and Surgeons, also at the Univ. Archives at UIC, provide valuable information about Van Hoosen's tenure at the college. Another collection of Bertha Van Hoosen Papers, containing scrapbooks and correspondence, is housed at the Medical College of Pennsylvania's Archives and Spec. Coll. on Women in Medicine. These archives also hold the papers of Rose V. Menendian, a surgeon trained by Van Hoosen. These papers include many letters from Van Hoosen. She published *Scopolamine-Morphine Anaesthesia* in 1915. Van Hoosen's numerous scientific articles on obstetrics and gynecology are published in the *Women's Medical Journal (WMJ)* and occasionally in other scientific journals. Her articles on opportunities for women in medicine are also found in the *WMJ*. Historians who have written about Van Hoosen include Judith Walzer Leavitt, who addresses Van Hoosen's advocacy of twilight sleep in "Birthing and Anesthesia: The Debate over Twilight Sleep," *Signs*, Autumn 1980; and Eve Fine, "Separate but Integrated: Bertha Van Hoosen and the Founding of AMWA," *Journal of the American Medical Women's Association*, September/October 1990. A biography of Van Hoosen appears in *NAW* (1980).

EVE FINE

VAN PAPPELENDAM, LAURA
February 10, 1883–February 10, 1974
ARTIST, TEACHER

The first of three children, Chicago artist Laura Van Pappelendam was born to a Dutch American family in the small town of Donnellson, Iowa. When she was still young, her parents, John and Alice Van Pappelendam, moved the family to Keokuk, Iowa, where her father established a real estate and insurance business. In 1904, two years after Van Pappelendam graduated from Keokuk High School, she enrolled in the School of the Art Institute of Chicago (SAIC), beginning her studies in the design department. During her second year she concentrated on courses in SAIC's academic department; and in the third year, after determining that she should prepare to teach art, Van Pappelendam began the training courses at SAIC's Normal School and received a teaching certificate in 1909.

Van Pappelendam immediately obtained a position as a summer school instructor in the design department of the Normal School at SAIC. She continued her own art education while she taught classes at SAIC, studying with renowned artists Karl Buehr and Nicholas Roerich. She also studied painting with Spanish impressionist Joaquin Sorolla y Bastida in 1911, while he was a visiting professor. Van Pappelendam took postgraduate work at SAIC from 1917 and studied with George Bellows in 1919. On June 18, 1926, SAIC awarded her the degree of Bachelor of Art Education, given to all graduates of the teacher training department who had also completed a year of academic work in education, English, history, and modern languages. Van Pappelendam concurrently took night and Saturday afternoon classes at the University of Chicago and received a Bachelor of Philosophy degree in 1929.

Van Pappelendam managed to balance a full career as a teacher at both SAIC and at the College of Education of the University of Chicago (1919–24) and in the University's newly established Department of Art (1924–48). During her fifty years as a teacher at SAIC, she taught a variety of subjects, including still-life painting, pottery, mechanical drawing, design, and construction and life drawing. Her commitment to SAIC and the museum was especially strong. During the 1930s she made numerous paintings of the interior of the Art Institute, documenting the installation of the 1933 Century of Progress art exhibitions. She enjoyed an excellent rapport with her students, who were drawn to her enthusiastic and vivacious personality. Known as "Miss Van" to students and colleagues alike, she once dressed as a Picasso portrait for a surrealist ball, a dramatic example of her sense of humor and style.

Although Van Pappelendam was well liked and respected as a teacher, she was best known as an artist and often felt that her demanding teaching schedule took time away from her painting. Her primary medium was oil paint, but she also worked in watercolors and experimented with printmaking. Her earlier paintings display a palette dominated by pastel colors, bright lighting, and the *plein air* and still-life subject matter of the American impressionists. However, Van Pappelendam did not limit herself to painting in one particular style; later work displays qualities gleaned from American, European, and Mexican modernists. Instead of abandoning skills that she learned, Van Pappelendam built upon and sometimes returned to techniques that were learned during her early development as an artist. She once stated that her choice of subject matter generally reflected an interest in depicting the "existing relations" (Jacobson, 130) of forms rather than a concern with making social comment or expressing personal ideas. Van Pappelendam's development as an artist was stimulated by new vistas and new techniques gleaned from a lifetime of study with other artists. Summers away from teaching were critical for this maturation.

Her first trip to Santa Fe, New Mexico, in the summer of 1920 began a pattern, as she found a small art colony at the foot of the Sangre de Cristo Mountains. Van Pappelendam returned to Santa Fe for the next seven summers. In the Southwest, she, like other American artists, came into contact with subject matter native to America. Van Pappelendam usually stayed with the painter Olive Rush, who had settled in Santa Fe in 1920. Rush introduced Van Pappelendam to potter Alice Clark Meyers; Florence Dibbell Bartlett, founder of the Museum of International Folk Art; art collector Mary Cabot Wheelwright; and other artists and writers in the area. Van Pappelendam returned to Santa Fe in the 1950s.

Van Pappelendam developed her use of color during these Santa Fe summers, an interest that had been first stimulated by her teacher Joaquin Sorolla y Bastida. In the 1930s, she spent her summers painting in Mexico; in Cuernavaca in 1930, she met Mexican muralist Diego Rivera. Studying with Rivera that summer, the student Van Pappelendam was not ready to return to teaching and requested a short leave from her responsibilities at SAIC, which she received from Dean Charles Fabens Kelley. It was a crucial time for her career as an artist, for Diego Rivera "opened [her] . . . eyes to new wonders" (Jacobson, 130). In Mexico she began to paint more expressively, showing a new approach to form, composition, and color as seen in *Fitted to a Lava Bed* (1930), *Magnolia Blossoms* (1930), and *Back of the Church* (1931).

In the late 1930s and early 1940s, family responsibilities called her back to her hometown of Keokuk, Iowa, where she painted in a converted garage and tended to her aunt and ill stepmother. It was during this period that she completed many paintings using the Maroger Medium, a process used by one of her professors. Jacques Maroger taught his students an oil emulsion medium used by the Dutch, Flemish, and Italian masters that he had rediscovered. When her stepmother's cancer was arrested in 1949, Van Pappelendam was free to go to Santa Fe again and did so for the following five summers. Here she returned to her earlier impressionist palette.

If the first milieu in which art educator Van Pappelendam drew her inspiration was the pioneering School of the Art Institute of Chicago, the second was the University of Chicago. Here she participated first as a student, then as a teacher, and finally as part of the broader cultural community interested in an agenda of national and international humanistic initiatives. Van Pappelendam was involved in the creation of both the Renaissance Society and the Department of Art at the University of Chicago. The society held lectures, concerts, and exhibits that, in the first fifteen years, were in keeping with the kind of idealist approach to art of AIC trustees Charles Hutchinson and Martin Ryerson and sculptor Lorado Taft. Important for Van Pappelendam, the Renaissance Society began to provide encouragement for the university to adopt as legitimate the inclusion of the study of art into the liberal arts curriculum. It was not until 1924 that all of the college's art interests were organized into one Department of Art, where Van Pappelendam was an instructor for twenty-four years.

One of the leading academic families at the University of Chicago interested in art and culture was that of economics professor John Ulrich Nef Jr. and his wife Elinor Castle Nef, who became a close friend of Laura Van Pappelendam. The Nefs and Van Pappelendam were active in the Renaissance Society, with Elinor Nef and Van Pappelendam serving on its board of directors consistently from 1915 through the 1950s. The Nefs supported Van Pappelendam's art career by helping her to exhibit and sell her work. They provided her with a place to live as a caretaker of their house and companion to Elinor Nef's mother. Through the Nefs, Van Pappelendam met French artist Marc Chagall.

The Nefs' interest in peace issues meshed with Van Pappelendam's Quakerism. Elinor Nef and Van Pappelendam traveled abroad in 1937 during the depths of the Great Depression. Signs of the rise of fascism left a profound impression on Van Pappelendam, who began to disclose strong feelings about warfare and military conscription. During the 1940s Van Pappelendam identified with her church's pacifist stance and antiwar activities; she also came to know about the Women's International League for Peace and Freedom through Elinor Nef. In his work as a scholar and chair of the Committee on Social Thought at the University of Chicago, John Nef focused on issues of militarism and the relationship of war and culture. Intrigued, Van Pappelendam later supported Nef's efforts to establish a Center for Human Understanding in Washington, D.C.

Van Pappelendam was an incredibly prolific artist, and her work was included in more than 250 exhibitions. At the Art Institute alone, her work was displayed in over sixty exhibitions, including one two-person show. She also exhibited at the Arts Club of Chicago, Findley Galleries, the Hyde Park Art Center, the Renaissance Society at the University of Chicago, Roullier Galleries, the South Side Art Association, and the Vanderpoel Memorial Art Gallery. Her works were shown through the Chicago Friends of Art, the Chicago Society of Artists, the Illinois Academy of Fine Arts, and the Western Society of Engineers. In the 1930s, Van Pappelendam's art was displayed in New York at the Whitney Museum of American Art, the Riverside Museum, the Academy of Allied Arts, Delphic Studios, and in a national art exhibition of American Art in Rockefeller Center. Her work was included in several national exhibits and twice exhibited in Dublin, Ireland.

Van Pappelendam received her first awards, the William O. Goodman Prize, for paintings that she exhibited in the *Art Students League Exhibitions* of 1917, 1918, and 1919. In 1921, she received two Honorable Mentions, one for *Old Spanish Porch*, shown at the *25th Annual Artists of Chicago and Vicinity Exhibition*, and one from the Chicago Society of Artists exhibit. In 1929, she was awarded a Recognition Prize by the South Side Artists Association for her painting *Yellow Walls*. Two years later, she won the coveted William Merritt French Memorial Gold Medal for *Magnolia Blossom* at the *44th Annual Exhibition of American Painting and Sculpture*. At the 1932 *Annual Exhibition of Artists of Chicago and Vicinity*, she received the Mr. and Mrs. Jule F. Brower Prize for *Banana and Geranium Plants*. In 1933, she was awarded the prestigious Mr. and Mrs. Frank G. Logan Prize for *Long Haired Cactus*, which was shown at the *Artists of Chicago and Vicinity* exhibit. In 1936, she won a silver medal from the Chicago Society of Artists for *An Old Church*. She was awarded the Clyde M. Carr Prize in 1942 for *At the End of the Porch*, which was exhibited at the *Artists of Chicago and Vicinity* exhibit. That same year, she won the Women Artists Salon of Chicago Prize for *Blue Flower Pots*. Her final award came in 1951, when she was given Honorable Mention from the Alumni Association of the School of the Art Institute of Chicago for *The Bailey Place on the Mississippi River*.

Van Pappelendam was an active member of the Chicago arts community and was involved in a number of arts clubs. She was an artist member of the Arts Club of Chicago, the Chicago Galleries Association, and the Chicago Society of Artists.

Van Pappelendam retired from teaching in 1959 and was subsequently named Professor Emerita. After her death in 1974 in a convalescent home in California, it was found that she had willed stock to SAIC in order to establish a scholarship fund now known as the Laura Van Pappelendam and Elinor Castle Nef Fund.

Van Pappelendam's work and influence has had a lasting effect both in Chicago and elsewhere. In March of 1988, the School of the Art Institute of Chicago, in conjunction with an Archives of American Art symposium about Chicago modern artists, planned a reunion for those who knew or studied with Van Pappelendam. In his book, *Over a Century, a History of The School of the Art Institute of Chicago 1866–1981*, Roger Gilmore wrote that Van Pappelendam's students used her techniques to teach their own classes. Edna McLeod, Van Pappelendam's niece, established a nonprofit organization, Laura Van, Inc., which serves to research Van Pappelendam's life and work, to coordinate exhibitions, and to establish scholarships and awards in her name. Since her death, new appreciation of Van Pappelendam as a western American artist resulted in her works being included in exhibits in the Autry Museum of Western Heritage (1995–96); Owings-Dewey Fine Art, Santa Fe, New Mexico (1996); and the Museum of Fine Arts, Santa Fe, New Mexico (1996); the Gilcrease Museum in Tulsa, Oklahoma (1996); and the Museum of Art, Brigham Young University, Provo, Utah (1996–97).

Sources. The informative "Resume of Laura Van Pappelendam," which was researched and compiled by Edna McLeod, is in the Art Institute of Chicago (AIC) Archives. Secretary's files that pertain to the Laura Van Pappelendam and Elinor Castle Nef Scholarship Fund as well as card files of prizes won in Chicago exhibitions are also located in the AIC Archives. The Ryerson and Burnham Libraries of the AIC have the exhibition catalogs of Chicago arts clubs and galleries, the AIC "Scrapbook" and Art and Artists of Chicago "Scrapbook." Articles about Van Pappelendam's exhibitions and work may be found in these scrapbooks as well as in her faculty file. Correspondence between Elinor Castle Nef, her husband John Ulric Nef Jr., and Laura Van Pappelendam is located in the John U. Nef Papers, UC Spec. Coll. The Alice Roullier Papers at the NL contain information regarding the Arts Club of Chicago exhibitions. Barton Faist, Chicago artist and collector, has a collection of Van Pappelendam's work and numerous anecdotes pertaining to Chicago art history. *Art of Today: Chicago 1933*, ed. J. Z. Jacobson (1932), contains an interview with Van Pappelendam and other contemporary Chicago artists. Issues of *Alumnus*, published by the School of the AIC in the winter of 1969, are valuable. Anne Felicia Cierpik, "The History of the Art Institute of Chicago from Its Incorporation on May 24, 1879, to the Death of Charles L. Hutchinson" (master's thesis, DePaul Univ., 1957), and *Over a Century, a History of The School of the Art Institute of Chicago 1866–1981*, ed. Roger Gilmore (1982), are good sources for historical information regarding the School of the Art Institute of Chicago. *Antiques and Fine Art* magazine, March–April 1991, published a substantial article about Van Pappelendam's life and work, "Laura Van Pappelendam: A Lively and Generous Spirit," by Sandra D'Emilio.

COLLEEN BECKER

VAN VOLKENBURG, ELLEN
October 8, 1882–December 15, 1979
THEATER COFOUNDER, ACTRESS, PRODUCER, DIRECTOR, WRITER

Ellen (Nellie) Louise Van Volkenburg, at thirty, became internationally known when she and her British husband, Maurice Browne, founded the Chicago Little Theatre, which fostered the American little theater movement. She also created the first serious children's theater in America, where she spread the art of marionette making. After the Chicago Little Theatre went bankrupt, she continued to perform, produce, direct, and write plays.

Born in Battle Creek, Michigan, Ellen Van Volkenburg was the only child of Frank Hoyt and Juliet (Cooper) Van Volkenburg. Her father, of Dutch descent, traveled for the meatpacking industry, bringing his family from Battle Creek to Fort Wayne, Indiana, and finally to Chicago, where they lived in an upper-middle-class, northside apartment. Because of her father's career demands, Van Volkenburg spent much of her childhood living in hotels. As a child, she could memorize a play verbatim upon hearing it once. She would silently sit at a performance, induce a trance, weep through the play and uncannily record each line, voice, and mannerism. She practiced her imitations on fellow hotel guests.

Van Volkenburg continued performing imitations while an undergraduate at the University of Michigan, where she was vice-president of the Comedy Club and participated in such student productions as *The Professor's Tragedy* at the Old Athens Theater in Ann Arbor. After she graduated in 1904, Van Volkenburg gained wide popularity as an important solo woman entertainer. She gave imitations of such famous stars as Maude Adams and Ethel Barrymore. In this type of performance, she reproduced every character and action in a play, with only one chair for a prop. Her mother traveled with her as she performed these one-woman shows.

Her personal and professional life would have been very different without Maurice Browne, a poet, dramatist, and scholar. They met when traveling in Florence, Italy, in 1910 and married June 1, 1912. Van Volkenburg and Browne opened the Little Theatre in Chicago in the fall of 1912 with a five hundred dollar check from a friend and well-wisher, Mary Blair, wife of banker Chauncey Blair. While giving theatrical performances at social affairs for Chicago's upper class, she had met Blair and other women who helped foster an art theater in the city, including Lolita Sheldon Armour, wife of J. Ogden Armour of the Chicago meatpacking industry, and MARY ALDIS, who had her own little theater in Lake Forest, Illinois.

The physical theater in the Fine Arts Building reflected a growing American interest in Asian art. For their programs Van Volkenburg and Browne used Japanese rice paper with cover designs by Raymond Johnson. Chinese tapestries and wood carvings decorated their tea room. Its stage was small—fifteen feet wide, eighteen feet deep, and less than twelve feet high—and it seated ninety-three. Van Volkenburg's mother, then known as "Mummy Van," worked at the theater's box office. Juliet (Cooper) Van Volkenburg continued to accompany her daughter when she performed with the touring company of the Chicago Little Theatre.

When the Little Theatre opened in October 1912 with Wilfrid Wilson Gibson's *Womenkind* and William Butler Yeats's *On Baile's Strand*, it functioned as an experimental and repertory theater and prided itself on being an artistic and intellectual center for Chicago. Many people came to the Sunday evening gatherings, including Theodore Dreiser, Clarence Darrow, Eugene Debs, Lincoln Steffens, and Emma Goldman. Poets, including HARRIET MONROE, Vachel Lindsay, Carl Sandburg, Arthur Dawson, and EUNICE TIETJENS, read there. The theater's goals were to introduce new authors, perform one-act experimental plays, and establish an American poetic drama. The theater served as a protest against nineteenth-century stagecraft with its idealized, unsubstantial imitation of reality.

Both Van Volkenburg and Browne were interested in dramatic line, form, and pattern and experimented with lighting as well as symbolic presentations. They had financial as well as artistic motivation for their innovations: having no money to buy floodlights or spotlights, they used dishpans and funnels, relying on the lights reflected from the theater's floor.

In the summer of 1913, Lolita Armour gave them one thousand dollars, and Harriet Edgerton gave them money for travel. They went to England, visited Browne's family, and then toured Europe. While visiting Munich, Germany, they met two sisters who gave occasional amateur marionette shows in Solln, a nearby town. These women, the Misses Jannsens, made their own puppets and inspired Van Volkenburg, changing the course of American puppetry. With the aid of Harriet Edgerton, Bettie Ross, Louise Mick, and puppet makers Carroll Friend and Kathleen Wheeler, Van Volkenburg developed shows that pleased both adults and children. Among her favorite puppet shows were *The Deluded Dragon* with Harriet Edgerton, first performed on February 20, 1915, and Edgerton's rendition of William Shakespeare's *A Midsummer Night's Dream*, first performed on April 25, 1916.

After Van Volkenburg and Browne opened the Chicago Little Theatre, she continued to travel and perform as a one-woman entertainer, introduced puppet theater into the repertory, and toured with the Little Theatre. In 1915, she traveled the United States with the Little Theatre, playing the role of Hecuba, one of her favorite parts, in Gilbert Murray's translation of Euripides' play, *The Trojan Women*. The press called her performance masterful. With dark eyes and high cheekbones, Ellen Van Volkenburg left a vivid impression as Hecuba. During the years of the Little Theatre, 1912–17, Van Volkenburg and Browne helped revive Greek drama, particularly Euripides' *Trojan Women* and *Medea*. They also brought European, English, and Irish theater to America, performing such plays as Henrik Ibsen's *Hedda Gabler*. They produced original drama such as Alice Brown's *Joint Owners in Spain* and Cloyd Head's *Grotesques*. Their interest in symbolic drama, puppets, and marionettes helped set the tone for other American art theaters.

The Chicago Little Theatre members attempted to establish their Chicago art theater on democratic lines. From the first year, the company had problems with Maurice Browne's authoritarian style. One of the actresses, ALICE GERSTENBERG, indicated that Ellen Van Volkenburg served as actress, director, financial manager, and peace-keeper, trying to keep dialogue open between Maurice Browne and many of their associates. Browne quarreled with the actors and with the management of the Fine Arts Building, which housed the theater. In addition, Van Volkenburg's marriage to Browne was increasingly troubled by his sexual exploits. These personal tensions contributed to the problems that plagued the company.

The Chicago Little Theatre needed the support of its wealthy backers, but some of the conservative contributors became unhappy with Van Volkenburg's and Browne's affiliation with the peace movement. The Carnegie Foundation, at the urging of JANE ADDAMS, had put up five thousand dollars to finance the Little Theatre production of the antiwar play, *The Trojan Women*. Sponsored by the Woman's Peace Party, the play was performed forty-two times in thirty-one cities to approximately thirty-three hundred people during the fifteen weeks in which the company traveled from Chicago to Baltimore, then San Francisco and other parts of the West Coast, and back to Chicago. After the United States entered World War I, many backers withdrew their financial support of the Little Theatre.

Of all the Little Theatre's original plays, only Cloyd Head's *Grotesques* was a substantial financial success. As a result, the theater closed and the Chicago Little Theatre declared bankruptcy in December 1917.

Van Volkenburg and Browne went west in 1918 to teach at the Cornish School, an arts academy in Seattle, Washington. They lived near a beautiful, isolated fjord in Nellita, a tiny settlement.

A year later Van Volkenburg revealed her ambivalent feeling toward Chicago. She believed that human-made places like Chicago were dreadful and found only the lake naturally beautiful. After 1919, she never lived in Chicago again.

She spent eight summers at the Cornish School, where she established a dramatic school and puppet theater. There, she set up the first marionette department in any school in the United States, and in the spring of 1918, she dramatized *Alice in Wonderland*. She also spent part of the school year teaching in Utah (1918), Oregon (1921), and Montana (1922), though for almost a decade the Cornish School was her base.

At the same time, she continued her career as an actress and director. Among many other appearances, Van Volkenburg played Clytemnestra in *Medea* at the Garrick Theatre in New York. On March 22, 1920, she played one of her other favorite roles, that of Nora in Henrik Ibsen's *The Doll House*. At the Garrick, she also played the title role in George Bernard Shaw's *Candida*. In January 1922, she produced *Mr. Faust* at the Provincetown Theatre in Cape Cod, Massachusetts. Van Volkenburg and Browne often worked together during the twenties and thirties. She and Browne directed the Seattle Repertory Company 1920–21, and in 1922 the Maurice Browne–Ellen Van Volkenburg Repertory Company in New York.

After moving west, she and Browne remained married but frequently did not live together. They legally separated on May 17, 1924, after Browne and another woman, Margaret-Ellen Janson, a California poet, had a child together. The divorce became final in 1926 on the grounds of willful desertion. Regardless of their problems, they maintained a personal as well as professional relationship throughout Browne's life.

Browne returned to England in 1927 to try to get his fi-

nances on track. His wealthy friends, Dorothy and Leonard Elmhirst, were willing to back his English drama ventures. They invited Van Volkenburg in 1927 to direct a play of her own choosing at Dartington, the Elmhirsts' residence in Totnes, Devon county. She came to England and directed *A Midsummer Night's Dream*. Browne's luck was improving; he had both financial backing and opportunity and used it to invite Van Volkenburg to direct Cecil Day Lewis's translation of Raul Raynal's *The Unknown Warrior* at the West End Theatre. The play was a success. Browne's next production, R. C. Sheriff's *Journey's End*, was so well received that he presented it around the world for almost four years. With the money he earned, he purchased the Globe and Queen's theaters and for a moment became the most powerful theater magnate in the English-speaking world.

In the autumn of 1929, Chicago gave him a hero's return. Van Volkenburg, back in Seattle, came to hear Browne praised as the Little Theatre's founder. Whatever her emotions at hearing Browne get so much credit for what was rightfully hers as well, Van Volkenburg did not protest. Mary Aldis protested for her in a letter on October 13, 1931, to Griffin Barry, who had written an article on Maurice Browne and the Little Theatre for the *Theatre Guild* magazine. Aldis corrected and enhanced his knowledge of Van Volkenburg's contributions and suggested that Barry write a companion piece on her. Barry never did.

In 1928, at the request of the Elmhirsts, Van Volkenburg returned to Dartington and again organized dramatic work there. She produced *Othello*. Constance Smedley described Van Volkenburg's showing of *Othello* at the Savoy Theatre in London, with Paul Robeson in the title role, as one of the finest productions of that play on the English stage. By October 1931, Van Volkenburg was director of productions for Maurice Browne, Ltd., and director of the London Theatre Company. Between 1920 and 1931, she had productions at the Globe, Queen's, Prince of Wales, Savoy, Apollo, and Fortune theaters. In 1927, she played Tekla in August Strindberg's *Creditor* at the Arts Theatre in London and the title role in *Candida* at the Greenwich Village Theatre two months later.

Van Volkenburg stayed true to her vision of an art theater. When the Globe did not function as an experimental theater, she and Richard Odlin remodeled a thirteenth-century barn into a suitable little theater. There, she continued experimenting with puppets and marionettes. Browne and Van Volkenburg fought about their increasingly different visions of what was possible in London's West End, but their careers remained interwoven. When the London Theatre company closed in 1934, Van Volkenburg went back to America and never worked in England again.

Van Volkenburg continued to act and produce. In the early 1940s she acted in the Pasadena Playhouse in California. She played the role of Genevieve Millward in *The Distaff Side* and she acted in *Arsenic and Old Lace*. In that decade she also produced *The Trojan Women* for the University of British Columbia and joined Eighteen Actors Inc.

At this point in her career, Van Volkenburg saw herself increasingly as a writer. On November 18, 1940, the *Los Angeles Times* wrote about her as the best-known woman stage producer and director in the world, but by this time Van Volkenburg was clearly involved in trying to write her own plays. One, dated

1943, copyrighted under a pseudonym, Emily Hoyt, was entitled *Ameriga Vespucci*. In this play, a woman, using any means she could to get to America, was rejected by the Puritans. Another play, written with Dorothy Crawford, *Nine Points of the Law*, was drafted about the same time. In 1946 they wrote a second play, *Kip*. About ten years later she dramatized Henry James's *The American*, which was produced in England in July 1969.

In the 1950s, Van Volkenburg was still involved in many projects. She directed Beatrice Straight in a Broadway production of *Eastward in Eden*. She helped Browne edit his autobiography and spent months in his English home. Regardless of tensions, Van Volkenburg remained loyal to Browne, contributing money to his household after World War II and providing moral support in his last years.

After Browne's death in January 1954, Van Volkenburg continued to work and travel. She lived in New York and Los Angeles, where for the last fifteen years of her life she was intimate with a woman, Jo H. Jordan, a counselor from Los Angeles. Jordan was her roommate and soulmate. Van Volkenburg died of a stroke in Los Angeles in 1979 and was buried in Marshall, Michigan, with her parents and her extended family.

Ellen Van Volkenburg, one of the most famous female producers of her time, was a woman with a photographic memory, a genius for mimicry, and a talent for acting and puppetry. As a cofounder of the impressive Chicago Little Theatre, she influenced the direction of American theater.

Sources. The Ellen Van Volkenburg papers are housed at the Univ. of Michigan, Spec. Coll. Library. The collection has many letters, diaries, scrapbooks, promptbooks, and clippings, and includes Constance Smedley's unpublished article, "Women Producers." Scrapbooks for 1906–41 are particularly helpful. Clippings from *Theatre Arts* magazine, May 1917, and from newspapers throughout the United States, 1924–40, appraise the Little Theatre and describe Van Volkenburg's talents. The papers contain an inventory of Van Volkenburg's manuscripts held by the repository. For information on Van Volkenburg's Chicago days, see letters and clippings at the CHS in the Chicago Little Theatre Collection and in the Cloyd Head and Alice Gerstenberg collections at NL in Chicago. Gerstenberg's lengthy, unpublished autobiography, "Come Back with Me," can be found at the NL. A book that offers a personal angle on Van Volkenburg's contribution to the theater world is *Miss Aunt Nellie, the Autobiography of Nellie C. Cornish*, ed. Ellen Van Volkenburg Browne and Edward Norhoff Beck (1964). This is her only published work. An interview article by Mme. Qui Vive, "The Most Remarkable Girl in Chicago: Ellen Van Volkenburg of the Marvelous Memory," in the Chicago *Sunday Record-Herald*, October 31, 1909, highlights her childhood and photographic memory. A later interview article in the same newspaper, February 22, 1914, by Mary O'Connor Newell, "How Success Has Come to the Little Theatre," gives a perspective on the Browne–Van Volkenburg public presentation of their shared work life. Although most books with information on Van Volkenburg focus on Browne, they are still useful. Among these are Sheldon Cheney's *The New Movement in the Theatre* (1914), Oliver Martin Saylor's *Our American Theatre* (1923), Maurice Browne's *Too Late to Lament* (1956), and Dale Kramer's *Chicago Renaissance* (1966). Other accessible and informative articles include Maurice Browne's "The Temple of a Living Art," *Drama*, November 1913; Bernard Dukore, "Maurice Browne and the Chicago Little Theater," *Theatre Survey*, vol. 3, 1962; Donald Tingley's "Ellen Van Volkenburg, Maurice Browne and the Chicago Little Theatre," *Illinois Historical Journal*, Autumn 1987; Charles Lock's "Maurice Browne and the Chicago Little Theatre," *Modern Drama*, vol. 31, 1988; and Douglas Clayton's "Yesterday's City: Temple of a Living Art," *Chicago History*, November 1993.

MARILYN J. ATLAS WITH KATHRYN L. BEAM

VICKERY, MABEL SLADE
September 13, 1854–August 22, 1944
EDUCATOR, SCHOOL FOUNDER

Mabel Slade Vickery, founder and headmistress of the Chicago Latin School, was born in Winchester, Massachusetts, to Jonathan A. and Esther (Bosworth) Vickery, whose ancestors were early New England settlers. Her father was an architect, and she had one brother and two sisters. Vickery's baptismal name was Mary Isabella, but she changed it to Mabel Slade when she was thirty. She was educated at Malden High School, Malden, Massachusetts, and Boston University, before she began to teach in 1880.

Until 1885 Vickery taught in the high school at Lynn, Massachusetts. During the early 1880s, many people in Massachusetts were concerned about school teachers' lack of preparation for their task. By 1884, the city of Lynn stressed the need to hire normal-school graduates and considered starting its own teacher-training program. Vickery probably saw the need for further preparation and, after leaving Lynn High School in 1885, entered the Salem (Massachusetts) Normal School. Her class had forty-four students, of whom she was the oldest. The Massachusetts normal schools required courses to be taken in all subjects taught in the common schools with the exception of foreign languages. Each student was required to complete two terms and to state in writing an intent to teach in the state's public schools.

At Salem Normal School, Vickery was chosen to compose the class song for graduation, a significant honor, and in 1890 she composed the ceremonial hymn for the alumnae triennial. After graduation from the school in 1885, Vickery became the principal of the Chatham (Massachusetts) Grammar School and then was principal of the Orange (Connecticut) High School for the 1887–88 school year.

While a student at Salem, Vickery made a study of schools in and around Boston, reviewing the various teaching techniques employed. She became interested in the Quincy System, made famous by retired U.S. Army Colonel Francis W. Parker, superintendent of the Quincy, Massachusetts, schools from 1875 to 1880. Parker was an educational reformer under whose supervision the Quincy school system became a model throughout the country. The governing principles of Parker's method were the abolishment of rote memorization—the long-time basis of American public school education—and the establishment of a child-centered curriculum. Colonel Parker's method offered a new way to approach the education of children. In 1883 Parker came to Chicago to head the Cook County Normal School. Because of Parker's association with the normal school, many Chicagoans became acquainted with the Quincy System, or as it was sometimes called, "Colonel Parker's Method."

In 1888, Vickery traveled to Chicago at the invitation of a group of well-to-do parents who sought a person trained in the new teaching methods of the Quincy System to prepare their sons for eastern colleges and boarding schools. The parents had contacted the Quincy superintendent of schools for a recommendation, and he suggested Vickery. She was hired for two years, and classes were held in the library of the home of manufacturer Eliphalet Blatchford, who lived in a wealthy area of Chicago just north of the city's booming commercial center. During the 1880s, Chicago was a rapidly growing city where enterprising men could often make fortunes easily, and they wanted elite schools for their children. Having started her school in the home of one of Chicago's leading families with the sons of civic leaders as pupils, Vickery had a source of students for her college preparatory school—the children of the city's newest and most successful entrepreneurs.

In 1890, when Vickery's first students left to attend eastern schools and the Blatchford home was no longer available for classes, publisher Alexander C. McClurg and his wife, Eleanor (Wheeler) McClurg, invited Vickery to use their house, not far from the Blatchford home, for teaching another small group of boys. In 1892, when the McClurgs moved to a new home nearby, Vickery's school moved there also. When the McClurgs left for Europe in 1894, Vickery had to move her school once again.

Robert Peck Bates, a young classicist, recently graduated from Trinity College in Hartford, Connecticut, arrived in Chicago in 1893 to work with Vickery. Together they established a demanding classical curriculum, hired more faculty, began developing plans for the school, and, in 1894, rented a small house not far from the school's previous location. At that time, the school had twenty-five students and seven teachers; in just three years, it outgrew its space and moved to a larger, rented place a few blocks away.

In 1896 at the suggestion of Harriet (Hammond) McCormick and ANITA McCORMICK BLAINE, classes for small girls and boys were begun, with Vickery in charge and Harriet and Mary Bradley engaged as teachers. The girls in these classes were the first to enter what would become the Chicago Latin School; they would be members of the girls' graduating class of 1907. Girls and boys continued to learn together at the school through the eighth grade, but they were separated into girls' and boys' divisions at the secondary level, a practice traditional at private preparatory schools. Vickery served as headmistress of the girls' division and Bates as headmaster of the boys' division. However, Vickery taught history in both divisions. She returned to the East as a special student at Harvard University during three summers, in 1895, 1897, and 1898; there she received a certificate in American history, preparing her to teach at the high school level.

In 1898 Vickery and Bates, with seventy-two students and a faculty of sixteen, incorporated their institution under the name the Chicago Latin School. By 1899 they had erected a permanent building for the school, remaining in their original location on Chicago's Near North Side. It opened in September 1899, with 125 students and twenty-one instructors and with Vickery and Bates as co-owners and co-principals.

The high school course of study that Vickery and Bates devised for the students was rigorous; it included foreign and classical languages, mathematics and sciences, English and American literature, and both ancient and modern history. Vickery and Bates intended that their students be thoroughly prepared for exacting eastern colleges, as their parents wished. Consequently, by its second decade, the Latin School was firmly established as one of the leading schools in Chicago, and the majority of its male graduates matriculated at Harvard, Yale, Princeton, and Cornell universities. Many of the girls who graduated from the school attended top-flight eastern women's colleges as well as coeducational colleges in the Midwest. Vickery and Bates added electives in manual training and crafts to their traditional classical curriculum. The inclusion of these subjects reflected Vickery's agreement with educators such as Parker and pragmatist philosopher John Dewey, then based in Chicago, who proposed a democratic education that combined "culture" and "useful work" for all students. These educators opposed a class-based separation of "culture" for the children of an elite and the manual skills associated with "useful work" for the children of the working class.

Vickery did not ignore students' need for exercise to develop their bodies as well as their minds, believing that students could learn better if they were healthy and fit. The physical education policy of the school also encouraged the formation of athletic teams and the development of body skills as preparation for athletic life in college. Besides a penchant for neatness and cleanliness, Vickery touted the virtues of fresh air. She insisted one could not study in a room with the temperature higher than sixty-eight degrees; on visiting a classroom, she went directly to the windows and threw them open.

One of Vickery's first female students described her headmistress as "quiet and unassuming, yet dominant in any situation. She was short and always wore her hat in the classroom. She worked long hours and was a marvel of endurance. Even in her seventies, I have often seen her climb the four flights of stairs with no appearance of exertion" (Wilkins, Margo Moss Archives, n.p.).

Vickery and Bates remained co-owners of the school until 1913, when she and several faculty members incorporated the girls' division as the Chicago Latin School for Girls, located in a new building. Vickery became owner and head of the girls' school, while Bates remained head and owner of the boys' Chicago Latin School.

In 1929, at age seventy-four, Vickery decided to retire. She sold the girls' school to parents, who incorporated it as the Girls Latin School of Chicago. Robert Peck Bates had already retired in 1926. That year the Chicago Latin School was sold to parents and incorporated as the Chicago Latin School for Boys. A larger building was constructed that was still part of the Latin School of Chicago in the 1990s.

In June 1929, the Alumnae Association of the girls' school held a reception honoring Vickery at the Fortnightly, a prominent Chicago women's club. Her portrait, by the eminent English painter Frank Salisbury, was unveiled at the gathering. It was given to the school by the alumnae in honor of Vickery's many years of service. Former students, faculty, and parents had a deep respect for her, and the line of guests at the reception extended for a half a block from the door of the Fortnightly. Vickery's striking portrait hangs in the Upper School building of the Latin School of Chicago.

Vickery's single-minded devotion to her school kept her from participating in activities not directly related to its administration and welfare. A sense of the meaning of Vickery's long career was given in the 1929 *Rostra*, the girls' school yearbook, which described the richness of Vickery's life in creating a school to fill a need, keeping high standards, and providing a firm foundation for the institution's future. After a long career dedicated to teaching, Vickery, who never married, retired to a home she shared with her sister in Natick, Massachusetts. She died there in 1944 at age eighty-nine, from the complications of old age, and was buried in Lindenwood Cemetery, Stoneham, Massachusetts, near her birthplace. In the 1990s, the parent-owned, coeducational Latin School of Chicago, created by the 1953 merger of the Girls Latin School of Chicago and the Chicago Latin School for Boys, remained the leading independent college preparatory day school that Vickery had developed from its beginnings.

Sources. The Margo Moss Archives at the Latin School of Chicago contain most of the available material on Mabel Slade Vickery: correspondence, mostly on business matters; Latin School catalogs and yearbooks; and ephemera. Also in the Margo Moss Archives are unpublished papers by Josephine Wilkins, the school's first historian. The first Chicago Latin School catalog (1899–1900) gives an overall look at the school—its classrooms, faculty, and curriculum—and its supporters and patrons. The yearbooks—*Sigillum* (Boys School), *Vita Schola* and *Rostra* (Girls School)—are often dedicated to Vickery and occasionally contain accounts of her achievements as founder and head. There is an entry on Vickery in Paul Gilbert and Charles Lee Bryson, *Chicago and Its Makers* (1929). Joan M. Maloney's *Salem Normal School 1854–1905* (1990) contains some material about Vickery as a student there and about the normal schools and public education of the time in Massachusetts. Several informative letters from Maloney are also on file in the Latin School Archives.

MARY ANN MCFARLANE

VITTUM, HARRIET ELIZABETH
February 14, 1872–December 16, 1953
SETTLEMENT HOUSE HEAD RESIDENT, SOCIAL REFORMER, SUFFRAGIST, POLITICAL AND CIVIC ACTIVIST

From 1904 to 1953, Harriet Elizabeth Vittum devoted her life to assisting the primarily Polish immigrant neighbors who were using the Northwestern University Settlement House (NUS) at Augusta and Noble Streets in the Chicago neighborhood of North West Town. On behalf of her neighbors she offered her services to city, state, and nation.

Vittum, known as Hattie, Miss Vittum, H.E.V. and H.V., was born in Canton, Illinois, to George Brown and Delia A. (Burrell) Vittum, who married in a Congregational service in 1866. She was the second child among brothers Frank, Edwin, and Karl. Her father, a prosperous merchant born in Canton, was descended from French Huguenots who had settled in Sandwich, New Hampshire. He attended Knox College in Galesburg, Illinois. Harriet Vittum's mother came west with her family from Auburn, New York, to Canton, where S. T. Burrell managed a train station and owned a hotel. Raised by civic-minded parents in a pleasant home, Vittum probably attended the Congregational Church; as an adult, the humanistic Vittum was not a regular churchgoer. Vittum graduated valedictorian of Canton Public High School in 1890. She was a dark-haired, dark-eyed girl with a tendency to plumpness and a serious face

with prominent features. She wore her hair pulled into a bun, a style she would retain. Although Vittum wrote tenderly about a future husband and her engagement ring in an August 5, 1898, letter intended for her mother, there is no record that she ever married.

During the decade of the 1890s, Vittum engaged in a variety of activities. She most likely trained as a nurse under a local doctor, as was the custom in rural communities; but by 1893, she was working at the Illinois Building of the World's Columbian Exposition in Chicago, where her father's cousin was an Illinois commissioner. After that she spent several years honing her clerical skills at the Illinois Children's Aid Society. In 1899, she was making use of her nursing skills as a nurse and supervisor at the Altruistic Hospital located within two rooms of her parental home. She assisted with two difficult surgeries to demonstrate Canton's need for a hospital.

In June 1903, Vittum was certified to teach respiratory and physical exercises at Chicago's Francis Marshall School, afterwards working for Dr. Henry B. Favill and his associates. Starting sometime in 1904, Vittum volunteered with a girls' evening program at Northwestern University Settlement (NUS) at the suggestion of a friend. She became a resident volunteer in her free time in 1905 and the following year, apparently, acted as temporary head resident on a part-time basis for the absent NUS head resident, Raymond Robins, until his resignation in 1907. That spring a woman was appointed head resident at NUS, and Vittum returned full-time to Favill. When the head resident resigned in the fall, Vittum accepted the modestly paid position from the NUS association council in October 1907. NUS was located in a 1.5-square-mile area of the impoverished 17th Ward, known for its many saloons, sweatshops, and slum housing. As a salaried employee, Vittum managed NUS and guided its association, clients, paid staff, residing workers, volunteers, and assisting organizations. Vittum was the ninth administrator of NUS since its founding in December 1891 by influential persons affiliated with Northwestern University (NU) in Evanston, Illinois; NUS itself had no official connection to the university. By 1901, NUS had moved for the fourth time to the building on Augusta. The architects' proposed Noble Street annex with gym and auditorium was not built because funding fell short.

The years between 1907 and 1916 were very active for Vittum. The friendly, capable, energetic head resident brought NUS stability and continuity while providing pragmatic leadership for its growth and development. Between 1907 and 1910, for example, she doubled the distribution of pasteurized milk by NUS to neighboring babies from 61,084 to 121,769 bottles, thereby expanding the Save the Babies campaign begun at NUS in 1898 in an effort to lower infant mortality. She canvassed the neighborhood for sick babies to be brought to the NUS dispensary and counseled mothers about sanitation and modern medical care.

In addition to having a hands-on relationship with the settlement's programs, Vittum participated in the broader reform community. She understood the need for political action and for the organization of workers in trade unions. Vittum was a loyal member of the Chicago branch of the Women's Trade Union League (WTUL), opposing poor working conditions, advocating the education and mobilization of women, and joining

FIG. 122. *Northwestern University Settlement House director Harriet Vittum, on the left, talks with Women's Trade Union League leader Margaret Dreier Robins, 1917.*

with such other women reformers, trade unionists, and head residents of Chicago settlements as MARGARET DREIER ROBINS, JANE ADDAMS, MARY McDOWELL, and AGNES NESTOR. Vittum also participated in the women's political reform culture that was so influential in implementing new social policy to address the challenges of industrial society. She was a founding director of the civic welfare–oriented Woman's City Club of Chicago (WCC), whose membership was a who's who of women reformers—LOUISE deKOVEN BOWEN, MARY WILMARTH, RACHELLE YARROS, HANNAH SOLOMON, ANNA NICHOLES, and others.

Vittum created additional facilities for NUS between 1910 and 1912. In lieu of a three-story annex, a basement gymnasium was built with a drop-down stage. The gym's flat roof was transformed into a children's playground. The first NUS recreational camp, the House in the Wood, was established on rented land. An adjacent house was remodeled to contain housekeeping and laundry training areas as well as a print shop. Dean Peter Lutkin of NU Music School helped establish a music program at NUS. Vittum encouraged the NUS clubs, federated as the Neighborhood Guild by Raymond Robins, to become a strong force connecting the neighborhood and the settlement.

After the Illinois legislature passed a partial state suffrage act on June 26, 1913, which extended the franchise to women and enabled them to vote in presidential and "virtually all municipal, county, town, and village offices" (Buechler, 178), Vittum began educating women in the 17th Ward about voting in the spring aldermanic election. Vittum was president of the Woman's City

Club of Chicago at the time; organized by city wards, the club was an extraordinary network linking activist women. Jane Addams urged Vittum to seek the 17th Ward aldermanic seat. Vittum ran as an Independent in an attempt to clean up political corruption. Her platform demanded settlement movement goals, including better schools and adequate sanitation. Her spirited campaign climaxed with one thousand girls and boys marching along with her to a rally, shouting, "We want Miss Vittum" ("1,000 'Kids' Shout for Miss Vittum"). The large independent vote demonstrated the clout of female politics. In a field of six candidates, she received 1,420 votes to the winner's 3,489.

Running on the Progressive Party ticket in the fall of 1914, both Vittum and Mary McDowell were candidates for the Cook County Board of Commissioners. The county board had mishandled county relief funds during a recent decline in the economy. The two women were backed "by a group who wanted them as experienced workers to disseminate facts about public institutions" (Cranston) in the hope of cleaning up politics. Neither won, but theirs was an audacious challenge. Vittum remained active with Raymond Robins on the Progressive [Party] State Senatorial Committee. She was a delegate to the 1916 Progressive Party Convention in Chicago, where Theodore Roosevelt declined the party's presidential nomination although he had been the unsuccessful presidential candidate on the Progressive Party ticket in 1912. Vittum, on behalf of the dissolved Progressive Party, interviewed Republican presidential candidate Charles Evans Hughes at his cottage in New York and found him an acceptable candidate.

In 1916, the Republican National Committee appointed Vittum to head its Woman's Bureau in Chicago to organize the vote for Hughes among the enfranchised women of the western states, including Illinois. Waging a strong campaign for Hughes, Vittum gained national prominence. Incumbent President Woodrow Wilson won, however, although by a narrow margin; he was helped by the votes of women who favored his campaign position of maintaining American neutrality in World War I.

The United States declared war on Germany in April 1917. Vittum organized NUS as a civilian center for the war effort. The settlement offered Red Cross classes and served as an induction center for the armed forces. Vittum traveled to other counties as a director of the Illinois Woman's Committee of the Council of National Defense, organizing county councils for the distribution and shipment of supplies overseas. During the war, NUS printed its own news bulletin, the *Neighbor;* it featured letters from the war front from NUS neighbors. In 1918, in the middle of her war efforts, Vittum lost her father, who died after a prolonged illness.

The postwar years and the 1920s failed to bring the nation back to the "normalcy" hoped for by many Americans. Instead, it was a time of economic problems, racial tensions, and changing values in the neighborhoods of American cities. In Chicago, southern black migrants faced segregated housing and discrimination. By 1919, the overcrowding of the Black Belt—the area on the city's South Side where African Americans were forced to live because white neighborhoods refused to rent or sell property to Blacks—created pressures on the housing market. Blacks attempting to move into all-white blocks near the Black Belt met with hostility and, increasingly, with violence as white property owners joined together in associations to maintain segregated housing patterns. "In the spring of 1919, the bombing of Negro homes and assaults on Negroes in the streets and parks became almost everyday occurrences" (Spear, 212). In the summer, when a black youngster swimming in Lake Michigan inadvertently crossed the "invisible" boundary line dividing Chicago's lakefront into black and white beach areas, he was stoned to death by white people. Police ignored the charges made by Blacks who witnessed the incident; an African American crowd attacked several white men, and soon white gangs retaliated by "beating, stabbing, or shooting thirty-eight Negroes who had accidentally wandered into white districts" (Spear, 214). The rioting that began on that hot Sunday afternoon in July continued into the week; by Wednesday evening, with no end in sight, Chicago Mayor William Thompson asked Illinois Governor Frank Lowden to send in the militia. The Chicago Race Riot of 1919, with violence on both sides, shocked liberals and conservatives. Vittum and Graham Taylor responded to the violence by calling for a conference to help reduce the heightened racial tensions. Courageously, Vittum marched with African American ADA McKINLEY, head resident of the South Side Settlement, along with Mary McDowell and Jane Addams, in a show of solidarity and in the belief that it was necessary to address the social injustices experienced by the black community.

During the 1920s, Vittum continued to provide leadership at NUS, to encourage the participation of women in politics, and to promote the well-being of the settlement movement through professional organizations. In 1920 she headed the Republican Party's Woman's Division. At the Republican National Convention held in Chicago in June 1920, General Leonard Wood was Vittum's choice to be nominated by the party as the candidate for the presidency. Wood had become an army surgeon after graduating from Harvard Medical School and had gained a national reputation by serving with distinction as military governor of Cuba from 1899 to 1902. Warren G. Harding received the nomination, however, and became the next president.

In the 1920s, under Vittum's leadership, NUS continued to provide clinics in nutrition, prenatal and well baby care. NUS converted a nearby building into a two-hundred-seat theater with Polish decor, the Guild Playhouse. The recreational camp House in the Wood was relocated to a north suburban forest preserve. Vittum also continued to encourage her settlement workers to reside in the house, a policy reflecting the philosophy of the founding generation of settlement house leaders. By 1930, however, it was becoming increasingly difficult to find workers willing to accept residency as a prerequisite for employment. In part, this change in attitude reflected the professionalization of the field of social work. Rather than a way of life for the settlement resident, the settlement house became a place of employment for a new generation who defined themselves as social workers. Vittum encouraged the residence concept and noted, "'Never a week goes by that we do not discuss at our dinner table some political situation in the neighborhood.' For Vittum, such conversation was 'very definite and a very vital part of settlement life'" (Trolander, 45). She saw the settlement house as more than a social agency delivering services to the immediate community. She continued to link the activities of the settlement with a broader agenda of civics and social reform. She believed, for example, in "bringing neighborhood political problems to the attention of her board" (Trolander, 56) and remarked in her article "A Time and Money Budget for a Department of Civics and Politics in a Settlement," published in the March 1930 issue of the *Neighbor,* that her board members "[were] very much interested in the political activities of the Settlement and would like to have [the settlement] do more" (quoted in Trolander, 56).

While settlements had always been concerned with the issues of food, jobs, and housing for the neighborhood's working poor and indigent, the economic conditions that challenged the United States during the Great Depression years were substantially different in nature and scope. Not all settlement head residents advocated New Deal policies; some, whose boards were conservative or whose budgets relied on funding from cautious or conservative Community Chests, felt constrained. The progressive Harriet Vittum had a liberal board and was in a position to advocate such measures as Social Security. Her support of major new legislation was only one aspect of her heightened activity to remedy economic and social conditions as the depression deepened. Before Franklin Delano Roosevelt's election in 1932, Vittum joined with other reformers and settlement workers in the Chicago Workers Committee on Unemployment (CWCOU), a group motivated by the extreme social dislocations brought about by the economic collapse of the country. She was a member of CWCOU's Advisory Committee, which also included JESSIE BINFORD and LEA DEMAREST TAYLOR. In January 1932, Vittum, Taylor, Karl Borders, and ES-

THER KOHN organized hearings to publicize the living conditions of the unemployed. Vittum was one of the head residents in Chicago and nationally who supported New Deal policies and actively participated in social action activities to empower the working class and the poor. After early relief measures and New Deal programs were put in place, CWCOU created grievance committees to investigate the complaints of the unemployed. Vittum and Taylor "helped the grievance committees gain access to the relief authorities" (Trolander, 98) so that those who were victims of administrative errors or oversights could have their situations rectified.

NUS provided to its neighbors food, candles for light, coal for heat, and temporary lodging for evicted families. A nearby building became Lincoln Lodge with a craft shop, club rooms, and other facilities for men and boys. Vittum and NUS participated in the government's Workers Education program, along with the University of Chicago Settlement and Chicago Commons. Workers Education provided classes for workers that encouraged them to organize and take political action. When a wave of strikes occurred across the nation in 1937, Chicago settlement workers, including Vittum, created the Citizens' Emergency Committee on Industrial Relations. The committee aimed to bring accurate information about industrial conditions and labor disputes to the general public. Vittum was also involved with initiatives to develop housing programs for low income citizens. For her advice to the Works Progress Administration (WPA) regarding federal housing needs, she was honored with a civic trophy for "rendering the most unselfish service to the city" (Douglas).

The international scene also engaged Vittum, especially when war broke out in Europe in 1939. Along with many citizens, she initially opposed American intervention. In early 1940 she was one of the organizers of the Roll Call of American Women; the group opposed U.S. involvement in any war not directly in defense of the country. Following the attack on the United States fleet in Pearl Harbor, December 7, 1941, Vittum wholeheartedly supported U.S. participation in World War II. NUS soon was busy with air raid drills, war stamp and bond sales, patriotic sings, and classes in civilian food stamp use. Hundreds of NUS neighbors served their country.

The postwar decade presented new, internal problems for NUS. The Lincoln Lodge was no longer rentable, and the theater building was in such poor physical condition that it was deemed beyond repair. Resident workers were aging; staffing problems had to be addressed; and Vittum, now age seventy-five, announced her pending retirement at the settlement's annual dinner in April 1947. Vittum wrote to a friend, "I am not going away because I want to leave . . . but I am getting old" (Vittum to Amelia Sharp, October 18, 1947, NUS Association records). On November 11, 1947, Vittum was elected by the main board to be honorary president in perpetuity of the auxiliary NUS board. At a testimonial dinner in honor of Vittum on November 11, 1947, Governor Dwight H. Green described her as one of the most effective lobbyists in the state for the interests of the people.

After forty years, the retired Vittum moved out of her third floor suite at NUS and into a small apartment in downtown Chicago. As she took the streetcar to NUS, Vittum was often seen with her pince-nez clipped to her customary brown dress and wearing a hat with decorations that evoked the fashions of an earlier era. Her days were busy; she served as a vice-president of the Woman's City Club, wrote community news columns, started her memoirs (none were ever found), attended meetings, and worked on a community housing plan. She celebrated her eighty-first birthday at NUS looking well and happy.

Ten months later, Vittum, in a semi-conscious state, was admitted to Passavant Memorial Hospital (formerly part of Northwestern Memorial Hospital) by her dear friend, a volunteer physician at the NUS pre-natal clinic, Augusta Webster. Vittum died of a cerebral hemorrhage. News of her death was reported with a banner headline in the *Chicago Daily News*, announcing, "Miss Vittum, 1st Lady of Needy Dies" (December 16, 1953). After lying in state at NUS, and following services in Chicago and Canton that were conducted by Congregational ministers, Vittum was buried in her family's plot at Greenwood Cemetery, Canton, Illinois.

Posthumously, Vittum was honored with editorials and memorial resolutions. A settlement endowment fund, a camp memorial lodge, and a twelve-acre Vittum Park in Chicago were dedicated to her memory. During her half century of involvement with NUS, most of her days were spent with thousands of her neighbors. Vittum's strengths were her love of people and her belief in the democratic process as the route to achieve social justice. She worked well with people of all classes, races, and ethnicities, excelling at networking and empowering others. Her innovative work was in the practice of community organizing. She knew her neighbors as a neighbor. A broad spectrum of people appreciated Harriet Vittum's life and work, including Miecislaus Haiman, the curator of the Polish Roman Catholic Union of America Archives and Museum, Chicago; Harold L. Ickes, former New Deal Secretary of the Interior; colleague Lea Demarest Taylor; and sociologist Emory S. Bogardus. They all identified her exceptional skills and her commitment to the people she served.

Sources. The papers of Harriet Elizabeth Vittum are part of the Northwestern Univ. Settlement Association records at Northwestern Univ. Library Archives, Evanston, Illinois. The collection includes Vittum's annual reports, essays, correspondence, case reports, scrapbooks, pictures, memorabilia, and issues of the *Neighbor*, an NUS newsletter. Harriet E. Vittum papers are also at UIC Spec. Coll. Articles about Vittum include Bernice Cranston, "Miss Vittum's Career Is One Long Crusade," *CT*, November 25, 1934; "1,000 'Kids' Shout for Miss Vittum," *Chicago Record Herald*, April 6, 1914; W. A. S. Douglas, "Harriet E. Vittum, N.U. Settlement Chief Selected as City's Most Useful Woman," *Chicago Herald and Examiner*, June 1, 1937; and Helen W. Carr, "Two Great Women," *Woman's City Club Bulletin*, Spring 1954. Mark Wukas, *The Worn Doorstep, Informal History of Northwestern University Settlement Association, 1891–1991*, ed. Doris Overboe and Ronald R. Manderschied (1991), provides useful background. Other books include Judith Ann Trolander, *Settlement Houses and the Great Depression* (1975); Steven M. Buechler, *The Transformation of the Woman Suffrage Movement: The Case of Illinois, 1850–1920* (1986); Allan H. Spear, *Black Chicago: The Making of a Negro Ghetto 1890–1920* (1967); and Allen F. Davis, *Spearheads for Reform: The Social Settlements and the Progressive Movement, 1890–1914* (1967, new edition 1984).

DORIS PICCINO OVERBOE

VONNOH, BESSIE ONAHOTEMA POTTER
August 17, 1872–March 8, 1955
SCULPTOR

Bessie Potter was the only child of Alexander C. and Mary "Molly" (McKenney) Potter. Born in Cleveland, Ohio, in 1836, Alexander Potter was of Irish descent. Mary Elizabeth McKenney's family had emigrated from Scotland several generations before her birth in Clarksfield, Ohio, in 1841. Married in 1861 in Maumee City, Ohio, at the McKenney family home, the Potters lived in Maumee City for eight years before moving to St. Louis, Missouri, where Bessie was born. Alexander Potter sold farm machinery. He died as a result of a railway accident when Bessie Potter was two years old.

After her father's death, Potter came down with an unknown illness resulting in paralysis. For the next eight years, she underwent painful medical treatments. When she was ten years old, her physician declared he could do no more for her. In "Tears and Laughter Caught in Bronze" (1925), Potter recalled that she heard his prognosis, but instead of dying, she slowly began to recover. "Why, no one ever understood. I only know that when all the treatments and fussing ceased I slowly began to mend" (p. 8). She later credited her illness with giving her "plenty of time to dream of beauty that is in the world" (quoted in Aronson, 15).

At age fourteen, Potter decided to become a sculptor. She and her mother had moved to Chicago by 1877, where her mother worked as a clerk to support them. Nothing is known of her early education, but eventually she attended Cook County Normal School. This was at a time when Colonel Francis W. Parker, an experimental educator, headed Cook County Normal. In the child-centered environment established there, it was possible for Potter to explore her creativity and contemplate a career in the arts. Both Parker, the principal, and Kristian Schneider, her teacher, encouraged Potter. Her first modeling teacher, Schneider was a German sculptor who later created ornamental models for architects Dankmar Adler and Louis Sullivan. Potter enjoyed these early modeling lessons, although she later remarked that she did not feel they were very challenging. She set up a studio in her home and started to get orders: a portrait of a house and a modeled head of a political figure for a cane.

When she was fourteen, she and her mother visited the shop of an Italian plaster caster, who introduced Potter to the sculptor Lorado Taft. Lorado Taft was so supportive of women in the arts that he has been referred to as "the father of Chicago's women sculptors" (Aronson, 27). Potter enrolled later that year in the School of the Art Institute of Chicago (SAIC), where Taft was an instructor. Because Potter's mother could only afford one year of SAIC tuition, Taft agreed to allow Potter to work as his studio assistant on Saturdays. Taft, one of the major sculptors of the Midwest, ran a large studio with many assistants who worked on many of his public sculpture commissions. Both in his art classes at SAIC and in his studio, Taft gave work to women artists. Soon after, Julia Bracken (see JULIA BRACKEN WENDT) joined the studio.

In 1891, Potter came to public notice for her work in student art exhibits. One sculpture in particular, a figure of a standing female nude, *Echo* (1891), received high praise for being as "subtly charming in conceit as it is excellent in execution"

(quoted in Aronson, 34). By June 1891, Potter had saved enough money to take a trip to New York City, where she met one of her idols, Augustus Saint-Gaudens, whose sculpture of Abraham Lincoln, *The Standing Lincoln*, in Chicago's Lincoln Park was completed in 1887. Lorado Taft had been enthusiastic when a committee of Chicagoans invited Saint-Gaudens to portray Lincoln because he, like Taft, was among the first group of American sculptors to depart from the neoclassical convention of portraying heroes in classical roles and, instead, showed them in natural poses with contemporary clothing. Bessie Potter was among the students in Chicago associated with Taft's and Saint-Gauden's new approach. When she returned to Chicago in the fall of 1891, Potter finished her studies at SAIC.

At this time she began making sculptures for the World's Columbian Exposition of 1893 with Taft's other students. Saint-Gaudens was influential in promoting Taft's work. The exposition offered opportunities for American artists, because there was great demand for architectural sculpture and decoration throughout the vast fairgrounds and buildings, as well as for art work that was displayed in the Fine Arts Building. Years later Potter remembered the thrill of being a part of this great endeavor. Although she had to ride to the exposition grounds in an unheated horse car, she "mounted the bumpy car each morning as if it were a chariot" (Vonnoh, 8). Potter and the other students were to help Taft in implementing his commissions on the Horticulture Building. When Lorado Taft asked if he could hire young women to help, architect Daniel Burnham, who was in charge of the entire plan for the exposition buildings, replied that Taft could employ anyone, even "white rabbits" (quoted in Aronson, 40), if they could do the work. The name stuck.

It is difficult to ascertain the full extent of Potter's contribution to the World's Columbian Exposition. Potter unsuccessfully entered the contest for the exterior sculptural decoration of the Woman's Building but received a commission, independent of Taft's studio, for the Illinois State Building, where she sculpted an eight-foot statue of *Art*, a figure holding a palette and brushes. Five other White Rabbits also received independent commissions, each artist receiving eight hundred dollars for her work, thus beginning their professional careers. Potter also exhibited two plaster busts in the Fine Arts Building of the exposition.

The exposure that Potter received as a result of her work at the exposition resulted in her participation in local art exhibitions beginning in 1892. At a Palette Club exhibit in 1892, Potter showed a bust, *Mrs. Charles Henrotin* (1892), of clubwoman ELLEN HENROTIN, an influential patron of culture in Chicago with close ties to BERTHA HONORÉ PALMER, chair of the Board of Lady Managers of the exposition. Besides giving Potter visibility invaluable for gaining patrons, the exposition also accorded her the opportunity to view the work of artists from around the world. Potter was particularly taken by small bronze figures by Prince Paul Troubetskoy, exhibited in the Italian section. These figures inspired the twelve-inch figures for which Potter would become noted. In 1894, Potter moved into her own studio in the Athenaeum Building, on the same floor with sculptors Lorado Taft, his sister Zulime Taft, Carrie Brooks, and Janet Scudder. Although Potter exhibited a plaster bust, *Portrait Bust—Mr. L. T.* [Lorado Taft] (c. 1893) at the Art Institute in October 1894, most of her time between 1893 and 1898 was devoted to creating more than one hundred plaster statuettes of women, which came to be called "Potterines." In these, she rejected neoclassism and, instead, added color to her sculptures and portrayed her subjects in contemporary, not classical, dress. The popularity of small terra-cotta figures unearthed at Tangara, Greece, probably provided a favorable climate for the appreciation of Potterines.

These plaster (and later bronze) portrait statuettes helped her attract patronage. Some of the prominent Chicagoans portrayed in these Potterines included: JULIA NEWBERRY (1894); Mabel E. Kohlsaat (1896), the daughter of E. Nelson Blake, president of the Chicago Board of Trade; the writer Hamlin Garland (1895); and Emily (Brown) Gross, the wife of multimillionaire real-estate developer Samuel Eberly Gross, portrayed with Susan B. Anthony (1896). Another prominent person who sat for a statuette was Caroline Ryerson, an active member of the Antiquarian Society, a women's club that procured works, especially pieces of decorative art, for the Art Institute. The relationship between women's clubs and women artists was crucial, because women artists were excluded from gentlemen's clubs, in which male artists could make important contacts with patrons. Potter's statuettes, though initially inexpensive at twenty-five dollars, increased in price as she gained patrons through word-of-mouth contacts.

Potter was of a larger art community that strove to create a new image of Chicago, no longer a frontier backwater but an internationally recognized city of sophistication. Following the World's Columbian Exposition of 1893, U.S. artists promoted American themes while continuing to admire French impressionism. Potter's contribution was to render urban women's images, in contrast to the familiar images of the American West popular in sculpture and paintings of the period. She and other artists, musicians, and writers formed a salon, the Little Room, which had one of its earliest meetings in her studio in 1894. Included, in addition to Potter and Lorado Taft, were painter Charles Francis Browne; architect brothers Irving K. and Allen B. Pond; writers Hamlin Garland, Henry Blake Fuller, and HARRIET MONROE; and theater director ANNA MORGAN. Garland and Fuller were part of the regionalist literary movement. Potter shared Garland's and Taft's love for impressionism. It was through her relationships with this community that Potter developed her style and her interest in portraying familiar Chicago subjects that were part of her personal experience.

In May 1895, Potter received a public honor from the Art Institute in partnership with the Arche Club, a women's organization concerned with art education. The club, which was composed of five hundred members, funded an AIC art lecturer, Mary H. Ford. Arche donated one hundred dollars to the AIC to be used to purchase works by a woman artist. The museum elected to use the funds to buy seven works by Potter: *Chrysanthemum Girl* (1894), *William B.* (1895), *Mildred* (1895), *A Summer Girl* (1894), *An American Girl* (1895), *Evelyn* (1895), and *Miss F* (1895). This opportunity was more important for the chance to display in the Art Institute collection than for the monetary compensation. The seven pieces, the first by a woman sculptor to be acquired by the AIC, were replaced with later Potters as her career developed.

After Potter's trip to Paris in the summer of 1895, she began to sculpt mothers and children, portraying the latter in a direct, natural manner that often showed them with thoughtful or serious expressions. *Mildred* (1895), the daughter of art collector Mary (Mrs. Chauncy J.) Blair, is an eight-and-one-half-inch-tall bust of a young girl with drapery around her shoulders. *The Twins* (1896), a double portrait on a single base, portrays Dorothy and Caroline, the daughters of Mr. and Mrs. Charles E. Kohl. It received honorable mention from the Arche Club Salon of 1897. In 1898, a *New York Times* critic characterized it as the "best of all her work" (quoted in Aronson, 133). A *Young Mother* (1896) shows the influence of French sculptor Auguste Rodin, whom Potter met, in the way that light plays off the surface of the work. In 1897, this statue won second prize for sculpture at the Tennessee Centennial Exposition in Nashville.

The years 1898 to 1900 were filled with professional recognition and personal transition. In 1898, Potter and Enid Yandell were admitted to the National Sculpture Society, the second and third women to receive this honor. In May 1898, Potter moved with her mother to New York City, one of a wave of successful artists who after 1894 had moved from the Midwest with their youth and artistic experimentation to the East Coast.

Potter married Robert Vonnoh in September 1899, culminating a friendship begun in Taft's studio before the exposition. Although some of her friends thought that the marriage would end her career, she managed to balance married life and sculpture with the help of her mother, who managed many of the day-to-day domestic duties. Robert Vonnoh was a successful painter and early American impressionist. The Vonnohs did not have any children. Potter Vonnoh referred to her work as "my bronze and marble babies. . . . I love them as much as if they were flesh and blood. . . . [They] never grow up, I have no heartaches and disappointments over them" (quoted in Connor and Rosenkrantz, 106).

Potter Vonnoh received many awards in the next twenty years. In 1904, she was awarded the Julia A. Shaw Memorial Prize by the National Academy of Design for her work *Enthroned* (1902). Two years later, she was elected the first full, permanent female member of this prestigious organization. Potter Vonnoh was commissioned to create a bust of Vice-President James S. Sherman (1909–11), now located at the Capitol. In 1913, First Lady Ellen Wilson invited Potter Vonnoh to display her art at the White House, the first American artist to exhibit there. The Vonnohs had become friends with the Wilsons, who were neighbors at their summer homes in Cornish, New Hampshire. From 1921 to 1928, the Vonnohs participated in joint exhibits. Bessie Potter Vonnoh's sculpture and Robert Vonnoh's paintings complemented each other thematically. After leaving Chicago in the nineteen-tens, she began placing children and adolescents in garden sculpture. One example is the (Theodore) Roosevelt Memorial near his burial place at the Roosevelt Bird Sanctuary in Oyster Bay, New York.

Tensions in the Vonnohs' marriage arose partly from Potter Vonnoh's close relationship with her mother. Until her death on January 11, 1932, Molly Potter lived with her daughter. In addition, the environments that Potter Vonnoh and Robert Vonnoh needed for their artistic creativity differed; Bessie Potter Vonnoh preferred the urban environment of New York and Paris, while

Robert Vonnoh wished to paint in rural Grez, France. Although they never divorced, the Vonnohs lived independently of each other from the middle 1920s until Robert Vonnoh's death on December 28, 1933. Following the deaths of her mother and husband, Potter Vonnoh was baptized and confirmed at the Episcopal St. Bartholomew's Church in Manhattan. Potter Vonnoh continued to exhibit her works until 1950. Upon her death in 1955, she was buried near Robert Vonnoh and Molly Potter in Duck River Cemetery in Old Lyme, Connecticut. She bequeathed to the Corcoran Gallery of Art in Washington, D.C., the bronzes of their choice.

Bessie Potter Vonnoh was important for Chicago and for American art as a whole. A woman of the Gilded Age, she emerged as an artist at a time in which Chicago was shaking off its frontier image and recreating itself as a city of culture and sophistication. Shaped by her experiences in the World's Columbian Exposition of 1893 and supported by the female network of women's clubs interested in mentoring women artists, Potter Vonnoh came to create art that would represent modern women and children. Instead of the large public art of her mentor Lorado Taft, Potter Vonnoh brought the naturalism of her generation of sculptors to the subject matter of domestic life.

Sources. Bessie Potter Vonnoh, "Tears and Laughter Caught in Bronze: A Great Woman Sculptor Recalls Her Trials and Triumphs," *Delineator,* October 1925, details much of what is commonly known about Potter Vonnoh's childhood and early art career. Julie Alane Aronson, "Bessie Potter Vonnoh (1872–1955) and Small Bronze Sculpture in America" (Ph.D. diss., Univ. of Delaware, 1995), is an invaluable, extensive biography, which is especially helpful in illustrating Potter Vonnoh's role in the World's Columbian Exposition and her early art career in Chicago. Chicago Art Institute Scrapbooks, 1891–1938, are on microfilm at the Harold Washington Library, CPL. These contain articles that chronicle Potter Vonnoh while a student at SAIC, her early exhibits, and World's Columbian Exposition experiences. Entries in Janis Connor and Joel Rosenkranz, *Rediscoveries in American Sculpture Studioworks 1893–1939* (1989), and Charlotte Streifer Rubinstein, *American Women Sculptors: A History of Women Working in Three Dimensions* (1990), provide detailed overviews of Potter Vonnoh's career. Rubinstein also places Potter Vonnoh within the context of her contemporaries in the Gilded Age. Jeanne Madeline Weimann, *The Fair Women* (1981), is useful for background information on the World's Columbian Exposition.

AMY C. SCHNEIDHORST

VRÁZ, VLASTA ADELE
June 18, 1900–August 22, 1989
JOURNALIST, LECTURER, RELIEF WORKER, COMMUNITY LEADER

Vlasta Adele Vráz, editor and copublisher of *Svornost* (Concord), the leading Czech newspaper in Chicago during the first half of the twentieth century, came from a prominent Chicago Czech American family. In 1875, her maternal grandfather, August Geringer, founded *Svornost*, the first Czech newspaper in Chicago and the first Czech daily paper in the United States. Through his newspaper, Geringer supported the founding of many of the important economic, cultural, and social institutions of the developing Chicago Czech community. Vráz was the daughter of Vlasta (Geringer) Vráz and Enrique Stanko

Vráz, the son of an Austro-Hungarian diplomat. E. St. Vráz was a prominent explorer, naturalist, writer, and lecturer, whom Vlasta Geringer met when she was studying in Prague (now capital of the Czech Republic). They were married in Chicago in 1897. Like Vlasta Vráz's grandfather and father, Vlasta Geringer Vráz was an active member of the Chicago Czech American community. She participated in many cultural activities in the city and organized aid from Chicago Czechs for Czech refugees in Vienna after World War I. Throughout her life, Vlasta Adele Vráz carried on a strong family tradition of activism on behalf of Czech immigrants in the United States and Czechs who remained in her family's former homeland.

Vráz was born in Chicago but spent several of her childhood years, beginning in 1907, in Prague. The Vráz family returned to Chicago in 1910. Because she was an outstanding student, the University of Chicago offered her a scholarship upon her graduation from Harrison High School in 1917. However, her uncle discouraged her from accepting the scholarship, arguing that since she was probably going to get married, a university education would be wasted on her. Thus, under family pressure, she turned down the offer, a decision that she later regretted. She was able to compensate for the lack of formal higher education because of her native intelligence and avid reading. She never married.

After high school, Vráz began to work full-time for *Svornost,* her family's newspaper. She also contributed articles to other newspapers, particularly *Amerikán,* a Czech-language paper developed by the *Svornost* staff for rural readers. Her work for *Svornost* continued throughout her active life. Vráz's grandfather Geringer and other *Svornost* editors were highly critical of the Austro-Hungarian empire's treatment of Czechs and Slovaks. Increasingly they agitated on *Svornost's* pages for Czech and Slovak independence and the establishment of a Czechoslovak republic. During the 1910s, Vráz's father traveled to Czech communities throughout the United States, speaking on behalf of Czech independence and encouraging American Czechs to support Czechs in their homeland in their struggle to establish a democratic state. Living as Vráz did in the midst of a family that was deeply committed to the Czech independence movement, Vráz became involved as well. Because of her intimate understanding of the political situation in both the United States and Europe, her regular weekly column reporting on and interpreting the movement, which appeared in the Sunday edition (*Nedělní Svornost*), became popular and highly regarded.

In 1921, after the establishment of the first Czechoslovak republic, Vráz's father settled in Czechoslovakia, and Vráz and her mother joined him there. The family participated in the rich intellectual life of their homeland and moved within an elite circle of friends, many of whom were the leaders of the republic. In his twenties and thirties, Vráz's father had been a pioneering explorer and naturalist who traveled in central Africa, equatorial America, and the South Sea region. He was a popular figure, somewhat of a hero to Czechs, and lectured widely on his experiences as an explorer. Based on his exploits, he wrote both scientific and popular books that his daughter translated from Czech into English. (She also translated other works from English to Czech.) While her father lived in Prague, Vráz acted as his secretary. At the same time she worked as a foreign correspondent for *Svornost* and contributed articles to magazines published in Prague.

After her father's death in 1932, Vráz and her mother remained in Czechoslovakia for several more years. Vráz wrote her father's biography *Život a cesty E. St. Vráze* (The life and travels of E. St. Vráz), a best seller published in Prague in 1937. During the 1930s, Vlasta Vráz became friendly with the family of Tomáš G. Masaryk, president of the Czechoslovak republic, and with Dr. Eduard Beneš, who succeeded Masaryk as president in 1935.

In the late 1930s, as a foreign correspondent for *Svornost* Vráz covered events in Czechoslovakia leading toward the fall of the country to Nazi Germany and the beginning of World War II. She reported on the Munich agreement of 1938 between Hitler and representatives of Great Britain and France, by which the Allied countries allowed Hitler's armies to occupy Sudetenland, an area of Czechoslovakia that bordered Germany. From the Sudeten region, the Germans launched a full-scale invasion of the rest of the country in March 1939. Vráz continued to report for *Svornost* during the first months of Nazi occupation; then she and her mother left for the United States.

Returning to Chicago in 1939, she became an editor and copublisher of *Svornost*. (*Svornost* remained in the Geringer family's hands until it was sold in 1947; by 1957 it had ceased to exist.) During World War II, Vráz aided the Czech government in exile. She also worked with the Voice of America and with Radio Free Europe and took a deep interest in furthering American-Czechoslovak relations. Vráz played an active role in American war efforts, lecturing both in English and Czech and participating in relief work for Czechoslovak refugees.

Upon her return to the United States, she met and became friends with Betka Papánek, a Chicagoan of Slovak parentage and the wife of Dr. Ján Papánek, one of the leaders of the Czechoslovak government in exile and, later, the Czechoslovak ambassador to the United Nations. In 1940, Vráz, Papánek, and Dr. Alice Masaryk, daughter of Tomáš G. Masaryk, organized Czech American women into Czechoslovak units of the American Red Cross. These Czech units worked for both the American Red Cross and the Czechoslovak Red Cross in exile. They raised funds to purchase medical supplies, sewed hospital gowns, folded bandages, collected wool for knitting socks, scarves, and mittens, and arranged to ship them first to France and later to England.

In recognition of her efforts during World War II, Vráz was appointed public relations director of American Relief for Czechoslovakia, an organization that served under President Franklin Roosevelt's War Relief Control Board. After the war ended, she returned to Prague in the summer of 1945 and worked there as an organizer and then as assistant director for American Relief for Czechoslovakia. One of the first foreign civilians to enter Czechoslovakia after the war, Vráz traveled throughout the war-torn country in an army jeep, assessing needs and arranging for supplies from the relief agency to be distributed. She was soon appointed field director, in complete charge of the relief agency's operation in Czechoslovakia. Under her guidance, more than four million dollars worth of food, medicine, clothing, and hospital equipment were brought to Czechoslovakia. Vráz also helped to organize a program of sup-

plementary school lunches for two hundred thousand children. In her relief work, she cooperated closely with the Czechoslovak ministries of health and social welfare and with city officials, relying often on the friendships and contacts she had made in Prague in the 1920s and 1930s. She was directed by her agency to set up a relief program based solely upon need, regardless of political pressures. The aid she delivered was to be understood as a gift from the Americans.

During the immediate postwar years, supporters of democracy within the Czechoslovak government were embroiled in a bitter struggle to retain their control of the country in the face of rising pressure from both the U.S.S.R. (Soviet Union) and the powerful communist party within Czechoslovakia itself. Vráz entered this struggle on the side of those who supported democracy, working to try to stop the country from becoming a communist state. From 1945 to 1948, her relief organization's headquarters in Prague became a rendezvous for those working to keep Czechoslovakia a democracy, looking to the United States for support. In this period she lectured on various American topics, including "The American War Effort" and "President [Franklin] Roosevelt," and led discussions at popular American Forums attended by large Czech audiences interested in life in the United States and in democratic government. These public forums often became the sites of impassioned debates between those who supported democracy and those who supported communism. She was also asked to lecture in other Czechoslovak cities by Friends of the U.S.A., an organization formed to counter the communist message of a group called Friends of the U.S.S.R.

Besides interpreting America to the citizens of Czechoslovakia, Vráz interpreted events taking place in Czechoslovakia to Americans. Vráz returned to the United States several times from 1945 to 1947 to lecture on the situation in Czechoslovakia. By the fall of 1947, Vráz had become a correspondent for the *New York Times*, reporting on the tense struggle developing in Czechoslovakia as communists began to take over the republic. In that year, Ján Masaryk (the son of Tomáš Masaryk), the Czechoslovak Minister for Foreign Affairs, presented Vráz with the Order of the White Lion, the highest civilian order awarded by the Czechoslovak Republic, for her efforts on behalf of the republic during and after the war.

When the Czechoslovak government finally became communist in February 1948, American relief efforts began to wind down. In spite of the fact that Vráz was an American citizen, she was arrested by the Czechoslovak secret police in April 1949, accused of espionage, and imprisoned in Prague's Pankrác prison. Urged by the combined efforts of Illinois Senator Paul Douglas and Illinois Congressman Adolph Sabath, the U.S. State Department exerted strong pressure on her behalf. She was released after a week and expelled from the country. Upon her return to Chicago, she spoke often to various community and women's groups and at churches and civic organizations about her life in what she termed a police state.

Turning her energy toward Czechoslovakians in the United States, Vráz became a leader of the Czechoslovak National Council of America, an organization founded in 1918 to promote the cooperation of Czech Americans for the preservation of democratic freedom. (The forerunner of this organization was the Czech National Council established in 1910 by Vráz's father.) She joined the council in 1956, working as an organizer and in public relations. Vráz's eminent position within the Czechoslovak community in the United States helped her to bring together the representatives of various waves of Czech immigrants in the groups of which she was a member. She could work cooperatively with the descendants of those coming in the early wave of immigration in the mid-nineteenth century, those who came to escape Nazi occupation in 1939, those who fled after the communist takeover in 1948, and, finally, those who came in 1968, following the events of "Prague Spring"—the invasion of Czechoslovakia by Warsaw Pact forces (the combined troops of the Soviet Union and its East European satellites). Descendants of the earliest immigrants sometimes viewed the successive waves of newcomers with suspicion. Vráz was capable of bridging these differences and bringing the groups together to work on common goals.

Her work for the council included editing two monthly publications: *The American Bulletin* (in English) and *Věstník* (in Czech). Because the Czechoslovak National Council of America had long felt a need to preserve the story of Czech and Slovak immigration and its contribution to life in the United States, Vráz compiled *Panorama*, a historical review of Czechs and Slovaks in America, published by the council in 1970. She served as vice-president of the organization and, from 1962 to 1970, as its president. After she retired from this position, she was named the organization's honorary president.

Vráz was also a member of the executive boards of the Czechoslovak Society of Arts and Sciences in America and of the American Fund for Czechoslovak Refugees, organized by Dr. Ján Papánek in 1948. The latter organization became one of the leading agencies helping Czechoslovak refugees, first in Europe and then in the United States. Vráz and others tried to raise funds to endow a chair of Czech and Slovak studies at the University of Chicago, but that effort failed.

During the 1950s, she continued to present Czechoslovak democratic interests to the American public, as she had during the previous decade. In 1956 she received a letter of commendation from Senator Paul Douglas for her devotion to Czechoslovak independence and liberal principles. In 1970 she was recognized for her concern and devoted service for Czechoslovak refugees by an official letter of appreciation from the president of the American Fund for Czechoslovak Refugees.

Vráz died at age eighty-nine, just months before the revolution that led to the reestablishment of the Czechoslovak Republic after more than forty years of communist control. Vráz was buried in the Bohemian National Cemetery on Chicago's northwest side. Shortly after her death, she was honored as a patriot and a great champion of freedom in a resolution of the Eighty-sixth General Assembly of the Illinois Senate. A few years later, the Chicago area chapter of the Czechoslovak National Council named itself after Vráz to memorialize one of its most influential leaders.

Sources. Material on Vlasta Adele Vráz can be found in the Geringer-Psenka-Vráz Family Papers at the CHS. The material includes correspondence, speeches, diaries, a brief history of Czech newspaper publishing in the United States, a short autobiographical sketch, and other items of interest. The Czechoslovak Heritage Museum, Library, and Archives, Oakbrook, Illinois, hold collections such as the papers of the Czecho-Slovak Protective Society, which give significant background information on the Czechoslovak community in the United States. Holdings include books by Vráz's father that give information about Vráz's early life and family. Vlasta Vráz, compiler, *Panorama: A Historical Review of Czechs and Slovaks in the United States of America* (1970), contains biographical articles on Vráz, her father, her maternal grandfather, other leaders in the Czechoslovak community in Chicago, as well as entries on such topics as American Relief for Czechoslovakia and the American Fund for Czechoslovak Refugees.

EVA ROCEK

WAITE, CATHARINE VAN VALKENBURG
January 30, 1829–November 9, 1913

SUFFRAGIST, LAWYER, JOURNALIST, EDITOR, PUBLISHER

Catharine Van Valkenburg Waite was a dedicated leader of the suffragist cause in Illinois from its inception. She donated her legal services to women who could not pay lawyers, and she published an influential legal journal advocating social and legal reforms. Her contemporaries also knew her as a prominent journalist and a successful businesswoman.

Van Valkenburg was born in Dumfries, Canada West (later Ontario), the eldest child and only daughter of Margaret A. (Page) Van Valkenburg, a Canadian by birth, and Joseph Van Valkenburg, possibly a farmer from Holland. The family moved to Denmark, Iowa, when Van Valkenburg was about seventeen. At nineteen she taught for a year, then in 1849 enrolled in the Female Collegiate Department of Knox College in Galesburg, Illinois. In 1852 Van Valkenburg transferred to Oberlin College in Ohio, entering as a fourth-year student in the female department's literary course. In that year she affiliated with the Congregational church. At Oberlin Van Valkenburg tutored students in elocution and helped to found a literary society. She graduated with honors the next year.

Van Valkenburg was twenty-five years old when she married Charles Burlingame Waite on April 26, 1854. Waite, five years her senior, was the son of Lucy (Clapp) Waite and Daniel D. Waite, a physician. When he was about sixteen years old, the family moved from western New York to settle near Chicago. Charles Waite entered Knox College in 1844. The following year, he went to Rock Island, Illinois, to study law. In 1846 he established a short-lived antislavery newspaper. Admitted to the Illinois bar in 1847, Charles Waite returned to Chicago in 1853 and became one of the city's most successful lawyers. The five surviving children of the six born of the marriage of Catharine and Charles Waite were Jessie T. (born 1856), Lucy Clapp (1860), Margaret (1862), Charles Lincoln (1865), and Joseph Van Valkenburg (1875).

In 1855 Illinois's first suffrage organization was founded in Earlville. Catharine Waite wrote the first plea for political rights for women published in Illinois, which appeared in the *Earlville Transcript* that year. Both Waites lectured on equal rights throughout the state. Catharine Waite continued to teach. Beginning in 1857 she taught for two years at Union Park Seminary in Chicago. The family moved to Hyde Park in 1859, where Waite established the Hyde Park Seminary for young women, which she conducted intermittently for eleven years.

In 1862 President Lincoln, with whom Charles Waite had ridden the judicial circuit in Illinois, appointed Charles Waite an associate justice of the Supreme Court of Utah Territory. Mormon settlers led to Utah by Brigham Young in 1847 had been in rebellion against federal authority. After more than two months of perilous travel by wagon train, the Waite family arrived in the Great Salt Lake Valley in July 1862. Soon Waite observed what she judged to be the misery of the Mormon women. When a Boston newspaper published "spicy letters" (*Adventures*, 77) by Waite's sister-in-law criticizing the Mormon practice of polygamy, the family was threatened with violence. By October 1862, after antipolygamy laws had been passed by Congress, federal troops were arriving in Utah Territory, and the federal judges were the target of open hostility. Charles Waite was threatened with hanging, and Catharine Waite, by then the only non-Mormon woman in town, learned how to use a six-shooter.

Many wives of polygamous men visited Catharine Waite secretly and described the cruelties they and their families endured. Waite defied Brigham Young to help these women. "Brigham is now my bitter enemy," Waite wrote, "and says he would rather have forty 'Gentile' men among his people, than one 'Gentile' woman. I like my life here. . . . There is just enough of danger to make it exciting and just enough of adventure to make it interesting" (*Adventures*, 119). Her concern for their plight prompted her to begin her legal education through reading the law under her husband's supervision. She began writing a book intended to alert the public to the "dangerous character [of the] religious monarchy . . . growing up in the midst of the Republic" (*NAW* [1971], 524).

Having found that the laws could not be enforced, and having held only one term of court, during which there were no cases on the docket, Charles Waite resigned his position. The Waites were living in Idaho City in 1865 when their first son was born. Charles Waite again risked personal violence when, as district attorney of Boise County, he opposed a newly organized committee of vigilantes.

Possibly because of the danger they encountered in the far western territories, the Waites returned to Hyde Park in 1866. That year Waite applied to study medicine at Rush Medical College. Refused admission, she reopened her seminary and continued the suffragist work begun a decade earlier. She also published *The Mormon Prophet and His Harem*, hailed as an authoritative history. Waite rewrote the book as a more personalized account in 1868. *Adventures in the Far West; and Life Among the Mormons* was published in 1882, the year Congress outlawed polygamy.

The Waites were among the founders of the Illinois Woman Suffrage Association (IWSA). In June 1868, Catharine Waite, along with MARY LIVERMORE and others, had formed a woman's club, the Chicago Sorosis, to promote women's welfare, among other goals. It was one of the first women's clubs in the United States. The group split, with the Livermore faction focusing its energy on gaining woman suffrage, in contrast to universal suffrage. In October 1868, MYRA BRADWELL issued a call for a Chicago woman's suffrage convention in *Chicago Legal News*, the law journal she edited and published with her husband James Bradwell. Susan B. Anthony and Elizabeth Cady Stanton, whom Catharine Waite came to count among her close friends, made their first tour through Illinois and other western states after the National Woman's Suffrage Convention was held in Washington, D.C., in January 1869. They spoke at the Chicago group's convention in February. There Charles Waite proposed several resolutions supporting women's rights. On February 12, 1869, the IWSA was founded with Mary Livermore as president.

Anthony and Stanton founded the National Woman Suffrage Association (NWSA) in May 1869 to achieve woman suffrage through a constitutional amendment. Their paper, the *Revolution*, condemned the proposed Fifteenth Amendment for not including woman suffrage and advocated more liberal divorce laws and other unpopular reforms. Six months later, Lucy Stone and others formed the more moderate American Woman Suffrage Association (AWSA), which supported the Fifteenth Amendment and advocated seeking suffrage through amending state constitutions. The "call" to join the AWSA was signed by Charles Waite, who was appointed a vice-president. Catharine Waite, however, remained loyal to the NWSA, primarily because of her friendship with Stanton and Anthony. Nonetheless, Myra Bradwell praised Catharine Waite as a moderate suffragist.

Catharine Waite was elected president of the IWSA in 1871, thwarting Livermore's attempt to affiliate IWSA with the AWSA. Waite ended her teaching career and toured Illinois in an effort to help organize suffrage societies throughout the state.

During the Illinois State Constitutional Convention that met from 1869 to 1870, which had been called to revise the 1848 document, the Waites and other women's rights advocates lobbied for inclusion of a woman suffrage amendment so that the (male) electorate could vote on it and other constitutional revisions. Catharine Waite responded to that effort's failure by testing personally the newly adopted Fifteenth Amendment of the United States Constitution. When she was refused voter registration by the Hyde Park board in November 1871 solely because she was a woman, Waite filed a petition to compel the board to register her. Charles Waite argued on his wife's behalf, but the Cook County court denied the plea and assessed her costs. After that, Charles Waite shifted his energies from law to scholarship.

In 1874, reflecting the suffrage movement's redirection toward more moralistic issues, Catharine Waite began a decade of editing the *Crusader*, a temperance paper. She also engaged in printing and publishing books under the imprint of C. V. Waite and Company. Newspaper columnist and suffragist ELIZABETH HARBERT listed Waite among the members of the Illinois Woman's Press Association in 1879 and later described her as among the most prominent journalists in the state. Harbert reported Waite's successful efforts as a businesswoman when Waite opened an office as a financial and real estate agent. Waite built several large apartment houses and managed extensive real estate interests.

Catharine Waite's commitment to suffrage did not wane, however. She remained in charge of the IWSA's legislative work until 1890. She served as chair of the Illinois Equal Rights Association's executive committee in 1879, when Harbert was president, and she was a delegate to the NWSA's June 1880 meeting in Chicago. In 1885, when the state organization focused on municipal suffrage, she was corresponding secretary of the influential Chicago woman suffrage association. As Waite continued active leadership of the state and local suffrage movements, her eldest daughter Jessie played a role in the national arena.

While Waite pursued her many interests, Charles Waite, a freethinker, spent a great deal of time over several years in the Library of Congress in Washington, D.C., researching *The History of the Christian Religion to the Year 200*, published by C. V. Waite and Company in 1881. Charles Waite embarked on a three-year study tour of Europe in 1884. The Waites' second daughter, LUCY CLAPP WAITE, was also in Europe at that time completing her medical studies.

Catharine Waite ceased editing the *Crusader* but continued to manage the publishing business as well as real estate interests. In 1885, at the age of fifty-six, Waite, who had read law for two decades and tried cases in courts of justices of the peace, enrolled in the Union College of Law, then the joint law department of the University of Chicago and Northwestern University. While a law student, Waite designed and supervised the construction of several apartment buildings, managed the building and printing businesses' finances, and raised young Joseph in

Charles Waite's absence. Waite graduated from law school in June 1886 and was admitted to the Illinois bar. She continued to practice law without charge for the benefit of women who could not pay lawyers.

Waite inaugurated the *Chicago Law Times*, published by C. V. Waite and Company, in November 1886. The quarterly carried the motto "The Machinery of law needs mending." In addition to articles on general legal, jurisprudential, historical, political, and sociological topics and biographical data about women lawyers, Waite published articles advocating reform of laws pertaining to the legal rights of women, insanity, abortion, and divorce. Contemporary reformers FRANCES E. WILLARD and Mary Livermore hailed the *Chicago Law Times* as an authority recognized in the United States, Canada, England, Scotland, and France. While serving as its editor, Waite was elected president of the Woman's International Bar Association in 1888. She ceased publishing the *Chicago Law Times* with the October 1889 issue.

Like many other Chicago women leaders, Waite was involved in planning for the World's Columbian Exposition. A prominent member of the Queen Isabella Association formed in 1889 to secure recognition at the 1893 Exposition of woman's achievement, Waite first suggested erecting a statue of Isabella. She believed, with the other Isabellas, that the queen of Castille and Aragon "had enabled Columbus to make his voyage and that she should be honored at the Fair" (Weimann, 28). Waite organized leaders by congressional districts "to enroll members at one dollar apiece and to sell shares at five dollars each to raise money for the statue of Queen Isabella" (Weimann, 29). The Isabellas hoped to raise sufficient funds also for a Woman's Pavilion, an international clubhouse, and assembly rooms. They did not succeed in building their pavilion or in completing a proposed bronze statue of Isabella, but they did erect a six-story building off the fairgrounds for their clubhouse and, next to it, a hotel for women visitors to the Exposition.

Around 1900, the Waites moved to Colorado. In 1903, Catharine Waite published *Homophonic Conversations*, an aid to the study of German, French, and Italian written jointly with her husband, and in 1904 they wrote and published *Thoughts Concerning a Common Language*, exploring a universal tongue. Catharine Waite, then age seventy-five, still practiced law and developed and managed real estate. She traveled in Europe during 1905–1906, also visiting Egypt and Palestine.

Charles Waite died on March 25, 1909. Catharine Waite was suddenly stricken while on a journey to her daughter Lucy's home in Park Ridge, Illinois, in 1913. She died that day of heart disease in her daughter's home. Lucy Waite wrote that her mother "preserved to the last a keen interest in all the live issues of the day" ("Catharine Van Valkenburg Waite," 2). Following a memorial service held by the Chicago Society of Rationalism, Waite's cremated remains were interred in Graceland Cemetery, Chicago.

Waite's friend and fellow lawyer CATHARINE McCULLOCH summed up Waite's independent, courageous, enthusiastic, and generous spirit when she wrote, "She did the thing she thought right, regardless of the powers that be" ("Catharine Van Valkenburg Waite," 1). As a leader in the women's rights movement, as a writer and editor with a reform agenda, and as a lawyer, Waite worked throughout her long life to help the disenfranchised.

Sources. Catharine Waugh McCulloch's undated three-page typescript, "Catharine Van Valkenburg Waite, Lawyer," in the Catharine Waugh McCulloch Papers (Series VI of the Mary Earhart Dillon Collection), SL, and Lucy Waite's undated brief typescript, "Catharine Van Valkenburg Waite," *Scrapbook*, CHS, written after her mother's death in 1913, provide insights into Waite's character and personal relationships. Catharine Waite's responses to the Oberlin alumnae questionnaire (1886–89, 1904, 1908) and Lucy Waite's response to the Oberlin questionnaire on deceased alumnae, 1916, are useful. Waite's book *Adventures in the Far West; and Life Among the Mormons* (1882) provides details about the Waites' years and the first Mormons in Utah, while the three volumes of *Chicago Law Times* (November 1886–October 1889) show Waite as a scholar, historian, and lawyer. Waite also published *The Mormon Prophet and His Harem* (1866) and, with her husband Charles, *Homophonic Conversations* (1903) and *Thoughts Concerning a Common Language* (1904). A thorough search of footnotes in Elizabeth C. Stanton, Susan B. Anthony, and Matilda J. Gage, eds., *History of Woman Suffrage*, vols. 2–5 (1881–1922) provides a sense of Waite's continuous involvement in the suffrage movement. The biographical essay on Waite by Dorothy Thomas in *NAW* (1971) is a strong anchor for a study of Waite's life. *The Transformation of the Woman Suffrage Movement: The Case of Illinois, 1850–1920* (1986) by Steven M. Buechler details the state and national context of the Waites' involvement in the suffrage movement. Jeanne Madeline Weimann, *The Fair Women* (1981), tells the story of the Queen Isabella Association.

CAROLE DIANNE SMITH

WAITE, LUCY CLAPP
March 7, 1860–December 16, 1943
SURGEON, HOSPITAL ADMINISTRATOR, AUTHOR

Lucy Clapp Waite, who practiced and taught medicine in Chicago, was born in the city, the third of six children and the middle sister of three daughters of Charles Burlingame Waite and CATHARINE VAN VALKENBURG WAITE. Her father, an agnostic and a freethinker, was a lawyer and judge. Her mother, who was refused admission to Rush Medical College in Chicago, became a lawyer, women's rights activist, and publisher. Her grandfather, Daniel D. Waite, was one of the early physicians in the city.

In 1880 Waite received a B.A. degree from the old University of Chicago, which closed in 1886. She then enrolled in Hahnemann Medical College, a homeopathic school, in Chicago, obtaining the M.D. in 1883 and entering medical practice. Homeopathy, developed in the early nineteenth century by the German physician Samuel Hahnemann, was based on treatment by the use of highly diluted drugs that caused in a healthy person the symptoms of the disease being treated in the patient. In May 1889, shortly after the devastating flood in Johnstown, Pennsylvania, she and Dr. FRANCES DICKINSON formed the Illinois Medical Women's Sanitary Association, which sent three women doctors to aid the distressed inhabitants. Waite decided to become a surgeon and gynecologist, and in the early 1890s, feeling the need for a regular medical degree, entered Harvey Medical College. She obtained her second M.D. in 1895, the year Frances Dickinson became president of the school. Waite later taught gynecological and abdominal surgery at Harvey.

At the same time that she was developing her career as a physician, Lucy Waite was also engaged in the suffrage movement with MYRA BRADWELL and others interested in the legal, political, and economic rights of women. These women and other well-known clubwomen and society leaders such as BERTHA HONORÉ PALMER had a keen interest in, if not a shared vision of, how women should be represented at the upcoming world's fair, a celebration of the four hundredth anniversary of Christopher Columbus's arrival in the Americas. From 1889, Chicagoans were deeply involved with efforts to have their city become the site for the projected World's Columbian Exposition in 1893. Bradwell and Palmer were among the Chicago women who took the initiative to make certain that women would be represented at the exposition. The official Board of Lady Managers, headed by Palmer, planned to show women's work in a separate building and hoped to remain neutral on the issue of women's right to vote. The Queen Isabella Association (QIA), founded in August 1889, of which Lucy Waite was a leading member, wanted to display women's achievements alongside men's. QIA members—many of whom were physicians, lawyers, and businesswomen—planned to place a statue of the monarch on the fairgrounds and to build a woman's pavilion. The QIA members also differed from the Board of Lady Managers in their support for suffrage and interest in raising the suffrage issue whenever possible. The QIA opened offices in other cities that were competing to be the site for the upcoming fair and organized itself along both geographic lines based on congressional districts and professional or activity interests.

In March 1890 Waite was appointed to a committee of the local QIA group to look into the possibility of holding international women's congresses at the fair. The next year Waite wrote an article in the *Queen Isabella Journal* linking Isabella, the fifteenth-century Spanish monarch, to American women's struggle for suffrage in the late nineteenth century. The Isabellas pointed out that Isabella used her own funds to support Christopher Columbus's explorations of the New World. Waite could understand how men might not wish to emphasize Isabella's major role or acknowledge how much her money made the development of the American continent possible, but she found it difficult to understand how women could do this and, also, oppose suffrage for themselves. In paying tribute to Isabella, American women were making the argument that they had an equal right, with men, "to this fair land"; and the World's Columbian Exposition, Waite believed, gave women the great opportunity "to prove their right of citizenship" ("Kinship of Isabella," 9).

At the same time that Waite was writing for QIA, she published a novel in 1891 about women physicians. *Doctor Helen Rand*, written under the pseudonym Lois Wright, A.M., M.D., told the story of Dr. Rand—thirty-one years old, the same age as Waite—her adult housemate, the homeopathic physician Kate Summerville, and the child Paul, who was Rand's son born out of wedlock. Rand had adopted him in order to raise him, since she felt she could not make herself known as his mother. The book was dedicated "in the name of Justice to Children . . . to woman's truest friend—the woman physician" (quoted in Beatty, 54). In the course of the book Waite criticized religious morality that stigmatized children of unmarried parents. She presented various contemporary views on the role of women in the home and in society.

In addition to QIA, Waite was active in the Chicago Woman's Club for twenty-four years (1894–1918), working in the Science and Philosophy Department. On March 7, 1894, Waite married Dr. F. Byron Robinson, an investigator into anatomical and surgical problems and a prolific writer. Waite had been his student and then became his colleague. The writings of each contain references to the work of, and help by, the other. Robinson requested that Waite retain her maiden name. Later the couple adopted a boy under the legal name of Ralph Waite-Robinson.

When Dr. MARY HARRIS THOMPSON, head of the Chicago Hospital for Women and Children, died suddenly in 1895, Waite was named to succeed her as Head Surgeon and Medical Superintendent of the hospital, renamed the Mary Thompson Hospital. To prepare for this appointment, she spent the next two years studying in Europe, primarily in Paris and Vienna. During Waite's absence, Dr. MARIA MERGLER held the position of head physician and surgeon. Waite's European teachers included the pioneering ovariotomist, Jules Pean, and the surgeon, Jean Pozzi, who helped establish the specialty of gynecology in France. While on the trip Waite attended the International Congress of Medicine in Moscow and visited several women physicians, including Dr. Marie Siebolt, the only woman practicing in Turkey. As a result of the visits, Waite wrote "Woman in the Medical Profession" in the 1897 issue of *Medical Herald*, discussing the status of women physicians in a number of countries and declaring that male biases kept women from becoming leaders in science. She prophesied for woman, "When the time shall come that not a vestige of sex aristocracy remains in the medical profession, when the mere fact of holding a medical degree makes her eligible to every medical institution and society in the land, . . . in view of her attainments in the past, . . . she will not be found wanting in scientific investigation and original research" (p. 452).

Upon her return in 1897 she took up her responsibilities at the Thompson Hospital, where she ran the city's major gynecological clinic. A capable administrator, she made the hospital a first-ranked institution in Chicago. She continued to practice medicine and was considered an accurate diagnostician and a skillful surgeon, noted for a low death rate in operations. A colleague, Dr. Nicholas Senn, called her "one of the ablest and most successful surgeons in the city" (quoted in Sperry, 63). She taught at the University of Illinois College of Medicine from 1900 to 1908 as professor of clinical gynecology and also instructed women medical students at Thompson Hospital.

She joined the Medical Women's Club of Chicago at its founding in 1903 and was active during its early years, when the organization focused on scientific interests. She served as president 1904–1905.

Throughout her life Waite wrote on a variety of subjects in medicine—gynecology, surgery, general medical topics, and women in medicine as both patients and physicians. Waite's knowledge of French and German enabled her to keep up with the European literature in gynecology and related subjects. This expertise was reflected in her articles in the medical literature.

Her first paper, in the *American Journal of Obstetrics*, 1893, discussed five cases of laparotomy, surgical section of the abdomen. In 1896 she published in the *Chicago Medical Recorder* a report on cases of removal of the uterus in bilateral diseases of the appendages. Her discussion of eighty-five vaginal hysterectomies without a death (*American Journal of Surgery and Gynecology*, 1899) described a contemporary controversy over the best surgical route, abdominal or vaginal, and based her preference for the vaginal route on better recovery prospects for patients. In her review of the status of surgical intervention in retroversions of the uterus, published in the *Journal of the American Medical Association* in 1905, she criticized the unnecessary performance of gynecological surgery and set criteria: operations necessary, procedures safe, and surgeries with a record of success. The next year, in *Medical Record*, she reviewed the characteristics of postsurgical shock and factors in its diagnosis.

Waite gave research reports on clinical procedures at international meetings, followed by publication. In 1905 she presented a paper, "Some Gynecologic Superstitions," at the Pan-American Medical Congress in Panama. Published that year in *American Medicine*, the analysis discussed superstitions of medical practitioners that made women victims of untrue theories and unclear methods. Again, Waite criticized unnecessary surgery based on false information about the female reproductive system. The next year, at the Fifteenth International Congress of Medicine at Lisbon, she spoke on the clinical significance of uterine deviations based on a study of three thousand cases; the report was published in 1906 in transactions of the congress.

Waite also explored medical topics outside gynecology. In 1905 she wrote "The Element of Truth in Mental Healing," published in the *New York Medical Journal*, describing the combination of both mental and physical aspects of an illness. She returned to literary publication in 1909, when she compiled *Gems from the Literary Works of Dr. Nicholas Senn*, excerpts from the travel writings of her friend and fellow surgeon.

Byron Robinson died in 1910; Waite continued working until her retirement around 1920. After retiring from medicine she published two more literary works. In 1923 she edited *Freethought Year Book; Selections from Pioneer Freethought Literature*, a calendar of daily quotations. Three years later she compiled *The Thomas Jefferson Year Book*, made up of a Jeffersonian quotation for each day of the year.

She lived in Park Ridge, Illinois, between 1913 and 1928, when she moved to Denver, Colorado, where her brother Charles lived. During the final fifteen years of her life she shared a house with another woman physician, Julia Downey Fitz-Hugh. Upon her death Waite was cremated at Fairmount Cemetery in Denver.

Lucy Waite made substantial contributions to gynecology and abdominal surgery in a multiple career that encompassed medical practice, teaching, hospital administration, and clinical research. Her achievements in medicine were complemented by her active concern for women's rights and her promotion of proper medical treatment of women.

Sources. Waite's article on the status and responsibilities of women, "The Kinship of Isabella of Castile to the Women of the Nineteenth Century," appeared in the *Queen Isabella Journal*, vol. 2, 1891. Her important studies in medicine include the following articles: "Five Cases of Laparotomy. With Macroscopical Examination of Specimens," *American Journal of Obstetrics*, vol. 28, 1893; "Removal of the Uterus in Bilateral Diseases of the Appendages: Report of Cases," *Chicago Medical Recorder*, vol. 10, 1896; "Eighty-five Consecutive Vaginal Hysterectomies without a Death," *American Journal of Surgery and Gynecology*, vol. 12, 1899; "The Present Status of Surgical Intervention in Retrodeviations of the Uterus," *Journal of the American Medical Association*, vol. 44, 1905; and "Shock," *Medical Record*, vol. 70, 1906. William K. Beatty's informative biographical essay, "Lucy Waite—Surgeon and Free Thinker," *Proceedings of the Institute of Medicine of Chicago*, vol. 45, 1992, includes a listing of twenty-one of Waite's publications. Two contemporary publications have additional information on Waite and her contemporaries: F. M. Sperry's *A Group of Distinguished Physicians and Surgeons of Chicago* (1904) and A. N. Waterman's *Historical Review of Chicago and Cook County*, vol. 1 (1908).

WILLIAM K. BEATTY

WALKER, NELLIE VERNE
December 8, 1874–July 10, 1973
SCULPTOR

Nellie Verne Walker was a prominent figure in the Chicago art world for more than forty years. Born in Red Oak in southwestern Iowa, she was a year old when her parents moved to Moulton, a small community in the south central part of the state. Walker's mother, Rebecca Jane (Lindsey) Walker, was a homemaker, whose forebears came before the American Revolution. Her father, Everett A. Walker, was a tombstone maker and real estate dealer. There were six children—four daughters and two sons; Nellie was the oldest.

Walker was drawn to her father's stonecutting workshop, where she learned to smooth and polish stone and to cut epitaphs and decorative borders for grave markers. During the summer of 1892, a year after her graduation from the local high school, Walker's father granted her request for a block of Bedford stone purchased for use as a monument base. She wanted to try her hand at carving a head of Abraham Lincoln. Using a picture of an engraving of Lincoln as a model, Walker created a credible likeness in only three weeks. She followed the engraving closely, including the angle of the head and the details of the clothing.

The Lincoln bust was shown in the Iowa Building of the 1893 World's Columbian Exposition, Chicago, identified as the work of a seventeen-year-old girl without formal training. During the week between Christmas and New Year's day preceding the exposition, Walker and her father toured the fairgrounds; he recalled that they appeared to his daughter like an "actual fairy land" (quoted in Noun, "Making Her Mark," 163). In May, after the exposition opened, Walker and her father returned to Chicago, where they spent six weeks. At this time Walker enrolled in an elementary class at the School of the Art Institute of Chicago (SAIC). Although eager to stay longer, Walker returned to Iowa because the family's financial resources were limited.

Back in Iowa and determined to become a sculptor, Walker learned typing and shorthand and got a job as a secretary for a lawyer in the nearby city of Ottumwa. Six years later she was able to set out for Chicago, with the help of a two hundred dollar loan from her employer. For the next four years Walker attended classes at SAIC and studied under Lorado Taft, whose openness

FIG. 123. *From left to right, Agnes Fromen, Hester Bremmer, Robert Tschaegle, Seth Belsey, Nellie Verne Walker, unidentified person, Leonard Crunelle, Mary H. Webster, Lorado Taft, Gertrude Strickler, Mabel Torrey, Betty Torrey, Fred Torrey, Ben Shute, Ruth Mose, Mrs. Gamache (housekeeper and cook), Enrique Alferez, at Midway Studios, 1929.*

to teaching female students had already attracted to his classes Evelyn Longman, Bessie Potter (see BESSIE POTTER VON-NOH), and Julia Bracken (see JULIA BRACKEN WENDT). Taft later recalled her determination and short stature; she was not more than four feet eight inches in height.

During this period Walker struggled to sustain herself. A job in the Art Institute library paid enough to cover her tuition, but the meager funds that she brought from home did not last long. When Evelyn Longman, Taft's assistant, left for New York in 1901, Walker replaced her, earning a small salary. Walker's secretarial skills also were useful with Taft's correspondence. At his request, she took over his lectures to Chicago school children, and from 1904 to 1906 Walker was an instructor in modeling at SAIC. It was in 1904 that Walker began to exhibit regularly at the Art Institute of Chicago (AIC). Lorado Taft was well known for his monumental, often symbolic, sculptures in the Beaux-Arts tradition. Walker also worked in this style, having been influenced by Taft—her mentor and teacher.

In 1903 and 1904 Nellie Walker was sculpting a portrait bust, *Governor Albert Baird Cummins*, in the Iowa state capitol in Des Moines, using a makeshift studio in the attic over the senate chamber. While working on the bust, Walker and her work-in-progress were caught in a fire in the house chamber. Since firefighters were too busy to save an unfinished work, Walker rushed upstairs to her smoke-filled studio and rescued the bust, an act of heroism recounted by the local Des Moines newspaper. Walker completed the commission but apparently it was never purchased. (Walker made a gift of the Cummins bust to the Iowa State Department of History and Archives in the 1940s.)

In 1902 Walker was asked to create a cemetery monument,

Winfield Scott Stratton, in memory of the Colorado Springs mining tycoon. To complete the piece, she quit her teaching position at SAIC and accepted Taft's offer of space in his studio in the Fine Arts Building near the Art Institute. Walker had ample facilities for the execution of large-scale sculpture; she also found herself in a building filled with artists' studios, literary salons, and musicians' rooms. Completed in 1905, the monument in Evergreen Cemetery, Colorado Springs, is of two veiled figures symbolic of charity, which are partially detached from a mass of granite. The Stratton commission was a turning point; Walker was recognized as a professional sculptor of merit when the Stratton monument was featured in *Art and Progress*, along with works by Augustus Saint-Gaudens and Daniel Chester French. Walker's piece was described as "Rodinesque . . . using rough blocks of granite from which dimly emerg[e] spirit figures" (Rubinstein, 122).

The Stratton memorial was the first of fourteen grave monuments that Walker sculpted during her career, including memorials in Cadillac and Battle Creek, Michigan; Marinette, Wisconsin; Minneapolis, Minnesota; Omaha, Nebraska; Baltimore, Maryland; and Chicago. "One wonders if Walker ever thought of herself as following in her father's footsteps—except in a more elegant manner" (Noun, 165).

In 1907 the state of Iowa commissioned Walker to make a portrait figure, *Senator James Harlan*, senator from Iowa. Completed in 1909, the full-length bronze is located in the Hall of Columns, the United States Capitol Building. Her career going well, Walker became affiliated with artistic and literary circles in Chicago and was elected to membership in the prestigious "Little Room," a select group of men and women artists, writers, and aspiring cultural leaders who met regularly in the Fine Arts Building. Her impressive achievements were capped by her first trip to Europe in 1910. She traveled as far as Constantinople.

Walker won national recognition in 1911 with her election to the National Sculpture Society. The only other Chicago member at that time was Walker's mentor, Lorado Taft. That same year she left her studio in the Fine Arts Building and joined Taft and other artists who had moved the previous year to a new studio space that Taft had erected on land belonging to the University of Chicago on its south campus.

The group of studios, all under one roof, were known as the Midway Studios because they were constructed on land that had once been the site of the famous Midway Plaisance of the 1893 World's Columbian Exposition. Each sculptor had a studio in which to live and work. Together they employed a cook, who prepared the midday meal and had other housekeeping responsibilities. At times there were as many as thirty or forty people at lunch, which was served in the large central hall, presided over by Taft at the head of the table. The monumental art works in progress overshadowed the group. Walker, a permanent resident, traditionally sat at the other end of the long table. "This is an ideal way to live," she told her niece, Genevieve Lewis Szaton, "no husband to please, no children to disturb one, good friends to converse with, who will give help when needed, yet all the privacy one could wish for" (quoted in Noun, 168). In addition to having this studio space, Walker was one of a group of painters, sculptors, and writers, including Taft, who owned Eagle's Nest, a camp on the cliffs of the Rock River near Oregon, Illinois.

Her best-known work in Iowa, *Chief Keokuk* (1913), Rand Park, Keokuk, Iowa, marks the burial place of the great chief and overlooks the Mississippi River. Walker's statue shows Keokuk in a heroic pose wearing his war bonnet of eagle plumes. The following year Walker made her second trip to Europe; financed in part by gifts from friends wanting to make sure her stay would be extended, the young woman sculptor met the seventy-three-year-old Auguste Rodin, whom she greatly admired. Walker planned to stay for two years and rented a studio in Paris. The outbreak of World War I cut short her visit.

Back in Chicago, Nellie Walker was one of the women who founded the Cordon, an arts club that would develop independence and protect personal expression. Members were chosen on the basis of achievement in the arts and the professions and included poet HARRIET MONROE, pianist FANNIE BLOOMFIELD ZEISLER, and novelist MARY BRADLEY. Nellie Walker served two terms as president of this organization. From 1917 to 1921, during the administration of Governor Frank O. Lowden, Walker served on the Illinois State Board of Art Advisors and in that role advised on public monuments, especially war memorials, which were popular following World War I.

Taft occasionally hired Walker to assist him with his commissions. In the 1920s Walker worked on the two large figures, *Moses* and *Socrates*, situated on either side of the entry to the courthouse in Jackson, Mississippi. She designed and modeled the figures. Also in the 1920s she did *Courage*, a statue placed in the courtyard of St. Luke's (Episcopal) Hospital, Chicago; *Her Son*, a composition of a mother and child that was exhibited at

AIC; and *Dr. William F. King*, a portrait bust of the former president of Cornell College, Iowa. In 1923 she finished two panels in low relief for the exterior walls of the library at Iowa State University, Ames. The panel at the north end featured figures symbolic of the activities of women students (art, home economics, literature); the panel at the south end depicted activities of men students (engineering, science, veterinary medicine, agriculture). All of the figures were draped in a classical manner. Walker also toured the Midwest as a lecturer for the Redpath Lyceum Bureau; her "Clay Talks" were popular; she demonstrated modeling a clay head, making a plaster cast, and cutting marble. By 1926 the prospect of several large commissions for the Taft group encouraged Walker to think seriously about owning her own cottage on Lake Michigan near Chicago. She wrote to her close friend, Chicago writer Henry B. Fuller, "Our sculpture factory has been running full-time and full-force. . . . We are now on the home stretch, with eight more figures to make in about six weeks. . . . It's been rather fun, although I do not know that I have ever been so tired evenings as I have since this work began" (quoted in Noun, 170).

Unfortunately, the stock market crash that hit the United States in 1929 and the Great Depression that followed meant that Walker's dream of a place on the southern shore of Lake Michigan was never realized. Personal losses and financial difficulties marked the 1930s. Although Walker never married, she had a close friend in Henry Fuller, who was a frequent visitor. His death in July 1929 "left a major void in her life" (Noun, 171). The death of Lorado Taft in 1936 was an even more severe loss; without Taft, Midway Studios seemed empty. Walker was one of five of Taft's associates named to complete unfinished commissions at the time of his death. The *Haym Salomon* monument was one of these commissions, and Walker sculpted the figure of Salomon.

Sculpture commissions declined for Walker during the 1930s. She refused to participate in the Works Progress Administration under President Franklin Roosevelt's New Deal. "I would starve before I would go to that bunch for help" (quoted in Noun, 171), she wrote to her friend, Mary Hunter of Des Moines, commenting about Roosevelt's programs for unemployed artists. The project in Chicago was in the hands of "an ultra modern advocate" (p. 171), she said, who would love nothing better than to be able to turn down older artists. Walker, a staunch Republican, viewed Roosevelt with great alarm. She feared that his second election in 1936 might be the last general election this country would ever see.

Walker received two commissions during the 1930s: an Iowa Woman Suffrage memorial panel, and a statue and panel commemorating the Lincoln family's journey from Indiana to Iowa. The suffrage memorial, completed in 1934, was a low relief panel in bronze honoring the women who worked for woman suffrage in Iowa. The panel was commissioned by the Iowa Woman Suffrage Commission and is located in the rotunda of the state capitol near the entrance to the House of Representatives. Walker depicted the long march of the suffrage battle, illustrating the successive generations of women who had been engaged in the fight for women's rights. The panel looked to the future, showing the passing of a torch to the next generation, symbolized by a young girl suggesting that others would follow.

In keeping with the theory of art practiced in her youth by artists influenced by the Beaux-Arts tradition, this modern theme was portrayed in classical terms, with the figures, identified by the symbols they carried, "clothed in long, flowing robes reminiscent of ancient Greek art" (Noun, 172).

The Abraham Lincoln monument, commissioned by the Illinois chapter of the Daughters of the American Revolution, was completed in 1937. Located close to Vincennes, Indiana, near the spot where the Lincoln family is thought to have crossed the Wabash River into Illinois, the monument is a ten-foot-high, twenty-six-foot-long relief panel carved out of Indiana limestone. Lincoln's family walks alongside an oxcart filled with belongings; overhead, a guiding angel points the way to Springfield, Illinois. A free-standing bronze figure of the young Abe Lincoln is in front of the panel.

Other works by Walker include a Polish-American war memorial in Chicago and *Memorial to the Soldiers of 1812* (1932), Historical Building, Springfield, Illinois. Walker's Chicago career ended in 1948 when the University of Chicago took over the land and buildings of Midway Studios. She had little income or savings, and, with failing eyesight, moved to Colorado Springs, Colorado, where her youngest sister lived. She spent her last years in the Myron Stratton Home; ironically, its patron, Stratton, was a member of the family that had given Walker her first professional commission in 1905. In good health, although nearly blind, Walker spent the next twenty-five years organizing her papers and memorabilia. Independent spirited until the end, she wrote her own obituary, gave instructions that no funeral be conducted after her death, and traded one of her sculptures, *St. Francis*, in exchange for cremation. She died in the Stratton Home, and her ashes are interred in the Oakland Cemetery, near Moulton, Iowa.

Nellie Verne Walker sculpted more than thirty-five public monuments, largely for sites in the Midwest and Colorado. Walker and her generation of professional women sculptors—*American Art Annual* lists more than one hundred such women in 1910—came from a variety of backgrounds. As activist women moved beyond the home to influence civic affairs, artists such as Nellie Walker reshaped public space to incorporate monuments designed and executed by women sculptors.

Sources. The Walker file at the Iowa State Hist. Soc. Library, Des Moines, contains correspondence, clippings, and niece Genevieve Lewis Szaton's manuscript, "Reminiscences," 1969. Walker correspondence is also at NL and in the American Archives of Art, Washington, D.C. There are several pamphlets in the pamphlet collection at Ryerson Library, Art Institute of Chicago (AIC). See the *Ryerson Index,* vol. 11, including AIC Scrapbook citations on Walker. Inez Hunt, *The Lady Who Lived on Ladders* (1970), is the most complete publication about Walker. See also Lorado Taft, "Women Sculptors of America," *Mentor,* February 1919; Ruth Helming Mose, "Midway Studio," *American Magazine of Art,* August 1928; Josephine Craven Chandler, "Nellie Verne Walker: An Appreciation," *American Magazine of Art,* July 1924; Ragna B. Eskil, "She Steps One Rung Higher," *Independent Woman,* January 1948; Louise Rosenfield Noun, "Making Her Mark: Nellie Verne Walker, Sculptor," *Palimpsest,* Winter 1987. Charlotte Streifer Rubinstein's *American Women Sculptors: A History of Women Working in Three Dimensions* (1990) includes the story of Walker and her generation.

LOUISE ROSENFIELD NOUN

WALLER, JUDITH CARY
February 19, 1889–October 28, 1973
BROADCAST PIONEER, RADIO EXECUTIVE

Judith Cary Waller was born in Oak Park, Illinois, the oldest of four daughters of Katherine (Short) Waller and John Duke Waller, a surgeon. Her maternal grandfather, Methodist minister William S. Short, was president of the Illinois Women's College in Jacksonville, Illinois (later MacMurray College), and her mother was a graduate of the college. Waller was educated in the public schools of Oak Park. After she graduated from high school in 1908 and spent the next year traveling in Europe, her family expected her to lead a life in society, but she wanted to be an independent self-supporting woman. In 1909 she took business courses, despite her father's opposition and his refusal to pay the costs. For several years she worked as a secretary at the advertising agency, J. Walter Thompson, in Chicago. Between 1918 and 1920, she served as office manager at Thompson's New York City office. Advertising was in its infancy, and Waller was on the ground floor of a new field, as she would be again in radio. At the advertising agency, she developed her writing, editing, and general business skills.

In 1922, as a result of personal contact with Walter Strong, business manager of the *Chicago Daily News*, Waller went to work for the radio station WGU, recently acquired by the newspaper. Radio stations in the early 1920s were usually owned by newspapers and were seen as outlets for reporters to air their stories and features. While showcasing newspaper stories, radio had no advertising, since the content highlighted the newspaper, the station sponsor. Strong asked Waller to take a job as the first general manager of WGU. When Waller admitted that she did not know anything about radio, Strong replied that no one else did either. Radio was uncharted waters; Judith Waller displayed her spunk by taking control of the station with the help of an engineer. She wore many hats: as writer, recruiter of talent, and announcer of the news.

Because radio was a new business, and its future success was unclear, women had opportunities to become managers, producers, writers, and announcers. Once the field became established, women participants often lost the most prestigious positions to men. In a 1933 article in *Radio Stars*, describing leading women pioneers, Waller's profile read: "If you had a promising social career, would you elect a business course instead of a coming-out party and be a stenographer instead of a social butterfly?" (Carroll, 88). Though the writer quickly acknowledged that Waller became the manager, not the stenographer, at WGU, her opening effectively demonstrated the mind-set of that period. Young women of the upper middle class, such as Waller, were not expected to enter the work world. Waller defied the social expectations of the time, improvised in a new position, and quickly developed a reputation as a determined and capable manager.

Precisely because radio was still a novel medium, many performers disdained it, others feared it, and still others were puzzled by its impact. Waller showed herself to be an astute observer of the radio scene. While the other Chicago radio station, KYW, played Tin Pan Alley songs, she offered classical music to listeners. Waller attracted the reluctant star of the Metropolitan Opera, soprano Sophie Braslau, to sing on the radio station by promising her free publicity in the *Chicago Daily News* for her upcoming concerts. Beginning with Braslau's appearance on April 13, 1922—the initial broadcast—Waller offered her audience arias and symphonies. Chicago Opera Company's MARY GARDEN sang on rival station WGN at a later time, demonstrating the success of Waller's innovation.

In October 1922, WGU changed its station letters to WMAQ, which remained the radio station's name through the 1990s. As manager, Waller enjoyed complete autonomy throughout the 1920s. Without advertising announcements and sponsors to influence her decisions, she could produce any shows she liked. Waller often spoke of her role as a radio pioneer and reminded audiences that radio was an instrument of democracy; in her opinion, public service, in its broadest sense, was the main purpose of this new medium. Waller envisioned radio to be both an elite and popular phenomenon, appealing to the minds and imaginations of all listeners. All programming, she believed, should engage people in a thoughtful and provocative manner.

Her innovative manner was quickly displayed. In the 1920s, Waller produced a play-by-play commentary of the University of Chicago's and Brown University's 1924 football match; she followed that sports event with a 1925 baseball game and scooped the other radio stations in the city by airing the 1925 inaugural events for President Calvin Coolidge. In her interest to include a wide array of international news, she took advantage of the latest technology so that *Chicago Daily News* foreign correspondent John Gunther could send a report straight from London. In 1926 she embarked on an experiment of broadcasting as a service to public schools by producing a series of programs for an elementary school in Chicago. By the end of the year, eleven schools were tuning in. This program was the forerunner of the *American School of the Air*, broadcast by the Columbia Broadcasting System (CBS) a few years later and continued until the mid-1930s. Waller had a comprehensive view of radio as a transmitter of all aspects of American cultural experience; sports, politics, education, and international affairs all shared air time. Thanks to her good relations with *Chicago Daily News* staff, she had access to news reporters who offered her programming ideas and took part in shows for WMAQ.

Known as a charming and discerning woman, Waller convinced the conductor of the Chicago Symphony Orchestra to play on WMAQ, the group's first performance on radio. Probably her best known discovery was the *Amos 'n' Andy* Show, which began to broadcast on WMAQ on December 4, 1928. The *Chicago Daily News* started the first comic strip featuring African American characters to coordinate with, and publicize, the new *Amos 'n' Andy* Show. At that time, WMAQ was a CBS affiliate. Waller went to New York City to try to interest the network in the show, but the CBS executive could not be persuaded that such a show would be successful. He told her: "I think you'd better go back to Chicago. It's very plain to see that you know nothing about radio" (Williamson, 112). This show, originally called *Sam 'n' Harry*, was broadcast on rival station WGN, and Waller believed that the two white men who played African American characters, Charles Correll and Freeman Gosden, had the makings of success.

She was right. Running six nights a week, the show treated African Americans in a derogatory, stereotypical, and humorous fashion. Amos was the trusting soul, while Andy was portrayed as avoiding work as often as possible. The images were a direct carryover from minstrelsy; although African American critics derided the show, audiences loved it. Within a year, *Amos 'n' Andy* had 60 percent of the audience. People flocked to buy radios so they could listen to the show. More importantly, perhaps, Waller had introduced a new kind of radio programming: ongoing situation comedy. Until that point, only individual discreet events were heard on the radio; new radio programmers all over the country scrambled to place ongoing situation comedies and domestic dramas on their stations.

In 1929 Judith Waller became vice-president and general manager of WMAQ. Though programming steadily broadened, she displayed her sense of the importance of educational and cultural shows by starting the *University of Chicago Round Table* in 1931. For the next two decades, listeners heard discussions with such prominent citizens as Margaret Mead, Eleanor Roosevelt, and many others.

In November 1931, the National Broadcasting Company (NBC) bought WMAQ, changing its status from a network affiliate to a totally owned outlet for a network. No longer would programming be aimed at an exclusively local market. The management of WMAQ was absorbed into that of NBC, and Waller's role and functions were reduced in programming as well as management. Instead of running the station, she became NBC's education director for the Central Division, a diminished and narrower role. While Waller continued to produce local programs for young people and schools, her future work focused on educational shows almost exclusively.

Waller persuaded the administrators of the Chicago school system in 1932 to bring radios into the classrooms to hear her educational programs. The plan was approved and quickly became a great success with several hundred schools, including some in neighboring states. As a broadcaster committed to the educational value of radio, Waller became active on the national scene when she was appointed in 1936 to the congressionally authorized Federal Radio Education Committee. The committee was formed to resolve conflicts between educators and commercial broadcasters. Earlier in 1930, she had helped to found the Institute for Education by Radio, clear evidence of her consistent interest in preserving the educational role of radio.

During the 1940s, NBC changed her title to public service director of the Central Division, but her main responsibilities remained the same. One new idea she implemented was the NBC Summer Radio Institute in conjunction with Northwestern University in Evanston, Illinois; students planning a radio career took summer courses in broadcasting. Waller relied on her many contacts to bring together an impressive array of experienced radio broadcasters to speak. She collated the written materials, contributed her own thoughts, and led the first session. The institute was so successful that the next year summer programs were started at the University of California, Los Angeles, and Stanford University.

Broadcasting in the Public Service became a 1943 compilation of the curricular materials written by Waller and others for the summer institutes. Three years later, she wrote a textbook,

Radio: The Fifth Estate, that included a section written by her as well as contributions by others. In the text, she stated, "Radio broadcasting is not just a business; it is also an art" (p. 3). The text remained a useful source for many years; a revised edition appeared in 1950. One section of the book dealt with public service programming, the area in which Waller had become particularly interested. While always recognizing the business aspect of radio, she deplored the excessive commercialism that became dominant. By the 1940s, radio had become a familiar and profitable medium in American society, and the educational and cultural aspects of radio programming had lost out to the entertainment and advertising content.

Waller, however, always displayed her determination to keep her ideals for radio before the professionals' eyes. At the twentieth-anniversary dinner of the Institute for Education by Radio, she gave the banquet speech and reminded the audience that such issues as the social responsibility of radio and television, contributions of the media to world understanding, and educational use of radio remained critical issues deserving serious attention.

Waller's ability to spot talent remained alive when in 1952 she selected Frances Horwich, dean of the School of Education at Roosevelt University, Chicago, to be Miss Frances on the children's television show *Ding Dong School.* It remained on television for years as one of the most beloved early children's shows. Indeed, Waller recognized the potential of television and worked for its development. In 1954, at the age of sixty-five, she retired from NBC only to continue her role as pioneer for the new medium of television. She became an advisor to Purdue University's educational television station, which planned to beam telecasts to schools from an airplane. She served on a committee of educators and television professionals to select the teachers for the televised lessons. The operation sent programming to about fifteen hundred schools in a six-state area. Waller became a speaker on the educational and cultural possibilities of television.

Waller lived in Evanston, Illinois, during her retirement, with a sister, Katherine Waller, often lecturing at Northwestern University and conducting television workshops. She died of a heart attack at the age of eighty-four.

Judith Waller was a pioneer in programming in the early years of radio broadcasting. Believing that commercial radio had a responsibility in education and public service, she successfully developed significant programs in both areas.

Sources: The Broadcast Pioneers Library at the University of Maryland at College Park Libraries has interviews made with Waller in 1951 and 1965. Waller's book, *Radio: The Fifth Estate* (1946) discusses her goals in radio. Mary E. Williamson, "Judith Cary Waller: Chicago Broadcasting Pioneer," *Journalism History,* Winter 1976–77, summarizes her career. For biographical essays, see *NAW* (1980) and June Sochen's sketch in *American National Biography,* ed. John A. Garraty and Mark C. Carnes (1999). Other useful sources are Catharine Heinz, "The Voice of Authority, or, Hurrah for Christine Craft," *Feedback,* Spring 1984; Catherine Heinz, "Women Radio Pioneers," *Journal of Popular Culture,* Fall 1978; and Iris Ann Carroll's article on women pioneers in the field, "Smart Women in Radio," *Radio Stars,* October 1933. An obituary appears in the *CT,* October 29, 1973.

JUNE SOCHEN

WALRATH, FLORENCE DAHL
August 18, 1877–November 7, 1958
PIONEER IN PRIVATE ADOPTION, AGENCY FOUNDER

Florence Walrath founded and headed the north suburban Cradle Society of Evanston, Illinois, from 1923 until 1950. A pioneer in the field of private adoption, she had no professional social work training, but under her leadership, the Cradle became one of the best-known private adoption agencies in the United States.

Florence Dahl, the daughter of Lawrence and Betsey Louisa (Anderson) Dahl, came from an Episcopalian family in Chicago that traced its ancestry back to the Mayflower. She attended North Division High School from 1892 to 1896, where she met William Bradley Walrath, her geometry teacher and future husband. Walrath had graduated from Northwestern University and Kent College of Law and was supplementing his new law practice by teaching in high school. They became engaged when Dahl was seventeen and married two years later, on June 29, 1897. The Walraths had two daughters, Hester and Helen, who were born twenty-two months apart.

Although she never clearly stated the reason, Florence Walrath taught her daughters at home until they were ten years of age. At that time she entered each of them in the fifth grade in the local public school. The girls each graduated from high school in three years and went on to college.

When her younger daughter was fourteen, Walrath gave birth to a son, William Bradley III. She then decided her son needed a playmate and the Walraths had their fourth child, Gretchen. Once again, Walrath tutored her young children at home until they reached ten years of age. They were a close family that traveled and shared activities.

Walrath's career in adoption work began in spring 1914, when her older sister's first baby died at birth and the mother expressed a wish to adopt a baby. Adoption was not a widespread practice at the time. Pregnant with her third child, Walrath decided to aid her sister. Worried that an adopted child might not measure up to their family's standards, Walrath carefully found a baby girl whom her sister and brother-in-law adopted and came to love like a child born to them.

Her family's experience with adoption, and Walrath's awareness of new scientific findings that proved newborns could survive on formula instead of mother's milk, led to her new conception of adoption. In addition, she learned that in some cases the birth mother was not the best person to raise her child. Walrath began to emphasize that, while the unwed mother's situation was not her fault alone, she should make the further sacrifice of putting her child up for adoption to give it the best chance in life. She moved away from fears of hereditary problems and argued that, not only was adoption a better solution to the problem of illegitimacy, it was the only solution.

Walrath came to believe that "parenthood [was] a spiritual relationship, a stewardship, which [began] after birth" ("The Cradle Story," 4). She concluded that every child, if placed in a proper, loving, normal home under the care of two responsible parents, would realize full potential.

As a result of Walrath's success in finding a baby for her sister, friends began to ask her to find babies for them. She became well-known by hospital staff at Chicago area hospitals as a person to call for the placement of unwanted babies in adoptive homes. Walrath took newborns to Evanston Hospital, where the infants would remain, usually for six weeks, until pronounced physically fit and ready for adoption. Walrath soon found that there were always more couples who wanted to adopt than there were available babies.

At first the Walraths paid the hospital costs for the babies during their stay at Evanston Hospital, but it became a heavy financial burden. The Walraths made arrangements with the hospital for three free beds; soon more were needed, and they set up a separate bank account or "emergency fund." Informal fundraising among social friends met some of the demand. The Walraths, however, looked for a larger endowment, hoping to find a patron who would endow eight beds in the pediatric department. Business owner Frank S. Cunningham took on the cause but was stymied by the hospital. One of its patrons had become convinced that Walrath's work was encouraging illegitimacy.

In 1923, when Walrath had already arranged eighty successful adoptions, it became clear that she desperately needed a place to care for the infants prior to their adoptions. Five prominent businessmen—Henry Dawes, Frederick Hossack Scott, Rollin A. Keyes, Sewell L. Avery, and Cunningham—each made a down payment of one thousand dollars to buy a building in Evanston. Thus the Cradle Society was established. The five, together with Florence Walrath and seven other patrons—all closely related by kinship or ties of friendship—constituted the society's board in the early days.

Walrath made the Cradle's policy on what constituted a baby suitable for adoption. The child had to be normal, its parents' history without any undesirable physical or mental conditions. Babies were placed under observation by medical and psychiatric experts for six weeks; any remediable physical defects would be corrected during this time. Walrath housed the "imperfect" babies separately and expressed some surprise that there were couples willing to adopt and love these infants despite their "handicaps." At the time of adoption, the birth records were sealed, and the birth mother was not told the final placement once the adoption was concluded. Walrath encouraged the adoptive parents to tell their child, as soon as comprehension was possible, that he or she had been chosen for adoption.

The Cradle Society expanded from its original 1923 building. Two more buildings were acquired. Initially the care provided by the society was superior to other institutional facilities. Its infant mortality rate from 1923 to 1927 was only 5 percent compared to a 10 percent rate for hospitals and orphanages. In 1927, however, an epidemic of gastroenteritis hit the Cradle and the agency's mortality rate rose to 10 percent. The source of the epidemic was located in the powdered milk fed the babies. The problem was solved by having the manufacturer develop a boilable product that could be sterilized without curdling. The technique led to formula sterilization processes in common use today.

Cradle physicians, led by GLADYS DICK, also pioneered an antiseptic technique to prevent cross-infection from handborne germs within the nursery. In July 1928, the Dick technique was implemented, and the morality rate dropped to 1 percent.

In 1931, after her youngest child left for college, Florence Walrath became the Cradle's full-time managing director while remaining an officer of the society. Though the costs of operating the agency rose enormously over the years, Walrath resisted accepting government funding, even during the Great Depression. By 1930, the Cradle spent forty-two thousand dollars a year caring for twenty-four babies.

The Cradle's aseptic techniques so dramatically controlled infant epidemics that they were copied by hospitals and other institutions. A new building, opened in 1939, was fitted out with a mechanical barrier to airborne germs and a germicidal light to destroy germs. Laudatory accounts of the Cradle's techniques began to appear in such national media as *Time* magazine and the *Saturday Evening Post*. An article appeared in *Collier's* magazine in 1939, however, accusing the Cradle of trafficking in babies. Professional social workers, already critical of many of the policies of the Cradle, took advantage of the publicity to charge Walrath and the society's directors with running a "closed corporation" ("Study of the Cradle," November 1940, Welfare Council Papers) primarily interested in securing adoptable babies for friends. The Cradle was accused of participating in an adoption racket—selling babies and giving preference to major contributors—because the society accepted contributions from adopting parents. Walrath vigorously denied all charges.

Professional social workers denounced Cradle staffers for their lack of experience and training in the child placement field, for giving some families preferential treatment in allowing them to adopt more than one child, and for not participating in professional conferences. One of the problems was that many of the Cradle workers were volunteers and, ironically, were not invited to such conferences.

The Cradle responded to the criticism by reiterating that it was a nonsectarian philanthropic organization supported by voluntary contributions from individuals and the fund-raising activities of its auxiliaries. It emphasized that it accepted no fees from the adopting parents or from the birth mother. It requested that the Council of Social Agencies make a study of its activities.

The Cradle attempted to inaugurate standard casework practice in its adoption work and to cooperate with professional adoption agencies. It was difficult for Cradle workers to reorient themselves since they remained isolated generally from association with other adoption workers. The agency also risked whatever good will it had built up, by experimenting with more professional practices when it asked out-of-state agencies to make child placement studies of homes in their locales. Such engagement in interstate placements contributed to the perception that the Cradle was still violating sound child welfare casework principles. Under Illinois state law prior to 1945, however, an adoption became final when the court passed on the qualifications of the adoptive parents without a waiting or trial period in which professional social workers had an opportunity to make home visits. This situation made Illinois, and the Cradle in particular, a mecca for couples anxious to adopt a child but residing in states with more stringent laws.

The Illinois adoption law passed in 1945 mandated a sixmonth trial period before an adoption could be made final. Each prospective home had to be visited and evaluated by a professional social worker. A supervisory visit was made before the decree of legal adoption could be entered in the court. The same process had to be repeated if a couple made additional adoptions.

Florence Walrath claimed to be pleased with the new requirements, but she also complained about the expense of professional social work and, in the last four years of her active involvement with the Cradle, four different directors of casework came and went, frustrated with Walrath's interference. The era drew to a close when Walrath retired at age seventy-three in 1950, twenty-seven years after she founded the Cradle. Her task had become more difficult in the years following World War II. Increasingly, the number of applications from couples seeking adoption outran the number of available babies. Publicly she credited the widening gap with the greater acceptability of adoption, but privately Walrath admitted that the spread of birth control practices had contributed to the shortage of adoptable babies.

Volunteers like Walrath found themselves displaced in the adoption field because their ideology had become passé. Walrath's core idea, that single mothers could not provide sufficient care for the normal development of a child, was increasingly disputed. Her notion of what constituted a family seemed old-fashioned. Likewise, her belief that the adopted child should never learn the identity of the natural parents also fell into disfavor.

In 1948 Florence Walrath moved to the Georgian Hotel in Evanston. It was five years since the death of her husband. In 1952, by then increasingly frail, she moved to the Mather Retirement Home, also in Evanston. Her condition deteriorated when, in 1954, she was injured in an automobile accident. The Cradle Society held a gala eightieth birthday celebration for Walrath in 1957. She died the following year. She had placed six thousand babies in homes and had pioneered in private child adoption prior to the professionalization and specialization of the field by both public and private agencies. The successful sterile procedures of the Cradle's research doctors dramatically controlled infant epidemics and became standard precautions in hospital pediatric units.

Sources. The Evanston Hist. Soc. has a clipping file on Florence Walrath and on the Cradle Society, some correspondence, speeches, and copies of articles, as well as Walrath's typescript, "The Cradle Story" (n.d.). The Illinois Children's Home and Aid Society Papers, UIC Spec. Coll., have Cradle Society correspondence. See "Study of the Cradle Made by the Council of Social Agencies at the Request of the Cradle," November 1940, Welfare Council Papers, CHS. Also see Paula F. Pfeffer, "Homeless Children, Childless Homes," *Chicago History*, Spring 1987.

PAULA F. PFEFFER

WANG, CHI CHE
October 30, 1894–October 10, 1979
BIOCHEMIST, RESEARCHER

Chi Che Wang, who conducted and directed research at hospitals in nutritional chemistry, was born in Soochow (Suzhou), China. The little known about her family came from her own reports. Her parents were educated by tutors, and Wang's mother and sister ran a school of two hundred students until it was closed when the Japanese invaded in 1939. Her father was a government official—described by Wang as a prime minister—who died at the age of forty-eight. Wang's parents sent her to the United States for education, and she graduated from Wellesley College, Wellesley, Massachusetts, with a B.A. degree in 1914. She remained in the United States for the rest of her life.

She came to the University of Chicago (UC) for graduate work, receiving an M.S. degree in chemistry in 1916 and a Ph.D. in nutrition and chemistry in 1918. Her colleagues at UC commented on "how small she was, and how much she knew and how deeply she could concentrate with all the noise going on in the laboratory" (Dye, 261). She studied in the Department of Home Economics at a time when the field was being developed at the university in graduate study and research. She was the first student to receive a Ph.D. under KATHARINE BLUNT, who became the informal head of the department in 1918 and built an outstanding research program. Wang's graduate studies also included one year at Johns Hopkins University in 1917 and summer work in microbiology at the University of Wisconsin. During graduate studies, she coauthored an article with Katharine Blunt, "Chinese Preserved Eggs-Pidan," the first of a number of research articles throughout her career that dealt with scientific topics drawn from Chinese culture.

Upon her arrival in Chicago, Wang made contact with the Chinese community. In 1916 she became one of the founders of the Chicago Chinese Women's Club, whose members included Dr. MARGARET LIN and businesswoman MANSIE O'YOUNG. Wang served as vice-president and social chair and was active in the group until 1926. She took pride in her Chinese heritage in a creative way. As a club activity, she wrote a play, "Chinese Joan of Arc," directing the performance and playing a role before an audience of nearly two hundred, most of them non-Chinese.

In later years she recalled her use of Chinese cooking for fund-raising for the Women's University Club of Chicago, a social group of which she was a member. At her booth, she arranged the preparation of some eight hundred meals with the assistance of six of the sixteen laboratory assistants whom she supervised at work.

Wang remained at UC until 1920 as an instructor and then moved to Michael Reese Hospital in Chicago as head of the Department of Chemistry at the Nelson Morris Memorial Institute of Medical Research, which had been established nine years earlier. This position was the first of several that engaged her in both research and administration of research at a hospital. In 1922 she was elected a fellow of the American Association for the Advancement of Science, based on her research. At Reese, supervising a staff of nine, she did research on metabolism, with a focus on obesity and on undernourished children, publishing more than forty articles. She remained at Reese until 1930, spending the last two summers as a researcher at the Woods Hole Marine Biological Laboratory in Massachusetts.

Wang moved in 1931 to Cincinnati, where she continued to work on her specialty in child metabolism. She was an assistant professor of biochemistry and director of the Metabolic Division of the Children's Hospital Research Foundation in the University of Cincinnati Medical College. Wang's research on the metabolism of children and adolescent girls included two discussions of the basal metabolism of Chinese children in the United States.

In 1940 she left Cincinnati to become a research chemist at the Northwestern Yeast Company in Chicago, attracted by an opportunity to work on vitamins. After three years she decided that she preferred an educational environment over a commercial one and in 1943 became an assistant professor of physiology at the Northwestern University Medical School. Her research headquarters were at Children's Memorial Hospital, where she was involved in a study of nephrosis in children. In 1946 she left Chicago for a year to do research at the Mayo Clinic in Rochester, Minnesota; she ran a biochemical research laboratory at St. Mary's Hospital, working on methods of analyzing blood chemistry. She then returned to Northwestern as associate professor. This time her base was at the Veterans Administration Hospital in Hines, Illinois, where she was in charge of the biochemical research laboratories.

Wang was aware of the limitations placed on women who wished to have careers in science and gave publicity to the work of science professionals. For five years she took part in a Woman's World's Fair in Chicago, where she set up demonstrations of the clinical laboratory procedures used in her research. Her laboratory assistants participated, and their booth generally had a full audience.

During her Chicago years, Wang was active in a Congregationalist church, where she taught Sunday school for five years. She had a strong interest in photography and always belonged to a camera club.

Although she served as vice-president of the Chicago Section of the American Chemical Society, Wang saw the restrictions imposed on women and turned them to advantage. The society allowed a woman member to be in charge of one meeting each year. When Wang became chair of that meeting, she arranged for a prominent woman chemist, Katharine Coward, a specialist on vitamins, to be guest speaker. She also took a term as vice-president of Sigma Delta Epsilon, the honorary society for women scientists, and was active in the honorary society for women chemists, Kappa Mu Sigma, where she was treasurer for three years.

In 1954, she left Chicago to become chief chemist in charge of the Clinical and Research Chemical Laboratory at the Veterans Administration Hospital in Topeka, Kansas. Her research here was very different from the earlier nutritional studies, dealing with clinical chemistry problems, including biopsies for liver cell necrosis.

She was forced to retire in 1961 because of a broken hip due to a fall. Five years later, in October 1965, she was in a serious car accident and broke both legs. Thereafter, she needed crutches to get around and could barely walk or stand without pain. Wang became seriously ill in 1976. Relatives and friends thought that she was dying, but she recovered and was able to return home. Three years later she died in a Topeka nursing home at the age of eighty-four, and her body was cremated.

By the end of her career, Chi Che Wang was considered "a biochemist of high repute" (Sheldrick, 89). Her excellent education and outstanding skills as a scientist enabled her to fashion a distinguished career in research and administration.

Sources. The Margaret Clapp Library Archives, Wellesley College, have reports from Wang on her work through 1970, including a bibliography of her published articles. Wang's authored or coauthored research articles, 1916 to 1960, appeared in professional journals, including *Journal of Home Economics, Journal of Biological Chemistry, Archives of Internal Medicine, American Journal of Diseases of Childhood,* and other periodicals in medicine and chemistry. The Northwestern Univ. Archives contain brief information forms from Wang for 1944–52. Biographical information appears in *American Men of Science* (1961) and in Marie Dye, *History of the Department of Home Economics, University of Chicago* (1972). Wang's work is mentioned in *Pioneer Women Teachers of Connecticut 1767–1970,* ed. Helen M. Sheldrick (1971). An obituary is published in the *Topeka Capital-Journal,* October 12, 1979.

ALETHA A. KOWITZ

WARD, WINIFRED LOUISE
October 29, 1884–August 16, 1975

PIONEER IN CREATIVE DRAMATICS AND CHILDREN'S THEATER During the first half of the twentieth century, Winifred Ward's imagination and energy moved creative dramatics into elementary schoolrooms across the country. The sparkling director who drew the children into the magic of theater also taught in the public schools and trained teachers all over the world. Many children's drama specialists in the 1990s claim to be "third generation Winifred Ward," meaning that they trained with Ward's students.

Ward spent her childhood in Eldora, Iowa. The youngest daughter of George William and Frances Allena (Dimmick) Ward, she attributed her love of theater to both her parents. Her father, an attorney and civic leader, had been an amateur actor in his youth. Her mother, a leader in local and statewide organizations, sometimes took her three daughters and a son on a winter sojourn to Washington, D.C., where she was born. It was on one of those visits that Winifred Ward saw her first professional theater, a play by Frances Hodgson Burnett.

Following her graduation from Eldora High School in 1903, Ward enrolled in Cumnock School of Oratory in Evanston, Illinois. She received a diploma in 1905 and returned to Eldora to teach declamation for two years. In 1907 she went back to Cumnock for another year of study and then spent eight years in Adrian, Michigan, where she taught reading, directed school plays, and coached both competitive speech and girls' basketball in public schools.

In 1916 Ward returned to the Chicago area to complete her education. Two years later the University of Chicago awarded her the Ph.B. (Bachelor of Philosophy) degree with honors in English and general literature. Her performance of Rudyard Kipling's "The Ballad of East and West" brought her the Florence James Adams Prize for Artistic Reading. Upon finishing her degree, Ward accepted a teaching position at the Cumnock School of Oratory, which in 1920 became the School of Speech at Northwestern University in Evanston, north of Chicago. Ward taught at Northwestern for the next thirty years.

Ward quickly achieved a reputation as an innovative teacher. In 1924 her duties expanded when Ralph Dennis, dean of the School of Speech and member of the local school board, proposed adding dramatics to Evanston's elementary school curriculum. The proposal passed, and Dennis recommended that Ward take charge of the program. The new position gave

Ward the opportunity to launch the field that she called "creative dramatics." She continued to teach at Northwestern and brought the university and the Evanston school district into a close collaboration that continued until 1966, sixteen years after her retirement.

Creative dramatics, as Ward defined it, included "all forms of improvised drama" (*Playmaking with Children*, 3), from story dramatization to pantomime, in which all the children took part in the creative process without consideration of an outside audience. In children's theater, on the other hand, even though children might appear in the cast, the main goal was to bring plays to child audiences. Ward distinguished between the terms because she thought that as part of their education, all children should have both experiences—participate in creative dramatics and also know how to enjoy theater as audience members.

In 1925, after a year of success with creative dramatics classes for seventh and eighth graders, Ward and her Northwestern colleagues, Ralph Dennis and Alexander Dean, founded a children's theater. Its financial support and personnel first came from Northwestern University and the Drama Club of Evanston; later the PTA (still later it became the National Parent Teacher Association) and the school district shared the funding costs.

On November 6, 1925, Jessie Braham White's *Snow White and the Seven Dwarfs*, under Ward's direction, opened at Northwestern University. During its third season the children's theater moved to Haven Junior High School. As time passed, performances were added at other junior high schools in the North Shore suburbs of Chicago. The company flourished as the Children's Theatre of Evanston until 1966, when local School District 65 assumed full financial and legal responsibility and renamed it Theatre 65.

With the staging of *Snow White*, Ward launched her plan to integrate university teaching with her work as an elementary school drama specialist. Beginning in 1925 she held three professional titles simultaneously: director of the Children's Theatre of Evanston, supervisor of Dramatics in the Evanston Public Schools, and instructor in Northwestern University's School of Speech. According to her detailed records, during the next twenty-five years she directed seventy-six plays, produced even more, and involved 118,000 individuals in the Children's Theatre of Evanston. In the schools she expanded creative dramatics to include both elementary and junior high school students. At Northwestern she taught aspiring professionals who helped make her theories known throughout the country; her student ALVINA KRAUSE later became a prominent teacher and director.

Ward began to receive national recognition in 1930. It was the sixth season for the Children's Theatre of Evanston, and Ward had commissioned *The Emperor's New Clothes* from CHARLOTTE CHORPENNING, a playwright and colleague at Northwestern. After a successful tour of the North Shore, Ward took the show to the National Theatre in Washington, D.C. The production played to wide acclaim, bringing distinction to Ward and propelling Chorpenning into her new career as the founding artistic director of the Goodman Children's Theatre in Chicago. For the rest of their careers, Chorpenning and Ward—known to their colleagues as Chorpie and Winnie—continued to work together.

In 1930 Ward also published her first book, *Creative Dramatics in the Upper Grades and Junior High School*. In it she acknowledged her debt to John Dewey. Like Dewey, she thought that the purpose of education was to help children learn to live richly at the present moment. Her book promoted her belief that drama taught children to be fully engaged in experience.

During the Great Depression, the Children's Theatre of Evanston held to a steady production schedule, a powerful index to the importance it had not only for children but also the adults in the community. People were eager to find ways to make their own entertainment. Creative dramatics made learning fun and taught children to rely on their imaginations, and children's theater provided a creative outlet for both children and the adults who worked with them.

In 1936 Ward attended the Moscow-Leningrad Theatre Festival, Leningrad, where some of the most innovative theater in the world was taking place. After the 1917 Revolution, the U.S.S.R. (Soviet Union) had established the first permanent children's theater in Europe. Ward had yearned to see the work of Natalya Satz, the renowned director of the Moscow Theatre for the Young Spectator. Upon returning from the U.S.S.R., Ward wore her satin Cossack blouse to class and regaled her students with descriptions of what she had seen, seeking to inspire them to learn from other cultures.

In 1939 Ward published *Theatre for Children*, a book designed to teach theater specialists how to direct for children. Its educational impact continued to be felt for the next twenty-five years. She also began to develop a national network of child drama teachers and in 1944 organized the first meeting of the Children's Theatre Conference (CTF) at Northwestern University. It continues to thrive as a branch of the American Alliance for Theatre and Education (AATE). During that same year, Northwestern presented her with an Alumni Merit Award. She revised *Creative Dramatics* into the book that became the standard text in the field, *Playmaking with Children* (1947). As CTF strengthened, she began to cultivate her professional alliances abroad, paving the way for the formation of an international professional association in child drama.

In 1950 Ward formally retired from Northwestern University, the Evanston Public Schools, and the Children's Theatre of Evanston. At commencement that year, Northwestern awarded her its highest honor, the Alumni Medal for Distinguished Service. As Professor Emeritus, she consulted, wrote essays, gave speeches, and served as a representative of children's theater at UNESCO (United Nation's Educational, Scientific and Cultural Organization). In 1952 she published *Stories to Dramatize*, a collection of folk tales. Widely praised, the book was distributed internationally. Lured back to teaching by Union Theological Seminary in New York City, Ward developed a course on religious drama and wrote essays on drama for religious publications.

Retirement brought Ward accolades and new responsibilities. She received the honorary degree Doctor of Humane Letters from three institutions: Adelphi University, Garden City, New York (1953); Western College for Women (now Miami University), Oxford, Ohio (1957); and Eastern Michigan University, Ypsilanti, Michigan (1971). She was awarded prizes from theater associations, served on several boards, and did volunteer work for the First Methodist Church in Evanston, the World Clothing Drive, and the Near East Foundation, as well as for her professional organizations.

In 1960 Ward collaborated with her former student Rita Criste, who had succeeded her at Northwestern and in the Evanston Schools, to produce a film, *Creative Drama: The First Steps*. That same year the U.S. Office of Education commissioned Ward to write *Drama with and for Children*, a pamphlet that went into three printings. Nearly five thousand copies were distributed.

In the mid-sixties both Northwestern and District 65 responded to the success of children's drama by making bureaucratic changes. In 1963, Rita Criste gave up the teaching of creative dramatics but continued to direct the Children's Theatre. By the time Criste retired from Northwestern in 1966, the three-part job Ward had developed forty years earlier had evolved into three full-time positions. Anne Thurman became creative drama supervisor for District 65; Barbara McIntyre took over Criste's job at Northwestern, and Jane Triplett became director of the Children's Theatre of Evanston, which she renamed Theatre 65. In the early seventies financial problems caused Theatre 65 to disband. For the next five or six years, creative dramatics flourished, but no children's theater toured the public schools. Within a few years, Thurman, who had studied with Ward, joined the Northwestern faculty. There she developed once more a children's theater company in the Ward tradition.

Throughout her career and long after retirement, Ward welcomed students and colleagues to her home in Evanston, an apartment she shared with her close friend, Hazel Easton. Ward and Easton, having met when they were new teachers at Cumnock, had begun rooming together in 1919 in a boarding house in Evanston. Eventually, they moved to an apartment and continued to teach together until 1935, when Easton left Northwestern to open a bakery. As devoted friends who shared a passion for child drama, Ward and Easton extended their influence far beyond the classroom. In their living room discussions of children's make-believe and dramatic play came alive. Their hospitality encouraged the growth of an international network of students, teachers, directors, and others who cherished the combination of children and playmaking.

Along with what she did for children, Ward was important in offering new opportunities in theater to women. Because of gender bias, talented women had found it difficult to be taken seriously as playwrights and directors in adult theater. By training performers and audiences for children's theater, Ward legitimated the field in the eyes of the artistic and academic establishments. Moreover, as her students grew into adulthood, they carried with them the expectation that women could be successful playwrights and directors.

After attending a concert in 1974, Ward suffered a stroke in her Evanston apartment. She died in August 1975, leaving Hazel Easton and a host of devoted friends and colleagues to carry on her work. The Winifred Ward Zeta Phi Eta Scholarship was established as a memorial in 1978, and in 1979 her papers were assembled at Northwestern University Archives.

Ward's legacy lives on. In the 1990s, Northwestern University brought plays to children of the North Shore, and aspiring teachers and directors received rigorous training in theater. In School District 65 specialists in creative dramatics taught every child from kindergarten through eighth grade. AATE cited Evanston as the cradle of creative drama, a cradle set in motion by Winifred Ward.

Sources. The most important resource for the student of Winifred Ward is the collection of her personal papers in the Northwestern Univ. Archives. The collection includes ten boxes, many of them containing scrapbooks and clippings about the Evanston Children's Theatre. The archives also hold copies of most works written by and about Ward, as well as photographs of her and her productions. For insight into her theories of child drama, the reader should consult Ward's own writings. In addition to her four major books cited above, including *Playmaking with Children* (1947), and her film script, Ward wrote two pamphlets and numerous articles. The most extensive treatment given to Ward appears in Jan A. Guffin, "Winifred Ward: A Critical Biography" (Ph.D. diss. Duke Univ., 1975), which provides a full bibliography of Ward's writings. For the history of Evanston Children's Theatre, see Kenneth Russell Hosie's "Theatre 65: Its Organization, Operation and Function as a Children's Theatre" (master's thesis, Pennsylvania State Univ., 1972). See also Ruth Beall Heinig's collection of articles, *Go Adventuring! A Celebration of Winifred Ward: America's First Lady of Drama for Children* (1977), and *Children's Theatre Review*, vol. 25, 1976, the Winifred Ward Memorial Issue. Ward is included in *NAW* (1980). In her book, *Northwestern University School of Speech: A History* (1981), Lynn Miller Rein places Ward in her professional context. A more recent biographical entry by Douglas Street appears in *Notable Women in American Theatre: A Biographical Dictionary*, ed. Alice M. Robinson, Vera Morory Roberts, and Melly S. Barranger (1989).

FRANCES FREEMAN PADEN

WARING, MARY FITZBUTLER
November 1, 1869–December 3, 1958
PHYSICIAN, CLUBWOMAN, ACTIVIST, EDUCATOR

The lives of African Americans were impacted by migration, urbanization, and war in the first three decades of the twentieth century, and, from within the black community, individual men and women emerged to aid in the construction of community life in northern cities. The presence and power of such women as Mary Fitzbutler Waring, through their vision, dedication, and energy, provided guidance during those tenuous times. She joined with a number of pioneering African American women of the early twentieth century whose voices were heard locally, nationally, and internationally as they proclaimed the gospel of racial uplift and equality.

Mary Fitzbutler was one of six children born to Henry and Sarah H. Fitzbutler. Migrating from Ontario, Canada, in 1872, the Warings settled in Louisville, Kentucky, where Mary Fitzbutler was born. This was also the place where Henry Fitzbutler, after he completed his studies at the medical school of the University of Michigan, established a medical college in 1888, the Louisville National Medical College, which was open to all, regardless of color. Mary Fitzbutler's own career unfolded as she saw her father's efforts to train young doctors, one of whom was her mother. These examples of service to others motivated Fitzbutler throughout her early education in the public schools of Louisville, her teacher training at the normal school, her graduation from Louisville National Medical College in 1898, and her completion of a degree in medicine from the Chicago Medical School in 1923.

In 1901, Fitzbutler married Frank Waring, an educator and activist who served as a high school principal. The Warings moved to Chicago. Frank Waring raised funds to support the Old Folks Home and was active in the Appomattox Club and the Grand Lodge of the Knights of Pythias. His work as activist and educator continued until his death in 1923.

Mary Waring was a teacher at Wendell Phillips High School before she practiced medicine in Chicago. Little can be found regarding her medical practice; because of racial, gender, and professional bias, many pioneering black and white women physicians combined their medical practices with community service work. Waring turned to the growing health needs of the black community. Many of her efforts to expand medical care and raise the consciousness of her community about health issues were directed through the activities of the National Association of Colored Women (NACW).

The NACW was founded in 1896 as an effort to organize and centralize the energies of the many local black women's clubs across the nation. These clubs responded to the violence and racial pressures experienced by the black population following the Reconstruction Era, when Jim Crow laws were passed in the wake of a U.S. Supreme Court ruling in 1883 that nullified the Civil Rights Act of 1875. This conservative trend culminated in 1896 with *Plessy v. Ferguson*, which "upheld state measures of discriminating against colored patrons on the railroads and established the 'separate but equal' doctrine" (Wesley, 24).

By the early 1900s, the gifts and visions of black clubwomen like Waring were put to use as they joined with other political and civic organizations in the black community to fight for equal opportunity for African Americans. Waring's early leadership in such organizations as the local Phyllis Wheatley Club and the Emanuel Settlement Day Nursery provided a much needed service to young women newly migrating to Chicago from the South. By locating housing and organizing vocational counseling and training, child care, and social activities, these and other black-initiated and black-run agencies addressed the serious needs of African American migrant women in their search for urban employment opportunities.

Waring's leadership moved beyond the local level when she was selected, in 1911, to serve as an alternate to represent the NACW at the executive session of the National Council of Women, the white counterpart of the NACW. Two years later she was elected as the corresponding secretary of the Illinois Federation of Colored Women. While continuing her local and statewide activities, Waring accepted an appointment to the position of chair of the NACW's Department of Health and Hygiene. She was also the editor of the NACW publication, *National Notes*.

From 1913 to 1930, as the growth of urban centers in the North provided jobs for many but also created massive health problems, Waring focused on the health problems of blacks. One of the first was the tuberculosis epidemic that afflicted thousands between 1913 and 1914. Waring sponsored a number of training sessions and health programs across the country, through regional and local black women's clubs, to address critical health concerns. Through her writings in *National Notes* she provided common sense information that stressed the need for sanitation in urban areas and for prevention programs.

In 1914, Governor Edward F. Dunne, confirming the Illinois Federation of Colored Women's Clubs' choice, appointed Waring to serve as one of the commissioners of the Abraham Lincoln Jubilee planned for the Illinois Exposition of 1915. Her appointment, in response to a resolution passed by the NACW to include a "colored woman" (quoted in Carney, 681) on the board, involved Waring in the planning and executing of a twenty thousand dollar event commemorating fifty years of progress of black women and men in Chicago. Waring wanted the event to be an opportunity for black and white viewers alike to see and appreciate exhibits of "'quality' work" (quoted in Carney, 681) by Blacks to illustrate the "gains made by the race in business, education, and manufacturing" (Carney, 681). The exposition served not only to dispel negative images and stereotypes but also to illustrate in a concrete way the motto of the NACW, "Lifting as We Climb," a theme of racial uplift and self-determination.

The Great Migration of southern Blacks to northern cities after World War I escalated the challenges to health, hygiene, and sanitation in the overcrowded, segregated "Black Belt" of Chicago. Waring continued to address these issues in a variety of articles in *National Notes*. "Census counts in the northern cities during the migration period showed that a greater number of women than men were making the journey from the South" (Giddings, 142). Black women were seeking employment opportunities in the textile, clothing, food, and tobacco industries. On the one hand, for the first time, "significant numbers of Black women were earning decent wages in the mainstream of the American labor force" (Giddings, 143), but "Black representation in the unions was very small," and, of this small number, "the number of Black women was negligible" (Giddings, 154). This swelling of employment numbers forced the NACW to deal seriously with the problems of black working women and, specifically, acceptance of black women in the labor unions.

Waring's personal campaign during this time of work and war continued to focus on health. At the eleventh biennial convention of the NACW in 1918, she introduced a proposal to include black Red Cross nurses in the war effort. On the local level, Waring continued in her role as educator and physician as she organized training classes for nurses in Chicago through the National Nurse Training Service; regionally, she instituted Red Cross training and classes in home care in St. Louis, Missouri, all in an effort to increase preventive and supplemental health care for African Americans.

By 1920, Waring had served the NACW as chair of its Department of Health and Hygiene and had been the editor of *National Notes* for seven years. She was treasurer of the Illinois Federation of Colored Women for three years. In the fall of 1920 she was elected one of three alternates of the then president, Mary B. Talbert, to represent the NACW at the International Council of Women in Christiana, Norway. Her international experiences were both expansive culturally and disheartening. When she and her black colleagues visited the American Women's Club managed by the Young Men's Christian Association in Paris, they were confronted with the same racial prejudices and inequities practiced at home. Waring wrote, "Now the prejudice of the United States is a disgrace to the country and the

Y.M.C.A. should let it be washed out by the broad expanse of water of the Atlantic and not introduce it into their private hostelries of Europe. . . . In Norway the women cannot understand this sort of thing and we have been treated with the greatest courtesy everywhere" (quoted in Carney, 682). Finding that Americans in Europe tenaciously held onto standards of inequality and segregation, Waring became even more committed to the uplift and integration of Blacks into the mainstream of American society.

In 1929, as the nation struggled to cope with the economic tragedies of the stock market crash and the Great Depression that followed, the NACW escalated its efforts to meet the needs of the black community. At the same time, internal problems among black clubwomen began to emerge. "Former NACW president Mary McLeod Bethune felt that the NACW's priorities were misplaced and had begun in 1928 to recruit supporters to form a new national organization. By 1930, plans for this group, which was to become the National Council of Negro Women (NCNW), were underway" (Carney, 682). Waring disagreed with this initiative, and "the mantle of leadership was passed on to her at a critical moment in the organization's history" (p. 683). Waring feared that the proposed NCNW would weaken the national black women's club movement. Advocating strengthening the NACW, she rose to the ranks of an executive officer when she served as vice president from 1930 to 1933 and then national president, serving two terms from 1933 to 1937.

During Waring's four years as president, the NACW continued to emphasize the traditional concerns of women that centered around home, family life, employment, and health. Waring also, through the pages of *National Notes*, remained a strong voice against the injustices of lynching and discrimination. In an era of rising violence against Blacks, defense of the Scottsboro boys became a rallying cry for African Americans as well as white reform and radical groups. Nine young black men were accused of raping two white women on a freight train near Paint Rock, Alabama, and were arrested on March 25, 1931. The Scottsboro boys—ages thirteen to twenty-one—went to trial without adequate legal representation and were quickly convicted on superficial evidence. All but one were sentenced to death. A struggle to free the young men was waged in the courts; the defendants' lawyers secured a new trial on appeal, which began on March 27, 1933. A month before the new trial, one of the young women repudiated the rape charge. Despite new evidence and a strong defense, the all-white jury delivered a guilty verdict. An Alabama circuit judge overturned the verdict and ordered a new trial. In 1934, in the midst of the Scottsboro case, Waring urged NACW members to "actively support the anti-lynching measure that was pending in the U.S. Senate and to join efforts to make segregation illegal" (Carney, 683). In 1937, at the conclusion of the final appeal, four of the nine defendants were released and the remaining five sentenced to lengthy prison sentences. That year Waring wrote an open letter to NACW members, soliciting their continued efforts to campaign for release of the five and thanking them for their ongoing support.

In 1935, Waring's address, "Women in Industry," at the nineteenth biennial convention reflected her continuing concern with the impact of the economic depression and the high level of black unemployment on the black community and black women workers. She advocated the hiring of Blacks as salespersons and attendants in the parts of the community where Blacks predominated. Waring also demonstrated diplomatic skills as the leader of the NACW when, in 1935, she helped avert a lawsuit against the association by the Ralph Printing Company. Unusual haste to complete a written history of the NACW for the 1933 convention had resulted in poor proofreading and additional costs. Waring stepped in to pay the balance of the expense while encouraging club members to squelch their criticism and support the effort regardless of the mistakes.

Waring had been a proponent of working with white women's organizations and had supported the NACW's affiliation with the National Council of Women, the predominantly white umbrella organization for women's clubs in the United States. Mary McLeod Bethune, already initiating the National Council of Negro Women, "supported withdrawal of the NACW from the predominantly White National Council of Women, although a Black clubwoman had recently been named a council vice-president" (Giddings, 211). Opposing this withdrawal, Waring, who had worked for integration, told the NACW, "My dear friends, *now* and *ever* let me admonish you not to burn the bridges over which you pass that those who come after may not cross" (quoted in Giddings, 212). The debate between Waring, who criticized Bethune before an NACW meeting, and Bethune reflected the historic tension between integrationists and separatists among black intellectuals. In spite of such controversies, Waring remained a strong and constant advocate for the racial uplift of African Americans through integration, not separation.

After her tenure as president of the NACW, Waring continued her work through the creation of clubs in other regions and her involvement in other organizations like the Chicago League of Women Voters, the National Republican League of Colored Women, the Delta Sigma Theta Sorority and the National Association for the Advancement of Colored People (NAACP).

At the age of eighty-nine, Waring died from complications associated with arteriosclerosis. Her funeral was at St. Thomas Episcopal Church, Chicago, and she was buried in Lincoln Cemetery, Worth, Illinois. She had no children, and her estate was divided among her two surviving sisters, two nephews, and two great nephews.

Waring left a lasting legacy to the African American community through her life's work. Her emphasis on the support and empowerment of African American women in both the home and workplace can be seen as a prelude to the work of contemporary black feminists. Through her efforts to unite across racial lines, she joined the cadre of later emerging black leaders who were committed to seeking equal opportunities through integration.

Sources. Correspondence, minutes, programs, articles, and other records from her work with the National Association of Colored Women (NACW) are in Lillian Serece Williams, consulting ed., *Records of the National Association of Colored Women's Clubs 1895–1992* (Microfilm, 1993–). Copies of *National Notes* are located in the Northwestern Univ. Library, Evanston, Illinois. Waring is listed in *Who's Who in Col-*

ored America (1941–44, 1950) and in *Notable Black American Women, Book II*, ed. Jessie Smith Carney (1996). Helpful studies of African American clubwomen include Paula Giddings, *When and Where I Enter: The Impact of Black Women on Race and Sex in America* (1984), and Charles Harris Wesley, *The History of the National Association of Colored Women's Clubs—A Legacy of Service* (1984). Information about African American women physicians can be found in Darlene Clark Hine, "Co-Laborers in the Work of the Lord. Nineteenth-Century Black Women Physicians," in *"Send Us a Lady Physician": Women Doctors in America, 1835–1920*, ed. Ruth J. Abram (1985), and in Herbert N. Morais, *History of the Negro in Medicine* (1920). The *Chicago Defender* mentioned Waring January 10, 1910, and the *CT* published her obituary December 6, 1958.

JULIA M. SPELLER

WARSHAWSKY, CELIA BURG
March 14, 1921–July 28, 1986
ADVOCATE FOR THE DEAF, TEACHER, POLITICAL ACTIVIST

Celia Burg and her twin sister, Julia, were born in Passaic, New Jersey, to Benjamin and Fanny (Cohen) Burg. The girls' birth was two months premature; they each had a profound hearing loss. Their parents never made them feel different from their older sister, Belle, or their younger sister, Jean. Celia and Julia Burg studied piano, guitar, violin, and dance. In order for the twins to learn the words to the music, Fanny Burg would turn up the volume of the phonograph and the girls would put their ears close to the speaker as their mother mouthed the words. The girls were always included when company came and were encouraged to take part in the conversation. Both their parents came from Russia and had strong accents; the twins learned to read lips of people with accents and were able to tell where people came from by their speech.

The twins attended public school and were both shy and nervous. They were avid readers, had very good language skills, and did much reading before class, so they had a good idea of what was being said. Since they were good at sports, the girls were popular in school. They had each other to practice with and, as early as seven years of age, were playing ping pong on the kitchen table.

Celia Burg got her first hearing-aid when she started high school. It was a device with a microphone, an ear mold, and two large batteries that went into a pocket on her leg. She took it off when she had her gym class so that the children would not make fun of her.

The girls had problems in high school. One teacher would walk around the room asking test questions, and when the girls asked her to stand in their line of vision, she yelled, "If you two gals don't understand me, you don't belong here" (letter from Julia Burg Mayes to Hope Bernstein, October 14, 1996). Since they could talk to each other by silently mouthing words, the twins were able to help each other through tests. Just before the Burgs graduated from high school, they heard about Gallaudet College, a school for the hearing impaired in Washington, D.C. Knowledge of sign language was a requirement to attend Gallaudet and they found a deaf night school teacher to teach them.

Immediately after high school graduation, they attended the New Jersey School for the Deaf, where they compressed two years of algebra into four months in order to pass the college entrance exams. Julia Burg passed and went on to Gallaudet, while

FIG. 124. *Advocate for the deaf Celia Burg Warshawsky, on the right, with twin sister, Julia.*

Celia Burg happily stayed at the School for the Deaf for one more year. In 1940, she followed her sister to Gallaudet, where she was a good student. Though she walked with a slight limp because of hip deterioration, she participated in tennis, fencing, and drama. She had a busy social life and met Leonard Warshawsky, another deaf student.

After graduating in 1945, Celia Burg went to Florida for one year to teach at the Florida School for the Deaf and Blind in St. Augustine. In 1946, she married Leonard Warshawsky and moved to Chicago. Unable to teach in the Chicago schools because she lacked several courses required for teacher certification, Warshawsky began work at Sears, Roebuck and Co. in the purchasing office. In a short time she was promoted to the advertising and sales promotion headquarters, where she served as secretary and senior clerical assistant to the assistant of audiovisual services. She also was a tutor for the Illinois Department of

Rehabilitation from 1953 to 1970 as well as a private tutor. Warshawsky began to participate in organizations for the hearing impaired.

Still interested in becoming a classroom teacher, Warshawsky worked toward obtaining her teacher certification. She enrolled in courses at Northwestern University, Evanston, Illinois, and at the University of Nebraska–Lincoln. In 1969, when Northwestern was changing its method of training teachers of the hearing impaired from oral communication (lip reading) to total communication (a combination of lip reading and sign language), Warshawsky was hired to teach sign language. After this teaching experience, and having completed the additional course work for her certification, Warshawsky was hired in 1970 to teach in the Hatch Elementary School, Oak Park, Illinois. She became the first hearing impaired person to teach in a public school in the state. Her classes were part of the program offered by the West Suburban Association for the Hearing Impaired.

Warshawsky was very influential in getting people in the region to sign and talk. When she began teaching, her students were still using the oral method of lip reading alone. Warshawsky taught by signing and talking, using key word concepts, lip reading, finger spelling and gesturing. She insisted on proper use of grammar, conjugation of verbs, and correct use of adjectives and adverbs. She taught in the West Suburban consortium for eleven years. After three years at Hatch, she taught at Willard School, River Forest (1973–76), and at Forest Road School, La Grange Park (1976–81).

In June 1971, she served as instructor at the Total Communications Institute at the University of Wisconsin–Milwaukee for day-school teachers of the deaf. She became very active in the Registry of Interpreters for the Deaf and was a strong advocate for the need of interpreters. Each state had a committee of deaf and hearing persons that rated people who wished to become interpreters. She was on the advisory board at the University of Wisconsin and traveled between Chicago and Milwaukee for many years.

Also in 1971, she became the educational chair for the Greater Chicago Parents of the Hearing Impaired. Warshawsky was involved with parents of deaf children even though she was not able to have children herself. Many parents did not want their children to use sign language in public. They felt that if their children went to an oral school, they would learn to talk. Warshawsky believed that this approach put deaf children at a great disadvantage. She wanted parents to learn sign language along with their infants. She knew parent-to-child teaching was very difficult, and she became an adviser on improving parent-child communication with hearing impaired children. She was honored by the Illinois Parents of the Hearing Impaired in 1985.

Warshawsky was a rare person among many who were hearing impaired in that she was never hesitant in communicating with the hearing world. She had some hearing and was able to speak understandably. Her clear and articulate speech attested to her determination to overcome her disability in order to achieve the goals she set for herself. When she was called upon to give public testimony, as she often did, before federal, state, and municipal agencies, she knew when it would be more effective to speak and when to use an interpreter. Warshawsky

urged the deaf to be aware of pending legislation that affected their needs and to write and call legislators to express their views.

Warshawsky became involved with the hearing as well as the non-hearing community. She was elected president of the Quota Club of Chicago, which was a social service club whose philanthropic interests included helping the deaf. Quota International chose her as the International Deaf Woman of the Year in 1983. In her acceptance speech, Warshawsky said that she had to be more than a teaching pioneer and more than a role model. "It was up to me to get involved in parent organizations, the deaf community, advocacy groups, coalitions for the disabled, not just deaf" (Speech to Quota International Convention).

When closed captioning became available on television networks in the 1970s and one of the networks refused to use it, Warshawsky organized a group to picket. Her sign read, "I still don't know who shot J.R." in reference to the popular television show (interview with Laurel Raci, October 10, 1996). Soon that network also started using closed captioning.

Celia and Leonard Warshawsky were founding members of the Chicago Hebrew Association of the Deaf, which began mainly as a social club. Warshawsky felt that there should be a religious element to the club, and the couple applied to Hebrew Union College, Cincinnati, Ohio, for a student rabbi to come once a month to their meetings. One student who came for three years and always stayed with the Warshawskys was Douglas Goldhammer. She taught him sign language and was a source of Goldhammer's inspiration to work with the deaf. When Rabbi Goldhammer was ordained, the club voted to become a synagogue and hired him to be the spiritual leader of Bene Sholom, Skokie, Illinois, the only full-time synagogue of the deaf in the United States. Warshawsky started a synagogue choir, becoming its director, and developed beautiful sign language for the liturgy.

Celia Warshawsky became active in the National Congress of the Jewish Deaf (NCJD) and worked to develop a prayer book, *Signs of Judaism*, which was used for many years. The purpose of the NCJD was to encourage Jewish deaf all over the United States to focus on their heritage and to keep their faith intact. Warshawsky was elected to the NCJD Hall of Fame in 1986.

Warshawsky was instrumental in gaining the enactment of Illinois legislation providing telecommunications devices for all deaf persons. In the 1980s, when American Telephone & Telegraph (AT&T) wanted to discard old Western Union teletypewriters, the company made them available to the deaf community. Celia and Leonard Warshawsky received one of the machines, which are like typewriters with modems that allow non-vocal communications over telephone lines. Believing the hearing impaired belonged in the mainstream of society, Warshawsky wanted everyone to have equal access to these devices. She appeared before the AT&T stockholders meeting, the Illinois Joint Commission on Public Utilities, and the Chicago Development Block Grant Fund hearings to advocate for these devices for the hearing impaired. This advocacy resulted in the passage of the Universal Telephone Services Protection Law of 1985 that provided Telecommunications Devices for the Deaf (TDD) at no cost to them. The legislation also established a statewide dual party relay system. The service was funded by a surcharge on all monthly telephone service. Warshawsky served on the Statewide Task Force created by the Illinois Commerce Commission to ensure that efficient and effective rules and regulations were developed to carry out this law.

Both Warshawskys were active in the National Fraternal Society of the Deaf (NFSD), a insurance company for the deaf, which also provided services and scholarships for its members. Celia Warshawsky was president of the women's division, and her husband served as grand secretary. She was named Frater of the Year and inducted into the NFSD Hall of Fame in 1982. Some other organizations in which she was active are the Chicago Club for the Deaf, the Sertoma Club, the Interpreter Training Program at Waubonsee Community College, and the Gallaudet Alumni Association. She worked with the City Wide College Program for the Handicapped, cochaired the Skokie Advisory Council on Disabilities, and was a member of the executive committee for the Decade of Persons with Disabilities.

Celia Warshawsky continued work in the larger community. In 1986, McDonald's Corporation wanted to produce a commercial showing hearing impaired students. The idea was to show that non-hearing people did the same things as hearing people. McDonald's contacted the Chicago Hearing Society, where Warshawsky was the first deaf-signing person on the board. A focus group of hearing and non-hearing persons was formed, and Warshawsky became a member of the group as well as a consultant for this successful project. She was the first deaf person to interpret at a criminal trial in Illinois. She participated in the training of police recruits undertaken by the Chicago Hearing Society to sensitize police to the communications of deaf persons.

Warshawsky was proud to be a deaf person. She had enthusiasm for living. She loved the theater and was a member of the advisory council for Chicago-land Advocates for Signed Theater. She also loved to travel and helped organize trips for the hearing impaired.

At the age of sixty-five, Warshawsky died suddenly of a massive heart attack. Although some members of the deaf community thought Warshawsky was often too assertive, so many people attended her funeral at Congregation Bene Sholom that nine interpreters were needed to sign the service. The executive director of the Chicago Hearing Society described Warshawsky as a "very dynamic person and a real leader. She fought locally and nationally for the disabled. She also worked for the educational rights of hearing-impaired children" (Heise). Following her death, as a memorial to her, the Chicago Hearing Society held Celia Warshawsky Training Workshops in 1987 and 1988 to encourage self-advocacy and to promote the development of skills needed to be an effective leader.

Celia Warshawsky's lifetime disability led her to her work as a teacher and as an advocate for improved technology for the hearing impaired. It also contributed to her role as a communicator between the hearing and deaf communities.

Sources. Julia Burg Mayes, Margate, Florida, wrote a letter to Hope Kell Bernstein on October 14, 1996, about her sister's life; Mayes provided a letter that Celia Warshawsky wrote to a friend in 1981, as well as Warshawsky's speech when she accepted the 1983 Quota International Deaf Woman of the Year Award. Chicago Hearing Society Papers, CHS, have the organization's newsletters and other materials. In 1996 and 1997, Hope Kell Bernstein conducted interviews with Julia Burg Mayes; Abberlae Rovell; Rabbi Douglas Goldhammer; the Racis, Laurel, Mitchell, and Don; Patricia Scherer; Jill Sahakian; Jean Modry; John B. Davis; and Garlene Lamb. Articles about Warshawsky include "Students Listen, Hear with their Eyes," *Oak Leaves*, May 17, 1972; "Celia Warshawsky, Friend, Advocate, Teacher," *The Frat*, September–October 1986 (National Fraternal Society of the Deaf, Mt. Prospect, Illinois); and Kenneth Heise, "Celia Warshawsky, Advocate for Deaf," *CT*, July 30, 1986.

HOPE KELL BERNSTEIN

WATSON SCHÜTZE, EVA LAWRENCE
September 16, 1867–May 20, 1935
PAINTER, PHOTOGRAPHER

Eva Lawrence Watson was born in Woodbridge, New Jersey, to Dr. John C. and Mary (Lawrence) Watson. It is not known how many siblings she had, though in correspondence she mentioned a sister. Her parents, both Scottish by birth, recognized Watson's artistic talent and enrolled her in the Pennsylvania Academy of Fine Arts in Philadelphia, Pennsylvania, from 1882 to 1889. There she studied painting and clay modeling with master nineteenth-century realistic painter Thomas Eakins and painter Thomas Anshutz. In autobiographical notes Watson made later in her life, she reminisced about this period: "after six years could draw and model, knew the 'human form,' hated the Classics especially Greek and Latin and the old Flemish masters. All seemed not art but artificial. Imaginative impulses all paralyzed—no outlet for creative impulses. Did not want to paint and 'copy nature'" (quoted in Block, 2). Following her studies, Watson worked for several years as a commercial artist; she reproduced "masterpieces of art" through the photogravure process and reported that she "nearly died of it!" (quoted in Block, 2).

Watson eventually left the commercial photogravure business and in 1894, renewed and invigorated by the possibilities she saw in photography, resumed her art making. Still a relatively new medium, photography was considered at the time to be useful for purposes of scientific exactitude and precise recording. Watson's interest in photography, however, was as an alternative to the process of copying nature; her interest in the medium was as a tool for self-expression. Watson's first exposure to photography may have been through her former instructor, Thomas Eakins, who had been using the camera as an artistic tool for several years.

Watson was described by a lifelong friend as "a little above the average height, slight of figure, rather pale, with earnest, searching eyes . . . quick and nervous of motion, reserved and self-reliant in bearing, and in speech quiet, thoughtful, and to the point" (Block, 3). From 1894 to 1896 Watson shared a studio in Atlantic City, New Jersey, with a colleague and former schoolmate, Amelia Van Buren. Here she developed a reputation as a highly paid artist/photographer, and in 1897 she opened her own studio in Philadelphia. Soon Watson's studio became a gathering place for the Philadelphia Naturalists, a group of photographers who sought to promote the recognition of photography as a fine art. The general name for this new movement was "pictorialism," or simply, "the Cause" (Block, 4).

During these formative years in Philadelphia, many of the qualities that would characterize Watson's ongoing work began to evolve, notably, a sensitivity to the aesthetics of form, light, and tonality—aspects disregarded in the more conventional photographic documents of the day.

Six of Watson's photographs were juried into the 1898 Philadelphia Salon, an annual exhibition of the Philadelphia Photographic Society. Until this year the salon had been under the control of the "rationalists," the scientific-minded bulwarks of the society. Seated on the 1898 jury, however, was Alfred Stieglitz, a photographer credited with spearheading the pictorial movement and in 1902 formalizing it into what came to be known as the Photo-Secession.

Following Watson's debut in the Philadelphia Salon exhibition, Stieglitz recruited her into his new movement, and for the next several years she played a key role in the development of "the Cause" as a lecturer, juror, and writer. She was elected into the Philadelphia Photographic Society in 1899 and, in 1901, joined The Linked Ring, a prestigious British organization of pictorialists. During this period, her work was included in every important pictorial exhibition in the United States and abroad and written about in major publications.

The opposing and more traditional photographic movement at the time consisted of the rationalists. This group maintained a view of photography that stressed representation and precise recording of the appearance of persons, places, and objects. The rationalists decried the pictorialists as "long haired" and their photography as "fuzzyography" (Panzer, 20). They denounced the jury of the 1900 Salon, on which Watson sat, accusing it of deluging the photographic public with bad photography and worse art.

In 1901, the rationalists won out over the pictorialists and regained control of the Philadelphia Salon. The members of the exhibition committee—pictorialists all—resigned, and began discussing the establishment of an independent pictorialist group similar to The Linked Ring. Watson was deeply immersed in these discussions, but in 1901, just as they became serious, her life took a dramatic turn. She married and moved to Chicago to join her husband, Martin Schütze, a young German lawyer. Schütze had been educated in Germany and received his Ph.D. from the University of Pennsylvania in 1899. From 1900 to 1901, he was instructor in German at Northwestern University.

After moving to Chicago, Watson Schütze remained active in the Photo-Secession for a short time, organizing, writing, exhibiting, and corresponding regularly with Stieglitz. In December 1902, Watson wrote to Stieglitz about her feelings of isolation as a singular force in fighting to have photographers recognized as artists, evidence of her efforts to expand the pictorialist cause into a movement of larger scope.

For reasons that are not altogether clear, the relationship between Stieglitz and Watson Schütze began to sour after the movement was formalized. Eventually she began to feel excluded from (perhaps even pushed out of) Stieglitz's New York circle and decided formally to leave the Photo-Secession in 1905.

Withdrawing from the movement she had helped to create, Watson Schütze shifted her attention to her new life in Chicago.

Her husband, Martin Schütze, had acquired a position as professor of German language and literature at the University of Chicago. The newlyweds settled in the South Side neighborhood of Hyde Park close to the university. Throughout the ensuing years of their marriage the couple shared a deep love, mutual respect, and many common interests. Martin Schütze was devoted to his wife and unequivocally supportive of her as an artist. They did not have children.

Shortly after moving to Chicago, Watson Schütze established a studio on the sunny top floor of the Fine Arts Building in downtown Chicago. The Fine Arts Building then housed a vibrant community of artists, musicians, actors, and women activists. Alfred Stieglitz's brother Julius, professor of chemistry at the University of Chicago and an amateur photographer in his own right, is thought to have been helpful in introducing Watson Schütze to the portrait-buying community in Hyde Park. This community included the young but nationally regarded faculty of the philosophy department at the University of Chicago, along with their families, and included the John Deweys, the George Herbert Meads, and James Hayden Tufts. In addition, at this time Watson Schütze made the acquaintance of JANE ADDAMS and others associated with the social settlement Hull-House. These individuals became not only subjects of Watson Schütze's photographs for many years, but also close and lasting friends of the Schützes. "Indeed, the spirit and friendship of Jane Addams and the Hull House group were of greatest importance to the people who [sic] Eva photographed. ELLEN GATES STARR bound Martin's [Schütze's] books of poetry; James Tufts and George Mead marched in suffrage parades with Jane Addams; Eva photographed her, conveying forcefully the sense of inward vision that governed her life" (Block, 13).

In her Chicago studio, Watson Schütze rekindled her interest in painting. Discovering that each medium benefited the other, she continued to work in both painting and photography for the rest of her career, with an emphasis on painting.

In 1902 Watson Schütze and her husband Martin were cofounders of the Byrdcliffe Arts and Crafts colony in Woodstock, New York. Watson Schütze acquired a second studio at Byrdcliffe in 1903 that she used for both photography and painting, spending long summers there, eventually staying six months a year in Woodstock. The Byrdcliffe arts and crafts colony attracted other Chicago artists, including Hull-House cofounder and bookbinder Ellen Gates Starr. Watson Schütze studied with Woodstock painter Thomas Schumacher, whose work she greatly admired, and she exhibited her paintings frequently in Chicago. While her photographs of this period survived, her paintings, described as "carefully composed, straightforward representational images" (Block, 21–22) have not surfaced.

Watson Schütze's health declined as she got older due to myocarditis, a chronic inflammation of the heart muscle. As Watson Schütze weakened and had to curtail her painting, she developed an interest in art history, theory, and criticism. Albert C. Barnes's book, The Art in Painting (1925), had a particular influence on her, inspiring her membership in the A. C. Barnes Foundation and her strong support of modern art. Watson Schütze's new interest constituted a philosophical departure from the notion of art as a means to beauty, transcendence, and the ideal that had characterized her pictorial photography. A similar shift in artistic expression was occurring on a broader level as well, as demonstrated by the Armory Show of 1913 in New York, which introduced America to postimpressionist, cubist, and futurist art.

Few members of the Chicago art scene were hospitable to the new works of modern art. Most art organizations were, like the Renaissance Society established in 1915 at the University of Chicago, deeply entrenched in a lingering nineteenth-century mindset and resistant to any modernist influence.

Watson Schütze was recruited as president of the Renaissance Society in 1929, a position she held until her death six years later. During her tenure, she became the force that transformed the group "from a largely amateurish, unfocused organization into an internationally recognized, truly vanguard institution advancing a rigorous modernist agenda" (Fulton, 11).

Watson Schütze's agenda was to educate Chicagoans about modern art. This mission was actualized through a progressive and focused program of exhibitions, lectures, films, and publications. Out of the society's publishing program came the first three books on modernism published in the United States: *Plastic Redirections in 20th Century Painting* (1934) by James Johnson Sweeney, an exhibition coordinator at the Renaissance Society; *The Meaning of Unintelligibility in Modern Art* (1934) by Edward Rothschild; and *Seurat and the Evolution of "La Grande Jatte"* (1935) by Daniel Catton Rich, which was still in progress at the time of her death.

Watson Schütze died of heart failure at the age of sixty-seven, before the fruits of her labor were realized. Eva Watson Schütze is buried at Oak Woods Cemetery in Chicago. At the time, the Renaissance Society was in the midst of developing what would be a pivotal exhibition of works of the French artist Fernand Léger, then relatively unknown. After opening in 1936, this exhibition traveled to the Museum of Modern Art in New York City, the Art Institute of Chicago, and the Milwaukee Art Institute, attesting to the integrity of Watson Schütze's vision.

Eva Watson Schütze's life and work reflected significant transitions in the world of art and photography during the late nineteenth and early twentieth centuries. Although she considered herself primarily a painter and secondarily a photographer, the majority of available information concerns her work in photography, and her paintings are nowhere to be found. In 1933, just two years before her death, Watson Schütze presented a paper entitled "Women in the Fine Arts" in which she delineated the incomplete history of women artists, covering twenty-five hundred years. The paper reads like a self-fulfilling prophecy considering that, despite the efforts of Watson Schütze and her husband to preserve something of her legacy as an artist, it nevertheless faded after her death. Yet, in the 1970s, material and information surfaced about the photographic work of this influential woman.

Sources. Archival collections containing material pertaining to Watson Schütze include the Martin Schütze Papers located in UC Spec. Coll. While most of these materials pertain to Martin Schütze, the papers include biographical notes he made with the intention of writing Watson Schütze's biography. Also contained in this collection is Watson Schütze's 1933 typescript paper, "Women in the Fine Arts." Fifty-four letters that Eva Watson Schütze wrote to Alfred Stieglitz during the formative years of the Photo-Secession are housed in the Stieglitz Archives, Collection of American Literature, Beinecke Rare Book and Manuscript Library, Yale Univ. The Woodstock Artists Association and the Woodstock Hist. Soc., both in Woodstock, New York, are good sources of archival information for her years at Byrdcliffe. In 1985 UC exhibited its collection of Watson Schütze's work; curator Jean F. Block's introductory essay in the exhibition catalog, *Eva Watson Schütze: Chicago Photo-Secessionist* (1985), is a good source of information on the artist's life and photography in Chicago. The Renaissance Society's archives are stored on microfilm at the Archives of American Art in Washington, D.C., and include detailed programming and administrative records from Watson Schütze's tenure as the society's president. Jean Fulton culled much of her information from this archive for her chapter, "A Founding and a Focus: 1915–1936," *A History of The Renaissance Society: The First Seventy-Five Years*, ed. Joseph Scanlan (1993), which examines Watson Schütze's role in this organization. There are several major collections of Eva Watson Schütze's photographs. The International Museum of Photography at the George Eastman House in Rochester, New York, has a well-rounded collection of more than fifty prints, including portraits of Thorstein Veblen and William Butler Yeats. UC Spec. Coll. holds about one hundred portraits, mostly of Watson Schütze's Chicago circle of friends and subjects. Other work is located in the private collection of Howard Greenberg/Howard Greenberg Gallery, New York, and in the Philadelphia-based private collection Miller-Plummer Collection of Photography. Many of Watson Schütze's writings on photography and the Photo-Secession were published in the periodicals *Camera Notes, Camera Work,* and *American Amateur Photography* between 1900 and 1904. Reviews of her work also appeared in these publications as well as in *Brush and Pencil.* Francis Benjamin Johnston's series, "The Foremost Women Photographers in America," featured Watson Schütze as one of seven photographers in the *Lady's Home Journal,* September 1901. In addition, brief sketches and references to Watson Schütze can be found in numerous books, including Philadelphia Museum of Modern Art, *Three Centuries of American Art* (1976); Mary Panzer's exhibition catalog, *Philadelphia Naturalistic Photography: 1865–1906* (1982); and Naomi Rosenblum's *A History of Women Photographers* (1994).

KAREN RUBY BROWN

WATTS, MAY PETREA THEILGAARD
May 1, 1893–August 20, 1975
NATURALIST, EDUCATOR, AUTHOR, ENVIRONMENTAL ACTIVIST

May Watts, a pioneer in conservation education and preservation of the natural landscape, was born in Chicago, the third child of four daughters of Hermann and Claudia (Andersen) Theilgaard. Her parents had immigrated and were married in the United States in 1886. Trained as a landscape gardener in Denmark, her father worked with one of Chicago's most famous landscape artists, Jens Jensen, on plantings in the Chicago Park District's public parks, until he suffered a severe sunstroke and had to take an indoor job at a sheet metal stamping factory. Her mother worked briefly outside the house as a maid, then remained a full-time homemaker.

Her father and his knowledge of plants made an initial, powerful impression on May Theilgaard that was to continue throughout her life. Later, she described gardening in the backyard of her childhood home side by side with her father as he taught her the names of plants—sometimes she learned their scientific names before the common ones—as one of her very

FIG. 125. *Naturalist May T. Watts at the Indiana Dunes, 1957.*

earliest memories. Learning and teaching became a common thread for all four Theilgaard daughters. Her sisters went on to become teachers in the Chicago public school system.

Soon after graduation from Lakeview High School in Chicago, Theilgaard took her first teaching job in a one-room schoolhouse in Midlothian, Illinois, when she was seventeen or eighteen years old. She was intent on continuing her own studies. Beginning in 1912, she attended the University of Chicago part-time and, like her two older sisters, financed her college education by concurrently teaching; she taught at grade schools in Arlington Heights, Illinois, and Wilmette, Illinois. Theilgaard traced her choice of college to a childhood ritual with her father, who, on Sunday afternoon walks with the family past the recently built University of Chicago, pointed at the school and said, "One day you will go there" (correspondence from Nancy Watts to Catharine Bell, June 5, 1995). Theilgaard took night and summer courses at the University of Chicago, where she was a student of Professor Henry C. Cowles, a specialist in the emerging science of ecology (then called natural sciences), who

had a profound influence on her career. Cowles's field-trip approach to teaching helped form the foundation for her own teaching trademarks many years later: a dynamic, interactive approach to learning, including hands-on nature hikes.

Theilgaard graduated from the University of Chicago on August 30, 1918, receiving a B.S. degree in botany and natural sciences with election to Phi Beta Kappa. She spent the next few years teaching at her alma mater, Lakeview High School. On December 27, 1924, May Theilgaard married Raymond Watts, a young engineer and aviator who became an enabler and expediter of her work, in addition to pursuing his own full-time career. He was completely supportive of Watts both personally and professionally.

In 1925, Watts returned to school to take classes at the School of the Art Institute of Chicago; she would later illustrate her writings. Watts was also a poet, and that same year, one of her works, "Vision," appeared in an anthology, *The Best Poems of 1925*, selected from British, American, and Irish periodicals. The following year she had Erica, the first of four children, then Nancy (born 1927), Tom (born 1929), and Peter (born 1937 with Down's syndrome, died 1947).

The family's move in 1927 to the developing Ravinia area of Highland Park, a suburb north of Chicago, sparked a decisive turn in Watts's career. All around her, she watched city people flocking to build new homes in this heavily wooded and wildflower-filled parcel of land. They bulldozed their lots and laid long carpets of green grass with no apparent regard for native plantings, resulting in what Watts described as geraniums planted on rectangular graves. She conducted an active campaign to teach her neighbors about the value of Ravinia's natural landscape for the nearly fifteen years her family lived in the area. Watts joined the Friends of Our Native Landscape, a local group that included Jens Jensen, Henry Cowles, and HARRIET MONROE, editor of *Poetry* magazine. In 1936, she wrote and illustrated the booklet, *Ravinia: Her Charms and Destiny*, which had a clear message that Ravinia's landscape must not be destroyed to plant lawns. Watts also lectured about native plantings and natural landscape at local garden clubs, published nature poems, booklets, and, in 1938, a children's book, *My Nature Book: Fun in the Out-of-Doors.*

Watts's lectures and writings caught the interest of a Lake Forest neighbor, Jean Morton Cudahy, daughter of Joy Morton, founder of the Morton Salt Company. Morton, who had a longstanding interest in arboretums, had founded the Morton Arboretum, a place to cultivate trees and shrubs for educational and scientific work, on his property in Lisle, Illinois, in 1922. After working there from 1939 to early 1941 as a part-time teacher of classes for the Garden Club of Illinois, Watts became, in 1942 when she was nearly fifty, the first, and for the next fifteen years the only woman in a professional position hired at the arboretum. For the next two decades she held the title of staff naturalist.

Over the years, her popular, year-round nature classes became a staple at the Morton Arboretum. Watts's class offerings and nature hikes embodied her scientific and creative talents, covering botany, ecology, and geology, as well as gardening, sketching, and poetry. The popularity of these classes was due to Watts's style—her animated storytelling, keen sense of humor, and magnetic personality. She reached thousands of people, from grade school students to families to teachers, inspiring their interest in nature with her charisma, warmth, and genuine fondness for her field. The intellectual grounding for her course came from her scholarship and breadth of scientific knowledge.

Watts made a distinct impression on and generated a devoted following of students, peers, and colleagues. Citing "her forthright sincerity and her deep insight into human nature, as well as the world around her," one journalist concluded that "no one can come in contact with her dynamic individualism for more than ten minutes without gaining a lasting impression" (Towsley, "Naturalist Extraordinary"). In the same article, Watts was physically described: "tall as a man, she has a regal carriage. Her eyes, with their X-ray quality, beget an honesty from those with whom she converses. Wearing tweeds, flat heels, no makeup and a crown of braids, she is striking in appearance."

Watts's arboretum work was significant not only directly, as her educational program became a model for other nature institutions across the country, but also in offshoots of writing and publishing. During her first six years at the arboretum, her writings included more than twenty articles in the *Morton Arboretum Bulletin of Popular Information* and articles in the national magazines *Nature* and *Better Homes and Gardens.*

Her personal and professional life were deeply intertwined. Raymond Watts took photographs for use in her slide lectures. With her husband's and children's strong interest and support, she expertly juggled her family and career by integrating the two, according to her daughter Nancy, by being inexhaustible. Her teaching and lectures and books and many other projects were part of family life. She found ways to let the children help, especially when they were in high school, and made her work seem fascinating and connected to them.

In the 1950s she and her husband established the Nature Study Guild to publish her series of tree, plant, and flower identification keys used in classes. Raymond Watts helped design the keys and handled most of the business end of this successful publishing venture.

At the same time Watts began working at the arboretum, her family moved to nearby Naperville to a house built in 1866. The imaginary evolution of the landscape of this house was the focus of a chapter in her first book, *Reading the Landscape*, published in 1957. The book received favorable reviews in the United States and the United Kingdom, was listed as a Book-of-the-Month-Club publication, and became required reading in university-level biology and ecology classes. Watts also hosted a concurrent series of nature classes on WTTW–Channel 11 entitled *Reading the Landscape.* Raymond Watts assisted by making props for the television series.

In 1961, Watts suffered a severe, temporarily paralyzing stroke. She retired from her full-time position at the arboretum and became naturalist emeritus. The retirement years that followed, which included several years of recovery from the stroke, were among her most productive. In 1963, in a letter to the editor of the *Chicago Tribune*, Watts proposed what became officially, in 1966, the Illinois Prairie Path, an unprecedented, nearly thirty-mile footpath through DuPage County. She led a determined, grassroots movement to turn the Chicago, Aurora, and Elgin interurban railway right-of-way into a nature trail connecting thousands of miles of Forest Preserve District land. "We are human beings. We are able to walk upright on two feet. We need a footpath," Watts wrote in her letter. "Right now the right of way lies waiting, and many hands are itching for it. Many bulldozers are drooling" ("Future Footpath?"). Her vigorous, successful efforts earned her much local and national attention as the founder of the Illinois Prairie Path.

Her husband died in 1966, following pneumonia and a stroke. Throughout the 1960s Watts continued to write, lecture, and teach. Her publications included a children's book, *The Doubleday First Guide to Trees*, numerous articles for local and national publications, and in 1966, a weekly column for the *Chicago Tribune*, "Nature Afoot."

In 1971, inspired by previous travel through Europe, Watts published *Reading the Landscape of Europe*. Under the title, *The Countryside Around Us*, the book was simultaneously published in England. That same year, Watts was selected to help cut a symbolic ribbon with the United States Secretary of the Interior at the opening of the National Trails System in Washington, D.C. There, Watts was given the 1971 National Trails Symposium Award of the U.S. Department of the Interior for her outstanding work in establishing the Illinois Prairie Path. That same year she also received a personal letter of commendation from the President of the United States, Richard M. Nixon.

Watts's achievements were recognized with numerous national, state, regional, and local awards and honors. Highlights included the 1954 Margaret Douglas medal for conservation education, the highest honor of the Garden Clubs of America; the 1963 dedication of the May Watts Reading Garden at the Morton Arboretum; a 1966 citation from the Illinois Parks and Recreation Association; the prestigious 1972 Arthur Hoyt Scott Garden and Horticulture Award, given by Swarthmore College in Pennsylvania for outstanding contributions to the art and science of gardening; and a 1972 citation from the Illinois House of Representatives. Additionally, May 1 was declared May T. Watts Day by the Mayor of Naperville, Illinois, in 1972.

Over the last years of her life, Watts's energy and passion for her work continued. She revised and expanded her first book, *Reading the Landscape*, which was published under the new title of *Reading the Landscape of America* in 1975. She continued to lecture and was at work on a new book when she died at home in her sleep at eighty-two years of age.

May Watts used her creative and scientific talents to teach others to understand, appreciate, and preserve nature, which she loved deeply. Her dedicated efforts were—and still are—instrumental in impacting the perspective of students, colleagues, and people around the world, as well as inspiring interest in the natural landscape of her own suburban backyard of Chicago. In honor of her gifted teaching, the May T. Watts School, an elementary school in Naperville, Illinois, was dedicated in 1989. Her Naperville home, after her death, housed the May T. Watts Society until that organization dissolved in 1996. Watts's tree, flower, and plant identification finder keys are still widely used in nature education programs; after she died, Watts was cremated and her remains buried in the family plot in Naperville. Her son, Tom Watts, took over the successful Nature Study Guild publishing company until his death in 1992. The company continues to operate under his daughter, Bridget Watts, and a reissue of *Reading the Landscape of America* was published in 1999. The Illinois Prairie Path is used by thousands of people each year, and Watts's insistence on valuing native plantings and natural landscape is one of the focal points of the environmental movement in Illinois and the United States. Her books *Reading the Landscape of Europe* and *The Countryside Around Us* remain on travelers' reading lists, while *Reading the Landscape* and *Reading the Landscape of America* were cited in the 1991 *Landscape Journal* by landscape writers, teachers, and designers as among the books that had most influenced their work.

Sources. The May T. Watts Papers and Archives are located at the Library of the Morton Arboretum, Lisle, Illinois. An extensive collection, they contain nearly all of her published works and a bibliography of her publications. The archives also include many of her illustrations, as well as photographs, personal correspondence, biographical information, award brochure tributes, and newspaper articles. The articles include May Watts's letter, "Future Footpath?" *CT*, September 25, 1963, and Genevieve Towsley, "Naturalist Extraordinary," *Naperville Sun*, October 10, 1961. Information on Watts's life and achievements came from correspondence to Catharine Bell from Carol Doty at the Morton Arboretum, May 8, 1995, and from her daughter, Nancy T. Watts, June 5, 1995. Richard A. Thompson, *Around the Arboretum* (1981), provides background.

CATHARINE BELL

WEISS, MARY CATHERINE BISHOP
December 11, 1930–October 8, 1966
MATHEMATICIAN

Mary Bishop, the younger child of Albert and Helen (Mercet) Bishop, was born in Wichita, Kansas, where her father, a West Point graduate and a former army colonel, was in the mathematics department at the University of Wichita. Albert Bishop was forced to leave the army because of the ill effects of having been gassed during World War I. This experience left him in poor health, and he died in 1932 at the age of fifty-one, when his daughter was barely a year and a half old and her brother, Errett Bishop, was four. Helen Bishop, who had been her high school's valedictorian, was deprived of a college education, because she could not afford tuition and there were no scholarships available to her. She trained as a nurse, a profession to which she did not feel well suited. After her husband's death, she and the two children moved to Florence, Kansas, where she had grown up on a farm. When Errett Bishop, who became a brilliant mathematician, entered the University of Chicago at the age of sixteen, the family moved to Chicago.

The University of Chicago gave its undergraduate degrees through the College, an institution founded by President Robert Maynard Hutchins and with a focus on a liberal arts curriculum. After attending the Laboratory School, a primary and secondary school attached to the University of Chicago, for a few years, Mary Bishop entered the College at the university on a scholarship at age sixteen.

At the Lab School and the university, Mary Bishop was drawn to mathematics. She was strikingly beautiful—tall, thin, with an expressive face, fair skin, dark hair, and penetrating eyes. She carried herself with a natural elegance and seemed oblivious of her attractiveness. In the College she met Guido Weiss in a chemistry class, and they quickly became good friends. They received Ph.B. degrees in 1949, and she and Guido Weiss were married one year later. They both became graduate students in mathematics at the university.

At this time the University of Chicago Department of Mathematics was considered by many in the field to be the best in the country. Mathematics was a graduate department, and the students who came from other colleges had previously taken the mathematics courses that were available in a traditional four-year program. The same graduate courses were taken by the graduates of the College, even though they had studied only two mathematics courses designed to give students an overall view of the subject. Along with the competitiveness of the department there was a feeling of camaraderie. Students, including the Weisses, and faculty saw each other frequently at the library, at daily afternoon teas, at lunches on campus, and in other informally organized student activities. Mary and Guido Weiss received M.S. degrees in 1952. Guido Weiss then worked with Professor Antoni Zygmund, a mathematician who made fundamental contributions to the area of harmonic analysis, in whose work both Weisses were interested and whose friendship both enjoyed.

During this period few women majored in mathematics at American universities. Women students who were inclined to mathematics were not likely to be encouraged to enter the field and were often discouraged. Feeling insecure about her mathematical abilities, Mary Weiss went to work for an insurance company. When she was asked to pass actuarial examinations, she took and passed all exams very quickly, in a period of six months. Her supervisors admitted that they had asked her to take the exams only because they thought that she could not do so. After an unhappy year and a half at the job, she left and worked from 1953 to 1955 on a University of Chicago project sponsored by the U.S. Air Force at the Museum of Science and Industry. The work involved problem solving in theory of probability. In 1955, after much persuasion by her husband and Zygmund, who thought very highly of her mathematical abilities, she returned to school as Zygmund's student. She was a "natural mathematician" (Guido Weiss, "Mary Catherine Bishop Weiss," 236), spending long hours, even days, in deep concentration on problems in which she was interested, oblivious of everything else. Mary Weiss received financial support from the university and finished the Ph.D. degree in 1957.

Guido Weiss had already received a Ph.D. and was on the mathematics faculty of DePaul University in Chicago. Mary Weiss joined the faculty there. She was an assistant professor at DePaul from 1957 to 1960. Mary and Guido Weiss were in the same area of mathematics and published articles together on lacunary series. They enjoyed a sabbatical leave in Buenos Aires and Paris in 1960–61. They both sought positions at excellent mathematics departments around the country. Guido Weiss received attractive offers, but Mary Weiss did not get a job offer for a long time. She resented these rejections, because she was aware of her strengths and abilities. Before the 1970s, it was difficult for women mathematicians to be hired by universities. They "found employment mainly at the women's colleges and small liberal arts colleges" (Grinstein and Campbell, x). Finally both obtained positions at Washington University in St. Louis, Missouri.

They moved to Washington University in 1961. Guido Weiss held a position as associate professor with tenure, while Mary Weiss was assistant professor and received tenure in two years. After the move, they separated, although they remained friends after their divorce. In 1963–64 she was visiting associate professor at the University of Chicago, where Professor Zygmund attempted, unsuccessfully, to get her a faculty position. The Chicago mathematics department had had no women on its faculty since 1946. In 1964 Mary Weiss was appointed full professor at DePaul University and spent the year 1964–65 there. She then went to Cambridge University, England, on a National Science Foundation fellowship. She was visiting associate professor at Stanford University in the spring of 1965.

Weiss worked in the area of harmonic analysis. The problems she worked on and her methods were sometimes described as hard analysis. She collaborated with prominent mathematicians. In her joint work and in her individual studies she attacked very difficult and challenging problems.

At the same time she was a devoted teacher, who shared her mathematical ideas with many graduate students. She maintained close ties with the University of Chicago and informally directed the research of several candidates there for the Ph.D. in mathematics.

Concerned with social and political issues, Weiss was active in Adlai Stevenson's unsuccessful campaign for the U.S. presidency in 1956. During the 1960s she supported the civil rights movement as a member of the Congress of Racial Equality; and she supported other related organizations. She also participated in early demonstrations against the war in Vietnam.

Upon her appointment to a professorship in mathematics at the new University of Illinois at Chicago, Mary Weiss returned to Chicago in the summer of 1966. She lived in Hyde Park, her old University of Chicago neighborhood. Weiss seemed to have a bright future ahead. She lived in her favorite city and had a secure position in an up-and-coming department with the promise of a brilliant career. Still, personal problems, anxieties, and bouts of depression, which had plagued her for years, remained. After teaching at Illinois for less than a month, she died of an overdose of sleeping pills at the age of thirty-five.

The proceedings of a mathematical conference at Southern Illinois University held six months after her death were dedicated to the memory of Mary Weiss and included a section of her dissertation research. Professor Zygmund wrote that she contributed "results of considerable and lasting value" (quoted in Haimo, xi) to her field. Her work "made a lasting impact in the fields of harmonic analysis and of real variable" (Haimo, v) and showed an exceptional intuition shared by few mathematicians. Her works are still inspiring to researchers in her field.

Sources. Vera Pless, who recalled her friendship with Mary Weiss at the University of Chicago, provided valuable information. In addition, Vera Pless and Bhama Srinivasan obtained important information in interviews with Guido Weiss on November 4, 1995, and Yoram Sagher on January 15, 1996, as well as from correspondence with Guido Weiss January 12, 1996, and February 26, 1998. Biographical information on Weiss appears in Guido Weiss, "Mary Catherine Bishop Weiss," in *Women of Mathematics: A Biobibliographic Sourcebook*, ed. Louise S. Grinstein and Paul J. Campbell (1987). This sourcebook also provides background information on the status of women in the field of mathematics in the twentieth century. Antoni Zygmund, "Mary Weiss," in *Orthogonal Expansions and Their Continuous Analogues: Proceedings of the Conference Held at Southern Illinois University Edwardsville, April 27–29, 1967*, ed. Deborah Tepper Haimo (1968), provides a discussion of Weiss's mathematical work and a bibliography of her publications; the volume includes an article by Mary Weiss based on her dissertation, "A Theorem on Lacunary Trigonometric Series."

VERA PLESS
BHAMA SRINIVASAN

WELGE, GLADYS
May 23, 1902–July 27, 1976
CONDUCTOR, VIOLINIST, TEACHER

Gladys Welge was born in Chicago, the second of two surviving children of Frederick and Fredericka (Aron) Welge. Her brother, Vernon, was seven years older than she. Although their parents were Chicago-born, both sets of grandparents had emigrated from Germany early in the nineteenth century. The family lived at various locations in Chicago, eventually settling in the Austin neighborhood.

Though neither parent had a college education or musical training, they encouraged both children to succeed in music. When young Gladys Welge was found playing with a box wrapped in string pretending it was a violin, her parents decided that she should have lessons. Welge learned quickly and soon was considered a child prodigy. At the age of nine, she appeared in recitals and concerts throughout the Midwest, giving as many as fifty concerts a year.

When Welge was seventeen, she and her brother opened the Welge School of Music in the family's home. Every room was used for music lessons. The school eventually attracted many students and employed fourteen teachers. Vernon taught piano and Gladys taught violin. She also led the student orchestra, her first conducting experience. In addition to frequent recitals at the school, there were annual recitals in downtown Chicago. Welge was a demanding teacher, who advised parents to discontinue lessons if students showed little effort or interest.

In 1918 Welge enrolled in the Chicago Musical College and, in 1922, earned a Bachelor of Music degree. She studied violin with Leon Sametini, music theory with Felix Borowski and Louis Saar, and conducting with Boston Philharmonic Orchestra conductor Ethel Leginska. For her outstanding violin performance, Welge received scholarships and a diamond medal. In 1924 she earned a Master of Music degree, with a major in violin performance.

In 1925 Welge married Otto Meyer, a clerk, whom she had met at the Lyon & Healy music store in Chicago. Meyer taught cello and tenor banjo at the Welge School of Music. The couple, who had no children, were divorced in 1927. After her divorce, Welge lived with her parents, first on Chicago's West Side, and later in a modest brick bungalow in the suburb of Oak Park, which bordered Chicago and was not far from the Welge School in the Austin neighborhood where Vernon Welge lived with his wife and children. When her mother became ill, Welge nursed her until her death in 1940. Thereafter, Welge lived with her father, caring for him until his death in 1953.

Having demonstrated her outstanding skill as a violinist, Welge was admitted in 1925 to membership in the newly formed

Woman's Symphony Orchestra of Chicago. In 1926 she was chosen as principal second violinist, a position she held for the next twelve years. This orchestra was one of the first of the all women's orchestras in the United States, organized at a time when, except for an occasional harpist, women were not permitted to audition for major orchestras. The board of directors and an auxiliary, fund-raising group were also composed of women. At first, the musicians received little, if any, pay. Later they became unionized and were paid union scale. The reputation of the Woman's Symphony Orchestra grew, and in 1933 and 1934 they performed for thousands at the Century of Progress Exposition.

Welge also served as finance secretary of the orchestra from 1920 to 1935. In 1930, she was named assistant conductor, a position she held for eight years. Her first performance on January 19, 1931, received rave notices from Chicago music critics.

In 1931 Gladys Welge also became affiliated with a Sunday School Orchestra that played for religious services and gave concerts. Under Welge's leadership, this group of thirty amateur and semi-professional players grew to more than seventy-five. In January 1933, the Oak Park Symphony, as it was now called, gave its first performance as a full orchestra, playing major symphonic works. The orchestra soon gained the support of the community. Welge remained active with it for two decades.

In the summer of 1936, Welge conducted the Woman's Symphony Orchestra in six concerts at Grant Park. Reviewing one of these concerts, the *Herald Examiner* reported, "She set herself a difficult assignment, presenting four movements of the *Scheherazade* . . . which are full of pitfalls and traps. This gifted and energetic woman escaped them all" (August 6, 1936). In 1937, her conducting was described as "strikingly forceful" and "dynamic" (*Evening American*, December 14, 1937). At the beginning of the 1938–39 season, Gladys Welge was appointed conductor of the Woman's Symphony Orchestra, replacing EBBA SUNDSTROM. The *Musical Leader* noted that her "authority, sense of interpretation, complete command of all sections of the orchestra" had created an ensemble of merit (January 28, 1939, 12). The orchestra was experiencing difficulties. Welge conducted only the first two concerts of the 1938–39 season. The following year, she was not listed with the orchestra in any capacity, and she never performed with them again.

In 1940, using Gladys Welge as an example, local newspapers countered remarks made in a radio broadcast by music critic Deems Taylor, who said that women conductors could not stand the physical strain and would not receive cooperation from men musicians. In reply, Welge noted that men had made up the greater part of the community orchestra's personnel during most of its life: "I am sure my musicians have no less respect for my knowledge of conducting and musicianship because I am a woman. They accept me as a person" (*Oak Leaves*, April 3, 1943). Welge's statement had originally appeared in an article, "A Civic Symphony Orchestra and a Woman Conductor," one of a series that she wrote for *Music Notes*, a publication of the Illinois Federation of Music Clubs.

Well-known soloists accepted Welge's invitation to perform with the Oak Park Symphony, among them pianists Percy Grainger and Eugene List, and Metropolitan Opera stars Licia Albanese and Helen Jepson. Grainger commented on the orchestra in 1943 that it was the "finest amateur orchestra I have heard. Miss Welge is a genius" (Symphony of Oak Park and River Forest program, April 7, 1944). Gladys Welge herself stated that a conductor should have "a thorough musical education, tremendous physical stamina, teaching ability, leadership and conducting technique," qualifications that must be "intensified for a woman" (*Oak Leaves*, October 13, 1949). Possessing these qualities, she was able to lead the orchestra through the difficult years of the Great Depression and World War II. In 1954, after twenty-two years as conductor of the Symphony of Oak Park and River Forest, Welge retired.

Simply dressed, rather short, her dark hair bobbed, Welge was described as outgoing, pleasant, and gregarious. Possessed with seemingly boundless energy and leadership ability, Welge was active in clubs and musical organizations. She was a charter member and president of the Oak Park Club of Zonta International. She formed Alpha Kappa, a music sorority for women, and belonged to Phi Beta, a national professional fraternity for musicians. Welge was a life member of the Chicago Federation of Musicians and of Organized Women Musicians. While continuing to concertize as a violinist and to teach privately, Welge opened her own music studio in Oak Park in 1941. For two years in the early 1940s, Welge served on the board of directors of the Illinois Federation of Music Clubs. As the state chair for orchestral promotion, she directed the organizing of orchestral groups in schools and towns throughout Illinois. For four years she was the head of the orchestra department in the Downer's Grove, Illinois, public schools. She also taught music at the Avery Coonley School in Downer's Grove for a short time.

In retirement she became Minister of Music at the Fontana Community Church in Fontana, Wisconsin, where she directed music for fifteen years. Welge spent her last years in Laguna Beach, California, where she was Minister of Music of the Neighborhood Congregational Church. She played principal violin with the Riverside Symphony and formed the Laguna Hills String Ensemble, an amateur group.

In 1973, Welge returned to Oak Park for a special award from the Symphony of Oak Park and River Forest as part of a celebration of the fortieth anniversary of the founding of the orchestra. There she conducted a short concert piece. She died of cancer in Laguna Beach at the age of seventy-four. Her body was cremated and interred at Mt. Emblem Cemetery in Elmwood Park, Illinois, next to the graves of her parents.

Gladys Welge played a visible and active role in the musical life of Chicago in the middle years of the twentieth century. At a time when women were just beginning to aspire toward careers as professional musicians and a few women were starting to dream of becoming conductors, Gladys Welge succeeded both as a professional violinist and as an orchestra conductor. Between 1919 and 1938 Welge helped to found a music school in the Austin neighborhood of Chicago; served as principal second violinist, assistant conductor, and conductor of the Woman's Symphony Orchestra of Chicago; and founded a community orchestra in Oak Park that she conducted for twenty-two years.

Sources. Robert Welge, nephew of Gladys Welge, and his wife, Sharon Welge, of Des Plaines, Illinois, provided a written account of the history of the Welge family. The Welges granted an interview, along with their cousin, George Rensch, who had taken lessons from Gladys Welge. Interviews also were obtained from some individuals who had worked with Gladys Welge as musicians or board members: Edith Prescott Crabbe of Maywood, Mildred E. Saliny of Oak Park, and Margery L. Neff of Oak Park. The Chicago Musical College of Roosevelt Univ. has records of Welge's admission and the degrees she earned. A photocopy of the Welge School of Music Catalog, obtained from Sharon Welge, gave information about the school. The programs of the Woman's Symphony Orchestra from 1926–48 are housed at the CHS. The complete programs of the Symphony of Oak Park and River Forest from 1933 to the present can be found at the Hist. Soc. of Oak Park and River Forest. The newspaper *Oak Leaves* is available at the Hist. Soc. of Oak Park and the Oak Park Public Library. Addresses and vital statistics about the Welge family are in Chicago directories of the period and census reports at NL. The CPL's Spec. Coll. yields some random issues of the *Austinite*. For background information on music and musicians of the period, *Étude* magazine and the *Musical Leader* magazine are valuable sources. "Women's Symphony Scores at Auditorium," in *Musical Leader*, January 28, 1939, describes Welge's conducting.

ELIZABETH TITUS REXFORD

WELLES, CLARA BARCK
August 4, 1868–March 14, 1965
SILVERSMITH, ENTREPRENEUR

Clara Barck Welles, founder of the Kalo Shop, a preeminent Chicago arts and crafts enterprise, was born in New York to immigrants John and Margaret (Bowman) Barck. By the late 1890s, when she enrolled in the School of the Art Institute of Chicago (SAIC), the family had moved to a farm in the state of Oregon. Barck graduated in 1900 with a degree in decorative design and joined other SAIC alumnae who were establishing craft studios, including BESSIE BENNETT. Barck opened the Kalo Shop in downtown Chicago near Bennett's silver shop. "Kalo" was an adaptation of the Greek word for beautiful. Barck was a proponent of the Arts and Crafts movement, a reform effort with origins in England. Advocating the abandonment of industrial production methods for a return to hand craftsmanship, followers of the movement also strove to bring beauty into the lives of ordinary people through the creation of attractive and affordable objects. Barck's approach, from the beginning, was to "enter the all-male arena of the large commercial concern" rather than produce "small articles for a restricted clientele" (Evans, 6).

The Kalo Shop was one of the first shops in Chicago specializing in arts and crafts products that were both beautiful and useful, as reflected in the motto: "Beautiful, Useful, and Enduring." During its first five years, the Kalo Shop produced objects in a variety of media, including burnt leather, textiles, and copper. Barck also began to exhibit her works at the Art Institute of Chicago's (AIC) annual exhibitions of decorative design that started in 1902. Barck was one of several SAIC decorative design alumni exhibiting in what later became known as exhibitions of applied art. The exhibitions were part of the general Arts and Crafts movement in Chicago and helped promote the works of regional artisans as well as the Arts and Crafts philosophy. From 1903 to 1907 Barck's designs were sold at the Kalo Shop's retail store in the Fine Arts Building, a center for artists, musicians, and writers.

Clara Barck married George Welles in 1905. He was a coal merchant and amateur metalworker and encouraged Barck Welles to produce metalwork exclusively. Welles closed her downtown shop and opened the Kalo Art Craft Community in the Welles's home in the Chicago suburb of Park Ridge. In addition to producing handwrought tableware and jewelry in copper and silver, the Kalo Community offered design classes and an apprenticeship program in metalsmithing to both men and women. Clara Welles taught some of the classes, which were attended mostly by women; silversmiths employed in the shop also taught. She initially employed one silversmith and several young women workers, known as "Kalo girls," and designed all of the products herself; she eventually expanded the Kalo Shop staff to twenty-five silversmiths. Welles also hired a number of skilled silversmiths who were Scandinavian immigrants. Although she hired women as full-time designers, generally she controlled the designs in her shop, allowing the younger designers to make new pieces under her supervision.

Welles took an active role in advancing woman suffrage and increasing women's participation in the arts. She headed the publicity committee of the Illinois Equal Suffrage Association. Welles led a musical band of Illinois suffragists in the woman suffrage parade held March 3, 1913, the day before the inauguration of Woodrow Wilson as president of the United States. She was a longtime member of the Cordon Club, an organization of about 550 women artists and art supporters founded in 1915 when the male Cliff Dwellers Club—a prestigious social club for the city's literary and art elite, including Hamlin Garland, Henry Blake Fuller, and Lorado Taft—refused to accept women members or establish a women's division. Welles was a member of the Municipal Art League, a society of individuals and clubs whose goal was the promotion of art in public space and the popularization of works by painters and sculptors. As an employer of immigrants and women, Welles achieved commercial success in her business at the same time that she established fair working conditions and expanded opportunities, a legacy in part of the Arts and Crafts movement's social ideals. Welles encouraged her staff members to improve their talents, and she took an interest in their lives beyond the workplace. At Christmas time, for example, she allowed craft workers at Kalo to produce presents for their families, using as much silver as they wanted.

After a divorce in 1914, Welles closed the Park Ridge training community and reopened the Kalo Shop in downtown Chicago with a first floor storefront salesroom and second floor workshop. The reorganization marked the end of the training community, since the shop became a commercial enterprise without classes and an apprenticeship system. That same year she opened a retail outlet in New York City. This return to an urban setting happened at the start of World War I; the shop faced shortages of both silver and male workers. Welles adapted to the new conditions by transforming the shop's production to small items that could be crafted by her team of designers, women who were already producing much of Kalo's jewelry items. The shop was run almost entirely by women during the war. When the War Department took over the North Michigan Avenue building in Chicago in 1918, Welles moved her business into the Fine Arts Building a few blocks south. The number of artists' studios in the Fine Arts Building made it Chicago's best-known art colony. It was a meeting place for many of the city's most influential women's clubs and organizations as well as a gathering place for writers, artists, and musicians. In 1918 she closed the New York City retail outlet.

In 1921 Welles moved the Kalo Shop to Chicago's Near

FIG. 126. *Silversmith Clara Barck Welles, second from left, with craftswomen in her Kalo Shop, 1914.*

North Side. Business fell off noticeably with this move away from Michigan Avenue. Finally, in October 1936 Welles returned to a more visible location, this time in the Railway Exchange Building near the Fine Arts Building, where the Kalo Shop remained until its closing in 1970.

In 1937 Welles was invited by the Metropolitan Museum of Art in New York City to submit representative pieces for an exhibition of contemporary design. The critics found the pieces "freshly creative," "definitely her own," and "emphatically American" (quoted in Darling, 55).

Welles retired to San Diego, California, in 1940, retaining ownership of the Kalo Shop. There she devoted time to the Travelers Aid Society and to the American Red Cross. In 1959 she transferred the Kalo Shop to four of her employees—Robert R. Bower, Daniel P. Pederson, Yngve Olsson, and Arne Myhre. The shop remained in operation until July 31, 1970, when it closed following the deaths of two of the four owners. Welles had died of natural causes in San Diego five years earlier. Her remains were cremated.

Welles owned the leading craft shop in silver and jewelry in Chicago for much of the twentieth century, and her high standards influenced a large community of Chicago metalworkers, many of whom she trained. The Chicago Historical Society mounted a comprehensive exhibit of Kalo silver in 1977. Antique dealers, museum curators, and collectors continue to regard pieces produced by Welles and her employees as some of the finest silver ever made in the United States.

Sources. The extensive Kalo Shop Papers, including many of the shop's working drawings, are at CHS. Kalo silversmith Robert R. Bower's letter to David A. Hanks, January 15, 1971, in the CHS collection, is particularly informative. The Art Institute of Chicago and the CHS have collections of Kalo silver. Useful studies of the Kalo Shop include Sharon S. Darling, *Chicago Metalsmiths: An Illustrated History* (1977); R. Tripp Evans, "A Profitable Partnership," *Chicago History*, Summer 1995. See also Perry R. Duis, "'Where Is Athens Now?' The Fine Arts Building 1898 to 1918," *Chicago History*, Summer 1997, for a discussion of the Fine Arts Building.

KRISTAN H. MCKINSEY

WELLS, DORA
October 4, 1862–April 5, 1948
HIGH SCHOOL PRINCIPAL, VOCATIONAL EDUCATION
ADVOCATE, REFORMER

Dora Wells was born in Montpelier, Vermont, the oldest daughter of Samuel and Mary P. (Leslie) Wells. She attended school in Montpelier, graduating from high school in 1880, and then went to Wellesley College. She received a B.A. degree in 1884. The next fall she began her career in education by teaching Latin, Greek, and chemistry for a year at Montpelier High School. In 1885, when Alice Freeman Palmer, then president of Wellesley, wrote to her about a job in a private school north of Chicago, Wells moved to the Midwest, but the school collapsed financially shortly after her arrival. She found a job as a high school principal in St. Peter, Minnesota, staying three years before going on to a principalship in Corry, Pennsylvania, for a year and a half. Wells then moved to St. Cloud, Minnesota, where in six years she was able to change a very poor school into one rated by the state university as a first-rate high school. Later Wells

FIG. 127. *Girls high school principal Dora Wells standing in front of her automobile, Chicago.*

commented that when she first arrived in St. Peter, she was "no more fit to be a principal of a high school than a kitten" ("Outline," 2), but the enormous expansion of schools to accommodate the settlement of the country required that teachers and principals learn their trade on the job.

Wells desired more education, however, and in 1896 began graduate work in political science and sociology at the University of Chicago, receiving an M.A. degree in 1897. She then taught history and civics for ten and a half years at Medill High School in an immigrant neighborhood on Chicago's Near West Side. She took pride in the fact that a number of her male students went on to successful careers.

In 1908, Wells was one of twenty Chicago high school teachers who were sent to study secondary education in England and Scotland for two months under the auspices of the National Civic Federation. Civic and business leaders as well as educators sought to develop a public school system that could address the needs of an industrial society whose population was largely immigrant or the children of immigrants. There were plans for a more centralized administration of the schools in Chicago, to be run by professionally trained educators; and different groups with interests in the outcome of educational planning debated the kind of education modern public schools should offer. After returning from Great Britain, Wells taught industrial history of the United States at Chicago Normal College from 1909 to 1911. There she was one of a committee of three who organized the "Chicago Course," which was studied by many principals, teachers, and normal school students. Later this course was revised for younger students and was required in the public schools where, in Wells's view, it "was a real stimulus in expanding [city planner Daniel] Burnham's ideal of 'the City Beautiful'" ("Outline," 3).

Wells's career spanned a period of spectacular growth in enrollment in the upper elementary grades and high school. When she began teaching, only 7 percent of American fourteen to seventeen year olds were enrolled in high school; by the time she retired, 51 percent of that age group attended school. This growth was a response to changes in the economy that reduced the demand for child labor, led to increases in family incomes that allowed families to forego children's wages, and promoted expansion in the number of white collar jobs for which high school could provide preparation. High school leaders began to question the value of the traditional academic curriculum, dominated by Latin, for the thousands of students who would not attend college. Assuming that many of the new clients of the high school would end up in industrial jobs, some educational reformers sought ways to make schooling more relevant.

Dora Wells was brought directly into the center of the new movement in 1911 when ELLA FLAGG YOUNG, superintendent of schools for Chicago, asked her to head a new school for girls in the city, a technical high school. Accepting the challenge, Wells implemented this new experiment and until her retirement in 1933, remained principal of the Lucy Flower Technical High School for Girls, named after child welfare leader LUCY FLOWER.

Technical, vocational, or industrial high schools providing training for employment were instituted in most cities during the early years of the twentieth century but were usually limited to boys. In founding Lucy Flower Technical, Ella Flagg Young was seeking to provide for girls an equivalent education to that provided for Chicago boys in the city's two large technical high schools—Richard T. Crane and Albert G. Lane. An equivalent education for girls was inherently problematic, since even innovators in female education assumed that for the vast majority, the long-range goal of women was marriage and homemaking and that work outside the home would be limited to a few years before marriage. Wells and Young knew this situation was not the reality for thousands of women who continued to work after marriage and motherhood. At the same time, the quality and economy of home life seemed threatened by urbanization and industrialization. Putting together these two concerns, Young and Wells came up with two different curricula for the Flower School. The minority of girls who would become teachers or those whose families could afford to keep them at home until they married took a four-year home economics course that included college preparatory work. The majority of girls enrolled in the two-year vocational course, which prepared them for jobs in sewing, dressmaking, and millinery—occupations close to the traditional female household skills.

The school remained heavily committed to this limited conception of women's vocational needs, even though Wells had hoped to prepare girls for work in photography and typesetting, fields in which there was some demand for women workers. Initially these subjects were not taught, nor were stenography and typing, skills that were beginning to provide women with new employment opportunities. After six years, enrollment at Lucy Flower Technical had not increased satisfactorily. A business curriculum was then introduced. Although it produced the desired increase in students, it was unaccountably discontinued ten years later.

The school began with seventy-six students and considerable fanfare in the press. It was, however, located in the old South Division High School building, a location that may have reflected the limitations of the school system's commitment to the idea of a girls' technical school. The South Division building had been abandoned and left vacant when, in the 1890s, construction of an elevated train along its back wall made it impossible to hear over the noise of passing trains. It was, as well, in a slum area. Four years later, obtaining little if any improvement, Lucy Flower Technical moved to the old Carter Elementary School on Chicago's South Side, a building in poor condition, not designed for the vocational courses offered, and overall so small that classes had to be held in portable units on the playground.

Limited facilities, however, did not daunt Wells or a growing band of commuting students who traveled from all over the city to the only public high school girls could choose to attend. A student who commuted from the Near North Side recalled that by the time she neared her destination, the only people on the train were Flower students and teachers. Few teachers or women drove cars at the time, so it was all the more remarkable when Dora Wells arrived from her Hyde Park home in her car.

In her daily life, Wells lived according to Ella Flagg Young's model for professional women who, she believed, should specialize like the men. Women teachers should not attempt to be housekeepers. Wells lived with her sister, Emma, a Wellesley graduate who was also a Chicago public school teacher. Both were tall, spare, elegant women who lived in a large apartment and always had a maid. The maid accompanied Dora Wells to Vermont for the summer vacation. The implication of the professional woman model was that some women should work as housekeepers for others. Initially, Wells thought that courses in domestic science might result in a higher status for women in this field, but this elevation was never realized.

In a different but related vein, Wells advocated domestic science education for presumably middle-class young women who were headed for a lifetime of marriage and family responsibilities but not work outside the home. Wells contemplated an ideal four-year course for such students that would include technical information about running a home. Certain courses were key to Wells's conception of a modern education for the majority of girls: management and use of money; the study of foods and their preparations, emphasizing the nutritional needs of children, adult workers, and the aged; sanitation; laundering; household chemistry; the uses of labor-saving machinery and devices; garment making; and house planning, including the placement of light, ventilation, plumbing, and heating. Other courses in academic subjects, the "worthy use of leisure," facts of sex hygiene, and training in personal ethics and social responsibility were critical because girls "should be made to see that [their] home[s]" were not limited to the walls of individual houses but that for each young woman "her home is the community in which she lives and to it she owes service" ("Fundamentals," 292).

Wells took the radical position that housewives should receive a wage for their labor. "I do not belittle love and devotion and self-sacrifice but I believe that the services of the wife and mother in the home should be clearly defined and be measured by a money standard" ("Fundamentals," 289), she wrote. She reasoned that measuring a woman's work this way would greatly raise the dignity of her service and help to stabilize the wages of women in other fields of labor. To Wells, then, technical education was not synonymous with vocational or job-oriented training. Lucy Flower Technical's mission included training for specific female-related occupations, but Dora Wells held a broader vision of its responsibility to educate the modern woman in the context of a definition of womanhood held by many of the Progressive Era female social reformers. Six years after the passage of the Nineteenth Amendment, Wells concluded that "equality does not mean identity" ("Fundamentals," 289) and that the "essentials" for women were determined by their sex, the factor that "must of necessity always dominate the life work of the majority of women" ("Fundamentals," 289). The challenge for society as a whole, and Lucy Flower Technical specifically, was to educate the girl for her role so well that the higher life of the family and the community would gain by the results.

By the mid-1920s, there were 550 students at Lucy Flower, the vast majority attending for only one or two years and only about one-tenth completing the four-year course. In both the vocational and academic programs, an effort was made to relate one course to another and to make all the work as practical as possible. Wells was particularly proud of the school lunchroom, which was run by students under the supervision of a "household science" teacher. Students planned the menu, did the marketing, prepared and served the food, and kept accounts. On the academic side, French students translated Molière's *Le bourgeois gentilhomme*, the 1924 senior class play. Sewing classes made the costumes, and art classes constructed the sets.

In the 1920s, about one-half of the students were African American, drawn from the black community north and east of the school. As both black and white students remember it, race was not an issue, though outside of school students went their separate ways, divided along the color line. Race relations at

Lucy Flower were unique for their lack of tension at a time when ugly incidents occurred at both Wendell Phillips and Englewood High Schools, where black enrollments grew during the late 1910s and 1920s. Graduates of Lucy Flower credited Wells's leadership with creating an atmosphere in which students felt they were part of an extended family.

In December 1927, Lucy Flower Technical High School finally moved into its new facility, a building across the street from the Garfield Park Conservatory on the city's West Side. By this time, Chicago provided three large well-equipped technical high schools for boys; at last, young women would have their chance too. The new school included rooms full of sewing machines and stoves. Special classes were fitted out for child care and beauty culture, and a dining room and sitting room offered space to practice the kind of entertaining believed to be the goal of middle-class family life. There were, however, no rooms for business machines, typesetting, or photography; there were no athletic fields or swimming pool. Technical education for girls reflected an ideology of traditional sex-role expectations. The school was popular with families looking for an all-girls' school, or an alternative to their neighborhood high school. By the time of Wells's retirement as principal in 1933, the student body numbered twenty-six hundred. The proportion of black students dropped dramatically with the move to the predominantly white West Side, but some African American students continued to attend, mostly commuting from the South Side.

At the end of Wells's career, the school was a genteel place where there were more art teachers than science teachers, where students coming from modest homes were impressed by the refined atmosphere. Wells impressed upon them the virtues of gentility as well as of study and hard work. Enrollment peaked shortly after Wells's retirement, as more and more girls chose to attend their neighborhood schools, which now taught office skills they could use in the growing white collar job market in which they would work before marriage.

The institution Wells had created was not, as she had hoped, the first of many such schools. Its success as a school of home economics was limited to that historical period during which most girls did not aspire to college and many parents were looking for a safe, single-sex school without tuition. In the long run, the need for the school disappeared as opportunities for women as office workers grew, interest in home economics waned, and at the same time, more Catholic families could afford all-girls Catholic schools. Lucy Flower Technical High School had provided an alternative, however. Many African American women in particular used it as a way out of the ghetto and, after World War II, into college.

Wells retired in 1933 at the age of seventy; thereafter she divided her time between the apartment she shared with her sister Emma in Hyde Park and her family home in Montpelier, Vermont. She remained active in education, serving as chair of the Education Committee of the Woman's City Club, as a member of the Citizens Schools Committee, and as head of the Legacy Committee of the Chicago Woman's Club, in which role she influenced the expenditure of the income from the club's Ella Flagg Young legacy on activities helpful to the Chicago public schools. She was awarded an Honorary LL.D. degree from Antioch College in 1935 for her service in secondary education. She died in Montpelier in 1948. Wells's great strength was her conviction that ordinary people deserve a good education and that girls should not be held back for the lack of it.

Sources. Biographical information is available in a typescript, "Outline of Educational Career of Dora Wells," at SL; a typescript is also located in the Lucy Flower Vocational High School. Published works by Dora Wells include "The Lucy Flower Technical High School," *School Review,* November 1914; "Fundamentals in a High School Course for Girls," *Chicago Schools Journal,* April 1926; and "Women as Educators," *Chicago Principals' Club Reporter,* May and June 1939. Numerous newspaper articles in the *CT, Chicago Daily News, Chicago Record-American,* published at the time of the school's founding, at Wells's retirement, and on her death, offer information. A special issue of the Lucy Flower High School newspaper, *Flower Echo,* October 4, 1948, includes many reminiscences. Further information about African American students at the school, based on interviews with eighty students who attended between 1913 and 1972, may be found in Nancy Green, "Remembering Lucy Flower Tech: Black Students in an All-Girl School," *Chicago History,* Fall 1985.

NANCY STEWART GREEN

WELLS, SARAJANE
December 8, 1913–January 10, 1987
RADIO ACTRESS, MUSEUM EDUCATOR

Sarajane Wells had two successful careers spanning forty-five years. As an actress, she was an award-winning star of many early shows during the golden age of radio serials and dramas. As one of the first educational directors of the Chicago Historical Society, she was a pioneer in the field of museum education, creating innovative programs to inform, entertain, and inspire children and adults.

Sarajane Wells was born in Owensboro, Kentucky, the daughter of Clark Lanier and Fern (Van Houtin) Wells. Her mother enthusiastically supported her childhood activities in dance, horseback riding, and acting, while her father, a stern but caring man, traveled the Midwest for the Fairbanks-Morse Scale Company. Ultimately, the family settled on Chicago's North Side, where Wells attended Senn High School. There she studied acting with drama teacher Melita Skillen, who had trained many young Chicago performers. In her last year at Senn, Wells answered a city-wide audition call for a new radio series, *Jack Armstrong, the All-American Boy,* "one of the greatest, longest-running juvenile adventures of all radio, . . . first heard on CBS from Station WBBM, Chicago, on July 31, 1933" (Dunning, 311). Robert Hardy Andrews, creator of the series, fashioned Jack Armstrong as "a super-athlete" (p. 311). Initially, Sarajane Wells was cast as the show's villainess, Gwendolyn Duval. Grateful she was selected, Wells was also surprised when the drama agent handling the auditions promptly took 10 percent of her pay. Unfair as this procedure seemed, it was the Great Depression, and Wells realized there were a hundred women waiting in line to replace her if she protested the rules.

After high school, while working first as Duval and then in the more prestigious role of Jack Armstrong's cousin, Betty Fairchild, Wells studied at the School of the Art Institute of Chicago from 1933 to 1935 and then attended Northwestern University for three years. Her portrayal of Fairchild lasted thirteen years. In the early episodes, the *Armstrong* series setting was Hudson High School, "which may have been named after the actual Hudson High School in Hudson, Minnesota, near Minneapolis" (Wells, 179). Jack Armstrong's athletic exploits were central to the plot, but in subsequent episodes, the plot shifted focus, and Armstrong and his cousins Billy and Betty began traveling the world, finding adventure at every turn.

Through the magic of radio, fifteen minutes a day, five days a week, in separate live broadcasts for the East Coast and the Midwest, plus prerecording electrical transcriptions for the West Coast, the *Armstrong* cast members scratched and clawed their way through jungles in the Philippines, climbed mountains in Tibet, hunted wildebeests on the African veldt, and fought off a seemingly inordinate number of Mongolian "war lords" (Wells, 179). The first director of the show was stern, and there were times, Wells recalled, when she went home crying, only to have her father remind her that "if [she did not] want to quit," she would have to "learn to take direction without tears" (Wells, 181). It was good advice; the director hired her for other roles in another afternoon show.

Systematically building a successful career and expanding into occasional nighttime dramas and commercial work, Wells joined with several of her fellow performers in 1937 to become charter members of the American Federation of Radio Artists (AFRA). She also became a member of the "Bridge Was Up" club, Chicago actors and actresses who, when they missed performances, used the excuse that one of the many movable bridges spanning the meandering Chicago River was in its upright position as they dashed from studio to studio.

On March 2, 1942, Wells married fellow actor Dolph Nelson. They had one child, a daughter, Stephanie. Wells remained with the *Armstrong* show until 1946 but simultaneously appeared as an ingenue in a number of daytime soap operas by the legendary writer, IRNA PHILLIPS. From 1938 to 1946, she appeared on Phillips's *The Guiding Light*, and from 1944 to 1949 on *The Woman in White*. During this period she also found time to appear in Phillips's *The Road of Life* and *The Right to Happiness*, along with brief roles in the popular serials *Ma Perkins*, *Mary Marlin*, and *The Romance of Helen Trent*. Wells felt her work on the soap operas was not as physically demanding as *Jack Armstrong*; for that show she needed to master a number of vocal techniques. The soaps, however, were emotionally stressful. As Mary Rutledge in *The Guiding Light*, or as the leading character, Eileen Holmes, in *The Woman in White*, Wells might be asked to perform the entire broadcast herself, using her voice, interpretation, and delivery to carry the characterization.

Wells's life and career underwent a significant change when, realizing that Chicago was losing ground as a radio production center, she made the decision to move to California to continue her career. Nelson traveled west first, and Wells followed in 1946 when *The Woman in White* show was transplanted to California. Nelson and Wells divorced in 1948. That year Wells began performing regularly in nighttime drama, and in 1949 she was a recipient of a prestigious Peabody Award for her performance in the NBC *University Theatre*'s dramatization of Ernest Hemingway's short story, "The Short Happy Life of Francis Macomber."

Notwithstanding Wells's success, work for actresses in radio began to diminish. Television was making serious inroads into radio's audience, and serial radio programs were dwindling. She did not consider television to be a viable option and returned to Chicago in the early 1950s. For a short time Wells worked in sales at a bookstore. In January 1953, she accepted a position as an associate at the Chicago Historical Society (CHS). Within a year, Sarajane Wells was the director of CHS's Education Department.

Wells's work at the CHS revolutionized the concept of educational programs for the historical society and other museums. In an era when many museums had hardly begun to develop programming for children, Wells made them her top priority and worked to change policies at the CHS. Drawing upon her acting skills and experiences, Wells developed unique and highly successful dramatic programs, hands-on exhibits, and visual tableaus. Under Wells's supervision, costumed performers added visually to the understanding of the lives of midwestern settlers in the museum's Pioneer Gallery. Folk singing, storytelling, and participatory skits entertained kindergarten and first grade children. Multi-screen slide presentations with sound and vocal effects, such as her presentation on the Great Chicago Fire of 1871, brought history to life with intensity and clarity.

An early project by Wells was the development of slide-talk assembly programs for school children. Often written by Wells in collaboration with her associate Fred Gothan, these audiovisual presentations focused on Chicago, Illinois, and American history. In addition to writing the presentations, Wells also functioned as narrator, director, and producer, teaching her staff the subtle nuances she had learned in years of radio performance. Wells also wrote and edited copy for materials that were distributed to Chicago area schools and students in hopes of promoting historical society attendance. Her efforts were successful, and the slide-talk performances more than filled the society's 440-seat auditorium.

Within five years of Wells's taking on a leadership role at CHS, her assembly programs attracted nearly thirty-one thousand students and interested adults to eighty-eight performances scheduled throughout the year. One year later, attendance was more than thirty-five thousand, and there were one hundred presentations. Nearly fifteen thousand students attended the historical society's 631 guided tours and gallery talks in 1958–59. During this period, Wells was struggling with a severe case of asthma that, on occasion, would impair her breathing and leave her seriously weakened. Her enthusiasm and organizational skills and the efficiency of her staff ensured the success of her department's projects. She developed a positive work ethic in her staff that helped them through their busy daily routine; they worked as "jacks-of-all-trades" able at any given moment to produce newsletters, develop scrapbooks, arrange assembly schedules, conduct "Summer Fun" activities, manage field trips, create coloring book competitions, coordinate film showings, and hold history quiz competitions for elementary school students. In addition, Wells promoted the CHS through numerous appearances on local radio and television programs. She also developed volunteer and docent programs, as well as "duo-tours" in the Chicago area, which coupled the Chicago Historical Society with another local museum, the Chicago Academy of Sciences.

Wells worked with other museums and participated in several organizations dedicated to educational programming in historical societies and museums in the Midwest and nationally. In the 1960s, she served as the chair of the education section of the American Association of Museums and was a member of the American National Committee for Education for the International Council of Museums.

Wells also found time to devote to her own Chicago neighborhood, Old Town in Lincoln Park. She chaired the Old Town Art Center (1960–62) and the Old Town Bal Masque (1961–62), a fund-raising event for the Old Town Triangle Association—her local community organization. Wells served on the board for the Triangle Association and for Chicago's Lincoln Park Conservation Association. She created a slide-talk presentation about the Old Town Art Fair, one of Chicago's oldest and most popular outdoor art exhibits. Interested in community improvement, Wells also campaigned to plant crabapple trees and participated in the local Whistle Stop crime prevention program.

In 1976, Wells was diagnosed with Alzheimer's disease. Two years later she stepped down from her position at the CHS and moved into another office in an attempt to organize her files. A year later she left the historical society, her capabilities diminished as the disease progressed. Wells struggled through the final portion of her life. She spent her last days in a nursing home, dying at the age of seventy-three.

Sarajane Wells broke new ground in communications, first in radio, and later in her imaginative approach to displaying and interpreting the American past. The presentations that she developed entertained and informed thousands of people in innovative ways.

Sources. Sarajane Wells's career at CHS can be traced through Education Department "Annual Reports." Joel Steinberg conducted interviews with Sarajane Wells's daughter, Stephanie Quan, on February 27, 1997, and with her CHS colleagues Theresa Krutz and Don Park on March 21, 1996. Information exists about the radio programs in which she performed, but there is minimal material about Wells or her actual performances. The best source is her own article, "Looking Backward: My Life in Radio," *Chicago History,* Fall 1978. Additional references to individual programs can be found in Frank Buxton and Bill Owen, *The Big Broadcast: 1920–1950* (1972); John Dunning, *Tune in Yesterday: The Ultimate Encyclopedia of Old-Time Radio* (1976); and Jim Harmon, *The Great Radio Heroes* (1967).

JOEL STERNBERG

WELLS-BARNETT, IDA BELL
July 16, 1862–March 25, 1931
JOURNALIST, SUFFRAGIST, CIVIL RIGHTS ACTIVIST

Cofounder of the National Association for the Advancement of Colored People (NAACP) and best known for launching the nation's first antilynching campaign from Memphis, Tennessee, Ida Bell Wells was the first of eight children born to James Wells, a carpenter, and Elizabeth (Arrington) Wells, a well-known cook in Holly Springs, Mississippi. Her parents worked for Spires Boling, a contractor and architect, as slaves and then as freed persons until 1867, when a dispute over voting rights prompted James to remove his family and work for himself.

Ida Wells attended Shaw University (later Rust College), established in 1866 by the Freedmen's Aid Society, in Holly Springs. Her self-described "butterfly existence" (*Crusade for Justice,* 16) abruptly came to an end in 1878, when both parents

FIG. 128. *Journalist and clubwoman Ida B. Wells-Barnett led a national antilynching movement as a young woman and continued to speak out against racism the rest of her life.*

succumbed to a yellow fever epidemic, forcing Wells to end her days as a student and teach in a rural school to support her two brothers and three sisters. About 1880, the disposition of the family was such that Wells could accept an aunt's invitation to move to Memphis, Tennessee, where she eventually secured a teaching position in the Memphis public schools.

Wells's activist career began in earnest on September 15, 1883, when, after being forcibly removed from the first-class Ladies Car on the Chesapeake, Ohio, and Southwestern Railway, she won suit against the railroad in the lower courts. (The decision would be overturned in the state supreme court in 1887.) A request to write about the experience for a Baptist weekly, the *Living Way,* marked the beginning of her journalistic career, during which her writings on politics, race matters, and advice columns under the name "Iola" were picked up by the *New York Freeman,* the *Gate City Press* (Kansas City, Missouri), and the *Fisk University Herald* (Nashville, Tennessee), among others. In 1889, the "Princess of the Press," as she was anointed by her colleagues, was elected a secretary of the Afro-American Press Association—the first woman to hold an office in the organization—and became a co-owner of the Memphis *Free Speech and Headlight*, a militant weekly. Two years later, Wells was dismissed from her teaching position after criticizing the school system for its inadequate facilities and instances of exploitative sexual relations between black female teachers and white board members.

Amidst growing racial tension in Memphis, a close friend of Wells, Thomas Moss, president of a black grocery cooperative, was lynched on March 9, 1892, with two other employees, Calvin McDowell and Henry Stewart. When the only arrests made for the crime were enraged black members of the community, she counseled armed self-defense, led a successful boycott of the city's trolley cars, and, in accordance with Moss's last words, encouraged thousands to abandon Memphis for the new territories opening up in the West.

The murders would also transform the journalist into one of the nation's first investigative reporters, as Wells began culling newspaper accounts, visiting sites, and interviewing witnesses to meticulously document that, as in the case of Moss, the growing number of lynchings was due to economic competition and racial "control"—not the oft-claimed charge that black men were being summarily killed for raping white women. Her May 21, 1892, editorial observing that "rapes" were in fact often consensual liaisons between white women and black men, resulted in her newspaper office's being destroyed and threats that she would be lynched herself if found in Memphis.

Wells moved to New York City, where she wrote articles in the *New York Age* on lynching. In October 1892, black women activists from New York, Boston, and Philadelphia, held a testimonial on Wells's behalf and raised money to publish her pamphlet *Southern Horrors*, which documented that of the 728 lynchings between 1884 and 1892, only a third of the victims were even accused of rape, much less guilty of it. The testimonial marked, as Wells noted, "the real beginning of the club movement among the colored women in this country" (*Crusade for Justice*, 81), which culminated in 1896 with formation of the National Association of Colored Women (NACW), the first national black woman's organization in the United States.

In 1893, Wells was invited to the British Isles by Isabelle Fyvie Mayo and Catherine Impey, coeditors of the journal *Anti Caste*, the publication of the Society for the Brotherhood of Man, to talk about lynching. After Wells returned to the United States in 1894, the campaign, widely covered in the British and American press, resulted in the formation of British antilynching committees made up of influential journalists, members of Parliament, and such prominent figures as the Duke of Argyle and the Archbishop of Canterbury. This development in turn spurred stateside attention to the issue, and such Americans as the labor leader Samuel Gompers and Woman's Christian Temperance Union president FRANCES E. WILLARD—despite an earlier confrontation with Wells—lent their names to the cause.

Between trips to England, Wells made an appearance at the 1893 World's Columbian Exposition in Chicago to protest the exclusion of African American contributions to the world and to distribute a pamphlet, *The Reason Why the Colored American Is Not in the World's Columbian Exposition*. It was published with the assistance of Frederick Douglass, who wrote an essay in the pamphlet as did Wells, and of Ferdinand L. Barnett, a widowed

lawyer with militant views, who was the founder of Chicago's first black weekly, the *Conservator*. By the time Wells was on her second tour of England, she was receiving letters of courtship from Barnett, and soon after her return, the two were married on June 27, 1895, in Chicago's Bethel African Methodist Episcopal Church.

A year later, Ferdinand Barnett was named assistant state's attorney and headed the Negro Bureau for the Republican presidential campaign. Also in 1896, the couple began their family with the birth of Charles Aked, followed by Herman Kohlsaat in 1897, Ida Bell Jr. in 1901, and Alfreda Marguerita in 1904. Although the birth of her children forced Ida to recede from the public periodically, compelling suffragist Susan B. Anthony to bemoan her "divided duty" (*Crusade for Justice*, 255), Wells-Barnett still maintained a strenuous schedule. In 1896, though still nursing her first-born, she stumped the state for the Women's Republican State Central Committee (upon its promise to provide a nurse at every stop). In the following year—through the Ida B. Wells Club, established in 1893—she helped establish the first black kindergarten in the city at Bethel Church. The lynching of a black South Carolina postmaster, Frazier Baker, in 1898 sent her, infants in tow, to Washington, D.C., where she was part of an Illinois delegation of civic leaders and congressional representatives who waited on President William McKinley. As one of the group's spokespersons asking for federal intervention, she made "a very clear and able presentation of the case and the President was much impressed by what she said," the Cleveland *Gazette* reported on April 9, 1898. Although the Justice Department took the unprecedented step of going to South Carolina to try the case, little could be done about the refusal of the jury to convict the perpetrators. Some months later, Wells-Barnett traveled to Virden, Illinois, when Governor John R. Tanner refused to give protection to two hundred black strikebreakers whom he characterized as "colored ex-convicts and scalawags" (Springfield, Illinois, *Record*, October 22, 1998). The black men had been shot at by white coal miners, and Wells-Barnett, despite her husband's being a state appointee, publicly criticized the governor and arranged that the men tell their side of the issue at two mass meetings in Springfield and Chicago, respectively.

Although she was sometimes depicted as being too individualistic to work with others, the formation of effective organizations to press protection and protest was important in her activist concerns. She welcomed the establishment of the Afro-American Council in 1898—in which she served as secretary and then as head of the Anti-Lynching Bureau—particularly in the wake of the Wilmington, North Carolina, riot that resulted in the death of several Blacks, the fleeing of thousands more, and the turning out of an interracial coalition of elected city officials. Both Barnetts would stop being active in the Afro-American Council only when Booker T. Washington's allies began to dominate it in 1902. By that time, Wells-Barnett was the most outspoken critic of Washington. As early as 1897, Wells-Barnett had argued that Washington was making a great mistake "in imagining that black people could gain their rights merely by making them factors in industrial life" (*Washington Colored American*, January 7, 1897). Perhaps she was most disturbed by the Tuskegee educator's oft-expressed view that the criminal behavior of Blacks was also responsible for lynching, and his implication that with sufficient funding he and Tuskegee could ameliorate such pathology. Between 1900 and 1904, Wells-Barnett also published views in direct contradistinction to Washington's in mainstream publications, including the *Independent*, *Arena*, and *World Today*.

Ideology was also responsible, in part, for Wells-Barnett's becoming inactive in the National Association of Colored Women, when, after its 1899 convention in Chicago, she unsuccessfully challenged the reelection of then Washington ally Mary Church Terrell as president. It would not be the last time the two prominent activists would cross swords.

In lieu of the other organizations, Wells-Barnett worked with the Equal Opportunity League, founded in 1903 by Chicago anti-Bookerite activists Charles E. Bentley and Edward H. Morris; and she continued to work with Illinois women's organizations, both black and interracial. Wells-Barnett believed that white women activists had an important role to play in terms of community uplift in general and lynching in particular, and therefore that it was important that black women "emancipate" their white sisters from prejudice. Wells-Barnett had longstanding memberships in the Illinois Equal Suffrage Organization and the Chicago Political Equality League. Although she was critical of JANE ADDAMS's views about lynching, Wells-Barnett made common cause with her on numerous occasions. In 1903, for example, she enjoined the Hull-House reformer to lead an interracial group that successfully put an end to pro-school-segregation articles in the *Chicago Tribune*.

Wells-Barnett served as vice-president of the Frederick Douglass Center established by CELIA WOOLLEY, a white Unitarian minister, writer, and settlement house worker. Wells-Barnett organized black women to help fund the center, and, Woolley, after some difficulty in finding a site where the owner would permit Blacks to meet, eventually found a building on Chicago's South Side. Subsequently, Woolley moved her own family into the center, which became the locus of black and white civic leaders who provided recreational and instructional facilities for young people, as well as of a forum for educational lectures and political speakers. By 1906, Chicago clubwoman FANNIE BARRIER WILLIAMS boasted that there were between three and four hundred black and white members, both women and men, as well as a woman's club, established the year before, numbering seventy women. On several occasions, Woolley and other white woman reformers of the center showed their courage when they refused to be intimidated by articles in the daily press denigrating the interracial teas that featured "White women and Negresses" (*Voice of the Negro*, December 1904). Nevertheless, the disaffection of Wells-Barnett began with the presumption on Woolley's part that a white woman should preside over the center's woman's club, then reached a climax when the president, Mary R. Plummer, implied that black criminality was largely to blame for the bloody Atlanta race riot of 1906. Similarly, Woolley probably showed evidence of a similar point of view, one revealed in her telling Booker T. Washington allies in Chicago that she thought W. E. B. Du Bois's poignant elegy, "The Litany of Atlanta," written in response to the violence, was "sickening" (S. L. Williams to Emmett J. Scott, October 22, 1906, Booker T. Washington Papers).

Of personal concern that year was her husband's unsuccessful campaign to become the first Black elected to a municipal judgeship. At first count, with the support of Chief Judge Harry Olson, and a brilliant record as states attorney, it appeared that he had eked out a narrow victory despite a virulently racist reaction to his candidacy. But the demand for a recount resulted in the finding that he had in fact lost by 304 votes out of a total of 200,000 cast. Wells-Barnett bitterly pointed out that the decisive reason for the margin of defeat was the antipathy of black ministers whom she had earlier antagonized and, though she does not mention it, who were also loyal to other factions of the party.

Subsequent issues in Chicago, such as the failure to stop a showing of Thomas Dixon's racist play *The Clansman* in the city's theaters despite the effort of Jane Addams, and nationally, such as the unjust dismissal of black soldiers after a riot in Brownsville, Texas, helped make the Springfield, Illinois, riot of 1908 a proverbial "last straw." Precipitated by a white woman's accusation of rape (later recanted), it resulted in the lynching of two Blacks and the deployment of five thousand militia to restore order. The Springfield riot held special significance. Although there had been such violence in the North before—including two 1903 lynchings in Belleville and Danville, Illinois, respectively—that this one took place in the home of Abraham Lincoln would awaken a neoabolitionist sentiment in the Northeast that challenged the accommodationist strategies of Booker T. Washington. In Illinois, a black legislator, Edward Green, was able to pass a bill that stipulated the removal of any law enforcement official who did not make adequate efforts to prevent the illegal removal of a prisoner under his "protection." The riot also led Wells-Barnett to organize the Negro Fellowship League in September 1908. The first meetings of the league were held in her home and were attended by young men from her Bible class at Grace Presbyterian Church.

Her hopes for an effective national organization to achieve equal rights for Blacks were no doubt buoyed by the "Call," which appeared in February of 1909 and called for a conference of progressive activists to be held in New York City. The author of the circular, which was distributed across the country, was Oswald Garrison Villard, son of the abolitionist William Lloyd Garrison and publisher of the *New York Evening Post*. According to Mary White Ovington—the New York settlement house worker who was a catalyst for the formation of what became known as the National Association for the Advancement of Colored People (NAACP)—eight Chicagoans signed the "Call." The group included three women: Jane Addams, who would later preside over the Chicago branch of the organization; MARY McDOWELL, the University of Chicago Settlement director; and Wells-Barnett, who was also the only African American in the city to respond to this first appeal. In May, Wells-Barnett attended the first conference, where she gave an address later published as *Lynching: Our National Crime*, which called for the implementation of a federal antilynching law.

Although the NAACP would subsequently take Wells-Barnett's lead and make lynching the focus of its concerns, Wells-Barnett's relationship with the civil rights organization was troubled from the beginning. Writing about the first meeting, W. E. B. Du Bois, the only black officer of the group, described a woman, undoubtedly Wells-Barnett, who, during the deliberations, jumped to her feet and exclaimed that their white supporters were being treacherous. Subsequently, Du Bois dropped her name from the "Founding Forty" list of the organization, explaining that he wanted to replace it with Charles Bentley's name, since he thought Wells-Barnett could be "represented" by Celia Parker Woolley of the Frederick Douglass Center. After the adverse reaction to Wells-Barnett's exclusion—particularly that of John Milholland, businessman and founder of the Constitution League, who volunteered to resign so that she might be put in his place—she was restored to the list and named a member of the executive committee. She spoke at the NAACP's meeting in May 1910, which formalized the organization. She also convinced the board to authorize her and Frances Blascoer, the secretary of the organization, to attend the National Association of Colored Women meeting in Louisville, Kentucky, to talk about the NAACP. Although her first appearance at an NACW conference in almost a decade met with enthusiastic applause at the beginning, Wells-Barnett's decision to call for a resolution to make the editor of the National Notes, the NACW organ, an elected instead of a perpetual office, elicited much vocal disapproval. The editor of the publication was Margaret Murray Washington, wife of Booker T. Washington. By the following year, Wells-Barnett complained of being excluded from the counsels of the NAACP and attenuated her relationship with it.

Wells-Barnett was more appreciated on other fronts. Between the two NAACP meetings, she had traveled to the scene of the lynching of "Froggie" James in November 1909 by a mob in Cairo, Illinois. There she was able to mobilize the support of reluctant black local leaders and successfully argue the legal case to deny Cairo's Sheriff, Frank Davis, from being reinstated by then Governor Charles S. Deneen, in accordance with the antilynching law passed after the Springfield riot. Understanding the important principle behind Wells-Barnett's achievement, the Chicago *Defender*, February 19, 1910, praised her as "the race's greatest advocate," and another black newspaper, the Springfield *Forum*, though lamenting that a woman was doing the work "naturally presumed to be that of the men," characterized Wells-Barnett as "the heroine of her age" and concluded that "the nation is better off for her having lived in it" (*Forum*, December 11, 1909).

The following year, it was Wells-Barnett who first alerted the community and served as liaison to Oswald Villard regarding the plight of Steve Green, an Arkansas tenant farmer who, after killing his landlord in self-defense, fled to Chicago. In August 1910, he was betrayed by an acquaintance, and a group of community leaders was able to prevent his extradition to Arkansas, where he faced certain death. For her role in the Green case, the Chicago *Defender* described her as "that watchdog of human life and liberty" (September 24, 1910).

When it became necessary for Green to hide from authorities, he found refuge in the new headquarters of the Negro Fellowship League located on South State Street. Wells-Barnett was able to acquire the space as a result of a public appearance in which she talked about the exclusionist policies of the Young Men's Christian Association (YMCA) and the need for an uplifting institution. After the speech, she was approached by Jessie Lawson, wife of *Chicago Daily News* publisher and YMCA

benefactor Victor Lawson, who agreed to fund a reading room. The three-story Negro Fellowship League building, which opened on May 1, 1910, was subsequently also used to lodge homeless men and provide job placement services; it also became the site for a number of black women's organizations, including the Ideal Woman's Club, of which Wells-Barnett was, in that year, listed as president.

One of the concerns of the club was woman suffrage; in the same year, Wells-Barnett founded the Women's Second Ward Republican Club, the stated purpose of which was "to assist the men in getting better laws for the race and having representation in everything which tends to the uplift of the city and the race" (*Broad Ax*, April 9, 1912). Meetings featured both black and white suffragists, and attendance reached two hundred. The timeliness and popularity of the suffrage organization was due, in part, to the burgeoning black population of the 2nd Ward, which in 1910 made up 25 percent of the 42,801 population and in five years would grow to 40 percent of the 63,342 residents in the ward. The group also reflected a new phase of the woman's suffrage movement that saw such organizations proliferate among Chicago's ethnic and working-class women.

Anticipating Illinois's becoming, in 1913, the first state east of the Mississippi to grant women the vote for presidential electors and township officials, Wells-Barnett organized the Alpha Suffrage Club in January of that year. The club, Illinois's first black woman's suffrage organization—and also the first to hold meetings in Bridewell prison for the edification of female inmates—soon grew to a membership of two hundred women. Wells-Barnett, with money raised from the club, went to Washington, D.C., to attend the National American Woman Suffrage Association's parade in March 1913—only to discover that the national organizers, for fear of alienating southern white suffragists, did not want Blacks to march. Refusing to accede to such a demand, Wells-Barnett waited for the parade to begin, then suddenly materialized from the crowd and determinedly took her place amidst the other Illinois suffragists. On either side of her were two supportive white members of the contingent: Belle Squire, who had helped Wells-Barnett organize the Alpha Suffrage Club, and Virginia Brooks, the acknowledged leader of the younger suffragists.

Back in Chicago, the Alpha Suffrage Club prepared for enfranchisement by using the block system to canvass the predominantly black wards to get women registered to vote in the aldermanic primary held February 1914. Although during the canvass the women were in some cases met with jeers and sarcasm, Wells-Barnett told them not to be intimidated and encouraged them to return to the neighborhoods. By the time of the election, three thousand women were registered in the 2nd Ward, and when their support for a black independent in lieu of the regular machine candidate nearly resulted in the latter's defeat, they got the attention of the political establishment. The near miss prompted the black Republican Oscar De Priest and the ward organization president, Samuel Ettleson, to promise the women that if they voted for the party regular, the Republicans would fill the next vacancy with a black candidate. True to their word, De Priest was nominated for the aldermanic seat for the following year, as were two other black candidates from other factions. Refusing to split the black vote, which would result in the election of a white Democrat, the Suffrage Club members had all three candidates come before them to seek their endorsement. They chose De Priest, and, on February 27, 1915, he won the Republican primary and subsequently became the first black alderman in the history of Chicago. De Priest praised the women's work and acuity that had given him a three thousand vote margin in a field of five. In return, Wells-Barnett had hoped that De Priest would support her husband, who was then in private practice, when he sought the judgeship again.

That Wells-Barnett was not attuned to the new era of machine politics was evident when, at the height of her political influence, she switched her support from the successful mayoralty candidate, William Hale Thompson—for whom she had been actively campaigning in the 1915 election—to Judge Harry Olson. The latter, like Ferdinand Barnett, belonged to the progressive wing of the Republican Party and had not only supported Ferdinand's candidacy but, with the termination of Lawson's financial support of the Fellowship League, had come to Wells-Barnett's aid. The judge had augmented Wells-Barnett's income by appointing her, in 1913, as an adult probation officer in the municipal courts, the first such appointment given to a person of color. The meaning of such monies to the Barnetts was evident in their legal and personal support for numerous individuals for whom they appeared before pardon boards, obtaining commuted sentences and even releases from prison. One of the most publicized cases, begun in 1915, was that of Joe Campbell, a Joliet prisoner accused of setting a fire that killed the warden's wife. While Campbell was awaiting execution, Wells-Barnett, convinced that his confession had been obtained by coercion and that he was innocent, took Campbell's case. She and her husband spent the next three years and much of Ferdinand Barnett's professional and personal resources to take the case all the way to the Illinois Supreme Court. In the end, Campbell's death sentence was commuted to life imprisonment.

The Barnetts' loyalty to Olson, despite his late and politically disastrous entrance into the race, resulted in Wells-Barnett's losing her appointment as an adult probation officer. The Negro Fellowship League was forced to move into smaller quarters. Although the struggle to keep it open was made even more difficult by competing organizations like the black YMCA and the Urban League, the Negro Fellowship League continued to be a base, until 1920, from which Wells-Barnett would meet the new challenges of the postwar years.

Coinciding with the death of Booker T. Washington in 1915 and the showing of D. W. Griffith's salacious film *Birth of a Nation*, the migration of African Americans—urged on by oppressive economic and social conditions in the South and job opportunities in the North—became, as one historian described it, "a mass movement" (Spear, 129). In Chicago alone, fifty thousand mostly poor, mostly uneducated Blacks made their way to the city's South Side between 1916 and 1919. The consequent racial upheavals found Wells-Barnett responding as she had in the past. In the immediate wake of the East St. Louis "massacre," where between fifty and one hundred Blacks were killed, Wells-Barnett, braving police barricades, traveled to the city, where she gathered first-hand information, published the victims' side of the story, and subsequently attacked the states attorney for fo-

cusing primarily on indictments against Blacks. In 1918, with little support from her more cautious peers, she determined to memorialize black soldiers in Houston, Texas, who had been courtmartialed and hung for firing on the city in response to white harassment. She passed out "Martyred Soldiers" buttons despite warnings from the Justice Department that she could be arrested under the new Espionage and Sedition laws. She implored Chicago city authorities—who had done little about the twenty-six bombings of the last two years aimed at black residences in once all-white neighborhoods and their realtors—"to set the wheels of justice in motion before . . . Chicago would be disgraced by some of the bloody outrages that have disgraced East St. Louis" ("Voice of the People," *Chicago Tribune*, July 7, 1919). Her words were a harbinger of things to come. Three weeks later in Chicago, the stoning and drowning of a black boy for swimming in a contested "white area" of Lake Michigan precipitated three days of violence that resulted in the death of 23 black and 15 white individuals and injuries to another 537 persons. In this case, she ended her participation in the Protective Association led by ministers and other civic leaders when they insisted on asking the same attorney general whom Wells-Barnett had criticized in East St. Louis to take over the Chicago investigations.

By this time, Wells-Barnett had cast her fate with more radical organizations, such as the National Equal Rights League, headed by journalist Monroe Trotter, and Marcus Garvey's Universal Negro Improvement Association (UNIA). In 1918, she was elected a UNIA delegate to the Versailles Peace talks held at the end of World War I in Paris, France. However, she was now marked as "a far more dangerous agitator than Marcus Garvey" by the Justice Department and denied a passport (Hill, 329).

A year after the Chicago riot, Wells-Barnett, amidst criticism that her activism undermined efforts by both local and national organizations such as the NAACP and the Urban League, was forced to close the Negro Fellowship League. In that year, she also became ill, and after being hospitalized, wondered, in her autobiography, if it was time to look out for her own personal interests instead of those of the race, which had drawn so much criticism and so little financial support. Perhaps her final answer was reflected in the last decade of her life. A year after she was hospitalized, Wells-Barnett went undercover to Little Rock, Arkansas, where she interviewed black union members sentenced to be executed for killing white persons in self-defense. Her articles on the men were published at a crucial time in the legal proceedings, which eventually led to commuted terms and the freeing of the men. In 1924, she was defeated by Mary McLeod Bethune for the presidency of the NACW. In the mid-twenties, she and other progressive black Illinois clubwomen supported A. Phillip Randolph's effort to unionize Blacks in his Brotherhood of Sleeping Car Porters and Maids, which went against the grain of most of Chicago's black leadership. In 1929 she was head of the Conference of Women's Republican Clubs, and in 1930 she ran, unsuccessfully, for a state senate seat as an independent.

At age sixty-nine, after a brief illness, Ida B. Wells-Barnett died of uremia, a kidney disease, at Dailey Hospital, Chicago, and was buried at Oak Woods Cemetery. Nine years later, as a result of an intensive campaign conducted by women's clubs and civic and social organizations, the Chicago Housing Authority changed the name of South Parkway Garden Apartments to the Ida B. Wells Garden Homes.

Sources. The Ida B. Wells Papers, including her diary, are in UC Spec. Coll. The Chicago Woman's Club records are at the CHS. Correspondence in the Booker T. Washington Papers, Library of Congress, has material about Wells-Barnett. The primary source of information on Ida B. Wells-Barnett's life is *Crusade for Justice: The Autobiography of Ida B. Wells* (1970), edited by her daughter, Alfreda Duster. Articles by Wells-Barnett were published in *New York Age*, the Chicago *Inter-Ocean*, the Chicago *Conservator*, and the *Independent*. Selected works by Wells-Barnett include "Afro-Americans and Africa," A.M.E. *Church Review*, July 1982; *On Lynchings: Southern Horrors* (1892); "Booker T. Washington and His Critics," *World Today*, April 1904; "How Enfranchisement Stops Lynchings," *Original Rights Magazine*, June 1910; "Lynch Law in All Its Phases," *Our Day*, May 1893; *The Reason Why the Colored American Is Not in the World's Columbian Exposition*, with Frederick Douglass, I. Garland Penn, and Ferdinand L. Barnett (1893); *A Red Record* (1895); "Lynch Law in America," *Arena*, January 1900; "Lynching and the Excuse for It," *Independent*, May 16, 1901; *Mob Rule in New Orleans* (1900); "The Negro's Case in Equity," *Independent*, April 26, 1900; "Our Country's Lynching Record," *Survey*, February 1, 1913; *The Arkansas Race Riot* (1922). Reports about Wells-Barnett's activities include untitled newspaper articles in the Cleveland *Gazette*, April 8, 1898; *Washington Colored American*, January 7, 1897; *Voice of the Negro*, December 1904; and the article, "Voice of the People," *CT*, July 7, 1919. Bettina Aptheker, ed., *Lynching and Rape: An Exchange of Views by Jane Addams and Ida B. Wells* (1977), includes Hull-House's head resident's views. Elisabeth Lasch-Quinn, *Black Neighbors: Race and the Limits of Reform in the American Settlement House Movement, 1890–1945* (1993), has an analysis of the mainstream settlement movement's relationship to Blacks, including a discussion of Jane Addams and Louise deKoven Bowen of Hull-House. Anna Massa, "Black Women in the 'White City,'" *Phylon*, Winter 1965, discusses the race issue and the politics of white clubwomen and black clubwomen during the World's Columbian Exposition. Works on black clubwomen include Elizabeth Lindsay Davis, *Lifting as They Climb* (1933) and *The Story of the Illinois Federation of Colored Women's Clubs* (1922); Stephanie J. Shaw, "Black Club Women and the Creation of the National Association of Colored Women," *Journal of Women's History*, vol. 33, 1991; Deborah Gray White, "The Cost of Club Work, the Price of Black Feminism," in *Visible Women: New Essays on American Activism*, ed. Nancy A. Hewitt and Suzanne Lebsock (1993); Anne Meis Knupfer, *Toward a Tenderer Humanity and a Nobler Womanhood: African American Women's Clubs in Turn-of-the-Century Chicago* (1996). Selected books and dissertations about black women in American history that include information on Ida B. Wells-Barnett are Paula Giddings, *When and Where I Enter: The Impact of Black Women on Race and Sex in America* (1984); Dorothy Sterling, *Black Foremothers: Three Lives* (1979); Mildred I. Thompson, *Ida B. Wells-Barnett: An Exploratory Study of an American-Black Woman, 1893–1930*, vol. 15 of *Black Women in United States History*, ed. by Darlene Clark Hine, Elsa Barkley Brown, Tiffany R. L. Patterson, and Lillian S. Williams (1990); Emilie Maureen Townes, "The Social and Moral Perspective of Ida B. Wells-Barnett as Resources for a Contemporary Afro-Feminist Christian Social Ethic" (Ph.D. diss., Northwestern Univ., 1989); Rosalyn Terborg-Penn, "Afro-Americans in the Struggle for Woman Suffrage" (Ph.D. diss., Howard Univ., 1977); Karen M. Mason, "Testing the Boundaries: Women, Politics, and Gender Roles in Chicago, 1890–1930" (Ph.D. diss., Univ. of Michigan, 1991); Wanda Hendricks, "The Politics of Race: Black Women in Illinois, 1890–1920" (Ph.D. diss., Purdue Univ., 1990). Works on the history of Blacks in Chicago include Charles Branham, "Black Chicago: Accommodationist Politics before the Great Migration," in *The Ethnic Frontier: Group Survival in Chicago and the Midwest*, ed. Melvin Holli and Peter d'A. Jones (1977); St. Clair Drake and Horace R. Cayton, *Black Metropolis: A Study of Negro Life in a Northern City* (1945); Allan H. Spear, *Black Chicago: The Making of A Negro Ghetto 1890–1920* (1967); Beth L. Bates, "The Unfinished Task of Emancipation: Protest Politics Come of Age in Black Chicago, 1925–1943" (Ph.D. diss., Columbia Univ., 1997). See also Robert A. Hill, ed., *The Marcus Garvey and Universal Negro Improvement Association Papers* (1983), and the articles in the Springfield, Illinois *Record*, October 22, 1898, and *Broad Ax*, April 9, 1912.

PAULA J. GIDDINGS

WENDT, JULIA BRACKEN
June 10, 1871–June 22, 1942
SCULPTOR

Julia Bracken, born in Apple River, Illinois, was the twelfth of thirteen children. Her parents, Andrew and Mary (McNamara) Bracken, were of Irish descent. Andrew Bracken is said to have worked on the railroad, but not much is known about him. The Brackens moved to nearby Galena, Illinois, soon after Julia Bracken was born. Details about Julia Bracken's formal education are hard to ascertain. However, it is clear where she learned and nurtured her artistic skills. Mary Bracken was supportive of her daughter's artistic endeavors at an early age. Bracken would make lizard, toad, and turtle figurines out of bread dough when her mother did the weekly baking. When baked, these figures became distorted and Bracken would be disappointed. However, Bracken soon discovered that the red clay found near her childhood home was perfect for sun drying. Bracken turned to creating clay figures that she would proudly present to her mother.

When Bracken was nine years old, her mother died. Bracken's older sisters, now busy taking care of the family, were not pleased to have Bracken playing in the mud and bringing her treasured figures into the house. In response, Bracken enthusiastically took up carving figures out of wood. As embellishment, Bracken rubbed the dye off the wallpaper in the living room to color the faces of her figures. Bracken's sisters noticed the wallpaper was fading more than it should have and put an end to Bracken's artistic pursuits.

Not receiving the support she needed, Bracken ran away from home at the age of thirteen. Later in life Bracken was reluctant to speak of this episode. In retrospect, she felt she had been too critical of her family, yet she had needed the freedom to become an artist. To earn a living, Bracken, who was barely past her own childhood, became a domestic in the home of Alice B. Stahl of Evanston, Illinois. Fortunately, Stahl recognized Bracken's talent and encouraged her. By the age of sixteen Bracken had earned her first commission as an artist. She carved the wooden pulpit at the Evanston Congregational Church.

Stahl paid Bracken's tuition so the aspiring artist could enroll at the School of the Art Institute of Chicago (SAIC). In 1887, Bracken began to study art under Lorado Taft at SAIC; soon she became an assistant in his studio. Taft supported women sculptors in his classroom as well as in his studio, and it was in Taft's studio that Bracken met sculptor BESSIE POTTER VONNOH.

Construction of the "White City"—the palatial exhibition halls and settings for the 1893 World's Columbian Exposition in Chicago—created many opportunities for American artists. Lorado Taft was influential in giving women artists opportunities to work on the sculpture and decoration needed in abundance at the exposition. Taft, commissioned to decorate the Horticultural Building, approached Daniel Burnham, the architect of the White City, and asked if he could hire women sculptors to assist him. Burnham's oft-quoted reply was that Taft could employ anyone capable of doing the work, even white rabbits. These "White Rabbits"—Janet Scudder, Carol Brooks, Enid Yandell, Bessie Potter Vonnoh, and Julia Bracken—formed a close bond. They rented a hotel room near the fairgrounds where they all lived together. As sculptor Janet Scudder describes, "It was a wholesome, happy, stimulating life" (Scudder, 58–59).

In addition to working on Taft's commissions, the White Rabbits were encouraged to seek independent commissions, which many of them, including Bracken, received. Although Bracken did not receive a commission for the much sought after Woman's Building, she was commissioned to do *Illinois Welcoming the Nation,* now permanently on exhibit in the Illinois state capitol in Springfield. Bracken also was commissioned to do *Faith,* one of six figures for the interior of the exposition's Illinois State Building.

By this time Bracken had reunited with her family and was caring for her father, who was terminally ill, and the orphaned children of one of her sisters, who had died. One reporter later wrote that "she gathered [the children] in and devoted her life to them" (James, 8). Although busy, Bracken still had time to fall in love. Bracken met painter William Wendt in 1893 when they lived down the hall from each other in Chicago. A German immigrant who had arrived in America at age fifteen, he was a self-taught painter attracted to Southern California landscapes. His work, *Montecito,* was shown at the Art Institute of Chicago (AIC). After their first meeting, Bracken immediately took a liking to Wendt but was determined to devote herself to her career and to the care of her nieces.

Bracken established her own studio in downtown Chicago, undertaking commissions such as *Monument to the 19th Illinois Volunteer Infantry* in 1897 for a Civil War monument in Chattanooga, Tennessee. In 1901, Bracken received recognition for her bas-relief *The Modern Prophets.* The reliefs, which included members of the Arts and Crafts movement, Leo Tolstoy, John Ruskin, and Thomas Carlyle, showed Bracken's connection to the Arts and Crafts movement in Chicago. Bracken became a leading figure in the Bohemia Guild in Chicago, a workshop following the precepts of the Arts and Crafts movement that was affiliated with the Industrial Art League. The Guild, located in downtown Chicago, was led by professional artists, including Julia Bracken, bookbinder Gertrude Stiles, and hand printer Frederic W. Goudy. It ran a school of Industrial Art and Handicraft in conjunction with the women's auxiliary of the Industrial Art League, which was a gathering place for individuals dedicated to the ideas of Carlyle, Ruskin, and William Morris, whose images in carvings by Bracken decorated the school.

In 1903, Bracken was appointed a staff sculptor for the Louisiana Purchase Exposition in St. Louis, Missouri, which was inaugurated the following year. Bracken was the only woman appointed to the staff; moreover, she was the only woman to have sculpture displayed in the exposition. Her most important commission was that of a statue, *James Madison,* the fifth president. True to Bracken's style, this sculpture portrayed James Madison very simply, pointing to the intersection of the Mississippi River and the Missouri River on a globe. One reviewer said of Bracken's contribution to the fair, "Her work honors woman; more, it honors sculpture" (Maxwell, 277).

When William Wendt moved to Los Angeles, California, in 1906, Bracken reconsidered her position on marriage. Deciding they could not live apart, Julia Bracken married William Wendt in 1906, and together they moved to the West Coast to pursue their careers. Many artists and critics, including Taft, felt that by leaving Chicago, Bracken Wendt was putting her husband's career before her own. On their arrival in California, the Wendts purchased a studio on Sichel Street. It had belonged to another California artist couple, Marion and Elmer Wachtel. Julia Bracken Wendt built the cabinetry and shelves and constructed her own armatures. She began the process of building a new reputation as a sculptor in California while maintaining her connections with the art world in Chicago. In 1908, Bracken Wendt spent the entire summer at work in Chicago. She completed several commissions, including a bronze tablet commemorating department store merchant and philanthropist Marshall Field for the Field Museum of Natural History, of which he was the major patron. She did a life-sized marble bust of Chicago physician and suffragist SARAH HACKETT STEVENSON, presently on display in one of the American art galleries at AIC.

In 1909, Bracken Wendt created a medallion for the Chicago Society of Artists. Emblazoned across the top of the medallion was the word "art," indicating that art was the highest of all human endeavors. The same year, AIC mounted a joint exhibit of the Wendts' works. William Wendt exhibited forty California landscapes, and Bracken Wendt exhibited sixteen plaster sculptures, including a bust of her husband. Bracken Wendt received so many commissions after this exhibition that she stayed in Chicago for most of the year to complete them.

In California, Bracken Wendt advocated equality for women artists as she had earlier in Chicago. In 1909, when a Los Angeles editor indicated that women should not be allowed to join a newly formed art club, Bracken Wendt was outraged. In response to his comment that women artists would try any means to infiltrate the organization, Bracken Wendt declared, "The fact is, the woman who succeeds in art must be too large to squeeze through 'loopholes' for she must be large enough to overlook the littleness of would-be men, and she must succeed not with their brotherly help but in spite of them" (*Los Angeles Times,* December 26, 1909). In 1911, Bracken Wendt again spoke out on equality. Under the pseudonym "Fern," she entered the California Political Equality League's poster contest. Bracken Wendt's poster shows Justice as a female figure holding a shield with a symbol that signifies the equality of male and female. The inscription reads, "Intelligence has no gender" (*Los Angeles Times,* April 23, 1911).

In February 1911, the Fine Arts League of Los Angeles commissioned Bracken Wendt to do a sculpture for the new Museum of Art, Science, and History. In order to complete this monumental task, Bracken Wendt again added on to her Sichel Street studio and hired some assistants. It took Bracken Wendt two years to complete her sculpture, which was entitled, appropriately, *Art, History, and Science* (1913). She was paid seventy-five hundred dollars for this commission. Art critic Anthony Anderson said of the sculpture, "Nothing can compare to its dignity, beauty, and significance. May the globe of light these figures lift up in the rotunda of the building be symbolic of the dawn of a new era [in Los Angeles culture]" (Anderson, "Art and Artists," *Los Angeles Times,* January 28, 1912). John W. Mitchell, president of the Municipal Art Commission, said, "They mark the beginning of an art life in this community that shall constantly strive to symbolize its artistic ideals and ambitions in concrete forms" ("Symbolic of Art Uplift," *Los Angeles Times,* May 31, 1914).

In 1915, the Pan-California Exposition came to San Diego, California. The exposition was a regional cultural fair celebrating San Diego's natural seaport and reflecting on the Spanish Mission influences in the city. In 1915, California was also host to the Panama-Pacific International Exposition in Los Angeles. The expositions were designed to complement one another. Bracken Wendt earned a gold medal for her work; this piece remains unidentified.

Although Bracken Wendt was becoming increasingly busy with work in Los Angeles, she and William Wendt had another joint exhibition in Chicago in 1921. Bracken Wendt taught sculpture for seven years at the Otis Art Institute (now the Otis-Parsons Institute), Los Angeles. In 1924 she finished an important public commission, *Lincoln,* a bronze half figure of the president, for Lincoln Park, Los Angeles. Bracken Wendt's love of local history and interest in the California art community was strong. She sculpted figures of "noted Angelenos such as *Charles Lummis* (Lummis House, Los Angeles), the defender and promoter of Native American and California culture, *Perry Widener, Frank Wiggins, Dean MacCormack, Charles Walton,* and *Judge William Rhodes Hervey* (the last three bronze busts are in the Masonic Temple, Los Angeles). She was working on a bust of *John Steven McGroarty* for Mission Playhouse, San Gabriel" (Rubinstein, 109). She was a leader in developing the California Art Society, and she served on the Municipal Arts Commission for three years. Julia Bracken Wendt closed her studio in 1936 and moved to Laguna Beach to join her husband, whose portrait she was working on at the time of her death. Bracken Wendt died in Laguna Beach, California, in 1942.

Many critics claim that if Bracken Wendt had remained in Chicago she would have had a more prestigious career. However, she defined her own career and was successful. Bracken Wendt came of age at the height of the woman's movement of the late nineteenth and early twentieth century. Her life and art reflected the values expressed in this first wave of women's activism as well as women's moral and political roles in the reformation of public life. Bracken Wendt's work is idealistic and neoclassical; her works reflect conceptions of womanhood that identify women as role models in both the domestic and public spheres and as upholders of civic and private virtue—not fragile, sentimental creatures on pedestals, but equal, independent persons capable of inhabiting all the places men traditionally had dominated, particularly the arts. Influenced by the Chicago Arts

and Crafts movement, the work of Lorado Taft, and the public art movement, Bracken Wendt believed there was "plenty of work to be done in the field of art, and room enough for all who have ability and are earnest workers" and that women did not want chivalry from male artists but had "every reason to expect justice" ("An Open Letter").

Sources. Julia Bracken Wendt's "An Open Letter" appears in Anthony E. Anderson's column, "Art and Artists," *Los Angeles Times,* December 26, 1909, and gives her views on women artists; she is quoted extensively in the *Los Angeles Times,* September 7, 1919, about her view of "the moderns." Contemporary articles about Julia Bracken Wendt include Anthony E. Anderson's column "Art and Artists" in the *Los Angeles Times* on September 16, 1906; September 6, 1908; January 31, 1909; August 29, 1909; December 26, 1909; January 28, 1912; and July 20, 1913. Three news articles of interest appear in the *Los Angeles Times,* April 23, 1911; May 31, 1914; and September 7, 1919. Articles in the *Graphic* appear May 11, 1907; July 18, 1908; August 15, 1908; June 26, 1909; October 15, 1910; April 1, 1911; March 8, 1913; and August 14, 1915. See also Everett C. Maxwell, "The Art of Julia Bracken Wendt, Noted Sculptures [sic]," *Fine Arts Journal,* November 1910; Landon Haynes, "Julia Bracken Wendt: California Women of Distinction," *Los Angeles Times,* March 9, 1924; and Eleanor Minturn James, "From Gingerbread Men to Sculpture," *Los Angeles Times,* January 5, 1930. Lorado Taft briefly discusses Bracken Wendt in *The History of American Sculpture* (1930). Janet Scudder, *Modeling My Life* (1925), describes the milieu of women sculptors at the end of the nineteenth century. Biographies of Bracken Wendt appear in Nancy Dustin W. Moure, *Dictionary of Art and Artists in Southern California before 1930* (1978); Esther Sparks, "Biographical Dictionary of Painters and Sculptors in Illinois, 1808–1945," 2 vols. (Ph.D. diss., Northwestern Univ., 1945); and Charlotte Streifer Rubinstein, *American Women Sculptors: A History of Women Working in Three Dimensions* (1990). For a description of Lorado Taft and the women sculptors in his Chicago studio, see Timothy J. Garvey, *Lorado Taft and the Beautification of Chicago* (1988). Eileen Boris, *Art and Labor: Ruskin, Morris, and the Craftsman Ideal in America* (1986), has a discussion of the Chicago Arts and Crafts movement.

KATHERINE CLARK

WHITE HORSE, CHAUNCINA YELLOW ROBE
December 28, 1909–June 13, 1981
COMMUNITY ACTIVIST, ADVOCATE FOR THE ELDERLY

Chauncina Yellow Robe White Horse was born in Rapid City, South Dakota. Her father was Chauncey Yellow Robe, a Lakota Sioux Indian from the Rosebud Reservation and nephew of Chief Sitting Bull. A graduate of Carlisle, the first federal (Bureau of Indian Affairs) Indian boarding school, Chauncey Yellow Robe was a respected educator and orator. In 1903, he was appointed disciplinarian (adviser) at the Rapid City Indian boarding school, where he worked for more than two decades. There, he met and married Lillian Springer, the school nurse, a woman of Swiss descent.

Chauncina Yellow Robe was the middle child of the three Yellow Robe children, all girls. The Yellow Robe sisters grew up in Rapid City at a time when the great majority of Indian people lived on reservations. They lived in an Indian boarding school but attended the local public high school. Chauncina, Rosebud, and Evelyn Yellow Robe benefited from, felt comfortable with, and were successful in both the Indian and non-Indian worlds. Rosebud Yellow Robe, the oldest, attended the University of South Dakota and became an educator. Evelyn Yellow Robe, the youngest, graduated from Mt. Holyoke College and completed an M.A. degree at Northwestern University. She taught English at Mt. Holyoke and Vassar and became a medical researcher.

As a young teenager, Chauncina Yellow Robe managed the household for her mother, who was disabled by arthritis. Upon graduation from Rapid City High School in 1928, the year her mother died, Chauncina Yellow Robe moved to the Rosebud reservation to live with a relative of her father. Chauncey Yellow Robe retired from the Bureau of Indian Affairs and moved to New York. Hoping to develop a truer picture of Indian people than movies portrayed, he took part in a 1929 motion picture depicting Indian life, *The Silent Enemy*, produced in conjunction with the American Museum of Natural History. He died of pneumonia in 1930.

That year, Chauncina Yellow Robe moved to New York City, where both of her sisters were living. She took college courses and hoped to become a lawyer but had to support herself. Jobs were scarce during the depression, but she managed to get a position at Macy's department store, where she worked her way up in sales. One day, she noticed that among a group of movers near their truck was an Indian man, Lee White Horse. At this time, the Indian population of cities, including both New York and Chicago, was very small, and it was unusual to meet another Indian. The two quickly got to know each other and soon after were married.

Lee White Horse, an Arapaho from Oklahoma, was involved in show business, performing with various groups as an archer. Chauncina became part of the act, serving as the target around which he shot. It was dangerous work, but she had confidence in him because, as she explained later, "He was my husband" (interview with Pat Tyson). The couple joined side shows and circuses, traveling to different places to perform. The White Horses continued to perform the act until some time shortly after World War II, when Lee accidentally shot Chauncina with an arrow. After the accident, they gave up the archery act but remained in show business through the 1950s.

Chauncina and Lee White Horse had three children: Chauncey, Robert, and Carmen. The family settled in Pittsburgh, where they experienced a tragic loss when Chauncey White Horse died in a motorcycle accident.

Seeking better opportunities for work, the White Horse family moved to Chicago around 1960. They came independently, but they arrived during a period when many Indians left their home reservations and moved to selected cities as part of the federal Bureau of Indian Affairs Relocation Program, initiated in 1952. Relocation was one aspect of the Termination Policy, which aimed at minimizing government responsibilities to Indian tribes by reducing the number and size of recognized tribes. This reduction was accomplished by terminating the special legal and political status of individual tribes (more than one hundred tribes were terminated before President Richard Nixon declared an end to termination) and by relocating tribal members from reservations into urban areas, where they could obtain employment and would forfeit rights and benefits owed to them by treaty. Chicago was one of five major cities selected for the relocation of Indian people. The Indian population of the city

grew significantly during the decade of the 1950s, when relocation was most active. The census count of American Indians in Chicago jumped from 775 in 1950 to 5,329 in 1960.

In Chicago, Chauncina White Horse found a job in advertising with the publisher R.R. Donnelley Corporation, where she worked until she reached the mandatory retirement age of sixty-five. For most of that time, her husband was in a wheelchair and unable to work, so she became the primary provider for her family. She spent weekends in the extensive outdoor market on Maxwell Street, where members of immigrant communities in Chicago came to buy and sell a variety of goods. Drawing on her own knowledge and experience, she demonstrated and sold herbs, liniments, and snake oil. There, she met Indian people from a number of tribes, who came to Maxwell Street to shop. The White Horse family kept up a strong relationship with those on their home reservations. They often visited and were visited by family and friends from the reservations; like other Indians in urban areas, they were bilocal.

Throughout her years in Chicago, Chauncina White Horse was involved in various American Indian community organizations and activities. Her contemporaries perceived her as a leader in the Chicago Indian community. They saw in Chauncina White Horse a woman who had strong opinions, was analytical, and who convinced others through reason. She served on the advisory board of St. Augustine's Center for American Indians, established in 1962 by the Episcopal Diocese of Chicago. Like many Indian people, she combined organized religion with native beliefs. St. Augustine's was a comfortable place for Chauncina White Horse and others to worship while celebrating their Indian identity.

A longstanding member of the Chicago American Indian Center, established in the early 1950s to provide support services to newly relocated Indians, she became an organizer of the Native American Committee Senior Program, which brought to Indian elders in Chicago some of the same services provided for elders on reservations. She stressed the need for such services, noting, "First Americans are the forgotten Americans, and of these the Older Indians are the most forgotten of all" ("Indians of Chicago," 87). The Senior Site at the American Indian Center looked to her as its founding inspiration; she spoke well and convincingly about the need for such a site and brought people together to make it happen. She secured funding to turn the concept into physical reality. Her advocacy at seminars and meetings throughout the country resulted in support both for the Chicago Center and for national programs such as low income housing assistance for Native American senior citizens.

Chauncina White Horse's work on behalf of American Indian elderly extended beyond the Chicago Indian community. In 1971, she was chosen to participate in a special session on Indian concerns in a White House Conference on Aging. For five years after that, she and others sought in vain to sustain national support for issues raised in that session. The resulting frustration led to the First National Indian Conference on Aging, sponsored by the National Tribal Chairman's Association and held in June 1976 in Phoenix, Arizona. Chauncina White Horse served on the planning committee for that meeting. She took a leadership role as fifteen hundred participants determined to establish the National Indian Council on Aging (NICOA) and elected her to its board of directors, a position she held for the rest of her life.

Chauncina White Horse served on the NICOA board as the Minneapolis Area representative, an area that included Chicago and Minneapolis as well as reservation communities. Although involved in Indian politics on the national level, she consistently represented the interests of Indian people in urban areas, including Minneapolis and Chicago. She reminded NICOA and its supporters that Indian people in urban areas had needs that were not met by local and state social service programs. Indeed, non-Indian social service agencies frequently refused to serve Indian people, assuming mistakenly that they received special tribal benefits. By the mid-1970s, the population of American Indian people in urban areas was approaching that on the reservations, yet federal programs, with some exceptions, focused on reservation communities alone.

At the same time, she became involved in a program in Chicago for young people. After retiring from Donnelley's in 1973, she worked as a counselor and job developer for Al Kobe (Chippewa), director of the new Indian Comprehensive Employment Training Act (CETA) program, "Indians for Indians." She believed strongly that Indian people could adapt and prosper in many different environments and should depend on each other for support. "Indians for Indians" reflected these goals. CETA was part of the federal Office of Equal Opportunity effort in the Civil Rights era to develop community programs. In her CETA work she gained a reputation for expecting the best from everyone and never excusing poor performance. She was a role model for Indian youth and was particularly successful in encouraging her clients to attend and stay in school.

In the late 1970s, she saw the value of recording the life experiences of transplanted older Indians. Elderly Indians, White Horse argued, were truly "transitional" people with "one foot in the tribal ways and one foot in the dominant white world" ("Indians of Chicago," 79). She saw these elders as "historians of some of the greatest changes regarding the American Indian coming into cities and looking for a better life" ("Indians of Chicago," 80). Her insistence on the importance of recording the experiences and perspectives of Indian elderly in Chicago resulted in the Chicago American Indian Oral History Project of the D'Arcy McNickle Center for the History of the American Indian at the Newberry Library, with interviews done in 1984, three years after Chauncina White Horse's death.

She was a prime mover in developing a Newberry Library conference, "Urban Indians," held in 1980; the proceedings, which appeared after her death, were dedicated to her as "an inspirational voice in the Chicago American Indian community and the moving force" (*Urban Indians*, dedication) of the conference. Chauncina White Horse felt it was important to capture the new urban experience of Indian people. She saw that Indian voices were lacking in the historical record, even where they were the most informed and experienced. She realized, furthermore, that while most Americans were at least familiar with the existence of reservations, few Chicagoans were even aware that American Indians were living in their city.

Chauncina White Horse died at the age of seventy-one at her home in Bensenville, Illinois, and was buried in Uniondale Cemetery in Pittsburgh, next to her son Chauncey. She had car-ried out her most influential community work in the last decade of her life. She is remembered nationally and locally for her work on behalf of American Indian elderly. NICOA continues as the solitary organization dedicated to the special issues of Indian elderly, who benefit from the advocacy work of Chauncina White Horse. She was a respected elder, committed to the welfare of the community, involved with its youth as she fought for its elderly, and able to communicate with and relate to non-Indian academics, politicians, and others.

Sources. Chauncina White Horse's article, "The Indians of Chicago: A Perspective," in NL for the History of the American Indian, Urban Indians: *Proceedings of the Third Annual Conference on Problems and Issues Concerning American Indians Today*, Occasional Papers Series, no. 4 (1981) counters articles on the disastrous state of Indian people in urban communities in the 1970s by profiling several older Indian people and listing many Indian community organizations in Chicago. Her work is noted in the published reports of the first two National Indian Conferences on Aging, *The Indian Elder, A Forgotten American* (1976) and *The Continuum of Life: Health Concerns of the Indian Elderly* (1978). NICOA newsletters include references to Chauncina White Horse: *NICOA News*, Fall 1979, provides a tribute to Chauncey Yellow Robe, her father, and describes her work for Indians. The Newberry Library Center for the History of the American Indian, Special Publication no. 1, *Chicago American Indian Oral History Pilot Project: Transcript Description and Index* (1984), and the following unpublished interviews provide information on Chauncina White Horse and context for understanding the community that she served: interview with Ada Powers, July 28, 1983, #012, and with Susan Power, September 26, 1983, #016, both in the Chicago American Indian Oral History Project, NL, and at NAES (Native American Educational Services) College Library, Chicago, Illinois. Terry Straus obtained further information in interviews in 1995 with Chauncina's son, Robert White Horse, a Bensenville, Illinois, resident; her friends, Inez Dennison and Pat Tyson in Chicago, and Father Peter Powell of St. Augustine's Center for American Indians, Chicago.

ANNE TERRY STRAUS

WICKER, IREENE SEATON
November 24, 1900–November 17, 1987
CHILDREN'S RADIO ENTERTAINER, RADIO AND TELEVISION ACTRESS

Ireene Wicker devoted her life to children's entertainment, first on radio during its golden age in the 1930s and 1940s and then on television, including some of the earliest experimental television shows. Known as "The Singing Lady," she was heard by millions of listeners for more than forty years.

Irene Seaton was born in Quincy, Illinois, to a family of Scottish descent. (She changed the spelling of her first name to Ireene early in her stage career.) She was the third of three children born to Margaret (Hunsaker) Seaton, a teacher, and Kenner Seaton, who worked for the Burlington Railroad for more than fifty years. Irene Seaton demonstrated theatrical talent early in life, performing in summer stock theater at age twelve. After graduating from Quincy High School, Seaton attended the University of Illinois at Urbana-Champaign, where she focused on the performing arts. She said that her family was against her choice of career.

In 1917, Irene Seaton married her college sweetheart, Walter Wicker, who later became a producer and actor in radio. His grandfather, Charles Gustavus Wicker, and his great-uncle Joel

FIG. 129. *Radio and television entertainer Ireene Wicker, "The Singing Lady," innovated children's programming.*

In 1930, Ireene Wicker starred in a children's radio show sponsored by the Kellogg Company, the breakfast cereal producer. Kellogg wanted a program with songs for children, but Wicker felt children enjoyed songs and stories in combination. For her audition, she dramatized "Twinkle, Twinkle, Little Star," adding original, imaginative stories and songs. She was a hit and debuted on radio WGN in Chicago in 1931 with *The Singing Lady*, writing her own adaptations and acting all the parts herself. *The Singing Lady* made its national debut on NBC, January 11, 1932, with Ireene Wicker as writer, star, and producer. She introduced Kellogg's new cereal, "Rice Krispies" to the country and influenced its commercial success.

Wicker's storytelling style was popular with children as well as parents, who appreciated its wholesome content, so different from other juvenile programming containing violence, stereotyping of indigenous peoples, and melodrama. A May 1935 article in *Radio Guide* described her as the "only radio entertainer whose program is officially recommended by the . . . Parent Teacher associations" (Thomas, 3). Wicker's approach to her work was connected with a deep respect for children, and she treated them as individuals with intelligence equal or superior to her own. She was an advocate for responsibility in broadcasting for children. "Give the children the thrills they want," she said, "but temper them with facts, probability, imagination and intelligence" (Siegel, n.p.).

More than twenty-five million children listened to her regularly. At the height of her popularity during the grim years of the Great Depression, Wicker received as many as one million fan letters a year. During the 1930s, the World Telegram Radio Editors' Poll chose *The Singing Lady* as the "Best Children's Show" for five consecutive years. She was ranked number one above *Dick Tracy*, *Little Orphan Annie*, and *The Lone Ranger*. She was selected by *Radio Stars* as one of nine outstanding women in the field of radio, awarded medals by *Parents' Magazine*, and endorsed by the General Federation of Women's Clubs. Wicker's programming included dramatization of such classic tales as *Alice in Wonderland* and *Jack and the Beanstalk*, biographical stories of great achievers in the arts such as Peter Paul Rubens, Wolfgang Amadeus Mozart, and Giuseppi Verdi. In addition she interviewed famous contemporaries, including Charlie Chaplin, Franklin D. Roosevelt, and Mary Pickford; they told stories of their childhoods.

The number of actors working in radio during this era was small. Wicker played as many as twenty-seven different roles each week, and, in 1936, *Radio Mirror* described her salary as the highest for a radio program by one woman. A typical day for the hard-working and successful Wicker began in her home office, where she did research and script writing with the help of her secretary. She then switched to her piano where, with her accompanist, she planned the music segments of her program. Then it was off to the Merchandise Mart studios for rehearsal and broadcast.

Radio performers often raced through the hallways of the Merchandise Mart in order to meet the complicated schedules of playing multiple roles in programs that were being broadcast simultaneously or close in time. Frequently, scripts were being completed just as actors grabbed them to read on the air. One of Wicker's most hectic days included her performance as the

Wicker, donated a parcel of land on the Northwest Side of Chicago, which came to be known as Wicker Park. Irene Seaton Wicker's mother-in-law, MARY WICKER, was an artist. Irene and Walter Wicker had two children, Walter Charles Jr. and Nancy.

Irene Wicker studied drama at the Goodman Theatre School, Chicago, from 1927 to 1930. She appeared in professional productions at the Goodman Theatre in 1929 and 1930. Roles were scarce, and Wicker was offered opportunities in traveling shows; but she did not want to leave her family. Instead, she reoriented her career toward the new field of radio, adding a third "e" to her name on the advice of a numerologist, who said this change would lead to great success. Thereafter she was known as Ireene Wicker.

Wicker prospered in the burgeoning radio environment. The first radio network was formed in Chicago by the National Broadcasting Center (NBC) in 1922, and Chicago became the center of radio broadcasting in the United States. Good facilities were available in Chicago; after 1936, with the completion of the twenty-four-story Merchandise Mart—at the time the world's largest building—many studios were located there. Chicago was the home of such nationally popular radio shows as *Fibber McGee and Molly*, *Amos 'n' Andy*, and many soap operas.

Singing Lady, followed by a cab ride to a different studio, where she acted the lead roles in scenes from *A Doll's House*, *Anna Christie*, and *The Life of Greta Garbo*.

In the 1930s, Wicker appeared in some of the first popular radio soap operas, sometimes working with her husband. *Today's Children* was set in a Chicago neighborhood and followed the story lines of several local families. At one time it was a top-rated series on daytime radio. Wicker also had roles in *Harold Teen* and *Judy and Jane*, soap operas broadcast in the 1930s.

Wicker was part of the early development of television, performing in several experimental programs broadcast over station WXAP, owned by the *Chicago Daily News*, with simultaneous voice broadcast over radio station WMAQ. In January 1931, she appeared in *The Maker of Dreams*, the first television drama synchronized with radio produced in the Midwest. That same year she appeared in a musical comedy TV show, *The Merry-Go-Round*. The television camera was stationary; when she played Puck in *A Midsummer Night's Dream*, with English actor, Sir Cedric Hardwicke, Wicker and the other actors had to crawl off the set because of the limitations of camera technology.

Wicker's life changed significantly in the late 1930s and early 1940s. She moved to New York City in 1936 at the request of her show's sponsor, the Kellogg Company. By 1937 *The Singing Lady* was seen four times a week on NBC. Wicker also had a thirty-minute Sunday show, *The Ireene Wicker Music Plays*, on the Mutual network. The plays were dramatizations for children of operas, folk legends, fairy tales, and children's classics, and her fellow actors included Don Ameche, Charita Bauer, John Houseman, Agnes Moorhead, and Everett Sloane. Shortly after the move to New York, Ireene and Walter Wicker were separated; their divorce was granted in October 1937, and Walter Wicker remarried in November. On January 11, 1941, Ireene Wicker married Victor Hammer, secretary-treasurer of the Hammer Art Galleries, New York City. Her son, Walter Charles Wicker Jr., age twenty, a volunteer fighter pilot with the American Eagle Squadron of the Royal Canadian Air Force, was killed during World War II in action over Dover, England, on April 27, 1942. Wicker was devastated by his death, which she said forever changed her outlook on life. In a speaking engagement before the convention for the Institute for Education by Radio, Wicker said, "'Children too . . . must know what men are fighting for and for what they also may be asked to lay down their lives'" (Heise). "'Write for children, too,' she told her audience, and then left sobbing. Only then did the people learn that her son had been killed the day before" (Heise).

In the late 1940s, as television became more popular, Wicker incorporated marionettes into *The Singing Lady* production. Wicker appeared on viewers' ten-inch screens dressed in a flowing gown and holding a magic wand. Pretty and diminutive at one hundred pounds, the elfin Ireene Wicker was the ideal teller of imaginative tales in the new entertainment medium.

It was ironic that Wicker, an entertainer who had won the respect of parents, youth, and professional educators for her wholesome approach to children's entertainment, became the victim of the redbaiting tactics of conservative ideologues. "During the 1950s, Red Channels [*sic*], a private blacklisting publication, charged that the actress had sponsored a re-election committee for a Communist councilman in New York" (Robertson). Wicker, whose political activities had been almost nonexistent, "denied she had even heard of the man" (Robertson). In the cold war, anticommunist paranoia of the era, the false accusation in *Red Channels* was distributed to commercial sponsors, advertising agencies, and producers. Wicker was labeled a communist sympathizer along with other personalities, including composer and conductor Leonard Bernstein, writer Dorothy Parker, and playwright Arthur Miller. Just weeks after her name appeared in *Red Channels*, the Kellogg Company canceled *The Singing Lady*, offering the excuse that her program appealed to a limited age group. *The Singing Lady* had one of the highest ratings of all children's television programs and Wicker actively attempted to get *Red Channels* to retract its accusation and clear her name. Instead, the publication questioned her patriotism and denied her request.

When the charges could not be proven, Wicker and her attorneys received a printed apology from *Red Channels* stating that she was not a communist sympathizer. A retraction was published November 1950, in *Newsweek* magazine, but it was too late. For the next two years no one would consider airing her show. She never again attained the same level of popularity or income for her work.

By 1953, Wicker was broadcasting a thirty-minute TV series called *Little Lady Story Time* on WABC–TV from New York. Reviews were good, including one by radio and television critic Judith Crist, who wrote, "Twenty years of storytelling have left Ireene Wicker . . . without loss of her girlish laughter, her ability to impersonate at least a dozen different characters in one story or her talent for enthralling the young in heart of all ages" ("Miss Wicker Storyteller to All Ages").

The greatest tribute to Wicker's accomplishments came in the 1960s when she received the George Foster Peabody Award for lifetime achievement and an Emmy Award from the Academy of Television Arts and Sciences. Wicker wrote children's books, including *The Singing Lady's Favorite Stories* (1934), *Young Music Makers: Boyhoods of Famous Composers* (1965), and *Young Master Artists: Boyhoods of Famous Artists* (1965); she recorded her *Singing Lady* repertoire on Record Guild of America, Decca, Riverside, and Mercury records.

In her later years, Wicker and her husband lived both in New York and Palm Beach, Florida, traveling extensively because of Victor Hammer's art business. In 1975, Wicker retired. She moved into a nursing home in Palm Beach in 1982, where she died of heart failure five years later. She was buried at Camp Point, Illinois.

Sources. Nancy Wicker has a collection of personal papers, correspondence, photographs, newspaper clippings, and a scrapbook documenting Ireene Wicker's life. Included in the collection is the typescript of a biography, "Ireene Wicker (Hammer) 'The Singing Lady'" by Nancy Wicker, n.d. An interview with Nancy Wicker was conducted March 23, 1994. Ireene Wicker's radio and television scripts are at the Broadcasting Museum, New York, New York. Articles about Wicker include Norman Siegel, "They Call Her Radio's 'One-Lady' Show," *New Jersey Ledger*, August 2, 1936; Lorraine Thomas, "Sing, Lady, Sing," *Radio Guide*, May 1935; [n.a.], "The Singing Lady Says . . . 'Children Respond to Honesty,'" *Women's Day*, August 1938; [n.a.], "How to Have That Career," *Radio Mirror*, October 1936; Val Adams, "The Singing

Lady Goes before the Cameras," *NYT*, July 17, 1949; Judith Crist, "Miss Wicker Storyteller to all Ages," New York *Herald Tribune*, October 18, 1953; [n.a.], "Brief Biographies—Ireene Wicker," *Chicago Daily News*, April 20, 1935; Ted Poston, "Only Sad Songs for Singing Lady as 'Red Channels' Plays off Key," *New York Post*, September 11, 1950; Karen Singer, "'The Singing Lady': A Superstar from Radio's Heyday," *Greenwich Time*, October 19, 1982. Obituaries are Kenan Heise, "Ireene Wicker Hammer, 'Singing Lady' of Radio," *CT*, November 19, 1987; Nan Robertson, "Ireene Wicker Hammer Dies, 86; Storyteller to Millions of Children," *NYT*, November 18, 1987; and Don Hayner, "Ireene Wicker Hammer, Radio's 'Singing Story Lady' of the 1930s," Chicago *Sun-Times*, November 19, 1987.

JILL SCHACTER

WICKER, MARY HACKNEY
November 10, 1854–September 3, 1942
PAINTER, SCULPTOR

Mary Hackney Wicker was a painter and sculptor who actively sought for herself many opportunities not usually available to women artists of her time. Born in Aurora, Illinois, Mary Hackney was the daughter of Benjamin and Lydia (Wightman) Hackney. Her father, son of a revolutionary war veteran, had moved to the Midwest from New York to capitalize on the boom in the railroad business. In Aurora, he was president of the Chicago Burlington and Quincy Railroad and the founder of Jennings Seminary. Her mother's family was from Rhode Island. Mary Hackney had two brothers.

Growing up in Aurora, Mae Hackney, as she was often called, was known at a young age for her interest in art. One of her earliest teachers, Wells Sawyer, became a lifelong friend and patron. Sawyer's daughter, Helen, was also a close friend and later became Hackney's traveling companion. After her mother died, Mary Hackney moved to Chicago to live with her brother Walter.

On December 27, 1893, Mary Hackney married Charles Gustavus Wicker Jr. Wicker's father, Charles Gustavus Wicker Sr., and his uncle began preliminary real estate development in what would become known as the Wicker Park neighborhood, where they donated a tract of land to the city for use as a public park. In the early years of her marriage, Mary Wicker continued to cultivate her interest in art, spending summers in Bay View, Michigan, where she painted some of her most beautiful watercolor landscapes and still lifes. On her honeymoon in Guadalajara, Mexico, Wicker made many studies of the chapels they visited, a subject that would appear later in her art. The Wickers' first son did not survive infancy. On July 19, 1898, Mary Wicker gave birth to a second son, Walter Charles Wicker, whom they called "Bobs."

Mary Wicker believed that in order to become a better artist, she had to go to Paris. At this time, Paris was still the undisputed capital of the art world, and most noteworthy American artists spent some time training there. Her decision to go to Paris was not easy, and she remained highly conflicted about uprooting her family to attain her goal. On the day of her departure for Paris, she wrote in her journal that ambition was "that most dangerous and subtle passion, which drives us on—goads us to do seemingly impossible things" (p. 1). Although married and a mother, Wicker had the support of her husband and, on March 26, 1906, she left Chicago with her son Bobs.

In Paris, Wicker immediately immersed herself in training. She enrolled Bobs in a private school so that she could devote herself to her work and found a room for herself in a hotel and later a pension. She took lessons with the noted teacher Jean Paul Laurens at the famed Académie Julian, a school popular with Americans studying abroad. Foreign study in the arts was limited for women at the time, since the École des Beaux-Arts was principally open to men and to French citizens. While exceptions were possible, a stiff examination determined admission; tuition was free. At the Académie Julian students had to pay tuition, but women, foreigners, French citizens, and students of all ages were admitted equally without any entry examination. Wicker sought to educate herself in the many aspects of French art, frequently visiting museums and exhibitions in Paris and traveling outside the city to visit the birthplace of the Barbizon school. Her early experience in Paris was one of shock, and she found it difficult to work. "I suppose that coming from *no* Art to *all* Art is such a violent change that it upsets us muchly" (Nancy Wicker scrapbook, 1), she noted in a letter to her sister-in-law, Caroline Wicker, on May 18, 1906. In the same letter, she observed, "I think the Art life of Paris is ideal but deadening after a time. . . . I believe that America will yet have a great Art of its own and we will have done our studying *here*."

Wicker traveled to Bruges, Belgium, where she worked in a studio that was located in the former home of the noted Dutch artist, Peter Paul Rubens. In Bruges, she studied the Dutch masters, and the effect was evident in the highly expressive style of her portraits. In September, Wicker's husband joined her, and together they traveled to Spain and northern Africa.

In Morocco she witnessed an Arab chieftain chained in the marketplace by the local authorities. Struck by his independent stance although a captive, she later recorded this memory in her painting, *The Arab*. The relatively short but critically important European studies and travels became the basis of some of Wicker's later works. As she wrote to her family in March 1907, "I think that I can paint every day for five years on the studies and ideas I have in mind" (Nancy Wicker scrapbook, 1). After nearly a year abroad, the Wickers returned to Chicago.

Mary Wicker's self-portrait, *Myself—Just Back from Paris* (1908) was one of the first pieces finished before personal tragedy imposed a period during which she ceased to exhibit her work, although she may have continued to paint. Not long after their return from Europe, on February 9, 1909, her husband was drowned in a boating accident off the coast of Florida.

It was not until the 1920s, after her son went to college, that Wicker began to travel again, find new subjects, recall some of her earlier memories on canvas, and exhibit widely. One of her most powerful works from this period was *The Arab*, based in part on the Moroccan marketplace memories of her trip to North Africa with her husband and in part on a study she made of a model at the Art Institute of Chicago (AIC). She soon started one of her most productive periods, having some of her greatest exhibition success in Chicago. In one of her earliest exhibitions, in 1924, the *Twenty-eighth Annual Exhibition by Artists of Chicago* at the AIC, she won two awards—the Roger's Park Women's Club prize and the Englewood Women's Club prize—for *Intérieur des Cloîtres*. She followed this success with entries at the *13th Annual Exhibition* of the Allied Artists of

America, Inc., in 1925; the National Academy of Design in 1929; the American Federation of the Arts traveling exhibition in 1929; the Pennsylvania Academy of Fine Arts in 1930; and the National Arts Club.

Contemporary critics commented favorably on Wicker's ability to handle a wide range of subject matter, from landscapes of exotic venues to penetrating psychological portrait studies. While her subjects were often fairly conservative, her style was not. In many of her works, Wicker used only a palette knife, creating a richly textured surface. A Parisian publication singled out her work shown at the National Academy and called her a genius with color. Eleanor Jewett, an art critic for the *Chicago Tribune*, compared her work to that of Marie Laurencin, a well-known French artist. Wicker's portraits, landscapes, and still lifes from the 1920s showed the influence of her European training and also that of her American teachers, who included Horsep Pushman, Leon Gaspard, Charles W. Hawthorne, George Brown, and Robert Henri.

Wicker contributed to the Chicago arts scene as a member of the Arts Club of Chicago, where her painting, *My Favorite Model*, was included in a 1928 exhibition of works by Arts Club members. She also exhibited at the Woman's World's Fair and Illinois Women's Athletic Club, both in 1928, and she made frequent contributions to the Hoosier Salon, a group of midwestern artists who modeled themselves after the French impressionists. Wicker maintained a studio in Chicago. While many of her works were portraits or landscapes of foreign subjects, she also created a few scenes of Chicago, including Grant Park, La Rabida, and Clark Street.

Although primarily a painter and watercolorist, Wicker also experimented with sculpture. She studied with Stanislaus Szukalski and exhibited her work *Opus II—Brahms* in the National Academy of Design's 1929 exhibition. This bronze sculpture was based on the *allegro appassionato* of the Brahms piece and was inspired by a Chicago Symphony Orchestra performance in 1928.

Stricken by arthritis, Wicker was unable to paint in her final years. She died in Providence, Rhode Island, and her remains were cremated at the Forest Hills Crematory, Forest Hills, Massachusetts.

Throughout her life, Mary Hackney Wicker maintained the independent and adventurous spirit she first demonstrated when she went to Paris as a young mother to study art. This spirit was evident not only in the way she sought out the best training for herself but also in the style of her art. Interest in her work has continued since her death; a portrait by Wicker was included in an exhibition in 1990, *A Taste for Elegance: American Artists Seek European Style*, at the Louisiana Arts and Science Center, Baton Rouge. Wicker's painting *The Arab* was chosen for a National Museum of Women in the Arts (NMWA) exhibition in October 1997 by the Illinois committee for the NMWA to represent Illinois women artists.

Sources. Many of Mary Wicker's papers, including twenty-two sketchbooks from all periods of her life and a journal that was written during her trip to Europe in 1906, are at CHS. Nancy Deborah Wicker, Mary Wicker's granddaughter, has two scrapbooks that contain copies of the original correspondence, personal papers, documents, and newspaper articles. The originals are also in Nancy Wicker's possession. Nancy Wicker wrote a brochure that contains memories of her grandmother and a partial list of works currently in her possession, December 1, 1992. There are 220 extant watercolors and paintings by Wicker. Fifteen of the paintings were donated by Nancy Wicker to CHS in 1991. The remainder are owned by Nancy Wicker or are in private collections. Nancy Wicker also has a collection of ninety-two greeting cards designed by Mary Wicker. Mary Wicker is listed in Daniel Trowbridge Mallet, *Mallett's Index of Artists* (1948); *Who Was Who in American Art*, ed. Peter Hastings Falk (1985); and *The Julian Academy: Paris 1868–1939* (1989). Her participation in exhibitions during her lifetime is documented in the registers of the Art Institute of Chicago, the National Academy of Design, the Arts Club of Chicago, and the Hoosier Salon, among many others. Wicker is mentioned in an article, "Rediscovering American Art," *Exhibit 104*, May/June 1981.

JODI LOX MANSBACH

WILLARD, FRANCES ELIZABETH CAROLINE
September 28, 1839–February 17, 1898
WOMEN'S RIGHTS AND TEMPERANCE REFORMER, AUTHOR, SPEAKER

Frances E. Willard was president of the Woman's Christian Temperance Union for nearly two decades, from 1879 until her death in 1898. As head of what was then the largest American women's organization and a reformer of international fame, Willard led her constituency in support of a broad reform agenda, ranging from temperance to women's rights to labor issues. Called America's "uncrowned queen" (Gordon, 314) during her lifetime, she was, in the estimation of her contemporaries, the most famous woman in the United States.

Willard was born into a western New York farm family of New England ancestry. Her father, Josiah Flint Willard (1805–68), and her mother, Mary Thompson (Hill) Willard (1805–92) had two children besides Frances who survived infancy: an older son, Oliver (1835–78), and a younger daughter, Mary (1843–62). Willard's family was a close-knit one for whom she had great affection. From childhood she admired her brother Oliver and appreciated his comradeship with her. Her sister Mary was her intimate—"her other self" (Gifford, "Writing Out My Heart," 15)—and Mary's early death at nineteen from typhoid fever brought great grief to the entire family. Her father's death from tuberculosis not long after was another difficult loss. Her mother remained her strongest supporter and guide throughout most of her life; Willard depended on her for wise advice and spiritual sustenance.

In 1841 the family moved to Oberlin, Ohio, where Willard's father began to prepare for the ministry at Oberlin College by entering its preparatory department. They moved again in 1846 to southeastern Wisconsin because of Josiah Willard's health; he was already showing signs of incipient tuberculosis.

Frances Willard spent the years from 1846 to 1858 on the family farm near Janesville, Wisconsin, reveling in what she later remembered as a carefree, country existence. Yet she acquired a love of learning and a sense of community responsibility during these early years that stayed with her throughout her life. Her parents revered education and they and their neighbors took a lively interest in the antislavery struggle and other social issues of the time. Her mother, in particular, loved literature, especially heroic poetry, encouraging her children to commit po-

FIG. 130. *Temperance and social reformer Frances E. Willard seated at her desk, c. 1888.*

FIG. 131. *International temperance leader and suffragist Frances E. Willard with Lady Somerset, her English counterpart, c. 1892.*

ems to memory and recite them. She also supported Willard's early efforts at writing, suggesting that she keep a journal and submit essays and stories to newspapers and magazines. Willard's father took civic duties seriously, serving a term in the Wisconsin state legislature and many years as a trustee of the Wisconsin Institute for the Blind. He also presided over the Wisconsin State Agricultural Society and held county and town offices.

Willard's mother, formerly an elementary school teacher, taught her two daughters at home until they were well into their teens. By January 1856 Willard's parents and neighbors established a one-room schoolhouse nearby, where she and her sister Mary studied for more than a year. Next, they attended for one term in 1857 the Congregationalist-founded Milwaukee (Wisconsin) Female College, where their Aunt Sarah Hill was teaching. But Willard's father preferred to send his daughters to a Methodist school, and in 1858, Willard and her sister entered North Western Female College, a secondary school in Evanston, Illinois, as boarders. Shortly afterward, her father leased his Wisconsin farm and entered a Chicago banking firm. The entire family moved to Evanston, a newly founded suburb of Chicago. There, the Willards quickly entered the lively intellectual, social, and religious life centering around the town's Methodist church and its three Methodist-related educational institutions: Northwestern University, Garrett Biblical Institute, and the female college. Willard and her sister attended their school as day students, and their brother, Oliver, enrolled at the biblical institute to become a Methodist minister.

Willard graduated from North Western Female College in June 1859 and began to teach school in Harlem (later River Forest), Illinois, in the early summer of 1860. For most of the next decade, she held a series of teaching positions in public schools in Illinois and Methodist-related secondary schools in Illinois, Pennsylvania, and New York. The Willard family's commitment to Methodism was strong, and Willard herself was a lifelong member of the denomination, joining the Evanston Methodist church in spring 1861 when she was twenty-one. Yet from her young adulthood, her Methodist enthusiasm was accompanied by a broad-minded, ecumenical spirit.

From early fall 1861 to winter 1862, Willard was engaged to Charles Fowler, a promising young Methodist minister and good friend of her brother Oliver. Their engagement was encouraged by family, friends, and the Evanston Methodist community. But Willard broke it off because she felt no physical attraction toward Fowler, although she admired, respected, and honored him. She was, however, deeply in love with her best friend Mary Bannister, who later married her brother Oliver. Although Willard wrote in her journal that her intense love for Bannister ended abruptly at the time of her sister Mary's death, she continued to form attachments to several women over her lifetime. Willard never married; instead she received emotional sustenance from her strong and abiding friendships with women who shared her spiritual life and her passion for reform.

From her early teens, Willard had longed to see the many famous sites in the "old world" (Gifford, "'My Own Methodist Hive,'" 95) that she and her family and friends had read about in magazines and books. She realized her dream of travel in her late twenties, when her friend Kate Jackson's father paid her way to accompany his daughter on a two-and-a-half-year tour of Europe and the Middle East. From spring 1868 to fall 1870, the two young women studied European history, culture, and languages, gathering knowledge they intended to use as teachers when they returned to the United States.

During these years, Willard's commitment to what she termed "the Woman Question" (Gifford, "'My Own Methodist Hive,'" 95) deepened as she observed the condition of women in Europe and the Middle East. She had supported woman suffrage from at least 1860, when she was twenty-one years old and read an essay by popular preacher Henry Ward Beecher entitled "Women's Influence in Politics" in the New York Independent, a Congregationalist weekly (February 16, 1860). Beecher strongly advocated the vote for women in this essay and Willard heartily agreed. She often recorded her dismay at women's educational disabilities, and her disagreement with societal expectations that married women would subdue any dreams they might have of careers or intellectual interests to their husbands' wishes and requirements. In spring 1868, as she and Jackson prepared for their European trip, they attended a lecture by Theodore Tilton, a newspaper editor and prominent women's rights speaker, on "The American Woman." Willard was inspired by Tilton's speech and wrote in her journal: "Some how since I heard Tilton lecture, my purpose is confirmed—my object in life clearer than ever before. What I can do in large & in little ways, by influence, by pen, by observation, for *woman*, in all Christian ways, that I will do. And may God help me!" (March 21, 1868, quoted in Gifford, "*Writing Out My Heart*," 265–66).

While in Paris, Willard and Jackson met with French and American women's rights supporters who were concerned about women's economic dependence on men. Willard began to analyze women's economic disabilities as well as their educational and political ones, realizing that overcoming women's second-class status meant reform in all areas of their lives. After her return from Europe in fall 1870, Willard crafted her observations on women's status in Europe and the Middle East into a lecture, "The New Chivalry," that she gave many times in the Chicago area to large and enthusiastic church audiences. In it she called on the chivalrous men of the "new world" to join with women in developing a new egalitarian relationship between the sexes; it would be in America, she insisted, and not in the "old world," that a new model of equality would emerge.

Willard realized from this experience of lecturing that she enjoyed public speaking and was good at it, but she still saw herself primarily as an educational reformer. She had spent much time studying the methods of educating women in the countries

she visited, at the request of friends back home who were working to found a college for women in Evanston. In early spring 1871, within a few months of her return to Evanston, Willard accepted the presidency of the Evanston College for Ladies, which was to be a sister institution of Northwestern University.

As president, she became well-known in the Chicago area and beyond, through her fund-raising efforts for the college as well as by her direction of it. She participated in the National Women's Congress in fall 1873, where she was elected a vice-president of the Association for the Advancement of Women formed at the congress. MARY LIVERMORE, a former Illinois suffrage leader who had recently moved to Massachusetts, introduced her to many eastern women's rights reformers. Livermore became a mentor of Willard's, often giving her the support and courage she needed to take liberal positions on women's rights. The friends and allies Willard made through the women's congress and other avenues were invaluable to her as she pursued her aim of working on behalf of women's independence.

When the Evanston College for Ladies united with Northwestern in fall 1872, Willard became dean of the women's division of the university. She remained dean until spring 1874, when she resigned in a disagreement with the university's administration over the governance of the women's division. Suddenly faced with the prospect of finding another position, Willard began to investigate possibilities, including the burgeoning temperance movement with which she had sympathized for many years.

During the winter of 1873–74, a Women's Crusade against liquor dealers had begun in Ohio and spread quickly throughout the northern United States. By summer 1874, a permanent organization, the Woman's Christian Temperance Union (WCTU), was launched. That same summer, Willard visited women temperance leaders in New York City and attended the first Gospel Temperance Camp Meeting in Maine. On her way home, she joined a band of Women's Crusade participants in Pittsburgh as they knelt praying outside a saloon in an attempt to persuade the saloon keeper to give up his trade. Willard was convinced that her future lay in temperance reform but worried that she would not be able to support herself and her mother through this work. She received a letter from Louise Rounds, a Chicago Women's Crusade leader, asking her to become president of the Chicago WCTU. With some hesitation, she accepted the offer and embarked on her reform vocation.

For the first year of her temperance work, Willard's WCTU activities focused on downtown Chicago, where she operated out of the Chicago WCTU headquarters, a rent-free office in the Young Men's Christian Association (YMCA) building. In the YMCA's Farwell Hall, she led daily evangelistic prayer meetings, exhorting drunkards to accept Christ and sign a temperance pledge. When not involved in saving souls, she expanded the scope of the Chicago WCTU by producing publicity, speaking on the organization's goals and methods, and raising money for its operation. Although she was somewhat successful in helping to fund the Chicago WCTU, she worked without a salary until she met MATILDA CARSE, a Chicago WCTU leader. Carse personally raised a salary of one hundred dollars a month in order to ease Willard's precarious financial situation. Carse's care for her young colleague was the beginning of a close working relationship that lasted throughout Willard's career in the WCTU.

As a delegate from the Chicago WCTU, Willard attended the first Illinois WCTU meeting in October 1874 and there devised a motto encapsulating the organization's mission—"For God and Home and Native Land"—that the state WCTU immediately adopted. It became the motto of the National WCTU (NWCTU) two years later. Representing the Illinois WCTU, Willard participated in the first national WCTU convention, which met in Cleveland, Ohio, in November 1874. Convention delegates elected her corresponding secretary of the NWCTU, with the task of traveling across the country, speaking and establishing local unions.

Through her work with local and state leaders, Willard rapidly became a power within the organization as the head of its more liberal wing. Her followers endorsed woman suffrage as a means of "Home Protection," a slogan Willard invented to signify that women's vote would be instrumental in passing legislation prohibiting the sale of liquor, thus protecting women from the effects of male drunkenness. Although she had worked closely and harmoniously with NWCTU president Annie Wittenmyer for two years, Willard's public advocacy of woman suffrage, beginning in summer 1876, caused a rift between the two officers. Wittenmyer and her conservative supporters opposed the vote for women, preferring to rely on women's influence through the traditional strategies of prayer and petition to bring about prohibition. Sensing that the time was not yet right to challenge Wittenmyer for the presidency of the NWCTU, Willard resigned her national office in fall 1877.

Even earlier, she had begun to work with Dwight L. Moody, a popular Chicago-based evangelist, traveling with him for several months on an eastern tour, where she led well-attended women's prayer meetings. At one of these, she met ANNA GORDON, a young Massachusetts woman. The two women quickly became close friends, and Gordon acted as Willard's personal secretary until Willard's death in 1898. Gordon efficiently managed all the details of Willard's busy life and was, as well, a companion whom Willard and her mother regarded as an integral part of the alternative family that they created for themselves during the 1870s.

After Willard left the Moody campaign in fall 1877, chafing under his narrow Protestantism and his limited understanding of women's roles in evangelism, Gordon accompanied her back to Evanston, where Willard launched her fight for woman suffrage. Willard, her mother, and Gordon considered Rest Cottage, the house Willard's father had built in the mid-1860s in Evanston, their family home. From the mid-1880s until the early 1890s, Rest Cottage was the center of NWCTU activity, serving as office and living quarters to the three women as well as several NWCTU staff members. It was a female household knit together by a shared spiritual and reform commitment, with Willard's mother as its head and heart.

Willard first tested the "Home Protection" ballot measure in Illinois in the mid-1870s by undertaking a petition campaign to persuade the Illinois legislature to pass a bill giving women the vote on whether liquor licenses could be issued in the state. WCTU women collected more than 175,000 signatures in support of the Home Protection ballot measure in spring 1879 and succeeded in getting a bill before the legislature, but it was defeated in the House and died in committee in the Senate. Nevertheless, the campaign was a triumph for Willard and the Illinois WCTU; they had managed to bring the issue of woman suffrage squarely before the state at a time when there was little other suffrage activity in Illinois.

Even though she remained out of the NWCTU spotlight for several years, Willard and her supporters kept agitating within the organization for woman suffrage. In 1879 she went as the head of the Illinois delegation to the NWCTU convention, where she was easily elected president, a victory for those who supported woman suffrage and intended to broaden the aims of the NWCTU. During the next several years, the WCTU under her direction grew from a small, struggling group focused on the single issue of temperance to a massive organization, numbering nearly two hundred thousand at the close of the nineteenth century. Its broad program of reform encompassed temperance; woman suffrage; women's economic and religious rights; the reform of the institutions of marriage, home, and family; and the support of measures advocated by the rising labor movement.

Willard understood her organization as a powerful vehicle for women's self-development. As a strong, independent leader who urged her constituency to move beyond women's familiar territory of home and church into a wider sphere, she was the WCTU's most powerful model of self-development. Convinced that women's superior morality mandated their entry into the male-dominated world of politics, government, and business in order to purify it and make it responsive to the needs of women and children, Willard set about to convince the WCTU. Her persuasive oratorical powers were legendary. She was a spellbinding speaker who could command her listeners' attention for hours on end and inspire them to realize that they were capable of wielding power they had never known they had.

Willard spoke to her mainly white, middle-class Protestant audience in a language they understood, that of evangelical Protestantism. She insisted that God called them forth to make the world better—a challenge they could not resist. And her WCTU followers believed her; she elicited enormous personal loyalty from them and sincere respect from many others, both in the United States and abroad. A diminutive figure with a sweet face and an ever-present pince-nez who dressed in a plain but pleasing manner, Willard did not threaten the women she sought to influence as did some of the women's rights reformers of the era. Yet over the course of her WCTU presidency, she proposed more and more audacious roles and activities for American women, moving the country's mainstream in a more liberal direction. Her rallying cry, which she embodied, was "Womanliness first—afterward what you will" (Bordin, *Frances Willard*, 9); it seemed on the surface a safe position. But in Willard's interpretation it was a blueprint for radical action.

Under her direction, the WCTU became a kind of school to train women for responsible participation in the public life of their country. By the early 1880s, she had gained the WCTU's endorsement of woman suffrage. She then began to urge its members to see themselves as a potentially powerful pressure group within national, state, and local party politics. She insisted that the WCTU could bring about changes in laws and government policies even before women gained the vote. Following her lead, WCTU women brought their considerable influence to bear on all levels of government by means of lobbying, forming coalitions of groups working for the same reform ends, and through more informal avenues of persuasion. At the same time, Willard and the WCTU continued to push for woman suffrage.

Much of Willard's coalition-building was done at the national level. In 1881, she labored to heal the rift the Civil War had created by going on a southern tour to encourage southern women to work with their northern sisters in the WCTU. Her 1883 "Western Round-Up" was her first concerted effort to organize WCTUs in the Far West. Eventually the WCTU widened its scope internationally with the founding of the World's WCTU in 1883. Meanwhile, Willard continued to build her reform network in Chicago and Illinois, becoming a member of several Chicago organizations working for women, including the Chicago Woman's Club, and state organizations such as the Illinois Woman's Press Association. In 1888, as president of the National Council of Women, a group organized during the fortieth anniversary celebration of the Seneca Falls declaration of women's rights, Willard pushed for women's coalitions in states and cities across the country.

She was instrumental in forming one such coalition in Chicago in June 1888, as seventy women's organizations responded to her call for local women's groups to join forces. During the summer, Willard agreed to be the president of what became the Woman's League of Chicago. In October 1888, at the League's first formal meeting, Willard gave a stirring address, "The Dawn of Woman's Day." In it she announced that "next to God, the greatest organizer on this earth is the mother." She called on Chicago's "mother-hearted women"—whether or not they were biological mothers—to mobilize the "resistless force of . . . aggregated motherhood" (*Our Day*, November 1888, 346–47) in order to address the deplorable conditions for women in the labor force. The Woman's League was apparently short-lived. Its successor, the Illinois Woman's Alliance, in which Willard was only peripherally involved due to the press of her national duties, was active for several years on the Chicago reform scene. The alliance implemented some of the investigations and changes she had advocated in her October 1888 speech to the coalition. Impressed and delighted by Chicago's female reform community, Willard dubbed the city a "paradise of exceptional women" (Bordin, *Frances Willard*, 150), a milieu in which she was proud to locate the national headquarters of the WCTU.

Willard's presidency of the National Council of Women marked the peak of her power and prestige as a reform leader. Throughout the 1880s, her organization carried out the "Do Everything" policy Willard had laid out for it in 1881. It became involved in myriad causes and reforms: from prison visiting to securing police matrons for women in jail, from the kindergarten movement to scientific temperance education in the public schools, from the right of women to preach to their right to have control of their own bodies, from arbitration as a way of settling labor disputes to calling for international arbitration as an alternative to war. Willard and other prominent WCTU leaders politicized their organization and shaped it into a strong force capable of setting reform goals and effecting them. Their leadership was recognized and heeded by a large segment of the American population as well as by millions of followers worldwide.

Drawing on the WCTU's increasing power and influence during the 1880s, Willard sought to enter the national political arena. She had been a longtime supporter of the Republican Party, believing in its commitment to reform since her father and other Evanstonians had joined it in the late 1850s. But she became disillusioned with the party's failure to champion woman suffrage and prohibition at the national level. Concluding that neither the Republican nor Democratic Party was likely to support woman suffrage or temperance in the near future, she worked throughout the 1880s to persuade the WCTU to throw its weight behind the rising Prohibition Party.

She did not accomplish this goal without a struggle, however. Some of the WCTU's finest leaders believed that it should remain nonpartisan, and others kept their allegiance to the Republican Party. A small minority, including Republican J. Ellen Foster, a lawyer from Iowa and one of Willard's most valued colleagues, left the WCTU in disagreement with Willard's partisan political stance and formed the Non-Partisan WCTU. Prominent woman suffragists such as Lucy Stone and her husband, Henry Blackwell, pointed out to Willard that in some states woman suffrage and temperance were championed by the Republican Party and urged her not to lend the WCTU's influence exclusively to the Prohibition Party. Willard was distressed by this criticism but kept her organization in the Prohibition Party ranks. As a member of the party's executive committee for many years, she argued for the continued inclusion of a woman suffrage plank in its platform and watched with apprehension as the party began to focus more and more during the 1890s on the single issue of prohibition.

During the 1880s Willard began to sympathize with the country's growing labor movement. For the first years of her presidency, she had concentrated on building the WCTU's strength and establishing it as a major force in reform. But as her organization consolidated its power, she turned her attention to the pressing problems of urban industrialization. Willard, like many other reformers, became increasingly alarmed at the great gap between rich and poor, owners and workers, that was developing during the last third of the nineteenth century. She began to seek solutions to the problems of the exploitation of workers and the poverty that resulted.

She was especially drawn to the Knights of Labor, then the largest labor organization, because its leader, Terence Powderly, endorsed both woman suffrage and temperance. Like Willard, he advocated arbitration between owners and workers rather than the use of violent means to obtain better conditions for workers, a position some rising socialist leaders supported. Furthermore, the Knights enthusiastically welcomed women into their ranks, which other unions did only reluctantly, if at all. In the mid-1880s, Willard became acquainted with Knights' leader ELIZABETH RODGERS, head of an all-woman local in Chicago. Willard introduced Rodgers, a working-class woman, to the members of Chicago's overwhelmingly middle-class women's reform network and asked Rodgers to inform them about the situation of working women.

In her annual addresses to the WCTU from the late 1880s on, Willard continually raised the issue of the growing inequity between rich and poor. She spoke about labor's attempt to redress this economic gap and her acute sense of the injustice present in the country's capitalist system. Searching for a way to confront the unjust economic situation in the United States, she considered various alternatives, including Nationalism, a form of nonviolent socialism described by economic reformer Edward Bellamy in his best-selling Utopian novel, *Looking Backward.* She recommended that WCTU members read Bellamy's book and form Nationalist clubs to study the cooperative state he proposed. In the early 1890s, she joined the Fabian Society, a British socialist group that worked, like Bellamy's Nationalists, for nonviolent change from private to state ownership of the manufacturing and transportation industries and of utilities.

In an attempt to bring together a reform alliance among the growing populist movement, labor groups, the Prohibition Party, and the WCTU, Willard joined with other leaders hoping to create a new political party that would mount a serious challenge to both Democrats and Republicans in the 1892 presidential election. Delegates from these groups met at the St. Louis Industrial Conference in February 1892 to hammer out a platform for the new party and to fuse the disparate factions into a cohesive organization. Willard used all her political skill and influence to lobby for woman suffrage and temperance planks, but she was unsuccessful. With this defeat, she reached the limits of her political power as the leader of a women's organization because she could not promise a bloc of voters in the November election. Some of the other leaders at the conference might have been sympathetic to her goals of woman suffrage and prohibition, but they could not afford to support an ally who was unable to deliver the vote.

During the 1890s, Willard's WCTU presidency became more troubled. Her organization felt pinched economically by the 1893 depression. Several financial ventures the WCTU had undertaken were on shaky ground, and the organization looked to Willard for rescue. At the same time, Willard had begun to spend at least half of every year in England, working with Isabel (Lady Henry) Somerset, the president of the WCTU's British counterpart, the British Women's Temperance Association, hoping to revamp that organization along the lines of the WCTU. Somerset and Willard had met in 1891 when Somerset first visited the United States to take part in the CTU annual convention. They quickly became good friends, and when Willard's mother died in summer 1892, Somerset invited Willard to be her guest in England while she recovered from her grief over her mother's death. The two leaders' friendship was stimulating to their reform work and emotionally satisfying but kept Willard from attending to the WCTU's growing problems. Her absence from the United States was sorely felt by her organization as disagreements arose between factions of national officers and Willard's leadership was challenged.

Furthermore, her constituency began to question her views. In the 1870s and 1880s, Willard had usually been able to persuade her organization to support her more radical positions. But by the 1890s she had moved far beyond most of the WCTU

membership by championing labor and espousing Christian socialism. She had also begun to assert that poverty was a main cause of intemperance rather than the other way around, as most Americans believed at the time. And she came to believe that temperance would never result from legislative action; instead it would come through education and training. Most WCTU members could not accept Willard's challenges to social and economic positions held by America's middle class, from which the WCTU's membership came. Her ideas were a threat to the very basis of the country's dominant capitalism, and all but a few of her followers were uncomfortable with the challenges that Willard posed to capitalist ideology.

All these factors combined to place great strain on Willard's relationship to her organization. Yet her constituency eagerly continued to support some of her causes during the 1890s. They rallied around her effort to rescue Armenian refugees from Turkish oppression, raising funds and agreeing to sponsor Armenian families in the United States. They mounted a huge drive securing 7.5 million signatures on the "Polyglot Petition," calling on the world's leaders to stop the global traffic in liquor and opium.

Willard continued to speak out boldly against Turkish oppression and on other issues of human rights abuse internationally, but she failed to attack white racism in her own country with similar forcefulness and moral clarity. During the 1880s and early 1890s, race relations in the United States had reached a nadir; Jim Crow laws, segregation, and white terrorism of African Americans had grown to dreadful proportions. By 1892, the number of lynchings had increased to its highest point. Antilynching campaigner IDA B. WELLS-BARNETT and other African American leaders looked to white reformers like Frances Willard, known internationally for her championing of human rights issues, to join with them in condemning lynching.

At the time, the WCTU was one of very few national organizations that welcomed African American members. Wells could reasonably expect Willard to take a strong stand against lynching. However, Willard equivocated, faced with both her moral obligation to denounce lynching as the worst excess of white racism and her need not to offend Southern WCTU leaders. Although she decried the vigilantism of lynching, she suggested that it was understandable as an action to protect white women from black men, an argument many Southerners, including some in the WCTU, used to condone lynching. In making such a statement, she showed her lack of understanding of the actual causes of lynching as well as her tendency toward compromise in order to please both sides in a controversy. Often in the past she had been successful at this tactic, bringing together disparate groups and factions to work toward common goals. But in this instance, Willard managed only to disappoint antilynching activists in the United States and Great Britain and compromise herself as a reformer. Her failure tarnished her reputation as a moral leader.

Willard became ill in the early 1890s, suffering from pernicious anemia, then a fatal disease. She struggled to keep up her hectic speaking and writing schedule and attempted to retain control of her organization from across the Atlantic, but she had lost her former buoyancy and energy. Even exercise regimes and diet could not return her to health. Throughout the decade, she grew weaker and more seriously ill. Finally, in New York City in early February 1898, she contracted influenza as she was ready to sail for England once more. Her body, frail and weakened by anemia, could not fight off the flu, and she died on February 17, 1898, at age fifty-eight, with her beloved Anna Gordon and other WCTU leaders at her bedside.

WCTU members were stunned at the news of Willard's death. Disagreements with their president were set aside as the organization joined the entire nation to mourn one of its most revered figures. Two thousand people jammed the Broadway Tabernacle in New York City to attend her funeral, and many thousands more gathered at the railway stations of towns and villages across the Midwest as her funeral train traveled toward Chicago. There she lay in state for a day at the Woman's Temple, the national headquarters of the WCTU, as an estimated twenty thousand people filed by to pay their respects. After a final service at the Evanston Methodist church, she was buried in her family's plot at Rosehill Cemetery on Chicago's North Side. A reformer to the last, Willard had requested Anna Gordon to carry out her wish to be cremated, then an innovative idea and one that repulsed Gordon, Isabel Somerset, and other close colleagues of Willard's. But loyalty to her friend's last wishes overcame Gordon's discomfiture with cremation and, a few weeks later, she arranged for Willard to be cremated and her ashes placed in her mother's grave as Willard had desired.

Often in her speeches and writings, Willard had proclaimed the imminent arrival of "the dawn of woman's day" with the fast-approaching twentieth century. The day that she envisioned might best be characterized by one of her favorite aphorisms, which she used over and over again to spur her organization on toward its goals: "Woman will bless and brighten every place she enters, and she *will* enter every place on the round earth!" (Willard, "The Work of the WCTU," 404). Through her impassioned leadership of the largest and most powerful women's organization of the time, Willard succeeded in making this slogan a reality for hundreds of thousands of women.

Sources. A large collection of Willard materials—correspondence, a fifty-volume journal, scrapbooks, copies of speeches and articles, etc.—is in the Woman's Christian Temperance Union (WCTU) archive, Frances E. Willard Memorial Library, National WCTU Headquarters, Evanston, Illinois. Much, but not all, of this material is on microfilm: Series III, *The Temperance and Prohibition Papers* (1977). The journal volumes and some other Willard material are microfilmed as an *Addendum* (Series V [1982]) and a complete transcription of the journal, produced by Carolyn De Swarte Gifford, is on deposit at the Willard Library. Other Willard papers at the Willard Library, discovered since the original microfilming project, have not been microfilmed. Correspondence from Willard can also be found in the papers of many late-nineteenth-century reform and religious leaders, for example, those of women's rights leaders Susan B. Anthony and Elizabeth Cady Stanton. An edition of Willard's journal has been published: Carolyn De Swarte Gifford, *"Writing Out My Heart": Selections from the Journal of Frances E. Willard, 1855–1896* (1995). Willard produced a copious autobiography: *Glimpses of Fifty Years: The Autobiography of an American Woman* (1889). She published many other books, including *Woman and Temperance* (1883); *How to Win: A Book for Girls* (1886); *Woman in the Pulpit* (1889); *Do Everything: A Handbook for the World's White Ribboners* (1895); *A Wheel within a Wheel* (1895, 1991); and, with Mary A. Liver-

more et al., *Woman of the Century* (1893). She wrote numerous articles for journals and newspapers, including the prominent reform journals *Our Day*, *Arena*, and *Dawn*, as well as *Union Signal*, the official newspaper of the WCTU, and other temperance papers, such as *Voice*, the New York-based organ of the Prohibition Party. She also authored many chapters in edited volumes, including "The Work of the W.C.T.U.," in Annie Nathan Meyer, *Women's Work in America* (1890). The Woman's Temperance Publishing Association, publishing arm of the WCTU, issued many booklets and pamphlets written by Willard; one of the most important, *A White Life for Two*, went through many reprintings. There have been a number of biographies of Willard, including Anna Gordon, *The Beautiful Life of Frances E. Willard* (1898), written from the perspective of Willard's loyal companion and including many memorials from international reform leaders; Ray Strachey, *Frances Willard: Her Life and Work* (1913), by the granddaughter of one of Willard's trusted lieutenants, who had access to many women who worked with Willard; Mary Earhart (Dillon), *Frances Willard: From Prayers to Politics* (1944), interpreting Willard as a powerful political figure and influential women's rights leader; and Ruth Bordin, *Frances Willard: A Biography* (1986), which incorporates new research in the history of alcohol in America and the growing field of women's history from the 1960s to the1980s into a portrait of Willard as a skillful and persuasive reformer. There have been several recent studies of Willard's rhetoric, including, Richard W. Leeman, *"Do Everything" Reform: The Oratory of Frances Willard* (1992), and Amy Rose Slagell, "A Good Woman Speaking Well: The Oratory of Frances E. Willard (Ph.D. diss., Univ. of Wisconsin—Madison, 1992). Slagell's dissertation contains a chronological listing of Willard's speeches and reproduces the full text of more than fifty. Elizabeth B. Clark, "The Politics of God and the Woman's Vote: Religion in the Suffrage Movement in America" (Ph.D. diss., Princeton Univ., 1989), compares Willard's and her organization's approach to suffrage with that of Elizabeth Cady Stanton and other suffrage organization leaders. Suzanne M. Marilley, "Frances Willard and the Feminism of Fear," *Feminist Studies*, vol. 19, 1993, examines Willard's political ideology and the rationale for the WCTU's support of woman suffrage, as does C. D. Gifford, "Wouldn't You Like to Vote as Well as Oliver: Frances Willard's Crusade for Women's Equality," *Humanities*, July/August 1995. For a discussion of Willard's religion, see C. D. Gifford, "'My Own Methodist Hive': Frances Willard's Faith as Disclosed in her Journal," in *Spirituality and Social Responsibility: Vocational Vision of Women in the United Methodist Tradition*, ed. Rosemary Skinner Keller (1993). C. D. Gifford, "For God and Home and Native Land: The WCTU's Image of Woman in the Late Nineteenth Century," in *Women in New Worlds*, ed. Keller, vol. 1 (1981), and C. D. Gifford, "Frances Willard and the WCTU's Conversion to Woman Suffrage," in *One Woman, One Vote*, ed. Marjorie Spruill Wheeler (1995), look at the changing understanding of womanhood within the WCTU, encouraged by Willard's leadership. C. D. Gifford, "Frances Willard and the Women's Movement in Illinois: The Ballot for Home Protection, 1874–1882," unpublished manuscript, 1995, details Willard's first campaign for woman suffrage. Ruth Bordin, *Woman and Temperance: The Quest for Power and Liberty* (1981), and Susan Dye Lee, "Evangelical Domesticity: The Origins of the WCTU under Frances Willard" (Ph.D. diss., Northwestern Univ., 1980), give an understanding of Willard's relation to her organization. Mari Jo Buhle, *Women and American Socialism, 1870–1920* (1981), chapter 2, places Willard within a radical reform tradition. Emilie M. Townes, "Because God Gave Her Vision: The Religious Impulse of Ida B. Wells-Barnett," in *Spirituality and Social Responsibility*, ed. Keller, and Carol Mattingly, *"Well-Tempered Women": Nineteenth Century Temperance Rhetoric* (1998), chapter 7, give accounts of Willard's clash with Wells-Barnett over Willard's equivocal stance on lynching, as does Bordin's biography.

CAROLYN DE SWARTE GIFFORD

WILLARD, FRANCES LANGDON
October 31, 1797–March 24, 1854

EDUCATOR

As an itinerant early schoolteacher and women's seminary principal, Frances L. Willard tried to raise the standards of education for women to meet the higher intellectual and moral demands of life in a new republic. She struggled to be economically independent as a single woman and was driven throughout her life to extend her vision of Protestant Christianity to others, especially those on the western frontier. She was born in Wallingford, Connecticut, the youngest of John and Huldah (Langdon) Willard's three children who survived infancy. Her father was a Congregational minister who served at Meriden, Connecticut, until 1802, when he moved his family to the backcountry at Lunenburg, Vermont. To supplement a meager local pastor's salary there, he conducted a traveling ministry under three different home missionary boards and practiced medicine as a self-taught physician.

Because the Willards had limited means, the children had fewer educational opportunities than their father, who graduated from Yale University. Frances Willard's brother, Julius Alphonso, apprenticed with an uncle to learn the drug and mercantile business; her sister, Elizabeth ("Eliza"), learned enough to teach school before marrying. Willard was strongly devoted to her father, "a man of eminent piety" (Frances L. Willard to National Popular Education Board, June 19, 1849, 3, National . . . Board Papers). She underwent a conversion experience in 1820 when religious revivals were spreading across New England, engaging the population in an awakened sense of religious purpose. Committed to perpetuating her father's influence but aware that the ministry and missionary fields were closed to her as a woman, Willard turned to teaching, a respectable profession for a single woman who dedicated herself to religious service.

Little is known about Willard's education. She grew up in an era of scarce, unsystematic, often short-lived, private schools of varying quality, especially for girls with limited means. She attended two summers at Hanover Academy in New Hampshire, receiving free board from relatives there. About 1829, she studied educational methods under the Reverend Samuel Hall at Concord, Vermont; he was an educational reformer and an American pioneer in teacher training and systematic methods of instruction. Her father, a local subscription school, and personal reading may have provided her only other training. She expressed familiarity with the practices of such better-known contemporaries in the emerging field of women's higher education as Sarah Pierce, Mary Lyons, Emma Willard, and Catharine Beecher. Between 1818 and 1831, Frances Willard taught girls for a year or less each at Columbia and Lancaster, New Hampshire, and Lunenburg, Vermont, and between one and two years each at Gorham, Maine, and Penn-Yan, New York.

From the late 1820s, concern about the trans-Appalachian frontier, stereotypically presumed to be morally destitute, grew rapidly among eastern Protestants. Organizations and individuals responded with plans to send church-affiliated settlers, especially teachers, west to promote and exemplify the benefits of Yankee culture and religion, as well as to counter the already existing Catholic presence. At Penn-Yan about 1829, Frances L.

Willard became convinced of the spiritual and literary needs of Mississippi Valley settlers and vowed to go west. She expected to leave New England in 1831 with her brother who, under the influence of Reverend Lyman Beecher of Boston, was emigrating with his family to Carrollton, Illinois. For unknown reasons, she instead returned to New York state to teach and head seminaries at Brownville and Adams, in Jefferson County, for five years. She expressed her continued zeal, however, for the western mission. By the end of 1835, she was in Illinois, teaching three girls in a family school at Monticello (later renamed Godfrey) near her brother, who by then had moved to Alton. On May 9, 1836, Willard opened a Female School in Chicago.

Willard's seminary in frontier Chicago was similar to most of those she had taught in before and would encounter later in life. She was directed by an all-male group of trustees that included Protestant ministers and civic leaders who recognized such a school as a community asset and most of whom had daughters to be educated. Because of the precarious business affairs of such schools, Willard commonly left a position in personal debt because school money was still owed to her. She worried, for years, about her continued inability to repay loans from her brother and a cousin. Trustees at Chicago went so far as to promise Willard the eventual security of public seminary buildings, including boarding facilities, to come from the income of a public school fund to be generated by government land sales. Upon arrival, however, she found that the nominal trustees, in view of the uncertainty of economic development, wanted her initially to take full financial responsibility. She had to collect fees and pay for salaries, equipment, and board for herself and assistants.

In Chicago, Willard at least did not have the burden of locating a suitable room or building to rent as a school. In 1835, John S. Wright, a young Yankee speculator, had built the town's first building specifically for school purposes. He did so at the urging of his mother, Huldah Wright, who also corresponded with Willard about starting the new seminary and was considered its patroness.

An advertisement for the school that appeared in the *Chicago American* as early as March 19, 1836, described the surprisingly advanced courses that Willard's own patchwork education had prepared her to teach. Assuming students already knew rudiments of reading and writing, Willard offered a basic program for girls ages eight to twelve, whom she considered most susceptible to educational influence: reading, writing, spelling and defining, geography, arithmetic, history, grammar, and composition. A more advanced level consisted of further arithmetic, ancient and modern history, bookkeeping, natural philosophy (physics or science), chemistry, rhetoric, logic, and intellectual and moral philosophy. For women desiring to qualify to teach, a special course of study was available. Ornamental skills more typical of an earlier generation of female schools—needlework, drawing, painting, and music—were offered at an extra charge. Since pupils ranged in age from five to older than twenty, teachers had to prepare for a wide range of learning levels.

Frances Willard tried, in all her schools, to gain authorization for a nonsectarian student body, daily Bible instruction, and prayer. At Chicago, pupils and parents were assured a program of religious instruction, with Christianity upheld as a model for behavior and character formation. In a wider sense, Willard's goal, as stated in her advertisement, was to give young ladies a broad education to "fit them for all the important duties of life they may be called upon to perform" (*Chicago American*, March 19, 1836).

Frances Willard's Chicago seminary began with seventeen pupils; within a month, it increased to thirty. By July an assistant was hired. Later a second assistant was recruited for a growing school. On October 28, 1836, fifty-seven students presented the results of six months of Willard's instruction at a public examination before an audience of four hundred at the Presbyterian church.

At first, Willard was favorably impressed with Chicago and hoped to make it a permanent home. She claimed more freedom from chronic lung problems and incapacitating nervous headaches than ever in her life. She praised the town's four Protestant clergy and declared to her brother that she liked everything about the growing city except its lack of religious fervor. The latter she attributed to enormous profits from land speculation and a craze to get rich that permeated society. After eight months, Willard was less enthusiastic. The cost of living in Chicago was high and housing scarce; finding respectable, religious families with whom to board out-of-town students, assistants, and herself was a constant problem. She despaired of having girls older than thirteen serious about studies, when their parents encouraged them to be active in the materialistic social life of a wealthy town. To Willard, the solution was to have students under her constant supervision in a boarding school, but she realized that the original plans for a public boarding school would not be realized.

The second year of the female seminary at the Wright building began in May 1837 under Louisa M. Gifford, a former Willard assistant. Frances Willard continued to teach elsewhere, despite a recurrence of old health problems during the previous, harsh Chicago winter. In July 1837, she tried a new strategy: in a rented house, she opened a school as well as her own boarding facility for out-of-town pupils, assistants, and "a few pious gentlemen" (Frances L. Willard to Julius Willard, October 4, 1837, 2, Samuel Willard Papers). Soon, several boarders became seriously ill, and she added nursing duties to her teaching, cooking, and general housekeeping. She acknowledged the help of good assistants and supportive citizens in keeping it all running. She was delighted to be settled in her own home, which, she declared, was "becoming the resort for the pious portion of [the] community" (Frances L. Willard to Julius Willard, October 9, 1837, 2, Samuel Willard Papers). While she was preoccupied with boarders' sickness in the fall of 1837, three other ladies' schools were begun in competition with hers. By the end of the following March, she had been through a severe lung illness and had given up housekeeping. In May 1838, she left school teaching in Chicago and spent the summer with her brother and his family in Alton.

Frances Willard next taught at Carrollton, Illinois, for two years. During this period she also attempted to establish a private boarding school at Upper Alton. The school lasted only through the summer of 1839 because of inadequate community support. In the winter of 1840–41, she taught at Russellville, in northern Alabama, in the family of a wealthy plantation owner who was building a girls' boarding school; when his business failed, she found a church school position beginning March 1841 at Tuscumbia, fifteen miles away. Five months later, an urgent letter from her sister, Eliza Parsons, about their mother's declining health summoned her back to Vermont; the two sisters shared nursing duty, and Willard taught one term in Danville, until Huldah Willard died in May 1842.

After an abortive attempt to establish a Lunenburg school, Willard set out in the fall of 1842 for North Carolina to combine teaching efforts in a log academy with her Connecticut cousin Olynthia Hart. Before she could leave New England, however, she had to halt four times and accept the hospitality of relatives while seeking treatment for lingering, incapacitating back pain, the result of lifting her bedridden mother. Nine months later, finally able to work again, she taught briefly at Durham, Connecticut, then Sing Sing and Haverstraw, New York, each time relinquishing her duties for lack of viable enrollments.

In 1844–45, Willard headed the female department at Black River Religious Institute, Watertown, New York, but she left because the minister-principal undermined her discipline by giving wealthier students preferential treatment. For the next several months, still nursing back problems, she stayed with a cousin, Dr. Augustus Willard, at Greene, New York, and taught at a small school there. On April 12, 1847, Frances Willard opened a ladies' school at Montrose, Pennsylvania, for five pupils, with a curriculum similar to the one she had offered at Chicago. Enrollment grew to sixty-five over the following months, but not without problems. Because she could not find help she considered competent, Willard cooked for four to six boarding pupils, as well as for her assistants. Competition from a nearby Catholic school and the local Baptists hurt the seminary. Living costs were high; community support was fickle, and the Montrose climate reactivated her pulmonary problems.

Willard's desire to be near her brother, as well as her acute awareness of advancing age and the fact that the East was overcrowded with teachers, made her increasingly look westward for some permanency throughout the 1840s. She even considered alternatives to teaching—supervising a boarding house, bookkeeping, and copy writing. Leaving Montrose in early 1849, Willard taught a summer term at Towanda, Pennsylvania; she then entered a six-week training program of the religiously oriented National Popular Education Board, an organization that helped match eastern teachers to frontier localities where they were needed. For reasons not known, Willard left before the end of the program and got to St. Louis on her own by November 9, 1849. After unsuccessfully seeking opportunities in that area, she returned to her former position at Carrollton, Illinois, for eighteen months. Her attempt to begin an academy at Peoria in 1851 was defeated by too much competition and poor arrangements. Following summer teaching at Canton, Willard began a new girls' school at Mount Vernon on August 25, 1851. It was at least partially publicly funded, but it was firmly backed, built, and furnished by a local merchant. Here, in the southernmost of her Illinois experiences, Willard found the residents of Tennessean background and some of her older students just beginning their education.

While teaching at Mount Vernon, she met the Reverend John Ingersoll, Presbyterian minister at Marion, a widower with grown children and an itinerant like herself; they were married August 3, 1852. Since the Mount Vernon employer held her to her contract for the next school session, the newlyweds settled for visiting each other when possible for a period of several months. In late 1853 illness again overtook Willard-Ingersoll, and she consulted several doctors for relief from dropsy or edema. Finally, she went to Alton to her brother Julius Willard, where she died March 24, 1854.

In spite of continual problems with health, constant debt and precarious financial independence, indifferent trustees, and competitive schools, Frances L. Willard was part of a group of early educators who extended the scope of female education beyond basic reading and writing and the more decorative domestic arts. Before teacher-training schools or even common schools could be taken for granted, she acquired the requisites to teach courses to girls that today would be considered secondary or even college level. According to her "Catalogue of Pupils," which spanned more than three decades, in ephemeral schools scattered over seven states, twenty-three towns, and hundreds of miles, she provided a moral example and opportunities for advanced training to at least twelve hundred girls and women. She also helped seventy-four to qualify to teach and fifty former teachers to upgrade their skills. If she did not succeed as well as such educators as Emma Willard and Mary Lyons, it may be because circumstances denied her supportive sponsors who could summon sufficient financing to get her enterprises through the first unstable years and put them on sound footing. Poor health was yet another chronic obstacle to securing the permanent home and opportunities to influence others that she doggedly pursued throughout her life.

Sources. Collections documenting Frances L. Willard's life include the Samuel Willard Papers, Illinois State Hist. Library, Springfield; Robert G. Ingersoll Papers, Ingersoll Family Papers, and Robert G. Ingersoll and Family, General Correspondence, all at Illinois State Hist. Library; and the Frances L. Willard Collection, CHS, which has her unpublished "Catalogue of Pupils," 1818–53. Other details about Willard appear in the Barbour Collection of Connecticut Vital Records (microfilm), Connecticut State Library, Hartford; Illinois Statewide Marriage Index, Jefferson County (microfiche), Illinois State Archives, Springfield; and National Popular Education Board Papers, Connecticut Hist. Soc., Hartford. Useful published works that illuminate Willard's role in Chicago's educational beginnings include Chicago Superintendent of Schools, *Annual Report* (1858); John S. Wright, *Chicago: Past, Present and Future* (1867); Alfred T. Andreas, *History of Chicago*, vol. 1 (1884); and Mary Ann Hubbard, *Family Memoirs* (1912). Contemporary newspapers, *Chicago Democrat* and *Chicago American*, have advertisements for Willard's schools. Studies that provide important context for Willard's life as an early-nineteenth-century single, religious, western, female professional educator include Thomas Woody, *A History of Women's Education in the United States*, vol. 1 (1929); Colin B. Goodykoontz, *Home Missions on the American Frontier* (1939); Polly Welts Kaufman, *Women Teachers on the Frontier* (1984); and Lee Virginia Chambers-Schiller, *Liberty: A Better Husband, Single Women in America, the Generations of 1780–1840* (1984). The *Alton [Illinois] Daily Morning Courier*, March 25, 1854, carried her death notice.

WILLA G. CRAMTON

WILLIAMS, FANNIE BARRIER
February 12, 1855–March 4, 1944
JOURNALIST, SOCIAL REFORMER, CIVIC LEADER, CLUBWOMAN

Fannie Barrier Williams, the second daughter and the last of three children of Anthony J. and Harriet (Prince) Barrier, was born in Brockport, New York. Her parents, as well as her grandparents on both sides of her family, were freeborn.

Anthony J. Barrier, a modestly prosperous barber who periodically supplemented his income moonlighting as a coal merchant, was able to purchase a home and provide his family with a comfortable middle-class lifestyle. A deeply religious and public-spirited man, he was a respected leader in the local white Baptist church, in which his family members were the only black members, and he was an active participant in the civic affairs of Brockport. Anthony and Harriet Barrier were a fairly educated couple who enjoyed "good books and the refinements of life" (Williams, "Autobiography," 91) and introduced their children to both.

Fannie Barrier received her early education in neighborhood schools, and she completed the academic and classical program at the State Normal School in Brockport in 1870. Following graduation, in keeping with her desire to do something important or extraordinary, Fannie Barrier joined the army of northern teachers who went to the South during Reconstruction to educate freedpeople.

Born and raised in an overwhelmingly white community in which she suffered little discrimination, Fannie Barrier was ill-prepared for the scalding racism and discrimination that she encountered in the South. These experiences provided a rude awakening to what it meant to be black and female in the South and crystallized for Barrier the fundamental issues related to the African American's struggle in the United States.

Fannie Barrier had some ability as a painter, and during her tenure in the South she decided to develop that talent. She succeeded in persuading a white art teacher to give her instruction, but since a condition of her admission was that she be screened off from the other students, she refused to attend. Instead, Barrier returned North, enrolling at the New England Conservatory of Music in Boston. Once again her ambitions and aspirations were obstructed by what she termed "the tyranny of a black complexion" ("Autobiography," 92). When some white students objected to her attendance, the principal advised Barrier that her presence imperiled the interests of the institution. Subsequently, Fannie Barrier found a teaching position in Washington, D.C., and entered the School of Fine Arts to perfect her skills as a portrait painter.

While living in Washington she met S. Laing Williams, a native of Georgia who held a political appointment in the U.S. Pension Office and who was a law student at Columbian University (later George Washington Law School). After graduating from law school with honors and completing several graduate courses, he married Fannie Barrier in 1887 in the home of her parents in Brockport, New York. The newlyweds moved to Chicago, where S. Laing Williams was admitted to the Illinois bar. With the assistance of Fannie Barrier Williams, who retired from teaching after her marriage, S. Laing Williams was able to establish a thriving legal practice.

The Williamses, who had no children, found their niche in Chicago's close-knit black community and joined the Unitarian All Souls Church of Jenkin Lloyd Jones. They became active in the civic life of the city and leaders in the struggle to uplift their race. Shortly after their arrival in Chicago in 1887, S. Laing Williams organized the Prudence Crandall Study Club, an elite literary society that limited membership to twenty-five and attracted some of the city's most socially prominent African Americans. Fannie Barrier Williams served as the head of the club's art and music department. She also aided her husband with other organizations that he founded and cofounded, including the Hyde Park Colored Voters Republican Club, the Taft Colored League, and the Black Diamond Development Company. She became actively involved in various aspects of the women's and social reform movements in Chicago and used her influence and associations in the interests of the disadvantaged. To this end she worked with groups regardless of color, and she had a degree of success in improving the lot of the downtrodden and in finding good employment for a few black women. Fannie Barrier Williams was an active member of the Illinois Woman's Alliance, an association of almost all Chicago women's organizations, and between 1891 and 1894 she held almost every office including vice-president and secretary. In 1894 she became the head of the Alliance's Committee on State Schools for Children.

When the Williamses arrived in Chicago, there was no hospital at which a black doctor held a regular staff appointment or had the privilege of performing operations, and none received black patients on an equal basis. In 1890 Emma Reynolds, a young black woman, was denied admission to every nurses' training school in the city because of her race. Reynolds's story, so similar to her own experiences, struck a responsive cord in Fannie Barrier Williams. Under the leadership of Dr. Daniel Hale Williams, Chicago's black community reacted to this incident by initiating a drive to create an interracial hospital. Out of her friendship with Dr. Williams and her interest in providing employment opportunities for black women and improving social services in the black community, Fannie Barrier Williams became a major force in the movement that culminated in the establishment of Provident Hospital and Training School in 1891. While the hospital served black and white patients, Williams advocated that the Training School for Nurses admit only black women. "There are other training schools for white women, but none at all for colored women. Why let white women take any of the few places we'll have open" (quoted in Hendricks, "Fannie Barrier Williams," 1261), she argued.

In 1904 the Williamses were instrumental in the founding of the Frederick Douglass Center, an experimental residential and recreational center designed to promote better race relations. Fannie Barrier Williams became one of the directors of the center in 1905 and supported the institution financially over the years. The Williamses were also long-standing members and supporters of the Abraham Lincoln Center, a social welfare agency sponsored by their church.

Williams was thrust into the national limelight in the early 1890s. As part of the planning for the 1893 World's Columbian Exposition, in 1890 the Fair Commission appointed a Board of Lady Managers whose task it was to approve applications for exhibition space in the women's pavilion. The conspicuous absence of African American women on the board or any provision for the inclusion of exhibits from black women infuriated a large segment of Chicago's black female population. An ad hoc group of black women presented to the Board of Lady Managers a resolution requesting that an office be established to collect exhibits from American "colored" women. The Fair Commission refused to create the suggested office; but as a conciliatory gesture, it agreed to appoint a black woman to assist in supervising the installation of exhibits in the Woman's Building. Fannie Barrier Williams, who was very well known by many of the prominent white women associated with the exposition, was the commission's choice for the position. She later served as secretary of the art department of the woman's branch of the congress auxiliaries for the fair and was invited to deliver two addresses at the Exposition.

Fannie Barrier Williams's first presentation, "The Intellectual Progress of the Colored Women of the United States since the Emancipation Proclamation," was given before the World's Congress of Representative Women in May 1893. A few months later she was one of five African American women to address the World's Parliament of Religions—her topic, "Religious Duty to The Negro."

Williams, an eloquent, impassioned, and forceful speaker, was soon in great demand as a lecturer. Between 1893 and 1908 she traveled extensively, speaking before women's clubs and other organizations. Williams was an accomplished musician, and she sometimes supplemented her lectures with concerts. Williams was also a reporter for the *Women's Era*, *New York Age*, and *Chicago Record-Herald*. Moreover, she was a frequent contributor to other newspapers and journals, and her articles appeared in several books. Williams assisted her husband with most of his scholarly works and also ghostwrote Booker T. Washington's biography of Frederick Douglass.

Williams was nominated in 1894 for membership in the all-white Chicago Women's Club (after 1895 the Chicago Woman's Club) by ELLEN HENROTIN, CELIA WOOLLEY, and Grace Begley. The resulting controversy over Williams's race received national attention. After fourteen months of bitter wrangling, in 1895 she became the first, and for thirty years remained the only, black member of the Chicago Woman's Club. During the same year she served as one of the National League of Colored Women's delegates to the Second Triennial Session of the National Council of Women held in Washington, D.C. She represented Illinois at the First Congress of Negro Women, which met in conjunction with the Cotton Exposition in Atlanta. There she presented a paper at the Frederick Douglass Memorial Service at which Booker T. Washington gave his historic "Atlanta Address." In fact, the influence of Washington's ideas on Williams's thinking was evident in her speeches and writings as early as 1896. Over the years the Williamses became close personal friends of Booker T. Washington and his family.

Williams played an active role in the black women's club movement in Chicago and in the founding of the National League of Colored Women (NLCW) in 1893. She was also instrumental in the establishment of the NLCW successor in 1896, the National Association of Colored Women (NACW). The Ida B. Wells Club, organized in September 1893 and named after its founder (see IDA B. WELLS-BARNETT), was the first black women's club organized in Chicago, followed by the Phyllis Wheatley Club in March 1896. Williams was a founding member of the Phyllis Wheatley Club, and she served as a teacher in the day nursery begun by the club in 1904. When this group opened the Phyllis Wheatley Home for Girls in 1908, Williams became a member of the board of directors, serving as its corresponding secretary. The club and home were named after the African American poet, who spelled her name Phillis Wheatley. When NACW held its first national meeting in Nashville, Tennessee, in 1897, ELIZABETH DAVIS, president of the Phyllis Wheatley Club, extended an invitation to the NACW to hold its 1899 national meeting in Chicago.

In February 1898, the pastor of Bethel African Methodist Episcopal Church called together a number of women interested in "improving social conditions" in Chicago's black communities, "advanc[ing] neighborhood fellowship, and "lend[ing] a hand to the unfortunate and those who need the active sympathy of earnest women" (Williams, "Chicago Report"). To this end the Chicago Women's Conference was formed. The work plan for this organization was developed by an Executive Committee, and Fannie Barrier Williams was elected head.

Williams and her husband increasingly became involved in national affairs. After Booker T. Washington founded the National Negro Business League in 1900, S. Laing Williams became a prominent member and was elected registrar for the league in 1901. Williams became an active supporter of the league, assisting her husband and presenting papers at the 1902 and 1904 annual conventions. When Washington's supporters assumed control of the Afro-American Council, a national civil rights organization, in 1902, Williams was elected corresponding secretary of the organization, succeeding Ida B. Wells-Barnett. Following her husband's appointment as assistant U.S. attorney in 1908, Williams wrote and lectured less often. After Woodrow Wilson's election in 1912, Booker T. Washington's influence in the White House declined and S. Laing Williams lost his government appointment. The Williamses became more active in the National Association for the Advancement of Colored People, and Fannie Barrier Williams engaged extensively in the woman suffrage movement.

After S. Laing Williams's death in 1921, Williams curtailed many of her activities. However, when Mayor William Hale Thompson appointed her to the Chicago Public Library Board in 1924, making her the first Black and the only woman on this policy-making body, she accepted. Williams served on the board from 1924 to 1926. When declining health forced her to resign, she moved back to her family's home in Brockport, New York. There she lived with her sister, Ella B. Barrier, until she died of arteriosclerosis at the age of eighty-nine.

Fannie Barrier Williams devoted her life's work to eradicating sexism and racism in the United States and to promoting social reforms that would enhance the well-being of the American people. Williams was an educated middle-class black female reformer, and her experiences were, in many respects, representative of African American women who came to the forefront of the struggle for gender and racial justice in the nineteenth century. At the same time, certain aspects of her life were unique to a small and often neglected segment of that population. Recog-

nizing this distinction, Williams suggested in 1904 that "no one but a colored woman, reared and educated as I was, can ever know what it means to be brought face to face with conditions that fairly overwhelm you with the ugly reminder that a certain penalty must be suffered by those who, not being able to select their own parentage, must be born of a dark complexion" (Williams, "Autobiography," 91).

Sources. There are Fannie Barrier and S. Laing Williams files in the Booker T. Washington Papers and materials on Williams in the Mary Church Terrell collection, both at the Library of Congress. Her columns in the *Women's Era,* the *New York Age,* and the *Chicago Record-Herald* as well as her articles in *The Voice of the Negro* are useful. The National Association of Colored Women's Papers are available on microfilm at the National Archives for Black Women's History, National Council of Negro Women, Washington, D.C.; they include Williams's "Chicago Report," 1899, reel 16. Williams's "A Northern Negro's Autobiography" appeared in the *Independent,* July 14, 1904. A general chronology of her life is provided in Wanda Hendricks, "Fanny Barrier Williams," *BWA.* Other writing by Williams include the following: "Social Bonds in the 'Black Belt' of Chicago," *Charities,* October 1905; *The Colored Woman and Her Part in Race Regeneration* (1900, reprinted 1969). Also see Elizabeth Lindsay Davis, *Lifting as They Climb* (1895); Allan Spear, *Black Chicago: The Making of a Negro Ghetto, 1890–1920* (1967); and Anne Meis Knupfer, *Toward a Tenderer Humanity and a Nobler Womanhood: African American Women's Clubs in Turn-of-the-Century Chicago* (1996). For an in-depth discussion of Fannie Barrier Williams and the World's Columbian Exposition of 1893, see Ann Massa, "Black Women in the 'White City,'" *Phylon,* Winter 1965.

JUNE O. PATTON

WILLIAMS, FLORENCE CHAPMAN
1884(?)–February 22, 1964
HEALTH EDUCATOR, ANTI-TUBERCULOSIS ACTIVIST

Florence C. Williams, a career health educator and public health field-worker, devoted more than fifty years of her life to the antituberculosis movement. Tuberculosis (TB) was the leading cause of death among all Americans in the late nineteenth century. By the early 1900s, however, the overall death rate from TB began to decline, except among black Americans, who were six times more likely to contract the disease and seven times more likely to die of it than white Americans. The roots of the higher incidence of tuberculosis among African Americans lay in such factors as poverty, substandard housing and diet, and inadequate access to health care. Florence Williams spent a lifetime combating this disparity, battling in the arenas of public health and education, community and social work, and the politics of race as it affected access to health care.

Scant information exists about Florence Chapman's early years. She was born in Washington, D.C., but the names of her parents are not known. On October 16, 1906, at age twenty-two, she married Theodore F. Williams in a ceremony conducted by an African Methodist Episcopal minister at the Raleigh, North Carolina, home of the groom.

Williams undoubtedly received her formal education prior to 1915, by which time she was working in the Division of Negro Health at the North Carolina State Board of Health. She may have attended the Miner Normal Teachers College in Washington, D.C.

In 1919 North Carolina granted Williams a leave of absence so that she could work with the Young Men's Christian Association (YMCA) in Europe. During World War I and the demobilization period that followed it, nearly thirteen thousand volunteers served as "secretaries" at the YMCA canteens and "huts" that supported the camps and leave areas of the American Expeditionary Forces. Although 140,000 black soldiers served overseas, the YMCA dispatched fewer than ninety black secretaries to assist these troops at their segregated camps, and most of these volunteers arrived after the fighting ended. In March 1919 Williams was one of sixteen "colored" women sent to assist the three who had been there during the war itself. She spent six months in the port city of St. Nazaire, the largest leave area in France and home to more than thirty thousand black troops. There she taught literacy and health classes, operated a library, prepared refreshments, and wrote letters to soldiers' families back home.

After serving in France, Williams returned to her position in North Carolina but was granted another leave of absence from 1922 to 1923 to attend Columbia University in New York, where she enrolled in a special health education program at Teachers' College. By 1924 she had come to the attention of the National Tuberculosis Association (NTA), then just beginning to recognize that TB patients were more likely to consult health professionals of their own race. Under the auspices of the NTA, Williams worked briefly as a health demonstrator in West Virginia and then joined the Arkansas Tuberculosis Association (ATA) as head of its Negro Education Program. Williams encountered the politics of race and poverty as she traveled the state with a black physician, Dr. Hugh A. Browne, setting up black clinics "side by side with white clinics in the field" (Erle Chambers to Dr. Michael Davis, September 1, 1931, Rosenwald Fund Archives). In characterizing the efficacy of their fieldwork, the executive director of ATA, Erle Chambers, pointed out the additional benefit in changing racial stereotypes and attitudes: "Dr. Browne is a whole interracial commission just as Mrs. Williams is" ("Report of Use Made of Rosenwald Fund," 1931, 5, Rosenwald Fund Archives). Chambers expressed to Dr. Michael Davis, medical director of the Julius Rosenwald Fund, her organization's hope that as a result of their work, "we may produce in the white group a finer spirit of service which will enable them to meet the Negro group squarely on the common ground of science and humanity as they have never done before" (Chambers to Davis, September 1, 1931).

From 1930 to 1934 Williams organized and directed a series of courses and programs at Arkansas State College for Negroes. Designed as a general health curriculum for the state's black teachers and county extension agents, a key component of these courses included teaching students how to identify active cases of TB and how to help prevent the disease from spreading in their own communities.

More recognition came to Williams during her decade in Arkansas than at any other time in her long career. In 1926 she journeyed to Belgium as a delegate to the International Board of Missions' Conference on Christian Education for Africa. She attended the White House Conference on Child Health and Protection in 1930, serving as a member of the School Child Committee and its Subcommittee on Negro Schools. The fol-lowing year, Williams participated in President Herbert Hoover's Conference on Home Building and Home Ownership, where, along with IRENE McCOY GAINES, she was one of twenty-two members of the Committee on Negro Housing. In 1934 she attended the National Conference on Fundamental Problems in the Education of Negroes, supported in part by the Chicago-based Rosenwald Fund, and was one of four who authored the Subcommittee Report on Child Health Problems.

In September 1931 Florence Williams's husband of nearly twenty-five years, Theodore F. Williams, died in Raleigh. For many of those years, the couple had lived apart while she pursued job opportunities outside of North Carolina. At the time of his death, Theodore Williams was fifty-six and a college professor.

As the full force of the Great Depression hit, funding for Williams's work grew precarious, and by 1934 Arkansas could no longer pay her salary. That same year the Chicago Tuberculosis Institute began discussing its need for a Negro Health Education Program, and at the urging of executive director Louise Sachs, the institute's board voted to engage Williams for a six-month period "to survey and outline a program for Chicago" ("Minutes," June 18, 1934, 2, Chicago Lung Association Papers). Her salary was "not to exceed $150 per month" (p. 2).

Upon reporting for duty at the institute in September 1934, Williams began the process of interviewing prominent leaders in the black community to solicit their advice. Working closely with Dr. Midian O. Bousfield, the only Black on the institute's board and later the medical director of the Rosenwald Fund, Williams assembled an impressive Advisory Committee on Negro Health Education. Composed of doctors, clergy, educators and social workers, journalists, and business and community leaders, the advisory committee helped Williams launch an ambitious agenda of educational initiatives in the city's teeming black districts. She organized early diagnosis clinics that offered skin testing and X-ray follow-up for those with positive tests, and she trained community volunteers to help her conduct house-to-house calls in targeted neighborhoods. She visited public and parochial schools, YMCAs, churches, and community centers, offering lessons about personal hygiene and prevention and early detection of communicable diseases exacerbated by overcrowded housing conditions.

Coincident with Williams's hiring, the institute's board approved the funds to conduct a survey documenting the extent of tuberculosis among Chicago's African American population. The report, prepared from 1935 to 1936, concluded that black mortality from TB was out of proportion to the population, and it documented that from 1930 to 1934, almost one-third of Chicago's TB deaths occurred among African Americans, even though Blacks represented just over 7 percent of the city's entire population. In addition to identifying city neighborhoods with high rates of TB, the study revealed that the machinery for finding cases in Chicago's black neighborhoods was woefully inadequate. It pointed to a lack of fieldwork and follow-up with active TB cases and noted that of the area's many hospitals treating TB patients, only a few treated African Americans. As Chicago's black population swelled throughout the 1930s and 1940s, TB statistics for African Americans remained grim. But in a letter to a colleague, Williams expressed concern that dwelling on morbidity and mortality rates could be counterproductive. While organizing a Negro Health Institute in 1937, she argued that the key to decreasing disease was identification, treatment, and education. "It isn't how much tuberculosis, or syphilis, etc. there is in a group, but do we have it, that matters, and if we have it what can we do to get rid of, or lessen it" (Williams to M. O. Bousfield, July 20, 1937, Rosenwald Fund Archives).

Working within the constraints of Chicago's racially segregated health and school systems meant that she confronted the issues of inadequate funding, personnel, and treatment facilities on a daily basis. In 1941, after seven years on the job, Williams's salary was raised to $185 a month and an additional nurse was hired to work with her in the black districts. The institute's annual budget for 1944–45, totaling more than $235,000, included just $4,560 for Negro Health Education, and most of that was for salaries. Municipal politics further complicated Williams's work. As a voluntary organization, the institute's primary missions were outreach and education. While tuberculosis testing, diagnosis, and research fell within its purview, treatment of active or "open" TB cases fell to the Municipal Tuberculosis Sanitarium (MTS). From its opening in 1915, the MTS was the city's largest and best TB hospital. A tax-supported institution, it was also a bastion of political patronage and racism, and its doors were closed to most Blacks. Provident Hospital attempted to serve the South Side of Chicago, but the TB ward at Cook County Hospital was the last stop for most black Chicagoans with advanced cases of the disease.

In the mid-1940s, a U.S. Public Health Service report harshly criticized the state of tuberculosis care and services in Chicago and Cook County. In its wake came both functional and financial reorganization, and slowly TB services began to improve. Williams assumed responsibility for running the institute's office on the South Side, where she oversaw TB testing efforts and educational programs. With the advent of public housing, she focused attention on the relationship between environment and disease, advocating on-site health centers and helping to establish prevention and health promotion programs at the Altgeld Gardens and Ida B. Wells housing projects, the latter named after IDA B. WELLS-BARNETT. In 1953 the Beta Iota Zeta chapter of Zeta Phi Beta sorority honored Florence Williams with its "Woman of the Year" award.

Williams's health began failing in the late 1950s, a few years before her retirement in 1961. She died at home three years later of coronary thrombosis and hypertension. Her death certificate noted her age as sixty-seven, but Williams was actually closer to eighty, having worked well into her seventies. Her need to support herself beyond age sixty-five and her desire to participate in a pension plan predicated on a maximum age limit may help explain the thirteen-year age discrepancy.

Since she left neither will nor heirs, the task of handling Florence Williams's final affairs fell to the Cook County Public Administrator. She had lived alone and frugally in a small and modestly furnished apartment in Chicago's Hyde Park neighborhood. At the time of Williams's death, her assets included $9,500, held in two savings accounts, and the balance of her pension fund, about $8,000. In the weeks and months after her death, the Public Administrator was unsuccessful in locating any relatives who might legally claim her estate. In December 1964 the Tuberculosis Institute of Chicago and Cook County

(the Chicago Tuberculosis Institute having changed its name in 1937) filed suit against the Cook County Public Administrator, claiming that it was entitled to Florence Williams's seventeen thousand dollar estate. The institute argued that it should be awarded Williams's money because she was a twenty-seven-year employee who received a pension upon retirement in 1961 and she "felt deeply indebted to the plaintiff for its non-discriminating policy towards negroes" (Williams's Case File #1038, "Complaint," December 2, 1964, 4). After two years of protracted legal wrangling, a settlement was reached between the institute and the county that deducted the legal fees for both parties from Williams's estate and then divided the remainder equally—half going to the institute and the other half to the county/state. At St. Mary Cemetery in Evergreen Park, Illinois, Florence Williams lies in a plot purchased by the Public Administrator and paid for with funds from her estate. No stone marks her final resting place.

Williams spent nearly half a century fighting "the white plague" on two fronts: persuading African Americans that they need not be afraid of testing or treatment and reminding white members of the health establishment that germs respect neither racial nor neighborhood boundaries. The development of potent antibiotics in the 1950s signaled that the battle against tuberculosis could be won. But absent a miracle cure for the social ills she fought throughout her career—racism, poverty, and inadequate access to housing and health care—Florence Williams died knowing that the war itself was far from over.

Sources. The papers of the Chicago Lung Association (CLA, formerly the Tuberculosis Institute) at the CHS span the years that Florence Williams worked there. Though the papers are incomplete and not inclusive of primary materials documenting the work of the Negro Health Education Department, the minutes of board meetings provide a general overview of Williams's work from 1934 to 1949. The CLA papers also include surveys and reports, including demographic and statistical studies, that document the incidence of tuberculosis in Chicago during the first half of the twentieth century. The Julius Rosenwald Fund Archives, Fisk University Library Spec. Coll., is a source for materials about several projects Williams worked on in Arkansas and Chicago, as well as about Midian O. Bousfield, M.D., who worked with Williams when she first came to Chicago. The Young Men's Christian Association of the U.S.A. Archives, at the Univ. of Minnesota, are a unique repository of primary and secondary sources about the organization's work during World War I. For information regarding Williams's estate after her death, see Florence C. Williams's Case File #1038, Office of the Public Administrator, Cook County, Illinois. Marian Nelson, "The Negro Tuberculosis Problem in Chicago," manuscript, 1936, American Lung Association Library in New York City, is informative. For background see David McBride, *From TB to AIDS: Epidemics among Urban Blacks since 1900* (1991), and Vanessa N. Gamble, compiler, *Germs Have No Color Line: Blacks and American Medicine, 1900–1940* (1989), a volume in the series *Medical Care in the United States: The Debate before 1940.* An excellent bibliography is *A History of Tuberculosis in the Black Community* (1975) compiled by Lenwood G. Davis. See also Lewis Hunt, *The People versus Tuberculosis* (1966). A documentary film by Diane Garey and Lawrence Hott, *The People's Plague* (Florentine Films, 1996), is essential viewing for anyone interested in the social and medical history of the rise, decline, and resurgence of tuberculosis in America.

TERRY J. FIFE

WILMARTH, MARY J. HAWES
May 21, 1837–August 28, 1919

SOCIAL AND CIVIC REFORMER, SUFFRAGIST, CLUBWOMAN

Mary Wilmarth played an active role not only in civic affairs but also on the political scene and in many of the social issues of her day. Mary J. Hawes was born in New Bedford, Massachusetts, the daughter of Shubael and Nancy B. (Smith) Hawes. She grew up in Newport, New Hampshire, where her sea captain father retired to become a farmer; she was educated at the Kimball Union Academy in Meriden, New Hampshire. On May 28, 1861, Mary Hawes married Henry Martin Wilmarth in New Bedford and joined him in Chicago, at that time a city of approximately 110,000 inhabitants.

Henry Wilmarth, a native of Newport, was born in 1837. His family, like that of his wife, can be traced back to seventeenth-century New England. In 1856, at the age of nineteen, Henry Wilmarth moved to Chicago, where he established H. M. Wilmarth and Company, manufacturers of gas lighting fixtures; he became a founder of Chicago's First National Bank and engaged in some real estate investments, all very successful ventures.

Shortly after arriving in Chicago, the Wilmarths became members of the First Presbyterian Church, where liberal theologian David Swing was minister. Their first home was on Michigan Avenue immediately south of Congress Street. According to contemporary newspaper accounts, Henry Wilmarth, joined by some of his neighbors, fought the Great Chicago Fire of 1871 with an abandoned fire engine and stopped the fire's progress southward, barely saving the Wilmarth home. It was the first house to escape destruction in that part of the city, while Terrace Row, the elegant block of homes just north of the Wilmarth house, went up in flames.

Henry Wilmarth died suddenly at his home in Chicago on February 27, 1885. The *Chicago Evening Journal* reported the cause of death as "paralysis," and it described him as "one of Chicago's most substantial capitalists and business men for nearly thirty years" (February 27, 1885). Seven years after Henry Wilmarth's death, the Congress Hotel Company expressed interest in building a hotel on the grounds of Wilmarth's home, and Mary Wilmarth leased the land to the company. When the Congress Hotel opened she moved in and lived there until her death in 1919.

Of the Wilmarths' three daughters, only Anna, the youngest, outlived her mother. Born in 1873, Anna Wilmarth attended the University of Chicago. She was married in 1897 to James Westfall Thompson, a young faculty member of the university's history department. Two years after they were divorced in 1909, she married Harold LeClair Ickes. She had known him, as well as James Thompson, from her student days at the university. By the time of their marriage Harold Ickes was an attorney actively involved in politics. ANNA ICKES, even more than her mother, was a political activist and reformer. She was involved in a variety of pursuits: among them were her roles in various prominent women's clubs; she was also a trustee of the University of Illinois and on the boards of the Chicago Home for the Friendless, the Chicago Regional Planning Association, and the Indian Rights Association. Starting in 1928, she became a three-term senator in the Illinois state legislature.

In Mary Wilmarth's early years, volunteerism meant that those who could afford to gave time and money to help others; those who could not gave personal service. The women were supportive of each other and worked in groups or through institutions, including churches. Although few had professional careers, many looked upon their club work and their philanthropic activities as careers and worked hard and seriously at them. It was taken for granted that women were not concerned with political reform but only with social issues, for example, improving garbage collection, the public schools, or police service. A few women, of course, were able to step out of these constraints and work for political reform. But in most cases, although a woman remained independent in her interests, the freedom of a woman to be involved in such activities depended on her husband's willingness to allow her to do so, or, if she was not married, on her father's. When the first women's clubs began to appear, many women were forbidden to join since most people believed in the adage that "woman's place is in the home" (Beadle, 18). Most of the women involved with the clubs were well-to-do and had the advantages of their husbands' and fathers' money, connections, and power.

Although Wilmarth began to volunteer from the time she first moved to Chicago, it was not until after her husband's death in 1885 that she began to play a very active civic role. She helped organize early women's groups. She was president of the Illinois branch of the Consumers' League; she was a friend and supporter of ELLA FLAGG YOUNG, the first female superintendent of the Chicago public schools; she also worked in close association with JULIA LATHROP, head of the Children's Bureau in Washington, D.C. She was involved with the Legal Aid Society and was a strong supporter of the Women's Trade Union League (WTUL), whose legal counsel was Harold Ickes. Wilmarth marched in the picket lines against Hart, Schaffner and Marx (HS&M) during the 1910 garment workers strike. As she frequently did for men and women who otherwise would have had to spend the night in jail, Wilmarth provided bail for the arrested HS&M pickets who could not do so themselves. For years she was part of a committee of women who lobbied department store managers to convince them to give their salespeople a half day off on Saturdays during the summer months. This goal was finally achieved in 1919, shortly before Wilmarth died.

She was an ardent suffragist yet recognized that woman's influence was limited at best. When William Hard's book *The Women of To-morrow* was first published in 1910, Wilmarth was particularly taken with the muckraker's last chapter, "Mothers of the World." She believed in its concern over the place of women and felt it was "a strong argument" for "equal suffrage" (*Annals of the Chicago Woman's Club*, 289). She obtained permission to reprint it and asked the Chicago Woman's Club to do so for "general distribution" (*Annals of the Chicago Woman's Club*, 289), which it did.

Wilmarth was interested also in the University of Chicago and gave the university money from time to time for special projects. She was generous in providing student loans and offering grants for various fellowships and scholarships as well as in outfitting the Reynolds Club, a student lounge, with reading material. In a letter written May 31, 1904, enclosing four hundred dollars to the university's Department of Household Administration for a year's fellowship, Wilmarth wrote: "I understand

FIG. 132. *Mary J. Hawes Wilmarth, in black dress, Jane Addams standing directly in front of her, with other unidentified women, en route to the Bull Moose (Progressive) Party convention, Chicago, 1912.*

that four hundred dollars will provide one scholarship for the ensuing year and am glad to offer that sum for the purpose. Intuition and common sense have been too long held adequate as an equipment for housekeeping. Knowledge should replace ignorance and I welcome the attention given the subject" (Wilmarth to Marion Talbot). She sent President William Rainey Harper one thousand dollars to be given to the University of Chicago Press to help with the expenses of publishing Professor James H. Breasted's Egyptian research. A few years later the university president, Harry Pratt Judson, in a letter dated August 25, 1908, asked her for a guarantee of one thousand dollars so that the press could afford to publish James Westfall Thompson's new book. She gave the money but was firm in her request that Thompson not be informed of her donation, perhaps because the marriage of Thompson and her daughter was breaking up. (They were divorced the following year.)

Women's clubs added much to the social and intellectual betterment of the city. In the late 1860s there were only a very few women's associations in existence throughout the country, but fifty years later more than a million women were involved in clubs. At the beginning these clubs were viewed as "study groups" (Campbell, 147) and were looked upon as vehicles for self-improvement in culture, literature, and art. The Chicago Women's Club (after 1895 Chicago Woman's Club) and the Woman's City Club of Chicago, however, looked toward "practical community work" (Campbell, 155).

Wilmarth was involved in a number of women's clubs—notably the Fortnightly, the Chicago Women's Club, and the Woman's City Club of Chicago—whose members were for the most part wives of wealthy philanthropists who were involved in reform and in trying to solve the city's civic problems. Wilmarth was a charter member and two-time president (1894–96, 1903–1904) of the Fortnightly, which was founded in 1873 by KATE NEWELL DOGGETT, its first president, as a literature

and discussion association to inculcate culture and intellectualism in women who had a desire to learn. It was one of the earliest of Chicago's women's clubs. The city's wealthier and more educated women were drawn to it. Many intellectuals and a number of professional women were among its members, and Chicago's civic and reform female leadership were also early members. While the club members did do some work in social justice and in furthering the arts and sciences, they rejected the idea of getting involved in public works or in many of the weightier social issues. A short listing of some of the scholarly papers Mary Wilmarth delivered at the Fortnightly in accordance with that club's mission indicates the scope of the literary culture offered: "The Cynics, the Epicureans, and the Stoics" (1877), "The Struggle between Paganism and Oriental Asceticism" (with Mrs. J. MacGregor Adams) (1880), "Spanish Oppression in the Netherlands" (1887), "The Philosophy of Balzac" (1891). In 1913, at a fortieth celebration of the Fortnightly's first meeting, Wilmarth spoke on the "Influence of the Society upon the Community" (1913).

Mary Wilmarth was also an active member of the Chicago Women's Club (CWC), founded by Caroline M. Brown, who became its first president. Organized May 17, 1876, the CWC became one of the largest women's clubs in the country. Its stated mission was to deal with civic problems, philanthropy, and reform issues. Unlike the Fortnightly, with its emphasis on literature, culture, and self-improvement, CWC efforts were mainly in practical work and social activism, which, within seven years of its founding, became its focus. In comparison to other women's clubs of the era, the CWC was more liberal on many issues, including race and suffrage. FANNIE BARRIER WILLIAMS became CWC's first African American member in 1895 after fourteen months of debate; for thirty years, she remained the only black member of the club. Activities were divided into departments: reform, home, education, philanthropy, art and literature (which, despite its name, worked to improve and beautify the city), and philosophy and science. A member was required to serve in one department, although she was allowed to participate in the activities of other departments. The CWC concept proved popular, and its membership increased rapidly. Starting with twenty-one women, by 1892 the members numbered 566, the largest of all Illinois clubs. By 1911 membership was limited to twelve hundred.

Many Fortnightly members also belonged to the CWC, which gave them a means for trying to correct the city's social and civic ills. Among those members who belonged to both were Mary Wilmarth, JULIA HOLMES SMITH, Ellen Mitchell, SARAH HACKETT STEVENSON, and ELLEN HENROTIN, "the five who seemed to be in *everything*" (Beadle, 50). When the Woman's City Club of Chicago was founded in 1910, many also joined that organization for the same reason.

There were a number of affiliated groups under the aegis of the CWC, such as the Physiological Institute, the Protective Agency for Women and Children, the Industrial Arts Association, the Political Equality League, the Society for the Promotion of Physical Culture and Correct Dress (of which Wilmarth was the second president). Among the issues for which CWC campaigned were leadership positions for women in the public school system (the appointment of Ella Flagg Young as superintendent of Chicago schools was credited to CWC's lobbying), a free kindergarten in the public schools for poor children (eventually adopted by the board of education for all children), appointment of a female physician to the Cook County Insane Asylum for Women (a successful campaign), manual training to be taught in the public schools (adopted), the appointment of a woman to the Chicago Board of Education (achieved in 1889 when Ellen Mitchell became the first female member of the board and confirmed three years later, after Mitchell's death, when she was succeeded by LUCY FLOWER). Members were creative in their ideas for change and were generally successful in their efforts, although sometimes it took decades to achieve the desired results.

Wilmarth served on a number of diversified committees in the CWC, from fashion to finding suitable club quarters to picking a design for a club pin. In 1889 she was appointed program committee chairperson. She delivered a paper on "A Better Chicago" at a CWC meeting. Mary Wilmarth, then, was part of a thriving culture of women's clubs whose interests were diverse and included the earliest collective efforts for social reform and the betterment and protection of women and children. She and her generation of organized clubwomen had begun to make the transition from women's work of benevolence and charity to the kind of political social reform undertaken by men and women activists during the Progressive Era and associated with the leadership of JANE ADDAMS.

Wilmarth met Jane Addams not long after Addams came to Chicago in January 1889. The two women developed a close friendship that lasted until Wilmarth's death thirty years later. Wilmarth was intrigued with Jane Addams's description of the settlement house she envisioned and became an early and enthusiastic supporter of both Addams and Hull-House. In due course she also became a trustee of both the Henry Booth House and the Frederick Douglass Center in Chicago. One of the first public meetings held to discuss Addams's ideas for the settle-ment house was held at Wilmarth's home. She became the first president of the original board of trustees of Hull-House, active in its projects, generous with financial support in a variety of ways. In the beginning, in order to reimburse those settlement house workers who could not afford to live and work at Hull-House, Addams used her own money. As the services being offered at Hull-House increased, it became necessary to find outside resources to meet the mounting financial needs. Wilmarth was one of those women called upon, and she paid fifty dollars per month directly to a specific worker. The financial situation eased somewhat with the incorporation of the Hull-House Associates in 1894, but there was always a continuing need for money. Whenever necessary, Wilmarth also would fund a teacher's salary, subsidize lectures, pay for equipment and projects—even, as in 1903, pledge to pay for the installation of fire doors. She introduced Addams and ELLEN GATES STARR, cofounder of Hull-House, to a number of the wealthier reform-minded clubwomen of Chicago, many of whom contributed large sums of money through the years, helping to make Hull-House the outstanding success it became. Besides its settlement house activities, Hull-House added impetus and purpose to the birth of the profession of social work.

Wilmarth worked with the diverse reformers, labor leaders, and intellectuals that gathered around Hull-House and seemed to have few compunctions about combining diverse people. When Hull-House held a reception for the anarchist Peter Kropotkin in 1891, Wilmarth, undeterred by the event's unpopularity, invited the socialist and philanthropist ANITA McCORMICK BLAINE to attend. She also invited President Harper of the University of Chicago to dinner at Hull-House to meet Kropotkin.

Wilmarth shared many of Addams's interests and became involved in many of Addams's projects. Her letters to Addams give some indication of the affection she felt toward her: "My Ever Dear!" is the salutation on a letter of July 28, 1908, which ends with "Yours with abiding love" (*Jane Addams Papers*). In a letter dated July 31, 1916, thanking Addams for dedicating one of her books to her, Wilmarth writes that there is no honor she could ever receive that would mean as much. She asks, "How did you ever think of so crowning me?" and closes with "Yours with love beyond any expression of it I have ever made" (*Jane Addams Papers*). On December 14, 1916, she calls Addams the "leader of us all" and ends her letter with "Yours to be led" (*Jane Addams Papers*).

Wilmarth sent Ellen Gates Starr to England to learn the art of bookbinding so that the skill could be taught at Hull-House. She also commissioned Starr to bring back an unbound Chaucer from William Morris's Kelmscott Press. Starr returned with the Chaucer, which included eighty-seven illustrations by Sir Edward Burne-Jones, in 1896. It was bound in the United States in crushed levant morocco by Peter Verlag. In 1899 Wilmarth presented the book to the Fortnightly, where it was displayed in the library of its clubrooms.

As plans for the 1893 World's Columbian Exposition began to take shape, it was apparent that women had been left out of the agenda, despite the lobbying of women's groups for their participation. The Chicago network of women reformers then took things into their own hands. MYRA BRADWELL urged Congress to hold the exposition in Chicago and was largely responsible for Chicago's being chosen as the site. A committee of women requested that Mayor Carter Harrison intervene in arrangements by asking the World's Columbian Exposition Commission to consider appointments for women, with the result that BERTHA PALMER was invited to head the Board of Lady Managers, making her the official hostess of the exposition. Nine CWC members served as lady managers on the board. Wilmarth, with Ellen Henrotin and Lucy Flower, then wrote to Palmer suggesting the inclusion of congresses to focus on areas of interest to women. The result was the establishment of 210 congresses under the aegis of the Woman's Branch of the Congress Auxiliary of the Columbian Exposition. Many members of the Fortnightly and the Chicago Women's Club were active in the auxiliary. Palmer became president of the body of congresses, with Henrotin vice-president and chief executive. Various women activists headed local congresses, including Mary Wilmarth (Education), Lucy Flower (Moral and Social Reform), Jane Addams (Social Settlements), and Ellen Henrotin (Labor).

At the same time Chicago and the nation were celebrating the four hundredth anniversary of Columbus's "discovery" of America, the country was beginning to suffer a severe depression, with three million unemployed and hundreds of bank failures. Labor strikes were taking place, and picketers were clashing with management and police. The next year there would be a march on Washington, D.C., with the unemployed demanding a public works program to create jobs. During the depression following the World's Columbian Exposition, CWC made it a point to supply employment for poor mothers. Both the CWC and later Hull-House were committed to experimenting with the best ways of finding social welfare methods that would most successfully create independence and improve conditions.

Women's work in reform was stimulated by the congresses held during the World's Columbian Exposition. Other initiatives in the political sphere also encouraged both women's heightened fight for suffrage and organized womanhood's entrance into politics, even before women obtained the vote. Mary Wilmarth, Jane Addams, and many of the leading figures in the settlement movement and the world of women's clubs lent their support to Progressive Era political initiatives from 1890 to 1920. Progressivism, a middle-class movement with a strong crusading spirit, aimed to create a better and more equal world and to help restore the essence of democracy. Its birth was a response to a major desire of many citizens for industrial reform. Among its other goals were woman suffrage, direct primaries, the ballot measures of initiative and referendum, child labor laws, establishment of the eight-hour day, and minimum wages for women. Such better government and civic organizations as the City Club of Chicago for men—founded in December 1903 so that members could assume full responsibility as citizens to promote policies, programs, and legislation to improve public welfare—had a female counterpart in the Woman's City Club of Chicago founded June 4, 1910. Both clubs were organized as municipal reform organizations on the principle that the citizens of a city are responsible for the welfare of the community in which they live. Their members were upper-middle-class city dwellers. The men were generally businessmen or professionals; the women were their wives and daughters, sisters and

mothers. Club members also came from the ranks of new women professionals, including social workers, settlement directors, physicians, and lawyers. Both organizations were nonpartisan.

Wilmarth was the first president of the Woman's City Club. She served for two terms, 1910–11 and 1911–12, after which she remained as honorary president through 1916. The Woman's City Club's goal was to increase a "sense of social responsibility for the safeguarding of the home and . . . the city" (quoted in Flanagan, 1032). The men's City Club wanted to train workers for the benefit of industry and opposed policies or programs deemed anticapitalist; they would not work with workers' groups or socialist groups. The Woman's City Club would work with unions and women's groups. They advocated government ownership of the telephones and other utilities. Some of the specific issues with which the Woman's City Club was concerned were housing, child welfare, woman's rights and suffrage, clean air, garbage and sewage disposal, public education, parks and playgrounds, courts, elections, and animal protection.

In 1912 Theodore Roosevelt formed the Progressive Party, whose campaign planks reflected the goals of the progressive movement. Anna Wilmarth Ickes and her husband Harold Ickes participated in the formation of the Progressive Party in Illinois. Jane Addams, a strong advocate for industrial reform, was active in the party, and Mary Wilmarth became an enthusiastic supporter. Wilmarth and Addams were the two delegates-at-large chosen from Illinois to attend the party's first national convention, held in August 1912 in Chicago, where they nominated Theodore Roosevelt for president and endeavored to pass the party planks. Wilmarth chaired the Educational Committee of the Jane Addams Chorus, which was organized to help the Progressive Party alert the public to its platform planks. It was affiliated with the Roosevelt Progressive Republican League and was an appeal to women to become actively involved in helping the party obtain its goals for all citizens. Choruses were formed throughout Illinois, with especially active groups in Chicago and its suburbs. Those members who could sing were asked to join a performing group. Although the party made some gains in 1912, it lost heavily in 1914; in 1916 Roosevelt declined its offer to nominate him again for the presidency. Soon afterward the party was dissolved. At the 1916 Republican convention held in Chicago, Wilmarth marched with a group of suffragists to present their arguments for the right of women to vote.

Wilmarth continued to support Jane Addams and a progressive agenda. Addams's pacifism during World War I brought her into conflict with many clubwomen and reformers. The "peace committee" (Linn, 331) of the CWC stopped meeting at Hull-House, and her talks on the war met with silence. Wilmarth, however, did not break with Addams.

Mary Wilmarth died at age eighty-two, three weeks after suffering a broken hip in a fall in her summer home in Lake Geneva, Wisconsin. Services were held there the next day and at her daughter's home in Hubbard Woods, in north suburban Winnetka, the following day. The private interment ceremony was held in Graceland Cemetery on Chicago's North Side.

A quiet and dignified woman with a fund of knowledge she generously shared, Wilmarth approached all issues with understanding and sympathy. Although she was interested and active in a variety of causes and creative in her ideas, she had none of the militancy, the aggressive intensity, many movement leaders exhibit. She was more of a follower than a leader. Her gentle humor and optimism about life benefited the movements she was involved in, as did her generosity, her gentleness, and kindness. She remained loyal to the causes she believed in and always argued for them when faced with opposition. She was devoted to Chicago and spared herself nothing to help the city. She worried about the children of the poor. In 1887, from her summer estate in Lake Geneva, Wilmarth organized the Lake Geneva Fresh Air Association, where economically depressed mothers and their children could spend some time in the country. She worked for improved child labor laws and better industrial conditions for workers. She was concerned about the hostile relations between Blacks and Whites.

In her eulogy, Jane Addams mentioned her close personal thirty-year friendship with Wilmarth, whom she described as having "a finely endowed and cultivated mind" and a "wisdom that brings humility" (Addams, 98). Addams said Wilmarth was "a center of spiritual power and intellectual life" (p. 105), with an air of "intellectual distinction" (p. 98). Her life, Addams continued, was "an unending commerce of fine deeds and great thoughts" (p. 108).

Sources. The CHS has the papers of the Chicago Woman's Club and the Woman's City Club of Chicago. UIC Spec. Coll. has the Hull-House Association Papers, the Jane Addams Memorial Collection, and *The Jane Addams Papers* (Microfilm Edition, 1985). UC Spec. Coll. has letters from Mary Wilmarth to William Rainey Harper, Henry Pratt Judson, and Marion Talbot in the Presidents' Papers 1889–1925. Biographical information is found in Jane Addams, *The Excellent Becomes the Permanent* (1932); James Weber Linn, *Jane Addams: A Biography* (1935); and the following autobiographical works by Harold L. Ickes: *The Autobiography of a Curmudgeon* (1943); *The Secret Diary of Harold L. Ickes*, vol. 1: *The First Thousand Days 1933–1936* (1953); *The Secret Diary of Harold L. Ickes*, vol. 2: *The Lowering Clouds 1939–1941* (1954). Information about Mary Wilmarth is included in the biography of her daughter in J. Leonard Bates, "Anna Wilmarth Thompson Ickes," *NAW* (1971). Works about the clubwomen movement include Henriette Greenebaum Frank and Amalie Hofer Jerome, *Annals of the Chicago Woman's Club for the First Forty Years of Its Organization, 1876–1916* (1916); Muriel Beadle, *The Fortnightly of Chicago: The City and Its Women 1873–1973* (1973). Articles and books about women's participation in progressivism include Barbara Kuhn Campbell, *The "Liberated" Woman of 1914: Prominent Women in the Progressive Era* (1976, 1979); Maureen A. Flanagan, "Gender and Urban Political Reform: The City Club and the Woman's City Club of Chicago in the Progressive Era," *American Historical Review*, October 1990; William Hard, *The Women of To-morrow* (1910, 1913); Robyn Muncy, *Creating a Female Dominion in American Reform 1890–1935* (1991); Kathryn Kish Sklar, "Comment: A Call for Comparisons," *American Historical Review*, October 1990. Also useful are Lana Ruegamer, "'The Paradise of Exceptional Women': Chicago Women Reformers, 1863–1893" (Ph.D. diss., Indiana Univ., 1982), and Kathleen McCarthy, *Noblesse Oblige: Charity and Cultural Philanthropy in Chicago 1849–1929* (1982). A conversation with scholar Barry Karl on the role of women in philanthropy was helpful. The following provide background information about Chicago history: Karen Sawislak, *Smoldering City: Chicagoans and the Great Fire, 1871–1874* (1995); Carl Smith, *Urban Disorder and the Shape of Belief: The Great Chicago Fire, the Haymarket Bomb, and the Model Town of Pullman* (1995); and Arthur Weinberg and Lila Weinberg,

Clarence Darrow: Sentimental Rebel (1980). Obituaries of Henry Wilmarth appear in the *Chicago Daily News*, February 28, 1885, and the *Chicago Evening Journal*, February 27, 1885. Obituaries of Mary Wilmarth appear in the *Chicago Daily News*, August 28, 1919; August 29, 1919; and in *CT*, August 29, 1919.

LILA WEINBERG

WILSON, HALENA
February 25, 1895–April 16, 1975
LABOR ACTIVIST, CIVIL RIGHTS ACTIVIST

Halena Wilson was born in Denver, Colorado, where she attended that city's public schools. Little is known about her family background and personal life. By the 1920s, Wilson (whose maiden name is not known) had moved to Chicago, where she married sleeping car porter Benjamin Wilson; they had no children. During that decade, she became an active member in the city's African American fraternal network. For a number of years, she served as Worthy Matron of the Order of the Star. Although she was a member of the Truth Seekers Liberal Church and served as a trustee for several years, her community activism did not center on the church. Rather, it was the labor movement, through the vehicle of the International Ladies' Auxiliary of the Brotherhood of Sleeping Car Porters, that fully engaged her attention for almost three decades before her retirement in 1957.

In the 1920s and 1930s, railroad sleeping car porters put the issue of African American trade unionism and civil rights squarely on the map of American labor and industrial relations. The Brotherhood of Sleeping Car Porters (BSCP), formed in 1925 and affiliated with the American Federation of Labor, fought a twelve-year battle for union recognition. Finally, in 1937, the Pullman company signed the first contract with the virtually all-black union. The brotherhood's achievements were tremendous: salaries went up, hours went down, job security improved, and grievance procedures partially protected worker's rights.

The brotherhood's success rested on a base of support provided by female relatives, allies, and railroad workers. The first Colored Women's Economic Council (the name given to the original chapters of brotherhood auxiliaries) was formed in New York in 1925, shortly after the founding of the brotherhood, while a Chicago council was formed the following year. In October 1931, Halena Wilson successfully ran for president of the Chicago branch, becoming that body's fifth president. At the suggestion of male brotherhood leaders, delegates to the first national conference of the numerous local Women's Economic Councils in September 1938 officially formed the International Ladies' Auxiliary, bringing together the various councils and auxiliaries under one organizational banner with its own constitution, regulations, and uniform program. At that gathering, Wilson became president of the newly formed auxiliary, composed of the wives, partners, and daughters of Pullman porters, as well as a number of Pullman maids. To a large extent, the auxiliary's history was shaped by Wilson's leadership, while Wilson's own public career centered on the brotherhood, its ladies' auxiliary, and the projects the two related organizations participated in or sponsored.

Although the Women's Economic Councils and the International Ladies' Auxiliary promoted by Wilson were completely

FIG. 133. *Halena Wilson, president of the Ladies Auxiliary, Brotherhood of Sleeping Car Porters and Maids, attending the Fifth Biennial Convention, Chicago, 1946.*

subordinate to the larger male Brotherhood of Sleeping Car Porters, Wilson believed strongly that the support of female family members was crucial to the brotherhood's success. Indeed, the auxiliary movement's stated purpose was to secure the active support of the porters' families for the brotherhood's cause. Labor unions—the BSCP in particular—constituted the "means through which a husband or father can be assured protection for his family and his home" (p. 1), Wilson argued in an article, "Brotherhood Auxiliary, Its Aim and Purpose," in the BSCP's monthly journal, *The Black Worker,* in February 1950. As she explained in a 1940 letter, the entire struggle was based on home and family; these responsibilities required a man to fight for a higher standard of living. Never questioning the sexual division of labor that relegated women to the home, Wilson repeatedly argued that women's domestic responsibilities necessitated their active support for the brotherhood. The well-being of the home and the future of the children were the responsibility of the porters' wives. "As wives," she told the assembled delegates to the BSCP biennial convention in 1944, "we need to understand and see some of the conditions under which our husbands

work. . . . We need to know how we can best strengthen them and thus make it possible for us to be able to plan for the future so that we can raise our children and to build strong, sound institutions for the future of our race" (*Report of Proceedings of the Fourth Biennial Convention,* 11).

The object of the auxiliary was to advance the economic, social, moral, and intellectual welfare of porters and their families through the promotion of women's involvement in brotherhood affairs, the cultivation of female leadership, and the development of a program of financial and organizational support of the brotherhood. The Women's Economic Councils and the auxiliary under Wilson's leadership offered concrete support for the efforts of Pullman porters to build and sustain their union. Tasks included extensive fund-raising and membership building through the organizing of teas, parties, and dances. In the brotherhood's early days, when it was "unable to pay rent, to pay telephone bills, to buy coal to heat their buildings," Wilson recalled at the brotherhood's 1948 convention, the "Ladies' Auxiliary, in every way imaginable was honorable and upright, and helped . . . to buy [necessary goods] and to provide finances" (*Report of Proceedings of the Sixth Biennial Convention,* 139) when needed. During the union's first decade, Wilson noted in her monthly column in the December 1951 issue of the *Black Worker,* the "lone Negro women's organization connected with labor to walk picket lines, to join mass demonstrations against the high cost of living, to advocate with other groups observance of meatless days in an effort to force prices down as well as obtain higher quality in Negro neighborhoods, to attend labor and legislative conferences as well as to take an active part in the Consumers Cooperative Movement" (p. 7).

The International Ladies' Auxiliary also engaged in civil rights activism within the organization's labor ranks and in the larger society. From at least the late 1930s onward, the Chicago branch under Wilson's leadership developed an extensive educational program aimed at porters, auxiliary members, their families, and the larger African American community; it included the sponsoring of local labor libraries, speakers, labor history classes, and Black History Week celebrations. From the 1930s to the 1950s, Wilson and the auxiliary continued to hold fund-raising events; raised money and donated clothing to several rural black schools in West Virginia; awarded scholarships to black women workers and auxiliary members, enabling them to attend trade union leadership training institutes; and made direct financial contributions to causes in civil rights. In the 1940s, Wilson and the auxiliary also helped to establish a Consumers Cooperative Buying Club and the Cooperative Union Eye Care Center, both in Chicago.

Wilson and her fellow auxiliary members actively protested racial discrimination in the job market, the armed forces, and the housing market. In 1941 and 1942, Wilson complained to city officials about the disproportionately high rents paid by black tenants for Chicago apartments. She called on her members to lobby on behalf of antilynching and anti–poll tax laws and for a passage of legislation creating a permanent Fair Employment Practices Committee to combat employment discrimination during and after World War II. She supported the March on Washington Movement that the brotherhood spearheaded in the first half of the 1940s to protest discrimination in wartime employment and the armed forces; Wilson and the Chicago auxiliary participated in the movement's mass demonstration and the "We Are Americans, Too" Congress against discrimination in employment and the armed forces held in June and July 1943. In 1954, the auxiliary made monetary contributions to the Montgomery, Alabama, bus boycott.

As president of the International Ladies' Auxiliary, Wilson served as a regular correspondent to the *Black Worker*. For almost two decades, she reported on the activities of the Chicago auxiliary, on the history of the trade union movement, and on larger issues of black women's contributions to and participation in the labor movement, and edited a page devoted to the local auxiliaries' activities. She frequently traveled across the United States and Canada, delivering speeches, organizing auxiliary chapters, reporting on their activities, and promoting the auxiliary's larger program.

Numerous other organizations and causes also absorbed Wilson's attention. In the 1940s, she served as an executive board member of the Chicago Women's Trade Union League and was an elected delegate to its Illinois State Legislative Conference in 1943. A strong believer in the cooperative movement, she was a member of the national Consumer Cooperative Council.

Wilson relinquished her position with the International Ladies' Auxiliary in 1957. Her health had deteriorated; she probably suffered a stroke in late 1956. In addition, brotherhood leaders reorganized the International Ladies' Auxiliary, which suffered membership loss as participants grew older or joined new organizations in the civil rights movement. The passenger railroad labor force, including BSCP, was also declining in numbers. The BSCP abolished the international aspects of the auxiliary and replaced its officers with brotherhood officials in 1957.

In subsequent years, Wilson continued to receive a pension from the brotherhood for her decades of past service. She died in Chicago at eighty years of age.

Halena Wilson campaigned on behalf of organized labor and for civil rights from the 1930s through the 1950s as the leader of the International Ladies' Auxiliary of the Brotherhood of Sleeping Car Porters. Her ideological vision combined her beliefs in the largely domestic character of women's roles with the necessity of women's activism in labor and rights movements.

Sources. Halena Wilson's organizational papers for the International Ladies' Auxiliary are included in the Papers of the Brotherhood of Sleeping Car Porters (BSCP), Chicago Division, at CHS. Among the papers is an untitled 1956 sketch of Wilson's life. The papers also have Wilson's speeches reprinted in *Report of Proceedings* of the brotherhood's annual and biennial conventions. The best study of the Ladies' Auxiliary and Wilson's leadership is M. Melinda Chateauvert, *Marching Together: Women of the Brotherhood of Sleeping Car Porters* (1998). A biographical entry on Wilson appears in *African-American Women: A Biographical Dictionary*, ed. Dorothy C. Salem (1993). In *Black Worker*, the monthly journal of the BSCP, Wilson edited a page devoted to the activities of the locals of the women's auxiliaries in the United States and Canada; numerous articles by Wilson appear in the journal. Also see Paula F. Pfeffer, "The Women Behind the Union: Halena Wilson, Rosina Tucker, and the Ladies' Auxiliary to the Brotherhood of Sleeping Car Porters," *Labor History*, Fall 1995, and "The Future of the Ladies Auxiliary," *Black Worker*, November 1957. An obituary was published in *Chicago Defender*, April 22, 1975.

ERIC ARNESEN

WIRTH, MARY BOLTON
December 21, 1898–February 6, 1976
SOCIAL WORKER, PUBLIC HOUSING AND RELOCATION OFFICIAL

Mary Bolton Wirth was a leader in the fields of public housing, social welfare, and race relations. Mary Bolton was born in Paducah, Kentucky. Her had family moved from North Carolina to nearby Symsonia by ox wagon in the 1840s. They had developed a settlement on one thousand acres, which included the Bolton school and cemetery. The Boltons also offered land to the community to be used as a "burying ground . . . 'for the benefit of the old School of Predestination Baptist [denomination] holding to the doctrine of unlimited predestation and Salvation by Grace in Time and Eternity'" (Wirth to the *Paducah News*, n.d., Mary Bolton Wirth Papers). Her grandparents worked the family farm, which was demolished in the 1940s. Her father, Valentine Lee Bolton, a harness salesman, once campaigned unsuccessfully for the office of sheriff of McCracken County. Valentine Bolton admired the views of William Jennings Bryan, political leader and orator, and was a strong supporter of women's rights. Her mother, Elizabeth Clark (Boaz) Bolton, a descendant of George Rogers Clark, the pioneer explorer, was a member of the Daughters of the American Revolution.

Valentine and Elizabeth Bolton's son, Lexington Lee, died at age five after receiving a diphtheria vaccine. Mary Bolton was born soon after and was considered a "replacement" (interview with Elizabeth Wirth Marvick) for her older brother, especially in her father's eyes. Valentine Bolton took a keen interest in his daughter's upbringing and encouraged her to take her studies seriously.

Bolton later attributed her strong interest in racial issues to her early, close relationship with her wet nurse, Lillian, who was quite likely African American. Bolton unofficially took the name Lillian as her own middle name in her nurse's honor. In keeping with their Baptist tradition, Mary Bolton's parents did not baptize her as an infant; later, as an adolescent, Mary decided not to join the church.

Mary Bolton attended public school through the twelfth grade in Paducah. Then, unlike most other young women in her community, she chose to pursue higher education away from home. Grown to her adult height of five feet, one inch, with long, thick dark hair worn in an upsweep, she enrolled at age seventeen at the University of Chicago. She went with her parents' ready agreement, since it was a Baptist-affiliated school. She arrived in Chicago suffering from a bout of malaria, which repeatedly flared up and interrupted her studies throughout her college career, requiring stays in the student infirmary.

While in college, Bolton was in sympathy with the few undergraduate student activists on the University of Chicago campus. Bolton disliked the rigid rules imposed on students, including mandatory chapel attendance four days a week, "enforced by the loss of one-half grade point for every four unexcused absences" ("These Are the Days," 29). Students were encouraged to demonstrate patriotism during World War I and this action also offended Bolton, who questioned the war and U.S. involvement. She sympathized with the few conscientious objectors on campus.

Bolton was deeply moved by one of the worst race riots in Chicago's history, which occurred in July 1919, just before her final college semester. The Hyde Park campus was near the Black Belt, the area where African American migrants from the South were forced to reside in congested and substandard buildings as a result of Chicago's segregated housing patterns. When a black youngster accidentally swam into an area of Lake Michigan claimed by white residents as an all-white beach, several of them stoned the African American to death while his friends watched. Despite the urging of many black witnesses, white police officers refused to arrest the white boys. Violence erupted among both African Americans and Whites; at the end of three days, 38 people of both races had died, 537 had been injured, and more than one thousand were left homeless. Bolton was appalled that most University of Chicago students returning to campus in the fall were either unaware of or undisturbed by these events. The effect of the events of the Chicago riot on Mary Bolton's later professional choices is clear, however.

Bolton earned a Bachelor of Philosophy degree in December 1919. She enjoyed studying German and met her future husband, fellow student Louis Wirth, at a social event held for German students who were part of a singing group. In 1921, when Bolton and Louis Wirth became engaged, he took her to Germany to meet his parents and to visit his family home. His parents were surprised that their son's future bride was not Jewish, but they readily accepted Bolton. The young couple married on February 14, 1922, and settled in Hyde Park, the university neighborhood where they remained most of their lives. Louis Wirth continued his studies at the University of Chicago, earning a doctorate in 1927. He was to become a noted professor of sociology at the university and an international leader in establishing the profession. They had two daughters, Elizabeth, born in 1925, and Alice, born in 1934; both attended the University of Chicago Laboratory Schools and the University of Chicago. The Wirths considered themselves agnostics but allowed their daughters to attend any religious service of their choosing.

Mary Bolton Wirth worked full time most of her adult life, with the help of her mother, who permanently resided with the young couple after the birth of their first child and provided much of the family's child care. Elizabeth Bolton returned to Paducah to visit her husband at regular intervals, and he came to Chicago occasionally.

Working briefly as a social caseworker for the United Charities of Chicago in 1922, Mary Wirth began her work as a probation officer for the Juvenile Court of Cook County in 1923. The court, established in 1899, pioneered in the treatment of troubled youth. Wirth continued her work there for more than a decade and gained prominence within the Chicago social work community. At the same time that she was raising a family and working in the field, Mary Bolton Wirth enrolled in graduate level studies at the University of Chicago in history, sociology, and social service, studying with EDITH ABBOTT and

SOPHONISBA BRECKINRIDGE at the School of Social Service Administration.

Wirth left the Juvenile Court in 1934, during the Great Depression, to organize the Social Service Department of the Chicago Works Progress Administration (WPA), at the personal invitation of Harry Hopkins, assistant to President Franklin D. Roosevelt. When the department, situated in a warehouse, first opened its doors, people seeking work flooded in, and the building had to be closed temporarily for fear of its collapse. As associate supervisor of the WPA division of employment for the Chicago office until 1938, Wirth oversaw the caseworkers who processed applications for the certification of low income families applying for relief. "The fact that there has been less discontent and trouble among WPA workers in Chicago than in most large cities is due in large part to the judgment with which . . . [Mary Wirth] handled . . . [her] part of the job" (Martha Phillips to Mary B. Wirth, October 7, 1937, Mary Wirth Papers), her supervisor wrote.

While employed with the Chicago office of the WPA, Mary Wirth met a young African American writer, Richard Wright, who was assigned to her WPA caseload. Wirth found the yet unknown Wright a job with a physician friend of hers. Later, Wirth referred Wright to the Writers' Project of the WPA, which her husband headed. The Wirths and Wright became lifelong friends, and the expatriate, now an internationally known writer who authored Native Son (1940), gave them a tour of Paris years later when they visited the city.

Mary Wirth served as the full-time executive secretary of the Chicago chapter of the American Association of Social Workers from 1939 to 1949. These were significant years for that professional organization, when major social policy decisions in the areas of health care, public housing, and aid to the children of unemployed parents were being elaborated at the federal and state levels. Social workers, whose daily experiences affected their views, attempted to inform the process. Wirth drafted a statement for the Chicago chapter that gained national exposure for its support of President Roosevelt's proposed Health Act, the purpose of which was to establish nationwide health care to meet the medical needs of all Americans, regardless of income.

During World War II, Wirth was appointed a medical field agent of the Selective Service System. She later received a commendation from President Harry S. Truman for her work in the area.

Wirth ended her professional employment in 1950 and did not return to the workplace until after her husband's death in 1952. At that time, Governor Adlai E. Stevenson asked her to serve temporarily as a consultant in social work for the State Reformatory for Women at Dwight, Illinois, to provide him with an assessment of conditions there. In 1953, Wirth took a full-time position as supervisor of the Community and Tenant Relations Division of the Chicago Housing Authority (CHA). Although she had no formal training in the area of public housing, much of her work drew on her strong communication and negotiation skills. Underlying all her actions and advice was a deep respect for individuals, regardless of the difficulties they encountered. Wirth and her husband shared a lifelong belief in urban renewal as the solution to many social ills. The problem of neighborhood gangs surfaced immediately at her job. She wrote in internal memos that building maintenance at the CHA projects was nonexistent, and tenants believed nothing could be done about the worsening conditions of neighborhood blight. In part the difficulties came from gangs. Records showed that things repaired in the past had immediately been broken by gangs. She wrote, "Vandalism was the catchword that explained everything. Noisy teenagers, robbery, and burglary were the order of the night" (memo, September 30, 1953, Mary Wirth Papers).

In her supervision of staff at the Jane Addams Homes, a public housing project on Chicago's Near West Side, Wirth frequently drew on the concept of the social worker as a professional who maintained extensive personal contact with clients. Wirth introduced forms and instituted procedures that required caseworkers to go beyond simple documentation of visits in their case reports, encouraging them to make the families they served come alive in their case reports through the use of anecdotal notes. In addition, she designed an experiment that was declared effective in dealing with multi-problem families and their destructive impact on public housing conditions. In this experiment, Wirth created a new staff position, a social work consultant, who determined a family's eligibility at the time of its application for housing. "These are not problem families," she wrote, "but individuals with problems" (handwritten notes, Mary Wirth Papers). Much of Wirth's energy went toward improving the housing conditions of families who were perceived as having a multiplicity of problems. "Everyone likes freedom—personal freedom," she said, "and housing projects should allow as much personal freedom as does not interfere with the freedom of others" (typed notes, 5, Mary Wirth Papers). She was critical of what she considered unnecessary housing authority restrictions placed on tenant families. "Put yourself in their place for a few seconds," she said. "How would you explain to your children that they cannot have a kitten, or a TV set?" (typed notes, 5).

While her primary focus was on low cost housing, she called for closer cooperation among welfare, housing, and urban renewal agencies to improve the living conditions of low income and displaced families. She noted that "rehabilitation is often made limited or impossible because of bad housing conditions, (yet) the demolition of slums and the provision of decent housing alone cannot be expected to cure the ills of the relocated slum dweller without additional welfare services" (typed draft of paper on cooperation and collaboration among social service agencies, 1, Mary Wirth Papers).

Wirth also spoke out forcefully in Chicago Housing Authority memos and reports against rigid rules that forced tenants who had improved their economic status to move from their project homes, uprooting them from the community and stability they had worked so hard to establish. Wirth appeared at many public programs, delivered numerous papers, and contributed to and authored several articles in the *Journal of Housing* from 1957 to 1965. She coauthored a conference paper with Philip Hauser, a colleague and sociology professor at the University of Chicago, in 1965, which appeared in an edited collection, *Poverty in America: Proceedings of a National Conference Held at the University of California, Berkeley, February 26–28, 1965.*

Wirth focused from 1959 through the early 1960s on the housing relocation needs of the elderly in her final place of full-time employment with the Chicago Urban Renewal Program,

where she continued her unrelenting fight for better, more humane conditions. "A sense of inferiority due to living in a substandard home," she said, "may often be a more serious health menace than any unsanitary conditions associated with housing" (handwritten notes, 2, Mary Wirth Papers).

Throughout her professional life, Wirth served as an adviser for many organizations and agencies, including the Advisory Board of the Cook County Department of Public Aid, the Advisory Committee of the Chicago Housing Authority, the Family Welfare Reviewing Fund of Chicago, the Welfare Council of Metropolitan Chicago, and the Southeast Commission. She also served as a consultant to the Community Renewal Program.

In the 1960s, she was as active in the local Hyde Park community as she had been across the city of Chicago. She was a founder of the Hyde Park Community Conference, a member of its Planning Committee, and a volunteer watcher in the housing court for the conference. She was also a founder of the Hyde Park Consumers Cooperative and a member of the Hyde Park Neighborhood Club. She served as a volunteer in special projects in the office of alderman Leon Despres, who wrote that she had a marvelous sense for uncovering facts, perceiving injustice, and marshalling data. She was active in the University of Chicago's Alumni Association, which in 1966 awarded her a Citation for Public Service.

In the 1950s and 1960s, Mary Bolton Wirth often noted the failures of such institutions as the juvenile justice system and public housing to maintain and expand their early promises of reform. She continued to work toward solutions and believed in the efficacy of committees of experts, community agencies, and citizens to organize and respond to urgent needs in society. Many of her recommendations seem prophetic, such as the release of self-sustaining public housing units to private investors; the relocation of low income families in scattered sites, including the suburbs; and the construction of solely low-rise and mid-rise housing projects, varying in size and blending into the surrounding community. She suggested that Chicago's Robert Taylor Homes, one of the largest high-rise low income projects in America, be organized into parts and that a few centrally located buildings sponsor a "college for tenants" (typed draft, untitled, undated, 1, Mary Wirth Papers). Every other building would attempt to attract middle income families with added amenities and tempting rents. Her expectation was that the higher standards of some could affect all. She blamed many intractable social problems on the flight of white residents from once stable neighborhoods when African Americans moved in, on real estate speculation, on discrimination on the part of lending institutions, and on the general racism that prevailed in American society.

Mary Bolton Wirth died of cancer in Berkeley, California, and was buried there. She was a strong advocate for the reform of programs and agencies established to help troubled youth, disadvantaged families, and the elderly. Wirth worked tirelessly to improve community services for those in need. She held several high-ranking positions in Chicago social service agencies and volunteered her advice and expertise to many civic and political organizations. She became deeply committed to social justice as a college student and continued to bring this passion to many causes throughout her life.

Sources. The Mary Bolton Wirth Papers are in UC Spec. Coll. The five boxes contain professional correspondence, drafts of published papers, certificates and notations of awards, and a few personal letters. They also include her notes and notebooks from readings, lectures, and seminars she attended. Several boxes contain Wirth's records from the Chicago Housing Authority and her work with the urban renewal agencies and housing for the elderly. Telephone interviews were conducted with Elizabeth Wirth Marvick, February 23, 1995, and Alice Wirth Gray, February 6, 1995. Among Wirth's publications are "Point-of-Entry Work with 'Problem Families' Proving Helpful," *Journal of Housing*, April 1957; with Philip M. Hauser, "Poverty in America: Relocation—Opportunity or Liability?" in *Poverty in America: Proceedings of a National Conference Held at the University of California, Berkeley, February 26–28, 1965*, ed. Margaret S. Gordon (1965); and "These Are the Days," *University of Chicago Magazine*, June 1968.

IRENE CLARE BECK

WOODS, SYLVIA GREEN
March 15, 1909–March 4, 1987
TRADE UNIONIST, POLITICAL ACTIVIST, RADICAL

A successful labor organizer and one of the first African American women to run for the Illinois General Assembly, Sylvia Woods agitated throughout her life for social and political reform. Her interview in the 1976 documentary film *Union Maids* strikingly portrays a radical's life and commitment to social justice.

Sylvia Green was born in New Orleans, Louisiana, where she lived with her mother, Lucinda Johnson; a stepfather, Mr. Johnson (first name unknown); and her younger brother, Joseph Johnson. She had an older brother, John Green. There is no information about Mr. Green, her birth father, but Sylvia Green wrote about her stepfather, a roofer and a union member of a segregated union. She reflected that even though it was segregated, it was better than no union at all because it ensured its members a higher pay rate than that of non-union workers. Sylvia Green had fond memories of Johnson and the way in which he illuminated her life with both a labor and a race consciousness.

As a child in New Orleans, she experienced racism, which like most black children, she did not understand. Writing later in an essay, "If I Had Known Then What I Know Now," in *Black Women in the Middle West Project*, she told of her displeasure at not being able to play in the park that she walked through every day to get to school because it was designated for white children only. She knew that her family paid taxes to support the park where she was unable to play and did not understand why she was prohibited from the park, its benches, and swings. One day after walking through the "white park," she vowed not to participate any longer in the morning school ritual of singing the "Star Spangled Banner." She was sent to the principal's office of the all-black segregated school she attended and questioned about her nonparticipation with the rest of the class. After explaining her reasons, the principal finally allowed her to practice her silence as long as she stood in the back of the class. At an early age Sylvia Green saw that "the land of the free and the home of the brave" was a contradiction.

Sylvia Green's experiences with racism were balanced by her exposure to Garveyism, a "grassroots black nationalist political movement . . . of racial pride and dignity" (*Encyclopedia of the American Left*, 253), which took its name from leader Marcus Garvey. A Jamaican, Garvey's militant program was popular in the United States from the mid-1910s through the 1920s. Sylvia Green's father, Mr. Johnson, was a Garveyite and often took her to meetings on Sundays at the local Longshoremen's (Union) Hall. In her essay, "You Have to Fight for Freedom" (*Rank and File*), she reminisced about how she enjoyed watching Blacks marching and singing while dressed in uniforms. It gave her a sense of pride and dignity to see Blacks uniting for freedom. She was impressed by the fact that the Garveyites wanted to leave America and return to Africa to experience the freedom they believed it was not possible to obtain in the United States. Her father wanted her to watch and listen to an African American woman who spoke every Sunday at the Longshoreman's Hall, believing that in order for Blacks to have freedom, they needed leaders with the capacity to speak out. He encouraged Sylvia Green to become such a speaker.

At age sixteen Sylvia Green married Henry Woods and the couple migrated to Chicago. They were part of the massive migrations of southern Blacks after 1900 who came to cities in the North in search of work and better opportunities. Unlike many southern Blacks from rural areas who had been displaced by the mechanization of cotton production, Sylvia Woods's background was urban, not rural. The crash of the stock market and subsequent breakdown of all sectors of the American economy in the Great Depression further deepened the economic crisis of African Americans both in the rural and urban South and in the cities of the North. Once in Chicago, Sylvia Woods found it difficult to secure a job that paid a decent wage. Woods, with much persistence, finally persuaded the Great Western Laundry company to hire her, despite her young age, to shake out clothes and linens. After learning every work assignment in the laundry, she demanded a higher wage. Woods's successful bargaining skills emerged and she received the raise she thought she deserved. Soon she organized the night shift laundry workers to pressure for an African American foreperson to represent them. She was taken home by the police after leading a demonstration at Great Western. Woods subsequently worked at two more laundries before she took a job at a Bendix Aviation plant on the West Side of Chicago during World War II.

Bendix was a "cost plus" contract plant that produced airplane carburetors for the government. The "cost plus" contract that Bendix Aviation held with the United States government guaranteed payments by the government no matter how much it cost to run the plant—plus a percentage of profit. According to Yolanda Hall, a lifelong friend and coworker of Sylvia Woods, African American workers were usually placed in less skilled jobs when hired at the factory. Woods, however, refused to work as a custodian and pressured the company until she was hired as a skilled worker to take burrs off carburetors. Later, Woods became a drill press operator. Hall noted that once hired, Woods tried to help those who lived in the community get a job at Bendix by giving them the correct "right" answers to put on the employment application. She wanted to see the people who lived in the neighborhood employed at the company that was in the middle of their community.

Again, Woods organized her peers. She helped organize United Auto Workers (UAW) Local 330 and served as shop com-

991

mittee representative and on the bargaining committee. In 1946 Woods led an ad hoc Council of Women Delegates in drafting a resolution that the UAW take a stand against sex discrimination in the workplace. Later, Woods ran for union office and was elected secretary-treasurer of UAW Local 330 for a two-year term. She had no previous experience as a treasurer but was very proud to hold that office and wanted to prove that, as a black woman with no previous bookkeeping or financial experience, she could perform the requisite duties of the office and perform them well. Hall said that 1943 to 1945 were intense years for the union because they were organizing the membership of the local at the same time that they were educating the employees and the union stewards. After the war, the plant closed and laid off all of its employees. Women employees, since they had done their part for the war effort, were encouraged to leave the work force so that men could return to their factory jobs. Woods and members of other UAW locals met to discuss strategies and to assist laid-off employees in filing for unemployment benefits.

The Woodses were able to buy a home on Chicago's West Side. Henry Woods worked at the Revere Copper and Brass company, a UAW shop. They belonged to the Greater Union Baptist Church, and Sylvia Woods was part of a nursing committee, ministering to ill congregants. The Woodses did not have any children, but they raised a nephew who had a close relationship to them.

Sylvia Woods turned to politics. In 1946, she became one of the first African American women to run for the Illinois General Assembly. Her opponents for state representative from the 21st District, Edward J. McCabe and Joseph L. Rategan, both Democrats, and Robert Petrone, a Republican, received 208,000 to her 8,000 votes. Petrone won with 83,000 votes. In 1946, successfully running for the Illinois General Assembly was difficult for a woman, and for a radical African American, an unlikely occurrence. Yet the fact that she received more than 3 percent of the vote showed that at least a small portion of her state legislative district heard her voice.

During the 1940s Woods was introduced to the activities of the American Communist Party (CP) by a coworker, and later she joined the party, becoming a lifelong member and educating black and white workers alike about their common enemy, capitalism. In the CP, she met and became friends with Geraldine and Claude Lightfoot and William and Louise Patterson. Her outspokenness was courageous, since activists on the Left had become the victims of government surveillance and repression. At the time, the Illinois Communist Party was led by African American Claude Lightfoot. Conservatives in postwar America targeted a broad range of political activists and trade unionists on the Left, and in the hysteria of the cold war era, U.S. Senator Joseph McCarthy and the House Un-American Activities Committee (HUAC) particularly focused on communists and communist sympathizers. Lightfoot's arrest in June 1956 under an indictment based on the Smith Act of 1940 was protested by CP members, civil libertarians, and progressives. The Lightfoot Defense Committee and other organizations such as the Chicago Joint Committee to Defeat the Smith Act worked to clear Lightfoot and the other Chicago defendants, Max M. Weiss, Fred M. Fine, and Gil Green. Sylvia Woods's political activism in the late 1950s and 1960s targeted all exploita-

tion and racism, which she as a communist saw in economic and class terms. Her concerns for the civil rights of African Americans were tied in with her advocacy of self-determination on the job for workers and with her interest in fighting poverty in the working-class and very poor neighborhoods of Chicago.

After her experiences at Bendix, Sylvia Woods studied nursing and health care practices at Richard T. Crane Junior College (later Malcolm X Junior College), a local city college on the Near West Side. She worked at various places for many years, including Cook County Hospital; and she organized workers and the community around medical concerns affecting the employees and the patients. Woods joined the Committee to Save Cook County Hospital, formed in 1977 when the Cook County Board of Commissioners convened a committee to make recommendations about the future of the hospital. At the time, its facility was one of two hospitals in the county that served the poor. Woods believed it was essential that the poor (and often primarily black families) in the community who could not afford medical services, and those who had lost medical insurance, had access to a public hospital. The employees of the hospital also wanted it to continue in order to maintain the community's economic stability; their jobs and secondary businesses with more jobs depended on the existence of the medical complex on the Near West Side.

During the 1970s, Woods participated in the movement to free political prisoners on the Left and in the civil rights and antiwar movements. Woods was a cofounder of the Chicago Defense Committee to Free Angela Davis; Davis was a Black Panther Party activist and member of the Communist Party. In 1970, Davis took up the cause of the Soledad Brothers, prison inmates who were charged with killing a guard, "and she became personally involved with their leader, George Jackson" (*Encyclopedia of the American Left*, 183). In August 1970 Jackson's brother Jonathan "sought to force the release of his brother by seizing hostages at the Marin County [California] courthouse" and in "the subsequent gunplay Jonathan and a judge were killed" (p. 183). Angela Davis was accused of involvement in the affair. When she was charged with conspiracy, kidnapping, and murder, "the entire civil rights and New Left movements were mobilized in her defense" (p. 183). In 1972, Angela Davis was acquitted of all charges.

Woods was a charter member of the National Alliance Against Racist and Political Repression (NAARPR); she and Charlene Mitchell—one of the organizers for the New York Defense Committee for Angela Davis—and other concerned activists and progressives held a three-day conference in Chicago to found the national watchdog organization. NAARPR wanted to ensure that political prisoners received fair treatment and due process in the courts; the organization also raised funds for their defense. Cases that NAARPR pursued included those of the Attica (New York State Prison) Brothers, Martin Sostre, Joanne Little, the Wilmington Ten (including Ben Chavis), and Delbert Tibbs.

Sylvia Woods mentored Mildred Williamson, a member of NAARPR and a community activist. Williamson said that Woods taught her everything she needed to know about organizing, "from dealing with the press to making pamphlets, to fund-raising" (interview with Williamson). Woods never gave up her organizing efforts, even during difficult political times, because she had faith in all people. Her early life did not provide experiences to build faith in white people, but she ultimately came to understand that "you have to have faith in [all] people, period. The whites, probably a lot of them feel towards blacks like I felt. But people, as a rule come through" (*Rank and File*, 129). Woods soon realized that color was not the issue and white people were not the enemy. The issue became class distinctions, and the enemies were the big corporations.

In 1976, filmmakers Julia Reichert, Miles Mogulescu, and James Klein interviewed Woods as one of the three principal figures in the award-winning documentary film *Union Maids*. Woods, along with other union activists Stella Nowicki (Vicki Starr) and Katherine Hyndman, gave accounts of union organizing and the life-threatening assaults they experienced during labor demonstrations in the 1930s and 1940s. In the film Woods explained that she joined the union to secure workers' rights. She understood the power of unity and thus involved herself in organizing workers where she was employed, at laundries in Chicago.

Woods was also interviewed for the film *Seeing Red* (1983); here she spoke about her involvement with communism. Woods claimed that as an auto worker she joined the communist movement because she was already marginalized by racism in America. She felt she had nothing to lose. Woods also cited her encounter with Federal Bureau of Investigation (FBI) agents as they followed many Communist Party members. She said that she did not refuse to talk with the FBI agents but did insist on talking with the agents only after they talked with her about the state of black people, especially black men, in America. In the Danish film, *The Long Shadows of the Plantation* (1979), Woods is the main person interviewed about life as a union organizer.

Soon after her husband's death in 1978, Woods moved into La Vista, a home for senior citizens on Chicago's Near South Side. Because of her past organizing experiences, she was very popular with the residents and soon was successful in coordinating various social events. Louise Leeks, a neighbor and friend of Woods at La Vista, commented that Woods, whom she remembered as a friendly and beautiful person, hated to leave the house on the West Side that she and her husband had purchased. Maintaining it, however, had become too much for her after his death. Sylvia Woods died at age seventy-seven from cancer.

Sylvia Woods fought for the freedom to speak, protest, and organize—not only for herself, but for all oppressed people. She was a lifelong radical, proud to be a "union maid." With an acceptance of the unfinished agenda that remained, she had the energy to commit herself again and again to working with progressive organizations on behalf of working-class people.

Sources. Three documentary films, *Seeing Red* (1983), *The Long Shadows of the Plantation* (1979), and *Union Maids* (1976), are significant and historic recorded interviews of Sylvia Woods. Alice and Staunton Lynd, eds., *Rank and File* (1973, reprint 1981), and Shirley M. Herd, Darlene Clark Hine, and Donald West, eds., *Black Women in the Middle West Project: A Comprehensive Resource Guide: Illinois and Indiana* (1986), have essays with quotes from Sylvia Woods. Interviews were conducted with Yolanda Hall, Louise Leeks, Vicki Starr (also known as Stella Nowicki), and Mildred Williamson. Josephine Wyatt,

Louise Leeks, and Martina McCain completed questionnaires. Useful books include Nancy F. Gabin, *Feminism in the Labor Movement: Women and the United Auto Workers 1935–1975* (1990); Robert A. Goldberg, *Grassroots Resistance, Social Movements in Twentieth Century America* (1991); Harry Haywood, *Black Bolshevik* (1978); Earl Ofari Hutchinson, *Blacks and Reds: Race and Class Conflict 1919–1990* (1995); Mari Jo Buhle, Paul Buhle, and Dan Georgakas, eds., *Encyclopedia of the American Left* (1992); and Jacqueline Jones, *Labor of Love, Labor of Sorrow: Black Women, Work, and the Family from Slavery to the Present* (1985).

MARIE E. HARDY

WOOLLEY, CELIA ANNA PARKER
June 14, 1848–March 9, 1918
MINISTER, RACIAL JUSTICE ACTIVIST, WRITER, CLUBWOMAN

Celia Parker Woolley was founder of the Frederick Douglass Center, Chicago, and one of the founding members of the National Association for the Advancement of Colored People (NAACP). She was born Celia Anna Parker to Marcellus Henry and Harriet Maria (Sage) Parker in Toledo, Ohio. Her father was an architect and religious freethinker from Sutton, New Hampshire, and her mother was an intelligent, well-read Episcopalian who was born in Middletown, Connecticut. Her parents had married on March 18, 1847, and settled in Toledo, Ohio. A year after Celia Parker's birth, the family moved west to Batavia, Michigan, a small town in the south central part of the state. Their final move in 1851 brought them to Coldwater, Michigan, the new county seat. Here Marcellus Parker found work designing and building many of the area's most important public and private buildings, including the new county courthouse and the library. He was elected an alderman to the city council. Like most middle-class white women of her day, Harriet Parker's life centered around family, but she found time to be an active member of several of Coldwater's literary clubs and circles. Shortly after the Parkers moved to Coldwater in 1851, their second daughter, Caramenceita, was born, followed five years later by a third daughter, Flora. Celia Parker's sisters died within days of each other in 1858, leaving Celia Parker to grow up an only child.

The happenstance of geographic location and parental theological beliefs made the Civil War a pivotal event in Celia Parker's life. The Parkers' modest two-story frame house was located halfway between downtown Coldwater and the railroad depot. It provided Celia Parker with a front row seat as men and horses left Coldwater for the battlefront. Inside the house, her parents praised Abraham Lincoln and the work of the abolitionists, especially Lucretia Mott and William Lloyd Garrison. These day-to-day political and social events combined to form a foundation for Celia Parker's later advocacy of racial justice.

The Parkers had the means and the desire to provide Celia Parker with a better education than that received by most young women of the era. In 1864, they sent her to the Lake Erie Seminary in Painesville, Ohio. She returned to Coldwater in September when the new Coldwater Female Seminary opened, and she was a graduate of its first class in 1867. Parker's participation in the graduation play and her graduation essay, "The Dove, the Cross and the Crown," read during the seminary's week-long, publicly held graduation exercises, provided early evidence of her lifelong intellectual interest in literature and theology.

Jefferson Henry (J. H.) Woolley, the son of Dr. George W. and Marietta (Royce) Woolley of Philadelphia, moved to Coldwater in 1867. He was a dentist and had come to Coldwater after practicing in Washington, D.C., and San Francisco. Celia and J. H. were married in 1868 and set up house in Coldwater. After her marriage, Woolley divided her time serving as secretary of the Ladies Library Association, helping to organize the Coldwater Suffrage Association, and writing and studying law with her friends Mrs. T. M. Kitchel and Carrie Perry. Her first literary success came in 1875 when the *Evening News* published her Thanksgiving story. A year later the Woolleys moved to Chicago.

Woolley wasted no time in taking advantage of the greater opportunities offered by Chicago. Within a year, she joined and presented her first paper before the Chicago Women's Club, an upper- and middle-class philanthropic, social, and civic reform organization founded in 1876. By 1888, Woolley was the club's president. Her work with the Woman's Social Science Association, whose leadership included suffragist and journalist ELIZABETH HARBERT, drew the attention of the local press, which abstracted her papers on dress reform and women's public speaking abilities. Word of Woolley's writing and speaking abilities spread, and in 1889, she was invited to join the Fortnightly, Chicago's oldest and most exclusive women's literary club, founded in 1873 by women's rights activist KATE NEWELL DOGGETT.

Woolley's writing career took off in 1877 with the publication of a small item on Chicago's liberal religious community in the *Index*, a Free Religious Association publication. She followed it with essays on a wide variety of topics, short stories, and poems in similar liberal religious publications. In the early 1880s, Woolley began writing for more secular periodicals, such as *Lippincott's Magazine* and *New England Magazine*. She reached a different audience in 1887 with the publication of her first novel, *Love and Theology*. It was well received, going into seven editions, two in hardcover and five in paperback under the title *Rachel Armstrong*. Woolley followed it with *A Girl Graduate* and *Roger Hunt*. All three used a romance story to present Woolley's concerns about women's rights, class stratification, social reform, and religious dogmatism.

Woolley's writing and lecturing career slowed in 1893 when the Geneva (Illinois) Unitarian Society unexpectedly called her to its pulpit. Woolley had been heavily involved in the Western Unitarian Conference since arriving in Chicago but had no theological school training and had not envisioned parish ministry as part of her career plans. Nevertheless, she accepted the challenge, and she, her husband, and their adopted son, Harry Shearer Woolley, moved to Geneva. Three years later, Woolley resigned the Geneva post in order to accept a call to the Independent Liberal Church in Chicago. In the fall of 1898, still grieving from her son's death in 1896 and shouldering new family responsibilities following her father's stroke, Woolley retired from parish ministry.

Woolley continued to press for women's rights and used her club ties as a means of gaining a public platform for her liberal political and social beliefs, as exemplified by being one of the founders of the Chicago Political Equality League. The league was a suffrage group originally organized by Woolley under the auspices of the Chicago Women's Club in 1894. In 1896, it became an independent entity with Woolley as its president.

Woolley returned to writing and lecturing full-time, and in 1903, she published her autobiographical work *The Western Slope*. In this book, she used reflections on her own life as a vehicle for examining society's successes and failures. According to Woolley, one particularly blatant failure of American society was the treatment of African Americans. Woolley's advocacy for African Americans had not ended with the Civil War. Her Chicago home was one of the few places where middle-class African Americans and European Americans regularly socialized together. Woolley's advocacy had a public dimension as well. During her presidency of the Chicago Woman's Club in 1888 (changed from Women's to Woman's in 1895), Woolley presented her friend FANNIE BARRIER WILLIAMS, a racial justice reformer, for membership. She and Williams faced tremendous opposition, but finally in 1896, Williams became the club's first African American member. By 1903, according to IDA B. WELLS-BARNETT, Woolley was "a very good friend of the race" (Aptheker, 55).

Woolley's commitment to African American rights entered a new phase in 1905. With input and funds from both African Americans and Whites, Woolley opened the Frederick Douglass Center on the edge of Chicago's Black Belt. It was modeled on her friend JANE ADDAMS's Hull-House, but according to Fannie Barrier Williams, unlike Hull-House, it was not organized to do slum work. Its target group was Chicago's small but growing African American middle class, and some of its first African American members were Fannie Barrier Williams and S. Laing Williams, Ida B. Wells-Barnett and F. L. Barnett. Woolley's hope was that the center would provide a common ground where educated African Americans and Whites could get to know each other. In her role as president and head resident, Woolley drew upon her vast political, social, and religious connections to secure jobs, letters of recommendation, and educational opportunities for individuals.

In 1909 the National Negro Conference met in New York City to address the status of African Americans since the collapse of Reconstruction. Woolley was invited to speak on the multi-dimensional nature of oppression, citing the interrelatedness of racial justice issues, women's rights, and the rights of labor. During the conference, Woolley was elected to the Committee of Forty on Permanent Organization, whose job was the formation of a national organization focused on racial justice issues. The Committee of Forty created the NAACP, and Woolley served on both its executive and general committees from 1911 to 1912.

With the development of Chicago branches of the NAACP and the Urban League in the late 1900s, the work of the Frederick Douglass Center waned. Woolley welcomed and supported the new organizations. In 1918, she gave rent-free office space in the center to the Chicago Urban League. The intention was that the league and the center would work together, but in February Woolley became ill. She died suddenly on March 9. Following her death, the center ceased to exist, and J. H. Woolley, who had supported his wife's work throughout their almost fifty years of marriage, gave the Urban League the center's three-story gray stone building. Woolley was cremated and her ashes were scattered on the grounds of Oak Woods Cemetery in Chicago.

Celia Parker Woolley dedicated her life to the goals of human equality and freedom. She lived her beliefs, acting as a bridge connecting Whites and African Americans, liberals and conservatives, society matrons and social reformers.

Sources. There is no collection of Woolley's personal papers, but material on her is available at Meadville-Lombard Theological School, Chicago, including the Jenkin Lloyd Jones Papers, and at the Coldwater Branch County Library, including the Coldwater Female Seminary files, Coldwater, Michigan. Unitarian Universalist Society Church Records are in Geneva, Illinois. Besides those mentioned above, Woolley's published works include two pamphlets, *The Ideal Unitarian Church* (1889) and *George Eliot: Suggestions for Clubs and Private Reading* (1890); and a play, *The Angel at the Gate* (1919). *Poole's Index of Periodical Literature* and *The Reader's Guide to Periodical Literature* list more than thirty poems, essays, and short stories written by Woolley between 1877 and 1915. Two local newspapers, *Courier* (Coldwater, Michigan) and *Coldwater Republican* are at the Coldwater Branch County Library on microfilm. Fannie Barrier Williams, "The Frederick Douglass Center," *Southern Plowman*, June 1906, and Celia Parker Woolley, "The Frederick Douglass Center, Chicago," the *Commons*, July 1904, are useful. Other sources include Herbert Aptheker, ed., *The Correspondence of W.E.B. Du Bois*, vol. 1 (1973); Charles Flint Kellogg, *NAACP: A History of the National Association for the Advancement of Colored People 1909–1920* (1967); Arvarh E. Strickland, *History of the Chicago Urban League* (1966); Muriel Beadle, *The Fortnightly of Chicago* (1973). A biography of Woolley appears in *A Woman of the Century: Leading American Women*, ed. Frances E. Willard and Mary A. Livermore (1893).

KOBY LEE-FORMAN

WYATT, EDITH FRANKLIN
September 14, 1873–October 26, 1958
NOVELIST, SHORT STORY WRITER, SOCIAL COMMENTATOR, LITERARY CRITIC

Edith Wyatt was a novelist and satirist whose comedies of manners contrast the city and the country, old money and new, the pioneer generation and their idle children. As a journalist, her interests expanded to include women's search for self-reliance through decent working conditions and woman suffrage. As a literary critic and reviewer, she read and commented on the works of men and women who would serve as role models of independence and of the equality of the sexes.

Edith Franklin Wyatt's father, Franklin Osmon Wyatt, came west from Vermont after marrying Marian LaGrange in Honesdale, Pennsylvania. Her mother, though primarily a homemaker, was a poet who privately published a volume of her poems, *Fragments of Family Life*, in 1929. Her father was a civil engineer building roads in Tomah, Wisconsin, when she was born there. She had two sisters, Faith and Phyllis. In 1877 the family moved to Dubuque, Iowa, where her father worked as a railroad and mining engineer. Later she wrote: "My father built the Turkey River railroad . . . and reorganized the regional river roads. As a child I used to love to go and listen to the engine bells and see the roundhouse and try to understand the switch track, and railroads, and steam engines, and the sights, sounds, and odors around them" ("Terrapin Ridge Leads Way to Historic Land," Wyatt Manuscripts). By 1884, Franklin Wyatt was oper-

ating the LaSalle County Carbon Coal Company, and the family was living in Chicago. Although she made her home in Chicago from 1884 until her death in 1958, her writing is suffused with her love of the land and her eloquence in describing prairies, cornfields, and valleys as well as the small-town cobbled streets, factories, and church spires of the Midwest. The rural scenes of Edith Wyatt's 1903 novel *True Love: A Comedy of the Affections* are located in LaSalle County.

Edith Wyatt began school in Dubuque (c. 1880) and graduated from Miss Rice's Higher School for Girls in Chicago. She attended Bryn Mawr College for two years (1892–94) and returned to Chicago to teach Greek for the next four or five years at the girls' school from which she had graduated. Her first publication, "The Wolf in Sheep's Clothing," a short story, appeared in 1898 in *New Stories from the Chap-Book*, published by the eminent Chicago publisher Herbert S. Stone. Her early career was marked by her success as a short story writer in such publications as *McClure's*, *Appleton's Magazine*, and the *Atlantic Monthly*. The stories that appeared in *McClure's* in 1899 and 1900 demonstrated a sense of humor, vivid character depiction, an eye for concrete detail of place and people, and a strong sense of what made Chicago the ethnically diverse and freewheeling place it was at the turn of the century. Wyatt's "Three Stories of Contemporary Chicago" (*McClure's*, 1900) caught the eye of renowned critic and novelist William Dean Howells, who wrote to her from his office at *Harper's Monthly Magazine*: "I have been reading your 'Three Stories of Contemporary Chicago Life [*sic*]' . . . with so much pleasure that I am going to ask you if you have possibly a novel on much the same ground, with characters as freshly and truthfully studied, which you could let me see with a view to its publication by Messrs. Harper & Brothers in book form" (November 7, 1900, Wyatt Manuscripts). Howells's public praise of her work continued until his death in 1920. Within a year of Howells's request Wyatt had assembled twenty-one short stories that were published by the editor S. S. McClure, in the volume *Every One His Own Way* (1901). In response, Howells announced that this young writer could now be included along with major Chicago writers Henry Blake Fuller, Will Payne, George Ade, and Robert Herrick as a defender of realism in Chicago.

By 1903 Wyatt had produced her first novel, *True Love: A Comedy of the Affections*. She had expanded her canvas to explore major themes first approached in the short stories. These themes included the city/village conflict, the contrast between the original settlers of Chicago and their children and grandchildren, the question of how social class differences were manifested, the importance of success in business for men and marriage for women, and the changes and redirections in urban society that had become visible in turn-of-the-century Chicago as immigration mushroomed. She also explored the question of "the New Woman" seeking equality with men in the home and the public world.

Wyatt's Chicago is not the alienating industrial jungle depicted by her contemporaries Upton Sinclair and Theodore Dreiser; it offers diversity and culture, but also overindulgence, snobbery, and complacency, which do not compare well with life in her small fictional town of Centerville. While her first collection, *Every One His Own Way*, focuses almost exclusively on

FIG. 134. *Novelist Edith Wyatt, in white dress seated in foreground, attends 75th birthday dinner for Mark Twain, Delmonico's Restaurant, New York, 1905.*

Chicago and the changes that can be seen taking place, the second volume, *True Love*, deepens the conflict by raising the question of what is being lost as the city replaces the village. Attention to this issue places Wyatt directly in the local color tradition of eastern writers Mary Wilkens Freeman and Sarah Orne Jewett and southerner Kate Chopin.

True Love is Wyatt's initial attempt to define how women's roles were changing and why it was becoming necessary to take a closer look at the institution of marriage. In this regard she can be seen as prefeminist in stance; if not ready to renounce marriage or challenge a male patriarchy, she does reject the traditional romantic heroine's qualities of submissiveness and flirtatiousness. Her heroine seeks equality in marriage, along with honesty and compatibility. In Wyatt's later essays—sociological and documentary studies of the lives of urban working women and farm women—and in her literary reviews of such unconventional heroines as novelist George Eliot, essayist Mary Wollstonecraft, and Russian revolutionary Catherine Breshkovsky, she shows herself committed to the radical stance of "the New Woman."

Wyatt continued to write stories, poetry, and children's tales in the 1920s and 1930s and published another novel, *The Invisible Gods*, in 1923. She remained an influential literary presence in Chicago through her activity as a founding board member of HARRIET MONROE's groundbreaking journal, *Poetry: A Magazine of Verse*, established in 1911. For many years, beginning in 1914, Wyatt was also on the board of the Society of Midland Authors, along with many other important Chicago writers.

After 1905, however, she turned increasingly away from fiction and toward social and political issues facing the country. In 1910 Wyatt had her first experience as a writer of documentary pieces. She was assigned by S. S. McClure to report the Cherry

Mine disaster in the Illinois coal fields, an area in which she had herself spent childhood summers. This article, published in *McClure's*, 1910, was the first of many to appear over the next thirty years in the *New Republic*, *McClure's*, and other journals. What seemed at first to be only a diversion into journalism became in many ways her life's real work. She evolved in her writing and political activities into a progressive activist and social commentator. The 1915 Eastland ferry catastrophe in the Chicago River, in which almost one thousand young working people, mostly women, drowned, prompted Wyatt's series of articles in Chicago newspapers, expressing outrage and calling for government action.

Both her journalistic writing and her numerous literary reviews from 1907 to the early 1950s show a preponderance of concern for the lives of women. In 1910–11 she and Sue Ainslie Clark spent time in New York City interviewing working girls in the garment trades. This activity resulted in the book *Making Both Ends Meet* (1911), which documented the hand-to-mouth existence, overwork, illness, and dismal working conditions of young women in New York City. Wyatt also reported on the New York cloak maker's strike (1911) and the Chicago garment workers' strike (1915). In 1916 she attended a suffragist convention in New Jersey and reported back in a series of Chicago newspaper articles and in the *New Republic*.

Her interest in women's lives was not restricted to the urban scene. In several major articles from 1914 to 1919, she addressed the strengths and contributions of women working on the land and described their unmet needs. In each piece she stressed women's search for self-reliance. In the same spirit of pursuing self-reliance, she often used her essays and reviews of literary works—in the *New Republic*, the *North American Review*, and *Poetry*—to highlight women who could serve as role models and men whose relationships with women demonstrated signs of support and mutual esteem. Some of the earlier essays are collected in *Great Companions* (1917). Her contribution to American literary criticism is marked by a breadth of knowledge of world literature, a sensitive understanding of how the lives and works of great literary figures are intermingled, and an abiding love and respect for the democratic spirit of American writers at their best.

Wyatt's activities were not limited to writing. She was connected with the Consumer's League fight for a Saturday half-holiday for department store employees and was the organization's vice-president in 1914–15. Her work on the board of directors of the Juvenile Protective Association from 1916 to 1921 brought her into conflict with municipal courts over the enforcement of laws for the protection of women and children. She was also active with the Illinois Children's Home and Aid Society as chair of the Colored Children's Auxiliary from 1921 to 1923. She taught classes in English to immigrants at Hull-House during the first decade of the twentieth century.

Wyatt remained unmarried and lived with her sister Faith, also unmarried, in various residences on the North Side of Chicago and in Pompano Beach, Florida. In 1953 they edited the unpublished writings of their recently deceased sister Phyllis Wyatt Brown. The volume was privately printed under the title *Twelve Hours Treasure*.

Continuing as an activist into her sixties and seventies, Wyatt devoted much of her time from 1938 until the late 1940s to developing a community garden in a vacant and unsightly lot adjacent to her apartment building in the Streeterville neighborhood, a block west of Lake Michigan. Begun by nineteen families who paid to have the corner cleared and covered with grass, it became a Victory Garden of vegetables during World War II, with more than eighty families involved in gardening. Afterwards the garden remained an oasis in the midst of a changing urban scene. Wyatt died in Chicago in 1958.

It was the ability to bring together in her writing and her life what was best in urban and rural culture that marked Edith Wyatt's extraordinary career. For most of her eighty-five years, she combined an impressive literary talent with an equally impressive commitment to social activism as a participant and a reporter.

Sources. The Edith Franklin Wyatt Manuscripts at NL include correspondence, first editions, and three boxes of published and unpublished works, including scrapbooks of her articles and reviews. A scrapbook contains an unidentified newspaper article, "Terrapin Ridge Leads Way to Historic Land," May 3, 1931. Besides the publications mentioned above, Wyatt's writings include *The Whole Family* (with William Dean Howells, Henry James et al.) (1907); *The Wind in the Corn, and Other Poems* (1917); *Art and the Worthwhile* (with Robert Morse Lovett et al.) (1929); *The Satyr's Children* (1939); and *Two Fairy Tales* (n.d). In addition to numerous reviews of her work at the time it was published, there have been only two critical articles devoted to Wyatt: a critical introduction by Babette F. Inglehart to a reprint of *True Love: A Comedy of the Affections* (1993) and Clara M. Kirk and Rudolph Kirk, "Edith Wyatt: The Jane Austen of Chicago," *Chicago History*, Spring 1971. This profile in part is drawn from Babette F. Inglehart, "Introduction," in Edith Wyatt, *True Love: A Comedy of the Affections*, copyright 1993 by the University of Illinois Press, used by permission. She is cited as a humorist in Martha Bruere, *Laughing Their Way: Women's Humor in America* (1934). William Dean Howells mentions her work in several columns: *Harper's Weekly*, May 2, 1903; *North American Review*, May 1903 and December 1916; and "Easy Chair," *Harper's Monthly*, March 1912.

BABETTE F. INGLEHART

YARROS, RACHELLE SLOBODINSKY

May 18, 1869–March 17, 1946

PHYSICIAN, SETTLEMENT HOUSE RESIDENT, LEADER IN SOCIAL HYGIENE AND BIRTH CONTROL MOVEMENTS

Rachelle Slobodinsky Yarros was born in Berdechev near Kiev in the Ukraine. Her parents, Bernice and Joachim Slobodinsky, were well situated financially. They provided her with an education in Russian schools and later hired tutors to instruct her in college-level subjects, because women were not allowed to enroll in Russian universities. The 1880s were a time of protest and political activism in Russia, as students, intellectuals, and workers reacted against the economic hardships, social inequities, and oppression of the tsarist system. While in her early teens, Slobodinsky became involved with the Nihilists, a radical Russian political group. Fearing arrest because of her risky political activities, she emigrated to the United States at eighteen years of age, accepting only enough money from her father to pay her passage. She supported herself by working for two years in a Rahway, New Jersey, sweatshop, where she headed an unsuccessful strike. Before beginning her studies in medicine, she worked as a typesetter.

Rachelle Slobodinsky became the first woman enrolled in the College of Physicians and Surgeons in Boston. During her vacations she did nursing in poorhouses. She continued her studies at the Women's Medical College of Pennsylvania, receiving an M.D. degree in 1893. She did a one-year internship at New England Hospital for Women and Children in Boston beginning in July 1893. Subsequently she completed further work in pediatrics at the New York Infirmary for Women and Children and at Michael Reese Hospital in Chicago.

During her internship at New England Hospital for Women and Children in Boston, she met and became friends with AL-ICE HAMILTON, also an intern. Both were unhappy with staff physicians' attitudes toward interns and the dearth of learning opportunities; both shared the views of second-generation women physicians that separatism and an exclusive concentration on women's health issues marginalized them.

Hamilton was impressed with her new friend's compassion for the poor. In 1893, Hamilton wrote that Slobodinsky's experiences working with the underprivileged led her to believe that "the only way in which people can reach the working classes is by living right among them and not letting them know for a while that you are not one of them" (quoted in Sicherman, 66).

On July 18, 1894, Rachelle Slobodinsky and Victor Yarros, also a Ukrainian émigré, were married in New York City. Yarros's work as a journalist and lecturer and his radical political philosophy attracted him to the political movements flourishing in Chicago, and the couple had moved there by1897. Rachelle Yarros became well established as a physician, while her husband pursued journalism and law. They had no children but later adopted a daughter, Elsie Donaldson.

Beginning in 1898, Yarros was an instructor and later an associate professor in clinical obstetrics at the College of Physicians and Surgeons of Chicago, which later became the University of Illinois College of Medicine. During her academic career she did groundbreaking work in obstetrical education and in teaching about human sexuality and contraception. From 1898 to 1910, she instructed both male and female medical students in obstetric care and home births in the college's so-called Department of Obstetrics in the Ghetto. Her facility with languages gained her access to the new immigrants; her knowledge and skill won her the respect of students and colleagues. This innovative program not only elevated the quality of obstetrical care available to the poor, it also improved and broadened the educational preparation of medical students.

From 1907 until 1927, Rachelle and Victor Yarros were residents of Hull-House. Yarros's life as a settlement-house resident confirmed her view that the ills of the body were rooted in social

FIG. 135. *Dr. Rachelle S. Yarros led the birth control movement in Chicago.*

ills. As her interest in her patients' social welfare grew, she joined forces with social workers and nurses in the community, particularly to address women's health needs and the problems of venereal disease.

A staunch advocate of birth control and sex education, Yarros was troubled by the issues surrounding abortion. While committed to a theoretical anti-abortion stance, she recognized that desperate women will take desperate measures, including suicide, to end unwanted pregnancies. Writing in 1916 in *Surgery, Gynecology and Obstetrics*, Yarros described the plight of these women and their children by citing poverty, infant mortality, the dangers of "quackery" and "involuntary motherhood" ("Some Practical Aspects of Birth Control," 189) as convincing arguments for reconsidering positions on birth control and abortion. Her personal experience with her patients' tragic situations had a profoundly disturbing effect on her. She redoubled her efforts to fight for sex education and accessible birth control services as a means of eliminating the need for abortion.

Yarros worked diligently with several civic organizations. In 1914 she was a founder of the American Social Hygiene Association, dedicated to eradicating venereal disease. During World War I, she delivered lectures for the Council of National Defense and served as lecturer for the National Young Women's Christian Association and the General Federation of Women's Clubs. She was the first vice-president of the Illinois Social Hygiene League established in 1915. That year Rachelle Yarros worked to establish a committee on birth control sponsored by the Chicago Woman's Club. In 1916 the Reform Department of the Chicago Woman's Club took up the subject of birth control and appointed Yarros to chair the Chicago Citizens' Committee. This committee later organized the Illinois Birth Control League (IBCL). Both groups were primarily concerned with education. In 1922, at the urging of Margaret Sanger, social activist and founder of the American Birth Control League that later became the Planned Parenthood Federation of America, members of the IBCL and others active in the birth control movement joined with Yarros to develop and staff Chicago's first birth control clinic, the second of its kind in the country. Sanger had organized the first clinic in New York City in 1916. The commissioner of health refused to grant the necessary license, however, even though Illinois law did not prohibit the dissemination of birth control information. The courts declared that the commissioner was within his rights to deny the license. In 1924, the IBCL opened a private medical center in the business district of Chicago, obviating the need for a license. Ultimately eight clinics served women in Chicago's neighborhoods. Mary Crane Nursery, a pioneering Hull-House effort to bring preschool education to neighborhood children, was the site of one clinic, successfully linking services for working mothers and their children.

In 1926, Yarros became professor of social hygiene, a position created for her by the University of Illinois College of Medicine in recognition of her contributions to the field of social hygiene and sex education. Although her male colleagues were reluctant at first to join Yarros in endorsing the tenets of the birth control movement, in 1929 eighteen Chicago physicians and faculty members of the medical schools at Rush, Northwestern, University of Chicago, and University of Illinois published a credo asserting the right of women to contraceptive information and devices. The credo showed Yarros's impact on the thinking of the medical community, emphasizing social as well as medical reasons for supporting women's right to birth control. Charles Sumner Bacon, her colleague and department head at University of Illinois College of Medicine and initially a skeptic regarding the safety of birth control methods, was among the signers.

The influence of the Hull-House approach to substantiating social problems through extensive and meticulous statistical documentation was apparent in Yarros's articles on the work of the medical centers. These clinics served many women, a large number coming from lower socioeconomic groups. Yarros reported that in 1929 the six clinics then open provided contraceptive advice to 1,340 women. Of that group, nearly all (96 percent) reported that they had used contraception successfully for one to fourteen months.

Yarros was a firm believer in the usefulness of research to undergird the cause of birth control. Hard data could answer objections raised by opponents and facilitate improvements in available methods and services. In an article written in 1931 in *Birth Control Review*, Yarros identified the utility of "systematic reporting based on experience with large numbers of cases, such as are treated by the birth control clinics conducted under proper supervision" ("Objections Disproved by Clinical Findings," 15). She was convinced that such documentation would focus physicians' attention on the birth control needs of women and families and reduce doctors' resistance to providing such services.

Firmly established in the medical community in Chicago and for a time president of the West Side branch of the Chicago Medical Society, Yarros did not hesitate to criticize her colleagues' attitudes and actions when she perceived them to be detrimental to the public good. In 1929, she resigned from the Chicago Medical Society to register her protest against its censure of the Illinois Social Hygiene League and the Illinois Public Health Institute and its expulsion of Dr. Louis Schmidt for advertising services to prevent venereal disease and for developing a mass-treatment approach for the prevention and treatment of venereal disease among the poor and working classes. In "Cost of Medical Care and the Controversy with the Chicago Medical Society" in *Medical Woman's Journal* (1929), Yarros wrote a scathing rebuttal of the society's action and urged the members to join forces with philanthropic and social agencies in the prevention of disease.

Under the aegis of the Illinois Social Hygiene League, Yarros created the nation's first premarital and marital counseling service in 1932. During the 1930s she was the Illinois League of Women Voters' Chairman of Social Hygiene. Her pioneering work in social hygiene brought her national prominence. She served as special consultant to the U.S. Public Health Service and the United States Interdepartmental Social Hygiene Board.

Yarros recognized that birth control information and devices were not sufficient for the social reform in sexuality that she envisioned. As a medical student she had worked with young prostitutes on the venereal ward at Tewksbury State Institution in Massachusetts during the summers of 1891 and 1892 and had become an early and vigorous advocate of sex education for adolescents. She had also seen at first hand the effect of syphilis on health and the price of sex ignorance. Yarros worked diligently with Hull-House and the Illinois Social Hygiene Society to establish sex education programs. Various educational methods were used, including lectures, discussions, small group meetings, and film. Accessibility was the keynote in Yarros's approach to sex education. She advocated that sex education programs be offered in locations where young people, especially young women, were likely to be found—in churches, at Hull-House programs, in factories, and in local park district field houses in the evenings and on weekends. These programs met with an enthusiastic response. The Chicago Church Federation endorsed Yarros's work, and she received cooperation from many civic groups and organizations, including the Chicago public schools.

Unlike many prominent proponents of birth control in the Progressive Era, Yarros rejected eugenics as an argument for providing birth control to the poor and the "defective" to prevent the submersion of the "better" classes. She displayed a rare glimpse of wry humor as she dismissed the viability of this position in her speech at Birth Control and National Recovery, a conference convened in Washington, D.C., by Margaret Sanger in 1934. Yarros expressed the hope that "this conference won't stress the privileged classes because we don't know who they are, and if we know now, we probably won't five years from now" (Chesler, 344–45). Her day-to-day experience with Hull-House neighbors provided ample evidence that sound character was not limited to the "better" classes.

In many of her writings, Yarros identified herself as a feminist physician. In her 1916 article, "Some Practical Aspects of Birth Control," she acknowledged the interconnectedness of the feminist movement, the changing roles and expectations of the modern woman, and attitudes toward birth control. Yarros pointed out that women were "unwilling to be subjected to involuntary motherhood" and felt they ought to have "the power of choice" (p. 189). She titled a book published in 1933 *Modern Women and Sex: A Feminist Physician Speaks*. Believing that knowledge was powerful and should be available to all, she published an inexpensive version in 1938 and retitled it *Sex Problems in Modern Society*.

During the 1930s Yarros and her husband, Victor, made several trips to Europe, including three visits to the Soviet Union. She noted mixed reactions in European capitals to social hygiene work, finding exemplary work being done in England and Germany and expressing great distaste for the practices at the Hospital Division at Saint Lazare Prison in Paris. She was much impressed with the Anti-Venereal Disease Institute in Moscow, which she described at length in her 1937 article, "Moscow Revisited: Social Hygiene 1930–1936." After a second visit, however, she was uneasy about the significant increase in social control exerted over women inmates of the institute.

Rachelle Yarros suffered a heart attack in 1939 and retired to Winter Park, Florida. In 1941, she and her husband moved to California. That year, in a tribute in the *Journal of Social Hygiene*, experts in the field acknowledged her guiding influence in sex education. Even in retirement, Yarros retained her interest in civic affairs through the League of Women Voters. In California, she chaired the Russian Relief Committee of La Jolla and served as vice-president of the San Diego Social Hygiene Association. Yarros also maintained a connection with a local Mother's Clinic. She died in San Diego of congestive heart failure and was cremated.

While she lived at Hull-House, Yarros became convinced that it was impossible to be a physician in isolation from the social ills that often underlie physical ills. She noted that many problems confronting women could be traced to ignorance, excessive childbearing, and exploitation. Summing up her position in the unpublished autobiography quoted in her April 1946 obituary in the *Journal of Social Hygiene*, she asserted: "the enlightened, socially minded doctor will sympathize with labor, with victims of exploitation and industrial autocracy, with the juvenile and adult delinquents who are the products of slums and blighted, ugly, depressing districts. He will work and fight for ripe and genuine reforms" (p. 185).

Throughout her life Yarros was active in all phases of the birth control movement. As a feminist, Yarros acknowledged that her work in the cause of birth control was fixed firmly in her day-to-day experience with the women who were served in the clinics and in her life as a resident of Hull-House. In 1943 Yarros wrote, "As I began, so shall I end. I am a feminist" ("Women Physicians and the Problems of Women," 29). Yarros made her experience a source of power and a catalyst for change in the cause of birth control.

Sources. Materials on Yarros's years at Hull-House and at the Univ. of Illinois Medical School are at UIC Spec. Coll. and UIC Library of Health Sciences. The Sophia Smith Collection, Smith College, Northampton, Massachusetts, holds documents related to Yarros's medical education at Women's Medical College of Pennsylvania. Archives and Spec. Coll. on Women in Medicine, Medical College of Pennsylvania, have correspondence between Yarros and the college and a list of her journal articles. The Countway Library, Harvard Medical School, has Yarros's surgery and maternity case notes from her internship at the New England Hospital for Women and Children, copies of annual reports of the Chicago Medical Centers, and some correspondence between Yarros in association with the Illinois Birth Control League and Dr. Norman E. Himes. Correspondence between Yarros and Margaret Sanger documenting Yarros's participation in regional and national conferences of the American Birth Control League is in the Margaret Sanger Papers at the Library of Congress. Yarros published numerous articles on birth control, social hygiene, and women in medicine; these include "Medical Women of Tomorrow," Medical Woman's Journal, June 1916; "Some Practical Aspects of Birth Control," Surgery, Gynecology, and Obstetrics, August 1916; "Experiences of a Lecturer," Social Hygiene, vol. 5, 1919; "Birth Control and Its Relation to Health and Welfare," Medical Woman's Journal, October 1925; "From Obstetrics to Social Hygiene," Medical Woman's Journal, November 1926; "Significance of Birth Control for Race Betterment," Medical Woman's Journal, 1928; "Objections Disproved by Clinical Findings," Birth Control Review, vol. 15, 1931; "Moscow Revisited: Social Hygiene 1930–1936," Journal of Social Hygiene, vol. 23, 1937; and "Women Physicians and the Problems of Women," Medical Woman's Journal, January 1943. A detailed analysis of the litigation between Yarros and Health Commissioner Herman Bundesen appears in Patricia Spain Ward's paper, "Should Chicago Have Birth Control Clinics? Dr. Rachelle Yarros versus Health Commissioner Herman Bundesen," manuscript, 1986, at UIC Library of the Health Sciences. Yarros's work with the medical centers in Chicago is chronicled in reports to the Birth Control Review beginning in March 1924 and discussed in detail in Patricia Spain Ward's "At the Eye of the Storm: Hull-House and the Chicago Birth Control Debate," presented in 1990 at Hull-House and the People's Health: A Public Humanities Symposium at University of Illinois at Chicago; a copy of the Ward paper is in UIC Spec. Coll. Documentation of Yarros's activities with the Illinois Social Hygiene League appears periodically in the Journal of Social Hygiene beginning in April 1919 and concluding with a memorial in October 1946. The April 1946 issue contains an obituary for Yarros. Yarros discusses her position on the controversy surrounding the Chicago Medical Society's expulsion of Dr. Louis E. Schmidt in "Cost of Medical Care and the Controversy with the Chicago Medical Society," Medical Woman's Journal, June 1929. Yarros's only book, Modern Women and Sex (1933), yields further insight into her work and thought. Biographical essays on Yarros appear in W. I. Trattner, Biographical Dictionary of Social Welfare in America (1986) and in NAW

(1971). References to Yarros and her role as physician, Hull-House resident, and social reformer appear in several works: Mary Lynn McCree Bryan and Allen F. Davis, 100 Years at Hull-House (1990); Ellen Chesler, Woman of Valor: Margaret Sanger and the Birth Control Movement (1992); David M. Kennedy, Birth Control in America: The Career of Margaret Sanger (1970); James Reed, The Birth Control Movement and American Society (1978); Carol Hadley Robinson, Seventy Birth Control Clinics (1930); Margaret Sanger, Margaret Sanger: An Autobiography (1938, reprinted 1971); and Barbara Sicherman, Alice Hamilton: A Life in Letters (1984). References to her journal articles and other professional activities are listed in Women in Medicine: A Bibliography of the Literature on Women Physicians (1977). Women of Hull-House, a videotape available from Jane Addams's Hull-House Museum, includes brief references to and photographs of Rachelle and Victor Yarros.

DIANE C. HASLETT

YOUNG, ELLA FLAGG
January 15, 1845–October 28, 1918
TEACHER, EDUCATIONAL REFORMER, ADMINISTRATOR

Ella Flagg Young, a prominent leader in turn-of-the-century progressive reform, spent her entire career in education, becoming the superintendent of the Chicago Public Schools from 1909 to 1915, the first woman to hold such an office in a large city. She was also the first woman to become president of the National Education Association. In Chicago, she worked with other women reformers, including JANE ADDAMS, CORNELIA DE BEY, and LUCY FLOWER in efforts to modernize the public schools, raise the quality of teacher preparation, and improve the working conditions of teachers. Young led the way in establishing innovative programs that met the needs of children growing up in an urban and industrial society. She was supported by women reformers against the politicians who controlled public education. Young joined with other suffragists in gaining the vote for women.

Born in Buffalo, New York, to working-class parents of Scottish descent, Ella Flagg was the youngest of three children. Her father, Theodore Flagg, was a skilled mechanic in sheet metal work, and her mother, Jane (Reed) Flagg, was a homemaker. Although her brother and sister attended a nearby grammar school, Ella Flagg remained at home. Her mother was convinced that her youngest child was physically weak and needed to have fresh air and sunshine, not confinement in a classroom. Flagg was a determined child, however, and by age eight or nine had learned by herself to read, much to the surprise of her mother.

When she was eleven, Flagg entered grammar school and became an eager student, following in her father's footsteps by excelling in mathematics. She completed the school curriculum by the age of thirteen, shortly before her family moved to Chicago. Her father hoped that job opportunities would be better in the rapidly growing Lake Michigan city. Ella Flagg planned to enter high school in Chicago. Unfortunately, Chicago school policy required all new students to complete one year of grammar school before becoming eligible to enroll in a high school. Grammar school was so boring and repetitious that Flagg withdrew after attempting to satisfy the high school entrance requirement.

When Ella Flagg reached the age of fifteen, one of her friends suggested she take the examination for teacher certification. Flagg successfully passed the examination but was too young to be a classroom teacher. The school superintendent allowed Flagg to enter the Normal Department of the Chicago High School, at the time, the sole teachers' training institution in the city. She finished the normal course in two years, during which time she arranged her own practice teaching by volunteering to assist in a second grade class. Such practice teaching was not yet required of teacher training, but Flagg's mother had expressed concern that her daughter had no practical experience with children and might be too severe in her expectations of them. Flagg's mother died two weeks after her daughter began her teaching career and did not witness Ella Flagg's teaching successes.

Flagg began teaching in a primary school in 1862. The following year she was promoted to head assistant (assistant principal today) of a larger grammar school. In 1865 she was asked to direct the new student teaching program for elementary teachers, "the small pre-collegiate 'practice school' newly opened at Scammon School" (Smith, "Ella Flagg Young and the Chicago Schools," 28).

In 1868 Ella Flagg married Chicago merchant William Young, a family friend who was considerably older than the young teacher. His health was poor and soon he moved by himself to a warmer climate, where he died in 1873.

Flagg Young taught high school mathematics for a year in 1871 and then became assistant principal of the normal department in 1872. By 1873, although her career was ascending, Ella Young had lost all of her family. Her brother died in a train accident in 1868; her husband died in 1873; and shortly after, her father and sister succumbed to pneumonia.

In 1876 Ella Flagg Young was appointed principal of the Scammon School, and three years later she was appointed principal of Skinner School, "one of the largest and most prestigious grammar schools in the city" (Smith, "Ella Flagg Young and the Chicago Schools," 28). She was one of the few women who had passed the principal's examination, since most women principals at the time held their positions without taking the certification examination required for men. She refused to accept special treatment because of gender and passed with high marks. She also started the Ella Flagg Young Club, an informal seminar for her teachers; they met in her home where they studied Shakespeare, Greek and modern drama, and other literary forms. She became known for allowing her teachers the freedom to develop their own teaching strategies.

Ella Flagg Young had several long-lasting friendships. William H. Wells, former superintendent of Chicago's schools, and his family were friends. In 1883, while principal of the Skinner School, Flagg Young met Laura Brayton, a new teacher there. The friendship grew over the years, and they traveled together, became roommates, and when Flagg Young was superintendent, Brayton became her personal secretary. In the fall of 1887, Flagg Young left the Skinner principalship to become an assistant superintendent in Chicago's schools. That year she addressed the National Education Association (NEA) convention, a predominantly male organization controlled by Nicholas Murray Butler, president of Columbia University; William Tor-

rey Harris, U.S. Commissioner of Education; and other prominent male educators known as the "Old Guard" (Smith, *Ella Flagg Young*, 164). In 1910 she would become the first woman president of the National Education Association.

Flagg Young continued to develop the teacher institutes she had begun at Skinner, but now she ran them for the whole district. She invited professors from the pedagogy and philosophy departments of the University of Chicago to speak to her teachers. Her methods excited interest and earned her respect; she was appointed to the state board of education and served from 1889 to 1909.

Graduate and professional preparation was becoming increasingly important for school administrators, and in 1895 Flagg Young entered a graduate program at the University of Chicago under the direction of the young John Dewey, who "had come to the University of Chicago in the summer of 1894, as head of the Departments of Philosophy, Psychology, and Pedagogy. In the fall of 1895, the University appropriated a thousand dollars to establish the educational laboratory he so earnestly desired" (De Pencier, 13), known as the Dewey or Laboratory School.

Flagg Young and Dewey quickly developed a friendship, and by 1899, she resigned her position as assistant superintendent to take up full-time graduate study. The arts faculty at the University of Chicago evaluated her prior academic study and determined it was the equivalent of a B.A. degree. Accepted in the Ph.D. program, she began teaching education courses at the university as an associate professorial lecturer in the Department of Education and helped to reorganize Dewey's laboratory school while she finished her doctorate. In 1900 she graduated with a Ph.D. magna cum laude, and her thesis was published in 1901 with the title *Isolation in the Schools*. It embodied her pragmatic philosophy as teacher and administrator.

Flagg Young taught education at the University of Chicago through 1904. During these years she also edited a professional journal, *Elementary School Teacher*, and continued to collaborate with Dewey, who believed that she was able to give practical substance to his pragmatic ideas because she had practiced pragmatism long before it became a formally conceived philosophical system. She was also one of the authors in the Contributions to Philosophy and Contributions to Education series (1901–1902) edited by Dewey. Flagg Young contributed three monographs to the series: *Ethics in the School*, *Scientific Method in Education*, and *Some Modern Types of Educational Theory*.

Politics in the Laboratory or Dewey School (now the Laboratory Schools of the University of Chicago) became intense in 1904; Dewey had appointed his wife, Alice Chipman Dewey, to be the principal, and she had reduced teacher salaries and initiated other unpopular policies. Flagg Young was swept into the controversy. In addition, President Harper pressured Flagg Young to teach more education courses at the same time that John Dewey expected her to reconcile conflicts at the Dewey School and continue to edit *Elementary School Teacher*. Consequently, in 1904, when Dewey left for Columbia University, a very weary Flagg Young decided to leave also.

Ella Young took a trip abroad in 1904; the principalship of the Chicago Normal School opened up and, upon her return in

1905, she took the position. She remained there until 1909, when she was unanimously appointed to the superintendency of the Chicago public schools by the board of education. At the Chicago Normal School, "Young thoroughly put into practice the pedagogical philosophy that she had learned and written about during her student years under Dewey" (Smith, "Ella Flagg Young and the Chicago Schools," 30).

In the late 1890s and early 1900s, a group of public school teachers had organized as the Chicago Teachers' Federation (CTF). Mainly comprised of elementary teachers, it was, in reality, a women's organization. In 1900, CTF leaders MARGARET HALEY and CATHARINE GOGGIN filed suit against the board of education on behalf of the union, charging that the board had rescinded promised salary increases. In 1904 the courts awarded the back pay, but it took two more years for the back salaries to be paid. Under the leadership of Margaret Haley, the CTF continued to gain political power. It affiliated with the Chicago Federation of Labor in 1902, although CTF members never approved of using the strike to gain advantage in their negotiations with the school board.

By the time Flagg Young was a candidate for the superintendency in 1909, many board members wanted the CTF's power to be curtailed. When Flagg Young was interviewed, the board asked her how she would deal with the CTF, and she answered "that she would treat the union as an 'educational institution'" (Smith, *Ella Flagg Young*, 152). The board wanted more equitable representation on the teachers' pension board. In return the board was willing to match dollar for dollar the teachers' contributions to their fund. Flagg Young thought that this was a reasonable plan. "Her answer was interpreted as tantamount to a promise. It may have been her greatest mistake to speak for a group like the CTF" (Smith, *Ella Flagg Young*, 152). Flagg Young was selected because she had good rapport with the teachers, and it was felt by board members that she could best handle the CTF.

The first two and a half years of Flagg Young's superintendency were successful ones in which the teachers and the board worked harmoniously under her direction. She characterized her leadership style as democratic efficiency; she managed to bring vocational education into all school levels; open the Lucy Flower Technical High School, a girls' vocational high school; offer courses in ethics, morality, and sex hygiene (called personal purity); and provide raises for the teachers.

Flagg Young's superintendency faced serious problems in the spring of 1912 when a new school board appointed by Mayor Carter H. Harrison Jr. began referring her recommendations to special committees before endorsing them. By the fall her recommendation for a reading series was not approved, and by December the board voted to take responsibility away from her for the course of study (which included the entire curriculum for the city schools). During the spring of 1913, the school board drafted a teachers' pension fund bill that would give the school board equal representation with the teachers on their pension board and provide for greater school board contributions to the fund. Young was asked to lobby the teachers to support this bill. Unfortunately, she failed to understand just how deeply the CTF distrusted the board, and the bill failed to gain enough support from teachers.

During the summer of 1913, Flagg Young decided that she was not working very effectively with the school board, and she tendered her resignation in August 1913. Mayor Harrison did not want this, nor did many of Chicago's citizens; consequently, the school board voted not to accept her resignation and she returned to office in the fall, assuming she had board support. Her greatest shock came that following December when she failed to be reelected superintendent.

Flagg Young was upset; she left the city over the holidays. Meanwhile, city-wide meetings were held, and a delegation of women led by Jane Addams called on the mayor to protest the board's action. Recently victorious in their battle for a state suffrage bill, two thousand women held a rally for Ella Flagg Young, whose support of women's political equality and her progressive education philosophy had made her extremely popular. Mayor Harrison called for some of her board opponents to resign, and finally a new school board voted to retain her, even though the old board had already elected the assistant superintendent, John D. Shoop, to succeed her. The board's attorney found a loophole in the election of Shoop: in the board's haste they failed to put a time limit on his term of office. Therefore, the new board was legally able to reinstate Flagg Young, so that by the time the schools reconvened after the holidays, she was back in office.

Controversy and conflict continued, however, and Flagg Young remained in the superintendency only until December 1915, when she retired. She spent four months in southern California, working on a book. Her plans were interrupted after the United States entered World War I. In 1917 she was asked to work for the Liberty Loan Committee in Washington, D.C., selling war bonds to support the country's efforts. In the fall of 1918 she contracted influenza while in Idaho working for the fourth Liberty Loan. She returned to Washington but developed pneumonia and died at the age of seventy-three. She was buried in Rosehill Cemetery, Chicago. "To Laura Brayton, confidant and personal secretary, Young left her personal property, twelve $1,000 bonds, and two-fifths of the yearly interest accrued on a trust fund established from the rest of her estate. . . . The other three-fifths interest went to each of three other friends" (Smith, *Ella Flagg Young*, 230).

Ella Flagg Young was a woman of significant accomplishments. She was the first woman to superintend a major school system and to receive the same salary as her male successor. She was the first woman to be elected to the National Education Association presidency. She was a pragmatist in her leadership style but committed to a progressive vision of public school education for a democracy. Jane Addams commented that Ella Young "had more general intelligence and character than any other woman . . . [she] knew" (quoted in *Chicago Tribune*, October 28, 1918).

Sources. Correspondence and papers pertaining to Ella Flagg Young are in the Presidents' Papers, 1889–1925, UC Spec. Coll., and the Chicago Teachers Federation files, CHS. Flagg Young's dissertation was published as *Isolation in the School* (1901), as part of the Contributions to Philosophy and Contributions to Education series that John Dewey edited. Her other titles in this series are *Ethics in the School* (1902), *Some Types of Modern Educational Theory* (1902), and *The Scientific Method in Education* (1902). She wrote many articles and papers, including those found in the *Proceedings and Addresses* of the National Education Association (1887–1917); her reports as superintendent are in the *Annual Reports* of the Chicago Board of Education, 1910–15. Joan K. Smith, *Ella Flagg Young: Portrait of a Leader* (1979), is the most complete discussion of Young's biography and career. See also Smith's article, "Ella Flagg Young and the Chicago Schools, 1905–1915, Progressive School Administration," *Journal of Illinois State Historical Society,* Spring 1980. An older work by a former student of Young is John T. Mc-Manis, *Ella Flagg Young and a Half-Century of the Chicago Public Schools* (1916). See Ida B. De Pencier, *The History of the Laboratory Schools: The University of Chicago, 1896–1965* (1967), for information on the early years of the Dewey School. There is a biography of Young in *NAW* (1971). An obituary appears in *CT,* October 27, 1918, and an article October 28, 1918.

JOAN K. SMITH

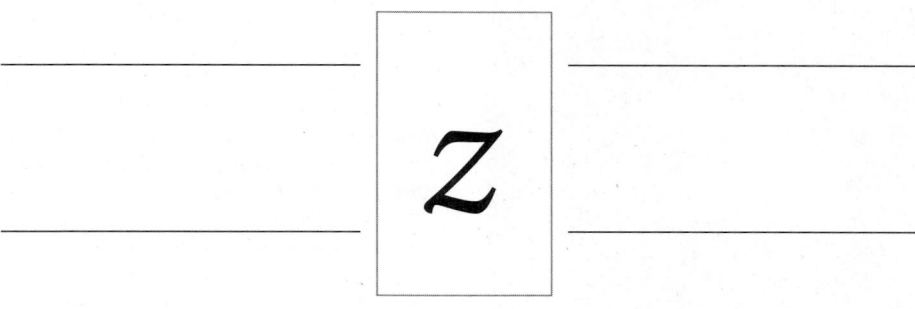

ZEISLER, FANNIE BLOOMFIELD
July 16, 1863–August 20, 1927

PIANIST, TEACHER

Fannie Bloomfield Zeisler, whose concert career spanned four decades and the music centers of Western Europe and the United States, was born in Austrian Silesia in the town of Bielitz, about 250 miles north of Vienna. Her father, Salomon Blumenfeld, was a retail merchant of modest means, and her mother, Bertha (Jaeger) Blumenfeld, came from a Jewish family of high social position. The two were incompatible and locked in a loveless and unhappy marriage. The family was living in poverty, and the younger of two sons was nine years old, when Fanny (changed to Fannie at age twelve) was born, a sickly infant described as suffering from anemia and nervousness. Growing up largely in the company of adults, the hyperactive child was reading at the age of four.

To escape a region devastated in 1866 by the Austro-Prussian War, the family left in the early summer of 1867 to join Bertha Blumenfeld's younger brother, Abraham Jaeger, in Appleton, Wisconsin. There, Salomon Blumenfeld worked in his brother-in-law's household-goods store. The business flourished, and the family moved on to Milwaukee in 1869 and then to Chicago in 1870, where Salomon Blumenfeld set up a dry-goods store near the central commercial district.

With the family's increased financial security, the boys were given music lessons, violin for the older Sigmund and piano for the younger Moriz. Fanny Blumenfeld, observing her brother Moriz's lessons with Bernhard Ziehn, began to teach herself to play the piano. At the age of seven she too began to study with Ziehn. On October 9, 1871, the family business was destroyed by the Great Chicago Fire; however, wholesalers Field & Leiter extended credit, and a new store was opened in November. Ziehn, who was less interested in teaching piano than in theory, turned Fannie Blumenfeld over to Carl Wolfsohn in 1874. Wolfsohn, founder of the Beethoven Society, allowed his advanced pupils to play at society programs. Consequently, Blumenfeld's first public appearance was for the Beethoven Society at its rooms on February 26, 1875. The tiny girl, who had to be lifted to the piano bench, played with a fluency of style and maturity of interpretation far beyond her years.

Blumenfeld graduated with honors from Moseley School, a public grammar school, in 1876. She then entered Dearborn Seminary, a private girls' school with mostly wealthy students. Suffering from chronic ill health and a lack of vitality, she was snubbed by her classmates as the only Jewish student and because she excelled in her studies. Life at home was chaotic; her estranged parents quarreled continually.

In 1877, Annette Essipoff, a well-known Russian pianist, gave a concert in Chicago and heard student auditions. She was very impressed with Fannie Blumenfeld's potential and urged that she go to St. Petersburg, Russia, to study with the great piano pedagogue, Theodor Leschetizky. Blumenfeld was determined to take advantage of this opportunity and persuaded her family to support the effort. In July 1878, she sailed with her mother and grandmother Jaeger for Europe. Her father and brother Sigmund moved to a boarding house, and her brother Moriz, who anglicized his name to Maurice Bloomfield, began postgraduate studies at Johns Hopkins University. The grandmother went to Galicia to live with a sister for the rest of her life, while Blumenfeld and her mother visited Bielitz to see cousins, including her future husband's siblings and cousin Moriz Rosenthal, who later became an outstanding concert pianist. Since Leschetizky was due to resettle in Vienna the following summer, Blumenfeld applied at the Vienna Conservatory, where she was accepted. Her health remained poor for the first two of five years she lived in Europe, as she suffered from anemia, indigestion, chronic constipation, and frequent violent headaches. In addition, she had a curvature of the spine, and a local surgeon advised her that she would not live to see twenty if she continued her piano studies. Leschetizky worried about her

FIG. 136. *Concert pianist Fannie Bloomfield Zeisler at piano, c. 1890s.*

unsatisfactory physical strength, but she pleaded so hard for lessons that he finally accepted her. She remained his pupil until 1883, when she returned to the United States to begin her professional career, using the name Bloomfield.

From 1883 to 1893, Bloomfield began building her reputation with concert tours in American cities. On October 18, 1885, she married lawyer Sigmund Zeisler, a political liberal who would serve as associate counsel in the Chicago Anarchists Case following the Haymarket riot in 1886. Sigmund Zeisler felt that once Fanny Bloomfield was married and had her first child, once she had tasted the hardships and sacrifices of a professional career, she would give it up and be content with home life. But he soon became convinced that their happy marriage could only be maintained by his supporting her dual roles as performer and homemaker. Their first child, Leonard, was born in 1886.

In 1884, Zeisler had joined the faculty at the School of Lyric and Dramatic Art, the beginning of a long-term commitment to teaching. She became active in the Illinois Music Teachers' Association and the Music Teachers' National Association. In 1888, leaving her son under her mother's care in Chicago, Zeisler again studied in Vienna with her mentor, Leschetizky, in master classes that included Annette Essipoff and Ignace Paderewski. After she returned home, Zeisler made annual win-

ter concert tours and spent the warm months at home systematically cleaning and mending everything in her house, mechanical tasks that she claimed rested her brain. She played with her son, attended social functions, and read a good deal. When she was not on tour, Zeisler taught piano classes at home, where each student had a half-hour lesson witnessed by classmates. Despite high tuition charges, she had more applicants than she could teach. She accepted only students who were talented and preparing to be professional musicians. Like her mentor, Zeisler stressed slow, careful practice and development of individual strengths rather than a prescribed method. Although outspoken in her criticisms and chary with praise, she inspired her students with such loyalty that they formed a Zeisler fan club.

In 1893, Zeisler and Paderewski appeared as solo artists at the World's Columbian Exposition in Chicago. Critics considered her "the greatest American woman pianist," but Zeisler sought a place as one of the "great living pianists" (Zeisler, biography, n.p.) without regard to gender. With that goal in mind, Zeisler made her first tour of German cities in the winter of 1893, gaining great acclaim for the perfection of her technique, the power of her tone, and the orchestral effects of her chords. Reviewers placed her among first-ranked performing pianists. Although depressed at being away from home and alone, she was an enormous success, playing before Johannes Brahms, Anton Bruckner, Leschetizky, and other important musical figures. Pianist and composer Anton Rubinstein remarked that there was not an artist in the world more talked of in Berlin than Zeisler. Unfortunately, she became ill and was forced to cancel the rest of the tour. The following winter she toured with her husband, playing for Richard Strauss, Gustav Mahler, and others.

A few months after the birth of her second child, Paul, in 1897, Zeisler debuted in London. There she was dubbed the "Duse of the Piano" (Zeisler, biography, n.p.). She declared that she would not have her son Paul growing up alone as had Leonard, and Ernest was born in 1899. While on tour, Zeisler often spent entire nights traveling back and forth from home just to spend a few hours with her children. When possible, she had a reception at home the last Wednesday of the month, where "Gentiles and Jews met and mingled on a plane of perfect social equality" (Zeisler, biography, n.p.) in a salon she maintained for twenty years. She believed that these social contacts could help eradicate anti-Semitism.

On March 24, 1900, she presented a twenty-fifth anniversary concert at Central Music Hall in Chicago. That season she made forty-three appearances. During the 1901–1902 season, she gave fifty-five concerts, many involving fatiguing train journeys with inadequate accommodations. The 1902 autumn tour included her debut in Paris, where she appeared before a hostile audience that objected to a soloist, expecting a program of orchestral music. Defiantly ignoring a storm of hisses, she began to play and soon wrung an ovation from the opposition.

A 1901 *Chicago Tribune* interview described the "intense forcefulness of the frail little woman. . . . At first glance the force, character and presence overshadowed the physical woman to such an extent as to be almost incongruous . . . olive complexion, with large, dark eyes, and with a student stoop at the shoulders, her voice naturally low, becomes almost strident at times under the influence of her interest and emotions" (quoted in Zeisler, biography, n.p.). Zeisler's intense individuality and absolute command of the keyboard exerted magnetic power over her audiences, and her ability to excite the highest critical and popular acclaim never waned throughout her career.

In 1905, Zeisler gave birth to a stillborn daughter when she went into premature labor after pulling a heavy sliding door. She also suffered hemorrhages in both eyes. The loss of this longed-for daughter, exacerbated by temporary near-blindness and self-blame for the early birth, brought about a deep depression from which she did not recover for more than a year.

After the season's absence in 1906, she was scheduled to appear with the Chicago Symphony Orchestra on February 22 and 23, 1907. Excitement was so great, however, that management took the unusual step of scheduling a third performance for the twenty-first, in anticipation of a huge demand for tickets. By 1908, she was limiting herself to thirty concert appearances per year. Recitals at Carnegie Hall in New York and Orchestra Hall in Chicago, and appearances with orchestras in cities from Boston to Minneapolis were annual events. In 1912 she made a winter concert tour of Germany, England, and France, after which she confined her appearances solely to American cities. She fell ill in 1917 with an unspecified malady and did not appear for three seasons. In her comeback concert at the age of fifty-seven, she played three concerti—Wolfgang Amadeus Mozart's D Major, Frédéric Chopin's F Minor, and Peter Ilyich Tchaikovsky's B-flat Minor—with the Chicago Symphony Orchestra under conductor Frederick Stock at a special concert on February 3, 1920. The program was a tour de force for the most hardy of performers, yet she rewarded the ardent applause with the scherzo from a concerto by Henry Litolff.

A huge celebration was planned for the 1925 Golden Jubilee of her first public appearance, including an Orchestra Hall concert, dinners at the Drake Hotel and the Cordon Club, luncheons at the Arts Club, the Chicago Woman's Club, the Piano Club of Chicago, and the Book and Play Club. For the concert, Zeisler played Ludwig van Beethoven's Andante in F as she had presented it in 1875, her beloved interpretation of the Robert Schumann Concerto in A Minor, and the Chopin F Minor concerto. In her honor, Illinois sculptor Loredo Taft unveiled a bust of Zeisler. *Chicago Evening Post* critic Karleton Hackett wrote, "No other resident artist has ever won the right to such an honor. . . . [She] has been one of the essential forces in our musical life" (Allais, 9). *Chicago American* critic Herman Devries expressed a contemporary bias in judging women performers, calling Zeisler a "prince of the pianoforte" because her talents were "too Olympian to be classed among the feminine exponents of her art" (Allais, 8).

The jubilee concert marked the end of her active musical career. She turned over the concert receipts, sixty-five hundred dollars, to the United Charities of Chicago for a Fannie Bloomfield Zeisler Musicians' Relief Fund. She spent a great deal of time and energy planning a celebration to unveil a monument in Vienna to her former teacher, Leschetizky. Her appearance at the ceremony in September 1926 was her last public act. Gradual heart failure resulted in her death the next year at her home in the Cooper-Carlton Hotel, and she was cremated at Oak Woods Cemetery, Chicago.

H. E. O. Heineman's editorial obituary in *Music Magazine* summed up Zeisler's impact on her adopted city: "Her life epitomizes . . . the development of music in Chicago and in the Middle West from the days when this city and this part of the country were just emerging from . . . pioneer life to the present time when the mere struggle with physical nature is no longer the almost sole occupation of the population. . . . [She carried] the name of Chicago . . . to the old centers of musical art in Europe where she was acclaimed as one of the great ones" (p. 5).

Sources. Although many articles written during Zeisler's lifetime used a hyphenated form of her name, virtually everything written since then has dropped the hyphen. Anecdotal accounts on the spelling change in her maiden name differ from public records. According to Sigmund Zeisler's typescript biography, found at the American Jewish Archives, Cincinnati, Ohio, Fannie Blumenfeld changed the spelling of her last name to Bloomfield in 1883 in order to match that of her brother, Maurice Bloomfield. The 1870 census places the entire family under "Bloomfield," but the family business is listed in the *Chicago City Directory* as S. Blumenfeld from 1871 to at least 1880. Sigmund Zeisler's typescript biography of his wife is rich in anecdotal information. A copy of the biography is included with correspondence, photographs, and programs in the Fannie Bloomfield Zeisler Papers at NL. Zeisler's career is treated in *NCAB* (1967), *NAW* (1971), and *Jewish Women in America: An Historical Encyclopedia*, ed. Paula E. Hyman and Deborah Dash Moore, 2 vols. (1997). Harold Schonberg's *The Great Pianists* (1963) has a good characterization of her training, style, and position in the history of music. Her teaching technique is discussed in Rowena Gailey, "A Little Lesson in Psychology," *Etude Music Magazine*, June 1937, and at greater length in Theodore Troendle's "How Fannie Bloomfield-Zeisler Taught," *Etude*, November 1929. Zeisler is the subject of many journal and newspaper articles, including "Woman in Music," *American Art Journal*, October 17, 1891; "Madness in Methods: A Symposium on Piano Playing," *Philharmonic*, April 1902; "Interview with Bloomfield-Zeisler," *Musical Courier*, April 4, 1906; and "Fannie Bloomfield-Zeisler," interview by G. Mark Wilson, *Musician*, October 1927. Paul Allais, compiler, *The Fannie Bloomfield Zeisler Golden Jubilee Celebration* (1925), eulogizes her performance and her importance in the musical world. H. E. O. Heineman's obituary, "An Individual Life and an Epoch," appears in *Music Magazine*, October 1927, a memorial issue for Zeisler.

DIANA HASKELL

List of Entries by Year of Birth

1781

OUILMETTE, ARCHANGE CHEVALLIER, 1781–1840

1797

WILLARD, FRANCES LANGDON, 1797–1854

1805–1819

GARRETT, ELIZA CLARK, 1805–1855
KINZIE, JULIETTE AUGUSTA MAGILL, 1806–1870
PORTER, ELIZA EMILY CHAPPELL, 1807–1888
HOGE, JANE CURRIE BLAIKIE, 1811–1890
MONHOLLAND, MOTHER MARY FRANCIS De SALES
    (Mary Monholland), 1816–1888
NEWBERRY, JULIA BUTLER CLAPP, 1818–1885
JONES, MARY JANE RICHARDSON, 1819–1910

1820–1829

HUBBARD, MARY ANN MILLS, 1820–1909
LIVERMORE, MARY ASHTON RICE, 1820–1905
O'BRIEN, MOTHER MARY AGATHA (Margaret O'Brien),
    1822–1854
STARR, ELIZA ALLEN, 1824–1901
HURLEY, SISTER MARY AGATHA (Eleanor Hurley),
    1826–1902
LAMB, MARTHA JOANNA READE NASH, 1826–1893
DOGGETT, KATE NEWELL, 1827–1884
THOMPSON, MARY HARRIS, 1829–1895
WAITE, CATHARINE VAN VALKENBURG, 1829–1913

1830–1839

BRADWELL, MYRA COLBY, 1831–1894
FASSETT, CORNELIA ADELE STRONG, 1831–1898
CULVER, HELEN, 1832–1925
GEHRING, SISTER WALBURGA (Eva Gehring),
    1832–1883
MILLER, EMILY CLARK HUNTINGTON, 1833–1913
STOCKHAM, ALICE BUNKER, 1833–1912
CARSE, MATILDA BRADLEY, 1835–1917
CORBIN, CAROLINE ELIZABETH FAIRFIELD,
    1835–1918
DRYER, EMMA, 1835–1925
McCORMICK, NETTIE FOWLER, 1835–1923
CHAPIN, AUGUSTA JANE, 1836–1905
CROUSE, RUMAH AVILLA HULL, 1836–1915
FLOWER, LUCY LOUISA COUES, 1837–1921
SMITH, AMANDA JANE BERRY, 1837–1915

WILMARTH, MARY J. HAWES, 1837–1919
SMITH, JULIA HOLMES ABBOT, 1838–1930
WILLARD, FRANCES ELIZABETH CAROLINE,
    1839–1898

1840–1849

RICHMOND, CORA LINN VICTORIA SCOTT HATCH
    DANIELS TAPPAN, 1840–1923
PUTNAM, ALICE HARVEY WHITING, 1841–1919
STEVENSON, SARAH HACKETT, 1841–1909
PULLMAN, HARRIET AMELIA SANGER, 1842–1921
HARBERT, ELIZABETH BOYNTON, 1843–1925
OWENS, FRANCES JOHNSTON (Genie), 1843–1903
COONLEY-WARD, LYDIA, 1845–1924
GESTEFELD, URSULA NEWELL, 1845–1921
YOUNG, ELLA FLAGG, 1845–1918
HALLOWELL, SARA TYSON, 1846–1924
PORTER, JULIA FOSTER, 1846–1936
CATHERWOOD, MARY HARTWELL, 1847–1902
HENROTIN, ELLEN MARTIN, 1847–1922
MARTIN, ELLEN ANNETTE, 1847–1916
RODGERS, ELIZABETH FLYNN, 1847–1939
FRACKELTON, SUSAN STUART GOODRICH,
    1848–1932
GLESSNER, FRANCES MacBETH, 1848–1932
SAMOLIŃSKA, TEOFILA CWIKLIŃSKA, 1848–1913
WOOLLEY, CELIA ANNA PARKER, 1848–1918
BROWN, CORINNE STUBBS, 1849–1914
HARRISON, ELIZABETH, 1849–1927
HOPKINS, JOSEPHINE EMMA CURTIS, 1849–1925
MEYER, LUCY JANE RIDER, 1849–1922
PALMER, BERTHA HONORÉ, 1849–1918
PELHAM, LAURA DAINTY, 1849–1924
POOLEY, GEORGIA BITZIS, 1849–1945
STEVENS, ALZINA ANN PARSONS, 1849–1900

1850–1859

HOLMES, LIZZIE MAY SWANK, 1850–1926
MORGAN, ELIZABETH CHAMBERS, 1850–1944
MERGLER, MARIE JOSEPHA, 1851–1901
MORGAN, ANNA, 1851–1936
SHAW, ANNIE CORNELIA, 1852–1887
SWEET, ADA CELESTE, 1852–1928
THOMAS, ROSE FAY, 1852–1929
EVERHART, MARY JANE, 1853–1928
GORDON, ANNA ADAMS, 1853–1931
PARSONS, LUCY E., 1853–1942
BURNHAM, CLARA LOUISE ROOT, 1854–1927
CROW, MARTHA FOOTE, 1854–1924

HULETT, ALTA MAY, 1854–1877
McDOWELL, MARY ELIZA, 1854–1936
VICKERY, MABEL SLADE, 1854–1944
WICKER, MARY HACKNEY, 1854–1942
DAVIS, ELIZABETH LINDSAY, 1855–1944
GOGGIN, CATHARINE, 1855–1916
LESLIE, AMY (Lillie West Brown Buck), 1855–1939
WILLIAMS, FANNIE BARRIER, 1855–1944
BARBE, LIZZIE T. SPIEGEL, 1856–1943
COBURN, ANNIE SWAN, 1856–1932
DICKINSON, FRANCES, 1856–1945
HULING, CAROLINE ALDEN, 1856–1941
CRADDOCK, IDA C., 1857–1902
HENRY, ALICE, 1857–1943
MOODY, HARRIET CONVERSE TILDEN BRAINARD,
   1857–1932
BENEDICT, ENELLA, 1858–1942
BUCKINGHAM, KATE STURGES, 1858–1937
LATHROP, JULIA CLIFFORD, 1858–1932
McCREA, ANNETTE E. MAXSON, 1858–1928
MYHRMAN, OTHELIA MÖRK, 1858–1936
SMITH, ELEANOR SOPHIA, 1858–1942
SOLOMON, HANNAH GREENEBAUM, 1858–1942
TALBOT, MARION, 1858–1948
BOWEN, LOUISE deKOVEN, 1859–1953
KELLEY, FLORENCE, 1859–1932
STARR, ELLEN GATES, 1859–1940

1860–1869

ADDAMS, JANE, 1860–1935
AHERN, MARY EILEEN, 1860–1938
DUDZIK, SISTER M. THERESA (Josephine Dudzik),
   1860–1918
GASTON, LUCY PAGE, 1860–1924
MONROE, HARRIET, 1860–1936
SPONLAND, SISTER INGEBORG, 1860–1951
WAITE, LUCY CLAPP, 1860–1943
HALEY, MARGARET ANGELA, 1861–1939
TRUE, CORINNE KNIGHT, 1861–1961
AMERICAN, SADIE, 1862–1944
BABER, ZONIA, 1862–1956
JACOBS-BOND, CARRIE, 1862–1946
KELLOGG TYLER, ALICE DeWOLF, 1862–1900
McCULLOCH, CATHARINE GOUGER WAUGH,
   1862–1945
PEATTIE, ELIA AMANDA WILKINSON, 1862–1935
WELLS, DORA, 1862–1948
WELLS-BARNETT, IDA BELL, 1862–1931
CLEARY, KATE McPHELIM, 1863–1905
JAQUES, BERTHA EVELYN CLAUSON, 1863–1941
PLATT, IDA, 1863–?
VAN HOOSEN, BERTHA, 1863–1952
ZEISLER, FANNIE BLOOMFIELD, 1863–1927
COOKE, FLORA JULIETTE, 1864–1953
FREER, ELEANOR EVEREST, 1864–1942
LIVSHIS, ANNA MINDLIN (Annie), 1864–1953
O'SULLIVAN, MARY KENNEY, 1864–1943

TROUT, GRACE WILBUR, 1864–1955
DE BEY, CORNELIA BERNARDA, 1865–1948
HEFFERAN, HELEN MALEY, 1865–1953
KERR, MAY WALDEN, 1865–1953
NICHOLES, ANNA E., 1865–1917
PERKINS, LUCY FITCH, 1865–1937
SHARP, KATHARINE LUCINDA, 1865–1914
BARTELME, MARY MARGARET, 1866–1954
BLAINE, ANITA EUGENIE McCORMICK, 1866–1954
BRECKINRIDGE, SOPHONISBA PRESTON, 1866–1948
CASSETTARI, ROSA, 1866–1943
CHMIELIŃSKA, STEFANIA, 1866–1939
DUMMER, ETHEL STURGES, 1866–1954
LATHAM, VIDA ANNETTE, 1866–1958
RICE, HARRIET ALLEYNE, 1866–1958
SCHMIDT, MINNA MOSCHEROSCH, 1866–1961
LOW, MINNIE F., 1867–1922
NELSON ROLLINS, IDA GRAY, 1867–1953
NEWBURY, MOLLIE NETCHER, 1867–1954
PALMER, PAULINE LENNARDS, 1867–1938
ROBERTSON, INA LAW, 1867–1916
SALAVA, BOŽENA, 1867–1960
WATSON SCHÜTZE, EVA LAWRENCE, 1867–1935
CARPENTER, HELEN GRAHAM FAIRBANK, 1868–1945
GYLES, ROSE MARIE, 1868–1949
HEDGER, CAROLINE, 1868–1951
McILVAINE, CAROLINE MARGARET, 1868–1945
McKINLEY, ADA SOPHIA DENNISON, 1868–1952
McMILLAN, M. HELENA, 1868–1970
ROBINS, MARGARET DREIER, 1868–1945
SIKES, MADELEINE WALLIN, 1868–1955
SMITH, MARY ROZET, 1868–1934
SUNDAY, HELEN AMELIA THOMPSON, 1868–1957
WELLES, CLARA BARCK, 1868–1965
ALDIS, MARY REYNOLDS, 1869–1949
ASHER, VIRGINIA HEALEY, 1869–1937
HAMILTON, ALICE, 1869–1970
LILLIE, FRANCES CRANE, 1869–1958
SLYE, MAUD, 1869–1954
WARING, MARY FITZBUTLER, 1869–1958
YARROS, RACHELLE SLOBODINSKY, 1869–1946

1870–1879

BENNETT, BESSIE, 1870–1939
HUMPAL-ZEMAN, JOSEFA VERONIKA, 1870–1906
MacLEAN, ANNIE MARION, 1870–1934
PETERSON, ANNA J., 1870–1952
CLARK, HERMA NAOMI, 1871–1959
EMANUEL, FANNIE HAGEN, 1871–1934
GRIFFIN, MARION LUCY MAHONY, 1871–1961
REIS, NANNIE ASCHENHEIM, 1871–1940
RICKERT, EDITH, 1871–1938
SLAGLE, ELEANOR CLARKE, 1871–1942
STEWART, ELLA JANE SEASS, 1871–1945
WENDT, JULIA BRACKEN, 1871–1942
ANDERSON, MARY, 1872–1964
CHENEY, FLORA SYLVESTER, 1872–1929

FISCHER, SISTER CELESTINE (Susanna Fischer), 1872–1953

GARNETT BUTLER TALLEY, ISABELLA MAUDE, 1872–1948

LAUDYN, STEFANIA (Laudyn-Chrzanowska), 1872–1942

McCORMICK, EDITH ROCKEFELLER, 1872–1932

VITTUM, HARRIET ELIZABETH, 1872–1953

VONNOH, BESSIE ONAHOTEMA POTTER, 1872–1955

CHORPENNING, CHARLOTTE BARROWS, 1873–1955

ICKES, ANNA WILMARTH THOMPSON, 1873–1935

LAUGHLIN, CLARA ELIZABETH, 1873–1941

PURVIN, JENNIE FRANKLIN, 1873–1958

SIMONS, MAY WOOD, 1873–1948

WYATT, EDITH FRANKLIN, 1873–1958

AMBERG, MARY AGNES, 1874–1962

ANDERSON, TENNESSEE CLAFLIN MITCHELL, 1874–1929

BEST, MARJORIE AYRES, 1874–1942

GARDEN, MARY, 1874–1967

REED, MYRTLE, 1874–1911

WALKER, NELLIE VERNE, 1874–1973

BLAKE, MARGARET DAY, 1875–1971

COFFEY, SISTER MARY JUSTITIA (Alice Marie Coffey), 1875–1947

KOHN, ESTHER LOEB, 1875–1965

LEMBERG, ROSA EMILIA CLAY, 1875–1959

LLOYD, LOLA MAVERICK, 1875–1944

SMITH, LUCY MADDEN, 1875–1952

ABBOTT, EDITH, 1876–1957

BINFORD, JESSIE FLORENCE, 1876–1966

BLUNT, KATHARINE, 1876–1954

BOYD, NEVA LEONA, 1876–1963

CARPENTER, RUE WINTERBOTHAM, 1876–1931

EVERLEIGH, ADA, 1876–1960

TUNNICLIFF, RUTH, 1876–1946

CURREY, MARGERY (Helen Marguerite), 1877–1959

FISCHER, MOTHER IMELDA (Elizabeth Fischer), 1877–1954

FULMER, HARRIET, 1877–1952

MARCY, MARY EDNA TOBIAS, 1877–1922

NANCREDE, EDITH de, 1877–1936

NATKIN, ESTHER WEINSHENKER, 1877–1928

OBERNDORFER, ANNE SHAW FAULKNER, 1877–1948

WALRATH, FLORENCE DAHL, 1877–1958

ABBOTT, GRACE, 1878–1939

DAHL, PETRA MARIE, 1878–1951

EVERLEIGH, MINNA, 1878–1948

FOLEY, EDNA LOIS, 1878–1943

GARDNER, HELEN, 1878–1946

HINMAN, MARY WOOD, 1878–1952

MALEK, LEONA ALFORD KRAG (Prudence Penny, Jean Prescott Adams), 1878–1951

O'NEILL, LOTTIE HOLMAN, 1878–1967

STANISIA, SISTER MARY (Monica Kurk, née Kurkowski), 1878–1967

FAIRBANK, JANET AYER, 1879–1951

JARRELL, SISTER HELEN, 1879–1951

JUDSON, CLARA INGRAM, 1879–1960

ROBERTS, LYDIA JANE, 1879–1965

1880–1889

KAUPAS, MOTHER MARIA (Casimira Kaupas), 1880–1940

MALONEY, ELIZABETH, 1880–1921

McCORMICK, RUTH HANNA, 1880–1944

NESTOR, AGNES, 1880–1948

CHRISTMAN, ELISABETH, 1881–1975

DICK, GLADYS ROWENA HENRY, 1881–1963

HENDERSON, ALICE CORBIN, 1881–1949

MURPHY, MOTHER EVELYN (Katherine Murphy), 1881–1955

ANDERSON JOHNSON, VIOLETTE NEATLEY, 1882–1937

BRADLEY, MARY HASTINGS, 1882–1976

FLOISTAD, BERTHA GRIMSTAD, 1882–1989

HUCK, WINNIFRED SPRAGUE MASON, 1882–1936

O'HANLON, SISTER MARY ELLEN (Catherine O'Hanlon), 1882–1961

POLACHECK, HILDA SATT, 1882–1967

THORNE, NARCISSA NIBLACK, 1882–1966

VAN VOLKENBURG, ELLEN, 1882–1979

BAKER, EDNA DEAN, 1883–1956

HEAP, JANE, 1883–1964

HOLT, NORA DOUGLAS, 1883–1974

NICE, MARGARET MORSE, 1883–1974

ROULLIER, ALICE, 1883–1963

TAYLOR, LEA DEMAREST, 1883–1975

VAN PAPPELENDAM, LAURA, 1883–1974

AUSTIN, RUTH INEZ, 1884–1990

BRIMSON, ALICE WORTHINGTON SMITH, 1884–1981

HUNCKE, OLGA HARRIET, 1884–1973

TIETJENS, EUNICE HAMMOND, 1884–1944

WARD, WINIFRED LOUISE, 1884–1975

WILLIAMS, FLORENCE CHAPMAN, 1884–1964

BOUSFIELD, MAUDELLE BROWN, 1885–1971

FERBER, EDNA, 1885–1968

GERSTENBERG, ALICE, 1885–1972

LEVITAS, MOLLIE SYBIL M., 1885–1984

MIRABELLA, ROSAMOND LIBONATI, 1885–1985

PALERMO, LUCY MARY RUSSO, 1885–1979

ANDERSON, MARGARET CAROLYN, 1886–1973

BARNES, MARGARET AYER, 1886–1967

HERSTEIN, LILLIAN, 1886–1983

KYRK, HAZEL, 1886–1957

LUNDE, LAURA HUGHES, 1886–1966

TORREY, MABEL LANDRUM, 1886–1974

ALSCHULER, ROSE HAAS, 1887–1979

AUSTIN, LOVIE (Cora Calhoun), 1887–1972

BULLOCK, CARRIE E., 1887–1962

KAWIN, IRENE, 1887–1976

BUTCHER, FANNY AMANDA, 1888–1987

DIECKMANN, ANNETTA MARIA, 1888–1974

FENBERG, MATILDA, 1888–1977

HYMAN, LIBBIE HENRIETTA, 1888–1969

LIN, MARGARET HIE DING, 1888–1973

PETRAKIS, STELLA CHRISTOULAKIS, 1888–1979

RUDOLPH, ANNE, 1907–1988
ARAI, JOAN FUJISAWA, 1908–1976
BLENDER, DOROTHEA PEARL, 1908–1972
GRIMM, EDITH RAMBAR, 1908–1984
MOORE GARBE, RUTH, 1908–1989
PAYNE, VIRGINIA, 1908–1977
ABERCROMBIE, GERTRUDE, 1909–1977
HALPERN, DINA, 1909–1989
WHITE HORSE, CHAUNCINA YELLOW ROBE,
    1909–1981
WOODS, SYLVIA GREEN, 1909–1987

1910–1919

DUNAYEVSKAYA, RAYA, 1910–1987
JACKSON, MAHALIA, 1911–1972
McGRATH, SISTER ALBERTUS MAGNUS (Marion Cecily
    McGrath), 1911–1978
PEBWORTH, MARY MARJORIE MULL, 1911–1967
PRINZ, TOBEY SILBERT SCHEIN, 1911–1984
BONDS, MARGARET ALLISON, 1913–1972
WELLS, SARAJANE, 1913–1987
SKENANDORE, AMY LEICHER, 1914–1990
STIGLER, ELISA, 1914–1973
CRILEY, FLORENCE LOUISE ATKINSON, 1915–1976
MENTSCHIKOFF, SOIA, 1915–1984
BRIGHT, ALICE MARY, 1917–1982
MURAKAMI, CHIYO KASHIWAGI, 1917–1990
ORMES, ZELDA JACKSON (Jackie), 1917–1985

ITO, MIYOKO, 1918–1983
KASSEL, MYRNA SIEGENDORF BORDELON,
    1918–1972

1920–1929

CARTER, VIVIAN, 1921–1989
WARSHAWSKY, CELIA BURG, 1921–1986
DAGENAIS, MARGARET MARIE, 1922–1983
McWHINNIE, MARY ALICE, 1922–1980
TUITE, SISTER MARJORIE, 1922–1986
FOX, CAROL, 1926–1981
PEURALA, ALICE MELICKIAN, 1928–1986

1930–1939

HANSBERRY, LORRAINE VIVIAN, 1930–1965
WEISS, MARY CATHERINE BISHOP, 1930–1966
MERRILL, IRIS BARBARA, 1934–1983

1940–1949

RIPERTON, MINNIE JULIA, 1947–1979

1950–1959

McCLAIN, LEANITA, 1951–1984
MARTINEZ, MARIA DIAZ, 1952–1990
SAUCEDO, MARIA del JESUS, 1954–1981

Photo Credits

FIGURES

1. Department of Special Collections, University of Chicago Library

2. Jane Addams Memorial Collection. Special Collections, The University Library, University of Illinois at Chicago

3. Jane Addams Memorial Collection. Special Collections, The University Library, University of Illinois at Chicago

4. Chicago Historical Society ICHi-19288

5. Jane Addams Memorial Collection. Special Collections, The University Library, University of Illinois at Chicago

6. Chicago Historical Society ICHi-27211

7. Marquette University Archives

8. The Schlesinger Library, Radcliffe College

9. Chicago Historical Society DN-084413, *Chicago Daily News* photo

10. Archives of the Billy Graham Center, Wheaton, Illinois

11. Chicago Historical Society ICHi-27209

12. Chicago Historical Society. Photographer Larson

13. Chicago Historical Society ICHi-09568

14. Chicago Historical Society DN-80817

15. Jane Addams Memorial Collection. Special Collections, The University Library, University of Illinois at Chicago

16. Chicago Historical Society

17. Constantin Brancusi (1876–1957), French, born in Romania, portrait of Rue Winterbotham Carpenter, charcoal and graphite, n.d., 64.5×45 cm. Gift of Mrs. Patrick C. Hill in memory of her mother, 1981.302. Photograph © 1997, the Art Institute of Chicago. All Rights Reserved

18. Chicago Historical Society. Photographer J. W. Taylor

19. Courtesy of Calumet Regional Archives, Indiana University Northwest

20. Chicago Historical Society ICHi-27206

21. Chicago Historical Society ICHi-27197

22. Chicago Historical Society ICHi-25869. Photographer Lil & Al Bloom

23. Chicago Historical Society ICHi-26297

24. Chicago Historical Society F38DA-P2C12. Photo courtesy Francis W. Parker Centennial Committee

25. Chicago Historical Society ICHi-27194

26. H. Rocher, "C. Adele Fassett." Office of the Architect of the Capitol. The Capitol, Washington, D.C.

27. St. Scholastica Priory Archives

28. Chicago Historical Society ICHi-30643

29. Courtesy of Gladys Wang

30. Photo by Charles Del Vecchio, 1978

31. State Historical Society of Wisconsin WHi(X22)9747. Photographer *Chicago Times Herald*

32. Chicago Historical Society DN-084803. Photographer *Chicago Daily News*

33. Chicago Historical Association ICHi-21346

34. Chicago Historical Society

35. Chicago Historical Society ICHi-30640

36. Chicago Historical Society ICHi-27208

37. Chicago Historical Society ICHi-30642. Photographer Moffett Studios

38. Chicago Historical Society. Photographer Mishkiss Studio, New York

39. Chicago Historical Society DN-001988. Photographer *Chicago Daily News*

40. Courtesy of Mater Dei Provincialate, Evansville, Indiana

41. Chicago Historical Society ICHi-27207. Photographer David B. Lannes

42. Chicago Historical Society

43. Courtesy of the National Woman's Christian Temperance Union

44. Jane Addams Memorial Collection. Special Collections, The University Library, University of Illinois at Chicago

45. Chicago Historical Society ICHi-16228

46. Photo courtesy National Portrait Gallery, Washington, D.C. Mary Fairchild MacMonnies, *Portrait de Mlle S. H.* (Sara Tyson Hallowell), 1886, oil on canvas, 111.8×97.2 cm (44×38 ¼ in), Robinson College, Cambridge University, Cambridge, England. Gift of Marion Hardy

47. Hogan Jazz Archive, Howard-Tilton Memorial Library Tulane University

48. National-Louis University

49. Courtesy of Hope Harshaw Evans

50. Courtesy of Tess Weiner

51. Chicago Historical Society ICHi-27210. Photographer Burke & Dean, Chicago

52. Department of Special Collections, The University of Chicago Library

53. Bohemian Women's Publishing Company Records. Special Collections, The University Library, University of Illinois at Chicago

54. Bohemian Women's Publishing Company Records. Special Collections, The University Library, University of Illinois at Chicago

55. Bohemian Women's Publishing Company Records. Special Collections, The University Library, University of Illinois at Chicago

56. Courtesy of Susan Lee Moy

57. Neg. No. 2A 23778. Courtesy Department of Library Services, American Museum of Natural History

58. Chicago Historical Society DN-Q-699. Photographer *Chicago Daily News*

59. Chicago Historical Society. Photographer Barnard

60. Chicago Historical Society DN-Alpha. Photographer *Chicago Daily News*

61. Jane Addams Memorial Collection. Special Collections, The University Library, University of Illinois at Chicago

62. Chicago Historical Society ICHi-10690

63. Jane Addams Memorial Collection. Special Collections, The University Library, University of Illinois at Chicago

64. Chicago Historical Society DN-009905. Photographer *Chicago Daily News*

65. Courtesy of Gladys Wang

66. Courtesy of Ann Lewin Diament

67. Chicago Historical Society DN-060956. Photographer *Chicago Daily News*

68. Chicago Historical Society ICHi-28793

69. Department of Special Collections. University of Chicago Library

70. Chicago Historical Society ICHi-14448

71. Chicago Historical Society DN-093741. Photographer *Chicago Daily News*

72. Jane Addams Memorial Collection. Special Collections, The University Library, University of Illinois at Chicago

73. Chicago Historical Society DN-4818. Photographer *Chicago Daily News*

74. Chicago Historical Society ICHi-09371

75. Sinsinawa Dominican Archives

76. Chicago Historical Society ICHi-16824

77. Courtesy of Ada S. McKinley Community Services, Inc.

78. Courtesy of Dr. Dolores J. McWhinnie

79. Chicago Historical Society

80. Department of Special Collections. University of Chicago Library

81. Courtesy of Sinsinawa Dominican Archives

82. Jane Addams Memorial Collection. Special Collections, The University Library, University of Illinois at Chicago

83. Chicago Historical Society DN-085128. Photographer *Chicago Daily News*

84. Chicago Historical Society ICHi-19928

85. Smithsonian Institute Archives, Record Unit 7150, American Ornithologists Union Collection, 1883–1978

86. © Mike Tappin

87. Jane Addams Memorial Collection. Special Collections, The University Library, University of Illinois at Chicago

88. Courtesy of Susan Lee Moy

89. Chicago Historical Society ICHi-30641

90. Courtesy Ida B. DePencier and Ann D. Carlson

91. Chicago Historical Society DN-063594. Photographer *Chicago Daily News*

92. Jane Addams Memorial Collection. Special Collections, The University Library, University of Illinois at Chicago

93. Courtesy Blair Perkins Grumman

94. Andrew T. Kopan Collection

95. Department of Special Collections, University of Chicago Library

96. Andrew T. Kopan Collection

97. Photo of Florence Price by G. Nelidoff, Chicago. Florence Price Papers, Special Collections Division, University of Arkansas Libraries, Fayetteville

98. Chicago Historical Society ICHi-27198

99. Department of Special Collections, The University of Chicago Library

100. Department of Special Collections, University of Chicago Library

101. Pavel Tchelitchew (1898–1957), American, "Alice Rouiller," pen and brush and red ink on buff board, 1935, 34.8 × 27.3 cm. Gift of Mrs. Alfred P. Shaw, 1976.647. Photograph © 1997, the Art Institute of Chicago. All rights Reserved

102. Chicago Historical Society DN-Alpha. Photographer *Chicago Daily News*

103. Chicago Historical Society DN-91344. Photographer *Chicago Daily News*

104. Special Collections and Archives, Knox College Library, Galesburg, Illinois

105. Jane Addams Memorial Collection. Special Collections, The University Library, University of Illinois at Chicago

106. Chicago Historical Society DN-060284. Photographer *Chicago Daily News*

107. Vivian G. Harsh Research Collection, Chicago Public Library

108. American Jewish Archives, Cincinnati Campus, Hebrew Union College, Jewish Institute of Religion

109. Courtesy of Carole Tormollan

110. Loyola University Chicago Archives, Leon T. Walkowicz Photo Collection

111. George Peter A. Healey, Eliza Allen Starr, 1861. Gift of Eunice Starr Wellington. The Snite Museum of Art, University of Notre Dame

112. Jane Addams Memorial Collection. Special Collections, The University Library, University of Illinois at Chicago

113. Chicago Historical Society DN-62357. Photographer *Chicago Daily News*

114. Chicago Historical Society DN-056700. Photographer *Chicago Daily News*

115. Archives of the Billy Graham Center, Wheaton, Illinois

116. Chicago Historical Society ICHi-27205. Photographer *Frankie & Johnnie*

117. Chicago Historical Society DN-54474. Photographer *Chicago Daily News*

118. University Archives, Iowa State University Library

119. Department of Special Collections, University of Chicago Library

120. Chicago Historical Society DN-008389. Photographer *Chicago Daily News*

121. Chicago Historical Society ICHi-27196. Photographer *Chicago American*

122. Chicago Historical Society DN-068176. Photographer *Chicago Daily News*

123. Department of Special Collections, University of Chicago Library

124. Courtesy of Julia B. Mayes

125. The May T. Watts Papers. The Morton Arboretum, Lisle, Illinois

126. Chicago Historical Society DN-063262. Photographer *Chicago Daily News*

127. Courtesy Nancy Stewart Green

128. Chicago Historical Society ICHi 12867

129. Courtesy Nancy Deborah Wicker

130. Courtesy of the National Woman's Christian Temperance Union

131. Courtesy of the National Woman's Christian Temperance Union

132. Jane Addams Memorial Collection. Special Collections, The University Library, University of Illinois at Chicago

133. Chicago Historical Society ICHi-24983

134. Chicago Historical Society ICHi-27195

135. Chicago Historical Society ICHi-26298. Photographer Moffett Studios

136. Zeisler Papers. The Newberry Library

COLOR PLATES

1. Milwaukee County Historical Society

2. Chicago Historical Society P&S-1960.0054

3. Chicago Historical Society 1881.13.14

4. Chicago Historical Society 1992.252.20

5. Chicago Historical Society 1992.252.?

6. The National Museum of Women in the Arts. Gift of Elizabeth Sita

7. William C. Seipp Fund, 1915.193. Photograph courtesy of The Art Institute of Chicago

8. The Art Institute of Chicago Purchase Fund, 1920.245. Photograph courtesy of The Art Institute of Chicago

9. Jane Addams Hull-House Museum. University of Illinois at Chicago

10. Jane Addams Hull-House Museum. University of Illinois at Chicago

11. Estate of J. C. Bulliet. Collection of Harlan J. and Pamela Berk

12. Collection of the Union League Club of Chicago

13. Collection of the Union League Club of Chicago

14. Gift of Mr. and Mrs. William J. Terrell Sr., 1991.160. © 2000, The Art Institute of Chicago. All Rights Reserved

15. Bridges Collection

16. Collection of Harlan J. and Pamela Berk

17. Bridges Collection

18. Collection of the Illinois State Museum

19. Collection of the Illinois State Museum

20. Bridges Collection

21. Margaret Dagenais Records. Loyola University Chicago Archives

22. Margaret Dagenais Records. Loyola University Chicago Archives

Editorial Board

Index of Contributors

Index

The main listing for each entry name shows the page numbers in bold. Pages for illustrations are in italics. Classification of entry names by occupation, activity, ethnicity, race, and religion is listed by topical word (e.g., educator, Irish American) followed by "entries" or "entry."

Book and Jacket Designer: Sharon L. Sklar

Copy Editors: Melanie Richter-Bernburg,

Miki Bird, and Carrie Jadud

Compositor: Graphic Composition, Inc.

Typefaces: Electra and Trajan

Book Printer: Maple-Vail Book Manufacturing

Jacket Printer: Pinnacle Press